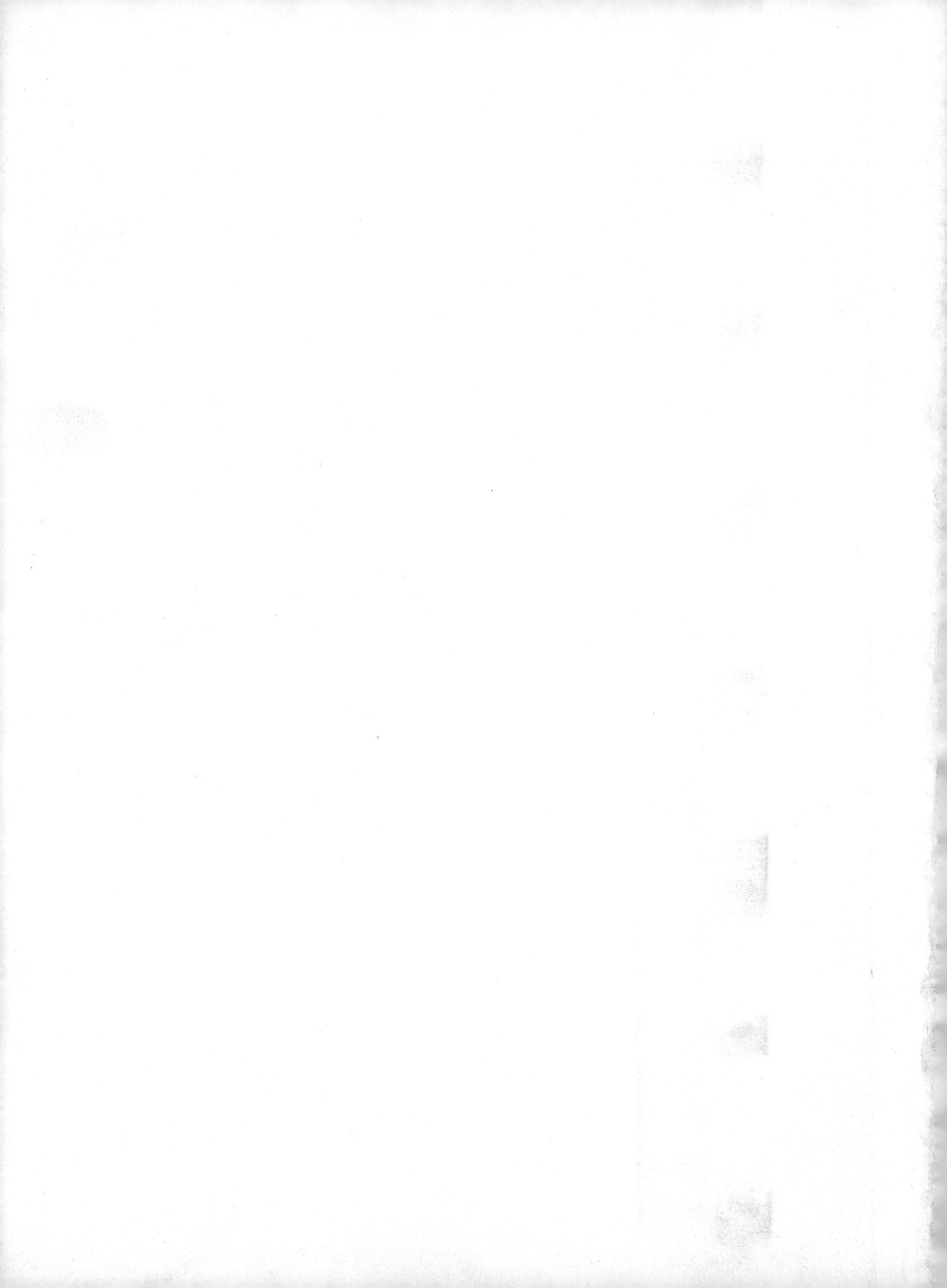

CDX Learning Systems™

FUNDAMENTALS OF

Mobile Heavy Equipment

Owen C. Duffy
Scott A. Heard
Gus Wright

JONES & BARTLETT
LEARNING

World Headquarters
Jones & Bartlett Learning
5 Wall Street
Burlington, MA 01803
978-443-5000
info@jblearning.com
www.jblearning.com

Jones & Bartlett Learning books and products are available through most bookstores and online booksellers. To contact Jones & Bartlett Learning directly, call 800-832-0034, fax 978-443-8000, or visit our website, www.jblearning.com.

Substantial discounts on bulk quantities of Jones & Bartlett Learning publications are available to corporations, professional associations, and other qualified organizations. For details and specific discount information, contact the special sales department at Jones & Bartlett Learning via the above contact information or send an email to specialsales@jblearning.com.

Production Credits
General Manager: Douglas Kaplan
Content Services Manager: Kevin Murphy
Senior Vendor Manager: Sara Kelly
Marketing Manager: Amanda Banner
VP, Manufacturing and Inventory Control: Therese Connell
Composition and Project Management: Integra Software Services Pvt. Ltd.
Cover Design: Scott Moden
Rights & Media Specialist: Robert Boder
Media Development Editor: Shannon Sheehan
Cover Image (Title Page): © Chris Henderson/Getty Images
Printing and Binding: LSC Communications
Cover Printing: LSC Communications

Library of Congress Cataloging-in-Publication Data unavailable at time of printing.

6048

Printed in the United States of America
25 24 23   10 9 8 7

BRIEF CONTENTS

CONTENTS

SECTION IV Wheeled Equipment and Attachments

SECTION V Track Drive Undercarriage & Working Attachments

SECTION VII Braking Systems

CONTRIBUTORS

Abraham Arispe
Tidewater Community College

Casey Elington
Western Technical College

Paul Losh
Lincoln College of Technology – Nashville, TN Campus

Stefan Liszka
Chisholm Institute

Tracy Sean McCrary
Gillette College – Northern Wyoming Community College District

Joseph Palecek
Gateway Technical College

Joseph Gingerich
Gillette College – Northern Wyoming Community College District

Andrew Kendall
College of Western Idaho

Larry Stremming
Vincennes University

Cole Eddy
Lincoln College of Technology – Nashville, TN Campus

Matthew Barnes
WyoTech – Laramie Campus

Duane Yachwak
Western Technical College

Jesse Kosten
Santa Rosa Junior College

Dan Hagaman
Lincoln College of Technology – Plainfield, NJ Campus

Steve Hancock
Parkland College

Steven Don
Montana State University Northern

Jon Wright
Western Dakota Technical Institute

SECTION I

Foundations & Safety

CHAPTER 1

Introduction to MORE Applications

Knowledge Objectives

After reading this chapter, you will be able to:

- **K01001** Classify off-road and mobile equipment according to application and industry.
- **K01002** Identify and describe the purpose and functions of off-road mobile equipment.
- **K01003** Identify design factors for the selection of mobile off-road equipment (MORE).
- **K01004** Outline and describe the job requirements of MORE technicians.
- **K01005** Describe and perform pre-start and walk-around inspections.
- **K01006** Identify the work and responsibilities of MORE technicians.

Skills Objectives

After reading this chapter, you will be able to:

- **S01001** Perform a pre-start and walk-around inspection of wheeled equipment.

▶ Introduction

For the past 10 years, the mobile off-road heavy equipment industry has had an annual growth rate of close to 6% worldwide. The equipment which includes a vast variety of machines ranging from bulldozers, pavers, excavators, backhoes, wheel loaders, graders, agricultural tractors, cranes, and forklifts is expected to have an 8.9% annual growth from 2015 to 2020 (**FIGURE 1-1**). Mining and material-handling equipment sales are expected to be even higher. And loaders, used primarily to move earth, are expected to account for more than 44% of the 2020 market revenue growth. The spinoff of such growth is an increased in demand for heavy equipment technicians. As new equipment is purchased to build our transportation infrastructure, extract resources, increase farm production, or refurbish old buildings, more technicians with an even greater array of skill sets are needed to service new technology.

▶ Skills and Responsibilities of MORE Technicians

K01006

Many skills useful just a few years ago are now outdated as new machine technologies to increase driver safety, comfort, machine productivity, and reliability are creating new competencies for technicians to adopt. Just a few examples of technological advancements include the use of machine telematics to monitor and control machine operations from a distance, advanced engine emission, fuel and control systems, and GPS guidance used by self-steering, autonomous and semi-autonomous driverless machines systems. Radical changes are taking place in the operation and control of hydraulic systems; the use of hybrid propulsion systems and advanced energy saving are some other technological

FIGURE 1-1 Example of the variety of equipment classified as off-road heavy duty using mobile hydraulic systems.

You Are the Mobile Heavy Equipment Technician

While performing a routine chassis lubrication of a wheel loader used in an underground mining operation, the shift crew leader announced it was time for a short work break. To keep your lever-operated hand-held grease gun clean while on break, you wrapped the gun in a cloth shop rag. To make sure you didn't misplace the grease gun, you then temporarily stored it inside the engine compartment since the access doors were open. However, while resting on your break, a supervisor walked by, noticed the grease gun, and reprimanded you for placing the grease gun where you thought it would be secure. Reflecting on the incident days and months later, you better appreciated the seriousness of the incident if the machine had been moved or you inadvertently left the grease gun in the engine compartment.

1. What might have happened to the grease gun and rag if they were left in the area of the engine compartment?
2. How different would a fire in the engine compartment of an underground equipment be compared to one above ground?
3. Is it likely that an operator pre-start inspection would have discovered a misplaced grease gun wrapped in a rag?

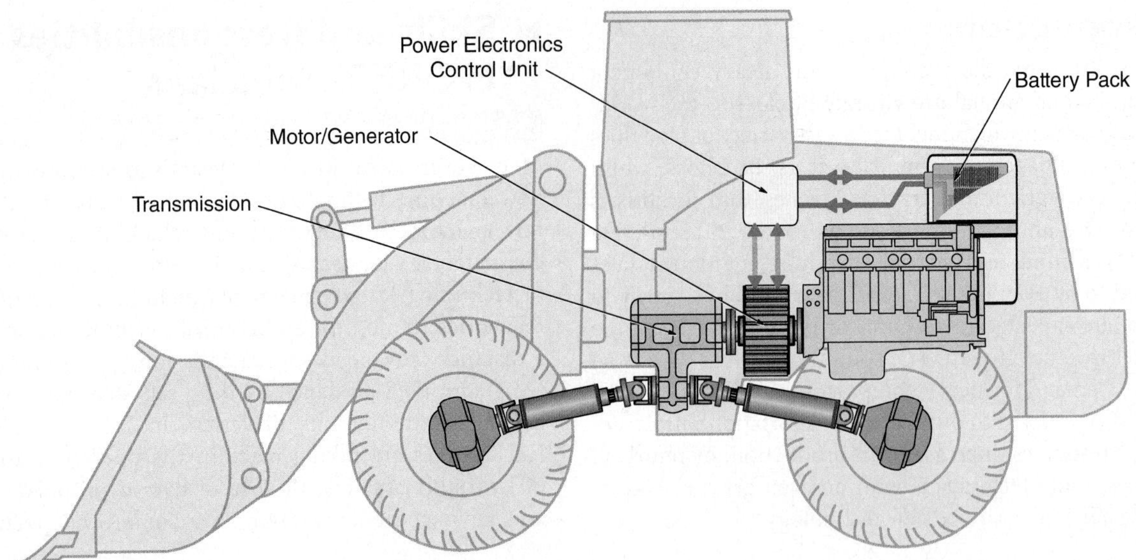

FIGURE 1-2 Hybrid machines such as this loader utilize an electric motor between the engine and transmission reducing both fuel consumption and emissions.

trends that technicians must master alongside traditional technologies (**FIGURE 1-2**). To meet these challenges, this chapter intends to help technicians begin to understand the field of off-road equipment service. It will identify what features help define off-road equipment to bring some order to the wide range of machines comprising the industry. Major technological milestones of the off-road equipment industry and factors that shape equipment design are also surveyed to provide a foundation for details of equipment construction and operation presented in later chapters. Finally, the chapter outlines heavy-duty (HD) off-road technician job descriptions and what expectations technicians can have in the industry.

▶ Pre-start Safety Inspection

K01005, S01001

It's important to ensure that whenever any machine is about to be used, it is mechanically safe and capable of performing the job it's designated to do. In fact, occupational health and safety laws in every jurisdiction require a procedure for inspecting, testing, and maintaining the safe operation of a vehicle on a daily basis. Furthermore, records must be kept of each inspection, including any notes made to identify items requiring maintenance actions. Each employee that uses a piece of equipment must perform a pre-start on that piece of equipment. This includes technicians. If a proper pre-start inspection was not performed, whoever was using the machine could be responsible for injuring themselves or someone else. Also, in some jurisdictions, it is a serious matter if a workplace safety inspector noted a defect with the equipment and a record on an inspection sheet or card was not made. To prevent the likelihood of a serious injury, fatality, or the loss of productivity due to equipment break down, it is important to first learn how to perform a pre-start inspection. These usually take 10 to 15 minutes depending on the type of equipment. Any user of the machine must also be properly trained to use the equipment and understand what is required to be inspected on the equipment. Generally, the steps outlined in **SKILL DRILL 1-1** are incorporated into all pre-start inspections.

SKILL DRILL 1-1 Pre-start Inspection

1. Inspect the area around the machines for:
   - tripping hazards
   - overhead hazards (i.e., loose rock, wires).

   Place at least two wheel chocks around the machine tires or track or ensure wheel chocks are in place. Stop and correct any hazards before proceeding further. If hazards cannot be corrected, they must be somehow controlled and noted on a safety inspection sheet or card.
2. Perform a visual circle check. Walk around the unit and check for:
   - damaged or worn parts/wires
   - wheel chocks
   - seat belts
   - housekeeping cleanliness
   - tire wear/pressure (visually)
   - fire hazards
   - overall condition of the unit.

   Check also that all parts, accessories, attachments, handles, and so on are attached in place and that nothing has come loose:
   - wheel nuts
   - hoses
   - electrical connections

SKILL DRILL 1-1 Pre-start Inspection (Continued)

- fire extinguisher
- fire suppression device.

Flammable materials near engine components create a high potential for fire, jeopardizing the safety of fellow workers, increasing downtime, and damaging to equipment. Make sure there are no dirty rags, lunch bags, spray paint cans, aerosol cans of any kind, or newspapers on the machine.

3. Check all levels, such as oil, coolant, and fuel levels. If the machine uses an automatic lubrication system, check the level of grease in the reservoir.
4. Start the equipment and inspect:
   - all lights
   - horns
   - temperatures/pressure gauges, and
   - other information systems.

   Record the hour meter reading on your pre-start checklist.
5. Perform another circle inspection while the equipment is running, and check for:
   - leaking hoses
   - leaking fuel lines
   - missing or damaged lights.
6. Test all operating systems:
   - back-up alarms
   - braking systems
   - steering
   - hoisting or hydraulic systems.

   After the machine has started and is being used, be aware of any changes in machine condition. For example, has the machine struck any object or been struck? Does the sound of the engine seem different? Are there any unusual smells? Are there any unusual noises or vibrations?

▶ What Is Mobile Off-Road Heavy Equipment?

K01002

Heavy equipment is a general term referring to a spectacularly diverse category of vehicles, operated off of roads and highways with purpose-built designs to perform a wide variety of industrial tasks. While the equipment may share many features of on-road vehicles constructed primarily to transport people and goods at high speeds, mobile, off-road heavy equipment functions in broad, non-transportation industry sectors, such as earth moving, mining, agriculture, construction, forestry, landscaping, and material handling. This category of machinery is also known by various other terms, such as heavy machine, heavy hydraulics, mobile hydraulics, construction equipment, or engineering equipment, and both rail and marine equipment are sometimes included in this category. A more authoritative definition for off-road equipment is provided by the Code of Federal Regulations (CFR), developed in the United States. This administrative legislation governing transportation defines off-road equipment as a vehicle having attached components designed to work in an off-road environment or designed to operate at low speeds, making them unsuitable for normal highway operation. Unloaded vehicle speeds should not exceed 45 mph, and there should be no capacity to carry occupants other than the driver and operating crew. In addition to those qualifications needed to classify a machine as off-road, the CFR adds that the machine may have at least one axle with a gross axle weight rating (GAWR) of 29,000 pounds or more and operates with limited speed (**FIGURES 1-3** and **1-4**). Note that recreational and sport utility vehicles that operate off-road would not fit this description and are regulated by different legislation.

FIGURE 1-3 The bulldozer is a classic example of an off-road machine. Its slow speed, capacity to move heavy loads, and use of tracks to navigate off-road terrain align with a definition of off-road heavy-duty equipment.

FIGURE 1-4 The mini-excavator, while not heavy in comparison to other off-road equipment, fits the CFR definition for off-road equipment.

While diverse in countless ways such as size, power, weight, function, and application, three things are distinctive about the off-road category of mobile equipment:

1. The use of fluid power attachments
Most types of off-road equipment use fluid power systems to operate equipment attached to the vehicle. **Fluid power** refers to both air and hydraulic systems transferring power to machine implements and accessories that perform the cutting, lifting, dragging, paving, sweeping, pushing, drilling, pumping, loading, digging, and dumping actions that off-road equipment is specifically designed for. Fluid power systems will use actuators that convert the energy in hydraulic fluid or compressed air into mechanical movement (**FIGURE 1-5**). Movement can be linear or rotational. Cylinders containing pistons are a common example of a linear actuator. Buckets, blades, harvesters, shovels, rippers, vibrating rollers, compacters, lifting forks, and brooms are just a few examples of equipment attached to off-road machines that use linear or rotary actuators (**FIGURE 1-6**). These additional accessories or implements create additional and unique power demands on the machine's engine not typically found in on-highway equipment, where the engine is used primarily for propulsion.
Fluid power not only operates equipment implements but also transfer force developed by the engine or electric motor to move the machinery. For example, engine-driven hydraulic pumps commonly supply the hydrostatic drive or hydraulic motors used by propulsion systems. The term **hydrostatic** refers to the transfer of energy through hydraulic fluids through flow and pressure (**FIGURE 1-7**). This is different from **hydrodynamic** systems, which convert kinetic energy contained in the hydraulic flow into mechanical movement. A fluid coupling, also known as a hydrodynamic clutch, is an example of a hydrodynamic device. Compressed air distribution systems are installed in underground mines to operate compressed air drive motors and implements. With the absence of electric sparks and noxious engine emissions, compressed air minimizes health and safety hazards to workers and the risk of explosion due to hazards from combustible gases and dust.
2. They are mobile
Off-road propulsion systems are unique and specially adapted to the operating terrain and other ground conditions where they are used. Soft, uneven, rugged ground conditions encountered while working in farm fields, forests, mines, or quarries or on an earth-moving project means that not only is the machine designed to maneuver well and supply extra traction force for moving loads but also that it should not sink or slip. Steering systems will commonly supply additional maneuverability in confined spaces. The work required of forklifts where the rear axle steers, or articulated loaders, are examples of a machine design adaptation for improved maneuverability (**FIGURE 1-8**). **Differential steering** (or skid steering), where one track will turn at a different speed than the other, provides even the largest machines with exceptional

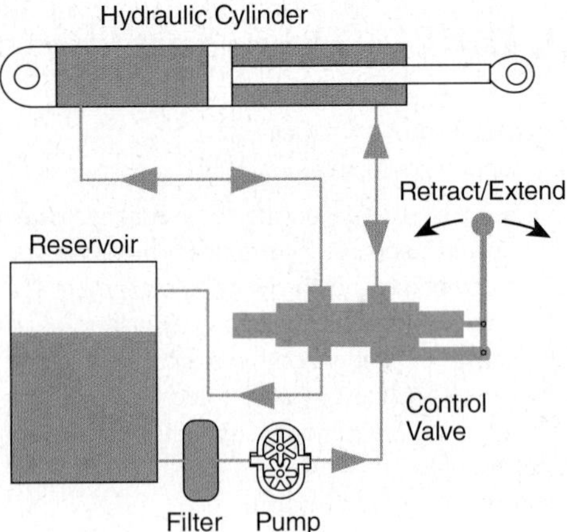

FIGURE 1-5 A simple hydraulic circuit. Actuators are devices that convert the energy of pressurized oil or air into movement. The hydraulic cylinder is an example of a linear actuator.

Changing Direction of Oil Flow to Control Valve

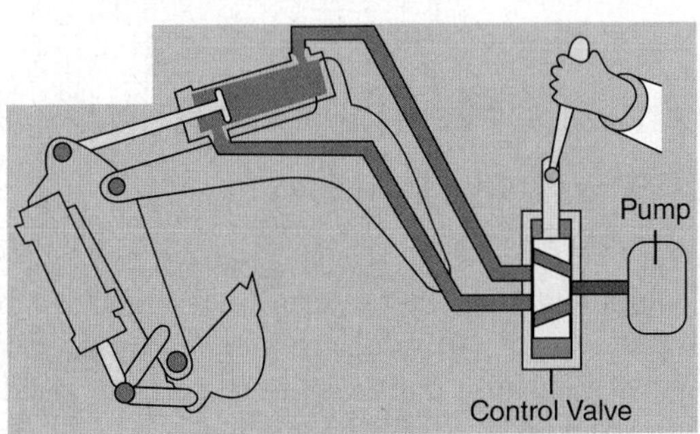

No Movement

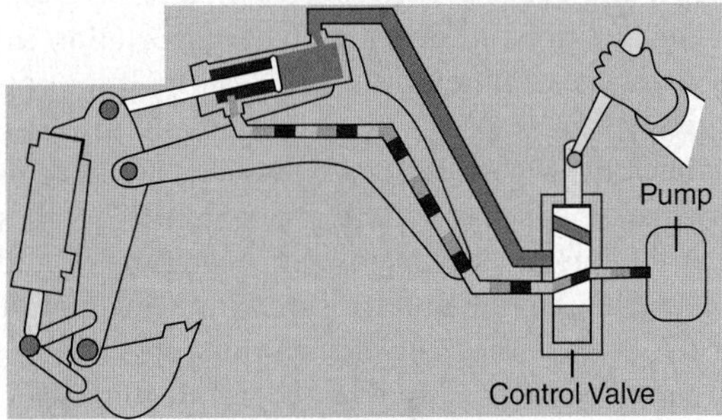

Retract Up

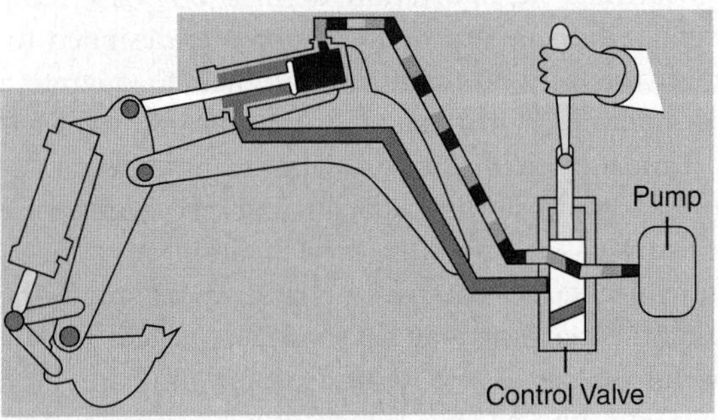

Push Down

FIGURE 1-6 Supplying pressurized oil to either side of the piston in this linear actuator causes the bucket to lift or lower.

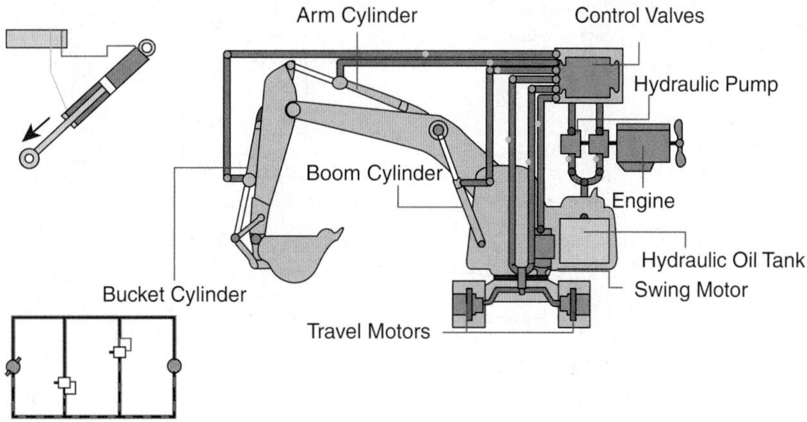

FIGURE 1-7 Hydraulic motors or travel motors are used to propel this excavator. "Hydrostatic drive" is the technical term given to rotary actuators used for a machine travel system. All other operations of the excavator are controlled using hydraulic devices.

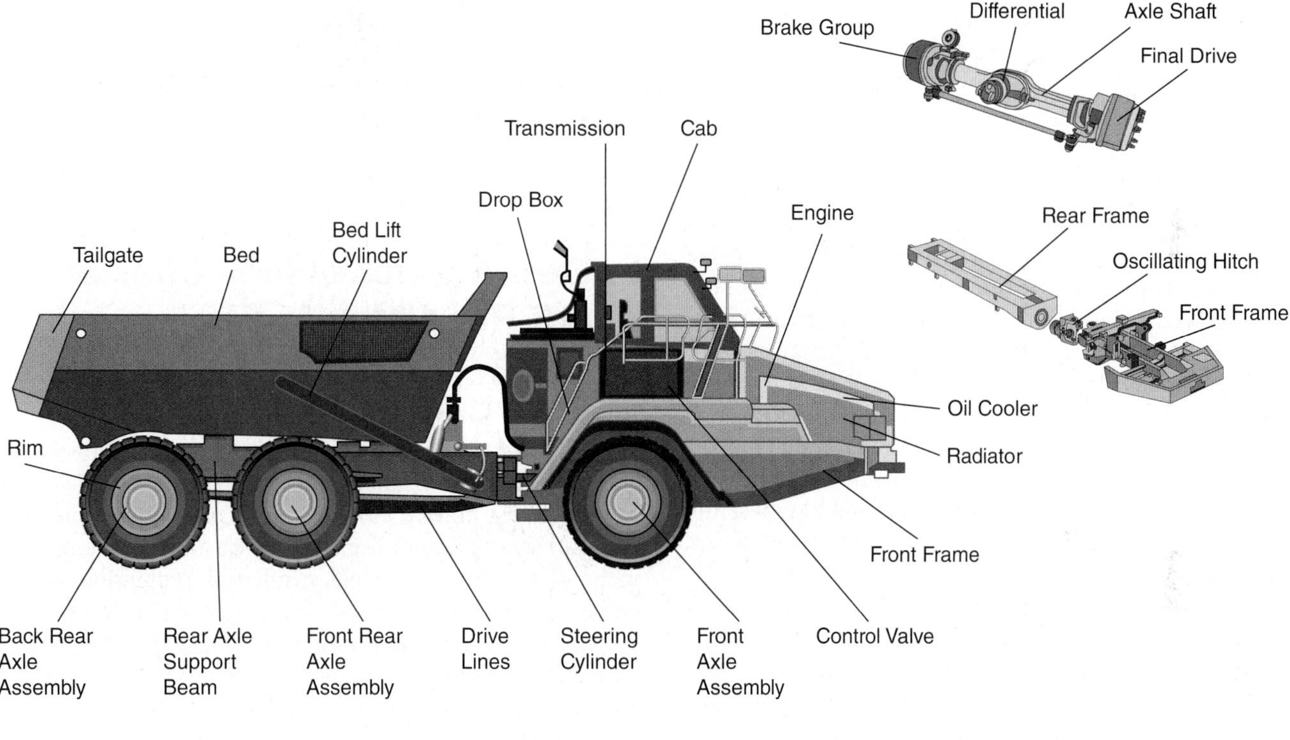

FIGURE 1-8 An articulated dump bends or articulates between the dump box and the cab. Bending gives the vehicle extra maneuverability around obstacles.

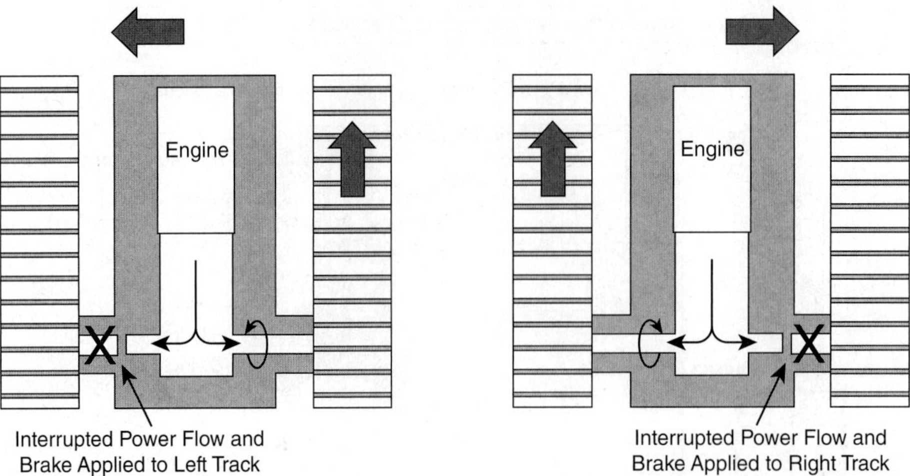

FIGURE 1-9 Differential steering, sometimes called skid steering, applies drive torque to one track while braking or reversing the direction of the opposite track.

maneuverability (**FIGURE 1-9**). Off-road vehicles are often stationary when working, and they infrequently exceed 10 mph or 6 km/hour when traveling.

3. They are self-powered
Off-road equipment is made mobile by drivetrain or propulsion systems, which are electric, hydraulic, or mechanical. In mechanical systems, a geared transmission, drive belts, or chains are used to transmit torque to wheels or the track undercarriage. Hydraulic force rotates drive motors in hydrostatic drive systems or couples engines with transmissions using torque converters or fluid clutches. Electric motors are more commonly used in emission-sensitive work environments such as underground mining or power lift equipment where exhaust from engines can harm workers. Hybrid electric drive systems have recently been developed and are used in excavators and bulldozers to reduce fuel consumption.

The term **prime mover** is a technical term that describes the principal device used to produce mechanical energy in off-road equipment, propelling the machine and supplying specialized equipment attachments. For example, a machine powered with only electricity to operate a motor would have its electric motor designated the prime mover. A diesel engine's high torque output, low fuel consumption, durability, and relatively low maintenance requirements make this energy source the prime mover of choice for HD off-road machines.

SAFETY TIP—Why Is HD Off-Road Equipment Painted Yellow?

Various colors and graphical symbols are used in many places on off-road equipment. Operating control symbols, instrumentation, and specific colors are used to designate functions or hazards in a universal language. The correct color can provide immediate information and warnings of hazards that are essential to work safety. Yellow is a color designated by OSHA—Occupational Health and Safety—as the basic color that should warn anyone and encourage them to exercise additional caution, and it marks physical hazards such as striking against, stumbling, falling, tripping, and "caught in between." Yellow is also one of the most visible colors in low light situations.

▶ Development Milestones of Off-Road Mobile Equipment

K01001

Internal Combustion Engines

The off-road heavy equipment industry is a relatively new enterprise. Until the beginning of the 1900s the use of machines to dredge, dig, thresh, plow, lift, haul, and reshape the natural landscape could not begin in earnest without the development of two key technologies: off-road propulsion systems and a mobile source of power. With the introduction of steam engines and later internal combustion engines such as the diesel engine, the centuries-old practice of using animal power to pull equipment, and humans to operate hand shovels or wheelbarrows, gave way to the use of far more powerful and increasingly sophisticated machines. Untethered from the need for wind power, water wheels, or even the use of animals, evolving engine technology at the turn of the last century dramatically accelerated the development of this new category of machines. Engines provided power to not only move the machines around off-road worksites but also to operate cables and fluid power systems for unique, purpose-built machines used to perform specialized jobs. Increasing engine power output provided the torque to perform more work in less time, multiplying machine efficiency. Using fluid power principles can produce extreme mechanical advantage which when harnessed, multiplies the mechanical power of an engine (**FIGURE 1-10**). For example, just under nine horsepower of hydraulic power is needed to lift five tons a height of one foot in three seconds (**FIGURE 1-11**).

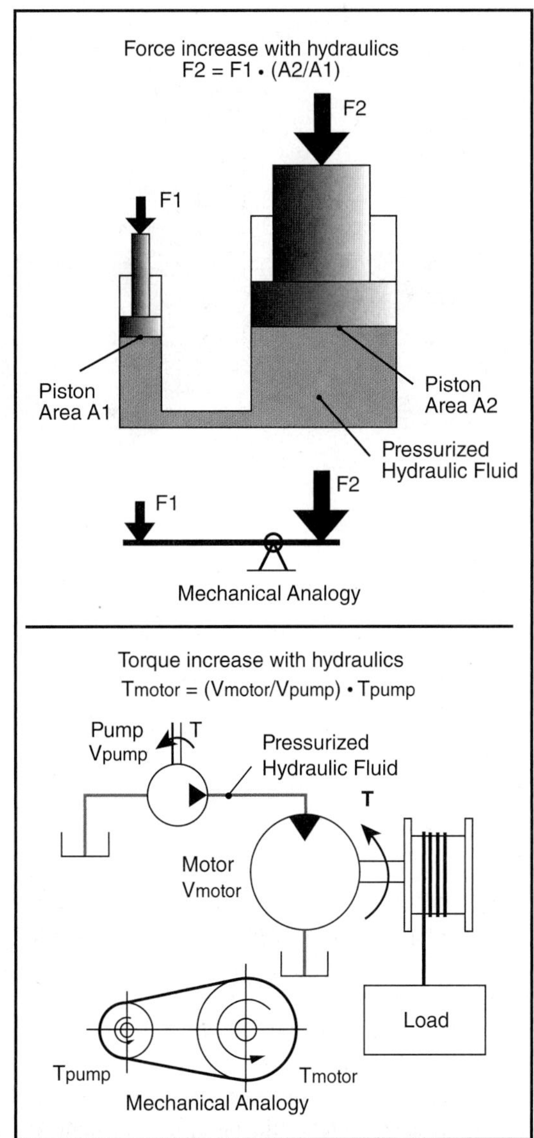

FIGURE 1-10 Note that using a small amount of force acting on the smaller piston's surface area can multiply the force exerted by the larger piston. The use of hydraulics enables the use of a high ratio of mechanical advantage.

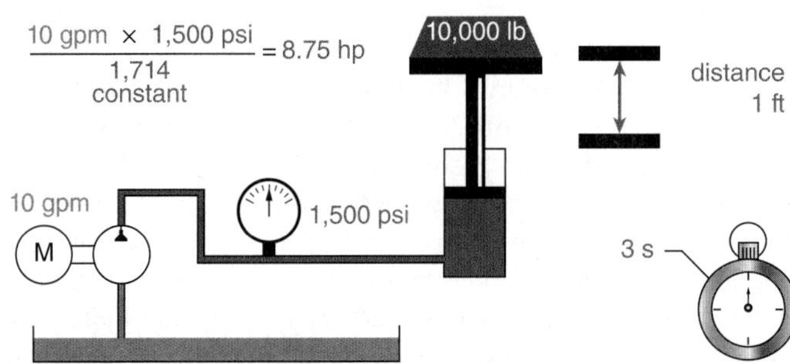

FIGURE 1-11 Calculating the conversion of horsepower to hydraulic power.

Track Undercarriage

Unique propulsion systems that have been better adapted to off-road use were a second major development that greatly advanced the evolution of mobile equipment. Off-road machinery is not designed to travel long distances carrying goods and people. Instead, the equipment typically moves more slowly over ground conditions such as farm fields, forests, mines, snow, mud, gravel, and rock and in loose dirt. Often requiring enormous traction force to push, carry, or dump heavy loads in these rugged, uneven terrains, equipment mobility is enhanced by transmitting traction force through continuous track-type or specialized wheeled-drive systems. Tracked machines, or crawlers as they are sometime called, are the best propulsion system for traveling over soft, loose, uneven ground conditions. Tracked equipment uses long rubber belts or linked metal plates called **track shoes** connected to produce a caterpillar-like movement (**FIGURE 1-12**). Track system components are collectively called the track **undercarriage**, which uses long rolling track to distribute heavy machine weight over a wide track shoe or belt width. Track systems have much more surface area in contact with the ground than the contact patch that wheeled equipment has equipment has with its use of rubber tires mounted on metal wheel rims. Multiplying track dimensions of width and length and then dividing the weight of even the heaviest of machines illustrates that a tracked machine has the advantage of providing lower **ground pressure**, which can easily be less than 10 psi. Low ground pressure track is better adapted to soft fertile soils of rich farmland and forests or to loose, soggy dirt and gravel. Not only would heavy machinery using track systems not easily sink, but the greater track surface area brought about by using the cleat-like features on track shoes and belts also provides greater traction force. These cleat like features found in track shoes are called **grouser** bars.

The first commercial continuous track vehicle was a steam-powered log hauler demonstrated in England in 1901. Just a few years later, Benjamin Holt purchased the patent rights for the track system and immediately applied the technology to tractors cultivating California farmland in the United States.

FIGURE 1-12 The track drive undercarriage on this bulldozer links metal track shoes together into a continuously rotating belt, which is used to propel the machine and provide additional traction force.

This early adopter of track drive undercarriage founded the Holt Manufacturing Company to produce tractors used for farming. In time, World War I British soldiers dubbed tanks using Holt's steel track drives Holt's tracked machines "caterpillars" because of the comparable movement of track drive propulsion. The name caterpillar stuck to Holt's equipment, which was later used when Holt merged with another company, the C.L. Best Tractor and formed Caterpillar Company in 1925. The versatility of tractors to navigate soft, churned ground encountered in logging and road-building operations led to the development of the military tank in World War I. During that conflict, Winston Churchill conceived of the idea of weaponizing the tractors while watching them haul equipment and supplies. Since that time, track drive propulsion became widely used by a huge variety of off-road machinery—in particular, by bulldozers.

Wide Base Pneumatic Tires

While many types of equipment use steel or rubber-belt continuous tracks systems to travel over severe service ground conditions, tires are used where higher speed or mobility is required. That development couldn't take place until the 1930s, when pneumatic tires were introduced. The first application of pneumatic tires for off-road equipment was in 1932 when an Allis Chalmers tractor in Waukesha Wisconsin had Firestone aircraft tires installed. Until then, the narrow, solid rubber tires used by on-road vehicles were quite useless. Wide steel or even wooden wheels with cleat-like projections were used instead of tires on tractors until specialized tire production got underway. However, since first being used on agricultural tractors in the 1930s, wide base pneumatic tires have become the dominant traction device for agricultural tractors and implements. Pneumatic tires' superior speed, maneuverability, and reliability in comparison to track drive undercarriage make them the preferred choice for agriculture applications. Rubber tires also demonstrate a 45% fuel economy advantage over slower moving, high-friction track drives. Newer rubber track systems, having many of the same advantages offered by metal track systems, are now ending the dominance of pneumatic tires in that category, enabling track drive to overcome the higher maintenance and initial acquisition cost associated with track undercarriage.

When using **ballast**, off-road tires offer more stability, which helps to prevent tire slippage in various soil conditions and to lower a machine's center of gravity (**FIGURE 1-13**). In addition to inflating the tire with air, adding ballast involves filling the tire to between 40% and 75% full with a liquid that will not freeze—or filling it with a denser mixture of water and calcium chloride slurry, providing even more weight. When used on equipment with tall tires and high axle clearances, the additional ballast helps prevent vehicle tipping. When filled with ballast, heavier tires are less prone to slipping, spinning, hopping, or axles lifting off the ground. The load-bearing capabilities of tires filled with ballast increases substantially over tires filled with only air.

Tire design for off-road equipment categorizes tires by service. Tread types are differentiated for use on hard-packed, soft, smooth, and rocky ground surfaces (**FIGURE 1-14**). Depending on the load they must support and the terrain encountered, each type of slow-moving equipment will have a unique tire designation.

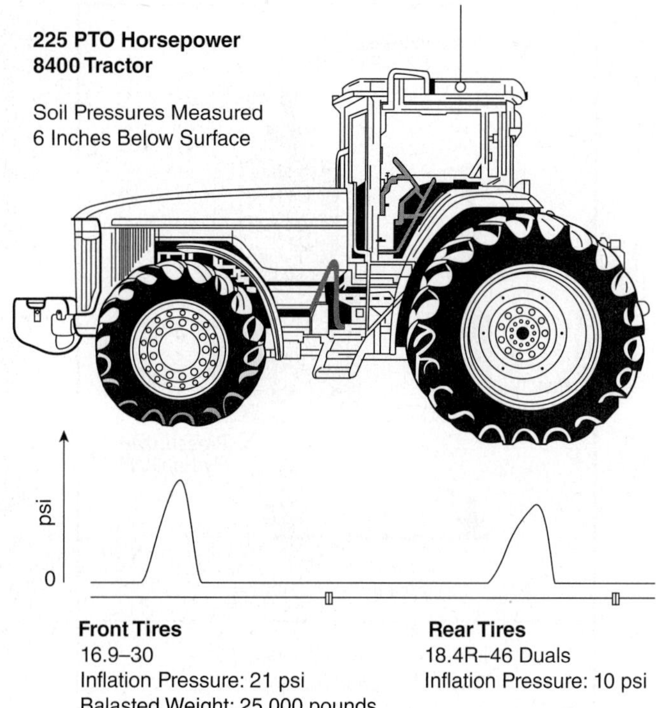

FIGURE 1-13 Tire ballast in these four tires is close to 12.5 tons. Ballast helps stabilize high center of gravity machines to prevent tipping and prevents tire slippage.

Replacement of Cable Systems with Mobile Hydraulic Systems

A third major technological development driving the evolution and sophistication of off-road machinery is the addition of hydraulic systems. Hydraulic systems on mobile equipment are used to transfer and control power on a wide variety attachments and implements. While hydraulic systems appear universal everywhere today, it wasn't until the 1960s that construction and agricultural equipment began to switch from using cable-operated systems. Bulldozer blades and excavator buckets all relied on winches and wire ropes that used mechanical clutches (**FIGURE 1-15**). Some older, lighter equipment relied on operators using tiresome hand cranks to manipulate cables. Development of new materials to fabricate hydraulic hoses such as nitrile rubber compatible with mineral oils was the first breakthrough to enable the use of mobile hydraulic systems. Water as a hydraulic medium corroded metals, and friction between seals and linear actuators quickly led to leaky seals. Steam had an identical problem. However, in the early 1950s, French equipment manufacturer Poclain and other European equipment manufactures introduced the first fully hydraulically operated machines.

Initial resistance to the use of hydraulics was high. The usefulness of hydraulic power was first demonstrated in 1936 on a Deere tractor. The mechanical rockshaft, a three-point hitch device connecting tractors to implements such as plows

	Surface	Tread form
(a)	Hard surfaces such as roads	Large area, shallow tread with "high" pressure
(b)	Normal agricultural work, dry soil	Heavy, intermediate depth tread
(c)	Soft, wet agricultural soils	Deep tread
(d)	Lawns, low sinkage is required	Wide, low pressure
(e)	Dry soil, heavy loads as in earthmoving	Tracks, as on a "crawler" tractor
(f)	Saturated, puddled soils	Metal cage, with angled lugs, alone or as extensions to normal tyres

FIGURE 1-14 Examples and applications of tread design used for off-road equipment applications.

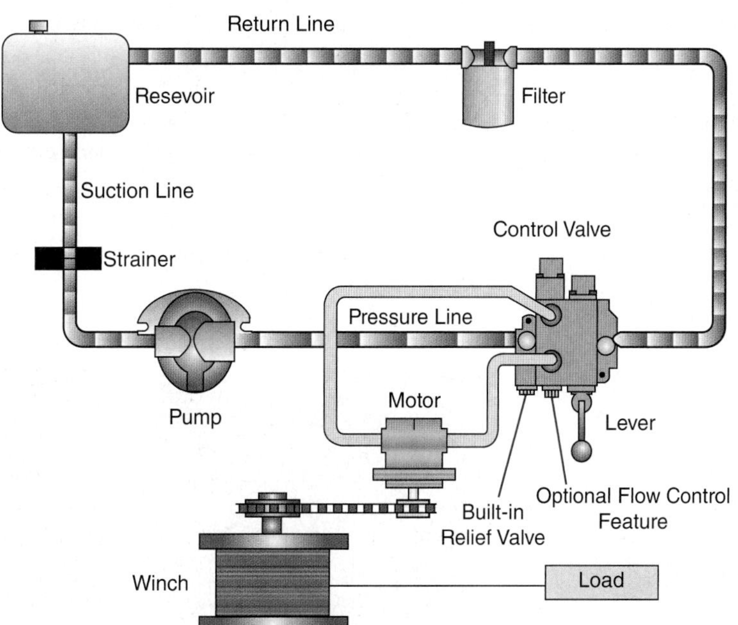

FIGURE 1-15 Hydraulic circuits replaced cable-operated movements of buckets blades. Instead of using a mechanical clutch, this cable winch is driven by a hydraulic motor.

or seeders, was replaced with a hydraulic rockshaft. The configuration provided a variable height and could change the angle of the implement relative to the tractor. The value of this hydraulic powered lifting device compelled all manufacturers to provide this feature, but the use of hydraulics did not quickly extend to other accessories. Problems with the earliest mobile hydraulic systems slowed rapid adoption of hydraulically operated implements and attachments. For example, early hydraulic hoses were prone to bursting, and operators perceived the first leaky hydraulic machines as dirty and underpowered. In addition to the need to constantly top up oil reservoirs due to oil loss through leakage, components operating in dusty, dirty conditions wore out quickly. This happened primarily because hydraulic systems required high filtering efficiency of hydraulic fluid to prevent premature system failures (**FIGURE 1-16**).

A second reason for slow adoption was that simple cable-machine designs combining levers, pulleys, gears, wheels, and inclined planes were still relatively easy to repair and powerful enough for most of the jobs at hand. The development of more sophisticated and innovative hydraulic systems with more must-have features drove change. For example, hydraulic cylinders enabled the application of a down force on a dozer blade for digging, rather than depending on gravity. Hydraulics' ability to transfer power through pipes and tubes to linear and rotary actuators led to equipment designs that became much more powerful, productive, efficient, and durable. A greater degree of machine control for raising and lowering implements also became possible, allowing greater precision while manipulating grader and dozer blades. Rotary power for functions such as fans, augers, saws, drills, and other traction motors could be introduced. Subsequent to refinements overcoming problems with early systems, operators rapidly adopted mobile hydraulics when they observed how blades, buckets, and booms could be moved more quickly and operated with greater force than what sluggish cables could manage.

The Advantages of Fluid Power Systems

Unleashed, the versatility and sophistication of mobile hydraulic systems has grown dramatically. Because chains, cables, sheaves, drums, friction clutches, gears, and hoisting engines were eliminated, equipment design could be simplified. In an excavator, the four cylinders that controlled the boom or stick and bucket are controlled by two joysticks today, and the operator's hand movements on each lever are instantly and accurately duplicated at the bucket. Early hydraulic systems operated with simple fixed-displacement gear pumps only actuated a single cylinder. Today, multiple hydraulic functions take place simultaneously, using vastly more efficient variable pressure and variable volume pumps. Early systems used hydraulic pressures topping out at 2,000 to 2,500 psi. High-energy flow losses took place when continuously pressurized hydraulic liquids converted pressure into heat using spring-loaded pressure-relief valves. Today, pressure-compensating and load-sensing hydraulic systems using variable displacement hydraulic pumps operate much more efficiently, using less fuel. Since the pumps supply only enough oil to maintain maximum system pressure, fuel

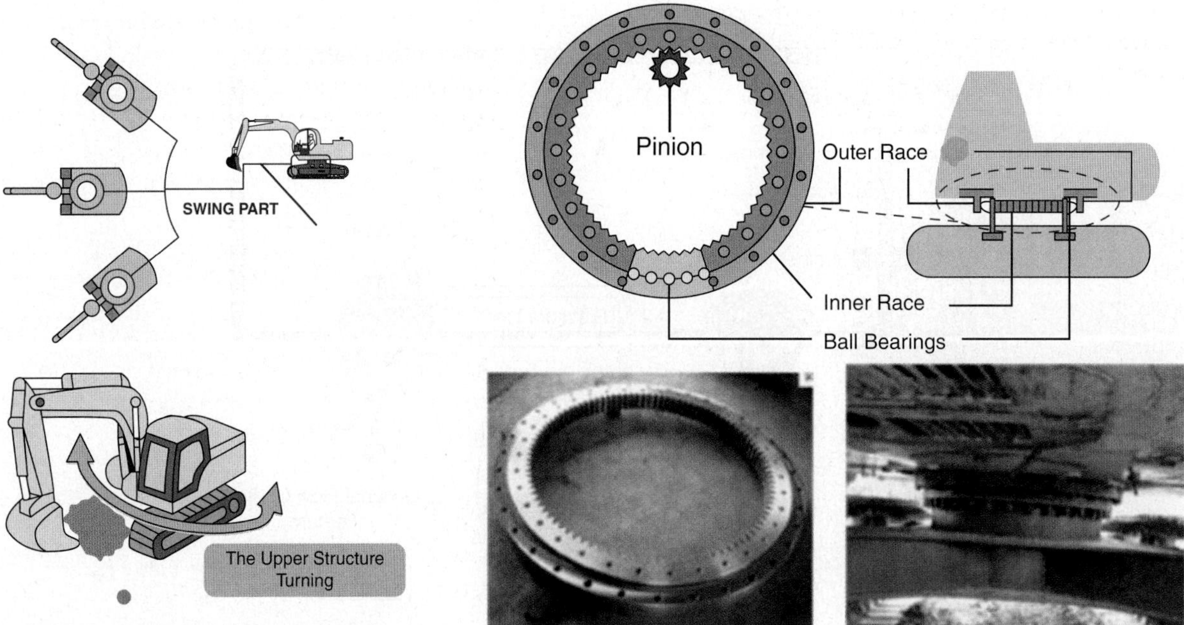
Swing Mechanism
Outer race fixed at upper structure turns with the "Pinion" that spins along with the inner race fixed at the lower structure.
The part between the outer Race and the inner Race turns smoothly on the ball bearings.
SWING PART
Pinion
Outer Race
Inner Race
Ball Bearings
The Upper Structure Turning

FIGURE 1-16 The earliest machines to convert to hydraulics were excavators. The upper house or structure rotates using a worm gear–driven slewing ring.

or electric energy is not wasted operating the hydraulic pump since excess fluid flow is not relieved and returned to a reservoir hydraulic pressure and returning it to a reservoir. Today, typical hydraulic systems on an excavator operates between 5,000 and 6,000 psi through smaller components operating with tighter tolerances. With higher pressures, the pistons in hydraulic cylinders and other actuators can move more quickly. Increased pressure and power enable machines like excavators or loaders to apply higher pressure to dig quickly in very hard ground. Tighter tolerances allow less dirt into the system and improve system durability. Hydraulic-powered attachments such as concrete breakers, grapple hooks, or augers are rapidly attached to equipment using hydraulic quick couplers, which connect and disconnect a sealing lock ring at a hose end to simplify attachment mounting (**FIGURES 1-17** and **1-18**).

FIGURE 1-17 This hydraulically operated plate packer attaches to a skid-steer loader. Hydraulic quick connectors are used to connect the hydraulic system.

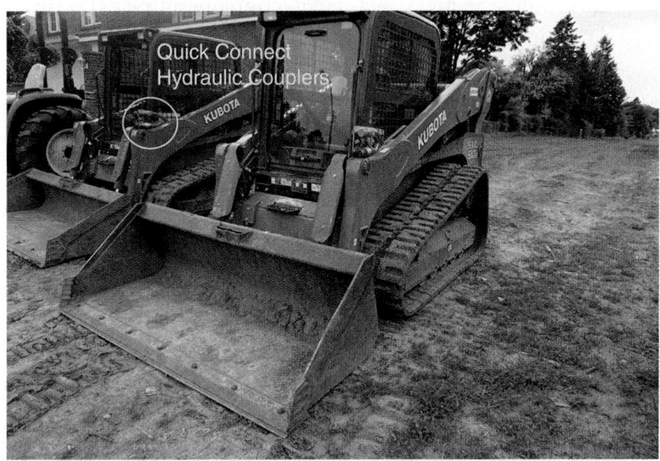

FIGURE 1-18 The quick connector on this skid-steer loader helps attach various implements, such as rotating brooms, hammers, brush cutters, or grapplers.

Smart Iron refers to machines operating with sophisticated electrohydraulic control systems. Hydraulic pumps with a programmable electronic control unit (ECU) have user interface software that allows technicians to quickly set up pump-specific parameters and make calibrated adjustments for machine behavior.

Onboard communication networks, which connect all of a machine's electronic control units to exchange information, introduce new levels of safety, efficiency, and enable the use of customizable features. These onboard networks have enabled the use of advanced telematics for communication between machines and remote monitoring at locations where real-time monitoring of the equipment operation takes place. Self-steering machines and both semi-autonomous and fully autonomous machinery are made possible using onboard network communication between control units for machine hydraulics, steering, engine, powertrain, and implements.

Mobile hydraulic systems offer a long list of advantages:

- Simplified operation—fluid power systems eliminate complex mechanical systems composed of cables gears, chains, belts, and camshafts.
- Long service life, which is the result of hydraulic fluid lubricating components and acting as a cooling medium.
- High horsepower-to-weight ratio—a 5 hp hydraulic motor can easily be held in the palm of your hand, whereas a 5 hp electric motor could weigh 40 lb (18.2 kg).
- Simplified system design—a single hydraulic pump or air compressor can supply power to many cylinders, rotary motors, or other actuators.
- Actuator force or rotational torque can be held constant.
- Pneumatic and hydraulic motors can produce high torque while operating at low rotational speeds without overheating.
- Safer operation in hazardous environments since they operate spark-free.
- An ability to tolerate high temperatures.
- Equipment and operator safety due to rapid-acting overload protection by means of pressure-relief valve.
- Simple displays of load force using a line pressure measurement device.
- Variable speed adjustment to machine drive speeds using hydrostatics and the capability to instantly reverse direction of movement.

Examining the differences between pneumatic and hydraulic systems, it can be noted that while air is capable of transmitting high force and torque, it has an advantage when used for rapid-acting, repetitive applications where direction of movement is frequently reversed. Since compressed air can absorb shock loads with a cushioning effect, it supplies a gentler and smoother application force in comparison to hydraulic or electromechanical actuators. Pneumatic systems can also provide improved control and precision when pressing or squeezing. Pneumatic systems cannot provide as high a force as hydraulic fluid can.

▶ Off-Road Machine Design

K01003

Demand for Equipment Productivity

The benefits of labor-saving productivity provided by off-road machines are impossible to overestimate. Off-road machines have been crucial for the development of modern infrastructure enjoyed by today's civilization. Equipment development has enabled enormous social change to take place, releasing workers from agricultural settings and many other labor-intensive endeavors and allowing them to move into cities to engage in other occupations. Without the invention of the simple farm tractor and a myriad of agricultural implements accompanying its evolution, it's difficult to imagine that we would have the stable and secure food supplies that we have today. In fact, it can be effectively argued that most of today's off-road machines found across the wide spectrum of equipment industry groups have their origins in modified agricultural tractors. The broad industry groups using off-road equipment include the following:

- agriculture
- forestry
- earth moving
- mining
- material handling.

Within each of these groups are many smaller, specialized sectors. Earth moving, for example, shares common types of construction equipment used by industries such as road building, landscaping, landfill, demolition, drilling, pipe laying, paving, and others. Mining also uses many machines identical to those used in earth moving but with unique adaptions for its specialized operating conditions. The most significant factor driving differentiation of the basic machine design is a demand for productivity. **Productivity** is measured over the course of an **operating cycle** (**FIGURE 1-19**). A generic operating cycle for many machines, such as a loader, excavator, or even a forklift, consists of three parts: loading, transporting, and unloading the material. Productivity is calculated by measuring the amount of material carried per cycle and dividing it by the total cycle time. Stated another way, machine productivity is like an equation for calculating power: the amount of work performed, divided by the time it takes to complete the work. Improving job performance or productivity is accomplished by either increasing the load-carrying capacity or shortening the cycle time.

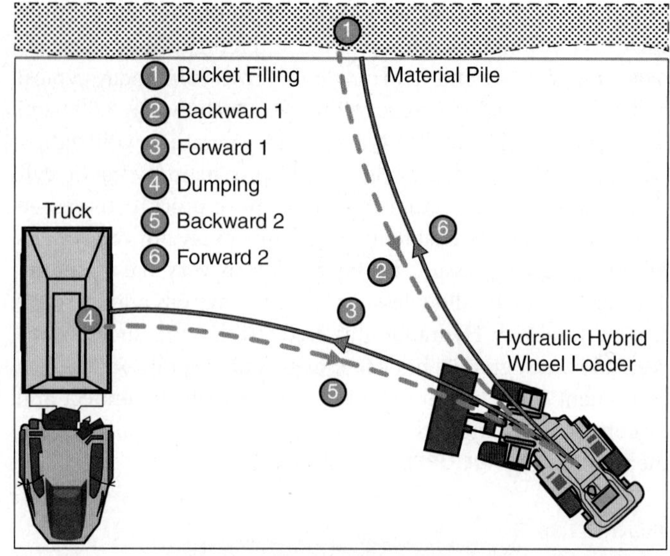

FIGURE 1-19 The operating cycle of a wheel loader consists of loading product into the bucket, traveling 25 meters backward, then 18 meters forward, and then unloading the material.

Other Factors Affecting Productivity

Since the evolution of off-road machines is driven primarily by productivity demands, various design features, implements, and accessories are integrated into purpose-built machines uniquely adapted for the operating conditions and tasks assigned to the machine (**FIGURE 1-20**). The following are some examples of factors influencing productivity:

1. Adding load carrying capacity of equipment is a major consideration. Bigger buckets and blades or wider tillers or mowers are examples of features to increase load-carrying abilities or the ability to do work. Clearly a larger cutting swath made by a wider mower blade will yield more productivity since more work is done during each pass through a field. However, load-carrying capacity puts further demands on the machine's power or engine size, frame, suspensions, tires, and so on.
2. Traction performance—machines depend on tires or track drive undercarriage to travel and navigate around obstacles. More work can be completed if the machine can push or pull greater weight or loads and/or move those loads faster. The terrain and the weight of the load are both considerations: Is it too soft for tires or hard enough to support the traction force of a machine and its weight?
3. Speed—the power of the prime mover, the choice of propulsion system, maneuverability, and the design of the accessories or implements used to cut, lift, grasp, or haul the load are among the many factors affecting operating cycle time. Anything that can get the job done faster will improve productivity. The use of more powerful hydraulic systems is an example of a feature that can further shorten the time needed to complete an operation.
4. Reliability, durability, and ease of maintenance—these factors are secondary to productivity demands but influence productivity since machines need to be available for as much up time or productive work as possible. These factors are significantly influenced by the skill of technicians and quality of maintenance programs.
5. Operator efficiency—the skill and ability of a machine's operator to remain focused on a task without fatigue can impact productivity. Improvements to cab layout and vehicle dynamic qualities can go a long way toward minimizing operator fatigue and to improving work safety while still increasing productivity. The ease of operation, quality of ride comfort, steering, instrument layout, suspensions, and

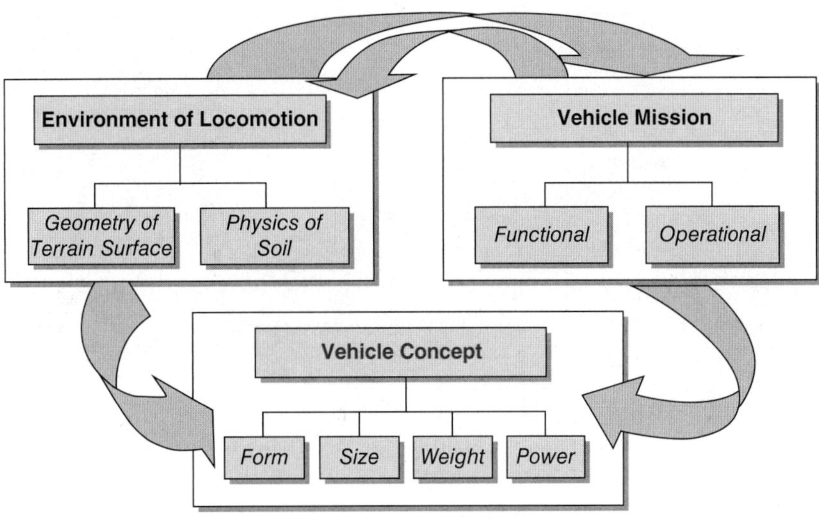

FIGURE 1-20 Factors influencing the design of off-road equipment.

cab environment may not be immediately thought of as important aspects of machine design, but they do affect an operator's ability to do a job well over a long shift. Being tired from stretching too far too frequently while operating controls; irritated due to poor sight lines, cab temperatures, dust, noise, or concern about risks to personal safety; distracted by the need to remain vigilant to too many warning lights, gauges, and awkwardly built levers, pedals, knobs, and switches definitely impacts machine productivity. The mandated use of **roll over protection systems (ROPSs)** and cab environment controls are not only essential to meet health and safety requirements for workers but can deeply affect how much work is performed by the end of the day.

Equipment Selection Factors

When selecting an off-road vehicle, the first question is where the machine will operate. Consider the following factors:

Maximum operating slope—a machine can be expected to operate anywhere from level ground to almost a vertical wall. If it must move up and down steep slopes, the torque applied through the wheels or track has to increase either through more powerful engines or through transmissions with greater mechanical advantages. If operated on steep slopes, the position of the machine's center of gravity must be considered to prevent overturning. Self-leveling cabs can extend the steepness of slope at which a machine operates. For example, in forest operations, tracked machines with self-leveling cabs are capable of operating on slopes up to 50% grade (**FIGURE 1-21**). Without self-leveling cabs, tracked equipment can operate on slopes up to 40%. Wheeled machines with higher centers of gravity should be restricted to slopes below 25%.

Obstacles—ground surface features, such as broken concrete, trees, landfill waste, boulders, stumps, logs, ditches, and mounds of material, can stop or slow a machine as it attempts to maneuver around the obstacle. Maneuvering will often require a small steering radius provided by steerable tires, skid-steer track, and articulated bodies, plus more traction force to account for steering resistances. If the distance between two obstacles is less than two vehicle lengths, it's best to adopt articulated steering. If obstacles such as boulders, stumps, or mounds of material are encountered, it's important that no interference between the obstacle and the bottom profile of the machine takes place that could cause a "hang-up" for a machine. Off-road vehicles may need to move at slow speeds through creeks or shallow ponds. Equipment should be designed to prevent water from entering or damaging any component of the vehicle.

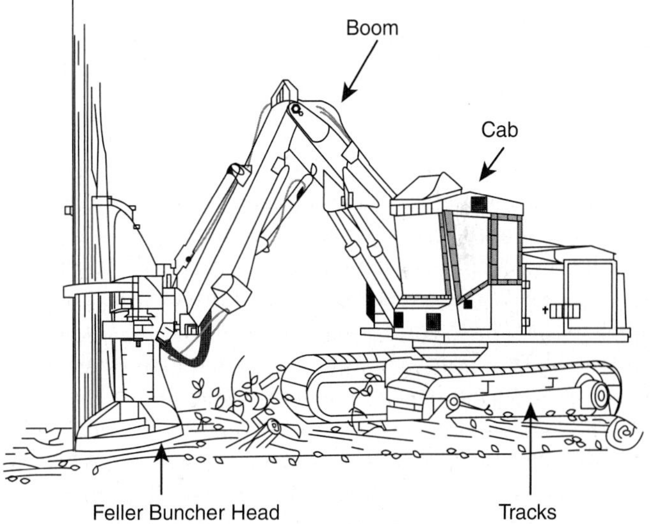

FIGURE 1-21 A common type of forest harvesting machine is a feller-buncher. It cuts and stacks tree trucks. These machines commonly use self-leveling cabs to operate on steeply sloped hill faces.

Driver visibility—several types of visibility are taken into account during vehicle design. Primary visibility refers to the operator's ability to see outside the cab in any direction, both near and far. Secondary visibility refers to how well the driver can monitor instruments and controls in the workplace and cab. Recognition distance or the distance a driver needs to recognize objects determines the maximum safe machine travel

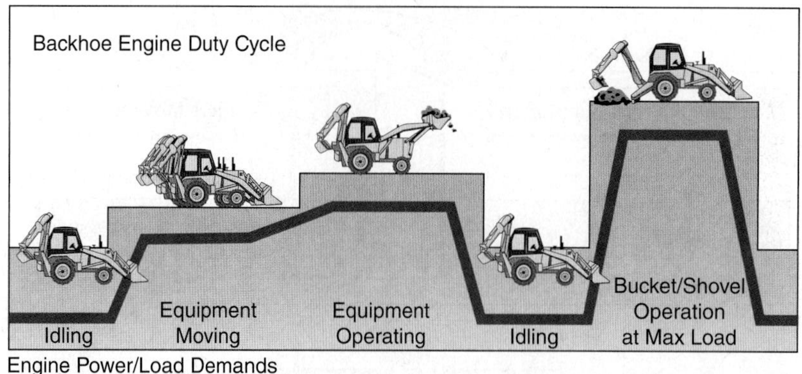

FIGURE 1-22 The engine operating cycle of a backhoe loader.

speed. Having a long recognition distance means lines of site and machine layout is particularly important for machines that travel fast. How fast a vehicle travels in turn influences the type and capacity of the braking system. Larger brakes with more safety features are needed by fast machines.

Engines—each off-road equipment application presents different mechanical and duty-cycle demands on the diesel engine (**FIGURE 1-22**). This variety of mechanical demands in turn requires a wide range of engines configured to power each different type of equipment. Engines will range in power from just 10 hp to thousands of horsepower. For example, Caterpillar's smallest mini-excavator weighs just over 1 ton at 2,060 lb (930 kg) and uses a 13 hp diesel engine. In contrast, Cat's largest model, the CAT 6090, which weighs in excess of 2,160,510 lb or 1,080 tons (979,990 kg), has a 4,500 hp engine and a bucket as large as 52.0 m^3. Operating requirements of off-road equipment mean these engines endure a more strenuous set of demands and duty cycles than on-highway equipment. For example, off-road equipment depends on its engines not only to propel the vehicle but to operate attachments like buckets, blades, and shovels. A backhoe may use the same engine as an electric generator, but the generator is used for extended periods at constant speeds and loads. In the loader, the duty cycle features frequent cycling between high engine speeds and loads, plus extended low-speed idling between tasks. Off-road vehicle propulsion requires an engine that's capable providing traction over a wide range of terrain profiles and physical conditions. Most off-road machines also use engine-driven hydraulic pumps to power the attachments in order to accomplish a specific task. These additional accessories create additional unique power demands on the engine that are not found in on-highway engines, where power is primarily used for propulsion.

Diesel engines are the workhorse for most of the off-road machines around the world. In 2003 in North America, diesel accounted for 67% of the engines used on farms, 100% of engines in construction, and 72% of engines in mining. In spite of the higher acquisition cost, diesel engines are used more often because they have the following advantages:

- higher torque output at lower engine speeds (**FIGURE 1-23**);
- superior fuel economy—smaller diesels will have 25–40% better fuel economy than spark-ignited engines, but larger turbocharged engines can achieve fuel efficiency more than 10 times that of spark-ignition engines;
- greater durability—in small to mid-range sizes, diesels will last 3–5 times longer than spark-ignition engines, sometimes lasting in tractors and bulldozers for as long as 20 to 30 years, and lasting for longer than 50 years in rail locomotives with engine speeds topping out at 110 rpm.

To lower fuel costs and reduce emissions, hybrid powertrains are frequently used. Hybrid off-road equipment creates synergies between hydraulics, engines, batteries, and electric motors. Flywheel and hydraulic-energy storage systems can produce more power with lower emissions and smaller engines while using significantly less fuel. One example is Caterpillar's D7E, a dozer that has a diesel-over-electric drivetrain. Advertised fuel savings of 10–30% are achieved, and some customers report even higher numbers. John Deere claims that its hybrid wheel loader gets 25% better fuel economy, while Komatsu has a hybrid excavator achieving 25–41% improved fuel efficiency. The hydraulic hybrid-design stores braking energy, and fluid

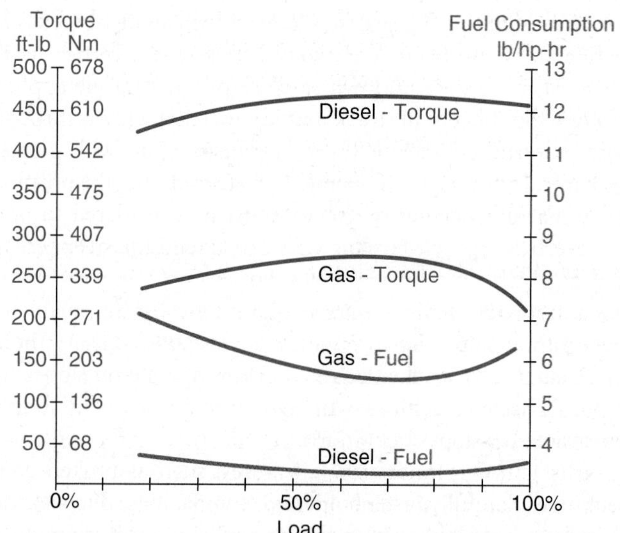

FIGURE 1-23 Diesel engines are used in almost all off-road diesel applications, primarily because they produce more power while burning less fuel than spark-ignition engines.

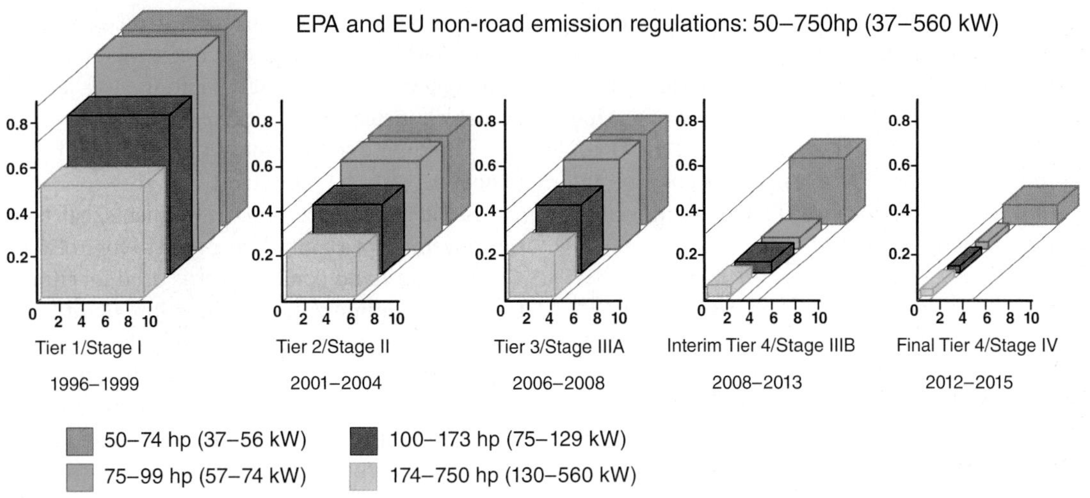

FIGURE 1-24 Emission standards for off-road diesel engines are organized into tiers. The level of permissible emissions and when the engines must meet targets for emission reduction depend on engine power output.

energy returning to the reservoir from cylinders retracting under the force of gravity or loads in hydraulic accumulators, which is used to accelerate the machine in subsequent machine cycles.

The use of gaseous fuels such as propane and natural gas is typically found in warehouse material-handling equipment like power lift or forklift machines. Low emissions from these engines compared to gasoline or diesel fuels is the primary reason for using these fuels. Acquisition costs are lower for equipment using engines based on popular spark-ignition, gasoline fuel designs. While not without hazards, gaseous fuels are stored and handled more safely and easily, compared to gasoline.

Engine Emission Standards

Since off-road diesel equipment covers a very wide variety of engines used in many different applications, emission standards harmonized around the world group engines into emission categories depending on power output. Emission standards are phased in depending on the engine horsepower and schedules, called "tiers." Tier 4 standards regulate the latest engines. The emission standards regulate nitrogen oxides (NOx), hydrocarbons (HC) or non-methane hydrocarbons (NMHC), carbon monoxide (CO), and particulate matter (PM), which is made up of mostly black soot (**FIGURE 1-24**).

Ergonomic Cab Design

Ergonomics refers to the study of human movement factors applied to workplace design to improve worker productivity while reducing the likelihood of injuries, such as repetitive strain. As mentioned earlier, the operator's cab is a workplace, and so functional considerations for the operators comfort and access to controls in the design of the cab are important to a machine's productivity. The operator's visibility, easy access to all controls, and safety are important for the operator to operate the machine at peak performance and productivity. Proper clearances between the operator and the machine components are necessary to provide access to and from the workplace. The Society of Automotive Engineers (SAE) outlines criteria for cab access systems in order to help minimize accidents and injuries to workers getting on or off or moving about while servicing or preparing to operate off-road machines (**FIGURE 1-25**).

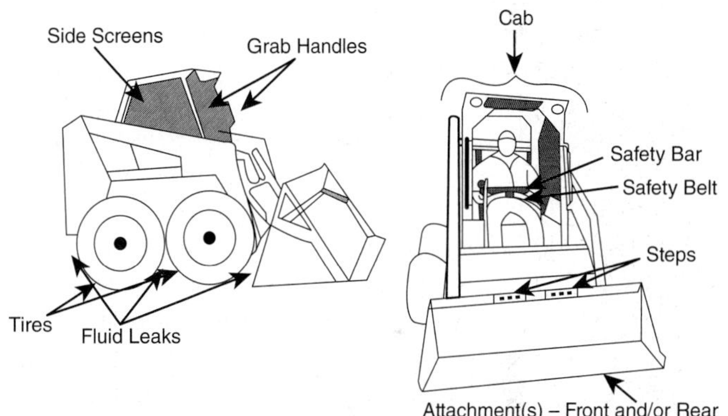

FIGURE 1-25 The presence and location of items such as grab handles and steps are important to minimize the probability of accidents for workers getting on and off the machine.

Information for dimensions and locations for steps, handrails, and handholds are included in the criteria.

Dimensions between the seat, instrument cluster, levers, and pedals are important for ease in manipulating operating controls. The SAE has developed a document called the "Recommended Practice, Instrument Face Design and Location for Construction and Industrial Equipment." The standard recommends grouping instruments:

- Group similar function instruments or controls on the panel.
- Make related groups of instruments equal in size.
- Design the panel as symmetrically as possible.
- Provide a central zone on the panel for the highest priority instruments. This is the arc lying within the 30° cone for easy eye movement, which is 380 mm wide at 700 mm from the operator's eye.
- Group the gauges in the priority zone horizontally and according to function with engine gauges to the left of the panel center and transmission gauges to the right. The panel center should be over the steering column or located around the tachometer or by a group of indicator lights.
- All remaining instruments should appear on either side of the priority group and keep their relative positions the same on all vehicles in the line.
- Controls on the instrument panel should also follow a standard for the whole line of vehicles. Universal symbols for operator controls have been standardized to achieve proper association between controls and displays.

Other industry standards for controls include the following:

When a foot-pedal control operates a clutch, it is actuated by the operator's left foot with the direction of motion forward and/or downward for disengagement.

Continuously used primary hand controls such as hand throttles, shift levers, and other control lever in tractors should be assigned to the right hand, and the left hand should remain available for steering at all times (**FIGURE 1-26**).

The engine speed hand-operated control should be located to operate with the right hand.

Rocker and toggle switch movements shall be consistent with the movement of a control lever used to control a similar function.

When a hand control lever is used for lift controls, implements, or equipment, the direction of motion is generally forward, downward, or away from the operator to lower the implement or equipment and rearward, upward, or toward the operator to raise the implement or equipment.

Note that there are two different standards used in excavators to control the boom and bucket, plus the direction of cab swing. The SAE standards (American) and International Standards Organization (European) both spread the four main digging controls between two x-y joysticks, with each standard using different forward and side movements controlling the boom and dipper cylinders in opposite directions. The x-y configuration enables an operator to control all four functions simultaneously. Switches are commonly used by electronically controlled joysticks to allow operators to select which control configuration they prefer to use (**FIGURE 1-27**).

Less frequently used controls such as those for power take-offs (PTO), clutch, parking brake, and differential lock should be designated for left-hand or left-foot operation.

- Use of color-coded hand controls are intended to help operators identify various types of controls. Red is used only for single-function engine stop controls (**FIGURE 1-28**).
- Orange is used only for machine ground motion controls, such as engine speed controls, transmission controls, parking brakes or park-locks, and independent emergency brakes.

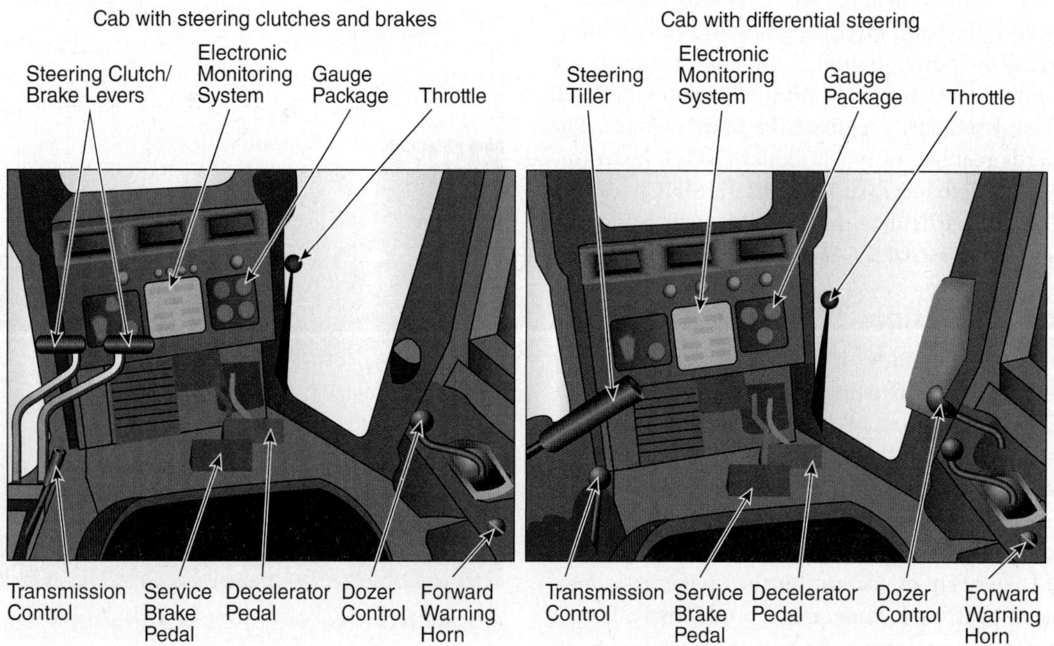

FIGURE 1-26 Comparing the cab control layout for a dozer with hydrostatic drive propulsion and one using clutches and brakes to control track differential speeds for propulsion and turning.

FIGURE 1-27 Joysticks in an excavator control the movement of the digging function and cab swing.

FIGURE 1-28 The use of universal symbols and color-coded controls in the instrument cluster of a backhoe loader.

- Yellow is used only for function controls that involve the engagement of mechanisms, such as power take-offs.
- Black or some other dark color to is used for all controls that have positioning and adjusting functions, such as steering, hydraulic control, implement hitch, seat adjustment, and machine lighting.

Off-road vehicles require lighting systems that allow safe operation during nighttime operation. For example, in agriculture there is a standard titled "Lighting and Marking of Agricultural Equipment on Highways" that specifies lighting and marking of equipment whenever it's operated or is traveling on a highway.

▶ What Does a Heavy Equipment Repair Technician Do?

K01004

Over the past decade, the heavy equipment industry, including construction equipment such as the backhoes, bulldozers, cranes, excavators, wheel loaders, graders, and forklifts, has achieved a nearly 6% annual growth rate worldwide. Construction of new transportation infrastructure, resource extraction, housing construction, and the refurbishing of older buildings has driven much of this industry growth. The spinoff is more jobs for heavy equipment technicians.

Job Description

Heavy equipment repair technicians install, maintain, and service off-road vehicles and equipment designed to accomplish a wide variety of tasks, such as transporting objects, lifting, plowing, drilling, and cutting. They may also be required to operate heavy equipment as part of diagnostic strategies outlined by a manufacturer. During maintenance and repair procedures, technicians test and adjust equipment; repair or replace defective parts, components, or systems; and diagnose faults or equipment malfunctions. They will also validate the correct operation of machinery, disassemble and reassemble heavy equipment and its components, order new parts and conduct inspections on machinery to ensure that it is properly functioning and complies with legislated safety or manufacturer standards. Technicians need to have the ability to write service reports, read and comprehend information in technical manuals, and interpret technical drawings of such things as schematics of electrical or hydraulic circuits.

Training of HD equipment technicians at vocational schools, colleges, and universities is aimed at producing competent technicians in a shorter time period than simply developing skills through practical experience alone could accomplish. To develop the best problem-solving skills, safe work practices, and repair techniques, vocational colleges concentrate on teaching principles of the construction, function, and operation of mobile off-road heavy equipment systems. Principles of science applicable to each subject and area of study supplement basic instruction, which are timelessly essential when analyzing problems and developing maintenance and repair techniques or strategies.

HD Equipment Technician Licensing

Unlike the repair industry for on-road vehicles, there isn't a mandatory or standardized certification that heavy equipment repair technicians are required to possess in every state or province. Instead, college diplomas, associate degrees, and certificates are available. Employers prefer individuals who have some understanding or background in mechanics and who are familiar with subject areas such as electrical systems, diesel engines, hydraulics, powertrains, brakes, and steering systems. In associate degree programs, students undertake a broad curriculum emphasizing mathematics, applied sciences, communications, marketing, logistics, industrial safety, law, and writing. Manufacturers also offer training programs, often in association with community colleges. While technician licensing is not mandatory, some equipment may need to be moved or operated during the service or repair process, which requires an operator's license. A further advantage for technicians is to hold a commercial vehicle driver license in addition to a regular driver's license, to operate truck trailer combinations when equipment is floated between a job and repair site.

New technologies to increase driver safety, comfort, machine productivity, and reliability are placing ever-increasing demands for greater technician skills. Technological advancements, including air-conditioned cabs, hydrostatic drives, automated transmissions, telematics, engine monitoring systems, and GPS guidance systems used by autonomous and semi-autonomous driverless machines systems, require new skill sets and knowledge. Industry growth, combined with the increased features, demands more technicians with greater skills and training in heavy equipment.

Where Do Technicians Work?

Heavy-duty equipment technicians are employed by companies that own and operate heavy equipment, heavy equipment dealerships, rental and service companies, construction contractors, forestry companies, mining companies, ski hills, and government departments that service and repair their own equipment. Technicians will also work in marine, oil and gas, material-handling, landscaping, and land-clearing industries. Many HD equipment technicians develop a wide range of skills and knowledge on a vast variety of equipment types and manufacturers.

In terms of working conditions, HD equipment technicians work in the full range of environmental conditions, including dealer repair centers, component rebuild shops service and shops owned by industry contractors. While one can expect to work primarily in well illuminated, ventilated, safe, clean shops with the latest service equipment, training, and service information systems, it is common to perform onsite equipment repairs. Since it is not always practical or possible to tow disabled equipment back to a shop, technicians should expect to work for long days at remote sites during inclement weather conditions. For example, in Canada in cold weather, broken down equipment is tented over during servicing. This may take place on the side of a steep hill, in a forest while repairing logging equipment, or alongside a busy right of way for a pipeline. In those situations, a technician will transport their entire toolbox and a large supply of parts potentially needed to repair a machine. Repairing track equipment may require digging and shoring up equipment with timbers to access the undercarriage for repairs.

A positive attitude toward adverse working conditions in the field is essential at times. Since work often requires standing, bending, crawling, lifting, climbing, pulling, and stretching, it's important for technicians to be in and maintain a good physical condition. The use of other senses, such as smell, hearing, and vision, are important when performing diagnostic work. While many people believe that because heavy equipment is large and heavy, proportionally more strength is required to complete tasks. This idea is not entirely correct. Heavier components and larger fasteners require different working techniques using specialized assistance form small cranes; hydraulic presses; larger, more powerful air tools; and even other equipment such as backhoes and forklifts. More often than not, the ability of technicians to develop a repertoire of creative or clever work techniques and employ a variety of power devices to overcome unique challenges working on heavy equipment is better and more often deployed by a skilled technician than simply using brute strength.

The size and complexity of off-road heavy equipment increases the potential for injury and threats to life and limb. For this reason, safe working practices critical. Technicians must be conscious of potential impact of their work on people, equipment, the work area, and environment. In recent years, greater emphasis is placed on the safe handling, disposal, storage, and recycling of toxic or environmentally hazardous materials such as coolant, oil, used filters, batteries, refrigerants, and dust from diesel particulate filters.

Technicians also need to possess the ability to work alone or as part of a team. There are often problems requiring collaboration between fellow technicians to solve or help perform physical tasks. The work many heavy-duty technicians perform presents some of the toughest challenges of any trade. The complexity and sophistication of many types of heavy equipment, particularly problems with contemporary hydraulic systems, place additional demands on the ability to think logically, methodically, and quickly. Given the cost of parts and the loss of production time that can run into thousands of dollars and hours, a dependable level of skill and competency is demanded from the best HD technicians. It's not surprising to find technicians with those rare combinations of skills to receive compensation commensurate with those abilities earning well above a six-figure annual income.

▶ Wrap-Up

Ready for Review

- ▶ Off-road equipment sales are undergoing steady growth, which will provide employment opportunities and demand and for new skills in the future.
- ▶ Off-road mobile equipment is defined as a machine having attached components, designed to work in an off-road environment or designed to operate at low speeds.
- ▶ Off-road machines have an unloaded vehicle speed that can't exceed 45 mph, and there should be no capacity to carry occupants other than the driver and operating crew.
- ▶ Most off-road equipment uses fluid power systems, which use either air or hydraulic force, to operate equipment attached to the vehicle.
- ▶ Off-road propulsion systems are unique and specially adapted to the operating terrain and other ground conditions where they are used. The systems provide extra traction over soft, uneven terrain while often performing heavy work.
- ▶ The major source of energy for propulsion on a machine is called the prime mover. Engines and electric motors are most often used as prime movers.
- ▶ Not only does the prime mover provide power to move the machines around off-road worksites, but it also operates cables and fluid power systems performing specialized jobs.
- ▶ Tracked machines, also called track undercarriage machines, use either steel plates or rubber belts that have the advantage of providing lower ground pressure for heavy machines to prevent them from sinking.
- ▶ Tracked machines provide additional traction force through cleat-like features on track shoes called grousers.
- ▶ The Caterpillar Company was cofounded by Benjamin Holt, who acquired the patents for the track-type undercarriage. The name Caterpillar was used to describe the machinery using track-type undercarriage.
- ▶ The first use of wider pneumatic tires on off-road equipment took place in the 1930s, and aircraft tires were first installed on an agricultural tractor.
- ▶ The use of extra weight for tire ballast to make a tire heavier adds stability, helps prevent machine tip-over, and increases traction force applied to the ground by the tire.
- ▶ The use of hydraulic fluid power on off-road equipment eliminated the use of cable systems on machines which simplified machine control operation.
- ▶ Hydraulically operated equipment meant that equipment could be operated much more simply, faster, and with greater force.
- ▶ The use of hydraulics enabled machines to force shovels and buckets into the ground rather than rely on the weight of gravity. Hydraulic attachments could be added to machines.
- ▶ Increasing equipment productivity drives machine design. Productivity is improved by increasing the load-carrying capacity and/or shortening the cycle time. Cycle time can be shortened by increasing machine travel or operational speed.
- ▶ Diesel engines are traditionally the preferred prime mover because they produce more power and use less fuel than other engines. Diesel engines also have greater durability.
- ▶ Emission standards for off-road equipment are established by horsepower ratings.
- ▶ To improve productivity and safety, machine cabs and controls use ergonomic designs with universal symbols and color coding on switches and controls. Cabs also have roll over protection for operators.

Key Terms

ballast The addition of weight inside a pneumatic tire that's used to give the machine additional stability and traction force. A common ballast material is a water and calcium chloride mixture.

differential steering or **skid steering** A steering principle where one track will turn at a different speed than the other, providing even the largest track-type machines with exceptional maneuverability.

fluid power Both air and hydraulic systems transfer power to machine implements and accessories performing work.

ground pressure The force measured in pounds per square inch (psi) a machine applies to the ground through its contact patch with a track or tire.

grouser A bar or cleat-like protrusion from a track shoe of a track-type undercarriage.

hydrodynamic A system that converts kinetic energy contained in hydraulic fluid flow into mechanical movement.

hydrostatic The transfer of hydraulic fluid energy from flow and pressure.

operating cycle The time that a machine requires to perform a specific operation such as fill and dump one bucket of material.

prime mover A technical term describing the principle device used to produce mechanical energy in off-road equipment, propelling the machine and supplying specialized equipment attachments.

productivity A measurement of machine power. Productivity is calculated by measuring the amount of work performed by a machine and dividing that by the time it takes to perform the work. Units for productivity vary and could range from tons of material moved per hour or how many trees are moved a minute.

track shoes Metal plates linked together to form the tracks of a track-type undercarriage system.

undercarriage The generic name given to all the components making up the propulsion mechanism for track drive equipment.

Review Questions

1. Which of the following machines is expected to have the highest sales growth in 2019?
   a. Bulldozers
   b. Asphalt equipment
   c. Forklifts
   d. Loaders
2. Telematics refers to
   a. wireless transmission of machine fault codes.
   b. monitoring and control of machine operations from a distance.
   c. self-steering equipment.
   d. GPS navigation.
3. Which of the following defines the features that classify off-road equipment?
   a. The Society of Automotive Engineers (SAE)
   b. The Code of the Federal Registry (CFR)
   c. The Environmental Protection Agency (EPA)
   d. The Equipment Manufacturers Association (EMA)
4. Which of the following best defines a hydrostatic drive system?
   a. Transmission of energy through flow and pressure
   b. Transmission of energy through fluid flow only
   c. The use of hydraulics motors in machinery
   d. The use of hydraulic pumps in machinery
5. Ground pressure refers best to which of the following?
   a. Downward force exerted by tires
   b. The weight per unit area or pounds per square inch (psi) exerted by machine track
   c. How soft or complaint a ground surface is
   d. The hardness of ground beneath track
6. The first use of track undercarriage anywhere was for a
   a. farm tractor.
   b. grader.
   c. excavator.
   d. log hauler.
7. Which of the following ground conditions is track-type undercarriage best suited for?
   a. Grass-covered fields
   b. Snow plow operations
   c. Mining
   d. Soft, loose sand, soil, or gravel
8. Tire ballast is designed to
   a. extend tire life.
   b. increase traction force and machine stability.
   c. seal tires to prevent leakage.
   d. freeze when the temperature gets cold.
9. How is machine productivity best measured?
   a. Over an operating cycle
   b. The amount of time it takes to perform a task
   c. The amount of load a machine can carry
   d. By using a stopwatch
10. Which off-road emission tier would include the latest diesel engines?
   a. Tier 1
   b. Tier 3
   c. Tier 4
   d. Tier 5

ASE Technician A/Technician B Style Questions

1. Technician A says that diesel engines are most commonly used by off-road machines since they have fewer maintenance requirements, such as the need to change spark plugs. Technician B says that diesel engines are used since they provide more power and use less fuel. Who is correct?
   a. Technician A
   b. Technician B
   c. Both Technician A and Technician B
   d. Neither Technician A nor Technician B
2. Technician A says hybrid off-road equipment is used to reduce fuel consumption. Technician B says that hybrids have reduced engine emissions. Who is correct?
   a. Technician A
   b. Technician B
   c. Both Technician A and Technician B
   d. Neither Technician A nor Technician B
3. Technician A says that the color red is used to designate engine shut-down controls. Technician B says yellow is used to identify an engine shut-down control. Who is correct?
   a. Technician A
   b. Technician B
   c. Both Technician A and Technician B
   d. Neither Technician A nor Technician B
4. Technician A says that excavators use joysticks with a standardized x-y pattern of control to rotate the operators cab and manipulate the bucket. Technician B says that joysticks can be configured to move the cab and bucket in one of two ways. Who is correct?
   a. Technician A
   b. Technician B
   c. Both Technician A and Technician B
   d. Neither Technician A nor Technician B
5. Technician A says that cable-operated equipment was replaced using hydraulic controls. Technician B says hydraulic systems replaced pneumatic systems on early equipment. Who is correct?
   a. Technician A
   b. Technician B
   c. Both Technician A and Technician B
   d. Neither Technician A nor Technician B
6. Technician A says that a hydraulic motor will weigh less than an electric motor. Technician B says that hydraulic control systems are smoother than pneumatic control systems because they can better absorb shock loading. Who is correct?
   a. Technician A
   b. Technician B
   c. Both Technician A and Technician B
   d. Neither Technician A nor Technician B

7. Technician A says that track drive systems were first invented and used in England. Technician B says that the Caterpillar Company invented track drive undercarriage. Who is correct?
   a. Technician A
   b. Technician B
   c. Both Technician A and Technician B
   d. Neither Technician A nor Technician B
8. Technician A says that one thing that all off-road equipment has in common is the use of hydraulic or air attachments used to perform a specialized task. Technician B says that all off-road equipment will have engines and an axle able to carry over 29,000 lb. Who is correct?
   a. Technician A
   b. Technician B
   c. Both Technician A and Technician B
   d. Neither Technician A nor Technician B
9. Technician A says that track drive machinery with differential steering is the most maneuverable steering system. Technician B says that machines with tires are better able to navigate around obstacles. Who is correct?
   a. Technician A
   b. Technician B
   c. Both Technician A and Technician B
   d. Neither Technician A nor Technician B
10. Technician A says that only diesel engine is considered to be a prime mover. Technician B says the electric motors and hydrostatic drives are prime movers. Who is correct?
   a. Technician A
   b. Technician B
   c. Both Technician A and Technician B
   d. Neither Technician A nor Technician B

CHAPTER 2
Identification & Classifications of MORE

Knowledge Objectives

After reading this chapter, you will be able to:

- **K02001** Categorize MORE according to operation, drive system, and function.
- **K02002** Describe construction features of various categories of MORE.
- **K02003** Explain terminology associated with the construction and operation of MORE.
- **K02004** Describe MORE attachments.
- **K02005** Identify common steering, propulsion, frame, and hydraulic systems and components.

Industry/Accreditation

After reading this chapter, you will be able to:

- **I02001** Communicate trade-related information using standard terms for components and operations.

Skills Objectives

After reading this chapter, you will be able to:

- **S02001** Start, operate, and shut down equipment.

Attitude Objectives

After reading this chapter, you will be able to:

- **A02001** Acquire correct service information for repair and maintenance procedures.

▶ Introduction

Anyone passing by a major construction project has no doubt witnessed many types and sizes of mobile off-road equipment (MORE) in use. Practically any construction-related need imaginable can be satisfied with some type of MORE. In addition to construction, other industries, such as forestry, mining, and agriculture, also benefit from the use of such heavy equipment. Some pieces of heavy equipment, such as a compactor, are designed for one specific purpose. Other types of equipment, such as an excavator, might be used for several different tasks. Additionally, many types of MORE can be fitted with attachments to further enhance the equipment's capabilities.

For service technicians to work safely and effectively on MORE, they must be familiar with the basic categories of equipment and understand what each type is used for. They also must recognize common features of MORE and understand how these machines are powered and operated. This chapter will identify basic MORE classifications and examine construction features found in these types of equipment. It also will describe common attachments, systems, and components associated with MORE and explain terminology pertaining to the construction and operation of the equipment.

▶ Basic Categories of MORE

K02001

MORE classifications can be based on different criteria. For example, equipment manufacturers might categorize their products according to the industry they serve, such as agriculture, forestry, or construction. Another classification method is based on the general purpose or function of the equipment. With this method, material-handling equipment would include machines such as cranes, forklifts, and knuckleboom loaders. The way equipment is propelled, or driven, is another method of classifying MORE. For example, track-mounted equipment would use metal or rubber crawler tracks to provide locomotion and include equipment such as dozers, excavators, and some types of cranes. Wheel-mounted equipment would use wheels or tires for mobility and include equipment such as loaders, graders, and haulers. Regardless of the classification method used, the same equipment will often fit into different categories. The equipment covered in this chapter is categorized by its use in excavation, earth moving and mining, grading and compacting, and hoisting and handling.

SAFETY TIP

Service technicians working at practically any work site are likely to encounter numerous types of MORE being operated at the same time. For this reason, technicians must be aware of the inherent hazards of working around heavy equipment and people. They must remain vigilant at all times to avoid accidents that could kill or injure themselves or other personnel or damage equipment.

Excavation Equipment

The Occupational Safety and Health Administration (OSHA) defines excavation as "Any man-made cut, cavity, trench, or depression in an earth surface formed by earth removal." Based on this definition, many organizations include mass excavation equipment such as excavators, backhoes, and trenchers in this category of MORE.

Excavators

An excavator is a piece of heavy equipment that is commonly used in earth-moving, trenching, and loading applications (**FIGURE 2-1**). It has a large **gooseneck boom** and bucket on the front of the machine that are mounted with an operator's cab onto a rotating platform. The platform, which can be rotated a full 360 degrees to enable the operator to swing the boom and bucket in any direction, is attached to an **undercarriage** that has crawler tracks or wheels that allow the excavator to be moved.

FIGURE 2-1 Typical excavator.

You Are the Mobile Heavy Equipment Technician

A customer calls and asks if you can come out to a construction site to check over an excavator that they are going to use for some demolition work. The customer says they haven't used this particular excavator in a while and wants you to check it over before they start the job to avoid any unnecessary downtime.

1. Why would you need to ask about the basic type of excavator?
2. Why would you need to ask about any special attachments being used on the equipment?
3. Would it be important to ask about the basic propulsion and control systems? If so, why?
4. Should you ask about any manufacturer's manuals for the equipment? If so, why?

FIGURE 2-2 Common track-mounted excavator applications: **A.** backfilling, **B.** lifting, **C.** trenching, and **D.** loading.

Two basic types of excavators are standard hydraulic excavators: track-mounted machines with crawler tracks and wheel-mounted excavators, which use rubber tires. Standard hydraulic excavators (usually just called excavators) have excellent stability and traction. They are available in many sizes and capacities, from mini excavators with engines of less than 20 hp (15 kW) to extremely large excavators with engines of several hundred hp (kW). Track-mounted excavators have several common uses (**FIGURE 2-2**).

Wheel-mounted excavators can perform the same basic jobs as track-mounted excavators. The major difference between the two is that a wheel-mounted excavator has axles with rubber tires instead of crawler tracks (**FIGURE 2-3**). Rubber tires are more suitable for operating on pavement or other surfaces that need to be protected.

Both track-mounted and wheel-mounted excavators are available as **telescoping boom** excavators (**FIGURE 2-4**). In other words, instead of using the common gooseneck boom and bucket arrangement, these excavators use a telescoping boom that can

FIGURE 2-3 Wheel-mounted excavator.

FIGURE 2-4 Telescoping boom excavator.

be extended outward and retracted. Telescoping boom excavators are commonly used in sloping and finish grading applications.

Backhoe Loaders

K02001

A popular piece of MORE that is similar to an excavator is a backhoe loader (**FIGURE 2-5**). In a typical configuration, a hydraulically operated excavating arm is mounted onto the rear of a rubber-tired tractor or, in some cases, a crawler (track-mounted) tractor. The backhoe part of the equipment is commonly used for small excavation work, digging manholes, and trenching. A loader bucket is attached to the front of the tractor. The front-end loader is often used for removing excavated soil, backfilling, and loading trucks. The tractor engine provides the power for the backhoe and the loader and enables the tractor to be maneuvered.

While backhoe loaders come in many sizes and models, they are generally smaller and less powerful than other types of excavating equipment. The boom has less swing than that of an excavator, but the backhoe's mobility and maneuverability make it a very useful piece of excavation equipment—especially in applications where larger excavators cannot be used.

FIGURE 2-5 Typical backhoe loader.

Trenchers

As its name suggests, a trencher is a type of MORE that is used to dig trenches for burying pipes, cables, culverts, and similar items. Many different types of trenchers are available, from small tractor-mounted versions to large track-mounted models. One common type of trencher called a **chain trencher** (**FIGURE 2-6**). It is a track-mounted trencher with a hydraulically controlled boom that can be lifted and lowered to control the depth of the trench. A chain with cutting bits travels around the boom to cut through hard soil and rock. Chains of different widths are available to cut narrow or wide trenches.

Another type of trencher is a **wheel trencher** (**FIGURE 2-7**). Instead of using a boom and cutting chain, a wheel trencher uses a wheel with teeth to dig through pavement or hard soil. Wheel trenchers come in many sizes, from small portable models like the one shown in Figure 2-7 to large track-mounted trenchers capable of cutting a trench 36 inches (91 cm) wide and up to 7 feet (2.15 m) deep.

Tractor-mounted trenchers are commonly used for burying utility lines at construction sites (**FIGURE 2-8**). In this application, a tractor pulls the trencher blade attachment to lay the cable.

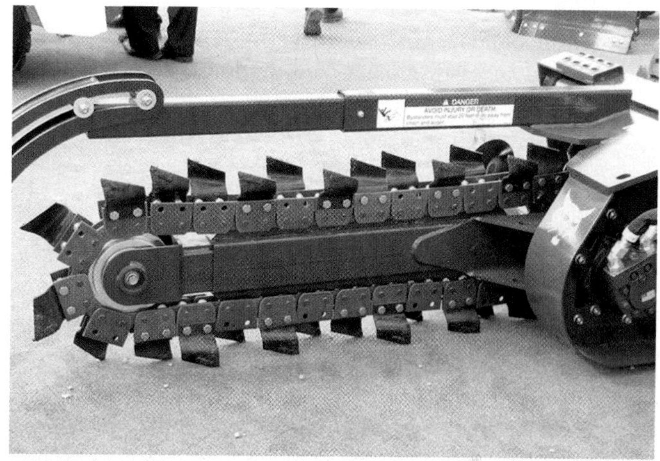

FIGURE 2-6 Track-mounted chain trencher.

FIGURE 2-7 Portable wheel trencher.

FIGURE 2-8 Tractor-mounted trencher.

FIGURE 2-9 Typical dozer.

Earth-Moving and Mining Equipment

Most of the MORE used for earth moving and mining is designed to move large amounts of soil or aggregate from one place to another. Typically, these pieces of equipment include dozers, loaders, and off-road dump trucks.

Dozers

A dozer, or bulldozer, is one of the most common pieces of MORE used in earth-moving and grading applications. The primary purpose of a dozer is to push large amounts of soil, aggregate, or other material. A typical dozer (**FIGURE 2-9**) is an extremely heavy piece of equipment that moves on crawler tracks and has a wide blade mounted on the front. The blade is controlled hydraulically, and it can typically be raised, lowered, angled, and tilted to accommodate specific needs.

As with most types of MORE, dozers come in a variety of sizes and models. Four basic types of dozers are shown in **FIGURE 2-10**: low-track dozers, which are commonly used for

FIGURE 2-10 Basic types of dozers: **A.** low-track crawler dozer, **B.** high-track crawler dozer, **C.** high-speed dozer, and **D.** wheel dozer with compactor wheels.

grading purposes; high-track dozers, which are typically used for pushing large amounts of material; high-speed dozers, which are known for their agility and speed during finish grading jobs; and wheel dozers, which have a steering wheel and operator controls similar to those of a truck.

Loaders

A loader is a type of MORE that has a large bucket mounted on the front of a machine that looks much like a dozer. However, while a dozer blade is designed to push material, a loader bucket is designed to be raised, lowered, and tilted so that it can scoop up material, transport it to a different area on the site, and dump it. One of the benefits of a loader is that the lifting arms for the bucket can lift the bucket high enough to dump material onto piles or into trucks.

Loaders come in many sizes and configurations. They can be track-mounted or wheel-mounted (**FIGURE 2-11**).

Another type of loader that is popular for small jobs, especially jobs in tight spaces, is a skid steer loader (**FIGURE 2-12**). Skid steer loaders typically have a relatively small diesel engine, a hydrostatic drive system, and a bucket. They are available as track-mounted or wheel-mounted machines, and they have a very small turning radius. Modern skid steer loaders have joysticks in the cab that enable an operator to control the loader movement and the bucket.

FIGURE 2-11 Common types of loaders: **A.** track-mounted loader and **B.** wheel-mounted loader.

FIGURE 2-12 Skid steer loader.

Off-Road Dump Trucks

Off-road dump trucks have the same fundamental purpose of any dump truck—to safely move large amounts of material from one place to another (**FIGURE 2-13**). However, the similarities end there. Off-road dump trucks are unlike any dump truck that is seen on the highway. In fact, because of their massive size, these trucks are prohibited from operating on a highway. Instead, they are rugged, heavy-duty machines built to withstand the challenging conditions of road-building, construction, and mining sites. Off-road trucks are loaded using various types of loaders or excavators. They are then driven to another area on the site where the truck's powerful hoist cylinders lift the body and dump the load.

SAFETY TIP

Operators have a very limited view from the cab of a haul truck. Any personnel or equipment must be a considerable distance away from the cab to be visible. Always use care when approaching or working around haul trucks.

FIGURE 2-13 Off-road dump trucks.

> **TECHNICIAN TIP**
>
> Operating an off-road dump truck requires special training and certification. Off-road trucks are vastly different from highway vehicles. Never attempt to operate any type of off-road truck without first completing the proper training.

Off-road trucks are usually divided into two basic types: **rigid-frame** trucks and **articulated-frame** trucks. A rigid-frame truck, which is sometimes called a rigid dump truck, a haul truck, or a mining truck, has a non-pivoting frame that supports the cab and the body (**FIGURE 2-14**). A typical rigid-frame truck has two axles—a front axle for steering the truck and a rear axle for transferring the engine's power to the wheels. Because of the massive amount of weight that a haul truck can carry and its need for stability, the rear axle usually has dual wheels on each side.

Rigid-frame trucks use large, powerful diesel engines with as much as 4,000 hp (2,983 kW) or more. Some of the largest rigid-frame trucks also have electric motors inside the axle at the rear wheels. In these trucks, the diesel engine drives an AC (alternating current) alternator or DC (direct current) generator that, in turn, powers the electric motors. This powertrain setup provides additional power to each drive wheel and helps with braking.

Articulated-frame dump trucks, or articulated haulers as they are often called, are typically smaller than rigid-frame trucks (**FIGURE 2-15**). They are designed more for maneuverability in rough terrain than for sheer hauling capacity. However, articulated-frame trucks are still large pieces of MORE. These trucks can have engines with over 600 hp (447 kW) and bodies that can haul over 60 tons (54 tonnes).

An articulated hauler has a permanent hinge, or pivoting point, in the frame. The pivoting point is located between the operator's cab and the dump body so that all of the hauler's wheels follow the same path. Most articulated-frame trucks have all-wheel drive with a front axle for steering and two rear axles for driving the vehicle. The steering and drive systems are controlled hydraulically.

FIGURE 2-14 Rigid-frame truck.

FIGURE 2-15 Articulated-frame truck.

FIGURE 2-16 Underground mining truck.

In mining applications, special articulated-frame trucks are used underground. The underground mining truck is much like an aboveground truck, but with a lower clearance (**FIGURE 2-16**). The height reduction is achieved by moving the operator's cab forward of the front axle. Most underground mining trucks have all-wheel drive and two axles (one front-steering axle and one rear axle). Their capacities are similar to aboveground articulated-frame trucks.

Grading and Compacting Equipment

Before roads can be paved or buildings and structures can be erected, it is necessary to establish a solid foundation of soil. This is often accomplished by using scrapers to move and disperse soil, graders to smooth the soil and create slopes and ditches, and compacters to pack the soil and create a firm surface.

Scrapers

A scraper is a type of MORE that is used to move large amounts of soil or aggregate from one place to another. While some smaller scrapers are towed behind a dozer or tractor, most large

FIGURE 2-17 Wheeled tractor scraper.

FIGURE 2-19 Motor grader controls are very sophisticated today featuring GPS guidance.

ones are self-propelled, rubber-tired models (**FIGURE 2-17**). These scrapers are commonly called wheel tractor scrapers.

An operator drives the scraper forward and uses the hydraulic controls in the cab to lower the scraping edge and the hopper, or bowl. The soil is scraped into the hopper. Once the hopper is full, it is raised and closed. The scraper is then driven to an area where the back of the hopper is opened, and the soil is dumped and dispersed.

Graders

A motor grader is a long, narrow piece of MORE that has rubber tires, a large diesel engine, and an adjustable blade that is used in many earth-moving, ditching, grading, and smoothing applications (**FIGURE 2-18**). Graders are operated hydraulically with power provided by engines that range from as little as 125 hp (93 kW) to well over 500 hp (373 kW). The blade length on a grader can range from about 12 ft (366 cm) to more than 24 ft (732 cm).

Two basic types of motor graders are rigid-frame graders and articulated-frame graders. Rigid-frame graders are typically smaller and older graders that have a single frame along the length of the machine. Most graders today are articulated-frame graders that have a pivoting point in the frame. The pivoting frame enables the grader to work at an offset angle. In other words, the part of the grader to the front of the pivot can travel along a different line than the section to the rear of the pivot. This feature improves the grader's maneuverability and makes it easier for the grader to perform certain tasks, such as cleaning out ditches. Grader controls these days are very sophisticated using GPS positioning for blade height and angle **FIGURE 2-19** shows a modern motor grader with GPS control.

FIGURE 2-18 Typical motor grader.

Compactors

Whenever soil is graded and dispersed over an area, it must be compacted before any type of structure is built on it or any type of pavement is applied to it. If the soil is not compacted, it will settle on its own over time. However, any structure or pavement that is placed over that soil will be unstable and crack. Compactors are types of MORE used to compact soil and speed up the settling process in a consistent manner. In most cases, compactors are self-propelled machines equipped with large rollers or tires that are driven back and forth over soil, gravel, or asphalt to compact the material. Four common types of "ride-on" compactors are steel-wheel rollers, pneumatic tire rollers, vibratory steel-wheel rollers, and sheepsfoot rollers (**FIGURE 2-20**). These compactors have a diesel engine and a steering wheel or joysticks for operator control. Some models have an articulated frame for better maneuverability.

Hoisting and Handling Equipment

Hoisting and moving loads is a common requirement at nearly every construction and forestry site. Three types of MORE used for lifting, moving, and loading components and material are cranes, forklifts, and knuckleboom loaders.

FIGURE 2-20 Common types of ride-on compactors: **A.** steel-drum roller, **B.** pneumatic tire roller, **C.** vibratory steel-wheel roller, and **D.** sheepsfoot roller.

Cranes

When it comes to lifting and moving loads at a construction site, few machines are more suitable than a crane. Cranes are heavy machines that use a boom, cables, and counterweights to lift and move heavy objects. The boom and the operator's cab are mounted onto a rotating platform that enables the crane to lift and swing a load in any direction. Cranes have powerful diesel engines and are available as track-mounted or wheel-mounted machines. The specific size and type of crane that is used depends on factors such as the weight of the load, the terrain at the site, and the mobility that is needed.

Track-mounted cranes are commonly referred to as crawler cranes (**FIGURE 2-21**). They can be used in many rough terrain applications. Most crawler cranes have joysticks for operator controls and a high-strength **lattice boom** that can be raised and lowered. Intermeshing steel rods give the lattice boom its strength.

Wheel-mounted cranes are also used in challenging off-road conditions. Some wheel-mounted cranes are called rough terrain cranes for that reason. As a general rule, wheel-mounted cranes are mobile and can be operated on highway when required, use a steering wheel for operator control, and have a telescoping boom instead of a lattice boom. **FIGURE 2-22** shows a heavy wheel-mounted crane.

Forklifts

Forklifts, or lift trucks as they are often called, are used not only in warehouse environments but also on construction sites

FIGURE 2-21 Track-mounted (crawler) crane with lattice boom.

FIGURE 2-22 Wheel-mounted crane with telescoping boom.

FIGURE 2-23 Rough terrain forklift.

to move palletized components, sections of pipe, and similar material from one place to another. A typical MORE forklift is commonly called a rough terrain forklift since it has large rubber tires that enable it to move over terrain that is not suitable for conventional forklifts (**FIGURE 2-23**). These forklifts have a large mast in front of the operator's cab that can be tilted forward and backward and a pair of steel forks that can be raised and lowered to lift, carry, and lower material. A diesel engine is mounted behind the operator's cab, and the vehicle is steered with the rear wheels.

A different version of a forklift that is often used on construction sites is a telehandler (**FIGURE 2-24**). A telehandler has a telescoping boom mounted onto the rear of the vehicle that can be extended and retracted to lift objects to greater heights and distances than a typical forklift.

Knuckleboom Loaders

Knuckleboom loaders are a common sight at logging operations. They look like excavators since they have a gooseneck boom that is mounted with an operator's cab on a rotating platform. However, instead of using a bucket at the end of the

FIGURE 2-24 Telehandler forklift with telescoping boom.

boom, knuckleboom loaders use a type of hydraulically powered claw called a **grapple**. The grapple enables the operator to grab logs and other objects and move them onto piles or logging trucks. Mobile knuckleboom loaders are typically track-mounted machines that can move over the rough terrain found at logging sites (**FIGURE 2-25**).

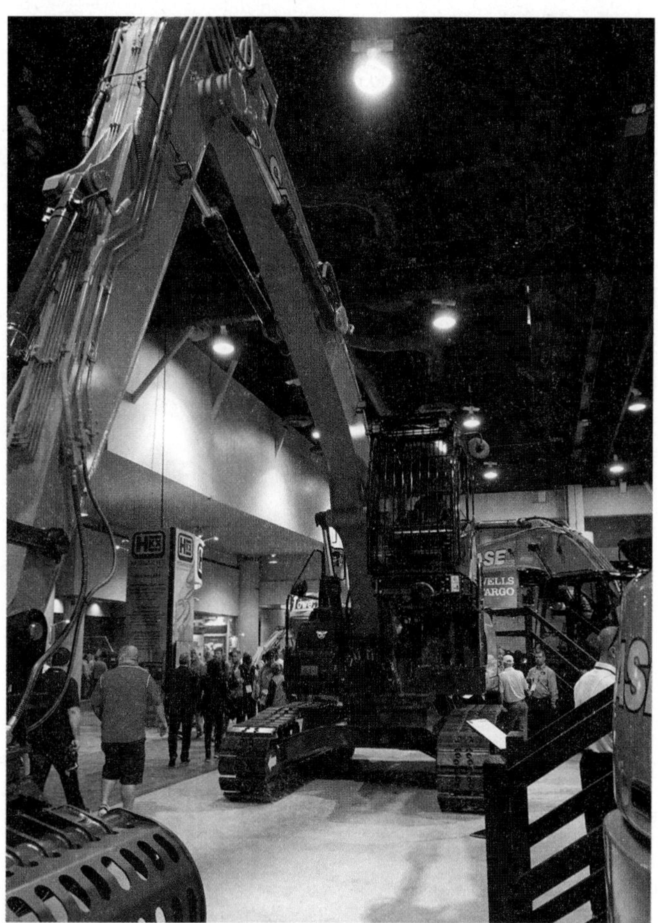

FIGURE 2-25 Track-mounted knuckleboom loader.

▶ MORE Construction Features

K02002

Machines found in any particular category of MORE share a lot of common features, even though they are manufactured by different companies around the world. Engines, powertrain components, operator controls, and other systems may differ somewhat from machine to machine, but the ultimate use and function of the equipment in that category will be the same.

Excavation Equipment Features

Excavation equipment, which includes machines like excavators and backhoe loaders, is designed to remove soil or other material from one area and place it in another area or into a truck. To accomplish this basic task, excavation equipment must have a powerful engine, a drive system, a steering system, some type of boom (gooseneck or telescoping) and bucket, a hydraulic system to power the boom and bucket, and operator controls to drive the equipment and control the operation of the boom and bucket.

> **SAFETY TIP**
>
> All types of MORE have safety features to protect the operator, the equipment, and other personnel and equipment in the area. Service technicians must be familiar with these safety features and always use them during any inspection and maintenance procedures.

The same major components and features of a standard hydraulic excavator can be found on any track-mounted hydraulic excavator, no matter the manufacturer or the size of the excavator (**FIGURE 2-26**).

Construction features for wheel-mounted excavators are very similar to those of standard hydraulic excavators (**FIGURE 2-27**). The main difference is the method of locomotion—in this case, rubber tires instead of crawler tracks. Outriggers are used on wheel-mounted excavators for added stability.

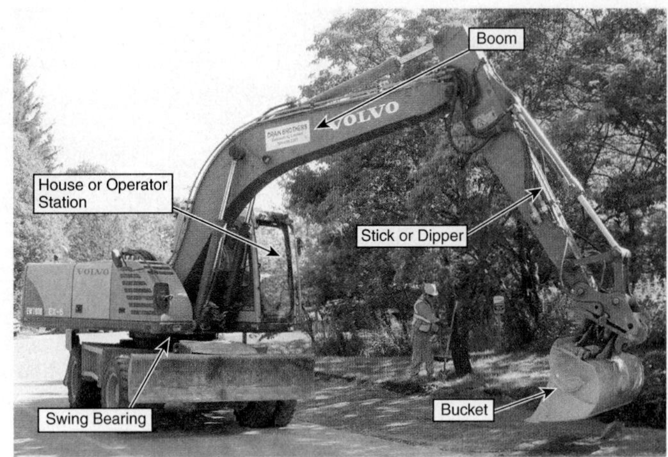

FIGURE 2-27 Major components of a wheel-mounted excavator.

As with excavators, backhoe loaders share many common features (**FIGURE 2-28**). In nearly every backhoe loader configuration, there is a front loader bucket that can be raised, lowered, and tilted; rubber tires for 2- or 4-wheel drive operation; outriggers to stabilize the machine; an excavating arm that consists of a boom and a stick; and a bucket mounted at the end of the excavating arm. A diesel engine powers the backhoe loader, and hydraulic controls enable the operator to drive the backhoe loader and operate the backhoe and the front loader.

Trenchers come in two basic forms: chain trenchers and wheel trenchers. Both types can be track-mounted or wheel-mounted machines. On a typical track-mounted chain trencher, the crawler tracks enable the trencher to move over rough terrain. The operator uses hydraulic controls to raise and lower the digging boom to the required depth and activate the rotation of the digging chain. The digging chain with teeth travels around the boom to cut through hard soil and rock. A device

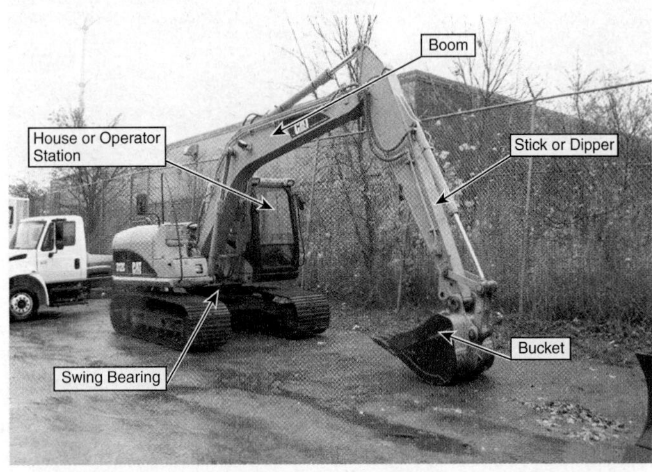

FIGURE 2-26 Major components of a standard hydraulic excavator.

FIGURE 2-28 Major components of a backhoe loader.

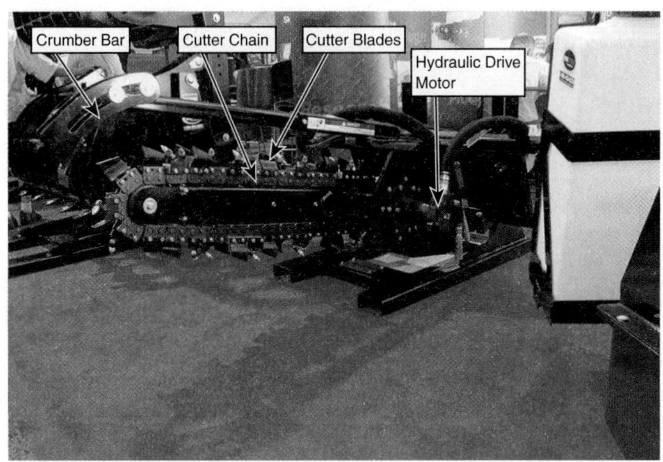

FIGURE 2-29 Major components of a chain trencher.

called a **crumber bar** follows the digging chain in the trench to prevent loose soil from collecting (**FIGURE 2-29**).

A wheel trencher shares most of the same basic construction features with the chain trencher. It simply uses a large wheel with teeth instead of a cutting chain to dig the trench.

Earth-Moving and Mining Equipment Features

MORE that is used for earth-moving and mining applications is designed to push, scoop up, and haul large amounts of material from one place to another. Common examples of earth-moving and mining equipment include dozers, loaders, and off-road dump trucks. Looking at each of these three types of equipment reveals common construction features.

A typical track-mounted (crawler) dozer has a heavy, wide blade at the front for pushing material. Hydraulic hoist cylinders are used to lift and lower the blade, and hydraulic blade angle cylinders are used to adjust the angle of the blade. All of the hydraulic controls for steering and operating the dozer are in the operator's cab. And a diesel engine provides the necessary power to drive all the systems (**FIGURE 2-30**).

FIGURE 2-30 Major components of a track-mounted (crawler) dozer.

Although other types of dozers are used regularly to meet specific needs, the basic features are essentially the same. Regardless of the size, manufacturer, and specific type of dozer being used, the primary purpose is still to push material.

Loaders look a lot like dozers, but their basic function is to scoop up material, transport it to a different area, and dump it. For this reason, a typical loader has a very large bucket mounted on the front and rubber tires that enable to machine to be driven around the site. A large diesel engine provides the power needed by the loader, and hydraulic controls inside the operator's cab make it easy for an operator to lift, lower, and tilt the bucket. While loaders can be track-mounted, most are wheel loaders with an articulating frame and a steering wheel for easy maneuvering (**FIGURE 2-31**).

Off-road dump trucks, especially rigid-frame trucks used in construction and mining, are enormous pieces of MORE. Even smaller versions of these trucks are huge. Rigid-frame trucks share many of the same major components (**FIGURE 2-32**). The operator's cab and the body are both attached to the rigid frame. The cab has a roll over protective system (ROPS) and a falling object protective structure (FOPS). Inside the cab are the controls

FIGURE 2-31 Major components of a wheel loader.

FIGURE 2-32 Major components of a rigid-frame truck.

needed to drive the truck and dump the body. Stairs provide access to the platform in front of the operator's cab, and railings surround the platform help to prevent falls. An extended section of the body, called the **canopy**, extends over the cab to protect the cab from falling material during loading and transport. Hydraulic hoist cylinders are used to raise and lower the body. The front axle is used to steer the truck while the rear tandem axle drives the truck.

Grading and Compacting Equipment Features

Grading and compacting equipment is used to move and disperse soil, smooth the soil, create slopes and ditches, and pack the soil firmly before any building or paving takes place. In most cases, these tasks are performed using scrapers, graders, and compactors.

Wheel tractor scrapers are heavy self-propelled machines with rubber tires, a scraping edge that can be raised and lowered hydraulically by the operator, and a large hopper (bowl) to collect the material scraped from the ground (**FIGURE 2-33**). The wheel tractor scraper pictured is a single tractor scraper. Scrapers are also available as a **tandem scraper**. Tandem scrapers have separate engines for the tractor section wheels and the scraper section wheels. Having separate engines provides greater power and traction in rough terrain.

Like most types of MORE, motor graders range in size and capacity. However, most graders share some common features. They are long, narrow machines with a front-steering axle and two rear drive axles, both of which have rubber tires. A large diesel engine located at the rear of the grader provides the power to drive the grader and operate the hydraulic systems. All graders have an adjustable blade used to move soil or aggregate; cut ditches; and mix, windrow, grade, and smooth material. The blade is attached to the grader with a drawbar and a circle, which are controlled with hydraulic cylinders to maneuver the blade vertically, horizontally, and at an angle to the frame. Modern motor graders have articulated frames that allow them to work at an offset angle. **FIGURE 2-34** shows the major components of a motor grader.

FIGURE 2-33 Major components of a wheel tractor scraper.

FIGURE 2-34 Major components of a motor grader.

FIGURE 2-35 Major components of a vibratory steel-wheel roller.

Compactors are familiar-looking machines used to compact soil or pavement and speed up the natural settling process. Most compactors are self-propelled machines that have a diesel engine, an operator's cab with a steering wheel and other controls, and some combination of large metal rollers or pneumatic tires at the front and rear of the machine. A vibratory steel-wheel roller has a device on each drum that generates vibration to further enhance the compaction capabilities of the machine (**FIGURE 2-35**).

Hoisting and Handling Equipment Features

Equipment used for lifting, moving, and loading components and materials include machines such as cranes, forklifts, and knuckleboom loaders. Each of these types of equipment must be able to safely lift heavy objects high into the air and, in most cases, transport those objects to another area of the work site.

Cranes are among the most common machines used to lift and move heavy objects. A typical track-mounted (crawler) crane uses a boom, cables, and counterweights to

FIGURE 2-36 Major components of a track-mounted (crawler) crane.

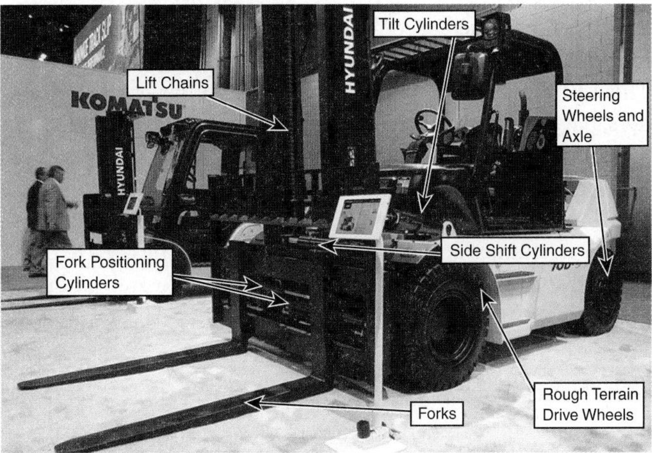

FIGURE 2-37 Major components of a rough terrain forklift.

accomplish this task. Most crawler cranes have large diesel engines, hydraulic systems, joysticks for operator controls, and a high-strength lattice boom that can be raised and lowered (**FIGURE 2-36**).

Forklifts are used to move palletized components, sections of pipe, and similar materials from one place to another. The major features and controls of a typical rough terrain forklift are similar to those of any off-road forklift (**FIGURE 2-37**).

▶ MORE Terminology

K02003

Service technicians working on MORE must be familiar with basic terminology used to describe the features and operation of heavy equipment. Many of the components that make up heavy equipment are often called by different names. Failing to understand MORE terminology puts technicians at risk of misidentifying equipment parts and misunderstanding operating practices when they communicate with equipment owners and operators.

Construction Terminology

There are many industry terms used to describe the construction features of mobile off-road equipment. The following list identifies some of the more common terms with which technicians should be familiar.

Apron—a movable section on the forward wall of a scraper's bowl that is used to close the bowl for transport after the bowl is full.

Automatic retarder control system—an electronic system used on an off-road truck that works with the engine brake and traction control system to slow the vehicle during downhill travel.

Cutting edge—on a motor grader blade, a sharp steel bar attached to the bottom of the moldboard that is used for cutting into the ground.

Dipper stick (or stick)—the section of the digging component of an excavator that connects the end of the boom to the bucket.

Grouser—on a dozer, a ridge or cleat across a track that improves the track's grip.

Haul truck—a common name used to describe a rigid-frame dump truck or a mining truck.

Hoe—any kind excavator that digs material by having its bucket pulled from front to back. The term "hoe" is also used to describe the entire assembly at the front of an excavator that consists of the boom, stick, and bucket.

Hoist cylinders—the hydraulic cylinders on an off-road truck that are used to raise and lower the dump body.

Knuckleboom—a term that is sometimes used to describe the pivot point between a gooseneck boom and a stick that resembles a knuckle.

Moldboard—on a motor grader blade, the long concave piece of metal on which the cutting edge is attached to push soil or aggregate.

Outriggers—stabilizing devices that can be extended from the front and rear sides of a piece of equipment to keep it from tipping or rolling.

Pad (or foot)—on a sheepsfoot roller, the part of the roller that projects outward from the drum and makes contact with the ground.

Platen—a flat plate that serves as the supporting base for the rotating platform of an excavator.

Sheepsfoot—a tamping roller in which projected pads (or feet) extend outward from the drum to compact soil.

Shooting-boom excavator—another name for a telescoping boom excavator.

Traction control system—a computerized system used on off-road trucks to divert torque from a spinning wheel to one or more of the other wheels to improve traction.

Turntable—the rotating platform of an excavator.

Upper carriage—the upper frame of an excavator onto which the turntable, engine, operator's cab, operator controls, and counterweights are attached.

Upper structure—the part of a telescoping boom excavator that includes the turntable, swing mechanism, counterweight, boom, and operator's cab.

Operation Terminology

As with construction feature terms, there are numerous terms used to describe aspects of equipment operation. Service technicians should be familiar with these terms. The following list identifies common terms associated with the operation of MORE.

Blade float—allowing the blade of a dozer to float over a surface to create a smooth finish.
Blade pitch—the angle at which a dozer blade is from vertical.
Blade tilt—the angle at which a dozer blade is from horizontal.
Crowd—to move the stick of a backhoe closer to the tractor or to force the stick into digging.
Curl—to rotate the bucket of a backhoe.
Dozing—the process of using the blade on a dozer to push material to a different place.
Draw—to move the stick of a backhoe back toward the operator.
Grubbing—to use a bucket to dig out roots and other buried material.
Haul road—a compacted dirt road over which off-road trucks and equipment travel to move material on and off site.
Reach—to extend the stick of a backhoe away from the cab.
Ripping—using a ripper attachment on the back of a dozer or grader to loosen hard soil or other material.
Scarifying—using a scarifier attachment on a motor grader to loosen soil in front of the blade.
Spoils—excavated material that is removed during a digging operation.
Undercutting—the process of digging material from beneath an excavator or from a bank or vertical face of a trench.

▶ Industry/Accreditation

I02001

The construction and operation terminology presented in the previous section is critical for service technicians working on mobile off-road equipment. Technicians must be able to accurately use terminology that is common in the trade and understand safety procedures that apply to this work. Federal and state agencies and industrial trade groups have developed standards over the years that technicians can use for source material:

- The Occupational Safety and Health Administration (OSHA) at www.osha.gov, which sets and enforces standards related to safety and equipment.
- The Mine Safety and Health Administration (MSHA) at www.msha.gov, which develops and enforces safety and health rules pertaining to mines in the United States.
- The Association of Equipment Manufacturers (AEM) at www.aem.org, which develops industry best practices, offers training, and maintains safety and technical information.

In addition, magazines covering heavy equipment and off-road equipment manufacturers typically have technical information available on their websites. Technicians working on MORE should exploit all available resources to ensure that they understand the terminology and regulations that apply to the trade.

▶ MORE Attachments

K02004

Like a car or truck, nearly every type of MORE has optional equipment and special attachments that can greatly enhance the equipment's capability. For instance, excavators and backhoe loaders can be fitted with different sizes and types of buckets, and dozers can use different types of blades. This section examines some of the more common attachments used on MORE.

SAFETY TIP

Attachments used on MORE must be compatible with the specific equipment. Using an incompatible attachment can be extremely dangerous because the attachment could fail and seriously injure personnel or damage equipment.

Excavation Equipment Attachments

Excavators are often used for demolition work. One attachment that enables an excavator to fulfill this task is a hydraulic breaker. This hydraulic attachment is used primarily for breaking boulders, pavement, concrete, and other solid objects (**FIGURE 2-38**).

Other common attachments that are used on excavators include demolition shears, which can be used to cut through steel bars and beams; cutter heads, which can be used to grind up brush, stumps, and trees; rippers, which can be used to break up hard soil; and grapples, which can be used to grab and place material (**FIGURE 2-39**).

SAFETY TIP

Whenever a cutter head, a hydraulic breaker, or demolition shears are used as attachments on an excavator, a steel cage must be used in the front of the operator's cab to minimize the risk caused by flying debris.

Backhoe loader attachments are similar to those used on excavators. For instance, most backhoes can be fitted with different types of buckets to make them a versatile choice for excavation jobs that do not require the power of larger

FIGURE 2-38 Hydraulic breaker attachment and bits for an excavator.

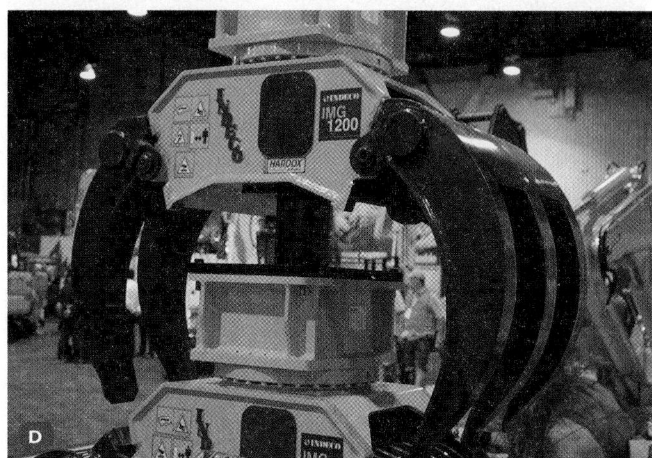

FIGURE 2-39 MORE attachments: **A.** demolition shears **B.** cutter head **C.** ripper attachment **D.** grapple.

excavators. They can also be used with rippers and hydraulic breakers. Two other attachments that are often used on backhoe loaders are auger attachments, which can be used to bore holes for posts or piers, and cold planer attachments, which can be used to grind paved surfaces (**FIGURE 2-40**).

Earth-Moving and Mining Equipment Attachments

As with most heavy equipment that uses buckets or blades, a dozer can be fitted with any one of several blade options, depending on the specific need. In addition, dozers often use

FIGURE 2-40 Backhoe loader attachments: **A.** auger **B.** cold planer.

ripper attachments to break up hard soil, winches to pull material and other equipment, and side booms to lay pipe or cable (**FIGURE 2-41**).

Loaders can use some of the same types of attachments that are used on backhoe loaders and excavators. For instance, various sizes and types of buckets are available, as are grapples, cold planers, and augers. Other attachments sometimes used on loaders include pallet forks, rotating brooms, and snow removal equipment.

Grading and Compacting Equipment Attachments

Two of the most common attachments used on motor graders are a scarifier and a ripper. Both of these attachments are used to break up hard soil, but a scarifier is located at the front of the grader ahead of the blade, whereas a ripper is located at the rear of the grader (**FIGURE 2-42**).

Hoisting and Handling Equipment Attachments

Equipment used for hoisting and handling material, including cranes, forklifts, and knuckleboom loaders, can be fitted with numerous attachments for special applications. For instance, cranes can use any of several types of hooks, grapples, and buckets to enhance their capabilities. They can also use pile driver attachments for driving posts or beams into the ground and wrecking balls to demolish buildings.

FIGURE 2-41 Dozer attachments: **A.** ripper **B.** winch **C.** side boom.

FIGURE 2-42 Motor grader attachments: **A.** scarifier **B.** ripper.

FIGURE 2-43 Forklift attachments.

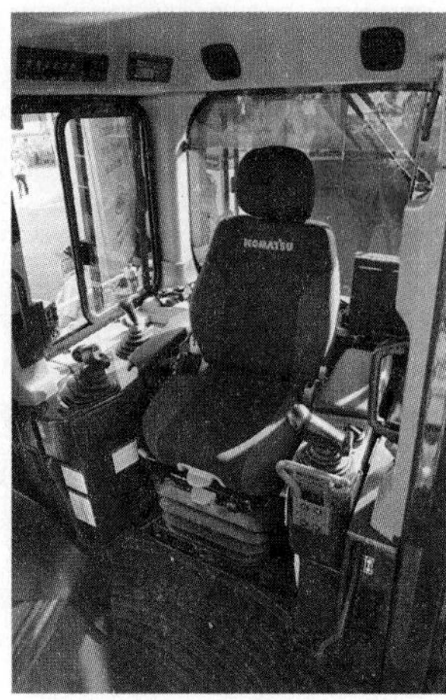

FIGURE 2-44 Operator controls in a modern hydraulic excavator cab.

Many of the attachments used on forklifts are designed to lift and carry specific shapes. For example, there are attachments for drums, rolls of paper, and blocks (**FIGURE 2-43**).

▶ MORE Systems and Components

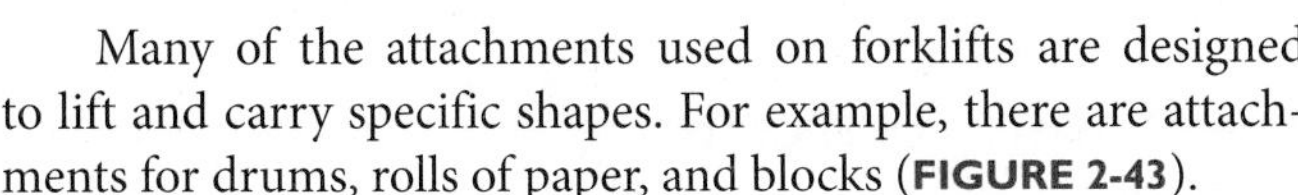

The safe and effective operation of mobile off-road equipment depends on many factors. Some of the most important factors pertain to the systems and components found on the different types of equipment. These systems include those associated with steering, propulsion, the frame, and hydraulics.

Steering Systems

The overall design of a piece of heavy equipment and the particular type of steering system built into the equipment dictates whether the operator will use a steering wheel, levers, and pedals, or a joystick (tiller), to control the equipment. As a general rule, older pieces of track-mounted equipment used levers and pedals that operated mechanically. Modern track-mounted equipment uses hydraulic and electronic controls—typically joysticks (tillers), switches, and foot pedals (**FIGURE 2-44**).

Wheel-mounted equipment is more likely to use a steering wheel and foot pedals that resemble those used in a truck. A modern wheel loader, for instance, has a steering wheel and pedals to drive the vehicle, as well as a joystick and switches to control the function of the loader (**FIGURE 2-45**). The steering system itself is hydrostatic and uses two hydraulic cylinders to control the vehicle.

Propulsion Systems

Older pieces of heavy equipment used diesel engines, manual transmissions, and crawler tracks or wheels to operate and move. Many of these machines still exist today, and new machines are still being produced with manual

FIGURE 2-45 Operator controls in a modern wheel loader cab.

transmissions—some of which have power reversers (power shuttles) and power shift options. Power reversers allow operators to change directions on a piece of equipment without having to use a foot clutch, stop the movement of the equipment, and manually shift into a forward or reverse gear. Power shift transmissions allow operators to change gears on the go without having to use a foot clutch.

Modern pieces of MORE use efficient diesel engines that range from 40 hp (30 kW) to about 600 hp (447 kW). These engines are often mated with heavy-duty (HD) hydrostatic transmissions that use pressurized fluid instead of gears to transfer power from the engine to the axles and wheels and provide infinitely variable speed. **FIGURE 2-46** shows a grader at work.

Equipment Frames

Different types of off-road equipment, such as dozers, graders, and trucks, are available with rigid frames or articulated frames (**FIGURE 2-47**). Choosing a frame for a piece of equipment depends on the strength, capacity, and mobility needed for the job. For instance, a rigid-frame haul truck in a mining application travels over established haul roads, so mobility is usually

FIGURE 2-46 A modern motor grader at work.

FIGURE 2-47 Rigid- and articulated-frame equipment: **A.** crawler dozer with rigid frame and **B.** wheel dozer with articulated frame.

not a mitigating factor. Brute strength, however, is a major concern. The capacity of a rigid-frame haul truck exceeds that of an articulated-frame truck. Articulated-frame trucks haul less, but they are very maneuverable and capable of traveling over muddy and rough terrain.

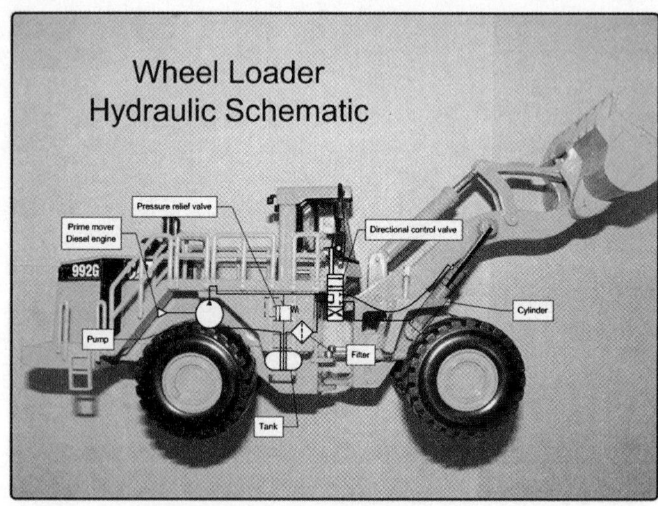

FIGURE 2-48 Wheel loader hydraulic system.

Hydraulic Systems

Hydraulic systems are one of the most important features on any kind of heavy equipment. A hydraulic system uses fluid power to greatly increase a machine's ability to lift, dig, grade, or perform other construction-related tasks. The system consists of many different components, including pumps, motors, valves, actuators, cylinders, and piping and hose (**FIGURE 2-48**).

By manipulating controls in the cab, an operator basically directs the flow of highly pressurized hydraulic fluid through the system to control the equipment.

SAFETY TIP

Working on or around hydraulic systems requires constant vigilance. The fluid in a hydraulic system is under great pressure and high temperature. Carelessly loosening a coupling or accidentally cutting a hose can release the fluid and subject personnel to serious injuries or burns.

▶ Attitude

A02001, S02001

Before starting, operating, or servicing any piece of MORE, it is important for technicians to be familiar with the equipment. This includes locating and reading any operator manuals and service manuals that may exist on site. Find out where those manuals are normally kept and take action to obtain the proper manuals for the equipment. If printed manuals are not available for the equipment, try to find electronic versions either from the client or online through the equipment manufacturer's website. It might also be possible to find the appropriate material by searching online. In some cases, it might be necessary to call the equipment manufacture to get the needed information. Whatever the means, it is important to ensure that the resource material being used matches the equipment being worked on. Follow the steps in **SKILL DRILL 2-1** to start, operate, and shut down a piece of MORE equipment.

SKILL DRILL 2-1 Starting, Operating, and Shutting Down Equipment

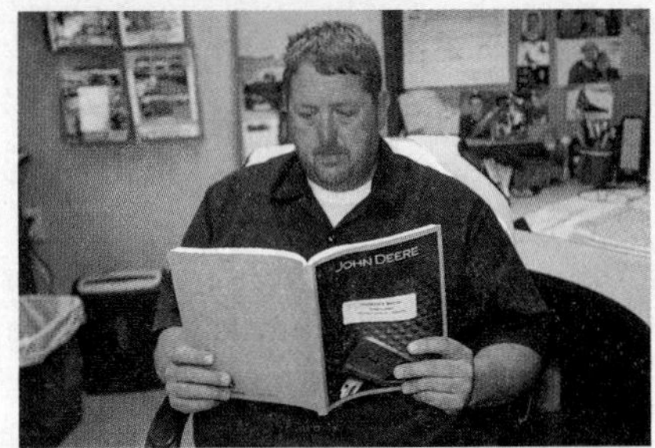

1. Obtain the necessary operator and service manuals that pertain to the equipment being serviced.

2. Perform a simple walk-around inspection of the equipment to ensure that there are no obvious problems, encroaching equipment, or personnel whose presence would prevent starting and moving the equipment.

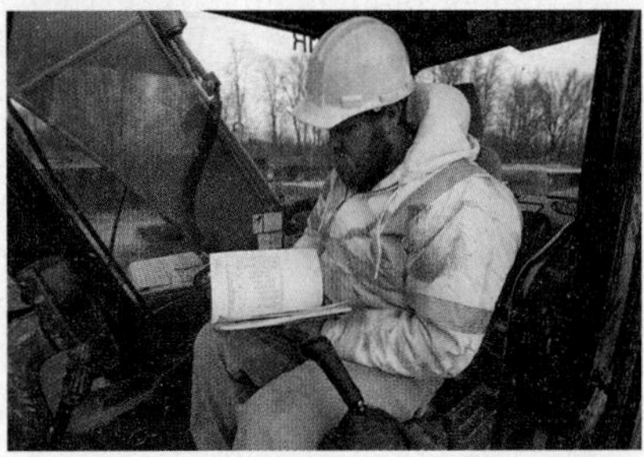

3. Enter the cab or operator area of the equipment and use the operator's manual to familiarize yourself with the layout and controls used to operate the equipment.

4. Following the guidelines in the operator's manual, complete the necessary steps to start the equipment.

5. Once the equipment has reached its normal operating temperature, follow the steps in the operator's manual to move and operate the equipment. Always pay attention to the surroundings when moving and operating any piece of equipment.

6. After moving and operating the equipment, follow the steps in the operator's manual to safely stop, shut down, and secure the equipment.

▶ Wrap-Up

Ready for Review

- MORE classifications can be based on different criteria, including which industry they serve, the general function of the equipment, the way equipment is propelled, or driven, and how the equipment is used.
- Many pieces of off-road equipment will often fit into several categories.
- An excavator is a piece of heavy equipment commonly used in earth-moving, trenching, and loading applications.
- Two basic types of excavators are standard hydraulic excavators: track-mounted machines with crawler tracks and wheel-mounted excavators, which use rubber tires.
- A typical backhoe loader has a hydraulically operated excavating arm mounted onto the rear of a rubber-tired tractor and a loader bucket attached to the front of the tractor.
- A trencher uses either a chain with cutting bits or a wheel with cutting teeth to dig trenches for burying pipes, cables, culverts, and similar items.
- A typical dozer, or bulldozer, is a heavy piece of equipment that moves on crawler tracks and has a wide blade mounted on the front to push large amounts of material.
- A loader has a large bucket mounted on the front that can be raised, lowered, and tilted so that it can scoop up material, transport it to a different area on the site, and dump it.
- A rigid-frame truck, which is sometimes called a haul truck or a mining truck, has a non-pivoting frame, a body, a front axle for steering, and a rear axle for transferring the engine's power to the wheels.
- An articulated-frame dump truck, or articulated hauler, has a pivoting point in the frame, is typically smaller than

rigid-frame truck, and is designed more for maneuverability in rough terrain than for sheer hauling capacity.

- An underground mining truck is much like an articulated-frame truck, but the operator's cab is moved forward of the front axle to give the truck a lower clearance.
- A scraper is a type of MORE that has a scraping edge that scrapes soil into a hopper so that it can be taken to another area to be dumped and dispersed.
- A motor grader is a long, narrow piece of MORE that has rubber tires, a large diesel engine, and an adjustable blade that is used in many earth-moving, ditching, grading, and smoothing applications.
- Motor graders can have rigid frames or articulated frames.
- Compactors are self-propelled machines equipped with large rollers or tires that are driven back and forth over soil, gravel, or asphalt to compact the material.
- Track-mounted (crawler) cranes have a high-strength lattice boom that can be raised, swung, and lowered to move heavy loads.
- Forklifts, or lift trucks, are used on construction sites to move palletized components, sections of pipe, and similar material from one place to another.
- A typical knuckleboom loader has a gooseneck boom with a hydraulically powered claw called a grapple that enables the loader to grab logs and other objects and move them onto piles or trucks.
- Machines found in any particular category of MORE share a lot of common features, even though they are manufactured by different companies around the world.
- A hydraulic breaker is an excavator attachment that is used primarily for breaking boulders, pavement, concrete, and other solid objects.
- A ripper is an attachment used on different pieces of MORE to break up hard soil.
- A scarifier is an attachment used on the front of a motor grader to break up soil ahead of the grader blade.

Key Terms

articulated frame A type of equipment frame that has a permanent hinge, or pivoting point, in the frame to enhance maneuverability.

canopy A part of the body of an off-road truck that extends above the cab to protect the operator from any falling material.

chain trencher A track-mounted trencher with a hydraulically controlled boom that uses a chain with cutting bits that travel around the boom to cut through hard soil and rock.

crumber bar A device on a chain trencher that follows the digging chain to prevent loose soil from collecting in the trench.

gooseneck boom A curved boom used on some types of equipment that connects to a dipper stick and bucket.

grapple A hydraulically powered claw that enables an operator to grab logs and other objects and move them onto piles or trucks.

lattice boom A type of boom commonly used on cranes that has a crisscross pattern of metal braces that enable it to lift heavy loads.

rigid frame A type of equipment frame that runs the full length of the equipment and has no pivoting points for articulation.

tandem scraper A type of scraper that has separate engines for the tractor section and the scraper section to provide greater power and traction for rough terrain.

telescoping boom A type of boom that can be extended outward and retracted.

undercarriage The lower frame of an excavator that supports the turntable and onto which the crawler tracks or wheels are attached.

wheel trencher A type of trencher that uses a large wheel with teeth to dig through pavement or hard soil.

Review Questions

1. The rotating platform on a standard hydraulic excavator can be rotated _____.
   a. 90 degrees
   b. 180 degrees
   c. 270 degrees
   d. 360 degrees

2. The primary purpose of a _____ is to push large amounts of soil, aggregate, or other material.
   a. scraper
   b. dozer
   c. loader
   d. telehandler

3. The height reduction of an underground mining truck is achieved by
   a. replacing the crawler tracks with small diameter tires.
   b. reducing the headroom inside the operator's cab.
   c. moving the operator's cab forward of the front axle.
   d. removing the crumber bar from the hopper.

4. Ditching, grading, and smoothing jobs are most likely to be accomplished using a(n) _____.
   a. motor grader
   b. tandem scraper
   c. mobile crane
   d. articulated loader

5. Wheel-mounted excavation equipment, such as excavators and backhoe loaders, use _____ for added stability.
   a. lattices
   b. outriggers
   c. crumbers
   d. canopies

6. A tandem scraper used in grading applications has two separate _____.
   a. scarifiers
   b. moldboards
   c. hoppers
   d. engines

7. The process of digging material from beneath an excavator or from a bank or vertical face of a trench is called _____.
   a. scarifying
   b. crowding
   c. undercutting
   d. grubbing

8. Which of the following excavator attachments can be used to cut through steel bars and beams during demolition work?
   a. Demolition shears
   b. Hydraulic breakers
   c. Cutter heads
   d. Grapple hooks
9. Side booms are best described as a type of
   a. forklift attachment used to maximize horizontal load control.
   b. haul truck attachment used to balance the body during unloading.
   c. backhoe loader attachment used to widen the equipment's stance.
   d. dozer attachment used to lay pipe or cable in trenches.
10. MORE engines are often mated with HD hydrostatic transmissions that use
   a. motor oil to power hydraulic valves and provide infinitely variable pumping.
   b. pressurized fluid to transfer power from the engine to the axles and wheels.
   c. hardened gears and shafts that directly drive planetary gear sets in the wheels.
   d. hydraulic cylinders located in the powertrain to move axles and wheels.

ASE Technician A/Technician B Style Questions

1. Technician A says the rotating platform on a standard hydraulic excavator is attached to an articulator beam that mounts to a chassis. Technician B says the rotating platform is attached to an undercarriage that has crawler tracks or wheels. Who is correct?
   a. Technician A
   b. Technician B
   c. Both Technician A and Technician B
   d. Neither Technician A nor Technician B
2. Technician A says the piece of equipment pictured here is a wheel-mounted excavator. Technician B says it is a skid steer loader. Who is correct?

   a. Technician A
   b. Technician B
   c. Both Technician A and Technician B
   d. Neither Technician A nor Technician B
3. Technician A says a hydraulically controlled boom that can be lifted and lowered is used to control the depth of a trench being dug by a track-mounted chain trencher. Technician B says the depth is controlled by cutting bits that can be extended and retracted. Who is correct?
   a. Technician A
   b. Technician B
   c. Both Technician A and Technician B
   d. Neither Technician A nor Technician B
4. Technician A says a loader is a piece of MORE that has a bucket designed to be raised, lowered, and tilted so that it can scoop up material, transport it to a different area on the site, and dump it. Technician B says a loader has a bucket designed to be raised, lowered, and tilted so that it can scoop up material and dump it into a truck. Who is correct?
   a. Technician A
   b. Technician B
   c. Both Technician A and Technician B
   d. Neither Technician A nor Technician B
5. Technician A says that the part of an off-road truck's body that extends above the cab to protect the operator from falling material is called the gooseneck. Technician B says the part of the body that extends above the cab is the canopy. Who is correct?
   a. Technician A
   b. Technician B
   c. Both Technician A and Technician B
   d. Neither Technician A nor Technician B
6. Technician A says a vibratory steel-wheel roller has a device on each drum that generates vibration to further enhance the compaction capabilities of the machine. Technician B says the device on each drum generates vibration to prevent seams from forming between different pavement layers. Who is correct?
   a. Technician A
   b. Technician B
   c. Both Technician A and Technician B
   d. Neither Technician A nor Technician B
7. Technician A says a flat plate that serves as the supporting base for the rotating platform of an excavator is called an apron. Technician B says the flat plate being referred to is called a turntable. Who is correct?
   a. Technician A
   b. Technician B
   c. Both Technician A and Technician B
   d. Neither Technician A nor Technician B
8. Technician A says one of the most common attachments used on a motor grader is a scarifier. Technician B says one of the most common motor grader attachments is a ripper. Who is correct?
   a. Technician A
   b. Technician B
   c. Both Technician A and Technician B
   d. Neither Technician A nor Technician B

9. Technician A says attachments that are designed for moving objects such as drums, rolls of paper, and blocks are most likely to be used on a crane. Technician B says attachments for moving drums, rolls of paper, and blocks are most likely to be used on a forklift. Who is correct?

a. Technician A
b. Technician B
c. Both Technician A and Technician B
d. Neither Technician A nor Technician B

10. Technician A says haul trucks used in mining applications typically have rigid frames because they travel over established haul roads with huge loads. Technician B says mining haul trucks typically have rigid frames because they require greater mobility than articulated-frame trucks. Who is correct?

a. Technician A
b. Technician B
c. Both Technician A and Technician B
d. Neither Technician A nor Technician B

CHAPTER 3

Shop and Machine Safety

Knowledge Objectives

After reading this chapter, you will be able to:

- **K03001** Identify workplace hazards.
- **K03002** Describe industry practices for hazard assessment and control procedures.
- **K03003** Describe safety regulations, procedures, and occupational safety standards.
- **K03004** Describe the responsibilities of workers and employers to apply emergency procedures.
- **K03005** Describe the roles and responsibilities of employers and employees with respect to the selection and use of personal protective equipment (PPE).
- **K03006** Describe how to prepare a machine to safely service and repair it.

Skills Objectives

After reading this chapter, you will be able to:

- **S03001** Demonstrate the correct use of personal protection equipment.
- **S03002** Select, use, and maintain appropriate PPE for worksite applications.

Attitude Objectives

After reading this chapter, you will be able to:

- **A03001** Develop positive tradesperson attitudes with respect to housekeeping, personal protective equipment, and emergency procedures.
- **A03002** Apply appropriate safety procedures to workplace practices.

▶ Introduction

You probably know someone who has been, or have heard of a situation where someone has been, involved in a work-related accident or mishap. Work-related accidents and mishaps can result in severe personal injuries, damage to valuable equipment, and even death. This causes physical, emotional, and financial hardships for people and their families, lost revenue and production for repair shops, decreased morale of coworkers, and unnecessary inspections and oversight by government and industry authorities. The career you have chosen as a heavy equipment repair technician comes with many potential hazards and risks that can be reduced, but not eliminated. It is important to learn about hazards so that you can identify them and act to protect yourself and your coworkers. Some hazards are obvious, such as machines falling from hoists or jacks, or tires exploding during inflation. Other hazards are less obvious, such as the long-term effects of fumes from solvents. There are many things to learn about safety in the heavy equipment shop, but it is impossible to cover every situation you will encounter. If not properly handled, these hazards can result in accidents and mishaps that may cause equipment damage, severe injury to yourself and others, and even death. The key factor to lower the risk of an accident or mishap is safety. **Safety** is the condition of being protected from, or unlikely to cause danger, risk, or injury to yourself or others. This chapter will discuss some of the fundamental knowledge, attitudes, and actions to take in order to maintain a safe working environment.

The History of Safety in the Workplace

During the Industrial Revolution of the 1700s and 1800s, many people transitioned from working on farms and in the home to working in large industrial factories. This exposed many people to machinery and environments with safety risks they were not familiar with. During this time, very little attention was given by employers, and employees, to safety practices and risk mitigation techniques. As a result, many people were severely injured or killed, for what we would consider preventable causes today. Eventually, due to a large outcry from workers and their families, government and industry authorities began to implement rules and regulations governing safety in the workplace. Workplace safety has come a long way from its beginnings during the Industrial Revolution. You would likely be appalled by the safety practices of an industrial factory during the 1700s or 1800s (**FIGURE 3-1**). History is very important to safety, because if we do not learn from past mistakes, we are likely to repeat them. Learning from your own past experiences and mistakes, as well as the experiences and mistakes of others, is crucial for the improvement of safety in the workplace over time.

Roles of Safety in the Workplace

To create and maintain a safe working environment, everyone must know their specific role, as well as the roles of others regarding safety. This extends all the way from employees, supervisors, managers, and company officers to vendors and government and industry authorities. **Occupational safety and health** is important to ensure that everyone can work without being injured. Governments will normally have legislation in place with significant penalties for those who do not follow safe practices in the workplace. Occupational safety and health is everyone's responsibility. You have a responsibility to ensure that you work safely and take care not to put others at risk by acting in an unsafe manner. Supervisors and managers have a responsibility not to expose employees under their responsibility to risks, without providing employees with knowledge of the risks and appropriate safety measures. Your employer also has a responsibility to provide a safe working environment.

FIGURE 3-1 Workplaces until the last hundred years or so were unsafe and dirty environments. Injuries and deaths in the workplace were commonplace.

You Are the Mobile Heavy Equipment Technician

You are assisting another technician with repairs to a tractor loader backhoe. One of the mechanical linkages on the rear shovel of the backhoe has cracked and needs to be welded. The other technician wants to use an electric arc welder to perform the repair with the linkage left in place, as removing it would be difficult and time-consuming. The area where you will be performing the repair is very busy, with many people working.

1. What types of hazards are present during a welding operation with an electric arc welder?
2. What types of personal protective equipment (PPE) should you both use to protect yourself from welding hazards?
3. What measures (if any) should be taken to protect other people in the area from welding hazards?
4. What (if any) preparations should be made to protect yourself, other people, and equipment before welding begins?

Government regulators have a responsibility to enforce the law. Because safety is everyone's responsibility, anyone has the authority to stop an operation that is unsafe, in order to make corrections.

The Role of Hazard Prevention and Control in Safety in the Workplace

Not all **hazards** and **risks** in the workplace can be prevented or eliminated. The key is to apply the appropriate **risk controls**, to minimize the risk to personnel and equipment from workplace hazards. When appropriate risk controls are in place to protect employees and equipment from workplace hazards, they benefit everyone involved. The benefits of an effective workplace hazard prevention and control system include:

- avoiding unnecessary injuries and illnesses to personnel
- minimizing or eliminate unnecessary safety and health risks
- minimizing decreased production due to lost time safety incidents
- minimizing downtime due to equipment damage from safety mishaps
- increasing employee health
- increasing employee morale and job satisfaction.

To create and maintain a safe working environment, both employees and management must be committed to safety. The largest factor that can affect safety in a positive or negative way is *you*. This requires you to have the correct knowledge so that you know what to do and for you to act on that knowledge by performing the action correctly. Most accidents occur because of human factors. This means an individual did not know the correct action to perform, or they did know the correct action but did not perform the action correctly. To ensure the safety of yourself and others, make sure you are aware of the correct safety procedures at your workplace. This means listening carefully to safety information provided by your employer and asking for clarification, help, or instructions if you are unsure how to perform a task safely. Always think about how you are performing shop tasks, be on the lookout for unsafe equipment and work practices, and wear the correct **personal protective equipment (PPE)**. PPE refers to safety equipment like safety footwear, gloves, clothing, protective eyewear, and hearing protection (**FIGURE 3-2**).

Know the location of emergency equipment like fire extinguishers, defibrillators, and first aid kits, as well as the designated **evacuation routes**. Evacuation routes are a safe way of escaping danger and gathering in a safe place where everyone can be accounted for in the event of an emergency. It is important to have more than one evacuation route in case any single route is blocked during the emergency. Your shop may have an evacuation procedure that clearly identifies the evacuation routes (**FIGURE 3-3**). The evacuation routes will often be marked with colored lines painted on the floors. Exits should be highlighted with signs that may be illuminated. Always make sure

FIGURE 3-2 PPE refers to safety equipment like gloves, safety-toe work boots, eye protection, and hearing protection.

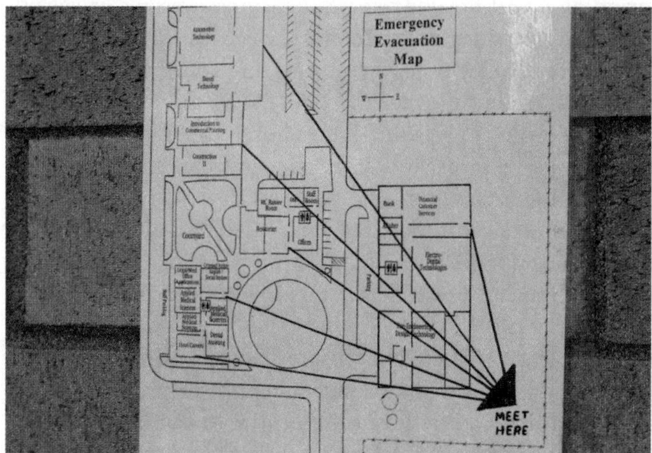

FIGURE 3-3 Your shop should have an evacuation route plan posted in several places throughout your shop.

you are familiar with the evacuation routes for the shop. Before conducting any task, identify which route you will take if an emergency were to occur. Muster points are usually identified outside of the shop and provide a safe gathering area where a designated individual can perform a roll call to ensure that everyone is accounted for.

> ▶ **TECHNICIAN TIP**
>
> Emergency Evacuation Routes and Exits: Keep emergency evacuation routes and exits clear of tools, equipment, parts, or machines. Never block, lock, or obstruct emergency exists. Doing so may prevent prompt evacuation in case of an emergency.

Remember that safety is everyone's responsibility! In this chapter, we will introduce the fundamental concepts of safety in the workplace, so that you will have the knowledge to work safely. It is up to you to take the correct actions to keep yourself and others safe in your workplace.

▶ Identification of Workplace Hazards

K03001

A **hazard** is anything that could hurt you or someone else, and most workplaces have them. It is almost impossible to remove all hazards in the workplace, but it is important to recognize and identify hazards and work to reduce their potential for causing harm by putting specific **hazard control measures** in place. Hazard control measures are processes and procedures put into place to reduce or eliminate the risk and/or severity of an accident or mishap. For example, operating a bench grinder poses several hazards. While it is not possible to eliminate the hazards of using the bench grinder, by putting specific hazard control measures in place, the risk of those hazards can be reduced. A risk analysis of a bench grinder would identify the following hazards and risks: a high-velocity particle that could damage your eyesight or that of someone working nearby; the grinding wheel breaking apart, damaging eyesight or causing cuts and abrasion; electrocution if electrical parts are faulty; heat or high-velocity particles damaging your hands; a risk to your hearing due to excessive noise; and a risk of entrapment of clothing or body parts through rotating machinery. To reduce the risk of these hazards, the following measures are taken: position the bench grinder in a safe area away from where others work; make sure electrical items are regularly checked for electrical and mechanical safety, when operating the equipment wear PPE such as protective eyewear, gloves, hearing protection, hairnets, or caps; do not wear loose clothing that can be caught in the bench grinder; and ensure that all guards and safety devices specified by the manufacturer are in place. Unidentified hazards have the greatest potential to cause a workplace accident or mishap. Therefore, it is important to have processes in place that constantly seek to identify new hazards in the workplace. At many shops, hazards may already be identified for you during training and new employee orientation. Hazards may also be identified for you through signage on specific machines or in certain areas where hazards exist. You may be educated on specific workplace hazards by shop safety managers or in periodic safety updates and memos. While many shops are very proactive in identifying hazards for their employees, this does not relieve each person of their responsibility for their own safety. Just as the hazards most likely to cause an accident or mishap are the unidentified hazards, so too the people most likely to be involved in an accident or mishap are those who do not familiarize themselves with their work environment and hazard related information.

Hazardous Environments

A **hazardous environment** is a place where hazards exist. Most workplaces have some type of hazards, but the type or hazard and severity of the risk can vary. For example, the risk to an employee in a coffee shop is quite different from the risk to an employee in a heavy equipment shop that repairs mobile off-road equipment. It is much less likely that an employee at a coffee shop may be killed due to not familiarizing themselves with the hazards in their working environment. In contrast, an employee at a heavy equipment shop with potentially dangerous equipment around, such as overhead cranes, equipment lifts and jacks, welding equipment, and power tools, has a much greater potential to be severely injured or killed by not familiarizing themselves with the hazards in the work environment. Your employer could identify every hazard with clear signage and invest heavily in an effective safety program, but if you do not familiarize yourself with the hazards of your work environment, you are a potential danger to yourself and others. An important first step in identifying hazardous environments is to familiarize yourself with the shop layout. If it is not already part of your employer's new-hire or onboarding process, ask your supervisor or another employee to provide a tour of the shop to you. Ask about, and pay attention to, the locations and types of hazards and their respective control measures: fire extinguishers, fire alarms, exhaust ventilation hoses, hazardous and flammable material storage, spill kits, and the location of material safety data sheets and other safety-related documentation. There may be special work areas that are defined by painted lines. These lines show the hazardous zone around certain machines and areas. If you are not working on the machines, you should stay outside the marked area. Study the various warning signs around your shop. Understand the meaning of the signal word, the colors, the text, and the symbols or pictures on each sign. Ask your supervisor if you do not fully understand any part of a sign. To identify hazardous environments, follow the steps in **SKILL DRILL 3-1**.

Hazard Signs

Always remember that a shop is a hazardous environment. To make people more aware of specific shop hazards, legislative bodies have developed a series of safety signs. These signs are designed to give adequate warning of an unsafe situation. Each sign has four components:

- Signal word: There are three signal words—danger, warning, and caution.

  Danger indicates an immediately hazardous situation, which, if not avoided, will result in death or serious injury. Danger is usually indicated by white text with a red background. See **FIGURE 3-4A** for an example of warning signage.

  Warning indicates a potentially hazardous situation, which, if not avoided, could result in death or serious injury. The sign is usually in black text with a yellow or orange background. See **FIGURE 3-4B** for an example of warning signage.

  Caution indicates a potentially hazardous situation, which, if not avoided, may result in minor or moderate injury. It may also be used to alert people about unsafe practices. This sign is usually in black text with a yellow background. See **FIGURE 3-4C** for an example of a caution sign.
- Background color: The choice of background color also draws attention to potential hazards and is used to provide contrast so that the letters or images stand out. For example, a red background is used to identify a definite hazard; yellow indicates caution for a potential hazard. A green background is used for emergency-type signs, such

SKILL DRILL 3-1 Identifying Hazardous Environments

1. Familiarize yourself with the shop layout. Study and understand the various warning signs around your shop. Identify exits and plan your escape route in case of emergency. Know the designated gathering point, and go there in an emergency.

2. Check the air quality. Locate the extractor fans or ventilation outlets, and make sure they are not obstructed in any way. Locate and observe the operation of the exhaust extraction hose, pump, and outlet used on a machine's exhaust pipes.

3. Check the location, type, and operation of fire extinguishers and fire alarms in your shop. Be sure you know when and how to use each type of fire extinguisher.

4. Find out where flammable materials are kept, and make sure they are stored properly.

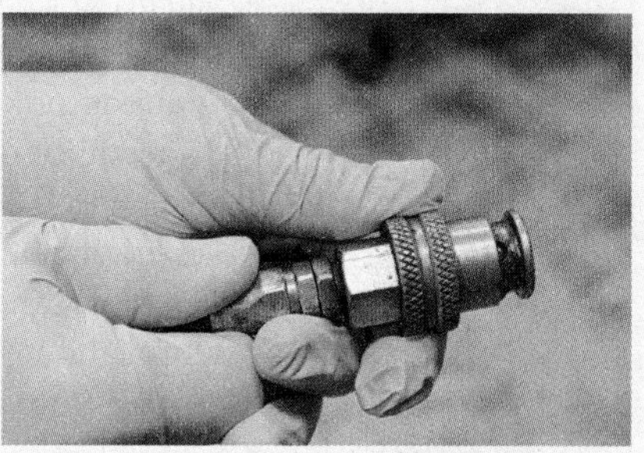

5. Check the hoses and fittings on the air compressor and air guns for any damage or excessive wear. Be particularly careful when troubleshooting air guns. Never pull the trigger while inspecting one: severe eye damage can result.

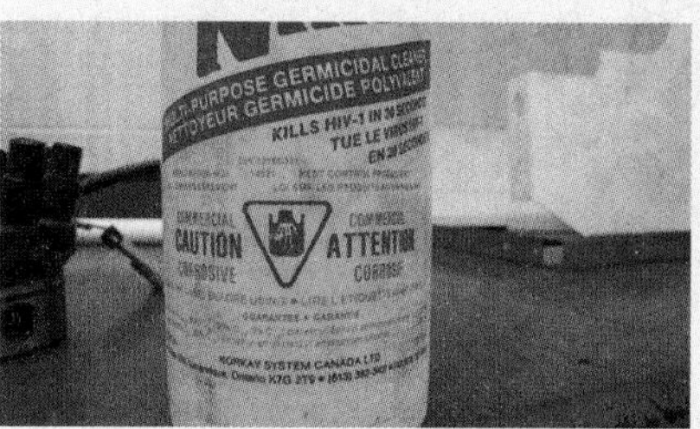

6. Identify caustic chemicals and acids associated with activities in your shop. Ask your supervisor for information on any special hazards in your particular shop and any special avoidance procedures that may apply to you and your working environment.

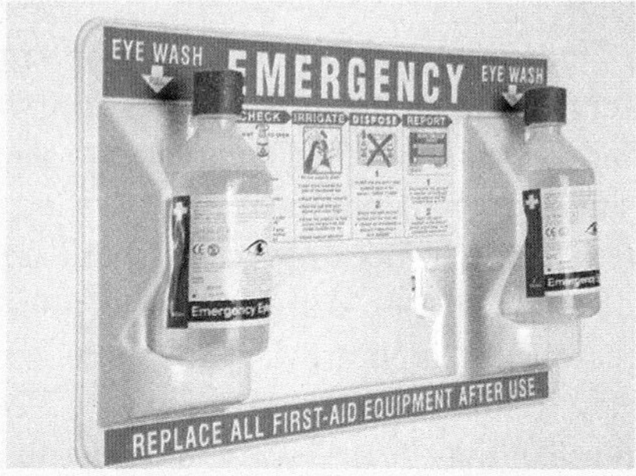

7. Identify the location and proper operation of the emergency eye wash station in your shop.

8. Identify the location, and verify the contents of the spill kits located in your shop.

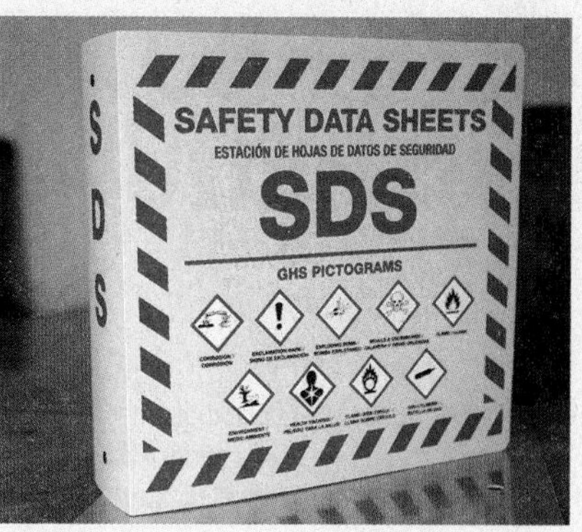

9. Identify the location of material safety data sheets and other safety-related documentation in your shop.

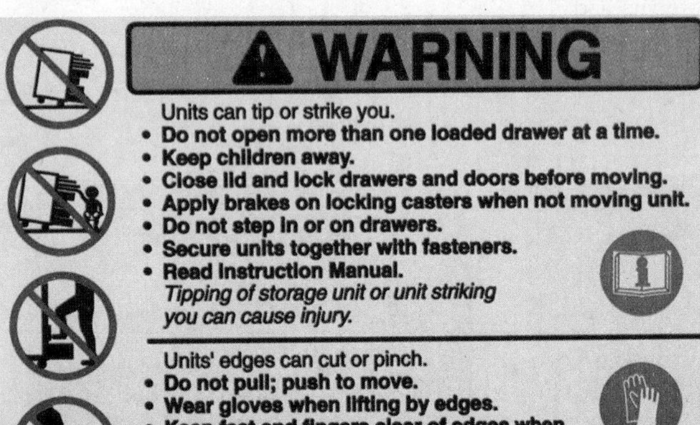

FIGURE 3-4 Standard Hazard Signage **A.** Danger is usually indicated by white text on a red background. **B.** Warning is usually in black text with an orange background. **C.** Caution is usually in black text with a yellow background.

as for first aid, fire protection, and emergency equipment. A blue background is used for general information signs.

- Text: The sign will sometimes include explanatory text intended to provide additional safety information. Some signs are designed to convey a personal safety message.
- Pictorial message: In symbol signs, a pictorial message appears alone or is combined with explanatory text. This type of sign allows the safety message to be conveyed to people who are illiterate or who do not speak the local language.

Safety Equipment

Shop safety equipment includes the following items:

- Handrails: Handrails are used to separate walkways and pedestrian traffic from work areas. They provide a physical barrier that directs pedestrian traffic and also provide protection from machine movements.
- Machinery guards: Machinery guards and yellow lines prevent people from accidentally walking into the operating equipment, or they indicate that a safe distance should be kept from the equipment.
- Painted lines: Large, fixed machinery such as lathes and milling machines present a hazard to the operator and others working in the area. To prevent accidents, a machinery guard or a yellow painted line on the floor usually borders this equipment.
- Soundproof rooms: Soundproof rooms are usually used when a lot of noise is made by operating equipment. An example is the use of a chassis dynamometer. A vehicle operating on a dynamometer produces a lot of noise from its tires, exhaust, and engine. To protect other shop users from the noise, the dynamometer is usually placed in a soundproof room to keep shop noise to a minimum.
- Adequate ventilation: Exhaust gases in shops are a serious health hazard. Whenever a machine's engine is running, toxic gases are emitted from its exhaust. To prevent an excess of toxic gas buildup, a well-ventilated work area is needed as well as a method of directly venting the machine's exhaust to the outside.
- Gas extraction hoses: The best way to get rid of these gases is with a suction hose that fits over the machine's exhaust pipe. The hose is attached to an extraction pump that vents the gas to the outside.
- Doors and gates: Doors and gates are used for the same reason as machinery guards and painted lines. A doorway is a physical barrier that can be locked and sealed to separate a hazardous environment from the rest of the shop or a general work area from an office or specialist work area.
- Temporary barriers: In the day-to-day operation of a shop, there is often a reason to temporarily separate one work bay from others. If a welding machine or an oxyacetylene cutting torch is in use, it may be necessary to place a temporary screen or barrier around the work area to protect other shop users from welding flash or injury.

▶ TECHNICIAN TIP

Stay alert for hazards or anything that might be dangerous. If you see, hear, or smell anything odd, take steps to fix it or tell your supervisor about the problem.

> ▶ TECHNICIAN TIP
>
> Whenever you perform a task in the shop, you must use personal protective clothing and equipment that are appropriate for the task and that conform to your local safety regulations and policies. Among other items, these may include the following:
>
> - work clothing, such as coveralls and safety toed footwear
> - eye protection, such as safety glasses and face masks
> - ear protection, such as earmuffs and earplugs
> - hand protection, such as gloves and barrier cream
> - respiratory equipment, such as face masks and respirators.
>
> If you are not certain what is appropriate or required, ask your supervisor.

Technical Manuals in Hazard Identification

Reading and familiarizing yourself with the **technical manual** for the equipment you are operating or servicing is vital to hazard identification. Equipment manufacturers may publish separate operating and servicing manuals, or they may be combined into a single text. Manufacturers include the most complete information on specific hazards and safety-related information in their technical manuals. Before operating or servicing any equipment, especially for the very first time, you should read and become familiar with the manufacturer's technical manual, paying attention to the hazards and safety-related information. The manufacture's technical manuals can be considered the most complete and correct information on the equipment, which include hazards and safety information. Not all hazards are marked with signage on the equipment itself, which is why it is important to read the technical manual and note any hazard and safety information. Periodically, manufactures may issue updates or supplements to their technical manuals, which may include hazard and safety-related information. Because of this, it is important to include any updates to technical manuals and publications as soon as they are released by the manufacturer. If a hard copy manual isn't available, one can often be obtained online and downloaded. Ensure that the manual that is downloaded is the exact one for the machine or equipment that you are working on. The information contained in the manufacturer technical manuals is one of your best tools to avoid workplace accidents and mishaps (**FIGURE 3-5**).

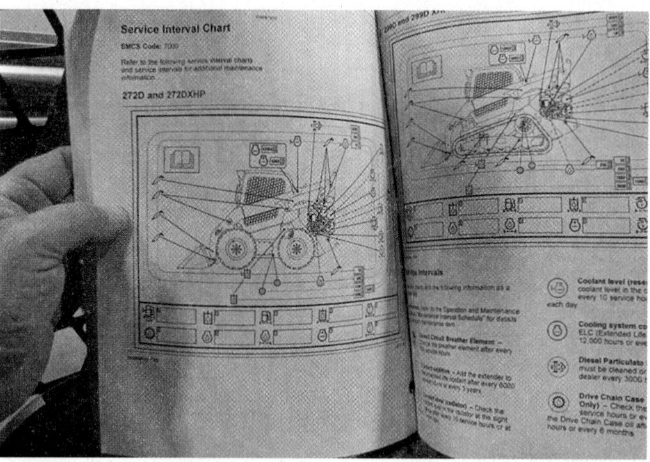

FIGURE 3-5 An equipment manufacturer's operating and repair manuals are a critical source for safety-related information and warnings.

Specific Machine and Shop Safety Hazards

When employed at a workplace that services automotive or mobile off-road equipment, there are some common hazards that may be present. In the next paragraphs, we will briefly discuss some of these common hazards.

Hazardous Materials

A **hazardous material** is any material that poses an unreasonable risk of damage or injury to persons, property, or the environment if it is not properly controlled during handling, storage, manufacture, processing, packaging, use and disposal, or transportation. These materials can be solids, liquids, or gases (**FIGURE 3-6**). Most shops use hazardous materials daily, such as cleaning solvents, spray paint, gasket cement, brake fluid, and coolant. Hazardous materials must be properly handled, labeled, stored, and cleaned in the event of a spill.

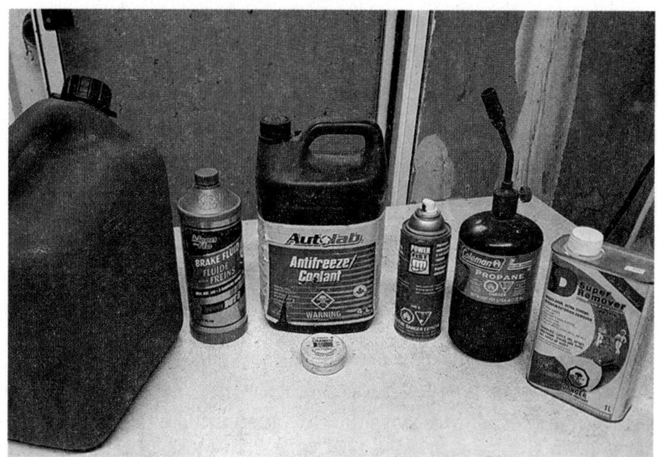

FIGURE 3-6 Hazardous materials can be liquids, solids, or gases. All hazardous materials are dangerous.

Hazardous Material Spill Kits

A **spill kit** is a kit used in workplaces that use or store liquid hazardous material and other liquids that require special cleanup procedures (**FIGURE 3-7**). These kits contain items needed in the cleanup of a liquid hazardous material spill. A spill kit may contain gloves, eye protection, rubber apron, absorbent pads, barrier materials, sand or other absorbent loose material. Ensure you know the location of spill kits in your shop. Spill kits should be inspected regularly and restocked as needed. Before using a spill kit to cleanup any liquid or hazardous material spill, read the **material safety data sheet (MSDS)** for the material and follow the cleanup and disposal instructions. If in doubt about proper cleanup and disposal procedures, contact the material manufacturer at the telephone number on the MSDS or the product label.

FIGURE 3-7 Spill kits should be located in areas where spills are most likely to occur.

▶ TECHNICIAN TIP

Hazardous material spill kits: The technician should know where the spill kits are in their work area. In the event of a spill, first clear the area. Next, read the **Safety data sheet (SDS)** for the spilled material to determine what to do in case of a spill and the proper way to clean up and dispose of the spilled material. If further details are needed, contact the material manufacturer at the telephone number listed on the SDS.

Material Safety Data Sheets

Hazardous materials are used daily and may make you very sick if they are not used properly. The manufacturers of all hazardous materials are required to provide an SDS also called an MSDS, which provides specific information on the hazards associates with the material. MSDS contain detailed information about the hazardous materials to help you understand how they should be safely used, any health effects relating to them, how to treat a person who has been exposed to them, and how to deal with them in a fire situation. An MSDS can be obtained from the manufacturer of the material. The shop should have an MSDS for each hazardous substance or dangerous product they have. In the United States, it is required that workplaces have an MSDS for every chemical on site. Whenever you deal with a potentially hazardous product, you should consult the MSDS to learn how to use that product safely. If you are using more than one product, make sure you consult all the MSDS for those products. Be aware that certain combinations of products can be more dangerous than any of them separately. MSDS are usually kept in a clearly marked binder and should be regularly updated as chemicals come into the workplace. See **FIGURE 3-8** for an example of an MSDS. Generally, the SDS must contain at least the following information:

- revision date
- material and manufacturer ID
- hazardous ingredients
- health hazard data
- fire and explosion data
- details about the material mixing or reacting with other materials
- special precautions.

Review the following figures for an example of an SDS. To identify information found on an SDS, follow the steps in **SKILL DRILL 3-2**.

Engine Exhaust Hazards

Running engines produce dangerous exhaust gases, including carbon monoxide and carbon dioxide. Carbon monoxide in even small concentrations can kill or cause serious injuries. Carbon dioxide is a greenhouse gas, and vehicles are a major source of carbon dioxide in the atmosphere. Exhaust gases also contain hydrocarbons and nitrogen oxides. These gases can form smog and cause breathing problems for some people.

Carbon monoxide is extremely dangerous, as it is odorless and colorless and can build up to toxic levels very quickly in confined spaces. In fact, it doesn't take very much carbon monoxide to pose a danger. The maximum permissible exposure limit (PEL) for **OSHA (Occupational Safety and Health Administration)** is 50 parts per million (ppm) of air for an eight-hour period. The National Institute for Occupational Safety and Health has established a recommended exposure limit of 35 ppm for an eight-hour period. The PEL is so low is because carbon monoxide attaches itself to red blood cells much more easily than oxygen does, and it stays with the blood cell. This prevents the blood cells from carrying as much oxygen, and if enough carbon monoxide has been inhaled, it effectively asphyxiates the person. Always follow the correct safety precautions when running engines indoors or in a confined space, including over service pits since gases can accumulate there. The best solution when running engines in an enclosed space is to directly couple the machine's exhaust pipe to an exhaust extraction system that will ventilate the fumes away from the enclosed space to the outside air (**FIGURE 3-9**). The extraction system should be vented to where the fumes will not be drawn back indoors, to a place well away from other people and other premises.

Do not assume that a gasoline engine fitted with a catalytic converter can be run safely indoors; it cannot. Catalytic converters are fitted into the exhaust system in a similar way as mufflers and have a ceramic core with a catalyst that when in operation, controls exhaust emissions through chemical reaction. Diesel trucks and machines equipped with after-treatment exhaust systems operate in much the same manner, and the same safety precautions should be taken with a running diesel truck or machine. They require high temperatures to operate efficiently and are less effective when the exhaust gases are relatively cool, such as when the engine is only idling or being run intermittently. A catalytic converter can never substitute for adequate ventilation or exhaust extraction equipment. In fact, even if the catalytic converter were working at 100% efficiency, the exhaust would contain large amounts of carbon dioxide and very low amounts of oxygen; neither condition can sustain human life.

SAFETY TIP

Do not operate gasoline/petrol or diesel engine equipment indoors without proper exhaust extraction hoses attached for ventilation.

SAFETY DATA SHEET

1. Identification

Product identifier	**Brakleen® Brake Parts Cleaner**
Other means of identification	
Product code	05089, 05089T, 85089, 85089AZ
Recommended use	Brake cleaner
Recommended restrictions	None known.

Manufacturer/Importer/Supplier/Distributor information

Manufactured or sold by:

Company name	CRC Industries, Inc.
Address	885 Louis Dr. Warminster, PA 18974 US
Telephone	
General Information	215-674-4300
Technical Assistance	800-521-3168
Customer Service	800-272-4620
24-Hour Emergency (CHEMTREC)	800-424-9300 (US) 703-527-3887 (International)
Website	www.crcindustries.com

2. Hazard(s) identification

Physical hazards	Gases under pressure	Compressed gas
Health hazards	Skin corrosion/irritation	Category 2
	Carcinogenicity	Category 1B
	Specific target organ toxicity, single exposure	Category 3 narcotic effects
Environmental hazards	Hazardous to the aquatic environment, long-term hazard	Category 2
OSHA defined hazards	Not classified.	

Label elements

Signal word	Danger
Hazard statement	Contains gas under pressure; may explode if heated. Causes skin irritation. May cause drowsiness or dizziness. May cause cancer. Toxic to aquatic life with long lasting effects.
Precautionary statement	
Prevention	Obtain special instructions before use. Do not handle until all safety precautions have been read and understood. Do not puncture or incinerate container. Do not expose to heat or store at temperatures above 49°C/120°F. Use with adequate ventilation. Open doors and windows or use other means to ensure a fresh air supply during use and while product is drying. If you experience any symptoms listed on this label, increase ventilation or leave the area. Avoid breathing mist or vapor. Avoid breathing gas. Wash thoroughly after handling. Wear protective gloves/protective clothing/eye protection/face protection. Avoid release to the environment.
Response	If on skin: Wash with plenty of water. If skin irritation occurs: Get medical attention. Take off contaminated clothing and wash before reuse. If inhaled: Remove person to fresh air and keep comfortable for breathing. Call a poison center/doctor if you feel unwell. If exposed or concerned: Get medical attention. Collect spillage.
Storage	Store locked up. Protect from sunlight. Store in a well-ventilated place. Exposure to high temperature may cause can to burst.
Disposal	Dispose of contents/container in accordance with local/regional/national regulations.

3. Composition/information on ingredients

Mixtures

Chemical name	Common name and synonyms	CAS number	%
Tetrachloroethylene	Perchloroethylene	127-18-4	90 - 100
Carbon dioxide		124-38-9	1 - 5

Specific chemical identity and/or percentage of composition has been withheld as a trade secret.

Material name: Brakleen® Brake Parts Cleaner SDS US

05089, 05089T, 85089, 85089AZ Version #: 02 Revision date: 08-07-2014 Issue date: 12-20-2013 1 / 9

FIGURE 3-8 An example of an SDS with key areas highlighted.

4. First-aid measures

Inhalation	Remove victim to fresh air and keep at rest in a position comfortable for breathing. Call a POISON CENTER or doctor/physician if you feel unwell.
Skin contact	Remove contaminated clothing. Rinse skin with water/shower. If skin irritation occurs: Get medical advice/attention. Wash contaminated clothing before reuse.
Eye contact	Rinse with water. Get medical attention if irritation develops and persists.
Ingestion	In the unlikely event of swallowing contact a physician or poison control center. Rinse mouth.
Most important symptoms/effects, acute and delayed	May cause drowsiness and dizziness. Headache. Nausea, vomiting. Irritation of eyes and mucous membranes. Irritation of nose and throat. Skin irritation. May cause redness and pain.
Indication of immediate medical attention and special treatment needed	Provide general supportive measures and treat symptomatically. Keep victim under observation. Symptoms may be delayed.
General information	IF exposed or concerned: Get medical advice/attention. Ensure that medical personnel are aware of the material(s) involved, and take precautions to protect themselves.

5. Fire-fighting measures

Suitable extinguishing media	Dry chemical, CO2, or water spray.
Unsuitable extinguishing media	Do not use water jet as an extinguisher, as this will spread the fire.
Specific hazards arising from the chemical	Contents under pressure. Exposure to high temperature may cause can to burst. When exposed to extreme heat or hot surfaces, vapors may decompose to harmful or fatal corrosive gases such as hydrogen chloride and possibly phosgene.
Special protective equipment and precautions for firefighters	Firefighters must use standard protective equipment including flame retardant coat, helmet with face shield, gloves, rubber boots, and in enclosed spaces, SCBA.
Fire-fighting equipment/instructions	In case of fire: Stop leak if safe to do so. Move containers from fire area if you can do so without risk. Containers should be cooled with water to prevent vapor pressure build up.

6. Accidental release measures

Personal precautions, protective equipment and emergency procedures	Keep unnecessary personnel away. Keep people away from and upwind of spill/leak. Keep out of low areas. Wear appropriate protective equipment and clothing during clean-up. Avoid breathing mist or vapor. Avoid breathing gas. Do not touch damaged containers or spilled material unless wearing appropriate protective clothing. Ensure adequate ventilation. Local authorities should be advised if significant spillages cannot be contained. For personal protection, see section 8 of the SDS.
Methods and materials for containment and cleaning up	Eliminate all ignition sources (no smoking, flares, sparks, or flames in immediate area). Keep combustibles (wood, paper, oil, etc.) away from spilled material. This material is classified as a water pollutant under the Clean Water Act and should be prevented from contaminating soil or from entering sewage and drainage systems which lead to waterways. Stop the flow of material, if this is without risk. Collect spillage. Wipe up with absorbent material (e.g. cloth, fleece). Clean surface thoroughly to remove residual contamination. For waste disposal, see section 13 of the SDS.
Environmental precautions	Avoid release to the environment. Contact local authorities in case of spillage to drain/aquatic environment. Prevent further leakage or spillage if safe to do so. Do not contaminate water. Avoid discharge into drains, water courses or onto the ground.

7. Handling and storage

Precautions for safe handling	Obtain special instructions before use. Do not handle until all safety precautions have been read and understood. Pressurized container: Do not pierce or burn, even after use. Do not use if spray button is missing or defective. Do not spray on a naked flame or any other incandescent material. Do not smoke while using or until sprayed surface is thoroughly dry. Use with adequate ventilation. Open doors and windows or use other means to ensure a fresh air supply during use and while product is drying. If you experience any symptoms listed on this label, increase ventilation or leave the area. Do not cut, weld, solder, drill, grind, or expose containers to heat, flame, sparks, or other sources of ignition. Use caution around energized equipment. The metal container will conduct electricity if it contacts a live source. This may result in injury to the user from electrical shock and/or flash fire. Avoid breathing mist or vapor. Avoid breathing gas. Avoid contact with eyes, skin, and clothing. Avoid prolonged exposure. Use only in well-ventilated areas. Should be handled in closed systems, if possible. Wear appropriate personal protective equipment. Observe good industrial hygiene practices. Avoid release to the environment. Do not empty into drains. For product usage instructions, please see the product label.
Conditions for safe storage, including any incompatibilities	Level 1 Aerosol. Contents under pressure. Do not puncture or incinerate container. Do not expose to heat or store at temperatures above 49 °C/120 °F. Do not handle or store near an open flame, heat or other sources of ignition. Exposure to high temperature may cause can to burst. Store in a well-ventilated place. Store away from incompatible materials (see Section 10 of the SDS).

8. Exposure controls/personal protection

Occupational exposure limits

US. OSHA Table Z-1 Limits for Air Contaminants (29 CFR 1910.1000)

Components	Type	Value
Carbon dioxide (CAS 124-38-9)	PEL	9000 mg/m3

FIGURE 3-8 (Continued)

10. Stability and reactivity

Reactivity	The product is stable and non-reactive under normal conditions of use, storage and transport.
Chemical stability	Material is stable under normal conditions.
Possibility of hazardous reactions	No dangerous reaction known under conditions of normal use.
Conditions to avoid	Heat, flames and sparks. Contact with incompatible materials. When exposed to extreme heat or hot surfaces, vapors may decompose to harmful or fatal corrosive gases such as hydrogen chloride and possibly phosgene.
Incompatible materials	Strong oxidizing agents. Strong acids. Strong bases.
Hazardous decomposition products	Hydrogen chloride. Trace amounts of chlorine and phosgene. Carbon oxides. Halogenated materials. Carbonyl halides.

11. Toxicological information

Information on likely routes of exposure

Inhalation	Prolonged inhalation may be harmful. May cause drowsiness and dizziness. Headache. Nausea, vomiting.
Skin contact	Causes skin irritation.
Eye contact	Direct contact with eyes may cause temporary irritation.
Ingestion	Ingestion of large amounts may produce gastrointestinal disturbances including irritation, nausea, and diarrhea.
Symptoms related to the physical, chemical and toxicological characteristics	May cause drowsiness and dizziness. Headache. Nausea, vomiting. Irritation of nose and throat. Irritation of eyes and mucous membranes. Skin irritation. May cause redness and pain.

Information on toxicological effects

Acute toxicity Narcotic effects.

Product	Species	Test Results
Brakleen® Brake Parts Cleaner		
Acute		
Dermal		
LD50	Rabbit	3305.1284 mg/kg estimated
Inhalation		
LC50	Rat	20.4779 mg/l, 4 Hours estimated
Oral		
LD50	Rat	2691.8162 mg/kg estimated

* Estimates for product may be based on additional component data not shown.

Skin corrosion/irritation	Causes skin irritation.
Serious eye damage/eye irritation	Direct contact with eyes may cause temporary irritation.
Respiratory sensitization	Not available.
Skin sensitization	This product is not expected to cause skin sensitization.
Germ cell mutagenicity	No data available to indicate product or any components present at greater than 0.1% are mutagenic or genotoxic.
Carcinogenicity	May cause cancer.

IARC Monographs. Overall Evaluation of Carcinogenicity

Tetrachloroethylene (CAS 127-18-4) 2A Probably carcinogenic to humans.

US. National Toxicology Program (NTP) Report on Carcinogens

Tetrachloroethylene (CAS 127-18-4) Reasonably Anticipated to be a Human Carcinogen.

Reproductive toxicity	This product is not expected to cause reproductive or developmental effects.
Specific target organ toxicity - single exposure	May cause drowsiness and dizziness.
Specific target organ toxicity - repeated exposure	Not classified.
Aspiration hazard	May be an aspiration hazard.
Chronic effects	Prolonged inhalation may be harmful. Prolonged exposure may cause chronic effects.

12. Ecological information

Ecotoxicity Toxic to aquatic life with long lasting effects. Accumulation in aquatic organisms is expected.

Product		Species	Test Results
Brakleen® Brake Parts Cleaner			
Aquatic			
Fish	LC50	Fish	19.1805 mg/l, 96 hours estimated
Components		**Species**	**Test Results**
Tetrachloroethylene (CAS 127-18-4)			

FIGURE 3-8 (Continued)

13. Disposal considerations

Disposal of waste from residues / unused products	This material and its container must be disposed of as hazardous waste. Consult authorities before disposal. Contents under pressure. Do not puncture, incinerate or crush. Do not allow this material to drain into sewers/water supplies. Do not contaminate ponds, waterways or ditches with chemical or used container. Dispose in accordance with all applicable regulations.
Hazardous waste code	D039: Waste Tetrachloroethylene F001: Waste Halogenated Solvent - Spent Halogenated Solvent Used in Degreasing F002: Waste Halogenated Solvent - Spent Halogenated Solvent

US RCRA Hazardous Waste U List: Reference

Tetrachloroethylene (CAS 127-18-4) U210

Contaminated packaging	Empty containers should be taken to an approved waste handling site for recycling or disposal. Since emptied containers may retain product residue, follow label warnings even after container is emptied.

14. Transport information

DOT

UN number	UN1950
UN proper shipping name	Aerosols, poison, Packing Group III, Limited Quantity, MARINE POLLUTANT
Transport hazard class(es)	
Class	2.2
Subsidiary risk	6.1(PGIII)
Label(s)	2.2, 6.1
Packing group	Not applicable.
Environmental hazards	
Marine pollutant	Yes
Special precautions for user	Read safety instructions, SDS and emergency procedures before handling.
Special provisions	Not available.
Packaging exceptions	306
Packaging non bulk	None
Packaging bulk	None

IATA

UN number	UN1950
UN proper shipping name	Aerosols, non-flammable, containing substances in Division 6.1, Packing Group III, Limited Quantity

15. Regulatory information

US federal regulations	This product is a "Hazardous Chemical" as defined by the OSHA Hazard Communication Standard, 29 CFR 1910.1200.

TSCA Section 12(b) Export Notification (40 CFR 707, Subpt. D)

Not regulated.

SARA 304 Emergency release notification

Not regulated.

US. OSHA Specifically Regulated Substances (29 CFR 1910.1001-1050)

Not listed.

US EPCRA (SARA Title III) Section 313 - Toxic Chemical: Listed substance

Tetrachloroethylene (CAS 127-18-4)

CERCLA Hazardous Substance List (40 CFR 302.4)

Tetrachloroethylene (CAS 127-18-4)

CERCLA Hazardous Substances: Reportable quantity

Tetrachloroethylene (CAS 127-18-4) 100 LBS

Spills or releases resulting in the loss of any ingredient at or above its RQ require immediate notification to the National Response Center (800-424-8802) and to your Local Emergency Planning Committee.

Clean Air Act (CAA) Section 112 Hazardous Air Pollutants (HAPs) List

Tetrachloroethylene (CAS 127-18-4)

Clean Air Act (CAA) Section 112(r) Accidental Release Prevention (40 CFR 68.130)

Not regulated.

Safe Drinking Water Act (SDWA)	Not regulated.
Food and Drug Administration (FDA)	Not regulated.

Superfund Amendments and Reauthorization Act of 1986 (SARA)

Section 311/312 Hazard categories	Immediate Hazard - Yes Delayed Hazard - Yes Fire Hazard - No Pressure Hazard - Yes Reactivity Hazard - No
SARA 302 Extremely hazardous substance	No

FIGURE 3-8 (Continued)

US state regulations

US. California Controlled Substances. CA Department of Justice (California Health and Safety Code Section 11100)

Not listed.

US. New Jersey Worker and Community Right-to-Know Act

Carbon dioxide (CAS 124-38-9)
Tetrachloroethylene (CAS 127-18-4)

US. Massachusetts RTK - Substance List

Carbon dioxide (CAS 124-38-9)
Tetrachloroethylene (CAS 127-18-4)

US. Pennsylvania Worker and Community Right-to-Know Law

Tetrachloroethylene (CAS 127-18-4)
Carbon dioxide (CAS 124-38-9)

US. Rhode Island RTK

Tetrachloroethylene (CAS 127-18-4)

US. California Proposition 65

WARNING: This product contains a chemical known to the State of California to cause cancer.

US - California Proposition 65 - CRT: Listed date/Carcinogenic substance

Tetrachloroethylene (CAS 127-18-4) Listed: April 1, 1988

Volatile organic compounds (VOC) regulations

EPA

VOC content (40 CFR 51.100(s))	0 %
Consumer products (40 CFR 59, Subpt. C)	Not regulated

State

Consumer products	This product is regulated as a Brake Cleaner. This product is not compliant to be sold for use in California and New Jersey. This product is compliant in all other states.
VOC content (CA)	0 %
VOC content (OTC)	0 %

International Inventories

Country(s) or region	**Inventory name**	**On inventory (yes/no)***
Australia	Australian Inventory of Chemical Substances (AICS)	Yes
Canada	Domestic Substances List (DSL)	Yes
Canada	Non-Domestic Substances List (NDSL)	No
China	Inventory of Existing Chemical Substances in China (IECSC)	Yes
Europe	European Inventory of Existing Commercial Chemical Substances (EINECS)	Yes
Europe	European List of Notified Chemical Substances (ELINCS)	No
Japan	Inventory of Existing and New Chemical Substances (ENCS)	Yes
Korea	Existing Chemicals List (ECL)	Yes
New Zealand	New Zealand Inventory	Yes
Philippines	Philippine Inventory of Chemicals and Chemical Substances (PICCS)	Yes
United States & Puerto Rico	Toxic Substances Control Act (TSCA) Inventory	Yes

*A "Yes" indicates that all components of this product comply with the inventory requirements administered by the governing country(s)
A "No" indicates that one or more components of the product are not listed or exempt from listing on the inventory administered by the governing country(s).

16. Other information, including date of preparation or last revision

Issue date	12-20-2013
Revision date	08-07-2014
Prepared by	Allison Cho
Version #	02
Further information	CRC # 491G
HMIS® ratings	Health: 2* Flammability: 0 Physical hazard: 0 Personal protection: B
NFPA ratings	Health: 2 Flammability: 0 Instability: 0

FIGURE 3-8 (Continued)

NFPA ratings

Disclaimer

CRC cannot anticipate all conditions under which this information and its product, or the products of other manufacturers in combination with its product, may be used. It is the user's responsibility to ensure safe conditions for handling, storage and disposal of the product, and to assume liability for loss, injury, damage or expense due to improper use. The information contained in this document applies to this specific material as supplied. It may not be valid for this material if it is used in combination with any other materials. This information is accurate to the best of CRC Industries' knowledge or obtained from sources believed by CRC to be accurate. Before using any product, read all warnings and directions on the label. For further clarification of any information contained on this (M)SDS consult your supervisor, a health & safety professional, or CRC Industries.

FIGURE 3-8 (Continued)

SKILL DRILL 3-2 Identifying Information on a Safety Data Sheet

1. Once you have studied the information on the container label, find the MSDS for that material. Always check the revision date to ensure that you are reading the most recent update.

2. Note the chemical and trade names for the material, its manufacturer, and the emergency telephone number to call.

3. Find out why this material is potentially hazardous. It may be flammable, it may explode, or it may be poisonous if inhaled or touched with your bare skin. Check the **threshold limit values (TLVs)**. The concentration of this material in the air you breathe in your shop must not exceed these figures. There could be physical symptoms associated with breathing in harmful chemicals. Find out what will happen to you if you suffer overexposure to the material, either through breathing it in or by coming into physical contact with it. This will help you take safety precautions, such as eye, face, or skin protection; wearing a mask or respirator while using the material; or washing your skin afterwards.

4. Note the **flash point** for this material so that you know at what temperature it may catch fire. Also, note what kind of fire extinguisher you would use to fight a fire involving this material. The wrong fire extinguisher could make the emergency even worse.

5. Study the **reactivity** for this material to identify the physical conditions or other materials that you should avoid when using this material. It could be heat, moisture, or some other chemical.

6. Find out what special precautions you should take when working with this material. This will include personal protection for your skin, eyes, or lungs, as well as storage and use of the material.

7. Be sure to refresh your knowledge of your SDS from time to time. Be confident that you know how to handle and use the material and what action to take in an emergency, should one occur.

Electrical Hazards

Many people are injured by electricity in shops. Poor electrical safety practices can cause shocks and burns, as well as fires and explosions. Make sure you know where the electrical panels for your shop are. All circuit breakers and fuses should be clearly labeled so that you know which circuits and functions they control (**FIGURE 3-10**).

In the case of an emergency, you may need to know how to shut off the electricity supply to a work area or to your entire shop. Keep the circuit breaker and/or electrical panel covers closed to keep them in good condition, prevent unauthorized access, and prevent accidental contact with the electricity supply. It is important that you do not block or obstruct access to this electrical panel; keep equipment and tools well away so

FIGURE 3-9 Exhaust extraction hoses should be vented so that the exhaust gases are not drawn back indoors.

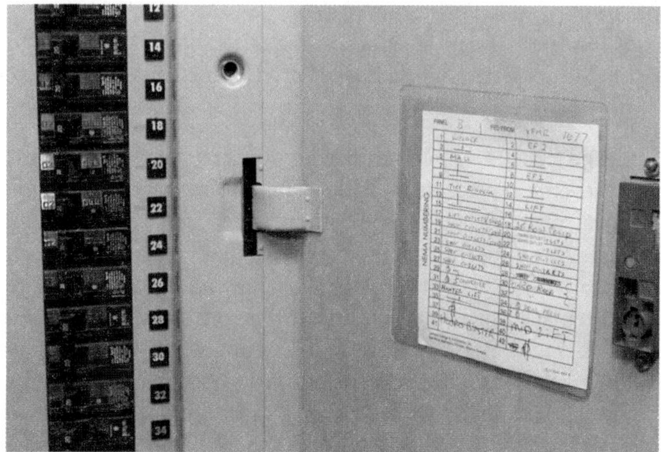

FIGURE 3-10 Electrical fuse panel—All fuses and switches should be clearly labeled with the circuits and functions they control.

emergency access is not hindered. In some localities, 3 ft (0.91 m) of unobstructed space must be maintained around the panel at all times. There should be enough electrical receptacles in your work area for all your needs. Do not connect multiple appliances to a single receptacle with a simple double adapter. If necessary, use a multi-outlet safety strip that has a built-in overload cut-out feature. Electric receptacles should be at least 3 ft (0.91 m) above floor level to reduce the risk of igniting spilled fuel vapors or other flammable liquids. Be sure that your shop has fire extinguishers rated to extinguish electrical fires and that you know where they are. Machines with high-voltage electric drive systems are becoming more common. Specific training and PPE is mandatory before a technician can work on a machine with high-voltage electric drive. *Never* work on live high-voltage equipment or machines.

Portable Electrical Equipment

If you need to use an extension cord, make sure it is made of flexible wiring—not the stiffer type of house wiring—and that it is fitted with a ground wire. The cord should be neoprene covered, as this material resists oil damage. See **FIGURE 3-11** for an example of a proper electrical extension cord.

Always check it for cuts, abrasions, or other damage. Be careful how you place the extension cord, so that it does not cause a tripping hazard. Also, avoid rolling equipment or machines over it, as doing so can damage the cord. Never use an extension cord in wet conditions or around flammable liquids. Portable electric tools that operate at 240 volts are often sources of serious shock and burn accidents. Be particularly careful when using these items. Always inspect the cord for damage and check the security of the attached plug before connecting the item to the power supply. See **FIGURE 3-12** for an example of a damaged electrical cord. Use 110 volt or lower voltage tools if they are available. All electric tools must be equipped with a ground prong or double-insulated. If they are not, do not use them. Never use any high-voltage tool in a wet environment. Air-operated tools cannot give you an electric shock, because they operate on air pressure instead of electricity; so they are safer to use in a wet environment. High-voltage equipment like welders or kidney loop filters may have long cords to allow them to be used throughout a shop bay. These cords must be inspected carefully, and extra protection should be used for them anywhere there is a risk of damaging the insulation on them.

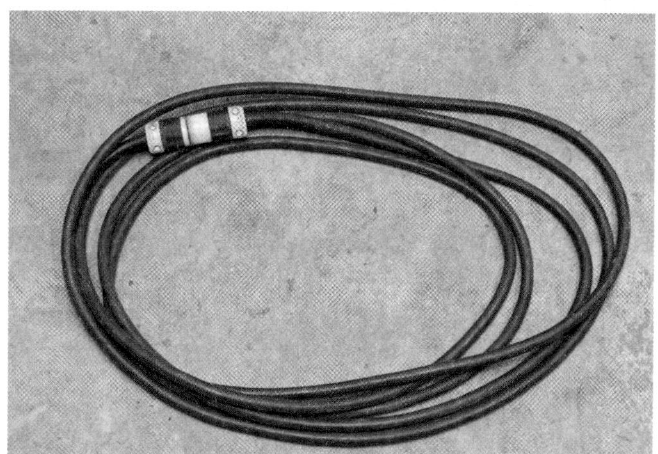

FIGURE 3-11 Extension cords—should be neoprene covered.

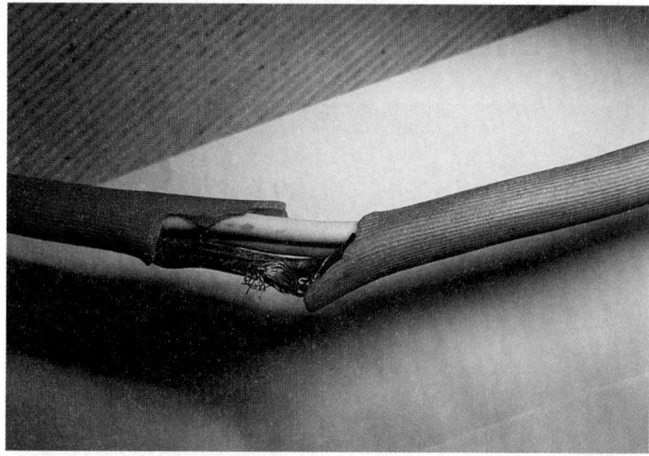

FIGURE 3-12 Never use an electrical cord if the insulation is damaged or cut.

SAFETY TIP

When the insulation has been cut or damaged on an electrical cord or the ground terminal is missing, it should be disposed of. Using electrical cords with damaged insulation or missing ground terminals may cause a shock, resulting in serious injury, fire, and even death.

Portable Shop Lights

Portable shop lights/droplights can be very useful tools to add light to a particular area or spot on the machine you are working on. Always make sure you follow the safety directions when using shop lights. They should have protective covers fitted to them to prevent accidentally breaking the lamp. If a lamp breaks, it can be an electrical hazard, particularly if a metal object comes in contact with exposed live electricity. For this reason, low-voltage lamps or lamps with fitted safety switches are often used in order to prevent accidental electrocution. Some shop lights are now cordless, particularly those with LEDs fitted as the light source. Cordless lights are a safe option because they isolate you from the high voltage. Electric droplights are a common source of shocks, especially if they are the wrong type for the purpose or if they are poorly constructed or maintained. All droplights should be designed in such a way that the electrical parts can never come into contact with the outer casing of the device. Such lights are called double-insulated. The bulb should be completely enclosed in a transparent insulating case or protected within a robust insulating cage. See **FIGURE 3-13** for an example of a proper droplight. The bulbs used in electric droplights are especially vulnerable to impact and must not be used without insulating cage protection. Incandescent bulbs present an extreme fire hazard if broken in the presence of flammable vapors or liquids and should not be used in repair shops. LED and fluorescent bulbs, while still hazardous, are much safer.

Fire Hazards

The danger of a fuel fire is always present in a repair shop. Most machines carry a fuel tank, often with large quantities of fuel on board, which is more than sufficient to cause a large, destructive, and potentially explosive fire. Take precautions to make sure you have the correct type and size of extinguishers on hand for a potential fuel fire. Make sure you clean up spills immediately and avoid ignition sources, like sparks, when in the presence of flammable liquids or gases.

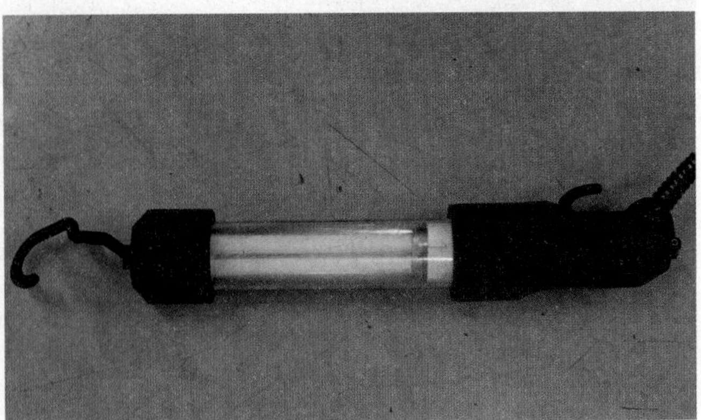

FIGURE 3-13 All droplights should be properly protected.

▶ TECHNICIAN TIP

Fire danger is always present in shops, particularly because of the amount of flammable liquids and materials used in shops and machines. Always be aware of the potential for a fire, and plan ahead by thinking through the task you are about to undertake. Know where firefighting equipment is kept and how it works. Many shops require the use of a fire watch person when "hot work" is being performed (torchworking, welding, or grinding). The person on fire watch is to be on lookout for signs of fire in the area while hot work is being performed and for up to one hour afterward.

Fuel Vapor Liquid fuel vaporizes to different degrees, especially when spilled, and the vapor is generally easy to ignite. Because fuel vapor is invisible and heavier than air, it can spread unseen across a wide area, and a source of ignition can be quite some distance from the original spill. Fuel can even vaporize from the cloths or rags used to wipe up liquid spills. These materials should be allowed to dry in the open air, not held in front of a heater element. Any spark or naked flame, even a lit cigarette, can start an explosive fire.

Spillage Risks Spills frequently occur when technicians remove and replace fuel filters. They also occur during the removal of a fuel tank sender unit, which can be located on the side or top of the fuel tank, without first emptying the tank safely. Spills can also occur when fuel lines are damaged and are being replaced, when fuel systems are being checked, or when fuel is being drained into unsuitable containers. Avoid spills by following the manufacturer's specified procedure when removing fuel system components. Also, keep a spill response kit nearby to deal with any spills quickly. Spill kits should contain absorbent material and barrier dams to contain moderate-sized spills.

Draining Fuel If there is a possibility of fuel spillage while working on a machine, then you should first remove the fuel safely. Do this only in a well-ventilated, level space, preferably outside in the open air. Make sure all potential sources of ignition have been removed from the area, and disconnect the battery on the machine. Do not drain fuel from a machine over an inspection pit. Make sure the container you are draining into is an approved fuel storage container (fuel retriever) and that it is large enough to contain all the fuel in the system being drained.

Using a Fuel Retriever The best practice for removing fuel from a machine's fuel tank is to pump it out with a fuel transfer pump. Ensure that the receiving container is clean if the fuel is to be reused, and ensure that it doesn't leak. Fuel transfer pumps can be electric or pneumatic. Check the service manual for details on how best to drain the fuel from the machine you are working on.

SAFETY TIP

Never weld anywhere near a gas tank or any kind of fuel line. Welding work on a tank is a job for specialists. An empty fuel tank can still contain vapor and therefore can be even more dangerous than one full of liquid fuel. Do not attempt to repair a tank yourself.

Toxic Dust Hazards

Toxic dust is any dust that may contain fine particles that could be harmful to humans or the environment. If you are unsure as to the toxicity of dust, then you should always treat it as toxic and take the precautions identified in the SDS or shop procedures. Brake and clutch dust are potential toxic dusts that repair shops must manage. The dust is made up of very fine particles that can easily spread and contaminate an area. One of the more common sources of toxic dust is inside drum brakes and manual transmission bell housings. It is a good idea to avoid all dust if possible, whether it is classified as toxic or not. If you do have to work with dust, never use compressed air to blow it from components or parts and always use PPE such as face masks, eye protection, and gloves. If you are cleaning up your area after a repair, do not dry sweep dust; instead, use a low-pressure wet cleaning method. Such methods include a soap and water solution used in a dedicated portable wash station, a low-pressure aerosol brake cleaning solution, or a pump spray bottle filled with water. You may also use a **HEPA** vacuum cleaner to collect dust and to clean equipment. HEPA stands for high-efficiency particulate absorption. HEPA filters can trap very small particles and prevent them from being redistributed into the surrounding air. After completing a servicing or repair task on a machine, dirt is often left behind. The materials present in this dirt usually contain toxic chemicals that can build up and cause health problems. To keep the levels of dirt to a minimum, clean up dirt immediately after the task is complete. The vigorous action of sweeping causes the dirt to rise; therefore, when sweeping the floor, use a soft broom that pushes, rather than flicks, the dirt forward. Create smaller dirt piles and dispose of them frequently. Another successful way of cleaning shop dirt is to use a water hose. The waste water must be caught in a settling pit and not run into a storm water drain.

Various tools have been developed to clean toxic dust from machine components. The most common one is the brake wash station. It uses an aqueous solution to wet down and wash the dust into a collection basin. The basin needs periodic maintenance to properly dispose of the accumulated sludge. This tool is probably the simplest way to effectively deal with hazardous dust because it is easy to set up, use, and store. Another such tool uses a vacuum cleaner that has a large cone attachment at the nozzle end. The base of the cone is open so that the brake assembly can fit into the cone. A compressed air nozzle, which is also attached to the inside of the cone, is used to loosen dirt particles. The particles are drawn into the cleaner via a very fine filter. Domestic vacuum cleaners are not suitable for this application because their filters are not fine enough to capture very small dust particles.

Used Engine Oil and Fluid Hazards

Used engine oil and fluids are liquids that have been drained from the machine, usually during servicing operations. Used oil and fluids will often contain dangerous chemicals and impurities and needs to be safely recycled or disposed of in an environmentally friendly way. **FIGURE 3-14** shows some of the equipment used to properly dispose of used oil. There are laws and regulations that control the way in which they are to be handled and disposed of. The shop will have policies and procedures that describe how you should handle and dispose of used engine oil and fluids. Be careful not to mix incompatible fluids such as used engine oil and used coolant. Generally speaking, petroleum products can be mixed together. Follow your local, state, and federal regulations when disposing of waste fluids. Used engine oil is a hazardous material containing many impurities that can damage your skin. Coming into frequent or prolonged contact with used engine oil can cause dermatitis and other skin disorders, including some forms of cancer. Avoid direct contact as much as possible by always using gloves and other protective clothing, which should be cleaned or replaced regularly. Using a barrier-type hand lotion will also help protect your hands, as well as make cleaning them much easier. Also, follow safe work practices, which minimize the possibility of accidental spills. Keeping a high standard of personal hygiene and cleanliness is important so that you get into the habit of washing off harmful materials as soon as possible after contact. If you have been in contact with used engine oil, you should regularly inspect your skin for signs of damage or deterioration. If you have any concerns, see your doctor.

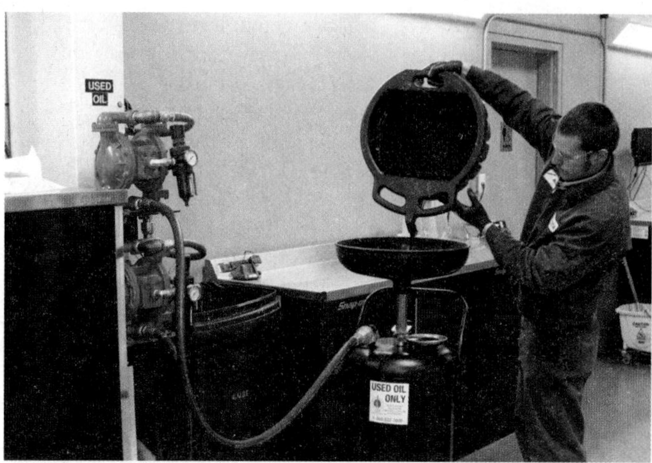

FIGURE 3-14 Used oil and fluids often contain harmful chemicals and contaminants and must be safely recycled and disposed of in an environmentally friendly way.

Identifying potential hazards is the most important part of safety in the workplace. You cannot protect yourself, or others, from hazards that you are not aware of. If you, or your shop management, don't identify the hazards in your workplace, they will not simply be ignored. Unless you identify hazards before an accident or mishap, hazards will tend to make themselves known in an unpleasant way.

▶ TECHNICIAN TIP

- Some machine components, including brake and clutch linings, contain asbestos, which, despite having very good heat properties, is toxic. Asbestos dust causes lung cancer. Complications from breathing in the dust may not show until decades after exposure.
- Airborne dust in the shop can also cause breathing problems such as asthma and throat infections.

- Never cause dust from machine components to be blown into the air. It can stay floating for many hours, meaning that other people will unknowingly breathe in the dust.
- Wear protective gloves whenever using solvents.
- If you are unfamiliar with a solvent or a cleaner, refer to the SDS for information about its correct use and applicable hazards.
- Always wash your hands thoroughly with soap and water after performing repair tasks on brake and clutch components.
- Always wash work clothes separately from other clothes so that toxic dust does not transfer from one garment to another.
- Always wear protective clothing and the appropriate safety equipment.

SAFETY TIP

Whenever using an atomizer with solvents and cleaners, make sure there is adequate exhaust ventilation. Wear appropriate breathing apparatus and eye protection.

▶ Hazard Assessment and Control Procedures

K03002

Develop a safe attitude toward your work. You should always think "safety first" and then act safely. Think ahead about what you are doing, and put in place specific measures to protect yourself and those around you. When you think ahead about what you are doing, you are conducting a hazard assessment. When you put into place specific measures to protect yourself and those around you, you are implementing control procedures. For example, you could ask yourself the following questions:

- What could go wrong?
- What measures can I take to ensure that nothing goes wrong?
- What PPE should I use?
- Have I been trained to use this piece of equipment?
- Is the equipment I'm using safe?

Answering these questions and taking appropriate action before you begin will help you work safely.

Most technicians working on **MORE** (mobile off-road equipment) machines will be required to complete a pre-job hazard assessment. This will be a standardized form with areas to fill in or check off to identify specific hazards related to the task being performed. The technician will also have to list ways to reduce risks and to list the types of PPE to be used. The forms (usually a pocket-sized card) will need to be carried with the technician and signed by their supervisor.

Industry Hazards Assessment and Control Processes

There are certain standard hazard assessment and control procedures and practices within industrial workplaces. For example, in the United States, the government regulator of safety in the workplace is OSHA, which has a six-step process for hazard identification and assessment:

1. Collect existing information about workplace hazards.
2. Inspect the workplace for safety hazards.
3. Identify health hazards.
4. Conduct incident investigations.
5. Identify hazards associated with emergency and non-routine situations.
6. Characterize the nature of identified hazards, identify interim control measures, and prioritize the hazards to control.

OSHA also has a six-step process for hazards prevention and control:

1. Identify control options.
2. Select controls.
3. Develop and update a hazard control plan.
4. Select controls to protect workers during non-routine operations and emergencies.
5. Implement selected controls in the workplace.
6. Follow up to confirm that controls are effective.

Another common process for hazard assessment and control is called **operational risk management (ORM)**. This comprises a simple five-step process:

1. Identify the threats or hazards.
2. Assess the risk.
3. Analyze the risk control measures.
4. Make control decisions.
5. Implement risk controls.
6. Supervise and review.

The above-mentioned hazard assessment and control processes allow a workplace to have a standardized and consistent approach to workplace hazards and safety. Employees with a safe attitude follow these approaches to hazard assessment and control without thinking about it. For example, before beginning work on a fuel tank, you may place a portable fire extinguisher nearby, in case a fire were to break out. This is a great example of performing a hazard assessment and implementing appropriate control measures.

Continuous Hazards Assessment through Shop Safety Inspections

Shop safety inspections are valuable ways of identifying unsafe equipment, materials, or activities so that they can be corrected to prevent accidents or injuries. The inspection can be formalized by using inspection sheets to check specific items, or they can consist of general walk-arounds where you consciously look for problems that can be corrected.

Some of the common things to look for are items blocking emergency exits or walkways, poor safety signage, unsafe storage of flammable goods, tripping hazards, faulty or unsafe equipment or tools, missing fire extinguishers, clutter, spills, unsafe shop practices, and people not wearing the correct PPE. Formal and informal safety inspections should be held regularly. For example, an inspection sheet might be used weekly or monthly to formally evaluate the shop, while informal inspections might be held daily to catch issues that are of a more immediate nature. During shop safety inspections, also look for hazardous practices committed by employees. Here are some items to pay attention to in your workplace.

Proper Ventilation

Proper ventilation is required for working in the shop area. The key to proper ventilation is to ensure that any task or procedure that may produce dangerous or toxic fumes are recognized so that measures can be put in place to provide adequate ventilation. Ventilation can be provided by natural means, such as by opening doors and windows to provide air flow for low-exposure situations. However, in high-exposure situations, such as machines running in the shop, a mechanical means of ventilation is required; an example is an exhaust extraction system. Areas where parts are being cleaned or areas where solvents and chemicals are used should also have good general ventilation, and if required, additional exhaust hoods or fans should be installed to remove dangerous fumes. In some cases, such as when spraying paint, it may be necessary to use a personal respirator in addition to proper ventilation.

TECHNICIAN TIP

Before beginning a task, research the proper ventilation procedure for working within the shop area. Use the correct ventilation equipment and procedures for the activities you are working on within the shop area.

Lifting

Whenever you lift something, there is always the possibility of injury; however, by lifting correctly, you reduce the chance of something going wrong. Before lifting anything, you can reduce the risk of injury by breaking down the load into smaller quantities, asking for assistance if required, or possibly using a mechanical device to assist you when you lift. If you must bend down to lift something, you should bend your knees to lower your body; do not bend over with straight legs, because this can damage your back (**FIGURE 3-15**). Place your feet about shoulder width apart and lift the item by straightening your legs while keeping your back as straight as possible.

FIGURE 3-15 Prevent back injuries when lifting heavy objects by crouching, with your legs shoulder width apart, standing as close to the object as possible, and positioning yourself so that the center of gravity is between your feet. Use your legs to lift the object, not your back.

SAFETY TIP

When lifting objects repeatedly, use a **back brace**. When lifting heavy or large objects get someone else to help.

Housekeeping and Orderliness

Good housekeeping is about always making sure the shop and your work surroundings are neat and kept in good order. Trash and liquid spills should be quickly cleaned up, tools need to be cleaned and put away after use, spare parts need to be stored correctly, and generally everything needs to have a safe place to be kept. You should carry out good housekeeping practices while working, not just after a job is completed. For example, get rid of trash as it accumulates, clean up spills when they happen, and put tools away when you are finished working with them. It is also good practice to periodically perform a deep clean of the shop so that any neglected areas are taken care of.

Slip, Trip, and Fall Hazards

Slip, trip, and fall hazards are ever present in the shop, and they can be caused by trash, tools and equipment, or liquid spills being left lying around. Always be on the lookout for hazards that can cause slips, trips, or falls. Floors and steps can become slippery, so they should be kept clean and have anti-slip coatings applied to them. High-visibility strips with anti-slip coatings can be applied to the edge of step treads to reduce the hazard. Clean up liquid spills immediately and mark the area with wet floor signs until the floor is dry. Make sure the shop has good lighting so that hazards are easy to spot, and keep walkways clear from obstruction. Think about what you are doing, and make sure the work area is free of slip, trip, and fall hazards as you work.

Most government legislation requires workers to wear fall-arrest harnesses if working at heights of 10 ft or more in an area that has no barricades or railings. There are many workplaces that have lower height thresholds for implementation of working at heights, such as 6 ft. There will be specific training required for working at heights to educate workers on things like proper harness usage, acceptable tie-off points, and acceptable documentation. Many situations will see a technician working at heights on a MORE machine. Always inspect the integrity of the tie-off points before connecting a fall-arrest harness to them.

Working on MORE machines often requires a technician to work on a jobsite. For construction sites and quarries, uneven ground and slippery conditions will introduce many slip and trip hazards. Extra caution needs to be taken when working on machines outside of the shop environment.

The safest workplaces have a high level of commitment from the employer by having standardized safety processes in place, proper safety equipment, as well as employees committed to safety. Safety is a continuous process that requires constantly assessing new hazards and implementing effective controls to maintain a safe working environment.

▶ Safety Regulations, Procedures, and Occupational Safety Standards

K03003, A03002

Safety regulations, procedures, and standards are important because they provide consistency by requiring everyone to follow the same set of rules governing their actions related to safety. Safety regulations, procedures, and standards also provide a way to share information about how to avoid past accidents and mishaps. This is done by including lessons learned from past accidents and mishaps at your workplace, or others, in the safety regulations, procedures, and standards of your shop. Most people can imagine how nonsensical it would be if every employee were injured performing the same repair procedure on a piece of equipment simply because no one communicated how to avoid the hazard that caused the injury. Safety regulations, procedures, and standards are effective at preventing accidents and mishaps because they communicate how to avoid and minimize certain hazards and injuries based on lessons learned from previous accidents and mishaps.

Next we will talk about three types of safety regulations, procedures, and standards:

- government and industry regulations, procedures, and standards
- shop policies, procedures, and standards
- equipment manufacturer policies, procedures, and standards.

Government and Industry Regulations, Procedures, and Standards

Most countries have government and industry entities that regulate certain aspects of safety and environmental issues in the workplace. The regulations, rules, processes, procedures, and standards set by government entities are usually a matter of law. Violations of these regulations can result in civil and sometimes criminal penalties for employees and the employer. Employees and managers should be familiar with government safety regulations as they apply to their workplace in order to prevent penalties – but most importantly to keep everyone safe. In addition to government regulators, many industries have entities that may set safety-related rules, regulations, and recommended practices. Some examples of these are the **Society of Automotive Engineers (SAE)** and the **National Institute for Automotive Service Excellence (ASE)**. While they do not usually carry the force of law, these entities can better determine how to apply safety and government safety regulations to your specific workplace. In the United States, there are two primary government agencies that you will need to become familiar with: **OSHA** and the **EPA**.

OSHA is a U.S. government agency that was created to provide national leadership in occupational safety and health. It finds the most effective ways to help prevent worker fatalities and workplace injuries and illnesses. OSHA has the authority to conduct workplace inspections and, if required, fine employers and workplaces if they violate OSHA regulations and procedures. For example, a fine may be imposed on the employer or workplace if a worker is electrocuted by a piece of faulty machinery that has not been regularly tested and maintained.

EPA stands for the Environmental Protection Agency. This federal government agency deals with issues related to environmental safety. The EPA (Environmental Protection Agency) conducts research and monitoring, sets standards, and can hold employees and companies legally accountable to keep the environment protected. Shop activities will need to comply with EPA laws and regulations by ensuring that waste products are disposed of in an environmentally responsible way, chemicals and fluids are correctly stored, and work practices do not contribute to damaging the environment. In addition, specific industries may have further regulatory entities they must answer to. For example, in the mining industry in the United States, **MSHA (Mine Safety and Health Administration)** sets additional rules and regulations that effect MORE (mobile off-road equipment) technicians. While the examples in this chapter refer to OSHA, MSHA, and the EPA, most countries have equivalent organizations. If you are in a geographic region outside of North America, you should check with your local government authorities for the appropriate regulations that apply to your location. Both OSHA and the EPA publish useful information related to safety and environmental friendliness in the workplace. If you are looking for information about safety or the environment in the workplace, the OSHA and EPA websites are a valuable source.

▶ TECHNICIAN TIP

Most workplaces are required to form a joint health and safety committee. The number of members is dependent on the number of employees that work on site. The committee is made up of supervisory staff and employees and is mandated to hold regular meetings to discuss health and safety concerns and put action plans in place to remedy and prevent problems.

Shop Policies, Procedures, and Standards

Shop policies and procedures are a set of documents that outline how tasks and activities in the shop are to be conducted and managed. They also ensure that the shop operates according to OSHA and EPA laws and regulations. A **policy** is a guiding principle that sets the shop direction, while a **procedure** is a list of the steps required to get the same result each time a task or activity is performed. An example of a policy would be an OSHA document for the shop that describes how the shop complies with legislation. An example of a procedure would be a document that describes the steps required to safely use a commercial vehicle hoist. Each shop will have its own set of policies and procedures and a system in place to make sure the policies and procedures are regularly reviewed and updated. Regular reviews ensure that new policies and procedures are developed and that old ones are modified in case something has changed. For example, if the shop moves to a new building, then a review of policies and procedures will determine which ones of them relate to the new shop, its layout, and equipment. In general, the policies and procedures are written to guide shop practice; help ensure compliance with laws, statutes, and regulations; and reduce the risk of injury. Always follow your shop policies and procedures to reduce the risk of injury to your coworkers and yourself and to prevent damage to property. It is everyone's responsibility to know and follow the rules. Locate the general shop rules and procedures for your workplace. Look through the contents or index pages to familiarize yourself with the contents. Discuss the policy and the shop rules and procedures with your supervisor. Part of the safety policies in most large shops are procedures and requirements for reporting hazards. It is the responsibility of all workers in a shop to identify and report hazards that haven't been previously reported. Once reported, the company must take action to reduce risks related to the hazard. Ask questions to ensure that you understand how the rules and procedures should be applied and your role in making sure they are followed.

▶ TECHNICIAN TIP

Machines often can't be brought to a repair shop and must be repaired on site. The technician assigned to the repair may be required to attend a site orientation seminar before being allowed to enter the customer's workplace. This seminar will make the technician aware of all site-specific safety policies, including information about fire escapes and PPE requirements and locations for first aid kits.

Equipment Manufacturer Policies, Procedures, and Standards

When you need information about a specific piece of equipment or machinery, you should consult the equipment manufacturer's information. Equipment manufacturers publish **operating manuals**, **repair and maintenance manuals**, and **technical and safety bulletins**. The manufacturer's information should be considered the most correct and authoritative information regarding the safe and proper operation, repair, and maintenance of that specific piece of equipment. Prior to operating, or repairing, an unfamiliar piece of equipment, it is good practice to consult the applicable manufacturer's operating or maintenance and repair manual. When reviewing the manufacturer's manual, pay attention to safety-related messages like danger, warning, cautions, and notices. The manufacturer knows better than anyone else how to safely and properly operate their equipment. It has often been said that workplace safety regulations, policies, and procedures are "written in blood." This means that they have been written and revised many times due to lessons learned from past accidents that have resulted in serious injuries and death to employees. It is much easier to learn from the past mistakes of others by following current workplace safety rules than by learning from your own mistakes.

▶ Emergency Actions and Procedures

K03004, A03001

If an accident or mishap occurs, it is important for both employees and the employer to know what to do. An accident or mishap can quickly become an emergency if not handled properly. An emergency is a serious, unexpected, and often dangerous situation requiring immediate attention. An emergency can cause serious equipment damage, personal injury, or even death if not properly addressed. It is critical that your shop educate all employees on how to handle emergency situations they may encounter. It is also critical that your shop has the appropriate emergency information and supplies readily available in a prominent location and that all employees know where these items are. An emergency situation can escalate quickly; it is vital that employees know where emergency items and instructions are before an emergency occurs. During an emergency, time lost attempting to locate fire extinguishers, emergency eye wash stations, emergency equipment shut down controls, first aid kits, and first aid instructions can result in further equipment damage or injury to personnel. In the next few paragraphs, we will discuss some common emergency situations and actions.

Equipment Emergencies

An equipment emergency can result in damage to equipment, shop facilities, hazardous material spills, and injury to personnel if not properly addressed. Some examples of equipment emergencies are a runaway diesel engine, malfunctioning welding equipment, shop crane failure, air compressor failures, leaking oil storage containers, and equipment fires. The best action taken to address equipment emergencies is prevention. Ensure that all equipment is maintained, inspected, and working properly. Remove malfunctioning equipment from service promptly. Ensure all safety and emergency devices are installed and work properly on equipment. Ensure employees know where emergency shutdown controls are, and ensure they are clearly visible. However, when an equipment emergency does occur, know how to address it by following these simple steps:

- Is the situation dangerous to people in the area?
  - If needed, evacuate all people in the area that could be effected.
- Is the situation dangerous to me?
  - If it is dangerous for me to enter the area, evacuate and contact emergency services.
- How do I stop the situation from getting worse?
  - If available, and safe to do so, use the emergency shutdown control at the equipment.
  - If not, attempt to shut down the equipment at the main electrical panel.
  - If possible, apply control measures to prevent further damage and risk to equipment.

When possible, we want to limit the damage caused by equipment emergencies. The most important action is to prevent injury to personnel. If you can safely address an equipment emergency, then do so. If addressing the equipment emergency would risk your safety, or the safety of others, evacuate and contact emergency services.

First Aid Emergencies

The following information is designed to acquaint you with basic first aid principles and the importance of first aid training courses. You will find general information about how to take care of someone who is injured. However, this information is only a guide. It is not a substitute for training or professional medical assistance. Always seek professional advice when tending to an injured person.

First aid is the immediate care given to an injured or suddenly ill person. Learning first aid skills is valuable in the workplace in case an accident or medical emergency arises. First aid courses are available through many organizations, such as the Emergency Care and Safety Institute (ECSI). It is strongly advised that you seek out a certified first aid course and become certified in first aid. The following information highlights some of the principles of first aid. In the event of an accident, the possibility of injury to the rescuer or further injury to the victim must be assessed. The first step is to survey the scene. While doing this, try to determine what happened, what dangers may still be present, and the best actions to take. Remove the injured person from a dangerous area only if it is safe for you to do so. When dealing with electrocution or electrical burns, make sure the electrical supply is switched off before attempting any assistance.

Always perform first aid techniques as quickly as is safely possible after an injury. When breathing has ceased or when the heart has stopped, brain damage can occur within four to six minutes. The degree of brain damage will increase with each passing minute, so make sure you know what to do, and do it quickly.

▶ TECHNICIAN TIP

There are three important rules of first aid:

1. Know what you must not do.
2. Know what you must do.
3. If you are not sure what procedures to follow, send for trained medical assistance.

First Aid Principles

Prompt care and treatment prior to the arrival of emergency medical assistance can sometimes mean the difference between life and death. The goals of first aid are to make the immediate environment as safe as possible, preserve the life of the patient, prevent the injury from worsening, prevent additional injuries from occurring, protect the unconscious, promote recovery, comfort the injured, prevent any delay in treatment, and provide the best possible care for the injured person. When attending to an injured victim, always send for assistance. Make sure the person who stays with the injured victim is more experienced in first aid than the messenger. If you are the only person available, request medical assistance as soon as reasonably possible. When you approach the scene of an accident or emergency, do the following:

1. Danger: Make sure there are no other dangers, and assist only if it is safe to do so.
2. Response: Check to see if the victim is responsive and breathing. If responsive, ask the victim if he or she needs help. If the victim does not respond, he or she is unresponsive.
3. Have a bystander call 911. If alone, call 911 yourself (or, if in another country, the relevant emergency assistance phone number).
4. If the victim is unresponsive and not breathing, place your hands in the center of the victim's chest and provide 30 chest compressions hard and fast (**FIGURE 3-16**).
5. Tilt the victim's head back and lift the chin to open the airway. Give one rescue breath lasting one second, take a normal breath for yourself, and then give the victim another breath lasting one second. Each rescue breath should make the victim's chest rise.
6. Repeat the compression and breath cycles until an **automated external defibrillator (AED)** is available or EMS (emergency medical service) personnel arrive (**FIGURE 3-17**).
7. Once an AED arrives, expose the victim's chest and turn on the AED. Attach the AED pads. Ensure that no one touches the victim. Follow the audio and visual prompts from the AED. If no shock is advised, resume CPR (cardiopulmonary resuscitation) immediately (five sets of 30 compressions and two breaths). If a shock is advised, do not touch the victim, and give one shock. Or, shock as advised by AED. Immediately resume 30 compressions and two breaths.

Bleeding

A wound that is severely bleeding is serious. If the bleeding is allowed to continue, the victim may collapse or die. Bleeding is divided into two categories: external and internal. **External**

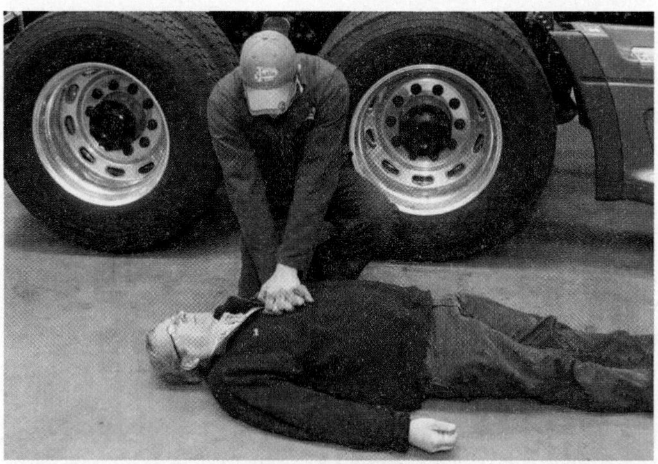

FIGURE 3-16 Chest compressions.

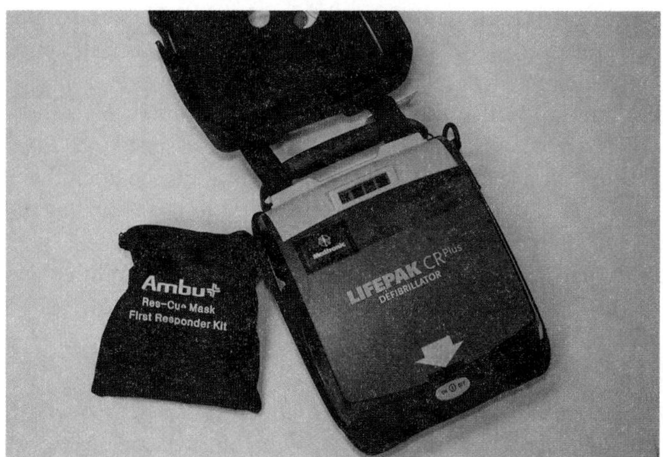

FIGURE 3-17 The use of an AED is taught in all certified CPR training classes.

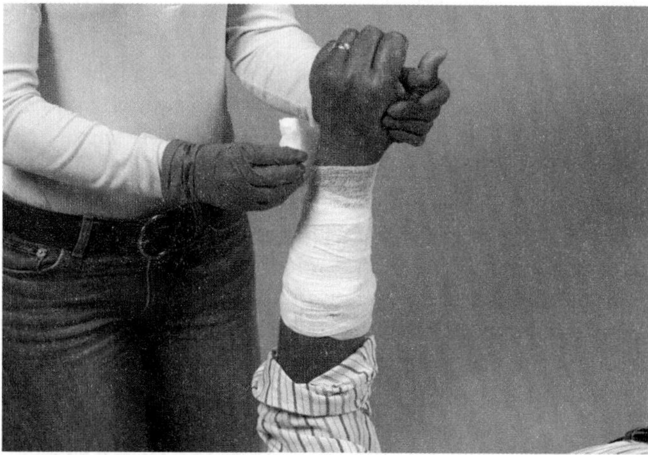

FIGURE 3-19 If blood soaks through the bandages, apply additional bandages on top of the existing ones.

bleeding is the loss of blood from an external wound where blood can be seen escaping. **Internal bleeding** is the loss of blood into a body cavity from a wound with no obvious sign of blood. Before providing first aid, make sure you are not exposed to blood. Wear latex gloves or an artificial barrier. Lay the victim down, then apply a gauze pad and direct pressure to the wound (**FIGURE 3-18**). Apply a pressure bandage over the gauze. If blood soaks through the bandage, apply additional dressings and pressure bandage (**FIGURE 3-19**). Call 911 if bleeding cannot be controlled. Give nothing by mouth to the victim and seek medical aid immediately. If an object punctures the victim's skin and becomes embedded in the victim's body, do not attempt to remove the object. Stabilize the object with a bulky dressing. Seek medical care immediately. If the injured person has internal bleeding, it may not be immediately obvious. Symptoms of internal bleeding are bruising, a painful or tender area, coughing frothy blood, vomiting blood, stool that is black or contains bright red blood, and passing blood with urine. To assist an injured victim with internal bleeding, lay the victim down, loosen tight clothing, give nothing by mouth, and seek medical aid immediately.

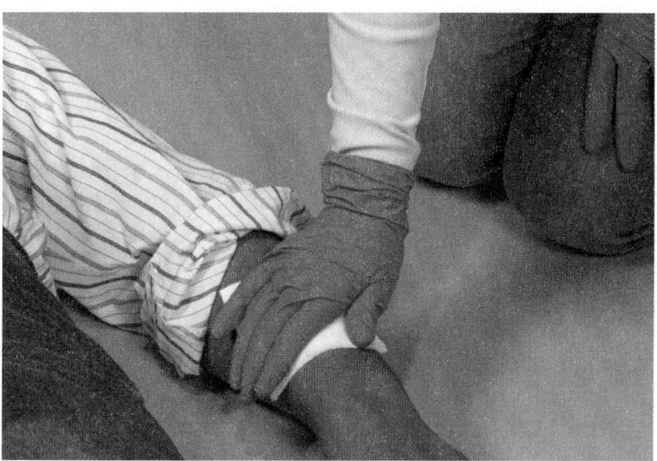

FIGURE 3-18 Apply a gauze pad, and direct pressure to the wound.

> **SAFETY TIP**
>
> During an emergency, never remove existing bandages and dressings simply because they are bleeding through. Always apply the new ones on top of the existing bandages. Removing existing bandages from an open wound will cause it to reopen and result in more bleeding.

Eye Injuries

Foreign objects can become embedded in the eye, or chemicals can splash into the eye. If an object penetrates and becomes embedded in the eye, do not attempt to remove it. Lay the victim down, stabilize the object with a bulky dressing or clean cloths, ask the victim to close the other eye, and call 911 (or the relevant emergency assistance phone number) (**FIGURE 3-20**). If an object is loose on the surface of the eye, pull the upper lid over the lower lid. Hold the eyelid open and gently rinse with water. Examine the lower lid by pulling it down gently.

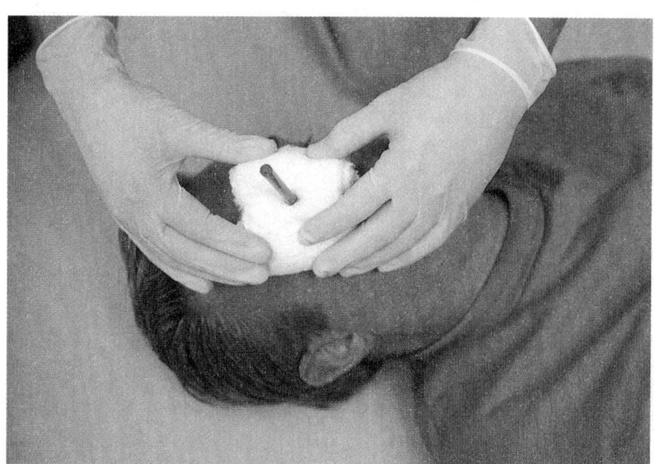

FIGURE 3-20 If an object penetrates and becomes embedded in the eye, stabilize the object with a bulky dressing, clean cloths, or a small foam cup. Then seek immediate medical attention. *Do not* remove the object.

If you can see the object, remove it with a moistened sterile gauze, a clean cloth, or a moistened cotton swab. Examine the underside of the upper lid by grasping the lashes of the upper lid and rolling the lid upward over a cotton swab. If you can see the object, remove it with a moistened sterile gauze or a clean cloth (**FIGURE 3-21**). If some chemical splashes into the eyes, you may be able to flush it out using an eye wash station (**FIGURE 3-22**). Hold the eye wide open and flush with warm water for at least 20 minutes, continuously and gently. Irrigate from the nose side of the eye toward the outside to avoid flushing material into the other eye. Loosely bandage the eyes with wet dressings. Call 911 (or the relevant emergency assistance phone number).

Eyewash Stations and Emergency Showers

Hopefully you will never need to use an eye wash station or emergency shower. The best treatment is prevention, so make sure you wear all the PPE required for each specific task to avoid injury. Eye wash stations are used to flush the eye with clean water or sterile liquid if you get foreign liquid or particles in your eye. There are different types of eye washers; the main ones are disposable eye wash packs and eye wash stations. Some emergency or deluge showers also have an eye wash station built in. When someone gets chemicals in their eyes, they typically need assistance in reaching the eye wash station. Take their arm and lead them to it. They may not want to open their eyes even in the water, so encourage them to use their fingers to pull their eyelids open. If a chemical splashed in their eyes, encourage them to rinse their eyes for 20 minutes. While they are rinsing their eyes, call for medical assistance.

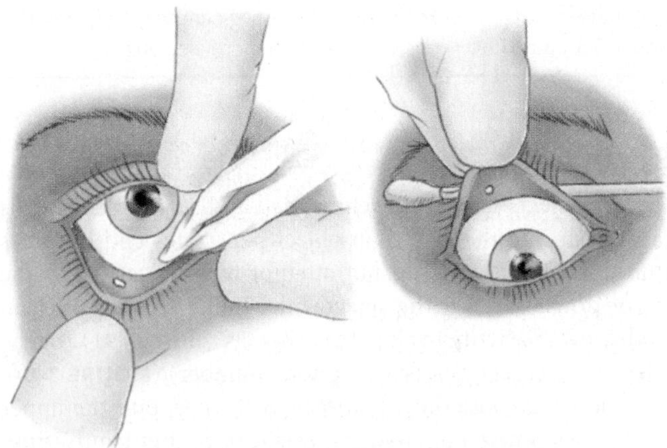

FIGURE 3-21 Locate and remove a foreign object from the eye.

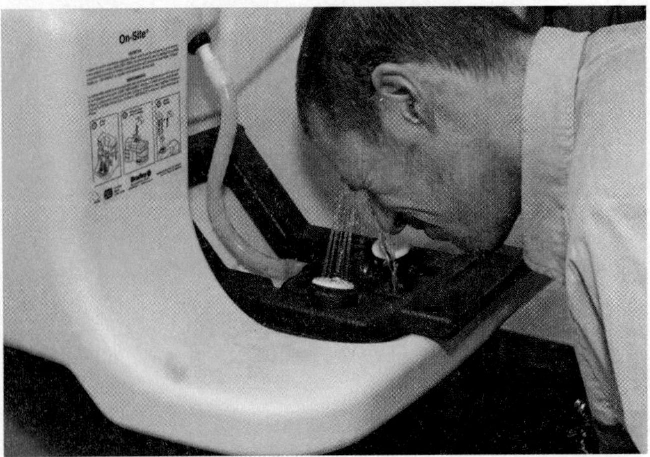

FIGURE 3-22 Emergency eyewash station: Flush out the eye to prevent chemical burns at an emergency eye wash station.

Fractures

A fracture is a broken or cracked bone. Always seek medical care for all fractures. There may be symptoms you are not aware of that may make the injury more complex than first thought. There are three types of bone fractures: A **simple fracture** involves no wound or internal or external bleeding; an **open fracture** involves bleeding or the protrusion of bone through the skin; and a **complicated fracture** involves penetration of a bone into a vital organ. The symptoms of a fracture include hearing a snapping noise when the injury occurred, pain or tenderness at or near the injury, inability to move the limb, loss of strength in the limb, shortening of the limb or an abnormally shaped limb, swelling and/or bruising around the area, and a grinding noise if the limb is moved. Allow the victim to support the injured area in the most comfortable position. Stabilize the injured part with your hands or a splint to prevent movement. If the injury is an open fracture, do not push on any protruding bone. Cover the wound and exposed bone with a dressing. Apply ice or a cold pack if possible to help reduce swelling or pain. Call 911 (or the relevant emergency assistance phone number) for any open fractures or large bone fractures. Do not move the victim unless there is an immediate danger. Be aware of the onset of **shock**, which may present as the victim vomiting or fainting. Shock is when the body's tissues do not receive enough oxygenated blood.

Sprains, Strains, and Dislocations

When a joint has been forced past its natural range of movement, or a muscle or ligament has been overstressed or torn, a sprain, strain, or dislocation may occur. A **sprain** occurs when a joint is forced beyond its natural movement limit. This causes stretching or tearing in the ligaments that hold the bones together. The symptoms of a sprain include pain and loss of limb function, with swelling and bruising present. When a sprain occurs, apply covered ice packs every 20 minutes, elevate the injured limb, and apply an elastic compression bandage to the area and beyond the affected area. You should always treat a sprain as a fracture until medical opinion says otherwise.

A **strain** is an injury caused by the overstretching of muscles and tendons. Symptoms of a strain are sharp pain in the area immediately after the injury occurs, increased pain when using the limb, or tenderness over the entire muscle. The muscle may also have an indentation at the strain's location. When a strain occurs, have the victim rest, elevate the injured limb, apply covered ice packs every 20 minutes, and apply an elastic compression bandage. A **dislocation** is the displacement of a joint from its normal position; it is caused by an external force stretching the ligaments beyond their elastic limit. Symptoms of a dislocation are pain or tenderness around the area, inability to move the joint, deformity of the joint, and swelling and discoloration over the joint. If a dislocation occurs, try to immobilize the limb and seek medical attention. Do not try to put the joint back in place.

Burns and Scalds

Burns are injuries to body tissues, including skin, that are caused by exposure to heat, chemicals, and radiation. Burns are classified as either superficial, partial thickness, or full thickness. Superficial burns, or **first-degree burns**, show reddening of the skin and damage to the outer layer of skin only (**FIGURE 3-23**). Partial-thickness burns, or **second-degree burns**, involve blistering and damage to the outer layer of skin (**FIGURE 3-24**). Full-thickness burns, or **third-degree burns**, involve white or blackened areas and include damage to all skin layers and underlying structures and tissues (**FIGURE 3-25**). Burns can be caused by excessive heat, such as from fire; friction, such as from a rope burn; radiation, such as from a welding flash or a sunburn; chemicals, including acids and bases; or electricity, such as from faulty appliances. Scalds are injuries to the skin caused by exposure to hot liquids and gases. The effects of burns and scalds can include permanent skin and tissue damage, blisters caused by damage to surface blood vessels, severe pain, and shock. Remove the victim from any danger. If clothing is burning, have the victim roll on the ground using the "stop, drop, and roll" method. Smother the flames with a fire blanket or douse the victim with water. For minor burns, cool the burn with cool water until the body part is pain free. After the burn has cooled, apply antibiotic ointment. Do not apply lotions or aloe vera. Cover the burn loosely with a dry, nonstick, sterile, or clean dressing. Do not break any blisters. Give an over-the-counter pain medication such as ibuprofen. Seek medical care. Any large or third-degree burn must be treated by a qualified medical practitioner. Serious burns include skin that is blackened, whitened, or charred; a burn that is larger than three-quarters of an inch (2 cm) in diameter; or a burn that is in the airway or on the face, hands, or genitals. When presented with such burns, call 911 immediately.

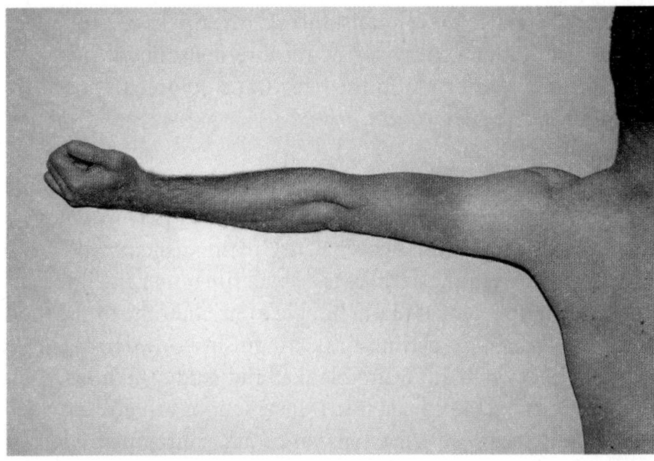

FIGURE 3-23 First-degree burn.

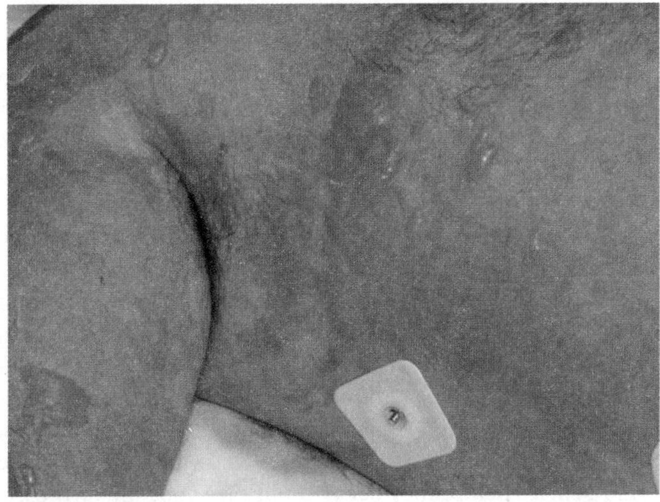

FIGURE 3-24 Second-degree burn.

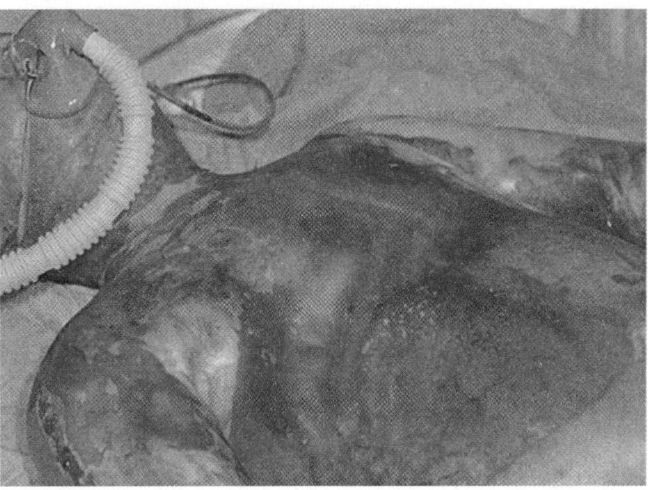

FIGURE 3-25 Third-degree burn.

Fire Emergencies

A fire is one of the most dangerous situations you may encounter in your shop. A fire can get out of control quickly. That is why it is important to know what to do in case of a fire emergency. If a fire occurs in your shop, clear everyone in the area and sound the alarm. Attempt to extinguish the fire only if it is small and under control. If you have any doubt about your ability to extinguish the fire quickly, evacuate the area and call emergency services.

Extinguishing Fires

Three elements must be present at the same time for a fire to occur: fuel, oxygen, and heat. The secret of firefighting involves the removal of at least one of these elements, usually the oxygen or the heat, to extinguish the fire. For example, a fire blanket when applied correctly removes the oxygen, while a water extinguisher removes heat from the fire. In the shop, fire extinguishers are used to extinguish most small fires. Never hesitate to call the fire department if you cannot extinguish a fire safely.

Fire Classifications In North America, there are five classes of fire:

- Class A fires involve ordinary combustibles such as wood, paper, or cloth.
- Class B fires involve flammable liquids or gaseous fuels.
- Class C fires involve electrical equipment.
- Class D fires involve combustible metals such as sodium, titanium, and magnesium.
- Class K fires involve cooking oil or fat.

Fire Extinguisher Types Fire extinguishers are marked with pictograms that depict the types of fires that the extinguisher is approved to fight (**FIGURE 3-26**):

- Class A: Green triangle
- Class B: Red square
- Class C: Blue circle
- Class D: Yellow pentagram
- Class K: Black hexagon

Fire Extinguisher Operation Always sound the alarm before attempting to fight a fire. If you cannot fight the fire safely, leave the area while you wait for backup. You will need to size up the fire before you make the decision to fight it with a fire extinguisher by identifying what sort of material is burning, the extent of the fire, and the likelihood of it spreading. To operate a fire extinguisher, follow the acronym for fire extinguisher use, PASS:

- Pull.
- Aim.
- Squeeze.
- Sweep.

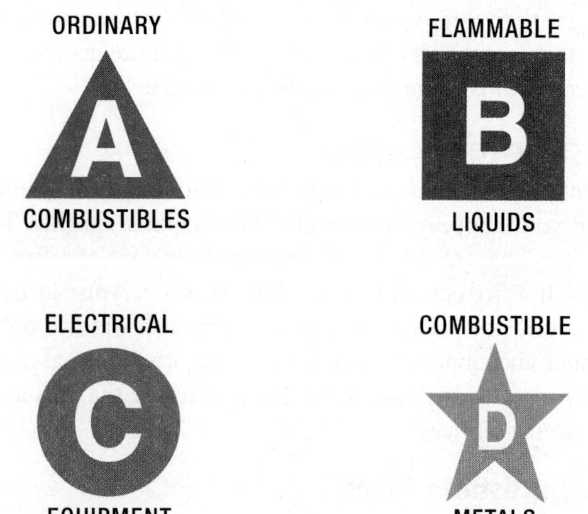

FIGURE 3-26 Fire Extinguisher–Type Labels—Fire extinguishers often include a shape as well as a letter to denote its classification.

Pull out the pin that locks the handle at the top of the fire extinguisher to prevent accidental use (**FIGURE 3-27A**). Carry the fire extinguisher in one hand, and use your other hand to *aim* the nozzle at the base of the fire (**FIGURE 3-27B**). Stand about 8–12 ft (2.4–3.7 m) away from the fire and *squeeze* the handle to discharge the fire extinguisher (**FIGURE 3-27C**). Remember that if you release the handle on the fire extinguisher, it will stop discharging. *Sweep* the nozzle from side to side at the base of the fire (**FIGURE 3-27D**).

Continue to watch and never turn your back to a fire. Although it may appear to be extinguished, it may suddenly reignite. If the fire is indoors, you should be standing between the fire and the nearest safe exit. If the fire is outside, you should stand facing the fire with the wind on your back so that the smoke and heat are being blown away from you. If possible, get an assistant to guide you and inform you of the fire's progress. Again, make sure you have a means of escape, should the fire get out of control. When you are certain that the fire is out, report it to your supervisor. Also, report what actions you took to put out the fire. Once the circumstances of the fire have been investigated and your supervisor or the fire department has given you the all clear, clean up the debris and submit the used fire extinguisher for inspection.

Fire Blankets **Fire blankets** are designed to smother a small fire and are effective at putting out a fire on a person. They are also used in situations where a fire extinguisher could cause damage. For example, if there is a small fire under the hood of a machine, a fire blanket might be able to smother the fire without running the risk of getting fire extinguisher powder down the intake system. Obtain a fire blanket and study the how-to-use instructions on the packaging. If instructions are not provided, research how to use a fire blanket or ask your supervisor. You may require instruction from an authorized person in using the fire blanket. If you do use a fire blanket, make sure you return the blanket for use or, if necessary, replace it with a new one.

The most important things that your employer can do to ensure that emergencies result in the least amount of equipment damage and injuries is to ensure that the shop has the proper equipment for emergencies, that employees have been trained properly, and that employees are given the proper information on how to handle emergencies. The most important thing that you can do is know how to handle emergencies before they occur. If you do not know how to handle an emergency before it occurs, you will not know how to handle the emergency when it happens. Know where the location of emergency devices such as fire extinguishers, fire alarms, spills kits, first aid kits, and emergency eye wash station are in your shop. Know how administer basic first aid during emergencies. Know where important emergency information is, such as SDS for hazardous materials. Knowing how to handle emergencies before they occur could save your life or the life of a coworker.

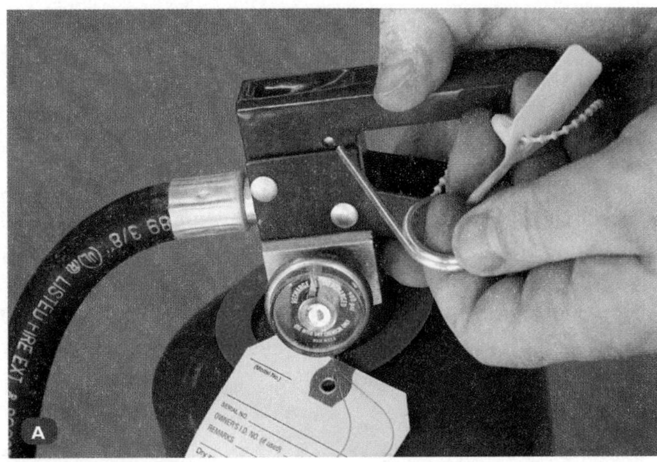

FIGURE 3-27 To operate a fire extinguisher, follow PASS: **A.** Pull, **B.** Aim, **C.** Squeeze, **D.** Sweep.

▶ Selection and Use of Personal Protective Equipment (PPE)

K03005, S03001, S03002

PPE is equipment used to block the entry of hazardous materials into the body or to protect the body from injury. PPE includes clothing, shoes, safety glasses, hearing protection, masks, and respirators (**FIGURE 3-28**).

Employee and Employer Responsibilities in Selecting and Using PPE

Employers are responsible for providing most of the PPE needed in the workplace. During new-hire orientation and onboarding, you may be advised that you are required to purchase certain PPE before starting work, such as steel-toe shoes and safety glasses. Employers are also responsible for providing training to employees on the proper PPE to wear or use for each work task and machine. This information should also be published in your shop safety policies and procedures. While it is your employer's responsibility to provide the proper PPE and inform you about how and where to use it, it is the employee's responsibility to ensure they wear or use the correct PPE when needed.

FIGURE 3-28 PPE includes clothing, shoes, safety glasses, hearing protection, dust masks, respirators, and fall protection harnesses.

An employee who is injured due to failure to use the proper PPE may be subject to disciplinary actions. Furthermore, most employers do not want to employ a person who has a consistent disregard for their own and others' safety.

Selecting the Appropriate PPE

Before you undertake any activity, think about all potential hazards and select the correct PPE based on the risk associated with the activity. For example, if you are going to change hydraulic brake fluid, put on some gloves to protect your skin from chemicals.

As you go through this chapter, you will learn how to identify the correct PPE for a given activity and how to wear it safely. The PPE you use must fit correctly and be appropriate for the task you are undertaking. For example, if the task requires you to wear eye protection and specifies that you should use a full-face shield, do not try to cut corners and only wear safety glasses. You also need to make sure the PPE you are using is worn correctly. For example, a hairnet that does not capture all your hair is not protecting you adequately.

Types and Uses of PPE

There are many types and uses of PPE. But they all have one thing in common: to prevent injury to the user. It is vital that you are familiar with the different types and uses of PPE. You will not always be told what type of PPE is best for a given situation. By knowing the various types of PPE and their uses, you can choose the best PPE for the task.

Protective Clothing

Protective clothing includes items like shirts, pants, shoes, and gloves. These items are your first line of defense against injuries and accidents and must be worn when performing any work. Always make sure protective clothing is kept clean and in good condition. You should replace any clothing that is not in good condition, since it is no longer able to fully protect you.

> ▶ TECHNICIAN TIP
>
> Each shop activity will require specific clothing depending on its nature. Research and identify what specific type of clothing is required for every activity you undertake. Wear appropriate clothing for various activities according to the shop's policy and procedures.

Work Clothing Always wear appropriate work clothing. Whether this is a one-piece coverall/overall or a separate shirt and pants, the clothes you work in should be comfortable enough to allow you to move, without being loose enough to catch on machinery. The material must be flame retardant and strong enough that it cannot be easily torn. A flap must cover buttons or snaps. If you wear a long-sleeve shirt, the cuffs must be close fitting, without being tight. Pants should not have cuffs, so that hot debris cannot become trapped in the fabric.

Taking Care of Clothing Always wash your work clothes separately from your other clothes. Start a new working day with clean work clothes, and change out of contaminated clothing as soon as possible. It is a good idea to keep a spare set of work clothes in the shop in case a toxic or corrosive fluid is spilled on the clothes you are wearing.

Footwear

The proper footwear provides protection against chemicals, cuts, abrasions, slips, and items falling on your feet. The soles of your shoes must be acid and slip resistant, and the uppers must be made from a puncture-proof material such as leather. MORE technicians almost always wear safety shoes with a steel cap to protect the toes (**FIGURE 3-29**). Always wear shoes that comply with your local shop standards.

Headgear

Headgear includes items like hairnets, caps, and hard hats. They help protect you from getting your hair caught in rotating machinery and protect your head from knocks or bumps. For example, your hard hat can protect you from bumping your head on a machine when the machine is raised on a hoist. It is also good practice to wear a cap to hold longer hair in place and to keep it clean when working under a machine. Some caps are designed specifically with additional padding on the top to provide extra protection against bumps.

Hand Protection

Hands are a very complex and sensitive part of the body, with many nerves, tendons, and blood vessels. They are susceptible to injury and damage. Nearly every activity performed on machines requires the use of your hands, all of which put you at risk of injury. Whenever possible, wear gloves to protect your hands. There are many types of gloves available, and their applications vary greatly. It is important to wear the correct type of glove for the various activities you perform.

Chemical Gloves Heavy-duty and impenetrable chemical gloves should always be worn when using solvents and cleaners. They should also be worn when working on batteries. Chemical gloves should extend to the middle of your forearm to reduce the risk of chemicals splashing onto your skin (**FIGURE 3-30**).

FIGURE 3-29 Safety footwear protects against chemicals, cuts, abrasions, slips, and items falling on your feet.

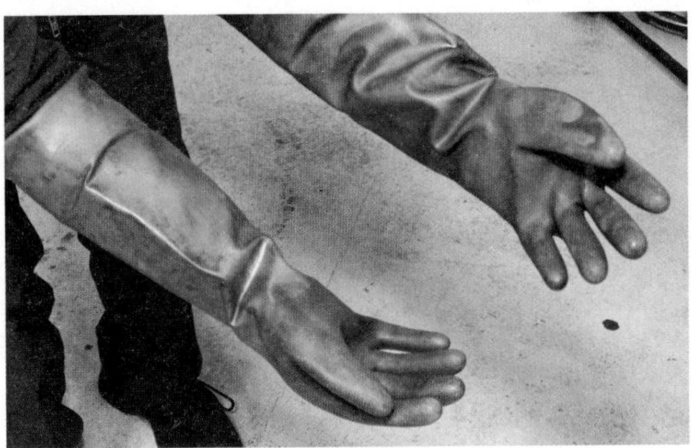

FIGURE 3-30 Chemical gloves should extend to the middle of your forearms to reduce the risk of chemical burns to your skin.

Always inspect chemical gloves for holes or cracks before using them, and replace them when they become worn. Some chemical gloves are also slightly heat resistant. This type of chemical glove is suitable for use when removing radiator caps and mixing coolant.

Leather Gloves Leather gloves will protect your hands from burns when welding or handling hot components (**FIGURE 3-31**). You should also use them when removing steel from a storage rack and when handling sharp objects. When using leather gloves for handling hot components, be aware of the potential for heat buildup. **Heat buildup** occurs when the leather glove can no longer absorb or reflect heat, and heat is then transferred to the inside of the leather glove. At this point, the leather gloves' ability to protect you from the heat is reduced, so you will need to stop work, remove the leather gloves, and allow them to cool down before continuing to work. Also, avoid picking up very hot metal with leather gloves, because it causes the leather to harden, making it less flexible during use. If very hot metal must be moved, it would be better to use an appropriate pair of pliers.

Light-Duty Gloves Light-duty gloves should be used to protect your hands from exposure to greases and oils (**FIGURE 3-32**). Light-duty gloves are typically disposable and can be made from a few different materials, such as nitrile, latex, and even plastic. Some people have allergies to these materials. If you have an allergic reaction when wearing these gloves, try using a glove made from a different material.

FIGURE 3-31 Leather gloves will protect your hands from burns when welding or when handling hot parts.

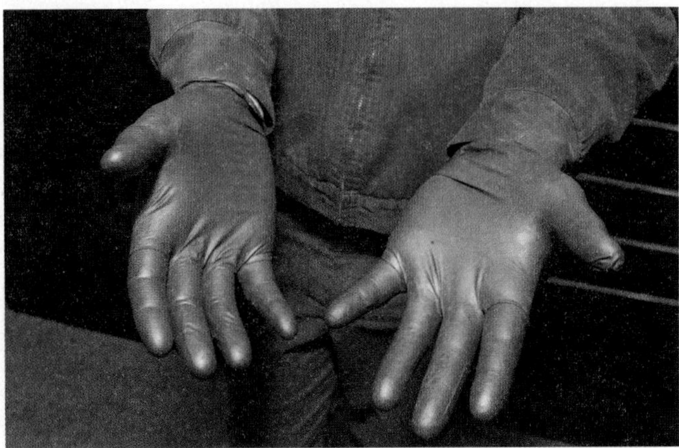

FIGURE 3-32 Light-duty gloves should be used to protect your hands from grease and oils.

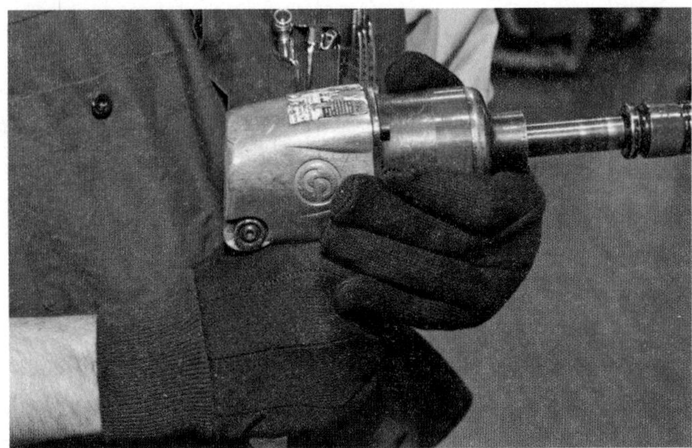

FIGURE 3-33 Cloth gloves work well in cold temperatures, so that cold metal tools do not stick to your skin.

General-Purpose Cloth Gloves Cloth gloves are designed to be worn in cold temperatures, particularly during winter, so that cold tools do not stick to your skin (**FIGURE 3-33**). Over time, cloth gloves will accumulate dirt and grime, so you will need to wash them regularly. Regularly inspect cloth gloves for damage and wear, and replace them when required. Cloth gloves are not an effective barrier against chemicals or oils, so never use them for that purpose.

Barrier Cream **Barrier cream** looks and feels like a moisturizing cream, but it has a specific formula to provide extra protection from chemicals and oils. Barrier cream prevents chemicals from being absorbed into your skin and should be applied to your hands before you begin work (**FIGURE 3-34**). Even the slightest exposure to certain chemicals can lead to dermatitis, a painful skin irritation. Never use a standard moisturizer as a replacement for proper barrier cream. Barrier cream also makes it easier to clean your hands because it can prevent fine particles from adhering to your skin.

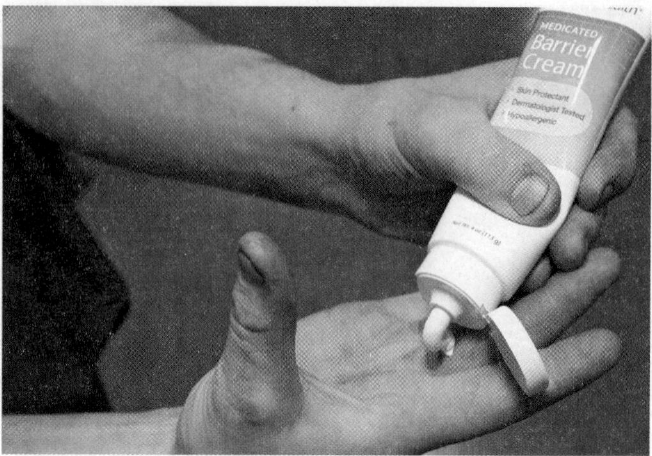

FIGURE 3-34 Barrier cream acts as a protective layer, preventing chemicals from being absorbed into your skin. It should be applied before starting work.

Cleaning Your Hands When cleaning your hands, use only specialized hand cleaners, which protect your skin. Your hands are porous and easily absorb liquids on contact. Never use solvents such as gasoline or kerosene to clean your hands, because they can be absorbed into the bloodstream and remove the skin's natural protective oils.

Hearing Protection

Ear protection should be worn when sound levels exceed 85 decibels, when you are working around operating machinery for any period of time, or when the equipment you are using produces loud noise. If you must raise your voice to be heard by a person who is 2 ft (0.6 m) away from you, then the sound level is about 85 decibels or more. Ear protection comes in two forms: One type covers the entire outer ear, and the other is fitted into the ear canal (**FIGURE 3-35**). Generally speaking, the in-ear style has higher noise-reduction ratings. If the noise is not excessively loud, either type of protection will work. If you are in an extremely loud environment, you will want to verify that the option you choose has a high enough rating. You can also use double hearing protection, by using both in-ear and over-the-ear devices.

FIGURE 3-35 Ear protection comes in two forms, in-ear protection fits in and conforms to the inside of the ear. Over-the-ear protection fits over the outside of the ears.

Breathing Devices

Dust and chemicals from your workspace can be absorbed into the body when you breathe. When working in an environment where dust is present or where the task you are performing will produce dust, you should always wear some form of breathing device. There are two types of breathing devices: disposable dust masks and respirators.

Disposable Dust Masks A disposable dust mask is made from paper with a wire-reinforced edge that is held to your face with an elastic strap. It covers your mouth and nose and is disposed of at the completion of the task (**FIGURE 3-36**). This type of mask should be used only as a dust mask and should not be used if chemicals, such as paint solvents, are present in the atmosphere.

Respirator A respirator has removable cartridges that can be changed according to the type of contaminant being filtered. Always make sure the cartridge is the correct type for the contaminant in the atmosphere. For example, when chemicals are present, use the appropriate chemical filter in your respirator. The cartridges should be replaced according to the manufacturer's recommendation to ensure their effectiveness. To be completely effective, the respirator mask must make a good seal on your face (**FIGURE 3-37**).

SAFETY TIP

A dust mask or respirator will filter out only particulate contaminates. They will not protect you in an atmosphere in which there is not enough oxygen to sustain life. In these cases, a closed respiratory system with its own oxygen supply must be used.

Eye Protection

Eyes are very sensitive organs, and they need to be protected against damage and injury. There are many things in the shop environment

FIGURE 3-36 A disposable dust masks covers both the nose and mouth and is thrown away at the end of the task.

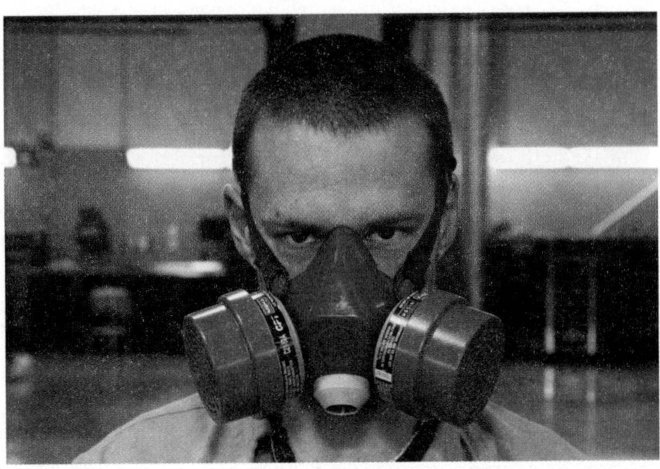

FIGURE 3-37 To be effective, the respirator mask must make a good seal on your face.

that can damage or injure eyes, such as high-velocity particles coming from a grinder or high-intensity light coming from a welder. In fact, the American National Standards Institute (ANSI) reports that 2,000 workers per day suffer on-the-job eye injuries. Always select the appropriate eye protection for the work you are undertaking. Sometimes this may mean that more than one type of protection is required. For example, when grinding, you should wear a pair of safety glasses underneath your face shield for added protection.

Safety Glasses The most common type of eye protection is a pair of safety glasses, which must be marked with "Z87" on the lens and frame. Check with your supervisor for the specific protective eyewear rating required at your job site. Safety glasses have built-in side shields to help protect your eyes from the side. Approved safety glasses should be worn whenever you are in a shop. They are designed to help protect your eyes from direct impact or damage from flying debris (**FIGURE 3-38**). The only time they should be removed is when you are using other eye protection equipment. Prescription and tinted safety glasses are also available. Tinted safety glasses are designed to be worn outside in bright sunlight conditions. Never wear them indoors or in low light conditions, because they reduce your ability to see.

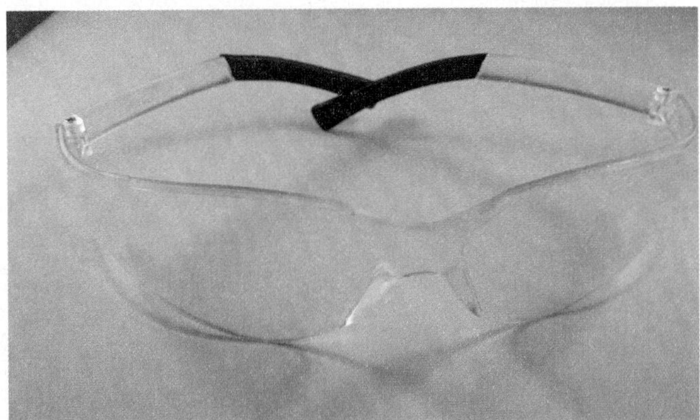

FIGURE 3-38 Safety glasses are designed to protect your eyes from direct impact or damage from flying debris.

Welding Helmets Wear a **welding helmet** when using or assisting a person using an electric welder. The light from a welding arc is very bright and contains high levels of ultraviolet radiation. The lens on a welding helmet has heavily tinted glass to reduce the intensity of the light from the welding tip, allowing you to see the task you are performing more clearly (**FIGURE 3-39**). Lenses come in a variety of ratings depending on the type of welding you are doing; always make sure you are using a properly rated lens. The remainder of the helmet is made from a durable material that blocks any other light from reaching your face. Welding helmets that tint automatically when an arc is struck are also available. Their big advantage is that you do not have to lift and lower the lens by hand.

Gas Welding Goggles **Gas welding goggles** can be worn instead of a welding mask when using or assisting a person using an oxyacetylene welder (**FIGURE 3-40**). The eyepieces are available in heavily tinted versions, but they are not as tinted as

FIGURE 3-39 The lens on a welding helmet is heavily tinted to reduce the intensity of the light from the welding arc, while still allowing you to see what you are doing.

FIGURE 3-40 Gas welding goggles can be used instead of a full-face welding helmet when using or assisting someone using an oxyacetylene welder.

those used in an electric welding helmet. There is no ultraviolet radiation from an oxyacetylene flame, so the welding helmet is not required. However, the flame is bright enough to damage your eyes, so always use goggles of the correct rating.

Full-Face Shield It is necessary to use a full-face shield when using solvents and cleaners, epoxies, and resins or when working on a battery (**FIGURE 3-41**). The clear mask of the face shield allows you to see all that you are doing and will protect your entire face from chemical burns should there be any splashes or battery explosions. It is also recommended that you use a full-face shield combined with safety goggles when using a bench or angle grinder.

Safety Goggles Safety goggles provide much the same eye protection as safety glasses but with added protection against harmful chemicals that may splash up behind the lenses of glasses (**FIGURE 3-42**). Goggles also provide additional protection from foreign particles. Safety goggles must be worn when servicing air-conditioning systems or any other system that contains pressurized gas. Goggles can sometimes fog up when in use; if this occurs, use one of the special anti-fog cleaning fluids or cloths to clean them.

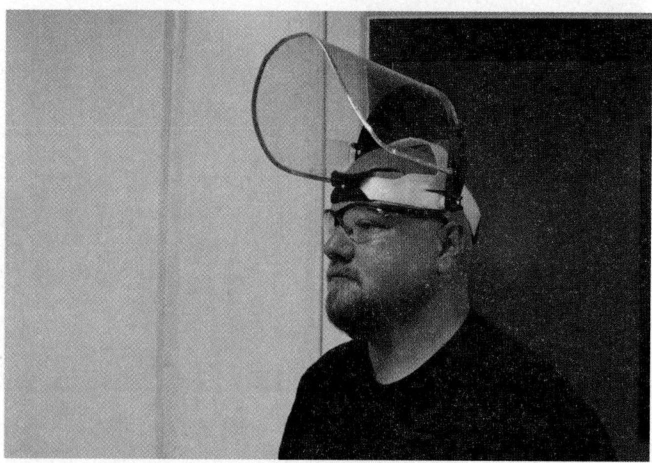

FIGURE 3-41 It is necessary to use a full-face shield when using a grinder, solvents and cleaners, epoxies, and resins and when working on a battery.

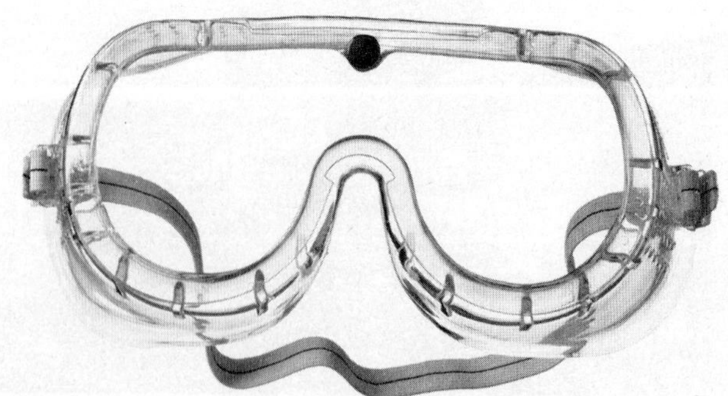

FIGURE 3-42 Safety goggles offer much the same eye protection as safety glasses but with the added protection of preventing liquids and debris from entering from the sides of the lens.

▶ TECHNICIAN TIP

Each lab/shop activity will require at least the safe use of safety glasses, clothing, and shoes depending on its nature. Research and identify whether any additional safety devices are required for every activity you undertake.

Hair Containment

It is easy to get hair caught in rotating machinery, such as drill presses or running engines, and it can happen very quickly. If your hair gets caught in the machinery, you can be pulled into the machinery and injured or killed. Hair should always be tied back and contained within a hairnet or cap. Your shop will have policies and procedures relating to appropriate hairstyles for shop activities. Research the policy and procedures to determine appropriate hairstyles for activities. Always wear your hair according to the policy and procedures. Use hairnets, caps, or elastic bands as required for each activity.

Watches and Jewelry

When in a shop environment, watches, rings, and jewelry present several hazards. They can get caught in rotating machinery, and because they are constructed mainly from metal, they can conduct electricity. Imagine leaning over a running engine with a dangling necklace: it could get caught in the fan belt and be ripped from your neck. Not only will it get destroyed, but it could also seriously injure you. A ring or watch could inadvertently short out an electrical circuit, heat up quickly and severely burn you, or cause a spark that may make the battery explode. A ring can also get caught on moving parts, breaking the finger bone or even ripping the finger out of the hand (**FIGURE 3-43**). To be safe, always remove watches, rings,

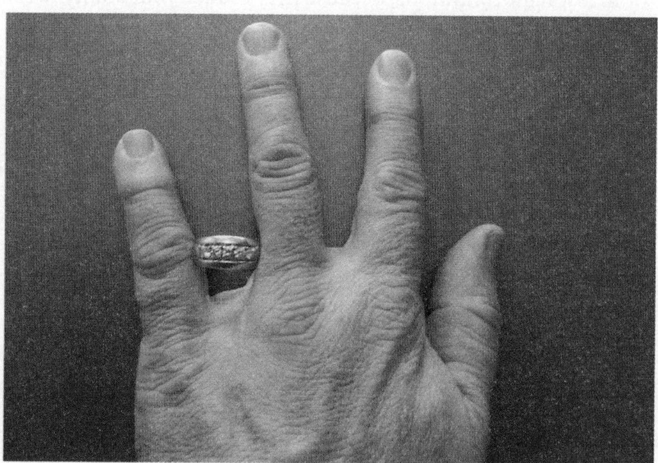

FIGURE 3-43 Wearing rings and other jewelry while operating machinery or lifting heavy items may cause severe injury.

and other jewelry before starting work. Not only is it safer to remove these items, but also your valuables will not get damaged or lost.

High-Pressure Fluid Injection Injuries

A specific type of hazard that a MORE technician should be aware of is high-pressure fluid. As a MORE technician, you will be working on and around various hydraulic and pneumatic systems under extreme pressures. It may be difficult to believe, but high-pressure equipment such as hydraulic lines, high-pressure grease guns, and high-pressure fuel injection systems have the potential to cause serious injury and even death. The pressure in these systems can be more than 12,000 psi. A small pinhole, or crack in a high-pressure hydraulic hose or fuel injection line, can cause fluid to escape at a velocity of over 600 ft per second. This causes a great deal of force in a small area that can act like a needle or a knife, puncturing gloves or outer garments and penetrating the skin. These high-pressure fluid injection injuries usually require emergency medical treatment. When the fluid enters the body, it kills tissue and gangrene will begin to occur if it is not treated. Fluid injection injuries are often painless and very small. Pain and swelling may not occur for several hours after the initial injury. Failure to seek medical help quickly may result in the need to amputate fingers and limbs. Furthermore, there is a risk of blood poisoning and bacterial infection (**FIGURE 3-44**).

What to do if you suspect a fluid injection injury If you suspect a person has a fluid injection injury get them to a hospital immediately. In addition, take the MSDS for the fluid with you and inform the medical staff that the injury may be a high-pressure fluid injection injury. Inform the hospital staff of the type of fluid and provide them with the copy of the MSDS.

How to prevent fluid injection injuries If the system must be pressurized to find the source of a leak, stand well away from the suspected leak area and wear the appropriate PPE, such as a full-face shield, thick gloves, and overalls. Use a piece of cardboard or wood, and place it near the suspected leak area until the location of the leak is detected. Do not place any part of your body near a potential high-pressure leak.

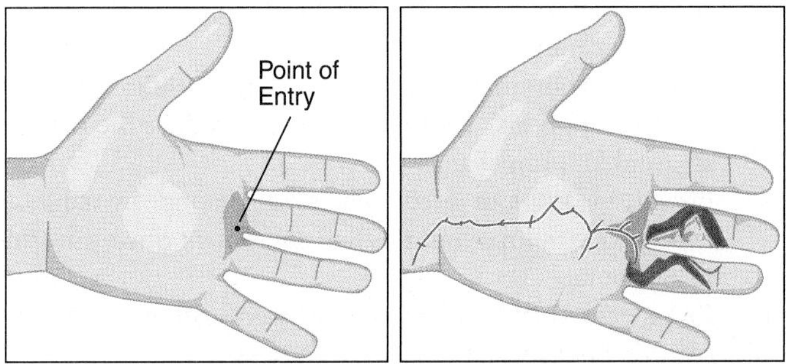

FIGURE 3-44 High-pressure fluid injection injuries can be overlooked and might appear harmless. But they require immediate surgery and can cause great damage to tissues if left untreated.

One of the easiest and most effective ways to protect yourself from injury is by using the appropriate PPE. Ensure that before performing a work task, or operating a machine, you research what, if any, PPE is required. Also, ensure that the PPE you are using meets applicable safety standards. It can be tempting not to use the proper PPE, to make working easier or speed things up—but the consequences can be severe.

▶ Safe MORE Service and Repair

K03006

MORE machines must be put into a safe condition when technicians are about to perform service or repair procedures on them. When a machine problem is being diagnosed, it will need to remain in a working condition and all applicable hazards related to a live running machine must be adhered to. This includes keeping all personnel clear of the danger zone, having spotters when travelling or working in close quarters, communicating with other machine operators that are close by, and ensuring the operator is familiar with operating the machine.

Once a machine is ready for servicing or having repairs performed on it, there are steps to take to make the machine safe to work on. This ensures that all sources of potential energy (hydraulic, electrical, and potential kinetic) on the machine are neutralized and/or unable to be released in an uncontrolled manner. The following examples are common practices used to make machines safe to work on. Always refer to the machines service information to be aware of all machine-specific procedures needed to put a machine into a safe condition.

Lock Out Tag Out

There will be variations of **LOTO (Lock Out Tag Out)** procedures for different shops, employers, and jurisdictions. However, the desired outcome of any LOTO system is to prevent unwanted start-up or movement of a machine while it is being worked on. Every technician must be aware of their company's LOTO policies and adhere to them. Disregard for LOTO procedures can be cause for dismissal or other types of discipline.

Today, almost all MORE machines will have a master disconnect switch that will have a lock hasp around it. It is usually part of the main battery ground circuit, and by turning off this switch and locking it out, the machine cannot be started. Every employee that works for a company that has a LOTO policy will have a personal lock with their identification on it. The worker must use their lock to lock out the machine they are working on, and they are the only ones that can normally remove it. If there is more than one technician working on a machine, a lock out box will need to be used. The box will contain the key for the lock on the machine, and it provides several locations for multiple technicians to apply their locks. Tagging out a machine involves placing a "Do Not Operate" tag on the machine to notify anyone that the machine is locked out, when it was locked out, and why it has been locked out (**FIGURE 3-45**).

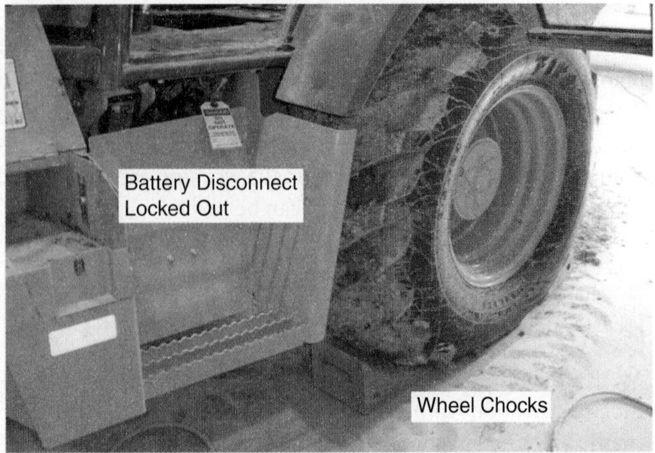

FIGURE 3-45 MORE machine that displays a "Do No Operate" tag and has wheel chocks applied.

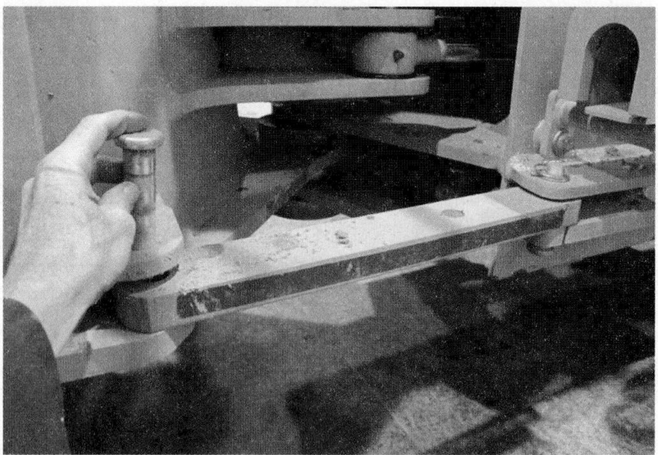

FIGURE 3-46 MORE machine that is having a steering lock applied.

Wheel Chocks

Wheel chocks are used in a repair shop to ensure a rubber-tired MORE machine doesn't roll in an uncontrolled manner. It is common practice that as soon as a machine is parked in a shop, wheel chocks are placed on both sides of one wheel (Figure 3-45).

Wheel chocks are available in a range of sizes for all sizes of machines.

Implement Locks

When working on MORE machines, it may be necessary to get into pinch points. These are areas where serious injury or death can occur if mechanical locks aren't put in place. For example, a tractor loader backhoe will have a boom cylinder lock that once installed with the boom raised will mechanically prevent it from lowering. Other common implement locks are for dump boxes on trucks and steering locks for articulated machines. These locks should always stay with the machine and are usually painted red to identify them (**FIGURE 3-46**).

Depressurizing Accumulators

Many MORE machines will have one or more hydraulic accumulators. These devices are designed to store pressurized hydraulic fluid and are part of steering, brake, or hydraulic systems.

Before work is done on these systems, these accumulators must be de-energized. Always refer to the machine's service information for the proper way to do this. For example, a brake accumulator could be bled down by pumping the brake pedal while monitoring system pressure.

De-energizing High-Voltage Electrical Systems

Some MORE machines will have high-voltage electric drive systems. There is a chance that even after the machine's engine is shut off, high voltage could be present.

To confirm that no high voltage is present, a detailed procedure must be followed. This includes very specific PPE for the task and includes training to know how to properly perform the task.

▶ Wrap-Up

Safety is an investment by both you and your employer, in you. If you do not consider safety worth investing your time, knowledge, and effort into, you or others around you will pay a high price at some point. Having a safe attitude is a cheap insurance policy against injuries, and it also demonstrates your professionalism.

Ready for Review

- It is everyone's responsibility to maintain a safe working environment.
- Anyone has the authority to stop an operation that is unsafe.
- Hazards should be identified before beginning a task or operating equipment.
- Attempt to eliminate a hazard or risk if possible; if not possible, apply risk control measures to reduce the risk of an accident or mishap.
- Effective workplace safety policies save money by reducing expensive employee injuries and equipment downtime due to accidents.
- Employees must know and abide by government and shop regulations, especially concerning safety.
- Employers are required to maintain copies of all MSDS for all hazardous substances they have on site.

- Employees should be aware of where MSDS are in their shop.
- Employees should be aware of the location of emergency equipment such as fire extinguishers, fire alarms, emergency eyewash stations, first aid kits, AEDs, and hazardous material spill kits.
- Employees must know what to do in an emergency before one occurs: There will not be enough time to learn what to do during an emergency.
- Employers are responsible for providing employees with the proper PPE in order to perform their jobs and for training them on the proper selection and use of PPE for the different tasks in the workplace.
- Employees are responsible for using the proper PPE to protect themselves and others from injury.
- *Do not* attempt to disable, remove, or cheat operator protection systems on machinery and equipment.
- Conduct a hazard assessment and read the operator or repair manual before operating or repairing any equipment you are not familiar with.
- MORE machines must be put in a safe condition prior to service or repairs being performed on them. This includes locking out the machine, using wheel chocks, and de-pressurizing accumulators.

Key Terms

Automated External Defibrillator (AED) A portable device that checks the heart rhythm and can send an electric shock to the heart to try to restore a normal rhythm. AEDs are used to treat sudden cardiac arrest (SCA).

National Institute for Automotive Service Excellence (ASE) An independent, nonprofit organization that seeks to improve the quality of automotive repair by testing and certifying automotive service professionals.

back brace A piece of PPE that protects the back by bracing, which is used when heavy or frequent lifting is involved.

barrier cream A cream that looks and feels like a moisturizing cream but has a specific formula to provide extra protection from chemicals and oils.

caution Indicates a potentially hazardous situation, which, if not avoided, may result in minor or moderate injury.

complicated fracture A fracture in which the bone has penetrated a vital organ.

danger Indicates an immediately hazardous situation, which, if not avoided, will result in death or serious injury.

danger zone Area of a machine where if a person were to have a body part during the machine cycle would incur injury.

dislocation The displacement of a joint from its normal position, which is caused by an external force stretching the ligaments beyond their elastic limit.

double-insulated Tools or appliances that are designed in such a way that no single failure can result in a dangerous voltage coming into contact with the outer casing of the device.

ear protection Protective gear worn when the sound levels exceed 85 decibels, when working around operating machinery for any period of time, or when the equipment you are using produces loud noise; also called hearing protection.

Environmental Protection Agency (EPA) A U.S. federal government agency that deals with issues related to environmental safety.

evacuation routes A safe way of escaping danger and gathering in a safe place where everyone can be accounted for in the event of an emergency.

external bleeding The loss of blood from an external wound, where blood can be seen escaping.

fire blanket A safety device designed to extinguish incipient (starting) fires. It consists of a sheet of fire retardant material that is to be placed over a fire in order to smother it.

first aid The immediate care given to an injured or suddenly ill person.

first aid kit A kit containing items needed to apply emergency first aid, such as bandages, gauze, medical tape, and other items.

first-degree burns Burns that show reddening of the skin and damage to the outer layer of skin only.

flash point The lowest temperature at which vapors of a volatile material will ignite when given an ignition source.

gas welding goggles Protective gear designed for gas welding, which provide protection against foreign particles entering the eye and are tinted to reduce the glare of the welding flame.

hazard Anything that could hurt you or someone else.

hazard control measures Actions taken to reduce, eliminate, or lessen the possible damage from hazards.

hazardous environment A place where hazards exist.

hazardous material Any material that poses an unreasonable risk of damage or injury to persons, property, or the environment if it is not properly controlled during handling, storage, manufacture, processing, packaging, use and disposal, or transportation.

headgear Protective gear that includes items like hairnets, caps, or hard hats.

heat buildup A dangerous situation that occurs when the glove can no longer absorb or reflect heat and heat is transferred to the inside of the glove.

HEPA (high-efficiency particulate absorption) A type of particulate air filter, which is effective at filtering out fine particles and dust.

internal bleeding The loss of blood into the body cavity from a wound, where there is no obvious sign of blood.

LOTO (Lock Out Tag Out) A system that must be adhered to that ensures a machine is safe to work on. The machine's energy sources are neutralized, and the machine is prevented from starting.

Material Safety Data Sheets (MSDS) Same as safety data sheets (SDS).

MSHA (Mine Safety and Health Administration) A U.S. federal government agency created to provide safety and regulatory enforcement in mining activities.

occupational safety and health A multidisciplinary field concerned with the safety, health, and welfare of people in the workplace.

Occupational Safety and Health Administration (OSHA) A U.S. federal government agency created to provide national leadership in occupational safety and health.

operating manual A manual published by an equipment manufacturer with information on how to safely and properly operate equipment.

operator protection systems Safety systems and devices designed to protect the operator of machinery from injury.

open fracture A fracture in which the bone is protruding through the skin or there is severe bleeding.

Personal Protective Equipment (PPE) Safety equipment designed to protect the technician, such as safety boots, gloves, clothing, protective eyewear, and hearing protection.

policy A guiding principle that sets the shop direction.

procedure A list of the steps required to get the same result each time a task or activity is performed.

reactivity The rate at which a substance will undergo a chemical reaction. The higher the reactivity, the faster it will chemically react.

repair and maintenance manual A manual published by an equipment manufacturer with information on how to safely and properly maintain, repair, and troubleshoot equipment.

respirator Protective gear used to protect the wearer from inhaling harmful dusts or gases. Respirators range from single-use disposable masks to types that have replaceable cartridges. The correct types of cartridge must be used for the type of contaminant encountered.

risk Exposing a person or a valuable item to danger, harm, or loss.

risk controls Measures or actions taken to reduce and control risk.

Society of Automotive Engineers (SAE) A U.S.-based, globally active professional association and standards developing organization for engineering professionals in various industries, including automotive; mobile, off-road equipment; commercial truck; and aerospace. It sets industry standards and regulations.

safety The condition of being protected from or unlikely to cause danger, risk, or injury to yourself or others.

Safety Data Sheets (SDS) Sheets that provide information about handling, use, and storage of materials that may be hazardous; also called material safety data sheets.

second-degree burns Burns that involve blistering and damage to the outer layer of skin.

shock Inadequate tissue oxygenation resulting from serious injury or illness.

simple fracture A fracture that involves no open wound or internal or external bleeding.

spill kit A kit or container containing items needed to clean up and control liquid and hazardous material spills.

sprain An injury in which a joint is forced beyond its natural movement limit.

strain An injury caused by the overstretching of muscles and tendons.

technical manual A collection of information (paper or electronic) containing specific technical data regarding how to properly operate, maintain, repair, or troubleshoot a piece of equipment. Technical manuals may also contain technical data on how to complete a task or procedure.

technical safety bulletins Documents periodically published and distributed by an equipment manufacturer, in which they identify a safety risk or hazard and how to properly control the risk or hazard.

third-degree burns Burns that involve white or blackened areas and damage to all skin layers and underlying structures and tissues.

Threshold Limit Value (TLV) The maximum allowable concentration of a given material in the surrounding air.

toxic dust Any dust that may contain fine particles that could be harmful to humans or the environment.

warning Indicates a potentially hazardous situation, which, if not avoided, could result in death or serious injury.

welding helmet Protective gear designed for arc welding; it provides protection against foreign articles entering the eye, and the lens is tinted to reduce the glare of the welding arc.

Review Questions

1. Which of these IS NOT a benefit of an effective workplace hazard prevention and control system?
   - **a.** It avoids unnecessary injuries and illnesses to personnel.
   - **b.** It increases employee morale and job satisfaction.
   - **c.** It allows employees to have a party when we reach 365 days with no lost time incidents.
   - **d.** It minimizes downtime due to equipment damage from safety mishaps.
2. Personal protective equipment (PPE) includes all of the following EXCEPT:
   - **a.** Safety glasses
   - **b.** Portable welding screen
   - **c.** Welding helmet
   - **d.** Steel-toe shoes
3. True or False. The most effective operator protection system is not to place your hand in the machine's danger zone.
   - **a.** True
   - **b.** False
4. Effective control measures to minimize the risk of an accident includes all of the following EXCEPT:
   - **a.** Your supervisor will tell you how to minimize all risks.
   - **b.** Read the manufacturer's operator manual before using equipment.
   - **c.** Conduct a walk-around inspection to ensure the machine is safe before operating.
   - **d.** Ensure all operator protection systems are in place and operating correctly before using equipment.
   - **e.** Read your shop safety policies before beginning work at a new job.

5. True or False. Guards on machinery can be removed to speed up production if you are confident you know what you are doing.
   a. True
   b. False
6. How long can a diesel engine be operated indoors before an exhaust extraction hose should be attached?
   a. The engine can be run indefinitely as long as the shop bay doors are opened.
   b. The engine can be run for up to 30 minutes.
   c. It depends on your shop policy.
   d. Gasoline and diesel engine equipment should not be run indoors without an exhaust extraction device attached.
7. There are three signal words: _______, ___________, and ______________.
   a. stop; warning; danger
   b. warning; general; danger
   c. danger; warning; caution
   d. caution; stop; danger
8. The maximum OSHA permissible exposure limit (PEL) for carbon monoxide is parts per million (ppm) of air for an 8-hour period.
   a. 20
   b. 30
   c. 40
   d. 50
9. Typically, there should be of unobstructed space around an electrical panel.
   a. 1'
   b. 2'
   c. 3'
   d. None of the choices is correct.
10. Which of the following bulb types presents an extreme fire hazard if broken in the presence of flammable vapors or liquids?
   a. Incandescent
   b. LED
   c. Fluorescent
   d. None of the choices is correct.

ASE Technician A/Technician B Style Questions

1. Technician A says that the press brake machine must be taken out of commission because the operator protection system has been disabled. Technician B says that he has never been injured, and it has always been like that. So, you should not have a problem operating the machine. Who is correct?
   a. Technician A
   b. Technician B
   c. Both Technician A and Technician B
   d. Neither Technician A nor Technician B
2. Technician A says that reading the equipment operating manual is not needed because all warnings are clearly posted on the machine itself. Technician B says that it is always good practice to read the operating manual before using unfamiliar equipment. Who is correct?
   a. Technician A
   b. Technician B
   c. Both Technician A and Technician B
   d. Neither Technician A nor Technician B
3. Technician A says that you should read the label on the product to determine what, if any, hazards it poses. Technician B says that you should read the MSDS on the product to determine what, if any, hazards it poses. Who is correct?
   a. Technician A
   b. Technician B
   c. Both Technician A and Technician B
   d. Neither Technician A nor Technician B
4. Technician A says that OSHA regulations are the most correct source of information about all safety-related processes and procedures that must be done in the shop. Technician B says that the equipment manufacturer operating and repair manuals are the most correct source of information regarding the operation of specific equipment. Who is correct?
   a. Technician A
   b. Technician B
   c. Both Technician A and Technician B
   d. Neither Technician A nor Technician B
5. Technician A says that you should read the label on the product to determine what, if any, hazards it poses. Technician B says that you should read the MSDS on the product to determine what, if any, hazards it poses. Who is correct?
   a. Technician A
   b. Technician B
   c. Both Technician A and Technician B
   d. Neither Technician A nor Technician B
6. Technician A says if the diesel engine is running "clean," you do not have to attach an exhaust extraction hose to run it indoors. Technician B says that you can operate a diesel engine indoors if there is proper ventilation, like having the bay doors open. Who is correct?
   a. Technician A
   b. Technician B
   c. Both Technician A and Technician B
   d. Neither Technician A nor Technician B
7. Technician A says that the best way to stop bleeding is to apply a tourniquet first. Technician B says that you should try to elevate, apply pressure, and use gauze and bandages before using a tourniquet. Who is correct?
   a. Technician A
   b. Technician B
   c. Both Technician A and Technician B
   d. Neither Technician A nor Technician B
8. Technician A says that should use a fire blanket to attempt to put out an engine fire. Technician B says that you use a

fire extinguisher to attempt to put out an engine fire. Who is correct?

a. Technician A
b. Technician B
c. Both Technician A and Technician B
d. Neither Technician A nor Technician B

9. Technician A says that you should use only a welding helmet during electric arc welding. Technician B says that you can use welding goggles for electric arc welding, as it is less restrictive and allows you to see your work material better. Who is correct?

a. Technician A
b. Technician B
c. Both Technician A and Technician B
d. Neither Technician A nor Technician B

10. Technician A says that you should use chemical gloves when handling grease and oils. Technician B says that you can use barrier cream when handling grease and oils. Who is correct?

a. Technician A
b. Technician B
c. Both Technician A and Technician B
d. Neither Technician A nor Technician B

CHAPTER 4

Bearings, Seals, Lubricants, Gaskets, and Sealants

Knowledge Objectives

After reading this chapter, you will be able to:

- **K04001** Describe and explain the purpose, operation, and construction of seals and bearings.
- **K04002** Outline the procedures used to install seals and bearings.
- **K04003** Describe and perform the steps used to adjust bearing preload.
- **K04004** Describe and perform the steps used to replace a seal.
- **K04005** Identify and explain causes of seal and bearing failures.
- **K04006** Outline and perform the steps required to replace a gasket.
- **K04007** Identify and describe the types and applications of sealants.
- **K04008** Identify and classify commonly used fluids and lubricants.

Skills Objectives

After reading this chapter, you will be able to:

- **S04001** Select and correctly use fluids and lubricants commonly used in the industry.
- **S04002** Select and use the proper tools for replacement of bearings and seals.

Attitude Objectives

After reading this chapter, you will be able to:

- **A04001** Locate and adhere to OEM service procedures for servicing seals, bearings and gaskets.

▶ Introduction

A typical heavy equipment machine will have many types of bearings, seals, gaskets, sealants, and lubricants. Together, these items are some of the most critical components in any piece of heavy equipment. These items allow other components to continue to operate properly, and without them, many other critical parts would fail quickly. Despite advances in material and construction, bearings, seals, gaskets, and lubricants are a point of considerable wear and stress and require periodic maintenance and repair. A heavy-duty equipment technician will spend a significant amount of time maintaining and servicing these components. You must be familiar with their purpose, operation, construction, types, and repair procedures to ensure they are serviced properly.

The History of Bearings, Seals, Gaskets, and Lubricants

The use of bearings goes back thousands of years, predating the Industrial Revolution of the 1700s. Some of the earliest known uses of bearings were in the form of wooden rollers supporting the moving of heavy objects. There also exist engineering drawings created by Leonardo da Vinci dating back to the 1400s and 1500s showing enclosed ball bearings. In fact, some wooden bearings are still in use today for certain applications. Seals have also been in use for thousands of years in various forms. Some of the earliest types of seals and gaskets consisted of simple rope coated in tar, pitch, or animal fats (also called tallow). In fact, rope seals still exist for some applications. During the era of the steam engine, a stuffing box (also called a packing seal, gland seal, or gland packing) was used to prevent leakage of fluid between sliding or rotating parts. Since World War II, mechanical seals have replaced the packing and gland seals in shaft sealing applications.

Prior to the widespread use of petroleum lubricants in the late 1800s, most lubricants were made of plant- or animal-based materials such as tar, pitch, plant and animal oils, and animal fats. During and after World War II, when synthetic oil and lubricant production became more widespread, it became possible to create lubricants and oils for almost any application. Since then, synthetic lubricants have become more specialized, and many equipment manufacturers use lubricants that have very specific properties and specifications. Therefore, it is crucial to verify that the lubricants you are using fulfill the specific equipment manufacturer's specifications as published in the manufacturer's service and repair manual. Failure to use the exact lubricants specified by the equipment manufacture can result in voided warranty, equipment damage, premature wear to components, and decreased operation efficiency.

▶ Purpose, Operation, and Construction of Seals and Bearings

K04001, A04001

Purpose of Bearings

Bearings play an important part in keeping heavy-duty (HD) equipment and machines working. They are designed to greatly reduce friction between moving parts by keeping them separated and allowing relative motion in the desired direction. If two parts are allowed to contact each other while there is relative motion, then the increase in friction will create heat. If enough heat is created, the parts will start to weld themselves together, similar to inertia welding. Bearings are also designed to constrain movement to only the desired direction and to support a load.

Operation of Bearings

Bearings reduce friction by using rolling elements such as rollers and balls in their construction. In slow **linear** movement applications, plain bushings can be used, which consist of materials that have a low **coefficient of friction** with one another.

Bearings are also designed to carry a load. A load can be applied to a bearing in either of two basic directions: radial and axial. **Radial** loads act at right angles to the shaft (bearing's axis of rotation). **Axial (thrust)** loads act parallel to the axis of rotation (along the shaft). See **FIGURE 4-1** for a good visual representation the loads on a bearing and shaft.

The ability of a bearing to carry a load is influenced by several factors, including the type of bearing (ball, roller, or bushing type), the number of roller elements, the type of material the bearing and roller elements are composed of, and the total surface contact area of all the roller elements. For example, due to a roller bearing's larger total surface contact area of the roller elements compared to an equivalently sized ball bearing, roller bearings are used for applications with higher radial loading. Overloading in the axial or radial direction of any type of bearing can cause deformation and premature bearing failure. For

You Are the Mobile Heavy Equipment Technician

You and another heavy-duty equipment technician are preparing to replace the left-side axle shaft seal on the rear differential of a hydraulic front end loader. This requires removing the entire axle shaft from the differential to complete.

1. What types of environmental and personnel hazards may be present during this repair operation?
2. What types of general or specialty tools may be required to properly complete this repair operation?
3. What are the critical areas to inspect in order to ensure the axle shaft seal will not fail again prematurely?
4. What (if any) manufacturer technical data should you look up before beginning the repair?
5. How do you determine what type, and specification, of axle fluid to use to refill the axle once the repair is complete?

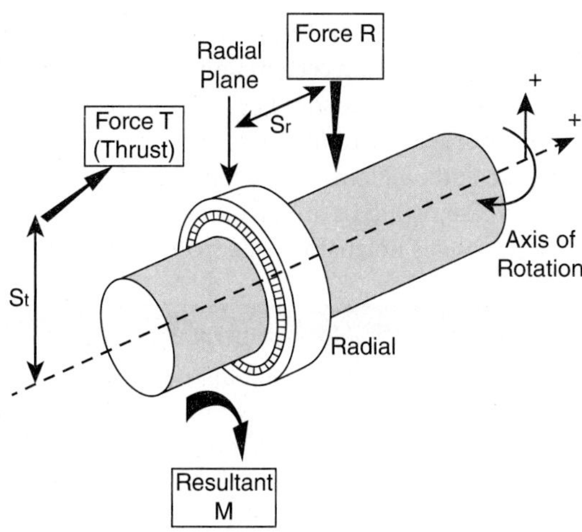

FIGURE 4-1 Axial and radial loads applied to a bearing and shaft.

FIGURE 4-2 A camshaft bearing is a type of friction bearing. It uses pressurized oil to provide a thin film of oil between the bearing's inner surface and camshaft, which the camshaft rides on. Notice the oil hole.

this reason, a heavy-duty equipment technician should pay close attention to bearing failures and determine the root cause of failure. If overloading or another external source caused a bearing to fail prematurely, the replacement bearing will also fail prematurely if the external cause of failure is not corrected.

Types and Construction of Bearings

Almost all bearings are made from metal, but some light-duty bearings could be non-metallic, such as wood or plastic. The size and type of bearing used mostly depends on the amount of load and speed during normal operation between the two parts that the bearing is separating. Next, we will explore several types of bearings, including their descriptions and applications.

Friction Bearings (Plain Bushings)

Friction Bearings, or Plain Bushings, can be used for slow, linear movement like an extendable backhoe stick; partial, slow rotation of components like bucket linkages; or very fast rotating components like engine camshafts (**FIGURE 4-2**).

A friction bearing is characterized by its lack of roller elements. It simply consists of a cylinder that surrounds a moving or rotating shaft. The bearing can be a split shell type, or a single piece construction. The bearing is designed to have a small gap between the inner bearing surface and the moving shaft to prevent metal-on-metal contact. In high-speed rotating applications, the air gap is filled with a high-pressure oil film, which the shaft rides on (**FIGURE 4-3**).

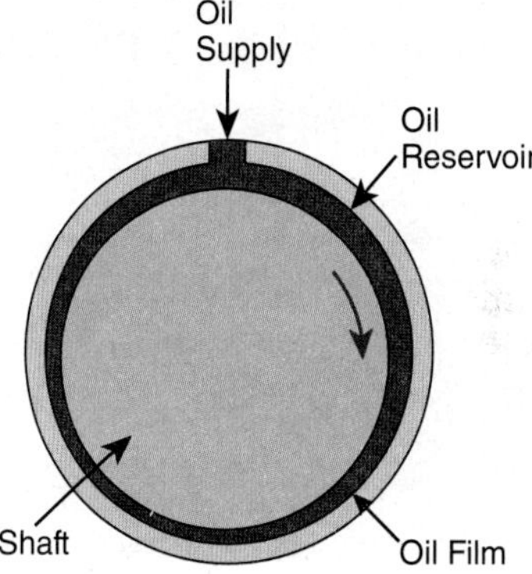

FIGURE 4-3 A camshaft bearing uses a thin film of pressurized oil to carry the load and act as a low friction bearing surface for the camshaft.

The bearing material is selected to provide a low **coefficient of friction**, good wear and fatigue strength, and an imbedded ability to resist damage to the bearing or shaft from particles. These bearings can consist of one or more types of materials sandwiched together to provide the desired characteristics. The dimensional tolerance, or gap, between the bearing inner surface and the moving shaft is critical. If the gap is too large, this will cause excessive shaft movement. In bearings that use high-pressure lubrication, this will cause a possible loss of the oil film between the bearing and the shaft and a possible loss of oil pressure at the bearing. If the gap is too small, this may result in metal-to-metal contact and excessive wear between the bearing and the shaft during expansion and contraction due to heat.

Plain Spherical Bearings

Plain spherical bearings are also a friction-type bearing in that they do not use roller elements, though there are spherical bearings that do use roller elements. This type of bearing is used in applications that require a mechanical linkage between two parts, but the angle between the parts varies or is not parallel or perpendicular to one another (**FIGURE 4-4**).

Some examples of plain spherical bearings are in tie rod ends used in steering systems (**FIGURE 4-5**). Because the angle between the steering linkage and the steering knuckle where the steering linkage attaches is not the same throughout the movement of the steering, a simple eyelet and pin cannot be used.

FIGURE 4-4 A plain spherical bearing. Notice the inner and outer rings and how the angle between the rings can vary.

FIGURE 4-5 Two plain spherical bearings used in a steering tie rod. Note the grease fittings.

Plain Spherical bearings allow the circle to be angled

FIGURE 4-6 A plain spherical bearing used in the eyelet ends of a hydraulic cylinder.

Other examples of plain spherical bearings include ball joints as well as spherical bearings placed into the eyelet ends of a hydraulic cylinder (**FIGURE 4-6**).

The plain spherical bearing consists of an inner spherical ring placed within an outer spherical ring and locked together so that the inner ring is held captive within the outer ring in the axial direction only. The inner ring is free to rotate and change angle radially (within certain limits based on the bearing design), but cannot move axially. The outer surface of the inner ring and the inner surface of the outer ring, called the raceway, slide against each other. Plain spherical bearings are either lubricated with a grease fitting or are of a maintenance-free design. This type of bearing is normally made from hardened steel.

> **TECHNICIAN TIP**
>
> "Maintenance-Free" Bearings & Joints: Do not assume just because a bearing or joint does not have a grease fitting that it is "maintenance-free" and does not require lubrication. Also, do not assume that because one bearing or joint on a piece of heavy equipment does not have a grease fitting, the entire piece of machinery is "maintenance-free" and requires no lubrication. Verify the proper lubrication points and schedule in the manufacturers service and maintenance manual or lubrication data plate.

Occasionally, plain friction bearings will be mounted on rotating shafts. They are typically installed in the bore, or housing, of a component with an **interference fit** so that the bearing remains stationary relative to the bore, or housing, it is mounted into. An interference fit, also called a **press fit** or **friction fit**, is a means of fastening two parts together so that they are in direct contact with one another and are held in place only by friction, or the tightness of the fit. The amount of friction between two surfaces is directly proportional to the force that presses them together. Because of this, a great deal of force is applied to install and uninstall interference-fit joints. However, if too much force is applied during installation and disassembly, the parts can deform and be damaged. Assembling components together using an interference fit requires using either a linear or a transverse method. In the linear method, a force is applied to the components linearly along the axis of the shaft to push the component onto the shaft using a **hydraulic press**, an **arbor press**, a **bearing driver**, or something similar. In the transverse method, either the outer part is expanded with heat or the inner part is shrunk by super cooling. The parts are then assembled and allowed to return to room temperature. As the parts return to room temperature, the gap between them closes and they touch one another. The resulting force between the parts is perpendicular, or *transverse*, and creates the friction needed to hold the parts tightly together. For bearing installation, this may require cooling the bearing or pressing the bearing into place with special tools. Bearing and component cleanliness is critical to proper installation. Bearing removal could require the use of special tools or procedures such as using a puller, press, or specific heating or cooling procedures and tools.

Rolling Type Bearings

Ball Bearings **Ball bearings** are typically used to allow independent rotation of a component and a shaft and could be used for low- or high-speed applications. They are designed to withstand mainly radial loads and limited axial loads. They are for relatively low loads because the load is concentrated on a few small spherical balls as the contact points. Ball bearings are characterized by the spherical ball rolling elements. Ball bearings are typically constructed of an assembly with an outer **race**, inner race, spherical balls, and a bearing cage. Bearing cages are meant to keep the rolling elements of the bearing separated and evenly spaced apart. Bearing cages can be made of light plastic, soft metal or hard, machined metal depending on the bearing design. The ball bearing races act as the surface that the spherical ball elements ride, or roll, on. The bearing races are made to specific dimensions and composed of specific materials, to provide an ideal surface for the ball bearings to ride on. In some cases, the ball bearing does not have its own race, but instead, it rides directly on the shaft or inside of a hole. In these cases, the shaft or hole surface that the bearing rides on is specifically machined to act as the race for the ball bearing. Ball bearing races will usually be an interference fit for either the outer diameter of the outer race or the inner diameter of the inner race. This means that removal or installation will require a gentle heating or cooling process or a special tool. Lower-speed ball bearings could be lubricated by grease, while medium- to high-speed usage bearings will be lubricated with oil. Ball bearing assemblies could also incorporate seals to keep contamination out and lubrication in. See **FIGURE 4-7** for an exploded view of a typical ball bearing assembly.

Roller Bearings **Roller bearings** are characterized by their cylindrical roller elements. They are used in applications where a shaft exerts high radial loads with minimal axial loads (10% of axial load). Like ball bearings, roller bearings will have an inner race, outer race, cylindrical roller elements, and bearing or roller cage. Roller bearings could come preassembled or have a separate outer race. Roller bearings can be used in partial rotation and full rotation and in low- to high-speed applications. Removing a roller bearing could require special puller tools or heating tools and procedures. Roller bearing installation could require gentle heating or cooling and/or special tools. Care must be taken to push or pull on the press-fit races only when installing. Depending on their application and speed, roller bearings could be lubricated by grease or oil.

Because they are designed to carry heavy loads, roller bearings are found throughout heavy-duty equipment applications. Some examples are in wheel bearings, axle bearings, and throughout transmissions and gearboxes. There are four main types of roller bearings: spherical, cylindrical, tapered roller, and needle bearings.

Spherical roller bearings are characterized by their barrel-shaped rollers. The rollers are narrow at the ends, and they bulge in the middle like a wooden barrel. They will handle some axial load and can tolerate slight misalignment of the two separated components. See **FIGURE 4-8** for a picture of a spherical roller bearing.

Cylindrical roller bearings are characterized by their cylinder-shaped roller elements. The axis of the rollers is parallel to the shaft. They are designed to carry heavy radial loads, and not axial loads. Any misalignment of the inner and outer bearing races will lead to excessive bearing wear and premature failure. This bearing type is the earliest and simplest type of bearing. A roller bearing can be as simple as wooden rollers placed under a heavy object. A typical application for a cylindrical roller bearing is to support the planet pinion gears in a planetary gear assembly used in final drives and power shift transmissions. See **FIGURE 4-9** for a picture of a typical cylindrical roller bearing.

Tapered roller bearings are characterized by the conical (cone-shaped) rollers (**FIGURE 4-10A**) that are arranged in at a *tapered* angle to the shaft so that the rollers form a cone shape around the shaft (**FIGURE 4-10B**).

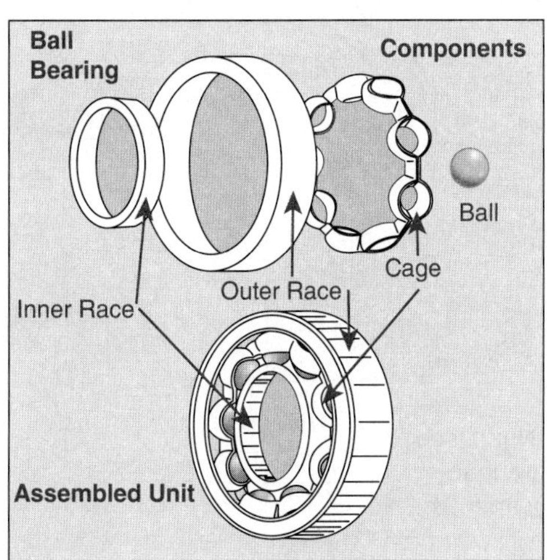

FIGURE 4-7 An exploded view of ball a bearing assembly.

FIGURE 4-8 A typical spherical roller bearing. Note the barrel-shaped rolling elements.

FIGURE 4-9 A typical cylindrical roller bearing. Note the cylinder-shaped rolling elements.

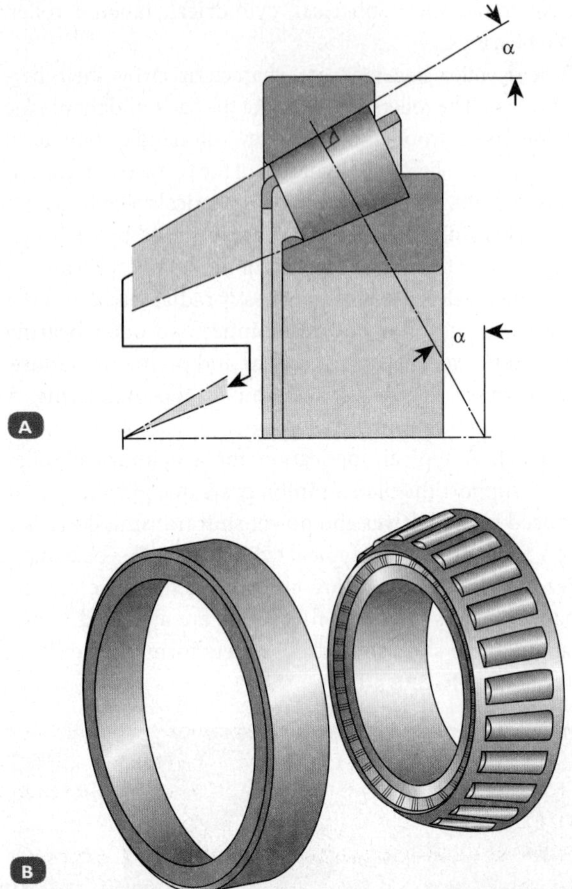

FIGURE 4-10 **A.** Notice the cone shape of the rollers in a tapered roller bearing. **B.** Notice the cone-shaped, or tapered arrangement, of all the roller elements.

FIGURE 4-11 A large pair of tapered roller bearings used in the planetary gear set of a final drive.

Because of their shape, tapered roller bearings can manage both axial (thrust) and radial loads. Typical applications for tapered roller bearings include wheel bearings, differential pinion gear shaft bearings and crown (ring) gear bearings, gear boxes, and many others. See **FIGURE 4-11** for a picture of a pair of medium-sized tapered roller bearings used in the planetary gear set of a final drive. Did you know that bearings in large industrial applications, such as power generation facilities, can be taller than a person and weigh tens of thousands of pounds?

Tapered roller bearings can be preloaded, which ensures the rollers are in full contact with the races all the way around the bearing. Tapered roller bearings will come as two separate pieces, commonly called a cup and cone. The cup is the tapered outer race, and the cone is an assembly of the tapered inner race with the rollers and a bearing cage.

Removing tapered roller bearings requires procedures similar to roller and ball bearing removals; however, bearing installation will require an adjustment procedure.

A common use for tapered roller bearings is using two bearings together to minimize the in-and-out axial movement of a shaft. A single tapered roller bearing will prevent axial movement in a single direction. However, if two tapered roller bearings are facing in opposite directions, they will restrict axial movement of a shaft in both directions. In this case, the combination of two tapered roller bearings and a preload force applied to the bearings will keep shaft axial movement to a minimum. This is a common arrangement of tapered roller bearings in differential pinion shaft bearings. The pinion shaft nut is used to apply the preload needed for the bearings. See **FIGURE 4-12** and **FIGURE 4-13** for how preload adjustments affect pinion shaft bearing applications.

Tapered roller bearing **preload** adjustment could involve adding or removing shims and/or a fastener torquing procedure. The goal of this procedure is to ensure that every roller is supporting an equal part of the load and that the amount of axial movement in the shaft is minimized. To confirm this, a specific rolling resistance must be created that equates to proper bearing preload. It is important throughout the bearing adjustment procedure to lubricate the rollers and to rotate the component to allow proper bearing seating to get an accurate reading. Preload measurement is usually accomplished by using a weight scale or torque wrench to measure the pounds or kilograms of

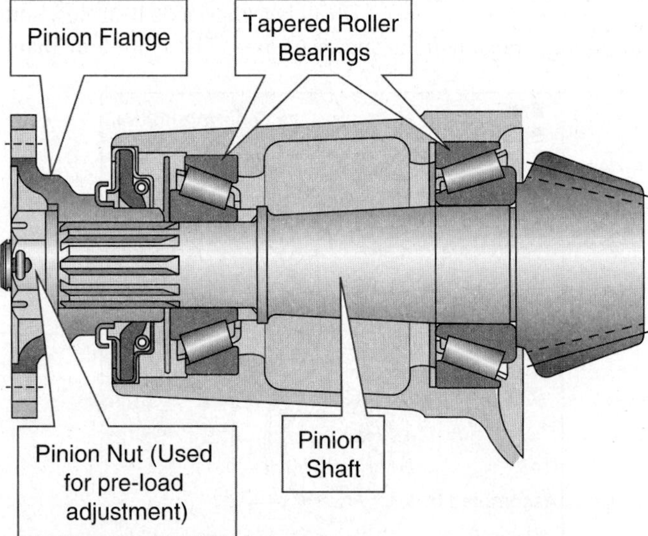

FIGURE 4-12 A differential pinion gear cutaway illustration showing the components.

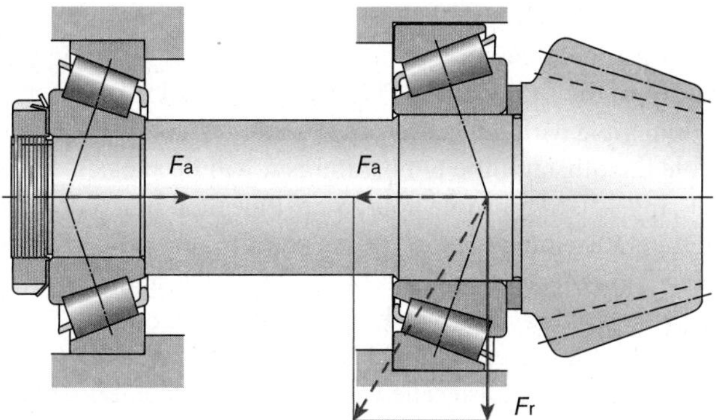

FIGURE 4-13 A cutaway illustration showing the axial (F_a) and radial (F_r) forces acting on the pinion shaft and roller bearings. The force F_a on the left side of the illustration is exerted by tightening the pinion shaft preload nut.

FIGURE 4-14 A leaking seal.

force required to rotate the supported component. The equipment manufacturer will publish specifications and procedures for preload adjustment.

Needle bearings are characterized by their thin (small diameter), long, and numerous roller elements. Needle bearings can be found in universal joint caps and the pilot bearing located on the input shaft of a manual transmission.

▶ TECHNICIAN TIP

Don't lose your bearings! Ball bearings, roller bearings, and especially needle bearings can have very small roller elements that are easily lost. Take care during removal and installation not to lose your rolling elements, and keep each bearing separate so that rolling elements from different bearings don't get mixed together.

Purpose of Seals

Seals play an important part in keeping heavy-duty equipment and machines working. A typical heavy equipment machine will use many different types of seals. Seals are necessary to keep fluids inside compartments, separated from another fluid, to seal pressurized or unpressurized air, or to keep dirt and environmental contaminants out of compartments. There are many different types and styles of seals, and they are made of many different types of materials.

A very common repair is to fix a fluid leak because of a failed seal, so it's important to understand the different types of seals and what they are made of. **FIGURE 4-14** shows a picture of a seal that's leaking fluid.

Operation of Seals

Seals simply act as a barrier to keep unwanted elements out of an area and keep the desired materials in. Seals can be grouped into two main categories: **static** and **dynamic**. Static seals work between two stationary components, such as a cylinder head and an engine block. Dynamic seals work between two components that move in relation to each other, such as a transmission input shaft and the transmission housing. It is obvious that a seal may be needed between two moving parts, because the parts must have a small gap between one another to move freely. However, someone may ask why two stationary parts cannot just be bolted directly together without the need for a seal. It may be possible to have two or more components made of the same material and having similar enough shapes to be bolted together and form a seal. In heavy-duty equipment applications, different materials and shapes are often used to manufacture components. Different materials have different rates of expansion (and to a certain degree different shapes) and contraction with changes in temperature. When two different materials are mated together, they may form a good seal at **ambient temperature**. However, when the temperature changes, they will expand and contract at different rates and will create a gap and *break the seal* at some point. Because of this, a suitable seal is used that will create a seal between the two components throughout the expected operating temperature range of the equipment.

▶ TECHNICIAN TIP

Be careful with that new seal! One of the most common causes of premature seal failure is damage caused to the seal during installation. Be very careful with new seals, as they are damaged easily. It is much easier to replace a new seal that became damaged as soon as the damage is detected. Once parts and components are reassembled and a leak is found upon repair verification, it becomes much more expensive and time-consuming to replace a new seal that was damaged.

Types and the Construction of Seals

There are far too many different types of seals to describe every one of them in this textbook. We will briefly review a few of the more common types of seals.

Static type seals can be broken down into different types of seals:

- O-rings
- D-rings
- X-rings
- backup rings
- flat rings.

Dynamic seals can be broken down into different types of seals:

- metal-to-metal piston ring–type seals
- taper faced metal-to-metal seals
- lip-type seals
- lip-type metal-supported seals
- spring-loaded lip-type metal-supported seals.

O-ring, D-ring, and Square-Ring Seals

These are flexible seals made from an elastomeric compound made of a base polymer that is mainly a natural or synthetic rubber. They will usually stay circular in shape in use but can sometimes fit into an odd-shaped groove or over a non-circular–shaped component. Their cross-section shape determines whether they are called an O-ring, D-ring, X-ring, or square-ring (**FIGURE 4-15**).

For the remainder of this section, all these seals will be called O-rings since they are the most common.

They are sized by their overall inside and outside diameter and cross-sectional diameter. Some different types of O-ring material are silicone, Buna-N, Viton, neoprene, and nitrile. The type of material a seal is constructed of is based on the type of fluid or gas it will be exposed to and the normal operating temperature of the fluid or gas. This means the seal material must be compatible with the substance it is in contact with and must be able to withstand the temperatures it will be subjected to. If an O-ring is used for some non-compatible fluid or gas or out of its temperature range, it can't be expected to seal properly. If an O-ring is overheated, it will become hard, crack, and allow fluid leak. Excessive heat is the leading cause of O-ring failure.

If an O-ring is used to seal two components, it will fit into a machined groove (also called a **gland**) on one component and should get compressed by about one-third of its diameter when the second component is fastened to the first to provide a positive seal (**FIGURE 4-16**).

O-ring seals that are used with fluid fittings can be used to fit over top of the fitting and seal against a beveled shoulder in a component when the fitting is threaded into it. O-rings could also seal the fitting on its face when they fit into a groove in the fitting.

Some O-ring–type seals that are used around the circumference of a shaft or cylinder rod will require a second ring, called a backup ring.

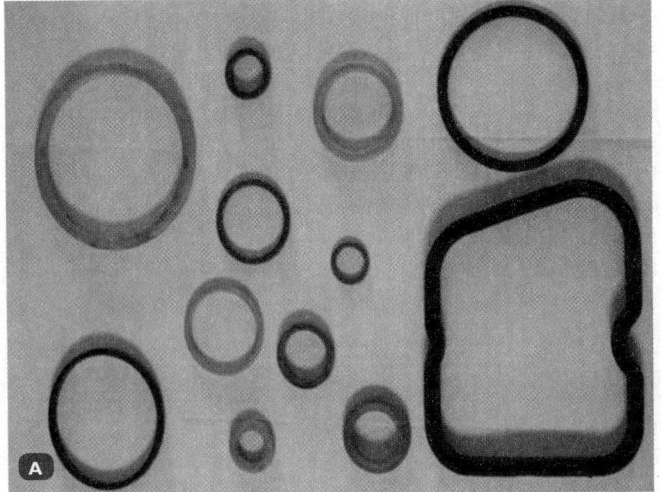

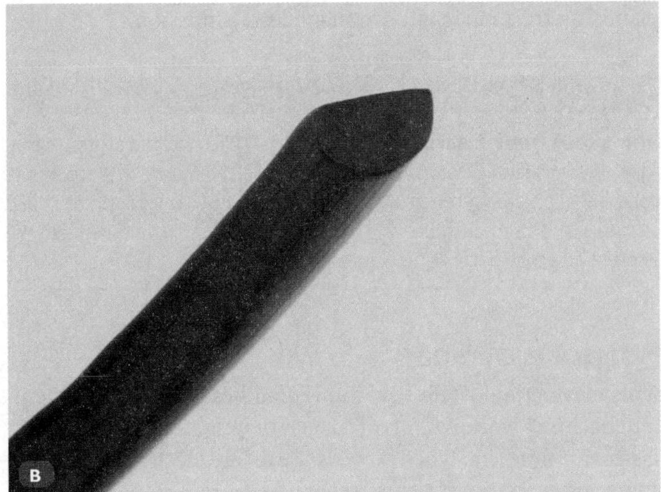

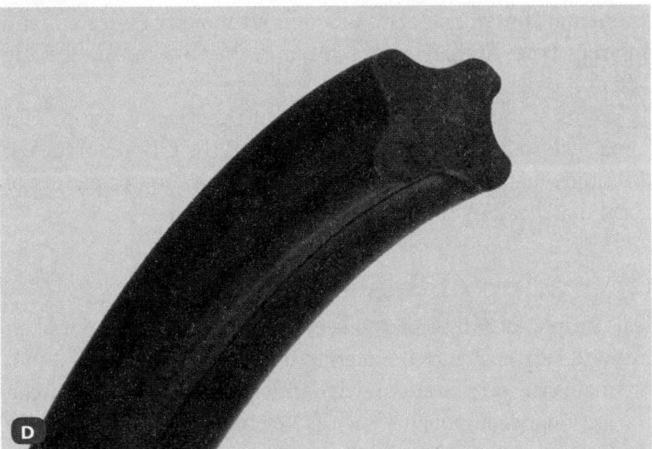

FIGURE 4-15 **A.** A variety of O-ring type seals. **B.** A cross-sectional view of a D-ring. **C.** A cross-sectional view of a square-ring **D.** A cross-sectional view of an X-ring.

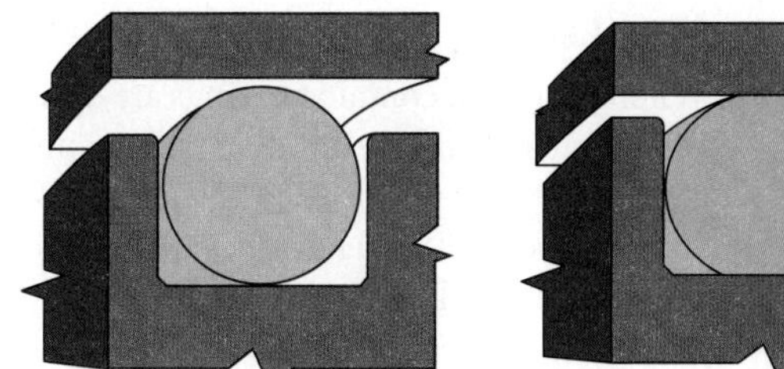
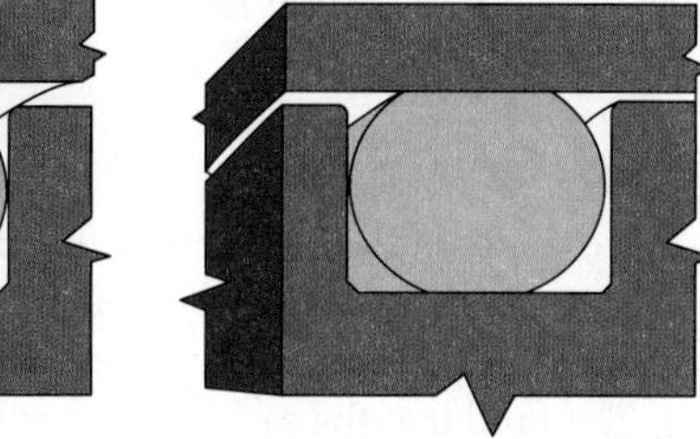

FIGURE 4-16 A cross-sectional view of static type O-ring seal before, during, and after compression with the mating surface. Notice how the compression at the top of the O-ring from the mating surface will cause the O-ring to fill the groove area.

This will be a harder, nylon material that is placed directly beside the O-ring to provide support for it in the O-ring groove around the outside circumference of a component.

Any time components are removed for repair or service, it is common practice to replace all O-ring–type seals. This is a cheap way to ensure there won't be any seal-related leaks. The groove that the O-rings fit into must be clean and free of corrosion, to ensure a proper and long-lasting seal.

▶ TECHNICIAN TIP

When replacing or reassembling components with seals and gaskets, always consult the equipment manufacturer's repair and service manual to determine which seals and gaskets require replacement once removed. Many seals and gaskets are "one-time-use" items and require replacement once disassembled or removed.

O-ring–type seals can be custom-made from bulk lengths. O-ring making kits will come with measuring and cutting tools and special adhesives to join the two ends of the O-ring.

Lip-Type Seals

Lip-type seals are designed to have one or more sharp elastomeric sealing surfaces creating a seal between the seal lip and the mating circumferential surface of a component or shaft. **Radial shaft seals** are a common type of lip seal. Some lip-type seals will rotate on a stationary shaft, whereas others will be stationary, with the shaft rotating inside the seal. Lip-type seals are usually dynamic seals, meaning that they will seal between two moving components or one stationary and one moving component. These seals can be made from different types of material, such as hard urethane, flexible rubber, or a combination of either one plus a steel backing support. Lip-type seals could have oil pressure acting on the lip to help apply more force to the lip and thereby create a more effective seal. See **FIGURE 4-17** for an assortment of lip-type seals.

Some lip-type seals will use spring pressure behind the lip to assist with creating a tighter seal. You should always check this type of seal after installation to make sure the spring is still in place (**FIGURE 4-18**).

Metal-supported lip-type seals will usually be installed with an interference fit into a recess in the component. The metal backing or support for this type of seal will usually have a soft vinyl-like coating on it that will fill any inconsistencies between the metal backing and the component it is installed into.

FIGURE 4-17 **A.** A variety of lip-type seals. **B.** Cross sections of lip-type seals.

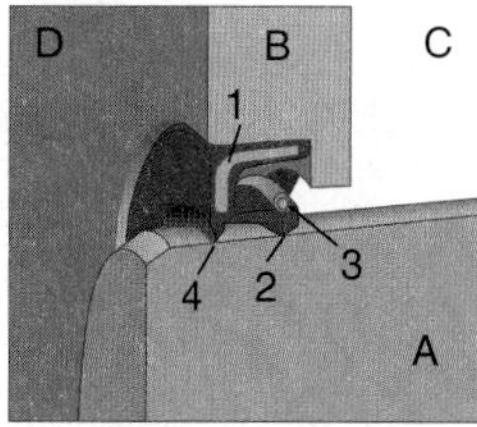

FIGURE 4-18 A radial shaft seal is a type of lip seal. Note the different seal parts labeled: **A.** Rotating shaft. **B.** Housing. **C.** Inside compartment (fluid filled). **D.** Housing face. **1.** Metal insert. **2.** Primary sealing lip. **3.** Spring. **4.** Dust seal lip.

Some lip-type seals will have their lips ride on a **wear sleeve**. The wear sleeve is a thin piece of hardened steel designed to wear down over time and should be replaced when the seal is replaced. This prevents the rotating motion from wearing down the actual components. Engine crankshafts will commonly use wear sleeves. Some lip-type seals and wear sleeves come as an assembly and must not be separated. They will require a special installation tool, and they are used mainly for rear crankshaft seals on engines.

Metal-to-Metal Face Seals

These are sometimes called duo-cone seals, and they feature two hard, special alloy metal rings that are precisely hardened and lap fitted. The hard smooth surfaces run against each other and create a seal on their faces. The fluid that the seal contains will provide some lubrication and cooling for the seal. They will have a large elastomeric O-ring seal behind them. The O-rings will keep pressure on the metal seals after component assembly, as well as complete a seal between the outer circumference of the metal seal and the component they are mounted in. One metal seal is stationary while the other rotates against it. This type of seal is most commonly used for wheel seals and or final drive seals. Duo-cone seals are very effective at keeping oil in and dirt out.

Duo-cone seals can be reused, provided they don't exceed recommended wear specifications and don't show other signs of failure like pitting or cracks. Wear on duo-cone seals is measured by seeing how wide the contact pattern is between the two metal parts.

Piston Ring–Type Seals

This style of seal is typically found in turbochargers and used to seal the turbo shaft. They are also found in torque converters and transmissions. They are a simple, hardened metal ring that creates a dynamic seal between two rotating parts and are very similar to piston rings. Care must be taken when installing this type of seal to not overstretch them or scratch them.

▶ Bearing and Seal Servicing

K04002, S04002

The following paragraphs will detail some of the methods and procedures used when replacing, removing, installing, and servicing seals and bearings.

Replacing Bearings

When parts that contain bearings are disassembled, the bearings can be reused and do not normally require replacement so long as they are still performing their function satisfactorily, pass a visual inspection, and feel smooth when rotated by hand. Do not unpackage new bearings until you are ready to install them. The packaging protects the bearings. New bearings should always be lubricated with the oil they will normally run in after they are installed. Ideally, you should wear latex gloves when handling new bearings because the moisture from your hands will start corroding the bearing. When reconditioning components with bearings, the bearings should be thoroughly cleaned with a water-free cleaning solvent like Varsol and inspected. Look for imperfections such as pitting, scoring, brinelling, corrosion, chipping, smearing, discoloration, and flaking of the surface. *Do not* blow-dry bearings with full shop air pressure, because this may over-speed the roller elements and cause damage.

When inspecting bearings, follow the procedures in **SKILL DRILL 4-1**.

Bearing Removal

The method for bearing and race removal depends on the method of installation. If the bearing is not an interference fit, then removal can be as simple as removing the fasteners and components, followed by the bearing and race. However, if the bearing and/or race was installed using an **interference fit**, then special tools and procedures are required for removal. The bearing race that is secured using an interference fit is called the **press-fit** race. The bearing race that is not secured using an interference fit is called the **slip-fit** race. Bearings may have one or both races that are press fit. Numerous tools and procedures are used to ensure safe and reliable bearing removal while minimizing the chance of damage to parts during removal. Damage to bearings, races, shafts, and housings can occur when the improper tools or methods are used. Some examples of incorrect tools and methods that may cause

SKILL DRILL 4-1 Inspecting Bearings

1. There are several ways to inspect bearings for serviceability and determine if a replacement is required:

- conducting a visual inspection of the bearings and races for signs of bearing failure (Looking)
- listening to the bearings and/or components move before or after disassembly for signs of bearing failure (Listening)
- feeling and/or measuring for excessive end play in the bearing before disassembly. Also, check for excessive play and looseness after disassembly between the bearing and race and the roller elements (feeling/measuring for end play).

2. Determine whether there is there a specific customer complaint or symptom that may be caused by a bearing failure—for example, excessive noise from the front wheel that gets louder on one side during a turn.

3. Listen for problems in the bearing before disassembly, if possible. Turn the shaft, or moving portion, and listen for any excessive noise from the bearing area, such as grinding, crunching, or scraping. Try to isolate any unusual noises as much as possible before determining whether the bearing requires replacement solely based on excessive noise when turning the bearing.

SKILL DRILL 4-1 Inspecting Bearings (Continued)

4. Feel for excessive end play, or looseness, in the bearing before disassembly, if possible. Grasp the shaft, or moving portion, by hand and move it vertically and horizontally. You can also check for excessive axial movement in the shaft by pushing and pulling the shaft, or moving portion, in and out. If needed, use a **dial indicator** to measure the specific amount of end play in the bearing. In general, any perceptible movement may be an indication of excessive looseness in the bearing. However, many equipment manufacturers publish specifications for looseness, or end play, allowable in the bearing. Refer to the equipment manufacturer's repair and service manual to determine whether there is a specification listing the allowable end play before recommending the replacement of a bearing. *Note:* You must measure end play with the bearing installed. End play cannot be measured once the bearing is removed.

If any of these conditions is detected, try to eliminate other causes by isolating the specific bearing, race, and shaft in question from other rotating parts and assemblies as much as possible. Then inspect the bearing and race visually for damage and replace as needed.

5. Feel for roughness when rotating the bearing. Bearings should turn smoothly and not have any roughness, heavy resistance, or jerking motion when turning.

If any of these conditions is detected, try to eliminate other causes by isolating the specific bearing, race, and shaft in question from other rotating parts and assemblies as much as possible. Then inspect the bearing and race visually for damage, and replace as needed.

6. Perform a visual inspection of a bearing and race to determine if there is a bearing or race failure causing a specific problem. Always clean the bearing before inspecting or reinstalling. When inspecting, the critical areas are the bearing rolling elements and the bearing races or **raceway**, so look for these specific indicators of a bearing or race failure, and replace if needed:

- pitting
- rust or corrosion
- scoring
- foreign debris damage
- nicks
- deformation to rollers, bearing cage, or race
- spalling
- damaged or broken cage or separators
- indicators of bearing overheating—brownish-blue or bluish-black coloring
- damage to integral seals
- imperfections seen or felt that require bearing and race replacement.

7. Note that bearings and races must be replaced as a set, do not replace one without also replacing the other.

damage include using hammers and drift pins, unevenly applying force, and incorrect or misaligned mounting or gripping locations.

▶ TECHNICIAN TIP

Due to the large amount of force required to remove and install interference-fit bearings, care should be taken. The bearings, races, shafts, and housing can be damaged if too much force or improper tools or methods are used to remove or install bearings and races. When removing or installing bearings or races, if it is requiring too much force without any movement, stop and try a different method. It is much better to stop and try a different method than to permanently damage an expensive shaft or housing.

Bearing removal could include using a puller, hydraulic or arbor press, internal bearing puller (a slide hammer type), heating or cooling, or other manufacturer-recommended tools.

Methods and Tools Not Recommended for Bearing Removal

Heavy-duty equipment technicians should always follow the specific equipment manufacturer's repair and service manual for the proper tools and procedures for bearing and race removal. Failure to follow the equipment manufacturer's service and repair manual may result is damage to bearings, races, seals, shafts, housings, and other parts. Furthermore, damages caused by not following the manufacturer's repair procedures is not covered by the manufacturer's warranty and may result is a declined warranty claim and a significant charge to the shop. There are several methods and tools that are frequently used to remove bearings and races, but they are not recommended:

- using a hammer and/or punch
- cutting the bearing with cutting equipment or a welding torch
- welding on the bearing and allowing it to cool to shrink it
- flame/torch heating.

Using a hammer and/or punch to remove bearings creates a large shock to the bearing, race, shaft, and housing, which may cause damage. Additionally, it applies an uneven amount of force in a concentrated area, which is not recommended. Cutting the bearing or race with cutting equipment or a welding torch is not recommended because doing so would have a high probability of damaging the shaft or housing. Welding on the bearing produces a great amount of heat in a small area and may damage the heat temper of other components. Flame heating also produces a great amount of heat. This will result in decreased life and weakness of shafts and housings. If heating or cooling of the bearing is required by the manufacturer, there are special tools designed to heat and cool bearings that should be used. Once again, always follow the equipment manufacturer's service and repair manual for specific bearing removal procedures.

Bearing Removal Tools

Bearing removal tools are defined by their type and maximum pulling force. The following special tools are used for bearing removal (**FIGURE 4-19**):

- hydraulic press
- arbor press
- mechanical two-jaw bearing puller
- mechanical three-jaw bearing puller
- hydraulic puller
- bearing separator or pulling plates.

Selecting the appropriate bearing removal tool depends on how well the part can be gripped and where (outside race, inside race, housing), how much reach and spread are needed, whether the component can be removed and moved to a press, and how much force is required for removal.

Hydraulic/Arbor Press A **hydraulic press** or an **arbor press** is an excellent tool for bearing and race removal and installation. It is safe when used properly, can apply a great deal of force in a controller manner, and minimizes the chance of damaging components. Furthermore, many accessories exist for presses to assist with bearing and race installation and removal. A press can be set up to support the bearing or race while the press forces the shaft out of the bearing or to support the shaft while the bearing is forced off. Always refer to the equipment

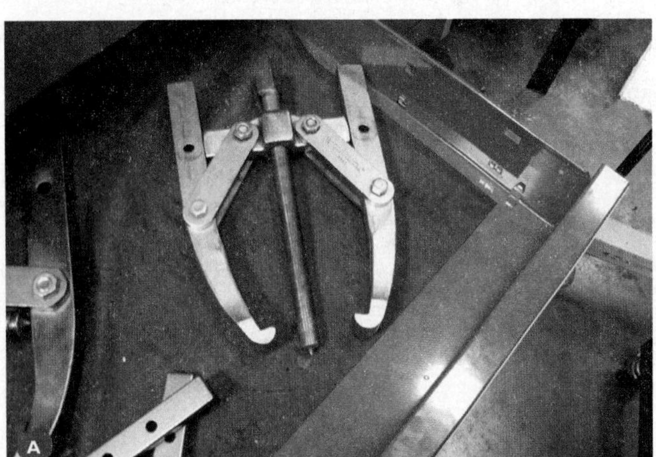

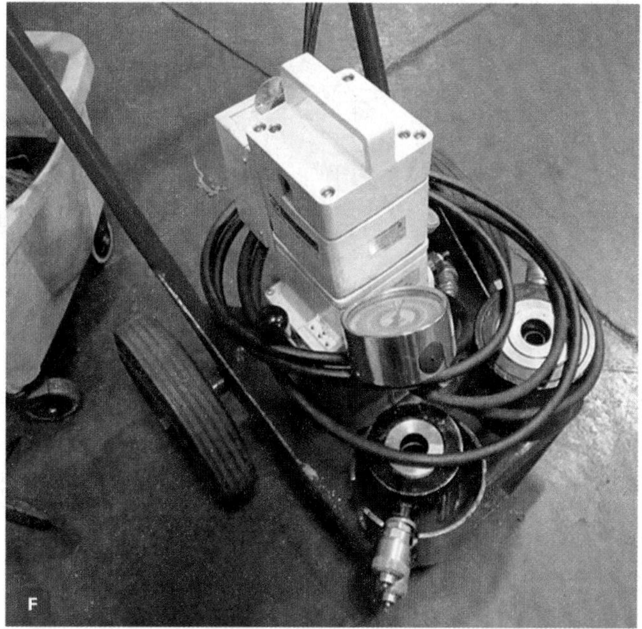

FIGURE 4-19 Special tools used for bearing removal: **A.** Two-jaw-type bearing puller. **B.** Three jaw bearing puller. **C.** Bearing separator/pulling plates. **D.** Hydraulic press. **E.** Arbor press. **F.** Hydraulic puller.

manufacturer's repair procedure in the maintenance and repair manual for specific steps and tools required for bearing and/or race removal. While the specific setup of the press will depend on the job, these basic principles can be applied:

1. Ensure the press is in good working order.
2. Clean all mounting and contact surfaces of the press, support blocks, rings, adaptors, and bearing and race components.
3. Support the bearing or race so that the forces do not go through the rolling elements and so that you achieve the maximum contact area with the bearing or race to evenly distribute the forces (**FIGURE 4-20**).
4. Ensure the mounting and supports are steady and will not slip.
5. Ensure the axis of the bearing/race/shaft will align with the axis of the ram from the press (**FIGURE 4-21**).
6. Slowly press the ram down, to take up all the slack and ensure the parts remain aligned.
7. Apply gradual force using the ram until the parts are free and separated.
8. *Note*: If the parts begin to deform, or it is requiring an excessive amount of force, *stop* and try a different method.

SAFETY TIP

When using a hydraulic or arbor press, use proper PPE such as safety glasses. If a part shatters, it can send sharp metal debris into your eyes if not protected. Avoid placing your hands or fingers near pinch points and do not grasp or hold parts to keep them aligned while applying pressure with the ram.

Bearing Pullers Bearing pullers are used when it is not possible or it is very difficult to remove the components and bring them to a press for removal. Jaw-type bearing pullers typically grip the bearing from the outside of the bearing. They can also be designed with reversible jaws to grip the bearing from the inside hole. Follow the equipment manufacturer's instructions as well as the bearing removal tool manufacturer's instructions when using pullers and other tools. When using bearing pullers, follow these basic principles in addition to the tool manufacturer's instructions:

- Ensure the jaws are fully engaged with the bearing press-fit race. If needed, use **adaptor plates**, also called **pulling plates**, to better grip the bearing and/or apply the force to the press-fit race. *Note*: Gripping the bearing by the slip-fit race when removing will cause all the force to go through the rolling elements and may result in damage to the bearing rollers and/or race.
- Ensure that the jaws will not slip and that they are aligned properly.
- Ensure the center forcing screw is properly aligned with the shaft. As the forcing screw is tightened, it must pull the bearing parallel to the shaft and not at an angle.
- Ensure that the bearing will not drop or fall once removed. If needed, use protection blankets or similar.

Internal Bearing Pullers The **slide hammer–type**, also called a **Blind hole bearing puller**, is a tool used when the outer bearing race is press fit into a housing (**FIGURE 4-22**).

As you can see from the image, it is not possible to grip the outside of the bearing, as it is press fit into the housing. Furthermore, the center shaft must be removed to use this tool. Follow these general steps when using this tool:

1. The tool is placed into the inner bearing hole.
2. The jaws are expanded so that they grip the bearing from the inside.

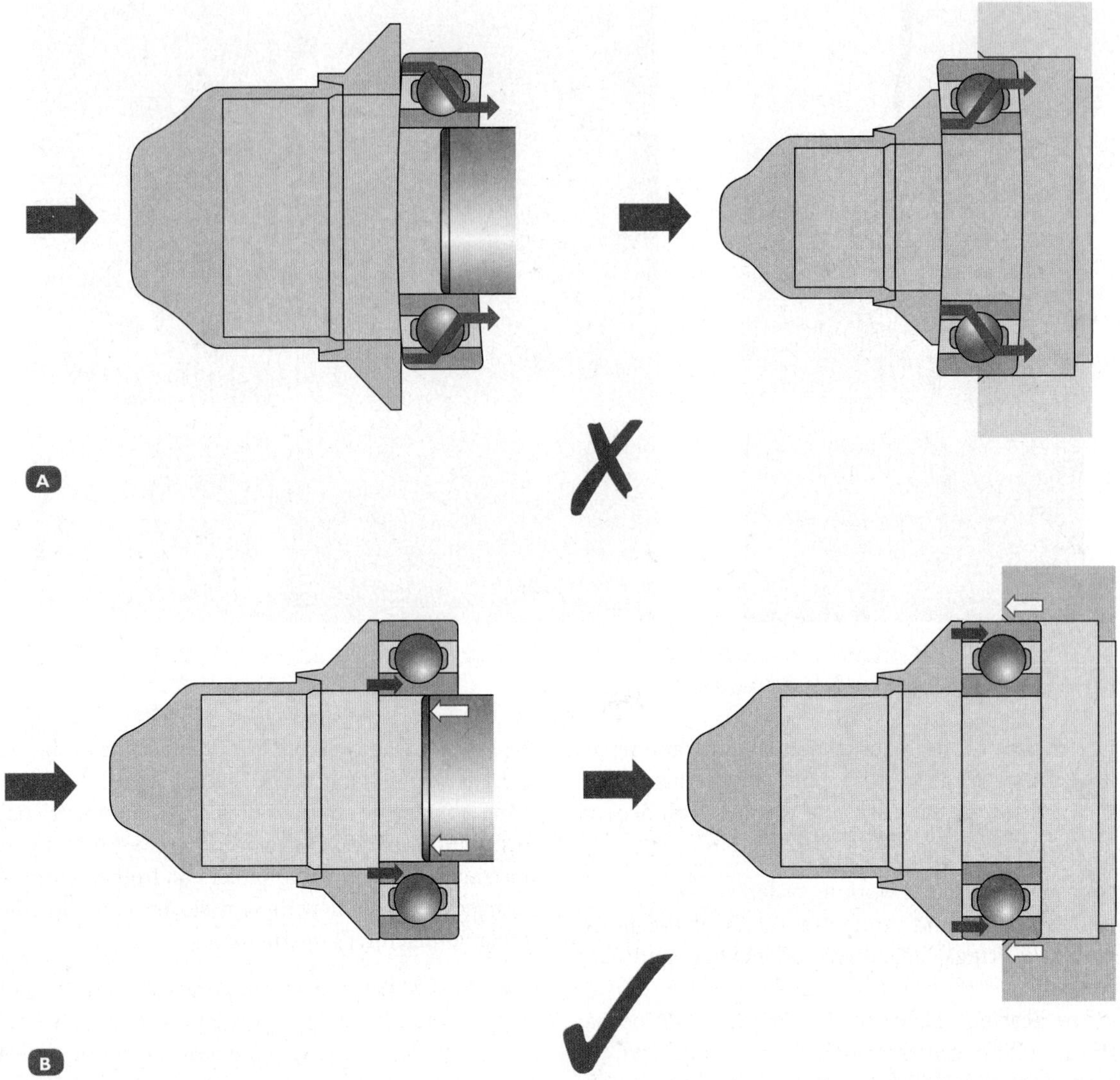

A

B

FIGURE 4-20 During bearing and race removal and installation, improper distribution of forces can result in bearing and race damage. Use appropriately sized blocks and rings for support to ensure the forces do not damage the bearing and race: **A.** Incorrect distribution of forces. **B.** Correct distribution of forces.

FIGURE 4-21 Ensure that the bearing/race has proper support and that the axis of the ram aligns with the axis of the bearing, race, or shaft.

FIGURE 4-22 A bearing race pressed into the housing.

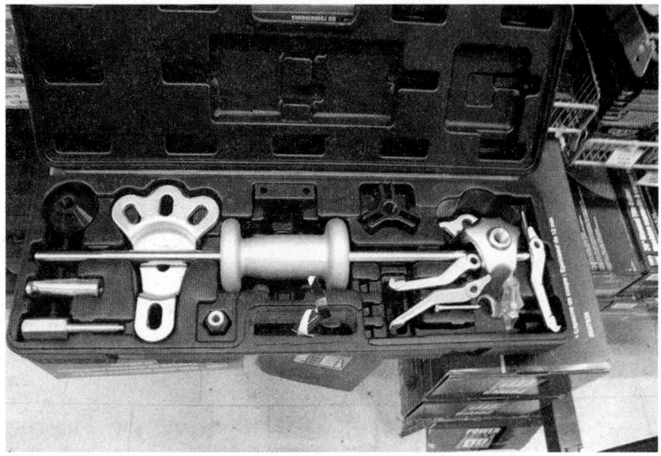

FIGURE 4-23 Slide hammer–type internal bearing puller. The puller is inserted into the bearing hole and expanded; then the bearing is removed.

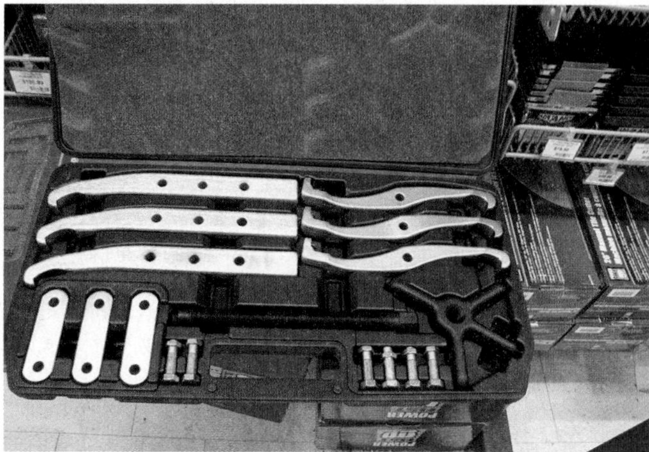

FIGURE 4-24 Internal jaw–type bearing puller tool.

3. The shaft is tightened. See **FIGURE 4-23** for a typical slide hammer internal bearing puller set.
4. The operator then uses a slide hammer action back and forth to force the bearing loose.
5. *Note*: This tool type applies a large amount of force in a quick shocking motion to the bearing, so attempt to use the minimum amount of force needed to loosen the bearing in order to prevent bearing damage.

Internal Jaw–Type Bearing Puller This tool has the jaws reversed from the outside jaw-type bearing puller, so that it grips from the inside of a hole. This type of puller has two or more jaws. The more jaws, the more evenly pulling forces are distributed and the better the puller assembly is kept in alignment. This method is usually preferred to the slide hammer type, as it applies force gradually and not in a shocking motion. The drawback to this type is that it may not be possible to use with smaller hole diameters (**FIGURE 4-24**).

Blind Housing Bearing Puller This tool is used where it is impossible to use traditional bearing pullers. This puller would be used in applications where the outer bearing race is press fit into the housing and the inner bearing race is press fit onto the shaft. In this circumstance, neither the outer nor the inner portion of the bearing can be gripped. This tool is used only as a last resort because it destroys the bearing and can create metal shavings during the attachment process that can fall inside the housing. The following are the steps to follow to attach and use this puller:

1. A drill bit is used to drill through the bearing cage in the raceway between two ball bearings. Depending on the tool, drill the bearing cage at two points, 180 degrees opposite of one another. *Note*: Extreme care must be taken to prevent any metal shavings from falling into the housing.
2. The bearing cage is then pulled apart enough to fit the puller ends into the bearing raceway.

FIGURE 4-25 Use bearing separator plates (also called pulling plates) to ensure the pulling forces are applied only to the inner press-fit bearing race.

3. The puller ends are inserted into the bearing raceway, then rotated to engage the raceway.
4. The puller is then assembled and the forcing screw is positioned to center on the shaft (or housing is some tools).
5. The operator tightens the forcing screw to take up all the slack and ensures the tool is properly aligned.
6. The forcing screw is tightened gradually to remove the bearing from the housing and the shaft.
7. The old bearing is discarded and replaced.

Bearing Separator Plates/Pulling Plates Bearing separator plates, or pulling plates, **FIGURE 4-25** are accessories typically used with bearing pullers. They are composed of a two- or three-piece metal design that is disassembled and placed around the shaft behind the bearing to be pulled. They are then reassembled and tightened. The outside of the plates has a specific area for a puller to attach firmly to. The center of the plates has a raised area that then contacts and surrounds the inner press-fit bearing race around the shaft. The plates allow for the pulling forces to be applied only to the press-fit inner bearing race. This prevents the pulling forces from going through the rolling elements and damaging the bearing, as would be the case if only the outer slip-fit bearing race were gripped. Refer to the tool manufacturer's specific instructions for how to mount and use the plates (Figure 4-25).

> **TECHNICIAN TIP**
>
> Bearing removal tools: When possible, grip the bearing at the press-fit portion of the bearing race when removing. This will prevent pulling forces from going through the bearing rolling elements and damaging the rollers or raceway. Pulling plates are an excellent way to ensure that the puller jaws have a good grip and that the pulling forces are placed on the press-fit inner race. If this is not possible, use the minimum amount of force to remove the bearing and thoroughly inspect after its removal for roller or raceway damage or deformation.

Bearing Cleaning

When you recondition components with bearings, the bearings should be thoroughly cleaned with a water-free cleaning solvent like Varsol and inspected (**FIGURE 4-26**). *Do not* blow-dry bearings with full shop air pressure, because this may over-speed the roller elements and cause damage. Follow these general steps to clean bearings:

1. Soak the bearings in a clean solvent bath filled with a recommended solvent for bearing cleaning. Soak overnight if possible. Keep the bearing off the bottom of the solvent bath, where dirt and debris accumulate.
2. After the bearing has been allowed to soak and loosen any dirt, debris, and old grease, rinse it in a bath of clean solvent.
3. Inspect to ensure all the dirt, debris, and old grease has been removed and the bearing is clean.
4. Allow the bearing to dry completely.
5. After drying, perform a thorough visual inspection. Rotate the bearing and rolling elements to verify proper operation.
6. Coat (or "pack") the bearing with the same type of lubricant that it will be running in when installed in the equipment. Ensure the entire bearing, rollers, and raceway are completely coated in lubricant. Consult the equipment manufacturer's maintenance and repair manual for the specific lubricant type. *Note*: Do not coat the bearing in any lubricant or grease other than what it will be operating in. Coating the bearing in a different grease or lubricant may result in contamination due to incompatible lubricant types from that which the bearing will be running in when installed in the equipment.
7. If the bearing will not be immediately installed in the equipment, wrap the bearing in waterproof paper and store in a paper box or another container.
8. *Note*: A bearing with a seal, or shield, on only one side should be cleaned and inspected just like an open bearing. A bearing with a seal, or shield, on both sides should not be washed or submerged in solvent. Simply wipe the outside clean.

It is common to use a **mechanical bearing packer** to coat the bearing and to force heavy grease throughout the bearing rollers and raceway (**FIGURE 4-27**).

Mechanical bearing packers are easy to use; they apply lubricant more uniformly; and they are cleaner than packing with your hands.

Bearing Installation

Proper bearing installation is one of the most critical areas to ensure a long life for a bearing. Improperly installed bearings are one of the leading causes of premature bearing failure. If the bearing is not properly installed by using the correct methods and tools, the improper installation will lead to premature bearing failure. Follow the specific equipment manufacturer's instructions for installing a bearing on a piece of equipment. There are two basic methods for installing bearings that have one or more press-fit races, and the specialized tools involved depend on these methods:

- cold mounting
- hot mounting.

FIGURE 4-26 Thoroughly clean bearings with a suitable solvent, then dry it and inspect it for damage before reusing it.

FIGURE 4-27 A mechanical bearing packer is very good at ensuring the bearing, rollers, and raceway are properly coated with lubricant before installation. They are also less messy, and faster than packing by hand.

Cold Mounting

Most bearings are installed using the cold-mounting method. In this method, the bearing is left at ambient temperature, and force is used to push the bearing onto the shaft or into the housing. This achieves a linear interference fit. As with bearing removal, great care must be taken to prevent damage to the bearing, races, shaft, and housing. There are two critical aspects of cold-mounting bearings.

1. Ensure the bearing is aligned properly. A bearing that is pressed on crooked, or that is misaligned, will fail prematurely and cause stress to other components. Hydraulic and arbor presses are great tools to ensure proper alignment during bearing installation.
2. Ensure the forces used to push the bearing on are concentrated on the press-fit bearing race only. Applying force to the slip-fit race will cause the pushing forces to go through the rolling elements and may damage the bearing rollers and raceway (**FIGURE 4-28**).

There are several types of bearing installation tools used in cold mounting. The following are the most commonly used tools:

- **bearing driver** (**FIGURE 4-29**)
- **hydraulic press** (**FIGURE 4-30**)
- **arbor press** (**FIGURE 4-31**).

The bearing driver kits consist of solid or hollow rings of multiple diameters, along with a cylindrical tube. One end of the tube fits into the driving rings, and the other end of the tube will be hit with a dead-blow hammer. It is important to select the driving ring with a diameter that will allow the forces to contact the press-fit race or both the press-fit and slip-fit races simultaneously. If a driving ring is selected and it contacts only the slip-fit race, damage to the bearing rollers and raceway may occur. It is also critical when mounting a bearing to ensure that the bearing and installation tool are perfectly square and that no misalignment occurs (**FIGURE 4-32**). Most bearing drivers can also be used as seal drivers.

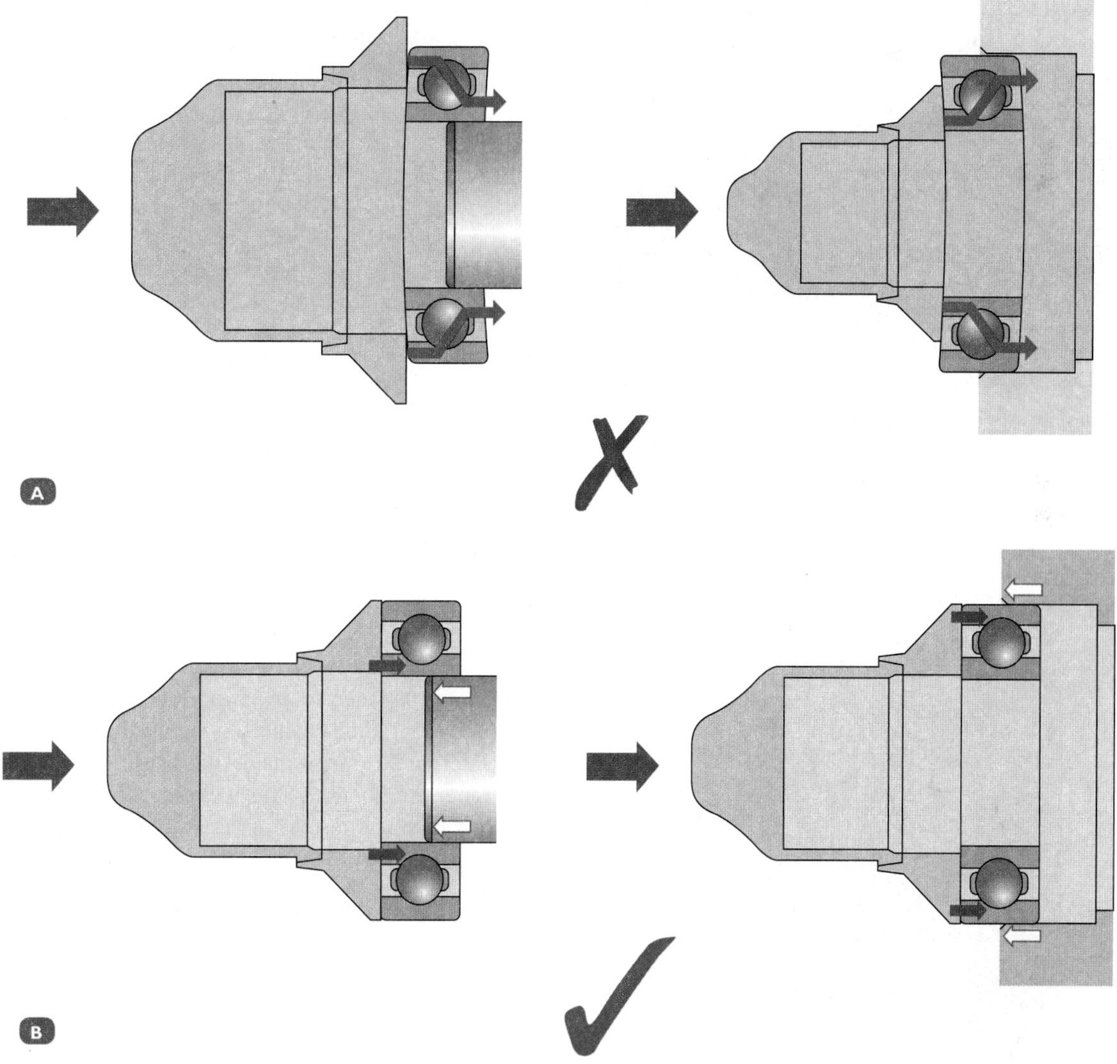

FIGURE 4-28 A. The incorrect distribution of forces and support for a bearing install and **B.** the correct distribution of forces and support for a bearing install.

FIGURE 4-29 Bearing driver kits come with multiple diameter driving rings. Use the appropriate ring size so that all the driving forces are applied to the press-fit race or both the press-fit and slip-fit race simultaneously.

FIGURE 4-30 Just as with bearing removal, a hydraulic press is an excellent tool for bearing installation.

FIGURE 4-31 As with bearing removal, an arbor press is an excellent tool for bearing installation.

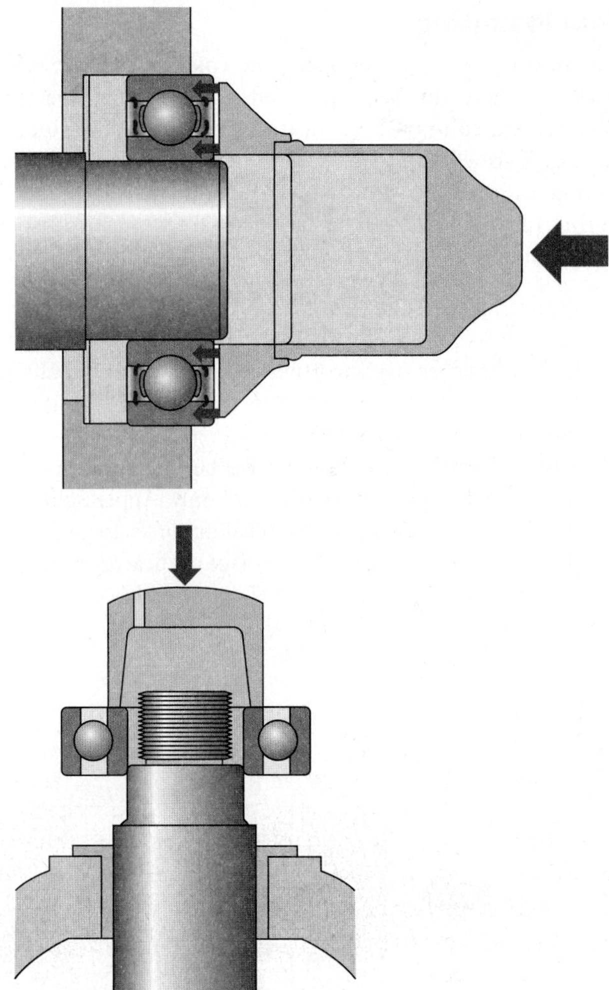

FIGURE 4-32 A bearing driver is used to install a press-fit bearing onto a shaft or into a housing. Ensure that the driving ring/adaptor is in contact with the press-fit race or both the press-fit and slip-fit race simultaneously to prevent bearing damage.

Tapered Shaft Bearing Installation

Bearings which are mounted onto a tapered shaft achieve their interference fit by being driven up the shaft. As the bearing is driven further up the shaft, the shaft diameter increases, and so the bearing fits more tightly, and more tightly onto the shaft. Care must be taken to avoid driving the bearing too far up the shaft. Driving the bearing too far up the shaft will remove all the internal clearance inside the bearing, between the rolling elements and the race. This will cause the bearing not to rotate freely, which will result in premature bearing failure and excess heat and friction (**FIGURE 4-33**).

Tapered Roller Bearing Installation

The installation of tapered roller bearings requires an adjustment called a **preload** adjustment. Tapered roller bearing preload adjustment could involve adding or removing shims and/or a fastener torquing procedure. The goal of this procedure is to ensure every roller is supporting an equal part of the load. To confirm this, a specific rolling resistance must be created that

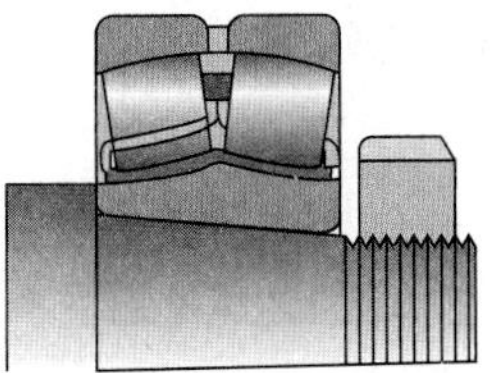
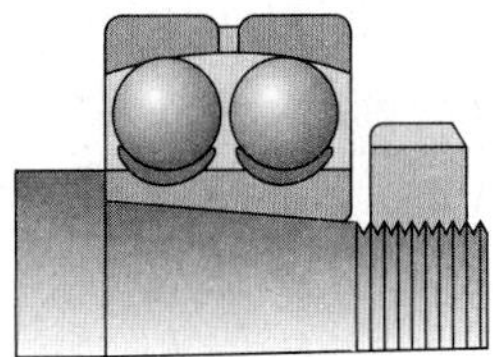

FIGURE 4-33 Bearings installed onto a tapered shaft must not be driven too far up the shaft. This removes all the internal clearance and will result in premature bearing failure.

equates to proper bearing preload. It is important throughout the bearing adjustment procedure to lubricate the rollers and to rotate the component to allow proper bearing seating in order to get an accurate reading. Preload measurement is usually accomplished by using a fish scale to measure the pounds or kilograms of force required to rotate the supported component. The force is then multiplied by the distance from the center of the component to the attachment point of the scale. As with all bearing installations, consult the specific equipment manufacturer's repair and service manual for instructions.

Super Cooling

Some repair procedures require parts to be cooled. Many bearing installations will be easier if the bearing or part that it is installed on is cooled. The bearing, or shaft, can be cooled to shrink it. When the bearing, or shaft, heats back up to ambient temperature, it will expand and achieve a transverse interference fit. This could be as simple as using a food freezer, or it could be more complicated and hazardous, such as when using dry ice or liquid nitrogen, to super cool parts. Special caution needs to be taken and PPE needs to be worn when using super-cooling equipment to prevent frostbite. Methods such as super-cooling or heating should be used only when specifically called for by the equipment or bearing manufacturer. In the event that the equipment manufacturer calls for these methods to be used in the repair manual, it is critical to follow the directions exactly to prevent damage or injury.

Hot Mounting

Hot mounting is used to achieve a transverse interference fit. Use this method when directed by the equipment manufacturer. This method is achieved by heating the inner race when press fit onto a shaft or heating the housing when press fit into the housing. Extreme care should be taken, as this method can cause personal injury, fire, and damage to bearings, shafts, and housings if done improperly or if the equipment or bearing manufacturer instructions are not followed. It is not recommended to use a heating torch, as this applies a great deal of heat to a small area and is a major fire hazard. When using these methods, wear the proper PPE and follow the tool and equipment manufacturer's safety precautions and instructions. It will be important to heat parts to a specific temperature and not overheat them; otherwise, the part's metallurgical structure will start to change and the part will likely fail prematurely. To prevent this, you should use a heat crayon that will indicate when the part is at a specific temperature. The crayon is rubbed on the part, and when

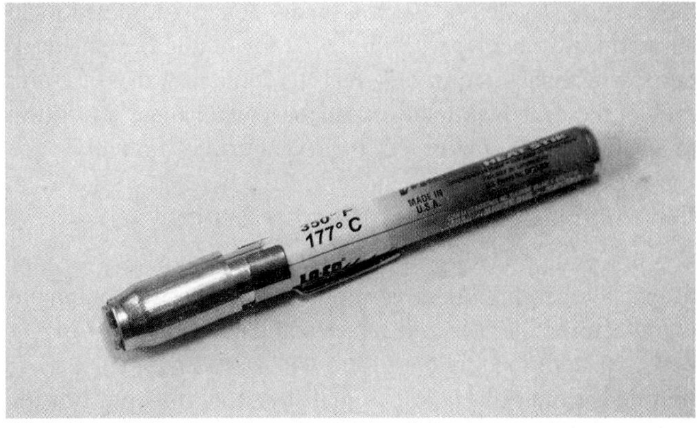

FIGURE 4-34 Temperature indicator sticks are made in multiple temperature ranges and are an excellent way to determine when a part reaches a certain temperature.

FIGURE 4-35 A variety of methods can be used to heat bearing for installation but the induction method is the best.

it melts, you know it is at the right temperature. Heat crayons come in different heat ranges (**FIGURE 4-34**).

A variety of methods can be used to heat bearings for installation. Propane torches, although they are not recommended, are still frequently used. This method of heating a bearing is highly inaccurate and can lead to premature bearing failure, so again, it is not recommended. A more reliable method of heating bearing is by using an oven because the temperature can be controlled and monitored. The most popular and the recommended method, which comes from bearing manufacturers, is induction heating. When heating bearings, it is important that the temperature does not exceed the maximum recommended by the manufacturers. Heat crayons like the one pictured in Figure 4-34 will melt at specific temperatures and indicate when the bearing has been heated sufficiently. **FIGURE 4-35** shows a variety of heating systems.

Once again, too much heat or heat in too small of an area can permanently change the metallurgical properties of the metal. This may not be visible, but it will weaken the parts and reduce their service life. Methods such as super-cooling or heating should be used only when specifically called for by the equipment or bearing manufacturer. In the event the equipment manufacturer calls for these methods to be used in the repair manual, it is critical to follow the directions exactly to prevent damage or injury.

General Bearing Installation Steps

The following process will provide general guidelines for how to install a bearing. As always, refer to the specific equipment manufacturer's service and repair manual for specific instructions. In addition, follow **SKILL DRILL 4-2** to practice your knowledge and skills is selecting the best tools for your bearing and seal replacement.

1. Work only with clean tools, clean hands, and clean surroundings to avoid damage to the bearing.
2. The shaft and housing bore should be inspected and verified to be clean, smooth, and free of any imperfections on the surfaces that the bearing or seals will contact.
3. Leave bearings in their packaging until they are ready for installation. Do not wash off the lubricant covering them unless it is incompatible with the lubricant the bearing will operate in.
4. Lubricate the race being press fit and the shaft or housing seat on which it will sit with the same lubricant the bearing will operate in.
5. Start the bearing on the shaft or in the housing with the rounded corner of the race going on first.
6. Using the bearing installation tool, apply uniform force only to the press-fit portion of the bearing. Ensure the tool is square and not at an angle.
7. Never hammer directly on races or rollers. Do not use a wooden or soft metal mallet, as chips and splinters may enter the bearing.
8. Use the minimum amount of force needed to seat the bearing.
9. Drive the bearing solidly up against the shoulder of the shaft and/or housing.
10. Lubricate the bearing prior to installation.

▶ Adjusting Bearing Preload

K04003

When tapered roller bearings are installed, they are required to be **preloaded**, which ensures the rollers are in full contact of the races all the way around the bearing. Applying a preload removes all the internal clearance, or space, between rollers and races in the bearings. When there is space, or clearance, between the bearing rollers and raceway, it has a negative preload. This is because there is no load, or force, on the bearing internal rollers and raceway. When the internal clearances in the bearing are zero, it has zero preload. All solid materials have some amount or crush, or elasticity to them—even hard metals. Because of this, you can create negative internal clearance in a bearing. This condition is having a preload, or force, on the bearing. So, a positive preload means the bearing has a negative amount of internal clearance between the rollers and raceway.

Of course, we don't want to crush the rollers and raceway by having too much preload. So, the right amount of preload is critical to proper bearing operation. Too little or too much preload may result in bearing damage, shaft damage, high heat and friction, and increased rolling resistance. Tapered roller bearing preload adjustment could involve using nuts, spacer sleeves, deformable sleeves (also called crush sleeves), adding or removing shims, and/or a fastener torquing procedure. The goal of this procedure is to ensure every roller is supporting an equal part of the load. To confirm this, a specific rolling resistance must be created that equates to proper bearing preload. It is important throughout the bearing adjustment procedure to lubricate the rollers and to rotate the component to allow proper bearing seating in order to get an accurate reading. Preload measurement is usually accomplished by using a fish scale to directly measure the pounds or kilograms of force required to rotate the supported component, or using by a torque wrench. The equipment manufacturer will publish specifications on the amount of preload and the procedures to adjust it in the repair and service manual. The specific steps to adjust preload depend

SKILL DRILL 4-2 Selecting and Using the Proper Bearing and Seal Installation Tools

As with most repairs, one of the most important things is using the right tool for the right job. Bearings and seals can be easily damaged by using the incorrect tools or methods for installation or removal. Have you, or has another technician you know, ever installed a bearing using a punch and a hammer or used a flame torch to install bearings?

Let's see if you can use the correct tools for the job.

1. Select a piece of heavy-duty equipment currently in your shop for service or repair.
2. Gather the needed information and look up in the manufacturer's service and repair literature the required tools, and removal and installation procedure for one of the wheel end bearing and seals. You could also look up an outer axle bearing or another shaft bearing.
3. Ask yourself these questions:
   - What tools are required to perform this job correctly?
   - Do I have the correct or equivalent tools specified by the equipment manufacturer?
   - Is the bearing a press-fit one? If so, is the outer or inner race, or are both races, press fit?
   - Will I need any accessories to my bearing and seal tools to work properly?
   - Will I need to do any adjustments once the bearing installation is complete?

on the equipment/bearing manufacturer. Generally, the technician will do the following:

1. Take initial measurements of preload or internal clearances to determine the appropriate crush sleeve, shims, and so on to use.
2. Assemble the bearings and components, rotating several times to seat the bearings.
3. When assembling a pinion bearing cage manufacturers will publish a specification as to how much pressure should be placed on the assembly with a press, (this pressure will represent the load placed on the bearings after final assembly).
4. Check the preload by measuring the turning resistance of the bearings using the equipment manufacturer's procedures (commonly by using a fish weight scale (**FIGURE 4-36**)).
5. The weight scale will indicate the pounds pulled, multiply this by the distance in inches from the center of the component to the edge where the string for the scale is attached, (this distance represents the lever length being used to turn the component); the result will be the inch pound rolling torque or preload of the component.
6. Compare actual measurement to specifications, and determine if adjustments are needed.
7. Adjust and repeat until preload is within specifications.

▶ Removal, Installation, and Replacement of Seals

K04004

Seals require much the same tools and techniques for installation as bearings. Just like bearings, the specific removal and installation process depends on the type of seal. Most seals will be damaged upon removal, or are one-time-use and must be replaced when removed for disassembly. Some of the more common seal removal tools are seal picks, and a seal removal tool (**FIGURE 4-37**).

Extreme care must be taken when installing and replacing seals to ensure they are installed properly and not damaged. Seals can be delicate and easily damaged. Keep new seals in their original container until just prior to installation to prevent damage. Seals should be lubricated with a compatible lubricant at the sealing and lip surfaces to prevent damage during installation. Seal installation can require tools as simple as a set of small picks or more specialized tools like a **seal driver** (**FIGURE 4-38**).

FIGURE 4-36 Measuring bearing preload using a torque wrench and a fish weight measuring scale.

O-Rings

Any time components are removed for repair or service, it is common practice to replace all O-ring–type seals. This is a cheap way to ensure there won't be any seal-related leaks. The groove that the O-rings fit into must be clean and free of corrosion to ensure a proper and long-lasting seal. O-ring seals should be lubricated when installed, and sometimes grease is used to hold the seal in place upon installation. You should also be sure they aren't twisted. Extra measures taken during installation to prevent the new O-ring from being damaged will reduce the likelihood of a time-consuming repair of a brand new seal leaking upon repair verification. A good set of **seal picks** will help with removing and installing O-ring seals.

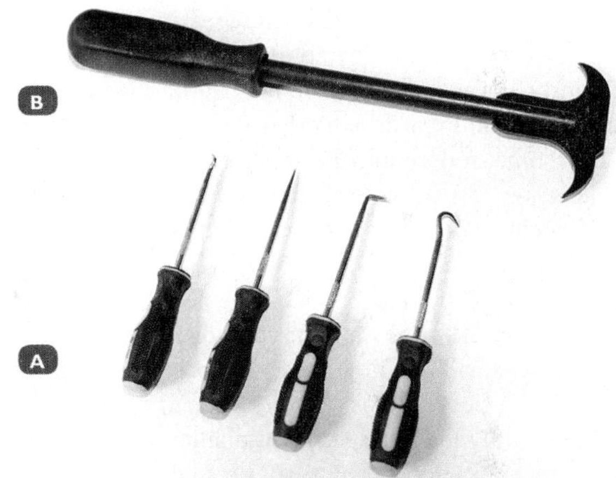

FIGURE 4-37 Seal removal tools: **A.** Set of seal picks. **B.** Seal removal tool.

FIGURE 4-38 Seal installation tools.

Lip-Type Seals

Lip-type seal installation can be tricky, and care needs to be taken not to damage the seal on installation. Depending on the type of lip-type seal, there could be several different installation procedures. Urethane or elastomeric lip-type seals that are installed on the inside of hydraulic cylinder head will need to be carefully folded without creasing the seal. This will effectively decrease the inside diameter of the seal, allowing it to fit inside the cylinder bore and then expand into the seal groove.

Metal-supported lip-type seals will usually be installed with an interference fit into a recess in the component. The metal backing or support for this type of seal will usually have a soft vinyl-like coating on it, which will fill any inconsistencies between the metal backing and the component it is installed into. The ideal way to install a metal-supported lip-type seal is with a seal installer tool that will center itself on the seal and apply pressure only to the outside diameter of the metal support. This tool will likely have a solid part in the center that allows the technician to drive the seal in with a hammer. Care needs to be taken when installing this type of seal to install it evenly and to stop driving when the seal has bottomed out. Removing lip-type seals could involve using heel bars or pry bars or involve drilling holes in the metal support and inserting screws that are pried on or pulled out with a slide hammer and a coarsely threaded adapter. Grooves or recesses for lip-type seals should be clean and dry before seal installation. The seal lip should be lubricated before component assembly.

Some lip-type seals will have their lips ride on a **wear sleeve**. The wear sleeve is a thin piece of hardened steel that is designed to wear over time and should be replaced when the seal is replaced. This prevents the rotating motion from wearing on the actual components. Wear sleeves are installed by gently heating them and using a special tool to slide them over the components they are protecting or pressed on by using special tools. When the sleeve cools, it will shrink onto the component for a tight fit. Engine crankshafts will commonly use wear sleeves. Some lip-type seals and wear sleeves come as an assembly and must not be separated. They will require a special installation tool, and they are used mainly for rear crankshaft seals on engines.

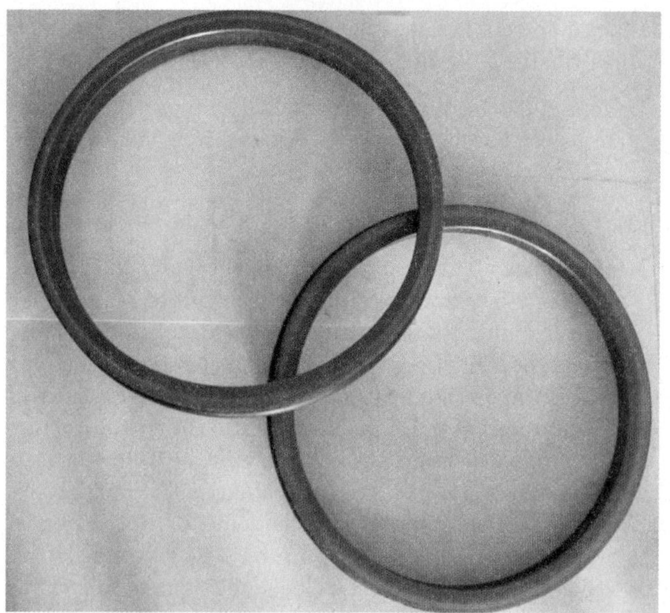

FIGURE 4-39 A metal-faced type of dynamic seal, sometimes called a duo-cone seal.

Metal-to-Metal Face Seals

These are sometimes called duo-cone seals. This type of seal (shown in **FIGURE 4-39**) is most commonly used for wheel seals and or final drive seals. Duo-cone seals can be reused provided that they don't exceed recommended wear specifications and don't show other signs of failure, such as pitting or cracks. Wear is measured with duo-cone seals by seeing how wide the contact pattern is between the two metal parts. Duo-cone toric O-ring seals must be completely dry and clean during installation; however, the metal faces must be lubricated before component assembly. Special installation tools are recommended to be used for installing these seals.

Piston Ring–Type Seals

This style of seal is typically found in turbochargers and used to seal the turbo shaft. They are also found in torque converters and transmissions. They consist of a simple hardened metal ring that creates a dynamic seal between two rotating parts and are very similar to piston rings. Care must be taken when installing this type of seal to not overstretch them or scratch them.

Many of the same techniques and tools for proper bearing removal and installation can be used with seals. Seals can require replacement when specified by the equipment manufacturer during the disassembly of other components or when they have failed. A seal can be considered to have failed when it is no longer performing its intended function. For a seal that is used to seal gases, when any amount leaks past the seal, it is considered to have failed. For a seal that is used to seal liquids, there can be several stages of failure: a seal can be weeping, have a leak to a drip, or have completely failed. How severe a seal leak can be before requiring replacement depends on the application and equipment manufacturer. For a seal that is used as a dust seal, to keep contaminants out, it would be considered to have failed when it is not keeping dust and contaminants out. A failed dust seal can allow foreign material to enter and contaminate internal components, such as bearings. Failed seals can also lead to cross-contamination of fluids from one machine component to another, eventually causing damage to other parts. Replacing a seal is much cheaper, and less time-consuming, than allowing a problem to persist and damage other parts and systems. Replace seals when

- seal replacement is required as part of another service procedure, as specified in the equipment manufacturer's service and repair manual
- the seal is leaking, or not performing its function
- the seal is damaged during removal or fails a visual inspection prior to reassembling components.

▶ Causes of Seal and Bearing Failures

K04005

Bearing Failures

Bearings rarely fail because of a design or manufacture defect. Machine design engineers select bearings for use based on normal operating loads and conditions, regular maintenance being done, and an expected lifespan. If the machine is operated, maintained, and repaired according to the manufacturer's recommendations, the machine's bearings should last several thousand hours. They usually fail because of one of the following causes:

- Overloading: For example, if a rock truck is constantly overloaded, this extra weight will overload the machine's wheel bearings and shorten their life (**FIGURE 4-40**) shows an overloaded bearing failure.
- Over-speeding: For example, if a machine gets stuck and one wheel receives all the speed from the differential, it will be over-speeding one wheel bearing and could cause it to fail.
- Contamination: Bearings need a specific type of clean lubrication and will fail if the lubrication is compromised because of contamination from dirt, water, metal, coolant, air, fuel, or other fluids (**FIGURE 4-41**) show contamination failure.

FIGURE 4-40 Bearing damage due to overloading.

- Misalignment: If the bearing isn't designed to handle misalignment, failure will occur if there are excessive and misdirected loads created because of this.
- Lack of lubrication: Low oil levels or lack of grease will cause shortened bearing life. Without lubrication, the metals will smear against one another (**FIGURE 4-42**).
- Improper installation: For example, bearings that are misaligned, improper tools damaging bearings or races, bearings not fully seated in housing or on shaft, and bearings with improper preload adjustment will fail prematurely (**FIGURE 4-43**).

It is important to look for external causes when a bearing fails prematurely. If the type of failure or an inspection of the failed bearing indicates a possible external cause, investigate it thoroughly. A new bearing that is installed when there was another cause for the bearing to fail will only result in a repeat failure. Until the condition that caused the bearing to fail is corrected, replacement bearings will fail again.

FIGURE 4-41 Bearing damage due to foreign debris contamination. This could be due to a failed seal allowed contaminants from the outside in or a mechanical failure in an inside component.

FIGURE 4-42 Bearings require lubrication. A loss or lack of lubrication will soon lead to catastrophic bearing failure and may cause additional damage as well.

FIGURE 4-43 Bearing damage due to improper installation is the most preventable cause. A hammer and drift punch is not a proper tool for installing most bearings.

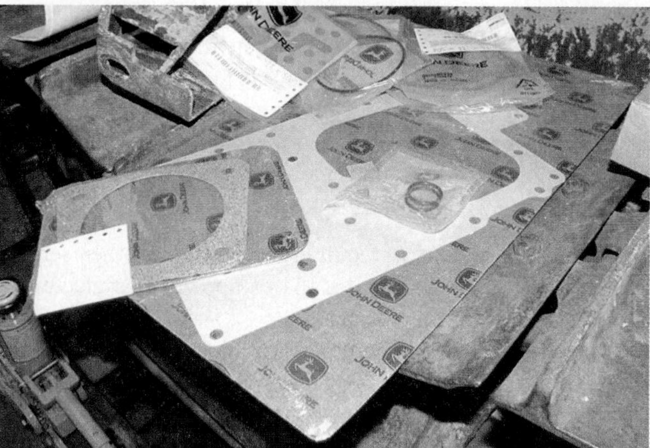

FIGURE 4-44 Gaskets come in all shapes, sizes, and materials.

Seal Failures

Seals can fail for numerous reasons. The most common cause of seal failure is excessive heat. Excess heat will cause the seal the shrink and harden, eventually leading to a leak. Here are some of the possible causes of seal failure:

- excessive heat
- use of fluids or additives incompatible with the seal
- shaft or housing misalignment
- shaft or housing sealing surfaces have imperfections
- shaft is bent or out of round
- bearing failure causing excess shaft movement
- excessive vibration
- improper installation tools or techniques
- inadequate lubrication
- foreign debris damage.

Just as in bearing failure analysis, seal failure may be caused by external factors. When replacing a failed seal, inspect the old one to determine the cause of failure. If you suspect something other than normal seal wear, look for other causes. If a seal has failed due to an external cause, such as excess shaft movement, replacing only the seal will not correct the problem.

▶ Gasket Servicing

K04006

Gaskets can be very simple in design and made from one type of material. They may need to seal almost no pressure, or they can be very complex multi-material structures that could be required to seal several thousand psi of pressure, such as when used for sealing between an engine block and its cylinder head. Gaskets can be made from materials such as paper, cork, plastic blends, steel, rubber blends, steel rubber laminations, and composite fiber blends. Gaskets should be designed to seal two stationary parts and the pressures that are built up inside one or more compartments. Although the components that a gasket is sealing are stationary the gasket must allow for slight relative movement created by temperature and or pressure changes. They should also allow for slight surface imperfections. See **FIGURE 4-44** for an example of an assortment of gaskets.

Most gaskets should be installed on clean, dry surfaces. This will require a thorough cleaning procedure of old gasket material. Appropriate care and PPE usage should be practiced when removing old gaskets. Care must be taken when cleaning old gasket material off metal surfaces. If you are too aggressive with your cleaning procedure, it is possible to remove metal from the component being cleaned. Some cleaning tools you may use for this include scrapers, knives, emery cloth, sandpaper, and fiber pads on pneumatic die grinders.

▶ Types and Applications of Sealants

K04007

Sealant is a substance that is applied in a liquid form to fill a gap between components, which then hardens to create a seal. Many people also refer to sealant as a liquid gasket. Sealant can fill crevices and sharp corners to create a seal in ways that a solid pliable gasket cannot. The heavy-duty equipment technician will become very familiar with many types of sealants, if they have not already. Each type of sealant is specifically engineered to operate in certain conditions. Sealants are selected and defined according to their characteristics. To select the appropriate sealant for a certain application, the following factors must be considered:

- What is the temperate range that the sealant must perform in?
- What solid materials will the sealant need to adhere to, to form a seal?
- What liquids and/or gases will the sealant be exposed to?
- What pressure range will the sealant need to perform under?
- How large of a gap, will the sealant need to fill to form a seal?
- How long does the sealant need to last?

- Does the sealant need to be flexible or hard?
- Are there restrictions on the type of material that the sealant can be composed of (for example, silicone-based sealants)?
- Where will the sealant be used (engine oil pan, transmission pan, gearbox cover, water pump, etc.)?

As you can see, selecting the correct sealant for an application involves many factors. Therefore, in most circumstances, the equipment manufacturer specifies the sealant to use for each application. The heavy-duty equipment technician should follow the instructions in the equipment manufacturer's service and repair manual when selecting the correct sealant. Failure to follow the manufacturer's requirements may result in using the improper sealant. A sealant that is improper for the application may not seal at all, may fail in a very short time, may not cure, or may cause contamination to other systems and parts, resulting in component damage. It is much easier and more economical to use the correct sealant in the first place than to have to disassemble and reseal components later. Sealants are used in most of the major systems in heavy-duty equipment, such as engines, transmissions, drivetrains, and body applications. In general, there are three types of sealants used in engine sealing applications (**FIGURE 4-45**):

1. RTV (room temperature vulcanizing) sealant
2. anaerobic sealant
3. pipe joint compound.

RTV sealant is pliable and the most commonly used sealant for most automotive and heavy-duty equipment applications. It is not suitable for extremely high temperatures, such as are found in exhaust systems or cylinder head gaskets. Anaerobic sealant can cure without the presence of oxygen. This is required because in some applications, once components are assembled the sealant will not be exposed to the atmosphere. Because of this if anaerobic sealant was not used, the sealant could not cure properly. Pipe joint compound can be used to seal connections in alternate-fueled engines. It is typically used with propane systems to seal threaded components that are under low gas pressure.

FIGURE 4-45 There are many different types of sealants.

▶ TECHNICIAN TIP

Sensors and sealants sometimes don't mix! Because of their nature, some material from a sealant will inevitably enter the systems, fluids, and gases that the sealant is exposed to, directly or indirectly. Because of this, the material the sealant is made of must be compatible with its application. For example, some types of silicone RTV sealant will damage oxygen sensors. Even when the sealant is used in an area of the engine not exposed to the exhaust fumes directly, the silicone will contaminate the oxygen sensors eventually. Silicone RTV used on an oil pan gasket will contaminate the oil, eventually entering the combustion chambers and then out the exhaust, contaminating the oxygen sensors. Follow the equipment manufacturer's specifications for the type of sealant to be used in each application.

▶ Fluids and Lubricants

K04008, S04001

Fluids are used in equipment for many purposes. Most fluids will be needed for lubricating system components. The fluid will create a film between parts that are moving in relation to each other, which prevents metal-to-metal contact of the components. Transmission fluid, for example, will keep shafts floating in a film of oil. This is called hydrodynamic suspension. Other fluids, like engine coolant, are used for cooling components, while yet others are needed for both lubrication and cooling. Hydraulic and brake systems use fluid for transferring energy, cooling, sealing, and lubricating.

It is very important to use the proper **viscosity**, type, and quality of fluid for each system. All systems on a piece of equipment are designed to be used with a fluid made to a certain standard. Most equipment manufacturers will have their own brand of fluids that have been made to their standards, and they will strongly recommend using their brand in their machines. They may also give minimum standards that an aftermarket fluid must meet if the owner wants to use another kind of fluid. If a piece of equipment is still under warranty, it is wise to use whatever fluids the equipment manufacturer recommends and keep records that can prove this fact in case there is a warranty dispute. Warranty claims can be denied based on the use of wrong fluids.

Fluid Viscosity

Fluid viscosity refers to a fluid's resistance to flow. When it comes to recommending proper fluid viscosities, equipment manufacturers will provide a viscosity chart with the equipment repair and maintenance guide. Fluid viscosity requirements will mandate changing the **ambient air temperature** (outside air temperature in the immediate vicinity of the machine). Generally speaking, as the ambient temperature where the equipment is working warms up from winter to summer, thicker fluids should be used, and the opposite is true from summer to winter. If the fluid is to stay in the compartment for 500 hours, you must try to roughly predict the highest and lowest temperatures that the equipment will be operating in and use the recommended viscosity for that temperature range.

Fluid viscosity is measured by standards set by two organizations: **SAE (Society of Automotive Engineers)** and **ISO (International Organization for Standards)**. Both organizations have developed test methods that measure the rate of fluid flow through a fixed orifice when it is at a certain temperature. The faster it flows, the lower its viscosity is or the thinner it is. It will be given a lower number that relates to the lesser amount of time it took to flow through the orifice. The opposite is true for a thicker fluid, and the longer it takes, the higher its viscosity number. To compare two fluids that you may be familiar with, think of water as a very low viscosity fluid and shampoo as a very high viscosity fluid. Typical SAE viscosity numbers for machine fluids range from SAE 0W to SAE 60. An SAE number that has a W following it has been tested at a lower temperature; the W stands for winter. ISO viscosity numbers (measured in VG, or viscosity grade) range from ISO VG 22 to ISO VG 100.

See **FIGURE 4-46** for a range chart of fluid viscosity to ambient air temperature, for several fluid types.

Fluid Viscosity Ratings

Gear oil has a different numbering system, which starts at SAE 75W and goes to SAE 140. Some fluids are called multi viscosity, such as 10W30 engine oil. They will act like a lower viscosity fluid when cold, which means they flow better but will resist thinning out when they warm up. This is done with additives called viscosity improvers. If a fluid thins out too much, it won't provide the proper oil film between rotating components. The product's viscosity rating will be identified on the product label (**FIGURE 4-47**). Here are some typical viscosity numbers for different fluid types:

- diesel engine oil—SAE 10W30 or 15W40
- hydraulic fluid—SAE 10W or ISO 32
- power shift transmission fluid—SAE30
- axle fluid—SAE 95
- final drive fluid—SAE 50
- brake fluid—10W.

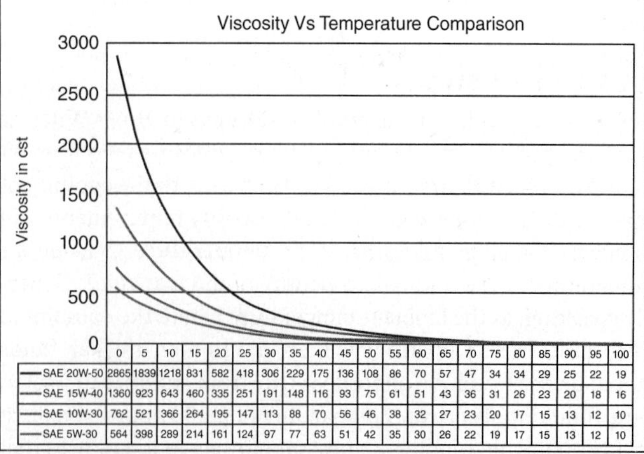

	0	5	10	15	20	25	30	35	40	45	50	55	60	65	70	75	80	85	90	95	100
SAE 20W-50	2865	1839	1218	831	582	418	306	229	175	136	108	86	70	57	47	34	34	29	25	22	19
SAE 15W-40	1360	923	643	460	335	251	191	148	116	93	75	61	51	43	36	31	26	23	20	18	16
SAE 10W-30	762	521	366	264	195	147	113	88	70	56	46	38	32	27	23	20	17	15	13	12	10
SAE 5W-30	564	398	289	214	161	124	97	77	63	51	42	35	30	26	22	19	17	15	13	12	10

FIGURE 4-46 Many types of heavy-duty equipment specify using different viscosity fluids at ambient air temperatures.

FIGURE 4-47 Viscosity ratings on multiple fluid types.

Fluid Additives

Equipment manufacturers will generally recommend that no aftermarket additives need to be added to any fluids for a machine. There are some exceptions to this, such as an axle that has friction material in it for an anti-spin (limited slip) device.

There are countless fluid additives available that their manufacturer's claim will improve performance, increase fuel economy, stop leaks, and lower emissions (**FIGURE 4-48**). In most cases, these additive manufacturers have not put in the engineering, research, and independent testing needed to determine the long-term

FIGURE 4-48 Some examples of the many type of fluid additives available; most are not recommended.

effects of these products on all the equipment types they could be used in. If the equipment manufacturer is not willing to allow these additives into their equipment during the warranty period, when they are responsible for paying for repairs, then you may want to think twice about using them when you, your customers, or your company are responsible for paying for the repairs.

Fluid Properties

Besides the viscosity grading of fluids, there are many other important properties a fluid should have before it can be used. Always check with the manufacturer's maintenance information to see the required fluid properties for any system. Other machine fluids and their properties follow.

Diesel Fuel

The type of diesel fuel recommended for a machine is determined by the manufacturer. Improper fuel used in a machine can cause filter plugging and many other fuel system component problems. Diesel fuel used in heavy equipment can fall under two classifications: (Number 1) diesel that has a lower viscosity and is used in the winter and (Number 2) diesel that is slightly higher in viscosity and used in the summer. Diesel fuel suppliers will adjust the viscosity of fuels as seasonal temperatures change.

Sulfur content in diesel fuel is very important with today's low emission engines. Most engines designed for North American use, now require the use of ULSD (ultra-low sulfur diesel) with a sulfur content of less than 0.0015% (15 ppm). Some fuels used in the past had sulfur contents over 1%.

Biodiesel has gained popularity lately and has been approved by most manufacturers to use if it meets recognized standards. The organic part of biodiesel is limited to no more than a small percentage (5–20%) of the diesel fuel content. Biodiesel is labeled B5 or B20 to identify the organic content. See **FIGURE 4-49** for how low sulfur diesel is identified at the fueling pump.

Water in diesel fuel can cause very expensive problems and should be kept to a specified percentage minimum. This

FIGURE 4-49 If the equipment requires low sulfur diesel fuel, it must be used to prevent damage. Additionally, if your equipment is capable of using biodiesel, you can use it to conserve resources.

is done with water separators and fuel tank drains. Fuel tanks on machines should be filled up as much as possible to reduce condensation buildup.

Engine Oil

Engine oil must do the following 10 things:

1. permit easy starting when cold
2. provide lubrication to moving engine parts and prevent wear
3. prevent metal-to-metal contact in pressurized friction bearings
4. protect against corrosion and rust
5. keep engine parts clean and move contaminants away from critical areas
6. reduce combustion chamber deposits
7. resist forming varnish and sludge deposits
8. cool engine parts by absorbing heat
9. seal in combustion chamber gases
10. not produce foam.

The ideal engine oil for any diesel engine will use a base oil combined with the proper additives, to address these 10 requirements. Using the oil recommended by the engine manufacturer in a machine is crucial for achieving the maximum service life from engine components that are in contact with the oil, as well as being able to maximize oil change intervals.

Some machines will come from the factory with break-in oil that will need to be changed at 250 hours of use.

Proper engine oil type is recommended by two characteristics. The is first viscosity, and the second is its rating according to **API (American Petroleum Institute)** or another engine oil property rating organization. Most major engine manufacturers will create their own oil standard. API has set engine oil standards for many years. They started in the mid-1900s by setting minimum standards that engine oil should meet. They looked for properties

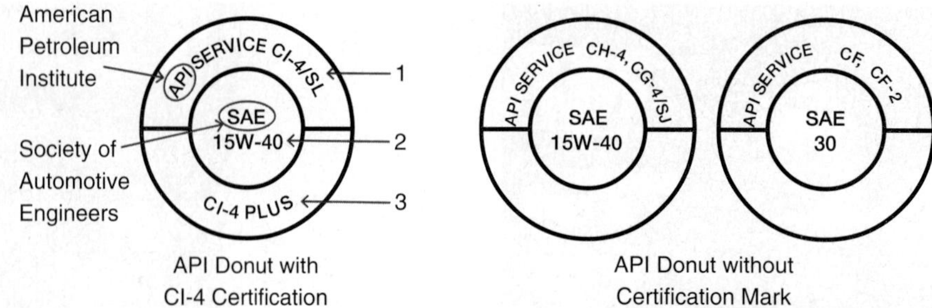

FIGURE 4-50 Ensure that the API rating on the engine oil used at least meets the equipment manufacturer's minimum requirements.

like antioxidation, antifoaming, and anticorrosion to help engine manufacturers get the most life and efficiency out of their engines. The first designation for gas engines was SA (S stands for spark ignition), and the first for diesel was CA (C standing for compression ignition). As engine technology moved forward, it put different demands on the engine oil, and every few years SAE would create a new minimum standard. As the new standards came out, the letter designation would change. Today's diesel engines will need from a CG-4 to a CJ-4 spec oil. See **FIGURE 4-50** to see the label API ratings of diesel engine oil.

Using the proper oil for today's low emission engines is critical to ensuring their longevity and staying within the low emission regulations. Synthetic engine oil can be used if it meets the recommended standards and is the proper viscosity. The main advantage of synthetic is its cold weather low viscosity or ease of flow ability in low temperatures and resistance to oxidation at high temperatures. All new oil is backward compatible, meaning the newest specification can be used for older engines as well.

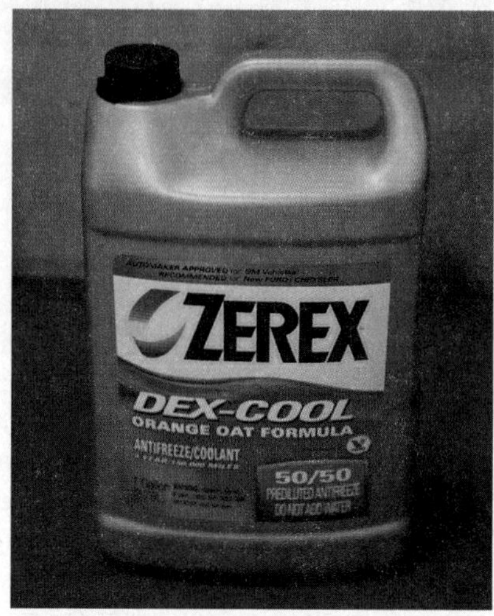

FIGURE 4-51 Diesel engine coolant.

Engine Coolant

Most diesel engine coolant is made up of three things: glycol, water, and additives. Water alone should never be used in a cooling system except in case of emergency. A minimum of 30% glycol/70% water should be used, and a more common mix is 50/50. Distilled or de-ionized water should be used if needed to top up but the safest way is to add a premixed coolant solution, which is usually 50/50.

Coolant additives will protect the metal surfaces that the coolant is exposed to by preventing foaming, rust, corrosion, liner pitting, and scale buildup. Additives will get depleted as the engine accumulates hours and will need to be topped up at certain service intervals.

Glycol in the coolant helps prevent freezing and boiling of the coolant. A 50/50 concentration will give a freeze protection down to –34°F (–36°C) and a boil protection of up to 223°F (106°C). Overconcentration of glycol (70% and higher) will start to decrease these properties. There are two main types of coolant used: coolants with an ethylene glycol base and those with a propylene glycol base.

Many machines come with long-life coolant commonly called ELC or extended-life coolant that will be able to stay in the machine from 6,000 to 12,000 hours with only additive top-offs. See **FIGURE 4-51** to see an example of a diesel engine coolant.

Engine coolant can also be sampled and analyzed. This is also good practice, especially if long-life coolant is expected to be in the system for five or more years.

Hydraulic Fluid

It has been said that the most important component in a hydraulic system is the hydraulic fluid. Hydraulic fluid has to clean, cool, lubricate, and seal the components it operates in, but its main function is to transfer energy. Hydraulic fluid in a high-pressure system will be compressed (roughly 1% for every 2,000 psi) and relaxed constantly. This will put an extra strain on the fluid.

The most common type of hydraulic fluid is the petroleum-based type and is usually called mineral oil, hydraulic oil, or just oil. It is the most economical and easiest to find. Some machine manufacturers will allow you to use or will recommend that diesel engine oil be used in the hydraulic system since many of the requirements that an engine oil must meet apply to hydraulic oil.

You will quite often see the letters AW associated with hydraulic oil. This stands for antiwear, and the oil will have a higher zinc and phosphorus content. Other additives in the oil will include detergents, rust inhibitors, antioxidants, and antifoaming agents.

To make a hydraulic fluid have a more stable viscosity over a wide range of temperatures, it will have viscosity improvers (VI) added.

Some machines can use water-based or glycol-based hydraulic fluids. These fluids are used for their fire-resistant properties. There are also biodegradable ester synthetic-based hydraulic fluids that are used for their environmentally friendly properties. These alternative fluids are much more expensive

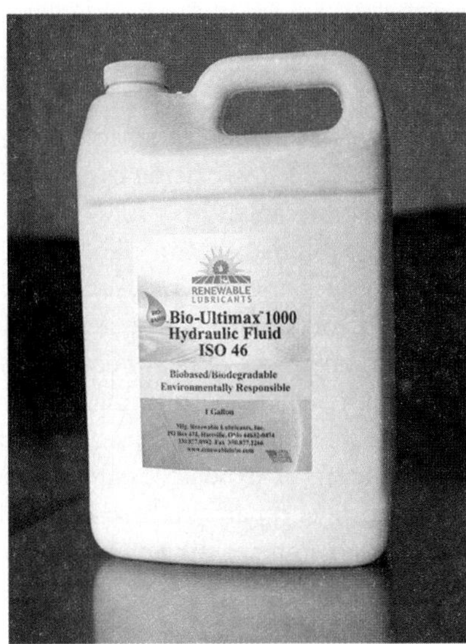

FIGURE 4-52 Biodegradable hydraulic fluid.

than mineral oil–based hydraulic fluids and will need special consideration for service intervals and filter compatibility. For example, bio-hydraulic oil is much more sensitive to water content and must be changed if water content exceeds 0.1%. See **FIGURE 4-52** to see a container of biodegradable hydraulic fluid.

Power Shift Transmission Fluid

Power shift, or automatic, transmissions have friction discs in them that require specific additives to allow them to function properly and last. Friction discs that run in fluid need an oil with friction modifiers added to it. Almost all power shift transmissions will have a torque converter driving it. A torque converter uses the fluid as a power transfer medium that relies on hydrodynamic principles. The fluid in a power shift transmission also needs to float rotating shafts, transfer heat, and provide anticorrosion, antioxidation, and antiwear functions. Using the incorrect fluid or having the transmission fluid become contaminated can damage the frictions discs and other parts inside the transmission. This could require a complete teardown and rebuild of the entire transmission. One power shift fluid specification that is required to be met by many manufacturers is Caterpillar TO-4 (**FIGURE 4-53**).

Axle and Final Drive Fluid

If the axle or final drive doesn't have friction materials in it that will be exposed to the lubricating fluid, it will likely require an oil classed as a gear oil. A common oil used for axles and final drives is classified as GL-5. Limited slip-type final drives with friction clutch discs usually require a limited slip additive to be added to the fluid.

Brake Fluid

Machines that have an automotive type of hydraulic brake system (master cylinder and wheel cylinders or calipers) will require a glycol-based brake fluid that will be either DOT 3 or DOT 5 specification. Brake fluid must be able to withstand extremely high temperatures and be able to absorb moisture (hygroscopic). Machines that use petroleum-based brake fluid may use oil from its hydraulic system or have its own brake oil reservoir. It will likely be a low viscosity fluid, like 10W.

FIGURE 4-53 Caterpillar TO-4 transmission fluid.

Grease

Grease is used to lubricate moving parts that don't have their own lubrication system. Grease is a lubricant that is usually used for slower moving parts exposed to high forces. It needs to be replenished regularly, because it will get squeezed out from between the parts it is lubricating and dry out.

Grease needs to do the following:

1. reduce friction and wear
2. provide corrosion protection
3. protect bearings from water and contaminants
4. resist leakage, dripping, and throw off
5. resist change in structure and consistency during usage
6. be compatible with seals.

Base materials for grease are mostly either petroleum, mineral, or synthetic with calcium, aluminum, or lithium as the thickener. Additives are then combined with the base material to provide all the qualities mentioned above. Grease additives may include

- oxidation inhibitors—which prolong the life of a grease
- EP (extreme pressure) agents—which guard against scoring and galling
- anticorrosion agents—which protect metal against attack from water
- antiwear agents—which prevent abrasion and metal-to-metal contact.

Grease specifications are mostly established by the **NLGI (National Lubricating Grease Institute)**. The required grease for machine lubrication can vary widely, but the most common type of grease used for lubricating the slow-moving high-force parts such as excavator boom, stick, and bucket pins is EP 2. Grease viscosity ranges from 000 (thinnest for extreme cold) to 6 (which is solid).

FIGURE 4-54 A wide variety of types of grease exist.

The most common grease viscosities are 1 (like soft margarine) and 2 (like soft peanut butter). Grease used in automatic greasers will be thinner (0 or 00) because it must flow through hoses, tubes, and valves. See **FIGURE 4-54** to see a variety of greases.

Follow **SKILL DRILL 4-3** to see if you can identify and select the correct fluids and lubricants.

As a heavy-duty equipment technician, you will be spending a lot of your time servicing bearings, seals, gaskets, and fluids for the equipment you service. These items are some of the most critical parts on any piece of heavy equipment. Failure to perform required maintenance, performing repairs incorrectly, or not detecting failures early with these parts can result in costly damage to other, more expensive parts and systems. Performing quality and proper repairs in these areas will reduce the probability of costly and embarrassing comeback repairs on the equipment you are servicing.

SKILL DRILL 4-3 Selecting the Correct Fluids

The most important thing about servicing fluids is selecting the correct fluid for the correct application. Incorrect fluids can result in expensive damage to major systems and parts, such as engines, transmissions, brakes, and hydraulic systems.

1. Select a piece of heavy-duty equipment currently in your shop for service or repair.
2. Gather the needed information and look up in the manufacturer's service and repair literature the proper fluid types, ratings, specifications, and capacities for each of the following fluids:
   - engine oil
   - transmission fluid
   - coolant
   - hydraulic fluid
   - final drive/axle gear oil.
3. Determine whether the manufacturer specifies that any fluids depend on other factors like ambient air temperature, type of use, hours or miles/kilometers on equipment, etc.
4. Now, research whether your shop has the correct fluids in stock or where they can be sourced from.

Wrap-Up

Ready for Review

- The largest single factor in premature bearing failures is improper installation.
- When installing an interference-fit bearing, place the driving forces onto the press-fit race or both the press-fit and slip-fit races simultaneously.
- Look for external causes for bearing and/or seal failure when they failure prematurely.
- When removing and reinstalling old bearings or seals, carefully inspect them and replace if they show signs of failure.
- Be careful not to install lip-type seals backward; this will cause premature failure.
- Bearing heating and super-cooling methods of interference-fit installation should be done only when called for in the equipment manufacturer's service and repair manual.
- New bearings and seals should be kept in their packaging until just prior to installation, to protect them.
- Some equipment manufacturers will specify different fluid viscosities and types depending on the ambient temperature outside where the equipment works.
- Always look up the equipment manufacturer's required types of fluids, lubricants, and sealants to ensure a proper repair and that no damage was incurred due to incorrect fluids and sealants.
- When a bearing preload adjustment is required with a repair, you must follow the equipment manufacturer's instructions carefully to achieve the correct amount or preload.
- Use safety glasses when removing and installing bearings.

Key Terms

adaptor plates An accessory for bearing removal and installations tools. The plates surround a shaft, and provide a surface for puller jaws to attach while also ensuring all the forces are placed at the inner press-fit race of the bearing.

arbor press A small hand operated press that uses mechanical leverage to apply a compressive force to a ram

National Institute for Automotive Service Excellence (ASE) An independent, nonprofit organization that seeks to improve the quality of automotive repair by testing and certifying automotive service professionals.

ambient temperature The temperature of the surrounding environment.

API (American Petroleum Institute) An organization in the United States that sets standards and standardized tests for petroleum products.

axial (thrust) Axial, or thrust, loads always act along the centerline of a shaft. So, they can only apply a force that moves a shaft in or out along its axis.

ball bearings A type of bearing which uses spherical balls as the rolling elements within a raceway, to reduce friction between moving parts. They are typically mounted between a shaft and stationary housing.

bearing A machine element that constrains movement to only the desired direction and reduces friction between moving parts.

bearing driver A tool used to install bearings, and sometimes seals, that applies a uniform amount of force to a targeted area of the bearing to drive the press-fit surface of a bearing onto a shaft or into a housing.

blind hole bearing puller A bearing removal tool that is used when the outer bearing race is press fit into a housing and can only be removed by placing a tool through the center, or blind, hole and pulling from the inside.

coefficient of friction A dimensionless physical value that describes the amount of force needed for one surface to slide against another. A ratio of the force needed to move one surface against another, divided by the force (or pressure) between the two surfaces. A higher value means the two surfaces have a greater amount of friction, or resistance, to movement between them.

cylindrical roller bearings Bearings that feature cylindrical rolling elements to reduce friction between moving parts. Roller bearings will have an inner race, outer race, bearing cage, and rollers. The axis of the rollers is parallel to the shaft. They are designed to carry heavy radial loads, not axial loads.

dial indicator A device for precision measurements used to measure small variations, such as end play, movement in a bearing, or run-out.

dynamic Objects that are dynamic are moving or changing.

friction bearing A plain bushing, or friction bearing, also called a plain bearing is a mechanical element used to reduce friction between rotating shafts and stationary support members or housings. They contain no rolling elements and are often lubricated with pressurized lubricant.

friction fit An interference fit, also called a press fit or friction fit, is a means of fastening two parts together so that they are in direct contact with one another and are held in place only by friction or by the tightness of the fit.

gland A recess, or gap, in a part where a seal or O-ring is placed to form a seal when two parts are brought together.

hot mounting A method of bearing installation in which heat is used to expand a bearing, and then the bearing is placed onto a shaft, where it cools and contracts. The bearing will then have a transverse interference fit.

hydraulic press A machine that uses a hydraulic cylinder to generate a compressive force.

interference fit An interference fit, also called a press fit or friction fit, is a means of fastening two parts together so that they are in direct contact with one another and are held in place only by friction or by the tightness of the fit. There is negative clearance between the interference-fit parts, so they must be pressed or forced together.

ISO (International Organization for Standards) An international body which sets standards for members, typically in engineering, mechanical, automotive, and aerospace areas.

linear Linear motion is a motion in a single dimension along a straight line.

Material Safety Data Sheet (MSDS) Same as safety data sheet (SDS).

mechanical bearing packer A tool that uses mechanical force to push grease into all a bearing's external and internal parts. Used to easily *pack* bearings with grease.

needle bearings Bearings that are characterized by their thin (small diameter), long, and numerous roller elements.

NLGI (National Lubricating Grease Institute) An industry organization in the United States that sets standards and rating for grease products.

Occupational Safety and Health Administration (OSHA) A U.S. federal government agency created to provide national leadership in occupational safety and health.

Personal Protective Equipment (PPE) Safety equipment designed to protect the technician, such as safety boots, gloves, clothing, protective eyewear, and hearing protection.

plain bearing A plain bushing, or friction bearing, also called a plain bearing is a mechanical element used to reduce friction between rotating shafts and stationary support members or housings. They contain no rolling elements and are often lubricated with pressurized lubricant.

plain bushings A plain bushing, or friction bearing, also called a plain bearing is a mechanical element used to reduce friction between rotating shafts and stationary support members or housings. They contain no rolling elements and are often lubricated with pressurized lubricant.

plain spherical bearings The plain spherical bearing consists of an inner spherical ring, placed within an outer spherical ring and locked together so that the inner ring is held captive within the outer ring in the axial direction only.

preload A condition in which a bearings internal clearances are completely removed by pressing the bearing against a shaft and/or housing, so that there is negative internal clearance. The bearing therefore has a *load* applied at all times to the rolling elements and raceway.

press fit An interference fit, also called a press fit or friction fit, is a means of fastening two parts together so that they are in direct contact with one another and are held in place only by friction or by the tightness of the fit. There is negative clearance between the interference-fit parts, so they must be pressed or forced together.

pulling plates An accessory for bearing removal and installations tools. The plates surround a shaft and provide a surface for puller jaws to attach to while also ensuring all the forces are placed at the inner press-fit race of the bearing.

race The area in which the rolling elements on a rolling bearing ride; also called a raceway.

raceway The area in which the rolling elements on a rolling bearing ride; also called a race.

radial Radial loads act from the center of a circle or shaft outwards. So, the load, or force, is always at a right angle to the circumference of the circle they are acting from.

radial shaft seals A seal used between cylindrical moving elements such as a shaft and a bore or housing; also called lip seals.

repair and maintenance manual A manual published by an equipment manufacturer with information on how to safely and properly maintain, repair, and troubleshoot equipment.

roller bearings Bearings that feature cylindrical rolling elements to reduce friction between moving parts. Roller bearings will have an inner race, outer race, bearing cage, and rollers. They may be straight or tapered roller bearings.

society of Automotive Engineers (SAE), SAE International A U.S.-based, globally active professional association and standards developing organization for engineering professionals in various industries, including automotive; mobile, off-road equipment; commercial truck; and aerospace. It sets industry standards and regulations.

seal A device used to join two or more parts together and prevent the leakage of liquids or gases and the introduction of contaminants.

slip fit A slip fit is when two parts fit together with positive clearance between them so that they will slip over one another.

spherical roller bearings Bearings that are characterized by their barrel-shaped rollers. The rollers are narrow at the ends, and they bulge in the middle like a wooden barrel. They will handle some axial load and can tolerate misalignment of the two separated components.

static Objects that are static are not moving or are not changing.

tapered roller bearings Bearings that are characterized by the conical (cone-shaped) rollers that are arranged in at a *tapered* angle to the shaft, so that the rollers form a cone shape around the shaft.

technical safety bulletins Documents periodically published and distributed by an equipment manufacturer that identify a safety risk or hazard and how to properly control the risk or hazard.

thrust loads Axial, or thrust, loads always act along the centerline of a shaft. So, they can only apply a force that moves a shaft in or out along its axis.

viscosity The state of being thick, sticky, or semi-fluid in consistency due to internal friction.

wear sleeve The wear sleeve is a thin piece of hardened steel placed over a rotating shaft that is designed to wear over time, and it should be replaced when the seal is replaced.

Review Questions

1. Some bearings will have a cage as part of their assembly that will
   a. help distribute oil evenly.
   b. keep dirt away from the rollers.
   c. help preload the bearing.
   d. keep the rollers or balls separated.
2. When installing some bearings, a fish scale is used to
   a. help torque the nut properly.
   b. measure the rolling resistance after it has been preloaded.
   c. weigh the balls or rollers before they are installed.
   d. weigh the torque wrench to make sure it's calibrated.
3. What must all gaskets allow for when creating a seal between two parts?
   a. Temperature changes that create part movement
   b. Negative pressure spikes
   c. Highly corrosive fluids
   d. Fastener de-torquing
4. Fluid viscosity is determined by
   a. boiling the fluid and measuring the thickness.
   b. pouring the heated fluid through a fixed orifice.
   c. freezing the fluid and measuring the thickness.
   d. vaporizing the fluid and measuring the density.
5. True or False. A flame torch is an acceptable method to heat a bearing for a hot mount interference fit?
   a. True
   b. False
6. API ratings for diesel engine oil start with a "C." What does the letter C stand for?
   a. Compression
   b. Combustion
   c. Centigrade
   d. Combination
7. A roller bearing is designed to support mostly which type/s of load/s?
   a. Radial load
   b. Axial load
   c. Both radial and axial loads
   d. horizontal loads
8. A typical ball bearing is designed to support mostly which type/s of load/s?
   a. Radial load
   b. Axial load
   c. Both radial and axial loads
   d. horizontal loads

9. A taper roller bearing is designed to support mostly which type/s of load/s
   a. Radial load
   b. Axial load
   c. Both radial and axial loads
   d. horizontal loads
10. Which of the following is not a type of o-ring seal?
   a. X-ring
   b. Square ring
   c. D-ring
   d. C-ring

ASE Technician A/Technician B Style Questions

1. Technician A says that the bearing puller should be attached with the jaws gripping the outside of the bearing and the forcing screw against the end of the shaft, to pull the inner press-fit bearing race off the shaft. Technician B says that you should use a pulling plate behind the bearing and attach the puller jaws to the plate. Who is correct?
   a. Technician A
   b. Technician B
   c. Both A and B
   d. Neither A nor B
2. Technician A says that you should use a wooden hammer and a soft brass punch to lightly tap the bearing on, alternating around the circumference in a star pattern to distribute the forces driving the bearing on. Technician B says that you should use a length of old pipe, whose diameter fits the press-fit bearing race, and a hammer to drive the bearing on. Who is correct?
   a. Technician A
   b. Technician B
   c. Both A and B
   d. Neither A nor B
3. Technician A says grease that is labeled EP means it can withstand extreme pressure. Technician B says automatic greasers will use a lower viscosity grease. Who is correct?
   a. Technician A
   b. Technician B
   c. Both A and B
   d. Neither A nor B
4. Technician A says that a diesel engine not rated to use B20 biodiesel could be damaged by using B20. Technician B says that an older diesel engine not rated to use ultra-low sulfur diesel fuel could be damaged if fueled with that type of fuel. Who is correct?
   a. Technician A
   b. Technician B
   c. Both A and B
   d. Neither A nor B
5. Technician A says that engine oil ratings are formulated by the Society of Automotive Engineers (SAE). Technician B says that engine oil ratings are established by the American Petroleum Institute (API). Who is correct?
   a. Technician A
   b. Technician B
   c. Both A and B
   d. Neither A nor B
6. Technician A says that the *tapered* in tapered roller bearings refers to the tapered, cone-style layout of the bearing rollers around the center of the bearing. Technician B says that the *tapered* in tapered roller bearings refers to the fact that the rollers themselves are cone-shaped or tapered. Who is correct?
   a. Technician A
   b. Technician B
   c. Both A and B
   d. Neither A nor B
7. Technician A says that an oil bath heater is acceptable to use for heating any bearing type for a hot mounting. Technician B says that it is always preferable to use a super-cooling method to shrink the shaft, as this has less chance of damaging the heat temper of parts. Who is correct?
   a. Technician A
   b. Technician B
   c. Both A and B
   d. Neither A nor B
8. Technician A says that sealant should be used where a gasket makes a very sharp curve on the engine oil pan, to achieve a better seal. Technician B says that you must make sure the chemical makeup of the sealant is compatible with that area of the engine. Who is correct?
   a. Technician A
   b. Technician B
   c. Both A and B
   d. Neither A nor B
9. Technician A says that for a tapered shaft bearing installation, you should drive the bearing up the shaft as far as it will go until it has no looseness in the bearing. Technician B says that there must be some amount of internal looseness in the bearing to run properly. Who is correct?
   a. Technician A
   b. Technician B
   c. Both A and B
   d. Neither A nor B
10. Technician A says that anaerobic sealant can cure without the presence of oxygen. Technician B says that anaerobic sealant means that you must have oxygen present for the sealant to cure. Who is correct?
   a. Technician A
   b. Technician B
   c. Both A and B
   d. Neither A nor B

CHAPTER 5

Tools and Fasteners

Knowledge Objectives

After reading this chapter, you will be able to:

- **K05001** Describe and explain the purpose and use of hand- and air-operated tools.
- **K05002** Identify tools and fasteners using correct industry terminology.

Skills Objectives

After reading this chapter, you will be able to:

- **S05001** Select, use, and maintain hand- and air-operated tools.
- **S05002** Select and use measuring tools according to their proper purpose, function, and procedure.

Attitude Objectives

After reading this chapter, you will be able to:

- **A05001** Organize and correctly store tools and fasteners with respect to good housekeeping.

▶ Introduction

The design of **mobile off-road equipment** (MORE) is the result of a number of engineering sciences. Not only are they structurally complex, but they also combine a number of unique characteristics, components, and ancillary equipment that unite to allow them to perform specialized tasks in some of the harshest environments. Engine blocks and components are made of metals that are able to withstand very high temperatures and stresses. Lubricants keep the engine with its cooling properties functioning smoothly by reducing friction on moving parts and allowing the engine to perform reliably. The vehicle body is made of materials that are durable and strong enough to withstand harsh conditions and repeated use. In addition to understanding the basic materials used in MORE construction and the fluids used to keep them operating safely and efficiently, technicians must know which tools to use for different types of service applications. Tools and equipment are vital components of an efficient and effective shop and/or field service operation. Nearly all repair tasks involve the use of some sort of tool or piece of equipment.

The vast majority of tools are designed to remove and install fasteners. Fasteners are designed to hold two or more components together. All types of MORE have hundreds and even thousands of parts and thousands of fasteners. These parts must be able to be assembled, from multiple components into one machine. In addition, these machines must be serviceable, which means the components must be able to removed and reinstalled. This requires the use of fasteners that allow for the easy assembly, removal, and installation of parts. Much of the work that goes into a part replacement is involved with the fasteners that attach the part to the rest of the equipment. Because of this, it is vitally important for the MORE technician to be familiar with fasteners, their uses, types, and special considerations.

In this chapter, you will learn about the basic tools and fasteners used in MORE and how to identify the correct tool and fasteners for a particular application, how to use the tool correctly, and how to clean, inspect, and store it properly after using it.

History of Tools and Fasteners

The use of simple tools can be traced back as far as Stone Age humans. In fact, tools were a critical part of the everyday life of early humans. This includes tools used as weapons and for leather working. Later, when humankind began to establish agriculture-based societies, tools used for agriculture, irrigation, weaving, and stone working were essential. Fasteners of various types have been used since the same time, although they have evolved to a more advanced degree. Early fasteners were as simple as wooden pegs hammered into holes in a pieces of wood to form a joint and later various types of metal nails. While the screw principle was first documented by Archimedes around 200 B.C.E., modern mass-produced threaded fasteners did not appear until the late 1700s. This invention was critical to the Industrial Revolution. The invention of a process to mass-produce high-quality metal threads in fasteners allowed larger, stronger, faster, and more precise machines. In fact, without the ability to create threaded fasteners, modern equipment and machinery would not be possible. Since the first introduction of humankind to simple tools and fasteners, we have advanced significantly to include power- and computer-operated tools (**FIGURE 5-1**).

▶ Purpose and Usage of Tools

K05001

A **tool** is a physical item used to do something or accomplish a goal. The purpose of a tool is to allow a person to perform a task that would be more difficult, time-consuming, dangerous, or impossible without that tool. Tools can be used to tighten or

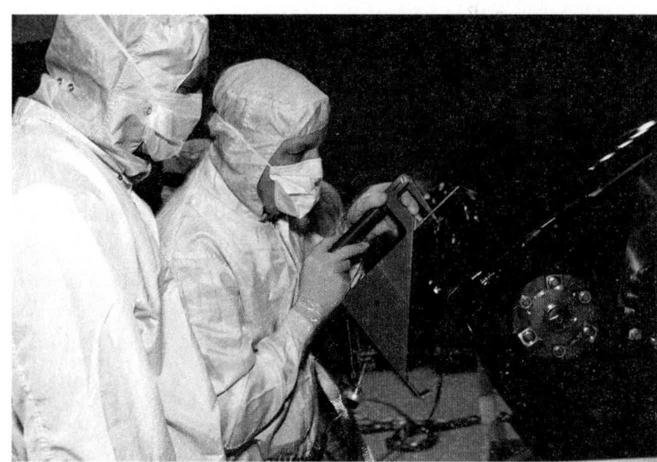

FIGURE 5-1 An example of advanced tools: a power-operated tool used by NASA in the assembly and servicing of the Hubble Space Telescope.

You Are the Mobile Heavy Equipment Technician

You are required to go out to a field service location to perform a repair on a piece of MORE that will require the removal and reinstallation of several parts to access the component that requires replacement.

1. What considerations should you make to ensure you select the proper tools to bring with you to the equipment site?
2. How can you determine whether any specialty tools or equipment may be required for the repair, before traveling to the job site?
3. Once at the equipment site, what (if any) preparation should you take to ensure that tools and fasteners do not get lost or misplaced?
4. After the repair is complete, what measures should you take to properly clean the repair site?
5. After the repair is completed, how can you ensure that no tools or equipment are left behind?

loosen fasteners, remove or install **press-fit** parts, or measure physical quantities such as distance, air or hydraulic pressure, vacuum, weight, force, torque, electrical voltage, power, current, and many others. When the proper tools are used for the proper applications, they can make accomplishing a task much easier. When used improperly, they can be a safety hazard.

Every tool has a proper application and a proper way to use it. The following paragraphs will provide some basic knowledge on the proper use of tools. A tool is used properly when it is used in the intended manner so that its user can accomplish its stated goal safely.

Basic Tool Preparation and Safety

Although it is important to be trained on the safe use of tools and equipment, it is even more critical to have a safe attitude. A safe attitude will help you avoid being involved in an accident. Technicians who think they will never be involved in an accident will not be as aware of unsafe situations as they should be, and such an attitude could lead to accidents. Therefore, as we discuss the various tools and equipment you will encounter in the shop, pay close attention to the safety and operation procedures. Tools are a technician's best friend, but if used improperly, they can injure or kill.

Work Safe and Stay Safe

Always think "safety first" whenever you use tools. There is nothing more important than your personal safety. If you use tools (both hand and power) incorrectly, you could potentially injure yourself and others. Always follow equipment and shop instructions, including the use of recommended **personal protective equipment (PPE)**. One of the characteristics of MORE is that they are big and heavy. Because of this, many of the tools used to service MORE are big, heavy, operated with a great deal of torque, and potentially dangerous. Accidents take only a moment to occur but can take a lifetime to recover from. You are ultimately responsible for your own safety, so remember to work safe and stay safe.

Handling and Using Tools Safely

Tools must be safely handled and used to prevent injury and damage. Always inspect tools prior to use, and never use damaged tools or any replacement tool. Check the manufacturer's documentation and the shop procedures or ask your supervisor if you are uncertain about how to use any tool. Inspect and clean tools when you have finished using them. Always return tools to their correct storage location. Some tools are heavy or awkward to use, so seek assistance if necessary, and use correct manual handling techniques.

▶ Tools and Equipment Fundamentals

K05001, S05001, S05002, A05001

Every tool is designed to be used in a certain way to do the job safely. It is critical to use a tool in the way it is designed to be used and to do so safely. For example, a screwdriver is designed to tighten and loosen screws, not to be used as a chisel. **Ratchets** are designed to turn **sockets** and are not to be used as a hammer. Think about the task you are undertaking, select the correct tools for the task, and use each tool for what it was designed for.

Identifying Metric and Imperial Designations

Many tools, measuring instruments, and fasteners come in metric and imperial sizes. Tools are identified as metric or imperial by markings that identify their sizes or by the increments on measuring instruments. Fasteners bought new will have their designation identified on the packaging. Other fasteners may have to be measured by a ruler or **vernier caliper** to identify their designation. Manufacturers' charts showing thread and fastener sizing will assist in identifying imperial or metric sizing.

To identify metric or imperial designations, follow these steps:

1. Examine the component, tool, or fastener to see whether any marking identifies it as metric or imperial. Manufacturer specifications and shop manuals may be referred to and may identify components as metric or imperial.
2. If no markings are available, use measuring devices to gauge the size of the item and compare thread and fastener charts to identify the sizing. Inch-to-metric conversion charts will assist in identifying component designation.

▶ TECHNICIAN TIP

The correct tools make you much more efficient and effective in performing your job. Without tools, it would be very difficult to carry out machine repairs and servicing. This is the reason many technicians invest thousands of dollars in their personal tools. If purchased wisely, tools will help you perform more work in a shorter amount of time, thereby making you more productive. Therefore, think of your tools as an investment that pays for itself over time.

Types of Tools

In this section, we will examine the following types of tools:

- hand-operated tools
- measurement tools
- air-operated (pneumatic-operated) tools.

▶ TECHNICIAN TIP

If you work in the field, it is extremely important to bring the proper tools with you to the job site. Failing to bring needed tools will increase repair time and cause you to have to make inconvenient return trips to retrieve the proper tools. The selection of your basic tool loadout will come only through experience performing service on the specific type of MORE equipment you work on. However, you can identify any specialty tools that may be required by reviewing the equipment manufacturer's service information for the expected repair before departing for the job site. You will find the added time establishing this habit will save you a lot of time and frustration in the long run.

Hand Tools

A large percentage of your personal tools will be hand tools. These are available in a variety of shapes, sizes, and functions, and like all tools, they extend your ability to do work. Over the years, manufacturers have introduced new fasteners, wire harness terminals, quick-connect fittings for fuel and other lines, and additional technologies that require their own specific types of hand tools. This means that technicians need to add tools to their toolboxes all of the time.

Wrenches **Wrenches** (often referred to as spanners in some countries) are used to tighten and loosen nuts and bolts, which are two types of fasteners. There are three commonly used wrenches: the **closed-end wrench**, the **open-end wrench**, and the **combination wrench**. The closed-end wrench fits fully around the head of the bolt or nut and grips each of the six points at the corners, just as a socket does. This is precisely the kind of grip needed if a nut or bolt is very tight, and it gives you a better chance of loosening very tight fasteners. Its grip also makes the closed-end wrench less likely than the open-end wrench to round off the points on the head of the bolt (**FIGURE 5-2A**).

The ends of closed wrenches are bent or offset so that they are easier to grip, and they have different-sized heads at each end. One disadvantage of the closed-end wrench is that it can be awkward to use once the nut or bolt has been loosened a little, because you have to lift it off the head of the fastener and move it to each new position. The open-end wrench is open on the end, and the two parallel flats grip only two points of the fastener (**FIGURE 5-2B**). Open-end wrenches usually have either different-sized heads on each end of the wrench or heads the same size but with different angles. The head is at an angle to the handle and is not bent or offset, so it can be flipped over and used on both sides. This is a good wrench to use in very tight spaces as you can flip it over at the end of its travel and get a new angle, so that the head can catch new points on the fastener. Although an open-end wrench often gives the best access to a fastener, it should not be used if the fastener is extremely tight, as this type of wrench grips only two points. If the jaws flex slightly or the flats do not fit tightly around them, the wrench could suddenly slip when force is applied. This slippage can round off the points of the fastener. The best way to tackle a tight fastener is to use a closed-end wrench to break the bolt or nut free; then use the open-end wrench to finish the job. The open-end wrench should be used only on fasteners that are no more than firmly tightened. The combination wrench has an open-end head on one end and a closed-end head on the other (**FIGURE 5-2C**). Both ends are usually the same size, so the closed end may be used to break the bolt loose and the open end to turn the bolt. Because of its versatility, this is probably the most popular wrench for technicians.

A variation on the open-end wrench is the **flare-nut wrench**, also called a flare-tubing wrench (**FIGURE 5-2D**). This type of wrench enables a better grip than the open-end wrench does because it grabs all six points of the fastener instead of only two. However, because it is open on the end, it is not as strong as a closed-end wrench. The partially open sixth side allows the wrench to be placed over tubing or pipes so that it can be used to turn the tube fittings. Do not use the flare-nut wrench on extremely tight fasteners because the jaws may spread, damaging the nut.

Another open-end wrench is the **open-end adjustable wrench, or crescent wrench**. This wrench has a movable jaw that by turning an adjusting screw can be adjusted to fit any fastener within its range. It should be used only if other wrenches are not available, because it is not as strong as a fixed wrench and thus could slip off of and damage the heads of tight bolts or nuts. Still, it is a handy tool to have because it can be adjusted to fit most fastener sizes.

A **ratcheting closed-end wrench** is a useful tool for some applications because it can be repositioned without having to be removed (**FIGURE 5-2E**). It has an inner piece that fits over and grabs the fastener points and is able to rotate within the outer housing. A ratcheting mechanism allows it to rotate in one direction and lock in the other direction. In some cases, the wrench simply needs to be flipped over to be used in the opposite direction. In other cases, it has a lever that changes the direction from clockwise to counterclockwise. Be careful to not overstress this tool by using it to tighten or loosen very tight fasteners, as the outer housing is not very strong.

There is also a **ratcheting open-end wrench**, which uses no moving parts. One of the sides is partially removed so that only the bottom one-third remains to catch a point on the bolt. The normal side works just like a standard open-end wrench. The shorter side of the open-end wrench catches the point on the fastener so that it can be turned. When moving the wrench to get a new bite, the wrench is pulled slightly outwards, disengaging the short side while leaving the long side to slide along the faces of the bolt. The wrench is then rotated to the new position and pushed back in so that the short side engages the next point. This wrench, like other open-end wrenches, is not designed to tighten or loosen tight

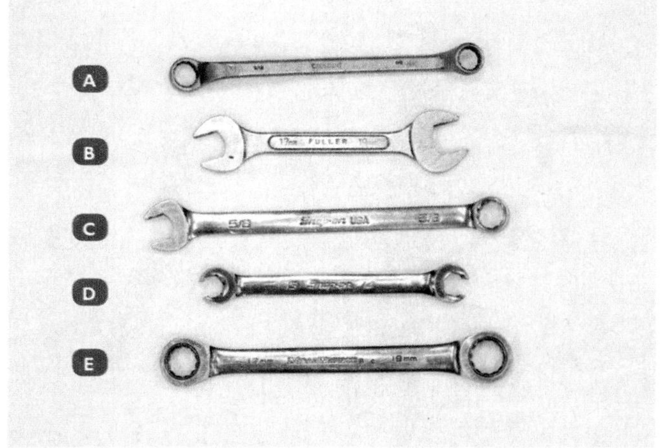

FIGURE 5-2 **A.** Closed-end wrench. **B.** Open-end wrench. **C.** Combination wrench. **D.** Flare-nut wrench. **E.** Ratcheting closed-end wrench.

fasteners, but it does work well in blind places where a socket or ratcheting closed-end wrench cannot be used.

The **pipe wrench** grips pipes and can exert a lot of force to turn them (**FIGURE 5-3A**). Because the handle pivots slightly, the more pressure put on the handle to turn the wrench, the more the grip tightens. The jaws are hardened and serrated, so increasing the pressure increases the risk of marking or even gouging the metal of the pipe. The jaw is adjustable, so it can be threaded in or out to fit different pipe sizes. Pipe wrenches are also available in different lengths, allowing increased leverage to be applied to the pipe.

A specialized tool called a **filter wrench** grabs fuel, oil, and coolant cartridge-type filters. The filter wrench provides extra leverage to remove a filter when it is tight (**FIGURE 5-3B**). These are available in various designs and sizes. Some filter wrenches are adjustable to fit many filter sizes. Note also that a filter wrench can be used to remove and tighten a filter. Always check the markings on a filter to determine how much farther a filter is rotated with a wrench after it has been hand-tightened.

Sockets Sockets are very popular because of their adaptability and ease of use (**FIGURE 5-4**). Sockets are a good choice when the top of the fastener is reasonably easily accessible. The socket fits onto the fastener snugly and grips it on all six corners, providing the type of grip needed on any nut or bolt that is extremely tight. They are available in a variety of configurations, and technicians usually have a lot of sockets so that they can access a multitude of tight places. Individual sockets fit a particular size of nut or bolt, so they are usually purchased in sets.

Sockets are classified by the following characteristics:

- metric or imperial depending on the equipment manufacturer
- size of drive used to turn them—½ inch, ⅜ inch, and ¼ inch are most common, while 1 inch and ¾ inch are common on HD off-road equipment
- number of points—6 and 12 are most common
- depth of socket—shallow and deep are most common
- thickness of wall—standard and impact are most common, while thicker-walled sockets are used for air-operated impact wrenches.

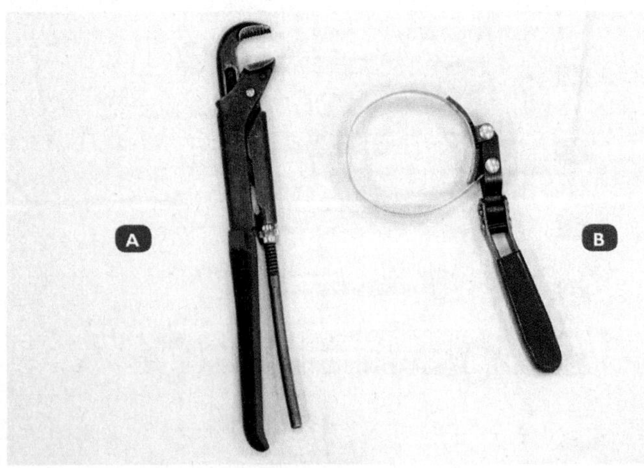

FIGURE 5-3 A. Pipe wrench. **B.** Oil-filter wrench.

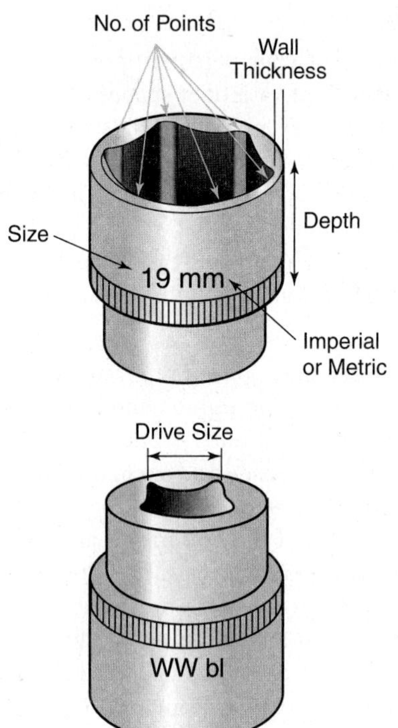

FIGURE 5-4 The construction of a socket.

Sockets are built with a recessed square drive that fits over the square drive of the ratchet or other driver. The size of the drive determines how much twisting force can be applied to the socket. The larger the drive, the larger the twisting force. Small fasteners usually need only a small torque, so do not use a drive larger than you need because too large a drive may impede the socket's access to the bolt. For fasteners that are really tight, an impact wrench exerts a lot more torque on a socket than turning it by hand. Impact sockets have thicker walls than standard wall sockets and have six points, so they can withstand the forces generated by the impact wrench as well as grip the fastener securely.

Both 6-point and 12-point sockets fit the heads of hexagonal shaped fasteners. Also, 4-point and 8-point sockets fit the heads of square-shaped fasteners. Because 6-point and 4-point sockets fit the exact shape of the fastener, they have the strongest grip on the fastener, but they fit on the fastener in only half as many positions as a 12-point or 8-point socket.

▶ TECHNICIAN TIP

When using a socket or wrench, if the nut or bolt feels like it is beginning to round the corners off, stop and change to a different socket. Try a socket with fewer points of grip, like a 6-point or a 4-point socket. This will grip better and prevent rounding off the nut or bolt.

Another factor in accessing a fastener is the depth of the socket. If a nut is threaded quite a distance down a stud, then a shallow-length socket will not fit far enough over the stud to reach the nut. In this case, a deep socket will usually reach the nut (**FIGURE 5-5A**). Turning a socket requires a handle. The most common socket handle, the ratchet, makes easy work of tightening or loosening a nut when not a lot of pressure is involved (**FIGURE 5-5B**). A ratchet may be set to turn in either direction and does not need much room to swing. It is built to be convenient, not super strong, so too much pressure could damage it. For heavier tightening or loosening, use a breaker bar because it gives the most leverage (**FIGURE 5-5C**).

When that is not available, a **sliding T-handle** may be more useful. With this tool, both hands may be used, and the position of the tee piece is adjustable to clear any obstructions when turning it (**FIGURE 5-5D**). The connection between the socket and the accessory is made by a square drive (**FIGURE 5-5E**). The larger the drive, the heavier and bulkier the socket. The ¼ inch drive is for small work in difficult areas. The ⅜ inch drive accessories handle a lot of general work where torque requirements are not too high. The ½ inch drive is required for all-round service. The ¾ inch and 1 inch drives are required for large work with high-torque settings.

Many fasteners are located in positions where access can be difficult. There are many different lengths of extensions available to allow the socket to be on the fastener while extending the drive point out to where a handle can be attached (**FIGURE 5-5F**). A **speed brace** or speeder handle is the fastest way to spin a fastener on or off a thread by hand, but it cannot apply much torque to the fastener; therefore, it is used mainly to remove a fastener that has already been loosened or to run the fastener onto the thread until it begins to tighten (**FIGURE 5-6A**). A **universal joint** takes the turning force that needs to be applied to the socket through an angle (**FIGURE 5-6B**).

Pliers **Pliers** are a hand tool designed to hold, cut, or compress materials (**FIGURE 5-7**).

They are usually composed of two pieces of strong steel joined at a fulcrum point, with jaws and cutting surfaces at one end and handles designed to provide leverage at the other. There are many types of pliers, including slip-joint, combination, arc joint, needle-nosed, and flat-nosed. Quality **combination pliers** (**FIGURE 5-8A**) are the most commonly used pliers in a shop. They are made from two pieces of high-carbon or alloy steel. They pivot together so that any force applied to the handles is multiplied in the strong jaws. Some pliers provide a powerful grip on objects, whereas others are designed to cut. Combination pliers can do both, which is why they are the most commonly used (please note that pliers are job-specific). Combination pliers offer two surface—one for gripping flat surfaces and one for gripping rounded objects—and two pairs of cutters. The cutters in the jaws should be used for softer materials that will not damage the blades. The cutters next to the pivot can shear through hard, thin materials, such as steel wire or pins.

Most pliers are limited by their size in what they can grip. Beyond a certain point, the handles are spread too wide or the jaws cannot open wide enough, but **slip joint pliers** overcome that limitation with a movable pivot. These are often called **Channellocks**, after the company that first made them. These pliers have parallel jaws that allow you to increase or decrease the size of the jaws by selecting a different set of channels. They

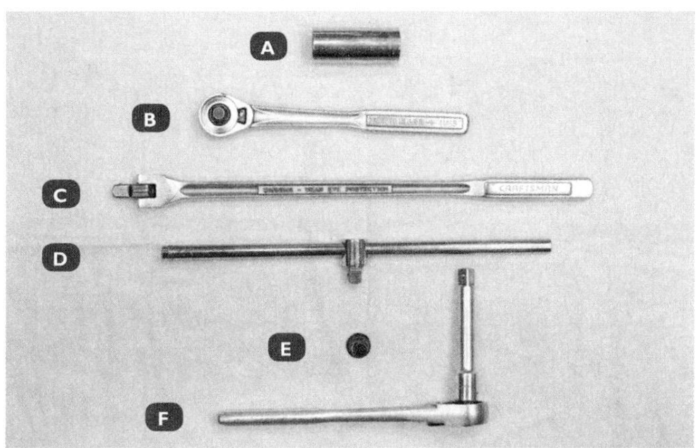

FIGURE 5-5 **A.** Deep socket. **B.** Ratchet. **C.** Breaker bar. **D.** Sliding T-handle. **E.** Square drive. **F.** An extension with a handle attached.

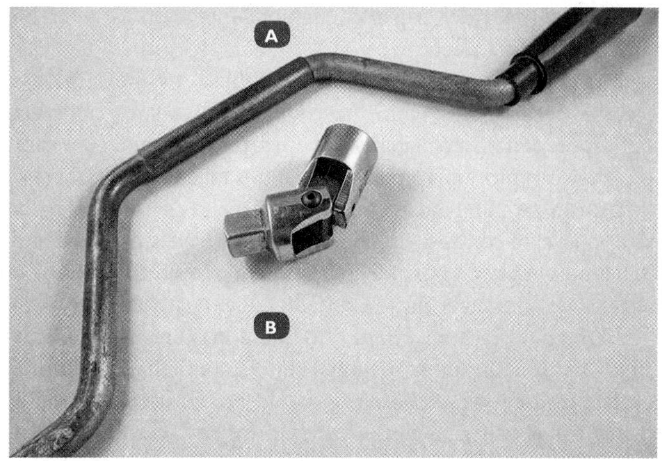

FIGURE 5-6 **A.** Speed brace. **B.** Universal joint.

FIGURE 5-7 Pliers are used for grasping and cutting.

are useful for a wider grip and a tighter squeeze on parts too big for conventional pliers.

There are a few specialized pliers in most shops. **Needle-nosed pliers**, which have long, pointed jaws, can reach tight spots or hold small items that other pliers cannot. For example, they can pick up a small bolt that has fallen into a tight spot (**FIGURE 5-8B**). **Flat-nosed pliers** have an end or nose that is flat and square; in contrast, combination pliers have a rounded end. A flat nose makes it possible to bend wire or even a thin piece of sheet steel accurately along a straight edge (**FIGURE 5-8C**).

Diagonal-cutting pliers (**FIGURE 5-8D**) are used for cutting wire or cotter pins. Diagonal cutters are the most common cutters in the toolbox, but they should not be used on hard or heavy-gauge materials, because the cutting surfaces will be damaged. End-cutting pliers, also called **nippers**, have a cutting edge at a right angle to their length (**FIGURE 5-8E**). They are designed to cut through soft metal objects sticking out from a surface.

Snap ring pliers have metal pins that fit in the holes of a snap ring. Snap rings can be of the internal or external type. If internal, then internal snap ring pliers compress the snap ring so that it can be removed from and installed in its internal groove (**FIGURE 5-8F**). If external, then external snap ring pliers are used to remove and install the snap ring in its external groove (**FIGURE 5-8G**).

SAFETY TIP

Always wear safety glasses when working with snap rings, as the rings can easily slip off the snap ring pliers and fly off at tremendous speeds, possibly causing severe eye injuries.

▶ TECHNICIAN TIP

When applying pressure to pliers, make sure your hands are not greasy; if they are, they might slip. Select the right type and size of pliers for the job. As with most tools, if you have to exert almost all your strength to get something done, then you are using either the wrong tool or the wrong technique. If the pliers slip, you will get hurt. At the very least, you will damage the tool and what you are working on. Pliers get a lot of hard use in the shop, so they do get worn and damaged. If they are worn or damaged, they will be inefficient and can be dangerous. Always check the condition of all shop tools on a regular basis.

Locking pliers, also called *vice grips*, are general purpose pliers used to clamp and hold one or more objects (**FIGURE 5-9**). Locking pliers are helpful because they free up one or more of your hands when working; they clamp something and lock themselves in place to hold it. They are also adjustable, so they can be used for a variety of tasks. To clamp an object with locking pliers, put the object between the jaws, turn the screw until the handles are almost closed, then squeeze them together to lock them shut. You can increase or decrease the gripping force with the adjustment screw. To release them, squeeze the release lever and they should then open up.

Cutting Tools **Bolt cutters** cut heavy wire, non-hardened rods, and bolts (**FIGURE 5-10A**). Their compound joints and long handles give the leverage and cutting pressure needed for heavy-gauge materials. **Tin snips** are the nearest thing in the toolbox to a pair of scissors (**FIGURE 5-10B**). They cut thin sheet metal, and lighter versions make it easy to follow the outline of gaskets. Most snips come with straight blades, but if there is an unusual shape to cut, there is a pair with left- or right-hand curved blades. **Aviation snips** are designed to cut soft metals (**FIGURE 5-10C**). They are easy to use because the handles are spring-loaded open and double-pivoted for extra leverage.

Allen Wrenches **Allen wrenches**, sometimes called Allen keys or *hex keys*, are tools designed to tighten and loosen fasteners with Allen heads (**FIGURE 5-11**). The Allen head has an internal hexagonal recess that the Allen wrench fits into. Allen wrenches come in sets, and there is a correct wrench size for every Allen head. They give the best grip on a screw or bolt of all the drivers, and their shape makes them good at getting into tight spots. Care must be taken to ensure that the correct size of Allen wrench is used; otherwise, the wrench and/or socket head

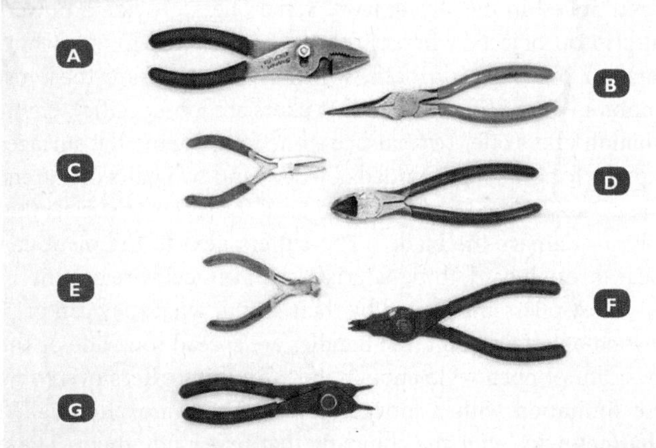

FIGURE 5-8 **A.** Combination pliers. **B.** Needle-nosed pliers. **C.** Flat-nosed pliers. **D.** Diagonal-cutting pliers. **E.** Nippers. **F.** Internal snap ring pliers. **G.** External snap ring pliers.

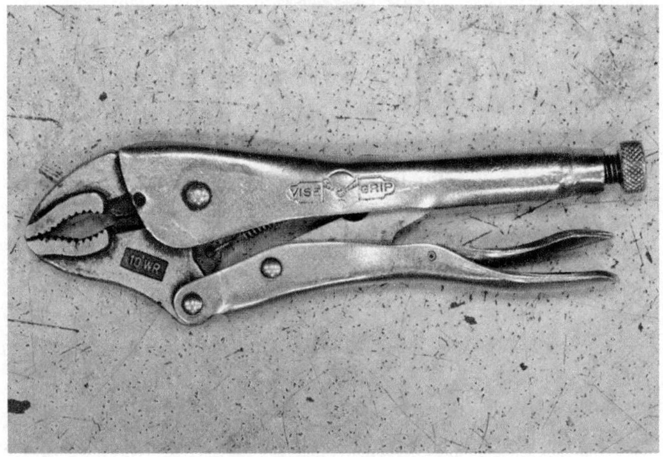

FIGURE 5-9 Locking pliers.

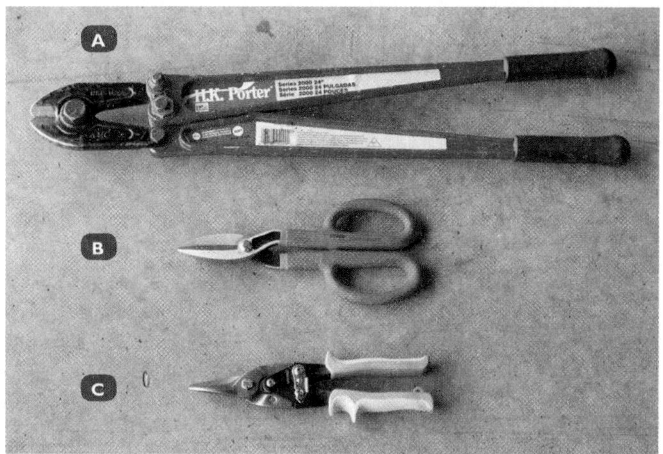

FIGURE 5-10 **A.** Bolt cutters. **B.** Tin snips. **C.** Aviation snips.

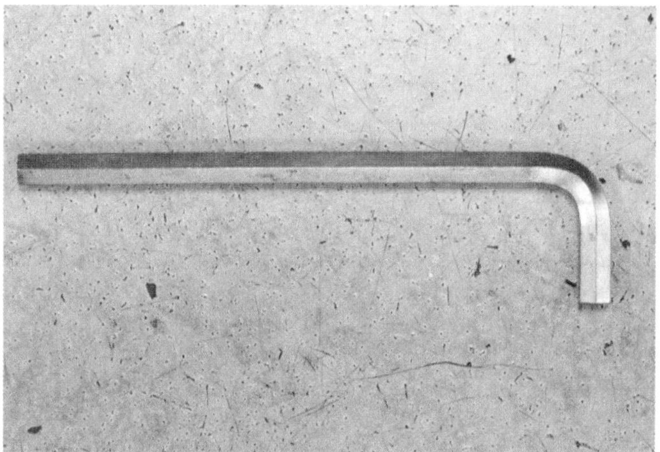

FIGURE 5-11 A typical Allen wrench.

will be rounded off. The traditional Allen wrench is a hexagonal bar with a right-angle bend at one end. They are made in various sizes in both metric and imperial. As their popularity has increased, so too has the number of tool variations. Now Allen sockets and T-handle Allen wrenches are available.

Screwdrivers The correct screwdriver to use depends on the type of slot or recess in the head of the screw or bolt and how accessible it is. Most screwdrivers cannot grip as securely as wrenches, so it is very important to match the tip of the screwdriver exactly with the slot or recess in the head of a fastener; otherwise, the tool might slip, damaging the fastener or the tool and possibly injuring you.

SAFETY TIP

When using a screwdriver, always check where the screwdriver tip could end up if it slipped off the head of the screw. Many technicians who have not taken this precaution have stabbed a screwdriver into or through their hand, thigh, or other body part.

The most common screwdriver has a flat tip, or blade, which gives it the name **flat-tip screwdriver** (**FIGURE 5-12A**). The tip

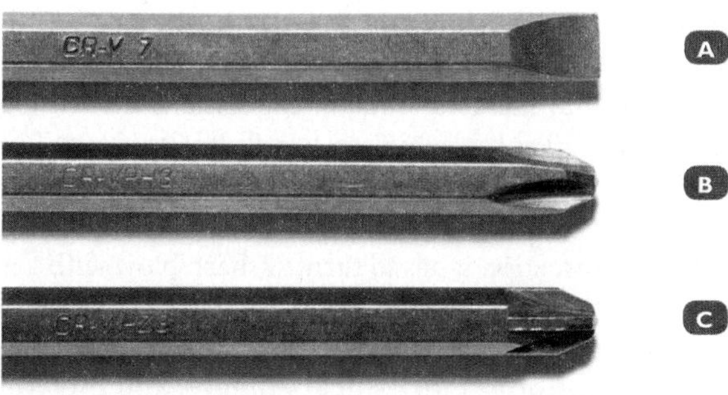

FIGURE 5-12 **A.** Flat-tip screwdriver. **B.** Phillips tip screwdriver. **C.** Pozidriv-tip screwdriver.

should be almost as wide and thick as the slot in the fastener so that the twisting force applied to the screwdriver is transferred right out to the edges of the head where it has the most effect. The tip should be a snug fit in the slot of the screw head. Then the twisting force is applied evenly along the sides of the slot. This will guard against the screwdriver suddenly chewing a piece out of the slot and slipping just when the most force is being exerted. Flat-tip screwdrivers are available in a variety of sizes and lengths, so find the right one for the job. If viewed from the side, the tip should taper slightly until the very end, where the tip fits into the slot. If the tip is not clean and square, it should be reshaped or replaced. When you use a flat-tip screwdriver, support the shaft with your free hand as you turn it (but keep it behind the tip). This helps keep the tip square on the slot and centered. Screwdrivers that slip are a common source of damage and injury in shops.

A screw or bolt with a cross-shaped recess requires a **Phillips screwdriver** or a *Pozidriv screwdriver* (**FIGURE 5-12B**). The cross-shaped slot holds the tip of the screwdriver securely on the head. The Phillips tip fits a tapered recess, whereas the Pozidriv fits into slots with parallel sides in the head of the screw (**FIGURE 5-12C**). Both a Phillips screwdriver and a Pozidriv screwdriver are less likely to slip sideways because the point is centered in the screw, but again, the screwdriver must be the right size. The fitting process is simplified for these two types of screwdrivers because four sizes are enough to fit almost all fasteners with this type of screw head.

The **offset screwdriver** fits into spaces where a straight screwdriver cannot and is useful where there is not much room to turn it (**FIGURE 5-13A**). The two tips look identical, but one is set at 90 degrees to the other. This is because sometimes there is room to make only a quarter turn of the driver. Thus the driver has two tips on opposite ends, so that offset ends of the screwdriver can be used alternately.

The **ratcheting screwdriver** is a popular screwdriver handle that usually comes with a selection of flat tips and Phillips tips (**FIGURE 5-13B**). It has a ratchet inside the handle that turns the tip in only one direction depending on how the slider is set. When set for loosening, a screw can be undone without removing the tip from the head of the screw. When set for tightening, a screw can be inserted just as easily.

An **impact driver** is used when a screw or a bolt is rusted/corroded in place, or overtightened, and needs a tool that can apply more force than the other members of this family (**FIGURE 5-13C**). Screw slots could easily be stripped with the use of a standard screwdriver. The force of the hammer pushing the bit into the screw, and at the same time turning it, makes it more likely that the screw will break loose. The impact driver accepts a variety of special impact tips. Choose the right one for the screw head, fit the tip in place, and then tension it in the direction it has to turn. A sharp blow with the hammer breaks the screw free, and then it can be unscrewed.

Magnetic Pickup Tools, Mechanical Fingers, and Mechanic's Mirrors **Magnetic pickup tools** and **mechanical fingers** are very useful for grabbing items in tight spaces. A magnetic pickup tool is typically a telescoping stick that has a magnet attached to the end on a swivel joint (**FIGURE 5-14A**).

The magnet is strong enough to pick up screws, bolts, and sockets. For example, if a screw is dropped into a tight crevice where your fingers cannot reach, a magnetic pickup tool can be used to extract it. Mechanical fingers are also designed to extract or insert objects in tight spaces (**FIGURE 5-14B**). Because they actually grab the object, they can pick up non-magnetic items, which makes them handy for picking up rubber or plastic parts. They use a flexible body and come in different lengths, but are typically about 12–18 inches (305 to 457 mm) long. They have expanding grappling fingers on one end to grab items, and the other end has a push mechanism to expand the fingers and a retracting spring to contract the fingers. Another tool that comes in handy is a mechanic's mirror. A **mechanic's mirror** is a small mirror on a stick that can be adjusted to view leaks, identify tags, and find dropped parts and tools. It can be placed into areas that are difficult to view or access.

TECHNICIAN TIP

The challenge is to get the magnet down inside some areas because the magnet wants to keep sticking to the sides. One trick in this situation is to roll up a piece of paper so that a tube is created. Stick that down into the area of the dropped part, then slide the magnet down the tube, which will help it get past magnetic objects. Once the magnet is down, you may want to remove the roll of paper.

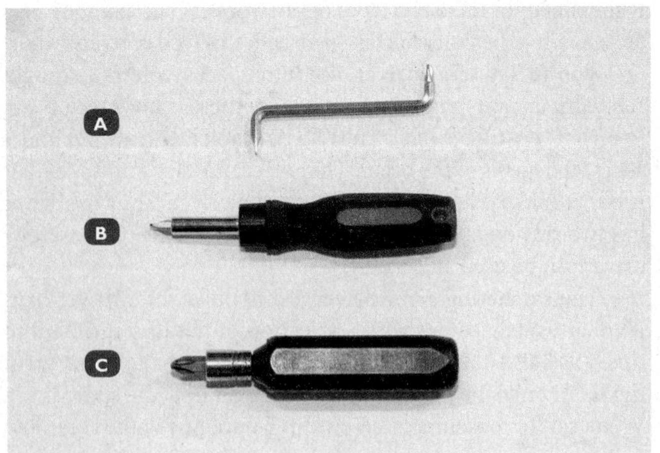

FIGURE 5-13 A. Offset screwdriver. **B.** Phillips tip screwdriver. **C.** Pozidriv-tip screwdriver.

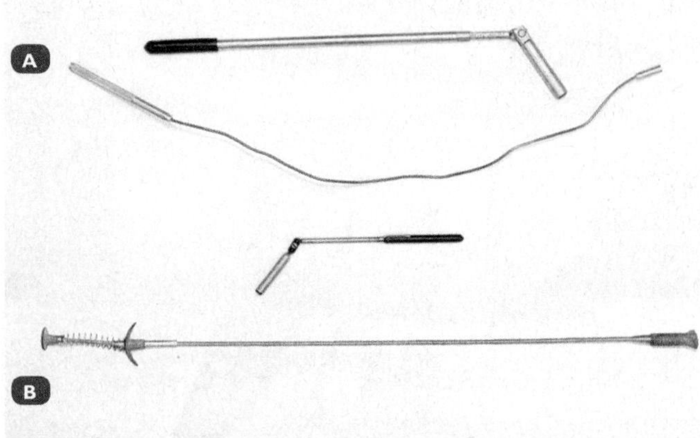

FIGURE 5-14 A. Magnetic pickup tools. **B.** Mechanical fingers.

Hammers Hammers are a vital part of the shop tool collection, and a variety are commonly used. The most common hammer in a shop is the **ball-peen (engineer's) hammer** (**FIGURE 5-15A**). Like most hammers, its head is hardened steel. A punch or a chisel can be driven with the flat face. Its name comes from the ball-peen or rounded face. It is usually used for flattening and **peening** a rivet. The hammer should always match the size of the job, and it is better to use one that is too big than too small.

SAFETY TIP

The hammer you use depends on the part you are striking. Hammers with a metal face should almost always be harder than the part you are hammering. Never strike two hardened tools together, as this can cause the hardened parts to shatter.

Soft-Face Steel Hammers feature a drop forged head specifically designed to mushroom when striking hard base materials; they are gaining popularity for added safety against chipping and spalling, which cause injury.

Hitting chisels with a steel hammer is fine, but sometimes you need to only tap a component to position it (**FIGURE 5-15B**). A steel hammer might mark or damage the part, especially if it is made of a softer metal, such as aluminum. In such cases, a soft-faced hammer should be used for the job. Soft-faced hammers range from very soft, with rubber or plastic heads, to slightly harder, with brass or copper heads. When a large chisel needs a really strong blow, it is time to use a **club hammer** (**FIGURE 5-15C**). The club hammer is like a small mallet, with two square faces made of high-carbon steel. It is the heaviest type of hammer that can be used one-handed. The club hammer is used in conjunction with a chisel to cut off a bolt where corrosion has made it impossible to remove the nut. The most common small-headed mallet in the shop has a head made of hard nylon (**FIGURE 5-15D**). It is a special purpose tool and is often used for moving things into place where it is important not to damage the item being moved. For example, it can be used to tap a crankshaft, to measure end play, or to break a gasket seal on an aluminum casing.

A **dead-blow hammer** is designed not to bounce back when it hits something (**FIGURE 5-15E**). A rebounding hammer can be dangerous or destructive. A dead-blow hammer may be made with a lead head or, more commonly, a hollow polyurethane head filled with lead shot or sand. The head absorbs the blow when the hammer makes contact, reducing any bounce back or rebounding. This hammer can be used when working on the machine chassis or when dislodging stuck parts.

SAFETY TIP

When using hammers and chisels, safety goggles must always be worn. In addition, watch fingers and hands around hammers and be careful of bounce back. Many embarrassing injuries occur while using hammers.

Chisels The most common kind of chisel is a cold chisel (**FIGURE 5-16A**). It gets its name from the fact that it is used to cut cold metals rather than heated metals. It has a flat blade made of high-quality steel and a cutting angle of approximately 70 degrees. The cutting end is tempered and hardened because it has to be harder than the metals to be cut. The head of the chisel needs to be softer so that it will not chip when it is hit with a hammer. Technicians sometimes use a cold chisel to remove bolts whose heads have rounded off.

A **cross-cut chisel** is so named because the sharpened edge is across the blade width. This chisel narrows down along the stock, so it is good for getting in grooves (**FIGURE 5-16B**). It is used for cleaning out or even making key ways. The flying chips of metal should always be directed away from the user.

▶ TECHNICIAN TIP

Chisels and punches are designed with a softer striking end than hammers. Over time, this softer metal "mushrooms," and small fragments are prone to breaking off when hammered. These fragments could cause eye injuries or other penetrative injuries to people in the area. Always inspect chisels and punches for mushrooming and dress them on a grinder when necessary.

Punches **Punches** are used when the head of the hammer is too large to strike the object being hit without causing damage to adjacent parts. A punch transmits the hammer's striking power from the soft upper end down to the tip that is made of hardened high-carbon steel. A punch transmits an accurate blow from the hammer at exactly one point, something that cannot be guaranteed using a hammer on its own.

When marks need to be drawn on an object such as a steel plate to help locate a hole to be drilled, a **prick punch** is used to mark the points so they will not rub off (**FIGURE 5-17B**).

They can also be used to scribe intersecting lines between given points. The prick punch's point is very sharp, so a gentle tap leaves a clear indentation. The center punch is not as sharp as a prick punch and is usually bigger (**FIGURE 5-17A**). It makes a bigger indentation that centers a drill bit at the point where a hole needs to be drilled. A **drift punch** is also called a starter punch because you should always use it first to get a pin moving (**FIGURE 5-17C**). It has a tapered shank, and the tip is slightly hollow so that it does not spread the end of the pin and make it an even tighter fit. Once the starter drift has got the pin moving, a suitable pin punch will drive the pin out or in. A drift punch also works well for aligning holes on two mating objects, such as a valve cover and cylinder head. Forcing the drift punch in the hole will align both components for easier installation of the remaining bolts. **Pin punches** are available in various diameters. A pin punch has a long, slender shaft with straight sides. It is used to drive out rivets or pins (**FIGURE 5-18A**). A lot of components are either held together or accurately located by pins. Pins can be pretty tight, and a group of pin punches is specially designed to deal with them. Special punches with hollow ends are called **wad punches** or **hollow punches** (**FIGURE 5-18B**). They are the most efficient tool to make a hole in soft sheet material, such as shim steel, plastic and leather, or (most commonly) in a gasket. When they are used, there should always be

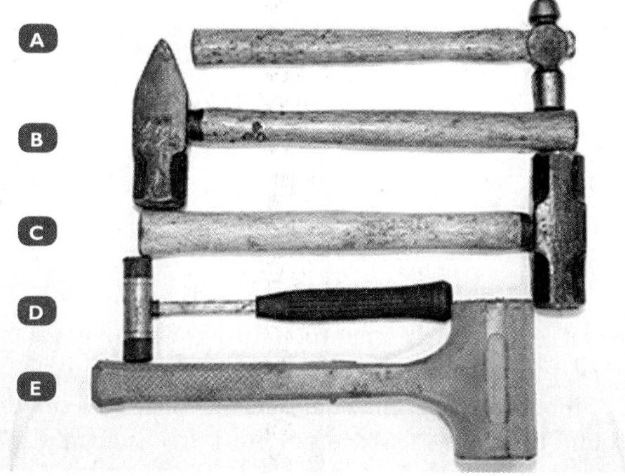

FIGURE 5-15 **A.** Ball-peen hammer. **B.** Steel hammer. **C.** Club hammer. **D.** Nylon/brass tip mallet. **E.** Dead-blow hammer.

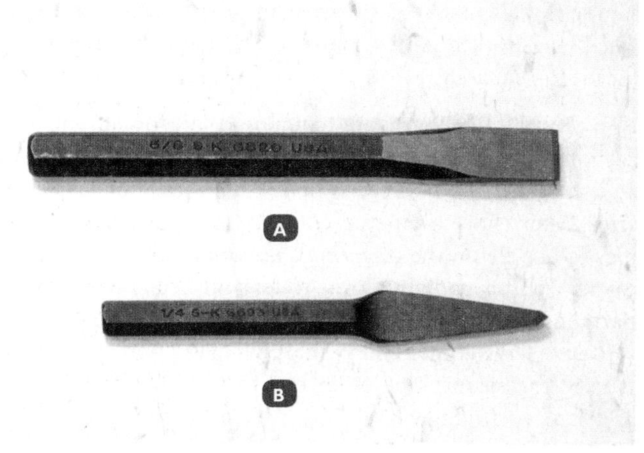

FIGURE 5-16 **A.** A cold chisel. **B.** A cross-cut chisel.

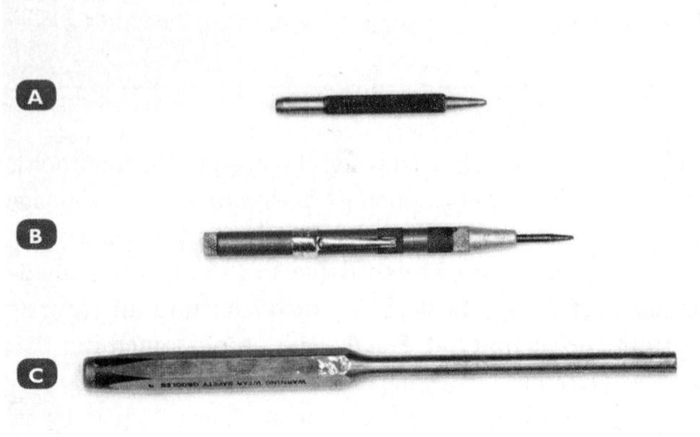

FIGURE 5-17 **A.** Center punch. **B.** Prick punch. **C.** Drift punch.

FIGURE 5-18 **A.** Pin punch. **B.** Wad punch. **C.** Number punch set.

a soft surface under the work, ideally the end grain of a wooden block. If a hollow punch loses its sharpness or has nicks around its edge, it will make a mess instead of a hole. Numbers and letters, like the engine numbers on some cylinder blocks, are usually made with number and letter punches that come in boxed sets (**FIGURE 5-18C**). The rules for using these punches are the same as for all punches: The punch must be square with the surface being worked on, not on an angle, and the hammer must hit the top squarely.

Pry Bars **Pry bars** are composed of forged, medium carbon, spring-like steel and are used as levers to move, adjust, or pry. Pry bars are available in a variety of shapes and sizes. Many have a tapered end that is slightly bent, with a plastic handle on the other end (**FIGURE 5-19A**). This design works well for applying force to tension belts or for moving parts into alignment. Another type of pry bar is the roll bar (**FIGURE 5-19B**). One end is sharply curved and tapered and is used for prying. The other end is tapered to a dull point and is used to align larger holes, such as transmission bell housings or engine motor mounts. Because pry bars are made of hardened steel, care should be taken when using them on softer materials to avoid any damage.

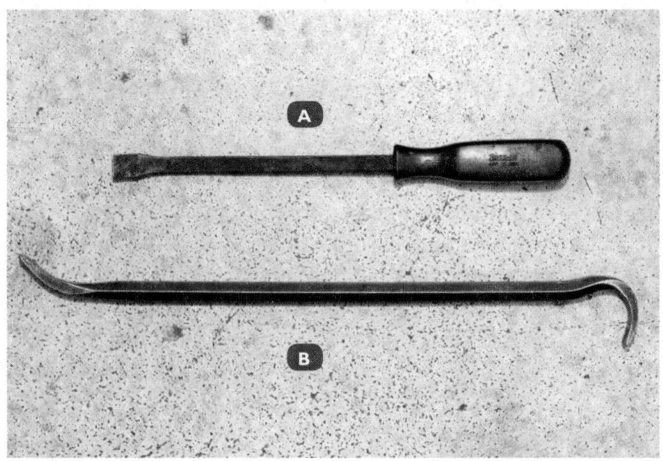

FIGURE 5-19 **A.** A pry bar. **B.** A roll bar.

FIGURE 5-20 A gasket scraper.

Gasket Scrapers A **gasket scraper** has a hardened, sharpened blade. It is designed to remove a gasket without damaging the sealing face of the component, when used properly (**FIGURE 5-20**). On one end, it has a comfortable handle to grip, like a screwdriver handle; on the other end, a blade is fitted with a sharp edge to assist in the removal of gaskets.

The gasket scraper should be kept sharp to make it easy to remove all traces of the old gasket and sealing compound. The blades come in different sizes, with a typical size being 1 inch (25 mm) wide. Whenever you use a gasket scraper, be very careful not to nick or damage the surface being cleaned.

▶ TECHNICIAN TIP

Many engine components are made of aluminum. Because aluminum is quite soft, it is critical that you use the gasket scraper very carefully so as not to damage an aluminum surface. This can be accomplished by keeping the gasket scraper at a fairly flat angle to the surface. The gasket scraper should also be used only by hand, not with a hammer.

Note: It is extremely important to always point gasket scrapers away from your body and hand while removing gasket material. Stubborn gasket material tends to stick unevenly in areas around bolt holes. Gaskets can break free suddenly and cause the scraper to overshoot the part being cleaned and can cause severe lacerations.

Files Files are cutting devices designed to remove small amounts of material from the surface of a workpiece. Files are available in a variety of shapes and sizes and degrees of coarseness, depending on the material being worked on and the size of the job. Files have a pointed tang on one end that is fitted to a handle. Files are often sold without handles, but they should not be used until a handle of the right size has been fitted. A correctly sized handle fits snugly without working loose when the file is in use. Always check the handle before using the file. If the handle is loose, give it a sharp rap to tighten it up, or if it is the threaded type, screw it on tighter. If it fails to fit snugly, you must use a different handle size.

SAFETY TIP

Hands should always be kept away from the surface of the file and the metal that is being worked on. Filing can produce small slivers of metal that can be difficult to remove from a finger or hand. Clean hands will help avoid slipping and lessen the corrosion caused by acids and moisture from the skin.

What makes one file different from another is not just the shape but also how much material it is designed to remove with each stroke. The teeth on the file determine how much material will be removed (**FIGURE 5-21**). Since the teeth face in one direction only, the file cuts in only one direction. Dragging the file backward over the surface of the metal only dulls the teeth and wears them out quickly.

Teeth on a coarse-grade file are longer, with a greater space between them. A coarse-grade file working on a piece of mild steel will remove a lot of material with each stroke, but it leaves a rough finish. A smooth-grade file has shorter teeth cut more closely together. It removes much less material on each stroke, and the finish is much smoother. The coarse file is used first to remove material quickly, then a smoother file gently removes the last of it and leaves a clean finish on the work. The full list of grades in flat files, from rough to smooth, follows (**FIGURE 5-22**):

- *Rough files* have the coarsest teeth, with approximately 20 teeth per 1 inch (25 mm). They are used when a lot of material must be removed quickly. They leave a very rough finish and must be followed by finer files to produce a smooth final finish.
- *Coarse bastard files* are still coarse files, with approximately 30 teeth per 1 inch (25 mm), but they are not as coarse as the rough file. They are also used to rough out or remove material quickly from a job.
- *Second-cut files* have approximately 40 teeth per 1 inch (25 mm) and provide a smoother finish than the rough or coarse bastard file. They are good all-around intermediary files and leave a reasonably smooth finish.
- *Smooth files* have approximately 60 teeth per 1 inch (25 mm) and are a finishing file used to provide a smooth final finish.
- *Dead-smooth files* have 100 teeth per 1 inch (25 mm) or more and are used where a very fine finish is required.

Some flat files are available with one smooth edge and are called *safe-edge files*. They allow filing up to an edge without damaging it. Flat files are fine on straightforward jobs, but you need files that work in some awkward spots as well. A **warding file** is thinner than other files and comes to a point; it is used for working in narrow slots (**FIGURE 5-23A**).

A **square file** has teeth on all four sides, so you can use it in a square or rectangular hole (**FIGURE 5-23B**). A square file can make the right shape for a squared metal key to fit in a slot. A triangular file has three sides (**FIGURE 5-23C**). Because it is

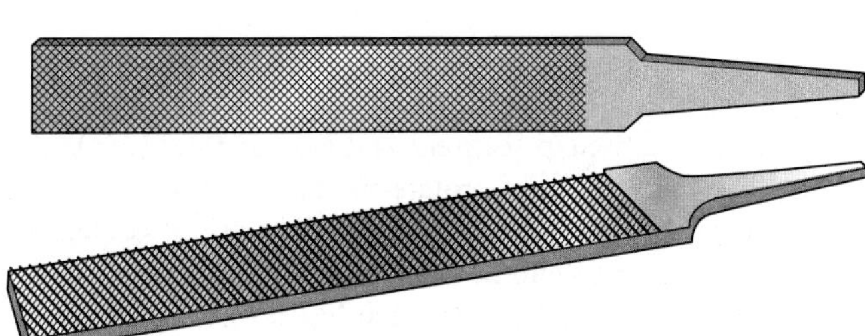

FIGURE 5-21 The teeth on a file.

FIGURE 5-22 Common flat files.

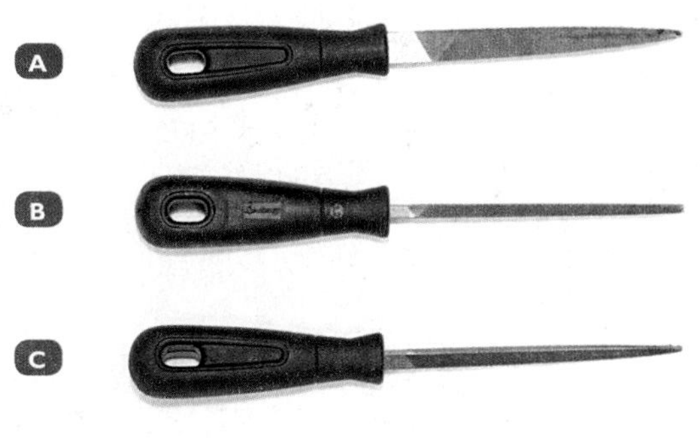

FIGURE 5-23 A. Warding file. **B.** Square file. **C.** Triangular file.

triangular, it can get into internal corners; it can cut right into a corner without removing material from the sides.

Curved files are either half-round or round. A half-round file has a shallow convex surface that can file in a concave hollow or in an acute internal corner (**FIGURE 5-24A**). The fully round file, sometimes called a *rat-tail file*, can make holes bigger. It can also file inside a concave surface with a tight radius. The thread file cleans clogged or distorted threads on bolts and studs (**FIGURE 5-24B**). Thread files are available in either metric or imperial configurations, so make sure you use the correct file. Each file has eight different surfaces that match different thread dimensions, so the right face must be used. Files should be cleaned after each use. If they are clogged, they can be cleaned by using a file card or file brush (**FIGURE 5-24C**). This tool has short steel bristles that clean out the small particles that clog the teeth of the file. Rubbing a piece of chalk over the surface of the file prior to filing will make it easier to clean.

Hacksaw The hacksaw is used for the general cutting of metals for a crude cut (**FIGURE 5-25**). The frames and blades are adjustable and rated according the number of teeth and hardness of the saw.

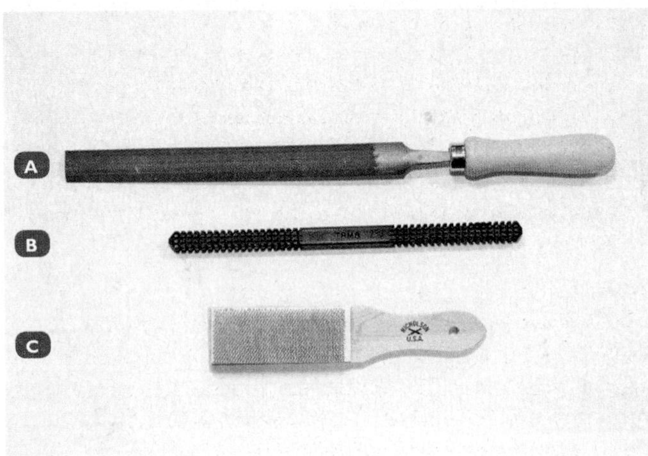

FIGURE 5-24 **A.** Curved file. **B.** Thread file. **C.** File card.

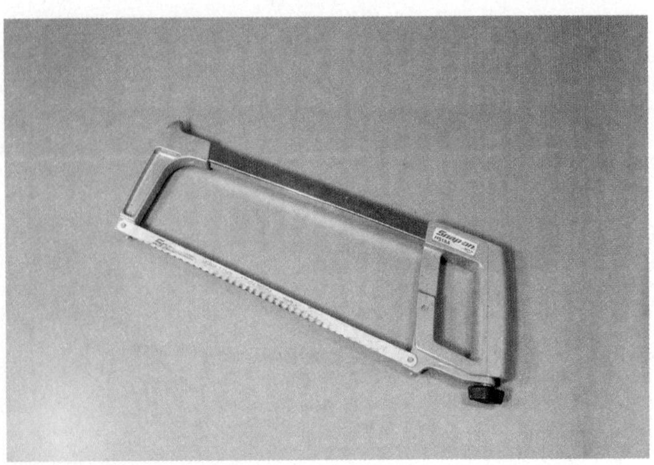

FIGURE 5-25 A hacksaw.

Clamps and Vices The **bench vice** is a useful tool for holding anything that can fit into its jaws (**FIGURE 5-26A**). Some common uses include sawing, filing, or chiseling. The jaws are serrated to give extra grip. They are also very hard, which means that when the vice is tightened, the jaws can mar whatever they grip. To prevent this, a pair of soft jaws may be fitted whenever the danger of damage arises. These are usually made of aluminum or some other soft metal, or they can have a rubber-type surface applied to them. When materials are too awkward to grip vertically in a plain vice, it may be easier to use an **offset vice**. The offset vice has its jaws set to one side to allow long components to be held vertically. For example, a long threaded bar can be held vertically in an offset vice to cut a thread with a die.

A **drill vice** is designed to hold material on a drill worktable. The drill worktable has slots cut into it to allow the vice to be bolted down on the table to hold material securely (**FIGURE 5-26B**). To hold something firmly and drill it accurately, the object must be secured in the jaws of the vice. The vice can be moved on the bed until the precise drilling point is located and then tightened down by bolts to hold the drill vice in place during drilling. The name for the **C-clamp** comes from its shape (**FIGURE 5-26C**). It holds parts together while they are being assembled, drilled, or welded. It can reach around awkwardly shaped pieces that will not fit in a vice. It is also commonly used to retract disc brake caliper pistons. This clamp is portable, so it can be taken to the work.

Taps and Dies **Taps** cut threads inside holes or nuts (**FIGURE 5-27A**). They are usually available in three different types. The first is known as a **taper tap**. It narrows at the tip to give it a good start in the hole where the thread is to be cut. The diameter of the hole is determined by a tap drill chart, which can be obtained from engineering suppliers. This chart shows what hole size must be drilled and what tap size is needed to cut the right thread for any given bolt size. Remember that if you are drilling a ¼ inch (6 mm) or larger hole, you should use a smaller pilot drill first. Once the properly sized hole has been drilled, the taper tap can tap a thread right through a piece of steel to enable a bolt to be screwed into it.

The second type of tap is an **intermediate tap**, also known as a *plug tap*, and the third is a **bottoming tap**. They are used to tap a thread into a hole that does not come out the other side of the material, called a blind hole. A taper tap is used to start the thread in the hole, and then the intermediate tap is used, followed by a bottoming tap to take the thread right to the bottom of the blind hole.

A **tap handle** (**FIGURE 5-27B**) has a right-angled jaw that matches the squared end that all taps have. The jaws are designed to hold the tap securely, and the handles provide the leverage for the operator to rotate the tap comfortably to cut the thread. To cut a thread in an awkward space, a T-shaped tap handle is very convenient. Its handles are not as long, so it fits into tighter spaces; however, it is harder to turn and to guide accurately. To cut a brand-new thread on a blank rod or shaft, a die (**FIGURE 5-27C**) held in a **die stock handle** (**FIGURE 5-27D**)

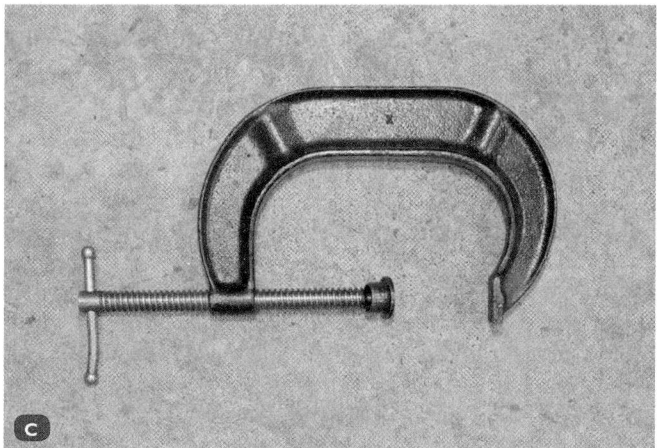

FIGURE 5-26 **A.** Bench vice, **B.** drill vice, and **C.** C-clamp.

is used. The die may be split so that it can be adjusted more tightly onto the work with each pass of the die, as the thread is cut deeper and deeper until the nut fits properly. The **thread chaser** is also common in the shop. It is hexagonally shaped to fit a wrench, and it is commonly used to clean up threads that are rusty or have been damaged.

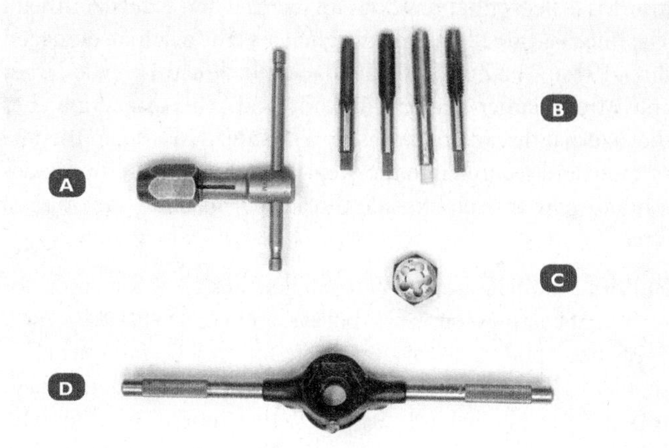

FIGURE 5-27 **A.** Tap handle, **B.** taps, **C.** die, and **D.** die stock handle.

Screw extractors are devices designed to remove screws, studs, or bolts that have broken off in threaded holes. A common type of extractor uses a coarse, left-hand tapered thread formed on its hardened body. Usually, a hole is drilled in the center of the broken screw, and then the extractor is screwed into the hole. The left-hand thread grips the broken part of the bolt and unscrews it. The extractor is marked with the sizes of the screw it is designed to remove and the hole that needs to be drilled. It is important to drill the hole carefully in the center of the bolt or stud in case you end up having to drill the bolt out. If you drill the hole off-center, you will not be able to drill it out all the way to the inside diameter of the threads, and removal will become nearly impossible.

Thread Repair **Thread repair** is used in situations where it is not possible to replace a damaged component. This may be because the thread is located in a large, expensive component, such as the engine block or cylinder head, or because parts are not available. The aim of thread repair is to restore the thread to a condition that restores the fastening integrity. It can be performed on internal threads, such as in a housing, engine block, or cylinder head, or on external threads, such as on a bolt.

Many different tools and methods can be used to repair a thread. The least invasive method is to reshape the threads. If the threads are not too badly damaged—for example, if the outer thread is slightly damaged from being started crooked (cross-threaded)—then a thread file may be used to clean them up or a restoring tool may be used to reshape them. Each thread file has eight different sets of file teeth that match various thread pitches. Select the set that matches the bolt you are working on and file the bolt in line with the threads. The file removes any distorted metal from the threads. File only until the bad spot is reshaped. The thread-restoring tool looks like an ordinary tap and die set, but instead of cutting the threads, it reshapes the damaged portion of the thread.

Threads that have substantial damage require other methods of repair. A common method for repairing damaged internal threads is a thread insert. Several manufacturers make thread inserts, and they all work in a similar fashion. The thread insert is a sleeve that has both an internal and external thread. The internal thread on the insert matches the original, damaged thread size. The hole with the damaged thread is made larger and a fresh, larger-diameter thread is cut. This thread matches the external thread on the insert. The thread insert can then be screwed and secured into the prepared hole. The insert provides a brand-new threaded inside thread that matches the original size.

Pullers **Pullers** are a very common, universal tool used for removing bearings, bushings, pulleys, and gears (**FIGURE 5-28A**). Specialized pullers are also available for specific tasks where a standard puller is not as effective. The most common pullers have two or three legs that grip the part to be removed. A center bolt, called a forcing screw or jacking bolt, is then screwed in, producing a jacking or pulling action, which extracts the part. **Gear pullers** come in a range of sizes and shapes, all designed for particular applications (**FIGURE 5-28B**). They consist of three main parts: jaws, a crossarm, and a forcing screw. There are generally two or three jaws on a puller. They are designed to work either externally around a pulley or internally. The forcing screw is a long, fine-threaded bolt that is applied to the center of the crossarm.

When the forcing screw is turned, it applies many tons of force through the component you are removing. The crossarm attaches the jaws to the forcing screw. There may be two, three, or four arms. If the crossarm has four arms, three of the arms are spaced 120 degrees apart. The fourth arm is positioned 180 degrees apart from one arm. This allows the crossarm to be used as either a two- or a three-arm puller.

FIGURE 5-28 **A.** Puller. **B.** Gear puller.

Flaring Tools A **tube-flaring tool** is used to flare the end of a tube so it can be connected to another tube or component. One example of this is where the brake line screws into a wheel cylinder. The flared end is compressed between two threaded parts so that it will seal the joint and withstand high pressures. The three most common shapes of flares are the **single flare**, for tubing that carries low pressures, such as a fuel line; the **double flare**, for higher pressures, such as in a brake system; and the ISO flare (sometimes called a bubble flare), which is the metric version used in brake systems (**FIGURE 5-29A**).

Flaring tools have two parts: a set of bars with holes that match the diameter of the tube end that is being shaped and a yoke that drives a cone into the mouth of the tube (**FIGURE 5-29B**). To make a single flare, the end of the tube is placed level with the surface of the top of the flaring bars. With the clamp screw firmly tightened, the feed screw flares the end of the tube. Making a double flare is similar, but an extra step is added, and more of the tube is exposed to allow for the folding over into a double flare. A double-flaring button is placed into the end of the tube, and when it is removed after tightening, the pipe looks like a bubble. Placing the cone and yoke over the bubble allows you to turn the feed screw and force the bubble to fold in on itself, forming the double flare. An ISO flare uses a flaring tool made specifically for that type of flare. It is like the double-flare process but stops with the use of the button. It does not get doubled back on itself. It should resemble a bubble shape when you are finished.

Pipe cutters are used to cut a tube to the correct length. These tools produce a cleaner cut because they have fewer burs on the outer surface of the tube (**FIGURE 5-29C**). A screw on the cutter tightens a cutting wheel that is rotated around the tube. The sharpened cutting wheel of a pipe cutter does the cutting. As the tool turns around the pipe, turning the screw increases the pressure, driving the wheel deeper and deeper through the pipe until it finally cuts through. There is a larger version that is used for cutting exhaust pipes.

Riveting Tools There are many applications for blind rivets, and various rivet types and tools may be used to do the riveting. **Pop-rivet guns** are convenient for the occasional riveting of light materials (**FIGURE 5-30**). A typical pop or **blind rivet** has a body, which forms the **finished rivet** and a **mandrel**, the latter of which is discarded when the riveting is completed (**FIGURE 5-31**). It is called a blind rivet because there is no need to see or reach the other side of the hole in which the rivet goes to do the work. In some types, the rivet is plugged shut so that it is waterproof or pressure-proof. The rivet is inserted into the riveting tool, which when squeezed, pulls the end of the mandrel back through the body of the rivet. Because the mandrel head is bigger than the hole through the body, it swells out as it comes through the body. Finally, the mandrel head will snap off under the pressure

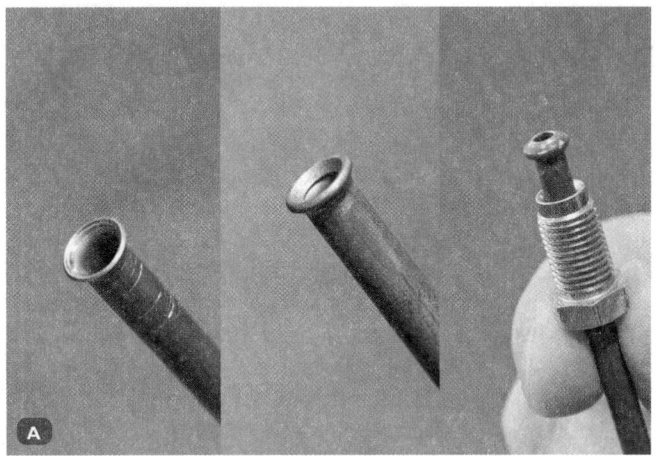

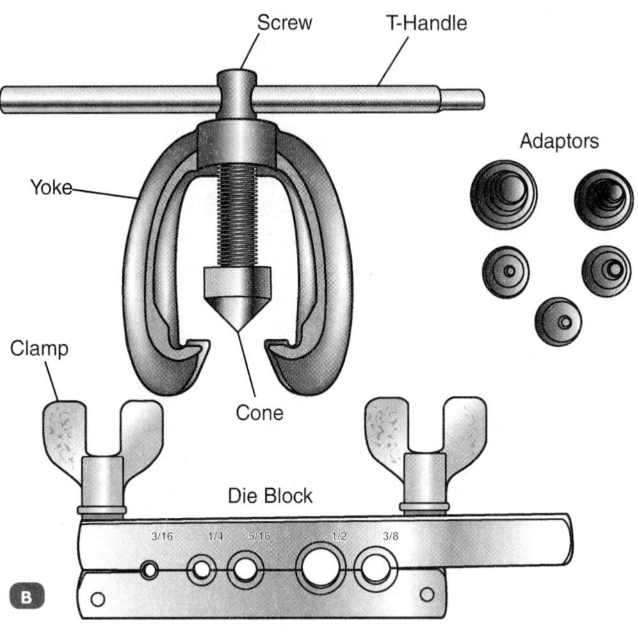

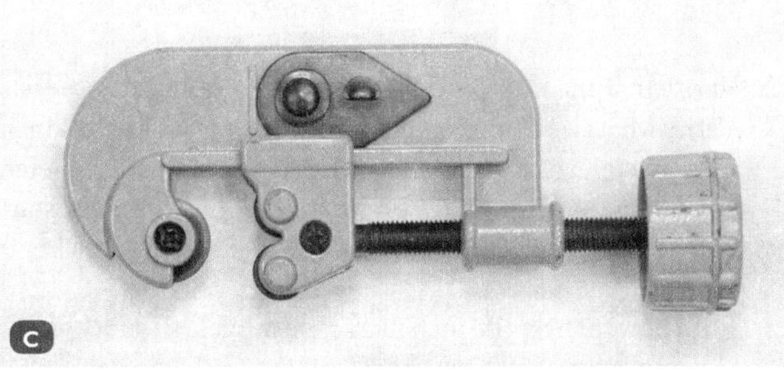

FIGURE 5-29 A. Single flare, double flare, and ISO flare. **B.** Components of a flaring tool. **C.** Tubing cutter.

and fall out, leaving the rivet body gripping the two sheets of material together.

Measurement Tools

Precision Measuring Tools MORE technicians are required to perform a variety of measurements while carrying out their job. This requires knowledge of what tools are available and how

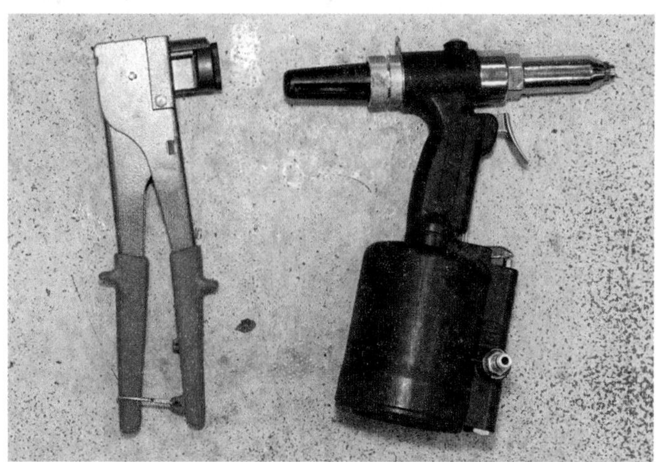

FIGURE 5-30 Pop rivet guns.

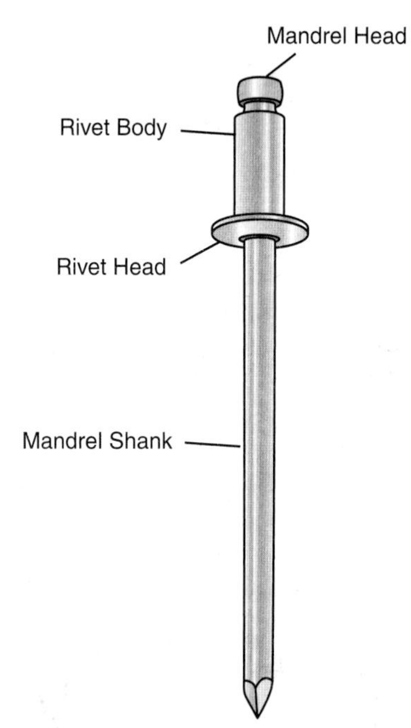

FIGURE 5-31 Anatomy of a blind, or pop, rivet.

to use them. Measuring tools can generally be classified according to what type of measurements they can make. A measuring tape is useful for measuring longer distances and is accurate to a millimeter or fraction of an inch (**FIGURE 5-32A**). A steel rule is capable of accurate measurements on shorter lengths, down to a millimeter or a fraction of an inch (**FIGURE 5-32B**). Precision measuring tools are accurate to much smaller dimensions: a micrometer, for example, can accurately measure down to $^{1}/_{1000}$ of a millimeter (0.001 mm) in some cases.

▶ TECHNICIAN TIP

The metric, also called the International System of Units (SI), and imperial systems are two sets of standards for quantifying weights and measurements. Each system has defined units. For example, the metric system uses millimeters, centimeters, and meters, whereas the imperial system uses inches, feet, and yards. Conversions can be undertaken from one system to the other. For example, 25.4 mm is equal to 1 inch, and

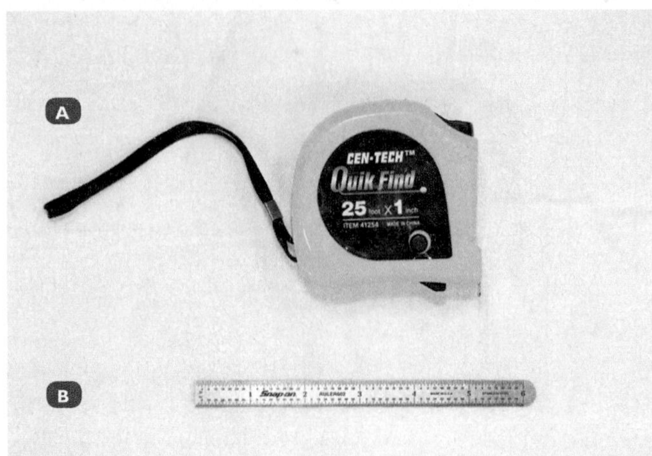

FIGURE 5-32 A. Measuring tape. **B.** Steel rule.

304.8 mm is equal to 1 foot. Tools that make use of a measuring system, such as wrenches, sockets, drill bits, micrometers, rulers, and many others, come in both metric and imperial measurements. In many countries, metric measurements are the standard. However, conversion tables can be used to convert from one system to the other if needed.

Measuring Tape Measuring tapes are a flexible type of ruler and are a common measuring tool. The most common type found in shops is a thin metal strip about ½ inch to 1 inch (13 to 25 mm) wide that is rolled up inside a housing with a spring return mechanism. Measuring tapes can be of various lengths, 16 to 25 feet (5 or 8 meters) and longer being very common. The measuring tape is pulled from the housing to measure items, and a spring return winds it back into the housing. The housing will usually have a built-in locking mechanism to hold the extended measuring tape against the spring return mechanism.

Stainless Steel Rulers As the name suggests, a stainless **steel ruler** is a ruler that is made from stainless steel. Stainless steel rulers commonly come in 12 inch, 24 inch, and 36 inch (30 cm, 61 cm, and 1 meter) lengths. They are used like any ruler to measure and mark out items. They are very strong, have precise markings, and resist damage. When using a stainless steel ruler, you can rest it on its edge so the markings are closer to the material being measured, which helps to mark the work precisely. Always protect the steel ruler from damage by storing it carefully; a damaged ruler will not give an accurate measurement. Never take measurements from the very end of a damaged steel ruler, as damaged ends may affect the accuracy of your measurements.

▶ TECHNICIAN TIP

Sometimes the end of your tape measure, or ruler, is damaged and you cannot reliably see the zero mark. If this is the case, simply start at the next whole number—for example, start at 1 inch or 1 cm. But don't forget to subtract that same number from the final measurement.

Outside, Inside, and Depth Micrometers Micrometers are precise measuring tools designed to measure small distances; they are available in both millimeter (mm) and inch (") calibrations. Typically, they can measure down to a resolution of $1/1{,}000$ of an inch (0.001") for a standard micrometer or $1/100$ of a millimeter (0.01 mm) for a metric micrometer. Vernier micrometers equipped with the addition of a vernier scale can measure down to $1/10{,}000$ of an inch (0.0001 inch) or $1/1{,}000$ of a millimeter (0.001 mm). The most common types of micrometers are the outside, inside, and depth micrometers. As the name suggests, an **outside micrometer** (**FIGURE 5-33A**) measures the outside dimensions of an item. For example, it could measure the diameter of a valve stem. The **inside micrometer** measures inside dimensions. For example, the inside micrometer could measure an engine cylinder bore (**FIGURE 5-33B**). **Depth micrometers** measure the depth of an item, such as how far a piston is below the surface of the block (**FIGURE 5-33C**).

The most common micrometer is an outside micrometer. The horseshoe-shaped part is the frame. It is built to make sure the micrometer holds its shape. Some frames have plastic finger pads so that body heat is not transferred to the metal frame as easily, because heat can cause the metal to expand slightly and affect the reading. On one end of the frame is the anvil, which contacts one side of the part being measured. The other contact point is the spindle. The micrometer measures the distance between the anvil and spindle, so that is where the part being measured fits. The measurement is read on the sleeve/barrel and thimble. The sleeve/barrel is stationary and has linear markings on it. The thimble fits over the sleeve and has graduated markings on it. The thimble is connected directly to the spindle, and both turn as a unit. Because the spindle and sleeve/barrel have matching threads, the thimble rotates the spindle inside of the sleeve/barrel, and the thread moves the spindle inwards and outwards. The thimble usually incorporates either a ratchet or a clutch mechanism, which prevents overtightening of the micrometer thimble when taking a reading. A lock nut, lock ring, or lock screw is used on most micrometers and locks the thimble in place while you read the micrometer.

To read a standard micrometer, perform the following steps:

1. Verify that the micrometer is properly calibrated.
2. Verify what size of micrometer you are using. If it is a 0–1 inch micrometer, start with 0.000. If it is a 1–2 inch micrometer, start with 1.000 inch. A 2–3 inch micrometer would start with 2.000 inch, and so on. (To give an example, let's say it is 2.000".)
3. Read how many 0.100 inch marks the thimble has uncovered. (Example: 3 × 0.100" marks = 0.300".)
4. Read how many 0.025 inch marks the thimble has uncovered past the 0.100 inch mark in step 3. (Example: 2 × 0.025" marks = 0.050".)
5. Read the number on the thimble that lines up with the zero line on the sleeve. (Example: 13 × 0.001" marks = 0.013".)
6. Lastly, total all the individual readings. (Example: 2.000" + 0.300" + 0.050" + 0.013" = 2.363".)

A metric micrometer uses the same components as the standard micrometer. However, it uses a different thread pitch

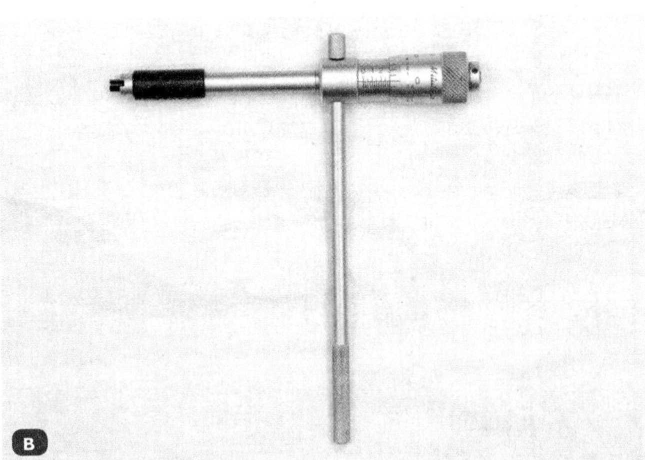

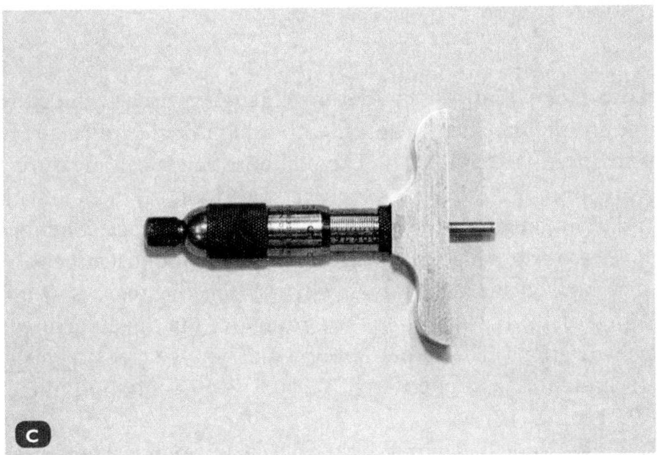

FIGURE 5-33 A. Outside micrometer. **B.** Inside micrometer. **C.** Depth micrometer.

on the spindle and sleeve. It uses a 0.5 mm thread pitch (2.0 threads per millimeter) and opens approximately 25 mm. Each rotation of the thimble moves the spindle 0.5 mm, and it therefore takes 50 rotations of the thimble to move the full 25 mm distance. The sleeve/barrel is labeled with individual millimeter marks and half-millimeter marks, from the starting millimeter to the ending millimeter, 25 mm away. The thimble has graduated marks from 0 to 49. Reading a metric micrometer involves the following steps:

1. Read the number of full millimeters the thimble has passed. (To give an example, let's say it is 23 mm.)
2. Check to see if it passed the 0.5 mm mark. (Example: 0.50 mm.)
3. Check to see which mark the thimble lines up with or has just passed. (Example: 37 × 0.01 mm = 0.37 mm.)
4. Lastly, total all the numbers. (Example: 23 mm + 0.50 mm + 0.37 mm = 23.87 mm.)

If the micrometer is equipped with a vernier gauge, meaning it can read down to $\frac{1}{1000}$ of a millimeter (0.001 mm), you need to complete one more step. Identify which of the vernier lines is closest to one of the lines on the thimble. Sometimes it is hard to determine which is the closest, so decide which three are the closest and then use the center line. At the frame side of the sleeve will be a number that corresponds to the vernier line. It will be numbered 1 to 0. Take the vernier number and add it to the end of your reading. For example: 23.77 + 0.007 = 23.777 mm.

For inside measurements, the inside micrometer works on the same principles as the outside micrometer, and so does the depth micrometer. The only difference is that the scale on the sleeve of the depth micrometer is backward, so be careful when reading it.

Using a Micrometer To maintain the accuracy of measurements, it is important that both the micrometer and the items to be measured are clean and free of any dirt or debris. Also, make sure the micrometer has been zeroed before taking any measurements. Never overtighten a micrometer or store it with its measuring surfaces touching, as this may damage the tool and affect its accuracy. When measuring, make sure the item can pass through the micrometer surfaces snugly and squarely. This is best accomplished by using the ratchet to tighten the micrometer. Always take the measurement several times and compare results to ensure you have measured accurately. To correctly measure using an outside micrometer, follow the guidelines in **SKILL DRILL 5-1**.

Telescoping Gauge For measuring distances in awkward spots, such as the bottom of a deep cylinder, the **telescoping gauge** has spring-loaded plungers that can be unlocked with a screw on the handle so that they slide out and touch the walls of the cylinder (**FIGURE 5-34**). The screw then locks them in that position, the gauge can be withdrawn, and the distance across the plungers can be measured with an outside micrometer or calipers to convey the diameter of the cylinder at that point. Telescoping gauges come in a variety of sizes to fit various sizes of holes and bores.

Split Ball Gauge A **split ball gauge (small hole gauge)** is good for measuring small holes where telescoping gauges cannot fit. They use a similar principle to the telescoping gauge, but the measuring head uses a split ball mechanism that allows it to fit into very small holes. Split ball gauges are ideal for measuring the wear on valve guides on a cylinder head.

SKILL DRILL 5-1 Precision Measurement Using an Outside Micrometer

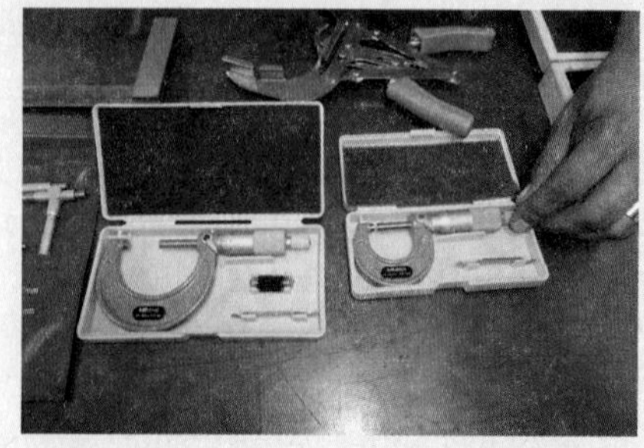

1. Select the correct size of micrometer. Verify that the anvil and spindle are clean and that it is calibrated properly.

2. Clean the surface of the part you are measuring.

3. In your right hand, hold the frame of the micrometer between your little finger, ring finger, and palm of your hand, with the thimble between your thumb and forefinger.

4. With your left hand, hold the part you are measuring and place the micrometer over it.

5. Using your thumb and forefinger, lightly tighten the ratchet. It is important that the correct amount of force is applied to the spindle when taking a measurement. The spindle and anvil should just touch the component, with a slight amount of drag when the micrometer is removed from the measured piece. Be careful that the part is square in the micrometer so that the reading is correct. Try rocking the micrometer in all directions to make sure it is square.

6. Once the micrometer is properly snug, tighten the lock mechanism so that the spindle will not turn.

7. Read the micrometer and record your reading.

8. When all readings are finished, clean the micrometer, position the spindle so that it is backed off from the anvil and return it to its protective case.

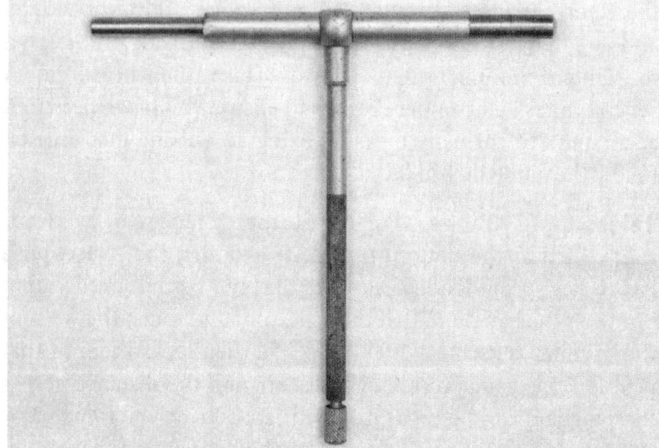

FIGURE 5-34 Telescoping gauge.

A split ball gauge can be fitted in the bore and expanded until there is a slight drag. Then it can be retracted and measured with an outside micrometer. Like some of the other measuring instruments discussed, the split ball gauge may have a dial or digital measurement scale fitted for direct reading purposes.

Dial Bore Gauge A **dial bore gauge** is used to measure the inside diameter of bores, with a high degree of accuracy and speed (**FIGURE 5-35**). The dial bore gauge can measure a bore directly by using telescoping pistons on a T-handle with a dial mounted on the handle. The dial bore gauge combines a telescoping gauge and dial indicator in one instrument. A dial bore gauge determines whether the diameter is worn, tapered, or out-of-round according to the manufacturer's specifications. The resolution of a dial bore gauge is typically accurate to $^{5}/_{10,000}$ of an inch (0.0005") or $^{1}/_{100}$ of a millimeter (0.01 mm).

To use a dial bore gauge, select an appropriately sized adapter to fit the internal diameter of the bore, and install it to the measuring head. Many dial bore gauges also have a fixture to calibrate the tool to the size you desire. The fixture is set to the size desired, and the dial bore gauge is placed in it. The dial bore gauge is then adjusted to the proper reading. Once it is calibrated, the dial bore gauge can be inserted inside the bore to be measured. Hold the gauge in line with the bore and slightly rock it to ensure it is centered. Read the dial when it is fully centered and square to the bore to determine the correct measurement. Store a bore gauge carefully in its storage box, and ensure the locking mechanism is released while in storage. Bore gauges are

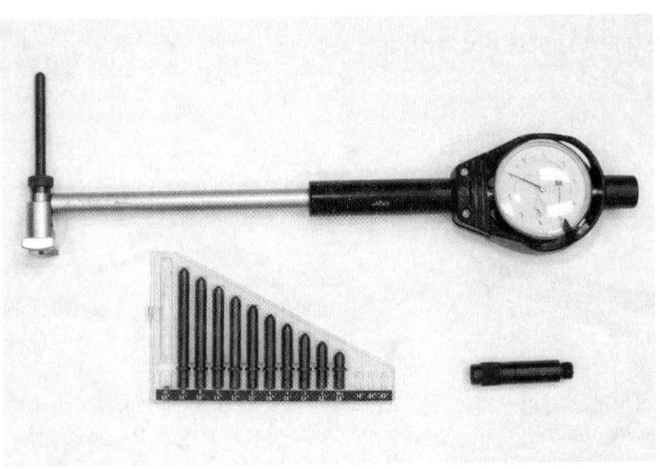

FIGURE 5-35 Dial bore gauge set.

available in different ranges of size. It is important to select a gauge with the correct range for the bore you are measuring. When measuring, make sure the gauge is at a 90-degree angle to the bore and read the dial. Always take the measurement several times and compare results to ensure you have measured accurately. To correctly measure using a dial bore gauge, follow the guidelines in **SKILL DRILL 5-2**.

Vernier Calipers Vernier calipers are a precision instrument used for measuring outside dimensions, inside dimensions, and depth measurements, all in one tool. They have a graduated bar with markings like a ruler. On the bar, a sliding sleeve with jaws is mounted for taking inside or outside measurements. Measurements on older versions of vernier calipers are taken by reading the graduated bar scales, while fractional measurements are read by comparing the scales between the sliding sleeve and the graduated bar. Technicians will often use vernier calipers to measure the length and diameter of bolts and pins or the depth of blind holes in housings. Newer versions of vernier calipers have dial and digital scales. The dial vernier has the main scale on the graduated bar, while fractional measurements are taken from a dial with a rotating needle. These tend to be easier to read than the older versions. More recently, digital scales on vernier calipers have become commonplace. The principle of their use is the same as any vernier caliper; however, they have a digital scale that reads the measurement directly.

Always store vernier calipers in a storage box to protect them and ensure that the measuring surfaces are kept clean for accurate measurement. If making an internal or external measurement, make sure the caliper is at right angles to the surfaces to be measured. You should always repeat the measurement several times and compare results to ensure you have measured accurately. To correctly measure using vernier calipers, follow the guidelines in **SKILL DRILL 5-3**.

Dial Indicators **Dial indicators** can also be known as dial gauges, and as the name suggests, they have a dial and needle where measurements are read. They have a measuring plunger with a pointed contact end that is spring-loaded and connected via the housing to the dial needle. The dial accurately measures movement of the plunger in and out as it rests against an object. For example, they can be used to measure the trueness of a rotating disc brake rotor. A dial indicator can also measure how round something is. A crankshaft can be rotated in a set of V blocks. If the crankshaft is bent, it will show as movement on the dial indicator as the crankshaft is rotated. The dial indicator senses slight movement at its tip and magnifies it into a measurable swing on the dial. Dial indicators typically measure ranges from 0.010 inch to 12 inches or 0.25 mm to

SKILL DRILL 5-2 Precision Measurement Using a Dial Bore Gauge

1. Select the correct size of the dial bore gauge you will use and fit any adapters to it.

2. Check the calibration and adjust it as necessary.

3. Insert the dial bore gauge into the bore. The accurate measurement will be at exactly 90 degrees to the bore. To find the accurate measurement, rock the dial bore gauge handle slightly back and forth until you find the centered position.

4. Read the dial to determine the bore measurement.

5. Always clean the dial bore gauge and return it to its protective case when you have finished using it.

SKILL DRILL 5-3 Precision Measurement Using Vernier Calipers

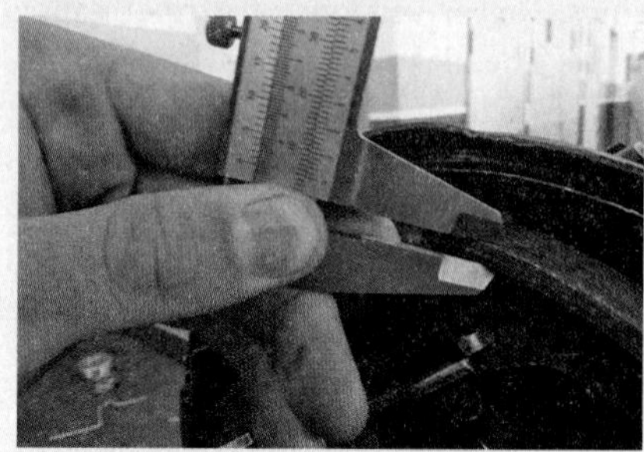

1. Verify that the vernier caliper is calibrated (zeroed) before using it. If it has not been zeroed, notify your mentor, who will get you a replacement vernier caliper.

2. Position the caliper correctly for the measurement you are making. Internal and external readings are normally made with the vernier caliper positioned at 90 degrees to the face of the component to be measured. Length and depth measurements are usually made parallel to or in line with the object being measured. Use your thumb to press or withdraw the sliding jaw to measure the outside or inside of the part.

3. Read the scale of the vernier caliper, being careful not to change the position of the movable jaw. Always read the dial or face straight on. A view from the side can give a considerable parallax error. A parallax error is a visual error caused by viewing measurement markers at an incorrect angle.

300 mm and have graduation marks of 0.0005 inch to 0.01 inch or 0.001 mm to 0.01 mm. The large needle can move numerous times around the outer scale. One full turn may represent 1 mm or 0.1 inch. The small inner scale indicates how many times the outer needle has moved around its scale. In this way, the dial indicator can read movement of up to 1 inch or 2.54 cm. Dial indicators can measure with an accuracy of 0.001 inch or 0.01 mm. The type of dial indicator you use will be determined by the amount of movement you expect from the component you are measuring. The indicator must be set up such that there is no gap between the dial indicator and the component to be measured. Most dial indicator sets contain various attachments and support arms so that they can be configured specifically for the measuring task.

Dial indicators are used in many types of service jobs. They are particularly useful in determining runout on rotating shafts and surfaces. Runout is the side-to-side variation of movement when a component is turned. When attaching a dial indicator, keep support arms as short as possible. Make sure all attachments are tightened to prevent unnecessary movement between the indicator and the component. Make sure the dial indicator pointer is positioned at 90 degrees to the face of the component to be measured. Always read the dial face straight on, as a view from the side can give a considerable parallax error. The outer face of the dial indicator is designed so that it can be rotated in such a way that the zero mark can be positioned directly over the pointer. This is how a dial indicator is zeroed. To correctly measure using a dial indicator, follow the guidelines in **SKILL DRILL 5-4**.

Straight Edge **Straight edges** are usually made from hardened steel and are machined so that the edge is perfectly straight. A straight edge is used to check the flatness of a surface. It is placed on its edge against the surface to be checked. The gap between the straight edge and the surface can be measured by using feeler gauges. Sometimes the gap can be seen easily if light is shone from behind the surface being checked. Straight edges are often used to measure the amount of warpage the surface of a cylinder head has.

Feeler Gauges **Feeler gauges** (also called *feeler blades*) are used to measure the width of gaps, such as the clearance between valves and rocker arms. Feeler gauges are flat metal strips of varying thicknesses. The thickness of each feeler gauge is clearly marked on each one. They are sized from fractions of a millimeter or fractions of an inch. They usually come in sets with different sizes and are available in metric and imperial measurements. Some sets contain feeler gauges made of brass. These are used to take measurements between magnetic components. If steel gauges were used, the drag caused by the magnetism would mimic the drag of a proper clearance. Brass gauges are not subject to magnetism, so they work well in that situation. Some feeler gauges come in a bent arrangement to be more easily inserted in cramped spaces. Others come in a stepped version. Two or more feeler gauges can be stacked together to make up a desired thickness. Alternatively, if you want to measure an unknown gap, you can interchange feeler gauges until you find the one (or more) that fits snugly into the gap, then total their thickness to measure the gap. In conjunction with a straight edge, they can be used to measure surface irregularities in a cylinder head.

If the feeler gauge feels too loose when measuring a gap, select the next larger size and measure the gap again. Repeat this procedure until the feeler gauge has a slight drag between both parts. If the feeler gauge is too tight, select a smaller size

SKILL DRILL 5-4 Precision Measurement Using a Dial Indicator

1. Select the gauge type, size, attachment, and bracket that fit the part you are measuring. Mount the dial indicator firmly to keep it stationary.

2. Adjust the indicator so that the plunger is at 90 degrees to the part you are measuring and lock it in place.

3. Rotate the part one complete turn and locate the low spot. Zero the indicator.

4. Find the point of maximum height and note the reading. This will indicate the runout value.

5. Continue the rotation and make sure the needle does not go below zero. If it does, reverse the indicator and re-measure the point of maximum variation.

6. Check your readings against the manufacturer's specifications. If the deviation is greater than the specifications allow, consult your supervisor.

SKILL DRILL 5-5 Selecting and Using Feeler Gauge Sets

1. Select the appropriate type and size of feeler gauge set for the job you are working on.

2. Inspect the feeler gauges to make sure they are clean, rust-free, and undamaged, but slightly oiled for ease of movement.

3. Choose one of the smaller wires or blades and try to insert it in the gap on the part. If it slips in and out easily, choose the next size up. When you find one that touches both sides of the gap and slides with only gentle pressure, then you have found the exact width of that gap.

4. Read the markings on the wire or blade and check these against the manufacturer's specifications for this component. If gap width is outside the tolerances specified, inform your supervisor.

5. Clean the feeler gauge set with an oily cloth to prevent rust when you store the set.

until the feeler gauge fits properly. When measuring a spark plug gap, feeler gauges should not be used, because the surfaces are not perfectly parallel, so it is preferable to use **wire feeler gauges**. Wire feeler gauges use accurately machined pieces of wire instead of metal strips. To select and use feeler gauge sets, follow the guidelines in **SKILL DRILL 5-5**.

Air-Operated Tools

As a technician, you will use **air tools** often. Air tools will make up an expensive and indispensable part of a technician's personal tools. As such, it is important to know their proper selection, usage, and care. Air tools, or pneumatic-operated tools, typically run at 120 psi (5.74 kPa), so exercise caution around them. Compressed air is transported through pipes and hoses. Air tools have quick-connect fittings so that various air tools can easily be used on the same air hose. Although there are several styles of quick-connect fittings, a shop usually uses one style throughout the entire shop. An **air ratchet** uses the force of compressed air to turn a ratchet drive (**FIGURE 5-36A**). It is used on smaller nuts and bolts. Once the nut has been loosened, the air ratchet spins it off in a small fraction of the time it would take by hand. The air ratchet also works well when there is not much room to swing a ratchet handle.

An **air nozzle** is probably the simplest air tool (**FIGURE 5-36B**). It simply controls the flow of compressed air. It is controlled by a lever or valve and is used to blast debris and dirt out of confined spaces. Blasting debris and dirt can be dangerous, so eye protection must be worn whenever this tool is used. Noise levels are usually high, so ear protection should also be worn. It is dangerous to use an air nozzle to clean yourself off. Its blast should always be directed away from the user and anyone else working nearby.

An **air hammer**, sometimes called an *air chisel*, is useful for driving and cutting (**FIGURE 5-36C**). The extra force that is generated by the compressed air makes it more efficient than a hand chisel and hammer. Just as there are many chisels, there are many bits that fit into the air hammer. Selecting which one to use depends on the job at hand.

An **air drill** has some important advantages over the more common electric power drill (**FIGURE 5-36D**). With the right attachment, an air drill can drill holes, grind, polish, and clean parts. Unlike the electric drill, it does not carry the risk of producing sparks, which is an important consideration around flammable liquids or petroleum tanks. An air drill does not trail a live electric lead behind it that could be cut and possibly cause shock and burns. Neither does it become hot with heavy use. The most common air tool in a repair shop is the **air-impact wrench** (**FIGURE 5-36E**). It is also called an *impact gun* or **rattle gun**, and it is easy to understand why when you hear one. Taking the wheels off a vehicle to replace the tires is a typical application for this air tool. Removing lug nuts often requires a lot of torque to twist the nuts free, and air-impact wrenches work well for that. The air-impact wrench may be set to spin in either direction, and a valve controls roughly how much torque it applies. It should never be used for the final tightening of wheel nuts. There is a danger in overtightening the wheel nuts, as this could cause the bolts to fail and the wheel to separate from the vehicle while it is moving. Another rule to remember about the air-impact wrench is that you must use special hardened impact sockets, extensions, and joints. The sockets are special heavy-duty, six-point types, and the flats can withstand the hammering force that the impact wrench subjects them to. Air can also be used to power a **grease gun**, which is used to lubricate components with grease fittings. The air power forces the grease through the aperture.

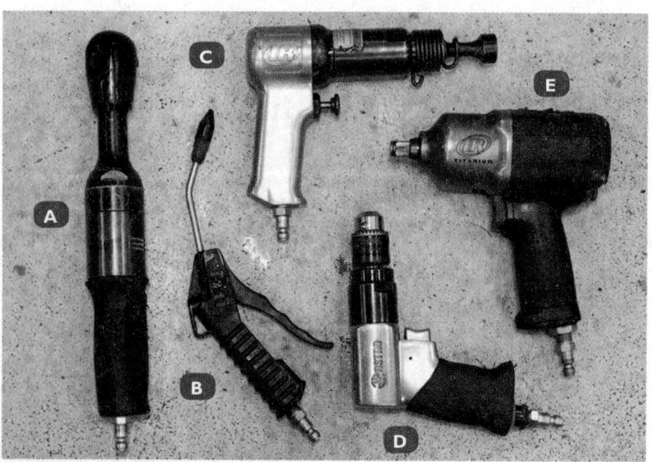

FIGURE 5-36 A. Air ratchet. **B.** Air nozzle. **C.** Air hammer. **D.** Air drill. **E.** Air-impact wrench.

It is critical for the MORE technician to be a subject matter expert on all different types of tools; including hand tools, air tools, precision measuring tools, and many other types of tools. You should be an expert on the proper selection, application and usage, and maintenance of tools. Having expert tool knowledge will save you an enormous amount of time, money, frustration, and possible equipment damage and injuries over your career. Follow **SKILL DRILL 5-6** to learn some techniques for the proper selection, usage, and maintenance of tools.

▶ Purpose, Usage, and Types of Fasteners

K05002

Locking devices or fasteners used in this industry are primarily designed to hold things in a particular location or to hold things together. These devices come in many forms, and depending on the particular application, one or more types of locking devices may be used. They can be in the form of a physical fastener or chemical adhesive. This chapter provides a description of the types of locking devices and fasteners found in MORE design equipment applications.

Types of Fasteners

There are many different fasteners used in equipment applications, including screws, bolts, studs, and nuts. Washers and chemical compounds can be used to help secure these fasteners.

Screws

Screws are generally smaller than bolts and are sometimes referred to as metal threads (**FIGURE 5-37**). They can have a variety of heads, they're used on smaller components, and their thread often extends right from the tip to the head so that they can hold together components of different thickness.

SKILL DRILL 5-6 Steps for the Proper Selection, Use, and Maintenance of Tools

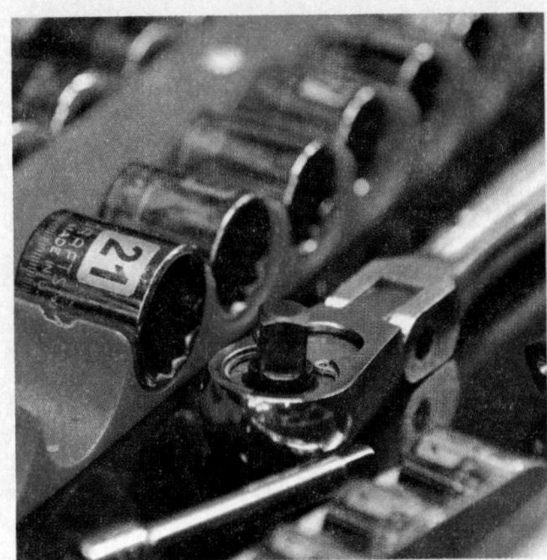

It is important to select, use, and maintain the proper tools when completing a job. Here are some basic tips and step-by-step procedures for ensuring your tools serve you well.

- Keep your personal tools organized and maintain an up-to-date inventory of your tools. A great way to accomplish this is to use foam inserts in your tool box drawers cut to the exact shape of each tool. This way you can easily know where the proper location for each tool is and when a tool is missing.
- Ensure you maintain your tools and any tools that have broken are separated from your working tools so that they can be repaired or replaced.
- Don't loan out tools to people you don't trust, but if you do, have them fill out a hand receipt to establish accountability for the tool.

Try these steps to see how well you can select and use the proper tools for a job. On your next repair job, do the following:

1. Before starting a job, look up the repair procedure in the manufacturer's technical information; pay attention to special tools referenced and what other tools you think you may need to accomplish the repair.

2. Determine whether your shop has the needed special tools (if any), and determine whether they are in proper working order and have been maintained.

3. Determine whether you have all the other tools to accomplish this job and that they are in proper working order.

4. Perform the repair job per the equipment manufacturer's instructions.

5. After the repair in completed, determine whether any tools require repair or maintenance.

6. Then return all tools to their proper location.

7. Evaluate the following:

- How much time did it take to properly check out and return tools?
- Did you have to go back and retrieve tools that you had not anticipated a need for before starting the repair? How much added time did this take?
- If you checked out any special shop tools, were they in proper working order and maintained when you got them?
- Did you, or your shop, not have some tools that you needed?
- Looking back on the repair, were there any tools you could have used that would have saved time or made the repair job safer?

It is important over time that you improve and learn more effective techniques in the selection, use, and maintenance of tools. Don't be the person who is struggling for hours to complete a repair when if you had the correct tool, you could accomplish in minutes.

FIGURE 5-37 Screws are generally smaller than bolts and are sometimes referred to as metal threads.

FIGURE 5-38 A. An Allen head screw and **B.** an Allen wrench set.

Different screws can be tightened with a range of tools. An **Allen head screw** has a recess for an **Allen wrench** (**FIGURE 5-38**). An Allen head screw is sometimes called a hex head screw. It usually screws into a hole rather than a nut, and it needs to be tightened with an Allen wrench.

FIGURE 5-39 A machine screw.

A **machine screw** has a slot for a screwdriver (**FIGURE 5-39**).

Screwdrivers come in many sizes, and you should always use the correct size of blade for the machine screw slot. There are several special screws that cut their own threads as they go. This is called *tapping a thread.* Pictured in **FIGURE 5-40A** is a **self-tapping screw**. It is made of hard material that cuts a

FIGURE 5-40 Self-tapping screws.

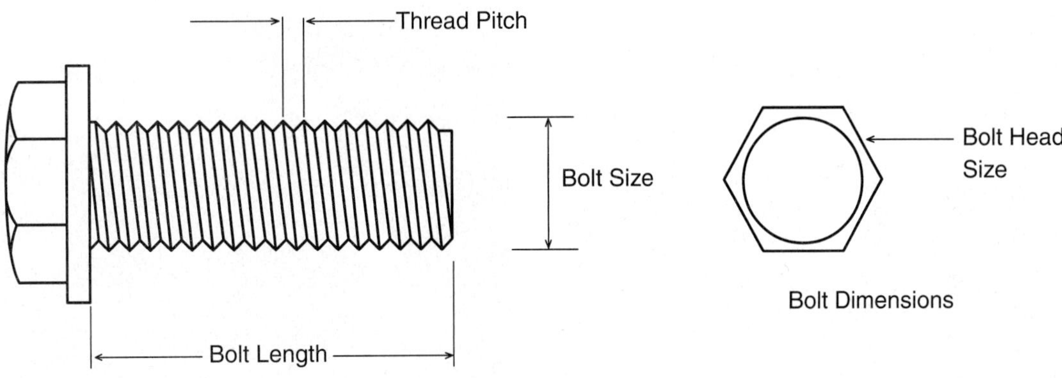

FIGURE 5-41 Bolt nomenclature.

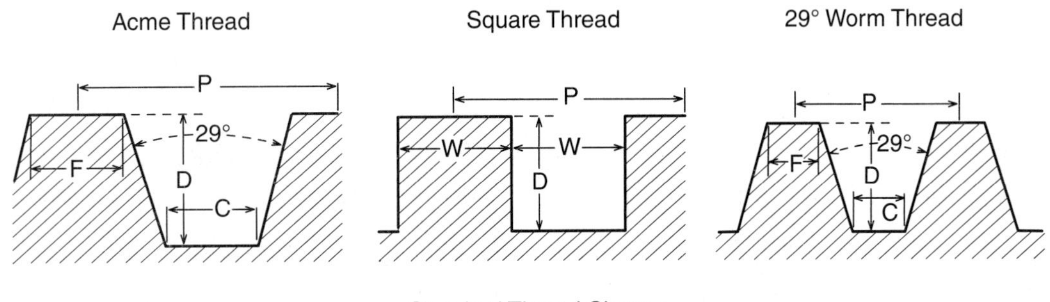

FIGURE 5-42 Standard thread shapes.

mirror image of itself into the hole as you turn it. The screw in **FIGURE 5-40B** is also known as a self-tapping screw, but it is designed for cutting and holding thin sheet metal, so it is often used on car bodies.

Bolts, Studs, and Nuts

Bolts, studs, and nuts are fasteners designed for heavier jobs than screws and tend to be made of metal or metal alloys. **Bolts** are cylindrical pieces of metal with a hexagonal head on one end and a thread cut into the shaft at the other end (**FIGURE 5-41**). They are often bigger than screws and are used for heavier jobs. Bolts are always threaded into a nut or hole that has an identical thread cut inside. The thread acts as an inclined plane; as the bolt is turned, it is drawn into or out of the matching thread.

▶ TECHNICIAN TIP

Threads are cut on screws, bolts, nuts, and studs and inside holes to allow components to be attached and assembled. There was a time when there were many different thread designs used throughout the world. Modern equipment still use a range of thread patterns, but due to standardization, it is getting much simpler (**FIGURE 5-42**). Nearly all the nuts, bolts, screws, and studs on a vehicle have a V-thread cut into them. A screw jack or a clamp has square threads cut into it. The square thread is more difficult to machine and is used mainly when rotational movement needs to be transferred into lateral movement—for example, the screw in a vice where the rotary movement of turning the handle is translated into the lateral movement of the jaws closing.

Nuts are often used with bolts. A nut is a piece of metal, usually hexagonal, with a thread cut through it to fit the bolt thread. The hexagonal heads for the bolt and nut are designed to fit tools such as combination wrenches and sockets (**FIGURE 5-43**).

Torx drivers are used for **torx screws**, which enable more tightening torque to be applied to a screw than a similar-sized hex head screw would without damaging the head. Because they better resist coming out, they are often found in engines or places with limited space and a compact screw head is required (**FIGURE 5-44**).

FIGURE 5-43 Bolts usually have hexagonally shaped heads.

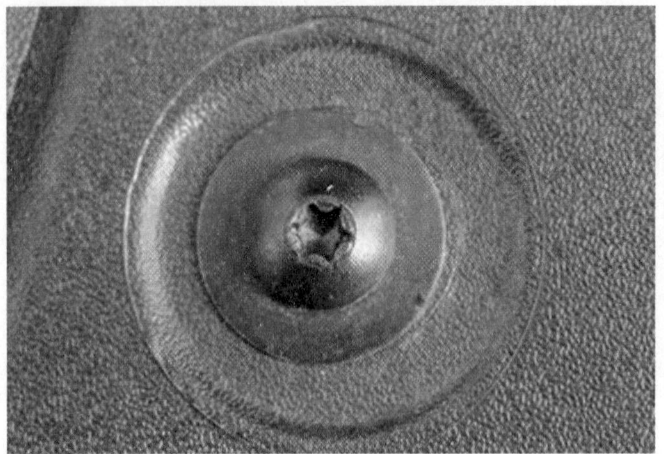

FIGURE 5-44 Torx screws are often found in places such as cylinder heads to engine blocks, where high-tightening torque is required and there is limited space for a larger fastener.

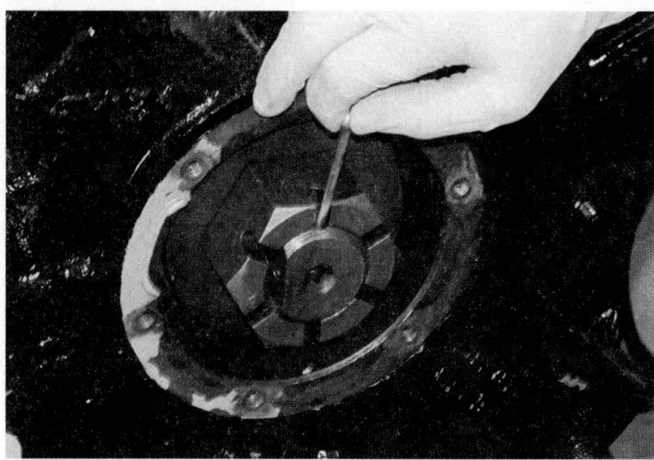

FIGURE 5-46 A castellated nut.

FIGURE 5-45 A self-locking nut is highly resistant to being loosened by engine vibrations.

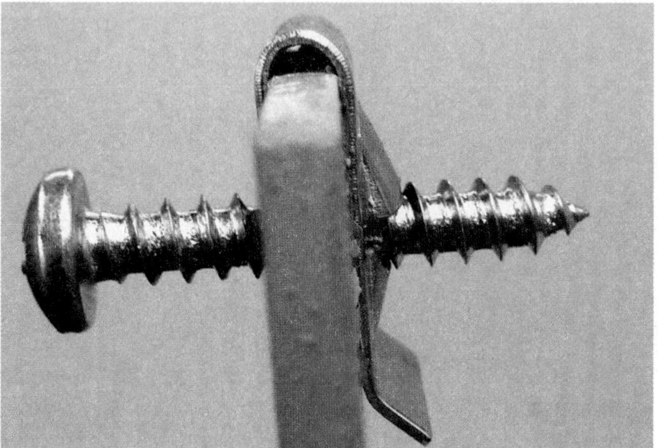

FIGURE 5-47 Speed nut.

There are many ways to keep the nut and bolt done up tightly. A self-locking or **nyloc nut** can have a plastic or nylon insert. Tightening the bolt squeezes it into the insert, where it resists any movement. The self-locker is highly resistant to being loosened by vibration between parts (**FIGURE 5-45**). Tightening this style of nut distorts the insert, so it provides its locking effect only the first time you use it. If you remove the nut, it should be replaced with a new one.

A **castellated nut** has slots like towers on a castle (**FIGURE 5-46**). When it is screwed onto a bolt that has been drilled in the right spot, a split pin can be passed through them both and then spread open to lock the nut in place. Castellated nuts are a very secure type of fastener used when safety is critical. They are also used when scheduled maintenance requires inspection and adjustments to take place for items such as front wheel bearings.

A **speed nut** is not as strong as the other types, but it can be a fast and convenient way to secure a screw (**FIGURE 5-47**). Once the speed nut has been started, it does not need to be held. These are often used in places like body component fixings. Some bolts and nuts need washers. Washers can be made from several materials depending on their application, including aluminum, copper, fiber, and steel.

Here are some brief descriptions of the more common washers:

- **Flat washers** spread the load of a bolt head or a nut as it is tightened and distribute it over a greater area (**FIGURE 5-48A**). This protects the surface underneath from being marked by the nut or head as it turns and tightens down. Flat washers should always be used to protect aluminum alloy.
- A **spring (lock) washer** compresses as the nut tightens, and the nut is spring-loaded against this surface, which makes it unlikely to work loose (**FIGURE 5-48B**). The ends of the spring washer also bite into the metal. Spring washers are used more for bolts and nuts.
- Screws mostly rely on smaller **serrated-edge shake-proof washers** (**FIGURE 5-48C**). The external ones have teeth on the outside, and the internal ones have teeth on the inside; one type has both.

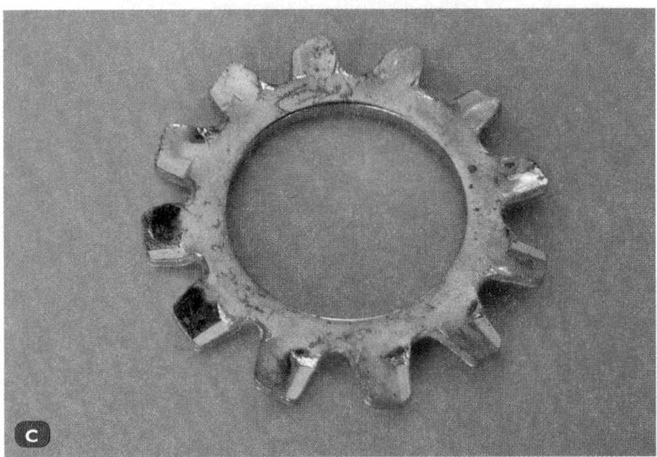

FIGURE 5-48 Types of washers: **A.** Flat washer. **B.** Spring washer. **C.** Serrated edge shake-proof washers. **D.** Spindle washer.

- **Spindle washers** are used behind a wheel bearing. The key or tab on the washer (**FIGURE 5-48D**) prevents the washer from spinning due to bearing rotation.

Often, the thread on a stud is only as long as it needs to be to tighten onto the nut or into the threaded hole. Some special versions have both a left- and right-hand thread on them. A **stud** (**FIGURE 5-49**) is like two bolts in one; for instance, an exhaust manifold on the cylinder head is normally located and held by studs and nuts. A stud does not have a fixed hexagonal head; rather, it is one continuously threaded piece. When a stud is used, it is threaded into one part, where it stays. The mating part is then slipped over it and a nut is threaded onto the end of the stud to secure the part. Studs are commonly used to attach an axle shaft flange to the hub, and they can have different threads on each end. Bolts, nuts, and studs can have either standard or metric threads. They are designated by their thread diameter, thread pitch, length, and grade. The diameter is measured across the outside of the threads; it is measured in fractions of an inch for standard-type fasteners and millimeters for metric-type fasteners. A ⅜ inch (9.5 mm) bolt has a thread diameter of ⅜ inch (9.5 mm); ⅜ inch (9.5 mm) is not the size of the bolt head.

FIGURE 5-49 A stud has threads on both ends.

The **standard (imperial) system** also uses a marking system to indicate tensile strength, as shown in **FIGURE 5-50**. This is a grade 5 bolt, which can be tightened to specific torque as specified by the manufacturer. **Torque** is a way of defining how much a fastener should be tightened.

The metric, or SI, system uses numbers stamped on the heads of metric bolts and on the face of metric nuts (**FIGURE 5-51**). Even

FIGURE 5-50 Tensile strength markings using the standard system—a grade 5 bolt.

FIGURE 5-51 Bolts and nuts are often marked to indicate how much torque can be safely applied to them. Markings using the metric system are shown here.

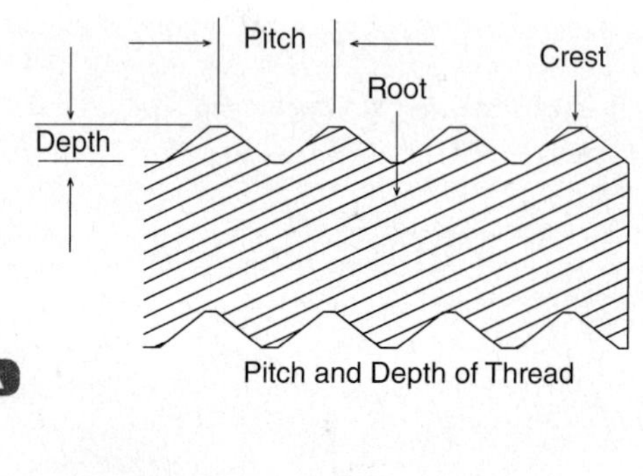

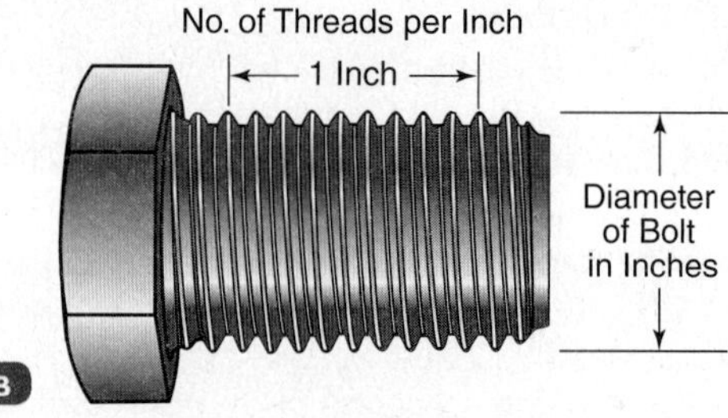

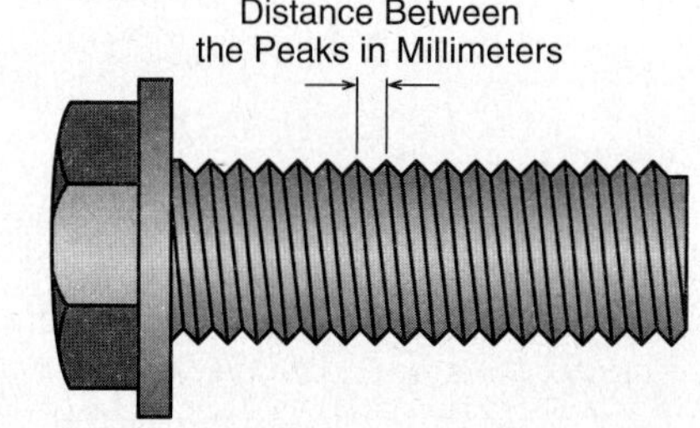

FIGURE 5-52 A. The terms when describing a thread are marked in this illustration. **B.** In the standard system, pitch is measured in threads per inch (tpi). **C.** In the metric system, the thread pitch is measured by the distance between the peaks of the threads in millimeters.

studs have a marking system to make sure they are not overstressed when you tighten them.

The numbers indicate the *tensile strength* of the bolt. The number does *not* mean the size of the bolt. *Note*: The distance between flats on the bolt or nut heads generally indicates the wrench size to be used. The number of threads along the length of a fastener is called **thread pitch** (**FIGURE 5-52A**). In the standard system, the thread pitch is measured in threads per inch (tpi), which is the distance between the peaks of the threads in inches (**FIGURE 5-52B**). Each bolt diameter in the metric system can have up to four thread pitches. Metric threads, designated with a capital M, are rated according to their outer diameter and their pitch (**FIGURE 5-52C**).

▶ TECHNICIAN TIP

The global version of metric is called the International System of Units, or SI. The standard system of inch-pounds is still used by some manufacturers, particularly in the United States. The metric system, however, has produced some competing classifications for fasteners. For example, metric hex cap screws may have three different standards:

1. DIN 931 (DIN 933 fully threaded)
2. ISO 4014 (ISO 4017 fully threaded)
3. ANSI/ASME B18.2.3.1M.

These three standards are interchangeable, differing primarily in the width across the flat dimensions.

The length of a bolt is fairly straightforward. It is measured from the end of the bolt to the bottom of the head and is listed in inches or millimeters. The grade of a fastener relates to its strength. The higher the grade number, the higher the **tensile strength**, which refers to how much tension it can withstand before it breaks. Tensile strength for fasteners is generally listed in pounds per square inch (psi) or megapascals (MPa) of bolt shaft area.

▶ TECHNICIAN TIP

Many bolts and nuts need to be tightened to a specified level—tight enough to hold components together but not so tight that the component or the fastener could fail. This force applied to a fastener used to tighten it is called the **torque specification**. Bolts and nuts are often marked with grades to indicate their strength, which determines how much torque can safely be applied to them. For example, a grade 8 bolt is stronger than a grade 5 bolt and can be tightened to a higher torque. The specific torque required for every bolt on the vehicle should always be obtained from the manufacturer's technical information system. Once bolts are tightened, there are different ways to ensure they stay tight. For example, a locking washer, a locking chemical compound, or a nylon locking device built into the nut may be used.

Fasteners and Torque

Fasteners are designed to secure parts that are under various tension and shear stresses. The nature of the stresses placed on parts and fasteners depends on their use and location. For example, head bolts withstand *tension stresses* by clamping the head gasket between the cylinder head and the block. The bolts must withstand the very high combustion pressures trying to push the head off the engine block in order to leak past the head gasket. An example of fasteners withstanding *shear stresses* is wheel studs and wheel nuts. They clamp the wheel assembly to the suspension system, and the weight of the vehicle tries to shear the lug studs. If this were to happen, the wheel would fall off the vehicle, leading to an accident. To accomplish their job, fasteners come in a variety of diameters and levels of hardness, which are defined in tensile strength grades. Fasteners with screw threads are designed to be tightened to a specific torque depending on the job at hand, the tensile strength or hardness of the material they are made from, their size, and the thread pitch. If a fastener is overtightened, it could become damaged or could break. If it is under-tightened, it could work loose over time.

Torque Charts

Torque specifications for bolts and nuts in vehicles will usually be contained within shop manuals. Bolt, nut, and stud manufacturers also produce torque charts, which contain all the information you need to determine the maximum torque of bolts or nuts (**FIGURE 5-53**). For example, most charts include the bolt diameter, threads per inch (mm), grade, and maximum torque setting for both dry and lubricated bolts and nuts (**TABLE 5-1**). A lubricated bolt and nut will reach maximum torque value at a lower setting. In practice, most torque specifications call for the nuts and bolts to have dry threads prior to tightening. There are some exceptions, so closely examining the torque specification chart is critical.

In the absence of torque specifications the values below can be used as a guide to the maximum safe torque for a specific diameter/grade of fastener. The torque specification is for clean dry threads, if the threads are oiled reduce the torque by 10%.

Bolt Diameter	Bolt Grade Marking									
	4.6		4.8		8.8		10.9		12.9	
	Maximum Torque		Maximum Torque		Maximum Torque		Maximum Torque		Maximum Torque	
	lb ft	Nm	lb ft	Nm	lb ft	Nm	lb ft	Nm	lb ft	Nm
M4	0.8	1.1	1	1.5	2	3	3	4.5	4	5
M5	1.5	2.5	2	3	4.5	6	6.5	9	7.5	10
M6	3	4	4	5.5	7.5	10	1.1	15	13	18
M8	7	9.5	10	13	18	25	26	35	33	45
M10	14	19	18	25	37	50	55	75	63	85
M12	26	35	33	45	63	85	97	130	111	150
M14	37	50	55	75	103	140	151	205	177	240
M16	59	80	85	115	159	215	232	315	273	370
M18	81	110	118	160	225	305	321	435	376	510
M20	118	160	166	225	321	435	457	620	535	725
M22	159	215	225	305	435	590	620	840	726	985

FIGURE 5-53 Torque specification chart.

TABLE 5-1 U.S. Bolt Torque Specifications

	SAE Grade	5 (Dry)	7 (Dry)	8 (Dry)
Bolt Diameter	Threads per Inch	Torque (lb-ft)	Torque (lb-ft)	Torque (lb-ft)
¼"	20	8	10	12
¼"	28	10	12	14
5/16"	18	17	21	25
5/16"	24	19	24	29
⅜"	16	30	40	45
⅜"	24	35	45	50
7/16"	14	50	60	70
7/16"	20	55	70	80
½"	13	75	95	110
½"	20	90	100	120
9/16"	12	110	135	150
9/16"	18	120	150	170
⅝"	11	150	140	220
⅝"	18	180	210	240
¾"	10	260	320	380
¾"	16	300	360	420
⅞"	9	430	520	600
⅞"	14	470	580	660
1"	8	640	800	900
1"	12	710	860	990

Torque Wrenches

A **torque wrench** is also known as a tension wrench (**FIGURE 5-54**).

It is used to tighten fasteners to a predetermined torque. It is designed to tighten bolts and nuts using the drive on the end, which fits with any socket and accessory of the same drive size found in an ordinary socket set. Although manufacturers do not specify torque settings for every nut and bolt, it is important to follow the specifications when they do. For example, manufacturers recommend a specific torque for cylinder head bolts. The torque specified will ensure that the bolt provides the proper clamping pressure and will not come loose, but will not be so tight as to risk breaking the bolt or stripping the threads (**FIGURE 5-55**).

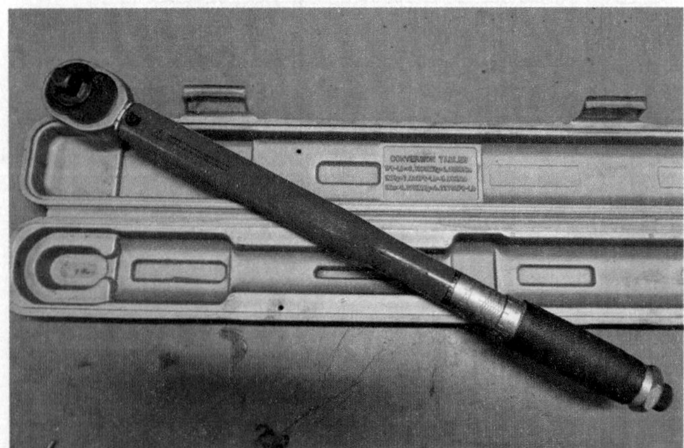

FIGURE 5-54 The torque wrench has an adjustable handle, which allows technicians to adjust to the correct tightening torque specification for the job.

FIGURE 5-55 The torque wrench is fitted over the wheel locking nuts and tightened to the specified torque.

The torque value will be specified in foot-pounds (ft-lb) or newton meters (N·m). The torque value is the amount of twisting force applied to a fastener by the torque wrench. For example, foot-pound (newton meter) is described as the amount of twisting force applied to a shaft by a perpendicular lever 1 foot (meter) long with a force of 1 pound (newton) applied to the outer end. A torque value of 100 ft-lb will be the same as applying a 100-pound force to the end of a 1-foot–long lever. (*One ft-lb is equal to 1.35 N·m.*) Torque wrenches come in various types: beam-style, clicker, dial, and electronic (**FIGURE 5-56**).

The simplest and least expensive is the *beam-style* torque wrench. It uses a spring steel beam that flexes under tension. A smaller fixed rod then indicates the amount of torque on a scale mounted to the bar. The amount of deflection of the bar coincides with the amount of torque on the scale. One drawback of this design is that you must be positioned directly above the scale so you can read it accurately. That can be a problem when working in a confined space. The *clicker-style* torque wrench uses an adjustable clutch inside that slips (clicks) when the preset torque is reached. You can set it for a particular torque on the handle. As the bolt is tightened, once the preset torque is reached, the torque wrench will click. This makes it especially useful in situations where the scale of a beam-style torque wrench cannot be read. The higher the torque, the louder the click; the lower the torque, the quieter the click. Be careful when using this style of torque wrench, especially at lower torque settings. It is easy to miss the click and then overtighten, break, or strip the bolt. Once the torque wrench clicks, stop turning it, as it will continue to tighten the fastener if you turn it past the click point. The *dial* torque wrench turns a dial that indicates the torque based on the torque being applied. Like the beam-style torque wrench, you must be able to see the dial to know how much torque is being applied. Many dial torque wrenches have a movable indicator that is moved by the dial and stays at the highest reading. That way, you can double-check the torque achieved once the torque wrench is released. Once the proper torque is reached, the indicator can be moved back to zero for the next fastener being torqued.

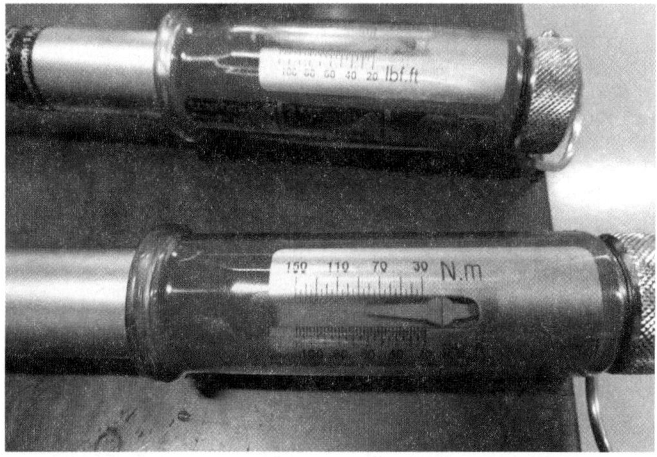

FIGURE 5-56 Torque wrench.

The *digital* torque wrench usually uses a spring steel bar with an electronic strain gauge to measure the amount of torque being applied. The torque wrench can be preset to the desired torque. It will then display the torque as the fastener is being tightened. When it reaches the preset torque, it will usually give an audible signal, such as a beep. This makes it useful in situations where a scale or dial cannot be read. Torque wrenches fall out of calibration over time or if they are not used properly, so they should be checked and calibrated annually. This can be performed in the shop if the proper calibration equipment is available, or the torque wrench can be sent to a qualified service center.

Most quality torque wrench manufacturers provide a recalibration service for their customers.

To help ensure that the proper amount of torque gets from the torque wrench to the bolt, support the head of the torque wrench with one hand (**FIGURE 5-57**).

When using a torque wrench, it is best not to use extensions. Extensions twist and deflect when used, which reduces the actual amount of torque applied to a fastener. If possible, use a deep socket rather than adding an extension. Torque is not always the best method of ensuring that a bolt is tightened enough to give the proper amount of clamping force. If the threads are rusty, rough, or damaged in any way, the amount of twisting force required to overcome thread friction increases. Tightening a rusty fastener to a particular torque will not provide as much clamping force as a smooth fastener torqued the same amount. All threads must be clean before tightening the fastener to a specified torque. This also brings up the question of whether threads should be lubricated. In most cases, the torque values specified are for dry, nonlubricated threads, but always check the manufacturer's specifications. When bolts are tightened, they are also stretched. If they are not tightened too much, they will return to their original length when loosened. This is called **elasticity**. If they continue to be tightened and stretch beyond their point of elasticity, they will not return to their original length when

FIGURE 5-57 Ensure the proper amount of torque gets from the torque wrench to the bolt by supporting the head of the torque wrench with one hand.

loosened. This is called the **yield point**. **Torque-to-yield (TTY)** means that a fastener is torqued to, or just beyond, its yield point. With the changes in engine metallurgy that manufacturers are using in modern vehicles, bolt technology has had to change as well. To help prevent bolts from loosening over time and to maintain an adequate clamping force when the engine is both cold and hot, manufacturers have adopted "stretch" or (TTY) bolts.

TTY bolts are designed to provide a consistent clamping force when tightened to their yield point or just beyond. It is important to note that in virtually all cases, TTY bolts cannot be reused, because they have been stretched into their yield zone and would very likely fail if re-torqued. Always check the manufacturer's specifications when doing this because some manufacturers say that the bolt must be changed once a maximum length has been reached. Another tightening procedure is the **torque angle** method. Torque angle is considered a more precise method to tighten bolts and is a multistep process (**FIGURE 5-59**). Bolts are first tightened to a specific torque, and then an additional number of turns, degrees of rotation, or flat rotation are made (**FIGURE 5-58**).

To use a torque wrench and torque angle gauge, follow the guidelines in **SKILL DRILL 5-7**.

FIGURE 5-58 Torque sequence.

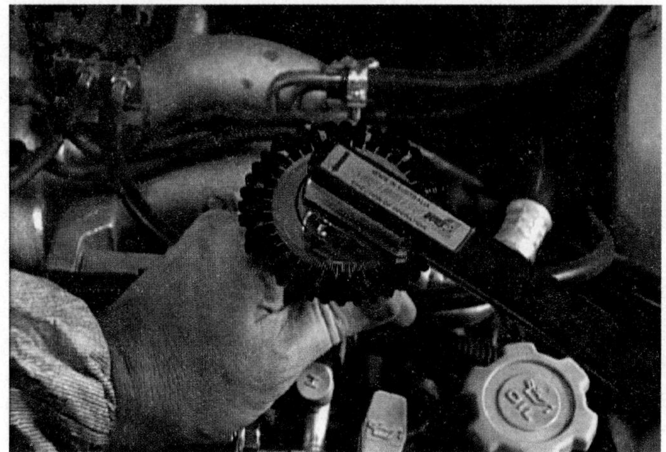

FIGURE 5-59 Angle gauge.

SAFETY TIP

For your safety,

- refer to the manufacturer's specifications when tightening fasteners
- return the torque wrench to its lowest setting when finished
- if replacing a fastener, make sure it has the correct tensile value for the task it will perform.

SKILL DRILL 5-7 Using a Torque Wrench and Torque Angle Gauge

1. Clean and install a bolt. Lightly tighten the bolt with a hand ratchet.
2. Check the specifications. Determine the correct torque value and sequence for the bolts or fastener you are using. This will be in foot-pounds (ft-lb) or newton meters (N·m). Also, check the torque angle specifications for the bolt or fastener and whether the procedure requires only one step or more than one step.
3. Tighten the bolt to the specified torque. If the component requires multiple bolts or fasteners, make sure to tighten them all to the same torque value in the sequence and follow the steps specified by the manufacturer. Some torquing procedures could call for four or more steps to complete the torquing process. For example, vehicle specifications as follows:
   a. Step 1: Torque bolts to 30 foot-pounds (40 newton meters).
   b. Step 2: Torque bolts to 44 foot-pounds (60 newton meters)
   c. Step 3: Finally, tighten the bolt a further 90 degrees.

▶ Wrap-Up

To become a successful MORE technician you must become an expert in tools, fasteners, and measuring equipment. Know how to select the proper tool for the job, how to use it, and how to maintain your tools. Your personal tools will likely become one of your largest financial investments, so take good care of them.

Ready for Review

- Tools and equipment should be used only for the task they were designed to do.
- Always have a safe attitude when using tools and equipment and wear necessary personal protection equipment.
- Do not use damaged tools; inspect them before using, then clean and inspect again before putting them away.
- Fasteners will use external markings to designate their grade and type of thread.
- Micrometers can be outside, inside, or depth.
- Gauges are used to measure distances and diameters; types include telescoping, split ball, and dial bore.
- Dial indicators are used to measure movement.
- A straight edge is designed to assess the flatness of a surface.
- Feeler blades are flat metal strips that are used to measure the width of gaps.
- Air tools use compressed, pressurized air for power; types include the air-impact wrench, air ratchet, air hammer, air drill, and blowgun/air nozzle.
- Sockets grip fasteners tightly on all six corners. Sockets are classified as follows: standard or metric, size of drive used to turn them, number of points, depth of socket, and thickness of wall.
- Threaded fasteners include bolts, studs, and nuts and are designed to secure vehicle parts under stress.
- Torque defines how much a fastener should be tightened.
- Flat washers spread the load on a bolt or nut.
- Metric bolts are sized and classified by millimeters in diameter and the distance in millimeters between the thread peaks.
- Imperial system bolts are sized and classified by the diameter and the number of threads per inch.
- Torque wrenches and torque angle gauges are used to ensure the bolts torque.
- TTY bolts are usually not reusable, because they stretch when they are tightened correctly.

Key Terms

air drill A compressed-air–powered drill.

air hammer A tool powered by compressed air with various hammer, cutting, punching, or chisel attachments. It's also called an air chisel.

air-impact wrench An impact tool powered by compressed air designed to undo tight fasteners. It's also called a rattle gun, or impact gun.

air nozzle A compressed-air device that emits a fine stream of compressed air for drying or cleaning parts.

air ratchet A ratchet tool for use with sockets powered by compressed air.

air tools A tool that is powered by compressed air, also called pneumatic tools.

Allen head screw Sometimes called a hex head screw, it has a hexagonal recess in the head that fits an Allen key. This type of screw usually anchors components in a predrilled hole.

Allen wrench A type of hexagonal drive mechanism for fasteners.

aviation snips A scissor-like tool for cutting sheet metal.

ball-peen (engineer's) hammer A hammer that has a head that is rounded on one end and flat on the other, which is designed to work with metal items.

bench vice A device that securely holds material in jaws while it is being worked on.

blind rivet A rivet that can be installed from its insertion side.

bolt A type of threaded fastener with a thread on one end and a hexagonal head on the other.

bolt cutters Strong cutters available in different sizes, designed to cut through non-hardened bolts and other small-stock material.

bottoming tap A thread-cutting tap designed to cut threads to the bottom of a blind hole.

C-clamp A clamp shaped like the letter C; it comes in various sizes and can clamp various items.

castellated nut A nut with slots, similar to towers on a castle, that is used with split pins; it is used primarily to secure wheel bearings.

closed end A wrench with a closed or ring end to grip bolts and nuts.

club hammer The club hammer is like a small mallet, with two square faces made of high-carbon steel. It is the heaviest type of hammer that can be used one-handed.

combination pliers A type of pliers for cutting, gripping, and bending.

combination wrench A type of wrench that has an open end on one end and a closed-end wrench on the other.

crescent wrench The open-ended adjustable wrench, or crescent wrench, which has an adjustable thumb wheel that moves the lower jaw to grip smaller or larger fasteners.

cross-cut chisel A type of chisel for metal work that cleans out or cuts key ways.

curved file A type of file that has a curved surface for filing holes.

dead-blow hammer A type of hammer that has a cushioned head to reduce the amount of head bounce.

depth micrometers A micrometer that measures the depth of an item such as how far a piston is below the surface of the block.

diagonal-cutting pliers Pliers for small wire or cable.

dial bore gauge A gauge that is used to measure the inside diameter of bores with a high degree of accuracy and speed.

dial indicators A dial that can also be known as a dial gauge, and as the name suggests, it has a dial and needle where measurements are read.

die stock handle A handle for securely holding dies to cut threads.

double flare A seal that is made at the end of metal tubing or pipe.

drift punch A type of punch used to start pushing roll pins to prevent them from spreading.

drill vice A tool with jaws that can be attached to a drill press table for holding material that is to be drilled.

elasticity The amount of stretch or give a material has.

fasteners Devices that securely hold items together, such as screws, cotter pins, rivets, and bolts.

feeler gauges Flat metal strips used to measure the width of gaps, such as the clearance between valves and rocker arms; also called feeler blades.

finished rivet A rivet after the completion of the riveting process.

flare-nut wrench A type of closed-end wrench that has a slot in the box section to allow the wrench to slip through a tube or pipe. It's also called a flare-tubing wrench.

flat-nosed pliers Pliers that are flat and square at the end of the nose.

flat tip screwdriver A type of screwdriver that fits a straight slot in screws.

flat washers Spread the load of bolt heads or nuts as they are tightened and distribute it over a greater area. They are particularly useful in protecting aluminum alloy.

gasket scraper A broad, sharp, flat blade to assist in removing gaskets and glue.

gear pullers A tool with two or more legs and a cross-bar with a center forcing screw to remove gears.

grease gun A device used to force grease into an item, usually a grease fitting. It can be powered by hand, compressed air, or electricity.

impact driver A tool that is struck with a blow to provide an impact turning force to remove tight fasteners.

inside micrometer A micrometer that measures inside dimensions.

intermediate tap One of a series of taps designed to cut an internal thread; also called a plug tap.

locking pliers A type of plier where the jaws can be set and locked into position.

machine screw A screw with a slot for screwdrivers.

magnetic pickup tools An extending shaft, often flexible, with a magnet fitted to the end for picking up metal objects.

mandrel The shaft of a pop rivet.

mechanical fingers Spring-loaded fingers at the end of a flexible shaft that pick up items in tight spaces.

mechanic's mirror A small mirror on a stick that can be adjusted to view leaks, identify tags, and find dropped parts and tools. It can be placed into areas that are difficult to view or access.

mobile off-road equipment (MORE) Mobile equipment designed specifically for off-highway use. Examples are front-end loaders, back-hoes, haul trucks, trenchers, mining equipment, etc.

needle-nosed pliers Pliers with long tapered jaws for gripping small items and getting into tight spaces.

nippers Pliers designed to cut protruding items level with the surface.

nut A fastener with a hexagonal head and internal threads for screwing on bolts.

nyloc nut Keeps the nut and bolt done up tightly; it can have a plastic or nylon insert. Tightening the bolt squeezes it into the insert, where it resists any movement. The self-locker is highly resistant to being loosened.

offset screwdriver A screwdriver with a 90-degree bend in the shaft for working in tight spaces.

offset vice A vice that allows long objects to be gripped vertically.

oil-filter wrench A wrench used to grip and loosen an oil filter. Not to be used for tightening an oil filter.

open-ended adjustable wrench The open-ended adjustable wrench, or crescent wrench, has an adjustable thumb wheel that moves the lower jaw to grip smaller or larger fasteners.

open-end wrench A wrench with open jaws to allow side entry to a nut or bolt.

outside micrometer A micrometer that measures the outside dimensions of an item.

peening A term used to describe the action of flattening a rivet through a hammering action.

personal protective equipment (PPE) Safety equipment designed to protect the technician, such as safety boots, gloves, clothing, protective eyewear, and hearing protection.

Phillips screwdriver A type of screwdriver that fits a head shaped like a cross in screws. It's also called a Phillips head screwdriver.

pin punch A type of punch in various sizes with a straight or parallel shaft.

pliers A hand tool with gripping jaws.

pop-rivet gun A hand tool for installing pop rivets.

press fit An interference fit, also called a press fit or friction fit, is a means of fastening two parts together so that they are in direct contact with one another and are held in place only by friction, or the tightness of the fit. There is negative clearance between the interference fit parts, so they must be pressed or forced together.

prick punch A punch with a sharp point for accurately marking a point on metal.

pry bars A high-strength carbon-steel rod with offsets for levering and prying.

pullers A generic term to describe hand tools that mechanically assist the removal of bearings, gears, pulleys, and other parts.

punches A generic term to describe a high-strength carbon-steel shaft with a blunt point for driving. Center and prick punches are exceptions and have a sharp point for marking or making an indentation.

ratchet A generic term to describe a handle for sockets that allows the user to select the direction of rotation. It can turn sockets in restricted areas without the user having to remove the socket from the fastener.

ratcheting closed-end wrench A closed-end wrench that has a ratcheting mechanism so that the tool does not have to be removed, to continue turning.

ratcheting open-end wrench An open-end wrench that can be moved slightly and then repositioned so that the tool does not have to be completely removed in order to continue turning it.

ratcheting screw driver A screwdriver with a selectable ratchet mechanism built into the handle that allows the screwdriver tip to ratchet as it is being used.

safe working load (SWL) The maximum safe lifting load for lifting equipment.

screws Usually smaller than bolts and are sometimes referred to as metal threads. They can have a variety of heads and are used on smaller components. The thread often extends from the tip to the head so they can hold together components of variable thickness.

screw extractor A tool for removing broken screws or bolts.

self-tapping screw A screw that cuts down its own thread as it goes. It is made of hard material that cuts a mirror image of itself into the hole as you turn it.

serrated-edge shake-proof washer A washer that is used to anchor smaller screws.

single flare A sealing system made on the end of metal tubing.

sliding T-handle A handle fitted at 90 degrees to the main body that can be slid from side to side.

snap ring pliers A pair of pliers for installing and removing internal or external snap rings.

socket An enclosed metal tube commonly with 6 or 12 points to remove and install bolts and nuts.

soft-face steel hammers A type of hammer featuring a drop forged head specifically designed to mushroom when striking hard base materials are gaining popularity for added safety against chipping and spalling causing injury.

speed brace A U-shaped socket wrench that allows high-speed operation. It's also called a speeder handle.

speed nut A nut usually made of thin metal; it does not need to be held when started, but it is not as strong as a conventional nut. It's a fast and convenient way to secure a screw.

split ball gauge (small hole gauge) A gauge that is good for measuring small holes where telescoping gauges cannot fit.

spring washer A washer that compresses as the nut tightens; the nut is spring-loaded against this surface, which makes it unlikely that it will work loose. The ends of the spring washer also bite into the metal.

square file A type of file with a square cross-section.

square thread A thread type with square shoulders used to translate rotational to lateral movement.

standard (imperial) Bolts, nuts, and studs can have either metric or imperial threads. They are designated by their thread diameter, thread pitch, length, and grade. Imperial measures are in feet, inches, and fractions of inches. Most countries use metric.

steel ruler A ruler that is made from stainless steel. Stainless steel rulers commonly come in 30 mm, 60 mm, and 1 meter lengths.

straight edges A measuring device generally made of steel to check how flat a surface is.

stud A type of threaded fastener with a thread cut on each end, as opposed to having a bolt head on one end.

tab washer A washer that gets its name from the small tabs that are folded back to secure the washer. After the nut or bolt has been tightened, the washer remains exposed and is folded up to grip the flats and prevent movement.

tap A term used to generically describe an internal thread-cutting tool.

tap handle A tool designed to securely hold taps for cutting internal threads.

taper tap A tap with a taper; it is usually the first of three taps used when cutting internal threads.

telescoping A gauge used for measuring distances in awkward spots, such as the bottom of a deep cylinder.

tensile strength The amount of force required before a material deforms or breaks.

thread chaser A device similar to a die that cleans up rusty or damaged threads.

thread pitch The coarseness or fineness of a thread as measured by the distance from the peak of one thread to the next, in threads per inch.

thread repair A generic term to describe a number of processes that can be used to repair threads.

tin snips A cutting device for sheet metal, which works in a similar fashion to scissors.

tool A physical item used to do something or accomplish a goal.

torque The twisting force applied to a shaft that may or may not result in motion.

torque angle A method of tightening bolts or nuts based on angles of rotation.

torque specification Describes the amount of twisting force allowable for a fastener or a specification showing the twisting force from an engine crankshaft, which is supplied by manufacturers.

torque-to-yield (TTY) A method of tightening bolts close to their yield point or the point at which they will not return to their original length.

torque-to-yield (TTY) bolts Bolts that are tightened using the torque-to-yield method.

torque wrench A tool used to measure the rotational or twisting force applied to fasteners.

torx bolt A type of screw with an internal or external six point star shaped head.

tube-flaring tool A tool that makes a sealing flare on the end of metal tubing.

universal joint A flexible joint that goes between two rotating shafts, allowing them to operate at different angles to one another.

vehicle hoist A type of vehicle lifting tool designed to lift the entire vehicle.

vernier caliper An accurate measuring device for internal, external, and depth measurements that incorporates fixed and adjustable jaws.

yield point The point at which a bolt is stretched so hard that it fails; it is measured in pounds per square inch (psi) or kilopascals (kPa) of bolt cross-section.

wad punch A type of punch, which is hollow, used for cutting circular shapes in soft materials, such as gaskets.

warding file A type of thin, flat file with a tapered end.

slip joint pliers Adjustable pliers with parallel jaws that allow you to increase or decrease the size of the jaws by selecting a different set of channels.

welding helmet Protective gear designed for arc welding; it provides protection against foreign articles entering the eye, and the lens is tinted to reduce the glare of the welding arc.

wrench A generic term to describe tools that tighten and loosen fasteners with hexagonal heads.

Review Questions

1. Torque values are measured in __________ meters.
   a. mega
   b. kilo
   c. pound
   d. newton
2. Which of the following are among the many different fasteners used in heavy-duty equipment applications.
   a. Screws
   b. Bolts
   c. Nuts
   d. All of the above
3. __________ strength refers to the amount of force a bolt can take before it fails.
   a. Shaft
   b. Thread
   c. Tensile
   d. Turning
4. Manufacturer's charts showing _____________ will assist in identifying standard and metric sizing.
   a. thread zoning
   b. Fastener sizing
   c. Both A and B
   d. Neither A nor B
5. The ________________ micrometer measures parts that are placed in between the anvil and spindle.
   a. inside
   b. outside
   c. depth
   d. standard
6. ___________ pliers, also called vice grips, are general purpose pliers used to clamp and hold one or more objects.
   a. Arc joint
   b. Locking
   c. Needle-nosed
   d. Flat-nosed

ASE Technician A/Technician B Style Questions

1. Technician A says that you would use an outside micrometer to measure the inside diameter of the bottom of a cylinder. Technician B says that you would use a dial bore gauge to measure the bottom diameter of a cylinder for out of round. Who is correct?
   a. Technician A
   b. Technician B
   c. Both A and B
   d. Neither A nor B
2. Technician A says bolt cutters cut hardened rods. Technician B says tin snips can cut thin sheet metal. Who is correct?
   a. Technician A
   b. Technician B
   c. Both A and B
   d. Neither A nor B
3. Technician A says if a fastener is overtightened, it could become damaged or could break. Technician B says if a fastener is under-tightened, it is likely to be satisfactory for reuse. Who is correct?
   a. Technician A
   b. Technician B
   c. Both A and B
   d. Neither A nor B
4. Technician A says torque specifications for bolts and nuts in vehicles will usually be contained within workshop manuals. Technician B says that in practice, most torque specifications call for the nuts and bolts to have oiled threads prior to tightening. Who is correct?
   a. Technician A
   b. Technician B
   c. Both A and B
   d. Neither A nor B
5. Technician A says one of the tools used to repair damaged bolt holes is the helical insert, more commonly known by its trademark, Heli-Coil. Technician B says Heli-Coils are made of coiled wire and are inserted into a tapped hole that is larger than the desired hole. Who is correct?
   a. Technician A
   b. Technician B
   c. Both A and B
   d. Neither A nor B

6. Technician A says the most commonly used pair of pliers in the shop is the needle-nosed plier. Technician B says the most common is the snap ring plier. Who is correct?
   a. Technician A
   b. Technician B
   c. Both A and B
   d. Neither A nor B
7. Technician A says that a drift punch is also named a starter punch because you should always use it first to get a pin moving. Technician B says a center punch centers a drill bit at the point where a hole is required to be drilled. Who is correct?
   a. Technician A
   b. Technician B
   c. Both A and B
   d. Neither A nor B
8. Technician A states that a tap handle has a right-angled jaw that matches the squared end that all taps have. Technician B states that to cut a thread in an awkward space, a T-shaped tap handle is very convenient. Who is correct?
   a. Technician A
   b. Technician B
   c. Both A and B
   d. Neither A nor B
9. Technician A says that you should use a depth gauge to measure the thrust end play in a shaft. Technician B says that you should use a dial bore gauge. Who is correct?
   a. Technician A
   b. Technician B
   c. Both A and B
   d. Neither A nor B
10. Technician A says that a Torx head fastener is shaped like a star. Technician B says that an Allen (hex) head fastener is shaped like a star? Who is correct?
    a. Technician A
    b. Technician B
    c. Both A and B
    d. Neither A nor B

CHAPTER 6

Oxyacetylene-Heating and Cutting Equipment

Knowledge Objectives

After reading this chapter, you will be able to:

- **K06001** Describe oxyacetylene equipment and components.
- **K06002** Explain safety regulations for heating, cutting, and welding of metals.
- **K06003** Describe oxyacetylene-heating, cutting, and welding processes.
- **K06004** Describe brazing and soldering processes.
- **K06005** Recommend correct repair techniques for welding metal using oxyacetylene equipment.

Industry/Accreditation

After reading this chapter, you will be able to:

- **I06001** Communicate trade-related information using standard terms for oxyacetylene-heating and cutting procedures.

Skills Objectives

After reading this chapter, you will be able to:

- **S06001** Demonstrate the proper procedures for cutting, welding, soldering, and brazing of metals.

Attitude Objectives

After reading this chapter, you will be able to:

- **A06001** Locate and follow appropriate safety procedures when heating, cutting, and welding metal.

▶ Introduction

The use of oxyacetylene equipment for heating, cutting, welding, brazing, and soldering metal is a common practice in many heavy equipment repair shops and industrial settings. Oxyacetylene cutting and welding is based on combining acetylene, which is a highly combustible gas, with oxygen to produce very high flame temperatures that are needed for metal working. Since oxyacetylene equipment does not require electricity and is commonly available in portable outfits, mobile off-road equipment (MORE) service technicians can take it onsite and use it for tasks such as heating and loosening rusted fasteners, cutting pieces of metal, and joining or patching metals. This chapter identifies and describes oxyacetylene equipment and explains safety regulations associated with using the equipment. It also describes heating, cutting, welding, brazing, and soldering processes performed with oxyacetylene equipment and examines some repair techniques that can be used for welding.

FIGURE 6-1 Typical oxyacetylene equipment.

▶ Oxyacetylene Equipment and Components

K06001

A typical oxyacetylene outfit consists of numerous major (standard) components, along with other supplemental components that enable technicians to operate the equipment safely and use the equipment for specific jobs.

FIGURE 6-2 Protective caps and cylinder valves.

Standard Equipment

The major components that make up a typical oxyacetylene outfit include an acetylene cylinder, an oxygen cylinder, a pressure regulator for each cylinder, a **flashback arrestor** on the outlet of each regulator, a hose for each gas, a **check valve** (or a second flashback arrestor) at the end of each hose, and a torch (**FIGURE 6-1**). Many oxyacetylene outfits used in the field are portable–that is, the cylinders and other components are placed on some type of wheeled cart that enables the equipment to be moved safely and easily.

The two cylinders hold the oxygen and acetylene gases under pressure. Each cylinder has a screw-on protective cap that should remain in place when the cylinders are not in use. Removing the protective caps reveals a valve on top of each cylinder that can be opened to allow the gas to flow from the cylinder and closed to shut off the gas flow (**FIGURE 6-2**).

Attached to each cylinder is a pressure regulator that has two pressure gauges (**FIGURE 6-3**). One gauge is called the **cylinder pressure gauge**. It shows how much pressure is in the cylinder. The other gauge is called the **working pressure gauge**. It shows how much pressure is in the hose, or line. The line pressure for each gas can be adjusted using an adjusting screw on the applicable pressure regulator.

Located between the outlet of the pressure regulators and the hoses that lead to the torch handle are flashback arrestors. Flashback arrestors are spring-loaded valves that prevent

You Are the Mobile Heavy Equipment Technician

You are called to a construction site to service a customer's dozer. While you are there, you notice a crack in a frame support underneath the dozer that requires removal before a replacement can be attached. Your service truck is equipped with a portable oxyacetylene cutting torch, so you know you'll be able to make the repair. But you have some questions.

1. Where might you find information about the proper gas pressure settings to use when cutting?
2. Is there a way to identify the proper size and type of cutting torch tip to use?
3. What safety precautions should you use when cutting off the frame member?

FIGURE 6-3 Pressure regulators and gauges.

FIGURE 6-4 Flashback arrestors.

backflow from the torch handle and hoses (**FIGURE 6-4**). More specifically, they prevent a flame from traveling back up the hose to the cylinders in the case of a **flashback**, which occurs when the oxygen and acetylene burn inside the torch handle. During a flashback, the gas flame enters into nozzle or torch and is accompanied by a loud popping sound or hiss. The flame will either extinguish or re-ignite at the nozzle. Flashback happens if the torch valve pressures are set lower than they should be for a particular tip, which produces low gas flow out of the tip. Flashback can also happen if cylinder pressures are too low, or if the torch tip becomes over heated such as when it is held too close to the work.

> ▶ TECHNICIAN TIP
>
> The use and locations of flashback arrestors and check valves on oxyacetylene equipment can vary. Flashback arrestors are positioned between the regulators and the hoses, and check valves are positioned between the hoses and the torch handle. Both flashback arrestors and check valves can be positioned between the regulators and the hoses. In an ideal situation, flashback arrestors are positioned between the regulators and the hoses and between the hoses and the torch handle. While both devices allow flow through the hoses in one direction only—from the cylinders to the torch handle—only a flashback arrestor can prevent a detonation wave caused by a flame inside the torch handle from traveling back up the hose and into the acetylene cylinder. It should also be noted that some torch handles have built-in flashback arrestors and check valves, making it unnecessary to use separate flashback arrestors and check valves at the torch handle.

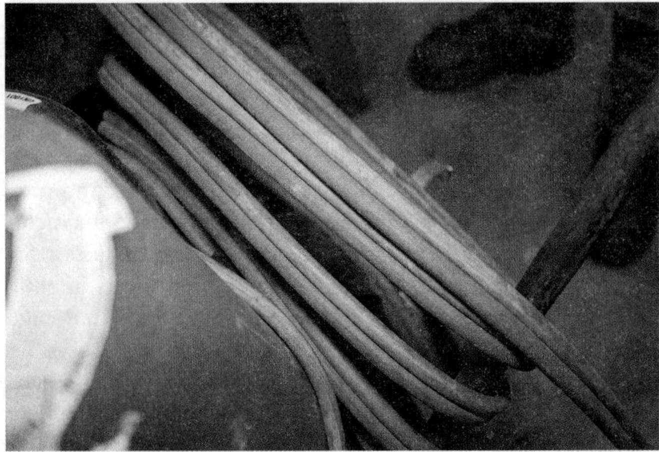

FIGURE 6-5 Twin-line oxyacetylene hose.

The hoses run from the flashback arrestors at the regulators to check valves (or a second set of flashback arrestors) on the torch handle. Different sizes and colors are used for the hoses, but a common convention is red for the acetylene hose and green for the oxygen hose (**FIGURE 6-5**). The oxygen and acetylene hoses are typically connected together for most of their length to form what is called **twin-line hose**.

> ▶ TECHNICIAN TIP
>
> Red and green hoses are typical for oxyacetylene equipment. However, a combination of red hoses is used for acetylene, and blue or black hoses are used for oxygen. To prevent gas connections from inadvertently becoming interchanged, acetylene gas connections use left-hand threads, while oxygen use right-hand threads. This means connections turn in two different directions for each gas when either tightening or loosening fittings. Left-hand threads will typically use a notch mark on the thread fittings.

The torch handle (or torch body) is the part of the equipment that the technician holds and moves about during operation. The torch handle usually has check valves or flashback arrestors screwed into it where the hoses connect. Gas flow control valves that can be used to adjust the flow of oxygen and acetylene are at the base of the handle. The top of the handle is threaded so that different tips and attachments can be installed for heating, cutting, and welding (**FIGURE 6-6**).

Tips and attachments provide an area for the oxygen and acetylene to mix and form a flame at the end of the tip. The tips and attachments used on the torch handle can vary a great deal, depending on the type of work to be done and the type and thickness of the metal being worked on. Torch tip manufacturers provide sizing charts that identify the

FIGURE 6-6 Torch handle.

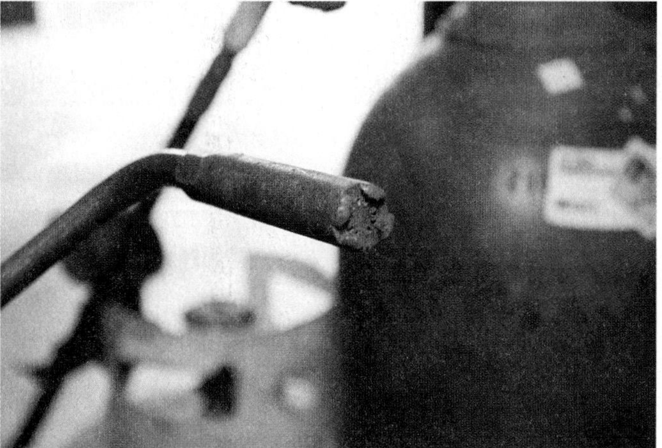

FIGURE 6-7 Torch with rosebud heating tip.

proper tip to use for various metal thicknesses. Such charts also specify the pressures to use for the oxygen and acetylene. Technicians should always follow the tip manufacturers' guidelines when selecting the appropriate tip for the work being performed.

As a general rule, welding tips and special heating tips called **rosebud** tips and **MFA** tips are used for heating metal (**FIGURE 6-7**). Heating tips have numerous holes in the end that produce multiple flames with a wide pattern suitable for heating metal. The flame is directed toward the area of the metal that must be heated. Once the metal is cherry red, it can be bent or otherwise manipulated. As with all tips, heating tips come in various sizes. Technicians should always use the heating tip recommended by the manufacturer.

Cutting metal typically requires a cutting attachment and a cutting tip (**FIGURE 6-8**). A typical cutting attachment has three pipes running to the nozzle—one pipe for oxygen, one pipe for acetylene, and one pipe for oxygen from the oxygen blast lever. When this type of torch is used, the metal to be cut is first heated by an oxyacetylene flame. Once the metal begins to melt, the oxygen blast lever is pressed to provide a high-pressure stream of oxygen to cut through the metal.

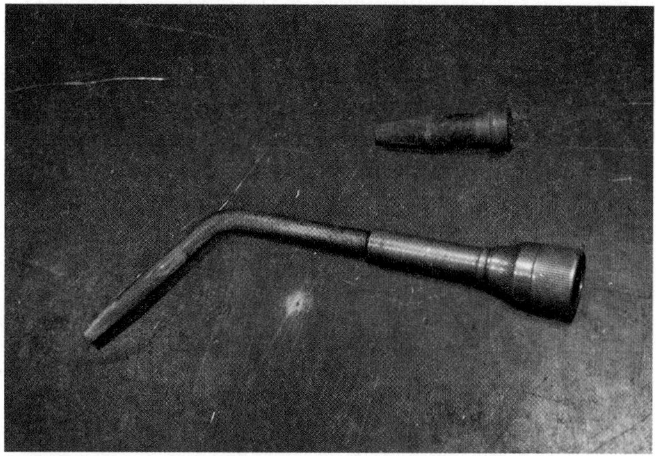

FIGURE 6-8 Torch with cutting attachment and cutting tip.

FIGURE 6-9 Torch with welding tip.

▶ TECHNICIAN TIP

When cutting metal that is greater than 8 inches (203 mm) thick, a dedicated cutting torch must be used instead of a torch handle with a cutting attachment and cutting tip. A cutting torch has the same oxygen and acetylene connections and valves as a typical torch handle, and it has an oxygen blast lever. It is simply built as a single torch that can be used in heavy duty operations.

A torch with a welding tip is used for welding metals (**FIGURE 6-9**). Unlike a cutting torch, a welding torch has no oxygen blast lever. A welding torch may not have any visible pipes running to the nozzle, or it may have only two pipes—one for oxygen and one for acetylene. As with a typical torch handle, a welding torch has gas flow control valves that enable a technician to adjust the flow of oxygen and acetylene.

▶ TECHNICIAN TIP

While a welding torch is designed to weld metal, it can also be used to heat small objects like fasteners that have rusted or seized up. This eliminates the need to change from a welding tip to a heating tip for a small job.

Supplemental Components

Excluding personal protection and safety equipment, there are numerous additional components and tools that are typically used with oxyacetylene equipment. For example, one or more wrenches are needed for loosening and tightening tip, torch, hose, regulator, and cylinder connections on oxyacetylene equipment (**FIGURE 6-10**). The cylinder valves are usually opened with knobs although smaller acetylene cylinders may be opened with a T-wrench. Other connector sizes can vary with the equipment. **FIGURES 6-10A** and **B** show typical oxyacetylene system connections.

A striker is a tool used to light the torch (**FIGURE 6-11**). When the two arms of a striker are squeezed together, the ends of the arms brush against a piece of flint and create sparks that ignite the oxyacetylene fuel. Most strikers use replaceable flints that can be purchased separately.

Tip cleaners are used routinely to remove buildup from cutting and welding tips that block or interfere with gas flow (**FIGURE 6-12**). A common tip cleaner tool has an array of round steel files, or **reamers**, to fit different tip orifice sizes. Most tip cleaner tools include a flat file that can be used to remove buildup on the outside of the tip. Using tip cleaners on a regular basis helps extend the life of the tip and maintain the proper flame pattern.

When oxyacetylene equipment is used to weld, braze, or solder two pieces of metal together, some type of filler metal must be used during the process (**FIGURE 6-13**). The specific filler metal that is used will depend on the metal being joined. Filler metal often comes in the form of filler rods. Gas welding rods range in size from 1/16-inch (1.6 mm) diameter to 1/4-inch (6.4 mm) diameter, with most rods being 36 inches (914 mm) in

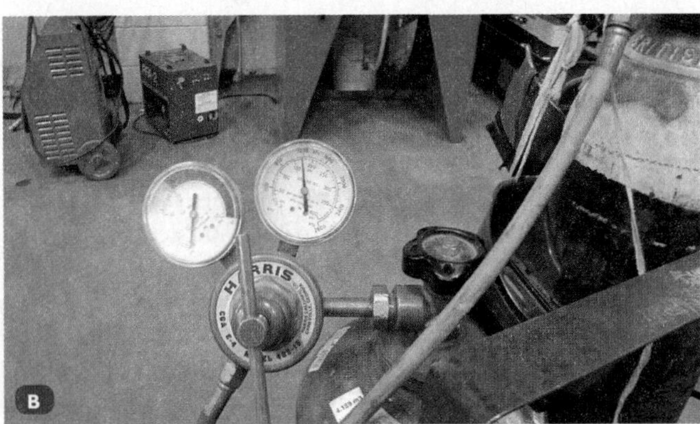

FIGURE 6-10 **A.** Oxygen bottle connections. **B.** Acetylene bottle connections.

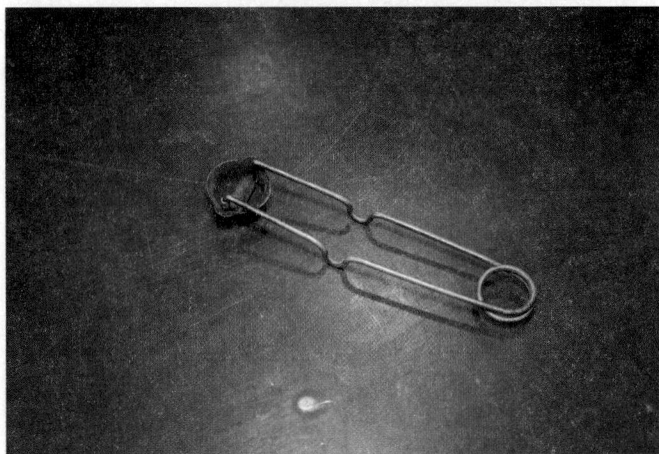

FIGURE 6-11 A striker.

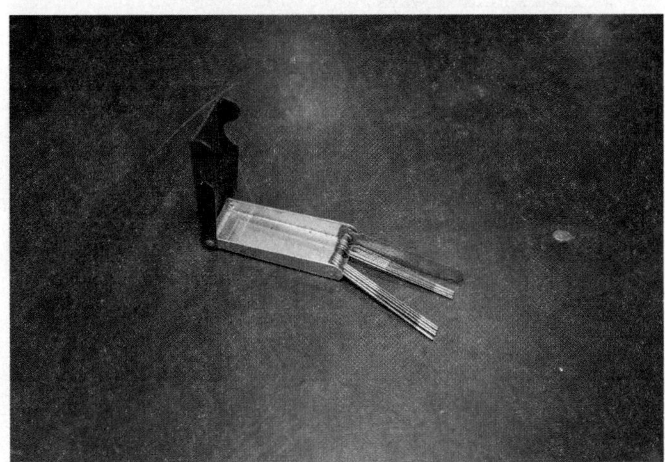

FIGURE 6-12 Torch tip cleaner tool.

FIGURE 6-13 Common filler materials.

length. Common welding rods used for filler material are available as carbon steel, aluminum, and various alloys, including bronze and copper. Filler metals used for brazing and soldering commonly include bronze, sliver solder and other alloys.

▶ Safety Regulations

K06002

Safety must be the first and foremost priority when working with oxyacetylene equipment. Cylinder pressures and flame temperatures alone pose significant hazards. The pressure inside a full cylinder of acetylene is approximately 250 psi (1,724 kPa), while the pressure in an oxygen cylinder is approximately 2,200 psi (15,168 kPa). When acetylene is mixed with oxygen, very high flame temperatures of 6,300°F to 6,800°F (3,480°C to 3,760°C) are produced. To ensure that they protect themselves and other personnel, technicians must follow safety rules related to clothing and protective gear, the work area environment, and the manner in which they use oxyacetylene equipment.

Personal Protective Equipment

Technicians should always wear appropriate personal protective equipment (PPE) when heating, cutting, or welding with oxyacetylene equipment (**FIGURE 6-14**). The exact protective equipment that is needed can vary according to regulations and company standards, the activity being performed, and the work environment.

As a general rule, the following PPE should be worn during oxyacetylene heating, cutting, and welding:

- A solid material (non-mesh) hat made of flame-retardant material. The bill of the hat should be facing to the rear.
- Tight-fitting welding goggles with the proper light-reducing shade for the work being done. The **American National Standards Institute (ANSI)** publishes a shade range guide for various types of welding and cutting activities in its *ANSI Z49.1* standard. A typical shade range for oxyacetylene work is from shade 3 to shade 6, but some heavy welding activities require a shade 8.

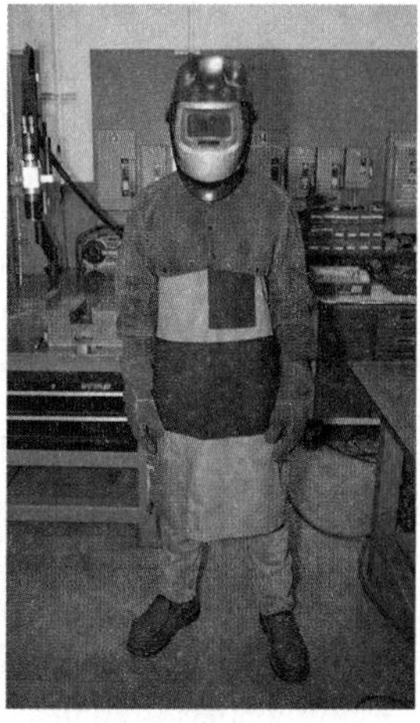

FIGURE 6-14 Typical personal protective equipment.

SAFETY TIP

Sunglasses should not be worn as a substitute for welding goggles because they do not filter the extreme ultraviolet light as effectively. In addition, the plastic used in the lenses of sunglasses will not protect your eyes from sparks.

- A face shield over the welding goggles to protect the face from flying sparks, debris, and heat.
- Earmuffs (or earplugs) to minimize noise and protect ear canals from sparks.

SAFETY TIP

In some applications, such as cutting or welding material overhead, a full leather hood with a properly tinted face plate is preferable to wearing separate welding goggles and a face shield. In addition, if a hard hat is required in the work area, the hard hat must be able to accommodate the face-shield and rear deflector attachments.

- A protective leather apron or, at a minimum, flame-retardant clothing capable of protecting against ultraviolet light and hot sparks. Shirts should have long sleeves; pants should have no cuffs; and jackets should have no pockets, where hot metal can collect.
- Long leather welding gloves to protect hands and arms.
- Leather work boots. The tongue and lace area of each boot should be tall enough to be covered by the pants legs. Otherwise, leather **spats** should be used to cover the front of the boots.

While working around the flames and high heat associated with oxyacetylene heating, cutting, and welding, technicians should not wear jewelry or body-piercing studs. These items can snag on equipment and absorb heat from the torch flame.

Breathing masks or respirators may be required when heating, cutting, or welding certain materials. For example, copper, lead, mercury, zinc, and other materials can produce toxic fumes when heated with a torch. For short-term exposure to some fumes, a technician may be safe using a high-efficiency particulate arresting (HEPA) filter or a metal-fume filter (**FIGURE 6-15**). But if a technician is exposed to such toxic fumes for a long period of time, a full-face supplied-air respirator (SAR) is necessary.

SAFETY TIP

Using oxyacetylene equipment to cut metal containing zinc, such as galvanized steel, may be prohibited in some locations because of the toxic nature of the fumes that are released in the process. Always verify whether flame cutting of galvanized steel is permitted, and if so, be sure to wear the appropriate breathing equipment.

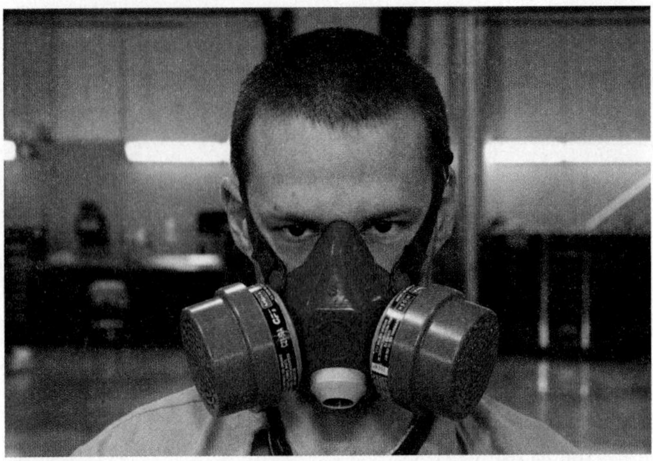

FIGURE 6-15 Worker wearing a respirator.

Work Area Safety

Whenever oxyacetylene equipment is used, there is an inherent risk of fire and explosion. To minimize these and other risks, technicians should always inspect and prepare the machinery or equipment to be worked on, as well as the work area and its surroundings before using oxyacetylene equipment. Maintaining a safe work area typically includes the following:

- Remove flammable materials such as rags, paper, boxes, and flammable liquids from the work area or shield them using a fire-resistant cover. Many work site fires are caused by cutting torches, so maintaining a neat and clean work area can greatly reduce accidental fires.
- Make sure that approved fire extinguishers are readily accessible before starting any heating, cutting, or welding operation.
- Make sure that oxyacetylene equipment is properly positioned at the work site to avoid trip hazards.
- Determine if the work area is a **confined space** or if it requires a hot-work permit or a fire watch. If so, follow all requirements and procedures for the site. Many sites require hot-work permits and fire watches, and failure to abide by these requirements can lead to serious injuries and penalties.
- Make sure that the work area is properly ventilated. This is especially true for confined spaces. Fans, exhaust hoods, and ventilated booths can all be used to provide the necessary ventilation.
- Do not use oxygen to ventilate a work area. Releasing a large amount of oxygen into the work space can cause rapid and uncontrolled combustion if a spark ignites flammable material. Oxygen should be kept away from petroleum products to prevent fire and explosions.
- Never release acetylene into a work area. Acetylene is lighter than air, and if it's mixed with air or oxygen, it can explode at lower concentrations than other fuels.

Safe Equipment Use and Storage

Technicians must follow appropriate safety guidelines when operating and storing oxyacetylene equipment.

Safe Equipment Use

Safe equipment use typically includes the following:

- Never use acetylene at a pressure above 15 psig (103 kPa).
- Turn regulator adjustment screws counterclockwise until they are free before opening cylinder valves. When opening cylinder valves, stand to the side of the regulators.
- Always use an appropriate striker to light the oxyacetylene torch. Never carry matches or gas-filled cigarette lighters or attempt to use them to light the torch. Using matches or lighters requires technicians to position their hand(s) too close to the torch tip. Plus, sparks can ignite matches and cause lighters to explode.
- Use caution when handling a lighted torch. Never point the torch flame toward a person or any flammable material in the area.
- If possible, place a heat shield behind the workpiece being heated, cut, or welded to protect other objects in the area from becoming hot. Also, use chalk or soapstone to write "HOT" on any hot metal to protect other personnel from touching it.
- Before heating, cutting, or welding any kind of tank, barrel, or pipe, make sure the container did not previously contain explosive, hazardous, or flammable materials. Always clean containers and fill them with water or purge them with an inert gas to prevent fire, explosion, or toxic fumes.
- While working, avoid breathing in cutting or welding fumes and smoke. Use a fan, if necessary, to divert the fumes and smoke. Wear an appropriate breathing apparatus to avoid toxic fumes when necessary.
- Never use oxygen to blow dust and dirt off clothing or equipment. Oxygen can remain trapped in clothing and ignite and burn rapidly if exposed to a spark.
- Ensure that all scrap metal or **dross** being discarded has cooled to a point where it does not pose a fire hazard.

Safe Equipment Storage

To minimize fire and explosion hazards, it is critical to follow safety guidelines related to the storage of oxyacetylene equipment that is not in use. Safe equipment storage rules include the following:

- Oxygen cylinders and acetylene cylinders must be stored separately (**FIGURE 6-16**). The cylinders must be kept at least 20 feet (6 meters) apart or separated by a wall that is 5 feet (1.5 meters) high with a minimum 30-minute burn rating. These safeguards are intended to prevent any small fire in the area from causing an oxygen cylinder safety valve to open and fuel an uncontrolled blaze.
- Cylinder storage areas must be located away from exits, halls, and stairwells to avoid blocking escape routes during an emergency. Cylinders should also be located where unauthorized personnel cannot tamper with them and in areas where they will not be affected by heat, radiators, furnaces, and welding sparks. Appropriate warning signs must be posted in the storage area.

FIGURE 6-16 Cylinder storage area.

- Empty cylinders should be stored separately from full cylinders. They can, however, be stored in the same room or area.
- All cylinders must be stored vertically, and their protective caps should be screwed on firmly.
- Because the cylinders store gases at high pressure, they must be secured with a chain or other device to prevent them from being knocked over accidentally. If an oxygen cylinder falls over and the main valve breaks, high-pressure gas inside the cylinder will enable it to become a missile with enough force to penetrate concrete block walls.

▶ Oxyacetylene Heating, Cutting, and Welding

K06003

The processes used to heat, cut, and weld metal using oxyacetylene equipment can involve connecting the components, setting up the equipment so that it can be operated safely and effectively, testing connections for leaks, adjusting the gas valves and regulators to the correct flows and pressures, lighting and adjusting the torch flame, and following the equipment manufacturer's recommendations for performing the appropriate task.

Initial Equipment Setup

If technicians are required to set up oxyacetylene equipment for use, they must follow all the applicable safety precautions, wear the appropriate PPE, and use the equipment manufacturer's guidelines for setup. Most of the initial steps for preparing oxyacetylene equipment to use for heating, cutting, and welding metal are basically the same. While there can be subtle differences in the equipment being used, most oxyacetylene equipment requires the following basic setup steps.

1. Carefully position the cart that is holding the oxygen and acetylene cylinders so that they are close enough for the hoses to reach the work but far enough away to avoid sparks, flames, and intense heat. Both cylinders must be upright and properly secured in the cart with a chain.
2. Before making any connections, clear the cylinder valves on both cylinders. First, remove the protective cap from the acetylene cylinder and place it where it will not be lost. Standing with the cylinder's outlet nozzle pointing away, use a T-wrench or other appropriate tool to briefly crack open the cylinder valve about a one-quarter turn counterclockwise. After a second or two, turn the valve clockwise to close it. Use a clean cloth to wipe out the inside of the valve nozzle to remove any remaining dirt or debris. Repeat the procedure for the oxygen cylinder to ensure that all debris has been cleared.
3. Attach the regulators to the cylinders. Turn the adjusting screw on the acetylene cylinder's valve outlet nozzle counterclockwise until no resistance can be felt. Place the regulator fitting inside the valve nozzle and use a wrench to tighten the regulator nut. Follow the same steps to attach the oxygen regulator to the oxygen cylinder valve. Remember that oxygen and acetylene fittings use right- and left-hand threads, respectively. Never use any oil to lubricate threads since high-pressure oxygen will ignite any oil and grease on the threads.
4. Install a flashback arrestor in each regulator outlet. Follow the equipment manufacturer's recommendations regarding the type and placement of flashback arrestors.
5. Connect the hoses to the flashback arrestors. The red hose should attach to the flashback arrestor on the acetylene regulator, and the green hose should attach to the flashback arrestor on the oxygen regulator. The acetylene hose has a notched fitting, which indicates it is a left-hand thread that must be turned counterclockwise to tighten. The oxygen fitting should be turned clockwise.

▶ TECHNICIAN TIP

New oxyacetylene hoses may have a powder lining the interior. If that is the case, the hoses should first be blown out before connecting. Hold the loose ends of the hoses so that they point away, open the acetylene cylinder valve, and turn the adjusting screw of the acetylene regulator clockwise until the working pressure gauge reads 10 psig (69 kPa). Allow the acetylene to flow out for two seconds, and then close the adjusting screw and the cylinder valve. Repeat the procedure for the oxygen hose.

6. Install a check valve or flashback arrestor between the end of each hose and the torch handle to prevent reverse gas flow (backflow). Make sure that the red acetylene hose is connected to the acetylene check valve and that the green oxygen hose is connected to the oxygen check valve.
7. Identify the proper torch handle for the job and attach it to the check valves on the hose ends. Make sure all connections follow the red and green color coding for hoses. Acetylene hoses and connections are all left-hand threads, while oxygen gas connections are right-hand threads. This means that the acetylene connections are made counterclockwise and the oxygen connections are made clockwise. All connections must be tightened using an appropriate wrench. Check for leaks with soapy water sprayed over all connections after gas pressure is supplied to the hoses.

8. Select the proper type of tip for the work being done. Check the condition of the tip and, if necessary, use a tip cleaning tool to clean the tip before use. Screw the tip onto the torch end and tighten it. The torch tip fitting allows the gas valves on the torch handle to be aligned for a comfortable, easily accessible working position.
9. Test all equipment connections for leaks with soapy water and check for gas leaks by observing whether bubbles appear on connections under gas pressure. Correct any leakage before proceeding further. To do this, first, close the oxygen and acetylene torch valves. Then, turn both valves clockwise to open them. Standing to one side, slowly open the oxygen cylinder valve about a half turn. Turn the adjusting screw for oxygen regulator until the working pressure gauge reads 20 psig (138 kPa). Then open the acetylene cylinder valve a quarter turn, and turn the acetylene regulator adjusting screw until the working pressure gauge reads 5 psig (35 kPa). Close both cylinder valves and watch the cylinder pressure gauges. If there is a drop in pressure on the gauges, there must be a leak. Retighten all the connection fittings and repeat the test. If a leak is still indicated, brush all the fittings and hoses with a **leak test solution** and watch for bubbles to appear at the leak site. If a leak cannot be corrected, replace the fitting, component, or hose as needed.

Heating

Using oxyacetylene equipment to heat metal requires the use of a heating tip that is appropriate for the metal being worked on. Rosebuds and MFA (multiple flame acetylene) tips are used in many heating applications, but technicians should always use the torch tips recommended by the equipment manufacturer. Technicians should also wear the proper PPE when preparing the equipment and heating metal.

The basic process for heating metal using oxyacetylene equipment is as follows:

1. Determine the type and thickness of the metal to be heated.
2. Follow the manufacturer's recommended heating tip size to select the proper tip for the job.
3. Inspect the heating tip for damage or plugged flame holes. Clean the tip with a tip cleaner if necessary.
4. Install and tighten the heating tip according to the manufacturer's instructions.
5. Close the oxygen and acetylene flow control valves on the torch handle.
6. Loosen (back out) the adjusting screws on the oxygen and acetylene regulators.
7. Stand to the side of the oxygen cylinder and slowly open the cylinder valve until the proper pressure is indicated on the regulator working pressure gauge. High gas pressure suddenly released from the cylinder can damage regulator components. Once the pressure on the cylinder pressure gauge rises, open the oxygen cylinder valve all the way. Opening the valve all the way backseats the valve to prevent oxygen leakage past the valve stem.
8. Stand to the side of the acetylene cylinder and slowly open the cylinder valve until the cylinder pressure gauge on the regulator displays the cylinder pressure. Do not open the acetylene cylinder valve more than one and a half turns. This enables the gas to be quickly shut off in the event of an emergency.
9. Open the oxygen flow control valve on the torch handle completely.
10. While the oxygen is flowing, tighten the adjusting screw on the oxygen regulator until the proper working pressure is displayed. Continue the oxygen flow for 10 seconds to purge the hoses and torch.
11. Close the oxygen flow control valve on the torch handle.
12. Open the acetylene flow control valve on the torch handle approximately one-eighth of a turn.
13. While the acetylene is flowing, tighten the adjusting screw on the acetylene regulator until the proper working pressure is displayed. Continue the acetylene flow for 10 seconds to purge the hoses and torch.
14. Close the acetylene flow control valve on the torch handle.

SAFETY TIP

Never let the acetylene working pressure rise above 15 psig (103 kPa). At pressures above 15 psig (103 kPa), acetylene can become unstable and explode.

15. Open the acetylene flow control valve on the torch handle approximately one-quarter of a turn.
16. Use a friction lighter to ignite the torch.
17. Use the acetylene flow control valve to increase the acetylene flow until the flame leaves the end of the heating tip and stops smoking. Then, decrease the acetylene flow until the flame returns to the tip.
18. Slowly open the oxygen flow control valve until a **neutral flame** is achieved. A neutral flame is characterized by one or more inner cones, which are light blue in color, surrounded by a darker blue outer flame envelope (**FIGURE 6-17**). This type of flame is achieved when the proper proportions of oxygen and acetylene are being burned. The lighter blue tip of the innermost cone is the hottest part of the flame. The neutral flame is the most commonly used oxyacetylene flame for heating, cutting, and welding.

FIGURE 6-17 Neutral flame.

19. Direct the torch flame onto the metal to be heated. Position the flame so that the tip of the inner cone is at the metal.
20. When the area of the heated metal to be bent turns cherry red, remove the flame and close the oxygen flow control valve and the acetylene flow control valve on the torch handle. Bend or manipulate the metal as needed. Be extremely careful to avoid being burned by the hot metal.

Cutting

Using oxyacetylene equipment to cut metal requires the use of a cutting attachment and cutting tip (or cutting torch) that is appropriate for the metal being worked on. Technicians should always use the cutting attachments and tips recommended by the equipment manufacturer. Technicians should also wear the proper PPE when preparing the equipment and cutting metal.

The basic process for cutting metal using oxyacetylene equipment is as follows:

1. Determine the type and thickness of the metal to be cut, and prepare the metal by removing any rust or debris. If necessary, mark the cutting line using a soapstone marker.
2. Follow the manufacturer's recommendations to select the proper cutting tip for the job.
3. Inspect the cutting tip for damage or plugged holes. Clean the tip with a tip cleaner if necessary.
4. Install and tighten the cutting attachment and tip according to the manufacturer's instructions.
5. Close the oxygen and acetylene flow control valves on the torch handle.
6. Loosen (back out) the adjusting screws on the oxygen and acetylene regulators.
7. Stand to the side of the oxygen cylinder and slowly open the cylinder valve until the proper pressure is indicated on the regulator working pressure gauge. Once the pressure on the cylinder pressure gauge rises, open the oxygen cylinder valve all the way.
8. Stand to the side of the acetylene cylinder and slowly open the cylinder valve until the cylinder pressure gauge on the regulator displays the cylinder pressure. Do not open the acetylene cylinder valve more than one and a half turns.
9. Open the oxygen flow control valve on the torch handle completely. Also, press and hold open the oxygen blast lever.
10. While the oxygen is flowing, tighten the adjusting screw on the oxygen regulator until the proper working pressure is displayed. Continue the oxygen flow for 10 seconds to purge the hoses and torch.
11. Release the oxygen blast lever and close the oxygen flow control valve on the torch handle.
12. Open the acetylene flow control valve on the torch handle approximately one-eighth of a turn.
13. While the acetylene is flowing, tighten the adjusting screw on the acetylene regulator until the proper working pressure is displayed. Continue the acetylene flow for 10 seconds to purge the hoses and torch.
14. Close the acetylene flow control valve on the torch handle.
15. Open the acetylene flow control valve on the torch handle approximately one-quarter turn.
16. Use a friction lighter to ignite the torch.
17. Use the acetylene flow control valve to increase the acetylene flow until the flame leaves the end of the heating tip and stops smoking. Then, decrease the acetylene flow until the flame returns to the tip.
18. Slowly open the oxygen flow control valve until a neutral flame is achieved.
19. Press the oxygen blast lever all the way down to check the flame pattern. The flame should have a long, thin cutting jet that extends as much as 8 inches (203 mm) from the cutting oxygen hole at the center of the tip (**FIGURE 6-18**). When the flame is correct, release the oxygen blast lever.
20. Position the torch perpendicular to the metal and approximately 1⁄16 inch (1.6 mm) above the surface of the metal. Continue heating the metal until it begins to melt.
21. Depress the oxygen blast lever and, once the flame pierces the metal, start moving the torch slowly along the cut line. The torch movement should be in whichever direction provides the best visibility.
22. When the cut is complete, release the oxygen blast lever, remove the flame from the metal, and close the acetylene flow control valve and the oxygen flow control valve on the torch handle. Be extremely careful to avoid being burned by the hot metal.

Welding

The basic concept behind oxyacetylene welding is to heat two pieces of metal (the work metal) enough to form a small puddle of molten metal between them. Filler metal, typically in the form of a welding rod, is then placed into the molten puddle where it melts and fuses the two pieces of work metal together.

Using oxyacetylene equipment to weld metal requires the use of a welding tip that is appropriate for the metal being worked on. Technicians should always use the welding tips recommended by the equipment manufacturer. They should

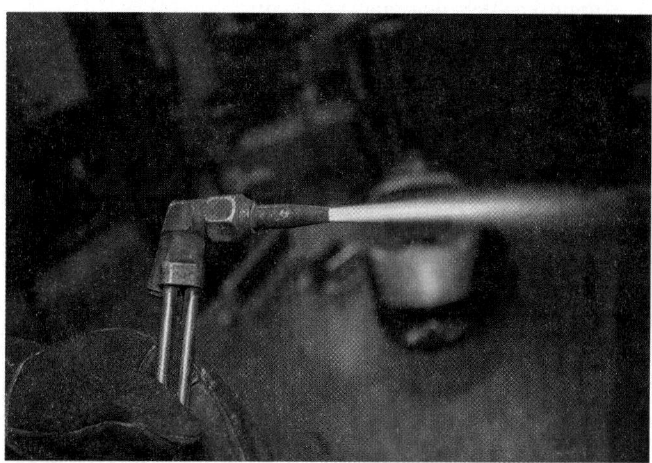

FIGURE 6-18 Torch flame with cutting jet.

also wear the proper PPE when preparing the equipment and welding metal.

The basic process for welding metal using oxyacetylene equipment is as follows:

1. Determine the type and thickness of the metal to be welded and prepare the metal by removing any rust or debris.
2. Follow the manufacturer's recommendations to select the proper welding tip for the job.
3. Inspect the welding tip for damage or plugged holes. Clean the tip with a tip cleaner if necessary.
4. Install and tighten the welding tip according to the manufacturer's instructions.
5. Close the oxygen and acetylene flow control valves on the torch handle.
6. Loosen (back out) the adjusting screws on the oxygen and acetylene regulators.
7. Stand to the side of the oxygen cylinder and slowly open the cylinder valve until the proper pressure is indicated on the regulator working pressure gauge. Once the pressure on the cylinder pressure gauge rises, open the oxygen cylinder valve all the way.
8. Stand to the side of the acetylene cylinder and slowly open the cylinder valve until the cylinder pressure gauge on the regulator displays the cylinder pressure. Do not open the acetylene cylinder valve more than one and a half turns.
9. Open the oxygen flow control valve on the torch handle completely.
10. While the oxygen is flowing, tighten the adjusting screw on the oxygen regulator until the proper working pressure is displayed. Continue the oxygen flow for 10 seconds to purge the hoses and torch.
11. Close the oxygen flow control valve on the torch handle.
12. Open the acetylene flow control valve on the torch handle approximately one-eighth of a turn.
13. While the acetylene is flowing, tighten the adjusting screw on the acetylene regulator until the proper working pressure is displayed. Continue the acetylene flow for 10 seconds to purge the hoses and torch.
14. Close the acetylene flow control valve on the torch handle.
15. Open the acetylene flow control valve on the torch handle approximately one-quarter of a turn.
16. Use a friction lighter to ignite the torch.
17. Use the acetylene flow control valve to increase the acetylene flow until the flame leaves the end of the heating tip and stops smoking. Then, decrease the acetylene flow until the flame returns to the tip.
18. Slowly open the oxygen flow control valve until a neutral flame is achieved.
19. Position the torch so that the tip of the inner cone of the flame is just above the surface of the metal to be welded. Heat the two metals along a narrow welding path until a puddle of molten metal forms.
20. Place the end of the gas welding rod into the puddle and slowly move along the welding path to fuse the two metal pieces together. The filler metal and the molten metal from the two workpieces form a **bead** (**FIGURE 6-19**).

FIGURE 6-19 Oxyacetylene torch welding.

21. When the weld is complete, remove the flame from the metal and close the oxygen flow control valve and the acetylene flow control valve on the torch handle. Be extremely careful to avoid being burned by the hot metal.

▶ Oxyacetylene Brazing and Soldering

K06004

Oxyacetylene equipment can be used for brazing and soldering metals. Unlike welding, where extremely high temperatures are used to melt the base metals and the filler metal so that they fuse together, brazing and soldering use lower temperatures that only heat the base metals but melt the filler metal to bond the base metals together.

Brazing

Brazing is a method used to join two pieces of metal together by heating the metal pieces and then melting a brazing rod to bond the workpieces together through **adhesion**. The brazing rod material melts at a lower temperature than the metal pieces being joined together. The molten filler metal flows into the gap between the metal pieces through **capillary action**, which is essentially the adhesive force exerted by the surface of a metal to attract a dissimilar metal over its surface. When cooled, the filler metal bonds the workpieces together.

Brazing operations require temperatures above 800°F (427°C), but not as high as those used for welding. The temperature must be high enough to melt the brazing filler metal rod but low enough to not melt the base metal workpieces. Since the workpieces themselves are never melted together (only bonded together by a filler metal), they can be the same type of metal or different types of metal. This is a key advantage of brazing.

In order for brazing to work effectively, two important criteria must be met: (1) the two base metal workpieces must be very closely fitted, and (2) they must be extremely clean. Research has shown that joint clearances between 0.0012 and 0.0031 inches (0.03 and 0.08 mm) are an ideal range for brazing. However, acceptable joint clearances for brazing operations can

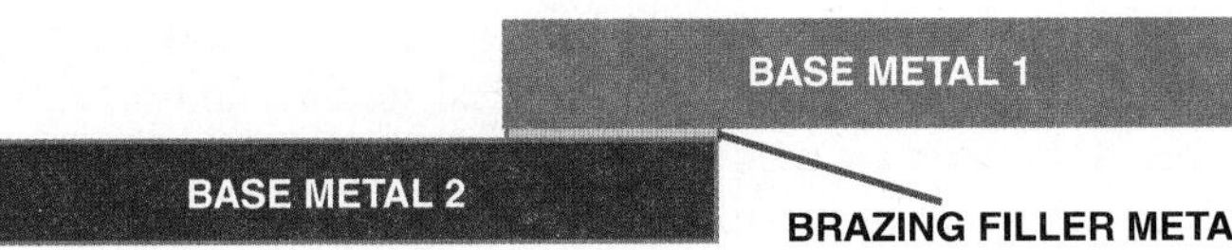

FIGURE 6-20 Brazed lap joint.

be as high as 0.024 inches (0.6 mm). Realistically, brazing two clean metal pieces that have been overlapped to form a lap joint should result in a very strong bond (**FIGURE 6-20**).

Proper cleaning of the base metal surfaces prior to brazing is usually accomplished using chemical solvents and/or abrasives. One important factor when using abrasives such as sandpaper to clean the metal surfaces is to maintain some roughness on the metal. Smoothing the metal surfaces too much interferes with the flow, or **wetting**, of the molten filler metal. A slightly rough surface provides better capillary action of the filler metal and, therefore, better joint strength.

In addition to cleaning the surfaces of the base metals, it is also necessary to maintain an environment that prevents oxides from forming on the metals when brazing is taking place. Preventing oxidation and removing contaminants during brazing operations is accomplished with **flux**. Flux comes in several forms, including paste, liquid, and powder, and it can be brushed on the metal surfaces being brazed (**FIGURE 6-21**). When heat is applied to the base metals, the flux melts and flows into the joint to remove impurities ahead of the filler metal. Many brazing filler metal rods have a flux coating or a flux core, which eliminates the need to add flux prior to brazing.

The basic process for brazing metal using oxyacetylene equipment is as follows:

1. Determine the type(s) of metal to be brazed and thoroughly clean the metal with a solvent and/or an abrasive pad.
2. Follow the equipment manufacturer's recommendations for selecting the proper welding tip and brazing filler metal rods for the job.

> **TECHNICIAN TIP**
>
> If the brazing filler metal rods being used have a flux coating or a flux core, it may not be necessary to use additional flux to clean the joint prior to brazing.

3. Inspect the tip for damage and clean it with a tip cleaner if necessary.
4. Install and tighten the tip according to the manufacturer's instructions.
5. Close the oxygen and acetylene flow control valves on the torch handle.
6. Loosen (back out) the adjusting screws on the oxygen and acetylene regulators.
7. Stand to the side of the oxygen cylinder and slowly open the cylinder valve until the proper pressure is indicated on the regulator working pressure gauge. Once the pressure on the cylinder pressure gauge rises, open the oxygen cylinder valve all the way.

FIGURE 6-21 Worker applying flux paste prior to brazing.

8. Stand to the side of the acetylene cylinder and slowly open the cylinder valve until the cylinder pressure gauge on the regulator displays the cylinder pressure. Do not open the acetylene cylinder valve more than one and a half turns.
9. Open the oxygen flow control valve on the torch handle completely.
10. While the oxygen is flowing, tighten the adjusting screw on the oxygen regulator until the proper working pressure is displayed. Continue the oxygen flow for 10 seconds to purge the hoses and torch.
11. Close the oxygen flow control valve on the torch handle.
12. Open the acetylene flow control valve on the torch handle approximately one-eighth of a turn.
13. While the acetylene is flowing, tighten the adjusting screw on the acetylene regulator until the proper working pressure is displayed. Continue the acetylene flow for 10 seconds to purge the hoses and torch.
14. Close the acetylene flow control valve on the torch handle.
15. Open the acetylene flow control valve on the torch handle approximately one-quarter of a turn.
16. Use a friction lighter to ignite the torch.
17. Use the acetylene flow control valve to increase the acetylene flow until the flame leaves the end of the heating tip and stops smoking. Then, decrease the acetylene flow until the flame returns to the tip.
18. Slowly open the oxygen flow control valve until a **carburizing flame** is achieved. Brazing can be performed with a neutral flame, but a carburizing flame is preferable. A carburizing flame is sootier and cooler than a neutral flame, which helps remove oxides from the surface of copper. A carburizing flame can be identified visually because its inner cone is longer and less defined than that of a neutral flame (**FIGURE 6-22**). To achieve a carburizing flame, simply adjust the flow control valves on the torch handle to provide a bit more acetylene than oxygen to the gas mix.
19. Direct the torch flame approximately 2 inches (51 mm) above the surface of the metal to be brazed, starting on each side of the joint and moving inward toward the joint.

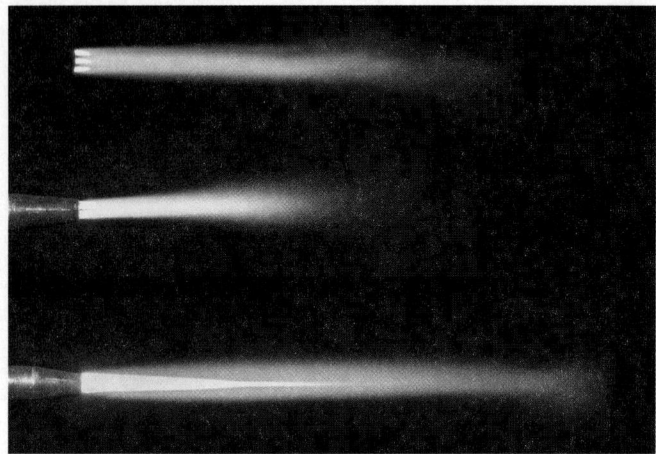

FIGURE 6-22 Carburizing flame compared to neutral flame.

20. Continue to heat the metal until it turns dark red, but stop before the metal shows signs of melting. Then, remove the torch flame from the metal.
21. Touch the tip of the brazing rod to the metal and observe the capillary action as the rod melts and the filler metal flows into the joint. When the joint appears to have been adequately filled, remove the brazing rod and close the oxygen and acetylene flow control valves on the torch handle. Be extremely careful to avoid being burned by the hot metal.
22. Allow the metal to cool, or dip it into water to hasten the cooling process. Remove any excess flux from the joint with a wire brush.

Soldering

Soldering is a method used to join two pieces of metal together by heating the metal pieces and then melting a soldering rod or soft solder material to bond the workpieces together through adhesion. The soldering material melts at a lower temperature than the metal pieces being joined together. The molten filler metal flows between the metal pieces through capillary action and, when cooled, bonds the workpieces together.

Soldering operations are typically done at temperatures around 500°F (260°C), since that is the temperature at which silver soldering rods melt. The temperature must be high enough to melt the soldering filler metal but low enough to not melt the base metal workpieces. Since the workpieces themselves are never melted together (only bonded together by a filler metal), they can be the same type of metal or different types of metal.

Because of the relatively low temperatures involved in soldering operations, soldered joints are among the weakest joints formed in oxyacetylene applications. However, if done properly, soldered joints can withstand a great deal of abuse and, in electrical applications, maintain electrical connectivity at terminals and connectors.

For soldering to work effectively, the two base metal workpieces must be very closely fitted—that is, they must have a well-defined seam—and they must be extremely clean. Joint clearances for most soldering jobs should be about 0.005 inches (0.13 mm). Proper cleaning of the base metal surfaces prior to soldering is usually done with chemical solvents and/or abrasives. If abrasives are used to clean the metal surfaces, it is desirable to maintain some roughness on the metal to enable the proper capillary action of the solder.

To prevent oxidation and remove impurities, flux should be applied to the metal during the soldering process. Some solder filler rods have a flux coating or a flux core, which can eliminate the need to add additional flux prior to soldering.

The basic process for soldering metal using oxyacetylene equipment is as follows:

1. Determine the type(s) of metal to be soldered and thoroughly clean the metal with a solvent and/or an abrasive pad.
2. Follow the equipment manufacturer's recommendations for selecting the proper welding tip and soldering filler metal rods for the job.
3. Inspect the tip for damage and clean it with a tip cleaner if necessary.
4. Install and tighten the tip according to the manufacturer's instructions.
5. Close the oxygen and acetylene flow control valves on the torch handle.
6. Loosen (back out) the adjusting screws on the oxygen and acetylene regulators.
7. Stand to the side of the oxygen cylinder and slowly open the cylinder valve until the proper pressure is indicated on the regulator working pressure gauge. Once the pressure on the cylinder pressure gauge rises, open the oxygen cylinder valve all the way.
8. Stand to the side of the acetylene cylinder and slowly open the cylinder valve until the cylinder pressure gauge on the regulator displays the cylinder pressure. Do not open the acetylene cylinder valve more than one and a half turns.
9. Open the oxygen flow control valve on the torch handle completely.
10. While the oxygen is flowing, tighten the adjusting screw on the oxygen regulator until the proper working pressure is displayed. Continue the oxygen flow for 10 seconds to purge the hoses and torch.
11. Close the oxygen flow control valve on the torch handle.
12. Open the acetylene flow control valve on the torch handle approximately one-eighth of a turn.
13. While the acetylene is flowing, tighten the adjusting screw on the acetylene regulator until the proper working pressure is displayed. Continue the acetylene flow for 10 seconds to purge the hoses and torch.
14. Close the acetylene flow control valve on the torch handle.
15. Open the acetylene flow control valve on the torch handle approximately one-quarter of a turn.
16. Use a friction lighter to ignite the torch.
17. Use the acetylene flow control valve to increase the acetylene flow until the flame leaves the end of the heating tip and stops smoking. Then, decrease the acetylene flow until the flame returns to the tip.
18. Slowly open the oxygen flow control valve and then adjust the two flow control valves so that a bit more acetylene than

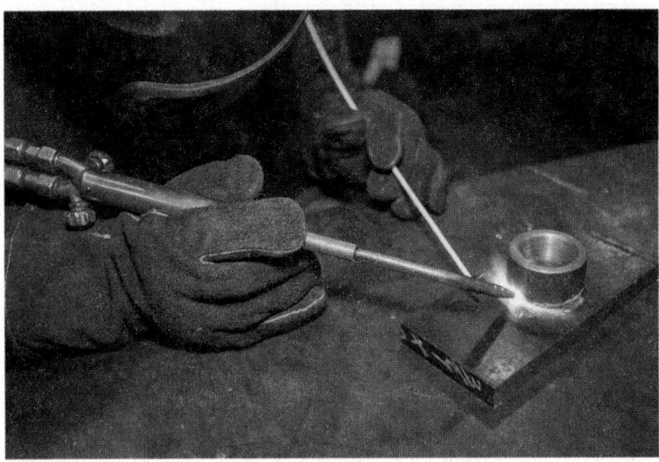

FIGURE 6-23 Soldering a pipe elbow.

oxygen is being provided to the gas mix and a carburizing flame is achieved.

19. Direct the torch flame approximately 2 inches (51 mm) above the surface of the metal to be soldered, starting on each side of the joint and moving inward toward the joint.
20. Continue to heat the metal until it turns red, but stop before the metal shows signs of melting.

> **TECHNICIAN TIP**
>
> Some metals might not turn red to indicate that they are hot enough for solder to be applied. In these cases, it is best to observe the condition of any flux that has been applied to the joint. When the flux melts and becomes clear, the joint is hot enough to melt the solder filler material.

21. When the base metal appears to be hot enough, remove the torch flame and touch the tip of the soldering rod to the metal (**FIGURE 6-23**). Observe the capillary action as the rod melts and the filler metal flows into the joint. When the joint appears to have been adequately filled, remove the soldering rod and close the oxygen and acetylene flow control valves on the torch handle. Be extremely careful to avoid being burned by the hot metal.
22. Allow the metal to cool or dip it into water to hasten the cooling process. Remove any excess flux from the joint with a wire brush.

Oxyacetylene Welding Repair Techniques

K06005

Numerous techniques can be used to make oxyacetylene welding applicable to many different applications. The specific technique used can depend on factors such as the type and thickness of the metal being welded, the type of preparation needed for the metal, and the positioning and movement of the welding torch and welding filler rod.

Base Metal Preparation

An important part of oxyacetylene welding repair involves preparing the metal to be welded. No matter how thin or thick the metal workpieces are, they need to be cleaned and properly positioned before welding begins. In some cases, it may be necessary to tack weld the workpieces to hold them in position for welding or to gap the pieces to allow for expansion and contraction. Thicker metals may have to be beveled to create a suitable joint for the welding bead (**FIGURE 6-24**).

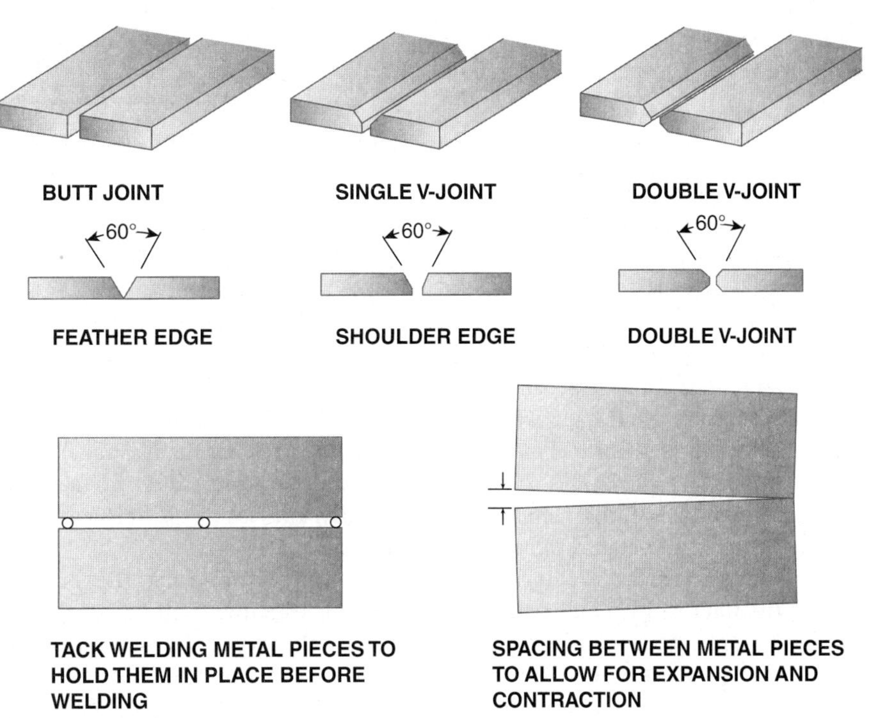

FIGURE 6-24 Preparing workpieces for welding.

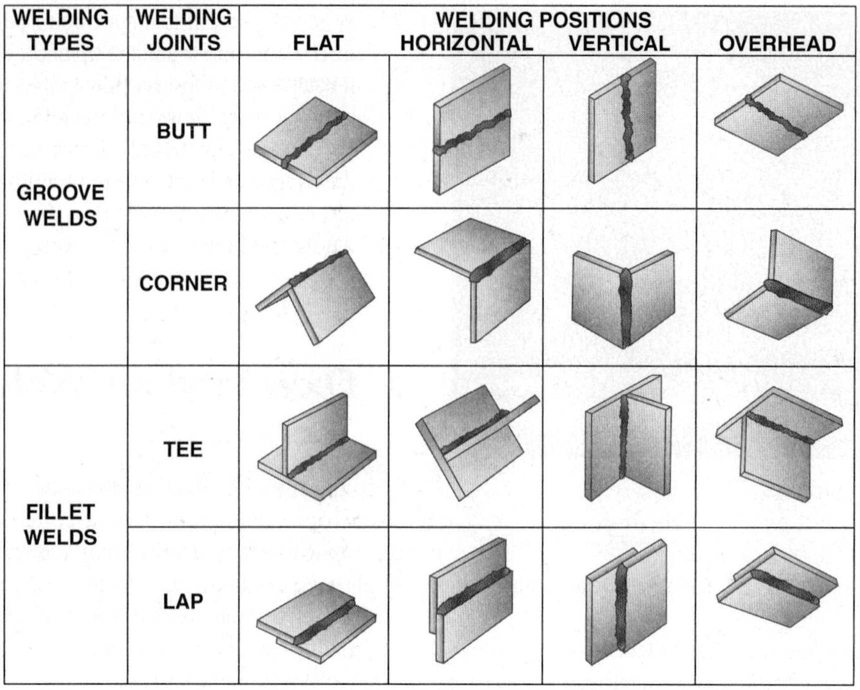

WELDING TYPES	WELDING JOINTS	WELDING POSITIONS			
		FLAT	HORIZONTAL	VERTICAL	OVERHEAD
GROOVE WELDS	BUTT				
	CORNER				
FILLET WELDS	TEE				
	LAP				

FIGURE 6-25 Welding positions, types, and joints.

Welding positions, welding types, and welding joints can vary from job to job (**FIGURE 6-25**). Four welding positions that service technicians are likely to use include flat, horizontal, vertical, and overhead. In addition, two common welding types are groove welds and fillet welds, and four common welding joints are butt, corner, tee, and lap.

Groove welds are done on beveled surfaces. This allows the molten base metal and filler metal to fill the prepared joint groove to create a strong connection. Fillet welds, on the other hand, do not require beveling. They are often performed on metal plates that are aligned perpendicular to one another.

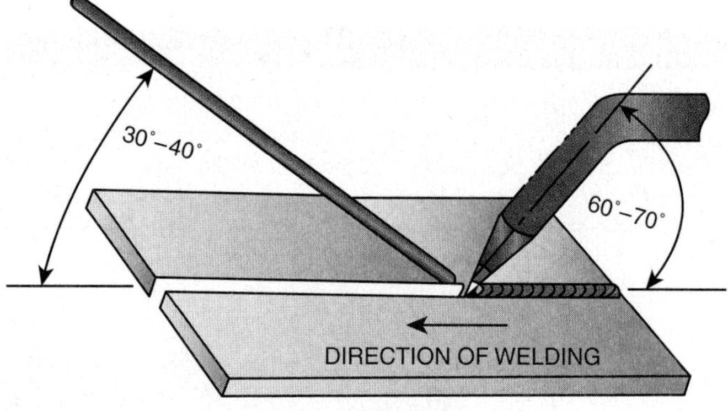

FIGURE 6-26 Forehand welding technique.

Forehand and Backhand Welding

There are two fundamental techniques used for oxyacetylene welding: **forehand welding** and **backhand welding**. These two techniques are referred to by numerous other names, as well. For instance, forehand welding is sometimes called the leftward technique, forward welding, push welding, puddle welding, and ripple welding. Backhand welding is sometimes called the rightward technique, backward welding, drag angle welding, and pull welding. Regardless of the name used, the two methods differ in several ways.

Forehand welding is best suited for welding metals that are relatively thin—typically less than one-eighth of an inch (or 3–5 mm) thick. With this technique, the welding torch is held in the right hand and the filler rod is held in the left hand. Welding begins on the right side of the seam and moves toward the left side of the seam (**FIGURE 6-26**). The torch flame is directed away from the finished weld and pushed in the direction of the welding, which allows it to preheat the joint before the filler rod is melted. The filler rod is angled toward the finished weld and moved in a backward and forward motion.

Backhand welding is typically used for thicker metals. With this technique, the welding torch is held in the right hand and the filler rod is held in the left hand. Welding begins on the left side of the seam and moves toward the right side of the seam (**FIGURE 6-27**). The torch flame is directed toward the finished weld and pulled in the direction of the welding. The filler rod is angled away from the finished weld and moved in a circular motion.

As a general rule, the backhand welding technique requires less filler material and gas usage while resulting in better weld properties than the forehand welding technique. And since many MORE welding jobs involve thick metals, service technicians are more likely to use this welding technique.

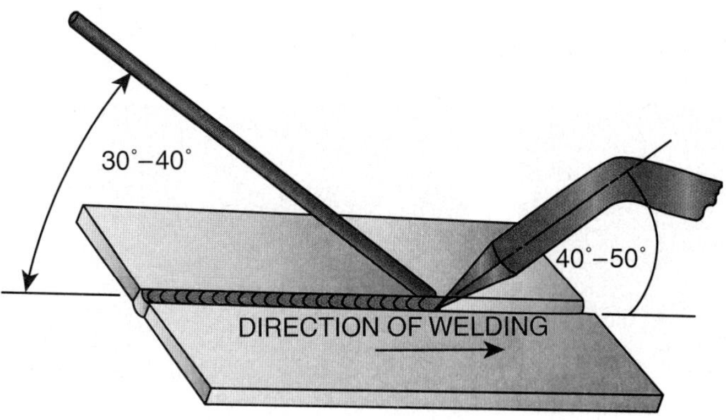

FIGURE 6-27 Backhand welding technique.

▶ Industry/Accreditation

I06001, S06001

The terminology associated with the composition and use of oxyacetylene equipment is critical for MORE service technicians. Technicians must be able to accurately use terminology that is common to the trade and understand safety procedures that apply to this work. Federal and state agencies along with industrial trade groups have developed standards over the years that technicians can use for source material:

- The Occupational Safety and Health Administration (OSHA) at www.osha.gov, which sets and enforces standards related to safety and equipment.
- The National Fire Protection Association (NFPA) at www.nfpa.org, a global nonprofit organization devoted to eliminating death, injury, property, and economic losses due to fire, electrical, and related hazards. See Standard 51, *Standard for the Design and Installation of Oxygen-Fuel Gas Systems for Welding, Cutting, and Allied Processes*; Standard 51B, *Standard for Fire Prevention During Welding, Cutting, and Other Hot Work*; and Standard 55, *Compressed Gases and Cryogenic Fluids Code*.
- The American Welding Society (AWS) at www.aws.org, a nonprofit organization with a global mission to advance the science, technology, and application of welding and allied joining and cutting processes, including brazing, soldering, and thermal spraying.
- The American National Standards Institute (ANSI) at www.ansi.org, an organization that oversees the creation, promulgation, and use of norms and guidelines that impact U.S. businesses. See Standard Z49.1 *Safety in Welding, Cutting, and Allied Processes.*

In addition, oxyacetylene equipment manufacturers and magazines covering the welding industry typically have technical information, including glossaries, available on their websites. Technicians working on MORE should exploit all available resources to ensure that they understand the terminology and regulations that apply to the trade. To correctly cut, weld, solder, and braze metals, follow the guidelines in **SKILL DRILL 6-1**.

▶ Attitude

A06001

Before setting up and using any type of oxyacetylene equipment, it is critical for MORE service technicians to be thoroughly familiar with the safety regulations and procedures that pertain to the equipment and its use for heating, cutting, and welding metal. This includes locating and reading any safety-related manuals that may exist on site. Find out where those manuals are normally kept and take action to obtain the proper manuals for the equipment. If printed manuals are not available for the equipment, try to find electronic versions either from the client or online through the equipment manufacturer's website. It might also be possible to find the appropriate material by searching online. In some cases, it might be necessary to call the equipment manufacture to get the needed information. Whatever means you use, it is important to ensure that the resource material being used matches the equipment and the procedures being performed.

SKILL DRILL 6-1 Cutting, Welding, Soldering, and Brazing Metals

1. Obtain and review the necessary manuals that pertain to safety practices and the PPE needed, the setup and operation of the oxyacetylene equipment, and the procedures to be used.

2. Using the equipment manufacturer's manuals, set up and leak test the oxyacetylene equipment, and gather the recommended attachments and tips needed to perform the work.

3. Following the equipment manufacturer's guidelines, set the pressures and flows for the oxygen and acetylene, light and adjust the torch to achieve the proper flame pattern, and position the torch flame to heat and cut through the metal.

(Continued)

SKILL DRILL 6-1 Cutting, Welding, Soldering, and Brazing Metals (Continued)

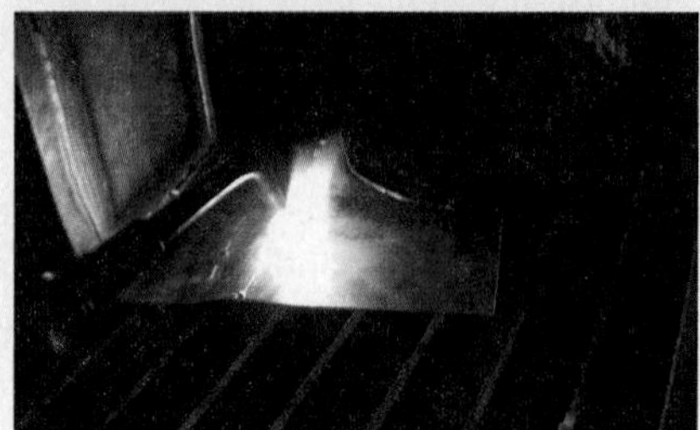

4. Following the equipment manufacturer's guidelines, set the pressures and flows for the oxygen and acetylene, light and adjust the torch to achieve the proper flame pattern, and position the torch flame and filler metal rod to heat and weld two pieces of metal.

5. Following the equipment manufacturer's guidelines, set the pressures and flows for the oxygen and acetylene, light and adjust the torch to achieve the proper flame pattern, and position the torch flame and filler metal rod to heat and fuse two pieces of metal.

6. Following the equipment manufacturer's guidelines, set the pressures and flows for the oxygen and acetylene, light and adjust the torch to achieve the proper flame pattern, and position the torch flame and filler metal rod to heat and braze two pieces of metal.

Wrap-Up

Ready for Review

- The major components that make up a typical oxyacetylene outfit include an acetylene cylinder, an oxygen cylinder, a pressure regulator for each cylinder, a flashback arrestor on the outlet of each regulator, a hose for each gas, a check valve (or a second flashback arrestor) at the end of each hose, and a torch.
- Each cylinder has a pressure regulator with two gauges: a cylinder pressure gauge that shows how much pressure is in the cylinder and a working pressure gauge that shows how much pressure is in the hose, or line.
- Flashback arrestors are spring-loaded valves that prevent a flame from traveling back up the hose to the cylinders.
- Check valves allow flow in one direction only.
- Oxyacetylene hoses are typically color coded: red for acetylene and green for oxygen. To prevent interchanging gas pathways through the equipment, acetylene connections use left-hand threads and oxygen right-hand threads.
- A torch handle usually has flow control valves for adjusting the flow of oxygen and acetylene and a threaded outlet for different tips and attachments for heating, cutting, and welding.
- There are many types of tips available for oxyacetylene torches, including those designed specifically for heating, cutting, welding, brazing, and soldering.
- Some common supplemental components used with oxyacetylene equipment include wrenches, strikers, tip cleaners, and filler metals.
- The pressure inside a full cylinder of acetylene is approximately 250 psi (1,724 kPa), while the pressure in an oxygen cylinder is approximately 2,200 psi (15,168 kPa).
- When acetylene is mixed with oxygen, very high flame temperatures of 6,300°F to 6,800°F (3,480°C to 3,760°C) are produced.
- Technicians should always wear appropriate PPE when heating, cutting, or welding with oxyacetylene equipment.
- Breathing masks or respirators may be required when heating, cutting, or welding materials that can produce toxic fumes when heated with a torch.
- To minimize the risk of fire and explosion, technicians should always inspect and prepare the machinery or equipment to be worked on, as well as the work area and its surroundings before using oxyacetylene equipment.
- If the work area is a confined space or if it requires a hot-work permit or a fire watch, follow all requirements and procedures for the site to avoid serious injuries and penalties.
- Make sure that the work area is properly ventilated by using fans, exhaust hoods, or ventilated booths.
- Always follow safety guidelines related to the storage of oxyacetylene equipment that is not in use.
- Oxygen cylinders and acetylene cylinders must be secured separately in a safe area at least 20 feet (6 meters) apart or separated by a wall that is 5 feet (1.5 meters) high with a minimum 30-minute burn rating.
- If technicians are required to set up oxyacetylene equipment, they must follow all the applicable safety precautions, wear the appropriate PPE, use the equipment manufacturer's guidelines for setup, and leak test all connections before use.
- Factors that must be considered during oxyacetylene-heating, cutting, and welding processes include the type

and thickness of the metal involved, the equipment manufacturer's recommendations for torch attachments and tips, the flows and pressures of the oxygen and acetylene, the torch flame profile, and the technique used to accomplish the task.

- Brazing is a method used to join two pieces of metal together by heating the metal pieces to above 800°F (427°C) and then melting a brazing rod to bond the workpieces together through adhesion.
- When brazing rod material melts, it flows into the gap between the metal workpieces through capillary action and, when cooled, bonds the workpieces together.
- A key advantage of brazing is that it can be used to bond together the same type of metal or different types of metal.
- Soldering is a method used to join two pieces of metal together by heating the metal pieces to about 500°F (260°C) and then melting a soldering rod or soft solder material to bond the workpieces together through adhesion.
- When soldering material melts, it flows between the metal workpieces through capillary action and, when cooled, bonds the workpieces together.
- Since the workpieces themselves are never melted together (only bonded together by a filler metal), soldering can be used to bond the same type of metal or different types of metal.

Key Terms

adhesion The bonding property that occurs when two metals are joined together using molten filler metal to fill the gap between them.

American National Standards Institute (ANSI) An organization that oversees the creation, promulgation, and use of norms and guidelines that impact U.S. businesses.

backhand welding A welding technique (also called the rightward technique, backward welding, drag angle welding, and pull welding) best suited for thick metals in which the welding torch is held in the right hand, the filler rod is held in the left hand, and the welding direction moves from the left side of the seam toward the right side of the seam.

bead The deposit of filler metal and/or base metal along a joint or seam that results from a welding process.

capillary action The ability of a liquid, such as molten filler metal, to flow into narrow gaps between two objects. The adhesive properties of a metal's surface for dissimilar metals are directly related to capillary action.

carburizing flame A torch flame that has an excess of acetylene in the oxyacetylene fuel mix and is characterized by a sootier flame using an inner flame cone that is longer and less defined than that of a neutral flame.

check valve A type of valve that allows the flow of gas or liquid in one direction only.

confined space An enclosed area that has limited space and accessibility and requires special safety procedures for entering into, working in, and exiting it.

cylinder pressure gauge The gauge on an oxygen or acetylene regulator that shows how much pressure is in the cylinder.

dross Oxidized and molten metal waste (slag) that is left over during oxyacetylene cutting and welding operations.

flashback An unintentional ignition of oxygen and acetylene inside a torch handle that, if left unimpeded, can travel backward through the torch, hoses, and regulators into the cylinders.

flashback arrestor A spring-loaded valve installed on oxyacetylene equipment as a safety device to prevent flame from entering the torch hoses and traveling backward to the cylinders.

flux A material that is used during brazing and soldering operations to prevent oxidation and remove impurities from the metals.

forehand welding A welding technique (also called the leftward technique, forward welding, push welding, puddle welding, and ripple welding) best suited for relatively thin metals in which the welding torch is held in the right hand, the filler rod is held in the left hand, and the welding direction moves from the right side of the seam toward the left side of the seam.

leak test solution A soapy liquid that, when placed on oxyacetylene equipment connections, can indicate leaks by bubbling.

MFA A shortened term for multiple flame acetylene torch tip, which is a type of oxyacetylene torch tip used for heating metal.

neutral flame A torch flame that has the correct proportions of oxygen and acetylene and is characterized by one or more inner cones, which are light blue in color, surrounded by a darker blue outer flame envelope.

reamer Any of several round steel files found on a tip cleaner tool and used to clean tip orifices.

rosebud A type of torch tip with numerous holes in the end that produce multiple flames with a wide pattern suitable for heating metal.

spats A type of PPE, often made of leather, worn over the laces and tongue of work boots to protect workers from hot metal.

twin-line hose Oxygen and acetylene hoses that are connected together for most of their length.

wetting The flow of molten filler material during brazing and soldering operations.

working pressure gauge The gauge on an oxygen or acetylene regulator that shows how much pressure is in the hose, or line.

Review Questions

1. Removing the protective cap from an oxygen or acetylene cylinder reveals a _____.
   a. flashback arrestor
   b. check valve
   c. pressure regulator
   d. cylinder valve
2. The proper tool to use for lighting an oxyacetylene torch is a _____.
   a. spatter
   b. striker
   c. flasher
   d. rosebud

3. According to the American National Standards Institute (ANSI), a typical shade range for protective goggles used in oxyacetylene welding is from _____.
   a. shade 0 to shade 2
   b. shade 1 to shade 3
   c. shade 3 to shade 6
   d. shade 9 to shade 15
4. If a technician is going to be exposed to toxic fumes for a long period of time during a cutting or welding procedure, the technician should wear a _____.
   a. full-face, supplied-air respirator (SAR)
   b. high-efficiency particulate arresting (HEPA) filter
   c. pure oxygen supply mask (POSM)
   d. dampened charcoal canister mask (DCCM)
5. Cracking open the oxygen and acetylene cylinder valves before setting up an oxyacetylene outfit is done to _____.
   a. reset the cylinder regulators
   b. clear the valves of debris
   c. premix and flame test the gases
   d. purge the work area
6. Cutting through a piece of thick metal typically requires a technician to _____.
   a. increase the acetylene pressure above 15 psig (103 kPa)
   b. introduce a separate inert gas to the welding puddle
   c. slowly push a reamer rod into the initial cut
   d. depress and hold the oxygen blast lever on the torch
7. When brazing is used to join together two base metal workpieces, the heat from the torch flame _____.
   a. melts only the base metal workpieces
   b. melts one base metal workpiece and the brazing rod material
   c. melts only the brazing rod material
   d. melts both metal workpieces and the brazing rod material
8. Soldering operations are typically done at temperatures around _____.
   a. 500°F (260°C)
   b. 800°F (427°C)
   c. 2,000°F (1,093°C)
   d. 3,000°F (1,649°C)
9. Groove welds are most likely to be done on _____.
   a. non-beveled surfaces
   b. perpendicularly aligned metal plates
   c. very thin metal sheets
   d. beveled surfaces
10. Which welding technique involves angling the torch flame toward the finished weld while angling the filler rod away from the finished weld?
   a. Leftward
   b. Backhand
   c. Forehand
   d. Push

ASE Technician A/Technician B Style Questions

1. Technician A says the working pressure gauge on an oxygen regulator indicates how much pressure is in the cylinder. Technician B says the working pressure gauge shows how much pressure is in the hose, or line. Who is correct?
   a. Technician A
   b. Technician B
   c. Both Technician A and Technician B
   d. Neither Technician A nor Technician B
2. Technician A says a rosebud tip is used for heating metal. Technician B says a rosebud tip is used for cutting metal. Who is correct?
   a. Technician A
   b. Technician B
   c. Both Technician A and Technician B
   d. Neither Technician A nor Technician B
3. Technician A says acetylene should never be used at a pressure above 25 psig (172 kPa). Technician B says acetylene should never be used at a pressure above 20 psig (138 kPa). Who is correct?
   a. Technician A
   b. Technician B
   c. Both Technician A and Technician B
   d. Neither Technician A nor Technician B
4. Technician A says oxygen cylinders and acetylene cylinders must be stored separately and kept at least 20 feet (6 meters) apart. Technician B says oxygen and acetylene cylinders must be stored separately and separated by a wall that is 5 feet (1.5 meters) high with a minimum 30-minute burn rating. Who is correct?
   a. Technician A
   b. Technician B
   c. Both Technician A and Technician B
   d. Neither Technician A nor Technician B
5. Technician A says the best flame to use for heating metal is a neutral flame. Technician B says the best flame for heating is a carburizing flame. Who is correct?
   a. Technician A
   b. Technician B
   c. Both Technician A and Technician B
   d. Neither Technician A nor Technician B
6. Technician A says to position the torch so that the tip of the innermost cone in the neutral flame is just above the metal to be welded. Technician B says the tip of the innermost cone in the neutral flame is the hottest part of the flame. Who is correct?
   a. Technician A
   b. Technician B
   c. Both Technician A and Technician B
   d. Neither Technician A nor Technician B
7. Technician A says brazing involves heating the base metal until it is hot and then melting a brazing filler metal rod to achieve capillary action. Technician B says brazing is done by using the torch to melt brazing filler metal onto a cool base metal to achieve acceptable cohesion. Who is correct?
   a. Technician A
   b. Technician B

c. Both Technician A and Technician B
d. Neither Technician A nor Technician B

8. Technician A says to always add flux to the metals being soldered, even when flux-coated or flux-core solder is being used. Technician B says if flux-coated or flux-core solder is being used, there is no need to add additional flux prior to soldering. Who is correct?
   a. Technician A
   b. Technician B
   c. Both Technician A and Technician B
   d. Neither Technician A nor Technician B
9. Technician A says the best welding technique to use for welding thin metal is the backhand method. Technician B says it is best to use the drag angle method or the pull welding method. Who is correct?
   a. Technician A
   b. Technician B
   c. Both Technician A and Technician B
   d. Neither Technician A nor Technician B
10. Technician A says four common welding joints are butt, corner, tee, and lap. Technician B says four common welding joints are smooth, crossed, lap, and overhead. Who is correct?
   a. Technician A
   b. Technician B
   c. Both Technician A and Technician B
   d. Neither Technician A nor Technician B

CHAPTER 7

Shielded Metal Arc, MIG, and TIG Welding

Knowledge Objectives

After reading this chapter, you will be able to:

- **K07001** Describe shielded metal arc welding (SMAW) equipment and components.
- **K07002** Explain safety regulations for welding of metals using SMAW.
- **K07003** Select and use mild steel electrodes for shielded metal arc welding.
- **K07004** Describe air-arc gouging.

Skills Objectives

After reading this chapter, you will be able to:

- **S07001** Differentiate between MIG, TIG, and stick welding procedures.
- **S07002** Demonstrate the proper procedures to weld mild steel with shielded metal arc.
- **S07003** Demonstrate the procedures to weld mild steel using wire feed processes (MIG, TIG).

Attitude Objectives

After reading this chapter, you will be able to:

- **A07001** Locate and follow appropriate safety procedures when welding metal.

Industry/Accreditation

After reading this chapter, you will be able to:

- **I07001** Communicate trade-related information using standard terms for SMAW welding.
- **I07002** Recommend correct repair techniques for welding metal using SMAW procedures.

▶ Introduction

Service technicians working on heavy equipment are almost certain to use shielded metal arc welding (SMAW) at one time or another. SMAW, often called stick welding, is the most common form of arc welding used on MORE (mobile off-road equipment) machines. Two other forms of arc welding that technicians might also encounter are gas metal arc welding (GMAW), which is often referred to as metal inert gas (MIG) welding, and, to a lesser extent, gas tungsten arc welding (GTAW), which is often called tungsten inert gas (TIG) welding.

For service technicians to work safely and effectively with arc welding equipment, they must be familiar with the basic types of equipment, recognize and follow all safety guidelines associated with the equipment, and know how to set up and use the equipment to accomplish the necessary task. This chapter describes SMAW, MIG, and TIG welding equipment, examines safety regulations that apply to arc welding, and describes how to use arc welding equipment for various welding applications.

▶ Shielded Metal Arc Welding (SMAW) Equipment and Components

K07001, S07001

Shielded metal arc welding (SMAW), or stick welding, is the most commonly used form of arc welding. Stick welding uses the intense heat produced by an electric arc that is created between a base metal workpiece and the tip of a filler metal electrode (welding rod). The heat from the arc melts the workpiece metal along the welding joint as well as the filler metal electrode. As a result, the metals form a molten pool in which they fuse together through **coalescence** to form a strong welded bond.

There are numerous reasons why stick welding is the most popular form of arc welding. The equipment is relatively simple and inexpensive, and it can be used on most common metals and alloys. In addition, stick welding is generally easy to learn, requiring only a moderate amount of practice. The filler metal electrodes used in stick welding are widely available and have a flux coating that protects against oxidation, so no additional flux or shielding gas is needed. Furthermore, stick welding equipment is portable, which makes it a good choice for field service applications and limited access areas. Stick welding can also be performed outdoors in less than ideal weather conditions (e.g., windy, damp conditions).

SMAW Equipment

The main components of a typical SMAW system include the welding machine, or **power source**, and its internal components; an electrode cable with an electrode stick holder, a work cable with a work clamp, a power supply cable that plugs into an electric outlet, an on/off power switch, an AC/DC (alternating-current/direct-current) output selector, and an amperage selector (**FIGURE 7-1**).

At its core, a basic stick welding machine like the type found in MORE maintenance facilities is essentially a **step-down transformer** that converts high-voltage, low-current AC power from a wall outlet (or engine) to a lower-voltage, higher-current AC or DC output. Any stick welder that provides DC output power includes a **rectifier** or some other means to convert the AC input power to a DC output. The AC/DC output selector allows a welding technician to select the form of output current. In addition, the amperage selector allows the welder to choose the amount of current needed for the welding operation (**FIGURE 7-2**).

FIGURE 7-1 Typical SMAW equipment.

You Are the Mobile Heavy Equipment Technician

A foreman at a construction site asks if you could weld a bracket that holds part of the blade adjustment mechanism on one of their crawler dozers. You think the bracket that the foreman is describing is near the engine compartment, but you won't know for sure until you see it. The foreman also mentions that the brackets appear to have been welded before. You'll need to take an arc welding rig to the site, but you have some questions to consider before you load up the equipment and go.

1. Would the thickness and type of metal that needs to be welded be a factor in which type of welding equipment you use?
2. Would the location of the bracket that needs welding pose any safety-related concerns?
3. Where might you find information about the proper electrodes and welding equipment settings to use during the welding job?
4. If the bracket broke at a previous weld, what might you need to carry to prepare for welding it again?

FIGURE 7-2 Output current controls on SMAW power source.

Stick welders can use a range of electrical power inputs, from 120V for small machines to 600V for large machines. In a typical configuration, a stick welder would convert an AC input power of 220V at 50 amps to a DC output of 25V at 125 amps. DC is the most common current used for stick welding. Unlike alternating current, DC flows in only one direction and results in easier arc starting and less sticking and spatter.

One critical aspect of SMAW is that the welding machine provides a **constant current** output. This means that the output current from the welding machine, which accounts for the intense heat at the arc, remains relatively constant even when there are variations in the welding conditions—such as when a welding technician varies the distance, or length, of the arc.

Another critical aspect of SMAW has to do with the **electrical polarity**, or the direction of current flow, in the welding circuit. The circuit starts at the power source (the SMAW machine) and includes the electrode cable and holder, the electrode, the base metal workpiece, and the work cable and clamp. When a DC output is used, one pole, or terminal, is always positive and the other pole is always negative. Connecting the electrode cable to the positive terminal of the SMAW power source and the work cable to the negative terminal of the power source sets up a **direct current electrode positive** (DCEP) connection (**FIGURE 7-3**). This is also referred to as a **reverse polarity** connection, and it is the most commonly used connection in stick welding because it provides the best welding results. Most electrodes are designed to be used in DCEP connections.

> ▶ TECHNICIAN TIP
>
> If stick welding is being performed on a machine that has its own electrical system, there is a risk that the large amount of electric current passing through the machine could damage the machine's electrical components. For this reason, service technicians should disconnect the machine's battery ground cable and all onboard electronic control modules prior to welding.

SMAW Components and Accessories

Good-quality stick welding is possible only when the correct electrode is selected and used. Electrodes are available in many different sizes, wire materials, and coatings. Electrode sizes for SMAW range from 1⁄16-inch (1.6 mm) to 3⁄8 inch (9.5 mm). The American Welding Society (AWS) provides a standard electrode classification system that service technicians should use

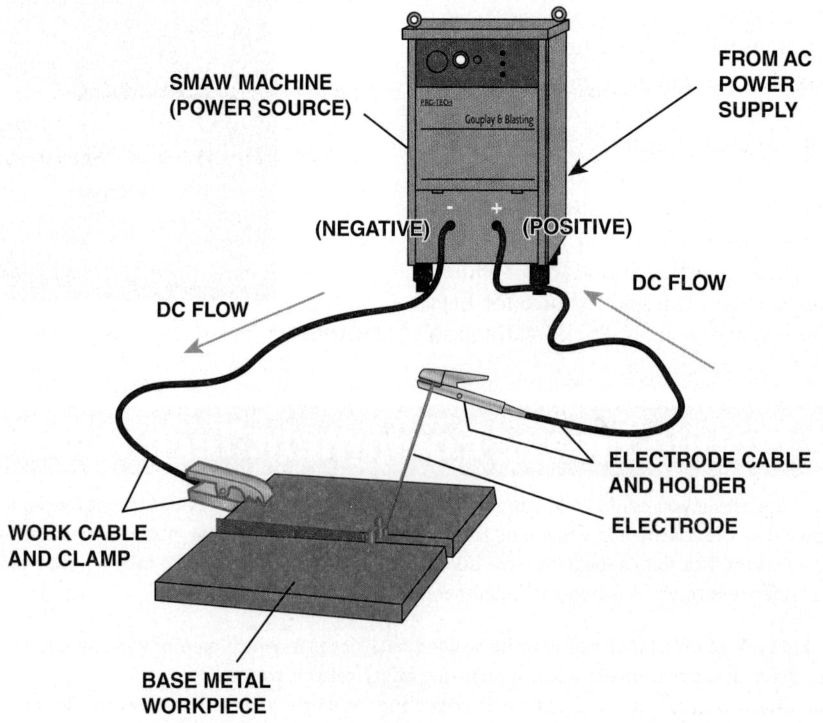

FIGURE 7-3 Welding circuit with DCEP connection showing current flow using electron theory.

TABLE 7-1 Common SMAW Electrodes

Standard AWS Electrode Name	Minimum Tensile Strength	Welding Positions	Flux Coating Material	Amount of Penetration	Output Current
E6010	60,000 psi (413,685 KPa)	All	Cellulose sodium	Deep	DC only
E6011	60,000 psi (413,685 KPa)	All	Cellulose potassium	Deep	DC/AC
E6013	60,000 psi (413,685 KPa)	All	Rutile potassium	Medium	DC/AC
E7018	70,000 psi (482,633 KPa)	All	Iron powder Low hydrogen	Shallow to medium	DC/AC

when selecting the proper electrode (**TABLE 7-1**). In this classification system, the electrode name is coded as follows:

- E = electrode
- the first two numbers = the tensile strength of the welded joint
- the third number = the acceptable welding position(s)
- the fourth number = the type of flux coating material, the amount of penetration, and the acceptable type of output current.

Since SMAW electrodes are consumed as they melt to provide filler metal, they must be replaced regularly. This is one disadvantage of stick welding when compared to other forms of arc welding.

In many stick welding jobs, the base metal workpieces being welded need to be held in place—at least until an initial weld has been completed. There are many types and sizes of clamps that can be used for this purpose (**FIGURE 7-4**). Some welding clamps are modified locking, or vise-grip, pliers. Other clamps are designed to hold workpieces at a 90-degree angle.

One drawback of stick welding relates to the **slag** that forms on the weld bead. This slag must be completely removed before another bead can be laid on top of the previous bead. Slag can be removed using a chipping hammer and a wire brush (**FIGURE 7-5**).

MIG Welding

One form of arc welding that service technicians might encounter is called gas metal arc welding (GMAW). This form of welding is often called metal inert gas (MIG) welding because it requires the use of a shielding gas to protect the weld from oxidation and contaminants in the surrounding air. The three most commonly used gases are argon, carbon dioxide, and helium. Depending on the metal(s) being welded, two of these gases are often mixed.

▶ TECHNICIAN TIP

MIG welding is not suitable for outdoor use. This is because MIG welding requires the use of shielding gases, and any wind at the welding site can interfere with the gas flow and leave the weld vulnerable to oxidation and impurities.

MIG welding was developed during the 1940s as a way of speeding up welding processes, especially for supplies and equipment needed during World War II. It is perhaps the easiest form of arc welding to learn. In addition, MIG welding can be used to join a wide variety of metals. However, MIG welding is best suited for thin or medium-thickness metals and is most commonly used in high-volume production applications. Plus, the need for one or more shielding gas cylinders makes MIG welding equipment less portable.

FIGURE 7-4 Welding clamps.

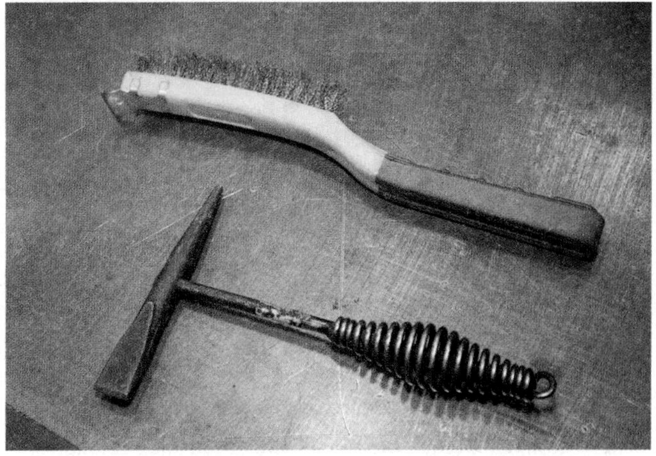

FIGURE 7-5 Chipping hammer and wire brushes for slag removal.

The basic equipment in a MIG welding outfit includes a welding machine, or power source; a shielding gas supply; an electrode wire feed reel, or spool; electrode wire; a welding gun; and a work return connection.

During operation, a technician presses a control switch, or trigger, on the welding gun to start the electric power, the electrode wire feed, and the shielding gas flow through a liner to the tip of the welding gun. The arc that is created at the tip of the welding gun produces intense heat—typically 6,000°F to 10,000°F (3,316°C to 5,538°C). This heat melts the base metal workpiece along the weld joint as well as the electrode wire. The shielding gas protects the molten weld pool so that the metals coalesce to form a strong weld. The work return, which is attached to the workpiece, completes the welding circuit back to the power source.

The power source of a MIG welding outfit converts AC power from an electrical source to DC output power. More specifically, the power source provides direct current, constant voltage power to the welding gun. The MIG welding process typically operates using a direct current electrode positive (DCEP) connection, also known as a reverse polarity connection.

Many types of electrode wire are available for MIG welding. Most electrode wire is available in one of four sizes: 0.024 inch (0.6 mm), 0.030 inch (0.8 mm), 0.035 inch (0.9 mm), or 0.045 inch (1.2 mm). Standards and recommendations have been developed over the years to help welders select the proper electrode wire for the type and thickness of the metal(s) being welded (**FIGURE 7-6**).

One of the most common electrode wire types used for general purpose welding of mild steel is ER70S-6. The designation for this electrode wire is based on the American Welding Society (AWS) A5.18 specification. Coding for the designation is as follows:

- ER = the filler metal can be used as an electrode or rod
- 70 = the tensile strength of the weld in 1,000 psi (6,895 KPa) increments or 70,000 psi (482,633 KPa) total
- S = the electrode wire is solid
- 6 = the chemical composition of the wire.

▶ TECHNICIAN TIP

The use of flux-core electrode wire is an option for MIG welding. Flux-core electrode wire eliminates the need for a shielding gas, which can improve the portability of the equipment. However, using flux-core electrode wire produces more slag. Most welders prefer to use solid-core electrode wire with a shielding gas.

TIG Welding

One form of arc welding that technicians could possibly encounter is gas tungsten arc welding (GTAW), which is often called tungsten inert gas (TIG) welding. TIG welding is most often used to weld thin pieces of metal, such as stainless steel or aluminum, but it can be used to weld many other types of metal, including steel, copper, brass, bronze, and numerous alloys. Service technicians do not often run into these applications, but they should be aware of how TIG welding works.

TIG welding uses a tungsten electrode to produce the electrical arc needed for welding. The tungsten electrode is not a consumable electrode as in other arc welding processes. Instead, it heats the base metal workpiece while a separate consumable tungsten filler rod is added to the weld puddle. An inert shielding gas is used to prevent oxidation and prevent impurities at the weld. Since two hands are needed to control the welding electrode and the filler rod, TIG welding is considered one of the more difficult arc welding methods.

The main components of a typical TIG welding outfit include a power source, a shielding gas cylinder with a regulator and valves, a coolant system (optional), a torch, a work cable and work clamp, and a foot-operated remote control (**FIGURE 7-7**). During operation, a welder starts the inert gas

Material	Suggested Wire Types, Polarity	Suggested Shielding Gases (Flow Rate of 20-30 cfh)	Wire Sizes (Diameters)	24 ga. (0.6 mm)	22 ga. (0.8 mm)	20 ga. (0.9 mm)	18 ga. (1.2 mm)	16 ga. (1.5 mm)	14 ga. (1.9 mm)	1/8" (3.2 mm)	3/16" (4.8 mm)	1/4" (6.4 mm)	5/16" (7.9 mm)
Steel	Solid Wire ER70S-6 (DCEP)	C_{25} Gas Mixture 75% Ar / 25% CO_2	.024" (0.6 mm)	2/28	2.5/30	2.5/30	2.5/35	3/50	3.5/65	4.5/90	5.5/100	---	---
			.030" (0.8 mm)	2/20	2.5/25	2.5/25	3/35	3/40	3.5/45	4.5/65	5.5/85	6.5/95	7.5/100
			.035" (0.9 mm)	---	2.5/20	2.5/20	3/25	3/30	3.5/35	4.5/55	5.5/65	6.5/70	10/80
	Solid Wire ER70S-6 (DCEP)	100% CO_2	.024" (0.6 mm)	---	---	3/25	3.5/30	3.5/40	4/45	4.5/60	5.5/90	---	---
			.030" (0.8 mm)	---	---	3/20	3.5/30	3.5/35	4/40	5/50	6/70	7/75	10/80
			.035" (0.9 mm)	---	---	---	3.5/20	4/25	4.5/30	5/45	5.5/50	7/65	10/65
	Flux Core E71T-11 (DCEN)	No Shielding Gas required. Good for windy or outdoor applications.	.030" (0.8 mm)	---	---	---	1/15	2/25	3/30	4/45	6/60	7/70	---
			.035" (0.9 mm)	---	---	---	1/15	2/20	3/25	4/40	6/55	7/60	10/65
			.045" (1.2 mm)	---	---	---	---	3/10	4/15	4.5/20	6/30	7/40	10/45
Stainless Steel	Stainless Steel (DCEP)	Tri-Mix 90% He / 7.5% Ar / 2.5% CO_2	.024" (0.6 mm)	---	---	3.5/35	4/35	4/45	4.5/65	5.5/90	6/100	---	---
			.030" (0.8 mm)	---	---	3.5/25	3.5/20	4/40	4.5/50	5/65	6/80	7/95	---
			.035" (0.9 mm)	---	---	---	3.5/25	4/35	4.5/45	5/55	6/65	7/85	---

Number on left of slash is voltage knob setting. **EXAMPLE: 4.5/65**

Number on right of slash is wire speed knob setting. **EXAMPLE: 4.5/65**

FIGURE 7-6 MIG electrode wire selection chart.

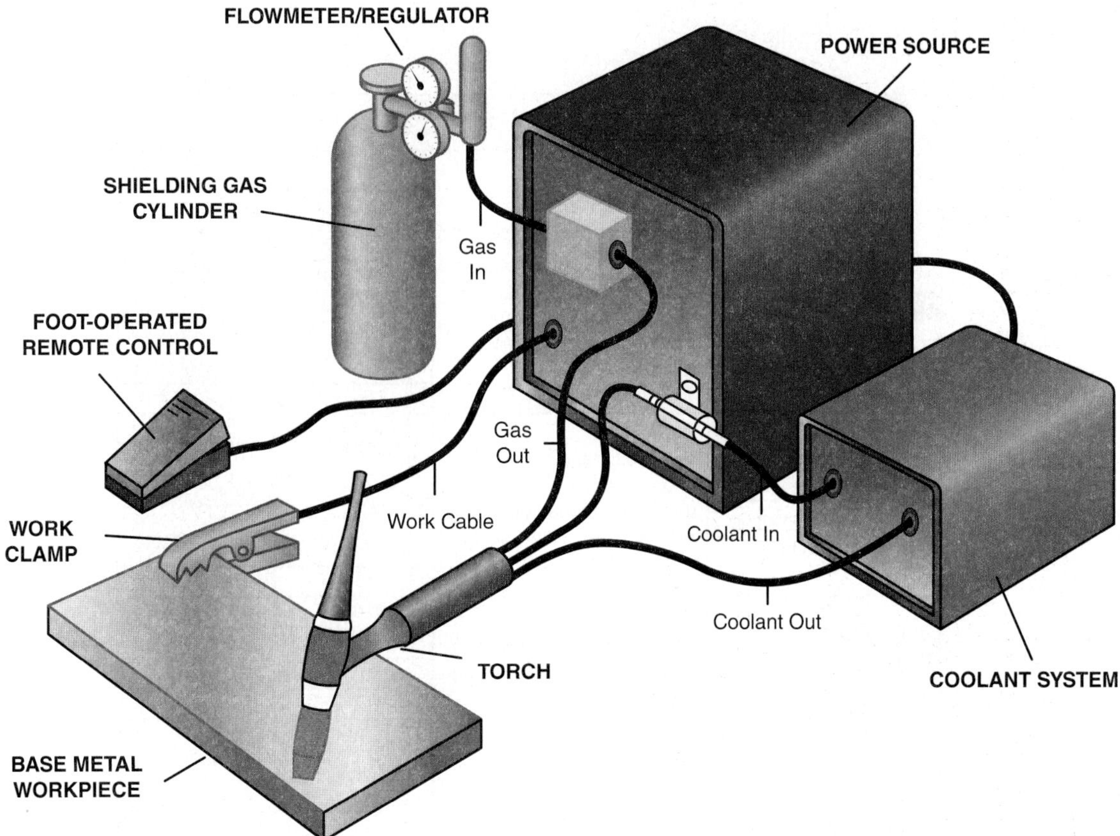

FIGURE 7-7 GTAW (TIG) welding equipment setup.

flow through the TIG torch and positions the torch just above the metal to be welded. The welder then uses the foot pedal control to start an arc at the tungsten electrode in the torch. When the base metal workpiece begins to melt, the welder then adds the tungsten filler metal rod at the arc to fill the welding joint. In some TIG welding setups, cooling water flows through the torch to prevent the tungsten electrode from overheating.

The tungsten filler metal rods used in TIG welding are classified by AWS A5.12 and color coded to help technicians identify the correct rod to use for the welding application (**TABLE 7-2**).

In order to differentiate between MIG, TIG, and stick welding procedures, follow the steps in **SKILL DRILL 7-1**.

▶ Safety Regulations

K07002

Safety must be the foremost priority when working with any type of arc welding equipment. The intense heat and light produced by an electrical arc can pose a significant hazard to welders and other workers in the area. In addition, working around high-voltage and high-current electrical equipment presents a constant risk of electrical shock or electrocution. To ensure that they protect themselves and other personnel, technicians must follow all safety rules related to clothing and protective gear, the work area environment, and the way they use arc welding equipment.

Personal Protective Equipment

Technicians should always wear appropriate PPE when using arc welding equipment (**FIGURE 7-8**). The exact protective equipment that is needed can vary according to regulations and company standards, the welding activity being performed, and the work environment, but all clothing and protective gear should be dry and free of holes.

As a general rule, the following PPE should be worn during arc welding activities:

- A solid material (non-mesh) hat made of flame-retardant material. The bill of the hat should be facing to the rear.
- A welding helmet or, at a minimum, tight-fitting welding goggles with the proper light-reducing shade for the work being done. The Occupational Safety and Health Administration (OSHA), the American National Standards Institute (ANSI), and the American Welding Society (AWS) publish shade range guides for various types of welding and cutting activities. OSHA's shade range guide for arc welding work is from shade 7 to shade 11, while ANSI and AWS guidelines recommend shade 10 to shade 14 (**TABLE 7-3**).

▶ TECHNICIAN TIP

Many welding helmets available today feature auto-darkening technology. When an arc is struck, the lens of the helmet darkens to its shade setting within fractions of a second.

TABLE 7-2 Tungsten Filler Rod Classifications

COMMON TUNGSTEN ELECTRODE TYPES & SIZES			
ISO 6848 COLOR CHART	TYPE	SIZE	
		INCHES	MILLIMETERS
2% Thorlated Red AWS A5.12 EWTh-2 ISO 6848 WT20	Good D/C are starts and stability, medium erosion rate, medium amperage range, medium tendency to spit.	.020 x 7"	0.5 x 175mm
		.040 x 7"	1.0 x 175mm
		1/16 x 7"	1.6 x 175mm
		3/32 x 7"	2.4 x 175mm
		1/8 x 7"	3.2 x 175mm
		5/32 x 7	4.0 x 175mm
0.8% Zirconiated White AWS A5.12 EWZr-8 ISO 6848 WZ8	Balls well, handles higher amperage than pure tungsten with less pitting, better arc starts and arc stability than pure tungsten.	.020 x 7"	0.5 x 175mm
		.040 x 7"	1.0 x 175mm
		1/16 x 7"	1.6 x 175mm
		3/32 x 7"	2.4 x 175mm
		1/8 x 7"	3.2 x 175mm
		5/32 x 7"	4.0 x 175mm
1.5% Lanthanated Gold AWS A5.12 EWLa-1.5 ISO 6848 WL15	Best D/C arc starts and stability, low erosion rate, wide amperage range, no spitting.	.020 x 7"	0.5 x 175mm
		.040 x 7"	1.0 x 175mm
		1/16 x 7"	1.6 x 175mm
		3/32 x 7"	2.4 x 175mm
		1/8 x 7"	3.2 x 175mm
		5/32 x 7"	4.0 x 175mm
2% Cerlated Gray AWS A5.12 EWCe-2 ISO 6848 WC20 (*Formerly Orange*)	Excellent arc stability. Low erosion rate, best at low amperage range, no spitting, good D/C arc starts and stability.	.020 x 7"	0.5 x 175mm
		.040 x 7"	1.0 x 175mm
		1/16 x 7"	1.6 x 175mm
		3/32 x 7"	2.4 x 175mm
		1/8 x 7"	3.2 x 175mm
		5/32 x 7"	4.0 x 175mm
Pure Green AWS A5.12 EWP ISO 6848 WP	Balls easy, tends to spit at higher amperages. Used for non-critical welds only.	.020 x 7"	0.5 x 175mm
		.040 x 7"	1.0 x 175mm
		1/16 x 7"	1.6 x 175mm
		3/32 x 7"	2.4 x 175mm
		1/8 x 7"	3.2 x 175mm
		5/32 x 7"	4.0 x 175mm

SKILL DRILL 7-1 Differences Between SMAW, MIG, and TIG

1. Using SMAW equipment manuals, carefully examine the SMAW equipment setup to identify the components and applicable settings involved in a stick welding process.

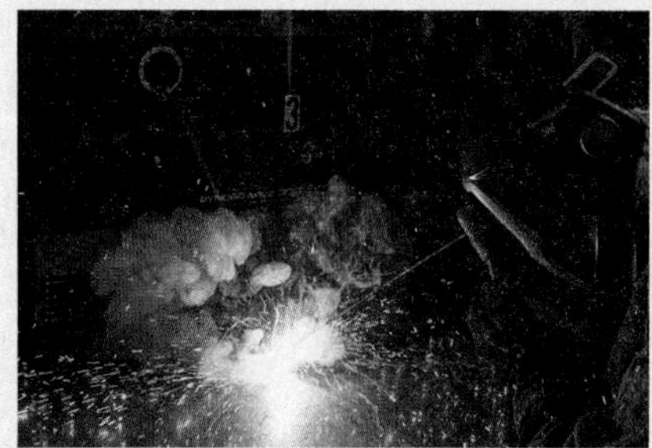

2. Wearing all the appropriate personal protective equipment (PPE), perform a test welding exercise using SMAW to familiarize yourself with the fundamentals of the stick welding process.

3. Using MIG welding equipment manuals, carefully examine the MIG equipment setup to identify the components and applicable settings involved in a MIG welding process.

SKILL DRILL 7-1 Differences Between SMAW, MIG, and TIG (Continued)

4. Wearing all the appropriate PPE, perform a test welding exercise using MIG equipment to familiarize yourself with the fundamentals of the MIG welding process.

5. Using TIG welding equipment manuals, carefully examine the TIG equipment setup to identify the components and applicable settings involved in a TIG welding process.

6. Wearing all the appropriate PPE, perform a test welding exercise using TIG equipment to familiarize yourself with the fundamentals of the TIG welding process.

FIGURE 7-8 Typical personal protective equipment.

SAFETY TIP

Sunglasses should not be worn as a substitute for welding goggles because they do not filter the extreme ultraviolet light as effectively. In addition, the plastic used in the lenses of sunglasses will not protect your eyes from sparks.

- A face shield over the welding goggles to protect the face from flying sparks, debris, and heat.
- Earmuffs (or earplugs) to minimize noise and protect ear canals from sparks.

SAFETY TIP

In some applications, such as welding material overhead, a full leather hood with a properly tinted face plate is preferable to wearing separate welding goggles and a face shield. In addition, if a hard hat is required in the work area, the hard hat must be able to accommodate face-shield and rear deflector attachments.

TABLE 7-3 Arc Welding Shade Range Guidelines

Operation	Electrode Size – inch (mm)	Arc Current (Amperes)	OSHA Minimum Protective Shade Number	ANSI & AWS Shade Number Recommendations*
Shielded Metal Arc Welding (SMAW)	Less than 3/32 (2.4)	Fewer than 60	7	-
	3/32–5/32 (2.4–4.0)	60–160	8	10
	More than 5/32–1/4 (4.0–6.4)	More than 160–250	10	12
	More than 1/4 (6.4)	More than 250–550	11	14
Gas Metal Arc Welding (GMAW) and Flux Cored Arc Welding (FCAW)		Fewer than 60	7	-
		60–160	10	11
		More than 160–250	10	12
		More than 250–550	10	14
Gas Tungsten Arc Welding (GTAW)		Fewer than 50	8	10
		50–150	8	12
		More than 150–500	10	14

- A protective leather apron or, at a minimum, flame-retardant clothing capable of protecting against ultraviolet light and hot sparks. Shirts should have long sleeves, pants should have no cuffs, and jackets should have no pockets where hot metal can collect.
- Long leather welding gloves to protect hands and arms.
- Leather work boots. The tongue and lace area of each boot should be tall enough to be covered by the pants legs. Otherwise, leather **spats** should be used to cover the front of the boots.

While working around the electricity and high heat associated with welding, technicians should not wear jewelry or body-piercing studs. These items can snag on equipment, absorb heat from the welding arc, and provide an unintended path for electrical current.

Breathing masks or respirators may be required when welding certain materials. For example, copper, lead, mercury, zinc, and other materials can produce toxic fumes when heated. For short-term exposure to some fumes, a technician may be safe using a high-efficiency particulate arresting (HEPA) filter or a metal-fume filter. But if a technician is exposed to such toxic fumes for a long period of time, a full-face, supplied-air respirator (SAR) is necessary (**FIGURE 7-9**).

Work Area Safety

Whenever arc welding equipment is used, there is an inherent risk of electrical shock, fire, and explosion. To minimize these and other risks, technicians should always inspect and prepare the machinery or equipment to be worked on, as well as the work area and its surroundings before using any arc welding equipment. Maintaining a safe work area typically includes the following:

- Remove flammable materials such as rags, paper, boxes, and flammable liquids from the work area or shield them using a fire-resistant cover. Many work site fires are caused by cutting and welding activities, so maintaining a neat and clean work area can greatly reduce accidental fires.

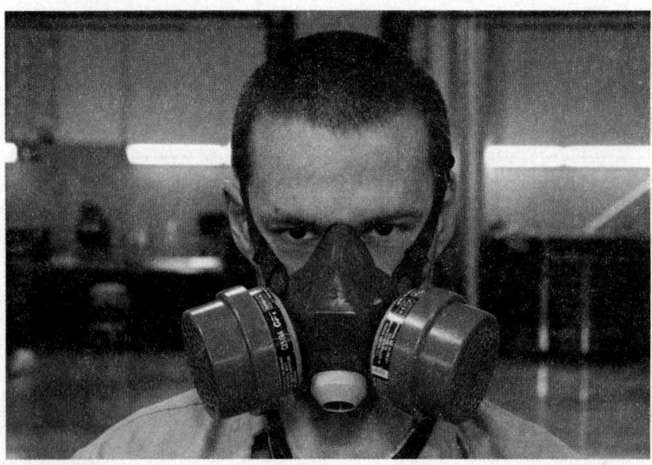

FIGURE 7-9 Worker wearing a supplied-air respirator (SAR).

- Set up flash shields or flash curtains to help isolate the intense light and heat of the welding area.
- Make sure that approved fire extinguishers are readily accessible before starting any welding operation.
- Make sure welding equipment is properly positioned at the work site and that all electrode and work cables are kept out of the way to avoid trip hazards.
- Determine whether the work area is a **confined space** or if it requires a hot-work permit or a fire watch. If so, follow all requirements and procedures for the site. Many sites require hot-work permits and fire watches, and failure to abide by these requirements can lead to serious injuries, penalties, and loss of equipment and structures due to fire.
- Make sure that the work area is properly ventilated. This is especially true for confined spaces. Fans, exhaust hoods, and ventilated booths can all be used to provide the necessary ventilation.
- Do not use oxygen to ventilate a work area. Releasing a large amount of oxygen into the work space can cause rapid and uncontrolled combustion if a spark ignites flammable material. Oxygen should be kept away from petroleum products to prevent fire and explosions.

Safe Equipment Use

Before starting any welding procedure, technicians must prepare the welding work area, properly set up the welding equipment, prepare the metal to be welded, and then follow appropriate safety guidelines for operating the welding equipment. Safe equipment use typically includes the following:

- While working, avoid breathing in welding fumes and smoke. Use a fan, if necessary, to divert the fumes and smoke. Wear an appropriate breathing apparatus to avoid toxic fumes when necessary.
- Never use oxygen to blow dust and dirt off clothing or equipment. Oxygen can remain trapped in clothing and ignite and burn rapidly if exposed to a spark.
- When using MIG welding equipment, do not press the control switch, or trigger, on the welding gun until you are ready to begin the welding process.
- Never point a welding gun toward others.
- Do not overuse welding equipment to a point where the equipment begins to overheat.
- Always connect the work cable clamp as closely as possible to the welding area to minimize the distance that the welding current has to travel.
- Ensure that all scrap metal or slag being discarded has cooled to a point where it does not pose a fire hazard.

▶ Shielded Metal Arc Welding of Mild Steel

K07003, S07002, S07003

Many of the welding activities that MORE (mobile off-road equipment) service technicians will encounter involve the use of SMAW on mild steel. Mild steel is basically a low-carbon

FIGURE 7-10 SMAW E6010 electrodes.

steel (0.25% or less carbon) that is used in countless everyday applications. It is not brittle. It can be heated and bent, as well as welded with relative ease. To achieve satisfactory results when welding mild steel, technicians need to follow the welding equipment guidelines for selecting the proper electrode and using the proper welding technique.

Selecting Mild Steel Electrodes

Selecting the proper electrode for SMAW is not particularly challenging. In fact, an E6010 electrode is perfectly capable of handling most general steel repairs that MORE service technicians are likely to face (**FIGURE 7-10**). The E6010 electrode is a good general purpose electrode that is available in various sizes to fit most SMAW needs.

There are, of course, other electrodes that might be more suitable for particular applications. Electrode manufacturers provide selection charts that technicians should always use for choosing the proper electrode (**TABLE 7-4**).

Welding Mild Steel

The amount of current (amps) needed to weld depends on numerous factors, including the thickness of the metal being welded, the diameter of the electrode being used, and the position being used during the welding process. As expected, thinner metals and smaller electrodes require less current than thicker metals and larger electrodes. Service technicians should always follow the electrode manufacturer's recommendations for equipment settings.

The basic procedure for welding mild steel using SMAW equipment is as follows:

Stick welding equipment setup and operation is as follows:

1. Ensure that the work area has been properly set up for the welding activity.
2. Determine the type(s) of metal to be welded and thoroughly clean the metal with a solvent and/or an abrasive pad to remove any rust or contamination. Ensure that the welding area and all materials are completely dry of water or any cleaning liquids that were used.
3. Use the electrode manufacturer's selection guide to select the proper electrode for the job.
4. Connect the electrode cable and the work cable to the welding machine in the proper position for the type of welding to be done (DC positive, DC negative, or AC).
5. Set the amperage on the machine according to the electrode manufacturer's guidelines.
6. Connect the work clamp to the base metal workpiece as close to the weld area as possible.
7. Put on all the appropriate PPE required for the job.
8. Turn on the welder and place the appropriate electrode into the electrode holder.

SAFETY TIP

If using a welding helmet that does not have an auto-darkening feature, be sure to lower the front of the welding helmet before initiating an arc to prevent eye damage.

9. Scratch or tap the tip of the electrode against the workpiece to start the arc.
10. Maintain the proper electrode angle, movement, and travel speed as the electrode is consumed.

▶ TECHNICIAN TIP

It may be necessary to adjust the amperage setting on the power source if the weld does not appear to be satisfactory. Follow the equipment manufacturer's recommendations if an amperage adjustment is needed.

11. When the electrode is almost completely consumed, quickly pull the electrode holder away from the weld to interrupt the arc.
12. Allow the bead to cool, and then completely remove the slag using a chipping hammer and a wire brush.
13. If additional beads are needed, repeat the process to initiate the arc and continue the welding. Be sure to remove the slag from each added bead before continuing.
14. When the welding job is complete, turn off the power source and remove the work clamp from the workpiece.

SAFETY TIP

Remember that the weld area will remain hot for quite a while. Allow ample time for the workpiece to cool before touching it. Also, any slag that has been removed from the bead(s) should be allowed to cool before it is disposed of.

In order to demonstrate the proper procedures for welding mild steel using shielded metal arc welding, follow the steps in **SKILL DRILL 7-2**.

In order to demonstrate the proper procedures for welding mild steel using wire feed processes (MIG, TIG), follow the steps in **SKILL DRILL 7-3**.

TABLE 7-4 SMAW Electrode Selection Chart

ELECTRODE SELECTION CHART

ELECTRODE	AC	DC *	POSITION	PENETRATION	USAGE
6010	NO	EP	ALL	DEEP	MIN, PREP, ROUGH, HIGH SPATTER
6011	YES	EP	ALL	DEEP	
6013	YES	EP, EN	ALL	LOW	GENERAL, EASY
7014	YES	EP, EN	ALL	MED	SMOOTH, EASY, FAST
7018	YES	EP	ALL	LOW	LOW, HYDROGEN, STRONG
7018AC	YES	EP	ALL	LOW	
7024	YES	EP, EN	FLAT HORIZ FILLET	LOW	SMOOTH, EASY, FASTER
Ni-Cl	YES	EP	ALL	LOW	CAST IRON
308L	YES	EP	ALL	LOW	STAINLESS

* EP = ELECTRODE POSITIVE (REVERSE POLARITY)
* EN = ELECTRODE NEGATIVE (STRAIGHT POLARITY)

DIAMETERS/AMPERAGES

1/16	3/32	1/8	5/32
X	40–85	75–125	110–165
20–35	40–85	75–125	110–165
20–45	40–90	80–130	105–180
35–60	80–125	110–165	150–210
30–50	65–100	110–165	150–220
30–50	65–100	110–165	150–220
X	100–145	140–190	180–250
X	50–70	65–85	100–140
X	40–80	75–115	105–160

SKILL DRILL 7-2 Welding Mild Steel with SMAW

1. Prepare the work area and the workpiece to be welded. Use appropriate manufacturers' guidelines to set up the welding equipment and select the proper electrode.

2. Put on all appropriate PPE needed for the welding task.

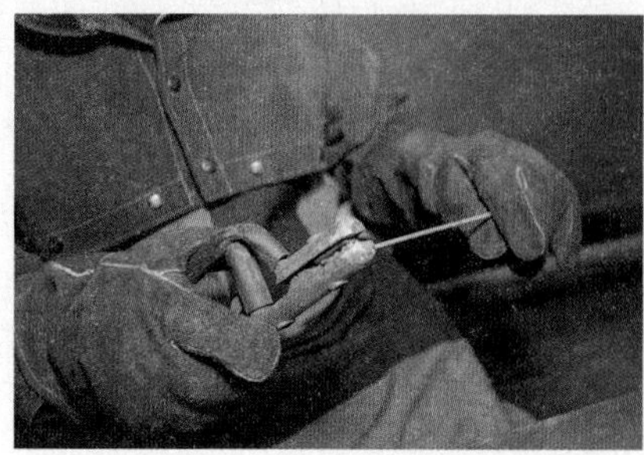

3. Turn on the welder and place the appropriate electrode into the electrode holder.

4. Scratch or tap the tip of the electrode against the workpiece to start the arc. Maintain the proper electrode angle, movement, and travel speed as the electrode is consumed. Replace consumed electrodes as needed.

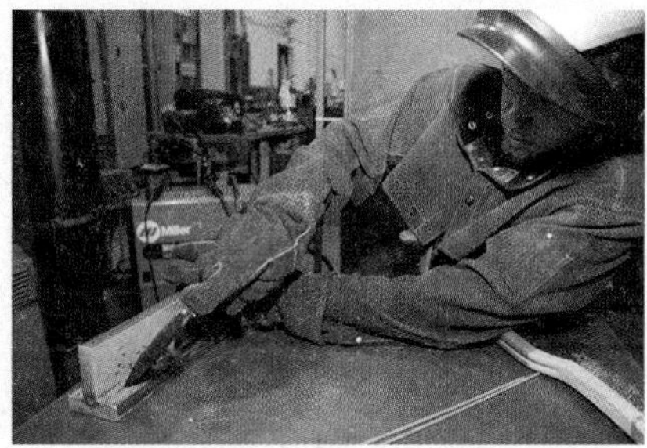

5. When the welding bead has been completed, allow it to cool, and then completely remove the slag using a chipping hammer and a wire brush.

6. After completing the welding job, shut down and disconnect the welding equipment and follow all safety precautions related to hot workpiece metal and slag.

SKILL DRILL 7-3 Welding Mild Steel with MIG and TIG

1. Prepare the work area and the workpiece to be welded. Use appropriate manufacturers' guidelines to set up the MIG welding equipment, select the proper electrode wire, and turn on the shielding gas.

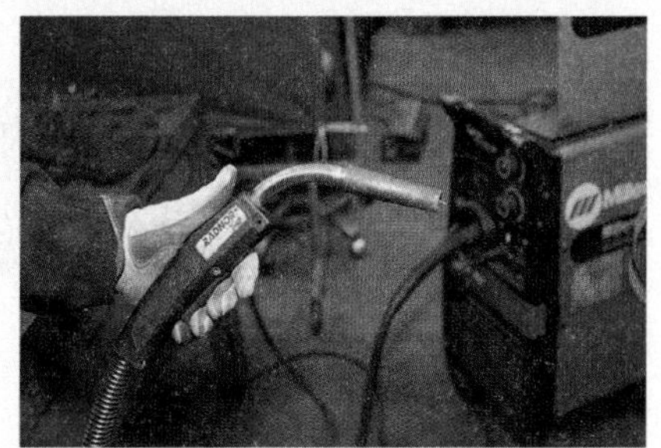

2. Put on all appropriate PPE needed for the welding task.

3. Position the electrode tip at the workpiece and press the control switch on the MIG welding gun to start the electric power, the electrode wire feed, and the shielding gas flow.

(Continued)

SKILL DRILL 7-3 Welding Mild Steel with MIG and TIG (Continued)

4. Slowly move the welding gun along the weld joint at the proper travel speed to allow the molten base metal and the filler metal to fill the joint.

5. Use the appropriate manufacturers' guidelines to set up the TIG welding equipment, select the proper tungsten filler metal electrode, and turn on the shielding gas.

6. Depress the TIG welder foot pedal to start an arc at the torch. When the base metal workpiece begins to melt, push the tip of a tungsten filler metal electrode into the arc to allow the molten base metal and the filler metal to fill the joint.

▶ Air-Arc Gouging

K07004

Air-arc gouging is a process in which metal is removed from a workpiece using the heat from a carbon or graphite electrode arc and a jet of compressed air to blow away the molten metal. Air-arc gouging is commonly referred to by several different names, including air-arc cutting, carbon arc cutting, or air carbon arc cutting (CAC-A). Regardless of the name, however, the process is the same. MORE service technicians might use this process for activities such as cutting off welded-on bucket cutting edges or tooth adapters and removing liners from haul truck boxes. A few special pieces of equipment are needed to perform air-arc gouging, and the technique used for the process is different from those used in other forms of metal cutting.

Air-Arc Gouging Equipment

Air-arc gouging requires three special pieces of equipment: an electrode cable and torch handle that can be hooked up to a compressed air hose, carbon/graphite gouging electrodes, and a source of compressed air (**FIGURE 7-11**).

The electrode cable has a fitting for connecting the hose from the compressed air source, which is typically an air compressor located nearby (**FIGURE 7-12**). The compressed air is

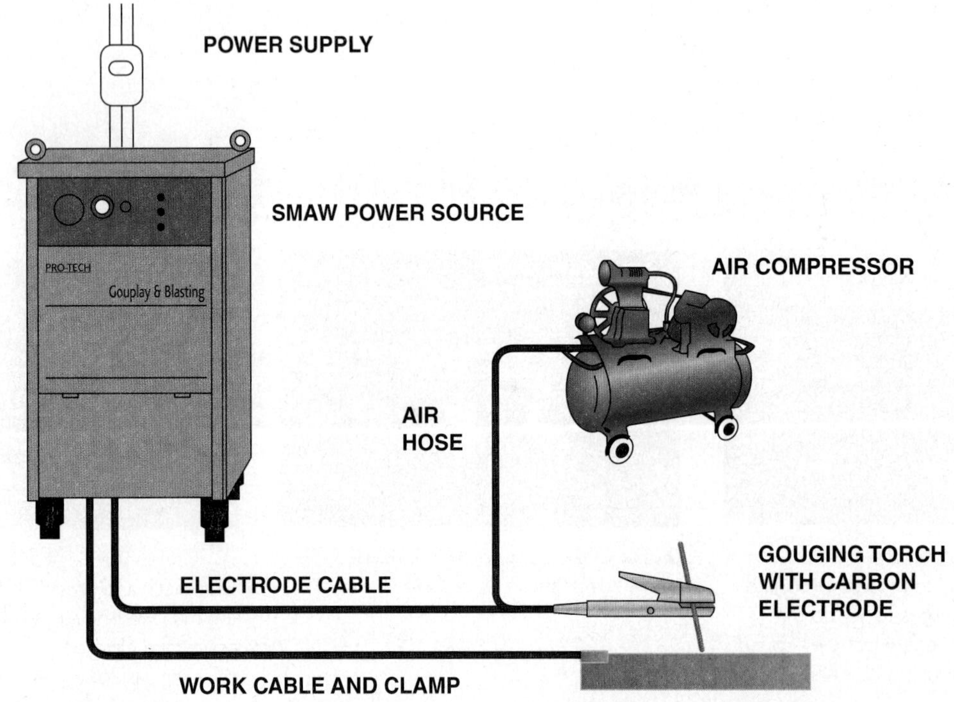

FIGURE 7-11 Air-arc gouging equipment setup.

FIGURE 7-12 Air-arc gouging electrode cable and torch.

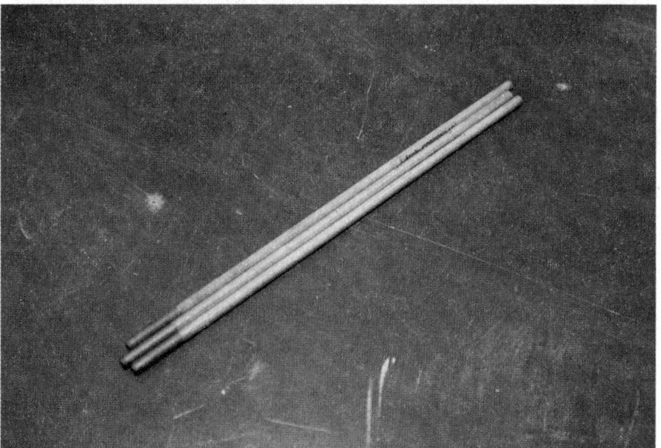

FIGURE 7-13 Air-arc gouging electrodes.

routed to the torch handle, which has small channels through which the air can flow to blow away the molted metal during the air-arc gouging process.

Electrodes used for air-arc gouging are much different from other welding electrodes. Gouging electrodes are available in a variety of sizes, and most of them are copper clad (**FIGURE 7-13**). They are typically a blend of carbon and graphite and are designed to produce the intense heat necessary for air-arc gouging. Technicians should always follow the electrode manufacturer's guidelines when selecting electrodes for air-arc gouging activities.

Air-Arc Gouging Process

Before an air-arc gouging procedure is performed, technicians must make sure that the work area is properly prepared for the intense sparks, noise, and fumes that will occur. The work area must be well ventilated and, if possible, partitioned from the surrounding area. The welding equipment must be properly set up according to the manufacturer's guidelines. The basic steps for an air-arc gouging procedure are as follows:

1. Use the electrode manufacturer's selection guide to select the proper gouging electrode for the job.
2. Connect the electrode cable and the work cable to the welding machine in the proper position according to the manufacturer's recommendations.
3. Set the amperage on the machine according to the electrode manufacturer's guidelines.
4. Connect the work clamp to the base metal workpiece as close to the gouging area as possible.
5. Connect the air hose from the compressed air source to the electrode cable for the gouging torch.
6. Put on all the appropriate PPE required for the job.
7. Turn on the welder and place the appropriate electrode into the electrode holder. Follow the electrode manufacturer's guidelines on how to position the electrode in the holder.

SAFETY TIP

If using a welding helmet that does not have an auto-darkening feature, be sure to lower the front of the welding helmet before initiating an arc to prevent eye damage.

8. Scratch or tap the tip of the gouging electrode against the workpiece to start the arc.
9. Squeeze the torch handle to allow the compressed air to blow away the molten metal from the gouging area.
10. When the electrode is used up, replace it with a new electrode. Continue this process until the gouging job is complete.
11. Turn off the power source and, if applicable, the air compressor. Remove the work clamp from the workpiece.

SAFETY TIP

Remember that the area of the workpiece around the gouge will remain hot for quite a while. Allow ample time for the workpiece to cool before touching it.

▶ Attitude

A07001

Before setting up and using any type of arc welding equipment, it is critical for MORE service technicians to be thoroughly familiar with the safety regulations and procedures that pertain to the equipment and its use for welding metal. This includes locating and reading any safety-related manuals that may exist on site. Find out where those manuals are normally kept, and take action to obtain the proper manuals for the equipment. If printed manuals are not available for the equipment, try to find electronic versions either from the client or online through the equipment manufacturer's website. It might also be possible to find the appropriate material by searching online. In some cases, it might be necessary to call the equipment manufacture to get the needed information. Whatever the means, it is important to ensure that the resource material being used matches the equipment and the procedures being performed.

▶ SMAW Terminology

107001

The terminology associated with the composition and use of SMAW equipment is critical for MORE service technicians. Technicians must be able to accurately use terminology that is common to the trade and understand safety procedures that apply to this work. Federal and state agencies, along with industrial trade groups, have developed standards over the years that technicians can use for source material:

- the Occupational Safety and Health Administration (OSHA) at www.osha.gov, which sets and enforces standards related to safety and equipment
- the National Fire Protection Association (NFPA) at www.nfpa.org, a global nonprofit organization devoted to eliminating death, injury, property, and economic due to fire, electrical, and related hazards
- the American Welding Society (AWS) at www.aws.org, a nonprofit organization with a global mission to advance the science, technology, and application of welding and allied joining and cutting processes–proper procedures for cutting or welding hazardous containers are described in the *American Welding Society (AWS) F4.1, Safe Practices for the Preparation of Containers and Piping for Welding and Cutting*
- the American National Standards Institute (ANSI) at www.ansi.org, an organization that oversees the creation, promulgation, and use of norms and guidelines that impact U.S. businesses—see standard Z49.1 *Safety in Welding, Cutting, and Allied Processes.*

In addition, SMAW equipment manufacturers and magazines covering the welding industry typically have technical information, including glossaries, available on their websites. Technicians working on MORE should exploit all available resources to ensure that they understand the terminology and regulations that apply to the trade.

▶ SMAW Repair Techniques

107002

An important part of SMAW welding repair involves preparing the metal to be welded. No matter how thin or thick the metal workpieces are, they need to be cleaned and properly positioned before welding begins. Often, welding clamps are needed to hold workpieces in place. In some cases, it may be necessary to tack weld the workpieces to hold them in position for welding or to gap the pieces to allow for expansion and contraction. Thicker metals may have to be beveled to create a suitable joint for the welding bead (**FIGURE 7-14**).

Welding positions, welding types, and welding joints can vary from job to job (**FIGURE 7-15**). Four welding positions that service technicians are likely to use include flat, horizontal, vertical, and overhead. In addition, two common welding types are groove welds and fillet welds, and four common welding joints are butt, corner, tee, and lap.

Groove welds are done on beveled surfaces. This allows the molten base metal and filler metal to fill the prepared joint groove to create a strong connection. Fillet welds, on the other hand, do not require beveling. They are often performed on metal plates that are aligned perpendicular to one another.

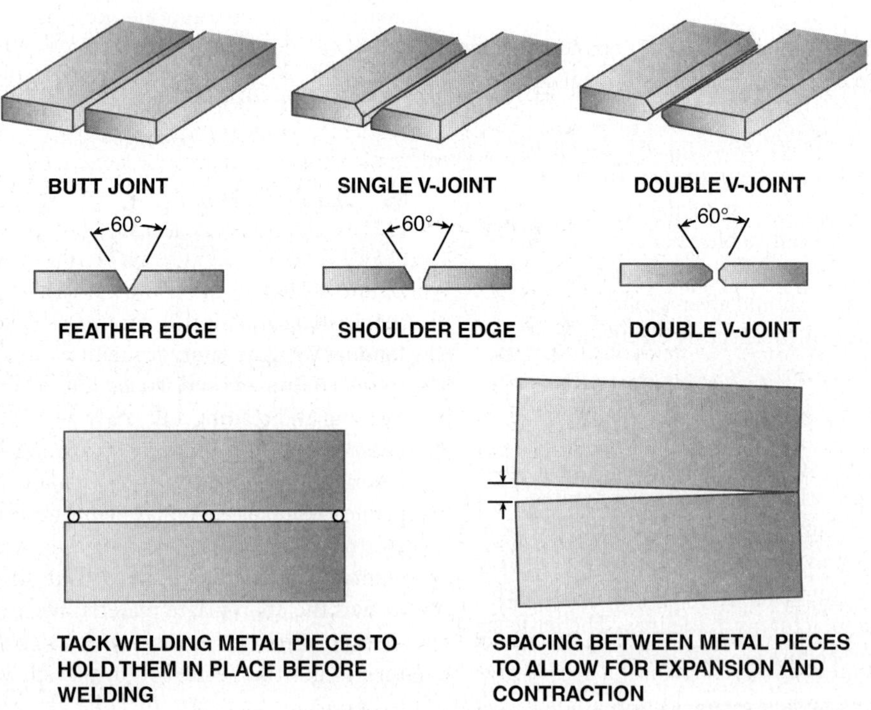

FIGURE 7-14 Preparing work pieces for welding.

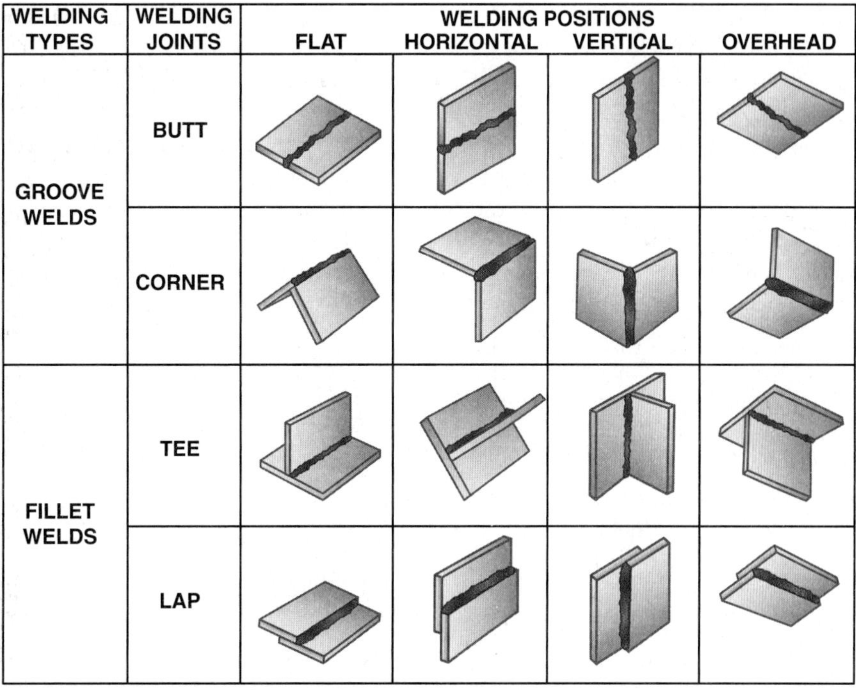

FIGURE 7-15 Welding positions, types, and joints.

▶ Wrap-Up

Ready for Review

- Shielded metal arc welding (SMAW), or stick welding, is the most commonly used form of arc welding.
- Stick welding uses the intense heat from an electric arc created between a base metal workpiece and the tip of a filler metal electrode (welding rod) to melt the metals so that they fuse together through coalescence to form a strong welded bond.
- Stick welding is a popular form of arc welding because the equipment is relatively simple and inexpensive; it can be used on most common metals and alloys; it is generally easy to learn; the filler metal electrodes are widely available and have a flux coating that protects against oxidation; and the equipment is portable, which makes it a good choice for field service applications and limited access areas.
- The main components of a typical SMAW system include the welding machine, or power source, and its internal components; an electrode cable with an electrode stick holder, a work cable with a work clamp, a power supply cable that plugs into an electric outlet, an on/off power switch, an AC/DC output selector, and an amperage selector.
- A stick welding machine is essentially a step-down transformer that converts high-voltage, low-current AC power from a wall outlet (or engine) to a lower-voltage, higher-current AC or DC output.
- Any stick welder that provides DC output power includes a rectifier or some other means to convert the AC input power to a DC output.
- The AC/DC output selector on a stick welder allows a technician to select the form of output power, while the amperage selector allows the welder to choose the amount of current needed for the welding operation.
- A typical stick welder can convert AC input power of 220V at 50 amps to a DC output of 25V at 125 amps.
- DC is the most common current used for stick welding because it flows in only one direction and results in easier arc starting and less sticking and spatter.
- An SMAW machine provides a constant current output, which means that the output current that accounts for the intense heat at the arc remains relatively constant even when there are variations in the welding conditions—such as when a welding technician varies the distance, or length, of the arc.
- In SMAW, connecting the electrode cable to the positive terminal of the power source and the work cable to the negative terminal sets up a direct current electrode positive (DCEP), or a reverse polarity, connection, which is the most commonly used connection in stick welding.
- Electrode sizes for SMAW range from 1⁄16-inch (1.6 mm) to 3⁄8 inch (9.5 mm), and the American Welding Society (AWS) provides a standard electrode classification system for service technicians to use when selecting the proper electrode.
- There are many types and sizes of welding clamps that can be used to hold base metal workpieces in place for welding.

- Slag that forms on a weld bead must be completely removed before another bead can be laid on top of the previous bead. Slag can be removed using a chipping hammer and a wire brush.
- Gas metal arc welding (GMAW), or metal inert gas (MIG) welding, requires the use of a shielding gas to protect the weld from oxidation and contaminants in the surrounding air.
- The three most commonly used gases in MIG welding are argon, carbon dioxide, and helium—or some mixture of them.
- MIG welding equipment includes a welding machine, or power source; a shielding gas supply; an electrode wire feed reel, or spool; electrode wire; a welding gun; and a work return connection.
- A control switch on a MIG welding gun starts the electric power, the electrode wire feed, and the shielding gas flow through a liner to the tip of the welding gun. The arc that is created melts the base metal workpiece and the electrode wire to form a molten weld pool where the metals coalesce to form a strong weld.
- Most MIG electrode wires are one of four sizes: 0.024 inch (0.6 mm), 0.030 inch (0.8 mm), 0.035 inch (0.9 mm), or 0.045 inch (1.2 mm).
- One of the most common electrode wire types used for general purpose MIG welding of mild steel is ER70S-6.
- Gas tungsten arc welding (GTAW), or tungsten inert gas (TIG) welding, is most often used to weld thin pieces of metal such as stainless steel or aluminum.
- TIG welding uses a non-consumable tungsten electrode to produce the electrical arc needed for welding.
- The TIG electrode heats the base metal workpiece while a separate consumable tungsten filler rod is added to the weld puddle. An inert shielding gas is used to prevent oxidation and prevent impurities at the weld.
- The main components of a typical TIG welding outfit include a power source, a shielding gas cylinder with a regulator and valves, a coolant system (optional), a torch, a work cable and work clamp, and a foot-operated remote control.
- Technicians should always wear appropriate PPE when welding with any type of arc welding equipment.
- Breathing masks or respirators may be required when welding materials that can produce toxic fumes when heated.
- To minimize the risk of fire and explosion, technicians should always inspect and prepare the machinery or equipment to be worked on, as well as the work area and its surroundings before using arc welding equipment.
- If the work area is a confined space or if it requires a hot-work permit or a fire watch, follow all requirements and procedures for the site to avoid serious injuries and penalties.
- Make sure that the work area is properly ventilated by using fans, exhaust hoods, or ventilated booths.
- Mild steel is basically a low-carbon steel (0.25% or less carbon) that is used in countless everyday applications.
- An E6010 is a good general purpose SMAW electrode for most steel repairs.
- Air-arc gouging is a process in which metal is removed from a workpiece using the heat from a carbon or graphite electrode arc and a jet of compressed air to blow away the molten metal.
- Air-arc gouging is commonly referred to by several different names, including air-arc cutting, carbon arc cutting, or air carbon arc cutting (CAC-A).
- MORE service technicians might use air-arc gouging for cutting off welded-on bucket cutting edges or tooth adapters and for removing liners from haul truck boxes.

Key Terms

coalescence The fusing together of two or more metals that occurs when the metals are heated to a point of liquefaction and, after cooling, are bonded together to form one continuous solid.

confined space An enclosed area that has limited space and accessibility and requires special safety procedures for entering, working, and exiting.

constant current The ability of a system to maintain a consistent current output even when there are voltage variations in the load.

Direct Current Electrode Positive (DCEP) The flow through an electrical circuit that is formed when an electrode cable is connected to the positive terminal of a power source and the work cable is connected to the negative terminal of the power source; also referred to as a reverse polarity connection.

electrical polarity The direction of current flow in an electrical circuit based on the fact that current flows from the positive pole, or terminal, to the negative pole.

power source A component in an arc welding system that converts AC input power into an AC or DC output at the appropriate voltage and current levels needed for the welding task.

rectifier A device that converts alternating current (AC) to direct current (DC).

reverse polarity The flow through an electrical circuit that is formed when an electrode cable is connected to the positive terminal of a power source and the work cable is connected to the negative terminal of the power source; also referred to as a direct current electrode positive (DCEP) connection.

slag Oxidized and molten metal waste that is left over from welding operations.

spats A type of PPE, often made of leather, worn over the laces and tongue of work boots to protect workers from hot metal.

step-down transformer A component that converts high-voltage, low-current AC power from a wall outlet (or engine) to a lower-voltage, higher-current AC or DC output.

Review Questions

1. In most SMAW applications, the welding machine power source converts high-voltage, low-current AC power to a _____.
   a. higher-voltage, lower-amperage AC output
   b. constant-voltage, constant-current output

c. lower-voltage, lower-current AC/DC output
d. lower-voltage, higher-current DC output

2. The amperage selector on a stick welding machine allows the welder to choose _____.
   a. the type of source power being provided to the welder
   b. the amount of current needed for the welding operation
   c. the speed at which the electrode wire is fed to the torch
   d. the voltage level flowing to the work cable and clamp
3. Connecting the electrode cable to the positive terminal of an SMAW power source and the work cable to the negative terminal of the power source sets up a(n) _____.
   a. direct current electrode negative (DCEN) connection
   b. alternating current inverse polarity (ACIP) connection
   c. direct current electrode positive (DCEP) connection
   d. alternating current straight polarity (ACSP) connection
4. In the American Welding Society (AWS) standard electrode classification system, the first two numbers in a stick welding electrode name indicate _____.
   a. the tensile strength of the welded joint
   b. the acceptable welding position(s) for the electrode
   c. the amount of penetration provided
   d. the type of flux coating material on the electrode
5. The three most commonly used gases in MIG welding are _____.
   a. nitrogen, oxygen, and helium
   b. argon, carbon dioxide, and helium
   c. carbon dioxide, acetylene, and argon
   d. helium, hydrogen, and carbon dioxide
6. Which arc welding process is most likely to require a filler metal electrode rod, a foot-operated remote control, and a coolant system?
   a. Shielded metal arc welding (SMAW)
   b. Gas metal arc welding (GMAW)
   c. Metal inert gas (MIG) welding
   d. Gas tungsten arc welding (GTAW)
7. If a technician is going to be exposed to toxic fumes for a long period of time during an arc welding procedure, the technician should wear a _____.
   a. full-face, supplied-air respirator (SAR)
   b. high-efficiency particulate arresting (HEPA) filter
   c. pure oxygen supply mask (POSM)
   d. dampened charcoal canister mask (DCCM)
8. During arc welding, where should the work cable clamp be connected?
   a. At least 12 inches (305 mm) from the welding area of the workpiece.
   b. To any dry wooden object in the vicinity of the welding area.
   c. As close as possible to the welding area of the workpiece.
   d. To a grounding buckle on the welder's leather apron.
9. How often should slag be removed during stick welding activities?
   a. SMAW does not create slag.
   b. Slag should be removed after every bead is laid.
   c. Never. Slag protects the weld from oxidation.
   d. All slag can be removed at once when the welding process ends.
10. What typically flows through the torch handle during an air carbon arc cutting process to remove molten metal?
   a. liquid coolant
   b. graphite powder
   c. carbon fibers
   d. compressed air

ASE Technician A/Technician B Style Questions

1. Technician A says the heat from a stick welder arc melts the workpiece metal and the filler metal electrode so that they fuse together through coalescence. Technician B says the metals fuse together through adherence. Who is correct?
   a. Technician A
   b. Technician B
   c. Both Technician A and Technician B
   d. Neither Technician A nor Technician B
2. Technician A says the filler metal electrodes used in stick welding require additional flux or a shielding gas. Technician B says SMAW electrodes already have a flux coating. Who is correct?
   a. Technician A
   b. Technician B
   c. Both Technician A and Technician B
   d. Neither Technician A nor Technician B
3. Technician A says a stick welding machine is essentially a step-up transformer. Technician B says the machine converts low-voltage, high-current AC power to a higher-voltage, lower-current AC or DC output. Who is correct?
   a. Technician A
   b. Technician B
   c. Both Technician A and Technician B
   d. Neither Technician A nor Technician B
4. Technician A says a stick welder that provides DC output power needs a rectifier or similar means to convert the AC input power to a DC output. Technician B says the only component needed to make the conversion is the electrode arrestor. Who is correct?
   a. Technician A
   b. Technician B
   c. Both Technician A and Technician B
   d. Neither Technician A nor Technician B
5. Technician A says the most commonly used circuit connection in SMAW is direct current electrode positive (DCEP). Technician B says the most commonly used circuit connection is reverse polarity. Who is correct?
   a. Technician A
   b. Technician B
   c. Both Technician A and Technician B
   d. Neither Technician A nor Technician B
6. Technician A says a type of arc welding that uses a shielding gas to protect an electrode wire that is continuously fed into the weld is called tungsten inert gas (TIG) welding.

Technician B says that type of arc welding is called gas tungsten arc welding (GTAW). Who is correct?

a. Technician A
b. Technician B
c. Both Technician A and Technician B
d. Neither Technician A nor Technician B

7. Technician A says ANSI and AWS guidelines for arc welding recommend the darkest lens available (shade 6) for eye protection. Technician B says ANSI and AWS guidelines recommend shade 10 to shade 14. Who is correct?
   a. Technician A
   b. Technician B
   c. Both Technician A and Technician B
   d. Neither Technician A nor Technician B
8. Technician A says the best way to ventilate a work area before and during a stick welding procedure is to use fans or exhaust hoods. Technician B says the way to purify and ventilate a work area is to release a long burst of oxygen from the SMAW cylinder. Who is correct?
   a. Technician A
   b. Technician B
   c. Both Technician A and Technician B
   d. Neither Technician A nor Technician B
9. Technician A says mild steel is easily welded using SMAW because the steel is not all that hard or brittle. Technician B says an E6010 electrode is suitable for most general mild steel repairs using SMAW. Who is correct?
   a. Technician A
   b. Technician B
   c. Both Technician A and Technician B
   d. Neither Technician A nor Technician B
10. Technician A says you have to use an inert gas, such as oxygen, to remove molten metal during an air-arc gouging process. Technician B says you should use compressed air. Who is correct?
    a. Technician A
    b. Technician B
    c. Both Technician A and Technician B
    d. Neither Technician A nor Technician B

CHAPTER 8

Principles of Hoisting, Rigging, and Slings

Knowledge Objectives

After reading this chapter, you will be able to:

- **K08001** Identify and describe the purposes, types, functions, and applications of lifting, rigging and blocking equipment.
- **K08002** Describe wire rope applications.
- **K08003** Discuss winch design, operation, and troubleshooting procedures.
- **K08004** Explain towing, transporting, and coasting precautions.
- **K08005** Describe proper lifting techniques and equipment according to occupational health and safety standards.

Skills Objectives

After reading this chapter, you will be able to:

- **S08001** Demonstrate manual lifting procedures using correct body mechanics.
- **S08002** Demonstrate inspection, testing, and operating procedures for lifting rigging and blocking equipment following manufacturers' recommended procedures and government regulations.

Attitude Objectives

After reading this chapter, you will be able to:

- **A08001** Locate and follow appropriate safety procedures when using lift equipment.

Industry/Accreditation

After reading this chapter, you will be able to:

- **I08001** Recommend equipment for lifting components and equipment.

▶ Introduction

This chapter introduces the mobile off-road equipment (MORE) technician to the principles of lifting, support using blocking and cribbing, and towing operations. We also specifically review the types of equipment used in hoisting, rigging, winching, towing, and blocking. This consists of a brief overview of the equipment, techniques, procedures, and safety-related information on these topics. The safe and proper procedures and use of many types of equipment used for lifting, rigging, hoisting, supporting, and towing requires specialized training and experience (**FIGURE 8-1**). This chapter is not a substitute for the proper training and experience required to safely and correctly operate this type of equipment.

SAFETY TIP

Lifting heavy objects is no joke! The larger and heavier an item is, the more inherent danger there is when undertaking a lifting operation. Always take the time to ensure you are properly trained and qualified, and follow safe practices when operating lifting, hoisting, rigging, and blocking equipment and devices.

FIGURE 8-1 The operation and use of most types of lifting, hoisting, towing, rigging, and blocking equipment and devices requires specialized training and experience. Failure to be properly trained and experienced when operating these types of equipment and devices may result in serious equipment damage, injury, and death to yourself and others!

FIGURE 8-2 The parts, components, and assemblies of MORE can weigh thousands of pounds, or hundreds of kilograms, requiring the use of specialized lifting equipment.

As mentioned previously, specialized training and instruction is required for most types of specialized heavy lifting, towing, and supporting equipment and devices. Because of this, we only briefly review self-powered equipment used for lifting, towing, and supporting heavy objects. The bulk of the information here focuses on the non-self-powered devices and equipment used for lifting and supporting heavy objects inside the MORE shop.

Typically, MORE is large, heavy, and bulky. As such lifting, towing, and supporting many MORE parts and components require specialized heavy-duty equipment and devices. Many of these parts and components can weigh thousands of pounds (or hundreds of kilograms), or even more (**FIGURE 8-2**).

As we go through the different objectives in this chapter, we will review the following:

- Lifting equipment and devices (hoisting, rigging, slings, wire rope/cables, and winches)

You Are the Mobile Off-Road Equipment Technician

You are replacing the dump bed on a 200-ton capacity Caterpillar 789D Mining Truck. You will be utilizing a certified and properly trained team to perform this lifting event and to operate a 100-ton capacity gantry in your shop, for removal. Once removed, the dump bed will have to be moved outside the shop and placed on a concrete pad to await reconditioning.

1. What are the critical weights and capacities that should be researched before planning this major lift event?
2. How can you determine if the proper lifting equipment and capacity are utilized?
3. How can you determine what lifting points to use on the dump bed?
4. How many lifting points should you use?
5. How do you determine which component is the limiting load factor in the operation?
6. When the dump bed is removed, should it rest directly on the ground?
7. How should the lift bed be supported to prevent damage to the concrete pad on the ground?

- Blocking devices (blocking and cribbing)
- Towing equipment and devices
- Proper lifting techniques for human manual lifting

To start, let's establish some definitions of the types of procedures and devices we are talking about. **Lifting equipment**, also known as lifting gear, is any equipment or devices used to lift a load vertically. This can include jacks, a block and tackle, vacuum lift, hydraulic lift, hoist, gantries, windlasses, cranes, forklifts, slings or lifting harnesses, rigging, wire rope/cables, and any other items used to lift a load vertically. Here, we refer to all types of equipment and devices used for lifting a load as lifting equipment.

In this chapter, we refer to all equipment and devices used to support a load in a stationary position as **blocking devices**, also referred to as **blocking** and **cribbing**. This includes blocking, cribbing, jack stands, timbers, dunnage, and any other devices or equipment designed to support a load in a stationary position.

Towing equipment and devices are any equipment or devices used to pull, or tow, a load horizontally. This includes towing ropes, cables, linkage devices, and any other devices used in the towing process.

In this chapter, we refer to manual lifting as lifting done by a person without the aid of mechanical devices. This may include a single person or multiple people. We also discuss here some safety equipment used in manual lifting.

History of Lifting, Blocking, and Towing Equipment

The simplest lifting device is the lever. Some of the earliest written accounts and drawings of a mechanical lever were from Archimedes in the 3rd century BCE. Although it is certain that levers and lifting devices have been in use for thousands of years prior to Archimedes, his writings and drawings are the earliest proof still existing of the mathematic principles of the lever. Although the actual devices and equipment used for lifting, blocking, and towing from ancient times may not survive today, signs of their use are clearly evident (**FIGURE 8-3**).

The laws of physics have not changed from ancient times until today. Heavy items still require mechanical lifting devices, proper blocking equipment to support their weight, and towing equipment to pull them horizontally.

▶ Purpose, Usage, and Types of Lifting and Blocking Equipment and Devices

K08001, S08001, S08002, A08001, I08001

Many different types of lifting devices are used in the MORE field. In most motive power applications, lifting devices are used on an occasional basis, but in heavy equipment they are essential, even to some tasks that would otherwise be considered relatively simple. With MORE, even removing the wheels of a machine can require extensive lifting equipment, as their wheel components can weigh thousands of pounds. The MORE technician must be able to use a variety of lifting equipment throughout the workday, from simply muscle power to operating large gantry cranes capable of lifting several hundred tons, and he or she must do so safely and with confidence. Next, we discuss some of the more common lifting systems.

Manual Lifting

The most elementary piece of lifting equipment is the muscle. But human muscles can be easily injured, affecting your ability to work. You can prevent many debilitating back and knee injuries by using proper lifting techniques. When bending down to lift an object, for example, always bend at the knees before attempting to lift. Never bend from the waist, which is the surest way to strain your back or, in a worst-case scenario, rupture a disc in your back. Place your feet on either side of the object you want to lift, and point them in the direction you wish to travel. If an item is too awkward or large for you to lift on your own, ask someone to help you lift it. To use correct manual lifting techniques, see the steps outlined in **SKILL DRILL 8-1**.

FIGURE 8-3 A. A replica lifting device from ancient Roman times. **B.** Ancient Egyptians using towing ropes and rollers to pull heavy stone blocks. The principles of lifting, blocking, and towing remain the same.

SKILL DRILL 8-1 Correct Manual Lifting Techniques

1. Plan your movement—what your path of travel while carrying the object will be.
2. Decide whether your item will require one person or two persons to carry.
3. Determine where the center of gravity of the object is; place the center of gravity closest to your body when lifting.
4. Check to see whether the item has handles; it is usually easier to use handles to lift an item.
5. Place your feet shoulder-width apart in front of the item.
6. Squat down, bending at the knees and hips only to grasp the item.
7. Look straight ahead, keep your back straight, chest out, and shoulders back.
8. Slowly lift by straightening your hips and knees. Keep your back straight and don't twist.
9. Hold the object as close as possible to your body, and carry at belly button level.
10. Set the load down carefully, squatting with your knees and hips while keeping your back as straight as possible.

Lifting Equipment and Devices

As stated in the introduction, lifting equipment, also known as lifting gear, is any equipment or devices used to lift a load vertically. This can include jacks, a block and tackle, vacuum lift, hydraulic lift, hoist, gantries, windlasses, cranes, forklifts, slings or lifting harnesses, rigging, wire rope/cables, and any other items used to lift a load vertically. Another word we need to define is **hoisting**. Hoisting is the action of lifting a load using cables or ropes. Although a load may be referred to as being "hoisted," when it is lifted vertically using cables or ropes, if the same load is lifted using hydraulic jacks (pushed up vertically), it is being lifted. For the purposes of this chapter, **rigging/rigging gear** are all the components used to attach the mechanical hoisting equipment to the load being lifted. This can include rope, wire rope/cables, slings, shackles, eyebolts, eye nuts, links, rings, turnbuckles, rigging hooks, compression hardware, rigging blocks, load-indicating devices, and precision load positioners. A person who specializes in the lifting and moving of heavy objects is called a **rigger**. Because riggers undergo a large amount of special training and education to safely and properly lift and support large and heavy items, they may be required for these critical jobs. The MORE technician can conduct lifting or supporting operations for smaller jobs when a rigger is not required. When in doubt about the safe and proper planning, application, and use of lifting and supporting equipment and procedures, refer to the machines service information or consult a certified rigger.

> ▶ TECHNICIAN TIP
>
> As a MORE technician, sometimes you need to have knowledge and responsibilities that may normally be handled by a dedicated specialist. Before undertaking a task outside of your normal knowledge and capabilities, ask yourself whether this operation may require a certified specialist or special training—and whether you are confident you can safely perform the task. Some lifting, towing, and blocking equipment and procedures may not require a special certification or a dedicated specialist to perform, but others do. Know your limits, and if in doubt, *stop*. Consult the equipment manufacturer's manual and industry or government regulations. It is better to take your time to ensure all aspects of a heavy lift are conducted properly by properly trained personnel. Failure to use proper techniques, procedures, equipment, and trained personnel can result in equipment damage, serious injury, or even death.

Selecting Appropriate Lifting Equipment

You may end up using many different types of lifting equipment in a shop. Lifting equipment is designed to lift and securely hold loads. Some examples of lifting equipment include vehicle hoists, floor jacks, jack or jack stands, engine and component hoists, mobile gantries, chains, slings, and shackles. Each piece of lifting equipment has a maximum weight it can support. The maximum operating capacity is usually expressed as the **safe working load (SWL)**. For example, if the SWL is 1 ton, the equipment can safely lift up to 2,000 pounds (907 kg). When using lifting equipment, never exceed its capacity, and always maintain some reserve capacity as an extra safety margin. In addition, you should use each piece of lifting equipment for its designed purpose only. For example, use a vehicle hoist only to lift equipment within its capacity. Using lifting equipment incorrectly may lead to equipment failure that can cause serious injury and damage.

The Safe Use of Lifting Equipment

In addition to double-checking safe working loads and using equipment only for its intended purpose, technicians can take several other steps to ensure a safe operating environment. These include testing and test certification. Requirements can vary by country and your local area, so be sure to check with your supervisor if you have any questions.

> SAFETY TIP
>
> Know which lifting equipment in your shop requires special training and/or certification. If you do not have the special training and certification to operate a piece of lifting equipment, *do not* operate it. Find a qualified person to operate the equipment and perform the task you need completed. These items require special training and certification for a reason; they can be extremely complex to operate and present a huge potential safety hazard.

> ▶ TECHNICIAN TIP
>
> When using multiple pieces of lifting equipment, the SWL (safe working load) is limited to the lowest rated piece of equipment. Remember, "A chain is only as strong as its weakest link." Consider the rigging such as the chains, cables, ropes, fittings, rings, the equipment tie-down

points, and the lifting equipment such as the hoist or crane you are using on a heavy lift. The lifting equipment's capacity is limited by the strength of the weakest single component. For example, a 5-ton chain with a 3-ton D-shackle has a maximum lifting capacity of 3 tons or less.

▶ TECHNICIAN TIP

Manufacturers supply operating information for lifting equipment, including the equipment's SWL. Check the lifting equipment's SWL, and compare it with the weight of the object or vehicle you intend to lift. Never exceed the SWL.

Testing Lifting Equipment

Lifting equipment should be periodically checked and tested to make sure it is safe, in accordance with local regulatory requirements. The testing should be recorded for each piece of lifting equipment, and the equipment should be clearly labeled with a sticker affixed to it that includes its inspection date and SWL. Inspections should identify any damage, such as cracks, dents, marks, cuts, and abrasions, which could prevent the lifting equipment from performing as designed. Refer to the manufacturer's manual to find out how often maintenance inspections are recommended. The time frame is usually every 12 months in the case of hoists and lifts, but may be longer for lifting equipment such as chains and slings. Always check local regulations to determine the requirements for periodic testing of lifting equipment.

Checking the Test Certificate

In most countries, lifting equipment is subject to statutory testing and certification. If this is the case where you work, the **test certificate** should be attached to or displayed near the lifting equipment (**FIGURE 8-4**).

Before using a piece of lifting equipment, make sure the most recent inspection recorded on the test certificate is within the prescribed time limit. If it is not, the test certificate has expired, and you should notify your supervisor.

Selecting Appropriate Lift Points

When dealing with lifting heavy objects, it is critical to lift the object using solid and secure lift points with enough capacity to lift the item without damage. In many cases, a lifting device is used that pushes the item up vertically, by using a jack between the ground and a suitable lift point under the equipment (**FIGURE 8-5**).

SAFETY TIP

Failure to utilize proper lift points may result in equipment damage or injury. Whether you are lifting from below using a jack, or from above using a hoist, ensure you use designated and proper lift points when available. Lifting a heavy item can place a lot of strain into a very small area, possibly resulting in failure of the lifting point. In the absence of a manufacturer's designated lifting point, utilize the strongest area available.

In these cases, look for a designated lift point first. If none is available, use the strongest part of the item. Other critical factors in selecting a good lifting point are looking for ones that will allow good positioning with the item's center of balance, and for one that has a stable part that will not move or slip on the jack.

Just as important as ensuring that the lifting points are strong enough to support the lift is making sure that the correct lifting point positioning is used. In explaining this, we need to define a few terms. The **center of gravity** (**CG**), also called the center of balance, of an object is the point, or position, at which the item's weight is evenly dispersed, and all sides are in balance. If the item were to be supported in a direct vertical axis from the center of gravity, it would balance perfectly. As the center of gravity is a position, it has units of length; inches, feet, meters, centimeters. The center of gravity of an object can be described as the distance from an arbitrary reference point on the item, to the center of gravity. The arbitrary reference point from where the center of gravity is measured is called the **reference datum line** (**RDL**). For instance, the manufacturer of a certain piece of heavy equipment may describe the item's center of gravity as being 200 inches

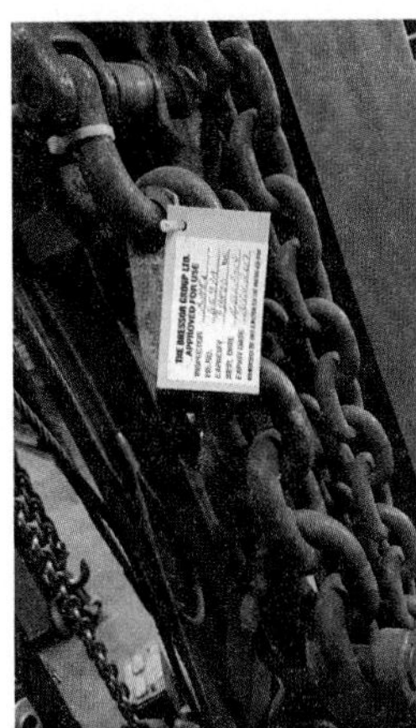

FIGURE 8-4 Compliance testing tags contain details of when the last test was done and when the next test is due.

FIGURE 8-5 Always identify and use the correct lifting points when lifting a heavy item. Consult the manufacturer's maintenance and repair manual if lifting points are not readily identified.

from the item's front end, where the manufacturer may define the "front end" as the point where the front of the machine protrudes the most, at a height of 24 inches above ground level. Where the reference datum line is on an item does not matter, so long as it is specifically defined and does not change.

The further away the item is supported from the vertical axis of the center of gravity, the more it has a tendency to rotate. The tendency of an item to rotate about a pivot is called torque.

Take the case where you are lifting an item by jacking from underneath. If the jack is placed at a lifting point not in the same vertical axis of the center of gravity, the item will tend to rotate as it is being lifted. In many cases, this is not desirable and creates an unstable condition. However, if the jack is placed at a lifting point that is in the same vertical axis of the item's center of gravity, it will lift straight up and not rotate. Therefore, it is important to know where the item's center of gravity is, before lifting. An item that is lifted by utilizing a poorly positioned lifting point can become unstable and fall.

The same principle applies to lifting an item from above by hoisting. If a single point chain or rigging is used, it must be placed in the same vertical axis as the item's center of gravity. If it is not, the item will rotate until the center of gravity of the item is in the same vertical axis as the lifting hook (**FIGURE 8-6**).

When lifting an entire piece of equipment, many times the center of gravity will be posted on the equipment itself or on a data plate. The center of gravity may also be listed in the manufacturer's technical manual. When the center of gravity is included on a data plate or in a technical manual, it is defined as a distance from the manufacturer's RDL. In many cases, the MORE technician will be utilizing lifting equipment to lift heavy parts and subcomponents of a larger piece of equipment. In these instances, the item's center of gravity is not predetermined, and MORE technicians must use their own best judgment on whether a more in-depth analysis must be done before undertaking the lift. Certain very large or heavy items are considered to entail a critical lift, which requires a specialist to perform. These types of lifts are not covered in this chapter. However, there are many heavy lifts that the MORE technician can do in the shop or field that do not require special certifications.

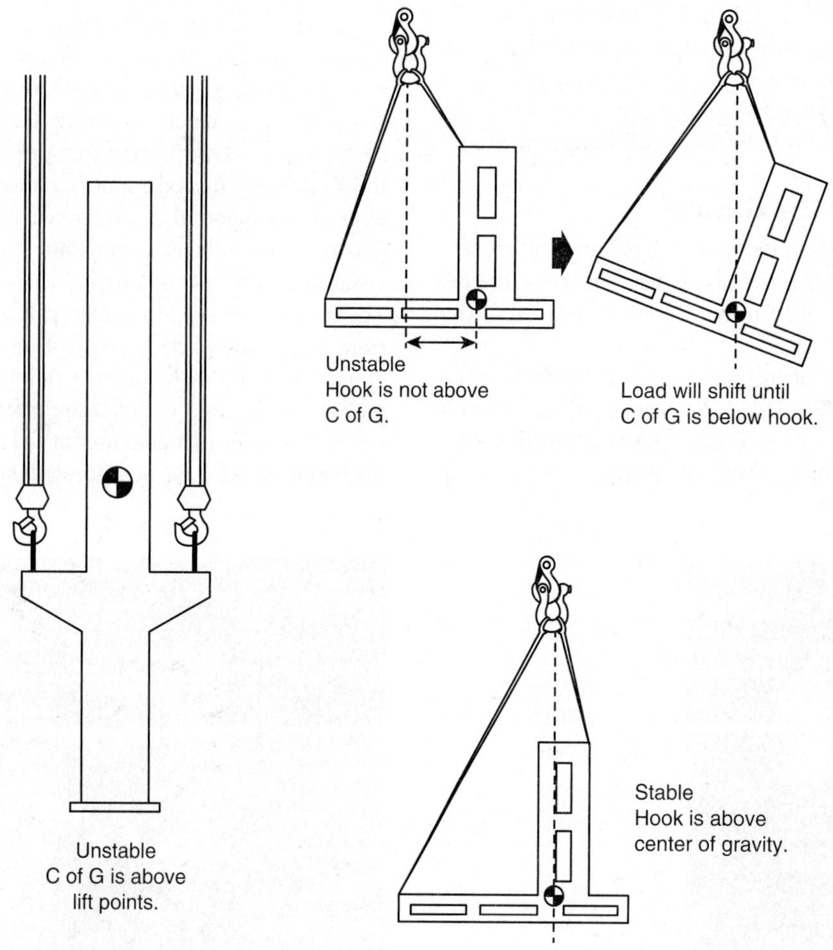
Unstable
Hook is not above
C of G.
Load will shift until
C of G is below hook.
Unstable
C of G is above
lift points.
Stable
Hook is above
center of gravity.
Effect of Center of Gravity on Lift

FIGURE 8-6 The position of the lifted item's center of gravity with respect to the lifting hook and lifting points is critical. Poor positioning will cause the load to shift and may result in equipment damage and injury.

In these cases, safety is paramount, especially where the item's CG is not known and therefore the load may be subject to shifting. Keep these criteria in mind when selecting your lifting points:

- When available, use the manufacturer's dedicated lift points.
- Ensure that the lifting points capacity is known and will not be exceeded.
- When lifting an item from below by jacking, use a lift point that is *below* the item's center of gravity.
- When lifting an item from above by hoisting, use a lift point that is *above* the item's center of gravity.
- When lifting using a single lift point, use a lift point in the same vertical axis as the item's center of gravity.
- When hoisting using two lift points, place them symmetrically the same distance apart from the item's center of gravity.
- When lifting an item by hoisting, keep the lifting hook in the same vertical axis as the item's center of gravity.

Types of Lifting and Moving Equipment

Once you have verified that a piece of equipment is safe to use, you can get to work. You will use your shop's lifting equipment not only to raise heavy components but also to move and lower pieces into place as well. Which equipment you use depends on a part's size, weight, and type, as well as the job you intend to perform. This section looks at several different types of lifting and moving equipment.

Chain Blocks and Mobile Gantry Cranes **Chain blocks** and mobile **gantry cranes** are often used together to lift larger components inside heavy equipment shops. Chain blocks can be attached to, and hang from, mobile gantries. Chain blocks lift parts, and mobile gantries move wherever the work needs to be done.

Chain blocks have a safety latch and hook fittings that attach to lifting points on a component. Once attached to a load, the chain block lifts large components when the technician pulls the chain through a rotating wheel. Mobile gantries can either be wheeled into place on a floor or are mounted on tracks near the roof of the shop and operated with hand controls that move the gantry into position and lower the chain block with a hook (**FIGURE 8-7**).

Both lifting devices relieve the technician of having to exert a lot of effort to remove heavy components and lower them into an area where they can be serviced or replaced. Carefully check the lifting hooks on these devices before use, to make sure the end of the hook hasn't opened beyond the standard limit. Inspect chains for any mud or grit, and examine safety latches to be sure they are working properly.

Slings and Shackles Slings are another type of lifting equipment. Technicians use them to lift and lower many things in the shop. For example, a transmission, engine, or differential can be lifted using these devices (**FIGURE 8-8**).

They can be made from strong webbing material, wire rope, or chain. Webbed slings have an eye at each end for the connection of shackles (discussed later in this section) to attach loads. Wire rope and chain slings may have any number of different fittings for different applications. Regardless of the sling type and its fittings, each will have a maximum working load that you cannot exceed. As with all lifting equipment, you must test slings regularly to ensure they are safe to use. If you suspect that any piece of lifting equipment is damaged, do not use it. Have it tested before placing it into service. Webbed slings are usually flat in appearance and made from strong synthetic materials such as polyester. Synthetic slings can be more susceptible to cutting or abrasive damage than harder materials, such as chains or wire, and should be checked before each use to ensure they are not damaged. Web slings are available in a variety of lifting capacities for different lifting tasks. When using synthetic slings, always ensure they are protected from sharp corners, which may damage the slings and reduce lifting capacity. Wire rope slings are made from many strands of fine wire and a core. The size, number, and arrangement of the wires determine the sling's lifting capacity. Wire rope slings are less susceptible to abrasion and cutting than synthetic slings, but

FIGURE 8-7 Gantry crane used for heavy lifting.

FIGURE 8-8 Chain-type slings and other heavy lifting components in a shop.

FIGURE 8-9 Chains can have many different types of fittings at either end.

always check them for any damage, such as kinks and broken or cut wires, as these will reduce their lifting capacity. Chains are made from hardened steel and are not as susceptible to damage as synthetic or wire rope slings. Chains can have several different types of fittings attached to the ends, such as eyes, shackles, and hooks (**FIGURE 8-9**).

Chains, like all lifting equipment, should be checked for damage before being used and regularly tested and tagged. Shackles are attached to slings and chains to use as connectors between a component and various applications, such as lifting equipment. See **FIGURE 8-10** for an example.

In lifting equipment, shackles are secured with a pin through the bottom of the shackle. Secure D-shackles, a common type of shackle, with a piece of wire through the shackle's eye, to lock the pin and prevent it from working loose. The same applies to bow shackles. As with all lifting equipment, inspect shackles to make sure they are in good condition and free from dirt and grime.

Jacks and Jack Stands Jacks and **jack stands** are used every day in heavy equipment shops to safely lift and support equipment. Although a jack is a lifting device, and a jack stand is a supporting device, we speak about both here as they are usually used and spoken about together. As with other shop equipment, before use it is important to check jacks and jack stands for safety reasons. If you suspect that they are faulty, *do not use them*. Take them out of service, and have them tested and serviced.

Jacks An equipment jack is a lifting tool that can raise part of an object from the ground prior to removing or replacing components, or raise heavy components into position. Jacks used for lifting heavy-duty equipment operate the same as the jacks you are probably familiar with, to lift vehicles. The only difference is, jacks used to lift heavy equipment are larger and have a greater lifting capacity (**FIGURE 8-11**). Although you can use a jack to raise and support a piece of equipment, you must not use an equipment jack to support the equipment's weight during any task that requires you to get underneath any part of it. For any shop tasks that call for you to crawl under a piece of equipment, only use a jack to raise the equipment so that it can then be lowered onto suitably rated and carefully positioned stable jack stands or blocking.

The three main types of jacks are the **hydraulic jack**, **pneumatic jack**, and **mechanical jack**. Hydraulic and pneumatic jacks are the most common types. They can be mounted on slides or on a wheeled platform. In hydraulic jacks, pressurized oil acts on a piston to provide the lifting action; in pneumatic jacks, compressed air lifts the vehicle; in mechanical jacks, a screw or gears provide the mechanical leverage required for lifting.

Different jacks are available for different purposes:

- *Floor jacks* are a common type of hydraulic jack that is mounted on four wheels, two of which swivel to provide a steering mechanism. The floor jack has a long handle that is used both to operate the jacking mechanism and to move and position the jack. Floor jacks have a low profile, making them suitable to position under vehicles.
- *Bottle jacks* are portable jacks that usually have either a mechanical screw or a hydraulic ram mechanism that rises vertically from the jack's center as you operate the handle. They are relatively inexpensive too automotive and may be provided with vehicles for changing flat tires.

Air jacks use compressed air either to operate a large ram or to inflate an expandable air bag rarely used to lift the vehicle. Often the air jack is fitted to a movable platform with a long handle.

FIGURE 8-10 D-shackles can be used to connect pieces of lifting equipment. Do not use D-shackles with an unknown lifting capacity/rating.

FIGURE 8-11 A jack should only be used to raise part of a piece of equipment enough to install jack stands, blocking, or other stable and proper supporting devices. *Never* work under a piece of equipment supported only by jacks or other lifting devices.

You use air jacks to lift vehicles as an alternative to floor jacks. Because they require a compressed air supply, air jacks are usually used in the shop rather than for mobile operations. An air bag–type jack can be especially useful in situations where a very low-profile jack is needed; the jack will sit on an uneven surface; or the load to be lifted must be spread out over a larger area of jacking surface.

- *Sliding-bridge jacks* are usually fitted in pairs to four post hoists as an accessory to allow the vehicle to be lifted off the drive-on hoist runways. Operated by a hydraulic mechanism or compressed air, sliding-bridge jacks use a platform mounted to a scissor-action jack to lift the vehicle along the length of the runway, thus making it more convenient to work on wheels and brakes. These types of lifting systems may be found in shops that cater to lighter pieces of more equipment.
- *Transmission jacks* are specialized jacks for lifting and lowering transmissions during removal and installation. Transmission jacks are usually mounted on a floor with wheels and have a large flat plate area on which the transmission rests securely. They are usually operated by a hydraulic mechanism but can also be powered by compressed air.

Jack Stands Jack stands, also known as just stands, are adjustable supports used with jacks. They are designed to support a machine's weight once it has been raised by a jack. They normally come in matched pairs and should always be used as a pair (**FIGURE 8-12**).

Jack stands are mechanical devices, meaning they mechanically lock in place at the height selected. Stands are load rated, so you should only use them for loads less than the rating indicated on the jack stand. They are very dependable if you use them properly.

Always grip jack stands by the sides to move them. Never grip them by the top or the bottom to move them, as they can slip and pinch or injure you. Check that a stand's base is flat on the ground before lowering a machine onto it; otherwise, the stand might tip over, causing the machine to slip off. Once you have the jack stands positioned correctly, you can lower the machine onto the stands and move the jack out of the way.

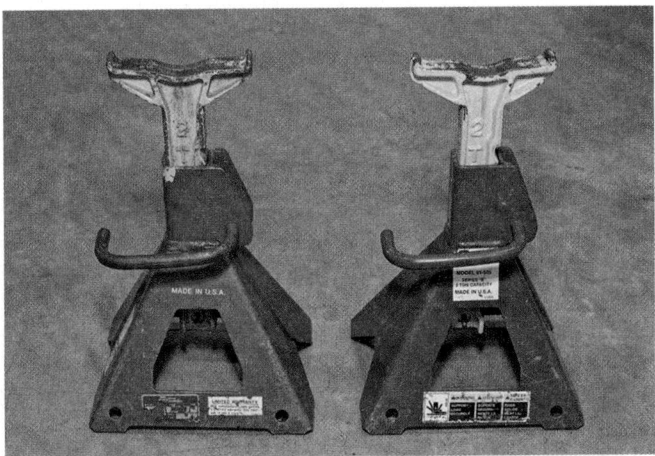

FIGURE 8-12 Always use jack stands in matched pairs.

SAFETY TIP

For safety's sake, always place the jack stand locking pins into the aligned holes of the jack stand frame and the movable support platform.

Jack stands provide a stable support for a raised machine that is safer than the jack because the machine cannot be accidentally lowered while the stands are in place. Once you are ready to lower a machine that is on stands, you first raise it again with a jack so you can remove the stands. Because lifting devices are also lowering devices, remember that it's unsafe to work underneath a machine that is supported only by a jack, because it could give way or be accidentally lowered. Never use stands for a job for which they are not recommended.

SAFETY TIP

Never support a machine on anything other than jack stands. Do not use wood or steel blocks to support a machine in the shop; the blocks might slide or split under the machine's weight. Do not use bricks or concrete blocks to support a machine either; they will crumble under the weight.

Using Vehicle Jacks and Jack Stands The weight of the machine you want to lift will determine the size of the jack you use. Always check the capacity of the jack before lifting a machine. If the end of the machine is heavier than usual, or if the machine is loaded, you need to use a jack with a larger lifting capacity. Make sure the stands are in good condition and that their size and capacity are adequate before you use them to support the machine. If they are cracked or bent, they will not support the machine safely. Always use matched pairs of jack stands. To lift and secure a machine with a floor jack and stands, follow the guidelines in **SKILL DRILL 8-2**.

Vehicle Hoists A **vehicle hoist** raises a whole vehicle off the ground so that a technician can easily work on the vehicle's underside. Although this type of lifting system is rarely encountered in a typical MORE shop, it is mentioned here to explain its use should you come across it in shops that also work on equipment transportation vehicles. The vehicle hoist is also useful for raising a vehicle to a height that eliminates the need for the technician to bend down. For example, when changing wheels, you can raise the vehicle to waist height to avoid excessive bending. Vehicle hoists are available in several different designs. They also come in a range of sizes and configurations to meet a shop's needs. For instance, some vehicle hoists are mobile, and others are designed for use where the ceiling height is limited. You can electronically link together some vehicle hoists to use on longer vehicles, such as trucks and buses.

Hydraulic Hoist One type of vehicle hoist, the **hydraulic hoist**, is very easy to use with most vehicles. You drive a vehicle onto a platform so that the wheels rest on two long, narrow platforms, one on each side of the vehicle (**FIGURE 8-13**). Next,

SKILL DRILL 8-2 Lifting and Securing a Machine with a Floor Jack and Stands

1. Position the machine on a flat, solid surface. Put the equipment into Neutral or Park, and set the emergency or hand brake. If applicable place wheel chocks in front of and behind the wheels that are not going to be raised off the ground.
2. Select two stands of the same type, suitable for the equipment's weight. Place one stand on each side of the vehicle at the same point, and adjust them so that they are both the same height.
3. Roll the equipment jack under the vehicle, and position the lifting pad correctly under the frame, crossmember, or specified jacking point. Turn the jack handle clockwise, and begin pumping the handle up and down until the lifting pad touches and begins to lift the equipment. If jacking on the chassis frame, always use a wooden block or similar device between the jack and the frame to protect the frame from gouges.
4. Once the wheels or tracks lift off the floor, stop and check the placement of the lifting pad under the machine to make sure there is no danger of slipping. Double-check the position of the wheel chocks to make sure they have not moved. If the machine is stable, continue lifting it until it is at the height at which you can safely work under it.
5. Slide the two stands underneath the machine, and position them to support the machine's weight. Slowly turn the jack handle counterclockwise to open the release valve, and gently lower the machine onto the stands. When the equipment has settled onto the stands, lower the jack completely, and remove it from under the equipment. Gently push the equipment sideways to make sure it is secure. Repeat this process to lift the other end of the machine.
6. When the repairs are complete, use the jack to raise the equipment off the stands. Slide the stands from under the machine. Make sure no one goes under the machine or puts any body parts under the it, as the jack could fail or slip.
7. Slowly turn the jack handle counterclockwise to gently lower the equipment to the ground. Return the jack, stands, and wheel chocks to their storage area before you continue working on the equipment.

FIGURE 8-13 This type of hydraulic hoist is rarely seen in shops that work exclusively on MORE.

the platforms are raised, taking the vehicle with them. The vehicle's underside is then accessible to the technician. Because the vehicle rests on its wheels on the hoist, you can't remove the wheels unless the hoist is fitted with sliding-bridge jacks.

Portable Lifting Hoists Another type of vehicle hoists is **portable lifting hoists**, or *portalift mobile hoists* as they are sometimes referred to. These offer a lifting system that is simple to operate and allow complete underbody access for maintenance and repair. Portalift hoists again are not very common in shops that work on heavy equipment. Portable lifting hoists do, however, provide shop flexibility as they are fully portable and can be easily moved to any area of a standard shop floor. You can raise or lower the hoist posts individually, in pairs, or all together. When used as a group, they are coupled together with cables to ensure that they operate in sync with one another, and the vehicle is raised equally on each leg of the hoist (**FIGURE 8-14**).

Many types have cable hangers allowing you to keep your cables off the shop floor. The vehicle being worked on can always be put in the best possible position to suit the type of work being done. This can save time and provides the correct working condition for the technician. The hoists can be set at the best height for the task being performed and for the individual technician doing the job. Some types of portable lifting

FIGURE 8-14 Portable lifting hoists, not common in MORE shops.

hoists have the controller on one of the pedestal legs, and others have a mobile controller that gives the operator complete lifting control away from the lifting zone. Both types of hoists have a remote pendant that allows the operator to safely inspect the lifting operation from any point around the vehicle.

Safety Locks Every vehicle hoist in the shop must have a built-in mechanical locking device so the vehicle hoist can be secured at the chosen height after the vehicle is raised. This locking device prevents the vehicle from being accidentally lowered and holds the vehicle in place, even if the lifting mechanism fails. You should never physically go under a raised vehicle for any reason unless the safety locking mechanism has been activated.

Ratings and Inspections All vehicle hoists are rated for a particular weight and type of vehicle. Never use them for any task other than that recommended by the manufacturer. Never use a vehicle hoist to lift a vehicle that is heavier than its rated limit. Most countries have regulations that require hoists to be periodically inspected, typically annually, and certified as fit for use. Before you use a vehicle hoist, check the identification plate for its rating, and make sure it has a current registration or certification label.

Engine Hoists **Engine hoists**, or mobile floor cranes, are capable of lifting very heavy objects, such as engines, while the engines are being removed from a machine or refitted. The engine hoist's lifting arm is moved by a hydraulic cylinder and is adjustable for length. However, extending the lifting arm reduces its lifting capacity because it moves the load farther away from the supporting frame. You can extend the supporting legs for stability, but the more you extend the arm and the legs, the lower the engine hoist's lifting capacity. The safe lifting capacity at various extensions is normally marked on the lifting arm. The engine or component to be lifted is attached to the lifting arm by a sling or a lifting chain. The sling and lifting chain must be rated as capable of lifting weights more than the engine or component being lifted and must be firmly attached before the engine hoist is raised. When the engine or other component has been lifted and slowly and carefully moved away from the machine, it should be lowered onto an engine stand or onto the floor (**FIGURE 8-15**).

FIGURE 8-15 A folded engine hoist. Engine hoists come in many sizes and lifting capacities.

FIGURE 8-16 Inspect to make sure all chains, fixtures, and riggings are in good condition.

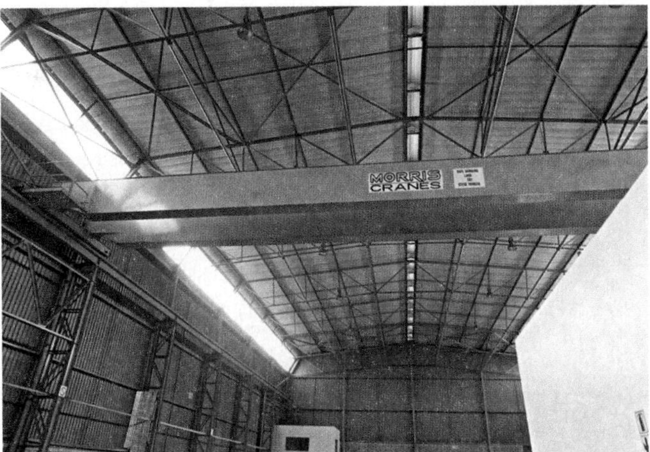

FIGURE 8-17 Overhead cranes are common place in heavy equipment shops.

The farther off the ground an engine is lifted, the less stable the engine hoist becomes. When using these types of hoists or cranes, always make sure that the slings and rope, cables, and chains that are used are compliant with relevant regulations and do not exceed the load ratings (**FIGURE 8-16**).

Overhead Cranes Many heavy equipment shops are equipped with **overhead cranes** (**FIGURE 8-17**).

These must be used in accordance with local regulations and with the correct slings, ropes, and chains. The crane is only as good as the slings connecting it to the equipment to be moved. Operate the crane smoothly, slowly, and with caution. Don't rush. Always ask for assistance if required. In many cases, two people will be required to operate an overhead crane—one to operate the crane, the other as a lookout—to watch the load and guide it if necessary.

SAFETY TIP

Never use a hoist to lift any weight greater than the lifting capacity of the hoist, sling, chains, or bolts.

Using Lifting Equipment

Like many shop activities, using lifting equipment involves managing risks. Think carefully about what you are going to do, plan your activities, and check the equipment to make sure it is safe to use.

Using Engine Hoists and Stands Engine hoists are capable of lifting very heavy objects, which make them suitable for lifting engines. Make sure the lifting attachment at the end of the lifting arm is strong enough to lift the engine and is not damaged or cracked. When attaching the lifting chain or sling to an engine, make sure it is firmly attached and that the engine hoist is configured to lift that weight. Make sure the fasteners attaching the lifting chain, or sling, have a tensile strength that is more than the engine's weight. To keep from overstressing the sling, leave enough length in the sling so that when the engine is hanging, the angle at the top of the sling is close to 45 degrees and does not exceed 90 degrees. In areas where space is limited for lifting, you should use a spreader bar to aid the lifting operation (**FIGURE 8-18**).

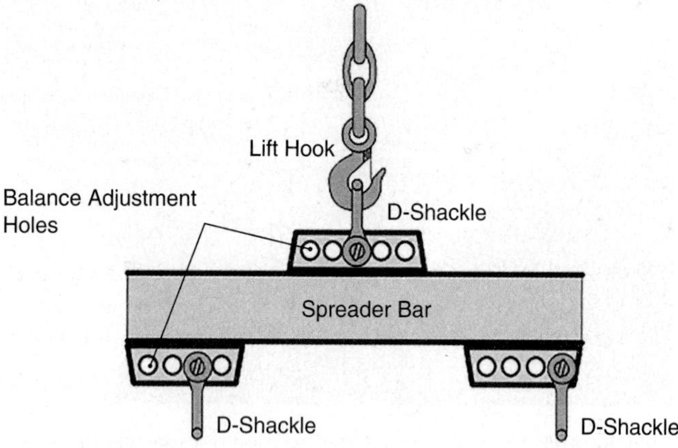

FIGURE 8-18 Spreader bars provide mounting points to spread the loads weight, some are also adjustable.

The bar is a straight piece of reinforced steel that bridges across the lifting eyes and is connected by D-shackles. The bar's center has a ring or D-shackle that is attached to the crane for lifting. If removing an engine from an engine bay, lower the engine so that it is close to the ground after removal. If the engine is lifted high in the air, the engine hoist will be unstable. When moving a suspended engine, move the engine hoist slowly. Do not change direction quickly because the engine will swing and may cause the whole apparatus to tumble. To use engine hoists and stands, follow the guidelines in **SKILL DRILL 8-3**.

> ▶ TECHNICIAN TIP
>
> - The engine hoist's load rating must be greater than the weight of the object to be lifted.
> - Never leave an unsupported engine hanging on an engine hoist. Secure the engine on an engine stand or on the ground before starting to work on it.
> - If using an engine stand, make sure it is designed to support the weight of the engine and that you have the correct number of bolts to hold the engine to the stand.
> - Always extend the engine hoist's legs in relation to the lifting arm to ensure adequate stability.

Lifting heavy items is inherently dangerous. It is important for the MORE technician to know the basic principles of lifting items safely and properly. It is also important to know the different types of lifting devices in your shop, which ones require special certification or training, how to inspect them for proper operation and safety inspection certifications, and how to operate them properly and safely.

> ▶ TECHNICIAN TIP
>
> When involved with a lift, never place yourself or a body part underneath the item being lifted or jacked during the lift. When overhead cranes are in use, stand well outside the danger area, and never stand

SKILL DRILL 8-3 Using Engine Hoists and Stands

1. Prepare to use the engine hoist. Lower the lifting arm, and position the lifting end and chain over the center of the engine.
2. Wear appropriate PPE, such as leather gloves, during the entire operation, beginning with inspecting the chain, steel cable, or sling, and bolts to make sure they are in good condition. Before you use the crane, make sure the chain or sling is rated higher than the weight of the item to be lifted. Also, ensure that the lifting arm is only extended to the length of its lifting capacity applicable to the weight of the item to be lifted. Only use approved lifting equipment—nothing homemade. Look carefully around the component that is about to be lifted, to determine whether it has lifting eyes or other anchor points.
3. If the engine or component has lifting eyes, attach the sling with D-shackles or chain hooks. If you need to screw in bolts and spacer washers to lift the engine, make sure you use the correct bolt and spacer size for the chain or cable. Screw the bolts until the sling is held tight against the component.
4. Attach the hoist's hook under the center of the sling, and raise the engine hoist just enough to lift the engine to take the slack up on the cable, chain, or sling. Double-check the sling and attachment points for safety. The engine's or component's center of gravity should be directly under the engine hoist's hook, and there should be no twists or kinks in the chain or sling.
5. Raise the engine hoist until the engine is clear of the ground and any obstacles. Slowly and gently move the engine hoist and lifted component to the new location with minimum ground clearance to prevent swinging and potential tilting of the whole crane.
6. Make sure the engine is positioned correctly. You may need to place blocks under the engine to stabilize it. Once you are sure the engine is stable, lower the engine hoist, and remove the sling and any securing fasteners. Finally, return the equipment to its storage area.

underneath an unsupported load. Only begin work underneath an item after it has been properly supported and all safety precautions inspected and followed. Always have an escape route planned when involved in a lift. Plan the fastest and most direct route to get out of danger should the equipment collapse, including a route that will be clear of any additional rolling or falling equipment should something go wrong.

Blocking Equipment, Devices, and Procedures

In this section, we examine the principles of supporting a heavy item by blocking, along with the associated blocking equipment and devices. Blocking can be defined as the procedures and devices used to support a load (**FIGURE 8-19**). Just as in lifting, when extremely heavy or large loads need to be supported, a specialist called a rigger can be used. Because riggers undergo a large amount of special training and education to safely and properly lift and support large and heavy items, they can be used for these critical jobs. The MORE technician can conduct a lifting or supporting operation for any job when a rigger is not required. When in doubt about the safe and proper planning, application, and use of lifting and supporting equipment and procedures—you must refer to the machines service information or a certified rigger.

For the case of the MORE technician, blocking is used to support a machine, component, or attachment before working on it—to prevent it from falling. Blocking is also used to support a concentrated load such as outriggers or to spread the load out when heavy items are resting on a surface. Because each job and application is different, only general safety and procedures can be suggested. Most equipment manufacturers' technical manuals will outline the specific procedures for blocking, and these should be followed. Here, we go over some basic principles.

Chocking

Chocks are blocks of material placed against a wheel to prevent undesired rolling movement. They should be constructed of a material that will not crush easily and of a size that the tire cannot roll over easily. Prior to lifting any wheeled piece of equipment, always chock in front and behind one of the tires to prevent unwanted rolling (**FIGURE 8-20**). Chocks should be placed on the downhill side of the vehicle. When possible, use two chocking points due to the weight shifting when the item is lifted. Also, ensure the item is locked out, to prevent anyone else from accidentally attempting to start or move the equipment.

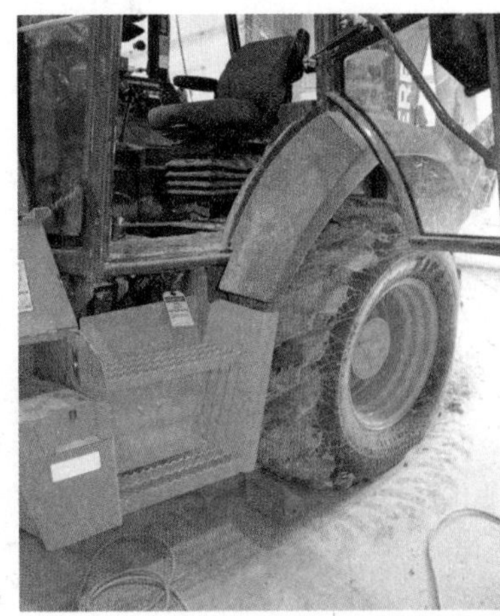

FIGURE 8-20 Chocking on both sides of the tire before lifting prevents unintended movement of the equipment during the lift.

Locking Lift Cylinders and Articulating Joints In-Place

Before jacking, lifting, or blocking a piece of equipment, ensure that hydraulic lift cylinders and articulating joints are mechanically locked in place to prevent movement. Never rely on the hydraulic pressure in a lift cylinder to prevent a part from falling (**FIGURE 8-21**). Furthermore, once a piece of equipment is raised to the desired height, *and before working underneath*, always ensure that buckets, forklift carriages, and other moveable equipment is blocked to prevent movement even in the event of a hydraulic system failure. When lifting equipment with articulating joints such as front-end loaders, or dump trucks in which the front and rear portion of the equipment has an articulating

FIGURE 8-19 Blocking can support an entire piece of equipment, a component, or an attachment while it is being serviced.

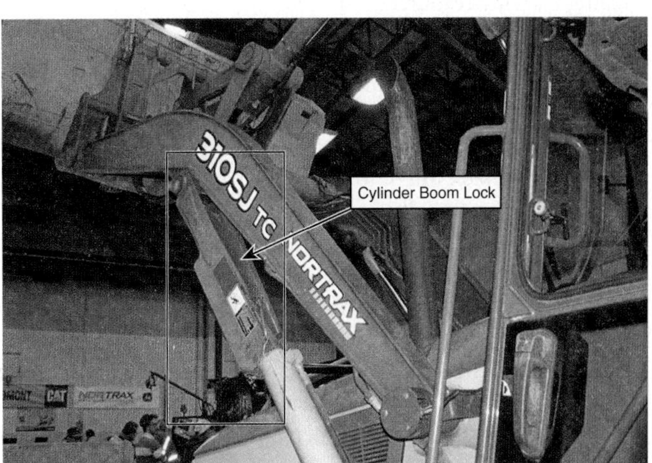

FIGURE 8-21 Always mechanically lock hydraulic lift cylinder in place before lifting a piece of equipment. Never trust your life to an O-ring!

FIGURE 8-22 When a machine's implement is rested on the ground, it should be extended so that it cannot move further.

joint, *always lock the articulating joint before lifting*. Failure to adhere to these rules has a very high likelihood of causing unintended equipment movement, possibly resulting in equipment damage, serious injury, or death.

If raising and locking the lift cylinder is not practical for the work being done, then the machine's implements should be rested on the ground so that they cannot move, as shown in **FIGURE 8-22.**

SAFETY TIP

Before working underneath any equipment, make sure it is properly supported. Inspect the blocking and/or supports, and check that wheels are chocked, articulating joints are locked, hydraulic lift cylinders are locked, *and* their ancillary equipment is supported. If something does not seem right, *stop* and check with a competent person or the equipment manufacturer's manual. Don't risk your life trusting someone else's improper work.

The following are some basic procedures to observe when blocking and supporting items. For further details, the machines service information or consult a certified rigger or rigging training resources.

- Use blocking when specified by the equipment manufacturer for a repair, and follow the manufacturer's instructions.
- Use blocking whenever working underneath a heavy item that has been lifted, to prevent it from falling if the lifting device were to fail.
- Use blocking whenever the weight of an item would cause damage to the item or the surface it rests upon. For example, do not lay an engine directly on the ground. Support it with blocking.
- Use blocking material that can withstand the concentrated load without deforming or splitting.
- The entire assembly of blocking equipment and materials is only as strong as the weakest part. *Ensure the materials and equipment selected can support a weight at least four times the weight of the item being supported.*
- Use blocking material that is square shaped and stable. Do not use round or triangular blocking.
- Park equipment on a flat, stable surface.
- Ensure chocks and parking brakes are used before lifting equipment.
- Inspect blocking equipment and materials for damage. Do not use blocking that is cracked or splintering.
- Use blocking materials that are at least twice as wide as they are tall, for stability.
- Use four points of contact when possible; if not, use at least two points of contact.
- When supporting equipment, ensure lift cylinders and articulating joints are mechanically locked to prevent shifting. *Never* rely on hydraulic pressure to keep an item from falling. (*Note:* The equipment manufacturer usually provides mechanical locking devices for this purpose.)
- Use blocking of the same material, type, and size so that the crush factor and capacity are uniform.

Just as with lifting, blocking and supporting equipment is both critical and a possible safety hazard. Ensure you follow the equipment manufacturer's recommendations when supporting an item. In addition, consult your shop's policy and procedure manuals and more experienced technicians when the need to block equipment arises. If you perform lifting and blocking duties often, ask your supervisor about specific training and technical resources to ensure you are complying with industry practices, the law, and safety regulations. Educating yourself on the proper techniques and equipment for blocking equipment will be time well spent.

▶ OSHA Standards for Proper Lifting Techniques and Equipment

K08005

As discussed previously, in the United States the government entity that sets rules for occupational health and safety is **OSHA (Occupational Safety and Health Administration)**. Because the operation of lifting devices can result in serious injuries and death, OSHA has many general and specific rules governing lifting and lifting devices. If you are working outside of the United States, consult your supervisor to determine what rules and standards must be followed for lifting and lifting equipment in your country. For the purposes of this chapter, we discuss OSHA and industry rules that apply in the United States.

First, let's set the proper attitude toward safety standards, OSHA, and other industry workplace safety and standards entities. Safety rules/regulations, OSHA, and other industry safety organizations are not your enemy or an impediment to getting the job done. They are your partner in ensuring the job gets done safely and correctly. Furthermore, you should take the rules, regulations, and advice of these entities seriously. Most of the safety rules and regulations exist because of a serious accident that caused damage to equipment or because someone was seriously injured or died. It would be accurate to say that safety regulations were "written in blood." Therefore, not following safety regulations puts yourself, your coworkers, and your equipment in danger.

Depending on what industry you are working in, as a MORE technician you may have to comply with additional industry regulations set by other government or industry entities. Consult with your supervisor to see what rules and regulations apply for lifting in your shop.

OSHA usually only sets general rules and regulations. It often defers the specifics of how to perform a task or operate a piece of equipment, or what technique or equipment to use, to the equipment manufacturer or another industry body more familiar with the exact situations a worker may encounter. Basically, following OSHA rules is not a substitute for following the equipment manufacturer's recommendations or being proficient in your job. OSHA often refers to the general duty clause listed in Section 5(a)(1) of the OSHA act, which states:

> Each employer shall furnish to each of his employees employment and a place of employment which are free from recognized hazards that are causing or are likely to cause death or serious physical harm to his employees.

Now, let's review two areas for which OSHA has some rules and guidelines for lifting.

OSHA Guidelines for Manual Lifting

OSHA has some published training material and guidelines for manual lifting. OSHA does not have specific rules for, for example, the maximum weight a single person should lift. According to training material for manual lifting on the OSHA website (https://www.osha.gov/SLTC/etools/electricalcontractors/supplemental/principles.html#lifting). The following are some basic techniques for manual lifting.

- The person's head is kept upright, looking straight ahead.
- When standing, the torso should not be bent more than 10–20 degrees from vertical. The natural curve of the spine is maintained.
- Pelvis and shoulders face straight ahead.
- Shoulders are relaxed and knees slightly bent.
- Do not leave items lying on the floor where they may cause a tripping hazard.
- Plan the route of travel and ensure it is clear *before* performing the lift.
- Lift within your *power zone*. The *power zone* is between mid-thigh and mid-chest height. This allows lifting with the least amount of effort.
- Use proper handholds on the items being lifted.
- Pulling is generally preferred to pushing and has a lower chance of injury.
- Rotation of tasks. Employees should rotate repetitive tasks that use different muscles to lower the chance of injury.

As concerns how much weight a single person should lift, OSHA published to its website a letter to clarify rules dealing with this subject (https://www.osha.gov/pls/oshaweb/owadisp.show_document?p_table=INTERPRETATIONS&p_id=29936). OSHA defers to the National Institute for Occupational Safety and Health (NIOSH). NIOSH has a model that helps to determine the risk of injury based on the weight being lifted and several other factors (http://www.cdc.gov/niosh/docs/94-110/). These are only voluntary guidelines though. The lifting equation establishes a maximum load of 51 lb (23 kg). For a manual lift of weights above 51 lb (23 kg), OSHA recommends using other means such as these:

- A two-person lift
- A mechanical lifting device
- Breaking down items into smaller pieces

Although it may seem embarrassing or unneeded to ask another person for help or to use a mechanical lifting device, it is preferable to being injured and in pain, and possibly out of work.

OSHA Rules for Lifting Equipment

Several OSHA regulations deal with lifting equipment, depending on the type. We review some basic OSHA rules for several types of lifting equipment. Remember, it is your responsibility to research and know the applicable OSHA, industry standards, and equipment manufacturer specific rules and regulations.

- **Overhead and Gantry Cranes** (OSHA Standard 1910.179, 1926.1438)
  - The rated load of the crane shall be plainly marked and visible.
  - Equipment and all rigging devices must comply with the manufacturer's recommendations.
  - Crane movement shall be clear of obstructions.
  - Functional inspection performed daily.
  - Full inspection performed should be monthly to every 12 months, depending on frequency of use.
  - Employee training is required.
- **Hoisting/Lifting Equipment with a Capacity of 2,000 lb or Less** (OSHA Standard 1926.1441)
  - The rated load should be marked on the lifting device.
  - Equipment and all rigging devices must comply with the manufacturer's recommendations.
  - Post-assembly, (after being attached to the load), inspection is required to verify that equipment and connections meet the manufacturer's specifications.
  - Employee training is required

You will notice that the common rules OSHA sets are that the personnel operating lifting equipment must be trained to use the equipment; the lifting capacity must be clearly marked; the equipment manufacturer's recommendations must be followed; the equipment and load (once connected) must be inspected; and the maximum working load capacities of any devices and equipment must not be exceeded.

When guidance is needed about specific lifting procedures, rigging equipment and best practices, consult the machines service information or a certified rigger. For further details, refer to the OSHA standards for the specific equipment you are using, any applicable industry standards, and the lifting equipment manufacturer's information.

▶ Wire Rope Application and Use

K08002

Wire rope is simply rope made from wire. A wire rope consists of several strands of metal wire twisted into a helix shape along its entire length. Because of its usefulness, wire rope is used in many applications (**FIGURE 8-23**). Wire rope is often called cable.

Wire rope was initially developed as an alternative to metal chains. In a metal chain, a single failure in one chain link causes a catastrophic failure. In wire rope, a single failure of a wire does not lead to a catastrophic failure, as it has many other wire and wire strands to share the load should one fail. In addition, because of the twisted wire, internal friction between the wires also prevents a catastrophic failure should a single wire break. The most common material for wire rope is steel. Wire rope is used in many applications such as guy wires to support large towers, in suspension bridges, and for lifting and hoisting in cranes and elevators. Wire rope is quite strong, comes in many sizes, can come in very long applications, and is resistant to abrasion and crushing. Some important limitations to wire rope are listed here:

- It must be kept from bending, twisting, or kinking.
- Sharp bends and contact with sharp edges can cause damage.
- Wire rope conducts electricity.
- It must be inspected periodically (prior to use in critical applications such as lifting and rigging).

See **FIGURE 8-24** for an illustration of the different designs of wire rope.

FIGURE 8-23 Wire rope is used all around us in many devices and equipment, from a window regulator in a passenger car to the supporting cables in massive suspension bridges.

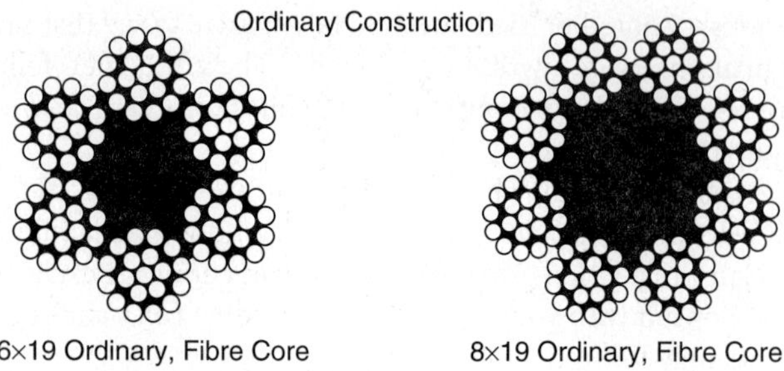

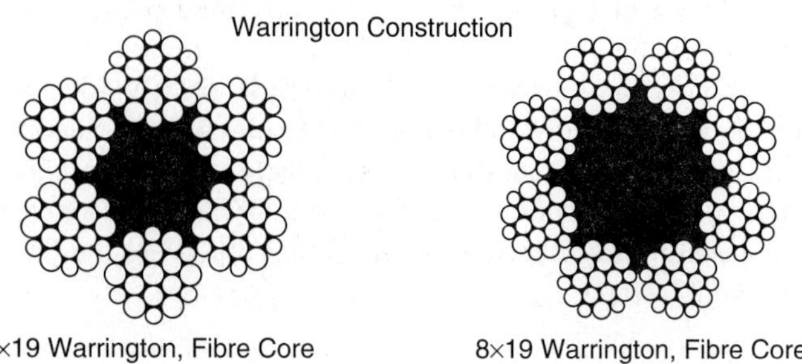

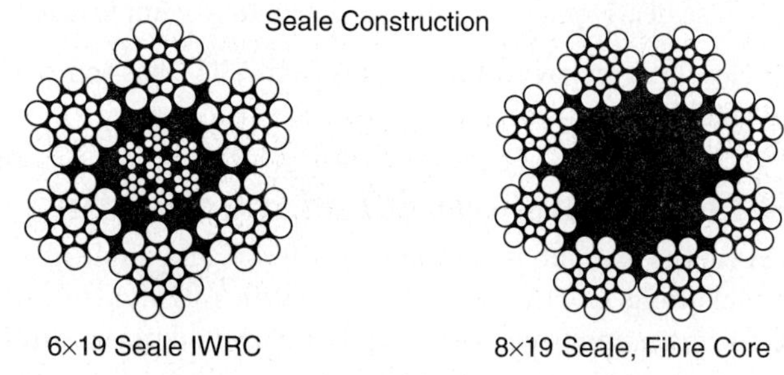

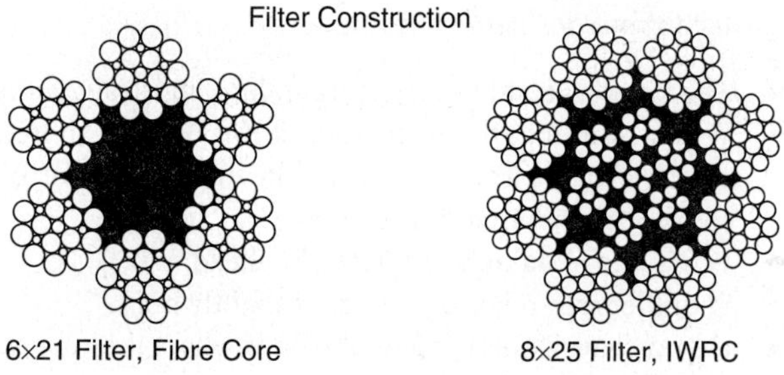

FIGURE 8-24 Wire rope comes in many designs.

Wire Rope End Terminations

A wire rope **end termination** is the treatment at the end or ends of a length of wire rope, usually made by forming an eye or attaching a fitting, and designed to be the permanent end termination on the wire rope that connects it to the load. Without the end terminations, the wire rope would not be able to connect to a load to perform a lift. The end terminations are just as important as the wire rope itself. An entire sling or rigging assembly is only as strong as the weakest part. Because of this, the end terminations and associated hardware can be a limiting factor on the safe working load (SWL) of an entire sling or lifting assembly. Only use wire rope and slings with end terminations that have been proof tested by the equipment manufacturer and that are created by a certified rigger. Personnel that assemble end terminations to wire rope and slings must have specific knowledge and training to ensure they are done properly. Many shop accidents have been caused by lifting sling failures due to end terminations assembled improperly and/or not proof tested. If in doubt as to whether a wire rope end termination was done properly, consult a rigging manual from a reputable industry authority or a wire rope manufacturer. A good general rule of thumb is, if the wire rope and/or sling does not have the manufacturer's tag, it should be suspect.

Wire Rope Inspection

Because wire rope has a finite lifespan and is susceptible to wear and failure, regular inspections, and the frequency and type of inspection, are mandated by government and industry safety agencies, for continued proper and safe operation. Failure to follow government and industry regulations regarding inspection may result in civil or criminal penalties. Consult your country and industry regulations about inspection of wire rope and lifting equipment. See **SKILL DRILL 8-4** for general information that can be used as a rough guide for inspecting wire rope used for horizontal pulling/towing and vertical lifting.

As with any MORE equipment and procedures, safety is paramount when using wire rope and cables. Many people have been injured and even killed because of improper use, application, and inspection of wire rope/cable. The proper use, application, and inspection of wire rope is not simple and requires special training and consulting technical data and manuals. Your proper knowledge will be the determining factor that ensures you can safely and properly use wire rope to perform your job. However, as stated previously, this chapter is not a supplement or replacement for proper technical training on the use, application, and inspection of wire rope and cabling.

SAFETY TIP

Only use wire rope, slings, and rigging hardware that has been proof tested by the equipment manufacturer, or a competent authority. *Do not use* homemade lifting equipment and hardware. Manufactured slings, hardware, and lifting devices are made using proven techniques and tested to ensure they can carry a specified load without failure or degradation. Homemade devices are not. Don't trust your lift to a homemade sling or end termination. A good rule of thumb: If it does not have the manufacturer's tag or stamping with the load rating on it—don't use it.

▶ Winch Design, Operation, and Troubleshooting

K08003, A08001

A **winch** is a mechanical device used to reel in (pull) or wind out (let out) horizontally a length of wire rope or chain. A winch used to vertically lift an object is considered a crane. Most

SKILL DRILL 8-4 Inspecting Wire Rope Applications Prior to Use (General External Physical Inspection)

1. Check wire rope for manufacturer's specification tag with name of manufacturer, date of manufacture, load capacity, and date of last inspection by a certified individual or authority. Do not use wire ropes or cables with an unknown load capacity.
2. If available, look up and utilize the specific inspection instructions from the cable manufacturer's website or technical data.
3. Visually inspect the end terminations and hardware for excessive corrosion and wear as well as for proper placement, tightness, breakage, or deformation. Repair or replace any end attachments showing signs of failure.
4. Ensure one end of the wire rope remains stationary. While wearing thick gloves, wrap a thick towel around the wire rope. Gripping around the towel and wire rope tightly, run the towel down the entire length of the wire rope to the end attachments. You will be able to feel any wires that have separated on the outside of the wire rope. Now, repeat the same thing, running the towel the other direction on the wire rope to the end. Note and mark any broken wires found. Although replacement guidelines for wire rope vary slightly with the design of the rope, a common replacement criteria would be if there are six or more broken strands in any one rope lay, any broken wires in the valley of the lays, (the inside), or any broken strands at an end termination.
5. While performing the above step, visually inspect the outside of the wire rope, paying attention to the following failure conditions:
   - Kinks
   - Birdcages
   - Core protrusions
   - Broken or frayed wires
   - Changes in wire rope diameter, indicating an internal core failure
   - Excessive wear and abrasion

   The above failures and or rope conditions are not repairable and depending on severity will require rope replacement.
6. Ensure the entire length of the wire rope/cable is inspected. If any failures or damage are found, consult the wire rope manufacturer's inspection criteria to determine whether replacement is needed.
7. *Important notes:* Some critical applications may require further inspection of the wire rope/cable, such as magnetic or other nondestructive inspection techniques. Consult the wire rope manufacturer's manual as well as applicable government and industry standards for more information.

FIGURE 8-25 A piece of mobile off-road equipment (MORE) with a winch.

winches utilize wire rope. We focus here on winches that utilize wire rope to move an item horizontally (**FIGURE 8-25**).

When conducting a winching operation, safety is paramount. Consult the winch manufacturer's technical manual for specific instruction on the proper use, inspection, and applications for the winch you are using. In addition, follow these basic rules when using a winch.

- Know the winch and the wire rope's rated capacity, and do not exceed it.
- Keep all nonessential personnel well away from any active winching operations.
- Designate a person in charge (PIC) for any winching operation. That person will be responsible for the overall safety and effective operation of the winching procedure.
- *Never* allow anyone to step over or under the winch's wire rope/cable during a winching operation.
- If needed, place a winch blanket on the cable to minimize snapback in the event of wire rope/cable failure.
- Ensure everyone has an escape route planned should the wire rope break during an operation.
- Ensure the wire rope was properly inspected prior to use.
- Use the shortest length of wire rope needed to perform the task. Longer lengths of wire rope have a greater danger area if they should break.

Improper spooling is a critical issue that can cause unneeded damage to the wire rope and result in unneeded hours to correct. Follow the winch manufacturer's instructions for how to spool/reel in the winch cable properly. Ensure that the wire rope has tension when it is reeled back into the spool. In addition, if the spool reel has grooves, follow the grooves when winding the spool. Ensure that when winding multiple layers of wire back into the reel, the layers do not get out of sync with the previous layer. The winding of the first layer is critical, as all the other layers will naturally follow. Ensure the first wind of the first layer is in the groove, pressed to the furthest outside of the spool flange. Then have each successive wind press close to the previous one without stacking on top of it. When the first layer is established properly, simply follow the bottom layer, and do not leave any gaps. If the wire rope gets out of sync, gently unwind the spool until the bad portion has been released. Then rewind the spool until all the cable has been placed properly on the spool.

▶ Towing, Transporting, and Coasting Precautions

K08004

As with most wheeled vehicles and equipment, MORE can unexpectedly break down and not be able to move under its own power. In addition, most MORE equipment cannot legally travel on the roadway, and so must be towed on a trailer to the site of operations. In this section, we discuss some basic precautions to towing, transporting, and coasting operations for MORE.

Due to the weight and complexity of the drive and steering systems of much MORE, there should be specific towing and transporting instructions from the equipment manufacturer. Whenever a piece of MORE must be towed or transported, you must consult the equipment manual for the equipment being towed, as well as the manual for the equipment selected to perform the towing or transporting. The primary goal of any towing or transporting operation is move the equipment without damage to either the towed or towing equipment, or injury to personnel involved.

SAFETY TIP

Before towing or transporting any MORE, consult the equipment manual for specific instructions and safety precautions. The equipment manufacturer has more knowledge than you regarding the proper towing and transportation of its equipment.

General Precautions for Towing Operations

For towing operations, following these basic guidelines in addition to the equipment manufacturer's manual.

- Always consult the equipment manufacturer's manual for specific instructions, required equipment, and safety precautions for the towed, towing, and any additional equipment before starting a towing operation.
- Ensure that the load ratings of all the towing attachments on the equipment to be towed, the equipment doing the towing, and any attaching devices is known.
- Ensure that load and capacity ratings are not exceeded.
- Ensure all nonessential personnel are kept clear of the operation.

- Ensure all essential personnel use the proper PPE.
- Ensure the brakes on the tow vehicle and trailer, towed vehicle, and other equipment are working before starting the operation.
- Maintain a reasonable and controllable speed.

General Precautions for Transporting Operations

When transporting MORE on a flatbed style or lowboy trailer, also known as a float, some additional precautions must be made. In this case, you must ensure that the MORE is securely fastened to the trailer using appropriate tie down. You must ensure that the equipment is restrained in place from any movement forward, backward (aft), vertically, and horizontally (sideways). Failure to adequately restrain the equipment to the trailer may cause the equipment to break loose during acceleration, deceleration, cornering, or going over a rise or bump. This can cause the equipment to fall off or impact the cab of the towing vehicle, resulting in serious equipment damage, personal injury, and even death.

You are probably already aware that the operator of a vehicle or piece of equipment is responsible to ensure that the load being carried is adequately restrained and secure.

Many countries' transportation industry standards set specific criteria for cargo restraint that must be applied to prevent movement. The **restraint criteria** are used to determine the proper amount of restraint that must be applied to a piece of cargo to prevent movement in the forward, rearward/aft, lateral, and vertical directions. The restraint criteria are given as a number followed by the letter "g" (example: 0.8 g). What this means is that the criteria references the normal acceleration due to gravity (g) on earth, which is 32.2 ft/s^2 (9.8 m/s^2). So, 0.8g would be 32.2 ft/s^2, multiplied by 0.8; which is 25.76 ft/s^2. This becomes the acceleration of mass due to gravity that must be restrained. The weight of an object (W) is its mass (M) multiplied by the acceleration due to gravity (g); $W = M \times g$. So, an item that weighs 75,000 lb and must be restrained in the forward direction to 0.8 g must only be restrained to 75,000 lb $\times$ 0.8 = 60,000 lb in the forward direction. If the restraint criteria were 1.0 g, then it would be 75,000 lb. If the restraint criteria were greater than 1.0 g, then it would be greater than 75,000 lb. This is used to determine that actual amount of restraint that must be provided by the restraint devices used. For transporting operations, follow these basic guidelines in addition to the information provided in the equipment manufacturer's manual.

- Always consult the equipment manufacturer's manual for specific instructions, required equipment, and safety precautions.

FIGURE 8-26 Proper restraints are essential when transporting equipment.

- Ensure that the capacity ratings of all the tie-down and restraint attachments, and tie-down devices are known.
- When determining actual restraint provided by the tie-down devices, the lowest rating of the attachment points or tie-down equipment will be used (a tie-down chain rated at 10,000 lb attached to a tie-down ring rated at 5,000 lb has a capacity of 5,000 lb).
- Always apply tie-down devices in symmetrical pairs (**FIGURE 8-26**).
- Do not mix and match tie-down device types in the same restraint direction (a nylon strap will stretch a different amount under load than a metal chain).
- Ensure the brakes on the tow vehicle and trailer, towed vehicle, and other equipment are working before starting the operation.
- Maintain a reasonable and controllable speed.
- Remember that with equipment on your trailer, your center of gravity will be higher, and the vehicle and trailer more prone to tipping over.

Coasting can be very dangerous, as it is often uncontrolled. Avoid coasting operations unless there is no other way to recover a piece of equipment. Because most MORE is very heavy, there are not many things that can stop or control a piece of MORE that is coasting uncontrolled. Perform a thorough operational risk management (ORM) analysis, and implement proper controls before performing any coasting operation. Try using another, larger, piece of MORE equipped with a winch to attach to the disabled equipment to slow and control it's decent rather than free fall coasting.

Wrap-Up

As you service MORE, you will be tasked to lift, tow, and move heavy equipment and parts. This carries inherent safety risks that can damage equipment, property, and result in injury to yourself and others. Ensure that you know the proper regulations, rules, equipment, and procedures to use. If you don't know, find out from a competent person or an authoritative source. Don't place yourself and others at risk by not knowing the correct way to perform a lifting, blocking, or towing operation. Conversely, don't place your life in someone else's hands without verifying everything has been done correctly.

Ready for Review

- Always use the proper lifting techniques when moving heavy objects.
- The safe working load indicates the operating capacity for lifting equipment.
- Lifting equipment includes vehicle hoists, floor jacks, jack stands, engine and component hoists, chains, slings, and shackles.
- Periodically check and test lifting equipment; consult the test certificate if available.
- Jacks can be classified by the type of lifting mechanism they use: hydraulic, pneumatic, or mechanical.
- Jack types include floor jacks, high-lift (farm) jacks, bottle jacks, air jacks, scissor jacks, sliding bridge jacks, and transmission jacks.
- Choose jacks according to size and lifting capacity.
- Jack stands support a vehicle's weight when it has been raised; always use jack stands in pairs.
- Vehicle hoists raise the vehicle to allow technicians underside access.
- Never use a vehicle hoist without activating the safety lock, or for lifting a vehicle heavier than the rated limit.
- Make sure a machine has enough clearance over the lifting mechanism.
- Engine hoists can lift heavy objects out of a machine and onto an engine stand.
- Check for damage before using an engine hoist, and make sure all components have the lifting capacity needed for the task.
- Always have a safe attitude when using tools and equipment, and wear necessary personal protection equipment.
- Always inspect lifting, rigging, and blocking equipment and devices prior to use.
- Never stand underneath an item being lifted.
- Always have an escape route planned should something go wrong during a lifting, towing, or coasting operation.
- Never sacrifice your body to save a piece of equipment from damage or falling.
- Don't exceed the rated capacity of a lifting, blocking, or towing device.

Key Terms

blocking Includes blocking, cribbing, jack stands, timbers, dunnage, and any other devices or equipment designed to support a load in a stationary position.

blocking devices Also referred to as blocking and cribbing. These include blocking, cribbing, jack stands, timbers, dunnage, and any other devices or equipment designed to support a load in a stationary position.

cable clip A device consisting of a U-bolt, a saddle, and two nuts, used to bind a loop at the end of a wire rope.

center of gravity (CG) Also called the center of balance. The center of gravity, or CG, of an object is the point, or position, at which the item's weight is evenly dispersed, and all sides are in balance. If the item were to be supported in a direct vertical axis from the center of gravity, it would balance perfectly.

chain blocks A chain block is a piece of equipment used to lift heavy items. The typical block, also known as chain falls, consists of two grooved wheels with a chain wound around them in the same fashion as a block and tackle. The chain wound around the two wheels creates a simple machine that uses the leverage and the increased lifting ability created by the two wheels to lift heavy weights.

chocks Blocks of material placed against a wheel to prevent undesired rolling movement.

cribbing Also referred to as blocking. This includes blocking, cribbing, jack stands, timbers, dunnage, and any other devices or equipment designed to support a load in a stationary position.

end termination The way the end of a wire rope is treated, usually by forming an eye that becomes the attachment for the wire rope.

engine hoist A small crane used to lift engines.

gantry crane A crane similar to an overhead crane except that the bridge for carrying the trolley or trolleys is rigidly supported on two or more legs running on fixed rails or other runway.

hoisting The action of lifting a load using cables or ropes.

hydraulic hoist A type of hoist that the vehicle is driven onto that uses two long, narrow platforms to lift the vehicle.

hydraulic jack A type of vehicle jack that uses oil under pressure to lift vehicles.

jack stands Metal stands with adjustable height to hold a vehicle once it has been jacked up.

lifting equipment Also known as lifting gear, any equipment or devices used to lift a load vertically. This can include jacks, a block and tackle, vacuum lift, hydraulic lift, hoist, gantries, windlasses, cranes, forklifts, slings or lifting harnesses, rigging, wire rope/cables, and any other items used to lift a load vertically.

mechanical jack A type of jack that utilizes mechanical power to provide lifting. A screw jack is a type of mechanical jack.

Occupational Safety and Health Administration (OSHA) The agency that assures safe and healthy working conditions by setting and enforcing standards and by providing training, outreach, education, and assistance.

overhead crane A crane with a movable bridge carrying a movable or fixed hoisting mechanism and traveling on an overhead fixed runway structure.

pneumatic jacks A type of vehicle jack that uses compressed gas or air to lift a vehicle.

portable lifting hoists A type of vehicle hoist that is portable and can be moved from one location to another.

Reference Datum Line (RDL) The arbitrary reference point from where the center of gravity is measured. Determined by the equipment manufacturer.

restraint criteria Used to determine the proper amount of restraint that must be applied to a piece of cargo to prevent movement in the forward, rearward/aft, lateral, and vertical directions.

rigger A person who specializes in lifting and moving heavy objects.

rigging/rigging gear All the components used to attach the mechanical hoisting equipment to the load being lifted. This can include rope, wire rope/cables, slings, shackles, eyebolts, eye nuts, links, rings, turnbuckles, rigging hooks, compressions hardware, rigging blocks, load-indicating devices, and precision load positioners.

safe working load (SWL) The maximum safe lifting load for lifting equipment.

test certificate A certificate issued when lifting equipment has been checked and deemed safe.

towing equipment and devices Equipment or devices used to pull, or tow, a load horizontally.

vehicle hoist A type of vehicle lifting tool designed any to lift the entire vehicle.

winch A mechanical device used to reel in (pull) or wind out (let out) horizontally a length of wire rope or chain.

wire rope clips Fitting for clamping parts of wire rope to each other.

Review Questions

1. Whenever possible, __________ points of contact should be used when blocking a piece of equipment.
   - **a.** two
   - **b.** one
   - **c.** three
   - **d.** four
2. When lifting an object using a hoist from above, the lifting devices should be attached ______________ the item's center of gravity.
   - **a.** above
   - **b.** below
   - **c.** on either side of
   - **d.** with no reference to
3. When an item is lifted from above using a two-chain hoist, with the chains at a 30-degree angle from the horizontal, the actual lifting capacity of the chains will be ____________ than if they were placed vertically.
   - **a.** less
   - **b.** more
   - **c.** the same
4. The actual lifting capacity of an overhead crane is limited by ____________.
   - **a.** the crane's capacity/rating
   - **b.** the rigging device(s) capacity/rating
   - **c.** the attachment points on the item being lifted
   - **d.** the lowest capacity/rating between the crane, rigging, and attachment points
5. When lifting an object using a jack from below, the jacking points are best if they are ______________ the item's center of gravity.
   - **a.** above
   - **b.** below the level of
   - **c.** on either side of
   - **d.** below and in line with
6. True/False. It is acceptable to mix types and materials of lifting and rigging equipment attached to the same load, if their capacity is not exceeded.
   - **a.** True
   - **b.** False
7. True/False. A lifting device with a capacity less than 2,000 lb does not require operator training.
   - **a.** True
   - **b.** False
8. When securing a piece of equipment for transportation onto a flatbed or lowboy trailer, ______________ restraint will prevent the item from tipping over and falling off the side of the trailer.
   - **a.** forward
   - **b.** aft/rearward
   - **c.** vertical
   - **d.** lateral
9. True/False. When a piece of equipment is properly restrained and secured for transportation onto a flatbed or lowboy trailer; the trailer with the equipment on it will be restrained from tipping over when going around corners.
   - **a.** True
   - **b.** False
10. Operators of lifting equipment are required to be knowledgeable of and adhere to which of the following standards and guidelines?
    - **a.** OSHA
    - **b.** The equipment manufacturer's
    - **c.** Industry standards
    - **d.** All of the above

ASE Technician A/Technician B Style Questions

1. Technician A says that wire rope must be inspected before use, and weekly. Technician B says that wire rope must be inspected before use and as often as the wire rope manufacturer, or government or industry standard requires. Who is correct?
   - **a.** Tech A
   - **b.** Tech B
   - **c.** Both A and B
   - **d.** Neither A nor B
2. Technician A says the parking brake must be applied before jacking a piece of wheeled equipment. Technician B says chocks must be installed in front of and behind a wheel before jacking a piece of equipment. Who is correct?
   - **a.** Tech A
   - **b.** Tech B
   - **c.** Both A and B
   - **d.** Neither A nor B
3. Technician A says that a wire rope can have broken wires along its length and still be useable. Technician B says that if there are broken wires at an end termination, the rope should be replaced. Who is correct?
   - **a.** Tech A
   - **b.** Tech B
   - **c.** Both A and B
   - **d.** Neither A nor B
4. Technician A says that you must still ensure that implements are supported, even with lift cylinder locks installed. Technician B says that because lift cylinder locks are installed, the implement is considered locked in place, and it is not necessary to support the implement. Who is correct?
   - **a.** Tech A
   - **b.** Tech B
   - **c.** Both A and B
   - **d.** Neither A nor B
5. Technician A says that articulating joints must be mechanically locked before lifting a piece of equipment. Technician B says that hydraulic lift cylinders must be mechanically locked or placed in the full down position prior to lifting a piece of equipment. Who is correct?
   - **a.** Tech A
   - **b.** Tech B
   - **c.** Both A and B
   - **d.** Neither A nor B
6. Technician A says that government standards such as OSHA are the most correct source of information on how to properly utilize a specific piece of lifting equipment. Technician B says that industry standards such as rigging manuals are the most correct source of information on how to utilize a specific piece of lifting equipment. Who is correct?
   - **a.** Tech A
   - **b.** Tech B
   - **c.** Both A and B
   - **d.** Neither A nor B

7. Technician A says that a noticeable change in the diameter of a length of wire rope may indicate internal failure and require replacement. Technician B says a length of wire rope that has a birdcage in it can be repaired by straightening and then wrapping the area in steel wire. Who is correct?
   a. Tech A
   b. Tech B
   c. Both A and B
   d. Neither A nor B
8. Technician A states that blocking is placed under an object to provide support. Technician B states that blocking is placed under an item to distribute the weight over a larger area. Who is correct?
   a. Tech A
   b. Tech B
   c. Both A and B
   d. Neither A nor B
9. Tech A says that you should not use a piece of lifting or jacking equipment with an expired test certificate. Tech B says that you should perform an inspection of all lifting and jacking equipment prior to use. Who is correct?
   a. Tech A
   b. Tech B
   c. Both A and B
   d. Neither A nor B
10. Tech A says that when towing a piece of heavy equipment, use the highest rated towing device you have available. Tech B says that you should consult the equipment manufacturer's manual and follow the specific procedures for towing. Who is correct?
   a. Tech A
   b. Tech B
   c. Both A and B
   d. Neither A nor B

D8
CAT
10
15
20
5
25
0
30
X 100
Steering
Fault
OK
Auto
WARNING

SECTION II

Electrical & Electronic Systems

CHAPTER 9

Principles of Electricity and Electrical Circuits

Knowledge Objectives

After reading this chapter, you will be able to:

- **K09001** Identify and explain the functions of the electrical elements of the atom.
- **K09002** Identify and describe conductors, insulators, and semiconductors.
- **K09003** Define and explain concepts of voltage amperage and resistance.
- **K09004** Describe the differences between the electron theory of current movement and the conventional current theory.
- **K09005** Describe the differences between alternating and direct current.
- **K09006** Describe the differences between electrical and electronic circuits.
- **K09007** Describe the heating effect of current in an electrical circuit.

Skills Objectives

After reading this chapter, you will be able to:

- **S09001** Differentiate between electrical units of measurement for voltage, amperage, resistance, and power.
- **S09002** Calculate energy consumption in a heating circuit.

▶ Introduction

Not long ago, a typical mobile off-road machine had fewer than 20 electrical circuits. Lighting, starting, and charging were the most significant electrical systems along with a few other electrical accessories like the horn and wipers. Today, the number of electrical circuits has increased into the hundreds, and very few mobile off-road machine systems operate without electronic control (**FIGURE 9-1**). Where the radio was once the most sophisticated electrical device, microprocessors containing millions of transistors control the traditional electrical systems, such as lighting and accessories, and the software contained in the control modules operates hydraulics, transmissions, engine, and onboard interactive display systems. Increasing sophistication of mobile off-road electrical systems include electronic machine and implement controls, hybrid electric powertrain, and telematics, which is monitoring and control of equipment using satellite, cell phone, and Internet-based equipment communication.

Today's electrical system components are no longer separated into distinct systems. Electronic control modules (ECMs) provide electrical signals to operate individual electrical components. The modules are then connected by onboard networks, enabling the control of the electrical system to be distributed over many electronic control modules (**FIGURE 9-2**). Networking electrical system components adds new equipment features that can enhance safety, performance, and operator comfort simply by adding only software and a twisted pair of wires to connect all the equipment ECMs. For example, receiving a hands-free cell phone call today could automatically mute the radio volume; leaving the operators seat will simultaneously engage the parking brake and disable the hydraulic implements; a grade control system using laser, sonic, and GPS technology provides in-cab guidance to operators. Electronic throttle control matches horsepower and torque to meet the demands of the application. Electrohydraulics provide superior implement control that reduces heat buildup and saves fuel.

FIGURE 9-1 Electronic controls extend to every machine system.

What is the point being made? The technology in today's mobile off-road electrical systems is both complex and sophisticated. More than ever, a successful and valued technician needs to have a sound understanding of electrical principles underlying mobile off-road electrical systems technology. Arguably, the technician's most essential skills are to understand principles of electricity, analyzing electrical problems and comprehending electrical system and component operation, plus knowing how to use test equipment to diagnose electrical problems.

▶ Electrical Fundamentals

K09001

Understanding the behavior of electricity can be more difficult than understanding mechanical concepts such as four-stroke cycle engine operation or braking fundamentals, because electricity itself cannot be seen, but its effects can be felt. At the same time, electricity is governed by the laws of science, so learning how electricity behaves can be approached in a logical manner, as with any other subject. By applying yourself, over time it will make more and more sense. This chapter explores basic principles about the nature of electricity and how it behaves. To get started, it is useful to know there are good analogies for how electricity behaves, which are helpful to understand different aspects of electricity's properties. Visualizing electrical concepts using these comparisons helps many learners to more easily understand electrical principles. In fact, one analogy is to think of electricity as nothing more than the movement of particles from one point to another. For example, imagine a line of marbles rolling through a tube or the flow of water through a pipe. The moving marbles or flow of water has energy that can be harnessed and made to

You Are the Mobile Heavy Equipment Technician

When measuring the amount of amperage drawn by a starting motor cranking, a 13.6L Deere PowerTech engine, a technician observed close to 900 amps of current were needed. The engine cranking speed was normal and close to 200 rpm, but the technician observed light smoke rising from some of the battery cable connections. After replacing all three batteries and making sure all batteries were fully charged, only 400 amps of current were needed to start the engine. The engine then cranked at close to the same speed as before the batteries were replaced.

1. Explain why the starting motor used more amperage before replacing the machine's batteries than after replacing the batteries.
2. If it were possible for the 12-volt starting motor to be used in a 24-volt circuit, what would you predict would happen to the amount of amperage drawn by the starting motor?
3. Explain why smoke was rising from the battery cable connections when the cranking amperage was high. Include the name of the applicable electrical law in your explanation.

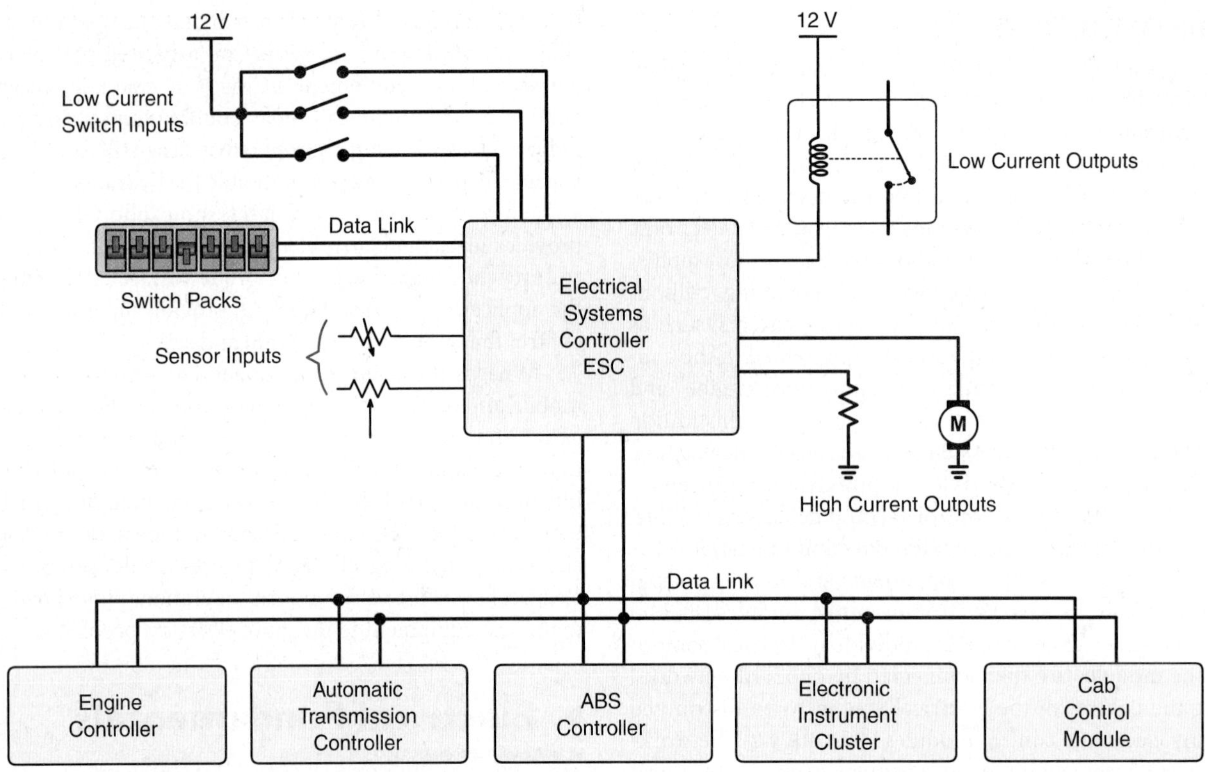

FIGURE 9-2 Contemporary mobile off-road machine system architecture. All electronic control modules are connected to an onboard machine network, which provides distributed control of the electrical system.

perform work or some specialized function. Electrical devices can extract the energy from moving particles (**FIGURE 9-3**). The energy can be converted into a variety of others forms such as light, heat, sound, electrical signals, or magnetic fields, which are then used to operate motors, solenoids, or relays. That is where some of electricity's magic comes in. Moving these electrical particles involves using positive and negative charges that are governed by basic **electrostatic theory**—unlike charges are attracted to one another (positive to negative), and like charges are repelled by one another (positive repels positive, negative repels negative) (**FIGURE 9-4**). These forces of charge repulsion and attraction are called electrostatic force and are foundational to produce the flow of electrical current and operate all electrical devices. Electrostatic forces of repulsion and attraction are incredibly powerful, and the energy they contain can be harnessed by electrical devices to perform work.

FIGURE 9-3 Electrical devices, such as this ECM, extract energy from moving particles.

Electrostatic Law Summary

- A proton's (+) charge repels another proton's (+) charge.
- An electron's (–) charge repels another electron's (–) charge.
- A proton's (+) charge attracts an electron's (–) charge.

As you continue, remember that electricity is the movement of charged particles from one place to another, pushed or pulled by electrostatic force.

Basic Electricity

All questions about the nature of electricity lead to the composition of matter. All matter is made up of atoms, as shown in **FIGURE 9-5**. Atoms are composed of electrons, protons, and neutrons. Positive electrical charges are found on protons, negative charges on electrons, and neutrons have no electrical charge. Neutrons and positively charged protons make up the nucleus of an atom. Neutrons are the electrical glue that

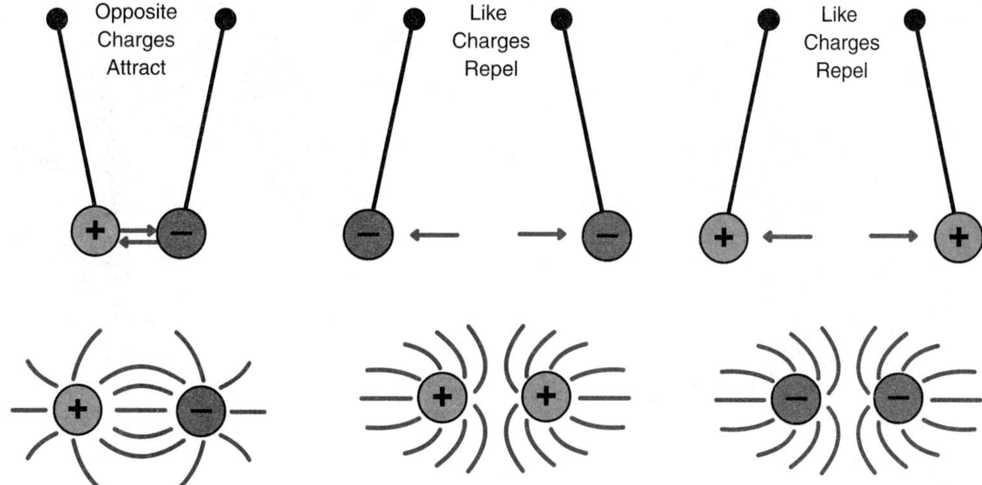

FIGURE 9-4 Summary of electrostatic laws.

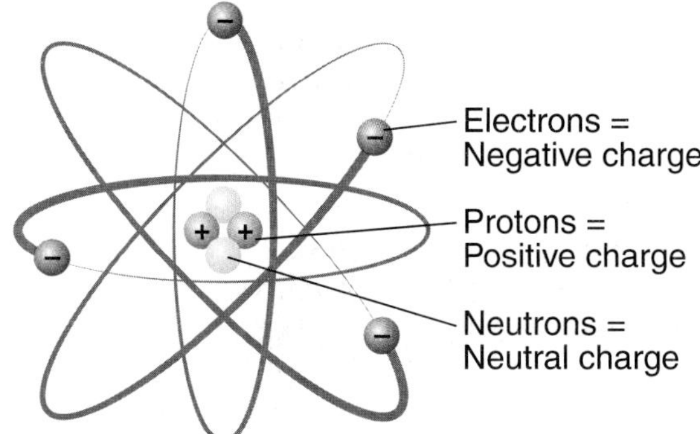

FIGURE 9-5 A model of the atom based on a 1910 understanding. The model is useful to understand electrical principles.

prevents the electrostatic forces of repulsion between the protons from bursting the nucleus. Moving around the outside of the nucleus are one or more negatively charged electrons. Electrons travel in different layers or shells around the nucleus. Each shell can contain only a specific maximum number of electrons.

With equal numbers of protons and electrons, the charges within an atom balance each other, leaving the atom with no overall charge. It is the goal of every atom to achieve this state of balance between the electrical charges. Only electrons can be removed or added to an atom, and not protons. If an atom loses or gains an electron, it is called an ion. The term "ion" simply means the atom has an imbalance of electrical charges due to the gain or loss of electrons. An atom with more electrons than protons has an overall negative charge and is called a negative ion. Ions are unstable, and the atom wants to return to a state where the electrical charges are balanced or neutral. In the case of a negatively charged ion, the presence of an extra electron causes the forces of repulsion to try to push the electron away from the atom, as illustrated in **FIGURE 9-6**. A deficiency of electrons gives the atom an overall positive charge and is called a positive ion. It is also not electrically balanced and will try to achieve a state of balance between the positive and negative charges and become neutral. In this case, the positively charged protons will pull on any available electron to return the atom to a state of balance between electrical charges.

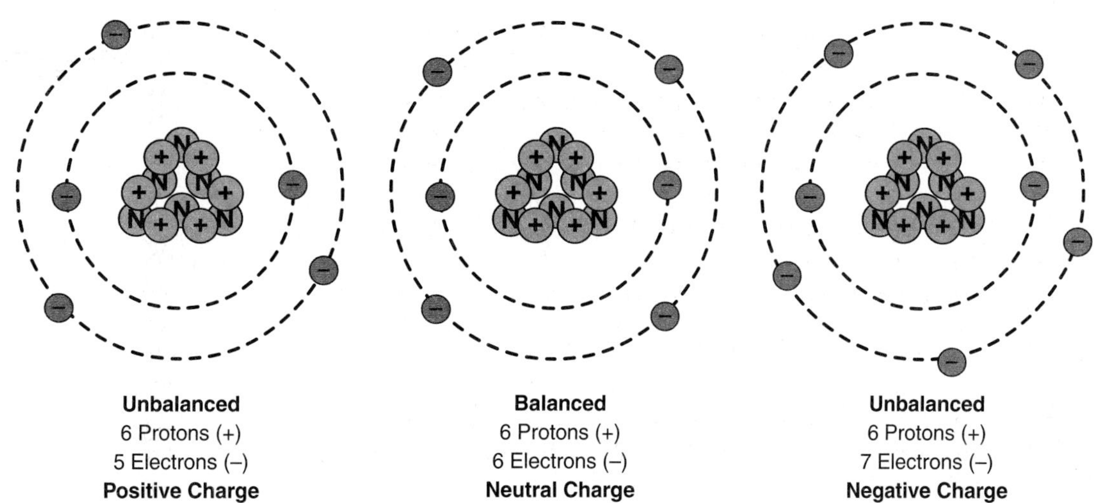

FIGURE 9-6 Imbalances between the number of electrons and protons produces an electrical charge.

If a negative ion and positive ion are close enough, the negative charge on the negative ion exerts a repelling force on the extra electron, causing it to be pushed away from its atom; at the same time, the positive ion exerts an attracting force on the extra electron. These forces of repulsion and attraction cause the electron to be pushed from one atom and pulled toward the positive atom, balancing the charges on both atoms. It is this movement of electrons from one atom to another that is called electricity.

▶ Conductivity

K09002

Not all atoms can give up or accept electrons easily. Materials that hold electrons loosely enable electrons in their outer shell to move easily. These materials are categorized as **conductors**, whereas materials that hold electrons tightly and prevent electron movement are called **insulators**. The electrons that are only loosely held by the positive charges in the nucleus can move when another force strong enough can overcome the forces of attraction holding an electron in the atom. In fact, atoms with the fewest electrons in their outer shell are the best conductors. Copper (Cu) is an example of a metal with only one electron in the atom's outer shell (**FIGURE 9-7A**). Because a single electron is held loosely by the nucleus, copper makes an excellent conductor. By contrast, argon (Ar) is a noble gas, meaning that it generally does not form molecules and so is an insulator (**FIGURE 9-7B**). Semiconductors such as silicon (Si) (**FIGURE 9-7C**) are discussed in greater detail in the section Semiconductors. **TABLE 9-1** shows how the conductivity of other metals compares to the conductivity of copper. Metals typically have lots of easily moved electrons, which make them good conductors. But it's not just metals that conduct electricity; liquids can too. Electrolytes are liquids that conduct electric current. The liquid inside a lead-acid battery is an example of where electrolyte is used. Under some circumstances, air and other gases can conduct electricity, which is seen when a spark crosses an air gap. The term "plasma" is used to describe ionized gases that conduct electrons.

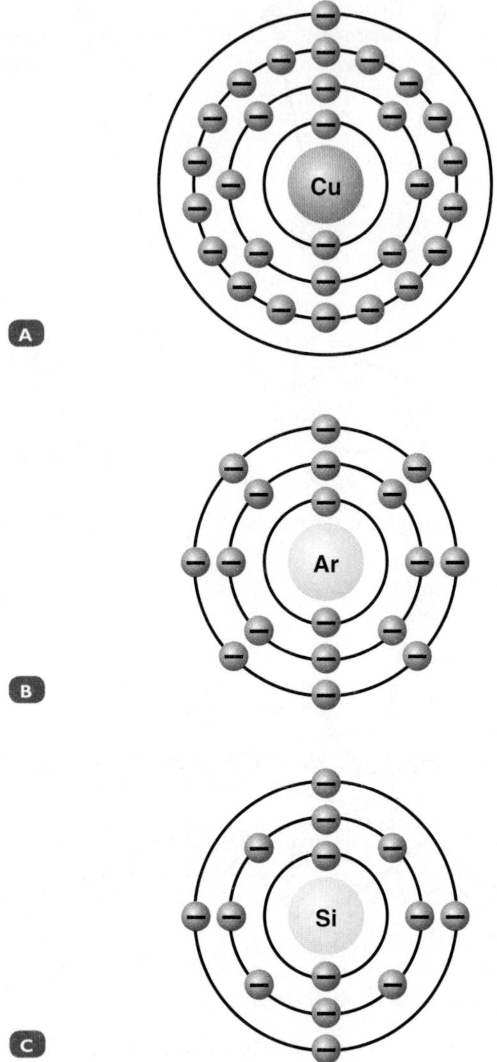

FIGURE 9-7 A. Conductor. **B.** Insulator. **C.** Semiconductor.

▶ Understanding Current

K09003, S09001

Understanding conductivity is the foundation for understanding the flow of electrical current. This section discusses the basics of current movement, how quickly electrical currents move, and in what direction.

Movement of Electric Current

The forces that can move electrons on or off an atom include the following:

- Light
- Heat
- Pressure
- Friction
- Magnetic fields
- Chemical energy

The force applied by each of these energy sources against an electron determines how fast an electron is moved from one atom to the next. This is like hitting a baseball (**FIGURE 9-8**). The harder the ball is hit, the faster it travels. As an electrical concept, the speed of electron travel from atom to atom is voltage. A **volt**

TABLE 9-1 Conductivity of Different Metals Compared to Copper

Conductor	Conductivity Compared to Copper
Silver	1.064
Copper	1.000
Gold	0.707
Aluminum	0.659
Zinc	0.288
Brass	0.243
Iron	0.178

is the unit used to measure the electrical potential difference between two points or electrical pressure (**FIGURE 9-9**). Higher electron **voltage** means the electrostatic forces pushing or pulling an electron are stronger. To understand better the concept of voltage and other characteristics of electrical current, the hydraulic model of electricity is a useful visualization. Essentially, the hydraulic model compares the flow of electricity to water movement through pipes and plumbing components. When using an analogy of electricity represented as water in a pipe, the concept of voltage is like pressure (**FIGURE 9-10**).

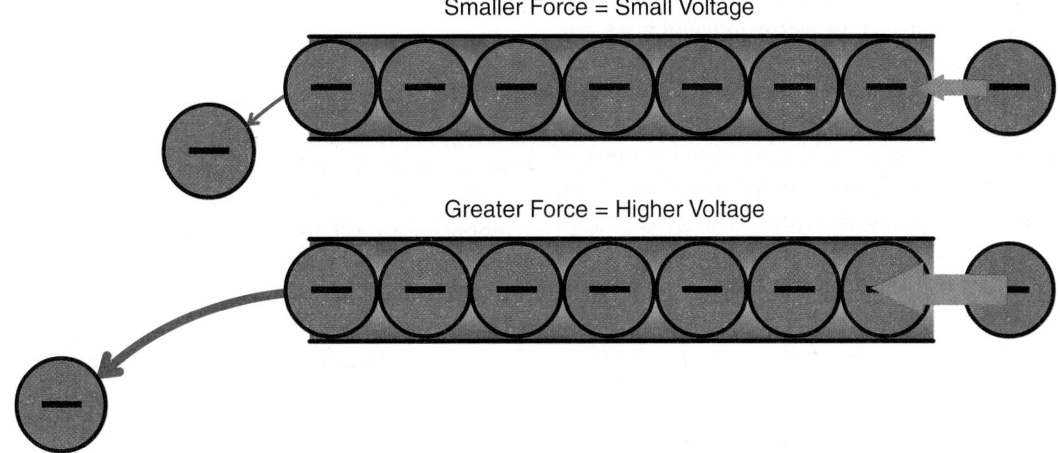

FIGURE 9-8 The force moving electrons through a circuit is voltage. The greater the force pushing the electrons, the higher the voltage.

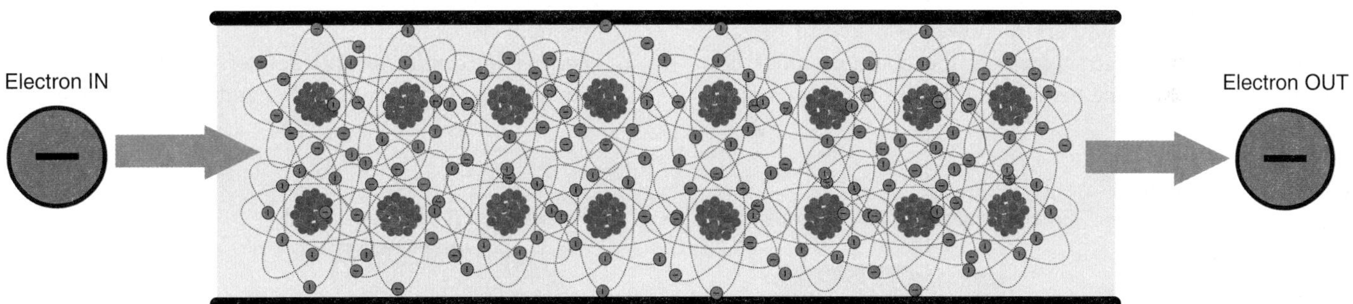

FIGURE 9-9 Electricity is the movement of electrons from atom to atom. The force moving electrons through a circuit is voltage.

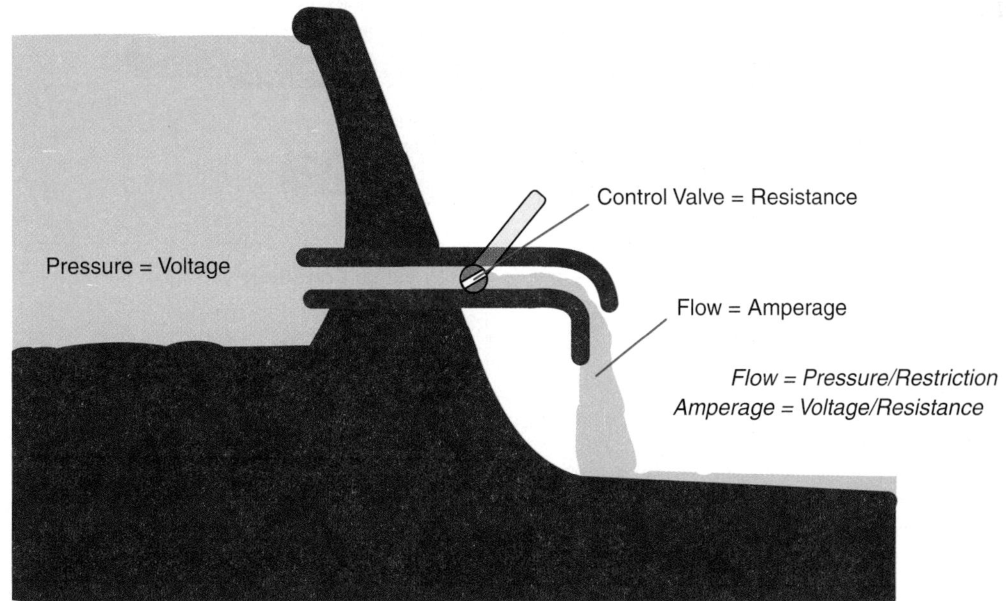

FIGURE 9-10 The concepts of electrical current flow: voltage, amperage, resistance.

Just as higher pressure in a pipe moves water faster, high voltage means electrons move with greater speed from atom to atom.

Amperage is another electrical term used to describe the movement of electrons or electrical current. The unit of measurement for amperage is the **ampere**. Although voltage can describe the average force of one or many electrons, amperage measures how many electrons are in movement at one time. When using the analogy of water in a pipe to describe the movement of electrons, amperage is like the number of gallons or liters moving past a point in the pipe per second of time. In a sense, amperage really describes the volume of electron flow. When describing the flow of electricity, a circuit's voltage and amperage together, the term "electric current" is used. Without both of these two electrical properties operating, there can be no electric current. No voltage means no pressure is available to push or pull electrons. No amperage means there are no electrons to move in a circuit. Please note, often the term "current" is used in some textbooks to describe amperage. Throughout this textbook, "current" describes the flow of electricity, which needs both voltage and amperage.

Together, the force of the electricity (volts) and volume of electrons moving in a circuit (amperage) function to perform work. To predict the amount of power available to perform work, a simple calculation answers the question about how much work can be done per second of time. Watts or wattage is the unit for measuring power. Wattage is a function of Voltage × Amperage, or Power = Volts × Amps. For example, if one wanted to find out how many amps are required to crank an engine over with a 10-horsepower starting motor, the calculation would be this: Because 746 watts is defined as being equal to 1 hp, 10 hp × 746 watts = 7,460 watts. If the available voltage is 12 volts, the equation would be:

$$7{,}460 = 12 \times \text{amps and } 7{,}460/12 = 621.6 \text{ amps}$$

Now this calculation does not take into consideration energy losses due to friction, circuit resistance, the efficiency of the starting motor, and so on. If 24 volts were available rather than 12 volts, the same power could be produced with half the amperage, or 311 amps. If only 6 volts were powering the starting motor, 1,243 amps would be needed.

Another important electrical concept is resistance. **Electrical resistance** is a material's property that reduces voltage and amperage in an electrical current. Electrical resistance is similar to the concept of friction. Like friction, which can slow objects down, anything that slows down the speed of electron movement is considered a **resistor**. Factors that determine the amount of resistance in a circuit include those listed in **FIGURE 9-11**.

1. *Type of material:* Conductors vary in the strength with which they hold electrons.
2. *Length of the conductor:* As length of a circuit or conductor increases, electrons travel farther and loose some energy.

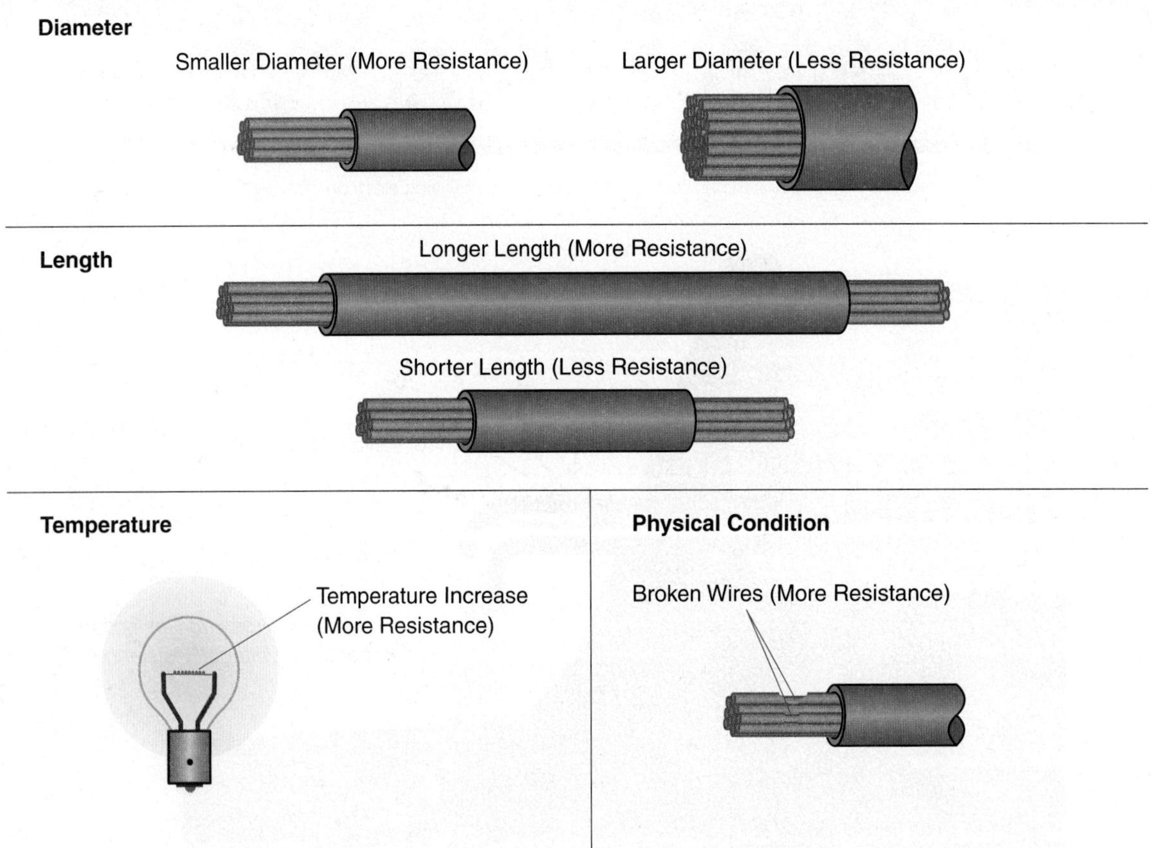

FIGURE 9-11 Factors affecting resistance in a circuit.

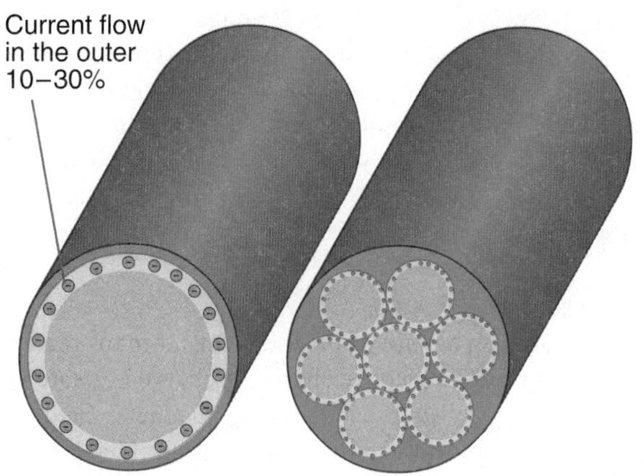

FIGURE 9-12 The forces of repulsion cause electrons to move to the outer surface of a conductor. Current flows in the outer 10–30%. Larger diameter wire and stranded wire with more surface area conduct current with less resistance.

3. *Diameter of the conductor:* The larger the conductor, the greater the capacity to carry current (**FIGURE 9-12**).
4. *Temperature of the conductor:* Electrons require more energy to move through a conductor as its temperature increases.

Resistors convert the energy in current flow to other forms of energy. Often resistance produces only heat. But electrical devices can also harness and convert electrical energy into other forms such as light, sound, movement, magnetism, and electrical signals carrying information. Electrical devices using electrical energy are called **loads** and always have some resistance (**FIGURE 9-13**).

The electrical unit for measuring the amount of resistance in a DC circuit is an **ohm**. The term is named after the person who discovered that 1 volt of electrical pressure is required to push 1 amp of current through a circuit if the circuit has a resistance of 1 ohm (**FIGURE 9-14**).

This relationship is known as **Ohm's law**. Stated mathematically, Ohm's law is:

$$\text{Voltage} = \text{Resistance} \times \text{Amperage}$$

Restating Ohm's law using a hydraulic analogy, 1 psi of water pressure is needed to push 1 gallon of water, in 1 second, through a pipe having a diameter of 1 inch.

Although the hydraulic analogy is not perfect, it provides a good visual image for remembering that, according to Ohm's law, increasing voltage in a circuit is like increasing water pressure. Just as more water flows through a pipe when water pressure is higher, more amperage flows through a circuit with higher voltage if the resistance or restrictions remain the same. Likewise, making a smaller restriction in a pipe is like increasing a circuit's resistance. Just as water pressure and volume drop in a narrower or restricted pipe, voltage and amperage are reduced with increased circuit resistance. The Greek letter omega (Ω) represents ohms, which is the unit used to measure resistance. Observing the relationship between the three factors of Ohm's law leads to the following conclusions:

If voltage is held constant in a circuit:
Amperage increases if resistance decreases.
Amperage decreases if resistance increases.

If resistance is held constant in a circuit:
Amperage will increase if voltage increases.
Amperage will decrease if voltage decreases.

If amperage is to remain the same in a circuit:
Voltage must increase if resistance increases.
Voltage decreases if resistance decreases.

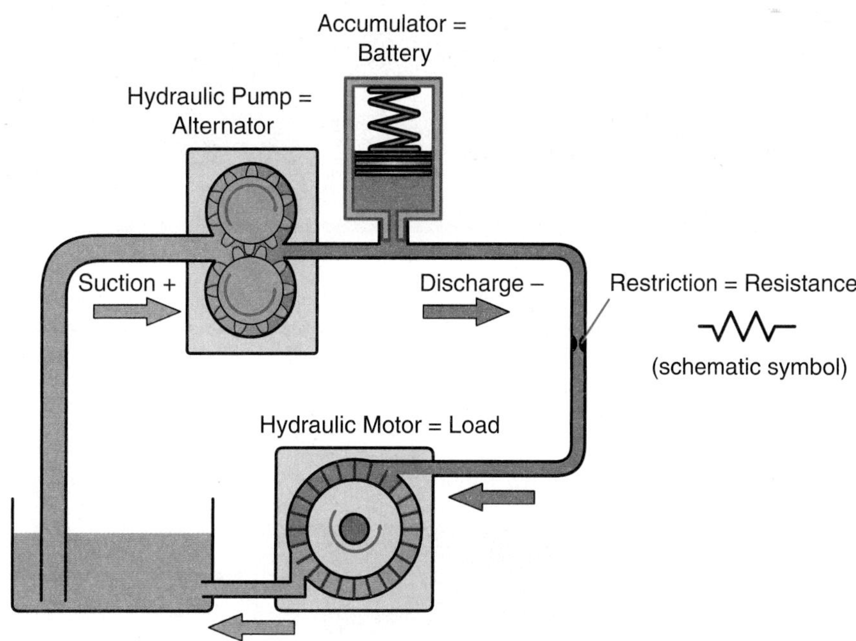

FIGURE 9-13 The analogy to resistance in the hydraulic model of current flow is a restriction in a pipe.

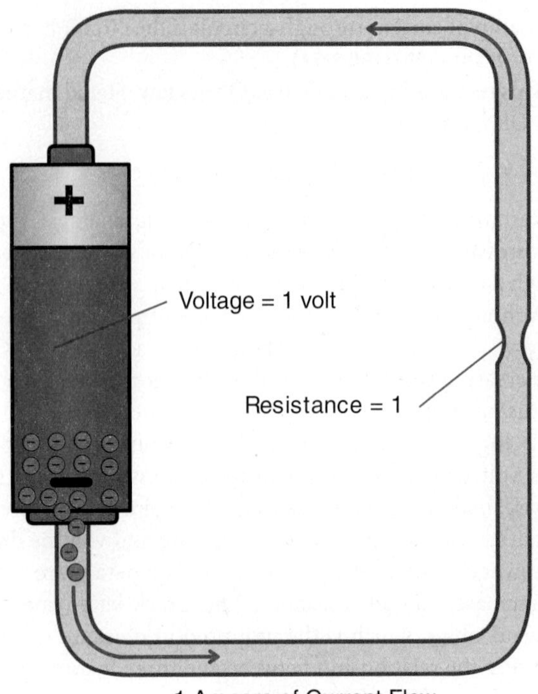

FIGURE 9-14 An ohm is the measuring unit for resistance. 1 volt of pressure is required to push 1 amp through 1 ohm of resistance.

Resistance produces a decrease or drop in voltage. That is a very important electrical concept to apply when troubleshooting problems in electrical circuits. An ohmmeter can be used to measure resistance, but learning how to measure voltage drop in a circuit with a voltmeter is one of the most helpful ways to identify unwanted resistance in an electric circuit. In off-road equipment, electrical system voltages are 12- or 24-volt systems; this means voltage is usually constant (except for battery or alternator failure), so resistance will be the main cause of low voltage issue within a circuit. Understating how to measure voltage drops is covered in the chapter Electrical Test Instruments.

▶ Direction of Current Flow

K09004

Only electrons can be moved on and off an atom to create either a negative or positive electric charge. A charge is created when a source of energy, such as a moving magnetic field, moves electrons from the outer shell of an atom. That movement changes the charge balance. Movement of electrons through a conductor continues to take place by using the electrostatic forces of either repulsion or attraction. For example, electrons on a negatively charged atom want to push the extra electron away. Positively charged atoms want to pull electrons onto the atom to balance the number of protons with electrons.

When areas of positive or negative charges are created, a pole, or polarity, is established. **Polarity** is simply the state of charge, either positive or negative. Polarity produces current flow (**FIGURE 9-15**). Electrons always move toward a positive pole and not the other way around. Areas of unbalanced electrical charges create either positive or negative poles (**FIGURE 9-16**). Polarity differences are also called potential differences and produce current flow.

The movement of negatively charged electrons to a positive charge is called the **electron theory of current movement**. It is actually not a theory, but a fact. The idea that electric current movement takes place when positive charges move to a negative pole is called **conventional current theory**. Conventional

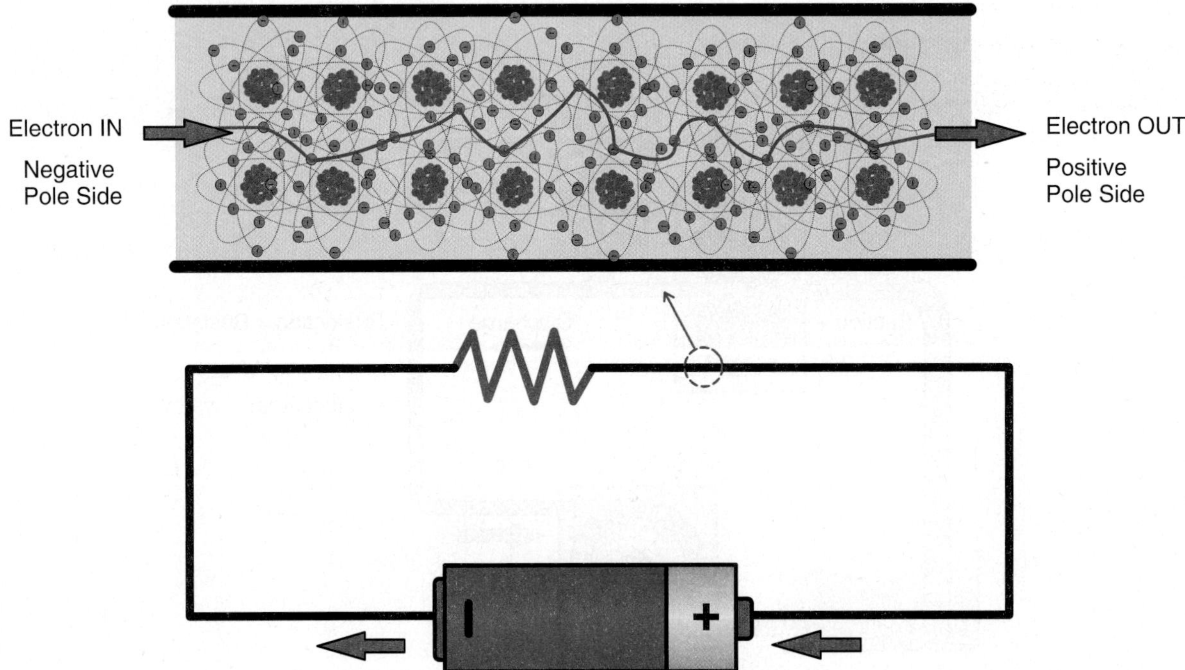

FIGURE 9-15 Polarity and electrostatic forces produce current flow.

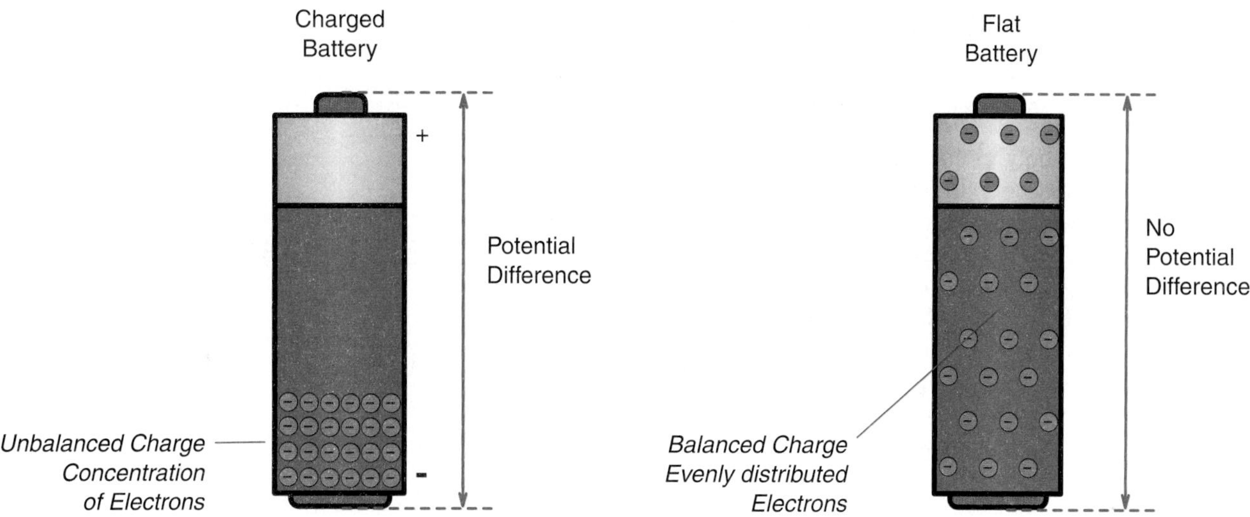

FIGURE 9-16 The pressure difference between poles produces current flow. The pressure difference is measured in volts.

current theory of electric charge movement was based on a 1910 model of the atom, which was incomplete. Later investigation found this idea was incorrect, and only negatively charged electrons moved in a circuit—in a negative to positive direction.

Many textbooks and training aids still used in trade occupations use conventional theory to explain electrical behavior. Trying to separate electron and conventional theory in practice can become confusing. However, the acceptance and use of either idea is generally not important for the technician. It is only important to remember that current flow is described by both concepts.

Nevertheless, technicians should be aware that some test instruments such as amp volt resistance (AVR) machines are designed presuming current flow is conventional (**FIGURE 9-17**). By contrast, **digital multimeters**, as shown in **FIGURE 9-18**, use electron theory, and the direction of current flow is generally provided by polarity indicators. Connecting the black or common lead of a meter to a positive voltage and the positive meter lead to a negative will cause the meter to display a negative symbol beside the number in the digital display. Diagnosing an unintended key-off current draw or parasitic current loss is one instance where it is important to note the direction of current flow; electron theory should prevail when trying to understand the problem.

Electron theory is also best used to describe the operation of semiconductors and more advanced electronic devices. Tracing current flow in wiring diagrams, however, is often easier using conventional theory. On circuit diagrams, the movement of current is often traced from the top left corner down to ground connections at the bottom of a page or PC screen.

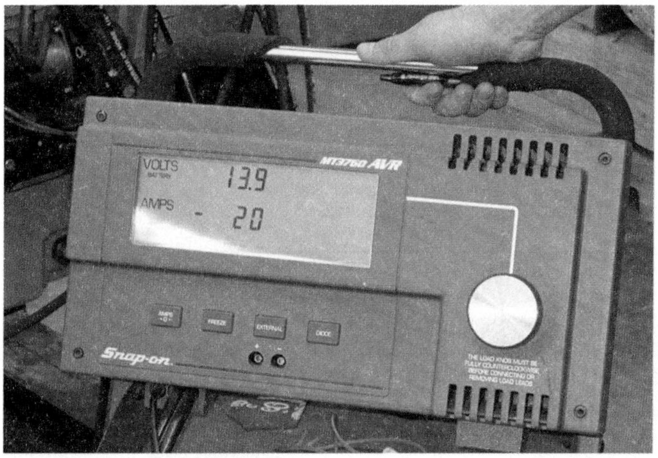

FIGURE 9-17 An amp volt and resistance (AVR) test instrument.

FIGURE 9-18 A digital multimeter displays electrical measurements in digits rather than using a sweeping needle.

▶ Direct Current and Alternating Current

K09005

When electrons move only in one direction in a circuit, the current is described as being **direct current (DC)**. In a DC circuit, electrons move continuously from negative to positive (**FIGURE 9-19**). When electrons are alternately pulled and pushed, it regularly changes the direction of current flow. That type of current flow is described as **alternating current (AC)** (**FIGURE 9-20**). When describing alternating current, the term "frequency" is used in addition to voltage and amperage. Frequency is measured by how often the alternating current changes direction. Units for frequency (direction changes per second) are called **hertz (Hz)**, which is another term for cycles per second. Plotting DC voltage on a graph produces a straight line, as shown in **FIGURE 9-21A**. Plotting AC voltage on a graph produces what is called a **sine wave** shape, illustrated in **FIGURE 9-21B**.

DC current flows only in one direction—from a positive to negative pole. A mobile off-road machine and its chassis are an example where DC current flow takes place (**FIGURE 9-22**). High concentrations of extra electrons at the negative polarity battery post travel through chassis ground cables to the machine circuits and electrical devices to reach the positive polarity battery post, which is deficient of electrons. Battery voltage, or potential difference, is determined by the comparing the overconcentration of electrons at the positive post and electron deficiency at the negative post. The greater the difference in electron concentration between the two points, the higher the battery voltage. How much resistance is present in the circuits between the positive and negative posts determines the volume of electrons that can flow—which is another way to describe amperage.

DC circuits are used in virtually all chassis circuits because a battery can easily store and supply DC current. But DC current has one major disadvantage: the farther it travels, the more resistance is present in the circuit. For example, if circuit amperage is high and correct size of wiring is not used, battery voltage can drop from 12.8 volts at a battery to just under 8 volts at the starter.

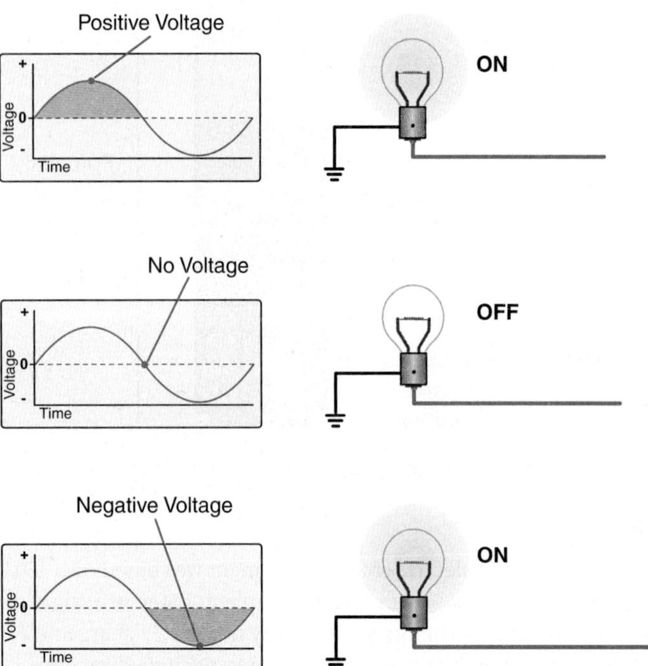

FIGURE 9-20 AC current changes direction. The number of times it changes per second is measured in hertz (Hz).

AC current is used to more efficiently power electric propulsion motors. AC current's main advantage is that it can be transmitted farther distances with less resistance and little voltage drop. Resistance is proportional to the frequency of AC polarity change. That is, the higher AC current's frequency, the less resistance AC current has in a circuit.

This property of AC current explains why it is used to transmit electricity to homes and industry over long distances with little power loss. Ohm's law does not apply to AC current flow except through resisters. The term "impedance" is used instead to describe resistance in AC circuits. AC current is a more

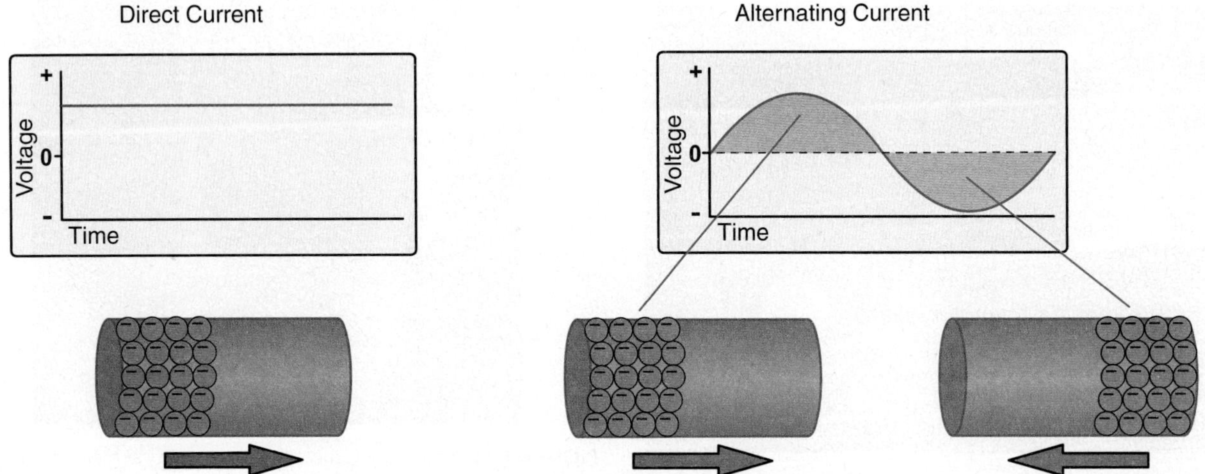

FIGURE 9-19 Current flow in one direction only is called direct current. Current flow that continuously changes direction is alternating current.

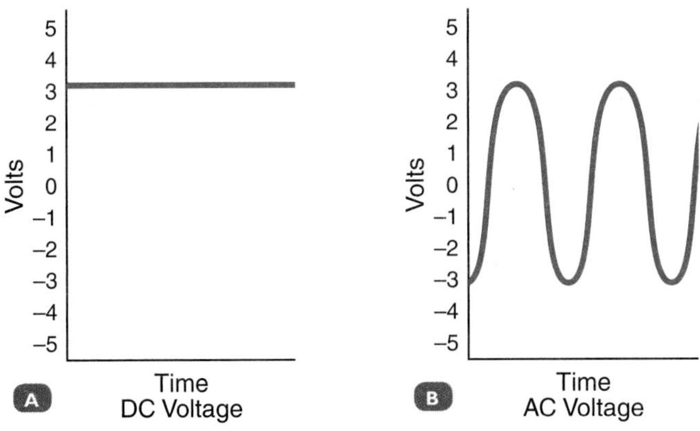

FIGURE 9-21A Waveforms. **A.** Direct current. **B.** Alternating current.

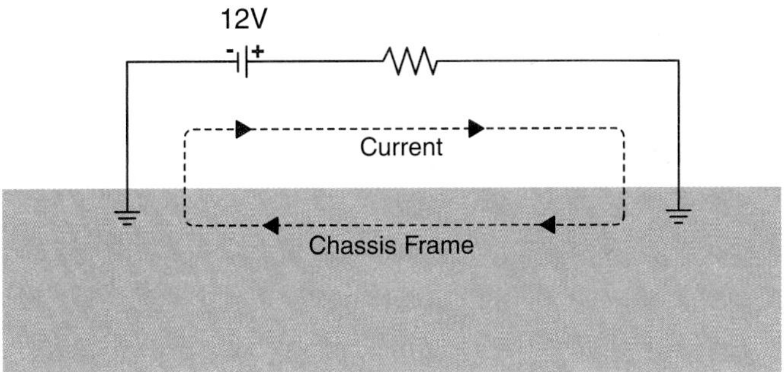

FIGURE 9-22 Machines use the frame as the ground or negative pole for the electrical system. A negative ground chassis reduces frame and body corrosion. Corrosion is more likely to take place on positively charged wires.

FIGURE 9-23 This variable reluctance sensor (VR) produces AC voltage. The waveform is displayed on a graphing meter.

efficient type of current to power electric motors, and using it simplifies motor construction. The speed of AC electric motors is also regulated by the frequency of AC current—higher frequency translates into faster motor speed.

Alternators produce AC current, which is then changed to DC current inside the alternator by a rectifier. To change DC current to AC current, a device known as a wave inverter, shortened to just **inverter**, is used. A variable reluctance–type sensor, such as the one shown in **FIGURE 9-23**, is used to measure wheel or engine speed and also can produce AC current.

▶ Heating Effect of Current

K09007, S09002

When an electric current travels through a bulb filament or an electric heating element, the filament or resistive element heats. Resistance in the elements converts electrical energy into heat energy. This observation is referred to as the "heating effect of current." As amperage and resistance increase, so does the heat produced, as shown in **FIGURE 9-24**.

So, why does the bulb filament heat and glow, but the wires connecting the bulb do not? The simple answer is that the narrowing of the circuit conductor causes collisions to take place between the electrons as they funnel into the circuit's restriction. Electrons, which are three times the size of protons, convert kinetic energy, present in electric current flow, into heat and light.

To understand this effect, think of a busy highway as traffic merges from six lanes to a single lane. The single lane cannot accommodate all the vehicles, so traffic must slow. Applying brakes reduces vehicle speed, much like voltage drop, and kinetic energy converts to heat due to friction between the brake drums, rotors, and friction material.

Fuses take advantage of this heating effect by using a narrow metal strip made of highly conductive material. When the amount of amperage exceeds a wire's ability to conduct the current without heating up, the strip melts to protect circuit wiring from burning. The amount of heat produced is directly proportional to the fuse's resistance, the time current flows, and the amount of amperage in the current. The transformation during heating is measured in joules. Mathematically, the relationship is described as:

$$H = I2Rt$$

where H is the heat output, I is the current (amps), R is the resistance in the circuit (ohms), and t is the time (seconds). So, if 2 amps pass through a wire with 25 ohms of resistance over the course of 1 minute (60 seconds), then the heat output is 6,000 joules.

Joule's law refers to the heating effect of electric current. It also helps explain why the seemingly small resistance of narrow wire having 0.01 ohm will drop voltage by only one-tenth with 1 amp of current but will completely burn if 750 amps of current pass through the connection, whereas a 00 gauge battery cable can easily handle the higher current load. The bigger cable with a larger cross-sectional area can conduct more amperage with less resistance because fewer collisions caused by cable narrowing will take place.

▶ Electrical Versus Electronic Circuits

K09006

Even though electricity is used to operate electrical and electronic circuits, the two types of circuit are not identical. What are the differences between electrical and electronic circuits? Electrical circuits usually conduct higher amounts of current

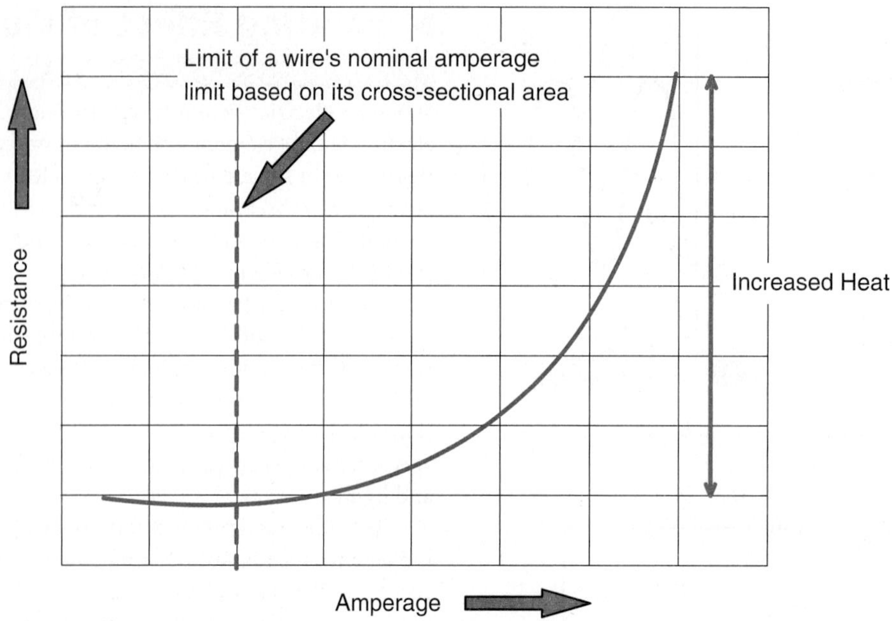

FIGURE 9-24 Exceeding the nominal amperage limit for a conductor will cause it to heat, and its temperature increases exponentially.

through heavier conductors and commonly operate devices such as solenoids, relays, motors, lights, and more. Electronic circuits use electricity to operate semiconductors such as transistors, integrated circuits, microprocessors, or microcontrollers. Electronic circuits use less amperage and often process electrical signals rather than perform the work of lighting, heating, and movement.

Semiconductors

Semiconductors are the most important type of material used to construct electronic devices. This material can have properties of both conductors and insulators and can switch back and forth between either state using small electrostatic charges. Early semiconductors were made from alloyed materials such as silicon or germanium. A very small quantity of another material added to silicon or germanium gives the new alloyed semiconductor its unique electrical properties.

Most semiconductors today are made from metal oxides. Metal oxide semiconductors are used in MOS-type transistors and microprocessors. MOS types have less resistance and conduct more current than the older semiconductor materials. Field effect transistors made from metal oxides are abbreviated **MOSFET** and are one of the most common types of transistors used in circuit boards by electronic control modules. **FIGURE 9-25** shows a MOSFET transistor.

Transistors can be used to switch current flow on and off and to amplify electrical signals. They are also used to construct logic gates in integrated circuits. Logic gates enable integrated circuits and larger microcontrollers and processors to perform mathematical calculations essential for the proper functioning of an ECM.

Two types of materials make up a basic semiconductor. One is a **P-type material**, which is made from material that can accept electrons. The "P" stands for positive because of its ability to accept and transport electrons. **N-type material** contains loosely held electrons, which explain why it's called "N," or negative, material. Both P and N materials are useless on their own, but when placed together, they can form diodes and transistors. Using MOS semiconductors, the material can even be arranged in a chip to function both as a resistor and capacitor which means that almost any type of circuit can be constructed from just this material.

FIGURE 9-25 MOSFETs and other MOS semiconductor devices are used in ECM circuit boards. This is an ECM from a Mercedes MB900 diesel engine, and the MOSFETs are output drivers.

▶ Wrap-Up

Ready for Review

- Today, the number of electrical circuits has increased into the thousands, and not a mobile off-road machine system is without electronic control.
- Electrical system components on mobile off-road machines are no longer separated into distinct systems. Electrical control is distributed over multiple electronic control modules (ECMs). ECMs are connected together to form onboard networks.
- It may be helpful to think of electricity as nothing more than the movement of specific particles from one point to another. The analogy of electric current flow using the hydraulic model is helpful to understand concepts of voltage, amperage, and resistance.
- The concept of voltage indicates the speed of electron movement from atom to atom. It is equivalent to the measurement of pressure in a pipe in pounds per square inch (psi).
- Amperage is a measurement of the number of electrons flowing past one point in a circuit during 1 second. It is equivalent to the measurement of flow or volume in a pipe in gallons or liters per second.
- Electrical resistance is similar to the idea of friction. Resistance slows down electron speed, which in turn reduces voltage and amperage.
- Forces of repulsion and attraction between electrons and protons are termed electrostatic force and are the primary type of energy contained in electricity used to perform work.
- Atoms are made of three fundamental particles: electrons, protons, and neutrons. Positive electrical charges are found on protons, negative charges on electrons, and neutrons have no electrical charge.
- Poles are areas of concentrated positive and negative electrical charges. Polarity is needed to produce electron flow.
- Ions are atoms with an imbalance of electrical charges due to the gain or loss of electrons.
- The flow of electrons from atom to atom is the basic concept of electricity.
- Current can be described as a function of voltage and amperage in a circuit—in other words, the speed and quantity of electron flow. Without either property, there is no flow of electricity in a circuit.
- The number of free electrons in an atom's valence ring determines how conductive the atom is. Fewer outer-shell electrons are associated with greater conductivity.
- Electron theory states that electrons move from negative to positive. Conventional theory states that electrons move from positive to negative. Both theories convey the idea of current flow, and each may in some instances be helpful when performing electrical diagnostic work.
- Electrical circuits usually conduct higher amounts of current through heavier conductors, and electronic circuits use electricity to operate semiconductors.
- The two fundamental types of current flow are direct current (DC) and alternating current (AC).
- Direct current has a constant polarity; alternating current has continuously changing polarity that produces a sine wave.
- Resistance is measured in ohms and depends on the type of material, its length, diameter, and temperature of the conductor.
- Good conductors have low resistance, and insulators have high resistance. Electrical energy lost through resistance is converted into heat.
- Semiconductors combine P-type and N-type materials.
- Semiconductors are very versatile materials and are used to make various electronic components. Their conductivity can be manipulated and precisely controlled using small electrostatic charges.

Key Terms

Alternating Current (AC) A type of current flow that continuously changes direction and polarity.

amperage The measurement of the quantity of electrons in electric current movement.

ampere (amp) The unit for measuring the quantity or numbers of electrons flowing past one point in a circuit per unit of time.

conductor A material that easily allows electricity to flow through it. It is made up of atoms with very few outer-shell electrons, which are loosely held by the nucleus.

conventional current theory The theory that the direction of current flow is from positive to negative.

digital multimeters An electronic test instrument.

Direct Current (DC) Movement of current that flows in one direction only.

electrical resistance A material's property that reduces voltage and amperage in an electrical current.

electron theory of current movement The movement of negatively charged electrons to a positive charge.

electrostatic theory The idea that like charges repel one another and unlike electrical charges attract.

ground The pathway through the chassis components, rather than insulated wiring for electrical current to move through a machine.

hertz (Hz) The unit for electrical frequency measurement, in cycles per second.

insulator A material that holds electrons tightly and prevents electron movement.

inverter A device that changes direct current into alternating current. Also called a *wave inverter.*

load A device in an electrical circuit with resistance.

MOSFET A field effect transistor made from metal-oxide semiconductor material.

N-type material Semiconductor material able to hold a small amount of extra electrons.

ohm The unit for measuring electrical resistance.

ohm's law A law that defines the relationship between amperage, resistance, and voltage.

polarity The state of charge, positive or negative.

P-type material Semiconductor material having electron deficiency or a place to hold additional electrons.

resistor A component designed to produce electrical resistance.

semiconductor A material that can have properties of both conductors and insulators and that can switch back and forth between either state, using small electrostatic charges.

sine wave The shape of an AC waveform as it changes from positive to negative, graphed as a function of time.

volt The unit used to measure potential difference, or electrical pressure.

voltage The speed at which electrons travel from atom to atom.

Review Questions

1. Which of the following statements is correct concerning conductivity?
   a. Copper makes an excellent conductor.
   b. Electrolytes are liquids that conduct electric current.
   c. The liquid inside a lead-acid battery is an example of where electrolyte is used.
   d. All of these are correct.
2. Which of the following is correct concerning electrostatic law?
   a. A proton (+) charge repels another proton (+) charge.
   b. An electron (–) charge repels another electron (–) charge.
   c. A proton (+) charge attracts an electron (–) charge.
   d. All of these are correct.
3. Which of the following is *not* correct concerning basic electricity?
   a. All matter is made up of atoms.
   b. Atoms are composed of electrons, protons, and neutrons.
   c. Positive electrical charges are found on protons.
   d. Negative electrical charges are found on neutrons.
4. Which of the following is *not* a factor that determines the level of electrical resistance?
   a. Type of material
   b. Length of the conductor
   c. Diameter of the conductor
   d. Weight of the conductor
5. Which of the following is *not* correct concerning movement of electric current?
   a. Watts or wattage is the unit for measuring power.
   b. Resistance produces a decrease or drop in voltage.
   c. Wattage is a function of Voltage × Amperage.
   d. Resistance is measured in amps.
6. Which of the following statements about Ohm's law is correct?
   a. If voltage is held constant in a circuit: amperage increases if resistance decreases; amperage decreases if resistance increases.
   b. If resistance is held constant in a circuit: amperage increases if voltage increases; amperage decreases if voltage decreases.
   c. If amperage is to remain the same in a circuit: voltage must increase if resistance increases; voltage decreases if resistance decreases.
   d. All of these are correct.
7. Which of the following statements is correct concerning semiconductors?
   a. Transistors can be used to switch current flow on and off and to amplify electrical signals.
   b. Transistors are used to construct logic gates in integrated circuits.
   c. Logic gates enable integrated circuits and larger microcontrollers and processors to perform mathematical calculations essential for the proper functioning of an ECM.
   d. All of these are correct.
8. Which of the following is *not* correct concerning semiconductors?
   a. Semiconductors are the most important type of material used to construct electronic devices.
   b. Semiconductors can have properties of both conductors and insulators and can switch back and forth between either state, using small electrostatic charges.
   c. Early semiconductors were made from alloyed materials such as silicon or germanium.
   d. Most semiconductors today are made from platinum or a silicone blend.
9. All of the following statements about the heating effect of current and fuses are true *except*:
   a. Fuses use a narrow metal strip made of highly conductive material.
   b. When the amount of amperage exceeds a wire's ability to conduct the current without heating up, the strip melts to protect circuit wiring from burning.
   c. Boyle's law refers to the heating effect of electric current.
   d. The amount of heat produced is directly proportional to the fuse's resistance, the time current flows, and the amount of amperage in the current.
10. Which of the following statements is correct concerning direct current and alternating current?
    a. When electrons move only in one direction in a circuit, the current is described as being direct current (DC).
    b. Plotting DC voltage on a graph produces a straight line.
    c. Plotting AC voltage on a graph produces what is called a sine wave.
    d. All of these are correct.

ASE Technician A/Technician B Style Questions

1. Technician A says there are two theories of current flow: the electron theory and the conventional theory. Technician B says it is only important to remember that current flow is described by both concepts. Who is correct?
   a. Technician A
   b. Technician B
   c. Both Technician A and Technician B
   d. Neither Technician A nor Technician B
2. Technician A says AC circuits are used in virtually all MORE machines circuits because a battery can easily store and supply AC current. Technician B says DC current is used to power hybrid-drive electric motors. Who is correct?
   a. Technician A
   b. Technician B
   c. Both Technician A and Technician B
   d. Neither Technician A nor Technician B
3. Technician A says AC current's main advantage is that it can be transmitted farther distances with less resistance and little voltage drop. Technician B says the term "resistance" is used with AC circuits as well as DC circuits. Who is correct?
   a. Technician A
   b. Technician B
   c. Both Technician A and Technician B
   d. Neither Technician A nor Technician B
4. Technician A says when an electric current travels through a bulb filament or electric heating element, the filament or resistive element heats. Technician B says resistance in the elements converts electrical energy into heat energy. Who is correct?
   a. Technician A
   b. Technician B
   c. Both Technician A and Technician B
   d. Neither Technician A nor Technician B
5. Technician A says electronic circuits use less amperage and often process signals rather than perform the work of lighting, heating, and moving. Technician B says electrical circuits usually conduct higher amounts of current through heavier conductors and commonly operate devices such as solenoids, relays, motors, lights, and more. Who is correct?
   a. Technician A
   b. Technician B
   c. Both Technician A and Technician B
   d. Neither Technician A nor Technician B
6. Technician A says metal oxide semiconductors are used in MOS-type transistors and microprocessors. Technician B says MOS types have less resistance and conduct more current than the older semiconductor materials. Who is correct?
   a. Technician A
   b. Technician B
   c. Both Technician A and Technician B
   d. Neither Technician A nor Technician B
7. Technician A says two types of materials make up a basic semiconductor. Technician B says the two types are R type and M type. Who is correct?
   a. Technician A
   b. Technician B
   c. Both Technician A and Technician B
   d. Neither Technician A nor Technician B
8. Technician A says today's electrical system components are no longer separated into distinct systems. Technician B says networking electrical system components provides the means for new machine features that can enhance safety, performance, and operator comfort. Who is correct?
   a. Technician A
   b. Technician B
   c. Both Technician A and Technician B
   d. Neither Technician A nor Technician B
9. Technician A says all questions about the nature of electricity lead to the composition of matter. Technician B says the movement of electrons from one atom to another is called electricity. Who is correct?
   a. Technician A
   b. Technician B
   c. Both Technician A and Technician B
   d. Neither Technician A nor Technician B
10. Technician A says metals typically have lots of easily moved electrons, which make them good conductors. Technician B says liquids cannot function as a conductor. Who is correct?
    a. Technician A
    b. Technician B
    c. Both Technician A and Technician B
    d. Neither Technician A nor Technician B

CHAPTER 10

Electrical Circuits and Circuit Protection

Knowledge Objectives

After reading this chapter, you will be able to:

- **K10001** Define and describe types of electric circuits.
- **K10002** Describe the relationship between voltage amperage power and resistance in electrical circuits.
- **K10003** Identify and describe the types and causes of electrical circuit failures.
- **K10004** Identify and describe types of circuit protection devices.
- **K10005** Identify and describe the operation of relays, magnetic switches, and solenoids.

Skills Objectives

After reading this chapter, you will be able to:

- **S10001** Inspect and test circuit protection devices.
- **S10002** Identify a resistive ground connection.

Introduction

Circuits are pathways made by electrical conductors that enable the flow of electrons. A variety of classifications are used to describe circuit configurations and failures. Most important for technicians to understand is how circuits are constructed. With that knowledge, a technician can properly analyze electrical problems, use correct diagnostic procedures with test instruments, and, of course, make accurate recommendations for repair, rather than guess at what may be wrong.

As shown in **FIGURE 10-1**, circuits consist of the following basic parts:

- Power source—in the form of a battery or alternator.
- Conductors—paths for electricity (e.g., wiring, printed circuits, chassis frame).
- Loads—the working devices that turn electrical energy into some other form of energy, such as lamps (light), motors (kinetic), radio (sound), glow plugs (heat), and more. Loads are considered the resistance of a circuit.
- Control—a device, such as a switch, that directs the flow of electrons though the circuit.
- Safety/circuit protection devices—fuses, circuit breakers, and virtual fuses, which protect the electrical system by interrupting the flow of current if the current flow becomes excessive.

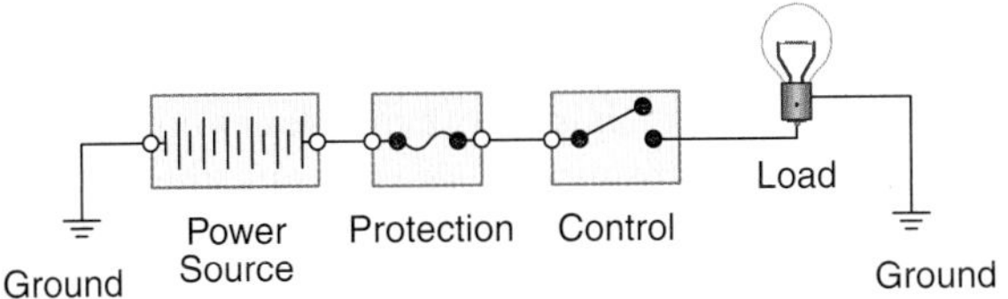

FIGURE 10-1 Minimum elements of a circuit include a power supply, circuit protection, control, and load.

Circuit Classification

K10001

Circuits found in mobile off-road equipment are classified three ways:

1. Operational state—open or closed
2. Arrangement—simple, parallel, series, combination
3. Failure mode—grounded, shorted, open, resistive, and intermittent circuit malfunctions

Operational State

"Open" and "closed" are the terms used to describe whether current is flowing through a circuit. An open circuit's electrical pathway is broken or unconnected (**FIGURE 10-2A**). This means current cannot flow because there is an open gap between two ends of the circuit. Current cannot move across the gap until the opening is closed.

A closed circuit has a complete electrical pathway for current to flow between the negative and positive terminal, as in **FIGURE 10-2B**.

> **TECHNICIAN TIP**
>
> Sleep or hibernation mode is a related term given to electronic control modules to describe a state where current flow is reduced after the ignition key is switched off or after a predetermined length of time has elapsed. Sleep mode reduces prolonged current drains from the battery.

Circuit Arrangement

Electric circuits are also classified according to the way electric components and loads are connected. Circuits on mobile off-road equipment are made from these types of arrangements:

- Simple
- Series

You Are the Mobile Heavy Equipment Technician

A motor grader has arrived at your shop with the request to install a wave inverter to enable the operator to charge cell phones and tablets and use laptop computers. The company wants you to supply 120 volts AC to a receptacle. Upon inspection, you find that the machine is equipped with a split voltage electrical system with a 24-volt alternator used to charge the batteries and supply the starter motor. An isolated ground is used on the rest of the motor grader, which uses 12 volts for all lights and accessories outside the engine compartment. When you ask the company representative what amount of amperage the company wants to supply the receptacle, the representative asks you to make a recommendation.

After researching the problem, you learn that the heaviest power users would be laptops consuming 3–5 amps to charge a dead battery. As you prepare quotes and recommendations for supplying the DC–AC converter, wiring them, and providing circuit protection to the inverters, you will need to consider the following:

1. What would be the maximum wattage required for the inverter? Assume there is no heat or other losses of electrical energy.
2. What would be the minimum fuse rating for the inverter using a single positive conductor if they were supplied either 12 or 24 volts?
3. What would be the minimum size of the conductors required if the inverters were connected to either a 12- or 24-volt power supply?

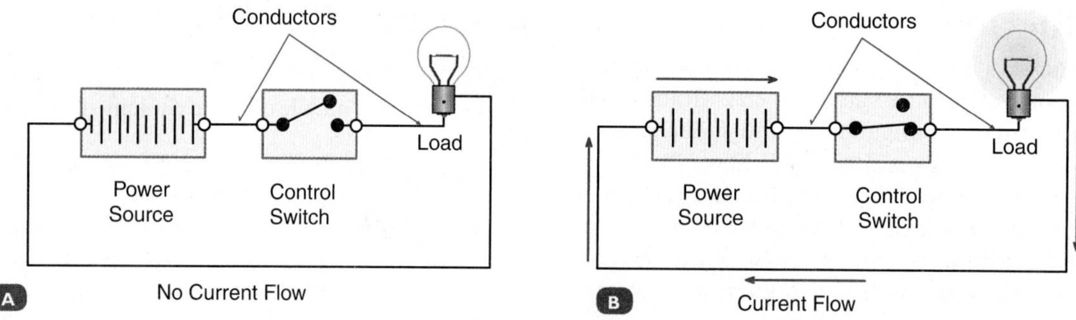

FIGURE 10-2 **A.** An open circuit has a broken electrical pathway. **B.** Closing the switch completes the electrical pathway.

- Parallel
- Series-parallel, also called combination circuits

Simple circuits are circuits that have only a power supply and a load. These are not used in mobile off-road equipment. This section, therefore, concentrates on series, parallel, and combination circuit arrangements.

Series Circuits

Series circuits are the simplest of circuits. In a **series circuit**, there can be multiple loads, but only one path for current to flow (**FIGURE 10-3**). Each device is connected like a chain, with all current flowing through one device after another. The defining characteristic of a series circuit is that only one single pathway exists for current to flow. The conductors, circuit protection device, loads, and source current are connected together, allowing current to move—but only through one path. If any part of the circuit is opened, such as when a lightbulb burns out, all current flow through the circuit stops.

The following features characterize series circuits:

- Only one single pathway exists for current to flow.
- The resistance of each load or device may vary, but the amount of current flowing through each will be the same.

The sum of the voltage drop across all loads is equal to the source voltage. This means all the voltage is used up pushing electrons through the loads. This observation is referred to as **Kirchhoff 's law** and is illustrated in **FIGURE 10-4**. The voltage drops across each of the loads will change if the resistance of the device or load is different from the others.

- At any given point in the circuit, the amperage is the same.
- The total circuit resistance is equal to the sum of each individual resistance.

Many machine circuits are series circuits. Switches, terminals, circuit protection, cables, and so on are common circuit components arranged in series (**FIGURE 10-5**). Identifying problems in series circuits often becomes a matter of measuring voltage drops to locate poor connections and deteriorated or defective components (**FIGURE 10-6**). A starter cable voltage loss test is one example of a test procedure using series circuit electrical principles to locate problems causing slow cranking. Excessive resistance at a starter cable connection due to corrosion will create a voltage drop and reduce the available voltage for the starter motor which results in slow cranking.

A starter motor circuit is a more complex example of a series circuit. Current passes from the chassis ground, the brushes, and field coils of the motor before entering the solenoid and then returning back to the battery. An open brush or coil will prevent the starter motor from turning because it is a series circuit.

Parallel Circuits

A more complex circuit than a series circuit arrangement is a **parallel circuit**. In a parallel circuit, there are multiple pathways for current flow, and all components are connected directly to

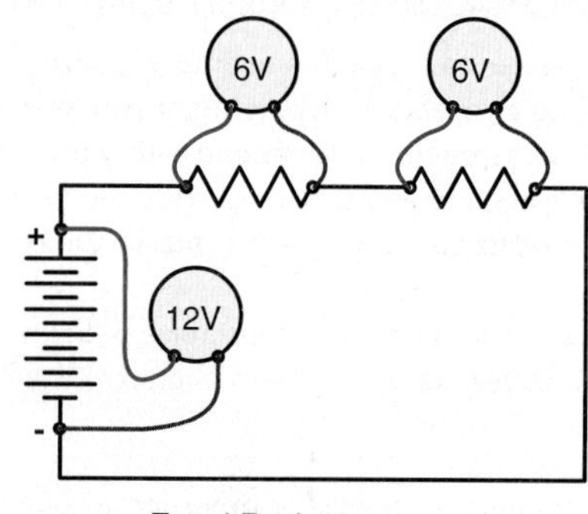

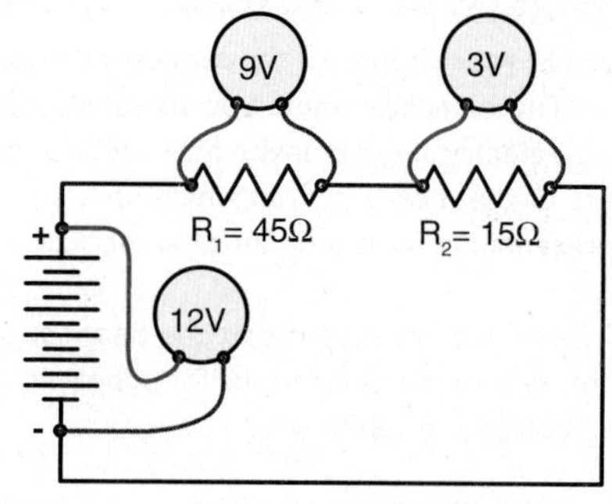

FIGURE 10-3 Observations for series circuits.

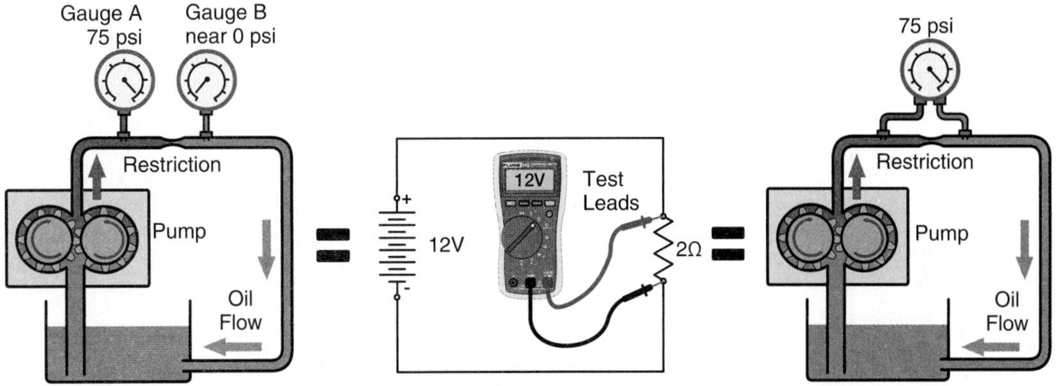

FIGURE 10-4 Voltage drop is the loss of voltage or electron pressure as current passes through a load. A voltmeter is used to measure the drop. Voltmeters measure a circuit's electron pressure differential. Note all the voltage is dropped after passing through the loads in a circuit.

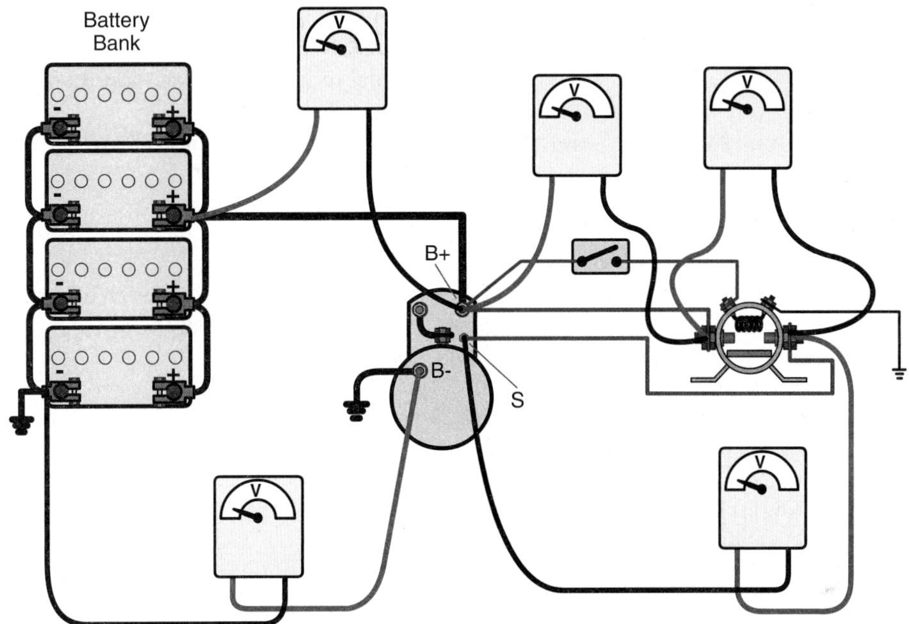

FIGURE 10-5 An example of how voltage drop testing can be used at various points for a starter circuit.

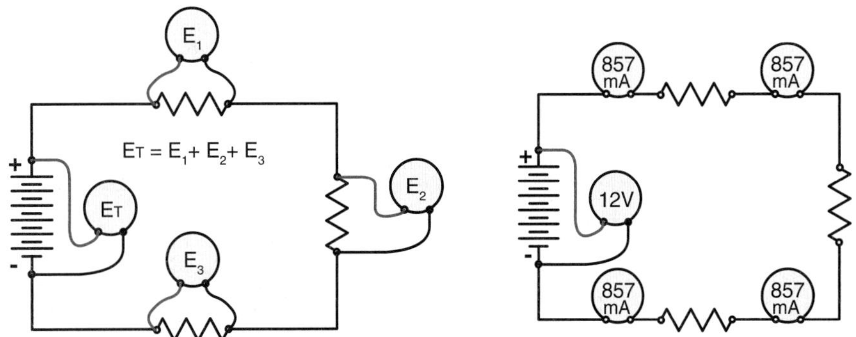

FIGURE 10-6 Understanding the behavior of voltage, amperage, and resistance in a series circuit. With each resistance, the voltage (electron pressure) drops. The voltage drop is cumulative and distributed across all the loads. Amperage (volume) in the circuit is dependent on total of circuit resistances. The amperage remains constant anywhere in the circuit.

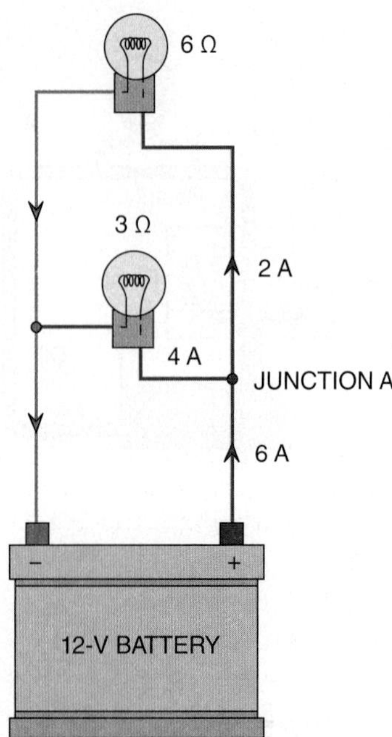

FIGURE 10-7 Parallel circuit with two loads that have different resistances and that create different current flows in each branch. Total flow is the cumulative of all parallel branch current flows.

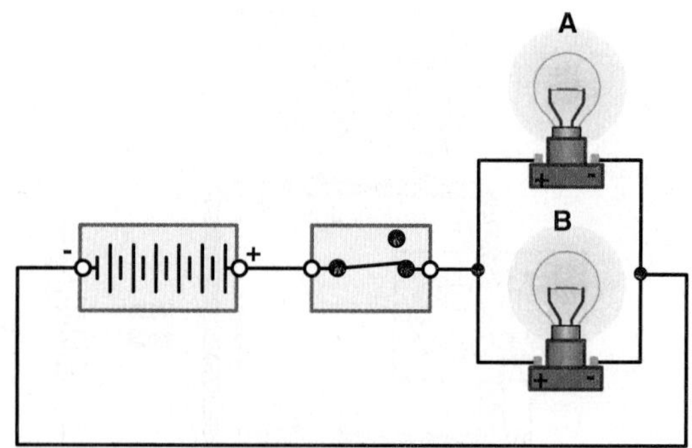

FIGURE 10-8 An example of a parallel circuit. Bulbs **A** and **B** are branches of the circuit.

the voltage supply. On paper, the schematic diagram of a parallel circuit resembles a ladder. The sides are sources of voltage—one is positive and the other negative. The ladder rungs are called branches. Because all branches connect to the same positive and negative current source, amperage in each branch can be different, depending on the branches' resistance. Adding the amperage in each branch will equal the total amperage in the circuit (**FIGURE 10-7**). Adding loads, however, lowers circuit resistance; the total resistance is always less than the smallest resistance in any branch.

In summary, a parallel circuit is characterized by the following:

- There are two or more pathways for the current (**FIGURE 10-8**).
- The voltage applied to each branch is the same throughout the circuit (**FIGURE 10-9**).

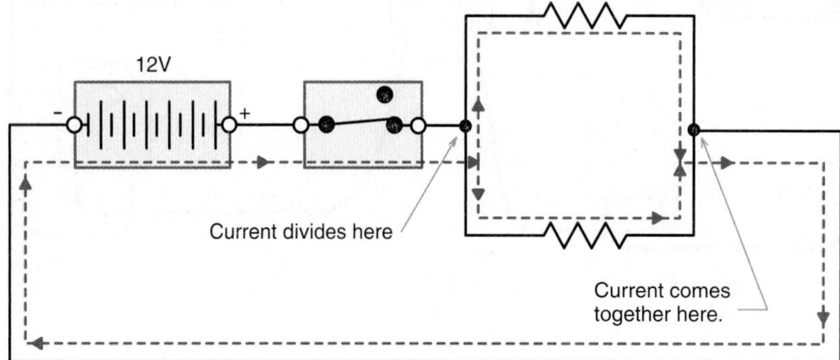

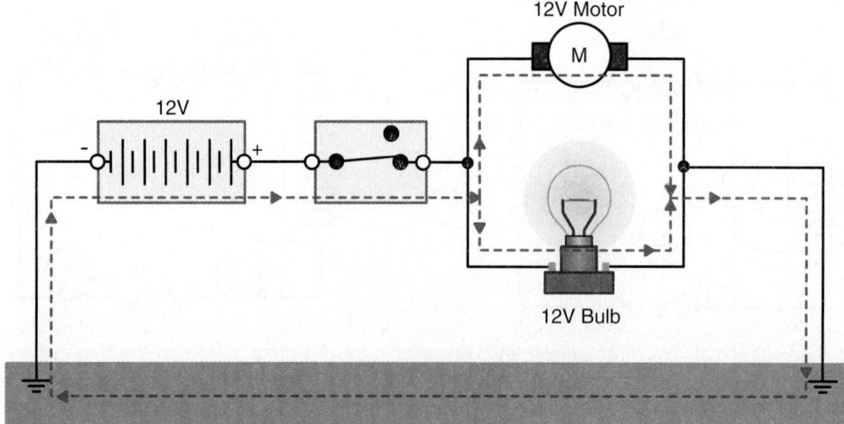

FIGURE 10-9 All loads in a parallel circuit receive the same voltage. The amperage used by each branch varies with the resistance in each branch.

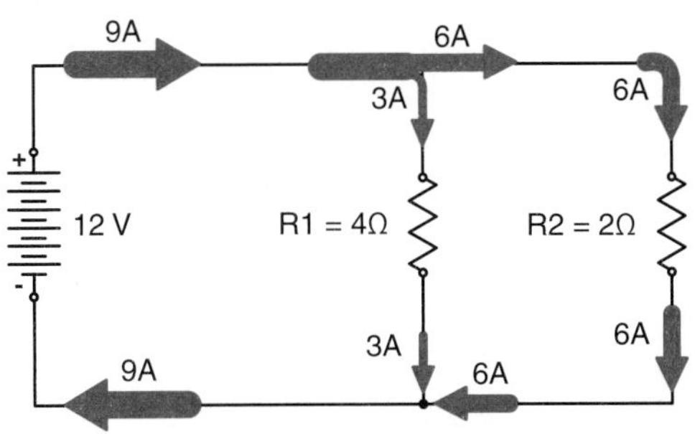

FIGURE 10-10 Amperage passing through each branch of a parallel circuit varies with the resistance.

- Amperage flow through each branch depends on its resistance. If the resistances in each branch are the same, the amperage will be the same.
- If one branch of the circuit is broken, current will continue to flow in the other branches.
- Total circuit resistance is always less than the resistance of the smallest resister (**FIGURE 10-10**).

Lighting circuits are common examples of parallel circuits. Machine work lights or taillight circuits are all connected in parallel with battery voltage applied to each bulb. Adding more lights creates more pathways for current to flow. This means amperage consumed in a parallel circuit will increase with every additional load (**FIGURE 10-11**).

Combination Circuits

Combination circuits, also called **series-parallel circuits**, use elements both of parallel and series circuits. These circuits are the most common ones used in mobile off-road machines. Typically, the power and control circuits are in series, but the loads are in parallel. When calculating or measuring voltage, amperage, and resistance, the rules for parallel and series circuits apply to each part of the circuit. That means the circuit must be subdivided into series and parallel circuits, and then calculations can be performed for each type of circuit.

▶ Current Flow in Circuits

K10002

Electrons making up current flow are not magically created by the circuit or power source. Only the electrons found in the conductors of a circuit move in a circuit. That means only the electrons already present in conductors, electrolyte, or devices of the circuit are put in motion. An analogy using a closed hydraulic system with a water pump shows that only electrons already present in the circuit are flowing (**FIGURE 10-12**). Consider hydraulic fluid that is pulled from a reservoir and put into motion. Fluid pressure and flow determine how much power the system has. Eventually the fluid pushed out the pump outlet returns to its inlet to keep the flow going. In the same way, electrons are pulled and pushed though conductors and loads in electric devices. The negative terminal pushes electrons, using electrostatic forces of repulsion, and the positive terminal pulls electrons by forces of electrostatic attraction. In a machine's electrical system, an alternator performs the same function as the fluid pump.

Resistance

Resistance refers to the force in a circuit that impedes or slows the transfer of electrons from one atom to the next. Explained another way, resistance is electrical friction. Resistance will lower both voltage and amperage in a circuit in proportion to the amount of resistance. Ohm's law mathematically describes the electrical relationship between voltage amperage and resistance.

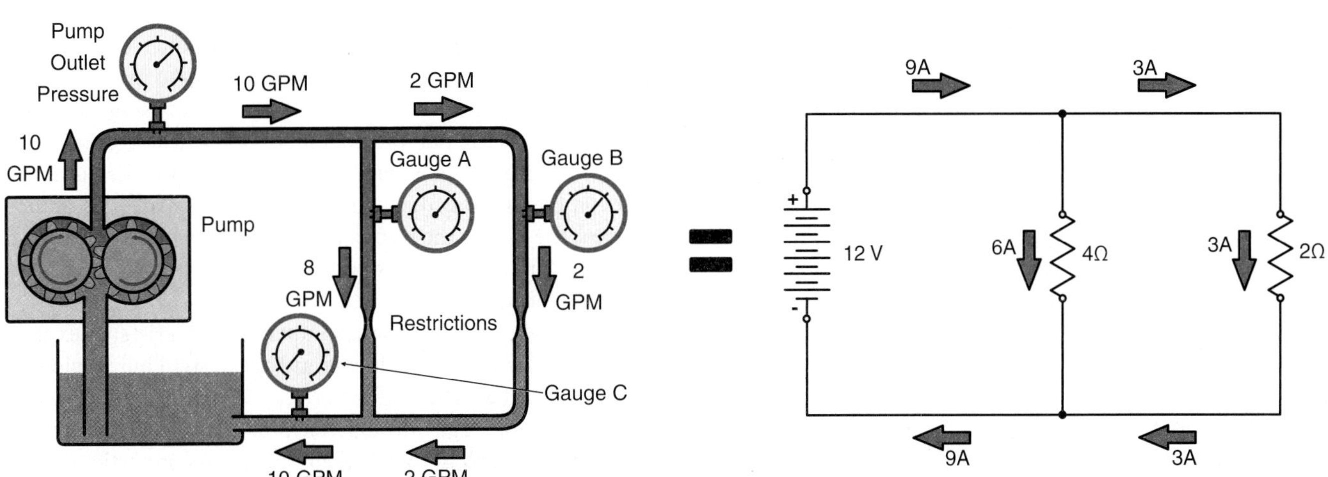

FIGURE 10-11 Comparing a hydraulic model of a parallel circuit with a schematic version. Note the same pressure is applied to all circuit branches, and the voltage drops to almost zero after passing through the loads.

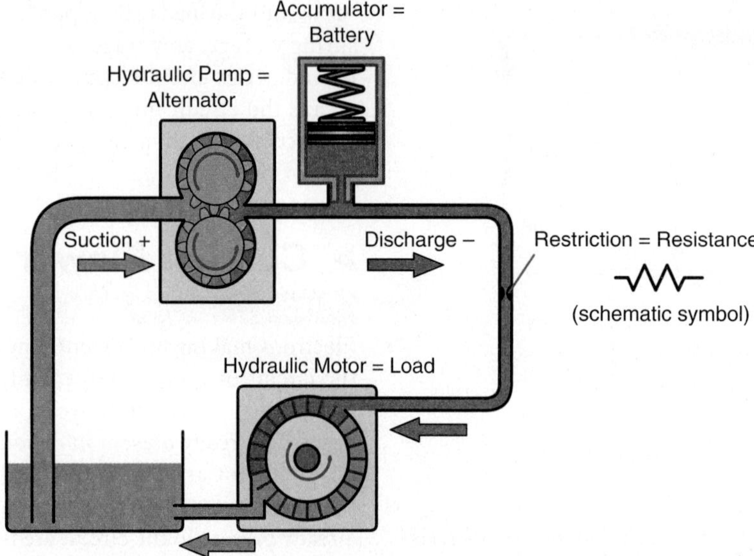

FIGURE 10-12 Current flow in a circuit is like a closed hydraulic system. Just as no new fluid is created in a hydraulic system, the conductors in the circuit are the only source of electrons. Loads use the energy in the flowing water and convert it to another form such as motion, sound, light, and heat.

> **TECHNICIAN TIP**
>
> Technicians rarely ever need to use an electrical formula to diagnose and repair a problem on mobile off-road equipment. And most instructors would agree that it is rare to perform mathematical calculations in the average repair facility. So, the question that naturally follows this observation is this: What is the point of learning formulas or performing calculations while learning about electrical systems? It is simply this: mathematics is another language that is effective in describing the behavior of electricity. Many learners who have struggled to understand electrical concepts have quickly grasped important insights while doing calculations using formulas based on electrical laws. Math is very often a shortcut to better comprehension of electrical subject matter.

Ohm's Law

Ohm's law defines the relationship between current, resistance, and voltage. Ohm's law calculations are seldom used by a technician, but comprehending the law's principles can help you better understand how electricity behaves. Working through calculations using Ohm's formula also enhances your intuitive understanding of electricity, which is invaluable when troubleshooting electrical circuits. The tradesperson's triangle in **FIGURE 10-13** is used to help calculate the values of voltage, amperage, or power. Placing your finger over the unknown value will help you determine whether the other two values should be multiplied or divided.

Ohm's law explains in mathematical language the relationship between amperage, voltage, and resistance in a circuit.

$$\text{Voltage} = \text{Amps} \times \text{Resistance}$$

Simply stated, 1 volt is required to push 1 amp of current through a circuit that has a resistance of 1 ohm. Ohms Ω are the unit used to measure resistance (**FIGURE 10-14**).

One application for Ohm's law is to calculate the voltage drop in a conductor for taillight wiring. All conductors have some resistance, so there will be a voltage drop through the wires going to the taillights at the rear of the machine. The amount of the drop depends on the amperage flowing through the circuit and the resistance of the wiring and connections. **TABLE 10-1** summarizes recommended wire gauge size required to minimize voltage drop.

Watt's Law

Watt's law, which is related to Ohm's law, explains the relationship between power, voltage, and amperage (**FIGURE 10-15**). Mathematically described, Watt's law is:

$$\text{Power (Watts)} = \text{Voltage} \times \text{Amperage}$$

With a constant system voltage, an increase in amperage through a circuit produces proportionally more power.

Heat is generally an unwanted by-product of resistance. Heat is produced as electron energy is lost due to resistance. Collisions occurring between electrons as they converge at "choke points" or resistive parts of a circuit produce heat. Increasing the amperage in a circuit is something like increasing the number of cars on the highway during rush hour—the greater the number of cars, the slower the traffic. More collisions between electrons take place in a crowded conductor, and electron energy is converted to heat.

This relationship between amperage and resistance explains why a thin wire can carry low-amperage current but would burn up (or at least overheat) if it were carrying excessive amperage. Excessive amperage through terminals and connectors produces heat, which in turn loosens electrical connections due to temperature cycling. Resistance in connections at the battery or

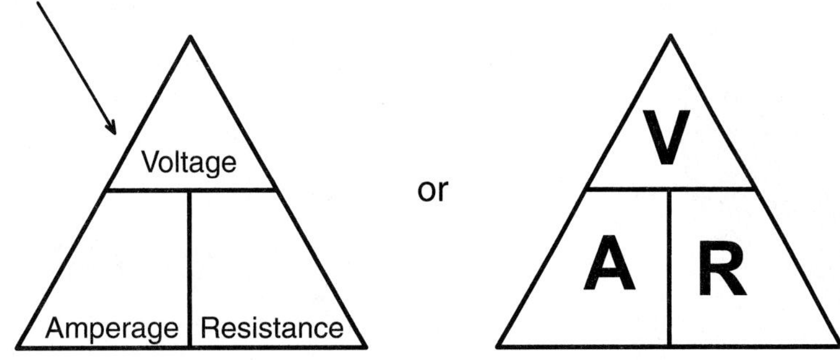
Ohm's Law states: Voltage = Amperage x Resistance
Arrange the variables into a "Tradeperson Triangle"
Voltage
Amperage
Resistance
or
V
A
R

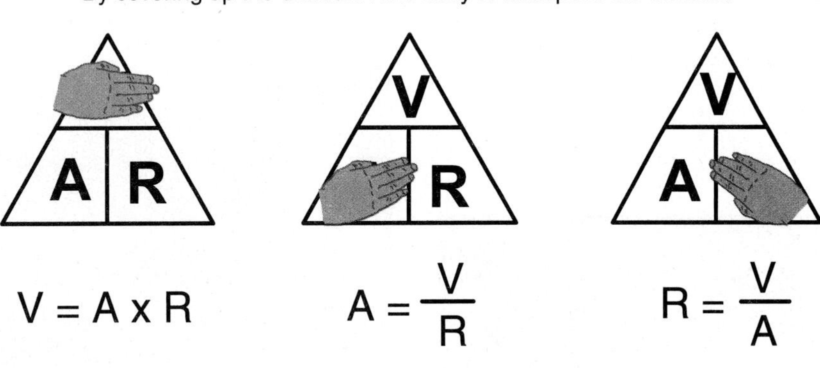
By covering up the unknown it is easy to transpose the formula.
A R
V R
V A
V = A x R
A = V/R
R = V/A

FIGURE 10-13 The tradesperson's triangle for calculating power.

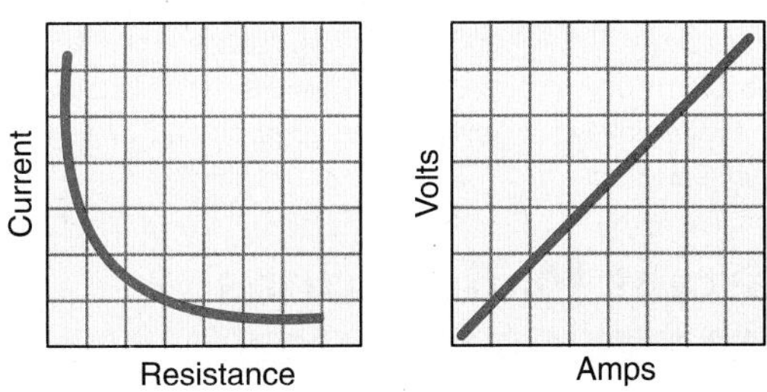
Current
Resistance
Volts
Amps

FIGURE 10-14 The relationship between volts, ohms, and amperage in Ohm's law.

in a starter motor circuit, which are undetectable with an ohmmeter, will show up as heat when a starter is cranking or when heavy loads are switched on in a machine. The most effective way to measure resistances in these circuits is to perform a voltage drop test when the high-amperage circuits are operating. Resistance will show up as voltage loss across resistive connections and components.

Advantages of the 24-Volt System

The 24-volt electrical systems used by many mobile off-road equipment machines have several advantages. First, by using

TABLE 10-1 Recommended Wire Gauges to Minimize Voltage Drop

Amperage	10 – Feet Gauge	20 – Feet Gauge	30 – Feet Gauge	50 – Feet Gauge	100 – Feet Gauge
1	18	18	18	18	18
2	18	18	18	18	16
3	18	18	18	16	16
5	18	18	18	14	12
10	18	16	14	12	10
25	16	12	10	8	6
50	12	10	8	6	2

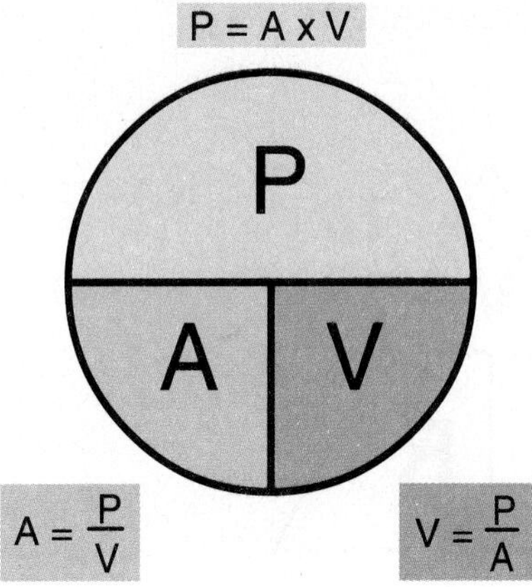

P = Power measured in WATTS
A = Amperes measured in AMPS
V = Electromotive Force measured in VOLTS

FIGURE 10-15 The relationship of power, voltage, and amperage according to Watt's law.

FIGURE 10-16 Electric motors are examples of constant power devices.

higher voltage, less amperage passes through a circuit to produce the same amount of power as a 12-volt circuit. For example, a device needing 120 watts of power would use 10 amps at 12 volts (Power = Amperage × Voltage). Electric motors are examples of constant power devices (**FIGURE 10-16**).

This means the number of watts they use to maintain speed is the same if circuit voltage and amperage change. For example, a 96-watt blower motor that is part of a 12-volt system has 8 amps flowing through it (Power = Volts × Amperage). At 24 volts, only 4 amps are required.

Reducing amperage through a circuit not only reduces resistance but also the size of conductors. Voltage drops in the system are reduced as well. More importantly, operating at 24 volts in comparison to at 12 volts gives an electrical system greater reliability. That is because heating and loosening of electrical connections are minimized. Finally, the size of components can be reduced, with increased power supplied by 24 volts (**FIGURE 10-17**).

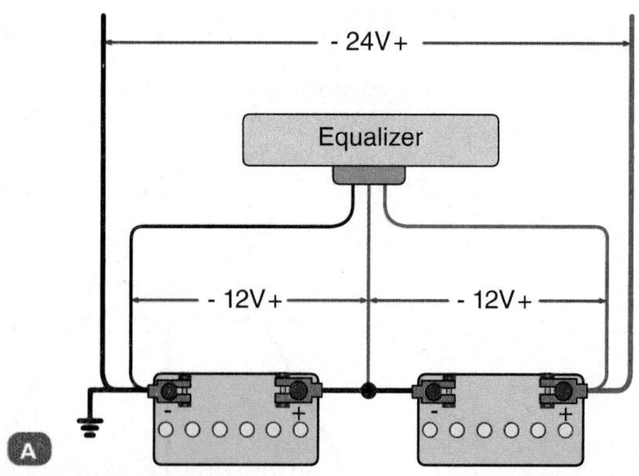

FIGURE 10-17 Many mobile off-road machines use 24-volt systems because of longer runs of wire and the greater use of electrical accessories such as lighting and ventilation. Voltage drops and electrical system problems due to high current flow are minimized. **A.** A battery equalizer allows voltage to split between 24-volt and 12-volt devices. **B.** A batter equalizer.

▶ Circuit Malfunctions

K10003

Just as there are categories for operational circuits, defective circuits have names based on failure mode. Classification of circuit malfunction can include the following:

- Opened
- Shorted
- Grounded
- High resistance
- Intermittent

Open Circuit Faults

When a circuit defect is caused by an opening in the electrical pathway, no current can flow through the circuit and this is considered to be an open circuit. Open circuits can be caused by a variety of problems, including poor ground or terminal connections, defective switches, and broken wiring (**FIGURE 10-18**). A fuse or circuit breaker that has opened due to excessive current flow creates an open, but the root cause of the problem is not the fuse.

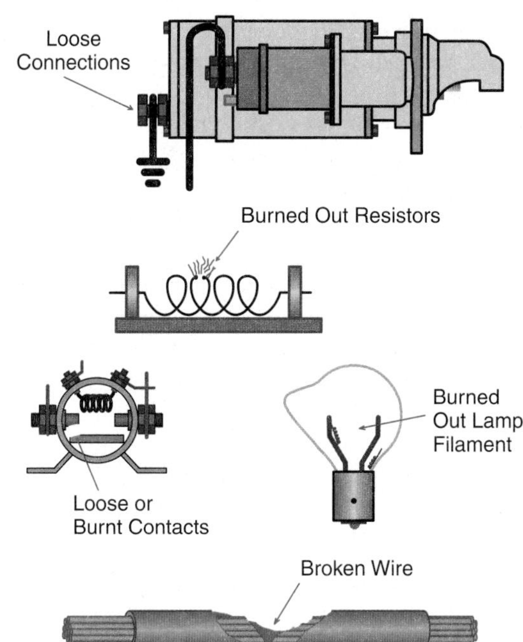

FIGURE 10-18 Causes of open and intermittent circuits.

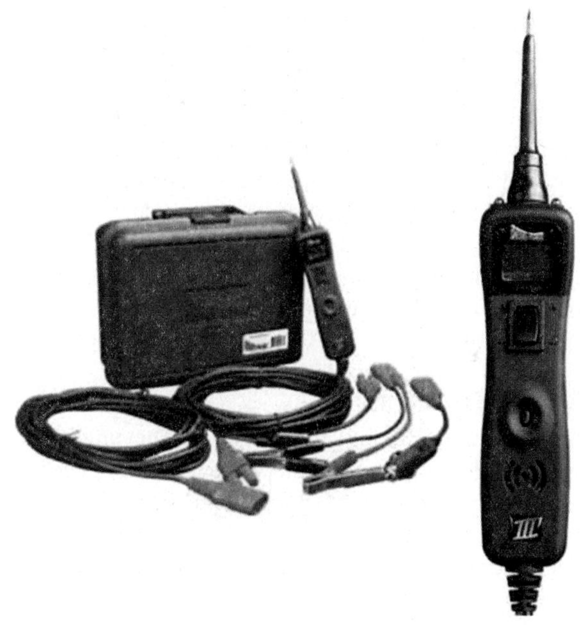

FIGURE 10-19 More advanced test lights are battery powered. Single probe tip can be used to determine polarity and detect ground, power, shorts, and breaks. Red LED indicates power; green LED indicates ground.

Where the open in the circuit occurs determines how the failure presents itself. For example, a broken wire to a single clearance light in a parallel circuit will have a different effect than a blown fuse. Depending on the type of fault, open circuits are typically detected using a multimeter or advanced test light to look for available voltage along the circuit (**FIGURE 10-19**).

High-frequency radio waves can be used to identify faults in bundles of wiring or in long runs of wiring hidden behind panels. A radio transmitter (**FIGURE 10-20**) installed in the fuse of an open or shorted circuit will emit short bursts of radio signals

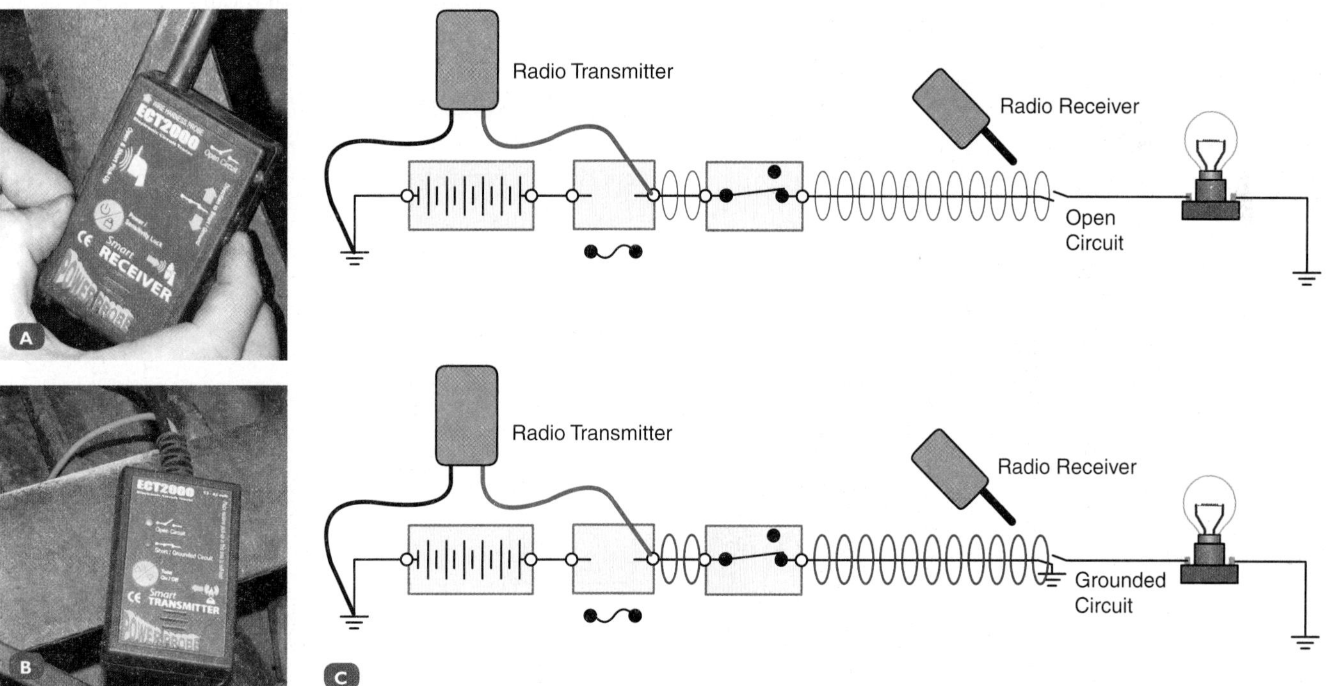

FIGURE 10-20 **A.** Radio receiver. **B.** Radio transmitter. **C.** This radio signal generator is designed to find opens, shorts, or grounded circuits without damaging the wire. A high-frequency signal is added into the circuit by connecting a transmitter. Moving the receiver in the vicinity of the wire will locate the break.

or low-voltage current into the defective circuit. The signal is not powerful enough to damage wiring, but open and shorts are located using a handheld radio receiver. A schematic diagram is useful when identifying open circuits to locate strategic points where circuit voltage can be measured using a multimeter. An ohmmeter can be used to find points where circuit continuity is lost only after the system is de-energized.

In onboard diagnostic system (OBD) circuits, the continuous component monitor constantly checks for open circuits by comparing signal out and return voltages.

Short Circuits

Short circuits are commonly thought of as the unwanted, high-amperage flow between battery power and negative ground. However, that type of fault is better described as a grounded circuit or short to ground. As its name suggests, a short is an electrical circuit that is formed between two points that bypasses the original current path, allowing current to flow through an unintended pathway (**FIGURE 10-21**). The current in a circuit will always try to find the path of least resistance.

A short may draw a higher or lower than normal amperage and simply be an unintended connection between two wires or circuits. A coil of wire (like one used in a solenoid or motor) is considered shorted if current does not pass through all the intended loops, but instead takes a shorter path. Another simple example of a short to power is a short between the brake light and running lights circuits. Stepping on the brakes would cause the running lights to illuminate, and vice versa. Some may call this a problem with current "backfeed," but it is more accurate to call it a short.

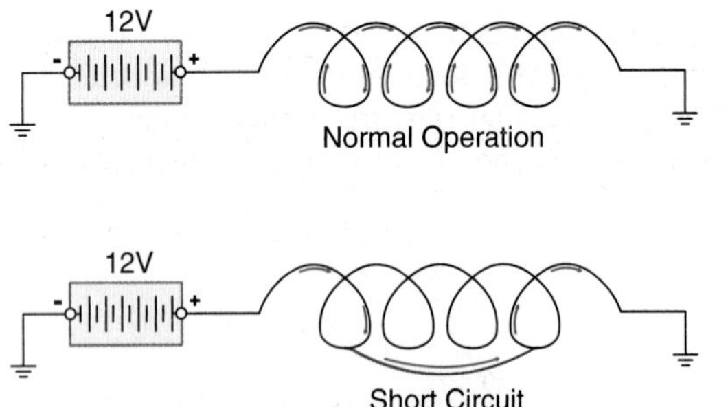

FIGURE 10-21 When current bypasses its intended load, it is referred to as a short circuit.

Onboard diagnostic systems that continuously monitor electrical signals from sensors and output devices will detect shorted conditions too. For example, if a three-wire sensor signal circuit is shorted to +5 volt reference voltage, it meets conditions required to generate the fault code "Sensor Input Voltage High" (**FIGURE 10-22**). The fault description "Sensor Input Voltage Low" is produced if either the sensor +5 volt supply is shorted to the sensor return circuit or the sensor signal wire is shorted to the sensor return circuit or to ground.

Grounded Circuits

A **grounded circuit**, sometime called a "dead short," is characterized by an unwanted low-resistance connection between battery positive power and chassis ground. Unlike the short-to-power malfunction, in all cases the short-to-ground will draw higher than expected current. A common example of a grounded circuit would be a battery or power cable insulation rubbing through against the negative ground chassis frame (**FIGURE 10-23**). The direct, low-resistance connection would cause high current flow resulting in blown fuse links and activation of other circuit protection devices or in the case of the battery cable rubbed through it could cause a fire due to the tremendous amount of current flowing through the cable.

High-Resistance Circuits

All circuits have a specific amount of resistance in them when new. High-resistance faults occur when the amount of resistance

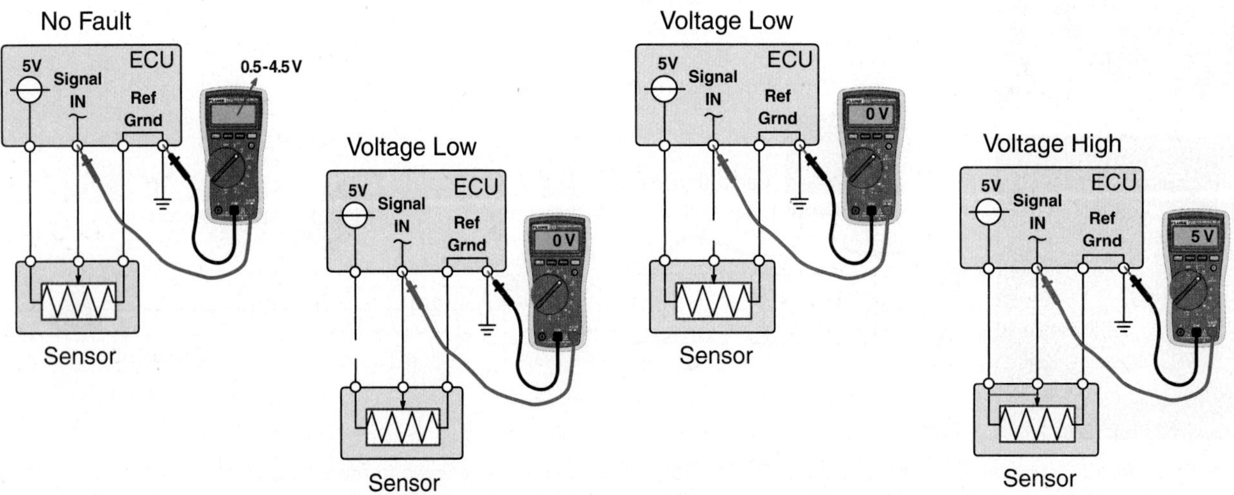

FIGURE 10-22 Sensor signal circuits are monitored by the onboard diagnostic system, which continually evaluates electrical system operation. Short circuits generate fault codes such as shorted high or low, or input voltage high or low.

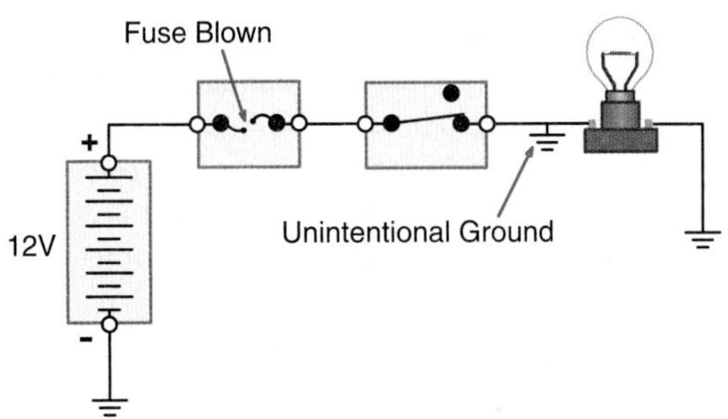

FIGURE 10-23 A grounded circuit fault occurring at a point after the protection device, but before the circuit load, results in an unintended low-resistance path to chassis ground. If the fuse or circuit breaker quickly opens when the control switch is closed, a grounded circuit is likely the cause.

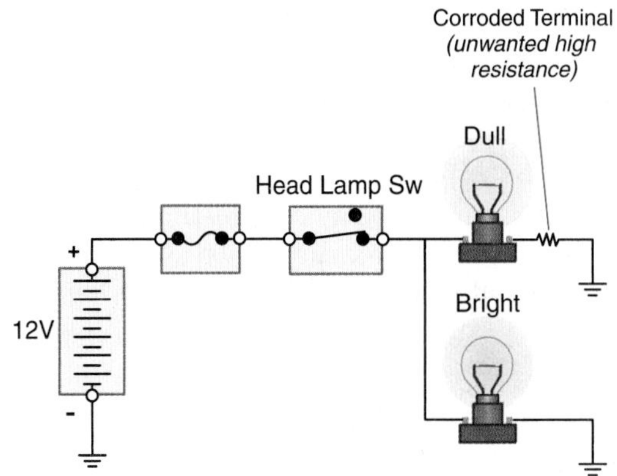

FIGURE 10-24 A poor ground is one cause of a resistive circuit.

increases above its originally intended value. When grounds or power connections in circuits have excessive resistance, circuits cannot function properly. These circuits can be referred to as being resistive. Circuits will also not operate properly if circuit components become excessively resistive. Dirty, corroded, or loose connections result in **resistive circuits** that do not allow components to properly operate. Battery terminals, lightbulb sockets, and connector sockets are common points for resistances to develop.

High current flow through a connection or circuit that has almost no resistance can turn highly resistive if high amperage passes through the connection.

Resistive ground connections can often be difficult to troubleshoot because circuits will find alternate grounds, or components will operate in very unusual ways. Double filament combined stop/tail bulbs are one common example of what is sometimes called a "backfeed" due to resistive grounds (**FIGURE 10-24**). A poor ground in the bulb socket of one lamp will cause the current to find a ground through the bulb on the opposite side of a machine. The taillights will flash alternately when the turn signal is on, and other bulb filaments will glow dimly even when they should not (**FIGURE 10-25**).

Intermittent Circuits

Intermittent circuits are characterized by an irregular interruption of current flow. Intermittent current flow through circuits is often attributed to vibration from a moving machine. An example is the connectors on the engine ECM, which receives a lot of vibration and has the strain of heavy wiring harnesses. Heat at terminal connections can cause continuous thermal cycling, and engine vibration can contribute to a momentary loss of continuity through a pin connection.

Overheated modules and coils are often another source of intermittent circuit problems. Heat causes resistance to climb in semiconductor devices as well as magnetic coils in solenoids or relays. If, after allowing modules or coils to cool, the devices or circuits operate, these heat-sensitive resistive components should be replaced.

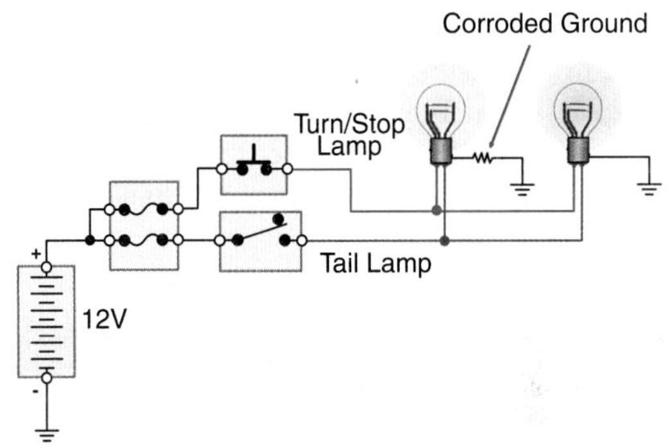

FIGURE 10-25 A resistive ground at the left 3157 stop/taillight bulb will cause a current to flow through the right bulb filaments as the circuit seeks a ground. The right bulb filaments will glow dimly because the circuit becomes a series circuit.

▶ Circuit Protection Devices

K10004

High-amperage flow through circuits produces resistance-induced heat. If excess amperage is allowed to pass through conductors, they can become overheated to the point where the insulation melts, and a fire can result. Circuits overloaded with current-hungry components or grounded circuits are the quickest way to cause damage to wiring and even start fires. So, to protect wiring harnesses and the safety of the machine's operator, circuit protection devices are used. A second reason for circuit protection is because damage to sensitive electronic components can also be caused by unintended reversal of battery polarity, such as when using booster cables. Third, excessive charging system voltage can also push more current through these devices and destroy them.

Traditional fuses, fuse links, and circuit breakers are connected in series and use heat produced from excessive current flow in faulty circuits to open the circuits. Fuses and circuit breakers will open overloaded circuits when amperage typically exceeds 10–15% of the fuse rating. This means a 20-amp fuse will open at 22–23 amps of current. Recently, network control of the electrical system in late-model equipment has enabled software control of current flow through circuits, introducing what is called the virtual fuse—circuit protection without a fuse.

Thermal Fuses

Thermal fuses come in many configurations (**FIGURE 10-26**). Three basic types of fuses are currently in use, which are opened by heat produced from resistance caused by high-amperage flow:

- Cartridge type
- Blade type
- Inline type

Cartridge fuses use strips of metal made in various thicknesses that are enclosed in a glass tube. The metal is manufactured to melt at a low temperature. If excessive current flows through the circuit, the fuse element melts at specific amperage due to the calibrated thickness of the metal strip. When inspecting the fuse to see whether it is blown, a break in the metal strip is observed in open fuse. A multimeter should read system voltage when both sides of an intact fuse are probed and the ignition switch is on. Cartridge fuses are seldom used on newer equipment.

FIGURE 10-26 Fuses come in many configurations.

Blade or spade-type fuses have blade-like metal lugs connected by a fusible metal wire. The compact, transparent plastic body allows more fuses to be inserted into a fuse carrier. There are two categories used: ATO and ATC series. The difference is whether the metal fuse wire is sealed or not. It is easy to check the integrity of the metal fuse wire using a multimeter set to DC volts to probe the metal spade ends. These are accessed from the back of the fuse. Breaks in the fuse wire are also visible through the transparent plastic body. Spade fuses are found in a variety of sizes and color-coded as well as numbered to indicate their maximum rated amperage (**FIGURE 10-27**).

Inline fuses are connected in series with the electrical devices needing additional circuit protection. A device may already be connected in a protected circuit but may have a lower tolerance for overcurrent or reverse polarity conditions. Electronic control modules (ECMs) are a common example of devices with inline fuses protecting the constant battery voltage supply line and supply of current from the ignition switch (**FIGURE 10-28**).

Low-amperage fuses are easily blown in overcurrent and reverse polarity conditions due to internal circuits using Zener diodes. These diodes allow supply current to go to ground under abuse conditions. Inline fuses are also used when adding electrical accessories to a circuit. Locating the fuses as close to the devices as possible shortens the time needed to blow the fuse. **TABLE 10-2** provides the recommended maximum fuse ratings for the corresponding wire size (per the American Wire Gauge [AWG] system).

Major Harness Protection

Fuses are used to protect individual circuits, but not necessarily major wiring harnesses. For those, fusible links are used. Fuse links are short sections of wire installed in series with larger diameter conductors. At one-quarter of the gauge of the main conductor, the fuse link will overheat and melt instead of the larger conductor when excessive amperage passes through the wire. This means brief overloads are possible with fuse links without causing current disruptions. Special plastic covers the link and will bubble when the link melts. Fuse links are effective

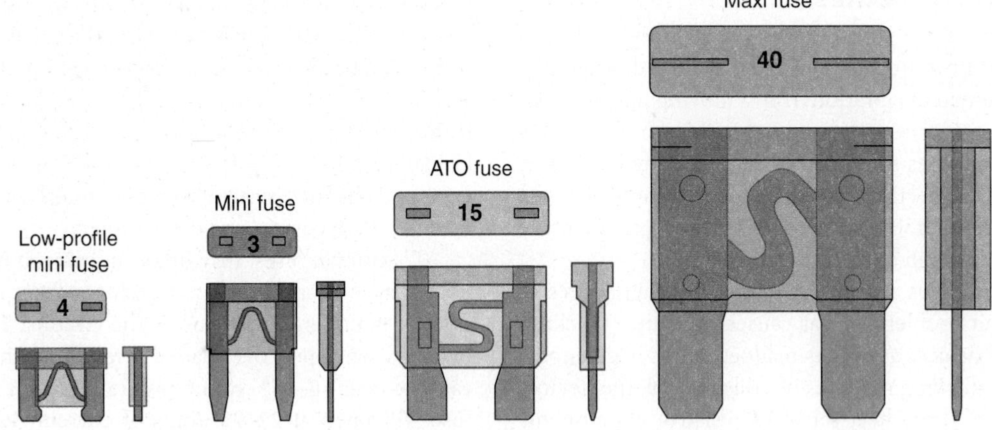

FIGURE 10-27 Thermal fuse types—mini, ATC, maxi, and AMG. Fuses are color coded to designate the maximum current.

FIGURE 10-28 Fuses at the battery box are usually protecting the power circuits to the engine ECM.

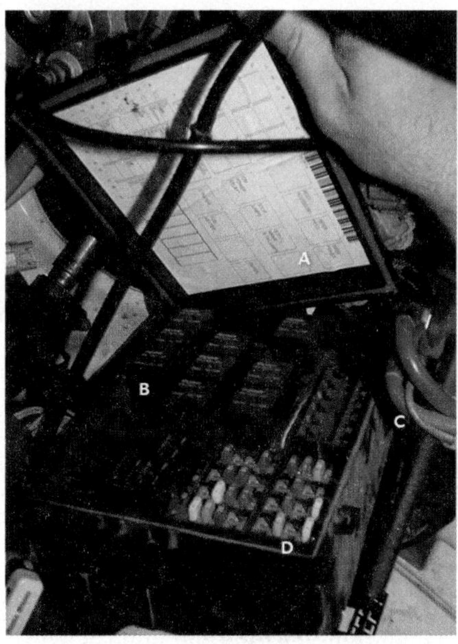

FIGURE 10-29 Power distribution boxes are the main location for circuit protection. The boxes break the electrical system into smaller and more numerous sections. Large electrical conductors do not pass through the occupant compartment, where potential fires can occur. **A.** Cover with component locator. **B.** Relays. **C.** Insulated positive cables. **D.** Blade-type fuses.

TABLE 10-2 Recommended Maximum Fuse Ratings by Wire Gauge

Wire Gauge (AWG)	Recommended Maximum Fuse Rating
00	400 amps
0	325 amps
1	250 amps
2	200 amps
4	125 amps
6	80 amps
8	50 amps
10	30 amps
12	20 amps
14	15 amps
16	7.5 amps

protection in major harnesses because limiting amperage in harnesses is not as critical as protecting them from overheating and burning.

Glow plug circuits, alternator battery cables, and major cab harness cables are a few examples where fuse links were once used. Fuse links are checked with a multimeter set to DC volts or by simply pulling the conductor where it usually attaches to a major battery terminal or starter cable connection. A link that stretches excessively like a rubber band is likely melted. Current should be found on both sides of an intact link if checked with a multimeter.

Maxi fuses have replaced fuse links as circuit protection devices. The use of power distribution boxes has broken down machine electrical systems into smaller and more numerous sections using shorter runs of wiring (**FIGURE 10-29**). It is easier to replace maxi fuses found inside distribution boxes, typically in sizes from 20 to 80 amps, which can protect several circuits. Larger specialized ratings are available from OEMs.

SAFETY TIP

When replacing blown fuses and circuit breakers, never install one with a higher amp rating. This could cause a wire or component to overheat and possibly cause an electrical fire. If a breaker or fuse is operating in an overloaded circuit, replace the wiring with a larger diameter, and then increase the rating of the circuit protection device.

Circuit Breakers

Circuit breakers are used in circuits where intermittent current overloads are common and where power must be rapidly restored, such as with wipers, headlights, and other lighting circuits. Unlike fuses, circuit breakers do not require replacement when they trip. Instead, they may either automatically reset or require a manual reset.

Typically, circuit breakers are made from bimetallic contacts connected in series with a circuit. These are strips of metal made from two different materials with different rates of expansion. When heated, the bimetallic strip bends and opens the contacts, disconnecting current flow from the circuit. Heat is produced when too much current flows through the bimetallic strip in the circuit breaker. In **Type 1 circuit breakers**, or automatically resetting breakers, current is restored when the bimetallic strip cools (**FIGURE 10-30**).

A circuit breaker can be a noncycling type too. Typically, those are **Type 2 circuit breakers**. One type is reset by removing the power from the circuit. A heating coil connected in parallel with the contacts is wrapped around a bimetal arm, keeping the arm hot and contacts disconnected after it has

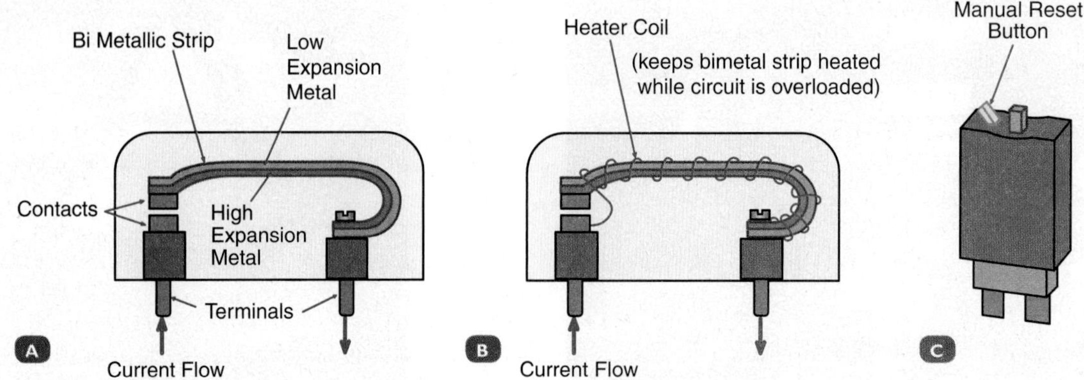

FIGURE 10-30 Three types of circuit breakers: **A.** cycling, **B.** noncycling, and **C.** manual reset. Bimetal strips of metal with different expansion rates bend when heated. Heat produced during high current flow causes contacts inside the breaker to open to protect the circuit wiring from overheating.

tripped. This current is not enough to operate a load, but the coil does continue heating the bimetal arm until power is removed. Another noncycling breaker is the **Type 3 circuit breaker**, which must be reset by depressing a reset button. The reset button pushes a spring back into position. That spring force holds the bimetal contacts open after the breaker has tripped. **TABLE 10-3** shows this classification for circuit breakers.

PPT Coefficient Fuses

A **polymeric positive temperature coefficient (PPTC) device**, commonly known as a **resettable fuse**, is a thermistor-like electronic device used to protect against circuit overloads. These devices are similar to nonlinear PTC thermistors. When heated while conducting excessive current, however, they quickly cycle between a conductive and nonconductive state until after current is removed or the device has cooled (**FIGURE 10-31**). Resistance in the device will suddenly increase to thousands of ohms.

Current trip ratings for PPTCs range from 20 mA to 100 A. Dozens of these devices are used in a single electrical control module to harden them against damage from shorts to power or ground, as well as other electrical faults in the external circuits they control.

Virtual Fuses

E-fuses are a more recent innovation in circuit protection. **E-fuses**, or **virtual fuses** as they are sometimes called, are software-controlled fuses that use **field effect transistors (FETs)**

TABLE 10-3 Classification of Circuit Breakers

Type 1	Automatically resetting—Will cycle the circuit breaker on and off until the overload condition is removed.
Type 2	Modified Type 1—Keeps the circuit breaker open until the overload condition is removed.
Type 3	A manual resetting thermal non-cycling circuit breaker—Remains tripped until the operator manually resets it by pushing a button located on the breaker.

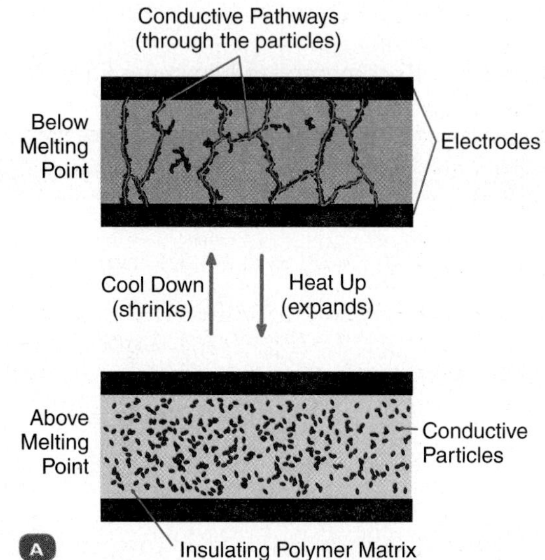

FIGURE 10-31 **A.** When heated while conducting excessive current, PPTCs quickly cycle between a conductive and nonconductive state until after current is removed or the device has cooled. **B.** Surface-mount resettable PTCs are used in this injector drive module. The fuses protect the sensitive microcontrollers against grounded circuits, reverse polarity, and electromagnetic interference.

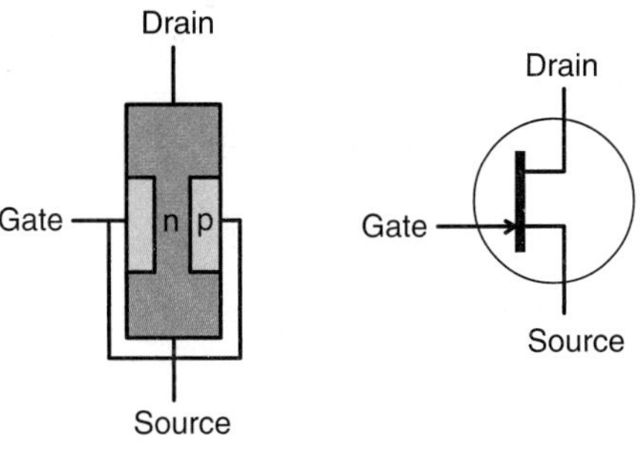

FIGURE 10-32 One of many types of FETs that can conduct high current flow with very little heating. By regulating the current applied to the gate, the amperage through the FET is controlled. Software enables programming of FET capabilities to act as virtual fuses or e-fuses.

for the circuit control device. The development of virtual fuses is important because it saves not only the cost of the fuse but also that of the fuse holder as well as the largest cost associated with using a traditional fuse—the wiring to and from the fuse.

Virtual fuses are now used in most power distribution modules in multiplexed electrical systems to enable programmable limits of amperage to body builder–installed circuits and any other machine circuits. Combinations of two FETs are used along with a signal from a microcontroller to establish a threshold for current transmission (**FIGURE 10-32**). These fuses are reset either when the ignition switch is turned off or when the FETs have sensed the overcurrent condition has ended.

▶ Inspecting and Testing Circuit Protection Devices

S10001, S10002

Protection devices are designed to prevent excessive current from flowing in the circuit. Protection devices such as fuses and fusible links are sacrificial, meaning that if excessive current flows, they will fail and must then be replaced. Circuit breakers can be reset. Once they trip, they either reset automatically or require a manual reset by pushing a button or moving a lever.

Fuses, fusible links, and circuit breakers are available in various ratings, types, and sizes, and must always be replaced with the same rating and type. In most machines, protection devices are located in the power battery positive side of the circuit. A blown or faulty fuse can be tested using a multimeter or test lamp. A good fuse will have virtually the same voltage on both sides. A blown fuse will typically have battery voltage on one side of the fuse and 0 volts on the other side. Fuses can also sometimes be visually inspected. This may require the removal of the fuse from the fuse holder. The fusible metal strip should be intact and, if measured by an ohmmeter, should have no, or very low, resistance. The contacts on both the fuse and the fuse holder should be clean and free of corrosion and should fit snugly together. To inspect and test circuit protection devices, follow the guidelines in **SKILL DRILL 10-1**. To identify a resistive ground connection, follow the steps in **SKILL DRILL 10-2**.

▶ Relays, Magnetic Switches, and Solenoids

K10005

Electrical circuits commonly use relays, magnetic switches, and solenoids as control devices to control the flow of current through a circuit.

Relays

A relay is a switch that uses a small amount of current to switch a larger amount of current. Locating a relay closer to a load requiring large amounts of current eliminates voltage drop caused by resistance from long runs of wires. Relays also eliminate the use of heavy conductors inside the cab of a machine, and that allows for safer operation.

SKILL DRILL 10-1 Inspecting and Testing Circuit Protection Devices

1. Identify the protection device to be inspected and tested. A fuse or circuit breaker is most commonly checked at a power distribution box or fuse panel.
2. Turn the ignition switch to the run or on position to supply power to the fuse.
3. Using a multimeter set to DC volts, probe the fuse or circuit breaker on each side (supply and load) to determine whether current is supplied to the device and whether current is available to the loads in the circuit.
4. If there is only power available to the circuit protection device and not to the load, the device is open. This requires replacement if it is a fuse or resetting the circuit breaker if possible. Fuse replacement is performed after identifying the cause for the overloaded circuit.

SKILL DRILL 10-2 Identifying a Resistive Ground Connection

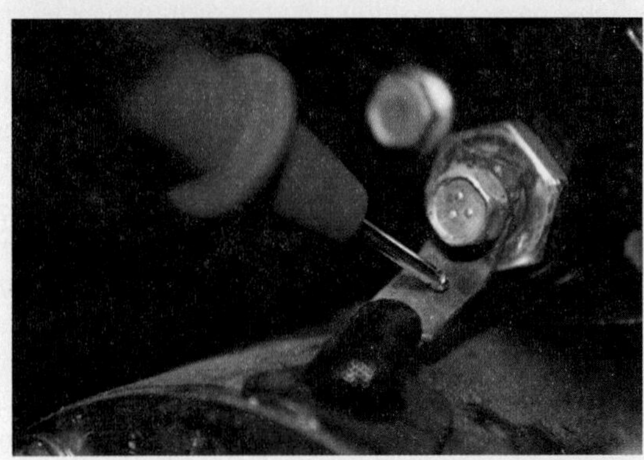

1. Locate a suspected ground connection. This is usually a bolt on a chassis or terminal on a wire lead attached to a stud.
2. Using a multimeter set to DC volts, place one lead of the voltmeter onto the chassis ground.
3. Place the other lead on the ground connection to the device that is not operating correctly.
4. Energize the device or operate the circuit.
5. If no fault exists, there should be no voltage displayed.
6. A reading of 0.5 VDC for a 12-volt system and 1.0 VDC for a 24-volt system indicates excessive resistance between the two leads of the multimeter.

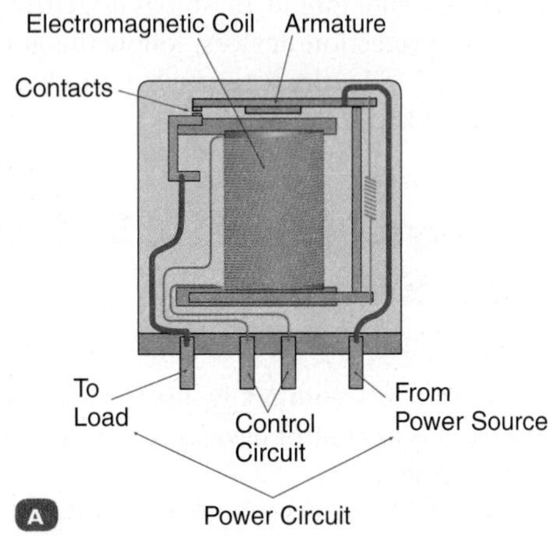

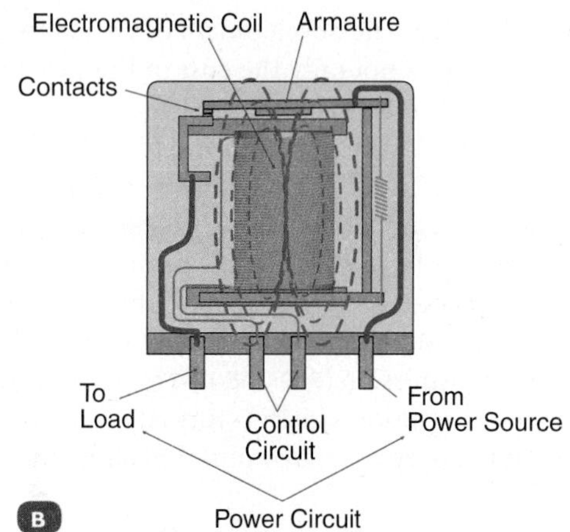

FIGURE 10-33 Operation of a relay with a single contact. **A.** Nonenergized with contacts open. **B.** Energizing the electromagnet with a small amount of electrical current closes the contacts, which can switch high-amperage current flow.

A typical relay has a control circuit and a load circuit. The control circuit is supplied current through a switch, which often is opened or closed by an ECM or the machine operator. Inside the relay, an electromagnetic coil pulls a set of contacts closed. It is across these contacts that a larger amount of current is switched. The relay's control circuit can be switched by supplying a power or ground to the relay. If an ECM supplies a positive voltage to control the relay, it is termed a pull-up circuit. If it supplies a ground, it is called a pull-down circuit.

International Organization for Standardization (ISO) relays, also called mini-cube relays, are the most common relays used today. See **FIGURE 10-33** and **FIGURE 10-34**.

The relay is standardized to be used across all equipment manufacturers, having standard pin numbers, functions, and dimensions to fit into a power distribution box. These can switch as much as 35 amps in a 24-volt system.

Because relays use electromagnetic coils, a large voltage spike is produced when the coils are de-energized. See **FIGURE 10-35** and **FIGURE 10-36**.

The rapidly collapsing magnetic field will move across the coil conductors, inducing over 200 volts. If the relay control circuit shares a voltage supply with the ignition switch or sensitive electronic component, electrical damage can occur. To prevent this, a diode or resistor connected in parallel across the

FIGURE 10-34 Mini ISO relays in a power distribution box. Current suppressed relays use a diode, resistor, and sometimes a capacitor to minimize a voltage spike produced through self-induction.

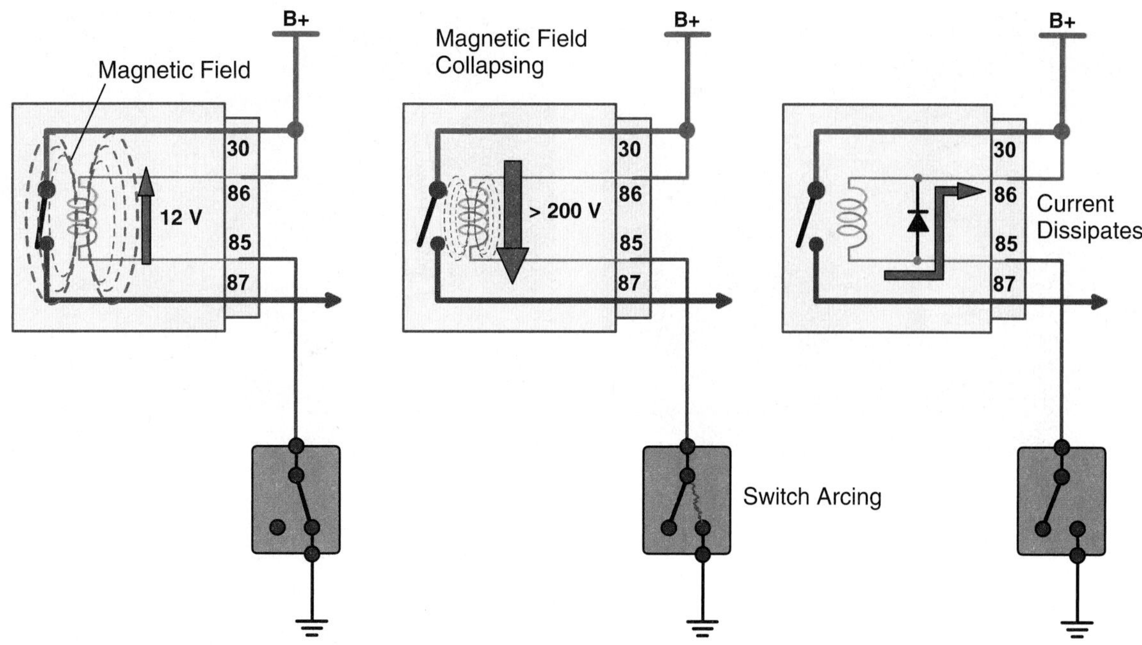

FIGURE 10-35 Self-induction inside a relay can supply a large voltage spike, which can damage sensitive electronic components. No conduction takes place through the diode during normal operation. High-voltage current moving in the opposite direction of the original current will forward bias the diode, and current dissipates through resistance in the circuit.

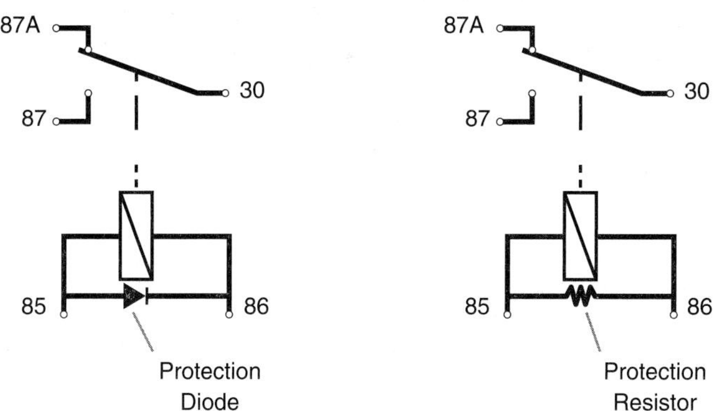

FIGURE 10-36 A resistor or a diode is used to suppress voltage spike produced through self-induction.

coil will provide an alternate pathway for the voltage spike to dissipate when the magnetic field collapses.

Magnetic Switches

Magnetic, or "mag," switches are identical in function to relays except that they switch even larger amounts of current and have atypical dimensions. See **FIGURE 10-37**.

Magnetic switches are also classified as continuous or intermittent duty service. When switching heavy amounts of current, such as to the starter motor solenoid, available battery voltage can drop. See **FIGURE 10-38**.

Low available voltage will reduce the magnetic field strength in the switch, causing the relay to "chatter" as it rapidly engages and disengages when the electrical system voltage drops.

To counter this effect, the electromagnetic coil windings are wound from heavier gauge wire. The result is fewer

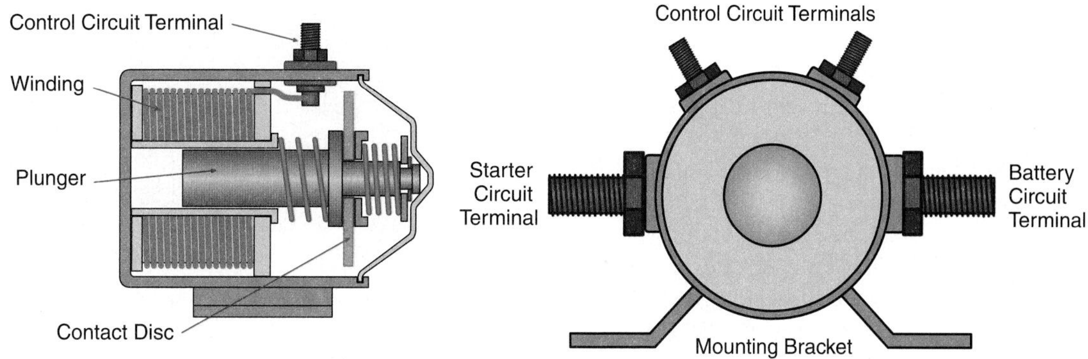

FIGURE 10-37 Construction of a larger magnetic switch used for switching large amounts of electrical current.

FIGURE 10-38 A. A magnetic switch used to switch high current flow to the **B.** starter solenoid. The chassis ECM supplies a ground to energize the control circuit.

FIGURE 10-39 A. The windings of intermittent duty mag switches are thicker. Thicker windings use more amperage but stay engaged longer when available battery voltage drops during cranking. **B.** Continuous duty relays use thinner, more resistive winding, which will not burn out due to high current flow.

coils but more amperage through the low resistance coil, which helps maintains magnetic field strength, as shown in **FIGURE 10-39**.

High-amperage flow through the winding causes the coil to quickly burn out after just a few hours of continuous operation. To prevent that, continuous duty relays are made from thinner wire with higher resistance. Although they can remain energized for longer periods of time, continuous duty relays are sensitive to voltage drop, leading to relay chatter.

> ▶ TECHNICIAN TIP
>
> Continuous and intermittent duty magnetic switches can look identical but will cause problems if not used in the correct application. Continuous duty relays when used to operate glow plug or starter motor solenoids will chatter during cranking. Intermittent duty relays will burn out if left energized for a few hours. Always verify the type of mag switch is meant for its intended applications.

Solenoids

Solenoids are devices with a movable core that converts current flow into mechanical movement (**FIGURE 10-40**).

Solenoids are used with starter motors to engage the drive mechanism while switching heavy current into the motor. They are also used to actuate door lock mechanisms, control air and hydraulic flow, move shut-off levers on fuel systems, and in any other place where electric control of mechanical movement is needed. See **FIGURE 10-41**.

Solenoids can be either pull-in type or push-and-pull type. In pull-type solenoids, an electromagnet pulls a soft iron core into the coil. To prevent a high amount of amperage being drawn by the solenoid and possibly burning out the coil, two coils are used. The first coil is a pull-in winding, which uses thick wire windings developing high magnetic field strength.

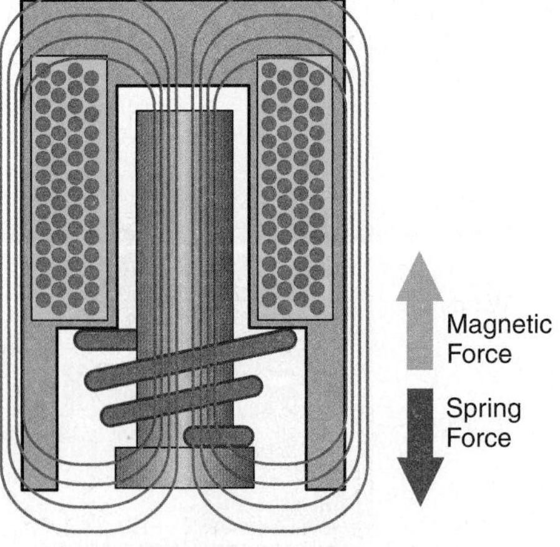

FIGURE 10-40 Solenoids may use a spring to return the actuator to a resting position.

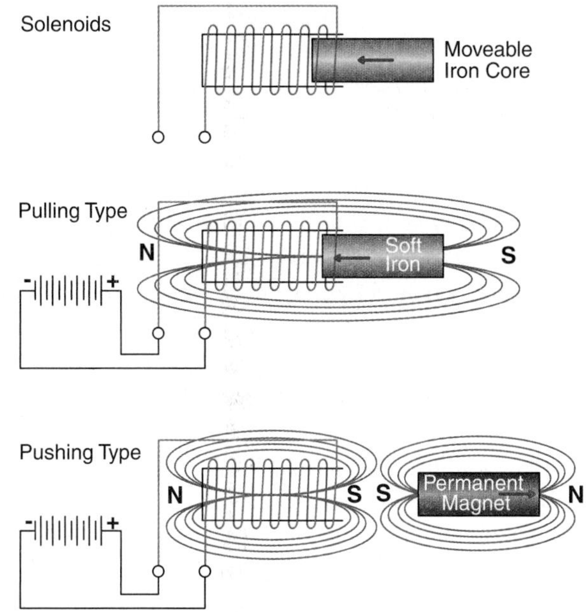

FIGURE 10-41 Push-and-pull–type solenoids. Reversing the direction of current flow through the winding changes its polarity. The magnetic actuator will be either pulled or repelled by the magnetic field.

A second hold-in coil "holds" the core in place after the pull-in winding is electrically disconnected. Solenoids of the push–pull type use a permanent magnet instead of an iron core to produce bidirectional movement. By changing the polarity of the coil, the magnetic field around the permanent magnet core can either repel or attract the coil.

> **TECHNICIAN TIP**
>
> It is important for the pull-in winding of a solenoid to be electrically disconnected after a solenoid is initially engaged. The thinner, more resistive windings of the hold-in winding will take over from the pull-in windings and keep the core engaged. If the solenoid remained engaged, the pull-in windings would burn out due to excessive current flow. Adjustment of solenoid travel is crucial to prevent this from happening by ensuring that the winding is not disconnected internally. Adjustable linkage on the solenoid plunger should be checked against the manufacturer's specifications (**FIGURE 10-42**).

FIGURE 10-42 This injection pump shut-off solenoid has a high-amperage pull-in and low-amperage hold-in winding to move the control rack from a no-fuel position.

Wrap-Up

Ready for Review

- A basic electrical circuit includes a power supply, a fuse, a switch, a load, and wires connecting them all together. More complex circuits also include circuit protection devices, a control device, and load and connecting wires.
- According to conventional theory of current flow, the positive power is the supply side of the circuit, and the ground is the return side of the circuit.
- Many machines connect the chassis and body to the negative battery terminal, which means most of the metal components on the machine are grounded.
- A component with no ground connection results in an open circuit and no current flow.
- There are three types of short circuit: short to ground, short to power, and unintended high resistance.
- An open circuit has infinite resistance.
- Unintended high resistance in a circuit causes a reduction in amperage in the circuit as well as a drop in voltage at the resistance.
- Volts, amps, and ohms are three basic units of electrical measurement.
- The higher the resistance, the less amperage that will flow in the circuit for any particular voltage.
- The lower the resistance, the higher the current flow in the circuit.
- Ohm's law is a mathematical formula that expresses the relationship among volts (V), amps (A), and ohms (R): A = V × R.
- Most of the time, when circuits fail, it is because the current flow is too low or nonexistent.
- Circuits come in two basic configurations—series circuits and parallel circuits. The two types can also be combined into what is called a series-parallel circuit.
- In a series circuit, if there is more than one resistance in the circuit, those resistances are connected one after the other; thus, the resistances add up.
- Excessively high current flow through circuits produces heat that has the potential to overheat conductors or

components to the point where the insulation melts, and a fire can result.

- Traditional fuses, fuse links, and circuit breakers are connected in series and use heat produced from excessive current flow in overloaded circuits to open the circuits.
- Protection devices are designed to prevent excessive current from flowing in the circuit.
- Protection devices such as fuses and fusible links are sacrificial, meaning that if excessive current flows, they will burn out and need replacement.
- Circuit breakers are resettable. A fuse or circuit breaker should be overrated by about 10–15% to prevent accidental tripping.
- Virtual fuses save not only the cost of the fuse but also that of the fuse holder and the largest cost associated with using a traditional fuse—the wiring to and from the fuse.
- A typical relay has a control circuit and a load circuit.
- Magnetic switches are identical in function to relays except that they switch even larger amounts of current and have atypical dimensions.
- Solenoids are devices with a movable core that converts current flow into mechanical movement.
- Solenoids can be either pull-in type or push-and-pull type. In pull-type solenoids, an electromagnet pulls a soft iron core into the coil. Solenoids of the push–pull type use a permanent magnet instead of an iron core to produce bidirectional movement.

Key Terms

circuit breaker A device that trips and opens a circuit, preventing excessive current flow in a circuit. It is resettable to allow for reuse.

combination (series-parallel) circuit A circuit that uses elements both of series and parallel circuits.

e-fuse A software-controlled fuse that uses field effect transistors for the circuit control device. Also called *virtual fuses.*

field effect transistor (FET) A unipolar transistor that uses an electric field to control the conductivity of a semiconductor material.

grounded circuit A circuit characterized by an unwanted low-resistance connection between battery positive power and chassis ground.

intermittent circuit A circuit characterized by uneven current flow.

Kirchhoff 's law A law that states that the sum of the current flowing into a junction is the same as the current flowing out of the junction.

parallel circuit A circuit in which all components are connected directly to the voltage supply.

polymeric positive temperature coefficient (PPTC) Device (resettable fuse) A thermistor-like electronic device used to protect against circuit overloads. Also called *resettable fuse.*

resistive circuit A circuit in which grounds and power connections cannot properly function due to overly high resistance.

series circuit The simplest type of electrical circuit, with multiple loads but only one path for current to flow.

short circuit An electrical circuit that is formed between two points, allowing current to flow through an unintended pathway.

thermal fuse A type of fuse opened by heat produced from resistance caused by high-amperage flow.

type 1 circuit breaker A cycling circuit breaker that automatically resets.

type 2 circuit breaker A noncycling circuit breaker.

type 3 circuit breaker A circuit breaker that requires manual reset.

virtual fuse A software-controlled fuse that uses field effect transistors for the circuit control device. A circuit protection strategy that monitors circuit amperage with software and shuts off the circuit when amperage exceeds a predetermined threshold. Also called *e-fuses.*

watt's law A law that defines the relationship between power, amperage, and voltage.

Review Questions

1. Which of the following are basic parts of an electrical circuit?
   a. Power source
   b. Conductors
   c. Loads
   d. All of the choices are correct.
2. Which of the following statements is/are correct concerning the term "operational state"?
   a. Open and closed are the terms used to describe whether current is flowing through a circuit.
   b. An open circuit's electrical pathway is broken or unconnected.
   c. An open circuit means current cannot flow because there is an open gap between two ends of the circuit.
   d. All of the choices are correct.
3. Which of the following is *not* correct concerning parallel circuits?
   a. There are two or more pathways for the current.
   b. The voltage applied to each branch is the same throughout the circuit.
   c. If one branch of the circuit is broken, current will continue to flow in the other branches.
   d. Total circuit resistance is always more than the resistance of the smallest resister.
4. Which of the following is/are correct concerning combination circuits?
   a. Combination circuits use elements in both parallel and series circuits.
   b. Combination circuits are the most common types used in mobile off-road equipment.
   c. Typically, the power and control circuits are in series, but the loads are in parallel.
   d. All of the choices are correct.

5. Which of the following is *not* correct concerning Ohm's law?
   a. Ohm's law is often used by a technician.
   b. An understanding of Ohm's law can help you better understand how electricity behaves.
   c. Ohm's law defines the relationship between current, resistance, and voltage.
   d. Simply stated, Ohm's law requires 1 volt to push 1 amp of current through a circuit that has a resistance of 1 ohm.
6. Why do machines often use a 24-volt system?
   a. Reducing amperage not only reduces resistance but also the size of conductors.
   b. Voltage drops in the system are reduced.
   c. Both A and B
   d. Neither A nor B
7. Which of the following are common points for resistances to develop?
   a. Battery terminals
   b. Lightbulb sockets
   c. Connector sockets
   d. All of the choices are correct.
8. Which of the following is *not* a type of thermal fuse?
   a. Cartridge type
   b. Modular type
   c. Blade type
   d. In-line type
9. Which type of circuit breaker must be reset by depressing a reset button?
   a. Type 1
   b. Type 2
   c. Type 3
   d. Type 4
10. Which of the following is/are correct concerning inspecting and testing circuit protection devices?
    a. Protection devices such as fuses and fusible links are sacrificial, meaning that if excessive current flows, they will blow or trip and have to be replaced.
    b. Circuit breakers can be reset.
    c. Fuses, fusible links, and circuit breakers are available in various ratings, types and sizes, and must always be replaced with the same rating and type.
    d. All of the choices are correct.

ASE Technician A/Technician B Style Questions

1. Technician A says circuits are pathways made by electrical conductors that enable the flow of electrons. Technician B says a variety of classifications are used to describe circuit configurations and failures. Who is correct?
   a. Technician A
   b. Technician B
   c. Both Technician A and Technician B
   d. Neither Technician A nor Technician B
2. Technician A says resistance is electrical friction. Technician B says resistance will lower voltage but in a circuit will not proportionately lower amperage to the amount of resistance. Who is correct?
   a. Technician A
   b. Technician B
   c. Both Technician A and Technician B
   d. Neither Technician A nor Technician B
3. Technician A says circuits found in mobile off-road equipment are classified in an operational state of open or closed. Technician B says circuits found in mobile off-road equipment are classified in the failure mode of blocked as well as shorted or open. Who is correct?
   a. Technician A
   b. Technician B
   c. Both Technician A and Technician B
   d. Neither Technician A nor Technician B
4. Technician A says a series circuit is a circuit with multiple loads and only one path for current to flow. Technician B says in a series circuit total circuit resistance is equal to the sum of the individual resistances. Who is correct?
   a. Technician A
   b. Technician B
   c. Both Technician A and Technician B
   d. Neither Technician A nor Technician B
5. Technician A says Watt's law, which is related to Ohm's law, explains the relationship between resistance and amperage. Technician B says increasing amperage through a circuit produces proportionally more resistance. Who is correct?
   a. Technician A
   b. Technician B
   c. Both Technician A and Technician B
   d. Neither Technician A nor Technician B
6. Technician A says a grounded circuit should not be confused with a "dead short," which is a different condition. Technician B says a common example of a grounded circuit would be a battery or power cable insulation rubbing against the negative ground chassis frame. Who is correct?
   a. Technician A
   b. Technician B
   c. Both Technician A and Technician B
   d. Neither Technician A nor Technician B
7. Technician A says when circuits are overloaded with current hungry components, or grounded circuits, it is the quickest way to cause damage to wiring, or even start fires. Technician B says a 20-amp fuse will open at 32–33 amps of current. Who is correct?
   a. Technician A
   b. Technician B
   c. Both Technician A and Technician B
   d. Neither Technician A nor Technician B
8. Technician A says fuse links are short sections of wire installed in series with larger diameter conductors. Technician B says when the gauge on the main conductor is at halfway, the fuse link will overheat and melt as excessive amperage passes through the wire. Who is correct?
   a. Technician A
   b. Technician B

c. Both Technician A and Technician B
d. Neither Technician A nor Technician B

9. Technician A says a polymeric positive temperature coefficient (PPTC) device is a thermistor-like electronic device used to protect against circuit overloads. Technician B says PPTCs are commonly known as manual resettable fuses. Who is correct?
a. Technician A
b. Technician B
c. Both Technician A and Technician B
d. Neither Technician A nor Technician B

10. Technician A says virtual fuses, or e-fuses, are a recent innovation in circuit protection. Technician B says virtual fuses are software-controlled fuses that use field effect transistors (FETs) as the circuit control device. Who is correct?
a. Technician A
b. Technician B
c. Both Technician A and Technician B
d. Neither Technician A nor Technician B

CHAPTER 11

Electrical Test Instruments

Knowledge Objectives

After reading this chapter, you will be able to:

- **K11001** Classify and identify the applications of electrical test instruments used in off-road mobile equipment service.
- **K11002** Describe the setup of a digital multimeter (DMM) and procedures for performing basic electrical measurements.
- **K11003** Describe the function and setup of a circuit tracer when performing basic electrical troubleshooting.
- **K11004** Describe the function and setup of graphing meters and oscilloscopes when performing basic electrical troubleshooting.
- **K11005** Describe the function and setup of electronic service tools when performing basic electrical troubleshooting.

Skills Objectives

After reading this chapter, you will be able to:

- **S11001** Check meter shunts.
- **S11002** Test electrical/electronic circuits and components using appropriate test equipment.

Introduction

Diagnosing and repairing electrical problems requires not only logic and deductive reasoning but electrical test tools too. A variety of electrical test instruments are needed, ranging from the simple test lights and electrical multimeters to more elaborate instrumentation for checking fault codes and viewing electrical signal wave forms.

Electrical Test Instruments

K11001, S11001

Self-Powered Test Light

Self-powered **test lights** are like regular test lights except that they contain a 1.5-volt battery (**FIGURE 11-1**).

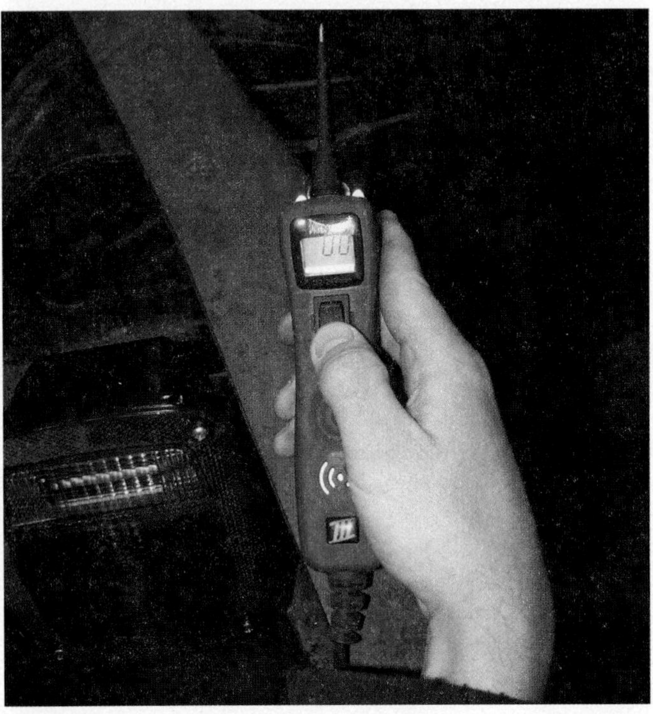

FIGURE 11-1 A self-powered electrical probe.

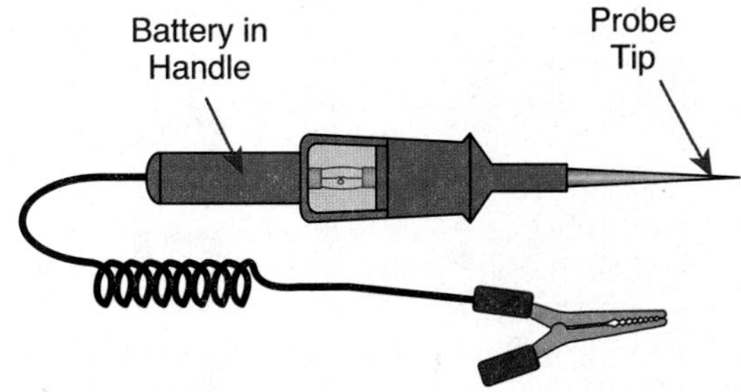

FIGURE 11-2 A self-powered test light can be used to find open, shorted, and grounded circuits after disconnecting the circuit from machine power and ground. The battery will supply the ground connection through the alligator clip.

Self-powered lights can be used to check for both open circuits and grounded circuits when either chassis power or ground is removed from the circuit (**FIGURE 11-2**).

The internal battery can supply current needed to illuminate the light. To check for an opening in a circuit, the machine battery is first disconnected. The light's alligator clip is connected to ground, and the circuit is probed sequentially from the switch or power supply to the load. Where the test light glows, the circuit is closed from machine ground to power. An open circuit prevents current from traveling from the ground to an insulated positive. For example, a broken wire between a heater blower motor and fuse will illuminate between the blower motor and break in the wire, but not after the break and before the fuse.

Grounded circuits are checked in a similar manner. While probing the circuit, its switches and connectors are opened. The light will stay illuminated in the section that is grounded. However, the light will go out after the section of circuit with an unintentional ground is disconnected. Self-powered voltmeters with probes are also useful for close-quarter probing of electrical circuits.

TECHNICIAN TIP

A 12- or 24-volt battery current will easily blow the bulb out of self powered test lights, so battery current should always be removed when

You Are the Mobile Heavy-Duty Technician

In the equipment fleet that you help maintain, quite a high number of wheel loaders are developing electrical short circuits, grounded circuits, and open circuits in the wiring connecting the operator's console to the rear lights. Many of the problems are likely the result of wiring being improperly secured, insulated, and tied at the factory. Repairing the wiring problem has become very time consuming, as several wiring circuits pass through the cab of the machine. Often, the panels must be removed to replace or repair the wiring. Even after replacing large sections of wiring between the body panels, many of these same wheel loaders require further repairs. Later repairs have to be made to the wiring that connects the signal and brake lights, as corrosion has taken place due to punctures from test lights. While reviewing maintenance strategies and procedures, consider the following:

1. What electrical test instrument would you recommend using to find shorts, grounded circuits, and open circuits behind the wheel loaders' body panels?
2. What electrical test instrument would you recommend for finding grounded circuits in the wiring between the lights and the grounded wire that is routed through the cab?
3. What maintenance recommendations would you make to prevent further repeat repairs of wiring after technicians have performed initial repairs?

using these lights. Although 1.5 volts is relatively low, it is still enough to damage computer circuits. Self powered test lights should never be used in electronic circuits using semiconductors—that includes sensors.

SAFETY TIP

High voltage from electric drives, the latest common rail injectors, and other electric systems can easily kill or cause serious physical harm if pierced by a technician. Always ensure appropriate power disconnect switches are removed when working around these circuits. Also, never pierce wiring covered in heavy protective loom or brightly colored insulation without first determining what voltage the conductors are carrying. The bright color and insulation often designate high voltage or sensitive circuits (**FIGURE 11-3**).

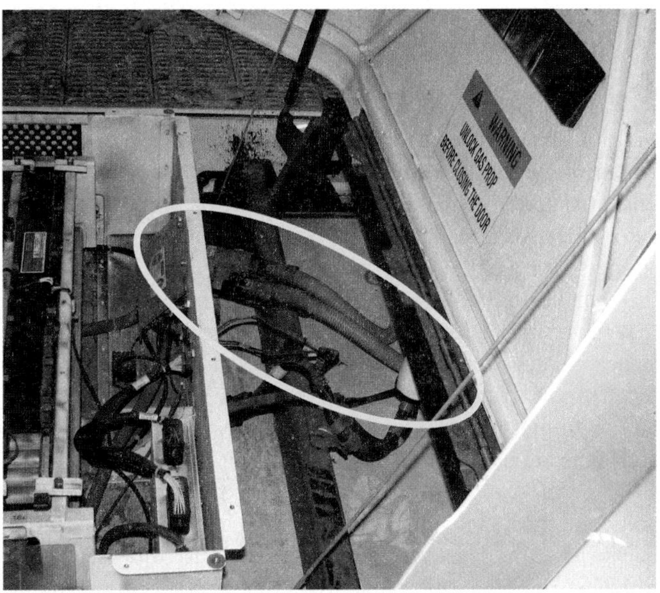

FIGURE 11-3 High-voltage cables such as those on electric-drive equipment have heavy protective insulation, which is brightly colored.

Self-Powered LED Test Lights

One of the disadvantages of incandescent test lights is that they can draw excessive current from a circuit to operate the bulb. In some cases, the additional load may damage a circuit. Using light-emitting diodes (LEDs) instead of an incandescent bulb overcomes this difficulty and adds capabilities to a test light. A popular type of LED test light is battery powered and has two LEDs—one red and the other green. With two LEDs, the technician can find out what the polarity of a circuit is as it's being tested. For example, if the light's alligator clip is connected to ground and the probe is connected to a positive polarity, the red LED comes on. A green light indicates it's a ground or connected to negative polarity. One disadvantage of LED lights is that they provide no indication of a circuit voltage and will be relatively bright between 1.5 and 3 volts. An incandescent light changes brightness depending on the circuit's voltage.

Multimeters

Multimeters are electrical measuring instruments combining functions of at least voltage, resistance, and amperage measurement into a single compact instrument. Digital multimeters are the most common category of multimeters and provide numerical displays of electrical data (**FIGURE 11-4**).

Analog meters use a sweeping needle that continuously measures electrical values (**FIGURE 11-5**).

Digital multimeters are almost exclusively used today because they are easiest to use and draw the least amount of current from circuits being measured. Sampling very little of a circuit's own current to take a measurement is a characteristic of **high-impedance multimeters**. High impedance refers to a meter's internal resistance to current flowing from a live circuit into the meter when measuring voltage and amperage. In sensitive electronic circuits, a test light or analog meter can act like a load and use too much current. The result is an overloaded or damaged circuit.

FIGURE 11-4 A digital multimeter with typical basic features.

FIGURE 11-5 An analog meter uses a needle and sweeping scale to measure properties of electrical current.

Basic Multimeter Electrical Measurements

Before using a multimeter, it is important to understand the basic measurements that it can produce. A multimeter measures resistance, continuity, voltage, and amperage:

1. **Resistance**—Measures circuit resistance in Ohms to determine whether it is within specifications. Wire coils and heating elements are examples of common devices where a measure of resistance determines serviceability. Open and short circuits are easily detected using the ohmmeter to measure resistance (**FIGURE 11-6**).
2. **Continuity**—Determines whether two points are electrically connected. Continuity is also valuable when checking for opens and shorts.
3. **Voltage**—Measurements are used to determine whether a component or circuit has the correct amount of available voltage. Measuring voltage drops in a circuit can help evaluate excessive resistance in high-amperage circuits such as the starting circuit. A voltmeter behaves like a pressure differential gauge by measuring the difference in electron pressure between two points in a circuit.
4. **Amperage**—Most measurements of amperage are performed at levels higher than multimeters can typically handle, so an inductance amp clamp is used instead. However, meters are usually capable of measuring up to 10 amps of current flow. Starter draw and alternator output are two common measurements of amperage regularly made using multimeters with an inductance clamp meter accessory.

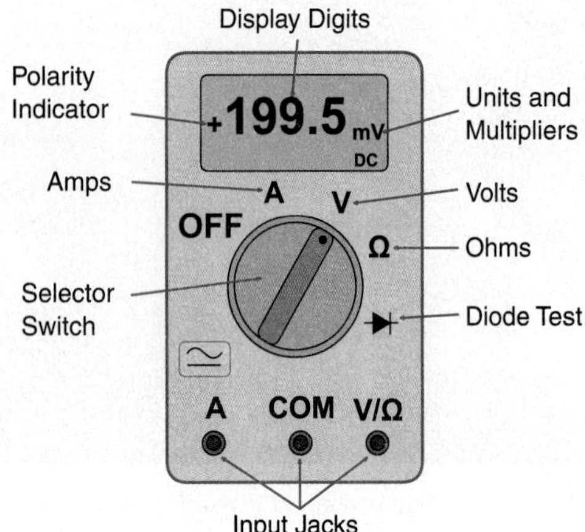

FIGURE 11-6 Features of a basic DVOM.

Multimeters may also perform additional electrical measurements including the following:

- Diode testing
- Frequency
- Capacitance
- Temperature
- Duty cycle
- Transistor testing
- Continuity tester with beeper Waveform display
- Engine RPM

Manual and Auto-Ranging Meters

Multimeters are available as auto- or manual-ranging types. An **auto-ranging multimeter** has fewer positions on its range selection knob. When set to amps, volts, or ohms, the meter automatically selects the correct range when meter test leads are connected to a circuit.

This feature contrasts with **manual-ranging multimeters** that must first be set to the correct range based on anticipated values measured. For example, the DC volts range of a manual meter may include a setting of 200 mV, 2 V, 20 V, 200 V, and 500 V. To measure 12-volt battery voltage, the range value just above the anticipated voltage is the 20-volt scale (**FIGURE 11-7**).

An auto-ranging meter would only require selecting DC volts, and the meter would do the rest. Auto-ranging meters can be slower to measure electrical values because they need time to adjust the operating range. As an alternative, auto-ranging meters can usually be set to operate as manual-ranging units.

With either automatic or manual-ranging meters, it is important to learn the electrical symbols and units of measurement listed in **TABLE 11-1**.

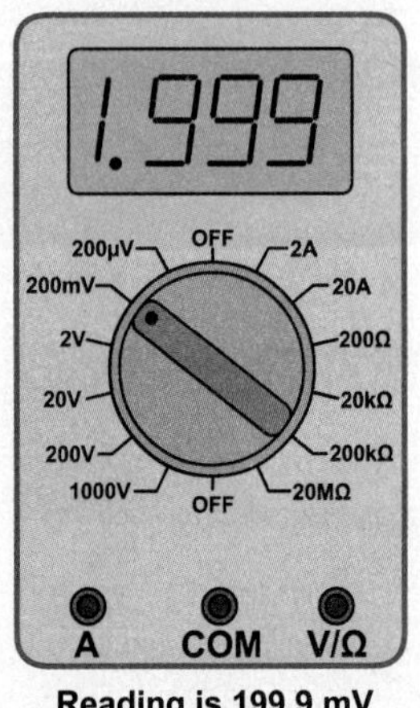

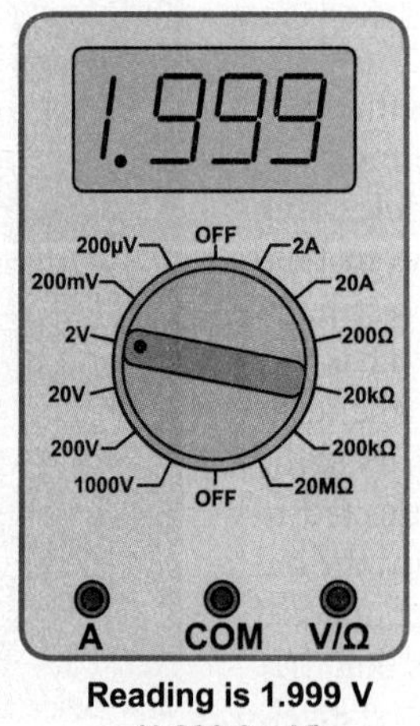

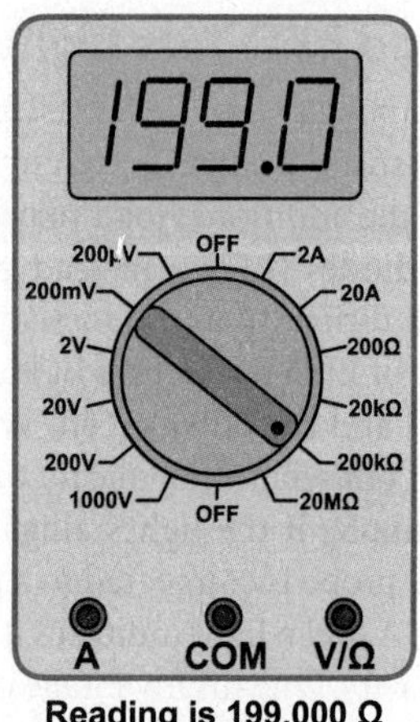

FIGURE 11-7 A manual-ranging meter will move the decimal point for many electrical measurements.

TABLE 11-1 Symbols and Meanings for Electrical Units of Measurement

Symbol	Meaning
M	Mega or million
K	Kilo or thousand
m	Milli or one thousandth
μ	Micro or one-millionth
V̄	V dc
Ṽ	V ac
mV	Millivolts (0.001 V or 1/1,000 V)
A	Amperage (amps)
mA	Milliamps (0.001A or 1/1,000 A)
μA	Microamps (0.000001 A or 1/1,000,000 A)
Ω	Resistance (ohms)
kΩ	Kilo-ohms (1,000 ohms)
MΩ	Megohms (1,000,000 ohms)
)))	Continuity beeper
Diode →⊢	Diode testing
Hz	Frequency (hertz, which is cycles/sec)
dB	Sound (decibels)
F	Capacitance (farad)
μF	Microfarads
nF	Nanofarads
Touch Hold & Auto HOLD	The last recorded stable reading
MIN MAX	Highest, lowest recorded readings
OL	Out of range

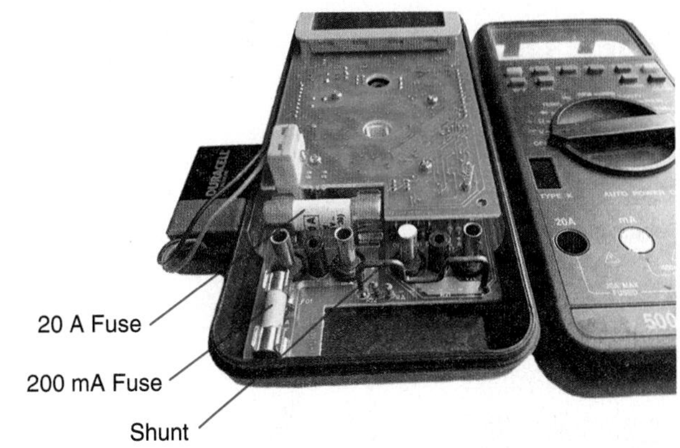

FIGURE 11-8 An ammeter shunt allows most of the current to pass through the shunt while allowing some small amount of current into the meter's measurement mechanism.

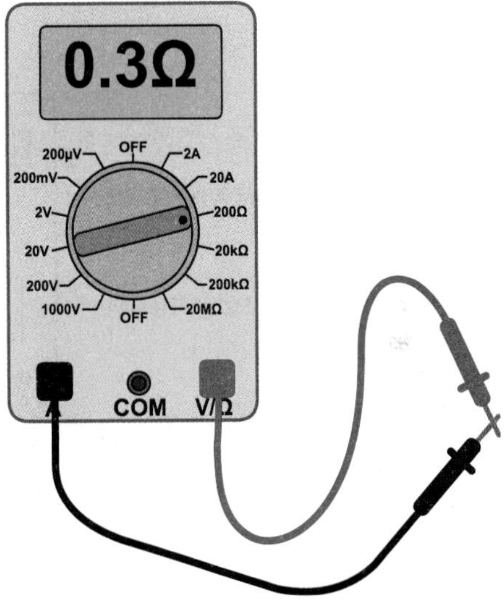

FIGURE 11-9 Checking the ammeter shunts should show continuity between the volts/ohm/amp red and amperage lead ports.

▶ TECHNICIAN TIP

When making measurements, and performing diagnostic tests with auto-ranging meters, the display may change continuously for some time until the correct range is established. If the measured value changes or test lead probes move too much, the meter may begin to auto-range once again. The process can lead to incorrect results if measurements are taken too quickly. Using the peak and hold feature or auto-hold will help to produce more accurate values. Otherwise, more patience and care is required when using these meters.

Meter Shunts

Before using a digital meter, one of the first things to check is whether its shunts or fuses are in place and functioning. Shunts are internal conductors with a small calibrated resistance, which directs some current flow into the meter when measuring amperage (**FIGURE 11-8**).

Almost all circuit current will pass through meter shunt, but some resistance is needed to send current into the measuring circuits of the meter. Shunts operate like fuses and have a maximum rating. A shunt should blow in an extremely short time if current exceeds the meter's capacity. If an ordinary fuse is used to replace a fast-blowing shunt, current will enter and damage the meter in the time it takes to open the ordinary fuse.

Shunts are checked by inserting the positive lead probe, while in the volt/ohm port, into the amperage probe port (**FIGURE 11-9**).

A meter set to check continuity or resistance should display continuity and some resistance. If two amperage ports are used on a meter, the larger amperage shunt will have a higher resistance than the low-amperage shunt. To check meter shunts, follow the steps in **SKILL DRILL 11-1**.

▶ Electrical Measurement with Multimeters

K11002, S11002

Multimeters are versatile instruments that allow the technician to take a variety of measurements. Three types of

SKILL DRILL 11-1 Checking Meter Shunts

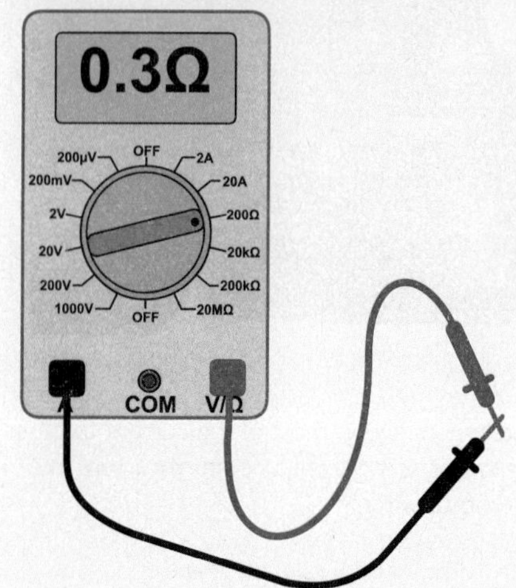

1. Plug test lead in volts/ohms input.
2. Select ohms' range.
3. Insert probe tip into mA input and read value. A small amount of resistance should be noted when probing the amperage inputs with the positive volt/ohm probe.
4. Insert probe tip into Amp input and read value. It should have a larger amount of resistance than the mA input.

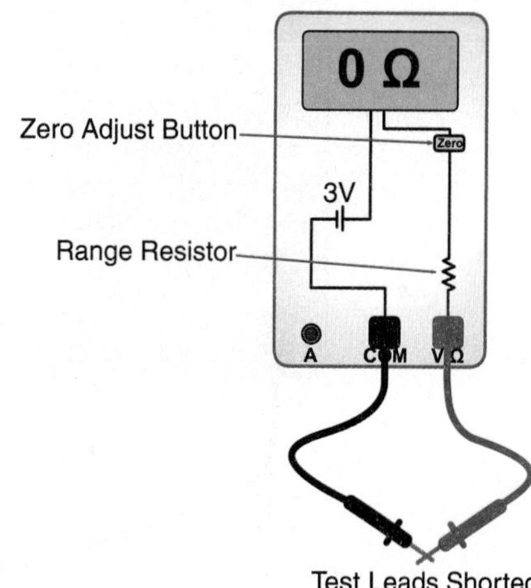

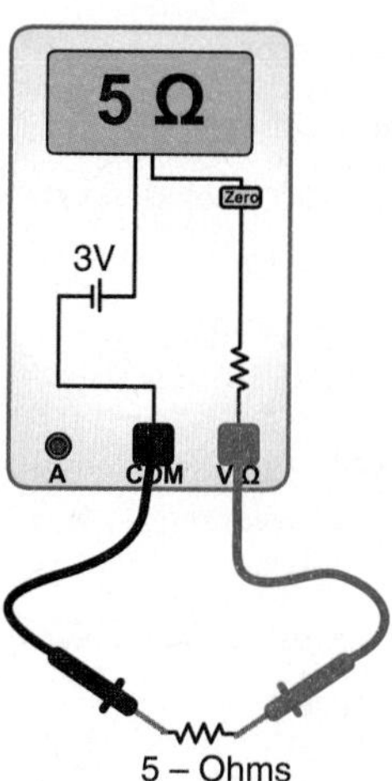

FIGURE 11-10 Ohmmeters use a small amount of current supplied by a battery to measure resistance. Voltage through the circuit is actually measured by the meter, which is reported in ohms. Voltage is proportional to circuit resistance.

measurements—voltage, resistance, and amperage—can be taken from circuits in three different ways. Understanding them is necessary to prevent meter damage and ensure accurate measurements.

Measuring Resistance—Ohmmeters

Measuring resistance is one of the most common functions of a multimeter, and many electrical diagnoses are made using an ohmmeter. By checking the resistance or circuit continuity with an ohmmeter, a circuit can be evaluated for shorts, opens, or high resistance. An ohmmeter uses a small amount of electrical current from an internal battery and sends it through a circuit or component.

The amount of current that flows through the component or circuit will depend on the circuit's resistance (**FIGURE 11-10**).

If the return current is high, the circuit resistance is low, and if the return current is low, the circuit resistance is high. Ranging the meter is done by using resistors to change the amount of current entering the circuit. This means that when selecting a meter range of higher resistance—for instance, 100 mega ohms rather than a 10-ohm scale—more current must leave the meter to pass through the highly resistive circuit (**FIGURE 11-11**).

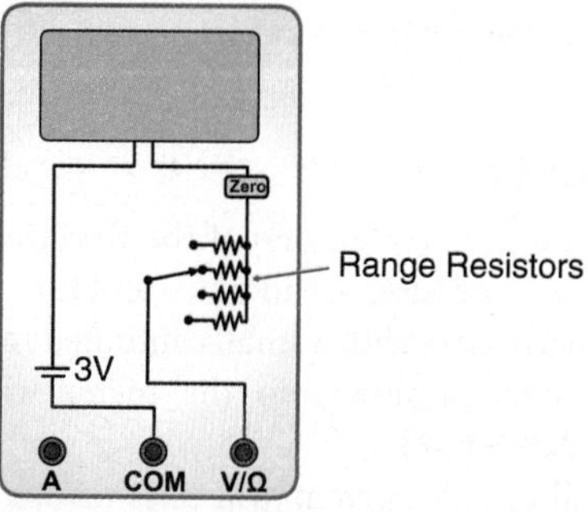

FIGURE 11-11 Manual or auto-ranging meters extend the range of the ohmmeter by substituting different resistances in series with the internal power source.

Because ohmmeters are self-powered, it is critically important to remember that ohmmeters should never be connected to a powered circuit. Connecting an ohmmeter into a powered circuit will blow the fuse or battery in the meter or otherwise damage the meter. Semiconductor circuits and sensors should not be checked with an ohmmeter, as the meter current may damage the device (**FIGURE 11-12**).

Ohmmeters are ineffective when checking for resistances in high-amperage, low-resistance circuits, such as when measuring battery cable voltage loss. Measuring voltage drop with a voltmeter when a circuit is operating is a more effective way of measuring resistances (**FIGURE 11-13**).

When measuring with an ohmmeter, it is important to observe how a meter displays in infinite resistance or an open circuit. Some meters will display either a 1 or 0 to indicate an open circuit (**FIGURE 11-14**).

It is important to understand also the range that the display is reporting. Million, thousand, and hundred are common ranges for an ohmmeter, and the displayed value may need to be multiplied by multimeter range.

When using an ohmmeter:

- The circuit must never be powered.
- The meter is connected in parallel across the circuit or component to measure the voltage dropped by the circuit resistance.
- It is not necessary to observe polarity when connecting test leads.

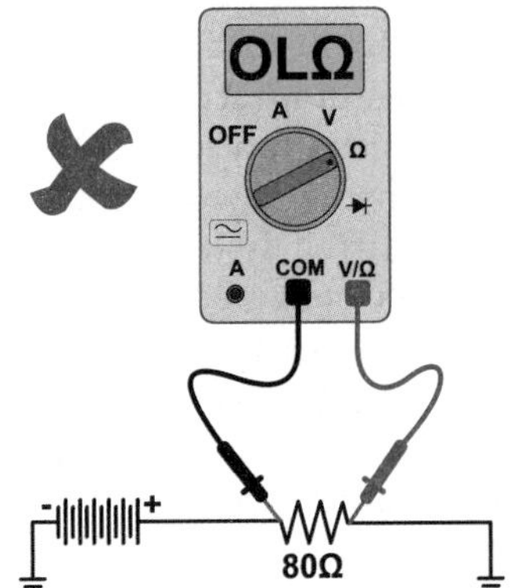

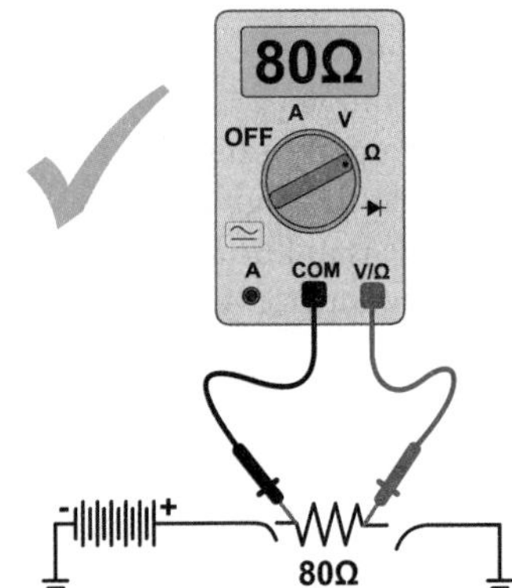

FIGURE 11-12 Because ohmmeters indirectly measure voltage, it is critical to remove power from a circuit before connecting the meter. Meter damage will occur otherwise.

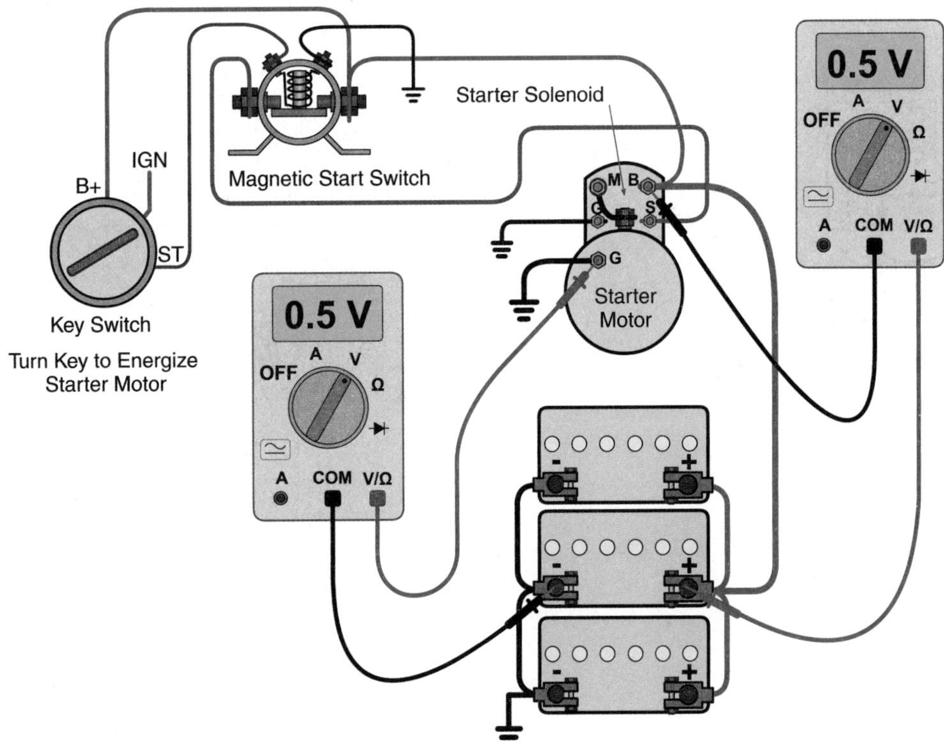

FIGURE 11-13 A voltmeter is best used to check for resistance in high-amperage circuits. Excessive voltage drop means the circuit has excessive resistance.

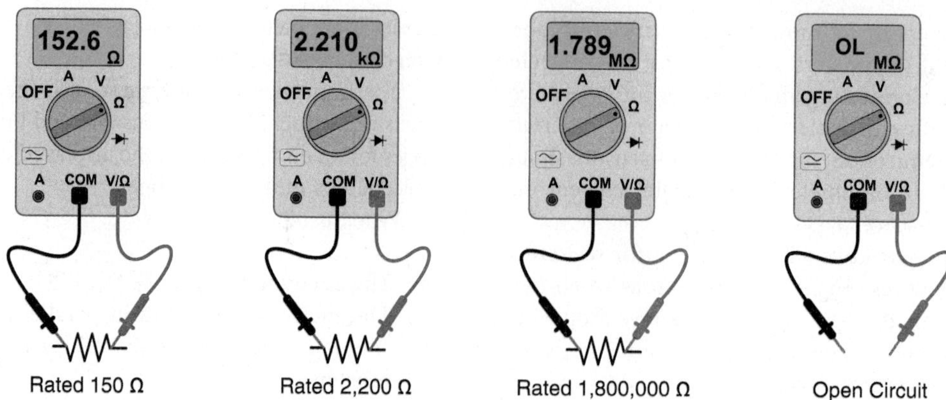

FIGURE 11-14 The ohmmeter display value may have to be multiplied to obtain the correct resistance value. On a 10k scale the number "1" would indicate a value multiplied by 10,000, meaning the actual value is 10,000 ohms.

- The positive test lead is connected to the ohms port and the negative lead to the common port of the meter.
- The meter needs to be properly ranged if not using an auto-ranging meter. Start at the highest range values and work down if the resistance is unknown.
- Not to be used with semiconductors and potentially inaccurate when testing diodes.

Measuring Voltage—Voltmeters

Voltmeters measure the difference in electrical pressure between two different points in the circuit (**FIGURE 11-15**).

Using a voltmeter is similar to measuring a pressure drop between two points. When measuring volts, the meter should be connected in parallel with the voltage source (**FIGURE 11-16**).

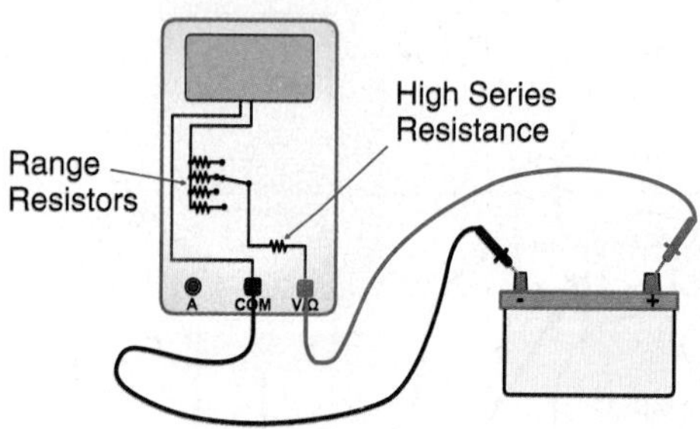

FIGURE 11-15 Only a small amount of current actually enters the voltmeter. Voltmeters with high internal resistance are called high-impedance meters.

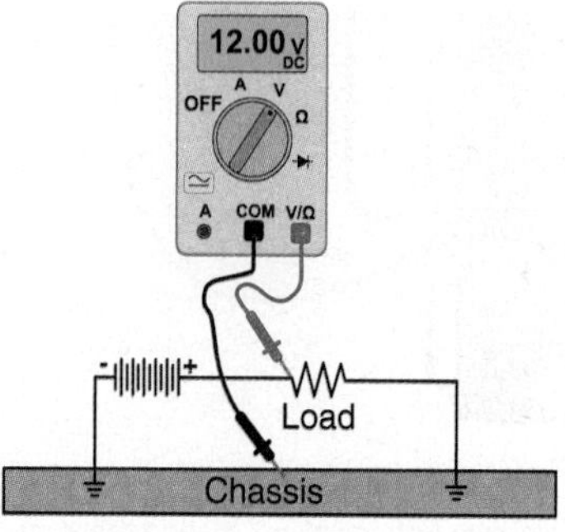

FIGURE 11-16 Voltmeters are connected in parallel in a circuit.

On mobile off-road equipment, you would commonly measure voltage drops across loads, determining whether there is sufficient voltage to a component, or measure sensor supply voltages. In any of these cases, the meter would be set to its 20 volts for 12-volt systems or 40 volts for 24-volt systems. Auto-ranging meters are set to the DC volts scale.

The positive meter lead probe is inserted into the volt-ohms port and the negative to the common port (**FIGURE 11-17**).

If the circuit polarity is not correctly observed (i.e., the negative probe is connected to the positive side of the circuit and vice versa), digital meters will show a negative volts symbol.

Best practices to use when measuring voltage include:

- Connecting the voltmeter in parallel with the circuit
- Observing polarity when measuring DC volts but not AC voltage (**FIGURE 11-18**)
- Ranging AC and DC volts separately
- When not using an auto-range meter, selecting the first voltage scale that is higher than the anticipated voltage; if unknown, starting at the highest scale
- Connecting the positive lead to volts/ohms port and the negative lead to common port
- Ensuring that the circuit is powered.

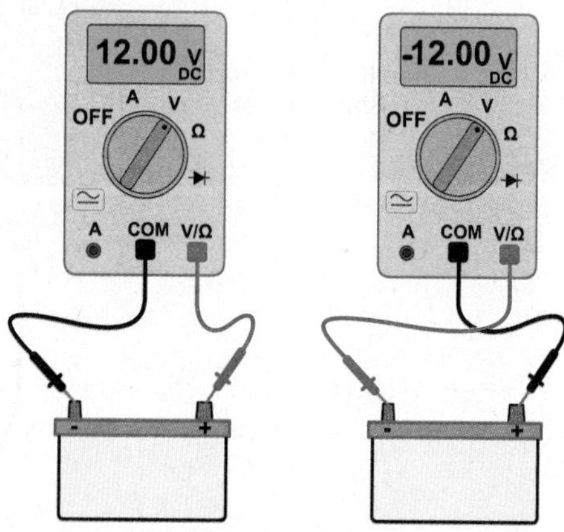

FIGURE 11-17 When connecting a voltmeter, the polarity of the meter and circuit should match. A polarity indicator uses electron theory and will show a meter is connected incorrectly to a circuit.

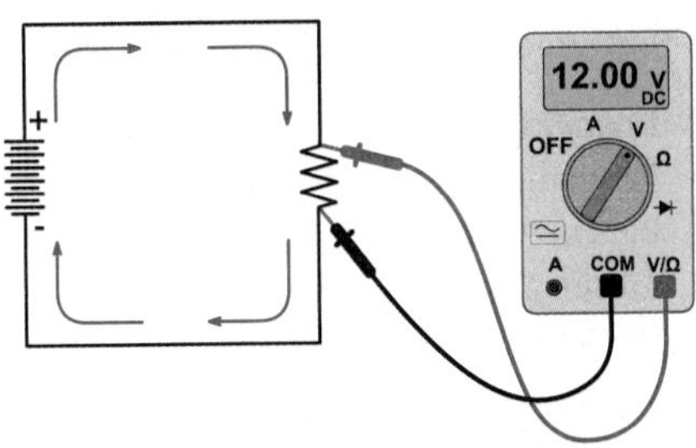

When measuring DC volts, the meter must be connected to the circuit with the correct polarity or the meter reading will be incorrect.

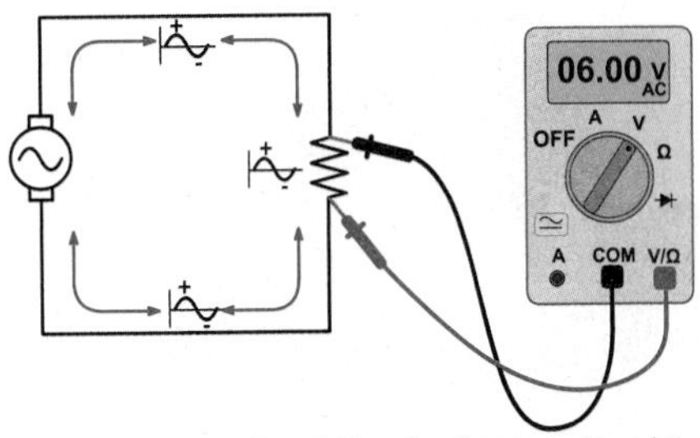

When measuring AC volts, the polarity of the meter to the circuit is unimportant and will not affect the meter reading.

FIGURE 11-18 Polarity does not need to be observed when measuring AC voltage.

TABLE 11-2 Multimeter Features to Protect Meter and User

Risk	Protection
Electrical arcing from transients high voltage sources (lightning, load switching)	Independent certification to meet CAT III-1000 V and CAT IV-600 V or higher
Voltage damage to meter while in continuity or resistance ranges	Overload protection in ohms up to the meter's volt rating.
Measuring voltage with test leads in amperage inputs	Fast blowing, high energy fuses rated to the meter's voltage rating. Use induction clamps to measure amperage
Shock from accidental contact with live components	Double insulated test leads, recessed and/or shrouded with finger guards

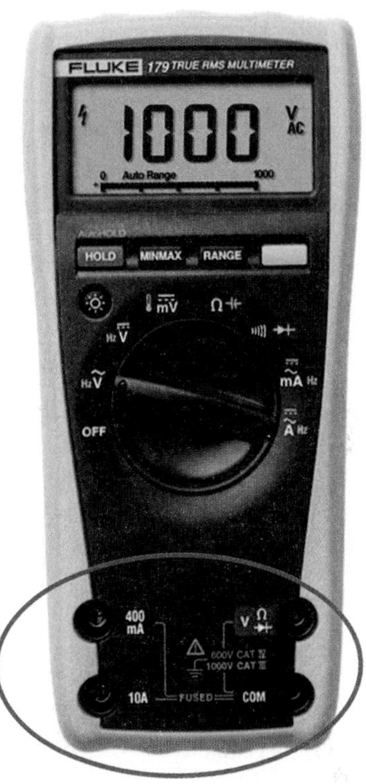

FIGURE 11-19 This meter has a safety rating of CAT III at 600 volts and CAT IV at 1,000 volts.

Voltmeters commonly include several protections against damage and safety risks (**TABLE 11-2**).

SAFETY TIP

Multimeters can and do blow up, causing personal injury and equipment damage. Safety features—such as using PTC thermistors in the ohmmeter, which become highly resistive when heated—are built into meters to limit damage to the meter. Voltage circuits are capacitive coupled, eliminating a direct connection to meter circuits. Low-impedance ammeters use **shunts** that blow when overloaded. Double insulation of meters, shrouded connectors, and the use of finger guards are other safety features. Check meters before using to see that insulation is not melted, cut, or cracked. Connectors and leads should not show any damage, such as insulation pulled away from end connectors. Probe tips should not be loose or broken off. Make sure the meter is safe for the application in which it is being used. IEC 61010 is a safety standard that establishes safety limits for meters. A Cat I meter in this standard, which is satisfactory for most technicians, should not be used to check voltages above 600 volts continuous, or 2,500 volts at peak. The top-rated CAT III meter can operate with 1,000 volts continuous and 8,000 volts transient peak (**FIGURE 11-19**).

Measuring Amperage—Ammeters

Ammeters measure the quantity of electrons flowing through a circuit per second of time. Amperage is the volume aspect of current flow, and voltage is the pressure of electrical flow. Measuring amperage requires that the circuit be broken and the meter placed in series with the circuit so that all the current flows through the meter shunts. See **FIGURE 11-20** and **FIGURE 11-21**.

Because all circuit current flows through the meter, the meter should never be connected to a current source in parallel, as it is the equivalent of shorting out a circuit. Two ports for the positive leads are commonly used to measure low amperage—milliamps, and amperage above 1 amp. Failure to move meter leads from low- to high-amperage ports will blow the meter shunt and may even damage the meter.

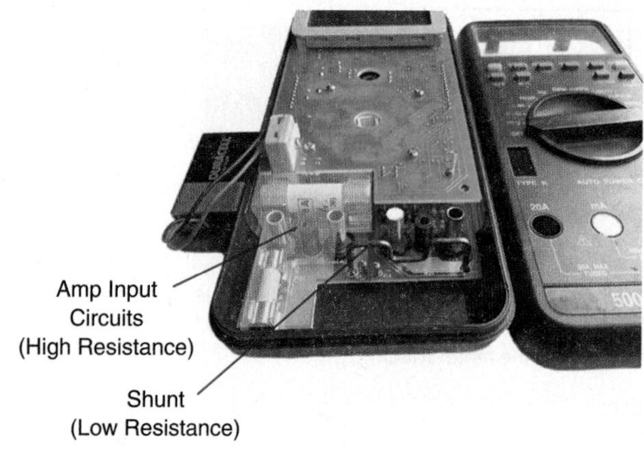

FIGURE 11-20 Ammeters use shunts that allow most circuit current to pass through the shunt rather than the meter.

Best practices to use when measuring amperage include:

- Ensuring that the circuit is powered.
- Ensuring that the ammeter is connected in series, causing all the current in the circuit to flow through the meter shunts.
- Observing polarity when measuring DC amperage (**FIGURE 11-22**).
- Choosing the correct shunt or port in the meter for connecting leads based on anticipated amperage. The common port is used for the negative lead, and A, mA and uA are used for the positive lead (**FIGURE 11-23**).
- When not using an auto-range meter, selecting the first amperage scale that is higher than the anticipated amperage; if unknown, start at the highest scale.
- When measuring more than 10 amps of current, use an inductive-type probe or dedicated amp clamp.

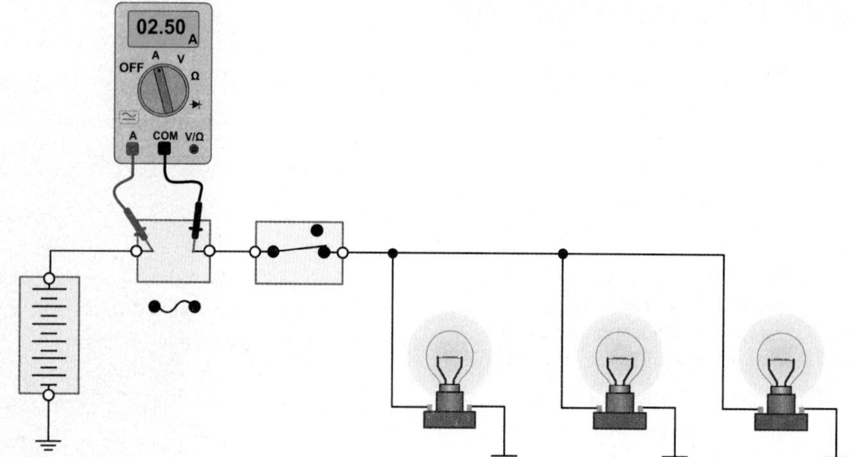

FIGURE 11-21 Connecting an ammeter in series to measure amperage.

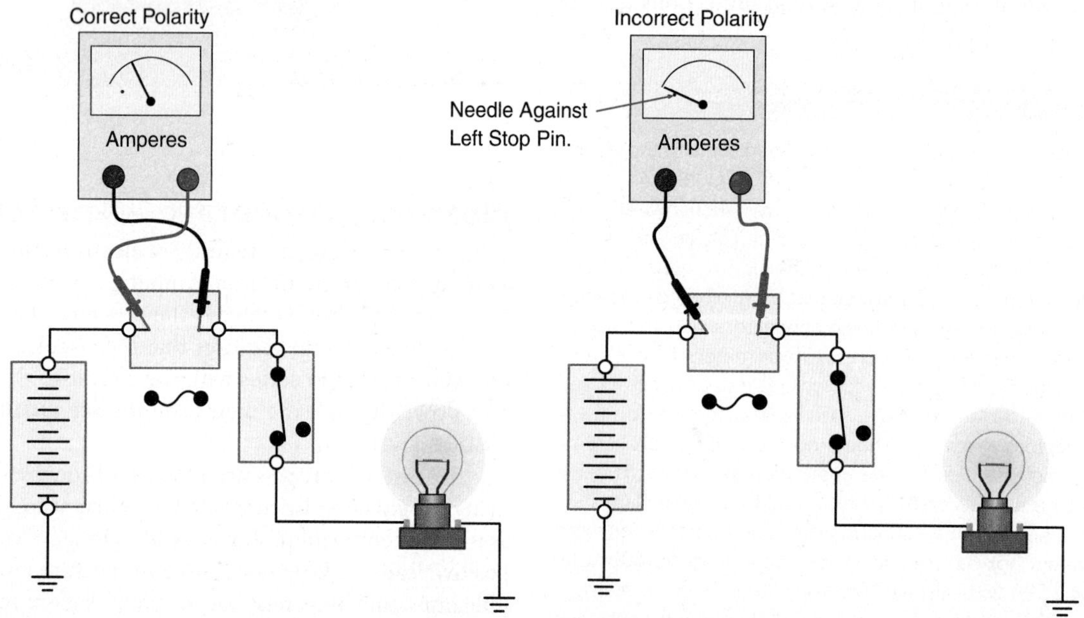

FIGURE 11-22 Ammeters require connection using correct polarity as noted using this analog ammeter. Digital meters will indicate the polarity is incorrect.

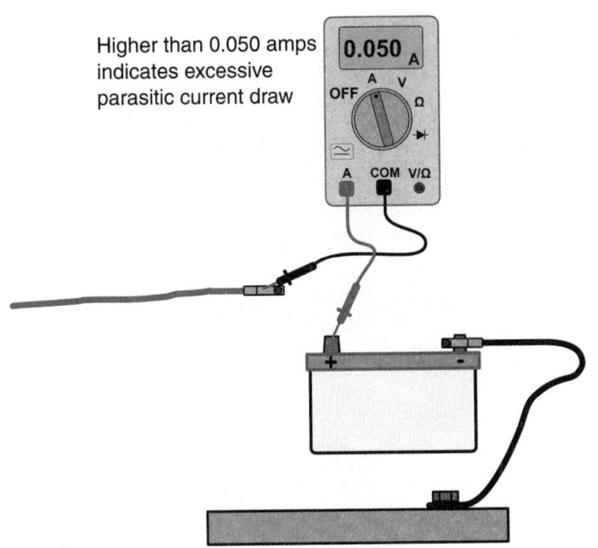

FIGURE 11-23 Connecting an ammeter in series to measure parasitic current draw that can drain a battery.

Inductive Amp Clamps

In powered circuits, **inductive amp clamps** placed around a conductor are used to measure amperage. These devices work by measuring a conductor's magnetic field strength, which is proportional to amperage (**FIGURE 11-24**).

While using an amp clamp, an electrical circuit does not need to be disturbed by connecting a meter in series.

Two types of amp or inductive clamps are used, which are connected to the voltage/common ports of a multimeter.

- Measuring AC only
- Measuring both DC and AC (**TABLE 11-3**)

Clamps that measure AC current use a current transformer built into the pickup. The alternating current passing through a conductor produces a magnetic field, which induces voltage through mutual induction into transformer windings. Using a specific turn ratio in the transformer, such as 1,000:1, voltage induced inside the transformer is calculated as a value for amperage. These clamps typically generate 1 millivolt per measured amp, which can be measured by the multimeter. DC clamps use Hall-effect technology. Hall-effect material found in these sensors changes their electrical resistance based on the strength of a magnetic field.

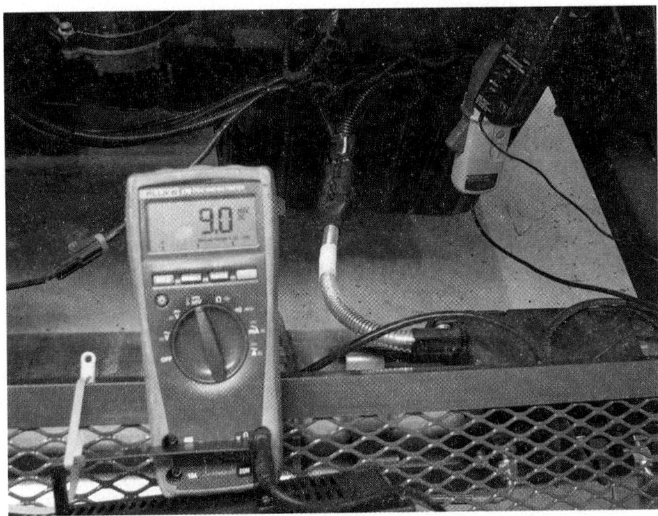

FIGURE 11-24 An inductive amp clamp measures the strength of the magnetic field around a conductor using a Hall-effect sensor. Magnetic field strength is proportional to amperage.

TABLE 11-3 Differences Between Features of an AC and an AC/DC Self-Contained Induction Clamp

Feature	AC	AC/DC
Output current	Current	Voltage
Scale factor	1 milliAmp per Amp	1 milliVolt per Amp
Sensor	Current transfer	Hall effect
Battery	No	Yes

Measuring Temperature

Multimeters use a thermocouple accessory to measure temperature by contact. Heating the thermocouple produces voltage proportional to temperature. **Type K thermocouples** are low-cost, general-purpose, temperature-sensing elements and are connected to the same meter terminals for measuring DC millivolts. Internal meter circuits convert the voltage measurements into a temperature reading.

Diode Scale

The low-voltage settings of an ohmmeter may not properly evaluate a diode, as a good silicon diode requires approximately 0.5–0.7 volt to forward bias or conduct current. Below this voltage, the diode may appear to block current in both directions. When placed in the diode range, a meter will put out higher voltage than the barrier voltage of 0.7 volt, to cause the diode to reverse and forward bias.

▶ Circuit Tracers

K11003

Circuit tracers, also called **wire tracers**, are electronic service tools used to trace a single wire over a distance where multiple wires are bundled, shorted, or open. Telephone companies once commonly used these to help field technicians locate problematic phone circuits. These units can identify wires deeply buried behind walls or in tightly bundled harness.

Several methods are used to identify circuit problems. Commonly though, one part of the signal tracing unit is clipped to a suspect wire and ground. When switched on, the unit injects a strong, two-tone square wave radio signal into the wire. The receivers consist of a sensitive radio with an audio amplifier and speaker. Slowly waving this device over a group of wires will detect where a conductor is located and where it ends. See **FIGURE 11-25** and **FIGURE 11-26**.

FIGURE 11-25 Using the circuit tracers after connecting the signal generator to a defective circuit.

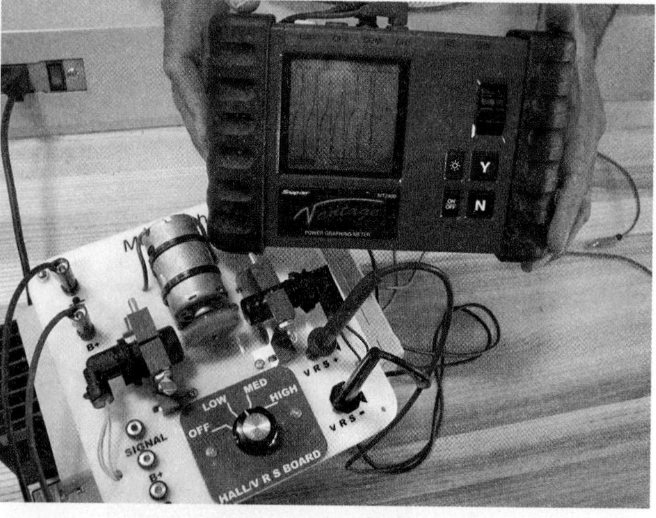

FIGURE 11-27 A graph of a pulse-width-modulated signal waveform obtained using a graphing meter.

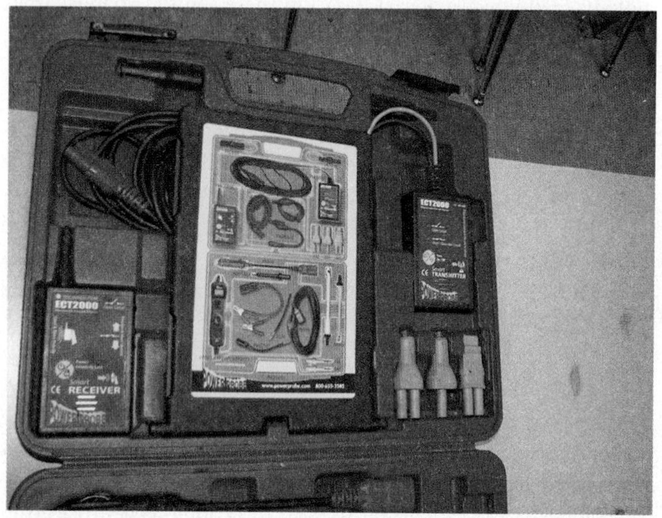

FIGURE 11-26 The transmitter and receiver of a circuit tracer used to trace electrical wires for open and short circuits.

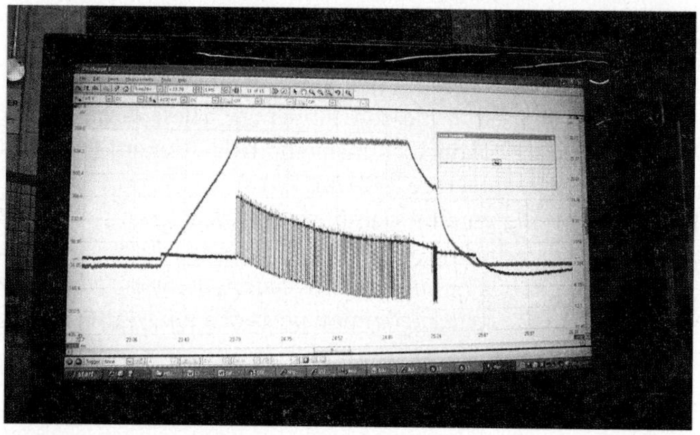

FIGURE 11-28 A graphical display of the electrical signal supplied to an injector using a Picoscope. Two channels measure voltage – blue trace, and amperage – red trace.

The intensity of the sound produced by the signal or the flickering of an LED light varies with proximity to the wire. The probe's tip is insulated for safety purposes.

▶ Graphing Meters and Oscilloscopes

KI1004

One of the latest diagnostic tools is a digital **graphing meter** used to analyze electrical waveforms produced by sensors, motors, actuators, and alternators. These test instruments plot an electrical value of a signal over time, displaying an easy-to-read graph with time on the x-axis and the signal value on the y-axis (**FIGURE 11-27**).

Component serviceability can be determined by analyzing the waveform or comparing it to known signals of good quality (**FIGURE 11-28**).

Component serviceability can be determined by analyzing the waveform or by comparing it to known signals of good quality. For example, a Hall-effect sensor may have intermittent problems that may not be detected by the machine's onboard diagnostic system. A faster-sampling graphing meter is better suited to detect a problem like this.

The life expectancy of an electric motor is another example of a component that can be evaluated by examining the small changes in current and voltage spikes caused by worn brushes. Scanners and OEM diagnostic software can also graph values captured by the ECM associated with a machine system, such as engine, transmission, hydraulic system, or body control, through the diagnostic connector. Dedicated graphing meters connect directly to a sensor, circuit, or component that requires testing. Whereas a single-channel graphing meter has only one input, two-, three-, and four-channel units have as many inputs and can graph the values together or on separate screens for comparative purposes. Oscilloscopes have more elaborate display modes to capture one-off signal glitches or jitter. Selectable signal triggers, sources, display rulers, slope measurement, and a wider variety of display options are also available with oscilloscopes.

When performing electrical circuit diagnostics, purpose-made jumper wires, fused jumper wires, and breakout boxes are helpful for quickly and effectively diagnosing problems without damaging wiring or connectors by back-probing or piercing wires (**FIGURE 11-29**).

A breakout box is connected in series with a major component or wiring harness to an ECM. Signals on each wire in the harness will correspond to a pin on the breakout box (**FIGURE 11-30**).

FIGURE 11-29 Terminal test kit for specific terminal types that will not damage wires or connectors while testing.

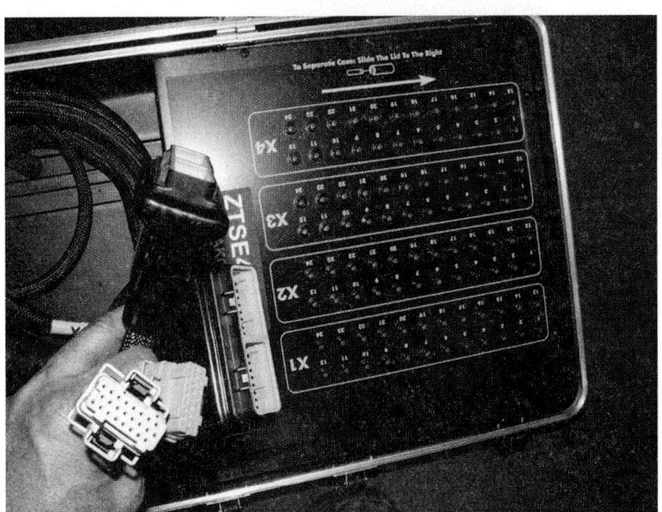

FIGURE 11-30 A breakout box with two matched connectors, female and male, connect in series to major wiring harnesses to perform pin-point diagnostic tests.

OEM templates, which are thin plastic sheets with printed numbers or letters, can be obtained to lay over the pins, helping to identify specific pin functions or circuit numbers. Smaller breakout harnesses, which connect to sensors or special wiring harnesses, are also useful to make pinpoint tests of circuits required by diagnostic procedures (**FIGURE 11-31**).

▶ Electronic Service Tools

K11005

A variety of OEM diagnostic software types are available and are used to read serial data from a machine data link connector. Most OEM diagnostic software is designed to run on a personal computer (PC) under Microsoft® Windows™ and, along with a data link adapter, the software can translate the serial data into a format that can be read by the technician. More sophisticated OEM diagnostic software uses bidirectional communication between the PC, communication adapter, and the machines ECM to send commands that can actuate output devices or cause the ECM to enter diagnostic routines such as performing cylinder cutout tests, solenoid function tests, and more.

SAE Requirements for Onboard Diagnostics

The SAE has developed onboard diagnostic (OBD) standards that most OEM diagnostic software use. These standards include the following:

1. Standards for 6- and 9-pin DLC connectors
2. J1978—describes the basic functions that an OBD scanner must support, including these:
   - Automatic hands-off determination of the communication protocol

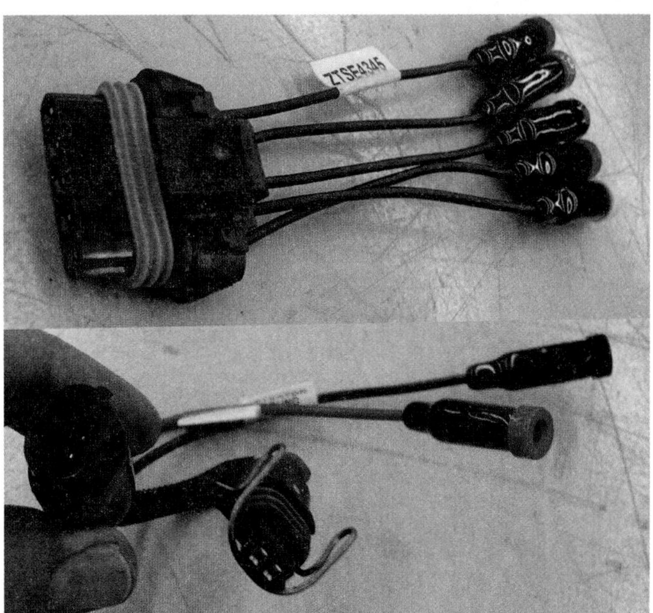

FIGURE 11-31 Purpose made jumper wires with terminal ends matching specific types of connector terminals are used to perform pin-point tests of voltage, amperage, and resistance.

- Obtaining and displaying the status of OBD evaluations such as supported and completed readiness or monitor tests and lamp MIL lamp status
- Obtaining and displaying diagnostic trouble codes (DTCs)
- Obtaining and displaying emissions-related data from engine parameters
- Obtaining and displaying emissions-related freeze frame data
- Clearing stored emissions-related DTCs, freeze frame data, and diagnostic test results.

3. J1979-02—describes diagnostic test modes for emission-related diagnostic data that can be displayed, including the following:
    - Request for current powertrain diagnostic data including engine parameters, MIL status, and readiness codes
    - Request for powertrain freeze frame data
    - Request emission-related powertrain DTCs
    - Clear/reset emission-related diagnostic information including MIL status, DTCs, freeze frame, and readiness codes
    - Request exhaust gas sensor monitor test results
    - Request latest onboard monitoring test results for noncontinuous monitor systems (i.e., after treatment catalysts, exhaust gas recirculation [EGR], misfire, etc.).
    - Request latest onboard monitoring test results for continuous monitor systems (i.e., comprehensive component monitor)
    - Can be used to request control of an onboard system and is manufacturer defined
    - This optional mode used to report machine information such as the serial number and possibly calibration information stored in the machine ECM
    - A display screen listing fault codes.

Additional OEM Diagnostic Software Functions

OEM diagnostic software can perform a variety of additional functions:

- *Bidirectional control*—can control selected equipment components or initiate systems actuator or diagnostic tests on command.
- *Graphical display*—can display real-time engine parameters or recorded data in a graphing format.
- *Help menu/trouble code library*—can guide a technician through certain procedures or has a built-in library of all the trouble codes.
- *Printer/Computer output*—connect to a printer or computer and prints or displays information from the machine.
- *Record/playback or snapshot mode*—can record a block of real-time machine system data and replay that information to assist in finding the root cause of a malfunction.
- *Reprogramming of machine ECM*—can perform off-board or onboard reprogramming of a machine's computer modules, specially the powertrain (ECM).
- *Scopes and meters*—can operate as a multimeter (measuring voltage, resistance, amperage, etc.).

Data Link Adapters

Data link adapters are used to translate serial data from the DLC into a format readable by a desktop or laptop computer. The adapter may connect to the PC using a cable connected to a serial port, USB port, or wirelessly over the Internet or Bluetooth communication (**FIGURE 11-32**).

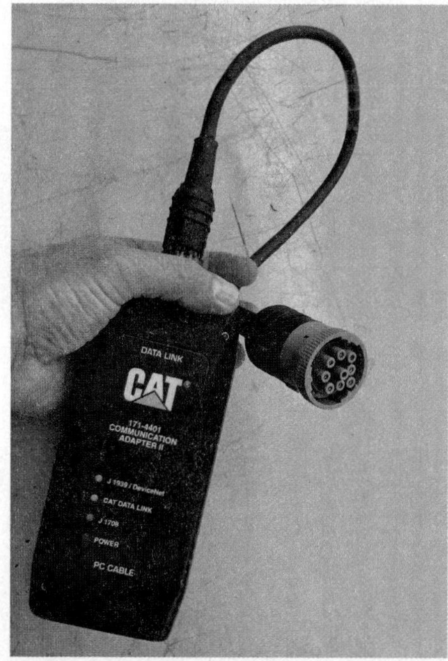

FIGURE 11-32 This data link adapter connected to the machine data link can translate DLC serial data into serial data readable by PCs or laptops. The adapter can communicate using a cable or with another adapter wirelessly over the same radio frequency as wireless Internet, or by using Bluetooth radio frequencies.

Wrap-Up

Ready for Review

- A variety of electrical test instruments are needed to diagnose and repair electrical problems.
- The simplest piece of electrical test equipment used to determine the presence or absence of current is a test light.
- Self-powered test lights are like regular test lights except that they contain a 1.5-volt battery.
- Multimeters are electrical measuring instruments combining functions of at least voltage, resistance, and amperage measurement into a single compact instrument.
- Multimeters can be analog, digital, or high impedance and come in auto-ranging and manual-ranging types.
- Before using a digital meter, one of the first things to check is whether its shunts or fuses are in place and functioning. Shunts are internal conductors with a small calibrated resistance, which directs some current flow into the meter when measuring amperage.
- By checking the resistance or circuit continuity with an ohmmeter, a circuit can be evaluated for shorts, opens, or high resistance.
- Ohmmeters are ineffective when checking for resistances in high-amperage, low-resistance circuits, such as when measuring battery cable voltage loss.
- Voltmeters measure the difference in electrical pressure or electron velocity between two different points in the circuit.
- Measuring amperage requires that the powered circuit be opened and the meter placed in series with the circuit so that all the current flows through the meter shunts.
- Inductive amp clamps are useful tools for measuring amperage without disturbing the circuit.
- Multimeters use a thermocouple accessory to measure temperature by contact. Heating the thermocouple produces voltage proportional to temperature.
- Circuit tracers are useful for identifying circuit problems in wires deeply buried behind walls or in tightly bundled harness.
- Graphing meters allow technicians to assess component serviceability by analyzing the waveforms.
- When performing electrical circuit diagnostics, purpose-made jumper wires, fused jumper wires, and breakout boxes are helpful for quickly and effectively diagnosing problems without damaging wiring or connectors by back-probing or piercing wires.
- A variety of OEM diagnostic software types are used to read serial data from a machine data link connector.

Key Terms

analog meter A meter that uses a sweeping needle that continuously measures electrical values.

auto-ranging multimeter A multimeter that has fewer positions on its range selection knob and will automatically select the correct range when meter test leads are connected to a circuit.

circuit (wire) tracer An electronic service tool used to trace a single wire over a distance where multiple wires are bundled, shorted, or open.

data link adapter A device used to translate serial data from the DLC into a format readable by a desktop or laptop computer.

graphing meter An electrical test instrument used to analyze waveforms and graphically plot an electrical value of a signal over time.

high-impedance multimeter A meter that samples very little of a circuit's own current to take a measurement.

inductive amp clamp A device that measures amperage by measuring a conductor's magnetic field strength, which is proportional to amperage.

manual-ranging multimeter A multimeter that must first be set to the correct range based on anticipated values measured.

shunts Internal conductors with small calibrated resistance and that direct current flow into the meter while measuring amperage.

test light The simplest piece of electrical test equipment, which consists of either a 12- or 24-volt incandescent lightbulb connected to an insulated lead and a sharpened metal probe.

type K thermocouple A low-cost, general-purpose, temperature-sensing element connected to the same meter terminals for measuring DC millivolts.

Review Questions

1. Which of the following statements about self-powered test lights is correct?
   a. Self-powered test lights are like regular test lights except that they contain a 1.5-volt battery.
   b. Self-powered lights can be used to check for both open circuits and grounded circuits when either chassis power or ground is removed from the circuit.
   c. The internal battery can supply current needed to illuminate the light.
   d. All of the choices are correct.
2. What is the usual capability of a multimeter to measure current flow in amps?
   a. 5 amps
   b. 10 amps
   c. 15 amps
   d. 20 amps
3. Which of the following is *not* correct concerning electrical measurement with multimeters?
   a. Three types of measurements—voltage, resistance, and amperage—can be taken from circuits in three different ways.
   b. An ohmmeter uses a small amount of electrical current from an internal battery and sends it through a circuit or component.

c. The circuit must never be powered when connected to an ohmmeter.
d. When using an ohmmeter, it is necessary to observe polarity when connecting test leads.

4. When using a manual-ranging multimeter, what range setting should be selected to measure 12 volts?
   a. 12 volt
   b. 18 volt
   c. 20 volt
   d. 24 volt
5. Which of the following statements about inductive amp clamps is correct?
   a. In powered circuits, inductive amp clamps placed around a conductor are used to measure amperage.
   b. These devices work by measuring a conductor's magnetic field strength, which is proportional to amperage.
   c. Both A and B
   d. Neither A nor B
6. Type K thermocouples are a(n) __________ temperature-sensing element.
   a. high-cost
   b. inefficient
   c. general-purpose
   d. rudimentary
7. Which of the following statements about the diode scale is correct?
   a. The low-voltage settings of an ohmmeter may not properly evaluate a diode, as a good silicon diode requires approximately 0.5–0.7 volt to forward bias or conduct current.
   b. Below 0.5–0.7 volt, the diode may appear to block current in both directions; when placed in the diode range, a meter will put out higher voltage than barrier voltage of 0.7 volt to cause the diode to reverse and forward bias.
   c. Both A and B
   d. Neither A nor B
8. Which of the following statements about graphing meters is *not* correct?
   a. One of the latest diagnostic tools is a digital graphing meter used to analyze electrical waveforms produced by sensors, motors, actuators, and alternators.
   b. Graphing meters plot an electrical value of a signal over time, displaying an easy-to-read graph with signal value on the x-axis and the time on the y-axis.
   c. Component serviceability can be determined by analyzing the waveform or comparing it to known signals of good quality.
   d. A Hall-effect sensor may have intermittent problems that may not be detected by the machine's onboard diagnostic system.
9. Which of the following statements about OEM diagnostic software is correct?
   a. A variety of OEM diagnostic software types are used to read serial data from a machine data link connector.
   b. The OEM diagnostic software is used to translate the serial data into a format that can be read by the technician.
   c. More sophisticated OEM diagnostic software uses bidirectional communication between the tool and the ECM to send commands that can actuate output devices or cause the ECM to enter diagnostic routines such as performing cylinder cutout tests.
   d. All of the choices are correct.
10. Which of the following is included in the SAE J1978 requirements?
    a. Obtaining and displaying diagnostic trouble codes (DTCs)
    b. Obtaining and displaying emissions-related data from engine parameters
    c. Both A and B
    d. Neither A nor B

ASE Technician A/Technician B Style Questions

1. Technician A says that self-powered test lights are like regular test lights except that they contain a 1.5-volt battery. Technician B says that self-powered test lights have to use the machine's battery power to function. Who is correct?
   a. Technician A
   b. Technician B
   c. Both Technician A and Technician B
   d. Neither Technician A nor Technician B
2. Technician A says that a popular type of LED test light is battery powered and has two LEDs—one red and the other green. Technician B says that the LED light will change brightness depending on the circuit's voltage. Who is correct?
   a. Technician A
   b. Technician B
   c. Both Technician A and Technician B
   d. Neither Technician A nor Technician B
3. Technician A says that multimeters are electrical measuring instruments combining functions of at least voltage, resistance, and amperage measurement into a single compact instrument. Technician B says that digital multimeters are the most common category of multimeters and provide numerical displays of electrical data. Who is correct?
   a. Technician A
   b. Technician B
   c. Both Technician A and Technician B
   d. Neither Technician A nor Technician B
4. Technician A says that a multimeter measures resistance, continuity, voltage, and amperage. Technician B says that the multimeter can be used to measure circuit resistance in amps to determine whether amperage is within specifications. Who is correct?
   a. Technician A
   b. Technician B
   c. Both Technician A and Technician B
   d. Neither Technician A nor Technician B
5. Technician A says that before using a digital multimeter, the first task is to check that its shunts and fuses are in place and functioning. Technician B says that shunts do not

operate like fuses and do not have a maximum rating. Who is correct?

a. Technician A
b. Technician B
c. Both Technician A and Technician B
d. Neither Technician A nor Technician B

6. Technician A says that the multimeter is connected in series with the circuit or component to measure the voltage dropped by the circuit resistance. Technician B says that the ohmmeter works well in testing semiconductors. Who is correct?
   a. Technician A
   b. Technician B
   c. Both Technician A and Technician B
   d. Neither Technician A nor Technician B
7. Technician A says that ammeters measure the quantity of electrons flowing through a circuit per second of time. Technician B says that measuring amperage requires that the circuit be broken and the meter placed in series with the circuit so that all the current flows through the meter shunts. Who is correct?
   a. Technician A
   b. Technician B
   c. Both Technician A and Technician B
   d. Neither Technician A nor Technician B
8. Technician A says that multimeters use a thermocouple accessory to measure temperature by contact. Technician B says that heating the thermocouple produces amperage proportional to temperature. Who is correct?
   a. Technician A
   b. Technician B
   c. Both Technician A and Technician B
   d. Neither Technician A nor Technician B
9. Technician A says that circuit tracers, also called wire tracers, are electronic service tools used to trace a single wire over a distance where multiple wires are bundled, shorted, or open. Technician B says that circuit tracers can identify wires deeply buried behind walls or in tightly bundled harness. Who is correct?
   a. Technician A
   b. Technician B
   c. Both Technician A and Technician B
   d. Neither Technician A nor Technician B
10. Technician A says that OEM software, along with a data link adapter, can translate the serial data from the machine ECU into a format that can be read by the technician. Technician B says that the DLC adapter may connect to the PC using a cable connected to a serial port, USB port, or wirelessly over the Internet or Bluetooth communication. Who is correct?
    a. Technician A
    b. Technician B
    c. Both Technician A and Technician B
    d. Neither Technician A nor Technician B

CHAPTER 12
Batteries and Battery Services

Knowledge Objectives

After reading this chapter, you will be able to:

- **K12001** Describe the purpose and applications of batteries.
- **K12002** Identify and describe the construction and types of lead-acid batteries.
- **K12003** Identify and describe the features of lithium, nickel-cadmium, and nickel-metal hydride batteries as well as ultracapacitors.
- **K12004** Identify and describe the purpose, operation, and application of battery types.
- **K12005** Define battery terminology, and explain battery ratings.
- **K12006** Recommend the correct size, type, and rating of replacement batteries.
- **K12007** Identify and explain chemical reactions in lead-acid batteries during charging and discharging.
- **K12008** Identify and explain the operation of battery isolators, low-voltage disconnect devices, charge equalizers, and battery management systems.
- **K12009** Identify safety equipment and safe work practices for servicing batteries.
- **K12010** Identify and describe failure modes of batteries.
- **K12011** Recommend battery replacement based on battery testing procedures.
- **K12012** Identify and describe the process of battery recycling.

Skills Objectives

After reading this chapter, you will be able to:

- **S12001** Inspect, clean, fill, or replace the battery, battery cables, clamps, connectors, hold-downs, and battery boxes.
- **S12002** Perform a battery state of charge test.
- **S12003** Perform a conductance test on a battery.
- **S12004** Perform a load test on a battery.
- **S12005** Charge a commercial battery.
- **S12006** Jump-start a commercial vehicle.
- **S12007** Measure parasitic draw on a battery.
- **S12008** Identify and test a low-voltage disconnect.

Attitude Objectives

After reading this chapter, you will be able to:

- **A12001** Locate and follow correct safety procedures and use personal protection equipment when serving electric motors.
- **A12002** Acquire correct service information for testing and maintenance of batteries.

▶ Introduction

Batteries are the most essential component in a vehicle's electrical system. Not only do batteries provide starting power for engines and operating electrical accessories, they play a critical role in proper operation and longevity of many other electrical components. The recent development of medium- and heavy-duty hybrid-drive vehicles adds to the battery's list of jobs: in addition to their traditional functions, batteries must now supply energy to electric drive motors and help recover energy during braking. Today's technicians need to know more than ever about the various types of batteries they will encounter and how those batteries work, as well as how to maintain, test, and work safely with them.

▶ What Is a Battery?

K12001

Batteries are not devices that store electricity. In reality, they convert chemical energy into electrical energy, and vice versa. When connected to an electrical load such as a light or electric motor, chemical reactions taking place inside the battery force electrons from the negative to the positive terminal of the battery, through the load. Flow of electricity ends when the electrical loads in the circuit deplete the battery's chemical energy. The single direction in which electrons flow during discharge means a battery is a source of direct current (DC).

▶ Battery Classifications

K12004

The industry classifies batteries into two basic categories: primary and secondary. In a **primary battery**, chemical reactions are not reversible, and the battery cannot be recharged. In contrast, **secondary batteries** are rechargeable (**FIGURE 12-1**). By reversing the direction of current and pushing electricity back into the battery, the "galvanic" chemical reactions that originally produced electrical current renew, allowing the secondary battery to be used over and over again. Secondary batteries based on the principles of galvanic reaction are the most practical for use in heavy equipment applications because they can be used repeatedly. (Technically a **galvanic reaction** is where the battery generates electricity when two dissimilar metals are placed in an electrolyte.)

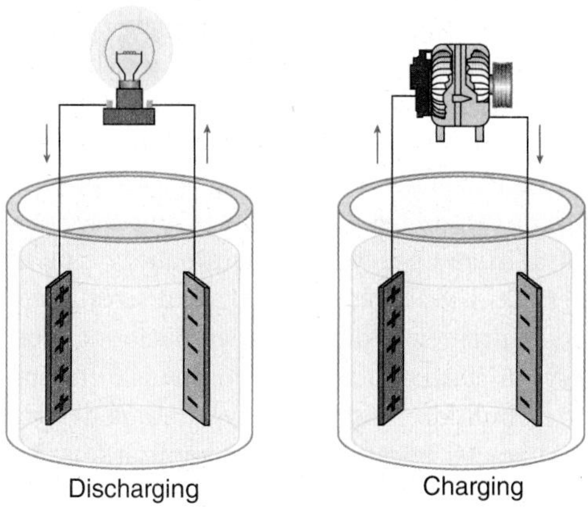

FIGURE 12-1 Secondary batteries can be repeatedly charged and discharged.

Galvanic Batteries

The term "battery" more accurately refers to a collection of electrochemical cells connected together. A medical experimenter named Galvani discovered more than two hundred years ago that two dissimilar metals placed in an electrolyte produce electricity. **Electrolyte** refers to any liquid that conducts electric current. For example, pure water does not conduct current. Tap water, however, does. That's because tap water often contains minerals and chlorine, which enable the movement of electronics, so tap water is an electrolyte. Water containing salt, acids, or alkaline substances is an even better conductor of electricity. The dissimilar metals placed in an electrolyte form electrodes, which are the points of the battery that create the positive and negative electrical poles. The chemical action between the electrolyte and electrodes strips electrons from one metal electrode and adds electrons to another electrode. This process develops the battery's polarity. After Galvani, another experimenter named Volta built the first battery when he alternately stacked copper and zinc plates separated with a piece of saltwater-soaked cardboard. Volta named it a "voltaic pile" after demonstrating its electrical properties.

You Are the Mobile Heavy Equipment Technician

As a technician with many years of service in your heavy equipment dealership, management has asked you to join the health and safety committee. Your experience working in a shop environment has made you conscious of the importance of using safe working practices and making workplace safety a top priority. One of the initiatives of the health and safety committee is implementing the best safety practices to use while working with batteries. In fact, development of an in-house policy in addition to OSHA requirements originates from a recent incident where an exploding battery injured one worker who was jump-starting a vehicle. As you consider the various procedures that your fellow workers should follow in the shop to avoid any accidents, injuries, or damage to customer vehicles and property, ask yourself:

1. What are the major safety issues related to working with batteries?
2. What protective equipment should we use when filling batteries or checking cell electrolyte with a hydrometer?
3. Can we outline a sequence of actions a technician should follow when jump-starting a vehicle?

A battery consists of two dissimilar metals: an insulator material separating the metals and an electrolyte, which is an electrically conductive solution. The material from which the electrodes are made and the type of electrolyte determine the voltage potential of a battery. The area of the plates making up each positive and negative electrode determines the capacity or amperage of a battery.

The traditional heavy equipment battery type is the lead-acid battery. It is available in a variety of sizes and designs to meet the requirements for various applications. For example, the battery for starting a vehicle's engine is different from the battery for a bulldozer. Each requires unique design and construction characteristics based on its applications. Batteries for having equipment using diesel engines supply high amperage to the starting motor for short periods of time. In contrast, a deep cycle battery's current is almost completely depleted, supplying smaller, continuous loads over longer periods of time.

▶ TECHNICIAN TIP

We can observe galvanic reactions in many places. Corrosion is one example of a galvanic reaction. The cooling system of an engine contains water (an electrolyte) and dissimilar metals like copper injector tubes, cast iron blocks, aluminum water pump housings, and so on. Metals losing electrons disintegrate while other metals remain unaffected. However, one can easily observe the electron transfer between the metals through coolant if you place a voltmeter with one lead in the coolant and the other on the engine block or other metal part. (Corrosion inhibitors in the cooling system work by minimizing the loss of electrons from metals.) Trailer manufacturers insulate aluminum side plates with a piece of nonconductive nylon or insulating tape to isolate the plate electrically from steel I-beams supporting the floor. For the same reason, when manufacturers place aluminum and steel disc wheels together on the same wheel end, they separate them with a plastic or nylon gasket to minimize the corrosion galvanic reactions cause.

Maintaining a strong negative ground on a vehicle minimizes chassis corrosion that galvanic reaction causes. You may notice most corrosion takes place at positive battery posts and at the end of non-insulated, positively charged wires. This happens because positively charged wire ends and battery posts are deficient of electrons. Oxygen and molecules in road salt are examples of substances that easily provide those electrons to electron-depleted metal and then bind electrically to positive terminals and wire ends. Some military equipment and off-road heavy equipment from Europe use a positive ground system to protect the exposed wiring on starters, alternators, and wiring harnesses from the effects of corrosion. Electrical system reliability is enhanced at the expense of chassis corrosion, which instead attacks large, heavy steel chassis components that can better withstand corrosion.

Because heavy equipment could have either a 12 V or 24 V system and all mobile equipment batteries are 12 V, this means that to power a 24 V system at least two batteries have to be connected together. You may find four or more batteries connected together on some machines. Therefore the term "battery system" is used. A battery system is needed for the following reasons:

1. To provide electrical energy to power electrical devices if the machine's engine is not running
2. To provide electrical energy to the starter to crank the engine
3. To provide electrical energy when the engine is running if the alternator can't satisfy electrical demand
4. To act like an accumulator to store and stabilize voltage

Thirty or 40 years ago, 6 V batteries were fairly common for heavy equipment electrical systems, but at least 99% of the machines today only use 12 V batteries. However, if the vehicle has more than one battery, it depends on how the batteries are connected as to how much voltage comes out of the battery system. Two 12 V batteries hooked in parallel (positive to positive and negative to negative) still produces 12 V, whereas two 12 V batteries connected in series produce 24 V. **FIGURE 12-2** demonstrates how two 12 V batteries are connected to make either a 12 V or a 24 V system. If you are replacing a set of batteries, make a sketch before removing any cables. Always disconnect and connect ground cables first and last, respectively.

Heavy equipment uses several types of batteries. Identify the conventional type by the removable caps over each cell that allow the technician to test and top up the electrolyte. The design of this style of battery allows a loss of electrolyte due to gassing that occurs when the battery charges. This style of battery is becoming increasingly less popular because of the higher maintenance required.

Another style is the low-maintenance battery that has removable caps; but because of different materials used for its plates, which reduce the gassing during the charging process, it rarely requires maintenance.

The most popular style of battery is the maintenance-free battery that is sealed for life. There is no way of checking or testing its electrolyte, and because of its different plate

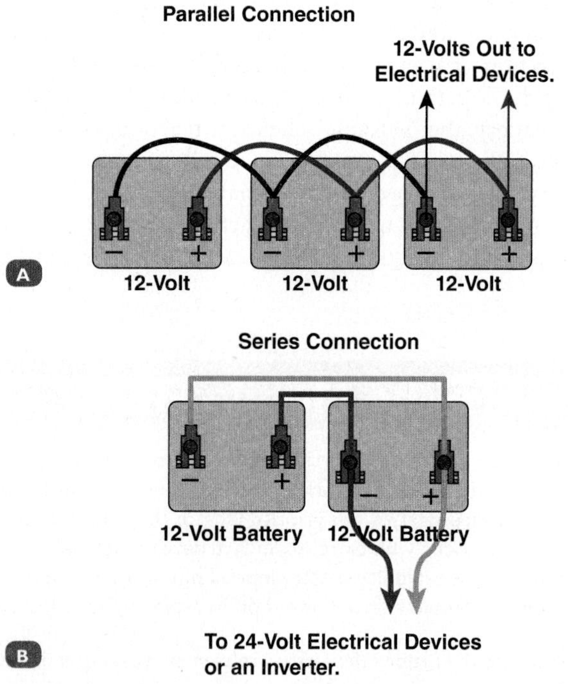

FIGURE 12-2 A. Batteries connected in a parallel configuration. **B.** Batteries connected in series.

material, it produces very little gas and therefore doesn't lose electrolytes.

Slowly gaining popularity are gel cells and glass mat batteries. These are a more expensive version of a maintenance-free battery that features a gel-type electrolyte and are supposed to be very durable. These batteries, however, come at a price premium and have special requirements when charging or boosting is required. We discuss the different types of batteries in detail later in this chapter.

SAFETY TIP

If you suspect a battery is frozen, *do not* boost or charge it until it is warmed up. If a battery's electrolyte freezes, it will likely distort the plates, which could cause an explosion if charged or boosted.

Electrolyte or battery acid is a very dangerous substance. If you get any on your skin, you should immediately flush the affected area with water. Always wear PPE (personal protection equipment). Baking soda neutralizes battery electrolyte. Every shop and service truck should have a box on hand. A solution of diluted ammonia and water also is effective and does not leave a powdery residue.

Battery Functions

Traditionally heavy vehicles have batteries similar to those we see in **FIGURE 12-3**, to provide starting current and operate electrical accessories if the engine is not running. And although supplying electric current for starting is the most obvious function for a battery, it's important to consider the other jobs the battery performs that are critical to proper electrical system operation. Battery functions on heavy-duty vehicles include those listed here:

1. **Providing electrical energy to the vehicle whenever the engine is not running.** When the engine is running, a properly designed and operational charging system supplies electrical current to meet most electrical demands and charge the battery. For today's heavy vehicles and equipment, the limitation on, or even elimination of, engine idle means batteries have to supply electrical current for prolonged periods to devices such as electrohydraulic pumps for hydraulic brakes, power steering, coolant pumps, and air-conditioning compressors. Heavy-duty equipment hybrid electric vehicles are now more commonplace. They are dependent on battery-supplied electrical current to operate all electrical devices, including electric drive motors and all electrical accessories, for much longer periods than conventional vehicles using accessories driven by an internal combustion engine.
2. **Providing electrical energy to operate the starter motor, ignition, and other electrical systems during cranking.** Other devices, such as hydraulic or air starter motors, could be used to start engines. However, even electronically controlled diesel injection systems require current to operate during cranking. With electric starter motors, batteries must be capable of delivering high current flow for short periods of time. Batteries used for cranking purposes have unique construction features and are commonly termed **starting, lighting, and ignition (SLI) batteries**. Diesel-powered equipment use multiple batteries, called a bank of batteries, connected in series or parallel to produce adequate starting current.

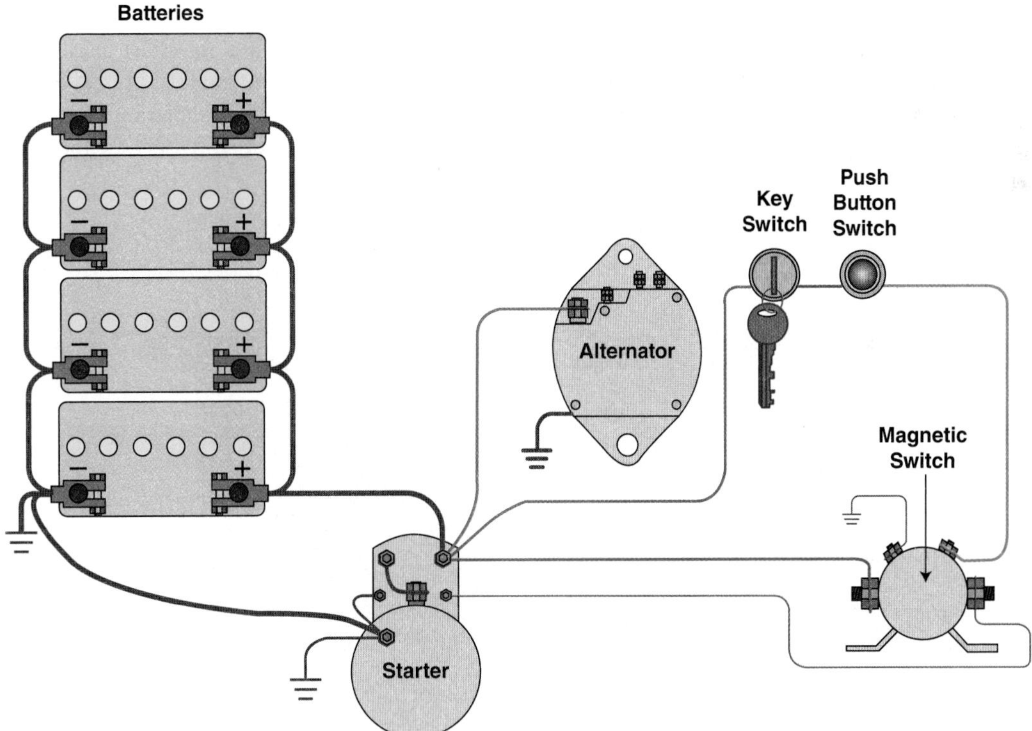

FIGURE 12-3 Batteries traditionally supply starter current and power to run electrical accessories when the engine is not running.

3. **Providing extra electrical power whenever power requirements exceed the output of the charging system.** High current demands are occasionally placed on the electrical system. For example, when an engine is idling, the charging system current output is low. Current flow to blower motors operating at high speed for heating or air conditioning systems, lighting circuits, and other electrical devices can exceed the output of the charging system. To maintain proper operation of these circuits, the batteries should be sized to provide adequate current.
4. **Storing energy over long periods of time.** Even when vehicles are not in use for extended periods of time, the battery is still expected to deliver current to start a vehicle. Today, heavy vehicles and equipment have numerous **key-off electrical loads.** These are current draws on the battery when the ignition is off. Also called **parasitic draw,** this battery current is required continually to operate vehicle security systems, GPS devices, and computer memory for multiple electronic control modules, entertainment systems, and other electrical accessories requiring constant power.
5. **Acting as an electric shock absorber for the vehicle's electrical systems.** The use of microprocessors and microcontrollers in almost every vehicle system makes today's heavy equipment sensitive to fluctuations in voltage. Operating on current in the millivolt range, stray and uneven electrical current can interfere with and even damage the operation of these sensitive electronic devices. The operation of common components such as alternators, switches, and electrical devices with inductive coils regularly produces this type of electrical interference. Batteries help minimize fluctuations in a vehicle electrical system by absorbing and smoothing variations in electrical current.
6. **Operating electric drive traction motors.** The development of hybrid electric vehicles (HEVs) has created new functions in addition to the traditional purposes of batteries. In HEVs, batteries must provide even higher amounts of current for longer periods of time to operate electric traction motors that propel the vehicle, as illustrated in **FIGURE 12-4**. HEVs require new battery chemistry and construction to extend battery life, reduce weight, increase energy density, charge more quickly, and discharge and charge more frequently while delivering higher amounts of current flow for extended periods of time. Batteries must accomplish these goals in the harsh operating environment and duty cycle of heavy equipment. At the same time, batteries must perform with greater and more consistent reliability than ever before. New types of batteries and battery management systems help meet these operational demands.

▶ Types and Classifications of Batteries

K12002

Batteries are generally classified by application. In other words, batteries are classified according to what they are used for and how they are made. Batteries are also classified according to the type of plate materials and chemistry used to produce current. Until recently, lead-acid batteries have been the only battery technology used in heavy equipment. Although the search for more durable and reliable lead-acid batteries has brought innovation to that category of batteries, the development of hybrid-drive vehicles has resulted in the introduction of different types of battery technology, such as nickel-metal hydride and lithium batteries. We discuss other chemistries in the Advanced Battery Technologies section.

Lead-Acid Batteries

Lead-acid batteries have been developed commercially for over 130 years and are a mature, reliable, and well-understood technology. They are also the most common battery used in the heavy equipment industry. Lead-acid batteries deliver high rates of current with a higher tolerance for physical and electrical abuse compared to other battery technology. These batteries

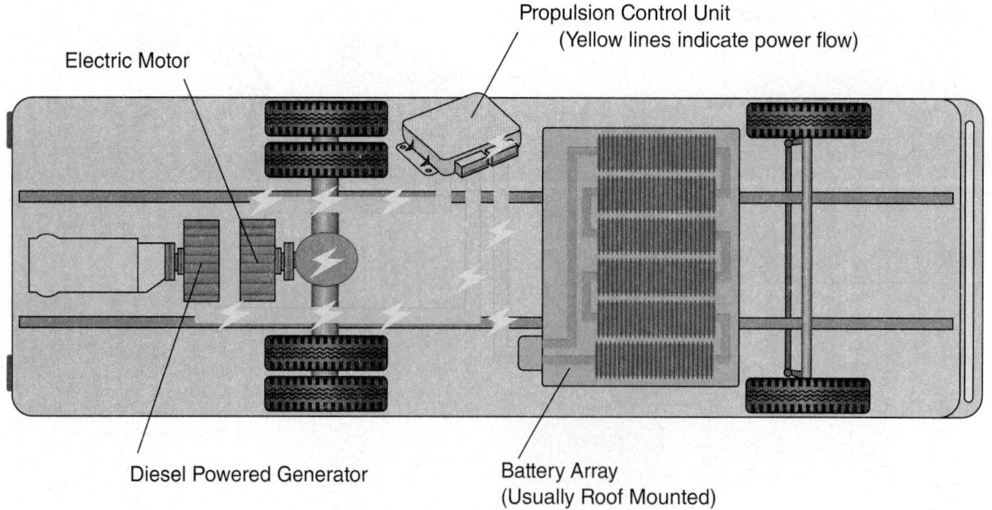

FIGURE 12-4 Batteries are now required to provide current to electric traction motors and store current produced during regenerative braking.

hold a charge well and when stored dry—without electrolyte—the shelf life is indefinite. Relatively simple compared to other battery technologies, lead-acid batteries are also the least expensive to manufacture in terms of cost per watt of power.

Contributing to the popularity of lead-acid batteries is the fact that they are available in a wide range of sizes and capacities from many suppliers worldwide. Manufacturers classify lead-acid batteries by their construction and application. Six types of construction are found on heavy equipment, but the basic chemical action is identical in all, including these:

- Flooded cell, including low maintenance (**FIGURE 12-5**) or maintenance free.
- Deep cycle flooded cell.

Valve-regulated lead-acid (VRLA) batteries, also called **sealed lead-acid** (SLA) or recombinant batteries, like the one shown in **FIGURE 12-6**, is a category that includes the following types:

- Flooded
- Gel cell
- Absorbed glass mat (AGM)
- Spiral cell (Optima® batteries)

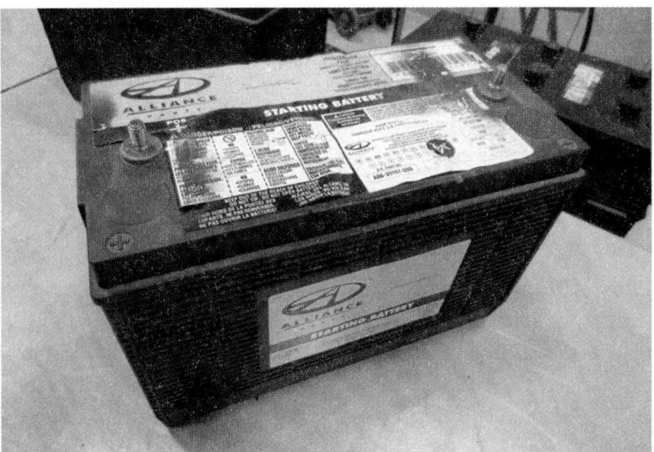

FIGURE 12-5 A typical low- or no-maintenance SLI battery.

FIGURE 12-6 A VRLA sealed battery.

Starting, Lighting, and Ignition Batteries (SLI)

Among the categories of lead-acid batteries, the most common use is for starting, lighting, and ignition (SLI). SLI batteries are designed for one short-duration deep discharge of up to 50% depth of discharge (DOD) during engine cranking. Discharging is quickly followed by a charging period, and the battery maintains a full charge. The operating requirements of an SLI battery are very different from those for **traction batteries** in hybrid electric vehicles, which are rechargeable batteries for propulsion. Although identical in appearance, SLI batteries are also constructed differently than deep cycle batteries.

Deep Cycle–Deep Discharge Batteries

Deep cycle batteries deliver a lower, steady level of power for a much longer period of time than SLI-type batteries. Furthermore, battery plate construction and charging and discharging characteristics of deep cycle batteries are different from SLI-type batteries. In heavy vehicles, deep cycle batteries supply current to constantly powered accessories like driver and vehicle communication devices. Deep cycle batteries also supply power to wave inverters, which in turn supply alternating current (AC) to appliances such as refrigerators, TVs, or laptop chargers. In addition, deep cycle batteries power accessory lighting, electric winches, and tailgates. This type of battery typically uses a battery isolator system that separates the main vehicle electrical system from the deep cycled battery circuit. The charging system replenishes the deep cycle battery charge, but the main vehicle electrical circuits cannot access it.

Battery Construction and Operation

The basic components of a battery are its case, terminals, plates, and electrolyte. Even though the construction of batteries can vary depending on their type and application, these basic components remain the same. It is important that technicians select the correct size, type, and construction for the application. Before selecting a battery for a particular application, the technician needs to answer a number of questions. For example:

- Is the starting battery or a deep cycle battery supplying electrical accessories?
- Is the battery working in extremes of temperature?
- Is it a high-vibration environment?
- What electrical load does the battery need to supply and for how long?
- What case and terminal configuration is required?

This section examines battery construction and discusses how those questions and their answers aid in the selection of the correct battery for an application. This section also explains the charge and discharge cycle of a battery.

Flooded Lead-Acid Batteries

Flooded lead-acid batteries refer to battery cell construction where the electrodes are made from thin lead (Pb) plates

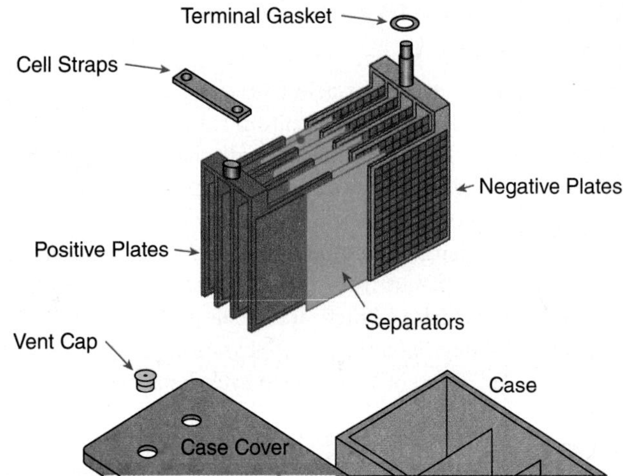

FIGURE 12-7 Typical plate arrangement in a wet cell battery.

submersed in liquid electrolyte. Two dissimilar compositions of lead form the positive and negative electrodes (**FIGURE 12-7**). Sponge lead, which is lead made porous with air bubbles, forms the negative plate. Lead dioxide (PBO_2) is the active material of the positive plate.

The electrodes and electrolyte of a lead-acid battery cell produce 2.1 volts. Connecting cells together in series allow a variety of output voltage. This means a fully charged 12-volt battery, in fact, produces 12.6 volts with no electrical loads by connecting six cells together. Twenty-four-volt systems are commonly used in heavy-duty off-road equipment and by the military. These combinations of 12-volt batteries connected in series produce 24 volts.

Adding Amperage and Voltage

The amount of amperage a battery supplies is a function of the surface area of the plates. To increase the amperage deliverable from a battery, the surface area or number of plates must increase. Plates connect together in parallel within each cell to increase the amperage or capacity of a battery. Positive plates connect only to other positive plates within each cell, and likewise with negative plates. Plate straps for each cell set of positive and negative plates join through a connector to another strap in adjacent cells. There are two rows of these intercell straps and connectors. In a 12-volt battery, six positive plate straps link in series to six negative plate straps, alternating a positive strap to a negative strap as each cell is connected (**FIGURE 12-8**). The last cell in the series circuit contains one of the battery posts, either positive or negative. Strap connections between the cells are made either through the cell partitions in the case or over the top of the partition.

Separator Plates

To prevent the battery positive and negative plates from touching and short-circuiting, manufacturers place separator plates between each plate in every cell. Separator plates are very thin, porous, glass-fiber materials that allow electrolyte to diffuse freely throughout the cell and at the same time prevent plate contact.

FIGURE 12-8 Interconnections between all six cells in a battery, showing the most negative and positive points of the battery.

▶ TECHNICIAN TIP

Manufacturers design and construct SLI batteries to deliver a short, high-amperage burst of current for starting. Using a deep cycle battery to replace an SLI battery can cause damage to starting motors and conductors through a condition known as low-voltage burnout. This happens when voltage drops very low while supplying high cranking amperage to the starting motor. Because the deep discharge battery cannot maintain as high an output voltage, the excessive amperage produces resistance and heat in motors, cables, and connection windings, leading to burnout.

Deep Cycle Versus SLI Battery Construction

Manufacturers design SLI batteries to produce a quick burst of energy for starting and should not be discharged less than 50% before recharging. Deeply discharging SLI batteries dramatically shortens their service life. Ideally, the longest service life is achieved when this battery is discharged no more than 5% and quickly recharged (**FIGURE 12-9**).

In contrast, deep cycle batteries are made for deep discharging by continuous but light electrical loads until completely

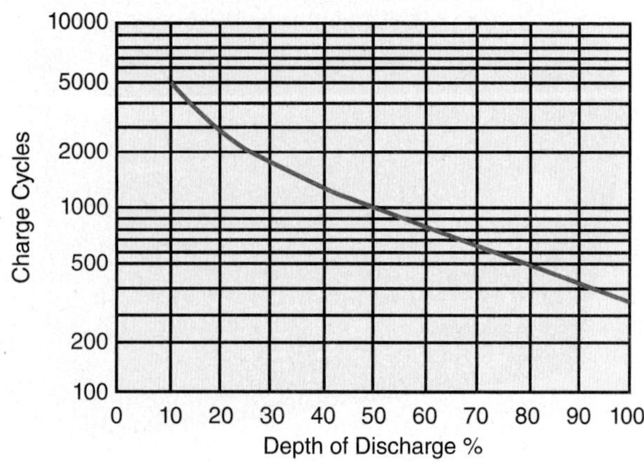

FIGURE 12-9 Deep discharging a battery shortens battery life.

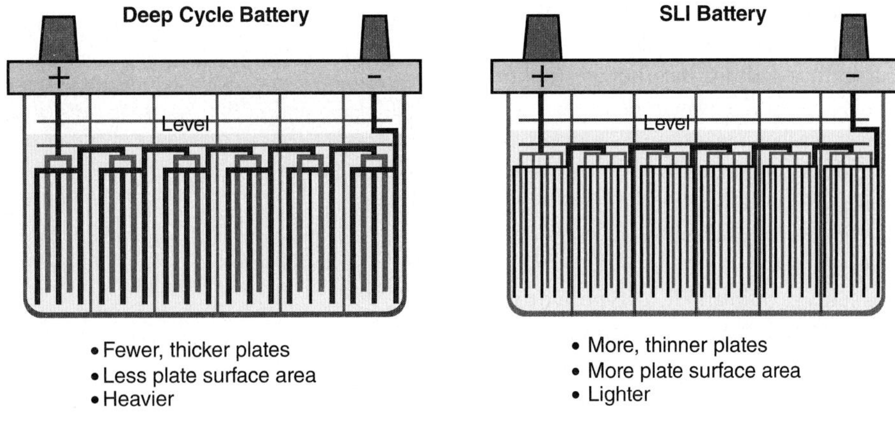

FIGURE 12-10 An SLI battery uses thinner plates.

discharged. To optimize SLI battery characteristics, plates are thin so that more plates fit in each cell. More and thinner plates translate into higher available amperage due to increased plate surface area. However, continuous discharge of SLI batteries for prolonged periods of time causes the current flow to overheat, distort, and warp the thin plates. Similarly, charging SLI batteries from a deeply discharged state can cause plates to overheat, dramatically shortening battery life. The primary difference between deep cycle batteries and SLI is the thickness of the plates (**FIGURE 12-10**). Deep cycle plates are thicker to resist distortion during a discharge/charge cycle. However, thicker plates mean fewer plates compared to an SLI battery with identical dimensions. Thicker plate batteries also have higher resistance during high-amperage charging and discharging in comparison to SLI batteries.

Electrolyte

Lead-acid battery electrolyte is a mixture of 36% sulfuric acid and 64% water. The specific gravity of water is 1.000. (**Specific gravity** is a measure of density.) Sulfuric acid has a specific gravity of 1.835, which means it is much heavier than water. Combined, the sulfuric acid and water solution has a specific gravity of 1.265. This makes it an electrolyte 1.265 times heavier than plain water. During charging and discharging, the specific gravity of the electrolyte changes. When discharging occurs, sulfate from the sulfuric acid enters both positive and negative plates. Oxygen also leaves the positive plate and combines with hydrogen left around in the electrolyte by the departing sulfate. This means the electrolyte has increasingly more water content and less acid during discharge, as **FIGURE 12-11** illustrates. The process reverses during charging when sulfate is electrically driven from the plates and renters the electrolyte. Measuring the specific gravity or density of an electrolyte, therefore, is a good measure of battery state of charge (SOC).

Manufacturers can make flooded cell batteries with or without an electrolyte. Dry batteries (without electrolyte) can be stored on the shelf for extended periods without the fear of sulfation and are lighter to transport. For this reason, electrolyte is often only added to the battery at the point of sale.

When the specific gravity of battery acid is too low, such as when a battery is discharged, it may freeze in colder climates. An electrolyte that has lost water and is therefore

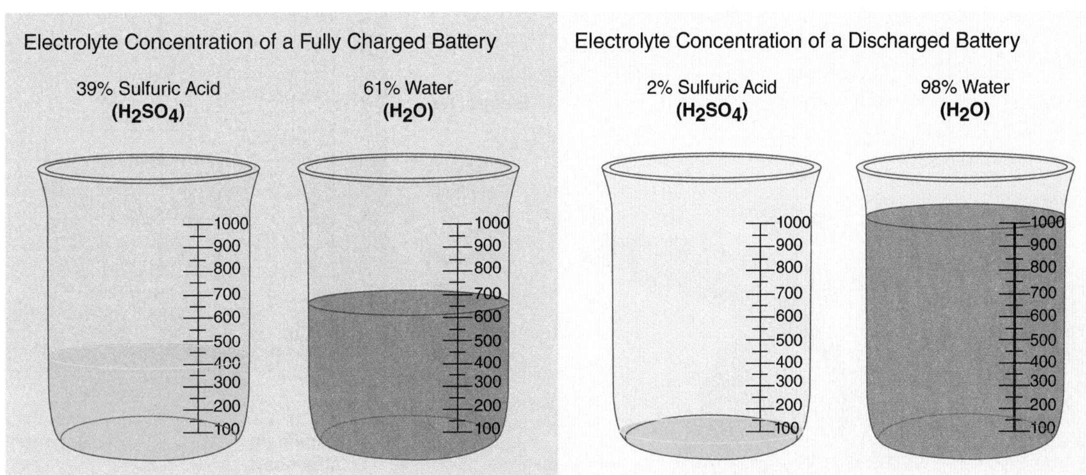

FIGURE 12-11 Electrolyte water and acid mixture for charged and discharged batteries.

overconcentrated with acid can accelerate corrosion of battery grids to which lead plate material is bonded.

It is important to note that sodium bicarbonate (baking soda, not baking powder) is an effective way to neutralize electrolyte spills. Using a power washer, for example, reduces the concentration of acid but does not neutralize it. Squirting a mixed solution of ammonia and water on spilled battery acid also neutralizes the acid. Water and ammonia also evaporates, leaving no mess to clean up.

Technicians can use a squeeze bulb and float-type hydrometer, like the one in **FIGURE 12-12A**, to measure the density or the specific gravity of liquids. Technicians can also use it to measure the specific gravity of batteries. A refractometer is an optical device that measures the density of coolant and battery electrolyte. When a drop of liquid is placed beneath the lens of the device and then held up against a bright light source, a graduated scale in the viewfinder indicates the battery's specific gravity. **FIGURE 12-12B** shows a refractometer. **TABLE 12-1** indicates the various specific gravity and voltage readings for flooded lead-acid batteries. Electronic hydrometers enable faster, temperature-compensated measurement of the battery's state of charge. Remember that battery acid is highly corrosive, so when using these devices, properly protect yourself by wearing eye protection, a rubber apron, and acid-resistant gloves, particularly when handling electrolyte.

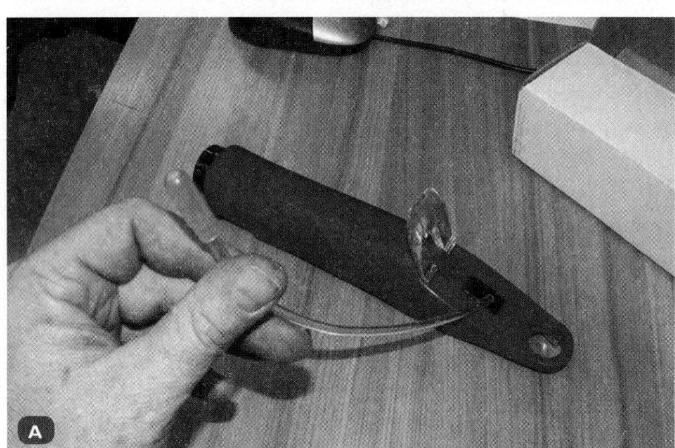

FIGURE 12-12 A. Typical hydrometer. **B.** Refractometer.

TABLE 12-1 State of Charge as Indicated by Specific Gravity and Voltage Reading for Flooded Cell Batteries*

Open Circuit Voltage	Specific Gravity	Percentage of Charge
12.65 or greater	1.265 (minimum)	100%
12.45	1.225	75%
12.24	1.190	50%
12.06	1.155	25%
11.89	1.120	0%

*AGM voltages will differ.

Battery Cases

The battery case is usually made of polypropylene. Ribbing and irregular features on the outside of the case increase the length of resistive electrical conductive pathways made when dirt and water accumulate on the case. These accumulations can allow current to drain from the battery posts. Each of the six cells in a 12-volt battery is sealed, and electrolytes cannot move between cells. A gap between the plates and the bottom of each cell forms a sediment trap, as **FIGURE 12-13** illustrates. The trap collects plate material that sheds during operation. Vibration and deeply discharging a battery accelerate the loss of plate material and reduce the battery's capacity. Without the trap, plate material accumulates and potentially short-circuits the plates, leading to rapid self-discharge of the battery.

During charging and discharging, the breakdown of water through a process called **hydrolysis** causes batteries to produce hydrogen and oxygen gas. These gases require venting and are an explosion hazard. In older flooded batteries, each cell had a cap to vent gases, add water to the electrolyte level, and permit the technician to inspect the electrolyte with a hydrometer.

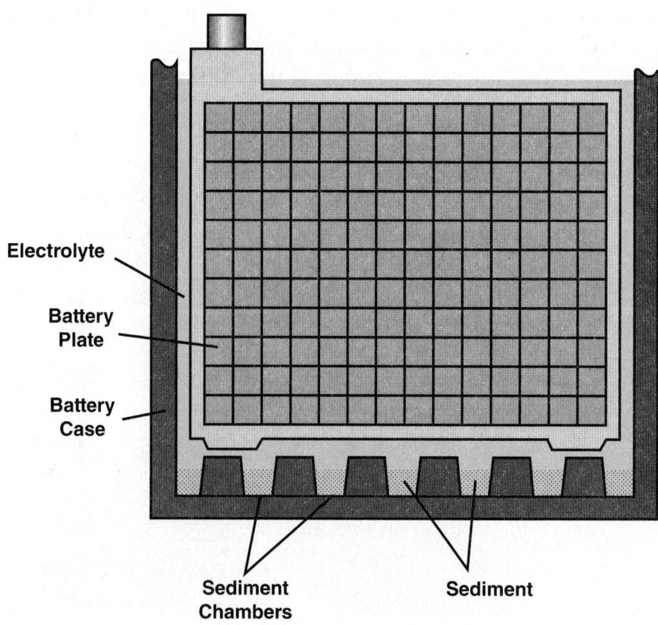

FIGURE 12-13 Typical sediment chamber in a flooded cell battery.

Low-maintenance batteries use a small, single vent near the top of the battery. The technician adds extra electrolyte to these batteries to compensate for water loss over the lifetime of the battery. Low-maintenance batteries have advanced plate material that result in less water loss than conventional flooded batteries. Nonetheless, a removable plug still allows access to the electrolyte during testing and servicing.

▶ Sizing and Terminal Configuration

K12006

Batteries for heavy equipment are available in a wide variety of sizes. Manufacturers build their batteries to an internationally adopted Battery Council International (BCI) group number. BCI group numbers are established according to the physical case size, terminal placement, terminal type, and polarity. For example, battery terminals used in medium- and heavy-duty applications use a top post, threaded stud, or "L" terminal, with combinations of each of these types. **TABLE 12-2** classifies various heavy-duty battery groups. Other designations relate to the battery terminal configuration, which refers to the shape and location of the positive and negative terminals on the battery, as **FIGURE 12-14** illustrates. Different types of battery posts are also available for batteries, including top post, threaded stud, side terminal, or "L" terminal, as well as combinations of each of these types.

▶ TECHNICIAN TIP

To help identification and prevent incorrect connection to post-type batteries, the positive terminal is 1/16" (1.6 mm) larger than the negative terminal. Because terminals are only soldered to the cell straps and

TABLE 12-2 Heavy-Duty Commercial Batteries Groups (12-VOLT)

BCI Group Size	Length (mm)	Width (mm)	Height (mm)	Length (inches)	Width (inches)	Height (inches)
4D	527	222	250	20 3/4	8 3/4	9 7/8
6D	527	254	260	20 3/4	10	10 1/4
8D	527	283	250	20 3/4	11 1/8	9 7/8
28	261	173	240	10 5/16	6 13/16	9 7/16
29H	334	171	232	13 1/8	6 3/4	9 1/8 10
30H	343	173	235	13 1/2	6 13/16	9 1/4 10
31	330	173	240	13	6 13/18	9 7/16

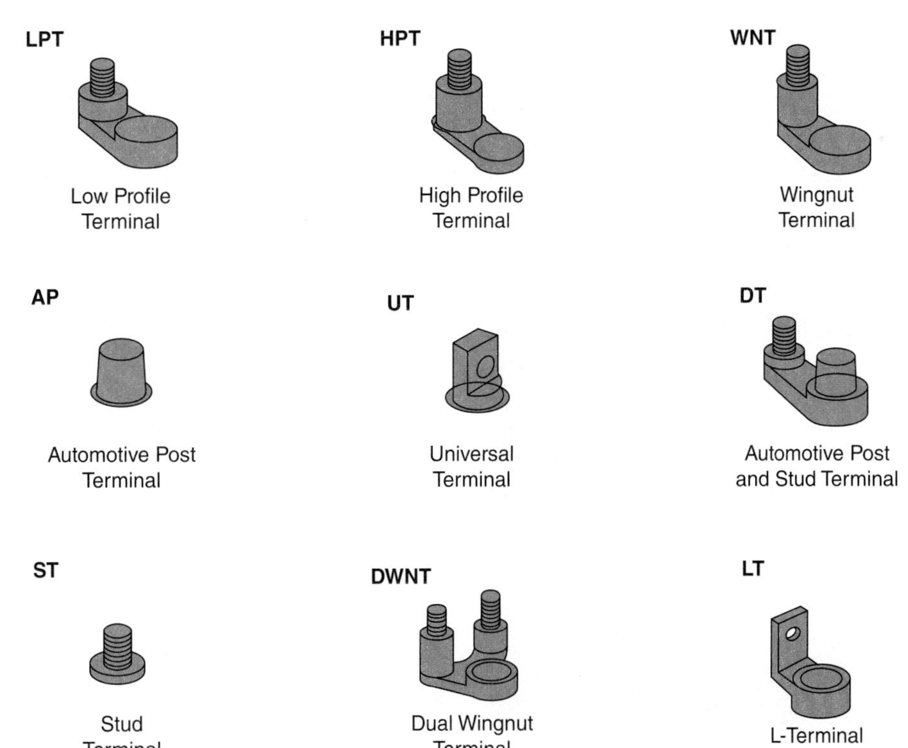

FIGURE 12-14 Typical types of layouts that use a lettering system for identification purposes.

anchored by the polyethylene case, they are vulnerable to damage if abused. Prying and hammering on posts are common types of abuse that break the seal between the post and case and damage the connection to the plate strap.

▶ Battery Ratings

K12005

The electrical capacity of a battery is the amount of electrical current a lead-acid battery can supply. The BCI and the Society of Automotive Engineers (SAE) establish common battery capacity ratings that North American manufacturers use. Technicians will encounter other rating systems depending on the origin of the vehicle and on some testing equipment, including the following:

- Japanese Industrial Standard (JIS)
- EN (European Norms) Standard
- DIN (Deutsches Institut für Normung)
- IEC (International Electrotechnical Commission) Standard

Several methods used to rate lead-acid battery capacity. The three most common are cold cranking amps (CCAs), cranking amps (CAs), and reserve capacity. **Cold cranking amps (CCAs)** is a measurement of battery capacity, in amps, that a battery can deliver for 30 seconds while maintaining a voltage of 1.2 volts per cell (7.2 volts for a 12-volt battery) or higher at 0°F (−18°C) (**FIGURE 12-15**). **Cranking amps (CAs)** measure the same thing, but at a higher temperature: 32°F (−0°C). A 500 CCA battery has about 20% more capacity than a 500 CA battery.

Reserve capacity is the length of time, in minutes, a battery discharges under a specified load of 25 amps at 26.6°C (80°F) before battery cell voltage drops below 1.75 volts per cell (10.5 volts for a 12-volt battery). This measure is modeled on estimates of how long an automobile could be driven after an alternator fails with electrical loads from headlights and other loads before the ignition system fails.

Amp-hour is a measure of a battery's capacity. Specifically, it is a measure of how much amperage a battery can continually supply over a 20-hour period without the battery voltage falling below 10.5 volts. Amp-hour is measured at 80°F (26.7°C)—the temperature at which lead-acid batteries perform best. A battery with a 200 amp-hour rating delivers 10 amps continually for 20 hours (20 hours × 10 amps). This is an important rating when selecting a deep cycle battery.

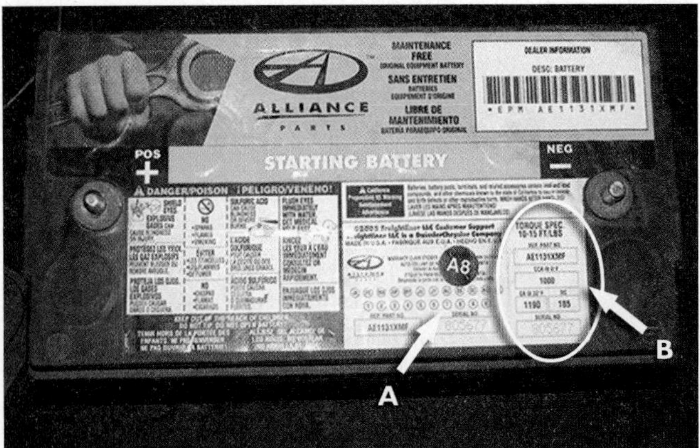

FIGURE 12-15 The battery's label indicates ratings. **A.** Date code. **B.** Battery ratings CCA, CA, and RC.

> ▶ **TECHNICIAN TIP**
>
> Early heavy-duty equipment vehicles with minimal electrical loads used 6-volt batteries for a 6-volt electrical system. In the 1950s, 12-volt systems and batteries became widely used. 24-volt systems are made from combinations of 12-volt batteries connected in series to produce 24 volts. Operating with higher voltages means less amperage flows through electrical circuits and connections yet they maintain the same power levels. With less amperage traveling through conductors, the reliability of the vehicle's electrical system improves because connections and cables do not heat nearly as much from high-amperage flow. The size of components and wire diameters are reduced as well.

Multi-Battery Configurations

Batteries can be connected together to supply either more amperage or more voltage. Diesel engines, which require high cranking torque, either connect batteries in parallel, like those in **FIGURE 12-16**, to supply more cranking amperage, or in series to supply higher voltage. For example, if two 600 CCA 12-volt batteries are connected in parallel, the batteries' potential output is 1200 CCA at 12 volts. If the batteries are connected in series, we add the batteries' voltage output together even though the cranking amperage remains the same. This means if two 600 CCA 12-volt batteries are connected in series, the batteries' potential output is 600 CCA at 24 volts.

Battery Selection

Factors that determine the battery rating required for a vehicle include those listed here:

- Current needed for key-off loads
- Current needed for operating electrical accessories
- The engine type (diesel or spark ignited)
- The engine size
- Climate conditions under which equipment must operate

In cold weather, battery power drops drastically because the electrolyte thickens and cold temperatures slow chemical activity inside the battery. Cold weather also makes engines harder to crank due to increased resistance from oil thickening. It is calculated that engine resistance increases between 50% and 250% in the winter compared to the summer, as **FIGURE 12-17** illustrates. Simultaneously, available battery current can drop by as much as 75%. As batteries age, their capacity drops too.

BCI estimates diesel engines require 220–300% more battery power than a similar gasoline engine. A typical 15L diesel engine today uses approximately 10,000 watts of current (or close to 12 horsepower) during cranking and initially needs 15,000 watts, or 20 horsepower. Vehicle manufacturers make

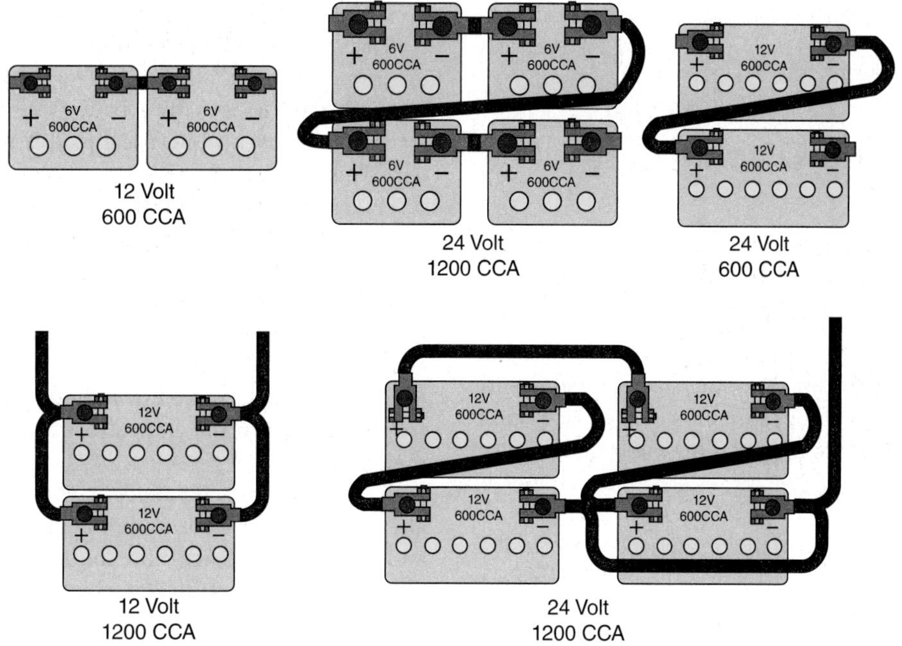

FIGURE 12-16 Typical battery bank configurations.

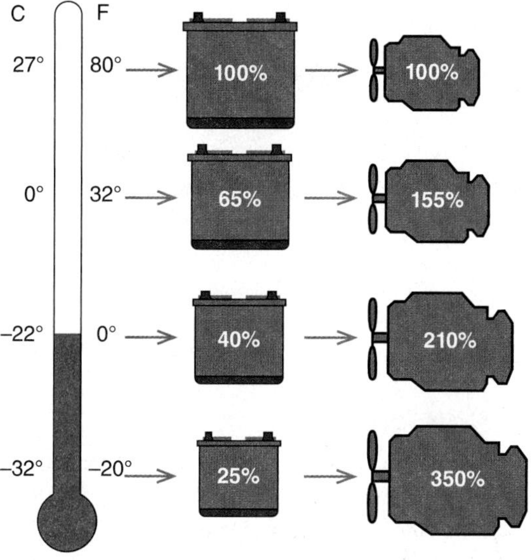

FIGURE 12-17 As temperature drops, engine rotation resistance increases, and battery chemical reactions slow.

recommendations about the capacity of batteries. The CCA rating of the battery is the most important rating considered when selecting batteries. Although selecting a battery with excessive current capacity might seem like a good idea, it is not. Extra capacity is expensive and high-amperage capacity available from batteries can lead to premature starter drive failure from excessive torque and damage from excessive amperage through starting circuit connections.

Equipment manufacturers use a number of variables when calculating battery capacity, but the most significant one is battery voltage at the end of engine cranking. Generally batteries are sized to ensure a minimum cranking voltage of no less than 10.5 volts after three consecutive cranking periods of 30 seconds, with a 2-minute cooldown period between each cranking period.

▶ TECHNICIAN TIP

Equipment with excessive battery capacity (too many CCAs) can lead to premature failure of the starter motor and starter drive due to excessively high torque. Excessive battery CCA increases the amperage through cables, connections, and starter circuit components, causing damage from resistance heating. However, inadequate battery capacity shortens battery life from deep discharging. Equipment may even fail to start in cold weather or as batteries age. Starter motors, cables, and circuits can be damaged from low-voltage burnout caused by undersized batteries.

Internal Resistance of Batteries

All electrical devices have internal resistance—even batteries. Not all battery types have the same internal resistance, however. A battery's internal resistance depends on the types of materials the manufacturer used to make the plates and the chemical composition of the electrolyte. A battery's internal resistance determines how quickly a battery can be charged or discharged.

Batteries with a relatively low internal resistance, such as a standard lead-acid battery, can be charged quickly, and they can also be discharged quickly to supply a lot of current over a short period of time. This makes them ideal for use as starter batteries in vehicles because they can supply the high-discharge current the starter motor requires to start the vehicle. Batteries are available with a lower internal resistance than that of a lead-acid battery, such as the newer lithium batteries now in battery banks for electric and hybrid vehicles. These types of batteries are more expensive than the standard lead-acid battery, and their lower internal resistance is generally not needed for everyday starter motor applications.

▶ Charging and Discharging Cycle

K12007

Battery plates are made of two different compositions of lead fabricated from paste bonded to lead alloy grids. The negative plate uses lead (Pb), and the positive plate uses lead peroxide (PbO_2). Antimony, calcium, or other metals are alloyed with the lead grid material to minimize corrosion that the lead acidic electrolyte can cause. Because the plates are made of dissimilar metals, the addition of electrolyte causes galvanic reactions in each cell.

In a fully charged condition, the positive plate material is predominantly lead peroxide (PbO_2), and the negative plate is sponge lead. The composition of the electrolyte is 64% water and 36% sulfuric acid. Chemical interactions between the plates and electrolyte strip electrons from the positive plate and add electrons to the negative plate, which produces a 12.6-volt difference between the battery terminals. A lead-acid battery remains in this condition without a load applied. However, due to activity of chemical reactions, a slow rate of self-discharge occurs, which eventually discharges the battery. This self-discharge rate is dependent on temperature and the selection of materials the manufacturer used during manufacturing. In hot climates, complete self-discharge is measured in weeks. In colder climates, cold slows down chemical reactions, so the self-discharge rate can take almost two years.

When a load is applied across the battery, electrons moving from the negative to the positive terminal accelerate galvanic reactions. **FIGURE 12-18A** illustrates this process. Both plates and the electrolyte composition change because of electron movement. Oxygen atoms in the positive plate move into the electrolyte while the sulfate part of the acid moves into the positive plate, changing the cell from lead peroxide (PbO_2) to lead sulfate ($PbSO_4$). On the negative plate, sulfate also moves into the plate material, forming lead sulfate ($PbSO_4$). The electrolyte becomes less acidic and turns to water as sulfate leaves and hydrogen in the electrolyte combines with oxygen driven from the positive plate.

Galvanic reaction in a battery stops under two circumstances. One is if the electrical load is removed from the battery. This halts chemical reactions when electrons move from one battery terminal to the other. Electron movement also stops when the positive and negative plates become saturated with sulfate in a process called **sulfation**.

When charging a lead-acid battery, the chemical reactions used to produce current are reversed, restoring the plate and electrolyte to its charged condition (see **FIGURE 12-18B**). While charging, sulfate is driven from both plates back into the electrolyte. Oxygen in the electrolyte recombines with the lead in the positive plate.

The chemical action occurs by connecting a charger or an alternator (DC current), stripping the positive post of electrons and forcing them back into the negative terminal. Charging voltage needs to be sufficiently high enough to overcome a battery's natural resistance to current flow. Most charging systems maintain a maximum charging voltage of approximately 0.5 volt above battery voltage. This explains why the charging system set point for most 12.65-volt batteries is around 14.2 volts. Higher voltage battery chargers push more current into the battery at a higher amperage.

> ▶ TECHNICIAN TIP
>
> If a battery is completely discharged, the similar chemical composition of both plates permits the battery polarity to reverse. If connected incorrectly to a charger or charging system, the battery charges up with reverse polarity. If an operator reconnects a battery with reverse polarity to a vehicle, the results are disastrous. Burnt wiring, blown fuses, and alternator damage quickly result, leading to a potential vehicle fire.

Plate Sulfation

Sulfate is driven off battery plates when charging, as **FIGURE 12-19A** shows. However, if a battery is left in a discharged state for a long period of time continually undercharged, or left partially charged,

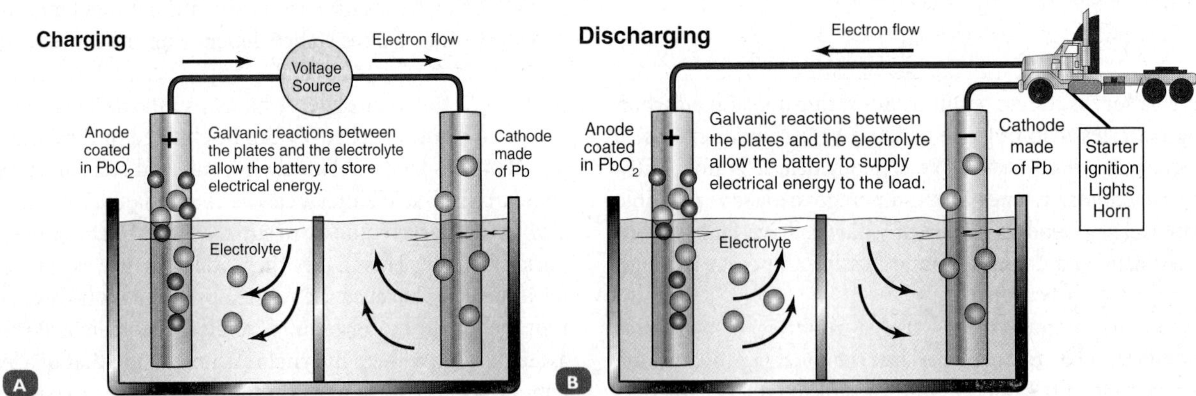

FIGURE 12-18 A. Charging cycle. **B.** Discharge cycle.

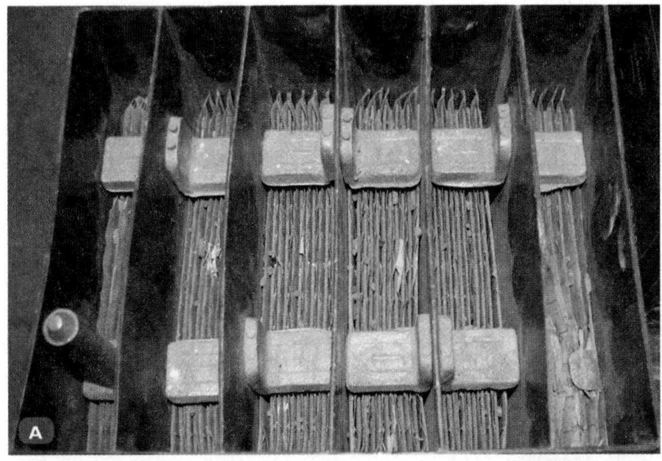

FIGURE 12-19 **A.** Normal plate condition. **B.** Sulfated plate.

the soft sulfate turns to a hardened crystalline form, as **FIGURE 12-19B** shows. Hard sulfate cannot be driven from the plates.

This means the battery cannot be recharged, and the remaining active plate material develops a high resistance to charging. The latest innovation to lead-acid battery technology incorporates black-carbon graphite foam into the plate paste to prevent sulfation damage. Graphite-foam carbon increases plate strength and surface area, which translates into greater power density and durability.

Gassing

During charging and discharging, water in the electrolyte breaks into its constituent hydrogen and oxygen. This process, called **electrolysis**, releases both gases. Electrolysis through the loss of water depletes battery electrolyte. If electrolyte is too low, the plates dry out, and the increased acid concentration of electrolyte permanently damages the grids. Severe **gassing** occurs when charging voltage pushes beyond 2.4 volts or when severe discharge takes place, such as when someone lays a wrench or piece of metal across battery terminals.

Low- and No-Maintenance Batteries

The use of antimony alloy in the plate grids of conventional flooded battery technology minimizes grid corrosion and allows these batteries to accept up to 10 times more overcharging than newer low- or no-maintenance batteries. Unfortunately, antimony-alloyed grids cause excessive gassing, resulting in substantial water loss. No- or low-maintenance battery technology solves that problem.

Introduced in the middle 1970s, no- and low-maintenance batteries reduce or eliminate the antimony content in grids. Manufacturers use calcium primarily now to replace antimony but they also use barium, cadmium, or strontium. No-maintenance batteries eliminate all the antimony, whereas low-maintenance batteries contain a reduced level of antimony content (approximately 2%). No- and low-maintenance batteries still require venting and need a large electrolyte reserve area above the plates to compensate for some water loss.

Another recent advance in grid composition involves manufacturers adding silver into the calcium-lead alloy. Silver alloy has a very high resistance to grid growth and corrosion. Thus, silver alloy significantly lengthens battery life in high-heat and severe-service conditions.

Some of the advantages of low- or no-maintenance batteries are presented here:

- Less water usage
- Less grid corrosion
- Less gassing
- Lower self-discharge rate
- Less terminal corrosion because less corrosive gas is emitted from the vents

The disadvantages of low- and no-maintenance batteries include the following:

- A lower electrical reserve capacity
- Often a shorter life expectancy
- Grid growth/expansion when exposed to high temperatures
- More quickly discharged by parasitic losses
- Difficulty accepting a boost when completely discharged

Although no-maintenance batteries contain a vent beneath the top cover, the battery tops are completely sealed. Delco, which introduced the first no-maintenance battery, uses a built-in hydrometer that has colored balls. These balls rise or fall in the electrolyte, depending on the electrolyte density, thereby providing an indication of the state of charge. To boost these batteries from a completely discharged state, a small charge is recommended for about 10 minutes to begin the hydrolytic process of breaking water into hydrogen and oxygen. After that, the batteries are capable of receiving a higher rate of charge.

Low-maintenance batteries may look completely sealed, but they usually have a means of adding water if required. Often the caps are concealed under a plastic cover that the technician removes to reveal cell caps that can be unscrewed (**FIGURE 12-20**).

The latest and most advanced commercial vehicle battery technology are **absorbed glass mat (AGM) batteries**. AGMs provide improved safety, efficiency, and durability over existing battery types. The electrolyte absorbs into a fine glass mat, as **FIGURE 12-21** shows, preventing it from sloshing or separating

FIGURE 12-20 The spiral cell Optima battery is an example of an AGM-type battery.

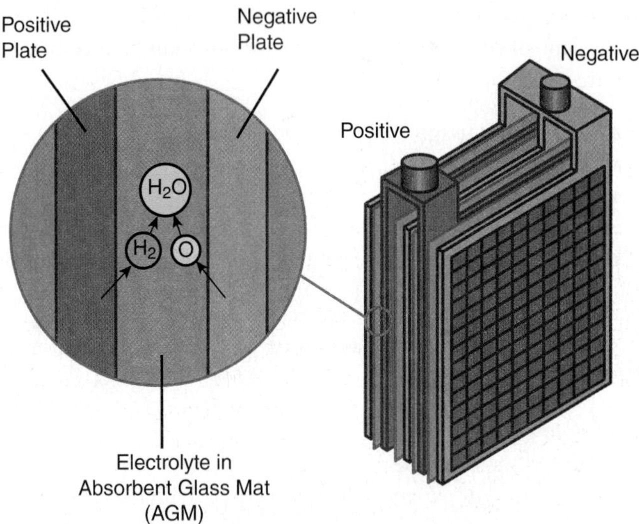

FIGURE 12-21 AGM batteries trap and recombine oxygen and hydrogen gases inside the glass mat next to the plates.

into layers of heavier acid and water. The fiber first helps by enhancing gas recombination rather than simply venting gas to the atmosphere and lowering electrolyte levels. AGM material also possesses low electrical resistance. As a result, it can deliver more cranking amperage and absorb up to 40% more charging current than conventional lead-acid batteries, leading to faster charging. Higher cell voltage and sensitivity to overcharging requires special service consideration.

▶ Advanced Battery Technologies

K12003

The demand for advanced battery technology in heavy equipment vehicles is growing. Several key factors are at play in determining which application of a variety of battery technologies to use on heavy equipment vehicles:

- Energy density (**FIGURE 12-22**)—expressed in watt-hour per kilogram (Wh/kg) and watt-hour per liter (Wh/l)

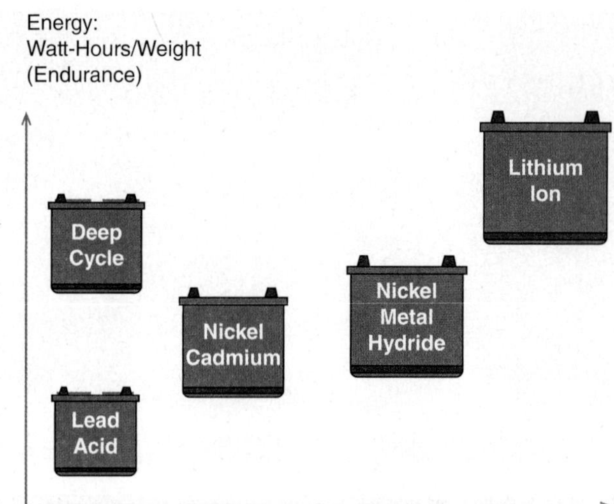

FIGURE 12-22 Comparing the energy density of various battery technologies. Lithium-ion produces the greatest amount of energy for the longest time per kilogram of weight.

- Life span—measured by the number of charge/discharge cycles as a function of depth of discharge
- The state of charge window—the availability of usable battery voltage
- Cost in dollars per kWh

Types of Advanced Batteries

The major battery technologies used in hybrid heavy equipment vehicles are nickel-metal hydride (NiMH), lithium, and lead-acid. Each technology has distinct capabilities, which we discuss in this section. **TABLE 12-3** compares the capacities of different battery types.

Nickel-Metal Hydride (NiMH) Battery

Manufacturers use **nickel-metal hydride (NiMH) batteries** not only in consumer electronics but also as a preferred battery chemistry for hybrid-drive vehicles. That is because NiMH batteries are relatively lightweight and have high power output and long life expectancy. Heavy-duty hybrids use these. NiMH batteries provide twice the energy storage of lead-acid by weight, but only half the power output—at 1.2 volts/cell compared to 2.1 volts/cell for lead-acid batteries. As **FIGURE 12-23** illustrates, a unique alloy of rare earth metal, which has an unusual ability to absorb hydrogen, forms the metal hydroxide negative electrode. The positive electrode is made of nickel oxide ($NiOH_2$). The electrolyte is composed of potassium hydroxide, which is an alkaline.

Lithium-Ion Batteries

Lithium-ion batteries were developed for use in the early 1990s. Lithium-ion (Li-ion) batteries are secondary batteries and are not the same as disposable, primary-type lithium batteries, which contain metallic lithium.

TABLE 12-3 Comparison of Properties for Different Battery Chemistries

Range			Energy Density		
Battery Type	**Voltage/cell**	**Cost Watt/hour**	**Watt-hour/kg**	**Joules/kg**	**Watt-hour/liter**
Lead–acid	2.1 volts	Lowest = 1	41	146,000	100
NiMH	1.2 volts	6 times lead-acid	95	340,000	300
Li–Ion	~ 4.0 volts	25 times lead-acid	128	460,000	230
Ultra capacitors	~ 2-3 volts	4–5 times lead-acid	30-60	–	–
Diesel Fuel	–	–	–	–	10,942

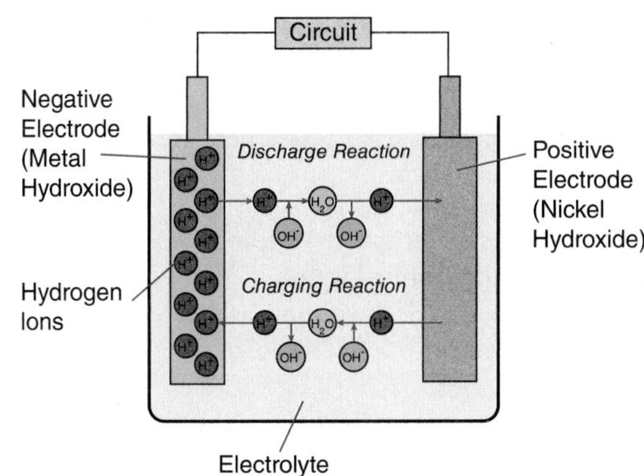

FIGURE 12-23 Chemical reactions in an NiMH type battery.

Like conventional batteries, Li-ion batteries have electrodes and use an electrolyte. Unlike conventional batteries, the chemical reactions in Li-ion batteries are not galvanic, and the material separating the electrodes is a gel, salt, or solid material. With no liquid electrolyte, Li-ion batteries are immune to leaking. Currently there are dozens of different cell chemistries used to produce lithium-ion batteries. The voltage, capacity, life cycle, and safety characteristics of a lithium-ion battery can change dramatically depending on the choice of material for the anode, cathode, and electrolyte. Regardless of their specific chemistry, lithium batteries have a higher energy density than other battery types such as lead-acid, nickel-cadmium, and NiMH, as **FIGURE 12-24** shows.

Popular Li-ion chemistries incorporate electrodes made from lithium combined with phosphate, cobalt, carbon, nickel, and manganese oxide.

Lithium-phosphate batteries ($LiFePO_4$ chemistry) are the most common lithium battery chemistry for use in heavy-duty hybrid and electric vehicles. The advantages to using lithium-ion batteries in vehicles include the following:

- The best power-to-weight ratio compared to other battery technology.
- Li-ion batteries have higher cell voltages, with as much as 5 volts in some designs. A typical cell voltage averages between 3.3 and 4.2 volts, which means fewer Li-ion cells are required to form high-voltage batteries. It also translates into fewer vulnerable and resistive cell connections and reduced electronics in the battery management system. One lithium cell can replace three nickel–cadmium (NiCad) or NiMH cells, which have a cell voltage of only 1.2 volts.

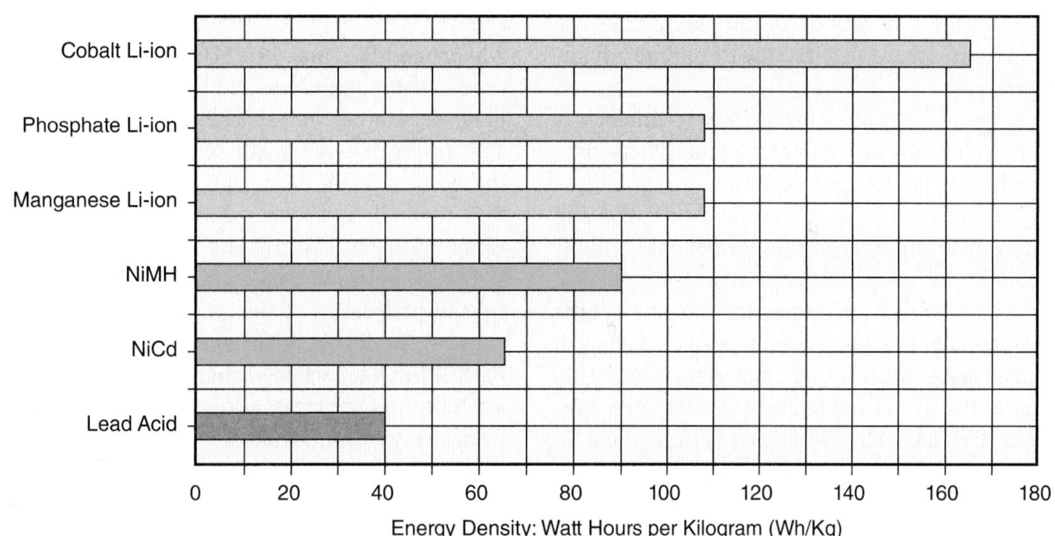

FIGURE 12-24 Comparing different lithium-ion battery energy densities with other battery types.

- Li-ion cells maintain a constant voltage for over 80% of their discharge curve. In comparison, conventional lead-acid batteries maintain voltage until only 50% discharged. Therefore, in a Li-ion battery, more stored energy is usable over longer periods to supply electrical accessories or to crank an engine frequently and faster, before becoming effectively discharged. It also means that a smaller capacity battery can supply a vehicle's power needs.
- Li-ion batteries operate well over wide temperature ranges: -60°F (-51°C) to 167°F (+75°C). Cold slows down chemical reactions in other battery technology. However, cold temperatures do not slow the nongalvanic reactions in Li-ion batteries.
- Charging characteristics of Li-ion batteries are superior to other batteries. In consumer electronic devices, Li-ion batteries have demonstrated the capacity to recharge as much as 90% within 5 minutes. That speed is a distinct advantage for the efficiency of regenerative braking used by electric and hybrid electric vehicles. Once charged, Li-ion batteries self-discharge at a very low rate.
- Li-ion batteries have low internal resistance and can discharge their current four times faster compared to lead-acid batteries. In addition, high discharge and charge rates do not wear out a Li-ion battery to the extent that charge and discharge cycles reduce the lifespan of other types of batteries. Currently, typical Li-ion batteries can withstand 1,200 charge–discharge cycles in comparison to 500–800 cycles for lead-acid and 1,500 for NiMH, as the chart in Figure 12-24 shows. Li-ion batteries last for millions of micro-discharge cycles. A micro-discharge cycle occurs when the charge is maintained between 40% and 80%. In contrast, lead-acid batteries last the longest only when discharged less than 5%.

Although Li-ion technology appears to have every advantage over other battery technology, Li-ion technology is restricted by a number of limitations. Extensive investment and research are currently aimed at correcting serious limitations to the use of Li-ion technology in heavy equipment applications. As a result, a variety of Li-ion chemistries are now competing for widespread use, each with unique advantages and disadvantages.

One disadvantage of current Li-ion battery technology is cost. Li-ion batteries currently cost eight times more than conventional lead-acid batteries for each kilowatt of power produced per hour. However, continuous innovation and increasing production are steadily dropping the price differential.

Chemical stability of Li-ion batteries is also a concern. High temperatures destroy some batteries, and they are known to overheat and even catch fire when overcharged or damaged. Complete discharge ruins other Li-ion batteries. The highly reactive chemistry of the Li-ion cell requires special safety precautions to prevent physical or electrical abuse of the battery. To maintain the cells within design operating limits, a microprocessor-controlled battery management system prevents damage and extends the life cycle of Li-ion batteries. Electronic controls add to production costs.

Valve-Regulated Lead-Acid (VRLA) Batteries

As mentioned, valve-regulated lead-acid (VRLA) batteries are sealed lead-acid batteries that do not have a liquid electrolyte and do not require the addition of water. This design has numerous advantages. Plate and electrolyte technology used in VRLAs result in lower self-discharge rates because VRLAs typically lose only 1–3% of their charge per month. This compares to lead antimony grid batteries having a self-discharge rate of 2–10% per week and with 1–5% per month for batteries using lead calcium grids.

Because VRLA batteries are completely sealed, they can be installed in any position without leaking—even under water. Sealing the battery eliminates the need to replenish the electrolyte or to check specific gravity. Battery state of charge is determined through voltage checks. Listed here are other advantages of VRLA batteries:

- No required specific gravity readings or adjustments
- No need to add distilled water
- No acid or lead to deal with in wash water
- No cable corrosion
- No tray corrosion
- No corrosive gas in battery compartment to damage electronics
- The longest service life of all battery types
- The highest cranking amps, even at low temperature
- The fastest recharge possible
- The highest vibration resistance
- 400 full cycles (80% DOD)
- Triple the life of traditional lead-acid batteries

The two common types of VRLA battery are absorbed glass mat (AGM) and gel. Additionally, a spiral cell battery, which is a variation of AGM technology, has actually become the more recognizable of the AGM-type batteries. We discuss each of these VRLA batteries in the following sections.

Absorbed Glass Mat (AGM) Batteries

Absorbed glass mat (AGM) batteries, as **FIGURE 12-25** illustrates, feature a unique and highly absorbent, thin glass fiber plate separator that absorbs the electrolyte like a sponge. The fiberglass-like plate separator, or mat, material gives the battery its AGM name. These batteries eliminate water loss through a process called oxygen recombination. No vents are used. Instead, the battery case is pressurized constantly to between 1 and 4 psi (6.9–27.6 kPa). Because of the special properties of the glass mat, pressurizing the battery causes 99%+ of the hydrogen and oxygen gases to recombine back into water when recharging. A piece of foil in place of a traditional vent cap allows the battery gases to vent only under severe conditions such as during overcharging when voltage is greater than 15 volts. If venting occurs, the battery is likely damaged, and the cell will dry out like any other cell. Charging above 2.7 volts per cell, the battery is severely damaged.

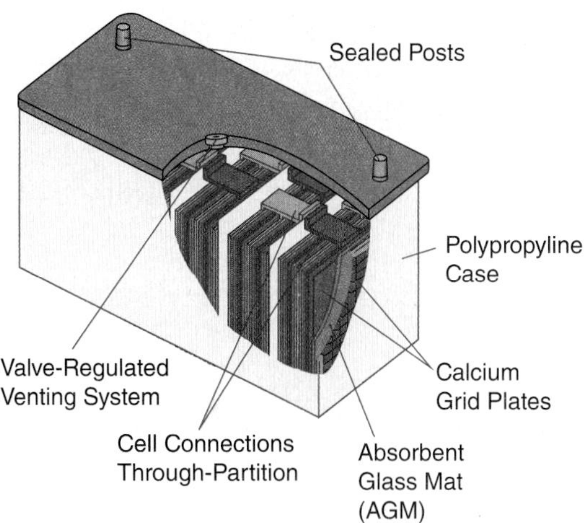

FIGURE 12-25 Construction details of a flooded absorbed glass mat (AGM) battery.

FIGURE 12-26 Technicians should use only microprocessor-controlled, or "smart," chargers to charge AGM batteries.

Advantages to AGM Batteries

AGM batteries have several advantages. Cell design places plates and separator mats closer together, which lowers the battery's internal resistance. A more efficient and faster chemical reaction between battery electrolyte and the plates can take place using the unique boron-silicate glass mat separator plate. Lower resistance and faster reactions means AGM batteries can charge at up to five times the rate of conventional lead-acid batteries. AGM cells produce slightly more voltage: 12.80–13.0 volts open-circuit voltage compared to 12.65 for conventional flooded lead-acid batteries. As a result, AGMs deliver more amperage at higher voltage when cranking. **TABLE 12-4** compares the state of charge and open-circuit voltage of flooded, gel, and AGM batteries.

Glass mat plate separators used in AGMs absorb mechanical shock better than other batteries. The vibration-resistant battery can therefore be used in operating conditions where other battery plates would quickly be destroyed. In one study, a fleet compared 68 trucks with conventional flooded batteries to 69 trucks with AGM batteries. Thirty-four months later, 113 of the flooded batteries had been replaced compared to eight of the AGM designs.

Service Precautions with AGM Batteries

AGM cells are extremely sensitive to damage from overcharging and require chargers that limit charging voltage to between 14.4 and 14.6 volts maximum at 68°F (20°C). Using conventional shop taper chargers, which can charge at up to 18 volts, will destroy an AGM battery. Sustained charging at 15 volts also causes the battery to overheat and gas excessively due to electrolysis. Instead, technicians should use a smart charger, such as the one in **FIGURE 12-26**. A **smart charger** is a battery charger with an internal microcontroller that regulates charging rates and times. It is an intelligent, temperature-compensated charger with an "AGM" setting. Because cell voltage is slightly higher for AGM batteries, a vehicle's charging system voltage may need adjustment to keep it in range between 13.8 and 14.4 volts maximum at 68°F (20°C) for optimum performance and service life. Voltage-regulator settings on some vehicles are too high for AGM batteries and may require adjustment. The higher open-circuit voltage also means that to prevent unequal charging and shortened battery life, operators cannot mix AGM batteries with other battery types. Without access to the electrolyte, AGM state of charge can only be determined by measuring battery voltage.

The depth of discharge also affects the life cycle of batteries. In general, the deeper the discharge between charges, the shorter the life cycle of batteries. **TABLE 12-5** compares the depth of discharge against the number of charge/discharge cycles that one can expect from different battery chemistry types.

TABLE 12-4 State of Charge Versus Open Circuit Voltage

	Open Circuit Voltage		
Charge	Flooded	Gel	AGM
100%	12.65	12.85	12.80
75%	12.40	12.65	12.60
50%	12.20	12.35	12.30
25%	12.00	12.00	12.00
0%	11.80	11.80	11.80

SAFETY TIP

AGM batteries are very sensitive to overcharging, as they will gas excessively and burst cell vents. Intelligent chargers that limit maximum charging voltage to 14.6 volts are required. Technicians should not use traditional taper chargers (used by most shops) that have an adjustable charging amperage setting to charge AGM batteries because taper chargers increase charging amperage to batteries by raising voltage to over 15 volts—and as much as 18 volts in some conditions.

Spiral Cell Optima Batteries

In the late 1980s, AGM battery technology advanced further with the introduction of spiral-wound plate technology.

TABLE 12-5 Comparison of Depth of Discharge Cycle to Battery Life for Different Battery Chemistries

Depth of Discharge	Gel: Cycle Life	AGM: Cycle Life	Flooded Lead-acid: Cycle Life	Li-ion	NiMH
100%	450	200	30–150	Potentially ruined/ damaged with some Li-ion chemistries	500–3,000 (demonstrated only)
80%	600	250			
50%	1,000	500	500	2,000	
25%	2,100	1,200			
10%	5,700	3,200	2,000	Millions +	300,000+ (demonstrated only)

FIGURE 12-27 A typical spiral-wound cell battery. Note the cylindrical cells.

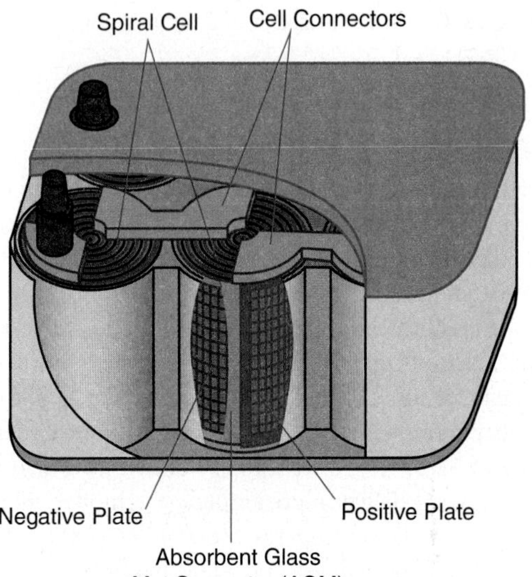

FIGURE 12-28 Spiral cell batteries are the more recognizable type of AGM battery technology.

FIGURE 12-27 shows a typical spiral-wound cell battery. **Spiral-wound cell batteries** are AGM batteries in every way except that the electrodes for each cell are not made of rectangular plates. Instead, two long, thin lead plates—the positive and negative electrodes—are coiled into a tight spiral cell with an absorbent microglass mat placed between the plates absorbing the electrolytes, as **FIGURE 12-28** illustrates. Replacing multiple plates with two coiled electrodes reduces internal battery resistance even further, thus enabling higher charging absorption rates for faster charging and higher discharge rates. These batteries also use higher internal gas pressures than other AGM batteries.

Manufacturers produce spiral cell batteries in three categories, designated by the color of the battery's top cover:

- Red top—a 12-volt SLI battery
- Blue top—a deep cycle battery
- Yellow top—a combination deep cycle and SLI or leisure battery

Gel Cell

Just as battery plate and grid materials technologies have advanced to allow more powerful, lighter, and longer-lasting lead-acid batteries, electrolyte technology has also evolved. In the mid-1960s, the industry introduced spill-proof batteries using gel cells. **Gel cell batteries** are created by adding silica powder to the electrolyte, which turns the liquid into the consistency of petroleum jelly, hence the name "gel cells." A fully charged gel cell battery has an open-circuit voltage of at least 12.85 volts and, like AGM cells, gel batteries are sensitive to overcharging and can be ruined by overcharging.

Ultracapacitors

Compared to more traditional capacitors, **ultracapacitors** are a new generation of high-capacity and high-energy density capacitors. Capacitors are electrical devices well known for their ability to store short bursts of electrical energy temporarily. For example, capacitors suppress and smooth voltage fluctuations, or ripple, from alternators. Capacitors also suppress radio static when connected across the power line-in. Ultracapacitors can supply large bursts of energy and quickly recharge themselves, which make them ideal for use in modern vehicles. Ultracapacitors are particularly advantageous in situations requiring regenerative braking and in frequent stop–start systems, such as in electric and hybrid vehicles.

Ultracapacitors have a very low internal resistance when compared to lead-acid batteries. Consequently, ultracapacitors deliver and absorb high-energy currents much more readily. In hybrid vehicles, using regenerative braking applications, typical batteries are slow to absorb a charge, thus limiting the maximum recovery of energy. Ultracapacitors do not have this problem and quickly recharge when depleted. This also makes them ideal for plug-in hybrid technology because they allow vehicles to recharge in seconds—not hours! Furthermore, unlike other battery technologies, continuous charge and discharge cycles do not wear out ultracapacitors. Whereas other battery technologies can be cycled between 200 and several thousand times, ultracapacitors can be cycled literally millions of times!

An ultracapacitor is constructed using two electrodes (plates), an electrolyte, and a separator plate, as **FIGURE 12-29A** illustrates. The dielectric material is double layered—not single as in conventional capacitors—and is made from a porous carbon. Although the construction features are similar to those of a galvanic-type battery cell, the method by which it stores electrical energy is different. Ultracapacitors store electrical energy within electrostatic fields (electrostatically) and do not produce electricity through electrochemical reactions. Like any capacitor, the main factors that determine how much electrical energy an ultracapacitor can store are as follows:

- Plate/electrode surface area—the greater the plate area, the higher the capacity.
- Distance between the plates—the closer the plates are, the higher the capacity.
- Electrical properties of the dielectric insulating layer separating the electrodes—some materials have better storage properties within capacitors than others.

A popular ultracapacitor type battery is the Maxwell ESM Ultra® series **FIGURE 12-29B**. Having the same dimensions as a group 31 battery, it can also produce 1800 CCA for 3 seconds and is unaffected by the cold. Three terminals are used: two are for charging the battery, and a third connects directly to the starter motor. An internal battery control module regulates the charging rate to each cell and performs diagnostic tests. Ultracapacitors are currently used to assist batteries for the first 1.5 seconds during cranking, where they can supply an additional 2,000 amps of current to supplement the starter batteries, as **FIGURE 12-30** illustrates. That supplement increases starter torque and speed when cranking amperage is highest during the initial starter engagement.

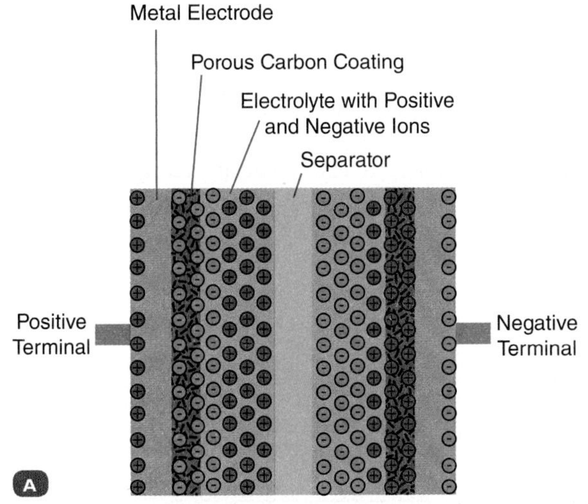

FIGURE 12-29 A. Construction of an ultracapacitor. **B.** Maxwell ESM Ultra series battery.

▶ Battery Management Systems

K12008

Battery failure is a costly service issue for heavy equipment. Weak batteries can lead to premature failure of starting and charging system components and loss of service caused by no-start conditions. The severe operating conditions and use of multiple batteries in many heavy equipment vehicles contribute to shortened battery life. Various electrical devices and systems that manage battery performance help minimize the expense and disruption due to battery failures. **Battery management systems (BMSs)** perform the following functions:

- Protect the cells or the battery from damage
- Prolong the life of the battery
- Maintain the battery in a state of charge to perform the work for which it is specified

The development of commercial hybrid-vehicle applications places more demands on batteries and requires sophisticated battery management systems for sensitive battery technology. Components of the battery management system include battery isolators, low-voltage disconnects, battery balancers and equalizers, and battery monitors. We discuss each of these components in the following sections.

Battery Isolators

Many heavy equipment vehicles use multiple batteries that we can separate according to function. For example, consider a

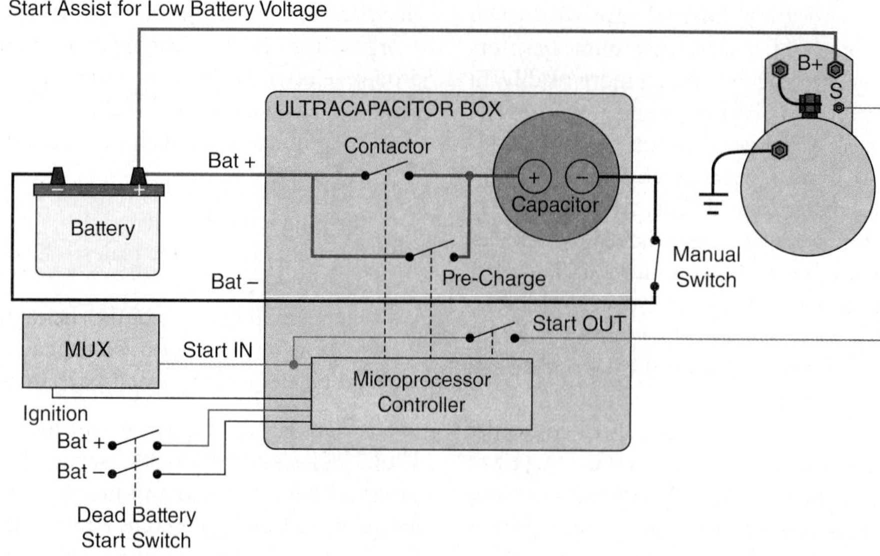

FIGURE 12-30 This ultracapacitor supplements the cranking current for a 24-volt battery, which reduces starting time.

vehicle with one battery bank of starting, lighting, and ignition (SLI) batteries for the starting and main vehicle operating system and another set of batteries for auxiliary deep cycle batteries for accessories or systems that operate after the engine shuts down. Permanently connecting all the battery banks in parallel could cause the SLI battery to become discharged if a continual electrical load is placed on the auxiliary deep cycle batteries for extended periods. This would prevent the vehicle from starting.

Battery isolator systems, or **split charge relays**, as **FIGURE 12-31** illustrates, enable the vehicle charging system to charge the auxiliary battery but electrically separate the auxiliary battery from the starting circuit when the engine shuts down. Separation of the main starting and auxiliary batteries can take place automatically during charging and discharging. Battery isolation systems range from simple, isolating solenoids or relays, to complex battery management systems that monitor charge rates and voltages for both the SLI and auxiliary batteries.

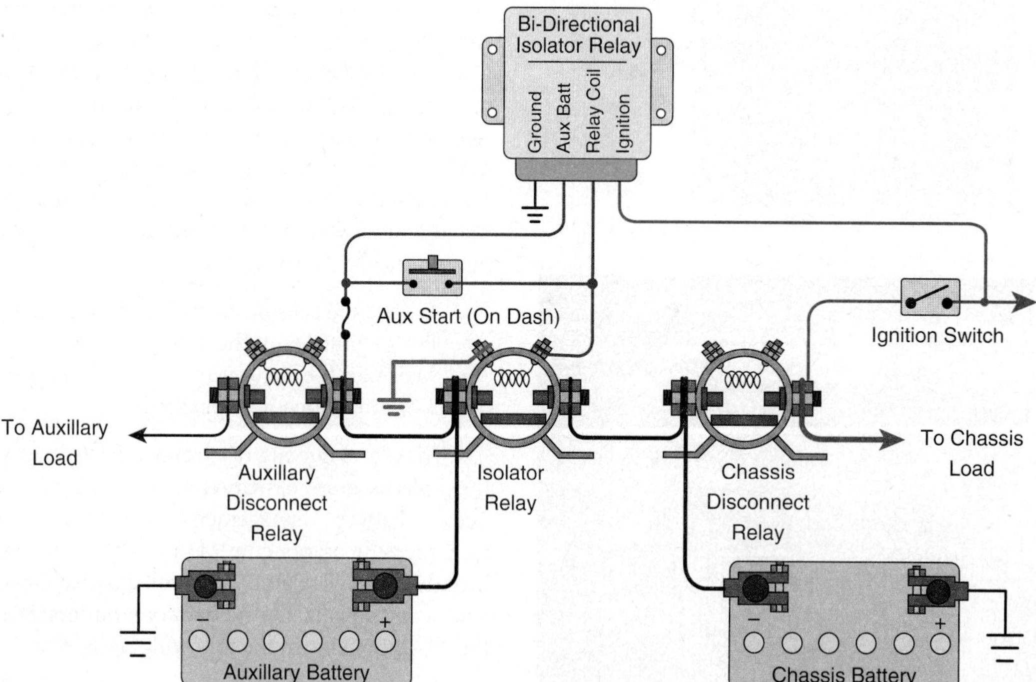

FIGURE 12-31 An isolator circuit ensures that auxiliary loads do not drain the chassis battery used for starting when the charging system is not operating. When the engine starts, the alternator charges both batteries, with the control module switching the isolator relay on and off under the appropriate conditions.

Low-Voltage Disconnect

Low-voltage disconnects (LVDs) monitor battery voltage and disconnect noncritical electrical loads when the battery voltage level falls below a preset threshold value. LVD devices preserve battery current to a level adequate to start the vehicle's engine when key-off loads or other parasitic draws are draining the battery. LVD devices then reconnect the electrical loads when the battery level is restored to a high enough voltage—for example, when the alternator begins charging above 12.6 volts. No intervention is required by the vehicle operator to protect the batteries, as the LVD automatically disconnects and reconnects the load. An audible warning typically alerts the operator before a disconnect event occurs, which is generally between 12.0 and 12.2 volts. LVDs can be integrated with the vehicle's power distribution system and progressively shed loads as battery voltage drops.

Battery Balancers and Equalizers

Higher cranking amperage and greater electrical loads in heavy-duty equipment require two or more batteries connected either in series for 24-volt electrical systems, or in parallel in 12-volt systems. Charging and discharging resistance changes with battery use and the electrical distance from the alternator. For example, longer battery cables and more electrical connections are almost unavoidable in many vehicles. This means one or more batteries in a bank get undercharged, which in turn leads to progressive plate sulfation. Sulfation, in turn, increases battery resistance, causing the battery to become weaker (**FIGURE 12-32**).

Balancers (sometimes called **battery equalizers**), as **FIGURE 12-33** illustrates, attempt to adjust battery voltage to compensate for unequal charges in multiple batteries. Equalizers are found in many commercial applications using 24-volt charging systems, including off-highway equipment.

In multiple battery configurations, whether connected in series or in parallel, batteries eventually charge and discharge unevenly, shortening battery life. For example, you may often discover that while testing two 12-volt batteries connected in parallel, one battery becomes completely dead while the other stays in good condition. When testing three batteries, one will be good, another fair, and the third defective. The defective battery is always the farthest from the alternator in terms of electrical distance.

There are two methods of correcting this common condition of unequal charge and discharge rates. One is to regularly rotate the batteries and exchange their positions in the configuration. Another method is to use a battery equalizer. Also, remember to check the equipment manufacturer's recommendation for connecting battery cables. Properly connecting cables is one way to minimize the charge and

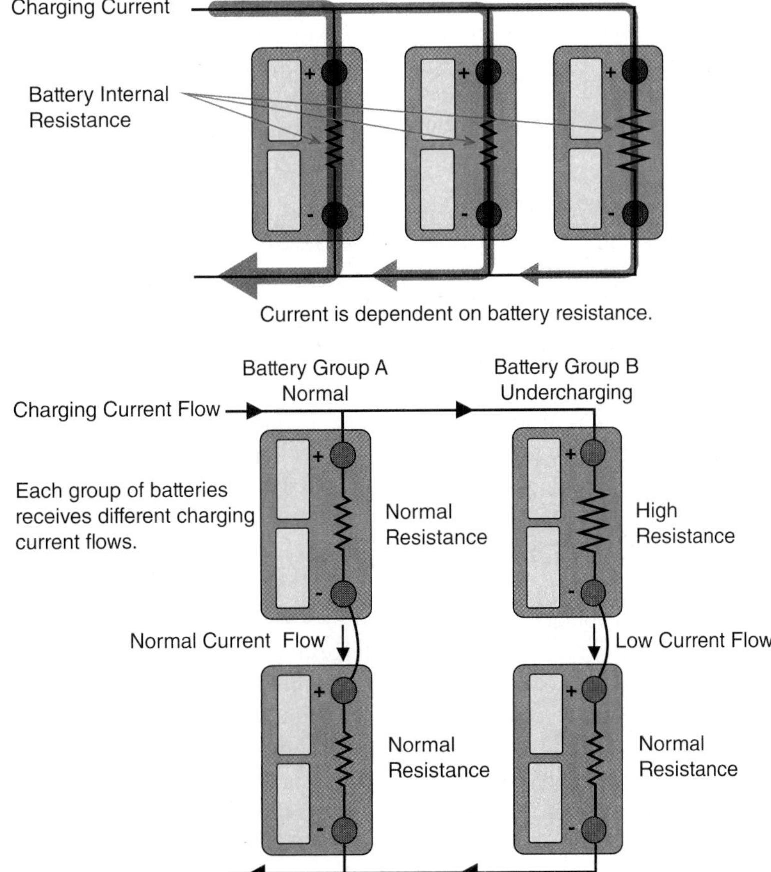

FIGURE 12-32 Batteries can develop unequal resistances with use.

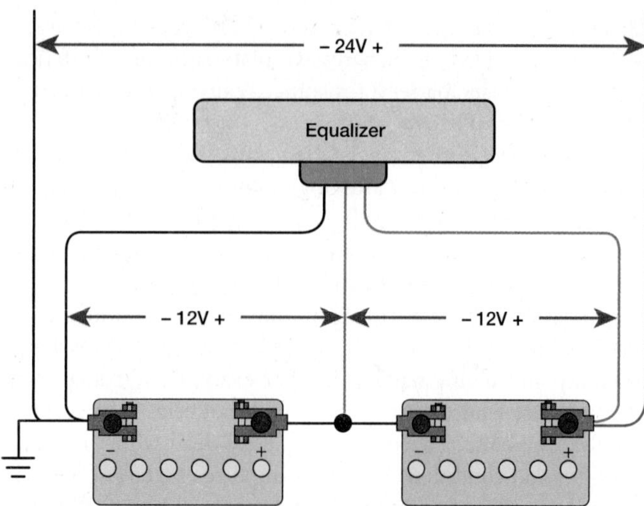

FIGURE 12-33 The equalizer controls the charging rate of two 12-volt batteries as well as evenly balances the current drawn from each.

discharge imbalances between batteries. Various configurations of charge equalizers enable the following:

- Charging 12-volt batteries from a 24-volt charging system
- Charging 24-volt batteries from a 12-volt charging system
- Charging series-connected 12-volt batteries at 24 volts and providing a 12-volt output for 12-volt chassis electrical loads
- Balanced battery charging of 12-volt batteries from 24 volts to within a difference of 0.1 volt
- Balanced draining of batteries to supply a 12-volt load so that each battery is depleted to within a difference of 0.1 volt

A common configuration has 12-volt batteries connected to the equalizer that interfaces the batteries with the 24-volt alternators, as **FIGURE 12-34** illustrates. The equalizer senses battery voltage and drives a higher charge rate into weaker batteries and less current into stronger batteries. The voltage balance and charge acceptance rate of each battery is kept to within 0.1 volt under light loads and within 0.5 volt at full loads. When the voltage of battery A is higher than that of battery B, the battery equalizer switches to standby mode. This means no power transfers from its 24-volt alternator input to its 12-volt output. If a 12-volt load is present, and battery A's voltage decreases to just below the voltage of battery B, the battery equalizer activates and transfers sufficient current from battery B to battery A, satisfying the load and maintaining an equal voltage and charge in both batteries.

More complex systems, like that in **FIGURE 12-35**, can have both battery isolation and battery equalization across multiple banks. For example, chassis batteries are isolated from each other when the alternator is not charging, but are connected together so both banks charge when the alternator is charging, and there is battery equalization for each bank.

Charge equalization is critical for series-connected battery cells in hybrid-vehicle applications. The higher voltage in

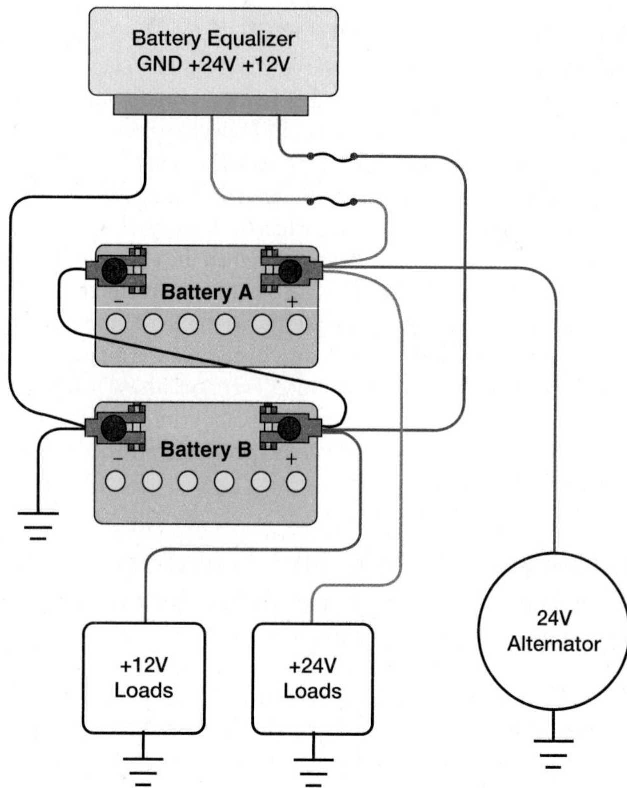

FIGURE 12-34 Battery equalizer used to ensure batteries within the bank remain charged with 12- and 24-volt mixed loads.

hybrid-drive systems requires very long series strings of batteries pushing battery performance to extremes. Without battery management systems incorporating charge equalization, battery banks would quickly fail.

Battery Monitors

Battery monitors in hybrid heavy equipment vehicles collect battery data for display to the operator and service technician. The data the monitors typically collect include the following:

- Temperature of each battery or pack
- Voltage of the pack
- Rate of charge or discharge

Hybrid Battery Management Systems

Hybrid-drive battery management is much more demanding than the previously described battery management devices. Batteries in these applications work in a demanding and harsh environment because of rapidly changing charging and discharging conditions, such as when the vehicle accelerates using electric motors and charges during regenerative braking. Li-ion and NiMH batteries best charge to between 40% and 70% of full capacity to allow absorption of current generated during braking and to extend their lifecycle. An on-board battery

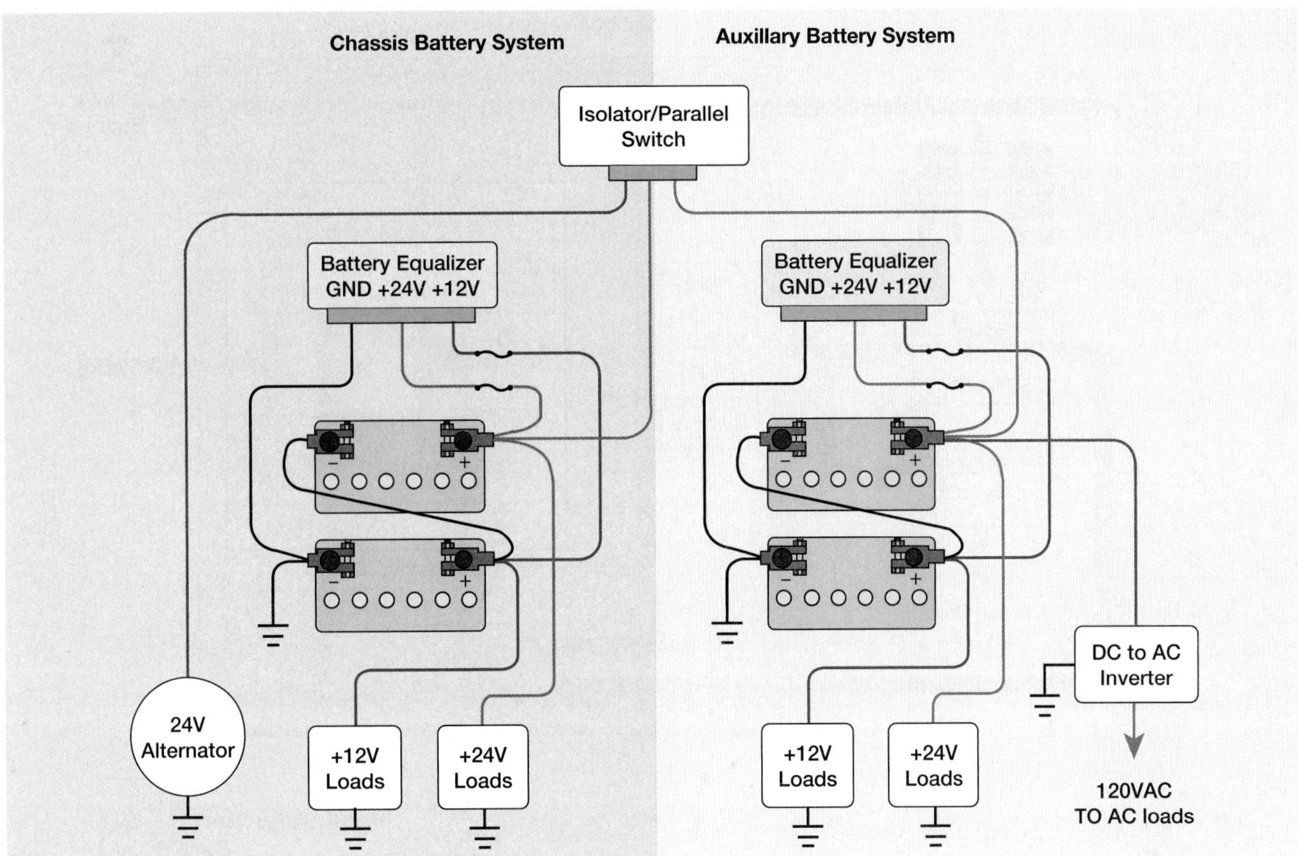

FIGURE 12-35 Schematic diagram of a battery equalizer combined with a battery isolator. The chassis system provides current to supply the starting motor batteries.

management system, like that in **FIGURE 12-36**, performs some, but not necessarily all, of the following functions:

- Monitoring the state of charge (SOC) of the battery and battery cells that compose the battery banks; this function is often the equivalent of a fuel gauge distance-to-empty reading
- Maintaining the state of charge (SOC) of all the cells with both voltage and amperage protection against overcharging and undercharge conditions
- Providing service and diagnostic information on the condition of the batteries and cells; this includes recording battery service and diagnostic data (battery voltage readings, temperature, hours, faults, out of tolerance conditions)
- Providing information for driver displays and alarms
- Providing an emergency protection mechanism in the event of damage, uncontrolled overheating, or other abuse condition
- Isolating the batteries or cells
- Charge equalization within the battery bank
- Adjusting the battery SOC to enable regenerative braking charges to be absorbed without overcharging the battery
- Communicating with the on-board vehicle network to receive information and instructions from other electronic vehicle-control units and responding to changes in the vehicle operating mode
- Calculating the optimum charging rate to each battery and/or cell
- Enabling adaptive strategies or emergency "limp home" mode in case of battery failure
- Providing reverse polarity protection
- Controlling temperature-dependent charging; some batteries can be damaged by charging when temperatures are lower than 32°F (0°C) or above 100°F (45°C)
- Providing discharge current protection to prevent damage to cell due to short circuits
- Providing depth of discharge cutoff

▶ Battery Servicing, Repair, and Replacement

A12002

Battery maintenance is often overlooked, and often the cause of a dead machine is the result of a lack of maintenance for the battery system. Simple things like checking electrolyte level, keeping the battery clean and secure, and checking and cleaning connections help get full life from a battery. If a large fleet of machines is able to get an extra season out of the battery in each machine because of a little extra maintenance, it could add up to thousands of dollars saved without including the cost of

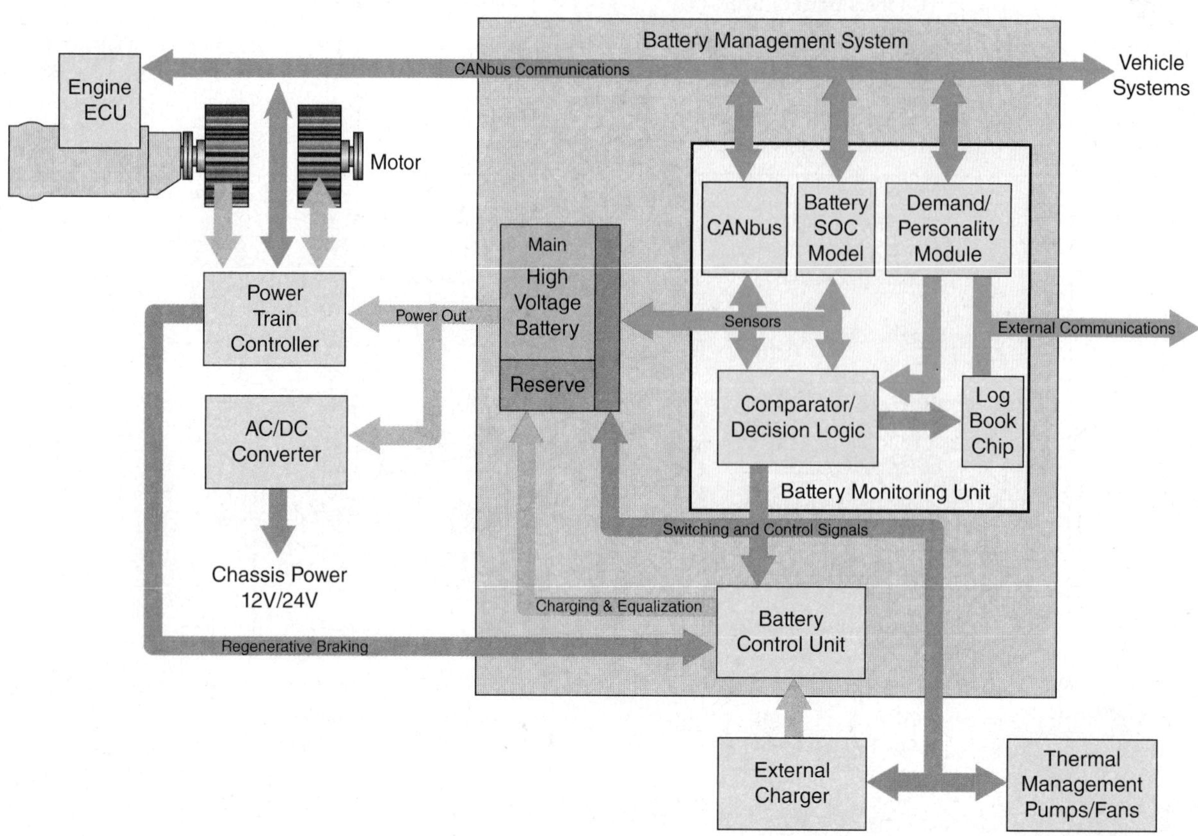

FIGURE 12-36 Diagram of the operation of a battery management system used in a hybrid-vehicle chassis.

machine downtime. There is also a huge environmental benefit to having batteries last as long as possible.

Because of the constant chemical-to-electrical change (self-discharge, discharge, or charge) and the harsh environment a battery must withstand in a machine (vibration, dirt, temperature extremes), the battery has a limited life. Proper care (cleaning, adding water, and charging) will extend the life of the battery.

Batteries should be the starting point when diagnosing complaints such as hard starting, slow cranking, or no-start complaints (**FIGURE 12-37**). Battery testing is also indicated when lights dim when an engine idles or when other electrical problems occur. Battery testing is also recommended whenever an alternator is replaced. Technicians use a variety of instruments and tools to evaluate the condition of vehicle batteries, and they use a number of procedures to service batteries during maintenance checks. This section covers these techniques.

Traditional comprehensive maintenance and testing of batteries include the following evaluation methods:

- Visual inspection, cleaning, filling, and battery replacement
- Checking that batteries are covered and secured in place
- Checking that cables ends are secure
- Checking that cables are not frayed or broken
- SOC testing using a voltmeter
- Cell voltage checks
- Load or capacity testing

FIGURE 12-37 Regular battery maintenance reduces downtime.

- Conductance or impedance testing
- Charging batteries
- Jump-starting vehicles
- Measuring parasitic draw

Technicians should evaluate batteries visually first before proceeding with any other significant tests. Visual checks include checking the electrolyte level, if possible. Most batteries today are sealed, or low- or no-maintenance type, which prevents this procedure.

Another basic maintenance task is to make sure the exterior case is dry and free of dirt. Dirt on top of the battery can actually cause premature self-discharge of the battery as current "leaks" across the path of dirt or grime. Grime and vapors from a battery can become conductive and drain the battery over time. To tell whether the surface of the battery is leaking current, use a digital volt-ohmmeter (DVOM), like the one in **FIGURE 12-38**, set to "Volts" to measure the voltage on the surface of the top of the battery. Do this by placing the black lead on the negative battery post and rubbing the red lead around the top of the battery, measuring the voltage present there. Any voltage exceeding 0.5 volt means you should wash down the battery with water. Do not use mixtures of diluted ammonia or baking soda, as they can enter the battery cells and contaminate electrolyte.

Terminals should be covered or protected to prevent corrosion, which eventually causes excessive resistance. Secure batteries against vibration, which can damage plate material, by inspecting machines' battery hold-downs regularly. Keep cable ends tight, and secure the cables so they do not rub against part of the machine and expose the wire. Machines have caught fire because of a battery or cable being loose and shorting out. **FIGURE 12-39** shows a properly secured battery.

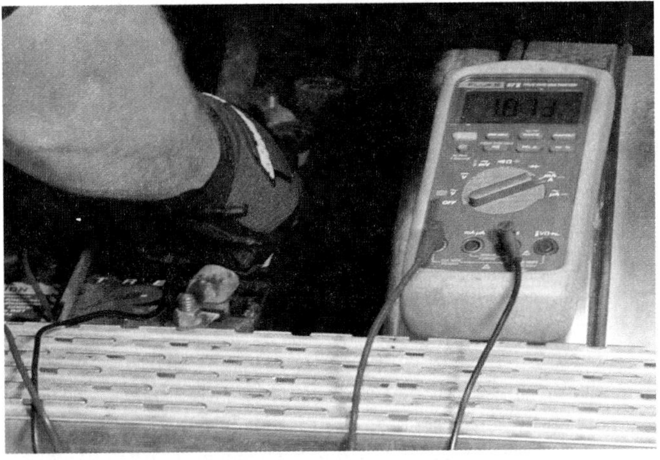

FIGURE 12-38 Measure voltage between points on the surface of the battery top to determine if there is any leakage current.

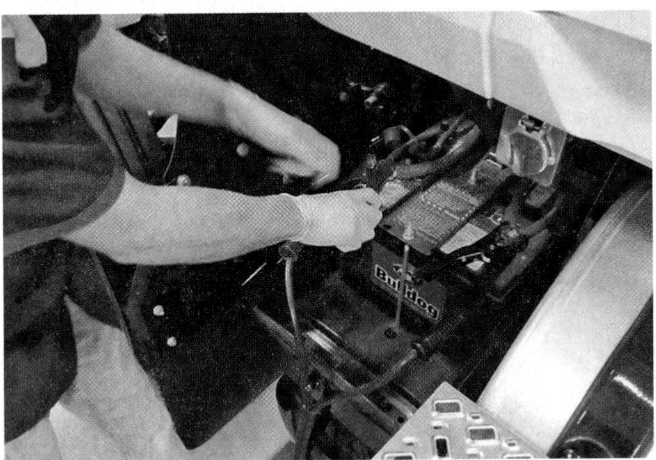

FIGURE 12-39 A properly secured battery.

Batteries should be fully charged to perform properly and to prolong their service life. A weakened battery causes the alternator to work harder charging batteries and shortens the alternator's life. Lower current level available to the starter leads to low-voltage burnout of the starter too. We cover state of charge in detail in the section Testing Battery State of Charge and Specific Gravity.

The section Battery Inspecting, Testing, and Maintenance covers several tests the tech can use to determine battery service life and identify reasons for battery failure. Load or capacity tests determine the ability of a battery to deliver cranking amperage, which we discuss in detail in the section Testing Battery Capacity. Conductance testing, or impedance testing, has replaced this method for evaluating battery capacity, which we cover in the section Testing Battery Conductance. Technicians do not perform testing for sulfation as part of a regular battery evaluation, but only to validate a diagnosis of sulfation. We discuss this procedure in the section Performing a Sulfation (3-Minute Charge) Test.

Parasitic draw testing and case drain or leakage testing are other means to detect conditions that cause batteries to lose their charge. A parasitic drain of battery current should be no more than 0.5 amp of current. Placing an inductive ammeter battery cable with all vehicle accessories off easily measures and detects excessive draw. Wet and dirty batteries leak voltage too. Placing one voltmeter lead on a battery post and the other lead on the case identifies voltage leaks exceeding 0.5 volt. Technicians should clean and dry battery cases to remove electrically conductive grime from the case. We discuss parasitic draw in greater detail in the section Measuring Parasitic Draw.

TECHNICIAN TIP

To prevent corrosion and resistance from developing at battery connections, you should apply treatments specifically designed to coat battery terminals. These treatments are not electrically conductive and do not attack cable insulating materials. Many other types of grease, such as chassis grease, are electrically conductive and lead to battery self-discharge and even corrosion of battery terminals.

Battery Service Precautions

K12009, A12001

The Prevent Blindness America organization recently reported that nearly 2,000 people in the United States suffer eye injuries every day. For this reason, safety should be the first priority when working around and servicing batteries. Batteries are dangerous for a couple of reasons. First, electrolyte inside lead-acid batteries is corrosive. Acid on skin, in eyes, on clothing, or on paint will burn, causing bodily harm and vehicle damage. Also, an explosive gas mixture consisting of hydrogen and oxygen is produced during charging and discharging of the battery. Follow these precautions to reduce the risk when working with batteries:

- Always wear protective clothing such as rubber gloves and goggles or full-face shields when handling batteries. When handling a battery or checking electrolyte levels, wear a rubber apron to protect clothing from splashed battery acid. If acid contacts your skin or eyes, flush with water immediately.

- Never wear any conductive jewelry (neck chains, watches, or rings) when working on or near batteries, as they may provide an accidental short-circuit path for high currents.
- Do not smoke, weld, or grind metal near batteries because sparks may ignite the explosive gas mixture.
- Never create a low-resistance connection or short across the battery terminals.
- Never disconnect a battery charger, jumper cables, or power booster from a battery when charging or jump-starting. Sparks will occur when disconnected and can result in battery explosions. Shut the power booster off. Disconnect the chassis ground clamp that is away from the battery first. Connect the ground clamp last when boosting.
- Charge batteries in a well-ventilated area. Always remove the negative or ground terminal first when disconnecting battery cables, because this procedure reduces the possibility of a wrench creating a short circuit between any positive voltage wiring and the chassis ground.
- Tighten all battery cable connections to the battery terminals properly. Loose connections are resistive and may cause sparks.
- Never set a wrench or other tool on a battery, as doing so can cause short battery terminals, leading to gassing, overheating, and an explosion in an alarmingly short period.

▶ TECHNICIAN TIP

Always connect and disconnect the main battery ground first. If there are other ground cables connected to the battery for the engine and other electronic control modules, connect these grounds last. When additional grounds are either connected or disconnected and you do not connect the main battery ground, voltage spikes could occur and may damage electronic control modules.

SAFETY TIP

Never allow a spark or flame around a battery, and never try to jump-start a frozen, faulty, or open-circuit battery; doing so could cause the battery to explode, causing injury.

▶ Causes of Battery Failure

K12010

According to several studies, batteries cause 52% of vehicle breakdowns or failures to provide service. Battery failures are by far the leading cause for service breakdowns, with tires being the next most common (15%), followed by engines (8%). The two most common complaints concerning batteries are that either they do not charge or do not hold a charge. Batteries may suddenly fail through the loss of a cell or because of open circuits within the internal connections. Plate deterioration through the gradual loss of capacity also causes batteries to fail slowly over time.

Sulfation

According to a study, of all lead-acid batteries customers returned to the manufacturer under warranty, close to half were found to have no defect. Of those found defective, sulfation caused close to 80%. You can observe sulfation when a white-colored substance coats and swells, as **FIGURE 12-40** shows. It occurs when batteries are subjected to prolonged undercharge conditions. During normal use, soft sulfate crystals form and dissipate as part of the normal charge and discharge cycle. During periods of prolonged undercharge, the sulfate converts to hard crystals and deposits on the negative plates. During subsequent charging, the hardened sulfate cannot be driven from the plate and reduces the active area of plate material. Sulfation also increases the internal resistance of a battery. This means higher charging voltage is needed to regenerate active plate material when charging. Pulse-type battery chargers have a setting for potentially reconditioning batteries that may have been sitting for periods of time in an undercharged state. Listed here are some common reasons for sulfation:

1. *Leaving batteries too long in a state of discharge:* Soft sulfation occurring during normal discharge turns to hard sulfate crystals over time. Batteries should be recharged as soon as possible after discharging. Key-off loads, also called parasitic drains, contribute to sulfation caused by prolonged discharge.
2. *Undercharging a battery:* High resistance at battery connections, particularly in batteries connected in series or parallel, leads to undercharging of cells. Incorrect charging system voltage can also cause undercharging.
3. *High ambient temperatures:* Temperatures in excess of 100°F (39°C) speed up chemical activity inside a battery, accelerating the self-discharge of a battery. Experts calculate that a new, fully charged, flooded battery would most likely not start an engine in as little as 30 days if exposed continuously to 110°F (47°C). Significantly higher rates of battery failures occur in warm regions of North America than in cold areas. To minimize self-discharge, store batteries in cool, dry places.
4. *Low electrolyte level:* Battery plates exposed to air dry out and prevent transfer of sulfate from the plate material back into electrolyte during charging. Adding acid to a battery does not recover a dead battery. Instead, it increases the concentration of sulfate in the battery.

FIGURE 12-40 Sulfate on the top of the plates of a lead-acid battery.

Performing a Sulfation (3-Minute Charge) Test

Use a 3-minute battery charge test to indicate sulfation. Perform this test as part of a regular battery evaluation, but only to validate a diagnosis of sulfation. This battery test requires you to charge the battery at 30–40 amps for 3 minutes, while measuring the battery voltage with the charger on. If the voltage rises above 15.5 volts, the battery is excessively resistive and is likely sulfated.

Vibration

Excessive vibration can cause open circuits in the internal battery connections; it can also produce "shed," or loose plate material, which settles to the bottom of the battery case. Shedding reduces the plate surface area and therefore reduces capacity. **Shedding** may also produce short circuits between the bottom of positive and negative plates.

Electrolyte Level and Condition

Low electrolyte level exposes the plates to air, preventing the transfer of sulfate from the plate material back into the electrolyte during charging. It is critical to maintain the correct acid–water mix of electrolyte. If electrolyte level is lost through evaporation, then add distilled water. If electrolyte is lost due to spillage, then top up the battery with electrolyte. Examine the electrolyte to detect damaged plates and grids. Gray or dirty electrolyte in any cell renders a battery defective. Although voltage and electrolyte readings may be satisfactory, contaminants, even in one cell, cause the battery to self-discharge quickly. Series connections between cells cause even one dead or defective cell to discharge all other cells in the battery. Check electrolyte condition at the same time you evaluate specific gravity.

Grid Corrosion

Grid corrosion, like that in **FIGURE 12-41**, takes place primarily in the positive grid and is accelerated by overcharging and high temperatures. When corrosion takes place, grid resistance increases during charging and discharging. Grids are the foundation and the electrical conducting layer for the battery plate.

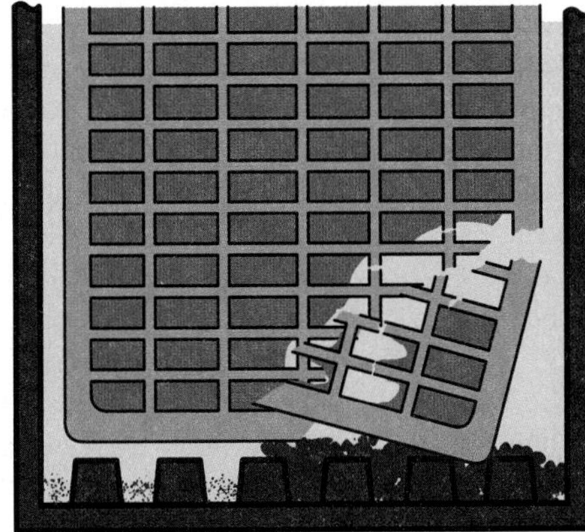

FIGURE 12-41 Corroded grids increase battery resistance, making the battery harder to charge and causing low supply voltage when cranking.

Although manufacturers alloy grids with antimony, calcium, or sometimes barium to minimize the corrosive effects of the electrolyte, grids do disintegrate. The mudlike lead paste attached to grids also falls apart when grids corrode.

▶ Battery Inspecting, Testing, and Maintenance

K12011; S12001, S12002, S12003, S12004

As noted earlier, batteries last longer if they are properly maintained. In fact, one of the most common causes of vehicle no-starts is dirty or corroded battery cables. Inspecting, cleaning, and filling (if not maintenance free) are common tasks that the technician should perform every 6 months to 1 year on top-post batteries, and 1–2 years on side-post batteries. During periodic maintenance, check batteries for proper ventilation. All slide mechanisms on battery trays should work properly. Inspect battery cables for rubbing or binding. Battery terminals should be tight and show no evidence of overheating. Always coat battery terminals with a dielectric sealer to prevent corrosion. Evaluate batteries visually first before proceeding with any other significant tests. Visual checks include these:

- Cracks
- Bulges—indicate batteries have either overheated or been frozen
- Cable connections—connections should be clean, tight, acid resistant, and show no signs of heat damage
- Battery hold-downs—loose or missing hold-downs cause plate shedding
- Dirty case—causes current to leak out of batteries
- Leaks
- Electrolyte level—level should be above the plates
- Electrolyte appearance—liquid should be clear; a brownish color may indicate damaged plates or contaminated electrolyte

To inspect, clean, fill, or replace the battery, battery cables, clamps, connectors, and hold-downs, follow the guidelines in **SKILL DRILL 12-1**.

Testing Battery State of Charge and Specific Gravity

Although the capacitance test is the industry standard to evaluate battery condition, technicians may still use other tests. One of those tests is the state of charge (SOC) test. As the term suggests, **state of charge** refers to the charge condition of the battery and is expressed as a percentage of a fully charged battery. In other words, SOC testing tells you how charged or discharged a battery is, not how much capacity it has.

A fully charged battery should have an open-circuit voltage of 12.65 volts. If the battery has been recently charged, a light load applied to the battery for a minute removes a surface charge. Open-circuit voltage is consequently affected by the battery specific gravity. About 1/12-volt change occurs for every 10°F below 80°F. **TABLE 12-6** shows SOC as indicated by specific gravity and voltage reading.

SKILL DRILL 12-1 Inspecting, Cleaning, Filling, or Replacing the Battery, Battery Cables, Clamps, Connectors, Hold-Downs, and Battery Boxes

1. Always remove the cable clamp from the negative terminal first. Then remove the positive terminal clamp. While they are disconnected, bend the cables back or, if necessary, tie them out of the way so that they cannot fall back and touch the battery terminals accidentally.
2. Remove the battery hold-downs or other hardware securing the battery. Depending on the type of vehicle, you will need to unbolt, unscrew, or unclip the restraint and move it away from the battery.
3. Keeping it upright, remove the battery from its tray and place it on a clean, level work surface. Visually inspect the battery for damage, cracks, bulges, loose or leaking posts, and so on. If you find any, you need to replace the battery.
4. Measure the voltage on the top of the battery with a DVOM. Place the black lead on the negative post and move the red lead across the top of the battery until you find the highest reading. The higher the voltage reading, the larger the potential drain.
5. Check the electrolyte level and its appearance.
6. Carefully clean the case of the battery, hold-downs, and battery tray and box either by (a) washing them or (b) wiping them down with damp paper towels if the battery and tray are not very dirty. It is best to wear rubber gloves while doing this, in case any corrosive electrolyte has leaked from the battery. Safely dispose of the paper towels.
7. Clean the battery posts or screw terminals with a battery terminal tool. On lead posts and terminals, the preferred tool is a scraper style, as it produces smooth surfaces that are more airtight when clamped together. Do not use the wire brush–style battery terminal tool, which leaves rougher surfaces that are more likely to corrode.
8. Clean the cable terminals with the same battery terminal tool or wire brush. Examine the battery cables for fraying or corrosion. If the damage looks extensive, replace the cables and terminals.
9. Reinstall the cleaned and serviced battery. Reinstall the hold-downs and make sure they hold the battery securely in position. If you need to install a new battery, be sure to compare the outside dimensions as well as the type of terminals and their locations prior to installation. These must meet the original manufacturer's specifications.
10. Reconnect the positive battery terminal and tighten it in place. Once the positive terminal is finished, reconnect the negative terminal and tighten it.
11. Coat the terminal connections with anticorrosive paste or spray to keep oxygen from the terminal connections. Verify that you have a good electrical connection by starting the vehicle.

TABLE 12-6 State of Charge as Indicated by Specific Gravity and Voltage Reading

Open Circuit Voltage	Specific Gravity	Percentage of Charge
12.65 or greater	1.265 (minimum)	100%
12.45	1.225	75%
12.24	1.190	50%
12.06	1.155	25%
11.89	1.120	0%

Voltage reading can also identify defective cells. Using a multimeter, place one meter lead on either terminal of the battery, and dip the other lead into battery electrolyte (if accessible). The meter should record a change of 2.1 volts for each cell when moving across the battery.

Measuring the density of electrolyte in each cell using either a bulb-type hydrometer or refractometer is the best way to evaluate the SOC. The specific gravity (SG) of electrolyte indicates the state cell charge. Cells should not have wide variations. If the SG reading between the highest and lowest cell is more than 0.050 point, the battery is defective. For example, if the highest SG is 1.265 points in one cell and only 1.210 in the lowest, the battery is scrap. **FIGURE 12-42A** and **FIGURE 12-42B** show two different tools technicians use to measure battery specific gravity. **FIGURE 12-42B** shows a refractometer.

Unlike the reading from a refractometer, you must correct the hydrometer's reading for electrolyte temperature. The density of battery electrolyte changes with temperature and 1.265 is only the density of electrolyte at 80°F (27°C). To correct for temperature effects on specific gravity, add or subtract 4 points to the reading either above or below 80°F (27°C) for every 10°F (6°C) temperature change. (For example, add 0.004 for temperatures at 70°F [21°C].) Because the hydrometer draws electrolyte into it to raise a float, the electrolyte level must be at least slightly above the top of the plates. If it is not, then you need to add distilled water and fully charge the battery. To perform a battery SOC test, follow the guidelines in **SKILL DRILL 12-2**.

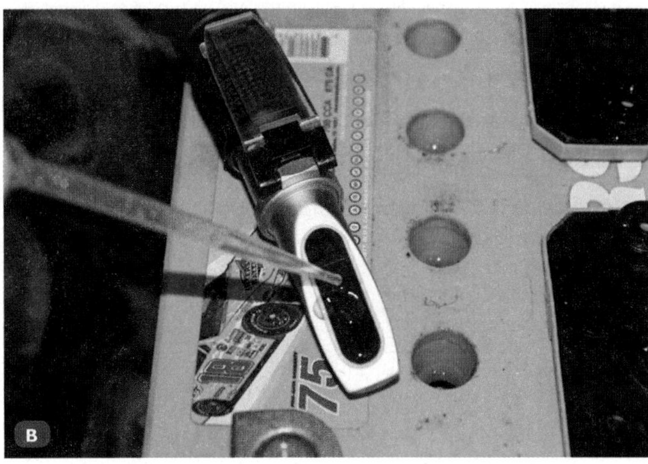

FIGURE 12-42 A. A hydrometer. **B.** A refractometer. You can use either to check the specific gravity of battery electrolyte in flooded cell batteries.

SKILL DRILL 12-2 Performing a State of Charge Test

1. If the battery is not a sealed unit, it has individual or combined removable caps on top. Remove them and look inside to check the level of the electrolyte. If the level is below the tops of the plates and their separators inside, add distilled water or water with a low mineral content until it covers them. Be careful not to overfill the cells; they could "boil" over when charging. If you add water, you need to charge the battery to ensure the newly added water mixes with the electrolyte before measuring the specific gravity.

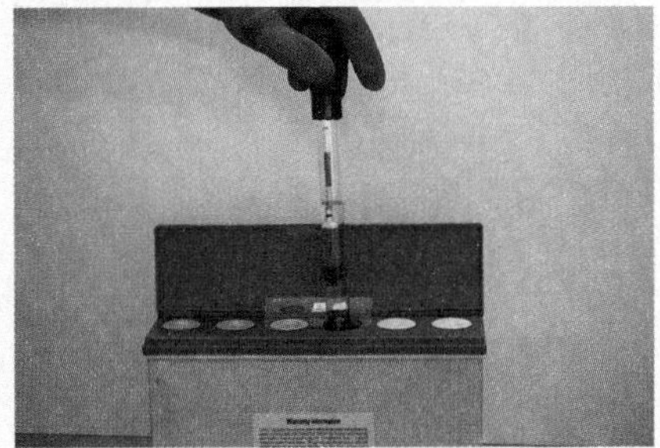

2. Using a hydrometer designed for battery testing, draw some of the electrolyte into the tester, and look at the float inside it. A scale indicates the battery's relative state of charge by measuring how high the float sits in relation to the fluid level. A very low overall reading (1.150 or below) indicates a low state of charge. A high overall reading (about 1.280) indicates a high state of charge. The reading from each cell should be the same. If the variation between the highest and lowest cell exceeds 0.050, the battery is defective, and you should replace it. Be sure to consult temperature correction tables if the battery electrolyte temperature is not at or around 80°F (27°C).

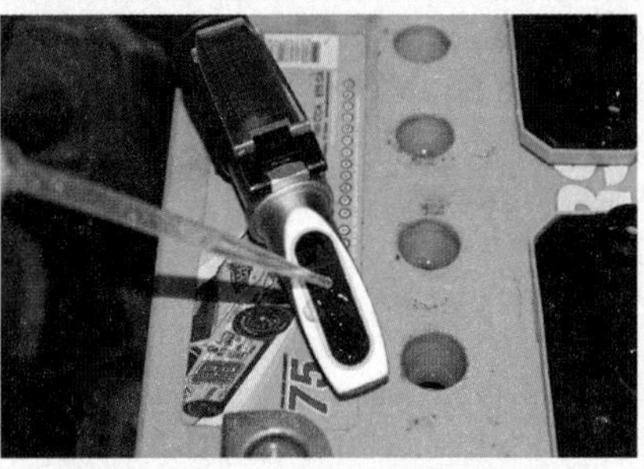

3. Using the refractometer, place one or two drops of electrolyte on the specimen window, and lower the cover plate. Make sure the liquid completely covers the specimen window. If not, add another drop of electrolyte:

- Look into the eyepiece with the refractometer under a bright light.
- Read the scale for battery acid. The point where the dark area meets the light area is the reading. Compare the readings with the values in step 2.

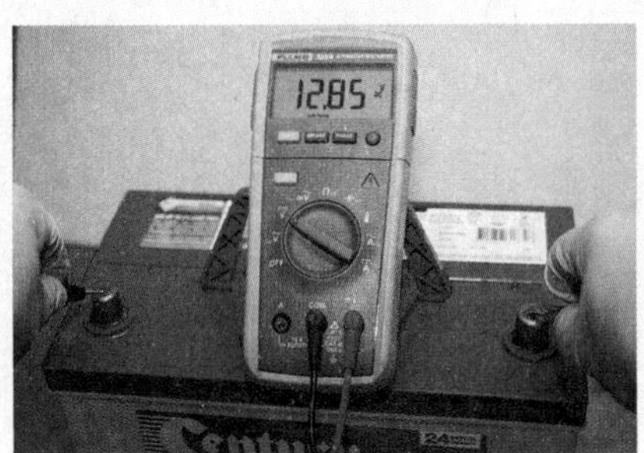

4. For open-circuit voltage testing with a DVOM, perform the following actions: (a) With the engine not running, select the "volts DC" position on your DVOM, and attach the probes to the battery terminals (red to positive, black to negative). (b) With all vehicle accessories switched off and the battery near 80°F (27°C), the voltage reading should be 12.65 volts if the battery is fully charged. This may be slightly lower at cooler temperatures.

> **TECHNICIAN TIP**
>
> When performing an SOC test, keep these tips in mind:
>
> - When filling a battery that is not fully charged, never fill it to the top of the full line, as charging the battery raises the electrolyte level.
> - Be aware that small amounts of electrolyte in the hydrometer may leak out, potentially damaging and corroding parts and battery terminals.
> - Do not inadvertently remove electrolyte from one cell or add it to another cell when testing; doing so causes incorrect readings.

Checking OCV (Open-Circuit Voltage)

Open-circuit voltage (OCV) is the difference of the electrical potential between the two terminals of a battery when the battery is disconnected from any circuit. Batteries should maintain an open-circuit voltage of 12.50 volts or greater. Use a voltmeter to check a battery's OVC.

To determine the stabilized open-circuit voltage, you need to remove the surface charge on the battery if the machine has been run in the last 10 hours. (If the machine has not been run for the last 10 hours, this step is not necessary.) To remove the surface charge, turn on three or four work lights (or any light load) and leave them on for 3–5 minutes. You can now check the battery. Place the negative lead of a multimeter on the negative terminal leaving the battery system and the positive lead on the positive terminal leaving the battery system. See **TABLE 12-7** to compare OCV to percentage charged.

Use a load tester to simulate placing a heavy load on a battery. Then check the OCV during and after you apply the load. The battery should have an OCV of at least 12.4 VDC before doing this test. The proper method is to apply a load equal to half the batteries CCA for 15 seconds and read the OCV at the end of the load test. If the battery voltage drops below 9.6 V, recharge and retest the battery. If it fails again, replace the battery.

Testing Battery Conductance

Evaluating a battery's condition using hydrometers, refractometers, and load testers provides reasonably accurate results if the technician uses the instruments correctly and the tech tests the battery under proper conditions. In the field, however, batteries often need charging for hours before the tech can test them, and SOC testing is time consuming.

TABLE 12-7 OCV Compared to Percentage Charged

Item	Measurement	Specification
Stabilized open circuit 12.5 volts or more	Percent charged	100
Stabilized open circuit 12.4	Percent charged	75
Stabilized open circuit 12.2	Percent charged	50
Stabilized open circuit 12.0	Percent charged	25
Stabilized open circuit 11.7 or less	Percent charged	0

In cold weather, testing on equipment outside presents other problems too. In the last 15 years, several rapid-test battery testers have emerged that eliminate the need for SOC and discharge-type testing. Referred to collectively as conductance testers, this equipment performs a measurement of the amount of active plate surface area available for chemical reaction. Active plate surface, as measured by conductivity, is a reliable indication of a healthy battery, as it corresponds directly to battery capacity. Also referred to as impedance testing, the AC equivalent to resistance, battery plate conductance declines as the battery fails.

All manufacturers are now requiring the use of a conductance test instead of a high-amperage load test in order for the company to consider warranty coverage. A **conductance test** determines the battery's ability to produce current. Many of the testers have integrated printers and, for the battery to be warranted, a printout of the test result has to accompany the battery return. Advantages of conductance testing are as follows:

- It does not require any battery discharge activity.
- It requires only minimal technician involvement, as the technician attaches only two clip-on connectors to the battery terminals during the test.
- It is fast—the tech can usually perform testing in less than 2 minutes.
- Low-frequency AC does not affect battery. Conductance testing does not prematurely age the battery.
- It is safe—it produces no heat or gassing.
- Technicians can repeat conductance testing immediately to verify the result.
- The technician can evaluate batteries in a state of discharge; some testers only require as little as 2 volts of battery voltage to qualify the battery
- All electrical standards testing organizations including Battery Council International (BCI) endorse the testing method.
- Printed read-outs can be supplied to the customer or to accompany warranty claims (**FIGURE 12-43**).

FIGURE 12-43 Printouts from a conductance tester.

The most common type of conductance tester works by applying an AC voltage of a known frequency and amplitude across the battery. A microprocessor inside the test unit interprets the battery's response to the signal. Conductance, or acceptance of the AC voltage, is measured by comparing the shape of the AC waveform exiting the battery to the waveform sent into the battery. The closer the waveforms match, the better the conductivity of the battery.

The most sophisticated testers today analyze lead-acid, Li-ion, and NiMH batteries, using a microprocessor containing algorithms that match waveforms from known battery configurations. These analyzers can identify not only the type and condition of a battery but also the manufacturer and other battery details. To conductance test a battery, follow the guidelines in **SKILL DRILL 12-3.**

TECHNICIAN TIP

Never use steel bolts, nuts, washers, and so on on battery terminals when using conductance testers. Instead, only use the lead adapters supplied with the conductance tester. The materials and any coatings on other hardware interfere with the signals sent through the battery and affect the tester's accuracy. Conductance testing is best suited for SLI batteries and may not provide accurate results for deep cycle batteries using thicker plate.

Testing Battery Capacity

Traditionally, the load test evaluates a battery's capacity, but the test has become less popular due to the overwhelming advantages of conductance testing.

The **load test** determines the ability of a battery to deliver cranking amperage and is based on the battery CCA rating. For example, a 1000 CCA battery can deliver 1,000 amps at −18°C, or 0°F for 30 seconds, while maintaining a voltage of 7.2 volts. During a load test, only half the CCA rating is applied as an electrical load for 15 seconds.

A battery must be at least 75% charged to perform a capacity test, so the technician must first evaluate SOC before proceeding. A carbon pile is used to simulate the high-amperage electrical load on the battery. At the end of 15 seconds, after one-half the CCA rating has been applied, battery voltage must not fall below 9.6 volts. If it does, the battery is scrap. Because temperature affects battery voltage, 0.1 volt is subtracted from the failure threshold voltage level of 9.6 volts for every 10°F below 70°F.

Another way to think of a load test is that you are testing the battery's ability to produce the high starting current while maintaining enough voltage to operate the engine's electronic control systems.

If the battery fails the load test after you have properly qualified its SOC, the battery should be discarded. Do not attempt to recharge and reload the test after it has failed the first time. To load test a battery, follow the guidelines in **SKILL DRILL 12-4.**

▶ Charging Batteries

S12005

Batteries go dead for a variety of reasons. Parasitic drains, self-discharge, or battery leakage are common reasons a battery may quickly lose its charge. A number of different chargers are available to recharge dead batteries, each with its own advantages and disadvantages.

Types of Battery Chargers

Differentiating between the types of battery chargers is useful for determining the best method for recharging a battery, given its condition and other operating variables. The most common types of chargers include constant-voltage chargers, constant-current chargers, taper-current chargers, pulsed chargers, and intelligent chargers.

- **Constant-voltage chargers**, like the one in Figure 12-43, are direct current (DC) power supplies that use a step-down

SKILL DRILL 12-3 Conductance Testing a Battery

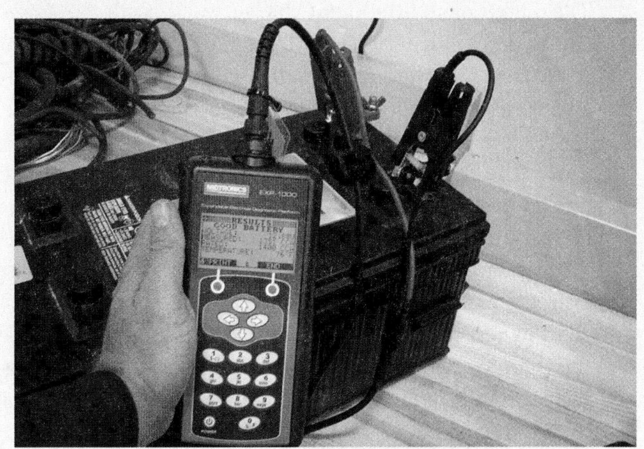

1. Consult manufacturers' procedures and guidelines for the battery you are to test and for the tester you are using.
2. Isolate batteries if they are connected in a bank so that you can test them individually.
3. Identify the type of battery, size, and voltage for input into the test unit.
4. Save information and input as required into the test unit.
5. Run the test.
6. Analyze the results by comparing them to manufacturer specifications.
7. Print or record results of the battery test. Repeat steps if multiple batteries are to be tested.

SKILL DRILL 12-4 Load Testing a Battery

1. With the tester controls off and the load control in the off position, connect the tester leads to the battery. Observe the correct polarity, and be sure the leads fully contact the battery terminals.
2. Place the inductive amps clamp around either the black or the red tester cables in the correct orientation.
3. Verify that the battery's state of charge is more than 75% before beginning the test. Also measure the battery's temperature to make any correction to the cutoff voltage threshold.
4. If you are using an automatic load tester, enter the battery's CCA and select "Test" or "Start." If you are using a manual load tester, calculate the test load, which is half of the CCA. Turn the control knob or press the "Start" button.
5. Maintain calculated load of 1/2 the CCA rating for 15 seconds while watching the voltmeter. At the end of the 15-second test load, read the voltmeter, and immediately turn the control knob off. At room temperature, the voltage must be 9.6 volts or higher at the end of the 15-second load. If the battery is colder than room temperature, correct the battery failure threshold voltage against temperature. Close to 1/10 volt lower is allowed for every 10°F below 70°F. Using the results from the test, determine any necessary action.

transformer and a rectifier to convert AC voltage to DC voltage for charging. As the name suggests, output voltage is constant between 13 and 14 volts. A manual switch may allow the voltage setting to increase or decrease to change the charge rate. These designs are found in inexpensive chargers, and the technician must use them with care because they can cause overcharging of batteries. **Trickle chargers**, which charge a battery at a low-amperage rate, are made following this design. Slow charging or trickle charging a battery is less stressful on a battery than fast charging because a low-amperage charge does not excessively heat and gas a battery.

- **Constant-current chargers** automatically vary the voltage applied to the battery to maintain a constant amperage flow into the battery. These vary the voltage to maintain the constant current into the battery as its resistance changes. Also called series chargers, several batteries can be connected together in series and charged together. These are premium, high-end chargers not commonly found in service facilities.
- **Taper-current chargers**, like that in **FIGURE 12-44**, are the chargers most commonly found in repair shops. Either constant voltage or constant amperage is applied to the battery through a manually adjusted current selection switch. Charger current only diminishes as the cell voltage increases. These chargers can cause serious damage to batteries through overcharging if the charge current is adjusted too high. Timers can automatically shut off the charger to prevent this condition.
- **Pulse type chargers** are recommended to recover sulfated batteries and send current into the battery in pulses of 1-second cycles. Varying the voltage and length of time a pulse is applied to the battery controls the charging rate. During the charging process, a short rest period of 20 to 30 milliseconds between pulses improves the quality of chemical reactions in the battery.
- The output of an **intelligent charger** varies with the sensed condition of a battery. This means the charger, like the one in **FIGURE 12-45**, monitors battery voltage and temperature and varies its output based on these variables. The charger also calculates the optimal charge current and varies it over the charging period, depending on the type of battery connected to it. Charging terminates when the voltage, temperature, or charge time indicates a full charge. VRLA batteries are best suited to these types of chargers. These chargers can be left connected indefinitely without overcharging, as they can maintain a float charge. This means the charging voltage floats at zero or a very minimal charge voltage until it senses that the battery voltage has fallen, and then resumes charging.

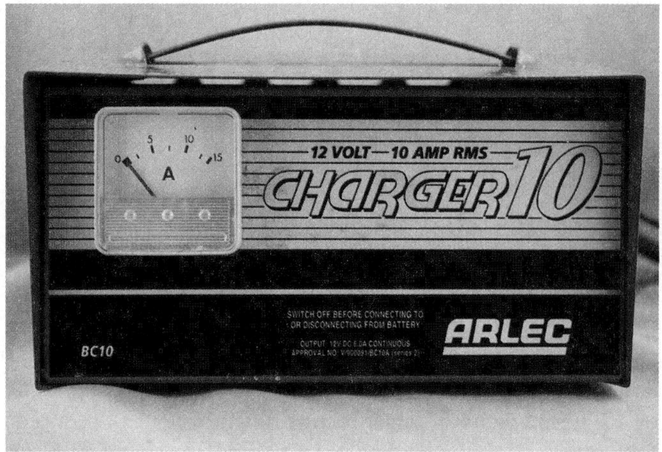

FIGURE 12-44 Take care with this type of basic constant-voltage charger to ensure overcharging does not occur.

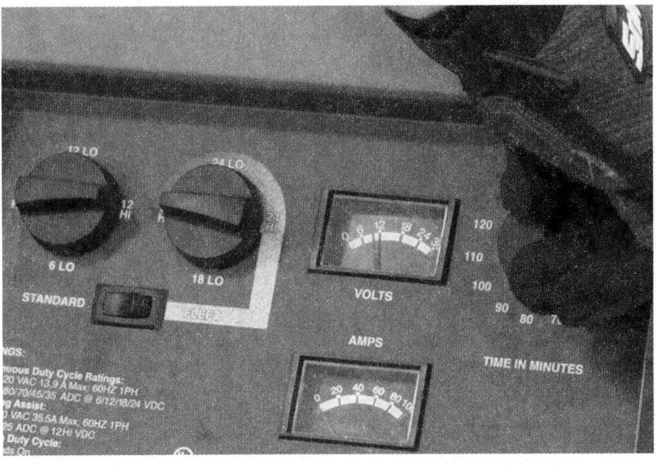

FIGURE 12-45 Note the timer on the right-hand side of this taper-current charger, to reduce the risk of overcharging.

FIGURE 12-46 This intelligent charger automatically controls the charge going to the battery. You can also select different battery types to ensure you are applying the correct charge rate for the battery you select.

Removing the negative battery terminal while charging a battery reduces the risk of burning up any electronic devices on the vehicle if the ignition key is on.

Charging Battery Banks: Series or Parallel

Manufacturers install multiple batteries in most heavy equipment vehicles to provide additional cranking amperage. Knowing how the batteries are connected together will determine how to properly connect a battery charger. Batteries can be connected in series or parallel. Batteries connected in series are connected in line with each other, with the positive of one connected to the negative of the other. Batteries connected in parallel are connected side by side, with positive connected to positive and negative to negative.

To charge a 24-volt set of batteries, you need a 24-volt charger to charge all the batteries at the same time. If you only have a 12-volt charger, you have two options: either charge one battery at a time, or reconnect the batteries so they are connected in parallel. To charge batteries, follow the guidelines in **SKILL DRILL 12-5**.

SKILL DRILL 12-5 Charging Heavy Equipment Batteries

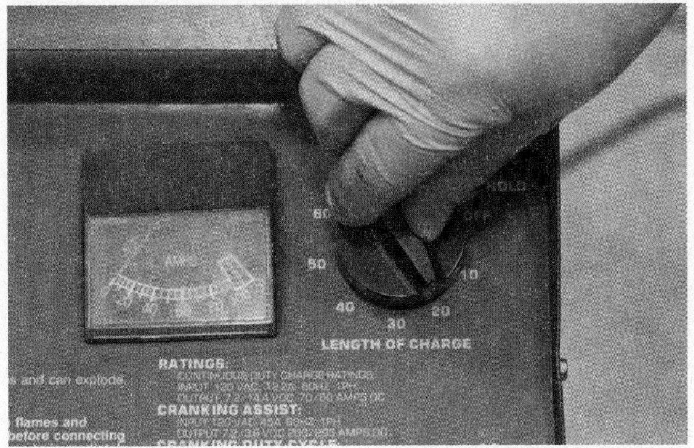

1. Determine the voltage of the system that needs charging. If you are charging a 12-volt battery, use the 12-volt setting on the charger. If you are charging a 24-volt battery, or two 12-volt batteries connected in series, use the 24-volt setting on the charger, if it has one.
2. Identify the positive and negative terminals. Never simply use the color of the cables to determine the positive or negative terminals; use the + and –, or the Pos and Neg, marks.
3. Visually inspect the battery to ensure there are no cracks, holes, or damage to the casing.
4. Verify that the charger is unplugged from the wall and turned off. Connect the red lead from the charger to the positive battery terminal. Connect the black lead from the charger to the negative battery terminal.
5. Check the settings on the charger, and verify that they are correct for what you are charging.
6. Turn the charger on, and select the automatic setting, if equipped. Select the rate of charge. A slow charger usually charges at a rate of less than 5 amperes. A fast charger charges at a much higher ampere rate, depending on the original battery state of charge; a fast charge should be carried out only under constant supervision.
7. Verify that the voltage and amperage the charger is putting out is proper.
8. Once the battery is charged, turn the charger off. Disconnect the black lead from the negative battery terminal and then the red lead from the positive battery terminal.
9. Allow the battery to stand for at least 5 minutes before testing the battery. Using a load tester or hydrometer, test the charged state of the battery.

SAFETY TIP

When connecting jumper cables, a spark almost always occurs on the last connection you make. That is why it is critical that you make the last connection on the chassis away from the battery and any other flammables. A spark also occurs when you disconnect the first jumper cable connection, so you also need to make that connection somewhere on the chassis.

- Keep your face and body as far back as you can while connecting jumper leads.
- Do not connect the negative cable to the discharged battery, because the spark may blow up the battery. Use only specially designed heavy-duty jumper cables to start a vehicle with a dead battery. Do not try to connect the batteries with any other type of cable.
- Always make sure you wear the appropriate personal protective equipment (PPE) before starting the job. Remember: batteries contain sulfuric acid, and it is very easy to injure yourself.
- Always follow any manufacturer's personal safety instructions to prevent damage to the vehicle you are servicing, and remember if you smell "rotten eggs" *do not* create any spark or flame, as you risk creating an explosion.
- The best practice to follow when charging a battery is "long and low." This means the longer time you take and the lower the amperage, the easier it is on the battery.

▶ Jump-Starting Equipment

S12006

Jump-starting a vehicle is the process of using one vehicle with a charged battery to provide electrical energy to start another vehicle that has a discharged battery. Because starting a vehicle requires a high amount of electrical energy, jump-starting a vehicle can put stresses on both vehicles. Taking your time when doing this not only ensures it is done safely, but it is also easier on both electrical systems. The ideal practice once the boosting cables are hooked up is to give the dead machine's battery plenty of time to be charged instead of just hooking up cables and immediately trying to crank the dead machine.

To jump-start heavy equipment vehicles, follow the guidelines in **SKILL DRILL 12-6**.

▶ Measuring Parasitic Draw

S12007

All modern vehicles have a small amount of current draw when the ignition is turned off. This charge runs some of the vehicle systems, such as various modules making up the on-board vehicle network. The vehicle computer systems also require a small amount of power to maintain the computer memory while the vehicle is off. The parasitic current draw should be a

SKILL DRILL 12-6 Jump-Starting Heavy Equipment

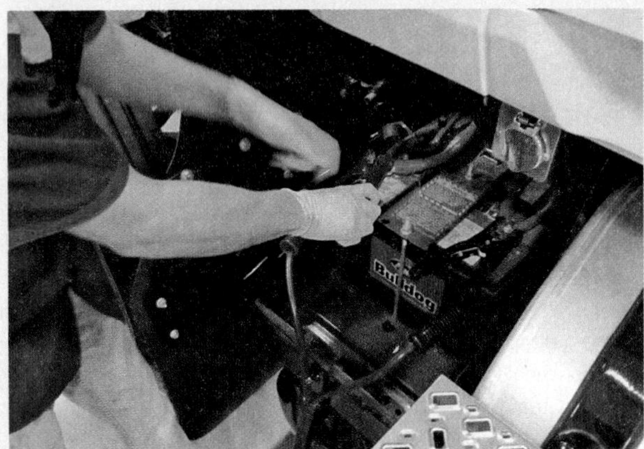

1. Position the charged battery close enough to the discharged battery that it is within comfortable range of your jumper cables. If the charged battery is in another vehicle, make sure the two vehicles do not touch.
2. Always connect the leads in this order:
   - First, connect the red jumper lead to the positive terminal of the discharged battery in the vehicle you are trying to start. The positive terminal is the one with the plus sign.
   - Next, connect the other end of this lead to the positive terminal of the charged battery.
   - Then connect the black jumper lead to the negative terminal of the charged battery. The negative terminal is the one with the minus sign.
   - Connect the other end of the negative lead to a good ground on the chassis of the vehicle with the discharged battery, as far away as possible from the battery.
   - *Do not* connect the lead to the negative terminal of the discharged battery itself; doing so may cause a dangerous spark.
3. Try to start the vehicle with the discharged battery. If the booster battery does not have enough charge or the jumper cables are too small in diameter to do this, start the engine in the booster vehicle, and allow it to partially charge the discharged battery for several minutes. Try starting the first vehicle again with the booster vehicle's engine running.
4. Disconnect the leads in the reverse order of connecting them. Remove the negative lead from the chassis ground away from the battery. Then disconnect the negative lead from the booster battery. Next remove the positive lead from the booster battery, and lastly disconnect the other positive end from the battery in the vehicle you have just started. If the charging system is working correctly and the battery is in good condition, the battery will recharge while the engine is running. *Note:* A deeply discharged set of batteries can cause the alternator to charge at an excessively high rate for too long, and damage to the alternator can occur.

relatively small amount of current, as excessive draw discharges the battery over a short amount of time.

Parasitic current draw does not necessarily immediately drop to its lowest level the instant the ignition is turned off. This usually occurs over a period of time as various systems go into hibernation or sleep mode, which can take up to a few hours. Consult the manufacturer's service information to determine the maximum allowable parasitic current draw and the time period, after the ignition is turned off, that it takes the modules to go to sleep.

Technicians can measure parasitic current draw in several ways. The most common is using an ammeter capable of measuring milliamps and inserting it in series between the battery post and the battery terminal. The ammeter is usually put in series with the negative battery lead. If the vehicle is equipped with systems or modules that require electronic memory to be maintained, follow the procedure for identifying modules that lose their initialization during battery removal, and maintain or restore electronic memory functions. Note that the timers may reset during the process of disconnecting the battery terminal and connecting the ammeter in series, so you may have to wait for the timers to go back to sleep. If you find excessive parasitic draw, disconnect fuses or systems one at a time while monitoring parasitic current draw to determine the systems causing excessive draw.

Disconnecting the battery can be avoided if a sensitive low-current (that is, milliamps) clamp is available. The low-amp current clamp measures the magnetic field generated by a very small current flow through a wire or cable. Placing the low-amp **current clamp** around the negative battery cable allows you to measure the parasitic draw. If you find excessive parasitic draw, disconnect fuses or systems one at a time while monitoring parasitic current draw to determine the systems causing the excessive draw. To measure parasitic draw with a parasitic load test, follow the guidelines in **SKILL DRILL 12-7**.

▶ Identify and Test Low-Voltage Disconnect (LVD) Systems

S12008

Low-voltage disconnect (LVD) systems disconnect a battery load when the voltage of the battery falls below a preset threshold. By doing this, they protect the battery from being excessively discharged and the vehicle from starting. The voltage threshold is normally set between 12.2 and 12.4 volts. Once the battery voltage rises above the set threshold, as it does when the vehicle starts and the alternator commences charging, the load reconnects automatically. In many cases, LVDs also incorporate an audible alarm and visual warning light to alert the operator before disconnection occurs.

LVDs are connected in series with the load. You test by varying the amount of input voltage around the threshold settings and checking the switching of the output or load to determine if the device switches on and off at the correct voltages. You can conduct testing on the vehicle or off the vehicle on a test bench. Test the LVD on the vehicle by monitoring the input and output, or load voltage, with a DVOM while placing a load across the battery to reduce battery voltage. At the threshold point, the device should turn the power off to the output or load. If two DVOMs are not available, you can use a test lamp to indicate when the output or load voltage drops away as the device switches off, although you should also check the output voltage at some point to ensure the load is receiving full battery voltage when the LVD has the load turned on. Compare the threshold voltages for turn on and off with the manufacturer's specifications. The units are usually sealed and are not serviceable, although some units may provide a means for adjusting threshold voltages.

You can also test the LVD off vehicle using a variable voltage power supply. When using a variable voltage power supply to test an LVD, you duplicate the connections made on the vehicle with the power supply taking the place of the battery. You must ensure that the power supply is capable of supplying enough current to operate the LVD and any load you connect to it on the bench. Once the unit is connected to the power supply and load, as per manufacturer requirements, you can slowly increase and decrease the power supply voltage to test the threshold voltages at which the LVD switches on and off the output or load. To identify and test a low-voltage disconnect system, follow the guidelines in **SKILL DRILL 12-8**.

▶ Recycling

K12012

Disposal is a critical issue at the end of every battery's service life. Batteries contain many environmentally damaging chemicals and neurotoxic lead. If they find their way into a landfill, the lead can contaminate the soil and groundwater. For this reason, recycling batteries is mandatory. Many municipalities require battery recycling and levy a "core charge" on every new lead-acid battery sold. The core charge is refunded if an old battery is brought in and exchanged for the new one. This process helps prevent people from discarding batteries in landfills. Check local laws and regulations to ensure that batteries are disposed of correctly.

SKILL DRILL 12-7 Measuring Parasitic Draw on a Battery

1. Research the parasitic draw specifications in the appropriate service information for the vehicle you are diagnosing. Typically this is between 0.035 and 0.050 amp (35–50 milliamps).
2. Connect the low-current clamp around (or insert the ammeter in series with) the negative battery cable, and measure the parasitic draw. Compare the parasitic draw with specifications.
3. Disconnect the circuit fuses one at a time to determine the cause of excessive parasitic current draw. Determine any necessary actions.

SKILL DRILL 12-8 Identifying and Testing a Low-Voltage Disconnect (LVD)

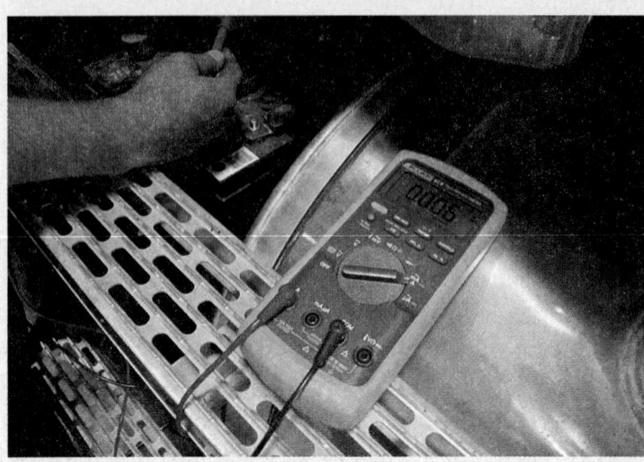

1. Research the LVD specifications such as the wiring schematic, device operation, and threshold voltages in the appropriate manufacturer's information.
2. Check the unit on the vehicle for appropriate power and grounds as per the manufacturer's specifications. If no battery voltage is present on the input side of the LVD, check fuses or circuit breakers for correct operation. Rectify any power or ground issues before proceeding to check LVD threshold voltages.
3. If you are testing the unit on a test bench, remove the unit from the vehicle, and connect both power and grounds to the unit as per manufacturer's specifications.
4. Connect a DVOM to the input or battery side connection of the LVD and a second DVOM or test lamp to the output or load-side connection. Note the voltage readings on both the input and output of the LVD.
5. Vary the battery voltage by connecting a variable load to the vehicle battery if testing in the vehicle, or adjust the voltage if using a variable voltage power supply for bench testing.
6. Note the DVOM readings of the threshold voltages from the input of the LVD as the unit turns the load, or output, on and off. Compare the voltage readings with manufacturer's specifications. If the unit does not meet specifications, adjust the threshold voltage if adjustment is possible. If the unit is not adjustable or cannot be adjusted to manufacturer's specifications, then you need to replace the unit.
7. Connect an appropriate load to the output, or load side, of the LVD, and recheck the threshold voltages to ensure the unit is capable of supplying the current with minimal voltage drop between the input and output, or load.
8. Check the operation of any warning lights or bulbs fitted to the unit, ensuring they turn and off as the output, or load, of the LVD is turned on and off. Report any recommendations, and return the unit to normal operation.

▶ Wrap-Up

Ready for Review

- There are two types of batteries. Primary batteries cannot be recharged; secondary batteries are rechargeable.
- Secondary batteries operate using the principles of galvanic reaction and are the most practical for use in heavy equipment vehicle applications.
- Through a galvanic reaction, electricity is produced when two dissimilar metals are placed in an electrolyte.
- Batteries have traditionally been used in heavy vehicles to provide starting current and operate electrical accessories if the engine is not running.
- Batteries are classified by use, application, and chemistry used within the battery. Although lead-acid batteries are most prevalent, hybrid-drive vehicles also make use of nickel-metal hydride and lithium batteries.
- Lead-acid batteries deliver high rates of current with a higher tolerance for physical and electrical abuse compared to other battery technology. These batteries hold a charge well and when stored dry—without electrolyte—the shelf life is indefinite.
- Regardless of battery construction, all batteries have the same basic components: case, terminals, plates, cell straps, and electrolyte.
- A starting, lighting, and ignition (SLI) battery can supply very high discharge currents while maintaining a high voltage, which is useful when cold starting. A lead-acid battery gives high power output for its compact size, and it is rechargeable.
- Starting, lighting, and ignition (SLI) batteries are designed for a single, short-duration, deep discharge during engine cranking. Deep cycle batteries provide lower amperage current continually for electrical devices and accessories.
- Lead-acid batteries can be manufactured with electrolyte or dry. Dry batteries can be stored on the shelf for extended periods without the fear of sulfation and are lighter to transport.
- During charging and discharging, batteries produce hydrogen and oxygen gas caused by the breakdown of water through a process called hydrolysis. These gases require venting and are an explosion hazard.
- Batteries can be configured into battery banks in cases where larger current or higher-voltage batteries are required.
- Battery temperature plays an important role in the performance of a battery, and lead-acid batteries have an

ideal operating temperature range. A battery's internal resistance depends on the types of materials used to make the plates and the chemical composition of the electrolyte. A battery's internal resistance determines how quickly a battery can be charged or discharged.

- Energy density, energy efficiency, life span, SOC window, and the cost in dollars per kWh are all factors in determining the battery technology to use on heavy equipment vehicles.
- The major battery technologies used in heavy equipment vehicles are nickel-metal hydride (NiMH), lithium, and lead-acid. Each technology has distinct capabilities.
- NiMH batteries are relatively lightweight and have high power output and long life expectancy, making them a preferred technology for hybrid-drive vehicles.
- Lithium-ion (Li-ion) batteries are secondary batteries. They are not galvanic, nor do they use an electrolyte solution. Rather, they use a gel, salt, or solid material that replaces electrolyte, so they are immune to leaking.
- Valve-regulated lead-acid (VRLA) batteries do not use a liquid electrolyte and are completely sealed. As such, they can be installed in any position without leaking.
- Absorbed glass mat (AGM) batteries use a pressurized battery case that helps recombine oxygen and hydrogen when the battery is recharged. These batteries have a lower internal resistance and a more efficient and faster chemical reaction.
- A spiral-wound cell battery is a special type of AGM battery that reduces internal resistance even further. Ultracapacitors can supply large bursts of energy and quickly recharge themselves—which make them ideal for use in modern vehicles. As such, they are particularly advantageous in situations requiring regenerative braking and frequent stop–start systems, such as in electric and hybrid vehicles.
- Compared to lead-acid batteries, ultracapacitors have very low internal resistance and are very quick to absorb a charge.
- To minimize and prevent battery failure, many vehicles incorporate a battery management system to protect the cells, prolong battery life, and maintain the battery in a state of charge.
- Battery isolation systems allow the multiple batteries in a battery bank to be separated according to function.
- When multiple batteries are connected in parallel, batteries eventually charge and discharge unevenly, shortening battery life. Batteries should therefore be rotated through the different positions in the battery compartment, or a balancer (equalizer) should be used to compensate for unequal charges in multiple batteries.
- Hybrid-drive battery management is much more demanding than the conventional battery management devices due to the harsher environment in which hybrid-drive batteries operate (e.g., rapidly changing charging and discharging conditions).
- Testing the batteries should be the starting point when diagnosing complaints such as hard starting, slow cranking, or no start; when lights dim when an engine idles or other electrical problems occur; and whenever an alternator is replaced.
- Keeping the battery and terminals clean is one of the best maintenance practices for batteries.
- Safety should be the first priority when working around and servicing batteries. The electrolyte inside lead-acid batteries is corrosive and can cause injury to skin and eyes, as well as damage to clothing and the vehicle's parts.
- Batteries also produce an explosive gas mixture of hydrogen and oxygen during charging and discharging.
- Batteries fail suddenly due to the loss of a cell or open circuits within the internal connections. Batteries also fail gradually through loss of capacity caused by age, sulfation, extremes in operating temperature, vibration, low electrolyte levels, and grid corrosion.
- Inspecting, cleaning, and filling (if not maintenance free) are common tasks that should be performed every 6 months to 1 year on top-post batteries and 1–2 years on side-post batteries.
- The reverse current flow can damage some or all of the electronic control units (ECUs) throughout the vehicle, so it is critical to connect the battery correctly to prevent sending the current in the reverse direction through the electrical system.
- The capacitance test is the preferred test of battery condition.
- State of charge testing indicates how charged or discharged a battery is. Low-maintenance or no-maintenance batteries may not provide access to the electrolyte in the cells for state of charge testing.
- Technicians use hydrometers and refractometers to measure the specific gravity of the electrolyte in the battery during an SOC test.
- Load testing has long been used to test a battery's capacity and internal condition, but is no longer used. Manufacturers now insist on conductance testing for batteries, particularly any battery returned under warranty.
- The types of battery chargers include constant-voltage, constant-current, taper-current, pulsed charger, and intelligent chargers.
- Even with the ignition turned off, all modern vehicles have a small amount of current draw used to run some of the vehicle systems, such as the on-board network modules.
- The parasitic current draw should be a relatively small amount of current, as excessive draw will discharge the battery over a short amount of time.
- Correct disposal of batteries by recycling them is good for the environment, and the precious metals can be reclaimed for reuse.

Key Terms

absorbed glass mat (AGM) battery A type of lead-acid battery that uses a thin fiberglass plate to absorb the electrolyte; this prevents the solution from sloshing or separating into layers of heavier acid and water.

amp-hour A measure of how much amperage a battery can continually supply over a 20-hour period without the battery voltage falling below 10.5 volts.

balancers A device designed to adjust battery voltage to compensate for unequal charges in multiple batteries; also called battery equalizers.

battery equalizers A device designed to adjust battery voltage to compensate for unequal charges in multiple batteries; also called balancers.

battery isolator systems A system designed to separate the main starting battery and the auxiliary battery; also called a split charge relay.

battery management system (BMS) A system of electrical devices used to manage battery performance.

cold cranking amps (CCAs) A measurement of the load, in amps, that a battery can deliver for 30 seconds while maintaining a voltage of 1.2 volts per cell (7.2 volts for a 12-volt battery) or higher at 0°F (−18°C).

conductance test A type of battery test that determines the battery's ability to conduct current.

constant-current charger A battery charger that automatically varies the voltage applied to the battery to maintain a constant amperage flow into the battery.

constant-voltage charger A direct current (DC) power that is a step-down transformer with a rectifier to provide the DC voltage to charge.

cranking amps (CAs) A measurement of the load, in amps, that a battery can deliver for 30 seconds while maintaining a voltage of 1.2 volts per cell (7.2 volts for a 12-volt battery) or higher at 32°F (−0°C).

current clamp A device that claps around a conductor to measure current flow. It is often used in conjunction with a digital volt-ohmmeter (DVOM).

deep cycle battery A battery used to deliver a lower, steady level of power for a much longer time.

electrolysis The use of electricity to break down water into hydrogen and oxygen gases.

electrolyte An electrically conductive solution.

flooded lead-acid battery A lead-acid battery in which the plates are immersed in a water-acid electrolyte solution.

galvanic reaction A chemical reaction that produces electricity when two dissimilar metals are placed in an electrolyte.

gassing A situation that occurs when overcharging or rapid charging causes some gas to escape from the battery.

gel cell battery A type of battery to which silica has been added to the electrolyte solution to turn the solution to a gel-like consistency.

hydrolysis The use of electricity to break down water into its oxygen and hydrogen gas components.

intelligent charger A battery charger that varies its output according to the sensed condition of the battery it is charging.

key-off electrical loads Machine electrical loads drawing battery current when the ignition is off.

load test A battery test that subjects the battery to a high rate of discharge; the voltage is then measured after a set time to see how well the battery creates current flow.

low-voltage disconnect (LVD) A device that monitors battery voltage and disconnects noncritical electrical loads when battery voltage level falls below a preset threshold value.

nickel-metal hydride (NiMH) battery A battery in which metal hydroxide forms the negative electrode and nickel oxide forms the positive electrode.

open-circuit voltage (OCV) The difference of the electrical potential between the two terminals of a battery when the battery is disconnected from any circuit.

parasitic draw An electrical load similar to a key-off electrical load except that the current draw is usually unintended or unwanted.

primary battery A battery using chemical reactions that are not reversible, and the battery cannot be recharged.

pulse-type charger A battery charger that sends current into the battery in pulses of 1-second cycles; used to recover sulfated batteries.

reserve capacity Refers to the length of time, measured in minutes, that a battery discharges under a specified load of 25 amps at 26.6°C (80°F) before battery cell voltage drops below 1.75 volts per cell (10.5 volts for a 12-volt battery).

secondary batteries A battery that produces electricity using reversible chemical reactions, allowing the battery to be recharged.

shedding A process that reduces the plate surface area and therefore reduces capacity. Shedding may also produce short circuits between the bottom of positive and negative plates.

smart charger A battery charger with microprocessor-controlled charging rates and times.

spiral-wound cell battery A type of AGM battery in which the positive and negative electrodes are coiled into a tight spiral cell with an absorbent microglass mat placed between the plates.

split charge relay A system designed to separate the main starting battery and the auxiliary battery; also called a battery isolator system.

state of charge test A test that indicates how complete the battery state of charge is, expressed as a percentage of a full charge.

sulfation Refers to a process where sulfate, originally contained in the electrolyte, becomes chemically bound to both battery plates

taper-current charger A battery charger that applies either constant voltage or constant amperage to the battery through a manually adjusted current selection switch.

traction batteries A type of battery construction, commonly used in hybrid electric vehicles, designed to deliver high-amperage loads to electric traction motors.

trickle charger A battery charger that charges at a low-amperage rate.

ultracapacitor A new generation of high-capacity, high-energy density capacitors.

valve-regulated lead-acid (VRLA) batteries A battery design using a gas-tight case that does not permit battery gases or electrolyte to leak from the battery except through a pressure-sensitive safety valve.

Review Questions

1. Which of the following is correct concerning battery classifications?
   a. Primary battery: chemical reactions are not reversible, and the battery cannot be recharged.
   b. Secondary battery: the battery is rechargeable.
   c. Both A and B
   d. Neither A nor B
2. Which of the following is correct concerning types and classification of batteries?
   a. Batteries are classified according to what they are used for and how they are made.
   b. Batteries are classified by the type of plate material and chemistry used to produce current.
   c. Both A and B
   d. Neither A nor B
3. Which of the following statements is correct concerning deep cycle–deep discharge batteries?
   a. Deep cycle batteries are used to deliver a lower, steady level of power for a much longer period of time than an SLI-type battery.
   b. Battery plate construction and charging and discharging characteristics of deep cycle batteries are different from those of SLI-type batteries.
   c. In heavy vehicles, deep cycle batteries are used to supply current to constantly powered accessories, such as driver- and vehicle-communication devices.
   d. All of the choices are correct.
4. Which of the following statements is correct concerning separator plates?
   a. To prevent the battery positive and negative plate from touching and short circuiting, separator plates are placed between each plate in every cell.
   b. Separator plates are very thin, porous, glass fiber plates allowing electrolyte to diffuse freely throughout the cell and at the same time preventing plate contact.
   c. Both A and B
   d. Neither A nor B
5. One of the characteristics of low- or no-maintenance batteries is __________.
   a. greater corrosion
   b. higher electrical reserve capacity
   c. lower water usage
   d. slow discharge rate due to parasitic loss
6. Which of the following statements is correct concerning battery selection?
   a. The CCA rating of the battery is the most important rating considered when selecting batteries.
   b. In colder weather, engines are also harder to crank due to increased resistance from oil thickening.
   c. BCI estimates diesel engines require 220–300% more battery power than a similar gasoline engine.
   d. All of the choices are correct.
7. Which of the following is *not* correct concerning lithium-ion batteries?
   a. Lithium-ion batteries have liquid electrolyte similar to lead-acid batteries.
   b. Currently there are dozens of different cell chemistries used to produce lithium-ion batteries.
   c. Regardless of their specific chemistry, lithium batteries have a higher energy density than other battery types, such as lead-acid, nickel-cadmium, and NiMH.
   d. Popular Li-ion chemistries incorporate electrodes made from lithium combined with phosphate, cobalt, carbon, nickel, and manganese oxide.
8. Which of the following is *not* correct concerning gel cell batteries?
   a. Gel cell batteries can be considered spill-proof batteries.
   b. A fully charged gel cell battery has an open-circuit voltage of at least 12.55 volts.
   c. Gel cell batteries are created by adding silica powder to the electrolyte, which turns the liquid into the consistency of petroleum jelly; hence the name "gel cells."
   d. Gel cell batteries are sensitive to overcharging and can be ruined by overcharging.
9. Which of the following is correct concerning valve-regulated lead-acid batteries (VRLA)?
   a. With a VRLA battery, there is no need to add distilled water.
   b. With a VRLA battery, there is no cable corrosion.
   c. With a VRLA battery, there is the longest service life of all battery types.
   d. All of the choices are correct.

ASE Technician A/Technician B Style Questions

1. Technician A says that hybrid electric vehicles are not commonplace in industrial settings, but are likely to be in the future. Technician B says that heavy equipment, particularly diesel-powered equipment, uses multiple batteries connected in series or parallel to produce adequate starting current. Who is correct?
   a. Technician A
   b. Technician B
   c. Both A and B
   d. Neither A nor B
2. Technician A says that a fully charged 12-volt battery is 12.00 volts. Technician B says that connecting cells together in series allows batteries to be produced in a variety of output voltage. Who is correct?
   a. Technician A
   b. Technician B

   c. Both A and B
   d. Neither A nor B
3. Technician A says that the primary difference between deep cycle batteries and SLI is the thickness of the plates. Technician B says that deeply discharging SLI batteries dramatically shortens their service life. Who is correct?
   a. Technician A
   b. Technician B
   c. Both A and B
   d. Neither A nor B
4. Technician A says that during charging and discharging, water in the electrolyte is broken apart into its constituent hydrogen and oxygen in a process called electrolysis. Technician B says if battery electrolyte is too low, the plates dry out, and the increased acid concentration of electrolyte permanently damages the grids. Who is correct?
   a. Technician A
   b. Technician B
   c. Both A and B
   d. Neither A nor B
5. Technician A says that the demand for advanced battery technology in commercial vehicles is growing. Technician B says that not only do the increasingly popular hybrid electric vehicles require advanced batteries, but heavy-duty commercial vehicles also have a greater need for electrical storage capacity to run accessories. Who is correct?
   a. Technician A
   b. Technician B
   c. Both A and B
   d. Neither A nor B
6. Technician A says that a smart charger is a battery charger in which microprocessors control charging rates and times. Technician B says that AGM state of charge can be tested with a battery hydrometer. Who is correct?
   a. Technician A
   b. Technician B
   c. Both A and B
   d. Neither A nor B
7. Technician A says that batteries should be the starting point when diagnosing complaints such as hard starting, slow cranking, or no start. Technician B says that dirt on top of the battery does not cause premature self-discharge of the battery. Who is correct?
   a. Technician A
   b. Technician B
   c. Both A and B
   d. Neither A nor B
8. Technician A says you should never create a low-resistance connection or short across the battery terminals. Technician B says to always wear protective clothing such as rubber gloves and goggles or full-face shields when handling batteries. Who is correct?
   a. Technician A
   b. Technician B
   c. Both A and B
   d. Neither A nor B
9. Technician A says that if electrolyte is lost due to spillage, then the battery should be topped up with electrolyte. Technician B says that if electrolyte level is lost through evaporation, then tap water should be added. Who is correct?
   a. Technician A
   b. Technician B
   c. Both A and B
   d. Neither A nor B
10. Technician A says that a fully charged battery should have an open-circuit voltage of 12.25 volts. Technician B says that if the battery has been recently charged, a light load applied to the battery for a few minutes will remove a surface charge.
   a. Technician A
   b. Technician B
   c. Both A and B
   d. Neither A nor B

CHAPTER 13

Electric Motors

Knowledge Objectives

After reading this chapter, you will be able to:

- **K13001** Identify and describe the applications of AC motors.
- **K13002** Identify and explain the difference between AC induction and synchronous motors.
- **K13003** Identify and describe the difference between single-phase and three-phase induction motors.
- **K13004** Describe and explain the construction, functions, applications, and operating principles of AC motors.

Skills Objectives

There are no Skills Objectives for this chapter.

▶ Introduction to Electric Motors

Manufacturers producing off-road heavy equipment use electric motors for electric-only propulsion and hybrid-drive systems combined with diesel engine (**FIGURE 13-1**). Electric-only systems using battery power are frequently used in forklifts and in electric powertrains for mining vehicles, and are moving the industry from reliance on underground diesel engines to zero-emission vehicles. Electric-drive and hybrid technology for the heavy construction market is relatively new, with the first hybrid tractors such as Cat's D7E and Komatsu's HB215LC-1 excavator appearing in 2010. However, diesel electric drives have been around since the 1930s and are the main propulsion configuration for locomotives and mining trucks hauling in high-production mining and heavy-duty construction projects (**FIGURE 13-2**). These machines haul anywhere from 40 to 100 tons of material in quarries or road-building work, using electric traction motors (**FIGURE 13-3**). The ultra-class trucks hauling 300–450 tons exclusively use diesel electric hybrid-drive systems. Technicians will encounter electric motors in other applications powering hydraulic pumps, steering systems, large hydraulic cooling fans, and driving compressors for air conditioning in operator cabs. Understanding electric motor operating principles and troubleshooting techniques is important, then, to a technician wanting a broad range of skills to diagnose and service problems caused by various types of electric motors and propulsion systems. In order to help build technician competencies associated with making repairs and giving service recommendations, this chapter examines the various applications of electric motors, their types, and the architecture of

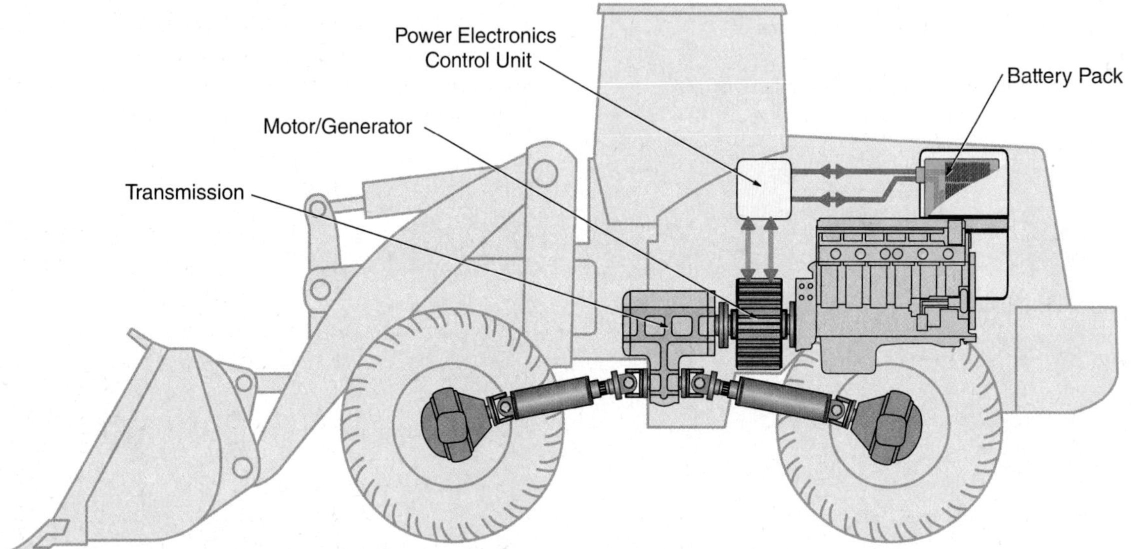

FIGURE 13-1 Many manufacturers are producing hybrid machines that use electric motors for propulsion, this strategy allows the engine to run at a more efficient RPM which saves fuel and therefore reduces emissions.

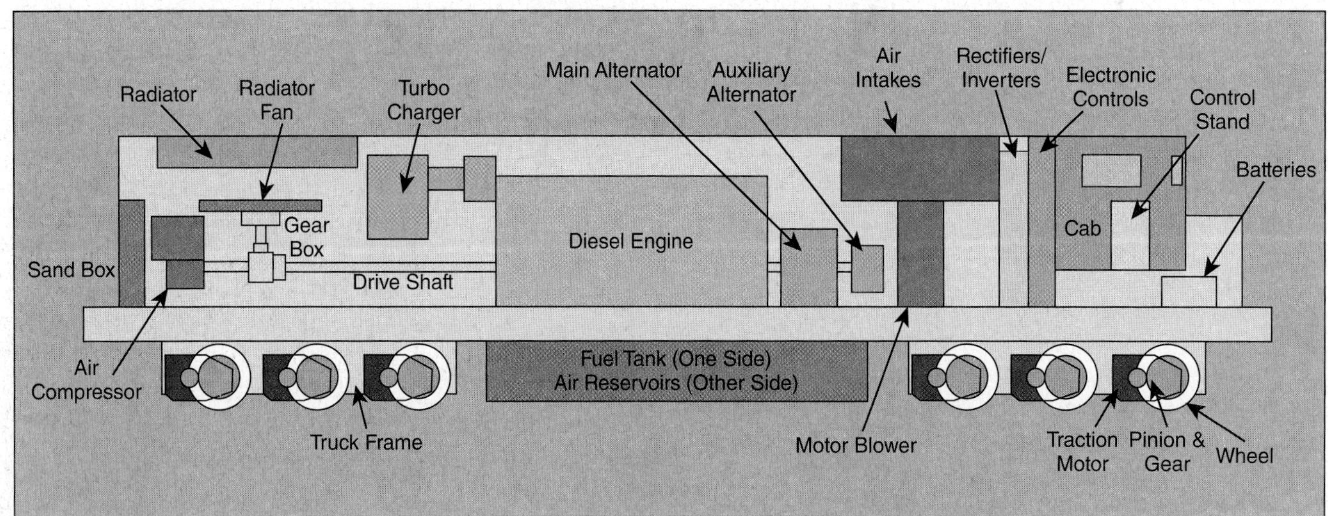

FIGURE 13-2 Locomotives use diesel electric generators to supply current to electric traction motors located at the wheels.

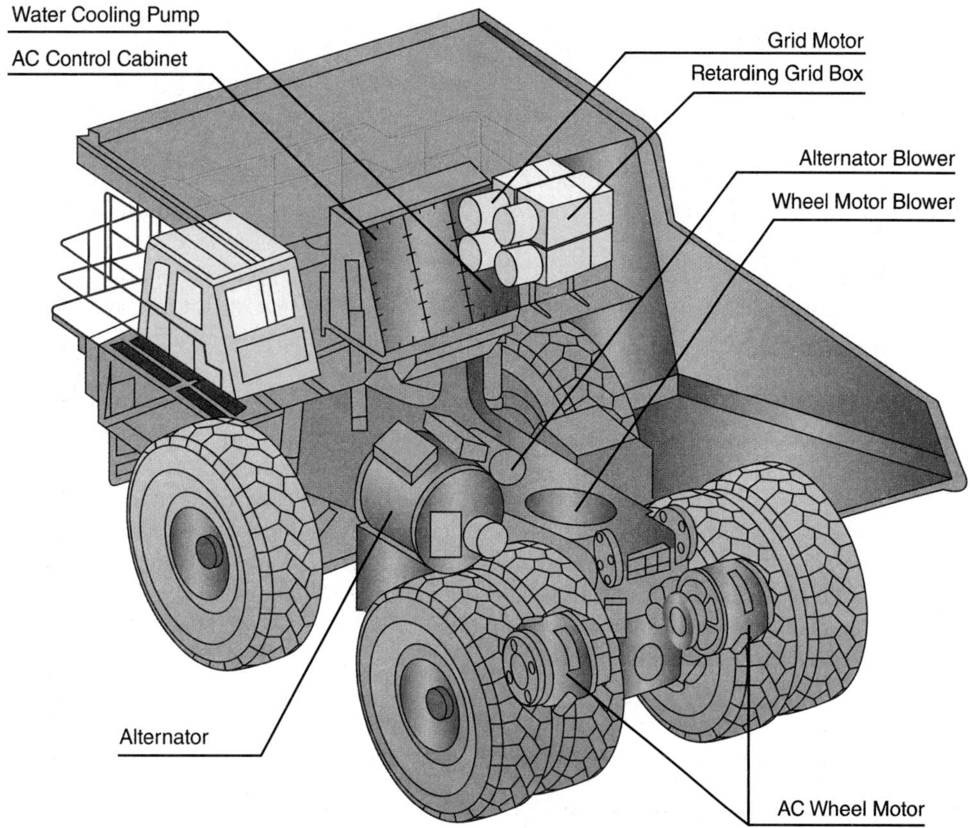

FIGURE 13-3 Diesel-driven AC generators supply current to electric drive motors of this truck.

electric-drive systems. Principles of operation of DC and AC motors, plus safety and service-related information, are covered to further enhance technical understanding and skills. Note that working with high-voltage electric current is potentially lethal. For this reason, electrical safety codes in most jurisdictions require technicians to have specialized electrician qualifications for working on circuits having more than 50 volts. Information in this chapter is to provide background information for understanding electric motors and servicing them in compliance with legislated safety and labor code standards.

▶ Advantages of Electric Motors

K13001

By definition, motors are devices that take any form of energy, other than combustion, and convert it into mechanical energy. Air, fluid, and vacuum are just a few of the different types of energy used to supply power to a motor. More specifically, electric motors use electrical energy and convert it into rotating mechanical energy. Because electric motors supply rotational energy like engines, they are used in place of engines and have advantages over engines. A few of these advantages include:

- Lower initial purchase cost and less complex construction
- More energy efficient than engines
- Fewer maintenance requirements
- Longer service life, as electric motors are designed for as many as 35,000 hours of operation
- Capable of producing maximum torque at low speeds and even stall speeds
- Smoother increase in speed and torque from 0 rpm to maximum
- Capable of providing retarding force to a machine
- Capable of generating electrical energy (when operating either as retarders or in a regenerative mode to charge batteries)
- Relatively inexpensive to operate—electricity is cheaper than liquid fuel such as diesel or gasoline
- Easier to start and simpler to operate—only a switch to turn on and off or an electronic controller is needed to regulate speed
- Capable of starting under a moderate load
- Capable of withstanding temporary overloaded conditions that severely reduce speed and may even stall the motor
- More compact in design, requiring smaller area and no additional support systems such as fuel tanks or radiators
- Low noise level
- No exhaust fumes
- Fewer safety hazards.

Auxiliary motors refer to motor functions driving auxiliary devices directly coupled, or driven by motors from a belt or gear drive. Examples of auxiliary motors include those driving air-conditioning compressors; cooling fans; and pumps for water, oil, or operating equipment such as hoisting devices. The use of auxiliary motors can promote more efficient engine operation. For example, when the AC compressor is driven electrically, it provides an acceptable reason for operators to shut off an engine during idling.

When used in a propulsion drive system, electric motors are referred to as **traction motors**. Combined with diesel electric-drive systems or hybrid-drive systems, motors are used to lower operating costs of traditional diesel equipment and reduce carbon emissions. In **series-type hybrid electric drive** systems where an engine drives a generator, which in turns supplies power to an electric motor, the bulk of efficiency gains is achieved by enabling the engine to work constantly within a narrow speed range.

Electric traction motors vary drive torque and speed to final drives with minimal change to the engine speed (**FIGURE 13-4**). Operating the engine inside a narrow speed range reduces fuel consumption because the speed range chosen is an optimal point of efficiency for an engine. In a series–parallel hybrid configuration, where the engine and motor combine to supply drive torque to supplement engine power output, electric motors can boost the drive torque from stand-still or add drive torque above an engine's base operating capabilities (**FIGURE 13-5**), Drive torque supplemented from an electric motor allows operators to obtain better engine response and encourages operation in a lower speed range. This in turn lowers power transmitted through the driveline and reduces fuel consumption.

FIGURE 13-4 Two electric motors and a smaller auxiliary motor located on top of this final drive supply propulsion force to an off-road machine.

Electric motors for battery electric machines such as forklifts or mine scooptrams for loading and hauling material are very power dense with high torque from a compact design. In the latest models, electric motors can produce three times the power of a comparable diesel 1.5-yard equivalent (**TABLE 13-1**). But the biggest benefit is that battery-powered equipment like this is the consequence of eliminating engine emissions. Diesel emissions are the major health hazard, and some mines have as many as 150 diesel machines working underground. According to one equipment manufacturer, several ventilation shafts, costing $50–100 million dollars each and needed to clear emissions, can be eliminated for underground mines. Additionally, 40–90% of total energy costs that are expended ventilating mines are substantially reduced when battery-powered electric-drive machines are used.

Diesel electric locomotives and heavy haul trucks popularized the use of electric-drive systems. Electric-drive motors simplified the way power is transmitted more efficiently to the wheels while greatly reducing maintenance requirements. Transmitting power through a transmission requiring an enormous number of gears and elaborate shifting mechanisms would be impractical (**FIGURE 13-6**). Braking and tire wear can be further reduced with electric drive motors. Braking and tire wear are reduced because the electric motor, when operated like a generator, can absorb energy and replace foundation brakes. Any electric motor, whether it is operated using AC or DC current, can also be used to generate current. A small amount

TABLE 13-1 Comparing Efficiency of Motors with Engines

Electric Motor	Diesel Engine	Gasoline Engine
50–95% efficient	40–55% efficient	2–35% efficiency

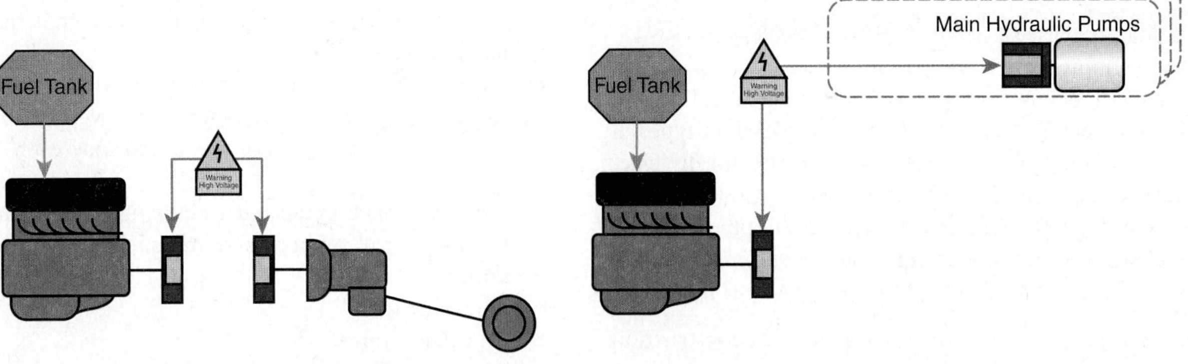

FIGURE 13-5 Configuration of a series-type hybrid powertrain and hydraulic system.

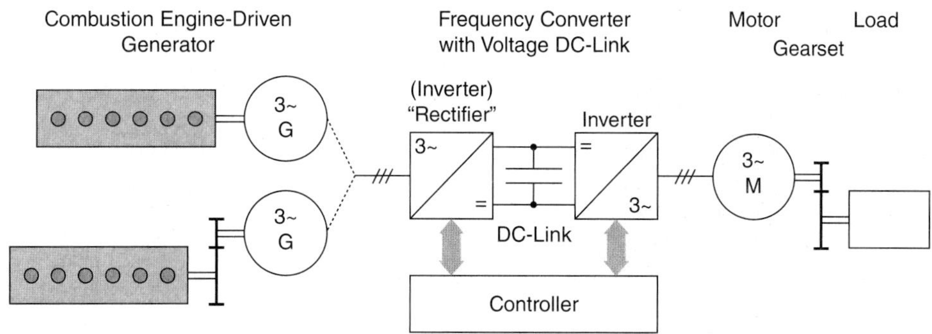

FIGURE 13-6 Locomotives and other diesel electric machines drive AC generators. AC current is converted to DC and then inverted again to AC to change voltage and frequency to better regulate propulsion motor operation.

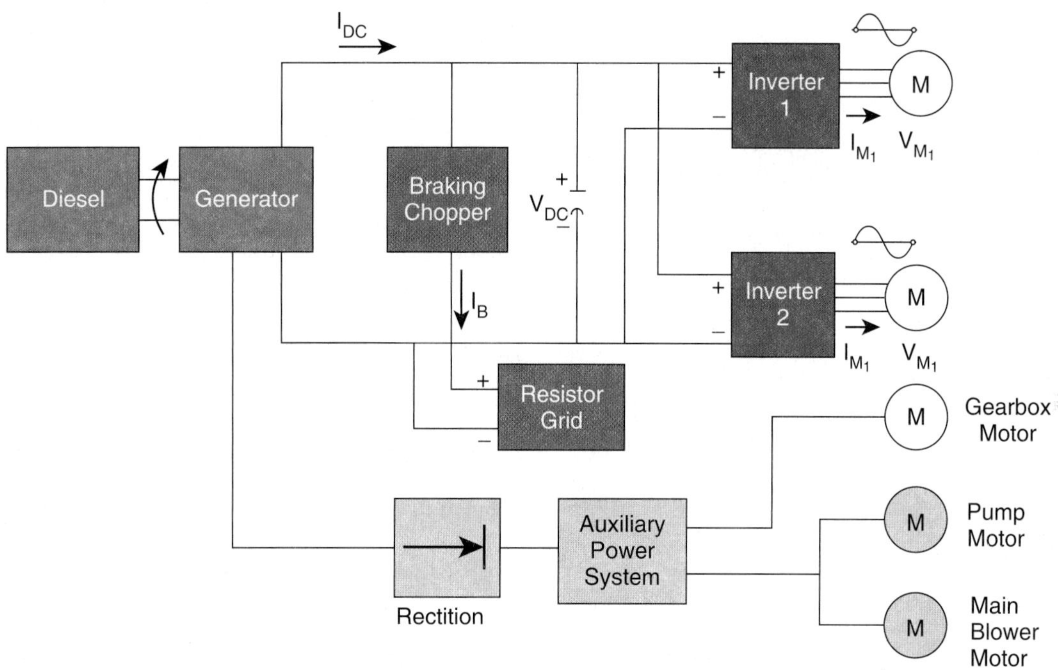

FIGURE 13-7 Any AC motor can be instantly converted to a generator and used as an auxiliary braking system. The retarder will often convert electrical energy to heat, using a resister bank.

of current supplied to the motor when it is being driven by a mechnical input will change it from motoring to electric power generation. When operated as a generator, the motor effectively turns into an energy absorbing brake, which in turn reduces foundation brake wear. When two drive motors are used to steer a machine, the differential torque control enhances turning capabilities and reduces tire wear. The generator function, which operates as an automatic retarder, can keep the machine within speed limits at all times. Anti-rollback supplied by the same retarder–generator function provides one-pedal control on hills and cruise control functions in both propel and retard operating modes (**FIGURE 13-7**).

When large lead-acid batteries are used on a machine such as an electric forklift, the batteries indirectly provide the benefit of providing more traction force to tires. Heavy batteries function as a counterweight to provide a stable counterbalancing force to oppose the lifted load.

▶ Classification of Electric Motors

K13002

The widest classification of electric motors is according to the type of electrical current used:

- Alternating current (AC) motors
- Direct current (DC) motors

Both types of motors are used in off-road machines. DC current motors are especially useful because they directly power through batteries. DC motor control is also simplified because speed and torque are controlled by varying current flow through motor windings, using a simple rheostat. A large variety of DC motor designs are used everywhere, from starting motors to blower motor fans, to powering pumps for fuel

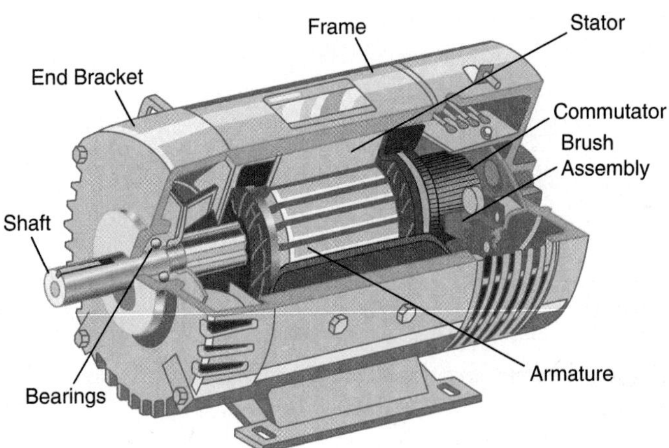

FIGURE 13-8 A cross-sectional view of a DC electric motor. Note the commutator and brushes.

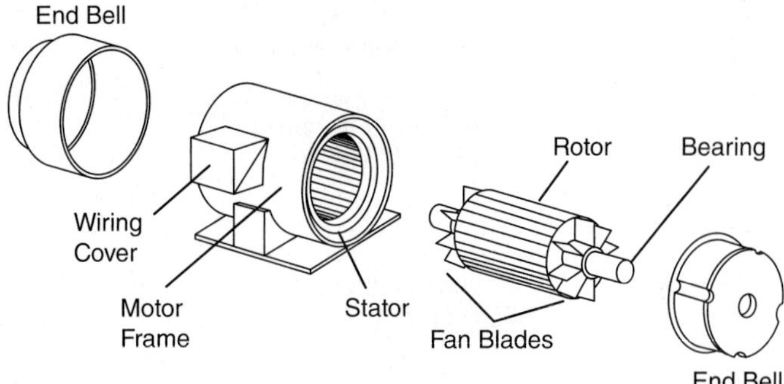

FIGURE 13-10 Major components of an AC induction motor.

or coolant (**FIGURE 13-8**). The arrangement of windings and whether they use permanent magnets generally classifies DC motors. The construction and operation of these motors is more extensively covered in Chapter 11. Although they have many applications, DC motors are generally not often used for propulsion systems, as they use a commutator and bushes to conduct current through the armature, the rotating part of the motor. Brushes eventually wear out, and the increased complexity of the motors makes them more expensive. Torque output compared to motor weight is less for DC motors (**FIGURE 13-9**).

AC Motors

AC motors are the most common type used for traction motors. One reason for the popularity is the AC motor has a simpler design with no moving parts to wear out except bearings supporting the motor shaft (**FIGURE 13-10**). Unlike DC motors, AC motors do not use commutators or brushes to switch the direction of current flow through an armature. Instead, the continuously changing polarity of AC current creates a rotating magnetic field movement inside an AC motor.

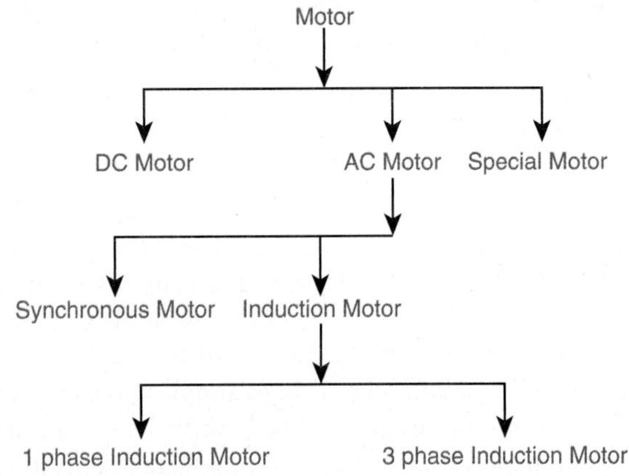

FIGURE 13-9 Classifications of electric motors.

A second major reason for using AC motors is the efficiency of AC current transmission. AC current is transmitted much farther than DC current, with little resistance. This property explains why municipalities use AC current to transmit electricity to homes and industry over long distances with comparably little power loss. To understand this, recall that electrons in AC current constantly moves back and forth in a circuit. There is no incremental forward movement of electrons in an AC conductor, unlike a DC conductor where electrons move continuously in only one direction—from negative to positive. In AC conductors, the movement of electrons cycle or pulses back and forth, causing the polarity of the conductor to continuously change (**FIGURE 13-11**). In one moment of time, electrons in an AC circuit are pulled and subsequently pushed, then pulled and pushed all over again. Power transmission of AC current in North America specifies a cycle switching time of 60 times per second for the push–pull polarity change of AC current. An electrical force exerting one push-and-pull cycle on the electrons produces a familiar sine wave if the circuit polarity is graphed over time. This continuously changing polarity of AC current, which can be 60 cycles per second, or 60 hertz (Hz), accounts for the efficiency of AC circuits. In AC circuits, electron energy isn't used up migrating electrons from one atom to the next along the length of the circuit to its end. Electrons in AC conductors stay in the same area. Resistance in an AC circuit, called **impedance**, is proportional to the frequency of polarity change. In fact, using higher frequency of polarity change or Hz reduces impedance or resistance in an AC circuit. In other words, the higher the AC current's frequency, the less resistance AC current has in a circuit.

Reduced circuit impedance and more efficient transmission isn't the only reason for using AC motors. The biggest advantage of AC motors is their simplicity. Because they have only one moving part, the rotor, they are more economical to build, operate more quietly with greater reliability. AC current simplifies motor construction by providing a constantly changing polarity. This eliminates the need for a commutator used in DC motors. In the most common AC motor designs, the AC current produces a continuously changing polarity of the magnetic fields inside the motor. AC current frequency regulates the speed of AC electric motors, with higher frequency corresponding to faster motor speed. This means AC motor speed control requires frequency regulation.

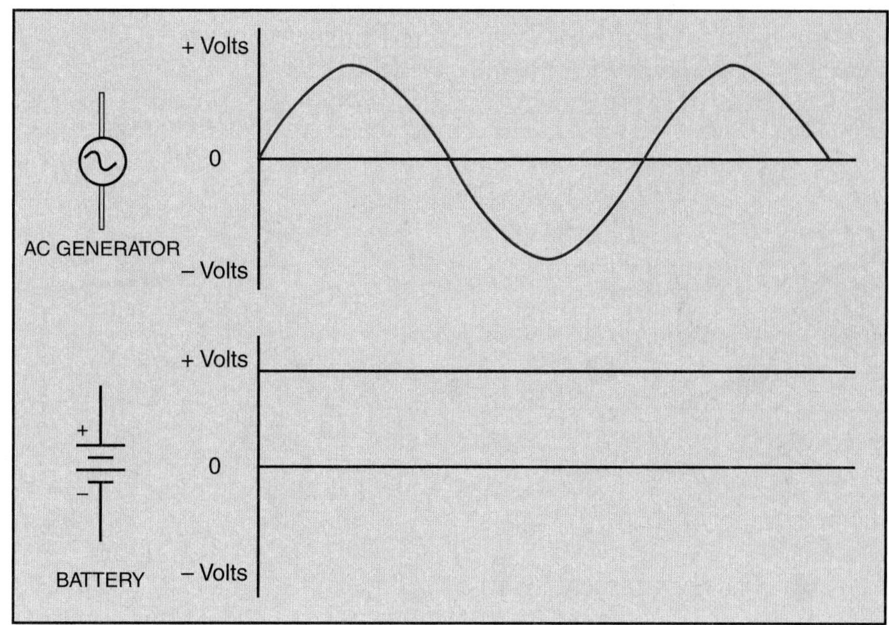

FIGURE 13-11 Comparing AC and DC electric current waveforms.

▶ AC Current Types

K13003

AC current has been used to power homes and industry since the 1890s, when industrialist George Westinghouse popularized the AC electric current type, invented by Nickolas Tesla. A major competitor using DC current also supplied electricity. Thomas Edison's, Edison electric company, later merged with another electric company to become General Electric, which competed with Westinghouse for domination of the power generation and supply. The current war fought between the two companies determined whether AC or DC current would ultimately be the electric current of choice for consumers and industry. The efficiency of AC current transmission won out, and AC current is delivered as two subtypes: single and three-phase current (**FIGURE 13-12**).

To diagnose the cause of a motor not starting, follow the steps in **SKILL DRILL 13-1**.

Single-Phase AC Current

Single-phase current, also known as house current, is used to power lights and small appliances. It's called single phase because of the use of two wires, one neutral and one power, which provide a pathway for electricity flow between them. The description of single phase is also derived from the appearance of the sine wave–shaped waveform of alternating current. Single-phase AC power voltage peaks at 90 degrees and 270 degrees when it completes a cycle time, measured in 360 degrees. This means at a starting point of 0 degrees, the voltage between the two wires is 0 volts and rises to +120 volts peak after 90 degrees. Voltage between the two wires falls to 0 volts after 120 degrees of cycle time and then peaks again to −120 volts after its polarity switches negative at 270 degrees of cycle time. Ninety degrees later, the current has a voltage of 0 volts before another cycle begins. Note that the peak voltage is briefly +120 volts during one cycle (**FIGURE 13-13**).

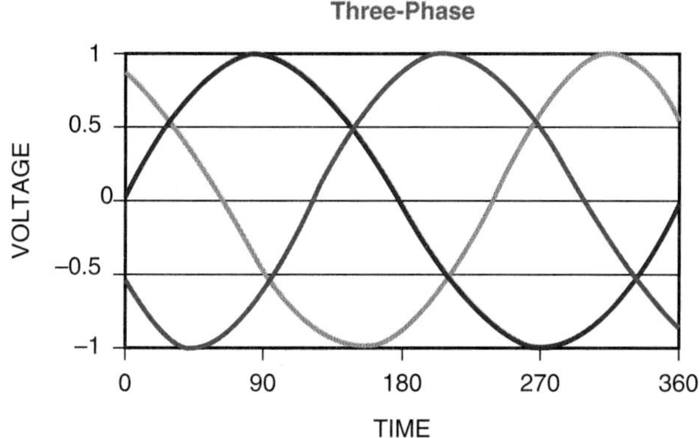

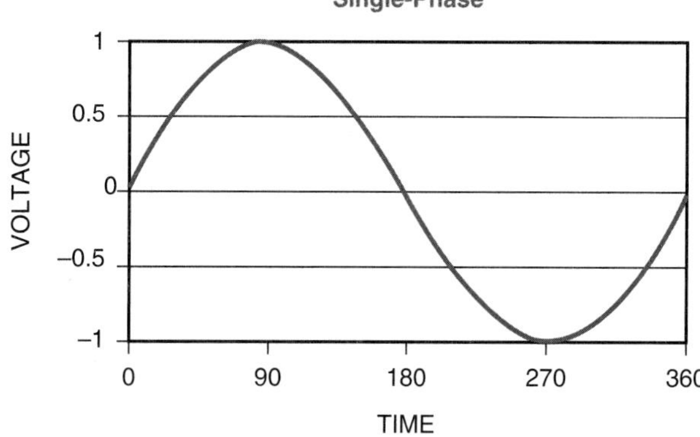

FIGURE 13-12 Single-phase versus three-phase current.

SKILL DRILL 13-1 Diagnosing a No-Start Split-Phase Motor

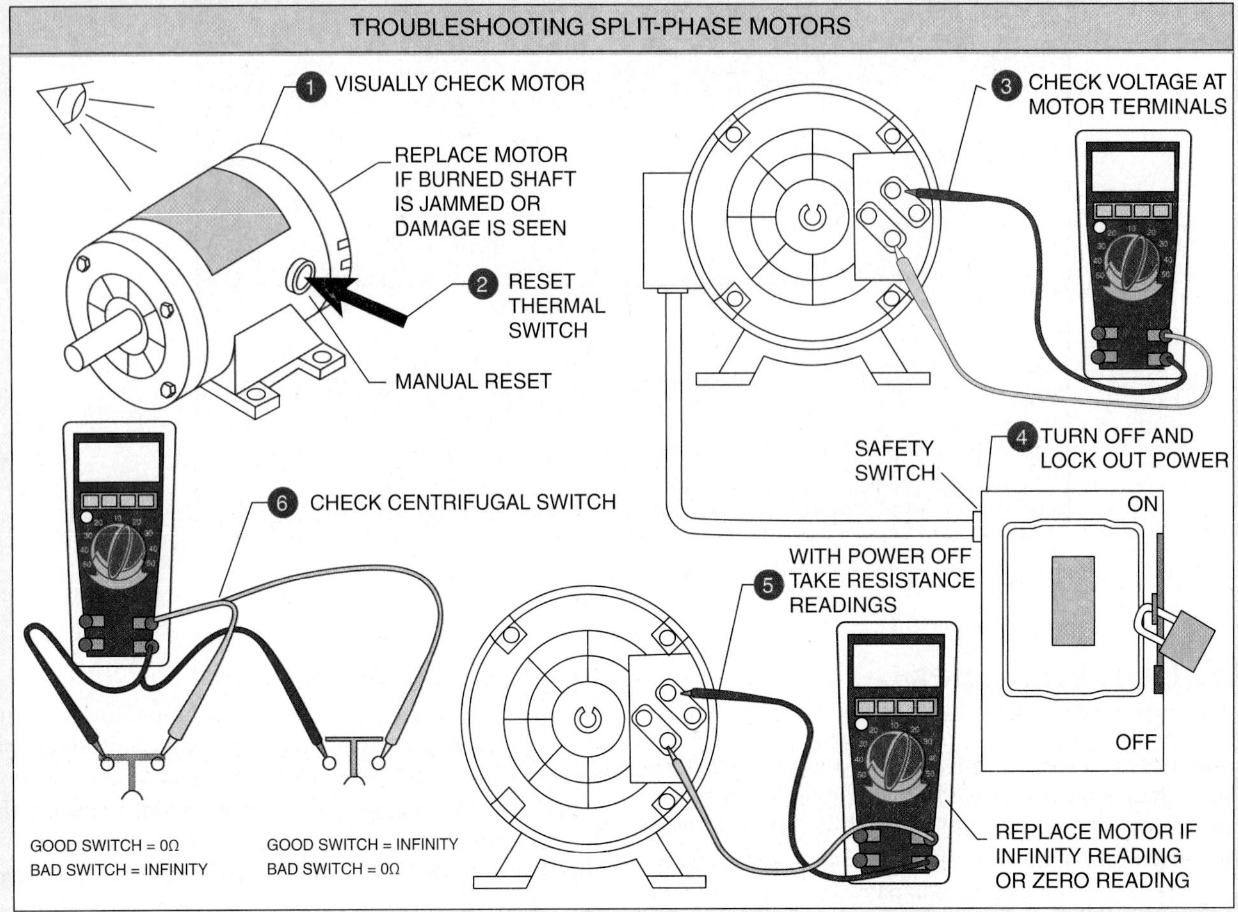

To troubleshoot a no-start condition of split-phase motor, use the following procedure as a general guideline:

1. Switch off the power to the motor, and lock out any electrical switch while working on the motor.
2. Visually inspect the motor for seizure, burned wiring, damage, or evidence the motor stator is burned out. Replace the motor if it is damaged.
3. Locate and inspect the motor thermal switch. Reset a manual thermal switch if it is tripped, and switch the motor on to recheck motor operation
4. If the motor remains inoperative, carefully check for line voltage at the motor's power terminals. Use a multimeter and set for AC voltage RMS. Alternatively, use an AC test light suited for the line voltage. If the voltage is not within 10% of the voltage listed on the motor's data plate, inspect the current supply line to the motor. If the voltage is adequate, switch off the power to the motor and lock out the switch.
5. With power switched off, use an ohmmeter to measure the resistance of the main and auxiliary windings by placing the meter leads across the power terminals of the motor. A minimum amount of resistance must be present. An ohmmeter measurement of 0 ohms resistance indicates an internal short circuit. A measurement of infinite resistance indicates a defective centrifugal switch, or open starting and main winding. The highest resistance reading is measured between the start and run terminals. A middle resistance reading is between the start and neutral terminals. The lowest resistance reading is between the run and neutral terminals.
6. If the motor leads have infinite resistance, remove the motor end cap or end bell. Visually inspect the centrifugal switch operation and for signs of burning or broken springs. Replace the switch if it is damaged. Check the switch operation by manually operating the switch while using a multimeter to determine whether it is opening and closing correctly.
7. Probe the motor leads at the centrifugal switch while checking to determine whether the resistance of the leads changes when operating the switch. If the resistance of the leads does not change when manually operating the switch, the motor is likely defective and should be replaced.

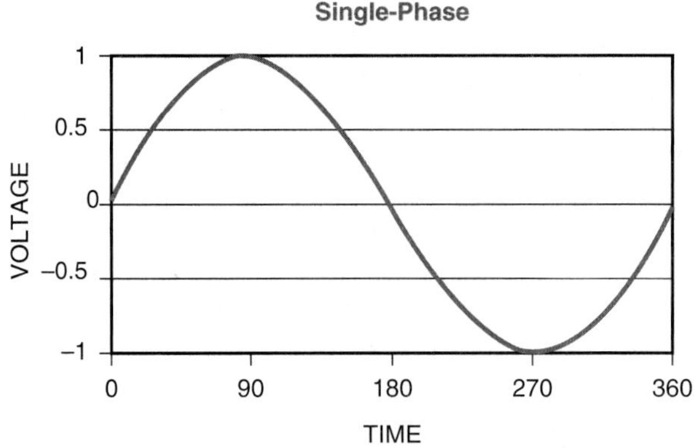

FIGURE 13-13 An AC sine wave shows the polarity peaks at 120 volts positive, falls to zero, then moves to −120 volts before returning to 0 volts at the end of the cycle.

Any other time, it is less than 120 volts, rising and falling as it approaches a polarity change. Voltage peaks and dips mean electric power is not supplied at a constant rate like DC current. The cyclical change in voltage and polarity of the power conductor takes place 60 times per second in North American power systems—50 times or hertz (Hz) in Europe. Single-phase conductors are color-coded according to electrical code for each country where the wiring is used. Generally, in North America, black is designated for power and white for the neutral conductor. In Europe, blue is neutral, with black or brown designated the power wire.

Single-phase current is adequate for operating electric motors up to about 5 horsepower. But the lower average voltage during a cycle means motors and other devices using single phase require more amperage to compensate for the lower peak average voltage compared to three-phase current described in the next section (**FIGURE 13-14**). Single-phase current is supplied at 120 or 240 volts, always using 0 volts as a reference. With 120 volts, the peak voltage is 120 volts measured from 0 volts to +120 volts, or 0 volts to −120-volt peaks. Similarly, 240 volts is measured from 0-volts to either positive or negative volt peak.

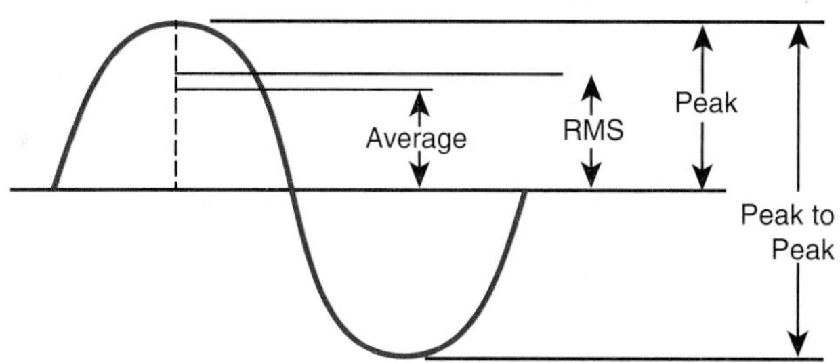

FIGURE 13-14 A single AC waveform only peaks two times during a cycle, and average voltage is less than its peaks.

> **TECHNICIAN TIP**
>
> **Measuring AC Voltage**
>
> It is not of everyday practical application, but AC voltmeters measure AC voltage using the **root mean square (RMS)** calculation. Stated mathematically: VAC = VRMS × √2. Because AC voltage peaks are not constant or continuous like DC current, the RMS measurement method provides a comparable measurement of AC current to DC current. The RMS value of AC voltage refers to the effective value of AC voltage or current and not the wave peak positive–to–wave peak negative difference in voltage. AC voltage calculated using RMS provides the equivalent AC voltage measurement to DC voltage that should have the same power or effect (**FIGURE 13-15**). For example, AC voltage measured using RMS method produces the same heating effect as DC current. This means a bulb connected to a 10 V RMS AC supply will shine with the same brightness when connected to a steady 10 V DC supply. This assumes the power source is a pure sine wave. Stated another way, the peak value of household voltage in North America is about 120 × √2, or about 170 volts measured from positive to negative voltage peak.

Three-Phase AC Current

Because AC current waveform has peaks and valleys, it contains less energy than DC current that remains constant. To improve the efficiency of devices using AC current, three-phase AC current can be used. Three-phase current provides more uniform delivery of current than single phase (**FIGURE 13-16**). Unlike single-phase current supplying AC using two wires, a neutral

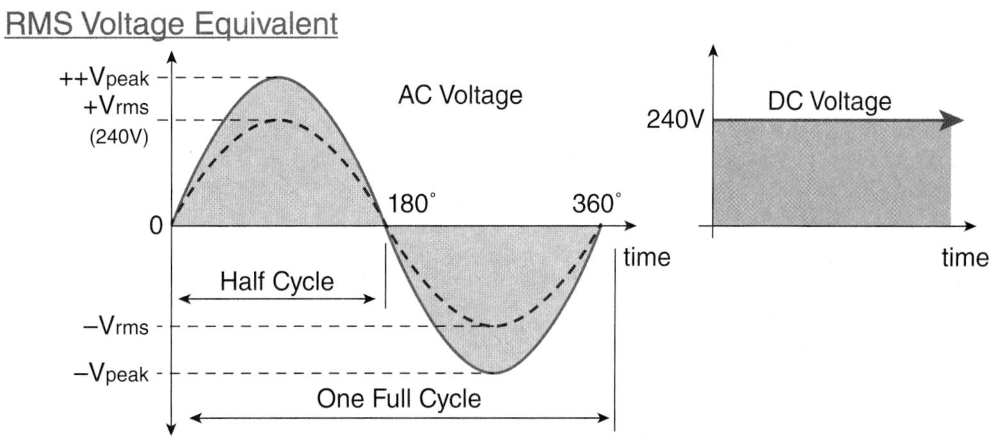

FIGURE 13-15 AC voltage is measured using an RMS calculation that gives it the same energy value as DC voltage.

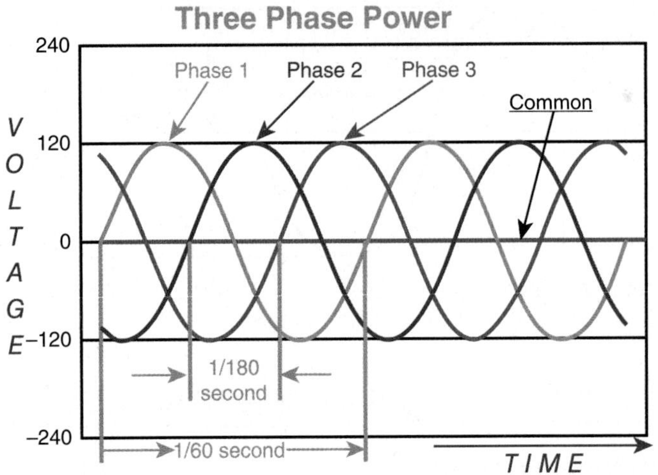

FIGURE 13-16 Three-phase current peaks more often per cycle than single phase.

and power wire and perhaps a third ground wire for safety, three-phase current uses five wires; three wires supply power, and the other two are a neutral and often a ground wire. When graphed over a 360-degree cycle time, three power wires, each 120 degrees out of phase with one another have entered the cycle. When a whole cycle of 360 degrees has completed, three phases of power have each peaked in voltage twice. That means there are six power peaks in three-phase current compared to just two in single-phase current. With a three-phase current supply, a steadier flow of power is delivered at a more regular rate, which contains more energy. Practically this means three-phase current can supply more power or energy per unit of time than single-phase current. When comparing motors, a single-phase 5 hp motor draws significantly more amperage than an equivalent 5 hp motor operating using three-phase motor, making three-phase power a more efficient choice for industrial applications.

To measure three-phase current draw, follow the steps in **SKILL DRILL 13-2**.

SKILL DRILL 13-2 Diagnosing Split-Phase Motor Capacitors

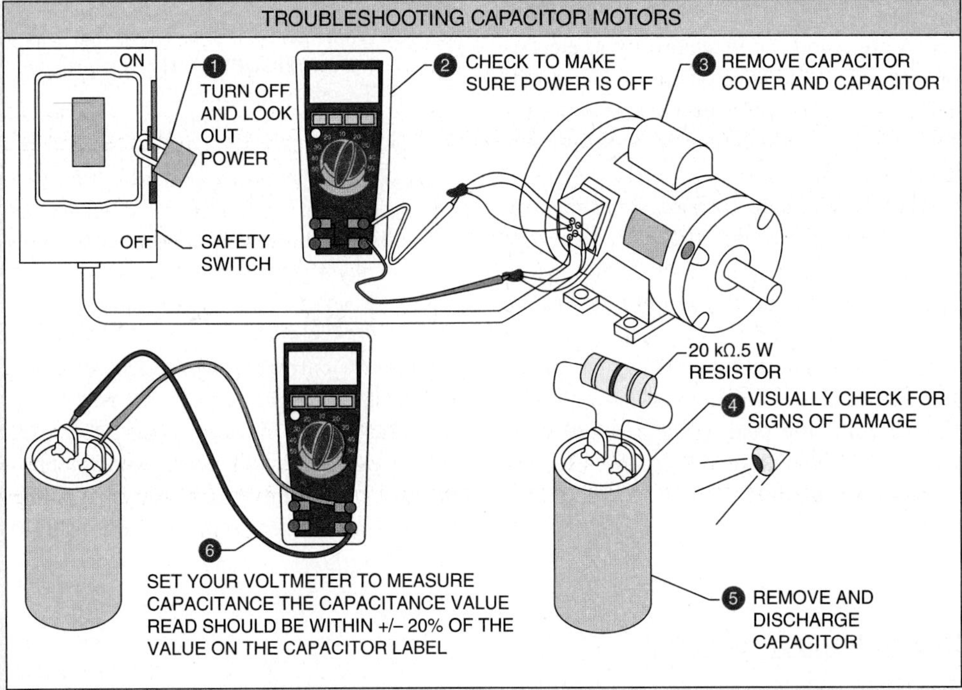

Starting capacitors are used by split-phase motors to initiate rotor rotation. A defective capacitor will prevent the motor from turning to start. However, manually turning the motor and causing it to rotate enables the motor to spin up to speed.

To troubleshoot a capacitor motor, use the following procedure as a general guideline:

1. Switch off the power to the motor and lock out any electrical switch while working on the motor.
2. Remove the cover of the starting capacitor that is usually located on the outside of the motor frame.
3. Visually inspect the capacitor for leaking oil, cracks, dents, or bulges. Replace the capacitor if any damage is observed.
4. Before a capacitor can be tested, any electrical charge it hold has to be drained by shorting the two terminals of the capacitor, using a resister and jumper wire. A capacitor in good working will hold a charge for days after the power is removed.
5. Use caution to avoid making contact with the capacitor terminals. A capacitor can be discharged while it is attached to the motor frame or disconnected. Connect a 20K ohm resister across the capacitor's two terminals, using a jumper wires. A good capacitor will produce

SKILL DRILL 13-2 Diagnosing Split-Phase Motor Capacitors (Continued)

a strong spark when its terminals are shorted together. Allow the charge to dissipate through the resistor for at least 5 seconds before disconnecting and removing the capacitor.

6. After a capacitor is discharged, measure the resistance of the capacitor, using an ohmmeter. Connect the ohmmeter leads to the capacitor terminals.

Good Capacitor: A good capacitor initially shows a low resistance reading that gradually climbs until the resistance is infinite. This happens because the small amount of current from the meter charges the capacitor, which progressively increases its resistance.

Defective Capacitor: A shorted capacitor has low or no resistance and remains like that when the meter is connected. A defective open capacitor shows infinite resistance even after it is discharged.

Three-Phase Conductor Color Codes

Conductors of a three-phase system are usually identified by a color code to allow technicians to calculate and evenly balance the loading or amperage drawn by each phase of a three-phase circuit (TABLE 13-2). Color-coding is also necessary to ensure the correct direction of rotation for motors. Rotation direction of three-phase motors is obtained by changing the connection of each phase to the motor stator windings. In addition to the superior efficiency, the ability to change direction of three-phase motors is an advantage and not something single-phase motors can perform. Each country uses its own color code to identify the phase of each conductor, and the neutral and ground circuits. Conductor colors conform to International Standard IEC 60446. However, the large discrepancy between color codes means it's very important to understand how to properly identify current phasing and related conductor color codes to prevent damage to circuits, devices, and anyone using the electrical devices. When the phases are connected correctly, current will never flow through the neutral wire that is also often connected to the ground wire in commercial or residential facility wiring. In the WYE phase distribution configuration most widely used in North America, three-phase current is designated 208Y/120 (FIGURE 13-17). This abbreviation means that the power line-to-line (L–L) voltage is 208 VAC in a WYE configuration and the line to neutral (L–N) voltage is 120 VAC (FIGURE 13-18). It is beyond the scope of this textbook to explain how to differentiate among other power distribution configurations and the techniques used to identify the line voltages.

TABLE 13-2 U.S. AC Power Circuit Wiring Color Codes

Function	Label	Color, Common	Alternative Color
Protective ground	PG	Bare, green, or green-yellow	Green
Neutral	N	White	Gray
Line, single phase	L	Black or red (2nd hot)	
Line, three-phase	L1	Black	Brown
Line, three-phase	L2	Red	Orange
Line, three-phase	L3	Blue	Yellow

NEMA Nomenclature for Electrical Connectors

When machines with electric motors are connected with cords, such as in underground mining, they use U.S. National

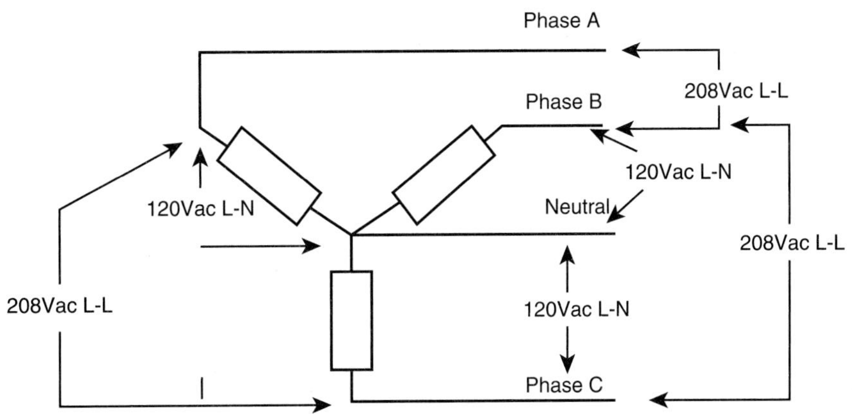

FIGURE 13-17 Connection points for a wye-wound three-phase motor.

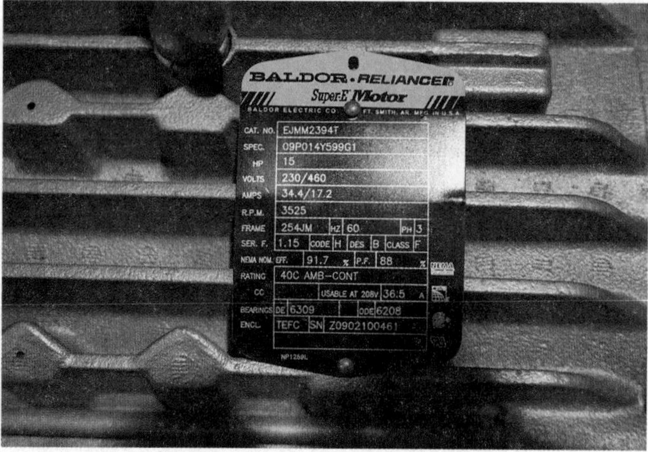

FIGURE 13-18 This electric motor tag contains information designating the motor as three-phase and listing the voltage at which the motor operates.

Electrical Manufacturers Association, or NEMA, compliant wiring devices. NEMA standard connectors are made in current ratings from 15 to 60 amps, with voltage ratings from 125 to 600 volts, each using various combinations of blade shapes dimensions, and orientation. The connector configurations use dimensions to design non-interchangeable plugs and receptacles unique for each combination of voltage, amperage, and grounding system. A simple alphanumeric code provides information about the number of current-carrying conductors, the application voltage, and whether it is used for single- or three-phase power (**FIGURE 13-19**). Letters at the beginning and end of the code are used to indicate whether the connector is a locking type and whether it is a male or female connector.

Twist lock devices all start with the letter "L," using curved-blades and twist-lock connectors (**FIGURE 13-20**). Twist-lock electrical connectors are required for heavy industrial and commercial equipment, to protect against accidental disconnection. After a twist-lock plug inserts into a twist-lock receptacle, the plug is twisted, and the curved blades latch into the receptacle. Unlatching the plug requires twisting the plug in the opposite direction.

Conductors

Orange insulation identifies all high-voltage conductors. This stands out on a machine and should alert technicians to potential danger. High-voltage conductors are also most likely the largest gauge wires on the machine: at least 2/0 gauge or larger. If they need to be larger than 4/0, they are identified by MCM numbers, such as 313 or 777. MCM is an abbreviation for "1000 circular mils." This equates to the cross-sectional diameter in mils. One mil is the equivalent cross-sectional area of a 0.001 in. diameter circle. If a wire is 313 MCM (KCmil), this equates to 313,000 mils.

These high-voltage conductors are multilayered, starting with the current-carrying copper core; then comes rubber insulation; then Mylar tape; then a braided, stainless steel grounding shield; and finally an outer orange nylon cover (**FIGURE 13-21**).

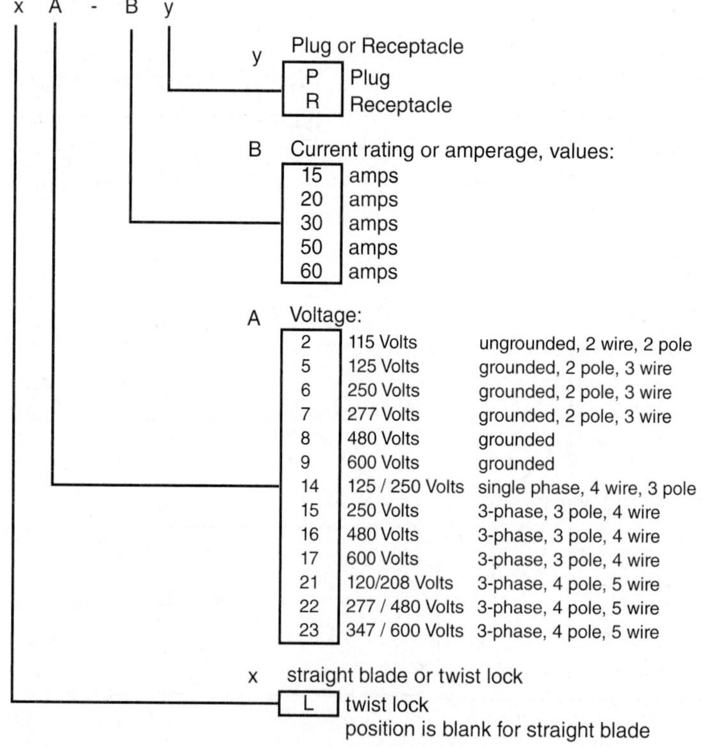

FIGURE 13-19 A NEMA chart identifying electrical socket and receptacle nomenclature.

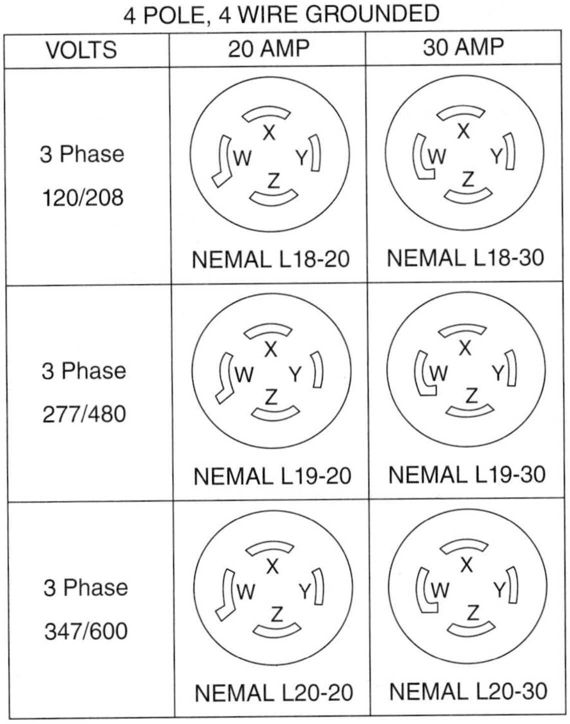

4 POLE, 4 WIRE GROUNDED

VOLTS	20 AMP	30 AMP
3 Phase 120/208	X W Y Z NEMAL L18-20	X W Y Z NEMAL L18-30
3 Phase 277/480	X W Y Z NEMAL L19-20	X W Y Z NEMAL L19-30
3 Phase 347/600	X W Y Z NEMAL L20-20	X W Y Z NEMAL L20-30

FIGURE 13-20 Shapes of various NEMA three-phase sockets.

FIGURE 13-21 Cross section of a high-voltage conductor.

▶ TECHNICIAN TIP

Servicing High Voltage Conductors

High-voltage conductors should never be modified and, if damaged, they should be replaced and never repaired (**FIGURE 13-22**). Conductors usually have heavy-duty connectors that must be torqued to specification to ensure they stay tight. If a connector comes loose, it will eventually start arcing, which causes a voltage drop that causes an operational problem and could end up burning off. Any time a high-voltage connector is assembled, it must be clean and dry. After the connection assembly is completed, the manufacturer may require an application of special sealant to minimize the likelihood of corrosion.

FIGURE 13-22 Example of high voltage conductors arranged in an insulated stand-off bracket.

▶ AC Motor Construction and Classification

K13004

All AC motors typically consists of two basic parts. The first is an outside stationary component, called a **stator**, that uses coiled wire supplied with alternating current to produce a magnetic field. The second moving component, called the rotor, is attached to the output shaft. Rotors correspond to an armature in a DC motor. Like all other electric motors, all AC motors use principles of magnetic repulsion to produce rotational movement (**FIGURE 13-23**). Magnetic fields in the rotor and stator oppose one another to produce rotational force (**FIGURE 13-24**). The rotor's magnetic fields are commonly created by permanent magnets, magnetic induction, or electromagnetic windings. The magnetic field of the stator winding can appear to have movement due to the use of alternating current. Remember that the direction of current flow in a conductor creates a magnetic field with poles, so a winding in the stator may have a north or south orientation depending on the direction of current flow produced by the continuous cycling of AC current. This means that in one moment, moment a single

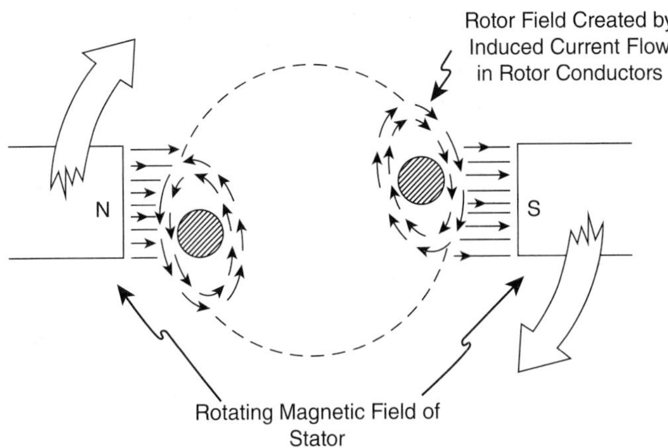

FIGURE 13-23 Electric motors operate using principles of magnetic repulsion.

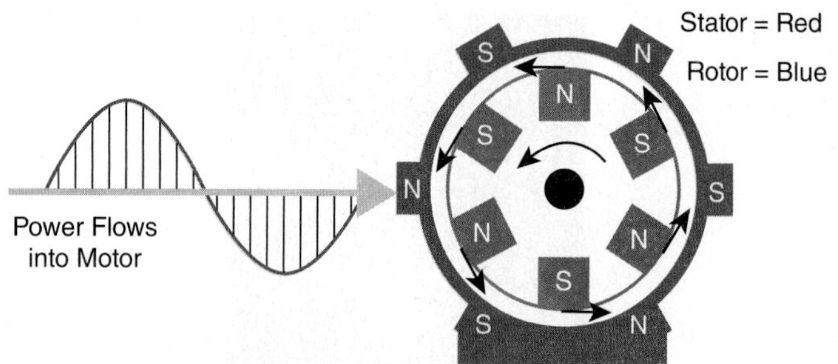

FIGURE 13-24 Magnetic poles in the rotor and stator simultaneously pull and push the rotor to produce rotation.

coil of wire may have its north pole oriented closest to the rotor and it's south pole orientated towards the outside circumference of the motor (**FIGURE 13-25**). When the direction or polarity of current flow changes 1/120th of a second later, the poles flip. This constant switching back and forth of magnetic poles 120 times a second during a 1-second cycle of a 60-Hz AC current appears as a rotating magnetic field moving around the circumference of the motor as magnetic poles alternate north to south and back again. Observing the apparent movement of magnetic field in relation to AC current polarity in the stator is important, to understand the operation of AC motors.

The two broad categories of AC motors examined in this chapter are classified as either induction or synchronous. Physically, these motors both have a wire-wound stator but are differentiated by the use of a wire-wound rotor used only in the synchronous-type motor. Each of these motors has various subtypes to provide such features as different starting characteristics, rotational speed, torque, and current consumption suitable for unique or specialized applications. The next section examines the construction and operation of these two basic categories of motors.

Induction Motors

Induction motors are the most commonly used type of AC motor. The motor's simple, rugged construction and relatively inexpensive manufacturing costs help popularize this motor used in light, medium, and heavy load applications from ½ hp to 500 hp. Induction motors are most commonly observed driving pumps, machine tools, compressors, conveyers, and large blower motors. Large electric motors driving loads at relatively constant speeds are typically induction-type motors. Both single-phase and three-phase induction motors are built. In addition to the number of power supply conductors, major differences between single-phase and three-phase motors are the use of specialized starting circuits or devices required by single-phase motors only, and the direction of rotation. Single-phase motors only turn in one direction, whereas three-phase motors operate in reverse and forward directions by switching the conductors supplying three phases of stator windings (**FIGURE 13-26**).

Induction motors use electric current in their rotor to produce magnetic fields, but rotors of induction motors are not connected to a supply of electrical current. There are some rare exceptions to this construction detail because unique motors have specialized speed regulation or soft start-up features, but the induction motor derives its name from AC current that is induced in the rotor conductors by the rotating magnetic field of the stator. In other words, induction motors are a broad category of motors having electric current induced in the rotor by magnetic induction (**FIGURE 13-27**).

Again, electric current is induced in the rotor by the changing stator magnetic fields. Magnetic fields in the stator, which continually switch due to the nature of AC current, in turn create magnetic fields in the rotor that automatically arrange themselves to oppose the magnetic fields of the stator. Interaction or

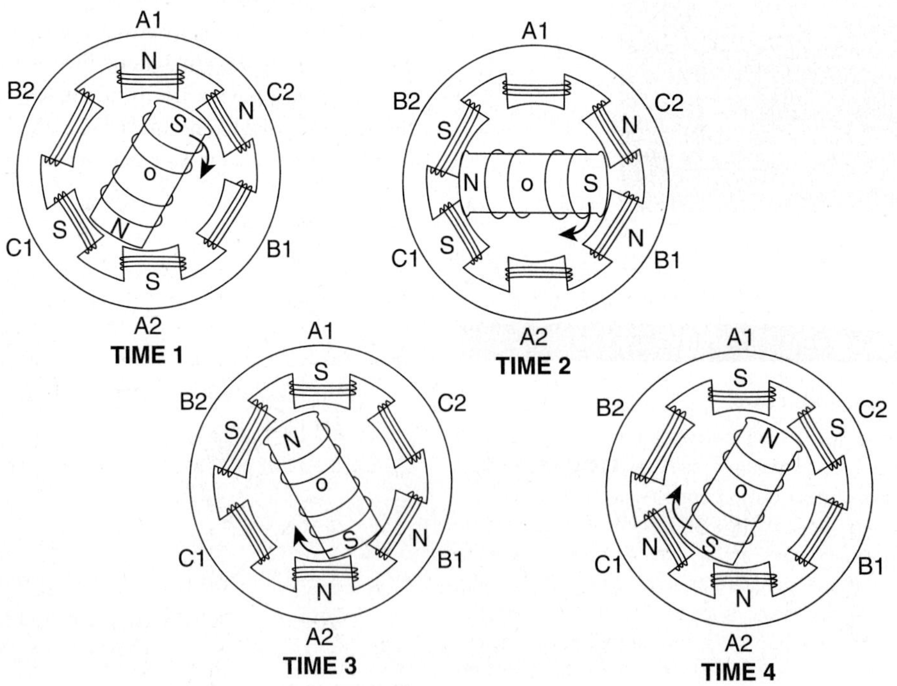

FIGURE 13-25 AC current in the rotor causes the poles to switch magnetic polarity every 120th of a second.

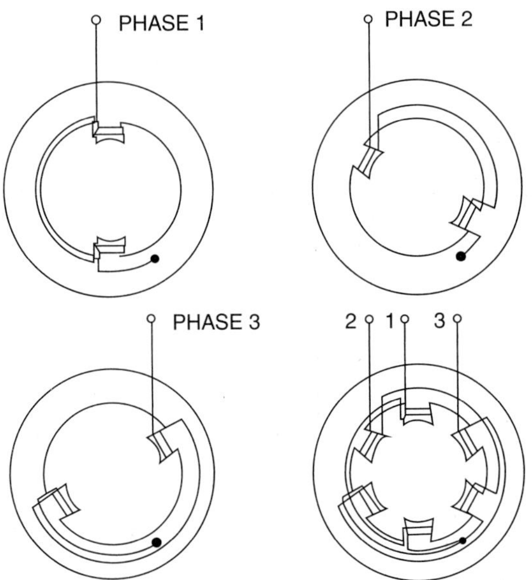

FIGURE 13-26 A three-phase stator has three separate circuits forming magnetic fields.

opposition between the magnetic fields in the rotor and stator causes the rotor to turn. To better understand this, remember that magnetic induction produces current flow the same way the secondary circuit of a two-winding transformer or ignition coil receives its power from the primary winding. As current flow in the primary winding builds up and expands it's magnetic field, the moving field cuts across the windings of the secondary coil, thereby inducing current flow in the secondary winding (**FIGURE 13-28**). Described another way, the induction motor can be considered a rotating transformer, where the primary winding is the stationary stator, but the secondary winding, the rotor, is free to rotate. Because electric current is only induced in the rotor, the induction motor does not require brushes. If an induction motor is compared to a DC motor, the DC motor can be called a conduction motor. Why? It is because brushes connect DC electric current flow to the armature windings through the commutator bars. Armature current is conducted in a DC motor, not inducted as in an AC induction motor.

It's important to remember that the polarity of the magnetic field induced in the rotor will always be opposite the polarity of the stator. **Lenz's law** summarizes this principle, stating that the

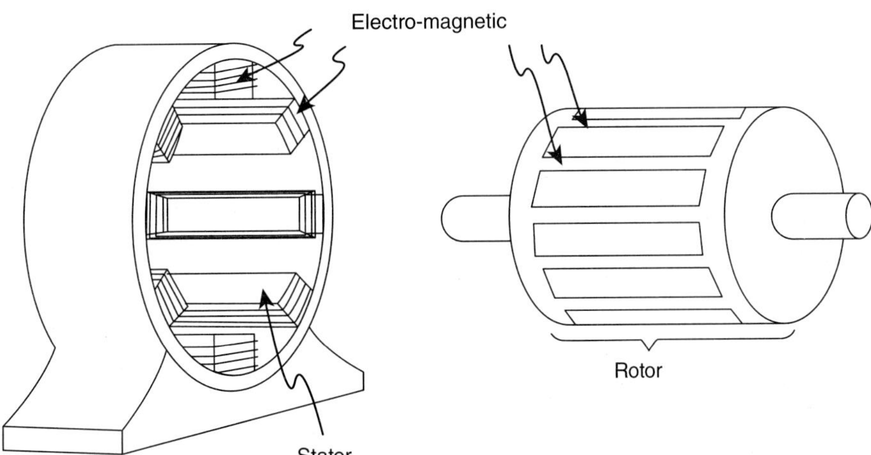

FIGURE 13-27 The magnetic field of the stator switches polarity and moves in and out from the motor centerline. The moving magnetic field induces current flow in the rotor bars.

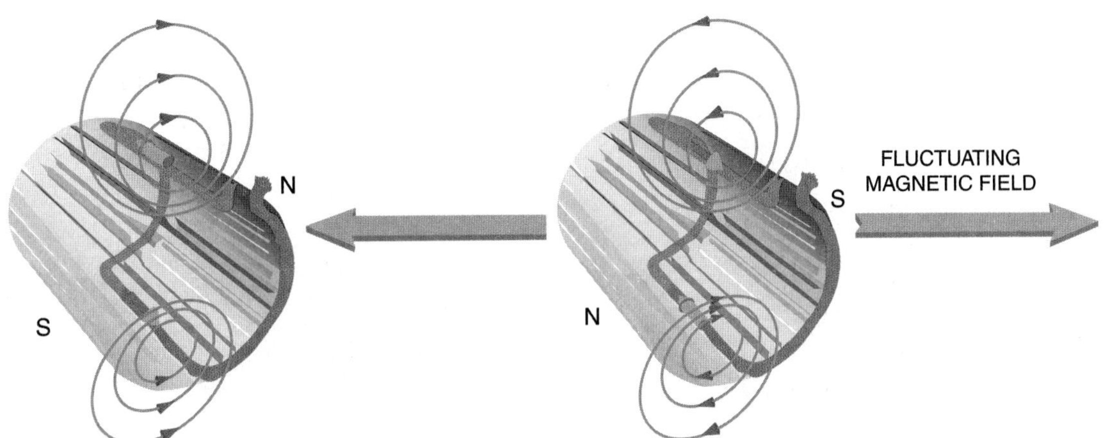

FIGURE 13-28 Current flow is induced in the rotor windings by the stator's moving magnetic field.

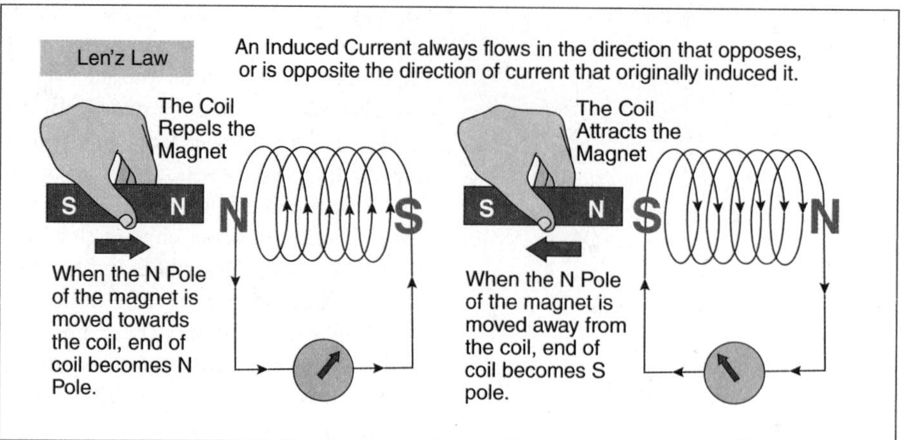

FIGURE 13-29 Lenz's law.

current induced in a circuit due to a change or movement of a magnetic field moves in a direction to build up a magnetic field with a polarity opposing the magnetic field of the original inducing current. Both magnetic fields in the rotor and stator exert a mechanical force against each other. (**FIGURE 13-29**).

Squirrel Cage Rotor

Close to 90% of induction motors use a **squirrel cage rotor**. Having a rotor with the simplest and most rugged type of construction, the squirrel cage rotor resembles an exercise wheel in a rodent cage. It consists of a cylinder with a laminated iron core having parallel slots along its axis for holding the rotor's conductors (**FIGURE 13-30**). The conductors are not wires, but heavy bars of copper or aluminum or alloys. Bars are placed in the slots and welded or bolted to two thick short-circuiting end rings. The end rings electrically connect the rotor conductors to one another to complete a circuit with other conductor bars in order to establish a magnetic field. No insulation is required between the laminated iron core and the conductor bars. This is because only low voltage current is induced in the rotor bars.

The rotor slots are usually cut at an angle to the shaft axis for two reasons. One is to help the motor run more quietly, because the magnetic fields are slightly skewed to offset alignment with the rotor field coils. This feature tends to reduce a vibration or magnetic hum as the rotor speed changes slightly every time the conductor bars align with the rotor magnetic field. A second similar reason is the skew of the conductor bars helps to prevent lock-up of the rotor bars with stator coils because of the potential for a synchronization of magnetic attraction forces that can take place when the motor initially starts or is heavily loaded.

Induction Motor Slip

It is impossible for the rotor of an induction motor to turn at the same speed as the apparent rotating magnetic field of the stator. If rotor speed and the apparent movement of the stators magnetic field were the same, so that the magnetic fields were directly opposite one another, no movement of the rotor could take place since both magnetic fields would lock the motor. A small angle or misalignment must exist between the rotor and the magnetic poles of the stator for two reasons. First, the difference in the angle is necessary to impart a push or repulsion force between the two opposing magnetic fields. The second, more important reason is that an angle must exist between the alignment of the rotor's conductor bars and stator field to induce voltage. If the magnetic field and the conductor bar are on the same plane or exactly parallel to one another, no induction can take place—there must be an angle for induction to take place. (**FIGURE 13-31**). As the angle between a conductor and magnetic field increase, more current flow is induced in a conductor. The greatest amount of current is induced at an angle of 90 degrees between the conductor and magnet. To maintain an angle, thus enabling the induction motor to run, the rotor must rotate at a speed at least slightly slower than that of the stator's

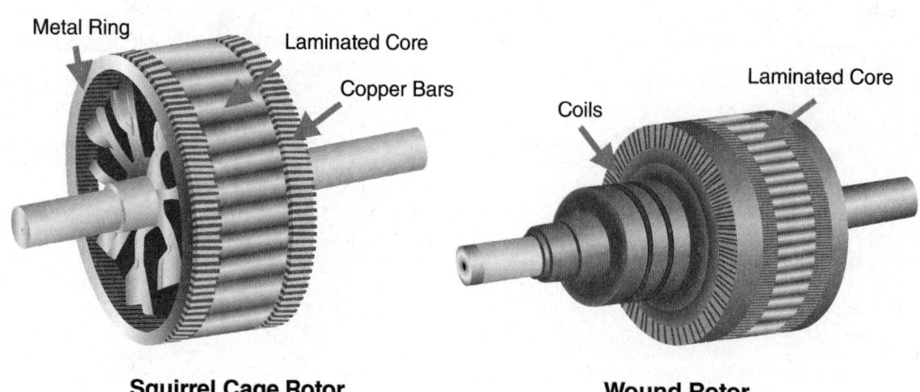

FIGURE 13-30 Comparing the squirrel cage rotor of an induction-type with a synchronous-type motor.

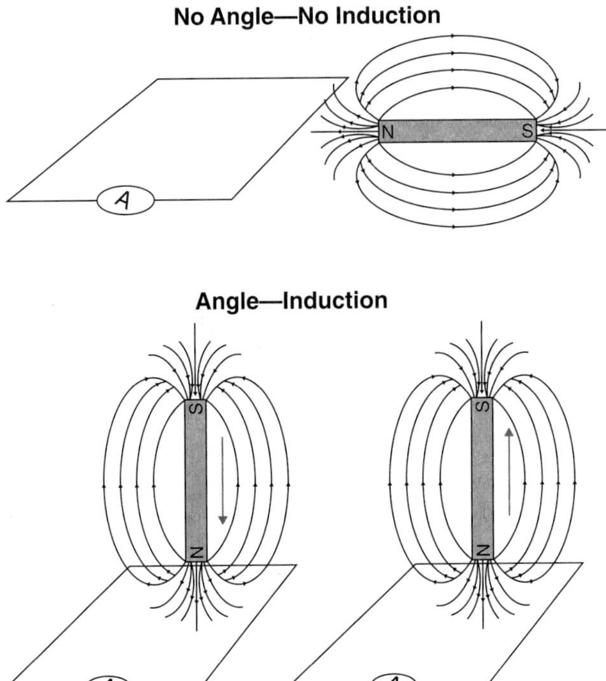

FIGURE 13-31 When the magnet is in the same plane or parallel to the conductor loop, no current is induced even if the magnet is moved closer and further away.

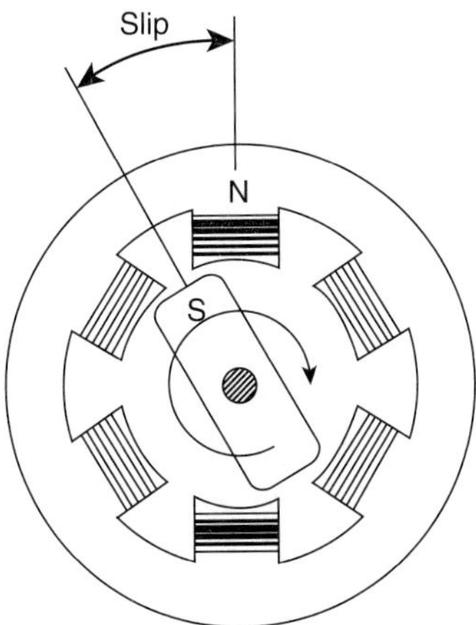

FIGURE 13-32 An angle between the magnet and conductor is required to induce current flow. The angle is called slip.

rotating magnetic field. This explains why actual induction motor speeds are always listed on a motor tag as 25, 50 or even 75 rpm below maximum no load speed. The difference between the speed of the rotating stator field and the rotor speed is called **slip** (**FIGURE 13-32**). The smaller the slip, the smaller the angle between the magnetic field and rotor conductor bars. Slip decreases the closer the rotor speed approaches the maximum motor speed. The speed difference, or slip, between actual and synchronized rotor-stator magnetic field speed movement varies from about 0.5% to 5.0%. Even with no load, some slip is present in an induction motor. Because induction motors do not allow the rotor and stator magnetic fields to synchronize speed, induction motors are also called **asynchronous**.

Slip is an important concept in understanding a motor's current consumption and how an induction motor varies its torque output in response to a load change. Consider first that rotor speed depends on the load applied to the rotor shaft, and the number of poles in a motor. As the load increases, the motor torque must increase to maintain speed. However, slowing the rotor increases the degree of slip. Slowing the rotor also increases the angle or misalignment between the stator magnetic field and magnetic field in the rotor conductors. Increased slip means more current is induced in the rotor because the angle increases between the conductor bars and the stator magnetic field. If more current is induced in the rotor, increased interaction takes place between more powerful rotor magnetic fields and the stator field. Hence, when slip increases, greater magnetic repulsion takes place to instantly increase motor torque. To obtain maximum interaction between the fields, the air gap between the rotor and stator is very small.

Consider too that current flow increases when a load resists rotor shaft rotation. This also is explained by the change in motor slip. As slip approaches near zero, and the rotor catches up to stator field speed, the rotor's magnetic field also induces current flow in the stator winding to oppose current flow through the stator. This takes place because the rotor field is cutting the stator windings faster and at a different angle than when greater slip is present. When the rotor's magnetic fields cut the stators, it produces a **counterelectromotive force (CEMF)** in the stator winding, which opposes current flow through the stator, thus increasing stator resistance to current. CEMF can increase only if the magnetic field cuts through the stator windings more quickly. Therefore, when heavier loads are turned by the induction motor, current flow increases because stator winding resistance caused by CEMF decreases. Only a slight change in speed is necessary to produce the usual current changes required to increase or decrease motor torque. As a result, induction motors are also called constant-speed motors.

Single-Phase Motor Starting Circuits

Single-phase motors will not operate from a stopped position unless they are provided some initial rotating force. When at a stopped position, the stator and rotor magnetic fields would lock together, north to south and south to north. If a single-phase motor described previously were put into operation, it would simply vibrate or hum. You would have to turn it by hand to get it to rotate. Once again, some slip or difference between the angles of magnetic fields is required, or a second magnetic field exerting its force on a portion of the rotor could unbalance the magnetic field. For this reason, single-phase, but not three-phase motors require a starting circuit. The purpose of the circuit or device is to create some unbalanced magnetic field over the rotor to begin to rotate the motor and produce slip. Motors with unique circuits and devices used to unbalance some of the magnetic fields in a **single-phase induction motor** lend the name **split phase** to single-phase motor operation. Split-phase motors are designed to use inductance, capacitance, or resistance to develop starting torque. Two common types of starting devices are examined next.

Capacitor-Start Motors

The most common first type of split-phase induction motor is the **capacitor-start type**. Three components are used: a capacitor; an additional winding, called the starting or auxiliary

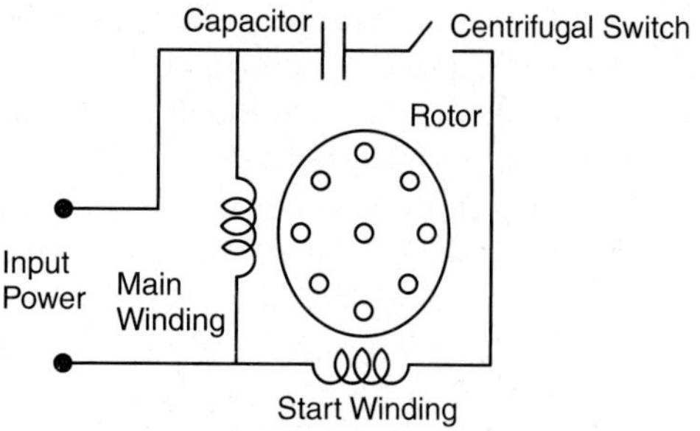

FIGURE 13-33 The arrangement of the capacitor, switch main, and starting windings of a capacitor start motor.

winding; and a switch, usually a centrifugal activated switch that closes when the motor stops and opens shortly after it starts. The starting winding is connected in parallel with the main winding but is placed physically at right angles to it. A 90-degree electrical phase difference between the two windings is produced by connecting the auxiliary winding in series with a capacitor and starting switch (**FIGURE 13-33**). When the motor is first energized, the starting switch is closed. This places the capacitor in series with the auxiliary winding. As the capacitor charges and discharges due to the polarity change of AC current cycle, the lead connected to the starting winding has the opposite electrical polarity of the electrical lead into the capacitor. When the proper capacitor is selected, it causes the current in the starting winding to lag the line voltage by about 45 degrees. The effect is that the main and starting windings are each 90 degrees magnetically out of phase with each other. The uneven distribution of magnetic forces exerted by the stator cause the rotor to rotate and speed up. When this happens, the centrifugal switch opens, disconnecting the capacitor. The motor then operates as a single-phase induction motor.

Because the auxiliary winding is only a light winding, the motor does not develop sufficient torque to start heavy loads. As a result, capacitive split-phase start motors are small horsepower motors.

Some heavier motors use a second capacitor, called a run capacitor, to enable two-phase motor operation. After the motor starts, the second capacitor is connected in series to another set of windings connected in parallel to the main windings, but physically offset by 90 degrees (**FIGURE 13-34**). The advantage of a two-phase motor is that single-phase current can be supplied,

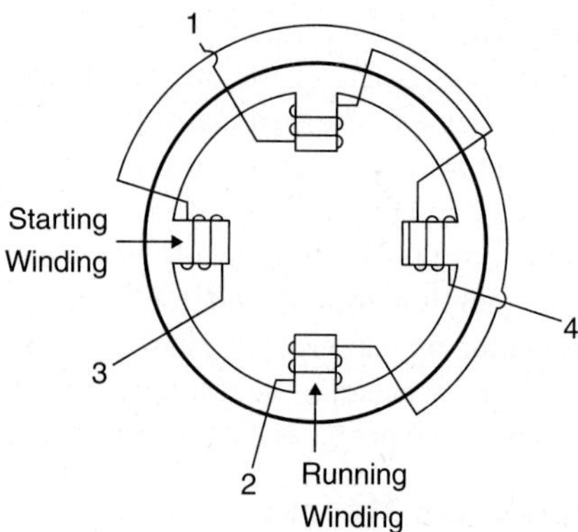

FIGURE 13-34 Starting winding and running winding are 90 degrees apart.

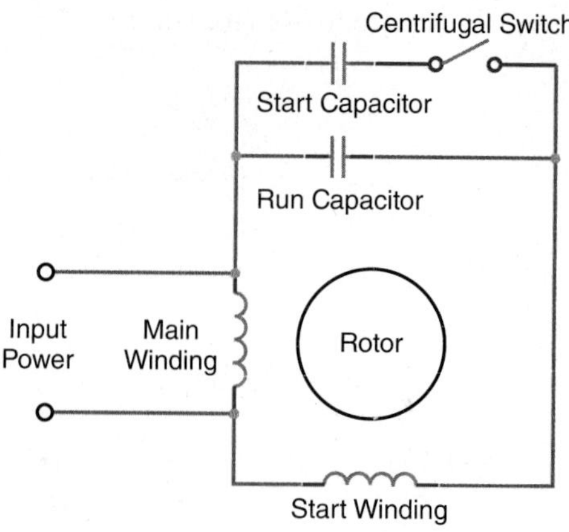

FIGURE 13-35 The arrangement of a run and start capacitor to give a motor two-phase operation.

but the motor's direction and speed can be regulated by a motor controller (**FIGURE 13-35**).

To inspect a motor capacitor, follow the steps in **SKILL DRILL 13-3**.

▶ TECHNICIAN TIP

Defective Capacitors

One of the most common complaints with single-phase motors is a motor that will not start turning or will run only after it's turned by hand. Low starting torque may prevent the motor from rotating and cooling, which opens a thermal protection switch. If the motor will not start, the cause is often a shorted capacitor, an open capacitor, or a capacitor that has a changed value due to deterioration. Capacitors have a limited life and require replacement after they have deteriorated. If a capacitor is short-circuited, constant current flow through the starting winding will cause the winding to overheat or burn out. In two-phase motors, a defective run capacitor will reduce motor torque, decrease maximum motor speed, or cause the motor to only speed up very slowly.

Resistance-Start Motors

Another type of split-phase induction motor is the **resistance-start motor**. Like the capacitor-start motor, the resistive-start motor also has a starting winding at 90 degrees to the main winding. The starting winding is switched in and out of the circuit just as it is in the capacitor-start motor. The difference is that the unbalance condition in the magnetic fields is produced by changing the resistance, or more correctly, the impedance of the windings is unequal. The main winding has a low resistance in contrast to the start winding, which has high resistance. During start-up, the **centrifugal start switch** closes and connects the start winding until the motor speeds up. Once the motor reaches a satisfactory speed, the centrifugal switch disconnects the starting winding from the power line, allowing the motor to continue to run as an induction motor. Resistance-start motors have even less start-up torque than capacitor-start motors.

Three-Phase Motors

Three-phase **squirrel cage induction motors** are widely used as large industrial drive units because they are rugged, reliable,

SKILL DRILL 13-3 Measuring Three-Phase Motor Current

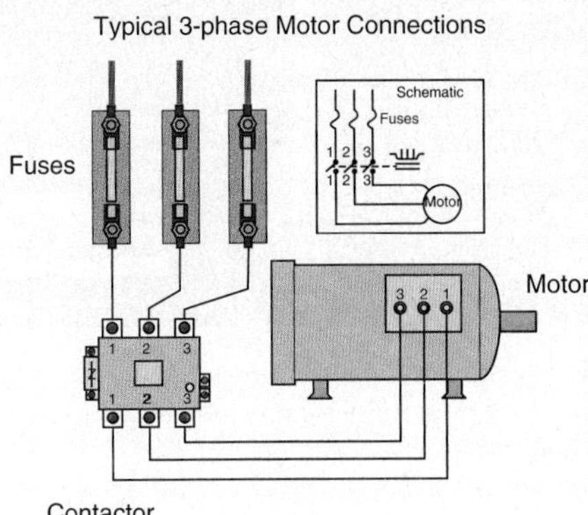

The procedure undertakes measuring the start-up and running current for a three-phase motor while it is connected to a load and comparing the measurements to the motor's data plate or specifications. As motors age, the amperage drawn generally rises because winding insulation resistance drops. Excess current consumption produces extra heat that must be dissipated or motor life is shortened. Uneven amperage drawn between each leg or phase of the motor indicates potential defects or imminent failure.

Note that this exercise is for informational purposes only and should only be done under the proper supervision and direction of a qualified electrician using prescribed tools and safety practices.

1. Inspect the appearance of the motor. Examine the frame for damage to the cooling fan blade or shaft. Manually rotate the motor shaft to check the bearing condition. Verify that the motor turns freely and smoothly.
2. Collect motor information from the data plate, noting amperage and voltage specification.
3. Measure the resistance between the motor frame and ground. Resistance should be less than 0.5 ohm.
4. Verify supply voltage when the motor is running, measuring the voltage between all legs or phases. The voltage should not vary more than 2% between each phase.
5. If correct voltage is present at the motor, measure the amperage of all three-phases of the motor with an inductive-type current clamp when the motor is under load. Looping the clamp around all three conductors should yield an amperage draw of zero amps because the direction of the magnetic field produced by each phase of current in each leg cancels the current induced by the magnetic fields of the other conductors in each leg cancels the draw of the others.
6. Add the amperage drawn by each phase of the motor, and compare with specifications listed on the motor data plate.

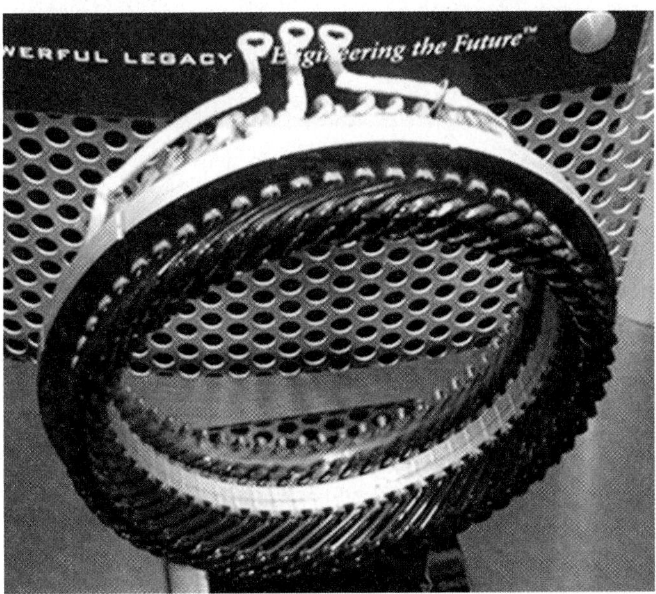

FIGURE 13-36 A three-phase motor stator.

and economical. Three-phase motors are similar in operation and construction to single-phase motors except for the stator. Rather than use a single winding, a three-phase motor uses three separate stator windings arranged 120 degrees offset from one another. Each of the windings is laid over the other and has a main power lead connected to it (**FIGURE 13-36**). All of the stator windings are connected to one another in one of two methods. The shape the connections form determines whether it is a **wye-wound** or a **delta-wound stator**. As the names suggest, a wye-wound stator has each end of the three windings connected to a neutral junction point. The other ends are connected to a power leads. A delta-wound stator connects each of the stator ends to form a triangle resembling the Greek letter delta (**FIGURE 13-37**).

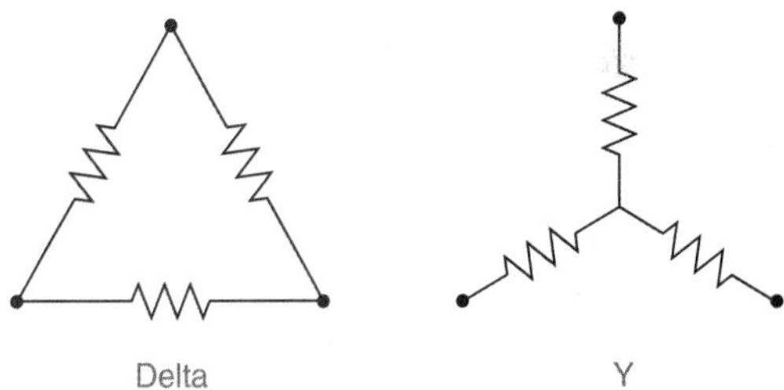

FIGURE 13-37 Comparing wye- and delta-wound stators.

Three of the most commonly used three-phase AC motors are designated as designs B, C, and D by the National Electrical Manufacturers Association (NEMA). They differ primarily in the value of starting torque and in the speed regulation near full load. Each of these designs employs the solid, squirrel cage–type of rotor, and thus there is no electrical connection to the rotor.

Motor Speed and Direction

The four-pole stator design with a synchronous speed of 1,800 rpm is the most common and is available in virtually all power ratings from ¼ hp to 500 hp. Single- and three-phase motor speed is calculated using the formula: rpm = (120 × AC frequency)/Number of poles in the motor:

$$1{,}800 \text{ rpm} = (120 \times 60)/4$$

Because the number of poles is fixed when the motor is built, the only way to change motor speed, whether it is single or three phase is to change the frequency of the AC current using a variable-frequency drive (VFD) motor controller. VFDs offer important energy savings when induction motors are used. Induction motors used in variable-torque centrifugal fans and pump and compressor load applications can reduce unnecessary energy consumption when turned slower.

There are, however, some exceptions to the four-pole design: 2-pole (3,600 rpm), 6-pole (1,200 rpm), 8-pole (900 rpm), 10-pole (720 rpm), and 12-pole (600 rpm) designs.

Because this category of induction motor has three phases or windings in the stator, the angles between the magnetic field of the stator and rotor can be electrically altered to reverse the direction of motor rotation. By simply reversing the power connections, the three-phase motor direction of rotation can be either forward or backward. Some motors may use a Hall-effect sensor called the **resolver** that measures the rotor position and speed for a motor controller to properly manage the motor operation. Because overspeed conditions will damage the motor if it is being driven during retarding mode operation, the resolver is a critical sensor for the motor controller to reduce current flow and shut down the system.

Induction Motors as Generators

The two types of motors most readily converted are three-phase squirrel cage induction motors and single-phase capacitor start single-phase induction motors. Turning the motors into generators for braking depends upon the degree of residual magnetism left in the rotor when motoring ends or the supply of current to the motor. By simply driving the motor with some current supplied to the stator, the motor operation will instantly switch to produce electricity. This current supplied to the stator can in turn produce magnetic fields in the rotor, causing the motor to produce alternating current. The frequency of alternating current depends on the speed at which the motor is driving. A three-phase motor will generate three-phase 60-Hz AC current when driven at 1,800 rpm. An AC current of 50 Hz is produced at 1,500 rpm. In generation mode, the maximum amperage is determined by the mass of the stator windings, the electrical load, and the torque driving the rotor at a precise 1,800 or 1,500 rpm. In retarding mode, the motor speed is irregular along with its generator frequency. Current must be rectified to DC current and then back to AC current to drive other electric motors.

Single-phase induction motors are used extensively for smaller loads, such as fans. Although traditionally used in fixed-speed service, induction motors are increasingly being used with variable-frequency drives (VFDs) in variable-speed service.

Synchronous Motor

Synchronous motors are another category of AC motors given the name "synchronous" because unlike asynchronous induction motors, the rotor always attempts to line up its magnetic poles with the rotating magnetic field in the stator. This means the motor does not operate with any slip and feature precise constant speed between no load and full load (**FIGURE 13-38**). The frequency of AC current maintains the motor's precise speed. For example, clock motors powered by AC current are a type of synchronous motor. Precision speed control allows these

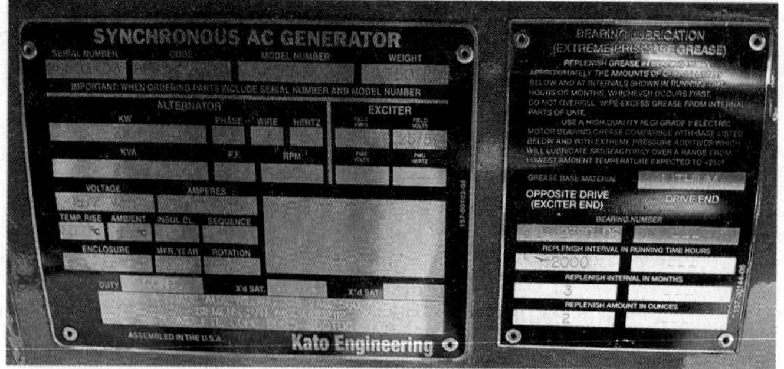

FIGURE 13-38 The specification plate for a synchronous motor for a mine truck. Note that the RPM is a precise 1,800 rpm to produce 60-Hz AC current.

FIGURE 13-39 This synchronous motor for a mine truck can operate as an AC generator.

motors to drive DC generators in welding machines that regulates the welding amperage. Synchronous motors are available in sizes up to 1,000 Hp and are more efficient than induction motors (**FIGURE 13-39**). They may be built as either single-phase or multiphase generator-motor machines. The brief description that follows is based on a three-phase design.

Synchronous motors are constructed with a stator of an induction motor but use a rotor like a DC motor. Unless the motor uses a permanent magnet rotor, DC current is supplied to a wire-wound rotor through slip rings on the rotor shaft. Like the stator of an induction motor, a synchronous motor is constructed from laminated stamped iron plates, which are slotted to receive the windings. The number of poles used in the stator is determined by the requirements of speed. More poles provide more speed, and vice versa. When supplied with three-phase current, the stator forms a magnetic field appearing to revolve at synchronous speed determined by rpm = 120 × Frequency/Poles. Synchronous motors can be electronically controlled to accelerate from zero to synchronous speed by changing the frequency of the stator current.

Energizing the stator with three-phase AC current produces a rotating magnetic field to revolve around the rotor. When the rotor is energized with DC current, the strong rotating magnetic field of the stator attracts the strong rotor field magnetized by DC current. The strong magnetic field on the rotor enables it to turn a load as it rotates in step, synchronized in speed with the stator's rotating magnetic field.

Unlike a three-phase induction motor, a synchronous motor cannot be started from a standstill by applying AC current alone to the stator. When AC current is supplied, the rotating magnetic field appears instantly and rotates too quickly past the rotor poles to allow it to move. In practice, the rotor is first repelled in one direction and then instantly in another. Torque is only available at synchronous speed, and without assistance, no starting torque is present.

To overcome the problem of no starting torque, large motors operating on commercial power frequency embed a squirrel cage–like induction winding in the rotor. The winding provides adequate torque for starting and acceleration and also operates to dampen motor speed oscillations. Once the rotor nears the synchronous speed, the synchronous rotor field winding is excited, pulling the motor into synchronization. Resistance in the stator circuit can also produce unbalanced magnetic fields needed to move the rotor, just as in single-phase motors. Passing rotor current through a bank of resisters like the resistive-start single-phase motor enables a control circuit to provide starting torque and change rotor speed (**FIGURE 13-40**). Very large motor systems may include an auxiliary starting motor that accelerates the unloaded synchronous motor before a load is applied.

Common Motor Enclosures

The housings around a motor that support and protect components vary depending on the degree of protection required. Open-type enclosures are made from light-gauge sheet metal surrounding the stator, with end plates to support the shaft bearings. The enclosure allows for excellent ventilation but offers little protection. A variation of the open enclosure protects more of the motor by providing ventilation openings only in the lower part of the housing so that liquids dripping from above cannot enter the motor. A protected enclosure has no provisions for ventilation and is called drip-proof. This type of enclosure may also be considered totally enclosed nonventilated (TENV). No openings are made in the housing, with no provisions made for ventilating the motor except for heat-radiating fins cast into the motor frame. Totally enclosed fan-cooled (TEFC) enclosures are like the TENV design, except a cooling fan is mounted at one end of the shaft to move air over the finned housing. TEFC-XP is an explosion proof design similar to the TEFC housing, except special protection prevents sparks from electrical connections or arcing brushes to ignite fires or causing explosions in hazardous environments.

A rough classification of motors by size is used to group motors of similar design:

- Subfractional horsepower: 1–40 millihorsepower (mhp) (0.75 to 30 W)
- Fractional horsepower: 1/20 to 1.0 hp (37 to 746 W)
- Integral horsepower: 1.0 hp (0.75 kW) and larger

Controls for AC Motors

Motor controls must perform several functions depending on the application, size, and the type of the motor involved. Small fractional or subfractional horsepower motors are usually started with a simple switch connecting the motor directly to the line voltage. Larger motors and motors on critical equipment require greater protection and include the following features:

- Ability to start and stop the motor
- Overload protection that would cause the motor to draw dangerously high current levels
- Overheating protection such as thermal switches that shut off power to overheated motors
- Personnel protection to prevent contact between people and hazardous parts of the electrical system
- Environmental protection controls for water levels, corrosive gases, liquids, explosive vapors, dusts, or lubricants
- Controls for regulating torque, acceleration, speed, or retarding functions of the motor
- Circuit protection of the conductors of the branch circuit in which the motor is connected.

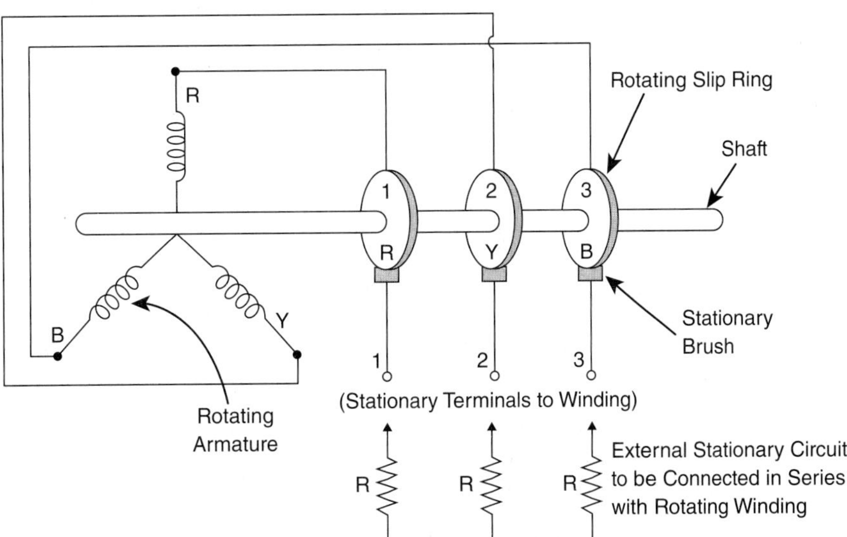

FIGURE 13-40 In a synchronous motor, starting torque and motor speed can be regulated by passing three-phase rotor current through a resister.

Wrap-Up

Ready for Review

- By definition, motors are devices that take any form of energy, other than combustion, and convert it into mechanical energy.
- The widest classification of electric motors is according to the type of electrical current used: alternating current (AC) or direct current (DC).
- AC current has been used to power homes and industry since the 1890s.
- Single-phase current, also known as house current, is used to power lights and small appliances. It is called single phase because of the use of two wires, one neutral and one power, which provide a pathway for electricity flow between them.
- To improve the efficiency of devices using AC current, three-phase AC current can be used. Three-phase current provides more uniform delivery of current than single phase. Unlike single-phase current supplying AC using two wires, a neutral and a power wire, with perhaps a third ground wire for safety, three-phase current uses five wires. Three wires supply power; the other two are a neutral and often a ground wire.
- All AC motors typically consist of two basic parts. The first is an outside stationary component called a stator that uses coiled wire supplied with alternating current to produce a magnetic field. The second moving component, called the rotor, is attached to the output shaft. Rotors correspond to an armature in a DC motor.
- Close to 90% of induction motors use a squirrel cage–type rotor.
- Induction motors are the most commonly used type of AC motor.
- It is impossible for the rotor of an induction motor to turn at the same speed as the apparent rotating magnetic field of the stator. The difference between the speed of the rotating stator field and the rotor speed is called slip. The smaller the slip, the smaller the angle between the magnetic field and rotor conductor bars. Slip decreases the closer the rotor speed approaches the stator field speed.
- Single-phase motors will not operate from a stopped position unless they are provided some initial rotating force.
- The most common first type of split-phase induction motor is the capacitor-start type. Three components are used. One is a capacitor; the second is an additional winding called the starting or auxiliary winding; and the third is a switch, usually a centrifugal activated switch that closes when the motor stops and opens shortly after it starts.
- Another type of split-phase induction motor is the resistance-start motor. The difference is that the unbalance condition in the magnetic fields is produced by changing the resistance, or, more correctly, the impedance of the windings is unequal. The main winding has a low resistance in contrast to the start winding, which has high resistance.
- Three-phase squirrel cage induction motors are widely used as large industrial drive units because they are rugged, reliable, and economical. Three-phase motors are similar in operation and construction to single-phase motors except for the stator. Rather than use a single winding, a three phase motors uses three separate stator windings arranged with a 120-degree offset from one another.
- Synchronous motors are another category of AC motors; they are given the name "synchronous" because, unlike asynchronous induction motors, the rotor always attempts to line up its magnetic poles with the rotating magnetic field in the stator.
- The housings around a motor that support and protect components vary depending on the degree of protection required. Open-type enclosures are made from light-gauge sheet metal surrounding the stator, with end plates to support the shaft bearings and allow ventilation. A protected enclosure has no provisions for ventilation and is called drip-proof.

Key Terms

asynchronous motor A category of AC motors, also known as an induction motor where the rotor speed and apparent speed of the magnetic field in the stator winding are not synchronized. Asynchronous motors operating speed is always less than maximum speed.

auxiliary motor A motor that drives auxiliary devices using a belt or gear drive or that is directly coupled.

capacitor-start motor A motor using a capacitor in series with the starter winding to put the starter winding 90 degrees out of phase with the main winding. Capacitor-start systems are required to begin rotor movement.

centrifugal start switch Used by split-phase motors to place a starter winding in series with the main winding during initial motor start-up when no rotor speed is present.

counterelectromotive force (CEMF) Electric current induced in a winding caused by the collapse of an adjacent magnetic field.

delta-wound stators A three-phase stator wiring configuration where the stator windings are connected at each end to form a triangle resembling the Greek letter delta.

impedance An electrical term to describe resistance in an AC circuit.

induction motor The most common type of AC motor, where the rotor current flow is induced by the stator's moving magnetic field; also called asynchronous motors.

Lenz's law A law of electromagnetism stating that the current induced in a circuit due to a change or a motion in a magnetic field is so directed as to oppose the change in flux and to exert a mechanical force opposing the motion.

resistance-start motors A type of split-phase motor with a starter winding used to initiate rotor rotation. A resister placed in series with the starter winding is used to unbalance motor magnetic fields to initiate rotor movement.

resolver A Hall-effect sensor used to measure the rotor position and speed for a motor controller in order to properly manage the motor operation in three-phase traction motors.

root mean square (RMS) A measurement method for AC voltage providing a comparable measurement of AC current to DC current. The RMS value of AC voltage refers to the effective value of AC voltage or current and not the wave peak positive–to–wave peak negative difference in voltage.

series-type hybrid electric drive A powertrain configuration where an engine drives only an electric generator, which in turn powers an electric motor.

single-phase current AC current that peaks two times during a cycle.

slip The difference between the speed of the rotating stator field and the rotor speed.

split-phase motor A single-phase motor with a starting winding used to initiate rotor movement.

squirrel cage rotor The type of construction used for rotors in an induction motor. In a squirrel cage rotor, the conductor bars are placed parallel to one another in a rotor cylinder. Ends of the conductor bar are connected with a shorting ring.

squirrel cage induction motor An AC motor with a rotor having solid condutor bars connected at each end with a shorting ring

synchronous motor A category of AC motors where the rotor and stator magnetic field revolve together at the same time.

traction motors Electric motors used in a propulsion drive system.

wye-wound stator A three-phase stator wiring configuration shaped like the letter "Y." Each end of a stator's three windings is connected to a neutral junction point. The other ends are connected to power leads.

Review Questions

1. Which of the following motors is the most common type of AC motor used?
   a. Synchronous
   b. Spilt-phase
   c. Capacitive-start
   d. Induction
2. Which of the following is true of a synchronous motor?
   a. Requires some degree of rotor slip to rotate
   b. Has a single layer of wire coils in the stator
   c. Uses a wire wound rotor
   d. Uses a squirrel cage–type rotor
3. Which of the following features does an asynchronous motor use?
   a. Only a single-phase stator winding
   b. Slip rings to supply current to the rotor winding
   c. A rotor speed matching the speed of the stator magnetic field
   d. A rotor requiring some speed slip to rotate
4. What determines the amount of slip needed by some AC electric motors?
   a. The number of stator poles
   b. The frequency of AC current
   c. The load applied to the rotor
   d. The angle of the magnetic fields
5. How is the direction of motor rotation changed in a three-phase induction motor?
   a. By changing the frequency of AC current
   b. By installing a capacitor in series with one of the main windings
   c. By installing a resister in series with one of the main windings
   d. By switching two of the power conductor connections supplying the motor
6. Which of the following motors uses a "run" capacitor?
   a. Synchronous motors
   b. Three-phase motors
   c. Two-phase motors
   d. Single-phase motors
7. What is the likely explanation for a motor to start rotating after it is turned by hand?
   a. A missing phase
   b. A shorted stator winding
   c. A defective rotor
   d. A defective capacitor
8. How many separate layers of stator windings are used by a single-phase motor?
   a. Not enough information
   b. One
   c. Two
   d. Three
9. What is the primary advantage of using battery-operated electric equipment in underground mines?
   a. The machines are less expensive to purchase.
   b. Batteries last longer than engines.
   c. Some ventilation shafts into the mine can be eliminated.
   d. There is better traction.
10. How do electric-drive machines reduce wear of brake friction material?
    a. The traction motor is switched from motor to generator operation.
    b. The electric motor is powered in a reverse direction.
    c. The brakes charge on-board batteries.
    d. Power is absorbed by AC–DC inverters.

ASE Technician A/Technician B Style Questions

1. Technician A says that diesel engines will last longer between overhauls compared to the life cycle of an electric traction motor used in a mining machine. Technician B says that electric motors can last longer than diesel engines. Who is correct?
   a. Technician A
   b. Technician B

c. Both A and B
d. Neither A nor B

2. Technician A says that electric motors are more energy efficient than gasoline engines. Technician B says that diesel engines are more efficient than gasoline engines. Who is correct?
   a. Technician A
   b. Technician B
   c. Both A and B
   d. Neither A nor B
3. Technician A says that single-phase motors are just as powerful as three-phase motors. Technician B says that three-phase AC hits peak voltage more times per second than single phase. Who is correct?
   a. Technician A
   b. Technician B
   c. Both A and B
   d. Neither A nor B
4. Technician A says that the wire windings in the rotor of an asynchronous motor are replaceable. Technician B says that asynchronous motors do not use wire windings in the rotor. Who is correct?
   a. Technician A
   b. Technician B
   c. Both A and B
   d. Neither A nor B
5. Technician A says that there is no such thing as two-phase electric current. Technician B says that an electric compressor motor is a two-phase motor and must be connected to two-phase current. Who is correct?
   a. Technician A
   b. Technician B
   c. Both A and B
   d. Neither A nor B
6. Technician A says that DC motors used as auxiliary motors are more popular because they last longer. Technician B says that DC motors are more popular because they have fewer parts and are more simply designed. Who is correct?
   a. Technician A
   b. Technician B
   c. Both A and B
   d. Neither A nor B
7. Technician A says that induction motor speed depends on the voltage powering the motor. Technician B says that single-phase motor speed depends on the amount of amperage the motor can handle. Who is correct?
   a. Technician A
   b. Technician B
   c. Both A and B
   d. Neither A nor B
8. Technician A says that using AC current is more efficient than DC current because it can be transmitted farther with less voltage drop due to resistance. Technician B says using AC voltage is less efficient because its direction changes 60 times per second. Who is correct?
   a. Technician A
   b. Technician B
   c. Both A and B
   d. Neither A nor B
9. While discussing possible causes for high voltage readings of 170 VAC at the connection to a single-phase motor, Technician A said that the voltmeter was not measuring AC current using the RMS method. Technician B said his meter was working properly and that the likely cause for the motor to burn out was 170 volts of single-phase current. Who is correct?
   a. Technician A
   b. Technician B
   c. Both A and B
   d. Neither A nor B
10. While discussing possible reasons for a motor to turn, but not reach correct operating speed, Technician B says that the starting capacitor of the two-phase motor was probably defective. Technician B said it was more likely a defective run capacitor. Who is correct?
    a. Technician A
    b. Technician B
    c. Both A and B
    d. Neither A nor B

CHAPTER 14

Starting Systems

Knowledge Objectives

After reading this chapter, you will be able to:

- **K14001** Identify and explain the function and operating principles of heavy-duty starting motors and circuits.
- **K14002** Identify and describe the types of starter motors.
- **K14003** Identify and describe the major components of a starting system.
- **K14004** Identify and explain the purpose and function of starting system control components.
- **K14005** Identify and describe the procedures for performing an on-machine starting system test.

Skills Objectives

After reading this chapter, you will be able to:

- **S14001** Measure starter draw.
- **S14002** Perform starter circuit cranking voltage and voltage drop tests; determine needed action.
- **S14003** Inspect and test components (key switch, push button, and/or magnetic switch) and wires and harnesses in the starter control circuit; replace as needed.
- **S14004** Inspect and test starter relays and solenoids/switches; replace as needed.
- **S14005** Remove and replace a starter motor and inspect the ring gear or flexplate.
- **S14006** Overhaul a starter motor.

▶ Introduction

Dozens of electric motors are found in mobile off-road equipment operating a variety of devices, from electric seats to fuel and coolant pumps, to fan blower motors and even instrument gauges. The largest of all these electric motors is the starter motor, like the one shown in **FIGURE 14-1**.

The starting system provides a method of rotating (cranking) the mobile off-road equipment's internal combustion engine (ICE) to begin the combustion cycle. The starter is designed to work for short periods of time and must crank the engine at sufficient speed for it to start. Modern starting systems are very effective provided that they are well maintained.

Understanding and maintaining starting systems is important because diagnosing "no-start" conditions is costly in terms of machine downtime and component costs if they are "over repaired" or haphazardly investigated. In fact, various manufacturers have noted that between 55% and 80% of all starters returned for warranty were not defective. Equipment and operator safety can be jeopardized if the starting system is not properly repaired and maintained. Interlocked circuits, which prevent the engine from starting under various operating conditions, and the high current supplied by multiple starting batteries are just two of the safety concerns with this system.

FIGURE 14-1 Typical starter motor cross section.

▶ Fundamentals of Starting Systems and Circuits

K14001

The starting/cranking system consists of the battery, high- and low-amperage cables, a solenoid, a starter motor assembly ring gear, and the ignition switch. On ECM-controlled starting systems, the ECM enables the operation of a relay to energize the starter circuit. Data supplied by other on-board network modules, along with control algorithms in the module, determine when and for how long the starter will crank. A control circuit determines when and if the cranking circuit will function.

During the cranking process, two actions occur. The pinion of the starter motor engages with the flywheel ring gear, and the starter motor then rotates to turn over, or crank, the engine. The starter motor is an electric motor mounted on the engine block or transmission. It is typically powered by a 12- or 24-volt battery and is designed to have high rotational torque at low speeds. The starter cables are the heaviest conductors in the machine because they carry the high current needed by the starter motor. The starter motor causes the engine flywheel and crankshaft to rotate from a resting position and keeps them turning until the engine fires and runs on its own.

High-compression-ratio diesel engines with large displacements require high amounts of electrical current, so multiple batteries are connected together to supply either more amperage or voltage. To supply more cranking amperage in a 12-volt system, batteries are connected in parallel. Adding more batteries connected in parallel increases the amount of amperage available for cranking, but the system voltage remains the same. Connecting batteries in series increases available voltage, but amperage supplied to the starter remains the same.

You Are the Mobile Heavy Equipment Technician

The cost of a no-start condition in the equipment you maintain is extraordinarily high. Equipment productivity, labor hours, and operator time are all lost. In addition, customer aggravation increases, as does the expense of resolving no-start conditions. At the specific direction from management to end or dramatically reduce the number of no-start complaints, you begin to analyze some of the common root causes of the starting system failures. Reviewing service records for the repaired equipment, you discover that the starting motors are frequently burned out, and cable terminals are loose and often burned as well. You also notice that there doesn't seem to be a specific preventative maintenance schedule in place to evaluate the condition of the starting system. It is only when the equipment does not start that the problems are identified, but that occurs too late to prevent disruption of operations. As you consider what steps to take to prevent the no-start complaints, answer the following questions.

1. Explain how the conditions that cause low-voltage burnout actually damage starting motors and starting-motor connections.
2. What maintenance practices would you recommend to prevent low-voltage burnout of starting motors and connections?
3. What trend would you observe regarding the voltage and amperage measurements made during a starter draw test if a starter were beginning to fail due to burnt brushes, armature, and field windings?

Demands on Today's Starting Systems

Today's off-road mobile equipment engines demand the most from starter motors because emission reduction strategies have increased engine cylinder pressures during cranking. Idle reduction policies require starters to more frequently crank warm engines, which are more mechanically resistive.

In spite of the increasing demands, new designs of starter motors and systems controls are enabling starters to last longer and increase output torque while substantially reducing motor weight. A typical example of this is the improvements and changes that have occurred to Delco Remy™ starter motors in recent times. The earlier Delco Remy™ 42MT weighed 58 lb (26 kg) (**FIGURE 14-2A**). The 39MT is the latest generation starter using a gear reduction planetary drive system to multiply torque output. The 39MT weighs approximately 30 lb (14 kg) or half the weight of the first generation of starters. Both starters are used on engines with 10 to 15-liter (L) displacement (**FIGURE 14-2B**). Minimum life expectancy for a starter now is 4 years, with 7,000 start cycles.

Most starting systems have only a single starter motor to crank the engine. In large displacement engines, such as locomotive diesel engines, where the starting demands are higher, two starter motors may be required to crank the engine over.

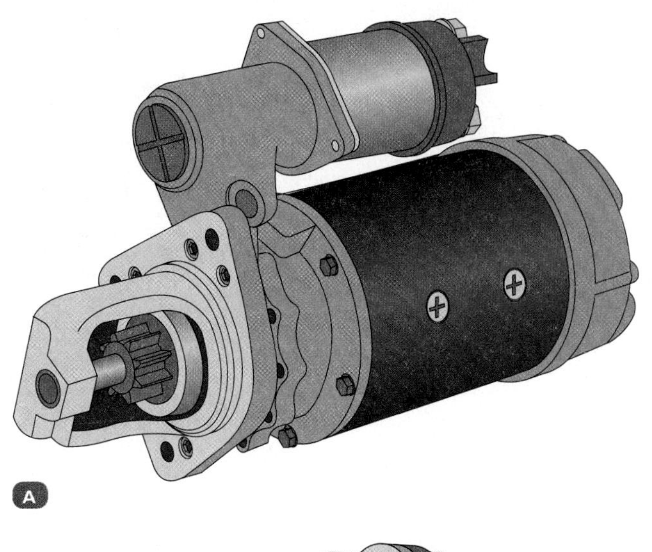

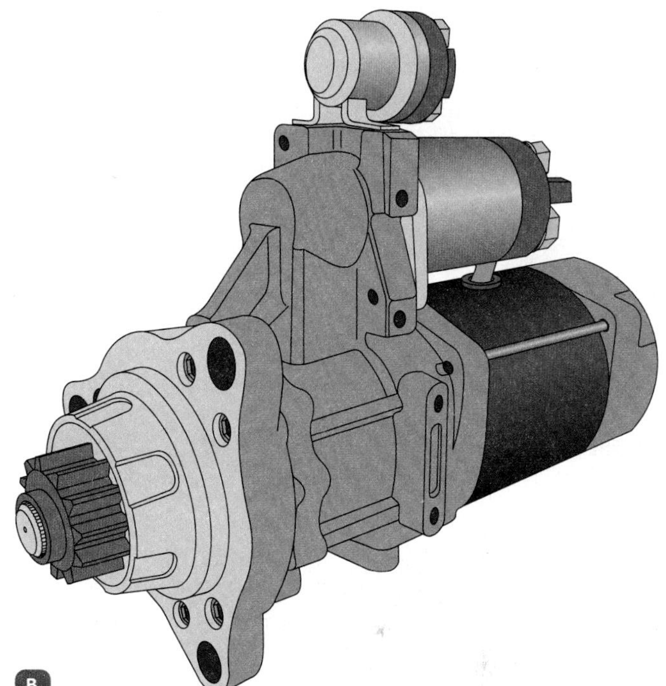

FIGURE 14-2 Two generations of improvements in starters. **A.** 42MT Direct Drive. **B.** 39MT Planetary Drive.

Starter Motor Classification

Electric starter motors were first installed in the 1912 Cadillac cars to replace hand-operated engine cranks. Although electric motors were invented decades before this, the concept that made electric starters practical was the idea of building motors to operate at high-amperage levels for a few seconds and not burn out. The Dayton Electric Company, later shortened and called DELCO™, pioneered the use of high-current-draw motors that enabled the starter to develop a tremendous amount of torque. The motors were unlike any compact electric motors of the day, which were all designed for continuous operation.

Using a small pinion gear, the starter motor rotates the engine through a ring gear attached to the flywheel. When the starter motor begins to turn, the pinion teeth quickly line up with the flywheel teeth and rotate the engine at a minimum of 125 rpm for a four-stroke diesel engine to an average of 200–250 rpm. In gasoline engines, the ratio between the flywheel ring gear and pinion gear is anywhere between 10 and 15:1. Diesel engines use 18:1 to 25:1, with 20:1 being most common.

Currently, there are three major categories of electric starters used in mobile off-road equipment.

- **Direct drive**: The motor armature directly engages the flywheel through a pinion gear. In this arrangement (**FIGURE 14-3**), the only gear torque multiplication is between the pinion gear and the ring gear.
- **Reduction gear drive**: The motor multiplies torque to the starter pinion gear by using an extra gear between the armature and the starter drive mechanism. The gear reduction allows the starter to spin at a higher speed with lower current while still creating the required torque through the reduction gear to crank the engine. The reduction drive of this type of starter motor is approximately between 3.3:1 and 5.7:1. These types of starters (**FIGURE 14-4**) can be identified by an offset drive housing to the motor housing.

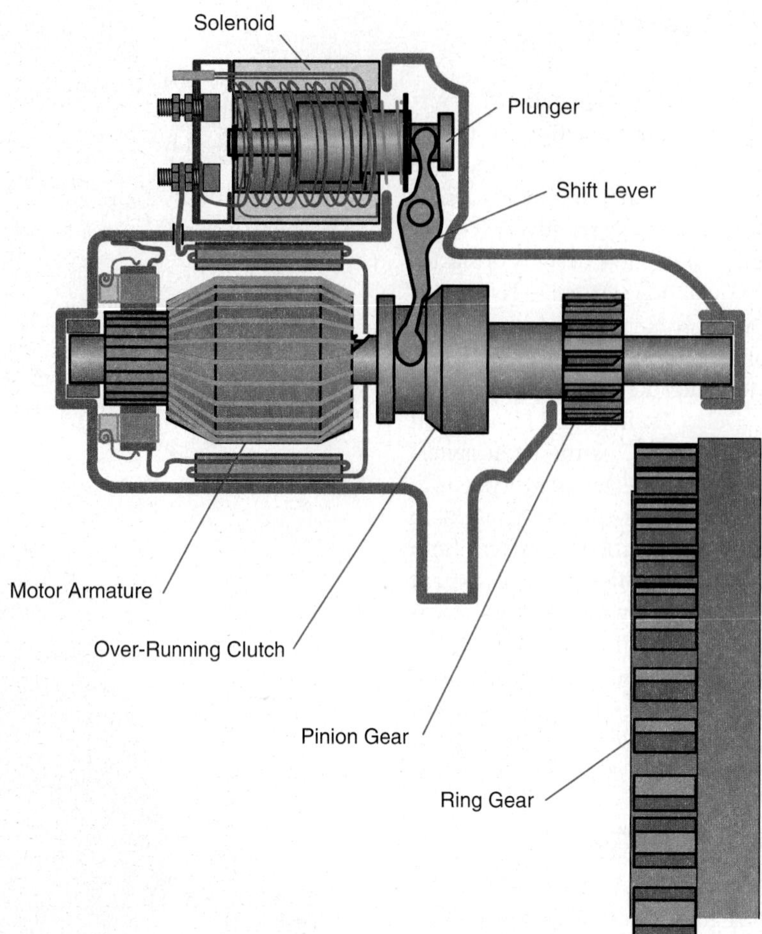

FIGURE 14-3 A typical direct-drive starter motor.

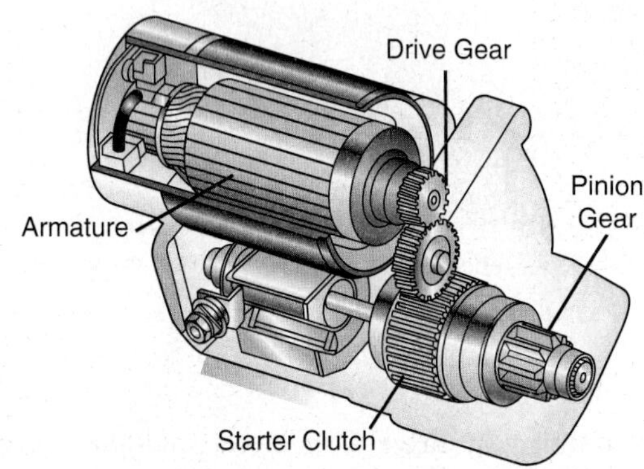

FIGURE 14-4 A typical reduction drive starter motor.

- **Planetary gear reduction drive**: Another type of gear reduction system, the planetary gear system (**FIGURE 14-5**), reduces the starter profile using a planetary gear set rather than a spur-type gears to multiply motor torque to the pinion gear. Gear reduction starters can reduce starter weight by more than 50%.

Direct-drive starters are becoming less common due to their larger size, heavier weight, and higher current requirements. The use of gear reduction and planetary gear reduction starter designs means the motor requires less current, is more compact, and is lighter—while increasing cranking torque. Higher motor speeds used in these units result in potentially less motor damage than direct-drive units because less current is needed to produce torque. The disadvantage of the smaller starter profile in comparison to direct-drive starters is the inability to tolerate high heat loads caused by prolonged engine cranking.

Pneumatic, or air, starters (**FIGURE 14-6**), are another type of starter motor used on some diesel engines. Without the need for batteries, air starting systems are lighter weight, and crank engines at faster speeds than electric starters can. Engines requiring higher cranking speeds, such as two-stroke Detroit Diesels, benefit from the use of air starters. Because air starters do not rely on batteries, high torque output in cold weather operation is instantly available.

The system consists of a geared air motor, starting valve, and a pressure tank. Compressed air from a dedicated reservoir tank is used to spin the motor after the operator pushes a spring-loaded, dash-mounted air valve. A set of reduction gears between the motor and pinion gears multiplies motor torque while engaging the flywheel ring gear. Once running, the engine recharges a dedicated starter air reservoir.

Hydraulic starting systems are another type of starter used on some diesel engines. They can be used to start engines up to

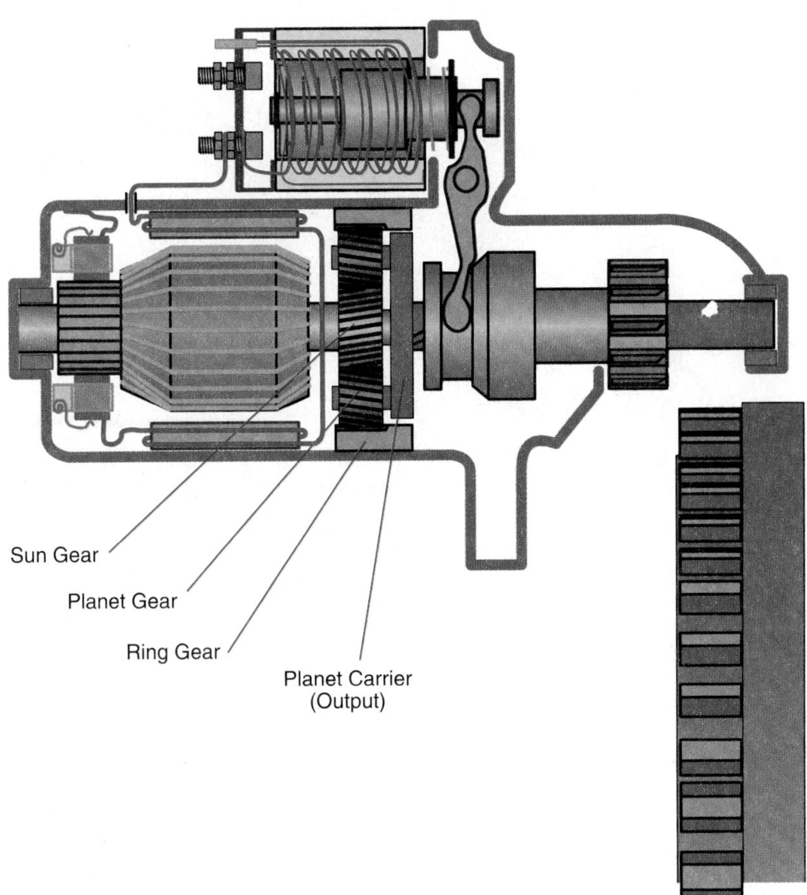

FIGURE 14-5 A typical planetary gear reduction drive starter motor.

FIGURE 14-6 A typical air starter.

80 liters in size. Hydraulic starters are most common in underground mining applications, offshore platforms, and other hazardous locations where it is important to reduce the risk of fire hazards. Like air starters, they are capable of higher cranking speeds and do not have electrical connections, which are prone to corrosion.

DC Motor Principles

All electric motors operate using principles of magnetic attraction and repulsion. Because like magnetic poles repel one another and unlike poles attract, it is possible to arrange magnetic poles within the motor to be continuously in a state of repulsion and attraction, which produces the motor action.

The magnetic fields are produced either by permanent magnets or electromagnets, which use coils or loops of conductors with electric current flowing through them to create magnetic fields. Two magnetic fields are required for motor action: one surrounds the motor armature and is called the field winding, and the other is in the rotating armature, as illustrated in **FIGURE 14-7**.

The magnetic field in the field is produced by permanent magnets, but in all heavy-duty applications by strong electromagnets. The armature's magnetic field is generated in loops of wire that form the armature windings. Motor action occurs through the interaction of the magnetic fields of the field coils and the armature, which causes a rotational force to act on the armature, producing the turning motion.

Heavy-duty starter motors use electromagnets in the field and armature windings, which are intensified by the low-reluctance, laminated, iron armature shaft and soft iron starter case. Motors used for smaller applications, such as blower and wiper motors, may use permanent magnets for the field and electromagnets for the armature. Permanent magnets used to replace electromagnets in the motor field are not used in medium or heavy-duty diesel engine starter applications.

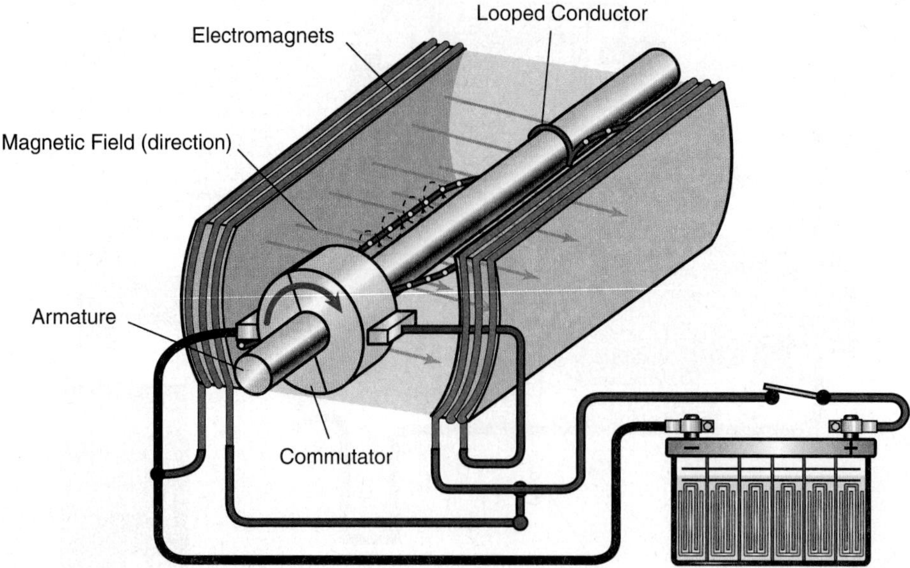

FIGURE 14-7 Basic direct-current electric motor operation. Two magnetic fields are required for motor action, one in the field and the other in the armature.

▶ Types of DC Motors

K14002

Direct current motors are categorized by the arrangement of electromagnetic circuits producing magnetic forces of repulsion and attraction. Common electric motor classification used in mobile off-road equipment is as follows:

- Series: Field and armature windings are connected in series. These motors develop the highest torque and are used as starting motors.
- Shunt (parallel wound): Field and armature windings are connected in parallel. These motors develop less torque but maintain a constant speed. They are often used as blower motors.
- Compound: Field and armature windings have both series and parallel connections. The motor has good starting torque and stable operating speed. These motors are commonly used in wipers and power seats.
- Stepper: The field is made from an electromagnet, and the armature has two or more coils that are energized by a microcontroller. These motors are used in instrument clusters gauges, actuators for turbochargers, and EGR valves, where high-precision movement is required.

Series Motors

The series and shunt motor are the two most common types found in the off-road industry. **FIGURE 14-8** shows the current flow circuits through a series and shunt motor.

Note the difference in the way the current flows through the fields. Series motors are called "series" because the field and armature windings are connected in series. So, current flows through the field windings first and then to the armature windings before leaving the armature through the positive brush. This means current first passes from the negative chassis ground, through a brush, and into the armature. Current leaves from another brush and passes into the field coils before returning to the battery positive. Because it is a series circuit,

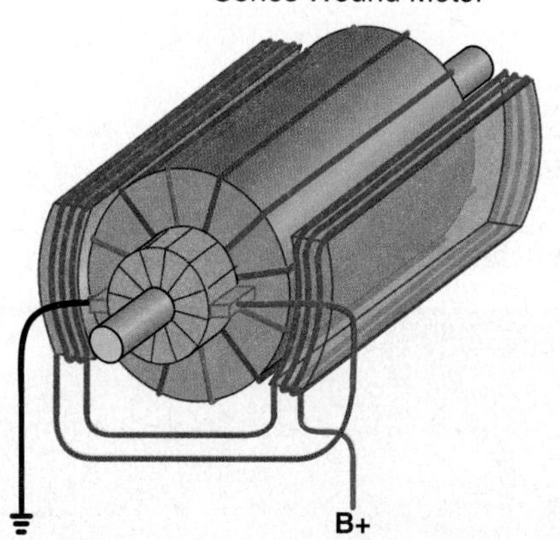

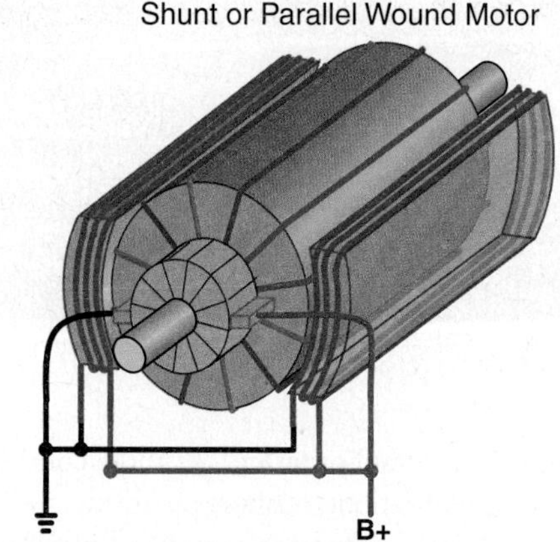

FIGURE 14-8 Typical circuits for basic series and shunt motors.

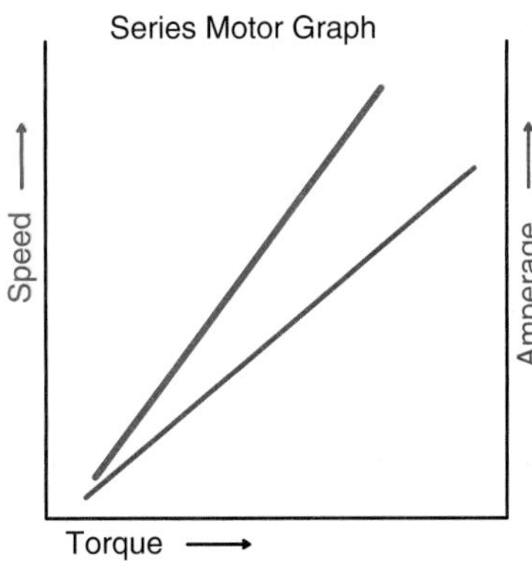

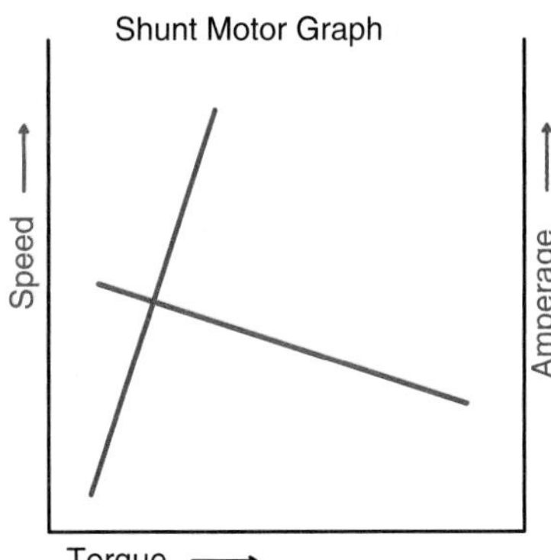

FIGURE 14-9 Comparing amperage drawn, speed, and torque of series and shunt motors.

any unwanted resistance inside the motor, whether it is a burnt contact or loose brush, will reduce current flow throughout the entire motor circuit.

Series-wound motors are primarily used in starter motors because they develop the greatest amount of torque at zero rpm, which is ideal for developing breakaway torque needed to crank a stopped engine. As magnetic field strength is always proportional to amperage and not voltage, the initial amperage drawn by a series motor produces the most torque. In comparison, shunt motors produce less torque than series motors but do not drop as much speed as torque requirements diminish. This makes them ideal for applications like blower motors (**FIGURE 14-9**).

Series Motor Current Flow

The current flow for a series motor (**FIGURE 14-10**) is as follows:

1. Current first enters the motor through the brush connected to negative chassis ground. Current passes through the armature via the commutator and leaves through the second brush connected to the field winding. A magnetic field is created in the armature.
2. Current passes through the windings of the field coils. The laminated iron making up the pole shoes intensifies the magnetic field strength. The direction the winding is wound around the pole shoe establishes the polarity of the pole shoe. The field windings are wound in directions opposite to one another to produce a like pole to the armatures, which always opposes the magnetic pole produced in the armature.

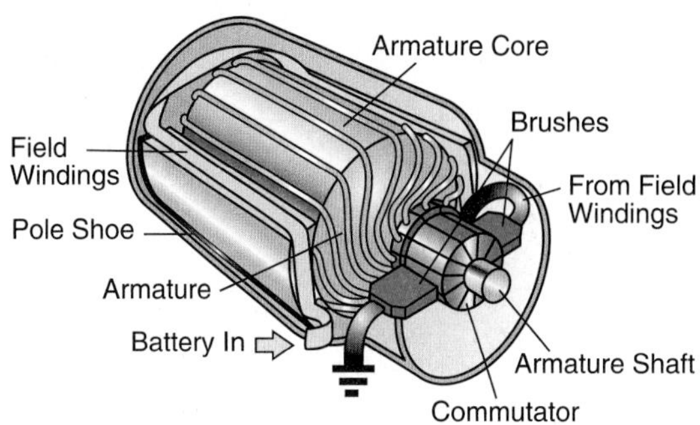

FIGURE 14-10 Current flow in a series motor and through the armature and fields in series.

3. The forces of repulsion between the field coil and armature cause the armature to turn.
4. Each armature winding is connected to a pair of segments on the commutator. The commutator turns with the armature, causing the stationary brushes to continuously connect with a new armature winding as the armature rotates. This arrangement enables the forces of repulsion to constantly reposition to maintain starter motor rotation.

Series Motor Operational Characteristics

Series wound motors also are self-limiting in speed due to the development of a **counter-electromotive force (CEMF)**. CEMF is produced by the spinning magnetic field of the armature, which induces electrical current flow in the opposite direction of battery current passing through the motor. Battery current and CEMF current both flow through a motor at the same time, but in opposite directions, which means CEMF provides resistance to battery current flow. It is important to observe that the faster the motor turns, the greater the CEMF, resulting in less current drawn from the battery. Higher voltage from cranking batteries produces greater motor speed and more CEMF. **FIGURE 14-11** illustrates the relationship between motor speed, torque, and amperage draw.

Consider the following relationship between armature speed, CEMF, amperage, and torque for a series starter motor:

- The faster the armature spins, the greater the CEMF current induced in the opposite direction of battery current flow.
- The starter draws less current from the battery as it spins faster due to CEMF resistance.
- Because less current is used at higher speeds, magnetic fields will weaken, and starter torque drops off.
- Slower motor speeds mean less CEMF resistance to battery current flow through the starter and results in higher battery amperage drawn by the starter.
- Greatest torque is produced at low speed because the motor will draw the highest amperage.

▶ TECHNICIAN TIP

Weak and discharged batteries are a starting motor's worst enemy because they can cause low-voltage burnout. Low battery voltage prevents the starter from spinning as fast as it should, which reduces CEMF—a

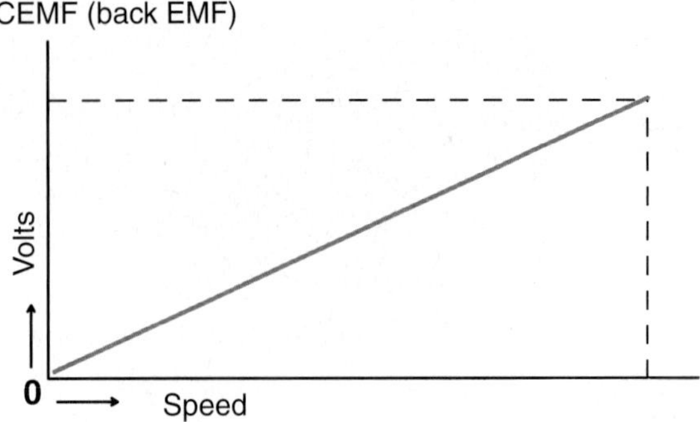

FIGURE 14-11 As motor speed increases, more CEMF is produced.

starter's internal resistance when operating. With lower internal resistance, the starter draws more amperage than it should, which leads to heat damage to starter windings, solenoids, and external circuits.

Amperage drawn by a starter at normal room temperature with a fully charged battery ranges from an average of 350 amps for a 7-liter engine to 800 or 900 amps for a 15-liter engine. Initial starting amperage is much higher because the engine is stopped and requires more torque from the starting motor to accelerate the engine from 0 rpm to cranking speed. Because of the high amperage drawn during cranking, the starter can only operate for short periods of time before cooling. Heat produced by continuous operation for any length of time will cause serious damage to the motor. Connections become loose and burnt. Some will even melt. Brushes and insulation will become burned, as well as motor windings. To help prevent heat damage, armature windings are brazed rather than soldered to the commutator. The starter must never operate for more than 30 seconds at a time and should rest for 2 minutes between extended crank cycles. This permits the heat to dissipate without causing damage to the starting motor.

Low-Voltage Burnout

Cranking an engine with low battery voltage causes one of the most damaging conditions for a starter. **Low-voltage burnout** occurs when excess amperage flows through the starter, causing the motor to burn out prematurely. When battery voltage is low, the starter will use even more amperage to rotate. This happens because starters are constant power devices. That is, starters will use any combination of voltage and amperage to produce the necessary output power, rated in watts. For example, if 7,200 watts of power is needed to operate a starter at 24 volts, 300 amps are required. If available battery voltage fell to 18 volts, then 400 amps would be needed according to Watts's law (watts = volts × amperage). Increasing amperage drawn from batteries, in turn, increases batteries' internal resistance. Increased circuit resistance through the battery causes available voltage to drop even further, which in turn increases the amperage needed to rotate the starter. Slower starter rotation means less CEMF is developed. Consequently, amperage through the starter climbs even more. To prevent damage from low voltage to the starter, cables, solenoid, and switches, several design and maintenance practices are required.

- Correct battery sizing: Batteries must be sized according to their CCA to maintain a cranking voltage of no less than 10.5 volts (for 12-volt systems) or 18 volts (for a 24-volt system) after three consecutive cranking periods lasting 30 seconds. The appropriate 2-minute cooling period is included in this estimation.
- Correct sizing of battery cables: Dedicated battery negative and positive cables are needed for heavier starting systems. Cable diameters should be sized for maximum amperage capacity using OEM recommendations. Double cables are needed when using four or more starting batteries.
- Using over-crank protection switches. Thermal protection switches may be located in the starter housing and connected in series with the starter solenoid ground circuit. When hot, the switch opens and prevents the starter solenoid from operating until the starter is sufficiently cooled.
- Using voltage-sensitive starter control circuit relays: Starter relays are produced that will disengage when battery voltage falls below a predetermined level, thus disconnecting the starter circuit. Alternatively, an electronic control module (ECM), which supplies current to energize the starter, can monitor battery voltage, enabling the ECM to disconnect the starter relay when battery current falls too low during cranking. Disconnect voltage is approximately 7.2 volts (12-volt system) or 14.4 volts (24-volt system).
- Using ultracapacitors: Ultracapacitors are a recent application of organic capacitors used to provide cranking assist to HD starters. Up to 1,800 amps of current can rapidly discharge for a brief moment to provide battery assist to the starting motor. As illustrated in **FIGURE 14-12**, ultracapacitors connected in parallel to the battery provide a high initial current to the starter to speed up the armature rotation. Supplementing the available amperage to the starter during the initial cranking period reduces the likelihood of a low-voltage burnout due to low CEMF when armature speed is reduced.

TECHNICIAN TIP

Battery capacity is specifically designed to meet the cranking requirements of the engine. An under-capacity set of batteries will *not* be capable of delivering the required current flow to the starter motor while still maintaining sufficient battery voltage. The batteries may cause low-voltage burnout of the starter and damage the starter circuit. It may also create a situation where there is insufficient voltage available to operate the engine's ECM during cranking. Although not as common a problem, excessive battery capacity can also damage the starter motor by supplying too much amperage while cranking. This can create a situation in which excessive torque is produced from the starter motor, damaging the starter drive and ring gear.

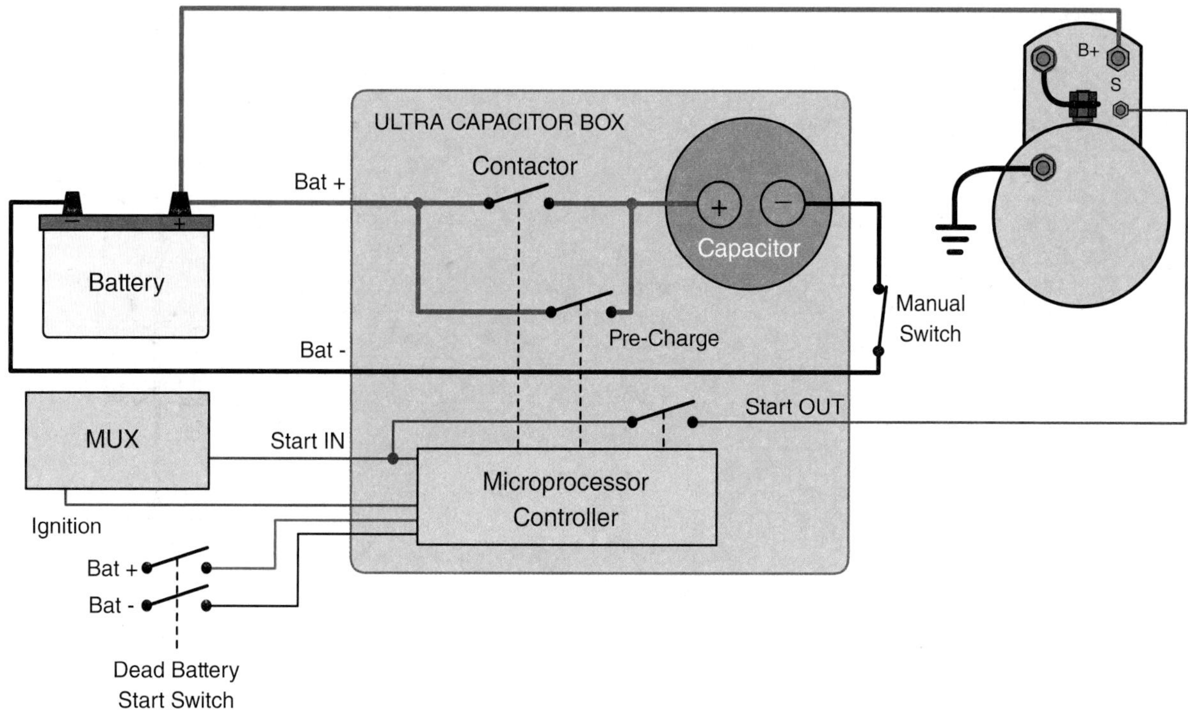

FIGURE 14-12 Power assist from ultracapacitors reduces the likelihood of low-voltage burnout.

▶ Components of Starters

K14003

Regardless of the motor design, a starter motor consists of housing, field coils, an armature, a commutator, brushes, end frames, and a solenoid-operated shift mechanism. Major variations between starters are in the starter drive mechanism. Some starters use a gear-reduction drive, whereas others use a direct-drive configuration. Still other starter motors, called axial starter motors, are a type of direct-drive starter. Axial starter motors use an axial sliding armature to engage the pinion with the flywheel. This type of starter is discussed later in this chapter.

Starter Housing and Field Coils

The starter housing, or frame, encloses and supports the internal starter components, protecting them and intensifying the magnetic fields produced in the field coils. Housings and pole shoes are made from soft iron, which conducts magnetic fields with less resistance than air or other materials, which concentrates the magnetic field produced in the fields, making a more powerful magnet. In the starter housing shown in **FIGURE 14-13**, field coils and their pole shoes are securely attached to the inside of the iron housing.

The field coils are insulated from the housing and are connected to a terminal, called the motor terminal, which protrudes through to the housing. Fields will have a north or south magnetic polarity facing inward or outward depending on the direction of current flow. The magnetic flux of the pole shoes is illustrated in **FIGURE 14-14**.

Field coils are connected in series with the armature windings through the starter brushes. In a four-brush starter motor, two brushes are used to connect the field coils to the armature and the other two brushes connect to ground to complete the series circuit.

FIGURE 14-13 A set of starter motor fields, windings, and housing.

Armature

The **armature** is the only rotating component of the starter. Armatures (**FIGURE 14-15**) have three main components: the shaft, windings, and the commutator.

Armature Shaft and Windings

Different from the thin wire used in shunt motors, armature windings are made of heavy, flat, copper strips that can handle the heavy current flow of the series motor. The windings are made of numerous coils of a single loop each. The sides of

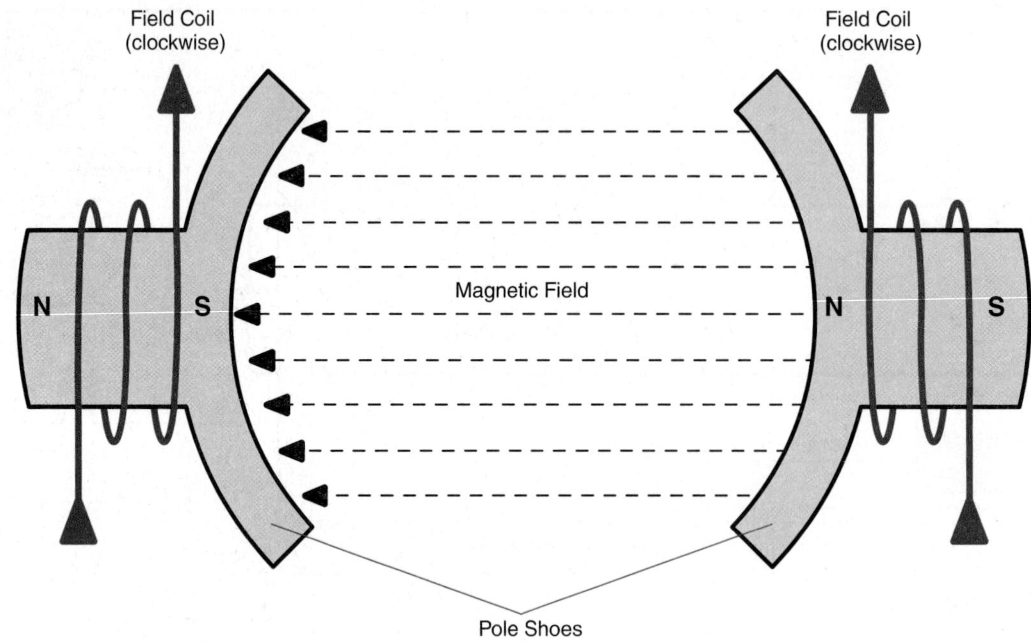

FIGURE 14-14 Field coils are wound around pole shoes, producing a north and south magnetic field.

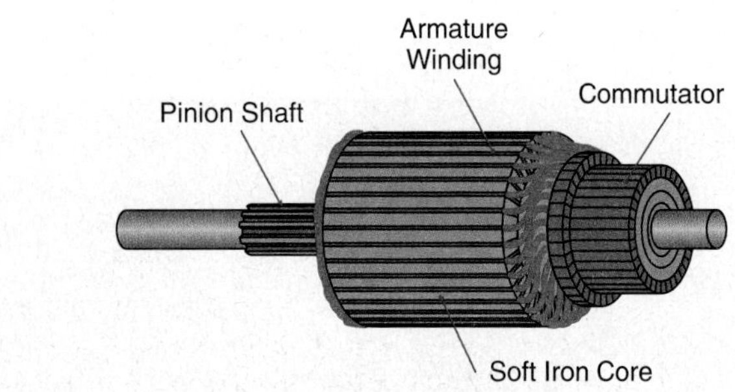

FIGURE 14-15 Features of an armature.

these loops fit into slots in the armature core or shaft, but they are insulated from it with insulating strips and varnish applied to the winding before placement. Each slot contains the side of one-half of a coil and is connected to a commutator segment. In a four-brush motor, the halves of a coil are wound at 90 degrees to each other. The coils connect to each other at the commutator so that current flows through all of the armature windings at the same time. This arrangement generates a magnetic field around each armature winding. The interaction between the armature and field windings' magnetic fields produces a torque or twisting force that turns the armature.

Commutator and Commutation

The commutator assembly is pressed onto the armature shaft. It is made up of heavy copper segments separated from each other and the armature shaft by insulation. The commutator segments connect to the ends of the armature windings. Starter motors have four or more brushes that ride on the commutator segments and carry the heavy current flow from the stationary field coils to the rotating armature windings via the commutator segments. A brush holder holds the brushes in position.

The commutator's role is to switch the direction of current flow through each armature coil as the armature rotates, thereby maintaining the rotary movement by ensuring the magnetic pole in the field winding is always the same as the pole in the armature winding opposite it. For a simple explanation of how a commutator works, consider a basic motor with a single loop of wire. When current flows in a conductor, an electromagnetic field is generated around it. If the conductor is placed in a stationary electromagnetic field with current flowing through the field in the opposite direction, the two magnetic fields will oppose one another, and the conductor will be repelled or pushed away from the stationary field. Reversing the direction of current flow in the conductor will cause the conductor to move in the opposite direction. This is known as the motor effect and is greatest when the current-carrying conductor and the stationary magnetic field are at right angles to each other.

By switching the direction of current flow through the conductor at the right time, the conductor can be continuously pushed away from one field winding and pulled toward another (**FIGURE 14-16**).

The turning motion is called the motor effect and causes the loop to rotate until it is at 90 degrees to the magnetic field. To continue rotation, the direction of current flow in the conductor must be reversed. A commutator is used to continually reverse the current flow to maintain rotation of the loop (**FIGURE 14-17**).

For example, a commutator consists of two semicircular segments that are connected to the two ends of the loop and are insulated from each other. Carbon brushes provide a sliding connection to the commutator to complete the circuit and allow current to flow through the loop. This continuously changing direction of current through the loop maintains a consistent direction of rotation of the loop. To achieve a uniform motion and torque output, the number of loops must be increased. The

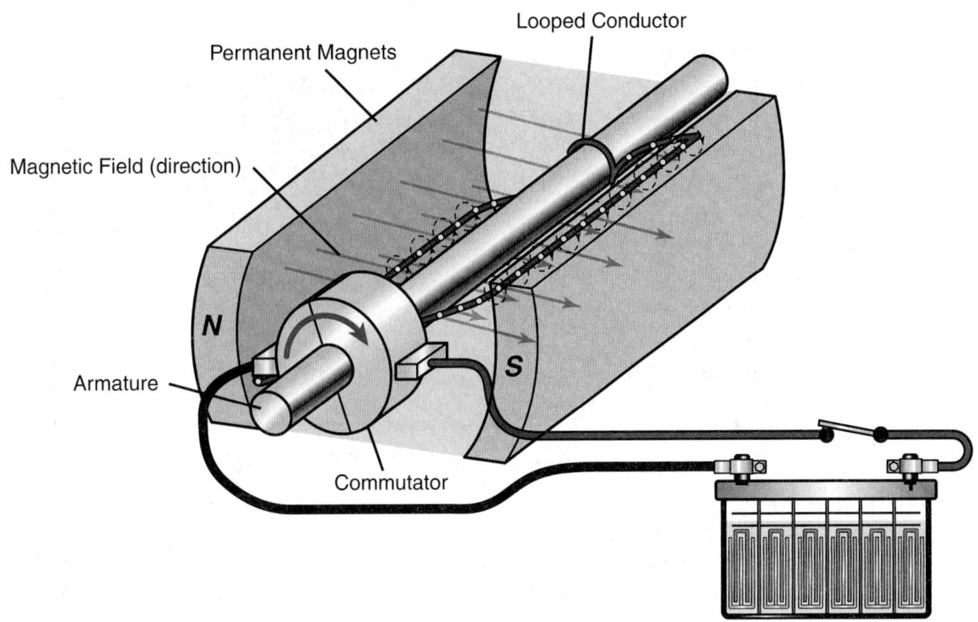

FIGURE 14-16 Simple single-loop motor and electromagnetic fields with commutator and brushes.

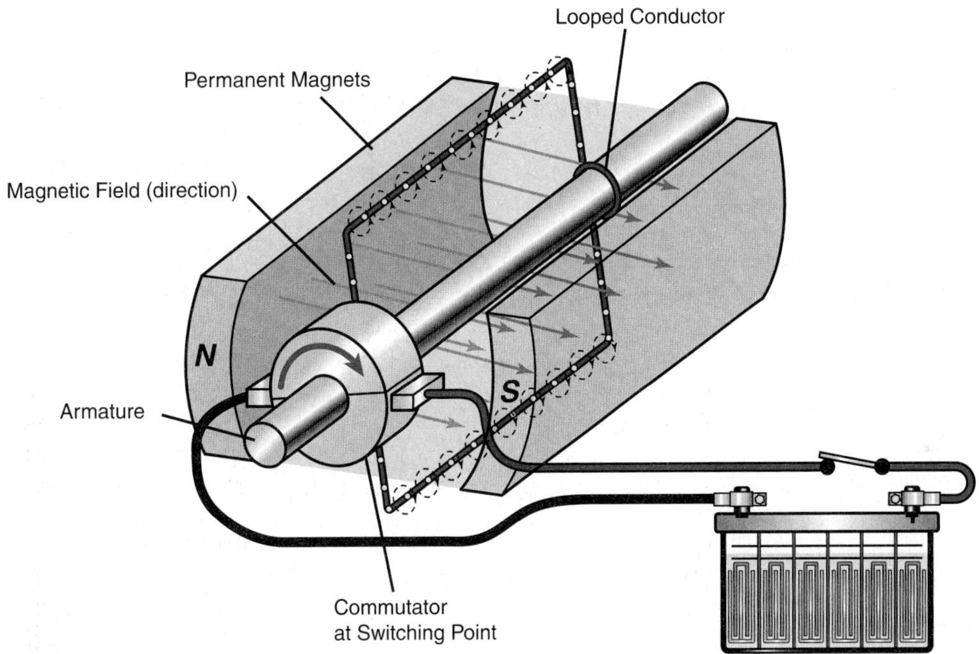

FIGURE 14-17 Simple single-loop motor and electromagnetic fields at the switching point of the commutator.

additional loops smooth out the rotational forces. A starter motor armature has a large number of conductor loops and therefore has many segments on the commutator. A simple multi-loop motor is depicted in **FIGURE 14-18**.

Solenoid and Shift Mechanism

The solenoid on the starter motor performs two main functions:

1. It switches on and off the high current flow required by the starter motor.
2. It engages the starter drive with the ring gear.

The solenoid-operated shift mechanism is mounted in a case that is sealed to keep out oil and road splash (**FIGURE 14-19**).

In direct-drive starters, the case is flange mounted to the starter motor case and contains two electromagnets around a hollow core. A movable iron plunger is installed in the hollow core. Energizing the electromagnets pulls the iron plunger, which in turn moves a shift lever, engaging the drive pinion gear (**FIGURE 14-20**).

At the same time, moving the iron core also closes a set of contacts to connect battery current with the motor terminal, directing full battery current to the field coils and starter

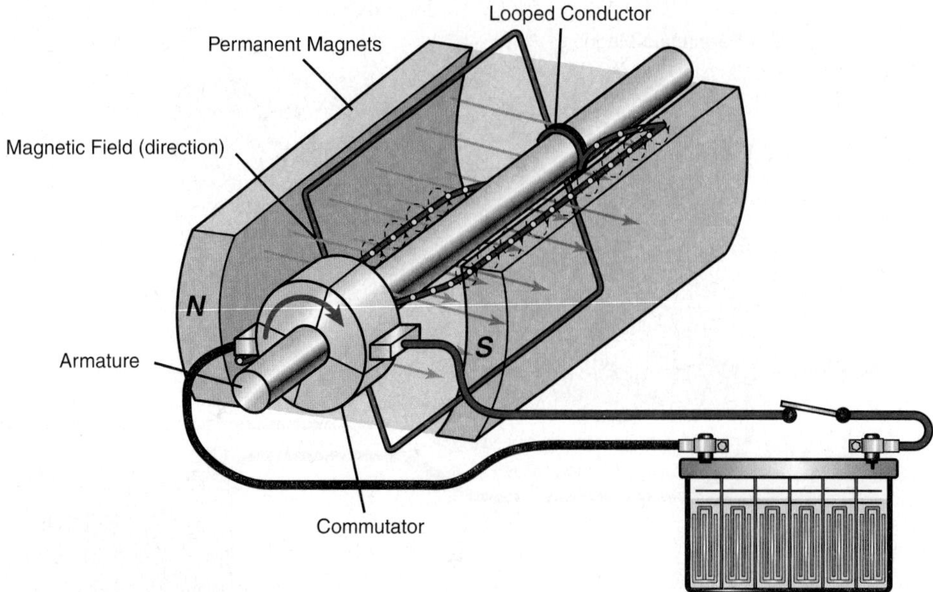

FIGURE 14-18 Simple multi-loop motor and electromagnetic fields with commutator and brushes.

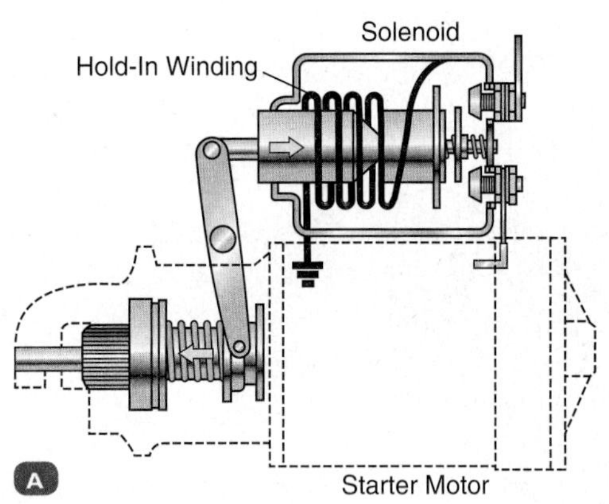

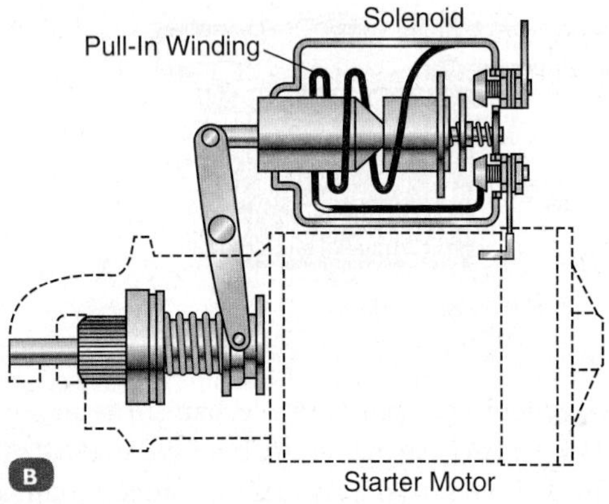

FIGURE 14-19 The solenoid uses two electrical windings. **A.** A hold-in winding. **B.** A pull-in winding.

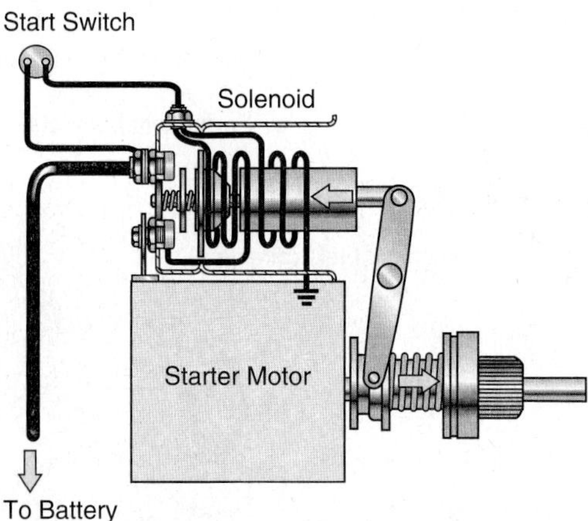

FIGURE 14-20 Solenoid starter contacts and starter drive linkage.

motor armature for cranking power. The starter pinion gear engages the flywheel ring gear before energizing the motor terminal to prevent damage to either gear from spinning teeth (Figure 14-20).

▶ TECHNICIAN TIP

A solenoid is an electromagnetic device that is used to perform work and has mechanical action. A solenoid is made with one or two coil windings wound around an iron tube. When electrical current is passed through the coil windings, it creates electromagnetic force that creates linear action, pushing or pulling an iron core. When the core is connected to a lever or other mechanical device, the solenoid can put this mechanical movement to practical use. For example, it may engage the pinion of the starter motor with the flywheel; shift gears in electronically controlled transmissions; shut off air, fuel, or oil supplies; engage engine and exhaust brakes; move the fuel rack in a diesel engine; and so on. Solenoids can also close contacts, such as the solenoid contact in a starter motor solenoid.

▶ TECHNICIAN TIP

Low battery voltage produces starter chatter—the rapid cycling of the solenoid plunger in and out of engagement. This happens because the thinner windings of the hold-in circuit are more sensitive to voltage drop than pull-in windings. When the solenoid closes the connection between the battery and motor terminal, the available voltage also drops due to the increased amperage flow from the battery.

Starter Drive Mechanisms

The starter drive transmits the rotational force from the starter armature to the engine via the ring gear that is mounted on the engine flywheel or torque converter. Armature rotation is transferred to the pinion gear through a variety of mechanisms.

Direct-drive starters, which diesel engines used exclusively for many decades, transferred torque directly to the pinion gear. Today, gear reduction starters using both planetary and spur-gear mechanisms have replaced direct drives. With a solenoid-actuated, direct-drive starting system, teeth on the pinion gear do not immediately mesh with the flywheel ring gear. If this occurs, a spring located behind the pinion gear compresses so that the solenoid plunger can complete its stroke. When the starter motor armature begins to turn, the pinion teeth quickly line up with the flywheel teeth, and the spring pressure helps them to mesh (**FIGURE 14-21**).

The pinion drive gear is attached to a roller-type, one-way (or overrunning) clutch that is splined to the starter armature, as in **FIGURE 14-22**.

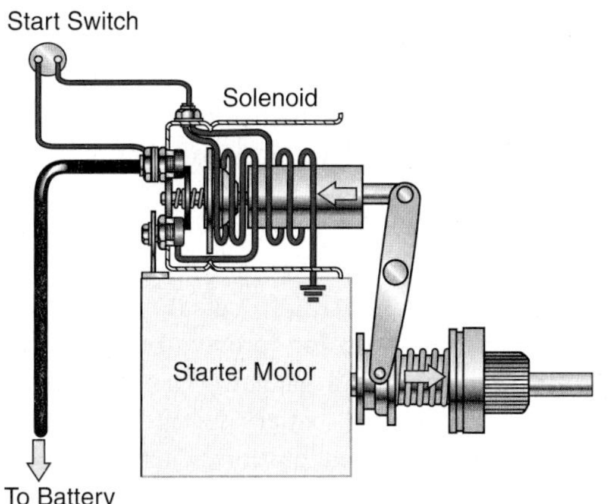

FIGURE 14-21 Both windings are energized, and the solenoid plunger is starting to move toward the cap.

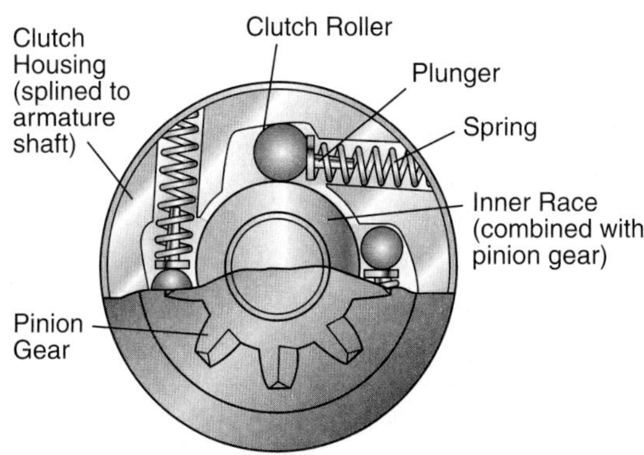

FIGURE 14-22 Starter drive one-way clutch.

A one-way clutch is in all pinion gears and operates like a ratchet to protect the starter motor. It drives when turned in one direction and slips when turned in the opposite direction. When the engine starts and runs, the starter motor would be damaged if it remained connected to the engine through the flywheel. The ring gear–to–pinion gear ratio, which multiplies starter torque, also multiplies the starter's speed when driven by the engine. At idle, with a 20:1 gear ratio, the starter's armature will turn 14,000 rpm or more, which will destroy the armature windings. To prevent this, the one-way overrunning clutch allows the pinion gear to spin—but not turn the armature if it remains or is accidentally engaged with the flywheel. When the solenoid is de-energized, the shift assembly is pulled away from the flywheel through spring pressure (**FIGURE 14-23**).

Most starters have a pinion clearance adjustment to ensure the pinion engages fully with the flywheel while maintaining a clearance from the drive end housing. Starter motors usually use one of the following three methods for providing pinion clearance adjustment, as illustrated in **FIGURE 14-24**. Proper adjustment of the mechanism is important to prevent damage to the flywheel teeth.

- An eccentric shift fork pin, which is turned until the correct pinion clearance is measured, and then locked off by a lock nut
- Shims, which are placed between the solenoid and housing to adjust pinion clearance
- A screw or nut on the solenoid core where it connects to the shift fork; tightening and loosening the screw or nut adjusts pinion clearance

▶ Starter Control Circuits

K14004

The starter control circuit, in its most basic form, has an ignition switch directly controlling the starter solenoid to operate the starter motor. In modern machines, the circuits are more

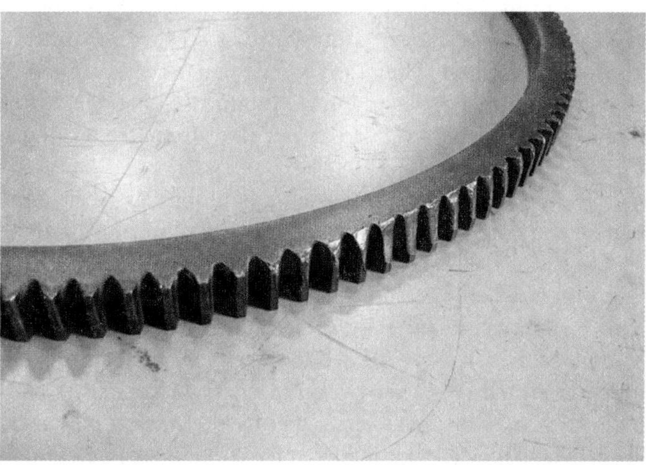

FIGURE 14-23 Ring gear damage can result from poorly adjusted pinion clearance or engagement of the pinion while the ring gear is rotating.

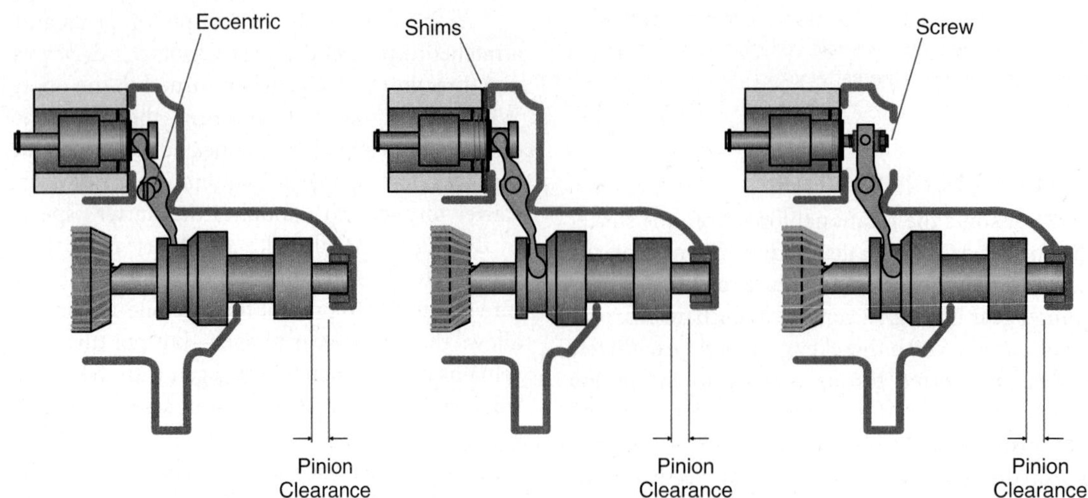

FIGURE 14-24 Typical methods of adjusting pinion clearance.

complex, as relays and control circuits, such as transmission neutral and clutch switches, are added to improve reliability and safety. The latest models of mobile off-road equipment use an electrical system control module, which interfaces with the machines on-board network that receives data from various sensors, to control the operation of the starter control circuit.

Solenoid Control Relay

Because it is neither practical nor safe to have large battery and starter cables routed in the cab of a machine, the starter control circuit allows the operator to use a small amount of battery current provided by the ignition switch to control the flow of a large amount of current in the starting circuit. The control circuit may also have a provision for locking out the starter engagement if the engine is running or the starter has overheated. Safety switches, also called neutral safety switches (**FIGURE 14-25A**), can be located in either of two places in the control circuit—interrupting either the ground or battery positive of the starter relay (**FIGURE 14-25B**). Placing the transmission in Park or Neutral, or depressing the clutch, closes the starter control circuit so current can flow to the relay switch. The safety switch can also be connected between the relay switch and its ground so that the switch must be closed before current can flow from the magnetic switch to ground.

ECM-controlled circuits use the ignition key as an input device and control the starter operation by supplying a ground to the starter relay. The starter relay is the point in the starting system where the control circuit and starter solenoid circuit join. Because starter solenoids can consume between 30 and 60 amps, relays are needed to switch low current from the ignition switch or starter button to energize the starter solenoid circuit. Starter relays are a type of intermittent duty relay. This means they are not intended for continuous operation or operation longer than a minute. The intermittent duty relay has heavy, large-gauge windings in the control circuit, capable of producing strong magnetic fields, which are less sensitive to voltage drop during cranking.

As there is a relatively high amount of amperage drawn by the starter solenoid itself, solenoid circuits have a minimum of one relay to switch current flow to the solenoid circuit. The relay may be controlled by a separate push button located in the dash or by an ignition key switch. On electronically controlled engines, it is more common to have the circuit controlled by a start button than the key switch. Having a start button prevents voltage drops through the switch. Likewise, a start button also prevents voltage spikes from the magnetic field collapse of the relay's coil, which could travel back to other ignition circuits through the key (**FIGURE 14-26**).

The ignition switch has other jobs besides controlling the starting circuit. The ignition switch normally has at least four separate positions: Accessory, Off, On (Run), and Start. There may be a separate position for "proving out," which test illuminates on-dash lights and gauges. When a machine has a push-button starter switch, battery voltage is available to the button switch only when the ignition switch is in the On position. When the starter pushbutton is pushed, current flows through the control circuit to the starter relay.

Relays use electromagnets to close contacts and act like a switch. Larger relays are sometimes referred to as "mag" switches.

Over-crank Protection (OCP)

Some starter motors are equipped with an **over-crank protection (OCP) thermostat**. The thermostat monitors the temperature of the motor (**FIGURE 14-27**).

If prolonged cranking causes the motor temperature to exceed a safe threshold, the thermostat will open the relay circuit, and the current to the solenoid is interrupted.

ADLO Lockout

Another device that may be used within the starter control circuit is **automatic disengagement lockout (ADLO)** (**FIGURE 14-28**).

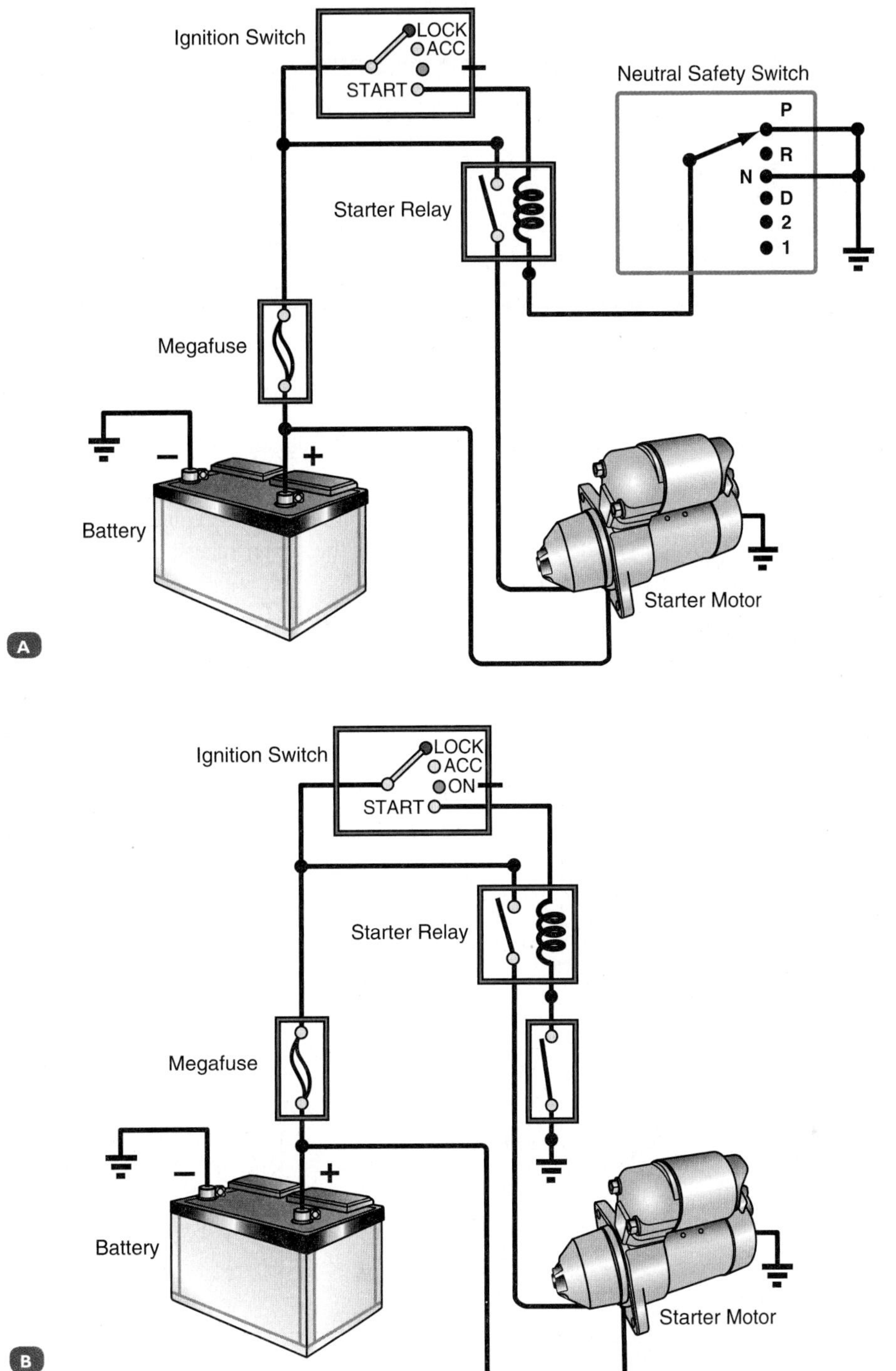

FIGURE 14-25 Basic starter control circuit. **A.** Neutral safety switch circuit. **B.** Clutch switch circuit.

The ADLO circuit prevents the starter motor from operating if the engine is running. It does this by using a **frequency-sensing relay** connected to the alternator, which detects AC current only when the alternator is charging. The ADLO relay contacts are connected in series in the starter motor control circuit. If the engine is running, the relay prevents starter engagement and disengages the starter if the key switch is left engaged too long after the engine starts.

Voltage-Sensing Relay

Because starters can be damaged from low battery voltage, some companies find the solution is to prevent the starter from cranking when the battery voltage is too low. This also has the additional benefit of preventing prolonged cranking. The voltage-sensing relay is connected in series to the solenoid control circuit. When the battery voltage drops below 7.2 volts

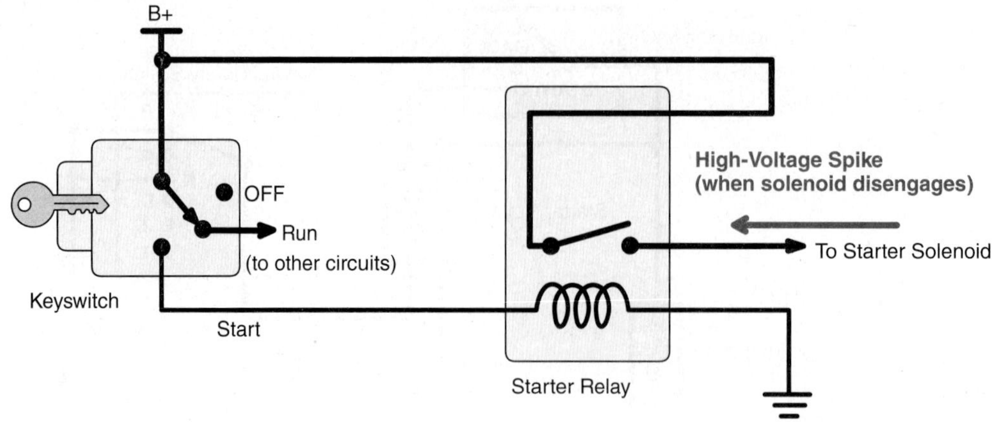

FIGURE 14-26 A relay prevents high-voltage spikes produced through self-induction in the solenoid from damaging the electrical system.

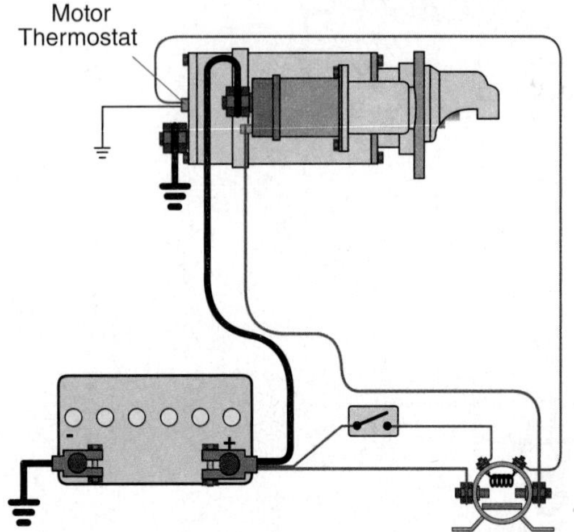

FIGURE 14-27 A thermostat switch monitors starter temperature and opens the starter circuit if the starter motor overheats.

while cranking, the voltage-sensing relay will typically open-circuit the starter relay circuit (**FIGURE 14-29**).

▶ Starting System Testing

K14005

The starting system requires testing when the engine will not crank, cranks slowly, cranks intermittently, or when the starter motor will not turn. Various manufacturers report that between 55% and 80% of defective starters returned for warranty work normally when tested. That points to poor or incomplete diagnosis of the starting and related systems and circuits. The starting system is just part of the overall machine's electrical and mechanical system. As such, there are areas of overlap between the various electrical and mechanical systems on the machine. For example, the starter system makes use of the batteries to supply power for starting, but the charging system has to

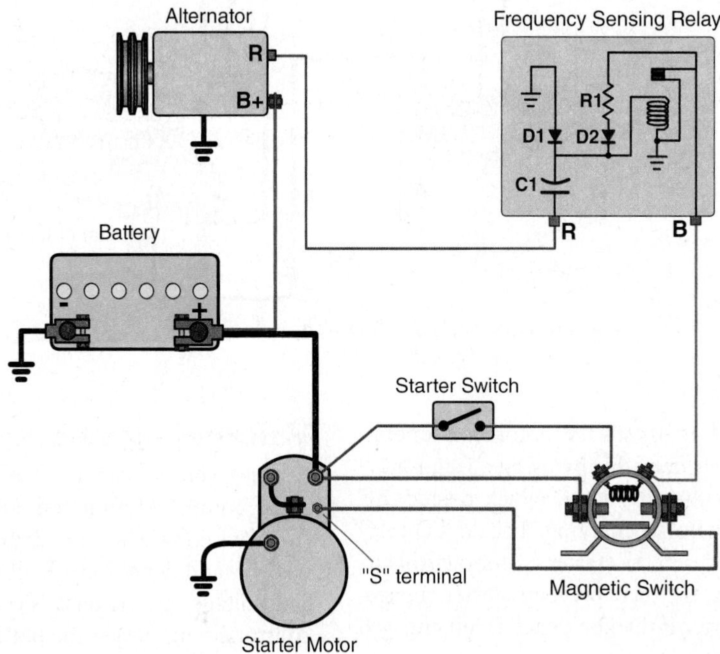

FIGURE 14-28 The ADLO relay senses alternator frequency and prevents the starter motor from operating while the engine is running.

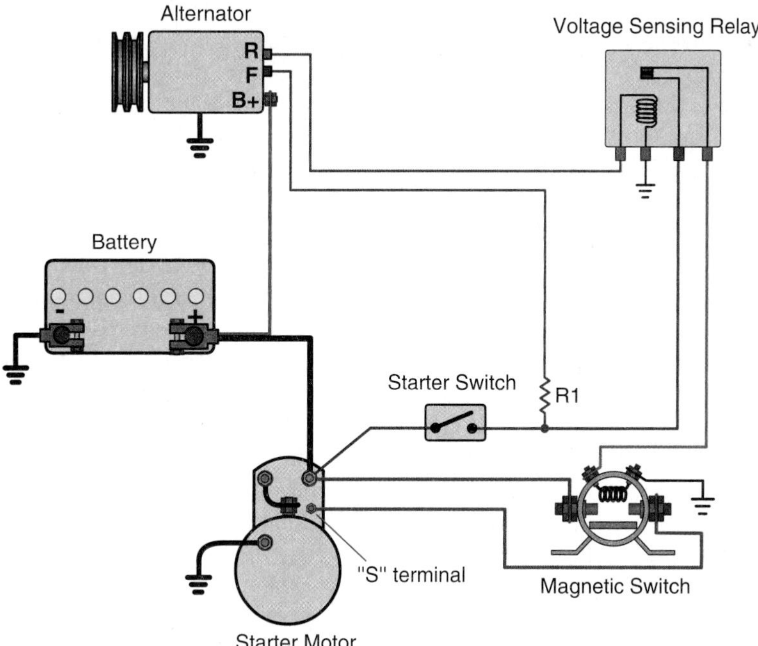

FIGURE 14-29 A low voltage-sensing relay can be connected in series with the starter control circuit to prevent the starter motor from operating if a low-battery-voltage condition occurs.

provide an adequate charge to ensure there is enough power to start the engine. At the same time, the engine's mechanical condition affects the load on the starter motor. So, when testing the starting system, also bear in mind that other electrical systems and mechanical items may require inspection to ensure a successful repair.

Because cranking torque produced from a starting motor is also affected by the condition and charge of the battery, the condition of the battery has to be qualified first before performing starting systems checks. Battery checks include the following:

- Verifying the battery voltage matches the voltage rating of the starter motor
- Ensuring that cranking amperage (CA or CCA) of the batteries meets or exceeds OEM recommendations
- Verifying that the state of charge is not lower than 50% and that open-circuit voltage is not less than 12.4 volts or 24.8 volts
- Measuring the batteries' capacity through load testing or conductance testing

For information on how to undertake battery checks, review the Servicing Batteries chapter.

▶ TECHNICIAN TIP

Low battery voltage and weak batteries are the primary cause of stress to starters and of excessive starter amperage draw. Faulty batteries also stress charging circuits, as an alternator is forced to continually charge a weak battery. Liquid starting aids can also produce engine "kickback" and apply extreme twisting forces to the motor. Heat from over-cranking and vibration from loose mountings are other leading causes of starter damage (**FIGURE 14-30**).

FIGURE 14-30 A burned solenoid contact disc caused by low available voltage.

Differentiating Between Electrical and Mechanical Problems

Whether a slow-crank or a no-crank condition, failure to crank over properly can be caused by electrical or mechanical problems. For example, slow cranking could result from an electrical fault such as high resistance in the solenoid contacts. This problem could be resolved by replacing the starter with a new or remanufactured unit. But the slow-crank condition could also be caused by a mechanical engine fault such as a spun main bearing that is causing a lot of drag on the crankshaft and preventing the starter from cranking it over at normal speed. In this case, the entire engine will have to be rebuilt.

As you can imagine, telling customers that they need a new starter motor when in fact they need a new engine (costing 10–20 times as much money) will not make them very happy with you. It is important to be able to differentiate between the two types of faults so that a wrong diagnosis can be avoided and the problem fixed appropriately the first time. Typical electrical problems that can cause starting system problems include loose, dirty, or corroded terminals and connectors; a discharged or faulty battery; a faulty starter motor; or a faulty control circuit.

Mechanical problems that may cause starting system problems include seized pistons or bearings, hydrostatic lock from liquid in the cylinder(s) (for example, a leaky fuel pressure regulator or water ingestion during off-road operation), incorrect injection or valve timing, a seized alternator or other belt-driven device, and so on. Gathering as much customer and equipment information as possible will assist in narrowing down the possible causes of the fault.

A slow-crank condition accompanied by a high draw could be due to a fault in the starter or to engine mechanical fault. If a mechanical fault is suspected, check the oil and coolant for signs of contamination. If the coolant and oil are mixing, suspect a head gasket or cracked head/block issue. If the oil and coolant are not contaminated, turn the engine over by hand to see if it is tight compared with a similar engine that is known to be good. If it is harder to turn than it should be, remove the accessory drive belt, spin each of the accessories, and try to turn the engine over again. If it is still hard to turn over, you will have to go deeper in your visual inspection and start disassembling components based on the information you have gathered along the way. For example, if the crankshaft cannot be turned a complete revolution, remove the injectors and see if liquid is ejected out of one or more cylinders. If so, the engine was hydrolocked, and you need to determine the cause. If no liquids are ejected, then you need to disassemble the engine further until you determine the cause of the mechanical resistance.

The important thing to remember is that slow-crank and no-crank conditions can be caused by both electrical and mechanical faults, so do not jump to conclusions. You need to identify the root cause of the fault through tests so that you can advise the customer on what is needed to repair the machine.

Starter Motor Tests

The inspection and measurement procedures used to diagnose starting system complaints should be symptom based. That is, a flow chart should be used to begin a proper sequence of pinpoint checks recommended by the OEM. Symptoms include intermittent and no start, slow cranking, prolonged cranking, starter chatter, and starter noise. Any diagnostic procedure should begin with qualifying the condition of the batteries and inspecting all battery cables, grounds, and connections. Information on how to undertake battery checks can be found in the Servicing Batteries chapter.

Listed here are some of the faults that may occur within the starter motor:

- Worn brushes: Intermittent starter operation or starter operation that resumes after it is tapped with a hammer indicates brushes with poor commutator contact. Poor contact could be due to weak spring tension after a brush wears out. Poor brush contact with the commutator can also be caused by loss of brush spring tension due to heating from excessively high-amperage flow—often because of prolonged cranking or low battery voltage. It can be evidenced by blued or even charred brush springs.
- Damaged field coils: Insulation can break down, causing shorts between coils or shorts to ground. This can be caused by age, contaminants breaking down the insulation, or excessive current flow. Excessive heat may also cause connections to be melted, creating additional resistance in the circuit.
- Damaged armature: An armature may have the commutator excessively worn or unevenly worn. The armature may also develop shorts between the windings, shorts to ground, and opens between windings and the commutator. A test instrument called a growler is used to test an armature.
- Worn bushings or bearings: Sintered brass bushings or, in some cases, bearings are used to suspend the armature in the starter case. Because motor efficiency is dependent on having the smallest clearance between the armature and field coils, any wear of bushing or bearings will cause contact between the armature and field coils. Worn bushing or bearings cause excessive current draw that can be observed during a starter draw test.

Use **TABLE 14-1** to assist in diagnosing starting system problems. Always consult manufacturers' information before commencing any work.

These tests are explained in the following sections:

- Available Voltage Test
- Starter Current Draw Testing
- Testing Starter Circuit Voltage Drop
- Inspecting and Testing the Starter Control Circuit
- Inspecting and Testing Relays and Solenoids

Available Voltage Test

If the starting system complaint is slow cranking, the available voltage test is recommended. This test measures the amount of voltage at the starter battery positive cable and ground stud on the starter, if equipped. Minimum available voltage to the starter must not fall below 10.5 volts after three consecutive cranking periods of 30 seconds, with a 2-minute cooling period between each cranking period. If the voltage falls below 10.5 volts, the electrical system may not have adequate current to energize injectors or operate ECMs, even though cranking speed is adequate.

To measure available voltage, first disable the engine from starting by removing a fuse for the ECM, disabling the shut-off solenoid, or by an alternative method. Then, connect a voltmeter between the starter ground stud and battery positive terminal on the solenoid. While cranking the engine, measure and record the amperage and voltage and evaluate the results.

TABLE 14-1 Starting System Diagnosis Chart

Concern	Possible Cause	Remedy
Engine cranks slowly, does not start	Discharged battery	Charge; test and replace if necessary
	Very low temperature	Allow battery to warm up; check circuits and battery
	Battery cables too small or poor connections	Install correct battery cables or clean and replace connections
	Defective starter motor	Test; repair or replace as needed
	Engine malfunction	Check engine for low oil or mechanical problems
Solenoid clicks, chatters	Loose or corroded battery terminals	Remove, clean, reinstall
	Battery discharged	Charge; test and replace if necessary
	Wiring problem inside solenoid	Replace solenoid
Lights stay bright, vehicle does not crank	Open circuit in starter	Disassemble and repair or replace starter
	Open circuit or high resistance in circuit	Check solenoid, relays, and neutral start switch or clutch switch; repair or replace if needed
	Open circuit in safety switch	Check; repair or replace switch
Lights dim greatly, vehicle does not crank	Discharged or malfunctioning battery	Charge and test battery; replace if necessary
	High resistance at battery connection	Clean and tighten terminal connections
	Loose or corroded battery terminals	Remove, clean, reinstall
	Very low temperature	Allow battery to warm up; check circuits and battery
	Pinion not engaging ring gear	Check for damaged parts and alignment of starter
	Solenoid engaged but not cranking	Check starter motor and connections
	Pinion jammed—starter and flywheel out of alignment	Check pinion and gear teeth
	Stuck armature in starter	Replace or repair starter
	Short in starter	Check engine for low oil or mechanical problem
	Engine malfunction	Charge and test battery; replace if necessary
Lights out, vehicle does not crank	Poor connection (probably at battery or earth)	Clean cable clamp and terminal; tighten clamp
	Open circuit	Clean and tighten connections; replace wiring if necessary
	Discharged or faulty battery	Charge and test battery; replace battery if necessary
Whine or siren sound just after starting	Overrunning clutch defective	Repair or replace as needed
	Solenoid plunger sticking	Repair or replace solenoid
	Weak return spring	Replace spring
	Damaged flywheel ring gear teeth	Remove and replace
	Pinion jammed, too tight—starter and flywheel out of alignment	Check pinion alignment with gear teeth; shim if necessary
Starter turns, engine does not	Pinion not engaging—starter and flywheel out of alignment	Check pinion alignment with gear teeth; shim if necessary
	Pinion slipping	Replace or repair starter
	Damaged flywheel ring gear teeth	Remove and replace
Pinion disengages slowly when engine starts	Solenoid plunger sticking	Repair or replace solenoid
	Overrunning clutch defective	Repair or replace as needed
	Weak return spring	Replace spring
	Pinion jammed, too tight—starter and flywheel out of alignment	Check pinion alignment with gear teeth; shim if necessary

▶ Starter Current Draw Testing

S14001

Testing starter motor current draw is the best indicator of overall cranking system performance. Manufacturers specify the current draw for starter motors, and any tests must be performed with a fully charged and correct capacity battery for the machine. Starter motors can be tested in two ways: on machine or off machine. The on-machine test is usually called a starter draw test, and the off-machine test is called a no-load test. Manufacturers provide specifications for one or both of the tests.

If the starting system complaint is slow cranking, a starter draw and available voltage test is recommended, using the following steps:

1. The engine is disabled from starting by removing a fuse for the ECM, disabling the shut-off solenoid, or by an alternative method.
2. A voltmeter is connected between the starter ground stud and battery positive terminal on the solenoid.
3. An inductive type amp clamp is placed over the either battery cable to the starter.
4. While cranking, the amperage and voltage are measured and recorded.

Results are compared with the manufacturer's specifications found in a shop manual. Properly charged batteries with adequate capacity should not allow available voltage to fall below 10.5 volts during cranking (**FIGURE 14-31**).

If cranking speed is low, and amperage measured is below normal but available voltage is high, the starting motor or starting circuit has high resistance. Worn brushes or loose or burnt internal connections could cause this condition.

If amperage drawn by the starting motor is high and available voltage low, the starter may be defective internally, the engine seizing or resistive, or the battery voltage low. Shorted field coils caused by the armature contacting the coils are a likely cause of an internal defect. Low available voltage to the starter may also be the cause. Undersized cables, loose connections, or a corroded and highly resistive connection reduce available voltage to the starter, causing excessive amperage draw. Each electrical connection and cable in the starter circuit has to be measured for voltage loss due to excessive resistance in this situation. Small resistances will become larger as amperage increases, predicted by Joule's heating law. Resistive wire or connections will drop voltage and heat up at the same time. By using a carbon pile to load cables and circuits to 500 amps, voltage loss should not total more than 5% in a 12-volt circuit (0.5 volt), with no more than 2% loss in any single cable.

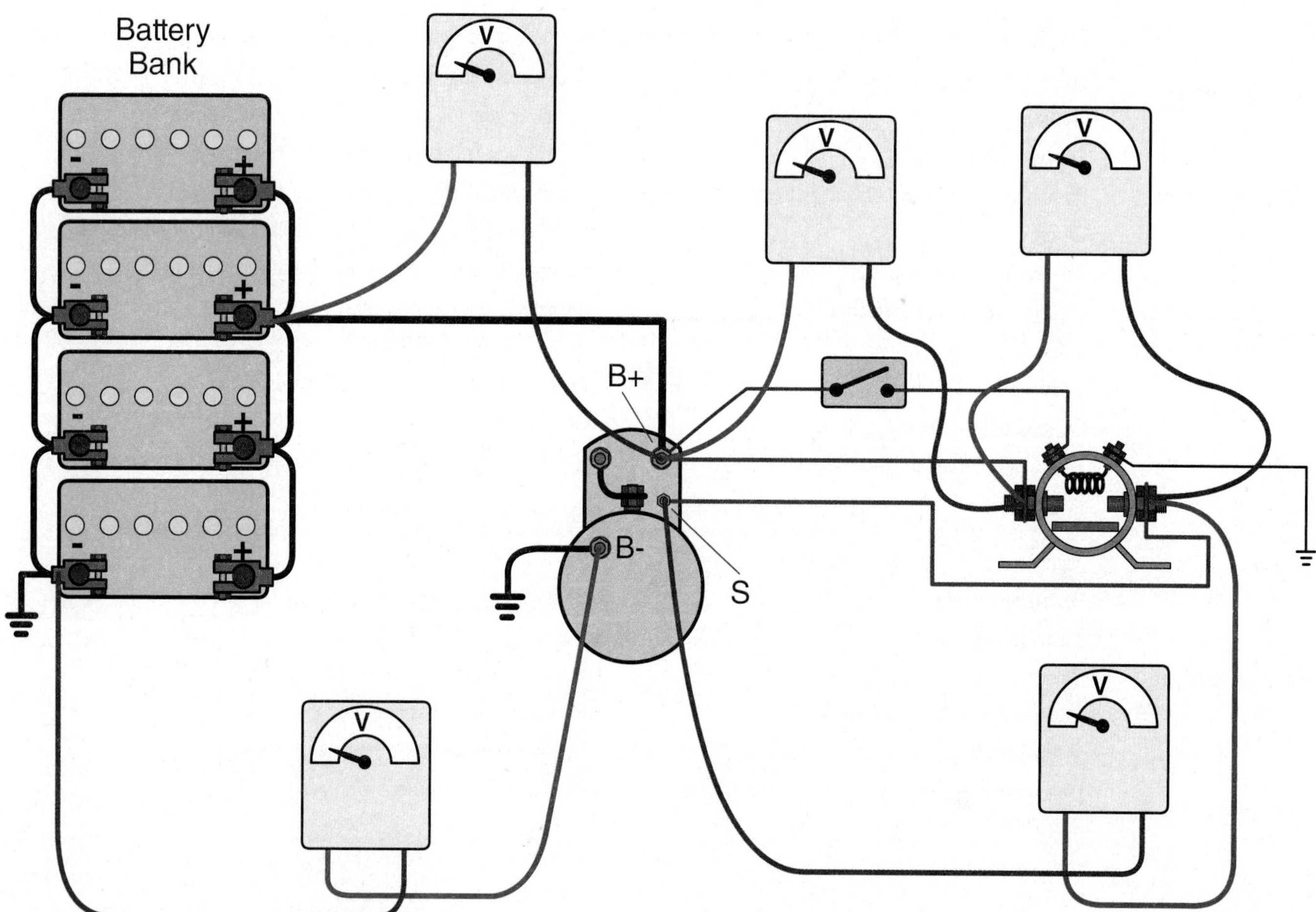

FIGURE 14-31 Positioning of the voltmeter to measure voltage drop across different parts of the starter circuit.

There is no "fixed" amount of amperage draw for each and every engine. However, no more than 1 amp per cubic inch of engine displacement should be observed. Manufacturers publish some guidelines for an engine or starter configuration. The amount of amperage used by a starter varies, however, due to the following reasons:

- Engine displacement—larger engines require more torque to turn and consequently more cranking amperage
- The compression ratio, which may change the amount of cranking torque
- The type of starter, direct drive or gear reduction, which changes the amount of amperage used.
- Mechanical condition of engine, which may be loose or tight due to varying mechanical conditions such as temperature, amount of lubrication, wear, bearing or piston seizure, ring condition, and combustion chamber deposits
- The starter drive-to-flywheel ratio
- The condition of the battery

To test the starter draw, follow the guidelines in **SKILL DRILL 14-1**.

▶ Testing Starter Circuit Voltage Drop

S14002

The electrical circuit of the starter motor consists of a high-current circuit and a control circuit. The high-current circuit consists of the battery, main battery cables to the starter motor solenoid, solenoid contacts, and heavy ground cables back to the battery from the engine and chassis. The control circuit activates the starting motor solenoid and can be ECM controlled. Voltage drop can occur across both the high-current and control circuits.

A voltmeter is used to measure voltage drop across all parts of the circuit. A voltmeter with a minimum/maximum range setting is very useful when measuring voltage drop because it will record and hold the maximum voltage drop that occurs for a particular operation cycle. Small resistance and poor connections are magnified when high amperage passes through the circuit—resistances that will not be observable when low amperage current passes through a circuit.

Voltage drop is tested while the circuit is under load. The voltmeter is connected in parallel across the component or part of the circuit that is to be tested for voltage drop. This means the voltmeter would be connected on either side of a terminal connection or either end of a cable. For example, to measure the voltage drop across a battery terminal, one voltmeter lead would touch the battery post, and the other end would touch the wire of the battery cable connected to the terminal, as close as possible to the post. When the starter is cranked, or a load applied through a carbon pile load tester, any resistance will be observed as a voltage reading. A high voltage reading indicates excessive resistance. Similarly, a voltmeter with long leads can be connected to each end of a battery cable. When the starter is cranked, cable resistance is observed with a voltmeter reading. In both cases, the voltmeter is simply measuring the voltage or pressure differential between two points.

To test starter circuit voltage drop, follow the guidelines in **SKILL DRILL 14-2.**

> **▶ TECHNICIAN TIP**
>
> A faulty battery affects voltage drop tests, so always ensure that the battery is fully charged and in good condition before performing tests.

▶ Inspecting and Testing the Starter Control Circuit

S14003

The starter control circuit activates the starter solenoid, and the starter solenoid activates the starter motor. If there is a problem in the starter control circuit, the machine will likely not

SKILL DRILL 14-1 Testing Starter Draw

1. Research the specifications for the starter draw test. Place an inductive-type amp clamp over either the positive or negative cable. It doesn't matter which starter cable is measured, as it is a series circuit, so amperage will be the same at any point in the circuit.
2. Connect the AVR voltmeter leads to the battery or at the starter.
3. Make sure all of the appropriate wires are inside the clamp and that the clamp is completely closed.
4. Disable the engine from starting by removing a fuse from the engine ECM or disabling the injection system shut-off solenoid.
5. With the engine disabled, crank the engine, and record the amps and volts as soon as the amps stabilize.
6. Compare the readings with the specifications, and determine any necessary actions.

SKILL DRILL 14-2 Testing Starter Circuit Voltage Drop

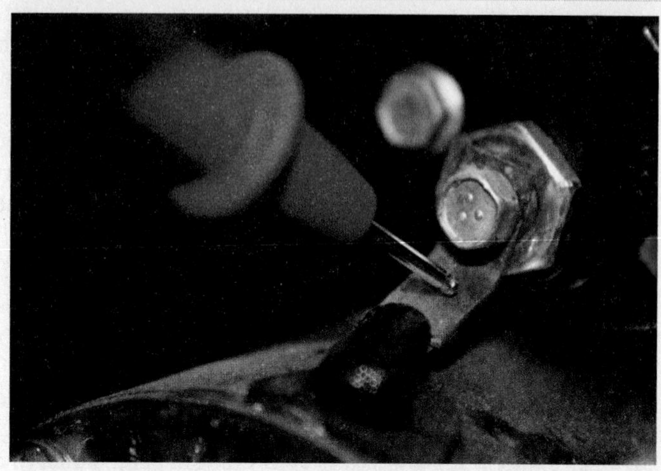

1. Set the DVOM to "Volts." Connect the black lead to the positive battery post and the red lead to the positive battery terminal on the starting motor.
2. Crank the engine, and read the maximum voltage drop for the positive side of the circuit. Connect the black lead to the negative battery post and the red lead to the negative terminal or starting motor ground stud. Crank the engine and read the voltage drop.
3. If the voltage drop is more than 0.5 volt on either side of the circuit, use the voltmeter and wiring diagram to isolate the voltage drop. Conduct further voltage drop tests across individual components and cables. Determine any necessary actions.

crank over at all, or maybe intermittently. The control circuit is made up of the battery, ignition switch, neutral safety switch (automatic equipment), clutch switch (manual equipment), starter relay, and solenoid windings. If the starter is controlled by the ECM, then you must be aware of all of the circuits, such as the immobilizer circuit and the ECM itself.

To inspect and test the starter control circuit, follow the guidelines in **SKILL DRILL 14-3**.

> **TECHNICIAN TIP**
>
> The starter relay bypass test is a quick method of determining whether the relay is operational. This test should be performed when the starter motor does not crank when the ignition is in the start position (or when the starter button is depressed). Connect a jumper wire between the battery and starter terminal on the relay. This connection bypasses the control circuit of the relay, so the engine should crank. If the engine cranks with the jumper installed, check to see whether current is supplied to the relay when the ignition key or starter button is in the crank position. If current is available to the relay, check the ground supplying the control circuit to determine whether it is properly connected or resistive. If the control circuit is properly energized and the starter cranks when the jumper wire is used, the starter relay is defective. If the starter motor still does not crank, check the cables and other circuits to the starter.

▶ Inspecting and Testing Relays and Solenoids

S14004

The starting system typically contains solenoids and relays that activate the control circuit. The solenoid is mounted on the starter motor, and one or more of the starter circuit relays are found on the starter, or firewall.

SKILL DRILL 14-3 Inspecting and Testing the Starter Control Circuit

1. Use a DVOM to measure voltage between the solenoid control circuit terminal on the solenoid (R) terminal and the housing of the starter while the engine is cranking.
2. If the voltage is less than 10.5 volts, measure the voltage drop between the R terminal and the relay.
3. If the voltage drop is less than 0.5 volt, measure the voltage drop on the ground side of the relay control circuit.
4. If the voltage drop is higher than 0.5 volt on either side of the circuit, use the wiring diagram to guide you in isolating the voltage drop on that side of the circuit. Continue conducting voltage drop tests across individual components and cables.
5. If the voltage drops are within specifications on both sides of the circuit, the resistance of the solenoid pull-in and hold-in windings must be measured. If out of specifications, the solenoid or starter motor and solenoid will have to be replaced.

Before performing any tests, ensure that the machine battery is charged and in good condition. The manufacturer's wiring diagrams should be checked to determine the circuit operation, identification, and location of all components in the starter circuit.

Relays must be tested in two or three ways, depending on the relay. The simplest test is to measure the resistance of the relay winding. If it is out of specifications, the relay will have to be replaced. If it is okay, the contacts must be tested for an excessive voltage drop. The best way to do this is by using an adapter that fits between the relay and the relay socket. This will allow the normal circuit current flow to flow through the contacts so that a voltage drop measurement can be taken. Any excessive voltage drop across the relay contacts will require the replacement of the relay. The last test is used only on relays with a suppression diode in parallel with the relay winding. Connect a reasonably fresh 9-volt battery across the relay winding terminals in one direction, and then switch polarity by turning the battery around. If the diode is good, the relay should click in one direction and not in the other. If it clicks in both directions, the diode is shorted. If it does not click in either direction, either the relay winding or the diode is open.

Solenoids are tested by measuring the voltage drop between the battery terminal and motor terminal. The first test to perform is a voltage drop test across the solenoid contacts. Place the red lead on the solenoid B–positive input and the black lead on the solenoid B–positive output. The voltage drop should be less than 0.5 volts for a 12-volt system and less than 1.0 volt for a 24-volt system. If not, replace the starter assembly. Testing of the solenoid winding requires partial disassembly of the solenoid. Therefore, it is usually best to disconnect the control circuit connector from the solenoid and use a jumper wire to activate the solenoid. If the solenoid and starter operate, there is probably a fault in the machine's control circuit that needs further testing. If the solenoid or starter does not work (and the circuit is grounded), then the starter is likely faulty and will have to be replaced.

To inspect and test relays and solenoids, follow the guidelines in **SKILL DRILL 14-4**.

▶ Removing and Replacing a Starter and Inspecting the Ring Gear or Flexplate

S14005

The starter motor will have to be removed to check for on-bench testing, poor drive engagement, or starter motor overhaul or replacement. The starter motor may be mounted in difficult-to-access locations. In some cases, other machine parts may have to be removed before the starter itself can be removed. Access to both the topside and underside of the machine may be required to remove mounting bolts. It may also be necessary to have another technician assist you to remove the heavy starter motor from machine.

To remove and replace a starter motor and inspect the ring gear or flexplate, follow the guidelines in **SKILL DRILL 14-5**.

SKILL DRILL 14-4 Inspecting and Testing Relays and Solenoids

1. To test a relay, measure the resistance of the relay winding, and compare with specifications. If the relay is out of specifications, replace it.
2. Use a relay adapter to mount the relay on top of the relay socket so you can check the control circuit wiring and perform voltage drop tests on the contacts.
3. Activate the relay while measuring the voltage across the relay winding. If it is near battery voltage, the control circuit wiring is okay.
4. Measure the voltage across the contacts with the relay not activated. This should read near battery voltage if both sides of the switched circuit are okay. If not, perform voltage drop tests on each side of the switch circuit.
5. Activate the relay while measuring the voltage drop across the contacts. If it is more than 0.5 volt, the relay will have to be replaced.
6. To test a starter solenoid, measure the voltage drop across the solenoid contact terminals with the key in the crank position. If it is more than 0.5 volt, replace the solenoid or starter assembly.
7. If the solenoid does not click with the key in the crank position, remove the electrical connection for the control circuit at the solenoid.
8. Use a jumper wire to apply battery voltage to the control circuit terminal on the solenoid and see if the solenoid clicks. If it does, then there is likely a fault in the control circuit wiring. If the solenoid still does not click (and the circuit is grounded), then the solenoid windings or starter brushes are likely worn (sometimes tapping on the starter while the key is turned to the crank position will free up the brushes enough that the pull-in winding can operate). Determine any necessary actions.

SKILL DRILL 14-5 Removing and Replacing a Starter Motor and Inspecting the Ring Gear or Flexplate

1. Locate and follow the appropriate procedure in the service manual.
2. Disconnect the battery ground and electrical connections to the starter motor.
3. Loosen the mounting bolts, leaving them in place until you are ready to remove the starter motor.
4. Remove the starter motor by supporting its weight while the mounting bolts are removed. You may need assistance to support the weight of the starter while this step is being conducted.
5. Examine the starter drive for any wear to the drive teeth.
6. Using a work light, inspect the ring gear or flexplate teeth for damage. Slowly turn the engine over while checking the ring gear or flexplate, ensuring the circumference is inspected. In difficult-to-see locations, an engine borescope may provide assistance. Report and report any damage to the ring gear.
7. Reinstall the starter motor by reversing steps 1 through 4 above.

▶ Overhauling a Starter Motor

S14006

Overhauling a starter motor requires the disassembly and checking of all component parts. The starter motor component parts should also be cleaned and replaced or repaired, and lubricated as necessary. Always mark the position of the housings in relation to each other before commencing disassembly. This ensures that the housings are correctly aligned when reassembled. Each starter motor is unique and may require slightly different disassembly and overhaul procedures. Always consult the manufacturer's procedures for the specific starter motor on which you are working.

Note that the assembly procedure is the reverse of disassembly. When assembling, be sure to correctly lubricate all lubrication points. Check the manufacturer's procedure for the lubrication points and type of lubricant.

Once the starter motor has been disassembled into its component parts, conduct the following tests for each component as follows:

- Solenoid:
  - Test the resistance and current draw of the pull-in and hold-in windings.
  - Check for the free movement of the iron core.
  - Check contacts and terminal end cap for wear and cracks. Make replacements if necessary.
- Drive and yoke:
  - Visually inspect the drive engagement yoke for wear and damage. Replace if there is excessive wear.
  - Check the drive clutch for slippage. If there is excessive slippage, replace the drive.
- Brushes:
  - Check the length of the brushes with the manufacturer's specifications and replace if necessary.
  - Check the brush springs for tension, brush movement in the brush holder, and the insulation of the brush holder.
- Field windings:
  - Visually check the insulation for cracks or damage. Check for short circuits through the field insulation and case by connecting a 110-volt test lamp between the field coil and case. If the lamp lights, there is a short circuit. If the field insulation fails, the field will have to be replaced or reinsulated.
- Armature:
  - Check the armature on a growler for shorts between windings. Using a thin metal strip, rotate the armature. A vibrating strip means the armature is shorted and requires replacement. However, before condemning it, check to ensure there are no shorts between the commutator segments. Retest if you find any.
  - Also check the armature insulation to ground using an insulation tester or the insulation tester fitted to the growler. Use an insulation test no higher than 110 volts for a 12- or 24-volt armature. Note that to pass an insulation test, the armature must be dry and free of contaminants.
  - If the armature fails either test, it must be replaced.
  - Machine the commutator in a lathe if it is worn.
  - Check the armature shaft for wear or damage to the bearing surfaces. Also check the drive splines for wear or damage. Check the laminations for damage. Check the shaft to ensure it is not bent. Check the windings to

SKILL DRILL 14-6 Overhauling a Starter Motor

1. Locate and follow the appropriate procedure in the service manual.
2. Remove the bearing end cap and circlip from the brush end.
3. Remove the solenoid and the yoke securing pin of the starter motor if it is fitted.
4. Remove the through bolts holding the starter motor together.
5. Prize the starter motor apart while checking for any remaining screws or bolts.
6. Remove the brushes from the brush holder if necessary.
7. Slide the armature out of the main casing.
8. Remove the drive circlip, and remove the drive assembly.
9. Clean, test, and inspect all component parts. Use specialized testers where necessary, for example, growler to test the armature, insulation tester to test fields and armature, and DVOM to check resistances of solenoid windings.
10. Replace any faulty components. You may need to arrange for the commutator to be machined to make it true.
11. Remove and replace the bushings into the end housing. Ensure bushes are pre-oiled if they are the sintered type. Bushings have to be driven or pressed out or using a bushings drift punch.
12. If the brushes require replacement, disconnect or desolder them, and replace them.
13. Reassemble the drive to the armature, ensuring it is appropriately lubricated.
14. Reassemble the armature into the main case, and locate the brushes. At this stage, the drive yoke and securing pin may have to be fitted. In some cases, the securing pin is not fitted until after the armature is in place.
15. Assemble the main case and end housing securing with the through bolts.
16. Reassemble the solenoid, its connections, and the brush end armature circlip. Ensure the appropriate lubrication if fitted.
17. Check to ensure that all components are fitted and the drive and armature are free to move.
18. Test the starter motor in the test bench.
19. Clean the work area, and return tools and materials to proper storage.

ensure they are not damaged or bent. Any damage to the above items means the armature should be replaced.

- Housings:
  - Check the housings for damage or wear. Replace if they are cracked or broken.
- Bushes:
  - Check the bushings for wear, using the armature bearing surfaces. Replace the bushings if they are worn.
  - When replacing bushings, use soft bush drifts to drive or press the bushes into and out of the housing.
  - Oil sintered bushings before fitting them into housing.
  - Some bushings may require machining to size once they are fitted into the housing.

Once the starter motor has been overhauled, it should be tested on a starter test bench with a full load if possible. If a full load test is not possible, conduct a no-load bench test as per the procedure in this chapter. To overhaul a starter motor, follow the guidelines in **SKILL DRILL 14-6**.

Engine and Starter Rotation

When observing engine rotation, many technicians often note the front engine pulley/harmonic balancer turns clockwise. However, not all engines are mounted in-line with the driveline (e.g., "V" drives). Some engines are mounted sideways in a machine, and some are mounted at the rear and sideways. Because there is an abundance of configurations including engines in machine applications, the SAE references engine rotation from the flywheel end of the engine. Most automotive style engines are left hand, or counterclockwise, rotation.

The location and position of the starter on the engine can determine which direction the engine is cranked. Starter drive mechanism and the cut of the teeth will be changed along with helix features of the armature that may move the drive.

Wrap-Up

Ready for Review

- The starting system provides a method of rotating (cranking) the machine's engine to begin the combustion cycle.
- Diesel engines require large starter current draw, so several batteries are often connected in parallel of series to increase available cranking amperage or voltage.
- New designs of starter motors and systems controls are enabling starters to last longer and increase output torque while substantially reducing motor weight.
- There are three major categories of electric starters used in off-road mobile equipment: direct drive, reduction, and planetary gear reduction.
- The three most common types of DC motors found in off-road mobile equipment are series, shunt, and compound motors.
- Series motors are called "series" because the current pathway through various components inside the motor is in series. Because it is a series circuit, any unwanted resistance inside the motor, whether it is a burnt contact

or loose brush, will reduce current flow throughout the entire motor circuit.

- Series wound motors also are self-limiting in speed due to the development of a counter-electromotive force (CEMF) that induces current in the opposite direction of battery current through the motor.
- Cranking an engine with low battery voltage is destructive to a starter motor.
- Regardless of the motor design, a starter motor consists of housing, fields, an armature, a commutator, brushes, end frames, and a solenoid-operated shift mechanism.
- Some starter motors are equipped with over-crank protection thermostats that will open the relay circuit and interrupt the current to the solenoid if prolonged cranking causes the motor temperature to exceed a safe threshold.
- Another protection device for the starter control circuit is the automatic disengagement lockout, which prevents the starter motor from operating if the engine is running.
- Dual-voltage systems allow the off-road mobile equipment to be started on 24 volts for improved electrical efficiency, and the other electrical loads operate on the more common 12 volts.
- The starting system is just part of the overall machine's electrical and mechanical system. As such, there are areas of overlap between the various electrical and mechanical systems on the machine.
- Whether a slow-crank or a no-crank condition, failure to crank over properly can be caused by electrical or mechanical problems. It is important to be able to differentiate between the two types of faults so that a wrong diagnosis can be avoided and the problem fixed appropriately the first time.

Key Terms

armature The only rotating component of the starter; has three main components: the shaft, windings, and the commutator.

automatic disengagement lockout (ADLO) A device that prevents the starter motor from operating if the engine is running.

counter-electromotive force (CEMF) An electromagnetic force produced by the spinning magnetic field of the armature, which induces current in the opposite direction of battery current through the motor.

direct drive A starter motor drive system in which the motor armature directly engages the flywheel through a pinion gear.

frequency-sensing relay A relay connected to the alternator that detects alternating current only when the alternator is charging.

low-voltage burnout A damaging condition for starter motors in which excess current flows through the starter, causing the motor to burn out prematurely.

over-crank protection (OCP) thermostat A thermostat that monitors the temperature of the motor and opens a relay circuit to interrupt the current to the solenoid if prolonged cranking causes the motor temperature to exceed a safe threshold.

planetary gear reduction drive A type of gear reduction system in which a planetary gear set reduces the starter profile to multiply motor torque to the pinion gear.

reduction gear drive A starter motor drive system in which the motor multiplies torque to the starter pinion gear by using an extra gear between the armature and the starter drive mechanism.

Review Questions

1. Which of the following statements about the starting/cranking system is correct?
   a. On ECM starting systems, the ECM controls the operation of a relay to energize the starter circuit.
   b. Data supplied by other on-board network modules, along with control algorithms in the module, determine when and for how long the starter will crank.
   c. A control circuit determines when and if the cranking circuit will function.
   d. All of the choices are correct.
2. In diesel engines, what is the most common ratio between the flywheel ring gear and pinion gear?
   a. 10:1
   b. 15:1
   c. 17:1
   d. 20:1
3. What is the minimum life expectancy for a modern starter?
   a. 2 years with 4,000 start cycles
   b. 3 years with 5,000 start cycles
   c. 4 years with 7,000 start cycles
   d. 5 years with 9,000 start cycles
4. Which of the following common electric motors develop the highest torque and are used as starter motors?
   a. Stepper
   b. Compound
   c. Shunt (parallel wound)
   d. Series
5. Which of the following statements concerning current flow for a series motor is correct?
   a. Current passes through the armature via the commutator and leaves through the second brush connected to the field winding.
   b. A magnetic field is created in the armature.
   c. Current passes through the windings of the field coils.
   d. All of the choices are correct.
6. Which of the following is *not* a component of a starter?
   a. Field coils
   b. Rotor
   c. End frames
   d. A solenoid-operated shift mechanism
7. Which of the following is *not* a main component of the armature?
   a. Shaft
   b. Body
   c. Windings
   d. Commutator

8. Which of the following statements about the commutator is correct?
   a. The commutator assembly presses onto the armature shaft.
   b. The commutator is made up of heavy copper segments separated from each other and the armature shaft by insulation.
   c. The commutator segments connect to the ends of the armature windings.
   d. All of the choices are correct.
9. Which of the following statements about starter control circuits is correct?
   a. In its most basic form, the starter control circuit has an ignition switch directly controlling the starter solenoid to operate the starter motor.
   b. In modern machines, the circuits are more complex, because relays and control circuits, such as transmission neutral and clutch switches, are added to improve reliability and the safety of machines.
   c. The latest models of machines use an electrical system control module, which interfaces with the on-board network that receives data from various sensors, and various sensors to control the operation of the starter control circuit.
   d. All of the choices are correct.
10. A possible cause of a solenoid clicking and chattering is ___________.
    a. loose or corroded battery terminals
    b. short in the starter
    c. an open circuit
    d. a slipping pinion

ASE Technician A/Technician B Style Questions

1. Technician A says that dozens of electric motors are found in off-road equipment operating a variety of devices from electric seats, fuel and coolant pumps, fan blower motors, and even instrument gauges. Technician B says that the largest of all these electric motors is the starter motor. Who is correct?
   a. Technician A
   b. Technician B
   c. Both A and B
   d. Neither A nor B
2. Technician A says that all electric motors operate using principles of magnetic attraction and repulsion. Technician B says that because like magnetic poles attract one another and unlike poles repel, it is possible to arrange magnetic poles within the motor to be continuously in a state of repulsion and attraction. Who is correct?
   a. Technician A
   b. Technician B
   c. Both A and B
   d. Neither A nor B
3. Technician A says that the series and shunt motor are the two most common types of motor found in the mobile off-road equipment industry. Technician B says that series motors are called "series" because the field and armature windings are connected in series. Who is correct?
   a. Technician A
   b. Technician B
   c. Both A and B
   d. Neither A nor B
4. Technician A says that series-wound motors also are self-limiting in speed because of the development of a counter-electromotive force (CEMF). Technician B says that CEMF is produced by the spinning magnetic field of the armature, which induces current in the same direction of battery current through the motor. Who is correct?
   a. Technician A
   b. Technician B
   c. Both A and B
   d. Neither A nor B
5. Technician A says that cranking an engine with low battery voltage causes one of the most damaging conditions for a starter. Technician B says that low-voltage burnout occurs when excess amperage flows through the starter, causing the motor to burn out prematurely. Who is correct?
   a. Technician A
   b. Technician B
   c. Both A and B
   d. Neither A nor B
6. Technician A says that the starter housing, or frame, encloses and supports the internal starter components, protecting them and intensifying the magnetic fields produced in the field coils. Technician B says that in the starter housing, field coils and their pole shoes are securely attached to the inside of the iron housing. Who is correct?
   a. Technician A
   b. Technician B
   c. Both A and B
   d. Neither A nor B
7. Technician A says that different from the thin wire used in shunt motors, armature windings are made of heavy, flat, copper strips that can handle the heavy current flow of the series motor. Technician B says that in a four-brush motor, the halves of a coil are wound at 60 degrees to each other. Who is correct?
   a. Technician A
   b. Technician B
   c. Both A and B
   d. Neither A nor B
8. Technician A says that the solenoid on the starter motor switches the high current flow required by the starter motor on and off. Technician B says that the solenoid on the starter motor engages the starter drive with the pinion gear. Who is correct?
   a. Technician A
   b. Technician B
   c. Both A and B
   d. Neither A nor B

9. Technician A says that the starter drive transmits the rotational force from the starter armature to the engine via the ring gear that is mounted on the engine flywheel or torque converter. Technician B says that in the past, gear reduction starters were used but that today, direct-drive starters have replaced them. Who is correct?
   a. Technician A
   b. Technician B
   c. Both A and B
   d. Neither A nor B

10. Technician A says that some starter motors are equipped with an over-crank protection (OCP) thermostat. Technician B says that the thermostat monitors the temperature of the motor. Who is correct?
    a. Technician A
    b. Technician B
    c. Both A and B
    d. Neither A nor B

CHAPTER 15
Charging Systems

Knowledge Objectives

After reading this chapter, you will be able to:

- K15001 Identify and explain the function and operating principles of the alternator.
- K15002 Identify and explain the construction and operation of the charging system.
- K15003 Identify and explain recommended procedures for diagnosing charging system complaints.

Skills Objectives

After reading this chapter, you will be able to:

- S15001 Replace a serpentine belt.
- S15002 Perform a charging system output test.
- S15003 Measure alternator output cable circuit voltage drop.
- S15004 Inspect, repair, or replace connectors and wires of charging circuits.
- S15005 Remove, inspect, and replace an alternator.
- S15006 Overhaul an alternator.

▶ Introduction

Compared with older off-road equipment, modern off-road equipment is increasingly dependent on electronic and electrical systems that require a constant and reliable supply of electrical power. As modern off-road equipment becomes more sophisticated, adding more comfort and convenience items, alternators are working harder than ever to keep up with the demands of the electrical system. For example, years ago a DC generator supplying 8–45 amps of current was all that was needed to operate lights, wipers, and the horn and to charge the batteries. Today, the average 12-volt electrical system loads for a late-model off-road machine may add up to as much as 150 amps at peak (**FIGURE 15-1**). Lighting, electronic powertrain and hydraulic controls, power accessories, communication, telematic systems, and many smaller electrical accessories add to the load carried by alternators on the newest machines.

Both alternators and DC generators produce electricity by relative movement of conductors in a magnetic field. That movement induces an electrical potential or voltage within the conductors. The key difference between an alternator and a DC generator is which component rotates or moves to generate electricity. In the DC generator, the conductors that generate power rotate as part of the armature, and the armature rotates within a magnetic field created by the stationary pole shoes. In the alternator, the magnetic field is created by the rotor, which rotates within the stationary stator windings to generate electricity there. In both cases, there is relative movement between the magnetic field and the conductors.

FIGURE 15-1 A typical off-road equipment alternator.

▶ Alternator Functions

K15001

The charging system provides electrical energy for all the electrical components on the machine. The main parts of the charging system, as illustrated in **FIGURE 15-2**, include the battery, the alternator, the voltage regulator (which may be integrated into the alternator), a charge warning light or voltmeter, and wiring that completes the circuits.

The battery stores an electrical charge in chemical form, acts as an electrical dampening device for variations in voltage or voltage spikes, and provides the electrical energy for cranking the engine. Once the engine is running, the alternator—which is connected to the engine and driven by a drive belt—converts some of the mechanical energy of the engine into electrical energy to supply energy to all the electrical components of the machine. The alternator also charges the battery to replace the energy used to start the engine. The voltage regulator circuit maintains the optimal battery state of charge by sensing and maintaining a required charging system output voltage.

Older machines have separate (discrete) regulators mounted on the firewall or frame. Later, charging systems included regulators that were incorporated inside the alternator. Electrical system control modules, or ECMs, are now used to regulate the charging system more efficiently by controlling alternator output based on a number of parameters, such as electrical loads, engine load and rpm, alternator capability, battery type and temperature, fuel economy benefits, and more.

Battery technology is also altering the charging requirements of alternators. For example, more OEMs are using absorbed glass mat (AGM) batteries now because AGM batteries are capable of absorbing an electrical charge of up to

You Are the Mobile Heavy Equipment Technician

There is an excavator that has had numerous service calls for jump-starting because the batteries often go dead. Service calls are taking place almost every day, causing a high level of aggravation to the customer and the service center where you work. On previous occasions, the batteries have been replaced. In addition, the charging system output has been measured and found to be OK. Furthermore, the presence of parasitic draws has been checked, and none were found. The excavator operator has often been blamed for the problems, assuming that they have left lights or other accessories on, draining the battery. Out of frustration, the service manager has asked you to accompany the excavator operator for a day to find out when the excavator batteries drain and whether electrical loads are left on. After the excavator has stopped for a 45-minute break, you find the batteries are dead. Checking the alternator, you discover that the back of the alternator where the rectifier bridge is located has become excessively hot to touch. Finally, the cause has been found. Before explaining the fault to the customer, you'll need to answer the following questions:

1. Why has the rectifier bridge of the alternator become hot to touch while the engine was shut down?
2. During previous checks of the charging system, what inspection procedure would have identified that fault?
3. What component has failed in the rectifier bridge? Be specific.

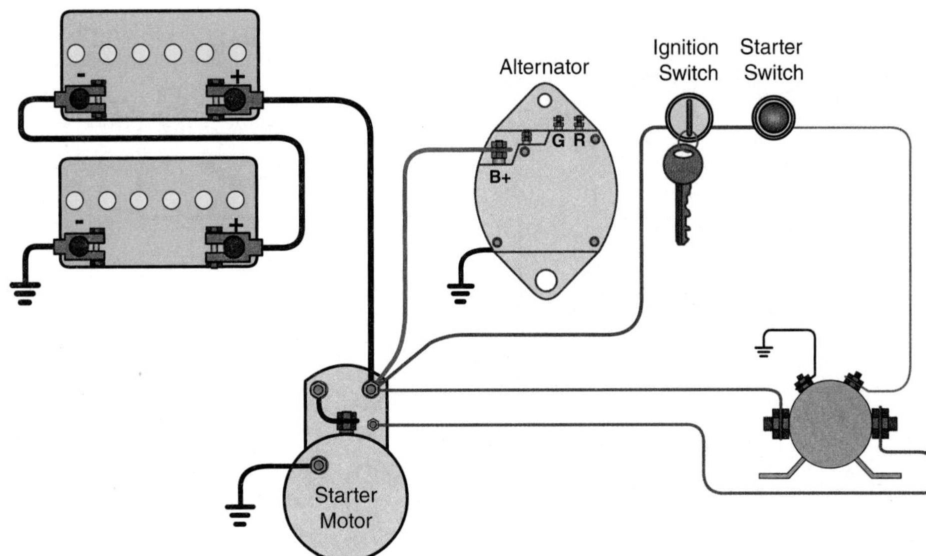

FIGURE 15-2 A typical 24 VDC charging system diagram.

five times faster than older flooded-type lead acid batteries. Different battery types and variations to cell chemistry also result in differences to required charging voltages, the charging voltage profile or the charge rate over time, and the state of charge voltage readings. Modern charging systems need to adapt to these various challenges, and in many cases, this is achieved through the use of electrical system control module (ECM) control over the charging system.

Alternator Advantages

Alternators have not always been used on mobile off-road equipment. Until the 1960s, DC generators were used to supply direct current to the electrical system and charge batteries. The current produced by DC generators became inadequate as machine electrical loads increased. Generators were especially inefficient at low speeds, leading to a discharged battery condition after long idle periods. The development of low-cost solid-state rectifiers in the 1950s made the use of alternating current "generators" (alternators) possible. Alternators are much more efficient at producing current than DC generators. Alternating current—not direct current—is produced inside an alternator. Several pairs of diodes, referred to as the rectifier bridge, have the job of converting AC current to usable DC current.

Thanks to solid-state electronics and circuitry, alternators have become the dominant design due to their superior operating characteristics compared to generators:

- Alternators weigh less per ampere of output.
- Alternators have fewer moving parts.
- Alternators can produce power at engine idle speeds; generators cannot.
- Alternators can be operated at much higher speeds.
- Alternators use a lighter rotor, compared to a heavy armature in generators.
- Alternators conduct less current through the brushes if equipped, thus reducing wear.
- Alternators do not require current regulators; they control their own maximum amperage output.
- Alternators will produce current when rotated in either direction. Polarity from generators will change when rotated in the opposite direction. Note that cooling fans in alternators can turn only in one direction.
- Alternators allow the reduction of battery capacity due to faster recharging rate.

Alternator Principles

The alternator converts mechanical energy into electrical energy by electromagnetic induction (**FIGURE 15-3**).

In a simplified version, a bar magnet rotates in an iron yoke, which concentrates the magnetic field. A coil of wire is wound around each end of the yoke. As the magnet turns, voltage is induced in the coil, producing a current flow. When the north pole is up and the south pole is down, voltage is induced in the coil, producing current flow in one direction. As the magnet rotates and the positions of the poles reverse, the polarity of the voltage reverses as well. As a result, the direction of current flow also reverses. Current that changes direction in this way is called alternating current (AC). In this example, the change in direction occurs once for every complete revolution of the magnet.

Alternating Current

The two most important parts in an alternator used to produce electrical current are the rotor and stator winding. The rotor contains a spinning electromagnet that induces current flow in the stator winding, which is made up of numerous coils of wire. By varying the current supplied to the rotor's electromagnetic coil, the strength of its magnetic field changes. The parts of the alternator are illustrated in **FIGURE 15-4** and will be discussed in detail in the section Alternator Components.

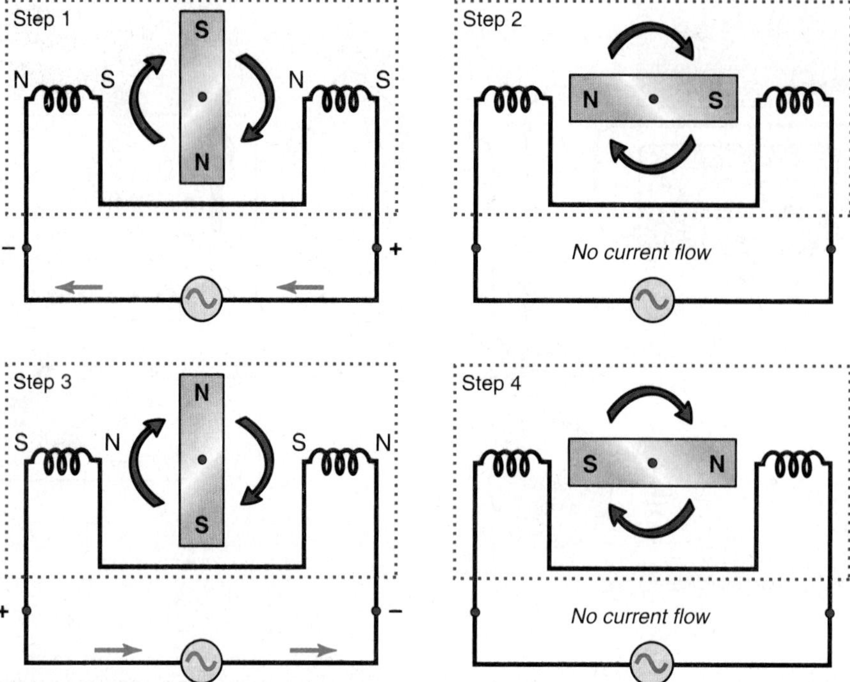

FIGURE 15-3 Electromagnetic induction.

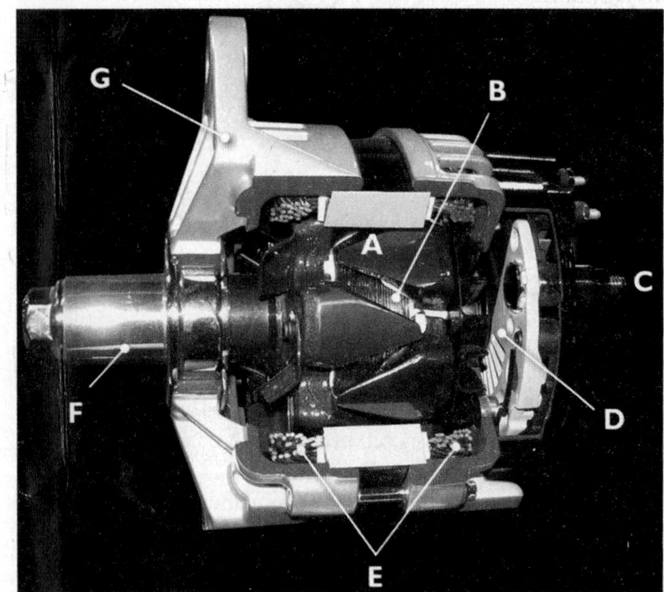

FIGURE 15-4 An alternator. **A.** Rotor. **B.** Rotor winding. **C.** Battery-cable connection. **D.** Rectifier bridge. **E.** Stator windings. (2). **F.** Rotor shaft. **G.** Ventilated aluminum housing.

The amount of current produced from an alternator is proportional to the following four factors. The first is the strength of the magnetic field in the rotor. Increasing the strength of the magnetic field increases the force pushing and pulling on electrons in a stator winding. Stronger magnetic fields in the rotor translate directly to higher output voltage and amperage. The second factor is the speed at which the magnetic field rotates. The third factor is the angle between the magnetic field and conductors in the stator. The last factor is the number and/or size of conductors cutting magnetic lines of force.

Maximum amperage output of an alternator is limited by the speed at which an alternator rotates. As the alternator spins faster, a counter electrical current is induced in the stator by the continuously changing polarity of AC current in the stator windings. This induced current, called the counter-electromotive force (CEMF), opposes any increase in current induced in the stator by the spinning rotor. At high alternator speeds, the CEMF, which is induced in the opposite direction of output current by changing AC current polarity, will begin to equal any increase to the induced stator current. The result is CEMF. CEMF acts to reduce the output current of the alternator. The faster the alternator turns, the higher the CEMF produced in the stator (**FIGURE 15-5**).

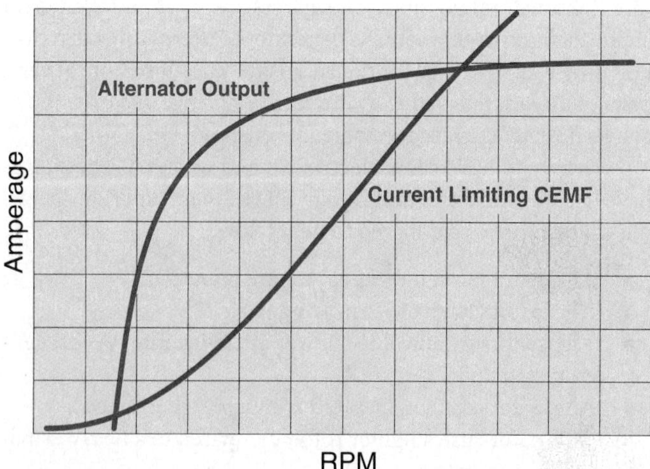

FIGURE 15-5 Chart showing alternator output and current-limiting CEMF.

Alternator Classification

Alternators can be categorized by a number of variables, including whether voltage regulation is internal or external; the diameter of the housing; whether the alternator is sealed, oil cooled, or externally air cooled; amperage output; charging voltage; manufacturer; and many other factors. The SAE (the American Society of Automotive Engineers) classifies alternator automotive mounting configurations into standards to enable the adaptation of alternators from all manufacturers to fit engines. Two common mounting types for alternators are a pad-mount alternator (**FIGURE 15-6A**) and a hinge-mount type (**FIGURE 15-6B**).

▶ Alternator Construction

K15002

Regardless of the alternator's classification, all alternators share common components. Major components of the alternator are illustrated in Figure 15-4:

- Rotor—a rotating electromagnet that provides the magnetic field to induce voltage and current in the stator.
- Brushes/slip rings—make an electrical connection to the rotor field coil to supply current from the voltage regulator.
- Stator—stationary coils of wire in which current and voltage is induced by the magnetic field of the rotor.
- Rectifier—converts the AC induced voltage and current into a DC output.
- Voltage regulator—controls the maximum output voltage of the alternator by varying the amount of current flow in the rotor and therefore the magnetic-field strength.
- Cooling mechanism (air and oil)—in the case of air cooling, additional airflow is provided through the use of a cooling fan.
- End frames and bearings—alternators have two end frames, which fit together to house the components into a single unit. One end frame contains the rotor, the drive end bearing, and drive mechanism (usually a pulley). The other end houses the stator rectifier regulator and brush assembly.
- Drive mechanism—in most cases, a pulley drive is used, but direct-gear drive mechanisms may also be employed.

FIGURE 15-6 A. Pad-mount alternator. **B.** Hinge-mount alternator.

Rotor

The rotor provides the rotating magnetic field that cuts the wire coils within the stator to induce the flow of electrical current in the stator. The rotor consists of an iron core that encloses a coil of many turns of wire. Each end of the wire coil is connected to one of two conductive slip rings on the rotor shaft. The wire coil and slip rings are electrically insulated from the rotor shaft. Energizing the rotor's wire coil with typically 2 to 5 amps produces an electromagnetic field beneath two halves of the soft iron core. These two halves are arranged into claws or pole pieces.

The pole pieces have two purposes. One is to intensify the electromagnetic field, and the other is to arrange magnetic lines of flux produced in the coil into poles on each claw of the rotor. Each of the claws or pole pieces will have a stationary pole that alternates in sequence with each pole piece as north and south. A heavy alternator has more pole pieces or "claws"—typically between 12 and 16. For heavy-duty alternators, 14 is a common number of claws. Passing current through the rotor coil magnetizes the rotor claws. Alternating poles of magnetism are formed north–south–north–south on the rotor.

The output of the alternator is determined by a couple of the alternator's physical features. The first is the size and number of windings in the stator that is cut by the magnetic lines of force. The second is the strength of the magnetic field of the rotor. Increasing or decreasing the current flow through the rotor winding will change the magnetic-field strength. Usually the maximum possible amperage is 5 amps or less. Controlling the strength of the magnetic field is the job of the voltage regulator. **FIGURE 15-7** illustrates how the current flows through the rotor.

Brushes and Brushless Alternators

Regulated current to the alternator rotor is supplied through a pair of graphite brushes sliding against slip rings on the rotor shaft. The slip rings and the coil are electrically insulated from

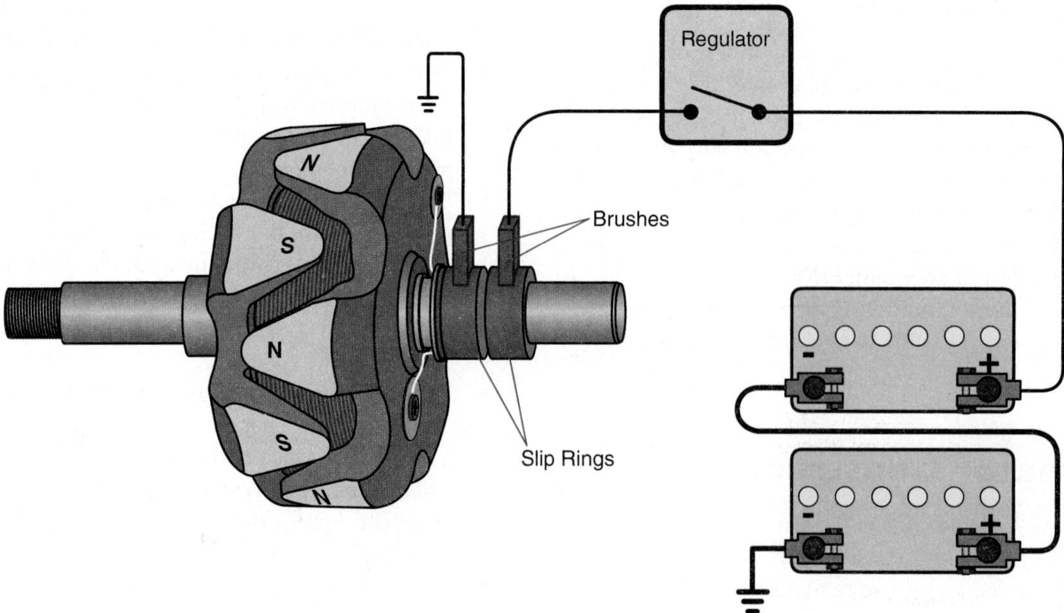

FIGURE 15-7 Current flow through the rotor.

the rotor shaft. Lightweight springs help the brushes maintain contact with the slip rings. Brushes are designed to provide many hours of service life, but they eventually wear out. Dirt, fluids, engine blowby, corrosion, and other substances can leave residues on the slip rings or gum up the brush holders, also preventing good contact.

The service life of heavy-duty alternators should ideally last as long as a machine's, accumulating hours of service of up to 20,000 hours. One way to extend the service life is by using brushless alternator designs, such as the one illustrated in **FIGURE 15-8**, to bypass the problems of using brushes.

Instead of locating the magnetic field coil inside a rotating rotor, these alternators use a stationary field winding bolted to the alternator end frame. The rotor's pole pieces rotate around the stationary coil. Brushes, therefore, are not required to deliver the current to the rotor. As a result, there is no need to service the brushes and slip rings.

Exciting the Alternator

While the voltage regulator will supply current to the rotor, some alternators require some residual magnetism on the rotor before current is generated. **Residual magnetism** refers to the small amount of magnetism left on the rotor after it is initially magnetized by the coil's magnetic field. Residually magnetized rotors will begin to induce current in the stator windings when the alternator starts rotating without any current passing through the rotor coil. The stator, in turn, supplies current to the voltage regulator through exciter diodes. Normal alternator operation using a regulator will resume once current is supplied to the regulator. This category of self-exciting alternators generally features a single heavy-gauge battery cable connecting the alternator to the machine batteries.

Self-exciting alternators do not require the use of a circuit but may require some initial current in the rotor's coil through the "R" terminal for the first time after installation or when the engine has been sitting without running for long periods. Often, equipment fitted with self-exciting alternators may require the engine rpm to be briefly increased after every start-up to initiate

FIGURE 15-8 A brushless alternator has rotating pole pieces around a stationary field winding. **A.** Rotor. **B.** Pole pieces (2). **C.** Stator windings. **D.** Stationary field coil.

charging. Using self-exciting alternators eliminates the need for a separate circuit from the key switch to the alternator and simplifies chassis wiring.

> **▶ TECHNICIAN TIP**
>
> Self-exciting alternators do not use a circuit connected to the ignition switch to switch on the voltage regulator and supply current to the rotor. Instead, they rely on residual magnetism found in the rotor after operating. If the alternator stays unexcited due to a prolonged shutdown period or after rebuilding, residual magnetism needs to be re-established. The "R" terminal is briefly energized with battery current using a jumper wire connected to the battery cable after the alternator starts. Once energized, the alternator will begin charging and should not need initializing with current again. Many alternators are regularly returned as defective because technicians are unaware of the procedure to excite the rotor initially.

Stator

The stator is made of loops of coiled wire wrapped around a slotted metal alternator frame. The laminated iron stator frame channels magnetic lines of force through the conductors, where current is induced by the spinning rotor. Because the wires are looped, with alternating magnetic north–south poles passing beneath the loops, alternating current is produced from the stator (**FIGURE 15-9**).

The windings are insulated from each other and also from the iron core. They form a large number of conductor loops, which are each subjected to the rotating magnetic fields of the rotor. The stator is mounted between two end housings, and it holds the stator windings stationary so that the rotating magnetic field cuts through the stator windings, inducing an electric current in the windings. To smooth the pulsating current flow, there are three distinct layers of windings offset 120 degrees in each layer from one another. This arrangement produces a more even flow of current from the alternator. The number of loops in each winding corresponds to the number of rotor poles. So, if the rotor has 14 poles, there will be 14 loops of wire in each of the three windings. Ultimately, the amount of amperage that the alternator is capable of producing depends on the mass of wire in the stator. A larger stator having more loops, more turns of wire in each loop, and/or thicker wire will have higher maximum output amperage than one with fewer loops, less wire, and thinner wire. **FIGURE 15-10** provides a side-by-side comparison of low- and high-output stators.

FIGURE 15-9 The stator consists of a cylindrical, laminated iron core, which carries the three-phase windings in slots on the inside.

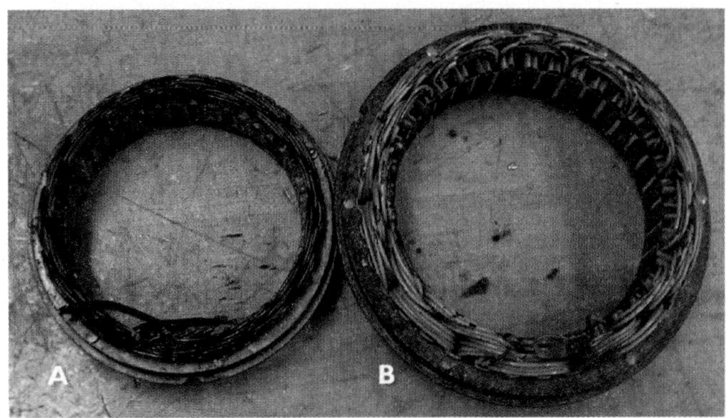

FIGURE 15-10 Comparison between **A.** a low- and **B.** a high-current output stator winding.

Phase Winding Connections

Two methods of connection can be used for the stator or phase windings: the Wye and Delta configurations. Both types of windings produce three-phase AC current, but voltage and amperage outputs differ. Windings connected in a Wye-type configuration have four connection points. As the name suggests, **Wye windings** resemble the letter "Y" (**FIGURE 15-11A**).

Three ends of each of the windings are connected to a point called the neutral junction. The other three free ends are connected to a pair of diodes in the rectifier bridge. The advantage of Wye windings is that they produce higher voltage at comparably lower rotor speeds. This means the alternator can begin charging a battery at lower engine speeds.

Delta windings, shaped like the symbol "delta," are more popular in alternators for diesel engines (**FIGURE 15-11B**). These windings have only three connection points. The three junction points between the windings are connected to a pair of diodes found in the rectifier bridge. Because stator windings are connected in parallel, the resistance of Delta windings is one third less than Wye windings. Although Delta windings do not produce as much voltage as Wye windings at the same low rotor speeds, they do, however, produce substantially more amperage. Delta-wound alternators are best adapted to supply higher amperage output to charge multiple batteries and the heavy electrical loads found in trucks, buses, and off-road machines. More importantly, the steady high-speed operation of diesel engines combined with the higher efficiency of delta-wound

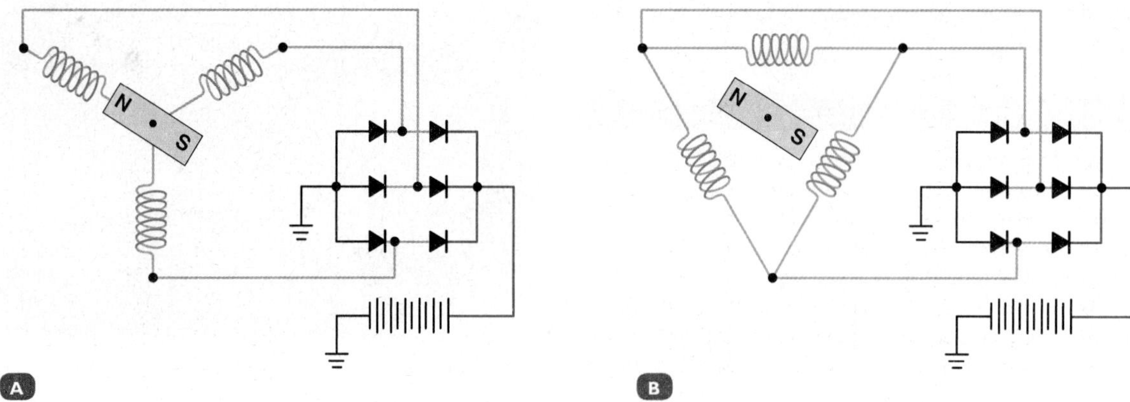

FIGURE 15-11 **A.** Wye-wound and **B.** Delta-wound stator configurations.

alternators at high speeds makes them better suited to use on diesel engines. Combination of Wye and Delta stators are rarely found in HD alternators.

Testing Stators

Stators, like rotors, are not normally serviced in a repair facility. However, when rebuilding, stators can be visually checked for burned, cut, or nicked winding laminations. Winding junction points are checked to ensure they are solid. Continuity should exist between all junction points of the stator. An amperage draw test of each winding can be performed to check the resistance and balance of each section of winding. No continuity should exist between the windings and alternator frame. As illustrated in **FIGURE 15-12**, a stator can be tested for short circuits and open circuits.

A leakage-to-ground test evaluates winding insulation and is also known as an insulation stress test. Stress testing involves passing high-voltage, low-amperage current through the windings. Any breakdown in insulation is detected when continuity exists between the windings and frame.

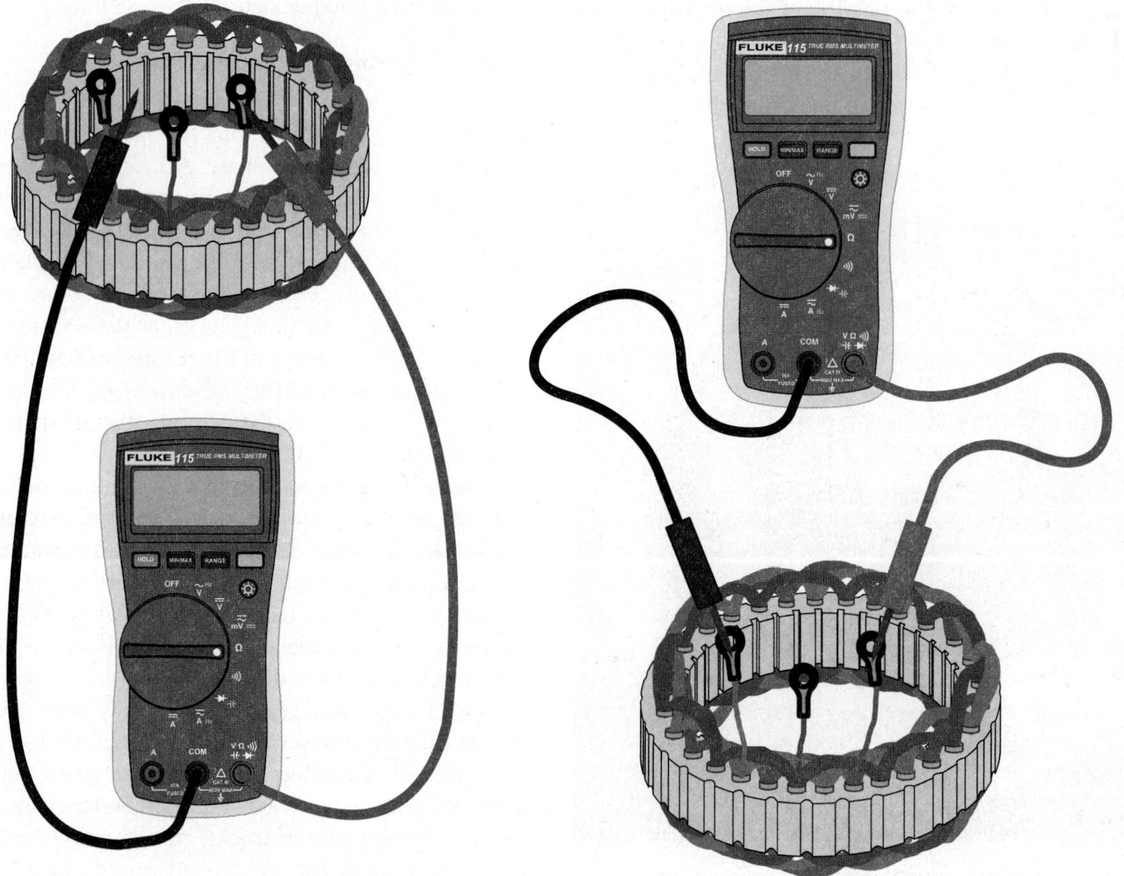

FIGURE 15-12 A stator can be tested for short and open circuits.

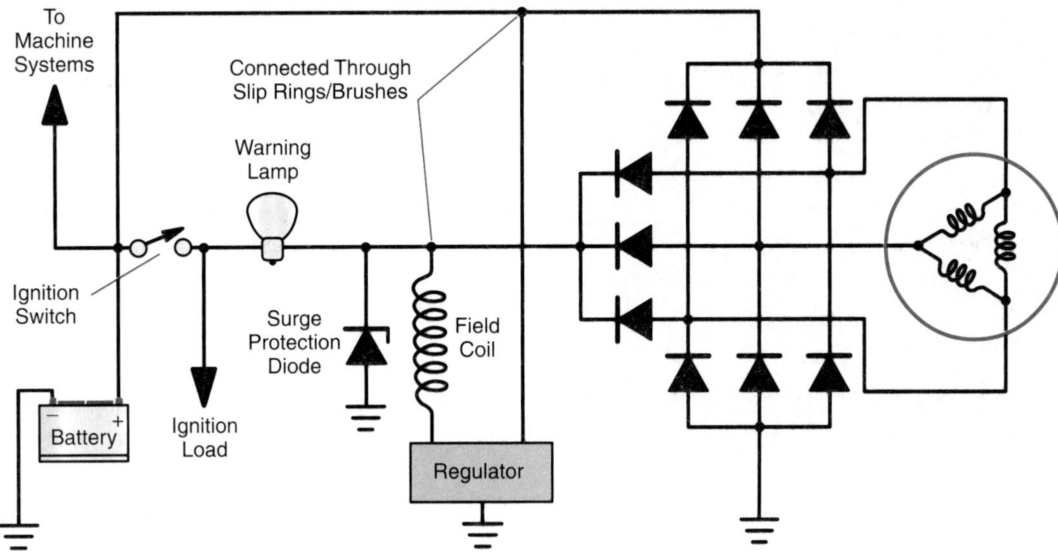

FIGURE 15-13 Current flow through a single phase in the forward direction.

Rectifier

Alternators produce alternating current, which is acceptable for operating many electrical devices. However, not all AC-operated devices are cost-effective to produce or efficient to operate on mobile equipment. AC current cannot charge a battery either. Converting the AC current to usable DC current is referred to as **rectification**.

AC current is induced in the stator due to the movement of the rotors' magnetic fields. Alternating north–south poles passing over windings will alternately push and pull electrons. Moving the electrons in two different directions gives stator current flow its AC characteristic. The speed at which the lines of force cut the conductors, the angle the magnetic field cuts the stator conductors, the number of conductors, and the wire gauge will determine the amount of amperage induced in the stator.

Two diodes are connected to each wire end of either Delta- or Wye-wound stators. Each stator winding will produce one of three phases of AC current (**FIGURE 15-13**).

So, a minimum of six diodes is required to completely rectify all three phases of AC into DC. The silicon diodes making up the rectifier behave like a one-way electrical check valve. The two diodes connected to each winding will allow either a positive or negative current potential to appear at the output of the rectifier. If only a single diode is used at the end of the windings, only half the AC sine wave will be rectified. Two diodes enable full wave rectification (**FIGURE 15-14**).

The top of the waveform is called the **alternator ripple**. A ripple that is consistent across each winding indicates that the stator windings and diodes are each creating current flow and voltage consistently. An inconsistent ripple indicates a fault in either the diodes or the stator windings. Study the illustrations carefully so that you understand the role the diode bridge plays in providing the relatively smooth DC output required by the machine's systems.

FIGURE 15-14 Diode trio supplies power to the rotor circuit in most alternators. **A.** Ignition terminal. **B.** Voltage regulator. **C.** Diode trio. **D.** Stator connections (3). **E.** Rectifier bridge. **F.** Negative ground connection. **G.** Positive battery terminal. **H.** "R" terminal.

Rectifier Diode Problems

Heat can cause premature failures of diodes (**FIGURE 15-15**).

Additional cooling of rectifier bridges can be accomplished with heavier diodes and heat sinks or by connecting diodes in parallel so that six rather than three pairs accomplish the work. Another problem facing an alternator occurs when the diodes become open or shorted. An internally shorted positive diode will cause a parasitic loss of battery current through the alternator when the engine is not running. This condition will also cause a loss of up to 67% of alternator output because it interferes with the rectification of current from two winding phases. Shorted diodes can be detected with an AC voltmeter measurement of alternator output. Generally, any more than 0.4–0.7 volts of AC current superimposed over the DC output indicate that AC current is passing through a shorted diode. Most dedicated

FIGURE 15-15 Rectifier in an alternator housing. Note the fins on the heat sink to remove heat.

alternator testing equipment will have a diode ripple feature that detects this large AC waveform and illuminates a diagnostic light on the machine. Graphing the alternator output with a graphing meter or oscilloscope and carefully observing the pattern also indicate the condition of the diodes. An open diode will not cause as much of a loss of output as a shorted diode—only up to 33% of output—but will cause increased fluctuations or pulsing of DC output current.

When measuring alternator output using an AC (not DC) voltmeter, AC current can normally be measured. An alternator with output voltage fluctuations between 13.9 to 14.2 volts DC, for example, will produce a 0.3-volt AC current. When graphed, the waveform looks like a ripple of a wave, hence the term AC ripple (**FIGURE 15-16**).

The voltage fluctuations are produced by the differences between the peak voltage of an AC sine wave and the minimum voltage found in the trough between sine waves (**FIGURE 15-17**).

AC ripple is suppressed by a capacitor inside the alternator and is absorbed by the battery. If AC ripple is too great, it leads to radio noise and electromagnetic interference (EMI) in many electronic control devices (**FIGURE 15-18**).

For example, an engine ECM may fail to function correctly, causing the engine to run rough. A powertrain module may even generate fault codes.

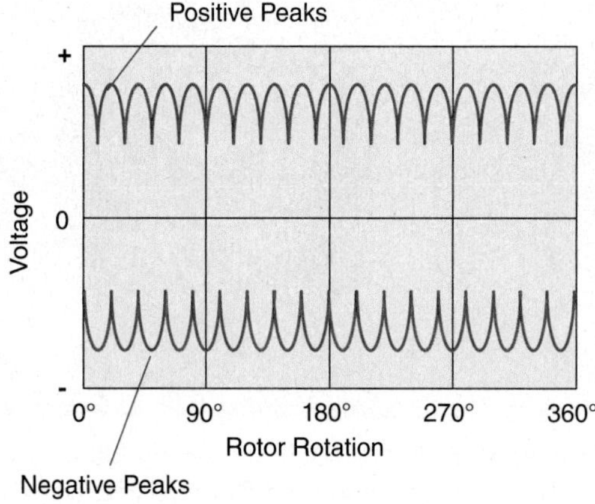

FIGURE 15-16 Typical alternator oscilloscope pattern showing AC ripple.

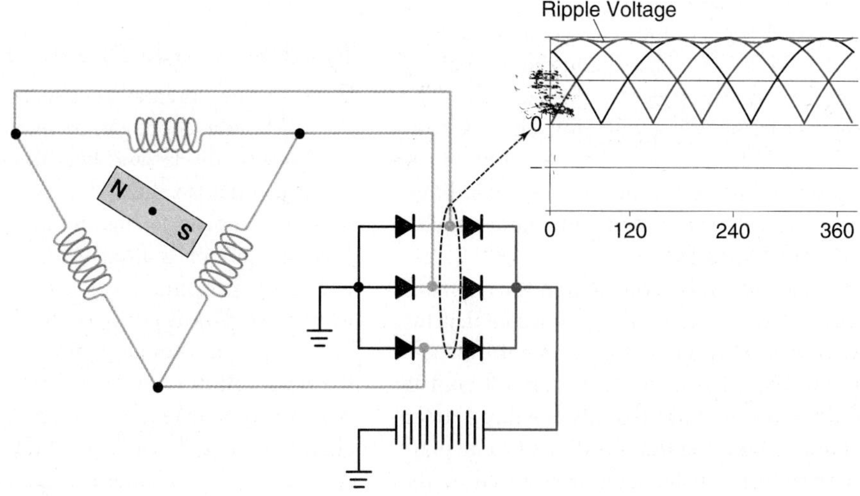

FIGURE 15-17 Three phases rectified.

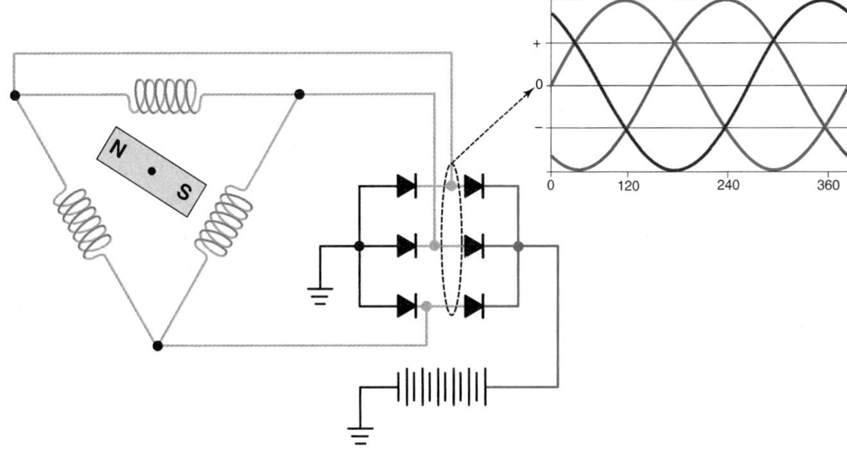

FIGURE 15-18 Three phases not rectified.

Smoothing Capacitors

Capacitors can be used to smooth alternator AC ripple and prevent EMI. In the alternator, one is connected across the output to act like an electric shock absorber. When the output voltage increases slightly, the capacitor will charge and absorb the new increase. When voltage drops, the capacitor will drain current back into the circuit, topping up the output voltage, and then the capacitor is ready for a new charge.

▶ TECHNICIAN TIP

A missing or defective alternator capacitor can cause radio noise and EMI interference with machine electronic modules. When checking for parasitic draws, the capacitor may give a false indication of current draw as it charges for a few seconds after the battery is disconnected. If batteries are disconnected for even a short time, they will spark when connected while the capacitor charges.

FIGURE 15-19 An external voltage regulator for a 24-volt alternator, with voltage regulator adjustment (circled).

Voltage Regulator

Voltage regulators are first classified as either external (**FIGURE 15-19**) or internal.

The majority of late-model alternators have internal regulators. Regulators can also be categorized by circuit connections used to supply current to the rotor used to induce "field excitation." Knowing the type of field excitation circuit used is helpful when developing diagnostic strategies for testing alternators:

1. A-type regulators regulate the field current by controlling the resistance through to ground. One rotor brush is connected to the alternator output or battery positive (B+), and the other is connected to ground through the regulator (**FIGURE 15-20**).
2. B-type regulators control the battery positive supply to the rotor. One brush is connected directly to negative ground, and the regulator varies battery positive voltage supplied to the other brush. B-type circuits are used only by external regulators. If the electronic regulator fails or develops a resistive ground due to corrosion, it commonly causes the alternator to overcharge, as system voltage is sensed through the ground and battery positive (**FIGURE 15-21**).
3. Isolated field-type of rotor excitation varies current through both the negative ground and battery positive (**FIGURE 15-22**).

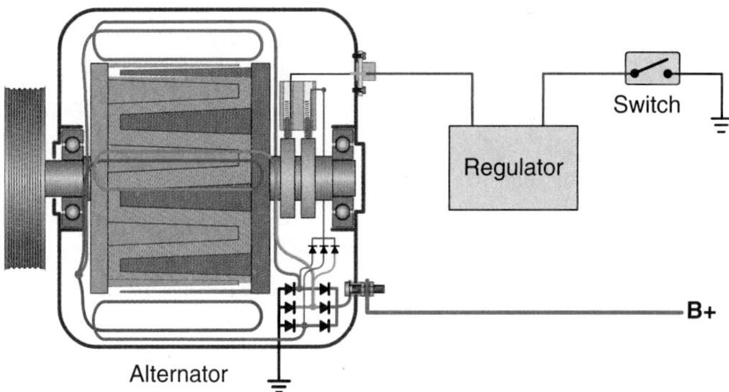

FIGURE 15-20 A-type regulator connection.

In systems-integrated (SI) series Delco alternators, current supplied to the regulator is provided by the diode trio. These

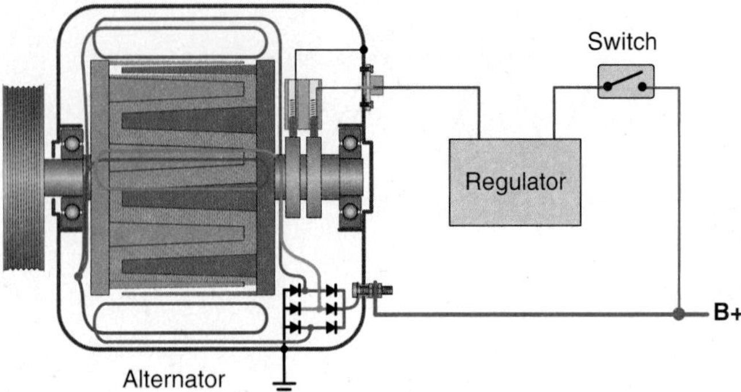

FIGURE 15-21 B-type regulator connection.

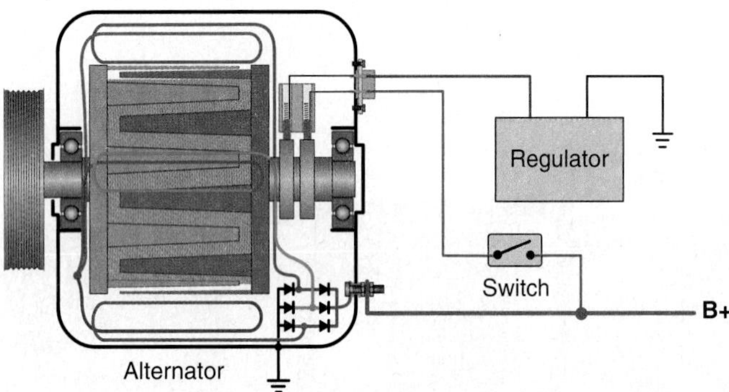

FIGURE 15-22 An isolated field alternator allows connection of either an A- or B-type regulator.

three diodes will perform single-phase rectification of each phase of the alternators' windings. Single-phase rectification means only a maximum of half the alternators' voltage output can excite the rotor.

Some voltage regulators use an analog voltage signal to modulate or change the strength of the magnetic field. This means that the current to the rotor continuously varies. As the alternator reaches its set point, the field current gradually diminishes. Digital regulators will use a pulse-width-modulated signal to control the magnetic-field strength. These alternators will have a duty cycle frequency interval of between 10 and 7,000 times per second. Within that frequency interval, the voltage regulator changes the length of "on-time" current applied to the rotor. Current is cycled on and off hundreds of times each second, and the duration of on-time increases as higher output is required.

Output current from an alternator varies with the strength of the rotor's magnetic field. Increasing or decreasing current flow through the rotor will change output. Low current through the rotor produces low output and vice versa with high current flow producing higher alternator output current. Changing electrical demands, varying engine speeds, and changing the battery state of charge all require rapid, continuous adjustments to output voltage.

Current or amperage regulation is a function of voltage regulation. To understand this, consider that an alternator's output depends on two factors: One is the regulator set point, and the other is the machine's electrical system's total circuit resistance. An electrical system with a battery in a low state of charge, and many other electrical loads switched on, has low resistance. Multiple current pathways exist, which lowers total circuit resistance. Low resistance permits high amounts of amperage to flow out of the alternator. (Remember Ohm's law: voltage = amperage × resistance.) Because the alternator is connected to all these circuits, the voltage regulator will supply the highest possible current flow to the rotor for maximum magnetic-field strength. As the batteries charge and some loads are turned off, less amperage is needed, because electrical system resistance increases. Because electrical system resistance increases, the system voltage will rise as amperage is reduced. When the system voltage reaches the alternator's set point, the voltage regulator will turn off the current to the rotor until the voltage falls again.

Stated another way, using power and Ohm's law (power = volts × amps), then if 1,200 watts of power are needed to supply the electrical system, the voltage amperage combination could be 85 amps at 14.0 volts or 100 amps at 12.0 volts.

Voltage regulators controlled by the ECM are commonplace. Using engine speed, air intake temperature and other variables, the ECM will adjust charging voltage to match battery temperature. To reduce drag when cranking, no field excitation takes place until after the engine starts. Once the engine is started, current output is slowly raised to minimize rough engine operation cause by heavy alternator loads. If battery voltage is too low, engine idle speed can be increased. Communication between the ECM and voltage regulator takes place over the controlled area network (CAN) (**FIGURE 15-23**).

Charging System Set Point

Alternators must be capable of controlling the output of the DC current. There must be enough current to adequately charge the batteries but not so much current that it causes damage to the machine's electrical system. Voltage regulation for 12-volt systems will establish a maximum charging voltage, known as the set point. Charging voltage set point averages between 13.5 volts and 14.6 volts. This is 1.5 to 2.0 volts above the 12.6-volt open-circuit voltage for a typical 12-volt battery. Also, 24-volt systems use 27 and 28.4 volts for a typical set point. It is always advisable to check manufacturer specifications for correct charging voltage ranges for the machine and operating conditions. Charging at voltages above 15 volts (12-volt system) and 31 volts (24-volt system) causes

- batteries to gas excessively
- batteries to overheat and lose electrolyte through electrolysis
- battery plates to shed grid material, buckle, and generally become damaged by heat as the temperature rises above 125°F (52°C)
- machine electrical systems, control modules, etc. to be damaged by high voltage
- premature and extensive bulb failure and LED light failure.

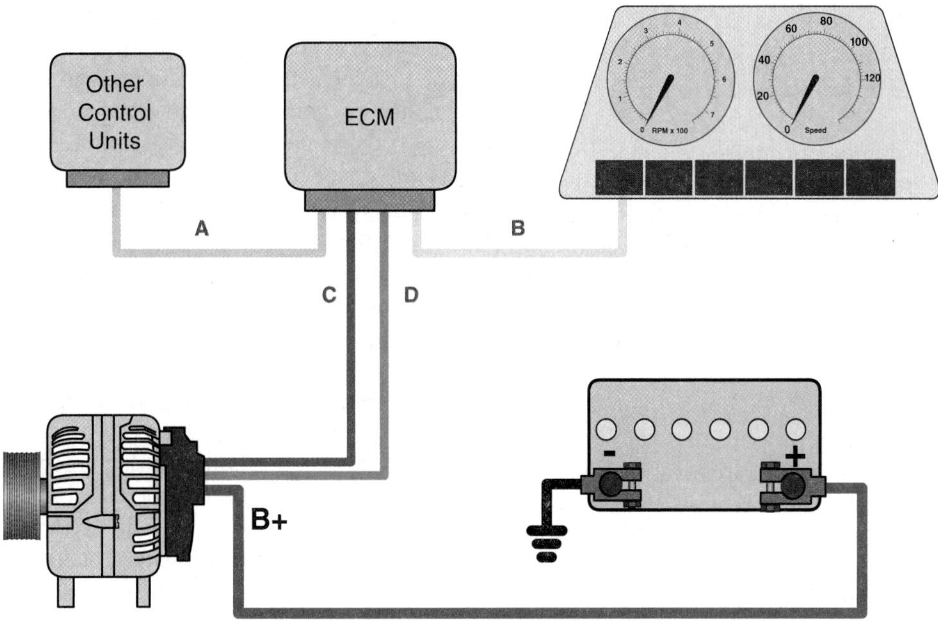

FIGURE 15-23 ECM controlled alternator. **A.** CANbus connection. **B.** CANbus connection to dash for charge lamp. **C.** Monitoring signal. **D.** Control signal.

Undercharging leads to battery plate sulfation and grid corrosion. This is a condition where sulfate deposited on the plates during discharge is left too long. If left long enough, sulfate turns to a hard-crystalline structure and cannot be driven off by charging. Multiple battery installations are especially vulnerable to the problems of uneven charge rates causing plate sulfation.

Factors affecting the precise set point include the following:

- *The type of batteries*—flooded batteries (standard lead acid) charge at lower voltages than no-maintenance or AGM batteries. AGM batteries are more easily damaged by overcharging.
- *States of battery charge*—discharged batteries have low resistance to current compared to charged batteries. AGM batteries can absorb 40% more current than flooded and low-maintenance batteries can.
- *Temperature*—battery resistance to charging increases as temperatures decrease. Temperature sensors in voltage regulators can adjust set points. To warm up the battery, Delco CS alternators charge at 16.5 volts for the first few minutes after start-up when the weather is cold.
- *Idle time*—low engine speed operation requires higher set points to keep batteries charged.

When operating in environments where a spark from an alternator's brush could trigger an explosion or cause a fire, the alternator is sealed and heat is radiated through the housing. Most alternators, however, rely on air to internally cool internal components (**FIGURE 15-24**).

If equipped with a cooling fan, the alternator must rotate in a direction that will push air through the unit. Today most cooling fans will push air through the alternator regardless of rotational direction.

FIGURE 15-24 A fan attached to rotor used to cool the alternator.

▶ TECHNICIAN TIP

The machine's electrical system can be severely damaged by high-voltage spikes if batteries are disconnected accidentally or intentionally while the alternator is charging. Since the rotor's magnetic fields do not disappear immediately and the battery is unable to absorb current, output voltage can suddenly rise to levels that can damage sensitive electronic devices. Some alternators include a **load-dumping** feature that temporarily suppresses these high-voltage spikes. This usually involves using specialized diodes in the rectifier bridges, which become resistive rather than conductive at a specific voltage level. The diodes are called **transient voltage suppression (TVS) diodes**. They will temporarily resist high voltage and automatically reset when the overvoltage goes away. Best practice is never to disconnect batteries when the engine is running.

Alternator End Frames and Bearings

The alternator housings support and enclose all of the alternator components and are typically constructed from aluminum (**FIGURE 15-25**).

Vents within the frames provide for a large amount of airflow to assist in dissipating heat. The housings accept the bearing assemblies, which support the rotor at the drive and slip ring ends. A pulley that is driven by a belt is mounted at the end of the rotor shaft. Most slip ring end frames also house the rectifier assembly. In some cases, the negative diodes are pressed into holes in the frame to provide a ground, while the positive diodes are mounted on insulated plates.

Drive Mechanism

A drive gear, rather than a pulley on rare occasions, is used to couple the alternator to the engine. It requires the alternator to be bolted directly to the engine in a location where a driving gear is available. This arrangement eliminates maintenance issues around belt tension and replacement but does require the alternator to be well sealed to prevent any oil leakage.

The correct gearing or pulley size needs to be selected for the alternator to ensure that the alternator does not overspeed at higher engine rpm but also produces enough output at idle to cater to electrical demand. Since an off-road diesel operates typically between 650 rpm and 2,100 rpm, a mechanical advantage between the alternator pulley and engine speed is needed to spin the alternator fast enough. Most larger alternators are limited to 8,000 rpm, which means the alternator drive ratio is precisely chosen to produce high output at idle yet stay below maximum speeds. This is particularly true because output curves tend to flatten out and brush and bearing wear increase with increasing speed. For large-bore diesel engines found in heavy off-road equipment, the driven ratio is approximately 2.7:1, which means that every engine rpm produces 2.7 rotor shaft revolutions. In recent years a ratio of 3:1 or even 3.1:1 is becoming common. At 2,000 rpm the alternator will turn 6,000 rpm. Some slow rpm diesels may use a ratio as high as 5:1 in comparison to smaller-capacity, higher-revving engines that use a ratio as low as 2:1.

V-type belts and pulleys have been the traditional method of driving alternators. However, to extend belt maintenance intervals, manufacturers have moved completely away from using V-type pulleys in favor of serpentine belts equipped with automatic tensioners (**FIGURE 15-26**).

A serpentine belt is a type of multi-rib belt that is long enough to drive multiple accessories. Due to the length of the serpentine belt and the number of accessories it drives, idler pulleys are required to ensure each pulley has enough wrap or surface contact with the belt. Serpentine belt systems reduce belt wear while improving the coupling force with multiple accessories.

Belt tensioners can be spring-loaded or hydraulic, and they can absorb some of the torsional vibration found in diesels as the crankshaft accelerates and decelerates with each cylinder power and compression event (**FIGURE 15-27**).

FIGURE 15-26 A multi-rib serpentine belt.

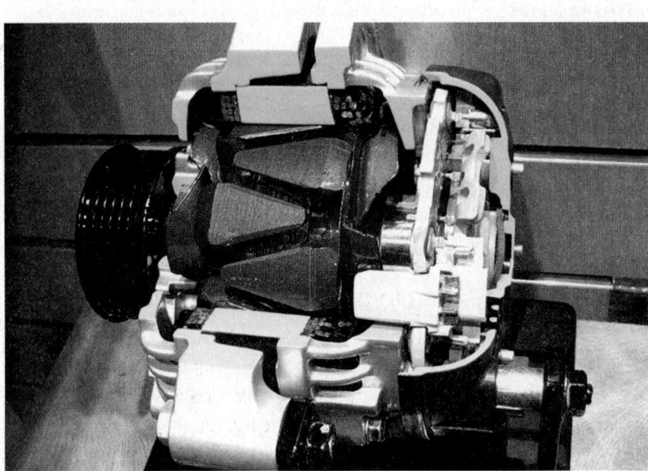

FIGURE 15-25 Alternator end frames enclose and support all components and allow for maximum airflow through the alternator to remove excess heat.

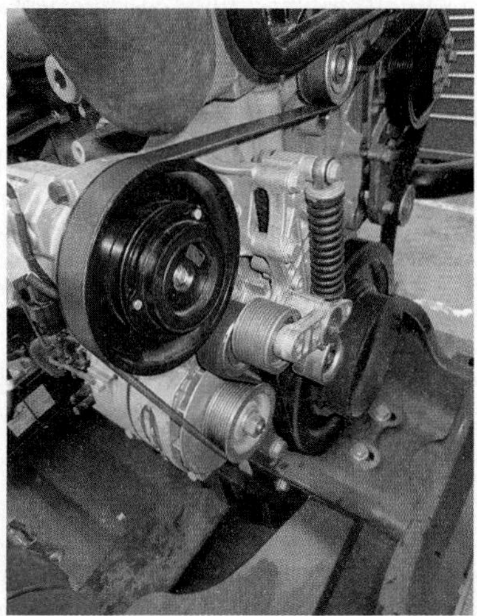

FIGURE 15-27 A belt tensioner ensures the correct tension is applied to the belt to prevent slippage.

The alternator drive belt bears the brunt of this damaging force occurring as the engine acceleration rate changes and the alternator's mass resists the speed change. When the belt and alternator speed are out of phase, the belt is snapped and slips. This force is magnified by the 3:1 drive ratio between the crankshaft and alternator pulley. To improve belt life and mechanical efficiency, it is becoming common to use **overrunning alternator decoupler (OAD)** pulleys rather than a conventional solid pulley and tensioner. An OAD pulley uses an internal spring and clutch system that allows it to rotate freely in one direction and provide limited, spring-like movement in the other direction. The pulley acts like a shock absorber, absorbing the force associated with belt accelerations and speed reversals, enabling the alternator to freewheel when the belt suddenly decelerates.

Alternator Wiring Connections

The terms and connections used in this section are ones commonly used for machines. Different manufacturers may use different socket arrangements, color codes, and naming conventions for the various terminals and connectors on alternators, so it is always important to check manufacturer's wiring diagrams and naming conventions for information. The wiring requirements for alternators are relatively simple. This is particularly true for internal regulator self-exciting alternators because they use only a single battery cable (**FIGURE 15-28**).

The battery positive cable is large, red gauge wire—#4AWG (American wire gauge) or larger. It connects to the battery terminal on the starter and has voltage present at all times. Some alternators, particularly high-output ones, will also have a ground or negative cable. A large-gauge wire (#4AWG or larger) is connected to battery or chassis ground (**FIGURE 15-29**).

This prevents the engine block from conducting hundreds of amps that the alternator may produce and minimizes voltage loss. A remote sensing connection will also be used on some alternators and will usually be marked on the back of the alternator with an "S" (**FIGURE 15-30**).

FIGURE 15-28 Self-exciting alternators typically have only a main battery connection.

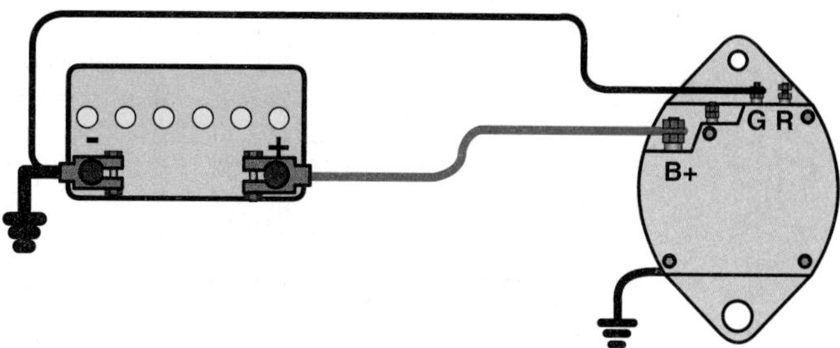

FIGURE 15-29 Circuit diagram for connection of self-exciting alternator.

The term **remote sensing** refers to the arrangement of directly connecting a terminal on the alternators voltage regulator to the battery in order to use battery voltage as reference point for regulating the alternator output voltage. This is different from simply using the large alternator to battery connection at the back of the alternator. Many alternators reference the battery positive connection at the alternator through this larger cable connection which often has lower voltage due to high amperage flow through the cable. Alternators that use **remote sensing** provide a more accurate direct reading of the battery at a regulator input terminal that is used for the regulator reference voltage. Remote sensing enables more accurate supply and adjustment of charging voltage to the batteries which help extend battery life. Without precise charging voltage supplied to the battery, its lifecycle is shortened through under and sometimes overcharging.

External regulator alternators will have additional connections to allow for field connections from the regulator to the alternator, as was shown in Figure 15-19. Provision for the connection of alternator warning lights may also be fitted to both internal and external regulator alternators.

Alternators that require external excitation will have an ignition excite or "I" connection. This small gauge wire has voltage present only when the ignition switch is in the run position. Current through this wire switches the voltage regulator on. In some machines built without voltmeters in the dash and equipped with an instrument cluster warning light, current will pass from the switch and to the light into the alternator regulator to provide initial excitation of the rotor's magnetic field. In most machines, however, voltmeters are used to indicate whether the charging system is properly functioning (**FIGURE 15-31**).

Another connection found on many alternators is the relay or "R" terminal. This terminal is connected directly to one phase of the stator winding. Because it is connected directly to the stator, it provides an AC signal whose frequency is related to the speed of the alternator. Because the speed of the alternator is related to engine speed, this signal can be used to operate a tachometer or an hour meter or to operate a frequency-sensitive starter lock out relay to disable the cranking circuit when the engine is running. Energizing or flashing this terminal, which is the temporary connection of battery voltage, is necessary on some self-exciting alternators in order to magnetize the rotor for

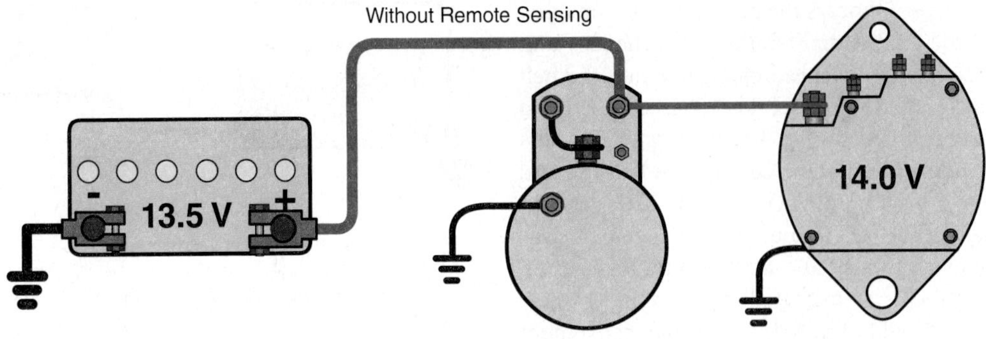

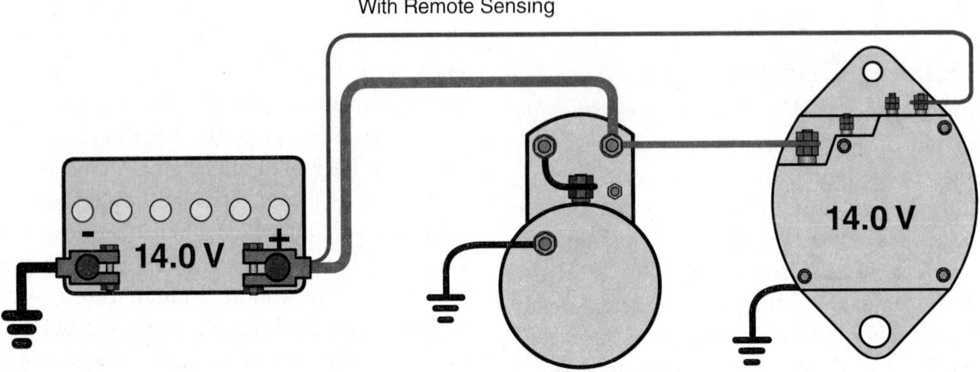

FIGURE 15-30 Remote sensing allows the voltage regulator to use battery voltage as a reference for alternator output voltage.

FIGURE 15-31 Instrument cluster warning light. When the alternator starts charging, charging voltage appears at the "I" terminal, which provides battery positive to both sides of the light and extinguishes the charging system warning light. In situations where a charge warning light is not required, an ignition feed may be directly connected to the "I" terminal.

initial start-up. Since the rotor is soft iron, the rotor will maintain this magnetism once it has been initially excited. However, after rebuilding or through prolonged inactivity, the rotor may lose the residual magnetism. For this reason, the relay terminal is needed on self-exciting single-wire alternators. This feature is common to some Bosch and Delco SI series alternators, which use voltage regulators.

▶ Charging System Diagnosis

K15003, S15001

When diagnosing charging system problems, always start with the battery. A weak or dead battery, corroded battery-cable connections, and/or damaged or worn components may cause a no-crank or slow-crank problem. Check for dirt buildup on the battery top, case damage, loose or corroded connections, or any other trouble that could drain the battery charge. Charging system malfunctions are often identified by battery condition. Use **TABLE 15-1** to assist in diagnosing charging system problems.

Always consult manufacturers' information before commencing any work.

Inspecting, Adjusting, and Replacing Alternator Drive Belts, Pulleys, and Tensioners

If a problem arises with an alternator, perform a visual inspection of its drive belts, pulleys, and tensioners. An index mark on a belt tension indicates whether the belt is too loose or too tight. Ideally, the tensioner arm should be centered between the two stop points on the tensioner bracket.

TABLE 15-1 Charging System Diagnosis Chart

Concern	Cause	Remedy
Overcharged batteries	Resistive voltage sensing lead contact at alternator or electrical system	Repair
	Open voltage sensing circuit	Repair circuit
	Defective voltage regulator	Replace regulator
	Improperly adjusted voltage regulator	Adjust regulator
	One shorted battery in a battery bank	Replace battery
Low voltage or no-charge condition	Loose drive belts	Tighten or replace belt as necessary
	Corroded, broken, burnt, or loose wiring connections	Repair connections
	Undersize battery cables	Install proper gauge cables
	Defective batteries	Replace batteries as required
	Batteries too far from sensing lead contact	Reposition
	Missing sensing lead contact	Repair contact
	Defective voltage regulator	Replace regulator
	Improperly adjusted voltage regulator	Adjust regulator
	Defective rectifier bridge; shorted or open diodes	Replace or overhaul alternator
No magnetic field at alternator	Poor contact between brushes and slip rings	Overhaul alternator/replace brushes
	Damaged or worn brushes/slip rings	Overhaul alternator/replace brushes
	No residual magnetism present in the rotor	Overhaul/replace alternator
	Defective or improperly adjusted regulator	Adjust or replace regulator as required
	Open, shorted, or grounded rotor winding	Overhaul alternator/replace rotor
	No ignition excitation of regulator	Check and repair connection
	No current feed to internal regulator	Check and repair connection

Preventive Maintenance Practices

When performing preventive maintenance, the following areas require attention.

1. Cleaning cable terminals, wiring, and alternator connection points or corrosion. Alternator surfaces should be cleaned until they are free of accumulations of dirt, grease, and dust. Air passages need to be unobstructed to allow air to easily pass through. All connection points must be clean and free from corrosion since voltage is sensed from between ground and battery positive.
2. Mounting brackets should be inspected for loose bolts and to allow correct belt alignment. Broken and loose mounting may indicate damage from engine torsional vibration. If other accessory drive system components are functioning correctly, a sturdier model of alternator may be required.
3. Condition of belts and belt tension. A loose belt will slip and cause undercharging. Tensioners must be correctly aligned operating perpendicular to the belt. Multi-grooved belts should be check for cracks, which may extend completely across the belt. The back side of the belt should not be worn and glazed.

FIGURE 15-32 Failure conditions for serpentine belts.

Belts can have several issues, as shown in **FIGURE 15-32**.

To replace a serpentine belt, follow the guidelines in **SKILL DRILL 15-1**.

SKILL DRILL 15-1 Replacing a Serpentine Belt

1. For safety reasons, disconnect the battery and lock out the machine. Inspect the belt for failure. Repair any condition causing belt contamination or failure due to misalignment.
2. Familiarize yourself with the belt routing. Draw a sketch, take a picture of the belt routing, or locate the belt routing diagram in a shop manual or on the radiator module.
3. Release the belt tension to remove the belt. To release belt tension, the automatic belt tensioner is retracted away from the belt using a wrench, socket wrench, 1/2" drive or 3/8" drive ratchet.
4. Inspect the drive belt pulley system for wear. Make sure the tensioner and the pulleys operate freely, without noise or looseness, and are in perfect condition. The tensioner pulley should contact the belt squarely; if not, the tensioner should be replaced. The installation of a belt kit containing a new tensioner and drive pulleys is recommended when replacing a belt at high accumulated mileage.
5. Before installing the new belt, inspect the alignment of the pulleys to prevent severe belt wear, damage, and belt noise.
6. Route and install the new belt according to the belt routing diagram. Align the belt ribs with the pulley grooves and ensure that the belt fits squarely on each pulley and all the belt grooves fit into the pulley grooves.
7. Release the belt tensioner once again to install the belt over the tensioner pulley. The automatic tensioner will apply the correct tension to the belt. When the installation tension is correct, unlock the machine, start the engine and observe if the belt drive and tensioning system is properly functioning.

▶ Charging System Output Test

S15002

Machine charging systems are voltage regulated, which means that the alternator will try to maintain a set voltage across the electrical systems. As electrical load current increases in the machine systems, voltage starts to drop. The voltage regulator senses this voltage drop and increases the current output of the alternator, which in turn increases system voltage to try to maintain the correct voltage in the system. The testing of an alternator output initially involves the testing of the system's regulated voltage using a voltmeter. Regulated voltage is the voltage at which the regulator is allowing the alternator to create only a small charge due to the battery being relatively charged, as evidenced by the greatly reduced current output.

Unless the batteries are deeply discharged, the equipment headlights should not dim at idle when the alternator is operating satisfactorily. To performance test the charging system, also called a set point test, alternator voltage and amperage is measured with the engine running at 1,000–1,500 rpm. With all the machine loads switched off and the batteries fully charged, alternator output should be 20 amps or less and voltage should be 13.8–14.4 volts for a 12-volt system. Also, 24-volt systems should charge between 27.8 and 28.4 volts. If the voltage is not within this range and the regulator not adjustable, the alternator is likely defective.

An alternator's performance is tested under load and measured while the engine is at 1,500 rpm. A carbon pile tester is connected to the batteries, and the system is loaded until it drops to 12.5 volts. At 12.5 volts, the amperage output from the alternator is also measured. Output should generally be within 10% of the alternator's maximum rating. This means that a 200-amp alternator should deliver at least 180 amps.

To differentiate between a defective regulator and the current generating section of an alternator, a full field test of the alternator is performed. This means that the voltage regulator is bypassed, and full battery voltage is supplied briefly to the rotor slip rings. The type of alternator circuit must be identified before performing this test.

"A" circuit alternators will ground one brush. In Delco alternators, ground is done by passing a screwdriver through the "D" tab at the back of the alternator. With the screwdriver against the alternator frame and the other end on a tab of the voltage regulator, a working alternator will begin to generate current. A voltmeter is used to measure output. If voltage rises, the regulator is defective and may be replaced instead of replacing the entire alternator.

"B" circuits will use a jumper wire connected to battery positive to full field. Isolated circuits will use two jumper wires. CAN-controlled alternators will provide diagnostic information needed to diagnose alternator problems. If current output does not rise after **full fielding**, it may indicate one of the following conditions:

- a shorted, open, or grounded rotor coil
- stator windings shorted, open, or grounded
- rectifier bridge shorted, open, or grounded.

To perform a charging system output test, follow the guidelines in **SKILL DRILL 15-2**.

SKILL DRILL 15-2 Performing a Charging System Output Test

1. Connect a charging system load tester to the battery with the red lead to the positive post, the black lead to the negative post, and the amp clamp around the alternator output wire.
2. Start the engine, turn off all accessories, and measure the regulated voltage at around 1,500 rpm. The regulated voltage is the highest voltage the system achieves once the battery is relatively charged, as evidenced by the ammeter reading less than about 20–30 amps when the amp clamp is around the alternator output cable. Typical regulated voltage specifications are wider than they used to be due to the ability of the electrical system ECM to adjust the output voltage for a wide range of conditions.
3. Operate the engine at about 1,500 rpm and either manually or automatically load down the battery to 12.5 volts or 25 volts for a 24-volt system. Measure the alternator amperage output. This reading should be compared against the alternator's rated output. Normally, the maximum output should be within 10% of the alternator's rated capacity. A hot alternator may have slightly lower results.

> **TECHNICIAN TIP**
>
> The battery, or battery terminals, should never be removed when the engine is running. Removing battery terminals on alternator-equipped machines may damage the alternator and sensitive electronic equipment fitted to the machine.

▶ Testing Charging System Circuit Voltage Drop

S15003

An excessive voltage drop in the charging system output and ground circuit tends to cause one of two problems: (1) The battery is not able to be fully charged because, although the alternator is producing the specified voltage, the voltage drop is reducing the amount of voltage to the battery, or (2) the battery is fully charged, but the alternator is working at a higher voltage to do so, potentially overheating it. Which of the two issues is occurring depends on where the voltage is sensed. If it is sensed at the alternator, then the battery will generally be undercharged. If the voltage is sensed at the battery, then the alternator will work at the higher voltage. Knowing the system will help you diagnose voltage drop issues in the output and ground circuits of the charging system.

The alternator cable voltage drop test is performed to test the positive cable for excessive resistance between the alternator and the batteries. With the engine running at 1,500 rpm and the alternator loaded to 75% of its output capacity, voltage is measured at the alternator and batteries. If the voltage difference is greater than 0.25 volts in a 12-volt circuit or 0.50 volts in a 24-volt circuit, all positive and ground wire cable connections should be checked. Acceptable cable voltage drop readings are less than 0.25 volts in 12-volt system and 0.50 volts in a 24-volt system. To test charging circuit voltage drop, follow the guidelines in **SKILL DRILL 15-3**.

SKILL DRILL 15-3 Testing Charging Circuit Voltage Drop

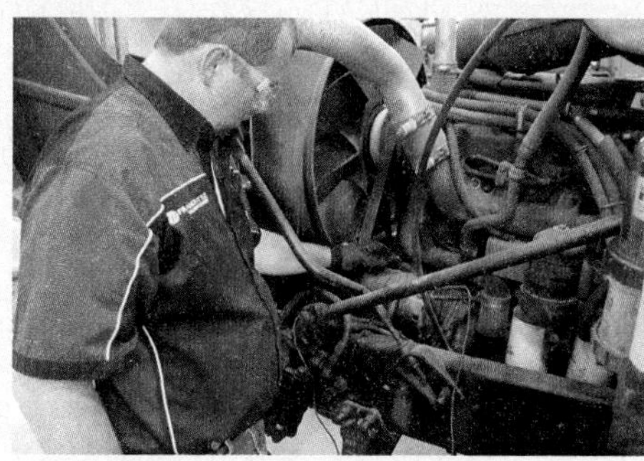

1. Set the digital volt-ohmmeter (DVOM) up to measure voltage, and select min/max if available. Connect the red probe of the DVOM to the output terminal of the alternator and the black probe to the positive post of the battery. The red probe goes on the positive battery post because, in this case, the alternator output terminal is higher voltage than the positive battery terminal. For the meter to read correctly, the leads need to be connected as listed.
2. Start the engine and turn on as many electrical loads as possible or use an external load bank to load the battery. Read the maximum voltage drop for the output circuit.
3. Move the leads to measure the voltage drop on the ground circuit by placing the black probe on the alternator case and the red probe on the negative terminal of the battery. With the engine running and the circuit still loaded, read the maximum voltage drop for the ground circuit.
4. If the measurements are excessive, check each part of the circuit for excessive voltage drops by slowly bringing the probes closer together on each section of the circuit. Determine any necessary actions.

Inspecting, Repairing, or Replacing Connectors and Wires of Charging Circuits

S15004

When you are diagnosing charging system problems, you should always make sure you visually inspect connectors and wires of charging circuits for tightness, wear, and damage. Check the connection on the voltage regulator and the alternator for loose electrical connections or shorted wires. Move the wires around while running the engine. If the warning lamp flickers or the ammeter instrument indicates incorrect charging, the problem is in the wire being jarred. You may need to perform a voltage drop test to check wiring along the charging system path. When replacing connectors and/or wires, always refer to the appropriate manufacturer's service manual for the exact procedure. To inspect, repair, or replace connectors and wires of charging circuits, follow the guidelines in **SKILL DRILL 15-4**.

Removing, inspecting, and Replacing an Alternator

S15005

During charging system tests, low-voltage and current output problems may indicate a defective alternator. If you find that the alternator is defective, it will need to be replaced. It is the rotors, brushes, stators, rectifier bridges, and cooling fans of the alternator that work together to create magnetic fields, produce current, and charge the system.

Alternators all operate on the same principle. There are, however, differences in their construction and style. Always refer to the appropriate manufacturer's service manual for the specific type and style of alternator. Follow the manufacturer's instructions when installing a new alternator. To remove, inspect, and replace an alternator, follow the guidelines in **SKILL DRILL 15-5**.

Overhauling an Alternator

S15006

Overhauling an alternator requires the disassembly and checking of all component parts. The alternator component parts should also be cleaned and replaced or repaired as necessary. The alternator is relatively simple to disassemble. You should always mark the position of the housings in relation to each other before commencing disassembly. This ensures that the housings are correctly aligned when reassembled.

Most alternators have the brushes inside the alternator, and they cannot be removed until the alternator is disassembled. However, some alternators have a brush box, which should be removed before the alternator is disassembled. Before commencing disassembly, check to see if the brushes can be removed while the alternator is in one piece. If so, undo the brush box and remove it. To disassemble the alternator, remove the through bolts with a suitable wrench or socket. Pry the housings apart; this may require a small pry bar to separate apart the housings, as they are usually a tight fit. When prying the housings apart, be careful not to damage any of the stator windings. The rotor will usually be attached to the pulley end housing. Once the alternator is separated into its two housings, further disassemble the alternator into its component parts. This may require the use of a soldering iron to remove the rectifier diodes and the brushes. The rectifier and main battery terminals will have a number of insulating bushings fitted to them. Be sure to note how the insulators are fitted for later replacement.

SKILL DRILL 15-4 Inspecting, Repairing, or Replacing Connectors and Wires of Charging Circuits

1. Locate and follow the appropriate procedure and wiring diagram in the service manual.
2. Move the equipment into the shop, apply the parking brakes, and chock the equipment's wheels. Observe lockout and tag-out procedures.
3. If the machine has a manual transmission, place it in "neutral." If it has an automatic transmission, place it in "park" or "neutral."
4. Trace the wiring harness from the alternator to the battery and around the engine bay.
5. Check the harness and connectors for wear, damage, and corrosion.
6. Disconnect the battery negative cable if repairs are necessary.
7. Repair damaged areas with replacement cables or connectors. Ensure all harnesses are secured to prevent abrasion or damage from vibration.
8. Reconnect all harness plugs and secure all connections.
9. Reconnect the battery negative cable.
10. Check the repair with a visual inspection and by running the machine.
11. Clean the work area and return tools and materials to their proper storage area.

SKILL DRILL 15-5 Removing, Inspecting, and Replacing an Alternator

1. Locate and follow the appropriate procedure in the service manual.
2. Move the machine into the workshop or safe work area, apply the parking brakes, and chock the machine wheels. Observe lockout and tag-out procedures.
3. If the machine has a manual transmission, place it in "neutral." If it has an automatic transmission, place it in "park" or "neutral."
4. Disconnect the battery from the machine.
5. Disconnect wires at the connector on the alternator. Make a note of the location and any special insulating washers.
6. Loosen bolts.
7. Slide the belt off the alternator.
8. Lift the alternator out of machine.
9. Place a new alternator onto the engine.
10. Hand screw the bolts without tightening; connect wires first if needed.
11. After checking the condition of the belt and replacing it if needed, slip the belt on each pulley and properly align the belt grooves with the alternator pulley grooves.
12. If required, adjust belt tension using a belt tension gauge.
13. Tighten the bolts.
14. Reconnect the battery.
15. Start the engine and verify that the alternator is charging.
16. Clean the work area and return tools and materials to their proper storage area.

Once the alternator has been disassembled into its component parts, conduct the following tests for each component:

- Housings
  - Clean and check housings for cracks. If they are damaged, replace them.
- Rotor
  - Check the resistance of the winding against the manufacturer's specifications. In some cases, it is also useful to check the current draw of the winding. Remember, the winding is inductive. This means it will produce a spark when power is connected or disconnected.
  - If the alternator has slip rings, check them for mechanical wear. If they are excessively worn, the slip ring assembly will need to be replaced. To do this, remove the coil wires and press off the old slip ring. Press on a new slip ring and reconnect the coil wires. You may need to machine a new slip ring in the lathe to produce a clean, round finish.
  - Check bearing surfaces and pulley retaining thread for wear. Replace the rotor if they are excessively worn.
- Diode rectifier
  - Check the diode rectifier with a diode checker. You can use a DVOM; however, a specialized alternator diode tester is recommended because it places a load on the diodes. Replace diodes if they fail the test. In some cases, individual diodes can be replaced. In others, the whole rectifier must be replaced as a unit.
- Regulator
  - Use a regulator tester to check the regulator. Each regulator tester is slightly different, although they perform the same job. Always check the manufacturer's specifications for the correct connections and procedure. Modern regulators are electronic and generally cannot be repaired. Replace the regulator if required.
- Brushes
  - If fitted, brushes should be replaced whenever the alternator is overhauled. Take care when reassembling the alternator to ensure the brushes are not damaged. Many alternators require the insertion of a pin to hold the brushes away from the slip rings as the alternator is reassembled.
- Bearings
  - Bearings should be replaced whenever the alternator is overhauled.
- Pulley and fan
  - Check the pulley and fan for wear, and replace it if necessary. When replacing the fan, ensure that it is replaced with one that operates in the same direction as the one removed.

Once the alternator has been overhauled, you will need to test it in an alternator test bench. Clamp the alternator securely in the test bench and make the electrical connections. Pay particular attention to the battery, regulator, and warning light to ensure they are connected as per the manufacturer's specifications. Run the alternator up to speed and make sure the warning light operates correctly, the alternator can generate its specified maximum current output, and the regulated voltage is within specifications. To overhaul an alternator, follow the guidelines in **SKILL DRILL 15-6**.

SKILL DRILL 15-6 Overhauling an Alternator

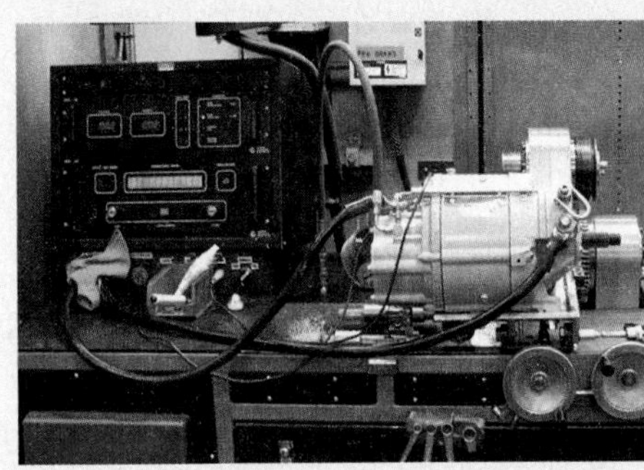

1. Locate and follow the appropriate procedure in the service manual.
2. Check to see if the brushes need to be removed first. If so, remove the brush box or regulator.
3. Remove the through bolts holding the alternator together.
4. Pry the alternator apart.
5. Disassemble the component parts from the housing. Take note of the placement of insulator bushes.
6. Clean, test, and inspect all component parts. Use specialized testers where necessary—for example, regulator tester, diode tester, and DVOM.
7. Replace any faulty components. If the slip ring assembly requires replacement, ensure the new slip ring is machined on the lathe.
8. Reassemble component parts into the housings.
9. Reassemble the alternator housings. Ensure the brushes are retained using a retaining pin to prevent damage to them.
10. Test the alternator in the alternator test bench. Ensure the warning light circuit is working and test for maximum current output and voltage regulation.
11. Clean the work area and return tools and materials to their proper storage.

▶ Wrap-Up

Ready for Review

- Both DC generators and alternators produce electricity by relative movement of conductors in a magnetic field. The key difference between an alternator and a DC generator is which component rotates or moves to generate electricity.
- The charging system provides electrical energy for all of the electrical components on the equipment. The main parts of the charging system include the battery, the alternator, the voltage regulator (which may be integrated into the alternator), a charge warning light or voltmeter, and wiring that completes the circuits.
- The alternator converts mechanical energy into electrical energy by electromagnetic induction.
- A single-phase stator has a single winding, which creates a single sine wave. In a typical equipment alternator, there are three separate coils of wire composing the stator.
- Alternators have a built-in maximum current limitation due to the CEMF in the stator coils.
- Brushless alternators have greater longevity than alternators with brushes.
- Alternators require an initial magnetic field to be produced within the rotor to initiate the process of generating electricity. Initial excitation can be either internal or external.
- Wye and Delta windings produce three-phase AC current, but voltage and amperage outputs differ according to speed and load. The Wye configuration produces higher voltage at lower rotor speeds.
- Alternators are much more efficient at producing current than DC generators are. Alternating current—not direct current—is produced inside an alternator.
- To change AC to DC, automotive alternators use a rectifier assembly consisting of two diodes for every phase of the stator winding.
- Alternators' voltage output is controlled by a voltage regulator. The voltage regulator regulates current output and limits the maximum charging system voltage.
- A significant amount of heat is produced within the alternator from the rectifier, stator, and rotor windings.
- Alternators can be driven by a pulley or direct drive through a gear.
- Equipment having high-current loads at idle or those with extra electrical loads can use two or more alternators.
- When diagnosing charging system problems, always start with the battery. A weak or dead battery, corroded battery-cable connections, and/or damaged or worn components may cause a no-crank or slow-crank problem.

Key Terms

AC ripple A pattern produced by voltage fluctuations from the alternator that create differences between the peak voltage of an AC sine wave and the minimum voltage found in the trough between sine waves.

alternator ripple The top of the waveform.

delta windings Stator windings in which the windings are connected in the shape of a triangle.

full fielding Making the alternator produce maximum amperage output.

load-dumping A feature that allows temporary suppression of high-voltage spikes.

overrunning alternator decoupler (OAD) A pulley that uses an internal spring and clutch system that allows it to rotate freely in one direction and provide limited, spring-like movement in the other direction.

rectification A process of converting alternating current (AC) into direct current (DC).

remote sensing Referencing the battery positive connection through an input terminal that is used for the regulator reference voltage.

residual magnetism The small amount of magnetism left on the rotor after it has been initially magnetized by the coil windings' magnetic field.

self-exciting alternator An alternator that relies on the residual magnetism found in the rotor after operating as a way to switch on the voltage regulator and supply current to the rotor.

sensing The voltage reference point the alternator uses for regulation of the output.

transient voltage suppression (TVS) diodes Specialized diodes in the rectifier bridge that become resistive rather than conductive at a specific voltage level.

wye windings Stator windings in which one end of each phase winding is taken to a central point where the ends are connected together.

Review Questions

1. Which of the following are functions of the battery?
   a. It stores an electrical charge in chemical form.
   b. It acts as an electrical dampening device for variations in voltage or voltage spikes.
   c. It provides the electrical energy for cranking the engine.
   d. All of the choices are correct.
2. Which of the following are correct concerning alternator principles?
   a. The alternator converts mechanical energy into electrical energy by electromagnetic induction.
   b. In a simplified version, a bar magnet rotates in an iron yoke, which concentrates the magnetic field.
   c. A coil of wire is wound around each end of the yoke; as the magnet turns, voltage is induced in the coil, producing a current flow.
   d. All of the choices are correct.
3. Which of the following is NOT an alternator classification?
   a. Externally air cooled
   b. Water cooled
   c. Sealed
   d. None of the above
4. Between ________and________ pole pieces or "claws" are found in the rotor of equipment alternators.
   a. 4; 8
   b. 8; 12
   c. 12; 16
   d. 18; 22
5. Which of the following is correct concerning phase winding connections?
   a. As the name suggests, Wye windings resemble the letter "Y."
   b. The advantage of Wye windings is that they produce higher voltage at comparably lower rotor speeds.
   c. This advantage means the alternator can begin charging a battery at lower engine speeds.
   d. All of the choices are correct.
6. Which of the following is correct concerning rectifier diode problems?
   a. Heat can cause premature failures of diodes.
   b. Additional cooling of rectifier bridges can be accomplished with heavier diodes and heat sinks or by connecting diodes in parallel so that six rather than three pairs accomplish the work.
   c. Both a and b
   d. Neither a nor b
7. Which of the following is correct concerning smoothing capacitors?
   a. Capacitors can be used to smooth alternator AC ripple and prevent EMI.
   b. In the alternator, one is connected across the output to act like an electric shock absorber.
   c. When the output voltage increases slightly, the capacitor will charge and absorb the new increase.
   d. All of the choices are correct.
8. Which of the following charging system set points is optimal for a 12-volt system?
   a. 12.6 to 12.9 volts
   b. 13.0 to 13.4 volts
   c. 13.5 to 14.6 volts
   d. 14.1 to 15.1 volts
9. Which of the following features does a remote sensing alternator use?
   a. An external voltage regulator
   b. A voltage regulator with an "R" terminal connected to the stator winding
   c. A direct connection between the battery and the voltage regulator
   d. A dash-mounted voltage regulator to indicate charging system output
10. Vents within the frames provide for a __________ amount of airflow to assist in dissipating heat.
    a. large
    b. steady
    c. small
    d. barely perceptible

ASE Technician A/Technician B Style Questions

1. Technician A says that today, the average 12-volt electrical system loads for a late-model machine add up to as much as 150 amps at peak load. Technician B says that both DC

generators and alternators produce electricity by relative movement of conductors in a magnetic field. Who is correct?

a. Technician A
b. Technician B
c. Both Technician A and Technician B
d. Neither Technician A nor Technician B

2. Technician A says that alternators have more moving parts than generators. Technician B says that alternators can produce power at engine idle speeds; generators cannot. Who is correct?
   a. Technician A
   b. Technician B
   c. Both Technician A and Technician B
   d. Neither Technician A nor Technician B
3. Technician A says that the two most important parts in an alternator used to produce electrical current are the rotor and stator winding. Technician B says that the rotor contains a spinning electromagnet that induces current flow in the stator winding, which is made up of numerous coils of wire. Who is correct?
   a. Technician A
   b. Technician B
   c. Both Technician A and Technician B
   d. Neither Technician A nor Technician B
4. Technician A says that the rotor is a rotating electromagnet field that cuts the wire coils within the stator to induce the flow of electrical current in the stator. Technician B says that the direct-gear drive mechanism is used in most cases but that a pulley drive may also be employed. Who is correct?
   a. Technician A
   b. Technician B
   c. Both Technician A and Technician B
   d. Neither Technician A nor Technician B
5. Technician A says that regulated current to the alternator rotor is supplied through a pair of graphite brushes sliding against slip rings on the rotor shaft. Technician B says that heavy-duty springs help the brushes maintain contact with the slip rings. Who is correct?
   a. Technician A
   b. Technician B
   c. Both Technician A and Technician B
   d. Neither Technician A nor Technician B
6. Technician A says that machines fitted with self-exciting alternators may require the engine rpm to be briefly increased after every start-up to initiate charging. Technician B says that using self-exciting alternators eliminates the need for a separate circuit from the key switch to the alternator and simplifies chassis wiring. Who is correct?
   a. Technician A
   b. Technician B
   c. Both Technician A and Technician B
   d. Neither Technician A nor Technician B
7. Technician A says that the stator is mounted between two end housings, and it holds the stator windings stationary so that the rotating magnetic field cuts through the stator windings, inducing an electric current in the windings. Technician B says that to smooth the pulsating current flow, there are three distinct layers of windings offset 60 degrees in each layer from one another. Who is correct?
   a. Technician A
   b. Technician B
   c. Both Technician A and Technician B
   d. Neither Technician A nor Technician B
8. Technician A says that stators are normally serviced in a repair facility. Technician B says that stators can be visually checked during rebuilding for burned, cut, or nicked winding laminations. Who is correct?
   a. Technician A
   b. Technician B
   c. Both Technician A and Technician B
   d. Neither Technician A nor Technician B
9. Technician A says that alternators produce alternating current, which can be used to operate many onboard electrical devices. Technician B says that converting the AC current to usable DC current is referred to as modulation. Who is correct?
   a. Technician A
   b. Technician B
   c. Both Technician A and Technician B
   d. Neither Technician A nor Technician B
10. Technician A says that voltage regulators are first classified as either external or internal. Technician B says that the majority of late-model alternators have external regulators. Who is correct?
    a. Technician A
    b. Technician B
    c. Both Technician A and Technician B
    d. Neither Technician A nor Technician B

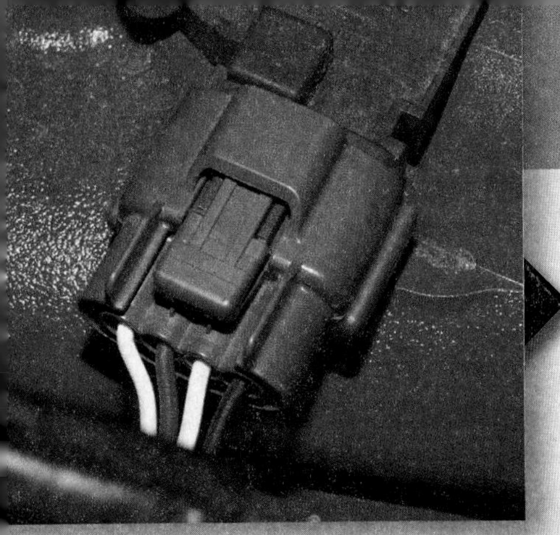

CHAPTER 16

Electrical Sensors, Sending Units, and Alarm Systems

Knowledge Objectives

After reading this chapter, you will be able to:

- **K16001** Identify and describe the functions, construction, and application of electronic sensors used to produce electrical signals for machine electronic control systems.
- **K16002** Identify and describe the operating strategies of electronic signal processing systems used in electrical system control on mobile heavy equipment.
- **K16003** Recommend and describe diagnostic procedures for sensors used in electronic control systems.

Skills Objectives

After reading this chapter, you will be able to:

- **S16001** Perform diagnostic procedures to evaluate the condition and operation of machine sensors, sending units, and warning systems.
- **S16002** Select and use the appropriate test instruments for evaluating the operation of sensors, sending units, and alarm systems.

▶ Introduction

Devices that convert one form of energy into another are called transducers. Sensors are a type of transducer that convert physical conditions or states into electrical data. Pressure, temperature, angle, speed, mass, etc. are just a few of the changing physical variables about which sensors supply electrical data to processors. A distinction is made between sending units and sensors. Sensors provide information to electronic control units, whereas sending units provide information to instrument gauges.

▶ Types of Sensors

K16001

An enormous number of sensor types exist to measure diverse types of data required by increasingly sophisticated machine management systems:

- accelerometers for machine dynamic control
- pressure sensors for engine oil, fuel, crankcase, and intake boost
- position sensors for machine speed, camshafts, crankshafts, and pedal position
- humidity sensors for adjusting air–fuel ratio control and cabin comfort control
- sunlight and rain/moisture sensors
- distance sensors for near obstacle detection and collision avoidance
- magnetoresistive (MR) sensors that use the earth's magnetic field to operate machine electronic compasses and navigation systems
- torque sensors
- fuel level sensors
- oil quality sensors
- temperature sensors
- coolant level sensors
- barometric pressure sensors
- mass airflow sensors
- engine knock sensors
- exhaust gas—NOx, ammonia, and oxygen sensors
- yaw sensors using the Coriolis effect to sense yaw rates
- global positioning sensors for GPS.

Active Versus Passive Sensors

All the types of sensors listed above are more simply classified other ways. For example, a sensor is considered active or passive depending on whether they use power supplied by the electronic control module (ECM) to operate. **Active sensors** use a current supplied by the ECM to operate while **passive sensors** do not (**FIGURE 16-1**).

Other classifications of sensors include the following:

- resistive sensors: rheostats, potentiometers, thermistors, piezoresistive sensors, and Wheatstone bridge pressure sensors
- voltage generators: oxygen sensors, NOx sensors, ammonia sensors, variable reluctance sensors, and piezoelectric sensors
- switches
- variable capacitance pressure sensors.

FIGURE 16-1 This opened pressure sensor is an active sensor. Note the integrated circuit used to change the sensed physical data into an electrical signal used by the ECM.

You Are the Mobile Heavy Equipment Technician

A customer has brought a wheel loader to your shop, complaining that the engine will occasionally not accelerate. Sometimes, after the throttle pedal is pushed multiple times, the engine will only idle. Other times the engine drops to idle while the machine is moving. Sometimes the problem corrects itself after the ignition key is cycled; other times the throttle starts operating correctly on its own. After checking for fault codes, you learn the machine has had codes erased by another technician. You suspect the problem is in the accelerator position sensor (APS), but you wonder if the problem could be in the wiring or the fuel system, or if it's a power derate condition caused by some other fault. After carefully inspecting the wiring harness and connectors to the APS, you believe they are in good condition. You connect a software-based diagnostic program to the machine data link to monitor the APS. There are three APS signals displayed with different voltages on each sensor. Consider the following questions as you proceed:

1. Does this APS use an idle validation switch?
2. What complaint would the operator have if one, two, or three of the APS voltages were incorrect?
3. How will you determine if the APS has a fault?

Reference Voltage

Reference voltage (Vref) refers to a precisely regulated voltage supplied by the ECM to sensors. Reference voltage value is typically 5 volts direct current (VDC), but some manufacturers use 8 or 12 volts. The use of a reference voltage is important in processor operation, because the value of the variable resistor can be calculated by measuring voltage drop when another resistor with a known voltage input is connected in series with it. In **FIGURE 16-2**, 5 Vref is used in the calculations performed by an ECM.

Reference voltage also supplies active sensors with current to operate integrated circuits contained inside the sensor. Switches will also use +5 Vref to signal the ECM.

Switches as Sensors

Switches are the simplest sensors of all, because they have no resistance in the closed position and infinite resistance in the open position. Switches are categorized as sensors whenever they provide information to an electronic control system. The data may indicate a physical value such as open or closed, up or down, high or low (e.g., a coolant level sensor or oil pressure switch), or it may indicate on and off (e.g., a brake light switch).

Switches as Digital Signals

The simplest digital signal is a single pole, single throw (SPST) switch. It is found in either an open or closed state. The on/off, open/closed state data provided by this switch can provide input information to an ECM required for decision-making. For example, the decision to start an engine based on whether a transmission is in neutral or the clutch is disengaged depends on the signal from a switch (**FIGURE 16-3**). A zero-volt signal would present as an open switch, while 12 volts would present as a closed switch. Ignition, brake, or door switches provide similar data to ECMs to answer simple yes or no, open or closed, on or off questions posed by operating software.

Pull-Up and Pull-Down Switches

Switches are further categorized by their connection to a current source and the ECM. When the switch is connected between the ECM and a battery positive, the switch is known as a **pull-up switch** (**FIGURE 16-4**).

Reference voltage also supplies active sensors with current to operate integrated circuits contained inside the sensor. Switches will also use +5 Vref to signal the ECM.

A circuit inside the module that is monitoring the switch connection will measure the voltage drop across a fixed resistor inside the ECM. The voltage data will provide information to processing circuits, which will determine whether the circuit or switch is open, closed, out of range, or shorted to ground.

A **pull-down switch** is connected between the ECM and a negative ground current potential (**FIGURE 16-5**).

When the switch is closed, ground current will flow into the ECM. A circuit inside the ECM monitoring the switch connection will also measure voltage drop across a fixed resistor. Once again, voltage data will provide information to processing circuits, which will determine whether the circuit or switch is open, closed, out of range, or shorted to a positive current potential.

Resistive Sensors

Resistive sensors are a class of sensors that will condition or change a voltage signal applied to the sensor. Many types of

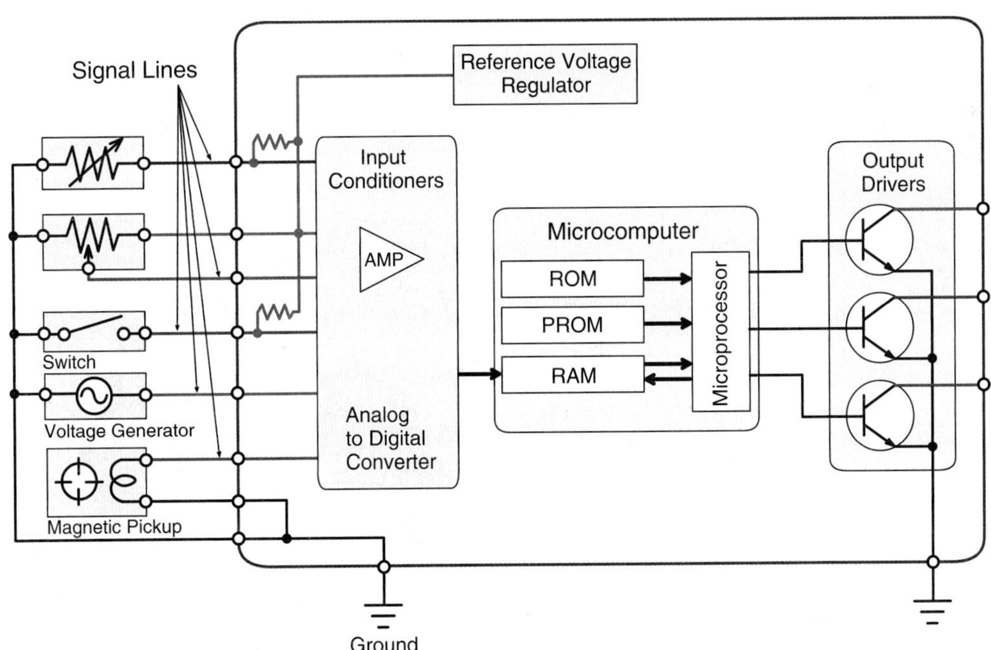

FIGURE 16-2 Reference voltage is supplied to power active sensors and to accurately calculate voltage drop across the sensor. The resistor in series with the reference voltage also limits current to the sensors.

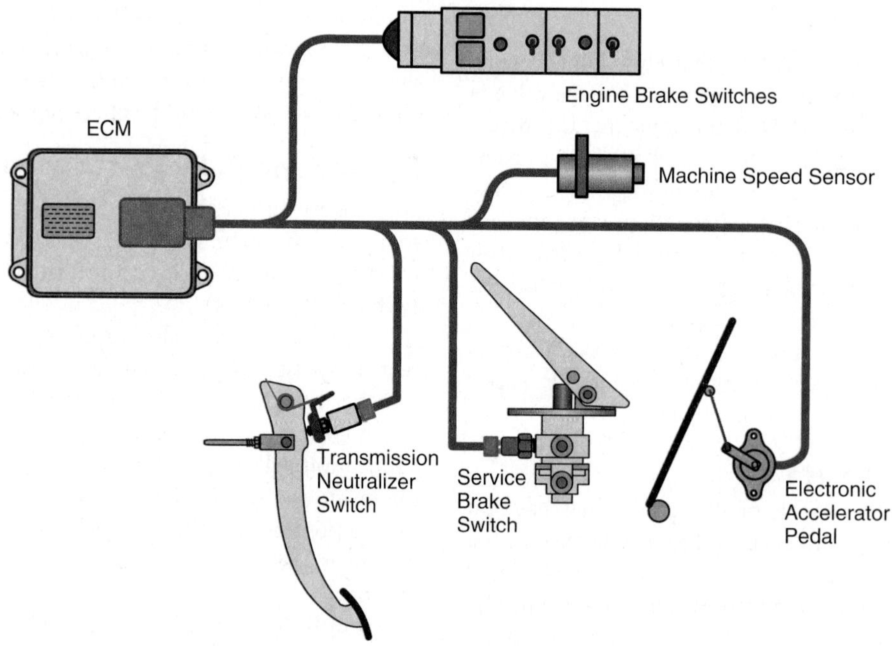

FIGURE 16-3 Examples of some basic switched inputs: clutch, brakes, power take-off, and proximity sensor switches.

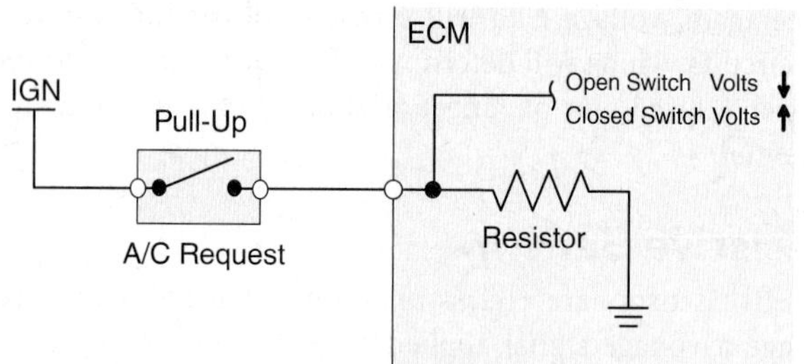

FIGURE 16-4 When a positive polarity is switched and supplied to the ECM, it is referred to as a pull-up switch.

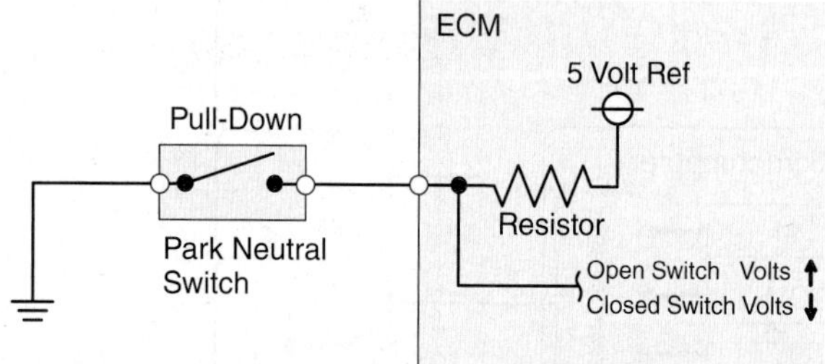

FIGURE 16-5 When a negative polarity is switched and supplied to the ECM, it is known as a pull-down switch.

resistive sensors exist, and pressure, temperature, and position sensors are the most common. Some of these sensors are three-wire active sensors.

Thermistors

A **thermistor** is a temperature-sensitive variable resistor commonly used to measure coolant, oil, fuel, and air temperatures. The name itself combines the words thermal and resistor. Thermistors are two-wire sensors that change resistance in proportion to temperature. This means thermistors provide analog data to processing circuits. When the sensor is measuring air temperature, such as in an intake manifold, the sensor is often constructed with a plastic body to minimize heat transfer from surrounding metal. When used to measure coolant or oil temperatures, the sensor element is enclosed in a brass case to make it more responsive to temperature change (**FIGURE 16-6**).

Thermistors are semiconductor devices with no moving parts. Two types of thermistors exist: negative temperature coefficient and positive temperature coefficient. In a negative temperature coefficient (NTC) thermistor, the resistance decreases as the temperature increases (**FIGURE 16-7**). In a

FIGURE 16-6 Three thermistor applications. **A.** For intake manifold temperature. **B.** For coolant temperature. **C.** For intake manifold temperature. Note the semiconductor material in the fast response, air-intake thermistor.

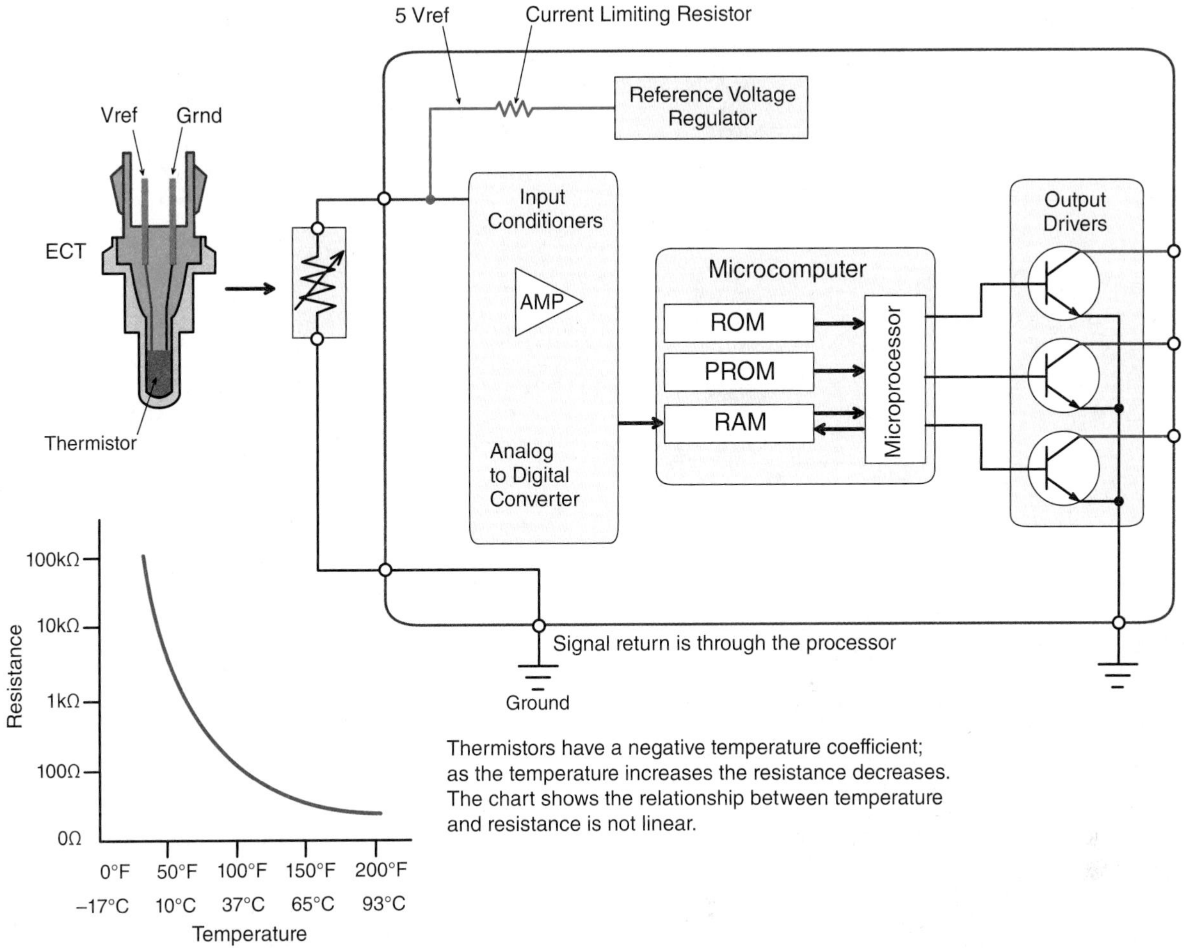

FIGURE 16-7 A thermistor circuit. Note the graph that illustrates the relationship between temperature and resistance.

FIGURE 16-8 Thermistors found in A. diesel particulate filters (DPFs) and B. selective catalyst reduction systems are often C. PTC thermistors. NTC thermistor material could not withstand the heat encountered when regenerating the DPF.

positive temperature coefficient (PTC) thermistor, the resistance increases as the temperature increases (**FIGURE 16-8**).

The most common type of thermistor is an NTC, in which the sensor's resistance goes down as the temperature goes up. So, when the sensor is cold, the sensor resistance is high and the ECM measures a lower return signal voltage in comparison to reference voltage. The voltage drop across the sensor is interpreted as a temperature value. Likewise, when the engine warms, the internal resistance of the sensor decreases and causes a proportional increase in the return signal voltage.

Rheostats

Rheostats are also two-wire variable resistance sensors. They are not commonly used as input devices to an ECM but are instead used to signal sending units such as for fuel level and oil pressure (**FIGURE 16-9** and **FIGURE 16-10**).

Rheostats use a variable sliding contact moving along a resistive wire. When current passes through the resistive wire, the sliding contact will conduct current flow from the wire. Current intensity at the sliding contact will vary depending on its position along the resistive wire.

Reference Voltage Sensors—Three-Wire Sensors

Three-wire sensors, regardless of how they appear or what function they perform, have a common wiring configuration: they all have ground, signal return, and positive voltage reference wire leads (**FIGURE 16-11**).

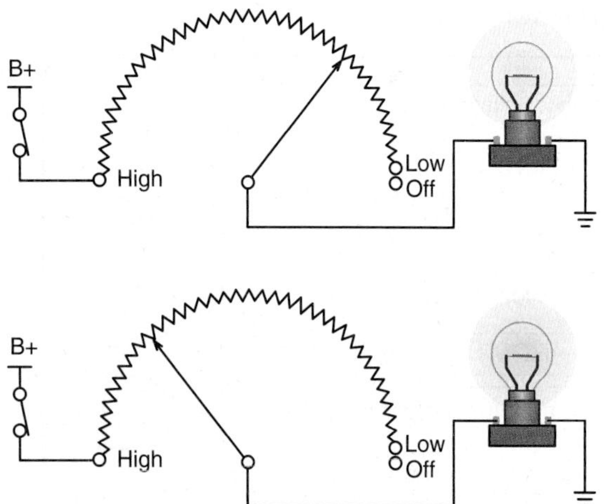

FIGURE 16-9 Operation of a rheostat controlling the intensity of a lightbulb.

FIGURE 16-10 A rheostat for a fuel level sending unit. The wiper-whiskers transfer current from one resistive track to another. Signal return is supplied by the wipers.

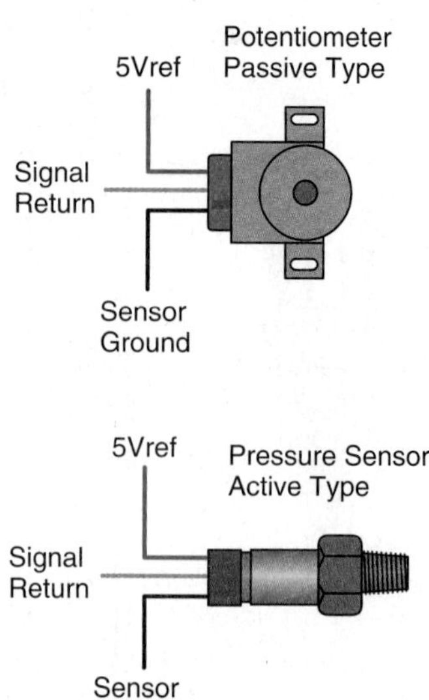

FIGURE 16-11 Three-wire reference voltage sensors have a ground, signal return, and positive voltage reference wire lead.

One wire provides reference voltage to the sensor. If it is an active sensor, reference voltage will supply current to operate an integrated chip inside the device. Reference voltage is also produced by the ECM as a comparison point for voltage calculations associated with sensor data.

The second sensor wire provides a negative ground signal through the ECM and not to engine ground. This ECM return or ground is also called zero-volt return (ZVR) and is identical to engine ground except that it is free of any type of electrical interference. Active sensors will use the ZVR or negative ground for the other source of current to operate the sensor. In resistive sensors, the ZVR acts as a reference point to measure voltage drop across the sensor.

The third wire is a signal return from the sensor. This circuit provides a positive voltage proportional to the physical value measured by the sensor. If pressure is the physical input measured, the signal wire data will carry an analog voltage signal proportional to pressure. Typically, low voltage of, for example, 0.8 volts will represent little to no pressure, while 3.9 volts will represent high pressure depending on the range of the sensor.

The advantage of using three-wire sensors is that they provide comprehensive diagnostic information about the sensor and its circuit operation. Sending units can be constructed with reduced complexity and expense and yet still provide the ECM with data to operate an engine, transmission, or other device. However, sending units lack the capability to self-monitor circuit operation. Consider an open or shorted to ground signal wire from a single-wire sensor. In this case, there is no means by which the ECM could accurately evaluate the situation. The wire could be broken or rubbed though, and still the unit voltage data received by the ECM would not be different from normal. It is very labor-intensive to find an electrical fault based on only an operational symptom—no fault codes or malfunction indicator lights are available to identify a circuit problem.

The ECM does have capabilities to monitor and diagnose two- and three-wire sensor circuits to an extent not possible with single-wire sensors. By monitoring the voltage range of the ground return path, signal voltage, and reference voltage, the ECM can determine whether the sensor and circuit are functioning correctly (**FIGURE 16-12**).

Sensor values can be compared with expected values to determine whether the data is rational. An explanation of how sensors and electronic circuits perform self-diagnostics and generate codes is covered in the Onboard Networks & Diagnostics Systems chapter.

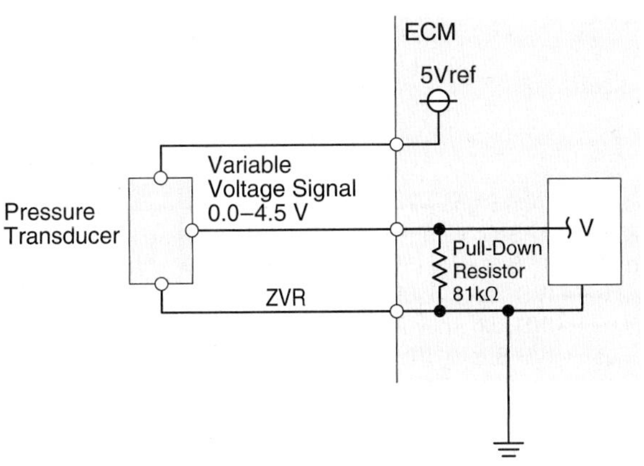

FIGURE 16-12 The ECM supplies the +5 Vref and ZVR ground. In this sensor, the ECM measures voltage between the + signal return and ZVR.

Potentiometers

Potentiometers are similar to rheostats in that they vary signal voltage depending on the position of a sliding contact or wiper moving across a resistive material. They are three-wire sensors with the signal wire connected to the internal wiper. Potentiometers supply analog data to processing circuits.

A common application of a potentiometer is a position sensor such as the throttle position sensor (TPS) (**FIGURE 16-13**).

This sensor is connected to a throttle pedal, lever, or dial and provides data regarding the operator's desired engine speed or power output by measuring pedal, lever, or dial angle or travel. The ECM will measure the voltage drop between the ground return circuit and the signal wire to calculate pedal, lever, or dial position. Voltage produced from the signal wire will be proportional to the pedal travel. This means that at idle or part throttle, the voltage at the signal wire will be low. Increasing pedal travel will produce increasing voltage to the signal wire as the sensor's internal wiper moves closer to the +5 Vref end of the resistive element. When the pedal returns to idle, the wiper will have less voltage because it is farther a way from the +5 Vref wire and because the current pathway is longer and therefore more resistive.

Idle Validation Switches and Throttle Position Sensors

A short circuit or incorrect data from the TPS, also called the accelerator position sensor (APS), can potentially cause the uncontrolled acceleration of an engine. For safety reasons, manufacturers will build an additional safety system to verify throttle position. One common throttle safety system is the **idle validation switch (IVS)**. This circuit uses two switches: at idle, one switch will be open and the other closed. Off idle, the switches change state, which means that the normally open switch closes and the normally closed switch opens (**FIGURE 16-14**).

This data is used by the ECM to verify that the operator has in fact moved the accelerator pedal and that the circuit is not malfunctioning. At idle, the state of the switch must correspond to the TPS voltage sensed by the ECM. If the expected position sensor voltage and IVS position do not match, the ECM will revert engine speed to idle or not allow the engine rpm to increase beyond idle speed.

Dual- and Multiple-Path Throttle Position Sensors

To improve the reliability of a TPS and validate accelerator position signals, some manufacturers are replacing the single

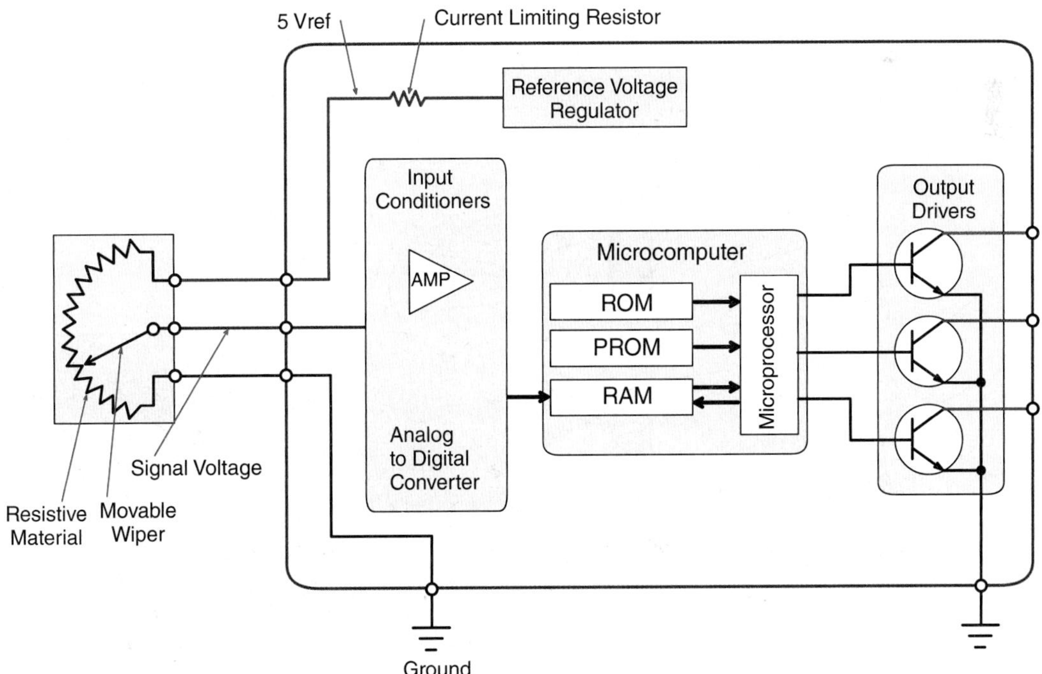

FIGURE 16-13 The TPS circuit commonly uses a potentiometer to measure throttle angle.

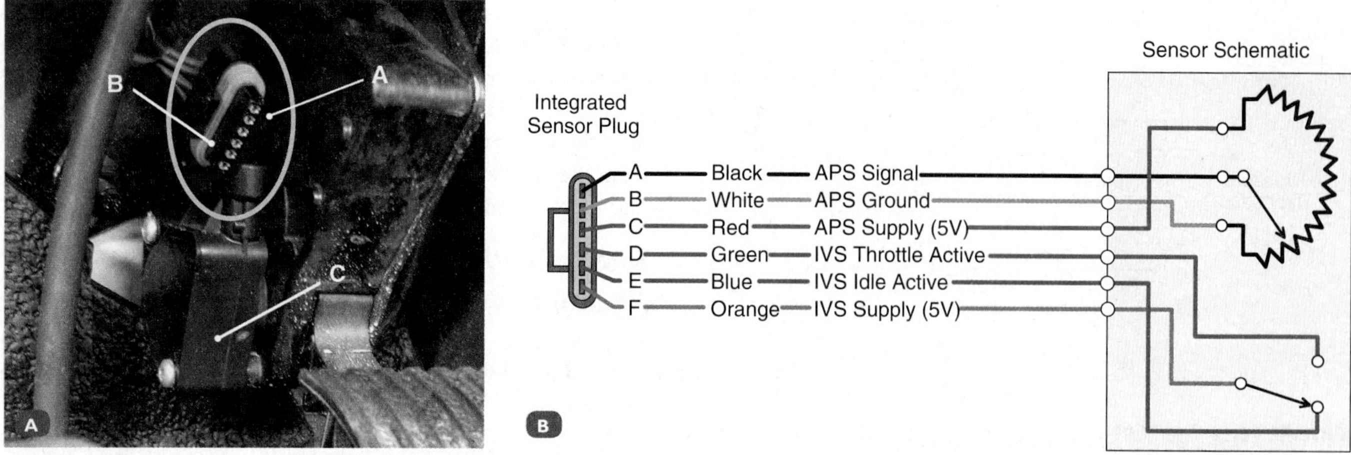

FIGURE 16-14 The IVS is usually integrated with the TPS. The IVS uses reference voltage and will switch the state of a normally open and a normally closed switch when moved off idle. **A.** Three sensor wires (A), three IVS wires (B), and the throttle position sensor (C). **B.** Color coding for integrated sensor plug.

TPS sensor track with a dual-track or even three-path TPS. The voltage of one sensor pathway is compared with another to verify that the sensor is operating within expected values (**FIGURE 16-15**).

If there is an unexpected difference between the voltage signals, the engine will only operate at idle speed. If one or even two of the resistive tracks wears out, the engine may still accelerate normally, but an APS fault is logged and the yellow fault warning indicator lamp will illuminate. Dual-path TPSs are potentiometers. Hall-effect TPSs are even more reliable because they have no moving parts. This TPS uses an alternating current (AC) magnetic field to induce current in a rotor moved by the throttle pedal. A circuit is used to convert the rotor's position into pedal position. This type of noncontact TPS sensor has no sliding friction parts to wear out (**FIGURE 16-16**).

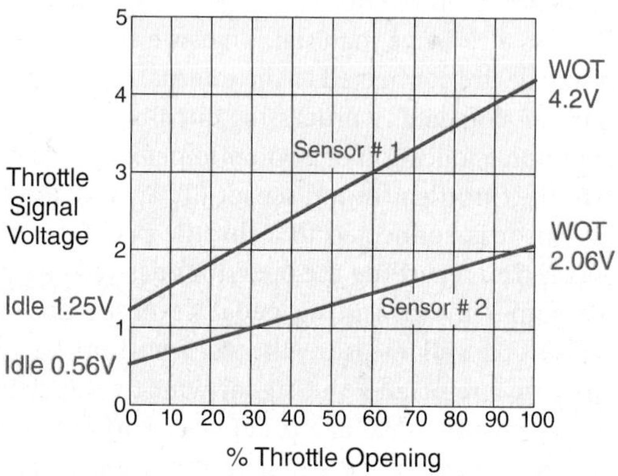

FIGURE 16-15 Voltages of accelerator position for the three-path sensor. Operating voltages are different for any given throttle angle. If one sensor fails, the other can supply a signal to operate the machine. If two signals fail, the machine will typically be only idle.

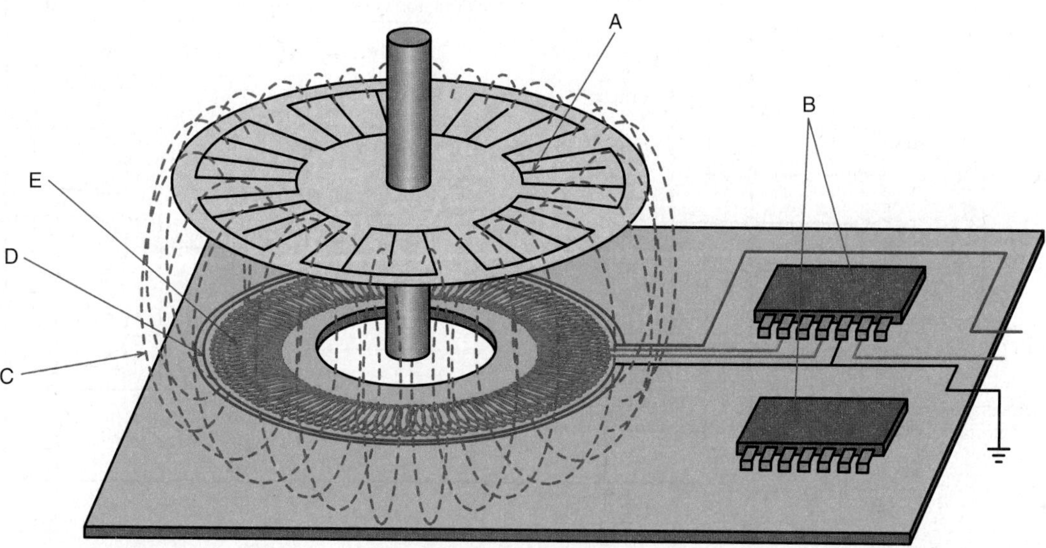

FIGURE 16-16 Hall-effect throttle position sensor (TPS). **A.** Conductive lamps in rotor. **B.** Integrated circuits, APP1 and APP2. **C.** Electromagnetic field lines of force. **D.** Stator excitation coils. **E.** Stator receiver coils.

Pressure Sensors

Pressure measurements, such as intake manifold boost, barometric pressure, and oil and fuel pressure, use two types of sensor technology: variable capacitance sensors and strain gauge resistive sensors. These are both active sensors that produce analog output signals.

Strain Gauges

A strain gauge measures small changes in the resistance of tiny wires caused by stretching or contraction. Construction of this type of pressure-sensing device uses resistive wires, called strain gauge wires, embedded in a flexible glass block. Behind the block may be a vacuum chamber to provide a reference point of zero for measurement of absolute pressure. If the device measures gauge pressure, the chamber will have atmospheric pressure as the reference value of zero.

When the glass plate flexes under pressure, the small resistive wires in it will change dimensions slightly. As the plate distorts due to pressure changes, it changes the resistance of the wires slightly (**FIGURE 16-17**).

A Wheatstone bridge electrical circuit, which measures changes in resistance of an unknown variable resistor, is used to measure this small change in resistance of the strain gauge wires (**FIGURE 16-18**).

By measuring this small change in the wires' resistance, the pressure applied to the plate is determined.

Piezoresistive Sensors

Piezoresistive sensors rely on the ability of certain mineral crystals to produce voltage or change resistance when compressed (**FIGURE 16-19**).

Rather than using a strain gauge wire construction, these sensors have a piezoresistive crystal arranged with a Wheatstone bridge to measure the change in resistance of the piezo crystal. These sensors produce analog electrical signals.

The advantage of these sensors is their ability to measure very high pressures. Because of the sturdiness of the crystal, piezo sensors are better adapted to measuring vibration and dynamic or continuous pressure changes. Knock sensors measuring abnormal combustion signals are a common application of piezoresistive

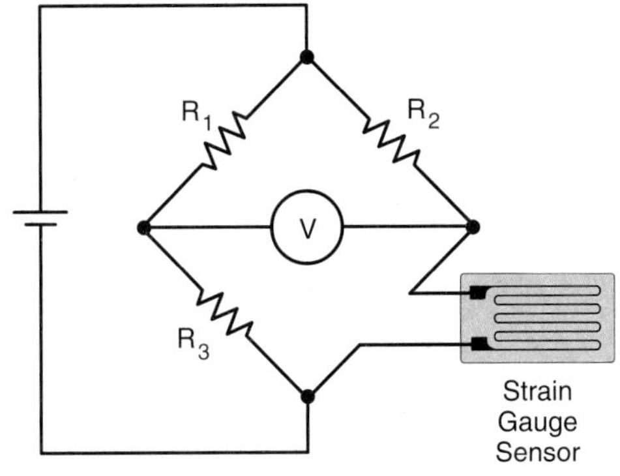

FIGURE 16-17 A strain gauge senses pressure via a wire embedded in glass or metal film that changes resistance as it is stretched under pressure.

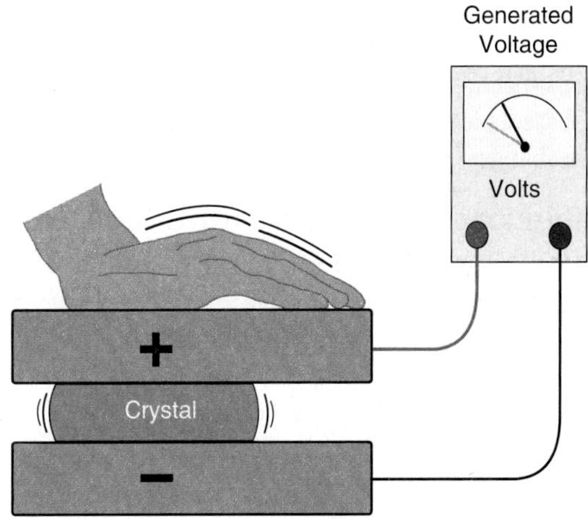

FIGURE 16-19 The piezoresistive principle.

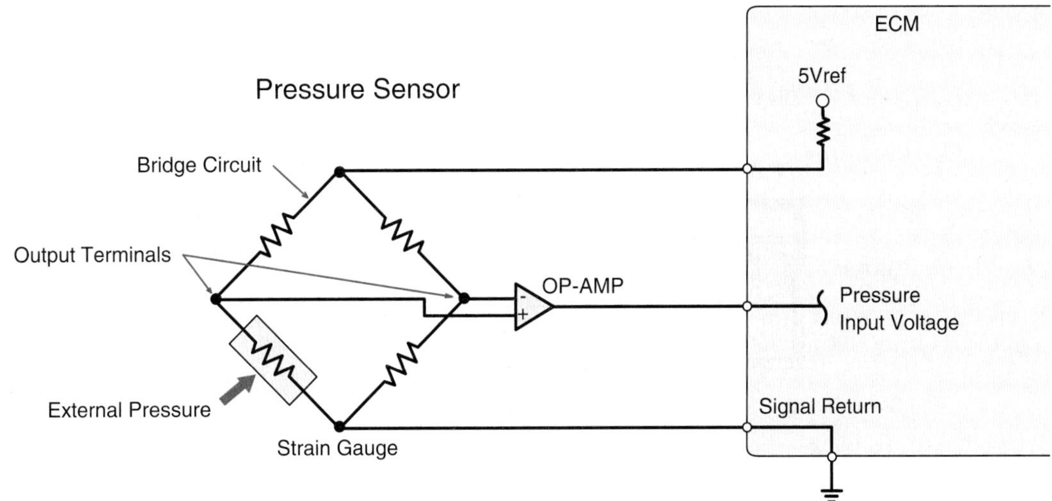

FIGURE 16-18 A Wheatstone bridge calculates the value of an unknown resistor using several other resistors of known fixed value.

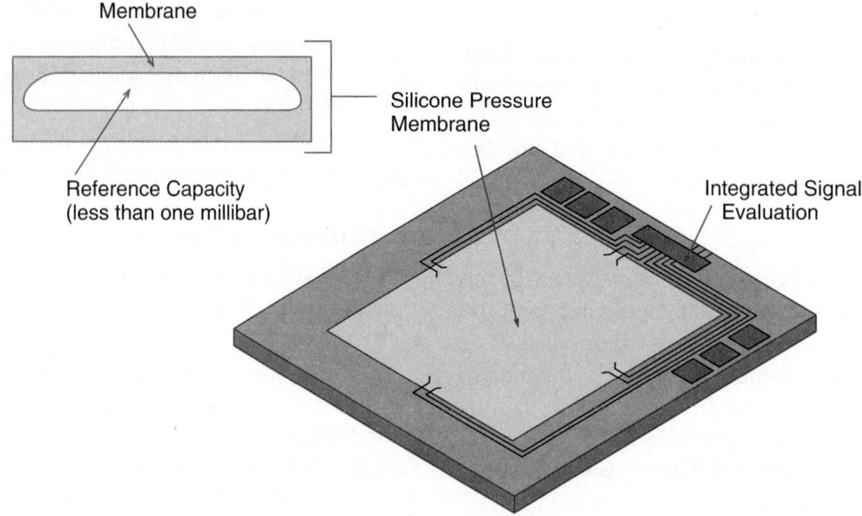

FIGURE 16-20 Construction of a silicon-based piezoresistive sensor. The silicone-ceramic material generates a voltage under pressure that is converted to an analog signal.

sensors. Another type of piezoresistive sensor uses mineral crystals arranged on a substrate of silicon (**FIGURE 16-20**).

The crystals behave as a semiconductor to produce electrical signals that are amplified and conditioned by internal circuits. Silicon-based piezoresistive sensors are very sensitive to slight pressure changes.

Variable Capacitance Pressure Sensor

A **variable capacitance pressure sensor** is an active sensor that measures both dynamic and static pressure. Though they are more expensive to manufacturer than a piezoresistive or strain gauge sensor is, the variable capacitance pressure sensor offers a greater range of measurement flexibility and more accurate readings. Because it is an active sensor, the stronger circuit signals to the ECM are not as vulnerable to voltage drop or electromagnetic interference.

Variable capacitance sensors use the distance between two plates, or dielectric strength, inside the sensor to measure pressure (**FIGURE 16-21**).

One plate diaphragm will move in response to intake manifold, oil, fuel, or some other physical pressure being measured. The other plate is fixed and has on one side a reference vacuum or pressure chamber to calibrate it for accurate pressure readings. As pressure increases or decreases, the distance between the two plates will change. An electrical charge is applied to the fixed plate, and the time it takes to charge the plate is measured. Charging time will change proportionally to the dielectric strength between the plates. An electronic circuit in the chip integrated inside the sensor measures the changing voltage/time value produced by the flexing plate and outputs an analog electrical signal of less than 5 volts.

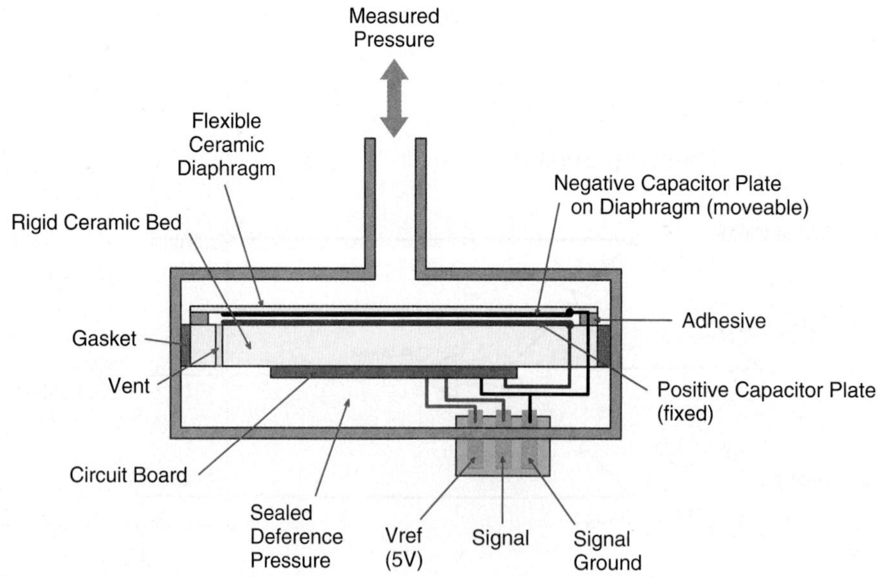

FIGURE 16-21 Cross section of a variable capacitance sensor.

Voltage Generators

This category of sensors is passive and produces an analog signal of varying voltage or AC frequency. Variable reluctance and galvanic sensors are two examples of voltage-generating sensors. While the gas sensors used on today's diesel engines are active sensors with modules that produce and condition signals, the operating principle is still a galvanic reaction that produces voltage. Exhaust stream gas sensors are used to measure oxygen, NOx, or ammonia gases in the exhaust stream. On diesel engines, data from oxygen sensors is commonly used to adjust exhaust gas recirculation (EGR) rates and sometimes to adjust the intake throttle plate position to control the operation of exhaust after treatment systems. Ammonia and NOx sensors are used to identify faults in the exhaust after treatment systems on most diesels from 2010 and later. Ammonia sensors are more frequently used on diesel engines from 2015 and later.

Variable Reluctance Sensors

Variable reluctance sensors are two-wire sensors used to measure rotational speed. Wheel speed, machine speed, engine speed, and camshaft and crankshaft position sensors are their most common applications (**FIGURE 16-22**).

Signals from the camshaft and crankshaft position sensors are used to calculate engine position for determining the beginning of engine firing order and injection timing. The camshaft gear has raised lugs that generate waveform signals to identify top dead center (TDC) for each cylinder. When graphed against time, the AC waveform produced by the sensor data is used to precisely calculate not only engine speed but also degrees of crankshaft rotation (**FIGURE 16-23**).

The ability of a material to conduct or resist magnetic lines of force is known as reluctance. Variable reluctance sensors use changing sensor reluctance to induce current flow by changing

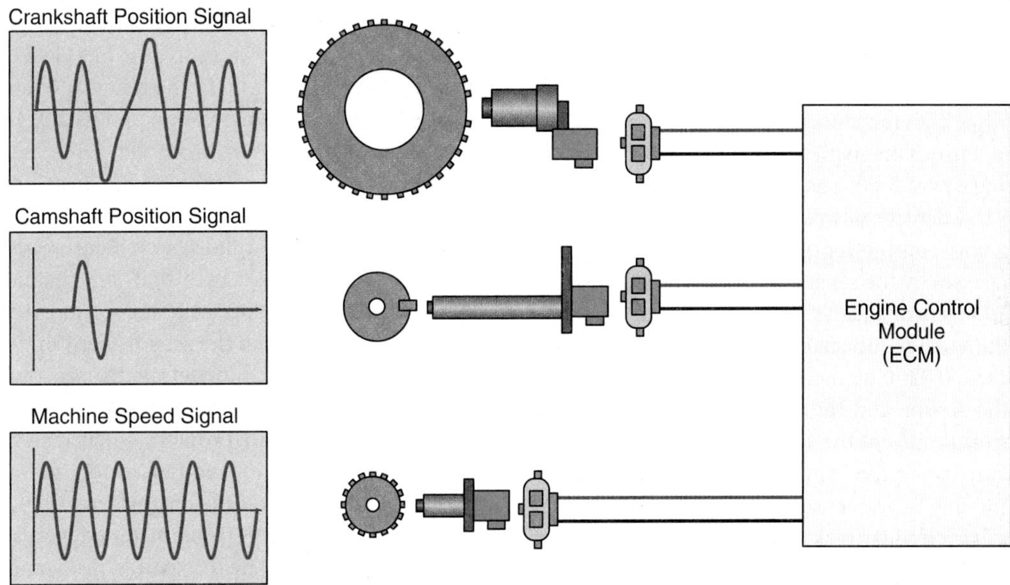

FIGURE 16-22 Common applications of variable reluctance sensors.

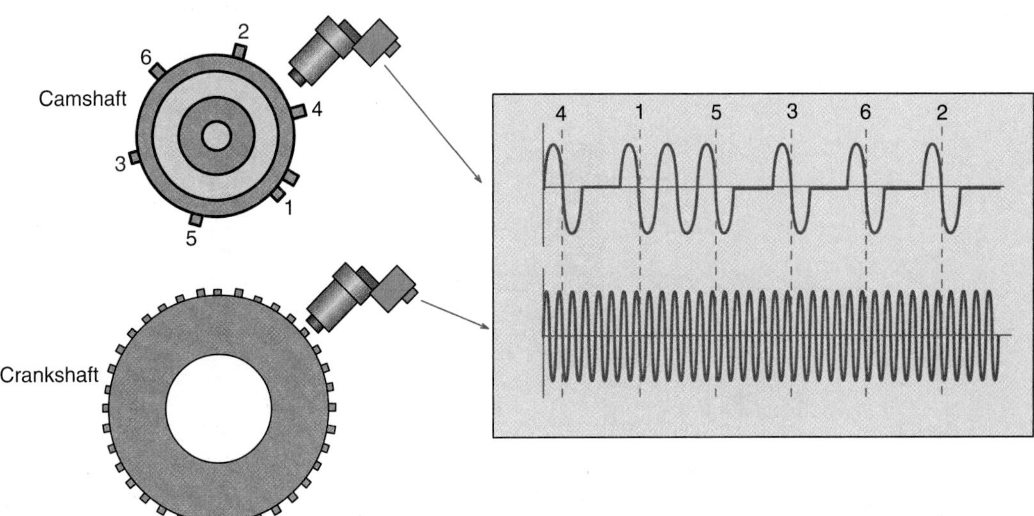

FIGURE 16-23 The tooth geometry of the crankshaft and camshaft sensors generates unique waveforms that identify cylinder-firing position and crank position.

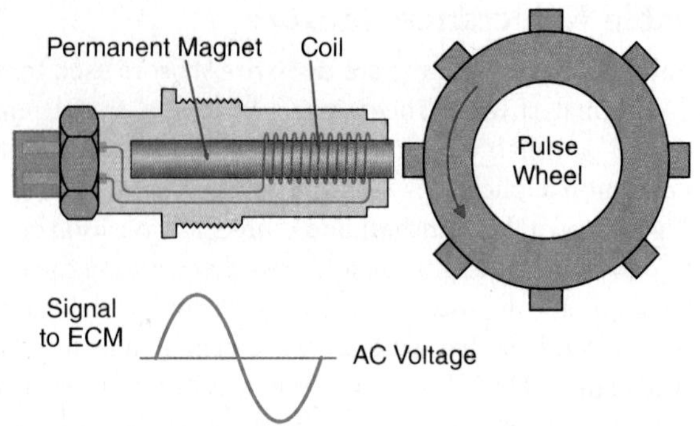

FIGURE 16-24 The reluctor ring helps the variable reluctance sensor generate an AC voltage signal.

magnetic-field strengths inside the sensor. A variable reluctance sensor is constructed with two main elements: a coil of narrow-gauge wire wrapped many times around a permanent magnet, and a reluctor ring (also called the sensor wheel, pulse wheel, or tone wheel), which has soft iron teeth and rotates on a shaft (**FIGURE 16-24**).

Because ferrous metals, particularly soft iron, have low reluctance and air has high reluctance to magnetic lines of force, the strength of the sensor's magnetic field expands and collapses as the reluctor ring's iron teeth pass across the sensor's magnet. By changing the density of magnetic lines of force, alternately expanding and contracting the magnetic field when a gear tooth or gap passes by the sensor, current is induced in the wire coil around the sensor magnet. Increasing reluctor wheel speed increases the voltage induced in the sensor. A small air gap of approximately 0.02–0.03 inch (0.51–0.76 mm) is maintained between the sensor and the reluctor wheel. Too much or too little air gap will prevent the sensor from detecting tooth movement. Software inside the ECM will detect and count the number of teeth passing by the sensor to calculate shaft speed.

If the processing circuits track how many teeth complete one rotation of the shaft, rpm is easily calculated. If the engine software can divide the number of teeth passing by the sensor per unit of time, it can precisely calculate the number of degrees of crankshaft rotation.

Hall-Effect Sensors

Like variable reluctance sensors, **Hall-effect sensors** are commonly used to measure the rotational speed of a shaft. Though they are more complex and expensive to manufacture than variable reluctance sensors are, Hall-effect sensors have the advantage of producing a digital signal square waveform and have strong signal strength at low shaft rotational speeds. This is especially useful when cranking an engine when engine rpm is slow. The durability and accuracy of the digital signal is preferred when more precise injection event timing is necessary, which is why most engines today use Hall-effect sensors.

The operation principle of a Hall-effect sensor is simple: Current flow through a Hall-effect material is made from semiconductive material that changes resistance in the presence of a magnetic field (**FIGURE 16-25**).

When current is applied to a Hall-effect material, no conduction occurs. However, in the presence of a magnetic field, the material will conduct current. The electrical signal output from the sensor material is analog, but circuits within the sensor will convert and amplify the rising and falling voltage into a square-shaped electrical waveform (**FIGURE 16-26**).

To produce the signal from the Hall-effect sensor, two configurations are used. The most common arrangement is the use of a metal interrupter ring or shutter and a permanent magnet positioned across from the sensor. Because ferrous metals have a lower magnetic reluctance than air, magnetic lines of force from a magnet placed opposite the sensor will flow through the metal shield rather than the sensor. Gaps in the interrupter ring will allow magnetism to penetrate the sensor, changing current flow through the Hall-effect material. Attaching the interrupter ring to a moving shaft provides rotational speed information to the control module. Another configuration for the Hall-effect sensor incorporates the magnet into the sensor itself. When a gear tooth or other ferrous metal trigger is present near the sensor, the magnetic field expands. Movement of the ferrous trigger or tooth away from the magnet causes magnetic-field contraction. This pulsing magnetic field generates the signal within the sensor (**FIGURE 16-27**).

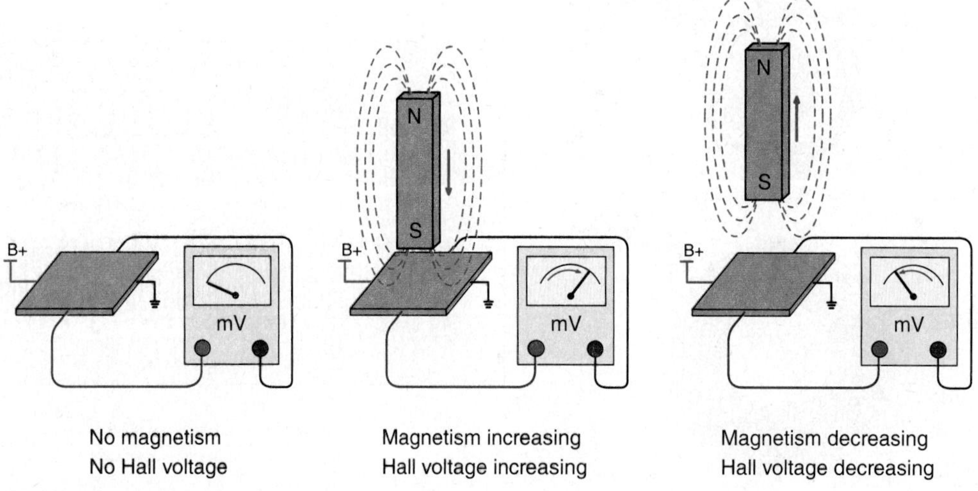

FIGURE 16-25 Hall-effect material is semiconductive and its ability to conduct electrical current changes in the presence of a magnetic field.

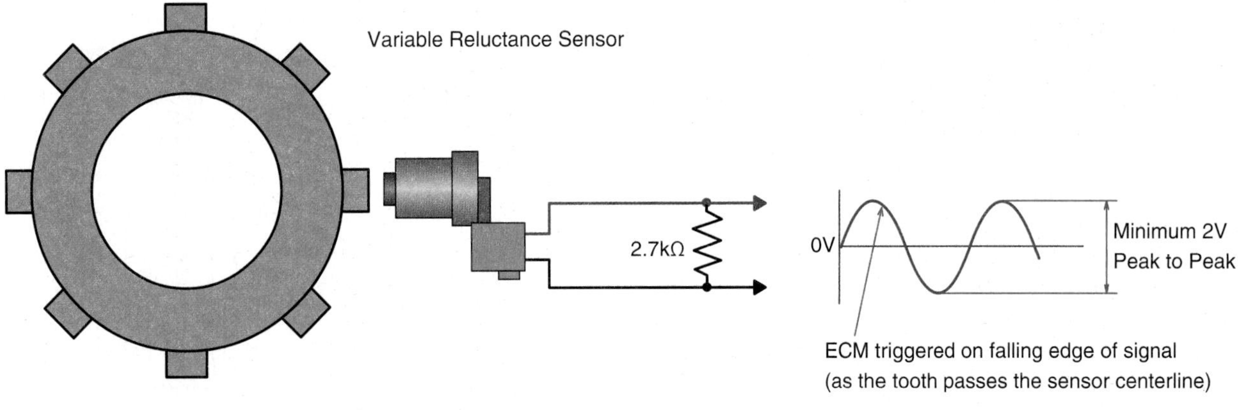

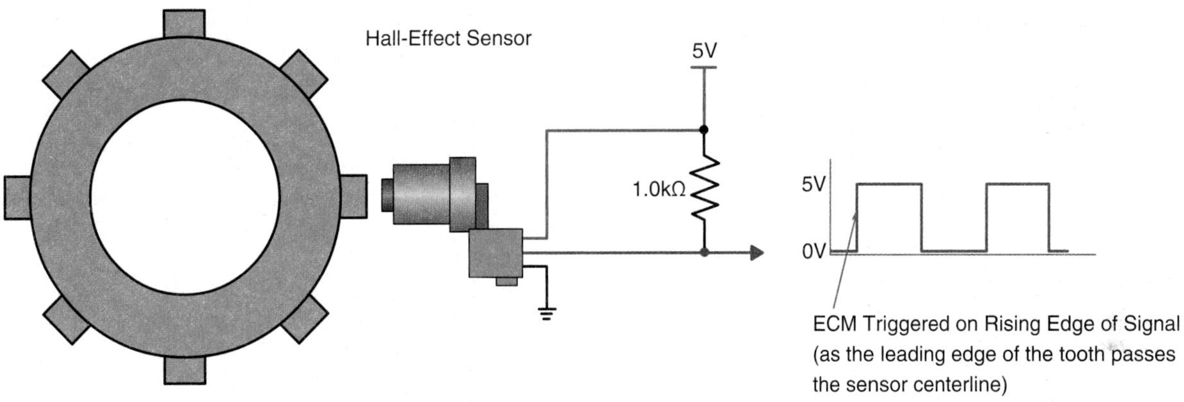

FIGURE 16-26 Comparing the signals of a Hall-effect sensor and variable reluctance sensor.

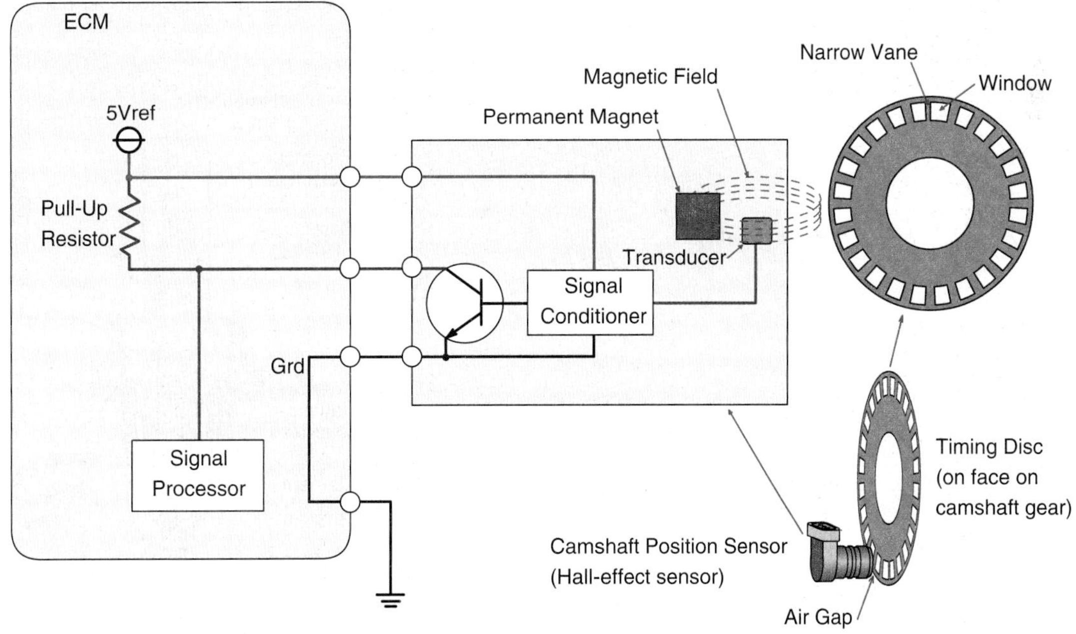

FIGURE 16-27 Operation of a camshaft position Hall-effect sensor using an internal permanent magnet.

Oxygen Sensors

Oxygen sensors are used to measure air–fuel ratio in order to calibrate EGR flow rates and air–fuel ratios for exhaust after treatment devices. Diesel engines use a heated planar, wide-band, zirconium-dioxide (ZrO_2) dual-cell oxygen sensor. This sensor technology is different from the narrow-band oxygen sensor technology used commonly on gasoline engines operating at stoichiometric air–fuel ratios. Wide-band oxygen sensors are used in diesel engines because they use lean-burn combustion systems, which normally leave an excess of air in the exhaust. Rather than producing a sharply falling and rising voltage near 0.5 volts, with 2% exhaust oxygen content found in gasoline engines, wide-band sensors produce a voltage proportional to a widely varying oxygen level (**FIGURE 16-28**).

The type of ceramic sensing element commonly used by wide-band sensors is a platinum-coated oxide of zirconium (ZrO_2). An important property of this ceramic is that it conducts oxygen ions when voltage is applied at high temperatures.

Diesel oxygen sensors are **wide-range planar sensors**, which means the sensing element is flat rather than thimble-shaped—that is, thimble-shaped like the sensors used on older gasoline-fueled engines (**FIGURE 16-29**).

They are also wide-band sensors, which means they generate a signal with a wide air–fuel ratio between 0.7:1 and infinity. When heated to over 1,200°F (700°C), the sensor becomes electrically conductive to oxygen ions. Because the oxygen content in the exhaust sample chamber is less than the oxygen concentration in the atmosphere, the oxygen content absorbed by the platinum coating on the ZrO_2 ceramic that contacts the exhaust and the coating that contacts the air will be slightly different (**FIGURE 16-30**).

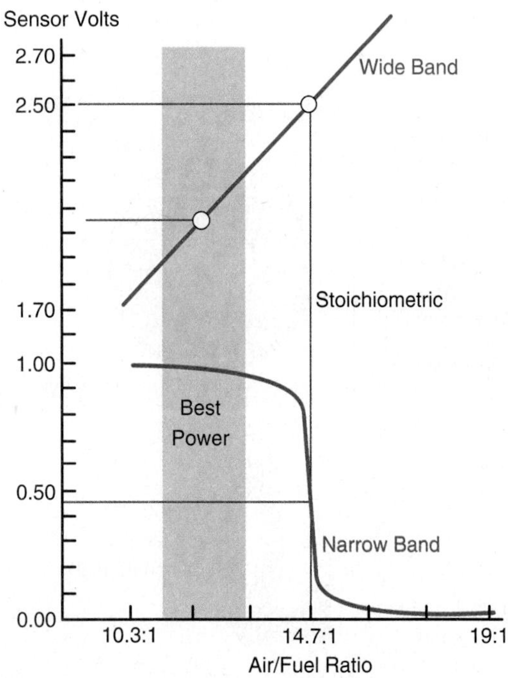

FIGURE 16-28 The voltage signal produced by a wide-band oxygen sensor. Note that unlike gasoline engine O_2 sensors, the current flow continues to increase past the stoichiometric ratio.

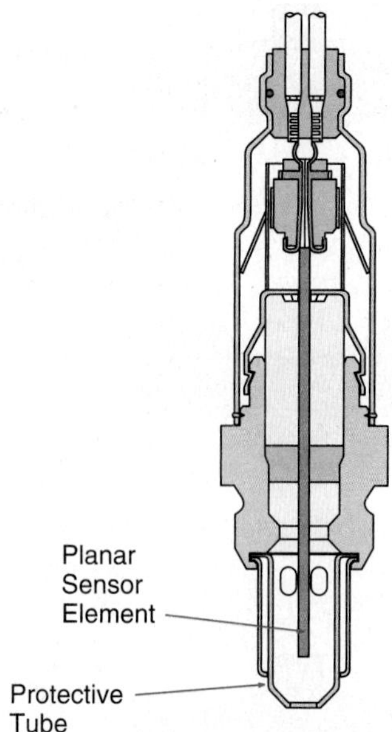

FIGURE 16-29 A cross section of a wide-range planar oxygen sensor.

This chemical difference in the sensor ceramic generates a voltage proportional to the oxygen content in the exhaust stream. The greater the difference in oxygen content, the higher the voltage. This voltage is produced because of the galvanic effect in which dissimilar metals in the presence of an electrolyte will produce electric current. Using the voltage produced across the two coatings, an amplifier circuit, called an oxygen pump cell circuit, will transfer excess electrons from the coating in the exhaust gas chamber to an electron-depleted electrode in the atmospheric reference chamber. The amount of current

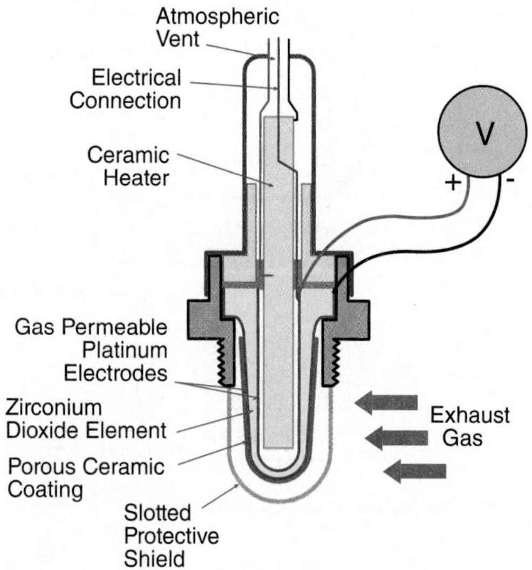

FIGURE 16-30 Voltage is generated when the oxygen composition of the platinum coatings on ZrO_2 is different due to a change in the relative oxygen content of the coatings.

used to transfer these electrons is proportional to air–fuel ratio, and a circuit will precisely calculate air–fuel ratios based on the amount of current required to balance the voltage differential.

NOx Sensors

NOx sensors are used to evaluate the operation of selective catalyst reduction (SCR) systems. These sensors measure NOx from the engine and NOx from the tailpipe, and they should verify a dramatic drop in NOx emissions. NOx sensors are constructed and operate similarly to wide-range planar oxygen sensors using ZrO_2 ceramic substrate, except different concentrations of alloys are used in the NOx sensor's platinum sensor walls. Also, NOx sensors include a chamber that first removes excess oxygen, then separates NOx into nitrogen and oxygen, and then pumps the resulting oxygen through the chamber walls. The two-chamber shape and the multilayered platinum element enable these sensors to differentiate with high precision oxygen ions originating from nitric oxide (NO) from among the oxygen ions present in the exhaust gas.

The NOx sensor's ZrO_2 chamber, which is the size of a thumbnail, is heated to 1,200°F (700°C). It is housed in a metal can that has a hole for exhaust gas entrance. The chamber walls break apart the NO into nitrogen and oxygen components. The amount of oxygen produced at this stage is proportional to the amount of NO. ZrO_2 ceramic substrate will pump oxygen through the wall when a current is placed on both sides of the chamber wall. As oxygen is pumped from the first chamber, the amount of oxygen can be measured as it passes through the wall of the second chamber because it generates a voltage proportional to its concentration. Because the oxygen ions originated only from NOx, an accurate measure is derived for NOx in the exhaust gas. A module connected to the sensor conditions the electrical signal to represent a value for the amount of NOx sensed in the exhaust stream (**FIGURE 16-31**).

Ammonia Sensors

A NOx SCR system used on late-model diesel engines involves injecting urea, a colorless and odorless liquid, into the exhaust stream. Once exposed to exhaust heat, the urea quickly breaks down to form ammonia, which reacts with NOx and renders it into harmless nitrogen, water, and oxygen molecules. However, ammonia is a noxious substance and should not escape into the atmosphere. The potential for ammonia to be released to the atmosphere has led to the required use of an ammonia sensor for most engines produced since 2014. The **ammonia sensor** provides data to the ECM that is used to determine whether excess ammonia is detected. Constructed like a wide-range planar NOx or oxygen sensor, an ammonia sensor uses an aluminum oxide substrate rather than a ZrO_2 planar element to detect and generate a voltage for ammonia in a range from 0 to 100 ppm.

Soot Sensors

Another new sensor introduced in 2014 is a particulate sensor, which measures any soot present in the exhaust. This sensor is a type of variable capacitance sensor that uses soot to change the dielectric strength between two charged plates. Increasing amounts of soot or particulate matter will reduce the dielectric strength and the electric charge that the plates can store.

Mass Airflow Sensors

The mass airflow (MAF) sensor is a device that measures the weight of air entering the engine intake. Its unique design also reports data about air density and, to some extent, the vapor content.

MAF sensors are common on engines operating at stoichiometric air–fuel ratios. However, on the diesel engines operating with an excess air ratio, the MAF is used as part of

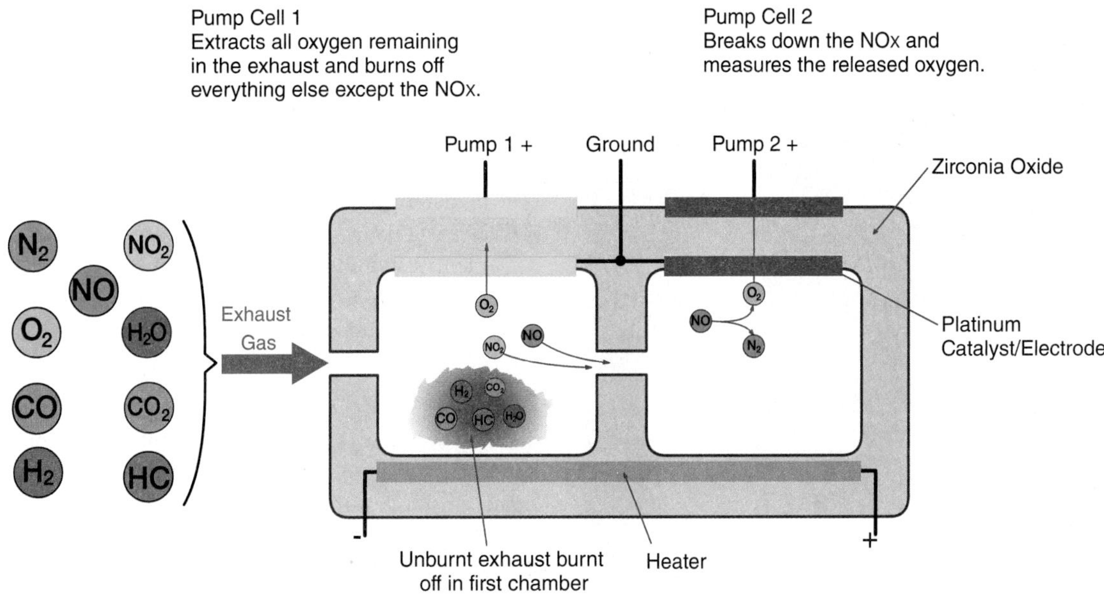

FIGURE 16-31 Operation of a NOx sensor. These sensors are also sensitive to any nitrogen in the exhaust stream and can detect ammonia gas as well.

the heavy-duty onboard diagnostics (HD-OBD) component monitor for the EGR. A variety of electrical signals originate from MAF sensors, but they all work using a hot-wire operating principle. Heated platinum wires or a thin film of silicon nitride embedded with several heated platinum wires are located in the intake air stream. A heating circuit maintains a fixed voltage drop across the wires, maintaining a constant resistance and temperature of the wires regardless of the airflow in the intake system. This means that if a voltage drop of 5 volts is maintained across the heated wire, more current needs to flow through the wire if it cools faster due to increased airflow. Similarly, if airflow drops, less current is needed to maintain the same voltage drop across the wire (**FIGURE 16-32**).

Circuits internal to the MAF measure the variation in current flow proportional to the cooling effect of air mass. Due to the large valve overlap characteristic of diesel engines, some intake air may be forced back out in pulses from the intake system. MAF sensors on some engines use a reverse airflow detection circuit. Because colder air is denser than warmer air, manufacturers will also use an air temperature sensor to provide additional data for calculations to compensate for the change in air mass (**FIGURE 16-33**).

Output Circuits

Output circuits, or output control devices, consist of display devices, serial data for network communication, and electromagnetic operator devices. The two basic types of operators are solenoids and relays. Injectors will use solenoids to meter fuel and adjust the timing of injection events.

Transistors inside the ECM are most often used to open or close circuits that control these operators. A small amount of current flowing from the microprocessor through the transistor base will control the output devices by supplying either a ground or battery current to complete a circuit (**FIGURE 16-34**).

Output drivers use field effect transistors (FETs) that are switched either on or off with very small voltages and produce little heat, which makes them ideal for output drivers.

FIGURE 16-32 Heated wires that change resistance as airflow across the sensor increases or decreases. Air mass is calculated based on how much electrical current is required to cancel the cooling effect of airflow across a heated wire.

FIGURE 16-33 A combination pressure and temperature sensor is used to calculate air mass entering an engine using a speed density algorithm. Note the two white signal wires.

▶ Sensors and Position Calculations

K16002

Engine control systems need to determine the correct cylinder and point in the combustion cycle for injection. In order to send an electrical signal to fire the injectors, the ECM needs to know two things:

1. *Crankshaft position.* The ECM must know the exact position of the crankshaft in reference to TDC—that is, the number of degrees the crankshaft has rotated since it turned past TDC.
2. *Cylinder identification.* This information is necessary to determine in which cylinder the injection event should take place, based on cylinder stroke position. Once the ECM can determine when the first cylinder has reached TDC compression stroke, it can use the engine firing order stored in memory to fire the remaining cylinders in the correct sequence. However, because the crankshaft rotates through 720 degrees of a four-stroke operating cycle, or two rotations of the crankshaft, cylinder stroke for any given cylinder can be determined only after the camshaft has passed through at least one revolution. To measure crankshaft position and identify cylinder stroke to begin a firing sequence, manufacturers have developed a number of strategies using either variable reluctance or Hall-effect sensors.

Single Engine Position Sensor

Teeth or raised lugs on a cam gear that turns at one-half engine speed can generate signals using a Hall-effect or variable reluctance sensor. A number of evenly spaced reluctor teeth, corresponding to the number of cylinders that an engine has, will produce a waveform or pattern that can be used to calculate the rotational velocity and engine position. This means that for every tooth that passes over the sensor, the ECM can calculate a specific number of degrees of crank or camshaft rotation has

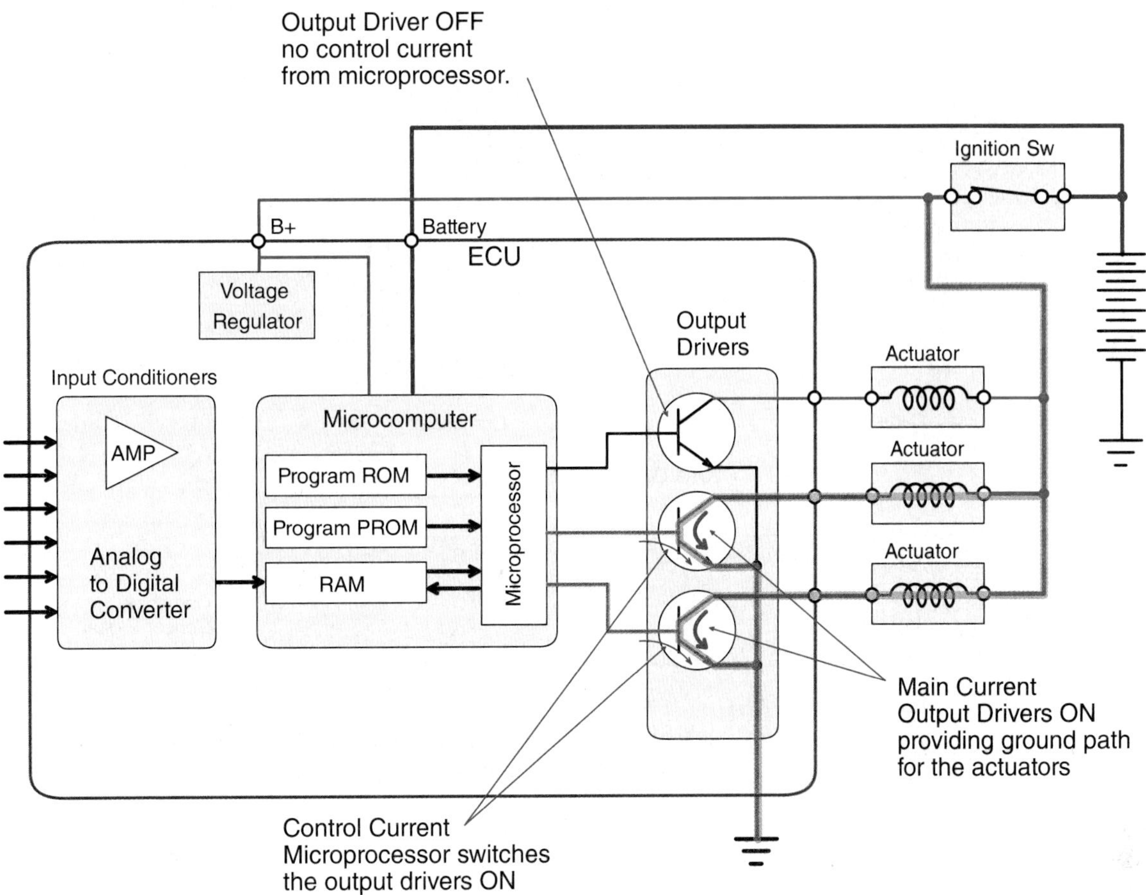

FIGURE 16-34 Transistors in the ECM control output devices by providing either a ground or a battery positive current to complete a circuit.

occurred. Counting the signals produced by reluctor wheel teeth and measuring the time elapsed between signals generated by the sensor allows the ECM to precisely calculate engine rotation in fractions of degrees.

Evenly spaced reluctor ring teeth or lugs, however, will not identify the cylinder stroke position. To identify TDC of the first cylinder's compression stroke, the cam gear may use an additional tooth or lug to identify the stroke position of each cylinder. A seventh tooth or lug on the cam gear of a six-cylinder engine could correspond to TDC of the first cylinder's compression stroke. Alternatively, a manufacturer may remove a tooth from a reluctor wheel. The longer time between two teeth is detected by the ECM's analysis of the sensor's waveform and will identify cylinder stroke as, say, TDC of the first cylinder (**FIGURE 16-35**).

Variations of this basic strategy include using one or two narrower teeth or an odd arrangement of teeth that corresponds to a particular engine position for a given waveform. It should be noted that the additional or missing tooth strategy may require as many as three crankshaft revolutions before the ECM can determine what the cylinder stroke position is.

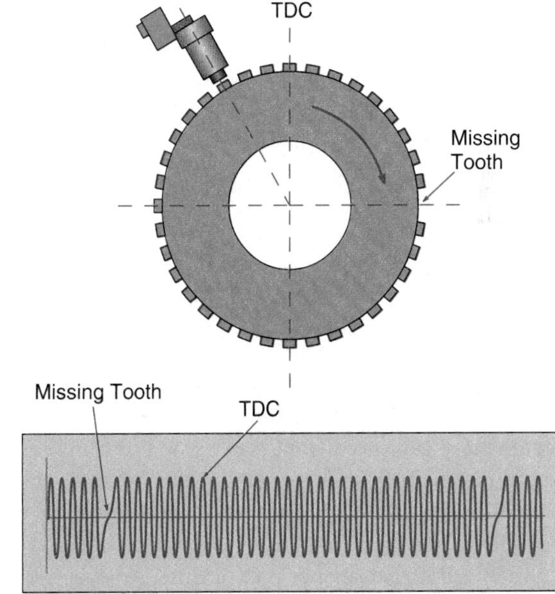

FIGURE 16-35 The waveform produced by a camshaft gear with a missing tooth on the signal generator wheel.

Using Two Sensors

A better strategy than using a single sensor on the camshaft is to use both camshaft and crankshaft position sensors. Using two sensors yields the advantage of improved precision in calculating crankshaft position. Using only the camshaft sensor, error is introduced due to backlash between the crankshaft

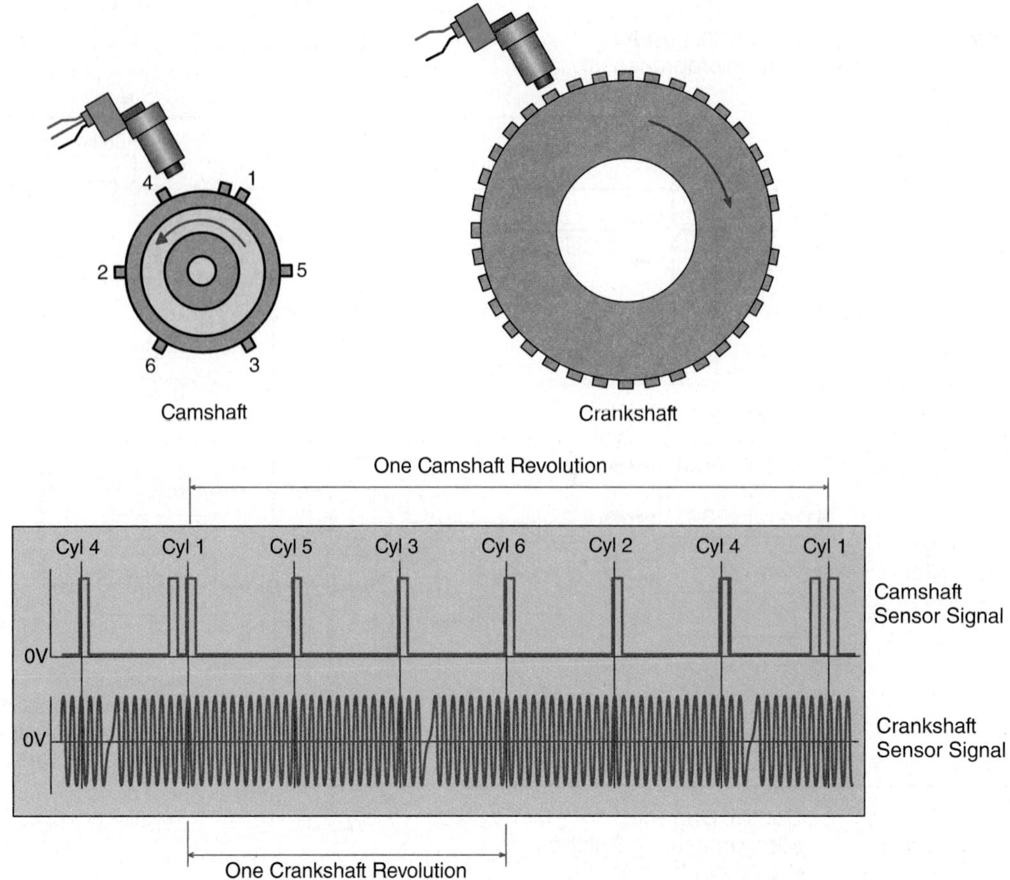

FIGURE 16-36 Two sensors produce crankshaft and engine position data with little error when compared to a single sensor on the camshaft. The camshaft reluctor wheel of a Hall-effect sensor produced the top waveform. A variable reluctance sensor generated the crankshaft waveform.

and camshaft gears. Worn gears can result in a significant amount of gear train backlash, producing unacceptable error in reporting crankshaft position. Using the crank sensor, the ECM can determine exactly where the position of the piston is (**FIGURE 16-36**).

Cylinder Misfire and Contribution Detection

The crankshaft of a diesel engine will speed up and slow down with each power and compression stroke in the engine. The waveform that is generated from the engine position sensor(s) can determine the rotational velocity of the crank. A cylinder that is misfiring or producing little power in comparison to the other cylinders will turn more slowly, resulting in fewer teeth passing the position sensor per unit of time. Analyzing sensor waveforms using edge detection software algorithms, the ECM can determine how much power each cylinder is contributing to overall performance. Similarly, a loss of compression in a cylinder results in less crankshaft deceleration during an operating cycle. The ECM may change injection quantities to even out cylinder contribution based on data from the crankshaft and camshaft position sensors.

▶ Sensor Fault Detection Principles

K16003, S16001, S16002

Technicians are often called upon to diagnose fault codes associated with sensors or sensor circuits. Understanding how sensor-related faults are detected and the diagnostic strategies used by an ECM will help you stay focused when performing pinpoint checks.

Sensors and Onboard Diagnostics

Electronic control systems have self-diagnostic capabilities to identify faults in circuits and sensors. Without the ability of an ECM to monitor circuit operation, diagnosing faults would become an extraordinarily difficult task, requiring the technician to manually perform voltage, resistance, and current measurements for every circuit, with the potential to produce a particular symptom of system malfunction. Waveforms from sensors producing varying frequencies, pulse width modulation, digital, or sine wave would also require a staggering amount of time and resources to analyze.

Because modern machines are required by emission legislation to monitor engine and other system operations for faults that could produce excessive emissions, evaluating sensor operation is a critical function of the HD-OBD system. There are three major categories of fault codes identified by engine manufacturer diagnostics (EMD) and HD-OBD:

1. *Out of range faults*. These faults primarily check sensor voltages, and in a few cases, they also check current draw to determine whether the sensor or associated circuits are open or have shorts. Voltages should be within 85% of reference voltage. That means for most sensors operating with a 5 Vref, signal voltages should not fall below 0.5 volts or above 4.5 volts (**FIGURE 16-37**).
2. *Rationality, plausibility, or logical faults*. Manufacturers use different terms to describe the same fault detection strategy whereby the validity or accuracy of sensor data is evaluated by comparing sensor voltages with expected values. Most often, sensor data from several more sensors or measurement systems is compared with data from a particular sensor to see if the data makes sense (that is, that it's logical or rational). Another name given to these types of faults is in-range faults, because the sensor could produce signal voltages that are not above or below a fault threshold voltage, but the sensor may have failed and is supplying incorrect data.
3. *Functionality faults*. HD-OBD systems are required to evaluate the operation of at least 12 to 14 other major emission systems, such as the exhaust aftertreatment, boost pressure, and EGR. Simple or elaborate fault detection strategies are used to check whether a particular emission system is functioning correctly. The major system monitors, as they are called, depend on sensor data to function, but they do not specifically check the sensor except to analyze the influence that sensor data has on a system. For example, if a system could not enter closed-loop operation because the sensor data was out of range, irrational, or had some problem with its operation, such as an abnormal operating frequency or switching time or a defective waveform, the sensor would be identified as having a fault. NOx sensor faults are a common example in which the sensor is working properly but, due to some other incorrect system function, the sensor is producing higher NOx levels, so the sensor is identified as defective. In other words, it is a concurrent code, not actually the fault the system has. In many cases, the NOx sensor is identified as being faulty, but although problems with a catalytic converter, EGR valve, or restricted air-intake systems will produce what appears to be an in-range fault, the problem actually lies outside the sensor.

Comprehensive Component Monitor

The comprehensive component monitor (CCM) is one of the system monitors required for OBD systems. It is a continuous monitor that constantly checks for malfunctions in any engine or emission-related electrical circuit or component providing input or output signals to an ECM. Electrical inputs and outputs are evaluated for circuit continuity and shorts by measuring voltage drops in a circuit. The monitor is also responsible for performing rationality checks of sensors. For example, if an oil pressure sensor indicated the engine had 40 psi (276 kPa) of oil pressure and the engine was stopped, the data would not make sense, and therefore a rationality fault would be stored. Another example would be that of a coolant temperature sensor that indicated the coolant was warm, say 140°F (60°C), but all other sensors such as oil, fuel, air inlet, and transmission temperatures were at −20°F (−29°C) and the engine had just started after cold soaking for 20 hours. Such a code could be triggered by plugging in a block heater, or it might indicate a defective sensor. Rationality codes need careful pinpoint diagnostic tests to determine whether a sensor is defective or some outside influence is affecting sensor data.

Outputs such as injector solenoids, relays, and dosing valves are evaluated by the CCM for opens and shorts by monitoring a feedback circuit from the FET, or "smart driver" associated with the output circuit. Smart FETs, as they are called, are FETs designed to supply data about the amount of amperage passing through the transistor gate (**FIGURE 16-38**).

These same gates can operate as virtual fuses that can disconnect power to the circuit if current flow is excessive. CCM codes use failure mode indicators (FMIs) developed by the International Society of Automotive Engineers (SAE) that indicate how an electrical circuit has failed (**TABLE 16-1**).

Out-of-range voltage codes that are the most common when sensors and circuits are open or shorted include FMI 3

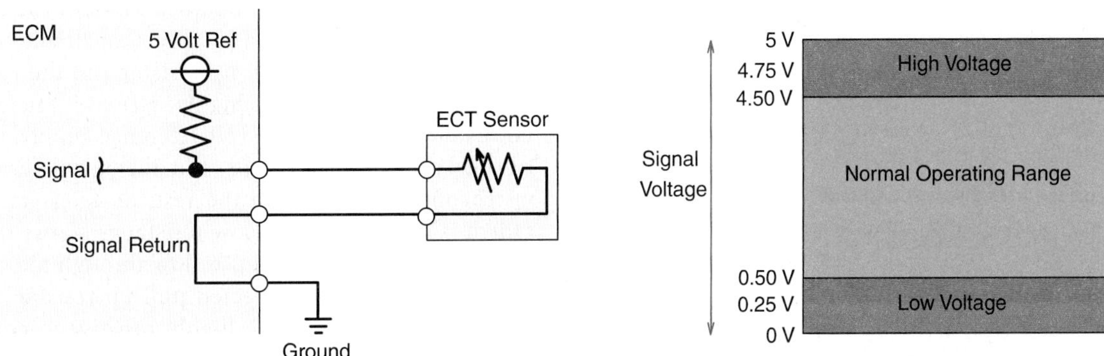

FIGURE 16-37 Out-of-range voltage codes on sensors are produced when the signal voltage falls outside 85% of reference voltage. This means signal voltages below 0.5 and above 4.5 typically trigger out-of-range voltage codes.

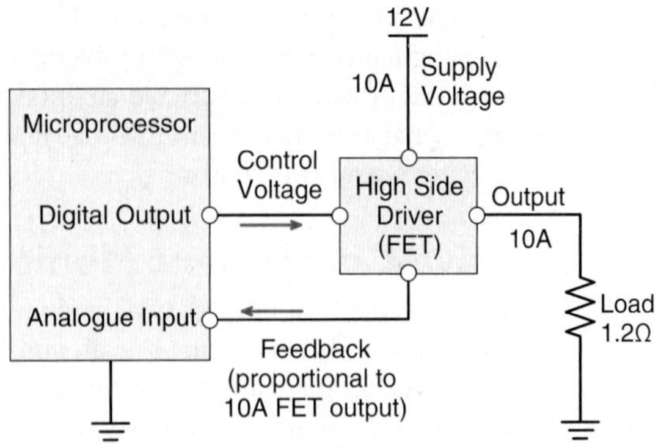

FIGURE 16-38 Smart FETs can provide feedback to the ECM about amperage moving through the transistor gate.

TABLE 16-1 American Society of Automotive Engineers (SAE) J1939 Failure Mode Identifier (FMI)

FMI	SAE Text
0	Data valid but above normal operational range—most severe level
1	Data valid but below normal operational range—most severe level
2	Data erratic, intermittent, or incorrect
3	Voltage above normal or shorted to high source
4	Voltage below normal or shorted to low source
5	Current below normal or open circuit
6	Current above normal or grounded circuit
7	Mechanical system not responding or out of adjustment
8	Abnormal frequency or pulse width or period
9	Abnormal update rate
10	Abnormal rate of change
11	Root cause not known
12	Bad intelligent device or component
13	Out of calibration
14	Special instructions
15	Data valid but above normal operating range—least severe level
16	Data valid but above normal operating range—moderately severe level
17	Data valid but below normal operating range—least severe level
18	Data valid but below normal operating range—moderately severe level
19	Received network data in error
20–30	Reserved for SAE assignment
31	Condition exists

and 4. J1587 and J1939 SAE rationality codes are 0, 1, and 2. J1939 also adds FMI codes 15–18, 20, and 21 for rationality-related faults. Codes 8–10 are used to report problems with waveforms from sensors or systems. Codes 5 and 6 are used by smart drivers that detect excessive or insufficient amperage in a circuit. Only FMI codes 11–14, 19, and 31 are not used by the CCM.

Circuit Monitoring—Voltage Drop Measurement

The way in which switch operation is monitored inside helps provide a foundation for other circuits to monitor sensors. Two basic types of switch inputs to the ECM are pull-up and pull-down switches. The terms “pull-up” and “pull-down” are often used to describe whether current through a circuit is supplied by the positive or negative current polarity. Pull-up means current is originating from a positive voltage source, and pull-down from a negative source. In the case of switches, pull-up switches supply a positive battery voltage input while pull-down supply a ground or negative voltage input (**FIGURE 16-39**).

Inside the ECM, a current-limiting resistor is connected in series with either of the switch types. This current-limiting resistor splits the voltage drop across the resistor and switch contacts. Voltage will drop across the current-limiting resistor when switch contacts are opened or closed. A high-impedance microcontroller capable of measuring voltage between an internal ECM ground and the resistor is connected in series with the current-limiting resistor, which enables a voltage reading. This means that voltage drop across the current-limiting resistor, whether it is a pull-up or pull-down switch, is measured by a voltmeter. Switch status (i.e., whether open or closed) is determined by measuring the voltage dropped across the current-limiting resistor.

Pull-Up Resistors

When two resistors are connected in series, the greatest voltage drop takes place across the resistor with the highest resistance. The second resistor will drop the remaining voltage in a circuit. This is predicted by Kirchhoff’s law, which states that the sum of the voltage drops in a circuit equals source voltage (**FIGURE 16-40**).

Because the microcontroller inside the ECM that measures voltage has very high resistance, it behaves like the largest of the resistors in a circuit. A pull-up resistor will have most voltage drop measured if the external circuit is open, because it places the microcontroller in series with the pull-up resistor. In this case, only a small amount of voltage is dropped by the pull-up resistor and the most voltage is dropped through the highly resistive microcontroller. For example, out of a +5-volt reference supply, the pull-up resister may drop 0.1 volts and the much more resistive microcontroller will drop the rest, or 4.9 volts. When the switch is closed, the very low resistance across the contacts will cause the most current to flow through the switch contacts and the series connected pull-up resistor. Almost no current flows through the highly resistive microcontroller, because the microcontroller is connected in parallel and has much higher resistance than the pull-up resistor and switch have, which are connected in series.

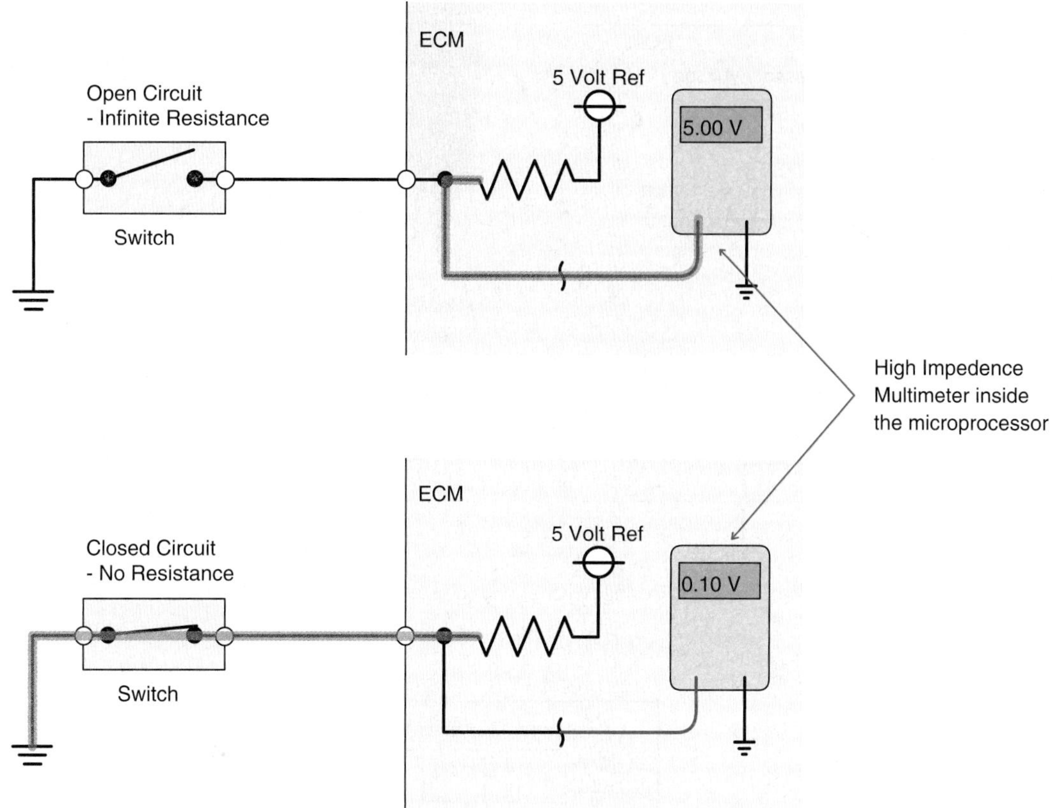

FIGURE 16-39 Pull-up switches supply a positive voltage to the ECM, while pull-down switches supply negative or ground.

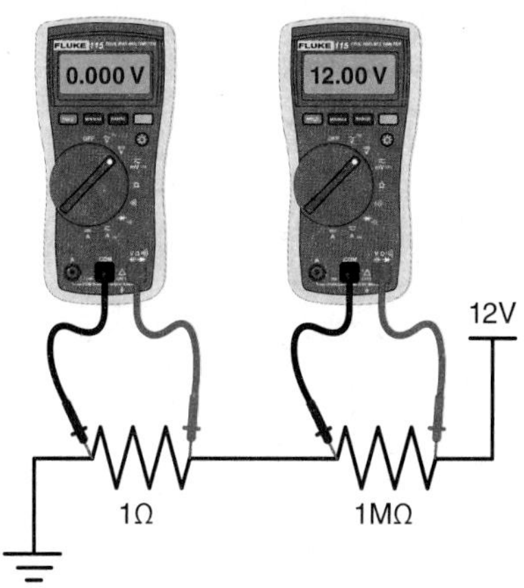

FIGURE 16-40 With two resistors connected in series, most voltage will drop across the resistor of higher value, which is predicted by Ohm's law (voltage drop = amperage × resistance).

Smart-Diagnosable Switches

Disconnected switches, shorted switch wiring, and resistive switch contacts cannot be diagnosed using open or closed diagnostic logic. To differentiate a disconnected switch from an open switch, resistors are placed in series or in parallel with the switch (**FIGURE 16-41**).

This enables the microcontroller to identify problems in the wiring between the switch and ECM for failures such as shorted to ground or open-circuited wiring. When properly connected in a functioning circuit, the resistor that is incorporated into the switch in series will have a calibrated resistance sensed by the microcontroller and measured as a specific voltage drop. If a switch has a resistor connected in parallel across its contacts, opening the switch provides a specific voltage drop measured by the microcontroller. If the switch wiring is shorted to ground or to battery positive or is simply disconnected, programmed logic within the microcontroller will identify the voltage reading as different from the switch resistance when opened or closed and log the appropriate fault code (**FIGURE 16-42**).

Pull-up resistors can be connected in series with the switches to further enhance the diagnostic capabilities of the microcontroller. Clutch, brake light, or AC pressure switches often use these arrangements because of their critical functions.

> ▶ TECHNICIAN TIP
>
> It is a very important and fundamental principle of electrical troubleshooting that when an ECM stores a diagnostic code, the code generally points to a problem somewhere in the circuit and not necessarily to the device connected to the circuit. If a code for a sensor is logged, further pinpoint testing using a diagnostic flowchart is required to properly diagnose the circuit.

Regulated Reference Voltage (Vref)

Regulated voltage supplied to sensor circuits (Vref) is important for several reasons. First, a stable and precise voltage is

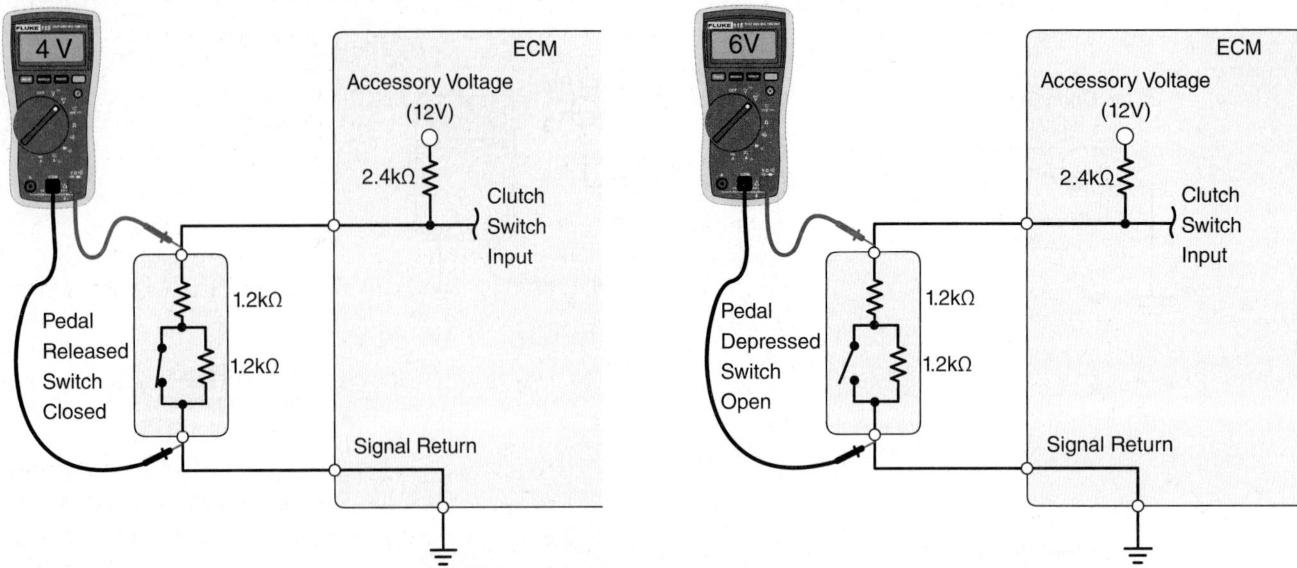

FIGURE 16-41 Placing resistors in series with opening and closing switches with different resistor values distinguishes switch status for each of these "smart switches."

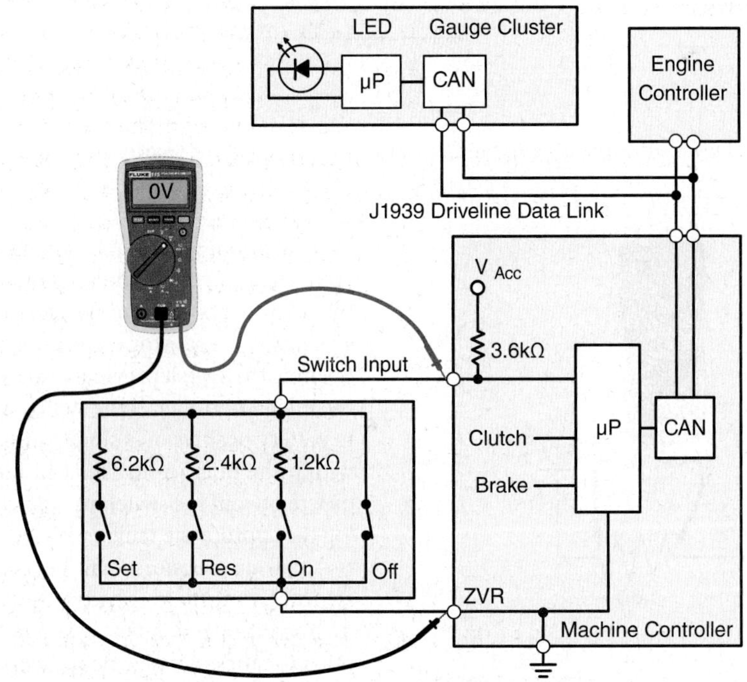

FIGURE 16-42 Resistors internal to the microcontroller are used to identify the different switches in a machine for proper control logic.

necessary for accurate voltage drop calculations used to determine the unknown resistance value of a sensor. Without the regulated voltage supply, changes in system voltage would produce sensor error. Current-limiting resistors are supplied a voltage lower than battery Vref to prevent excessive current flow through the microcontroller circuit if wiring becomes shorted. Vref values are typically 5 volts. (There are some exceptions: Caterpillar uses 8 volts on some control systems.) An internal ground called ZVR is just as important. All sensors using reference voltage return current through the control module and not to chassis ground. Variations in voltage at chassis ground would produce error in voltage drop calculations, resulting in incorrect signal voltages. The internal ground is also filtered and "cleaned," meaning it is free of electromagnetic interference.

▶ TECHNICIAN TIP

Just as Vref to sensors and switch circuits is regulated to typically +5 volts, a regulated ground circuit is provided through control modules. All sensors using reference voltage need a regulated ground return circuit through the control module and never to machine ground in order to prevent electrical interference and variations to voltage measurements. The control module in turn is connected to machine ground, which is the only way the electronic control system can function effectively.

Two-Wire Pull-Up Circuit Monitoring

To identify faults and measure signal voltage, thermistors are often connected to internal pull-up resistors. Thermistors are variable resistors that change resistance with temperature. These temperature-sensing devices are monitored for the following:

- resistance to validate normal signal voltage and detect out-of-range faults
- opens, either internal or in the circuit wiring
- shorts to power
- shorts to ground.

Like switches, the control module will measure voltage drop across an internal current-limiting pull-up resistor to calculate voltage drop across a thermistor. NTC thermistors increase resistance when they become colder and decrease resistance when they become warmer. Measuring temperature is performed by calculating the voltage drop across the thermistor connected in series with the pull-up resistor. As the resistance of the thermistor increases, less voltage is dropped across the pull-up resistor and more across the thermistor. The microcontroller will measure more voltage drop across the pull-up resistor when the thermistor becomes less resistive. Unwanted extra resistance in the circuit will produce a higher voltage drop across the sensor, generating colder temperatures. An open circuit (high resistance) will read the coldest temperature possible. Circuit-monitoring fault detection is typically designed to recognize sensor resistance values within approximately 85% of the voltage supplied from the pull-up resistor to be within normal range, and voltage readings outside of that range are recognized as abnormal (**FIGURE 16-43**).

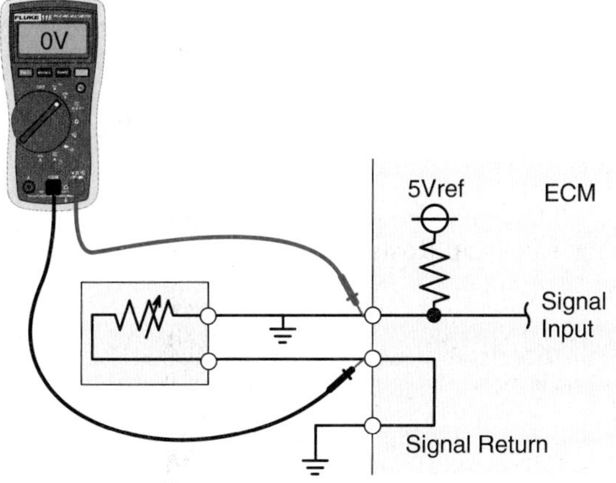

FIGURE 16-43 Circuit monitoring of thermistors involves measuring the voltage drop after a pull-up resistor. Fault code reports out-of-range signals at approximately 85% of Vref. This FMI 3 description is voltage high or shorted high.

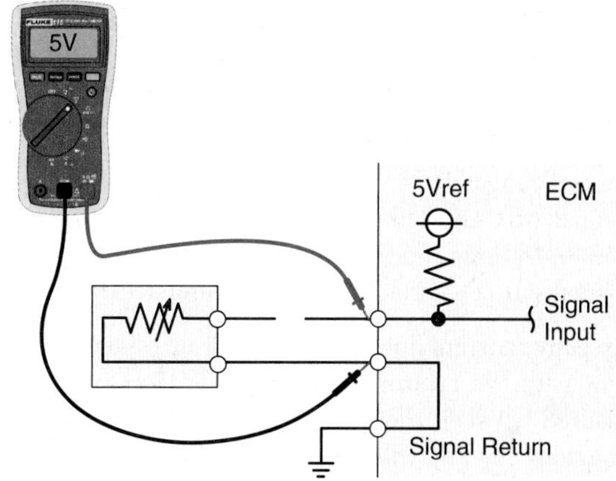

FIGURE 16-44 A thermistor with an SAE fault code of FMI 3: voltage high, shorted high.

The normal signal range used to diagnose most sensor circuits covers the entire operating range of the sensor signal, and the circuit should always have some resistance, whether hot or cold. A disconnected sensor will have infinite resistance, and no voltage is dropped across the thermistor. In these circumstances, the voltage reading by the circuit's microcontroller will see maximum voltage between its internal ground and the current-limiting resistor. An open sensor or disconnected open wiring will produce an SAE fault code description of "out-of-range high or shorted high" (FMI 3) (**FIGURE 16-44**).

The manufacturer and SAE FMI code descriptions point to the higher voltage sensed by the microcontroller because no voltage is dropped by the disconnected or open thermistor circuit and all voltage is now dropped by the microcontroller. Note that the sensor signal wire that is shorted to positive battery voltage or another +5-volt supply will generate an identical fault code as an open-circuited signal wire (**FIGURE 16-45**).

The logic used by the microcontroller that senses no or little voltage drop across the pull-up resistor could be caused by a positive voltage supply shorted to the signal wire. The ZVR could also be open and produce the same voltage readings by the microcontroller. Both conditions require appropriate pinpoint testing to isolate the fault.

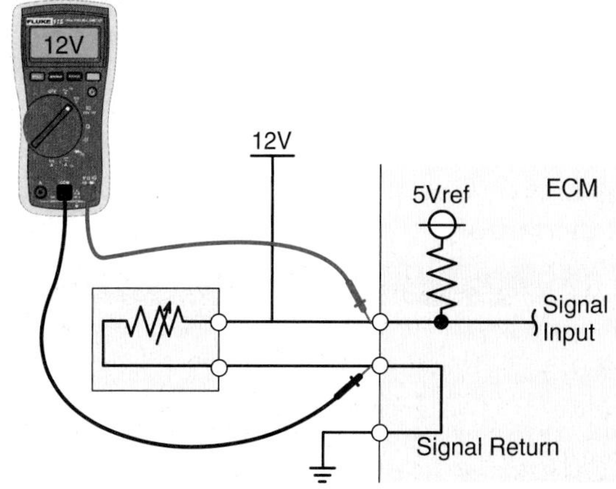

FIGURE 16-45 A thermistor with an SAE fault code of FMI 3: Shorted high, voltage high.

If a thermistor signal wire is rubbed through and making contact to machine ground, more current will flow through the signal circuit and the fault code description typically includes the following:

- out-of-range low or shorted low (FMI 4)
- signal wire shorted to sensor return or battery negative (manufacturer code)
- signal source shorted to ground (manufacturer code).

Excessive current flow across the pull-up resistor connected in series with the grounded circuit means low or no voltage is measured between the pull-up resistor and the signal wire. Because most current will flow through the short to ground, little current will flow through the microcontroller, and the voltage drop will be less than 0.5 volts. This explains why the code description given is out-of-range low or shorted low (FMI 4). Diagnostic logic programmed into the microcontroller points to a short to ground, causing excessive voltage drop across the current-limiting resistor of more than 85% of the voltage supplied to the resistor (**TABLE 16-2**).

Manufacturers can go beyond SAE minimum standards for reporting faults using J1939 protocols and add additional fault code descriptions using their own coding system. In the case of the disconnected thermistor, an enhanced code could carry a code description such as "signal wire shorted to sensor supply," "short to battery volt," "signal source shorted to voltage source," "open return," or "signal circuit."

▶ TECHNICIAN TIP

Pressure, temperature position, and other sensors can share a +5Vref or ZVR wire. Return is the equivalent to machine ground through the control module, which is free of electromagnetic interference and is regulated to provide the cleanest signal path. Problems in the reference voltage or signal return path can cause unusual problems and multiple fault codes from all the sensors. "Shorted high or low" and "voltage high or low" are typical fault code descriptions produced if sensors share common Vref and ZVR pathways. This happens because the voltage supplied to the sensors has changed. Less than +5 volts or the absence of a ZVR distorts the ECM's ability to properly sense correct signal voltages. If the return is connected to machine ground, voltage fluctuations and electromagnetic interference can sometimes distort electrical signals and measurement of voltage drops across the sensor circuits. A single defective sensor may have an internal short circuit to ground and +5 volts, which can interfere with the operation of all sensors. Disconnecting a defective sensor can sometimes cause the multiple fault code to disappear. The use of an LED diode installed in series with the ZVR circuit at each sensor can detect a malfunctioning circuit or device because the polarity-sensitive LED will light both directions when connected to the defective sensor.

▶ TECHNICIAN TIP

Just because a control module does not log a fault code does not mean that no problems exist in the electronic control system. Because the normal signal range (within 85%) used to diagnose most sensor circuits spans the entire operating range of the sensor, it is possible for the sensor to produce a signal that does not measure the actual operating condition and therefore will not be identified with a fault code. A good strategy to identify problems is to monitor signal voltage using a scanner or software data list while comparing observed values with expected values reported in a shop manual.

▶ TECHNICIAN TIP

Quick-testing to determine whether a fault code is generated by defective wiring, pin connectors, or a sensor can be performed using jumper wires. While monitoring sensor signal voltage using an electronic service tool, the signal voltage values should change when either disconnecting the sensor or jumping sensor signal wires to ZVR or +5 Vref. If no change is observed when momentarily grounding the signal wire or supplying the signal wire with +5 Vref, the wiring or pin connections in the circuit are suspect. Some manufacturers recommend using a calibrated resistor in series with the jumper wire when performing these tests, in order to prevent damage to sensitive control modules.

Three-Wire Sensor Circuit Monitoring

Three-wire circuits, whether digital or analog, passive or active, use a reference voltage, signal, and ZVR wire, also referred to as ground return by some manufacturers. Voltage out-of-range faults (FMI 3 and 4) are detected when the signal voltage from a sensor typically exceeds the 0.5–4.5 volts out-of-range fault threshold (**TABLE 16-3**).

TABLE 16-2 Out-of-Range Voltage Fault Code Descriptions Using a Pull-Up Resistor (i.e., two-wire NTC thermistor)

Condition	Observation	Code Description
Sensor disconnected	Signal voltage higher than 4.5 volts	FMI 3: Out of range high, shorted high
Signal wire shorted to positive voltage (12v battery or +5 volts reference)	Signal voltage higher than 4.5 volts	FMI 3: Out of range high, shorted high
Sensor open	Signal voltage higher than 4.5 volts	FMI 3: Out of range high, shorted high
Sensor signal wire shorted to ground	Signal voltage lower than 0.5 volts	FMI 4: Out of range low, shorted low
Sensor internally shorted to ground or ZVR	Signal voltage lower than 0.5 volts	FMI 4: Out of range low, shorted low

TABLE 16-3 Out-of-Range Voltage Fault Code Descriptions Using a Pull-Down Resistor (i.e., three-wire potentiometer)

Condition	Observation	Code Description
Sensor disconnected	Signal voltage lower than 0.5 volts	FMI 4: Out of range low, shorted low
Signal wire shorted to positive voltage (12v battery or +5 Vref)	Signal voltage higher than 4.5 volts	FMI 3: Out of range high, shorted high
Sensor open	Signal voltage lower than 0.5 volts	FMI 4: Out of range low, shorted low
Sensor signal wire shorted to ground	Signal voltage lower than 0.5 volts	FMI 4: Out of range low, shorted low
Sensor internally shorted to ground or ZVR	Signal voltage lower than 0.5 volts	FMI 4: Out of range low, shorted low

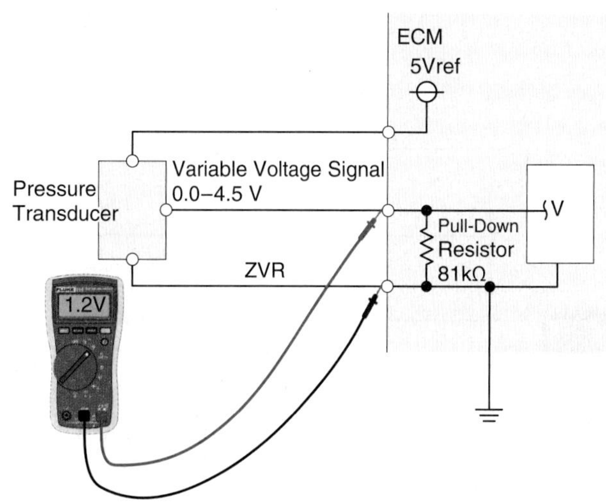

FIGURE 16-46 A low-bias sensor using a pull-down resistor. The sensor voltage is measured across the pull-down resistor.

The majority of three-wire sensors typically measure signal voltage between the positive voltage on the signal wire and the ZVR wire across a pull-down resistor (**FIGURE 16-46**).

However, some active three-wire sensors such as Hall-effect sensors and several manufacturers of pressure sensors supply variable resistance ground path for a +5 Vref from the ECM through the sensor's ZVR (**FIGURE 16-47**).

In this case, measuring signal voltage with three-wire sensors involves using a pull-up or pull-down resistor located in the ECM. In the case of a circuit using a pull-down resistor, a voltage-measuring microcontroller connected in parallel across the pull-down resistor measures voltage drop across the resistor between the positive signal wire and the negative ZVR. Because there is only one pull-down resistor, all the voltage supplied by the signal wire will be dropped across the pull-down resistor. This means that a defective active type sensor will have a fault code of FMI 4 for low voltage or shorted low if the +5 Vref and ZVR circuits are open (**FIGURE 16-48**).

Because no current is supplied to the active sensor with either an open Vref or ZVR, internal sensor circuits cannot operate and supply a varying signal voltage. Voltage in this case would be 0, which is below the 0.5-volt fault threshold for low

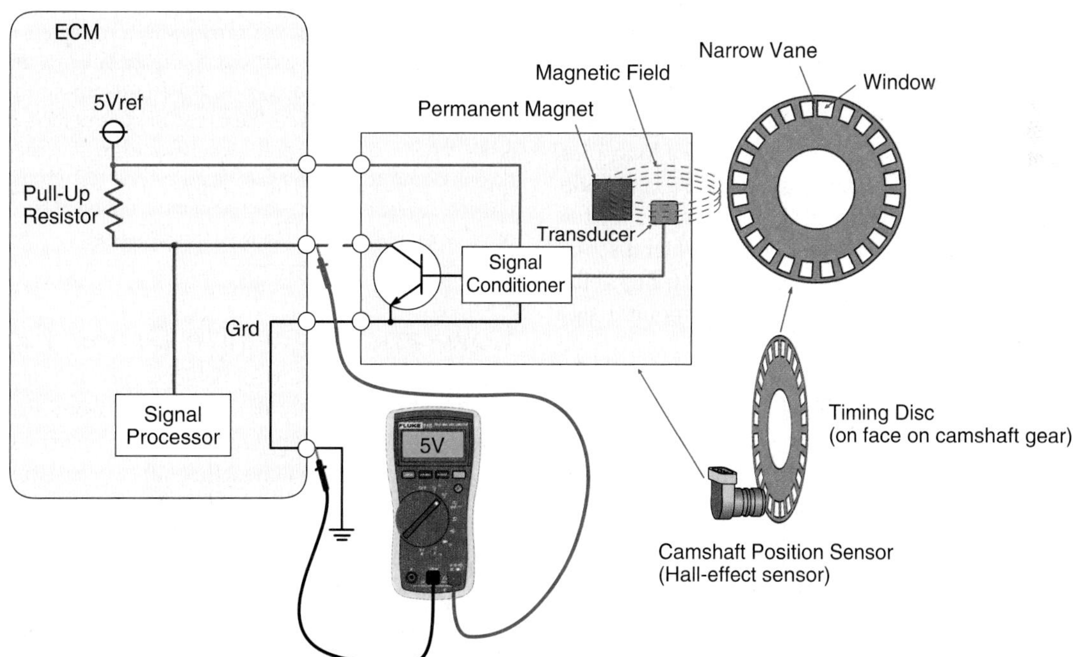

FIGURE 16-47 This Hall-effect sensor supplies a ground path through the sensor for signal voltage. Disconnecting the sensor produces an out-of-range +5 volts signal, which makes it a high-bias three-wire active sensor. Grounding the signal wire produces a 0-volt signal.

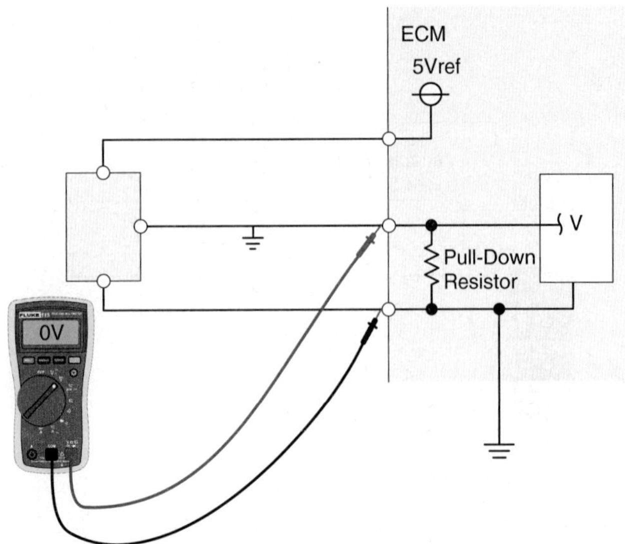

FIGURE 16-48 A signal wire of a three-wire active sensor shorted to ground produces a fault code of FMI 4: shorted low, voltage low.

voltage. A short to ground signal wire will produce an identical shorted-low, voltage-low FMI fault code.

If the sensor supplies a ground path for a signal circuit from the ECM containing a pull-up resistor carrying +5 volts, a disconnected sensor will produce a voltage high, shorted high FMI fault code. In this instance, the active sensor cannot work and provide an electronically variable resistance to ZVR for the current supplied through the pull-up resistor. This means the microcontroller will see +5 volts on the signal wire and produce a fault code of FMI 3: voltage high, shorted high—as illustrated in Figure 16-47.

High- and Low-Bias Sensors

Whenever a sensor is disconnected or open, the out-of-range voltage code will be either out-of-range high or out-of-range low. If the arrangement of the pull-up resistor causes signal voltage to go high when disconnected, it is considered a high-bias resistor. That is, it has a bias or tendency to produce a fault code of out-of-range high, voltage high, or FMI 3. If the tendency for a sensor circuit is to produce a voltage-low code when disconnected, it is considered a low-bias sensor. Generally, high-bias sensors use a pull-up resistor and low-bias sensors monitor signal voltage with a pull-down resistor.

Circuits using pull-up and pull-down resistors have the added advantage of limiting excessive current flow to a sensor to protect the wiring, sensor, or control module if a short to ground or battery positive takes place. Excessive current flow from an internally shorted sensor or Vref wires would be lowered by the resistors when a fault condition exists. By limiting excessive current flow during shorted conditions in sensor circuits, Vref and ZVR circuits are protected as well.

More comprehensive circuit monitoring also takes place between the Vref and ZVR in some but not all control systems. Open, shorted to ground, or shorted to voltage source or resistive circuit pathways result in fault codes for these circuits. Because ZVR is common to the sensors, problems with the reference voltage to a specific sensor circuit may be all that is detected.

▶ TECHNICIAN TIP

After performing a repair to an electronic control system, the repair should be validated before returning a machine to service to confirm the fault code does not reappear. In HD-OBD systems, repair validation requires operating the circuit or device under the enabling conditions for a major system monitor to run and obtain a system readiness code. Make sure the conditions to operate the device or run the monitor are met during the testing procedure. These procedures are outlined in the service manual. Double-check that no codes are pending or waiting to illuminate a malfunction indicator lamp (MIL). Occasionally, diagnostic codes can be set during routine service procedures or by problems outside the electronic control system. Always clear codes and confirm that they reappear prior to circuit troubleshooting. Comprehensive monitor codes on HD-OBD equipment often require only cycling the ignition switch on and off after a repair is completed to extinguish the MIL light.

▶ TECHNICIAN TIP

Tools required for fault isolation pinpoint testing include a digital volt-ohmmeter (DVOM) and some test leads or jumper wires. Proper break-out harness or pin connectors are needed to access the various connectors and components to be tested. Using improper tools can result in damage to pins and connectors and faulty meter readings, causing misleading diagnoses and producing even more diagnostic codes.

▶ TECHNICIAN TIP

If an intermittent fault is suspected, a physical check of the suspect circuit can be performed by flexing connectors and harnesses at likely failure points while monitoring the circuit with a multimeter or oscilloscope. Graphing meters with glitch testing capabilities can identify and record the circuit fault in microseconds. If the problem is related to temperature, vibration, or moisture, the circuit or control module can be heated, lightly tapped, or even sprayed with water to simulate the failure conditions. Some testing software features pull test capabilities, which can provide an audible alert when brief interruption in circuit voltages takes place when pulling or bending wiring harnesses.

Low- and High-Side Driver Faults

A large variety of electrical devices, such as relays, motors, and injectors, depend on current supplied from a control module to operate. When supplying a negative polarity or ground to a device, current is switched through a transistor called a low-side driver. Similarly, switching transistors supplying positive DC voltage are referred to as high-side drivers. Two techniques are used to detect opens, shorts, high resistance, and excessive current draw in these circuits. Current-limiting resistors used to measure voltage drop in the output circuit, much like in sensor circuits, are used to evaluate circuit performance. Another method involves direct measurement of output current using smart FETs (**FIGURE 16-49**).

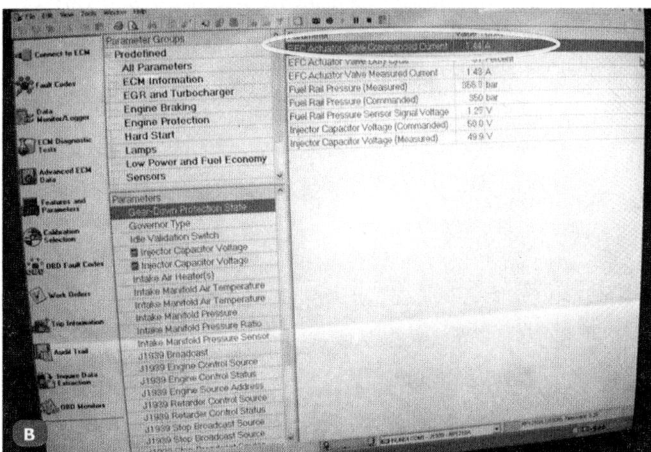

FIGURE 16-49 **A.** The rail pressure is controlled by the electronic fuel control valve. **B.** Amperage to the valve is measured by feedback from FETs inside the ECM.

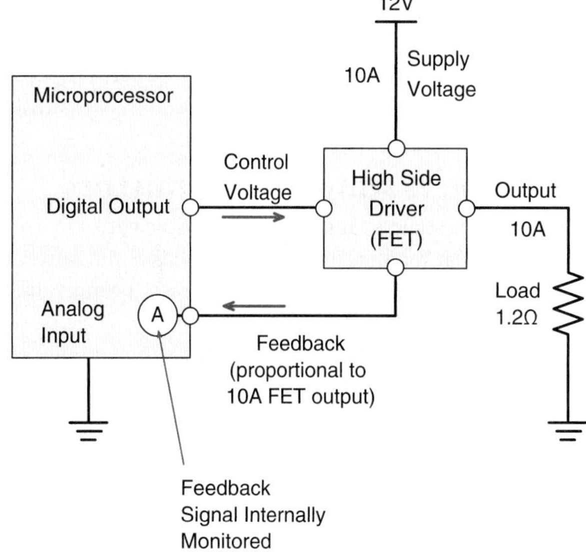

FIGURE 16-50 Circuit monitoring of FET output drivers for self-diagnostic fault monitoring.

In these circuits, the drain-to-source current flows are measured through a special feedback circuit to the microcontroller. Time on and amperage are used to set fault codes. FMIs 5 and 6 are produced when amperage exceeds out-of-range thresholds. FMI 5—current below normal or open—is produced if little or no amperage flows through the output circuit. FMI 6—current above normal or grounded—indicates a short to grounded circuit with high current flow (**FIGURE 16-50**).

For example, an injector that is supplied 2 amps at 70 volts using a high-side driver would be considered open if no current flowed or considered shorted to ground if amperage exceeded, say, 5 amps.

▶ TECHNICIAN TIP

To validate a repair, start the engine and let it idle for one minute. The ECM will turn off the red MIL light whenever the diagnostic monitor has run. If it is a CCM evaluating electrical circuits, the light will switch off immediately when this diagnostic monitor runs and passes. For other faults, the ECM will turn off the MIL after three consecutive ignition cycles in which the diagnostic runs and passes.

Maintenance of Sensors

The onboard diagnostic system capabilities are limited and can only narrow a fault to a circuit or system. After that, the technician must identify what the nature of the problem is that produced the diagnostic fault code. Servicing of sensor faults involves performing pinpoint electrical tests and making other observations to identify precisely where and what caused the fault. This stage of diagnostic testing is called off-board diagnostics.

Diagnostic Testing of Pressure Sensors

Diagnostic tests of pressure sensors are similar to other strategies for evaluating three-wire sensors. Onboard diagnostic systems will identify problems in the circuits. Scan tools can then measure real-time data to observe abnormal but in-range functional problems and retrieve fault codes associated with the circuits (**TABLE 16-4**).

Pinpoint tests using break-out harnesses are performed on live circuits too. Resistance tests are used to identify shorted or open wires in harnesses to these sensors. However, because these are active sensors with sensitive electronic circuits, it is not possible to perform resistance tests on the sensors themselves.

TABLE 16-4 Fault Code Descriptions for a Two- or Three-Wire Sensor

Condition	Observation	Code Description
In-range voltage but signal not valid	No rationality or plausibility when data compared with normal system behavior or other sensor inputs	In-range fault

SAFETY TIP

Never use a 12-volt jumper wire connected to battery positive to quickly check sensor harnesses. The ECM can easily be damaged by this method.

Diagnostic Testing of Thermistors

The range of resistance values of a thermistor varies by manufacturer and what temperature range the sensor measures. The change in resistance is not linear or directly proportional to temperature, either (**TABLE 16-5**).

At the low and high ends of a temperature range, small changes in temperature produce large changes in resistance, while changes in midrange temperature values produce smaller changes to sensor resistance. Several temperature and resistance values are supplied by the manufacturer to properly evaluate a thermistor when testing the use of an ohmmeter.

Diagnostic Testing of Variable Reluctance Sensors

Variable reluctance sensors are two-wire passive sensors. The coil of wire surrounding a magnet should be tested for continuity and should have its resistance measured. Resistance is high because there are hundreds of wire winding turns and the wire diameter is very small. The output of the sensor can be measured with an AC voltmeter. As the reluctor speed increases, the voltage produced by the sensor will rise proportionately.

A broken magnet will cause a low voltage reading. Likewise, an improper air gap between the sensor and reluctor will cause sensor output failure. Iron filings at the magnet of the sensor will also cause an inadequate change in sensor reluctance, generating insufficient voltage. Simply removing, cleaning, and reinstalling the sensor can sometimes correct inadequate or erratic sensor signals.

Variable reluctance sensor operation can often be evaluated from a scan tool or waveform graphing meter. For example, if an engine speed sensor is defective, engine speed data cannot be observed from a scanner. Graphing meters can compare known good sensor waveforms with observed waveforms to detect sensor faults.

TABLE 16-5 The Inverse and Nonlinear Relationship Between Temperature and Resistance of a Thermistor

Temperature		Resistance
°Celsius	°Fahrenheit	Ohms
100	210	185
70	160	450
38	100	1,600
20	70	3,400
−4	40	7,500
−7	20	13,500
−18	0	250,000
−40	-40	100,700

Diagnostic Testing of Hall-Effect Sensors

Diagnostic testing of Hall-effect sensors will follow similar diagnostic strategies for any other three-wire active sensor (**FIGURE 16-51**).

Out-of-range faults on the sensor can be pinpoint tested with a voltmeter by first verifying that +5 Vref and ZVR are available to the sensor (**FIGURE 16-52**).

After disconnecting the sensor and harness plug, quickly check to differentiate between a defective sensor and defective wiring harness by shorting the +5 Vref to the signal return circuit. While monitoring sensor voltage using software or a scanner connected to the diagnostic data link connector, the

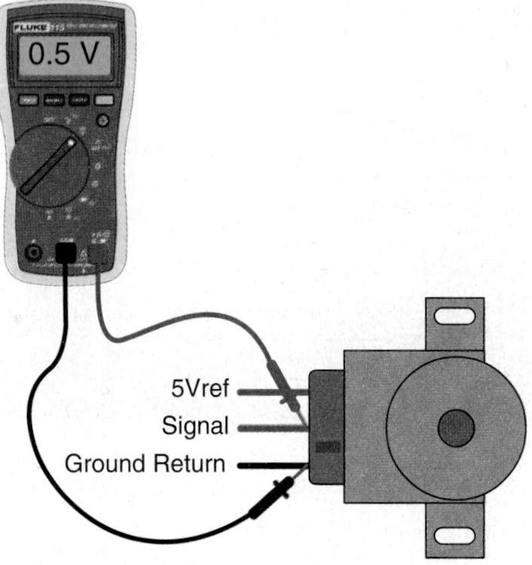

FIGURE 16-51 Signal voltage when pinpoint testing is always measured between the ground return and signal wire for all sensors.

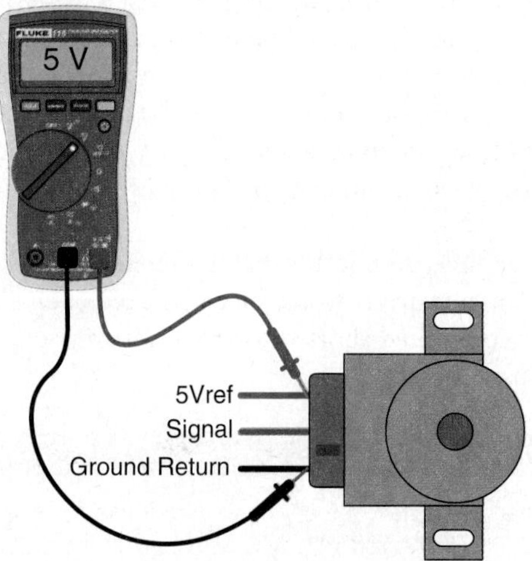

FIGURE 16-52 Confirming the availability of +5 Vref is an important step in pinpoint diagnostics to isolate a fault; 5 volts can be measured from either chassis ground or sensor ground return. To confirm both signals are accurate, measure ground return and +5 Vref.

signal voltage will show 5 volts or an "on" state. If there is no change in the voltage, the wiring harness or connector plugs are likely defective. Shorts of any of the circuit wires to ground, to battery voltage, or to one another are checked using either an ohmmeter when the machine battery is disconnected or measuring voltages in the sensor harness when the circuit is live.

Another important check of Hall-effect sensors is made using a graphing meter. Sometimes the circuit board within the sensor can fail and produce a waveform unrecognizable to the ECM, such as when the edges of a normally square waveform are not sharp and well defined. This often happens during a hot soak period, and the machine will not start until the engine cools. A graphing meter allows examination of the waveform for comparison between known good waveforms.

Diagnostics of Mass Airflow Sensors

MAF sensors produce waveforms or data that can be observed by using a graphing meter. Sensor operation can also be monitored using a scanner, OEM software, or a multimeter with a break-out harness. Diagnostics of MAF sensors will follow those of any three-wire active sensor. It is also important to remember that turbulence and airflow velocity variations can give false signals. For example, dirty heater wires, hot film, or film wires can cause incorrect readings. Screens placed inside the sensor to reduce turbulence can catch debris. These parts will require cleaning or replacement to restore proper operation. If the heater wire is intermittently breaking open, tapping the sensor to disconnect the wire will reveal the glitch if the sensor output is observed on a graphing meter or scanner.

▶ Wrap-Up

Ready for Review

- Devices that convert one form of energy into another are called transducers. Sensors are a type of transducer because they convert physical conditions or states into electrical data. Pressure, temperature, angle, speed, and mass are just a few of the physical variables about which sensors supply electrical data to processors.
- A sensor is considered active or passive depending on whether it uses power supplied by the ECM to operate.
- Reference voltage refers to a precisely regulated voltage supplied by the ECM to sensors. It is significant to processor operation because the value of the variable resistor can be calculated by measuring voltage drop across the resistor with a known input voltage.
- Other classifications of sensors include resistive sensors, voltage generators, switch sensors, variable capacitance pressure sensors, and piezo-pressure and piezoresistive sensors.
- Switches are the simplest sensors of all because they have no resistance in the closed position and infinite resistance in the open position. Switches are categorized as sensors whenever they provide information to an electronic control system.
- The simplest digital signal is a single pole, single throw (SPST) switch. It is found in either an open or a closed state.
- When a switch is connected between the ECM and a battery positive, it is known as a pull-up circuit. A pull-down circuit is constructed when current to the switch is connected between the ECM and a negative ground current potential.
- Resistive sensors belong to the class of sensors that condition or change a voltage signal applied to the sensor. Many types of resistive sensors exist.
- A thermistor is a temperature-sensitive variable resistor commonly used to measure coolant, oil, fuel, or air temperature. The most common type of thermistor is an NTC thermistor.
- Rheostats are two-wire variable resistance sensors. They are not commonly used as input devices to an ECM, but instead are used for sending units such as fuel level, oil pressure, and some temperature gauges.
- Three-wire sensors, regardless of how they appear or what function they perform, have a common wiring configuration. The first wire provides reference voltage to the sensor. The second wire provides a negative ground signal to the ECM. The third wire is a signal return from the sensor. The advantage of using three-wire sensors is that they provide comprehensive diagnostic information about the sensor and its circuit operation.
- Potentiometers are similar to rheostats in that they vary signal voltage depending on the position of a sliding contact or wiper moving across a resistive material. However, they are three-wire sensors with the signal wire connected to the internal wiper. Potentiometers supply analog data to processing circuits.
- Pressure measurements such as intake manifold boost, barometric pressure, and oil and fuel pressure use two types of sensor technology: One is a variable capacitance sensor and the other uses strain gauge resistive sensors. These are both active sensors that produce analog output signals.
- Strain gauge measurements record small changes in the resistance of tiny wires caused by the stretching or contraction of the wires.
- Piezoresistive sensors rely on the ability of certain mineral crystals to produce voltage or change resistance when compressed. Rather than using a strain gauge resistor wire construction, these sensors use a

piezoresistive crystal arranged with a Wheatstone bridge to measure the change in resistance of the piezo crystal. The advantage of these sensors is their ability to measure very high pressures.

- A variable capacitance sensor is an active pressure sensor used to measure both dynamic and static pressure.
- Voltage generators are passive and produce an analog signal of varying voltage or AC frequency.
- Variable reluctance sensors are used to measure rotational speed. Wheel speed, machine speed, engine speed, and camshaft and crankshaft position sensors are common applications of these sensors.
- A material's ability to conduct or resist magnetic lines of force is known as reluctance. Variable reluctance sensors use changing sensor reluctance to induce current flow by changing magnetic-field strengths inside the sensor.
- Like variable reluctance sensors, Hall-effect sensors are commonly used to measure rotational speed of a shaft. Though they are more complex and expensive to manufacture than variable reluctance sensors are, they produce a digital signal square waveform and have strong signal strength at low shaft rotational speeds.
- Oxygen sensors are used to adjust EGR flow on diesels and exhaust oxygen content for exhaust after treatment devices.
- NOx sensors are constructed and operate similarly to wide-range planar oxygen sensors, except that different concentrations of alloys are used in the sensor walls.
- Constructed like a wide-range planar NOx or oxygen sensor, an ammonia sensor uses an aluminum oxide substrate rather than a ZrO_2 element to detect and generate a voltage for ammonia in a range from 0 to 100 ppm.
- The mass MAF sensor measures the weight of air entering the engine intake. Its unique design also reports data about air density and, to some extent, the vapor content.
- MAF sensors are common on engines operating at stoichiometric air–fuel ratios. However, on diesel engines operating with an excess air ratio, the MAF is used as part of the HD-OBD component monitor for the EGR. A variety of electrical signals originate from MAF sensors, but they all work using a hot-wire operating principle.
- Output control devices consist of display devices, serial data for network communication, and operators—electromagnetic devices that transform electrical current into movement. Two basic types of operators are solenoids and relays.
- ECMs need to determine the correct cylinder and point in the combustion cycle for injection. To send an electrical signal for firing the injectors, the ECM needs to know two things: crankshaft position and the stroke that a cylinder is on.
- Using teeth or raised lugs on a cam gear that turns at one-half engine speed can generate engine position data using a Hall-effect or variable reluctance sensor.
- A better strategy than using a single sensor on the camshaft is to use both a camshaft and crankshaft position sensor. Using two sensors yields the advantage of improved precision in calculating crankshaft position.
- The crankshaft of a diesel engine will speed up and slow down with each power and compression stroke in the engine. The waveform generated from the engine position sensor(s) can determine the rotational velocity of the crank. Analyzing sensor waveforms using edge detection software algorithms, the ECM can determine how much power each cylinder is contributing to overall performance.
- A thermistor's resistance value varies by manufacturer and the substance being measured.
- Variable reluctance sensors are two-wire passive sensors. The output of the sensor can be measured using an AC voltmeter. As the reluctor speed increases, the voltage produced by the sensor will rise proportionately.
- Hall-effect sensors can be tested and diagnosed in a similar way to any three-wire active sensor.
- MAF sensors produce waveforms that can be observed by using a graphing meter. Sensor operation can also be monitored by using a scanner or a multimeter. Diagnostics of MAF sensors follow those of any three-wire active sensor.

Key Terms

active sensor A sensor that uses a current supplied by the ECM to operate.

ammonia sensor A sensor used in selective catalyst reduction (SCR), which provides data to the ECM that is used to determine whether ammonia values are out of anticipated range.

Hall-effect sensor A sensor commonly used to measure the rotational speed of a shaft; they have the advantage of producing a digital signal square waveform and have strong signal strength at low shaft rotational speeds.

idle validation switch (IVS) A circuit used for safety reasons that is used to verify throttle position.

NOx sensor A sensor that detects oxygen ions originating from nitric oxide (NOx) from among the other oxygen ions present in the exhaust gas.

passive sensor A sensor that does not use a current supplied by the ECM to operate.

piezoresistive sensor A sensor that uses a piezoresistive crystal arranged with a Wheatstone bridge to measure the change in resistance of the piezo crystal; these sensors are adapted to measuring vibration and dynamic or continuous pressure changes.

potentiometer A variable resistor with three connections: one at each end of a resistive path, and a third sliding contact that moves along the resistive pathway.

pull-down switch A switch connected between the ECM and a negative ground current potential.

pull-up switch A switch connected between the ECM and a battery positive.

reference voltage (Vref) A precisely regulated voltage supplied by the ECM to sensors; the value is typically 5 VDC, but some manufacturers use 8 or 12 volts.

rheostat A variable resistor constructed of a fixed input terminal and a variable output terminal, which vary current flow by passing current through a long resistive tightly coiled wire.

thermistor A temperature-sensitive variable resistor commonly used to measure coolant, oil, fuel, and air temperatures.

variable capacitance pressure sensor An active sensor that measures both dynamic and static pressure.

variable reluctance sensor A sensor used to measure rotational speed, including wheel speed, machine speed, engine speed, and camshaft and crankshaft position.

wide-range planar sensor A type of sensor technology that uses a current pump to calculate relative concentrations of oxygen, nitric oxide, and ammonia in exhaust gases.

Review Questions

1. Which type of input sensor is used by the engine management system and uses power supplied by the machine's ECM?
   a. Active
   b. Passive
   c. Inactive
   d. Delta
2. The use of a reference voltage is important in engine computer processor operation, because the value of the variable resistor can be calculated by measuring which of these values when another resistor with a known voltage input is connected in series with the variable resistor?
   a. Increase in voltage
   b. Voltage drop
   c. Amperage drop
   d. Decrease in resistance
3. To make sure that an engine fuel system drivability malfunction is identified and repaired correctly, always refer to ________.
   a. aftermarket service manuals
   b. diagnostic trouble code (DTC) diagnoses
   c. aftermarket training manuals
   d. OEM owners' manuals
4. Which of these is LEAST LIKELY to be used as a potentiometer in a diesel engine management system?
   a. Throttle position sensor (TPS)
   b. Accelerator pedal position (APP) sensor
   c. Accelerator position sensor (APS)
   d. Mass air flow (MAF) sensor
5. Which of these devices measures small changes in the resistance of tiny wires caused by stretching or contraction?
   a. Strain gauge
   b. Wire gauge
   c. Potentiometer
   d. Thermometer
6. ________ voltage is a precisely regulated voltage supplied by the ECM to sensors.
   a. Supply
   b. Reference
   c. System
   d. Control
7. A ________ switch is connected between the ECM and a negative ground current potential.
   a. pull-down
   b. pull-up
   c. resistive
   d. conductive
8. A two-wire sensor that changes resistance in proportion to temperature is called a ________.
   a. variable resistor
   b. thermistor
   c. capacitor
   d. transistor
9. Consider an active-type pressure sensor that uses a pull-down resister to identify signal faults. What fault code will likely be reported if the Vref wire is broken?
   a. Voltage high or shorted high
   b. Voltage low or shorted low
   c. Missing Vref
   d. Voltage high shorted low
10. Which of these sensor designs has the advantage of producing a digital signal square waveform and has strong signal strength at low shaft rotational speeds?
    a. Variable reluctance
    b. Voltage generating
    c. Variable capacitance
    d. Hall effect

ASE Technician A/Technician B Style Questions

1. Technician A says that passive sensors are not used in today's machine management systems. Technician B says that active sensors use current supplied by the ECM to operate. Who is correct?
   a. Technician A
   b. Technician B
   c. Both Technician A and Technician B
   d. Neither Technician A nor Technician B
2. Two technicians are discussing engine management input sensors. Technician A says that switches are the simplest sensors of all because they have no resistance in the closed position and infinite resistance in the open position. Technician B says that a zero-volt signal would present as a closed switch, while 12 volts would present as an open switch. Who is correct?
   a. Technician A
   b. Technician B
   c. Both Technician A and Technician B
   d. Neither Technician A nor Technician B
3. Technician A says that a knock sensor measuring abnormal combustion signals is a common application of piezoresis-

tive sensors. Technician B says that silicon-based piezoresistive sensors are very sensitive to slight pressure changes. Who is correct?
   a. Technician A
   b. Technician B
   c. Both Technician A and Technician B
   d. Neither Technician A nor Technician B
4. Technician A says that a defective mass airflow sensor can be diagnosed by using a graphing meter and inspecting the waveform that it produces. Technician B says that only the ECM can identify a faulty sensor. Who is correct?
   a. Technician A
   b. Technician B
   c. Both Technician A and Technician B
   d. Neither Technician A nor Technician B
5. Technician A says that if a problem is related to temperature, vibration, or moisture, the circuit or control module can be heated, lightly tapped, or even sprayed with water to simulate the failure conditions. Technician A says that a graphing meter with glitch testing capabilities can identify and record a circuit fault in microseconds. Who is correct?
   a. Technician A
   b. Technician B
   c. Both Technician A and Technician B
   d. Neither Technician A nor Technician B
6. Technician A says that switches are categorized as sensors whenever they provide information to an electronic control system. Technician B says that switch data may indicate a physical value such as open or closed, up or down, or high or low, or it may indicate on and off. Who is correct?
   a. Technician A
   b. Technician B
   c. Both Technician A and Technician B
   d. Neither Technician A nor Technician B
7. Technician A says that disconnecting a high-bias sensor will likely produce the fault code description "voltage high or shorted high." Technician B says that the fault code most likely reported by a disconnected high-bias sensor is "voltage low or shorted low." Who is correct?
   a. Technician A
   b. Technician B
   c. Both Technician A and Technician B
   d. Neither Technician A nor Technician B
8. Technician A says that wide-band oxygen sensors produce a voltage proportional to a specific exhaust gas oxygen level. Technician B says that oxygen sensors are used to measure air–fuel ratio in order to calibrate EGR flow rates and air–fuel ratios for exhaust aftertreatment devices. Who is correct?
   a. Technician A
   b. Technician B
   c. Both Technician A and Technician B
   d. Neither Technician A nor Technician B
9. Two technicians are discussing variable reluctance sensors. Technician A says that a broken magnet in the sensor will cause a low voltage reading. Technician B says that excessive air gap between the sensor and reluctor will cause sensor output failure. Who is correct?
   a. Technician A
   b. Technician B
   c. Both Technician A and Technician B
   d. Neither Technician A nor Technician B
10. Technician A says that *out-of-range faults* check sensor voltages and, in a few cases, current draw to determine whether the sensor or associated circuits are open or have shorts. Technician B says that *rationality faults* use a detection strategy whereby the validity or accuracy of sensor data is evaluated by comparing sensor voltages with expected values. Who is correct?
   a. Technician A
   b. Technician B
   c. Both Technician A and Technician B
   d. Neither Technician A nor Technician B

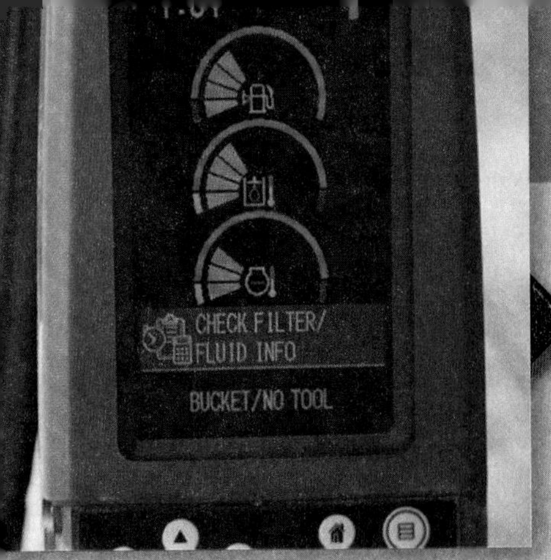

CHAPTER 17

Electrical Instrumentation and Alarm Systems

Knowledge Objectives

After reading this chapter, you will be able to:

- **K17001** Identify and describe the construction and operation of warning devices and gauge systems.
- **K17002** Describe the operation of capacitance and resistive touch driver information screens.
- **K17003** Describe procedures to inspect, test, and adjust gauge sending units and circuits.

Skills Objectives

There are no skills objectives for this chapter.

▶ Introduction

Instrument gauges, warning lamps, and operator information centers enable the operator to monitor the machine's operating condition, the status of equipment, and safety systems. The types of displays, warning lights, and gauges differ widely among machines and manufacturers but can be categorized according to common gauge groups, sensing, and input systems. For example, monitoring engine operation involves measuring the pressure and temperature of parameters of the lubrication, cooling, and air induction system. Charging voltage and amperage of the electrical system, fuel level, air pressure, engine, and machine speed are other common gauge systems. Warning lights for systems ranging from torque converter temperature, hydraulic oil filter bypass, low fuel, low air pressure, glow plug, parking brakes, etc. are used in situations where limited but simplified information is useful. Newer digital instrumentation has superior accuracy plus built-in self-diagnostic capabilities, offering the operator confidence that gauges and warning systems are operational. Operator display and input systems connected to the machine network provide informational capabilities far beyond previous instrumentation design.

▶ Warning Lights and Gauges

K17001

Warning Lights

Warning lights provide easily understood information to alert the equipment operator to potentially dangerous operating conditions (**FIGURE 17-1**).

Low air pressure, park brake on, low diesel exhaust fluid, powertrain oil temperature, etc. are activated a number of ways:

- mechanical ground switches
- electronic switches
- voltage drop circuits.

The charging system indicator light is an example of a light operated through voltage drop (**FIGURE 17-2**).

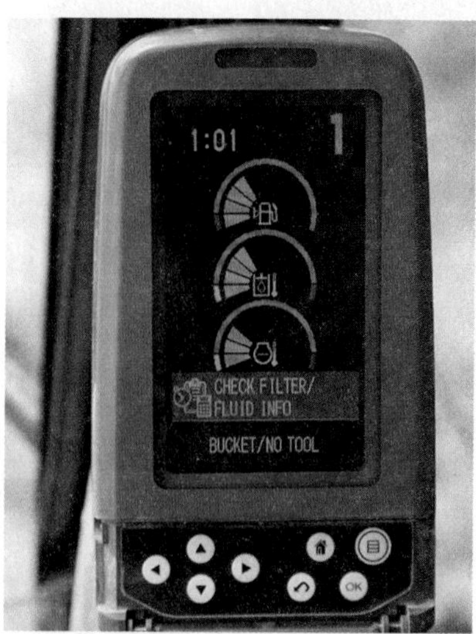

FIGURE 17-1 Warning lights.

After the engine starts and the alternator begins charging, battery voltage and charging system voltage are applied to both terminals of a bulb. If battery voltage is equal to or becomes higher than the charging system voltage, the voltage differential will cause the light to illuminate.

Mechanical ground switches are used to indicate low fluid levels, low-pressure warning systems, or differential engagement locks (**FIGURE 17-3**).

Normally closed pressure switches opened with mechanical, air, or oil pressure provide a path to ground to illuminate a bulb (**FIGURE 17-4**).

Electronic switches found in electronic control modules are the most common way warning lights are illuminated in today's machines. If a condition is sensed to which the operator needs to be alerted, the module has control logic to supply a ground or battery voltage to the light.

Prove-Out Sequence

In order to validate the correct operation of a warning light, the instrument cluster is designed to illuminate a bulb for several

You Are the Mobile Heavy Equipment Technician

A late-model machine has arrived at your shop with several complaints related to the electrical system. One complaint is that the check engine light is continuously illuminated. Another is that the instrument gauges go to zero and sweep from zero to full scale and then back again to a correct reading while operating. Other times the instrument gauge cluster does not move at all when the machine is started and running. In addition to requesting that the electrical problems be corrected, the operator expresses concern about running out of fuel if the gauges are not reading accurately. Having time-sensitive construction deadlines, an incorrect fuel reading for a fuel tank that is empty would be financially disastrous to the company.

As you proceed to diagnose the problem, you discover that lightly pulling on the wiring harness connected to the gauge cluster duplicates the complaint about the gauges sweeping from zero to full scale and back again to a correct reading again. Consider the following to predict what you think the technician will write on the work order:

1. Explain why the gauges complete a full-scale sweep when electrical power is interrupted.
2. What is potentially the simplest procedure the technician could use to identify the problem illuminating the check engine light?
3. Outline a procedure the technician could use to validate the correct gauge readings for the fuel level.

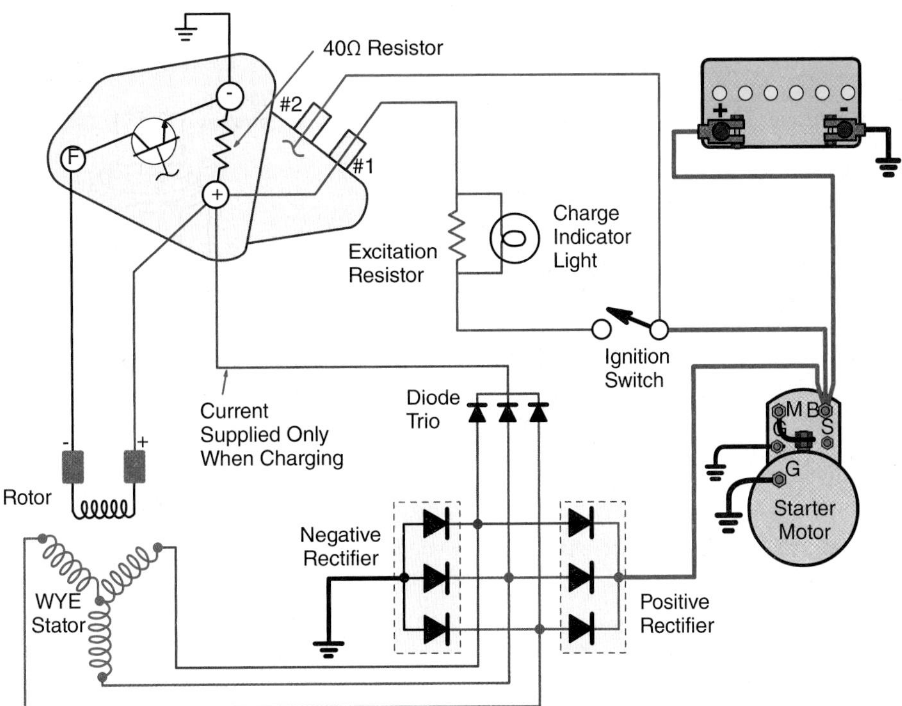

FIGURE 17-2 Alternator voltage regulators provide a ground path for a bulb when not charging and supply battery + current when charging to the warning light bulb terminal to extinguish the light.

FIGURE 17-3 A water in fuel sensor is a mechanical float-type switch in this diesel fuel filter. Denser water will raise the float fluid level sensor and ground the signal wire. **A.** Fuel filter. **B.** Internal electric float. **C.** Water in fuel sensor signal wire.

brief seconds with the key on and engine off or during key-on engine cranking (**FIGURE 17-5**).

If the engine starts, the bulb may remain lit until proper operating conditions are met, such as correct oil pressure is reached, the emissions system is operational, or coolant level is satisfactory. That sequence is called a **prove-out sequence**.

In older machines, the ignition key will supply a circuit to provide a ground and/or positive battery voltage path to illuminate instrument warning lights. Control modules will perform the same function during key-on events. The malfunction indicator lamp (MIL) and check engine lamp (CEL) will illuminate for approximately three to five seconds during engine start-up and then extinguish. If there are active fault codes, the lights will switch back on after start-up. Gauge cluster pointers may perform a full sweep of the gauge, from minimum to maximum, back to minimum, and then to received value. This prove-out sequence enables the operator to have confidence in the correct operation of the gauge unit.

Blink codes are used by some manufacturers to provide fault code data for a specific system. These codes are derived by counting the number of flashes from a warning lamp and observing longer pauses between the light blink. For example, OEM-specific powertrain codes, engine fault codes, or platform control fault codes may be either two or three digits in length. The fault code of 32 is displayed by three light blinks in quick succession, followed by a short pause and two more blinks. A longer pause will separate multiple codes when available for display.

Gauge Operating Systems

Common gauge systems use the following technologies:

- mechanical (direct reading)
- bimetallic
- electromagnetic
- stepper motor
- digital display.

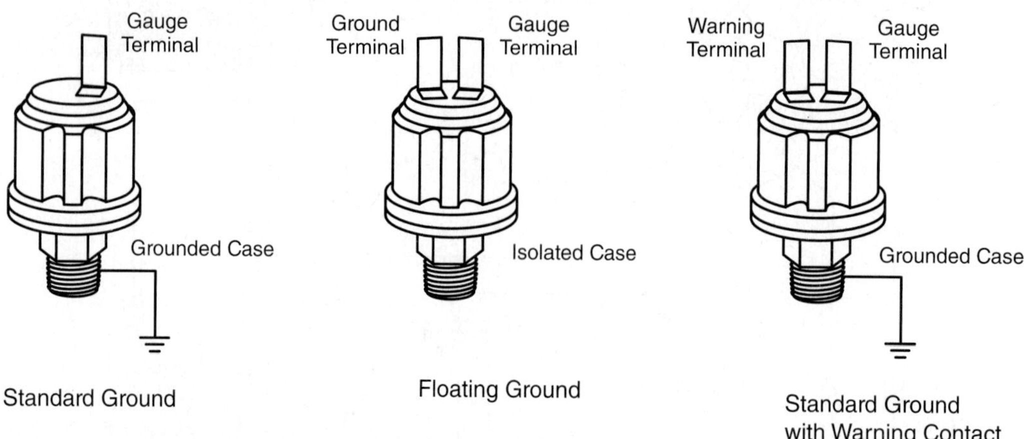

FIGURE 17-4 This normally closed hydraulic or air pressure switch is opened with pressure and closed when pressure is too low. A calibrated internal spring will allow the switch to complete a ground circuit when pressure drops below a preset amount.

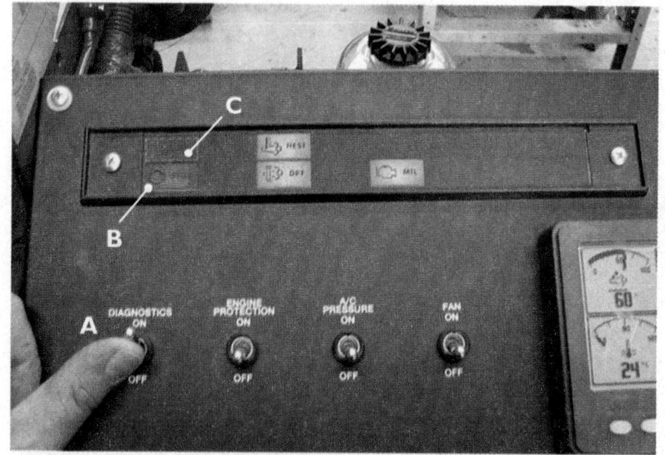

FIGURE 17-5 All warning lights will illuminate during the initial key-on period, to ensure the bulbs are functioning. The engine warning and stop lamp will blink OEM (original equipment manufacturer) flash codes when prompted by a diagnostic switch. **A.** Blink code diagnostic switch. **B.** Stop engine light red. **C.** Warning light—yellow.

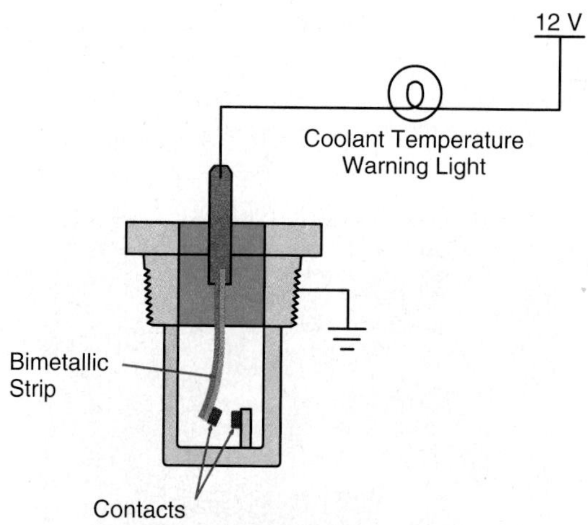

FIGURE 17-6 Bimetallic gauge operation. Bending of the bimetal strip changes the position of the pointer.

Mechanical Gauges

Mechanical direct-reading gauges are not electrical, since they depend on cables, air, or fluid pressure to operate. Speedometers operated by cables and oil pressure read by bourdon tube gauges are examples of direct-reading mechanical gauges.

Sending units are used in electrical instrumentation to convert pressure and temperature into analog signals used by instrument gauges. Sending units differ from sensors in that they are electromechanical devices, whereas sensors are non-mechanical electronic devices. Pressure and temperature switches will often operate warning lights.

Bimetallic Gauges

Bimetallic gauges work by heating metal strips, which bend and move a gauge pointing needle (**FIGURE 17-6**).

Two dissimilar pieces of metal are bonded together into a strip, much like a circuit breaker, and they expand at different rates as when heated. Heat produced through resistance of a wire coil wrapped around the bimetal strip is proportional to current flow (**FIGURE 17-7**).

Current supplied by a sending unit changes the position of the pointing needle attached to the bimetal strip. Because machine voltage fluctuates with changes to electrical loads and charging system output, a voltage regulator is required to maintain consistent gauge readings. Commonly, another bimetallic-type device will hold voltage supplied to gauges and sending units to between approximately 5 and 10 volts. The instrument voltage regulator (IVR) will use a bimetal arm with a set of breaker points that open and close rapidly when heating and cooling, in order to maintain instrument gauge voltage.

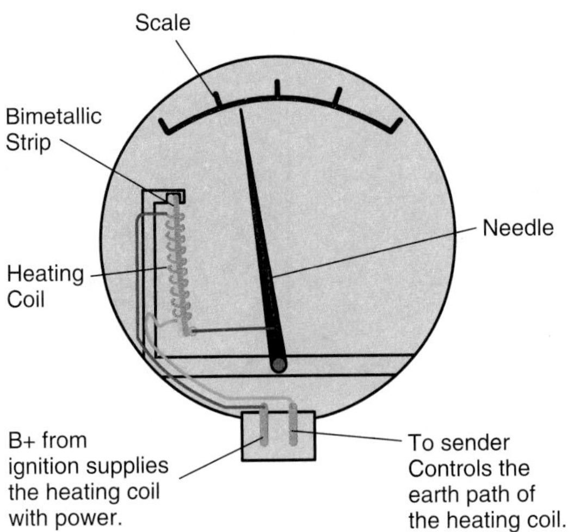

FIGURE 17-7 Construction and operation of a bimetal fuel gauge. Dissimilar metals expand at different rates when heated. The rheostat in the fuel tank controls current flow through the heater element.

D'Arsonval Gauges

D'Arsonval gauges are a type of electromagnetic gauge that moves a pointing needle directly proportional to current flow through an electromagnet attached to the pointer (**FIGURE 17-8**).

Needle deflection is controlled by current in the coil, which changes magnetic-field strength interacting with the fields of two permanent magnets fixed on either side of the coil. A larger flow of current produces a magnetic field that opposes one of the permanent magnet's fields and is attracted to another. Voltmeters are an example of a gauge that can use D'Arsonval movement. Other gauges using a D'Arsonval movement require a voltage regulator to maintain consistent readings.

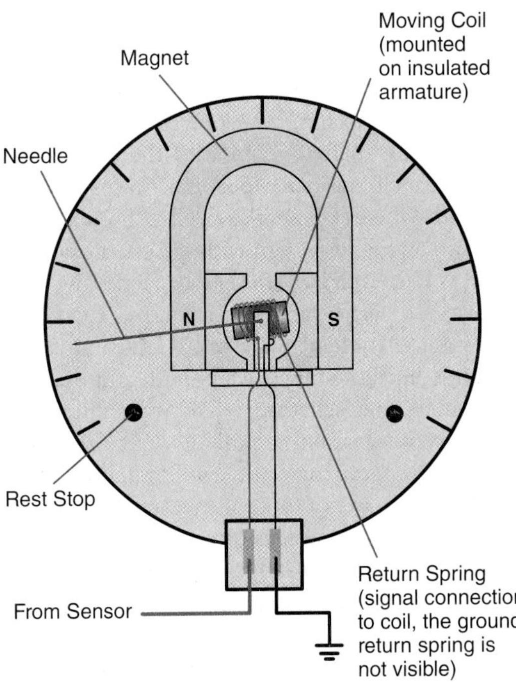

FIGURE 17-8 D'Arsonval movement gauges use a coil mounted between two permanent magnets. Changes in the coil's magnetic-field strength pull it toward one magnet and push it away from the other, causing rotation of the needle movement. A small light spring can return the pointer to a rest position.

Two- and Three-Coil Movements

Variations of the D'Arsonval movement use a pointer with a permanent magnet rather than an electromagnet. Two or three electromagnetic coils surround the pointer to rotate the gauge. Two-coil designs require a voltage regulator to maintain consistent readings, as charging voltage varies, while three-coil designs generally do not (**FIGURE 17-9**).

Both these gauges are more accurate than D'Arsonval movement gauges and are unaffected by temperature. In the two-coil gauge design, the field coils are wound in series but in opposite directions. This places a north and south pole on maximum and minimum reading sides of the pointer's magnet. Regulated ignition current is supplied to one end of the series coil, and the ground pathway is through a sending unit. Increasing current flow through the coil will intensify the forces of repulsion in one coil and attraction in the other. Pointer rotation takes place as magnetic-field strength increases or decreases proportional to current flow in the coils. In the **three-coil gauge** design, a coil is placed at the minimum and maximum reading ends of the pointer's rotation (**FIGURE 17-10**).

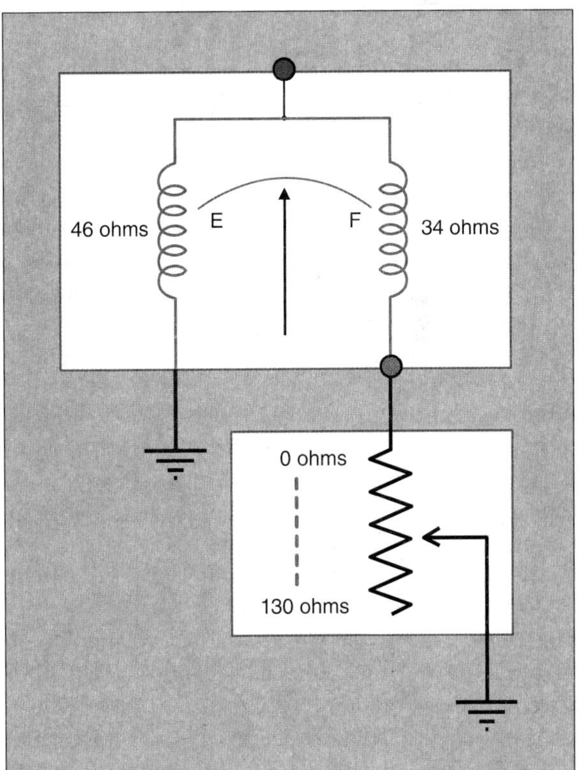

FIGURE 17-9 Two-coil gauges are connected to battery + in parallel but wound in the opposite direction. The ground of one coil is connected to a rheostat that changes the current passing through the coil and its magnetic-field strength. The needle is pulled to the coil with the strongest magnetic-field strength.

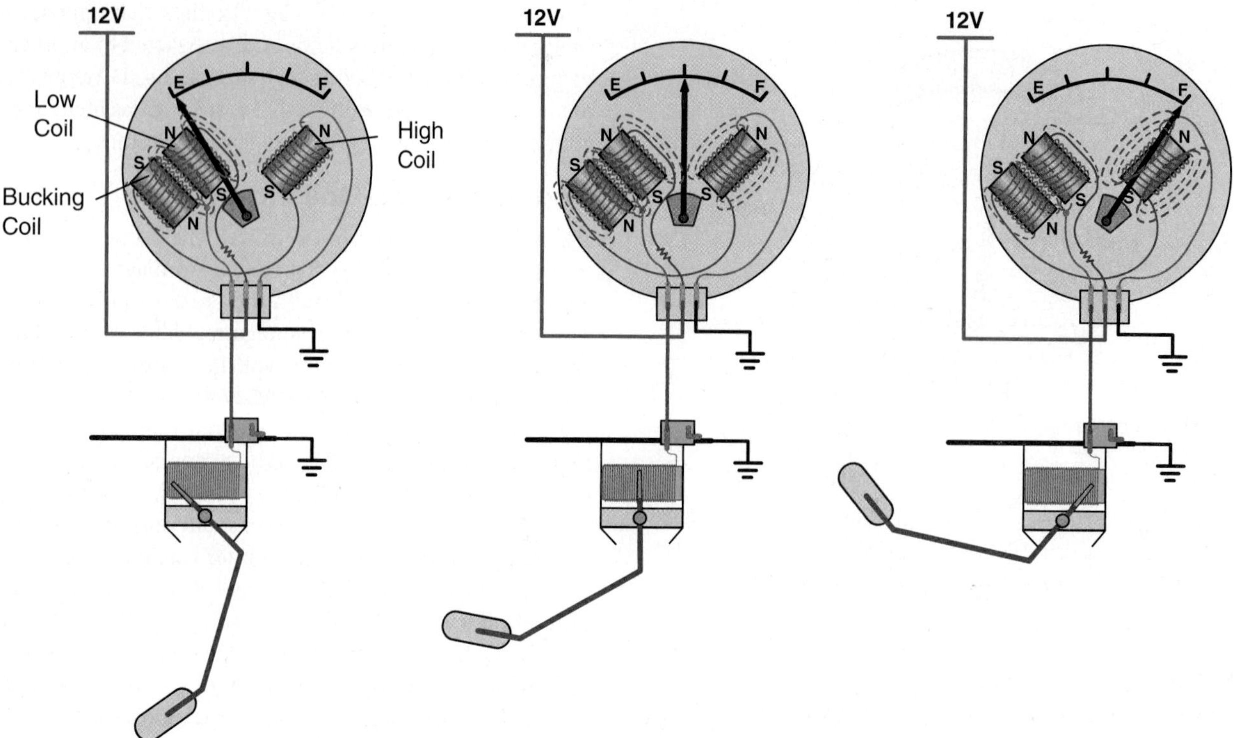

FIGURE 17-10 Operation of a three-coil design gauge. The bucking coil progressively cancels the effect of the minimum reading coil as less current passes through the sending unit.

A third coil, called a bucking coil, is placed between the minimum and maximum gauge reading. Ignition current passes through all three coils, which are wound in series. Two ground connections are supplied to the coil. One is at the end of the maximum coil, allowing all current to pass through all three coils. The other is a ground supplied through a sending unit. This ground connects to the gauge at a point between the minimum and bucking coil. Current flow passes through all three coils when resistance through the sending unit ground path is high. The maximum reading coil exerts the greatest force to pull the pointer magnet in that direction, as the minimum reading and bucking coil are wound in opposite directions to cancel each other's magnetic field. However, decreasing resistance through the sending unit permits more current to pass through the minimum reading coil, which progressively cancels out the effect of the bucking and maximum reading coil with decreasing sending unit resistance.

Stepper Motor Design

By far, **stepper motor gauges** are the most commonly used gauge technology in late-model instrument gauge clusters. The use of stepper motors to rotate pointers for analog displays bypasses the problem of inaccurate readings from bimetallic and electromagnetic coil gauges caused by voltage fluctuations, temperature changes, and oil leaks from fluid-dampened gauge clusters. This inexpensive and unique category of electric motors can precisely control the pointer rotation by dividing full motor rotation into a large number of fine resolution steps. Most gauges have 3,060 possible steps of positions between zero and full-scale deflection. Speedometers, odometers, pressure, and temperature gauges will use stepper motors to accurately display data. Stepper motors are brushless, DC electromechanical devices that generally use a permanent magnet shaft surrounded by two or more pairs of electromagnetic coils. Energizing one or more of these field coils will cause the shaft to align with the coil, pulling and holding the shaft in a stationary position. To continue rotating the shaft, another field coil next to the first is energized, causing the shaft's magnet to realign with the energized coil while the first coil is deenergized. Alternately energizing and deenergizing coils in a particular sequence moves the shaft in the desired direction in incremental steps. A large number of steps make the gauge appear to move in a smooth motion. The speed of rotation can be precisely controlled by changing the rate at which coils are switched on and off. A particular sequence of energizing and reenergizing of coils will pull and/or push the shaft in a full 360 degrees of rotation, but full rotation is unnecessary because the gauge sweeps through only 270 degrees for its minimum and maximum range. During start-up, gauge calibration and operation are checked by having the gauge sweep through its entire range, returning to zero, and then rotating to the correctly sensed position. A Hall-effect sensor and magnet built into the gauge are sometimes used to identify the full range of needle sweep.

Unipolar Stepper Motor

Two common types of stepper motors are used for instrument gauges: unipolar and bipolar motors. The unipolar stepper

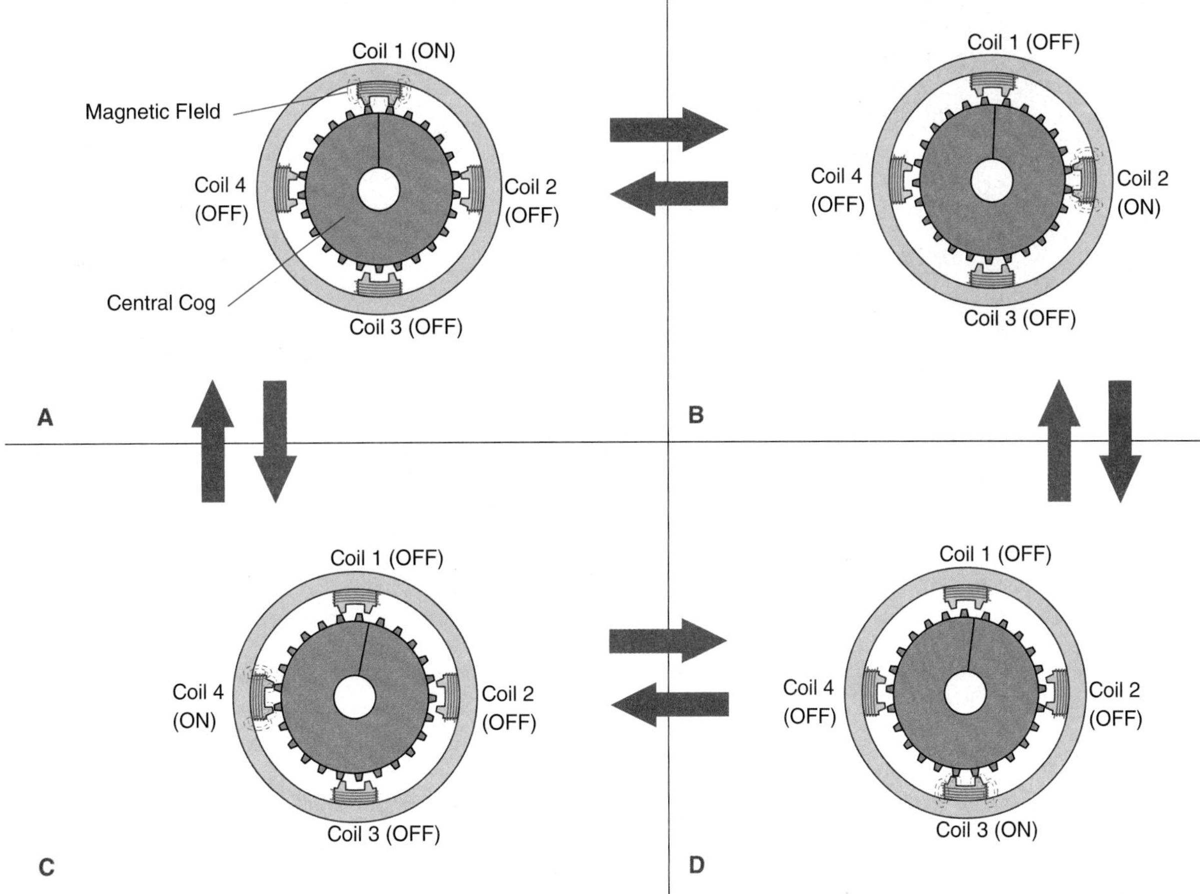

FIGURE 17-11 Unipolar motor operation. **A.** The upper electromagnet (1) is activated, and the teeth of the central cog line up accordingly. **B.** The upper electromagnet (1) is deactivated, and the right one (2) is turned on. The closest cog teeth then jump to line up with this new magnetic field. This causes a step turn of 1.8 degrees if there are 200 step turns. **C.** The right electromagnet (2) is deactivated and the lower one (3) is turned on. The cog teeth then jump to line up with the bottom electromagnet. This causes another step. **D.** The lower electromagnet (3) is switched off and the left (4) electromagnet is switched on. The cog teeth then jump to line up with the left electromagnet, producing another step.

motor is identified by its five or six wires that connect four field coils. The ends of all the coils have one common connection that is supplied power, giving the motor the name unipolar stepper because power is always supplied to this single point to form magnetic poles in the field coils. The other coil ends are connected to driver circuits of a microcontroller. Using digital logic and microcontrollers, the field coils are switched on and off to rotate the motor forward or backward or to hold the shaft (**FIGURE 17-11**).

TABLE 17-1 shows the steps used to rotate a four-pole unipolar stepper motor. A constant battery positive or ground is supplied to the coils while a ground or positive current source is switched on and off to rotate the motor.

TABLE 17-1 Steps Used to Rotate a 4-Pole Unipolar Stepper Motor

Step number	Coil A	Coil B	Coil C	Coil D
1	5-volts	0	0	0
2	0	0	5-volts	0
3	0	5-volts	0	0
4	0	0	0	5-volts
5	5-volts	0	0	0

Bipolar Stepper Motor

Unlike unipolar steppers, bipolar stepper motors have no common connection between the motor stator. Instead, coils used in the stator are independent sets of coils that enable a change in current polarity (**FIGURE 17-12**).

By measuring the resistance between the lead wires, bipolar steppers are distinguished from unipolar motors since any two pairs of wires will have equal resistance and no continuity between the coils in the stator (**FIGURE 17-13**).

Like unipolar motors, digital logic will energize the motors to produce desired motor travel characteristics. Torque is increased in bipolar motors at the expense of finer steps to produce rotation. Adding a second wire to each pair of coils in a unipolar motor allows half the coil to be energized, producing

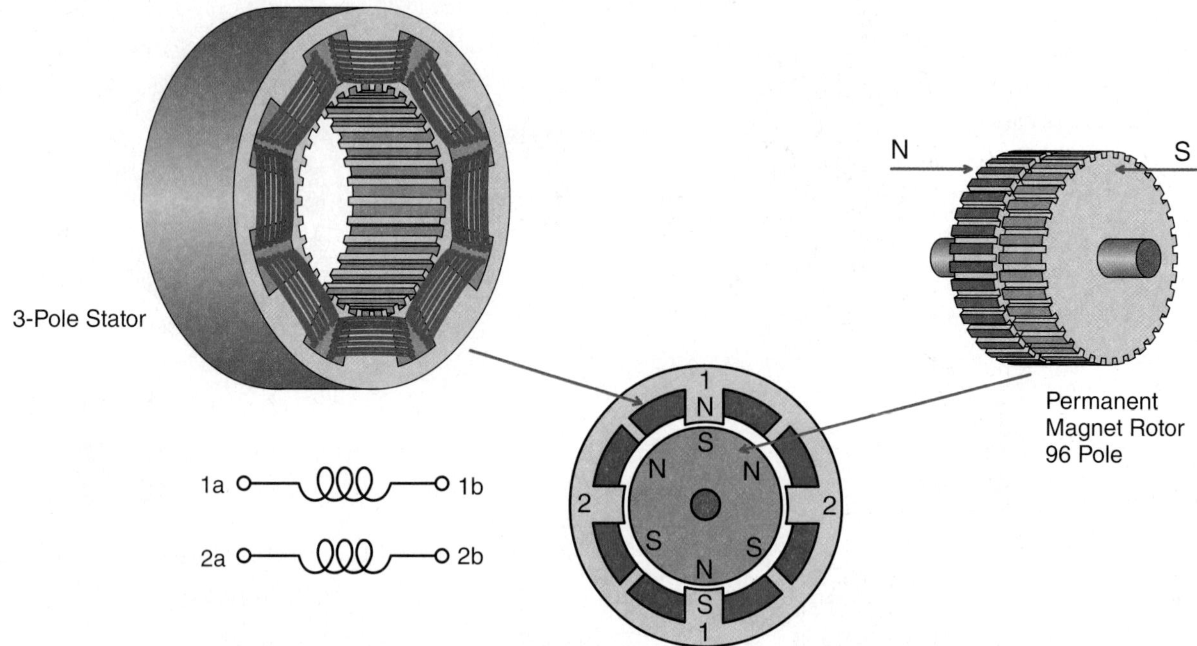

FIGURE 17-12 Some bipolar motor designs use permanent magnet rotors. Bipolar motors are capable of reversing current polarity across their coils, while unipolar motors cannot.

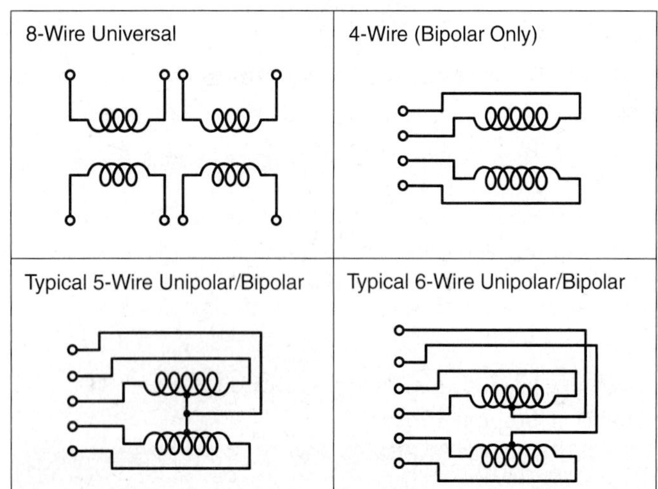

FIGURE 17-13 A variety of wiring combinations exist for various stepper motors. Stepper motor coils are energized one at a time or in pairs to increase torque output. Exhaust gas recirculation (EGR) motors are another application on diesel engines for stepper motors.

even finer steps of rotation. Directional changes are capable in both unipolar and bipolar stepper motors.

Digital CAN Gauges

Digitally driven gauges, networked gauges, or intelligent gauges are designed to display information broadcast over the communications. These gauges, which can use stepper motors or LCD/LED displays, are wired directly to the CANbus (controller area network bus). Circuits inside the gauges eliminate the need for a graphic label, interface module, or other device to drive them. Custom programming of the gauge at the manufacturer level is required to translate the programmable group message (PGM), which contains messages for multiple gauges in order to provide the proper interpretation or user-defined values (**FIGURE 17-14**).

Entire instrument clusters rich with data are now operated using CAN-driven data generated by control modules throughout the machine. Just two wires connecting the instrument panel gauge clusters to the CAN network are all that is necessary to display machine data and gauge information, provide fault codes, and display warning lamps.

FIGURE 17-14 A CAN-driven gauge will display data available on the machine network. CAN displays are both input and output devices. Menu buttons allow the operator or technicians to access a variety of data sets.

Speedometers

Speedometers electronically measure the driveshaft, wheel, or transmission shaft speed by counting a series of electrical pulses produced per mile or kilometer of distance traveled. A variable reluctance sensor is a toothed metal wheel typically placed at the transmission shaft to measure drive line speed, which corresponds to road speed.

Earlier equipment enables customized calibrations for the various chassis pulse counts using **data inline package (DIP) switches**. These are small slide switches located at the rear of the speedometer head, placed in either the on or off (1 or 0) position. Circuits inside the speedometer convert the number of received speed sensor pulses to a pulse count per mile that varies with wheel speed.

While DIP switches are set at the factory for an original equipment pulse count, switches may need to be reset if the drive line components, such as tire size or rear axle ratios, have changed from those originally installed on the machine. Procedures to adjust the DIP switches are outlined in service manuals and usually involve plugging variables for tire size or rolling radius and rear axle into a formula to determine the settings (**FIGURE 17-15**).

Inaccurate or fluctuating speedometer readings can be caused by other systems associated with the speedometer signal. Interference can originate from the engine/transmission signals and controllers, the alternator, and other charging system components. Alternating current ripple from the alternator can also induce electrical interference with speedometer signals.

Manufacturers currently use unique, proprietary software and diagnostic and maintenance tools that enable access to the machine speed settings within certain limits to accommodate changes in tire size or rear axle ratio and to adjust the speedometer calibration.

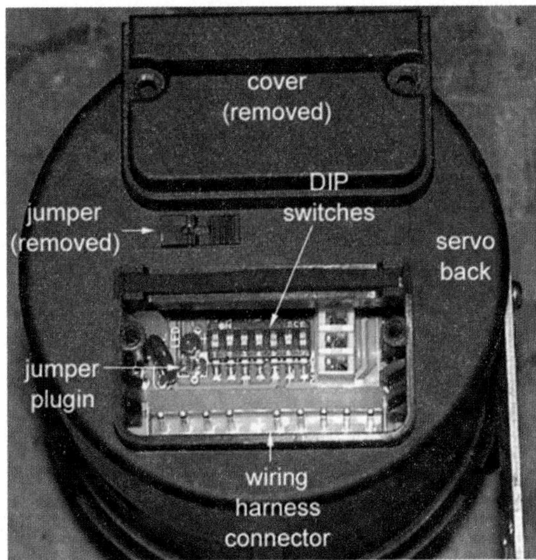

FIGURE 17-15 A speedometer with DIP switches is used to calibrate the display with pulses per mile from the speed sensor. Tire sizes and rear axle ratio require different DIP switch settings.

> **TECHNICIAN TIP**
>
> Most speedometers have tolerances of ±10% due primarily to variations in tire diameter. Sources of error due to tire diameter variations include wear, temperature, pressure, machine load, and nominal tire size. Machine manufacturers usually calibrate speedometers to read slightly higher than actual road speed by an amount equal to the average error. This practice eliminates potential liability caused by speedometers that display a lower speed than the actual road speed of the machine. GPSs can be used to validate the calibration of a speedometer. Failures or interference with signals from the variable reluctance speed sensor are best analyzed using a wave-form meter. Comparing the observed signal pattern with known good quality wave forms can identify potential problems with the speed signal.

Tachometers and Odometers

Tachometers used to observe engine speed are constructed and operate almost identically to speedometers. Variable reluctance or Hall-effect sensors are used to generate signals to the tachometer head. The engine control module (ECM) counts all of the pulses from both the speedometer and tachometer to track overall distance traveled by machine and engine. Several times per second in networked machines, the ECM sends out a packet of information consisting of a header and speed-distance data. The header is identifying the accompanying data packet as a distance or speed reading that can be read by the tachometer or odometer. Distance traveled may also be stored in an instrument cluster control module. In networked machines, trip values stored in the ECM are compared with an instrument cluster control. This means that if an attempt is made to roll back the odometer, the value stored in the ECM will not correspond and will generate a fault code.

▶ Operator Information Screens

K17002

Most operator information displays offered in machines today display engine rpm, fluid levels, fluid temperatures, warning lights, transmission speed and direction, and some basic diagnostic information or codes on liquid crystal displays (LCDs). Enormous amounts of other information systems can be added to the list: object detection warning, fuel consumption, action warning, outside temperature, telematics, and after treatment information. A variety of options are available to navigate the operator's information display menu: odometer buttons, the turn-signal wiper stalk, or a touch screen.

Liquid Crystal Display

LCDs use a compact passive display technology and consume little current to operate. Passive display means that LCDs do not emit light but instead use ambient light around the display to reflect images. The displays are made of several layers. An important one contains the liquid crystal, which is an organic substance having a liquid form with a crystal molecular structure (**FIGURE 17-16**).

The liquid is made of rod-shaped molecules that are arranged in a parallel lattice-like structure—a property that makes crystal transparent. However, an electric field can be used to control arrangement of the molecules. To do this, LCD

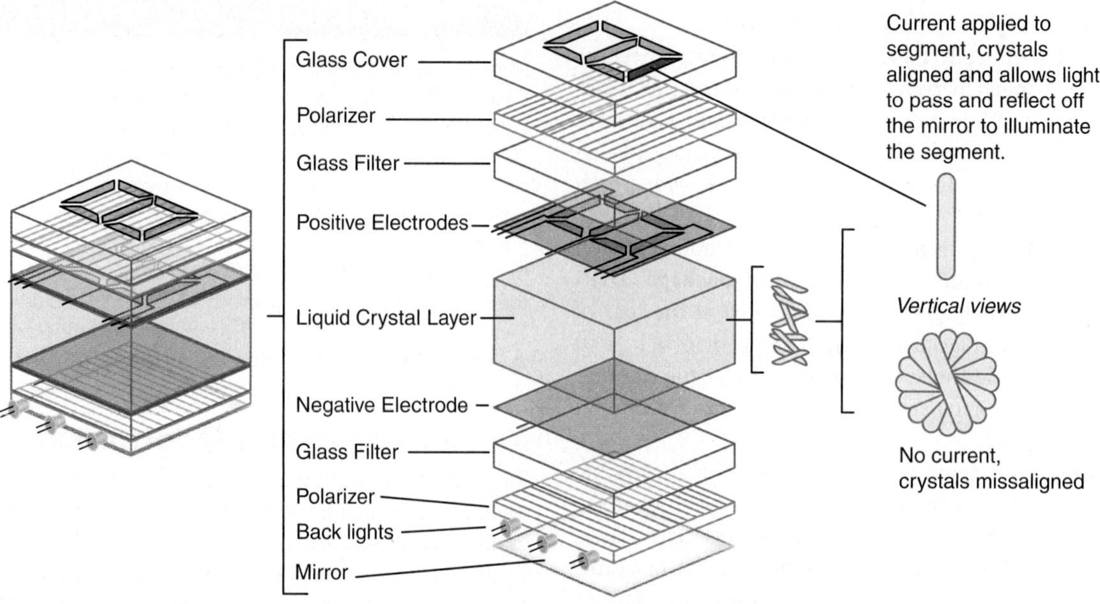

FIGURE 17-16 LCDs do not emit light but reflect it. Electric current passing through layers of glass distort liquid crystals, which allows light to either pass through and be reflected from the rear polarizer (on) or block light and reflect light from the top polarizer (off). Light reflected from the rear polarizer hits a dark gray or black surface. Light reflected from the top polarizer layer is silver or light gray.

glass has transparent electrical conductors embedded into each side of the glass, which are in contact with the liquid crystal fluid. Made of indium-tin oxide (ITO), the liquid crystal molecules will rotate in the direction of the electric current when it passes through the glass. When this happens, incoming light can pass through the glass and is reflected off a silver, gray, or black reflector surface, called the rear analyzer. What is observed is a black or gray character on a silver background taking the shape of the LCD cell. When the current is switched off, the molecules revert back to a twisted, light-blocking structure that reflects ambient light back to the observer, resembling a light gray or silvery image. Using multiple selectable current pathways through the glass and selectively applying voltage to the current paths, a variety of patterns can be achieved.

Resistive Touch Screens

All touch screen devices digitize the input from finger contact using an *x*-*y* coordinate. This means that there is a unique input determined by how far the contact is from the horizontal screen bottom or vertical side (**FIGURE 17-17**).

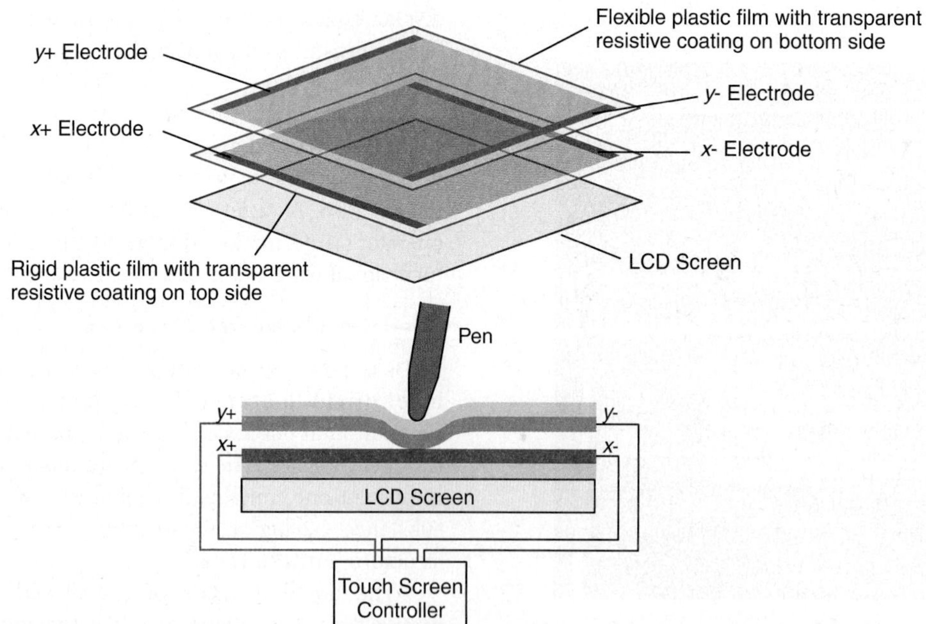

FIGURE 17-17 Resistive-type touch screens plot the location of a finger or stylus by plotting coordinates using a resistive film screen material. A unique resistance value on a screen is generated by pressing one current-carrying resistive film against another.

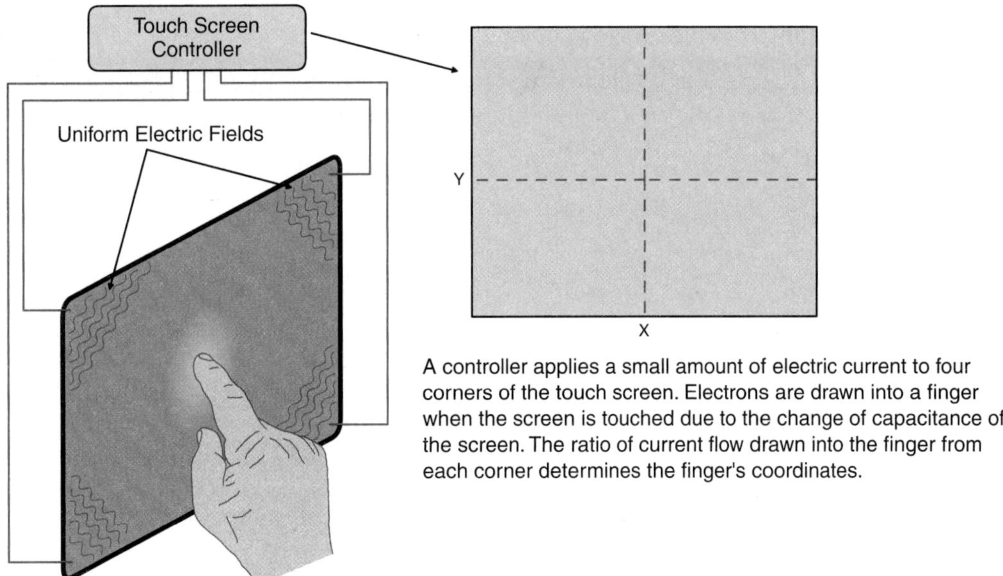

Touch Screen Controller
Uniform Electric Fields
Y
X
A controller applies a small amount of electric current to four corners of the touch screen. Electrons are drawn into a finger when the screen is touched due to the change of capacitance of the screen. The ratio of current flow drawn into the finger from each corner determines the finger's coordinates.

FIGURE 17-18 Operation of a capacitive touch screen.

Two types of technology used to sense the coordinates are capacitance and resistive touch screens.

Resistive touch screens are composed of two flexible transparent sheets lightly coated with an electrically conductive yet slightly resistive material. The sheets are separated by an air gap or microdot that closes like a switch when finger, object, or other pressure is applied to the screen. A unique voltage value is sensed by conductors placed at the *x-y* coordinate edge of the screen. Signal voltage is translated into coordinates, and an input command goes to the screen microcontroller. The resistive touch screen's advantages include its low cost, scratch resistance, durability, and capacity to operate in all climate conditions. Input can be made using either a finger or stylus.

Capacitance Touch Screens

Capacitance touch screens use two transparent plates as well. However, they use only one electrically charged layer that is typically a glass panel with a transparent coating of indium metal (**FIGURE 17-18**).

When a finger is placed on the screen, it draws electrons from that specific point on the charged plate by changing the dielectric strength of the air gap, electrically separating the plates. A unique voltage signal is sensed by conductors on the *x-y* axis of the screen. The signal varies in strength from left to right and up and down, proportional to where the contact was made. A microcontroller works out the *x-y* position based on the voltage signal caused by a change of plate capacitance produced by finger contact. If gloves—such as thin latex examination gloves, which prevent electron movement—are used, the screen will not operate. Nor will it operate if a stylus is used, and the screen is confused under wet or high humidity conditions. Capacitance-type touch screens, however, permit dual-finger touch processes and do not require as much pressure as resistive screens.

▶ Troubleshooting Instrument Gauge Problems

K17003

Technicians must be able to accurately diagnose gauge problems. A guide to troubleshooting gauge problems is in **TABLE 17-2**.

Sending Units

Sending units are electromechanical devices that convert pressure or fluid level into a variable voltage signal. Sending units are different from sensors, which are low-voltage electronic devices with no moving parts. Most sending units are a variable resistive type (**FIGURE 17-19**).

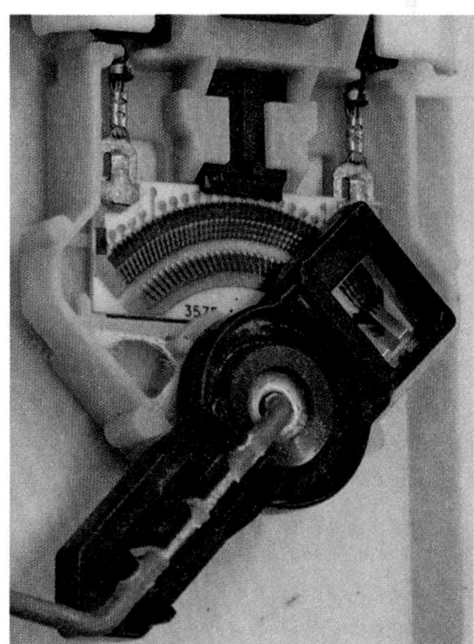

FIGURE 17-19 A rheostat used for the sending unit of a fuel tank.

TABLE 17-2 Troubleshooting Instrument Gauge Problems

Symptom	Possible Cause	Diagnostic Strategy
Gauges do not repond with a prove-out sequence when ignition is switched on.	Missing or broken ignition or ground wire	Check for power and grounds to instrument cluster.
	Blown fuse	Check fuses and breakers.
	Defective stepper motor	Continuity checks of stepper motor.
Erratic gauge readings	Loose connections at sender unit and/or gauge	Verify connections.
	Poor, loose, or resistive grounds	Measure resistance of sending unit and compare with specifications.
	Defective sending unit or gauge	Evaluate gauge during prove-out. Stepper motor gauges should smoothly sweep from min. to max. values then to minimum before moving to sensed value.
Gauge stays at minimum or maximum value all the time (i.e., fuel empty, no oil pressure, low coolant temperature)	Sender unit wire disconnected or open circuited	Verify oil pressure with master mechanical gauge. Visually check fuel tank level. Verify engine temperature using an infrared thermometer.
	Sender unit wires shorted to ground	Remove sender wire. Check harness isolate shorts to ground and repair.
	Sender unit defective, (i.e., broken unit, missing or leaking float, internally shorted to ground)	Measure resistance of sending unit over its full range. Check float.
	Defective gauge	Supply a calibrated resistance to sending unit lead to evaluate gauge. Ground out sending unit wire to observe whether gauge moves. Disconnect sending unit wire to observe whether gauge moves.
No data on CAN instrument gauge display	Pinched, shorted, or open CAN bus to instrument cluster	Check CAN signal to clusters using oscilloscope. Measure CAN power and ground with voltmeter.
	Missing terminating resistors	Measure CAN signals using a voltmeter. Measure resistance of CAN line batteries disconnected.

The fuel tank sending unit, for example, uses a resistive wiper mechanism. An electrical whisker or brush moves along a resistor track depending on the fuel level. Low-voltage current originating through the instrument panel fuel gauge passes through the resistor track and then through to ground via the whisker. Oil pressure sending units use a flexible bellow also containing a whisker that passes along a resistor track. Pressure below the bellows moves the whisker along the resistive track to supply a ground (**FIGURE 17-20**).

Current to the sending unit is also supplied by the gauge. With less resistance in the sending unit, more current passes through the gauge to deflect the pointer between minimum and maximum readings. Temperature sending units use a wax pellet similar to the design of a coolant thermostat. As temperature changes, the wax pellet will expand or contract. A disc over the wax pellet acts like a whisker to change the resistance of the current pathway through an internal resistive track. Electronic modules are available to convert variable voltage values into digital signals for use by digital gauges.

Diagnosing Sending Units and Gauges

Resistive-type gauges are quickly checked by opening the circuit to the sending unit or by grounding the sending unit lead. When a circuit is opened, circuit resistance becomes infinite and will move a gauge to either its minimum or maximum reading. If that does not happen, the circuit to the gauge or the gauge itself is defective. Grounding the lead wire to the sending unit should move the gauge to a maximum or minimum value too. The type of gauge construction—D'Arsonval, two-, or three-wire—will determine in which direction the gauge will move when opened or grounded. A gauge testing unit can evaluate gauge accuracy by supplying a resistance of known value to the circuit and then observing whether the gauge pointer is positioned where expected. The accuracy of a fuel gauge is ideally evaluated using this method. The resistance of a sending unit measured with an ohmmeter can determine whether its resistance is within the range expected for a given pressure temperature or liquid level (**FIGURE 17-21**).

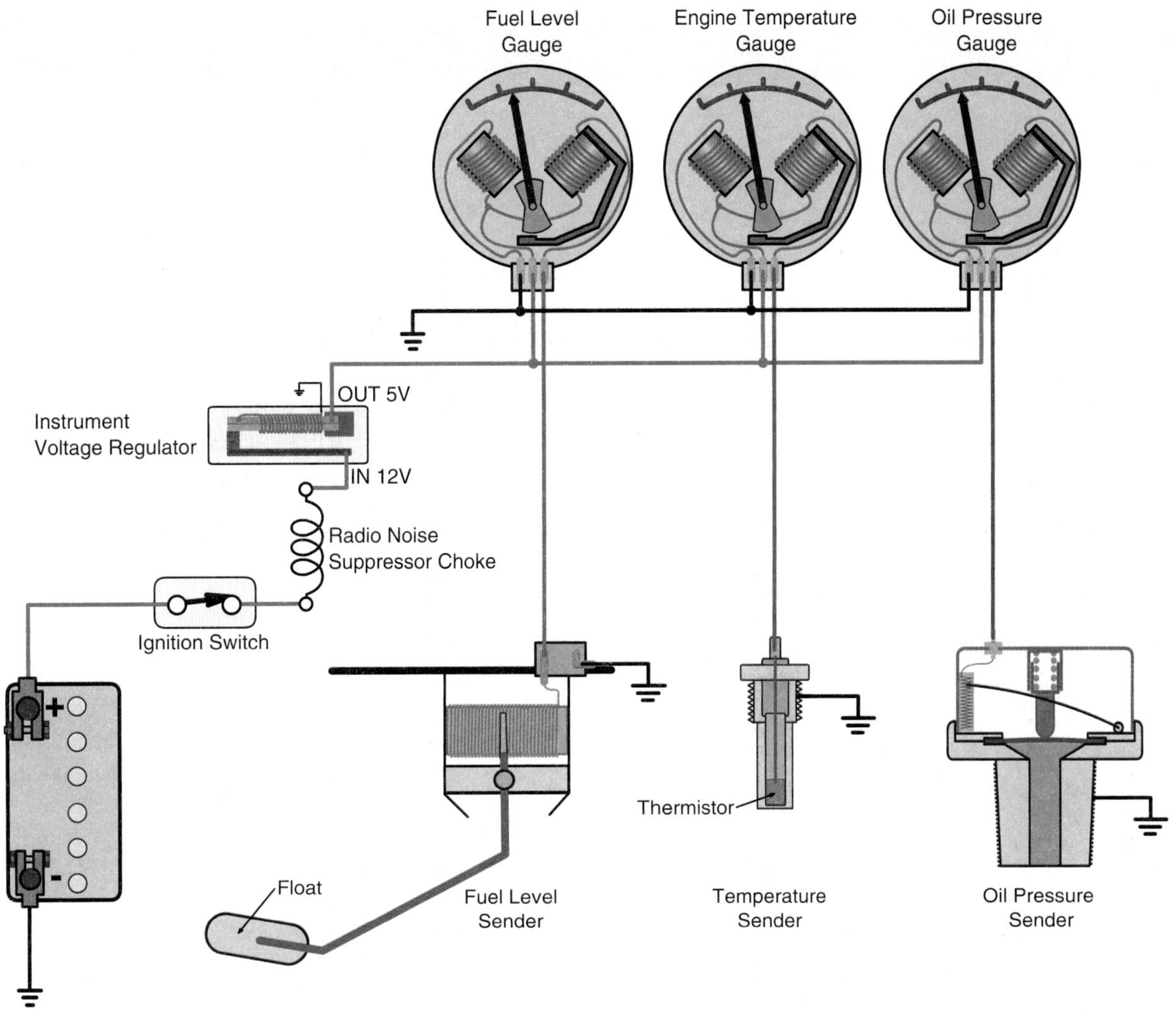

Fuel Level
Gauge
Engine Temperature
Gauge
Oil Pressure
Gauge
OUT 5V
Instrument
Voltage Regulator
IN 12V
Radio Noise
Suppressor Choke
Ignition Switch
Thermistor
Float
Fuel Level
Sender
Temperature
Sender
Oil Pressure
Sender

FIGURE 17-20 Construction of a variety of sending units with two-coil gauges. Note the voltage regulator used to maintain consistent gauge readings when charging system voltage varies.

59.70 Ω
Slowly move the float arm from full to empty

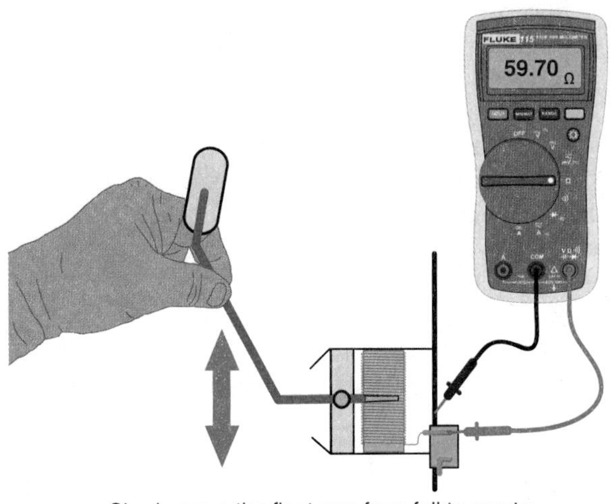

FIGURE 17-21 Measuring the resistance of a fuel sending unit.

It's important to verify the ground supplied to the sending unit is good, as this will interfere with sending unit resistance values. Some sending units are designed with two terminals, one of which provides a dedicated ground for the gauge circuit.

▶ TECHNICIAN TIP

Low or no resistance of a sending unit to ground through the engine block, transmission, or axle case is critical for accurate gauge operation. Undiagnosed resistive grounds can often lead to unnecessary replacement of sending units and gauges. Always check the continuity of a major component case or block-to-chassis ground as part of a diagnostic pinpoint test. The use of Teflon tape can also interfere with sending unit continuity. Use liquid thread sealer rather than tape to prevent thread leakage. Because gauges often operate at low voltage, never touch the sender lead to ignition +12 volt.

▶ Wrap-Up

Ready for Review

- Instrument gauges, warning lamps, and operator information centers enable the operator to monitor the machine's operating condition, the status of equipment, and safety systems.
- Warning lights provide easily understood information to alert the operator to potentially dangerous operating conditions.
- Mechanical switches, called sending switches, are used to indicate low fluid levels, low air pressure warning systems, or power divider engagement locks.
- Electronic switches found in electronic control modules are the most common way warning lights are illuminated in today's machines.
- To test the correct operation of a warning light, machines use a prove-out sequence in which the instrument cluster illuminates the warning lights for several brief seconds with the key on and engine off or during key-on engine cranking.
- Manufacturers use blink codes to provide fault code data.
- Gauge systems are designed to inform the driver about a developing problem by displaying a representation of a physical measure of system conditions (pressure, temperature, or fluid level).
- Common gauge systems are mechanical, bimetallic strip, electromagnetic, stepper motor, and digital display.
- For gauges to work accurately, they require voltage regulators to supply a steady current and smooth out variation from the alternator and from accessory systems being turned on and off.
- Stepper motors increase the precision of the pointer rotation on a gauge and can be either unipolar or bipolar.
- Most speedometers have tolerances of ±10% due primarily to variations in tire diameter. Sources of error due to tire diameter variations are wear, temperature, pressure, machine load, and nominal tire size.
- Today's machines include data displays that allow the operator to view engine rpm, fluid levels, fluid temperatures, warning lights, transmission speed and direction, and some basic diagnostic information. Many of these displays use liquid crystal technology.
- Touch screens can use resistive or capacitance touch technologies.
- Machines use a number of different types of gauge sending units, including thermistors and variable resistors.
- Electrical problems such as a blown fuse, faulty wiring, gauges, or sender units can result in faulty gauge readings.

Key Terms

bimetallic gauge A gauge in which two dissimilar pieces of metal are bonded together and expand at different rates when heated, thereby converting the heating effect of electricity into mechanical movement.

blink code A method of providing fault code data for a specific system that involves counting the number of flashes from a warning lamp and observing longer pauses between the light blinks.

capacitance touch screen A display screen that uses two transparent plates, one of which is electrically charged.

D'Arsonval gauge A type of electromagnetic gauge that moves a pointing needle directly proportional to current flow through an electromagnet attached to the pointer.

data inline package (DIP) switches A small slide switch located at the rear of the speedometer head placed in either an on or off (1 or 0) position.

prove-out sequence A sequence in which the warning lights for several brief seconds with the key on and engine off or during key-on engine cranking.

resistive touch screen A display screen composed of two flexible, transparent sheets lightly coated with an electrically conductive yet slightly resistive material.

three-coil gauge A gauge in which three field coils are wound in series, with a coil at minimum reading, one at maximum reading, and one between the two.

Review Questions

1. Which of the following statements about instrumentation is correct?
   a. The type of displays, warning lights, and gauges differ widely among machines and manufacturers but break down into common gauge groups, sensing, and input systems.
   b. Monitoring engine operation involves measuring the pressure and temperature of parameters of the lubrication, cooling, and air induction system.
   c. Charging voltage and amperage of the electrical system, fuel level, air pressure, engine, and machine speed are other common gauge systems.
   d. All of the choices are correct.
2. Which of the following is the most common method of illuminating warning lights in today's machines?
   a. Voltage drop circuits
   b. Pneumatic switches
   c. Mechanical ground switches
   d. Electronic switches
3. Which of the following statements about the prove-out sequence is correct?
   a. In older machines, the ignition key will supply a circuit to provide a ground and/or positive battery voltage path to illuminate instrument warning lights.
   b. In order to validate the correct operation of a warning light, the instrument cluster is designed to illuminate a bulb for several brief seconds with the key on and engine off or during key-on engine cranking.

c. If the engine starts, the bulb may remain lit until proper operating conditions are met, such as when the correct oil pressure has been reached.
d. All of the choices are correct.

4. Which of the following is NOT a technology used with common gauge systems?
a. Electromagnetic
b. Stepper motor
c. Bi-electrical
d. Digital display

5. Mechanical gauges may depend upon _______ to operate.
a. cables
b. air pressure
c. fluid pressure
d. All of the choices are correct.

6. How much voltage is supplied to gauges and sending units?
a. Between 0.5 and 1 volts
b. Between 1.5 and 2 volts
c. Between 3 and 4 volts
d. Between 5 and 10 volts
e. All of the choices are correct.

7. What is an example of a gauge that can use D'Arsonval movement?
a. Ammeter
b. Voltmeter
c. Fuel pressure
d. Water temperature

8. Which of the following statements about two- and three-coil movements is correct?
a. Variations of the D'Arsonval movement use a pointer with a permanent magnet rather than an electromagnet.
b. Two or three electromagnetic coils surround the pointer to rotate the gauge.
c. Two-coil designs require a voltage regulator to maintain consistent readings because charging voltage varies, but three-coil designs generally do not.
d. All of the choices are correct.

9. How many possible steps of positions do most stepper gauges have?
a. 1,530
b. 2,400
c. 2,800
d. 3,060

10. The unipolar stepper motor can be identified by its _____ wires that connect _____ field coils.
a. 2 or 3; 2
b. 4; 4
c. 5 or 6; 4
d. 7 or 8; 4

ASE Technician A/Technician B Style Questions

1. Technician A says warning lights can be built into gauges or mounted in a dedicated panel in the instrument. Technician B says warning lights require a power feed and ground for the light to illuminate. Who is correct?
a. Technician A
b. Technician B
c. Both Technician A and Technician B
d. Neither Technician A nor Technician B

2. Technician A says normally closed pressure switches opened with air or oil pressure provide a path to ground to illuminate a bulb. Technician B says normally opened pressure switches opened with air or oil pressure provide a path to ground to illuminate a bulb. Who is correct?
a. Technician A
b. Technician B
c. Both Technician A and Technician B
d. Neither Technician A nor Technician B

3. Technician A says that after the engine starts and the alternator begins charging, charging system voltage is applied to both terminals of a bulb. Technician B says the charging system indicator light is an example of a light operated through voltage drop. Who is correct?
a. Technician A
b. Technician B
c. Both Technician A and Technician B
d. Neither Technician A nor Technician B

4. Technician A says the malfunction indicator lamp (MIL) and check engine lamp (CEL) will illuminate for approximately three to five seconds during engine start-up and then extinguish. Technician B says if there are active fault codes, the lights will switch back on after start-up. Who is correct?
a. Technician A
b. Technician B
c. Both Technician A and Technician B
d. Neither Technician A nor Technician B

5. Technician A says stepper motor gauges reduce the problems associated with inaccurate readings from bimetallic and electromagnetic coil gauges caused by voltage fluctuations. Technician B says stepper motors are brush-type DC electromechanical devices that generally use a permanent magnet shaft that is surrounded by more than two pairs of electromagnetic coils. Who is correct?
a. Technician A
b. Technician B
c. Both Technician A and Technician B
d. Neither Technician A nor Technician B

6. Technician A says speedometers electronically measure the driveshaft speed by counting a series of electrical pulses produced per mile or kilometer of distance traveled. Technician B says two wires connecting the instrument panel gauge clusters to the CAN network are all that is necessary to supply the data necessary to display machine data and trip information, provide fault codes, and display warning lamps. Who is correct?
   a. Technician A
   b. Technician B
   c. Both Technician A and Technician B
   d. Neither Technician A nor Technician B
7. Technician A says gauge senders output an electronic signal based on an electrical input. Technician B says electronic modules are available to convert variable voltage values into digital signals for use by digital gauges. Who is correct?
   a. Technician A
   b. Technician B
   c. Both Technician A and Technician B
   d. Neither Technician A nor Technician B
8. Technician A says electrical problems such as a blown fuse, faulty wiring, gauges, or sender units can result in a faulty gauge reading. Technician B says machines use only one type of gauge sending unit. Who is correct?
   a. Technician A
   b. Technician B
   c. Both Technician A and Technician B
   d. Neither Technician A nor Technician B
9. Technician A says that if a gauge does not respond during a prove-out sequence, a blown fuse is the problem. Technician B says erratic gauge readings could be caused by resistive grounds. Who is correct?
   a. Technician A
   b. Technician B
   c. Both Technician A and Technician B
   d. Neither Technician A nor Technician B
10. Technician A says you should use an ohmmeter when checking for smooth operation of a fuel sender unit. Technician B says the fuel sender unit should be reconnected to the fuel gauge to check for full-range operation only after removing it from the tank. Who is correct?
    a. Technician A
    b. Technician B
    c. Both Technician A and Technician B
    d. Neither Technician A nor Technician B

CHAPTER 18

Principles of Machine Electronic Control Systems and Signal Processing

Knowledge Objectives

After reading this chapter, you will be able to:

- **K18001** Identify and explain the advantages of electronic signal processing over mechanical system control.
- **K18002** Identify and describe the operating principles of electronic signal-processing systems used in electrical system.
- **K18003** Identify and describe the types of electrical signals and associated terminology.
- **K18004** Identify and describe the functions, construction, and application of electronic control modules.

Skills Objectives

There are no skills objectives for this chapter.

▶ Introduction

Today's machine systems found on mobile off-road equipment are most often controlled by electronic systems, and technicians are just as likely to use a computer as they are to use a wrench to service them. Most machine systems cannot operate without complete or at least some degree of electronic control. This has not always been the case. Before the use of electronic controls, mechanical devices such as levers, springs, linkage, gears, cables, or bellows controlled system operation. Electronic systems using microcontroller- and microprocessor-based control now provide operational capabilities far exceeding any mechanical system capabilities and can do this with greater precision, efficiency, and reliability. The dominance and sophistication of electronic control makes skill development related to servicing this technology one of the most important priorities for successful technicians. Understanding the operating principles of electronic control systems is foundational for choosing diagnostic strategies, using service tools effectively, and making sound repair recommendations.

▶ Benefits of Electronic Control

K18001

Electronic control offers many benefits to today's mobile off-road equipment, including increased power and efficiency, enhanced reporting capabilities, telematics, increased safety, programmable features, and self-diagnostic capabilities.

Increased Power and Efficiency

Diesel engines were the some of the first machine systems transformed by electronic controls (**FIGURE 18-1**).

Engines had reached their limit of efficiency, and the next logical step was to apply electronic controls already used on gasoline engines. The immediate benefits of these refinements to engine operation are lower engine emissions, improved fuel economy, increased reliability, and enhanced performance. Smarter engines continue to deliver ever-increasing power from smaller displacements, quieter operation, and longer service intervals, in addition to needing less maintenance. The increased costs of some of these features are offset through improved engine efficiency. Many of the electronic control systems have in fact lowered the cost of machine production while adding more features with improved operating benefits. In comparison to mechanical controls, electronic controls enable far greater flexibility to adjust fuel injection metering, injection rate, and timing over a large number of operating conditions. When engine operational problems leading to excess emissions do occur, self-monitoring and self-diagnostic capabilities of electronic controls can identify the problem, alert the operator, and revert to operating modes that minimize noxious emission production.

TABLE 18-1 shows the increase in power output per cubic inch of displacement and lowering of emissions achieved through advanced technology and electronic control of the fuel system.

Information Reporting Capabilities

Life cycle costs of operating machines with these engines is further reduced through the ability of the engine control systems to interface with tablets and Windows-based diagnostic and service software. Service technicians can access a wealth of diagnostic and service data much faster and with more precise detail than before (**FIGURE 18-2**).

Operational reports from the machine ECM extracted during scheduled maintenance intervals report details such as diagnostic fault codes, fuel consumption, idle time, emission system performance, and machine abuse statistics (**FIGURE 18-3**).

Telematics

In addition to the obtaining machine and operational information downloaded at scheduled maintenance intervals, ECM data can be collected and modified by other means (**FIGURE 18-4**).

When equipped with the correct machine interface devices, machine and engine diagnostics can be performed from distant locations. Telematics, a branch of information technology, uses specialized telecommunication applications for the long-distance transmission of information to and from a machine (**FIGURE 18-5**).

You Are the Mobile Heavy Technician

A number of machines have arrived at your shop with a list of apparently unrelated complaints: machine speed display that begin to bounce at 10 mph (16 kph), automatic transmissions that shift erratically, dozens of hydraulic codes for components and circuits that have no faults, and rough-running engines. On one of the machines, when performing some pinpoint tests with a digital multimeter, you accidentally set the meter to read alternating-current (AC) and not direct-current (DC) voltage. You are surprised to discover close to 4 volts of AC current are superimposed on the system's 12-volt DC current. Realizing that the only component that could produce AC current is the alternator, you disconnect the alternator and find the AC voltage has disappeared along with the unusual electrical system complaints. To repair the problem, the alternator is replaced and so are the machine's batteries, which all tested defective. As you prepare to document the diagnosis and justify the replacement of the parts on the work orders, consider the following questions:

1. What shop equipment could be used to capture and record the AC voltage signal frequency and waveform to document the problem?
2. Would the electronic control module (ECM) be processing the correct data from some sensor inputs if AC voltage accompanies the DC voltage inputs? Explain your answer.
3. After gaining the experience repairing these machines, what checks would you recommend in future for diagnosing electrical problems that may be related to electrical signal interference?

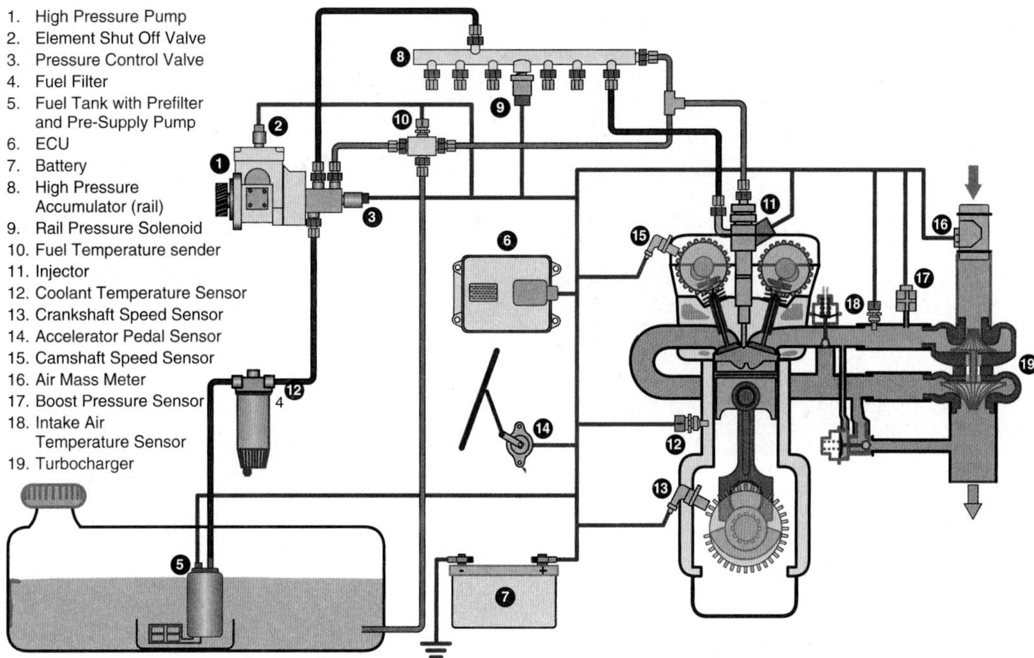

FIGURE 18-1 An overview of components used for the engine management system of a common rail diesel engine. Extensive use of electronics translates into precise control of combustion events for low emissions, superior performance, and fuel efficiency.

For example, when machines are equipped with radio-, satellite-, or cellular-based communications, a technician or equipment manager can remotely monitor any information about the machine, engine, or product the machine is carrying that is available from the machine network data link connector. Messages can be sent back and forth between the machine and a central location. For example, if the amount of fuel consumed is above normal, necessary steps can be taken to rectify equipment or operator error. A GPS can report machine location to an equipment manager, as well as log hours of run time. A fault code can be evaluated to determine whether immediate repairs are needed. For large operations, short-range wireless technology allows diagnostics and the programming of machines when they need a service or program update for increased productivity.

SAFETY TIP

The use of electronic engine and machine management provides for enhanced machine and occupant safety and security. If a machine's load is in danger, sensors and the machine control system can alert the operator. Engine systems can be monitored for operating conditions that have destructive potential. Low oil pressure, high intake, or coolant temperatures are commonly monitored conditions that can initiate an adaptive response to prevent catastrophic failure or damage. Dangerous operating conditions can trigger the engine to shut down, derate power, or simply warn the operator. The microprocessor powertrain control makes it possible to build in features that will protect the powertrain from damage due to excessive torque or speed as well. Hard braking and speeding are other measurable conditions monitored by management systems to ensure road safety.

TABLE 18-1 Increase in Power Output per Cubic Feet of Displacement

Engine Model	1988—7.3L IDI Diesel	2015—6.7L Powerstroke
Horsepower	180 hp	440 hp
Torque	338 ft/lb @ 1,600 rpm	860 ft/lb @ 1,600 rpm
NOX emissions	2.5 grams/bhp	0.07grams/bhp
Intake air flow @ 3,330 rpm	360 cubic feet/minute	732 cubic feet/minute
Exhaust flow @ 3,300 rpm	1,080 cubic feet/minute	1,499 cubic feet/minute
Fuel system	Mechanical distributor pump	Bosch piezoelectric injectors CP4.2 Common Rail Pump Electronic

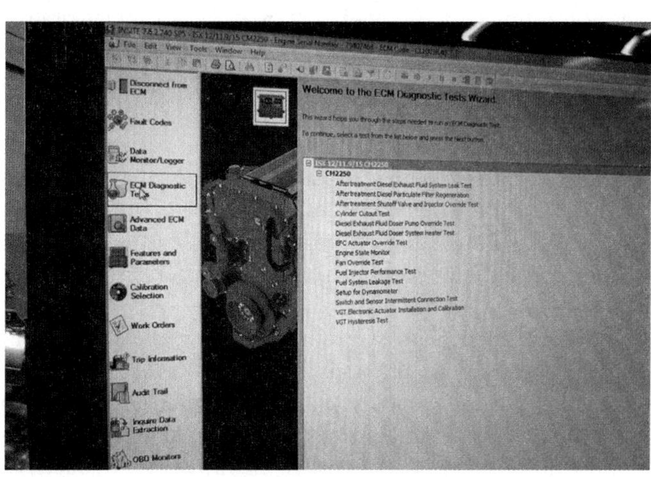

FIGURE 18-2 Screen shot with a menu of the various diagnostic routines available to troubleshoot engine operation.

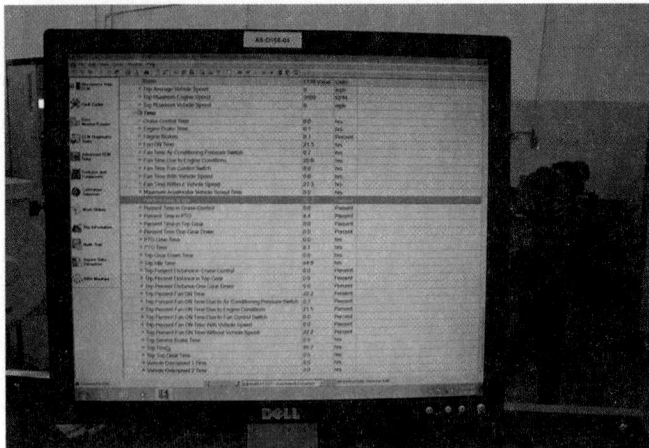

FIGURE 18-3 Machine information is data produced from monitoring machine operation, such as fuel filter hours, transmission shifting patterns, idling characteristics, hard braking.

FIGURE 18-4 The instrument cluster can provide information to the operator about a variety of machine operating conditions.

Programmable Machine Features

Service technicians and operators can take advantage of programmable electronic controls. Programmable software provides flexibility to engines, transmissions, and implements for adapting to specific job applications, which enhances machine productivity, longevity, and operator comfort. Programmable changes may include things as simple as idle shut-down timers or maximum vehicle speed limits to adding safety interlocks that prevent the vehicle from moving if a door is open, a boom is raised, or outriggers are extended (**FIGURE 18-6**).

Power and torque-rise profiles are easily altered electronically. Depending on the application, it is beneficial to performance and fuel economy to have maximum torque appear over different rpm ranges. Instead of replacing an injection pump and turbocharger to change engine power characteristics, electronically controlled engines are recalibrated with new software instructions. In a few minutes with some keystrokes, a stock machine can be reprogrammed to operate for a customer-specific application.

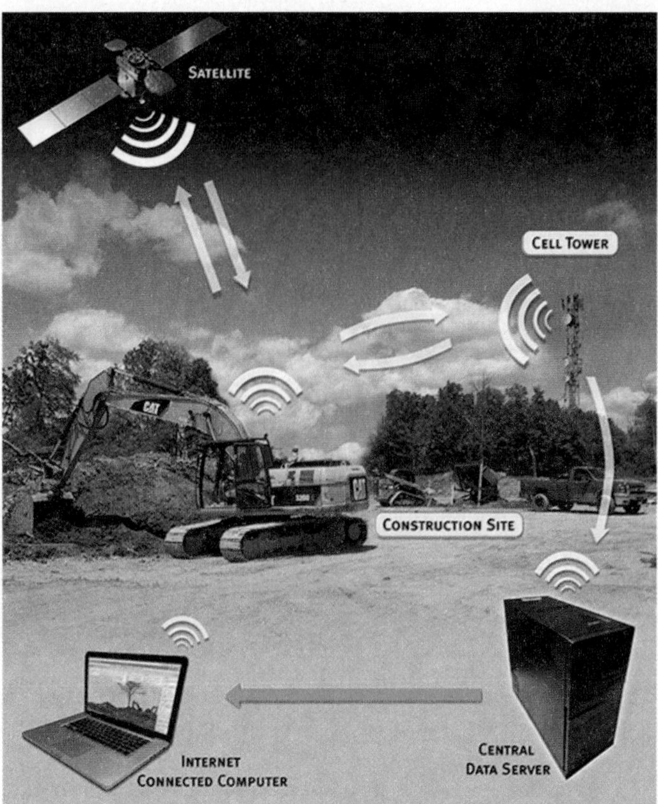

FIGURE 18-5 Telematics uses satellite communication or cell phone technology to interface with the onboard machine network. Any network data can be read and sent to a remote monitor, reporting diagnostics and other service-related information.

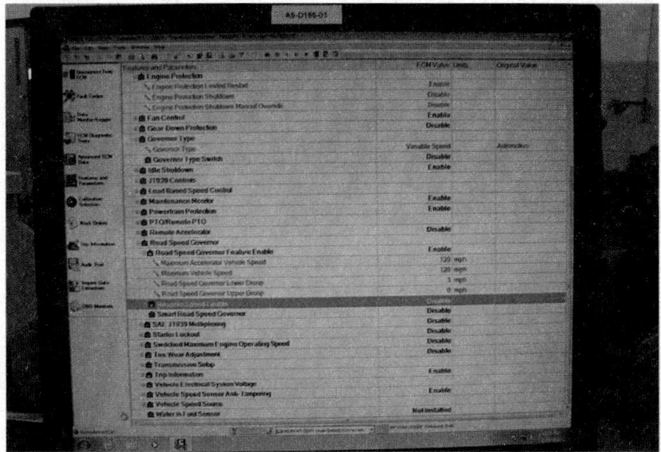

FIGURE 18-6 A screenshot from Cummins' service information system, called INSITE, displaying some of the programmable engine parameters.

Self-Diagnostic Capabilities

Electronic systems do not have many moving parts to wear out, but the systems can be complex. Diagnostics on electronically controlled machine systems can be performed easily, often with fewer tools and in less time than on mechanical systems. When something goes wrong with a component or circuit, it can be extremely time-consuming and difficult to identify the problem without some built-in self-diagnostic capabilities. Built into electronic control systems is a self-monitoring function with capabilities to check the operation of circuits and electrical devices and determine whether voltages are out of range, whether the sensor data is likely correct, and whether the system is functioning properly. Problems are quickly identified as they occur. The presence of faults is communicated through the malfunction indicator lamps. An engine may even lose power or derate to prevent excessive emission production and engine damage and provide an incentive to have the condition repaired. Electronic service tools assist the technicians in performing off-board diagnostics—that is, perform pinpoint checks to precisely identify system faults. Software-based diagnostics deliver huge amounts of data about system operation, enabling service technicians to identify problems more quickly than they could with mechanical systems. Since modules, sensors, and actuators are more compact, they can be replaced quickly with minimal training and experience required.

▶ Elements of Electronic Signal-Processing Systems

K18002

At first glance, the operation of electronic control systems looks mysterious, using a variety of sensors, wires, electrical actuators, and electronic modules moved with invisible electrical signals. However, to understand how electronic control systems operate, it is helpful to observe that any system functions can be broken down into three major divisions:

- sensing
- processing
- output or actuation (**FIGURE 18-7**).

Sensing Functions

Sensing functions collect data about operational conditions or the state of a device by measuring some value, such as temperature, position, speed, pressure, flow, angle. Sensors are devices designed to collect specific data in an electronic format.

Processing

Processing refers to the control system element that collects sensor data and determines outputs based on a set of instructions or program software. Operational algorithms, which are simply mathematical formulas used to solve problems, are included in the software that determines the steps taken when processing electrical data.

Outputs

The outputs of a system are functions performed by electrical signals produced by the processor. These may be signals to operate anything, including a digital display of numeric or alphabetic information, current to operate solenoids or injectors, actuators, motors, lights, or other electromechanical devices (**FIGURE 18-8**).

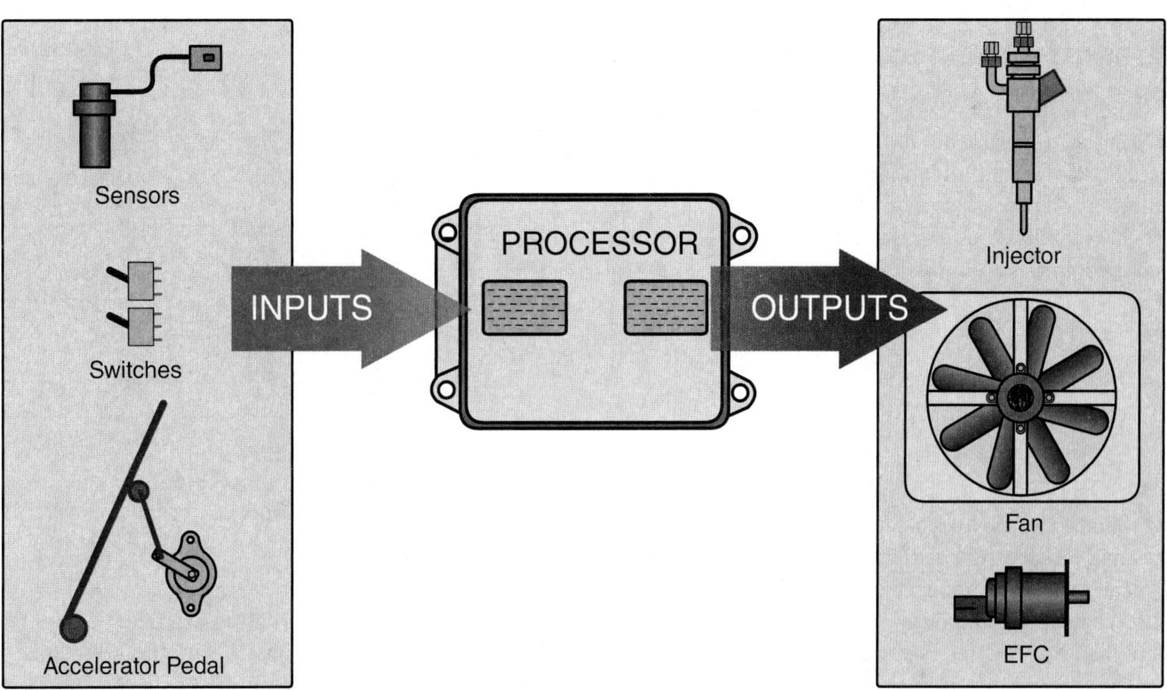

FIGURE 18-7 All engine management systems process electrical signals in three distinct stages: data collection from sensor inputs; data processing inside an ECM; and output devices, which are electrically operated.

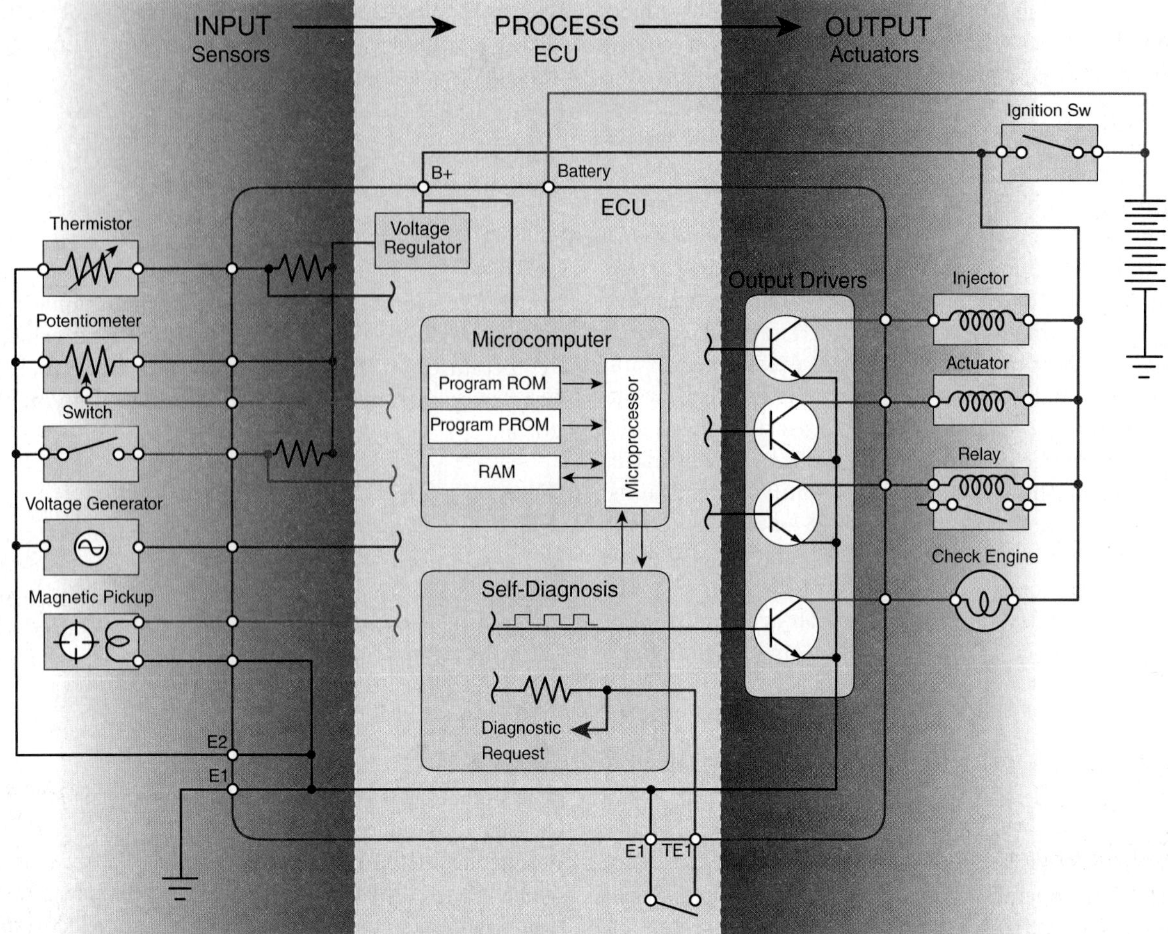

FIGURE 18-8 Three stages of signal processing. Sensors form input signals, and software-controlled microprocessors are used to make decisions after interpreting data, while electrically operated output devices carry out instructions of the processor.

▶ Types of Electrical Signals

K18003

Before looking at the elements of the electronic management system, it is first important to look at types of electrical signals used in information processing systems (**FIGURE 18-9**).

There are three types of electrical signals commonly used as either inputs or outputs in electronic engine control applications:

- analog
- digital
- **pulse-width modulation** (PWM).

Analog Signals

An **analog signal** is electric current that is proportional to a continuously changing variable. Analog signals then will have a changing value of voltage, amperage frequency, or amplitude. For example, temperature changes continuously. A thermometer measuring temperature change can represent every possible temperature with the movement of liquid in a glass or a hand on a dial. An analog electrical signal would represent the smallest change in temperature proportional to the movement of liquid or hand on the dial.

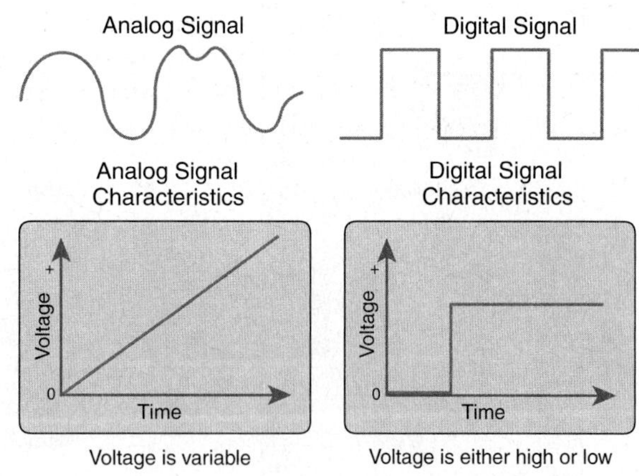

FIGURE 18-9 Electrical signal waveforms of two basic types of electrical signals: digital and analog.

Measurement of alternating electrical current is another example of an analog signal. Variable-reluctance-type sensors, such as transmission output shaft speed or some engine position sensors, will produce an alternating current. Changing shaft speed or engine speeds will continuously alter the

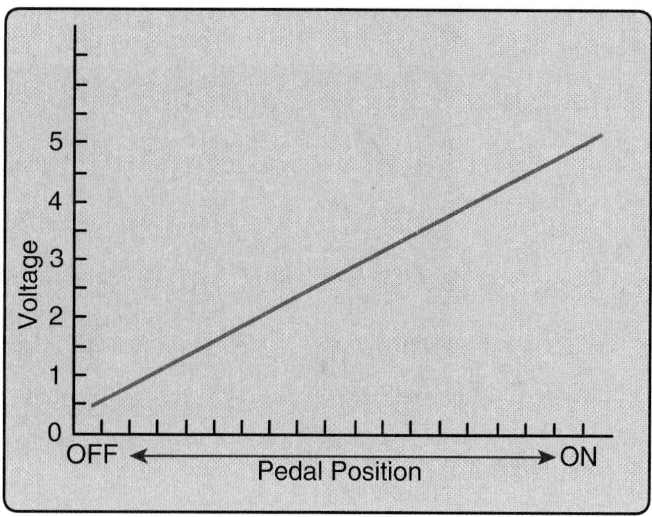

FIGURE 18-10 The signal voltage from this throttle position sensor is a type of analog data. An infinite number of values for voltage exist between idle and wide open throttle.

frequency of current polarity change that is leaving the sensor. The intensity of the voltage will further continuously vary with speed.

A throttle position sensor is another example where analog data can be collected. The electrical signal produced by the sensor varies proportionally to pedal angle. A continuously changing voltage output from the sensor will vary with the driver input (**FIGURE 18-10**).

Outputs can be analog as well. The intensity of a light or sound from an output device, such as a lamp or speaker, can be reproduced by varying the voltage and frequency of an electrical signal. A light is dimmed or brightened by increasing or decreasing current to a bulb. An analog signal representing sound produces loudness and pitch by varying the voltage and frequency current to a speaker.

FIGURE 18-11 This digital multimeter data represents resistance as a fixed, precise value. Smaller changes in resistance—several places to the right of the decimal point—are not easily measurable without the meter.

Digital Signals

In contrast to analog signals, **digital signals** do not vary in voltage, frequency, or amplitude. Instead, they are electrical signals that represent data in discrete, finite values. This means that the data is broken down into separate or smaller meaningful values. For example, the movement of hands on an analog clock will represent time in every possible value. However, a digital watch represents time in infinite values, such as seconds. A digital multimeter represents data the same way. The numerical display for an electrical measurement is represented as a fixed number (**FIGURE 18-11**).

In contrast, an analog meter would measure the same electrical value using a sweeping needle on a scale. A more common understanding of digital signals describes them representing data using only two conditions or values. This can be on or off, yes or no, 1 or 0, open or closed, up or down, etc. Binary code is an example of a digital signal. Every number from 0 to infinity and the letters of the alphabet are represented by a combination of 0s and 1s. Binary code easily lends itself to use in microprocessor circuits, where processing large amounts of alphabetic or numerical data, represented in strings of 0s or 1s, is performed.

Computerized powertrain management systems process information electronically using digital signals and binary code. This means that all information, whether analog or alphabetic, is converted into 1s and 0s. Using long strings of 1s and 0s may seem cumbersome, but just as Morse code tapped out on telegraphs could send information using only dots and dashes, the 1s and 0s of binary code can satisfactorily convey all kinds of information (**FIGURE 18-12**).

The difference between digital and Morse code is in the speed and accuracy of electronic processing. Processing millions and billions of 1s and 0s per second is something digital electronics can do to compensate for the cumbersomeness of using only 1s and 0s to communicate alphanumeric data.

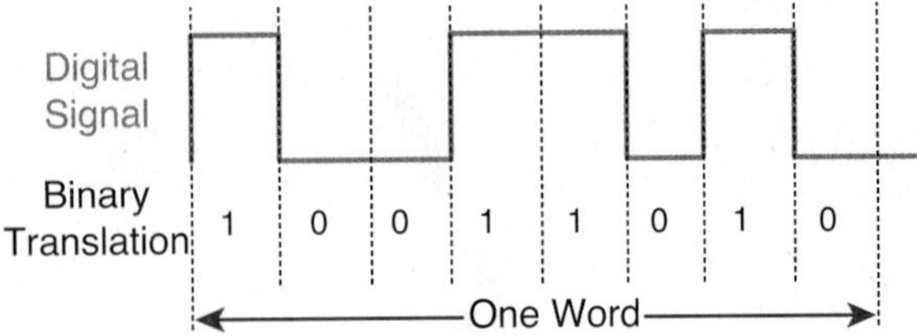

FIGURE 18-12 A bit is the smallest piece of digital information that is either a 1 or a 0. A byte is a unit of 8 bits. Binary code represents letters and numbers in strings of 1s and 0s. Digital data can be represented as 0s and 1s.

Bits and Bytes

A **bit** is a shortened term for binary digit. This is the smallest piece of digital or binary information and is represented by a single 0 or 1. As illustrated in Figure 18-12, a **byte** is a combination of 8 bits.

The speed data that is processed in the engine control module, also called ECM or ECU (engine control unit), is measured in bits. The number of bits it can process during one central processing unit (CPU) clock cycle classifies powertrain ECMs and computers. Desktop or laptop computers often use 64-bit processors. A Pentium IV processor is 32 bits, whereas a late model ECM will have 16-bit or 32-bit capability. A 3.0 MHz processor will have 3 million clock cycles per second, which means a 32-bit processor processes 96 million bits of data per second. While the clock speeds and bit size of the processors in an engine ECM are smaller than they are in an average desktop, so is the programming code. The capabilities of an engine ECM may appear to lag a personal computer (PC), but the PC operates using hundreds of complex software programs. An engine, implement or powertrain control microprocessor that operates using only one program with much simpler software code to process information and produce output signals has enormous processing capability (**FIGURE 18-13**).

Today's machine processors have many times the digital processing capabilities of the onboard computers used to send Apollo rockets to the moon.

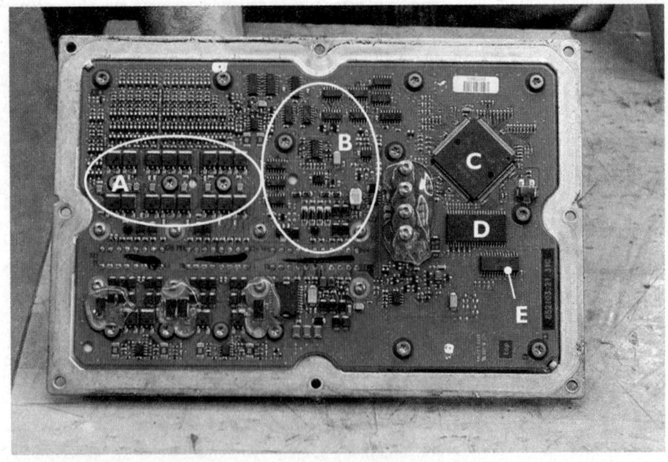

FIGURE 18-13 This injector driver uses a 32-bit microprocessor and a number of microcontrollers to operate the fuel injectors in an engine. **A.** FET transistor output drivers. **B.** DC-DC voltage step-up. **C.** Microprocessor. **D.** Memory. **E.** Microcontroller CAN transceiver.

Serial Data

While discussing binary code and digital signals, it is useful to understand what serial data is. The term "serial data" originates from the way data is transmitted. It is in series, one bit after another along a single or pair of wires. When serial digital data is transmitted using a pair of wires, each wire will transmit a voltage pulse represented as a rectangular waveform. The wires will have a **differential voltage**, which means the voltage on the wire pair is a mirror opposite voltage when transmitting serial data (**FIGURE 18-14**).

A large differential voltage pulse represents a 1, while a small differential voltage pulse represents 0. Serial data is used to transmit information from one electronic module to another. Onboard data networks share information and control machine operation using serial data. More important to the technician, electronic service tools will use serial data to receive and send data. The rate at which serial data is transmitted is referred to as the baud rate. **Baud rate** refers to the number of data bits transmitted per second.

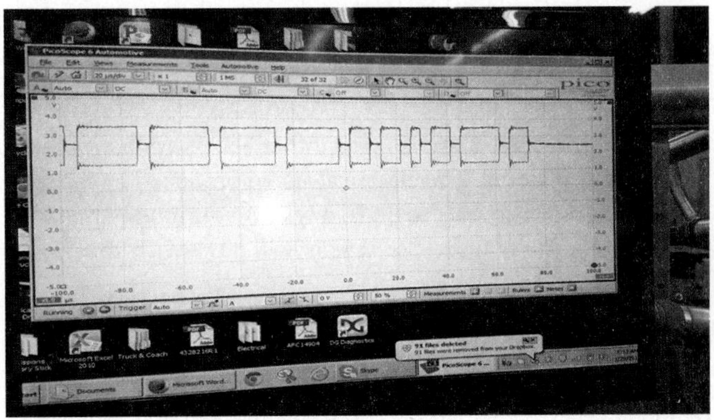

FIGURE 18-14 A J-1939 datalink waveform showing data. Serial data transmits a series of 1s and 0s and has a digital form. The wide part of the waveform represents 1 or a string of 1s, while the narrow part of the waveform represents 0 or a string of 0s.

Analog to Digital Conversion

Because electronic processing units can only handle binary digital data, analog signals are converted to digital signals in a process called **analog to digital conversion** (**FIGURE 18-15**).

To convert analog signals to digital binary information, special circuits, known as buffers or analog to digital (AD) converters, are used (**FIGURE 18-16**).

To convert an analog signal, the electronics do a couple of things. First, the changing analog signal is sampled or divided up into segments, like a loaf of bread. In one second of time, the varying analog signal could be sampled 10, 100, or even 1,000 times (**FIGURE 18-17**).

Each of these segments will represent a specific voltage value. The finer or more accurate the processor wants the data to be, the more frequent the sampling rate, resulting in

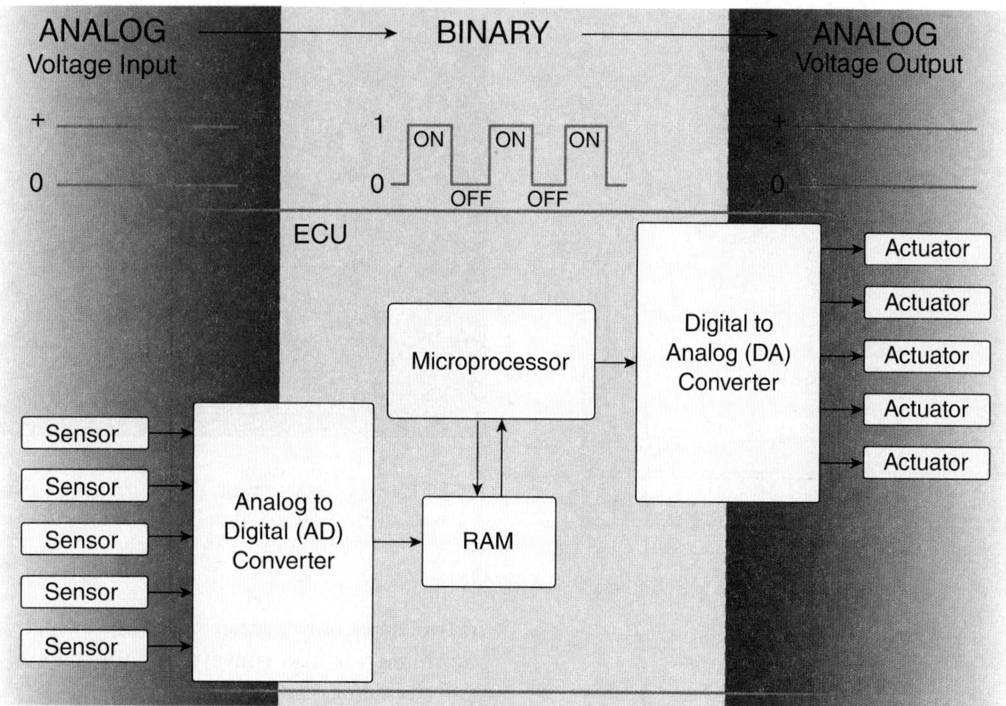

FIGURE 18-15 Analog to digital conversion occurs in the input circuits of the ECM. Digital to analog signal conversion may also occur in the output circuits of the ECM.

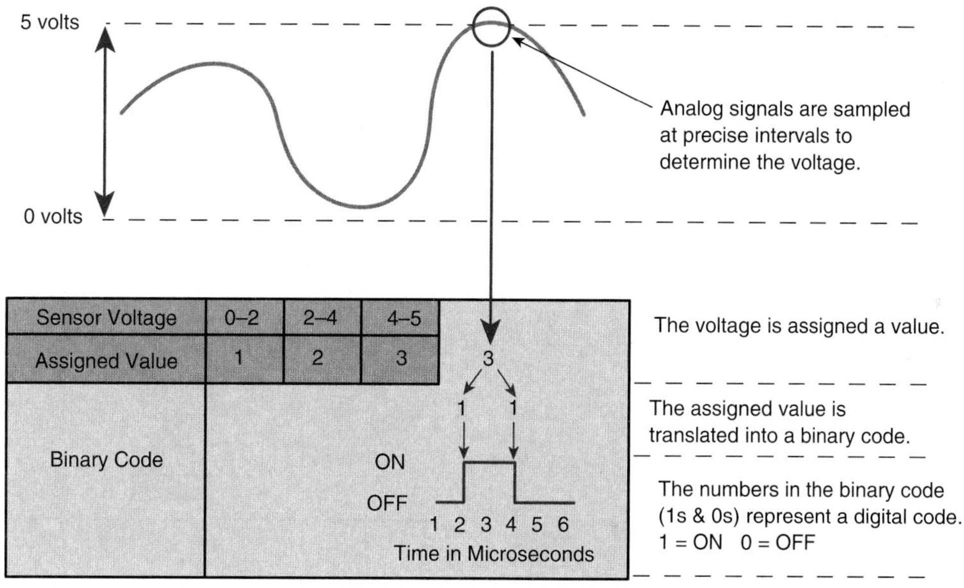

FIGURE 18-16 An analog to digital (AD) conversion. An analog waveform is sampled and measured many times a second to generate a digital representation of the waveform. This process is identical to forming MP3 files. The more frequently the signal is sampled—128K, 256K, or more—the higher the signal quality.

better signal resolution or fidelity. Each of the segments will be assigned a digital value that is translated into a binary number. MP3 files are an example of an analog (wave file) to digital conversion. A digital wave file could be sampled 64K times a second or 128K times a second or more. Higher fidelity—the faithfulness to the original analog signal—is achieved at the more frequent sample rate.

▶ TECHNICIAN TIP

The current used in the electronic control systems is generally DC voltage. Radio frequency interference (RFI) induced into the system by magnetic fields of high-voltage power lines, radio transmitters, and even a microwave would be AC voltage. The signal-processing systems of ECM input conditioning circuits generally recognize and ignore these types of signals. This does not mean all electromagnetic interference

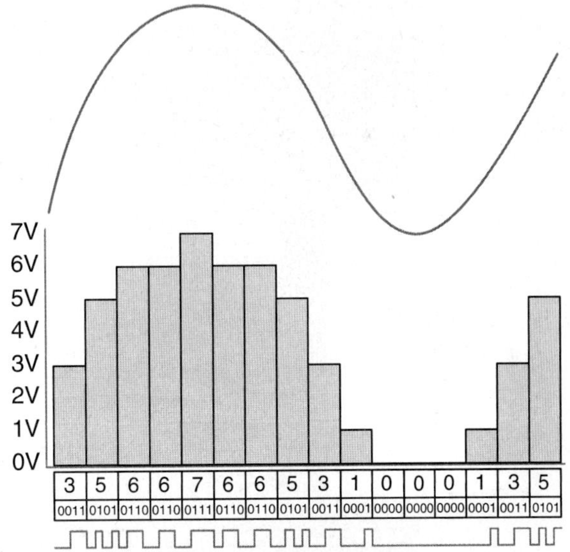

FIGURE 18-17 Analog signals from engine sensors are converted into digital signals for processing by the ECM.

FIGURE 18-18 A pulse-width–modulated signal displayed on a graphing meter. Notice that the width of the pulses is similar.

goes unnoticed. Magnetic fields can induce voltage in signal wires and cause confusion for signal-processing units producing numerous types of unintended consequences.

Pulse-Width Modulation

An electrical signal that shares similar characteristics with both a digital signal and an analog signal is the pulse-width–modulated (PWM) electrical signal (**FIGURE 18-18, FIGURE 18-19, FIGURE 18-20**).

PWM refers to a signal that varies in "ON" and "OFF" time. That means it is digital in one aspect because it represents data in two states only—either on or off, or high or low. However, information is also conveyed by the amount of time the signal stays on or off. Time on or off is variable, which gives it an analog characteristic. The units for measuring pulse width are always expressed in units of time. Time is the measure of how long the signal is high or on.

To understand PWM, consider a light illuminated by a PWM signal. In one second of time, the light may be cycled on and off once. If the signal is applied for one-quarter of a second, the pulse width would be 0.25 seconds wide (**FIGURE 18-21**).

Common examples of devices using PWM signals are solenoids, injectors, and light circuits. A PWM signal is typically reported in milliseconds. PWM signals are commonly used as an output signal of an ECM. For example, the current supplied to a fuel injector or the pressure regulator of a HEUI or common

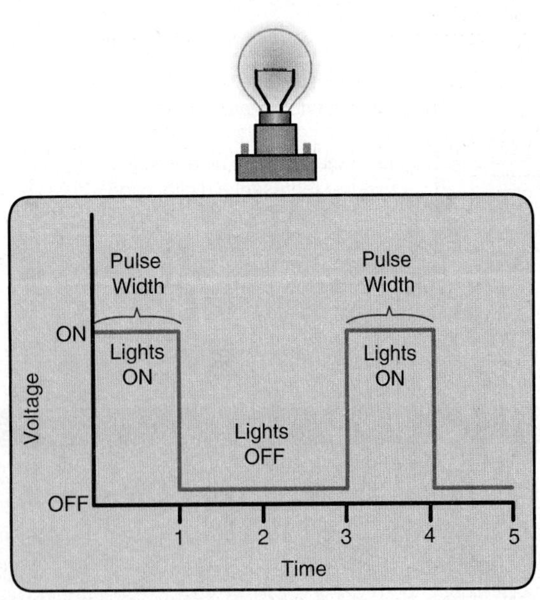

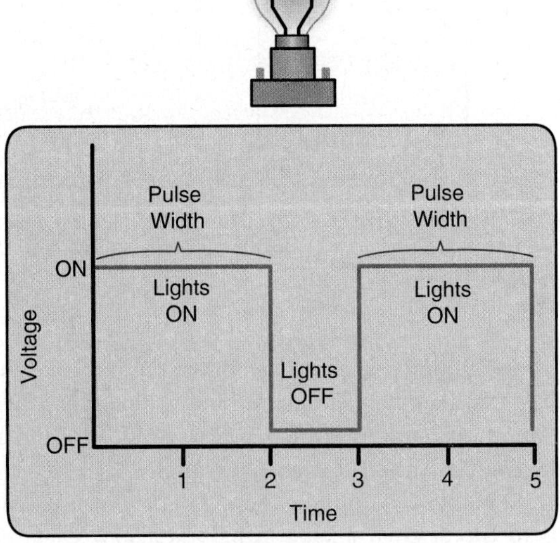

FIGURE 18-19 The longer the pulse width, the brighter the light, since more current flows through the circuit when pulse-width on-time lengthens.

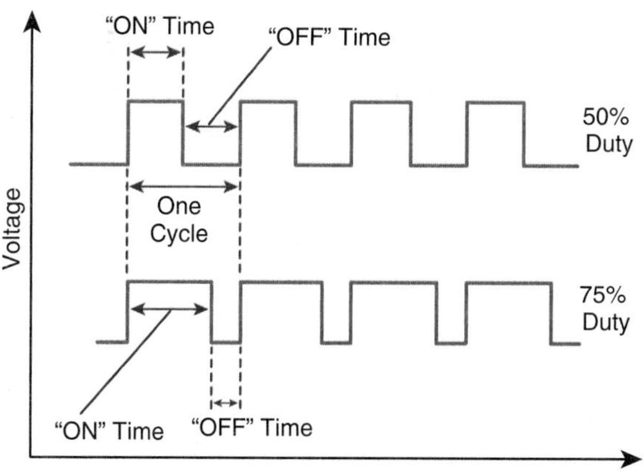

FIGURE 18-20 Duty cycle is a comparison of on-time to off-time in one cycle. A cycle can be 1 second, 500 ms, or any length of time, but the cycle time is fixed when measuring pulse width.

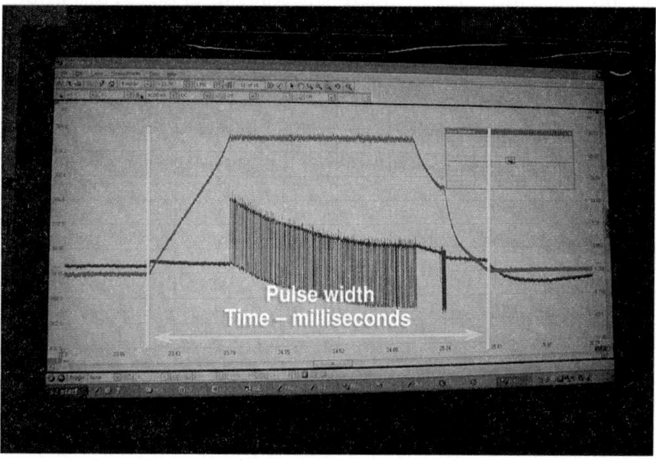

FIGURE 18-21 The pulse width of the energization-time of an injector solenoid is measured in milliseconds.

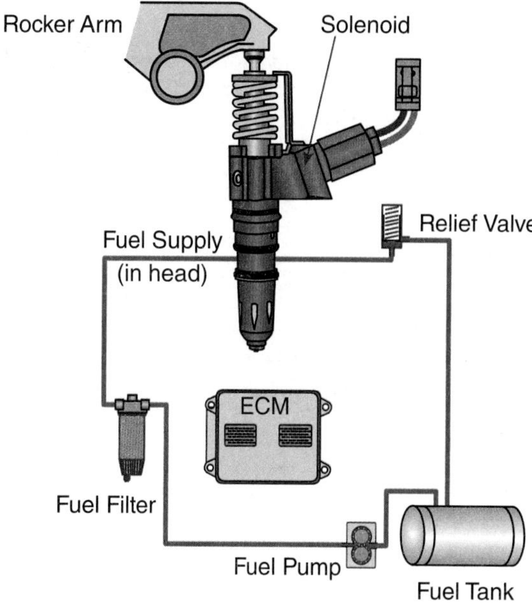

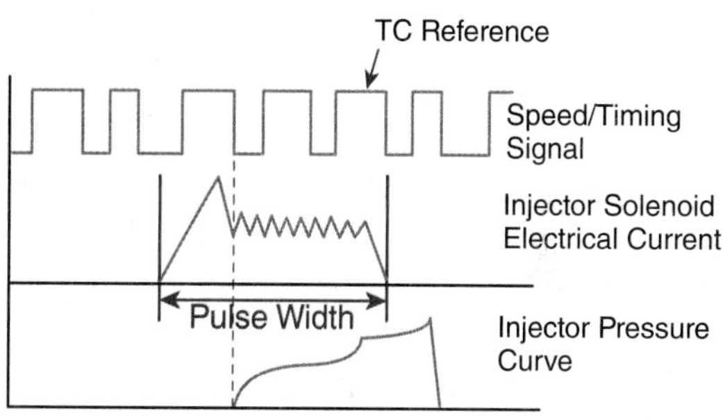

FIGURE 18-22 Varying the length of time electrical current energizes an injector solenoid will change the quantity of fuel injected into a cylinder.

rail pump is changed by varying the on-time of the electromagnetic control valve (**FIGURE 18-22, FIGURE 18-23**).

Output drivers of microprocessors are types of switches, usually switching transistors, which produce PWM signals to operate devices in an "ON" or "OFF" state (**FIGURE 18-24** and **FIGURE 18-25**).

The microprocessor device can also easily vary the duration-time of a driver opening and closing.

Sensors can input PWM signals, and solenoids can receive PWM signals. If a coil receives a PWM signal, it will be like getting an average voltage that is below the maximum voltage based on the amount of on-time or the duty cycle. Some manufacturers use sensors that use PWM signals to transmit data. One manufacturer that uses a lot of PWM signaling will pulse the signal at either 500 Hz or 5,000 Hz. PWM signals can come from position, level, pressure, and temperature sensors or can be an ECM output to a proportional solenoid. Caterpillar uses throttle position sensors that will transmit throttle position data using PWM signals. This type of data is unaffected by voltage drops encountered through long runs of wiring harnesses and multiple connectors between the sensor and ECM.

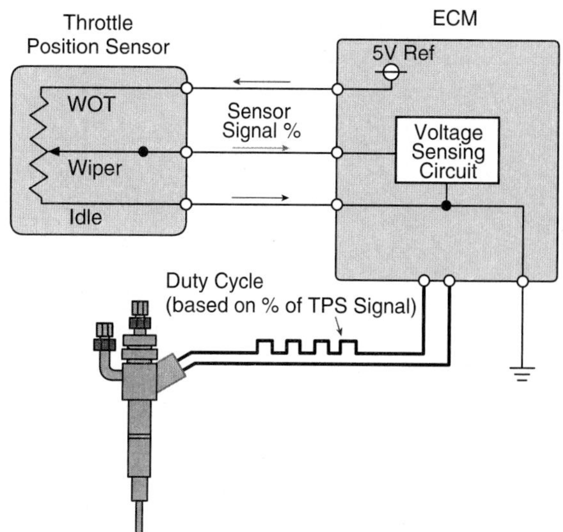

FIGURE 18-23 The ECM will use the throttle position sensor as one of many sensors to calculate the pulse width applied to an injector solenoid.

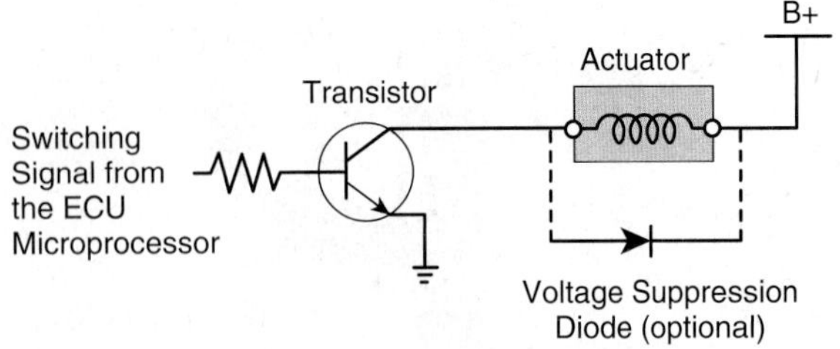

FIGURE 18-24 An output driver of an ECM is usually a switching-type transistor. When the microprocessor applies a small amount of current to the base of the driver, a larger amount of current flows through the transistor to the output device.

Duty Cycle

Related to the term "pulse width" is duty cycle, illustrated in Figure 18-20. **Duty cycle** is another unit for measurement for PWM signals. While a pulse width is measured in time, duty cycle is measured as a percentage—on-time versus off-time. Duty cycle refers to the percentage of time that a PWM signal is high or on, in comparison to off-time (**FIGURE 18-26**).

One on- and off-time for a PWM signal represents one cycle. Duty cycle units are expressed as a percentage of cycle time. For example, if the pulse width is 0.8 seconds and the off-time is 0.2 seconds, a cycle is 1 second in length. This means the duty cycle is 80%. A 100% duty cycle means the signal is on all the time, while a 0% duty cycle is off. Another way of expressing this relationship is signal off-time versus on-time. A signal that is applied for three-quarters of a cycle is 75% duty cycle.

The difference between duty cycle and PWM is where the signal is used. Duty cycle is commonly used to measure the time a signal is applied to an output device operating at a fixed frequency, whereas pulse width measures a signal applied to devices operating at a varying frequency interval. For example, an engine may speed up and slow down, so the pulse width or time that an injector is energized will vary with speed. It is practical to measure actuation time only, since it is difficult to always know the frequency of a cycle—rpm, in this instance. Depending on engine speed, 10 or 20 injections may take place in 1 second, making it practical to measure only pulse width.

Consider, however, an electrohydraulic pressure regulator. This device will have a PWM signal applied to close a valve and increase pressure. Removing the signal will cause pressure to decrease. The time the signal is applied is broken into fixed time intervals. Therefore, a solenoid for this device may be on for 0.20 seconds out of fixed 1-second intervals. This would give it a pulse width of 0.20 seconds but a duty cycle of 20%. Pulse width could increase or decrease with a changing duty cycle (**FIGURE 18-27**).

To practically interpret system operation, a measurement of duty cycle is more meaningful.

Frequency

Frequency is the number of events or cycles that occur in a period, usually one second. The units of measure for frequency are **hertz (Hz)**, which is the number of cycles per second. A

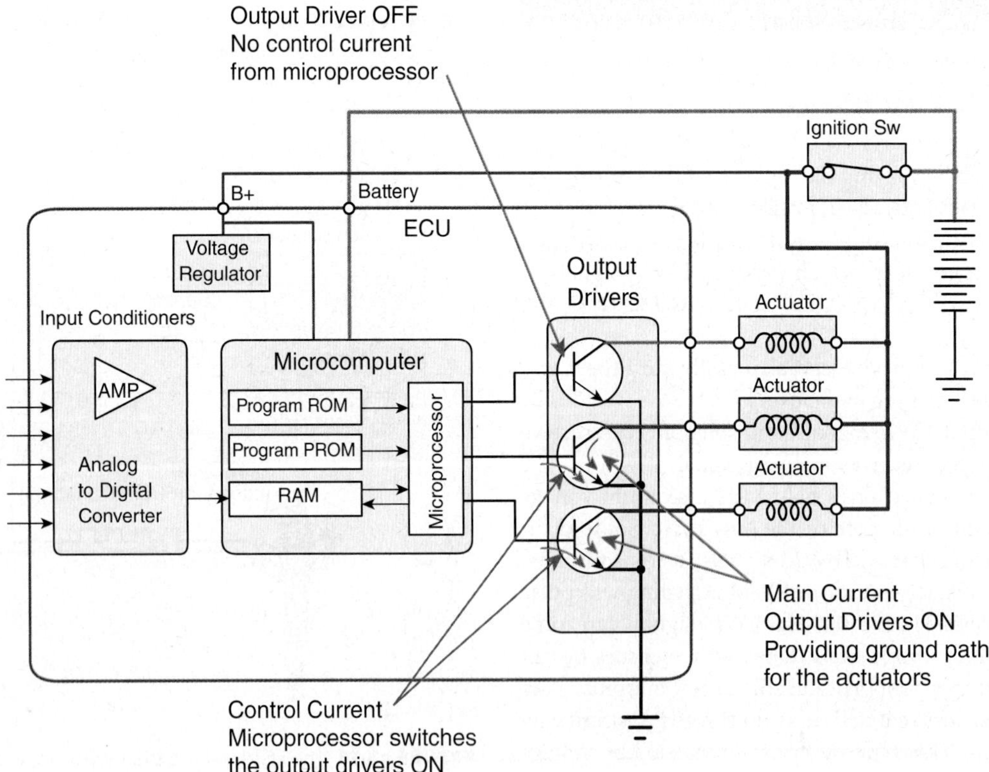

FIGURE 18-25 The microprocessor controls the operation of the output drivers, which switch current flow on and off to electrical devices.

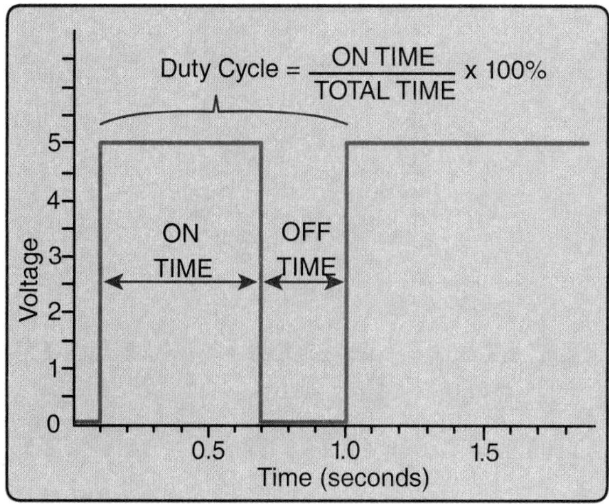

FIGURE 18-26 The measurement units for a PWM signal can also be a duty cycle. Duty cycle is expressed as a percentage of on-time versus off-time.

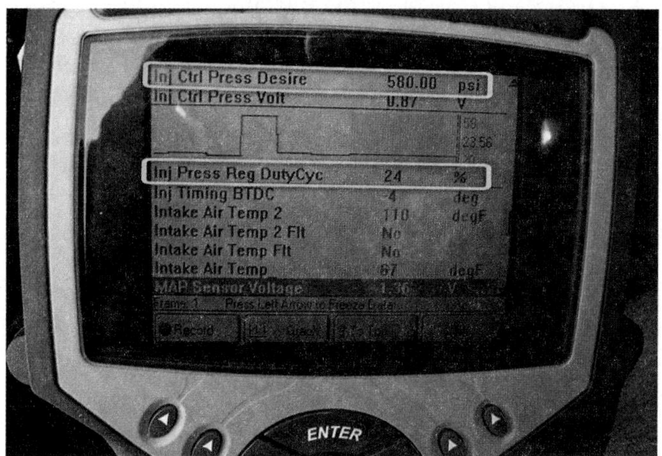

FIGURE 18-27 The duty cycle of this injection control pressure regulator for a HEUI fuel system is graphed and measured in duty cycle.

common application for frequency measurements is for alternating current. When current switches from positive to negative, one cycle has completed (**FIGURE 18-28**).

▶ Processing Function

K18004

Processing electronic signals used in machine electronic control management systems is the function of ECMs. Referred to as the electronic control module (ECM), a microprocessor or microcontroller is the heart of the control unit. Made from hundreds if not hundreds of thousands of transistors contained in a semiconductor chip, the integrated circuit chips making up microprocessors and various controllers will contain a minimal amount of memory plus input and output circuits. Microprocessors have more memory, which gives them the capability to perform advanced calculations and follow software-based instructions (**FIGURE 18-29**).

In contrast to microprocessors, microcontrollers are less capable and carry out more limited and only specific functions built into the chip design. Microcontrollers are usually not programmable. An ECM will contain several types of memory, output drivers that control the operation of electrically operated devices such as injectors and relays as well as complex signal conditioning circuits for information processing functions. An ECM will contain a transceiver, which enables it to receive and send communication signals to an onboard network.

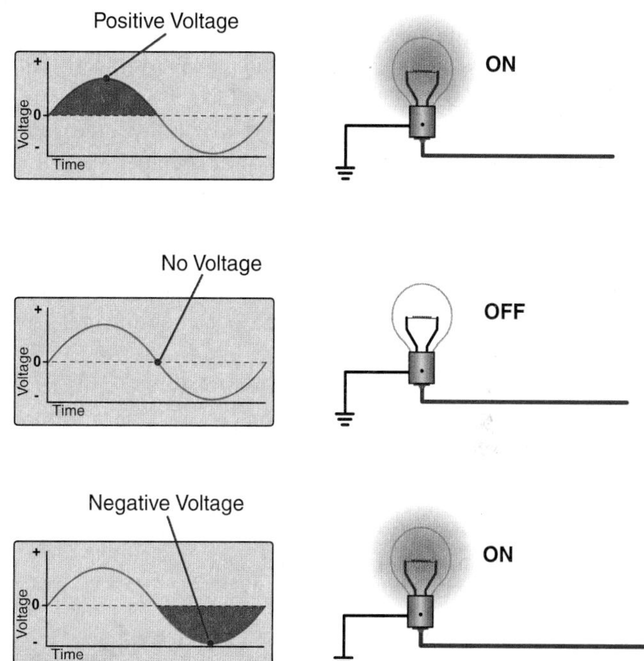

FIGURE 18-28 Frequency refers to the number of times a cycle occurs. Hertz refers to the number of times the cycle occurs in 1 second.

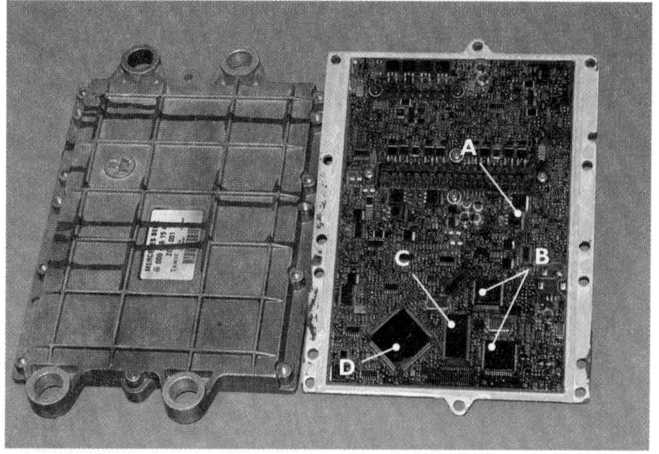

FIGURE 18-29 Integrated circuits used on a late model engine control module. **A.** Microcontroller. **B.** RAM (random access memory) and ROM (read-only memory). **C.** Flash memory. **D.** Microprocessor.

Several types of integrated circuit devices or "chips" are on board a typical ECM, which are essential to processing and ECM operation:

- the clock
- microprocessor
- microcontrollers
- analog to digital converted (AD converter)
- memory.

CPU Clock

The clock is an oscillator inside the microprocessor that controls how fast instructions stored in memory are processed (**FIGURE 18-30**).

It is like the drum beat that controls the pace of the work in the microprocessor. The clock speed is measured in hertz (or megahertz or gigahertz). With each cycle of the clock, the microprocessor will perform a set of tasks. Obviously, the faster the clock speed, the greater number of instructions processed per second.

Computer Memory

Several types of memory are used in an ECM, depending on its application. Some memory is used to store data from sensors since the ECM cannot process all sensor data simultaneously (**FIGURE 18-31**).

Other types of memory are required to store the instructions for operating the microprocessor. This memory would store software code to give the ECM its unique operational characteristics. Common categories of memory include

- read-only memory (ROM)
- random access memory (RAM)
- programmable read-only memory (PROM)
- **electrically erasable programmable read-only memory (EEPROM)**
- flash memory or non-volatile RAM (NVRAM), which is a ROM/RAM hybrid that can be written to but which does not require power to maintain its contents.

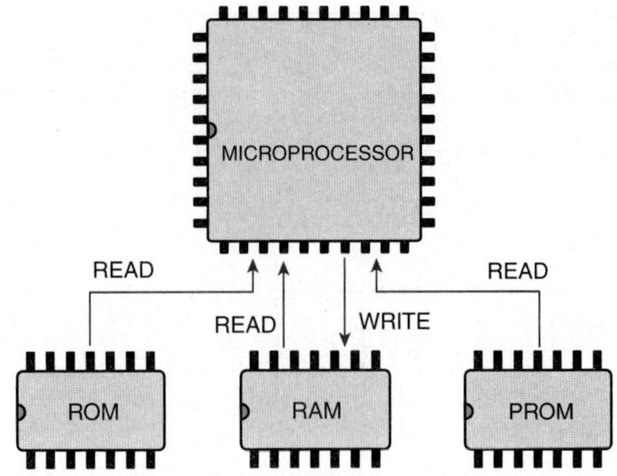

FIGURE 18-31 Several types of memory support the processing functions of the microprocessor. **Programmable read-only memory (PROM)** stores specific operational instructions.

Read-Only Memory (ROM)

Read-only memory (ROM) is used for permanent storage of instructions and fixed values used by the ECM that control the microprocessor. Information stored in the ROM would include algorithms such as how to calculate the pulse width for the injectors or the horsepower ratings for the machine. Other fixed values

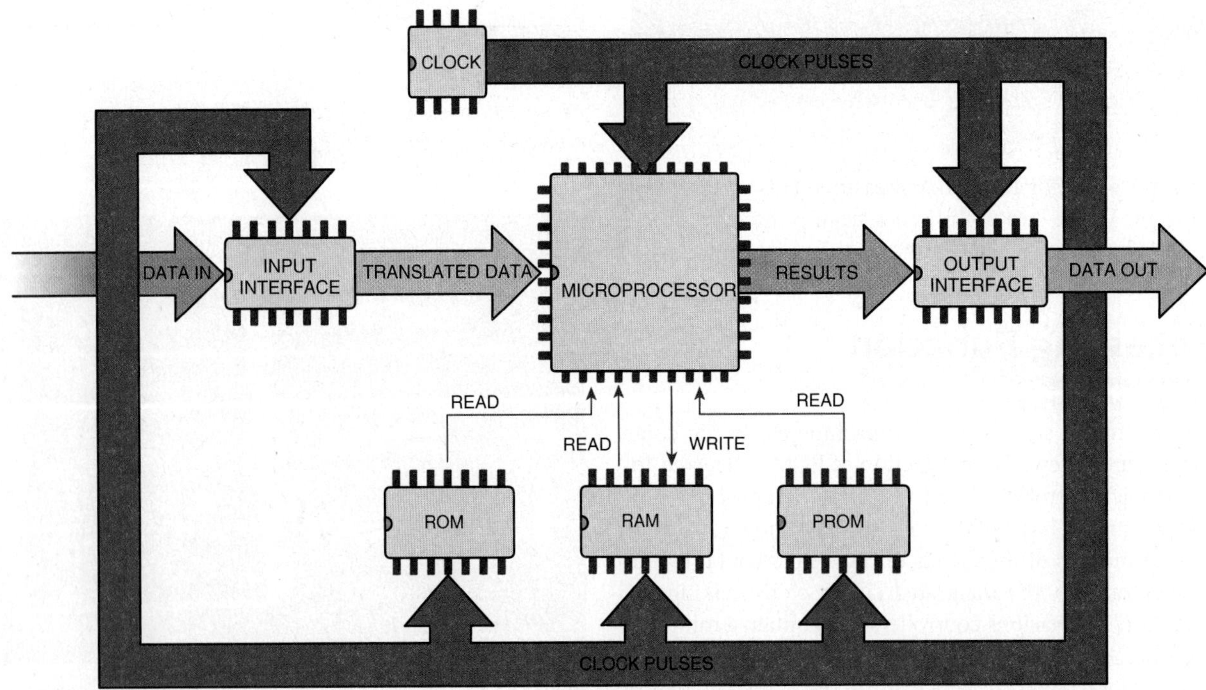

FIGURE 18-30 The CPU clock controls the pace of calculations inside the microprocessor. Each device inside the microprocessor waits for the clock to signal the executions of a particular instruction.

would identify a maximum engine rpm, the temperature value for an engine overheat condition, the type of transmission, or the type of implement system. The ECM reads the instructions, but it cannot rewrite or change the instructions contained in ROM. ROM data is stored by the manufacturer. ROM memory is permanent and is not lost even if power to the computer is interrupted. This means the memory is **non-volatile** (**FIGURE 18-32**).

Random Access Memory (RAM)

Random access memory (RAM) is a temporary storage place for information that needs to be quickly accessed. Input data from sensors is commonly stored in RAM, awaiting processing by the ECM. RAM memory is both readable and writable. Most RAM memory is designed to be lost when power is interrupted, such as turning the ignition key off. That is why RAM is often referred to as temporary storage of memory. However, RAM can be stored in the ECM after the key is shut off. Non-volatile RAM holds its information even when the power is removed. **Volatile RAM** will be erased when the power is removed. If volatile RAM receives its power from the ignition key, its memory is lost when the ignition is turned off. If battery power is used to keep the RAM memory intact when the key is off, it is also known as **keep alive memory (KAM)**.

EEPROM and Flash Memory

Electrically erasable programmable read-only memory (EEPROM) was developed to allow manufacturers to change the software operating the ECM electronically rather than physically fix it into the ECM during its design and construction.

In recent years, flash memory, which is non-volatile EEPROM memory has become the most common type of memory used in ECMs. This is almost identical to the type used on a USB memory stick. It has enormous shock resistance and durability and can withstand intense pressure, extremes of temperature, and immersion in water, which are conditions sometimes found in mobile off-road equipment. It also offers the convenience of easily reprogramming or recalibrating the ECM, also known as **flashing** or flash programming. Flash programming involves the installation of look-up tables in the ECM. Look-up tables are used by the ECM to solve mathematical problems called algorithms. An example of a simple algorithm would solve the problem of how fast the machine is traveling. The mathematical formula for speed would be distance/time. More complex algorithms involve calculating how much fuel to inject, when to inject fuel, or how long the injector should be energized. The look-up table provides specific data to help solve the problems for a specific engine.

▶ TECHNICIAN TIP

Microcontrollers and microprocessors are types of integrated circuits. The distinction between them is related to their capabilities. Engines, transmissions, and implement ECMs use microcontrollers. This is a special-purpose processor with limited capabilities, designed to perform a set of specific tasks. Reading sensor data and using logic gates to perform calculations and determine outputs required for the application such as energize a relay or injector solenoid are examples. Executing instructions stored in the memory of EEPROMs enhances the function of sophisticated microcontrollers. The controller's tasks, however, are limited to a specific application such as controlling the engine's operation. In contrast, a more sophisticated engine, implement, or other ECM use microprocessors are capable of executing logic and supporting a larger number of devices making up the ECM. Microprocessors will also use an operating system such as Windows, Linux, or Android, enabling the addition of multiple software programs to handle a larger variety of tasks.

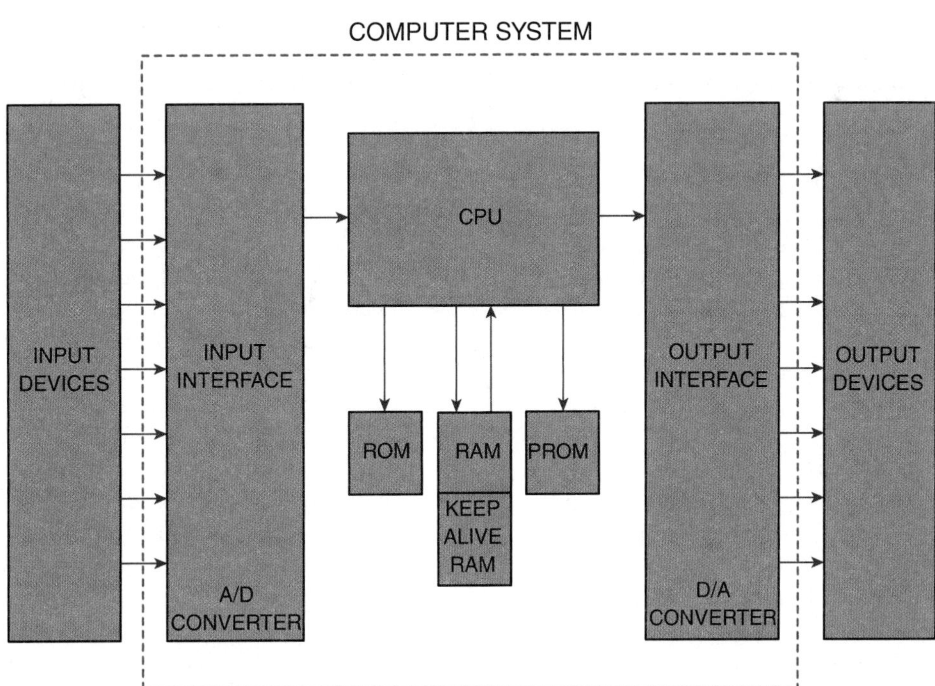

FIGURE 18-32 Non-volatile memory means the information is not lost when power to the ECM is disconnected or the ignition is switched off. Keep alive memory refers to memory that is retained only due to a constant supply of current to the ECM when the ignition is switched off.

▶ Wrap-Up

Ready for Review

- Electronic systems using microprocessor- and microcontroller-based controls provide operational capabilities far exceeding any mechanical system. The dominance and sophistication of electronic control makes developing skills related to servicing this technology one of the most important priorities for successful technicians.
- Diesel engines were the first machine systems transformed by electronic controls. The immediate benefits of these refinements to powertrain control include lower engine emissions, improved fuel economy, increased reliability, and enhanced performance.
- Service technicians can access a wealth of diagnostic and service information much faster and with more precise detail than before.
- Telematics, a branch of information technology, uses specialized applications for long-distance transmission of information to and from a machine. Messages can be sent back and forth between the machine and a central location.
- The use of electronic engine and machine management provides enhanced machine and occupant safety and security.
- Programmable software provides flexibility to engines, transmissions, and implements to adapt to; adapting to specific job applications; and enhanced machine productivity, longevity, and operator comfort. Programmable features include idle shut-down timers, implement controls, maximum machine speed limits, and safety interlocks that prevent the machine from moving if the parking brake is on, a boom is raised, or outriggers are extended.
- Built-in electronic control management systems allow machines to check the operation of circuits and electrical devices, evaluate the rationality of data, and identify problems as they occur. The presence of faults is communicated through the malfunction indicator lamps, cab displays, electronic service tools, or Windows-based diagnostic software.
- Electronic control systems can be broken down into three major divisions: sensing, processing, and output or actuation.
- Sensing functions collect data about operational conditions or the state of a device by measuring some value, such as temperature, position, speed, pressure, or flow.
- Processing collects sensor data and determines outputs based on a set of instructions or program software.
- The outputs of a system are functions performed in response to electrical signals produced by the processor.
- Three types of electrical signals commonly used as either inputs or outputs in electronic engine control applications are analog, digital, and PWM.
- An analog signal is an electric current that is proportional to a continuously changing variable.
- In contrast to analog signals, digital signals do not vary in voltage, frequency, or amplitude. Instead, they are electrical signals that represent data as binary values, such as on or off, 0 or 1, yes or no, up or down, open or closed.
- Binary code is an example of a digital signal. "Bit" is a shortened term for binary digit. This is the smallest piece of digital or binary information and is represented by a single 0 or 1. A byte is a combination of 8 bits.
- Serial data is used to transmit information from one electronic module to another. Onboard data networks share information and control machine operation using serial data.
- Because electronic processing units can only handle binary digital data, analog signals are converted to digital signals by special circuits known as buffers or AD converters.
- An electrical signal that shares similar characteristics with both a digital and analog signal is the PWM electrical signal. PWM refers to a signal that varies in on- and off-time. A PWM signal is typically measured in milliseconds (ms).
- Duty cycle is another unit of measurement for PWM signals, and it refers to the percentage of time a PWM signal is on versus the time it is off. Duty cycle is commonly used to measure the time a signal is applied to an output device operating at a fixed frequency, whereas pulse width measures a signal applied to devices operating at a varying frequency interval.
- Frequency is the number of events or cycles that occur in a period. The unit of measure for frequency is hertz (Hz), which is the number of cycles per second.
- ECMs are microprocessors or microcontrollers that process electrical signals. Several types of integrated circuit devices on board a typical ECM are essential to processing and ECM operation.
- The CPU clock is an oscillator inside the microprocessor that controls how fast instructions stored in memory are processed. It is like the drum beat that controls the pace of the work in the microprocessor. The clock speed is measured in hertz (or megahertz or gigahertz).
- Several types of memory are used in an ECM, depending on its application. Some memory is used to store data from sensors because the ECM cannot process all sensor data simultaneously. Other types of memory

are required to store the instructions for operating the microprocessor.

- Common categories of memory include ROM, RAM, PROM, EEPROM, and flash memory (a ROM/RAM hybrid that can be written to but does not require power to maintain its contents).

Key Terms

analog signal An electric current that is proportional to a continuously changing variable.

analog to digital (AD) conversion The process when an analog waveform is sampled and measured many times a second to generate a digital representation of the waveform.

baud rate The rate at which serial data is transmitted.

bit The smallest piece of digital information, which is either a 1 or 0.

byte A unit of 8 bits.

differential Refers to the voltage difference on a wire pair when one wires voltage is the mirror opposite voltage. A wide separation between the voltage pulses represents a 1 and a narrow separation represents a 0.

digital signals Electrical signals that represent data in discrete, finite values. Digital signals are considered as binary, meaning it is either on or off, yes or no, high or low, 0 or 1.

duty cycle The percentage of time a PWM signal is on in comparison to off-time.

electrically erasable read-only memory (EEPROM) Non-volatile memory technology that is used to store operating instructions or programming for an ECM.

flashing Reprogramming or recalibrating the ECM. Information is stored in the ECM's memory.

frequency The number of events or cycles that occur in a period, usually 1 second.

hertz (Hz) The unit for electrical frequency measurement, in cycles per second.

keep alive memory (KAM) Memory that is retained by the ECM when the key is off.

microcontroller A special-purpose processor with limited capabilities, designed to perform a set of specific tasks.

non-volatile memory Memory that is not lost when power is removed or lost.

programmable read-only memory (PROM) Memory that stores programming information and cannot be easily written over.

pulse-width modulation (PWM) An electrical signal that varies in on- and off-time.

random access memory (RAM) A temporary storage place for information that needs to be quickly accessed.

read-only memory (ROM) Memory used for permanent storage of instructions and fixed lookup table values used by the ECM that control the microprocessor.

telematics A branch of information technology that uses specialized applications for the long-distance transmission of information to and from a vehicle.

volatile memory A type of data storage that is lost or erased when the ignition power is switched off.

Review Questions

1. Which of the following is a benefit of electronic control?
   a. Increased power and efficiency
   b. Programmable features
   c. Self-diagnostic capabilities
   d. All of the choices are correct.
2. Which of the following statements about information reporting capabilities is correct?
   a. The life cycle cost of operating machines with these engines is further reduced through the ability of the engine control systems to interface with tablets and both diagnostic and service software.
   b. Service technicians can access a wealth of diagnostic and service data much faster and with precise detail than before.
   c. Trip reports from the machine ECM extracted during scheduled maintenance intervals report details such as diagnostic fault codes, fuel consumption, idle time, emission system performance, and machine abuse.
   d. All of the choices are correct.
3. Which of the following statements about safety is correct?
   a. If a machine is involved in an accident, a call can be made to an emergency dispatch.
   b. Engine systems can be monitored for operating conditions having destructive potential.
   c. Hard braking and speeding are other measurable conditions monitored by management systems to ensure safety.
   d. All of the choices are correct.
4. Which of the following is NOT correct concerning self-diagnostic capabilities?
   a. Diagnostics on electronically controlled machine systems can be performed easily, often with fewer tools and in less time than they can be on mechanical systems.
   b. The presence of faults is unable to be communicated through the malfunction indicator lamps.
   c. Electronic service tools assist the technicians in performing off-board diagnostics—that is, performing pinpoint checks to precisely identify system faults.
   d. Because modules, sensors, and actuators are more compact, they can be replaced quickly and with minimal training and experience required.
5. What type of data is collected by the sensing functions of the electronic control system?
   a. Temperature
   b. Pressure
   c. Both A and B
   d. Neither A nor B

6. What are some examples of outputs of the electronic control assembly?
   a. Current to operate solenoids or injectors
   b. Current to operate actuators
   c. Current to operate lights
   d. All of the choices are correct.
7. Analog signals can have a changing value of ________.
   a. voltage
   b. amperage frequency
   c. amplitude
   d. All of the choices are correct.
8. "Bit" is a shortened term for binary digit; a byte is a combination of ________ bits.
   a. 2
   b. 4
   c. 6
   d. 8
9. Which of the following statements about analog to digital (AD) conversion is correct?
   a. Because electronic processing units can only handle binary digital data, analog signals are converted to digital signals.
   b. To convert analog signals to digital binary information, special circuits, known as buffers, or analog to digital (AD) converters, are used.
   c. Both A and B
   d. Neither A nor B
10. Which of the following is NOT correct concerning duty cycle?
   a. Duty cycle is another unit for measurement for PWM signals.
   b. Duty cycle units are expressed as a percentage of cycle time.
   c. A 100% duty cycle means the signal is off.
   d. Duty cycle refers to the percentage of time a PWM signal is high or on in comparison to off-time.

ASE Technician A/Technician B Style Questions

1. Technician A says that most machine systems operate with at least some degree of electronic control. Technician B says that understanding the operating principles of electronic control systems is fundamental for choosing diagnostic strategies. Who is correct?
   a. Technician A
   b. Technician B
   c. Both Technician A and Technician B
   d. Neither Technician A nor Technician B
2. Technician A says that diesel engines were the first machine systems transformed by electronic controls. Technician B says that smarter engines deliver ever-increasing power from smaller displacements. Who is correct?
   a. Technician A
   b. Technician B
   c. Both Technician A and Technician B
   d. Neither Technician A nor Technician B
3. Technician A says that telematics uses specialized telecommunication applications for the long-distance transmission of information to and from a machine. Technician B says that telematics is not capable of transmitting information on fault codes. Who is correct?
   a. Technician A
   b. Technician B
   c. Both Technician A and Technician B
   d. Neither Technician A nor Technician B
4. Technician A says that technicians can take advantage of programmable electronic controls. Technician B says that power and torque-rise profiles cannot be altered electronically. Who is correct?
   a. Technician A
   b. Technician B
   c. Both Technician A and Technician B
   d. Neither Technician A nor Technician B
5. Technician A says that electronic control systems use a variety of sensors, wires, electrical actuators, and electronic modules moved with invisible electrical signals. Technician B says that the three major divisions of electronic control systems are sensing, processing, and output. Who is correct?
   a. Technician A
   b. Technician B
   c. Both Technician A and Technician B
   d. Neither Technician A nor Technician B
6. Technician A says that processing refers to the control system element that collects sensor data and determines outputs based on a set of instructions or program software. Technician B says that operational algorithms are included in the software that determines the steps taken when processing electrical data. Who is correct?
   a. Technician A
   b. Technician B
   c. Both Technician A and Technician B
   d. Neither Technician A nor Technician B
7. Technician A says that a bench signal is one type of electrical signal commonly used in electronic engine control applications. Technician B says that an analog signal is one type of electrical signal commonly used in electronic engine control applications. Who is correct?
   a. Technician A
   b. Technician B
   c. Both Technician A and Technician B
   d. Neither Technician A nor Technician B
8. Technician A says that, in contrast to analog signals, digital signals vary greatly in voltage, frequency, or amplitude. Technician B says that the binary code does not lend itself to use in microprocessor circuits, where processing large amounts of alphabetic or numerical data, represented in strings of 0s or 1s, is performed. Who is correct?
   a. Technician A
   b. Technician B

c. Both Technician A and Technician B
d. Neither Technician A nor Technician B

9. Technician A says that serial data is used to transmit information from one electronic module to another. Technician B says that baud rate refers to the number of data bits transmitted per minute. Who is correct?
   a. Technician A
   b. Technician B
   c. Both Technician A and Technician B
   d. Neither Technician A nor Technician B

10. Technician A says that a pulse-width–modulated electrical signal is an electrical signal that shares similar characteristics with both a digital signal and an analog signal. Technician B says that common examples of devices using PWM signals are solenoids, injectors, and light circuits. Who is correct?
    a. Technician A
    b. Technician B
    c. Both Technician A and Technician B
    d. Neither Technician A nor Technician B

CHAPTER 19
Onboard Networks Systems

Knowledge Objectives

After reading this chapter, you will be able to:

- **K19001** Identify and explain the purpose of onboard communication networks.
- **K19002** Identify and describe the construction of onboard communication networks.
- **K19003** Identify and describe the principles of onboard communication networks and multiplex communication technology.
- **K19004** Identify and explain the purpose, function, and application of distributed network control systems.
- **K19005** Describe and explain common diagnostic and service procedures for onboard machine networks.

Skills Objectives

After reading this chapter, you will be able to:

- **S19001** Check for completion of HD-OBD monitors for an engine.
- **S19002** Diagnose an HD-OBD–related fault code using diagnostic trees, appropriate code priority, appropriate flow charts, and pinpoint tests.
- **S19003** Perform a terminating resistor check.
- **S19004** Measure resistance of terminating resistors
- **S19005** Perform pinpoint voltage tests on a data link connector (DLC).
- **S19006** Check for shorts in the controlled area network.

▶ Introduction

Electrical systems on modern machines are becoming increasingly complex with the addition of a range of electronic and accessory systems, such as global positioning systems, Bluetooth systems, security systems, heated seats, and automatic climate control systems. Many of these systems are controlled by onboard computer systems. Increasingly, the electrical and electronic assemblies are interconnected through machine onboard data networks that require diagnosis. The technician requires an in-depth knowledge of these systems, including how they operate and are interconnected through the machines onboard network. Diagnosing a machine fault requires the use of dedicated diagnostic tools that communicate with the machine's electronic control units. Connecting a diagnostic scan tool or a personal computer to a machine allows the technician to monitor data from sensors or control certain components actions.

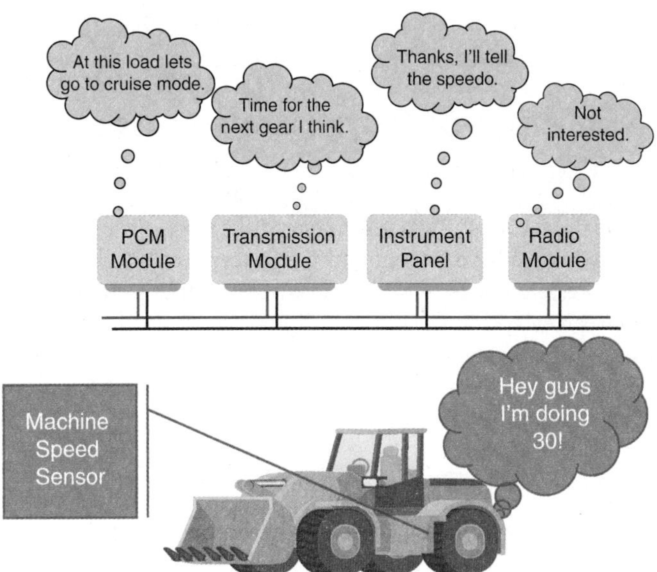

FIGURE 19-1 A networked system allows data to be sent over the system to all modules. The ones that need to know that information act on it, and the rest ignore it.

▶ Machine Onboard Networks

K19001

Today's mobile off-road equipment can have as many as 30 onboard electronic control modules monitoring and controlling the machine's systems, and these have increased the need for interaction between the machine's systems and components. For example, many systems must know the speed of the machine, such as instrument panel for the speedometer, transmission for gear selection, radio for speed-sensitive volume control, etc. (**FIGURE 19-1**).

Most often, the **typology** refers to the physical shape of the way a network is connected. Star network interconnections are shaped just like that—with star-shaped interconnections. It is the same way for most of the other sensors and systems as well.

Onboard machine networks are formed by connecting machine electronic control modules to one another to communicate and exchange information.

In concept, a machine network is somewhat like a social network, in which people are connected through websites or organizations that allow them to exchange information and collaborate to accomplish tasks or reach goals otherwise unachievable when unconnected. The idea of "the whole being greater than the sum of its parts" applies to machine networks too. Extensive use of microprocessor-based controls applied to nearly every machine system can also be leveraged with network communication to provide a huge number of benefits not possible with modules and devices left unconnected.

Communication takes place between all the modules and devices connected to the network by using an electrical signal-processing strategy called multiplexing. **Multiplexing** simply refers to a concept where transmission of more than one electrical signal or message takes place over a single wire or pair of wires. In modern machines, thousands of messages are exchanged every second over onboard networks. Originally devised to eliminate bulky wiring harnesses, multiplex communication across modules and other network devices has made onboard networks practical. Networking between modules enables customization of a machine's electrical system, providing new operating features, enhanced diagnostic capabilities, and simplified repair procedures. A good

You Are the Mobile Heavy Equipment Technician

After arriving at a customer's yard for a service call, you are asked to diagnose the problem with a brand-new excavator. The machine will start and run, but the engine will not accelerate above idle speed. After the engine is started, a red warning light immediately flashes for 30 seconds before the engine shuts down. You perform typical visual inspections of the machine, inspecting the exhaust systems and wiring harnesses and checking for fuel coolant, air, and oil leaks. According to the dash gauge and visual verification, the diesel exhaust fluid (DEF) tank is three-quarters full. Nothing seems amiss, but you realize that certain emission-related faults and engine-protection-system–related faults will produce these symptoms. Finding the fault that is specifically causing the severe engine power derate conditions and shutdown is challenging. Before performing any further steps, consider the following:

1. What are two procedures that can be used to retrieve fault codes, other than using OEM (original equipment manufacturer) or other types of diagnostic software?
2. Explain why the red engine warning lamp—the stop engine lamp—is flashing before the engine shuts down.
3. Are fault codes retrievable from this machine without OEM software? Explain your answer.

understanding of machine network construction, operation, and diagnostic techniques is critical for technician success.

▶ Network Construction and Classification

K19002

All networks have in common the concepts of interconnected modules, the use of serial data to enable digital communication between each module, and time division multiplexing as a communication strategy. However, there are a multitude of different networks types, each constructed differently, and each with its own unique characteristics.

The following are the most basic ways that onboard communication networks can be categorized:

1. *Typology*—typology describes how modules are connected to one another (**FIGURE 19-2**).

   Most often, the typology refers to the physical shape of the way a network is connected. Star network interconnections are shaped just like that—with star-shaped interconnections (**FIGURE 19-3**).

   Ring and bus networks are other common layouts of connection configurations for the channels exchanging data. The word "bus," when used in network typology, describes a network connection that looks just like a bus route. These configurations feature two-way traffic and "bus stops" along the way, which are electronic control modules. The J-1939 network used by all off-road equipment uses a bus-type typology.
2. *The physical layer*—this refers to how the network hardware is constructed. For example, most networks use twisted wire pairs, but some use single wires, connect wirelessly, or even communicate using fiber optics. Standards exist for each type of network, such as how many nodes (number of modules) can connect, the type of connectors used, the lengths of the network wires.
3. *Network protocol*—this refers to the rules or standards used to communicate over the networks. Communication standards, device naming, definitions, fault code structure, and the physical layer are examples of network elements governed by rules within a specific protocol. Mobile off-road equipment manufacturers have in the past used different protocols, many of which were written in the manufacturer's own proprietary language. Most of the mobile off-road equipment industry currently follows controller area network (CAN) standard protocol ISO11783 or SAE J1939 for agricultural and off-road equipment. Emission regulations legislate the use of network communication protocols.
4. *Centralized or distributed control*—networks may also be classified by (1) whether network operation is dependent on one master module directing the operation of several other slave module or (2) whether control of the machine's electrical system is shared among the machine's ECMs. Master-slave networks are referred to as centralized network control. The master module will send serial data to various other less sophisticated control modules, which contain only microcontrollers, to carry out instructions. The master module will make requests for information and sends commands to be executed by a slave module. A slave module responds only to requests by the master or central control module (**FIGURE 19-4**).

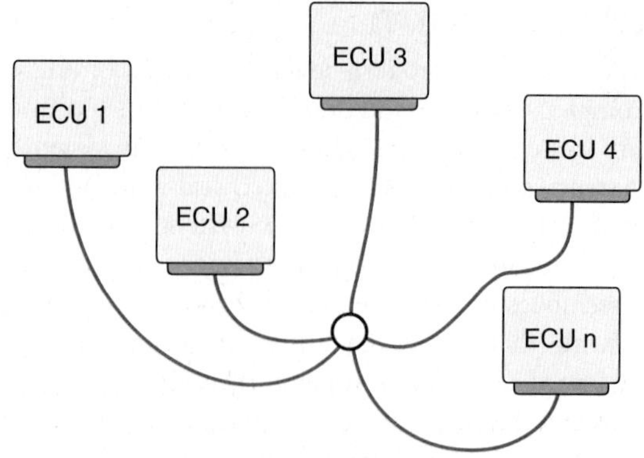

FIGURE 19-2 The typology of a star network is shaped like a star.

Distributed networks control machine operation and the electrical system using several to dozens of modules, all sharing information and sending output signals to electrical devices (**FIGURE 19-5**).

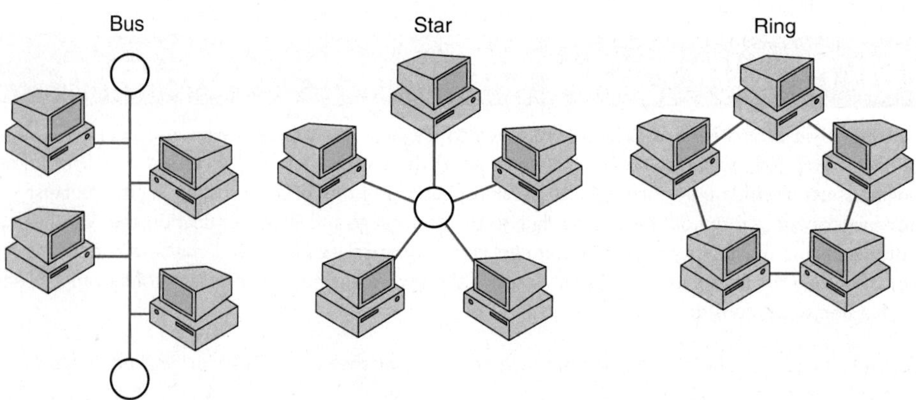

FIGURE 19-3 Network typology refers to the shape taken by the module interconnections.

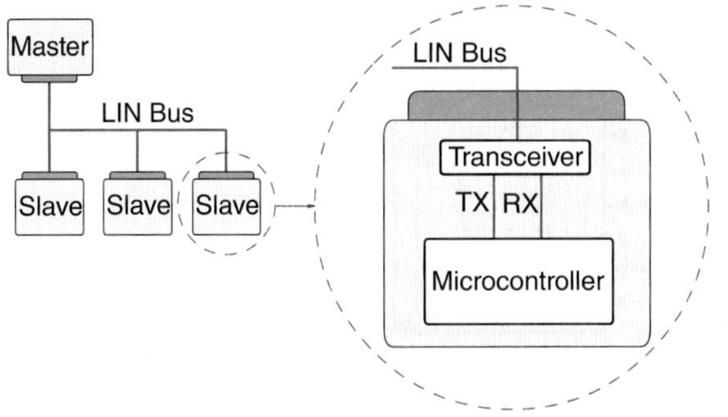

FIGURE 19-4 A local interconnect network (LIN) uses a centralized control.

Most late-model machines have, in fact, multiple onboard networks using a combination of network types.

Networks are also constructed based on organizational priorities. Modules are grouped by a machine's area or function, such as those involved in engine, transmission, implement, climate control, instrumentation, entertainment devices, or body electrical control. Not all information has high priority. For example, information that affects machine or occupant safety, such as the hydraulic system, engine, or transmission, will not always share the same network as one involving data exchange for the climate control or onboard entertainment system. Still, some information needs to be exchanged between the networks. To enable communication between different onboard networks, a **gateway module** is used (**FIGURE 19-6**).

The job of this module, as the name suggests, is to translate communication between different networks that operate by using different protocols or speeds. Without the gateway module, access to networks through the DLC using electronic service tools would not be possible.

▶ Time Division Multiplexing

K19003, S19001, S19002

Communication between modules and network devices typically takes place over a single wire or pair of wires connected to each module. When paired together and connected in parallel to all modules in the network, the typology forming the communication pathway is called a **data bus**. Information is communicated digitally by using a series of 1s and 0s that represent numbers and letters. The digital communication used by onboard networks is similar to the electrical language of Morse code. Under this system, communication took place over a pair of telegraph wires using a series of dots and dashes. Both Morse code and onboard networks use what is called binary code, which means there are only two choices or types of information—0 or 1, dot or dash. The biggest difference is the speed at which the data is exchanged. Digital modules communicate much faster than Morse code; the increased speed is made possible through the use of digital electronics.

It may be puzzling to understand how only the same two wires connected to each module can send and receive information, apparently simultaneously, especially considering the enormous volume of data passing over the networks. If communication took place simultaneously, the positive and negative voltage pulses representing 0s and 1s would collide, canceling one another or generally becoming garbled, a lot like a noisy classroom when everyone is speaking at once and thus no one is understood.

However, using an electrical signal communication strategy called multiplexing overcomes the problem. The type of multiplexing used in onboard networks works by dividing the time available to each network module or device to transmit and listen to information. **Time division multiplexing (TDM)**

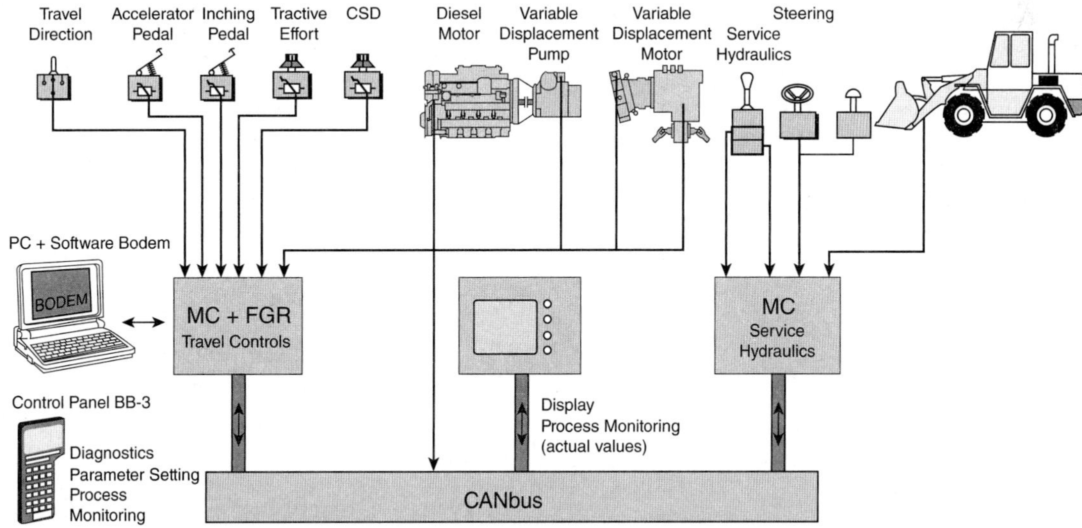

FIGURE 19-5 A J-1939 network uses distributed control of the machine's electrical system.

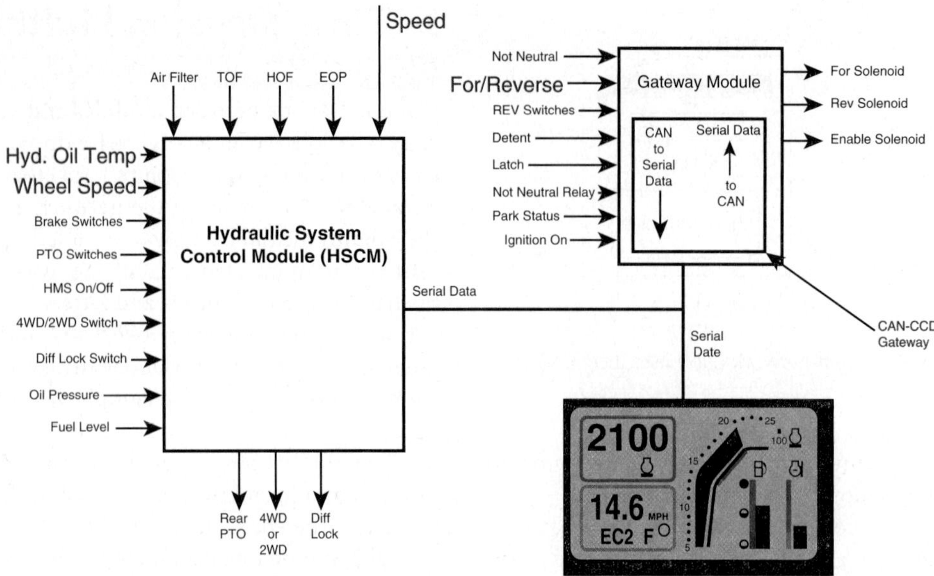

FIGURE 19-6 A distributed control network using a gateway module to translate between each network.

Image Provided As Courtesy of John Deere.

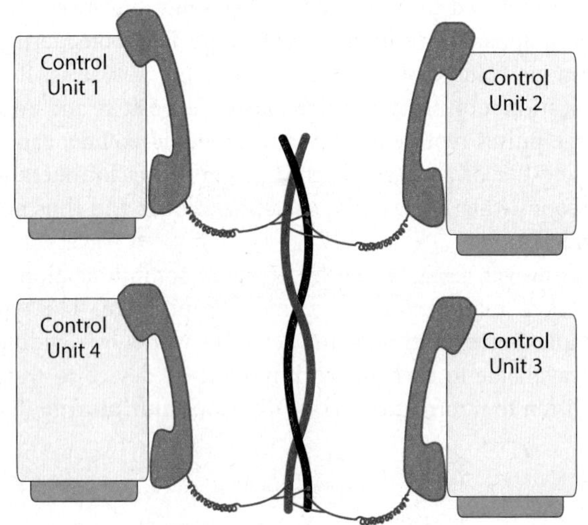

FIGURE 19-7 Time division multiplexing (TDM) is like a phone call where modules share a phone extension.

requires that the modules and other devices take turns, sharing the data bus communication pathway (**FIGURE 19-7**).

Only one module is allowed to talk, and all other modules must listen until it is their turn to talk. This should remind you of a well-ordered classroom where there is cooperation around communication and no one interrupts anyone else until they are finished speaking. Data transfer back and forth along the data bus does not take place simultaneously, but each device transmits and receives data by cooperating to time-share a common signal path (**FIGURE 19-8**).

The speed at which the data exchange takes place makes communication appear to occur simultaneously, although it does not.

Multiplexing Advantages

Multiplexed communication was originally designed to eliminate bulky wiring harnesses. Years ago, machines used a point-to-point electrical connection method that meant switching on a single light required a circuit connecting the battery to a fuse, a switch, wires connecting the switch to the light, a connection to chassis ground, and an operator to decide to switch the light on. Regardless of where the light and the switch were located, wire connected each terminal of the light or lighting circuit. Every electrical device operated this way.

Understandably, point-to-point wiring technique results in very large, heavy wiring harnesses throughout the machine. Each connection in the circuit and length of wire also produce electrical resistance and a source of potential failure. Corrosion, loose connections, and chafed wiring were common electrical system failures, and the technique created a notoriously unreliable system that was difficult to troubleshoot.

Point-to-point wiring construction created unique problems for machines. Many feet of electrical wire were needed to control the electrical systems. Adding electrical relays to operate other simple 12/24-volt circuits built further complexity into the electrical system, which accounted for as much as one-half of engineering time and a large percentage of a machine's assembly cost.

To eliminate the problems created by point-to-point wiring and relay logic systems, bulky wiring harnesses were replaced by electronic, microprocessor-controlled lighting modules strategically positioned near the light circuits or other electrical devices.

Additional multiplexing advantages include the following:

- software control of the electrical system
- enabled onboard diagnostics
- ease of connecting electronically controlled accessories and features
- reduction in number of sensors.

Software Control of Electrical System

When using networks, electrical system complexity is absorbed by software instead of a huge array of hardwired components and circuit boards. The electrical system occupies

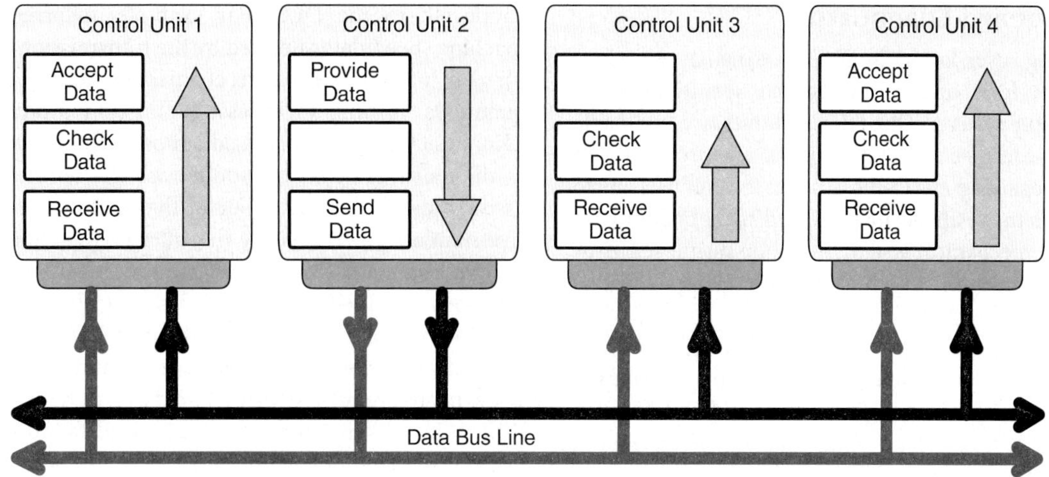

FIGURE 19-8 The rule of TDM multiplexing allows only one module to send information, and the remaining modules receive.

less space; is lighter in weight; and is easier to design, install, troubleshoot, and repair. An estimated two-thirds reduction in manufacturing cost and assembly time is achieved through the use of multiplexed network communication. The newest machine communication networks permit enhanced features and control of every electrical subsystem, from machine lighting and cab controls (e.g., wipers, HVAC, windows) to every chassis electrical accessory. Multiplexed networks also allow precise electrical control of implement controls, transmissions, instrument gauges, air- and hydraulic-operated accessories, global positioning, and engine and transmission operations (**FIGURE 19-9**.)

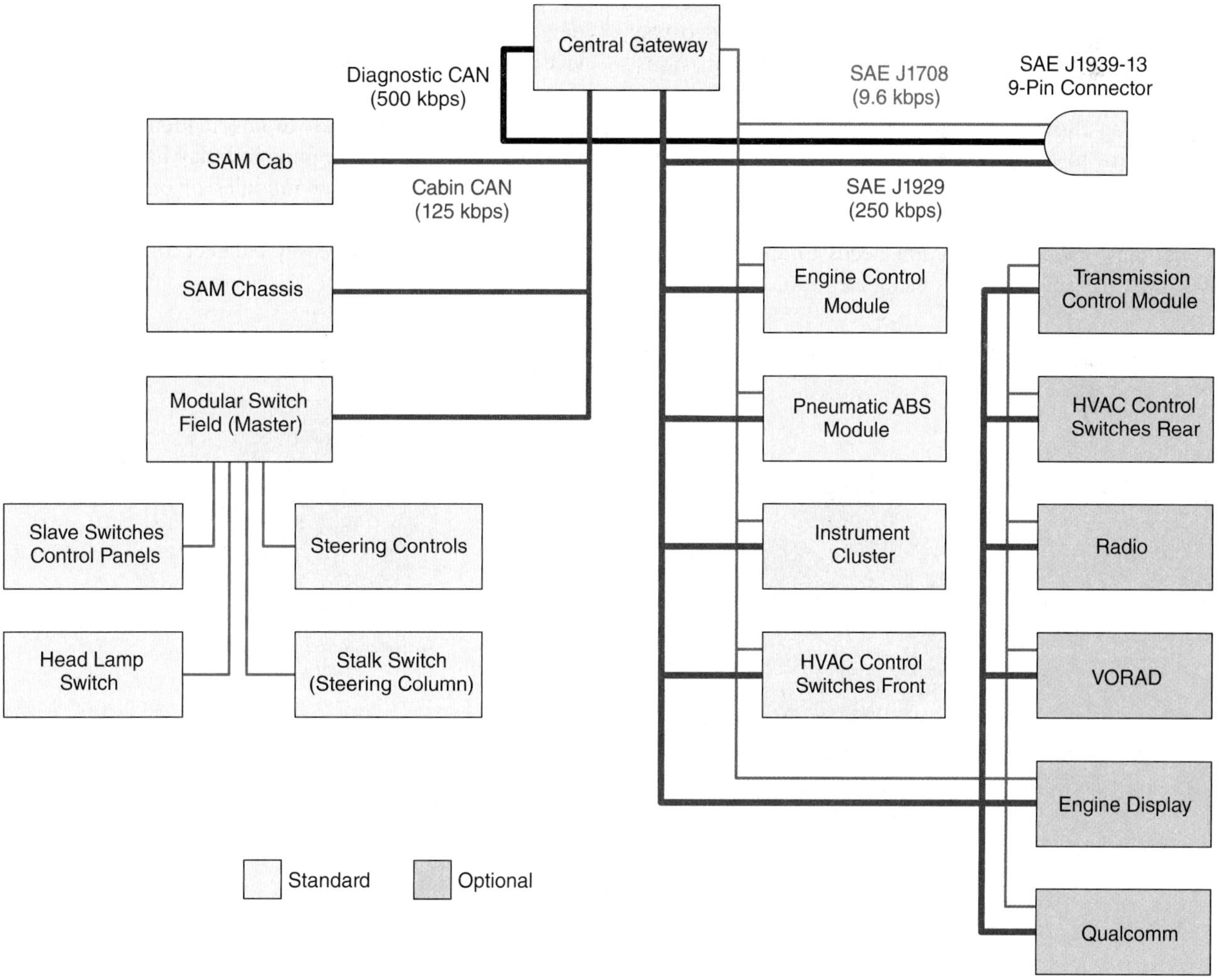

FIGURE 19-9 A gateway module enables communication between different onboard networks.

Enabling Onboard Diagnostics

Legislation setting ever-lower limits on exhaust emissions required a greater level of precision in the operation of the diesel fuel injection system. Those lower limits are attainable only through the extensive use of electronics. The problem with diagnosing and repairing electronic systems in comparison to mechanical ones is the relatively invisible and silent operation of electricity. Broken mechanical systems are often diagnosed visually or with mechanical tools such as pressure gauges and dial indicators.

However, a defective engine sensor or broken wire in a harness is not so easily detected, and it can be a time-consuming operation to diagnose based on only symptoms and a multimeter. Self-monitoring or self-diagnostic capabilities are, therefore, built into electronic control systems to help technicians perform faster diagnostic checks and repairs. Electronic control modules can easily evaluate the voltage and current levels of circuits to which they are connected and determine whether the data makes sense and is in the correct operational range. These self-diagnostic capabilities are referred to as **onboard diagnostics (OBD)** systems.

All electronically controlled engines, powertrain components, and implement controls have built-in self-diagnostic capabilities. To communicate this data to an electronic service tool from even a single module requires the use of duplex or **bidirectional communications**, meaning two-way multiplex communication. As modules for transmissions, braking, and other electronic controls are added, network communication allowed these modules to communicate fault codes and data to a single diagnostic data link connector (DLC) (**FIGURE 19-10**).

Because a variety of modules can impact the machine's emissions, network communication needs to and does make it easy to identify specific faults using electronic service tools connected to the DLC. For example, incorrect or missing machine speed data supplied by the transmission control module can interfere with correct injection timing and injection quantities, leading to excessive emission production. When a malfunction is detected, diagnostic information is stored in the machine's control module, which identifies the fault to assist in diagnosis and repair of the malfunction. The legislative standard developed by the International Society of Automotive Engineers (SAE) is referred to as heavy-duty onboard diagnostics (HD-OBD). This same legislation regulates the construction of a mandatory onboard network to access emission-related information. The OBD standard has many network-related requirements, all intended to reduce the cost and difficulties of repairing emission-related failures by independent repair facilities. Consequently, fault code reporting, the configuration of the DLC, communication language, and other network characteristics associated with emission control systems are standardized.

Ease of Connecting Electronically Controlled Accessories and Features

Machine accessories can be added at the factory or during aftermarket installation without any complex programming or equipment modification by using onboard networks. Connecting the device to the machine can occur automatically or by using service programming software. When a network-compatible accessory connects to a network, its presence is recognized and the network will provide access to information it needs to perform its job. This is much like plug-and-play hardware for personal computers. Remote power modules or other modules can be programmed to function per customized specifications, allowing machine builders to easily connect to the electrical system (**FIGURE 19-11**).

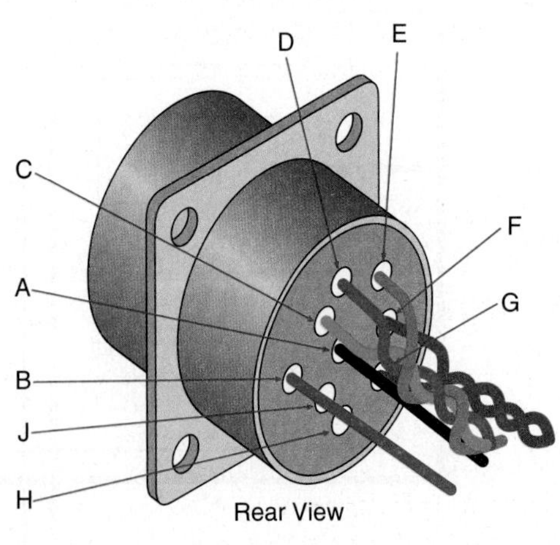

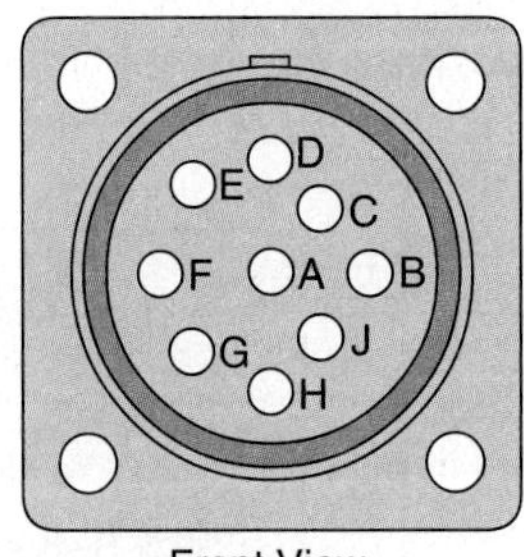

A Battery Ground
B 12V DC
C J1939 Data Link (+)
D J1939 Data Link (–)
E J1939 Shield
F J1587 Data Link (+)
G J1587 Data Link (–)
H Plug
J Plug

FIGURE 19-10 The 9-pin DLC enables service tool communication with the machine network.

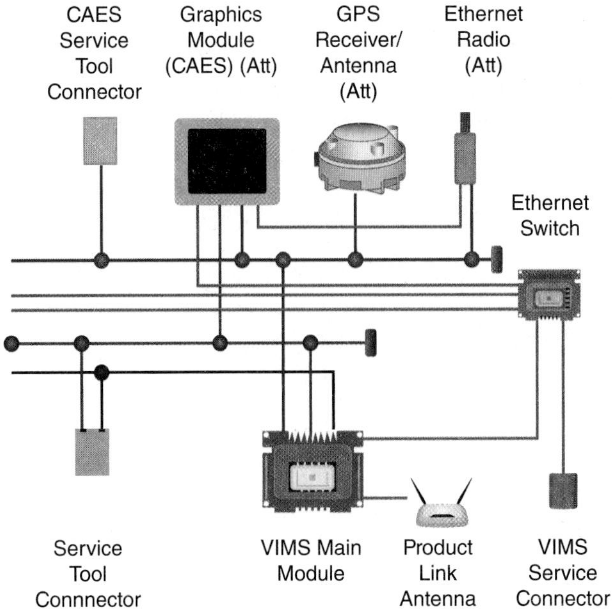

FIGURE 19-11 Electronic controlled accessories that can be connected to the machines network.

> **SAFETY TIP**
>
> On J-1939 CAN networks, any module connected to the network must be certified as compatible. Non-compatible modules may work, but they can cause unusual, and even catastrophic, problems. For example, security systems or remote starters connected to the network or networked devices, such as door locks and starting/ignition circuits, can suddenly and unexpectedly cause a machine to stop operation. "Footprint errors" are also produced when incompatible devices are connected to the network. Any affected module must be completely reprogrammed. Even engine ECMs, which are reflashed or recalibrated with modified performance modifications, can send incorrect information over the network, adversely affecting machine operation.

> **TECHNICIAN TIP**
>
> The use of electronic service tools such as scanners, PCs, and other devices to communicate with modules connected to the machine network is critical to the diagnosis and repair of emission-related faults. Fault codes, communication language, and other features of the onboard network are standardized by EPA (Environmental Protection Agency) legislation to make it easier for technicians to repair a wide variety of machines with a minimum amount of electronic service tools. The right to repair aspects of the EPA legislation enabled aftermarket tool manufacturers—not just the OEMs—to supply service tools to communicate with the network.

Reduction in Number of Sensors

Sensor data can be shared across many devices connected into a network. This network feature eliminates duplication of sensors needed for a module. A simple example is the use of a machine speed sensor. This data is required in many places by various devices. The instrument gauge cluster, transmission, and engine all require machine speed data, as does the entertainment system, which might lower or raise the radio volume depending on road speed. Using one electronic module to sense and process speed sensor data and then distribute the information over the network reduces the construction cost and associated wiring required to connect a sensor to each device that needs road speed data. Note also that the information-processing capabilities are distributed over many modules, which enhances the power of the total network. Instead of numerous modules performing the same task—such as processing speed data—only one module does it, which frees the processors in other ECMs to perform different work.

Other Network Outputs and Inputs

Multiplexed components on networks also include the following:

- instrument panel and gauge clusters
- odometers, now with digital LCD displays that can serve as a numeric fault code reader
- operator monitor
- cellular antenna system
- global positioning systems (GPS)

Multiplex switch packs permit dash switches to connect to the network with a twisted pair data bus. A variety of resistors and diodes within switch packs create a unique identifier for each switch, allowing them to be mapped to a unique function on the network (**FIGURE 19-12**).

This means that when accessories are installed, holes do not need to be cut into the dash, nor do new circuits need to be made. Outputs will originate from chassis or cab modules.

Power distribution modules incorporating inputs and power outputs with 20 amps or more of current-carrying capacity are useful programmable output devices. Modules containing **field effect transistors (FETs)**, which operate like a combined solid-state relay and a circuit breaker, also have virtual fusing for circuit protection. When current is applied to the gate, an FET can switch current flow like a regular switching transistor. However, a fourth leg or terminal on an FET allows monitoring of current levels through the FET. This means that if the programmed maximum current is exceeded, the current flow will switch off the FET.

▶ Controlled Area Networks

K19004, S19003, S19004

The term **controlled area networks (CAN)** describes a distributed network control system. This means no single central control module is used. Instead, each module or node on the network has processing capabilities that can initiate electrical control for faster response and also synchronize their operation with other network modules. Therefore, each module on the network has memorized the rules of what it has to do and what the rules are for doing it. Because the network has no central control, the connected components will still operate in the event that parts of it are severed.

CANs are the most widely used type of network for integrating powertrain operation of all the latest machines. These

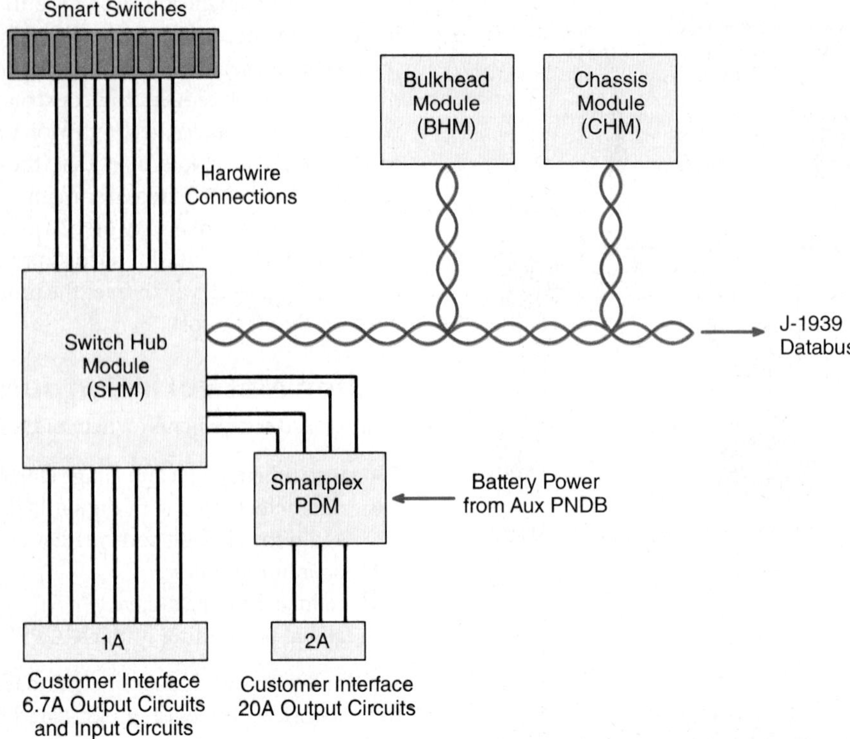

FIGURE 19-12 Programmable switch packs enable the customization of switch functions.

networks are often integrated in local area networks (LANs), which are machines using multiple types of networks on a single chassis, such as optical or other specialized proprietary networks connecting manufacturer-specific equipment. Because there is no central control module coordinating communication or controlling network devices, each network module has built-in processor capabilities to process input and output data while simultaneously receiving and transmitting data to the network. A built-in clock and transceiver in each CAN module helps synchronize multiplex communication between modules, so each takes an appropriate turn using the data bus to send and receive messages.

Other processing functions built into every CAN module allow it to interpret other network communication data and control the messages it sends to the data bus. This degree of sophistication makes CAN nodes more expensive to build. Other onboard networks are built to reduce costs and increase CAN speed.

J-1939 Versus J-1708/1587

Two different types of CANs used by mobile off-road equipment are the SAE network standards J-1939 and J-1587/1708. The J-1587/1708 CAN is identified by the six-pin DLC. It is an older network that transmits data at the relatively slow speed of 9,600 bits/second. J-1708 refers to the standards for the physical layer or just specifications for data bus construction. J-1957 has standardized fault codes and uses an SAE set of rules to govern the communication over the J-1708 physical network. The J-1708 data bus

- contains two twisted wires using 18-AWG that are color-coded orange and green
- links all electronic modules on the machine
- communicates at 9,600 bits per second (bps)
- transmits at a maximum distance of 131 feet (40 meters)
- connects up to 20 modules or nodes.

Beginning in 2001, J-1939 began replacing the J-1708 standard for data bus. The J-1939

- uses two twisted wires of 18 AWG that are color-coded yellow and green
- connects only modules that are compatible with the J-1939 standard
- requires terminating resistors
- communicates at 256,000 bps
- transmits at a maximum distance of 131 feet (40 meters)
- connects up to 30 modules or nodes
- stub connections to the twisted wire backbone are limited to 3 feet (1 meter) in length.

J-1939 defines not only the construction of the data bus but also all features and characteristics of the network. Contrasted to J-1957/1708, J-1939 is like high-speed Internet access compared to dial-up in terms of the amount of data carried per second. J-1587 and J-1939 use serial data communication protocols, which have similar characteristics but which differ in relation to rules about such things as message structure, transmission speed, connectivity hardware configuration, and diagnostic fault codes.

Serial Communication

Serial communication is like electronic Morse code. Instead of dots and dashes, however, 0s and 1s are transmitted in a series, one after another, using voltage pulses. As there is only one

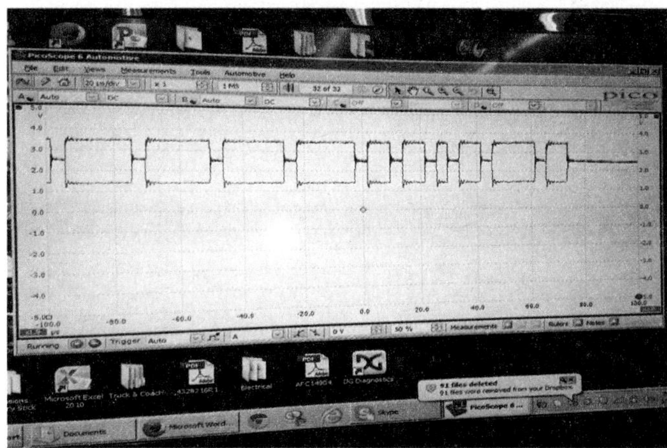

FIGURE 19-13 A serial data waveform from a J-1939 network.

path, data is transmitted one bit at a time, one bit after another, or in series (**FIGURE 19-13**).

A positive voltage of anywhere between 2 and 8 volts in comparison to a pulse of lower voltage would represent a 1. No voltage—or voltage close to 0 and no higher than +1.5 volts—represents a 0. Voltage on the paired wires is a mirror opposite to produce a sharp, crisp differential voltage that is easily understood by the modules (**FIGURE 19-14**).

Using differential voltage and twisting the wires minimize electromagnetic interference (EMI) in the wires, also called electrical noise, in wiring carrying serial data.

J-1939 communications have two wires: one wire, called CAN-hi, has a more positive voltage than the other, called CAN-lo. Each wire will have a mirror opposite charge of the other when communication takes place.

Twisted Wire Pair Data Buses

Wires are twisted to minimize electromagnetic interference caused by magnetic fields and radio waves (**FIGURE 19-15**).

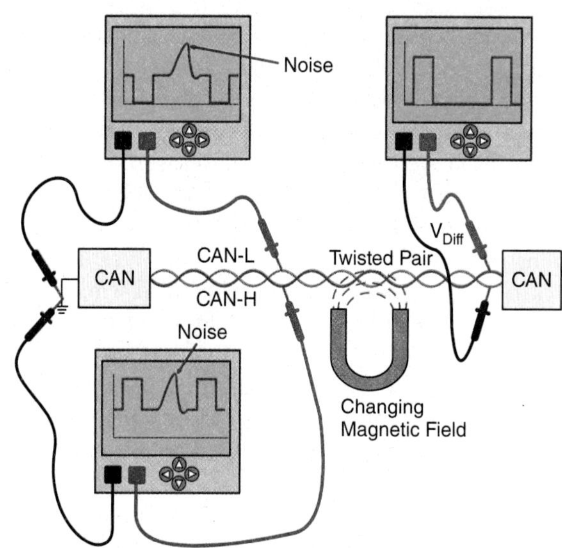

FIGURE 19-15 EMI sources that can affect the data bus. Differential voltage transmission minimizes signal interference.

For example, magnetic fields from starters, electric motors, injectors, or radio signals from CB (citizens band) radios can penetrate the wires and induce voltage. Distortions to voltage signals can garble or change network messages. A cancelation effect is achieved using differential voltage signals, as the two wires carry equal and opposite voltage polarity. When the signal reaches its destination, network modules detect the voltage difference between the two wires to determine whether the signal is a 1 or 0. This type of interpretation of the signal is known as **differential mode transmission**, and it provides a crisp, clear waveform. Note that J-1587/1708 networks reference the CAN voltage from ground and that the differential voltage measured between the two CAN wires is slightly higher than it is in J-1939 signals.

EMI introduced into the wires tends to affect both wires equally when wires are twisted together five turns per inch or

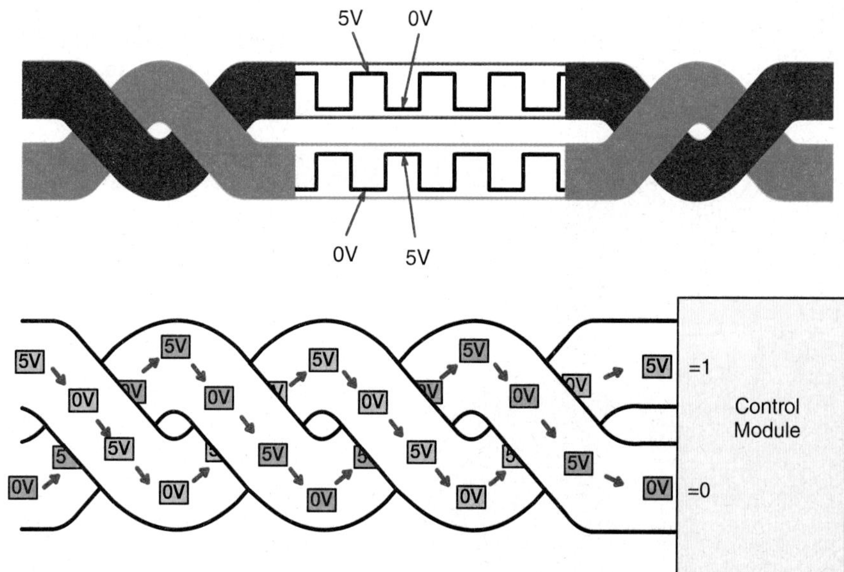

FIGURE 19-14 Differential voltage, or differential mode transmission, of serial data ensures that a clear, crisp electrical signal is transmitted over the data bus.

two turns per centimeter. The low-voltage signal of the CAN data bus is even more susceptible to EMI due to the transmission speed of 256 kbps to 800 kbps. Not only are wires twisted together to resist induction of current, but on earlier machines, they were also covered in a metal foil to absorb EMI signals. A third wire attached to the foil drains away induced current flow in the foil to ground. This is similar to the use of the braided shielding wire used on TV cable. With the TV cable, the inner wire carries the signal and the outer braided wire shields the inner cable from interference that would produce a static-filled, distorted picture.

To further minimize signal distortion, at each end of the J-1939 CANbus, there is a 120-ohm resistor that extinguishes multiplex voltage signals to prevent their reflection through the data bus (**FIGURE 19-16**).

Similar to a lightbulb, which converts current to heat and light, resistors absorb signals to increase transmission speed on the data bus. The J-1939 data bus also minimizes distortion of data caused by EMI interference. On a CAN, the CAN-H (high) wire is yellow and carries positive voltage (CAN+). The green wire, CAN-L (low) (CAN–), is negative. Signals could be transmitted over a single wire; if one of the wires were broken or grounded out, using the voltage-differential mode of transmission would provide a better signal quality capable of very high rates of data transmission.

CAN+ and CAN– wires provide 60 ohms of resistance. Disconnecting either of the terminating resistors causes the bus resistance to rise to 120 ohms. If the resistance of the data link is 120 ohms, then either there is an open circuit somewhere or a terminating resistor is missing. Pinched, cut, or shorted data bus wires will extinguish any network communication. The outer foil should have continuity with chassis ground and none to either of the twisted wire pair. Repairs to the bus need to be performed according to prescribed manufacturer procedures. Field experience has demonstrated that if only one J-1939 terminating resistor is missing, the network or machine will likely not have any operational problems. However, if both terminating resistors are missing, no communication is possible (**FIGURE 19-17**).

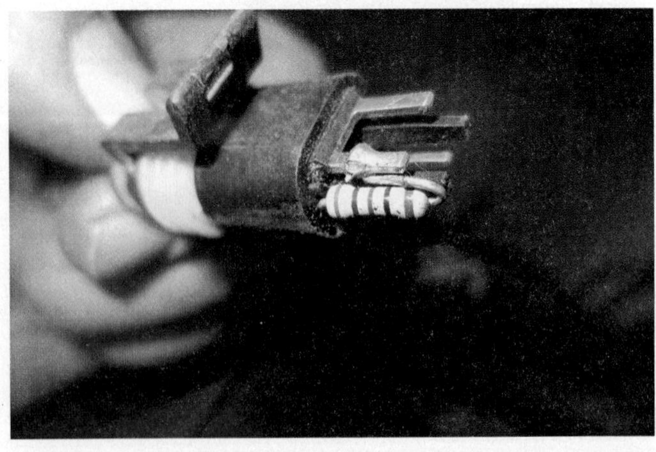

FIGURE 19-16 A terminating resistor for a J-1939 network.

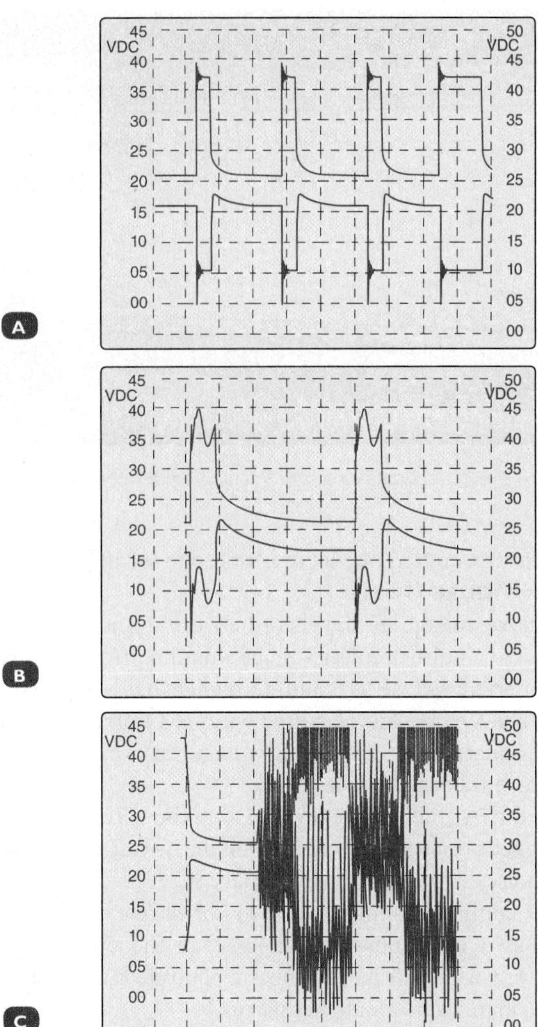

FIGURE 19-17 Waveforms when resistors are missing from a J-1939 data bus. **A.** Two resistors. **B.** One missing resistor. **C.** No resistors (all resistors missing).

To measure the resistance of terminating resistors, follow the steps in **SKILL DRILL 19-1**. Note that you should perform this test only after disconnecting the batteries.

> **TECHNICIAN TIP**
>
> Only one connection to ground should be made on the J-1939 drain wire. If more than one connection is made to ground, the outer shielding can become a circuit pathway. This will in turn intensify EMI interference if electrical current moves through the drain conductor.

Network Messages

Using CAN networks is like shouting a message in a well-ordered room crowded with people. Everyone can hear the message, but not everyone will respond or is permitted to speak at once because of message rules. Using the CAN protocols, however, is not as potentially confusing as a room full of shouting people. Instead of people, modules are communicating with one another operating under a strictly defined set of rules to

SKILL DRILL 19-1 Measuring Resistance of Terminating Resistors

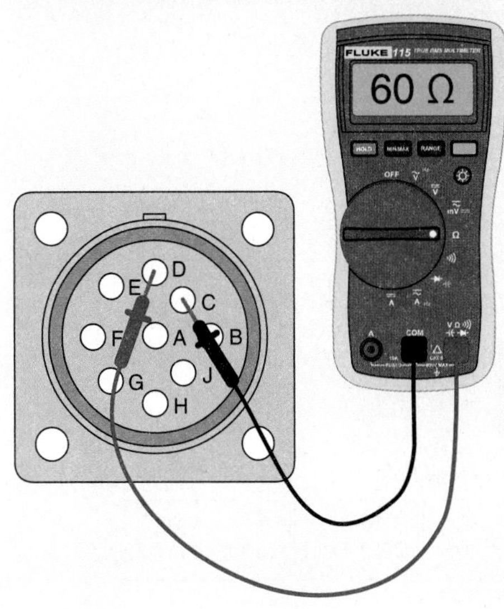

1. With the ignition off, disconnect the batteries.
2. Connect the leads of a digital multimeter to pins C and D of the 9-pin diagnostic connector.
3. Set the multimeter to read in ohms.
4. Measure and record the resistance. Normal resistance should be 60 ohms; 120 ohms indicates one missing resistor; 45 ohms indicates an extra resistor. With both resistors removed, there should be a high resistance of more than 10k ohms, but not infinite resistance.

control communication. To accomplish this, data carried on the CANbus has four distinct message formats:

1. Dataframe—its message format is something like this:
   a. "Hello, everyone. Here's some information labeled X. I hope it's useful!"
2. Remote frame—its message format is something like this:
   a. "Hello, everyone. Can somebody please send the information labeled Y?"
3. Error frame—its message format is something like this:
   a. (Everyone out loud) "Can you repeat that?" This message is sent by modules that do not understand a message if the information is garbled or is not sent according to rules.
4. Overload frame—its message format is something like this:
   a. "I'm a very busy at the moment with the GPS module, sending something more important. Could you please wait another moment?"

Using these message formats that determine which module is transmitting or receiving data, problems with message transmission are eliminated while communicating huge quantities of information.

Message Format

Messages sent and received over the network are constructed in frames and have a maximum message length of 130 bits. This maximum message length is, by digital data standards, short. A short message ensures the wait time for each message is as brief as possible. Each of the above message types is further divided into sections. Examples of frame sets included in the above message include a start frame, which indicates the start of the message. Another frame identifies the type of message, such as whether it is from the engine or transmission, and how important or what priority it has. For example, slow-changing data, such as coolant temperature, would have less priority or urgency than, say, a wheel lock-up event reported by the ABS (antilock brake system). Another frame within the message provides the actual data that is of interest to the modules, such as machine speed or whether the air conditioning is on or off. Finally, a couple of other frames are used to indicate the end of a message (**FIGURE 19-18**).

All modules acknowledge the receipt of information transmitted from a specific module by indicating there were no corrupted messages. This is like ending a telephone call with the message, "Did you hear what I said? Everyone says OK and goodbye."

No centralized special software controls the network communication. Operating instructions are imbedded in the memory chips used by the CAN module connected to the network. Manufacturers supplying devices connected to the network must ensure the devices are constructed to design specifications that make them network compatible. This enables the use of the plug-and-play feature of the network.

Data Bus Arbitration

Deciding which messages have priority to transmit over the network to prevent data collision between positive and negative signals is called **arbitration**. As soon as the data bus is free (i.e., the telephone line is not busy), each node or module can begin transmitting information. If two or more modules start transmitting at once, the message format decides which message has access to the data bus. For example, a wheel lock-up event or a traction control module message indicating excessive wheel slip will have priority on the data bus to supply information to the engine ECM and reduce power output. Modules with

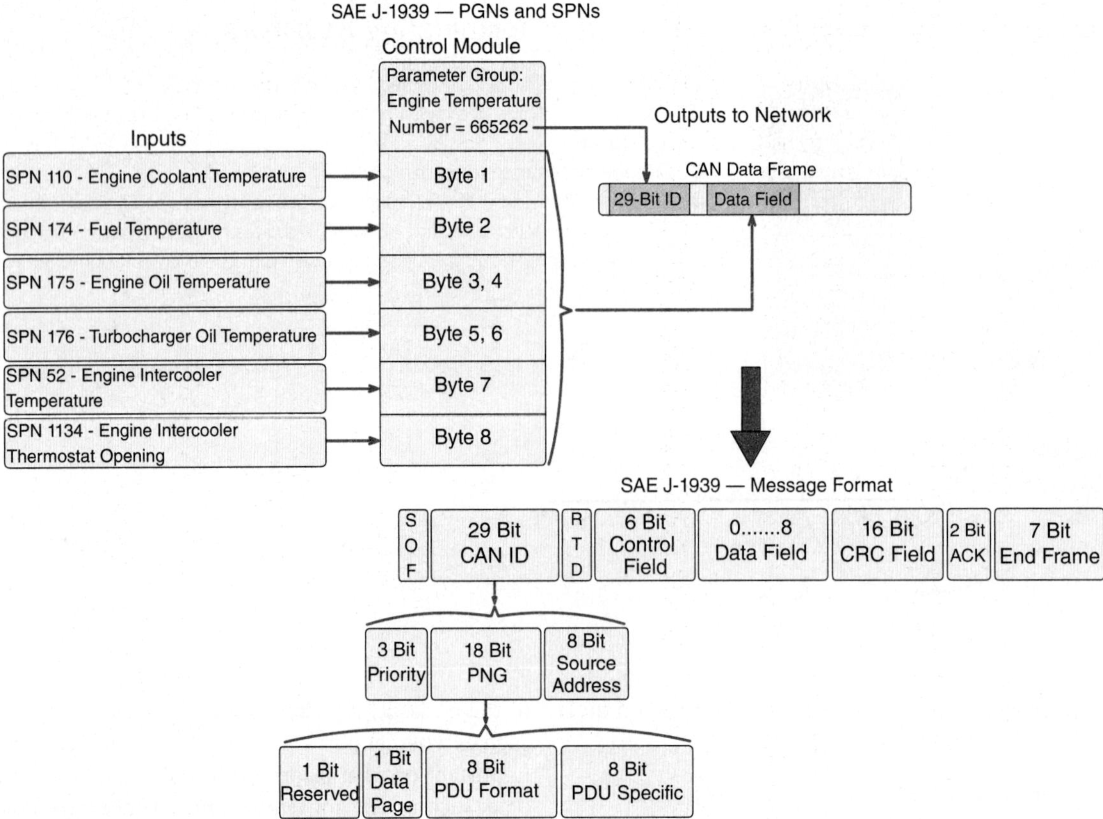

FIGURE 19-18 Construction of a J-1939 network message. Message information also includes whether the data is a fault code or simply system information.

lower priority messages automatically switch from transmitting to receiving and repeat their transmission as soon as the bus is free again.

Gateways—Joining Multiple Networks Together

Today, multiple networks exist on most machines. Rarely does contemporary equipment use only a single CAN for powertrain- and emission-related functions. The reason for multiple networks is primarily cost. Modules used on CANs have far more sophisticated microprocessors, software, and related electronics to operate on these networks with the complexity of communication protocols characteristic of CAN. Manufacturers can produce less-expensive, less-sophisticated modules, nodes, or devices for centrally controlled networks than they can for distributed CANs. Furthermore, manufacturers will often use their own in-house or proprietary networks for controlling unique OEM electrical devices on the network.

Many manufacturers often use **ladder logic**, a software-based control system that replicates relay-based electrical system operation. Where wiring diagrams once depicted battery current flow through electrical connections and devices and showed relays switched open or closed, ladder logic shows rules for software logic to control devices. For example, to operate a starting motor, the electrical system control software would need to confirm that a specific set of conditions is met by verifying a set of true/false statements, such as the following set:

- The ignition switch is in the start position = true/false.
- The transmission is in neutral = true/false.
- Battery voltage is above 10.6-volts = true/false.
- The hydraulic lockout is on = true/false.

Wireless Network Communication

Cell phone and Bluetooth technology are two additional methods of network communication that use wireless network interface. A Bluetooth-equipped phone, when recognized by the network, will turn down the volume of a radio and even transmit the call to the entertainment system or a headset for hands-free communication. Similarly, many aftermarket consumer devices such as navigation systems, entertainment devices, security alarms, media players, and pagers can be connected to the machine network with a touch of a button, or even with voice commands. Bluetooth communication technology is used to connect these devices to the networks and supply information for them to operate properly or to enhance functionality. Cell phone technology is also used

FIGURE 19-19 Telematics solution for remote monitoring.

in system interface. **FIGURE 19-19** shows a telematics technology that continuously transmits network information from a variety of modules to a central dispatch, where the data is monitored.

The machine network modules provide many features:

- remote machine diagnostics
- remote door unlocking
- locating lost or stolen machines
- remote ignition lock-out if the machine is stolen
- remote monitoring of payload data such as: tons per hour, total tonnage, overload warnings and cycle times
- the real-time positions, speed, status, and activities of a machine.

Bluetooth Technology

Bluetooth is a short-range wireless technology that can automatically connect a device to a network. Cell phones are a common application for Bluetooth technology, used to connect a phone with the audio system using the onboard network. Many machines today are equipped or retrofitted with a wireless communication module connected to the data bus of the onboard machine network to communicate with Bluetooth and other radio devices, such as key fobs and cell networks. Instead of using wires to communicate with the network, Bluetooth devices (such as cell phones) use radio frequencies. Communication from the cell phone to network is also multiplexed over a wide number of shifting radio frequencies. Frequency shifting happens much like changing the radio station several times every second, with both the network and the cell phone simultaneously exchanging data on different frequencies. To start a connection, the Bluetooth device will send a signal on a predefined radio frequency, telling the wireless module or node that it wants to communicate. The module, in turn, will send back a mathematical formula to the Bluetooth device telling it which frequencies to use and when. Communication can then begin between the wireless **network node** and the Bluetooth device. The communication formula that determines which radio frequencies to use and when to use them is constantly updated during the interaction.

▶ Diagnosing Network Communication Problems

K19005, S19005, S19006

Problems on networks commonly originate from the following causes:

- shorted or defective CAN modules
- shorts to ground, power or CAN-H and CAN-L wires
- missing terminating resistors
- additional terminating resistors.

When network problems are present, the symptoms can vary widely from machine to machine, depending on the fault and manufacturer. The machine may not start at all or may accelerate slowly (if it accelerates at all), the transmission may not shift properly, lights may be out, etc. (**FIGURE 19-20**).

Disconnecting modules one by one can help identify a module that is shorting out the CANbus. But the best diagnostic routine to identify a network problem is to perform resistance and voltage checks of the CANbus at the DLC. The HD-OBD system monitors the CANbus voltage and will report network faults if the voltage measurements are not correct or if there is a problem with the data. The failure of a service tool to communicate with the DLC requires a check of the voltage on the CAN pins, which should be a minimum of 1 volt. After disconnecting the batteries to remove all machine power, resistance checks of the terminating resistors can be performed. Too many or too few resistors will give an incorrect resistance reading. The proper resistance should be close to 60 ohms.

To perform a DLC voltage check, follow the steps in **SKILL DRILL 19-2**. This test checks whether enough voltage is available on the DLC CAN lines to transmit data. And to check for shorts in the CAN, follow the guidelines in **SKILL DRILL 19-3**. Again, perform this test only after disconnecting the batteries.

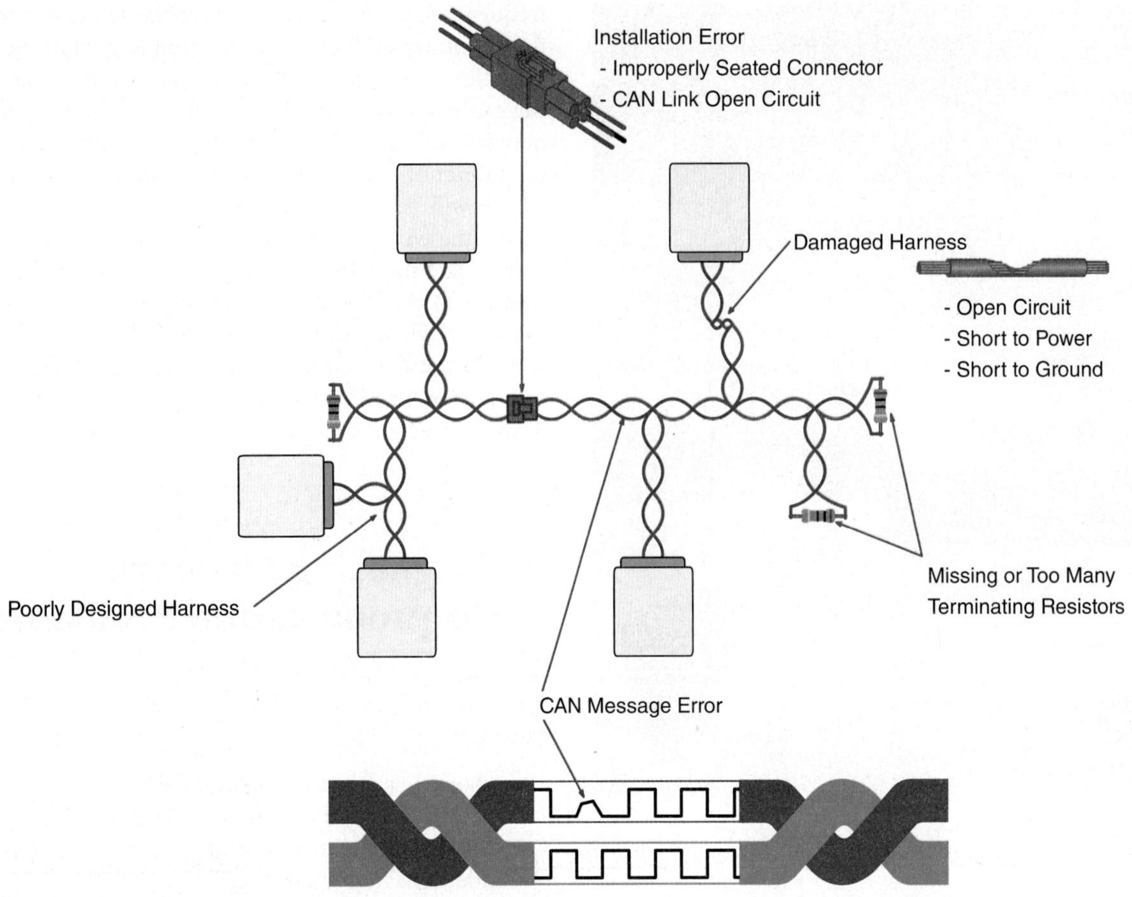

FIGURE 19-20 CANbus defects.

SKILL DRILL 19-2 Performing a DLC Voltage Check

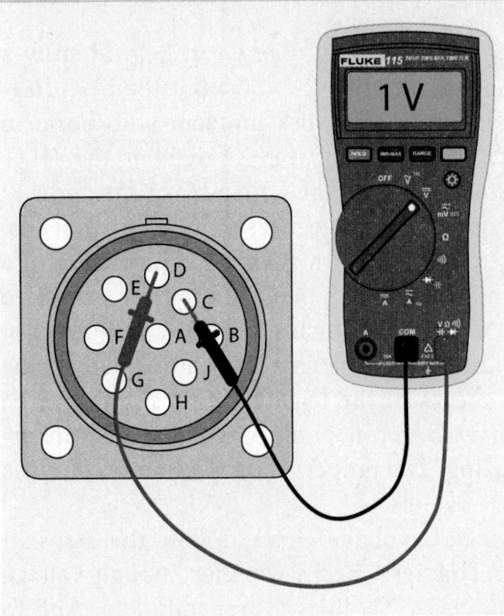

1. Set the digital multimeter (DMM) to read in ohms.
2. With the ignition on, connect the leads of a DMM to pins C and D of the 9-pin diagnostic connector.
3. Measure and record the voltage. The voltage should be more than 1 volt. If not, there is no network communication taking place.

SKILL DRILL 19-3 Checking for Shorts in the CAN

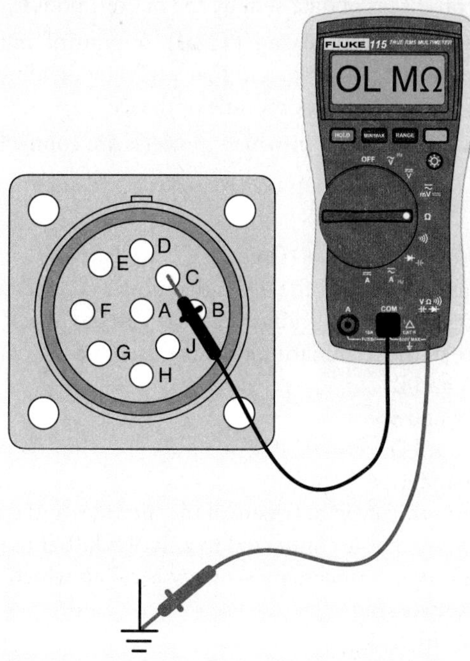

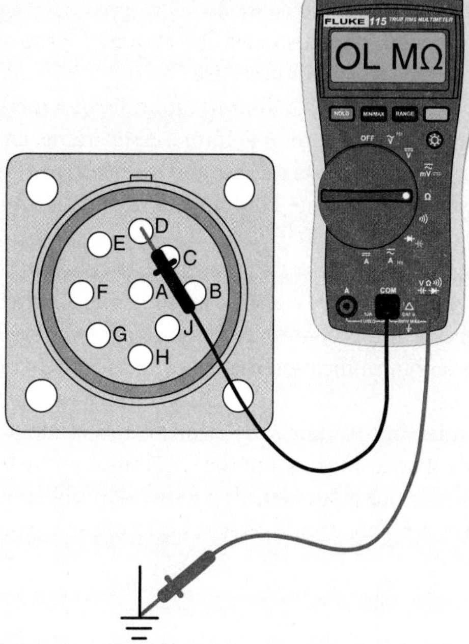

1. With the ignition off, disconnect the batteries.
2. Connect one lead of a DMM to pin C of the 9-pin diagnostic connector.
3. Connect the multimeter lead to chassis ground.
4. Set the multimeter to read in ohms.
5. Measure and record the resistance.
6. Connect one lead of a DMM to pin D of the 9-pin diagnostic connector.
7. Connect the other multimeter lead to chassis ground.
8. Measure and record the resistance. The resistance between chassis ground and pin C and D should be infinite or out of limit.

▶ Wrap-Up

Ready for Review

- Onboard machine networks are formed by connecting machine electronic control modules to one another to communicate and exchange information.
- Communication takes place between all the modules and devices connected to the network through the use of an electrical signal-processing strategy called multiplexing.
- Onboard networks can be categorized by typology, their physical layer, their network protocol, or by whether they have centralized or distributed control.
- Networks are formed based on organizational priorities, with modules grouped by area or function, such as those involved in engine, transmission, implement, climate control, instrumentation, entertainment devices, or body electrical control.
- The type of multiplexing used in onboard networks works by dividing the time available to each network module or device to transmit and listen to information. Only one module is allowed to talk, and all other modules must listen until it is their turn to talk.
- Advantages of multiplexing include the software control of the electrical system, enabling onboard diagnostics, ease of connecting electronically controlled accessories and features, and a reduction in the number of sensors.
- Controlled area networks are the most widely used type of network for integrating the machine operation of all the latest equipment.
- Two different types of CANs used by mobile off-road equipment are the SAE network standards of J-1939 and J-1587/1708.
- In serial communication, one wire, called CAN-hi, has a more positive voltage than the other, called CAN-lo. Each wire will have a mirror opposite charge of the other when communication takes place.
- Wires are twisted to minimize electromagnetic interference caused by magnetic fields and radio waves.

To further minimize signal distortion, at each end of the J-1939 CANbus there is a 120-ohm resistor that extinguishes multiplex voltage signals to prevent their reflection through the data bus.

- Network signals are distorted and slowed if terminating resistors are missing or defective.
- Data carried on the CANbus has four distinct message formats: data frame, remote frame, error frame, and overload frame. Messages sent and received over the network are constructed in frames with a maximum message length of 130 bits.
- Messages are prioritized to prevent data collision between positive and negative signals canceling one another.
- Cell phone and Bluetooth technology are two levels of network communication that use a wireless network interface.
- Disconnecting modules one by one can help identify a module that is shorting out the CANbus, but the best diagnostic routine to identify a network problem is to perform resistance and voltage checks of the CANbus at the DLC.

Key Terms

arbitration The process of deciding which messages have priority to transmit over the network to prevent data collision between positive and negative signals canceling one another.

bidirectional communication Two-way multiplex communication.

Bluetooth A short-range wireless technology that can automatically connect a device to a network.

controlled area networks (CAN) A distributed network control system in which no single central control module is used.

data bus The typology that forms the communication pathway of modules in a network.

differential mode transmission A situation in which network modules detect the voltage difference between two wires to determine if a signal is a 1 or a 0.

field effect transistor (FET) A unipolar transistor that uses an electric field to control the conductivity of a semiconductor material.

gateway module A module that translates communication between different networks that operate with the use of different protocols or speeds.

ladder logic The designed-in logic of a circuit that determines what activates a specific circuit.

multiplexing Transmission of more than one electrical signal or message takes place over a single wire or pair of wires.

network node A point on a network.

onboard diagnostics (OBD) Self-diagnostic capabilities of electronic control modules that allow them to evaluate voltage and current levels of circuits to which they are connected and determine whether data is in the correct operational range.

serial communication Communication using 0s and 1s to transmit data in a series, one bit after another in sequence.

serial data Pieces of data sent by the master module.

time division multiplexing (TDM) A type of multiplexing used in onboard networks and that works by dividing the time available to each network module or device.

typology The manner in which modules are connected to one another.

Review Questions

1. What terminals of the 9-pin diagnostic connector are connected to a digital multimeter (DMM) to check the resistance of the terminating resistors used for the CANbus?
   a. A and B
   b. 14 and 16
   c. C and D
   d. 3 and 4
2. Communication between all the modules and devices in a machine that is connected to a network that uses an electrical signal-processing strategy is called which of these?
   a. Networking
   b. Multiplexing
   c. Communication
   d. Linking
3. The rules or standards used to communicate over the networks are called ________.
   a. network protocol
   b. typology
   c. physical protocol
   d. CAN (controller area network)
4. Electronic control modules can easily evaluate the voltage and current levels of circuits to which they are connected and determine whether the data makes sense and is in the correct operational range. These self-diagnostic capabilities are referred to as which of these?
   a. CAN (controller area network)
   b. OBD (onboard diagnostics)
   c. network protocol
   d. typology
5. All networks have in common the concepts of interconnected modules. The use of ________ enables digital communication between each module and time division multiplexing as a communication strategy.
   a. scan tools
   b. multiplexing
   c. serial data
   d. parallel data
6. When paired together and connected in parallel to all modules in the network, the typology forming the communication pathway is called a ________.
   a. bus
   b. network
   c. system
   d. circuit

7. What requires the modules and other devices to take turns, sharing the data bus communication pathway?
   a. Data sharing
   b. Time division multiplexing
   c. A network
   d. A circuit
8. When using networks, electrical system complexity is absorbed by the ________ instead of a huge array of hard-wired components and circuit boards.
   a. computer
   b. controller
   c. network
   d. software
9. All electronically controlled engines and powertrain components have built-in self-diagnostic capabilities. To communicate this data to an electronic service tool from even a single module requires the use of ____________.
   a. bidirectional communications
   b. a factory scan tool
   c. direct communication
   d. a personal computer
10. Self-diagnostic capabilities are referred to as which of these?
   a. Diagnostic circuit check
   b. Off-board diagnostics
   c. Onboard diagnostics (OBD)
   d. Diagnostic control

ASE Technician A/Technician B Style Questions

1. Two technicians are discussing checking the voltage at the 9-pin diagnostic connector or datalink connector (DLC). Technician A says that voltage is checked with the ignition on at terminals C and D. Technician B says that the voltage at terminals C and D should be at least 12.6 volts. Who is correct?
   a. Technician A
   b. Technician B
   c. Both Technician A and Technician B
   d. Neither Technician A nor Technician B
2. When inspecting for shorts on the CANbus, Technician A says that neither CAN-H nor CAN-L should have continuity with chassis ground. Technician B says that only the CAN-L should have continuity with ground. Who is correct?
   a. Technician A
   b. Technician B
   c. Both Technician A and Technician B
   d. Neither Technician A nor Technician B
3. Technician A says that to check for fault codes, only a scanner or personal computer connected to the data link connector can retrieve codes. Technician B says that fault codes could also be retrieved from an instrument cluster display. Who is correct?
   a. Technician A
   b. Technician B
   c. Both Technician A and Technician B
   d. Neither Technician A nor Technician B
4. Two technicians are discussing machine serial data communication. Technician A says that the advantages of multiplexing include software control of the electrical system, enabling onboard diagnostics, the ease of connecting electronically controlled accessories and features, and a reduction in the number of sensors. Technician B says that controlled area networks are the most widely used type of network for integrating powertrain operation of all the latest machines. Who is correct?
   a. Technician A
   b. Technician B
   c. Both Technician A and Technician B
   d. Neither Technician A nor Technician B
5. Technician A says that in serial communication, one wire, called CAN-H, has a more negative voltage than the other, which is CAN-L. Technician B says that each wire will have a mirror opposite charge of the other when communication takes place. Who is correct?
   a. Technician A
   b. Technician B
   c. Both Technician A and Technician B
   d. Neither Technician A nor Technician B
6. Two technicians are discussing machine serial data communication and networks. Technician A says that data carried on the CANbus has four distinct message formats: data frame, remote frame, error frame, and overload frame. Technician B says that cell phone and Bluetooth technology are two levels of customization realized using a wireless network interface. Who is correct?
   a. Technician A
   b. Technician B
   c. Both Technician A and Technician B
   d. Neither Technician A nor Technician B
7. Technician A says that broken mechanical systems are often diagnosed visually or with mechanical tools such as pressure gauges and dial indicators. Technician B says that self-monitoring or self-diagnostic capabilities are, therefore, built into electronic control systems to help technicians perform faster. Who is correct?
   a. Technician A
   b. Technician B
   c. Both Technician A and Technician B
   d. Neither Technician A nor Technician B
8. Technician A says that wires are twisted to minimize electromagnetic interference caused by magnetic fields and radio waves. Technician B says that network signals will never be distorted and slowed if terminating resistors are missing or defective. Who is correct?
   a. Technician A
   b. Technician B
   c. Both Technician A and Technician B
   d. Neither Technician A nor Technician B

9. Two technicians are describing the use of electronic service tools. Technician A says that all fault codes, communication language, and other features of the onboard network are standardized by EPA legislation. Technician B says that only the equipment manufacturer's specific scan tool or software can read the legislated fault codes. Who is correct?
   a. Technician A
   b. Technician B
   c. Both Technician A and Technician B
   d. Neither Technician A nor Technician B

10. Technician A says that disconnecting modules one by one can help identify a module that is shorting out the CANbus. Technician B says that the best diagnostic routine to identify a network problem is to perform resistance and voltage checks of the CANbus at the DLC. Who is correct?
   a. Technician A
   b. Technician B
   c. Both Technician A and Technician B
   d. Neither Technician A nor Technician B

CHAPTER 20

Onboard Diagnostic Systems

Knowledge Objectives

After reading this chapter, you will be able to:

- **K20001** Identify and describe the principles of onboard diagnostic (OBD) systems.
- **K20002** Identify and describe features of onboard diagnostic and off-board diagnostic strategies.

Skills Objectives

There are no skills objectives for this chapter.

▶ Introduction

Technicians servicing today's machines will be just as likely to use a computer as a screw driver to perform repairs. Electronic systems using microprocessors control cab, engine, implements, and drivetrain systems and provide operational capabilities far exceeding any mechanical system—and with greater precision, efficiency, and reliability.

Although electronics offer many advantages over mechanical controls, a new challenge is to quickly identify and repair any failure in systems that operate with increasing invisibility by using electronic signals and software-based operating systems. To prevent a problem as simple as a broken wire from requiring a huge number of labor hours to identify and repair, electronic systems have self-diagnostic capabilities. These self-diagnostic capabilities extend to the emission systems, which also must operate flawlessly in order for the normal service life of the machine to maintain almost undetectable emission levels from the latest engines.

▶ Fundamentals of Onboard Diagnostics

K20001

The dominance of electronics makes skill development related to servicing electronic control technology one of the most important priorities for successful technicians. Understanding the operating principles of electronic control systems is foundational for choosing diagnostic strategies, using service tools effectively, and making sound repair recommendations. Nowhere are these skills more important than in comprehending and troubleshooting the operation of the OBD system. This unique system is responsible for maintaining a machine's compliance with emission standards. The comprehensive monitoring of the machine performed by the OBD system means electronic-related faults requiring service will be identified by the OBD system.

Development of Onboard Diagnostics

The term OBD has two meanings for the technician. The simplest, most familiar definition is the diagnostic function of electronic control systems to identify or self-diagnose system faults and report fault codes. The second meaning is the legislated standards for maximum machine emissions levels. The legislation also establishes requirements for maintaining the lowest machine emissions and alerting the operator if any fault occurs that could potentially cause emissions to increase above specific thresholds or levels.

Onboard Diagnostics

Emission standards established for off-road diesels, beginning in late 1994, have required a level of precision for engine control that is possible only through the extensive use of electronics. Electrical devices now perform the work once done by fuel system camshafts, levers, springs, flyweights, and other assorted mechanical devices. Because of the invisible nature of electronic signals and the operation of microprocessors executing thousands of lines of software code, many hours would be spent to identify simple problems, such as a broken wire or faulty sensor, if these systems did not have self-diagnostic capabilities. This self-diagnostic capability, referred to as the OBD system, was originally developed by manufacturers to enable technicians to service electronic controls. When a malfunction is detected, diagnostic information is stored for retrieval by a technician to assist in the diagnosis and repair of the malfunction (**FIGURE 20-1**).

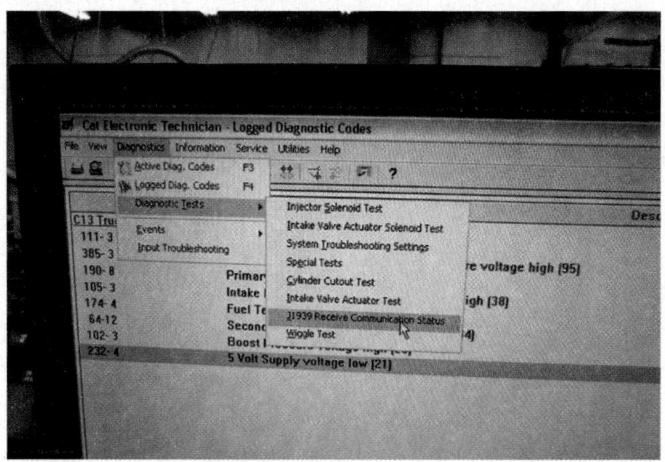

FIGURE 20-1 Use OBD to identify and report fault codes.

You Are the Mobile Heavy Equipment Technician

You are at a customer's yard to diagnose a problem with a brand-new wheel loader. The starter cranks, but the engine will not start. You perform typical visual inspections of the machine, examine the fuel system and engine wiring harnesses, and check for leaks. Nothing seems amiss, but you realize that the check engine light stays on. It would not take long to change the fuel filters out, but if they are not the problem, warranty would not pay for them. You know that an engine position sensor and its circuit could cause this problem, so consider the following:

1. What two procedures, other than using original equipment manufacturer (OEM) or other diagnostic software, can you use to retrieve fault codes?
2. Explain why the check engine lamp stays on.
3. Are SAE J-1939 fault codes retrievable from this machine without OEM software? Explain your answer.

▶ Self-Diagnostic Capabilities and Approaches

K20002

Electronic systems do not have many moving parts to wear out, but the systems can be complex. When something goes wrong with a component or circuit, identifying the problem without some built-in self-monitoring and self-diagnostic capabilities can be extremely time-consuming and difficult. Consider what steps would be needed to identify a problem as simple as a bent pin on a control module or a broken or worn wire on today's machines. Many hours, if not days, would be needed to trace every individual circuit while performing voltage and resistance checks. With built-in self-monitoring functions, electrical systems can check circuits and electrical devices, evaluate the accuracy of sensor data, and identify problems as they occur. The system records and reports when, where, and how faults occurred, enabling diagnostics on electronically controlled machine systems to be performed easily, often with fewer tools and in less time than on mechanical systems.

The system can take one of two self-diagnostic approaches to identifying faults. The system can either use traditional self-diagnostic strategies or use a model-based approach.

Traditional self-diagnostic strategies focus on specific areas of machine control, such as the engine, transmission, and implement control. In machines where only a few control modules are used and communicate with one another, out-of-range-type fault codes and off-board fault isolation methods are adequate.

System self-diagnostic checks are generally performed by the self-monitoring system by range checking sensors or circuit data. For example, if the signal voltage produced by a coolant temperature sensor exceeds the limits of normal operation, the system will generate an out-of-range electrical fault code (**FIGURE 20-2**).

A problem with allowing the system to generate fault codes based on simply range checking a sensor or circuit for correct electrical values is that the code will point to a general circuit problem that requires off-board pinpoint testing to determine whether it is the sensor, wiring, or even a disconnected or missing sensor. As system complexity evolved, the technician performed off-board diagnostics after the onboard system identified a fault. Using flow charts for a specific diagnostic code (e.g., troubleshooting diagnostic trees) in more sophisticated electronic control systems became more time-consuming and sometimes ineffective, resulting in a high number of "no fault found responses."

Manufacturers have also discovered incorrect component replacements and increased warranty costs are associated with a high reliance on off-board diagnostic testing by technicians even using the appropriate service literature. Furthermore, even with a fault code, from a sensor as simple as the coolant temperature, it could be a cooling system problem and not a sensor fault. The cooling system operation could be out of normal operating range and yet a coolant temperature sensor fault code is generated, but it's the system and not the sensor operating incorrectly.

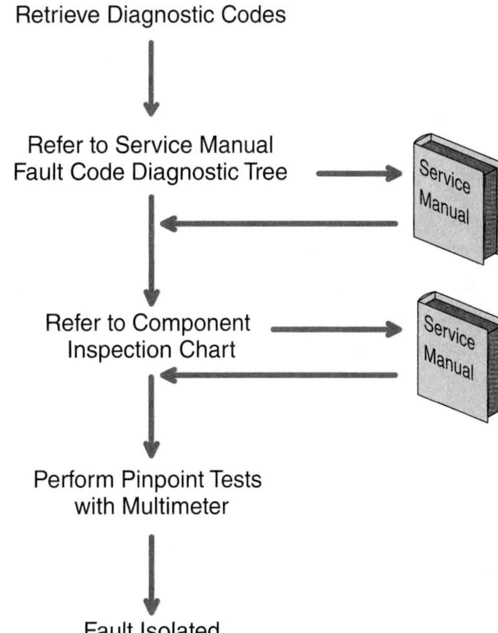

FIGURE 20-2 Older OBD systems monitored electrical circuits and reported out-of-range voltage signals as electrical faults. Newer systems monitor overall system behavior, comparing it to models of expected behavior, in addition to out-of-range circuit faults.

To correct the shortcomings of range-check-only diagnostic systems, *model-based diagnostics* compare system and component behaviors to expected patterns of operation. In addition to fault detection and isolation, the model-based approach also analyzes and categorizes the fault by using advanced algorithms. System problems are generally identified without interfering with system operation by substituting suspected data from a sensor or device with a backup or default data set.

Diagnostic Definitions

A variety of terms are used to categorize abnormal system operation.

1. **Fault**: A fault is a deviation of at least one characteristic property of the system from its standard behavior. Low battery voltage, excessive oil pressure, and a missing sensor input are examples of faults. Depending on how quickly a fault occurs and whether it persists, faults are classified in four categories:
   - *Active*: This type of fault is currently taking place and is uninterrupted in action. Sudden component or circuit problems are generally active faults. An illuminated malfunction indicator light (MIL) or check engine light (CEL) indicates an **active fault**.
   - *Historical:* This type of fault, which is also called inactive or logged, took place at one time but was corrected and is no longer active. A sensor that was temporarily disconnected is an example of a **historical fault**. Amber check engine lights can also indicate the presence of historical faults.

- *Intermittent:* This type of fault is not ongoing and can be both active and historical. Loose connectors or poor pin contact can cause an **intermittent fault**.
- *Incipient:* This type of fault is the result of system or component deterioration. An exhaust particulate filter filling with ash is an example of an **incipient fault**.

2. **Failure**: This refers to a fault that permanently interrupts a system's ability to perform a required function under specified operating conditions. Open or shorted circuits, cylinder misfires, or a seized variable geometry turbocharger (VGT) actuator are examples of failures. Failures produce active fault codes.
3. **Disturbance**: This is an unknown and uncontrolled input acting on the system. Electromagnetic interference, loss of mass, fluid or gas leakage from a hydraulic or pneumatic system, or excessive mechanical friction are examples of unknown or uncontrolled disturbances affecting system inputs. Low coolant level in a system without a level sensor could be an example of a disturbance.
4. **Fault detection**: This is a diagnostic strategy to determine whether faults are present in the system. An electronic control module will continuously check for voltage drops for all input and output circuits. Emissions system monitors are typical examples of a fault detection strategy used to evaluate a system's operation based on a model of expected behavior compared with actual performance of individual components or systems.
5. **Fault isolation**: This involves determining the location of the fault. Fault isolation is best accomplished using a diagnostic fault tree supplied by the manufacturer (**FIGURE 20-3**). Examples of fault isolation include pinpoint electrical testing using a voltmeter, an ohmmeter, or commanding actuator tests.
6. **Fault accommodation**: This happens when a fault is detected. Fault accommodation, which is also known as an adaptive strategy, reconfigures the system operation or substitutes suspect data with default data to maintain normal system functionality even with the fault. This strategy is also called fault healing. One example is a newer engine that continues to run after it has lost data from a defective crank or the cam position sensor. The control modules will substitute a value derived by using data from the other sensor to keep the engine running, although not as well. For example, defective mass air flow sensor data could be replaced by intake manifold pressure and temperature data.

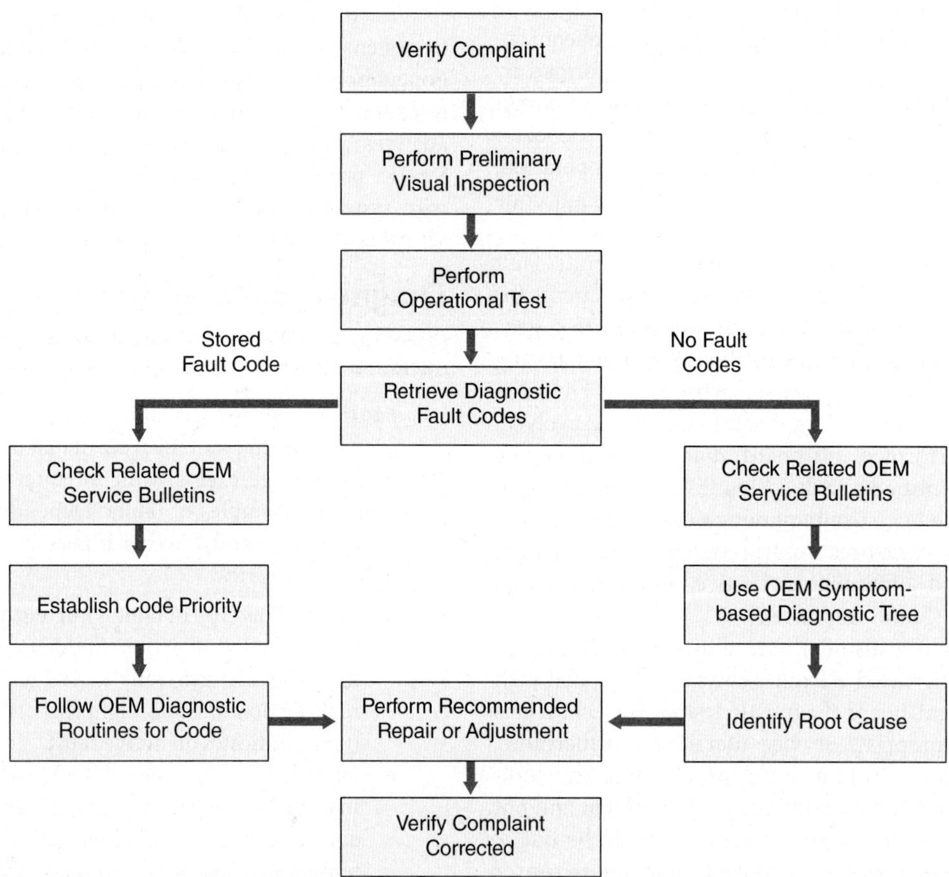

FIGURE 20-3 Use diagnostic fault code trees after retrieving a fault code, in order to complete appropriate checks. When multiple codes are set, observe code priority.

> ▶ TECHNICIAN TIP
>
> Adding auxiliary heaters for passenger compartments can cause the cooling system monitor to indicate a fault. Taking heat out of the cooling system during engine warm up will delay the time to warm up, which will illuminate the MIL.

Maintaining OBD

Maintaining the OBD system is critical in order to identify and address machine system deterioration and remedy failures. Technicians must understand how to use off-board diagnostics and interpret readiness and diagnostic trouble codes in order to diagnose a system properly and make appropriate repairs.

Off-Board Diagnostics

When electrical faults or system problems occur in machine control systems, electronic control modules log **diagnostic trouble codes (DTCs)** in the system memory, which are read through an instrument display cluster, also called a **blink code**, or retrieved by a scanner or personal computer connected to the machine DLC. OBD is the self-diagnostic checks by the control modules that measure circuit voltages, resistances, rationality, and other variables. More sophisticated OBD systems monitor system behavior to detect smaller faults faster. **Off-board diagnostics** and repair occur when the technician retrieves codes and machine data as a starting point to diagnose system problems. During off-board diagnostics, the technician may monitor system operation, perform actuator tests, pinpoint electrical tests, and inspect components. Remotely assisted diagnostics using **telematics** is also a type of off-board diagnostics. Telematics is a branch of information technology that uses specialized applications for the long-distance transmission of information to and from a machine (**FIGURE 20-4**).

Readiness Code

Depending on the OEM, some provision is made to validate whether a component or emissions system generating a DTC has been repaired or corrected. After a repair has been made, operating the machine under conditions that cause an emissions system monitor to self-check validates whether a successful repair has been completed. An OBD service tool displays a readiness code indicating that a monitor has completed its functionality test and that no fault was found. Each monitor requires a unique set of machine operating conditions to be met before it can properly run and evaluate the performance of an emissions system.

When an OBD readiness code validates the system that has been repaired, no other fault codes associated with the system should be active. However, a message such as "system not ready," "monitor incomplete," or "monitor not run" is displayed if the repair is not successful or if the emissions system has not met the conditions needed to enable the monitor to run.

> ▶ TECHNICIAN TIP
>
> After repairing a fault associated with the engine or power train, the codes should be cleared and the machine tested, which involves operating the machine under the conditions necessary for a monitor to run (i.e., operating temperature). Recheck the machine for codes after the test, before returning the machine to the customer. The monitor associated with the repaired fault should indicate it has "run" or is "ready."

Emissions System Deterioration

The OBD is primarily an emissions-driven diagnostic system. For diesel engines, the threshold for alerting the operator and setting a fault code generally occurs any time a condition is sensed that could cause noxious emissions to exceed the legislated federal test protocol (FTP) emissions standards 1.5 times. Higher thresholds are used for aftertreatment systems, with progressively lower threshold standards for the latest machine models. While malfunctions in the engine cause excessive emissions, problems with other machine systems can also cause the machine to exceed the threshold for emissions. Adaptive strategies can compensate for system deterioration. For example, wastegated turbochargers

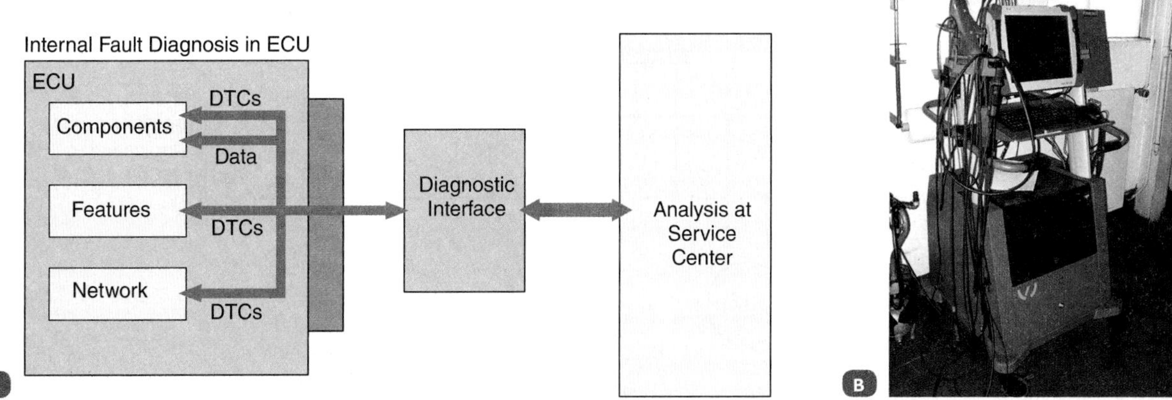

FIGURE 20-4 Performing off-board diagnostics involves isolating a fault based on fault code information.

have metal springs in their actuators. Heat and time will weaken the springs, so closed-loop feedback between the wastegate and the boost pressure sensor compensate for system deterioration. Common rail injectors are regularly checked using zero-fuel adaptation, which automatically updates the calibration file during engine deceleration.

Diagnostic Trouble Codes

The OBD system sets three types of codes: A, B, and C. Type A DTCs are the most critical emissions-related faults and will illuminate the MIL with only one occurrence. If a Type A code is set, the OBD can store it several ways. Type A codes are generally stored in the engine control module (ECM) historical memory. To help the technician diagnose the problem, the code has a failure record associated with it, such as a time and date stamp of when the last failure occurred, whether the code occurred since the last code clearing event, or whether the failure has occurred during the current ignition cycle. Furthermore, Type A codes have freeze-frame data, which is a record of all other sensor data occurring when the fault was detected.

Type B codes are emissions-causing faults that are less serious than Type A faults and must occur at least once on two consecutive trips before the MIL will illuminate. The MIL will also go out if a Type A or Type B DTC problem does not reoccur after a predetermined number of warm up/cool down cycle (e.g., 3–5 warm up/cool down cycle—which varies by OEM).

Type C DTCs are non-emissions-related codes, or enhanced codes. Enhanced codes also cover non-emissions-related failures that occur outside the engine control system.

Freeze-Frame Data

The freeze-frame data the ECM stores will provide a snapshot of the engine operating conditions present at the time the malfunction was detected. This information should be stored when a pending DTC is set. If the pending DTC matures to a MIL-on DTC, the manufacturer can choose to update or retain the freeze-frame data stored in conjunction with the pending DTC. Likewise, any freeze-frame data stored in conjunction with a pending or MIL-on DTC should be erased upon erasure of the DTC.

OBD Emissions Codes

The OBD executive is an element in the emissions system's operational strategy that manages the DTCs and operating modes for all diagnostic tests related to emissions systems. It can be referred to as the "traffic cop" of the diagnostic system, managing DTC storage and MIL illumination. Note that the HD-OBD MIL light is yellow, unlike the light-duty OBD-II system, which is red.

Control modules that contribute to maintaining emissions compliance must be connected to the controller area network bus (CANbus) using SAE J-1939 standards for communication and network operation (**FIGURE 20-5, FIGURE 20-6**).

CANbus modules performing emissions diagnostics will include the following types:

- engine ECM
- machine electronic control unit
- aftertreatment control module

FIGURE 20-5 HD-OBD data can be accessed from the CANbus through the data link connector.

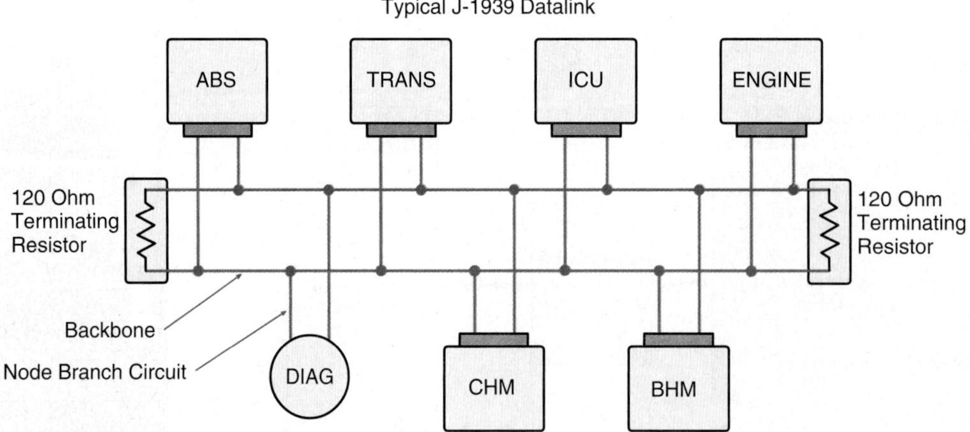

FIGURE 20-6 A CANbus connects machine modules and communicates using multiplex signals.

- aftertreatment NOx sensors
- engine VGT
- EGR control module
- implement
- transmission.

Two protocols typically exist for identifying fault codes on machine systems. The first is J-1587 using a J-1708 two-wire data bus. J-1587 began being used by heavy-duty and most medium-duty vehicles built after 1985. Up to 1995, individual OEMs used their own unique diagnostic connectors. J-1587, used primarily from 1996 to 2001, is easily identified by the six-pin diagnostic connectors. Beginning in 2001, most OEMs switched to a more sophisticated J-1939 standard, which can be recognized by a nine-pin diagnostic connector. Both the J-1587/1708 and the J-1939 network connections are found in the nine-pin DLC. A specific standard exists in both protocols for identifying faults detected by the CANbus modules. Machines built using ISO standards used by European manufacturers use a different type of connector. If a machine is built and does not require meeting minimum emission standards, no particular type of diagnostic connector is required.

> **TECHNICIAN TIP**
>
> To validate a repair for a fault detected by the comprehensive component monitor (CCM), start the engine and let it idle for one minute. The ECM will turn off the yellow MIL when the diagnostic monitor has run. If a CCM is evaluating electrical circuits, the light will switch off after the MIL has been illuminated for five seconds. For other faults, the ECM will typically turn off the MIL after three consecutive ignition cycles that the diagnostic monitor runs and passes.

Proprietary Blink and Flash Codes

Manufacturers are not bound to report faults by exclusively using CANbus codes. Specialized equipment and systems can use proprietary codes, meaning that the OEM is free to define its own non-emissions-related fault codes. Blink codes are dash lights that will blink, or flash, proprietary fault codes usually by using the red and amber warning lights.

Two- and three-digit codes commonly report faults. A typical arrangement to obtain blink codes based on a proprietary code will require switching on a diagnostics switch. A warning lamp flashes to indicate a fault code. Next, the stop lamp flashes out the hundredth, tenth, and single digits of the fault code. A short pause separates the flashing of each digit, and a longer pause separates codes. Warning lamps may switch between active and inactive codes by flashing either the red warning light for active or the yellow warning light for inactive. If no fault codes are active, the warning lamps remain lit. Some manufacturers may not use a diagnostic switch to obtain blink codes. Instead, the ignition key is switched on and off in a specific sequence to produce diagnostic blink codes. Rather than using a diagnostic switch, other machines may require creating the correct conditions—such as key-on engine-off (KOEO), park brakes set, or depressing switches—to prompt blink codes. Instrument clusters are network devices that can also receive and report fault codes in the absence of a readily available service tool.

J-1587 Fault Code Construction

The SAE (American Society of Automotive Engineers) developed the fault code reporting standard, referred to as J-1587. Six- and nine-pin diagnostic connectors carry J-1587 codes, but six-pin connectors do not include J-1939, the latest protocol. J-1587 fault codes are specifically constructed to help technicians easily isolate faults. The codes have four parts:

1. message identifier (MID) (also called module identifier)
2. parameter identifier (PID)
3. system identifier (SID)
4. failure mode identifier (**FIGURE 20-7**).

Other fault code identifiers specific to an OEM may include the following:

- Proprietary parameter identification (PPID) is an OEM identification of a parameter or value used only by that manufacturer.
- Proprietary subsystem identification description (PSID) is an OEM-unique component identification.

A **message identifier (MID)** identifies which module is reporting the fault. MIDs are the first byte or character of each message that identifies which control module on the J-1587 serial communication link originated the information. A standard list of message or module identifiers exists for all machines regardless of manufacturer.

1. A **system identifier (SID)** indicates a specific failed component or replaceable subsystem associated with a fault. There are several SIDs.
2. A **parameter identifier (PID)** is a value or identifier of an item being reported with fault data. J-1957 uses hundreds of PIDs.
3. The **failure mode identifier (FMI)** describes the type of failure detected in the subsystem and identified by the PID or SID. The FMI and the PID or SID, not both, combine to form a J-1957 diagnostic code. The general format of a fault message is MID-PID/SID–FMI.

   Now consider code 128-101-002. It breaks down as follows:

- 128: engine
- 101: intake boost pressure
- 002: data erratic, intermittent, or incorrect.

  OEM proprietary fault codes would include the following:

- 54: Detroit Diesel
- 84: Caterpillar
- 115: Cummins.

J-1939 Fault Code Construction

J-1939 codes have a construction similar to J-1957 but are far more comprehensive. J-1939 uses the CANbus protocol, which

Construction of J-1587 fault codes

Module Identifier — Subsystem Identifier — Failure Mode Indicator

MID	PIP/SID	FMI
128	110	000

MID (examples)
128 – Engine
130 – Transmission
136 – Brakes (ABS)
137 – Trailer (ABS)

PID/SID (examples)
110 – Coolant Temperature
183 – Fuel Rate (instantaneous)
190 – Engine Speed

FMI	Fault Description
00	Data Valid but Above Normal Operating Range
01	Data Valid but Below Normal Operating Range
02	Data Erratic, Intermittent or Eratic
03	Voltage Above Normal or Shorted High
04	Voltage Below Normal or Shorted Low
05	Current Below Normal or Open Circuit
06	Current Below Normal or Grounded Circuit
07	Mechanical System Not Responding Properly
08	Abnormal Frequency, Pulse Width, or Period
09	Abnormal Update Rate
10	Abnormal Rate of Change
11	Failure Mode Not Identifiable
12	Bad Intelligent Device or Component
13	Out of Calibration
14	Special Instructions
15	Reserved for Future Assignment by SAE

FIGURE 20-7 Construction of J-1587 fault codes.

permits any electronic control module to transmit a message over the network when the bus is idle or not transmitting other information. Similar to J-1957, every message includes an identifier that defines who sent it, what data is contained within the message, and the priority, or seriousness, of the fault or problem. Instead of a PID and SID, J-1939 uses only a **suspect parameter number (SPN)** (**FIGURE 20-8**).

FIGURE 20-8 J-1939 codes on a dash-mounted device the operator uses to check codes. Note the occurrence count ("OC: 1") in the top right corner of the screen. **A.** Suspect parameter number. **B.** Fault code identifier.

The SPN is the smallest identifiable fault. Next, a failure mode indicator (FMI) notes the type of failure that has been detected.

The **source address (SA)** field designates the control module that is sending the message table (**TABLE 20-1** and **TABLE 20-2**).

TABLE 20-1 J-1939 SAs

SID	Description
1	Engine
3	Transmission
11	Brakes

TABLE 20-2 Comparing J-1939 and J-1587 Fault Codes

J-1939	J-1957
Source address (SA)	Message identifier (MID)
Suspect parameter number (SPN) (thousands of combinations)	Parameter identifier (PID) (hundreds of combinations)
N/A	System identifier (SID)
Fault mode indicator (0–31)	Fault mode indicator (0–15)

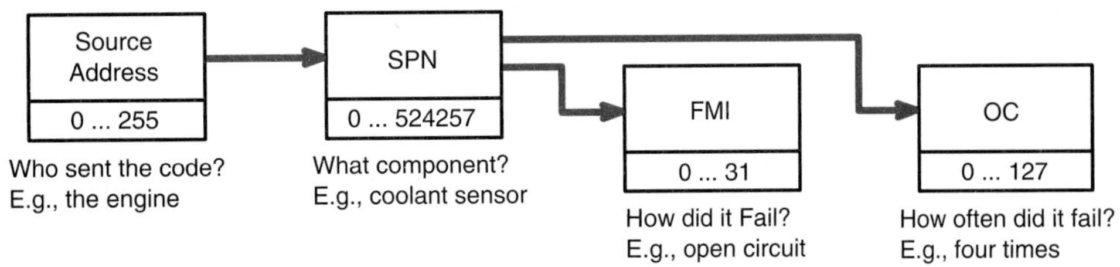

FIGURE 20-9 A J-1939 code uses SPNs and FMIs. An occurrence count (OC) may accompany the code on OEM software.

Suspect Parameter Number

The suspect parameter number (SPN) combines elements of J-1957 PIDs and SIDs. The SPN is used for multiple diagnostic purposes:

- identifying the least repairable subsystem that has failed
- identifying subsystems and/or assemblies that may not have completely failed but may be exhibiting abnormal operating performance
- identifying a particular event or condition that requires reporting
- reporting a component and nonstandard failure mode (**FIGURE 20-9** and **TABLE 20-3**).

J-1939 FMI

The FMI defines the type of failure detected in the subsystem identified by an SPN. The failure may not be an electrical failure but may instead be a subsystem failure or condition needing to be reported to the service technician and, perhaps, the operator. Conditions can include system events or statuses (**TABLE 20-4** and **TABLE 20-5**).

Occurrence Count (OC)

The OC represents the number of times a fault combination of SPN/FMI has taken place.

TABLE 20-3 Example SPNs

SPN	Description
031	Transmission range position
156	Injector timing rail 1 pressure
190	Engine speed
512	Driver's demand engine—percent torque
513	Actual engine—percent torque
639	J-1939 network
899	Engine torque mode
1483	Source address of controlling device for engine control
1675	Engine starter mode
2432	Engine demand—percent torque

TABLE 20-4 SAE J-1939 FMIs

FMI	SAE Text
0	Data valid but above normal operational range—most severe level
1	Data valid but below normal operational range—most severe level
2	Data erratic, intermittent, or incorrect
3	Voltage above normal or shorted to high source
4	Voltage below normal or shorted to low source
5	Current below normal or open circuit
6	Current above normal or grounded circuit
7	Mechanical system not responding or out of adjustment
8	Abnormal frequency or pulse width or period
9	Abnormal update rate
10	Abnormal rate of change
11	Root cause not known
12	Bad intelligent device or component
13	Out of calibration
14	Special instructions
15	Data valid but above normal operating range—least severe level
16	Data valid but above normal operating range—moderately severe level
17	Data valid but below normal operating range—least severe level
18	Data valid but below normal operating range—moderately severe level
19	Received network data in error
20–30	Reserved for SAE assignment
31	Condition exists

Parameter Group Number

SPN, source addresses, and FMI information are part of a larger J-1939 message called the **parameter group number (PGN)**. PGN information includes commands, data, requests,

TABLE 20-5 Comparison of J-1939 SPN and J-1708/J-1587 Fault Codes

Description	J-1939		J-1708/J-1587	
	PGN	SPN	MID	PID
Percent load at current speed	61433	92	128	92
Engine speed (rpm)	61444	190	128	190
Distance	65248	245	128	245
Engine hours	65253	247	128	247
Coolant temperature	53262	110	128	110
Oil temperature	65262	175	128	175
Fuel delivery pressure	65263	94	128	94
Oil pressure	65263	100	128	100
Speed	65265	84	128	84
Fuel rate	65266	183	128	183
Instantaneous fuel economy	65266	184	128	184
Ambient air temperature	65269	171	128	171
Turbo boost	65270	102	128	102
Air filter differential pressure	65270	107	128	107
Exhaust gas temperature	65270	173	128	173
Net battery current	65271	114	128	114
Battery voltage	65271	168	128	168
Transmission oil temp	65272	171	128	171
Brake application pressure	65274	116	128	116
Brake primary pressure	65274	117	128	117
Brake secondary pressure	65274	118	128	118
Hydraulic retarder pressure	65275	119	128	119
Hydraulic retarder oil temperature	65275	120	128	120
Fuel level	65276	96	41	96

acknowledgments, and negative acknowledgments, and fault codes. The package of serial data is transmitted over the CANbus. SPNs are assigned to each individual parameter within the PGN. This means each PGN will contain a different set of SPNs. For example, PGN 61444 is the electronic engine controller 1. Hundreds of possible messages can originate from this component because of the number of sensors and the complexity of the system and its operation (**FIGURE 20-10** and **TABLE 20-6**).

PGN 614444 includes the following SPNs:

- engine torque mode
- operator demand engine—percent torque actual engine—percent torque
- engine speed
- engine starter mode
- engine demand—percent torque.

Message Priority

To prevent message signals from canceling out one another, signal collisions are avoided through an arbitration process that takes place while the PGN identifier is transmitted. The lower the first number is in the message, the greater importance attached to the information, requiring all other modules to listen while the information is transmitted:

- Highest priority: This is used for situations that require immediate action by the receiving device in order to provide safe vehicle operation (e.g., braking systems). This level of priority is used only in safety critical conditions.
- High priority: This is used for control situations that require prompt action in order to provide safe vehicle operation (e.g., a transmission performing an upshift, which requires a change in engine speed to control gear synchronization of damage to clutch packs) (**TABLE 20-7**).

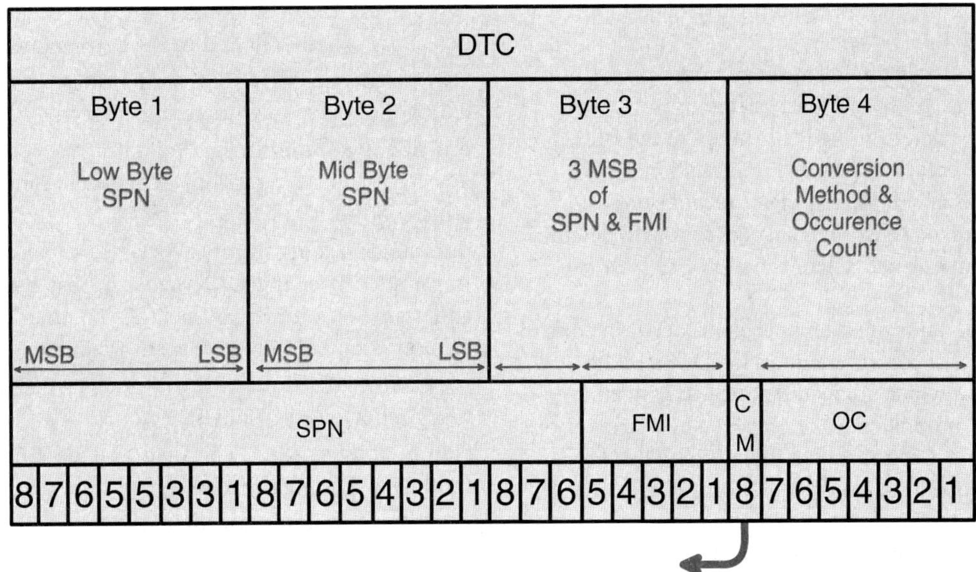

FIGURE 20-10 A J-1939 fault code is 29 bits long. The check sum (CM) field is a function of the other numbers in the code. If another module reads the code and the CM does not match, the data is rejected.

TABLE 20-6 Example PGNs

PGN	Description
61441	Electronic Brake Controller 1 (EBC1)
61442	Electronic Transmission Controller 1 (ETC1)
61444	Electronic Engine Controller 1 (EEC1)
65225	Service Information (SERV)

TABLE 20-7 Priority Fault Codes

Priority	Description
1 and 2	Reserved for messages that require immediate access to the bus
3 and 4	Reserved for messages that require prompt access to the bus in order to prevent severe mechanical damage.
5 and 6	Reserved for messages that directly affect the economical or efficient operation of the vehicle
7 and 8	All other messages not fitting into the previous priority categories

▶ Wrap-Up

Ready for Review

- Understanding the operating principles of electronic control systems is foundational for choosing diagnostic strategies, using service tools effectively, and making sound repair recommendations.
- Emission standards established for off-road diesels beginning in the late 1994 have required a level of precision for engine control that is possible only through the extensive use of electronics. Electrical devices now perform the work once done by fuel system camshafts, levers, springs, flyweights, and other assorted mechanical devices.
- Electronic systems do not have many moving parts to wear out, but the systems can be complex. When something goes wrong with a component or circuit, identifying the problem without some built-in self-diagnostic capabilities can be extremely time-consuming and difficult.
- With built-in electronic self-monitoring functions, electrical systems possess the capability to check the operation of circuits and electrical devices, evaluate the rationality of data, and identify problems as they occur.
- Traditional self-diagnostic strategies focus on specific areas of machine control, such as the engine, implement, and transmissions.
- Model-based diagnostics compare system and component behaviors to expected patterns of operation.
- A fault is a deviation of at least one characteristic property of the system from its standard behavior.
- A failure is a fault that permanently interrupts a system's ability to perform a required function under specified operating conditions.

- A disturbance is an unknown and uncontrolled input acting on the system.
- Fault detection is a diagnostic strategy to determine whether faults are present in the system.
- Fault isolation is determining the location of the fault.
- When a fault is detected, fault accommodation, which is also known as an adaptive strategy, reconfigures the system operation or substitutes suspect data with default data to maintain normal system functionality even with the fault.
- When electrical faults or system problems occur in control systems, electronic control modules log DTCs in the system memory, which are read through an instrument display cluster or blink codes or retrieved by a scanner or personal computer connected to the machine DLC.
- The SAE developed the fault code reporting standard, referred to as J-1587.
- J-1939 uses the CANbus protocol, which permits any electronic control module to transmit a message over the network when the data bus is idle or not transmitting other information. Every message includes an identifier that defines who sent it, what data is contained in the message, and the priority, or seriousness, of the fault or problem.

Key Terms

active fault A fault that is currently taking place and uninterrupted in action.

blink code A method of providing fault code data for a specific system, which involves counting the number of flashes from a warning lamp and observing longer pauses between the light blinks.

diagnostic link connector (DLC) The connection point for electronic service tools used to access fault codes and other information provided by chassis electronic control modules.

diagnostic trouble code (DTC) A code logged by the electronic control module when electrical faults or system problems occur in commercial vehicle control systems.

failure mode identifier (FMI) The type of failure detected in the SPN, PID, or SID.

historical fault A fault that took place at one time but that is now corrected and no longer active.

incipient fault A fault that is the result of system or component deterioration.

intermittent fault A fault that is not ongoing and can be both active and historical.

message identifier (MID) also called module identifier The electronic control module that has identified a fault. J-1587 protocols use MIDs.

off-board diagnostics Procedures to isolate a fault based on fault code information, including retrieving fault code information, monitoring system operation, performing actuator tests and pinpoint electrical tests, and inspecting components.

onboard diagnostics (OBD) Self-diagnostic capabilities of electronic control modules that allow them to evaluate voltage and current levels of circuits to which they are connected and determine whether data is in the correct operational range.

OBD manager Software that identifies fault codes and ensures emissions systems are operating correctly.

out-of-range monitoring Validating sensor data to verify that a system is operating within an expected range for a given operating condition.

parameter group number (PGN) A package of serial data transmitted over the CAN network that includes SPN, source addresses, and FMI, as well as commands, data, requests, acknowledgments, negative acknowledgments, and fault codes.

parameter identifier (PID) A value or identifier of an item being reported with fault data.

source address (SA) The field that designates which control module is sending the message.

suspect parameter number (SPN) A numerical identifier that defines the data in a fault message and the priority of the fault.

system identifier (SID) A fault code used by J-1587 protocols that identifies which subsystem has failed.

telematics A branch of information technology that uses specialized applications for the long-distance transmission of information to and from a vehicle.

Review Questions

1. Emission standards established for off-road diesels began in ______.
   a. 1994
   b. 1992
   c. 2001
   d. 2014
2. The OBD (onboard diagnostics) system can take one of two self-diagnostic approaches to identifying faults. The system can either use traditional self-diagnostic strategies or use ________.
   a. a manufacturer-based approach
   b. a model-based approach
   c. manufacturer-based diagnostics
   d. case-based reasoning
3. ___________ is/are an adaptive strategy that reconfigures the system operation or substitutes suspect data with default data to maintain normal system functionality even with the fault.
   a. Fault codes
   b. Fault accommodation
   c. Fault detection
   d. Disturbance
4. System self-diagnostic checks are generally performed by limit checking of __________ or circuit data.
   a. circuits
   b. sensors
   c. controllers
   d. monitors
5. Data from a sensor as simple as the coolant temperature are even more critical to operation because ________ that

evaluate emissions-control devices will run only after an engine has reached operating temperature.

a. monitors
b. circuits
c. sensors
d. controllers

6. In the OBD system, a __________ is a deviation of at least one characteristic property of the system from its standard behavior.

a. monitor
b. fault
c. defect
d. failure

7. What type of OBD fault is not ongoing and can be both active and historical?

a. Incipient
b. Controlling
c. Intermittent
d. Constant

8. What is an unknown and uncontrolled input acting on the OBD system?

a. Failure
b. Disturbance
c. Fault
d. Monitor

9. This type of fault is currently taking place and is uninterrupted in action.

a. Failure
b. Disturbance
c. Active
d. Incipient

10. A message identifier (MID) identifies which ________ is reporting the fault.

a. component
b. sensor
c. switch
d. module

ASE Technician A/Technician B Style Questions

1. Two technicians are discussing OBD for machines. Technician A says that the simplest, most familiar definition is the diagnostic function of electronic control systems to identify or self-diagnose system faults and report fault codes. Technician B says the OBD will only send blink codes to the display. Who is correct?

a. Technician A
b. Technician B
c. Both Technician A and Technician B
d. Neither Technician A nor Technician B

2. Technician A says that a fault is a deviation of at least one characteristic property of the system from its standard behavior. Technician B says that a historical fault took place at one time and can never be active again. Who is correct?

a. Technician A
b. Technician B
c. Both Technician A and Technician B
d. Neither Technician A nor Technician B

3. Technician A says that an incipient fault is not ongoing and can be both active and historical. Technician B says that an incipient fault is a fault that is the result of system or component deterioration. Who is correct?

a. Technician A
b. Technician B
c. Both Technician A and Technician B
d. Neither Technician A nor Technician B

4. Technician A says a suspect parameter number (SPN) is a fault code used by J-1587 protocols that identifies which subsystem has failed. Technician B says a system identifier (SID) is a numerical identifier that defines the data in a fault message and the priority of the fault. Who is correct?

a. Technician A
b. Technician B
c. Both Technician A and Technician B
d. Neither Technician A nor Technician B

5. Technician A says that some manufacturers may use their own codes because they are not bound to CANbus. Technician B says that all manufacturers must use CANbus. Who is correct?

a. Technician A
b. Technician B
c. Both Technician A and Technician B
d. Neither Technician A nor Technician B

6. Technician A says that a system identifier (SID) indicates a specific failed component. Technician B says that a parameter identifier (PID) is a value or identifier of an item being reported with fault data. Who is correct?

a. Technician A
b. Technician B
c. Both Technician A and Technician B
d. Neither Technician A nor Technician B

7. Technician A says that J-1939 uses the CANbus protocol, which permits any electronic control module to transmit a message over the network. Technician B says that J-1939 still uses parameter identifier (PID) as a value or identifier of an item being reported with fault data. Who is correct?

a. Technician A
b. Technician B
c. Both Technician A and Technician B
d. Neither Technician A nor Technician B

8. Technician A says that the suspect parameter number (SPN) combines elements of J-1957 PIDs and SIDs. Technician B says that the SPN is used for multiple diagnostic purposes. Who is correct?

a. Technician A
b. Technician B
c. Both Technician A and Technician B
d. Neither Technician A nor Technician B

9. Two technicians are discussing J-1939 fault code construction. Technician A says that parameter group number (PGN) information includes commands, data, requests, acknowledgments, and negative acknowledgments, and

fault codes. Technician B says that parameter group number (PGN) information includes commands, data, and requests only. Who is correct?

a. Technician A
b. Technician B
c. Both Technician A and Technician B
d. Neither Technician A nor Technician B

10. Two technicians are discussing J-1939 fault code construction. Technician A says that to prevent message signals from canceling out one another, signal collisions are avoided through an arbitration process. Technician B says that high priority is used for control situations that require prompt action in order to provide safe vehicle operation. Who is correct?

a. Technician A
b. Technician B
c. Both Technician A and Technician B
d. Neither Technician A nor Technician B

CHAPTER 21
Automated Machines, Telematics, and Autonomous Machine Operation

Knowledge Objectives

After reading this chapter, you will be able to:

- **K21001** Identify and describe the types, functions, and applications of autonomous and self-steering machines.
- **K21002** Identify and describe the purpose, function, construction, and operating principles of autonomous drive systems.
- **K21003** Identify and describe principles of machine position estimation, perception, and site mapping.
- **K21004** Identify and describe principles of machine motion planning.
- **K21005** Identify and explain the principles, types, and applications of vehicle telemetry.
- **K21006** Outline the principals involved in the integration of global positioning system (GPS) signals to autonomous machine control systems.
- **K21007** Explain the purpose, operation, and construction of autosteering, braking, and throttle output components.

Skills Objectives

After reading this chapter, you will be able to:

- **S21001** Perform OEM recommended diagnostic tests of autonomous drive control systems.
- **S21002** Locate and follow OEM service procedures for servicing autonomous drive systems.

▶ Applications of Autonomous and Self-Steering Machines

K21001

Automation, which is the use of control systems reducing or eliminating human intervention to operate machinery, is a rapidly evolving technology sector that has made its way into the off-road equipment industry. While on the road self-driving autonomous automobiles and trucks have received considerable media attention, the innovations are not new in comparison to off-road machinery. For years before the availability of a single autonomous car or truck for purchase by consumers, remote-controlled, self-steering, self-navigating, semi-autonomous, and fully autonomous off-road equipment was already being used in the agricultural, forestry, construction, and mining industries. In fact, many of the technologies and operational concepts used by on-highway vehicles were pioneered during the development of off-road equipment having various levels of driver-assisted, autonomous-operation capability. Farm tractors, mine trucks, and bulldozers with fully autonomous control systems—that is, off-road equipment capable of sensing its environment and navigating without human input—have been on the market since 2013 (**FIGURE 21-1**). Off-road products like these place fully autonomous off-road machines at least seven of eight years ahead of when the first fully autonomous cars are expected in the showrooms. **Fully autonomous operation**, the most advanced category of equipment without direct human "hands-on control," has evolved from a technological history of machines with **global positioning system (GPS)** guidance and self-steering systems used for over two decades.

For even longer than the use of semi-autonomous or even autonomous machine operation, mining equipment has regularly used simpler remote-control capabilities. These remote-control systems where an operator can use a set of controls that electronically duplicates actual machine controls enable operators to work at a distance and avoid potentially hazardous worksite conditions. Instead, radio signals transmitted over no further than line of site or Internet-based communication over even further distances can transmit operator commands to the machine without any detectable lag.

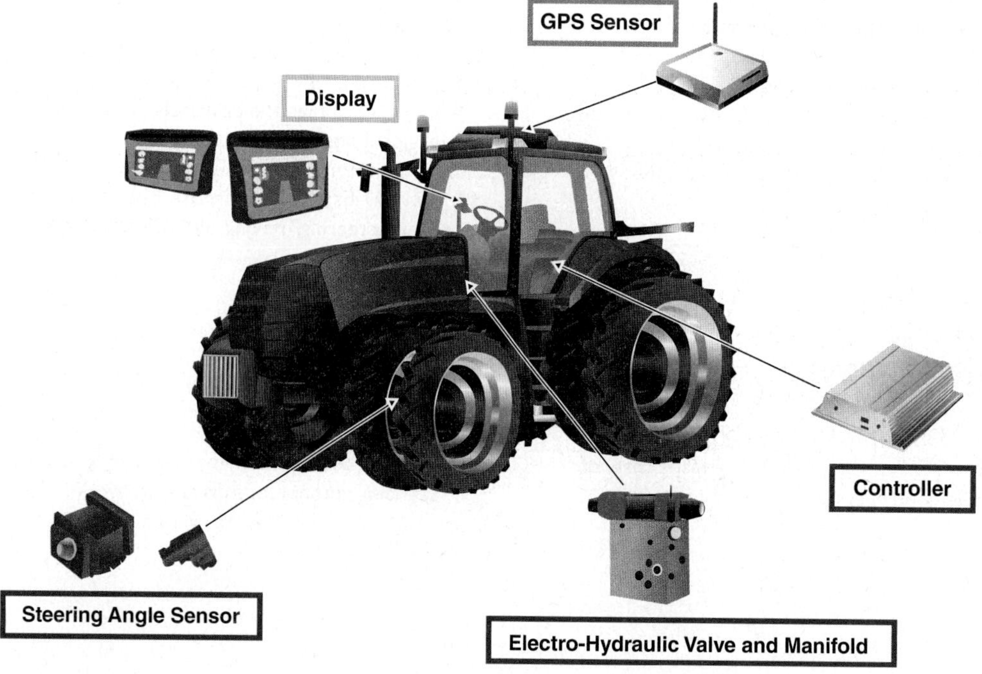

FIGURE 21-1 Major components of an automated guidance system found on an agricultural tractor.

You Are the Mobile Heavy Technician

Working at a construction business with a wide mix of earth-moving and excavating machines, you are tasked with retrofitting several pieces of older equipment with new telematics- and GPS-based technology to improve machine efficiency and better invoice working hours on the job. For this pilot program, you area allocated one wheel loader, an excavator, and two bulldozers and are requested to research and develop potential technical solutions for each of the machines. As you prepare your proposal, consider the following topics to compare solutions for each machine:

1. Outline the benefits to the operation for providing telematics and machine location data?
2. What types of retrofit components may be required for each machine to provide an indicate-only type of **computer-aided earth-moving system (CAES)**?
3. What are the advantages and disadvantages of single and dual GPS antenna/receiver systems?

Even without the use of sophisticated semi-autonomous and fully autonomous control, equipment operations are rapidly incorporating advanced electronic communications into machinery. The integration of **telematics**—that is, the transmission and receiving information from remote objects over cell phone or satellite communication networks—is widely recognized as delivering a tremendous number of benefits for technicians and equipment managers. Using telematics, machine data combined with GPS signals capable of tracking and navigating equipment anywhere, is viewed through web portals after it's analyzed with special software applications. The analysis supplies subscribers with an enormous amount of decision-making information related to operating more productive machines maintained with superior management, service, and maintenance practices (**FIGURE 21-2**).

Automated machine operation, remote-control, operator-assisted control, and the use of telematics encompass varying levels of sophistication and integration into machine systems. To help technicians understand these systems in order to effectively diagnose and service the equipment, this chapter will identify and examine machine technologies essential for enabling, remote-controlled, semi-autonomous, and fully autonomous machine operation. Operating principles of automated machine steering, positioning based on GPS signals, environment sensing, object detection, implement control, information processing, and interconnected machine networks are several of the major topics covered in this chapter. Highlighted too are various OEM machine management system software suites used to service what many today refer to as "smart-iron" (**FIGURE 21-3**).

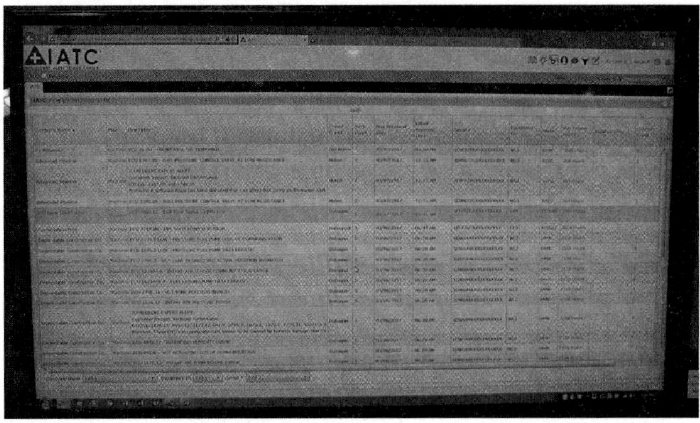

FIGURE 21-2 Diagnostic information transmitted from the machine helps technicians remotely diagnose a problem and determine what parts to bring on a service call.

▶ An Overview of Automated Machine Operation

K21002

Operating any type of off-road equipment is an extremely demanding task. The operator must not only safely steer, brake, and turn over rugged, unmarked pathways but also perform these tasks well while controlling implements, blades, and other attachments. In addition to the high level of skill that operators need to operate the machine implements, they must ensure that during repetitive tasks, they remain attentive and are

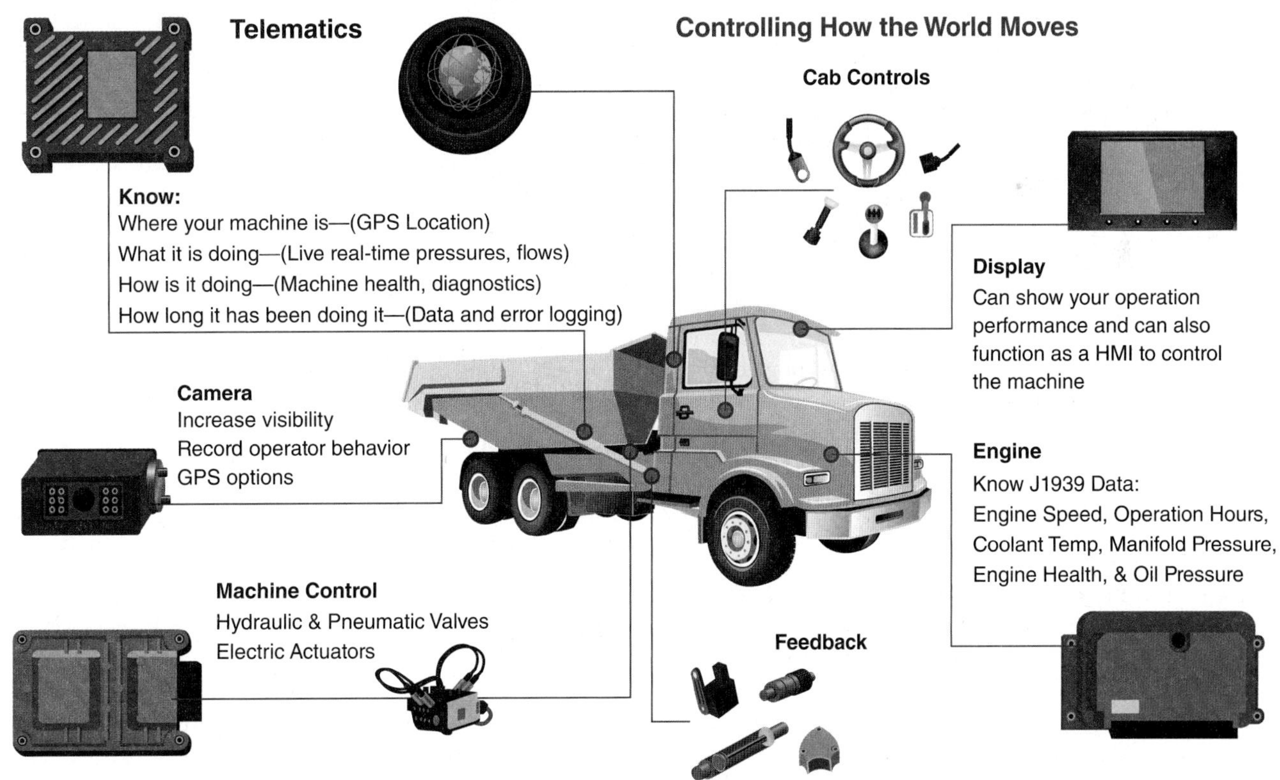

FIGURE 21-3 Key technologies of "smart iron" or the connected machine.

productive. Efficient operations are achievable only when the machine and operator are working quickly, at the highest skill level, using the least amount of fuel, and minimizing the likelihood of any potential damage to the machine, with little to no downtime. That means interruptions to the work cycle are kept to a minimum and that operations can take place during the day and night regardless of whether the work site is busy; crowded with other equipment and people; or noisy, dusty, and poorly lit. These demands impose enormous expectations that even the most skilled operator cannot deliver. Any kind of assistance or control method of safely reducing the amount of human intervention can only help to improve productivity and safety.

Overall, automating off-road machine functions has tremendous potential to increase productivity and improve the quality, accuracy, and precision of work. Automating machine steering, navigation, positioning, object avoidance, implement control, or any driving function can also increase worker and site safety, extend machine durability, and provide a wealth of features and data to equipment managers. When applied to off-road equipment, the greatest advantages of automation are not only increased production efficiency but also reduced labor cost. With various degrees of automation, machines can operate longer and faster. Rather than replace operator labor, automating simpler tasks allows operators to turn their attention to more critical, complex functions. At least, the learning curve for new operators can be reduced.

Machine automation doesn't always imply fully autonomous operation. Instead, it refers to varying degrees of machine operation performed without human intervention. Each off-road equipment industry has its own unique priorities in terms of automating functions. This means each application's system will use different types of sensors and programming objectives. In agriculture, a field tractor should not run over crops; it should minimize overlaps and skips while seeding, fertilizing, applying pesticides, or cultivating while the operator continuously monitors equipment performance. Tractors tow implements, and work is performed during the night. For a farm tractor, automating priorities are precise navigation, object recognition of plants and field hazards, and self-steering capabilities. Mining operations use machines to break and remove rock, then stockpile ore and waste materials. These sites are inherently dangerous since equipment runs through narrow tunnels, accompanied by blasting dangers, wall collapses, and explosion hazards. Automating machine functions that remove the operator from the cab can greatly improve worker safety (**FIGURE 21-4**). In mining, remotely operated mining equipment controlled by an operator at an offsite location that uses cameras and other sensors is an automation priority.

More elaborate machine operation is demanded by earth-moving equipment. The latest automated construction equipment uses bulldozers with automatically controlled blades that move to match digital 3D CAD drawings (**FIGURE 21-5**). CAESs integrate GPS data into a machine's hydraulic controls and guidance to autonomously operate a machine's hydraulic implements, such as buckets, shovels, booms, sticks, and blades. As the worksite features change, the machine transmits data about the work it has completed to enable software to update worksite maps, rendering the latest terrain and site conditions. The enormous increase in machine productivity using CAES means that precision blade or implement control using GPS locating services is a priority accessory for most new off-road equipment.

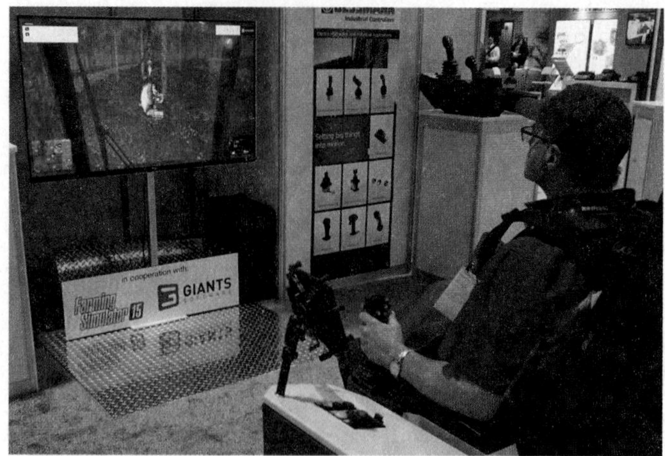

FIGURE 21-4 Remote control minimizes operator safety hazards while simultaneously providing a more comfortable and productive work environment.

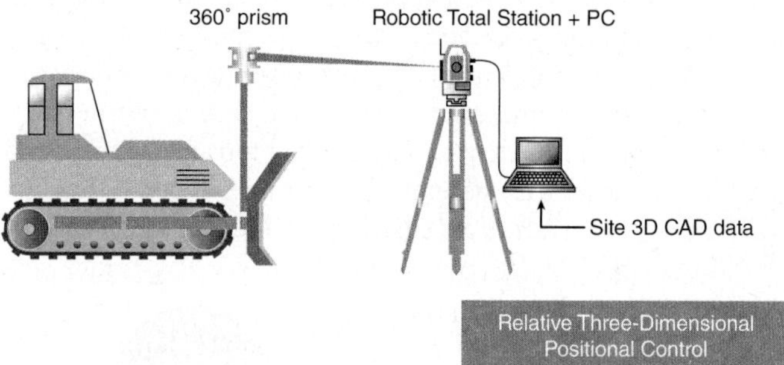

FIGURE 21-5 3D site drawing can be transmitted to a machine for precision blade control.

Whether it's on the farm, in the forest, underground, or clearing dirt for a roadway, the telematically connected machine can transmit diagnostic data. Machine position and usage is easily tracked by OEM software. Popular examples of machine monitoring and control software include Caterpillar's Cat Command System, Komatsu's Intelligent Machine Control, Case's SiteWatch, and John Deere's WorkSite. The following are functions common to equipment management software:

- identifying equipment abuse of improper machine operation prior to failure
- performing remote software upgrades to eliminate the need for technician service calls

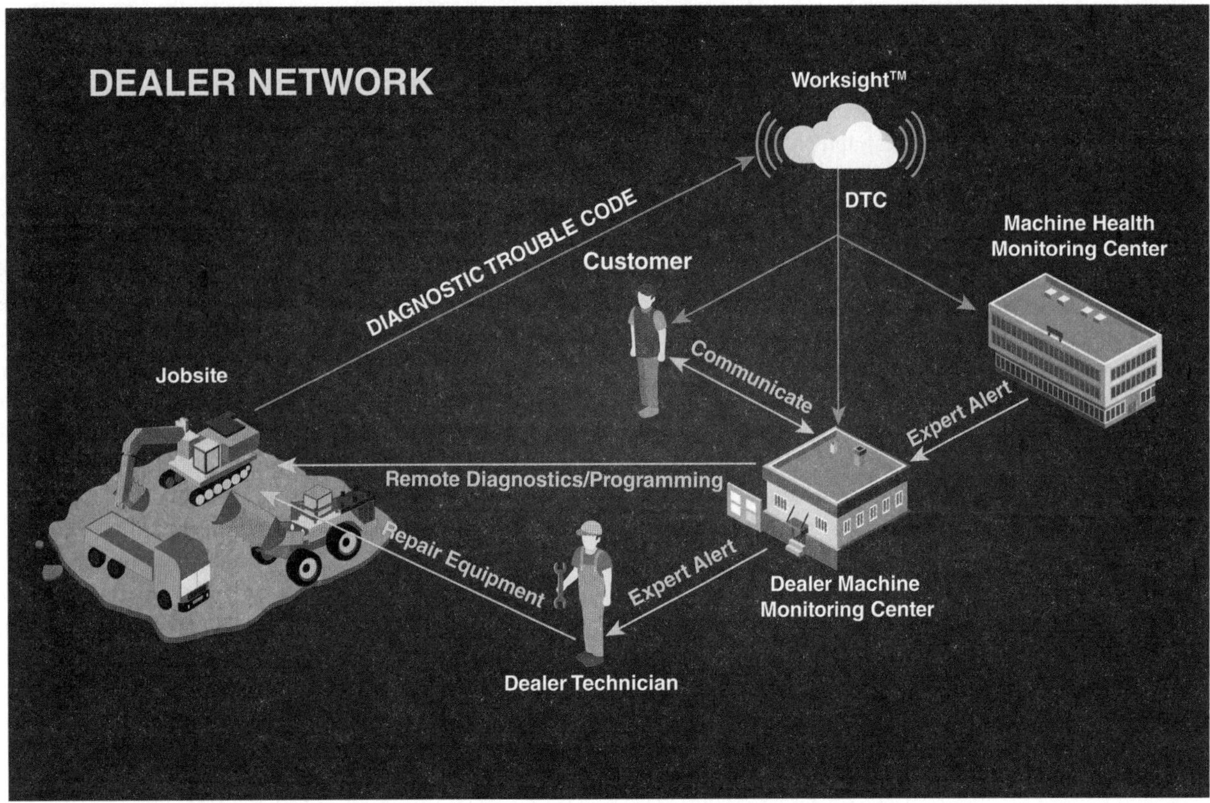

FIGURE 21-6 The typology or shape of connections for a telematics machine monitoring software suite.

- dispatching technicians with the correct parts to make a service call
- locating missing equipment moved outside a jobsite with GPS geofence notifications.

Machine data can be collected and typically transmitted via the Internet or cell phone signals to supply any measurable machine data, including information from engines, powertrains, work implements, hydraulic system controls, or machine positions (**FIGURE 21-6**). The technology that enables data collection and electronic transmission for display on a remote computer screen or web page is called telematics. Data about fuel consumption, fuel level, and pending faults can enable scheduling for refueling or service. Reporting various temperature, speed, and pressure data to equipment management software can relieve an operator's attention for more important work (**FIGURE 21-7**).

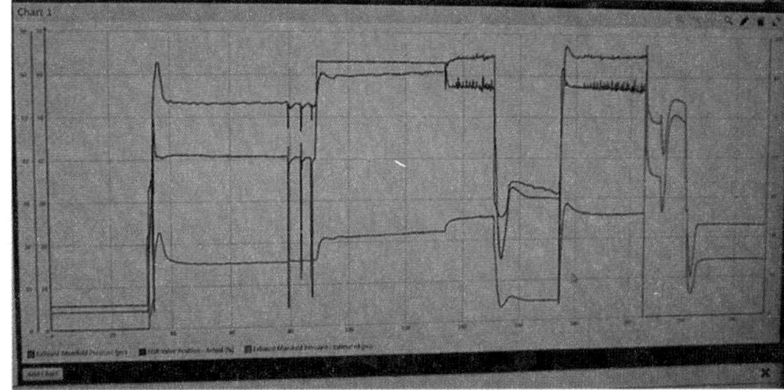

FIGURE 21-7 A telematics system transmitted this recording of a fault associated with a machines exhaust gas recirculation (EGR) system for analysis by a technician.

▶ Classifications of Autonomous Systems

K21003

Defined in the simplest way, automation is the use of control systems to reduce or eliminate human intervention. The term "autonomous" encompasses a wide range of technology applicable to the entire machine or its subsystems. An example of automated subsystem is parking, braking, collision avoidance, and driver assistance systems that can to some degree automatically intervene to prevent or reduce damage and injury during an emergency. Goals of fully autonomous equipment control take the operator completely out from behind the wheel and even eliminate the cab. Equipment is aware of its position and surroundings and able to adapt to changing conditions. Specific tasks performed by the machine are automatically accomplished with precision. Automated equipment designs provide a greater opportunity to improve energy efficiency many times over current benchmarks while producing zero emissions, with the bonus of never having an accident or causing an injury. Even though the machine may have full autonomous capability, human behavior can be integrated into machine operations. For example, machines that are aware of an operator's workloads or shift change time can drop off an operator and pick up another at a predetermined time and place. This feature, called **Humans in the Loop (HITL)**, includes people who provide assistance with autonomous function or other machine support, such as a repair technician.

There is no formal classification system yet for categorizing the level of off-road machine automation, but there is some correspondence to on-road, autonomous, or self-driving vehicle categories defined by the SAE (International Society for Automotive Engineers), which encompass some or all of these levels of automation. In 2014, **SAE J-3016** was adopted into legislation for on-highway vehicles. It classifies vehicle automation into five categories depending on the level of human control or intervention.

Autonomous Vehicle Standard

Level 0: Automated system has no vehicle control but may issue warnings.

Level 1: Driver must be ready to take control at any time. Automated system may include features such as adaptive cruise control (ACC), parking assistance with automated steering, and lane keeping assistance (LKA) Type II in any combination.

Level 2: The driver is obliged to detect objects and events and respond if the automated system fails to respond properly. The automated system executes accelerating, braking, and steering. The automated system can deactivate immediately upon takeover by the driver.

Level 3: Within known, limited environments (such as freeways), the driver can safely turn their attention away from driving tasks, but must still be prepared to take control when needed.

Level 4: The automated system can control the vehicle in all but a few environments, such as severe weather. The driver must enable the automated system only when it is safe to do so. When enabled, driver attention is not required.

Level 5: Other than setting the destination and starting the system, no human intervention is required. The automatic system can drive to any location where it is legal to drive and make its own decisions.

Types of Off-Road Autonomous Control Systems

The term "autonomous vehicle control" is generally understood to be similar to levels 3 through 5 of the J13016 standard, but in off-road machines these same designations have not yet developed. Driver-assisted control is taken to mean semi-autonomous control, and there are various degrees of capabilities and technological sophistication within that category. However, decades before Google and Uber ever fielded a self-driving car, agricultural equipment manufacturers like John Deere were marketing self-driving machinery. In fairness, the development pathway for autonomous and semi-autonomous machines has comparatively fewer obstacles. Using automated machinery on private property rather than in a complex environment of roadways traveled at high speeds meant reduced legal liability to manufacturers over concerns about errant equipment. Since agricultural fields have fewer potential obstacles that a street or highway filled with other machines and people operating at high speeds, the potential hazards to navigate are comparatively limited. Unlike streets and highways, detailed maps of rural fields with relatively straight rows of crops are not necessary, and equipment needs to move more often only in straight lines and turn after reaching the end of each row. The absence of regulations over autonomous and semi-autonomous off-road vehicles, such as those used in farming, has also helped the machinery to quickly become adopted onto the farm.

A more functional method to categorize or designate the types of semi-autonomous and autonomous machinery for tasks such as farming, earth-moving, and other off-road applications is to describe the equipment in terms of its use in steering, navigating, object recognition, and integrating machine control functions. Each has a different level of human control or need for supervision and approaches the question about what method best enables human interaction to make the machine more productive and reliable for any given task. These broad categories include the following:

1. Remote control (RC)

   RC is a control system that removes the operator from the machine whenever the working conditions pose safety hazards. An equipment operator instead stands in line of sight or has direct visual contact while using the remote control to operate the machine (**FIGURE 21-8**).

2. Telematics or tele-operated control

   Telematics refers to technology that sends, receives, and stores machine information through telecommunication devices such as radio, wireless Internet, and satellite or cell phone signals. While telematics has traditionally

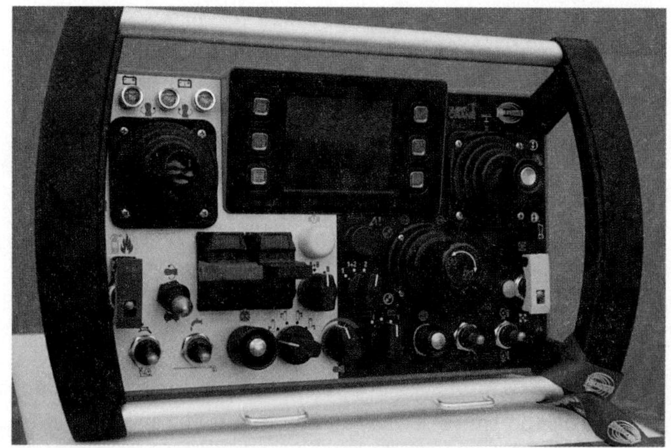

FIGURE 21-8 A remote-control panel wirelessly communicates with the machine. Controls on the machine are duplicated using the remote-control panel used by the operator.

involved taking equipment or vehicle information and transmitting it to a website where it can be viewed, two-way or bidirectional telematics communications enables the operator to control machines at a further distance than line-of-site remote control. Machine-to-machine communication is also accomplished using telematics communication principles.

3. Self-steering control

   Self-steering machine control refers to a collection of early stand-alone driver-assisted guidance control technologies that use external physical guidance devices such as foam markers, light ropes, inductive wires, or reflective tape. An electric motor–driven steering wheel or electrically controlled hydraulic steering control valve enables hands-off steering control of the machine. An automatic sensing system will use the physical marking system to provide a path for a machine to follow. Another method is to use a dead reckoning navigation system. This navigating system calculates a machine's current position by using a previously determined position or coordinating and updating that position based on known or estimated speeds over time. **Dead reckoning systems** depend only on vehicle sensors such as speed, steering angle, and even a magnetic compass. A radio-operated node or signal transmitter may provide a reference point. Prior to the introduction of GPS systems, agricultural vehicles used self-steering guidance systems for **precision farmer techniques**, which are techniques developed to precisely cultivate, seed, fertilize, and harvest crops. To install an assisted steering system motor, follow the steps in **SKILL DRILL 21-1**.

4. Self-steering + GPS navigation

   The GPS, which uses satellites to identify positioning and to navigate, have introduced much of the potential growth in off-road equipment automation. Introduced in the early 1990s for civilian use after being formerly used exclusively by the military, GPS navigation is used to provide a critical navigational input to microprocessor-controlled steering equipment. Again, these steering systems use electric motors driving the steering wheel, steering gears, or the electrohydraulic controls of the steering hydraulics. With accuracy to within ½ inch or 2 cm of a machine's position, these systems are often called integral autosteer and are regarded as the most accurate way to control the machine. The technology is commonly available as a retrofit, but virtually all manufacturers offer it as a machine accessory option, installed at the factory.

5. Self-navigation + object avoidance system

   With advancements in more powerful image-recognition software, position sensors, cameras, and laser perception systems, off-road machinery can integrate data acquired from the worksite with decision-making programing. The latest automation systems can gather, analyze, and

SKILL DRILL 21-1 Installing an Assisted Steering System Motor

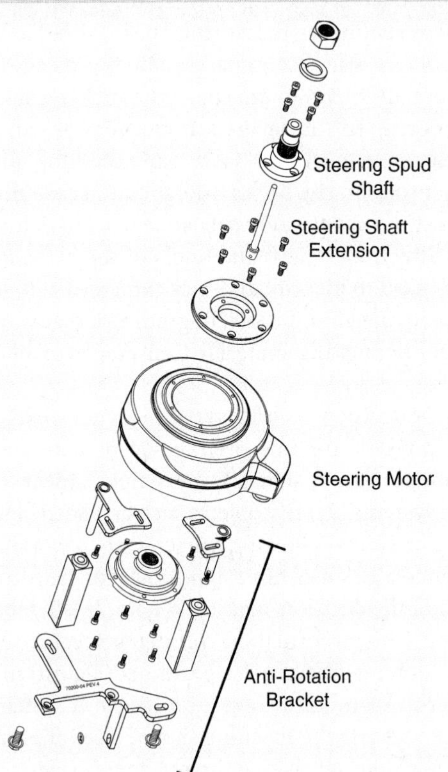

A popular GPS-controlled assisted steering system requires installing an anti-rotation bracket and a drive motor in the steering column. The following are general steps for installing the steering motor of a Trimble EZ EZ-Pilot-assisted steer system:

1. Disassemble the steering column by removing brackets and necessary covers to install the anti-rotation bracket. The bracket is used to support the steering motor on the steering shaft.
2. Install the anti-rotation bracket onto the steering column.
3. Loosen and remove the steering wheel from the splined steering shaft.
4. Assemble the EZ-Pilot drive motor by fastening the splined lower plate adapter to the bottom of the motor.
5. Fasten the anti-rotation pins to bottom plate of the motor at 11 and 1 o'clock positions.
6. Place the motor assembly onto the steering shaft with the motor's connector at a 2 o'clock position. The splines of the motor adapter and steering shaft must align. The anti-rotation pins on the bottom of the motor should be at the 12 o'clock and 3 o'clock positions. Do not force the motor onto the steering shaft. Instead, wiggle the motor while gently pushing downward.
7. Install a split lock washer and hex nut to hold the motor onto the steering shaft. Torque all hardware.
8. Rotate the motor and then slide the square anti-rotation tubes onto the anti-rotation pins.
9. Install the additional steering shaft telescopic extension rod. The rod has a threaded end that tightens onto the original steering shaft.
10. Lock the extension rod with a set screw against the flat side of the steering column shaft.
11. Bolt the upper motor adapter and the spud shaft to the top of the motor.
12. Reinstall the steering wheel onto the splined spud shaft using anti-seize compound on the threads.
13. Install the nut and lock washer and torque to specification.
14. Install the GPS antenna, control module, emergency shutdown switch, alarm, and display.
15. Calibrate the unit.

interpret machine and site information to operate actuation systems responsible for moving the machine while performing specific operations. These systems consist of different navigation systems, equipment sensors, actuators, and microprocessor control units synchronized to form an autonomously operated machine. Most importantly, a system to detect and analyze objects using one or more technologies such as a sonar, radar, LIDAR (a laser device operating long similar principles of a radar), or a stereo color camera is integrated into the machine control system.

6. Platooning—machine-to-machine communication

   Platooning is a machine-to-machine or inter-vehicle communication system that currently improves productivity by enabling a single operator to control the operation of multiple machines in an agriculture field operation. Most often used in machines operating on large farm fields, operators are relieved of tedious, repetitious driving routines and can instead concentrate on ensuring the accuracy of the work performed by the machines. Using autosteering, cruise control, and braking functions, one or more autonomous agriculture machines with a specific amount of lateral and longitudinal offset follow a lead machine. That means a lead machine with an operator overseeing the movement of all the machines in the field will have several other machines follow the lead tractor at a fixed space and distance. An arrangement like this is referred to as a platooning system. Platooning is enabled by connecting machines together using a **wireless CAN bridge**. The CAN bridge is the machine-to-machine communication systems collecting data from the **controller area network (CAN)**bus (shortened to CANbus) in one machine and wirelessly transmitting the information to the CANbus in the trailing machine (**FIGURE 21-9**). The CANbus contains data transmitted by every control module, including vehicle speed.

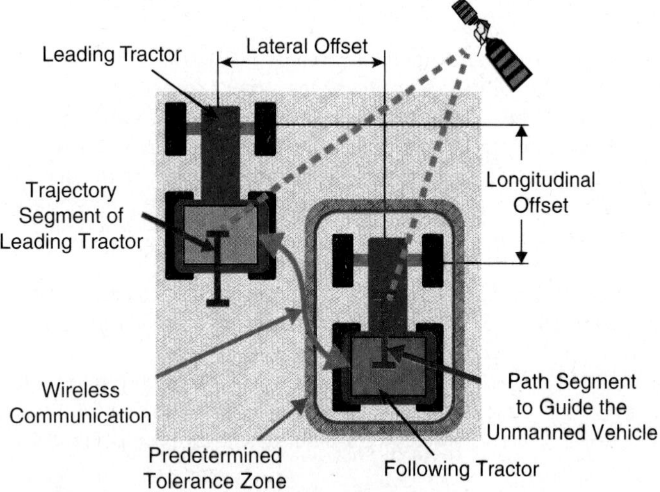

FIGURE 21-9 Platooning transmits CAN data from the lead machine to the trailing machine to maintain a precise lateral offset and distance of the trailing machine behind the lead unit.

To coordinate machine positioning, the geographical position of the lead tractor is transmitted continuously by wireless modems to the trailing machine to provide locating reference points to the trailing machine. Using the navigation coordinates of the lead machine, a path is planned for the trailing machine to follow at the specific calculated speed and steering angle relative to the lead machine. To ensure the operator-less trailing tractor follows the correct course, software with speed and motion control algorithms are built into the machine control modules. To install a CAN bridge with GPS, follow the steps in **SKILL DRILL 21-2**.

Automated System Architecture

To understand the operation of various levels of automated machine operation, it's important to identify the building blocks of any automated system (**FIGURE 21-10**). There are three critical elements of automated system architecture:

1. sensing-perception
2. decision-making or processing
3. actuation or output.

Sensing function responsibility is to collect information from the environment using a variety of sensors. The types of sensors can include cameras for image collection, GPS, and inertial guidance systems that sense machine and implement position. **Inertial guidance systems** are navigation systems used when GPS or communication with a base station is unavailable to track machine position and orientation relative to a known starting point, orientation, and velocity. Inertial guidance systems use dead reckoning navigation, which uses machine sensors or instruments measuring speed, direction, and rate of acceleration. A simple compass would be an example of an instrument used by an inertial guidance system. Not only are sensors needed for navigation, but they are also specifically adapted for a machine's task. An excavator, for example, will use sensors on the boom and stick to sense the position of the bucket. A road grader will use sensors to determine the position, direction, height and angle of the blade or moldboard. Sensors used to identify and pick tomatoes will be different from those involved in the task of grading a roadway, cutting down a tree, or moving material to a conveyor belt (**FIGURE 21-11**).

The processing or decision-making system is often sophisticated software responsible for interpreting sensor data and providing an appropriate output signal. For example, **object or collision avoidance systems** identify objects such as a deep hole capable of damaging or even swallowing a machine or a worker. The system may event read a speed limit sign. Object or collision avoidance is the job of the decision-making system. It will take sensor data and process the information through a specific set of procedures, rules, or mathematical algorithms (algorithms are mathematical formulas used to solve a problem). A system response determines whether the machine should steer around an object, stop the machine, or change the machine speed if it is not traveling at the correct velocity. Software algorithms may determine the difference between picking or ignoring a tomato

SKILL DRILL 21-2 Installing a CAN Bridge with GPS

CAN bridges wirelessly connect a machine's controlled area network to a wireless local area network (WLAN) or a cellular or Bluetooth network. They can also be used to connect machine-to-machine CAN networks such as those needed for configuring lead and trailing machines into platoons. The CAN bridge module interface connects to the machine and is configured with a PC that is running software designed to select and modify module features. When connected to a WLAN, network devices such as computers, smartphones, or tablets can manage and evaluate CAN data through a bidirectional communication enabled by the module. CAN bridges serve as a replacement for a CAN cable for more efficient and dependable communication between a machine and management tools.

The following is an overview of basic installation instructions for a CAN bridge module:

1. Unpack the unit and identify plugs for the power supply, antenna, and CAN connector.
2. Mount the module in the chassis and connect the main power harness to the chassis constant battery and switched battery supply. Do not install an external ground, since it may interfere with the reverse-polarity protection circuits.
3. Ensure the device is switched off and then connect the network data bus to a stub connecter having CAN-L and CAN-H signals. Ensure that the polarity of the network signal matches the units CAN-H and CAN-L connector.
4. Ensure that the device's power supply is switched off and connect the GPS, 3G cellular, or combination antenna cable to the module.
5. To maximize the performance of the GPS receiver, mount the GPS antenna in a place where it has an unobstructed view of the sky and is level with the horizon. If more than one antenna is used, mount them least 2 m away from each other to minimize interference.
6. Connect CAN module to a PC and establish a connection between the module and PC.
7. Configure the CAN bridge for various options, such as the types of devices it can communicate with and the Internet, cellular, and telematics service providers.

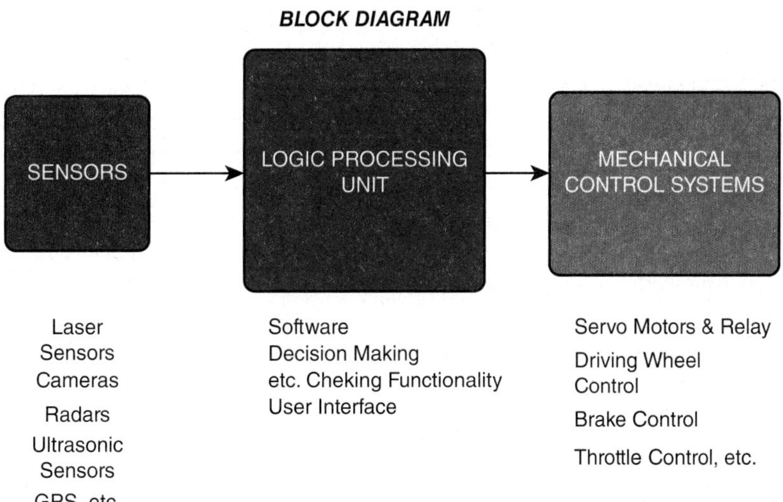

FIGURE 21-10 Three major elements making up system architecture for any level of autonomous machine operation.

based on the object size and color. A tree may be harvested if it fits the appropriate algorithm for selection based on diameter and location.

After processing system sensor data, decisions are made and output signals or messages are transmitted to the actuation systems when required. The machine may need to change direction or speed based on information processed by the decision-making system. The machine may also require moving a hydraulic cylinder to change the position of a grader blade, dump a bucket, or change the angle of a towed implement. Electrical signals from the processing system's electronic control units are converted by the actuation system into

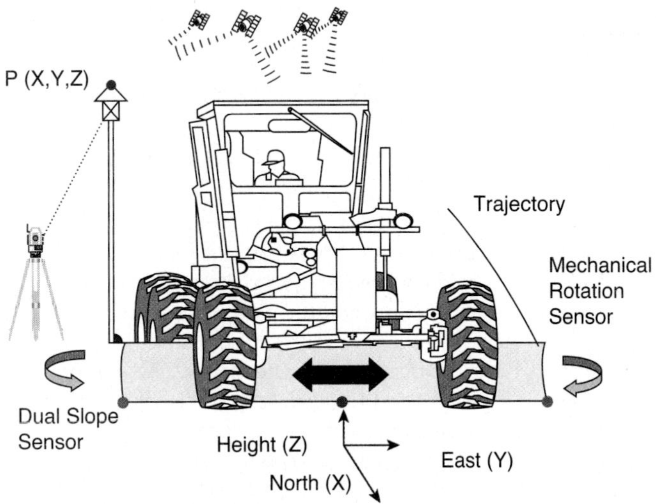

FIGURE 21-11 A GPS transmitter mounted on a pole and attached to the blade of a grader can sense place movement in three axes—*x*, *y*, and *z*. The input is used to change blade position as well as navigate the machine.

FIGURE 21-12 This electric-over-hydraulic control valve manifold interfaces with a CAN-controlled electronic module. Signals from the CAN network, including remote signals, will actuate any type of hydraulic controls.

the appropriate type of output (**FIGURE 21-12**). When a change is made, the sensing system will observe the new data and provide feedback to the processing system about whether the change is accurately following the direction given by the decision-making system. This process where the operation of an output device is monitored by a sensor is called **closed-loop control** or closed-loop feedback (**FIGURE 21-13**). If the system actuator's response is not correct, the sensing system provides the feedback to the decision-making system to make further corrections or supply a different output signal or message.

▶ Enabling Technologies for Machine Automation

K21004, S21001

Composing the elements of automated machine system architecture is another layer of technologies that are selected, arranged, integrated, and synchronized to form the whole automated machine. A detailed description of each of the following technologies common to most automated machines forms the scaffolding used to build machine architecture. This more fundamental layer of technology forming machine architecture includes the following networks.

Onboard Networks

Onboard machine networks are formed by connecting various machine electronic control modules to communicate and exchange information (**FIGURE 21-14**). One of the primary reasons for first constructing onboard networks is to reduce the need for complex wiring and redundant sensors. Sensor data collected by individual modules can be shared across a large number of devices connected into a network. This network feature eliminates the duplication of sensor input and associated wiring supplying each module needing the data. Connecting the

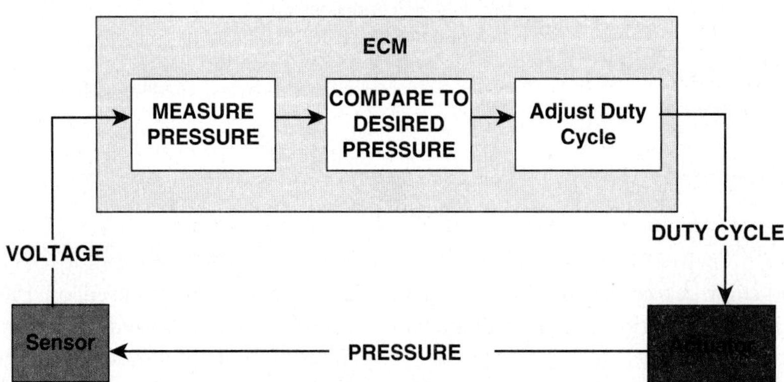

FIGURE 21-13 Principle of closed-loop feedback. A sensor will measure an actuator or output pressure or position. The engine control module (ECM) makes adjustments to the actuator to correct any deviation from commanded position or pressure.

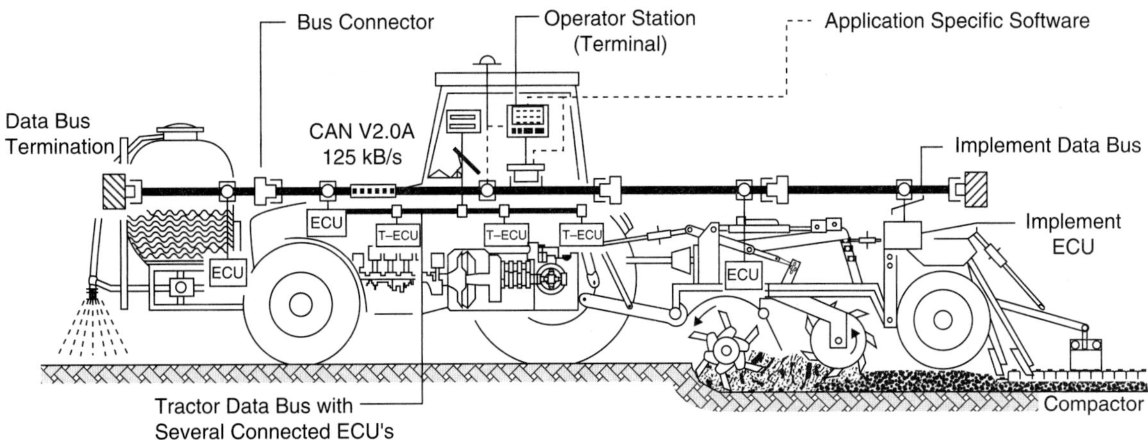

FIGURE 21-14 Multiple electronic control units are connected with a pair of wires to form an onboard machine network.

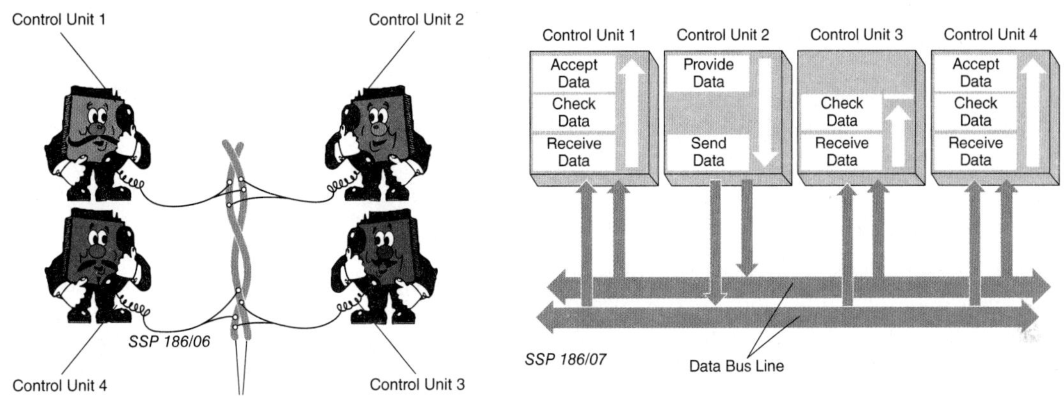

FIGURE 21-15 Communication principles of time division signal multiplexing over an onboard network. To prevent signal collisions, one module transmits information at a time while the others listen.

modules together using a pair of wires common to all the modules also eliminates the need for point-to-point wiring. The pair of wires called the data bus operates like a party line telephone system (**FIGURE 21-15**). A simple example of how onboard networks simplify electrical system wiring and sensor redundancy is the use of an engine speed sensor. These data are required in many places by various devices, such as the instrument gauge cluster, transmission, hydraulic control system, and other modules. The transmission needs it to calculate shift schedules and the hydraulic control system to match engine speed with hydraulic loads. Using one electronic control module to sense and process speed sensor data and then distribute the information over the network reduces the construction cost and associated wiring required to connect an engine speed sensor to each module requiring speed data. Note too that the information-processing capabilities are distributed over many modules, which enhances the power of the total network. Instead of numerous modules performing the same task—such as processing speed data—one module alone does it, which frees the processors in other ECMs to perform work.

The idea of "the whole being greater than the sum of its parts" applies to vehicle networks. Connecting modules together to share information makes it possible to customize many additional operational features. This idea of a vehicle network is somewhat similar to social networks, where people are connected through websites or organizations to exchange information and even collaborate to accomplish tasks or reach goals otherwise unachievable when unconnected. Extensive use of microprocessor-based controls applied to nearly every machine system can also be leveraged using network communication to provide a huge number of benefits not possible with modules and devices left unconnected.

Information is digitally communicated across onboard networks by using a series of 1s and 0s, representing numbers and letters. Each module transmits a 0 or 1 using a brief positive and negative voltage pulse. However, if voltage pulses were simultaneously transmitted together over a single wire pair, the voltage representation of 0s and 1s would collide and cancel out one another. Information would become garbled, a lot like a noisy classroom when everyone is speaking at once and no one is understood. To prevent this, an electrical signal communication strategy called multiplexing overcomes the problem of signal collision and cancellation. **Multiplexing** simply refers to a concept where the transmission of more than one electrical signal or message takes place over a single wire or pair of wires. In current models of machines, thousands of messages are exchanged every second over onboard networks using serial data—that is, data consisting of 1s and 0s sent one after another in series, transmitted by various control modules. Multiplexing used by onboard networks works by dividing the time available to each network module or device to transmit and listen to information. Time division multiplexing (TDM) requires the modules and other devices take turns sharing the communication pathway. Only one module is allowed to talk and all other modules must listen until it is their turn to talk. This is like a well-ordered classroom where there is cooperation around communication and the rule is no one interrupts someone else until they are finished speaking. Data transfer back and forth along the data bus does not take place simultaneously but each device transmits and receives data by cooperating to time-share a common signal path. The speed at which the data exchange takes place makes communication appear to take place simultaneously but it is in fact not.

Time division multiplexed communication strategy is not unlike Morse code using a sequence of dots and dashes to represent any letter or number combination. The biggest difference between the serial data of on board networks and Morse code is the speed the data is exchanged. Modules communicate much faster than old Morse code through the use of microprocessor electronics.

Controller Area Networks

The term "controlled area networks (CAN)" describes a distributed type of network communication control system. This means that no single central control module is used on a machine. Instead, each module or node on the network has processing capabilities that can not only initiate electrical control for faster response but also synchronize their operation with other network modules. This means each module on the network has memorized the rules of what it has to do and the rules for doing it. Because the network has no central control, parts of it can be severed and the connected components will still operate. CANs are the most widely used type of network used to integrate all operations of all the latest machines. CAN networks are often integrated in local area networks (LANs), a term which refers to a vehicle having multiple types of networks, such as optical or proprietary networks connecting manufacturer-specific equipment. Since there is no central control module coordinating communication or controlling network devices, each network module has built-in processor capabilities to process input and output data while simultaneously receiving and transmitting data to the network. A built-in clock and transceiver in each CAN module helps synchronize multiplex communication between modules so that each takes an appropriate turn using the data bus to send and receive messages. Other processing functions built into every CAN module allow it to interpret other network communication data and control what messages it sends to the data bus.

The CANbus

Electronic control modules can be connected in a variety of ways. **Network typology** refers to a term describing how modules are connected to one another. Most often, the typology refers to a physical shape of the way a network is connected (**FIGURE 21-16**).

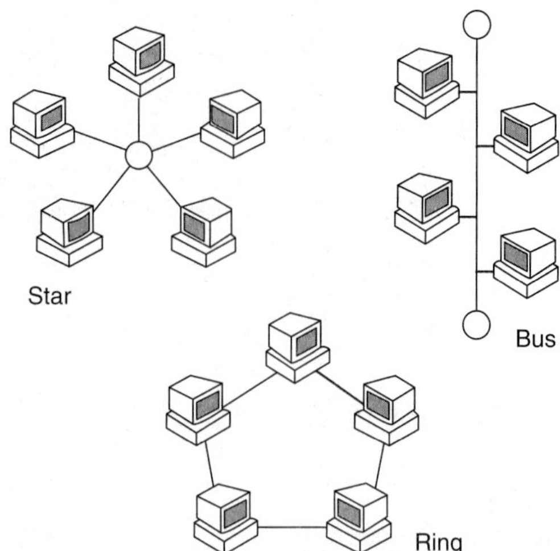

FIGURE 21-16 Network typology refers to the shape of the connections formed between network modules.

A star network's interconnections are shaped just like that—a star. Ring and bus networks are other common shapes or layouts of connection configurations for the channel's exchanging data. The term "CANbus" when used in network typology describes network connection that look just like a bus route on a street with two lanes for traffic. The street also has bus routes and bus stops along the way, which are electronic control modules.

Since there is only one path for electrical signals to travel on the CANbus—that is, one street—data are transmitted one bit at a time, one after another, or in series. A positive voltage of anywhere between 2 and 8 volts in comparison to a pulse of lower voltage would represent a "1." No voltage on either wire is "0." Voltage on the paired wires is a mirror opposite to achieve a sharp crisp differential voltage that is easily understood by the modules (**FIGURE 21-17**). Using differential voltage and twisting the wires minimize electromagnetic interference (EMI) in the wires, also called electrical noise, in wiring carrying serial data.

One wire is called CAN-H, which has a more positive voltage than the other, which is called CAN-L. Each wire will have a mirror opposite charge or polarity of the other when communication takes place. The **differential voltage** provides the best method for transmitting signals without noise.

Differences Between J-1939-2 CAN and ISO 11783 CAN Networks

There are a number of CAN networks used by off-road machinery, which differ primarily according to the rules, also called protocols, used to transmit and receive messages. A network layer is a term used to describe the ways these protocols organize sets of rules together. For example, protocol layers set rules for constructing connectors, how many modules can be connected, how far they can be separated, how fast messages should be transmitted, what diagnostic information should look like, etc. For off-road machines, three protocols are primarily used. One protocol primarily for machines built in North America is the SAE-developed **J-1939-2** network used by agricultural and forestry vehicles, and the **J-1939** network

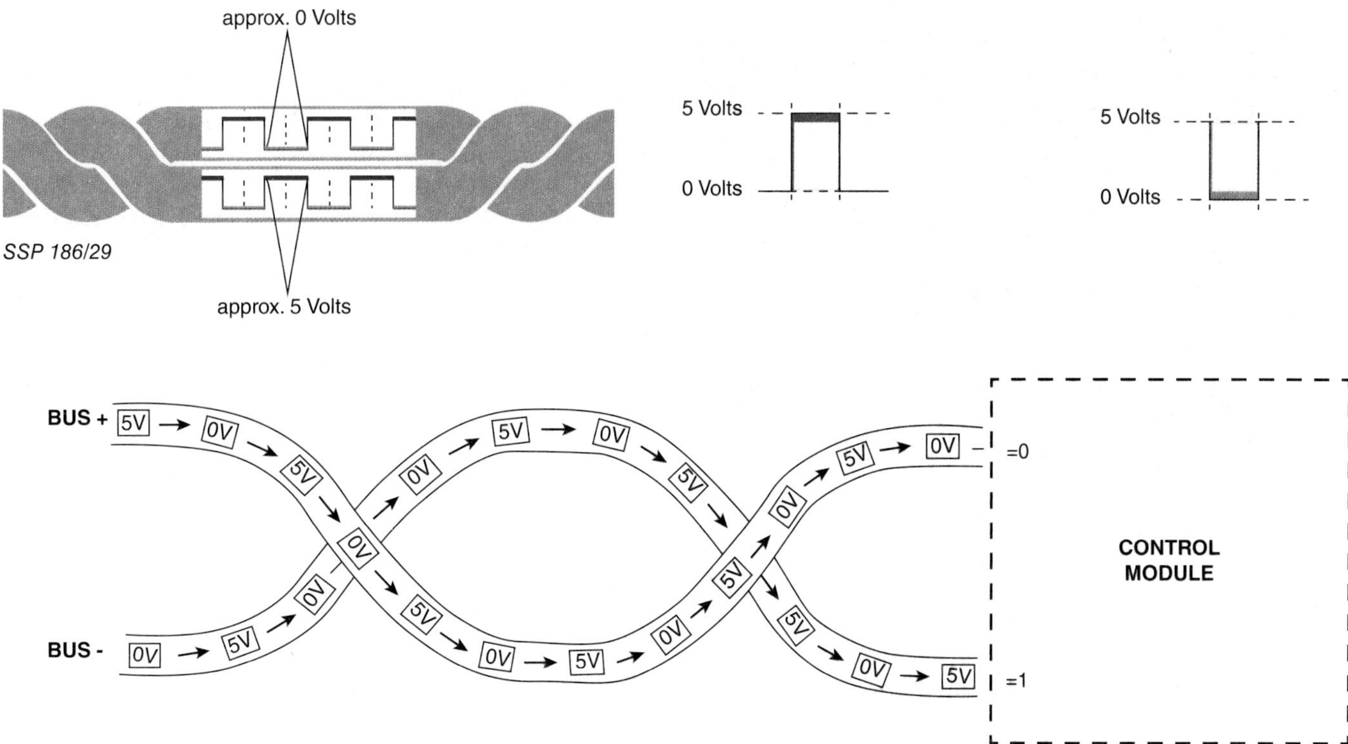

FIGURE 21-17 Principle of differential voltage transmission. A series of 1's and 0's is transmitted over the data bus contains digital information.

for off-road HD commercial vehicles uses a bus-type typology. The other is **ISO11783** series, also called an ISO-bus, developed in Germany and used primarily by European agriculture and forestry machines. All three standards—J-1939, J-1939-2, and ISO11783—are international standards and similar in defining the methods and protocols for data transfer between sensors, actuators, and control modules, as well as information storage and display units regardless of whether they are mounted on the machine or on implements. The J-1939-2 and ISO11783 are serial data network protocols that prescribe communication standards for forestry or agricultural tractors and mounted, semi-mounted, towed, or self-propelled implements such as cultivators, sprayers or harvesting machines. The data link connector is the easiest way to distinguish between each network. J-1939 uses a 9-pin connector, while ISO has a unique combination of power ground and data bus connectors (**FIGURE 21-18** and **FIGURE 21-19**).

Several features are unique to ISO11783. One is the provision for the addition of a **virtual terminal** in the cab of a machine (**FIGURE 21-20**). The virtual terminal is a screen mounted in the tractor used to allow the operator to control connected implements. Modules on ISO-bus machines can

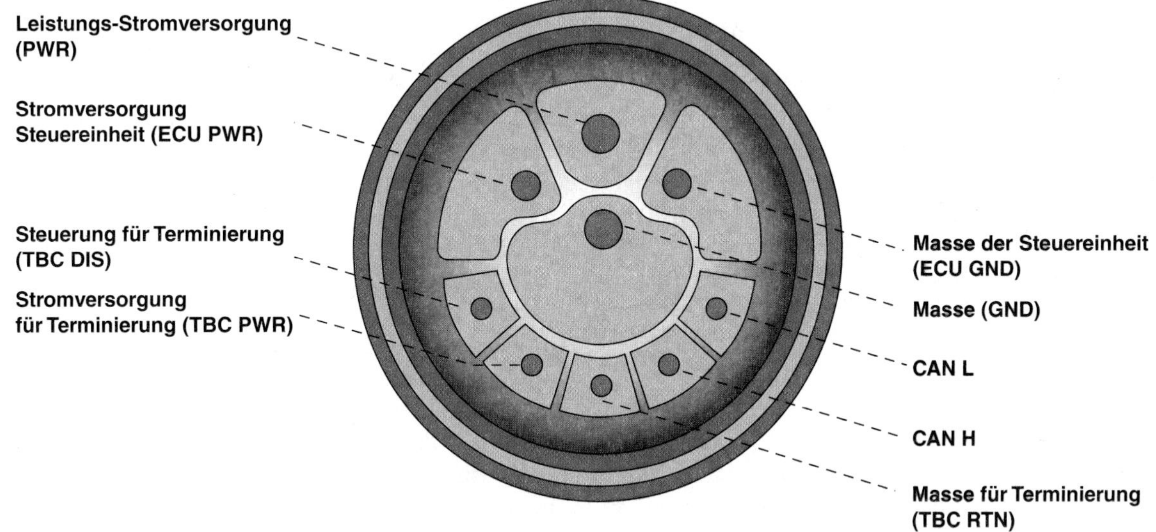

FIGURE 21-18 The configuration of the ISO 11783 data link connector.

FIGURE 21-19 A J-1939 data link connector.

FIGURE 21-20 A virtual terminal in the cab of a machine displays information transmitted over the CAN.

transmit what are called virtual objects along the CANbus to be displayed on the virtual terminal. The objects are visual representations of the implement or device controlled by the module. Multiple implements can be displayed on a single screen, which makes the use of the virtual terminal important in agricultural applications since it eliminates any separate implement control unit or its wiring unnecessary; one terminal allows the operator to control all of the implements. The J-1939-2 standard has similar capabilities but is less sophisticated in its support of the virtual terminal than the ISO-bus.

Telematics Standards

Other important additions to the ISO-bus standard include enabling the use of standardized telematics across all manufacturers. The interoperability of devices used on various OEM CAN networks is important to supporting customers by delivering basic telematics data in a standard format. Without this standardization, companies with mixed fleets of machines made by Cat, Komatsu, or Deere would need to use a separate provider to analyze telematics data. Extensible markup language (XML), a programming language used by ISO-bus that defines a set of rules for coding documents in a format that is both human readable and machine readable, is a differentiating feature of ISO 11783 from J-1939.

▶ Global Positioning Systems

K21006

The GPS, also called the **global navigation satellite system (GNSS)**, is a worldwide radio-navigation system that has had a tremendous impact on the advancement of automated machine guidance and navigation. To carry out precision-farming techniques or have machines operate on a construction site to dig, shape, and grade surfaces, precise machine positions that are accurate to fractions of an inch are necessary. GPS has provided this capability since the mid-1990s, when the navigation system built originally in the 1970s for the American military was opened up to civilian use. Several other GPS systems are operated by other nations and used by machines in North America and around the world. For example, Russia has a system called GLONASS; Europe has the Galileo System; Japan has the Quasi-Zenith Satellite System (QZSS); and China has the Compass System. Each system's fundamental operational concepts are the same but have slightly unique position-sensing advantages for equipment depending on where it is located. But most GPS systems on today's machines use dual frequency receivers receiving two GPS signals. When referenced together, the signals are integrated and the accuracy of each system is significantly enhanced.

Identifying Global Positions

Inexpensive GPS receivers, which are often integrated into the onboard network, are essential for any application requiring navigation or position-sensing capabilities. In North America, the GPS system consists of a constellation of 30 satellites orbiting the earth with 24 or more satellites visible to receivers on earth (**FIGURE 21-21**). To identify any position on earth, a GPS receiver needs to receive signals from three or more of these satellites. To do this, a mathematical concept called **triangulation** is used. Triangulation works when a receiver connects with signals transmitted from each satellite at precisely the same time. Since the satellites are located at different distances from the receiver, the signals will arrive at slightly different times (**FIGURE 21-22**). A time stamp on each signal allows the receiver to calculate how far it is from each satellite. By subtracting the time the signal was transmitted from the time it was received, the GPS receiver can measure the distance between it and each satellite. If the GPS receiver also knows the exact position of the satellites when the signals are transmitted, the intersection point of signals form a three-dimensional (3D) position with calculated coordinates indicating how far east or west (longitude) and north or south (latitude) the receiver is from the

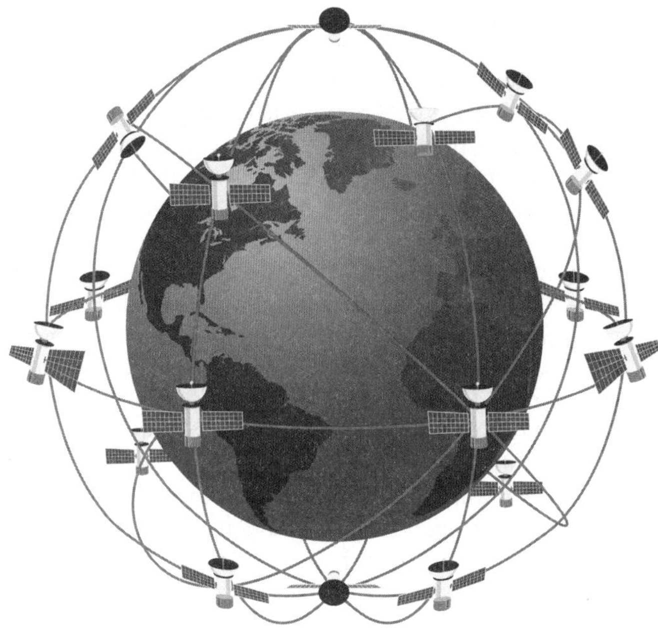

FIGURE 21-21 GPS, or global positioning system, is a generic term for satellite-based communication, which can be used for identifying machine position and navigation.

satellite. Additionally, the altitude or height above sea level of the receiver is calculated. Without signals from at least three different satellites, significant error has to be factored into the receiver's location (**FIGURE 21-23**). For example, if the receiver is located at a high altitude and three signals are not received, the receiver may use sea level as a reference point for location and locate the receiver a distance at least equal to the altitude away from the actual location.

GPS Signal Information

Note that the receiver needs to determine the location of the GPS satellites to calculate a position relative to the satellites. Two types of satellite data are required by the GPS receiver: the almanac and the ephemeris. The almanac and ephemeris contain information about the orbital information and location of the satellites. Both sets of data are transmitted intermittently by the GPS satellites, which are collected and stored by the GPS receiver. Unfortunately, this information is not continuously updated, and the receiver may need as long as 15 minutes to update almanac data and two hours for ephemeris information. Without the information, the receiver cannot accurately locate a position, which explains why sometimes it takes a long time to initially start up a GPS receiver.

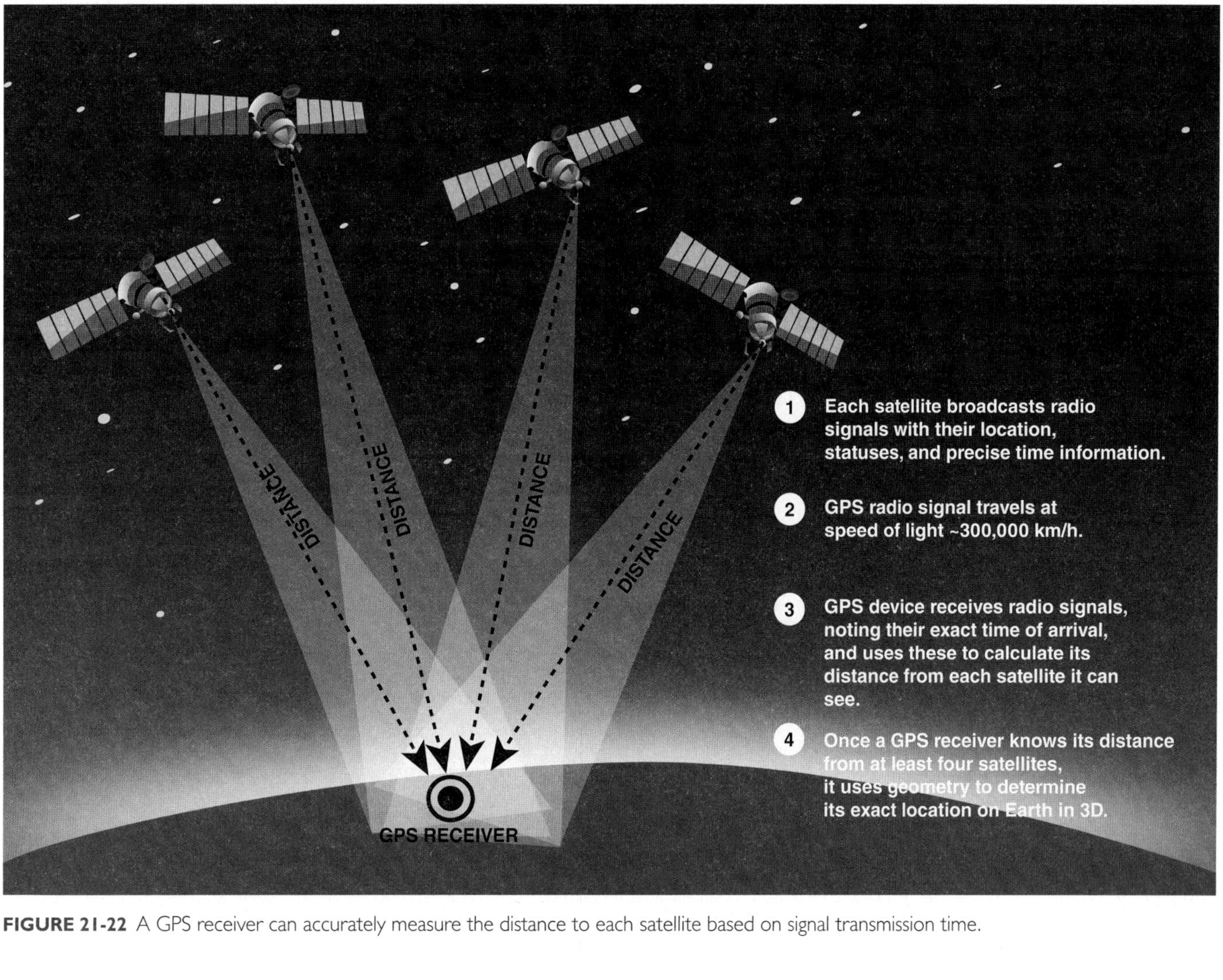

DISTANCE
DISTANCE
DISTANCE
DISTANCE
GPS RECEIVER
1 Each satellite broadcasts radio signals with their location, statuses, and precise time information.
2 GPS radio signal travels at speed of light ~300,000 km/h.
3 GPS device receives radio signals, noting their exact time of arrival, and uses these to calculate its distance from each satellite it can see.
4 Once a GPS receiver knows its distance from at least four satellites, it uses geometry to determine its exact location on Earth in 3D.

FIGURE 21-22 A GPS receiver can accurately measure the distance to each satellite based on signal transmission time.

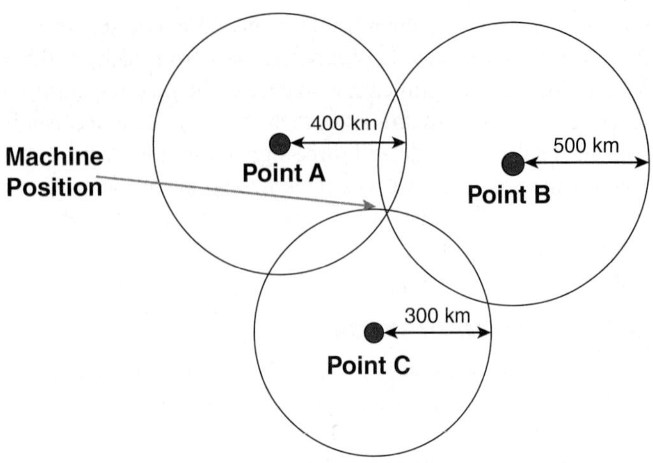

FIGURE 21-23 Triangulation—the use of three different angles to estimate position—is used to geo-locate a machine.

The terms "hot start" and "cold start" when used in relation to GPS devices refer to whether the receiver has recent almanac and ephemeris information. If the most recent information is not available, it is a cold-start condition. Assisted GPS or A-GPS used by cell phones will collect the almanac and ephemeris data more quickly from computer servers connected to the Internet rather than from satellite transmissions.

GPS Signal Correction Systems

Conventional GPS data can provide positional accuracy to within 10 m. Disturbances in the atmosphere, accuracy of GPS clocks, and satellite data can skew accurate positioning. To correct this problem and provide precise location, GPS units will have signals corrected using at least one of several supplemental ground-based reference stations. When the precise position of a ground station is known, data from ground reference stations are transmitted to the GPS receiver in order to apply a correction factor. These supplemental correction systems are needed to obtain positional accuracy to less than ½ inch or 1.27 cm for CAESs or machinery operating in farm fields navigating between rows with similar positional accuracy. Differential global positioning system (DGPS) wide-area augmentation system (WASS), **real-time kinematic (RTK)**, and dual frequency receivers are terms used to categorize supplemental GPS technology to correct satellite GPS error. These systems are privately owned but provide satellite differential correction subscription services used to improved positional accuracy to the decimeter or less than ½ inch (**FIGURE 21-24**).

On jobsites where equipment uses GPS to guide and control precision grading or asphalt paving, a radio base station or two supplemental rover devices help correct the GPS signal supplied to machine controllers. These generally provide even more precision for the geometry needed to accurately measure vertical dimensions. A GPS base station that receives satellite signals makes any necessary corrections to satellite signals and then transmits the corrections factors to GPS receivers on machines. Using the base station to correct satellite signal error, machines can operate from 6 to 9 miles away and maintain reception of the base station's signals.

GPS and GNSS Application

When considering applications for GPS, the first association is to a cell phone map app or a navigation system integrated into the dash of a car's or a truck's media system, providing the driver

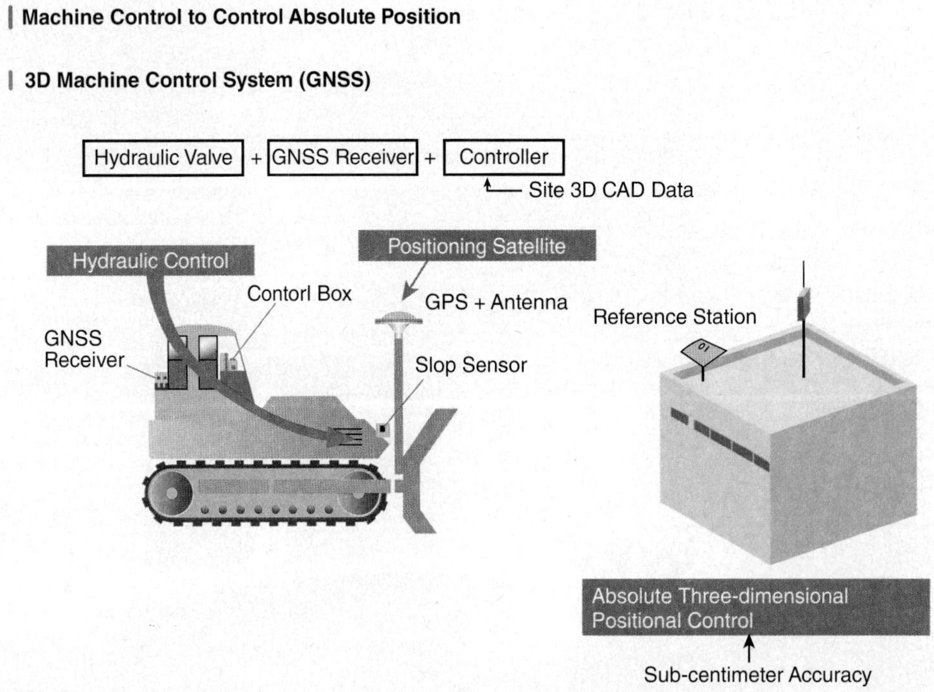

FIGURE 21-24 Satellite GPS requires assistance to more precisely locate machine implements and blades using a correction factor supplied by fixed point, land-based signals system.

with turn-by-turn directions. However, GPS has turned into an extremely valuable technology for off-road equipment.

GPS is used to locate and track equipment. A compact GPS receiver and radio transmitter tracking device can be connected into the onboard network and recognized like any other module. After that, it can then be used to locate the equipment and plan route activity. Since theft is a bigger concern with off-road equipment because it is often easier to steal than on-road vehicles and is far more expensive to replace, GPS can provide **geofencing** capabilities. With geofencing, a manger can be alerted to the movement of a machine outside a particular geographical area or expected operating hours. The same module can provide telematics data to a service provider, where machine data and statistics can be easily viewed on a website even though the equipment is half way around the world.

In most instances, the GPS device will use the equipment's battery current, but it can be configured to use its own internal power source that can last up to seven years. The device will transmit status updates when certain events, such as starting the engine, are triggered—as well as location updates at regular intervals, which are normally every two minutes.

CAESs are GPS-based earth-moving equipment that can use satellite data to compute the positions of machines, blades, and implements by using GPS antennas mounted on equipment. Project-specific design information stored in an onboard computer is used to compare the precise position of the earth-mover's blade, boom, stick, shovels or buckets against site-design coordinates. Machine operation is controlled according to a stored 3D map in order to cut, fill, or dig to a profile that exactly matches the X-Y-Z coordinates on a digital topographic plan. This eliminates the requirement to survey and stake a site and resurvey to measure progress.

The big players in the 3D GPS grade-control market are Topcon, Trimble, and Leica Geosystems.

Indicate and Automatic Mode

Machines equipped with GPS/GNSS have two options when using satellite positioning. One is indicate mode, which uses data produced during machine operation to provide the feedback to the operator who controls blades, shovels, or implements control. During **indicate-only mode**, the final contours of the work site are displayed on the cab terminal screen. When grading, the operator has to manually adjust the elevation and slope of the blade to match the plan, and the GPS only provides the operator with feedback about grading or digging information on a cab terminal (**FIGURE 21-25**).

In the second option or fully **automatic mode**, the machine's hydraulics are electronically controlled with no driver intervention make blade or implement adjustments. Most GPS guidance systems also provide the operator with the ability to define a specific grade elevation or grade angle without a specific design.

GPS Hydraulic Interface

A fully automatic CAES requires the GPS guidance system to be integrated into the machine's hydraulic implement controls. OEMs currently produce machines with these controls already

FIGURE 21-25 This GPS CAN logging module connects satellite communication to a machines CAN network supplying GPS data to the CAN network.

built in as an option. Aftermarket retrofit kits are also available, which enable the conversion of a machine into a fully automatic control. To interface or connect the GPS to the machine's implement controls, one of two methods may be used. The first is relatively simple if the machine is built using electric-over-hydraulic (EH) implement controls. In this instance, the GPS system can supply an input lever with electrical signals connected in parallel with the machine's implement lever. The signal from the retrofit GPS control module interprets the electrical signals as a lever command supplied by the operator and moves the hydraulic control accordingly. The second method for integrating GPS in the machine's hydraulic system on older or simpler designs is by adding a second pilot hydraulic valve in parallel with the machine's pilot hydraulic valve. This second valve is controlled by or integrated with data from the GPS CAN module and moves the hydraulic valve, thereby regulating the implement according programmed instructions and feedback from the blade, bucket, or implement position supplied by sensors or GPS devices (**FIGURE 21-26**).

Blade and Implement Positioning Systems

To provide an adequate set of data to the GPS's CAES blade, bucket, or implement position, it needs to provide feedback to the GPS control module. This is accomplished in several ways.

1. Installation of at least one GPS antenna/receiver mounted on the machine's blade. The machine will also have a GPS receiver and a radio. This enables the operators to use an indicate-only system to view two-dimensional (2D) site cross sections, elevations, and blade position diagrams. The

FIGURE 21-26 A. An electronic control module connected to the CAN network can operate pilot control valves in this hydraulic manifold. **B.** A control valve manifold assembly having electronically controlled pilot valves paralleling lever controlled valves.

machine's location relative to the site can also be mapped. However, side-to-side blade position is not precisely indicated. Machine position is determined, but not its orientation on the jobsite. However, a separate angle sensor can be incorporated into the machine to calculate the machine's slope. Furthermore, the accuracy of this system is dependent on the use of a site base station to provide correction factors. When a base station is used, the accuracy of an indicate-only system improves to approximately within 2–3 cm (**FIGURE 21-27**).

2. Installation of two GPS receivers on the top of masts of a blade or implement provides an accurate 3D, left–right, horizontal and vertical position of the blade. Using only one GPS receiver limits how the guidance system can sense the machine's position relative to the site design. Using two GPS receivers supplies the guidance system with two points of position, allowing it to calculate what angle the machine is on relative to the site plan. The GPS receivers allow the system to measure the machine's blade location within 1–2 cm accuracy for precise blade control and machine guidance. When grading, cross-slope information on steep slopes is provided even in high vibration environments. The front-to-back and side-to-side position of the machine can be integrated into tracking and guidance software (**FIGURE 21-28**).
3. **Inertial measurement systems** where **inertial measurement unit (IMU) sensors** are attached to the body of the machine, blade, or implement. When attached to the machine body, the positioning or spatial data as well as the known dimensions of the machine, enable the system to precisely calculate the position of a cutting blade at all times. IMUs and software model information provide a precise X-Y-Z position of the blade relative to the design

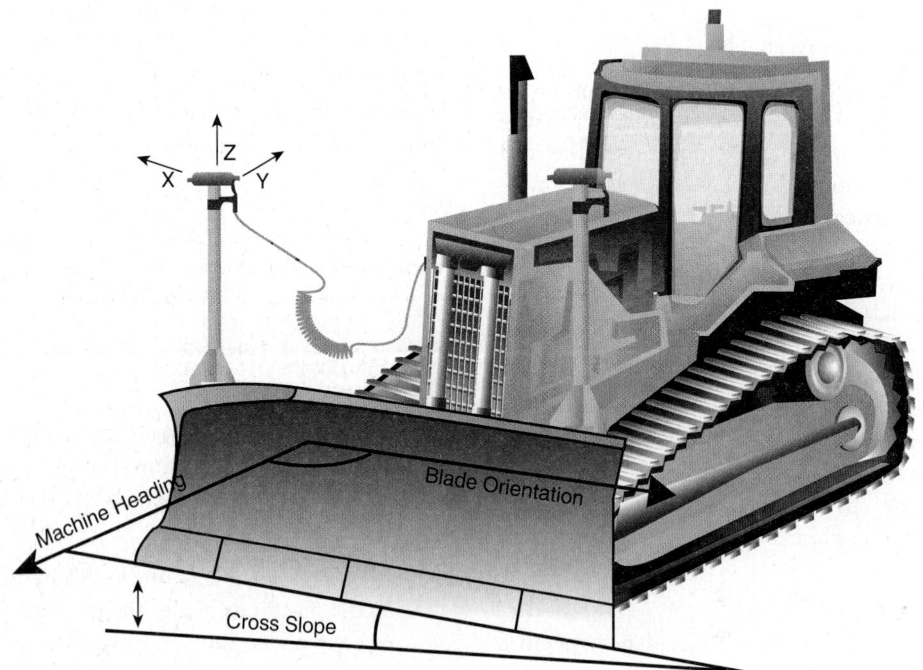

FIGURE 21-27 The use of one GPS antenna/receiver located on a machine blade provides 2D data.

FIGURE 21-28 Dual GPS antennas not only identify bucket and blade position but a machines centerline in relation to 3D site maps.

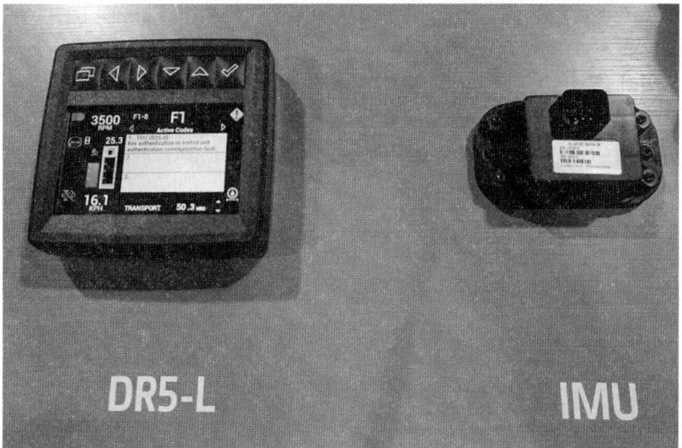

FIGURE 21-29 An inertial mass unit senses machine, implement boom or stick movement which is wirelessly transmitted to a control unit.

surface. IMUs communicate with each other as much as 100 times a second to provide a faster 3D mapping and machine response. Machines using IMUs are commonly referred to as "mast-less" GPS/GNSS systems (global navigation system) (FIGURE 21-29). However, IMUs will transmit information to the CAN, where it is integrated into the machine control system operating hydraulics and navigation or positioning systems.

4. Since GPS masts on the boom and stick are not practical, excavators use GPS technology along with **rotating ring laser angle sensors** integrated into the machine's boom, stick, and bucket. These sensors are a variety of IMU sensors and generally combine a ring-shaped arrangement of a laser with mirrors and a specialized laser light sensor or catcher that detects movement. Laser IMUs are sophisticated optical sensing devices that use a laser, two mirrors, and photo diodes that depend on principles of light diffusion (shifts from red to blue wavelengths) to detect speed and direction of movement. Data from these IMU sensor setups allow the operator to see how deeply they are digging and compare the actual bucket location to 3D topographical site designs on the cab terminal GPS display. Semi-automatic excavators will allow the machine to automatically raise the bucket to maintain the predetermined hole depth and will have an autostop function to prevent the bucket and boom function from lower beyond the predetermined hole depth (FIGURE 21-30).
5. Three **light bars** mounted in the machine cab of earthmoving machines can provide vertical and horizontal indicate-only guidance to the operator. Bright green indicates "on grade," and amber indicates "above" or "below" grade. In agriculture tractors, light bars can help a tractor steer between rows of crops accurately to prevent over-spraying or seeding errors.

> ▶ TECHNICIAN TIP
>
> The two most common failure points on GPS systems are (1) the cables connecting GPS antennas to control modules and (2) cab terminals that are improperly sealed, allowing water, dirt, and other elements into the units. Units are equipped with onboard diagnostic systems to identify problems. But since GPS antennas are expensive and prone to theft, most operators remove the antennas at the end of a shift to prevent theft. This situation creates significantly more wear and tear on coaxial cables connections to the units. To reduce downtime, spare antenna cables are commonly kept in stock, and terminal connections should receive a light coating of dielectric grease to prevent corrosion.

GPS System Limitations

While GPS systems can boost productivity by 30% or more, the acquisition cost on a large new machine equipped from the factory can be \$100,000 per machine. Retrofit GPS systems are available for lower costs on some machines and are transferrable from machine to machine. GPS cannot alone enable fully autonomous machine navigation and must be supplemented with other sensing systems.

When used, the GPS unit must have an unobstructed site line through the sky to satellites in order for signals to reach the antenna. This means GPS will not work underground or in street canyons where buildings obstruct signals. At high altitudes and latitudes, the satellite signals can weaken due to the orbital pathways used by satellites. The Russian-built GLONASS system using satellites located higher above the earth, which provides better coverage in these circumstances.

Strong electromagnetic waves can interfere with GPS signals as well. Unusual solar activity or high-voltage power lines, for example, can block satellite signals if machinery is operating beneath power lines.

Radar

Radar is an acronym for radio detection and ranging. It is a familiar technology with many applications that not only detects objects but also determines their distance, angle, and velocity relative to the radio transmitter. Just as light can be absorbed or reflected from the surface of an object to make it visible, radar uses electromagnetic waves reflected from an

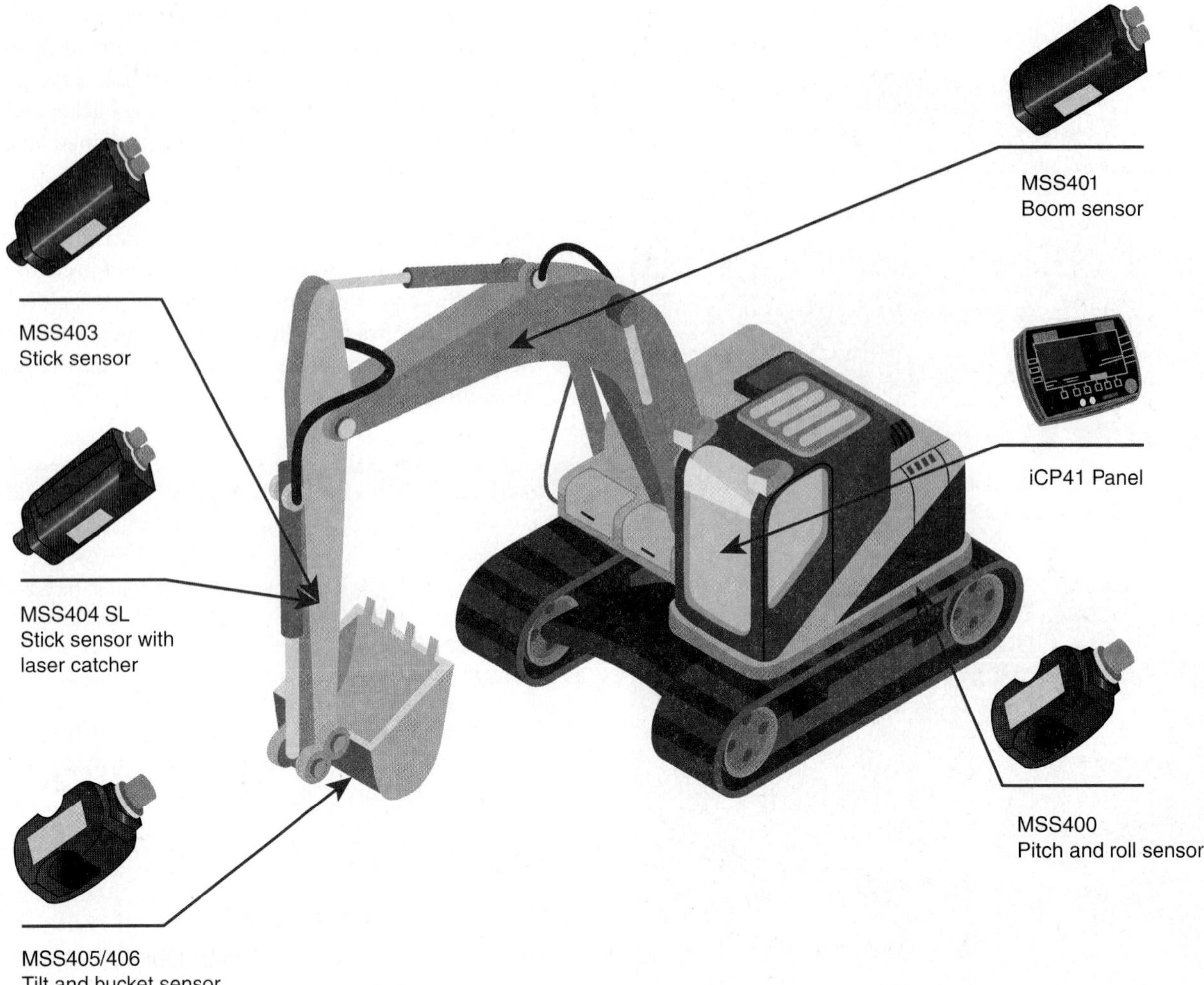

FIGURE 21-30 Laser sensors on the boom and stick provide precise machine coordinates for topographical 3D excavating.

object to make it visible to a radio receiver. A typical radar system will act as a transmitter and receiver of radio waves by sending pulses of radio waves for a few milliseconds and then stopping to listen for reflections of radio waves from an object. The radio receiver and signal processor analyzing the reflected radio waves can determine properties of the object, such as whether it is soft like a human being or hard like concrete. The time it takes for bounced signals to reach the receiver will provide information about the object's location and speed relative to the radar (**FIGURE 21-31**). A common application for simple radar devices is to measure ground speed (**FIGURE 21-32**).

Radar is preferred in guidance and navigation systems because it's computationally lighter than a camera and uses far less data than a **lidar** (radar using light detection principles). That means that comparatively less powerful computers are required to process and interpret the information from the radar. While radar signals are less accurate than others at detecting an object's position, radar can work better in more difficult conditions, such as in snow, rain, fog, and darkness. Additionally, various levels of automation will depend on radar to "cross-validate" or double-check what other sensors are seeing in order to predict motion or an object's properties. For example, a green tarp spread on a field or over the ground may be recognized by a camera as grass or a hazard to avoid. Radar, however, can differentiate the object from grass by characteristics of the signal that bounce off the tarp. Furthermore, when a tarp covers a hole or piece of equipment, the radar has the capability to see around or below the tarp.

Lidar

A new sensor technology often used in conjunction with radar is lidar. Lidar is an acronym for light detection and ranging, using pulsed laser beams rather than radio waves to measure distances. Using ultraviolet, visible, or near infrared light, it scans the environment to image a wide range of materials and objects. Metal, rocks, rain, chemical compounds, aerosols, and even clouds are scanned, and 3D images are produced by lidar. When combined with other data from radar, cameras, and GPS, high-resolution images containing enormous amounts of data can be used to navigate a machine as well as provide input to any other automated activity.

A lidar instrument consists principally of a laser redirected with a rotating mirror, which is used to scan the surrounding

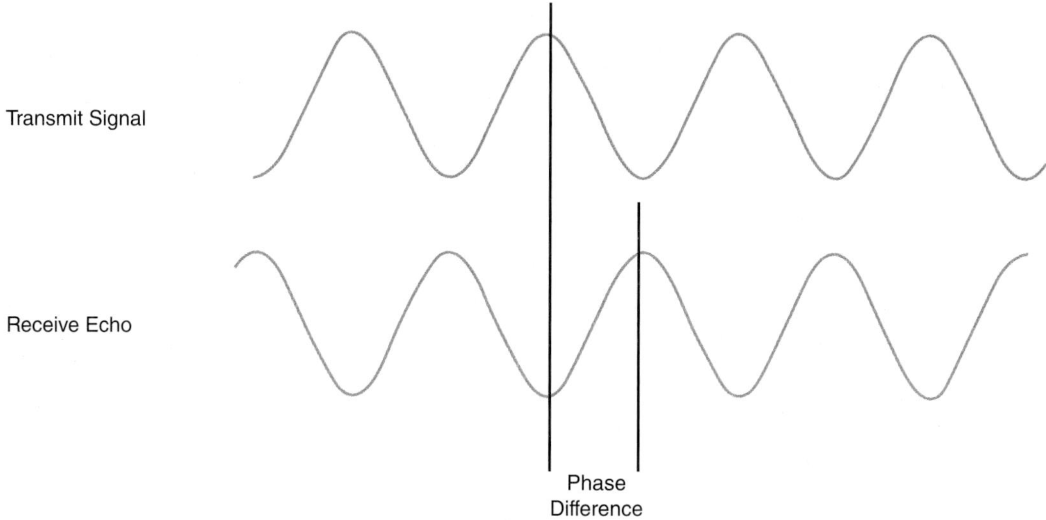

FIGURE 21-31 Radar and sonar calculate distance and speed based on the time difference between a wave emission and reflection.

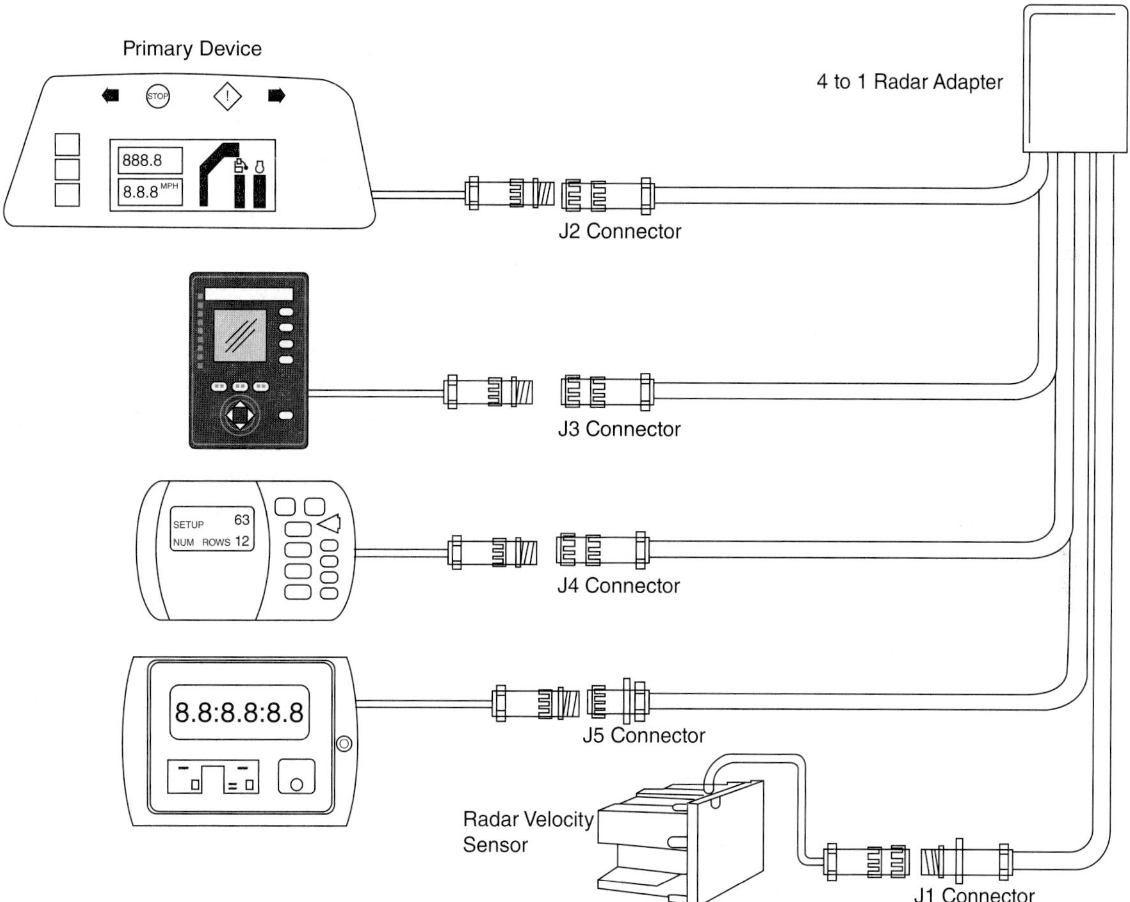

FIGURE 21-32 The four-to-one radar adapter allows one radar velocity sensor to provide a ground speed signal for a maximum of four separate devices, such as a control system, an instrument package, spreader, and a planter monitor.

environment. It is accompanied by a light-detecting receiver or scanner. A pair of lasers that beam light from the instrument through a mirror directs the beams at different angles to form a wide field of view called a layer. Each layer of a lidar is called a channel, and the signal from each individual channel creates a contour line. The rapidly rotating lidar mirror scans a 3D image of the surrounding environment from the contour line, much like an optical scanner. Adding more layers to a lidar improves its resolution, and many of today's lidars are produced with 16, 32, and 64 laser channels.

Lidar is currently an expensive technology: a 16-channel product costs close to $8,000. Adding multiple lidars to a machine makes the system even more costly to acquire. However, one collision avoidance systems application currently used by Volvo construction equipment uses a two-channel lidar and combines the data with three RGB (red, green, and blue) cameras. A terminal screen inside the cab provides the operator with a display showing the machine's location and the presence of other machines and pedestrians. If **RFID (radio frequency identification)** tags are embedded in the vests of workers, the cab terminal flashes and broadcasts a warning sound from the direction where a potential collision is detected.

When GPS signals are lost due to obstructions, the lidar can be used to guide a machine until the signals is re-established. Lidar sensors can also detect the edges of crop rows and distinguish crops from weeds and other foliage, which has great value for object detection systems.

Computer Stereo Vision

A machine's perception system needs to identify objects as well as gauge their speed and direction. To avoid the problem of producing what are called false negative detection (blindness to an object) and false positive detection (nonexistent ghost objects), more than one object sensing system should be used. Cameras provide a good method to cross-check or validate data from other sensors to prevent a catastrophe if a dangerous obstacle is not detected. Cameras are also relatively inexpensive. And unlike lidar, which see just gray scale images, cameras can see color that helps accurately classify or identify an object. This means cameras can see hazard flashers, clearance lights, brake lights, turn signals, and any other light on other vehicles. For reading road signage, a camera detecting red, green, and blue (RGB) is the best technology. In order to measure distance, two cameras or **stereo cameras** are necessary.

There are several drawbacks to camera technology. One is the difficulty of processing the amount of information produced by a camera that uses software. Cameras are computationally intensive. Lighting variations, such as when objects move into a shadow, can confuse cameras as well. This means they should have additional lighting to work well and not rely on just reflected light sources (**FIGURE 21-33**).

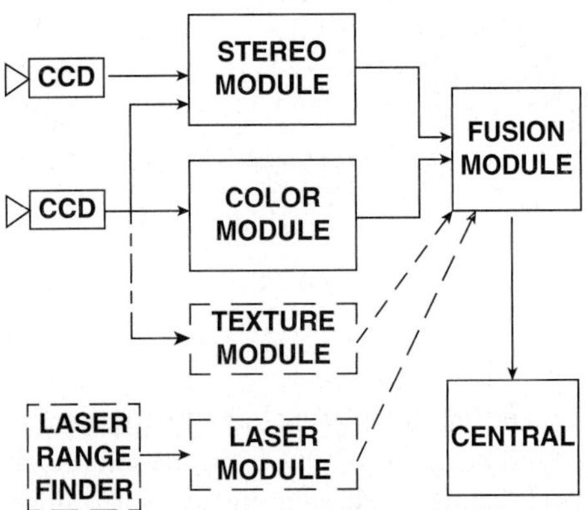

FIGURE 21-33 A schematic view of processing functions using color cameras integrated with an automated navigating system.

Two cameras providing binocular vision are required to measure depth or provide stereo vision using the principle of parallax. With parallax estimates, the shift in location of an object as seen between two different camera angles enables the calculation of a precise distance of an object from the cameras. Cameras can supply not just images but also software that can perform two basic types of analysis of the data. One is machine vision, which refers to a simple analysis of digital images to identify features, edges, detect motion, and motion parallax, depends on two cameras or binocular images to estimate distance. A tomato-picking robot uses edge, shape, and color information to locate the tomato and stereo vision for depth.

Another capability provided by binocular camera vision is computer vision. **Computer vision** refers a more difficult challenge of recognizing and interpreting the significance of objects. For example, differentiating between a human and a lamp post is more difficult than simply locating the two different objects. Even more difficult is discerning where the human's attention is and whether they are walking into a machine's path.

Radio Frequency Identification

While not directly integrated into automated machine technology, radio frequency identification (RFID) technology is used on the connected machine and work site. Tags are typically attached to equipment as part of an inventory tracking system and can be associated with telematics data. Safety systems used on machinery can sense RFID tags attached to worker clothing and can be used to alert a machine to the proximity to a worker.

RFID technology uses electromagnetic fields to automatically identify and track objects attached to tags. Information about the object, such as a blade or machine, is electronically stored on the tag and can be read by an RFID reader. RFID technology can be classified into two basic types—passive and active. Passive tags are powered as they collect energy from a nearby RFID reader's radio wave emissions. The RFID tag reader will ask the tag to supply information using radio signals containing electromagnetic energy to interrogate the tag. This energy is used to power up the tag and supply data to the reader. To work, then, a passive RFID must receive a radio signal with a power level approximately a thousand times stronger than that used for signal transmission. Naturally, these tags have an effective working range of just 3 feet and are susceptible to electromagnetic interference. However, newer tags using ultra-high-frequency signal readers are reported to operate up to 80 feet. A subset of RFID passive technology is seen in credit cards using near field communication chips (NFC). These cards contain a more secure type of RFID technology, but the principles are identical.

Active tags have an internal power supply, such as a battery, and can operate at hundreds of meters from the RFID reader. Unlike a passive RFID tag, an active RFID periodically transmits an identification signal. Bluetooth devices and Internet routers can read data from active tags. These types of tags do require battery replace from time to time (**FIGURE 21-34**).

RFID active tags can be simple, costing just a few cents, or more complex devices. The tag requires an integrated circuit for collecting and processing information, plus radio circuits

FIGURE 21-34 Inside an active type RFID tag.

FIGURE 21-35 An RFID tag attached to a machine blade used to identify equipment.

for receiving and transmitting radio signals. To collect DC power from a tag reader signal, passive tags will temporarily store DC current too. RFID tag memory can be either fixed with only a factory-assigned serial number or programmable memory that has a read/write capability. Specific equipment or object data can be written to the programmable RFID tag (**FIGURE 21-35**).

▶ Telematics

K21005

The term telematics is a combination of telecommunications and informatics—the science of processing data for storage and retrieval. Telematics is a technology field encompassing wireless communication, telecommunications, machine technology, onboard networks, and the use of the Internet. Essentially, it collects information from a machine or piece of equipment and sends it to a website, where it can be viewed and analyzed. Telematics systems installed on machines typically combine GPS technology with a communication connection to the onboard network to locate the machine, monitor its operation, and log and report data through Wi-Fi or cellular networks. A set of data from telematics systems is typically accessed through a subscription-based website providing data on one or more machines made by different original equipment manufacturers (OEMs). Equipment manufacturers are installing telematics systems as standard equipment on an increasing number of their products each year.

Common data points include

- GPS location
- fuel consumption
- idle time
- fault codes and warning messages for remote diagnostics
- engine hours
- route activity
- driving behavior
- vehicle utilization
- distance.

Using telematics systems to record simple factors such as machine hours and to measure idle time enables equipment managers to maintain preventive maintenance schedules, increase security through GPS location and geofencing, and use geofencing to help allocate machine time costs to a particular jobsite. Far more advanced analytics of machine operation can be achieved by adding additional sensors beyond all the sensor data available to the onboard network.

Until 2010, each OEM had its own unique telematics standard, which meant that a Deere, Cat, or Komatsu telematics provider couldn't provide information to the same owner for other machines in the fleet. The Association of Equipment Management Professionals (AEMP) developed the industry's first telematics standard for off-road heavy equipment. This meant that regardless of the machine brand, its telematics modules could supply equipment data to a single web-based telematics provider. This meant that telematics data wasn't limited to a single brand of machine used with a mixed-brand fleet of other equipment. Caterpillar, Komatsu, Volvo CE, John Deere Construction & Forestry, OEM Data Delivery, Navman Wireless, Topcon, and Trimble are able to deliver basic telematics data in a standard XML format (a programming language used by the Internet).

Telematics Standards

The **AEMP Telematics Data Standard** also provided the end user with the freedom to use one telematics service provider to retrieve data from any other rather than require a unique provider for each brand of machine. Version 1.2 of the standard includes 19 data fields in addition to SAE and ISO-bus fault code reporting capability. Some types of equipment are not yet covered by the standards, such as some agriculture equipment, cranes, mobile elevating work platforms, air compressors, and other niche products.

Telematics Modules

Telematics equipped machines will use an onboard electronic control module to collect, store, and transmit machine data over cellphone networks. However, most advanced modules have support for other wireless communication options, such as Wi-Fi, classic Bluetooth, and Bluetooth low energy. Both Bluetooth and Wi-Fi can operate concurrently since the modules will internally switch between Bluetooth and Wi-Fi when needed, to prevent any simultaneous radio transmissions. Modules are designed to provide both wired and wireless access to the CAN network of a machine through WLAN/Bluetooth (**FIGURE 21-36**).

▶ Remote Control

K21007

Remote controls operating diesel-powered load-haul-dump (LHD) vehicles first appeared in underground mines beginning in the 1970s. Today, they are used on many types of construction equipment in order to enhance operator safety and improve production efficiency. On worksites where the operator may be in potentially more danger due to conditions such as falling debris, steep slopes, or unusually dusty conditions, operators can remove themselves from the machine and operate it at a safer distance. A safer distance may be line of site, where the operator controls the machine using an alternate duplicate set of controls while watching the machine. For some remote-controlled machines needing to operate beyond the range of line of sight, video cameras can be mounted on the machine to enable the operator to observe what the machine is doing and how it is responding to inputs from remote controls. Since remote controls do not provide an operator with feedback such as hearing and feeling how the engine and hydraulic controls are responding to inputs, advanced use of additional sensors on the machine can be used to record and transfer information to a clean, quiet, climate-controlled remote workstation (**FIGURE 21-37**). System information such as engine or machine travel speed, system pressure and temperature values, machine and position derived from pitch, and yaw and roll sensors can report orientation. Workstations can use remote-control software so that the operator can view equipment action with a 3D display. Built-in mechanisms in the machine controls can even provide mechanisms for force feedback on acceleration, braking, and the bucket operation to enhance the ability of an operator to work remotely.

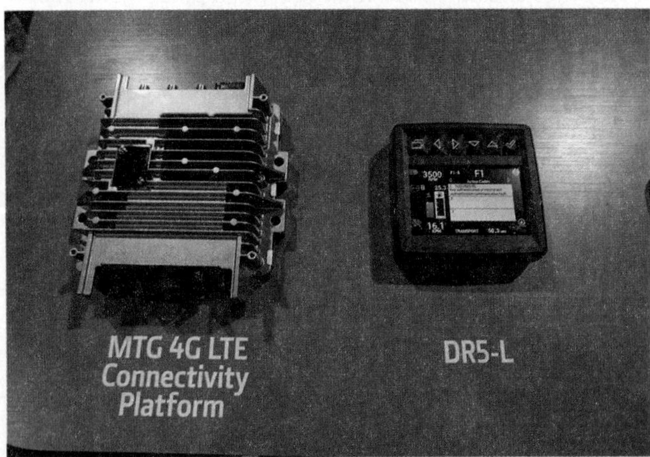

FIGURE 21-36 A cellular network combined with Internet connectivity connects to the machines CAN network to supply telematics suppliers with data.

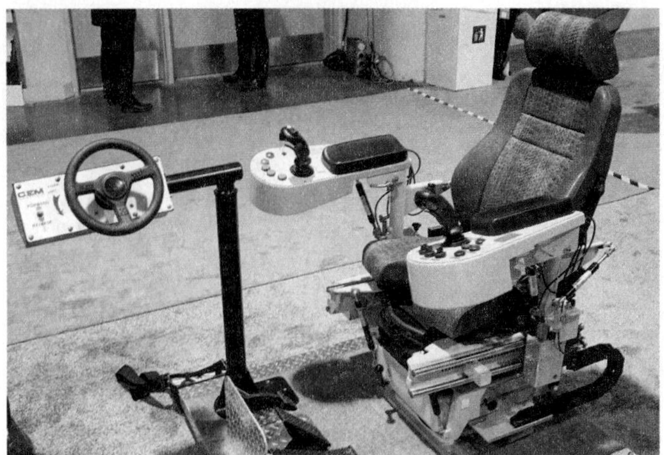

FIGURE 21-37 A remote-control work station duplicates machine controls to enable remote operation. Note the seat mechanism, which moves back and forth to provide sensory feedback from the machine.

Radio Control

Early portable remote-control receiver and transmitter units used coded radio signals to prevent unintentional operation of other equipment or interference from nearby radios transmitters. This meant the radio frequencies of the transmitting and receiving radio had to match to work. The receivers were electrically connected with a machine's electric, hydraulic, or pneumatic systems to control functions such as steering, braking, and load handling. While most systems still depend on radio signals to conduct two-way exchanges of information, the signals are digitized for safety reasons and to exchange more data than analog signals can allow. Digitizing the radio signals enables very secure transmitter/receiver communication, which can tolerate high levels of interference. They also permit bidirectional communication to allow the transmitter to validate correct data transfer between the machine and remote controls. In underground mining, the signals are typically sent over Wi-Fi routers using Internet protocols.

On any jobsite or fleet operation, it's important that remote controls have a standardized configuration in terms of how they control work for forward, reverse, and left and right orientation as well as for emergency stop, fire suppression, and other buttons or joystick controls. Mixing transmitters with a different

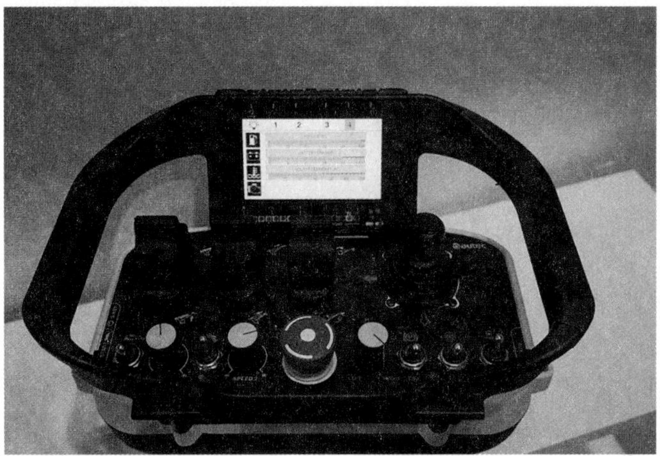

FIGURE 21-38 This radio remote-control unit has a large red emergency stop button.

set of controls can lead to errors when operators move between different controls. When the joysticks of a remote console are released, no forward or reverse signals are transmitted and the machine should immediately stop rather than roll on. Controls will use an emergency stop switch that shuts down the machine when it is pushed (**FIGURE 21-38**).

When used by an operator for line of site, portable transmitters should contain a tilt switch that ensures the transmitter will stop the machine if the operator were to trip and fall. Tilt switches should deactivate the machine when the control held by the operator moves more than 30 degrees or more from level.

Software such as Cat's Command for underground mining is capable of three levels of operational control, which is enhanced with video from onboard cameras to provide a real-time view of the machine location and operation.

Basic or tele-remote mode allows the operator to control the machine through line of sight. In copilot mode, the operator can monitor equipment locations in a mine plan and by using joysticks to give the machine directional input. Onboard perception systems such as radar, combined with radio network infrastructure providing a mine map, enable the machine to self-steer along a safe path. The most advanced element of control, namely autopilot, allows the machine to autonomously dump and return to the operator, who takes over control of the loading process. Zones within the mine operations area can be configured to regulate machine speed and to establish boundaries at required points. At any time, full operator control of the system can be obtained through tele-remote mode.

Converting a machine to remote operation is relatively simple in the latest models. On smaller Cat construction machines, such as skid steers, approximately an hour is required to install Cat's RemoteTask system. With the system—developed in collaboration with TORC Robotics, Inc. (TORC)—the machine can switch from manual to remote mode at the turn of a key switch. The system is transferrable between units.

▶ Automated Steering

K21007

An automatic guidance system is similar to a manual guidance system, except that the task of steering is done not by the operator but instead by an application-specific computer that operates machine controls by using special algorithms. To engage the system, the operator will commonly push an engagement switch to allow the system to take control, thereby self-navigating or guiding the vehicle along a calculated safe pathway. Manual control is resumed by simply moving the steering wheel, which is sensed by a pressure change in the hydraulic steering circuits. When autosteering is engaged, the steering controller sends signals to the steering system actuators. The machine path is cross-checked for accuracy using an anticipated GPS position for the vehicle's position. A steering angle sensor measures the turning angle of the steerable wheels, to provide closed-loop control to the steering controller (**FIGURE 21-39**).

Typical Components of Modern GPS Automatic Guidance Systems

Vehicle steering actuators such as the manual override detector receive electrical signals from the steering controller. In wheeled machines, the steerable front wheels will change angle or direction. Tracked machines will alter the speed of the tracks and move the machine according to principles of differential steering. Hydraulic actuators are typically linear actuators or proportional electrohydraulic valves mounted in hydraulic manifolds. A sensor integrated into the control valve body is called **a linear voltage differential transformer (LVDT)**. Essentially, the sensor supplies a voltage signal corresponding to a change in length. When proportional electrohydraulic valves are used, the movement of the spool valve is proportional to the amount of electrical current passed though the sensor's armature coils. As electric current flow increases or decreases through the sensor, spool valve movement is sensed, which in turn is used to calculate the change in the direction and rate of flow to an actuator. In hydrostatic drive machines using hydraulic drive motors at each wheel or track final drive, oil flow through proportional hydraulic control valves using LVDT sensors can differentially steer a machine.

Another type of valve used in steering systems is a closed-loop control valve that also uses a LVDT to measure and precisely position a spool valve. When the spool valve position matches a commanded position, it will cause the machine to steer in a particular direction. Using closed-loop spool position control enables very precise and consistent valve positioning relative to the flow of electrical current (**FIGURE 21-40**).

Primarily for safety reasons, steering interface controls use a manual override system to sense when the operator is providing a steering input by moving the steering wheel of the machine. A pressure sensor in the steering load sense line or a flow sensor that monitors flow in or out of the steering control valve will trip the system and disable the automated guidance system. Steering angle sensors mounted directly in the steering

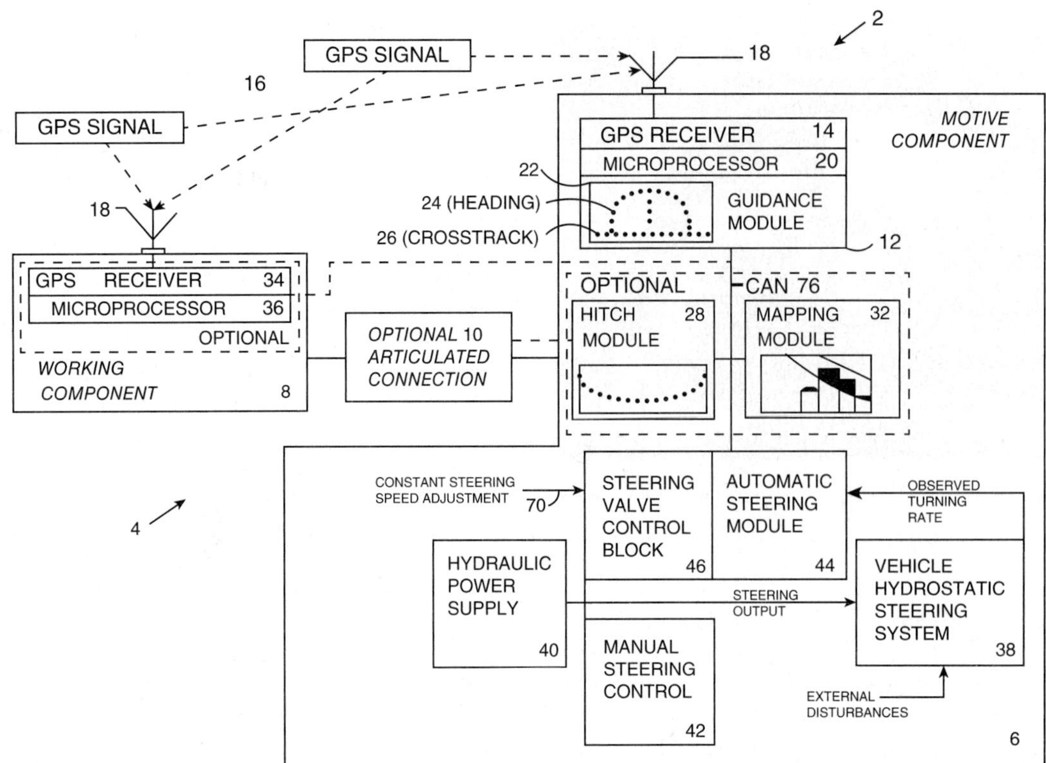

FIGURE 21-39 A functional schematic of a GPS-controlled steering system that includes implement steering through the hitch integrated into the tractor's steering control.

FIGURE 21-40 This electronically controlled servo valve controlling pressure, direction or force uses a dual 2–stage pilot valve with closed-loop feedback of the spool valve. Both the pilot valve and spool valve maintain precise position control using linear voltage differential transformers (LVDTs) located at the right die end of the valves.

FIGURE 21-41 Eaton's new wireless steering control valve is intended for autonomous machine control. The wireless transceiver is located on the right of the valve block.

column can perform a similar role whenever the steering wheel is moved by the operator.

CAN-Based Steering

Over the last few years, machines are increasingly equipped with steer-by-wire CAN-controlled steering systems. Inputs are supplied not only through the sensors of the steering control module but received from other modules on the machines, such as from implement control modules. These systems have the advantage of not requiring a parallel and redundant hydraulic system to support both manual and automated steering (**FIGURE 21-41**).

Electric Motor–Driven Steering Wheels

Electric motor drive systems that turn the steering wheel use GPS automated guidance strategies. An example of this system is the Trimble EZ-Steer, introduced in 2004. In the Trimble system, the steering shaft in the steering wheel column is turned

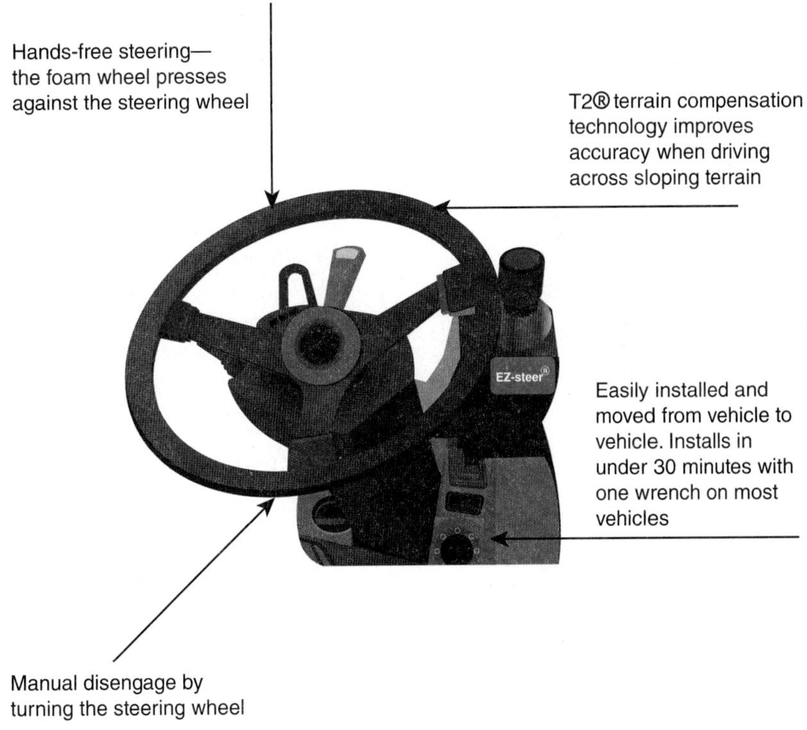
Hands-free steering—
the foam wheel presses
against the steering wheel
T2® terrain compensation
technology improves
accuracy when driving
across sloping terrain
EZ-steer
Easily installed and
moved from vehicle to
vehicle. Installs in
under 30 minutes with
one wrench on most
vehicles
Manual disengage by
turning the steering wheel

FIGURE 21-42 Trimble's EZ-Steer system uses a foam roller on an electric motor to operate the steering wheel.

by a small electric motor. These systems are sometimes called assisted steering systems and have become enormously popular as easy-to-install, retrofit systems (**FIGURE 21-42**).

Installation time is short, because it has few parts and does not require advanced skills. Systems such as EZ-Steer are easily transferred from one machine to another. One drawback of the torque output from an electric motor drive system is that it requires more time to turn a vehicle at a given angle than when using a hydraulic or steer-by-wire system. As a result of a slower turning and correction speed, there is lower accuracy than with hydraulic drive-by-wire systems. Manual override of these systems is achieved by monitoring current flow to the electric motor. Resisting motor direction, such as when the operator grabs the wheel and turns it in another direction, causes the electrical current flow to sharply increase to the motor. In that case, the control module detects this above-normal current flow and disconnects the motor.

Linear Sensors and Smart Cylinders

Linear movement sensors use a variety of technologies to transform length change into a voltage signal. A common approach converting length to voltage is to use a variable-resistance linear potentiometer. One advantage of these types of sensors is that they are typically easier to fasten on the cylinder than steering linkage, which leads to more accurate position measurement. Another variation of linear sensors is the smart cylinder. These cylinders locate the position sensor inside a hydraulic steering cylinder. Replacing a conventional hydraulic linear-actuated cylinder with a smart cylinder enables the use of a voltage signal to provide closed-loop feedback to the controller regarding steering angle (**FIGURE 21-43**).

• Lower energy consumption

FIGURE 21-43 An electric linear actuator provides closed-loop feedback regarding steering position.

Terrain Compensation

Terrain compensation is important to autoguidance systems to compensate for the effect that varying terrain altitudes can have on the machine's position as measured by the GPS receiver. The effect of roll can be very significant when the GPS antenna is mounted on the cab roof. If uncorrected, rolling and changes in altitudes can become a major source of steering error.

Error takes place often because GPS coordinates are measured at the roof of the vehicle and not at the ground where work is performed. Working side slopes or when the machine is tilted to the left or right causes an antenna, installed at a height of 3 m (about 9 ft), to translate 1 degree of roll into 5 cm (about 2") at ground level. When terrain compensation correction is applied, the vehicle's roll, yaw, and pitch (also referred to as the vehicle's attitude) can be measured and corrected (**FIGURE 21-44**).

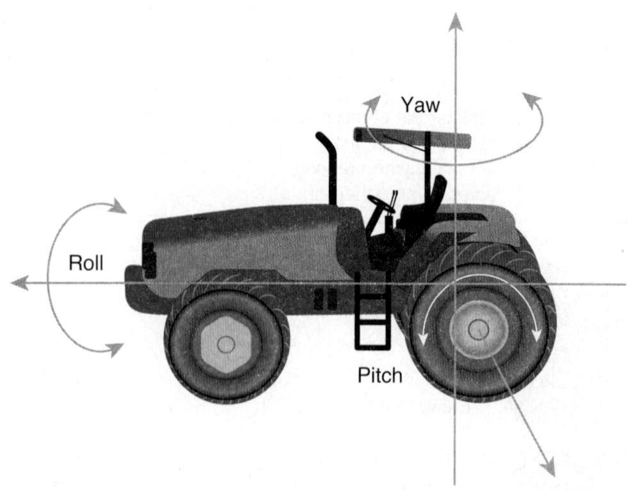

FIGURE 21-44 Yaw pitch and roll interfere with the GPS's capability to accurately sense machine position.

▶ Machine Safety with Radio and Other Wireless Technology

S21002

Technicians can be expected to install or repair a variety of technologies that use wireless radio communication. When servicing machines, the following guideless are important.

1. Wi-Fi safety
   - Do not install a retrofit self-steering or autosteer device on a machine or use automated applications where life depends on the proper (fault-free) operation of the device.
   - Do not enable autosteer or other automated applications unless adequate wireless network availability such as WLAN/Bluetooth is available. Failures or malfunctions of the device can lead to erroneous data transmission.
   - Never depend entirely on wireless devices for essential communications, because data transmission cannot be guaranteed at all times and under all conditions.
   - Do not use wireless devices in safety-related applications, since most devices that operate using radio signals are not approved for use in safety-related applications.
   - Do not operate a wireless device until systems are checked for conformity with legal requirements.
   - Wireless devices must not be allowed to operate until after qualified technicians and electricians with advanced knowledge of vehicle and CAN electrical systems have inspected them.
2. Antenna safety—dangers due to absorption of radio frequency (RF) energy

   Mobile communication devices may pose a health risk when operated in the close proximity of an operator. Energy in the radio waves is suspected of producing negative impacts on human health. The following lists some precautions to exercise during equipment retrofits:
   - Install the antenna(s) used for wireless devices, to provide a separation distance of at least 20 cm (8") from all persons.
   - Do not operate wireless devices in conjunction with and do not co-locate them with any other antenna or transmitter.
3. Electronic equipment interference

   Electronic equipment can cause dangerous interference from RF energy. Wireless devices receive and transmit RF energy when switched on. Interference can occur if they are used near to TV sets, radios, computers, or equipment that is inadequately shielded from RF energy. Follow any special regulations, and always switch off the wireless unit wherever it is forbidden to use (i.e., during blasting operations) or when you suspect that it may cause interference or damage.
4. Machine wiring guidelines
   - To protect wiring installation and other electrical wiring harnesses from mechanical abuse, run wires in flexible metal or plastic conduits.
   - Use wire rated for 85°C (185°F), with abrasion-resistant insulation, whereas wire rated for 105°C (221°F) should be used near hot surfaces.
   - Use a wire size that is appropriate for the current capacity of the module connector.
   - Separate high-current wires, such as solenoids, lights, alternators, or fuel pumps, from sensor and other induction-sensitive input wires.
   - Run wires along the inside of, or close to, metal machine surfaces where possible. This provides an EMI/RFI shield that minimizes the effects of electromagnetic interference.
   - Do not run wires near sharp metal corners. Use rubberized grommets to protect wiring routed around sharp bends and corners.
   - Do not run wires near hot machine members.
   - Provide strain relief for all wires.
   - Avoid running wires near moving or vibrating components.
   - Ground electronic modules to a dedicated conductor of sufficient size that is connected directly to the battery (−).

Wrap-Up

Ready for Review

- Automation, which is the use of control systems that reduce or eliminate human intervention to operate machinery, is a rapidly evolving technology sector that has made its way into the off-road equipment industry.
- Farm tractors, mine trucks, and bulldozers with fully autonomous control systems have been on the market since 2013.
- Mining equipment has used remote-control systems where an operator can use a set of radio controls that electronically duplicate actual machine controls, enabling operators to work at a distance and avoid potentially hazardous worksite conditions.
- Smart-iron refers to off-road equipment that integrates some level of telematic, semi-autonomous, or fully autonomous machine control.
- Automating machine steering, navigation, positioning, object avoidance, implement control, or any driving function can also increase worker and site safety, extend machine durability, and provide a wealth of features and data to equipment managers. Any degree of automation can allow the operator to pay more attention to complex machine tasks.
- Machine automation doesn't always imply fully autonomous operation. Instead, it refers to varying degrees of machine operation performed without human intervention.
- Telematically connected machines can transmit machine data collected from the onboard CAN, where it can be collected, analyzed, and viewed through an Internet portal. Data are typically transmitted via the Internet or cell phone signals and includes any measurable information on the machine, such as GPS data, fault information, and data from engines, powertrains, work implements, and hydraulic system controls.
- Onboard machine networks are important for enabling technology for autonomous machine operation. Onboard networks are formed by connecting various machine electronic control modules to communicate and exchange information.
- One of the primary reasons for constructing onboard networks is to reduce the need for complex wiring and redundant sensors. Sensor data collected by individual modules can be shared across a large number of devices connected into a network.
- Onboard networks enhance machine engine control unit (ECU) information-processing capabilities that are distributed over many modules, which enhances the power of the total network. Instead of numerous modules performing the same task—such as processing speed data—one module does it, which frees the processors in other ECMs to perform work.
- The SAE and ISO have established standards for onboard network design and function. While both standards are similar in operation, they use different data link connectors, software, and communication protocols.
- GPS systems use satellites to accurately identify the position of a machine. More precise locations of implements, blades, booms, and machine sticks require a land-based fixed location signal to correct error in GPS signals that are derived only from satellites. The signal correction generally requires a subscription from a signal or telematics service provider.
- GPS units must have unobstructed site lines through the sky to satellites for signals to reach the antenna. This means that GPS will not work underground or in street canyons where buildings obstruct signals.
- GPS modules connected to the CAN enable machine systems to integrate GPS data into machine hydraulic control, steering, and navigation functions.
- Autonomous control systems used by off-road equipment include varying levels of technology and operating strategies:
    - remote control (RC) using line-of-site radio signals
    - telematics or tele-operated control
    - self-steering control
    - self-steering + GPS navigation self-navigation + object avoidance system
    - platooning—machine-to-machine communication.
- Machines equipped with GPS/GNSS have two options when using satellite positioning. One is indicate mode, which uses data produced during machine operation to provide the feedback to the operator who controls blades, shovels, or implements control. In the second option, or fully automatic mode, the machine's hydraulics are electronically controlled with no driver intervention to make blade or implement adjustments.
- Installation of one GPS antenna mounted on the machine's blade enables the operator to use an indicate-only system to view site cross sections in 2D, elevations, and blade position diagrams. Machine position is determined, but not its orientation on the jobsite.
- Installation of 2 GPS receivers on the top of masts of a blade or implement provides an accurate 3D, left–right, horizontal and vertical position of the blade. Two GPS receivers supply the guidance system with two points of position, allowing it to calculate what angle the machine is at relative to the site plan.
    - Two GPS receivers allow the system to measure the machine's blade location within 1–2 cm accuracy for precise blade control and machine guidance.
- A CAES enables the GPS guidance system to be integrated into the machine's hydraulic implement controls.
- Inertial measurement systems use IMU sensors attached to the body of the machine, blade, or implement. When

attached to the machine body, the positioning or spatial data and the known dimensions of the machine enable the system to precisely calculate the position of a cutting blade at all times.

- IMU sensors using laser technology are used on excavators since using GPS masts on the boom and stick of an excavator is not practical.
- LVDT sensors provide closed-loop feedback control for steering and hydraulic system control valves. Essentially, these sensors supply a voltage signal corresponding to a change in length.
- Electric motor drive systems can be retrofitted to machines, which turn the steering wheel using GPS automated guidance strategies.
- Terrain compensation is important to autoguidance systems for them to compensate for the effect that varying terrain altitudes can have on the machine's position as measured by the GPS.
- When installing antennas, receivers, and network modules for retrofit systems, caution must be used to prevent interference caused by the energy from radio signals and to protect the operator from unnecessary exposure to radio energy.

Key Terms

AEMP telematics data standard A communication protocol enabling telematic end users with the freedom to use only one telematics service provider for different brands or makes of machinery.

automatic mode The machine's hydraulics are electronically controlled with no driver intervention to make blade or implement adjustments.

automation The use of control systems that reduce or eliminate human intervention to operate machinery.

binocular cameras Elements of an object detection system required to measure depth or provide stereo vision using the principle of parallax.

CANbus A two-wire network typology that connects modules in parallel.

closed-loop control A process where the operation of an output device is monitored and controlled by a sensor that provides feedback directly to an electronic control unit.

computer-aided earth-moving system (CAES) Integrates GPS data into the machine's hydraulic controls and guidance to autonomously operate a machine's hydraulic implements, such as buckets, shovels, booms, sticks, and blades. As the worksite features change, the machine transmits data about the work it's completed to enable software to update worksite maps, rendering the latest terrain and site conditions.

computer vision A more difficult challenge of recognizing and interpreting the significance of objects using binocular cameras.

controller area networks (CAN) A distributed type of network communication control system. This means no single central control module is used on a machine. Instead, each module or node on the network has processing capabilities that can not only initiate electrical control for faster response but also synchronize their operation with other network modules.

dead reckoning systems Are a navigation system that depends on only vehicle sensors such as speed, steering angle, and even a magnetic compass to guide a machine. A radio-operated node or signal transmitter may provide a reference point.

differential voltage A signal processing technique used on CANs to transmit serial data with the least amount of signal noise.

fully autonomous A machine control system capable of sensing its environment and navigating without human input.

global positioning system (GPS) also called the global navigation satellite system (GNSS) A worldwide radio-navigation system using satellites to communicate with earth-based radio receivers.

geofencing A feature provided by a telematic service supplier to alert a subscriber to movement of a machine outside a particular geographical area or during expected operating hours.

humans in the loop (HITL) People who provide assistance with autonomous function or other machine support, such as a repair technician.

indicate-only mode A computer-aided earth-moving technique that supplies machine data to a cab terminal, providing feedback about the position of a blade or implement.

inertial guidance systems A type of machine navigation that uses a known starting point, orientation, and velocity to guide a machine. Inertial guidance systems use onboard sensors or instruments that measure speed, direction, and rate of acceleration.

inertial measurement units (IMU) sensors Sensors attached to the body of the machine, blade, or implement. When attached to the machine body, the positioning or spatial data and the known dimensions of the machine enable the system to precisely calculate the position of a cutting blade at all times.

ISO11783 also called ISO-bus A network protocol developed in Germany and used primarily by European agriculture and forestry machines.

J-1939-2 An SAE network protocol used by agricultural and forestry vehicles.

J-1939 An SAE network protocol for off-road HD commercial vehicles

linear voltage differential transformer (LVDT) A linear hydraulic control sensor that supplies a voltage signal corresponding to a change in actuator length. When proportional electrohydraulic valves are used, the movement of the spool valve is proportional to the amount of electrical current passed though the sensor's armature coils.

lidar An acronym for light detection and ranging, which uses pulsed laser beams rather than radio waves to measure distances.

multiplexing A concept where the transmission of more than one electrical signal or message takes place over a single wire or pair of wires.

object or collision avoidance systems Systems that identify objects such as a boulder or a deep hole capable of damaging or even swallowing a machine.

platooning A method of controlling the operation of multiple machines performing the same tasks in a farm field with a single lead machine. Platooning is enabled through machine-to-machine communication or an inter-vehicle communication system and uses only a single operator to control the operation of multiple machines in an agriculture field operation.

precision farmer techniques Farming strategies that use technology such as automated machinery to precisely cultivate, seed, fertilize, and harvest crops.

radar An acronym for radio detection and ranging. It detects objects and determines their distance, angle, and velocity relative to the radio transmitter.

real-time kinematic (RTK) or dual frequency receivers GPS receivers that use a subscription-based signal correction for satellite GPS. RTK can provide positional accuracy to the decimeter or ½ inch on a year-to-year basis.

remote control A machine control system where an operator can use a set of controls that electronically duplicates actual machine controls, enabling the operator to work at a distance.

RFID technology Electromagnetic fields that automatically identify and track objects attached to tags. Information about the object, such as a blade or machine, is electronically stored on the tag and can be read by an RFID reader.

rotating ring laser angle sensors A positional type IMU sensor integrated into the machine's body, boom, stick, and bucket. There are a variety of IMU sensors, but are generally a rotation ring laser combined with mirrors and a specialized laser light sensor or catcher that detects movement.

SAE J-3016 The SAE standard that classifies the level of autonomous control of on-highway vehicles.

smart-iron Off-road equipment integrating some level of telematic, semis autonomous, or fully autonomous machine control.

telematics The transmission and reception of information from remote objects. Typically, GPS signals and onboard network data are transmitted over cell phone or satellite communication systems. The data are analyzed to supply machine information through a web portal.

terrain compensation A feature used by autoguidance systems to compensate for the effect of machine roll, pitch and yaw that varying terrain conditions can have on the machine's altitude position as measured by the roof mounted antenna of a GPS receiver.

triangulation A method using three or more satellite signals to locate position. Triangulation works when a receiver connects with signals transmitted from each satellite at precisely the same time. Since the satellites are located at different distances from the receiver, the signals will arrive at slightly different times.

virtual terminal A screen mounted in the tractor used so that the operator can control connected implements. Modules on ISO-bus machines can transmit what are called virtual objects along the CANbus to be displayed on the virtual terminal.

wireless CAN bridge A connection between the controlled area network of one machine and another. Platooning uses the CAN bridge for machine-to-machine communication, collecting data from the CANbus in one machine and wirelessly transmitting the information to the CANbus in the trailing machine.

Review Questions

1. An automated off-road machine describes off-road equipment that ______________.
   a. is capable of sensing and navigating its environment without human input
   b. is remote controlled
   c. has telematic capabilities
   d. has reduced requirements for human control
2. Which of the following descriptions best describes how the blade or bucket is controlled on a machine that has a computer-aided earth-moving system (CAES)?
   a. The blade or bucket is automatically guided using telematic signals transmitted from a base station.
   b. In automatic mode, the operator manipulates hydraulic controls while guided by a cab terminal.
   c. A 3D site plan will automatically guide the machine to shape site contours.
   d. A 3D site plan will either guide the operator or automatically control the bucket or blade.
3. Which of the following standards is used to designate a machine's level of autonomous capabilities?
   a. J-1939-2
   b. J-3016
   c. ISO11783
   d. There is no standard for off-road machinery.
4. Which of the following technologies will be used by a machine using a dead reckoning navigational system?
   a. A GPS receiver
   b. Vehicle speed sensor
   c. A CAN bridge
   d. Cellular, Bluetooth or a WLAN connection
5. Which of the following technologies is essential in order to enable platooning of machines?
   a. Radar
   b. Lidar
   c. A CAN bridge
   d. Radio remote control
6. What is the minimum number of satellites signals a GPS receiver needs to identify the location of a machine?
   a. 30
   b. 4
   c. 3
   d. 1
7. To obtain positional measurement accuracy from a GPS system required for machine navigation and positioning

buckets or blades to an accuracy of less than a ½ inch (1.27 cm) error, which of the following is required?
 a. Signals from four or more satellites
 b. Two GPS receivers
 c. A subscription service to correct satellite signal error
 d. Two different GPS systems such as GLONASS or Galileo
8. To accurately position the centerline of a machine used by computer-aided earth-moving systems, which of the following is a minimum technology requirement?
 a. A single GPS receiver
 b. Inertial measurement unit (IEU) sensors
 c. Electric-over-hydraulic controls
 d. Two GPS receivers
9. Closed-loop feedback control of linear type actuators often use ___________.
 a. linear voltage differential transformer (LVDT) sensors
 b. inertial measurement unit (IMU) sensors
 c. radio controls
 d. a pair of CAN bridge modules
10. Terrain compensation feature for GPS-guided machines is necessary to ___________.
 a. correct for steering error caused by machine roll, pitch, and yaw
 b. provide accurate measurement of machine position for collision avoidance systems
 c. identify GPS satellite errors
 d. correct for position error when changing altitude

ASE Technician A/Technician B Style Questions

1. Technician A says that the biggest advantage of automating machines is that operator labor is no longer required. Technician B says that automated machines enable the operator to turn their attention to more critical, complex functions. Who is most correct?
 a. Technician A
 b. Technician B
 c. Both Technician A and Technician B
 d. Neither Technician A nor Technician B
2. Technician A says that a machine with telematics capability can transmit GPS data wirelessly only if it is linked to a Wi-Fi network. Technician B says a machine with telematics capability will transmit machine and GPS data wirelessly over cellular, satellite, Wi-Fi, and even Bluetooth signals. Who is most correct?
 a. Technician A
 b. Technician B
 c. Both Technician A and Technician B
 d. Neither Technician A nor Technician B
3. Technician A and B were discussing the reason for a fully autonomous mine truck to drive to a fuel pump island half way into a work shift. Technician A says that it was likely due to a low fuel level. Technician B says it demonstrates the need for autonomous machines to have a human in the loop. Who is most correct?
 a. Technician A
 b. Technician B
 c. Both Technician A and Technician B
 d. Neither Technician A nor Technician B
4. Technician A says that closed-loop control of an actuator requires a sensor to monitor the actuator position. Technician B says that closed-loop control of an actuator is performed by the ECM, which supplies signals used to position the actuator. Who is most correct?
 a. Technician A
 b. Technician B
 c. Both Technician A and Technician B
 d. Neither Technician A nor Technician B
5. Technician A says that in North America, satellite signals from Russian and American military satellites are used to navigate and locate machine positions. Technician B says that only GPS signals from American satellites are used by machines in North America and around the world. Who is most correct?
 a. Technician A
 b. Technician B
 c. Both Technician A and Technician B
 d. Neither Technician A nor Technician B
6. Technician A says that computer-aided earth-moving systems (CAESs) operating with indicate-only capabilities automatically guide buckets and blades of machinery using 3D maps of a construction site. Technician B says that the automatic mode of a CAES provides an operator with site contour images on a cab terminal, which is used to guide the movement of the machine. Who is most correct?
 a. Technician A
 b. Technician B
 c. Both Technician A and Technician B
 d. Neither Technician A nor Technician B
7. While discussing the advantages of retrofitting equipment with telematics modules, Technician A said that a subscription for each brand of manufacturer is required for the machines. Technician B said that only one subscription service is required to view telematic data for all the company-owned machines. Who is most correct?
 a. Technician A
 b. Technician B
 c. Both Technician A and Technician B
 d. Neither Technician A nor Technician B
8. Technician A says that electronic control modules on a CAN share signal transmission time over the data bus. One module will transmit while all other modules listen. Technician B says the CAN is able to potentially handle both the transmission and reception of data simultaneously from all modules. Who is most correct?
 a. Technician A
 b. Technician B
 c. Both Technician A and Technician B
 d. Neither Technician A nor Technician B

9. Technician A says that different network communication protocols are used on equipment made for European and North American markets. Technician B says that there are two different North American network protocols established by the SAE: J-1939 and J-1939-2, with the later used by agricultural and forestry equipment. Who is most correct?

a. Technician A
b. Technician B
c. Both Technician A and Technician B
d. Neither Technician A nor Technician B

10. Technician A says that the use of two GPS receivers can provide the most precise machine position data for construction, farming, and forestry equipment. Technician B says that excavators cannot use a GPS mast like a bulldozer blade can and therefore cannot use CAES to locate the position of the boom and stick. Who is most correct?

a. Technician A
b. Technician B
c. Both Technician A and Technician B
d. Neither Technician A nor Technician B

CAT

SECTION III

Fluid Power

CHAPTER 22

Fundamentals of Hydraulics

Knowledge Objectives

After reading this chapter, you will be able to:

- K22001 Describe the fundamentals of hydraulics.
- K22002 Define hydraulic system terminology.
- K22003 Describe the advantages and disadvantages of hydraulic systems.
- K22004 Describe Pascal's law.
- K22005 Describe Bernoulli's principle.
- K22006 Describe the measurement units used for hydraulic systems.
- K22007 Describe how pressure and flow are created in a hydraulic system.
- K22008 Describe positive and negative pressures.
- K22009 Identify organizations that govern hydraulic system design and safety.
- K22010 Describe safety concerns unique to hydraulic systems.

Skills Objectives

After reading this chapter, you will be able to:

- S22001 Calculate pressure, force, and area.
- S22002 Release pressure from a hydraulic reservoir.

▶ Introduction

This chapter introduces the fundamental concepts of hydraulic systems and explains terminology specific to hydraulic systems. It describes the advantages and disadvantages of hydraulic systems, explains Pascal's Law, and covers common measurement units used for hydraulic systems. Pressure and flow are defined and explained, as well as positive and negative pressure.

Finally, it covers the organizations that govern industrial standards for hydraulic systems and safety concerns that are specific to hydraulic systems.

▶ Fundamentals of Hydraulics

K22001

Mobile heavy equipment machines rely on hydraulic systems to power and/or control many of the machines' systems. A machine's **prime mover** (typically a diesel engine, but could be an electric motor or other type of internal combustion engine) is used for power input to drive the system's pump and an actuator (cylinder or motor) is the power output of a **hydraulic system**. Hydraulic fluid is used to transfer energy throughout the system.

▶ TECHNICIAN TIP

Fluid power is a term that is used to sometimes describe energy transfer systems that use a fluid to transfer energy. Most people only consider hydraulic systems as a fluid power system; however, technically a pneumatic or air system is also a fluid power system.

Many of today's machines feature hydraulic systems that use computers and electronic systems and can share information with other machine systems. Advanced hydraulic systems are covered in later chapters, but the fundamental principles of how hydraulic systems function must be understood before moving into more complicated hydraulic systems. The basic principles of fluid flow and pressure can be applied to several other machine systems as well, and a sound knowledge of hydraulic fundamentals will be invaluable when it comes time to diagnose many different machine system problems. Therefore, it is critical that the information in this chapter is absorbed and understood before moving on.

Hydraulic systems were introduced to mobile off-road equipment several decades ago to eliminate mechanical systems that performed basic tasks like lifting a dozer blade or moving an excavator bucket. These mechanical systems were slow, hard to control, and required a great deal of maintenance. See **FIGURE 22-1** for an older machine with a mechanical implement system. Hydraulic systems are a key part of machines, from small skid steer equipment to massive mining shovels that can fill their buckets with over 30 tons of material, as shown in **FIGURE 22-2**.

FIGURE 22-1 An older machine with a mechanical implement system.

FIGURE 22-2 A massive mining shovel loading a haul truck.

You Are the Mobile Heavy Equipment Technician

You are given a job to diagnose a hydraulic problem on a large wheel loader. The loader has a lot of hours on it but has been serviced regularly since it was new. Approximately three months ago, its tilt cylinder failed and was replaced with an exchange unit.

There have been intermittent hydraulic system issues since then, and the last shift it worked, the operator reported the boom fell onto the side of a truck he was loading. It is also reported to have all functions working slower than normal. It is your job to confirm there is a legitimate problem and correct it.

1. What information would you want to have to start your diagnosis?
2. What are some basic tools you might need?
3. What are three possible causes for these problems?

Hydraulic fluid **flow** and **pressure** are managed by system components to achieve the design parameters set by manufacturers' engineers. These parameters are based on values that a machine needs to achieve such as maximum lifting/digging force, maximum travel speed, or maximum swing torque. The maximum values are limited by prime mover horsepower ratings, hydraulic system design, system adjustments, and structural strength of machine components.

Hydraulic fluid flow is created by the systems' pump(s), and as **pump** flow is directed to an actuator, the result is a physical motion of either a cylinder rod moving or motor shaft turning. A wide variety of machine components can be attached to either cylinder rods or motor shafts. See **FIGURE 22-3** for a backhoe bucket linkage attached to a hydraulic cylinder.

Fluid pressure in the system increases as resistance to actuator motion increases. If system pressure can overcome the load on the actuator, motion will continue; however, if the load increases beyond maximum pressure capabilities of the system, the actuator stops moving or stalls.

To put this in real terms, if an excavator is digging into a pile of loose gravel, there will be very little resistance, and its actuators will keep moving as the operator fills the bucket. However, if the same machine is used to dig wet clay, resistance will be much higher, and at some point, one or more of the machine's actuators will likely stall or stop moving because the hydraulic system pressure can't overcome the resistance.

A properly designed and maintained hydraulic system will provide thousands of hours of operation provided the operator follows recommended operating guidelines, and manufacturer's maintenance guidelines are followed.

Force Multiplication in a Hydraulic System

Hydraulic systems can be compared to mechanical systems that use **mechanical advantage** to multiply force through leverage.

Mechanical linkages can be used to multiply force when the principles of mechanical advantage are applied. A small input force applied can be multiplied several times if the pivot point is moved closer to the output. **FIGURE 22-4** shows how a lever can be used to increase force.

FIGURE 22-3 A backhoe bucket linkage attached to a hydraulic cylinder.

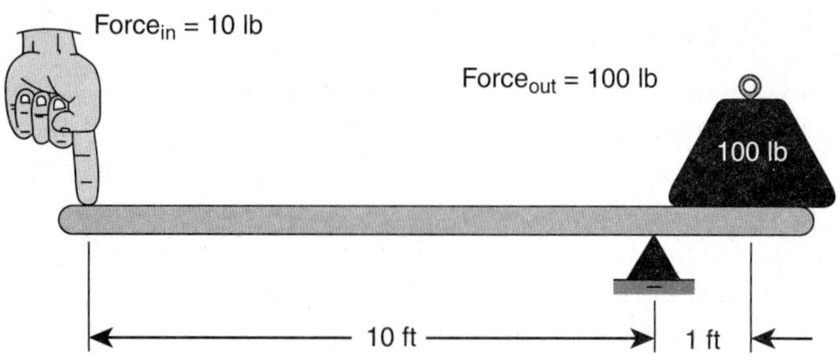

FIGURE 22-4 How a lever can increase force.

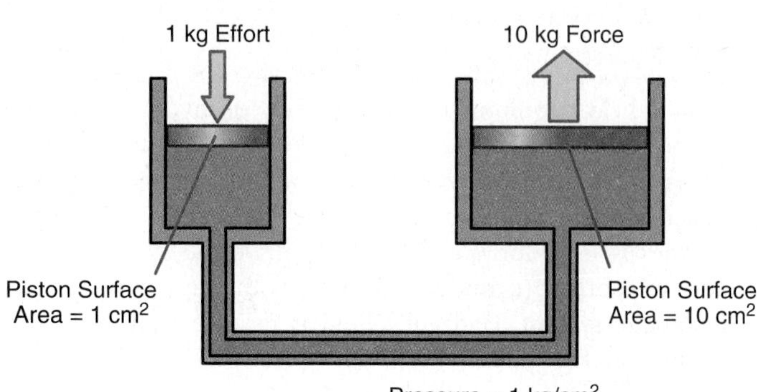

FIGURE 22-5 How force multiplication occurs in a hydraulic system.

The working hydraulic pressure contained in the system is applied to all internal surfaces it contacts. Input forces can be multiplied by simply increasing the surface area of the actuator (output component) that is exposed to the working hydraulic pressure.

This is similar to how **force multiplication** occurs in a mechanical system. See **FIGURE 22-5** to visualize force multiplication in a hydraulic system.

When system pressure is applied to larger surface areas, greater output force is created.

The trade-off that results when force multiplication occurs is that actuator speed and travel is reduced. This is also like a mechanical lever whereby as the pivot point is moved closer to the output the output travel distance is reduced in comparison to the input travel applied and the input vs. output speed differential increase.

▶ Hydraulic System Terminology

K22002

Hydraulics is a general term applied to the study of **fluids** (**liquid** or **gas**), typically in an enclosed system. Hydraulic **fluid power** is a specific area of hydraulics in which a liquid is used to transmit energy and power to one or more **actuators** to provide a force to move a load. Such systems are often referred to as *hydraulic systems*.

Flow in a hydraulic system refers to the movement of fluid within the system and is measured in units of volume per one unit of time. Most commonly **gallons per minute (gpm) or liters per minute (lpm)** are used to measure flow.

Pressure in a hydraulic system is created by the resistance against fluid flow. It is measured in units of force applied to one unit of area. Pounds per square inch (psi) or kilograms per square centimeter (kg/cm^2) are common units of hydraulic system pressure measurement. However, there are other units of pressure measurement, such as inHg (inches of mercury), inH$_2$O (inches of water), atm (atmospheres), bars, and kPa (kilopascals).

Hydrodynamics refers to the study of hydraulic systems where a high volume of fluid is in motion at a high velocity in an enclosed but loosely sealed system, and how the fluid acts on components in that system. A powertrain torque converter is a good example of a component that relies on fluid in motion to transfer energy. These systems rely more on fluid inertia than fluid pressure.

Hydrostatics refers to the study of fluid in an enclosed and tightly sealed system where the fluid is at rest and either under pressure or not. Machines that use fluid power to drive tracks or tires are quite often referred to as having hydrostatic drives. Although this is not in line with the true definition of "hydrostatic," the term is used frequently.

Pumps are needed in any hydraulic system to produce fluid flow, and without flow, no work can be accomplished.

Actuators are the output components that receive fluid flow and convert it into motion. Cylinders produce linear motion for tasks like lifting dozer blades up and down, whereas motors produce rotary motion, for example, to make tracks rotate.

Pneumatics is a specific area of hydraulics in which a gas (usually air) is used to transmit energy and power to one or more actuators to provide a force to move a load. Pneumatic systems are mostly limited to use in brake systems on some MORE machines; however, some rock drills are completely pneumatically powered.

▶ Advantages and Disadvantages of Hydraulic Systems

K22003

The fundamental operating concept of all hydraulic systems is the use of fluid to transfer energy. One of the main advantages of hydraulic systems is that they can be designed to move very heavy loads by applying hydraulic pressure to the movable part of an actuator.

Mechanical linkages are unnecessary within a hydraulic system, as fluid can be routed anywhere on a machine through tubes and hoses. Fluid power is then used to transfer the required force from the component exerting the initial force (pump) to the component exerting the moving force (actuator).

Hydraulically powered equipment also has the advantage of having fewer exposed mechanical parts that can wear and break down. Hydraulic systems are self-lubricating and compact, with high power density, and rely on multiplication of forces, whereby a small force can control large forces.

There are also disadvantages to hydraulic systems, such as the potential for equipment failure when hoses fail and the hydraulic fluid leaks. However, the disadvantages are far outweighed by the advantages of these systems.

Advantages of Hydraulic Systems

The following list summarizes the main advantages of hydraulic systems:

- **Reduced maintenance:** Hydraulic systems do not require complicated systems of gears, cams, cables, or linkages, and the wear and distortions associated with these components is dramatically reduced.
- **Precise control:** Position, speed, and other control parameters can be controlled very precisely and can be performed the same way repeatedly.
- **Immediate reaction:** Because hydraulic fluid is practically incompressible, when an operator moves a joystick to actuate a hydraulic function, the system reacts almost immediately. This is unlike a pneumatic system, which reacts with a delay because gases are compressible.
- **Multiplication of force:** Hydraulic system force multiplication allows for relatively small actuators at the point of force application, compared to other types of systems.
- **Flexibility:** Components can be conveniently located at widely separated points.
- **Construction:** Although numerous components may be required, some of which can be complicated, the actual construction of a system is simple.
- **Seamless speed control:** Speed variations can be accomplished without shifting gears or interrupting the power flow.
- **Ability to turn corners:** Fluid conductors can be designed to transmit fluids up, down, and around corners, without significant losses in efficiency. See **FIGURE 22-6**.

Disadvantages of Hydraulic Systems

The following list summarizes the main disadvantages of hydraulic systems:

- **High pressures:** Hydraulic systems require strong components that are precisely machined to withstand the high fluid pressures applied to them.

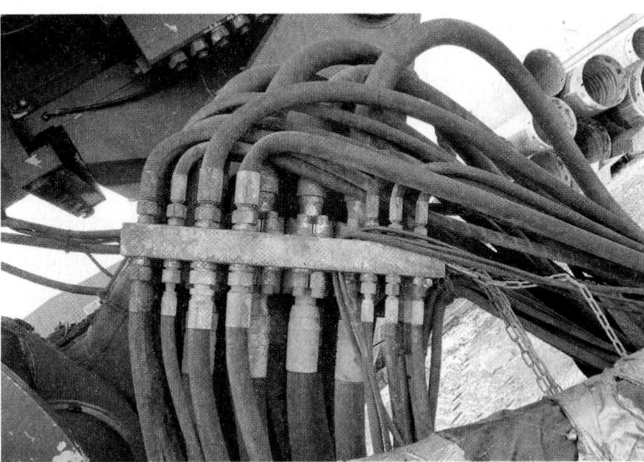

FIGURE 22-6 How hoses can direct fluid flow around a corner.

- **Relatively low efficiency:** Naturally occurring internal leakage in components (particularly pumps and hydraulic motors), as well as pressure losses in valves and piping, leads to lower overall system efficiencies compared to most other types of power transmitting systems.
- **Cleanliness requirements:** To ensure long component life and optimum efficiency, hydraulic fluids must be kept extremely clean and free of contaminants.
- **Safety:** High-pressure fluids can be a serious safety hazard in the case of hose ruptures or broken tubes and fittings.
- **Fire hazard:** All hydraulic fluids are flammable to a certain extent. Fluids must not be exposed to open flames or high-temperature heat sources.
- **Environmental hazard:** Hydraulic leaks can be damaging to the environment, and proper disposal of hydraulic fluids can be costly.
- **Leaks:** Fluid leaks and spills can be hazardous. **FIGURE 22-7** shows a hydraulic leak.

▶ Pascal's Law and Hydraulic Systems

K22004

The operating principles of today's hydraulic systems are embedded in the scientific principles of **Pascal's law**, which dates from the 1600s. To this day, even the most sophisticated modern equipment still operates on these principles. Pascal's law is described in the following section.

Pascal's Law

In the 1600s, Blaise Pascal observed the effects of pressure applied to a fluid in a closed system. Pascal's law states that pressure applied to a confined liquid is transmitted undiminished in all directions and acts with equal force on all equal areas, and at right angles to those areas.

This means that pressure exerted on a confined fluid at rest is transmitted equally in all directions, is the same at any point in the liquid, and is exerted at right angles to the walls of the container.

FIGURE 22-7 Hydraulic fluid leak.

If you were to fill a glass wine bottle to the top with water and force a cork into the bottle, you would be increasing pressure throughout the entire inside of the bottle. The pressure would be transferred by the water to the entire inside of the bottle and would act at right angles to the inside bottle surface.

If you could put a gauge in different locations around the bottle, you would see the pressure is the same anywhere you measured it. Because liquids are practically incompressible, the pressure would rise quickly if you kept pushing the cork, and eventually a weak spot in the bottle would fail. **FIGURE 22-8** demonstrates how pressure is created in a sealed container.

Taking hydraulic braking systems as an example, Pascal's law is the operating principle behind this everyday application. Pressure that develops in the master cylinder is transmitted through the hydraulic braking system as long as the system remains closed and has no leaks. At the actuators (brake calipers or wheel cylinders), there is a resistance to fluid flow as the fluid moves the brake component and pressure builds. **FIGURE 22-9** shows how fluid pressure is transferred through a hydraulic brake system.

In a closed system, hydraulic pressure is transmitted equally in all directions throughout the system. What happens to the pressure levels if there is a leak in the system? According to Pascal's law, a substantial leak will prevent the pressure from building up because there is very little resistance to flow. The result is that the pressure within the whole system will be equally low. This means that the vehicle may lose some or all of its braking ability if a leak develops, as pressure cannot be developed. **FIGURE 22-10** shows what happens to pressure in a hydraulic brake system when a leak develops.

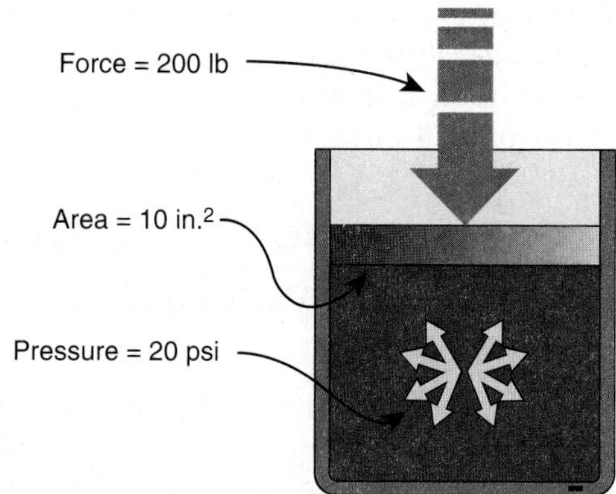

FIGURE 22-8 How pressure is created in a sealed container.

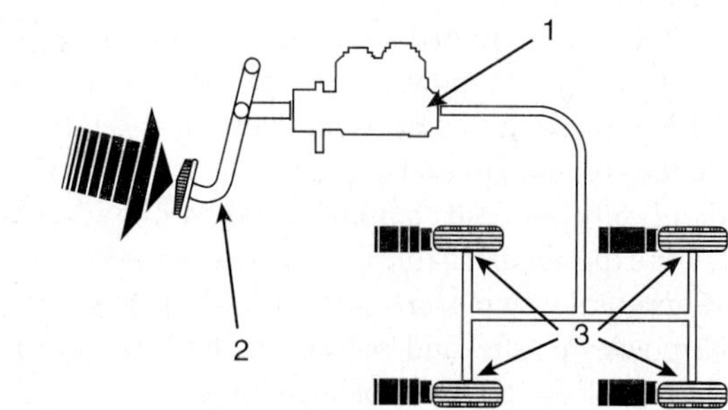

FIGURE 22-9 How fluid pressure is transferred through a hydraulic brake system.

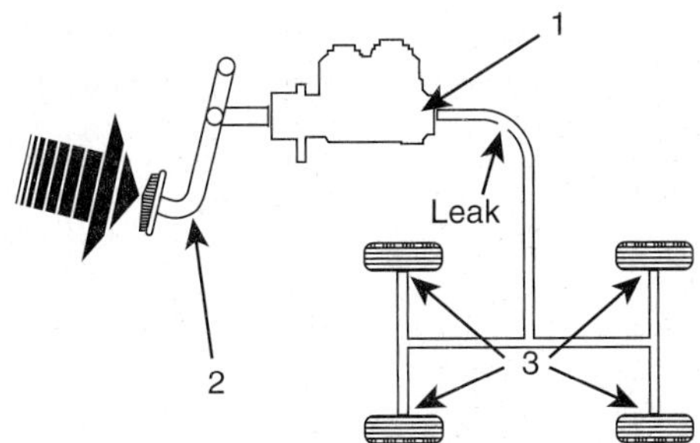

FIGURE 22-10 How pressure drops in a brake system when a leak develops.

Pascal's law also helps in diagnosing problems with hydraulic systems. For example, in the case of a brake system, if the brake pedal is squishy (soft or spongy), there is a good chance that the hydraulic braking system has air in it. This is because air is compressible and has to be removed by bleeding it out. If the brake pedal slowly sinks to the floor, there is likely a small leak in the system that must be found. If the vehicle pulls to one side, it could be that a brake hose is plugged or a line pinched, and is not allowing fluid to transfer pressure to one of the brake units.

To demonstrate Pascal's law, follow the guidelines in **SKILL DRILL 22-1**.

▶ Bernoulli's Principle

K22005

The principle is named after Daniel Bernoulli, who published it in his book *Hydrodynamica* in 1738. Bernoulli's principle states that a rise in pressure in a flowing fluid must always be accompanied by a proportionate decrease in the speed, and conversely an increase in the speed of the fluid results in a decrease in the pressure. As oil flows through a system and is made to speed up, there will be a pressure drop, and inversely, if the speed of oil flow decreases, its pressure will increase.

A practical application of this principle for technicians would be when they are replacing a hose or tube on a machine. Care must be taken to ensure the replacement hose or tube is the same inside diameter as the one being removed. Otherwise, a pressure drop or increase will occur and may affect system performance. Dramatic changes in fluid velocity across a valve may create force imbalances on the valves spool and result in erratic operation.

▶ Measurement Units for Hydraulic Systems

K22006

Both metric (International System of Units, or SI) and/or Standard (Imperial) measurement units can be found in manufacturers' service information when hydraulic system values are being discussed. The units used usually relate to where the machine was designed and/or manufactured and the common measurement system used by the manufacturer. Some examples are listed in **TABLE 22-1**.

> ▶ TECHNICIAN TIP
>
> To get an understanding for the different measurement units that manufacturers may use, do an Internet search for the machine specifications for a new excavator. You should be able to download a brochure that shows the specifications for the machine's hydraulic system. Compare a few different manufacturers' excavators to see what units are used. This will also give you an idea as to what normal pressure and flow settings are for new machines. Try comparing other types of machines' hydraulic system specifications.
>
> Several online tools and smartphone apps are also available to use for unit conversion if the measuring device you are using does not correspond to the service information you have.

SKILL DRILL 22-1 Demonstrating Pascal's Law

For this procedure, you need the following tools, materials, and equipment:

- Small hydraulic cylinder with a trunnion, clevis, or pivot mount to allow the cylinder to be suspended, and a pivot eye on the end of the rod
- Frame from which to suspend the cylinder
- Hand pump with pressure gauge
- Pressure gauge
- T-fitting for attaching the hand pump and the pressure gauge to the rod-end port of the cylinder
- Weights and chain or cable to suspend the weights from the cylinder
- Spanners and wrenches of appropriate sizes
- Pencil
- Paper
- Safety glasses or goggles
- Gloves

1. Put on safety glasses or goggles, and gloves.
2. Assemble the test setup.
   a. Suspend the cylinder from the frame.
   b. Insert the tee fitting into the rod-end port of the cylinder.
   c. Attach the pressure gauge and the hand pump to the T-fitting.
4. Demonstrate Pascal's law.
   a. Attach a light weight to the cable or chain attached to the cylinder rod.
   b. Use the hand pump to suspend the weight above the floor.
   c. Record the pressure on both pressure gauges (hand pump and cylinder).
   d. Lower the weight to the floor.
   e. Attach additional weights to the cable or chain.
   f. Use the hand pump to suspend the weights above the floor.
   g. Record the pressure on both pressure gauges.
   h. Repeat several times, using increasing weight.
   i. Report your conclusions.
   j. Clean work area, and return tools and equipment to proper storage.

TABLE 22-1 Common Measurement Units for Hydraulic Systems and Abbreviations

Pressure	
Unit	**Abbreviation**
Pounds per square inch	Psi
Kilograms per square centimeter	Kg/cm^2
Pascal	Pa, kPa, hPa
Inches of water	inH_2O
Bar	bar
Inches of mercury	inHg
Atmosphere	Atm
Flow	
Unit	**Abbreviation**
Liters per minute	lpm
Gallons per minute	gpm
Speed	
Unit	**Abbreviation**
Feet per second	fps
Meters per second	mps

▶ Hydraulic Pressure and Flow

K22007

One critical point to remember when trying to understand the operating principles of a hydraulic system is this: pumps create fluid flow, not pressure. The pressure in a hydraulic system is determined, for the most part, by the load the system must move. There is also inherent resistance to flow created by all the components that are part of the system. All hoses, valves, tubes, filters, coolers, and actuators naturally have a resistance to flow in them. This value is usually insignificant and should be acceptable if the system is designed properly, but it can be excessive under certain circumstances such as extreme cold weather. The hydraulic fluid's **viscosity** (resistance to flow) is also a factor to consider when looking at residual pressure (no load pressure) in the system.

The load on an actuator creates a resistance to pump flow, and that in turn develops the working pressure in the system. As loads change during a typical work cycle, the system pressure changes. As loads increase, resistance to flow increases, and an increase in system pressure follows. When the load on an actuator decreases, then a reduction in system pressure follows. Maximum system pressure is limited by a main relief valve, to keep pressure values to a safe limit. See **FIGURE 22-11** for a large load on a hydraulic actuator. Pressure is measured in units of force per one unit of area (**pounds per square inch or kilograms per square centimeter**).

Force is the outcome of fluid pressure being applied to an actuator (cylinder or motor). A cylinder outputs a linear force when fluid pressure is applied to its piston, and a motor outputs a rotary force (torque) when it receives pump flow. Linear force is measured in pounds, kilograms, or newtons, and rotary force is measured in foot-pounds (ft-lb) or newton meters (N·m)—the amount of rotational force 1 foot or 1 meter from the center of the rotary actuator shaft.

FIGURE 22-11 An actuator with a large load on it.

Varying amounts of mechanical force can be extracted from a single amount of hydraulic pressure. Because pressure is force per unit area (e.g., 3.45 bar, or 50 pounds per square inch [psi]), the same pressure applied over different-sized surface areas will produce different levels of force. See **FIGURE 22-12** to visualize how system pressure can act on several actuators and produce different force outcomes.

Engineers apply hydraulic principles to create varying amounts of mechanical force in hydraulic braking systems. As a practical example, this principle allows engineers to design automotive brakes to have a precise amount of braking force at each wheel. For instance, the front wheels on some front-wheel drive vehicles can produce up to 80% of the vehicle's stopping power because of the weight distribution and weight transfer. For these vehicles to brake smoothly, more pressure must be applied to the front brake units than the rear brake units. This is accomplished through the front and rear brake pistons. The larger brake pistons on the front wheels give greater mechanical force and braking power to the front wheels.

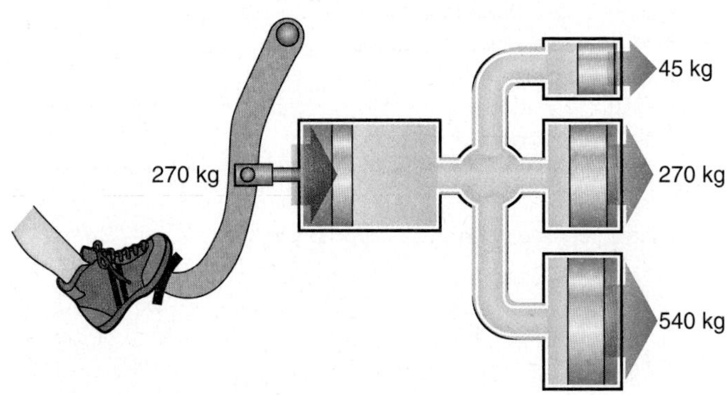

FIGURE 22-12 How one pressure can act on several actuators, with different force outcomes.

▶ TECHNICIAN TIP

Keep in mind when thinking about automotive brake systems that there is very little fluid flow required to make the brakes work. There will be a small clearance between the wheel brake friction material (brake pads or shoes) and the rotating member (rotor or drum) and only a small amount of fluid is needed to move the friction material against the rotating member. This is one type of hydraulic system that relies more on pressure than flow to achieve its designed performance outcome.

Figure 22-12 illustrates a hydraulic system that has cylinders of different sizes. When the brake pedal is pressed, the force against the piston in the master cylinder applies pressure to the brake fluid. Because the wheel brake actuators are being forced against a stationary object, as input force increases, then fluid pressure increases in direct proportion.

This same pressure is transmitted equally throughout the fluid, but each output piston develops a specific amount of **output force**, depending on its diameter (surface area). The top cylinder is smaller than the master cylinder, so the amount of force it exerts will be less than the force applied to the master cylinder. The middle cylinder is the same size as the master cylinder, so its output force will be the same. The bottom cylinder is larger than the master cylinder, and so its force will be greater.

▶ TECHNICIAN TIP

Input force, output force, and working pressure are optimized during the design of the hydraulic system, based on a specific equipment application. This is one reason why it is never acceptable to arbitrarily substitute hydraulic components from another piece of equipment.

Flow Rate and Speed of Actuator

The speed at which a load can be moved depends on the delivered flow rate and the size of the actuator that is receiving the flow. Hydraulic oil must circulate within a system for it to transmit energy to the working components. Without oil flow, most systems cannot work. Hydraulic flow is normally produced by using a positive displacement pump. This type of pump is discussed in detail in an upcoming chapter; however, a positive displacement pump produces fluid flow any time it is being driven.

Hydraulic fluid flow occurs when there is a pressure differential. In other words, fluid always flows toward a lower pressure in a manner similar to how a river flows to a lower elevation. At a pump's inlet, a low pressure is created when the pump starts turning, and this forces fluid that is in the reservoir to move into the pump. Once it leaves the pump outlet, the fluid then continues flowing through the system toward the reservoir that is at a lower pressure. At the pump outlet, fluid is at a higher pressure because of the system pressure created by the load, and the fluid flows toward a lower pressure at the reservoir. **FIGURE 22-13** depicts how oil flows from high pressure to low pressure.

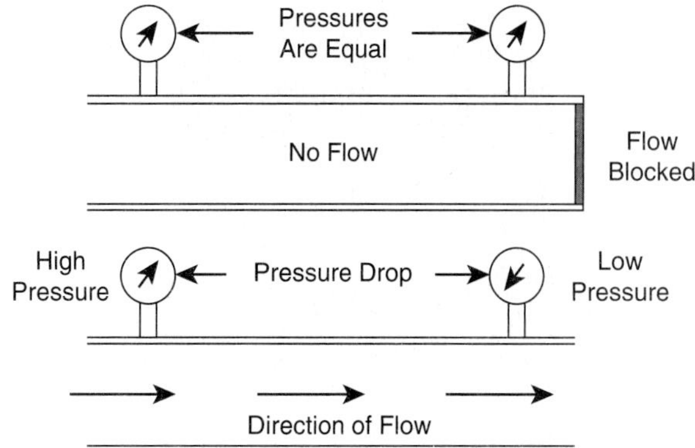

FIGURE 22-13 How oil flows from high to low pressure.

Three main points are critical to understanding hydraulic flow:

1. For a hydraulic system to create work, the hydraulic fluid must apply pressure to an actuator. An actuator is a device that converts fluid power to mechanical power, like a hydraulic cylinder or rotary motor. For instance, on a dozer the lift cylinder controls the up/down movement of the blade. Fluid pressure applied to the cylinder piston moves the rod into the cylinder, which in turn lifts the blade. The amount of pressure needed to lift the blade is determined by the weight of the blade and the size of the cylinder piston.
2. The rate of flow to an actuator is measured in liters per minute (lpm) or gallons per minute (gpm), and the flow rate determines the speed of the actuator. The flow is delivered by the pump.
3. The actuator speed changes when the rate of flow to the actuator changes. Speed of a linear actuator is measured in feet per second (fps) or meters per second (mps) while rotary actuator speed is measured in revolutions per minute (rpm).

When the flow rate to a linear actuator is increased, rod travel speeds up, and if the flow rate to a rotary actuator is increased, its output shaft speeds up. For example, to lift a dozer blade faster, there has to be a higher rate of fluid flow delivered to the cylinders from the pump.

▶ Positive and Negative Pressure

K22008

All hydraulic system pressure is measured in comparison to either atmospheric pressure or a perfect vacuum. Atmospheric pressure at sea level is 14.7 psi (1.01 bar, or 101.35 kPa), which is the weight of the column of atmospheric air that is applying force to a 1-inch square area at sea level. If exposed to the atmosphere, most gauges read 0 at sea level and approximately room temperature. The face of the gauge may say "psig," which stands for psi gauge.

If a gauge is calibrated to be an absolute gauge, it would read 14.7 psi at sea level. Although these gauges aren't as popular as psig gauges, you might see "psia" on the face of an absolute gauge to indicate how it is calibrated.

If you measured system pressure anywhere between the pump outlet and the work port of an actuator, you would read

FIGURE 22-14 A gauge that can read both positive and negative.

a positive pressure. That is, it would be above 0 psig. Negative pressure occurs when fluid pressure falls below 0 psig. There should only be two places in a system where a negative pressure occurs—at the pump inlet and under some circumstances in an actuator when the load overcomes the oil supplied to it. Negative pressure is sometimes referred to as vacuum (in reality it's a partial vacuum), and a pump inlet line is sometimes called a suction line.

See **FIGURE 22-14** to look at a gauge that can read positive and negative pressure.

▶ Organizational Bodies Governing Industrial Standards

K22009

Several international bodies maintain standards for hydraulic systems and components. These organizations ensure that safety is maintained for those working in the industry by ensuring that the design and manufacture of the equipment and components used in different systems meet the minimum specifications for the applications in which they are deployed.

ASTM International

ASTM International, formerly the American Society for Testing and Materials, develops voluntary consensus standards of quality, safety, and market access across a broad range of industries.

American National Standards Institute

The American National Standards Institute (ANSI) oversees the creation and dissemination of norms and guidelines for business and is involved in accreditation of standards-based programs. ANSI is the U.S. representative to the ISO.

International Organization for Standardization

The International Organization for Standardization (ISO) is the world's largest developer and publisher of international standards. ISO is a nongovernmental organization comprised of representatives from the national standards institutes of numerous countries throughout the world.

Joint Industrial Council

Though the Joint Industrial Council (JIC) is now defunct, the organization's hydraulic standards are still widely recognized and frequently referenced, and persist in legacy parts codes and schematics. There is one commonly used series of metal to metal angled face connectors that are referred to as JIC.

Society of Automotive Engineers

The Society of Automotive Engineers (SAE) is an international association of engineers and related technical experts. SAE develops voluntary consensus standards for the aerospace, automotive and commercial vehicle industries.

▶ Calculating Force, Pressure, and Area

S22001

This section describes the relationship between force, pressure, and area. It reviews Pascal's law and provides the formulas, with examples, that you will need to be able to calculate force in both a single-acting cylinder and a double-acting hydraulic cylinder. To make calculations regarding pressure or force of a hydraulic cylinder, you first need to determine the area of the piston.

Area of Circles

Linear actuators (cylinders) transfer fluid power in a hydraulic system using pistons, which consist of a circular surface (piston head) moving within a sealed cylinder. The piston is connected to a rod that moves in and out of the cylinder. The piston surface area is an essential part of force, pressure, and speed calculations. To understand how to make calculations for actuator force, pressure, and speed, one much first understand the properties of circles. There are three main measurements of a circle: the radius, the diameter, and the circumference.

Radius

The radius is a line from the center of the circle to its boundary and is denoted with a lowercase *r*. In hydraulics applications, the radius often must be derived from the diameter of the piston or the bore of the cylinder. See **FIGURE 22-15** for the different measurements of a circle.

Diameter

A diameter is a line that crosses a circle passing through the center and is denoted with a lowercase *d*. The diameter of the piston or bore of the cylinder is usually a known quantity.

Circumference

The circumference is the distance around the outside of a circle and is denoted with a capital *C*.

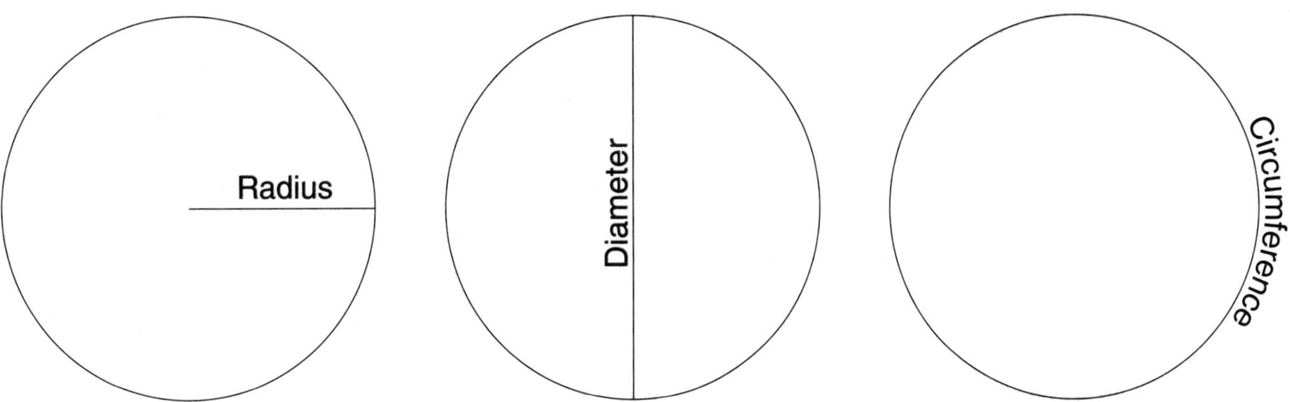

FIGURE 22-15 The three different measurements of a circle.

Circumference is not normally considered when it comes to calculating hydraulic system equations. The circumference of the piston can be calculated using the following formula: $C = \pi d$.

Relationship Between the Parts of a Circle

There are mathematical relationships between different parts of a circle. These relationships can be used to calculate an unknown value if two other values are known.

Diameter and Radius

The diameter of a piston is twice the length of the radius, which is expressed as $d = 2r$.

The radius of a piston is half the length of the diameter, which is expressed as $r = \frac{d}{2}$.

The circumference of a circle divided by its diameter equals pi (π):

- Pi is a Greek letter that is represented by the symbol π.
- $\pi = 3.1415927$ ... (*Note:* The ellipses (...) means that the number goes on into infinity.)
- If you take the circumference of any circle and divide it by its diameter, you will always get this number, no matter what size the circle is.

Calculating the Area of a Circle

The formula for calculating the area (A) of a circle is $A = \frac{\pi d^2}{4}$ or πr^2.

All answers must be in square units, such as in.^{2}, cm^2, and mm^2.

Example 1

Calculate the surface area of a piston, using radius (r), as depicted below:

$r = 3$ cm
$r^2 = 9$ cm
$A = \pi r^2$
$A = 3.14 \times 9$ cm
$A = 28.27$ cm^2

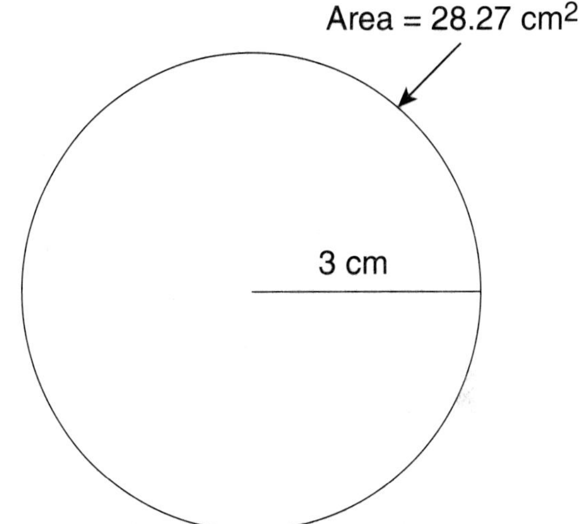

FIGURE 22-16 A circle with a radius of 3 cm and an area of 28.27 cm^2.

FIGURE 22-16 shows a circle divided into squares that represent one square centimeter each.

Example 2

Calculate the surface area of a piston, using diameter (d), as depicted below.

$$d = 15 \text{ cm}$$

$$A = \frac{\pi \times (15)^2}{4}$$

$$A = \frac{\pi \times (15 \times 15)}{4}$$

$$A = \frac{\pi \times 225}{4}$$

$$A = \frac{3.14159 \times 225}{4}$$

$$A = \frac{706.85775}{4}$$

$$A = 176.71 \text{ cm}^2$$

Formula for Pascal's Law

Pascal's law states that pressure applied anywhere to a body of fluid causes a force to be transmitted equally in all directions.

To solve for force, Pascal's law may be mathematically expressed as:

$$F = p \times A$$

where:

F = Force
p = Pressure
A = Area

(Force = Pressure multiplied by Area)

This may be inverted to solve for pressure:

$$p = F \div A$$

(Pressure = Force divided by Area)

Force is measured in kilograms (kg); area is measured in square centimeters (cm^2); and pressure is measured in kg/cm^2, or bar if working in SI (metric) units. In the imperial system, force is measured in pounds (lb), pressure in pounds per square inch (psi), and area in square inches ($in.^2$).

Calculating Force Output in a Single-Acting Cylinder

Single-acting cylinders only have one port in their barrel to allow fluid to apply pressure to the bottom of its piston.

1. First calculate the area of the piston, using the following formula:
   - Area (A) equals π (or pi) multiplied by the square of the piston's radius (r):
   - $A = \pi r^2$
     Note: In hydraulics applications, the diameter of the piston (same as cylinder bore) is often known. Use the bore, or interior diameter of the cylinder, to calculate the radius.
   - Radius is half the diameter (d) of the cylinder, or:

     $$r = -\frac{d}{2}$$

   - Though usually calculated in terms of radius, area can also be calculated in terms of diameter, as follows:

     $$A = \frac{\pi \times d^2}{4}$$

▶ TECHNICIAN TIP

The decimal representation of π is infinite and therefore must always be approximated. Always approximate π consistently throughout an equation or series of equations. Note that rounding π to two places of decimals (3.14) is adequate for illustration purposes; for real-world applications, greater precision (3.14159 ...) may be required.

2. To use a cylinder's area to solve for force (or pressure), using Pascal's law, follow the steps in the following examples.

Example 1

Determine the force produced by a cylinder with a 5 cm diameter if the operating pressure is 140 bar (143 kg/cm^2). Use your calculator when plugging in π, rather than the rounded number; that is, 3.14159 ...

- Use the formula $F = p \times A$.
- Pressure (p) is a known quantity: 140 bar.
- Calculate area (A), using the diameter of the cylinder (d):

$$A = \frac{\pi d^2}{4}$$

$$A = \frac{\pi (5)^2}{4}$$

$$A = \frac{\pi 25}{4} = \frac{78.5}{4}$$

$$A = 19.625 \text{ cm}^2$$

- Plug pressure (p) and area (A) into the formula, and solve:

$$F = p \times A$$

$$F = 140 \text{ bar} \times 19.625 \text{ cm}^2$$

$$F = 2747.5 \text{ kg}$$

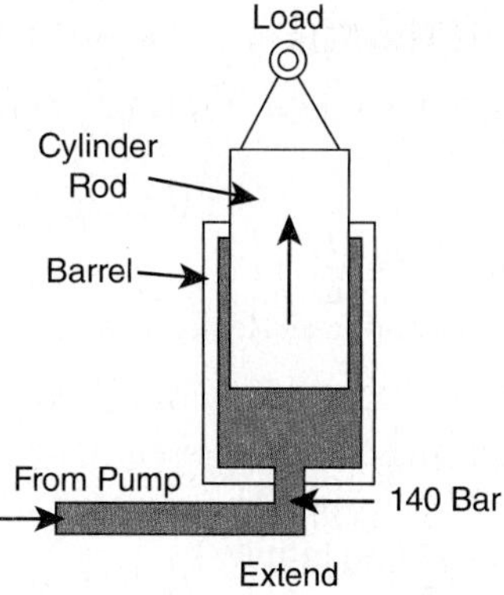

Single-acting cylinder with a 5 cm diameter piston and having a pressure of 140 bar applied to it.

Example 2

Determine the pressure required for a cylinder with a 7.62 cm bore to move a 5,500 kg load.

- Use the formula $F = p \times A$.
- Load (F) is a known quantity: 5,500 kg.
- To find the formula for calculating pressure, divide both sides by A:

$$F = pA$$

$$\frac{F}{A} = \frac{pA}{A}$$

$$\frac{F}{A} = p$$

$$p = \frac{F}{A} \text{ or } p = F \div A$$

- Calculate area (A), using the bore/diameter of the cylinder.
- Plug in the values to calculate the pressure.

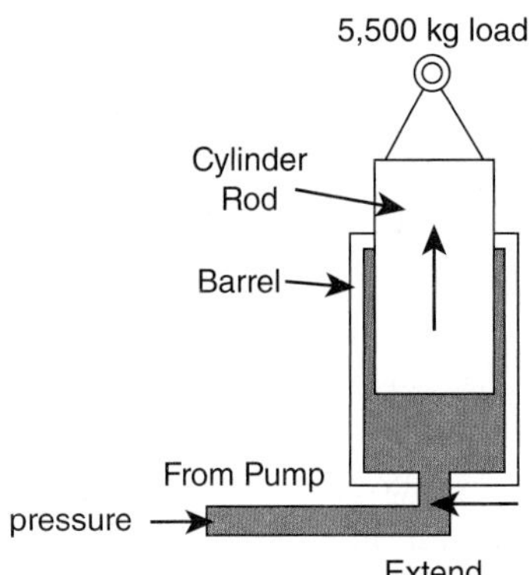

Single-acting cylinder with a 7.62 cm bore moving a load of 5,500 kg.

Calculating Force in a Double-Acting Cylinder

In a double-acting cylinder, force capability is different on extension versus retraction. On retraction, the area subjected to hydraulic pressure is less than on extension because the area taken up by the rod is not used to move the load. On extension, the effective area is the entire face of the piston; on retraction, the **effective area** is the piston area minus the rod area.

▶ TECHNICIAN TIP

To prevent confusion, use subscript to distinguish multiple related terms (A_{rod} versus A_{piston}) in an equation.

1. To calculate the effective area on extension (entire face of piston), use the formula:

$$A_{piston} = \frac{\pi d^2_{piston}}{4}$$

2. To calculate the extension force, use the formula:

$$F_{extension} = p \times A_{piston}$$

3. To calculate the effective area on retraction (piston area minus rod area), use the formula:

$$A_{effective} = A_{piston} - A_{rod}$$

4. The rod area is calculated like the piston area:

$$A_{rod} = \frac{\pi d^2_{rod}}{4}$$

5. To calculate the retraction force, use the formula:

$$F_{retraction} = p \times A_{effective}$$

Example 1

Determine the extension and retraction force capabilities of a double-acting cylinder if the cylinder bore is 7.62 cm and the rod diameter is 2.54 cm. The pressure available is 100 bar.

1. **Calculate extension force.**
   - Calculate extension force, using the formula:

$$F_{extension} = p \times A_{piston}$$

   - Pressure is a known quantity: 100 bar.
   - Calculate area (A), using bore/diameter of cylinder (d):

$$A_{piston} = \frac{\pi d^2_{piston}}{4} = 45.6 \text{ cm}^2$$

   - Plug in the values to calculate the extension force:

$$F_{extension} = p \times A_{piston}$$
$$= 100 \times 45.6$$
$$= 4{,}560 \text{ kg}$$

2. **Calculate retraction force.**
   - Calculate retraction force, using the formula:

$$F_{retraction} = p \times A_{effective}$$

   - Calculate effective area, using the formula:

$$A_{effective} = A_{piston} - A_{rod}$$

   - First, calculate piston area and rod area:

$$A_{piston} \text{ (solved above)} = 45.6 \text{ cm}^2$$

$$A_{rod} = \frac{\pi d^2_{rod}}{4} = \frac{\pi (2.54)^2}{4}$$

$$A_{rod} = 5.07 \text{ cm}^2$$

   - Then plug in the numbers to determine effective area:

$$A_{effective} = A_{piston} - A_{rod}$$
$$A_{effective} = 45.6 \text{ cm}^2 - 5.1 \text{ cm}^2$$
$$A_{effective} = 40.5 \text{ cm}^2$$

   - Plug in the values to calculate retraction force.

$$F_{retraction} = p \times A_{effective}$$
$$F_{retraction} = 100 \text{ bar} \times 40.5 \text{ cm}^2$$
$$F_{retraction} = 4{,}050 \text{ kg}$$

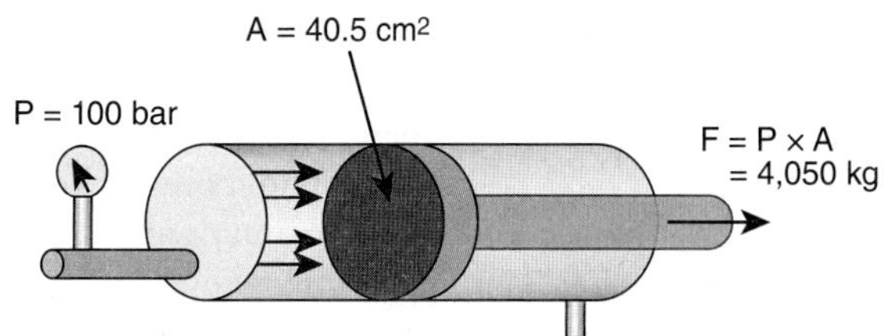

Double-acting cylinder with a piston diameter of 7.62 cm and a rod diameter of 2.54 cm, with 100 bar pressure applied to it.

You can conclude from these calculations that the cylinder has roughly 500 kg less retraction force than extension force because of the smaller surface area that the fluid pressure can be applied to.

Example 2

Determine the pressure required for the double-acting cylinder in Example 1 to extend and retract a 6,800 kg load.

- Area of the piston is a known quantity (from Example 1):

$$A_{\text{piston}} = 45.6\ \text{cm}^2$$

- Remember that $p = F \div A$

$$p_{\text{extension}} = F \div A_{\text{piston}}$$

$$p_{\text{extension}} = \frac{6{,}800}{45.6}$$

$$p_{\text{extension}} = 149\ \text{bar}$$

- Calculate the retraction pressure, using the effective area ($A_{\text{effective}}$) from Example 1 (40.52 cm^2):

$$p_{\text{retraction}} = F \div A_{\text{effective}}$$

$$p_{\text{retraction}} = \frac{6{,}800}{40.5}$$

$$p_{\text{retraction}} = 168\ \text{bar}$$

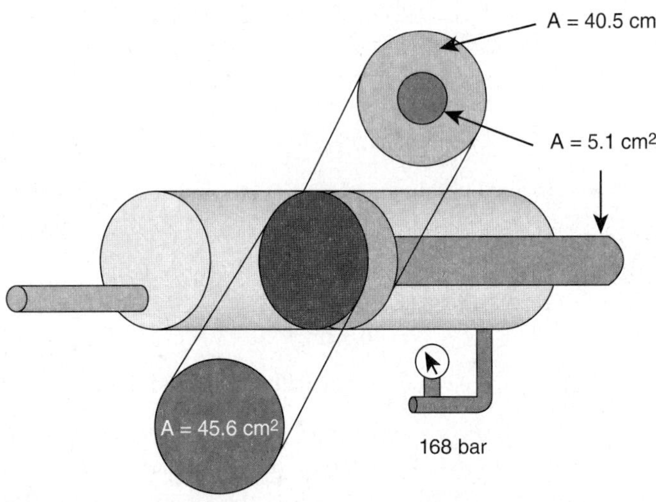

Double-acting cylinder with a 6,800 kg load on it and the pressure needed to move it.

You should conclude from these calculations that as the load on the cylinder increases, there must be a proportionate increase in pressure applied to the piston to move the load.

Practice using the $F = P \times A$ formula with your own piston dimensions, loads, and pressure values. This will help you understand the relationship between force, pressure, and area.

▶ Safety Concerns Related to Hydraulic Systems

K22010

Minor injuries, such as burns, and serious injuries or even death have resulted from technicians not being aware of potential dangers inherent to hydraulic systems. Hydraulic systems use hot, high-pressure fluids to transfer large amounts of energy, and personal harm can occur quickly if a technician isn't proactive in preventing an accident.

Incidents can happen because of improper testing methods or use of improper test equipment, such as using underrated hoses or gauges. Use of inadequate replacement parts such as hoses, seals, or tubes can result in the rupture of these components, and not only the escape of hot, high-pressure fluid but also the sudden uncontrolled movement of machine components could have disastrous results. A little common sense and proper use of PPE will go a long way to keeping you and your coworkers safe when working on hydraulic systems. You should always refer to the specific manufacturer's service information for the machine before performing any servicing or repairs to hydraulic systems.

These safety concerns also apply to hydraulic tools such as presses, which can operate at extreme pressures. You will see lots of warnings and cautions on machines and in service information so don't overlook them and become another statistic. Here are a few types of specific safety concerns that you should be aware of and some tips that help you avoid injuring yourself or others.

Oil Injection

Heavy equipment hydraulic systems operate at high pressures that are typically around 3,000–5,000 psi and can sometimes exceed 10,000 psi. This high pressure can be used to perform many high-force machine operations, but if that pressure is allowed to escape, and your skin or other body parts are exposed to it, some very serious consequences can occur. Skin can be punctured easily by high-pressure fluid, and if hydraulic fluid gets into your bloodstream, there is a good possibility of getting blood poisoning, which in turn could lead to death.

If you are looking for the source of a hydraulic leak on a machine and see oil dripping, this should raise a red flag for you. Although the oil looks like it is dripping harmlessly, it may in fact be spraying out under high pressure and waiting to do harm if you put your hand in its path. Be very cautious, and use a piece of cardboard, rubber, or wood to identify where the leak is originating. See **FIGURE 22-17** for a warning label for oil injection injury.

An oil injection accident is very serious and can easily result in an amputated limb or worse. To see the result of an oil injection injury, see **FIGURE 22-18**.

Trapped Pressure

Pressure can be trapped inside many hydraulic components even after the machine is shut off. If you need to replace a hose,

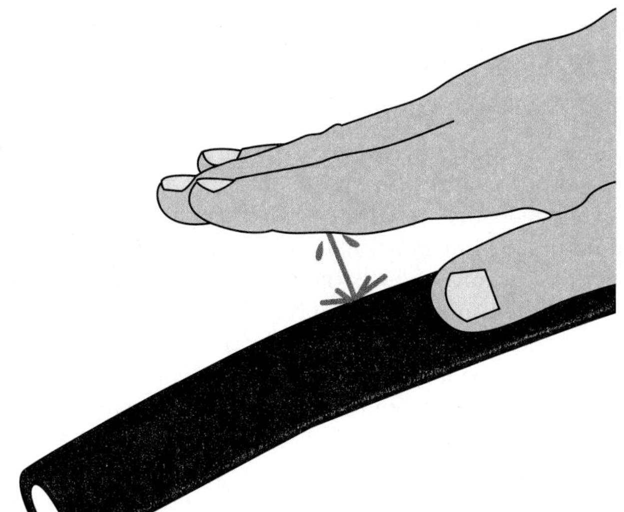

FIGURE 22-17 A warning label for oil injection injury.
Image Provided As Courtesy of John Deere.

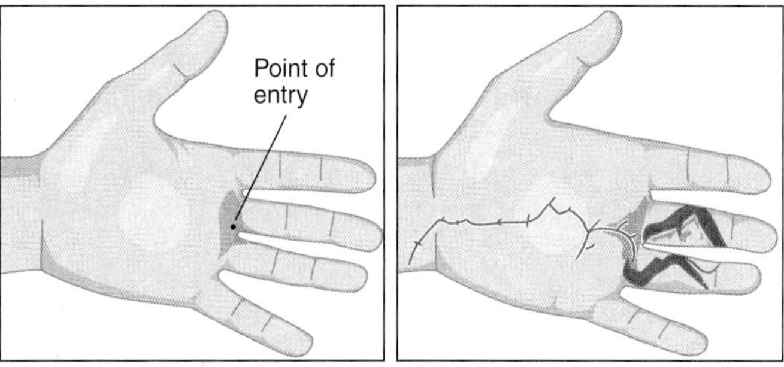

FIGURE 22-18 An oil injection injury.

tube, or other component at any time, the pressure inside that component must be reduced to safe levels. This may not be easy to do, and you should always refer to the appropriate service manual for proper procedures. Releasing pressure or bleeding off pressure can be very dangerous if done improperly. Always keep in mind, if you are releasing trapped hydraulic pressure, there's a good chance that some part of the hydraulic system is going to move.

SAFETY TIP

Always refer to the machine manufacturer's service information to learn how to release pressure safely. In some cases, you may need special tooling to safely release trapped pressure. Follow these procedures carefully and completely to ensure the safety of you and your coworkers.

Once you confirm all system pressure is released, perform appropriate lockout and tagout procedures for the particular machine you are working on. This procedure should follow all company and government requirements.

Crushing Hazards

A crushing hazard is present on a machine where there is the potential of machine components that can move and squeeze or crush you or your body parts. A good example of the pivot point or articulation joint of an articulated steering wheel loader. If a machine has hydraulic functions that can create crushing hazards, you must be very wary that you do not put yourself in a vulnerable position when working on the hydraulic system. Make sure any component that could move and cause a crushing injury will be mechanically held in place. Steering locks and boom cylinder supports are two examples of mechanical locks that must be installed if you're going to be working near crushing hazards.

Burns

Hydraulic systems can generate high amounts of heat, and this should be another safety concern for the technician. Burns to your body can occur at just over 100°F (38°C). You need to make sure that you take precautions to avoid getting burnt if you are servicing or repairing a hydraulic system that has just recently been operating. You should consider using a heat gun to ensure safe component temperature before proceeding. At times it will be unavoidable to work on a machine with hot hydraulic fluid, and if this is the case, you should use the proper PPE to keep yourself protected.

SAFETY TIP

Testing or adjusting a running piece of equipment should be avoided, but sometimes it is necessary to do so. If you need to work on a running machine, your senses should be on high alert. If someone else is running the machine you are working on, you must keep clear communications with that person to let him or her know what you want done. This is sometimes difficult, as a running machine can be very noisy, but the person operating the machine must be absolutely sure about what is required. If you are unsure of the operator's capabilities, stop and find someone whom you feel confident with. Even the smallest mistake when working on a running machine could be deadly.

Slips and Falls

Hydraulic fluid is slippery by nature, and if that fluid is leaked onto a surface that is walked on or a grab handle that is needed, a slip hazard is created. This could be a problem not only with a machine operator slipping and falling, but also for the technician at risk from fluid that has spilled or sprayed as a result of servicing or repairing the hydraulic system. Hydraulic leaks in a machines cab can create slip hazards. Make sure that all spilled fluid is cleaned up, and leaks that create slip hazards are repaired.

Fire Hazards

Hydraulic fluid is usually mineral-based oil, which is flammable. More than one machine has caught fire and burnt up because of a hydraulic leak that has either been sprayed onto a turbocharger or ignited by welding sparks or a torch. You need to be careful when welding or using a torch on a machine that has a hydraulic leak.

FIGURE 22-19 shows a fire hazard warning you may see on a machine.

FIGURE 22-19 Fire hazard warning that could be found on a machine.
Image Provided As Courtesy of John Deere.

Additional Hydraulic Safety Tips

- Release pressure from any accumulator before disconnecting lines.
- Never mix brands of connectors, hoses, or tubes, or otherwise combine hydraulic components with incompatible specifications.
- Never tighten leaking connectors while the system is under pressure.
- Always use hydraulic equipment and tooling for its intended purpose, according to manufacturer's specifications.
- Clean parts with a non-**volatile** cleaning solution.

▶ De-energizing a Hydraulic System

S22002

When de-energizing a hydraulic system, several steps should be followed in order to ensure that it is not accidentally re-energized. Anyone affected by the equipment shutdown should first be informed, and then the equipment should be shut down according to normal operating procedures. The power to the equipment should be turned off at the source, and any dedicated lockout devices specific to the system should be utilized. For MORE, this usually means preventing the diesel engine from being started by locking out the starting system.

The system should be de-energized using any bleed valves designed for the purpose (if fitted), and pressure-monitoring devices such as pressure gauges should be used to ensure that the system is safe. Many newer machines incorporate pressure sensors in their hydraulic systems, and system pressure can be read on the machines display or with a connected laptop computer.

Finally, a restart attempt should be made to confirm that all power is off, and a "Do Not Operate" tag secured to the power source, using a nylon cable tie.

To de-energize a hydraulic system, follow the guidelines in **SKILL DRILL 22-2**.

SKILL DRILL 22-2 De-energizing a Hydraulic System

1. Communicate the system shutdown to all affected personnel.
2. Shut down system according to normal operating procedures.
3. Turn off the power at the source.
4. Lock out energy sources, using dedicated lockout devices specific to the system.
5. Release all sources of stored energy, using bleed valves designed for that purpose.
6. Confirm de-energization with pressure gauges.
7. Attempt to restart machine to confirm power is off; return switch to "off" position.
8. Secure tag ("Do Not Operate") to the power source, using a nylon cable tie.

▶ Wrap-Up

Ready for Review

- Typically, a diesel engine is used to drive a hydraulic system pump, and the output component is an actuator. Fluid is used to transfer energy.
- Hydraulic systems were incorporated into off-road equipment many years ago to replace mechanical systems that required high maintenance and were hard to control.
- A pump is used to create fluid flow, and the flow is sent to actuators (cylinders or motors), where it is converted to mechanical motion.
- Resistance to fluid flow caused by loads on actuators creates pressure in the system.
- Forces can be multiplied in hydraulic systems by increasing the surface area of the movable surface in the actuator. System pressure that is applied to a larger surface area increases force output.
- Flow in a hydraulic system is measured in units of volume per unit of time (gpm or lpm).
- Pressure is measured in units of weight or force per unit of area (psi or kg/cm^2).

- Pumps create hydraulic fluid flow for the system to use.
- Actuators receive fluid flow and convert to either linear or rotary motion.
- Hydraulic systems have several advantages over mechanical systems, such as flexibility, simplicity, and seamless speed control.
- Some examples of disadvantages of hydraulic systems are fire hazards, high-pressure fluid hazards, and cleanliness requirements.
- Pascal's law is a fundamental principle for hydraulic systems and states that pressure applied to a fluid in one part of a closed system will be transmitted without loss to all other areas of the system.
- Bernoulli's principle states that an increase in the speed of a fluid occurs simultaneously with a decrease in pressure or a decrease in the fluid's potential energy, and the inverse occurs in fluid as speed slows.
- Many different units of measure are used for hydraulic systems, such as psi, gpm, and fps.
- Pressure in a hydraulic system is created by resistance to fluid flow. The main source is the load on an actuator, but all components in the system will create some resistance to flow.
- Force is the resulting output of an actuator that has fluid flow directed to it. A cylinder's rod moving is applying a force to what it is connected to.
- System pressure can be applied to different-sized actuators to create different output forces.
- Actuator output speed is directly dependent on the rate of flow it receives and the size of the actuator.
- Atmospheric pressure is the weight of a 1-inch square column of air at sea level and is equivalent to 14.7 psi.
- Most gauges account for atmospheric pressure and read 0 psi at sea level, but some are called absolute and read 14.7 psi at sea level.
- Negative pressure (less than atmospheric) should only occur in two places in a hydraulic system (pump inlet and supply side of an actuator if the load overtakes pump supply).
- Several international bodies maintain standards for hydraulic systems and components, such as ANSI, ASTME, and ISO.
- To calculate the force a cylinder can create when fluid is delivered to it, you need to know its piston diameter and the pressure being applied to it. $F = P \times A$.
- The area of a circle can be calculated if you know either the piston diameter or radius, using the formulas $A = \pi r^2$ or $A = (\pi d^2)/4$.
- Safety concerns related to hydraulic systems include oil injection, trapped pressure, crushing hazards, burns, slips and falls, and fire hazards.

Key Terms

actuator A mechanism that provides force to move a load. It converts fluid flow into either linear or rotary motion.

effective area the area of a piston that fluid pressure can act on to move a load.

flow Hydraulic pumps create fluid flow. The movement of fluid in a hydraulic system is measured in gpm or lpm.

fluid A substance, such as liquid or gas, that flows and easily changes shape.

fluid power an energy transfer system that uses a fluid as its medium.

force multiplication The force advantage that can be gained at the actuator in a hydraulic system.

gallons per minute or liters per minute Two common units of measure used to quantify fluid flow in a hydraulic system.

gas A state of matter characterized by low density, easy compressibility, and a tendency to diffuse readily and uniformly.

hydraulic system An energy conversion system that uses a hydraulic fluid to transfer power output from a prime mover to actuators that perform work.

hydrodynamics The study of hydraulic systems where a high volume of fluid is in motion at a high velocity.

hydrostatics The study of fluid in an enclosed system where the fluid is at rest.

liquid A fluid that has a definite volume, but no shape. Liquid takes on the shape of its container, up to that volume. For most practical purposes, liquid is incompressible.

mechanical advantage The process of using a device to get more output force than the amount of input force, with the trade-off being that the input distance is proportionately longer than the output distance.

output force Resulting force from a linear actuator that comes from the working pressure applied to the surface area of its piston, expressed as pounds, newtons, or kilograms.

Pascal's law The law of physics that states that pressure applied to a fluid in one part of a closed system will be transmitted equally to all other areas of the system.

pounds per square inch or kilograms per square centimeter Two common units of measure used to quantify pressure in a hydraulic system.

pressure The result of resistance to fluid flow.

prime mover The initial source of energy in a system; a machine that transforms energy from thermal, electrical, or pressure form to mechanical form.

pump The component in a hydraulic system that receives power from a prime mover and produces fluid flow.

viscosity The measurement of the resistance of a liquid to shear (the resistance of a fluid to flow at a given temperature).

working pressure The pressure within a hydraulic system while the system is being operated.

Review Questions

1. Mobile heavy equipment machines rely on __________ systems to power and/or control many of the machine's systems.
   a. electronic
   b. electrical
   c. hydraulic
   d. rotational

2. Hydrodynamics refers to the study of hydraulic systems where a ____ volume of fluid is in motion at a ____ velocity in an enclosed system, and how the fluid acts on the components in that system.
   a. high, low
   b. high, high
   c. low, low
   d. low, high
3. All of the following are advantages of using hydraulically powered equipment, *except*:
   a. having fewer exposed mechanical parts that can wear and break down.
   b. being self-lubricating and compact.
   c. having no chance of equipment failure.
   d. relying on multiplication of forces, whereby a small force can control large forces.
4. Pascal's law states that "the pressure applied to a fluid in one part of a closed system will ____________________ of the system."
   a. be transmitted without loss to all the other areas
   b. be transmitted with loss to all the other areas
   c. not be transmitted to other area
   d. be transmitted to only another specific area
5. According to Bernoulli's principle, a rise in pressure in a flowing fluid must always be accompanied by a ________________ in the speed.
   a. sudden decrease
   b. proportionate decrease
   c. sudden rise
   d. proportionate rise
6. Whether metric or standard measurement units are used is usually determined by all of the following *except*:
   a. where the machine was designed.
   b. where the machine was manufactured.
   c. where the machine was tested.
   d. the common measurement system used by the manufacturer.
7. When the flow rate to a linear actuator is increased, rod travel will ______________.
   a. speed up
   b. slow down gradually
   c. not be affected
   d. drop exponentially
8. If a Technician measured system pressure______________, they would read a positive pressure.
   a. at the pump inlet
   b. anywhere between a pump outlet and a work port of an actuator
   c. in an actuator when the load overcomes the oil supplied to it
   d. the tank outlet for the pump
9. Which is the world's largest developer and publisher of international standards?
   a. American National Standards Institute
   b. International Organization for Standardization
   c. American Society for Testing and Materials
   d. Joint Industrial Council
10. Which of the following is a good practice?
   a. Do not release pressure from any accumulator before disconnecting lines.
   b. Tighten leaking connectors while the system is under pressure.
   c. Clean parts with a volatile cleaning solution.
   d. Make sure any component that could move and cause a crushing injury will be mechanically held in place.

ASE Technician A/Technician B Style Questions

1. Technician A says the term used for the component that drives the hydraulic system is "prime mover." Technician B says that a pump is an example of a power output component. Who is correct?
   a. Technician A
   b. Technician B
   c. Both A and B
   d. Neither A nor B
2. Technician A says pressure in a hydraulic system is created by pump flow. Technician B says forces can be multiplied in a hydraulic system. Who is correct?
   a. Technician A
   b. Technician B
   c. Both A and B
   d. Neither A nor B
3. Technician A says flow can be measured in psi. Technician B says pressure can be measured in gpm. Who is correct?
   a. Technician A
   b. Technician B
   c. Both A and B
   d. Neither A nor B
4. Technician A says hydraulic system pumps create pressure. Technician B says hydraulic system pumps create force. Who is correct?
   a. Technician A
   b. Technician B
   c. Both A and B
   d. Neither A nor B
5. Technician A says Pascal's law refers to pressure in a sealed system. Technician B says Pascal's law refers to the result of changing speed of hydraulic fluid. Who is correct?
   a. Technician A
   b. Technician B
   c. Both A and B
   d. Neither A nor B
6. Technician A says the output speed of an actuator is dependent on fluid pressure only. Technician B says the output speed of an actuator is dependent on the rate of fluid flowing to it and its size. Who is correct?
   a. Technician A
   b. Technician B
   c. Both A and B
   d. Neither A nor B
7. Technician A says the retract force from a double-acting cylinder will always be less than the extend force given the same

pressure applied. Technician B says a single-acting cylinder only produces force when it extends. Who is correct?

a. Technician A
b. Technician B
c. Both A and B
d. Neither A nor B

8. Technician A says there are only European organizations to oversee technical and safety standards for hydraulic systems. Technician B says there are only American organizations to oversee technical and safety standards for hydraulic systems. Who is correct?
   a. Technician A
   b. Technician B
   c. Both A and B
   d. Neither A nor B
9. Technician A says that to find a value for force, you need to divide pressure by area. Technician B says to find the value for force, you need to multiply pressure by the area. Who is correct?
   a. Technician A
   b. Technician B
   c. Both A and B
   d. Neither A nor B
10. Technician A says oil injection injuries can be life threatening. Technician B says trapped oil pressure is always easy to release. Who is correct?
    a. Technician A
    b. Technician B
    c. Both A and B
    d. Neither A nor B

CHAPTER 23

Hydraulic Components—Principles of Operations

Knowledge Objectives

After reading this chapter, you will be able to:

- **K23001** Identify different types and applications of hydraulic systems used on mobile off-road equipment.
- **K23002** List the components of a basic hydraulic system.
- **K23003** Explain the operating principles of hydraulic system components.
- **K23004** Describe the operating principles of a basic hydraulic system.
- **K23005** Identify basic hydraulic schematic symbols.

Skills Objectives

After reading this chapter, you will be able to:

- **S23001** Calculate cycle time and horsepower requirements for hydraulic systems.
- **S23002** Draw a hydraulic schematic of a basic circuit using common symbols.

▶ Introduction

As mentioned in the previous chapter, a hydraulic system is an energy conversion system that begins with the mechanical power output from a rotating prime mover and uses hydraulic fluid to transfer energy to an actuator. The actuator then transfers the energy in the hydraulic fluid back to mechanical energy. The actuator could provide either linear (cylinder) or rotary (motor) motion.

A basic hydraulic system must have a minimum number of components to complete this energy transfer, and this chapter identifies those components and explain their operating principles.

One of the tasks a mobile off-road equipment (MORE) technician performs is diagnosing a hydraulic system problem. To do this, the Technician must be able to read and understand hydraulic schematics. Hydraulic symbols are used to make a hydraulic schematic, and these symbols are identified in this chapter. Another task a Technician may be asked to do is to add or customize existing hydraulic circuits to a machine. This requires reading or making schematics, and this chapter discusses reading and making schematics.

▶ Types and Applications of Hydraulic Systems Used for Mobile Off-Road Equipment

K23001

Types of Hydraulic Systems

A few different types of hydraulic systems are used on MORE machines. It is important to be able to understand the differences among them.

Open-Loop Hydraulic Systems

Most hydraulic systems used for implement control (blade, bucket, moldboard, etc.) that use linear actuators are considered to be open-loop systems. Open-loop hydraulic systems are ideal for these applications because of the flexibility they allow designers to have when designing hydraulic systems.

In **open-loop** hydraulic systems, the pump supply oil comes from the **reservoir** (tank). The pump then sends it to a directional control valve, where it either returns to the tank or is sent to an actuator. If oil is sent to an actuator, there will be return oil from the actuator that goes back to the tank through the directional control valve. The oil can then go back into the pump inlet. The oil going to the pump always starts at the reservoir and eventually "loops" its way back to the reservoir. The loop is considered to be open because the oil can return to the tank from several sources (directional control valve, actuators, pressure relief valves, etc.). See **FIGURE 23-1** for a schematic of a basic open-loop hydraulic circuit.

Closed-Loop Hydraulic System

In contrast with an open-loop system, in a **closed-loop** system the pump directly feeds a rotary actuator (motor), which negates the need for a directional control valve. The pump outlet sends fluid to the actuator inlet, and the return from the actuator goes directly back to the pump inlet. To reverse direction of the motor, the pump has to reverse flow direction, so it must be a bidirectional pump (to be discussed later). Because of normal internal leakage of the pump and motor, the loop has to be charged (kept full) with oil. A charge pump delivers oil from a reservoir to the closed-loop low-pressure side. Closed-loop hydraulic systems are quite often referred to as hydrostatic systems, and commonly used to generate machine travel. **FIGURE 23-2** shows a closed-loop hydraulic circuit.

Open- and Closed-Center Systems

There are also hydraulic systems that are called open center and closed center. This refers to the type of directional control valve that is used in the system. **Open-center** systems have pump oil flowing through their directional control valves all the time. When the actuators aren't being supplied oil, the pump flow is returned to the tank through the valve. These systems usually have fixed displacement pumps that always pump oil when they are rotating. An open-center directional control valve is depicted in **FIGURE 23-3**.

You Are the Mobile Heavy Equipment Technician

You are given the task of installing a hydraulic attachment on a 40-ton excavator. The machine owner requires a swivel bucket on the machine for a certain job coming up. A swivel bucket has an extra pivot point and uses an extra hydraulic cylinder to make it pivot. The excavator is not plumbed for any attachments, so you will have to install hoses and tubing all the way from the control valve to the end of the stick. It appears as though the main control valve has an extra spool for an attachment, but its outlet ports are blocked off. The owner bought the swivel bucket used, and there are no specifications with it.

1. What information would be helpful to know before starting this job, to ensure proper hydraulic operation of the bucket after it is installed?
2. What information do you need to know in order to buy the correct hoses, tubes, and fittings for the installation?
3. If you found a hydraulic schematic for the excavator, would that help with the install?
4. Once you have the swivel bucket installed, could you expect another type of attachment to work properly if you replaced the swivel bucket with it?

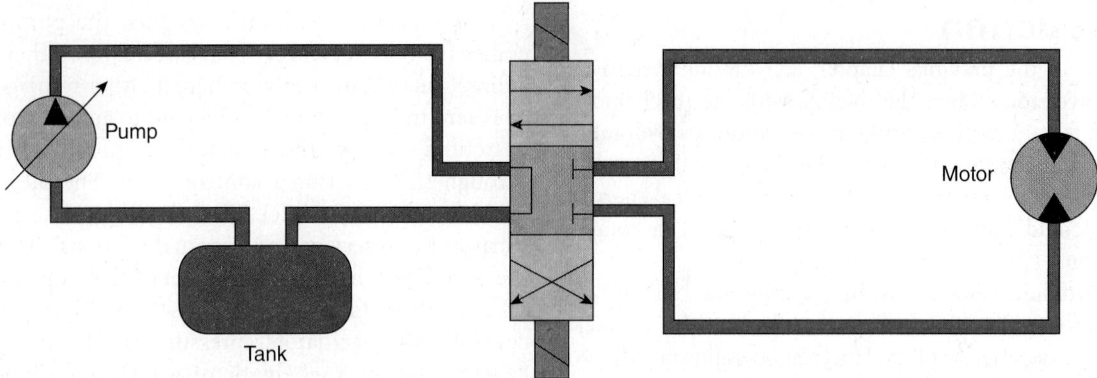

FIGURE 23-1 Schematic of a basic open-loop hydraulic circuit.

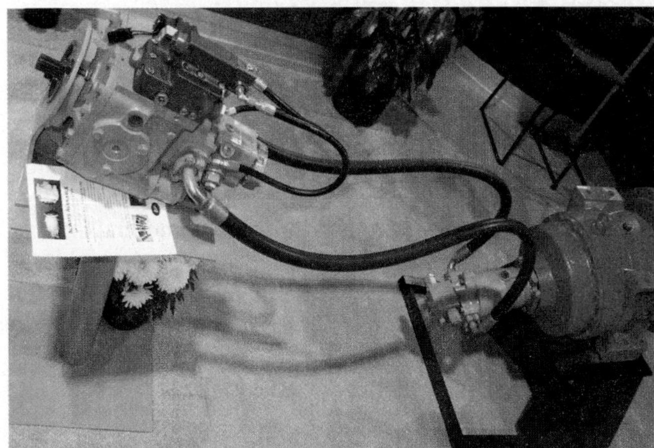

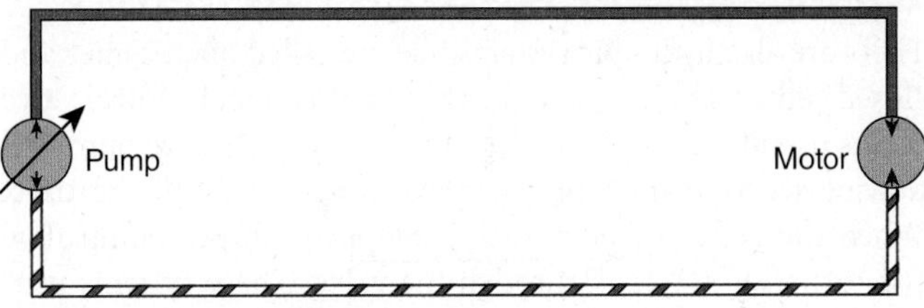

FIGURE 23-2 Closed-loop hydraulic circuit.

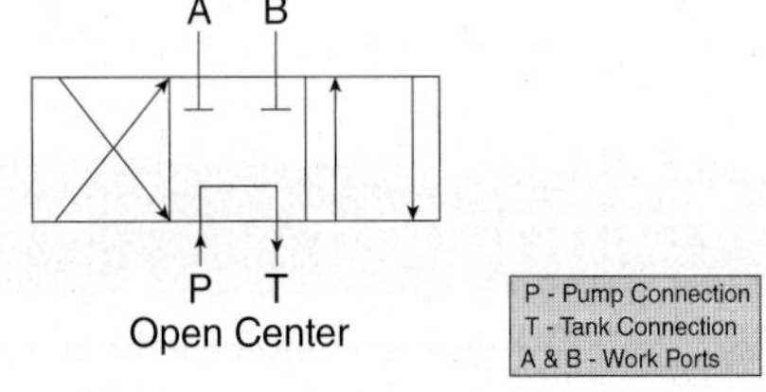

FIGURE 23-3 Open-center directional control valve.

Closed-Center Systems

In **closed-center** systems, directional control valves block pump oil flow and only redirect it when there is a request to send oil flow to one or more actuators. These systems are usually used with variable displacement pumps where flow can be shut off when there is no need to move actuators. See **FIGURE 23-4** for an example a closed-center directional control valve.

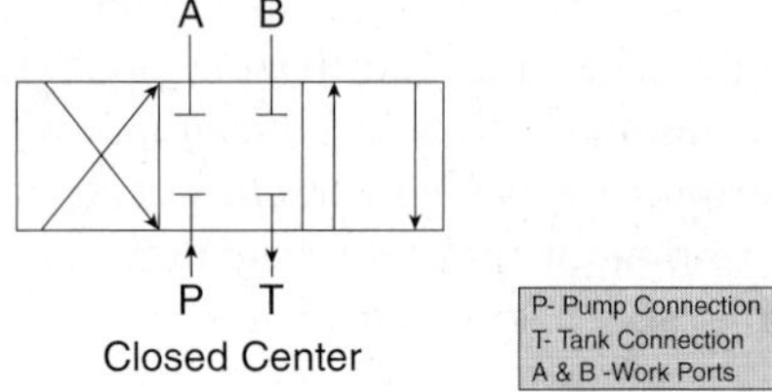

FIGURE 23-4 Closed-center directional control valve.

Applications of Hydraulic Systems on Mobile Off-Road Equipment

Common applications for hydraulic systems on MORE are for controlling machine implements such as loader buckets, dozer blades, dozer rippers, and haul truck dump bodies. These systems mainly need the motion and force from linear actuators either to directly move a machine component or indirectly move through a mechanical linkage. **FIGURE 23-5** shows a variety of machine implements powered by linear actuators.

There are many other machine systems that need rotary motion such as augers, track drives, and upper structure swing drives. **FIGURE 23-6** illustrates machine systems driven by rotary actuators. Rotary actuators produce torque output when oil is delivered to them.

Examples of Hydraulic Systems Found on Heavy Equipment Machines

The following are a few examples of different machines and the functions that hydraulic systems perform on them:

- Cranes—boom lift/lower, winch turning, swing rotation
- Earth movers—bowl lift/lower, ejector forward/back, apron up/down, steering, brakes
- Haul trucks—box lift/lower, steering, brakes
- Pavers—machine travel, belt rotation
- Fork lifts—forks, lower and tilt, steering, brakes
- Aerial lifts—boom lift, travel
- Excavator—boom up/down, stick in/out, bucket open/close, travel

FIGURE 23-5 A variety of machine implements powered by linear actuators.

FIGURE 23-6 Machine systems that are driven by rotary actuators.

- Loaders—boom up/down, bucket open/close, steering, brakes
- Compactor—steering, travel, vibration
- Backhoe—front boom up/down, front bucket open/close, rear boom up/down, rear stick in/out, rear bucket open/close, rear boom swing, steering, brakes.

Many machine attachments are hydraulically powered as well, such as hammers, brooms, and clam buckets and can use either linear or rotary actuators.

▶ Components of Basic Hydraulic Systems

K23002

To make a basic functional hydraulic system, you would need at least the following components: prime mover, reservoir, pump, directional control valve, pressure relief valve, actuator, hydraulic fluid, filter(s), and fluid conductors.

These components should be matched for both flow and pressure capacity to ensure system efficiency, smooth operation, and maximum longevity. Equipment manufacturer's engineers and designers must design the complete system so that its components work together. To design a hydraulic system, engineers start with determining the needs for actuator output in terms of force output (**linear actuators**) or torque output (rotary actuator) requirements. This determines actuator size and system pressure requirements. Then actuator speed requirements would be established, and this would determine system flow requirements. This includes **rod speed** parameters for linear actuators and output shaft rpm parameters for rotary actuators.

Finally cycle time and stroke length requirements have to be considered for a linear actuator. This also influences maximum flow requirements and, in turn, prime mover horsepower sizing. Hydraulic reservoir sizing could be determined at this point as well.

Mismatching hydraulic system components can lead to inefficiency, poor performance, or premature failures. For example: A pump's output specifications are 10 gpm flow at 2,500 psi while turning at 2,000 rpm. If it was installed into a system that had a working pressure of 3,500 psi, and its linear actuator needed 15 gpm to achieve a minimum **cycle time**, there would be complaints of a slow hydraulic system, and the pump may fail or at least not last for as long as it was originally designed to. If the cycle time is out of specification, the operator will complain that it is too slow or to jerky.

▶ TECHNICIAN TIP

When diagnosing some hydraulic problems, one of the basic checks to perform is to measure cycle time, that is, the time that a cylinder rod needs to travel one full stoke. A specification in the machine's service information will state what the cycle time should be. The specification will be given in seconds and have a minimum and maximum limit. An example is a bucket cylinder on an excavator that should have a cycle time of 5.5 seconds, extending plus or minus 0.5 second.

The following sections are an introduction to the components required for a basic hydraulic system. Power transfer in a hydraulic system can be understood by looking at **FIGURE 23-7**. The chapters that follow go into more detail about the construction features and types of hydraulic system components as well as how to maintain and repair them.

▶ Operating Principles of Hydraulic System Components

K23003, S23002

This section will discuss the basic operating principles of MORE hydraulic system components. Many of these components will be thoroughly looked at in chapters that follow. The intent here is to give an introduction to their operation.

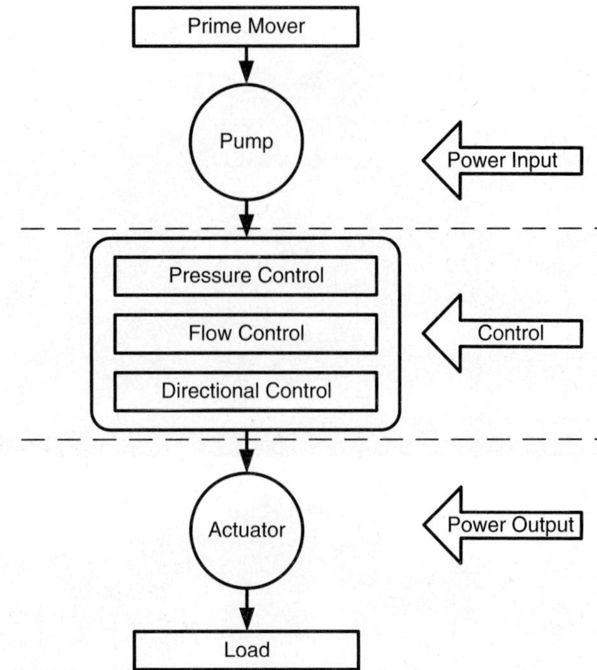

FIGURE 23-7 Power transfer in a hydraulic system.

Prime Mover

A machine's prime mover is used for the primary power source for a variety of machine systems, such as drivetrain, electric, and hydraulic.

Almost all MORE uses a diesel engine for their prime mover power. Diesel engines provide high torque and fuel-efficient operation at relatively low rpms, which helps ensure longevity of the components they drive. A diesel engine's high torque and low rpm output works well with most hydraulic systems, but systems that use variable displacement pumps that don't rely solely on pump rpm to determine hydraulic flow output are ideal matches for diesel engines. Pump input rpm can be made to vary from the prime mover rpm by transferring it through a set of fixed ratio gears. A pump drive gear set usually makes the pump turn faster than the prime mover. **FIGURE 23-8** shows a hydraulic pump connected to a prime mover.

Some machines are designed to have their diesel engines run at a steady rpm, but most diesel engine–powered machines normally have an rpm range between 700 rpm and 2,000–2,500 rpm. Depending on the type of pump used, engine rpm has a great influence on pump flow output.

Some large mining equipment, such as drills and shovels, may use electric motors for their prime mover that run at a fixed rpm, whereas some small machines could use gasoline- or propane-powered engines.

Reservoirs

A reservoir is a tank used to store the system fluid. The hydraulic reservoir holds excess hydraulic fluid to accommodate volume changes caused by cylinder extension and contraction, temperature-driven expansion and contraction, and leaks. The reservoir is also designed to aid in separating the air from the

FIGURE 23-8 Hydraulic pump connected to a prime mover.

FIGURE 23-9 A typical hydraulic reservoir.

fluid and to work as a heat exchanger to shed heat from the hydraulic fluid. Heavier contamination particles will also settle out in the bottom of the tank. See **FIGURE 23-9** for a typical hydraulic reservoir.

Reservoirs are usually mounted close to the machines pump(s) to reduce the chance of restricting the pump inlet. They are ideally mounted above the pump so gravity can assist in supplying fluid to the pump, but this may not be possible. The weight of hydraulic fluid above the pump inlet can be used to create "head pressure" to ensure a steady supply of oil gets to the pump.

They are usually fabricated from plate or formed steel, but some smaller machines have plastic hydraulic tanks. Some tanks supply more than one hydraulic system on a machine with the same oil, or they could even be partitioned to contain separate oils. Almost all tanks are constructed with baffles to slow down the return oil flow when it reaches the tank. This helps prevent turbulence in the oil and reduces the chance of air reaching the pump inlet.

Some tanks could have return filters to filter return oil or suction screens to keep large contamination out of the pump inlet.

Hydraulic tanks can be vented or pressurized. **Vented tanks** have breathers on top that allow filtered atmospheric air into them as the oil level changes due to actuator position or heat expansion. **FIGURE 23-10** illustrates a hydraulic tank breather.

FIGURE 23-10 Hydraulic tank breather.

Pressurized tanks take advantage of the pressure caused by expanding oil to create pressure in them. They sometimes use an external pressurized air supply from a pneumatic system or the diesel engine's intake air system to apply pressure to the inside of the tank. Pressurized tanks provide a higher positive pressure to the pump inlet.

Hydraulic tanks almost always provide an easy way for the operator to check the fluid level. Usually this is done by checking a **sight glass** on the side of the tank, but it could also be by using a dipstick. Most new machines also have a sensor that monitors fluid level and/or temperature. **FIGURE 23-11** shows a typical sight glass.

Hydraulic Pumps

A hydraulic pump converts mechanical rotary motion from the prime mover (the electric motor or internal combustion engine) to hydraulic power to operate the system. Hydraulic pumps produce the oil flow that is needed to move actuators (cylinders or motors). See **FIGURE 23-12** for a typical hydraulic pump.

There are two basic categories of hydraulic pump: **nonpositive displacement pumps** (also known as dynamic pumps) and **positive displacement pumps**. Pump displacement refers to the amount of fluid that a pump moves or displaces during one rotation of its driveshaft.

You may see a nonpositive displacement–type pump used as a charge pump in a hydraulic system. A charge pump in this case is for "charging" another pump's inlet with oil. Nonpositive displacement pumps have relatively large clearances between the rotating member and their housing and mainly use centrifugal force to move fluid. An engine coolant pump is a good example of this type of pump. Nonpositive pumps are not capable of maintaining high systems pressure because as loads increase, fluid can bypass inside the pump.

Positive displacement–type pumps are used for mobile equipment because they provide flow whenever they are turning and constantly back up the flow of oil leaving the pump. As actuator loads increase and system pressure increases, positive flow is needed to overcome the load and keep the actuator moving. If for some reason the flow of oil from a positive displacement pump gets totally blocked, a catastrophic failure will occur. These pumps must have very close tolerances (between 0.002" and 0.005" is common) between the rotating members inside the pump, as they rely on the fluid viscosity to create a seal between the members. **FIGURE 23-13** portrays a cutaway view of a multi-section hydraulic pump.

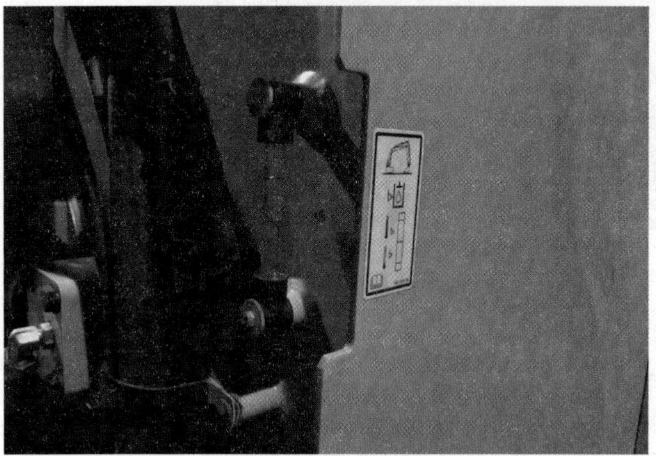

FIGURE 23-11 A typical hydraulic reservoir sight glass.

> **TECHNICIAN TIP**
>
> Keep in mind when servicing or repairing hydraulic pumps that they *must* always have an unrestricted supply to their inlet and must *never* have their outlet blocked. If either of these conditions is not met, pump failure will occur. Hydraulic pumps are also highly sensitive to contamination, and great care must be taken to ensure only clean oil enters the pump.

Hydraulic pumps must withstand high pressures and temperatures. Their housings can be made from machined cast aluminum or steel, and their rotating parts inside the housing are machined and hardened steel alloy. Proper clearances are critical to pump efficiency and longevity. As pumps

FIGURE 23-12 A typical hydraulic pump.

FIGURE 23-13 Cutaway view of a multi-section hydraulic pump.

wear, they become less efficient because less flow is produced per revolution, and this leakage turns into heat.

Pumps used on hydraulics equipment are positive displacement pumps. There are various types of positive displacement pumps—gear pumps, vane pumps, and **piston pumps**. Each type has distinct construction features and operating principles.

Fixed displacement pumps produce the same volume output per revolution, whereas **variable displacement pumps** can vary their output. Gear-type pumps are always fixed displacement–type pumps. For example, if a fixed displacement pump has a displacement of 25 cc/revolution and turns at 1,000 rpm, it will in theory produce a flow rate of 25 lpm. Another pump that has a displacement of 5 cubic inches/revolution and turns at 1,000 rpm will produce a theoretical flow rate of 21.6 gpm. These theoretical calculations don't take into account flow losses that naturally occur and increase with pump wear.

If a variable pump had a maximum displacement of 50 cc/revolution and was turning at 1,500 rpm, the maximum flow rate it could produce at that speed would be 75 lpm. It could also be controlled to produce any flow less than that.

Pump Types

MORE machines use a variety of hydraulic pumps. Several factors influence a manufacturer's decision on which type of pump to use. Some factors are cost, noise limitation, pressure limitations, flow limitations, and expected durability. The following sections discuss the most common pump types found on MORE machines.

Gear Pumps

Gear pumps are the simplest in design because they only contain two moving parts. There are two types of gear pumps: internal gear and external gear. External gear pumps are most common and have two gears with equally spaced teeth on the outside of their shafts that rotate inside the pump. One gear is driven by a splined or keyed shaft, and as it is driven, it drives the second gear inside the pump housing. When the pump starts to rotate, a low pressure is created at its inlet port, and hydraulic oil moves from the tank into the pump. The oil then is carried around the inside of the pump in the space between the teeth on each gear and the inside of the housing. As the oil reaches the pump outlet port, it leaves the pump and enters the system. **FIGURE 23-14** depicts a gear pump disassembled.

FIGURE 23-14 A gear pump disassembled.

Vane pumps

Vane pumps have multiple sliding vanes that are carried around in a rotor driven by the pump shaft. These parts of the pump rotate inside a cam ring that allows the vanes to move in and out of the rotor. As the vanes move, they create a changing volume between them. When a vane passes by the inlet port, oil moves into the pump because of the expanding size of the volume between vanes, which creates a lower pressure than the reservoir. Once the vanes pass the widest part of the cam ring and the volume starts decreasing, the oil is forced out the pump outlet and into the rest of the system. See **FIGURE 23-15** for an illustration of a vane pump rotor and cam ring. Vane pumps can be balanced (two inlet ports and two outlet ports) or unbalanced and can be fixed or variable displacement.

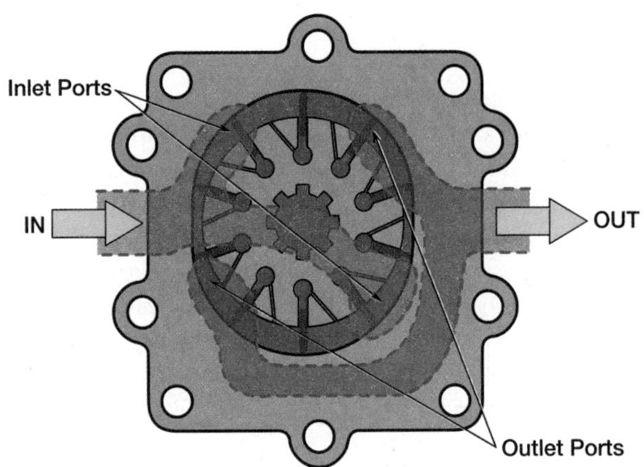

FIGURE 23-15 A vane pump rotor and cam ring.

Piston Pumps

Piston pumps are the most complex type of pump and can be either fixed or variable displacement, which makes them ideal

FIGURE 23-16 The cylinder block, pistons, and swashplate from a piston pump.

for a wide range of applications. This type of pump has a set of pistons that are carried around in a block that is driven by the pump shaft. The pistons have shoes that ride on a swashplate. A fixed displacement pump has a swashplate that is fixed at a certain angle (a few degrees from 90 to the centerline of the shaft). The swashplate angle determines the stroke length, which in turn determines the pump displacement. A variable displacement pump has a movable swashplate. As the swashplate moves, the pump displacement changes. **FIGURE 23-16** illustrates a piston pump's cylinder block, pistons, and swashplate.

Hydraulic Valves

Valves are constructed in a wide variety of configurations to meet different needs within hydraulic circuits. They can be assembled in blocks or modules, or can work alone. Whether used to relieve pressure or to meter hydraulic fluid to actuators, each valve is critical to the operation of all hydraulic equipment. Hydraulic valves can have housings that start out as cast steel or aluminum blocks that are then machine finished. Internal valve components start out as steel alloy materials that are finely machined and finished. Examples of different types of hydraulic valves and their functions include the following.

FIGURE 23-17 Main relief valve that is part of a directional control valve assembly.

Pressure Control Valves

Pressure control valves can limit system pressure or circuit pressure. They are usually adjustable and are set to keep pressures to a safe level to prevent component failure. See **FIGURE 23-17** for a main relief valve that is part of a directional control valve assembly. Normally, pressure control valves are held closed by spring pressure.

Flow Control Valves

Flow control valves control the flow rate of the fluid to the actuators so they operate at the proper speed. Flow control valves can be manually adjusted or actuated by hydraulic oil.

Directional Control Valves

Directional control valves direct the fluid to and from the actuators. Main control valves can have several sections or separate control valves combined into one housing, or they can be standalone components. Pilot control valves are a type of directional valve actuated by joysticks, and direct a much lower pressure oil to a main control valve to control its actuation.

Directional control valves can be controlled manually, electrically, pneumatically, or hydraulically. See **FIGURE 23-18** for an example of a directional control valve that is manually actuated.

SAFETY TIP

If you are required to adjust pressures in a hydraulic system great care must be taken to ensure pressures don't exceed maximum allowable limits. Excessive system or circuit pressures can cause sudden component failure, which can lead to a dangerous high-pressure leak. If a technician is exposed to a high-pressure leak, there is a great risk of an oil injection injury. These injuries are very serious and can lead to death.

Hydraulic Actuators

Actuators convert fluid energy back into mechanical energy to move a load. They can come in two forms: linear actuators (such as hydraulic cylinders, or rams), or rotary actuators (hydraulic motors).

FIGURE 23-18 A directional control valve that is manually actuated.

FIGURE 23-19 A linear actuator on a machine.

Hydraulic Cylinders

Hydraulic cylinders, or rams, receive hydraulic fluid from a directional control valve and transfer fluid in motion into linear mechanical motion. This is why they are called linear actuators. They are used to do everything from steering wheel loaders or lifting dump bodies on haul trucks, to moving the buckets of giant shovels in open-pit mines. In fluid power mechanics, the hydraulic cylinder enables the lifting of heavy components or materials in mobile equipment applications.

Hydraulic cylinders are made up of a barrel, a piston and rod assembly, and a head. The head and barrel make a sealed container in which the piston and rod assembly moves. The barrel is stationary and usually attached to the machine with a steel pin while the end of the rod is attached to a movable component. See FIGURE 23-19 for a linear actuator on a machine.

There are several variations of linear actuators, such as single acting, double acting, telescoping, and double rod. **Double-acting cylinders** are the most common design. They are sometimes called differential cylinders because their rod takes up space in the cylinder and creates a speed and force differential as the rod moves in and out of the barrel. Oil is directed into the cylinder through one of two ports at opposite ends of the barrel, and this oil is applied to either side of the piston. The oil flow acts on one side of the piston to move it and the rod, which in turn moves the load. See FIGURE 23-20 for an illustration of the components that make up a double-acting linear actuator.

All linear cylinders rely on a series of seals to keep fluid from leaking both internally and externally. Barrels start out as steel tubes that are finished internally to a crosshatched pattern with a specified roughness. Barrel bottom ends are usually welded on or threaded on and machined to receive pins. Rod end caps or heads are usually bolted to the barrel. Rods have a chrome finish that can be damaged fairly easily, and the rod end is usually welded to the rod. Pistons can be threaded onto the rod or held on with a large nut or bolt.

Hydraulic Motors and Rotary Actuators

Typically, hydraulic motors provide continuous rotary motion, whereas rotary actuators (sometimes called oscillators) provide a limited rotation, usually up to a maximum of 720 degrees.

A **hydraulic motor**, or actuator, is similar in construction to a hydraulic pump. But whereas pumps convert mechanical rotary motion to hydraulic power, the rotary actuator reverses the process by using the hydraulic power to create rotary

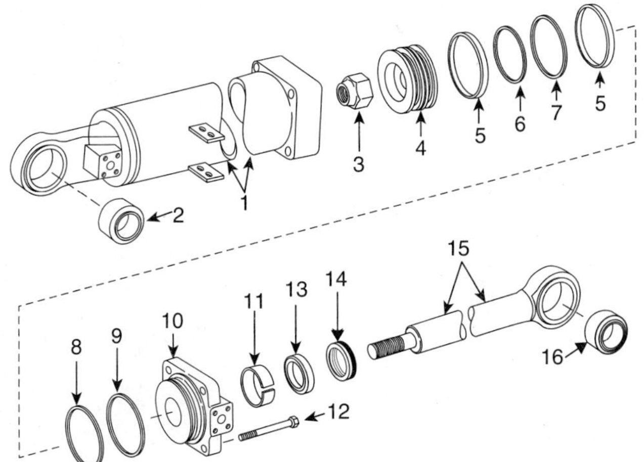

FIGURE 23-20 Double-acting linear actuator components.

mechanical motion. As with pumps, there are many different designs of hydraulic motors in order to best match specific applications. Hydraulic motors are available in fixed and variable displacement configurations and are almost always bidirectional to provide forward and reverse motion. By simply reversing flow to the motor, the output shaft rotation is reversed.

One common application for a rotary actuator is for producing travel torque for either a wheel-type or track-type machine. Another use is to turn the upper structure of an excavator or crane. See **FIGURE 23-21** for rotary actuators that drive the swing mechanism for a large crane.

Some types of hydraulic motors are gear, axial piston, bent axis piston, cam lobe, and gerotor. They all have precision-machined internal components and seals that are susceptible to contamination. Input flow is applied to movable components inside the motor, which in turn creates rotation that is transferred to the motor's output shaft. Most hydraulic motors have three ports to allow fluid movement in and out of them: two work ports and a third port to allow internal leakage to drain. See **FIGURE 23-22** for a cutaway view of a **bent axis motor** with a brake assembly integrated.

FIGURE 23-21 Rotary actuators that drive the swing mechanism for a large crane.

FIGURE 23-22 Cutaway view of a bent axis motor with a brake assembly integrated.

Hydraulic Filters

Filters are an important part of a hydraulic system because they remove damaging contaminants from the hydraulic fluid. Hydraulic systems are very sensitive to any form of **contamination** (liquid, solid, gaseous), and some solid contaminant particles can be microscopic in size. To keep fluid contamination to a safe level, several different styles of filters can be used in hydraulic systems to prevent contamination from damaging internal components. The most common type of filter is one that uses a filter media (mesh, cellulose, or synthetic) to capture contamination. They can be **spin on-type filters** that are replaced as a unit, or cartridge type that only have the element replaced. See **FIGURE 23-23** for some typical spin-on filters and a cutaway view of a spin-on hydraulic filter.

Filter efficiency refers to how effective the filter's contaminant capture is versus the extent to which it restricts flow. Filter assemblies have a bypass feature that allows flow past the filter if it becomes too restricted because of contaminant loading. Many filter assemblies will alert the operator if the bypass opens.

FIGURE 23-23 Typical spin-on filters and a cutaway view of a hydraulic spin-on filter.

Anytime the bypass for a filter opens, the machine should be stopped safely to prevent system damage.

Contamination can be removed from a hydraulic system by filters located at six different points within the system:

1. **Tank breather filter:** Large volumes of air can move in and out of a hydraulic tank. The air has to be filtered to remove water and dust particles before they contaminate the fluid. In addition, vapors released to the atmosphere from the hydraulic oil have to be removed to prevent air pollution.
2. **Case drain filter:** These are sometimes used to filter internal leakage oil from pumps and motors.
3. **Suction filter:** Suction filters or lines range from a coarse strainer of 250 microns (60 mesh) to a fine element of 25 microns (550 mesh). Suction filters clean the oil before it enters the pump, but they can also restrict flow if they are clogged or if the oil is too thick. Restricting oil flow to a pump will cause damage to it.
4. **Pressure filter:** A pressure filter or line can be installed between the pump and the directional control valves to remove fine particles, down to 3 microns (4,800 mesh) in some systems.
5. **Return filter**: A return filter filters the oil returning to the tank from the valves and actuators. Keeping the fluid in the hydraulic tank clean of contaminants is important so that the contamination doesn't get sent back through the system. See **FIGURE 23-24** for a return cartridge–type filter.
6. **Off-line filter:** The filtration system filters only part of the system's oil flow, so a dedicated pump and filtration system can be installed. Components can be smaller, and the finest of filters can be used without affecting the performance of the main system. These filters are sometimes called kidney loop filters.

FIGURE 23-24 A return cartridge–type filter.

> **TECHNICIAN TIP**
>
> A common task that a technician will perform on MORE is changing hydraulic filters. When doing this for the first time on a certain type or model of equipment, you should always refer to the maintenance guide for the machine. There could be one or two filters in locations on the machine that are not easy to find. You also need to take care that all pressure is released before removing filters or else you risk creating an environmental or safety hazard. **FIGURE 23-25** depicts an example of a warning found on a machine.

FIGURE 23-25 Warning found on a machine.

Lines and Fittings

Lines and fittings carry the fluid from the reservoir to the pump and on to the remaining system components through a combination of rigid steel tubing and flexible hose assemblies. Lines and fittings are also sometimes called **fluid conductors**.

When working with hoses and tubes, it is particularly important to understand how hoses are made, how they are fitted, and what their ratings mean. Flexible hose assemblies allow movement of actuators, reduce the transmission of vibrations, and absorb pressure spikes better than comparable rigid steel tubing. A hydraulic hose is constructed from layers of material selected to meet the required operating pressure and to be compatible with hydraulic fluids and applications. Hoses and tubes used on an excavator are shown in **FIGURE 23-26**.

Rigid steel tubes assist in cooling the fluid, are cost effective, and take up less space than comparable flexible hoses. The size of the internal bore of the tube or hose is important in facilitating the efficient flow of the hydraulic fluid. If the internal diameter is too small, then the flow will be restricted and will become turbulent. This also leads to excessive heat buildup in the fluid, which increases inefficiency. The correct internal diameter creates a smooth flow, described as **laminar flow**. Although desirable, laminar flow is often difficult to achieve in mobile hydraulic systems.

To achieve a constant oil flow rate within a circuit, three different factors have to be considered:

1. The supply from the tank or reservoir to the pump is subject to very low pressures and requires a large internal diameter to allow free flow of oil to the pump inlet.

FIGURE 23-26 Hoses and tubes used on an excavator.

2. Tubes or hoses subject to high pressure can be considerably smaller in diameter than pump supply hoses and will still maintain laminar flow.
3. Fluid returning from the directional valves to the tank or reservoir is subject to an intermediate pressure and requires an intermediate diameter.

Hydraulic fittings come in a wide variety of styles, types, pressure ratings, and sizes. As with hoses and tubes, great care must be taken when replacing fittings to ensure they are rated for the pressure they will be exposed to. They must also be compatible with the hoses and fittings they are connecting, or sudden failure is quite possible. See **FIGURE 23-27** for a variety of hydraulic fittings.

When replacing a hose or tube, it is always best to go with an original specification part or an oversize part, if unsure. Required pressure ratings for hoses and tubes must always be matched or exceeded when replacing hoses or tubes. **FIGURE 23-28** illustrates hoses marked with specifications and ratings.

FIGURE 23-27 A variety of hydraulic fittings.

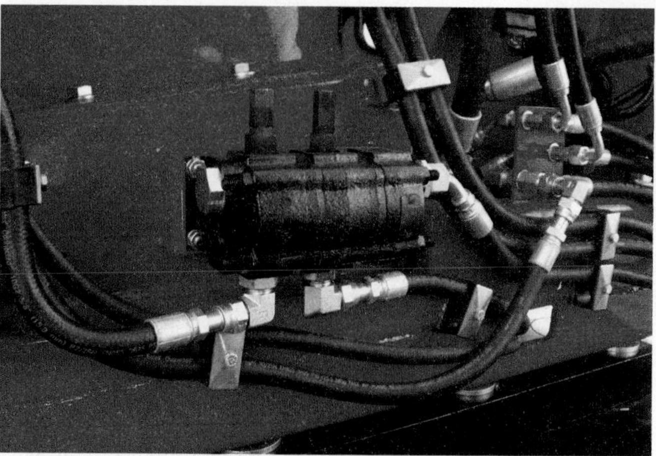

FIGURE 23-28 Hoses marked with specifications and ratings.

Some other components that may be found in hydraulic systems, but that are not necessary for all systems, are accumulators, heaters, and coolers.

Accumulators

A hydraulic **accumulator** is capable of storing hydraulic energy. It can perform a number of functions when used in a hydraulic system, including the following:

- Acting as an emergency power source in the event of pump or engine failure
- Providing a pressure source to hold loads in place with the pump shut down
- Providing additional hydraulic energy during peak load demand and recharging during low-demand periods, just like a battery and alternator in a car
- Removing pressure and flow pulsations created by actuators or pumps
- Providing fluid flow to supplement the pump in order to increase actuator speed
- Acting as a shock absorber for an actuator (an accumulator can operate faster than a relief valve)
- Operating as part of a suspension system for a vehicle or machine
- Starting up an emergency lubrication system
- Acting as part of an engine starting or cranking system for marine or mining applications.

A hydraulic fluid cannot be compressed or changed chemically. Therefore, for a hydraulic accumulator to work, the hydraulic energy must be changed into mechanical or pneumatic energy.

There are three types of hydraulic accumulators; each accomplishes energy storage in a different way:

- **Weighted accumulators** make use of a hydraulic cylinder lifting a weight, either directly or through a lever. The weight acts on the fluid, and the energy stored can be retrieved when needed. These are rarely found on today's machines.
- **Spring-loaded accumulators** replace the weight with a spring, usually the coiled compression type. Using a spring

FIGURE 23-29 Examples of hydraulic accumulators.

FIGURE 23-30 A hydraulic cooler.

reduces the physical size of the accumulator assembly. This type of accumulator is not very common.

- **Compressed-gas accumulators**, also known as hydropneumatic accumulators, replace the coiled spring with a gas. Oxygen or air is not suitable, as it may cause combustion, but nitrogen, which is almost inert in its natural diatomic state, is commonly used.

See **FIGURE 23-29** for Examples of hydraulic accumulators.

Heaters and Coolers

Heaters and coolers help to regulate hydraulic fluid temperature. These **heat exchangers** either put heat into the hydraulic fluid or remove it. To maintain fluid temperatures within the required operating range, an oil cooler may be required to dissipate waste heat that is generated by the hydraulic system. The quantity of waste heat increases as the components wear; therefore, the maintenance of the cooling circuit becomes more important as running hours accumulate on hydraulic components.

Two types of oil coolers can be found on MORE:

- The liquid-cooled type, usually used in torque convertor systems and marine applications
- The air-cooled variant, the most common in mobile equipment for hydraulic systems.

Air-cooled hydraulic oil cooler circuits operate with a design similar to that in an engine cooling system. Oil is circulated through small tubes with fins that dissipate heat to the surrounding air. A fan is used to keep air flowing past the cooler. See **FIGURE 23-30** for a hydraulic cooler.

More elaborate systems can feature a thermostatic or pressure-based bypass valve that directs cold fluid directly to the reservoir. As fluid temperature rises and viscosity reduces, a greater volume of fluid is passed through the cooler.

Hydraulic fluid heaters are found on machines that work in extreme cold environments and are used to maintain a minimum oil temperature and viscosity. They can be diesel-fired heat exchangers similar to supplementary engine coolant heaters or electric elements that could use a generator to keep them warm.

Identifying and Locating Hydraulic Component of MORE

To identify and locate hydraulic components on MORE, follow the steps in **SKILL DRILL 23-1**.

SKILL DRILL 23-1 Identifying and Locating Hydraulic Components on MORE

1. Go to one piece of MORE, and perform the required LOTO procedures to be sure the machine is in a de-energized state. Record the make, model, and hours on the machine.
2. If necessary, carefully open or remove access panels, to view hydraulic system components.
3. Locate the following hydraulic components on the machine: prime mover, pump, reservoir, directional control valve, one actuator, and one filter.
4. Describe the location of each component in relation to front/back, left/right of the machine and other machine components.
5. Give a brief description of each component.
6. Is the system an open-loop or closed-loop hydraulic system?
7. Are there any other hydraulic components on the machine, such as accumulators or heater/coolers?
8. Are there any safety warnings on the machine related to the hydraulic system?
9. Replace or close all access panels on the machine.
10. Remove all LOTO devices.

▶ Operation of a Basic Hydraulic System

K23004

A good example of a simple basic hydraulic system complete with prime mover is a hydraulic **wood splitter** powered by a gasoline engine. See Figure 23-30 for a typical gasoline-powered wood splitter. Although a wood splitter isn't considered to be a mobile off-road machine, its hydraulic system makes a great representation of a single circuit hydraulic system that could be found on MORE.

A wood splitter is used to split round 16–24" lengths of wood into smaller pieces, for firewood, that are easier to handle (**FIGURE 23-31**). It has one circuit or function. A wedge is attached to the end of the rod of its double-acting cylinder, and as the wedge gets pushed into the piece of wood that is held stationary, the wedge splits it.

A typical wood splitter produces 20 tons of linear force, good enough to split most hardwood easily. It uses a 6–8 horsepower prime mover that runs at a steady rpm, and therefore the pump supplies a steady flow to the circuit. The small gasoline engine drives a pump through a coupler. The pump is supplied oil from a reservoir to its inlet and sends oil to a directional control valve. The pump is a fixed displacement gear-type pump, which means as long as it is turning, it is moving oil, and the rate of oil flow is dependent on rpm.

FIGURE 23-31 A typical gasoline-powered wood splitter.

▶ TECHNICIAN TIP

Most wood splitters use a two-stage pump (one that has two sections) that delivers flow from both sections to the actuator when there is no load on it for faster actuator movement. There is an unloader valve in the pump that redirects flow from one of the sections back to the pump inlet when system pressure increases. This occurs when the wedge moves into the log. To keep things simple for now, we will assume the pump is a single-stage or single-section type. See **FIGURE 23-32** for a two stage pump. If you are not familiar with how a wood splitter operates, simply search the Internet to find a video of one at work. Keep in mind that there are many variations of these machines, so try to look for a simple single-function wood splitter.

FIGURE 23-32 Typical two-stage pump.

The directional control valve is an open-center type, which means when it's in neutral, it allows pump flow to pass through it and return to the tank through a filter. However, as soon as the operator moves the lever for the valve, its spool shifts and pump flow is redirected to the actuator. Pump flow now moves the piston in the cylinder, and the rod that is attached to the piston moves. Oil on the other side of piston also has to move, and it is returned back to the tank through the control valve. It passes through the return filter before it gets to the tank. For any open-loop hydraulic circuit that uses a fixed displacement pump, this is a typical path for the oil to circulate.

Just like any hydraulic system, pressure in the system is dependent on the load on the actuator. If the rod is moving out without any resistance, then pressure will be very low. If a log is placed on the bed and the operator keeps the lever shifted to move the rod and split the wood, then pressure will rise in an amount directly proportional to how much resistance the piece of wood creates. For example, a piece of soft wood may only require 1,000 psi to keep the rod moving, but a knotty piece of hardwood may stall (stop moving) the rod. If this happens, the pressure relief valve must open or else the engine would stall. When the pressure relief valve opens, the fluid continues flowing to the reservoir, and the engine keeps running, although it will be under maximum load.

To reverse the direction of the wedge once a piece of wood is split, the operator moves the lever on the directional control valve in the opposite direction. The spool inside the valve shifts, and pump oil is directed to the rod end of the cylinder. Oil now acts on the rod side of the piston and forces the piston and rod back into the cylinder. Once the wedge is drawn back, another piece of log can be placed on the table to be split by the next rod stroke.

The speed at which the rod moves is dependent on the amount of oil flow sent to it by the pump. Rod speed is measured in ft/sec or m/sec. Pump output is measured in gpm (gallons per minute) or lpm (liters per minute).

Oil pressure acting on the cylinder is dependent on the amount of resistance the rod encounters. Maximum pressure is limited by the pressure relief valve that is in the directional control valve.

▶ Calculating Cycle Times and Hydraulic Horsepower

S23001

If we use the above example of the wood splitter, we can take a look at how much horsepower is required to drive the pump and how fast the rod can cycle. Cycle time refers to the time it takes a cylinder rod to move a full stroke either extending or retracting.

To calculate cycle time, you need to know a few values. First, you have to know the cylinder dimensions to be able to calculate the volume of oil needed to move the rod a full stroke.

Once cylinder volume is determined and pump flow is known, cycle time can be calculated.

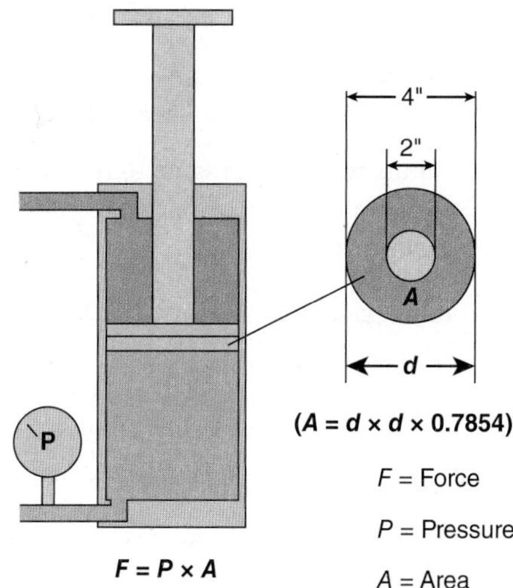

FIGURE 23-33 Dimensions of the cylinder.

Example 1

See **FIGURE 23-33** for an illustration showing the dimensions of the cylinder.

If a wood splitter has a cylinder with a piston diameter of 4" (radius is 2"), a rod diameter of 2" (radius is 1") and a stroke of 24", what is the volume of oil needed to cycle the rod?

Volume of head end of cylinder
(volume below piston when it's fully extended) $= A \times L$

$$\text{Area of piston} = \pi r^2$$
$$= 3.14 \times 2^2$$
$$= 12.56 \text{ in.}^2$$

$$\text{Volume of cylinder below piston} = A \times L$$
$$= 12.56 \text{ in.}^2 \times 24''$$
$$= 301.44 \text{ in.}^3$$

Therefore, it would take just over 300 in.^{3} of oil to fully extend the rod from the fully retracted position.

To calculate the volume of oil needed to retract the rod from fully extended, the volume that the rod takes up must be subtracted from the volume above the piston.

$$\text{Volume of rod} = A \times L$$
$$A = \pi r^2$$
$$A = 3.14 \times 1^2$$
$$A = 3.14 \text{ in.}^2$$
$$V = A \times L$$
$$V = 3.14 \text{ in.}^2 \times 24''$$
$$V = 75.36 \text{ in.}^3$$

Volume of oil needed to retract piston fully =
Total volume above piston—rod volume

$$= 301.44 \text{ in.}^3 - 75.36 \text{ in.}^3$$
$$= 226.08 \text{ in.}^3$$

If the pump produces 10 gpm, how fast would the rod fully extend?

Cycle time extend = Volume of oil needed/Pump flow × 60

Because the units must be the same to find an answer, you first need to convert oil volume from in.^{3} to gallons. There is 231 in.^{3} per U.S. gallon of oil.

Volume (gallons) = Volume (in.^{3})/231

= 301.44/231

= 1.3 U.S. gallons

Cycle time extend = 1.3 gallons/10 gpm × 60

= 7.8 seconds

Cycle time retract = Volume of oil needed/Pump flow × 60

Volume (gallons) = Volume (in.^{3})/231

= 226.08 in.^{3}/231

= 0.98 gallons

Cycle time retract = 0.98 gallons/10 gpm × 60

= 5.9 seconds

The difference in cycle times from extend to retract is roughly 1.9 seconds. This is because the volume that the rod takes up is not needed to move the piston. See **FIGURE 23-34** for an illustration of the example.

To calculate how much theoretical horsepower is needed to drive a pump, you need to know the maximum pressure the system is limited to and the maximum flow output of the pump. The formula for calculating hydraulic horsepower is psi × gpm/1,714.

Hydraulic horsepower = psi × gpm/1,714

= 3,000 psi × 10 gpm/1,714

= 17.5 hp

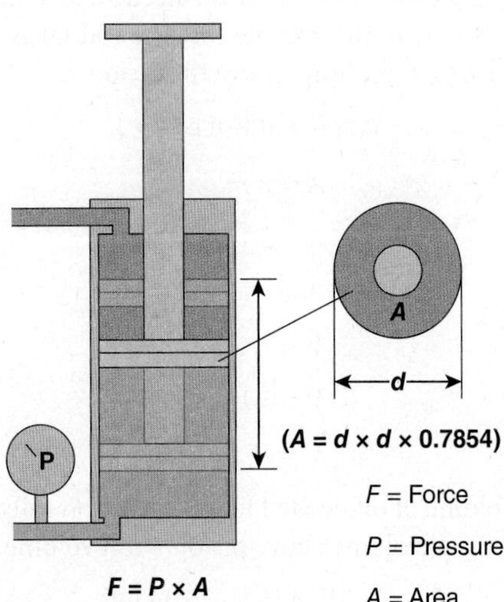

FIGURE 23-34 Cycle times.

> **TECHNICIAN TIP**
>
> Hydraulic systems are generally about 85% efficient, which means that the output energy value is only 85% of the input energy value. The 15% loss is mainly due to heat loss, which is a result of friction created by fluid flowing through the system. Friction creates heat, which in a hydraulic system is wasted energy because it simply dissipates to the atmosphere and performs no work.

For example, the wood splitter above requires a theoretical 17.5 hp prime mover based on a given flow output and the system's pressure. However, due to flow losses (inefficiencies), we will assume the system is only 85% efficient; therefore, it will require slightly more than 17.5 hp to drive the pump.

Prime Mover Requirements

As mentioned previously, most wood splitters use a two-section pump that diverts part of the pump flow when the system pressure increases. It uses a pump unloader valve to do this, but why is this feature used?

If pump flow at high pressure is reduced, the prime mover can be downsized, and instead of needing a 17.5 hp gasoline engine to drive the pump, a much smaller prime mover is needed. Also, for better machine operation if the rod slows down when the load increases, the operator will have better control.

Therefore, if half of the pump flow is diverted when pressure increases, then the prime mover size would decrease by one-half.

Hydraulic horsepower = Flow × pressure/1,714

= 5 gpm × 3,000 psi/1,714

= 8.75 hp

System Pressure Requirements

To calculate the maximum pressure at which the wood splitter needs to operate in order to produce 20 tons of force, you only need to know the piston area. Because Force = Pressure × Area, this can be easily calculated by reworking the formula:

$F = P \times A$

$P = F/A$

$P = 20$ tons/12.56 in.^{2}

$P = 40{,}000$ lb/12.56 in.^{2}

$P = 3{,}185$ psi

Therefore, if the relief valve was set at 3,200 psi, the wood splitter could produce approximately 20 tons of force on extend.

Calculating Cycle Times

To calculate cycle times, follow these steps:

1. Determine cylinder extend volume: Piston area × Stroke length
2. Calculate cycle time for extend: CT = Extend volume/pump flow × 60

3. Determine cylinder retract volume: Effective area × Stroke length
4. Calculate cycle time for retract: CT = Retract volume/pump flow × 60.

Example 1

A cylinder has a piston diameter of 20 cm, a rod diameter of 10 cm, and a stroke of 100 cm. What are the extend and retract times if a pump supplies 50 lpm to the cylinder?

Example 2

A cylinder has a piston diameter of 6.4", a rod diameter of 4.2" and a stroke length of 17". What are the extend and retract times if a pump supplies 28 gpm to the cylinder?

Calculate the hydraulic horsepower the following systems produce:

▶ Basic Hydraulic Schematic Symbols

K23005

Technicians who service and repair MORE will at some point need to read and understand a **hydraulic schematic**. This could be to assist with diagnosing a hydraulic system problem or to help with connecting a hydraulic attachment to a machine. Hydraulic schematics are similar to electrical schematics in that standard graphic symbols are used to represent machine components; they are not accurate as far as spatial relationship, and they can sometimes be color-coded. Hydraulic schematics can be used to trace oil flow through a system and to see what components are part of either one circuit or the entire system.

Schematics can come in paper or electronic formats. It's very important to find the exact schematic for the machine you are looking for because hydraulic systems can change drastically from one machine model to another, and even between machines that are of the same series production.

Look at **FIGURE 23-35** to see a schematic representation of the wood splitter that was discussed previously. This is a very simple schematic and very easy to interpret. More complex multi-circuit hydraulic systems could have their hydraulic schematics spread over several pages and have many more complex symbols.

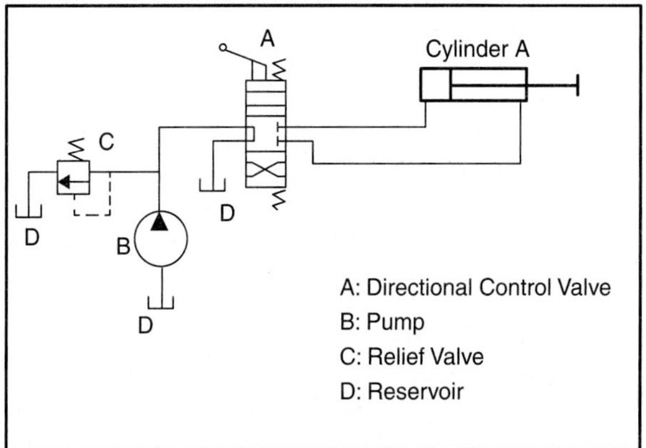

FIGURE 23-35 Schematic for a typical wood splitter.

The graphic symbols for fluid power systems and components, and the terms used to describe them, are standardized throughout the world by the ISO, with additional input from the ANSI.

Some manufacturers may use slight variations of these symbols, but they should be recognizable as symbols for the components they are representing.

Some basic shapes are the starting point for symbols used to identify hydraulic components such as the ones listed here:

Circle—pump or motor
Square—valve
Rectangle—multi-position valve or linear actuator
Diamond—fluid conditioner
Lines—hoses or tubes
Oval—accumulator

Additions to these basic symbols make up the majority of common hydraulic symbols. One common symbol that can be used with many other component symbols is a spring symbol, which is simply a series of horizontal or vertical zigzag lines. Chapter 33 for more details on hydraulic symbols and schematics.

Pumps and Motors

The symbols for pumps and motors start with a circle to indicate rotary motion. Triangles are added, and their orientation indicates fluid flow direction, which in turn shows whether it is a pump or motor. Solid triangles indicate fluid pumps (hydraulic pumps), and hollow triangles indicate a pneumatic pump (air compressor). Two triangles in a circle indicate a bidirectional component. A diagonal arrow through the symbol denotes that the component is a variable displacement type. Otherwise, you would assume it is fixed displacement. See **FIGURE 23-36** for the common symbols for pumps and motors. Two or more circles that are together indicate a multi-section pump.

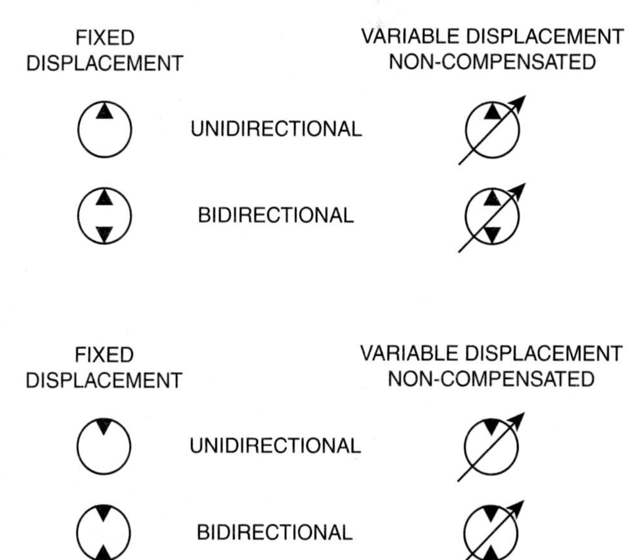

FIGURE 23-36 Common symbols for pumps and motors.

Valves

Valve symbols start with a square box, and as lines, arrows, and spring symbols are added, the type of valve is indicated. They will be shown in their unactuated, or at rest, state (machine off).

Pressure and Flow Control Valve Symbols

Common single box symbols are pressure relief valves, flow control valves, and pressure reducing valves. A square box will have other lines and arrows added to it to indicate how the valve functions. See **FIGURE 23-37** for some examples of pressure and flow control valves.

Directional Control Valve Symbols

Directional control valves are drawn as more than one square box joined together. The number of boxes indicates how many positions the valve can be in, and lines drawn parallel to the boxes indicate whether the valve is variable. The most common directional control valves have two, three or four positions.

The number of ports the valve has is shown by lines connected to one of the valve boxes, demonstrating the number of ways that oil can flow in and out of the valve body. Usually this is the "neutral position" for the valve, or the position when it is not being actuated.

Symbols will also be added to the ends of the valve to indicate how the valve is actuated (manually, electrically, pneumatically, or hydraulically).

A very common directional control valve is the three-position, four-way valve. **FIGURE 23-38** shows the symbol for a three-way, four-position, hydraulically actuated directional control valve.

Linear Actuator Symbol Symbols

Schematic symbols for linear actuators (cylinders) are rectangular in shape, with two lines at 90 degrees to each other, indicating the rod and the piston. A single-acting cylinder has just one port, and a double-acting cylinder has two. One variation of a basic cylinder symbol includes a cushioning cylinder. See **FIGURE 23-39** for common linear actuator symbols.

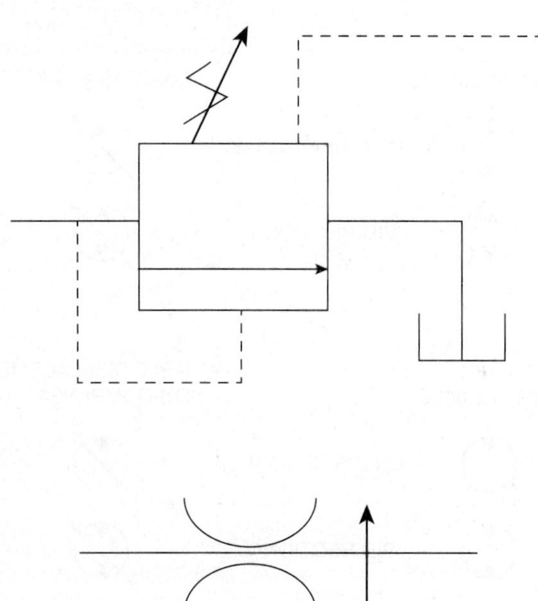

FIGURE 23-37 Examples of pressure and flow controls valves.

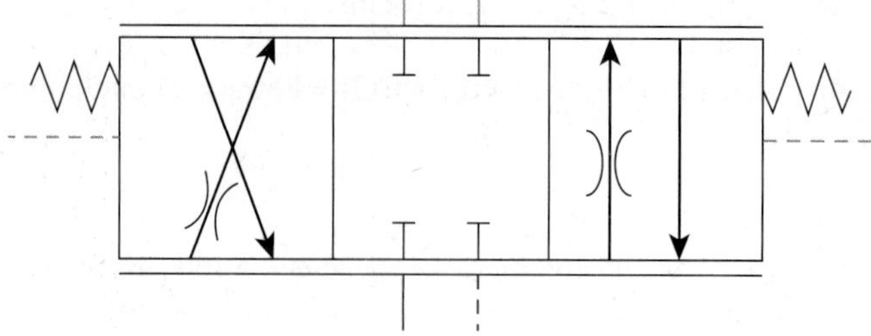

FIGURE 23-38 A three-way, four-position, hydraulically actuated directional control valve.

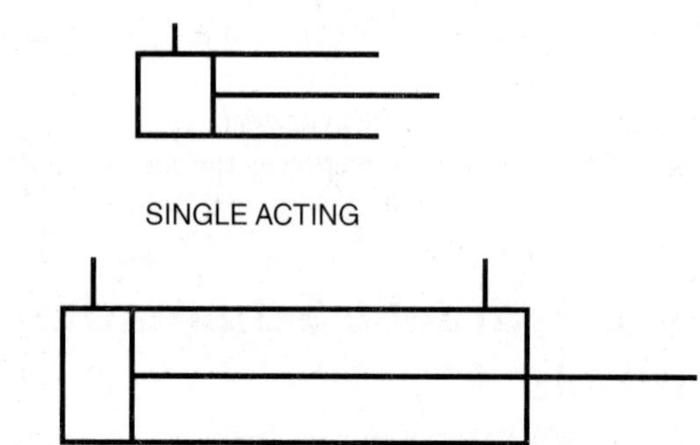

FIGURE 23-39 Common linear actuator symbols.

Fluid Conditioner Symbols

The basic shape used to represent fluid conditioners (filters, screens, heaters, and coolers) is a diamond. Lines and triangles are added to the diamond to indicate whether it is filtering, heating, or cooling oil that flows through it. **FIGURE 23-40** gives symbols for fluid conditioners.

Hydraulic Line Symbols

MORE has a wide variety of hydraulic hoses, tubes, and fittings to route hydraulic oil to and from all the hydraulic components on the machine. If you look at a hydraulic schematic, you will get the impression that most hydraulic lines are the same. To simplify a schematic, almost all hydraulic lines are drawn with two or three different symbols. Some schematics may include colored line symbols to indicate pressure or return lines, but most use black coloring for all lines. Lines that connect can be indicated by a dot where they cross. See **FIGURE 23-41** for a few examples of common symbols used for lines. Generally speaking, solid lines indicate pressure lines; dashed lines indicate pilot pressure lines; and dotted lines indicate drain lines. However, MORE manufacturers use a wide variety of line symbols.

Other Hydraulic Symbols

Some less common symbols you may see on a hydraulic schematic can be used to represent components such as accumulators, check valves, orifices, switches, gauges, couplers, and enclosures. See **FIGURE 23-42** for some other less common hydraulic symbols.

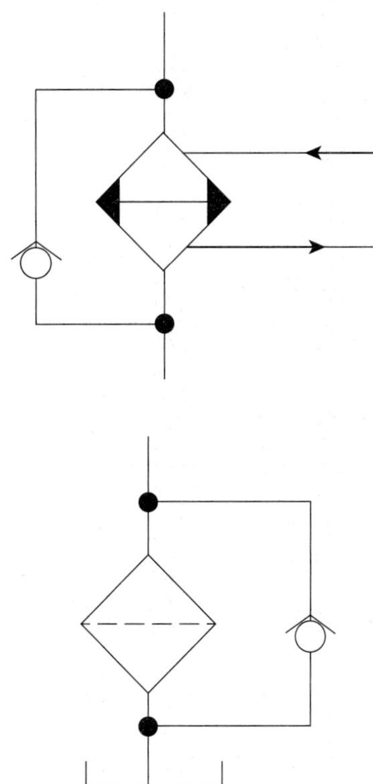

FIGURE 23-40 Symbols for fluid conditioners.

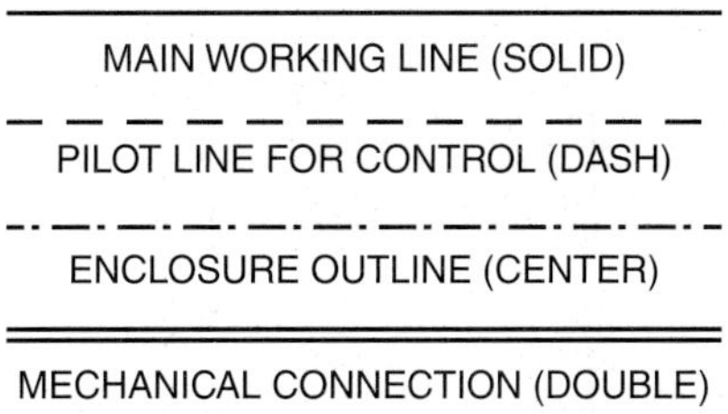

MAIN WORKING LINE (SOLID)

PILOT LINE FOR CONTROL (DASH)

ENCLOSURE OUTLINE (CENTER)

MECHANICAL CONNECTION (DOUBLE)

FIGURE 23-41 Common symbols used for lines.

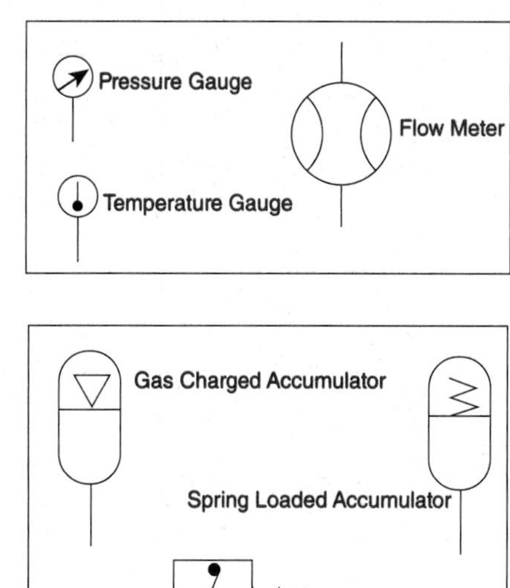

FIGURE 23-42 Other less common hydraulic component symbols.

MORE Hydraulic System Schematics

FIGURE 23-43 shows one section of a schematic for the hydraulic system of an excavator, as well as more schematic symbols. There are a variety of different symbols representing different components. Can you tell what components each of the symbols represents?

Some tasks may require a MORE technician to draw a hydraulic schematic. This could be for diagnosing problems or for installing hydraulic attachments on machines. **SKILL DRILL 23-2** gives you some practice drawing a hydraulic schematic.

Use of a pencil and ruler is recommended, and when finished, you should be able to trace oil flow through the system as if it were operating. Although there are many approaches to drawing circuit diagrams, very general step-by-step guidelines are provided in the following procedure. Add detail to the directional control valve.

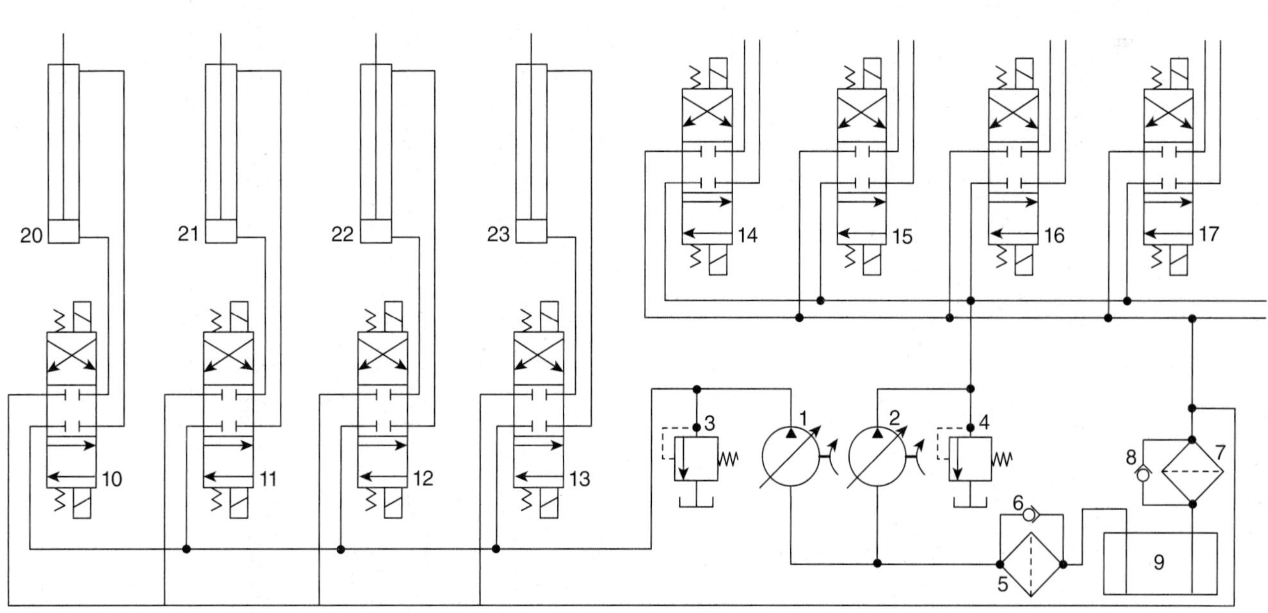

FIGURE 23-43 One section of an excavator schematic and more examples of symbols.

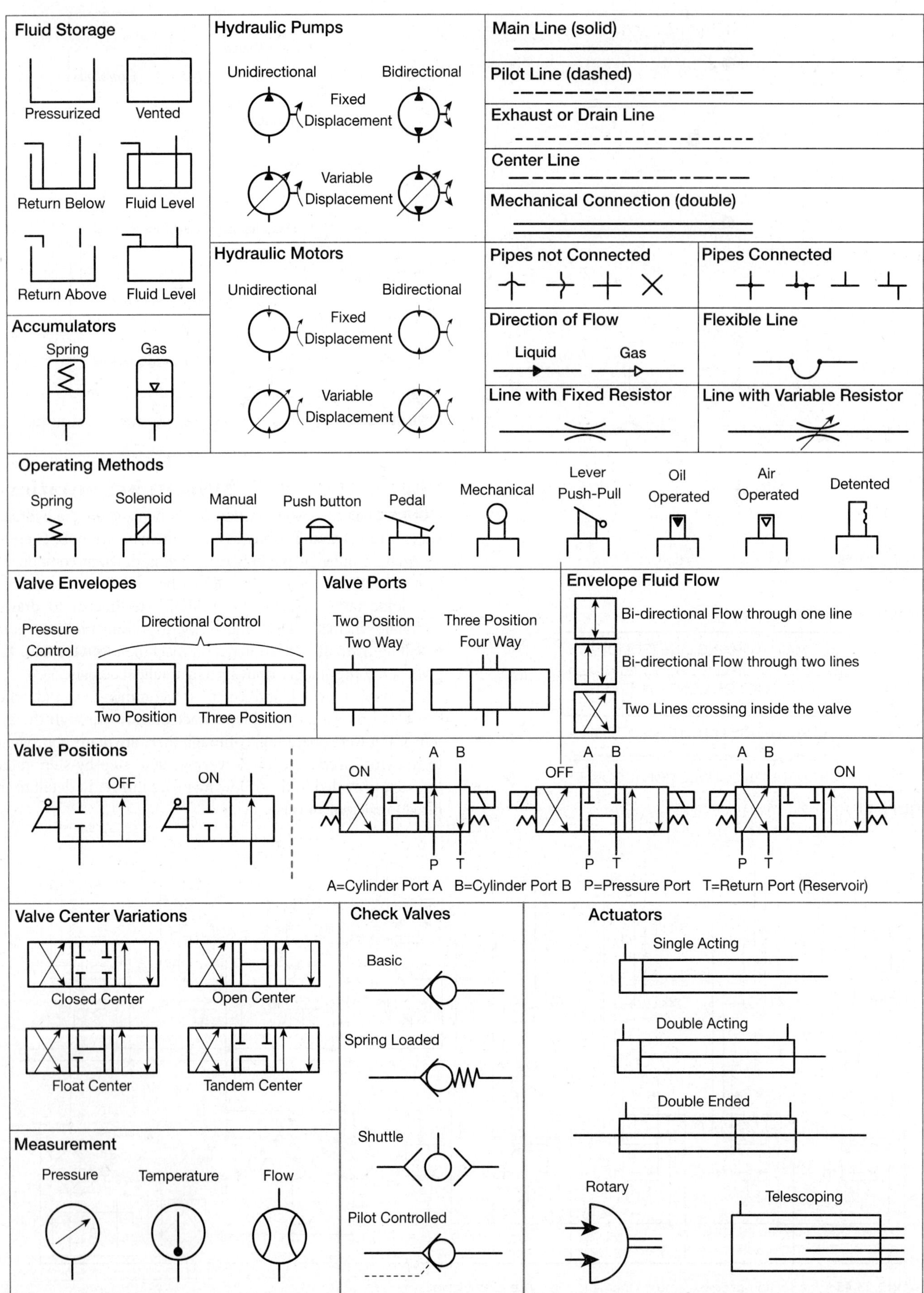

FIGURE 23-43 (Continued)

SKILL DRILL 23-2 Drawing a Hydraulic Schematic of a Basic Circuit Using Common Symbols

1. Start with the pump symbol connected to the reservoir.

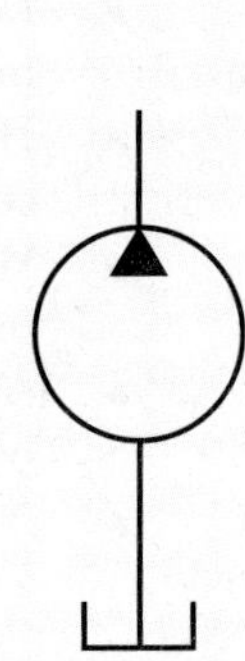

2. Add the pressure line from the pump outlet.

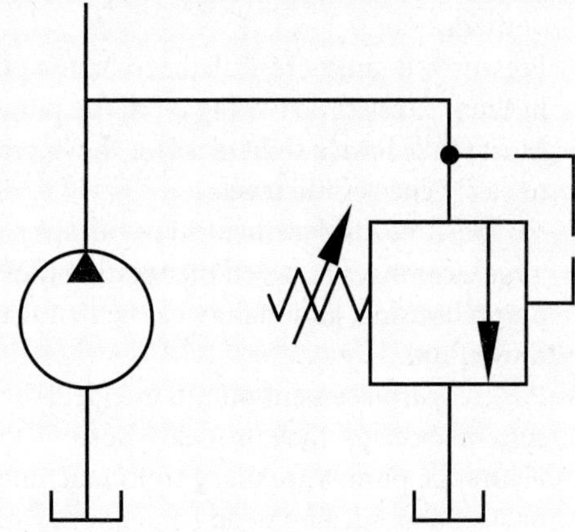

3. Show a relief valve attached to the pressure line.

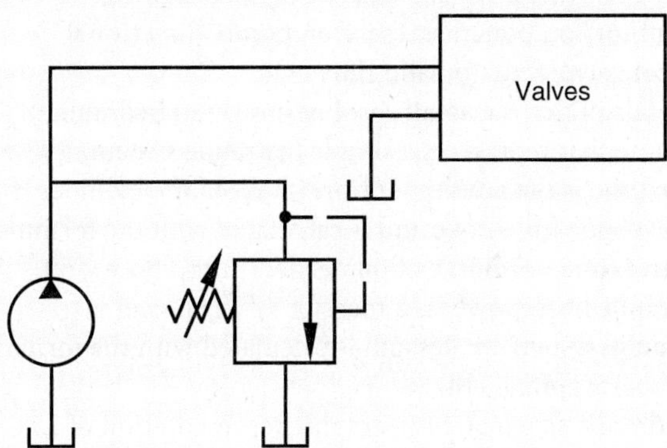

4. Draw directional control, flow control, and any pressure control valves as they should appear in the actual operating circuit to achieve the desired operation of the circuit.

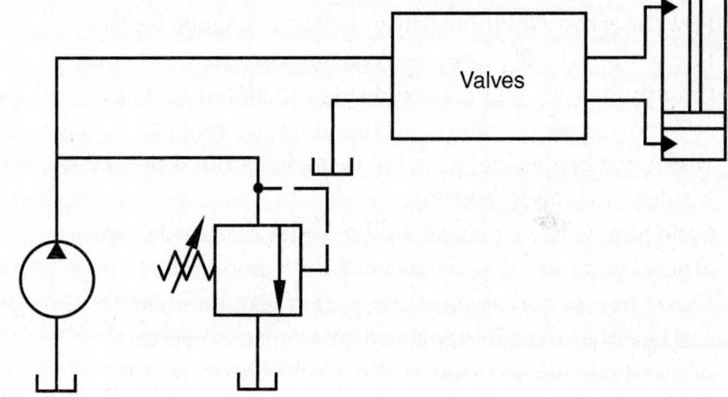

5. Draw the actuator(s).

▶ Wrap-Up

Ready for Review

- In an open-loop hydraulic system, the pump's oil supply originates at the reservoir, and pump flow eventually returns to the reservoir.
- In a closed-loop hydraulic system, the pump directly feeds a rotary actuator (motor), which negates the need for a directional control valve.
- In a closed-center hydraulic system, pump oil is blocked at the directional control valve. These systems are usually used with a variable displacement pump.
- Open-center systems have a directional control valve that allows pump flow through them.
- MORE uses hydraulic systems to generate linear or rotary forces and can be used to power many different functions such as lift booms, tilt buckets, steer machines, turn belts, turn fans, and turn winches.
- Hydraulic system components must be matched for flow and pressure capacity so they work together with smoothness and efficiency.
- Cycle time is a measure of a linear actuator's rod travel for a full stroke.
- A hydraulic system needs a prime mover to power it, and the most common type for MORE is a diesel engine. An electric motor could also be used.

- A reservoir is a tank used to store the system fluid. Reservoirs can be made of plate steel or plastic and are usually mounted close to the pump.
- Vented tanks allow atmospheric air to move in and out of them.
- Pressurized tanks are sealed and have a positive pressure in them to assist delivering oil to the pump inlet.
- Most tanks have a sight glass for the operator or technician to easily check fluid level.
- Nonpositive displacement–type pumps have relatively large clearances between the rotating member and the pump housing, and mainly use centrifugal force to move fluid.
- Positive displacement pumps are ideal for hydraulic systems because they provide a positive flow to the system.
- Hydraulic pumps are made from machined cast aluminum or steel and must be strong enough to withstand high system pressures and temperatures.
- There are various types of positive displacement pumps: gear pumps, vane pumps, and piston pumps.
- Fixed displacement pumps produce the same amount of flow for each revolution. The only way to change the flow rate of this type of pump is to change its rpm.
- Gear pumps are simple fixed displacement pumps with two moving parts: input shaft drives an external gear, which drives a second gear. Oil is carried around the inside of the pump housing.
- Vane pumps have multiple sliding vanes that are carried around in a rotor that is driven by the pump shaft.
- Piston pumps are the most complex type of pump and can be either fixed or variable displacement. A series of piston are carried around in a block, and an angled swashplate creates a pumping effect and determines pump displacement.
- Hydraulic valves are constructed in a wide variety of configurations to meet different needs within hydraulic circuits.
- Pressure control valves are used to manage pressure levels in hydraulic circuits or systems.
- Flow control valves control the flow rate of the fluid to the actuators so that they operate at the proper speed.
- Directional control valves direct the fluid to and from the actuators.
- Actuators convert fluid energy back into mechanical energy to move a load.
- Hydraulic cylinders receive hydraulic fluid from a directional control valve and transfer fluid in motion into linear mechanical motion.
- Linear actuators main components are barrel, head, piston, rod, and seals.
- Hydraulic motors receive oil from pumps or directional control valves and convert fluid flow into rotary motion; they can reverse direction if flow direction is reversed to them.
- Hydraulic motors can be fixed or variable displacement.
- Some types of hydraulic motors are gear, axial piston, bent axis piston, cam lobe, and gerotor.
- Filters are necessary to keep damaging contamination out of hydraulic fluid.
- There are several types of filters, such as tank breathers, return filters, and pressure filters.
- All system pressure must be released before changing hydraulic filters.
- Lines and fittings connect all system components and must be sized to allow smooth (laminar) flow.
- Hoses allow movement between movable and stationary components.
- Hydraulic fittings come in a wide variety of styles, types, pressure ratings, and sizes.
- All replacement lines and fittings have to be proper pressure rated and proper internal size.
- Accumulators can store hydraulic energy and are used for a variety of purposes in hydraulic systems. Three different types of accumulators are weighted, spring loaded, and pneumatic.
- Heaters and coolers are used to regulate fluid temperature.
- A basic hydraulic system must have the following minimum components: reservoir, pump, directional control valve, actuator, and filter.
- A wood splitter is a small gasoline-powered hydraulic machine that represents a simple hydraulic system.
- Cycle time is the amount of time it takes for a cylinder rod to travel one full stroke and is calculated with the formula: Control time = Volume of oil needed/Pump flow × 60.
- Hydraulic horsepower is a measure of the power a hydraulic system creates and is calculated with the formula Hp = psi × gpm/1,714.
- A hydraulic schematic is a graphic representation of a hydraulic system or circuit.
- Hydraulic symbols represent different hydraulic components and start with basic shapes such as circles, squares, rectangles, and triangles.

Key Terms

accumulator Hydraulic energy storage device.

bent axis motor One type of hydraulic motor that has a set of pistons and cylinder block inside it that receive oil flow and create torque.

closed center Hydraulic systems that have directional control valves that block pump oil flow.

closed loop A classification of a hydraulic system that has the pump outlet oil flowing directly to an actuator inlet.

contamination A damaging substance in hydraulic fluid.

cycle time A measure of the time it takes a cylinder rod to travel one full stroke.

directional control valves Direct the fluid to and from the actuators.

double-acting cylinders Most common type of cylinder, has a rod that can be powered both ways.

filters Component that removes damaging contaminants from the hydraulic fluid.

fixed displacement pumps Produce the same volume of flow per revolution.

fluid conductors Another term for tubes, hoses, and fittings that hydraulic system fluid flows through and that connects components.

flow control valves Control the flow rate of the fluid to the actuators so they operate at the proper speed.

gear pumps Two types—internal and external; external gear hydraulic pumps.

heat exchanger Heaters and coolers found in hydraulic systems.

hydraulic cylinder, or ram A device that uses hydraulic fluid flow and converts it to linear mechanical movement.

hydraulic motor Creates rotary motion when it receives oil flow.

hydraulic schematic A paper or electronic drawing that uses symbols to represent components; together they represent a machine's hydraulic system.

laminar flow Term used to describe smooth, nonturbulent flow.

linear actuators Receive oil from the directional control valve and convert oil flow into linear motion.

nonpositive displacement Types of pumps that have loose-fitting internal components and use centrifugal force to move fluid at low pressure.

open center Hydraulic systems that have pump oil flowing through their directional control valves all the time.

open loop A classification of a hydraulic system that has its pump inlet oil come from the reservoir, and all system flow returns to the reservoir.

piston pumps The most complex type of pump, and can be either fixed or variable displacement. Swashplate angle determines pump displacement.

positive displacement pumps Hydraulic pumps that have close internal clearances and will always move oil when they are turning.

pressure control valves Used to manage pressure levels in hydraulic circuits or systems.

pressurized tank Hydraulic tank that has positive internal pressure.

reservoir A tank used to store the system fluid.

return filter A filter used to clean oil before it returns to the tank.

rod speed A measure of how fast a linear actuators rod moves. Usually measured in fps (feet per second) or mps (meters per second).

sight glass A feature of a hydraulic tank to visually check fluid level.

spin on–type filters One-piece filter assembly.

spring-loaded accumulator A type of hydraulic fluid energy storage device that uses a spring to provide mechanical energy.

vane pumps Have multiple sliding vanes that are carried around in a rotor that is driven by the pump shaft.

variable displacement pumps A type of pump that can vary its displacement independently of its shaft speed.

vented tank Hydraulic tank that allows atmospheric pressure in; it uses two external gears to move oil around the inside of the pump housing.

wood splitter A gasoline-powered hydraulic machine that is used to split round pieces of wood into smaller pieces for firewood.

Review Questions

1. Mobile off-road equipment systems mainly need the motion and force from __________ actuators to move a machine component either directly or indirectly through a mechanical linkage.
   a. oscillator
   b. linear
   c. rotary
   d. frequency
2. Four technicians (Tech A, Tech B, Tech C, and Tech D) decide to build a basic functional hydraulic system. Tech A gathers prime mover, reservoir, and pump. Tech B gathers directional control valve, pressure relief valve, and actuator. Tech C gathers hydraulic fluid, filter(s), and fluid conductors. Tech D gathers relay, electric motor, lithium-ion battery, soldering machine, and soldering lead. Which technician's materials are required to build a functional hydraulic system?
   a. Tech A, B, and C
   b. Tech A and B
   c. Tech D, C, and B
   d. Tech A, B, C, and D
3. What is cycle time?
   a. Time that a piston takes to complete one stroke
   b. Time taken to complete one full cycle of fuel intake
   c. Time that a cylinder rod needs to travel one full stroke
   d. Time that a linear rod needs to travel one round
4. Diesel engines provide _______ torque and fuel-efficient operation at relatively _____ rpm's, which helps ensure longevity of the components they drive.
   a. high, high
   b. high, low
   c. low, high
   d. low, low
5. What is the normal rpm range for most diesel engine–powered machines?
   a. 500–2,500 rpm
   b. 700–2,500 rpm
   c. 800–2,000 rpm
   d. 600–2,000 rpm
6. In a hydraulic cooler, a thermostatic or pressure-based bypass valve directs cold fluid directly to the reservoir. As the fluid temperature ________ and viscosity ________, a greater volume of fluid is passed through the cooler.
   a. rises, increases
   b. rises, decreases
   c. drops, increases
   d. drops, decreases

7. Which of the following is *not* true with respect to a wood splitter?
   a. The small gasoline engine drives a pump through a coupler.
   b. The pump is a fixed displacement gear–type pump, which means as long as it is turning, it will be moving oil, and the rate of oil flow is dependent on rpm.
   c. The pump is supplied oil from a reservoir to its inlet and sends oil to a directional control valve.
   d. A loader valve in the pump directs flow from the pump inlet back to one of the systems when air pressure decreases.
8. Some basic shapes are the starting points for symbols used to identify hydraulic components. Which of the following symbol and hydraulic component are correctly matched?
   a. Square—valve
   b. Diamond—pump or motor
   c. Oval—hoses or tubes
   d. Circle—fluid conditioner
9. Two triangles in a circle indicate a:
   a. bidirectional component.
   b. variable displacement component.
   c. fixed displacement component.
   d. unidirectional component.
10. An operator can check the fluid level in a hydraulic tank by all of the following, *except* a:
    a. sight glass.
    b. sensor.
    c. dipstick.
    d. scanner.

ASE Technician A/Technician B Style Questions

1. Technician A says an open-loop hydraulic system has its pump output flow directly to a motor. Technician B says a closed-loop hydraulic system needs the pump inlet to be connected to the reservoir. Who is correct?
   a. Technician A
   b. Technician B
   c. Both A and B
   d. Neither A nor B
2. Technician A says an open center hydraulic system is usually paired with a fixed displacement pump. Technician B says a closed center hydraulic system is usually paired with a variable displacement pump. Who is correct?
   a. Technician A
   b. Technician B
   c. Both A and B
   d. Neither A nor B
3. Technician A says a hydraulic cylinder is sometimes called a rotary actuator. Technician B says a rotary actuator provides torque output when oil is delivered to it. Who is correct?
   a. Technician A
   b. Technician B
   c. Both A and B
   d. Neither A nor B
4. Technician A says a basic hydraulic system includes a pressure relief valve. Technician B says an accumulator is always part of a basic hydraulic system. Who is correct?
   a. Technician A
   b. Technician B
   c. Both A and B
   d. Neither A nor B
5. Technician A says some MORE uses solar power for their prime mover. Technician B says a diesel engine is the most common prime mover found on MORE. Who is correct?
   a. Technician A
   b. Technician B
   c. Both A and B
   d. Neither A nor B
6. Technician A says a vented tank uses an external pressure source to keep the tank pressurized. Technician B says a pressurized tank is used to help ensure a good supply of oil to the pumps inlet. Who is correct?
   a. Technician A
   b. Technician B
   c. Both A and B
   d. Neither A nor B
7. Technician A says vane pumps have two main rotating components (rotor and vanes). Technician B says a piston pump's displacement is determined by its swashplate angle. Who is correct?
   a. Technician A
   b. Technician B
   c. Both A and B
   d. Neither A nor B
8. Technician A says a properly sized hydraulic conductor will not provide laminar flow. Technician B says it is acceptable to undersize hoses and lines when replacing them. Who is correct?
   a. Technician A
   b. Technician B
   c. Both A and B
   d. Neither A nor B
9. Technician A says to calculate hydraulic horsepower, you need to know what type of pump is used. Technician B says to calculate cycle time, you need to know the setting of the main relief valve. Who is correct?
   a. Technician A
   b. Technician B
   c. Both A and B
   d. Neither A nor B
10. Technician A says the graphic symbol for pumps and motors starts with a square box. Technician B says that linear actuator symbols are based on a circle shape. Who is correct?
    a. Technician A
    b. Technician B
    c. Both A and B
    d. Neither A nor B

CHAPTER 24
Hydraulic Reservoirs

Knowledge Objectives

After reading this chapter, you will be able to:

- **K24001** Explain the purpose and fundamentals of hydraulic reservoirs.
- **K24002** Describe the types and construction features of hydraulic reservoirs.
- **K24003** Describe the principles of operation of hydraulic reservoirs.

Skills Objectives

After reading this chapter, you will be able to:

- **S24001** Identify the types and construction features of hydraulic reservoirs.
- **S24002** Inspect hydraulic reservoirs, following manufacturers' recommended procedures.
- **S24003** Perform a reservoir drain and cleanout procedure, following manufacturers' recommendations for hydraulic reservoirs.

▶ Introduction

A hydraulic reservoir has a simple function and doesn't get much attention in terms of service or repair. However, there are some important points to understand about reservoirs.

A hydraulic reservoir is a tank used to store the system fluid. It holds a specific amount of hydraulic fluid to accommodate volume changes in the system and performs a variety of other not-so-obvious important functions. This chapter describes the construction features and functions of hydraulic reservoirs and identifies the types of reservoirs and their uses. It goes on to describe the external and internal components of a properly designed reservoir and explains its functions. The chapter concludes with describing procedures to inspect, drain, clean out, and refill hydraulic reservoirs.

FIGURE 24-1 Typical hydraulic reservoir.

▶ Purpose and Fundamentals of Hydraulic Reservoirs

K24001

All hydraulic systems found on MORE machines have a reservoir. A technician won't spend a lot of time working on them, but there are a few important points to keep in mind when it comes time for a service or during some diagnostic procedures.

Hydraulic Reservoir Functions

The functions of a hydraulic reservoir consist of one or more of the following: holding an adequate supply of hydraulic fluid and conditioning the fluid (including heating, cooling, dehydration, deaeration, and separating of contaminants from the fluid). Each of these functions is described in detail in this section. **FIGURE 24-1** illustrates a typical hydraulic reservoir on MORE.

The reservoir's primary function is to provide a constant supply of hydraulic fluid for the system's pump(s) and components. The reservoir holds excess hydraulic fluid to accommodate volume changes from cylinder extension and contraction, temperature-driven expansion and contraction, and minor leaks. The reservoir can also function as a simple oil cooler to dissipate waste heat.

The reservoir is also designed to aid in conditioning by removing contaminants. One contaminant—water—can have a severe effect on hydraulic systems that are not designed to use water-based fluids; this is known as hydration, and some systems could be fitted with **dehydration** units to assist in the removal of water from the fluid. Air is another enemy of hydraulic systems, and reservoirs also aid in separation of air from the fluid. They assist in the removal of the air, or **deaeration**, by giving the fluid time to rest and allow the air to separate (rise and escape). Reservoirs can also help separate dirt and other particulates from the oil, as these solids will generally settle to the bottom of the tank.

Many reservoirs used on MORE contain return filters that filter returning oil just before it joins the oil that is in the tank.

Another feature that may be found in a hydraulic tank is an oil heater.

▶ Types and Construction Features of Hydraulic Reservoirs

K24002

Different types of machines have different types of hydraulic reservoirs. They are constructed differently and have different features that a technician should be aware of. The next section discusses the main types and features of hydraulic reservoirs.

You Are the Mobile Heavy Equipment Technician

The shop you are working at just had a large wheel loader brought in with a complaint of recurring hydraulic problems. You hear that several months prior it had a cylinder fail, and debris from the failure has been circulating through the system, causing problems. The system filters and oil have been changed several times, but a variety of operational problems continue. You have been assigned to make this loader operate as it should. Answer the following questions to simulate working through this situation:

1. What other information would be helpful to know in relation to the cylinder failure?
2. What recommendations would you make to the customer to repair this problem?
3. What tools, parts, and equipment might you need to complete the repairs?
4. What would you do to the reservoir as part of the repair?

Types of Hydraulic Reservoirs

There are two main types of reservoirs, vented and pressurized.

Vented reservoirs

In a **vented reservoir**, also called a breathing reservoir, the reservoir is open to the atmospheric pressure so that, as the fluid level changes because of the operation of the system actuators, atmospheric air enters and leaves the reservoir. Most MORE machines have differential cylinders that have different volumes of oil on either side of their piston. When the rods on these cylinders move, they either take more oil out of the reservoir or put more oil into it.

The other factor that changes fluid volume in a reservoir is oil temperature. For example, a 20°C increase in oil temperature will increase its volume 14%. When the oil cools, the opposite reaction occurs, and the oil contracts.

Vented reservoirs rely on atmospheric pressure and the weight of the oil (head pressure) to push the oil into the pump inlet. **Head pressure** is the pressure that develops at the bottom of a column of a liquid, and for hydraulic oil it is approximately 0.4 psi for every 1 foot of height.

These types of reservoirs must have a breather/filter that removes dust and moisture from air entering the tank. These breathers can be a separate part, but many vented tanks have their breathers built into the filler cap. See **FIGURE 24-2** for an example of a vented (or breathing) reservoir.

Pressurized Reservoirs

A **pressurized reservoir** is a sealed compartment that doesn't need a large breather. Therefore, atmospheric air doesn't usually enter the reservoir as the fluid level changes during system operation.

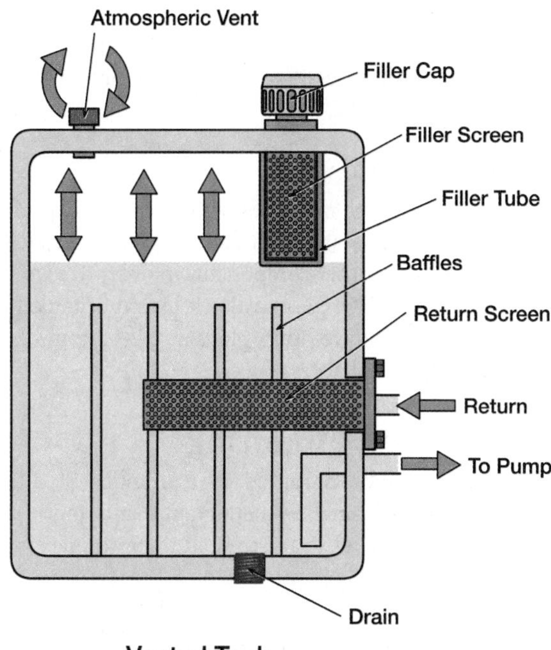

FIGURE 24-2 Vented reservoir.

Because the pressurized tank is completely sealed, atmospheric pressure does not affect the pressure in the tank. However, when the oil circulates through the system, it absorbs heat and expands. The expanding oil compresses the air in the tank above the oil and in turn creates a pressurized air volume above the oil. The pressurized tank forces the oil out of the tank and into the pump inlet.

Some machines have pressurized tanks that use an external pressurized air source to charge the tank with air pressure. The source could be the machine's pneumatic system that has a pressure regulator to reduce pressure to the tank, or a line coming from the engine's turbocharger outlet. Either source will provide low-pressure air (10–25 psi) to the hydraulic tank to assist in providing oil flow to the pump's inlet.

These types of reservoirs use a combination vacuum breaker and pressure relief valve to maintain a low level of pressure in the tank. It opens if the pressure drops below 0.5 psi (3.45 kPa) in order to allow air in. This is the vacuum break function and prevents any chance of starving the pump of oil. It is the only time the breather is needed.

The pressure relief portion will open between 10 psi (70 kPa) and 30 psi (207 kPa), depending on its spring pressure. This prevents excessive pressure in the tank that could cause it to bulge or leak.

These simple **vacuum breaker/pressure relief valves** can malfunction and be the cause of many problems such as bulging tanks, starving pumps, or malfunctioning valves. **FIGURE 24-3** depicts a pressure relief vacuum breaker valve.

> **TECHNICIAN TIP**
>
> Vented reservoirs have breather filters to prevent contamination such as dust and moisture in the atmosphere from entering the system. They must be serviced regularly and are often forgotten when a machine is being serviced.

Not changing breather filters can lead to expensive repairs. If a breather gets severely plugged, this could cause pump starvation, which can result in catastrophic failure. **FIGURE 24-4** depicts a reservoir breather that is overdue for service.

FIGURE 24-3 A pressure relief vacuum breaker valve.

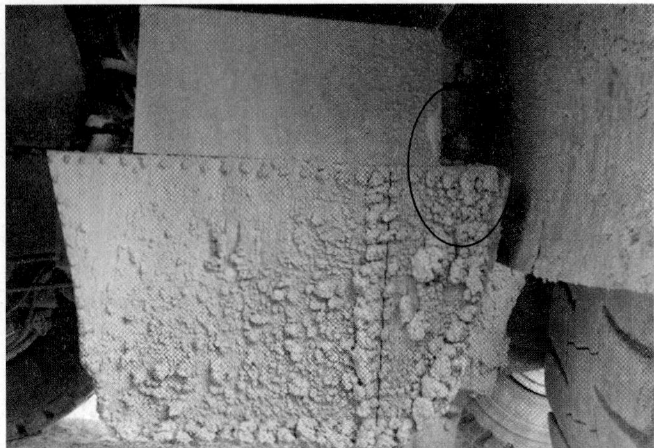

FIGURE 24-4 A reservoir breather that is overdue for service.

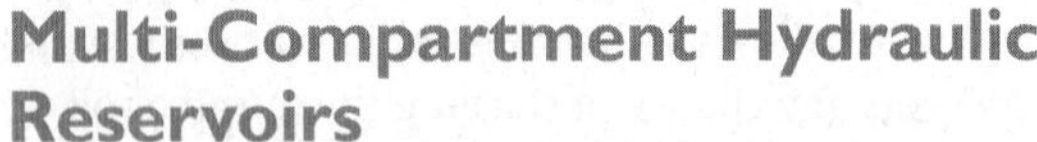

Multi-Compartment Hydraulic Reservoirs

Some machines have separate hydraulic reservoirs for their different systems such as steering, brakes, and implement. If there are space limitations on the machine, then designers sometimes combine two or three reservoirs into one housing. Although the outside housing looks like one large reservoir, internal walls divide the tank into separate compartments. See **FIGURE 24-5** for an example of a multi-compartment reservoir.

> **▶ TECHNICIAN TIP**
>
> When filling different compartments for a multi-compartment reservoir, take extra care to ensure the correct oil goes into each compartment. For example, one compartment could be for brake oil, and one could be for hydraulic oil. There are likely different requirements for the different oils, and mixing them up could lead to expensive problems.

Construction Features of Hydraulic Reservoirs

For machines where space is a premium, part(s) of the frame may be used as hydraulic reservoirs, but most machines use a stand-alone, separate tank. **FIGURE 24-6** shows a machine with a typical hydraulic reservoir. Hydraulic reservoirs can be fabricated to fit anywhere on a machine that makes efficient use of space, if this is a concern. They are quite often used as steps or mounting points for steps and handrails.

FIGURE 24-5 A multi-compartment reservoir.

FIGURE 24-6 A machine with a typical hydraulic reservoir.

Hydraulic reservoirs are made from different materials, but the most common ones are formed plate steel or molded plastic.

Steel reservoirs

Plate steel is a common construction material for reservoirs. Most tanks are made from 3/16" plate steel that starts out in large sheets that are then cut into pieces and formed or welded to make sections. Sections can then be welded together or bolted together. Some tanks are two-piece assemblies that can be disassembled by splitting them in half; where the two halves are sealed with a gasket; others have **access covers**, which are necessary to gain access to internal tank components during a maintenance or repair procedure.

Some tanks even have directional control valves mounted inside them. This will necessitate tank disassembly if there are repairs needed to the valve.

Plastic Reservoirs

Many smaller machines or machines with limited free space have molded plastic hydraulic tanks, as this style of tank can be manufactured to fit around other components in order to save space. **FIGURE 24-7** shows an example of a plastic hydraulic tank. Plastic tanks may or may not have drain plugs at the bottom of them and may or may not have access covers.

Hydraulic Tank Mounting

Hydraulic tanks can be mounted in a number of different manners. Lighter and smaller metal tanks and most plastic tanks can have light metal straps to hold them in place, with a threaded tightening mechanism to tighten the straps. A rubber cushion on the metal straps stops wear caused by vibration.

Larger plastic tanks or plastic tanks that are unusually shaped have threaded metal inserts molded into them so threaded fasteners can secure them to the machine.

FIGURE 24-7 A plastic hydraulic tank.

Many larger tanks need some fairly hefty mounts to keep them securely in place. Once the tank is full of hydraulic oil, a tank with a 30-gallon capacity can easily weigh several hundred pounds. Hydraulic tanks on large mining machines can easily weigh several tons (tonnes).

Some tanks are mounted rigidly to the machine's frame, whereas others could be mounted with rubber vibration isolators. **FIGURE 24-8** shows an example of a hydraulic tank mount.

Hydraulic Tank Sizing

A rule of thumb for engineers that design hydraulic systems for MORE is that the tank capacity should be 1.5–2 times the system's pump flow. In other words, if an excavator has a pump flow output of 100 lpm, it should have a tank that holds at least 150 liters of oil.

> **TECHNICIAN TIP**
>
> All vented reservoirs, regardless of size, must include enough empty space above the oil to allow for changes in the fluid level as the system is operated. Overfilling reservoirs, which reduces the void above the oil level, can lead to bulging tanks and or expensive damage.
>
> Always follow manufacturer's recommendations when filling or topping up a hydraulic reservoir.

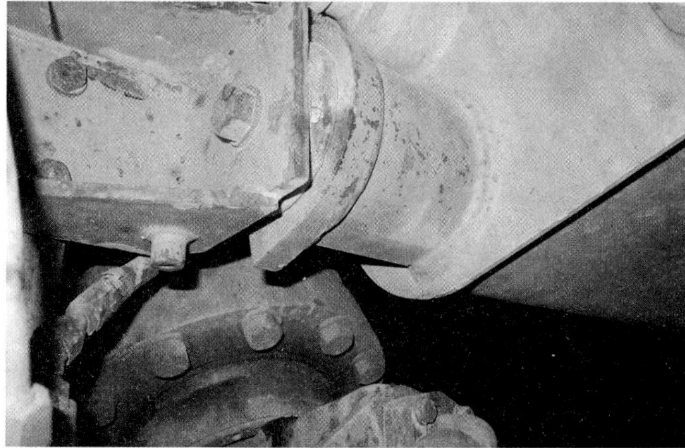

FIGURE 24-8 Hydraulic tank mount.

Hydraulic Reservoir Components

Reservoirs are made up of two categories of components besides the tank itself: the external components, which are required to contain the hydraulic fluid and manage tank pressure; and the internal components, which are primarily designed to provide the supply of, and control the return of, the fluid in the system. **FIGURE 24-9** depicts the components of a typical hydraulic reservoir. External components are indicated in black, and internal components are indicated in purple.

External Reservoir Components

The following list identifies the external components and provides a description of their specific purposes.

Filler Cap The **filler cap** is where fluid is added to the reservoir; it is usually located on the top of the reservoir but could be located on its side. The cap has a rubber seal that should seal tightly when closed. Caps can be threaded or similar to an automotive radiator cap (quarter-turn lock type) and many styles are antivandalism types. They can be lockable or provide a means to lock the cap with a padlock. **FIGURE 24-10** illustrates a lockable filler cap.

Breather Filter The breather filter prevents **contamination** from entering the reservoir with air that enters as the reservoir "breathes." There are many different styles of breathers found on vented reservoirs. **FIGURE 24-11** shows a typical breather.

Sight Glass The sight glass or oil level gauge allows for quick and easy checking of the fluid level. They come in different styles (round or cylindrical), and some reservoirs have more than one. Some are used to indicate a safe starting level range and a normal machine running range. Some sight glasses can also be combined with a temperature gauge. Sight glasses can,

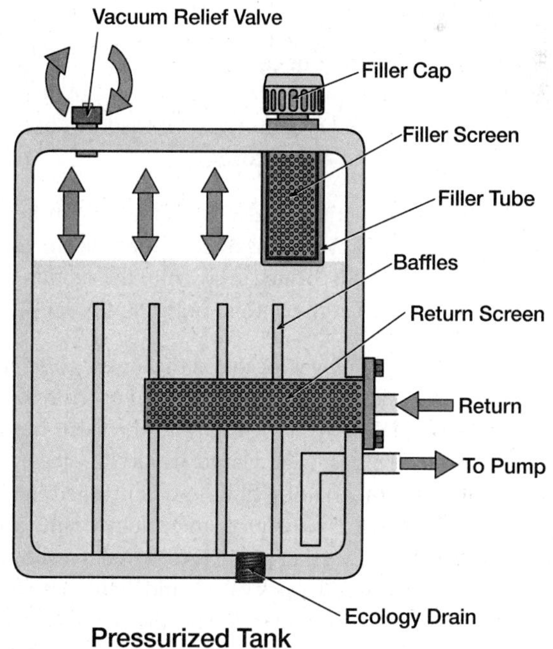

FIGURE 24-9 Components of a typical hydraulic reservoir.

FIGURE 24-10 A lockable filler cap.

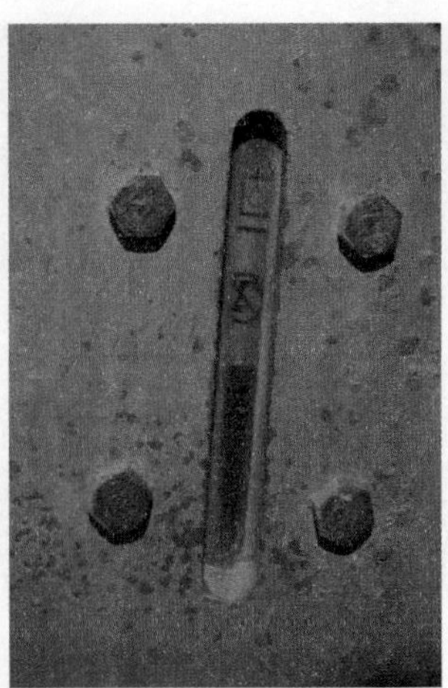

FIGURE 24-11 Typical breather.

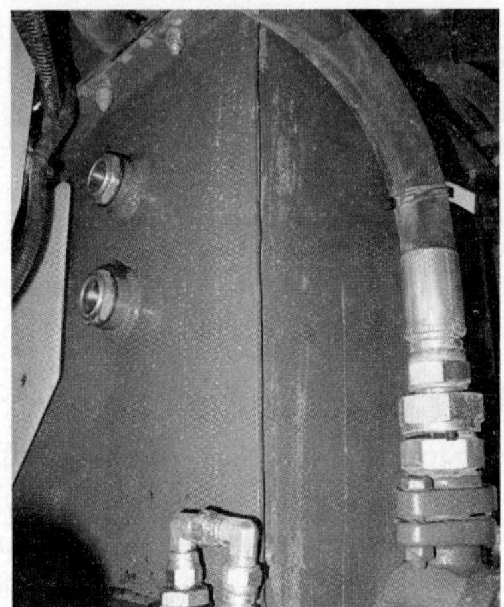

FIGURE 24-12 A variety of sight glasses.

however, be a source of leaks and need to be protected from damage. See **FIGURE 24-12** for a variety of sight glasses.

Access Cover The access, or cleanout, cover can be removed to inspect and clean the inside of the reservoir. It can be sealed with a gasket or O-ring and is another possible source of a leak. **FIGURE 24-13** illustrates an access cover.

Dished Bottom Sometimes called the sump, the dished, or tapered, bottom allows water and solids to settle to the lowest point in the reservoir and is located away from the suction tube. The tank drain is located at the bottom of the sump.

Drain Plug The drain plug is located at the lowest point of the reservoir and allows settled water to be drained or the reservoir to be emptied completely, if needed. Drain plugs can be NPT plugs or O-ring face plugs. Many larger reservoirs feature an **ecology drain valve** for draining fluid in a controlled manner to prevent spills. **FIGURE 24-14** depicts an ecology drain valve.

To use an ecology valve, first a plug is removed to expose the valve (a simple spring-loaded check valve), and then a pipe nipple is threaded into the valve that slowly opens the check valve. The further the check valve is opened, the faster the oil drains. To stop draining, you simply back out the nipple to close the valve.

FIGURE 24-13 Access cover.

Internal Reservoir Components

The following list identifies internal reservoir components and provides a description of their specific purposes:

Suction Tube The suction tube provides fluid flow from the reservoir to the pump. It should be well below the minimum

FIGURE 24-14 An ecology drain valve.

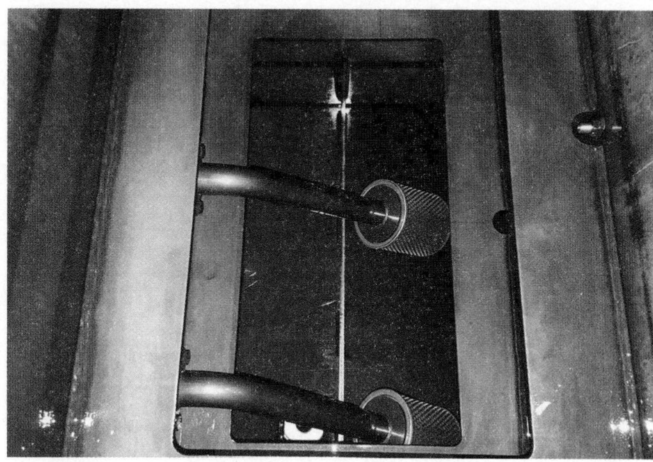

FIGURE 24-15 A tank with two return screens.

fluid level but far enough above the floor of the reservoir that it will not allow settled dirt and water to be picked up and carried to the pump. It should be located away from the return to prevent oil from going directly into the pump from the return. When inspecting the inside of a reservoir, check to be sure the suction tube is secure. A cracked suction tube can cause a pump to fail or create other operational problems due to aerated oil.

Suction Screen A **suction screen** is a coarse screen on the end of the suction line that provides the first line of filtration for the fluid going to the pump. It is often referred to as a "rock stopper." These screens can be a source of problems if they become plugged with contamination or cold oil.

Return Tube The return tube directs fluid from the system back to the reservoir, normally terminating well below the reservoir fluid level but slightly above the bottom of the tank. It should also be located away from the suction inlet. The tube is often cut at a 45-degree angle to slow the fluid as it enters the reservoir and prevent churning and foaming.

Return Screen **Return screens** can be found inside a reservoir and, in the oil returning to the tank from the system, are designed to stop any large contamination from entering the tank and reaching the pump inlet. **FIGURE 24-15** shows a tank with two return screens.

If there is a component failure, these screens must be removed and cleaned or replaced. **FIGURE 24-16** illustrates a screen with contamination from a cylinder failure.

FIGURE 24-16 A screen with contamination from a cylinder failure.

Return Filter Many larger machines have hydraulic tanks with return filters mounted inside the tank. This not only saves space but also eliminates the possibility of filter housings being damaged. It also provides a guarantee of clean oil returning to the tank. Some larger machines like mining shovels can have 12 or more return filters in their tanks. **FIGURE 24-17** depicts a return filter for a hydraulic tank.

FIGURE 24-17 Return filter.

SAFETY TIP

Before servicing return filters in tanks, be certain all tank pressure is released. This is particularly important when the hydraulic oil is hot. Although tank pressure is fairly low, a large volume of oil can leave the tank quickly if permitted, and hot oil can cause severe burns to exposed skin.

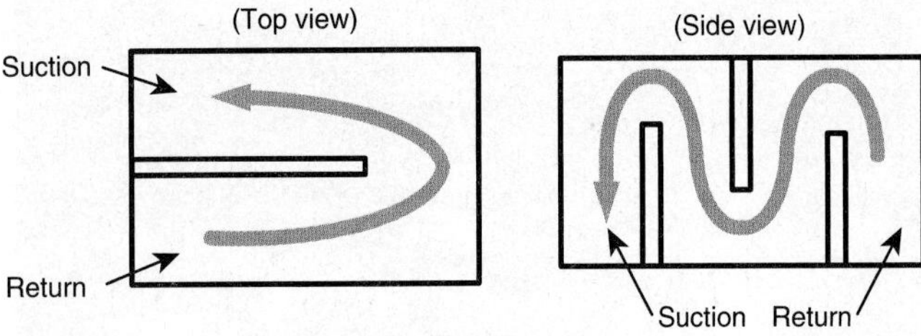

FIGURE 24-18 Examples of baffle configurations.

Baffle The **baffle** is a barrier separating the return line from the pump suction line. It is designed to force the fluid to stay in the reservoir longer so that the reservoir functions of cooling, deaeration, dehydration, and contaminant settling can take place. Baffles redirect oil flow to slow it down in a design similar to a maze. See **FIGURE 24-18** for examples of baffle configurations.

Hydraulic Fluid Level Sensor Many newer and larger MORE machines have fluid level sensors in their tanks. Sensor operation is discussed in other chapters, but its purpose is to alert the operator when the tank is fluid level is low. These sensors could trigger a light on the dash, log a fault code, prevent the machine from starting, or derate it and put into a safe shutdown mode.

Hydraulic Fluid Temperature Sensor Newer MORE machines have hydraulic temperature sensors that monitor fluid temperature in the tank. They are used to alert the operator when the hydraulic oil is too hot and could derate the machine or be used to speed up a cooling fan. These sensors could also be used to detect extremely cold oil at start-up, and this may log a fault code or keep the engine at a low power setting until the oil warms up.

Reservoir Location

Most mobile equipment manufacturers are forced by the design and space available to mount the reservoir wherever the designer can find room. This is often not the ideal location. Ideally the tank should be mounted above the pump inlet to take advantage of head pressure the oil height creates, but this is sometimes hard to accomplish. The other main consideration is for the distance from the reservoir to the pump inlet to be kept as short as possible. **FIGURE 24-19** shows a hydraulic tank location on a high track dozer.

Other factors such as accessibility for checking fluid levels and servicing are also considerations for designers.

▶ Principles of Operation of Hydraulic Reservoirs

K24003

The operation of a hydraulic tank is fairly simple: provide an ample supply of noncontaminated hydraulic fluid to the machine's hydraulic pumps for proper system operation. Hydraulic tanks must also provide a means to easily check fluid level and a way to top off oil and change it. If there are filters located inside the tank, there has to be easy access to them.

FIGURE 24-19 Hydraulic tank location on a high track dozer.

Hydraulic tanks assist with conditioning the fluid by helping to cool it and clean it. Cooling is accomplished by heat transfer through the walls of the tank. This is called convection, and as air passes by the warm tank, heat is transferred to it from the tank. Some tanks have heaters mounted to them if the machine is to be used in an extreme cold environment. These can be electric resistive–type heaters that are mounted in or on the tank or diesel fired heaters that use engine coolant as a medium to heat the hydraulic oil. **FIGURE 24-20** illustrates a hydraulic tank heater.

Tanks can clean fluid by allowing the larger particles to drop out of the fluid before the fluid gets back to the pump inlet.

A vented tank relies on the head pressure of the fluid and atmospheric pressure to maintain a steady flow of oil to the pump inlet. For a pressurized tank, it relies on pressure built up in the tank, combined with the head pressure of the oil volume in the tank, to supply the pump with oil.

Free flow of return oil must also be provided, or circuit operational problems can arise. If oil cannot return from a circuit to the tank, pressure will build up and cause problems such as valves sticking.

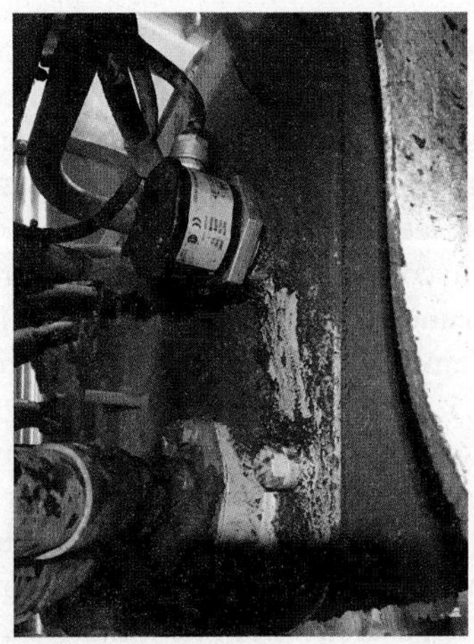

FIGURE 24-20 Hydraulic tank heater.

▶ TECHNICIAN TIP

Although not a very common occurrence, restricted oil return can cause hydraulic circuit problems. Don't forget to check for excessive restrictions in return lines to the tank as a cause of hydraulic problems.

One contractor had several older excavators converted to telescoping cranes, and one had a recurring problem of the winch motor not stopping when the machine was cold. This actually caused a lot of damage to the machine more than once. In the end, it turned out the company that did the modifications put too small of a fitting in the return line at the tank from the joystick pilot valve. When the oil was cold, it couldn't return fast enough and would back pressure up to the control valve, and made the valve stick open. This led to a dangerous situation by having the winch turn by itself.

⚠ WARNING

HYDRAULIC TANK

RELIEVE TANK PRESSURE WITH ENGINE OFF BY REMOVING CAP SLOWLY TO PREVENT BURNS FROM HOT OIL.

FIGURE 24-21 Warning sign on a hydraulic tank.

▶ Identify the Types and Construction Features of Hydraulic Reservoirs

S24001

The most common tasks you will perform that are related to reservoirs are checking oil level, topping up the oil, and changing the oil. Being able to identify the type of hydraulic reservoir a MORE has and how to maintain it is an important skill to have and will help keep you safe.

If you are asked to top off a reservoir, it is important that you identify the type of reservoir the machine has and the correct way to check fluid level. The safest way to do this is to reference the machine's service information. If the machine manual describes the safe procedure for releasing pressure from the tank, then it must be a pressurized tank. If there is no mention of releasing pressure prior to opening the tank, caution should still be used, even though the tank is likely a vented tank. There is a possibility that the tank breather is plugged and could allow pressure to build in the tank.

To know whether the reservoir is vented or not, look for a breather on the tank or a remote mounted breather. If it appears the breather is simply a filter and there are no pressure relief valves incorporated, the tank is likely a vented style.

However, the safest bet is to assume the tank is pressurized and slowly remove the cap while listening for pressure escaping and feeling the resistance of the cap.

Look for warning decals near the filler cap and pay attention to them. See **FIGURE 24-21** for an example of a warning sign on a hydraulic tank.

Release Tank Pressure

Before hydraulic fluid can be added to a tank the pressure in the tank must be released safely. Before attempting to release tank pressure, you should always check the fluid level to try to determine if the tank has been overfilled. If you suspect it has been overfilled, take extra caution when removing the filler cap. Also make sure the machine is in the correct service position. This will ensure the tank level is not too high.

FIGURE 24-22 Automotive style filler cap.

The two main methods for releasing tank pressure include using a pressure bleed-off device (button on the tank pressure relief valve or a turn of a ball valve handle) until pressure is heard to stop relieving or *slowly* removing the filler cap. When removing a threaded cap, first back it off one turn and listen. If you feel some resistance and hear pressure escaping, then wait until all pressure is released before removing the cap completely. When removing a half-turn locking filler cap, start turning it counterclockwise until it stops (this style of cap is similar to an automotive-type radiator cap). This is usually about a quarter turn. Wiggle the cap and listen for pressure escaping. When pressure stops, push the cap down and turn in a counterclockwise direction, and then remove cap. When all pressure is released, the cap should turn freely. **FIGURE 24-22** depicts an automotive-type filler cap.

▶ Inspect Hydraulic Reservoirs Following Manufacturers' Recommended Procedures

S24002

Part of a machine's regular maintenance is checking fluid levels, which includes the hydraulic fluid. It is important to know the proper machine positioning and fluid conditions before determining whether the fluid level is correct.

Some machines have to be put into a specific service position to get a correct fluid level. For example, in an excavator there could be different positions in which the boom, stick, and bucket can be placed. These positions put their cylinders at different points in their travel, which in turn means more or less oil in the cylinders versus the reservoir. There will likely be a decal on the machine near the sight glass, or a picture in the maintenance manual, to illustrate the proper machine positioning. It is safer to verify the correct position than assume it is right. Improper positioning can result in oil levels that are too high or too low. **FIGURE 24-23** shows a decal for proper positioning of an excavator for checking hydraulic fluid level.

Fluid condition can also be checked visually by looking at the sight glass. Discoloration of fluid could indicate contamination or overheating, whereas foaming or aeration are indications the system is ingesting air, a pump inlet restriction; a return tube is broken; or one of the tank baffles has failed.

Other inspection points related to a reservoir are checking its mounts for integrity or missing fasteners; checking for leaks; and checking the sight glass, breather, and filler cap for damage. Some more in-depth inspections may include removing the access cover and looking inside the tank for faults such as broken or cracked return tubes, plugged return screens, damaged inlet tubes, plugged inlet screens, or damaged or loose baffles.

SAFETY TIP

Hydraulic oil operating temperature is normally around 150°F (66°C). This is hot enough to cause moderate to severe burns. Try to get an accurate reading of oil temperature before working on any hydraulic system. The oil temperature can usually be read through the machine's cab display and should govern the level of PPE needed to work safely.

FIGURE 24-23 A decal for proper positioning of an excavator for checking hydraulic fluid level.

▶ Perform a Reservoir Drain and Cleanout Procedure Following Manufacturers' Recommendations for Hydraulic Reservoirs

S24003

At a certain point in a machine's life, typically at 2,000 hours or yearly, it will require a hydraulic oil change. This is usually a fairly routine procedure, but to ensure hydraulic system component longevity, it is important to follow all steps in the machine's service information.

Hydraulic Oil Change

The following procedure describes a generic hydraulic oil change for a large excavator:

1. Operate the machine to warm up the oil. This is particularly important if a machine has been sitting in a cold environment for a long period. This will not only speed up the draining process, but there will also be more contaminants that drain out with the oil.
2. Put the machine into service position. For different machines, this means different things. For all machines, this means grounding all implements, but for other machines like excavators, the boom stick and bucket may have to be put in a particular position to service the machine. **FIGURE 24-24** illustrates how one excavator should be positioned to be serviced.
3. Perform LOTO procedures appropriate for the worksite and legal jurisdiction.
4. Wear appropriate PPE to protect yourself, including gloves to prevent burns if the oil is over 100°F (66°C).
5. Make sure drain plug is accessible and the draining container has sufficient capacity.
6. Make sure the correct quantity and specification of hydraulic fluid is available.
7. Release pressure from the tank slowly and carefully.
8. Drain oil from tank.
9. Drain oil from pump inlet tube.
10. Install drain plugs with new O-rings, and torque to spec.
11. Fill tank to full mark, and perform pump bleeding procedure. To bleed air from pumps, connect a laptop to the machine, and disable the fuel injection system. Loosen the bleed screw at the filter base of the case drain filter. Crank over the engine until steady, air-free oil comes from bleed screw. Tighten the bleed screw.
12. Check oil level in tank and top off if needed.
13. Start the machine and run at low idle for 5 minutes.
14. Increase rpm to 1,200 rpm, and cycle implements slowly.
15. Put machine back to service position, and check oil level. Top off, if needed.

FIGURE 24-24 How one excavator should be positioned to be serviced.

▶ TECHNICIAN TIP

Most hydraulic reservoirs have a coarse screen under their filler cap that is meant to stop larger objects or contamination from entering the tank when it is being filled or topped off. It is very tempting to remove these screens because it slows down the flow of oil entering the tank. Try to avoid this temptation because you run the risk of allowing foreign material to enter the system. **FIGURE 24-25** shows the screen found under a filler cap.

Hydraulic Tank Cleanout

One less common task that may be performed is a hydraulic tank cleanout. This may never be part of a regular maintenance interval, but should be part of the procedure after a catastrophic hydraulic component failure. The consequences of not performing a proper tank cleanout after a component failure can be extremely expensive and cause a lot of downtime.

1. Drain the tank as per machine manufacturer's service information.
2. Remove inspection access cover (may require tank removal). **FIGURE 24-26** depicts a tank with an inspection cover.
3. Use a flashlight and or remote camera to inspect all areas of the tank.
4. If large metal particles are found, remove them with a magnet.
5. For smaller particles, use a good-quality parts cleaner to flush contaminants out the reservoir drain. Be aware of the possible buildup of toxic or flammable fumes when cleaning in a confined space. Consult the MSDS sheet for the cleaner you are using, and abide by its instructions.
6. Use a lint-free rag to clean all inside surfaces.
7. Clean or replace all screens.
8. Install the access cover with a new gasket or seal.
9. Refill the hydraulic tank, and perform any air bleeding procedure as required.

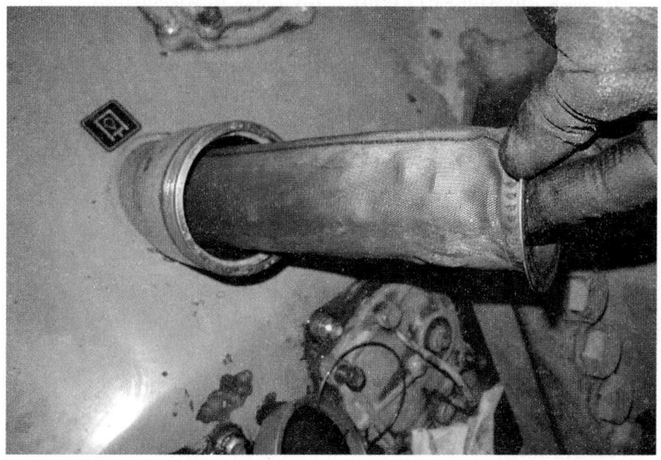

FIGURE 24-25 Screen found under a filler cap.

FIGURE 24-26 A tank with an inspection cover.

▶ Wrap-Up

Ready for Review

- The hydraulic reservoir or tank has a simple job—to supply the hydraulic system with clean, noncontaminated oil.
- The tank must hold an adequate supply of hydraulic fluid and condition the fluid (including heating, cooling, dehydration, deaeration, and separating of contaminants from the fluid).
- Vented reservoirs allow atmospheric air into the tank as fluid levels change. Breathers filter the air as it enters the tank.
- Pressurized tanks are sealed and use the pressure created by the expanding oil in the tank to generate pressure in the tank. They have a vacuum breaker/pressure relief valve to limit tank pressures.

- Multi-compartment tanks have one housing divided internally to supply different systems (steering, implement, and brakes, for example).
- Hydraulic tanks can be fabricated from plate steel or molded plastic and can be made to fit almost anywhere on a machine.
- Two-piece tanks are sealed with a gasket.
- Access covers allow technicians to inspect and maintain the inside of a tank.
- Hydraulic tanks are usually mounted rigidly to the machine's frame; however, sometimes rubber mounts are used.
- External tank components can include filler cap, breather, sight glass, access cover, dished bottom, and drain plug.
- Internal tank components can include suction tube, suction screen, return tube, return screen, return filter, and baffle.
- Hydraulic tanks can be located anywhere on a machine but should be placed close to the pump.
- Head pressure is created by the weight of oil acting on the bottom of the container holding it. Hydraulic oil produces approximately 0.4 psi for every 1 foot of height.
- Vented tanks supply oil to the pump's inlet, using head pressure and atmospheric pressure.
- Pressurized tanks supply oil to the pump's inlet, using pressurized air on top of the tank and head pressure of the oil.
- Free flow of return oil must be provided by the tank.
- Extra care must be taken when removing a filler cap on a hydraulic tank. Release pressure slowly and completely before removing cap. Always refer to the manufacturer's service information for the correct procedure.
- Make sure the machine's implements are in the correct position before checking hydraulic fluid levels.
- The first step to perform when changing hydraulic oil is to warm up the oil.
- Make sure to follow pump bleeding procedures closely, if required, after a hydraulic oil change.
- When performing a hydraulic tank cleanout, use lint-free rags for cleaning the inside of the tank.

Key Terms

access covers Necessary to gain access to the inside of a hydraulic tank.

baffle Partitions in tanks to help slow down the return oil before it gets to the suction tube.

contamination Anything (solid, liquid, air, heat or chemical) that is not a part of the original fluid formulation.

deaeration The removal of excess air from the fluid.

dehydration The removal of water from the fluid.

ecology drain valve A type of drain that provides a way to control the oil flow when draining the tank.

filler cap Allows oil to be added to the tank.

head pressure The pressure created by the weight of a liquid.

pressurized reservoir A pressurized tank that is completely sealed. Pressure in the tank is increased by the volume increase of the oil as it heats up or from an external pressurized air source.

return screen Coarse screen that stops large contaminants from entering the tank with the return oil.

suction screen Coarse screen that stops large contaminants from entering the pump inlet.

vacuum breaker/pressure relief valves Used on a pressurized tank to minimize vacuum and pressure levels in the tank.

vented reservoir Reservoir that is open to the atmosphere so that, as the fluid level changes due to operation of the system actuators and fluid temperature, atmospheric air enters and leaves the reservoir.

Review Questions

1. A hydraulic reservoir is a tank used to store _______.
   a. compressed air
   b. unused oil
   c. system fluid
   d. coolant
2. The hydraulic reservoir can function as a _______________________.
   a. simple oil cooler to dissipate waste heat
   b. leak identifier to identify any leaks in the system
   c. filter to remove contaminants
   d. power-generating system for attenuators
3. What do vented reservoirs rely on to push the oil into the pump inlet?
   a. Weight of the oil
   b. Temperature of the oil
   c. Viscosity of the oil
   d. Type of the oil
4. _______________ pressure in the hydraulic reservoirs is the pressure that develops at the bottom of a column of liquid.
   a. Tail
   b. Head
   c. Liquid
   d. Base
5. Pressurized reservoirs use a combination vacuum breaker and pressure relief valve to maintain a low level of pressure in the tank. The vacuum breaker opens if the pressure drops below ________ psi, to allow air in.
   a. 0.6
   b. 0.7
   c. 0.5
   d. 0.4
6. The pressure relief portion of a pressurized reservoir will open between ____ psi and ____ psi, depending on its spring pressure.
   a. 10, 20
   b. 10, 30
   c. 5, 20
   d. 5, 30

7. If a breather filter gets severely plugged, it could lead to ______________, which further leads to a catastrophic failure.
   a. reduced torque
   b. emptying of the fuel
   c. pump starvation
   d. engine stopping
8. Hydraulic tanks assist with conditioning the fluid by helping to cool it and clean it. Cooling is accomplished by __________.
   a. heat transfer through the walls of the tank
   b. the cold water present beneath it
   c. the carbon monoxide present in the air
   d. the coolants mixed in the tank
9. If oil cannot return from a circuit to the tank, __________________ and cause problems such as valves sticking.
   a. oil weight can increase
   b. pressure will go down
   c. oil viscosity can decrease
   d. pressure will build up
10. Discoloration of hydraulic fluid could indicate __________.
   a. overheating.
   b. the system is ingesting air.
   c. a pump inlet restriction.
   d. the return tube is broken.

ASE Technician A/Technician B Style Questions

1. Technician A says all hydraulic tanks are pressurized. Technician B says all hydraulic tanks are vented. Who is correct?
   a. Technician A
   b. Technician B
   c. Both A and B
   d. Neither A nor B
2. Technician A says all tank breathers filter the air that passes through them. Technician B says a pressurized tank requires a pressure relief valve. Who is correct?
   a. Technician A
   b. Technician B
   c. Both A and B
   d. Neither A nor B
3. Technician A says a multi-compartment tank only supplies one system with oil. Technician B says multi-compartment tanks contain an oil supply for two or more systems. Who is correct?
   a. Technician A
   b. Technician B
   c. Both A and B
   d. Neither A nor B
4. Technician A says common materials for tank construction are molded plastic, aluminum, and steel. Technician B says most tanks don't need access covers. Who is correct?
   a. Technician A
   b. Technician B
   c. Both A and B
   d. Neither A nor B
5. Technician A says hydraulic tanks should ideally be mounted above the pump. Technician B says a hydraulic tank minimum size is always based on the weight of the pump. Who is correct?
   a. Technician A
   b. Technician B
   c. Both A and B
   d. Neither A nor B
6. Technician A says the filler caps can be lockable. Technician B says the inlet tube should be located next to the return tube. Who is correct?
   a. Technician A
   b. Technician B
   c. Both A and B
   d. Neither A nor B
7. Technician A says if an inlet screen gets plugged, it won't cause any problems. Technician B says a plugged return can cause operational problems. Who is correct?
   a. Technician A
   b. Technician B
   c. Both A and B
   d. Neither A nor B
8. Technician A says to release the pressure in a tank, it's better to remove the cap as fast as possible. Technician B says you should always make sure the machine's implements are in the correct position before checking hydraulic fluid level. Who is correct?
   a. Technician A
   b. Technician B
   c. Both A and B
   d. Neither A nor B
9. Technician A says the first step when performing a hydraulic oil change is to warm up the oil. Technician B says hydraulic oil can't get hot enough to burn you. Who is correct?
   a. Technician A
   b. Technician B
   c. Both A and B
   d. Neither A nor B
10. Technician A says a pump bleeding procedure is sometimes necessary after changing hydraulic oil. Technician B says it's important to have the correct oil quantity and specification on hand before draining the old oil. Who is correct?
   a. Technician A
   b. Technician B
   c. Both A and B
   d. Neither A nor B

CHAPTER 25
Hydraulic Pumps

Knowledge Objectives

After reading this chapter, you will be able to:

- **K25001** Explain the purpose and fundamentals of hydraulic pumps.
- **K25002** Identify the types and construction features of hydraulic pumps.
- **K25003** Describe the principles of operation of hydraulic pumps.
- **K25004** Calculate pump displacement, flow, and horsepower for hydraulic pumps.
- **K25005** Recommend reconditioning or repairs for hydraulic pumps.
- **K25006** Describe the common causes of pump failure.

Skills Objectives

After reading this chapter, you will be able to:

- **S25001** Diagnose hydraulic pump problems.
- **S25002** Recondition a hydraulic pump, following manufacturer's service information.
- **S25003** Remove and install a hydraulic pump following manufacturer's service information.

▶ Introduction

Hydraulic pumps are literally the heart of any hydraulic system. The heart in your chest is a vital organ that pumps blood to all parts of your body, and a hydraulic pump is also a vital component, needed to circulate hydraulic fluid throughout a hydraulic system.

Just as our bodies would not function properly without a healthy heart, the same holds true for hydraulic systems and their pumps. Hydraulic fluid must be circulated throughout the system in order to transfer power from the prime mover to an actuator, and the hydraulic pump is the component that creates fluid flow.

Hydraulic pumps have precisely machined internal components that will work for thousands of hours as long as the pump is operated within its design parameters (pressure and temperature limits) and the system fluid is kept in good condition. Hydraulic pumps are costly to manufacture because of the close tolerances of their internal parts. They are one of the most expensive components of the hydraulic system, and in many cases of the whole machine, and the machine owner will not be happy if a hydraulic pump has to be replaced before its expected lifetime is up. Pump failures can be very costly in terms of parts and labor costs, but, more importantly, the machine downtime is very expensive. Catastrophic pump failures could cause a machine to be out of commission for weeks.

No matter how well they are looked after, all pumps will at some point wear out and/or fail. It is the job of the MORE technician to decide when a pump should be replaced, reconditioned, or repaired. Diagnosing hydraulic pump problems can be difficult, but with a solid knowledge of how pumps function and their components, a technician can confidently determine whether a hydraulic system problem is being caused by a pump, and can take steps or make recommendations to avoid a costly failure or to restore the hydraulic performance of a machine.

This chapter discusses the main types of pumps found in MORE hydraulic systems, how they are constructed, and how they operate. It also explains calculating pump output values and diagnosing, testing, and replacing pumps.

▶ The Purpose and Fundamentals of Hydraulic Pumps

K25001

The purpose of a hydraulic pump is to provide the machine's hydraulic system with the required flow of hydraulic fluid so the system can function as it was designed. The fluid flow is ultimately used by the actuator(s) in the system to perform work. This is how energy is transferred in a hydraulic system. A hydraulic pump is an **energy conversion** machine that changes the rotating mechanical power output from the prime mover (usually a diesel engine, but it could be any type of internal combustion engine or an electric motor) into hydraulic fluid power.

Pumps do not produce pressure; they only produce flow. However, the flow they produce must overcome the pressure developed in the system, which results from the resistance to flow. This resistance is primarily caused by the load the system is designed to move. Some examples of loads a MORE machine encounters are a hydraulic crane lifting a 20-ton pipe; an excavator digging into frozen ground; a wheel loader filling its bucket with wet sand; a scraper unloading a bowl of heavy earth; and a container handler lifting a 40-foot loaded container. **FIGURE 25-1** shows a heavy bucket of earth being picked up by a loader.

FIGURE 25-1 A heavy bucket of earth being picked up by a loader.

You Are the Mobile Heavy Equipment Technician

The company you are working for has a fleet of construction equipment that is fairly current, but some machines are getting older, and the owner is debating whether to sell them or recondition them. There are several excavators that have logged over 15,000 hours and have never had their main hydraulic pumps reconditioned.

It is your job to assess the main pumps on these machines and obtain quotes on replacing with exchange pumps or reconditioning them yourself. You need to know the following:

1. Are there any other sources for the pumps other than the manufacturer dealer?
2. What kind of warranty will they give on the pumps?
3. What tooling/equipment would you need to make an accurate assessment of the pumps?
4. Do you have the skill and experience to do this safely?
5. What tooling/equipment do you need to recondition the pumps yourself?
6. Is there a clean environment in the shop to do this?

Resistance to pump flow is also created by all the system components that the oil flows through, such as valves, hoses, tubes, fittings, and actuators. The combined system pressure from the load and system components works its way back to the pump outlet; this makes it seem like the pump is producing pressure, but it really is just providing flow to try to keep the system's actuators moving in order to overcome the load.

All pumps operate using the same principles of fluid mechanics, even though they can have very different internal mechanisms. Through the rotation of the internal mechanism, the pump volume is increased at the pump inlet. This creates a low-pressure area at the inlet, allowing fluid to be pushed into the pump by atmospheric pressure, pressure in the tank, head pressure, or a combination of these. That fluid is then carried through the pump to its outlet port, where the action of the internal mechanism decreases the volume in the pump, forcing the fluid out through the outlet port. Because hydraulic fluid cannot be compressed, it must flow out the pump outlet. With each pump revolution, more fluid is moved through the pump, which pushes the previous volume through the system and in turn creates a continuous flow of oil.

In essence, the **pressure differential** created at the pump inlet moves oil into the pump from the reservoir, and another pressure differential, between the pump outlet and the reservoir where the oil eventually returns, keeps the oil flowing through the system. Remember that a pressure differential is needed to make fluid flow in a sealed system. This principle aligns with the thought that oil always flows through the path of least resistance.

Hydraulic pumps can be found almost anywhere on MORE machines and are a critical component to keep the machine performing as expected. By understanding the different types of hydraulic pumps, how they work, and how to recondition them, you will become a valuable technician.

Pump Pressure Rating

Engineers that design hydraulic systems on MORE must match the pump to the system requirements in terms of flow output and pressure capacity. The pump must be able to withstand the maximum system pressure that would normally be felt at the pump outlet, plus a safety factor of approximately 20%. The pump **pressure rating** is expressed in psi, bar, mPa, or kg/cm^2.

Exceeding a pump's pressure rating reduces the pump's life expectancy or could result in a pump failure such as shaft breakage or housing fracture.

> **TECHNICIAN TIP**
>
> When replacing a hydraulic pump on any MORE machine, a technician usually just uses a part number from the manufacturer's service information to get the right pump. However, in certain situations it may be necessary to try to match an OEM pump with a pump from another supplier. In this case, the OEM specifications of the pump should be matched as closely as possible.

Pump Displacement

One of the specifications of hydraulic pump output is its displacement. This is a calculated theoretical number that states the volume of oil a pump will move or displace during one revolution of the pump's driveshaft. It is not a completely accurate indication of how much fluid the pump moves, because no pump is 100% efficient. All pumps have some internal leakage even when they are brand new, and this leakage reduces the theoretical displacement. Internal leakage increases with pump wear.

Pump displacement is stated in cubic inches per revolution (CIR) or cubic centimeters per revolution (CCR).

Pump Flow Output

Another pump performance measurement is the flow it produces per unit of time. It can be calculated using the pump's displacement figure and a simple formula.

$$Q = D \times \text{rpm}/K$$

where:

Q = **Pump output flow**
D = Pump displacement
rpm = Shaft input speed
K = Unit conversion factor

If pump displacement is given in cubic inches, then the unit conversion factor is 231. This is how many cubic inches are in a gallon of oil. This makes the resulting pump flow unit gallons per minute.

If the displacement is given in cubic centimeters, the unit conversion factor is 1,000 since there are 1,000 cubic centimeters in 1 liter of oil. This gives a result in liters per minute.

The flow can be measured in (U.S.) gallons per minute (**gpm**) or liters per minute (**lpm**). Actual pump flow is a measured value and is a true indication of how much oil the pump can move. It is measured at certain fluid conditions such as oil temperature and oil pressure.

TABLE 25-1 provides an example of a set of ratings for a small gear pump.

Types and Construction Features of Hydraulic Pumps

K25002

There are two general categories of hydraulic pumps: nonpositive displacement pumps (also known as dynamic pumps) and positive displacement pumps.

TABLE 25-1 Ratings for a Small Gear Pump

Displacement	Maximum Continuous Pressure	Maximum and Minimum Speed	Maximum Continuous Flow
1.22 in.^{3}/rev	3,150 psi	3,200–3,500 rpm	16.9 gpm

Nonpositive Displacement Pumps

A nonpositive displacement, or dynamic, pump is designed with a loose-fitting rotating component (impeller) inside its housing. When the impeller rotates as the pump shaft is driven, it creates a low pressure at its inlet that directs inlet flow to the center of the impeller. The impeller then moves the fluid out of the pump housing at a high velocity.

Because there is a lot of clearance between the impeller fins and the pump housing, if the pump outlet were blocked, flow would stop while the impeller kept turning. This is where the term "nonpositive" comes from.

As a result of their design, the output flow rate decreases as the system pressure increases. This type of pump would not be effective for a MORE hydraulic system that needs to overcome high resistances or loads. These pumps are primarily used as fluid transfer pumps and charge pumps rather than fluid power pumps.

An engine coolant pump is a good example of this type of pump. It works on centrifugal fluid flow principles and creates a high flow, but cannot overcome even low pressure.

FIGURE 25-2 is an example of a nonpositive displacement pump.

Positive Displacement Pumps

A positive displacement pump is designed in such a way that a buildup of pressure at the outlet has little effect on the output flow rate of the pump. Most fluid power pumps used on MORE are this type. The flow out of the pump is constantly pushed downstream by more flow, and a constant flow is created as the pump is continuously driven.

Because of the tight clearances inside positive displacement pumps, fluid does not have the chance to leak back through the pump. In fact, if pump flow output of a positive displacement pump were blocked, a serious pump failure would occur or the prime mover would stop turning. Remember that fluid is virtually incompressible, and if a pump is rotating, fluid has to keep moving through the pump or else serious consequences occur.

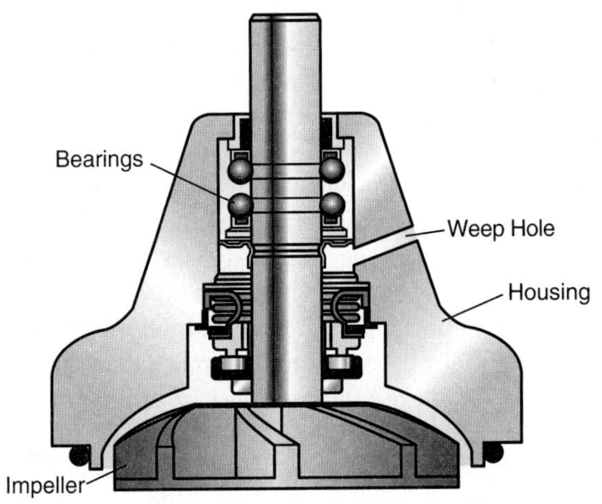

FIGURE 25-2 Nonpositive displacement pump.

Fixed Displacement

Fixed displacement types of pumps produce the same flow output for each revolution that the pump driveshaft makes. In other words, it "displaces" the same amount of oil for every pump rotation. The only way to change the flow output of a fixed displacement pump is to change the speed of its driveshaft (pump flow is measured in terms of time: gpm or lpm). The main types of fixed displacement pumps found on MORE machines are gear, vane, and piston. Both vane- and piston-type pumps have variations that can be either fixed or variable displacement pumps.

Variable Displacement

Variable displacement pumps are able to change the amount of fluid they pump per revolution, independently of the speed they are turning. They have mechanisms that can alter the pump displacement to make them more efficient, as only the required amount of flow is produced for the task at hand. Piston pumps are the most common type of variable displacement hydraulic pump found on MORE.

Types of Positive Displacement Pumps

There are three main categories of positive displacement pumps found on MORE: gear pumps, vane pumps, and piston pumps, whose operation is discussed in detail in later sections of this chapter. Each type has distinct construction features and can be used for different applications (see **TABLE 25-2**).

Gear Pumps

Gear pumps are typically limited to operating pressures of 241 bar (3,500 psi) and are used in many different applications on MORE, where a fixed displacement (or a constant amount of fluid for each revolution) is required. They are usually part of an open-center system and can come in a wide range of displacements.

Gear pumps have a simple design, which makes them relatively inexpensive, and are also fairly forgiving when it comes

TABLE 25-2 Positive Displacement Hydraulic Pump Categories

	Fixed Displacement	Variable Displacement
Gear Pumps		
External	X	
Internal	X	
Vane Pumps		
Balanced	X	
Unbalanced	X	X
Piston Pumps		
Axial—in-line	X	X
Bent axis	X	X
Radial	X	X

to contaminated oil, which makes them very durable. Two types of gear pumps can be found on MORE: internal gear and external gear.

External Gear Pumps

External gear pumps utilize two equal-sized gears on shafts that are in constant mesh. The gear teeth are on the outside of the shaft, which gives this pump its name. One gear has an extended driveshaft and is mated to the power source, which is either an internal combustion engine or electric motor. These pumps can be driven directly by a prime mover, a power take-off drive, driven by another powertrain component (torque converter) or driven from the back of other pumps. **FIGURE 25-3** illustrates a gear pump driven by another type of pump.

The shaft can be externally splined to mate with an internal spline in a gear or keyed to accept a gear. The shaft can also be tapered with a key slot to accept a gear that is tapered and locked to the shaft with a key. If a gear is installed on a pump shaft, the fastener must be torqued to specification. **FIGURE 25-4** depicts an external gear pump with a gear drive.

The gear driven by the power source is called the drive gear, and the second gear is called the driven gear or idler gear. The

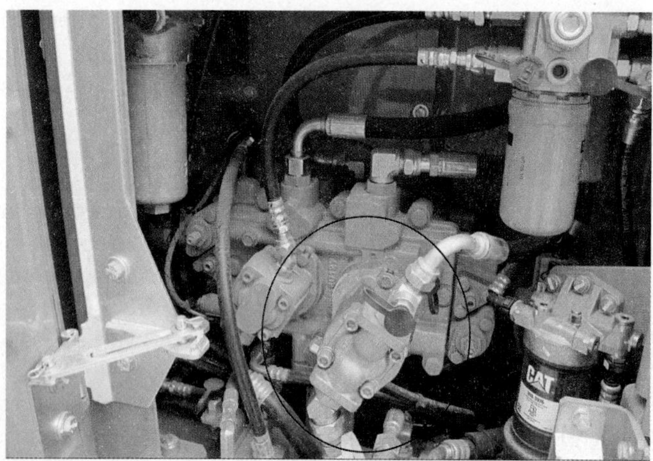

FIGURE 25-3 A gear pump driven by another type of pump.

FIGURE 25-4 External gear pump with a gear drive.

FIGURE 25-5 Locations for measuring clearance in a gear pump.

gears revolve inside a close-fitting housing, and the fluid is carried around in the space between the gear teeth. The gear shafts rotate inside plain bushings or roller bearings that are pressed into the pump housings.

A typical new pump clearance between the teeth tips and pump housing is 0.005–0.008". The tips of the teeth rely on a film of oil to maintain a seal with the outer housing to prevent internal leakage. **FIGURE 25-5** shows an external gear pump, clearance between the teeth tips and the housing is critical. Because of their design, gear pumps can be described as having a pulsating oil flow compared to vane or piston pumps, which have a constant flow.

In larger external gear pumps, the ends of their gears ride against brass endplates that have grooves to retain oil so as to maintain a film of oil. The brass endplates are a replaceable component that allows the housing to be reused, and can be replaced, whereas smaller pumps rely on a small clearance between the gear ends and the housing itself. **FIGURE 25-6** provides an exploded view of a typical external gear pump. The gear pump consists of (1) seal retainers, (2) seals, (3) seal backups, (4) isolation plates, (5) spacers, (6) a drive gear, (7) an idler gear, (8) a housing, (9) a mounting flange, (10) a flange seal, and (11) pressure balance plates, on either side of the gears.

Gears and their shafts are made from forged and precision-machined hardened steel, and gear pump housings can be made from machined aluminum or cast steel. Housings are manufactured in at least two pieces that are held together with fasteners and sealed with O-rings. Pump driveshafts are typically sealed with two lip-type seals. Housing sections usually use dowels to keep them accurately lined up, and pump sections can be held together with long bolts or studs. **FIGURE 25-7** portrays a gear pump housing cutaway showing a dowel.

The pump housing must have an **inlet port** and an **outlet port**, and typically the outlet port is smaller than the inlet. Some gear pumps may have a third port, a case drain port.

External gear pumps can also be multi-section, which means there are two or more pumps piggybacked to each other and driven by the same power source. Multi-section pumps can share a common inlet port. They can also provide drive to other

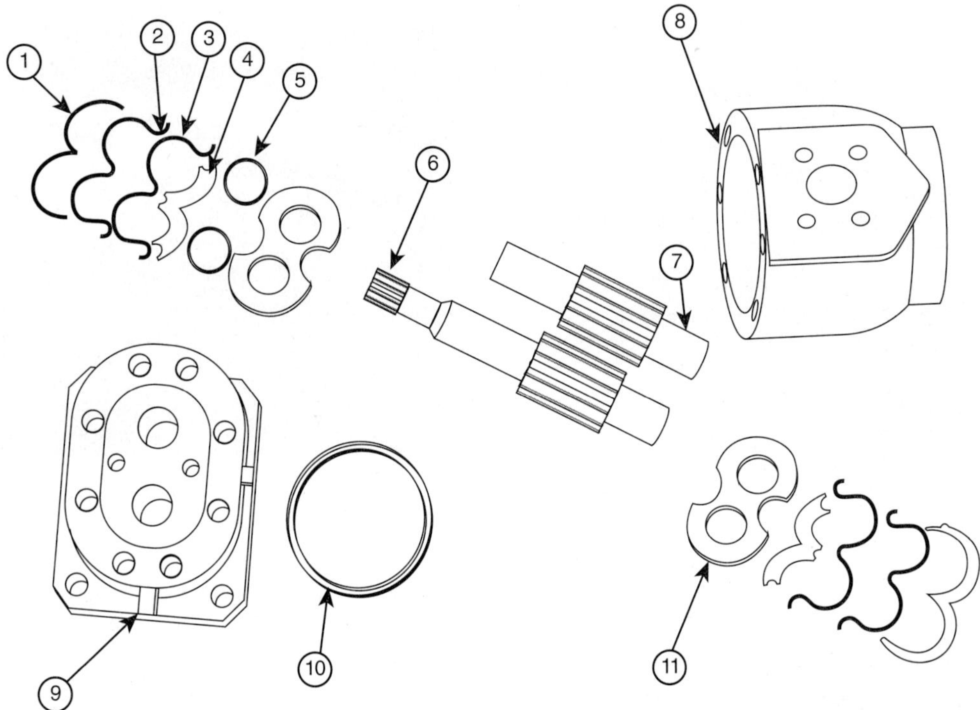

FIGURE 25-6 Exploded view of a typical external gear.

FIGURE 25-7 A gear pump housing cutaway showing a dowel.

FIGURE 25-8 A multi-section external gear pump.

types of pumps, such as vane and piston. **FIGURE 25-8** shows a multi-section gear pump.

Internal Gear Pumps

Internal gear pumps are sometimes used for low-flow and low-pressure systems on MORE, such as pilot oil or brake systems on small machines. They can also be used as charge pumps to deliver pressurized oil to another, larger pump's inlet. They feature two intermeshing gears that rotate on different centers: the outer with internal gear teeth, and the inner with external gear teeth. The inner gear is driven by a shaft and carries the outer gear (ring gear) with it inside the pump housing. The pump housing also has a crescent-shaped stationary spacer that keeps the gears partially separated at the lower part of the housing. An internal gear pump is shown in **FIGURE 25-9**. The interaction between the inner and outer gears create a pumping action as they rotate together.

Gerotor Internal Gear Pumps

This type of pump is similar to the internal gear pump and is sometimes called a conjugate curve gear pump because of the unique shape of the gear teeth. The main differences between the two types of internal gear pumps are the shapes of the gear teeth and the absence of the crescent-shaped spacer in the gerotor pump. A driveshaft rotates the inner gear, and the outer gear is carried around with it; the interaction between the two gears creates a pumping action. **FIGURE 25-10** depicts a gerotor internal gear pump.

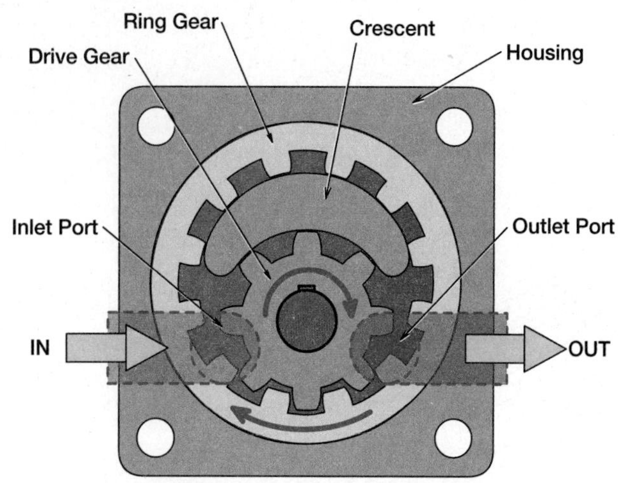

FIGURE 25-9 Internal gear pump.

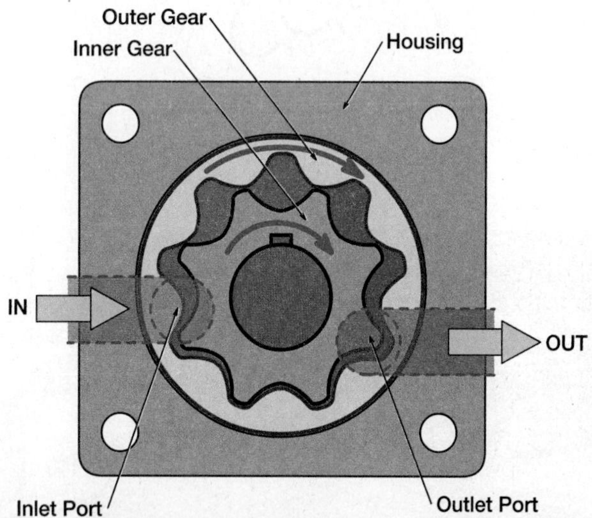

FIGURE 25-10 Gerotor-style pump.

Vane Pumps

Vane pumps are typically limited to operating pressures of 241 bar (3,500 psi) and are used in a variety of applications on MORE, such as small to medium-sized wheel loaders and bulldozers for their main implement functions (boom, bucket, blade control). Vane pumps sustain internal damage fairly easily. In **FIGURE 25-11**, an assembled vane pump is illustrated.

FIGURE 25-11 An assembled vane pump.

A vane pump's main parts consist of a housing, cam ring, rotor, vanes, and shaft. A cam ring (can be called a displacement ring) is held stationary in the pump housing, and the pump shaft rotates the rotor inside the cam ring. The rotor has slots that allow the vanes to slide in and out it, and the rotor and vanes are sealed on the end with end plates or flex plates.

> **TECHNICIAN TIP**
>
> In most vane pumps, the ends of the vanes are tapered. If you are reconditioning a vane pump, care must be taken to ensure the vanes are installed the right way. If one or more vanes are put in backward, the pump will not produce full flow because there will be a dead spot wherever the vanes are reversed. If a cartridge assembly is replaced, an arrow on the component will indicate shaft rotation direction, and care must be taken to make sure it is installed in the correct orientation.

Two ports in the rotor and pump housing allow the hydraulic oil to enter and exit the pumping area of the pump (some styles of vane pump rotors have two inlet and two outlet ports). The pump housing has at least two pieces that are sealed with an O-ring and fasteners. The rotor also has internal ports to allow pressurized oil behind the vanes, which forces the vanes out against the inner surface of the cam ring. The pump housing is machined cast steel, and the shaft and cartridge components are machined and hardened steel alloy.

The pumping action of vane pumps is created by the changing volume between the sliding **vanes**. Sliding vane pumps are quieter and have lower flow pulsations than gear pumps. A small amount of ring and vane wear can be compensated for by the sliding vanes. There are three main types of vane pump: unbalanced fixed displacement, unbalanced variable displacement, and balanced fixed displacement. Some vane pump assemblies are multi-section, which means more than one cartridge assembly is housed in the same pump assembly housing. The separate cartridges are driven by a common shaft and can share a common

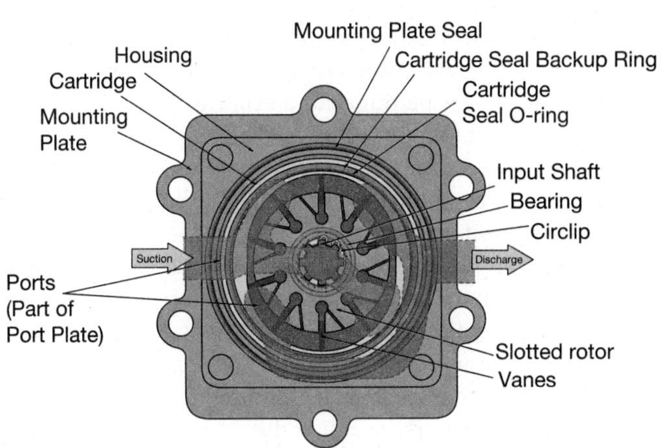

FIGURE 25-12 A cutaway of a vane pump.

FIGURE 25-13 A piston pump.

inlet port. Most vane pumps are easily serviceable because if internal pump problems are found, the pump cartridge assembly can be replaced. The cartridge consists of the support plates, the cam ring, the flex plates, the slotted rotor, and the vanes.

Both the fixed and variable vane pumps use common part terminology **FIGURE 25-12** shows a cutaway view of two section vane pump. Each type of vane pump will have a multi section housing, drive shaft, shaft support bearings, seals and cartridge/s that consists of: a cam ring, slotted rotor, end plates and vanes.

Some vane pump assemblies are multi-section, which means more than one cartridge assembly is housed in the same pump assembly housing. The separate cartridges are driven by a common shaft and can share a common inlet port.

Some vane pumps have a variable displacement capability. Variable vane pumps have a cam ring that is movable and can pivot to adjust the displacement of the pump. The cam ring is moved by an actuator piston that is controlled by a valve that is part of the pump control mechanism. The pump control could be hydraulically or electrically actuated.

Piston Pumps

Piston pumps are a common type of hydraulic pump that can be found on just about any type of MORE. They can be used for a wide variety of hydraulic systems that require medium to high pressure (3,000 to 6,000 psi) and a wide range of flow requirements. They are used to supply flow to circuits that use rotary actuators such as cooling fans, conveyors, augers, travel drives, and swing drives or circuits that use linear actuators (cylinders) such as blade lift, bucket curl, box hoist, or steering.

They can operate more efficiently with high and low shaft speeds than gear pumps and can tolerate higher pressures over longer periods. **FIGURE 25-13** illustrates a piston pump.

With proper maintenance and use, piston pumps can easily last over 20,000 hours, but if poor maintenance or operating practices are used, early catastrophic failures can be very expensive. Pump failures can also lead to system contamination and many other ongoing problems if pump debris gets sent through the system.

Piston pumps typically operate at pressures of 345 bar (5,000 psi) or higher and are used in applications such as implements, steering, brakes, and suspension systems. They come in three arrangements—**axial piston, bent-axis**, and radial piston pumps; however, radial piston pumps are not very common and are only briefly discussed here. Axial and bent axis piston pumps can also be referred to as straight housing and angled housing, respectively, and both types can be variable displacement type.

All styles of piston pumps have reciprocating pistons that move in and out of a barrel (cylinder block). Each pump has a method of turning rotary shaft motion into reciprocating piston motion. The internal mechanisms that make the pistons move are what differentiate the types of piston pumps. It is the reciprocating piston motion that creates fluid flow.

Axial Piston Pumps Construction

The main components of an axial piston pump are shaft, bearings, seals, cylinder block, pistons with slippers, port plate, **swashplate**, and housing. **FIGURE 25-14** portrays the main components of an axial piston pump.

FIGURE 25-14 Main components of (1) a piston pump, (2) the housing, (3) the shaft, (4) the pistons, (5) the port plate, (6) the barrel, and (7) the swashplate.

The pump housing has a flange machined on the shaft end to provide a mounting surface to mate with the component that drives it. They usually mount with two threaded fasteners, but some pumps use four. Axial piston pumps can also drive other pumps.

Axial piston pumps have their pistons arranged parallel to the pump shaft. A set of pistons is carried around in the barrel (sometimes called the cylinder block) in a series of evenly spaced bores. The bores and pistons are machined and polished together to achieve very close tolerances. So much so, that when reconditioning a piston pump it is not a good practice to mix up pistons and bores.

The splined pump shaft drives the barrel. The **port plate** is held stationary on the head of the pump and directs oil in and out of the barrel to ports in the housing. These kidney-shaped ports allow hydraulic lines to connect to the pump housing for inlet and discharge. The mating surfaces of the port plate and barrel are lap finished. The condition of these surfaces is critical for preventing excess internal leakage. The pump relies on a film of oil between these two components to create a dynamic seal that must contain maximum system pressure within the pumping mechanism. The slippers have a series of grooves that retain some oil that is used for lubrication between the slippers and the swashplate.

TECHNICIAN TIP

Lap finishing is a process that creates a flat and true surface to ensure a complete seal. When pump components are manufactured, lapping is done on a machine. To recondition the barrel and or port plate, it is possible to hand-lap them to remove minor scratches. Hand-lapping requires a perfectly flat surface, a large sheet of fine emery cloth and mineral spirits. The cloth is placed on the flat surface, rough side up, and soaked with mineral spirits. The component to be lapped is then worked in a figure eight pattern, with light down pressure, until an even finish is obtained.

Great care must be taken when handling components with lapped surfaces, as they are easily damaged.

The swashplate is at the opposite end of the barrel, and it stays in contact with the piston slippers because of a retaining plate. Each piston has a slipper on its ball end to enable a pivoting action to always keep the slipper following the swashplate's angled surface. The slipper faces have grooves to retaining lubricating oil.

The angle of the swashplate converts the rotary motion of the barrel and pistons into a reciprocating motion as the pistons are carried around in the barrel. The shaft is supported by bearings and is sealed with two lip-type seals. A weep hole between the seals will permit an external leak if one of the seals fail.

Piston pumps have many precisely machined and finished components that must maintain a close tolerance with each other. These tolerances are taken up with a thin film of oil that creates a seal between the components. The pump housing is machined from cast steel, and all other components are hardened and machined steel alloy. The piston slippers and their mating port place surface are usually made from a brass alloy to reduce sliding friction, as there is a lot of motion and contact between these two components.

Some leakage is permitted and expected between the components, but if it becomes excessive, the pump's efficiency drops off and may necessitate repairs or replacement. These close tolerances between pump components make all piston pumps particularly sensitive to contamination.

The pump housing has a third port that allows internal leakage to return to the tank (**case drain** leakage). Some pumps have pressure and temperature sensors as well. **FIGURE 25-15** shows three piston pumps and the hoses connected to them.

Variable displacement axial piston pumps change the angle of their swashplate to change their displacement. They typically have a piston push on one side of the swashplate, and it can pivot on stub shafts that ride in bearings. The piston receives oil from a pump control valve that can be electronically controlled.

Bent Axis Piston Pump Construction

The second most common type of piston pump is the bent axis, which shares many of the same components as the axial type but creates piston movement in a different manner. Common internal components include pistons, barrel, port plate, shaft, bearings, seals housing and head. In addition to these components, connecting links and a retainer plate are needed to join the pistons to the shaft assembly to transfer torque between the shaft and pistons.

The barrel centerline and shaft centerline are at an angle to each other and as the shaft rotates the angle creates a piston reciprocating motion since the pistons are moved in and out of the barrel as the assembly rotates. Component materials are the same as axial piston pumps and contamination will quickly degrade the pumps efficiency.

FIGURE 25-16 depicts a bent axis pump.

Variable displacement bent axis piston pumps use a piston to move their barrel, which in turn varies the pump displacement. The piston receives oil from a valve that can be electronically controlled.

FIGURE 25-15 Three piston pumps and the hoses connected to them.

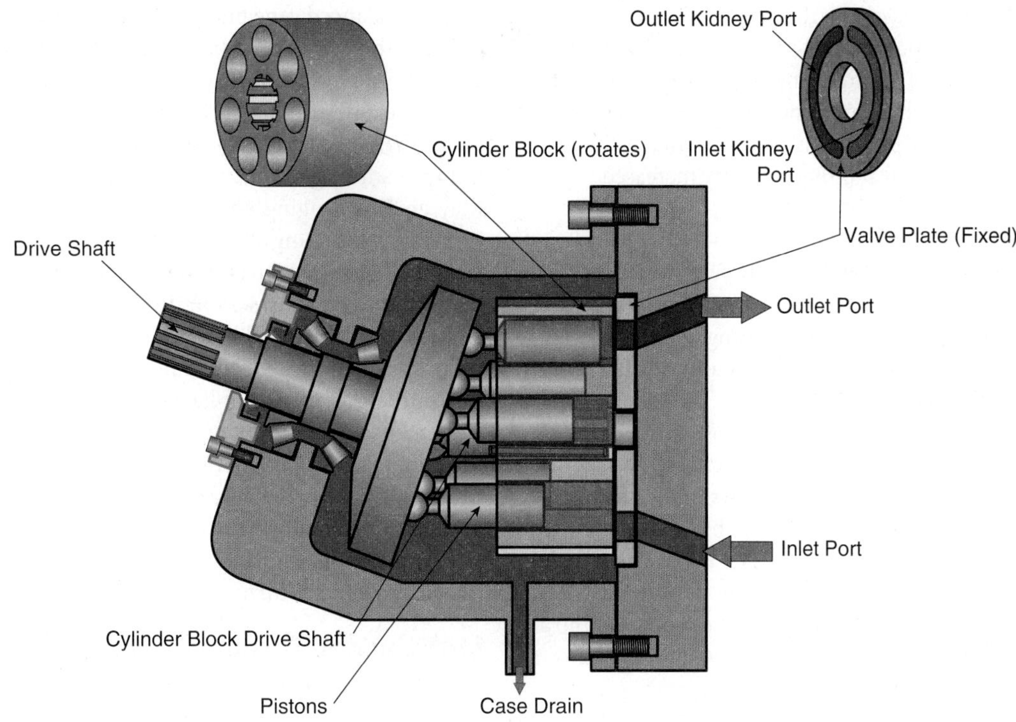

FIGURE 25-16 A bent axis pump.

▶ Operation of Hydraulic Pumps

K25003

Hydraulic pumps can be either fixed or variable displacement. All variations of gear pumps are fixed displacement, but vane and piston pumps can come in fixed or variable configurations. Fixed displacement pumps can only vary their flow output by their shaft turning at different speeds. They are simpler in construction, but their fixed output can lead to system limitations and inefficiencies.

Variable displacement pumps require extra control mechanisms, which can lead to reduced reliability, but they provide increased system flexibility and efficiency.

Whatever type of pump is used for a hydraulic system, its basic function is still to provide the flow required to make the system function as designed.

Gear Pump Operation

The two main types of gear pumps (internal and external gear) share some common principles of operation but are still quite different in the way they move hydraulic fluid. The next two sections describe how each type works.

External Gear Pump

The main components that make a gear pump move oil are its housing; drive gear (driven by the shaft); driven gear; and pressure plates, if present. As they rotate, the gear teeth separate at the pump inlet, allowing fluid to be forced into the pump from the reservoir. Oil floods the inlet of the pump, and once the teeth move past the pump inlet port, a sealed chamber is created. Remember, although there has to be a small clearance between the gear teeth and the pump housing, the viscosity of the oil creates a dynamic seal to effectively make a small, sealed, individual chamber.

The oil is carried around the inside of the pump housing, in the spaces between the gear teeth and the pump housing, to the outlet port. The ends of the pump housing or replaceable end plates complete the sealed chamber at the ends of the gears. The meshing of the teeth forces the fluid out through the outlet port and into the system. Because oil cannot be compressed, it must leave the pump through the outlet port. **FIGURE 25-17** illustrates how oil flows through an external gear pump.

Some external pumps have small lubrication passages to the bearings that feed them a small amount of oil; otherwise, the bearings rely on internal leakage oil for lubrication. As output pressure

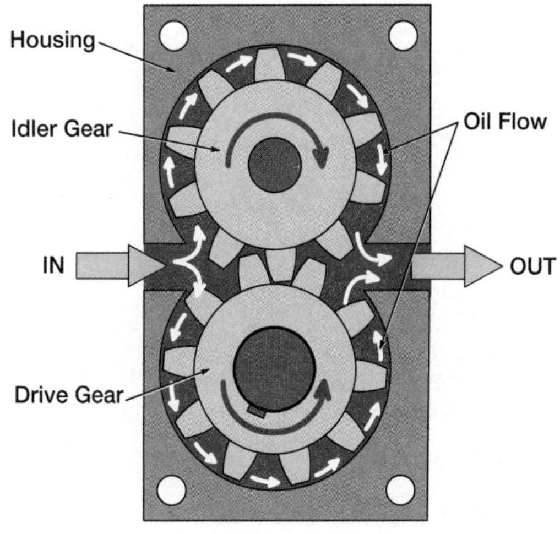

FIGURE 25-17 How oil flows through an external gear pump.

rises, more side thrust is placed on the gears and shafts because the oil is resisting being pushed downstream out of the pump, and the reacting force tries to spread the gears apart. If oil condition is poor (overdue for change, wrong viscosity, overheated, or contaminated) and output pressure is near maximum, then the possibility of bearing-to-shaft scuffing is greatly increased.

Internal Gear Pumps

The pump shaft drives the inner external gear, which in turn drives the outer external gear. The outer diameter of the outer gear is free to rotate inside the pump housing, with a thin film of oil separating the two components. The pump's ports are part of the pump's end housing.

Interaction between the two gears creates an expanding chamber at the pump inlet. This makes oil flow from the tank into the pump, to eliminate any voids. As the gears rotate, they move past a crescent-shaped barrier located in the housing, which separates the pump into two chambers. The oil that is trapped in the two chambers now moves toward the pump outlet, and because the oil can't be compressed, it is forced out of the pump as the pumping chamber decreases in volume. **FIGURE 25-18** shows how an internal gear pump works.

Gerotor pumps are similar in construction to internal gear pumps, but without the crescent-shaped barrier in the housing. They function with the same principles as the previously discussed internal gear pump. An expanding and contracting pumping chamber created by the interaction of the pumps gears creates fluid movement.

Vane Pump Operation

There are three variations of vane pumps: unbalanced fixed displacement, unbalanced variable displacement, and balanced fixed displacement. Variable displacement vane pumps are rarely used for MORE hydraulic systems.

The main difference between balanced and unbalanced vane pumps is the shape of the **cam ring** (sometimes called the stator ring). A balanced vane pump has an elliptically shaped cam ring, whereas the unbalanced pump has a round cam ring. However, the operating principle of all types of vane pumps is similar.

Vane pumps transfer oil through the action of movable vanes that are carried around in slots in the rotor inside of the pump's cam ring. As the vanes move up and down in the rotor, they create changing volumes between adjacent vanes. As the individual pumping chambers between two vanes expand in size, they also move past the inlet port, and oil is pushed into the pump from the reservoir. Rotation continues; the inlet port is then covered; and the pumping chamber is sealed until the first vane uncovers the outlet port. At this point, the vanes start to contract into the rotor because of the shape of the cam ring. This reduces the pumping chamber size and forces the oil out the pump outlet port and downstream into the system. The ends of the rotor and cam ring are sealed with end plates that are also pressurized to maintain a tight seal.

Variable displacement vane pumps have a cam ring that is movable, which in turn controls pump displacement.

Unbalanced Fixed Displacement Vane Pump

The unbalanced vane pump's rotor is mounted off center within the cam ring. As the pump shaft starts to rotate and turn the rotor, the vanes move out against the cam ring because of centrifugal force. As soon as oil starts to flow out of the outlet port, resistance to flow builds pressure, which is sent back through the rotor to passages under the vanes. This pressure keeps the vanes out against the cam ring to maintain oil flow. **FIGURE 25-19** demonstrates how oil pressure keeps vanes out against the cam ring.

Larger pumps may use a rocker spring, which transmits the force of one vane onto another. The volume of oil varies between each pair of vanes as the rotor rotates, moving oil from the inlet port to the outlet port. Pressure acts on only one side of the rotor; therefore, the forces acting on the shaft and bearings are unbalanced, and this can reduce the service life of

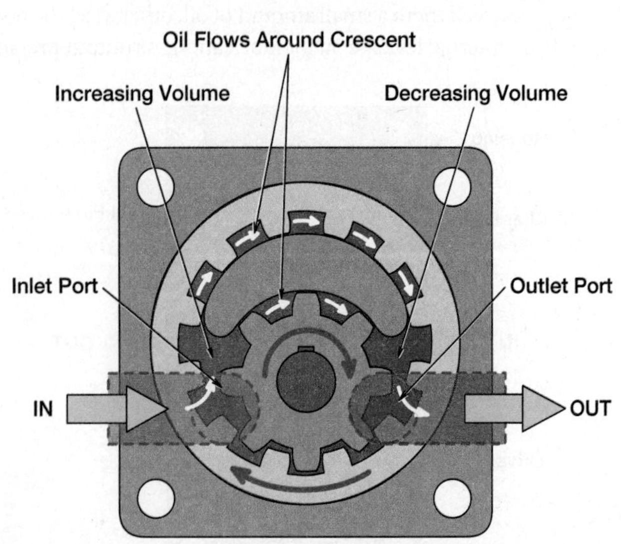

FIGURE 25-18 How an internal gear pump works.

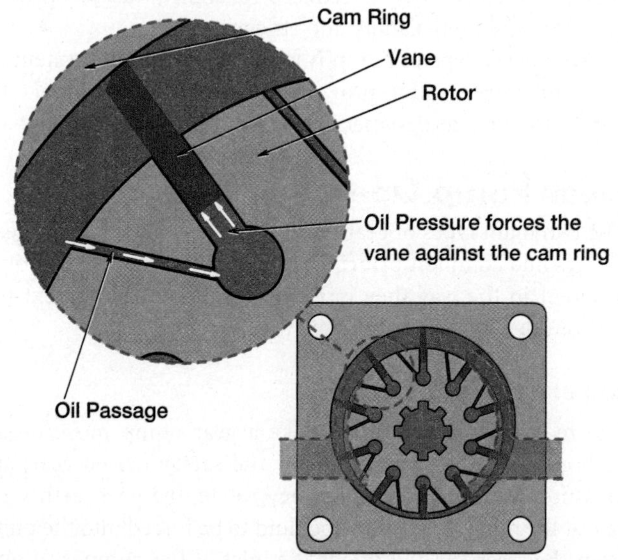

FIGURE 25-19 How oil pressure keeps vanes out against the cam ring.

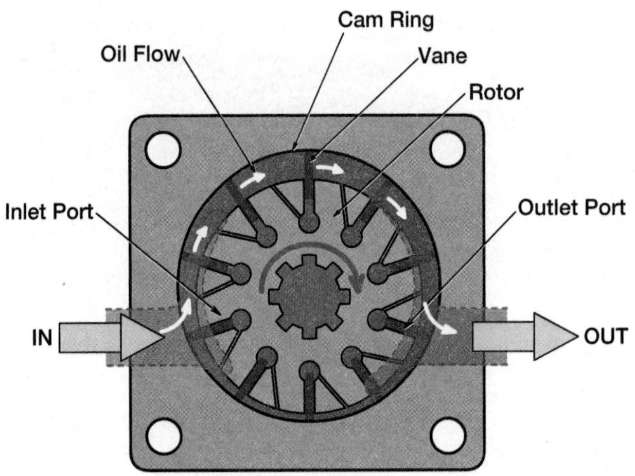

FIGURE 25-20 Unbalanced vane pump.

the unit at high pressures. Because of pressure limitations with this style of pump, they are only used for lower pressure applications on MORE. **FIGURE 25-20** shows an unbalanced vane pump.

Balanced Fixed Displacement Vane Pump

Balanced sliding vane pumps have a similar rotor and vane assembly as other styles of vane pumps, but the stator ring has an elliptical shape, which forms two pumping chambers opposite each other. This construction balances the load on the rotor shaft and bearings. Because of the even loading on the pump rotating components, this style of pump has a greater life expectancy. This is the most common arrangement for vane pumps found on MORE, and they have efficiencies of over 90% when new. Another beneficial feature of vane pumps is that they can compensate for wear on the vane tips and cam ring by simply allowing the vanes to move out further. See **FIGURE 25-21** for an example of a balanced fixed displacement pump.

Unbalanced Variable Displacement

A variable displacement vane pump moves the stator ring by using a small linear actuator that is contained in the pump housing. As the offset rotor rotates, the vanes make contact with the stator ring, thus creating less than atmospheric pressure at the inlet of the pump and allowing the pump to draw in fluid. If the stator ring moves to a point that centers the rotor within the housing, the volume between the vanes will remain the same all around the rotor, and the unit will stop pumping oil. The stator ring can be positioned anywhere between this zero-flow position and the maximum-flow position. This style of vane pump is not very common on MORE. **FIGURE 25-22** shows a variable displacement vane pump.

Piston Pump Operation

Piston pumps are found in medium- to high-pressure systems that may require any amount of flow and will maintain a constant, regular oil flow as needed. They operate with 90% efficiency, at high and low shaft speeds, and can tolerate high pressures over long periods; they are also generally less noisy than gear pumps. Internally they have many close-fitting moving parts, which make them costly and sensitive to contamination.

The main operating principle behind any type of piston pump is the creation of a reciprocating action by a series of pistons in a cylinder assembly. When a piston is moving down in its cylinder, oil is pushed into the cylinder from the reservoir, and when the same piston moves up, it pushes that same volume of oil out of the cylinder, out of the pump, and downstream into the system. The reciprocating action is timed to occur when the piston is exposed to either an inlet port or an outlet port.

Most piston pumps have between seven and nine pistons, and as the pump shaft turns, the pistons are all set in motion. The constant pumping action of all pistons creates a smooth steady flow of outlet oil.

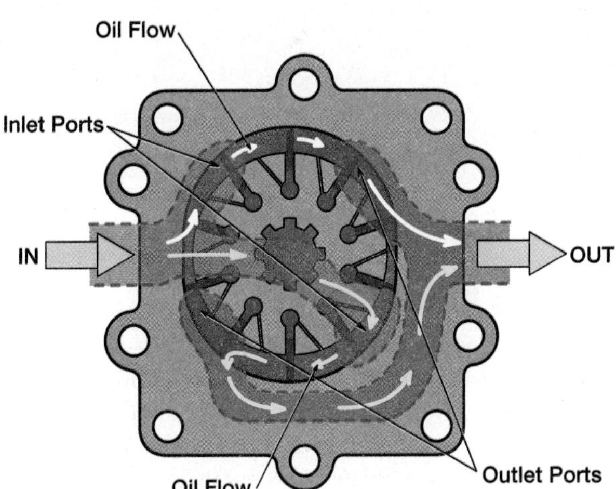

FIGURE 25-21 Balanced fixed displacement vane pump.

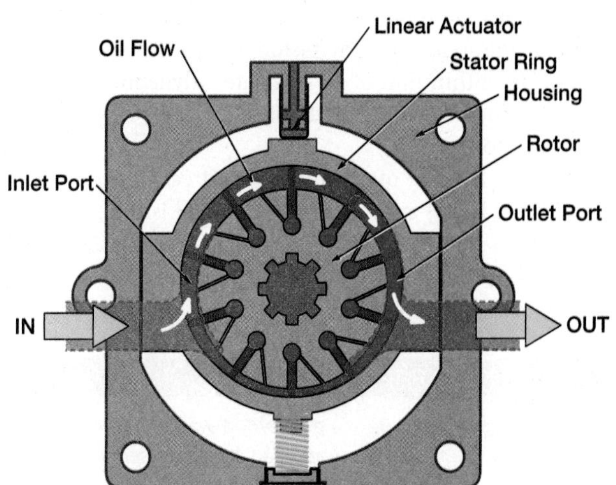

FIGURE 25-22 Variable displacement vane pump.

Piston pumps can easily operate at maximum pressures of 345 bar (5,000 psi) or higher. They come in three different arrangements: in line axial, bent axis, and radial (radial piston pumps are rarely found on MORE). The arrangement of the three types of piston pumps is summarized here:

- **In-line axial piston pumps:** In in-line piston pumps, the pistons operate parallel to the axis (driveshaft) of the pump.
- **Bent axis piston pumps:** In bent axis piston pumps, the pistons operate at an angle to the axis (driveshaft) of the pump.
- **Radial piston pumps:** In radial piston pumps, the pistons operate perpendicular to the axis of the pump. The piston arrangement is similar to that found in a radial internal combustion engine.

Axial Piston Pumps

Axial piston pumps have a rotating barrel assembly (cylinder, cylinder block) that is driven by the pumps shaft and contains an odd number of pistons (usually seven to nine). As the barrel is rotated, it carries the pistons with it. The barrel has a finely machined and finished surface, at the opposite end to the shaft, that mates with a port plate (sometimes called a valve plate). See **FIGURE 25-23** for a barrel and piston assembly. The port plate is stationary and aligns with the inlet and outlet ports in the pump head (end of the housing opposite from the shaft). The port plate allows oil transfer in and out of the pump. **FIGURE 25-24** shows where a port plate is located in the pump.

The angled swashplate located at the shaft end of the barrel actuates piston movement. As the barrel rotates and carries the pistons with it, the pistons' slippers follow the swashplate. The angle of the swashplate creates the reciprocating motion of the pistons in and out of the barrel. At any given time, half of the pistons are pulling away from the inlet port, allowing fluid to be pushed into the pump, and the other half are pushed in toward the outlet port, forcing fluid out of the pump and into the system. Pump displacement is determined by piston diameter and piston stroke.

Each piston can have a number of metal sealing rings, similar to an automotive engine piston, but most rely on close tolerances and a thin film of oil to create a dynamic seal between the piston and its cylinder. **FIGURE 25-25** depicts three different styles of pistons.

A small amount of oil will leak past each piston and from between the barrel and port plate. This oil is called case drain oil; it eventually fills the pump housing and must be allowed to drain. A third port in the pump housing provides a way to drain the case drain oil back to the tank.

> **TECHNICIAN TIP**
>
> Measuring case drain oil flow is a common way to find out whether a pump has excessive internal wear. Manufacturer's service information will provide specifications for maximum allowable case drain leakage, which can also be measured with a pressure gauge in some cases. Case drain pressures are normally very low.

FIGURE 25-23 A barrel and piston assembly.

Bent Axis Piston Pumps

Bent axis pumps operate in the same way as in-line axial piston pumps in that they use the reciprocating motion of pistons to create oil flow. The biggest differences in design are that a the barrel of a bent axis pump is on a different axis than its shaft, and there is no swashplate. The pump shaft drives the barrel through a mechanical link that provides an angled torque transfer. The pistons are driven by their ball ends, which are turned by the drive plate, and the barrel turns in unison with

FIGURE 25-24 Port plate location.

FIGURE 25-25 Three different styles of pistons.

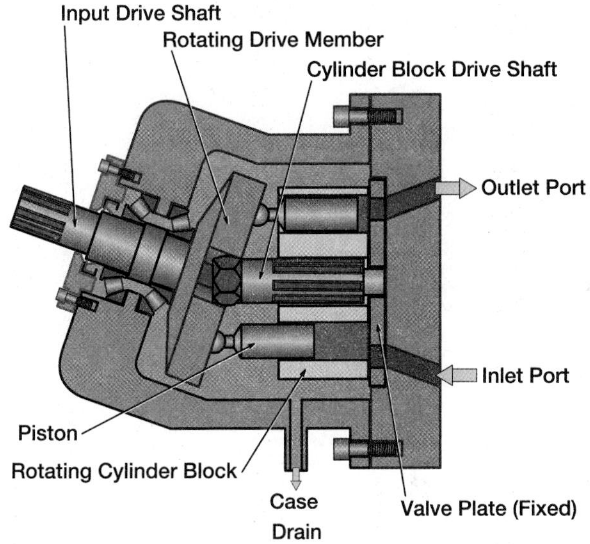

FIGURE 25-26 A simplified illustration of a bent axis pump.

the pistons. The ball ends are held to the drive plate by a retaining plate. Piston stroke movement occurs when the shaft rotates the barrel assembly, and the piston connecting rods move the pistons up and down in the barrel. **FIGURE 25-26** is a simplified illustration of a bent axis pump.

Bent axis pumps are commonly found on excavators in a variable displacement configuration and usually as a double-pump assembly (two pumping units in one housing). **FIGURE 25-27** provides an exploded view of a bent axis double pump.

Variable Displacement Piston Pump Operation

Piston pumps can have a variable displacement capability. Variable displacement pumps have a mechanism that allows the pumps displacement to be changed to match flow output to system needs. These pumps are designed to significantly increase system efficiency by providing only the flow that is required by the machine operator to actuate a cylinder or motor at the speed desired. Very little excess flow is wasted by using a variable displacement pump. Fixed displacement pumps can only vary flow output by having their shaft speed changed, and this is not always practical for a machine that needs its prime mover to drive other machine systems. Variable displacement pumps can change their flow output no matter what the shaft speed is.

Although there are several different types of variable displacement pumps, the most common ones found on MORE are axial piston and bent axis piston. Variable displacement pumps can be easily controlled by an ECM that is likely one of several machine ECMs that are part of the machine's multiplexing network. These electronic pump control systems can work in harmony with the machine's engine ECM in particular, to vary pump flow with engine load in order to make the machine more efficient.

Variable Displacement Axial Piston Pumps

A variable displacement axial piston pump is designed to deliver oil flow on demand through a series of reciprocating pistons housed in a rotating cylinder. In a fixed displacement axial piston pump, as described earlier in this chapter, the swashplate is held at a fixed angle to the pump. This provides a fixed piston stroke per shaft revolution.

For a variable displacement axial piston pump, the stroke length of its pistons is controlled either hydraulically or electronically by a control cylinder that is attached to a yoke that moves the swashplate. The yoke (swashplate) angle varies the piston stroke, increasing or decreasing pump displacement. An external screw mechanism is used to limit the swashplate maximum angle. **FIGURE 25-28** shows a variable displacement axial piston pump.

The swashplate pivots in the pump housing, either on stub shafts or on a saddle, and its angle can be controlled several ways. The simplest way is to have a spring trying to keep it at maximum angle and a hydraulically actuated piston (commonly called an actuator piston or control piston) trying to reduce the angle. Oil is supplied to the piston from one or more valves that are part of a pump control circuit. The simplest pump control circuit reduces pump flow only when pressure rises to relief valve setting. This valve is called a high-pressure cutoff valve.

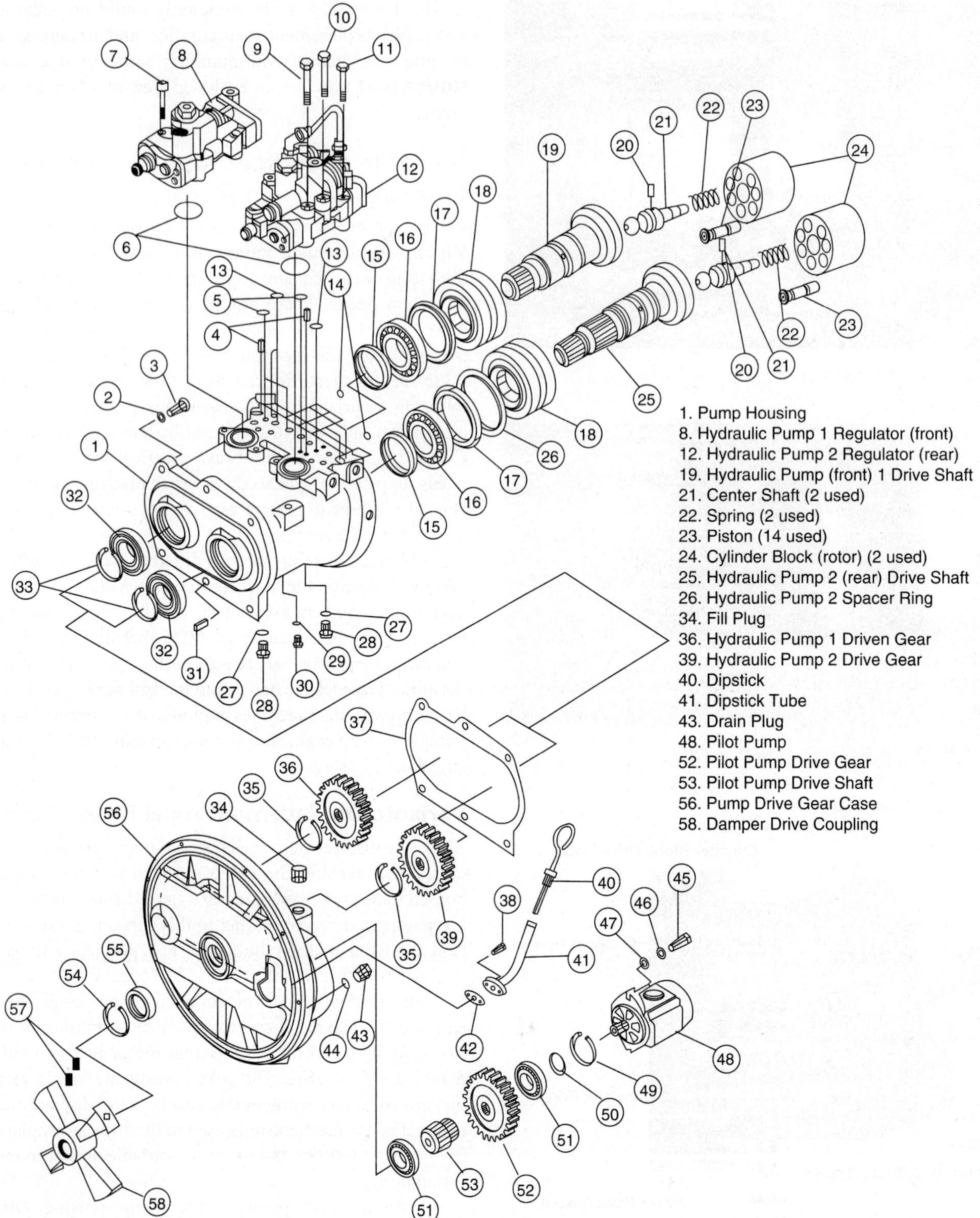

FIGURE 25-27 Exploded view of a bent axis double-pump assembly.

Image Provided As Courtesy of John Deere.

Changing the pump's swashplate from minimum toward maximum angle is referred to as **upstroking** the pump. An axial piston pump that is at maximum stroke has its pistons travel in and out of the cylinder block the greatest distance possible. This is limited by a maximum displacement stop that is sometimes adjustable.

When a pump's swashplate is at maximum and starts to move toward minimum angle, it is said to be **destroking**. It destrokes when the system is trying to reduce flow. Axial piston pumps never completely destroke because there is always a small internal leakage that must be overcome. The system pressure that is created when the pump is at minimum swashplate

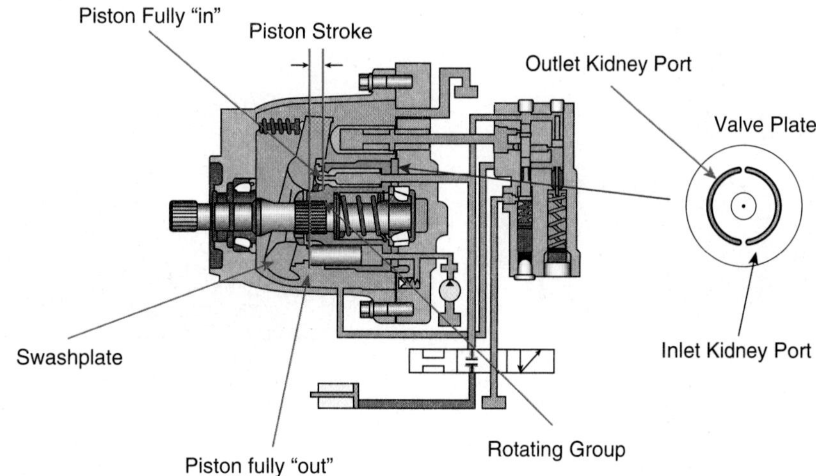

FIGURE 25-28 A variable displacement axial piston pump.
Image Provided As Courtesy of John Deere.

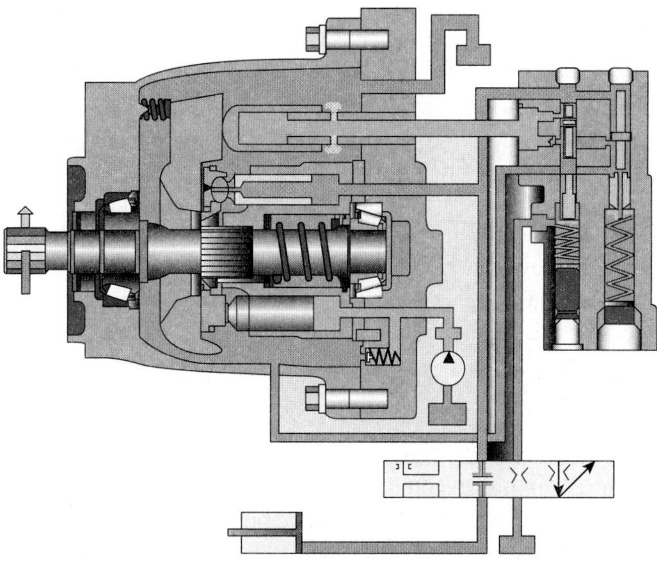

FIGURE 25-29 An axial piston pump at minimum angle.
Image Provided As Courtesy of John Deere.

angle is typically called standby pressure. **FIGURE 25-29** shows an axial piston pump at minimum angle.

Variable Displacement Bent Axis Piston Pumps

As described earlier, in a bent axis piston pump, the pistons and barrel are driven at an angle to the pump's shaft. Fixed displacement bent axis pumps have a fixed angle between the shaft and pistons, whereas the variable displacement style provides a means to change the angle between these two main components.

The pistons are driven by their ball ends, which are turned by the drive plate that is driven by the pump shaft, and the cylinder block is also driven by the pump shaft. The ball ends are held to the drive plate by a retaining plate. As the cylinder block changes angle in relationship to the pump driveshaft, the stroke of the pistons changes. The block has a concave end that moves along a curved end plate opposite to the driveshaft end. The end plate is also called a valve plate or port plate.

The closer the cylinder block and the shaft axis are together, the more minimal will be the pump's relative piston travel, and the pump flow will be at minimum. When the pump's control valve piston moves a pin, the pin then moves the cylinder block to a greater angle, and the pistons travel farther in the block. This increases the effective stroke of the pistons, and the pump flow output increases. The end of the cylinder block is lap finished and mates with the valve plate. The valve plate has inlet and outlet ports to direct oil in and out of the cylinder block from the pump housing ports. **FIGURE 25-30** illustrates a bent axis piston pump at minimum and maximum displacement angles. Bent axis variable displacement pumps can be electronically controlled just like axial piston pumps. They are commonly used for providing oil flow for excavators and are usually found as a tandem side-by-side pump in a common housing.

▶ Hydraulic Pump Performance Calculations

K25004

When working with hydraulic pumps, you may need to make various calculations to determine hydraulic pump displacement, theoretical flow rate, volumetric efficiency (VE), and pump power. Equations and examples are included here.

▶ TECHNICIAN TIP

If a customer wants to add a hydraulic attachment to a machine, the technician needs to know certain information about the attachment in order to be able to recommend whether the machine is capable of handling the attachment or whether hydraulic system modifications have to be made.

The attachment's flow and pressure requirements have to be satisfied or the attachment will not operate as designed. In some cases, a pump may have to be added, or an existing pump may have to be replaced with one that delivers more flow or can withstand higher pressures.

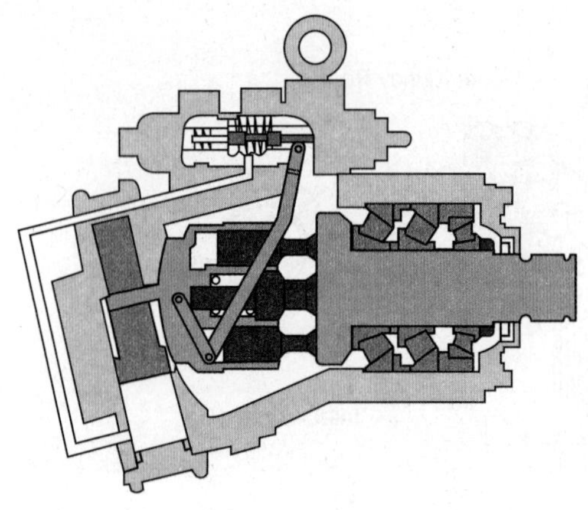

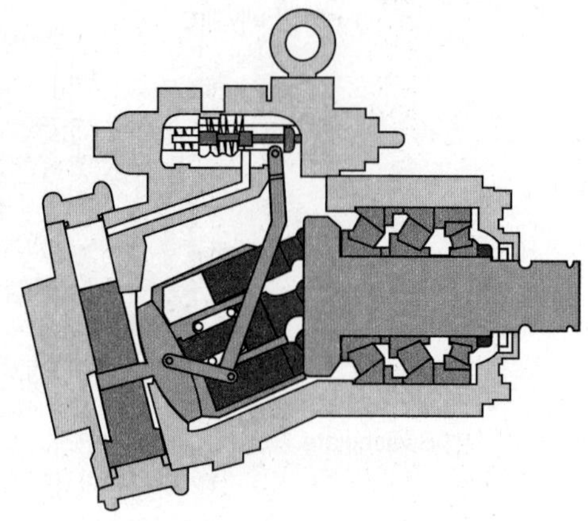

FIGURE 25-30 A bent axis piston pump at minimum and maximum displacement angles.

Calculating Hydraulic Pump Displacement

Pump displacement is commonly shown on the pump identification tag. If you need to calculate hydraulic pump displacement, use the following formula:

$$d = \frac{\text{Factor} \times Q}{N}$$

where:

d = Displacement, in cubic centimeters per revolution (cm^3/rev, or cc/rev) or cubic inches per revolution (in^3/rev)
Q = Pump flow rate, in liters per minute (lpm) or gallons per minute (gpm)
N = Pump speed, in revolutions per minute (rpm)
Factor = 1,000 for metric units and 231 for imperial units (U.S. gallons)

Example

A pump that is rotating at 1,000 rpm is producing a flow rate of 20 lpm. What is the displacement?

$$d = \frac{1{,}000 \times 20}{1{,}000} = 20 \text{ cm}^3\text{/rev}$$

Calculating Hydraulic Pump Theoretical Flow Rate

The **theoretical flow rate** of oil is calculated from two values: (1) the pump's displacement, which is commonly shown on the pump's identification label; and (2) the input shaft speed of the pump.

To calculate hydraulic pump theoretical flow rate, use the following formula:

$$Q = \frac{N \times d}{\text{Factor}}$$

where:

Q = Pump flow rate in liters per minute (lpm) or gallons per minute (gpm)
N = Pump speed in revolutions per minute (rpm)
d = Displacement in cubic centimeters per revolution (cm^3/rev, or cc/rev) or cubic inches per revolution ($in.^3$/rev)
Factor = 1,000 for metric units and 231 for imperial units (U.S. gallons)

Example 1 (metric)

A 20 cc pump whose input shaft is operating at 1,000 rpm will, in theory, deliver 20,000 cubic centimeters (cm^3) of fluid per minute. Dividing 20,000 by 1,000 converts the answer to liters per minute (lpm). Therefore, a 20 cc pump operating at 1,000 rpm will theoretically deliver 20 liters of fluid per minute.

This is expressed by the equation:

$$Q = \frac{1{,}000 \times 20}{1{,}000} = 20 \text{ lpm}$$

Example 2 (imperial)

A 1.22-cubic inch pump operating at 1,000 rpm will deliver 1,220 cubic inches ($in.^3$) of fluid per minute. There are 231 cubic inches in a U.S. gallon. (This example uses U.S. gallons. Note that there are 277.42 cubic inches in an imperial gallon.)

This is expressed by the equation:

$$Q = \frac{1{,}000 \times 1.22}{231} = 5.28 \text{ gpm}$$

Converting gpm to lpm

To compare these two answers, use the conversion:

3.79 liters = 1 U.S. gallon
5.28 gpm × 3.79 = 20.01 lpm

The difference in the answers is due to rounding off the various results to two decimal points.

▶ TECHNICIAN TIP

The flow rate formula and examples determine the *theoretical* flow rate. The *actual* flow rate can be determined only by using a flow meter to measure it. **Flow meters** are often used for diagnosing hydraulic system problems.

Calculating Pump Volumetric Efficiency

Volumetric efficiency is the comparison of theoretical pump flow to the actual flow that can be measured. For example, a 20 cc hydraulic pump, when manufactured, is calculated to have a theoretical oil displacement of 20 cubic centimeters (cm^3) per shaft revolution (cm^3/rev, or cc/rev).

However, most hydraulic components are not internally 100% leak-free. This may be by design, to provide lubrication, or it may be the result of the limitations of the materials used. Components also expand and contract with temperature changes, so it is difficult to maintain the close tolerances required to prevent leakage.

A pump manufacturer quotes the volumetric efficiency of a pump as at a specified pressure and using a known viscosity of oil. Hot, thin fluid at high pressure will produce more leaks, and reduced volumetric efficiency, than a cold fluid at low pressure. Different fluids, temperature, and pressure affect the volumetric efficiency, and increased pump wear, reduced oil quality, and raised operating temperatures reduce measured efficiency.

To calculate volumetric efficiency (VE), use the following formula:

$$\text{VE} = \frac{\text{Actual flow rate}}{\text{Theoretical flow rate}}$$

Example

A pump of 20 cc displacement would, if rotated at 1,000 revolutions per minute (rpm), theoretically deliver a flow of 20,000 cm^3 or 20 liters per minute (lpm). If a flow test is performed on this pump, the result may be correct at a low pressure of 50 bar, but at a higher pressure of 150 bar, internal leakage will be more apparent, and the measured flow will be reduced to 19 lpm, for example.

If the actual (measured) flow of 19 lpm is divided by the theoretical flow rate of 20 lpm, it can be calculated that this pump has 95% volumetric efficiency:

$$\text{VE} = \frac{19}{20} = 0.95 \text{ or } 95\%$$

Calculating Hydraulic Pump Power Output

A hydraulic pump converts mechanical energy into hydraulic energy. The maximum hydraulic power available from a fixed displacement pump can be calculated by multiplying the maximum system pressure by the actual flow when measured at maximum pressure, and factoring in a constant value. Similar calculations can be made for variable pumps.

For fixed displacement pumps, pressure and flow rate are multiplied together (Power = Pressure × Flow rate) and divided by a constant conversion factor. For metric unit calculations, use the formula:

$$\text{kW} = \text{Pressure in bar} \times \text{Flow rate in lpm} \div 600$$

Or:

$$\text{kW} = \frac{p \times Q}{600}$$

where:

kW = Output power in kilowatts
p = Pressure in bar
Q = Flow rate in liters per minute (lpm)
600 = Metric conversion factor

For U.S. unit calculations, use the formula:

$$\text{HP} = \text{Pressure in psi} \times \text{Flow rate in gpm} \div 1{,}714$$

Or:

$$\text{HP} = \frac{p \times Q}{1{,}714}$$

where:

Hp = Output power in horsepower
p = Pressure in pounds per square inch (psi)
Q = Flow rate in U.S. gallons per minute (gpm)
1,714 = U.S. conversion factor

Example

A 20 cc displacement pump is measured to deliver 19 lpm at the maximum system pressure of 150 bar. To calculate output power:

$$\text{kW} = 150 \text{ bar} \times 19 \text{ lpm} \div 600$$

Or:

$$\text{kW} = \frac{150 \times 19}{600} = \frac{2{,}850}{600} = 4.75 \text{ kW}$$

To calculate the mechanical power required to drive the hydraulic pump, the mechanical and volumetric efficiency have to be factored in. Energy lost due to internal fluid leakage, mechanical friction, and noise can reduce overall pump efficiency to between 80% and 90%.

For this example, a figure of 90% will be used:

$$\text{kW} = 150 \text{ bar} \times 19 \text{ lpm} \div 600 \times 0.9$$

Or:

$$\text{kW} = \frac{150 \times 19}{(600 \times 0.9)} = \frac{2{,}850}{540} = 5.28 \text{ kW}$$

This example shows that a pump requires 5.28 kW of mechanical power to create 4.75 kW of useful hydraulic power.

▶ Diagnosing Hydraulic Pump Problems

S25001

At some point in a technician's career, he or she will be required to diagnose a hydraulic system performance problem. This chapter looks briefly at hydraulic pump diagnostics and repair.

Many hydraulic performance symptoms may indicate that the pump is faulty, but without a proper diagnostic procedure, the pump should not be condemned. Countless hydraulic pumps have been changed needlessly over the years, as this seems to be an easy fix for many hydraulic problems. However, because the pump is most likely the most expensive hydraulic component on the machine, a definitive pump performance test should be performed before replacing a pump.

Diagnosing or troubleshooting a hydraulic system problem is no different than any other system troubleshooting procedure. The following steps should reaffirm a typical diagnostic procedure for any system problem:

1. Gather information from the operator and/or machine.
2. Know the system.
3. Confirm the problem.
4. Following the service information troubleshooting procedures for the particular machine should lead to an accurate conclusion.

Once it is determined that the pump is a possible legitimate cause of the system problem, pump testing can begin. Starting with simple visual checks, you would look for the following:

- Pump housing discoloration, indicating overheating
- Oil condition (discoloration, indicating overheating or contamination)
- Any loose fasteners for either the pump mount or pump inlet plumbing
- A case drain filter; remove the filter and then cut it open. **FIGURE 25-31** depicts a filter cut open.

If preliminary checks reveal nothing abnormal, further investigation could include running the machine and listening for unusual noises or feeling for vibrations.

The next stage of pump testing involves checking pump output pressures and flows. Special tooling and equipment could be required for this and must be inspected to ensure it is in good condition before it is installed and used.

If there is a complaint about a lack of hydraulic actuator power, the system pressure setting should be checked, and if it is found to be lower than specification, this could be caused by the pump. If the pump is fixed displacement and is severely worn internally, there could be enough oil bypassing to cause a low system pressure.

If the pump is a variable displacement type, the pump control mechanism should be checked. Newer machines could have in-cab displays with menus that, when scrolled through, could display system pressure. Otherwise, you will need to install a gauge at the pump outlet.

SAFETY TIP

All gauges and hoses used for checking system pressure must be rated for pressure above expected maximum pressure. This ensures a safety factor to prevent serious injury if a gauge or hose were to fail.

If there is a slow function complaint, the pump flow output should be measured. A flow meter must be installed in the pump output line, and certain conditions must be met to properly measure pump flow. **FIGURE 25-32** shows a flow meter used for pump testing.

Testing Hydraulic Pumps

Two important tests can be performed when testing hydraulic pumps: the no-load flow rate test and the flow/pressure profile test. The following example is for a fixed displacement pump mounted on a test stand, but the same test can be completed with the pump on the machine. This is a generic example; always follow the pump or machine manufacturer's specific test procedures for the pump you are testing.

FIGURE 25-31 Case drain filter cut open.

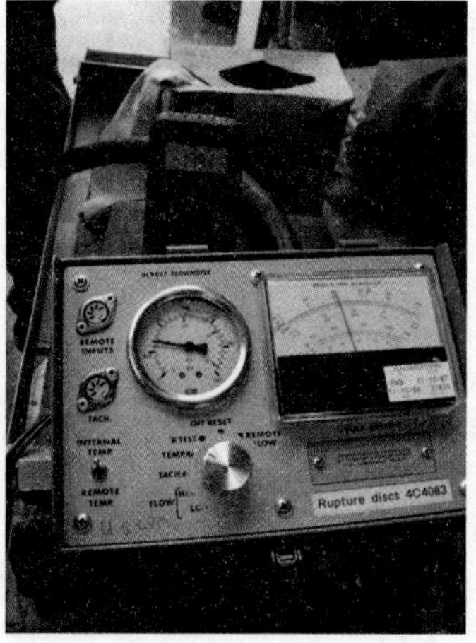

FIGURE 25-32 A flow meter used for pump testing.

▶ TECHNICIAN TIP

One common quick assessment for piston or vane pumps that a technician can perform is to measure case drain pressure or flow when the pump is under load. If the pump is worn or damaged, an excessive amount of oil will leak into the pump housing from the pump assembly. The test could be as simple as allowing the case drain oil to flow into a pail and timing how fast the pail fills.

SAFETY TIP

Testing pumps with flow meters can be dangerous because you are creating high pressure and high flow. Remember that there must always be a functional relief valve between the pump outlet and the flow restrictor.

For this procedure, you need the following tools, materials, and equipment:

- Hydraulic stand with the pump mounted
- Flow meter with integrated pressure gauge and restriction valve
- Properly rated hoses and fittings to complete the installation
- Appropriate wrenches and spanners
- Pencil and graph paper
- Manufacturer's data for the pump
- Safety glasses or goggles
- Gloves

Follow these steps:

1. Put on PPE: safety glasses or goggles, gloves, and so on.
2. Install the flow meter.
   a. Install the flow meter in series between the pump outlet and the tank.
   b. Open the restriction valve completely.
   c. Ensure oil viscosity is correct, and its temperature is within the specified range (usually 125–160°F [53–71°C])

The no-load flow rate test consists of the following basic steps:

1. Run pump at full rpm with no resistance in the test system.
2. Use a flow meter to measure the pump output.
3. Compare actual output to manufacturer's data.

The flow/pressure profile test consists of the following basic steps:

1. Run pump at full rpm.
2. Close the flow meter restriction valve to increase the system pressure in 7-bar (100 psi) increments.
3. Record flow rate at each increment, up to maximum system pressure.
4. Plot the results.
5. Compare with manufacturer's data.

FIGURE 25-33 depicts a technician adjusting the restriction valve on a flow meter while reading a digital pressure gauge.

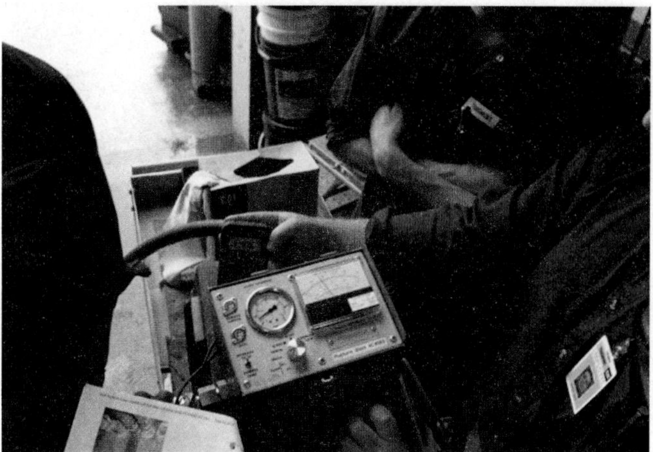

FIGURE 25-33 A technician adjusting the restriction valve on a flow meter while reading a digital pressure gauge.

Based on the findings of these two tests, you may conclude that the pump has some internal defects. A pump could have several different kinds of deficiencies, depending on its type, or it could just have overall excessive wear in critical areas that allows oil to leak internally or bypass.

▶ Hydraulic Pump Reconditioning and Repairs

K25005

Pump test results may indicate that a technician will need to recommend next steps as to whether a pump is reconditioned or replaced. Most manufacturers have guideline documentation to assist the technician with assessing pump condition and determining whether any pump components or a complete pump can be reused. These guidelines usually include measurement tolerances for pump components, such as shaft diameter, bearing diameter, clearance dimensions, and mounting flange trueness. They also include visual guides for defects such as scoring, discoloration, scratches, cracks, and pitting.

Determining whether a pump can be reconditioned or repaired is usually left to a technician with experience in reconditioning hydraulic components. However, by closely following pump manufacturers' reconditioning guideline information, any technician should be able to confidently assess a pump's condition. Serious financial consequences result if a pump is put back into service in a substandard condition, because a pump failure leads to damage to other components and more downtime.

Other factors as well influence a decision on whether a pump should be reconditioned, such as how urgent the need is to get the machine up and running, parts availability, whether a machine will be kept or sold, parts cost, and technician skill.

Some circumstances may require pump replacement rather than pump reconditioning. Some equipment dealers may have exchange pumps you can use to speed up getting a machine back in service, and these pumps could come with a reasonable cost and warranty. **FIGURE 25-34** illustrates an exchange hydraulic pump.

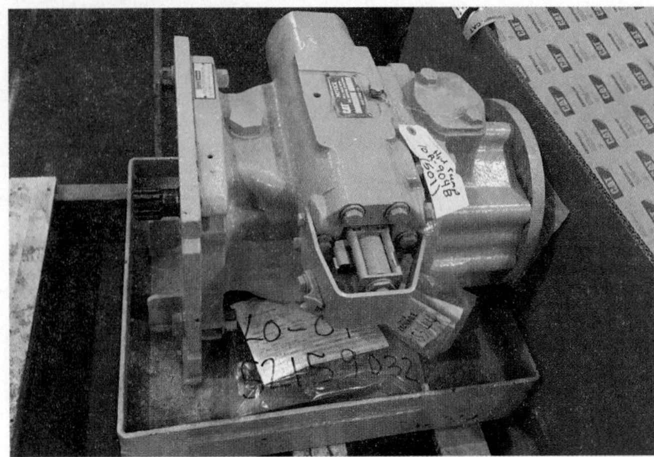

FIGURE 25-34 An exchange hydraulic pump.

▶ Common Causes of Pump Failure

K25006

Depending on the seriousness of the failure, a failure analysis may be required to find the root cause of the problem. If a machine has warranty coverage, the pump will be covered for the manufacturer's defects. It is also critical to avoid repeat failures when hydraulic pumps are repaired or replaced because of the expensive consequences associated. Pump inspections, installation, and maintenance procedures should be followed carefully to avoid some of the common causes of pump failure. These include the following:

- Contaminated fluid (the most common cause of pump failure)
- Cavitation
- Aeration
- Incorrect fluid
- Low oil level
- Excessive system pressures
- Restricted case drain lines
- Abuse and incorrect operating procedures such as stalling implements and overheating oil, insufficient oil warm-up, excessive pump speed, or incorrect adjustments).

These problems can all be avoided by keeping the equipment regularly serviced and maintained, and operating within the system's designed capacity.

▶ TECHNICIAN TIP

Contaminated fluid is the most common cause of pump failure and can include water, fuel, air, dirt, or metal contamination. Regular oil sampling can detect fluid contamination; the source of the contamination must be detected and corrected before changing the fluid, in order to stop a repeat occurrence.

Pump Cavitation

Cavitation is the formation of air or gas bubbles at the inlet of the pump. This leads to the collapse of air and gas bubbles in the pump, which creates a distinctive noise and a very destructive force. The noise has been described as sounding like marbles passing through the pump. This destructive force can be equivalent to well over 5,000 psi.

Pump housings and rotating components can be quickly destroyed if cavitation is severe enough and occurs long enough.

Causes of Pump Cavitation

Cavitation results from a restriction in the pump suction line, creating a high negative pressure in that line. Cavitation makes vapor bubbles form in the fluid, which then implode and erode metal components. True cavitation can be caused by a clogged suction filter, items stuck in the suction line, a kinked suction line, a collapsed hose line, a suction line that is too small or too long, or a plugged reservoir breather.

Effects of Pump Cavitation

When reconditioning a pump, it is important to inspect it for signs of cavitation because the effects can be extremely damaging to the system. Some of the effects of pump cavitation are listed here:

- Excessive pump noise
- Excessive pump wear due to bubbles and cavities imploding and damaging the pump components
- System contamination due to debris from pump component damage.

See **FIGURE 25-35** for an illustration of a pump swashplate that shows evidence of cavitation.

Fluid Aeration

Fluid **aeration** is caused by excessive air in the hydraulic fluid. It can be caused by a low fluid level, leaking fittings in the suction line, leaking actuator seals, new components being installed without being filled with fluid, tank baffle failure, wrong viscosity of fluid, or overheated fluid.

Aeration can be detected by looking at the reservoir sight glass or looking into the tank. If the oil is foamy looking, it is

FIGURE 25-35 A pump swashplate that shows evidence of cavitation.

aerated. This can be a damaging condition to the pump because the oil loses its lubricating properties, and if severe enough, it can cause pump failure.

▶ Reconditioning Hydraulic Pumps

S25002

Reconditioning hydraulic pumps can be a fairly simple task, or it can also be one of the more complicated tasks a technician will perform. This depends on the type of pump and how in-depth the repair is. Do not attempt to recondition a hydraulic pump unless you have read through the entire procedure, have the necessary tooling and equipment, and are confident in your abilities to work to a high standard.

If a pump is required to be reconditioned to "as-new" condition, then strict repair guidelines must be followed.

▶ TECHNICIAN TIP

Always have a well-lit and clean workspace available before starting to recondition a hydraulic pump. Plenty of bench space and lots of covered parts baskets are necessary as well. Clean lint-free rags and a good-quality camera are also a must.

The following is an example of a procedure to recondition an external gear pump. This typically happens in four steps: disassembly, parts assessment, parts ordering, and reassembly. **FIGURE 25-36** shows a hydraulic pump being worked on.

Part 1 Disassembly

1. Take a picture of the pump before cleaning, to inspect for signs of leakage or damage.
2. Completely clean the exterior of the pump.
3. Mark the pump housing for orientation before disassembly.
4. Slowly and methodically disassemble the pump, following manufacturer's service information.
5. Inspect pump components during disassembly, looking for damage and wear.

Part 2 Parts Assessment

1. Once the pump is completely disassembled, thoroughly clean and inspect all parts for damage and wear.
2. In particular, look at gear teeth condition, interior of pump housing, bearings, shafts, and O-ring grooves.
3. Insert shafts into pump housing, and measure tooth-to-housing clearance

Part 3 Parts Ordering

1. Only OEM parts should be ordered from the equipment dealer.

Part 4 Assembly

1. Replace all bearing and seals. If plain bearings are used, pay attention to bearing split orientation (should be opposite high-thrust area).
2. Install new or reused shafts in one-half of pump housing with clean oil.
3. Ensure shafts turn freely.
4. Assemble pump housing with new seals, and slowly tighten fasteners in small steps. Check that the shaft turns freely after each step.
5. Rotate the driveshaft while pouring a small quantity of clean oil into the pump inlet.
6. Seal the pump inlet and outlet until the pump is to be tested or installed on machine.

▶ Remove and Install a Hydraulic Pump, Following Manufacturer's Service Information

S25003

Hydraulic pump removal and replacement is a common procedure for technicians to perform. Important generic steps should be followed for removing and installing a pump, but specific procedures for the particular pump and machine must also be followed. **FIGURE 25-37** shows a technician removing a hydraulic pump.

FIGURE 25-36 A hydraulic pump being worked on.

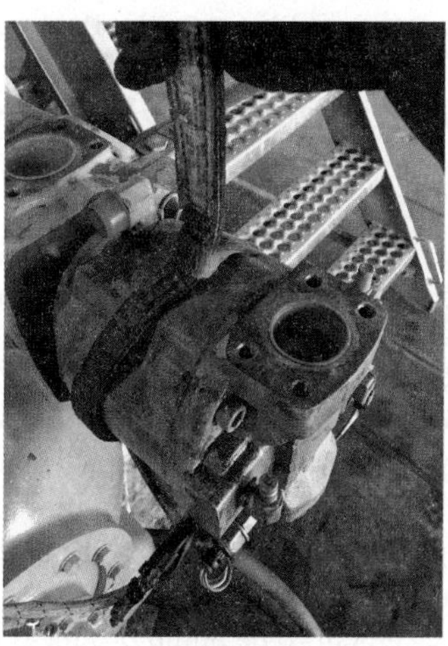

FIGURE 25-37 A technician removing a hydraulic pump.

The following is an example of a procedure to remove and install a hydraulic pump:

1. Before pump removal, thoroughly clean the work area.
2. Put the machine in service position, and utilize appropriate LOTO procedure.
3. Lower oil level and shut off supply or block off the pump inlet.
4. Remove any guarding or shrouds to gain access to the pump.
5. Remove the pump inlet, outlet, and any other lines or wiring
6. Seal off pump inlet and outlet lines
7. Remove the pump, using appropriate lifting device for the weight of the pump.
8. Inspect the pump driving mechanism.
9. Clean the pump mounting area.
10. Install the new pump mount seal, and lubricate the pump shaft.
11. For pumps with a case drain, fill the pump housing with clean oil.
12. Install the pump by mating the shaft to the drive, and slowly draw pump into the drive with fasteners,
13. Tighten the mounting fasteners to the proper torque.
14. Install all lines to the pump with new seals that are lubricated.
15. Top off the oil level, open the tank supply, or unblock the inlet.
16. Perform the pump bleeding procedure carefully, following machine service information.
17. Start the machine and run at low idle for 5 minutes, checking for leaks and listening for unusual noises.
18. Increase engine RPM to half speed, and slowly work implements, one at a time, to circulate oil.
19. Check the fluid level and top off, if needed.
20. Start the machine and check for leaks.
21. Slowly increase the engine RPM to high idle, and slowly move all implements.
22. If the system seems normal, start stalling implements to warm up oil (no more than 10–15 seconds).
23. Check system pressures and actuator cycle times, and recheck fluid level.

▶ TECHNICIAN TIP

If the pump was replaced due to a catastrophic failure, extra steps *must* include draining and cleaning out the tank, changing all filters, and using cleanout filters if available. Very close monitoring of the replacement pump and fluid condition will ensure replacement pump longevity.

▶ Wrap-Up

Ready for Review

- Hydraulic pumps are the heart of any hydraulic system and must function properly for a hydraulic system to work as designed.
- Hydraulic pumps provide flow to actuators and convert prime mover power into fluid power.
- System pressure is mostly created by the load that an actuator is trying to overcome.
- Pump inlet exposes an increasing volume, which reduces pressure and allows the tank to push oil into the pump.
- A decreasing volume at the pump outlet forces oil out into the system.
- Because hydraulic fluid cannot be compressed, it must leave the pump and flow toward the tank.
- Pumps must withstand full system pressure plus a safety factor.
- Pump displacement is the maximum volume of fluid a pump can move in one revolution and is a value calculated in either cubic inches or centimeters.
- Pump flow output is the amount of flow a pump produces per unit of time (gpm or lpm).
- A nonpositive displacement pump cannot produce flow when outlet pressure increases. It may be used for charging the inlet of a hydraulic pump.
- A fixed displacement–type pump produces the same amount of oil flow each revolution.
- A variable displacement–type pump can vary the amount of flow output without changing shaft speed.
- Three types of positive displacement pumps are found on MORE: gear, vane, and piston,
- External gear pumps are fixed displacement, simple, durable pumps that rely on a film of oil between the housing and gear teeth to create a seal.
- Internal gear pumps have a driven external gear meshing with an internal gear to create oil flow.
- Vane pumps feature sliding vanes that are carried around the inside of a cam ring in a rotor that is driven by the pump shaft.
- Piston pumps are commonly used on MORE and use a series of pistons that reciprocate in a barrel that is driven by the pump shaft to create fluid movement.
- The two common types of piston pumps found on MORE are in-line axial and bent axis.
- Piston pumps can be variable or fixed displacement type, and they rely on close tolerances to obtain high efficiency. This makes them sensitive to contamination.
- Axial piston pumps need the swashplate to create reciprocating piston motion, whereas bent axis pumps rely on connecting links and the barrel angle.
- Piston slippers are on the ends of the pistons and guide the piston around the swashplate.
- Piston pumps have a third port to drain internal leakage that is called the case drain port.

- External gear pumps transfer oil from their inlet to their outlet by trapping a volume of oil between each pair of gear teeth and the housing.
- When system pressure reaches maximum for a system with an external gear pump, a high side load is created on the pump shafts.
- Internal gear pumps transfer oil between the intermeshing teeth of their internal gear and external gear.
- Gerotor pumps are a variation of internal gear pump.
- Vane pumps have sliding vanes that create either expanding or retracting spaces between them as they rotate inside the cam ring profile.
- The most common type of vane pump found on MORE is the balanced fixed displacement type.
- Balanced vane pumps have two inlet and two outlet ports.
- Piston pumps are highly efficient and provide smooth, consistent flow from a compact design.
- Variable displacement pumps are used to make a more efficient hydraulic system and only provide flow when requested.
- Depending on the style of pump, different mechanisms are actuated to change the displacement of the pump.
- Axial piston pumps have a pivoting swashplate that changes their displacement, whereas bent axis piston pumps have a mechanism that moves their barrel to change the angle in relation to the pump's shaft.
- Variable pumps can be electronically controlled by an ECM that is part of a machine's electronic network that makes the machine more efficient.
- Variable displacement bent axis pumps change their displacement by pivoting the barrel assembly. A greater angle to the pump shaft increases displacement.
- Sometimes it may be necessary to calculate pump-related values to determine hydraulic pump displacement, theoretical flow rate, volumetric efficiency (VE), and pump power.
- Proper pump diagnostic procedures will prevent needless pump replacements.
- Two common pump tests are the no-load flow test and the flow/pressure profile test. The results are compared to factory specifications, and a decision is made as to next steps.
- Based on test results, recommendations are made to the machine owner as to whether the pump should be reconditioned or replaced.
- Cavitation is a fluid condition that is caused by a restricted pump inlet line and can be very destructive.
- Aeration is a fluid condition that is caused by excessive air in the system.
- Reconditioning hydraulic pumps requires a clean, well-lit workspace. The technician may need special tooling and must follow the manufacturer's service information closely.
- Care must be taken after installing a hydraulic pump to perform initial start-up procedures exactly as instructed by the manufacturer's service information.

Key Terms

aeration A condition caused by excessive air in the system fluid.

axial piston Pistons are parallel to the pump shaft and a swashplate creates piston movement.

bent axis Piston centerlines are at an angle to the pump shaft.

cam ring In a balanced vane pump the cam ring is elliptical in shape and makes the vanes move.

cartridge assembly Another term for the pumping assembly inside a vane pump.

case drain Another name for internal leakage oil that piston pumps have drained away.

cavitation A condition caused by a restricted pump inlet and is a destructive force that can cause severe damage to pumps.

destroking The action a variable pump makes to reduce its displacement.

energy conversion A pump converts mechanical energy into fluid energy.

external gear pump A simple design that features one drive gear meshed with a driven gear. Oil is transferred from the pump inlet to its outlet between adjacent gear teeth and the inside of the housing.

flow meter A testing tool that will measure the flow output of a hydraulic pump.

gerotor A variation of an internal gear pump.

gpm Gallons per minute (usually US gallons).

inlet port An opening in the housing that allows oil in from the tank.

internal gear pumps Another type of gear pump used for low flow and lower pressure applications.

lpm Liters per minute.

outlet port An opening in the housing that allows oil to leave the pump and move downstream through the system.

port plate Component in piston pumps that direct oil in and out of the barrel to and from the housing.

pressure differential The pump creates a pressure differential at its inlet and once it is pushed out of the pump it flows toward the tank which is another pressure differential.

pressure rating Pumps must withstand maximum system pressure plus a safety factor.

pump displacement Volume of fluid a pump can move in one revolution.

pump output flow The amount of flow a pump produces for a given amount of time

swashplate Component in an axial piston pump that creates reciprocating piston motion.

theoretical flow rate A calculated value that uses pump displacement and pump speed to determine a 100% efficient pump's output.

upstroke The term used to describe the action of increasing the displacement of a variable pump.

vanes The movable part of a vane pump the creates fluid flow.

volumetric efficiency A calculated value using the actual flow output of a pump and its theoretical output value that determines how efficient the pump is.

Review Questions

1. A hydraulic pump is an energy conversion machine that changes the __________ power output from the prime mover (usually a diesel engine, but could be any type of internal combustion engine or an electric motor) into ______________ power.
   a. rotating mechanical, hydraulic fluid
   b. hydraulic fluid, rotating mechanical
   c. hydraulic fluid, electrical
   d. electrical, hydraulic fluid
2. How is the pressure created in a hydraulic system?
   a. With the help of a pump
   b. By the viscosity of the liquid
   c. By resistance to flow of the liquid
   d. By a vacuum created in the system
3. A nonpositive displacement, or dynamic, pump is designed with a loose-fitting rotating component (impeller) inside its housing. When the impeller rotates as the pump shaft is driven, it creates a ______ pressure at its inlet that directs inlet flow to the _____ of the impeller.
   a. high, corner
   b. low, center
   c. low, corner
   d. high, center
4. What will happen if the pump flow output of a positive displacement pump gets blocked?
   a. A serious pump failure will occur.
   b. The prime mover keeps turning.
   c. The pump is not affected.
   d. There will be lower efficiency.
5. In variable displacement bent axis piston pumps, if the cylinder block and the shaft axis are close to one another, the pump's relative piston travel is __________ and the pump flow will be at _________.
   a. minimal, maximum
   b. minimal, minimum
   c. maximum, minimal
   d. maximum, maximum
6. For an external gear pump, as ______________________, more side thrust is placed on the gears and shafts because the oil is resisting being pushed downstream out of the pump, and the reacting force tries to spread the gears apart.
   a. output pressure drops
   b. output pressure rises
   c. input pressure drops
   d. input pressure rises
7. Identify the formula to calculate hydraulic pump displacement.
   a. $d = (\text{Factor} \times Q)/N$
   b. $d = \text{Factor} \times Q/N$
   c. $d = (\text{Factor} \times N)/Q$
   d. $d = \text{Factor} \times N/Q$
8. Which of the following is a nonvisual defect?
   a. Scoring
   b. Scratches
   c. Discoloration
   d. Pressure buildup
9. All of the following are common causes of pump failure, *except*:
   a. cavitation.
   b. aeration.
   c. incorrect fluid.
   d. high oil level.
10. Aeration may be caused by __________.
    a. overheated fluid
    b. a clogged suction filter
    c. items stuck in the suction line
    d. a leaking pressure hose

ASE Technician A/Technician B Style Questions

1. Technician A says the hydraulic pump only produces flow. Technician B says pressure in the system is mainly created by the load. Who is correct?
   a. Technician A
   b. Technician B
   c. Both A and B
   d. Neither A nor B
2. Technician A says pump inlet pressure must always be slightly positive. Technician B says there are occasions where the pressure at the pump outlet could read negative. Who is correct?
   a. Technician A
   b. Technician B
   c. Both A and B
   d. Neither A nor B
3. Technician A says pump displacement can be calculated to give a value of either gallons per minute or liters per minute. Technician B says most pumps produce roughly 1 gallon of flow per revolution. Who is correct?
   a. Technician A
   b. Technician B
   c. Both A and B
   d. Neither A nor B
4. Technician A says fixed displacement pumps produce the same volume of oil each revolution. Technician B says a variable displacement pump only varies its displacement when its shaft speed varies. Who is correct?
   a. Technician A
   b. Technician B
   c. Both A and B
   d. Neither A nor B
5. Technician A says internal gear pumps are variable displacement. Technician B says external gear pumps are fixed displacement. Who is correct?
   a. Technician A
   b. Technician B
   c. Both A and B
   d. Neither A nor B

6. Technician A says vane pumps have a rotating cam ring. Technician B says a vane pump can be variable displacement. Who is correct?
  a. Technician A
  b. Technician B
  c. Both A and B
  d. Neither A nor B

7. Technician A says a gerotor pump is a type of piston pump. Technician B says a rotary piston pump is the most common piston pump for MORE. Who is correct?
  a. Technician A
  b. Technician B
  c. Both A and B
  d. Neither A nor B

8. Technician A says variable displacement axial piston pumps feature a movable swashplate. Technician B says a variable displacement bent axis pump has a movable barrel. Who is correct?
  a. Technician A
  b. Technician B
  c. Both A and B
  d. Neither A nor B

9. Technician A says most fixed displacement pumps are controlled by an ECM. Technician B says a variable displacement piston pump always produces some flow. Who is correct?
  a. Technician A
  b. Technician B
  c. Both A and B
  d. Neither A nor B

10. Technician A says one of the common pump tests is called the zero swashplate calibration. Technician B says as a pump's internal leakage increases, its efficiency increases. Who is correct?
  a. Technician A
  b. Technician B
  c. Both A and B
  d. Neither A nor B

CHAPTER 26
Hydraulic Valves

Knowledge Objectives

After reading this chapter, you will be able to:

- **K26001** Explain the purpose and fundamentals of hydraulic valves.
- **K26002** Describe the principles of operation of hydraulic pressure control valves.
- **K26003** Describe the principles of operation of hydraulic flow control valves.
- **K26004** Describe the principles of operation of hydraulic directional control valves.
- **K26005** Describe the common causes of valve failures.
- **K26006** Recommend reconditioning or repairs of hydraulic valves.

Skills Objectives

After reading this chapter, you will be able to:

- **S26001** Identify the types and construction features of hydraulic valves.
- **S26002** Inspect, diagnose, and adjust hydraulic valves.

▶ Introduction

Hydraulic valves are constructed in a wide variety of configurations to match different needs within hydraulic circuits. They can be assembled in blocks or stacked together, or they can work alone. Whether used to relieve pressure or to deliver hydraulic fluid to actuators, each valve is critical to the operation of the hydraulic system it is part of. Hydraulic valves usually don't require service and are normally expected to last thousands of hours, providing that the hydraulic fluid they require is properly maintained. They usually only get attention from technicians when there are hydraulic system problems such as leaks, or pressure or flow issues.

This chapter discusses the main types of valves that can be found on MORE and their operation, and includes procedures for adjusting system and circuit pressure and diagnosing valve-related problems. Common types of valve failures and valve reconditioning are also discussed.

Keep in mind that hydraulic valves can be found in other machine systems such as power shift transmissions, hydraulic braking systems, and diesel engine fuel systems, so the knowledge gained by the reader of this chapter can be put to use in other areas.

▶ Purpose and Fundamentals of Hydraulic Valves

K26001

All hydraulic systems require a series of **valves** to control the fluid flowing between the pump, tank, and actuators. Once the hydraulic fluid leaves the pump outlet, it has to be controlled by valves in order to be able to harness the energy in it and make the systems' actuators perform the work the machine operator is expecting. A valve is a component that changes the condition of the hydraulic fluid it comes in contact with, in terms of pressure, flow, or direction.

To control the power output of the system, the hydraulic pressure has to be controlled; to control the speed of an actuator (rod speed or motor shaft speed), the rate of oil flow has to be controlled, and to control the direction of actuator movement, the direction of oil flow to the actuator has to be controlled.

Valves for the most part should be invisible and maintenance-free to the machine operator, with the exception of controls in the machine cab. For an operator to control the machine's hydraulic system, levers, pedals, switches, knobs, and touch displays in the cab can be used mainly to control fluid direction, but they may also allow the operator to change pressures and flows.

Newer machines incorporate electronic controls and monitoring of hydraulic systems that include electronically actuated pressure, flow, and direction control valves.

▶ Types and Construction Features of Hydraulic Valves

S26001

Three main classifications of valves are used to control oil pressure, oil flow quantity, and oil flow direction in a MORE machine hydraulic system: pressure control valves, flow control valves, and directional control valves.

These different types of valves can work individually or be combined with other types of valves in a combination valve or a main control valve assembly. Some valves are mounted to, or part of, other hydraulic components such as pumps, motors, or cylinders.

Individual and integrated control valves use either cast steel bodies that are machined to accept different valves or machined aluminum blocks with cartridge valves to incorporate pressure control, flow control, and directional control valves into a single, compact unit. **FIGURE 26-1** shows a control valve assembly. This is a main control valve for a newer dozer and incorporates a combination of directional control valves, pressure control valves, and flow control valves.

You Are the Mobile Heavy Equipment Technician

The company you work for owns several large excavators of the same make and model, but with a wide range of hours on them. The older excavators in the fleet have started to have recurring leaks at the main control valve.

The equipment manager is becoming concerned about the machine downtime that is accumulating, and the site foremen are concerned with the environmental damage the leaks are creating.

You have been assigned to come up with a fix for the older machines with recurring leaks and to try to prevent the newer ones from starting to leak. Rank the following pieces of information in order of importance to you for working toward a solution to this problem, and describe where would you find this information.

1. Maintenance records of the machines
2. The names of the operators
3. The size of the buckets that the machines have on them
4. Recent repair history for the machines
5. Is there still warranty on the machines?
6. Any diagnostic codes that are logged or active
7. How much the main control valve weighs
8. Where the leaks are originating

FIGURE 26-1 Control valve assembly.

The majority of all types of valves must have at least one movable component (the exception to this is a fixed orifice). This can be a ball, poppet, piston, or spool. When these components are moved or shifted by spring pressure, oil flow or oil pressure there is a port uncovered to change the state of the valve. When valve components shift, they are said to change position.

To make these movable valve components function, a spring usually holds the ball, poppet, piston, or spool in place, and either hydraulic pressure or flow will move the valve component in the opposite direction. The spring may be adjustable with either shims or a **threaded adjuster**. **Shims** are thin round pieces of metal that are placed in the spring cavity of a valve to change the tension of the spring. Shims typically come in thicknesses that range between 0.003" and 0.030".

Some valves are electrically actuated with solenoids that are used to overcome the spring force.

Hydraulic valves have at least two ports, and some have more than five ports, that allow hydraulic oil into and out of the valve.

Valve components are precisely machined and hardened to ensure close tolerances and component longevity. Most internal seal areas rely on metal-to-metal contact to create a leak-free seal or a thin film of oil to create a dynamic seal. These seal areas are critical to the valve's integrity and should be focused on when inspecting a valve. These areas also make hydraulic valves susceptible to fluid contamination; this emphasizes the need to keep the fluid passing through them clean.

O-ring seals keep the hydraulic oil contained internally and may be used to keep the oil separated between different sections of the valve. Spool-type valves with exposed ends have lip-type seals at the spool ends to keep dirt out of the valve.

> **TECHNICIAN TIP**
>
> Hydraulic valve internal components are finely machined and finished parts that must be treated gently when they are being handled. To maintain leak-free operation both internally and externally, valve sealing surfaces must be true and free of scratches, burrs, or nicks. Some tolerances are so fine that all parts must be warmed to the same temperature before assembly, and the valves must be assembled in warm oil. When assembling valves, always coat surfaces with clean hydraulic oil before assembly.

Principles of Operation of Pressure Control Valves

K26002

Oil pressure in both a circuit and the entire system has to be controlled to specific pressure levels to prevent component damage and allow the system to work as designed. Pressure control valves are mainly controlled by spring pressure that is usually adjustable, but they could be electronically or hydraulically controlled.

The main types of pressure control valves are as follows:

- **Pressure-relief valves:** Pressure-relief valves limit the maximum operating pressure in the system and provide a safety valve to prevent system over-pressurization, which could lead to component damage and or injury.
- **Unloading valves:** Unloading valves are remotely piloted (controlled by a pressure somewhere else in the system) valves that divert pump flow to the tank so that the pump operates at low pressure when certain pressure conditions are met in the system.
- **Sequencing valves:** Sequencing valves are remotely piloted valves that are used to control the sequence, or order of operation, of a series of actuators in the system.
- **Pressure-reducing valves:** Pressure-reducing valves lower the maximum pressure that can occur in a portion or branch of a system.
- **Brake valves:** Brake valves provide back pressure to limit speed on a hydraulic motor operating an over-running load (such as a piece of earth-moving equipment going downhill).
- **Counterbalance valves:** Counterbalance valves provide a back pressure to hold a vertical load in place until certain pressure requirements are met.

Pressure-Relief Valves

Pressure-relief valves are pressure-limiting devices used to protect hydraulic systems and their components. They are available in a number of configurations to meet the hydraulic circuit's requirements. For example, a relief valve that regulates the whole system pressure (**main relief**) is designed to operate at a higher flow rate and more frequently than one that is intended to protect a hydraulic cylinder from intermittent shock loads (**line relief**). Main relief valves are typically found immediately downstream from the pump outlet before the first directional control valve. Line relief or circuit relief valves can be found between a directional control valve and an actuator. See **FIGURE 26-2** for the different locations where a pressure-relief valve can be found in a system.

> **TECHNICIAN TIP**
>
> Most MORE hydraulic systems have more than one pressure-relief valve. It is important that these relief valves are adjusted to have their relief settings far enough apart in terms of pressure so the valves don't interact with one another when they open. They should be set at least 200 psi apart to prevent system instability.

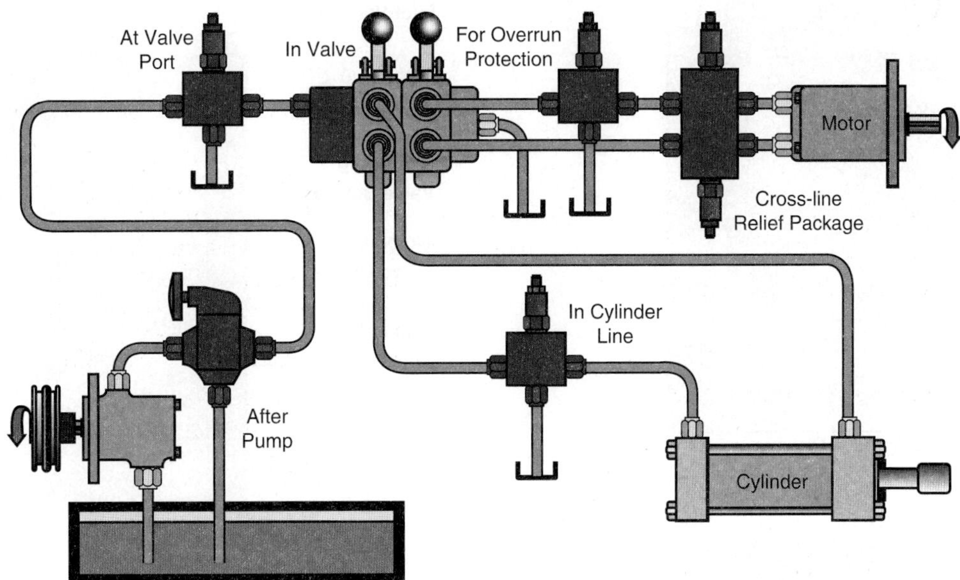

FIGURE 26-2 Different locations a pressure-relief valve can be found in a system.

There are two types of pressure-relief valves: direct acting and pilot operated.

Direct-Acting Relief Valves

The simplest type of pressure control valve is the **direct-acting relief valve**, which is sometimes called a simple relief valve. The four main parts of it are spring, body, poppet or ball, and adjuster (shims or screw). These can all be separate parts in a cast body. or a preassembled thread-in assembly that can be part of a manifold valve or an actuator. Direct-acting relief valves have two ports: one to allow oil pressure to be sensed at the ball or poppet, and another to allow oil to drain to the tank when the valve opens. See **FIGURE 26-3** for a direct-acting ball-type relief valve.

Circuit oil pressure is exposed to the ball or poppet, which is held on its seat by the spring. The valve is normally closed and opens when oil pressure gets high enough to overcome the spring pressure.

In order for the valve to remain open, the pressure at the valve inlet must remain at the pressure setting of the valve; therefore, the fluid going back to the tank does so at a high pressure drop across the relief valve, creating a great deal of heat. The valve remains open until the system pressure drops below the pressure setting of the spring.

FIGURE 26-3 A direct-acting ball-type relief valve.

Spring pressure is adjustable with either a threaded adjuster or shims.

The point at which a relief valve first unseats is called its cracking pressure, and a direct-acting relief valve has a relatively wide range of pressure, from cracking pressure to the pressure needed to fully open it (**pressure override**). For example, it could crack at 2,000 psi and be fully open at 2,200 psi. For this reason, direct-acting relief valves are usually only used for low-flow, noncritical circuits.

See **FIGURE 26-4** for a simple poppet-type relief valve at cracking pressure and fully open pressure.

Pilot-Operated Relief Valves

A **pilot-operated relief valve** is a two-stage valve that uses internal pressure or a remotely sensed **pilot pressure** to operate a small pilot section of the valve. When this pilot section opens, it relieves pressure on the back side of the unloading valve. This allows the unloading valve to open so that the main system flow is directed past the unloading valve and back to the tank. The valve remains open until the system pressure drops below the pilot pressure required to operate the valve. See **FIGURE 26-5** to see a pilot-operated relief valve.

This type of relief valve has a much narrower range of pressure between cracking pressure and fully open pressure (pressure override). For example, if the pilot valve opens at 2,000 psi, then the unloading valve will be fully open at 2,050 psi. Only a light spring is required to keep the unloading valve on its seat because oil pressure acts on its back side to keep it seated as well. An orifice in the unloading valve allows system pressure to transfer to the back side of the valve.

The relief pressure can be adjusted on this type of valve by changing the pilot poppet spring pressure with either shims or a threaded adjuster.

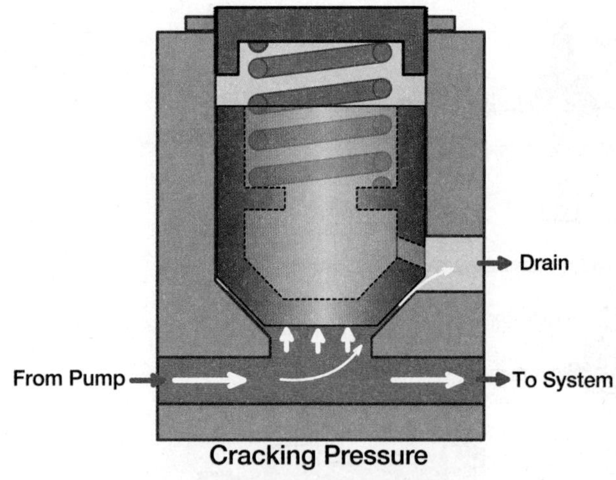

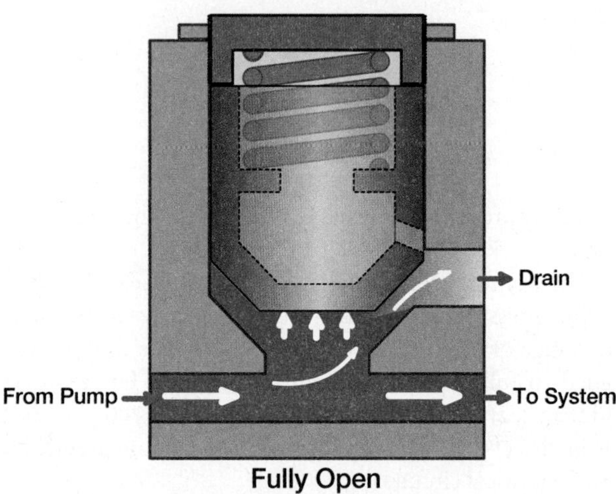

FIGURE 26-4 A simple poppet-type relief valve at cracking pressure and fully open pressure.

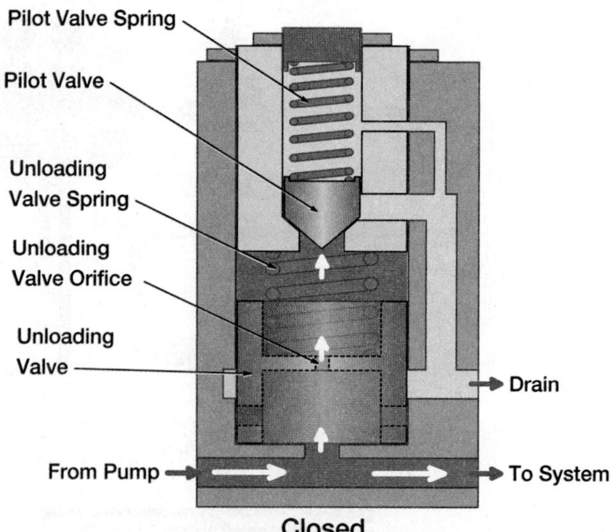

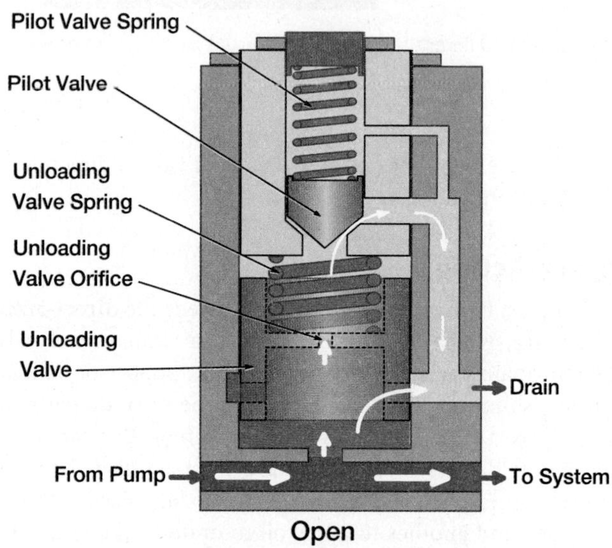

FIGURE 26-5 Pilot-operated relief valve.

> **TECHNICIAN TIP**
>
> When relief valves open, a great amount of heat is generated due to the oil flowing through a small opening at a high-pressure drop. This can be a good thing if you want to warm up the oil during a cold machine start-up. However, running a system over relief pressure on a hot day will quickly lead to overheated oil.

For example the formula BTU/hr = psi × gpm × 1.5 can be used to calculate how much heat is generated. If we use a main relief valve that is set at 2,500 psi and dumps 20 gpm to the tank, and use the formula to find how much waste heat is generated, we find 75,000 BTU/hr is generated. This is more than enough heat to keep an average house warm in the winter!

FIGURE 26-6 depicts the symbol used to represent an adjustable relief valve.

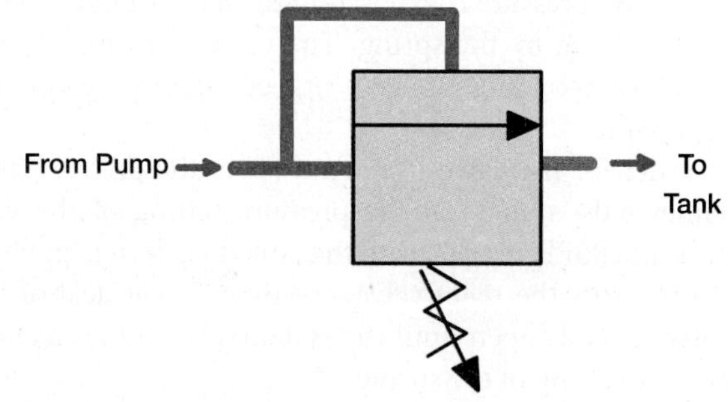

FIGURE 26-6 Symbol for an adjustable relief valve.

Unloading Valves

Some hydraulic systems use a two-section pump or two separate pumps to provide flow for one system. To make the system more efficient during high-pressure periods, a **pump unloading valve** is used to dump one pump's flow to the tank. During low-pressure operation (low load), flow from both pumps is combined to give fast actuator movement. The action of the unloading valve allows the prime mover to be downsized because there isn't a simultaneous high-flow and high-pressure condition. Heat loss is also greatly reduced as there isn't a great amount of flow being relieved at high pressure.

The valve senses system pressure and opens or closes based on the pressure level of the system. An unloading valve senses the system pressure away from the valve. There must be a **check valve** in-line between the two pump outlets to prevent the primary pump flow from dumping to the tank when the unloading valve opens. See **FIGURE 26-7** to see an unloading valve in a circuit.

Unloading valves can also be used in accumulator charging circuits. Accumulators are covered in detail in another chapter, but for now just know that they have to get charged with pressurized oil to a certain pressure level. See **FIGURE 26-8** for a simple schematic that shows an unloading valve in an accumulator charging circuit.

A check valve between the unloading valve and the accumulator isolates the portion of the system containing the accumulator from the unloading valve. Pressure on the accumulator side of the check valve is sensed through a remote sensing line and used to open the unloading valve. When the unloading valve opens, it allows pump flow to return to the tank at a low-pressure drop. This prevents the heat generation caused by the high-pressure drop that occurs across relief valves.

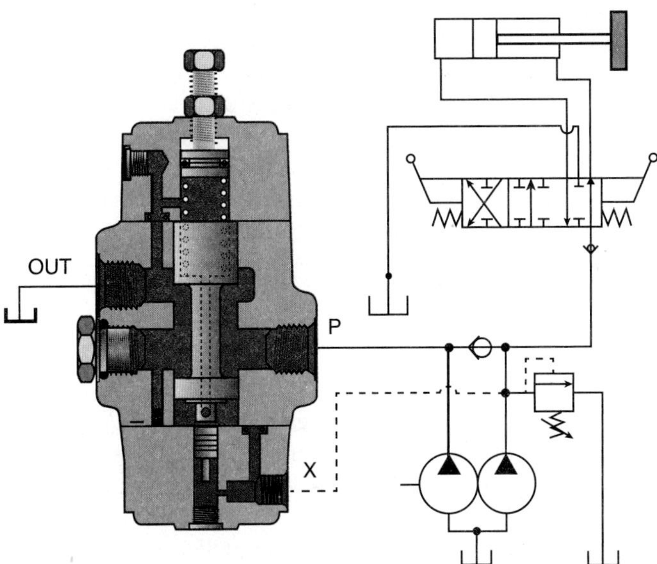

FIGURE 26-7 An unloading valve in a circuit.

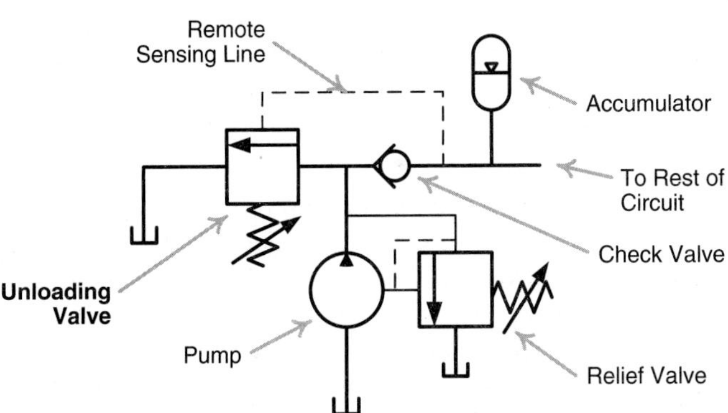

FIGURE 26-8 An unloading valve that is part of an accumulator charge circuit.

The symbol for an unloading valve is identical to the one used for a relief valve.

Sequencing Valves

Some machines have several hydraulic actuators that have to work in a specific sequence to perform the work they are designed to. An example is a hydraulic rock drill that has multiple lengths of drill steels that can be connected together to keep the drill bit from going further into the ground. To add additional drill steels, a sequence of separate actions has to happen in a specific order. Sequence valves could be used to ensure this happens correctly.

A **sequencing valve** is used in parallel circuits—such as a circuit containing two cylinders that must operate in a specific order—to ensure that the correct operating sequence is obtained. The sequencing valve is placed in the pressure line going to the cylinder that will operate second in the sequence. **FIGURE 26-9** illustrates a schematic that shows a sequence valve.

After the first cylinder has completed its operation, the pressure in the line to the second cylinder begins to increase. When the pressure in this line reaches the pressure setting of the sequencing

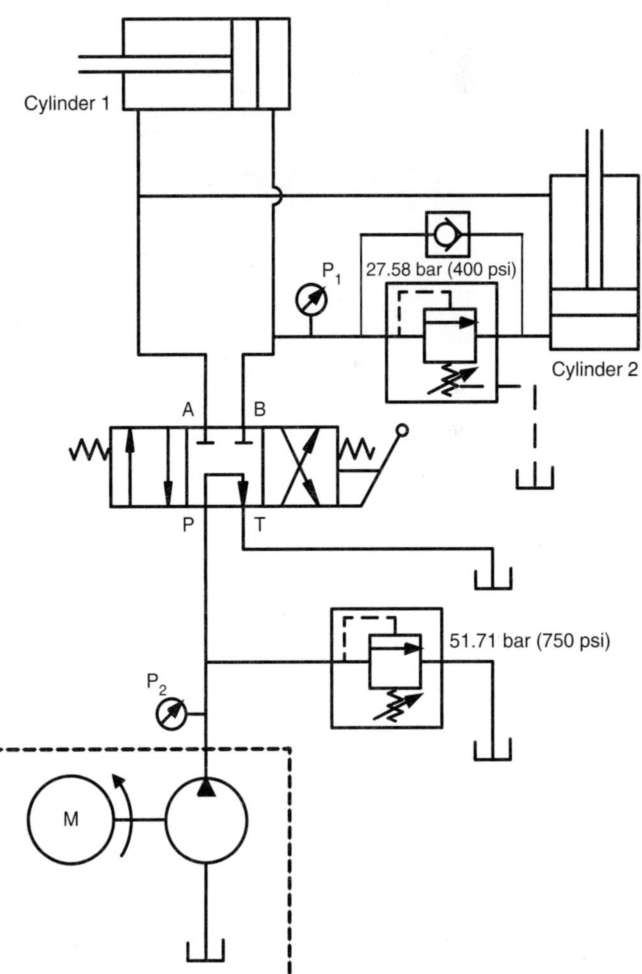

FIGURE 26-9 A schematic showing a sequence valve.

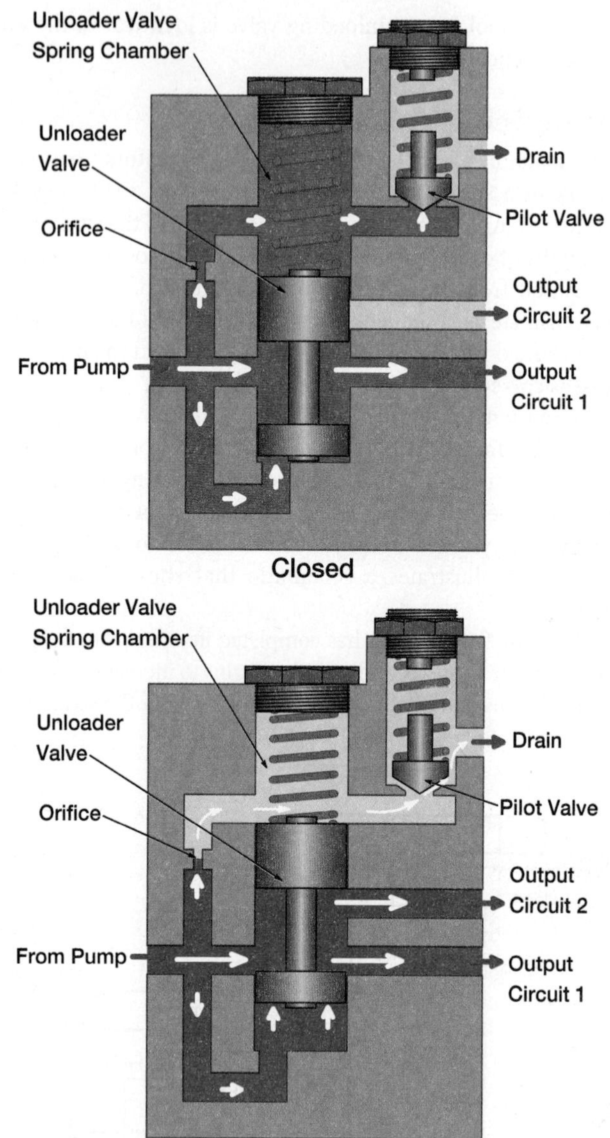

FIGURE 26-10 A sequence valve closed and open.

valve, the valve opens, allowing fluid to flow to the second cylinder. **FIGURE 26-10** shows a sequence valve closed and open.

A sequence valve is very similar to a pilot-operated pressure-relief valve, except that instead of dumping flow to the tank when it opens, it sends oil to another actuator. **FIGURE 26-11** depicts the symbol that represents a sequence valve.

Pressure-Reducing Valves

A pressure-reducing valve limits the pressure downstream of the valve in order to control the maximum pressure that portion of the system can experience. A typical example of where a pressure-reducing valve is used on a MORE machine is for the supply of pilot oil for a machine's pilot oil system. The pressure limit for these systems is typically 500 psi, and rather than have a dedicated pilot oil pump, some machines divert some

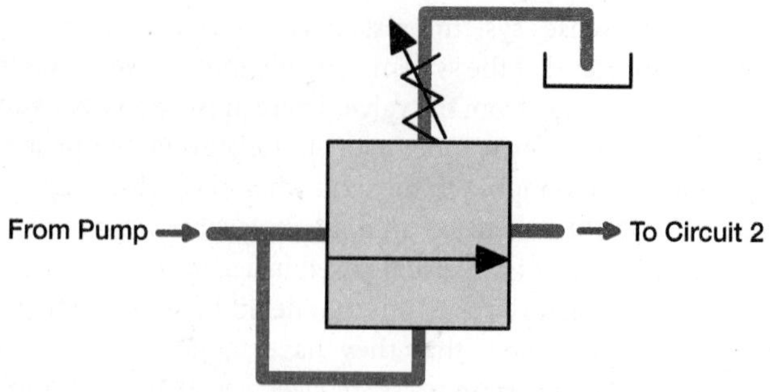

FIGURE 26-11 Symbol that represents a sequence valve.

flow from the main pump and use a **pressure-reducing valve** to limit the pressure in that circuit to a lower level.

Some machines may have an auxiliary circuit that operates at a lower pressure than the main system, and a pressure-reducing valve could be used there as well. A pressure-reducing valve in a system is shown in **FIGURE 26-12**. Unlike pressure-relief valves that are normally closed valves, pressure-reducing valves sense the pressure at their outlet and use that pressure to close the valve mechanism. **FIGURE 26-13** shows a pressure-reducing valve in its pump start-up state and its normal operating state. This is the only pressure control valve that operates in this way. All the others sense pressure either at their inlets or remotely and use that pressure to open the valve mechanism. A pressure-reducing valve can be used to limit the pressure available to a single actuator or to an entire branch of a system. It is adjusted by changing spring tension with either shims or an adjusting screw. **FIGURE 26-14** gives the symbol that represents a pressure-reducing valve.

Load Control Valves

Load control valves are used to limit actuator movement when the load on the actuator tries to create unwanted and/or uncontrolled actuator movement. Common applications for these valves are crane boom lift circuits, where the load tries to create a boom drift (boom cylinder leaks down); aerial work platform lift circuits; telehandler circuits (boom, telescope, stabilizers); backhoe stabilizer circuits; and some travel motor circuits (where the machine tries to overrun the fluid available due to the machine traveling downhill).

Load control valves are sometimes referred to as lock valves because they can hydraulically lock a cylinder in place. A few variations of load control valves can be found on MORE machines such as the ones discussed next.

Counterbalance Valves

These valves are used in circuits with open-center directional control valves and vertical cylinders, either to hold a load in place without risk of drifting or to precisely control the descent when lowering the load. Counterbalance valves are placed as closed as possible to the cylinder or directly on the cylinder. **FIGURE 26-15** illustrates a counterbalance valve used on a crane boom cylinder. By locating it on the cylinder, the risk of line failure and rapid uncontrolled movement of the load is eliminated.

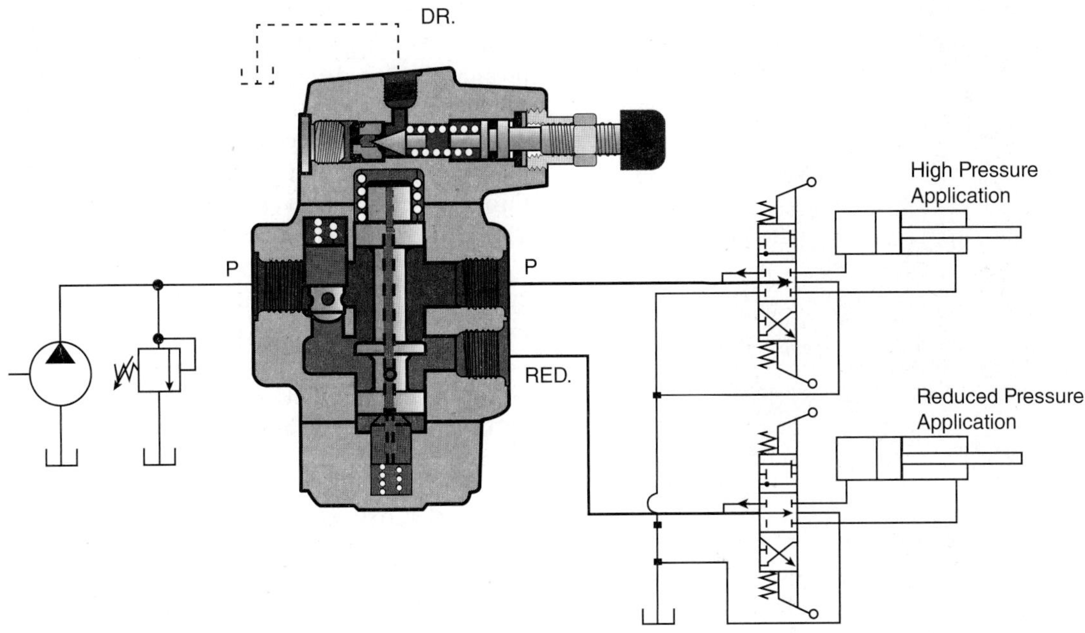

FIGURE 26-12 A pressure-reducing valve in a circuit.

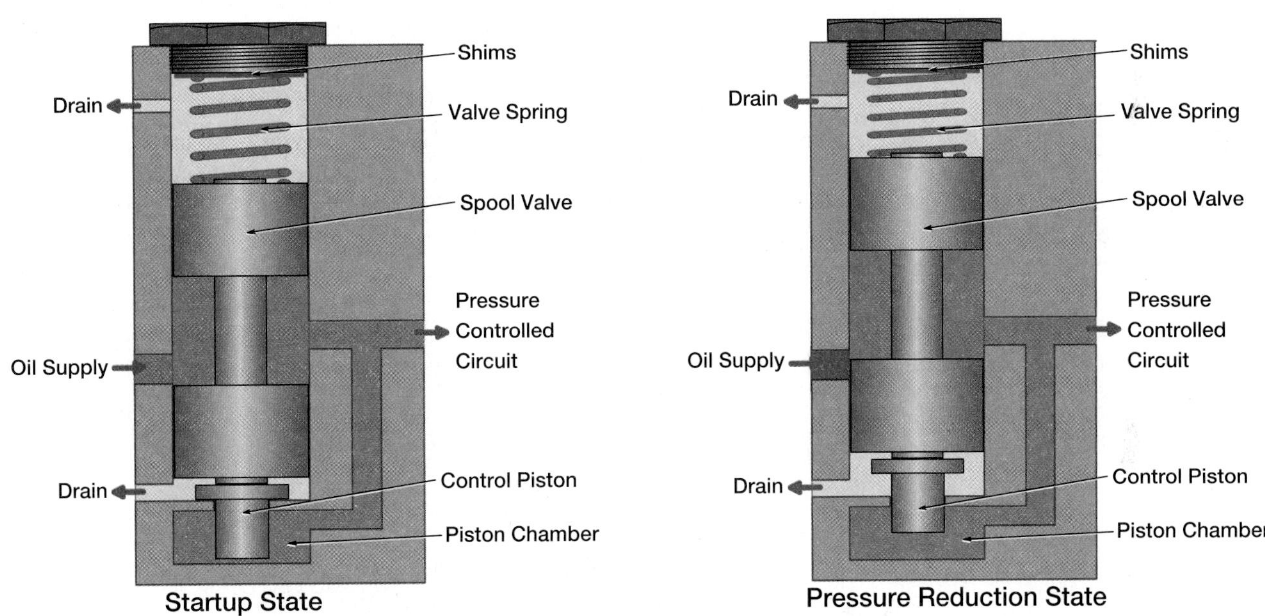

FIGURE 26-13 A pressure-reducing valve in its pump start-up state and its normal operating state.

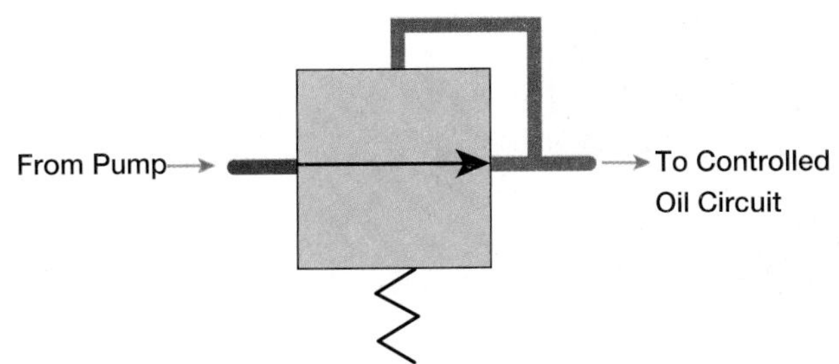

FIGURE 26-14 The symbol that represents a pressure-reducing valve.

SAFETY TIP

MORE machines that are used for critical lifts have counterbalance valves on their boom cylinders. Critical lifts are considered to be tasks that lift loads near people and have a high potential for personal or property damage should something go wrong. Many excavators are used for critical lifts when they really shouldn't be because of the absence of counterbalance valves on their boom cylinders. If a line to a boom cylinder on an excavator fails during a critical lift, the boom will drop in an uncontrolled manner and create a high risk of injury or death. Aerial work platforms, telehandlers, and man baskets use counterbalance valves as well.

FIGURE 26-15 Counterbalance valve used on a crane boom cylinder.

A counterbalance valve is a normally closed valve that locks hydraulic fluid in the cylinder with a movable piston to keep the cylinder's rod stationary until the valve is opened. Spring pressure keeps the valve closed, and this stops the cylinder rod from moving. The spring is adjustable in order to provide pressure adjustment if needed. These valves typically have a machined aluminum or cast steel body with separate piston, spring, and adjuster. They have two ports, and some valves have the piston, spring, and adjuster as a thread-in assembly.

When oil is sent to the opposite end of the cylinder, it tries to move the cylinder piston down in the cylinder. This creates a rapid pressure increase on the opposite side of the piston because the oil is trapped by the counterbalance valve. This pressure is sensed in the counterbalance valve on the opposite end of the spool from the spring. Once pressure increases enough to move the spool against the spring pressure, oil can leave the cylinder through the counterbalance valve and return through the directional control valve to the tank. This provides a smooth, controlled rod retraction.

As soon as the directional control stops sending oil to the cylinder, pressure drops in the counterbalance valve, and it immediately closes to trap oil in the cylinder again.

Counterbalance valves also have a check valve that is used as a bypass valve to allow free flow in the opposite direction. **FIGURE 26-16** portrays a counterbalance valve in a circuit with a cylinder and an overrunning load.

Vented Counterbalance Valves

These load control valves are almost identical to counterbalance valves, except that the spring chamber is vented or allowed to drain to the tank. This prevents any chance of back pressure influencing the spring behind the valve's piston. Load control valves are typically used with closed-center directional control valves that could possibly create some back pressure in the counterbalance valve if the spring chamber was not vented. In **FIGURE 26-17**, a vented counterbalance valve is used.

Pilot-Operated Check Valves

These valves are a simpler way to hold actuator rods in place when sudden and uncontrolled movement could create a hazard. A common application for this type of valve is for machines that have stabilizers (legs) that have to stay extended when the machine is operating. Cranes, backhoes, and telehandlers all have stabilizer legs that use pilot-operated check valves. **FIGURE 26-18** shows a stabilizer cylinder with two lock valves connected to its ports. Pilot-operated check valves have a cast steel or

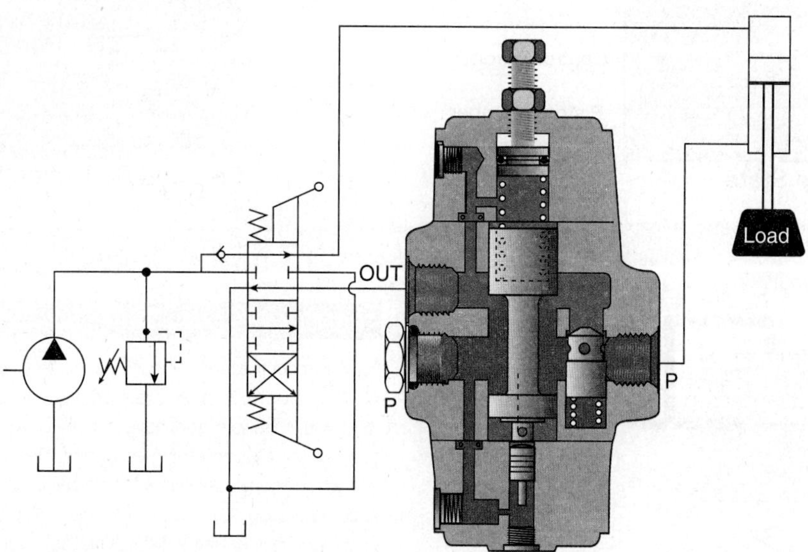

FIGURE 26-16 A counterbalance valve in a circuit with cylinder and an overrunning load.

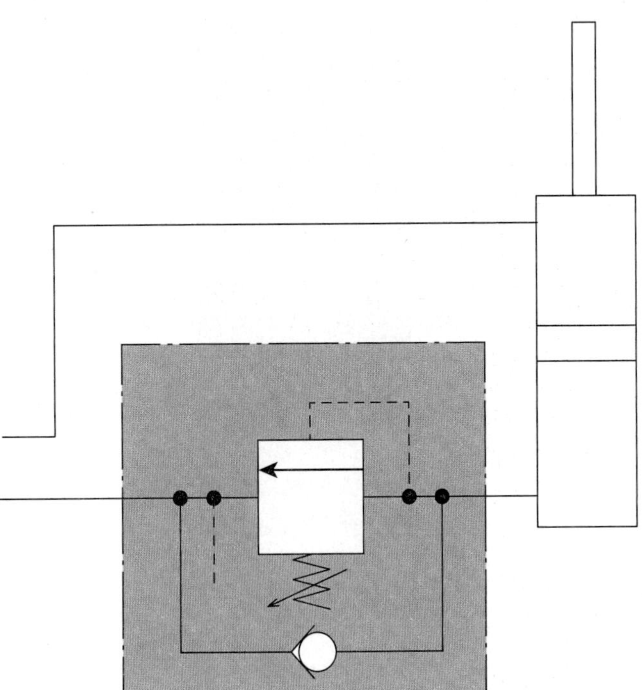

FIGURE 26-17 A vented counterbalance valve.

aluminum body, a check valve, two springs, a piston, and a rod. They have two ports: one for the cylinder and one for the directional control valve. In FIGURE 26-19, a pilot-operated check valve allows oil flow through the check valve to the cylinder.

Oil flows past the check valve freely in one direction, but as soon as the flow stops, the check valve closes and traps the oil in the cylinder in order to hydraulically lock the rod in place.

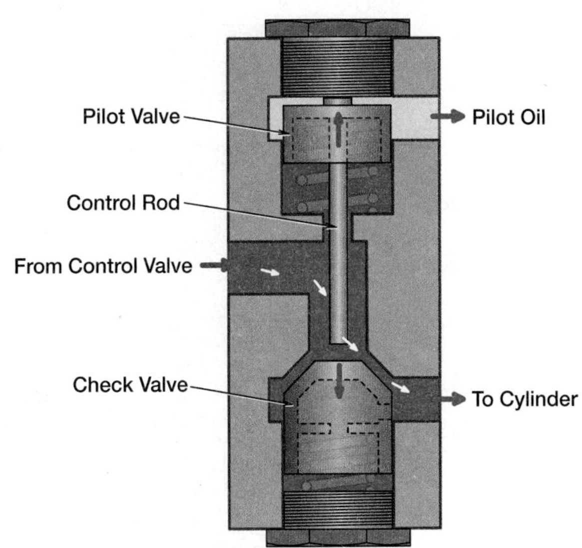

FIGURE 26-19 A pilot-operated check valve allowing oil flow through the check valve to the cylinder.

In FIGURE 26-20, a pilot-operated check valve is in the closed position. For example, imagine a crane's stabilizer leg extending to lift the crane off the ground and oil flowing into the head end of the cylinder freely. FIGURE 26-21 shows a crane stabilizer extended.

When the operator wants to retract the cylinder rod, the oil flow is reversed from the directional control valve and flows into the opposite end of the cylinder (rod end in this example). Pressure quickly rises in the head end of the cylinder because it is locked by the pilot-operated check valve. This pressure is sensed in the pilot oil chamber and acts on

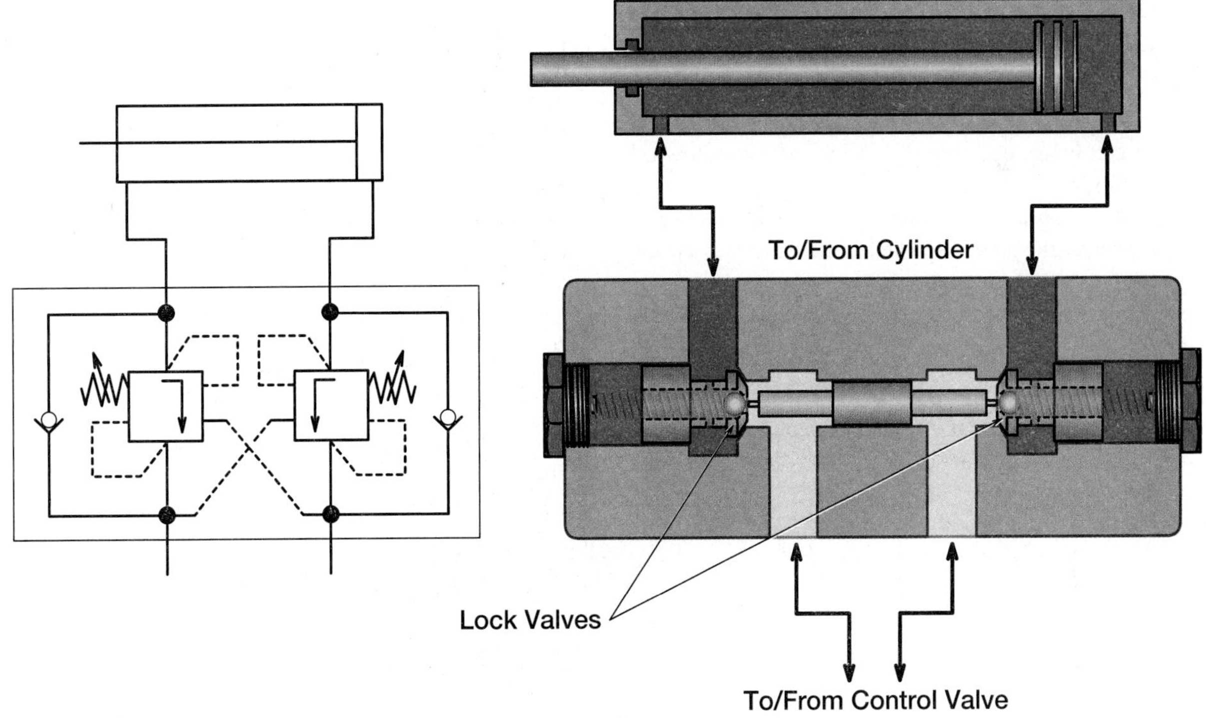

FIGURE 26-18 A stabilizer cylinder with two lock valves connected to its ports.

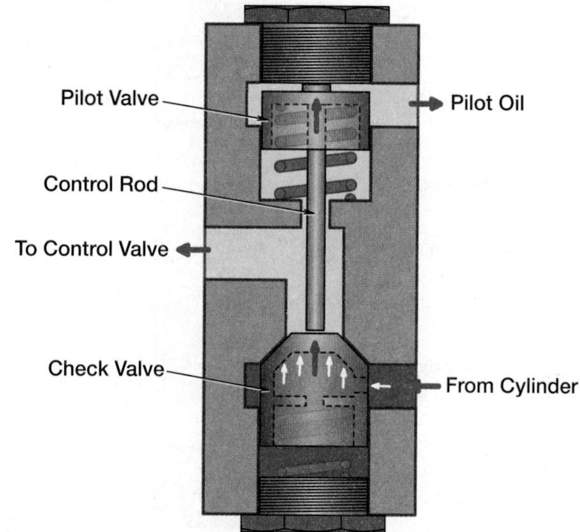

FIGURE 26-20 A pilot-operated check valve in the closed position.

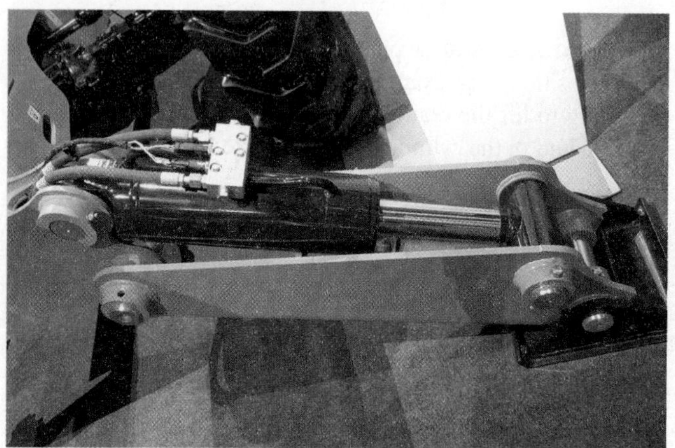

FIGURE 26-21 A crane stabilizer extended.

the pilot valve against spring pressure. This pushes the rod against the check valve, opening the check valve to allow oil to leave the cylinder.

The **pressure ratio** for how much pressure it takes to open the check valve versus the pressure locked in the cylinder is usually between 3:1 and 4:1. This means that if there are 1,200 psi locked in the cylinder, it would take approximately 400 psi to open the check valve. **FIGURE 26-22** depicts a pilot-operated check valve in the reverse flow position.

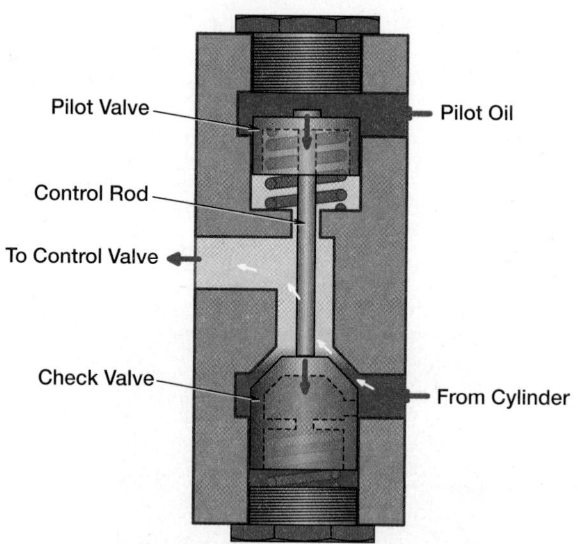

FIGURE 26-22 A pilot-operated check valve in the reverse flow position.

Brake Valves

Brake valves provide back pressure to limit speed on a hydraulic motor operating with an overrunning load (such as a piece of earth-moving equipment going downhill). A **brake valve** uses pressure inputs from both upstream and downstream of the hydraulic motor to adjust the position of the valve's moving mechanism and thus control the flow of oil through the valve. This action limits the rotating speed of the motor and uses it as a hydraulic brake to control the speed of the machine. **FIGURE 26-23** is an illustration of a circuit schematic that includes a brake valve. The pressure downstream of the motor is sensed at the inlet of the valve, just as in a relief valve. The pressure upstream of the motor is sensed through a remote sensing line. This is the only pressure control valve that uses two different pressures to adjust the valve mechanism.

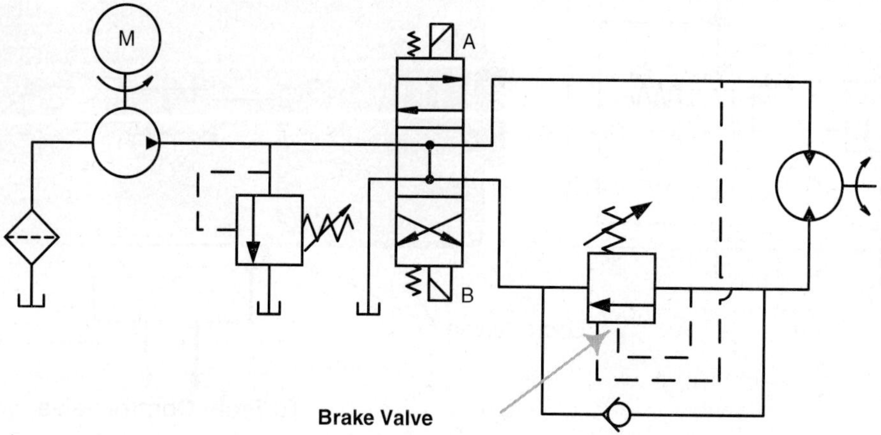

FIGURE 26-23 A circuit schematic using a brake valve.

SAFETY TIP

Extreme caution must be used when working with load control valves because of the potential for high pressures that may be trapped behind them. If one of these valves has to be adjusted or changed, all machine manufacturer's service procedures *must* be closely followed to reduce the risk of sudden pressure release.

▶ Operating Principles of Hydraulic Flow Control Valves

K26003

Flow control valves are used to adjust the flow rate to parts of the system, or the whole system, independently of what the directional control valve does. Flow control for a hydraulic system or circuit consists of controlling the volume of oil flow in or out of the system or circuit.

Flow control components reduce flow below the pump output flow rate or split it into two or more circuits. Some flow could be sent to the tank through a relief valve.

Placement of Flow Control Valves

Flow control valves can be used in three different locations relative to the actuator to control the actuator speed: meter-in, meter-out, and bleed-off. See **FIGURE 26-24** for the different locations where flow controls can be found.

Meter-In

In a meter-in system, the valve can be placed so that it controls the flow rate going into the actuator. The valves can be placed on either the cap end or the rod end of a cylinder to control its extension or retraction speed. They can also be placed on both ends to control the speeds in both directions. Similarly, valves can be placed on either or both sides of a hydraulic motor to control the speed in either or both directions of rotation.

▶ TECHNICIAN TIP

Check valves must be used in conjunction with the meter-in and meter-out flow controls so that fluid flowing in the reverse direction in the line can bypass the valve. The direction of the installation of the check valve determines whether the valve is a meter-in or meter-out valve.

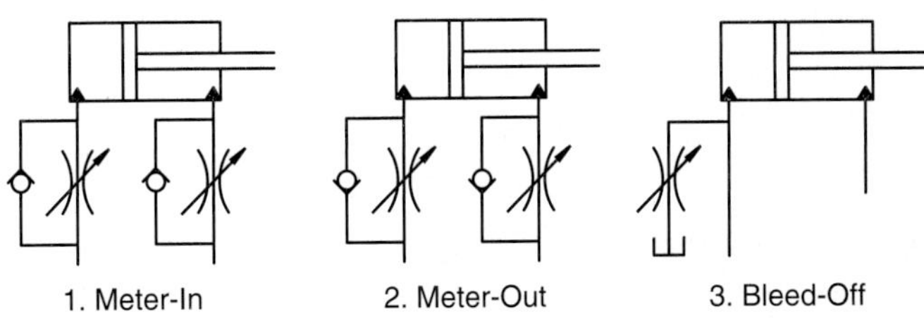

FIGURE 26-24 Different locations where flow controls can be used.

Meter-Out

In a meter-out system, the valve can be placed so it controls the flow rate leaving the actuator. Valves can be placed on either the cap end or the rod end of the cylinder to control its extension or retraction speeds. They can also be placed on both ends to control the speeds in both directions. Similarly, meter-out valves can be placed on either or both sides of a hydraulic motor to control the speed in either or both directions of rotation.

▶ TECHNICIAN TIP

When using either meter-in or meter-out flow control, the flow not used to operate the actuator is dumped back to the tank through the relief valve at relief valve pressure. This results in high heat generation and high power loss.

SAFETY TIP

If a cylinder is used to lower a vertical load, meter-out flow control is required. If the rod of the vertical cylinder is pointed downward, very high pressures may be experienced in the rod end of the cylinder. This is called *pressure intensification* in the rod end. It can result in blown rod pressure seals or even a bowed or split cylinder.

Bleed-Off

A bleed-off system allows fluid flow not needed to drive the actuator to be bled off and dumped directly back to the tank at low pressure. Unlike the meter-in and meter-out systems, which can be used on both sides of the actuator in the same system, the bleed-off system can be used on only one side, either the cap end or rod end of cylinder, or one side of a hydraulic motor.

Flow Control Component Types

These can be categorized into three groups: noncompensated flow controls, pressure-compensated flow controls, and flow dividers.

Noncompensated Flow Controls

Orifices Controlling flow in a hydraulic circuit can be accomplished in several ways.

The simplest way is by installing a fixed orifice. **FIGURE 26-25** displays the symbol used to represent a fixed orifice. When an orifice is installed, the orifice presents a higher than normal restriction to the pump flow. The higher restriction increases the oil pressure, which causes some of the oil to take another path.

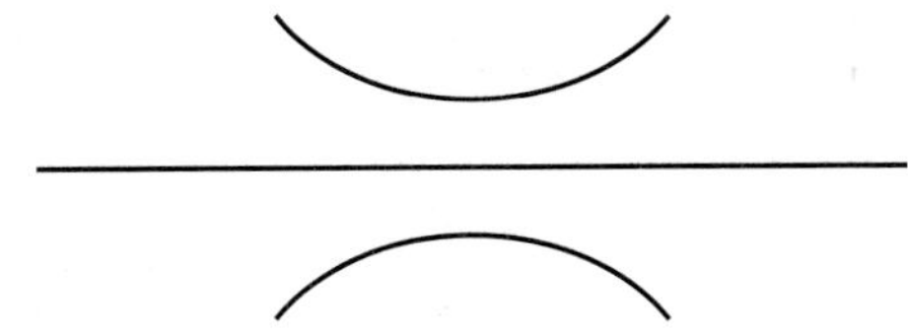

FIGURE 26-25 Symbol used to represent a fixed orifice.

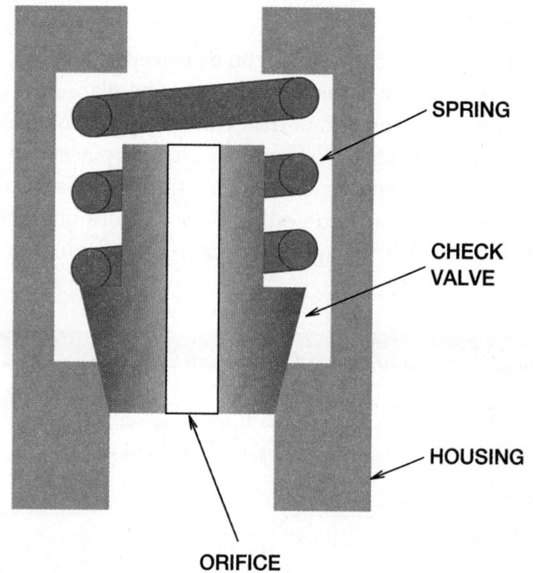

FIGURE 26-26 Fixed orifice in a check valve.

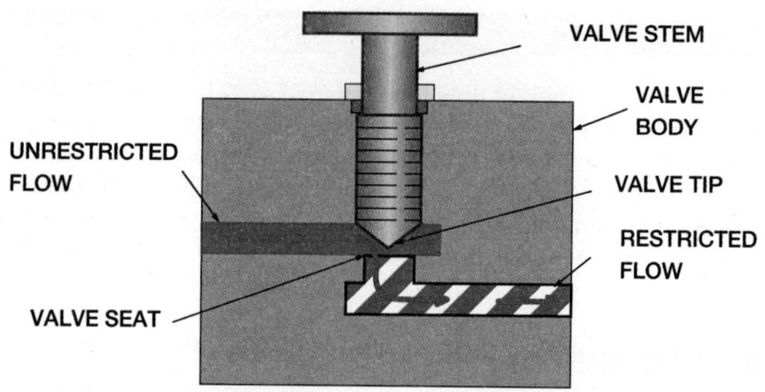

FIGURE 26-27 A needle valve.

The path may be through another circuit or over a relief valve. However, the oil flow that leaves the orifice is less than the flow trying to enter it.

The amount of oil flowing through an orifice is dependent on three factors: the size of the orifice, oil temperature, and the pressure drop across the orifice. An increase in oil flow through an orifice will result from either a larger orifice, warmer oil (lower viscosity), or a larger pressure drop across the orifice. **FIGURE 26-26** presents a fixed orifice in a check valve. This flow control component allows free flow in one direction and restricted flow in the opposite direction.

Needle Valves

Needle valves are also a simple type of flow control valve and are a variable orifice, but once they are adjusted and locked, they become a fixed orifice. Needle valves use a threaded and tapered device (needle), which is moved closer to or farther away from its tapered seat to adjust the size of the flow opening and, consequently, the flow rate through the valve. The head of the valve is normally designed with an adjusting lockable knob or screw. See **FIGURE 26-27** for a needle valve. The flow through the valve is dependent on the valve design, the size of the opening (valve adjustment), and the pressure drop across the valve (inlet pressure minus the outlet pressure). **FIGURE 26-28** shows needle valve positions and the symbol for a variable orifice.

Pressure-Compensated Flow Control Valves

Pressure-compensated flow control valves feature a movable internal mechanism (spool or piston) that attempts to maintain a constant flow through the valve regardless of the input pressure or the actuator load pressure.

The moveable spool has an internal flow orifice that is sized to allow a certain flow through it. A spring keeps the spool pushed to one end of the housing, and as oil flow increases, it uncovers a drain port. The spring value and orifice size should balance and allow a constant flow through the valve by draining more or less oil to the tank. A constant pressure drop across the valve is maintained, which in turn maintains a constant flow through the valve. **FIGURE 26-29** depicts a pressure-compensated flow control valve and the symbol that represents it.

The flow through these valves is dependent on the valve design and the valve adjustment (spring tension), which can be adjusted with shims or a threaded adjuster. Some pressure compensated flow control valves can also incorporate pressure-relief valves. In **FIGURE 26-30**, a pressure-compensated flow control valve with a pressure-relief valve incorporated is shown.

Flow Dividers

Flow dividers can be placed in a circuit to split or divide oil flow into two or more paths. There are variations of flow dividers: some always divide flow evenly, some divide flow unevenly, and some prioritize flow to one circuit, with a second one getting any leftover flow.

One example of where you might find a flow divider is a tree harvester that must have separate functions that are

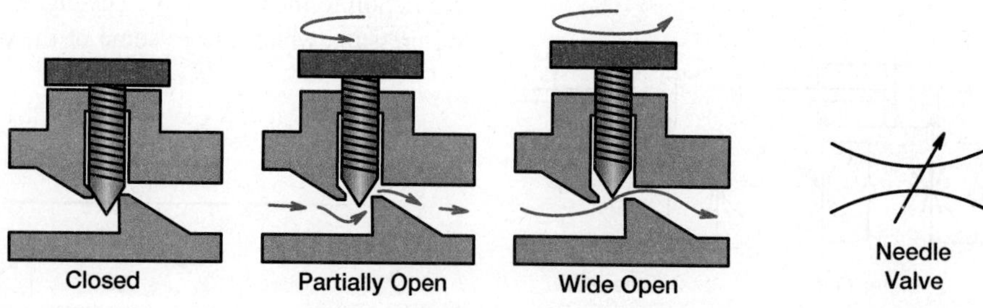

FIGURE 26-28 Needle valve positions and the symbol for a variable orifice.

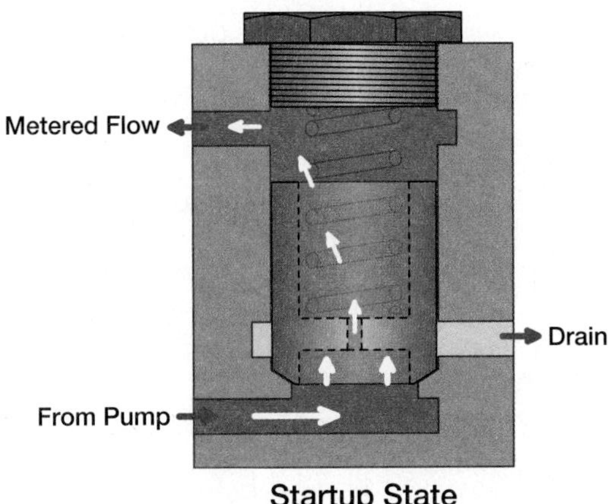

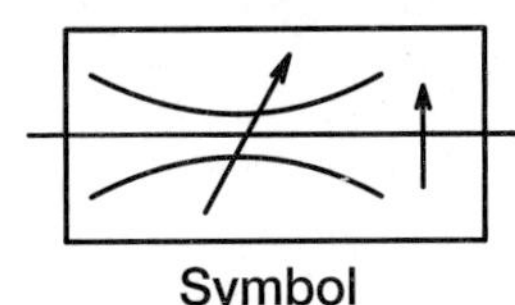

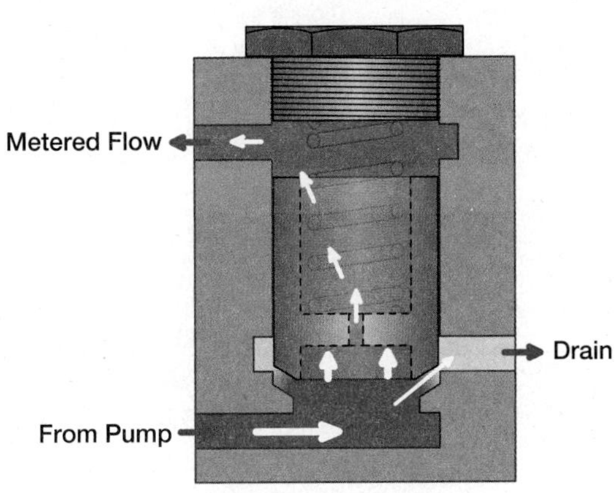

FIGURE 26-29 A pressure-compensated flow control valve and the symbol that represents it.

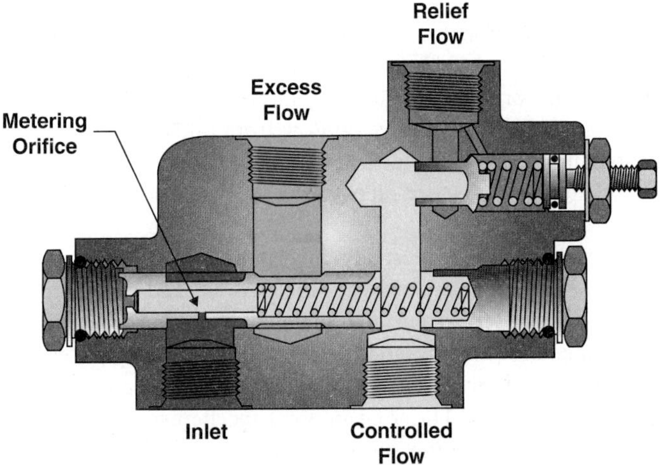

FIGURE 26-30 A pressure-compensated flow control valve with a pressure-relief valve incorporated.

FIGURE 26-31 A tree harvester that requires a flow divider.

supplied from the same circuit run at the same speed. This could be a conveyor and saw for example. See **FIGURE 26-31** for a tree harvester that requires a flow divider.

Spool-Type Priority Flow Dividers

If two parallel hydraulic circuits share one pump's flow, but one circuit is more critical than the other, a priority flow divider is provided to satisfy the flow requirements of the critical system first. This valve has a movable spool that has a fixed orifice and is held to one end of the valve housing by spring pressure. There are three ports in the housing: one inlet from the pump and two outlets to the circuits (priority and secondary). **FIGURE 26-32** illustrates a priority flow divider.

The size of the fixed orifice determines the flow to the priority circuit, with the secondary outlet getting the remainder of the flow. This device will always ensure that the priority circuit is supplied in the event that there is not sufficient flow for both circuits. This type of flow divider can be pressure compensated as well.

Pressure-Compensated, Proportional, Spool-Type Flow Dividers

Proportional flow dividers are used to equalize the flow to two actuators to ensure that they operate at the same speed. In a pressure-compensated, spool-type flow divider, pressure

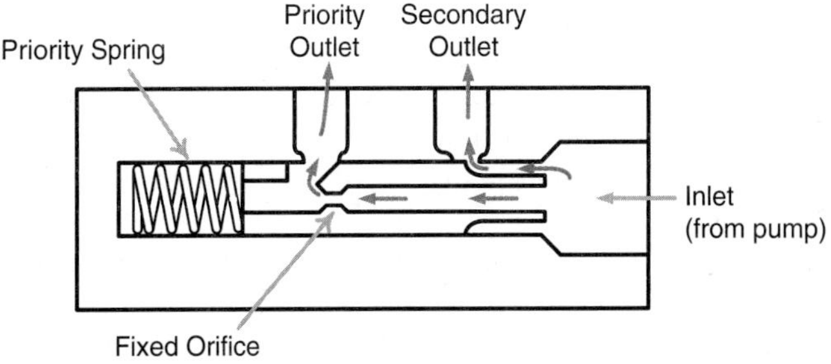

FIGURE 26-32 A priority flow divider.

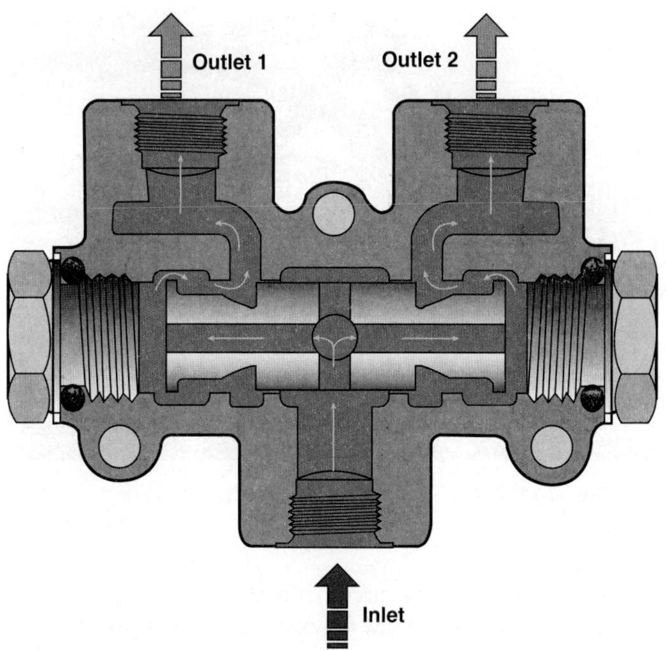

FIGURE 26-33 A spool-type flow divider.

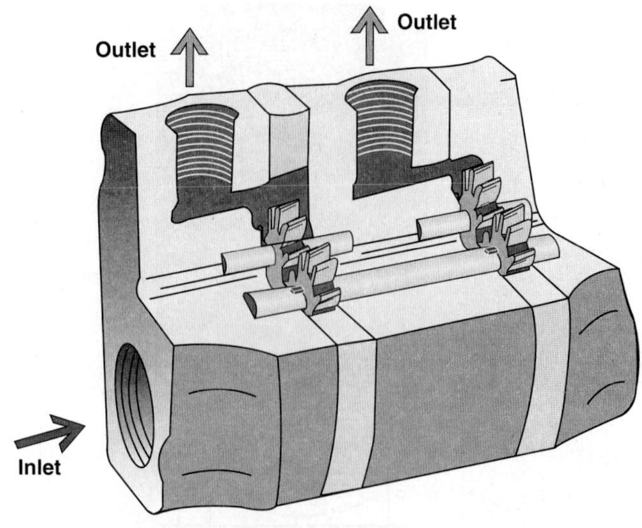

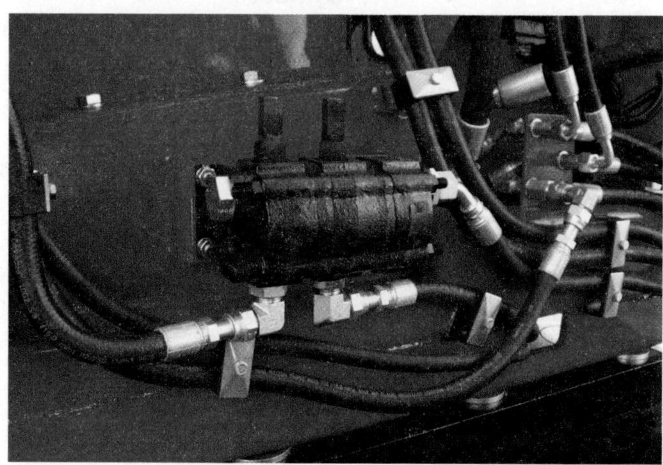

FIGURE 26-34 A gear-type flow divider.

imbalances in the system automatically position a sliding spool. These pressure imbalances occur at the outlet ports to the actuators due to the load or other factors, but the flow balance stays equal. **FIGURE 26-33** shows a spool-type flow divider.

Gear-Type Flow Dividers

A gear-type flow divider uses two hydraulic gear motors that are mechanically linked so that they must turn at the same speed. They are driven by the flow from the system pump, which enters the divider through a single inlet port.

The two motors act as metering devices and provide equal flows to the two outlet ports. They are contained in a single housing and look very similar to a multi-section gear pump, except there is no input shaft. See **FIGURE 26-34** to see a gear type flow divider.

▶ Principles of Operation of Hydraulic Directional Control Valves

K26004

Directional control valves (DCVs) determine the path and or direction that the oil flow takes through the system, and are important components of a hydraulic system. They can be simple one-way check valves with one moving part, or complicated and very expensive mechanisms with many moving parts.

They allow operators to control actuator movement speed and direction by directing oil flow to one or more actuators. All machines have more than one implement function that has to be moved with a hydraulic actuator (rubber-tired dozers being the exception because the blade lift/lower function is the only circuit). Directional control valve assemblies control two or more circuits and can be a stacked assembly made up of individual sections or machined from a one-piece steel casting or aluminum block. They receive oil flow from one or more pumps, distribute the flow to machine actuators when commanded to do so, and receive return oil from the actuators, which they then direct back to the tank.

DCV assemblies usually incorporate different types of valves, such as check valves, relief valves, and flow control valves, when they are part of a main control valve. They can be controlled in several different ways: manually (linkage or cable), hydraulically, electrically, or pneumatically (not common on today's machines). Different internal mechanisms are used to direct oil flow, but the spool type (sectional and monoblock types) is by far the most common in MORE hydraulic applications, with cartridge-type valves becoming more popular in recent years. **FIGURE 26-35** depicts a large monoblock control valve assembly.

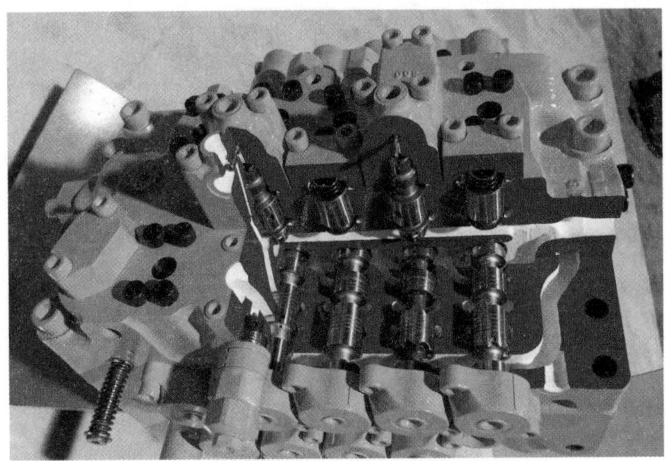

FIGURE 26-35 A large monoblock control valve assembly.

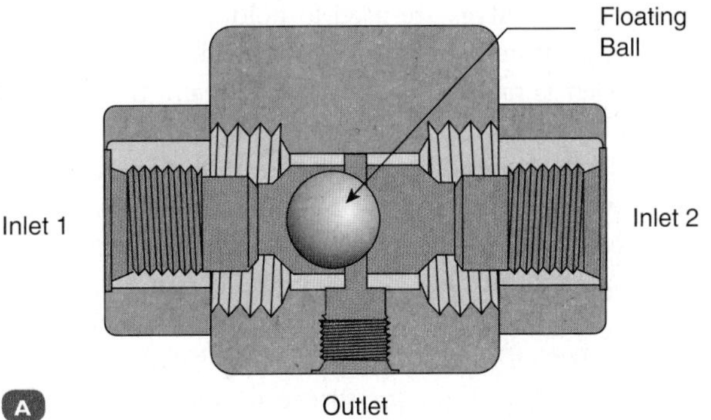

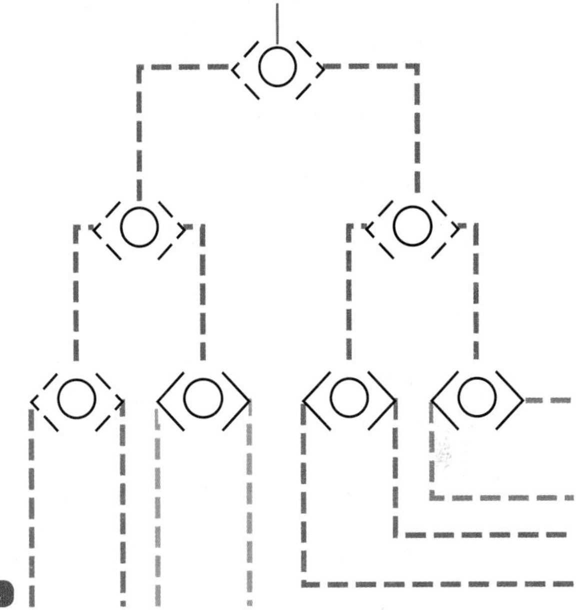

FIGURE 26-36 A. A shuttle check valve. **B.** A series of shuttle check valves connected together.

Check Valves

Check valves are used to prevent flow in one direction but allow free flow in the opposite direction. They are considered to be directional control valves because they affect the flow direction of oil in the circuit they are in. Two or three ports allow fluid to enter and leave their housing and one movable component. Check valves are a common part of MORE hydraulic systems, and few variations are discussed next.

Shuttle Check Valves

Shuttle check valves have three ports: two inlet and one outlet. They have a ball that moves freely in a housing and seals one of two ports when it is seated by the higher pressure oil flow from one of the inlets. **FIGURE 26-36A** shows a shuttle check valve. Oil can enter one of two inlet ports and exit the outlet port. They are usually connected with two or more other shuttle check valves and are used to send the highest working pressure to a pump control valve. A series of shuttle check valves connected together are displayed in **FIGURE 26-36B**. This arrangement senses the work port pressure and sends the highest pressure to the pump control valve.

In-Line Poppet–Type Check Valves

Some circuits require having a check valve to allow flow in one direction but prevent it from flowing in the opposite direction. They have a light spring in them to assist with seating the poppet. See **FIGURE 26-37A** to understand how a poppet-type check valve works. Poppet-type check valves have a machined housing and two threaded end caps that are sealed with O-rings; one has the poppet seat machined into it. A pressure and flow rating is stamped on these valves, and should not be exceeded. See **FIGURE 26-37B** for a poppet-type check valve.

Other Types of Check Valves

Check valves can be found in main control valve assemblies and are used for different functions, but their operation is still the same, even though they might go by different names.

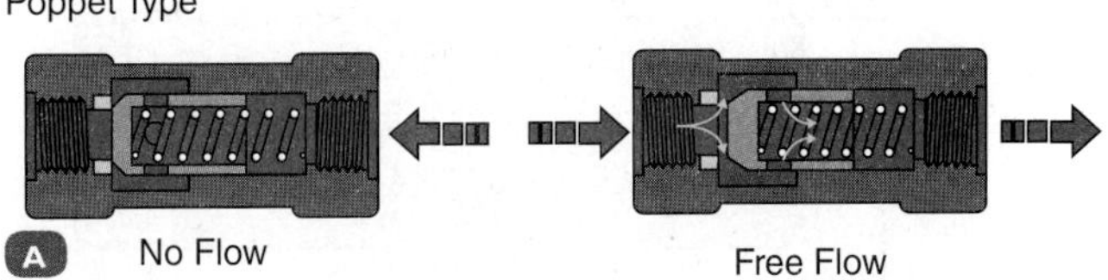

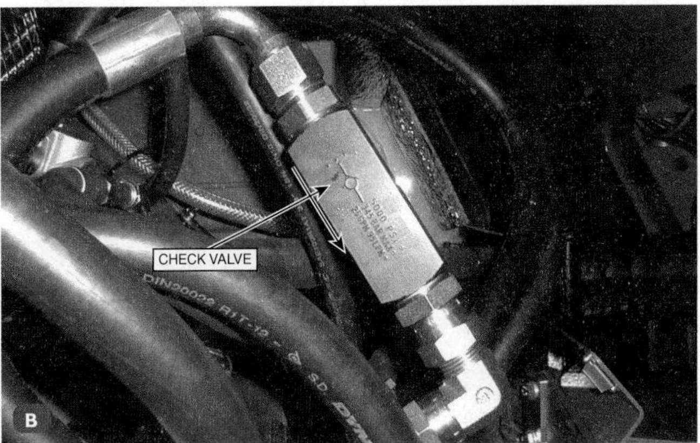

FIGURE 26-37 A. A poppet-type. **B.** check valve.

Load check valves are used to hold a load in place until pressure is great enough to move the load. For example, if a loaded bucket is raised and then stopped, and the directional control valve is brought back to neutral, the load check will seat to hold the boom in place. When pump flow attempts to move the boom cylinder rods out to lift the load again, it will have to open the load check valve first. This prevents the load from dropping slightly before the pump flow can start lifting it. **FIGURE 26-38** demonstrates how a load check valve works.

Anticavitation valves are check valves that allow tank oil to flow into an actuator if the pressure in the cylinder drops below tank pressure. This could happen when a load tries to move an actuator faster than the pump can supply oil to it. These valves, sometimes called makeup valves, are normally held closed by a light spring and circuit pressure. See **FIGURE 26-39** for an illustration of a makeup valve closed and open. **Pilot-operated check valves** are often referred to as lock valves because a common application for them is to lock a cylinder in place in order to eliminate a drift problem. This type of check valve has a piston that moves a rod to open the check valve and hold it open as long as pilot pressure is applied to the piston. **FIGURE 26-40** depicts a pilot-operated check valve.

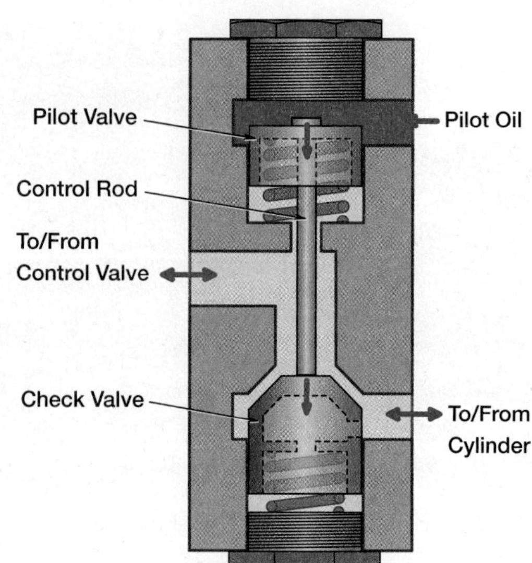

FIGURE 26-40 Pilot-operated check valve.

Directional Control Valve Configurations

Directional control valves are needed to direct pump oil flow to actuators and direct return oil to the tank from the actuators.

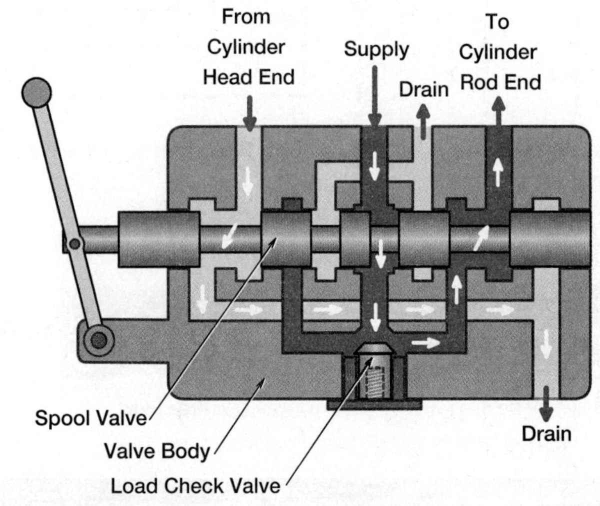

FIGURE 26-38 How a load check valve works.

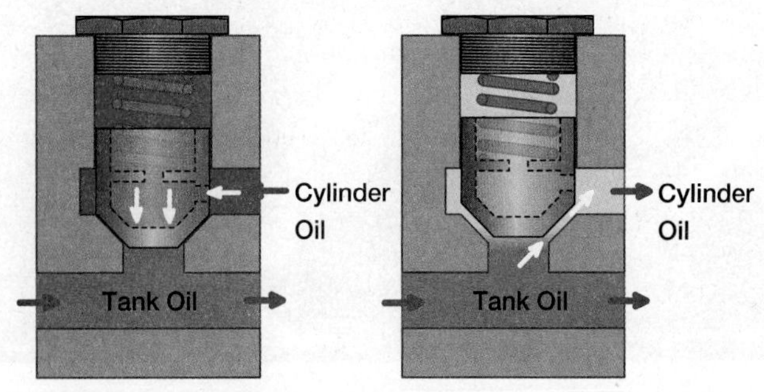

FIGURE 26-39 A makeup valve in the closed and open positions.

Ports allow hoses and tubes to connect the valve to the pump, tank, and actuators. Each section of a DCV has two main external ports, called A and B, that allow oil transfer to an actuator (cylinder or motor). DCVs also have internal or external ports to transfer oil into and out of the valve section to and from the pump and tank. Even though check valves are considered to be directional control valves, when technicians talk about a DCV, they are usually talking about a valve as described above.

The most common type of directional control valve found on MORE is the cast housing and spool type. The other main type is the cartridge type. All types can be classified by several characteristics, including construction type, center flow type, flow rating, pressure rating, number of circuits, type of actuation, and type of pressure protection.

Typically, directional control valve assemblies supply at least two circuits and could supply over 10, depending on the type of machine and the locations of the pump, the cab, and the actuators. Some MORE machines have more than one DCV assembly. For example, a backhoe loader typically has two directional control valve assemblies: one for the backhoe and one for the front loader. **FIGURE 26-41** shows the DCV assemblies on a backhoe loader.

Directional Control Valve Housing Types

There are three main types of DCV housings: one piece, or monoblock; sectional; and cartridge.

Larger DCVs that are used on high-flow machines like excavators are almost always made from one-piece cast steel bodies (monoblock); however, many smaller machines, like skid steers, can have monoblock-type DCVs as well. The number of circuits that a DCV supplies is referred to as the number of sections it has. In **FIGURE 26-42**, a four-section monoblock style of DCV is depicted. Cartridge-type valves are discussed in a later section, but they feature either thread-in or slip-in valve assemblies that can be DCVs. The cartridge housing is made from a solid piece of machined steel or aluminum.

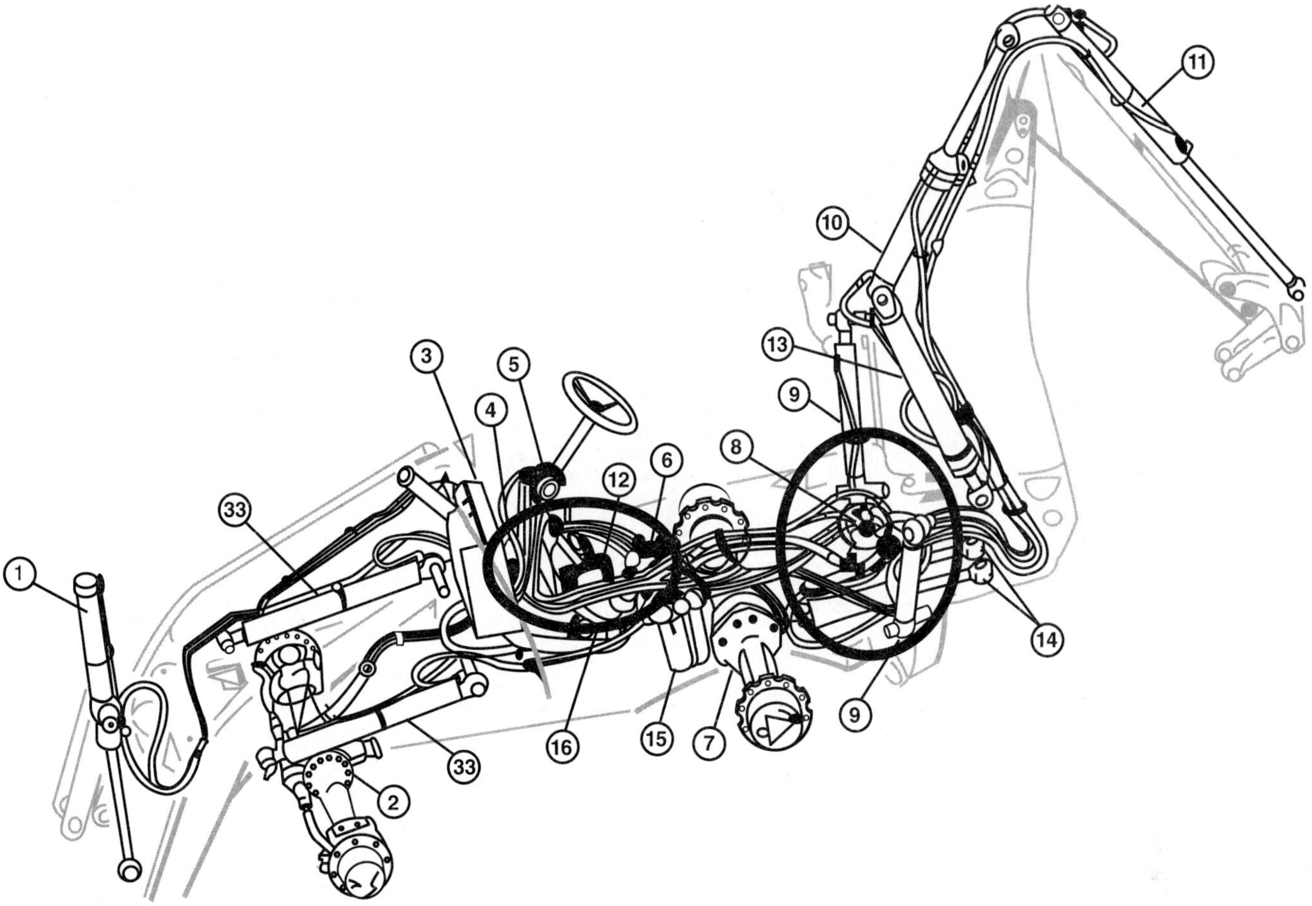

FIGURE 26-41 DCV assemblies on a backhoe loader.
Image Provided As Courtesy of John Deere.

FIGURE 26-42 A four-section monoblock style of DCV.

Directional Control Valve Positions

DCVs have movable spools or pistons that cover and uncover ports internally as they are moved to different positions. As the internal ports are covered and uncovered, the oil flow changes its path through the valve. The simplest DCV is one with two positions that redirects oil flow from either the pump to an actuator, or the actuator to the tank. This DCV has three ports, and the spool moves to join either the P and A port or the P and T port. Although not a very practical valve, this is an example of a simple type of DCV.

Different configurations of valves are based on the number of positions the spool can move to. MORE machines typically have DCVs with three or four positions; however, it is possible to see some with two or five positions. Valves with three or more positions have a neutral position that determines whether the valve is open center (pump oil goes to the tank) or closed center (pump oil is blocked). Unless indicated or stated that the valve is variable, it is assumed the positions are on/off or full flow/no flow. A variable valve allows a gradual increase/decrease in flow between positions. This is indicated by two horizontal lines on the outside of the valve symbol.

A three-position DCV has a neutral position and two positions that send pump oil to either of the A or B ports that are connected to an actuator. If you think of a dozer with a ripper, its DCV would have a three-position valve for raise, lower, and hold for the ripper lift function. **FIGURE 26-43** demonstrates how a three-position DCV can redirect oil when shifted.

A fourth position is sometimes used for a float position. Most dozers have a float position for the blade lift circuit. When the control lever is moved fully forward, the spool is shifted to let the A and B ports join, which allows the blade lift cylinder piston to "float" freely in the barrel. This lets the weight of the blade follow the contours of the ground when back blading. Many wheel loaders also have a float position for the boom circuit.

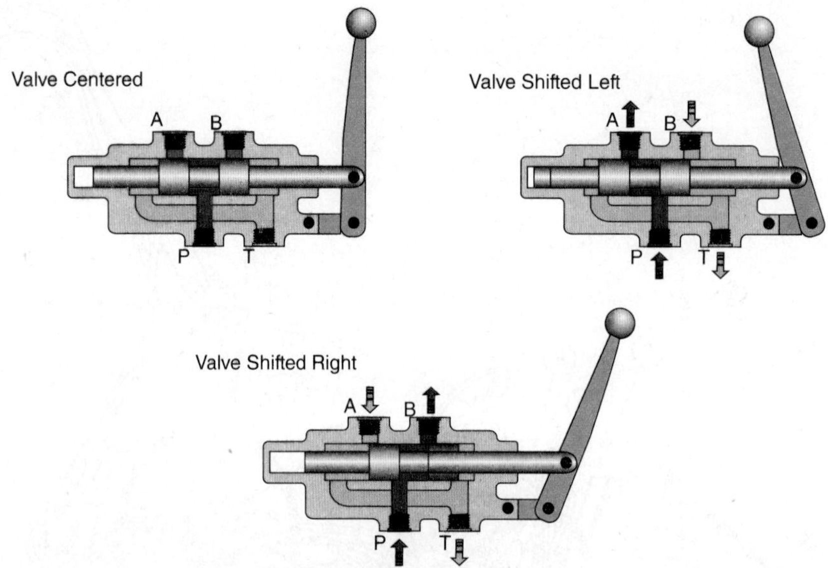

FIGURE 26-43 How a three-position DCV can redirect oil when shifted.

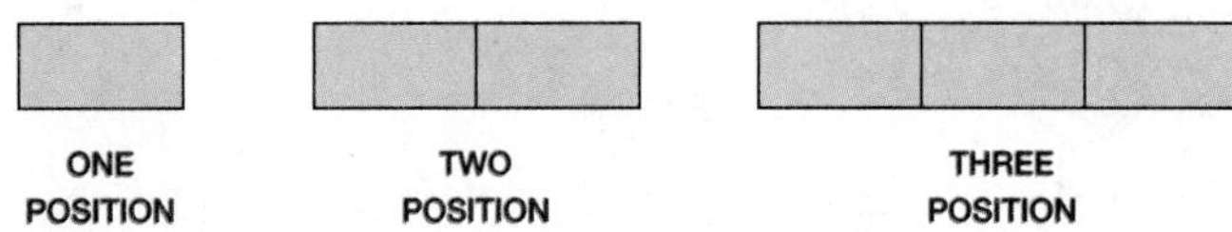

FIGURE 26-44 The symbols that represent one-, two-, and three-position valves.

Symbols for DCVs use individual boxes to represent the number of positions they have. Therefore, a three-position DCV symbol would have three boxes. The symbols in **FIGURE 26-44** represent one-, two-, and three-position valves.

A valve with a **regenerative** function sends return oil that normally goes to the tank back to mix with pump oil, so it would look like P to A and B to A. **FIGURE 26-45** is a schematic of a circuit using a DCV with a regenerative section. A regenerative function provides fast movement to an actuator when it is needed and pump oil volume can't satisfy the supply requirements.

Spool-Type Directional Control Valves

The most common type of DCVs are spool type, and both monoblock and sectional-type DCVs are spool type. **Spool** refers to the round shape of the movable part of the valve, which is a long, cylindrical, machined, and polished precisely fit piece. When assembled, there should only be a very small clearance (5–10 microns) between the bore of the housing and the outside diameter of the spool. In fact, the clearance is just enough to allow a film of oil between them. This film of oil is expected to both lubricate the spool as it moves and create a seal, as this is the only seal to separate working pressure and tank pressure in the valve.

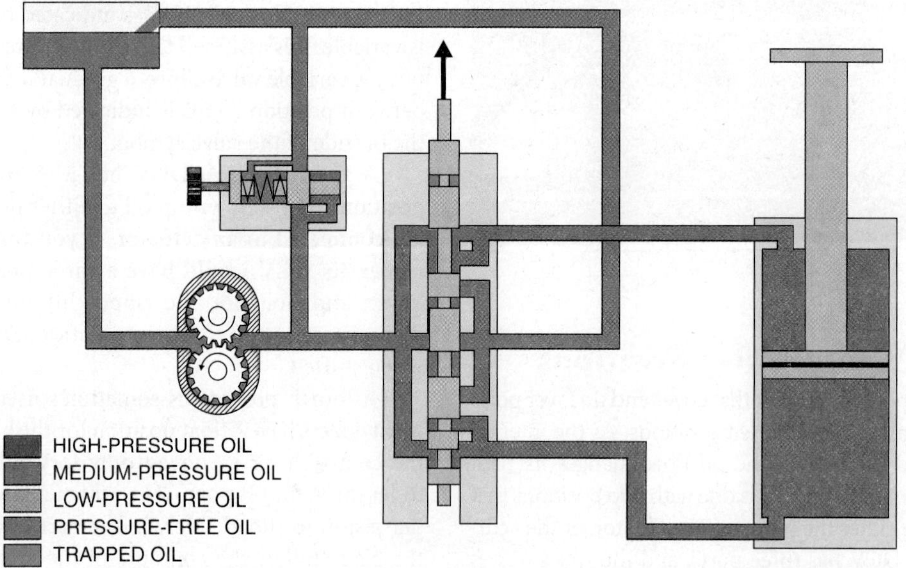

FIGURE 26-45 A schematic of a circuit using a DCV with a regenerative section.

FIGURE 26-46 A valve body with threaded ports.

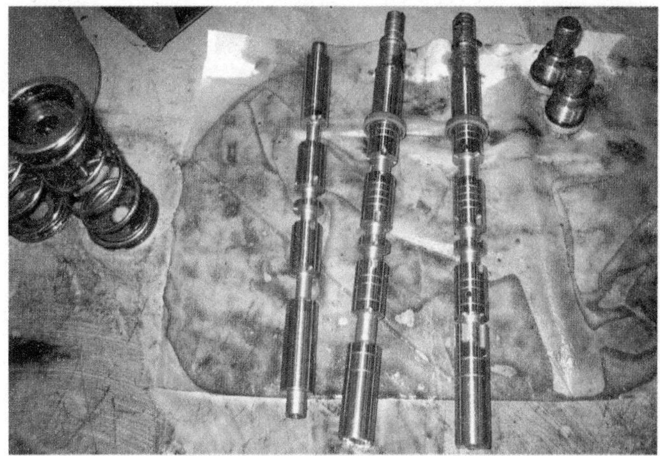

FIGURE 26-48 Three spools from a three-section DCV.

FIGURE 26-49 An individual section from a sectional DCV.

The body is a cast steel block that is machined and honed to accept the spool, and is sometimes heat treated for longevity. The external mating surfaces for the A and B ports are either threaded or machined flat, depending on the type of hose or tube that will be mated to them. See **FIGURE 26-46** for an example of a valve body with threaded ports.

▶ TECHNICIAN TIP

The number of ports that one section of a DCV has is another way to describe it. The typical DCV is a three-position, four-way valve. The positions are neutral: pump oil sent to A port; pump oil sent to B port. The four-way part refers to how many ports or "**ways**" oil can flow into or out of the valve (pump, tank, A port, and B port). **FIGURE 26-47** demonstrates how the number of "ways" are represented for a DCV.

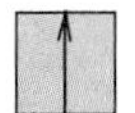

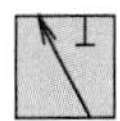

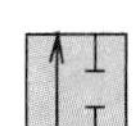

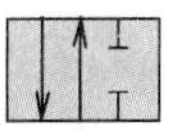

TWO-WAY THREE-WAY FOUR-WAY SIX-WAY

FIGURE 26-47 Different "ways" that are represented for a DCV.

DCV spools have two main surfaces that oil is exposed to. Their larger diameters are called lands, and these surfaces have small grooves machined into them that retain some oil for lubrication and sealing purposes. The lands create a seal in the valve, providing that the clearance between the spool and the bore in the valve body is not excessive or damaged. This dynamic seal is all that separates work port pressure and tank pressure, and can be in excess of a 5,000 psi difference.

SAFETY TIP

Some internal leakage is allowed in a DCV because it is not a 100% seal, and this is one reason why heavy implements may drift down over time. This is a normal occurrence, and if there are no other load-holding valves in the system, it is expected that a slow drift will occur. This is why a technician should *never* rely on the hydraulic system to hold implements in the air when servicing or repairing them. *Always* use a mechanical lock to keep implements from moving when working on or near components that are suspended hydraulically.

The smaller diameters in between the **lands** are called **grooves** and allow oil flow between the valve ports when the valve is shifted. In **FIGURE 26-48**, notice the differences between the three spools from a three-section DCV.

Sectional DCVs are made up of two or more individual sections that are bolted (stacked) together. Each individual section is a cast and machined body with smooth surfaces to seal with adjacent sections, and is bored to accept a spool. Sectional DCVs also have an A and B port to connect hoses or tubes to an actuator. **FIGURE 26-49** shows an individual section from a sectional DCV.

DCV spools themselves can have many variations among the different types, and even within the same DCV. One common feature found on spools is metering notches. **Metering notches** provide a smooth transition between open and closed positions. They are slots machined into the spool land area and can look like coin slots or be semicircular. A spool with metering notches is depicted in **FIGURE 26-50**.

Directional Control Valve Center Flow Patterns

The internal passageways in a DCV determine the type of system that a hydraulic circuit is by the way pump oil can flow through the valve or is blocked as it gets to the valve.

FIGURE 26-50 A spool with metering notches.

Open- and closed-center systems were referred to in earlier chapters, and these terms describe whether pump flow is blocked at the DCV or whether it can flow through it. Typically, open-center valves are used with fixed displacement pumps, and closed-center valves get oil supplied to them from variable displacement pumps. FIGURE 26-51 illustrates an open-center DCV.

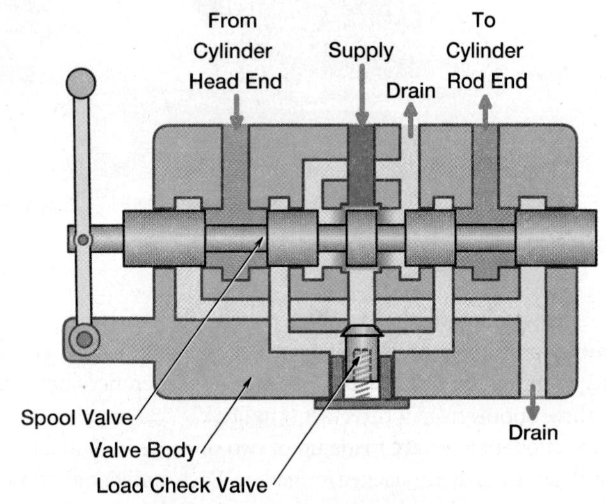

FIGURE 26-51 An open-center DCV.

CLOSED CENTER

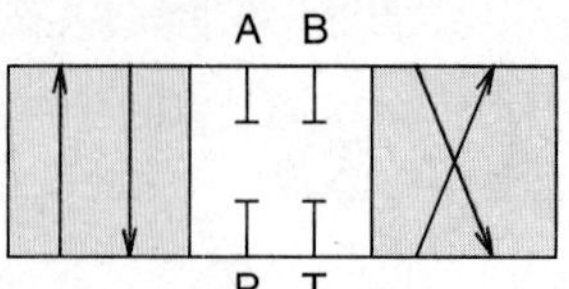

TANDEM CENTER (CATERPILLAR OPEN CENTER)

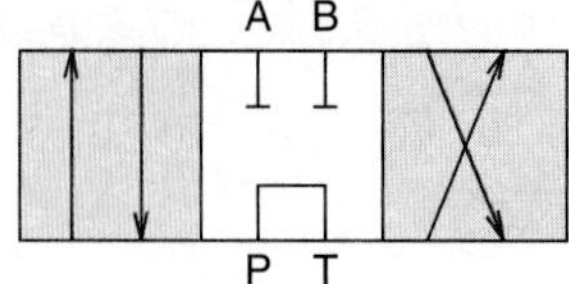

OPEN CENTER

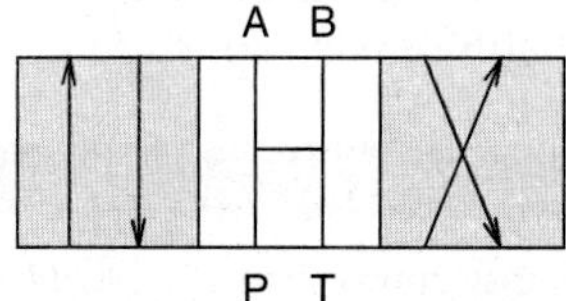

FIGURE 26-52 Three common DCV center sections are represented with a symbol.

A third type of **flow pattern** possible for a DCV is called tandem center. It is similar to an open-center valve in that the pump and tank are open to each other, but the A and B ports are blocked off. FIGURE 26-52 depicts how the three common DCV center sections are represented with a symbol. A fourth type of DCV center typically used with hydraulic motors is called a motor spool. It allows free flow between the A and B ports and can be either closed or open center in terms of the pump and tank ports.

Directional Control Valve Actuation Method

DCVs are the interface between the operator and the hydraulic system and need to receive input from the operator to get actuated. DCVs can be actuated in several ways—manually, hydraulically, electrically, or pneumatically—and they are kept centered with springs. Pneumatically actuated DCVs were used on some older machines but are seldom found on machines still in operation.

Some DCVs have a detent mechanism on one end of the spool. This is a spring-loaded mechanism used to hold the spool in place until moved by the operator. A typical function for a detent is to hold the spool in the **float** position, which for dozers and loaders occurs when the control lever is pushed to the furthest ahead position. FIGURE 26-53 shows common ways to actuate DCVs.

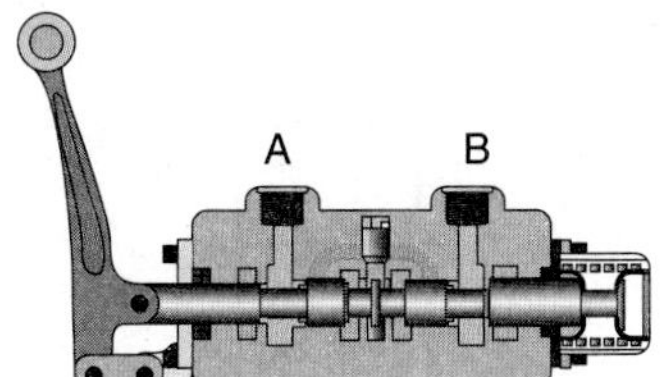

Manually Operated, Spring Centered

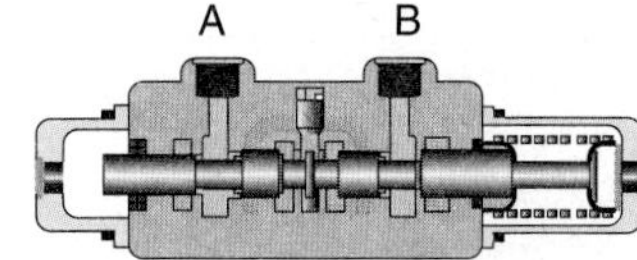

Hydraulic Pilot Operated, Spring Centered

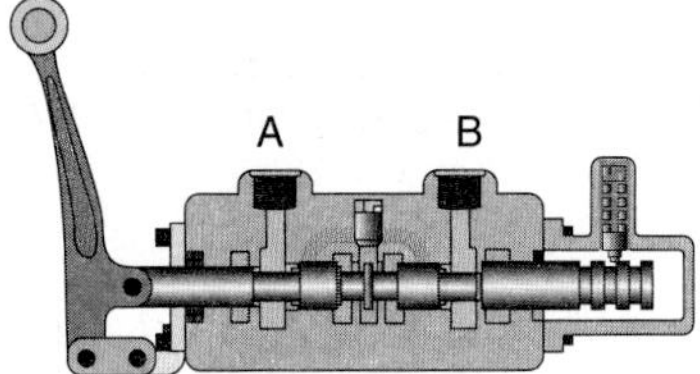

Manually Operated, Detented

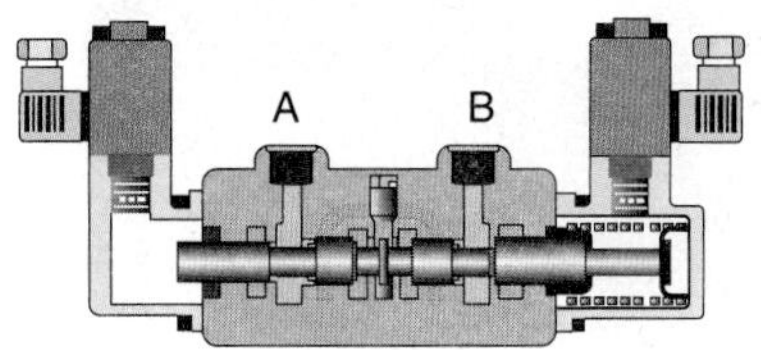

Electro-Hydraulic Pilot Operated, Spring Centered

FIGURE 26-53 Common ways to actuate DCVs.

FIGURE 26-54 Control levers for a mechanically actuated backhoe control valve.

Mechanically Actuated Directional Control Valves

Older and or simpler machines use mechanically actuated DCVs. This could be a lever- or pedal-actuated mechanical linkage that is directly connected to the spool or a cable assembly that is moved by a lever. Linkages and cables can be simple and inexpensive ways to move DCV spools, but they are also vulnerable to wear and adjustment problems in comparison to hydraulic and electric actuation. **FIGURE 26-54** shows the control levers for a mechanically actuated backhoe control valve.

Hydraulically Actuated Directional Control Valves

To reduce operator effort when controlling DCVs, a low-pressure hydraulic system controlled by the operator can be used, and its hydraulic outputs will actuate the DCV by shifting spools. It is commonly called a **pilot oil** system. Pilot oil systems typically are limited to 500 psi and can be supplied oil from a dedicated pump or from a pressure-reducing valve that takes oil from the main pump. A joystick and pilot control valve are shown in **FIGURE 26-55**.

FIGURE 26-55 Joystick and pilot control valve.

The valve assemblies used in the cab for pilot systems are called poppet valves. As an example, an excavator with pilot controls has left and right pilot control valves. The right pilot control sends oil to the boom and bucket main control valve spools, and the left pilot control sends oil to the stick and swing main control valves. Each one of these valves is topped by a joystick, below which are two or four poppet valves.

As the operator moves the joystick, a poppet valve gets pushed down or pulled up (two-poppet valve), and it meters some pressurized pilot oil to the end of the main control valve. The main control valve is then shifted against spring pressure and allows oil from the main pump to flow to the actuator it is controlling.

Electrically Actuated Directional Control Valves

Many newer machines feature joysticks controlling position sensors that in turn send signals to an ECM. The ECM then sends an electrical signal to a **proportional solenoid** valve on the DCV that meters low-pressure oil to the ends of the DCV spool. The low-pressure oil then shifts the spool to allow main pump oil flow to reach the actuator it is controlling. **FIGURE 26-56** shows an electronic joystick, ECM, and main control valve with proportional solenoids. This is considered to be an electrohydraulic system. For a variety of DCV actuator symbols, see **FIGURE 26-57**.

FIGURE 26-56 An electronic joystick, ECM, and main control valve with proportional solenoid.

DCV Symbols

DCV symbols start with one or more boxes to represent the number of boxes; then each box is filled in to show how the oil flows in each position. The ends of the boxes are marked with actuator symbols, and if the valve is variable, two horizontal lines are drawn along both sides of it. **FIGURE 26-58** depicts a variety of DCV symbols.

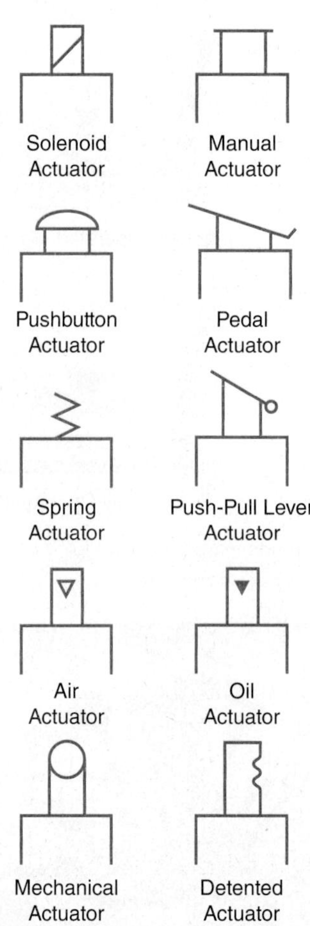

FIGURE 26-57 A variety of DCV actuator symbols.

Cartridge Valves

Cartridge valves are a variation of hydraulic valves that have many benefits compared to valve assemblies that have cast bodies, and/or they are custom made for particular machines. "Cartridge" refers to a valve assembly that is produced as a complete unit that can be replaced easily and is usually a throwaway item. These cartridge valves are installed into a machined block that make up a control valve assembly. A cartridge-type control valve could have as few as 1 cartridge or could have 10 or more cartridges of different types and styles.

Cartridge valves are less expensive to produce, reduce the chance of leaks when compared to sectional valves or valves that are connected by tubes or hoses, and can be used for a wide variety of machine models, with only minor modifications needed. The bores for cartridge valves employ a common design specification to make them universal across a wide variety of sizes. Larger diameter valves provide larger flow volumes, if needed, for different applications. **FIGURE 26-59** illustrates a cartridge-type control valve.

Cartridge valves are a replaceable part of a cartridge valve block assembly. When diagnosing a hydraulic problem, it's easy to swap cartridge valves if there is more than one of the same type in a block. If the problem moves when the valve is swapped, then you would know the cartridge valve is defective.

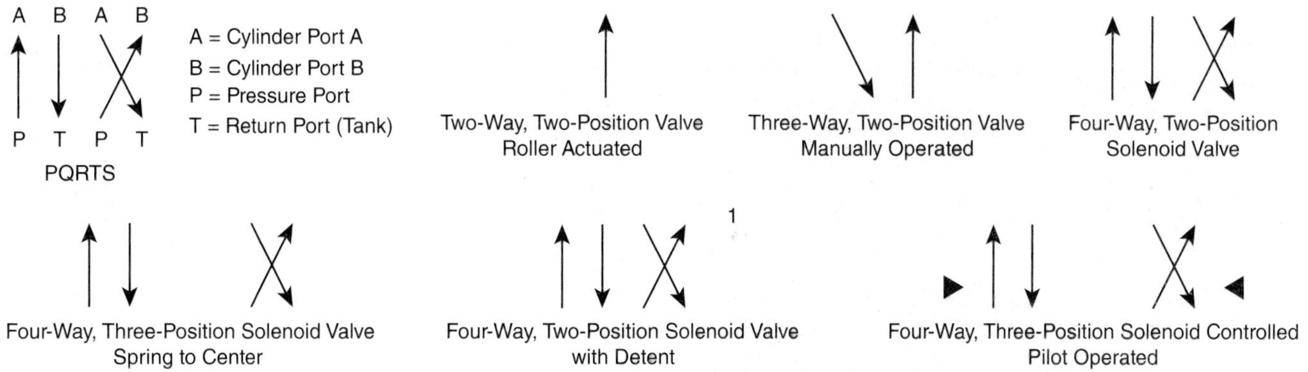

FIGURE 26-58 A variety of DCV symbols.

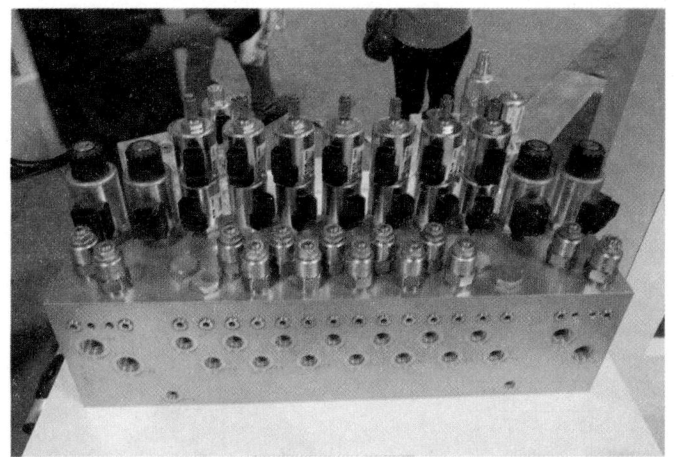

FIGURE 26-59 A cartridge-type control valve.

FIGURE 26-60 A typical cartridge valve.

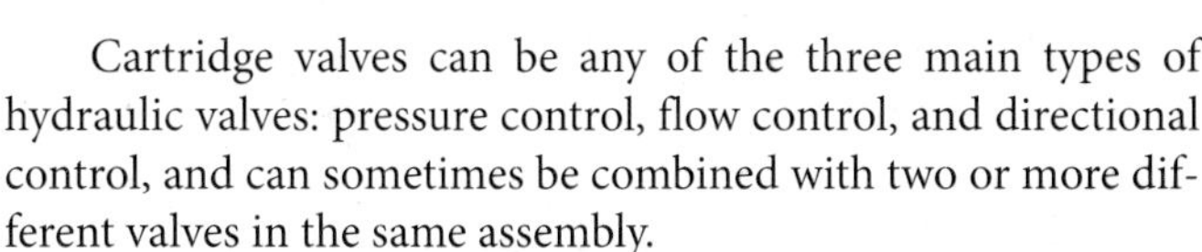

Cartridge valves can be any of the three main types of hydraulic valves: pressure control, flow control, and directional control, and can sometimes be combined with two or more different valves in the same assembly.

Cartridge control valve assemblies start with a solid block of either aluminum or steel and are machined to accept either thread-in or slip-in valve assemblies. Cross drilling passages join the valves in the block with each other, A and B ports, or pump and tank oil. The cross drillings take the place of hoses, tubes, and fittings that would normally be used to join traditional cast body valves that are separated.

FIGURE 26-60 shows a typical cartridge valve. Another benefit of not having valves separated by conductors is a gain in efficiency because of the reduction of heat loss.

Cartridge valves can be used by themselves or combined with many other types and styles of valves in a manifold. They can also be mounted to another component such as a cylinder or motor. In **FIGURE 26-61**, a cartridge valve is mounted on a cylinder. The majority of cartridge valves used on MORE machines are solenoid operated and can be either on/off valves or proportional. On some cartridge valves, two solenoids actuate an on/off–type valve.

One option found on cartridge valves is a function that allows the valve to be actuated manually if there is a problem with its solenoid. Proportional valves receive signals from an ECM that can vary the actuation of the valve.

FIGURE 26-61 A cartridge valve mounted on a cylinder.

The two main types of cartridge valves are thread-in and slip-in. More details on both styles are presented next.

Thread-In Cartridge Valves

Thread-in cartridges are preassembled valves with external threads to mate with threaded bores in the manifold. Grooves hold O-rings in place that create a seal on smooth bore surfaces in the body. **FIGURE 26-62** depicts a thread-in cartridge valve

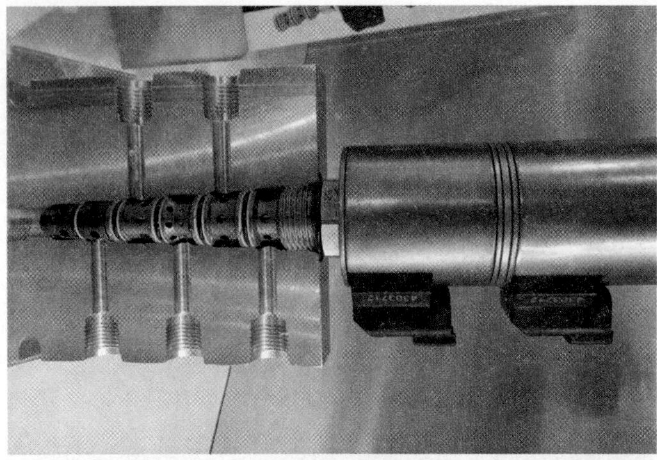

FIGURE 26-62 A thread-in cartridge valve with two solenoids.

FIGURE 26-63 A cartridge-type thread-in valve with the solenoid removed.

assembly with two solenoids. This type of valve is threaded into the valve body and must be torqued to specification. Many thread-in–type valves have a threaded adjustment mechanism to adjust spring pressure. Some thread-in valves are solenoid actuated and have electric coils that fit over the top part of the thread-in assembly. See **FIGURE 26-63** for a cartridge-type thread-in valve with the solenoid removed. When an electrical signal is sent to energize the coil, a magnetic field is created, and the valve core reacts by moving and actuating the valve.

Thread-in–type cartridge valves can be one of three styles: spool, poppet, or ball. **FIGURE 26-64** illustrates these three types of thread-in cartridge-type valves. One example of a common thread-in **cartridge-type directional control valve** is the four-way, three-position, solenoid-actuated valve. It could be used for many applications found on a MORE machine, but one example is to control the quick coupler cylinder on an excavator. The operator moves a locking toggle switch in the cab, and an electrical signal is sent to one of the solenoids on the cartridge valve. This shifts the valve spool and allows pump oil to flow to one end of the coupler cylinder to lock or unlock the coupler. **FIGURE 26-65** shows a four-way, three-position, solenoid-actuated valve.

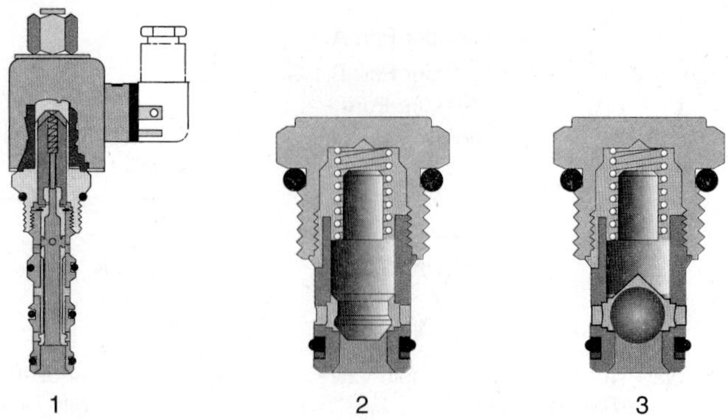

FIGURE 26-64 The three types of cartridge valves.

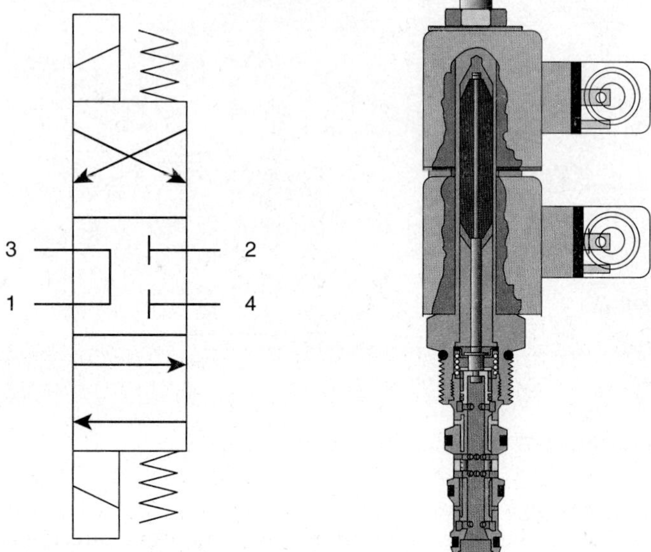

FIGURE 26-65 A four-way, three-position. solenoid-actuated valve.

SAFETY TIP

Use extreme caution when removing a cartridge-type valve because there may be high pressure trapped behind the valve. Follow all pressure release procedures as described in the machine's service information.

Slip-In Cartridge Valves

A second type of cartridge valve is the slip-in type. "Slip in" refers to the way the valve mates with the manifold it is part of. Rather than threads retaining the cartridge valve in the manifold, this type of valve has fasteners to hold the valve in place. See **FIGURE 26-66** for a slip-in–type of cartridge valve. Slip-in cartridge valves have all the same characteristics as the thread-in–type in that they can control pressure, flow, or direction. In some slip-in type valves, a cover houses part of the valve assembly such as a spring adjuster or even a complete valve subassembly like a relief valve. **FIGURE 26-67** shows a slip-in cartridge valve with a cover that houses a solenoid directional control valve.

FIGURE 26-66 A slip-in type of cartridge valve.

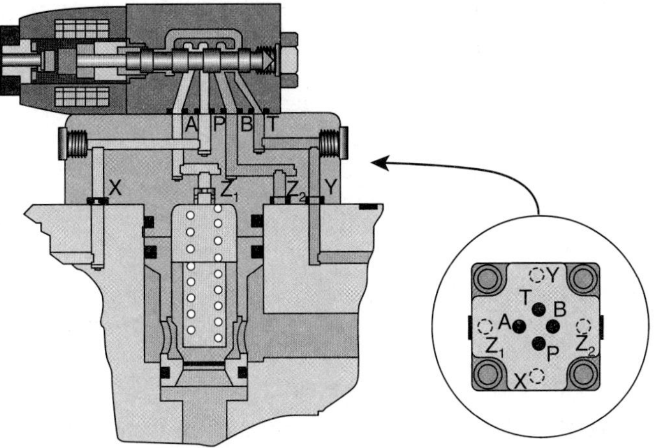

FIGURE 26-67 A slip-in cartridge valve with a cover that houses a solenoid directional control valve.

▶ Common Causes of Valve Failures

K26005

As mentioned earlier in the chapter, hydraulic valves typically provide many thousands of hours of service without the need for major service or repairs; outside of occasional adjustments or leak repairs, they may never be touched by a technician. Design improvements and material technology have dramatically increased valve reliability over the years. The biggest factor in achieving maximum life of hydraulic valves is to maintain fluid condition as per the manufacturer's recommendations. This includes fluid cleanliness, proper viscosity for operating ambient temperature, proper fluid properties/specifications, and keeping fluid temperature within proper range.

There are several possible causes of valve failures, but the most common is fluid contamination. Fluid contamination can cause spool sticking due to very small clearances between the valve spool and its housing. For example, typical clearances are between 5 and 10 microns in spool valves, so any contamination

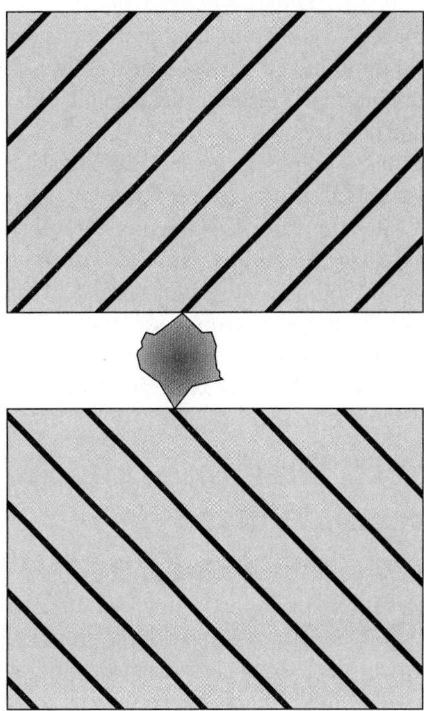

FIGURE 26-68 An example of contamination in a valve.

that can get between the spool and its body could cause the spool to stick. This condition is called silting and can lead to uncontrolled actuator movement if the spool sticks in an actuated position. **FIGURE 26-68** gives an example of contamination in a valve. Larger solid particles can also jam spools, poppets, and balls if they get caught between the movable part of the valves and either its body or seat.

Other Causes of Valve Failures

Outside of contamination as the most common type of valve failure, the following are also possible causes:

1. Seal failure results in oil bypassing internally or leaks externally. Overheated oil, improper installation, damage from other valve components, or improper seal can all be causes of seal failure
2. Misalignment can also cause spools or poppets to stick and jam. Improper installation or excessive wear can cause misalignment.
3. Improper adjustment will result in improper circuit operation.
4. Overheating fluid can cause valves to jam or wear excessively. Overheated oil can be caused by improper pressure settings, overloading the machine, plugged oil cooler, or a defective fan.
5. Broken or weak springs occur because many valves use springs to return them to one position or to hold them closed, and springs can fail completely or lose tension over time, resulting in improper valve operation.
6. Seat damage occurs in valves that use poppets and balls and that have seats that must have a true concentric sealing surface. Contamination or improper adjustment can damage valve seats and cause internal leakage and improper valve operation.

7. Spool or poppet damage happens when movable valve parts are damaged by contamination, improper assembly/installation, or improper operation. Scoring of spools or poppets can cause internal leakage or sticking and leads to improper operation of valve.
8. Valve actuator failure occurs for directional control valves, or any other valve that receives actuation, when the device that actuates the valve fails, leaving the valve inoperable. Reasons include coil failure—if a valve is electrically actuated, the coil can fail internally; pilot oil system failure—could be caused by pressure problem or pilot control problem; and mechanical actuator failure—linkage or cable broken or sticking. All of these lead to a valve that will not actuate.

▶ Inspect, Diagnose, and Adjust Hydraulic Valves

S26002

Hydraulic valves are a key part of any hydraulic circuit or system, and when that system isn't working properly, quite often a technician will have to inspect, diagnose, and adjust one or more valves. The following section looks at common procedures that a technician may perform.

Inspect Hydraulic Valves

Common reasons for inspecting hydraulic valves include improper circuit operation, hydraulic leaks, overheating hydraulic oil, and internal valve condition.

Improper Circuit Operation

Simple visual checks can reveal causes for improper operation. For example, if a valve is mechanically actuated, look for damage or problems with linkages or cables. One easy check is to disconnect the mechanism at the valve and see whether it is free from the valve to the lever or pedal.

Hydraulic Oil Leaks

External leaks can be found by looking for where the clean oil is coming from. The valve may have to be cleaned first, and then you may have to run the machine. Internal leaks are more difficult to find because the leak will usually find its way back to the tank.

▶ TECHNICIAN TIP

Never use cold water to clean a hydraulic valve that is hot. This may cause the valve to distort and jam up, which could lead to damaging the valve.

SAFETY TIP

Always use caution when looking for leaks on a running machine. High-pressure oil will be present, and proper PPE should be used to prevent injury. If the machine has to be operated, make sure there is enough clearance around it, and keep all other personnel away from the area.

Internal oil leaks can be hard to find because small cracks can create internal leaks, and some valve bodies have lots of small cavities. Bore cameras can help you find cracks or other defects in valve bodies.

Overheating Valve

Inspecting a valve for overheating is fairly simple. Look for signs of discoloration to either the paint on it (severe overheating) or even whether the dirt accumulation on it is a different color from the rest of the machine.

▶ TECHNICIAN TIP

To detect overheated components, a small adhesive-backed temperature indicator strip can be fixed to the component. These are color-coded with a range of temperatures, and a small box will turn black to indicate the highest temperature the component has registered. **FIGURE 26-69** shows a temperature indicator strip.

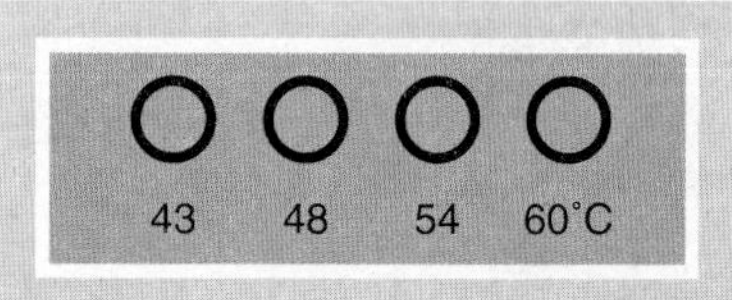

FIGURE 26-69 A temperature strip.

Internal Valve Damage and Wear

If a valve is disassembled, close inspection of the components can reveal light to heavy scoring, damaged seat, general wear, signs of fluid contamination or signs of overheating. Valve internal components should have a consistent finish on them, free of scoring or scratching. To inspect the internal components of a hydraulic valve, a well-lit and clean work bench must be available. See **FIGURE 26-70** for an example of a valve disassembled for inspection.

FIGURE 26-70 A valve disassembled for inspection.

Diagnose Hydraulic Valves

Some hydraulic circuit or system operational problems lead to the necessity of diagnosing hydraulic valves for proper operation. Inspecting valves was covered in the previous section, and external inspection should be the first step of any diagnostic procedure. Diagnostic procedures for hydraulic valves vary depending on the type of valve (pressure, flow, or directional).

Diagnosing Pressure Controls Valves

To determine whether a pressure control valve has a problem, the system or circuit pressure must be measured upstream from the valve for a pressure-relief valve and downstream for pressure-reducing and sequence valves.

SAFETY TIP

Because of the risk of severe injuries that can occur when pressure testing hydraulic systems, *all* manufacturer's service procedures must be strictly followed, and all test equipment must be checked for damage and adequate pressure rating.

Make sure all conditions are met for testing the valve, such as oil temperature, machine function, and engine speed. Install a pressure gauge and/or fittings that are known to be accurate in the correct location, and follow all safety procedures as stated in the machine's service information.

When testing a pressure-relief valve, it is usually necessary to block flow past the valve so that the valve opens. The valve's opening pressure is then measured close to the flow inlet to the valve and compared to a specification. When testing a pressure-reducing valve, it is necessary to install a gauge just past the valve. Run the machine to provide flow through the valve, and then read the pressure gauge.

Diagnosing Flow Control Valves

Flow control valves can be diagnosed with **flow meters** or a stopwatch, because correct flow equates to correct actuator speed. When measuring flow with a flow meter, all test equipment and fittings must be inspected for damage and pressure ratings. It is important that all diagnostic steps are followed and test conditions met.

Adjusting Hydraulic Control Valves

Many hydraulic valves can be adjusted to change either hydraulic pressure or flow. Main system relief pressure for simple systems is adjusted at the main relief valve; other types of more complex systems could have their relief pressure adjusted at the main pump.

Manually actuated DCVs can be adjusted to ensure the spool is in neutral when the control lever is in neutral. A threaded adjuster on the end of the spool valve provides some movement to center the valve. Some valves can be adjusted by changing shim thickness, whereas others are changed with a threaded adjuster.

FIGURE 26-71 An adjustable pressure-relief valve.

Adjusting Main Relief Pressure

Two methods can be used to adjust main relief pressure: shims and a threaded adjuster. Both methods change spring tension in the valve assembly, which in turn changes relief pressure. Adjusting pressure with shims requires partial disassembly of the valve, and threaded adjuster changes can be done with an Allen key or screwdriver and wrench.

Line relief or circuit relief pressure adjustment can be performed in a similar manner to adjusting main relief pressure. Usually, line relief pressure is a few hundred psi higher than main relief. Therefore, the first step is to increase the main relief pressure higher than what is expected for line relief pressure. Once the main relief is set higher, circuit relief can be checked and adjusted to specification. The last step is to adjust the main relief pressure to specification. See **FIGURE 26-71** for an adjustable pressure-relief valve.

SAFETY TIP

Use extreme caution when adjusting relief pressure. If pressure is accidently raised too high, there is risk of component failure as well as the possibility of sudden release of hydraulic oil under pressure.

▶ Recommend Reconditioning or Repairs of Hydraulic Valves

K26006

When it is determined that a hydraulic valve is defective, through a proper diagnostic procedure, a technician must determine whether the valve can be reconditioned or repaired. Depending on the complexity and type of repair needed, it may be necessary to replace the valve, as some repairs are cost prohibitive.

If a valve is leaking externally, it may simply require resealing. Care must be taken to inspect all sealing surfaces for damage, rather than simply replacing a seal. Lubricate seals before assembly, and torque all fasteners to proper specification. When resealing a multi-section directional control valve, extra care must be taken in torquing tie-rod fasteners to avoid

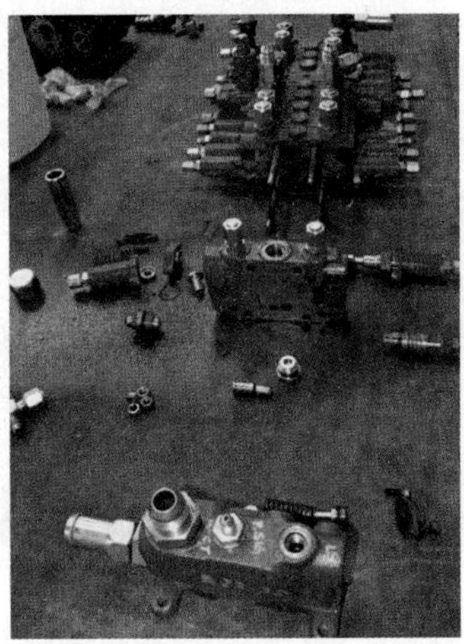

FIGURE 26-72 A multi-section directional control valve.

spool binding. **FIGURE 26-72** presents a multi-section directional control valve disassembled. Thread-in cartridge valves can be resealed or replaced easily.

Spool type valves are usually lap fitted when manufactured, to ensure close tolerances and smooth operation. For spool-type valves other than large monoblock multi-section valves, if either a spool or its body is damaged, the complete valve assembly will have to be replaced.

The exception to replacing spool valve assemblies is large multi-spool DCVs. Because these valves can be very expensive (most are well over $25,000), some minor repairs to their spools or bores are possible. Spools that are scored can be spray welded, ground, and lapped fitted to restore clearances. Valve bodies can be weld repaired and honed, provided damage is not too severe.

To disassemble, inspect, and reassemble a directional control valve, follow the steps in **SKILL DRILL 26-1**.

SKILL DRILL 26-1 Disassembling, Inspecting, and Reassembling a Directional Control Valve

The following procedure is a task that may be required for a couple of reasons, but is not one that is very common. If the DCV is a sectional type, there could be leaks between the sections, or one section might have to be replaced, or severe contamination has been flowing through the system.

1. Cap all open ports, and clean the exterior of the valve.
2. Place valve on a bench covered with clean rags or cardboard.
3. Take several pictures of the valve, and mark all plugs, valves, and so on, that have to be removed.
4. For a sectional valve, remove tie-rod bolts or studs, and separate all sections.
5. For a monoblock type valve, remove all valves, plugs, and spool covers.
6. Remove spools; handle and inspect these carefully. Inspect the valve body carefully.
7. For sectional valves, disassemble one section at a time and inspect carefully.
8. Note any damage or defects, and recommend repair.
9. Thoroughly clean all valve parts.
10. Put the valve assembly together in reverse order, carefully ensuring all parts fit properly. Replace all seals and use hydraulic oil to lubricate all parts at assembly. Ensure spools move freely in bores, and torque all valves and fasteners to specification while following any torquing sequence provided.

▶ Wrap-Up

Ready for Review

- Hydraulic valves are needed to control oil pressure, flow amount, and flow direction in a hydraulic system.
- Main control valve assemblies can have a combination of all three types of valves.
- The majority of all types of valves have at least one movable part inside them—a ball, piston, poppet, or spool.
- Valves typically have between two and five ports to allow oil flow in and out of the valve.
- Spring pressure and/or oil flow hold the movable parts in place or force them to move.
- Internal valve components are precisely machined and hardened to ensure complete sealing and long life.
- Hydraulic fluid must be kept clean to prevent damage and wear to hydraulic valves.
- Pressure control valves manage hydraulic pressure in either circuits or complete systems.
- Pressure control valves are mainly controlled by spring pressure that is usually adjustable, but they could be electronically or hydraulically controlled.
- Pressure-relief valves are pressure-limiting devices used to protect hydraulic systems and their components.
- Direct-acting relief valves are simple normally closed valves that have a wide range of pressure between cracking and fully open. They are spring or shim adjustable.
- Pilot-operated relief valves are two-stage relief valves that use either internal or an external pressure to open a pilot valve that then opens the main unloading valve.
- Unloading valves are used to divert pump flow to the tank when system pressure increases.

- Sequence valves are used to ensure two or more actuators operate in a specific sequence.
- Pressure-reducing valves are used to provide a lower pressure circuit in a hydraulic system. They are normally open valves that close to reduce pressure.
- Load control valves are used to hold or lower, in a controlled manner, a suspended load supported by a cylinder.
- Counterbalance valves hold a suspended load in place until pressure on the opposite side of the cylinder rises high enough to open the valve. They are usually mounted directly on a cylinder like a boom cylinder.
- Vented counterbalance valves have their piston chamber vent to the tank to avoid any influence by back pressure.
- A brake valve is used in a rotary actuator circuit to limit speed when the load tries to overspeed the motor.
- Flow control valves reduce or redirect oil flow from one part of a circuit to another.
- Flow control valves can be either meter-in, meter-out, or bleed-off.
- Three types of flow control valves are noncompensated, pressure compensated, and flow dividers.
- Orifices and needle valves are noncompensated flow control valves and will create a pressure drop as they restrict flow.
- Pressure-compensated flow control valves feature a movable spool that maintains a constant pressure drop across it in order to maintain a constant flow.
- Flow dividers can split one source flow into two or more separate flows equally, with priority or a set ratio.
- Directional control valves can be simple check valves or complex, multi-section, very expensive valve assemblies.
- Check valves allow flow in one direction but block it in the opposite direction.
- Several types of check valves can be found in MORE hydraulic systems, such as shuttle check, in-line check, load check, pilot-operated check, and anticavitation valves.
- Directional control valves with movable spools redirect oil between the pump tank and an actuator.
- DCVs can be part of a main control valve assembly that houses several different types of valves.
- DCV positions refer to the number of positions the movable part of the valve can move to.
- A three-position DCV is the most common configuration for a MORE machine (raise, lower, hold). Sometimes a fourth position is used for float (A to B).
- A regenerative position allows return oil from the actuator to join pump flow.
- A spool-type DCV has a cast steel body with passages cast in it that allow oil transfer.
- Each spool has lands that create a seal in the valve body bore and grooves that allow oil to flow past it.
- The term "ways" refers to the number of ports one section of a DCV has. A common DCV is a four-way valve (pump, tank, A, and B).
- A DCV center section flow pattern determines the type of system it is part of. The two main types are open center and closed center.
- DCVs can be actuated by several methods: mechanically, hydraulically, electrically, or pneumatically.
- Mechanical DCV actuation can start with a lever or pedal and transfer through linkage or cable to the spool.
- Hydraulic actuation is performed with a low-pressure system called a pilot oil system.
- Electrical actuation can be performed by on/off solenoids or proportional solenoids.
- Cartridge valves can be pressure, flow, or directional types, and are preassembled valves that are thread-in or slip-in style.
- Contamination is the most common cause of valve failure.
- To diagnose a pressure control valve, pressure gauges have to be installed downstream from the valve, and specific test conditions must be met.
- To diagnose a flow control valve, a flow meter, stopwatch, or photo tach should be used.
- Some expensive and larger spool valves can be reconditioned.

Key Terms

anticavitation valves Check valves that allow tank oil to flow into an actuator if pressure falls below tank pressure.

brake valve A valve used to limit motor speed when a load tries to overrun it.

cartridge-type directional control valves A style of DCV that has a thread-in or slip-in cartridge that is part of a solid block of machined steel or aluminum.

cartridge valve A type of preassembled valve that is easily serviceable; two types are thread-in and slip-in valves.

check valve A simple valve that allows flow in one direction but blocks it in reverse flow.

direct-acting relief valve A simple normally closed valves that opens when oil pressure overcomes its spring pressure.

float A fourth DCV position that allows free flow between an actuator's A and B ports.

flow divider A component used to split one source flow into two or more separate flows.

flow meter A measuring instrument used to measure oil flow when diagnosing flow problems.

flow pattern Each DCV center section has a certain flow pattern type based on whether flow is allowed between P, T, A, and B or blocked between them.

grooves The smaller diameter part of a valve spool that allows oil to flow past it and through the valve when it is shifted.

lands The larger part of a valve spool that creates a seal in the valve body.

line relief valves Valves that limit system pressure in one section of a circuit.

load check valve A valve used to hold or lower a load in a controlled manner that is supported by a cylinder. Different types of counterbalance valves include counterbalance valves, vented counterbalance valves, brake valves, and pilot-operated check valves.

main relief valves Valves that limit system pressure in a complete system.

metering notches Grooves or notches in lands of spool valves that allow gradual metering of oil to or from an actuator when a valve is shifted.

pilot oil A term to describe a low-pressure oil system used to actuated the spools in a DCV.

pilot pressure A lower pressure hydraulic system that controls a higher-pressure and higher-flow hydraulic system.

pilot-operated relief valve A two-stage relief valve that provides a narrow pressure override.

pressure-compensated flow control valves Valves that maintain a constant pressure drop and flow across them.

pressure override The difference in pressure between a relief valve opening (cracking) pressure and its fully open pressure.

pressure ratio A term used to describe the difference in pressure required to open a valve versus the pressure locked behind it.

pressure-reducing valve A valve that provides a lower pressure for part of a hydraulic system.

pressure-relief valves Valves that limit pressure in one part of a circuit or a complete system.

proportional solenoid Some electrically actuated valves feature proportional solenoid valves that are controlled by an ECM.

pump unloading valve A valve used to divert pump oil flow during high pressure periods to reduce heat and load on the prime mover.

regenerative Another type of DCV position that allows return oil from the actuator to join pump oil going to the other side of the actuator.

sequence valve A valve to ensure two or more cylinders connected in series operate in a specific sequence.

shims Thin round pieces of metal used to adjust spring tension in a hydraulic valve.

shuttle check valve A type of check valve with three ports that sends the higher of two pressures to another component.

spool The name for the movable part of a DCV valve that blocks oil flow and allows oil flow when shifted.

threaded adjuster A mechanism used to adjust spring tension in a hydraulic valve.

valve A component that changes the condition of the hydraulic fluid it comes in contact with, in terms of pressure, flow, or direction.

ways A term used to describe the number of ports that one section of DCV has on its external surface. A four-way valve is commonly used for MORE (ports for pump, tank, A, and B).

Review Questions

1. A valve is a component that changes the condition of the hydraulic fluid it comes in contact with in terms of all of the following, *except*:
   a. pressure.
   b. viscosity.
   c. flow.
   d. direction.

2. Pressure control valves are mainly controlled by ____________________, but they could also be electronically or hydraulically controlled.
   a. diodes
   b. spring pressure
   c. relay
   d. centrifugal force

3. Which of the following is *not* a type of pressure control valve?
   a. Pressure-relief valve
   b. Brake valve
   c. Counterbalance valve
   d. Meter-out valve

4. ____________________ control valves are used to adjust the flow rate to parts of the system, or the whole system, independently of what the directional control valve does.
   a. Flow
   b. Pressure
   c. Viscosity
   d. Heat

5. Flow control valves can be used in three different locations relative to the actuator, to control the actuator speed. Identify the location where the flow control valve is *not* used.
   a. Meter-in
   b. Meter-out
   c. Bleed-on
   d. Bleed-off

6. Which is the most common type of directional control valve found on MORE hydraulic applications?
   a. Electrical type
   b. Stacked type
   c. Spool type
   d. Manual type

7. Typical clearances are between 5 and 10 microns in spool valves, so any contamination that can get between the spool and its body could cause the spool to stick. This condition is called ____________________.
   a. spinning
   b. sticking
   c. slitting
   d. silting

8. ____________________-type valves are usually lap fitted when manufactured, to ensure close tolerances and smooth operation.
   a. Spool
   b. Gate

c. Plug
d. Pinch

9. Which of the following is *not* a type of DCV housing?
a. Monoblock
b. Multi-block
c. Sectional
d. Cartridge

10. Which of the following allow oil flow between the valve ports when the valve is shifted?
a. Lands
b. Spools
c. Grooves
d. Notches

ASE Technician A/Technician B Style Questions

1. Technician A says hydraulic control valves only control pressure and flow. Technician B says hydraulic control valves only control direction. Who is correct?
a. Technician A
b. Technician B
c. Both A and B
d. Neither A nor B

2. Technician A says a hydraulic valve could have a ball, piston, poppet, or spool inside it. Technician B says all hydraulic valves have three ports. Who is correct?
a. Technician A
b. Technician B
c. Both A and B
d. Neither A nor B

3. Technician A says a direct-acting relief valve is mostly used for main system pressure control. Technician B says a pilot-actuated relief valve has a narrow pressure override. Who is correct?
a. Technician A
b. Technician B
c. Both A and B
d. Neither A nor B

4. Technician A says a load control valve is sometimes called a lock valve. Technician B says brake valves perform a braking action for cylinders. Who is correct?
a. Technician A
b. Technician B
c. Both A and B
d. Neither A nor B

5. Technician A says a needle valve is a pressure-compensated flow control valve. Technician B says one type of flow divider is similar to a gear pump. Who is correct?
a. Technician A
b. Technician B
c. Both A and B
d. Neither A nor B

6. Technician A says a load check valve locks a cylinder in place until pressure on the opposite side of it opens the valve. Technician B says a load check valve keeps a cylinder with a load on it from lowering before pump flow can raise it. Who is correct?
a. Technician A
b. Technician B
c. Both A and B
d. Neither A nor B

7. Technician A says a directional control valve that is a three-way valve has three ports. Technician B says a directional control valve with a float position will likely be a fourth position. Who is correct?
a. Technician A
b. Technician B
c. Both A and B
d. Neither A nor B

8. Technician A says cartridge valves are only used as directional control valves. Technician B says cartridge-type pressure control valves can't be adjusted. Who is correct?
a. Technician A
b. Technician B
c. Both A and B
d. Neither A nor B

9. Technician A says silting can cause spool sticking. Technician B says an internal valve leak is easier to find than an external valve leak. Who is correct?
a. Technician A
b. Technician B
c. Both A and B
d. Neither A nor B

10. Technician A says a pressure control valve can be tested with a flow meter. Technician B says a pressure control valve can only be adjusted with shims. Who is correct?
a. Technician A
b. Technician B
c. Both A and B
d. Neither A nor B

CHAPTER 27
Hydraulic Actuators

Knowledge Objectives

After reading this chapter, you will be able to:

- **K27001** Explain the purpose and fundamentals of hydraulic actuators.
- **K27002** Describe the principles of operation of hydraulic actuators.
- **K27003** Describe the types of actuator seals, the materials from which they are made, and their handling and installation.
- **K27004** Describe the common causes of actuator failure.
- **K27005** Understand torque in relation to actuators.
- **K27006** Recommend reconditioning or repairs following manufacturer's recommendations for hydraulic actuators.

Skills Objectives

After reading this chapter you will be able to:

- **S27001** Identify the construction features and types of hydraulic actuators.
- **S27002** Calculate the force or pressure of a hydraulic cylinder.
- **S27003** Calculate hydraulic cylinder speed.
- **S27004** Calculate hydraulic motor power.
- **S27005** Inspect, test, and diagnose hydraulic actuators following manufacturer's recommendations.

▶ Introduction

This chapter describes the two types of actuators, their common identifying symbols, and their functions and applications. It also identifies the parts of each type of actuator and discusses the mounting of actuators, describes the seals used on the different types, and explains the causes of actuator failure. The chapter provides detailed coverage of the mathematical formulas for calculating cylinder force, pressure, and speed. The chapter also covers the concept of torque and the formulas for calculating hydraulic motor power and efficiency.

▶ Purpose and Fundamentals of Hydraulic Actuators

K27001

Hydraulic actuators convert fluid energy into mechanical energy to move a load. MORE (mobile off-road equipment) manufacturers use two types of actuators on their machines: linear actuators, such as hydraulic cylinders (sometimes called rams); and rotary actuators that are more commonly called hydraulic motors.

Hydraulic Cylinders

Hydraulic cylinders, or rams, are linear actuators: they provide for a linear form of energy transfer to produce either linear or angular motion. In fluid power systems, the hydraulic cylinder, which houses the piston and rod, enables the lifting or moving of heavy components and materials in mobile heavy equipment applications (**FIGURE 27-1**). They have three basic parts, a barrel, rod, and piston (**FIGURE 27-2**), and come in various types: single-acting and telescoping cylinders, double-acting cylinders, and double-rod cylinders.

Oil flow to a cylinder starts at the hydraulic pump, which delivers oil to a directional control valve and then to the hydraulic cylinder where it acts on the **piston**. The piston then makes the rod move, and the oil on the opposite side of the piston flows back to the reservoir. Typically the rod has an eyelet welded to it and is pinned to a moveable implement, so as the rod moves, the implement moves. An excavator stick cylinder is a good example of this, where it has the barrel pinned stationary to the boom, and the rod pinned to the end of the stick. As oil is supplied to the cylinder piston, travel is transferred through the rod and makes the stick move back and forth. In some cases, the rod is stationary, and the barrel moves as oil flows into the cylinder. This arrangement is sometimes found on excavator boom cylinders.

FIGURE 27-1 A hydraulic cylinder used to move an excavator stick.

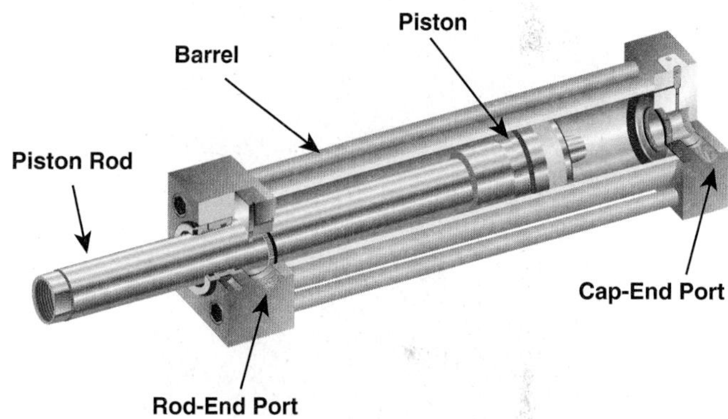

FIGURE 27-2 The basic components of an actuator: rod, barrel, and piston.

You Are the Mobile Heavy Equipment Technician

As a MORE (mobile off-road equipment) technician you work for a contractor that owns several skid steer loaders. The machines are used for snow clearing and have hydraulic snow blower attachments that replace the machines' buckets when there are large snow accumulations. The snow blowers rely on hydraulic motors to spin augers that throw the snow a fair distance away. The company's equipment manager has asked if it is possible to make the snow blowers move the snow further. It is your job to investigate all options to make the machine more effective at moving snow.

Answer the following questions related to the above scenario:

1. What would you need to know in relation to the machines existing hydraulic system that would allow you to calculate the theoretical speed of the snow blower?
2. How could you safely measure the speed of the snow blower?
3. What considerations would need to be made if the hydraulic system is modified to increase the speed of the snow blower?
4. What options are available to increase the speed of the snow blower?

Single-Acting and Telescoping Cylinders

Telescoping cylinders have multisection rods consisting of a two- to five-section assembly. They are used where long rod travel is needed and space is limited. Each succeeding section is smaller in diameter than the next one. As the rod sections extend, they start with the largest diameter first, and each smaller-diameter section follows.

In a single-acting cylinder, the oil flows into only one side of the cylinder to extend the rod. Cylinders return to their original positions by gravity usually, or a spring (**FIGURE 27-3**). These cylinders have limited uses on mobile off-road equipment (MORE).

Telescoping Cylinders

Telescoping cylinders can be single-acting (power up) or double-acting (power up and down) cylinders that have two or more rod sections that are extended **sequentially** (**FIGURE 27-4**). For MORE machines, they are mostly used in vertical to near vertical applications for single-acting cylinders, while a double-acting cylinder could be used for any position.

FIGURE 27-3 One possible application for a single-acting cylinder.

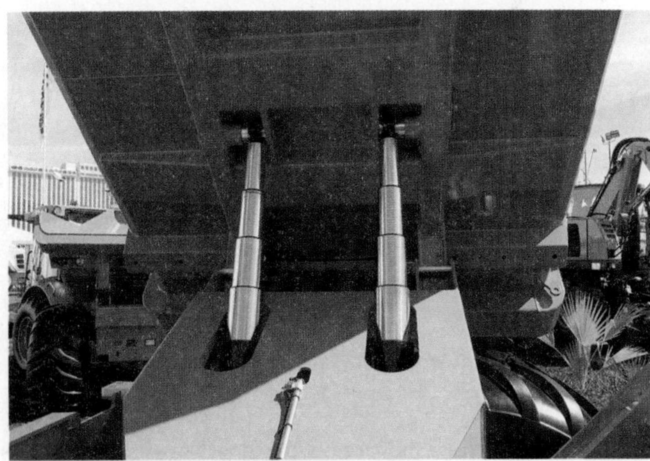

FIGURE 27-4 A pair of telescoping cylinders.

Oil flows into the bottom of the cylinder to extend the rod sections, and the weight of the boom and/or load causes the rod sections to retract. Single-acting telescoping cylinders only require one oil port at the base of the barrel.

On MORE such as haul trucks or articulating trucks, telescoping cylinders are used for hoisting and lowering the machines box or bed. They are usually double acting because these machines sometimes must have down pressure to lower the box if the machine is not level.

Double-Acting Cylinders

Double-acting cylinders have two oil ports. Supply oil flows into the barrel end port to extend the cylinder's rod, and oil flows into the cap end port to retract the rod (**FIGURE 27-5**). An example of an application of a double-acting cylinder is one that lifts and lowers a loader boom. Depending on which port receives oil flow from the pump, the rod us either forced out of the barrel or retracted into the barrel, which in turn raises or lowers the loader boom.

Rotary Actuators and Hydraulic Motors

Typically, hydraulic motors provide continuous **rotary** motion, whereas rotary actuators provide a limited rotation, usually up to a maximum of 360 degrees. They provide for a rotary form of energy transfer to produce rotary motion, providing torque as the force output to the load. Hydraulic motors are almost identical to hydraulic pumps in their construction and components (**FIGURE 27-6**). Pumps create fluid flow when their shaft is driven, whereas motors create torque when they receive oil flow. They provide continuous rotation using fluid power input to provide mechanical power output. In contrast, a hydraulic pump uses mechanical power input to produce fluid power output. Most hydraulic motor applications require rotation in both directions, and these motors are considered to be bidirectional.

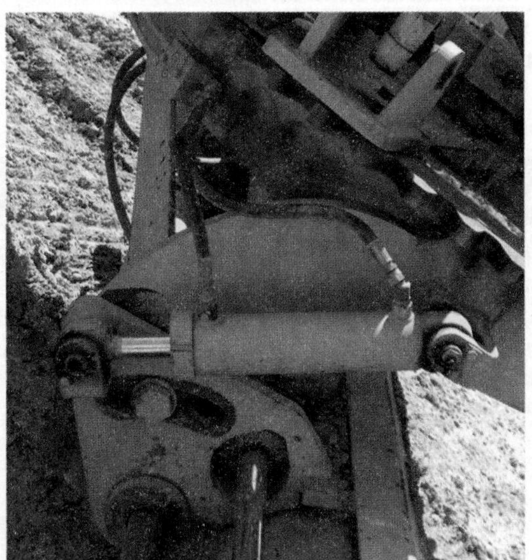

FIGURE 27-5 A double-acting cylinder.

FIGURE 27-6 A hydraulic motor used to drive the upper structure of a crane.

▶ TECHNICIAN TIP

Hydraulic motors are almost identical in construction to hydraulic pumps. Refer to Chapter 25, "Hydraulic Pumps," for detailed information about hydraulic pumps.

Hydraulic Actuator Symbols

FIGURE 27-7 shows the actuator symbols that hydraulic circuit diagrams use.

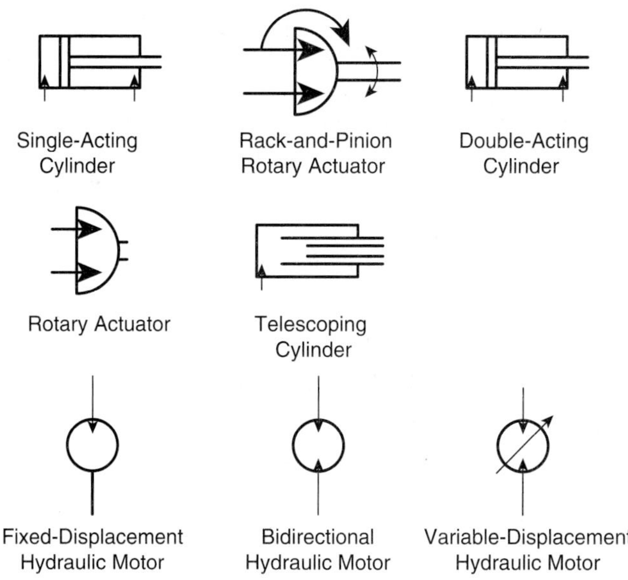

FIGURE 27-7 Symbols for common types of hydraulic actuators.

▶ TECHNICIAN TIP

Many variations on these basic symbols exist. However, the basic symbol for a linear actuator starts with a rectangle, and the one for rotary actuators starts with a circle. Perform a simple keyword search online for additional examples.

▶ Functions and Applications of Hydraulic Actuators

S27001

This next section discusses where hydraulic actuators may be used on MORE machines and how the operate.

Hydraulic Cylinders

MORE machine manufacturers use hydraulic cylinders for everything from steering and hoisting the box on haul trucks to moving the bucket on giant shovels in open-pit mines. Hydraulic cylinders can provide either linear or angular motion through the linkage they are attached to. Cylinders that provide linear motion (**FIGURE 27-8**) mount rigidly so that they cannot move from their original alignment. All motion resulting from their extension or retraction is linear and along the centerline of the cylinder.

Cylinders for angular motion are **trunnion** or **clevis** mounted so that the cylinder is free to pivot from its original alignment. This allows the load to move in an arc. An example of an application of **angular** motion is a bucket cylinder on an excavator, where its rod end eye moves through an arc as it extends and retracts.

Hydraulic Motors

As with hydraulic pumps, manufacturers use different designs of hydraulic motors to provide the best match for specific applications. Hydraulic motors provide continuous rotary motion and are available in fixed- and variable-displacement arrangements. They can also be bidirectional, meaning their output

FIGURE 27-8 Example of a hydraulic cylinder, on a scraper, that provides linear motion.

FIGURE 27-9 Cooling fan motor.

shaft can rotate clockwise or counterclockwise. Manufacturers use them in a wide range of applications:

- Internal and external gear types are designed for low-speed, high-torque applications to drive components directly, for example, in propulsion wheels, conveyors, and road brushes.
- Vane types are used on a hydraulic crane or arm, along with a grapple, clamshell bucket, or any other attachment that requires rotary motion to assist in positioning.
- In-line axial and bent-axis piston types can either be used where high speed with low torque is needed, such as a cooling fan motor, or they can be used where low speed and high torque are needed, such as traction drive motors for dozers. **FIGURE 27-9**.

▶ Hydraulic Actuator Construction

K27002

The construction of single- and double-acting cylinders is similar, but they operate differently. In the single-acting cylinder, power assistance is in only one direction and relies on the weight of the load to return it to the original position. The double-acting cylinder design provides power assistance in both directions and is not load dependent.

Both types of cylinder are constructed in a similar way; that is, each has a cylindrical **housing**, commonly called the barrel, that enables mounting to a secure location, fixing it at one end. Barrels can be a one- or two-piece design, with a separate rod end cap. The barrel end that is opposite of the rod end is called the head end and is usually welded to the barrel. It typically has a means to mount the cylinder to a fixed part of the machine and is usually machined to accept a bearing.

The rod cap's main functions are to enclose the barrel at one end and to guide the rod as it moves. For most linear actuators used on MORE machines, the rod cap is bolted or threaded to the barrel. Some machines use lighter-duty cylinders that have barrels with separate caps at both ends that are held together with tie rods. A static seal and O-ring combination between the barrel and the cap(s) seals the cap(s) to the barrel. The bottom end of the cylinder (opposite of the rod end) is usually called the head end.

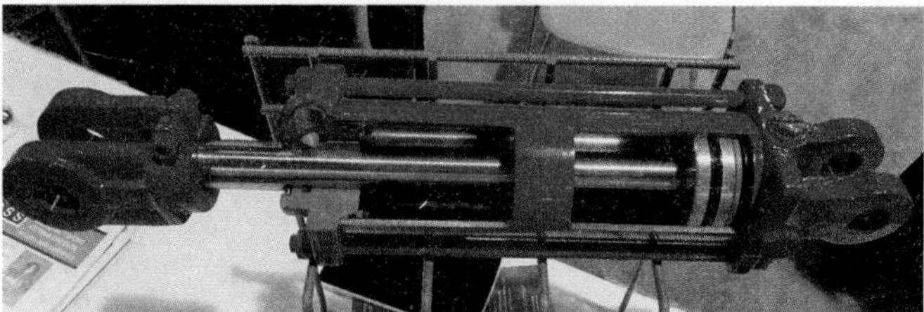

FIGURE 27-10 Cutaway view of a hydraulic actuator.

The barrel has a bore that is machined and honed inside it, within which a close fitting piston can move. Connected to the piston is a chrome plated **rod** that transfers piston movement, thereby providing linear movement to anything that is attached to the end of the rod (**FIGURE 27-10**). The rod is mated to the piston with a large threaded nut, large bolt, or a series of smaller bolts. Machined grooves on the piston accept seals and wear rings. The cylinder rod cap also has grooves machined into it to accept seals and a wear ring. The wear rings help prevent metal-to-metal contact between the piston and barrel, and the piston and rod cap.

The opposite end of the barrel from the cap is the rod cap. It is usually fastened to the barrel with a series of bolts, and a machined and sealed bore allows the rod to travel through the center of the barrel. The rod cap creates a sealed chamber, and the piston divides the chamber into two separate chambers that change in volume as the piston is moved along the barrel. Smaller cylinders have rod caps that thread into the barrel. Either type of rod cap must have seal(s) between it and the barrel to create a sealed chamber at the top of the cylinder.

Single-acting cylinders have a **vent** at the rod end to allow the cylinder to remain at atmospheric pressure on the rod side of the piston.The vent has a screen or filter to stop moisture and contamination from entering the cylinder.

FIGURE 27-11 shows the parts of a single-acting cylinder, and **FIGURE 27-12** depicts the parts of a double-acting cylinder.

Vane-Type Actuators

Manufacturer's construct vane-type rotary actuators (**FIGURE 27-13**) similar to vane type pumps. The vane motor is an alternative solution to the external gear actuator manufacturers use for high-speed, low-torque applications. Like a vane pump,

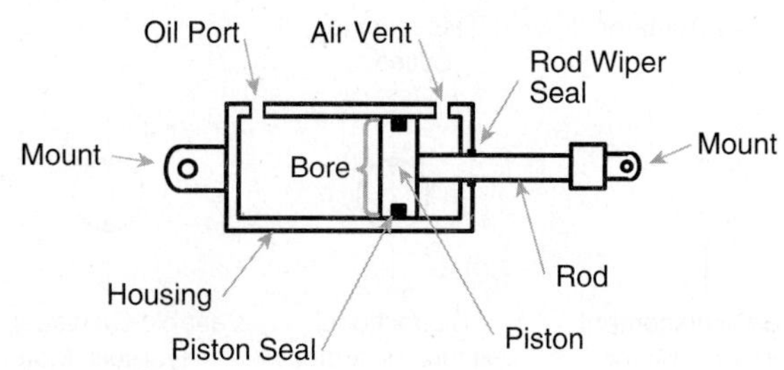

FIGURE 27-11 Single-acting cylinder construction.

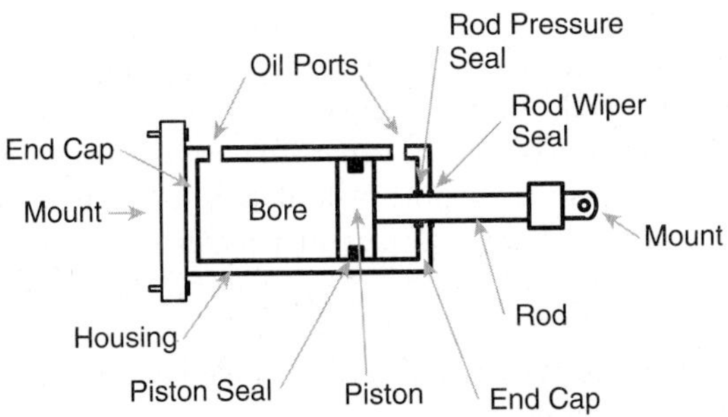

FIGURE 27-12 Double-acting cylinder construction.

FIGURE 27-13 Cutaway view of vane-type rotary actuator.

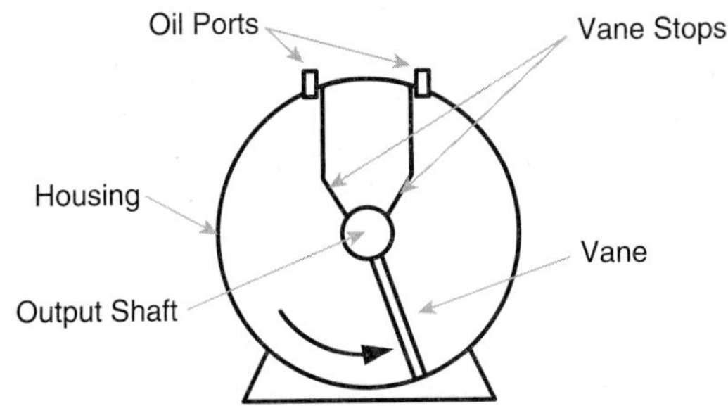

FIGURE 27-14 Vane-type rotary actuator construction.

it is constructed of vanes that rotate inside a cam ring and are guided by close fitting slots in the rotor. The center of the rotor is splined to an output shaft that turns as a result of fluid flow to the motor. Fluid enters the oil port on one side of the motor and leaves from the oil port on the opposite side (**FIGURE 27-14**).

FIGURE 27-16 Rack-and-pinion rotary actuator construction.

Vane motors usually have springs under the vanes to keep them out against the cam ring.

Rack-and-Pinion Rotary Actuators

There are two variations of rack-and-pinion rotary actuators. In the one in **FIGURE 27-15**, two opposing single-acting linear actuators attach to a common piston rod, or **rack**. **Teeth** machined into the rack piston rotate a pinion gear when the pistons move back and forth, according to which end of the piston hydraulic fluid is applied to. Rotation can be less or greater than 360 degrees. The second type has a barrel with a rack gear on the outside of the barrel (**FIGURE 27-16**). It is a double-rod type where both rods are fixed to the machine, and as oil is sent to one end of the cylinder, the barrel moves along the piston.

Hydraulic Motors

Hydraulic motors receive oil flow from the pump and convert this flow into mechanical torque that is transferred out the motors shaft. The types of motors that could be found on MORE machines include internal gear, external gear, vane, and piston.

In an external gear type hydraulic motor (see **FIGURE 27-17** for an example of an external gear type motor), the hydraulic fluid enters the inlet port and acts on the gear faces inside the pump housing, forcing the gears to turn. It then leaves through the outlet port on the opposite side of the housing. The driving

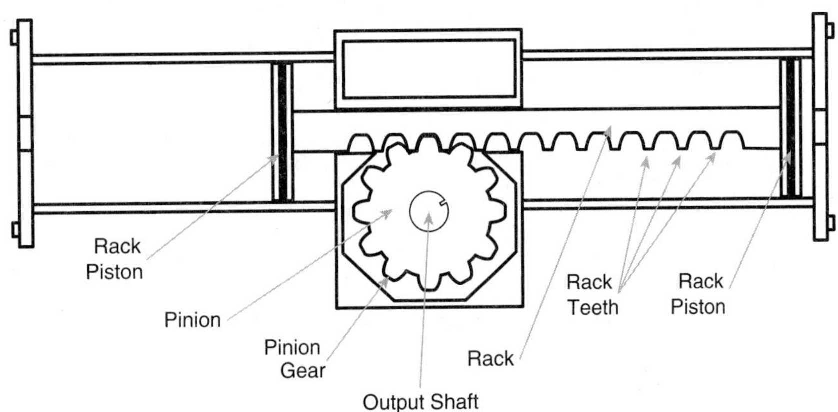

FIGURE 27-15 Cutaway view of rack-and-pinion rotary actuator.

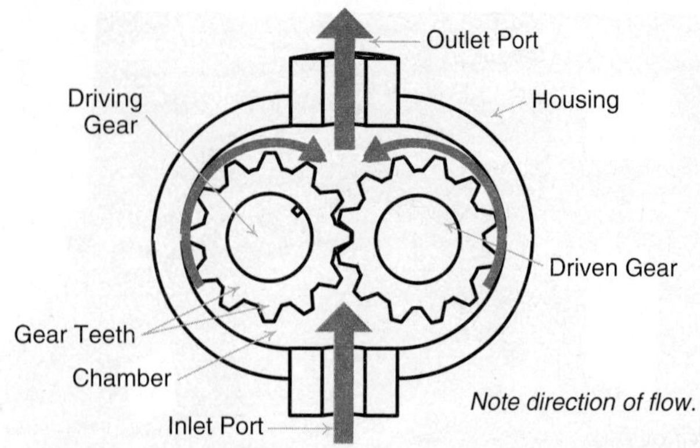

FIGURE 27-17 The parts of an external gear hydraulic motor.

gear drives the output shaft via a keyway to drive the component the motor is rotating. The driven gear acts as an idler in this example.

Hydraulic system motors can be axial piston, bent axis piston, or cam lobe–type motors, and smaller machines can also use gerotor or geroller motors.

Motors are rated by the amount of fluid it takes to create one shaft revolution (similar to pump ratings—the amount of oil flow created by one shaft revolution) or by their rpm output per flow rate received. The other important rating is the maximum torque output capability. For example, a fixed displacement motor for a broom attachment has an rpm output of 1,000 rpm per 36 gpm) and a maximum torque of 1,250 ft-lb at 2,500 psi.

Axial Piston Motor

Many MORE hydraulic systems use axial piston motors to convert fluid flow to mechanical rotation. This type of motor is similar in construction to axial piston pumps that create flow in that they use a swashplate, pistons, and cylinder block to convert fluid flow to shaft rotation for torque output. The opposite is true for an axial piston pump; it uses piston movement to create fluid flow.

Physically it is hard to tell the difference between an axial piston pump and motor. This is true for most pumps and motors that operate on the same principle.

Oil flows into one of the two main ports of the motor housing and goes through a port plate that is stationary. The port plate has a lap-finished surface that mates with the cylinder block. As the oil flows into the cylinder block, it pushes half of the pistons down the swashplate while the other half of the pistons move up the swashplate and push oil out the other main port. As the pistons push down the swashplate, they carry the cylinder block with it. The block then drives the output shaft of the motor.

> **TECHNICIAN TIP**
>
> The Internet offers many animations of hydraulic motor operation available for viewing. You can find one of the best examples of this at http://www.poclain-hydraulics.com/portals/0/tools/training/pompes/Pompe_circuit_ferme 2.swf. Check this one out or find others that will help you visualize how a hydraulic motor works.

This style of motor can be fixed or variable displacement. An example of this is a motor in a track loader that has a requirement of 3.5 cubic inches per revolution for low speed (maximum displacement) and can change to a displacement of 2.0 cubic inches per revolution for high speed (minimum displacement).

An axial piston motor can also be bidirectional. This means pump flow can be sent to either of two ports, and by switching the flow between ports, the motor shaft rotation reverses.

To change displacement, this type of motor has a control piston to move the swashplate to either minimum or maximum displacement. The oil pressure to do this comes from a solenoid valve on the motor or one that is mounted remotely. **FIGURE 27-18** shows a cross section of a variable displacement axial piston motor.

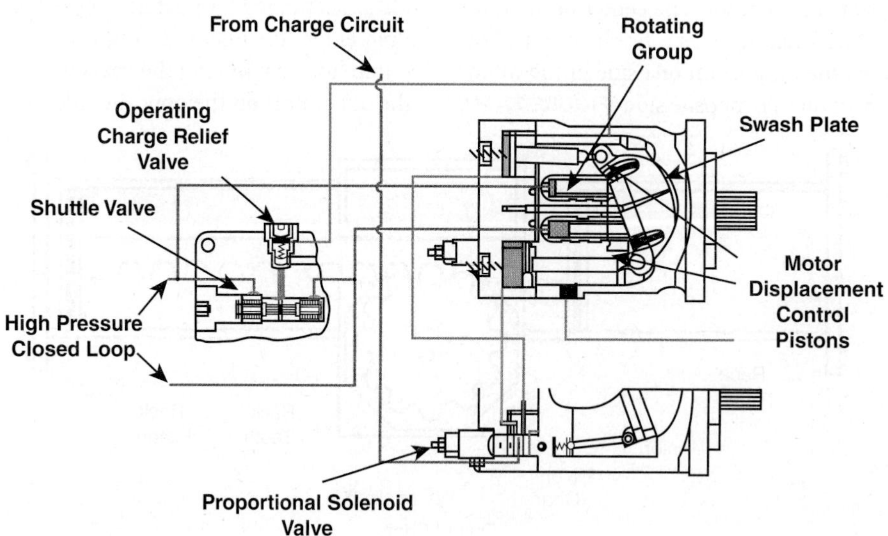

FIGURE 27-18 Variable displacement axial piston motor.

Image Provided As Courtesy of John Deere.

Bent Axis Motor

The cylinder block centerlines of bent axis motors are at an angle to the output shaft centerline. Two tapered roller bearings in the housing support the motor's shaft assembly. The cylinder block and pistons drive the motor.

The pump sends oil into the motor through the inlet port of the housing, and it goes through the port, past a bearing plate, and into the valve segment. The valve segment has two slots to allow oil to transfer between the bearing plate and pump housing end cap. The bearing plate provides a bearing surface between the rotating cylinder block and the nonrotating valve segment. The valve segment is able to move a few degrees if the motor is a variable displacement type; otherwise, it is fixed. The valve segment has a stub shaft protruding from it that fits into a bearing in the end of the cylinder block. This supports the cylinder block in the housing.

For a variable displacement motor, the opposite side of the valve segment has an outward curved shape that matches to a bearing surface on the bottom of the motor end housing. When oil feeds into the cylinder block where the pistons are at the top of their stroke, the oil forces the pistons down into the barrel for half of the motor's rotation. When oil pressure forces the pistons down, this makes the cylinder block rotate.

The cylinder block connects to the motor's shaft with a synchronizing shaft with two sets of three evenly spaced rollers protruding out from it. The rollers fit into grooves in the shaft assembly and the cylinder block. This is similar to a type of constant velocity joint for a front-wheel drive car. A spring on the inside of the shaft assembly keeps the cylinder block seated against the bearing plate and valve segment.

The bottoms of the pistons have a ball-shaped end and are supported in the shaft assembly in sockets. **FIGURE 27-19** shows an exploded illustration of a bent axis piston motor.

A variable bent axis motor has minimum and maximum displacement stops to stop the movement of the barrel between two points. There is a servo piston with a recess in it where the pin from the back of the valve segment engages. When the motor's displacement control (electric solenoid controlled) sends oil to one end of the servo, it moves, and moves the cylinder block with it, to move toward a lower displacement. This is the high-speed, low-torque mode for the motor. A spring returns the piston when the displacement control drains the oil.

Cam Lobe Motor

Also called a radial piston motor, a cam lobe motor uses a series of eight pistons, oriented in a radial arrangement in a carrier, with rollers attached to their bottom ends. The carrier turns the output shaft for the motor. Cam lobe motors can be bidirectional and are commonly found as the output for hydrostatic drive systems.

The pistons move in and out of the carrier as the rollers ride around the inside of an internal cam. The internal cam has six

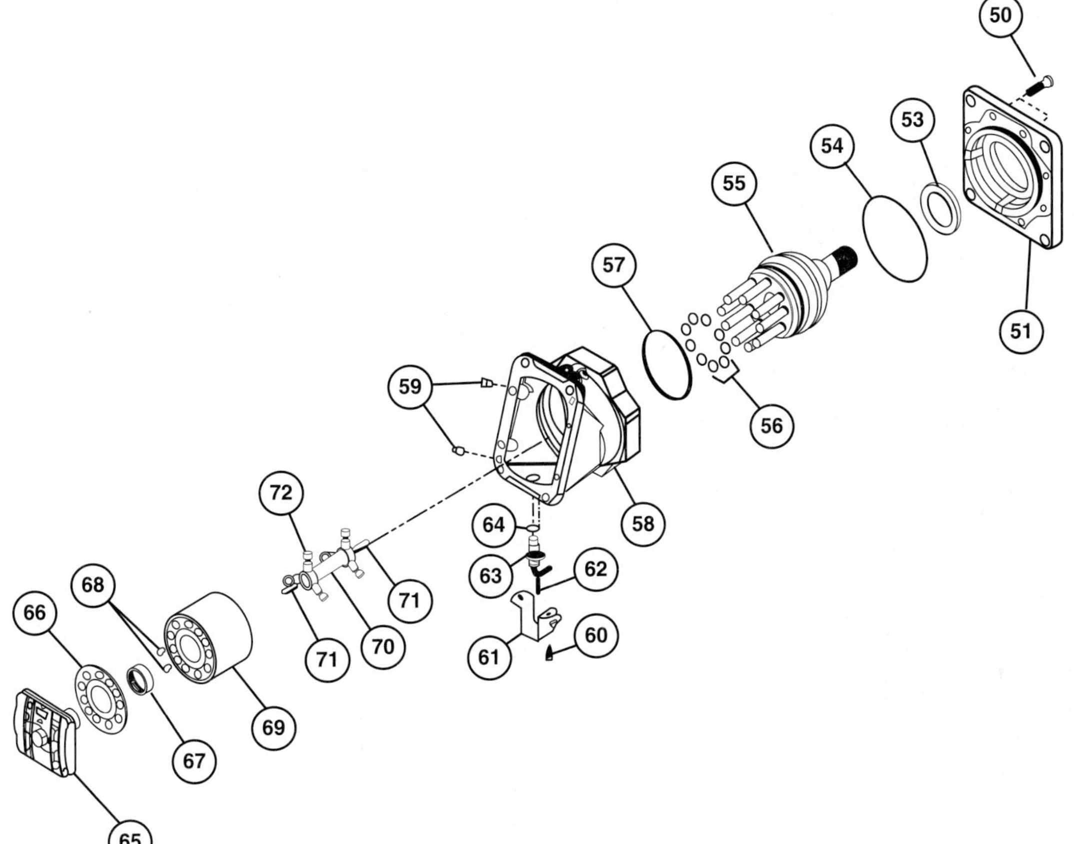

FIGURE 27-19 Exploded view of bent axis piston motor.

Image Provided As Courtesy of John Deere.

equally spaced lobes on the inside diameter of the cam ring. Oil pressure feeds into the motor housing through one of two ports. The other port directs oil out of the motor. The ports feed oil to a manifold that has passageways machined into it. These manifold passageways connect to ports on the outer circumference of the manifold. Six ports connect to one of the main motor ports, and six ports connect to the other main port. When the system pump supplies oil to one of the motor's main ports, the manifold can send oil to four of the pistons at any time. The other four pistons align with the return port. The remaining four ports are blocked off temporarily. To start the motor turning, the oil pressure pushes four pistons and rollers down cam lobes, and because the pistons are in bores in the carrier, the carrier rotates. The other four pistons are also carried around and ride up cam lobes. This pushes oil out of the carrier through the manifold and out of the motor into the low-pressure side of the loop. Once the motor starts turning, all pistons constantly move in and out of the carrier and ride up and down the cam profiles.

As you can imagine, port timing is critical to the operation of this style of motor because there must be a seamless transition between the oil flow in and out of the motor to the pistons that are either pushing down cam lobes or returning back into the carrier. **FIGURE 27-20** shows a cross section of a cam lobe motor.

Orbital Motor

Lighter duty hydraulic systems sometimes use an orbital motor to convert fluid flow into mechanical torque. Also called gerotor and geroller motors, the several variations of these motors fall into three main groups: disc valve, spool valve, and valve in star. These different types of orbital motors relate to how the oil is distributed within the motor as it moves to and from the main ports.

The motors all work on the same principle of having an inner and outer rotor with coarse "teeth," or lobes. The inner rotor has one less tooth than the outer rotor, and their centers are offset. The outer rotor's center is on the same axis as the output shaft, and the inner rotor's axis is offset from the outer rotor's axis.

As oil enters the motor, it goes into a small chamber between inner and outer rotor teeth. The applied pressure makes the rotors turn as the chamber expands. The expanding chamber reaches a maximum volume. As rotation continues, chamber volume decreases, forcing fluid out of the chamber and out the return port. The process occurs constantly for each chamber, providing a smooth pumping action. If oil is sent to the opposite port, the motor turns in the opposite direction if the motor is a bidirectional type.

The inner rotor has internal splines that drive an externally splined drive shaft. The splines are machined to allow the offset between the inner rotor and the output shaft as rotation occurs. This shaft is sometimes called a cardan shaft.

A geroller motor has rollers on the ends of the outer rotor teeth to reduce friction and improve longevity. The inner rotor has one less lobe than the rollers so that one lobe is always in full engagement with the rollers at any one time. This allows the rotor lobes to slide over the rollers, creating a seal to prevent pressure oil from returning to the inlet side of the motor. This change causes the orbiting gerotor to make as many power strokes as it has teeth for every revolution of the output shaft. The six-tooth gear shown makes six power strokes while the output shaft turns once. **FIGURE 27-21** shows a geroller type motor.

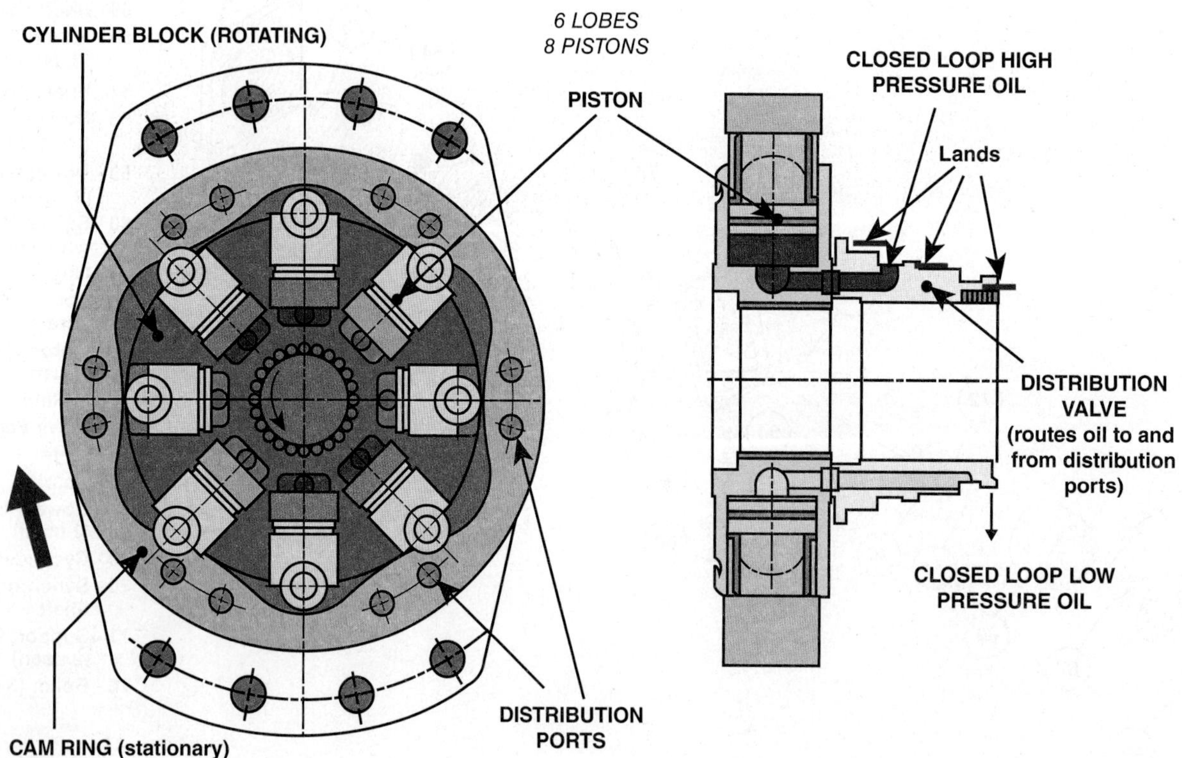

FIGURE 27-20 Cam lobe motor.

Image Provided As Courtesy of John Deere.

Gerotor motors give at or near full torque from about 25 rpm and normally do not go higher than 250 to 300 rpm. Maximum output torque relates directly to the width of the gerotor element, which may be as narrow as 1/4 in. (6.35 mm) to 2 in. (51 mm). Pressure ratings as high as 4,000 psi (276 bar) are common from most manufacturers.

Some gerotor motors have a selector valve that changes the internal rotary valve output to feed only half the chambers, causing the motor to run at twice the speed and half the torque.

Mounting of Hydraulic Actuators

Use or application determines mounting of actuators. Mechanisms that produce linear motion use threaded fasteners to mount the barrel to a frame with **flanges** on the barrel (**FIGURE 27-22**). Typically, the head end and rod end have self-aligning bearings that are pin-mounted to the machine or the implement. Manufacturers typically mount mechanisms that produce angular motion with trunnions or clevises, through which bolts attach them to the machine (**FIGURE 27-23**).

FIGURE 27-22 Barrel flange mounting.

▶ Seals on Hydraulic Actuators

K27003

Seals are critical when it comes to maintaining hydraulic equipment, no matter what the application (**FIGURE 27-24**). Machine downtime can be more expensive than the actual cost of repair, so it is cost-effective for the technician not to take shortcuts during repairs or maintenance of machinery, and to always check the condition of seals.

Seal Types

Manufacturers use various types of seals in hydraulic actuators (see **FIGURE 27-25**), including these listed here:

- **O-rings:** O-ring seals are used for static applications where two parts mate and are fastened together. They can

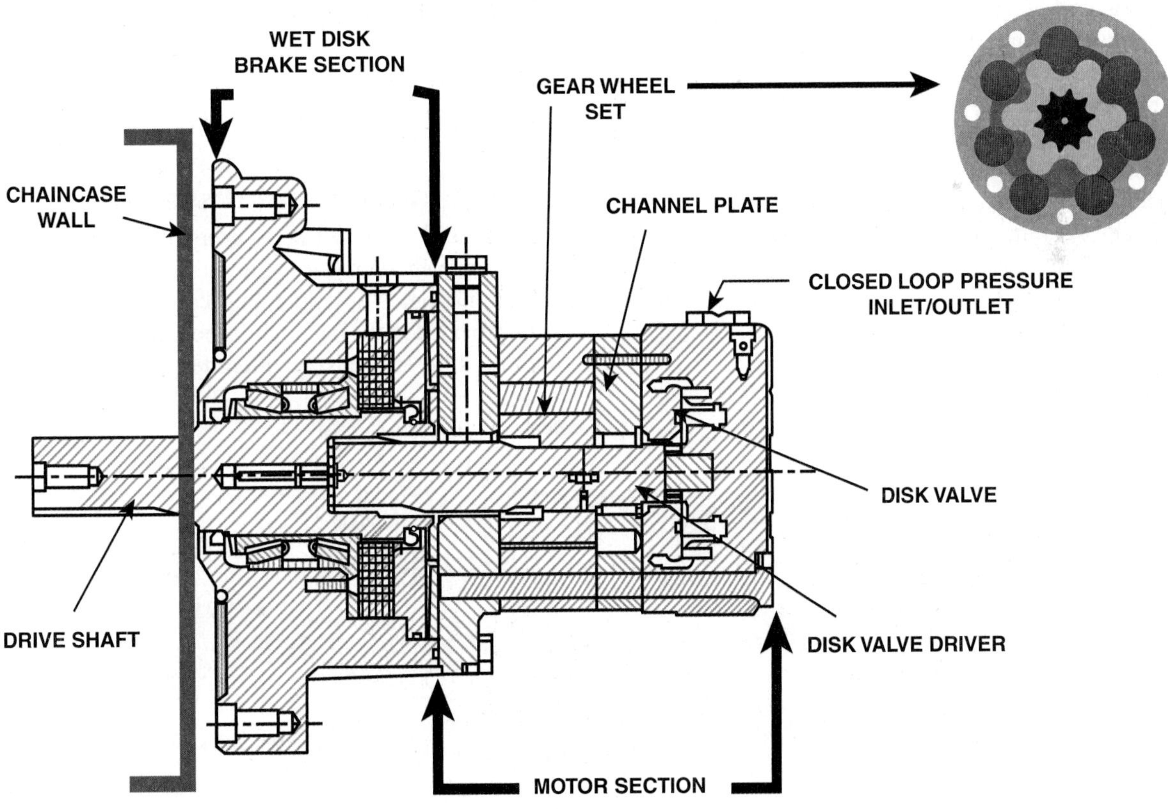

FIGURE 27-21 Geroller motor.

Image Provided As Courtesy of John Deere.

FIGURE 27-23 Clevis mounting.

withstand pressures of 5,000 psi (345 bar) or more. Manufacturers use O-rings as seals to close off passageways in actuators, preventing the loss of hydraulic fluid. Applications include: sealing cap to barrel, sealing motor housings together, and sealing hoses to cylinders.

- **Piston rings:** Similar to engine piston rings, piston ring type seals produce the least friction but are prone to leakage. They are used for creating a dynamic seal where two parts are in relative motion to each other. They can sometimes be found on the pistons in piston motors.
- **Cup seals:** These high-pressure seals are very tolerant of out-of-round cylinder barrels. Cup seals seal in only one direction, so two seals are needed. Some arrangements can work with systems dealing with pressures up to 6,000 psi (420 bar).
- **Lip seals:** These are available as either V-ring (chevron) or U-ring types. These are commonly used for sealing cylinder rods to rod caps, pistons to barrels, and motor shafts to housings.
- **T-seals:** T-seals require backup rings to seal. These are available for both rod and piston sealing applications, and manufacturers use them for pressures up to 6,000 psi (420 bar). The T-seal is designed as a retrofit arrangement for conventional O-ring seals and eliminates "spiral" or "twisting" seal failures that can occur when O-rings are used against a dynamic surface.

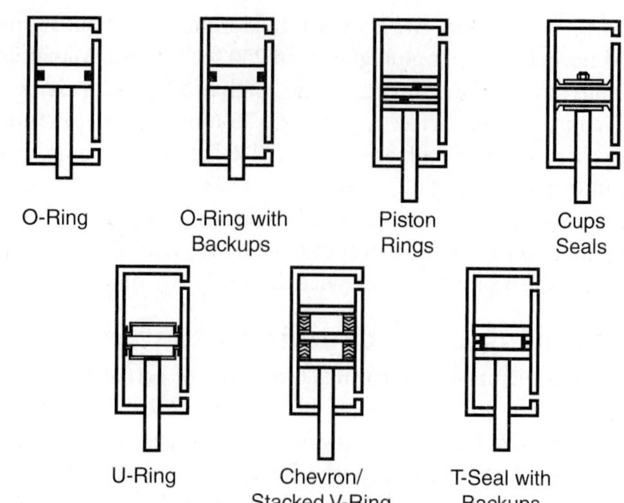

FIGURE 27-25 Seal types.

Seal Materials

Manufacturers make seals primarily from the following types of material:

- **Elastomeric:** A natural or synthetic material that has particular elastic characteristics and the ability to return to its original shape after a deforming force is removed.
- **Metallic**: Composed of metal and hard-wearing by definition.
- **Composite**: Comprised of several substances, with a range of durability and wear characteristics.
- **Fiber wear rings:** Made from a variety of materials, such as fiberglass, silica, and rubber, for use on pistons, to keep the piston centered in the bore, which prevents metal-to-metal contact between piston and barrel.

Seal Handling and Installation

HDETs need to install seals properly, using the appropriate tools to prevent damage, and in a clean environment to prevent contamination. When changing seals, you must change all the seals provided in the kit, not just those that appear to be leaking, because different seals are often dependent on one another as

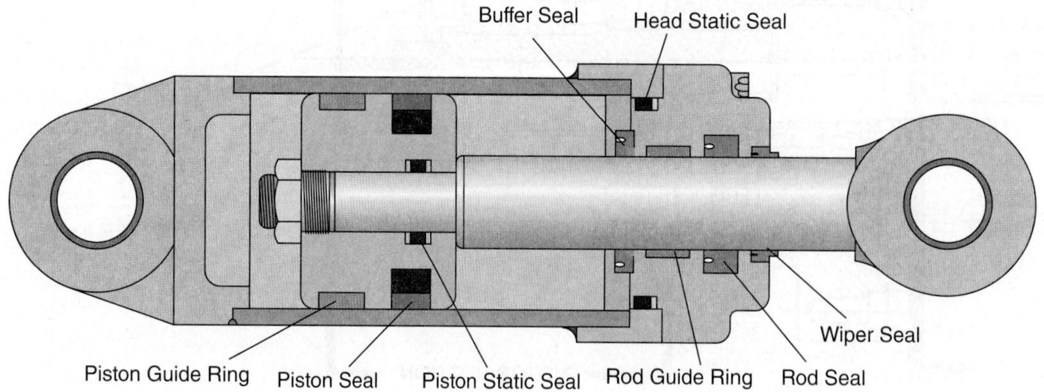

FIGURE 27-24 Seal use on a hydraulic cylinder.

FIGURE 27-26 Seals come in a range of types and sizes, and their use depends on the application.

part of a complete assembly. Lubricate all components during assembly, as most seals can be damaged when moving against a dry surface, even for a short a period of time (**FIGURE 27-26**).

SAFETY TIP

Do not use sharp tools for installation.

Common Causes of Actuator Failure

K27004

Hydraulic actuators may fail due to the following causes:

- Leaking piston seal
- Leaking rod seal
- Defective rod wiper seal

  Note: A defective wiper seal will often cause a leaking piston seal, a leaking rod seal, or a **scored** cylinder barrel because it allows contamination to enter the cylinder.

- Scored cylinder barrel
- Nicked or damaged rod
- Bent rod

See "Testing, Diagnosing, and Trouble-Shooting Actuator Problems" in this chapter for the causes and solutions to these issues.

Calculating the Force or Pressure of a Hydraulic Cylinder

S27002

To make calculations regarding pressure or force of a hydraulic cylinder, first determine the area of the piston. This section describes the relationship between force, pressure, and area. It reviews Pascal's law and provides the formulas, with examples, that you need to calculate force in both a single-acting cylinder and a double-acting cylinder.

Pascal's Law

Pascal's law, the principle of transmission of fluid pressure, states that pressure applied anywhere to a body of fluid causes the pressure to transmit equally in all directions. To solve for force, Pascal's law may be mathematically expressed as:

$$F = p \times A$$

where:

F = Force
p = Pressure
A = Area

(Force equals Pressure multiplied by Area.) This may be inverted to solve for pressure:

$$p = F \div A$$

(Pressure equals Force divided by Area.)

Force is measured in kilograms (kg), and area is measured in square centimeters (cm^2). Pressure is measured in bar. In the imperial system, force is measured in pounds (lb), pressure in pounds per square inch (psi), and area in square inches ($in.^2$).

Calculating Force in a Single-Acting Cylinder

1. First calculate the area of the cylinder, using the following formula:
   - Area (A) equals π (or **pi**) multiplied by the square of the cylinder's radius (r): $A = \pi r^2$

     Note: In hydraulics applications, the diameter of the cylinder (the **bore**) is often known. Use the cylinder bore, to calculate the radius.
   - Radius is half the diameter (d) of the cylinder, or: $r = \dfrac{d}{2}$
   - Though usually calculated in terms of radius, area can also be calculated in terms of diameter, as follows:

$$A = \frac{\pi \times d^2}{4}$$

TECHNICIAN TIP

The decimal representation of π is infinite and therefore must always be approximated. Always approximate π consistently throughout an equation or series of equations. Note that rounding π to two places of decimals (3.14) is adequate for illustration purposes; for real-world applications, greater precision (3.14159 ...) may be required.

2. To use a cylinder's area to solve for force (or pressure), using Pascal's law, follow the steps in the examples below.

Example 1

Determine the force produced by a cylinder with a 5 cm diameter if the operating pressure is 140 bar.

- Use the formula $F = p \times A$.
- Pressure (p) is a known quantity: 140 bar.
- Calculate area (A), using the diameter of the cylinder (d):

$$A = \frac{\pi d^2}{4}$$

$$A = \frac{\pi (5)^2}{4}$$

$$A = \frac{\pi\, 25}{4} = \frac{78.5}{4}$$

$$A \approx 20 \text{ cm}^2$$

▶ TECHNICIAN TIP

The ≈ symbol means "equals approximately," which in Example 1 means the number 20 cm^2 is a round number. To write π without rounding (when using the π key on a calculator for example), use "3.14159 …"

- Plug pressure (p) and area (A) into the formula, and solve:

$$F = p \times A$$

$$F = 140 \text{ bar} \times 20 \text{ cm}^2$$

$$F = 2{,}800 \text{ kg}$$

Example 2

Determine the pressure required for a cylinder with a 7.62 cm bore to move a 5,500 kg load.

- Use the formula $F = p \times A$.
- Load (F) is a known quantity: 5,500 kg.
- To find the formula for calculating pressure, divide both sides by A:

$$F = pA$$

$$\frac{F}{A} = \frac{pA}{A}$$

$$\frac{F}{A} = p$$

$$p = \frac{F}{A} \text{ or } p = F \div A$$

- Calculate area (A), using the bore/diameter of the cylinder.
- Plug in the values to calculate the pressure.

Calculating Force in a Double-Acting Cylinder

In a double-acting cylinder, force capability is different on extension versus retraction. On retraction, the area subjected to hydraulic pressure is lower than on extension because the area taken up by the rod is not used to move the load. On extension, the effective area is the entire face of the piston; on retraction, the effective area is the piston area minus the rod area.

▶ TECHNICIAN TIP

To prevent confusion, use subscript to distinguish multiple related terms (A_{rod} versus A_{piston}) in an equation.

1. To calculate the effective area on extension (entire face of piston), use the formula:

$$A_{piston} = \frac{\pi d^2_{piston}}{4}$$

2. To calculate the extension force, use the formula:

$$F_{extension} = p \times A_{piston}$$

3. To calculate the effective area on retraction (piston area minus rod area), use the formula:

$$A_{effective} = A_{piston} - A_{rod}$$

4. Calculate the rod area like the piston area:

$$A_{rod} = \frac{\pi d^2_{rod}}{4}$$

5. To calculate the retraction force, use the formula:

$$F_{retraction} = p \times A_{effective}$$

Example

Determine the extension and retraction force capabilities of a double-acting cylinder if the cylinder bore is 7.62 cm and the rod diameter is 2.54 cm. The pressure available is 100 bar.

1. **Calculate extension force.**
   - Calculate extension force using the formula:

$$F_{extension} = p \times A_{piston}$$

   - Pressure is a known quantity: 100 bar.
   - Calculate area (A), using bore/diameter of cylinder (d):

$$A_{piston} = \frac{\pi d^2_{piston}}{4} = 45.6 \text{ cm}^2$$

   - Plug in the values to calculate the extension force:

$$F_{extension} = p \times A_{piston}$$
$$= 100 \times 45.6$$
$$= 4{,}560 \text{ kg}$$

2. **Calculate retraction force.**
   - Calculate retraction force using the formula:

$$F_{retraction} = p \times A_{effective}$$

   - Calculate effective area using the formula:

$$A_{effective} = A_{piston} - A_{rod}$$

- First, calculate piston area and rod area:

$$A_{piston} \text{ (solved above)} = 45.6 \text{ cm}^2$$

$$A_{rod} = 5.07 \text{ cm}^2$$

- Then plug in the numbers to determine effective area:

$$A_{effective} = A_{piston} - A_{rod}$$

$$A_{effective} = 45.6 \text{ cm}^2 - 5.07 \text{ cm}^2$$

$$A_{effective} = 40.53 \text{ cm}^2$$

- Plug in the values to calculate retraction force:

$$F_{retraction} = p \times A_{effective}$$

$$F_{retraction} = 100 \text{ bar} \times 40.53 \text{ cm}^2$$

$$F_{retraction} = 4{,}053 \text{ kg}$$

▶ Calculating Hydraulic Cylinder Speed

S27003

The speed at which a cylinder extends or retracts is a function of the flow rate of oil entering (or, in some cases leaving) the cylinder. The following calculations are for the flow rate entering the cylinder.

Find the speed, or velocity (v), of a cylinder using the formula:

$$v = \frac{Q}{6A}$$

where:

Q = Flow rate, in liters per minute (lpm), or gallons per minute (gpm) for imperial units
A = Area available, in square centimeters (cm²), or square inches (in.²) for imperial units
v = Velocity, in meters per second (mps), or feet per second (fps) for imperial units
6 = Factor (3.12 for U.S. gallons)

Double-Acting Cylinder

The following example describes how to determine the extension and retraction speeds of a double-acting cylinder with a given bore and a given flow rate.

Example

Determine the extension and retraction speed of a double-acting cylinder that has a 7.62 cm bore and a 5 cm rod if the flow rate available is 15 lpm.

1. **Calculate extension speed.**
   - Remember that the extension speed calculation uses the full piston area. Therefore:

$$A_{piston} = \frac{\pi d^2_{piston}}{4} = \frac{\pi (7.62)^2}{4}$$

$$= 45.6 \text{ cm}^2$$

   Therefore, the extension speed is:

$$v_{extension} = \frac{Q}{6A_{piston}} = \frac{15}{6 \times 45.6}$$

$$= 0.055 \text{ mps}$$

2. **Calculate retraction speed.**
   - In retraction, the area available for the fluid to act on is the effective area—that is, the area of the piston minus the area of the rod.
   - The area of the piston, calculated above, is 45.6 cm².
   - The area of the rod is:

$$A_{rod} = \frac{\pi d^2_{rod}}{4} = \frac{\pi (5)^2}{4} \approx 20 \text{ cm}^2$$

   - Therefore the effective area is:

$$A_{effective} = 45.6 \text{ cm}^2 - 20 \text{ cm}^2 = 25.6 \text{ cm}^2$$

   - Therefore the retraction speed is:

$$v_{retraction} = \frac{Q}{6A_{effective}} = \frac{15}{6 \times 25.6 \text{ cm}^2} \approx 20 \text{ cm}^2$$

$$= 0.1 \text{ mps}$$

▶ TECHNICIAN TIP

General Observations Regarding Hydraulic Cylinder Force, Pressure, and Speed

You can draw the following conclusions regarding cylinder force, pressure, and speed from the examples provided:

- A double-acting cylinder has more force capability on extension than on retraction for any given pressure.
- A double acting cylinder has a faster retraction speed than extension speed for any given flow rate.
- The force a cylinder produces is purely a function of pressure. Flow rate is not considered.
- The speed of operation of a cylinder is purely a function of flow rate. Pressure is not considered (assuming that there is sufficient pressure to move the load in the first place).

▶ Understanding Torque

K27005

Rotary actuators produce a different kind of output force than linear actuators. This rotational force about an axis is known as **torque**.

- **Linear** force is the pushing or pulling of an object.
- Torque is the twisting or rotating force applied to rotate an object about an axis.

In the metric system, force is measured in kilograms (kg). Torque is measured in newton meters (N·m).

Torque Definitions

A newton meter (N·m) is the twisting force that a lever 1 m long with a force of 1 N applied to the end of the lever applies to a shaft.

In the imperial system, force is measured in pounds (lb) and torque is measured in foot-pounds (ft-lb) or inch-pounds (in-lb). These terms are equally acceptable expressed as pound-feet (lb-ft) or pound-inches (lb-in). A foot-pound (ft-lb) is the twisting force that a lever 1 foot long with a 1-pound mass on the end applies to a shaft. To change in-lb to ft-lb, divide by 12 (1 ft = 12 in.).

Torque Conversions

1 N·m = 0.74 ft-lb
1 N·m = 8.85 in-lb
1 ft-lb = 1.35 N·m
12 in-lb = 1 ft-lb
1 in-lb = 0.08 ft-lb

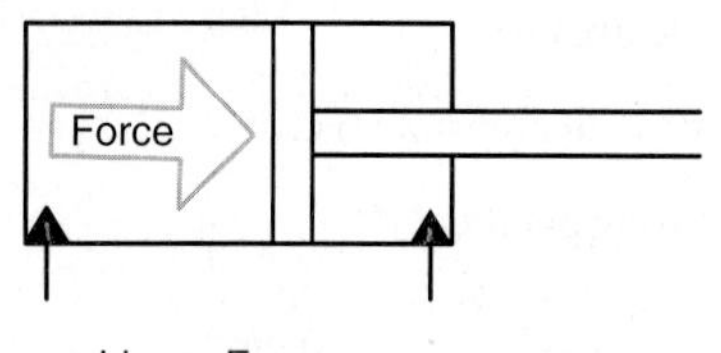

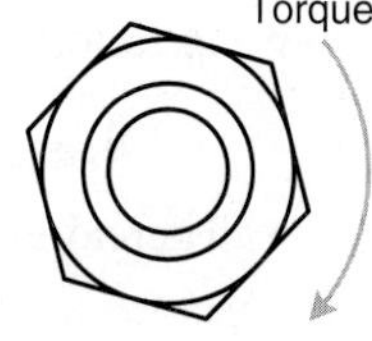

Rotary Actuator Torque Calculations

Rotary actuators do not produce linear force as cylinders do. These actuators produce rotary force, or torque, as their output force.

Calculate torque, or rotary force, with the formula:

$$\text{Torque} = \text{Force} \times \text{distance}$$

or

$$T = F \times d$$

where:

T = Torque, in newton meters (N·m)
F = Force, in newtons (N)
d = Distance, in meters (m)

If the force to rotate the nut is applied a distance of 0.2 m from the center point of the nut, and a force of 900 newtons (N) is applied, we can calculate the torque applied to the nut as follows:

$$\text{Force} \times \text{Distance} = \text{Torque}$$

$$F \times d = T$$

$$900 \text{ N} \times 0.2 \text{ m} = 180 \text{ N·m}$$

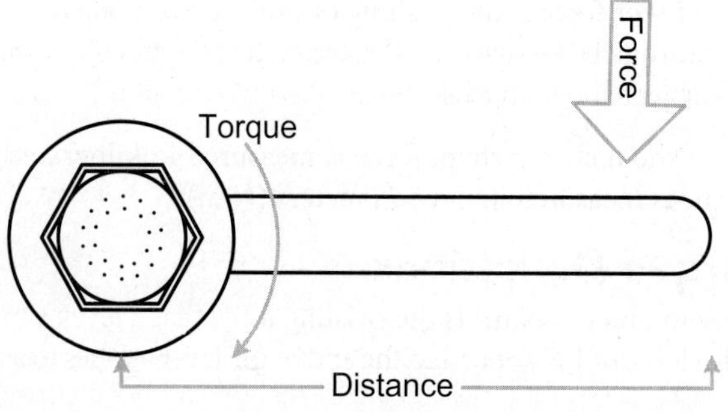

▶ Hydraulic Motor Calculations

S27004

Calculating Power

To calculate the output power output of a hydraulic motor, use the following formula:

$$p = \frac{T \times N}{9{,}549}$$

where:

p = Output power, in kilowatts (kW), or horsepower (Hp) for imperial units
N = Shaft speed, in revolutions per minute (rpm)
T = Output torque, in newton meters (N·m), or foot-pounds (ft-lb) for imperial units
9,549 = Factor (5,252 for imperial units)

Example

Find the output power of a hydraulic motor operating at 2,400 rpm with an output load of 95 N·m.

$$p = \frac{T \times N}{9{,}549} = \frac{95 \times 2{,}400}{9{,}549} = 24 \text{ kW}$$

▶ Testing, Diagnosing, and Trouble-Shooting Actuator Problems

S27005

Monitoring noise, drifting, leakage, and power loss helps prevent component failure and downtime. In most cases, simple observation of operating conditions can lead you to the proper corrective actions.

Leaks

The following may cause rod leaks in actuators:

- Pressure too high
- Damaged rod or rod bearing
- Fluid contamination
- Extreme temperatures
- Chemicals

Fluid Contamination

Contaminated fluid can cause the rod seal to fail prematurely. Abrasive particles suspended in fluid can damage the piston rod surface and the seal. A bad wiper seal can draw airborne contamination into a cylinder. Water can contaminate in mineral oil systems. This affects the fluid's lubricity and can cause seal materials to "age harden" at temperatures more than 149°F (65°C). Hydrolysis can affect polyurethane seals in high water-based fluids at temperatures above 122°F (50°C). This can lead to a loss of tensile strength and hardness, which can cause the rod seal to leak fluid.

Air can contaminate fluid, which in turn can cause damage to piston rod seals. Pressure shocks in systems with rapid cycling speeds may cause air bubbles to become charged with heat energy, often called "dieseling." This happens particularly in rod-up (vertical) applications in which a fast increase in hydraulic pressure causes localized, intense heating of bubbles on the primary seal's lip. Air in the fluid may also intensify the transmission of vibration, which may lead to other forms of failure.

Hydraulic fluid by nature contains air that cannot be removed. But this is not a problem. Leaks and damage occur when bubbles come out of the solution. Bubbles are caused by overloads, decompressing too fast, and extreme flow through too small of a port. If a cylinder is installed and bled correctly, but continues to experience air problems, one of these causes is probably the cause. This is especially true with water glycol fluids, for they can dissolve more air than mineral oil fluids.

High-Pressure Leaks

High-pressure leaks rarely occur with today's polyurethane seals. Leaks as a result of inadvertent high pressure on the piston can occur with seals made of other material. Severe, "meter-out" flow restriction at the head end of a cylinder that has an oversized piston rod can subject the seal to a back pressure equal to two times system pressure. If the equipment continues to operate in this condition, it can cause the seal to deteriorate quickly due to excessive friction, primary seal extrusion, and even rod cartridge or retainer failure.

Cylinder Drifting

Some conditions of a hydraulic circuit cause an actuator cylinder to drift when the cylinder's four-way control valve is in the center, neutral location. The reason is an unbalance between areas across the piston. Oil under pressure that leaks across the spool of the four-way valve puts pressure unequally on parts of the piston, which creates a force unbalance. This can cause undesirable piston movement unless there is adequate reactionary or dead load against the rod to restrain the piston drift. Internal oil leakage may also cause drifting (see below).

> ▶ TECHNICIAN TIP
>
> You can hear piston seal leakage and sometimes feel it on the barrel. Internal leakage also causes the temperature to increase in the cylinder. For example, if there are two blade-lift cylinders on a dozer, and in one of them a leaky piston seal has caused drift, that cylinder will be hotter than the other one.

Piston Seal Leakage

If the gravity or reactionary load is pulling the rod out, it is impossible to assemble the external circuit so that there is no drift in either an open- or closed-center system. Although leak-tight piston seals can prevent cylinder drift from a reactionary load on the piston rod or valve spool leakage, sometimes drift caused by leakage across the valve spool may persist, and you must replace the piston seals.

If the reactionary or gravity load pushes against the piston rod, you may be able to use a high-quality four-way valve with blocked cylinder ports in neutral to minimize drift. With no intensified pressure in the rod end of the cylinder, pilot pressure from the blind end of the cylinder does not permit a lock or check valve to close, allowing flow in either direction.

Piston seal leakage is a major problem in closed-center systems; sometimes it is almost impossible to reduce cylinder drift completely. Valves and cylinders for these types of systems must have extremely low leakage ratings.

> ▶ TECHNICIAN TIP
>
> Most manufacturers' service information includes allowable specifications for cylinder drift rates. For example, 1 inch in 5 minutes may be acceptable. Generally if you can see a cylinder drift, it is excessive.

Abnormal Noise

Cavitation (bubbles in the hydraulic fluid) or aeration (air mixed into the hydraulic fluid) are common causes of abnormal noise around actuators.

Cavitation happens when the volume of the hydraulic fluid that the actuator is demanding exceeds the volume the system can supply. The absolute pressure in the system then falls below the hydraulic fluid's vapor pressure. This causes vapor cavities to form in the fluid that implode when compressed, and a knocking sound results.

Cavitation can erode metal parts, which damages components and contaminates the hydraulic fluid. In some cases, this can lead to parts failure. Cavitation can happen anywhere in a hydraulic circuit, but the most likely place is at the pump. A restricted intake line or plugged inlet strainer can cause the hydraulic fluid in the line to vaporize. It is important to keep strainers and filters clean. If the intake line has a gate-type isolation valve, the valve must be open fully. A closed valve vibrates, causing noise. A restricted or collapsed intake line between the pump and reservoir can also cause noise. Replace worn intake lines.

> ▶ TECHNICIAN TIP
>
> If a load moves the rod faster in the cylinder than the pump can supply fluid to the cylinder, this can create voids and cavitation.

Aeration can cause knocking and banging noises as it compresses, then decompresses while circulating through the system. You may also notice fluid foaming and system damage that is a result of overheating, loss of lubrication, and burnt seals.

Air comes into the system via the pump inlet. Make sure all fittings and clamps are secure, and intake lines are not collapsed or brittle. Check to make sure there is enough fluid in the reservoir. Low fluid can cause a vortex to develop, which allows air into the pump. Air can also enter through the pump's shaft seal. Replace a leaking seal.

Low Power

Low power is a good indication that something is not right with the system. Low power means slower operation and longer cycle times. Flow determines the actuator's response and speed. Loss of speed means flow loss.

> **TECHNICIAN TIP**
>
> Low power and low speed are two different problems. Low power results from a pressure loss such as a seal bypassing or a system pressure problem. Low speed is a result of loss of flow or low flow. Internal leakage could cause this, or a supply problem could be the reason.

Hydraulic fluid can escape because of internal or external leakage. A leaking hose is obvious, but hidden internal leaks can happen in valves, in the actuator itself, or in a pump. When you have an internal leak, you have reduced pressure. This generates heat. You can use an infrared thermometer to identify parts that have internal leaks. If this is not revealing, try a hydraulic flow tester.

Internal leaks spontaneously increase heat on components and on hydraulic fluid. When the temperature of the fluid goes up, the fluid's viscosity goes down. With a decrease in viscosity, we see an increase in internal leakage. Internal leaks cause heat to increase, which causes fluid temperature to increase. Catching this damaging cycle early saves component wear and downtime.

▶ Inspection and Repair Procedures

K27006

Disassembling, Inspecting, and Reassembling a Hydraulic Cylinder

To disassemble, inspect, and reassemble a hydraulic cylinder, follow the guidelines in **SKILL DRILL 27-1**.

Testing a Cylinder for External and Internal Leakage

To test a cylinder for external and internal leakage, follow the steps in **SKILL DRILL 27-2**.

> **SAFETY TIP**
>
> HDETs must be aware of the hazards of working with hydraulic fluid and strictly adhere to safety precautions when working on any hydraulic system.
>
> - Hydraulic fluid passes through extremely small openings in an operating system. The fluid is under high pressure, often exceeding 5,000 psi.
> - The HDET must wear PPE (personal protective equipment) when performing maintenance on hydraulic systems. This must include eye protection and gloves.
> - Temperature of hydraulic fluids is between 165°F and 185°F (74°C and 85°C), created from pressure when hydraulic systems operate. This presents a burn hazard.
> - Hydraulic oil is also a fire hazard. When the oil ignites, it can be fatal or produce severe burns.
> - Search for small leaks by running a piece of wood or cardboard along a hydraulic hose. Do not search for leaks using your finger or hand. At high pressure, hot hydraulic oil can puncture gloves and penetrate several inches into soft tissues. Hydraulic oil, soft-tissue penetration can only be removed surgically.

Inspecting and Replacing Seals

To inspect and replace a seal, follow the steps in **SKILL DRILL 27-3**.

SKILL DRILL 27-1 Disassembling, Inspecting, and Reassembling a Hydraulic Cylinder

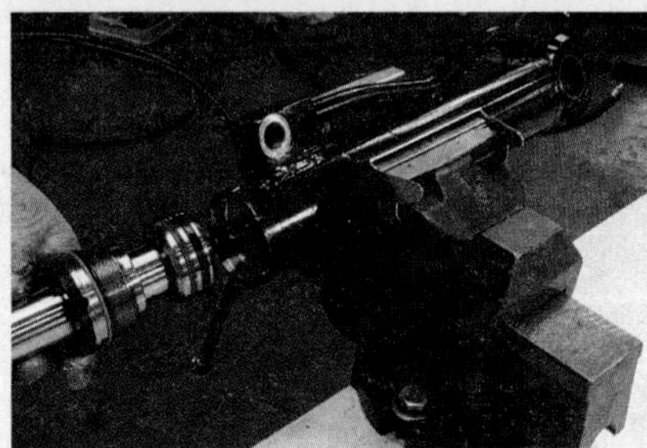

For this procedure, you need the following tools, materials, and equipment:

- Appropriate-sized wrenches
- Cylinder
- Replacement piston seal
- Replacement rod seal
- Replacement wiper seal
- A scribe
- Safety glasses or goggles
- Gloves

1. Put on safety glasses or goggles, and gloves.

2. Disassemble the cylinder.
   - **a.** Use the scribe to place match marks on the end caps.
   - **b.** Use appropriate wrenches to remove the end cap.
   - **c.** Remove the piston and rod assembly from the cylinder barrel.
   - **d.** Have your instructor check your work.

3. Inspect the cylinder.
   - **a.** Inspect the outside of the barrel for rust, dents, and other signs of damage and deterioration.
   - **b.** Inspect the bore for rust, corrosion, wear, scarring, and damage to the finish.
   - **c.** Inspect the rod for rust, corrosion, wear, scarring, and damage to the finish.
   - **d.** Have your instructor check your work.

4. Reassemble the cylinder.
   - **a.** Remove the old piston seal.
   - **b.** Carefully install a new piston seal onto the piston.
   - **c.** Carefully insert the rod assembly into the cylinder barrel.
   - **d.** Install a new rod seal (if used).
   - **e.** Make sure orientation is correct (lip is out) and that the seal is square to the rod.
   - **f.** Install the end cap.
   - **g.** Align the match marks.
   - **h.** Torque the bolts according to the manufacturer's instructions.
   - **i.** Have your instructor check your work.
   - **j.** Clean the work area, and return tools and equipment to the proper storage area.

SKILL DRILL 27-2 Testing a Cylinder for External and Internal Leakage

For this procedure, you need the following tools, materials, and equipment:

- Appropriate-sized wrenches
- Cylinder
- Double-acting cylinder
- Cylinder test fixture capable of holding a pressurized cylinder
- Safety glasses or goggles
- Gloves

1. Put on safety glasses or goggles, and gloves.
2. Test for external leakage.
   a. With the cylinder installed on the machine or test fixture, apply pressure and visually inspect the cylinder for leakage around the rod at the end cap.
   b. Repeat for several different positions.
   c. Have your instructor check your work.
3. Test for internal leakage.
   a. Install the cylinder on the test fixture, leaving the line to one side of the cylinder unconnected. *Note:* Pressurize only one side of the cylinder at a time.
   b. Bleed air from the side of the cylinder that will be pressurized.
   c. Apply pressure.
   d. Observe the open outlet for any leakage flow.
   e. Repeat for several cylinder extensions.
   f. Remove pressure.
   g. Disconnect the line to the cylinder and reconnect to the other side.
   h. Repeat steps (b) to (f) for the other side of the cylinder.
   i. Have your instructor check your work.
   j. Clean the work area, and return tools and equipment to the proper storage area.

SKILL DRILL 27-3 Inspecting and Replacing Seals

For this procedure, you need the following tools, materials, and equipment:

- Appropriate-sized wrenches
- Replacement seals
- Seat tools
- Lubricant
- Cylinder
- Scribe
- Pencil or pen and paper
- Safety glasses or goggles
- Gloves

1. Put on safety glasses or goggles, and gloves.
2. Disassemble the cylinder.
   a. Use the scribe to place match marks on the end caps.
   b. Use the appropriate wrenches to remove the end cap.
   c. Remove the rod assembly from the cylinder barrel.
3. Inspect the seals. *Note:* After inspecting the seals, record their condition on a piece of paper.
   a. Inspect the piston seals, and observe their condition. *Note:* If the piston seals are damaged, inspect the cylinder barrel to determine whether there are rough spots that could have caused the damage.
   b. Inspect the backup rings (if present), and ensure that they were installed properly. Note their condition.
   c. Inspect the rod seal (if used) and observe its condition. *Note:* If the rod seal is damaged, inspect the cylinder rod to determine whether there is damage to the rod that could have caused damage to the rod seal.
   d. Inspect the wiper seals and note their condition.
4. Replace seals, as necessary, according to the manufacturer's specifications.
   a. Remove the old piston seal.
   b. Carefully install a new piston seal and backup ring (if required) onto the piston.
5. Reassemble the cylinder.
   a. Carefully insert the rod assembly into the cylinder barrel.
   b. Install a new rod seal (if used). Make sure that the orientation is correct (lip is out) and that the seal is square to the rod.
   c. Install the end cap.
   d. Align the match marks.
   e. Tighten the bolts evenly on the end caps.
   f. Have your instructor check your work.
   g. Clean the work area, and return tools and equipment to their proper storage.

▸ Wrap-Up

Ready for Review

- Hydraulic actuators convert fluid energy into mechanical energy to move a load.
- The two types of actuators manufacturers use on heavy equipment vehicles are linear actuators and rotary actuators.
- Linear actuators provide a linear form of energy transfer to produce either linear or angular motion.
- Linear actuators have three basic parts: a barrel, a rod, and a piston.
- Linear actuators can be single acting and telescoping, or double-acting cylinders.
- Rotary actuators provide a rotary form of energy transfer to produce rotary motion.
- Hydraulic motors provide continuous rotary motion, whereas rotary actuators provide a limited rotation.
- The three types of hydraulic motors are gear, vane, and piston.
- An actuator's single-acting cylinder power assistance is in only one direction, relying on the weight of the load to return it to the original position.
- A double-acting cylinder provides power assistance in both directions and is not load dependent.
- Seals are a large part of the proper upkeep of actuators on heavy equipment vehicles.
- Pascal's law is the principle of transmission of fluid pressure and states that pressure applied anywhere to a body of fluid causes a force to transmit equally in all directions.
- Excessive and unusual noise, drifting, leakage, and power loss are the main concerns when troubleshooting, diagnosing, and repairing actuators.

Key Terms

angular Consisting of, or forming, an angle.

bore The inside diameter of a tube.

clevis An eye in a hydraulic mount, which secures with a bolt.

composite Composed of several substances.

elastomeric A natural or synthetic material that returns to its original shape after a deforming force is removed.

flange A ring or collar that increases strength and provides a place to attach other objects.

housing An enclosed case for a mechanism.

linear Extending or moving in one dimension only.

metallic Composed of metal.

pi The ratio of the circumference of a circle to its diameter; represented by the Greek letter π.

piston A solid disk that moves within a tube (or cylinder) under fluid pressure.

rack A bar with teeth; used with a pinion to convert linear to circular motion.

rod The moving part of a cylinder.

rotary Turning, or capable of turning, on an axis.

scored Notched, scratched, or incised.

seal Something used to completely close a gap, seam, or opening.

sequentially Operating in a series, or in logical order.

teeth Uniform projections in a piece of machinery that engage and transfer motion to or from a complementary piece of machinery.

telescoping Extending from a series of nested sections.

torque A measurement of rotational force.

trunnion Paired cylindrical projections for support, as on a cannon.

vent An opening that releases or discharges a fluid or gas.

Review Questions

1. Which of the following is not a true statement?
   a. In a single-acting cylinder, oil pressure flows into only one side of the cylinder, normally to extend it.
   b. A telescoping cylinder has two or more sections that extend sequentially.
   c. A double-acting cylinder has two oil ports that are used to extend and retract the cylinder.
   d. When a hydraulic motor's shaft turns, it produces a constant flow of oil.
2. Which one of these is *not* a type of hydraulic motor?
   a. Double acting
   b. Axial piston
   c. Bent axis
   d. Cam lobe
3. Which statement is true regarding hydraulic actuators?
   a. Hydraulic actuators convert fluid energy into mechanical energy to move a load.
   b. Manufacturers use three main types of actuators on heavy equipment machines.
   c. All hydraulic actuators produce both linear and rotary motion.
   d. None of the above
4. Choose the true statement or statements about linear actuators.
   a. They are also sometime called rams.
   b. One type is called external gear.
   c. Their force output is measured in ft-lb.
   d. The effective area of the piston considers the rod length.
5. Choose the true statement about hydraulic motors.
   a. They provide a rotary form of energy transfer.
   b. They have unlimited speed.
   c. They provide continuous linear motion.
   d. Their force output is measured in kilograms.
6. Choose the true statement about hydraulic motors.
   a. They use mechanical power input to provide fluid power output.
   b. They always rotate in one direction.

c. They use fluid power input to provide mechanical power output.
d. All of the above

7. Which of these are common symptoms of problems with hydraulic cylinders?
a. Leakage
b. Drifting
c. Excessive noise
d. All of the above

8. Which of the following is not a common cause for actuator failure?
a. Leaking piston seal
b. Fractured rod
c. Scored cylinder barrel
d. Leaking rod seal

9. Which of the following would increase the force output of a linear actuator?
a. Increase the oil flow rate to the cylinder.
b. Increase the piston diameter of the cylinder.
c. Increase the rod diameter.
d. Decrease the cylinder length.

10. Which of the following terms are related to hydraulic motors?
a. Linear
b. Rod
c. Swashplate
d. Bent axis

ASE Technician A/Technician B Style Questions

1. Technician A says manufacturers use only linear actuators on heavy equipment machines. Technician B says manufacturers use only rotary actuators. Who is correct?
a. Technician A
b. Technician B
c. Both A and B
d. Neither A nor B

2. Technician A says in single-acting telescoping cylinders, the cylinder returns to its original position by the weight of the load. Technician B says a double-acting cylinder rod retracts by oil flow. Who is correct?
a. Technician A
b. Technician B
c. Both A and B
d. Neither A nor B

3. Technician A says rotary actuators provide continuous rotary motion. Technician B says hydraulic motors provide a limited rotary motion. Who is correct?
a. Technician A
b. Technician B
c. Both A and B
d. Neither A nor B

4. Technician A says seals for cylinders can be made from elastomeric or composite material. Technician B says seals for cylinders can be made from metallic material or fiber material. Who is correct?
a. Technician A
b. Technician B
c. Both A and B
d. Neither A nor B

5. Technician A says applications for O-ring seals in actuators are limited to sealing the cap to the barrel. Technician B says manufacturers use O-ring seals only for sealing motor housings together and sealing hoses to cylinders. Who is correct?
a. Technician A
b. Technician B
c. Both A and B
d. Neither A nor B

6. Technician A says you should replace all seals when you service hydraulic actuators. Technician B says you need to replace only the worn seals. Who is correct?
a. Technician A
b. Technician B
c. Both A and B
d. Neither A nor B

7. Technician A says actuators fail on heavy equipment because of leaking seals. Technician B says rotary actuators fail because of a damaged or bent rod. Who is correct?
a. Technician A
b. Technician B
c. Both A and B
d. Neither A nor B

8. Technician A says Pascal's law is the principle of transmission of fluid pressure and it is expressed mathematically as $F = p \times A$. Technician B says Pascal's law is the principle of fluid pressure action and is expressed as $A = p \times F$. Who is correct?
a. Technician A
b. Technician B
c. Both A and B
d. Neither A nor B

9. Technician A says the force a cylinder produces is a function of pressure. Technician B says the force it produces is the function of pressure and flow rate. Who is correct?
a. Technician A
b. Technician B
c. Both A and B
d. Neither A nor B

10. Technician A says that when you inspect a hydraulic cylinder for damage and wear, you only need to check for leaks and inspect the outside of the cylinder. Technician B says you check for leaks, inspect the outside and inside of the cylinder, and inspect the rod. Who is correct?
a. Technician A
b. Technician B
c. Both A and B
d. Neither A nor B

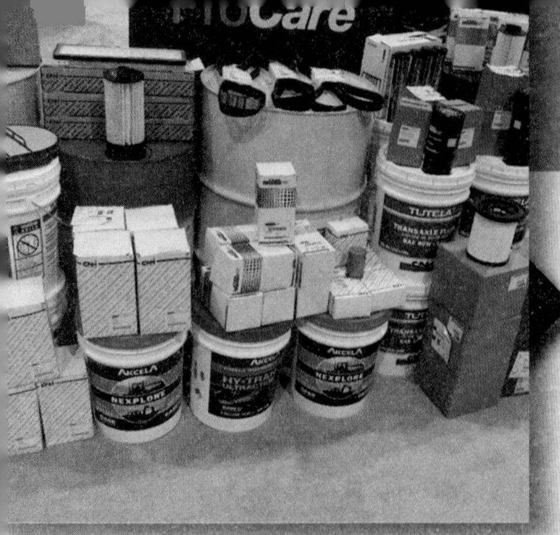

CHAPTER 28

Hydraulic Fluids and Conditioners

Knowledge Objectives

After reading this chapter, you will be able to:

- **K28001** Explain the purpose and fundamentals of hydraulic fluids.
- **K28002** Identify the composition and properties of hydraulic fluids.
- **K28003** Explain the purpose and fundamentals of hydraulic fluid conditioning.
- **K28004** Describe the function and construction features of hydraulic fluid filters.
- **K28005** Discuss the function and construction features of hydraulic coolers and heaters.

Skills Objectives

After reading this chapter, you will be able to:

- **S28001** Perform external filter hydraulic fluid cleanup.

▶ Introduction

The importance of using the proper hydraulic fluid and keeping it properly conditioned cannot be emphasized enough when discussing hydraulic systems and how to maximize the longevity and performance of all machine hydraulic system components.

Knowledge of hydraulic fluid properties such as viscosity and antiwear additives is an important part of being a good technician. A common task most MORE technicians perform is changing or topping up hydraulic fluid. Putting the right fluid in the machine's hydraulic tank, according to manufacturer's service information for the current operating conditions, is critical. Understanding fluid specifications that are found in the machine's maintenance manual is imperative.

Fluid conditioning refers to filtering, cooling, and heating the fluid. Proper fluid conditioning will keep the hydraulic fluid in optimum condition until it is time to change it, which could be after over 6,000 hours in some cases. Fluid contamination is the biggest cause of failed hydraulic system components, and correct filtration will drastically reduce that factor.

When it comes time to change hydraulic filters, a technician usually uses the part number from the machine's parts book to get the right filter. However, there could be times when it is necessary to add filters to a system or to use different filters instead of the original ones. A solid understanding of how filters work, the different types of filters, and where they should be placed in the system is important for any MORE technician to know.

MORE machine hydraulic systems generate excessive heat that must be transferred out of the fluid before it becomes damaging to the fluid or other system components. MORE machines are also found working in extreme climates, such as very hot and very cold conditions. Almost all machines require coolers to keep component temperature below critical temperatures, and some may also need fluid heaters to keep fluid temperatures above levels that start to affect the fluid's ability to flow properly.

Hydraulic fluid coolers are a common and important part of most hydraulic systems. Fluid must not overheat, or it will start to break down and loose vital properties, which could lead to premature failure of system components.

This chapter discusses the purpose of hydraulic fluids, hydraulic fluid properties, and the construction and operation of fluid conditioners (filters, heaters, and coolers).

▶ Purpose and Fundamentals of Hydraulic Fluids

K28001

Hydraulic fluids play a very important role in all hydraulic systems, and in fact, it can be said the fluid is the most important component in a hydraulic system. **Hydraulic fluid** truly is the lifeblood of any hydraulic system.

There are five main purposes hydraulic fluid serves in a hydraulic system: to provide an effective transfer of power; to lubricate all moving parts in the system; to clean all components internally; to transfer heat to help regulate system temperature; and to maintain an effective seal in some parts of the systems.

Power Transfer

As described in previous chapters, a hydraulic system is an energy conversion machine that uses hydraulic fluid to transfer energy. A prime mover drives a pump that transfers energy into the fluid, and the fluid then applies the energy to one or more actuators (cylinder or motor) that convert the fluid energy back into mechanical power.

To transfer power effectively, the fluid must be virtually **incompressible**.

Most liquids will compress slightly under pressure, and hydraulic fluid is no different, with the rule of thumb being roughly 1% per 3,000 psi.

As you can imagine, if a machine has an operating pressure of 5,000 psi and cycles from 0 to relief pressure on a regular basis, there will be a small spring effect because of the

You Are the Mobile Heavy Equipment Technician

You are a technician working for a smaller forestry contractor that has a mixed fleet of machines, from small skid steer loaders with simple hydraulic systems to harvesters that have very complex electrohydraulic systems. There are also different makes of machines in the fleet. Recently, a hydraulic pump failed on a machine that was designed and manufactured in Europe. This machine requires a specific type of biodegradable hydraulic oil. The failure occurred just after an operator had topped up the oil with a different kind of oil after a hose failure. This pump failure was very expensive not only for the parts needed but for downtime it caused as well. It is suspected that the use of a non-specified oil was the result of the pump failure.

To avoid a repeat failure, the equipment manager has asked you to come up with a solution. The following options are possible solutions:

1. Put a different lock, for which only technicians have a key, on the hydraulic cap.
2. Educate all operators about the type of hydraulic oil to use for the machine they are running.
3. Contact the machine manufacturer to see whether there is an alternative oil that could be used for all machines in the fleet.
4. Sell all machines that can't use a universal hydraulic fluid that is compatible with the one used by the majority of the fleet.
5. See whether there are any additives that could be used with the most common hydraulic oil to make it conform to the oil used in other machines.

Choose which options you would implement and explain why.

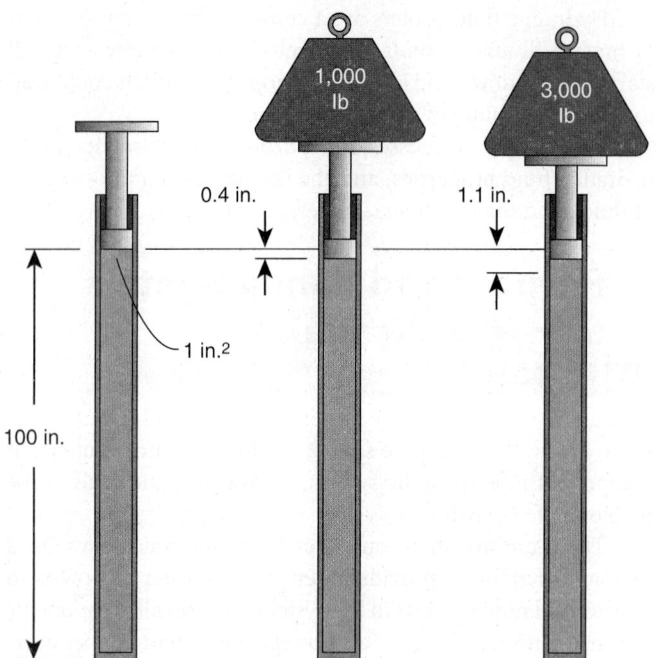

FIGURE 28-1 An example of how hydraulic fluid compresses.

FIGURE 28-2 The result of a lack of lubrication.

fluid compressing and expanding. Over time, this may degrade the fluid and will add to some heat buildup in the fluid, but a high-quality hydraulic fluid will resist degradation and perform flawlessly for thousands of hours. The noncompressibility or "stiffness" of hydraulic fluid leads to fast response and positive power transfer. **FIGURE 28-1** provides an example of how hydraulic fluid compresses.

Component Lubrication

Even simple hydraulic systems have many moving internal parts that have to be lubricated. Another job of hydraulic fluid is to provide lubrication to the moving parts in the system. Ideally. the fluid will keep the parts separated by a film of oil, a condition called **full film lubrication**. Under operating conditions, the film of oil can be as thin as 1 micron thick.

Typical hydraulic component clearances measured in microns are vane pump (vane tip to outer ring) 0.5–1; gear pump (gear to side plate) 0.5–5; servo valves (spool to sleeve) 1–4; piston pump (piston to bore) 5–40; actuators 50–250.

One **micron** is one-millionth of a meter, or 0.000039". The smallest particle a human eye can see is roughly 40 microns.

When components are manufactured, there should be enough clearance for a film of oil to separate them. However, as pressure builds and parts are in relative motion to each other, the film may be partially penetrated. This condition is called **boundary lubrication** and is just 0.05 micron thick. If contact occurs in a few small areas of a component with a few high spots (asperities) on its surfaces, no major damage will occur. However, if the fluid properties for antiwear aren't adequate, more contact will occur, which could lead to galling and significant metal transfer between two parts of a component. This in turn can quickly lead to component failure. **FIGURE 28-2** demonstrates the results of a lack of lubrication.

Cleaning

All hydraulic systems generate some contamination as they wear, and there will be other types of contamination in the fluid as well. Another function of the system's fluid is to carry this contamination to the system filters, where it can be left behind. Solid particles are the most common type of contamination. Another example is excessive air in the fluid. Air is a contaminant in hydraulic fluid and is transported to the reservoir, where it can disperse before being sent through the system again.

Several types of hydraulic fluid additives are meant to reduce or prevent contamination as well.

Cooling

Hydraulic fluid naturally absorbs heat as it flows past system components that generate heat, such as pumps, valves, and actuators. The fluid then transfers excessive heat to all other components that are cooler than the fluid, such as tubes, hoses, fittings, reservoirs, and coolers.

> **TECHNICIAN TIP**
>
> Hydraulic fluid can also transfer heat into system components for cold start-up. If a machine has a tank heater, first the fluid in the reservoir is warmed up and then transfers heat into other components as it circulates through the system. A careful warm-up procedure after a cold start-up warms the oil up, which in turn warms up all components it circulates through.

Sealing

Many hydraulic system components have large pressure drops across their surfaces or between two adjacent components. The parts could be stationary, such as a valve spool in its housing, or could be moving, such as the teeth on a gear pump's gear.

The lands on a valve spool could be separating high pressure oil at 5,000 psi and tank oil pressure at atmospheric pressure. The only barrier between these two pressures is a thin film of oil that creates a seal between the valve spool and its housing. All pumps rely on a thin layer of hydraulic fluid to create a seal between rotating and stationary internal components.

As clearances become greater due to component wear, and as the hydraulic fluid becomes "worn out," it becomes more difficult for the fluid to keep the seal intact.

▶ Composition and Properties of Hydraulic Fluids

K28002

Machine manufacturers are very specific about the properties of the hydraulic fluid that can be used for their hydraulic systems. When a hydraulic system is designed to accomplish specific tasks, the machine pressure and flow values are determined, and then components are selected to produce those requirements. Hydraulic system components are manufactured from a variety of materials, machined to extremely close tolerances, and finished to a defined roughness. For the components to achieve a desired lifespan without major repairs, designers have to determine the ideal hydraulic fluid that should be used in the system. Most components are expected to last between 15,000 and 20,000 hours, and to reach these expectations or even surpass them, it is imperative that the proper fluid be used.

Recently, one of the front-line wheel loaders for a large mining operation reached 40,000 hours with the original hydraulic pumps! This could not have been achieved without the use of an approved hydraulic fluid and regular service.

A variety of **fluid properties** have to be considered before a hydraulic fluid is used for a MORE machine. See **FIGURE 28-3** to see a container of hydraulic fluid that shows its fluid properties.

FIGURE 28-3 A container of hydraulic fluid that shows its properties.

Viscosity

A hydraulic fluid's viscosity is the most important property to consider when selecting a fluid to use for a MORE machine. Viscosity of hydraulic fluid is a critical property because a fluid with the proper viscosity flows easily through the system, without creating large pressure drops, because of its low resistance to flow. Proper viscosity fluid also lubricates components correctly because it can easily reach all areas of high importance, such as port plates in piston pumps or valve spools. Correct viscosity fluid also provides improved machine efficiency because power isn't consumed in just trying to circulate fluid.

Hydraulic fluid with too low viscosity will not lubricate internal components properly, and as pressures increase, so does the likelihood of metal transfer between two components. Conversely, hydraulic fluid that has a high viscosity rating will not flow to all areas of the system that need lubrication, and again there is a strong possibility component failure will result.

A fluid's viscosity is defined as its resistance to flow at a given temperature. A low-viscosity liquid is water, which flows easily at any temperature above freezing, and a high-viscosity liquid is honey, which flows very slowly at room temperature and even more slowly as it gets cooler. Temperature has the greatest influence on a fluid's viscosity, although pressure can change a fluid's viscosity. The viscosity of a hydraulic fluid doubles for every 5,000 psi it is subjected to.

Comparing two common oils that may be used in MORE machines and that are on the opposite ends of the viscosity range, think about ATF (automatic transmission fluid) and SAE 50 oil (like 80W90 gear oil). ATF has a viscosity that is very low and pours like milk even when cold, while gear oil pours slowly even at room temperature, and almost turns solid in extremely cold weather. Hydraulic fluid viscosity is a lot closer to ATF than gear oil. **FIGURE 28-4** demonstrates different viscosity oils pouring at low temperature. Machine manufacturers provide viscosity charts in their maintenance manuals so the machine owner and/or technician performing service on the machine will know the correct viscosity of hydraulic fluid to put in the machine, for the ambient air temperature range that the machine is expected to work in.

FIGURE 28-4 A demonstration of different oil viscosity oils pouring at low temperature.

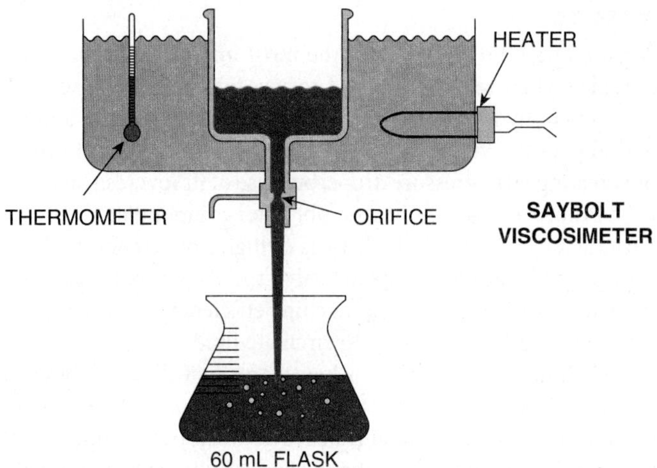

FIGURE 28-5 A test instrument for measuring fluid viscosity.

Several different methods are used to test fluid viscosity, but the most common way is to measure the time it takes a specific quantity of fluid at a specific temperature to flow through a specific-sized orifice or capillary. **FIGURE 28-5** shows a test instrument for measuring fluid viscosity.

Two different test categories are **kinematic** (fluid flow caused by gravity) and absolute (the force or time it takes an object to flow through a fluid). The tests are performed when the fluid is at an exact temperature. The most common units for the different test are kinematic-centipoise (cP) and absolute-centistoke (cSt). Saybolt Universal Seconds (SUS) is another less common measurement you might see for viscosity.

▶ TECHNICIAN TIP

The most common tool of measuring viscosity is the **Saybolt Viscosimeter**. The Saybolt Viscosimeter was invented by and named after George Saybolt. The Saybolt Viscosimeter unit of measurement is the Saybolt Universal Second (SUS). In the original viscosimeter, a container of fluid was heated to a specific temperature. When the temperature was reached, an orifice was opened and the fluid flowed out of the container and into a 60 mL flask. A stopwatch was used to measure the time it took to fill the flask. The viscosity was recorded as the number of seconds the flask took to fill at a given temperature. If a fluid, when heated to a temperature of 75°F (24°C), took 115 seconds to fill the flask, it's viscosity was 115 SUS @ 75°F (24°C). If the same fluid was heated to 100°F (38°C) and took 90 seconds to fill the flask, its viscosity would be 90 SUS @ 100°F (38°C).

Because hydraulic fluid doesn't usually need to be changed for at least 2,000 hours, the ambient temperature range the machine is working in can be extreme, depending on where the machine is working. This could be a range from −40°C to 40°C (−40°F to 104°F). **FIGURE 28-6** shows a **viscosity chart** for hydraulic fluid for a MORE machine.

Viscosity Index

This number given to a fluid indicates how its viscosity changes with temperature. The test temperatures are 40°C (104°F) and 100°C (212°F). A consistent viscosity over a wide range of temperatures is a desirable trait in a hydraulic fluid. A lower number indicates the fluid will exhibit a wide change in viscosity as it changes temperature. For example, a fluid with a **viscosity index** of 50 or lower would be very thick when cold but would flow easily when warmed up. Conversely, a fluid with a viscosity index of 100 or greater would flow very consistently throughout the range of temperatures. Synthetic fluids typically have a high viscosity index number that reflects their excellent flow stability over a wide range of temperatures.

Viscosity improvers increase a fluid's viscosity index number.

SAE Viscosity Ratings

The Society of Automotive Engineers have been testing and rating automotive and MORE fluids for many years. A standard they established many decades ago was the viscosity rating for automotive engine oil (SAE J300), which established testing procedures and created viscosity ratings for lubricating oil used in internal combustion engines. The same

	ISO 22 (HVG)	ISO 32 (HVH)	ISO 46 (HVI)	ISO 68 (HVJ)
ISO VG (ASTM D 2422)	22	32	46	68
Kinematic Viscosity @100°C cSt (ASTM D 445)	5.2	6.5	8.5	11.2
Kinematic Viscosity @40°C cSt (ASTM D 445)	23.6	31.8	46.7	68.5
Viscosity Index (ASTM D 2270)	161	165	161	155
Flash Point °C (°F) (ASTM D 92)	228 (442)	224 (435)	246 (475)	252 (486)
Fire Point °C (°F) (ASTM D 92)	242 (468)	246 (476)	266 (511)	270 (518)
Pour Point °C (°F) (ASTM D 97)	−49 (−56)	−46 (−51)	−44 (−47)	−41 (−42)
Four-Ball Wear Test (ASTM D 4172)				
(40 kg, 1,200 rpm, 75°C, 60 min.)	0.42	0.42	0.41	0.41
Copper Strip Corrosion Test 100°C, 3hrs. (ASTM D 130)	1A	1A	1A	1A
Foam (ASTM D 892, Sequence I, II, & III)	0/0, 10/0, 0/0	0/0, 10/0, 0/0	0/0, 10/0, 0/0	0/0, 35/0, 0/0
Demulsibility (ASTM D 1401)	40-40-0 (20)	40-40-0 (25)	40-40-0 (20)	40-40-0 (20)
Seal Tests Elastomer SRE-NBR 1, 100°C, 168 hrs. (ASTM D 471)	Pass	Pass	Pass	Pass
Rust Testing				
Distilled and Salt Water (ASTM D 665A & B)	Pass	Pass	Pass	Pass
KRL Shear Test, 15% Max KV loss, Stay-in-Grade	Pass	Pass	Pass	Pass

FIGURE 28-6 Viscosity chart for hydraulic fluid for a MORE machine.

Recommended Lubricant Viscosities

For Use at Outside Temperatures from –55°C (–67°F) to +20°C (+68°F)										
Outside Temperature	**°F**	–67	–58	–40	–22	–4	+14	+32	+50	+68
	°C	–55	–50	–40	–30	–20	–10	0	+10	+20
Hydraulic System	SAE SPO0W-20									
	SAE SPC5W-20									
	SAE 5W-20									
	SAE 10W									
	SAE 10W-30									
	SAE 15W-40									

Bar spans read from the chart gridlines: SAE SPO0W-20, –35°C to +10°C; SAE SPC5W-20, –30°C to +20°C; SAE 5W-20, –25°C to +10°C; SAE 10W, –20°C to +20°C; SAE 10W-30, –20°C to +20°C; SAE 15W-40, –15°C to +20°C.

FIGURE 28-7 A viscosity rating for a Caterpillar wheel loader.

system is also used for other MORE machine fluids, such as powertrain fluids and hydraulic fluids.

SAE viscosity ratings start with two test standards. Summer (warm ambient temperatures) ratings are tested at 212°F (100°C) and winter (cold ambient temperatures) ratings are tested at 0°F (–18°C). Common summer **SAE viscosity ratings** are SAE20, SAE30, and SAE50, which are based on centistoke values. Common winter SAE ratings are 5W, 10W, 15W, and 20W ("W" stands for winter). Lower SAE numbers relate to a fluid that flows more readily at lower temperatures than one with a higher SAE number.

A popular SAE viscosity rating for hydraulic oil is 10W. This has been a preferred viscosity rating for Caterpillar hydraulic systems for many years. **FIGURE 28-7** presents a viscosity chart for a Caterpillar wheel loader.

Engine oils are typically multi-viscosity oils such as 10W30 or 14W40. They include viscosity improvers to provide flow to critical engine parts at cold start-up but then provide high load protection after the oil heats up and its viscosity lowers. You may occasionally see a multi-viscosity fluid recommended for hydraulic systems, but these are usually a second choice after a monograde fluid.

> **TECHNICIAN TIP**
>
> Some manufacturers allow the use of engine oil in machine hydraulic systems. Engine oils have many similar properties to hydraulic fluids, and older machines with low-pressure and low-flow systems are able to run engine oil in their hydraulic system.

ISO Viscosity Ratings

A second common viscosity rating found on many hydraulic fluid containers is the ISO classification. **ISO viscosity ratings** are based directly on the fluid's kinematic viscosity rating that uses centistokes as the measurement unit. The test temperature is 40°C (104°F), which falls between the SAE test temperatures of summer and winter (100°C [212°F] and 18°C [0°F], respectively).

ISO viscosity ratings for MORE machines usually range between 22 and 68, with 32 being a very common selection for machines in most of North America. See **FIGURE 28-8** for a viscosity chart for ISO grades.

Other Hydraulic Fluid Properties

Besides viscosity, many other fluid properties have to be considered when selecting a hydraulic fluid for use in a machine, including lubricity, pour point, oxidation resistance, rust and corrosion resistance, demulsibility, fire resistance, and flash point.

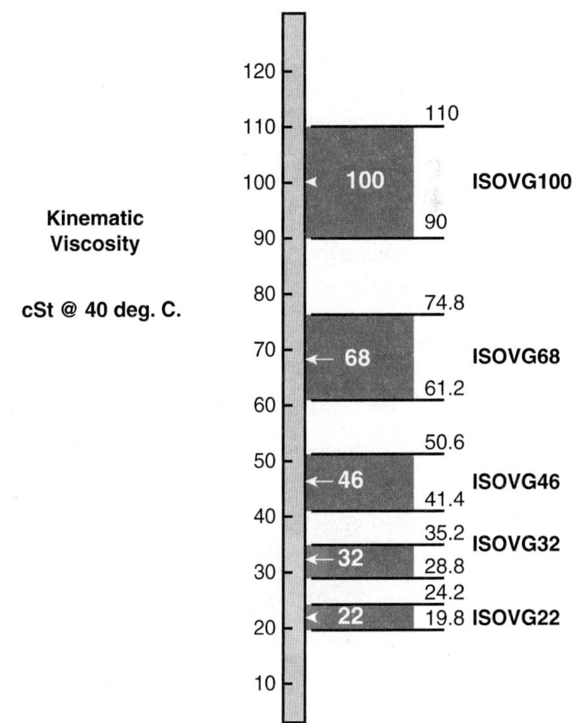

FIGURE 28-8 Viscosity chart for ISO grades.

Additives are chemical substances added to the base fluid to counteract specific conditions a hydraulic fluid may suffer from over its intended life.

Pour Point

Pour point is the lowest temperature at which a hydraulic fluid will flow. If a MORE machine is to be operated in extremely cold environments, this is one fluid specification that has to be carefully considered. A rule of thumb is that the pour point of a hydraulic fluid should be 20°F below the lowest temperature a machine will be exposed to. If the fluid used meets or exceeds this pour point value, the chance of cold oil starvation and lack of lubrication in critical areas should be eliminated.

Demulsibility

Demulsibility describes the ability of a fluid to separate water from itself. Water in hydraulic fluid has many negative effects and a fluid with good demulsibility properties is desirable.

Flash Point

A hydraulic fluid will be rated as to the point at which it first ignites when exposed to an ignition source typically between 200°F and 500°F (93°C and 260°C). This is of particular importance if fire-resistant fluids are a jobsite stipulation for the machine.

Fluid Degrading Conditions

Many negative conditions related to hydraulic fluid condition can occur. Hydraulic fluid additives are able to counteract most, if not all, conditions during the fluid's normal lifespan, but these additives will eventually drop out and leave the hydraulic system components vulnerable to damage and excessive wear.

Oxidation

Oxidation is a chemical combination of hydraulic fluid and oxygen that can create a shortened lifespan for petroleum- and vegetable-based fluids. Oxidation of fluid causes a buildup of varnish, gum, and sludge on components, which leads to excessive wear and sticking of valves. The condition is accelerated by high temperatures.

Oxidation can be visually detected as a darkening of fluid. **FIGURE 28-9** provides an example of fluid oxidation.

FIGURE 28-9 An example of fluid oxidation.

Rust and Corrosion

Rust occurs when ferrous material (iron and steel) combine with oxygen; corrosion is a chemical reaction between a metal and an acid. Acids in hydraulic fluid originate from water, and water also creates rust.

Water can enter hydraulic fluid systems in a variety of ways (tank breather, pressure washing, past leaky cylinder seals) and must be removed when levels are excessive. Water removal is discussed later in the chapter.

Foaming

Hydraulic fluid always has a certain amount of air content in it. If it is kept to a minimum safe level (8–10%) it will not cause negative performance or degrade the hydraulic fluid. However, excessive air in hydraulic fluid leads to foaming of the fluid and can have some serious consequences for a hydraulic system. A loss of power due to the compression of air is one effect of foaming fluid. A lack of lubrication is another serious result. Foaming can be seen in sight glasses for reservoirs and should be corrected as soon as it is detected. Antifoaming additives work to keep foaming from occurring.

Hydraulic Fluid Additives

To prevent hydraulic fluid degradation, fluid suppliers combine **additives** with the base fluid, to combat the negative conditions described above as well as others.

Additives are usually less than 10% of the volume of the base stock of oil. Antifoaming, antiwear, and anticorrosion additives are all commonly found in hydraulic fluid.

Most hydraulic fluids are formulated to be antiwear. The common additive that makes a fluid antiwear is ZDDP (zinc dialkydithiophosphate). This sulfur/phosphorous-based compound bonds to metal surfaces and provides a barrier between two surfaces that would otherwise come into contact.

These additives become depleted over time and necessitate a fluid change. Additives are also damaged by excessive heat, water, and chemical contamination.

▶ TECHNICIAN TIP

Some aftermarket fluid additive suppliers make claims regarding the use of their product, ranging from increased power to reduced fuel consumption. These additives may have limited benefits, but the normal recommendation from MORE machine manufacturers is to avoid using supplemental additives in hydraulic fluid.

Hydraulic Fluid Base Types

Hydraulic fluid can be based on a few different fluids. The main factors in determining which fluid to use for a machine are manufacturer's recommendation, cost, compatibility, environmental considerations, flammability properties, and availability. Base fluids include petroleum fluids, synthetic fluids, biodegradable fluids, and fire-resistant fluids. Technicians should always refer to the machine's service information or contact the dealer to ensure the correct fluid is used for the hydraulic system of any machine.

Petroleum-Based Hydraulic Fluid

Most hydraulic fluids used in MORE machines are based on crude oil-sourced mineral oil. Base stocks are refined from crude oil, and additives are added to it to enhance the performance and longevity of the oil.

The advantages of **mineral oil**-based hydraulic fluid are low cost, universal availability, good lubricity, and low toxicity. Most mineral oil-based hydraulic fluids are blended with antiwear additives to enhance component longevity. Some low-pressure systems allow the use of ATF (automatic transmission fluid), especially if there is a combined reservoir that supplies the transmission and hydraulic system. One downfall of ATF is its susceptibility to high temperatures.

Most equipment manufacturers have their own brand of hydraulic fluid that they recommend for use in their machines. It is developed and formulated based on the requirements for lubricity, antiwear, anticorrosion, air separation, flash point, and pour point. This should be the first choice for top off or replacement fluid when a machine is within its warranty period. There are minimum requirements for other fluids to meet should the machine owner want to use a non-OEM brand hydraulic fluid.

Some equipment manufacturers allow engine crankcase oils to be used for machine hydraulic systems, and common SAE grades are CF-4, CG-4, and CH-4. However, because engine oil has detergent additives that could cause foaming, caution should be used before adding an engine oil to a hydraulic system. **FIGURE 28-10** illustrates a hydraulic fluid container for mineral oil-based fluid.

Synthetic Hydraulic Fluid

A **synthetic hydraulic fluid** is a fluid created from an artificially created chain of molecules that are precisely arranged to provide excellent fluid stability, lubricity, and other performance-enhancing characteristics. Their high viscosity index (VI) provides excellent flow predictability over a wide range of temperatures. Synthetic hydraulic fluids are good choices where extreme low ambient temperatures and/or elevated temperatures and pressures are present.

Polyalphaolefin (PAO), alkylated naphthalene (AN), and ester base stocks are common types of fluid bases used to formulate a synthetic hydraulic fluid. There are some disadvantages to these fluids, including high cost and potential incompatibility with certain seal materials.

Biodegradable Hydraulic Fluid

Many jobsites where MORE machines are found working are regulated by strict environmental laws. Part of the regulations for the machines working within these jurisdictions is that their hydraulic fluids must be environmentally friendly. Biodegradable hydraulic fluids are becoming more popular because of the need for leaks not to cause harm to the environment.

These fluids are usually based on rapeseed oil or canola oil, and although they have limitations when compared to mineral oil-based fluids, most machine manufacturers allow them to be used without performance restrictions. There may be a reduced fluid change interval in some cases, and they are usually more expensive than mineral-based fluids. They also have limitations for cold weather use because of the base oil's higher viscosity. **FIGURE 28-11** shows a pail of biodegradable hydraulic fluid.

Fire-Resistant Hydraulic Fluid

Many jobsites where MORE machines are found working are regulated closely, and one of the stipulations for the machines working on a site might be that they must have fire-resistant hydraulic fluid in their system (underground mining machines, for example).

A fire in an underground mine is very dangerous, so most underground mining operations require the use of fire-resistant hydraulic fluid in their machines. Fire-resistant hydraulic fluids are sometimes referred to as high water-based fluids (HWBF).

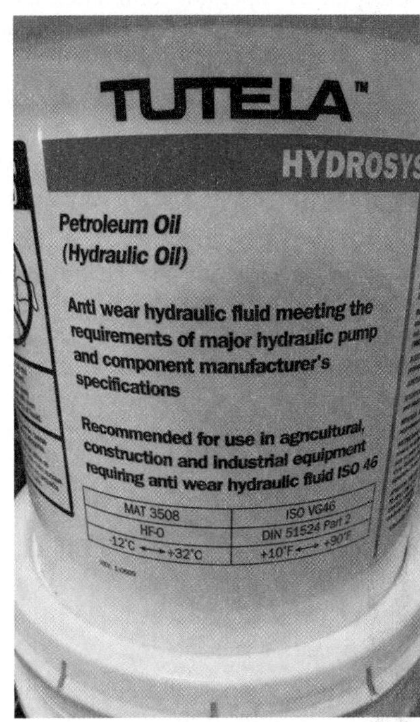

FIGURE 28-10 A hydraulic fluid container for a mineral oil–based fluid.

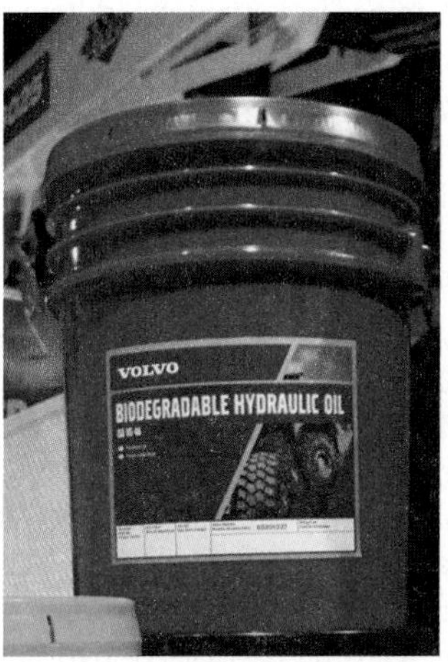

FIGURE 28-11 A pail of biodegradable hydraulic fluid.

The three basic types of **fire-resistant fluids** are water-glycols, water-oil emulsions, and synthetics. Water-glycol fluids contain 35% to 50% water (water inhibits burning), glycol, and a water thickener. Additives are added to improve lubrication and to prevent rust, corrosion, and foaming. Water-glycol fluids are higher viscosity than oil and may cause pump cavitation when cold. Extra warm-up procedures may be needed.

These fluids may react with certain metals and seals and cannot be used with some types of paints.

Water-oil emulsions are the least expensive of the fire-resistant fluids. A similar amount (40%) of water is used to that used in water-glycol fluids, to inhibit burning. Water-oil emulsions can be used in typical hydraulic oil systems. Additives may be added to prevent rust and foaming. Certain conditions call for synthetic fluids to be used to meet specific requirements. The fire-resistant synthetic fluids are less flammable than petroleum-based fluids and more suitable for used in areas of high pressure and elevated temperature. Many times, fire-resistant fluids react to polyurethane seals and may require that special seals be used.

▶ Purpose and Fundamentals of Hydraulic Fluid Conditioning

K28003

This chapter started off by saying that hydraulic fluid is the most important component in a hydraulic system. To keep the fluid within its required parameters so as to ensure component protection, the fluid must be conditioned or maintained while it is in the machine. Hydraulic fluid contamination has to be reduced and fluid temperature managed. To reduce contamination to acceptable levels, several types and levels of filtration may be needed. Heaters and coolers are also used to manage fluid temperature.

Fluid Contamination

Hydraulic fluid contamination is the leading cause of component failure by a wide margin. Most estimates are between 70% and 85% of component failures are caused by fluid contamination.

There are many sources of contamination; even new oil from a sealed container is contaminated beyond the minimum cleanliness requirements of most equipment manufacturers. However, with proper filters in place that get serviced regularly and with the use of manufacturer-specified fluid, most contamination can be maintained at a safe level.

Solid Contamination

Solid contamination can be in several forms, such as hard particles like metal, carbon, and silica; and soft particles such as rubber, fibers, and microorganisms.

Particle sizes are generally measured on the micrometer scale. One micrometer (or "micron") is one-millionth of 1 meter, or 39 millionths of an inch (0.0000394"). The limit of human visibility is approximately 40 μm (micrometers). Keep in mind that most damage-causing particles in hydraulic or lubrication systems are smaller than 14 μm. Therefore, they are microscopic and cannot be seen by the unaided eye.

> ▶ TECHNICIAN TIP
>
> Some examples of substances and their relative sizes are a grain of table salt—100 microns, or 0.0039"; human hair—70 microns, or 0.0027"; milled flour—25 microns, or 0.0010"; red blood cells—8 microns, or 0.0003"; bacteria—2 microns, or 0.0001".

Particles can be grouped into two size categories called silt and chip. Silt particles are 5 microns or less, and chip particles are 5 microns and larger in size. Silt particles build up and cause valve sticking and component overheating, and chip particles cause surface damage to components.

Clearances in Hydraulic Components

Very small clearances must be maintained between the internal components of hydraulic system components (pumps, valves, and actuators) in order to be able to seal and separate high and low pressure. As clearances increase, internal leakage increases, fluid overheating increases, and system efficiency decreases. The possibility of excessive contamination has the biggest influence on whether internal clearances are maintained. **FIGURE 28-12** provides examples of typical clearances found in hydraulic components. Contamination that is too large to fit between two components will not cause wear or cause them to stick, but it can plug orifices. However, contamination that is just slightly smaller than the clearance gets between the components' internal parts and cause wear and jamming. **FIGURE 28-13** demonstrates how assorted size particles interact with component clearances.

Gaseous Contamination

Excessive air in hydraulic fluid is unacceptable and will cause deficient performance due to it being easily compressible. One of the advantages of a hydraulic system is its positive, predictable, and quick response to operator commands. Excessive air in the hydraulic fluid results in a spongy feel instead of a stiff feel.

Aeration of hydraulic fluid can result from many system deficiencies such as leaks at the pump inlet line, tank baffle failure, and poor fluid condition.

Air in a liquid system exists in either a dissolved or entrained (undissolved, or free) state. Dissolved air may not pose a problem, providing it stays in solution. When a liquid contains undissolved air, problems can occur as it passes through system components. Pressure changes can compress the air and produce a large amount of heat in small air bubbles. The heat destroys additives, and the base fluid itself.

An 8–10% air content is an acceptable air saturation level for hydraulic systems and varies with atmospheric pressure levels and types of fluids. There are two types of air content in hydraulic systems: entrained air and free air.

- **Free air** forms large bubbles in the fluid and can be trapped at high points or pump cases in a system. It can be catastrophic to components such as pumps and actuators because no lubrication is occurring.
- **Entrained air** is dispersed throughout the fluid and forms bubbles from a few microns in size to ones that are visible. It gives hydraulic fluid a foamy appearance. An example of hydraulic fluid with excessive air in it is shown in **FIGURE 28-14**.

COMPONENT	CLEARANCE LOCATION	MICRONS	INCHES
Gear Pump	Gear to side plate	1/2–5	0.00002–0.0002
	Gear tip to case	1/2–5	0.00002–0.0002
Vane Pump	Tip of vane	1/2–1	0.00002–0.00004
	Sides of vane	5–13	0.0002–0.0005
Piston Pump	Piston to bore	5–40	0.0002–0.0015
	Valve plate to cylinder	1/2–5	0.00002–0.0002
Servo Valve	Orifice	130–450	0.005–0.018
	Flapper wall	18–63	0.0007–0.0025
	Spool sleeve	1–4	0.00005–0.00015
Control Valve	Orifice	130–10,000	0.005–0.4
	Spool sleeve	1–23	0.00005–0.0009
	Disk type	1/2–1	0.00002–0.00004
	Poppet type	13–40	0.0005–0.0015

FIGURE 28-12 Typical clearances found in hydraulic components.

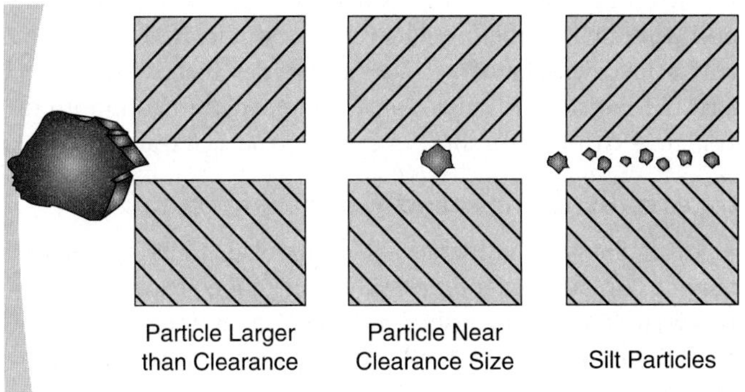

FIGURE 28-13 How assorted size particles interact with component clearance.

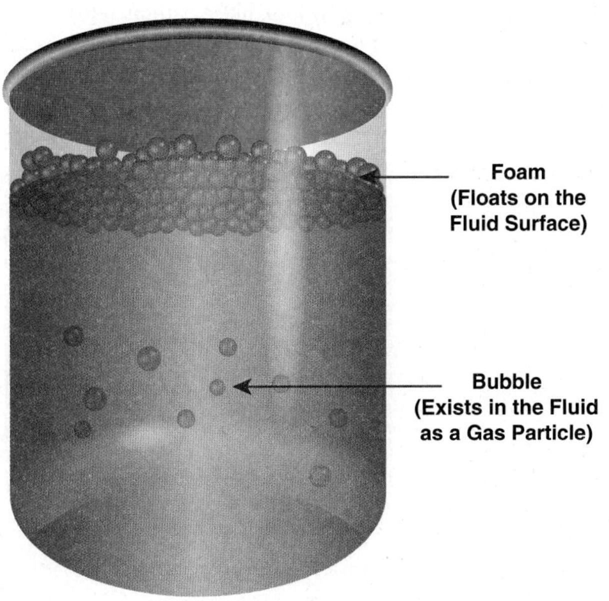

FIGURE 28-14 An example of hydraulic fluid with excessive air in it.

Liquid Contamination

Water is the most common type of liquid contamination found in hydraulic systems, but other types include diesel fuel, coolant, or engine oil. Water can enter a hydraulic system from several sources such as leaky cylinder seals, missing filler cap, or the tank breather, or from careless pressure washing of components.

Water has the most negative effect on petroleum-based hydraulic fluids.

Just like other contaminants, small levels of water in hydraulic oil can be tolerated, but the saturation point of hydraulic fluid is 300 ppm, or 0.03%. This is the level of water content that an oil-based hydraulic fluid can sustain without it starting to create negative effects on the system.

Excessive water content can cause viscosity changes, increased oxidation, additive dropout, and acid formation.

Water content in hydraulic oil can be in three forms: **free water** (water that separates from the oil easily and settles to the bottom of the tank); emulsified water (water that has combined with the oil and gives a milky appearance); and water in solution (not readily visible until oil cools). See **FIGURE 28-15** for a sample of hydraulic oil with excessive water in it.

▶ TECHNICIAN TIP

Most technicians assume new oil from either 20 L (5 gal) pails or from shop reels would be fine to pour or pump into a machine's hydraulic reservoir. However, according to most sources, this new oil is a source of contamination, and depending on the cleanliness requirements for the machine it is going into, it will likely contaminate the system. The new oil has traveled through hoses, pipes, and fittings before getting to its final container or dispenser and has picked up contamination along the way.

To be sure that doesn't occur, new oil should be filtered through an external transfer filter cart before it enters a machine's hydraulic system.

FIGURE 28-15 A sample of hydraulic oil with excessive water in it.

FIGURE 28-16 A cylinder rod seal leaking.

Contamination Sources

Hydraulic fluid contamination originates from a variety of sources that fall into the following categories: built-in contamination, external contamination, internally generated contamination, and maintenance-generated contamination.

Built-In Contamination

During the manufacture of all hydraulic components, a lot of contamination is created. Processes such as welding, grinding, honing, machining, heat-treating, and painting all generate contamination of some form. If the component manufacturer has high-quality control standards during and after manufacturing, leftover contamination ending up in a hydraulic system will be minimal. Final cleaning of components and a thorough inspection are critical steps toward achieving reliable system operation from the new oil. However, this is not always the case and one of the most likely periods to have a contamination related failure is in the first few hours of running a new system or after a major component has been replaced.

Replacement hoses and fittings are another common source of built-in contamination if they aren't properly cleaned or installed. New oil (top off or refill) could also be considered built-in contamination because it is usually not as clean as it should be.

External Contamination

External contamination is anything foreign that enters the hydraulic system and can cause a problem. It includes airborne solid particles (dust, dirt) and water (most common), but other substances such as metallic particles, chemicals, and microorganisms also contribute to hydraulic fluid degradation.

The three most common points for external contamination to enter a hydraulic system are tank breather, cylinder rod seals, and filler cap opening.

Tank breathers must allow air to transfer in and out of a vented reservoir to compensate for the changing fluid level in the tank. The breather should incorporate a filter that cleans the air before it enters, but breathers quite often get damaged or left off. A proper breather filter stops any contamination that is smaller than 3 microns in size. Breathers can also include moisture removal elements.

Cylinder rods are coated with a thin layer of hydraulic fluid as they move into the atmosphere, which attracts dust. As the rod moves back into the cylinder, the contamination is washed off it. Different rod seals are more effective at wiping off hydraulic fluid before it leaves the cylinder and before dust enters the cylinder. If you see a cylinder that is leaking oil past the rod seal, it is also transferring contamination into the system. **FIGURE 28-16** shows a cylinder rod seal leaking.

Internally Generated Contamination

As hydraulic systems operate and accumulate hours, the internal moving components (pumps, valves, cylinders) experience normal wear that sees them shed material. Under normal operating conditions (normal temperatures and pressures) and if the system's fluid and filters are maintained as recommended, the level of internally generated contamination will stay within safe limits.

The two time periods that normally see an excessive amount of internally generated contamination are the first few hours after the system is first put to work and the time after the component's expected lifespan. A graph constructed to track particle accumulation over time would typically look like a bathtub. **FIGURE 28-17** gives an example of such a graph. Excessive fluid contamination leads to more internally generated contamination because the fluid is wearing out components as it circulates and creating a snowball

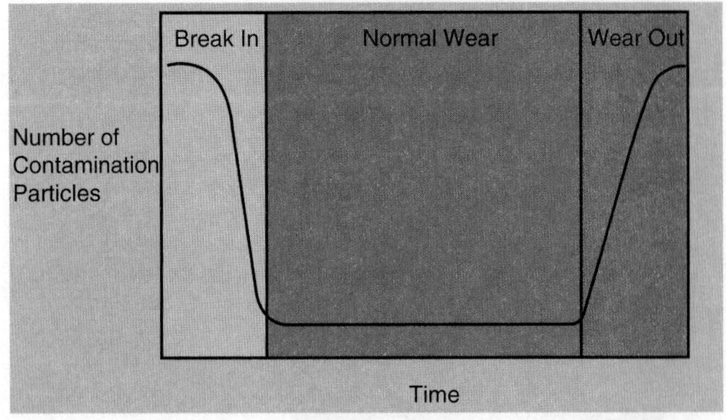

FIGURE 28-17 A graph that tracks particle contamination over time.

effect. Some factors that increase internal particle contamination are overheated hydraulic fluid; wrong viscosity fluid; high-pressure spikes; and fluid contaminated with air, water, or other chemicals.

Maintenance-Generated Contamination

If a hydraulic system could remain sealed for its lifetime, there would be a noticeable reduction in the amount of contamination that it was exposed to. Regular maintenance is a necessary part of keeping the system fluid within specified cleanliness limits as well as maintaining good fluid properties. If a technician uses best practices when it comes to servicing a hydraulic system, there should not be a marked increase in contamination. Some examples of practices that increase contamination are listed here:

1. Leaving components exposed to the atmosphere
2. Installing dirty components (hoses, filters, pumps, etc.)
3. Allowing dirt or water into the reservoir
4. Leaving hoses loose on the pump inlet
5. Changing components unnecessarily when diagnosing faults
6. Not filtering new oil before adding or refilling the tank
7. Not storing hydraulic fluid properly.

Some examples of best practices that avoid increasing contamination when maintaining or servicing hydraulic systems are these:

1. Sealing and capping all component ports, hoses, tubes, and fittings that could be exposed to the surrounding environment
2. Cleaning all components just prior to installation
3. Cleaning and drying all components before disassembly
4. Only replacing components that are faulty
5. Tightening all hoses and fittings properly and replacing all seals that are removed
6. Filtering new oil before topping up the tank or refilling it
7. Storing all hydraulic fluid in clean, sealed containers in a cool dry location.

Hydraulic Filters

Fluid filters are required in any hydraulic system to remove solid contamination from the fluid. Many variations of filters are found in hydraulic systems, and they can be located in several different places.

A hydraulic filter should be specified for the system it is part of in terms of contamination holding capacity and filtration levels. Filtration is always a balance between removing as much contamination as possible but not restricting fluid flow too much. When flow is restricted, a pressure drop occurs, and an increase in temperature follows.

ISO Fluid Cleanliness Code

In the mid-1970s, a **fluid cleanliness code**, ISO 4406, was established by ISO (International Organization for Standardization) to create a standard measuring system for hydraulic fluid cleanliness. Cleanliness is measured by taking a sample of fluid and counting the number of particles in three distinct size categories. It doesn't distinguish what the particles are made of—only their size. It has since been updated to ISO 11171 to reflect a more accurate test with slightly different particle sizing.

The test method uses specialized optical instruments to count the number of particles. The typical sample size is 100 mL and of that the number of particles per 1 mL that fit into three particle size categories is measured. The size categories are 4, 6, and 14 microns, and the number of particles that are equal to or larger in diameter than these three sizes is given a number. The more particles in each size category, the higher the number. **FIGURE 28-18** presents the ISO cleanliness code chart.

An example of a typical sample measurement would be 18/16/13. If applied to the size categories 4/6/14 microns, this translates to 1,300–2,500 particles that are 4 microns or bigger

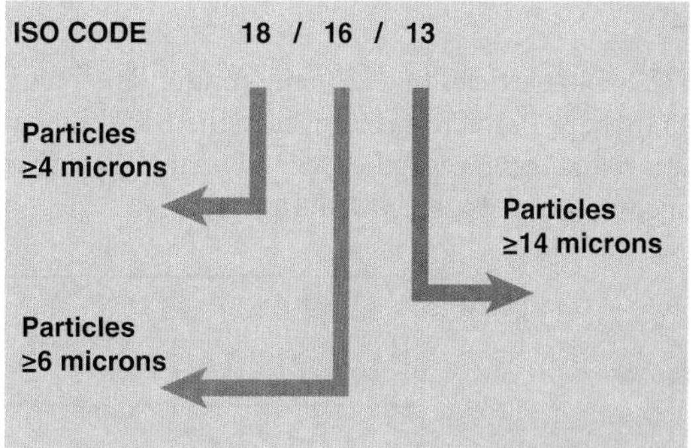

ISO Classification & Definition		
Range number	Micron	Actual Particle Count Range (per mL)
18	4+	1,300–2,500
16	6+	320–640
13	14+	40–80

Scale Number	Particles per mL More Than	Less or Equal
22	20,000	40,000
21	10,000	20,000
20	5,000	10,000
19	2,500	5,000
18	1,300	2,500
17	640	1,300
16	320	640
15	160	320
14	80	160
13	40	80
12	20	40
11	10	20
10	5	10
9	2.5	5
8	1.3	2.5
7	0.64	1.3
6	0.32	0.64

FIGURE 28-18 The ISO cleanliness code chart.

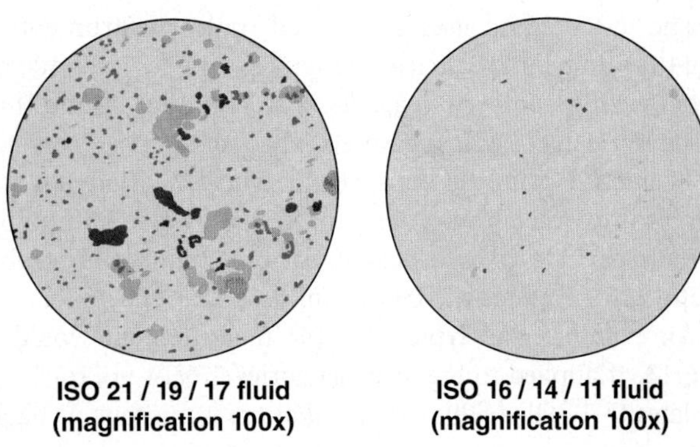

FIGURE 28-19 Two samples with distinct levels of contamination.

in size; 320–640 particles that are 6 microns or larger and 40–80 particles that are 14 microns or larger in the 1 milliliter sample.

For a visual comparison between two samples with distinct levels of contamination, see **FIGURE 28-19**.

> **TECHNICIAN TIP**
>
> Different system components are able to tolerate assorted sizes of contamination without any damage caused. Generally speaking, the components in low-pressure and low-flow systems can withstand higher levels of contamination than those in high-pressure, high-flow systems. For example, gear pumps are fairly forgiving, but servo valves are sensitive to any contamination. See **FIGURE 28-20** for a chart that outlines acceptable contamination levels for different components.

Types of Wear

Many types of wear can occur in a hydraulic system. The main types are as follows:

- Abrasive wear—Hard particles bridge two moving surfaces, scraping one or both.
- Cavitation wear—Restricted inlet flow to pump causes fluid voids that implode, causing shocks that break away critical surface material.

PUMPS			
Pressure	**<2,000 PSI <140 Bar**	**<3,000 PSI 210 Bar**	**<3,000 PSI >210 Bar**
Fixed Gear	20/18/15	19/17/15	18/16/13
Fixed Vane	20/18/15	19/17/14	18/16/13
Fixed Piston	19/17/15	18/16/14	17/15/13
Variable Vane	19/17/15	18/16/14	17/15/13
Variable Piston	18/16/14	17/15/13	16/14/12
VALVES			
Pressure		**3,000 PSI 210 Bar**	**>3,000 PSI >210 Bar**
Directional (solenoid)		20/18/15	19/17/14
Pressure (modulating)		19/17/14	19/17/14
Flow Controls (standard)		19/17/14	19/17/14
Check Valves		20/18/15	20/18/15
Cartridge Valves		20/18/15	19/17/14
Screw-In Valves		18/16/13	17/15/12
Prefill Valves		20/18/15	19/17/14
Load-Sensing Directional Valves		18/16/14	17/15/13
Hydraulic Remote Controls		18/16/13	17/15/12
Proportional Directional (throttle) Valves		18/16/13	17/15/12*
Proportional Pressure Controls		18/16/13	17/15/12*
Proportional Cartridge Valves		18/16/13	17/15/12*
Proportional Screw-In Valves		18/16/13	17/15/12
Servo Valves		16/14/11*	15/13/10*
ACTUATORS			
Pressure	**<2,000 PSI <140 Bar**	**3,000 PSI 210 Bar**	**<3,000 PSI >210 Bar**
Cylinders	20/18/15	20/18/15	20/18/15
Vane Motors	20/18/15	19/17/14	18/16/13
Axial Piston Motors	19/17/14	18/16/13	17/15/12
Gear Motors	21/19/17	20/18/15	19/17/14
Radial Piston Motors	20/18/14	19/17/15	18/16/13
Swashplate Design Motors	18/16/14	17/15/13	16/14/12

FIGURE 28-20 A chart that outlines acceptable contamination levels for different components.

- Fatigue wear—Particles bridging a clearance cause a surface stress riser that expands into a spall due to repeated stressing of the damaged area.
- Erosive wear—Fine particles in a high-speed stream of fluid eat away a metering edge or critical surface.
- Adhesive wear—Loss of oil film allows metal-to-metal contact between moving surfaces.
- Corrosive wear—Water or chemical contamination in the fluid causes rust or a chemical reaction that degrades a surface.

Wear can also be broken down into how it occurs. **Two-body wear** occurs when two components that are moving in relation to each other come into contact by breaking through the lubrication barrier. The contact is called abrasion and leads to galling when material is transferred or broken off. The broken off pieces then become contamination.

Three-body wear occurs when a piece of contamination gets between two moving components and creates more surface erosion and wear. **FIGURE 28-21** is an example of three-body wear.

Hydraulic Fluid Heaters

As mentioned earlier, fluid viscosity is most affected by temperature. Machines that work in extreme cold environments can be equipped with hydraulic fluid heaters to improve fluid viscosity during cold periods of operation.

The goal of a hydraulic heater is to raise the temperature of the hydraulic fluid to at least 20°F above its pour point. This is a critical temperature and should prevent fluid starvation.

Hydraulic heaters function by using resistive electrical elements, resistive electric blankets, or heat exchangers through which coolant is circulated.

Hydraulic Fluid Coolers

Hydraulic fluid should be kept below a prolonged operating temperature of 150°F (66°C) for it to maintain its critical properties. As ambient air temperatures climb, and as system pressures and flows increase when the machine is put to work, heat is transferred to the hydraulic fluid. If heat isn't transferred out of the fluid, it will keep building up and eventually start to break the fluid down.

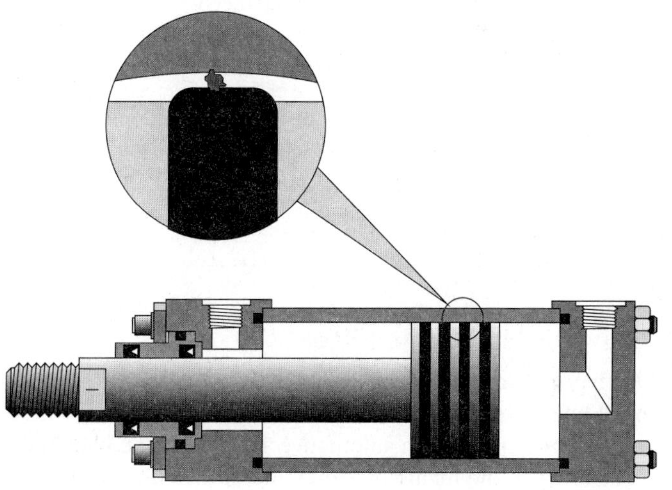

FIGURE 28-21 An example of three-body wear.

FIGURE 28-22 A hydraulic cooler on a machine.

Almost all machines produced today have hydraulic coolers to help limit the maximum temperature the fluid reaches.

Most coolers are airflow type and very similar to engine coolant radiators. **FIGURE 28-22** shows a hydraulic cooler on a machine.

▶ Function and Construction Features of Hydraulic Fluid Filters

K28004

As mentioned previously, fluid filters are a vital component of any hydraulic system. Without any filtration, the system fluid would eventually become contaminated and start to wear all components that it flows past. This also occurs if there is a filter in the system, but it isn't serviced regularly. Most filters have a **bypass valve** to allow flow even if the filter gets plugged. This prevents fluid starvation, even though the fluid isn't getting cleaned.

For any hydraulic system, it is critical that the right filtration is used at the right location. Filtration is always a balance between efficiency (stopping contamination from circulating) and flow restriction. Filter size equates to contamination holding capacity.

Filter Types

Filters can be categorized in several ways, such as by their location, construction type, pressure rating, flow rating, particle size, what they remove, and capacity to filter contamination. They can be grouped into three pressure ratings: low pressure—up to 350 psi, or 24 bar; medium pressure—up to 2,000 psi, or 138 bar; and high pressure—up to 6,500 psi, or 450 bar. Flow ratings in all pressure groups can be as high as 200 gpm with medium pressure filters reaching 300 gpm flow ratings.

Tank Breather

Air must be transferred in and out of vented hydraulic tanks as fluid levels fluctuate in the tank. To separate moisture and dirt from atmospheric air, a tank breather mounted to the tank provides the tank with clean air. Tank breathers typically catch contaminants as small as 3 microns in size.

This filter is often forgotten during services but should be replaced or cleaned on a regular basis. **FIGURE 28-23** depicts a tank breather that hasn't been service for a long time.

Breathers are quite often throwaway filter assemblies, but they can also be part of the filler cap.

Hydraulic Screens

Screens can be found in several locations in a hydraulic system such as for the pump inlet, return line in the tank, and in the filler neck of a tank. They can also be part of a filter assembly that is mounted in the tank. In this case, the screen is used as a prefilter for a cartridge filter that fits inside the screen. Screens are sometimes called strainers and are designed to catch relatively large debris and stop it from traveling through the system.

Screens can be used for negative pressure on the pump inlet or for high pressure with a pump outlet flow going through them. Most hydraulic pump manufacturers do not recommend the use of any filter or screen on the pump inlet, to reduce the chance of cavitation.

Screens are made from a metal mesh that is reinforced and could incorporate one or more permanent magnets. If used for a pump inlet filter, a screen has large openings to prevent flow restriction to the pump inlet. The mesh size relates to the number of openings per square inch. A 60-mesh **screen** has 60 openings per square inch and, depending on the wire size, has an approximately 238-micron opening. A 100-mesh size has 149-micron openings, and a 200 mesh has 74-micron openings. As mesh size goes up, the size of the opening goes down. A high-pressure screen assembly is shown in **FIGURE 28-24**.

Screens can be stand-alone filters when used as pump inlet filters, or can be a cartridge-style filter held in a housing, if used as a high-pressure filter. Screens can be washed and reused if not damaged.

FIGURE 28-23 A tank breather that hasn't been serviced for a long time.

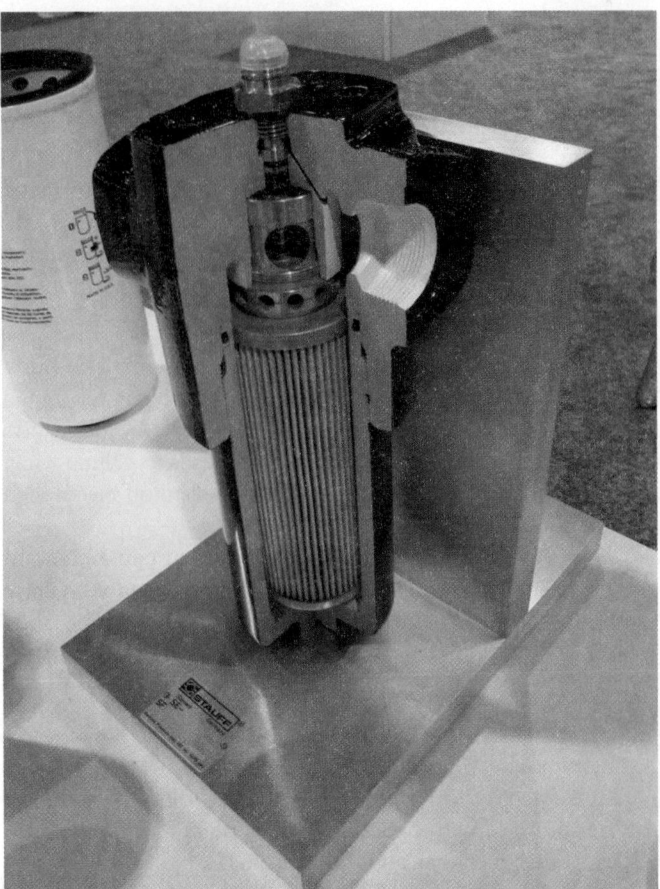

FIGURE 28-24 A high-pressure screen assembly.

> **TECHNICIAN TIP**
>
> A large wheel loader was having recurring hydraulic problems that started from a cylinder failure that sent debris throughout the system. To put a stop to the problem, a thorough investigation was ordered by the shop supervisor, which led to the hydraulic tank being removed. Inside the tank were two return screens, through one of which all the oil flow from the main control valve was flowing. After removing the screen, the problem was evident. The screen had caught the debris from the cylinder failure, which had never been removed and cleaned out. Subsequently the oil flowing through the screen was constantly churning the debris, and it eventually wore holes in the screen and got out of the screen. It then circulated back through the system and caused many ongoing problems. In **FIGURE 28-25**, a damaged return screen is shown.

Spin-On Hydraulic Filter

One type of hydraulic filter is the spin-on type, which has its own metal housing sealed and crimped onto a female threaded base. A spin-on filter is like an automotive-style engine oil filter but is made to withstand higher pressures and flows. These filters are a replaceable assembly with a filter element inside the metal housing.

FIGURE 23-25 A damaged return screen.

The inside element is a **pleated** multilayer configuration; fluid flows through it from the outside toward the center. The filter element usually has several layers, starting with a screen around the outside to stop large particles from damaging inner parts of the element. There may be up to four layers made of a variety of materials, with many variations to these inner layers. The inner layers are called the filter media and provide the filter with its efficiency at capturing contamination and maximum flow rating. **FIGURE 28-26** shows a cutaway of a spin-on hydraulic filter.

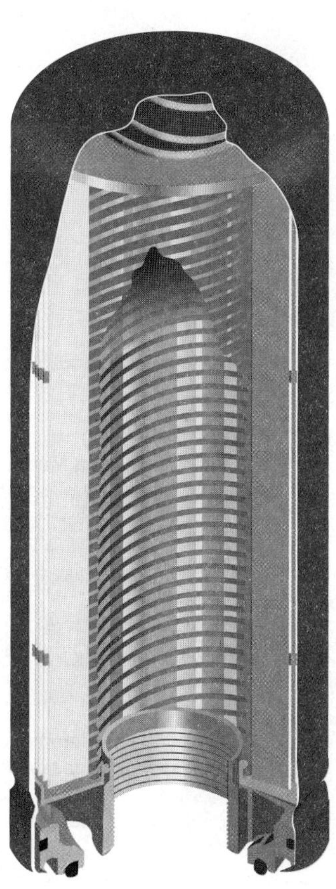

FIGURE 28-26 Cutaway of a hydraulic spin-on filter.

Spin-on–type hydraulic filters come in many sizes, flow ratings, pressure ratings, and efficiency ratings. The original filter should be rated for the system flows and pressures along with the expected fluid viscosity and ambient temperatures. Occasionally it may be necessary to deviate from the original filter in cases where pump flow is increased, fluid viscosity changes, or system pressure changes. Always check with the machine manufacturer before putting on a different filter. Cleanout filters may be available for post-failure cleanout. These will plug up fast and should only be left on for a brief period.

Spin-on filter bases contain bypass valves and may have bypass indicators that are visual or electrical devices. **FIGURE 28-27** depicts a spin-on filter with a bypass valve and switch.

TECHNICIAN TIP

It is normal for a filter bypass to open when a machine starts up after it has been sitting in cold weather for a few days. This is usually an indication that the filter is starting to get plugged, and it shouldn't keep bypassing for more than a few minutes or once the fluid viscosity lowers.

Machines with electronic monitoring systems will light up an indicator to make the operator aware that a filter is bypassing.

Cartridge

The other main type of hydraulic filter is the cartridge type. It has a separate filter element called the cartridge that either fits inside a reusable metal housing that mounts to a base that can be

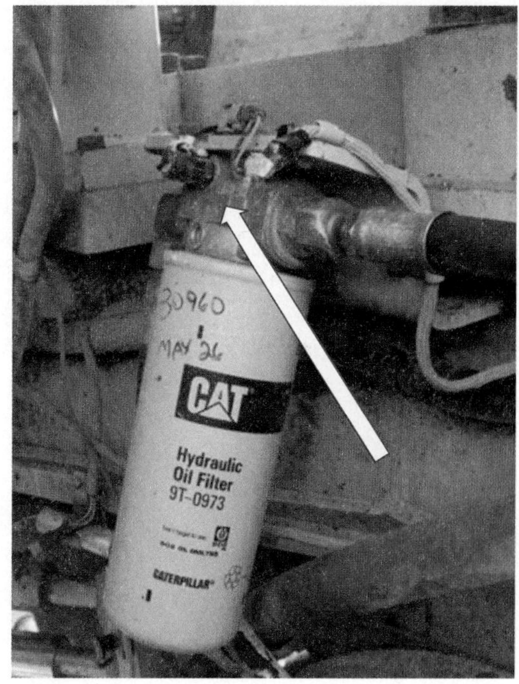

FIGURE 28-27 A spin-on filter with a bypass valve and switch.

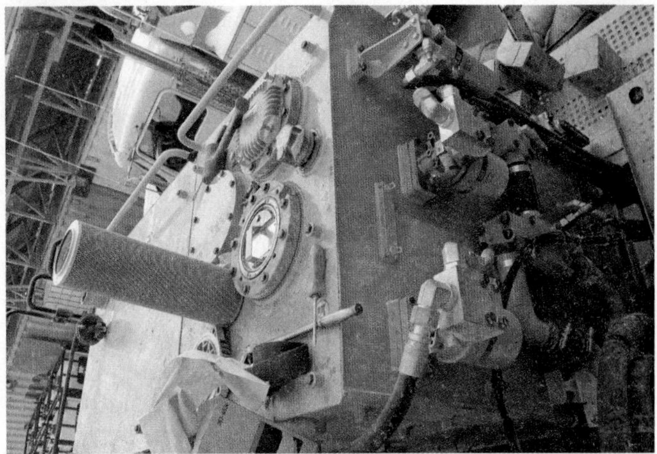

FIGURE 28-28 A cartridge filter that is inside an excavator's hydraulic tank.

mounted anywhere on the machine, or into a round sub-housing in the hydraulic tank. FIGURE 28-28 shows a cartridge filter that is inside an excavator's hydraulic tank.

Cartridge filters are usually used as return filters that accept fluid returning to the tank and clean it before it gets to recirculate. However, they can also be pressure filters. As pressure filters, they usually have a canister mounted to a base that holds the replaceable filter element. See FIGURE 28-29 to see a cartridge filter used as a pressure filter.

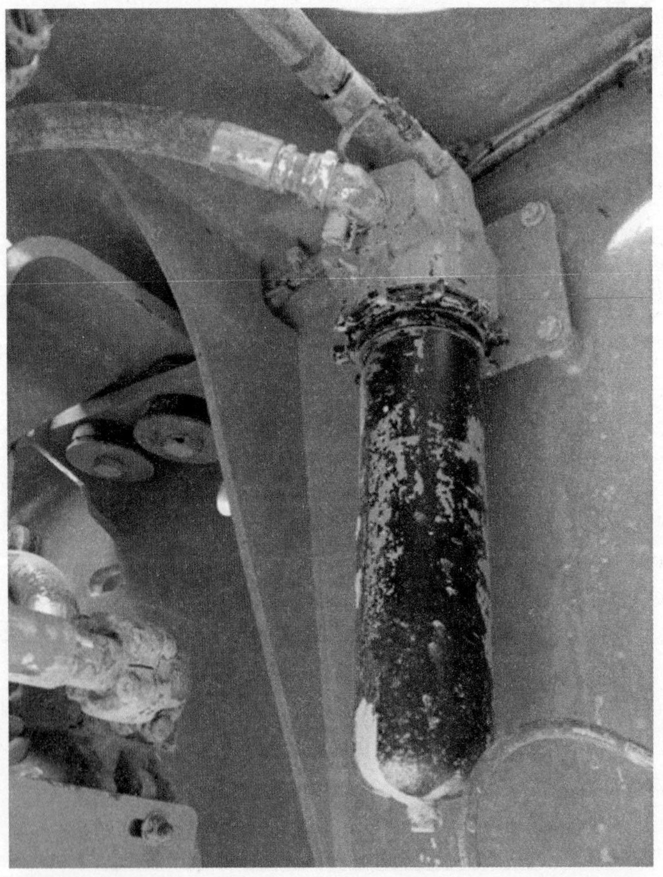

FIGURE 28-29 A cartridge filter used as a pressure filter.

Filter Media

Filter media is the actual material that captures contamination and keeps it from flowing through the system. In either spin-on or cartridge-type filters, it is pleated (folded) to get the maximum possible surface area exposed to the fluid. The media used in hydraulic filters has to be reinforced and supported to avoid damage and rupture. See FIGURE 28-30 for an example of a typical hydraulic filter media layering.

The media is bonded at both ends to end caps that are then sealed in the filter housing. Filter media comes in two general types—cellulose and synthetic (often called fiberglass)—and some are a blend of the two compounds. These types of media are depth media because they force the fluid to flow through and around the microscopic fibers, and this action allows the media to capture contamination.

Cellulose is a paper-based material and is acceptable for low-pressure, low-flow filtration. Cellulose is not compatible with non–petroleum-based fluids and will swell up and create flow blockage.

Synthetic media is generally superior to cellulose in consistency and efficiency but is more expensive. FIGURE 28-31 displays a comparison between cellulose and fiberglass media magnified.

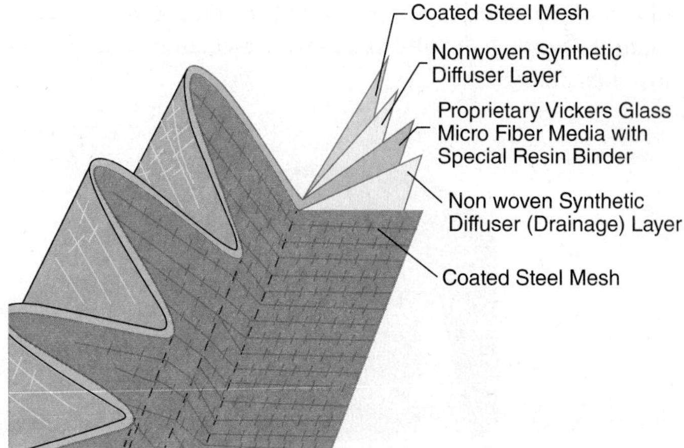

FIGURE 28-30 An example of a typical hydraulic filter media layering.

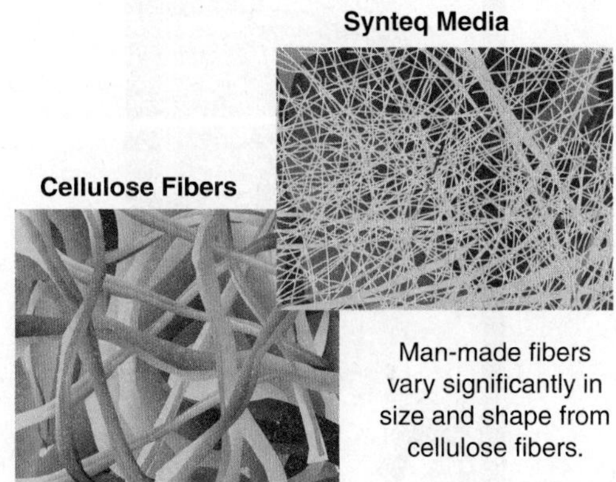

FIGURE 28-31 A comparison between cellulose and fiberglass media magnified.

Filter Indicators

Spin-on filters bases contain bypass valves that allow the hydraulic fluid to bypass them when the filter element gets plugged. Although this means that unfiltered fluid will flow past the filter and through the system, the bypass valve prevents over pressurization of the filter and the risk of a leak. Many filter bases also incorporate filter indicators to show when the filter is either plugged or close to needing a change. Filter indicators can be simple color-coded plungers (green is good; red means plugged) that work on the pressure differential of the fluid going across the filter, or can be a gauge. **FIGURE 28-32** shows a filter indicator gauge.

Another type of filter indicator is one that either turns on a light on the dash or sets a code, or both. This type of indicator uses a pressure switch located in the filter base that sends a signal to an ECM. The ECM then sends a signal to a light on the dash or logs a fault code. Some machines can be programmed to derate the engine if the hydraulic filter becomes plugged.

Kidney Loop Filter

Some other terms for a **kidney loop filtration** machine are filter cart, portable filter, off-line filter, external filter, and oil purifier/dehydrator. The term "kidney loop" comes from a medical procedure performed on people with defective kidneys. The patient's blood is circulated through an external filter to clean out impurities that would make the patient sick. The same procedure is done to a machine's hydraulic system when a kidney loop machine is connected to it.

FIGURE 28-32 A filter indicator gauge.

It may be necessary to perform extra filtration on a machine's hydraulic fluid in certain situations. These include after a catastrophic failure; after a major fluid contamination; or after a filter has failed, to extend the life of the fluid.

The many variations of kidney loop machines include size, flow rate, portability, manual or automatic operation, water removal function, and particle counter display.

Water removal from hydraulic fluid is performed by lowering the pressure to a negative value and heating the fluid to "boil off" the water. This is done with a dehydrator machine. In **FIGURE 28-33**, we see a kidney loop filter that includes a water removal feature. Kidney loop machines need regular maintenance, and their filters should not be allowed to become plugged.

> ▶ TECHNICIAN TIP
>
> Excessive water content in a hydraulic system can cause many problems. Another option to remove it, besides changing the fluid, is a hydraulic fluid **dehydrator**, a machine that is able to remove water from hydraulic fluid and that usually includes fluid filtration as part of its function.

To remove water from hydraulic oil, it may be necessary to install a dehydrator machine. It is similar to a kidney loop

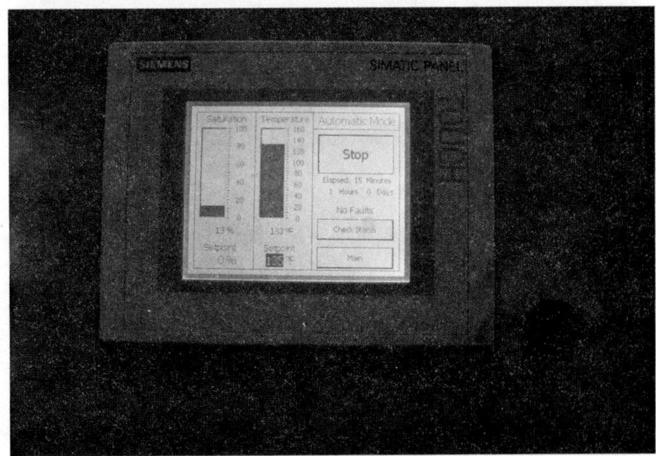

FIGURE 28-33 A kidney loop filter that includes a water removal feature.

machine but uses a vacuum pump to lower the pressure of the fluid in the machine and raise the temperature high enough to boil off the water in the fluid.

Filter Ratings

Filters are rated according to the flow they can accommodate, the pressure drop they create, and their effectiveness at capturing particles (efficiency). Solid particle contamination in fluid is measured by micron size. One micron is one-millionth of a meter, or 0.000039". The smallest particle a human eye can see is roughly 40 microns, and many filters capture particles as small as 5 microns. Some cleanout filters collect particles as small as 2 microns.

An ideal filter would not create an excessive pressure drop and would hold all normal contamination expected to accumulate within a service interval. There is always a trade-off between a filter's efficiency and its ability to allow unrestricted oil flow through it. If a filter captures too much contamination, it will become plugged, and its bypass valve will open, allowing unfiltered fluid to circulate through the system.

Two previously common ratings for filter efficiency—nominal and absolute—are not very accurate and should not be relied on. The more accurate and consistent way to measure filter efficiency is with a standardized test that compares the amount of contamination in the fluid before it gets to the filter and how much leaves the filter. A sophisticated test rig is used with a test dust that is of a specific size, and as the fluid flows through the filter, the number of dust particles are measured before and after the filter. The result is calculated as a Beta ratio. The size of the test particles defines the efficiency of the filter.

Filtration ratio (ßn)—The ratio of the number of particles greater than a given size upstream of the test filter divided by the number of particles of the same size downstream of the test filter. The Beta ratio is then used to calculate the filter efficiency with this formula:

$$\text{Efficiency} = B - 1/B \times 100$$

The Beta ratio is only valid if it includes the size of the test particles. See **FIGURE 28-34** for a comparison of filter efficiencies.

There are several other testing standards for filters such as ISO 16889—filter capacity and efficiency; ISO 2942—structural test; and ISO 2941—collapse strength.

Filter Locations

Filters can be used in several different locations throughout a hydraulic system. Depending on where they are located and their purpose, they will have different construction features. Simple low-pressure and low-flow systems usually have one return filter, whereas high-pressure, high-flow systems can have five or six different filters throughout the system.

Pump Inlet

Locating a filter of any kind at the inlet of a pump is debatable in terms of risk versus reward. In theory, the inlet oil should

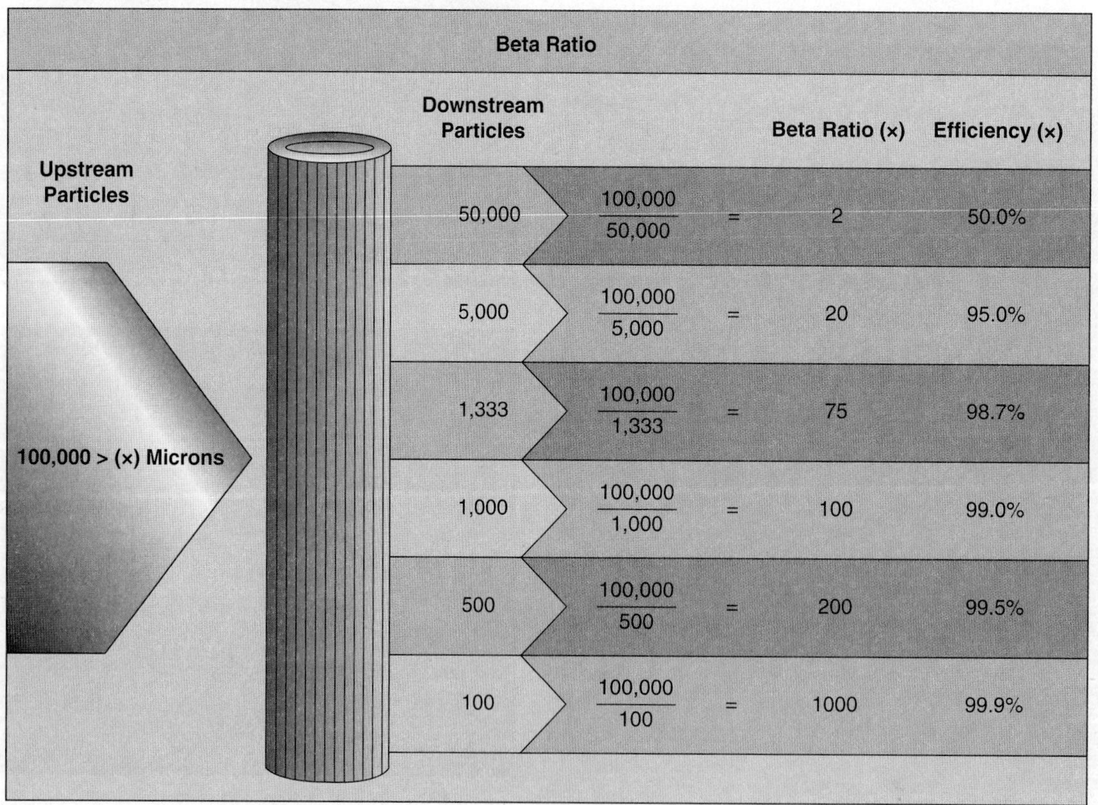

FIGURE 28-34 A comparison of filter efficiencies.

be filtered before it gets to the pump, and a screen is the least intrusive method. The risk is that if the screen gets plugged, it will cause a restriction to the pump inlet and create a cavitation scenario that could lead to a pump failure. The reward is that any large contamination that is in the tank will be stopped at the screen before it gets to the pump inlet.

It is rare to find a screen at the pump inlet, and if there is one, it is usually a pump that has a positive pressure fluid supply to the pump.

Return Filter

The most common location for a filter in an open-loop system is between the main control valve and the tank. A filter placed here will catch the majority of the internally generated contamination before it can return to the tank and get recirculated through the systems.

Pressure Filter

A filter placed between the pump outlet and the main control valve will be subject to system pressure and must be made to withstand pressure spikes that may occur. These filters catch any debris leaving the pump and keep it from being sent through the system.

Case Drain Filter

For machines that have high-flow and high-pressure systems, like larger excavators and shovels, the machine manufacturer might install filters in the return lines from the pumps' and motors' case drain lines **FIGURE 28-35**.

▶ Functions and Construction Features of Hydraulic Fluid Heaters and Coolers

K28005

The purpose of hydraulic fluid heaters and coolers was discussed previously, and now we look at the operation and construction of these components.

Hydraulic Fluid Heater Function and Construction

Some worksites are located where there are extreme cold temperatures. Northern latitudes or higher elevations can see temperatures well below freezing (0°C, or 32°F). Some fluid viscosities can flow at subfreezing temperatures, but when temperatures fall to the −30°F (−34°C) range and a machine's hydraulic system is operated with cold oil, severe internal damage can occur.

Many operations leave machines running just to keep machine fluids circulating in an attempt to keep them a little warm. Another option is to install fluid warmers on the machine. These include hydraulic fluid heaters, of which there are a couple of distinct types: electric-powered and coolant heat exchangers.

Electrohydraulic fluid heaters can be either the immersive or blanket type. Immersive fluid heaters mount to the tank and have a heating element that is contact with the fluid in the tank. When powered, the element heats up and heats the hydraulic fluid in the tank. If the machine is off, a natural circulation will occur as warm fluid rises. Electrohydraulic fluid heaters have to be powered by an AC power source (120 VAC or 240 VAC). Blanket-type electric heaters are either epoxied to the bottom of the tank or wrap around the tank. **FIGURE 28-36** illustrates a blanket-type hydraulic tank heater.

Hydraulic fluid heaters can also be heat exchangers that use engine coolant to warm the machines' hydraulic fluid. The coolant can come from the engine that is heated by running the engine or by a diesel-fired coolant heater. The warm coolant is circulated through a heat exchanger (thin wall tube) that is placed in the bottom of the tank.

Hydraulic heaters should be thermostatically controlled to avoid overheating the hydraulic fluid.

Hydraulic Fluid Cooler Function and Construction

Almost all machines have some type of hydraulic fluid cooler to transfer heat out of the fluid. Fluid that is overheated for a

FIGURE 28-35 A case drain filter.

FIGURE 28-36 A blanket-type hydraulic tank heater.

FIGURE 28-37 A typical hydraulic fluid cooler.

FIGURE 28-38 A hydraulic filter that has collected a lot of metal.

prolonged period starts to degrade quickly, which in turn puts all other system components at risk. Two kinds of fluid coolers may be found on MORE machines—coolant cooled and air cooled.

Coolant-cooled hydraulic fluid coolers aren't very common because the engine coolant is hotter than what the hydraulic fluid should be. However, if a hydraulic system shares fluid with a transmission, it may use a coolant-cooled fluid cooler.

Air-cooled fluid coolers are typically similar in appearance to engine coolant radiators and usually have aluminum cores. Aluminum is an excellent conductor of heat, and the core has thin fins, which air passes over in order to transfer heat to the atmosphere from fluid that flows through them. **FIGURE 28-37** shows a typical hydraulic fluid cooler.

▶ Perform a Post-Failure External Filtration Procedure

S28001

At some point in a technician's career, he or she will participate in repairing a hydraulic system because of a major component failure. Any component failure can cause long-lasting problems if a proper system cleanup isn't performed. To avoid a repeat failure, it is crucial that the system gets properly cleaned out. In **FIGURE 28-38**, a hydraulic filter has collected a lot of metal.

This job may include removing hoses, tubes, and fittings, and flushing them with mineral-based solvents. Minimum cleanout steps include draining the fluid, inspecting the inside of the tank, cleaning any screens in the system, and replacing *all* filters.

After running the machine for a brief time, it would be wise to check contamination levels with a live particle counter or an oil sample. Depending on the results of the fluid monitoring, it may be necessary to perform a kidney loop filtration procedure. To perform a system cleanout for a post-failure, pre-start-up external filtration procedure, follow the steps in **SKILL DRILL 28-1**.

SAFETY TIP

When a machine is connected to a filter cart or kidney loop machine, some extra hazards are created that the technician needs to be aware of. Hoses run from the machines hydraulic system to the kidney loop machine. The kidney loop machine also has to be powered, and most machines are at least 240 VAC, so the cord is both a trip hazard and a shock hazard. No heavy or sharp objects should be placed on or dragged over the electrical cord for the unit.

SKILL DRILL 28-1 Performing a System Cleanout

1. Drain as much fluid as possible from the tank, pumps, motors, cylinders, valves, and lines. Replace all plugs and lines with new O-rings or gaskets.
2. Replace all filters. Use high-efficiency cleanout filters if available.
3. Clean all screens with mineral spirits.
4. Open tank and clean with mineral spirits and lint-free rags. Close the tank, using a new cover O-ring or gasket.
5. Refill the hydraulic tank with the correct type and viscosity fluid (check maintenance manual).
6. Carefully perform any pump or motor bleeding procedures prior to starting.
7. Crank engine with no fuel several times to ensure pumps are getting fluid, before starting.
8. Top off the hydraulic tank if necessary.
9. Start the machine and let it idle for 5 minutes while you check for leaks and listen for noises at pump.
10. Increase rpm to 1,000, and slowly work functions without bottoming them out.

SKILL DRILL 28-1 Performing a System Cleanout (Continued)

11. Continue cycling actuators for 20–30 minutes.
12. Stop the machine.
13. Connect the kidney loop filter machine to the hydraulic tank so it draws from the bottom of tank and returns to the top.

14. Turn on the machine and monitor the particle counter.

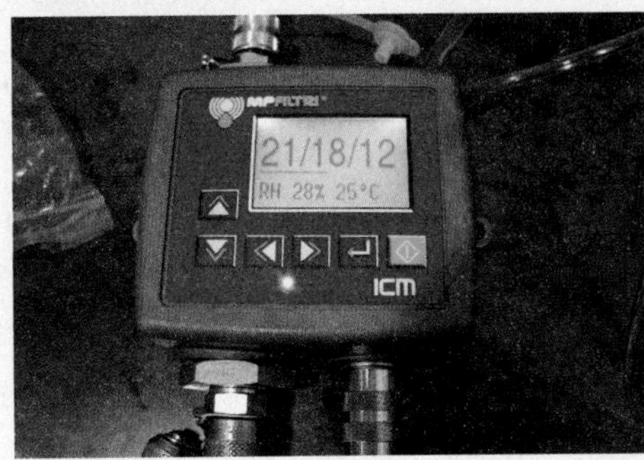

15. Stop the kidney loop machine when the ISO code reaches the desired value.
16. Start the machine and cycle the actuators while monitoring the particle counter.
17. If the ISO code goes above a set value, perform steps 14, 15, and 16 until the particle counter stays below set limit,

> **TECHNICIAN TIP**
>
> Oil sampling is a way to get an indication of fluid condition in machine fluid compartments. For hydraulic systems, an oil analysis readout is an important way to monitor the hydraulic system condition.

Fluid sampling is a routine task that all MORE technicians will perform during machine servicing or as part of a diagnostic procedure. Obtaining a hydraulic fluid sample can be done in three ways: midstream drain sample, vacuum pump sample, and live sample. Taking a live sample is ideal and will give the most accurate results. In **FIGURE 28-39**, a sample port for a hydraulic system can be seen.

FIGURE 28-39 A sample port for a hydraulic system.

Wrap-Up

Ready for Review

- "Fluid conditioning" is a term that refers to filtering, cooling, and heating hydraulic fluid.
- Hydraulic fluid is the lifeblood of any hydraulic system.
- Five main purposes hydraulic fluid serves in a hydraulic system are to provide an effective transfer of power; lubricate all moving parts in the system, clean all components internally, transfer heat to help regulate system temperature, and maintain an effective seal in some parts of the system.
- Incompressibility of hydraulic fluid makes a hydraulic system respond quickly and positively.
- Full film lubrication keeps two moving components apart with a thin film of fluid.
- Boundary lubrication allows occasional contact between two moving components.
- Hydraulic fluid cleans and cools as it circulates through the system.
- Hydraulic fluid is used to seal many components in a system.

- Hydraulic fluid properties must be carefully considered before adding fluid to a system.
- Viscosity is the most important property and refers to a fluid's resistance to flow. It is mostly influenced by temperature.
- Fluid viscosity is measured by timing how fast a specific quantity of fluid at a specific temperature flows through a fixed orifice.
- Viscosity charts show the proper viscosity that a fluid should have according to ambient temperatures that the machine will be working in.
- Viscosity index is a measure of stability in a fluid's viscosity as it changes temperature. Higher numbers equate to less change.
- SAE viscosity ratings are measured at 212°F (100°C) in summer and 0°F (−18°C) in winter.
- ISO viscosity ratings are tested at 40°C (104°F) and range from 22 to 68.
- Other fluid properties include lubricity, pour point, oxidation resistance, rust and corrosion resistance, demulsibility, fire resistance, and flash point.
- Oxidation is a chemical reaction between the hydraulic fluid and oxygen, and leads to varnished components.
- Foaming can occur if the air content of a hydraulic fluid is too high.
- Additives in hydraulic fluid are critical to provide antiwear and antifoaming properties and corrosion resistance.
- Base fluids for hydraulic fluid include petroleum fluids, synthetic fluids, biodegradable fluids, and fire-resistant fluids.
- Petroleum-based fluids are refined from crude oil.
- Synthetic fluids are artificially created and feature a high-viscosity index.
- Biodegradable fluids are based on rapeseed or canola oil and can be used in environmentally sensitive areas.
- Fire resistant fluids have a high-water base and are commonly used in underground mining machines.
- Fluid conditioning is needed to keep hydraulic fluid clean and keep its temperature regulated.
- Different types of contamination in hydraulic fluid are solid (dirt, metal, rubber), gaseous (air), and liquid (water, diesel fuel).
- Water content in hydraulic oil can be in three forms: free water, emulsified water, and water in solution.
- Hydraulic fluid contamination can originate from built-in contamination, external contamination, internally generated contamination, and maintenance-generated contamination.
- ISO cleanliness code is a way to accurately measure how much solid particle contamination is in hydraulic fluid.
- Two-body wear occurs between two moving components that break through the fluid film barrier.
- Solid contamination can create three-body wear.
- Screens are used to catch relatively large particles.
- Spin-on filters are one-piece, throwaway filters that filter from the outside to the center and have bypass valves in their base.
- Cartridge-type filters have a replaceable element that is sealed in a reusable housing.
- Filter media is the material that the filter element is made from and can be cellulose or synthetic.
- Cellulose media is not compatible with non–petroleum-based fluids.
- Synthetic media is sometimes called fiberglass media.
- Kidney loop filter machines can be called off line filters, external filters, and portable filters.

Key Terms

additives Chemical compounds added to the base hydraulic fluid intended to combat many fluid degrading conditions (foaming, rust, corrosion, viscosity breakdown).

boundary lubrication When two moving components come into contact occasionally by breaking through the fluid film.

bypass valve A valve incorporated into a filter base that opens to allow fluid flow when pressure increases due to filter plugging

cartridge filters Filters that have replaceable elements that are sealed in reusable housings.

dehydrator A device used to remove water from hydraulic systems. It lowers the pressure to a negative value and then raises the temperature to "boil off" the water.

demulsibility The ability of a fluid to separate water from itself.

entrained air Air that has mixed with hydraulic fluid and is circulated through the system.

filter media The material that the filter element is made from, which can be cellulose or synthetic.

fire-resistant fluids Three main types are water/glycol, water emulsion, and synthetic based fluids. Different seals and filters will likely be needed in the system.

fluid cleanliness code An ISO-established code to accurately measure solid particle contamination.

fluid conditioning Refers to filtering, cooling, and heating of hydraulic fluid.

fluid properties There are several properties of hydraulic fluid that have to be considered before adding fluid to a system.

free air Air is a contaminant in a hydraulic system, and free air is not mixed with the fluid.

free water Water that hasn't combined with hydraulic oil and will settle to the bottom of the tank.

full film lubrication When two moving components are separated by a thin film oil fluid.

hydraulic fluid The medium that flows through any hydraulic system. There are many types of hydraulic that can be found in MORE machines.

incompressible The property of a hydraulic fluid that is desirable to make the system responsive (hydraulic fluid is slightly compressible).

ISO viscosity ratings A viscosity rating at 40°C (104°F) that ranges from 22 to 68 for common fluids.

kidney loop filtration A separate filter machine that is connected to the hydraulic system to perform an extra cleaning.

kinematic One method of testing fluid viscosity.

micron A unit of distance measurement for microscopic particles. One micron is equivalent to one-millionth of a meter.

mineral oil A type of base fluid derived from crude oil.

oxidation A condition that results from the combination of hydraulic fluid and oxygen and heat.

pleated Describes how filter media is folded when it is formed into an element

SAE viscosity ratings A viscosity rating at 212°F (100°C) and 0°F (−18°C). SAE 20 and SAE 10W are common ratings.

Saybolt Viscosimeter A test instrument used to measure fluid viscosity.

screen A coarse filter that can be used for pump inlet, return, or pressure filtration.

synthetic hydraulic fluid Created from a manmade chain of molecules that result in a high-viscosity index, which is excellent cold weather use.

three-body wear Occurs between two moving components and solid contamination.

two-body wear Describes wear between two moving components that break through the fluid film barrier.

viscosity chart Can be found in the maintenance guide to show the proper fluid viscosity for hydraulic fluid according to ambient temperature.

viscosity index The measure of the rate of change in a fluid's viscosity as its temperature changes.

Review Questions

1. Hydraulic fluid serves all of the following functions in a hydraulic system, *except*:
   a. lubricating all moving parts in the system.
   b. removing contaminants from the system.
   c. transferring heat to help regulate system temperature.
   d. maintaining an effective seal in some parts of the systems.
2. To transfer power effectively in a hydraulic system, the fluid must ________________.
   a. have high boiling point
   b. be virtually incompressible
   c. be easily compressible
   d. have low boiling point
3. A hydraulic fluid's viscosity ______ for every 5,000 psi it is subjected to.
   a. doubles
   b. triples
   c. reduces by one-fourth
   d. reduces to half
4. Viscosity index is a number given to a fluid to indicate how its viscosity changes with______________.
   a. repeated use
   b. volume
   c. temperature
   d. pressure
5. Hydraulic system components (pumps, valves, and actuators) must maintain very small clearances between their internal components to be able to seal and separate high and low pressure. As clearances increase, all of the following happen *except*:
   a. Internal leakage increases.
   b. Fluid overheating increases.
   c. System efficiency decreases.
   d. Viscosity of fluid decreases.
6. Most filters have a ______________ to allow flow even if the filter gets plugged. This prevents fluid starvation, even though the fluid isn't getting cleaned.
   a. bypass window
   b. bypass valve
   c. suction pump
   d. alternative valve
7. All of the following are pressure ratings for a filter, *except*:
   a. 350 psi or 24 bar.
   b. 8,500 psi or 586 bar
   c. 2,000 psi or 138 bar
   d. 6,500 psi or 450 bar
8. Air-cooled fluid coolers are typically similar in appearance to engine coolant radiators and usually have ________ cores.
   a. silver
   b. copper
   c. aluminum
   d. lead
9. Machine fluids can be kept warm by all of the following methods, *except*:
   a. leaving the machine running.
   b. installing an electric-powered heat exchanger.
   c. using a coolant heat exchanger.
   d. adding hot fluid to the already present fluid.
10. The most common location for a filter in an open-loop system is __________.
    a. between the main control valve and the tank.
    b. inlet of a pump.
    c. between the pump outlet and the main control valve.
    d. in the return lines from the pumps.

ASE Technician A/Technician B Style Questions

1. Technician A says one of the main functions of a hydraulic fluid is to cool components. Technician B says hydraulic fluid can compress up to 10%. Who is correct?
   a. Technician A
   b. Technician B
   c. Both A and B
   d. Neither A nor B
2. Technician A says the SAE viscosity rating has both summer and winter ratings. Technician B says ISO viscosity ratings are tested at 40°C (104°F). Who is correct?
   a. Technician A
   b. Technician B
   c. Both A and B
   d. Neither A nor B

3. Technician A says boundary lubrication keeps all components separated. Technician B says full film lubrication maintains a film thickness of 0.001" at all times. Who is correct?
   a. Technician A
   b. Technician B
   c. Both A and B
   d. Neither A nor B
4. Technician A says hydraulic fluid additives can improve a hydraulic fluid's viscosity index. Technician B says a sulfur/phosphorous additive can improve anti wear properties. Who is correct?
   a. Technician A
   b. Technician B
   c. Both A and B
   d. Neither A nor B are correct
5. Technician A says water content in hydraulic fluid can reach 10% before it causes problems. Technician B says any air in hydraulic fluid is bad. Who is correct?
   a. Technician A
   b. Technician B
   c. Both A and B
   d. Neither A nor B
6. Technician A says the ISO cleanliness code takes into account the fluid's viscosity. Technician B says a lower ISO code number means the fluid is cleaner. Who is correct?
   a. Technician A
   b. Technician B
   c. Both A and B
   d. Neither A nor B
7. Technician A says tank breathers can help keep water out of tanks. Technician B says as mesh size goes up it can stop smaller particles. Who is correct?
   a. Technician A
   b. Technician B
   c. Both A and B
   d. Neither A nor B
8. Technician A says a cartridge filter is only used for low-pressure applications. Technician B says a filter bypass valve will open when the filter gets plugged. Who is correct?
   a. Technician A
   b. Technician B
   c. Both A and B
   d. Neither A nor B
9. Technician A says a filter Beta ratio rating is only valid if it includes micron size. Technician B says a filter's dirt holding capacity is measured in gpm. Who is correct?
   a. Technician A
   b. Technician B
   c. Both A and B
   d. Neither A nor B
10. Technician A says to remove water from hydraulic fluid a dehydrator will raise the fluid pressure and lower the temperature. Technician B says one type of fluid heater uses a diesel burner directly on the bottom of the hydraulic tank. Who is correct?
   a. Technician A
   b. Technician B
   c. Both A and B
   d. Neither A nor B

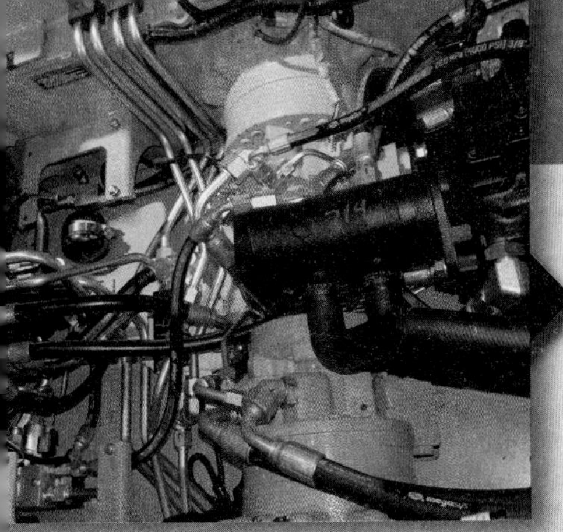

CHAPTER 29
Hydraulic Conductors and Connectors

Knowledge Objectives

After reading this chapter, you will be able to:

- **K29001** Explain the fundamentals of pressure in a hydraulic system.
- **K29002** Discuss the safety requirements for hydraulic system conductors and connectors.
- **K29003** Describe the construction features of hydraulic tubes.
- **K29004** Describe the construction features of hydraulic hoses.
- **K29005** Explain working pressure safety factor and burst pressure ratings for hoses and tubes.
- **K29006** Explain conductor sizing for proper fluid velocity.
- **K29007** Describe common conductor failures.
- **K29008** Describe the different types of hydraulic fittings found on MORE machines.
- **K29009** Describe the construction features of hydraulic seals.
- **K29010** Describe construction features of hydraulic quick couplers.

Skills Objectives

After reading this chapter, you will be able to:

- **S29001** Demonstrate how to replace a hydraulic hose using the STAMPED method.
- **S29002** Demonstrate how to remove and replace the O-ring of a flanged fitting.

▶ Introduction

Mobile off-road equipment (MORE) will have a wide array of hydraulic system arrangements on them. These systems can be used to control implements such as a blades and buckets, control steering systems, and braking systems, and many drivetrain systems will incorporate hydraulic systems. See **FIGURE 29-1** for a variety of MORE machines.

Each of these hydraulic systems will have a minimum number of components: pump(s), filter(s), actuators(s), a reservoir, and a directional control valve. All of these components need to be connected so that hydraulic fluid at operating temperature can pass between them at maximum pressure and flow without leaking internally or externally. This is the job of hydraulic fluid conductors, connectors, and seals.

The terms "conductor" and "connector" refer to any hose, tube, seal, or fitting that is part of a machine's hydraulic system and has hydraulic fluid flowing through it or past it. Hydraulic tubes and hoses will sometimes also be referred to as hydraulic lines.

It is particularly important to understand the characteristics and applications of the different types of **conductors**, **connectors**, and seals; how they are made; and what their ratings mean. This chapter describes the types and characteristics of rigid and flexible lines as well as appropriate line selection for various applications. It discusses line sizing and provides related information on velocity, pressure ratings, and burst pressures. It goes on to cover the various styles of hydraulic fittings and their uses, as well as hose ends and their characteristics.

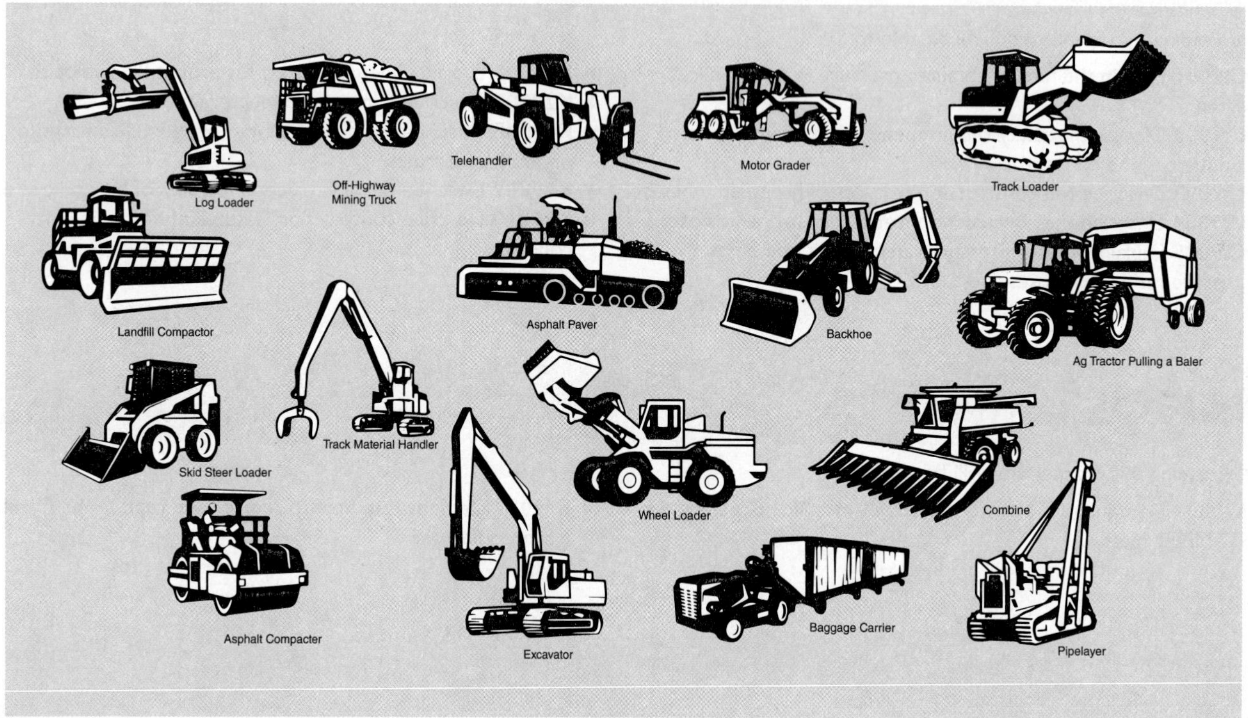

FIGURE 29-1 Heavy-duty equipment.

You Are the Mobile Heavy Equipment Technician

You are a technician working for a mid-sized general contractor with a variety of small- to medium-sized MORE machines. The fleet is about 10 years old, and the owner wants to bid on a job that is located near a waterway. One of the stipulations in the work contract is that all machines must have their hydraulic systems filled with biodegradable hydraulic fluid. The machines also must have all tubes, hoses, and connectors inspected, and the ones that appear to have any defects must be replaced. Any quick couplers would also have to be replaced to reduce the chance of leaks. All fluid conductors must be compatible with biodegradable hydraulic fluid as well.

Your job is to prepare a quote for replacing the fluid in the machines and any hoses or quick couplers that need to be replaced. Answer the following questions related to this task:

1. Where would you find the correct information regarding allowable biodegradable hydraulic fluids that could be used?
2. Where would you find the correct refill quantities for the machine's hydraulic systems?
3. What is the easiest way to get the correct hose replacement for a machine?
4. What key information would you need to know to get the correct hose replacement for a machine?
5. What would you have to know about the quick couplers to ensure you replace them with the correct ones?
6. Would there be anything else that would need to be changed after changing the hydraulic fluid?

Finally, it includes instructions on fabricating hydraulic hoses and connectors and the proper routing of hydraulic lines.

▶ Hydraulic Pressure in a Closed System

K29001

"Hydraulics" is a general term applied to the use of fluids (liquid or gas) to transfer energy in an enclosed system. Hydraulic fluid power is a specific area of hydraulics in which liquid pressure is transmitted from a pump to one or more **actuators** that provide a physical force to accomplish mechanical work. As shown in **FIGURE 29-2**, the pressure in the system is the same throughout the system, and the force that the fluid exerts to the surrounding conductor is equal. In hydraulic conductors, **static working pressure** means the pressure applied is constant.

Advantages of Hydraulic System Conductors and Connectors

One of the main advantages of a hydraulic system when compared to a mechanical system is that mechanical linkages for transferring power are eliminated. Tubes and flexible hoses can be used almost immediately to transfer the required fluid energy from the initial application force to the actuator exerting the activating force, even when there is considerable distance between the application and actuation.

Through the use of conductors and connectors that can transfer massive amounts of hydraulic energy, many mechanical components (shafts and U-joints; chains and pulleys; wire rope; and shafts and gears) can be eliminated. This greatly reduces maintenance since moving mechanical parts will require regular attention.

With the use of conductors and connectors, hydraulic energy can be transferred at an infinite number of angles (measured in degrees), around corners, and over great distances.

Disadvantages of Hydraulic System Conductors and Connectors

There are disadvantages to hydraulic system conductors and connectors, such as the potential for equipment failure and personal injury or death when hoses fail and the hydraulic fluid leaks. Still, the disadvantages are far outweighed by the advantages of these systems.

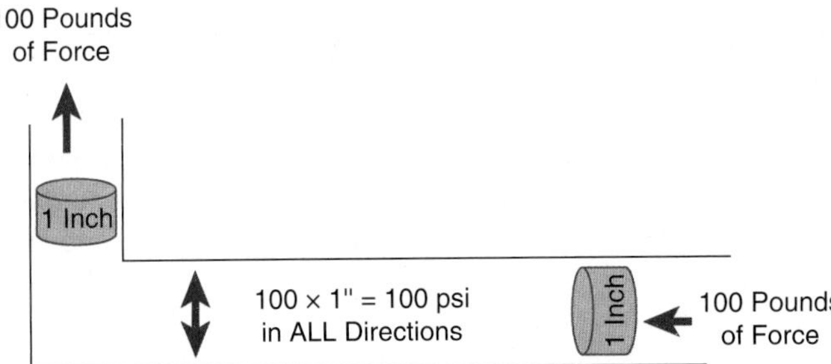

FIGURE 29-2 Equal pressure.

The following list summarizes the main disadvantages of hydraulic system conductors and connectors:

- *Safety*: High-pressure fluids create a safety hazard in the case of hose, seal, or tubing failures. The fluid itself can cause serious injury or death, and components can move in an uncontrolled manner.
- *Fire hazard*: All hydraulic fluids will burn under certain circumstances. Leaking conductors and connectors may expose fluid to open flames or high-temperature heat sources.
- *Leaks*: Fluid leaks and spills can be hazardous to the environment.

SAFETY TIP

Hydraulic systems operate under high pressures and high temperatures. Follow the manufacturer's recommendations to relieve all pressure in the system prior to servicing or repairing conductors and connectors. Service technicians must be constantly aware of the dangers associated with hydraulic fluid. If a hydraulic line or hose bursts, the hot fluid can cause severe burns, and it can be injected into the body. Always follow safe work practices when working around any parts of a hydraulic system.

▶ Safety Requirements for Hydraulic System Conductors and Connectors

K29002, S29001

FIGURE 29-3 shows some of the many safety labels posted on hydraulic equipment. Hydraulic systems can create hot, high-pressure fluids to transfer large amounts of energy. There is a high potential for injury or death if a technician isn't proactive in preventing accidents.

Use of inadequate or low-quality replacement hoses, seals, or tubes can result in these components rupturing and allow not only the escape of hot high-pressure fluid but also the sudden, uncontrolled movement of a machine, which could have disastrous results. A little common sense and proper use of personal protective equipment (PPE) will go a long way to keeping a technician safe when working on hydraulic systems. Also, always refer to the machine's specific manufacturer's service information before performing any servicing or repairs to hydraulic systems. There are many warnings and cautions on the machines and in service information that must be followed. There are also a few specific safety concerns to be aware of when working with hydraulic system conductors and connectors.

Trapped Potential Energy

Many hydraulic systems use accumulators that store high-pressure fluid. Be aware of any accumulator in the system before servicing or repairing it. Ensure all pressure is bled off before opening the system. Also, many hydraulic systems use spring pressure. Be very careful when working with springs that are not relaxed.

Crushing Hazards

It is very important that a machine be secured from uncontrolled movement when working on hydraulic components.

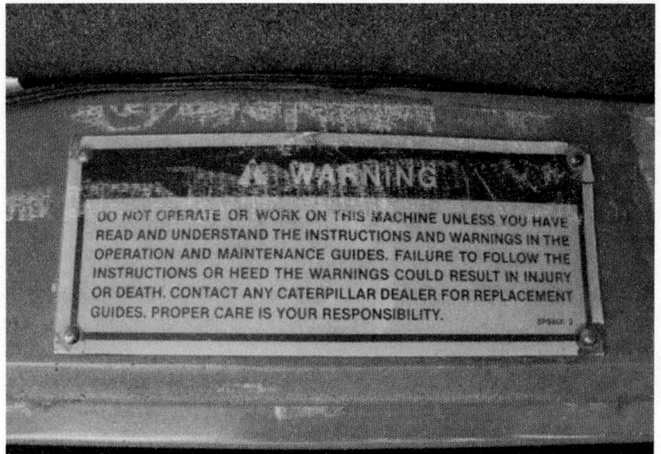

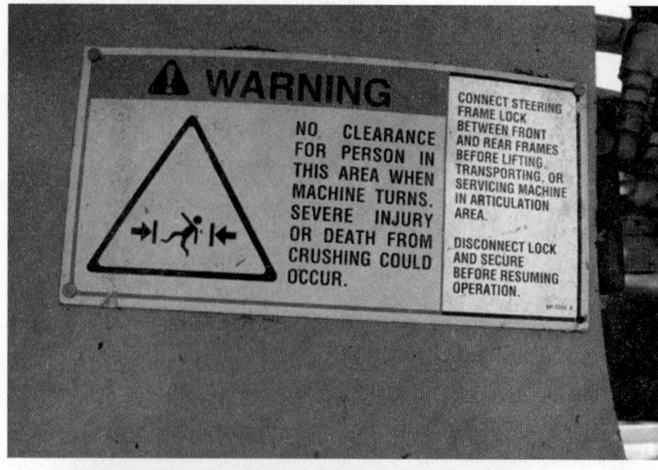

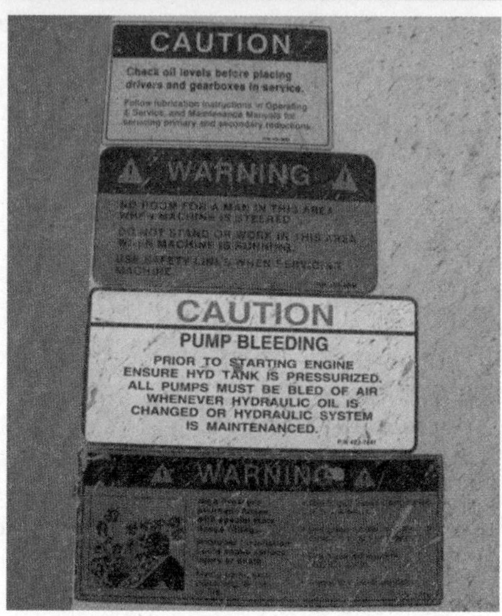

FIGURE 29-3 Safety labels.

This means using wheel chocks, proper lifting and blocking techniques, and tooling. Proper lockout/tag-out procedures must also be used when working on braking systems.

Burns

Hydraulic components can get very hot and need to be handled with care if the machine has been working recently. Again, appropriate PPE must be worn.

Slips and Falls

When working on a hydraulic system and therefore having to climb up and down from the machine's cab with tools and gauges, try to prevent falling by keeping three-point contact and by using fall restraint harnesses when necessary. Clean all fluid spills immediately to avoid a slip hazard.

Fire Hazards

Hydraulic fluid is often mineral-based oil, which is flammable. There has been more than one machine that catch fire because a hydraulic leak that has either sprayed onto a turbocharger or been ignited by welding sparks or a torch. Hydraulic line, cylinders, motors, and pumps can also become hot enough to ignite components, so be aware of high system temperatures.

Environmental Concerns

Hydraulic systems are sealed systems, and if the system is intact, there are minimal environmental concerns. However, actions taken by a technician may cause a fluid leak by opening a system. All fluid leaks *must* be contained! Drain buckets or trays, and use fluid-adsorbent cloth and a floor-dry material to contain leaks. The result of not containing fluid leaks can be very harmful to the environment and very costly. Cases of fines of $20,000 per square foot of contamination have been reported.

▶ Construction Features of Hydraulic Lines

K29003

As shown in **FIGURE 29-4**, hydraulic fluid is distributed between components through a combination of rigid steel **tube** and flexible hose assemblies. The term "hydraulic lines" refers to rigid and flexible fluid conductors that provide a means for fluid transfer between components.

Both rigid tubes and flexible lines have their respective advantages, and their use depends on the particular application.

FIGURE 29-4 Excavator with both rigid tubing and flexible hoses.

FIGURE 29-5 Alloy steel pipe.

Flexible hose assemblies allow actuators to move, can reduce the transmission of vibrations, and absorb pressure spikes better than comparable rigid steel tubing. Rigid steel tube assemblies can assist in cooling the fluid, are more durable, and take up less space than comparable flexible hoses.

Rigid Hydraulic Line

There are two types of rigid fluid conductors, defined by terms that are sometimes confused: pipe and tubing. The main differences between pipe and tubing are their construction materials and applications.

Hydraulic Pipe

Seamless alloy steel pipe is rigid and can be used only to carry hydraulic fluid for long straight runs. Cold-drawn precision seamless pipe is specially designed to withstand high-static (stationary fluid) and high-dynamic (fluid that is flowing) loads. To prevent rusting, pipe and fittings are constructed of corrosion-resistant steel alloys similar to those shown in **FIGURE 29-5**. They are also painted on the outside surface to protect exposed metal.

This type of conductor is not commonly found on MORE machines. One example of where pipes may be used would be a machine with a long stick, such as an excavator configured with long demolition arms. Since there could be straight lengths of 30 feet or more, pipe runs would be a more cost-effective choice.

Pipe is used mostly for transferring water, air, or steam in commercial and industrial stationary applications.

> ▶ TECHNICIAN TIP
>
> Never use **galvanized** pipe or fittings for hydraulic system applications. The coating can react with the hydraulic fluid and come off the pipe walls and fittings, causing contamination and damaging components.

Hydraulic Tubing

MORE machines will have preformed tube assemblies that are part of their hydraulic system. They are used for connecting components together and usually have a flexible hose attached to at least one end. Tube assemblies are rigid and are mounted solidly to a machine component, like a cylinder or a stick. Their pre-shaped tube will have ends welded on to accept connections to other components or conductors. Tubing can also be used for straight runs. Tubing is normally made from highly ductile, annealed material that makes it easy to bend and flare if needed. Tubing does not have the rigidity of pipe and so may be bent and shaped to accommodate the installation on the machine.

For MORE machines, the manufacturer will install preformed tube assemblies with welded-on flange ends to mate the tube to either a component (pump, valve, actuator) or hose(s). Tube assemblies are the preferred conductor when two components are stationary or when a hose isn't necessary. See **FIGURE 29-6** for a tube assembly.

FIGURE 29-6 A hydraulic tube assembly.

Tube dimensions are typically available in 1/16-inch increments from 1/8-inch up to 1 inch **outside diameter (OD)**, and in 1/4-inch increments above 1 inch. Hydraulic tube is sized by its external diameter.

Tubing dimensions are normally specified by **diameter nominal (DN)** in metric or **nominal tube size (NPS)** in inches. A table of specifications that defines the outside diameter, wall thickness, and **inside diameter (ID)** for a specific **working pressure** is illustrated in **TABLE 29-1**.

Note that the wall thickness increases as the ID decreases.

Tube assemblies require clamping that is effective in reducing vibration and eliminating any opportunity for cracking or rubbing on other tubes. See **FIGURE 29-7** for an excavator boom with a multitude of hydraulic tubes on its boom.

Tube Ends

Hydraulic tubes will have either welded-on ends or flared ends that allow them to mate with a hydraulic component (pump, valve, or actuator), a hose, or another tube. Welded-on ends usually accept a split flange–type connector that uses a seal to

TABLE 29-1 Tubing Specifications

Inch Tubes				
			Design Working Pressure (4:1 Design Factor) PSI	
Tube OD (inch)	Wall Thickness (inch)	Tube ID (inch)	Steel 1010	Stainless 304 & 316
1/8	0.028	0.069	6650	10000
1/8	0.035	0.055	8450	12700
3/16	0.035	0.118	5450	8200
3/16	0.049	0.090	7850	11800
1/4	0.028	0.194	3100	4650
1/4	0.035	0.180	3950	5950
1/4	0.049	0.152	5750	8650
1/4	0.065	0.120	7800	11750
1/4	0.083	0.084	9950	15000
5/16	0.035	0.243	3100	4650
5/16	0.049	0.215	4500	6750
5/16	0.065	0.183	6150	9250
5/16	0.083	0.147	8000	12050
5/16	0.095	0.123	9150	13800
3/8	0.035	0.305	2550	3850
3/8	0.049	0.277	3650	5550
3/8	0.065	0.245	5000	7550
3/8	0.083	0.209	6550	9900
3/8	0.095	0.185	7600	11450
3/8	0.109	0.157	8750	13200
1/2	0.035	0.430	1850	2800
1/2	0.049	0.402	2700	4050
1/2	0.065	0.370	3650	5500
1/2	0.083	0.334	4800	7200
1/2	0.095	0.310	5550	8350
1/2	0.109	0.282	6450	9750
1/2	0.120	0.260	7200	10800
1/2	0.148	0.204	8950	13450
5/8	0.035	0.555	1500	2200
5/8	0.049	0.527	2100	3200
5/8	0.065	0.495	2850	4300
5/8	0.083	0.459	3750	5650
5/8	0.095	0.435	4350	6550
5/8	0.109	0.407	5050	7600
5/8	0.120	0.385	5600	8450
5/8	0.134	0.357	6350	9550
3/4	0.035	0.680	1200	1850
3/4	0.049	0.652	1750	2600
3/4	0.065	0.620	2350	3550
3/4	0.083	0.584	3050	4600
3/4	0.095	0.560	3550	5350
3/4	0.109	0.532	4150	6200
3/4	0.120	0.510	4600	6900
3/4	0.148	0.454	5800	8700
7/8	0.035	0.805	1050	1550
7/8	0.049	0.777	1500	2200
7/8	0.065	0.745	2000	3000
7/8	0.083	0.709	2600	3900
7/8	0.109	0.657	3500	5250
7/8	0.120	0.635	3900	5850
1	0.049	0.902	1300	1950
1	0.065	0.870	1750	2600
1	0.083	0.834	2250	3400
1	0.095	0.810	2600	3900
1	0.109	0.782	3000	4550
1	0.120	0.760	3350	5050
1	0.148	0.704	4200	6350
1	0.188	0.624	5500	8250
1-1/4	0.065	1.120	1350	2050
1-1/4	0.083	1.084	1750	2650
1-1/4	0.095	1.060	2050	3050
1-1/4	0.109	1.032	2350	3550
1-1/4	0.120	1.010	2650	3950
1-1/4	0.188	0.874	4300	6450
1-1/4	0.220	0.810	5100	7700
1-1/2	0.065	1.370	1150	1700
1-1/2	0.083	1.334	1450	2200
1-1/2	0.095	1.310	1700	2550
1-1/2	0.109	1.282	1950	2950
1-1/2	0.120	1.260	2150	3250
1-1/2	0.134	1.232	2450	3650
1-1/2	0.220	1.060	4150	6300
1-1/2	0.250	1.000	4800	7250
2	0.065	1.870	850	1250
2	0.083	1.834	1100	1600
2	0.095	1.810	1250	1850
2	0.120	1.760	1600	2400
2	0.134	1.732	1800	2700
2	0.220	1.560	3050	4600

Information from Parker Hannifin Industrial Tube Fittings, Adapters and Equipment Catalog 4300

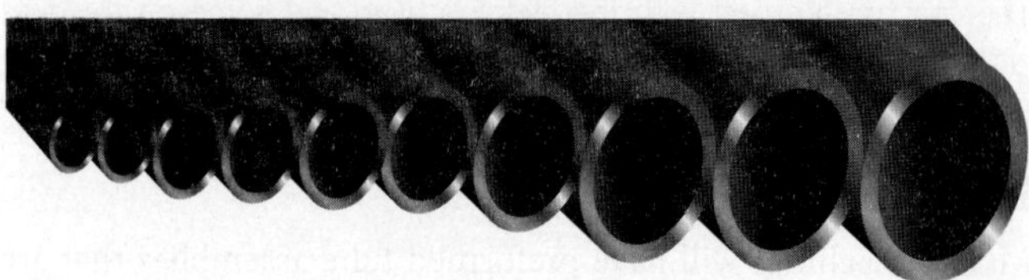

FIGURE 29-7 An excavator boom with a multitude of hydraulic tubes on its boom.

create a leak-free connection, while a flared end will use a large nut to seat a metal-to-metal sealing surface together. For example, the tube assembly in Figure 29-6 has split flange–type ends.

Specific types of sealing connections will be discussed later in this chapter.

▶ Construction Features of Hydraulic Hoses

K29004, S29002

Hydraulic hoses play a huge role as a conductor for hydraulic fluid on MORE machines. They can be used for pump inlet lines where there could be negative pressure to applications where there is over 6,000 psi present. See **FIGURE 29-8** for a variety of hoses found on a scraper.

They can also have lengths that range from a few inches to over 50 feet, again depending on the application. One example of a machine with several very long hydraulic hoses is a vertical boring machine, whose drilling head must travel up to 35 feet up and down a mast. See **FIGURE 29-9** for a vertical drilling machine.

FIGURE 29-8 A variety of hoses found on a scraper.

FIGURE 29-9 Vertical drilling machine.

Flexible hoses are ideal for use where excessive vibration is present or where there is relative movement between components on a machine. Hydraulic hose construction provides for movement between the ends of the hose and slight expansion and contraction in diameter. One example of this is the base of the boom on an excavator. To provide fluid flow out to the stick and bucket cylinders and any attachment that may replace the bucket on the machine, there needs to be a set of hoses that connect the tubes going up the boom to the tubes going to the main control valve on the machine. See **FIGURE 29-10** for a set of hoses at the base of an excavator boom. This set of hoses will be expected to go through hundreds of thousands of flex cycles over their lifetime without failure as the boom is raised and lowered.

Machines with multi-function attachments, like drill heads, that need to be oriented in a wide range of working angles will

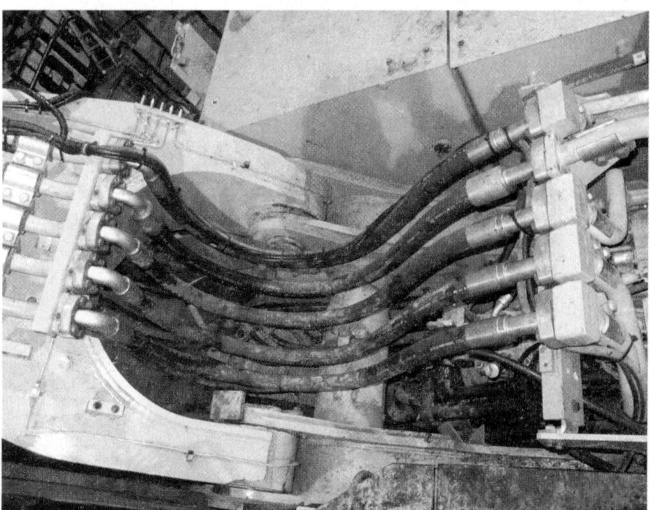

FIGURE 29-10 A set of hoses at the base of an excavator boom.

FIGURE 29-11 A drilling machine with a large bundle of hoses supplying its mast.

FIGURE 29-12 Hoses with standard identification on them.

need many hoses to supply hydraulic fluid to a wide variety of actuators to allow a wide range of motion. See **FIGURE 29-11** for a drilling machine with a large bundle of hoses supplying its mast.

Hydraulic Hose Standards

Hoses used on MORE machine hydraulic systems are constructed to international standards that define construction, dimensions, and pressure and temperature specifications. There are three organizations that set these standards: the Society of Automotive Engineers (SAE), based in North America; the Committee for European Normalization (CEN), based in Europe (CEN standards are identified on a hose by the letters "EN"); and the International Standards Organization (ISO). See **FIGURE 29-12** for an example of hoses with standard identification on them.

SAE 100R standards

TABLE 29-2 lists various SAE hose standards that describe material and construction by the Society of Automotive Engineers (SAE) and describes their construction. SAE standard J517 identifies the 100R hose series, which ranges from 100R1 to 100R18. The number designation following the "R" does not identify the number of reinforcement layers, but rather the specific requirement of a type of hose.

EN 850 Standards

EN standards are similar to SAE standards but are typically 30% higher for maximum working pressure; therefore, most manufacturers will install hoses that meet EN standards. EN hose standards fall into five general categories, which are based on hose construction (number or spiral wraps and type of material for layers). Each of the five general categories has sub-categories that further define the hose construction and pressure ratings. The appropriate rating is printed on the side of the hose. See **FIGURE 29-13** for an example of standard EN 854.

Hydraulic hoses found on MORE machines produced in North America have the following characteristics:

- They must comply with SAE J517 hydraulic hose standards.
- They are of the 100R-series, designated as 100R1, 100R2, etc., depending on materials and construction.
- They are designated by a dash number that indicates the inside diameter of the hose in sixteenths of an inch (multiples of 1.58 mm). For example, a –8 (dash 8) hose has an eight-sixteenths (one-half-inch) ID.

TABLE 29-2 SAE 100 Table

SAE Number	Inner Tube	Reinforcement	Cover
SAE 100R1	Synthetic rubber	1 High-tensile steel coating	Synthetic rubber
SAE 100R2	Synthetic rubber	2 Wire braids 2 Spiral plies 1 Wire braid	Synthetic
SAE 100R3	Synthetic rubber	2 Textile braids	Synthetic
SAE 100R4	Synthetic rubber	Braided textile fibers or spiral-body wire	Synthetic
SAE 100R5	Synthetic rubber	1 Textile braid 1 High-tensile steel wire braid	Cotton braid
SAE 100R6	Synthetic rubber	1 Textile braid	Synthetic rubber
SAE 100R7	Thermoplastic	Synthetic fiber	Thermoplastic
SAE 100R8	Thermoplastic	Synthetic fiber	Thermoplastic
SAE 100R9	Synthetic rubber	4 Spiral plies wrapped in alternating directions	Synthetic rubber
SAE 100R10	Synthetic rubber	4 Spiral plies of heavy wire wrapped in alternating directions	Synthetic rubber
SAE 100R11	Synthetic rubber	6 Spiral plies of heavy wire wrapped in alternating directions	Synthetic rubber

EN 854 — Fabric Braided Hose

Type 1TE — This hose shall consist of an inner tube of oil resistant synthetic rubber, one braided ply of suitable textile yarn and an oil and weather resistant synthetic rubber cover.

Type 2TW — This hose shall consist of an inner tube of oil resistant rubber, two braided ply of suitable textile yarn and an oil and weather resistant synthetic rubber cover.

Type 3TE — This hose shall consist of an inner tube of oil resistant synthetic rubber, three braided ply of suitable textile yarn and an oil and weather resistant synthetic rubber cover.

Type R6 — This hose shall consist of an inner tube of oil resistant synthetic rubber, one braided ply of suitable textile yarn and an oil and weather resistant synthetic rubber cover.

Type R3 — This hose shall consist of an inner tube of oil resistant synthetic rubber, two braided ply of suitable textile yarn and an oil and weather resistant synthetic rubber cover.

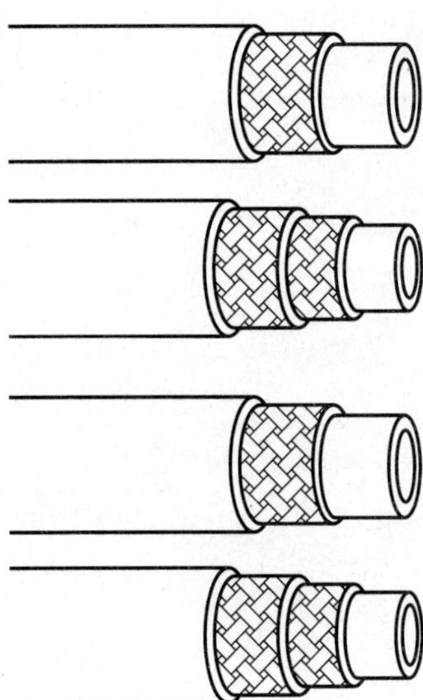

FIGURE 29-13 An example of standard EN 854.

Hose Construction

Hydraulic hoses are constructed in layers, starting with an inner tube that must be compatible with the hydraulic fluid flowing through the system. Reinforcement layers are added next to help the inner tube withstand the required pressures. Reinforcement layers are usually spiral-wound wire but could be a fibrous material. Special application hose that must be non-conductive cannot use wire reinforcement. An outer layer completes the hose assembly. See **FIGURE 29-14** for how a hydraulic hose is constructed.

Lower-pressure (up to approximately 2,500 psi) hoses will have one or two layers of reinforcement, while high-pressure hoses (up to 6,000 psi) may have up to six layers of reinforcement.

> **TECHNICIAN TIP**
>
> A common way to describe hydraulic hose construction is "two wire," "three wire," or "six wire." This refers to the reinforcement layers that a hose has.

Hose guarding

Hoses may need extra protection from external factors that may cause damage or wear to the hose. This could be caused from where they are located and rubbing on other components, rubbing on other hoses or tubes, or damage from mud or gravel that the machine may be working with. Hose guarding could be stiff plastic wrap, Kevlar cloth, or coiled spring steel. See **FIGURE 29-15** for a hose with guarding.

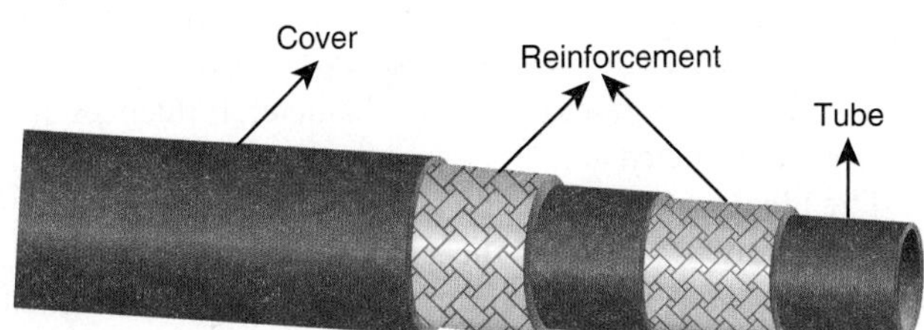

FIGURE 29-14 How a hydraulic hose is constructed.

Hose Ends

For hoses to be able to connect to either hydraulic components (pumps, valves, or actuators), tubes, or other hoses, they must have ends that allow this. Hose ends can be crimped on with special tooling. This makes the hose a onetime use component. See **FIGURE 29-16** for a hose crimping machine. There are also two-piece reusable hose ends that can be either pressed together with special tooling/equipment or threaded together. There is a wide variety of types of hose ends to create a seal between the hose and whatever it is connected to.

FIGURE 29-15 Hoses with guarding.

FIGURE 29-16 A hose crimping machine (SH photo).

▶ Working Pressure and Burst Pressure Ratings for Conductors

K29005

When a hydraulic system is designed, the component and conductor internal dimensions and wall strength are essentially determined by tubing flow capacity in **gallons per minute (gpm)** or liters per minute and working pressures in pounds per square inch or kilopascals. When the conductor working pressure is mentioned in its ratings, the pressure value is referring to the maximum pressure that may be expected when the system is operating normally. This typically ranges between 3,000 and 5,000 psi. Burst pressure in conductor ratings refers to a safety factor that allows the conductor to withstand a short duration pressure spike. For hoses, the burst pressure is usually four times the working pressure, and for tubing, the burst pressure can be from three to six times the working pressure.

Metric sizes are not direct equivalents to the imperial sizes in either size or capacity, but there is little difference between the maximum working pressure of the metric size and its closest equivalent imperial size. For example, a 12 mm OD by 2 mm wall tube is expressed as a 12 × 2 tube, which has a working pressure of 254.89 bar (3,697 psi). Its closest inch equivalent is a $^1/_2$-inch by 0.083-inch tube, which has the same working pressure. See **TABLE 29-3** for some examples of metric tubing sizes and their working pressures.

TABLE 29-3 Examples of Metric Tubing Sizes and Their Working Pressures

Tubing OD × Wall Thickness (mm)	Working Pressure (bar)	Working Pressure (psi)
8 mm × 1 mm	333.91	4,843
8 mm × 2 mm	539.86	7,830
8 mm × 2.5 mm	649.83	9,425
12 mm × 1.5 mm	189.95	2,755
12 mm × 2 mm	254.89	3,697
12 mm × 2.5 mm	319.92	4,640
15 mm × 1 mm	184.92	2,682
15 mm × 1.5 mm	279.93	4,060
15 mm × 2 mm	335.91	4,872
15 mm × 2.5 mm	408.86	5,930
22 mm × 1 mm	124.93	1,812

▶ TECHNICIAN TIP

Tubing manufacturers provide specific data on their products. When replacing tubing, always refer to the manufacturer's data to ensure that you make the correct selection.

▶ TECHNICIAN TIP

Never use copper tubing for hydraulic system applications. It is too weak to withstand the pressure.

▶ Conductor Sizing

K29006

Fluid flow is measured in gallons per minute or liters per minute, and the velocity that it flows through a conductor at for a given flow rate is dependent on the cross-sectional area of the inside of the conductor. If a line narrows, there is a pressure increase before the restriction and the speed of the flow (velocity) increase. As the line widens, there is a pressure drop and the speed of the flow decreases. For example, if the inside diameter of a conductor is reduced by 50%, the area that fluid can flow through is reduced by a factor of four. This would create a large restriction that in turn creates a large pressure drop after the restriction and a large increase in fluid velocity through the restriction. This results in excessive heat generated and a loss of efficiency. See **FIGURE 29-17** for an illustration showing how a conductor's inside diameter influences fluid pressure and velocity.

The ideal maximum fluid velocity in a conductor differs depending on the part of the circuit the conductor is in. Conductors should be sized to provide proper fluid velocity when flow is at its maximum. For example, pump inlet lines should be large enough to create no more fluid velocity than

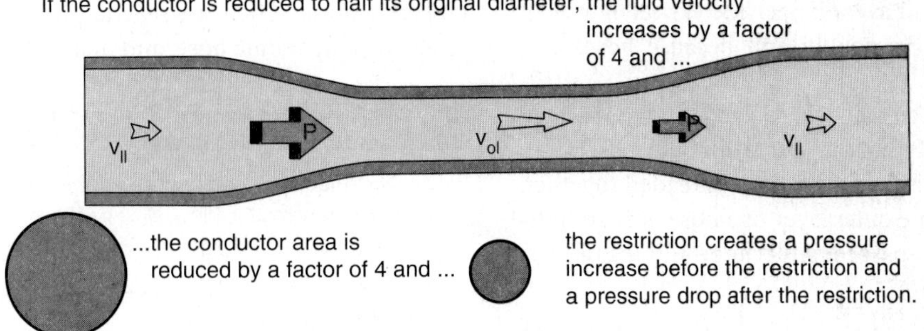

If the conductor is reduced to half its original diameter, the fluid velocity increases by a factor of 4 and ...
...the conductor area is reduced by a factor of 4 and ...
the restriction creates a pressure increase before the restriction and a pressure drop after the restriction.

FIGURE 29-17 The inside diameter of a conductor influences fluid pressure and velocity.

4 feet/sec; return lines should be large enough to create no more fluid velocity than 15 feet/sec; and pressure lines should be large enough to create no more fluid velocity than between 15 and 25 feet/sec.

If you are in doubt as to the size of conductor to install on a MORE machine's hydraulic system, first determine when part of the circuit it is part of, then refer to a chart like **FIGURE 29-18**. This type of chart is called a nomograph.

▶ TECHNICIAN TIP

When determining line size, always select the same size or one size up. Never use a smaller size, because it will cause a restriction to flow, higher fluid velocity, and a turbulence in the line.

Although desirable, laminar flow (non-turbulent) is difficult to achieve in mobile hydraulic systems. A compromise is required between the physical space available and the function of the tube or hose. For example, within a circuit, there are three different conditions and three different flow rates.

1. The supply from the tank or reservoir to the pump is subject to very low pressures, and the flow rate is the slowest, but it requires a large internal diameter conductor to allow fluid to flow freely to the pump inlet.
   - If the supply line is a hose, it must be reinforced so that it doesn't collapse (**FIGURE 29-19**).
2. Flow rate out of the pump is high and lines subject to high pressure can be considerably smaller in diameter than pump supply hoses and will still maintain laminar flow.
3. Fluid returning from the directional valves to the tank or reservoir is at a fairly low flow rate and pressure, so a larger diameter line is required.

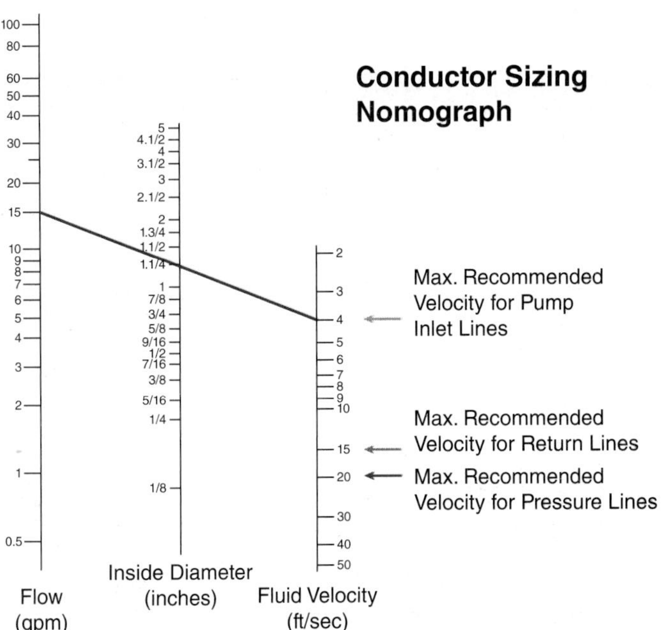

FIGURE 29-18 Nomograph for fluid conductors.

▶ Conductor Failures

K29007, S29001

Hydraulic conductors (tubes and hoses) are designed to withstand a limited number of pressure cycles under normal expected working conditions. Normal working conditions include maximum levels for fluid pressure and temperature (both ambient

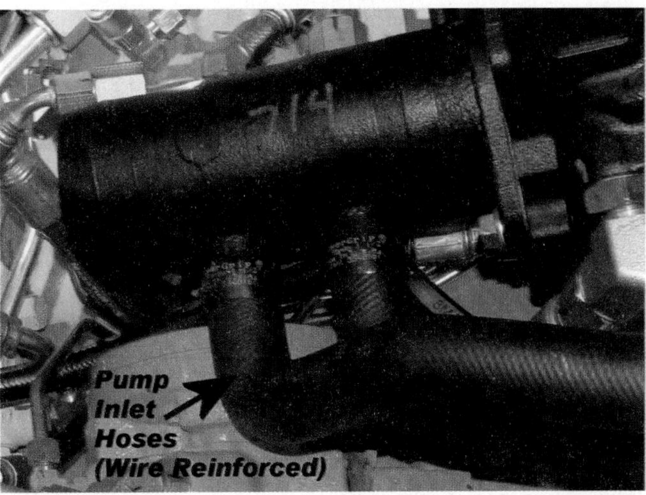

FIGURE 29-19 Pump inlet hose.

and fluid). Hydraulic tubes have a longer life expectancy than hoses have because of their rigidity and because hoses flex under pressure changes.

Tube assemblies will likely fail where flange ends have been welded on and at tight bends that can create thinner walls. Hoses can fail where their ends are crimped on or threaded together. If there is a bubble under the outer layer of a hose, it is an indication that fluid has flowed past the inner tube and that a hose failure is imminent.

Conductors can fail because of overpressurizing or improper installation. Most conductor failures are a result of them rubbing against something or something rubbing against them. See **FIGURE 29-20** for a failed hose that has rubbed on something.

Conductors must be installed properly to ensure they have a chance to achieve their expected longevity. This includes ensuring they are not twisted, are not kinked, don't need to be pried into place, and are clamped appropriately. See **FIGURE 29-21** for several hoses that have been moving in their clamps and have wires exposed.

Conductor Replacement

One of the most common tasks a MORE technician will perform is repairing hydraulic leaks, and a big part of that includes replacing hoses. There are several points to keep in mind when replacing a hydraulic hose, and many relate to safety.

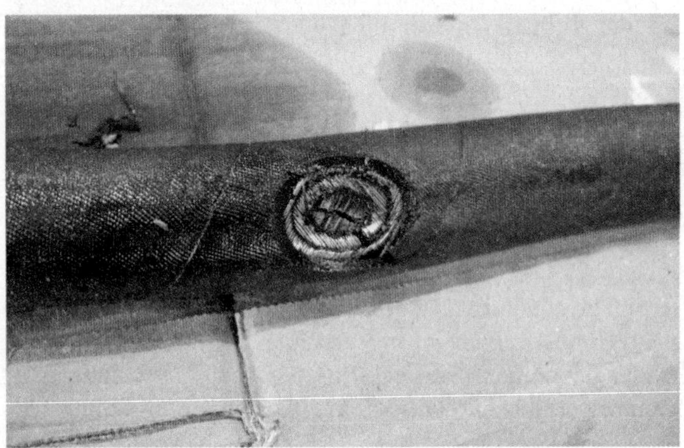

FIGURE 29-20 A failed hose that has rubbed on something.

FIGURE 29-21 Several hoses that have been moving in their clamps and have wires exposed.

SAFETY TIP

Never begin loosening a conductor until there is confirmation of zero pressure in the circuit. Follow all service information to achieve this. It may include the following steps:

1. Lower all implements to the ground.
2. Release tank pressure.
3. Cycle all controls with the key on and engine off.
4. Install mechanical locks if applicable.
5. Use appropriate blocking or stands if needed.
6. Bleed off pressure from all accumulators.
7. Lock out and tag out the machine.
8. Use appropriate PPE.

The best way to ensure the proper replacement conductor is installed to match pressure and flow conditions is to use the machine's parts book and order it by part number. If the parts book isn't available, look for a part number on the tube or hose. If that fails, then for replacing a hose as a last resort, use the STAMPED method.

As illustrated in **FIGURE 29-22**, when replacing a section of a hydraulic hose, use the **STAMPED** method to choose the correct replacement hose.

If the hose is damaged and the layline is not readable, the STAMPED method may be used by measuring the overall length of the hose, then cutting the old hose, looking at the construction of the hose, and measuring the ID. Also, prior to cutting, take note of the coupling orientation. Noting this will make it easier to build a replacement and match the couplings to mating ports. In addition, the maximum temperature of the fluid that will be flowing in the hose must be considered. To replace a damaged hose using the STAMPED method, follow the steps in **SKILL DRILL 29-1**.

▶ TECHNICIAN TIP

When replacing a hose, always use the same manufacturer because, as stated in *SAE J273, Recommended Practices*, "Hose from one manufacturer is not usually compatible with another."

▶ TECHNICIAN TIP

Always base the conductor selection on working pressure, never on burst pressure.

▶ Hydraulic Connectors

K29008

Hydraulic connectors provide a means for fluid conductors to be connected to each other and to other components. They can also be called hydraulic fittings. Their purpose is to create a leak-free connection and be able to withstand the fluid pressure, flow, and temperature they are exposed to. Hydraulic **fittings**

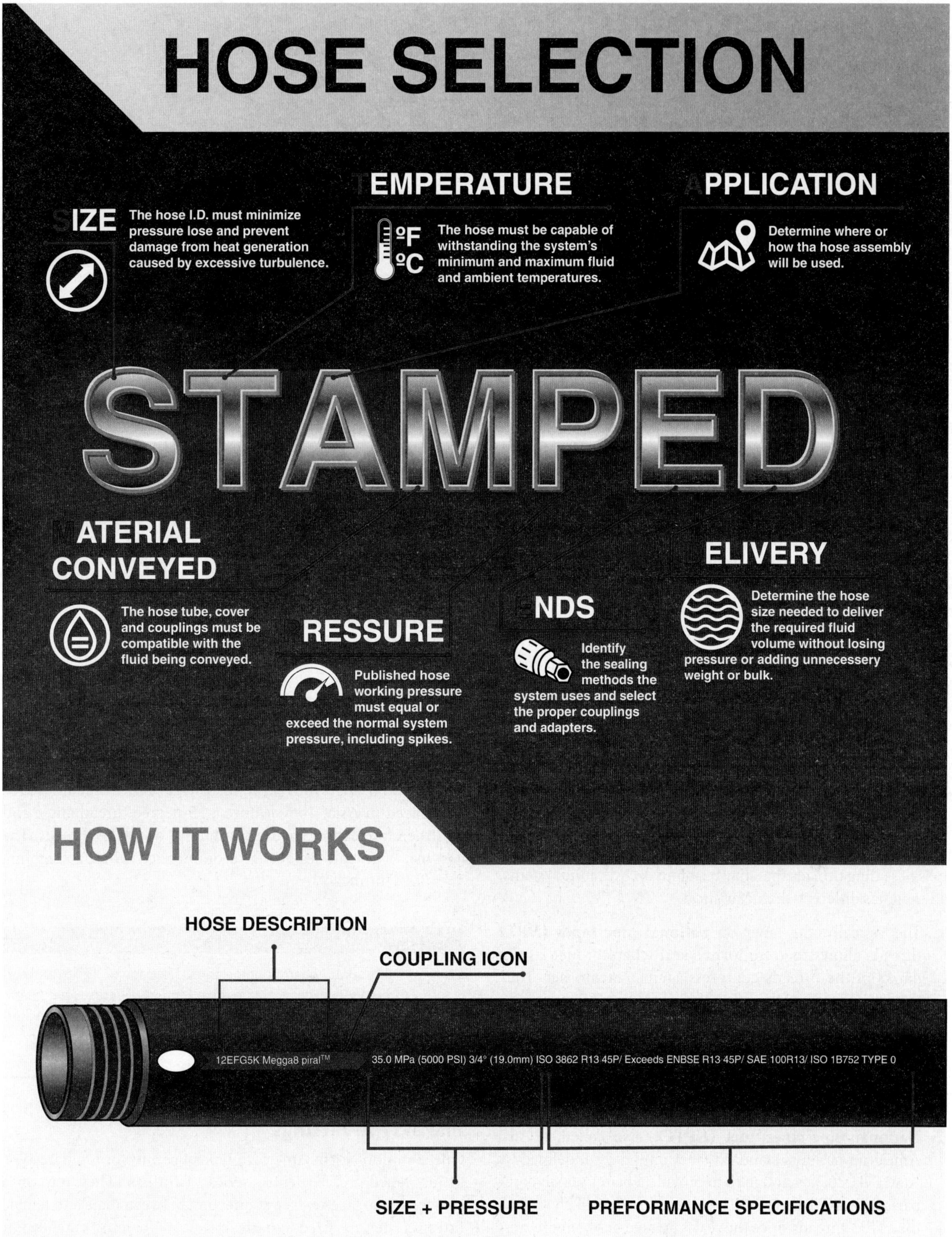

HOSE SELECTION

IZE

The hose I.D. must minimize pressure lose and prevent damage from heat generation caused by excessive turbulence.

EMPERATURE

The hose must be capable of withstanding the system's minimum and maximum fluid and ambient temperatures.

PPLICATION

Determine where or how tha hose assembly will be used.

STAMPED

ATERIAL CONVEYED

The hose tube, cover and couplings must be compatible with the fluid being conveyed.

RESSURE

Published hose working pressure must equal or exceed the normal system pressure, including spikes.

NDS

Identify the sealing methods the system uses and select the proper couplings and adapters.

ELIVERY

Determine the hose size needed to deliver the required fluid volume without losing pressure or adding unnecessery weight or bulk.

HOW IT WORKS

HOSE DESCRIPTION

COUPLING ICON

12EFG5K Megga8 piral™ 35.0 MPa (5000 PSI) 3/4° (19.0mm) ISO 3862 R13 45P/ Exceeds ENBSE R13 45P/ SAE 100R13/ ISO 1B752 TYPE 0

SIZE + PRESSURE

PREFORMANCE SPECIFICATIONS

FIGURE 29-22 STAMPED method of hose identification.

SKILL DRILL 29-1 Replacing a Hydraulic Hose

For this procedure, you will need the following tools, materials, and equipment:

- correct replacement hose with fittings
- hand tools, including wrenches and screwdrivers
- safety glasses or goggles
- gloves.

1. Put on gloves and safety glasses or goggles.
2. Make sure hydraulic pressure in the circuit is at zero.
3. Isolate the hose to be replaced and remove the hose.
4. Follow the information stamped on the hose:
   a. Read the hose description.
   b. Read the size and pressure rating.
   c. Read the hose rating.
   d. Select a proper replacement hose from the catalog of the original hose supplier.
   e. Install the replacement hose, properly routing using the standoffs and proper torque of the connectors.
   f. Check hydraulic fluid level.
   g. Start the machine, warm up the hydraulic fluid, and slowly increase the pressure in the circuit for the replacement hose.

are categorized by how they seal to each other when mated or to another hydraulic component, such as a hose, pump, valve, or actuator. The general categories of fittings are classified by how they seal: metal-to-metal seal; thread-to-thread seal; and O-ring-to-metal seal. The term "fitting" can refer to hose ends, tube ends, adapters, plugs, and caps and can be interchanged with the term "connector." Most machines will use a combination of two or more types of fittings throughout their hydraulic system. It is important to understand how fittings create a seal and how to identify the different types of fittings.

Metal-to-Metal-Type Fittings

This type of connection relies on a tight interference fit between the two parts of the connector. This can be a threaded connection or a flare-type face-to-face connection. They can be found for creating seals in low- to medium-pressure systems (1,500–3,000 psi) and used with hoses, tubes, and adapters.

Pipe-Thread Fittings

Pipe threads for hydraulic systems are designed to create a seal between the male and female threads. There are three different types of sealing threads that may be found on hydraulic systems, and each has different characteristics.

1. Theoretically, the taper on **national pipe taper (NPT)** threads allows them to form a seal when torqued as the flanks of the threads compress against each other. They feature a 60-degree thread angle. In reality, NTP threads do not seal well without the help of thread sealants, because the threads seal only on their flank and a spiral leak path is available at the thread root. NPT is suitable for lower system pressures and is found mainly in MORE machines produced in North America.
2. **National pipe-taper fuel (NPTF)**, also called dryseal American national standard taper pipe thread, defined by ASME B1.20.3, is designed to provide a better seal in comparison to NPT threads. The threads are less likely to leak than NPT threads since the seal is created between the crest and root of the mating threads. However, they may leak if the fittings are coupled and uncoupled more than once. Both NPT and NPTF threads have a taper of ¾ inches over 1 foot of length and are sized in 1/8-inch increments. Compare NPT and NPTF threads in **FIGURE 29-23**.
3. British standard pipe tapered (BSPT) is a third type of tapered thread fitting, which is popular with MORE machines produced in Asia. They feature a 55-degree thread angle and therefore cannot be used with NPT or NPTF threads. The use of thread sealant is recommended when assembling BSPT fittings.

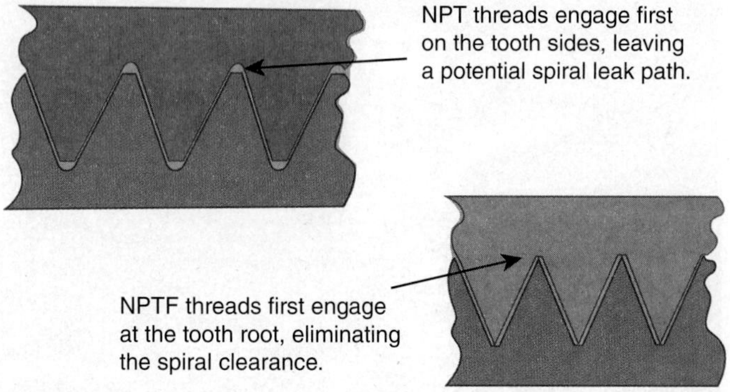

FIGURE 29-23 NTP and NTPF.

> **TECHNICIAN TIP**
>
> Care must be taken when applying thread sealant or Teflon tape to tapered threads. An excessive amount of either will create a contaminant in the hydraulic system. Apply only enough to cover the mating threads of the fitting. Never allow the sealant or tape to enter the hydraulic system.

Flare-Type Fittings

One common North American type of connector is a flare-type fitting called JIC 37-degree series of fittings. They rely on a tapered metal face-to-face connection between male and female fittings. They are sized in dash sizes of 1/16-inch increments. For instance, a –8 fitting would have a ½-inch inside diameter, and a –16 fitting would have a 1-inch inside diameter.

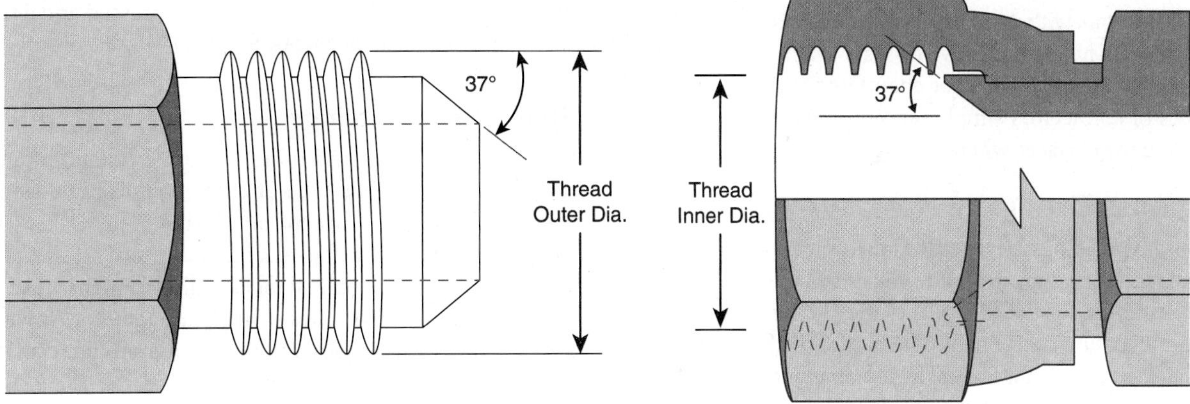

FIGURE 29-24 Flare fitting assembly.

The **JIC 37 Degree Flare (SAE J514)** connection will be found in many MORE hydraulic systems applications. Both the JIC male and JIC female components have a 37-degree flare seat and straight threads, as shown in **FIGURE 29-24**. The connection is held together mechanically by the torque on the straight threads of the female swivel nut.

The flared end of the metal tube provides a seating surface for a leak-tight seal. As shown in Figure 29-24, the male end of a fitting with the same flare angle threads into the female fitting, and the angles of the two tapered surfaces form a leak-proof seal. There is also a 45-degree flare fitting, but it is not very common on MORE machines.

Metric Fittings

A second common type of flare fitting is called metric. They have an inverted flare that creates a seal when the female swivel nut is tightened onto the male counterpart. A 24-degree angle at the sealing face creates a seal when torqued. There are three types of female nuts that could be used to mate with the male metric fitting. See **FIGURE 29-25** for a metric 24-degree fitting.

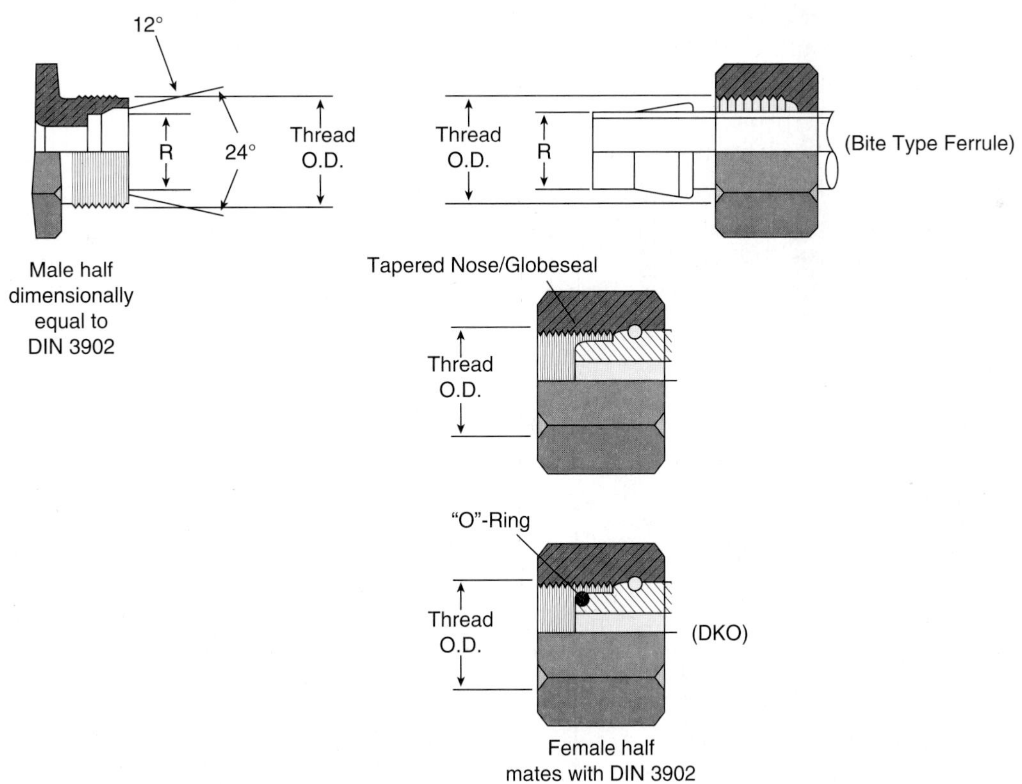

FIGURE 29-25 A metric 24-degree fitting.

Seal-Type Fittings

O-ring-type fittings are very common on MORE hydraulic systems. They can withstand very high pressures and rely on an O-ring that is held in a groove or seats against a shoulder to create a seal against a flat-face or chamfered surface. Servicing these types of connectors simply requires replacing the O-ring and cleaning the surfaces where the O-ring sits.

O-ring Boss Fittings

O-ring boss-type fittings are threaded into a female mating thread. They can have either a groove below the nut where an O-ring sits or a nut push on a washer that pushes the O-ring into a tapered groove in the mating component. The part of the female component with a tapered seat for the O-ring is sometimes referred to as a boss. These fittings are most commonly found installed in actuators and valves. See **FIGURE 29-26A** for an O-ring boss-type fitting.

O-ring Face Fittings

O-ring face fittings are common with many manufacturers for small- to medium-sized hoses and can seal very high pressures. The male part of the connector is threaded externally and has a machined groove on its face that accepts an O-ring. The female part of the connector (usually a hose or tube) has a swivel nut on it that gets torqued to the male fitting. Once tightened, the O-ring is compressed and a tight seal is created. See **FIGURE 29-26B** for an O-ring face-type fitting.

Split Flange Fittings

High-pressure hoses and tubes can quite often be found with split flange ends. This type of connector has one side with a machined groove to accept an O-ring. The O-ring will get compressed against a flat-machined surface to create a leak-free seal. Two-piece split flanges will clamp the hose or tube against the flat surface (most likely an actuator, valve, pump, or reservoir). The flanges pull down on a shoulder on the hose or tube.

Flange-type connectors are typically welded to the tube and, as shown in **FIGURE 29-27**, create a seal with O-ring or **D-ring** seals.

Flange connectors may be of a four bolt design and have two pressure ratings. **Code 61** is the standard series, and **Code 62** is the "6,000 psi" series. The design concept for both series is the same, but the bolt hole spacing and flanged head diameters are larger for the higher-pressure, Code 62 connection. The flat

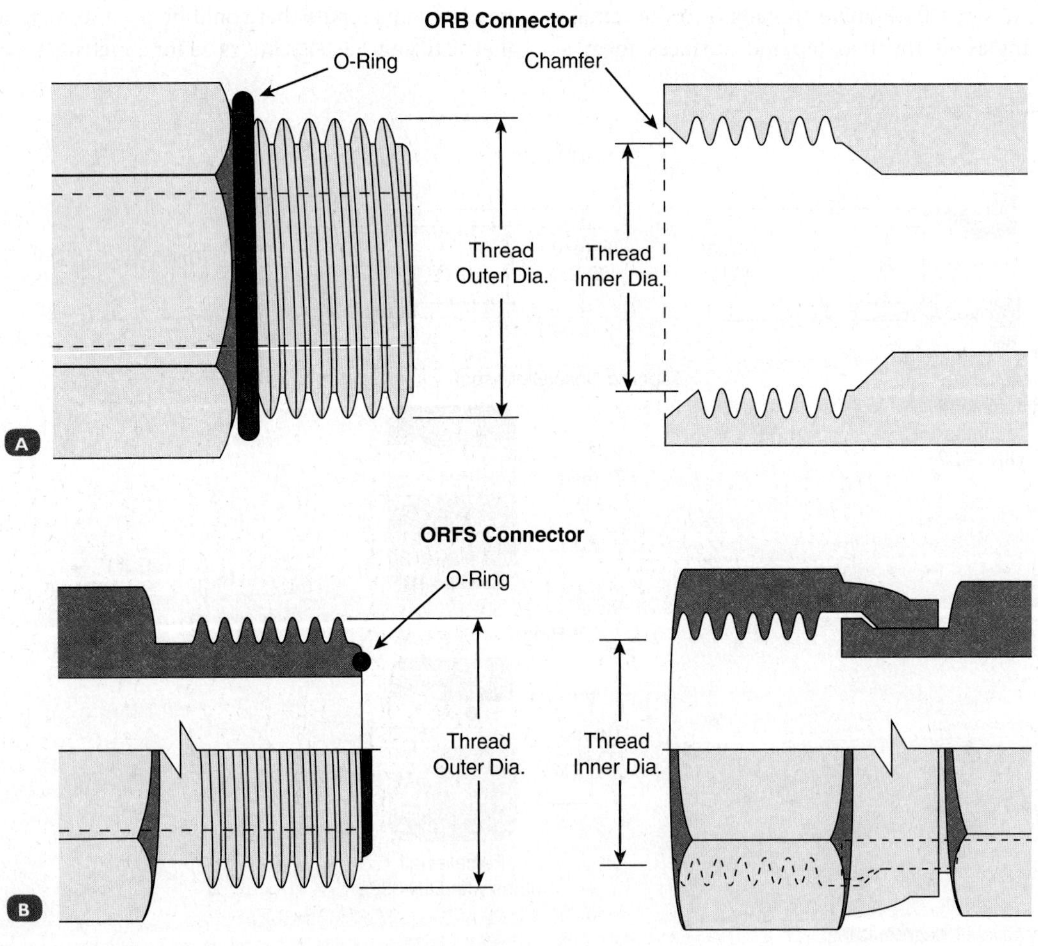

FIGURE 29-26 A. O-ring boss–type fitting. **B.** O-ring face–type fitting.

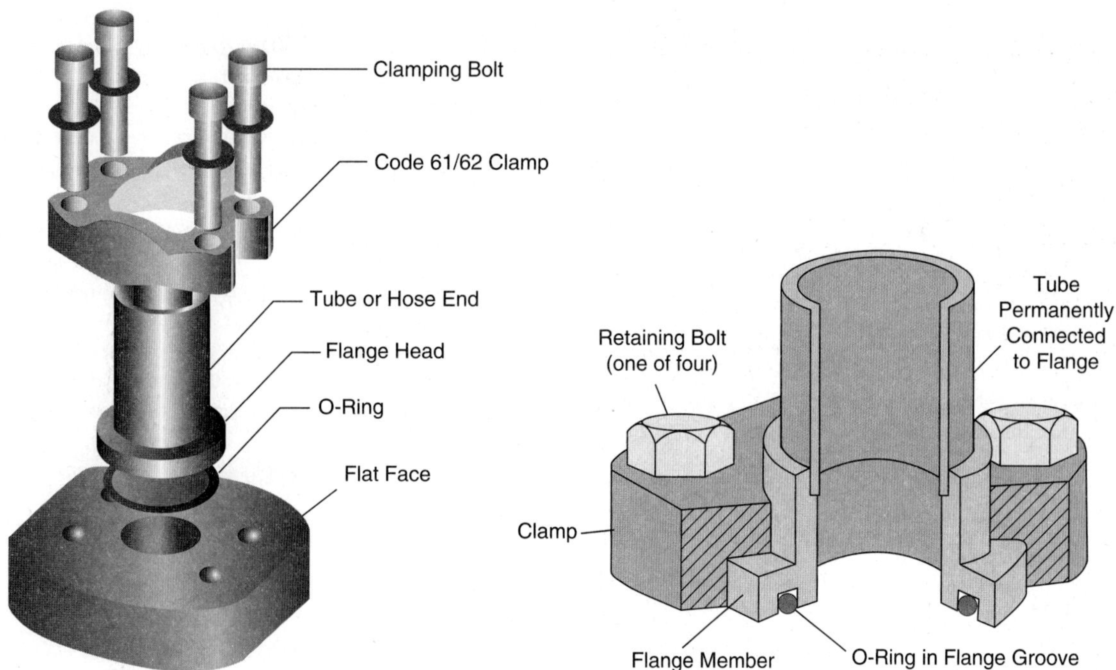

FIGURE 29-27 Flange fitting assembly.

face is an unthreaded hole with bolt holes in a pattern around the port. The flanged head is grooved for an O-ring, and it has either a captive flange or split flange halves with bolt holes to match the port. The seal takes place on the O-ring, which is compressed between the flanged head and the flat surface surrounding the port. The threaded bolts hold the connection together.

Fitting Identification

To properly identify a hydraulic fitting, a technician would first determine the type of fitting it is: metal-to-metal type, thread-to-thread type, or O-ring type. For flare-type fittings, an angle gauge would be used to measure the seat angle. To measure the size of the fitting, a caliper is used to measure either the inside diameter or the nut size at the flats. See **FIGURE 29-28** for a digital caliper being used to measure a fitting. A thread pitch gauge may also be needed to identify the thread pitch.

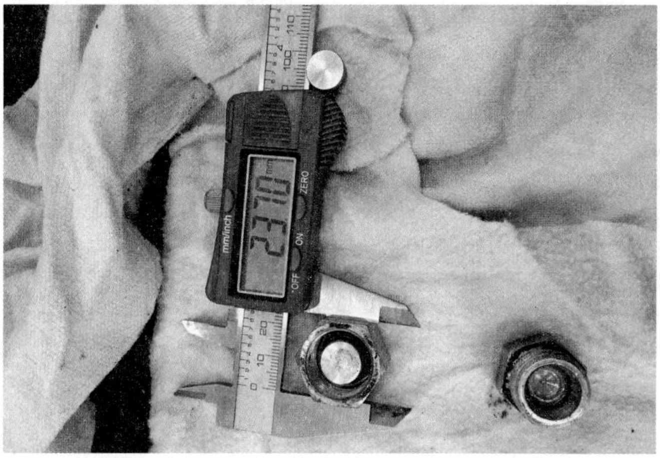

FIGURE 29-28 A digital caliper being used to measure a fitting.

▶ Construction Features of Hydraulic Seals

K29009, S29002

Hydraulic seals play a very important role in MORE hydraulic systems. They are the difference between a dry, leak-free system and one that is damp, dripping, or spraying hydraulic fluid out of it. There are two main types of seals used in hydraulic systems: static and dynamic. Dynamic seals are required when there is relative motion between two components and hydraulic fluid needs to be kept inside the system or kept separated. A typical application for a dynamic seal is one used for a hydraulic cylinder that seals the rod as it moves in and out of the barrel. Static seals are used to create a seal between two stationary components, such as a hose and a cylinder or the mating parts of a two-part connector. See **FIGURE 29-29** for an O-ring seal kit.

FIGURE 29-29 An O-ring seal kit.

SKILL DRILL 29-2 Removing and Replacing the O-Ring of a Flanged Fitting

For this procedure, you will need the following tools, materials, and equipment:

- flange fitting with O-ring
- replacement O-ring
- clamping bolts
- wrenches of the type and size to fit the clamping bolts
- cleaning solvent
- safety glasses or goggles
- gloves.

1. Put on gloves and safety glasses or goggles.
2. Release pressure in circuit following manufacturer's service information.
3. Remove and replace the O-ring.
   - **a.** After releasing system pressure, remove the clamping bolts.
     Note: Never loosen a fitting or clamp without releasing pressure first.
   - **b.** Separate the tube and O-ring assembly from the face.
   - **c.** Remove the old O-ring.
   - **d.** Inspect the surfaces of the face and flange head for scratches, scoring, or gouging.
   - **e.** Clean the face and flange head.
   - **f.** Lubricate the new O-ring with system fluid.
   - **g.** Replace the O-ring in the flange groove, ensuring that it seats completely.
   - **h.** Tighten the clamping bolts gradually and evenly in a "cross pattern."
   - **i.** Finish tightening the clamping bolts to the specified torque.

Fluid conductors and connectors have a wide variety of seals needed to keep fluid in and contamination out. O-ring seals are the most common type and have a circular cross section; however, there are many more shapes that seals could be (D-ring, X-ring, and O-ring with back up). There is also a wide variety of materials that seals could be made from, such as Buna-N, Viton, and silicone. Ensure the seal material is compatible with the fluid being used in the system. The safest bet when replacing any seal is to find the replacement part number and order it from the dealer for the machine manufacturer. Seal dimensions are measured at their overall diameter and their cross-section diameter. To remove and replace the O-ring of a flanged fitting, follow the steps in **SKILL DRILL 29-2.**

▶ TECHNICIAN TIP

Always replace all seals when repairing or replacing conductors or connectors. Lubricate O-rings with the fluid that is in the system before installation.

▶ Construction Features of Hydraulic Quick Couplers

K29010

Many MORE machines' hydraulic systems will come with quick couplers to allow hydraulic attachments to be connected to them. See **FIGURE 29-30** for a skid steer loader with a tree spade attachment that requires hydraulic fluid flow delivered

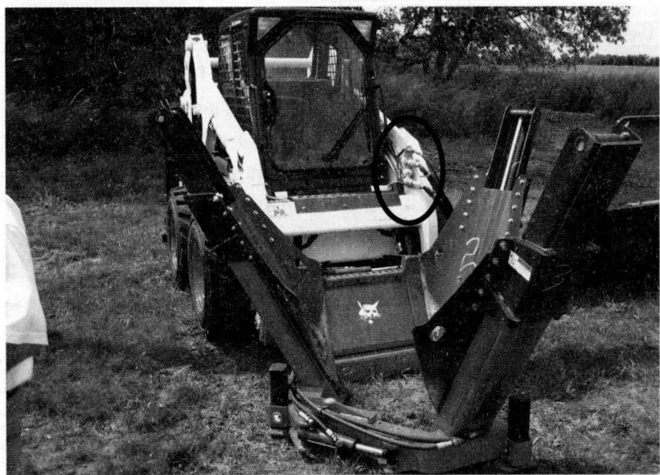

FIGURE 29-30 A skid steer loader with a tree spade attachment that requires hydraulic fluid flow delivered through quick couplers.

through quick couplers. Quick couplers will come in a wide variety of styles and sizes. The following are some general types: thread-together type, ball-latch type, and flat-face type. Hydraulically, they are simply one-way check valves that remain closed until coupled together. They will have a spring-loaded check valve in both the male and the female coupler. See **FIGURE 29-31** for a cross-sectional view of a set of quick couplers. Quick couplers can be a source of leaks and an easy place for contamination to enter the system. If couplers have protective caps when not in use, they should be used to prevent contamination entry. See **FIGURE 29-32** for a set of quick couplers with protective caps installed.

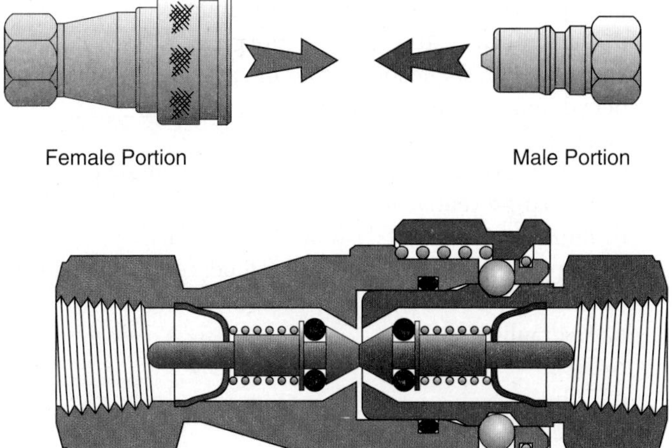

FIGURE 29-31 A cross-sectional view of a set of quick couplers.

FIGURE 29-32 A set of quick couplers with protective caps installed.

▶ Wrap-Up

Ready for Review

- Hydraulic fluid conductors on MORE machines may include pipe, tubing, and hoses, which are integrated by a variety of connectors.
- These hydraulic systems transport pressurized hydraulic fluid from the system's pump to the actuators that convert the pressure into mechanical motion or force.
- To work properly, these systems of conductors and connectors must provide leak-free full flow of the pressurized fluid from pump to actuator.
- Hydraulic pressure inside a conductor exerts equal pressure against the walls of a conductor.
- Safety requirements for working on a hydraulic system must be followed.
- The characteristics of a hydraulic fluid are lubricity, compressibility, and environmental compatibility.
- Working pressure must always be determined so that the conductor material's strength is greater than the maximum system working pressure, including pressure spikes. A conductor's burst pressure is typically six times greater than working pressure.
- Hose standard SAE J517 provides general, dimensional, and performance specifications for the most common hoses used in hydraulic systems.

Key Terms

actuator The component of a machine that is responsible for transferring hydraulic pressure to move or control a mechanism.

burst pressure The extreme pressure (typically six times more than working pressure) where a conductor may be expected to fail.

chafing Abrasion caused by mechanical friction.

Code 61 The standard series flange connector.

Code 62 The "6,000 psi" series flange connector.

conductors A pipe, tube or hose that carries fluids.

connectors A device that joins two pieces of pipe, tubing, or hose together.

D-ring A ring shaped higher in the middle and lower on the ends to eliminate performance degradation as the valve cycles in the reverse direction.

diameter nominal (DN) Tubing dimensions specified in metric.

fittings Components that couple conductors. Fittings are categorized by shape and function, such as tees, unions, and elbows.

galvanized Steel that has been coated with a layer of zinc to protect it from corrosion.

gallons per minute (gpm) The flow rate of a fluid measured in the number of gallons through a conductor in a minute.

inside diameter (ID) The wall-to-wall measurement on the inside of a conductor.

JIC 37-degree flare (SAE J514) Society of Automotive Engineers standard for flare connectors (male and female). Both the JIC male and JIC female components have a 3-degree flare seat and straight threads. The male and female flare seats seal when the 37-degree faces of the same size and thread style are engaged.

laminar flow The smooth movement of a fluid within a conductor.

national pipe taper (NPT) A standard for tapered thread of a pipe.

national pipe-taper fuel (NPTF) A type of thread designed to provide a leak-free seal in pipe connections; also called dryseal.

nominal tube size (NPS) Tubing dimensions specified in inches.

noncompressibility A fluid, unlike air, does not compress under pressure.

O-ring A ring that has a round cross section designed to be seated in a groove and compressed during assembly between two or more parts, creating a seal at the interface.

O-ring boss (ORB) A connector that has an O-ring on the male half of the connector and a chamfer on the female half to accept the O-ring. When the connection is tightened, the O-ring is compressed into the chamfer, making the seal, and the applied torque holds the connection together.

O-ring face seal (ORFS) The ORFS connector has the O-ring at the end of the male half of the connector and a straight thread. The female contact has a flat surface and a straight thread. A seal is formed when the O-ring in the face of the male end is compressed onto the machined flat surface female seat. The female nut mechanically holds the connection.

outside diameter (OD) The measurement of a cylindrical tube between opposite points on the external surface.

STAMPED A system of hose selection which stands for size, temperature, application, material conveyed, pressure, ends, delivery.

static working pressure The force acting on a conductor inner surface.

tubing A fluid conductor that may be bent and shaped to accommodate the installation on the machine. Tubing dimensions are typically available in 1⁄16-inch increments from 1⁄8 inch up to 1 inch outside diameter (OD) and in 1⁄4-inch increments above 1 inch.

turbulence A disturbed moving stream of fluid flow.

Velocity The speed of a fluid in a specified direction.

viscosity The quality of a fluid's thickness and resisting tendency to flow.

working pressure The normal operating pressure of a system or component.

Review Questions

1. Which of the following is *not* an advantage of hydraulic conductors?
   - **a.** They are designed to never fail.
   - **b.** They can allow fluid flow around corners.
   - **c.** They can allow fluid flow over long distances.
   - **d.** They can replace many types of mechanical devices.
2. Hydraulic systems can pose all of the following hazards, *except* ____________.
   - **a.** crushing hazards
   - **b.** burns
   - **c.** slips and falls
   - **d.** toxic gases
3. Why should one be aware of any accumulator in the system before servicing or repairing it?
   - **a.** Accumulator parts are not easily available in the market.
   - **b.** Accumulators have low pressure, which creates a vacuum.
   - **c.** Accumulators store high-pressure fluid.
   - **d.** Accumulators store low-pressure gases.
4. One of the most effective means of ensuring the reliability of hydraulic systems is through ____________.
   - **a.** discarding dysfunctional systems
   - **b.** avoiding operating them at constant maximum pressure
   - **c.** regular preventive maintenance
   - **d.** immediate repair of dysfunctional systems
5. Which of the following types of fluid conductor allows movement between two components?
   - **a.** Hydraulic hose
   - **b.** Pipe
   - **c.** Tube
   - **d.** Coupler
6. Working pressure ____________.
   - **a.** should be equal to burst pressure
   - **b.** should be more than burst pressure
   - **c.** should be less than burst pressure
   - **d.** should be equal to zero
7. Hose pressure burst factor should be _____ times more than the working pressure.
   - **a.** seven
   - **b.** four
   - **c.** three
   - **d.** six
8. Hydraulic hoses are designated by a dash number that indicates the inside diameter of the hose in ____________ of an inch.
   - **a.** sixteenths
   - **b.** tenths
   - **c.** fourteenths
   - **d.** elevenths
9. Identify the tools required to remove and replace the O-ring of a flanged fitting.
   - **a.** Wrench and seal pick
   - **b.** Hammer and cutting plier
   - **c.** Solvent and screw driver
   - **d.** Screw driver and hammer
10. Code 61 and Code 62 pertain to ____________.
    - **a.** ORB connectors
    - **b.** ORFS connectors
    - **c.** flange connectors
    - **d.** flare pipe connectors

ASE Technician A/Technician B Style Questions

1. Technician A says even minor fluid leaks or spills are hazardous. Technician B says minor fluid leaks are simply a part of equipment operation. Who is correct?
   - **a.** Technician A
   - **b.** Technician B
   - **c.** Both Technician A and Technician B
   - **d.** Neither Technician A nor Technician B
2. Technician A says the goal of a maintenance program for a hydraulic system is to preserve the performance

of the system and reduce operating and repair costs. Technician B says the service technician must understand and be able to perform regular hydraulic system maintenance service. Who is correct?
a. Technician A
b. Technician B
c. Both Technician A and Technician B
d. Neither Technician A nor Technician B

3. Technician A says hydraulic hoses normally consist of three to eight layers: an inner tube of synthetic rubber or thermoplastic; one or more reinforcement layers made of steel or textile braid; and an outer cover made of synthetic rubber or thermoplastic. Technician B says hydraulic hoses are designated by a dash number that indicates the inside diameter of the hose in sixteenths of an inch. For example, a –8 (dash 8) hose has an eight-sixteenths (one-half inch) ID. Who is correct?
a. Technician A
b. Technician B
c. Both Technician A and Technician B
d. Neither Technician A nor Technician B

4. Technician A says that galvanized pipe should be used for hydraulic systems. Technician B says that a hydraulic tube helps cool the fluid flowing through it. Who is correct?
a. Technician A
b. Technician B
c. Both Technician A and Technician B
d. Neither Technician A nor Technician B

5. Technician A says smaller line ID causes higher fluid velocity. Technician B says all locations in the system must have the same line sizes. Who is correct?
a. Technician A
b. Technician B
c. Both Technician A and Technician B
d. Neither Technician A nor Technician B

6. Technician A says working pressure is the *minimum* pressure at which the line was designed to operate. Technician B says working pressure is *well below* the limit of design tolerances. Who is correct?
a. Technician A
b. Technician B
c. Both Technician A and Technician B
d. Neither Technician A nor Technician B

7. Technician A says NPTF threads are more likely to leak than NPT threads. Technician B says uncoupling and then recoupling an NPTF-threaded fitting may cause leakage. Who is correct?
a. Technician A
b. Technician B
c. Both Technician A and Technician B
d. Neither Technician A nor Technician B

8. Technician A says to prevent chafing, external hose guarding should protect a hose in an area where it may contact moving machinery. Technician B says hoses should not be clamped, to allow for free movement. Who is correct?
a. Technician A
b. Technician B
c. Both Technician A and Technician B
d. Neither Technician A nor Technician B

9. Technician A says hydraulic lines should be kept away from hot components such as exhaust systems. Technician B says to leave extra length in hoses to accommodate length changes when the hose is pressurized. Who is correct?
a. Technician A
b. Technician B
c. Both Technician A and Technician B
d. Neither Technician A nor Technician B

10. Technician A says the use of inadequate or low-quality replacement hoses, seals, or tubes can result in minor to significant hydraulic fluid leaks. Technician B says that the proper use of personal protective equipment (PPE) is mandatory when working on hydraulic systems. Who is correct?
a. Technician A
b. Technician B
c. Both Technician A and Technician B
d. Neither Technician A nor Technician B

CHAPTER 30
Hydraulic Accumulators and Accessories

Knowledge Objectives

After reading this chapter, you will be able to:

- K30001 Define accumulator safety precautions.
- K30002 Explain the purpose, fundamentals, construction features, and types of hydraulic accumulators and hydraulic components.
- K30003 Understand the symbols for accumulators, coolers, and heaters.

Skills Objectives

After reading this chapter, you will be able to:

- S30001 Service a gas-charged accumulator.
- S30002 Pressurize a spring-loaded accumulator and test for leaks.
- S30003 Inspect, test, and clean an air-cooled cooler.
- S30004 Inspect, test, and clean a water-cooled cooler.
- S30005 Inspect an electric heater and test the element.

▶ Introduction

K30001

A hydraulic accumulator (**FIGURE 30-1**) is a pressure storage reservoir in which hydraulic fluid is held under pressure. An external source of fluid flow supplies fluid to one side of the accumulator while a second internal energy source applies pressure to the fluid. The internal source can be a spring, a raised weight, or a compressed gas. The majority of accumulators used on MORE (mobile off-road equipment) machines are gas type.

Accumulators store hydraulic energy and can perform a number of important functions in the hydraulic system. Some MORE machines will have several accumulators as part of different hydraulic systems—systems such as braking, steering, implement, or drivetrain.

Each of three types of hydraulic accumulators varies in construction and operation, but they all perform the same function: to provide pressurized fluid for a variety of reasons. Each type does this in essentially the same way. They can also be used in some cases to provide a spring or cushion effect.

This chapter describes the types and functions of accumulators, including a detailed discussion on the three main types, and explains the safety precautions HDETs (heavy-duty equipment technicians) need to follow when working with accumulators. The chapter then describes the purpose and functions of oil coolers, the operation of the two main types, and common sources of cooler failure. Finally, we discuss hydraulic heaters; their purpose, functions, and types; and common sources of failure.

FIGURE 30-1 Hydraulic accumulators.

▶ Types of Accumulators

K30002

In the following sections, we discuss the purpose, fundamentals, construction features, and types of hydraulic accumulators and hydraulic components.

The following are the three types of accumulators:

1. In *gas-charged accumulators*, also known as *hydropneumatic accumulators*, a precharge of inert gas provides the force needed to pressurize the fluid in the accumulator, and the energy stored can be retrieved when needed.
2. *Spring-loaded accumulators* replace the gas with a spring—usually the coiled compression type—and the spring provides the force on the piston needed to expel the fluid from the accumulator.
3. With *weight-loaded accumulators*, a hydraulic cylinder lifts a weight, either directly or through a lever. The weight provides the force needed to expel the fluid from the accumulator. These are found mainly in industrial hydraulic systems since they are not practical for mobile machine applications.

You Are the Mobile Heavy Equipment Technician

You are a technician working for a mid-sized general contractor with a variety of small- to medium-sized MORE excavators. The company has won a demolition job, and the equipment manager has requested that you check the accumulator precharge for all excavators and their hammer attachments. Answer the following questions related to this task:

1. Which of the following types of gas-charged accumulator would you expect to service?
   a. piston-type gas-charged accumulator
   b. bladder-type gas-charged accumulator
   c. diaphragm-type gas-charged accumulator
2. Where would you locate the correct service procedure for these accumulators?
3. What safety precautions need to be observed when servicing this accumulator?
4. What key information would you need to know to service the accumulator?
5. What PPE (personal protection equipment) is needed to service the accumulator?
6. What tooling would you need to service the accumulators?
7. How are gas-charged accumulators tested?

Functions of Accumulators

Accumulators perform four main functions:

1. *Providing a secondary fluid flow*: Accumulators can provide an emergency fluid flow to a system, which is commonly used for steering and brake system backup on MORE machines. For example, one or more accumulators can be used to provide a temporary oil flow to a brake system for a machine if its prime mover or brake pump fails. This allows the machine to be stopped safely when a brake fluid supply problem occurs. Steering oil supply can also be fed from accumulators if the engine-driven pump stops to allow the machine to be operated safely until it is brought to a stop.
2. *Absorbing shock*: Accumulators can act as shock absorbers for actuators. For example, wheel loaders can have a ride control option that tees in accumulators to the head end of their lift cylinders. This provides a spring action when the machine is traveling and can allow the machine to travel faster on uneven ground.
3. *Maintaining steady pressure*: Accumulators remove pressure and flow pulsations that actuators or pumps create. Pressure spikes are reduced to help reduce shock loads on components.
4. *Providing supplementary flow*: Accumulators provide supplementary flow by storing energy for use when the system pressure is less than that of the energy stored in the accumulator. They then release the stored energy to support the system at that time. Some excavators use accumulators to provide a supplementary swing motor and are part of a hydraulic hybrid system.

They can provide additional energy during peak load demand and recharge during low demand periods, just like a battery and alternator in a car. One example of this is an excavator hydraulic hybrid system that stores energy when the machine is slowing down while swinging. This energy is then used to assist in swinging the machine. For mining and other heavy equipment applications, accumulators can also act as part of an engine cranking system.

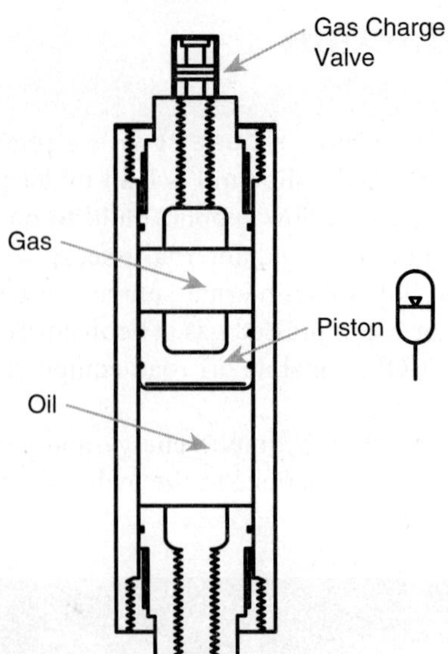

FIGURE 30-2 A piston-type gas-charged accumulator.

Gas-Charged Accumulators

Gas-charged accumulators take advantage of the compressibility of gas to supply energy for the side of the accumulator opposite to the fluid side. Oxygen and air are not suitable for use in gas-charged accumulators, because they may cause an explosion if they come into contact with the hydraulic fluid. Manufacturers instead use *nitrogen*, which is almost inert in its natural state. (An inert gas is a gas that does not undergo chemical reactions or change under different sets of conditions, such as temperature change.) Suppliers use gas-charged accumulators in many different applications.

Types of Gas-Charged Accumulators

The following are types of gas-charged accumulators:

- A *piston-type gas-charged accumulator* has a cylindrical body with a piston separating the hydraulic fluid and the gas (**FIGURE 30-2**). One or more seals on the piston keep the hydraulic fluid and gas separated. The piston moves up and down in the accumulator as fluid moves in and out. When precharging a piston-type accumulator, there must not be any fluid on the opposite side of the piston, so that it can be bottomed out in the cylinder. For piston-type accumulators, hydraulic system fluid flows into one end of the cylinder and moves the piston toward the gas side, which compresses the gas. Once the nitrogen gas has been compressed and the oil on the opposite side has been trapped in the accumulator, a potential energy is available for use when required.
- A *bladder-type gas-charged accumulator* uses a bladder made from a rubber-like material to separate the fluid and the gas and to provide the force needed to expel the fluid from the accumulator (**FIGURE 30-3**).

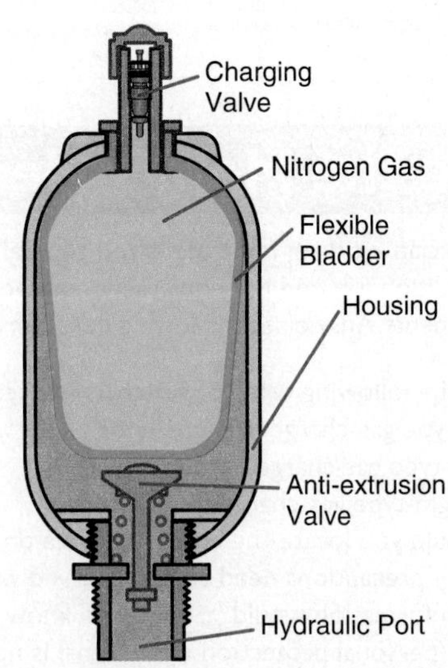

FIGURE 30-3 A bladder-type gas-charge accumulator.

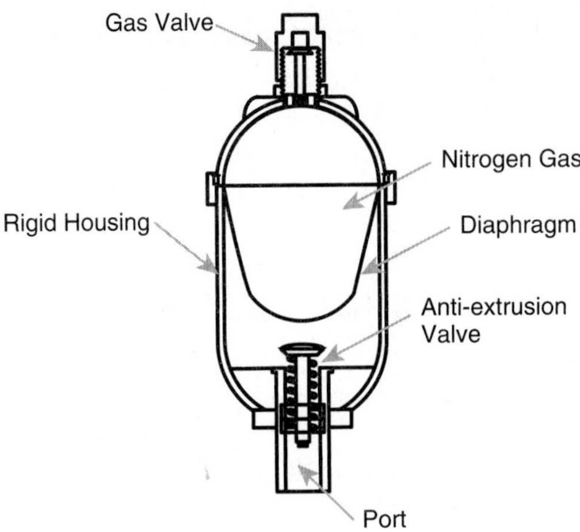

FIGURE 30-4 A diaphragm-type gas-charged accumulator.

- A *diaphragm-type gas-charged accumulator* has a two-piece spherical or cylindrical body with a diaphragm separating the fluid from the gas (**FIGURE 30-4**).

SAFETY TIP

Precharge gas-type accumulators only on the machine. Do not precharge an accumulator on the bench and then install it on the machine. Do not precharge an accumulator with nitrogen pressure beyond the accumulator's maximum pressure. You can find the maximum pressure on the accumulator housing. Always refer to the machine's service information for precharge pressure limits.

Characteristics of Gas-Charged Accumulators

No matter the type, gas-charged accumulators all exhibit the same operational characteristics:

- They are all charged with nitrogen or argon as the charge gas.
- They cannot supply a constant pressure all the time.
- Their oil volume depends on the physical size of space available in the oil volume side of the accumulator.

SAFETY TIP

Never use oxygen or air to charge accumulators! Using oxygen or air could result in an explosion if it comes into contact with the fluid. Air also can contain water vapor, leading to rust and eventual failure.

Gas-Type Accumulator Precharging

Pneumatic accumulators need a precharge of nitrogen gas that is applied with a charging kit and nitrogen cylinder. Depending on the type of pneumatic accumulator, nitrogen gas is precharged on one side of a piston, bladder, or diaphragm. The charge level is specified in the machine's service information and will have an ambient temperature factor included.

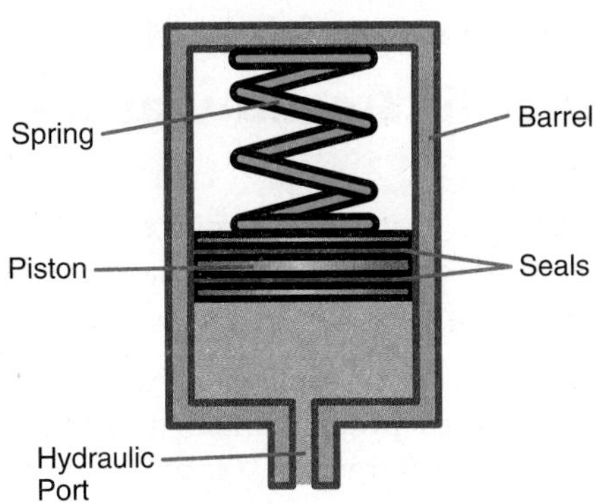

FIGURE 30-5 A spring-loaded accumulator.

Spring-Loaded Accumulators

A spring-loaded accumulator has a cylindrical body with a piston to separate the fluid and the mechanical energy force. A strong spring provides the force on the piston to expel the fluid from the accumulator (**FIGURE 30-5**). This kind of accumulator cannot supply a constant pressure; nor can it use all the fluid from the accumulator, because some fluid must remain in the accumulator to enable the accumulator to provide pressure to the system.

Weight-Loaded Accumulators

A weight-loaded accumulator has a cylindrical body with a piston separating the fluid from the mechanical energy force. A weight on top of the piston (or a very heavy piston) provides the force on the piston to expel the fluid from the accumulator (**FIGURE 30-6**). This type of accumulator is often constructed in place because of its large size.

Unlike gas-charged and spring-loaded accumulators, weight-loaded accumulators provide a constant pressure and therefore allow the use of all the fluid from the accumulator.

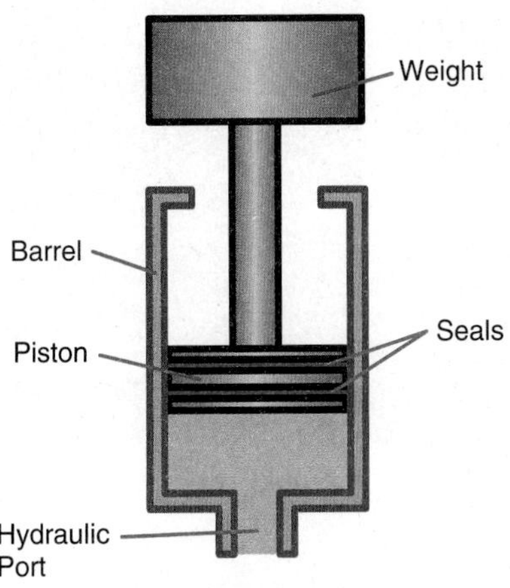

FIGURE 30-6 A weight-loaded accumulator.

▶ Safety Precautions for Hydraulic Accumulators

K30001, S30001, S30002

Accumulators store energy and therefore can pose significant safety hazards. Make sure you understand the hazards, and always follow appropriate safety precautions:

- Operate the entire system without the pump running, to discharge stored hydraulic fluid from the accumulator before removing it from the system.
- Always precharge the gas side of an accumulator according to the manufacturer's instructions.
- Too high or too low a precharge can cause damage to the accumulator, interfere with the proper functioning of the accumulator, and reduce the life of the accumulator.
- Never charge an accumulator higher than the pressure that the manufacturer recommends.
- Always use an inert gas, such as nitrogen or argon, to charge an accumulator.
- Never use oxygen. Using oxygen could result in an explosion if it comes into contact with the fluid.
- Never use air to charge an accumulator, since air can contain water vapor and sufficient oxygen to cause an explosion.
- Water vapor can also cause the accumulator to rust and eventually weaken to the point of structural failure.
- Before disassembling an accumulator, release both the gas and hydraulic pressures.
- Use extreme care in removing the springs from spring-loaded accumulators.

SAFETY TIP

Before disassembling the accumulator, ensure that the pressure on both the fluid and the gas sides of the accumulator is completely discharged. Use gauges to confirm that both sides of the accumulator are completely discharged.

Servicing and Testing Hydraulic Accumulators

To service a gas-charged accumulator, follow the steps in **SKILL DRILL 30-1**.

To pressurize an accumulator and test for leaks, follow the steps in **SKILL DRILL 30-2**.

▶ Hydraulic Oil Coolers

S30003

To maintain fluid temperatures within the required operating range (typically a maximum of 160°F), an oil cooler (**FIGURE 30-7**) is usually required to dissipate any excessive heat that the hydraulic system generates. The quantity of excessive heat increases as the components wear, so ongoing maintenance of the cooling circuit is important. Most machines produced today will have a hydraulic oil cooler as part of the machine's cooling package. However, some machines will have a standalone cooler with its own cooling fan. Since heavy equipment generally moves slowly, the machine's cooling system can't rely on ram air to dissipate heat from the coolers, so fans driven by hydraulic motors will create enough airflow to make the cooler effective.

SKILL DRILL 30-1 Servicing a Gas-Charged Accumulator

For this procedure, you need the following tools, materials, and equipment:

- a gas-charged accumulator suitable for repairing
- manufacturer's instructions for repairing the accumulator
- proper valves and gauges for recharging the accumulator
- nitrogen source for recharging
- appropriate wrenches
- safety glasses or goggles
- gloves.

1. Put on gloves and safety glasses or goggles.
2. Discharge the pressure on both the gas and fluid sides of the accumulator. Install pressure gauges to confirm that both sides have discharged.
3. Disassemble the accumulator in accordance with the manufacturer's instructions.
4. Inspect the accumulator in accordance with the manufacturer's instructions.
5. Reassemble the accumulator in accordance with the manufacturer's instructions and the equipment specifications.
6. Charge the accumulator with nitrogen in accordance with the manufacturer's instructions and the equipment operational specifications.
7. Clean the work area, and return tools and equipment to their proper storage area.

SKILL DRILL 30-2 Pressurizing a Spring-Loaded Accumulator and Testing for Leaks

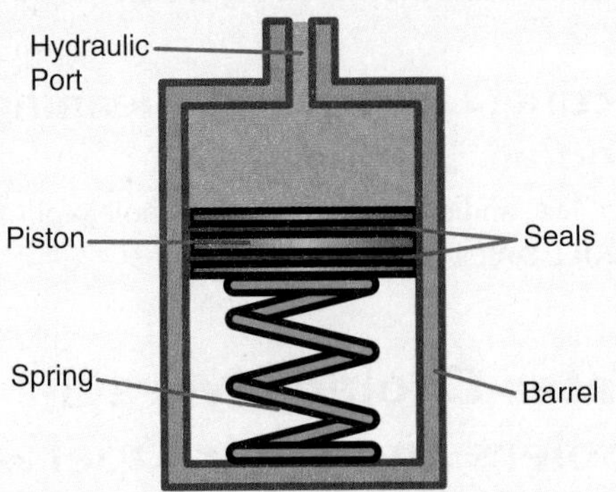

For this procedure, you need the following tools, materials, and equipment:

- a spring-loaded accumulator suitable for repairing
- hydraulic test stand with appropriate valving and connections for installing the accumulator
- test gauge to fit the accumulator fill valve
- manufacturer's instructions for testing the accumulator
- appropriate wrenches and spanners
- safety glasses or goggles
- gloves.

1. Put on gloves and safety glasses or goggles.
2. Mount the accumulator on the test stand.
3. Start the test stand and charge the fluid side of the accumulator to the desired pressure.
4. Test for and note any leaks present in the system.
5. Shut down the test stand and observe the pressure gauges for losses of pressure.
6. With the test stand shut down, completely discharge the fluid side of the accumulator.
7. Clean the work area, and return tools and equipment to their proper storage area.

FIGURE 30-7 A hydraulic oil cooler.

> **TECHNICIAN TIP**
>
> In some cold-weather conditions, the heat exchanger stops or reduces fluid viscosity from reducing, so that the hydraulic system operates within a given temperature range.

The purpose and main functions of a hydraulic fluid cooler are as follows:

- to remove excessive heat from the hydraulic system and increase fluid and component life
- to prevent excessive operating temperatures
- to prevent losses and inefficiencies in various hydraulic components due to fluid viscosity changes.

Most hydraulic oil cooler systems operate with a design similar to an engine cooling system. When the hydraulic fluid is cold, a thermostatic or pressure-based bypass valve directs cold fluid directly to the reservoir. As fluid temperature rises and viscosity reduces, a greater volume of fluid passes through the cooler. The thermostatic valve is essential for the system to work properly.

Types of Oil Coolers

Two types of oil coolers can be found on MORE machines:

1. *Air-cooled oil coolers* are the most common type that manufacturer's use in mobile equipment. Air-cooled oil coolers use air moving across the cooler to remove heat from the hydraulic fluid.
2. *Water-cooled oil coolers* are the type of oil cooler that manufacturers use in torque convertor, or hydraulic retarder systems and marine applications. Water-cooled oil coolers use coolant flowing through tubes to remove the heat.

> **TECHNICIAN TIP**
>
> Even though the second type of hydraulic cooler is called "water cooled," there should never be only water flowing through it. If this type of cooler is found on a MORE machine, it will have engine coolant flowing through it, which is a combination of coolant and water. Straight water would result in corrosion in the cooler and the possibility of damage from freezing.

Air-Cooled Coolers and Their Operation

Air-cooled coolers are like conventional engine coolant radiators in vehicles, but they contain hydraulic fluid in place of coolant. They consist of the following:

- a top tank, which holds incoming hot hydraulic fluid
- a radiator-like device consisting of a core with fins (typically aluminum) attached to tubes through which air passes to cool the hydraulic fluid
- a bottom tank, which holds the cooled hydraulic liquid (**FIGURE 30-8**).

This type of cooler will usually have a cold oil bypass valve to prevent cold-weather damage.

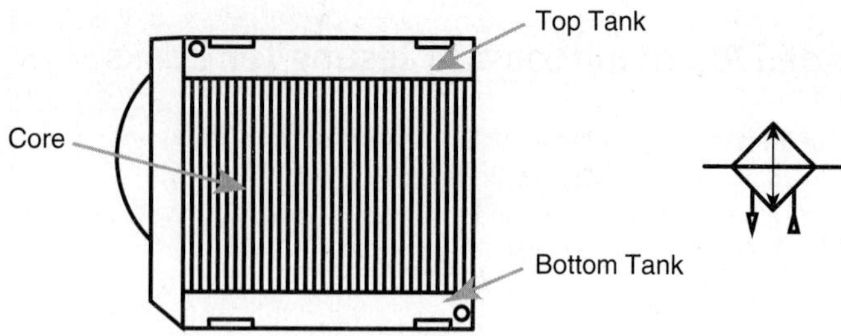

FIGURE 30-8 An air-cooled cooler.

The thermostat is normally located in the reservoir in hydraulic systems. The fluid passes from the top tank, through the core, to the bottom tank, which holds cooled hydraulic fluid and passes it back to the system.

Operationally, the greater the difference between the temperatures of the air and the hydraulic fluid and the higher the air flow through the cooler, the more effective the cooler is; therefore, coolers should always be located in a position where maximum cool airflow is assured.

Electrically or Hydraulically driven fans cool most coolers on MORE machines. Varying the speed and/or reversing the fan can help to self-clean the fins on the cooler.

Inspecting, Testing, and Cleaning an Air-Cooled Cooler

To inspect, test, and clean an air-cooled cooler, follow the guidelines in **SKILL DRILL 30-3**.

▶ Water-Cooled Hydraulic Coolers and Their Operation

S30004

Manufacturers design water-cooled coolers to maintain fluid temperatures within the required operating range—like their air-cooled counterparts. These coolers consist of a shell, or outer casing, which provides the flow path for the hydraulic fluid; tubes, which provide the flow paths for the cooling water;

SKILL DRILL 30-3 Inspecting, Testing, and Cleaning an Air-Cooled Cooler

For this procedure, you need the following tools, materials, and equipment:

- air-cooled cooler
- hand tool set
- service manual, if available
- solvent
- lint-free workshop towels
- caps for covering fluid ports
- hydraulic power supply capable of providing hydraulic fluid at the rated pressure and flow capacity of the cooler
- test bench control valve
- pressurized air supply
- water tank
- safety glasses or goggles
- gloves.

1. Put on gloves and safety glasses or goggles.
2. Clean the cooler.
   - **a.** Install caps to cover the fluid ports.
   - **b.** Remove any caked-on dirt and mud from outside the cooler. *Note*: Care must be taken with pressure washer not to damage fins.
   - **c.** Use solvent to remove any residual grease or film from external surfaces.
   - **d.** Allow the solvent to dry.
   - **e.** Remove the caps on the fluid ports.
   - **f.** Flush the unit with solvent.
   - **g.** Have your instructor check your work.
3. Inspect the cooler.
   - **a.** After completing each point in the inspection, briefly note the condition of the components.
   - **b.** Examine the external welds and joints for any signs of cracking.
   - **c.** Examine the fins for damage.
   - **d.** Examine the fittings for damage.
   - **e.** Have your instructor check your work.
4. Test the cooler.
   - **a.** Connect the cooler to the hydraulic power supply.
   - **b.** Slowly increase the pressure on the inlet side of the cooler, and slowly close the test bench control valve until you attain the rated test pressure according to manufacturer's specifications.
   - **c.** Examine the cooler for leaks, paying close attention to the areas near welds, joints, and fluid fittings.
   - **d.** Note any leaks.
   - **e.** Open the load valve.
   - **f.** Supply the cooler with fluid flow at a flow rate equal to its rated capacity.

SKILL DRILL 30-3 Inspecting, Testing, and Cleaning an Air-Cooled Cooler (Continued)

g. Allow the fluid to circulate until the operating temperature has been reached.
h. Measure the differential pressure across the cooler with the manufacturer's specified flow rate.
i. Record and compare to the manufacturer's specifications. *Note*: Excessive differential pressure is an indication of internal blockage. If pressure is too great, examine internal surfaces for blockage.
j. Have your instructor check your work.

5. Inspect the cooler with an alternative inspection method.

In situations where a hydraulic power supply is not present, use this alternative method to effectively inspect a cooler.

a. Remove the cooler from the system.
b. Drain all hydraulic fluid from the cooler.
c. Plug the outlet of the bottom tank with a short piece of hose with a pressure plug in it.
d. Submerge the cooler in a water tank.
e. Connect a regulated air supply to the inlet line of the top tank.
f. Activate the air supply and watch the water for bubbles that indicate leaks in the system.
g. Continue to test until you are certain that there are no leaks or until you have isolated all leaks.
h. Repair the leaks as required, or replace cooler if the damage is beyond repair. *Note*: A radiator repair shop can repair leaks in the fin-like cooling structure, and you can solder or braze the core and both tanks to repair them.
i. Have your instructor check your work.
j. Reinstall all components.

6. Clean the work area, and return tools and equipment to their proper storage area.

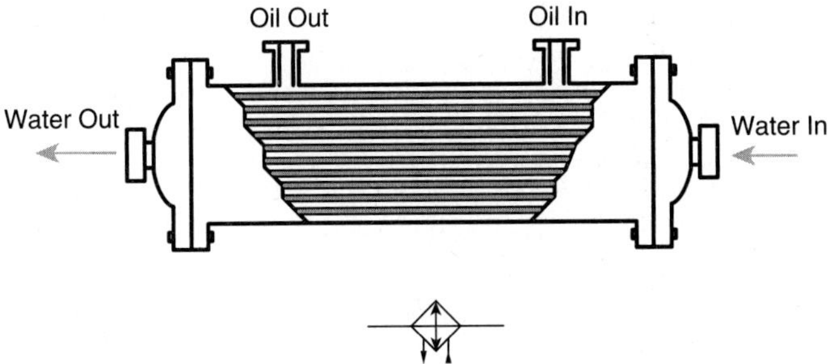

FIGURE 30-9 A water-cooled cooler.

and end caps, which direct the water to and from the tubes. A common way of describing them is according to their construction, and they are often known as "shell and tube coolers." The tubes run through the shell and allow the coolant to pass from the inlet at one end cap of the shell casing and out of the outlet at the other end cap. In some arrangements, the coolant flows through the shell while the oil flows through the tubes (**FIGURE 30-9**).

Operationally, the greater the temperature difference between the temperatures of the hydraulic fluid and the coolant, the more effective the cooler is. The coolant flow should be between one-quarter and one-half of the hydraulic fluid flow rate.

Also called bundle-type coolers, water-cooled coolers are seldom used for hydraulic system coolers and are found mainly in powertrain systems.

Inspecting, Testing, and Cleaning a Water-Cooled Cooler

To inspect, test, and clean a water-cooled cooler, follow the guidelines in **SKILL DRILL 30-4**.

Common Sources of Oil Cooler Failure

The HDET needs to perform oil cooler installation and maintenance procedures carefully to avoid some of the common sources of cooler failure:

- The cooling fins on air-cooled units are clogged with dirt and debris.
- The cooling fins are bent and damaged, restricting air flow.
- The radiator tubes are covered with dirt and debris.
- The cooling fan fails.
- The air is too hot.
- The air flow is too low.
- The water tubes or the shell on water-cooled units are clogged with sediment and debris (known as fouling).
- Water/coolant leaks into the fluid.
- Fluid leaks into the water.

TECHNICIAN TIP

Manufacturers use bypass valves to ensure that fluid can flow around the cooler in the event the water tubes or shell becomes clogged.

Hydraulic Heaters

S30005

To prevent high-pressure losses due to thick and heavy fluid flow through pipes and system components, manufacturers may use a heater (also called a *heat exchanger*) to raise the temperature of the fluid, which lowers its viscosity. In extreme climates, a heater can also warm the fluid to the desired operating temperature before starting the system during cold weather.

SKILL DRILL 30-4 Inspecting, Testing, and Cleaning a Water-Cooled Cooler

For this procedure, you need the following tools, materials, and equipment:

- appropriate shell and tube cooler
- manufacturer's data for the cooler
- water vat
- low-pressure air supply with pressure gauge
- caps and plugs needed to connect the air supply to the oil parts of the cooler
- hydraulic power unit
- hydraulic pressure gauges
- fittings needed to connect the power supply and gauges to the oil ports of the cooler
- appropriate wrenches and spanners
- safety glasses or goggles
- gloves.

1. Put on gloves and safety glasses or goggles.
2. Clean the cooler.
   a. Install caps to cover the fluid ports.
   b. Remove caked-on dirt from the outside of the cooler.
   c. Use solvent to remove residual grease from the external surfaces.
   d. Have your instructor check your work.
3. Inspect the cooler.
   a. After completing each point in the inspection, briefly note the condition of the cooler.
   b. Examine the external welds and joints for any signs of cracking.
   c. Check the assembly bolts for tightness.
   d. Examine the fittings for damage.
4. Test the cooler for internal leaks.
   a. Install an end cap on one oil port.
   b. Install a fitting for the air connection to the other oil port.
   c. Connect the air connection to the regulated air supply.
   d. Submerge the cooler in the water vat and allow any trapped air to escape.
   e. After all trapped air has escaped (the bubbling has stopped), turn on the air supply and adjust the air pressure to 10 to 20 psi (0.69 to 1.38 bar).
   f. Watch for a steady stream of bubbles coming from the water ports. *Note:* The stream of bubbles indicates internal leakage between the oil and water sides of the cooler. Do not use the cooler if this occurs.
   g. Have your instructor check your work.
5. Test the cooler for excessive pressure drop.
   a. Install hydraulic fittings on the oil ports of the cooler.
   b. Install pressure gauges on both the inlet and outlet oil ports.
   c. Turn on the hydraulic power unit and adjust the flow to the maximum flow for the cooler.
   d. Check the pressure drop across the cooler. *Note:* Check the cooler technical information for the allowable pressure drop—usually 20 to 30 psi (1.38 to 2.07 bar).
   e. Shut down the hydraulic power supply and disconnect the cooler.
   f. Have your instructor check your work.
6. Clean the work area, and return tools and equipment to their proper storage area.

Types of Heaters

Manufacturers use two types of heaters in hydraulic systems:

1. *Electric heaters* use electric heating elements to add heat to the hydraulic fluid (**FIGURE 30-10**). They are usually 240 VAC powered and can therefore present a high-voltage shock risk.
2. *Heat exchangers* (**FIGURE 30-11**) use heated air or liquid (usually engine coolant) to add heat to the system fluid, similar to a water-cooled cooler. Some heat exchangers will use the engine coolant from the prime mover, while others will have a diesel fuel-fired heat exchanger to heat the coolant before it then heats the hydraulic fluid.

▶ TECHNICIAN TIP

Consult the manufacturer's data before adding a heater to the system. Too high a temperature can overheat the fluid and in turn cause damage to hydraulic system components.

Common Sources of Heater Failure

HDETs should perform heater installation and maintenance carefully, to avoid some of the common sources of heater failure:

- The electric heating element fails.
- The electric heating element overheats the hydraulic fluid.
- The oil leaks into the heating fluid.
- The heating fluid leaks into the oil.

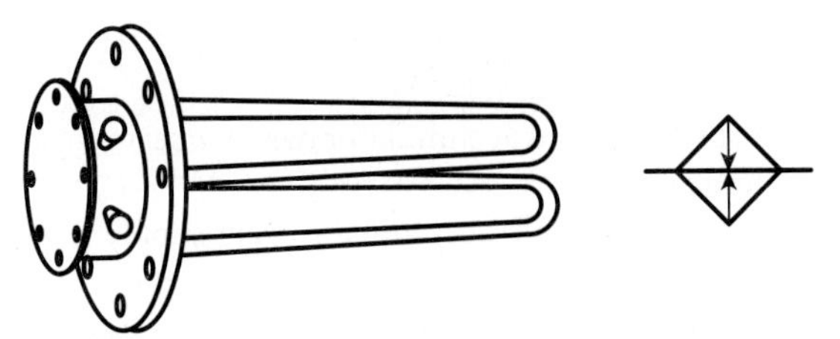

FIGURE 30-10 An electric heater element.

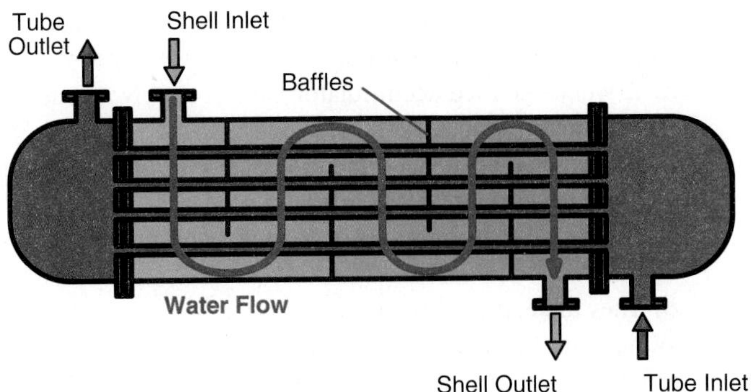

FIGURE 30-11 A hydraulic heat exchanger.

▶ Symbols for Accumulators, Coolers, and Heaters

K30003

FIGURE 30-12 shows some common symbols for accumulators, coolers, and heaters.

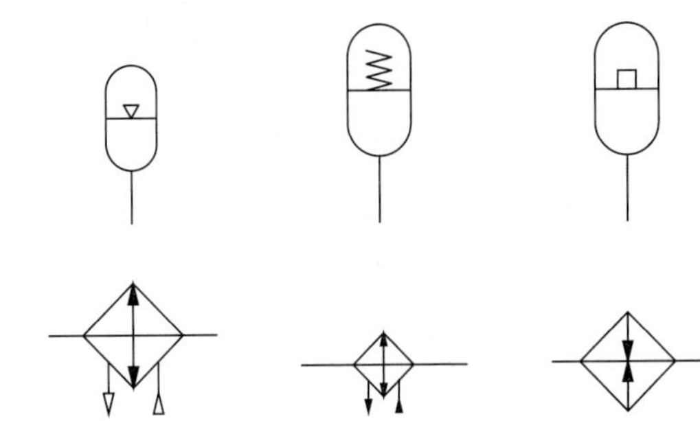

FIGURE 30-12 Common symbols for accumulators, coolers, and heaters.

▶ Wrap-Up

Ready for Review

- A hydraulic accumulator is a pressure storage reservoir in which a noncompressible hydraulic fluid is held under pressure, which an external source applies.
- For a hydraulic accumulator to work, the hydraulic energy must be converted into mechanical or pneumatic energy, since hydraulic fluid cannot be compressed or changed chemically.
- In a gas-charged, bladder-type accumulator, hydraulic fluid passes into the bladder at system pressure. The bladder is filled with gas, the fluid at system pressure compresses the gas, and the pressure in the bladder increases.
- In a gas-charged accumulator, the gas becomes even more compressed when the pump in the system pressurizes the fluid. If the system pressure drops because of a system failure, then the pressure in the bladder becomes higher than the pressure in the system. It is this pressure that provides the power to the system.
- There are three types of a hydraulic accumulators: gas-charged type, spring-loaded type, and weight-loaded type.
- In gas-charged accumulators, the gas provides the force needed to expel the fluid from the accumulator, and the energy stored can be retrieved when needed.
- Spring-loaded accumulators replace the gas with a spring—usually the coiled compression type—and the spring provides the force on the piston needed to expel the fluid from the accumulator.
- With weighted accumulators, a hydraulic cylinder lifts a weight, either directly or through a lever. The weight provides the force needed to expel the fluid from the accumulator.
- Accumulators perform four main functions: storing energy, absorbing shock, maintaining pressure, and providing emergency flow.
- Manufacturers use nitrogen (or argon) in gas-charged accumulators, never air or oxygen.
- There are three kinds of gas-charged accumulators: piston, bladder, and diaphragm.
- Gas-charged accumulators cannot supply a constant pressure all the time, and they cannot use all the fluid from the accumulator, because some fluid must remain in the accumulator to enable the accumulator to provide pressure to the system.
- Spring-loaded and weight-loaded accumulators have a cylindrical body with a piston to separate the fluid and the mechanical energy force.
- A spring-loaded accumulator cannot supply a constant pressure; nor can it use all the fluid from the accumulator, because some fluid must remain in the accumulator to enable the accumulator to provide pressure to the system.
- Weight-loaded accumulators provide a constant pressure and therefore allow the use of all the fluid from the accumulator.
- Accumulators store energy and therefore can pose significant safety hazards.
- To maintain fluid temperatures within the required operating range, an oil cooler may be required to dissipate the waste heat that the hydraulic system generates.

- Oil coolers remove heat from the hydraulic system, which helps avoid losses and inefficiencies in various hydraulic components, and it helps increase fluid life.
- There are two types of oil coolers: air-cooled coolers and water-cooled coolers.
- Air-cooled coolers are like conventional radiators in vehicles, but they contain hydraulic fluid in place of coolant.
- Water-cooled coolers consist of a shell, or outer casing, which provides the flow path for the hydraulic fluid; tubes, which provide the flow paths for the cooling water; and end caps, which direct the water to and from the tubes.
- To prevent high-pressure losses due to thick and heavy fluid flow through pipes and system components, manufacturers use heaters to raise the temperature of the fluid, which lowers its viscosity.
- The two types of heaters in hydraulic systems are electric and heat exchanger units.

Key Terms

bladder An inflatable bag, or sack, that contains fluids or gas.

diaphragm A flexible partition separating two cavities.

heat exchanger A device that transfers heat from one fluid to another without allowing the fluids to mix.

heater A device for adding heat to hydraulic fluids.

hydraulic accumulator A pressure storage reservoir in which a noncompressible hydraulic fluid is held under pressure, which an external source applies.

inert gas A gas that does not undergo chemical reactions or change under different sets of conditions, such as temperature change.

oil cooler A device that reduces the temperature of the hydraulic fluid in the system.

radiator A device that transfers heat from a fluid within to a location outside.

thermostat An automatic device for regulating temperature.

Review Questions

1. Which of these is a type of accumulator?
   - **a.** Gas charged
   - **b.** Spring loaded
   - **c.** Weight loaded
   - **d.** All of the above
2. Which of these is a function of an accumulator?
   - **a.** To store energy
   - **b.** To absorb pressure shocks
   - **c.** To supply fluid flow for emergencies
   - **d.** All of the above
3. Which of these is a true statement about types and characteristics of gas-charged accumulators?
   - **a.** Gas-charged accumulators are usually charged with oxygen.
   - **b.** The types of gas-charged accumulators include piston, vane, and diaphragm.
   - **c.** The bladder in a bladder-type accumulator provides the force needed to expel the fluid from the accumulator.
   - **d.** A bladder-type accumulator can supply a constant pressure.
4. Which of the following characteristics are true for spring-loaded accumulators?
   - **a.** A spring-loaded accumulator has a barrel to separate the fluid and the gas.
   - **b.** A spring-loaded accumulator can supply a constant pressure.
   - **c.** A strong spring provides the force on the piston to expel the gas from the accumulator.
   - **d.** None of the above.
5. Which of the following characteristics of are true for weight-loaded accumulators?
   - **a.** A weight-loaded accumulator cannot supply a constant pressure.
   - **b.** A weight-loaded accumulator is often constructed in place because of its large size.
   - **c.** All the fluid from a weight-loaded accumulator cannot be used.
   - **d.** They are easy to disassemble.
6. Which of the following are true statements concerning safety precautions when working with accumulators?
   - **a.** Always discharge stored hydraulic fluid from the accumulator before removing it from the system by operating the entire system with the pump running.
   - **b.** Too high a precharge can cause damage to the accumulator, interfere with the proper functioning of the accumulator, and reduce its life.
   - **c.** Accumulators are safe to work on as long as the machine is shut down.
   - **d.** Always use oxygen to charge an accumulator.
7. Which of the following are true statements concerning the functions of a cooler?
   - **a.** It removes heat from the hydraulic system and increases fluid and component life.
   - **b.** It prevents excessive operating temperatures.
   - **c.** It prevents losses and inefficiencies in various hydraulic components.
   - **d.** All of the above.
8. Which of the following are types of coolers?
   - **a.** Air cooled
   - **b.** Water cooled
   - **c.** Oil cooled
   - **d.** All of the above
9. Which are true statements regarding the function of air-cooled coolers?
   - **a.** A core is a radiator-like device through which air passes to cool the hydraulic fluid.
   - **b.** The top tank holds cooled hydraulic fluid.
   - **c.** The bottom tank holds incoming hot hydraulic fluid.
   - **d.** All of the above.
10. Which of the following are true about the components of water-cooled coolers and their functions?
    - **a.** The shell provides the flow path for the hydraulic fluid.
    - **b.** The tubes provide the flow paths for the cooling water.
    - **c.** The end caps prevent water and oil from mixing.
    - **d.** None of the above.

ASE Technician A/Technician B Style Questions

1. Technician A says a hydraulic accumulator holds a non-compressible hydraulic fluid under pressure. Technician B says an external source supplies fluid pressure in a hydraulic accumulator. Who is correct?
   a. Technician A
   b. Technician B
   c. Both Technician A and Technician B
   d. Neither Technician A nor Technician B
2. Technician A says hydraulic accumulators store hydraulic energy. Technician B says hydraulic accumulators help regulate the temperature of hydraulic fluid. Who is correct?
   a. Technician A
   b. Technician B
   c. Both Technician A and Technician B
   d. Neither Technician A nor Technician B
3. Technician A says accumulators remove pressure that actuators create. Technician B says accumulators can act as shock absorbers for actuators. Who is correct?
   a. Technician A
   b. Technician B
   c. Both Technician A and Technician B
   d. Neither Technician A nor Technician B
4. Technician A says gas-charge accumulators are charged with air. Technician B says gas-charge accumulators are charged with nitrogen. Who is correct?
   a. Technician A
   b. Technician B
   c. Both Technician A and Technician B
   d. Neither Technician A nor Technician B
5. Technician A says spring-loaded accumulators supply a constant pressure. Technician B says with weight-loaded accumulators, the hydraulic accumulator piston lifts a weight. Who is correct?
   a. Technician A
   b. Technician B
   c. Both Technician A and Technician B
   d. Neither Technician A nor Technician B
6. Technician A says manufacturers use air-cooled oil coolers in marine applications and torque converter systems. Technician B says that as fluid temperature rises and viscosity reduces, a greater volume of fluid passes through the cooler. Who is correct?
   a. Technician A
   b. Technician B
   c. Both Technician A and Technician B
   d. Neither Technician A nor Technician B
7. Technician A says air-cooled coolers use hydraulic fluid to help cool accumulators. Technician B says the thermostat in an oil cooler is normally located in the reservoir in hydraulic systems. Who is correct?
   a. Technician A
   b. Technician B
   c. Both Technician A and Technician B
   d. Neither Technician A nor Technician B
8. Technician A says manufacturers use bypass valves to ensure fluid can flow around the cooler if the water tubes or shell become clogged in a water-cooled cooler. Technician B says the bypass valve prevents cold-weather damage. Who is correct?
   a. Technician A
   b. Technician B
   c. Both Technician A and Technician B
   d. Neither Technician A nor Technician B
9. Technician A says you operate the entire system without the pump running to discharge stored hydraulic fluid from the accumulator before removing it from the system. Technician B says you always precharge the gas side of an accumulator according to the manufacturer's instructions. Who is correct?
   a. Technician A
   b. Technician B
   c. Both Technician A and Technician B
   d. Neither Technician A nor Technician B
10. Technician A says you can charge an accumulator higher than the recommended pressure. Technician B says you only use an inert gas, such as nitrogen or argon, to charge an accumulator. Who is correct?
    a. Technician A
    b. Technician B
    c. Both Technician A and Technician B
    d. Neither Technician A nor Technician B

CHAPTER 31
Hydrostatic Drives

Knowledge Objectives

After reading this chapter, you will be able to:

- **K31001** Explain the purposes and fundamentals of hydrostatic drives.
- **K31002** Describe the principles of operation of hydrostatic drives.

Skills Objectives

After reading this chapter, you will be able to:

- **S31001** Identify the types and construction features of hydrostatic drives.
- **S31002** Inspect, test, and diagnose hydrostatic drives following the manufacturer's recommended procedures.
- **S31003** Recommend reconditioning or repairs by following the manufacturers' recommendations for hydrostatic drives.

▶ Introduction

Hydrostatic drive systems have been used to propel heavy equipment machines since the 1950s. Small machines, such as skid steer loaders, first used hydrostatic drive systems after the original friction clutch drive system proved to be inadequate. These four-wheeled machines have separate drives for the left and right sets of wheels. To steer a skid steer loader left, the two left wheels slow down while the right two pull the right side of the machine ahead, thus skidding the machine around a corner. To steer right, the opposite actions must occur.

The work cycle of a skid steer loader proved to be a perfect application for a hydrostatic drive system. A skid steer loader spends a lot of time cycling between forward and reverse through a normal work cycle.

To increase productivity, there was a need for a drivetrain system that would provide a fast and easy transition between forward and reverse. There was also a need for the drivetrain to provide lots of power so that the machine could fill its bucket quickly. The last requirement was to have a machine that would be able to steer quickly and smoothly. A hydrostatic drivetrain would satisfy all three of these needs.

The first hydrostatic drive systems had simple manual controls, and its smooth operation provided seamless tight turning with plenty of power, which worked perfectly for this type of machine. Also, because of the machine's small size, the compact components of a hydrostatic system were a good match for this drivetrain application. Hydrostatic drive is still the preferred choice for skid steer machines and many other MORE (mobile off-road equipment) machines. See **FIGURE 31-1** to see a collection of skid steer machines that use hydrostatic drive.

This chapter will focus on **closed-loop** hydrostatic systems that propel machines. Closed-loop systems feature a pump that sends fluid directly to a motor, and the return fluid from the motor goes directly back into the pump. Some fluid will leak out of the loop (internally in pumps, motors, and valves) along the way and is replaced by a charge pump. Some fluid is intentionally bled out of the loop as well, for cleaning and cooling purposes.

FIGURE 31-1 A collection of skid steer machines that use hydrostatic drive.

Some machines, such as wheel-type or track-type excavators, will use open-loop hydrostatic systems to propel them. An **open-loop** hydrostatic system is one that has a pump that gets its fluid from the tank and sends it to a directional control valve that is part of a main control valve assembly. The directional control valve is actuated by the operator to send the pump flow to either of two ports of a travel motor. The travel motor will then rotate, and its shaft will drive a gear reduction (final drive) that will drive the machine's track or axle.

In this chapter, the principles and fundamentals of closed-loop hydrostatic drives will be discussed. The chapter will look at different variations of hydrostatic drives, how they are controlled and how common problems are diagnosed when the system isn't operating properly. The chapter will wrap up by discussing the reconditioning and repairs of hydrostatic drive components.

You Are the Mobile Heavy Equipment Technician

You are a MORE technician working for a sewer and water main contractor that has a large fleet of machines. The company has over a dozen crews, each of which includes the following machines: an 80-ton crawler crane; a 90-ton excavator; a 4-yard track loader; a 3-yard rubber-tired loader; a sheep foot compactor; and a 45-ton excavator. The track loaders are hydrostatic drive machines and are a mix of three generations of the same model.

You have been called to a jobsite to check out a drive problem on a track loader there. This track loader is having an intermittent problem, with one track driving slower than the other. You are familiar with the older generation track loaders but haven't spent a lot of time on the newest version. To get this problem diagnosed and repaired, answer the following questions:

1. What would be the first step in diagnosing the problem?
2. Could connecting a laptop help to diagnose the problem?
3. What are some basic checks you could perform to assist in diagnosing the problem?
4. What are three questions you would ask the operator?
5. What are three possible root causes of this problem?
6. How would you confirm that the problem has been fixed?

> ▶ TECHNICIAN TIP
>
> The term "**hydrostatic**" actually refers to fluids at rest, and in that sense, it is a misleading name to give to a fluid power system that creates motion. However, the term has been related to fluid power drive systems for many years and will continue to be for years to come.

▶ Purpose and Fundamentals of Hydrostatic Drives

K31001

A hydrostatic system is a type of hydraulic system that relies on variable pump output flow to control the speed and direction of the system's hydraulic motor(s). Hydrostatic systems use only hydraulic motors for actuators; therefore, the system's mechanical output is always rotational.

As with any hydraulic system, a hydrostatic drive uses a hydraulic pump driven by a prime mover (typically a diesel engine) to convert mechanical energy into fluid energy. The fluid flow from the pump is sent directly to a hydraulic motor, and from the motor it returns to the pump inlet, which makes this is a closed-loop hydraulic system. There are no directional control valves needed to divert pump flow.

The motor's internal components receive the fluid, and the interaction between the fluid flow and the motor's internal elements makes the motor's output shaft rotate. The motor converts the fluid energy back into mechanical energy. Once the fluid has done its job in the motor, it leaves the motor and is then sent back to the pump inlet. This fluid flow continues in a loop if the pump keeps moving fluid. See **FIGURE 31-2** to see how fluid flows between a pump and motor.

The direction and amount of flow output of the pump determines the direction and speed output of the motor's shaft. The rate and direction of fluid flow from the pump is controlled by the machine's operator. The pump or pumps used are described as bidirectional variable displacement. This means that the pump can vary its output flow volume and change the flow direction so that its output flow is independent of its input shaft speed and direction of rotation.

The amount of torque output created in a hydrostatic drive system depends on the load that the drive system is trying to overcome. As the load increases, the system fluid pressure must increase to overcome the load. For example, a track-type loader with a hydrostatic drive that is traveling with its bucket in the air will not need a high amount of torque to drive its tracks. However, when the bucket is dropped and the operator wants to fill it with some material, there needs to be a high amount of torque to keep the machine moving. The hydrostatic system pressure increases to produce more driving torque to keep the machine moving. If a gauge was reading system pressure, it may change from 500 to 5,000 psi between the two different conditions. See **FIGURE 31-3** to see a track loader filling its bucket.

If the same machine's operator wants to change travel speed from slow to fast, then the hydrostatic pumps will be controlled to increase the flow rate. If a **flow meter** was measuring the output of the pumps, it may read a change from 5 to 40 gpm (gallons per minute) under these two different conditions (slow to fast). If the pump flow is reduced to 0 gpm, then the motor shaft will stop turning and the machine will stop moving. This is considered to be neutral.

Hydrostatic Drive System Overview

Hydrostatic drive systems are sometimes also called hydrostatic transmissions because they transmit torque from the machine's prime mover (diesel engine) to tracks or wheels. A mechanical drivetrain can change the speed and torque of the machine's diesel engine output to increase torque and reduce the speed

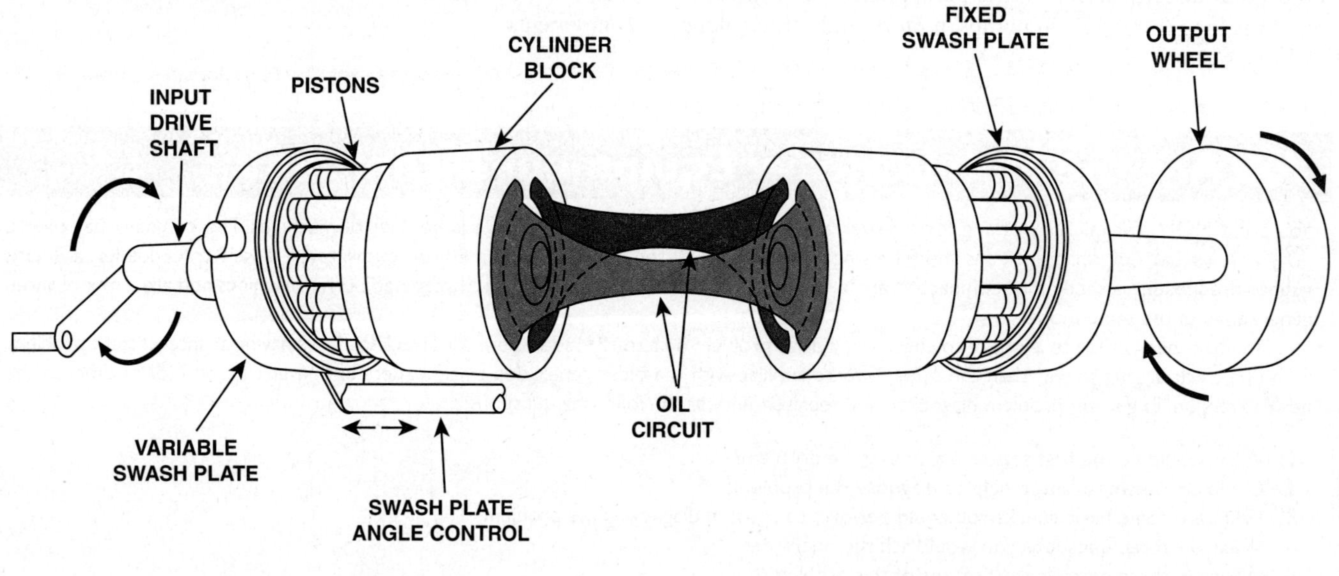

FIGURE 31-2 How fluid flows between a pump and motor.

Image Provided As Courtesy of John Deere.

FIGURE 31-3 A track loader filling its bucket.

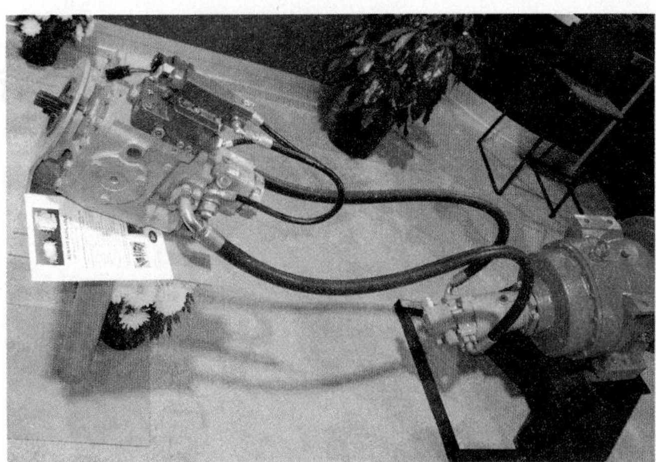

FIGURE 31-5 Pump and motor connected with hoses to make a closed-loop hydrostatic drive system.

of the drivetrain's output. It does this with combinations of gear ratios in different components that work to slow down rotational speed and increase rotational torque.

The hydrostatic transmission does this with one or more pumps, one or more motors, and hydraulic fluid. If you were to compare the interaction of a pump and motor to a mechanical gear set (pinion and crown gear), the pump would be the drive gear (pinion) and the motor the driven gear (crown). See **FIGURE 31-4** to see a crown and pinion gear set.

The ratio of a gear set is fixed and is based on the number of teeth on the drive and driven gears. The relationship between a pump and motor is infinitely variable and based on the pump output flow versus motor displacement. When the flow output of the pumps is varied, it is like changing the gear ratio of a gear set. Some hydrostatic systems can vary this relationship even farther by having a variable displacement motor.

Reverse rotation in a mechanical transmission is obtained by adding an idler gear between an input gear and an output gear. A hydrostatic transmission provides **reverse rotation** by simply changing the direction of fluid flow going to the motor. The flow reversal is enabled by using a bidirectional pump (to be discussed later).

FIGURE 31-4 A crown and pinion gear set.

By varying the flow, a hydrostatic system will be able to make the machine change directions and speeds or steer in a seamless manner. By having the output of the pump go directly to the motor, this is a closed-loop system. There is no need for directional control valves to meter the flow of fluid or to change the direction that it flows with a hydrostatic system, because fluid flow quantity and direction are controlled by changing the bidirectional pump output. See **FIGURE 31-5** to see a pump and motor connected with hoses to make a closed-loop hydrostatic drive system.

The majority of fluid that leaves the motor will then return to the pump inlet. All hydrostatic systems will need a **charge pump** that supplies makeup fluid to replace fluid that escapes the loop because of leakage. A certain amount of internal leakage is normal and is needed to lubricate, cool, and clean the internal pump and motor components. However, if this leakage becomes excessive, then there will be a loss of efficiency, which equates to lower torque and speed output. The charge fluid circuit will have a filter and possibly a fluid cooler as part of it to clean and cool system fluid.

When compared to mechanical-style drivetrains, hydrostatic drives offer many advantages. For example, one advantage is similar to why electric drives are gaining popularity, and that is that the prime mover (diesel engine) can be operated in a narrow rpm range and can therefore be designed for optimum efficiency with minimum emissions.

See **TABLE 31-1** for more advantages and disadvantages of hydrostatic drivetrains.

Hydrostatic System Braking

Hydrostatic systems can also naturally provide **dynamic machine braking** (driveline braking), which means the need for a service brake system is eliminated on most hydrostatic machines. Because of the closed-loop arrangement, there is nowhere for the fluid on the high-pressure side of the loop to go as long as the relief valve doesn't open. If the weight of the machine starts to push the machine, then the motor becomes a pump. The pump will provide a braking action because its shaft will resist turning faster because of the resistance of the engine.

TABLE 31-1 Advantages and Disadvantages of Hydrostatic Drivetrains

Hydrostatic Advantages	Hydrostatic Disadvantages
Seamless transition of speeds and directions	Components are sensitive to contamination
Allows engine to run at a steady rpm for improved efficiency and lower emissions	Components are expensive and require special tooling to repair and adjust
Track machines can power both tracks on turns	Can require specialized diagnostic tooling to troubleshoot problems
Excellent power to weight ratio	Less efficient because of internal heat loss
Locations of main components are very flexible	
Provides dynamic braking	
Can be stalled without damaging components	
Allows for counter-rotation of tires or tracks for spot turns	

One manufacturer's crawler dozer machine will also use one of its implement hydraulic pumps to provide an extra load on the engine when extra braking effort is needed. This system will run the pump's output through a restriction, thereby putting a load on the engine and therefore making the engine resist being driven by the hydrostatic system even more.

There will still be a need for a spring-applied parking brake system because hydraulic pressure will leak off over time. Hydrostatic systems will usually have the parking brake that is incorporated with the motor to give a braking effect on the final drive input. The brake release fluid circuit is usually part of the hydrostatic system's charge fluid system. See **FIGURE 31-6** for a cutaway view of a hydrostatic motor and brake assembly.

Hydrostatic Controls

The operator controls the pump and thereby controls the hydrostatic systems, which can be done in many ways, including using mechanical linkages or cables that are hand or foot controlled (used for lower flow and pressure systems), pilot fluid-actuated pumps that are **joystick** controlled, and electrical/electronic controls that are joystick or pedal controlled. These different operator controls will make the machine move from neutral in either direction at infinitely variable speeds (to a maximum limited speed) and could also steer the machine, depending on the type of steering system used for the machine. See **FIGURE 31-7** to see a joystick for a small track dozer that has a hydrostatic drive system.

FIGURE 31-7 Joystick for a small track dozer that has a hydrostatic drive system.

FIGURE 31-6 A cutaway view of a hydrostatic motor and brake assembly.

Hydrostatic Drive Configurations

There are many different configurations of hydrostatic drive systems, and a few examples are discussed here. These drive systems could be used to propel machines to well over 20 mph, as well as generate high torque at low speed. Some hydrostatic systems can be used to steer a machine, and some motors are variable displacement to give an extra-high-speed/low-torque or low-speed/high-torque feature. See **FIGURE 31-8** for a basic layout of a hydrostatic drive for a track machine.

Small machines (with less than 50 hp) that use a hydrostatic system may use an arrangement that combines the pump and motor into one housing. This could even be housed with a differential. One example of this type of machine is the agricultural-based utility tractor. This is commonly called a **hydrostatic transmission**, though some multi-pump assemblies are also called hydrostatic transmissions. This compact design

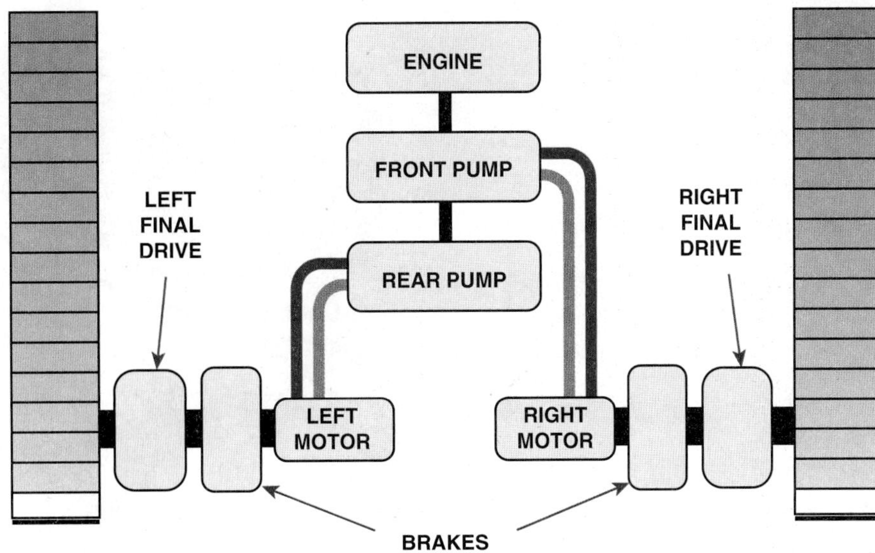

FIGURE 31-8 Basic layout of a hydrostatic drive for a track machine.
Image Provided As Courtesy of John Deere.

FIGURE 31-9 A hydrostatic drive utility tractor.

works well for small equipment, and its seamless operation makes it very user-friendly. See **FIGURE 31-9** for a hydrostatic drive utility tractor.

This type of unit will use passageways in the transmission housing to transfer fluid flow. All other hydrostatic systems use pumps and motors that are separate, and the fluid flows between them through hoses, tubes, and fittings.

Although the compact design of hydrostatic systems is ideal for smaller machines where space can be limited, many medium and large machines will also use hydrostatic systems to drive their tracks or wheels. Because of the excellent torque multiplication capabilities of hydrostatic drives, some track-type tractors with over 400 hp engines have their tracks driven with hydrostatic drive systems. With the addition of one or more gear reductions past the hydrostatic motor(s), these machines can produce massive amounts of drive torque.

One manufacturer makes a wheel loader that has a 340 hp engine driving one pump that drives two motors. These motors then drive a transfer case that sends torque to the front and rear axles via drive shafts. See **FIGURE 31-10** for hydrostatic drive arrangement for a wheel loader.

Hydrostatic systems can be used to drive a variety of wheel-type machines, such as skid steers, forestry machines, wheel loaders, the front wheels of a grader, telehandlers, and pavement grinders. Machines with drums (compactors) will also use hydrostatic drive systems to rotate the drum. Hydrostatic drives can also be used to drive track-type machines, such as bulldozers, track loaders, paving machines, drilling machines, and track-type skid steer machines. Almost all small- and medium-sized track machines have had their drivetrains evolve from mechanical to hydrostatic over the last 20–30 years.

While the majority of hydrostatic systems are used for machine travel, they can be used for other functions that need rotation. An example of this is the differential steering system used on some larger track-type tractors. They use the motor of a hydrostatic system to give the needed rotational torque to steer the machine by rotating a set of gears.

For machines that need to drive the left- and right-side wheels or tracks independently of each other (skid steer machines, track-type tractors, and track loaders), they will use an arrangement that features two pumps and two motors. One pump will send fluid to the left-side drive motor, and the other pump supplies the right-side motor. The motors will then typically drive an input to a gear reduction whose output then drives a sprocket to turn a track. These machines will use the speed differential between the left- and right-side track drives to steer the machine. The tracks or tires can even be driven in opposite directions to provide spot turning or counter-rotation. The motors for small skid steer machines drive a sprocket that in turn drives a chain that transfers drive to the wheels.

Dual pump and dual motor arrangements are called **dual-path hydrostatic systems**. Some large track machines will have each pump split its flow and send fluid to two motors for each track. The motors will drive a gear reduction to further slow

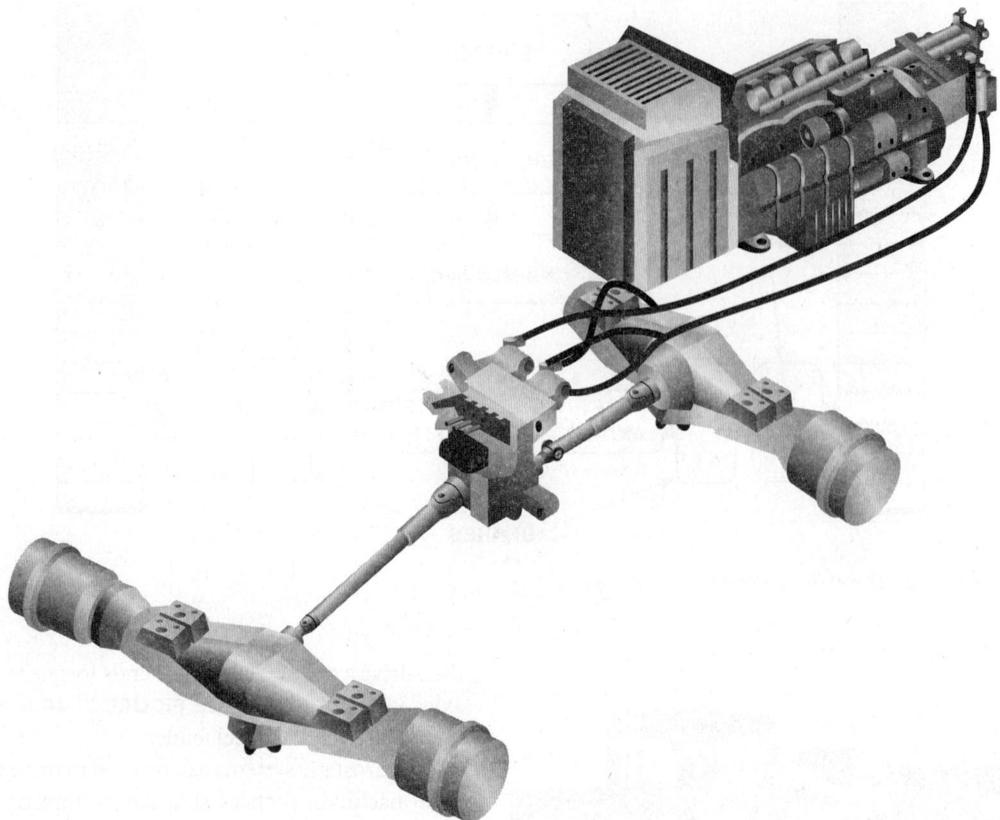

FIGURE 31-10 Hydrostatic drive arrangement for a wheel loader.

FIGURE 31-11 A dozer that has a dual-path hydrostatic drive system.

down rotation and increase torque. See FIGURE 31-11 to see a dozer that has a dual-path hydrostatic drive system.

Hydrostatic machines that feature a driven steering axle can have a driven solid (non-steering) axle or use articulated steering, which can have a variety of pump and motor arrangements. For example, a small articulating wheel loader may have one motor directly drive the front axle and one motor directly drive the rear axle. These motors will be driven by the same pump and rotate at the same speed.

Another articulated machine that is driven hydrostatically is a drum-type compactor. This machine will use one pump to drive one motor that drives the drum and another pump to drive one motor to drive the rear axle or two motors to drive the rear wheels.

A telehandler that is driven with a hydrostatic system will have front and rear steering axles and use one pump to drive one motor. The motor will drive one axle through a set of gears, and there will be a drive shaft that is driven by the first axle, which will send torque to the other drive axle.

As you can tell, there may be a wide variety of hydrostatic arrangements that all use the closed-loop pump/motor system for propelling machines. However, the same basic components are used for the hydrostatic portion of all hydrostatic drive arrangements: one or more bidirectional variable displacement pumps sending fluid to one or more fixed or variable displacement motors.

Dual-Path Hydrostatic System

Many hydrostatic drive machines will need two hydraulic motors to propel them and in turn two pumps to supply fluid to the two motors. This can mean that the two motors drive separate axles, final drives, or chain drives. This is considered to be a dual-path hydrostatic system.

The main components of a typical dual-path system are two pumps and two motors. The output of the motors will transfer torque into a gear reduction to further increase torque and decrease speed. The output of the gear reduction will then drive the machine's tracks or wheels. The pumps will be able to discharge fluid in either of two directions, which will make the motors turn their output shaft in either direction and will then change the direction of the machine's travel. A pump used for a hydrostatic system is considered to be bidirectional. Its shaft will be turned in only one direction by the machine's engine, but because of its design, it will be able to send fluid out either of two ports. This means the pump's inlet and outlet can trade places. Likewise, the motors will have two ports that can be either an inlet or an outlet.

The speed of the machine's travel is changed by changing the flow volume output of the pumps (remember the phrase "flow makes it go"). By varying the flow output volume of the pump, the speed output of the motors is changed. Simple systems will use fixed displacement motors, but many other systems will use dual displacement or variable displacement motors. The motor speed can be calculated by knowing the flow volume going into the motor and the motor displacement, then using the following formula:

$$\text{Motor rpm} = \text{flow (gpm)} \times 231/\text{motor displacement (cubic inches per revolution)}$$

Here is an example of this formula: a motor that drives the wheels of a skid steer machine has a displacement of 25 cubic inches per revolution and has a flow of 30 gpm going to it. Using this formula, you would calculate that its shaft would turn at 277 rpm.

▶ Principles of Operation of Hydrostatic Drives

K31002

To understand how fluid flows in a simple manually controlled hydrostatic system, we will look at a skid steer loader's system. The operation of this machine's hydrostatic system is typical of how a simple hydrostatic system works. It is considered to be a dual-path system because there are two pumps and two motors. It is really two separate hydrostatic systems that use a common fluid, charge fluid system, hydraulic tank, filtration, and fluid cooler. See **FIGURE 31-12** for the dual-path hydrostatic arrangement of a typical skid steer.

This machine has two flywheel-mounted bidirectional variable displacement axial piston pumps that supply fluid to two geroller-type motors. Types of pumps and motors will be discussed later in the chapter. The motors then send torque to sprockets and chains to drive the machine's wheels. The speed and direction of each drive sprocket is changed by the operator's moving joysticks back and forth that are connected to the pump swash plates. As the operator adjusts the swash plate angles, the pump flow output to the motors change. This will change the speed and direction of the left and right wheels independently, to speed up, slow down, steer the machine, or perform a **spot turn**.

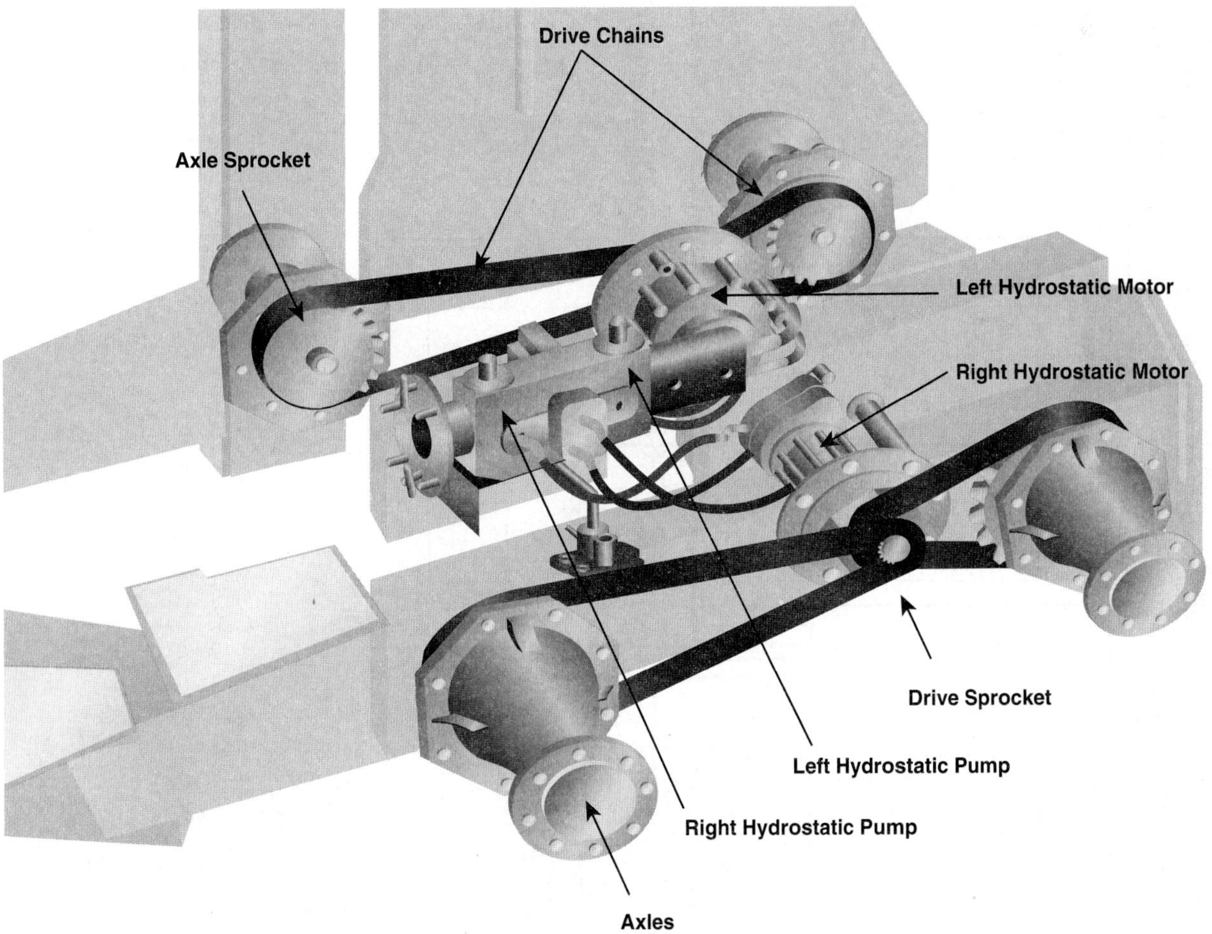

FIGURE 31-12 Dual-path hydrostatic arrangement of a typical skid steer machine.

Image Provided As Courtesy of John Deere.

There is another fixed displacement pump on this machine that is used for the machine hydraulic functions (boom and bucket). The pump is also used to supply charge fluid for the hydrostatic system. This machine uses a common reservoir, cooler, and filter for both the hydraulic and hydrostatic systems. This is a common arrangement for many small skid steer machines. See **FIGURE 31-13** for the schematic of a skid steer hydrostatic system.

Refer to the **schematic** and follow the path of fluid flow for the high-pressure closed-loop circuit. If you look at the right pump (4), imagine it is sending fluid out its top line to the right motor (7). Let's say the machine direction that this fluid flow creates is forward. The fluid would enter the motor and cause its shaft to rotate, leave the motor, and then head back to the pump. If there was a high enough resistance to stop the shaft, then pump outlet pressure would rise quickly and the relief valve (57) near the pump would open. This would route the pump output fluid back to the low-pressure side of the pump through the inlet side makeup valve (57). These valves (57) are actually **combination valves** that act as both a relief valve and a check valve, depending on whether they are exposed to fluid pressure on the high-pressure side or the low-pressure side of the loop.

When pressure builds in the high-pressure side of the loop, it is sensed at the end of the shuttle valve (61), which is part of each motor. The shuttle valve then shifts to allow some of the return fluid to pass by the shuttle valve, where it is sensed at the flushing relief valve. This is a low-pressure relief valve that will open to allow some fluid to flow through an orifice and into the motor housing. The fluid flow will then go through the pump housing to help cool it and then go to the tank. This valve is sometimes called a **flushing valve** and provides a constant flow of fluid going to the tank to cool and lubricate the motor and pump when the pump is moved from neutral. This valve will also keep a minimum amount of fluid pressure in the low-pressure side of the closed loop. The flushing relief valve is usually set 20–50 psi lower than charge pump relief, which is typically in the 200–350 psi range.

Because there is also a loss of fluid in the loop from internal leakage past the pump and motor rotating elements, as well as the controlled loss through the flushing valve, there must be a constant supply of fluid to replenish this fluid at the low-pressure side of the loop. This fluid is supplied by the fixed displacement gear pump (that is also the implement

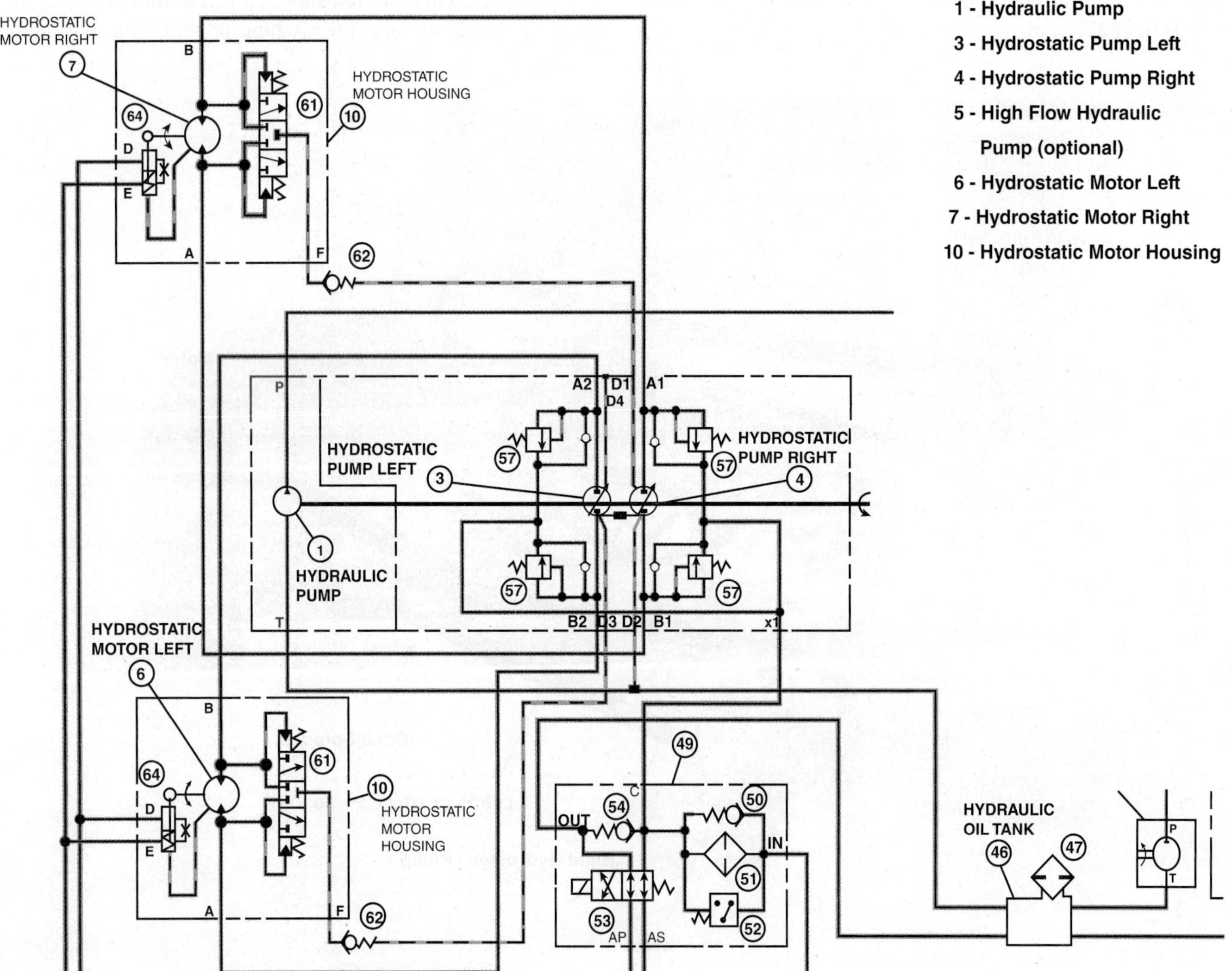

FIGURE 31-13 Schematic for a skid steer hydrostatic system.

pump for this machine) through the **makeup valves** (57) (part of the combination valves) in the hydrostatic pump housing. These are simple check valves that open to allow fluid into the pump inlet side if the return fluid pressure from the motor falls below **charge pressure**. The valves close when the pump port switches to a pump outlet port and the flow reverses, which causes the pressure to rise. This part of the system is needed to prevent pump cavitation and is common to any hydrostatic system. The charge fluid supply circuit is called such because the fluid charges the inlet side of the pump. It also keeps all parts of the system full of fluid, circulates fluid to help cool and lubricate components, and keeps back pressure on the pump's pistons when the pump is in neutral. Charge pump pressure is typically limited to between 200 and 350 psi, depending on the manufacturer, and is limited by a charge relief valve. When the charge relief valve opens, it will dump the pump flow back to the tank.

The gear pump flow for this system first goes to supply the implement functions (boom, bucket, and auxiliary) of this machine and then flows through the cooler and filter before it becomes available for charge fluid.

Larger hydrostatic systems will have a dedicated charge pump that is used for supplying charge fluid and one or more pump to supply the hydraulic system flow requirements. These machines will also likely have a dedicated hydrostatic fluid tank so that if there is a catastrophic failure, then there won't be cross-contamination between the two systems. Charge fluid can also be used for brake release fluid, pump servo controls, pilot controls, fan drive, and any other low-pressure hydraulic functions.

As you can see by the pump symbols on the schematic, the pumps are **variable displacement bidirectional**, which means they can send fluid out either one of two ports. If the pump (7) sent fluid out the bottom line, this would make the motor rotate in the opposite direction from what was just discussed. This would also shift the shuttle spool in the other direction but would still send some of the motor exhaust fluid out past the flushing valve to keep the motor cool and clean. The pump's main port that was the pump's outlet for forward is now the pump inlet. The opposite check valve would let charge fluid into the inlet of the pump. Now if the high-pressure side of the loop got high enough, the opposite relief valve would open.

To change the output of the pump, the operator of this machine would move the joystick from neutral, and the farther it was moved, the more flow the pump would produce. This would make the motor turn faster, and if the operators wanted to turn the machine, they would move the joysticks independently to change the speed differential of the machine's wheels. For spot turns, the left and right wheels could be turned in opposite direction or counter-rotate. Pump operation will be discussed further later in the chapter. See **FIGURE 31-14** for an illustration of a hydrostatic pump assembly.

The swash plate controls are the two square trunnions protruding from the top of the pump assembly. These trunnions are part of the pump's swash plates. The operator's joysticks are connected to a linkage that will connect to the square trunnions and will transfer back and forth movement of the joysticks to a partial rotary motion of the swash plate. As mentioned at the start of this section, this machine is a dual-path hydrostatic system. This means that the left joystick will control the rear pump's swash plate, which will make the left wheels rotate. The right joystick controls the front pump's swash plate and makes the right wheels turn.

Single-Path Hydrostatic System

To see the hydrostatic system for a small wheel loader that uses one pump and one motor, refer to **FIGURE 31-15**. As you can see, the hydrostatic pump (8) and charge pump are engines driven at the back of the machine. Hoses connect the pump to the motor (14). The motor is mounted on the rear axle (11), where it sends torque into a gear reduction. The output of the gear reduction then drives the rear axle, and a drive shaft transfers torque to the front axle (17). This would be considered a single-path hydrostatic system. See **FIGURE 31-16** for a schematic of a single pump and single motor hydrostatic system for a small wheel loader.

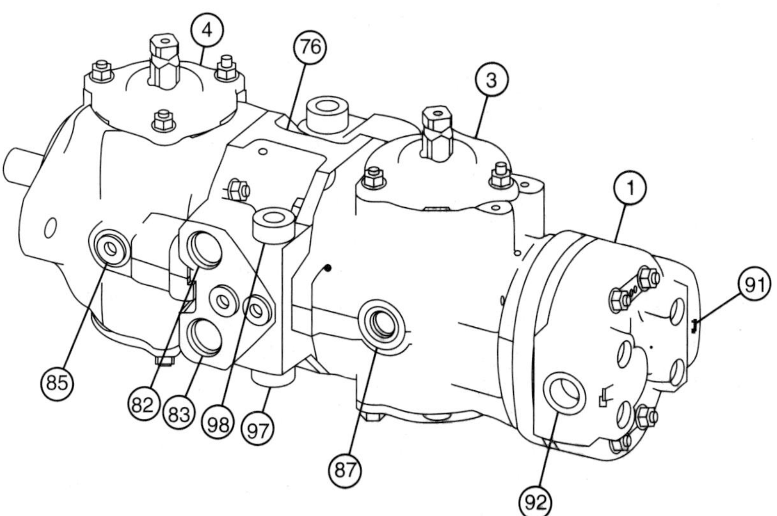

FIGURE 31-14 Hydrostatic pump assembly.

Image Provided As Courtesy of John Deere.

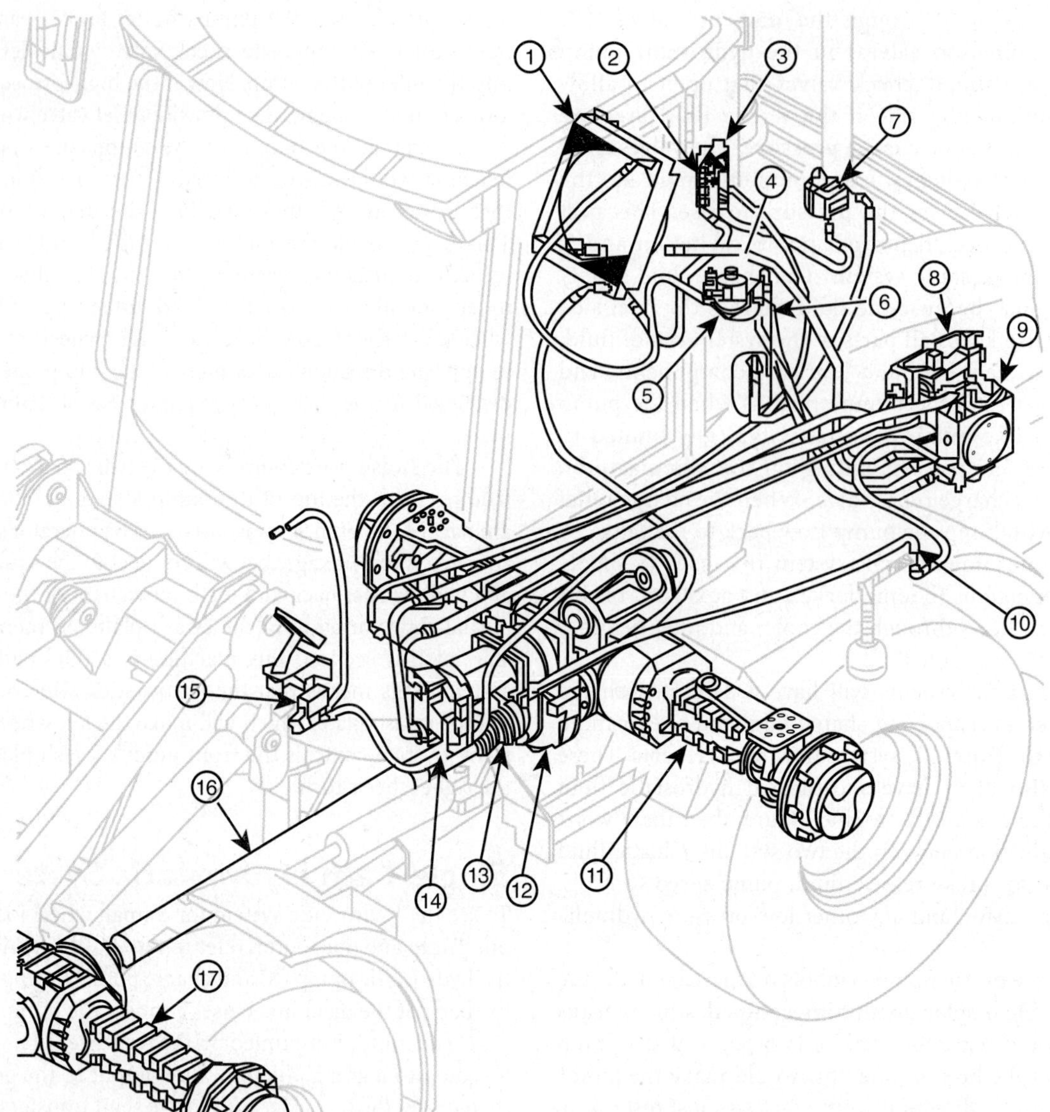

FIGURE 31-15 The hydrostatic system for a small wheel loader that uses one pump and one motor.
Image Provided As Courtesy of John Deere.

This is a simple hydrostatic system that features an electronically controlled pump and a two-speed motor. There is a charge pump that will provide a steady supply of makeup fluid.

▶ Types and Construction Features of Hydrostatic Drives

S31001

There are many variations of hydrostatic drive systems, but many of them have components in common. This section will discuss the main components and subsystems that are found in many hydrostatic drive systems.

Pump Drives

If a hydrostatic machine has more than one pump, it may have a pump drive. This is a set of gears in a separate housing that divides the engine input into two or more splined outputs. Pump drives will have their own fluid to lubricate the gears and bearings. See **FIGURE 31-17** for a pump drive. Larger pump drives will have a dampening device between the flywheel and the pump drive input gear.

Some smaller hydrostatic pump assemblies will be belt driven. The pumps could also be piggybacked (one pump drives the other) on each other and driven from the flywheel. The pumps' shaft could also provide drive to other machine pumps or to the system **charge pump**. See **FIGURE 31-18** for two hydrostatic pumps that are piggybacked.

Hydrostatic System Filtration

As is the case with hydraulic systems, hydrostatic drive systems use the mantra "clean, clean, clean." Hydrostatic systems must have the fluid flowing through their circuits, cleaned to a minimum specific level of cleanliness. This is usually set to an **ISO 4406** standard of 22/18/13 or lower and is dependent on the types of components used (see Chapter 23).

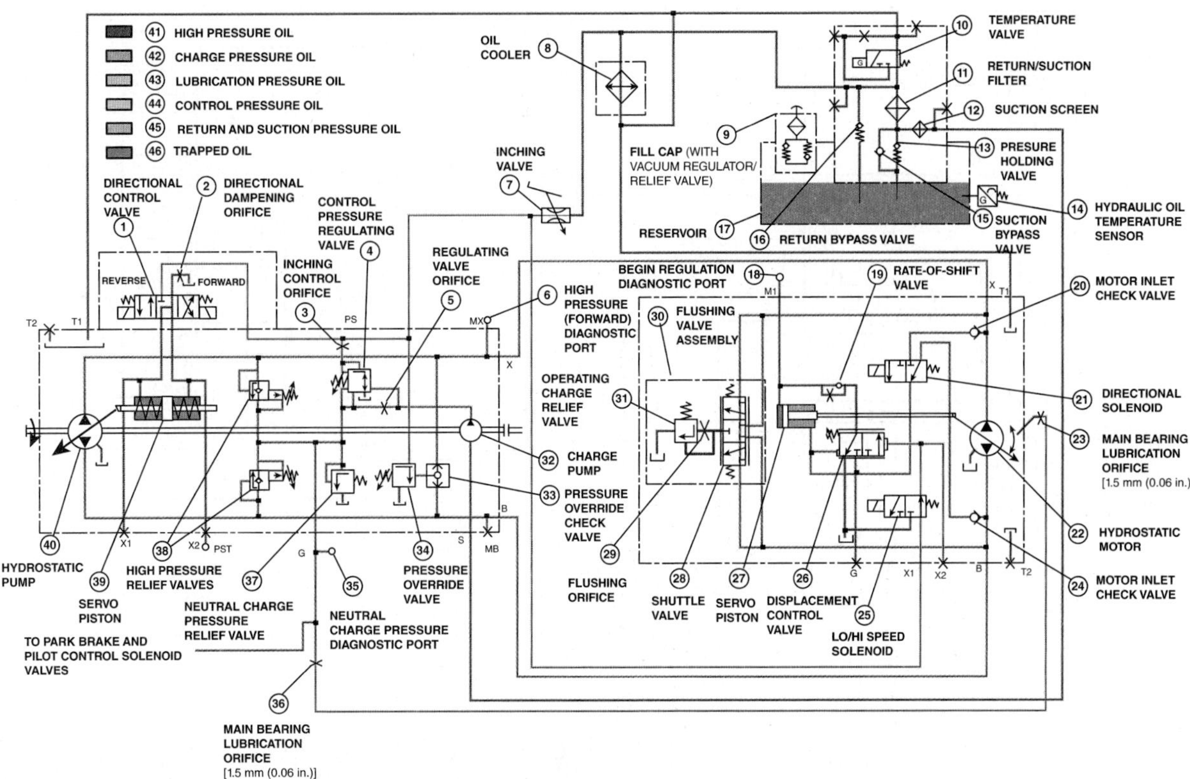

FIGURE 31-16 Schematic for a single-path hydrostatic system for a small wheel.

Image Provided As Courtesy of John Deere.

FIGURE 31-17 Pump drive.

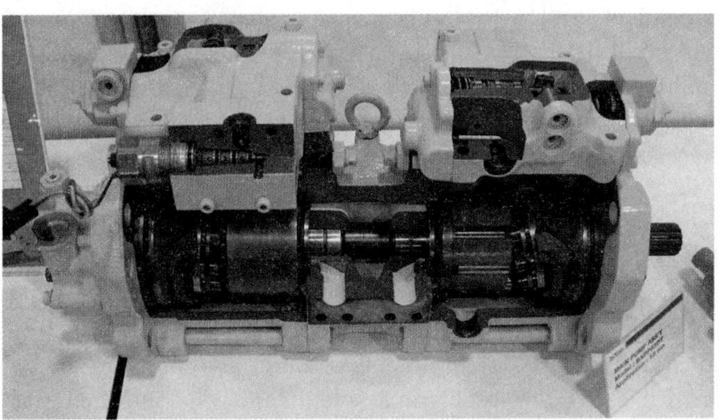

FIGURE 31-18 Hydrostatic pump arrangement.

Higher-pressure and higher-flow systems will require components with smaller internal clearances, which will require cleaner fluid.

There will be a main filter for all systems, and it is almost always located directly downstream from the charge pump. Some systems will also use a charge pump inlet filter, sometimes called a suction filter, and have their case drain flow filtered. Pump inlet filters will be the coarse mesh–type that won't cause a restriction but will stop large contamination from entering the pump.

All filters should be equipped with filter bypass valves to ensure fluid flows even if the filter becomes plugged due to contamination or fluid viscosity is too high. See **FIGURE 31-19** for a fluid filter arrangement of a hydrostatic system.

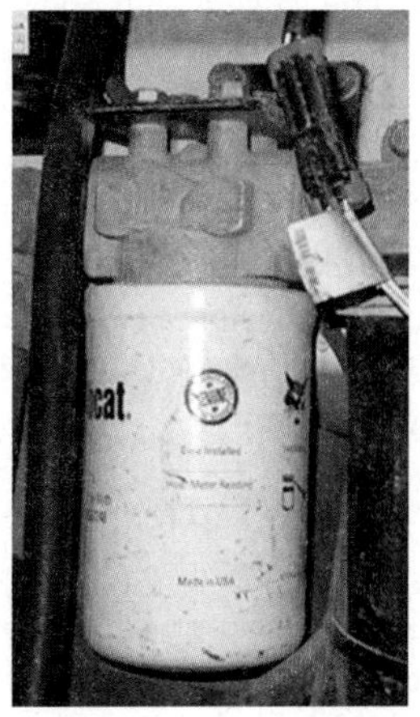

FIGURE 31-19 An oil filter.

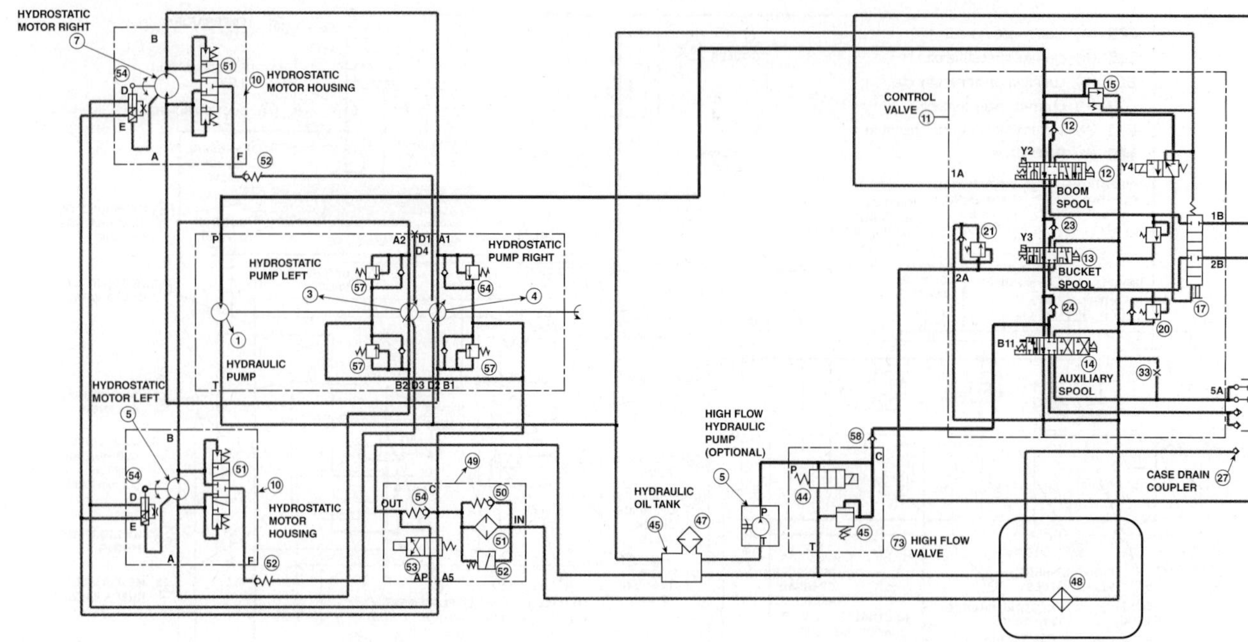

FIGURE 31-20 Schematic with fluid cooler.

Hydrostatic System Cooling

Because hydrostatic systems operate with very high pressures, there will be a great amount of heat created that needs to be managed. The fluid will need to be kept well below 180°F (82°C) to ensure that the fluid doesn't start to break down. Fluid will be directed to a fluid cooler that has air pushed past it by a fan. The cooler will have a series of tubes that divide the fluid flow from one side to the other, and the tubes will have small external fins on them that dissipate the heat from the fluid to the surrounding air. See **FIGURE 31-20** for a schematic with fluid cooler.

The fan could be engine driven by belts, but it will likely be driven by a hydraulic motor that is part of the charge fluid circuit. For simple systems, this will be a fixed displacement motor, but for many systems, there will be a variable displacement motor, and the circuit could provide a means to reverse the rotation of the motor. This is done to clean out any accumulated debris on the cooler fins.

Cooling circuits may have a **bypass valve** to allow cold fluid to bypass the cooler. The valve would open when the pressure climbs at the cooler inlet to prevent cooler damage. The valve is likely set to open at around 30 psi.

Some systems will have a cooler bypass valve that is electronically managed to make the return fluid bypass the cooler before it reaches the tank. This will help to bring the fluid up to operating temperature faster and prevent high pressures during cold fluid operation. See **FIGURE 31-21** to see a machine's hydraulic fluid cooler and fan.

FIGURE 31-21 A machine's hydraulic fluid cooler and fan.

Hydrostatic Fluid Tank

Hydrostatic system reservoirs are sized to provide the proper volume of fluid to keep the pumps and motors supplied with clean and cool fluid. Most small- to medium-sized machines will share the same fluid for both the hydraulic and the hydrostatic systems, while larger machines will have a dedicated hydrostatic fluid tank. The tank will have a level check device (sight glass, dipstick) for the operator to monitor the fluid level. The dipstick or sight glass level marks may be temperature dependent to allow for fluid expansion when it warms up. Some tanks will have a sensor to warn the operator of low level and could also have a temperature sensor in them. The tank should have a breather to prevent a vacuum being created that could starve the charge pump inlet.

Case Drain Circuit

Hydrostatic system pumps and motors will usually have a case drain circuit that allows internal leakage to return to tank. Cooling and cleaning of this fluid flow is important since it is the main way to clean and cool system fluid. Case drain fluid pressure should never exceed 60–70 psi for most systems and will quite often have a much lower maximum pressure. Otherwise, shaft seals and housing gaskets on the pump or motor could be damaged. Motor flushing valves may be used to increase the flow of case drain fluid for more effective cleaning and cooling. Measuring case drain flow is a common diagnostic test that indicates the condition of pump and motor internal components.

Hydrostatic Fluid

It is sometimes said the most important component in a hydrostatic or hydraulic system is the fluid. When engineers design a system, they will recommend a specific type and viscosity of fluid. The fluid will need to have oxidation, rust, and foam **inhibitors** in it to protect the hydrostatic system components and ensure their longevity. Only the specified fluid as stated in the machine's maintenance guide should be used. Always check with the equipment's dealer before deviating from recommended fluid types or viscosity. Never mix different types of fluids. Fire-resistant and biodegradable fluids may be allowed for some systems, but always check with the manufacturer to be sure that it's acceptable. Hydrostatic fluid will virtually be the same as that used in hydraulic systems, and for many machines, it will be the same fluid. A typical viscosity for hydrostatic fluid at an ambient operating temperature of 20°C to −40°C is SAE 10W. In some cases, approved engine oil can be used.

Operator Controls

Operator controls for hydrostatic machines vary greatly, from mechanical foot pedal controls to electronic joysticks. Only the simplest and smallest machines will still use mechanical controls today. For example, some skid steer loaders will use hand levers that convert forward and backward movement through linkages or cables into swash plate angle changes. If the machine's hydrostatic system is used for steering, then the operator controls will need to control left and right machine movement as well as forward and reverse. See **FIGURE 31-22** to see a set of manual controls for a skid steer loader.

Pilot controls will use low-pressure fluid that is typically around 300–400 psi maximum to feed fluid to pilot the joystick control valves. As the operator moves the joystick, this fluid pressure is metered at various lower pressures according to how far the joystick is moved and sent to the pump control piston. The joysticks have two or four poppet valves, depending on whether there are one or two pumps. Electronic joystick controls are simply **position sensors** and will be an input to an engine control module (ECM).

Hydrostatic Electronic Control Systems

There has been a trend over the last several years where more machines with hydrostatic systems are being managed by an electronic system. Hydrostatic electronic control systems will be multiplexed with one or more machine ECMs. **CANs** (controller area networks) enable sharing of information from sensors by all ECMs on the machine, and this will allow the machine to be more efficient by being able to manage the engine output most effectively. There will also be the capability to create operator warnings if the system operates outside of set parameters, and it will allow a technician to diagnose problems and make adjustments.

To manage the hydrostatic drive system, there will need to be a number of input sensors and switches to the ECM that may include joystick position, an FNR (forward-neutral-reverse) switch, a swash plate position sensor, a fluid temperature sensor, an engine speed sensor, a motor speed sensor, a fluid-level sensor, a filter bypass switch, a park brake switch, a charge pressure sensor, a throttle position sensor, and a seat switch. These inputs send electrical signals to the ECM that get processed and compared to stored information in the ECM memory.

The ECM then sends a signal out to a variety of actuators. The main outputs are the solenoids that will control the pump swash plate angle and the motor displacement. Some other outputs include park brake solenoid, pilot enable solenoid, fan drive solenoid, a CAN signal, and an operator indicator, warning lights, or a display.

The electronic control system will also provide a way to connect an electronic diagnostic tool through a diagnostic connector port. See **FIGURE 31-23** for a communication adapter connected to a hydrostatic machine.

FIGURE 31-22 A set of manual controls for a skid steer loader.

FIGURE 31-23 A communication adapter connected to a hydrostatic machine.

Hydrostatic System Components

The next section of this chapter will look at the different components that may be found in a hydrostatic drive system.

Hydrostatic Pumps

The purpose of the main pump/s in a hydrostatic system is to create fluid flow that gets sent directly to one or more motors. The motors will convert this flow into mechanical rotation.

The pump's shaft is externally splined and turned by the machine's prime mover's flywheel through a coupler, spline, or pulley and belt. Whenever the pump is not in neutral and turning, the pump will create a lower pressure at one of its two main ports and will make the fluid on that side of the loop flow into the pump. This inlet fluid is supplied by the return fluid from the motor and the charge pump. The fluid pushed into the pump is then sent out the pump's outlet by the pumping element to the motor through the high-pressure side of the loop.

Main hydraulic pumps that are used in hydrostatic drive systems will be bidirectional variable displacement–type pumps. This means they can send fluid out either one of their two main ports even though their drive shaft is turning in one direction. They differ from the pumps described in the pumps chapter that are used for hydraulic systems because those pumps had ports that are dedicated to being inlet or outlet and, therefore, could send fluid out only one port (outlet). This unidirectional style of pump will be used for the charge pump in a hydrostatic drive system. See **FIGURE 31-24** for a variable displacement bidirectional pump.

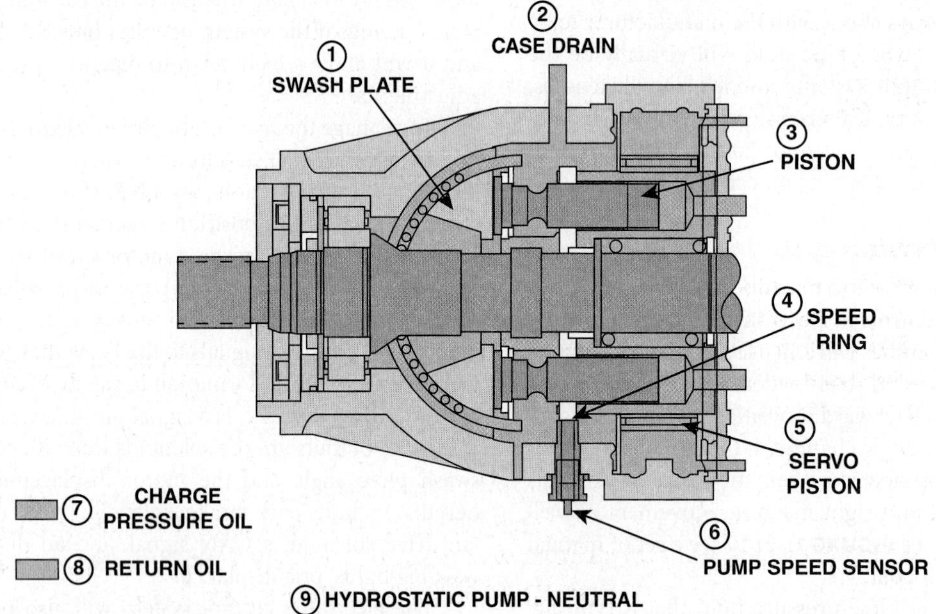

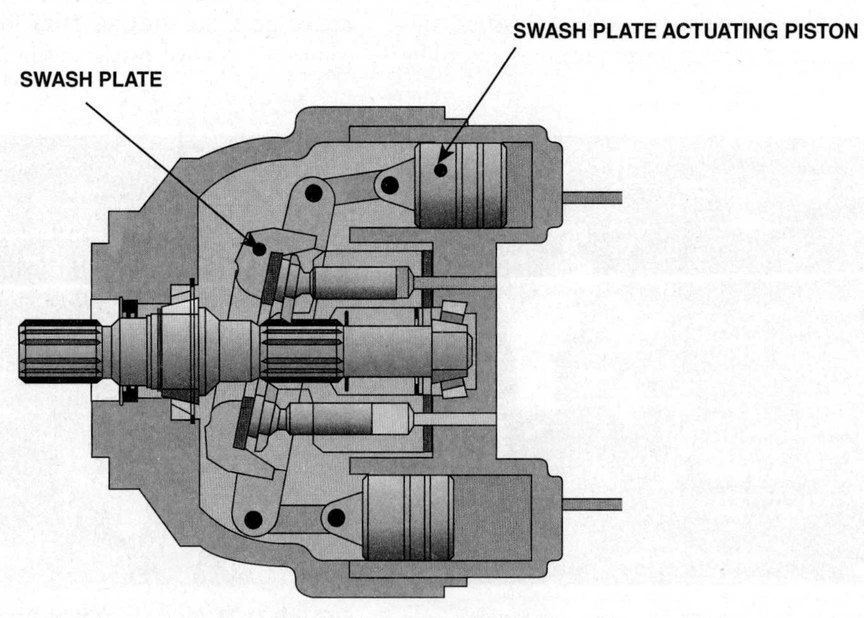

FIGURE 31-24 A variable displacement bidirectional pump.

Image Provided As Courtesy of John Deere.

The main style of pump used for hydrostatic systems is the **axial piston**.

The pump shaft is driven by the prime mover, suspended by bearings in the pump housing, and drives a cylinder block. The cylinder block is rotated by the shaft and has seven to nine bores, each of which carries a piston around inside of it. The bottom of the steel pistons is shaped into round balls, and over the ball, a brass slipper is fitted that pivots with the tilting swash plate. The brass slippers move around the face of the swash plate and are guided by a retaining plate so that they stay at the same angle as the swash plate. Sometimes swash plates can also be called cam plates. See **FIGURE 31-25** for a disassembled piston pump.

As the **swash plate** is angled, it will make the pistons move in and out of the cylinder block while the block is rotated by the shaft. A typical maximum inclination of 15 degrees means the piston travels the greatest distance when the swash plate is tilted 15 degrees away from being perpendicular to the centerline of the pump shaft. The end of the cylinder block opposite the piston slippers is lap finished to a stationary port plate that allows fluid in and out of the block. The port plate lines up with the two ports that are part of the pump's housing.

Axial piston pumps can change their displacement per revolution and flow direction by changing the swash plate angle. Pump rotation speed will also affect the flow output of the pump. Generally, hydrostatic pumps will be run at a fixed rpm that is usually the machine engine's high-idle rpm. This will allow engineers to design the engine to provide maximum performance and low emissions at this speed.

Changing the pump swash plate angle changes the piston effective stroke, which changes the pump's displacement and ultimately changes the machine's travel speed and direction. When a pump is in neutral, the swash plate is at a 90 degree angle to the pump drive shaft. This means there is no axial movement of the pistons as they rotate around the drive shaft in the cylinder block, and therefore, there is no fluid flow from the pump. As the swash plate angle is changed, the pistons will start to move up and down inside the cylinder block.

> **TECHNICIAN TIP**
>
> The easiest way to picture piston movement is to think of a child's manually powered merry-go-round that you might see in a city park. See **FIGURE 31-26** for a merry-go-round. If one person on the ride is spinning around while the ride is level, they wouldn't be moving up and down. If there were a way to tilt the ride, then that person would be moving up and down as they spin around the ride's axis.

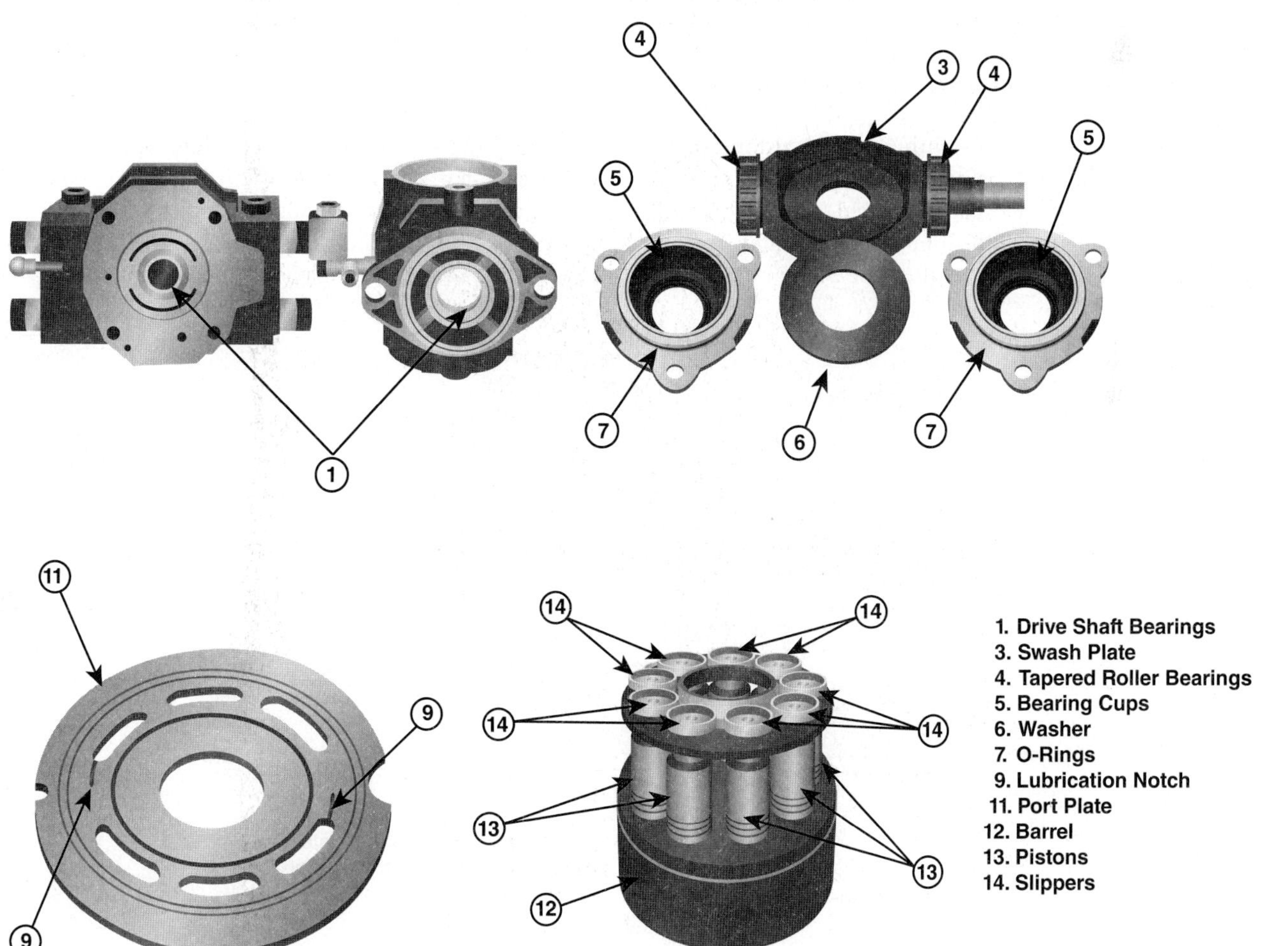

FIGURE 31-25 A disassembled piston pump.

Image Provided As Courtesy of John Deere.

FIGURE 31-26 A merry-go-round.

To relate this to the axial pump operation, focus on one piston through one revolution with the swash plate at its maximum angle. The pump's two ports are half-moon shaped and are separated. As the piston moves from one port to another, it will be moving from its lowest to highest position in the cylinder block. This will be when the piston is pushing fluid out of the pump through almost half of one revolution. As the piston continues through its second half of the revolution, it will move from the highest to the lowest position, and this will be when it creates a low pressure on top of it to bring fluid in through the other half of the port plate. See **FIGURE 31-27** for the different stages of piston travel during shaft rotation.

Once you are comfortable with a single piston's operation, imagine all the pistons going through the same constant motions as the pump shaft is turned. This action will create a constant flow of fluid from the pump inlet and out the outlet. As mentioned, this is when the pump swash plate is at a maximum angle. As the angle decreases, the piston travel decreases and, therefore, the pump's displacement per revolution decreases. When the swash plate then moves past neutral, it will start to send fluid out the opposite port as the inlet and outlet ports trade places. This will in effect reverse the flow of the pump. Then as the swash plate continues to increase its angle, the flow volume will increase in the opposite direction.

Swash plates can be supported by trunnions that rotate in bearings in the pump housing. The bearings can be needle-type or tapered roller–type. Swash plates can also be supported by a semicircle saddle arrangement that allows the swash plate to pivot as it is pushed around the saddle. This is also sometimes called a cradle-bearing arrangement, and it will have a U-shaped roller bearing for the curved swash plate to ride on. See **FIGURE 31-28** for a pump with a saddle-type swash plate pivot. The saddle-type swash plate will provide a more robust support and is controlled by a servo piston.

Lower flow axial piston pumps can be controlled manually with linkage that connects the joysticks to the swash plates. This is a less expensive and simpler way to control hydrostatic pumps. As pumps get bigger and produce higher flows, it becomes harder to manually control the swash plate. This means there needs to be hydraulic assistance to change the swash plate angle. This change can be done with one or more servo pistons that are connected to the swash plate, which will move the swash plate when fluid pressure is applied to the servos. See **FIGURE 31-29** for an axial piston pump that has a servo piston to move its swash plate.

The pump's servo pistons get fluid sent to them from a displacement control valve. This valve can be manually shifted or moved with solenoid-controlled fluid pressure. As it is shifted, it will send fluid to one of the servo pistons to change the swash plate angle, or if there is one servo piston, it

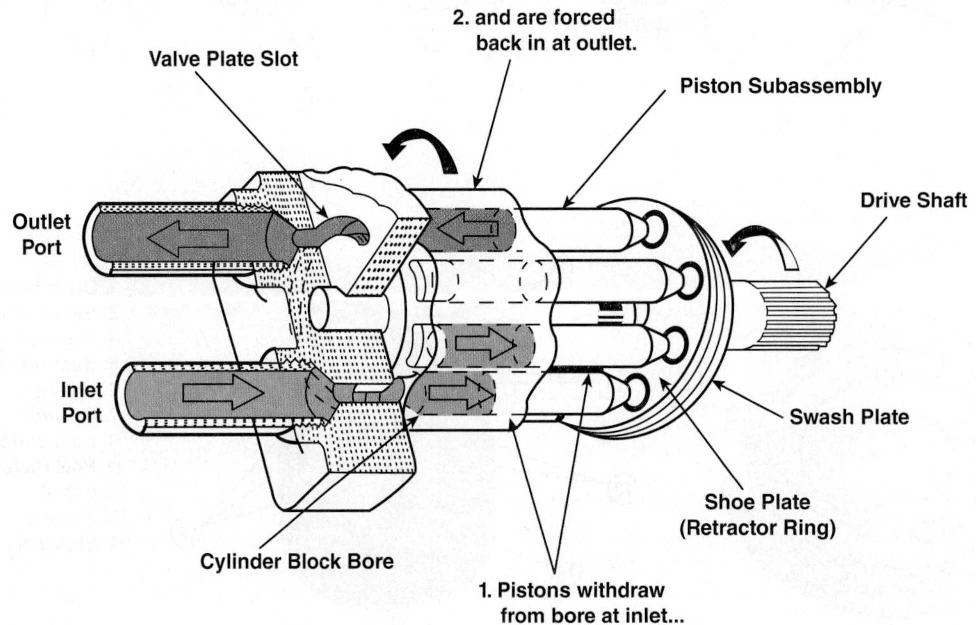

FIGURE 31-27 Different stages of piston travel during shaft rotation.

FIGURE 31-28 A pump with a saddle-type swash plate.

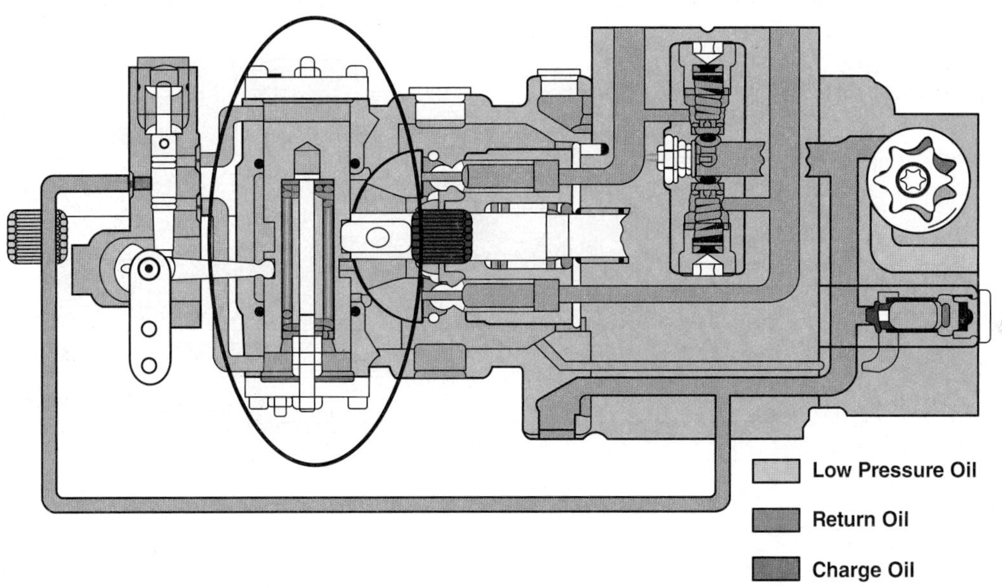

FIGURE 31-29 An axial piston pump that has a servo piston to move its swash plate.

Image Provided As Courtesy of John Deere.

will send fluid to one end of the piston. Most pumps will have this valve mounted on the pump housing.

Because hydrostatic system pressures can reach over 6,000 psi, the pump's pistons and barrels need to have very close tolerances to seal this pressure. They will be lap finished to provide between 5 and 15 microns of clearance. Some pistons will have seals that ride in grooves on their outer circumference to seal the pressure on top of the piston. Even though new pumps have small clearances, there will still be a certain amount of leakage that needs to be drained back to the tank. The pump housing will have a port to allow this fluid to return to the tank. This is called the case drain port.

These pumps will need a way to limit the maximum angle that the swash plate can tilt. For the mechanically actuated swash plate pump, this can be an external linkage adjustment. For servo-controlled swash plate pumps, the servo piston movement is limited by mechanical stops. This will limit the movement of the swash plate. Both types of swash plate limiters are adjustable, which allows the maximum pump flow (motor speed) to be set. Some pumps will also have adjustable internal mechanical stops.

There will also be a way to adjust the neutral point for the swash plate angle. Again, depending on the type of swash plate control, this will be either a mechanical linkage adjustment or a servo piston adjustment. More details will be discussed on this later.

Servo Control Valves

To manage pump flow from a hydrostatic pump that is not mechanically controlled, there needs to be a control valve arrangement that can send fluid to the pumps' servo pistons, which in turn will move the pump swash plate. The servo piston will be mechanically connected to the swash plate either through a linkage or directly with a pin that slides in a slot in the servo piston. There are many variations of pump servo control valves, and only a few will be discussed here. Pumps can use either one or two servo pistons to move the swash plate.

Servo control valves can be manually actuated spool valves or spool valves that are moved with pilot fluid that is controlled with electrically actuated solenoids. Manually controlled valves will likely be spring centered or cable controlled, and as the operator moves an FNR control, this will move the spool from neutral. The spool valve will allow charge pressure fluid to go to one end of the pump's servo piston. The spool will also allow the fluid at the other end of the servo to be returned to drain. This happens with a single servo piston pump control.

The spool will also be moved by a feedback link that is connected to the swash plate. The feedback link will re-center the spool after the swash plate has moved, and if the operator control is left in one position, the spool will slightly meter fluid to the servo to keep the swash plate at a desired angle. See **FIGURE 31-30** for a manually controlled servo control valve.

If the pump is electronically controlled, there will be two solenoids (forward and reverse) that get energized individually and by an electronic system that outputs a pulse-width modulation (PWM) signal or by potentiometers that send a variable voltage signal. The solenoid armature will move proportionately to the value of the signal sent to it. The armature movement will shift a valve that directs fluid to one end of the pump servo piston, which will cause swash plate movement.

Another variation of electrical/electronic pump servo controls is one that uses a linear torque motor that uses two solenoids to move a flapper valve. When the flapper valve moves, it will send charge fluid to either end of a displacement control valve spool. This will shift the spool and send charge fluid to either end of the swash plate servo piston to move the swash plate. There is a feedback linkage that connects the swash plate and spool valve. This will center the spool to stop and hold the swash plate in place if the operator's demand requires this. Deere calls this the pressure control pilot (PCP) valve. See **FIGURE 31-31** for a pump control valve that uses a flapper valve as the displacement control valve.

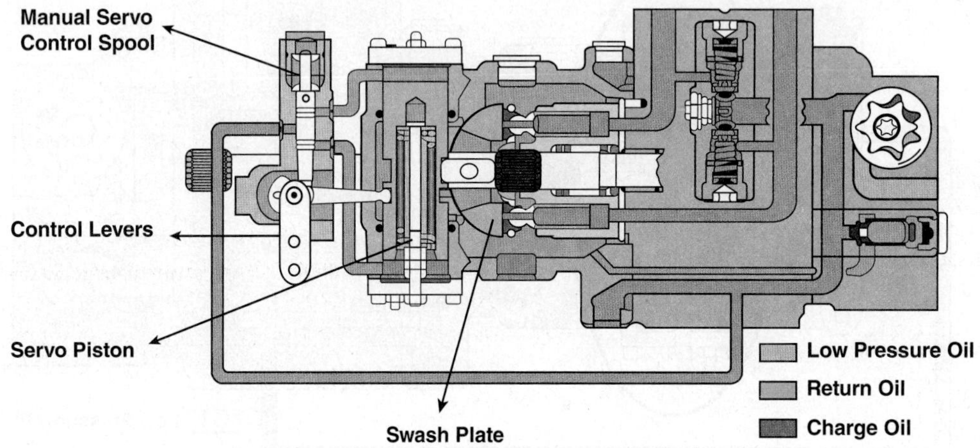

FIGURE 31-30 A manually controlled servo control valve.

Image Provided As Courtesy of John Deere.

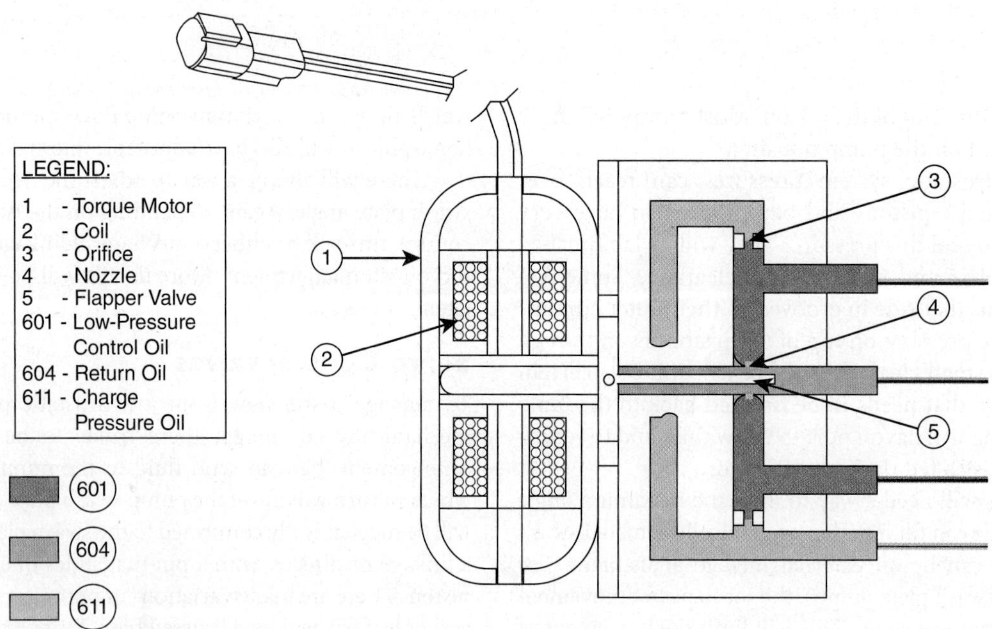

FIGURE 31-31 A pump control valve that uses a flapper valve as the displacement control.

Image Provided As Courtesy of John Deere.

Motors

Hydrostatic system motors receive fluid flow from the pump and convert this flow into mechanical torque that is transferred out the motor's shaft and sends torque toward the machine's final drive mechanism. Hydrostatic system motors can be one of several types: axial piston, bent axis piston, and cam lobe-type motors, and smaller machines can also use geroller motors. Piston' motors that are fixed displacement have their swash plate set at one angle that will usually give a low-speed/high-torque output.

Many hydrostatic systems will feature variable displacement motors that will provide multiple travel modes from high torque/low speed to high speed/low torque. To change to high speed, the motor displacement will need to decrease. Doing so increases the output shaft revolutions per unit of fluid flow to the motor. As a result, it decreases output torque and increases motor shaft speed.

All motors will incorporate a flushing valve or case drain port to allow a constant flow of cooling and cleaning fluid flow out of the loop on the low-pressure return side after the fluid leaves the motor element. There will also be a normal amount of internal leakage that also needs to be returned to the tank.

Most motors will incorporate a parking brake into their housing that will lock part of the rotating assembly to the housing. These are typically spring-applied hydraulically released multidisc brakes.

▶ TECHNICIAN TIP

Pump and motor displacement is measured by the volume of fluid that a pump produces per revolution or the volume of fluid that a motor needs for it to turn one revolution. This is typically measured in cubic inches per revolution (CIR) or cubic centimeters per revolution (CCR).

Motors, like pumps, are rated as to their displacement per revolution as well as their maximum pressure capability. For example, a variable displacement motor for a compact wheel loader can have a maximum displacement of 4.8 CIR (80 CCR), can have a minimum displacement of 2.0 CIR (34 CCR), and is able to withstand a working pressure of 7,000 psi.

Some machines that have a dual-path system will use a flow divider to equalize flow to the left and right motors. This will give the same effect as a differential lock that is used in a mechanical drivetrain. The flow divider ensures that the left and right motors turn at the same speed.

Axial Piston Motor

Some hydrostatic systems will use axial piston motors to convert fluid flow to mechanical rotation. This type of motor is very like the axial piston pumps that are used to create the flow for the system in that they use a swash plate, pistons, and cylinder block to transfer piston movement created by fluid flow to shaft rotation for the motor output. The opposite is true for an axial piston pump that uses piston movement to create fluid flow.

Judging by physical appearance, it would be hard to tell the difference between an axial piston pump and motor. This is true for most pumps and motors that operate on the same principle.

Fluid is sent into one of the two main ports of the motor housing and goes through a stationary port plate. The port plate has a lap-finished surface that mates with the cylinder block. As the fluid flows into the cylinder block, it will push on half of the pistons down the swash plate while the other half of the pistons are moving up the swash plate and pushing fluid out the other main port. As the pistons are pushed down the swash plate, they carry the cylinder block with it. The block then drives the output shaft of the motor. The fluid that leaves the motor returns to the pump inlet.

This style of motor can be fixed or variable displacement. To vary the displacement of an axial piston motor, its swash plate angle will need to be changed. If the motor is a two-speed type, it will likely default to the low-speed/high-torque mode, which means its swash plate angle will be at maximum, and therefore, it will be at maximum displacement. A fluid signal is sent to a servo piston in the motor that will move the swash plate to a smaller angle. An example of this is a motor used for a track loader that has a displacement of 3.5 cubic inches for low speed (maximum displacement) and can change to a displacement of 2.0 cubic inches for high speed (minimum displacement).

To change displacement, this type of motor will have two control pistons to move the swash plate to either minimum or maximum displacement. The fluid pressure to do this can come from a solenoid valve on the motor or one that is mounted remotely. See **FIGURE 31-32** for a cross-sectional illustration of a variable displacement axial piston motor.

Bent Axis Motor

Bent axis motors have their cylinder block centerlines at an angle to the output shaft centerline. The motors' shaft assembly is supported by two tapered roller bearings in the housing and is driven by the cylinder block and pistons.

Fluid is sent into the motor through the inlet port of the housing and goes through the port, past a bearing plate, and into the valve segment. The valve segment has two slots to allow fluid to transfer between the bearing plate and pump housing end cap. The fluid acts on the end of the pistons and pushes them out of the barrel, which in turn creates the rotation of the shaft.

The bearing plate provides a bearing surface between the rotating cylinder block and the nonrotating valve segment. The valve segment will be able to move a few degrees if the motor is a variable displacement type; otherwise, it is fixed. The valve segment has a stub shaft protruding from it that fits into a bearing in the end of the cylinder block. This will support the cylinder block in the housing. See **FIGURE 31-33** for a cross-sectional illustration of a bent axis motor.

A variable displacement bent axis motor has the opposite side of the valve segment, featuring an outward curve shape that is matched to a bearing surface on the bottom of the motor end housing. When fluid is fed into the cylinder block, where the pistons are at the top of their stroke, the fluid will force the pistons down into the barrel for half of the motor's rotation.

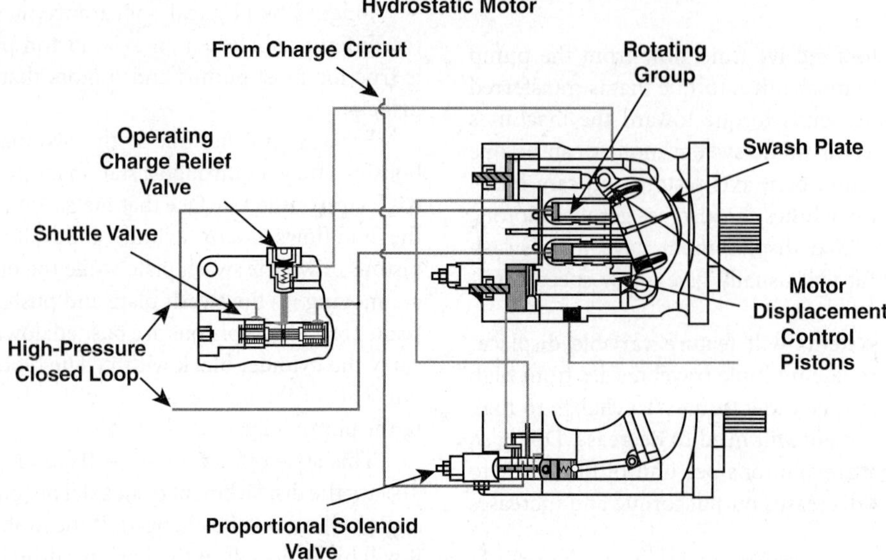

FIGURE 31-32 A cross-sectional illustration of a variable displacement axial piston motor.
Image Provided As Courtesy of John Deere.

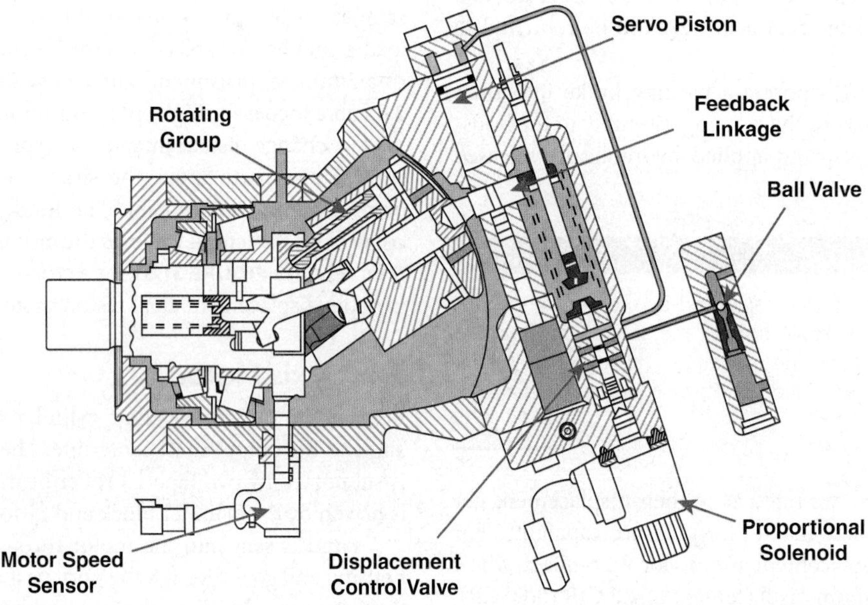

FIGURE 31-33 A cross-sectional illustration of a bent axis motor.
Image Provided As Courtesy of John Deere.

The pistons have a head with a groove that locates a seal to keep the fluid from leaking between the cylinder block and piston. When the pistons are forced down by fluid pressure, this will make the cylinder block rotate.

The cylinder block is connected to the motor's shaft with a **synchronizing shaft** with two sets of three evenly spaced rollers protruding out from it. The rollers will fit into grooves in the shaft assembly and the cylinder block. This is similar to a type of constant velocity joint that is used for a front-wheel drive car. There is a spring on the inside of the shaft assembly that will keep the cylinder block seated against the bearing plate and valve segment.

The bottoms of the pistons have a ball-shaped end and are supported in the shaft assembly in sockets. See **FIGURE 31-34** for an exploded illustration of a bent axis piston motor. A variable bent axis motor will have minimum and maximum displacement stops to physically stop the movement of the barrel between two points. There will be a servo piston with a recess in it where the pin from the back of the valve segment is engaged. When the motor's displacement control (which is controlled by electric solenoid) sends fluid to one end of the servo, it will move the cylinder block with it to move toward a lower displacement. This will be the high-speed/low-torque mode for the motor. A spring will return the piston when the displacement control drains the fluid.

Cam Lobe Motor

A **cam lobe motor**, also called a radial piston motor, uses a series of eight pistons that are oriented in a radial arrangement

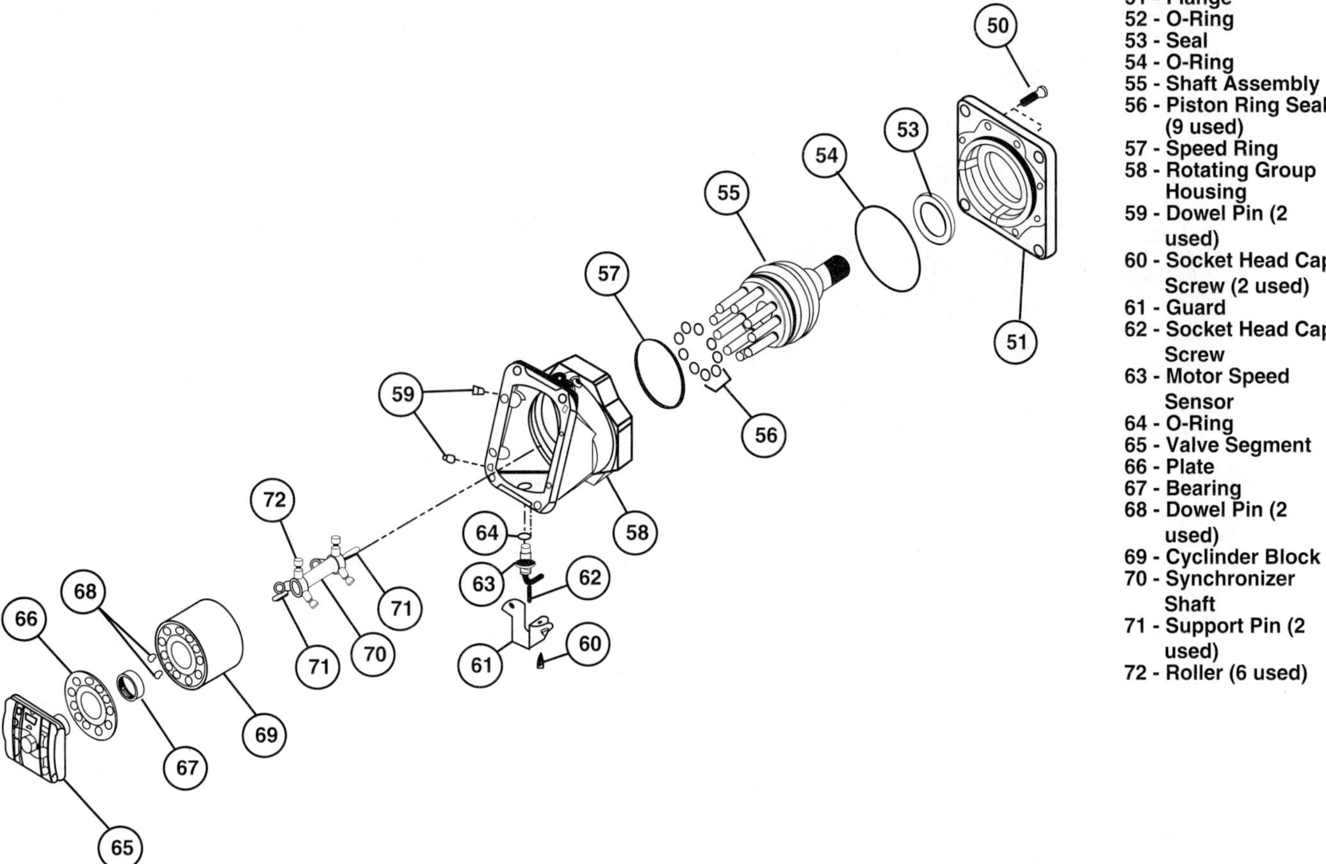

FIGURE 31-34 An exploded illustration of a bent axis piston motor.

Image Provided As Courtesy of John Deere.

in a carrier and have rollers attached to their bottom end. The carrier turns the output shaft for the motor.

The pistons will move in and out of the carrier as their rollers ride around the inside an internal cam. The internal cam has six equally spaced lobes on the inside diameter of the cam ring. Fluid pressure is fed into the motor housing through one of two ports. The other port will direct fluid out of the motor. The ports feed fluid to a manifold that has passageways machined into it. These manifold passageways connect to ports on the outer circumference of it. There are six ports connected to one of the main motor ports and six ports connected to the other main port. When fluid is supplied by the system pump to one of the motor's main ports, the manifold will be able to send fluid to four of the pistons at any time. The other four pistons will be aligned with the return port. The remaining four ports are blocked off temporarily. To start the motor turning, the fluid pressure pushes four pistons and rollers down cam lobes, and because the piston is in bores in the carrier, the carrier will rotate. The other four pistons are also carried around and will be riding up cam lobes. This will push fluid out of the carrier through the manifold and out of the motor into the low-pressure side of the loop. Once the motor starts turning, all pistons are constantly moving in and out of the carrier and riding up and down the cam profiles.

As you can imagine, port timing is critical to the operation of this style of motor because there needs to be a seamless transition between the fluid flow in and out of the motor to the pistons that either are being pushed down cam lobes or are returning back into the carrier. See **FIGURE 31-35** for a cross-sectional illustration of a cam lobe motor.

Cam lobe motors can also be dual displacement motors. If the same amount of fluid flows to the motor but is supplying only half the pistons, then the motor will turn at twice the rpm. This is done by supplying pressure fluid to only half of the pistons. The other half receives only charge pressure fluid. This is done by moving a displacement control valve, which will switch half of the discharge ports from high-pressure pump flow to charge fluid pressure.

Orbital Motor

Lighter-duty hydrostatic systems will sometimes use an orbital motor. There are several variations of these motors that can also be called gerotor and geroller motors, but they fall into three main groups: disc valve, spool valve, and valve in star. These different groups of orbital motors relate to how the fluid is distributed within the motor as it moves to and from the main ports.

They all work on the same principle of having an inner and outer rotor with coarse "teeth" or lobes. The inner rotor will have one fewer tooth than the outer rotor, and their centers will

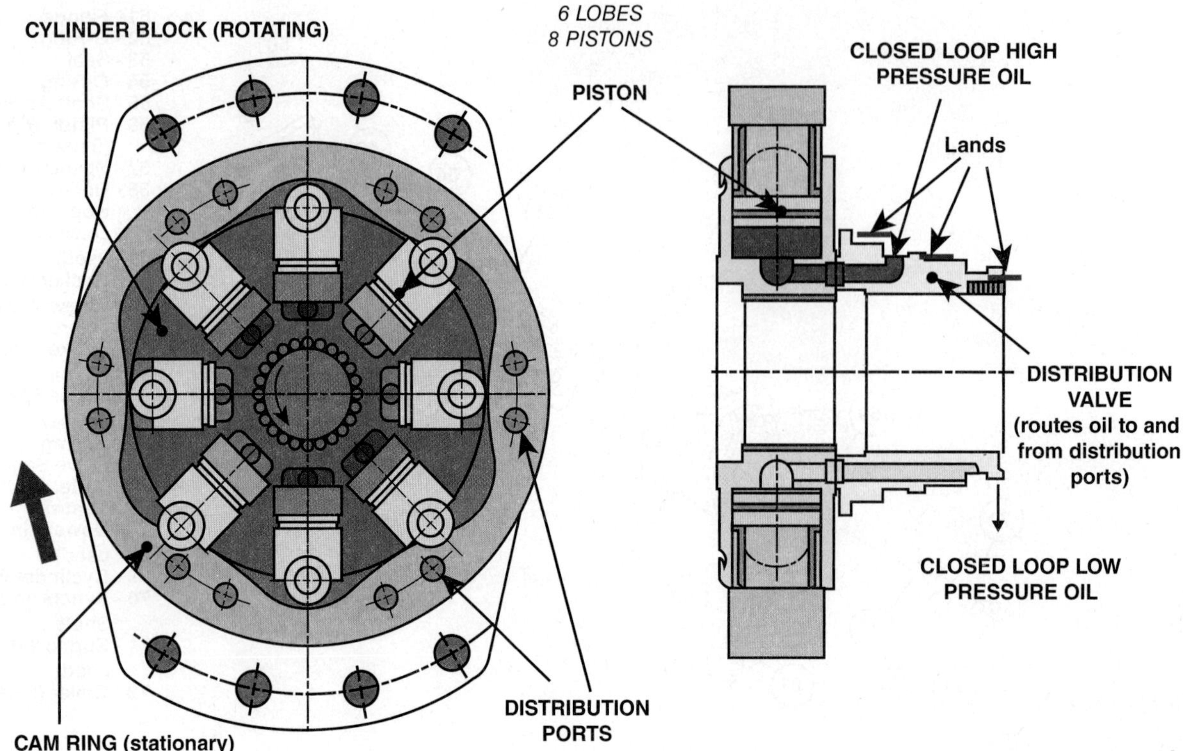

FIGURE 31-35 A cross-sectional illustration of a cam lobe motor.
Image Provided As Courtesy of John Deere.

be offset. The outer rotor's center is on the same axis as the output shaft, and the inner rotor's axis will be offset from the outer rotor's axis.

As fluid is sent into the motor, it will enter a small chamber that is created between inner and outer rotor teeth. The applied pressure will make the rotors turn as the chamber expands. The expanding chamber will reach a maximum volume. Then as rotation continues, chamber volume decreases, forcing fluid out of the chamber and out the return port. The process occurs constantly for each chamber, providing a smooth pumping action. If fluid is sent to the opposite port, the motor will turn in the opposite direction.

The inner rotor has internal splines that will drive an externally splined drive shaft. The splines will be machined to allow the offset between the inner rotor and the output shaft as rotation occurs. This shaft is sometimes called a Cardan shaft.

A geroller motor will have rollers on the ends of the outer rotor teeth to reduce friction and improve longevity. The inner rotor has one less lobe than the rollers so that one lobe will always be in full engagement with the rollers at any one time. This allows the rotor lobes to slide over the rollers, creating a seal to prevent pressure fluid from returning to the inlet side of the motor.

This change causes the orbiting gerotor to make as many power strokes as it has teeth for every revolution of the output shaft. The six-tooth gear shown makes six power strokes while the output shaft turns once. See **FIGURE 31-36** for a geroller-type motor.

These motors can also be equipped with a flushing port to allow fluid to circulate within the closed-loop circuit to aid in cooling and cleaning. Gerotor motors produce close to full torque from about 25 rpm and normally do not go higher than 250–300 rpm. Maximum output torque is directly related to the width of the gerotor element. Pressure ratings as high as 4,000 psi are common from most manufacturers. Some gerotor motors can have a selector valve that changes the internal rotary valve output to feed only half the chambers, causing the motor to run at twice the speed and half the torque.

Charge Pump

Charge pumps used in hydrostatic systems will be fixed displacement low flow units. Smaller systems will use gerotor-type pumps, while most others use gear-type pumps. These pumps can also supply fluid for other systems, such as main implement, brake release, or pilot fluid.

They are usually mounted on the back of one of the main hydrostatic pumps. The main pump shaft will continue through the pump housing and have either an internal or an external spline on it. The charge pump is driven either directly or by a coupling from the main pump shaft. The supply fluid to the charge pump could come from an internal passage in the main pump, or it could be an external line.

Charge pump flow is typically 20% of the volume of the main pump's flow.

Pump and Motor Ratings

An important rating for pumps and motors that are used in hydraulic and hydrostatic systems is displacement. This can be measured in cubic inches per revolution (CIR) or cubic

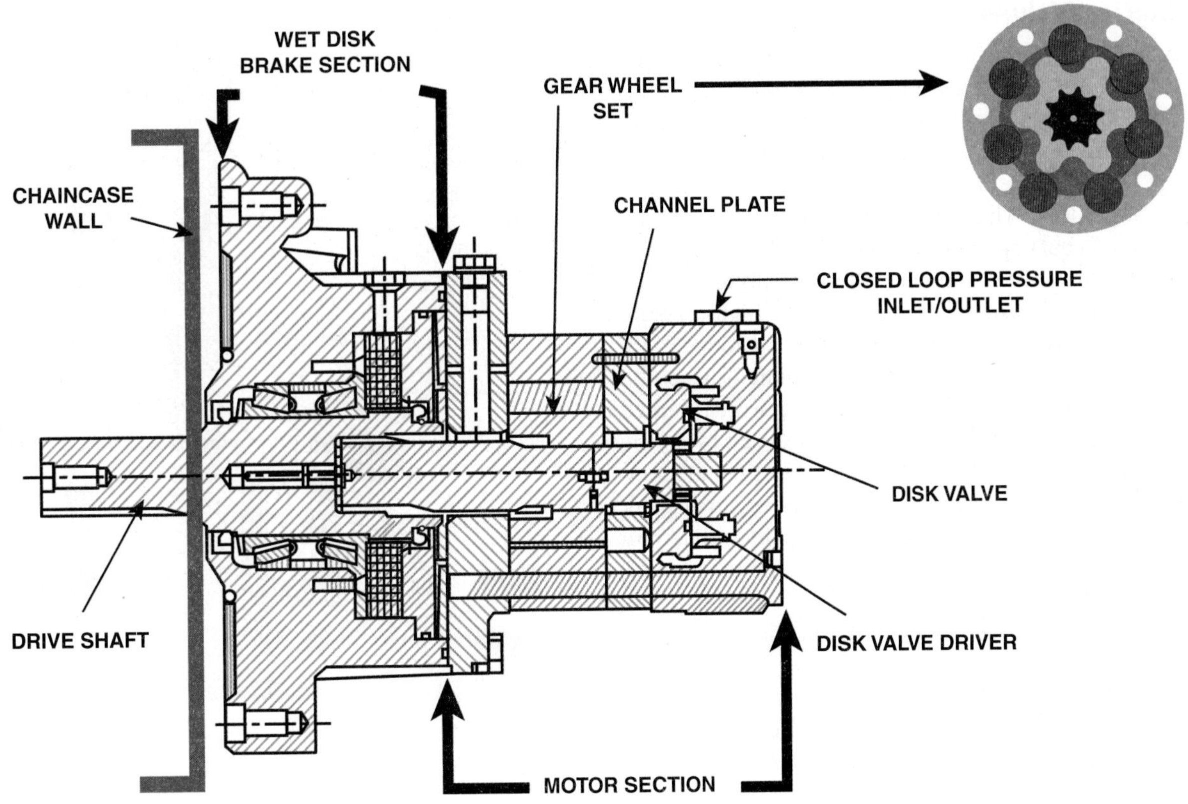

FIGURE 31-36 A geroller-type motor.

Image Provided As Courtesy of John Deere.

centimeters per revolution (CCR). For a pump, its displacement rating is the volume of fluid it can move during one revolution of its shaft. For a variable displacement pump, this will range from zero and increase to its maximum rating. All pumps for hydrostatic systems are axial piston–style, and their displacement is based on swash plate angle.

Motor displacement refers to the amount of fluid required to rotate its output shaft one revolution. Motors can be fixed or variable displacement (they will never go to zero displacement).

The torque of the motor's output shaft is determined by knowing its displacement per revolution and the pressure of the fluid going into the motor. The fluid pressure will be created by the resistance on the shaft, and the resistance is created by the load on the wheels or tracks. Remember that pressure is created by the resistance to flow. The following is the formula for motor torque output:

$$\text{Torque (inch pounds)} = \text{psi} \times \text{displacement (CIR)}/2\pi$$

An example for this would be a motor that is used to drive one set of wheels for a skid steer. If it has a displacement of 25 CIR and the fluid pressure is 5,000 psi, then by using this formula to calculate the torque output of this motor, you would find it produces just fewer than 20,000 in-lb or approximately 1,600 ft-lb of torque. The maximum pressure will be limited by pressure relief valves in each half of the closed loop.

When calculating hydrostatic system values, there needs to be a consideration of the amount of internal leakage within the pumps and motors of the system to get an actual value that can be expected. Like hydraulic systems, this leakage is the inefficiency of the system and is usually 15–20%. This inefficiency will decrease the speed of the motors and when factored into calculations will give a more realistic value of the actual motor speed.

This leakage from the pumps and motors needs to be sent to the tank, and this is done through ports in the housing. This fluid flow is commonly called case drain fluid and can sometimes be measured during a troubleshooting procedure that checks for pump and motor wear. As pumps and motors wear, their case drain flow and pressure increase.

Pumps are usually rated for the maximum rpm that their shafts should rotate at. Motor speed is determined by the rate of fluid flow applied to it. The rpm of a motor can also be calculated by knowing its displacement and how much fluid is flowing to it. The following is the formula for motor rpm:

$$\text{rpm} = \text{flow} \times 231/\text{displacement}$$
(if displacement is given in CIR).

Hydrostatic System Valves

There are several important valves that are needed to control the fluid flow and pressure in a hydrostatic drive system. Even simple hydrostatic systems need crossover relief valves to limit high pressure in the high-pressure side of the loop and make up valves to allow charge pressure fluid into the low-pressure side of the loop.

Combination Valves

Almost all hydrostatic systems use combination or multifunction valves on each side of the closed loop. These are a combination of relief and makeup (check) valves and are sometimes called **crossover relief valves**. Every hydrostatic system will need a high-pressure relief and a makeup valve as part of each side of the closed loop. These valves are usually threaded into the pump housing but appear on a schematic as being separate.

If a pump is upstroked to provide fluid flow to one port of a motor, then one side of the loop becomes the high-pressure side. This side needs to have its pressure limited to a certain level to prevent component and conductor failure. This could be from 4,000 to 7,500 psi or higher. The high pressure is sensed at the normally closed poppet, which is held closed by spring pressure. If the pressure exceeds the spring value, then the poppet opens and allows the fluid to go to the low-pressure side of the loop. This will happen if the load on the machine's drivetrain is so great that it stops the motor's output shaft and the pump is still trying to produce flow.

The **makeup valve** part of the combination valve opens to allow charge pressure fluid into the low-pressure side of the loop. It is a simple check valve that opens to prevent cavitation and the fluid from overheating. The makeup fluid is to replenish fluid lost to drain from component leakage and from flow through the flushing valve.

These valves are usually nonadjustable and must be replaced if found to be defective. See **FIGURE 31-37** for the combination valves (1) used for a pump assembly.

Flushing Valves

Flushing valves are designed to supply a constant controlled flow of fresh fluid into the closed loop for cooling and cleaning purposes. Because a hydrostatic system operates with a closed loop, there is only a small amount of leakage fluid that needs to be replenished. If there were no flushing valve, then the fluid in the closed loop would eventually overheat and break down. By draining a constant flow of fluid out of the loop, the charge pump will be continuously renewing this fluid with clean, cool fluid from the tank. This constant drain flow is created by the **flushing valve**, located on the motor housing. The flushing valve is sometimes called a hot fluid purge valve and must be set at a lower pressure than the charge relief valve. See **FIGURE 31-38** for a flushing valve.

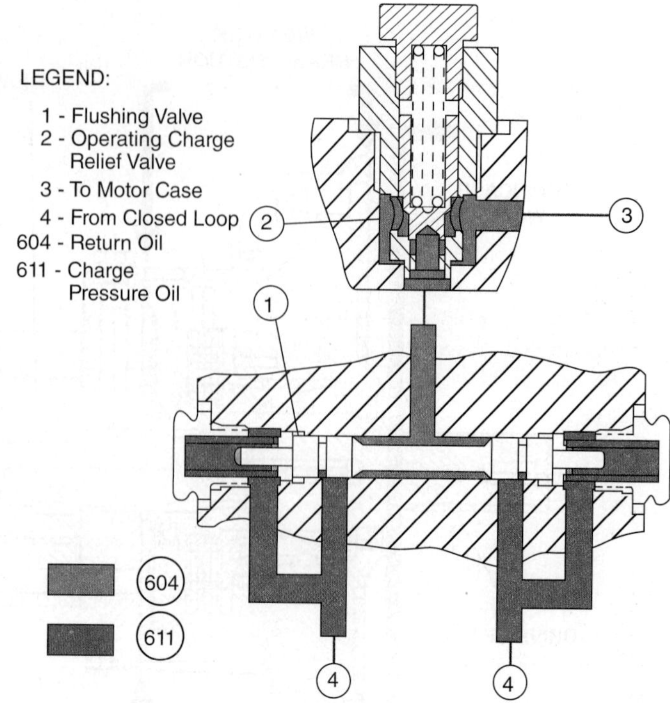

FIGURE 31-38 Flushing valve.

Image Provided As Courtesy of John Deere.

You can how see the valve will get shifted when the high-pressure side of the loop is sensed at the end of the spool and shifts it. It is important that the flushing valve pressure is set below the charge relief setting; otherwise, they won't provide a steady flow of fluid. The flushing valve is usually set around 30 psi lower than the charge relief, and this is not normally adjustable. For example, if there is a leakage drain of 3 gpm from the pump and 3 gpm from the motor and the charge pump is producing a flow of 12 gpm, then there will be a constant flow of 6 gpm through the motor housing when the flushing valve is shifted. This flow will carry away heat from the motor and pump to the fluid cooler or the tank.

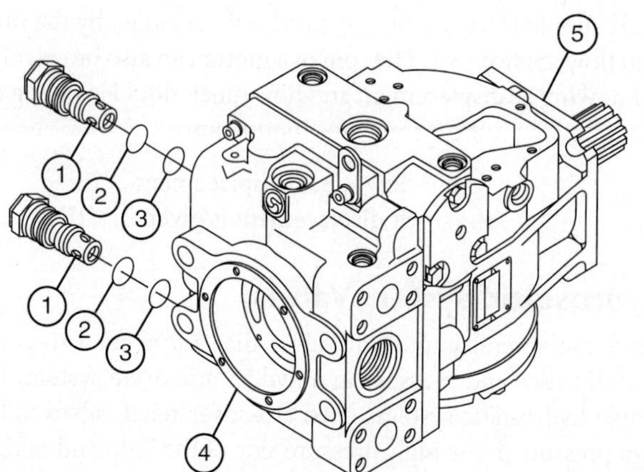

FIGURE 31-37 Combination valves used for a pump assembly.

Image Provided As Courtesy of John Deere.

Charge Relief

The charge fluid system needs to have a relief valve to limit its pressure. This will be a simple direct-acting poppet-type valve that will be part of the pump assembly if the charge pump is part of the pump assembly. The charge pressure relief setting is adjustable and is usually easily checked through a pressure tap.

Flow Divider

Some machines that use hydrostatic systems with individual left and right travel motors may use a flow divider between the pump and motors. It will ensure either all wheels or both tracks get equal fluid flow when needed. This will be necessary when the machine is traveling in muddy or slippery conditions. If one pump is supplying two motors, the majority of the flow will go to the motor with the least resistance. If the machine is turning, this flow priority will allow a speed difference between the left and right drives, much like a differential. However, if the machine starts to spin one drive, then all the fluid flow will go to that drive, and then the machine will get stuck. The flow divider will act like a differential lock to give equal flow to both drives.

Brake Release Valves

Parking brake release valves are usually solenoid-actuated on/off directional control–type valves. The brake release circuit will usually be supplied fluid from the charge pump flow. When the operator wants to release the parking brake, a rocker or toggle switch is moved to send an electrical signal to the solenoid. This will move a plunger that allows fluid to flow to the spring-applied brake piston to compress the spring and release the brakes. See **FIGURE 31-39** for a brake release valve.

▶ Inspect, Test, and Diagnose Hydrostatic Drives

S31002

At some point, a MORE technician will need to diagnose an operational problem with a hydrostatic drive. The next section will discuss common problems that could be reported, initial inspections, and some common testing and diagnostic practices used to find the cause of the problem.

Operational Problems

Operational complaints for hydrostatic machines can be grouped into a few categories:

- Machine won't drive
- Machine is slow
- Drive is weak
- No reverse or forward
- Machine won't travel straight
- Hydrostatic fluid overheating

Some other, less common problems include noisy vibrations, strange smell, too much power, and too fast. But it's not very likely that a technician would ever hear the last two complaints, since to an operator, most machines are never powerful enough or fast enough.

Inspect Hydrostatic Drives

An initial inspection would include the following:

1. Check for leaks. Look under the machine for drips and clean wet streaks on dirty machines.
2. Check oil level. Be aware of conditions needed for proper oil level (cold or warm oil, stopped or running).
3. Check oil condition (color, foaming, milky).
4. Check track tension (if applicable). Refer to operator's manual for correct tension.

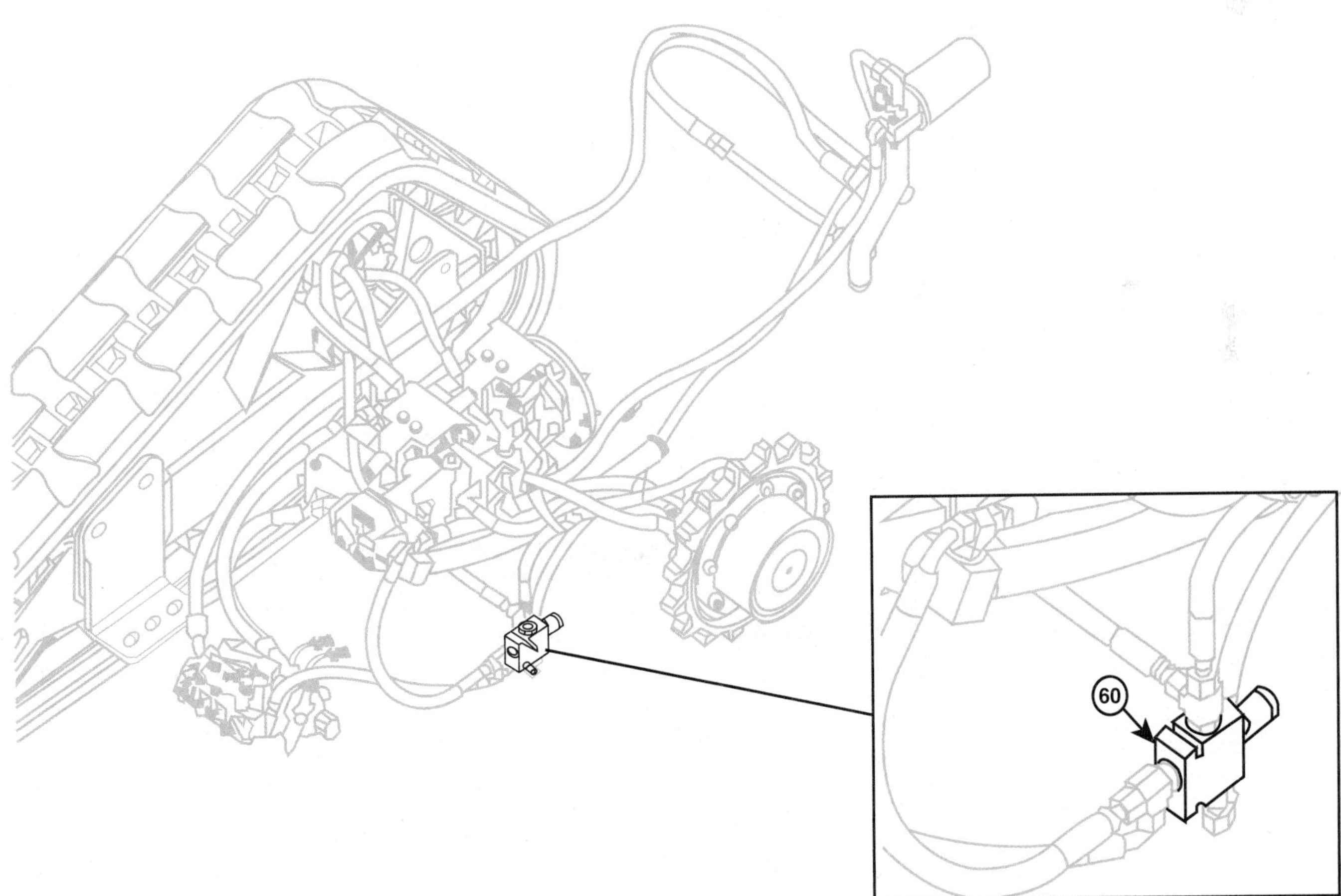

FIGURE 31-39 Brake release valve used on a skid steer loader.

5. Check tire pressure (if applicable). Refer to operator's manual for correct inflation pressure.
6. Check controls. Hand or foot controls should move freely with no stickiness.
7. Look for any damage to hydrostatic components.
8. Look for any other machine system problems (leaks, engine smoking, undercarriage damage).

FIGURE 31-40 A case drain filter with metal contamination.

SAFETY TIP

Never use your bare hands to check for a hydraulic leak. Even an innocent-looking leak can come from a high-pressure spray. High-pressure fluid injection injuries can result in severe injury or death. When checking for leaks, always wear a heavy-duty glove on your hand and use it to hold a piece of cardboard that can reveal a leak. Never grab a hose that may have a leak; the high-pressure oil could easily penetrate skin and light gloves.

Diagnose Hydrostatic Drive Problems

Hydrostatic system troubleshooting is similar to hydraulic system diagnostics because the same general principles of fluid power apply to both:

1. If there is a speed problem, there is likely a lack of flow.
2. If there is a weak drive problem, there is likely a lack of pressure or an internal leakage problem.

The technician would start by verifying the complaint. This may mean that you need to read the operator's manual to understand how the machine should work properly. Many problems will be specific to a given condition, and this will need to be reproduced to perform a proper diagnosis. For example, if a problem is related to the system fluid temperature being at a certain level, then you will need to match this, such as by getting the fluid up to 160°F.

Similar to all troubleshooting procedures, don't overlook the simple checks:

- Check fluid level and condition.
- Check for fault codes if applicable.
- Check for external leaks.
- Check for physical damage to components.
- Check track tension for track drive machines.
- Check tire pressure for wheeled machines.
- Check operator controls and the interlock system for proper operation.

▶ TECHNICIAN TIP

Hydrostatic drive systems can be very complicated even though they rely on basic closed-loop fluid power principles. To assist a technician with understanding fluid flow through a system, it is helpful to have a schematic. Hydrostatic system schematics will use the same symbols as hydraulic schematics and can come in paper or electronic versions.

If there is a speed problem, most manufacturers will provide a test procedure to confirm whether there is a problem. In general, this involves getting the fluid to operating temperature first, ensuring that the engine rpm is as specified and that the controls are functioning properly. The machine's brake system must also be confirmed to be released completely. Track machines also must have proper track tension because tracks that are too tight will rob horsepower and cause weak or slow travel.

Wheel or track speed can be measured with different methods and mainly depends on the size of the machine. For skid steer loaders with wheels, they can be put on stands, and the wheel speed is measured with a photo tachometer. Larger machines may have speed specifications that see a measured distance that has to be covered within a certain time window (200' in 22 seconds, for example).

System pressure is usually tested by keeping the brakes applied and trying to drive the machine while monitoring the high-pressure side values. Test ports can be used to check hydrostatic system pressures. Case drain pressure or flow could be tested and compared to specifications. If the results exceed specifications, this would indicate internal wear, which most often leads to pump or motor replacement. If there is a case drain filter, the filter can be removed, cut open, and inspected. The case drain filter will provide an indication of any wear conditions that are occurring in the system. See **FIGURE 31-40** for a case drain filter with excessive debris accumulated.

▶ TECHNICIAN TIP

Strange things can happen. This is a true story.

A technician was called to a hydrostatic drive track loader that was said to have a bad transmission fluid leak. An initial inspection didn't reveal anything obvious, but it was clear the hydrostatic fluid was low. After topping it up with 5 gallons of fluid, the technician ran the machine and checked for leaks again. Once again, there was nothing leaking. The technician told the operator to keep running the machine but to keep a close watch on the fluid level and look for any signs of leakage.

The technician returned the next day to find the level low, added another 5 gallons, checked for leaks, and repeated his instructions to the operator.

This went on for another six days before a leak finally appeared. It was coming from a door hinge fastener on the machine's main frame! The technician finally realized what was happening, and this was confirmed when the machine was sent to the shop for repairs.

One of the track motor's brake housings developed a crack, so the fluid was leaking into the cavity of the main frame of the machine. There was no way to confirm this until the fluid started leaking out of the frame.

Needless to say, the inside of the frame will never rust out.

Hydrostatic System Adjustments

There could be adjustments made to hydrostatic systems that will restore proper operation. One common adjustment that is made to hydrostatic pumps is neutral adjustment. This will ensure that the machine doesn't creep when the travel controls are in neutral.

If a machine has left and right drives and isn't driving straight when requested, then a tracking adjustment may be needed. This will match the speed of both sides to make the machine travel straight. This could be a linkage adjustment for machines with simple controls or could be an electronic **calibration** procedure performed with a computer. See **FIGURE 31-41** for a computer being used to calibrate a hydrostatic drive system.

For machines with mechanical linkage, the procedure of neutral adjustment would lengthen or shorten the linkage between the pump swash plate trunnion and the levers or foot pedals.

The following is an example of a calibration procedure performed on a medium-sized skid steer loader that has an electronically controlled hydrostatic system. This is a dual-path system with two pumps and two motors. This procedure is performed whenever a pump, motor, or ECM is replaced or when there are complaints about machine tracking (not going in a straight line when requested). This procedure will ensure that the systems ECM electrical signal outputs for controlling the pump's hydraulic flow outputs produce the expected results at the wheels.

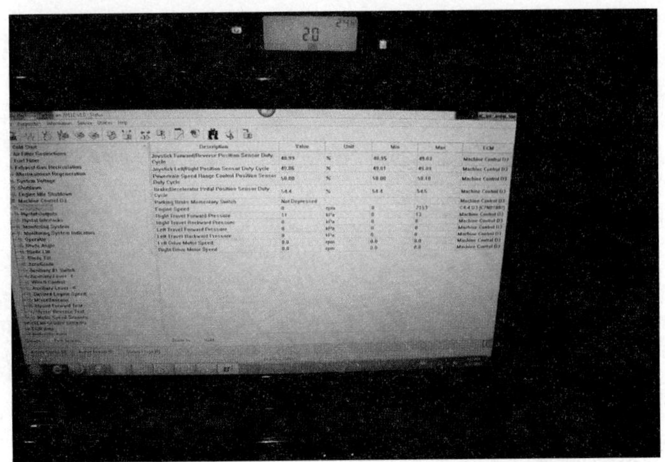

FIGURE 31-41 A hydrostatic drive system being calibrated.

The machine must be placed on jack stands. *Do not* raise the machine higher than needed to clear the floor. Barricade the area so that no other personnel can get close to the machine when the calibration is being performed. To perform a calibration procedure on an electronically controlled hydrostatic system, follow the steps in **SKILL DRILL 31-1**.

SKILL DRILL 31-1 Performing a Calibration Procedure

1. Warm hydrostatic fluid to at least 130°F.

2. Turn on ignition but do not start machine.

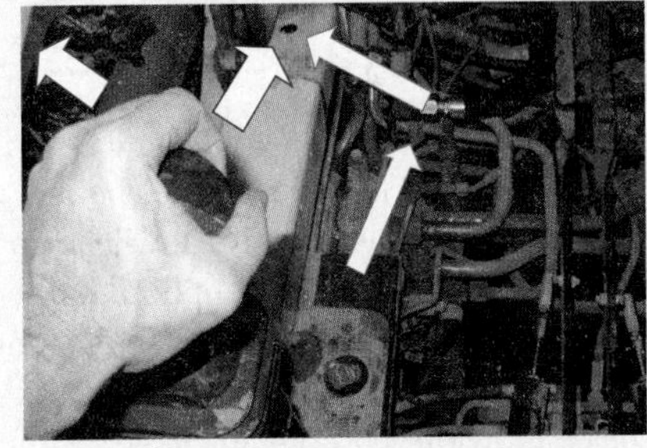

3. Move left joystick to farthest left and forward position and hold.

4. Press the "Press to Operate" button.

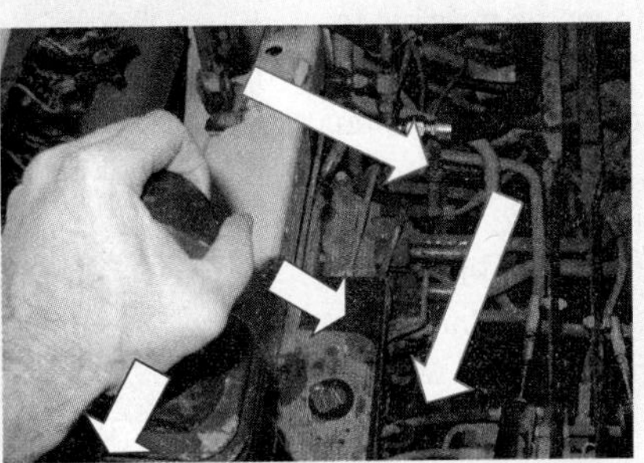

5. Move the left joystick to the back and right and hold.

6. Press the "Press to Operate" button.

(Continued)

SKILL DRILL 31-1 Performing a Calibration Procedure (Continued)

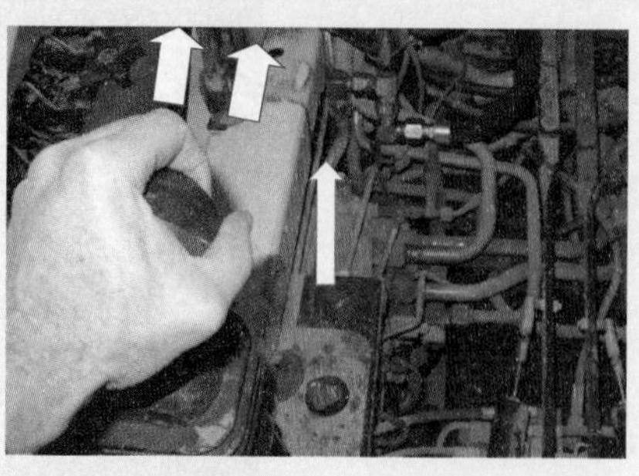

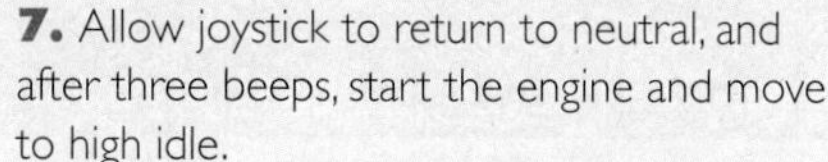

7. Allow joystick to return to neutral, and after three beeps, start the engine and move to high idle.

8. Move joystick to full forward and hold (wheels will rotate slightly forward up to five times, then rotate at full speed, and then finally stop).

9. Release joystick when a beep is heard.

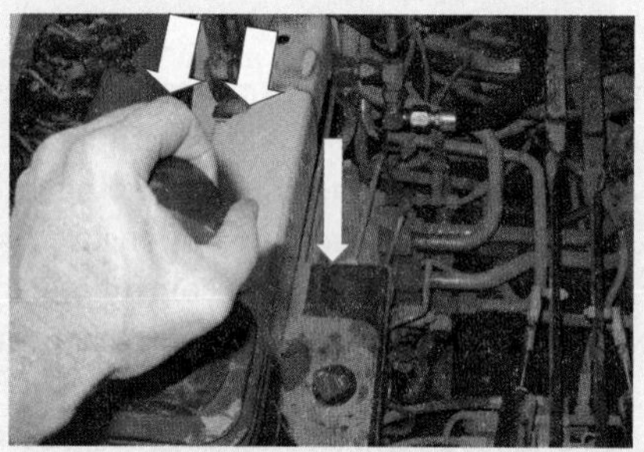

10. Move joystick to full reverse and hold (wheels will rotate slightly forward up to five times, then rotate at full speed, and then finally stop).

11. Release joystick when a beep is heard.

12. Calibration is now complete.

▶ Reconditioning or Repairs Following Manufacturers' Recommendations for Hydrostatic Drives

S31003

Once a diagnosis has been made and it is confirmed that one or more components is defective, it will be up to the machine owner to decide on the best repair option. In the end, the decision will be to repair or replace either the entire pump assembly or just the rotating group (pistons and cylinder block). It may be possible to replace individual pistons for larger pumps, but most likely for smaller pumps, it's only possible to buy the rotating group as an assembly.

There will be several factors that will influence the decision: component or parts availability, technician skill level, existing or required warranty, importance of machine, how well equipped the shop is, and how long the machine will be owned for.

Component Repair

Pump and motor repairs should be performed only if there is a clean, well-lit shop that has the necessary tools to complete the repair. The technician should also be comfortable with these types of repairs and with using measuring tools because the decision to reuse many parts will be based on precise dimensions.

Pump and Motor Repair

The following is a summary of a typical repair for a piston pump (could also be for a piston motor). During disassembling perform an initial inspection of parts for unusual wear or damage. See **FIGURE 31-42** to see a piston pump partially disassembled.

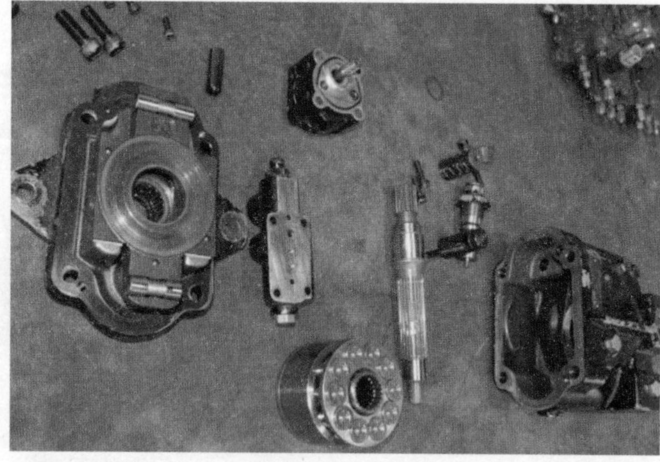

FIGURE 31-42 A piston pump partially disassembled.

Pump Disassembly

1. Thoroughly clean exterior of pump.
2. Mark housing for realignment.
3. Remove any valves from pump.
4. Remove pump head.
5. Remove swash plate actuator pistons and springs.
6. Remove port plate.
7. Remove bearing from shaft.
8. Remove rotating group from housing (cylinder block and pistons).
9. Remove shaft from rotating group.
10. Remove all bearings and seals.
11. Remove swash plate from cylinder block.
12. Remove pistons from cylinder block.
13. Remove pistons from retainer plate.
14. Remove retaining ball from cylinder block.
15. Use a press to compress spring in cylinder block; remove snap ring; slowly release spring and remove.
16. Disassemble valve(s), using caution due to stored energy with springs.

Piston Pump Component Inspection and Evaluation

1. Thoroughly inspect all components for excessive wear, scratches, scoring, and discoloration.
2. Pay particularly close attention to the port plate, cylinder block mating to port plate mating surface, pistons, and piston bores.
3. Check specifications for wear tolerances of pump components.
4. Confirm all measuring tools are accurate and zeroed.
5. Coat all components that will be reused with hydraulic oil, wrap in lint-free cloth, and store in a cool dry place.

Piston Pump Assembly

1. Ensure that all components are clean, work bench is clean and free of clutter, and surrounding work area is clean.
2. Reverse the disassembly process and apply hydraulic oil to all internal components before assembly.
3. Do not overheat bearings when installing them.
4. Torque all fasteners.
5. Check that pump rotates with an even amount of resistance.

Other Hydrostatic Drive System Component Repair

Hydrostatic drive valves may occasionally need to be repaired, but this will be limited to mainly repairing leaks and replacing broken springs since most internal valve parts are lap fitted to the housing. Hydrostatic drive controls will on rare occasion need repair. Mechanical linkages will wear and become sloppy, cables may stretch or break, and electronic joysticks may fail internally.

The most common repair a technician will perform on hydrostatic drive systems are fixing leaks. This ranges from tightening hoses, replacing O-rings, replacing hoses, and replacing tubes. When replacing a hose, ensure that the new hose is rated for at least as much pressure as the original.

Hydrostatic System Post-repair Start-Up

Once a hydrostatic system has been repaired, you will need to follow a specific procedure when first starting and running the machine to avoid a repeat failure or causing another type of failure. Always check the machine manufacturer's service information for this procedure. Ensure that pump or motor housings are filled with clean fluid before starting the machine. The pump inlet must always have all air bled from it to ensure that it gets a solid supply of fluid at first cranking. All filters should be replaced before starting, and fluid cleanliness should be confirmed, or the fluid should be replaced to be sure.

In the event of a catastrophic failure, you may need to dismantle the entire system and clean all components. Sometimes a **kidney loop** procedure will need to be done as well. This means filtering the system fluid with an external filter and monitoring contamination levels until they fall within an acceptable range. See **FIGURE 31-43** to see an external filter and particle counter.

There may be cleanout filters available to be installed for initial start-up. These filters will have finer micron ratings to capture smaller contaminants. Theses filters will plug up faster and will need to be changed within the first 10 hours of operation.

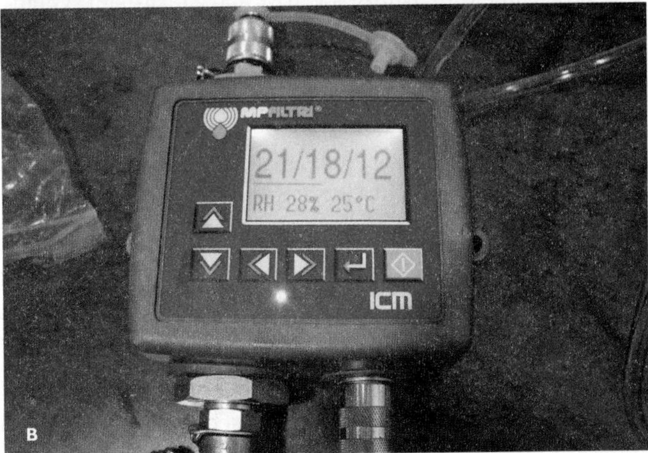

FIGURE 31-43 An external filter and particle counter.

▶ Wrap-Up

Ready for Review

- A skid steer machine uses a hydrostatic system to provide quick direction transition, smooth turns, and plenty of power to fill the bucket.
- A closed-loop hydrostatic system is one that sends pump output flow directly to a motors inlet, and the return from the motor goes directly to the pump inlet.
- Reverse rotation is enabled by reversing the pump flow to the motor.
- A charge pump is needed to maintain a constant supply of fluid in the closed loop since some fluid is lost through leakage and for cooling and cleaning.
- Hydrostatic machines provide dynamic braking, which eliminates the need for service brakes; however, a parking brake is necessary.
- Operators control hydrostatic systems by controlling pump flow.
- Housings with a double pump assembly or with the pump and motor in them could be called a hydrostatic transmission.
- Hydrostatic drive systems that use two pumps and two motors to drive either two sets of wheels or tracks are called dual-path hydrostatic systems.
- Schematics are used to trace fluid flow through a hydrostatic system. Written symbols and lines represent different components. Electronic versions can be used instead of paper copies.
- Combination valves are both high-pressure relief and check valves.
- Makeup valves allow fluid into the low-pressure side of the closed loop.
- Charge pressure is the level of pressure that the charge pump outlet is limited to.
- Larger hydrostatic drive systems will likely have a dedicated charge pump, whereas smaller systems may use the implement pump flow to supply the charge circuit.
- A machine with hydrostatic drive and a dual-path system will be able to counter-rotate or spot turn.
- Single-path hydrostatic systems have one pump driving one motor. The drive output of the motor could be divided through gear sets and shafts or other mechanical devices.
- Pump drives can rotate more than one pump and be either a set of gears in a lubricated housing or a belt drive arrangement.
- Hydrostatic system cooling is provided by an air-cooled heat exchanger that has a fan moving air past it. The fan is usually driven by a hydraulic motor.
- Hydrostatic fluid tanks provide a supply of fluid to ensure the system fluid stays clean and cool.
- Bypass valves allow fluid to flow past coolers when cold oil can't flow through them or past filters when they become plugged.
- Hydrostatic fluid tanks will have sight glasses and could have level and temperature sensors.
- A case drain circuit routes leakage from pumps and motors to the tank. It will provide cleaning and cooling to the fluid as well.
- Hydrostatic fluid is the most vital component of the hydrostatic system. Viscosity is critical, and fluid specifications must meet all minimum requirements as specified by the manufacturer.
- Operator controls can vary from mechanical (cable, linkage) to pilot oil and electronic joystick.
- Pilot oil controls are a low-pressure system to control pump output, and electronic joysticks are position sensors that send a signal to an ECM.
- Electronic hydrostatic controls can be part of a CAN.
- Axial piston pumps are the most common type used for hydrostatic drive systems.
- Axial piston pumps vary their displacement and flow direction by changing the angle of the swash plate.
- When the swash plate is at 0 degrees, the pump will not produce flow and it is neutral.
- Pump swash plates can be controlled with mechanical linkage, hydraulically or electrohydraulically.
- Pump servo control valves are needed to send oil to the pump servo piston in order to control pump flow output. There are many variations of servo control valves.
- An axial piston motor is very like an axial piston pump and can be fixed or variable displacement, depending on whether their swash plate is movable.
- Bent axis motors are like bent axis pumps and can also be fixed or variable, depending on whether their cylinder block is movable.
- Cam lobe motors have a series of pistons that follow the profile of an internal cam to create torque from oil flow.
- Orbital motors are used in smaller hydrostatic drive machines and are sometimes called geroller or gerotor motors. They have two rotating members that rotate on different centers and create torque by accepting fluid flow into an expanding chamber.
- Motors will be rated by displacement, maximum pressure, and maximum speed.
- The formula for motor torque: torque (inch pounds) = psi × displacement (CIR)/2π.
- The formula for motor speed: rpm = flow × 231/ displacement (if displacement is given in CIR).
- Charge pumps are needed in hydrostatic drives to replenish any fluid lost from the main loop because of component leakage or cooling and cleaning leakage.
- Hydrostatic drives can use many different types of motors (axial piston, bent axis piston, cam lobe, gerotor, geroller).
- Common operational problems associated with hydrostatic systems could include machine won't drive;

machine is slow; drive is weak; no reverse or forward; and machine won't travel straight.

- Simple inspections can include checking oil level, looking for leaks, checking controls, and checking track tension.
- Track or wheel speed can be measured by different methods, such as by using a photo tachometer.
- Case drain pressure or flow could be measured to get an indication of the internal condition of pumps and motors.
- Hydrostatic drive system adjustments included neutral adjustment and tracking adjustment (to make dual-path hydrostatic system machine travel straight). Adjustments could be made mechanically or with a laptop.
- Pump and motor repair should be done by a technician who is confident using fine measuring tools in a clean, well-lit workspace.
- Repairing leaks is a very common task related to hydrostatic drives.
- Always fill pump and motor housings with clean fluid prior to start-up following a replacement.

Key Terms

axial piston The style of pump that is most commonly used for hydrostatic drives.

bypass valve A valve used in filter bases or near coolers that will open to provide flow when pressure becomes too high. This will occur when a filter becomes plugged or cold fluid can't flow through a cooler.

calibration A procedure performed to match electronic input and output values to ECM software.

cam lobe motor A type of motor, sometimes called a radial piston motor. A series of pistons ride around an inside cam and create torque from fluid flow.

CAN A distributed network control system in which no single central control module is used. When two or more ECMs are connected, they can communicate over a network.

charge pressure Controlled pressure for the charge pump outlet that can feed the low-pressure side of the closed loop.

charge pump A fixed displacement pump that is needed to replenish the fluid that leaves the loop due to component leakage and due to cooling and cleaning intentional leakage.

closed loop A hydraulic system that has the pump outlet flow going directly to the motor and the return fluid from the motor going directly to the pump inlet.

combination valves Pressure relief valves and check valves in one housing. They can open to relieve high pressure to prevent damage or open to allow fluid in to the closed loop if pressure drops too low.

crossover relief valves Valves in the system that will relieve high pressure on one side of the loop if pressure gets too high.

displacement The volume rating used for pumps and motors that determines how much fluid it takes to create one rotation of a motor and how much fluid a pump moves per revolution, measured in cubic inches per revolution (CIR) or cubic centimeters per revolution (CCR).

dual-path hydrostatic systems A drive system that uses two pumps and two motors to drive either two sets of tracks or wheels.

dynamic machine braking Hydrostatic drive machines provide natural braking because of the closed-loop system.

fixed displacement motor Simple hydrostatic drive systems use a motor that will only produce a constant rotational speed if a constant supply of fluid is sent to it.

flow meter A tool used to measure fluid flow in a hydraulic system.

flushing valve A valve usually on the motor that allows a small amount of fluid out of the system for cleaning purposes.

hydrostatic Fluid at rest and is the term associated with hydraulic closed-loop drive systems.

hydrostatic transmission A pump and motor are combined into one housing. Sometimes double-pump assemblies in one housing are called hydrostatic transmissions as well.

inhibitors Additives used to prevent the degrading of system fluid under normal circumstances.

ISO 4406 A fluid cleanliness code used to determine the level of contamination in system fluid.

kidney loop An external filtration machine that is sometimes connected to a hydrostatic drive system to clean contamination out of the fluid.

joystick A term used to describe hand levers that could be used to control hydrostatic systems.

makeup valves Valves in the system that allow charge fluid into the closed loop if the pressure on the low side drops below the charge pressure setting.

open loop Hydraulic system that has the pump inlet fluid supplied from the tank and fluid leaving the directional control valve returning to tank.

pilot controls One type of operator control that uses low-pressure fluid to control pump output.

position sensors Electronic joysticks are really position sensors that send a signal to an ECM.

pump drive Some hydrostatic drive systems that have more than one pump may use a pump drive to rotate their pumps.

reverse rotation Hydrostatic drives provide reverse by reversing the flow of the pump.

schematic A roadmap that represents all components in a hydrostatic drive system. Fluid flow can be traced through the system by studying the schematic.

single-path hydrostatic systems Hydrostatic drive systems that use one pump to drive one motor.

spot turns A machine whose left and right tracks or tires rotate in opposite directions.

variable displacement bidirectional A term that describes the type of pump used for hydrostatic drive systems.

swash plate Component in an axial piston pump that provides variable displacement.

servo pistons Pistons used to hydraulically adjust swash plate angle.

servo control valves Valves that are electronically controlled by the operator and in turn control a pump servo piston that changes pump output.

synchronizing shaft Part of a bent axis motor that connects its cylinder block to the output shaft.

Review Questions

1. The most common purpose of most hydrostatic drives is to __________.
   a. propel heavy equipment machines
   b. power hydraulic implements
   c. create high hydraulic pressure
   d. create a vacuum
2. The compact components of a hydrostatic system were a good match for the drivetrain application in the first hydrostatic drive systems because of the machines' __________.
   a. large size
   b. high speed
   c. low speed
   d. small size
3. Hydrostatic fluid is supplied by the fixed displacement gear pump through the __________.
   a. makeup valves
   b. flushing valves
   c. relief valves
   d. bypass drive
4. Which valves act as both a relief valve and a check valve, depending on whether they are exposed to fluid pressure on the high-pressure side or the low-pressure side of the loop?
   a. Shuttle valves
   b. Combination valves
   c. Flush relief valves
   d. Inlet side makeup valves
5. Which of these is a set of gears in a separate housing that divides the engine input to it into two or more splined outputs?
   a. Pump drive
   b. Skid Steer
   c. Track loader
   d. Compactor
6. The purpose of a bypass valve is to __________.
   a. add feedback to the system
   b. remove excess pressure from the system
   c. allow cold fluid to bypass the system
   d. allow hot air to bypass the system
7. Which of these is a good practice while checking leaks in machines?
   a. Put your bare hand under the machine and check if you can feel the leak.
   b. Check for abnormal vibrations when the system is on.
   c. Check for abnormal temperatures in the machine.
   d. Look under the machine for drips and clean wet streaks on dirty machines.
8. If there is a __________ problem in the hydrostatic drive, there is likely a lack of flow.
   a. vibration
   b. speed
   c. temperature
   d. friction
9. All of the following factors factor into the decision to repair or replace either the entire pump assembly or just the rotating group, *except* __________.
   a. the credibility of the manufacturer
   b. technician skill level
   c. existing or required warranty
   d. importance of machine
10. A/an __________ loop means filtering the system fluid with an external filter and monitoring contamination levels until they fall within an acceptable range.
    a. open
    b. closed
    c. kidney
    d. filter

ASE Technician A/Technician B Style Questions

1. Technician A says all hydrostatic drive systems are open loop. Technician B says all hydrostatic drive systems have variable displacement motors. Who is correct?
   a. Technician A
   b. Technician B
   c. Both Technician A and Technician B
   d. Neither Technician A nor Technician B
2. Technician A says gerotor pumps are used only for main pumps on smaller machines. Technician B says all hydrostatic drive systems use bidirectional pumps. Who is correct?
   a. Technician A
   b. Technician B
   c. Both Technician A and Technician B
   d. Neither Technician A nor Technician B
3. Technician A says a special directional control valve is used to create reverse drive. Technician B says hydrostatic systems need charge pumps to replenish internal leakage. Who is correct?
   a. Technician A
   b. Technician B
   c. Both Technician A and Technician B
   d. Neither Technician A nor Technician B
4. Technician A says flushing valves let a steady amount of fluid out of the loop for cleaning and cooling. Technician B says bidirectional motors provide a high-speed reverse. Who is correct?
   a. Technician A
   b. Technician B
   c. Both Technician A and Technician B
   d. Neither Technician A nor Technician B

5. Technician A says it is possible to see a belt-driven hydrostatic pump. Technician B says hydrostatic drive systems can be part of a large dozer's steering system. Who is correct?
   a. Technician A
   b. Technician B
   c. Both Technician A and Technician B
   d. Neither Technician A nor Technician B
6. Technician A says a crossover relief valve will limit the pressure in the high side of the loop. Technician B says charge pressure should be within 100 psi of main system pressure. Who is correct?
   a. Technician A
   b. Technician B
   c. Both Technician A and Technician B
   d. Neither Technician A nor Technician B
7. Technician A says a flow divider will provide high and low speed like a two-speed axle. Technician B says it is possible for a hydrostatic machine to have its tracks turning in opposite directions. Who is correct?
   a. Technician A
   b. Technician B
   c. Both Technician A and Technician B
   d. Neither Technician A nor Technician B
8. Technician A says one of the easy and common checks to do is a calibration. Technician B says a slow drive problem is likely a pressure problem. Who is correct?
   a. Technician A
   b. Technician B
   c. Both Technician A and Technician B
   d. Neither Technician A nor Technician B
9. Technician A says connecting a kidney loop to a machine is an effective way to clean out the system. Technician B says fluid cleanliness is not as important in hydrostatic systems as it is in hydraulic systems. Who is correct?
   a. Technician A
   b. Technician B
   c. Both Technician A and Technician B
   d. Neither Technician A nor Technician B
10. Technician A says track tension should be checked prior to diagnosing a hydrostatic drive problem. Technician B says a machine that is constantly tracking will make it hard to drive straight. Who is correct?
   a. Technician A
   b. Technician B
   c. Both Technician A and Technician B
   d. Neither Technician A nor Technician B

CHAPTER 32
Advanced Hydraulics

Knowledge Objectives

After reading this chapter, you will be able to:

- **K32001** Explain the operation of open and closed center hydraulic systems.
- **K32002** Describe the operation of a variable displacement pump control valve.
- **K32003** Explain the operation of a load-sensing hydraulic system.
- **K32004** Explain the operation of pressure- and flow-compensated hydraulic systems.
- **K32005** Describe the operation of pilot-controlled hydraulic systems.
- **K32006** Explain the purpose and fundamentals of electronically managed hydraulic systems.
- **K32007** Describe the principles of operating electronically managed hydraulic systems.
- **K32008** Describe the operation and construction features of a typical excavator hydraulic system.

Skills Objectives

After reading this chapter, you will be able to:

- **S32001** Identify the construction features of electronically managed hydraulic systems.
- **S32002** Inspect, test, and diagnose an electronically managed hydraulic system.

▶ Introduction

From reading earlier chapters, you should already know the basic principles of simple hydraulic systems and how they convert mechanical energy to fluid energy and back to mechanical energy to perform work. The components of a simple system were also described, as was how they work together to transfer energy through fluid. This energy is converted into either motion or heat. It is the energy that is converted into heat that equates to a loss of efficiency or is simply wasted energy. This would be similar to the heat energy that is created when a machine brakes and is dissipated to the atmosphere. Heat in a hydraulic system is created by fluid flowing through conductors and components and through internal leakage, where fluid leaks past component parts like pistons, seals, and valve spools. By reducing unnecessary fluid flow, energy efficiency is increased.

This chapter will discuss how hydraulic systems have evolved into higher pressure and higher flow systems while also becoming more energy efficient and easier to operate. By reducing unnecessary flow and lowering effort of operator controls both of these objectives can be realized. These gains in system efficiency and the ease with which they are operated however have added some complexity to hydraulic systems.

▶ TECHNICIAN TIP

There can also be efficiencies gained by reusing return fluid that still has kinetic energy in it, rather than just dumping it back to the tank. Excavators are good examples of where this fluid "recycling" can improve a machine's efficiency. When an excavator's boom is lowered quickly as the machine is returning to dig a deep hole, there is a lot of fluid escaping the bottom of the boom cylinders in a hurry due to the weight of the boom, stick, and bucket forcing the boom cylinder pistons down. The fluid leaving the head end of the boom cylinders is more than enough to fill the void in the rod end of the cylinders, and this fluid is redirected there instead of going to the tank. If this feature weren't used, the pump would be required to supply this fluid. This can be accomplished with internal passages in the main control valve. This function is called boom down regeneration by some manufacturers.

FIGURE 32-1 An excavator with an advanced hydraulic system.

Plenty of ongoing research focuses on where to get even more efficiency gains in hydraulic systems. See **FIGURE 32-1** for an excavator with an advanced hydraulic system. It is estimated that if all working hydraulic systems were able to realize a 10% efficiency gain, this would save $9.8 billion worth of fuel per year. This research is focused on reducing heat losses so that a higher percentage of fluid power energy is used to perform work and send oil back to the tank with as little energy in it as possible.

A direct relationship to fuel savings can be made since the machine's prime mover (diesel engine) output will be used more efficiently. The chapter will also look at electrohydraulic systems, their construction features, how they operate, how to diagnose problems with them, advantages and disadvantages, and how they integrate with other machine electronic systems. The need to understand both basic hydraulic principles and more advanced systems and components by today's MORE (mobile off-road equipment) technician is mandatory.

This chapter is meant to give you the knowledge of how common hydraulic system components work individually and together in an advanced hydraulic system and what to do if they aren't working properly. There is no way to cover all the

You Are the Mobile Heavy Equipment Technician

You are a technician working as an apprentice at a dealership for one of the main machine manufacturers. You are assigned to perform a pre-delivery inspection (PDI) on a new 75-ton excavator. Part of the inspection includes ensuring that all hydraulic control functions are working properly.

This machine has an electrohydraulic system that includes electronic joysticks, electronically actuated directional control valves and electronic pump controls. As you are going through the checks provided by the manufacturer, you notice that the heavy-lift mode doesn't seem to be working.

Answer the following questions in relation to this problem:

1. How would you know what the heavy-lift function should change in terms of hydraulic performance on this machine?
2. How would you confirm that there is a real problem with this function?
3. What simple checks might you perform to start diagnosing this problem?
4. What tools or equipment might be needed to diagnose this problem?
5. How could you confirm that any repairs you performed solved the problem?

variations of components and systems for advanced hydraulics in this chapter, but if the concepts of how fluid pressure and flow work together to perform work in an advanced system are mastered, then you should be able to understand how almost any system functions. If you can understand how a system functions, then you should be able to diagnose problems with it and repair or adjust system components to restore the system to its intended performance level.

▶ Open Center Versus Closed Center Hydraulic Systems

K32001

Generally speaking, **open center hydraulic systems** use fixed displacement pumps to create their flow, while **closed center hydraulic systems** almost always use variable displacement pumps. There are exceptions to this distinction, such as some medium-sized excavators that use open center directional control valves with variable displacement pumps and closed center systems that use fixed displacement pumps with unloading valves.

Open center and closed center refer to the types of directional control valve used for the system and whether pump flow can flow through the center of it or not when the valve spools are in neutral.

Simple Open Center Hydraulic System

Simple open center hydraulic systems are often controlled by the operator, with direct mechanical linkage moving directional control valves, and they generally have pressures no higher than 3,000 psi. Their pumps are fixed displacement and have outputs of less than 25 gpm. An example of this would be a log skidder with manual controls and no auxiliary circuits. Its only hydraulic functions are blade lift/lower and winch rotation. This would be a low-flow and low-pressure simple system. See **FIGURE 32-2** for a log skidder with a simple hydraulic system. Its fixed displacement pump will send oil to an open center directional control valve that can actuate one or two circuits (blade and winch). The pump output flow can move more than one actuator at a time, but doing so requires the operator to manually meter pump flow between the two circuits.

FIGURE 32-2 Log skidder with a simple hydraulic system.

The full output volume from the pump will be constantly moving through the system, and even when the directional control valve is in neutral, there will be enough resistance to the flow to create some pressure. This will in turn be a load on the prime mover and generate heat due to friction of the fluid moving through conductors and components. These conditions both result in a loss of efficiency.

As machine and hydraulic component design has evolved, hydraulic systems have been designed to provide higher pressures and higher flows that are also easier to control by the operator. Several factors have influenced this newer and more advanced hydraulic system: the need to reduce operator fatigue and increase comfort, equipment manufacturer competition, the need for higher fuel efficiency, and tighter regulations on diesel exhaust emissions. There is much research and development going on presently to increase **fluid power system efficiency**, and there are huge potential gains. These efficiency gains will include pump design changes, control valve changes, and more electronic monitoring and control.

Only the most basic small machines today will use a simple hydraulic system as described above. Even most skid steer machines will feature pilot-operated hydraulic controls at minimum and could include variable displacement pumps with pump control valves, closed center direction control valves with flow compensators, or electronically controlled pump controls.

An open center type of system refers to one that uses a directional control valve having a passage (open center) to allow the flow from the pump to flow through it and on to the tank when the control valve is in neutral. There will likely also be a parallel passage to allow oil flow to other functions when one function is being actuated. See **FIGURE 32-3** for an illustration of an open center hydraulic system. Directional control valve types were discussed in Chapter 26. See **FIGURE 32-4** for the schematic for a machine with an open center hydraulic system. Since a fixed displacement pump moves its full displacement of oil as soon as it's turning, it has to be used with an open center control valve. Some systems will use a combination of two or more fixed displacement pumps to provide system flow. In this case, a pump unloading valve can divert the flow from one pump and direct it to the inlet of the other pump(s) or back to the tank. Even if an **unloading valve** is used, there is still some wasted energy because the full flow of oil from the pump is not doing any useful work. A pump unloading valve will sense higher system pressure and divert the flow of the second pump to reduce the load on the engine. The second pump flow is needed for higher flow demand conditions. See **FIGURE 32-5** for a double pump with unloader valve arrangement.

Closed Center Hydraulic Systems

Closed center directional control valves are designed to stop the flow of pump oil at the valve inlet until there is a need to move an actuator. This will reduce heat loss in the system. This type of

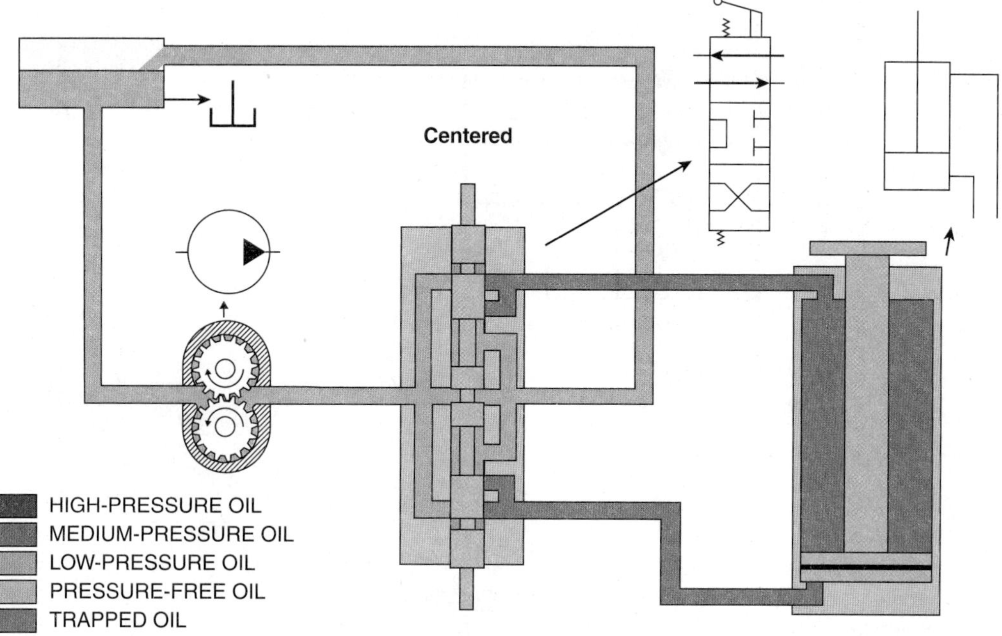

FIGURE 32-3 An illustration of an open center system.

Image Provided As Courtesy of John Deere.

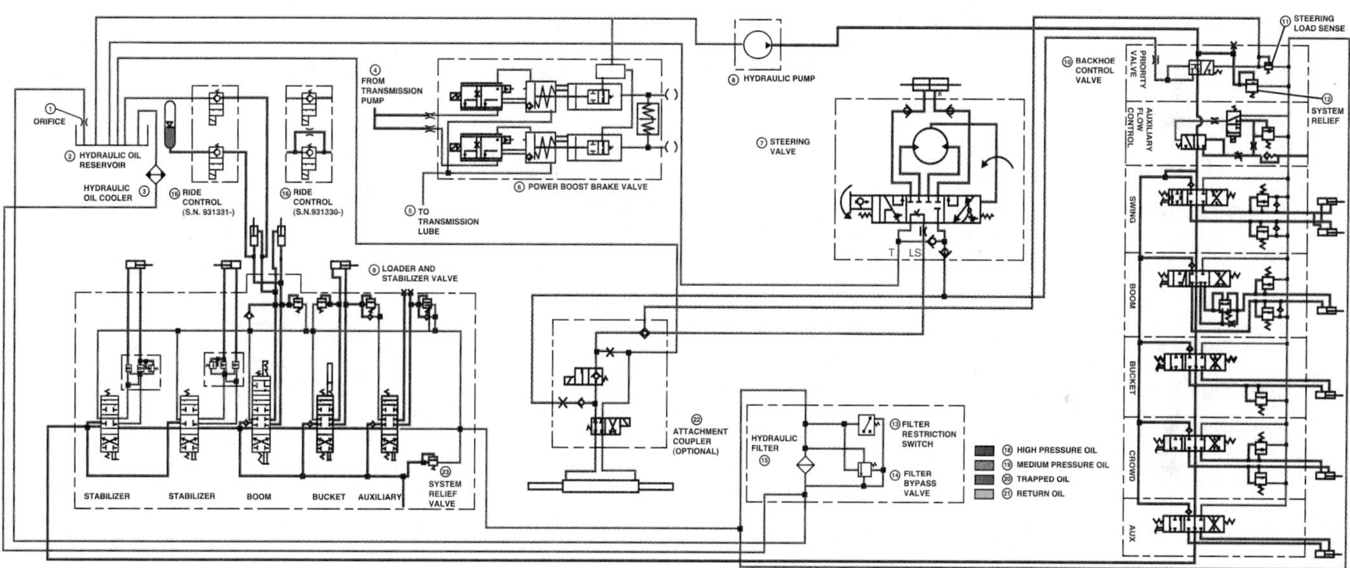

FIGURE 32-4 The schematic of a machine with an open center hydraulic system.

Image Provided As Courtesy of John Deere.

valve would ideally be used with a variable displacement pump since the pump can be "turned off" when there is not a high flow demand. See Chapter 25 for more information on variable displacement pumps.

A machine that has higher flow requirements will typically use a variable displacement pump with a closed center directional control valve to save on **flow losses**. For machines that require only low-flow and low-pressure hydraulic systems, an open center system is sufficient. However, if the machine designer wants to increase flow and reduce flow losses, then a variable displacement pump and closed center directional control valve must be used. Flow losses occur when oil leaks past internal components, such as pump pistons, cylinder seals, and motor components. These types of failures represent an unwanted pressure drop that also creates heat.

Another energy loss occurs when fluid is sent through conductors (hoses, tubes, and fittings) and components and the friction of the oil flowing through the inside of the conductors and components creates heat. This heat is a direct loss of energy and leads to inefficiency for a hydraulic system. Heat losses can be directly related to wasted horsepower by using the following formula: heat (BTU/hour) = flow (gpm) × pressure drop (psi) × 1.5.

Variable displacement pumps will be able to reduce their flow output no matter what speed their drive shaft is turning. By reducing the flow output when it's not needed, the system efficiency raises because of the reduced flow losses.

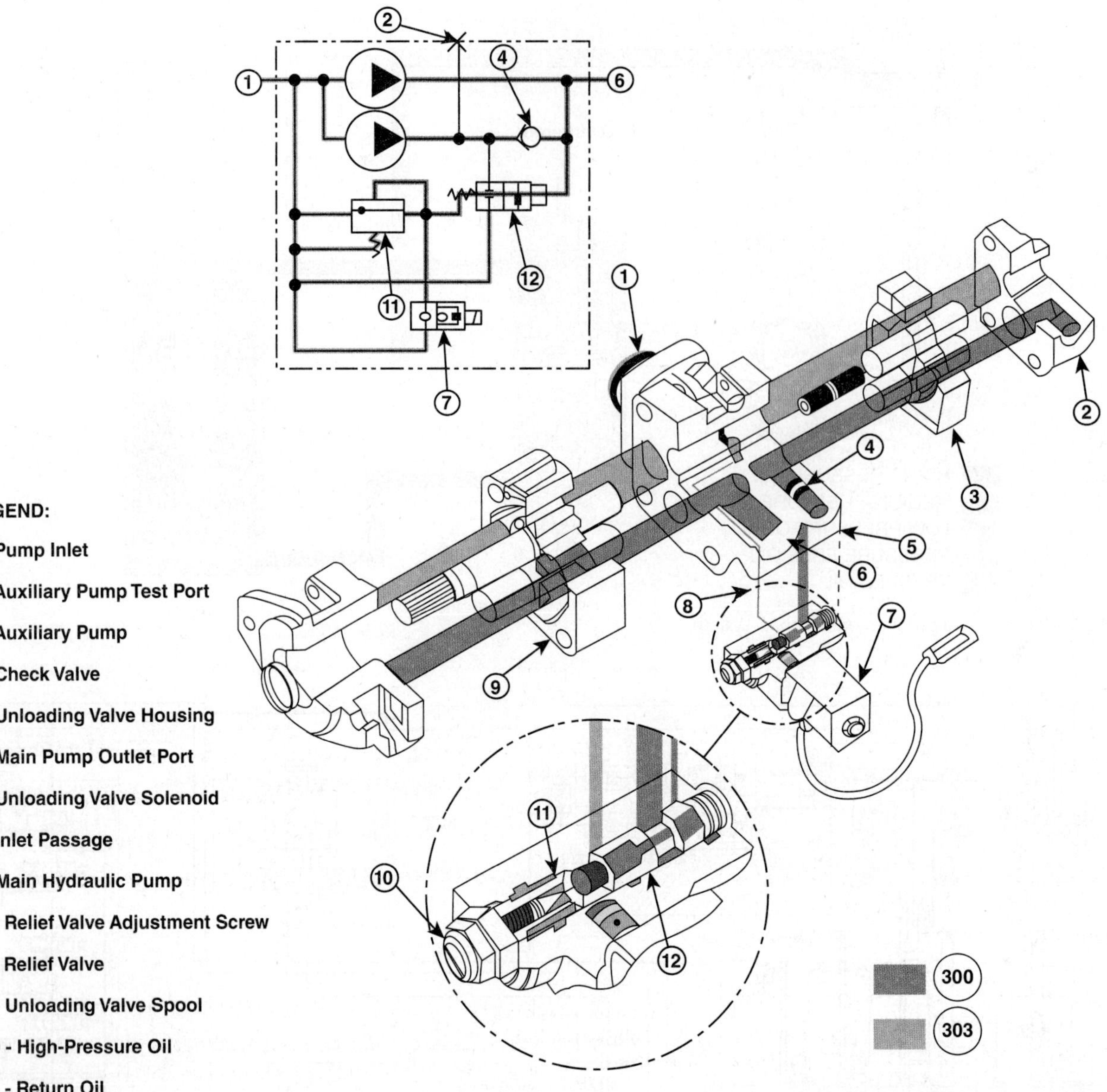

FIGURE 32-5 Pump and unloader valve.

Image Provided As Courtesy of John Deere.

> **TECHNICIAN TIP**
>
> As system leakage increases the pump must move more fluid to accomplish the same amount of work. The extra flow that is created but doesn't contribute to actuator movement is wasted energy (system inefficiency). A small amount of internal leakage is expected and is normal, even for a brand new system. When leakage exceeds a maximum limit, then it becomes a problem.

▶ Variable Displacement Pump Controls

K32002

Advanced hydraulic systems are designed to be more efficient by regulating the pump flow to deliver just enough oil to satisfy system loads and operator demands. There are many variations of systems to do this, but the goal is to provide only the pump flow to meet systems demands. Through the use of a **variable displacement pump** and a pump control valve, this is easily accomplished. The pump control valve can have a variety of different inputs, but its main output is used to hydraulically move the swashplate (axial piston pump) or cylinder block (bent axis piston pump) and vary the output of the pump. Oil pressure is applied to a piston (actuator), which then moves, and its movement will mechanically destroke the pump. See **FIGURE 32-6** for a variable displacement pump's actuator. Note that axial piston pump swashplates can sometimes be referred to as camplates.

Pump control valves are mounted to the pump and their actuator piston is mechanically connected to the pump swashplate or cylinder block. There are several different styles of pump control valves, and each one will have different inputs (i.e., electrical or hydraulic) that influence their internal mechanisms, which in turn direct oil pressure to their actuator piston.

FIGURE 32-6 A variable displacement pump's actuator.

Some pump control valves will have feedback linkage that gives a direct response from the pump swashplate or cylinder block. See **FIGURE 32-7** for a pump control valve for a bent axis pump.

Here are some examples of different sources of oil pressure that will act on the pump regulator valve spools:

1. Pump output oil from the main control valve—for some systems, pump oil will normally flow through a passage in the main control valve. This oil will be sent to the pump control valve through an orifice. If one of the main control valve spools is moved, the oil pressure to the pump control valve is decreased, and this will upstroke the pump. This oil pressure is proportional to the amount of oil sent to a function. The increase or decrease of this oil pressure will shift a spool in the pump control valve against spring pressure. The spool shifts to direct oil to the actuator piston or drain it away. This will move the actuator piston and change the pump output.
2. Average pump outlet pressure—for an excavator that has two main pumps, it is critical the pump control system considers the output of both pumps. Finding the output is done with a set of orifices and check valves. This pressure also moves the pump control valve spool to direct oil to the actuator piston or drain it away.
3. Solenoid-controlled engine speed sense oil—the hydraulic/engine controller will have an engine speed sensor as an input. One of its outputs, based on engine speed and programmed memory, will be a voltage signal to a proportional solenoid. This solenoid will allow oil to be sent to the pump regulator valve or drain it away. This is another way of regulating the pump output and is regulated based on engine speed.

Even though both pumps operate independently, there is a limit to how much horsepower one pump can take. This is usually 85% of the available engine horsepower. See **FIGURE 32-8** for a pump control valve that is used on an excavator.

▶ Load sensing

K32003

Changing the flow of a variable displacement pump to meet system demands will require a way to monitor the pressure of each circuit in the machine's main hydraulic system. This is the **load-sensing** function of an advanced hydraulic system, and it's one way to improve the systems efficiency. Once the load is sensed in each circuit and compared to other circuits, the highest load or pressure that is sensed will determine how much flow the pump produces.

If there is no load, such as when the controls are in neutral, then the pump will destroke and produce just enough flow to create standby pressure. This **standby pressure** will likely be 200–300 psi and will make the system more responsive since the pump is producing a small amount of flow at all times. If there were no standby pressure, the system would seem sluggish and lazy. This would put a slight load on the pump, but it would be almost insignificant.

As soon as a directional control valve has been moved and a circuit load has been created, this is sensed, and then a signal is sent to the pump control valve. The pump control valve will now upstroke the pump to provide enough flow to meet the pressure demand in the circuit.

Load sensing can be done hydraulically or electronically. Until fairly recently, any machine that featured load sensing did so hydraulically, but electronic load sensing is now becoming more common.

Hydraulic Load Sensing

The key to a load-sense system is the ability to monitor the pressures in each circuit. The following is a discussion on one type of hydraulic load-sense system. This system starts with cross-drilled passages in the main control valve. These passages will connect all work ports, but through the use of a series of check valves, they will allow only the highest pressure to be sent to the flow/pressure compensator. See **FIGURE 32-9** for a load-sense passage in a control valve.

> ▶ TECHNICIAN TIP
>
> Load-sense check valves have a simple assembly, with two inlet passages and one outlet. Work port pressure from one circuit is allowed into the inlet passages. The higher pressure will move the check valve ball onto the seat at the opposite end of the valve assembly. This pressure can now leave the valve and be sensed at another check valve or move to the pump control valve. See **FIGURE 32-10** for a control valve section with a load-sense passage represented schematically.

Because of the load-sense system and the action of the pump control valve, the pump flow will always be creating more pressure than the system load. For example, if the load on one circuit is 2,000 psi and the **margin spring pressure** is 450 psi, then the pump will provide the correct amount of flow to create 2,450 psi at its outlet. With a load-sense network, if another function is used on this same machine and it creates a load of 3,000 psi, then the pump must upstroke to give enough flow to

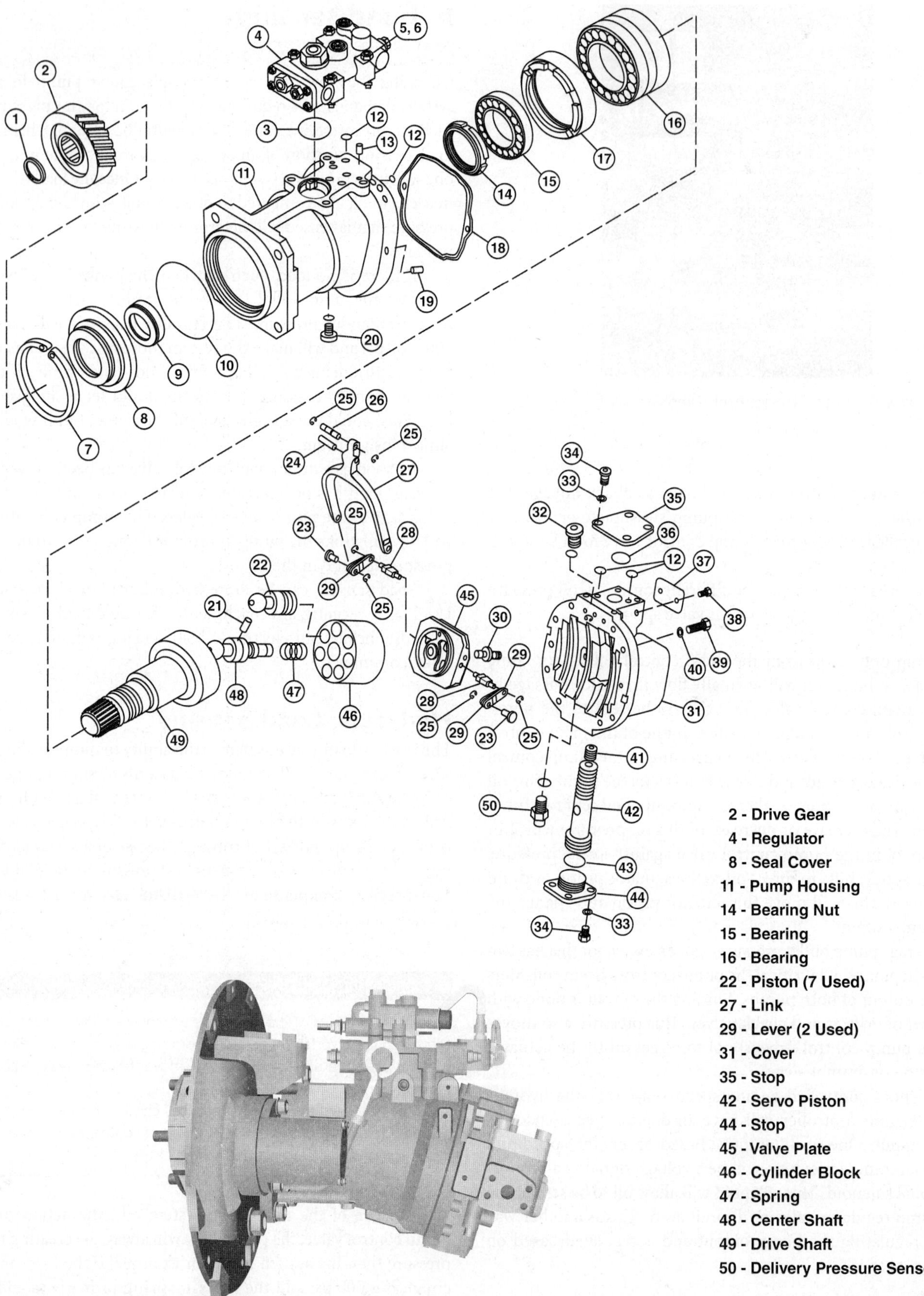

FIGURE 32-7 Bent axis variable displacement pump with a pump control valve or regulator (4).

Image Provided As Courtesy of John Deere.

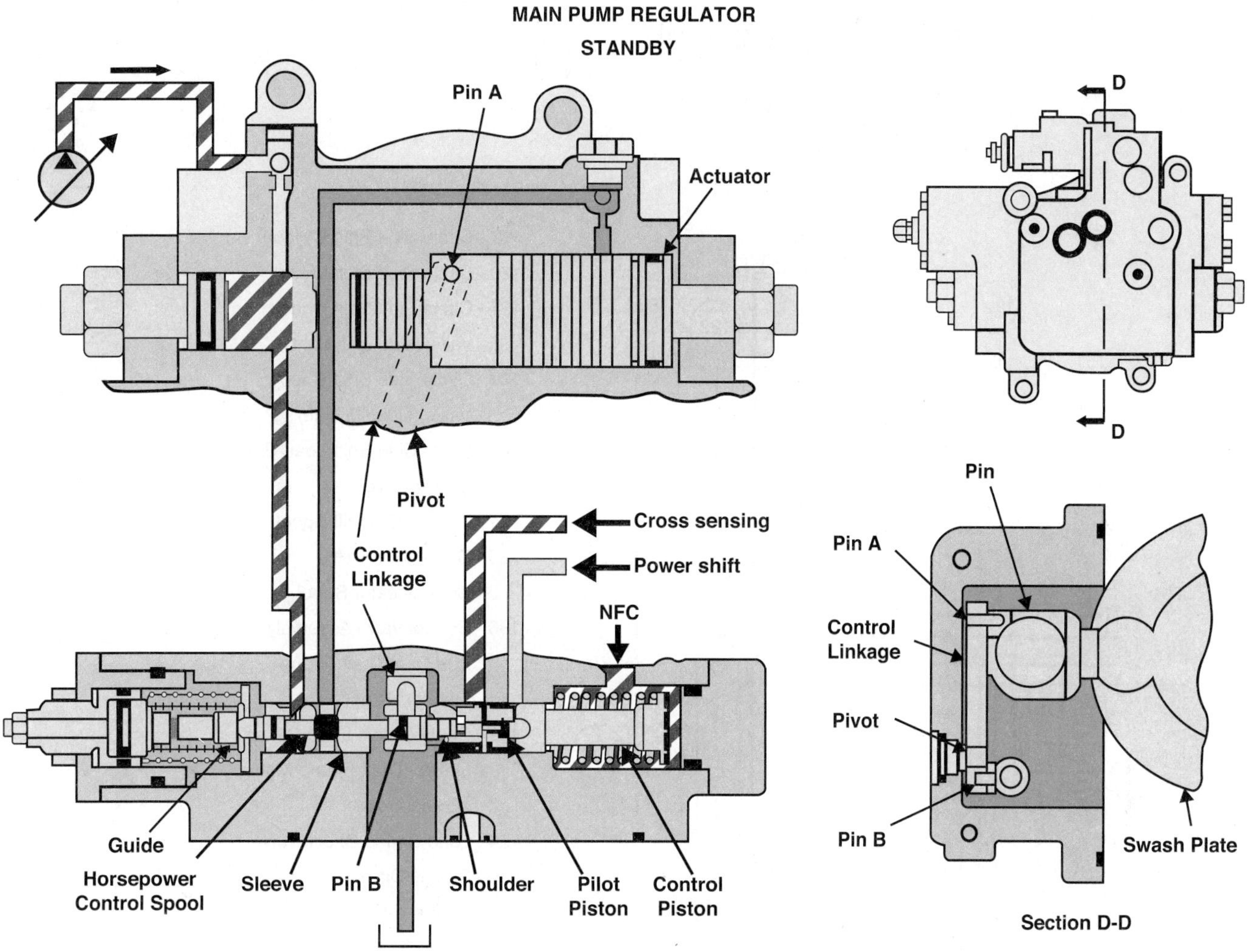

MAIN PUMP REGULATOR
STANDBY

Pin A
Actuator
Pivot
Control Linkage
Cross sensing
Power shift
NFC
Guide
Horsepower Control Spool
Sleeve
Pin B
Shoulder
Pilot Piston
Control Piston
D
D
Pin
Pin A
Control Linkage
Pivot
Pin B
Swash Plate
Section D-D

FIGURE 32-8 A pump control valve that is used on an excavator.

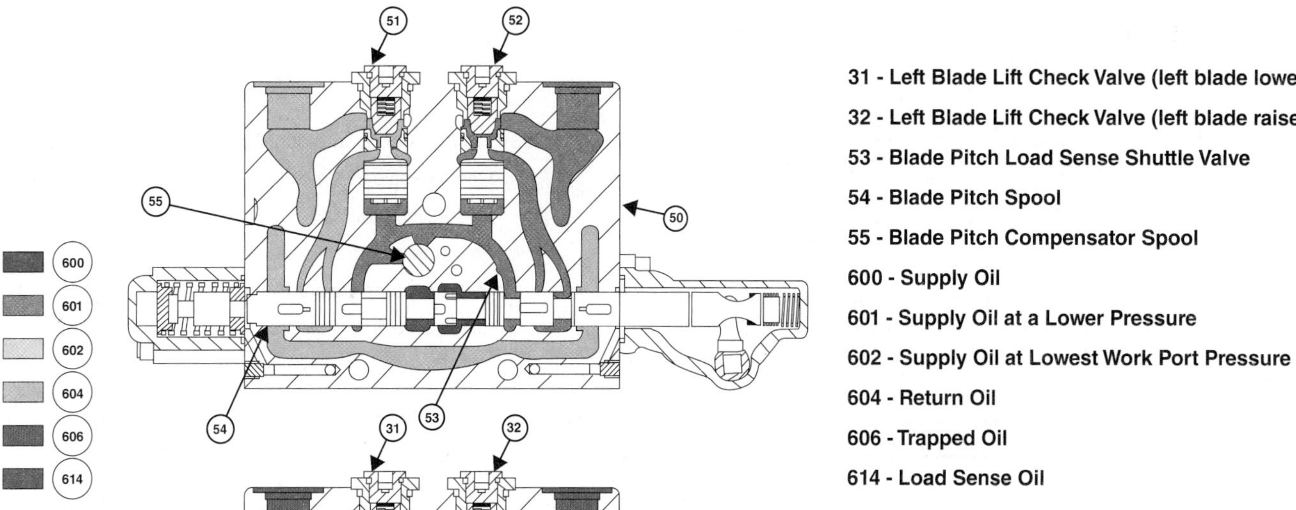

FIGURE 32-9 A load-sense passage (denoted by 614 coloured oil).

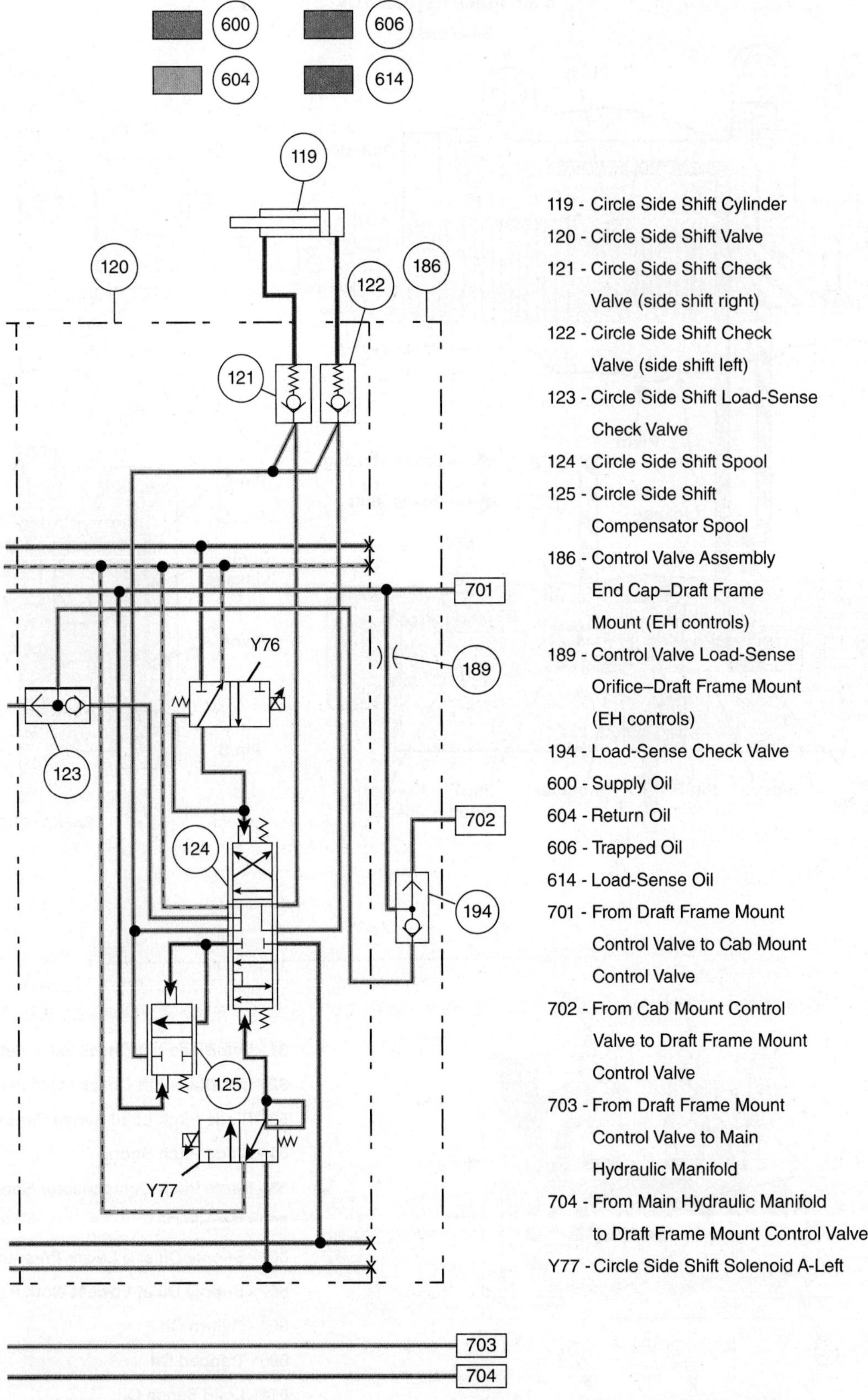

FIGURE 32-10 Hydraulic schematic of a Control valve section with a load-sense passage.

Image Provided As Courtesy of John Deere.

create the additional pressure. The pump outlet pressure would now be 3,450 psi.

Electronic Load Sensing

Newer, advanced hydraulic systems with load-sensing features will use pressure sensors in the main individual work ports to monitor circuit pressure. See **FIGURE 32-11** for a main control valve with pressure sensors for load sensing. The signals from the pressure sensors will be an input to the hydraulic system ECM (electronic control module). The ECM will then take the highest reading of all work port pressures and create an output signal that gets sent to the pump control valve. The pump control valve then reacts to the signal to set the pump displacement to produce a flow that will result in the desired output pressure. This pressure will be slightly higher than the highest work port pressure.

▶ Pressure- and Flow-Compensated Hydraulic Systems

K32004

What is compensation in terms of hydraulic systems? Compensation is a mechanism used to make up for some real or imagined deficiency (loss of pressure or flow). In practical terms, it is a monitoring and control system that maintains a level of flow output that will always satisfy the demands of the operator up to maximum pressure and flow output levels.

An important step in making hydraulic systems more efficient is to make the pump provide only the amount of flow that is necessary to do the work required.

> ▶ TECHNICIAN TIP
>
> It is important to remember when trying to understand this system that the basic fact is that pumps create flow and not pressure. Pressure is created by the resistance to flow.

FIGURE 32-11 A main control valve with pressure sensors for load sensing.

Non-compensated Hydraulic System

Before we discuss non-compensated hydraulic systems, let's first look at a system that uses a fixed displacement pump and an open center control valve. If the pump is turning at 2,000 rpm and producing 20 gpm, this quantity of oil is always being sent out the pump outlet. If the machine operator wants to move a cylinder slowly, then a directional control valve spool is moved to send some of this oil to the cylinder. If the demand is for 5 gpm, for example, then the other 15 gpm has to return to the tank. If the load on the cylinder creates a pressure of 2,000 psi, this is the pressure the pump has to overcome to keep the cylinder moving. Even though the operator wants only 5 gpm to move the cylinder a certain speed, the pump is still moving 20 gpm at 2,000 psi. See **FIGURE 32-12** for an illustration of the system as described above.

This means the pump is producing 15 gpm of oil at 2,000 psi for no reason. As you learned in Chapter 4, hydraulic horsepower is calculated by multiplying flow and pressure and then dividing the result by 1,714. To see how much horsepower is wasted in this example, simply multiply 15 gpm by 2,000 psi and divide by 1,714. You will find 17.5 hp is wasted just to do the 5.8 hp worth of work the operator wants (5 gpm × 2,000 psi/1,714). This doesn't include the extra 15% that the pump has to produce to overcome its own inefficiency.

By using a variable displacement pump that can provide only the amount of flow needed to satisfy the work being done, a lot of horsepower is saved. This translates directly into fuel savings since the prime mover has to do less work to drive the pump. Along with fuel savings, a great deal of exhaust emissions is not produced. In the above example, the 17.5 hp can be saved by reducing the pump flow to only the quantity necessary to move the cylinder (5 gpm). There is also much less heat generated in the system, which leads to reduced cooler sizes and increases the life of the system oil and the hoses.

If a pump is capable of being controlled so that it will produce only the flow that is needed based on the system load, this system is called a load-sensing pressure-compensated system.

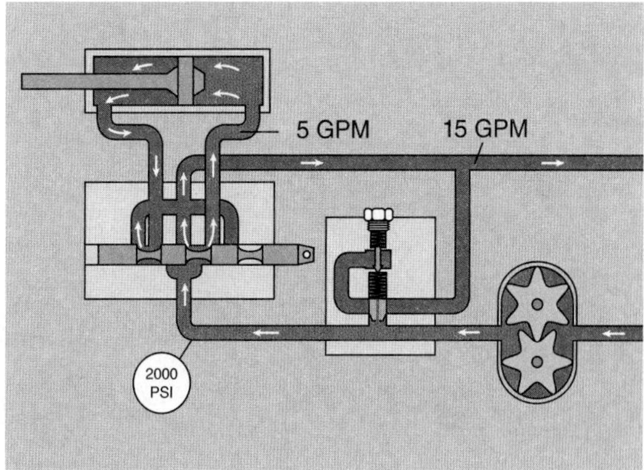

FIGURE 32-12 An illustration of a non-compensated hydraulic system.

High-Pressure Compensation

If a system is using a variable displacement pump, it needs to be able to reduce the pump flow when high-pressure conditions occur; otherwise, a major component failure is likely to occur. To prevent component failure, a variable displacement pump with a **high-pressure compensator** valve (sometimes called a pressure limiter or high-pressure cut-off valve) is used to reduce pump flow. This will monitor pump outlet pressure and send oil to the pump control piston to destroke the pump when maximum system pressure has been reached. The high-pressure cut-off valve will have an adjustable spring that pushes on a spool. Pump outlet oil works on the other end of the spool. If the oil pressure overcomes the spring pressure, the spool will move and uncover a passage. This passage allows oil to get to the pump control piston and destroke the pump.

This is the simplest type of pressure compensation system, and it is simply compensating for or adjusting the pump flow when the system pressure reaches a maximum value set by the spring pressure. See **FIGURE 32-13** for a high-pressure compensator destroking a pump.

> ▶ TECHNICIAN TIP
>
> All pressure-compensated systems will also have a main relief valve to limit maximum pressure. This may seem redundant, but if there were a malfunction with the pump control, the separate main relief valve would serve as a backup to keep pressure levels to a safe limit. The valve will usually be set 200–300 psi higher than the pressure compensator on the pump to avoid any interaction between the two.

Pressure and Flow Compensation

A pressure- and flow-compensated system is one that will provide oil pump oil flow based on the working pressure of the highest working circuit pressure. For example, if a backhoe is digging a trench and the operator is using the swing, boom, stick, and bucket functions simultaneously, the pump will try to satisfy the circuit that has the highest pressure. This could be any one of the four circuits, and it will be constantly changing in accordance with what the operator wants the machine to do. The point to remember is that the pump control compensator is designed to always make the pump provide enough flow to slightly exceed the pressure and flow demands of the circuit with the greatest needs.

This is usually a few hundred psi higher than what is needed. The difference in working pressure and pump output pressure is sometimes called the differential pressure or margin pressure and can range from 200 to 450 psi, depending on the manufacturer's specifications.

This margin pressure is added to the highest load-sense (working) pressure and is sent to the pump control piston, where it manages pump swashplate or cylinder block angle and therefore pump flow output.

The pump control valve will have two spools in it. One is the high-pressure compensator, and the other is the pressure/flow compensator (sometimes called margin spool or load-sense spool). The pump control valve is mounted directly to the pump.

The **pressure/flow compensator** has a light spring that acts on one end of a spool valve. The other end of the spool has the pump outlet oil acting on it. When a load-sense signal is sent to the flow compensator spool, it enters the

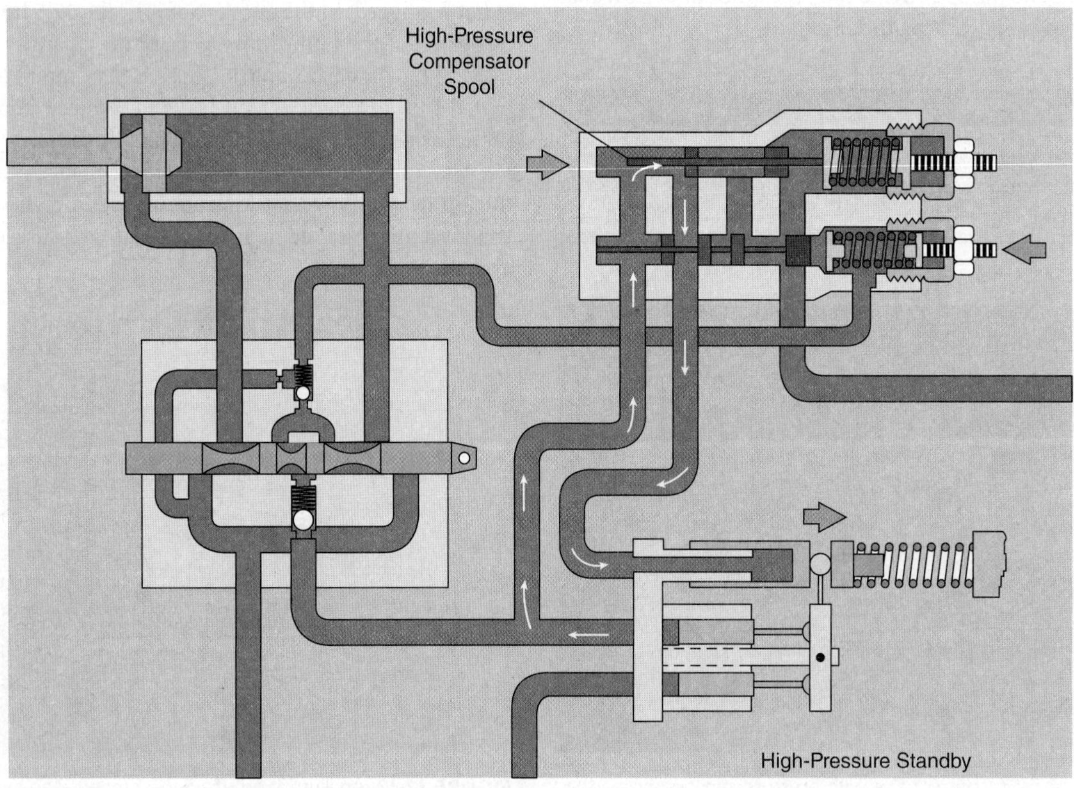

FIGURE 32-13 A high-pressure compensator destroking a pump.

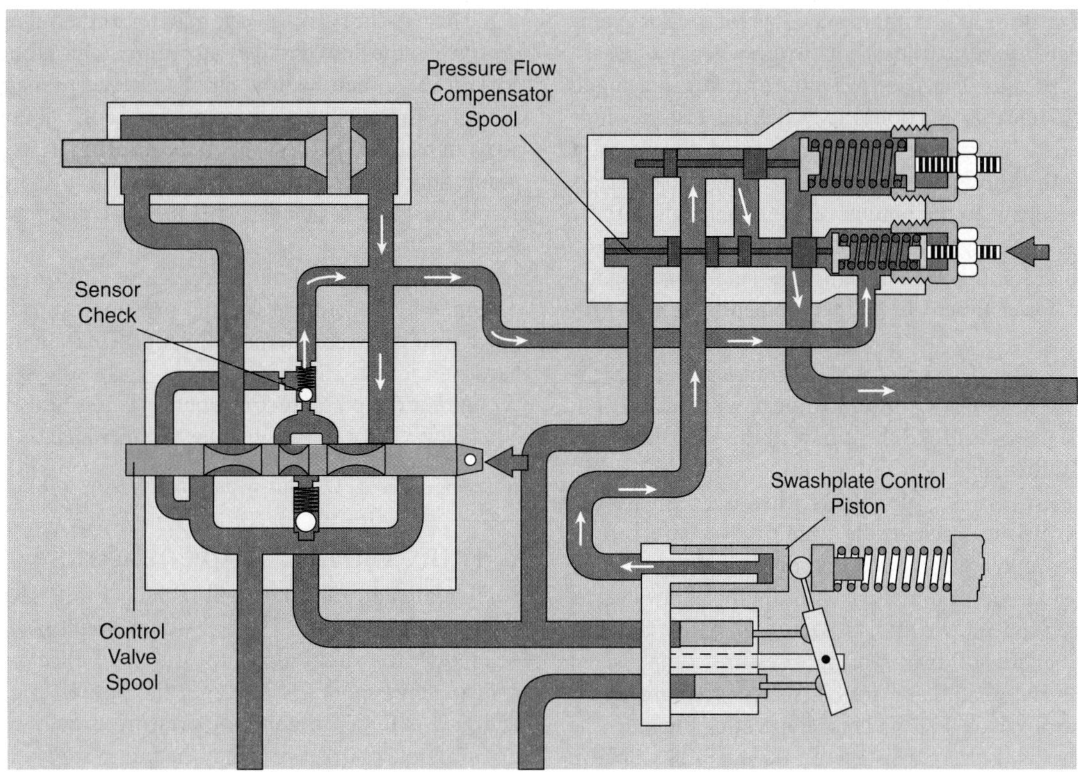

FIGURE 32-14 A variable displacement pump controlled by a pressure/flow compensator.

spring chamber, where it combines with the spring pressure. This combined pressure moves the spool to allow oil to be metered to the pump control piston. See **FIGURE 32-14** for a variable displacement pump controlled by a pressure/flow compensator.

Most axial piston pumps will have two pistons that control the swashplate: a bias piston and a control piston (sometimes called an actuator piston). When the pump is at rest and not turning, the bias piston and spring will keep the swashplate at maximum angle. As the machine is started and the pump turns, it immediately begins to pump oil. If the control valves are in neutral, this flow is blocked and then pressure rises. This pressure is sensed in the control valve load-sense passages and sent to the pump control valve, where it enters the chamber that is opposite of the spring chamber for the load-sense spool. Once the spring pressure is overcome (200–450 psi), the spool shifts to allow oil flow out of the control valves and into the actuator piston for the pump swashplate. The actuator piston is usually twice the diameter of the bias piston so that it can overcome the combination of the bias piston and bias spring. This will move the pump's swashplate and adjust the pump flow to give just enough flow to overcome the margin spring setting.

The result of pump flow in this condition is standby pressure. Standby pressure will be the pressure the pump flow creates when the directional control valve is in neutral and the pump is destroked. Standby pressure will be the pressure setting of the flow compensator valves spring, and the result is that the pump creates just enough flow to overcome any internal leakage. Standby pressure will make the system more responsive when moving a control lever from neutral. See **FIGURE 32-15** for an axial piston pump with a pressure compensator valve.

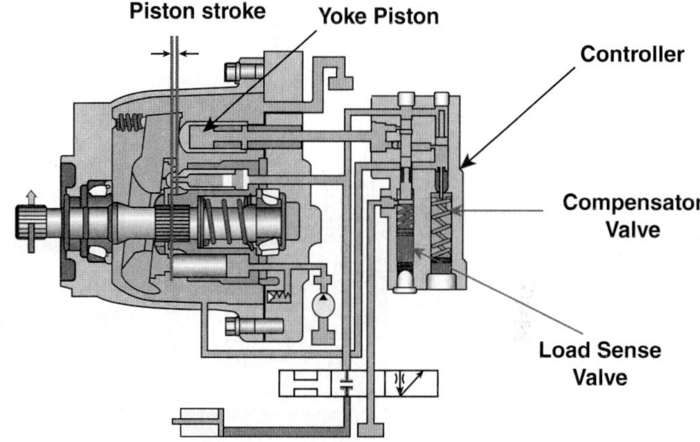

FIGURE 32-15 Axial piston pump with a pressure compensator valve.

Now that the pump is turning and its flow is creating standby pressure, it is ready to **upstroke**. As soon as the operator actuates a directional control valve to actuate a cylinder or motor, the pump flow will be able to go and do some work. The circuit pressure will now rise based on the resistance in the circuit. At this point, there needs to be a load-sensing system to control the pump flow based on what the circuit demands are.

An additional pump control that appears on some machines is called a torque-limiting compensator. In operation, most pumps will be required to produce only high flow at lower system pressure or lower flows at maximum system pressure. For example, if you think of how a backhoe loader works when it is trenching, the highest pressure is needed when the operator is trying to fill the bucket. While this function is activated, there isn't a whole lot of flow needed. Then once the bucket is filled, the operator will want to get the bucket out of the trench, swing it to one side, dump it, and return it to the bottom of the trench. All of these actions would require high flow and low to medium pressure.

There are instances where high flow and pressure are needed at the same time, but this combination is not very common.

A **torque limiter** will prevent a high-pressure and high-flow demand on the pump at the same time. It will sense output pressure and start to destroke the pump as the pressure starts to get close to either high flow or high pressure. Since hydraulic horsepower is pressure × flow/1,714, then if a reduction of either of these can be reached, the prime mover size can be reduced to save initial machine cost and operating costs. To see a variable displacement piston pump with a pump control valve, including torque control, see **FIGURE 32-16**.

Another benefit of load-sensing pressure-compensated systems is the fact that there are consistent pressure drops across the control valves. This will make operating the machine much easier because of the consistent feel the operator will have regardless of the amount of oil flow moving past the directional control valve spool.

The pressure drop always equates to the value of the spring pressure in the flow/compensator spool. This is because past the control valve there will be circuit or load pressure and before the valve there will be pump pressure. For example, if the load pressure is 2,000 psi and the margin spring is 300 psi, then the pump flow will create 2,300 psi. This will give a pressure drop across the valve of 300 psi. This pressure difference will always stay the same.

This contrasts with an open center and fixed displacement system, which will have varying pressure drops based on how much flow is directed across the spool. This will make the valves harder to actuate smoothly.

A reduced pressure drop equates to less heat loss and higher efficiency as proven by the following formula:

$$\text{BTU/hour} = \text{psi drop} \times \text{flow} \times 1.5.$$

Circuit Flow Compensator

Some main control valves will include a flow compensator for each section or circuit. The individual circuit flow compensator will reduce the pump supply pressure to the section's directional control valve spool. By reducing the pump supply pressure, it will also maintain a constant pressure drop across the directional spool regardless of what the pump supply is. This means the actuator speed is more dependent on spool movement and not just pump flow.

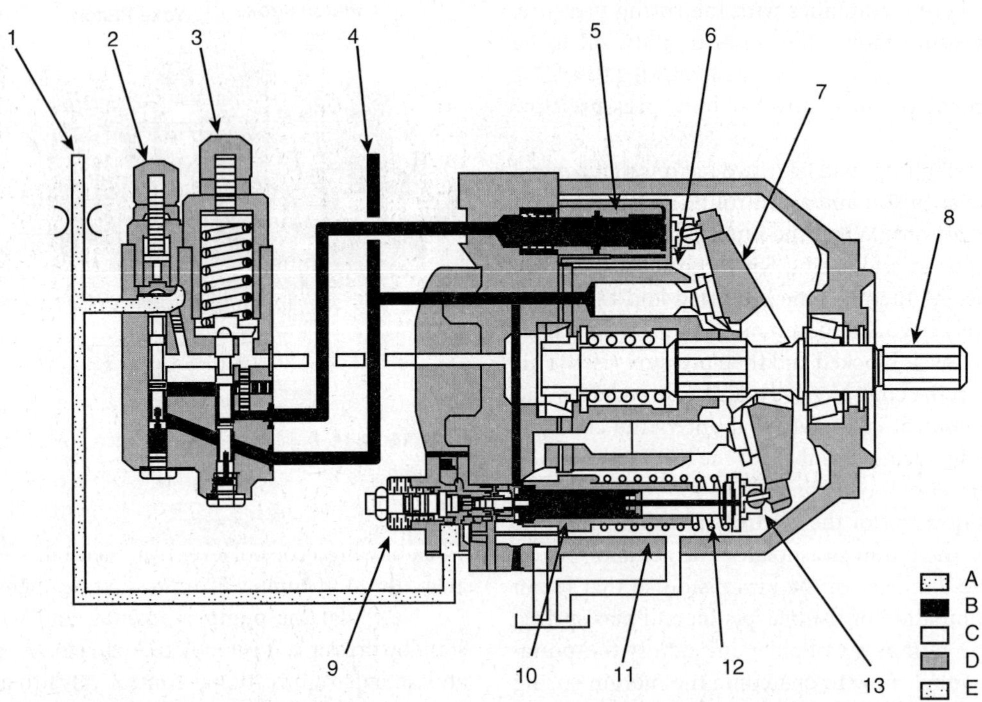

FIGURE 32-16 Pump with torque control.

Image Provided As Courtesy of John Deere.

It does this by having load-sense pressure added to the spring pressure on one side of a spool and the pump supply pressure on the opposite end of the spool. Therefore, the pressure drop across the spool is maintained at the value of the spring pressure. An example of this pressure is 50–100 psi. This compensator action will result in an actuator movement that is smooth and predictable.

Some flow compensators will meter flow after it leaves the directional control valve spool. When the pump can supply the total flow demand for all circuits, the circuits will not slow down. When the pump cannot supply the flow demand, the flow is divided proportionally between the activated circuits. The active circuits will move at a slower rate of speed because of the reduced flow of oil in each circuit.

This metering of pump flow between circuits in high-demand conditions is done with flow compensator valves for each circuit. The compensator valve meters pump flow after it leaves the spool and then directs it back past the spool to the work port for the circuit. See **FIGURE 32-17** for a directional control valve with a flow compensator.

Circuit Pressure Compensator

A pressure compensator could be located in each of the main control valve sections, before the control valve spool. The pressure compensator regulates the oil flow rate passing through the spool so that the differential pressure in the circuit before and after the spool is kept constant.

This will reduce the effort needed to move the directional control valve spool and lower the pressure drop, which lowers the heat generated. Less heat generated equates to higher efficiency.

▶ Hydraulic Pilot Controls

K32005

One of the first advances to make hydraulic systems easier to operate was the addition of **pilot controls**. Mechanically actuated directional control valves inherently require a higher amount of physical effort to move the valve spools and can cause operator fatigue. Pilot controls eliminate much of this manual effort.

Pilot controls use a low-pressure and low-flow system that is controlled by hand levers or foot pedals manipulated by the operator, and they will in turn control the machine's main high-pressure and high-flow system. This is similar to an electrical circuit that uses a relay to control a high current circuit with a low current circuit.

As flow volumes increase across a directional control valve spool, flow forces acting on the spool become harder to overcome. The result of these increased forces means that levers have to be longer in order to gain a mechanical advantage strong enough to move the spool. The result again is increased operator fatigue, which in turn leads to lost productivity. See **FIGURE 32-18** for a comparison of manual controls versus pilot controls for a backhoe.

Pilot oil systems overcome this problem by using hydraulic pressure to directly move the main directional control valve spools.

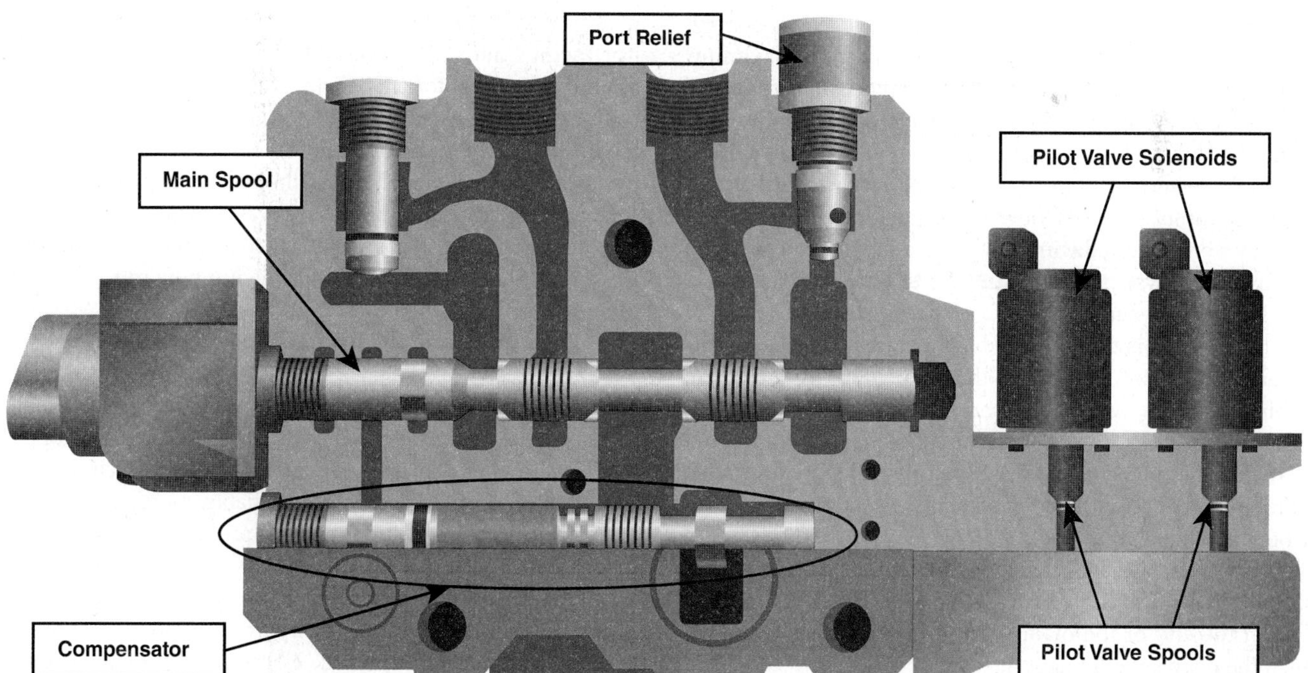

FIGURE 32-17 Directional control valve with a flow compensator spool.

Image Provided As Courtesy of John Deere.

FIGURE 32-18 Manual versus pilot controls.

Pilot control systems have the operator joysticks control **poppet valves**, which get supplied low-pressure (a maximum of 300–400 psi) oil from a dedicated pump or from oil that is diverted from the main system and reduced in pressure. See **FIGURE 32-19** for a cross section of a pilot control valve. Pilot system oil pressure is limited by a pilot oil relief valve that will be able to dump excess oil flow to the tank, or it can be controlled by a pressure-reducing valve that is supplied oil from the main hydraulic system. See **FIGURE 32-20** for a schematic of a dozer hydraulic system that uses a pilot oil system.

This pilot oil is then metered by operator-controlled poppet valve movement and sent to the main control valve of the machine, where it acts on the end of the main control valve spools to shift them. The distance the spool moves is in proportion to the amount of pressure that is acting on it. The resistance on the spool that creates this pressure is the centering spring on the opposite side of the spool.

When the joystick is returned to its neutral position, spring force will return the poppet valve to neutral. This will drain the oil from the end of the main spool, and the spring force will return the main spool to neutral.

The pilot oil system supply can also be used for other functions, such as releasing brakes, running a fan motor or an air-conditioning compressor motor.

▶ Purpose and Fundamentals of Electronically Managed Hydraulic Systems

K32006

Electronically managed hydraulic systems have been in use on MORE machines for a number of years now. Improvements in electronic component design and manufacturing and in the need to increase efficiency in hydraulic systems have made the integration of electronics into hydraulic systems commonplace in today's machines. An electronically managed hydraulic system uses an ECM to manage or control hydraulic functions and operator input used as one of several inputs. System monitoring is also managed by the ECM. The ECM compares the input signals to stored information and produces output signals to control electrohydraulic devices like pumps and valves.

▶ TECHNICIAN TIP

Electronically managed hydraulic systems can also be called electrohydraulic systems. The term indicates a hydraulic system that combines the use of electronic components. For the remainder of this section, the term "electrohydraulic" will be used.

"Electrohydraulic" is a general term that could include any hydraulic circuit that uses electrical components. However, a more specific way to define the term is to say that it is a hydraulic system that includes electronic components such as ECMs and sensors, as well as operator inputs like electronic joysticks that are inputs to the system controller.

Before electrohydraulic systems became popular, hydraulic systems relied on the operator to control and monitor them. Controlling a basic hydraulic system relies on the operators' senses (touch, hearing, and smell) to provide feedback from the system. Sounds from the engine and pump, feeling from the controls, and smells of hydraulic leaks or overheated components would hopefully trigger a reaction to change operation before there was a major problem. This of course relied on the operator to pay attention to warning signs and to be experienced in knowing how to react in case of a problem.

Older, non-electrohydraulic systems were also not very efficient. A lot of fluid flow was wasted, which put unnecessary loads on the prime mover. The prime mover would have to be oversized to compensate for this, which increased operating costs (higher fuel and maintenance costs). Machine owner demands for more efficient, more reliable, more powerful, and easier to operate hydraulic systems pushed manufacturers to incorporate electronics into hydraulic systems.

This is a natural progression for hydraulic systems since it provides a way to include the hydraulic system with the rest of the machine's multiplexed, electronically controlled systems. There are many benefits of this integration: allowing the hydraulic system to create fault codes, allowing technicians to monitor live pressures and flows for diagnostic and

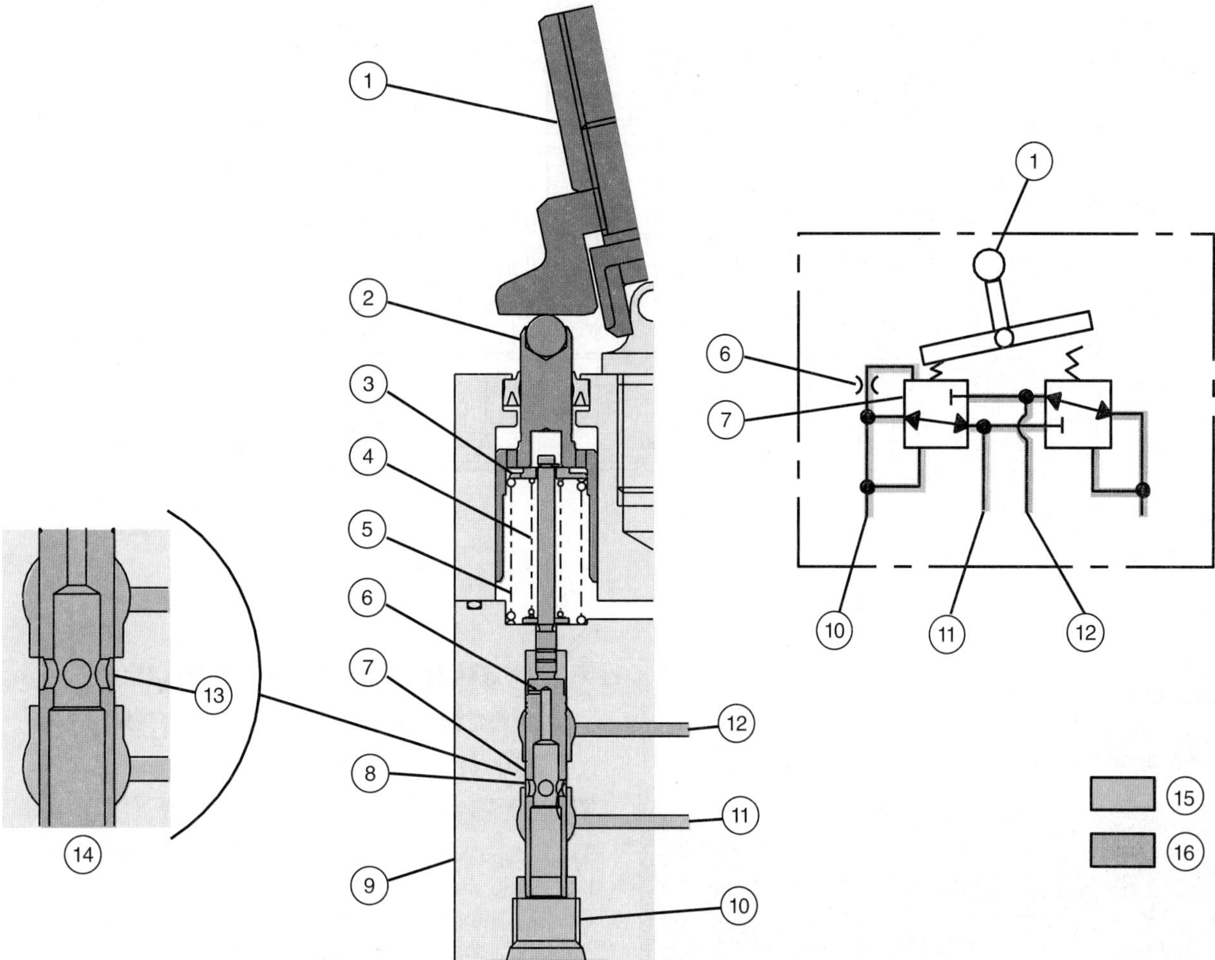

FIGURE 32-19 Pilot control valve.

Image Provided As Courtesy of John Deere.

calibration procedures, allowing the engine to react quickly to changing hydraulic loads, allowing the system to learn how the machine is typically operated, and allowing operators to tailor the system to work most efficiently within the typical operating conditions. See **FIGURE 32-21** for two machines of the same size: the first with no electronics and the second with an electrohydraulic system. There would be several distinct differences between these two machines: The newer machine would be quieter, easier to operate, more fuel efficient, more powerful, and more comfortable for the operator. However, it would be more complex, and problems would not be as easy to diagnose without a laptop computer. There would also be no direct feel for the hydraulic controls for the operator.

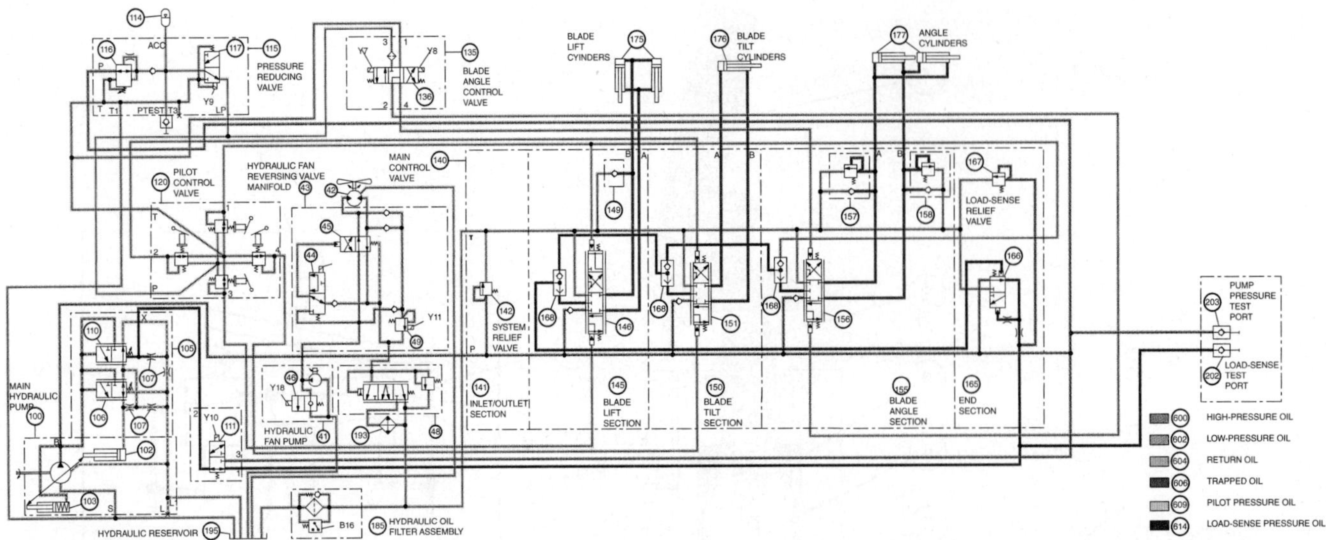

FIGURE 32-20 Dozer hydraulic system.

Image Provided As Courtesy of John Deere.

FIGURE 32-21 Two machines of the same size: the first with no electronics and the second with an electrohydraulic system.

> **TECHNICIAN TIP**
>
> A true electronically managed hydraulic systems will be completely "fly by wire." This term comes from the aviation industry when airplanes first used pilot controls that were simply inputs to an ECM and the ECM actually controlled the functions that made the plane fly.

▶ Principles of Operating Electronically Managed Hydraulic Systems

K32007

The main electrical/electronic components of an electrohydraulic system are the controller (ECM); pressure, flow, temperature, and position sensors; operator inputs, such as electronic joysticks, engine speed control, and work mode switch; and ECM outputs, such as solenoid-operated pump control, electrically actuated directional control valves, operator display, and variable relief valves. All of these components are connected together with wires and connectors.

A wide variety of information can be gathered by input sensors and operator controls. This information is processed by the ECM and compared to stored programming data (software). The ECM will then control the pump output with an electronic signal and control directional control valves by energizing solenoid valves. See **FIGURE 32-22** for an example of inputs, the hydraulic controller, and outputs for a skid steer loader.

Electrohydraulic systems will be part of the machine's complete electronic system. This means that all sensor information can be shared with other machine ECMs, such as engine, powertrain, braking, and any others that may be part of the machine's **CAN (controller area network) system.** See **FIGURE 32-23** for how a hydraulic controller is part of a machine's CAN system.

One example where shared information can benefit the overall machine operation is during a cold start. The engine ECM will see that the hydraulic fluid temperature is –20°C, for example, and will keep the engine in a derated condition until the hydraulic fluid temperature reaches –10°C. Pump damage could be prevented by having the engine derated, and if the same machine didn't have this feature, it would be up to the operator to perform a recommended warm-up procedure before putting the machine to work. This likely wouldn't

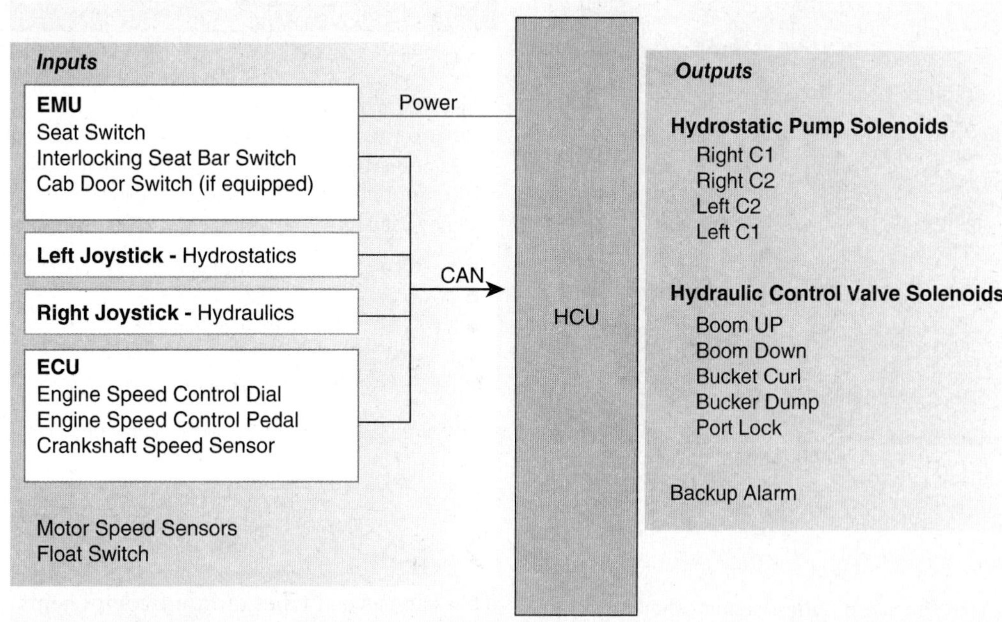

FIGURE 32-22 Inputs, outputs, and hydraulic controller for a skid steer loader.

Image Provided As Courtesy of John Deere.

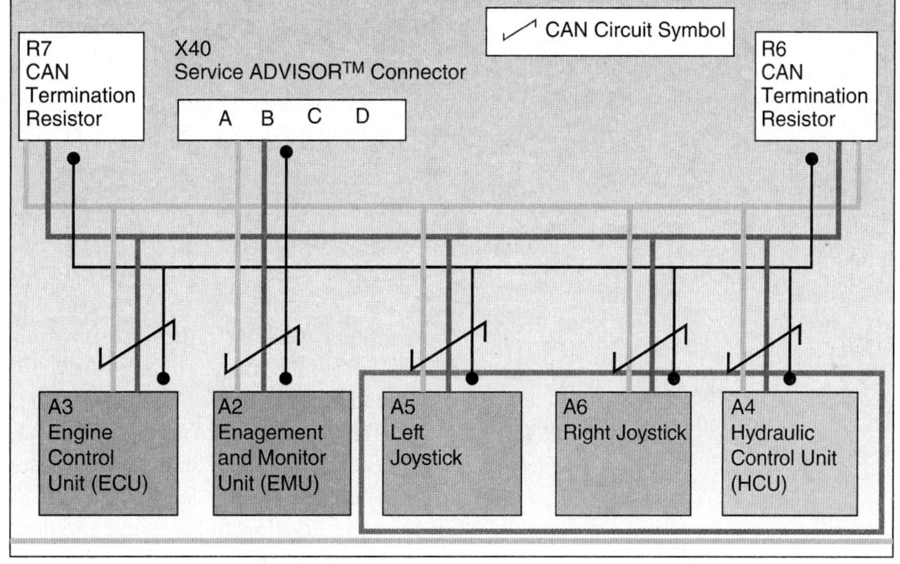

FIGURE 32-23 How a hydraulic controller is part of a machine's CAN system.

Image Provided As Courtesy of John Deere.

happen, and component damage risk would increase greatly. See **FIGURE 32-24** for a technician repairing a dozer in extreme cold conditions.

▶ TECHNICIAN TIP

One manufacturer currently produces an excavator that incorporates a hydraulic hybrid system into its swing circuit. This system includes an electronic control and monitoring system that makes the hybrid operation seamless and invisible to the machine operator.

During swing braking in a non-hybrid machine, the circuit is closed by the main control valve spool and oil pressure rises to open a relief valve, where it then returns to the tank. This creates a braking effect and slows the rotation of the upper structure of the machine. To capture the energy of this normally wasted fluid, the hybrid system uses this fluid to charge a set of accumulators. Once the accumulators have been charged, the pressurized fluid can be sent to the swing circuit when the machine starts to swing again. This reduces the load on the engine since it doesn't have to drive a pump to supply this fluid.

The following section looks at the individual components of an electrohydraulic system.

Electrohydraulic Controller

The controller is also commonly called the **ECM (electronic control module)** and can be considered to be the brains of

FIGURE 32-24 A technician repairing a dozer in extreme cold conditions.

the system. It performs the same duties as any other machine ECM in that it will gather information from sensors, process this information, and compare it to stored programming. It will then send out electrical signals to actuators. If you read Chapter 18, you should recognize this arrangement as the ECM inputs, information processing, and signal outputs.

Similar to home computers and the computers most of us carry around in our pockets, the ECMs found on today's machines have computing speed and power that is exponentially greater than ECMs of only a few years ago. During this time, their physical size has shrunk as well. Some hydraulic systems will have multiple controllers, and some valves will have controllers mounted directly to them. See **FIGURE 32-25** for a controller for an electrohydraulic system.

Electrohydraulic controllers will be part of the machine's CAN system, which will usually have at least four ECMs (engine, transmission, hydraulic, and machine) and possibly eight or more that are connected together with a data link. This electronic network allows communication between ECMs and the sharing of sensor information.

FIGURE 32-25 A controller for an electrohydraulic system.

▶ TECHNICIAN TIP

ECU, ECM, or other?

Different manufacturers will have different names for the electronic control devices they use. Whatever the term, they all more or less perform the same function of processing information from inputs and sending out command signals to outputs. The following are common terms that could be used for control modules:

- ECU—electronic control unit
- ECM—electronic control module
- HCM—hydraulic control module
- PCM—powertrain control module
- CCU—chassis control unit.

From here on, the term *ECM* will be used when talking about a machine's electronic control unit.

Inputs

There are several types of **input components** that can be part of electrohydraulic systems, such as sensors, switches, joystick controls, and touch screens. These different inputs can deliver different types of signals to the hydraulic ECM, such as analog, digital, and PWM (pulse-width-modulated) type.

Sensors

Sensors send a variable signal to an ECM. This could be any type of changing condition, such as position, temperature, speed, fluid level, or pressure. See **FIGURE 32-26** for a variety of sensors.

The follow are some examples of sensors the ECM will need information from:

1. Engine speed sensor needs to be monitored because much of the purpose of an electrohydraulic system is to keep the engine working in its ideal rpm and power range.
2. Pump outlet and circuit pressure will also need to be measured and reported to the ECM. The load-sensing feature of an electrohydraulic system needs to have system pressure monitored.
3. There could be oil temperature sensors in one or more areas. These may be needed to allow the ECM to decide whether it should allow full pressure and flow if the system oil is too hot or too cold.

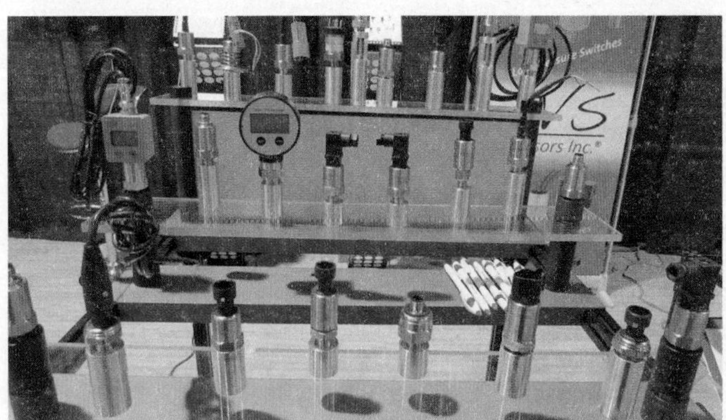

FIGURE 32-26 Various types of sensors.

4. Hydraulic tank oil level sensors are needed to alert the operator of low oil levels, because if the level is critically low, it could derate or even put the machine into a shutdown condition.
5. Position sensors could be needed to convert the operator inputs (levers or pedals) to an electronic value to the controller. They can also be used to tell the controller where the actuators are in their travel. For example, a loader boom sensor will tell the controller when the boom is close to the ground during a boom lower function so that it can slow the boom down. Some cylinder position sensors can be inside the cylinders to give an accurate indication of rod position.
6. Speed sensors could be used to monitor motor speeds of rotary actuators. See **FIGURE 32-27** for a Hall-effect speed sensor.

Switches

There will likely be several switches that are controlled by the operator: auxiliary flow control, work mode settings, engine speed control, a switch to disable pilot oil, and others.

The switches could be separated on an armrest or dashboard or combined into a keypad within arm's reach of the operator. See **FIGURE 32-28** for an operator display with switches.

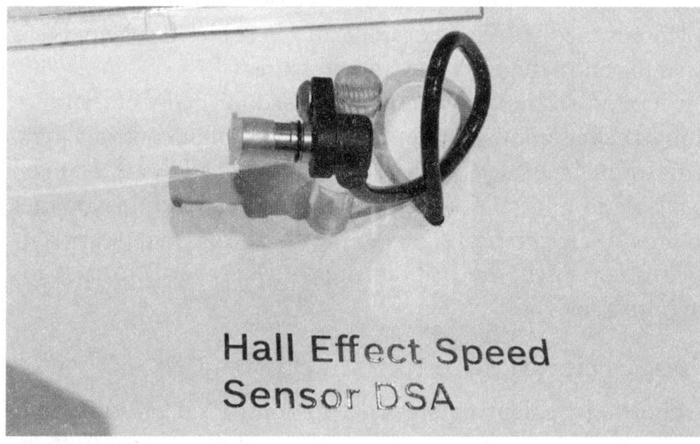

FIGURE 32-27 Hall-effect speed sensor.

FIGURE 32-28 Operator display with switches.

Joysticks and Pedals

The main electrohydraulic inputs for operator controls are joysticks and pedals. These operator-controlled devices will produce electrical signals that are sent to the ECM via the CAN network. Electronic controls eliminate mechanical or pilot controls and greatly reduce the number of moving parts.

Joysticks can be simple potentiometer-type, two-axis devices or multi-function controls with switches and thumbwheels included. For example, graders without steering wheels will have a pair of joysticks that can control up to five functions each. See **FIGURE 32-29** for the joystick for a grader.

Pedals that are part of an electrohydraulic system can control a variety of different functions, such as track travel, engine rpm, and auxiliary functions. Pedals are usually connected to a potentiometer, which will send a variable signal to the ECM dependent on pedal position. See **FIGURE 32-30** for a pedal used for an electrohydraulic system.

Display Screens

Newer machines may have touch screens that can display information and be used as an input by the operator or technician to influence the electrohydraulic system. Operators can use it to switch modes of machine hydraulic function, and technicians can use it to display electrical values when diagnosing a problem. See **FIGURE 32-31** for a touch screen.

FIGURE 32-29 The joystick for a grader.

FIGURE 32-30 A pedal used for an electrohydraulic system.

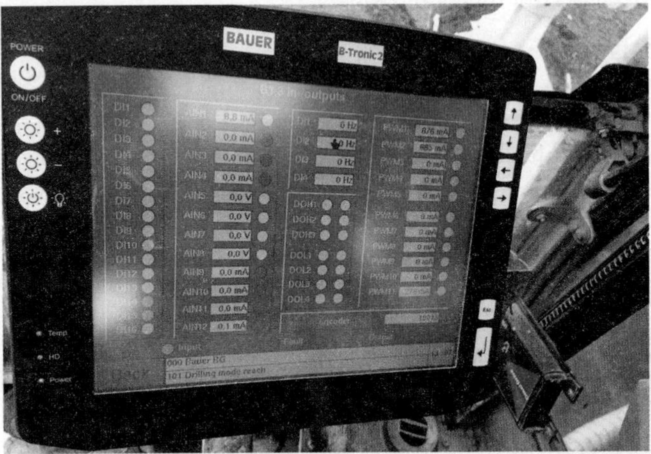

FIGURE 32-31 Touch screen.

Outputs

Electrohydraulic system **outputs** are used to control system flow and pressure. They can also be electronic signals to other ECMs and/or machine displays. Main control valve spools can be actuated with pilot oil that is controlled by proportional solenoid valves. These valves get an electrical signal from the ECM based on operator inputs, engine operating conditions, and stored programming.

Many main control valves will have pilot oil pressure applied the ends of the spools at all times. This pressure, along with spring pressure, keeps the spool centered. To move a spool, the ECM will energize a solenoid on the opposite end of the spool, which will open a passage to tank.

Pump controls are electrically controlled in electrohydraulic systems by using **proportional solenoid valves**. See **FIGURE 32-32** for an electrohydraulic main control valve with proportional solenoids.

On/Off Solenoid Valves

Simple low-flow and low-pressure circuits could use on/off solenoids to control pump oil flow to an actuator and return its oil back to the tank.

FIGURE 32-32 An electrohydraulic main control valve with proportional solenoids.

They will have a coil of wire that gets energized from an ECM, which will create a magnetic field that pulls a spool plunger into the solenoid body. When this happens, the spool opens passages in the valve body that it is part of. The passages allow oil to flow as described above. When the coil is deenergized, there will be a spring to return the spool to its normal position.

These valves could also be used to send pilot oil to one end of a main control valve spool. In this case, there will be a pair of solenoids used. This is an example of where on/off solenoids are used to control higher flows and pressures.

On/off solenoids could also be used for many other functions, such as allowing pilot oil to flow to pilot control valves. This would be a safety feature that would not allow any oil to be available to pilot oil joysticks until certain conditions are met to provide an electrical signal to the on/off solenoid (seat occupied, door closed, seat belt done up, etc.). See **FIGURE 32-33** for an on/off solenoid.

Proportional Solenoids

Proportional solenoids are used to control oil pressure and/or flow based on a pulsed electrical signal that is sent to them from an ECM. They can be found as part of main control valves,

FIGURE 32-33 An on/off solenoid.

pump control valves, and distributed control valves. When the signal is pulsed on and off quickly, the output from the driver is called a PWM signal.

A proportional solenoid will have a plunger that is held in either a normally closed or a normally open state by a spring. When the solenoid's coil of wire is energized with a PWM signal, it will become a magnet that will move the plunger. The amount of movement of the plunger will be determined by the amount of current sent to the solenoid, so these valves are infinitely variable.

A PWM signal is a series of on-and-off voltage pulses that are varied by a transistor. The frequency of the signal can range from 400 to 5,000 Hz. The amount of on-time versus off-time will determine the amount of current sent to the coil and the strength of the magnetic field, which will determine how far the coils plunger travels. See **FIGURE 32-34** for a piston pump with proportional solenoids.

▶ TECHNICIAN TIP

There are three terms that you may hear when electrohydraulic systems are being discussed. The terms "hysteresis," "dither," and "stiction" are likely unfamiliar, so an explanation of each follows:

Hysteresis

In electrohydraulic control systems, a certain result is expected from a certain input, and the same input may produce two different results, depending on whether the input level increases or decreases. This difference is the hysteresis. For example, a 500 mA signal to a proportional solenoid valve may produce 100 psi. If it changes to 1,000 mA to give 200 psi and then is reduced to 500 mA again, the result may be 105 psi. The 5 psi difference is hysteresis. Electrohydraulic controls have to consider the hysteresis factor of components.

Stiction

When a spool valve or plunger is stationary, it wants to stay stationary. This is called stiction. Many electrohydraulic controls will slightly pulse an electronic signal to the valve actuator to slightly oscillate the valve to prevent stiction.

Dither

A solenoid valve is made to oscillate slightly in order to prevent the spool it is controlling from sticking or to reduce stiction.

FIGURE 32-34 Piston pump with proportional solenoids.

Deere/Husco-Distributed Valve System

An example of a true, complete, multiplexed electrohydraulic system is the latest generation of John Deere backhoes that feature the TMC-distributed valve system (TMC stands for total machine control).

The operator inputs for the hydraulic system consist of a pair of joysticks that are electronic inputs to an ECM that is part of the joystick assembly. Each backhoe cylinder has an electronically controlled valve assembly mounted directly to the cylinder. Each valve has an ECM mounted directly to it. The valve assembly has four proportional solenoid poppet valves that are ECM controlled to give almost infinite control of oil flow to the cylinder. These valve assemblies have a pump supply and tank return line to route oil to and from them.

This system relies on the software programmed into the ECMs to make the cylinders function as requested by the operator's joystick inputs. See **FIGURE 32-35** for a Deere backhoe with TMC.

▶ Excavator Hydraulic Systems

K32008

Excavators are popular and versatile machines that were once fairly simple machines, with regard to hydraulics. However, they have become increasingly complicated in an effort to make them more efficient, more powerful, faster, and easier to operate. Most excavators produced today will have either a full electrohydraulic system or a combination of a conventional hydraulic system and an electrohydraulic system. This section of the chapter will focus on the main hydraulic functions of a modern excavator, particularly electrohydraulic features.

Excavator hydraulic systems have some unique features that should be highlighted. The main functions or circuits of an excavator are boom, stick (sometimes called arm), bucket, swing, and travel. Smaller excavators will typically feature a blade and a boom swing function as well. Most excavators will also have at least one auxiliary circuit for an attachment, like a hammer or swivel bucket. See **FIGURE 32-36** for an excavator with an advanced electrohydraulic system.

FIGURE 32-35 Deere backhoe with TMC.

FIGURE 32-36 An excavator with an advanced hydraulic system.

Any attachment added to a machine can be electronically controlled, usually with a button, trigger, thumb wheel, or pedal. The flow and pressure limits for the attachment can be preprogrammed either through an interactive display in the cab or by connecting a laptop computer.

A typical medium to large excavator (a machine of 15 to 90 tons) will have two high-flow main pumps that supply the oil flow to the main circuits mentioned above and a third pump to supply oil to a pilot system or an auxiliary function. If the third pump instead supplies an auxiliary function, then a fourth pump will be needed to supply pilot oil. Smaller excavators with blade, boom swing, or auxiliary functions will need a third pump to supply these circuits and a fourth pump for pilot oil, or they could use a pressure-reducing valve for pilot oil. See **FIGURE 32-37** for the main pump assembly for a medium-sized excavator.

The main pumps will each be dedicated to specific circuits, but there will be control valves that will allow both pump flows to combine for certain circuit conditions. An example of this is for the boom-up function when the machine is trenching and two pump flow is desired to get the bucket out of the trench quickly.

Pump control valves can get signals from different sources, and different manufacturers will call these sources different things. Many pump control valves now are electronically controlled to give the ECM full control of pump displacement.

There are different sources of oil pressure that will act on the pump regulator valve spools:

Pump output oil from the main control valve—for some systems, pump oil will normally flow through a passage in the main control valve. This oil will be sent to the pump control valve through an orifice. If one of the main control valve spools is moved, the oil pressure to the pump control valve is decreased, and this will upstroke the pump. This oil pressure is proportional to the amount of oil sent to a function. The increase or

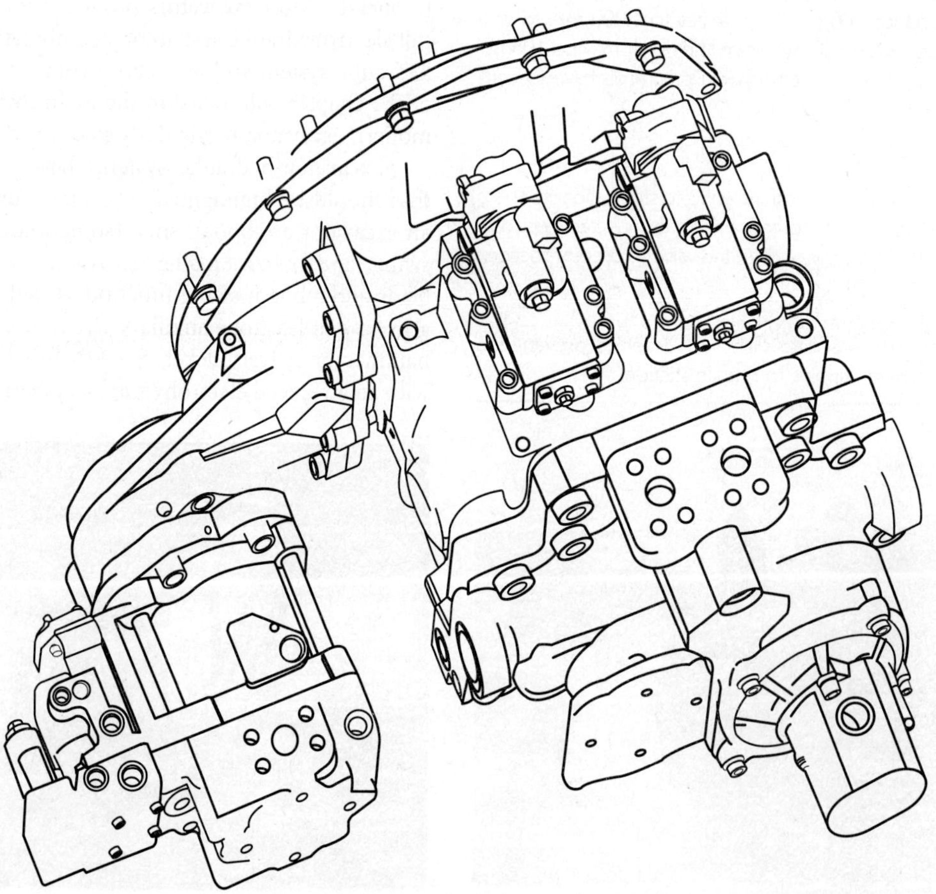

FIGURE 32-37 Pump assembly for a medium-sized excavator.
Image Provided As Courtesy of John Deere.

decrease of this oil pressure will shift a spool in the pump control valve. The spool shifts in order to direct oil to the actuator piston or drain it away. This will move the actuator piston and change the pump output.

Average pump outlet pressure—for an excavator that has two main pumps, it is critical that the pump control system considers the output of both pumps. This is done with a set of orifices and check valves. This pressure also moves the pump control valve spool in order to direct oil to the actuator piston or drain it away.

Solenoid-controlled engine speed sense oil—the hydraulic/engine controller will have an engine speed sensor as an input. One of its outputs, based on engine speed and programmed memory, will be a voltage signal to a proportional solenoid. This solenoid will allow oil to be sent to the pump regulator valve or will drain it away. This is another way of regulating the pump output based on engine speed.

Even though both pumps operate independently, there is a limit to how much horsepower one pump can take: usually 85% of the available engine horsepower.

A typical pump control valve will send oil pressure to an actuator piston that is mechanically controlling the displacement of the pump with a linkage attached to the piston. If the pump is an axial piston type of pump, it will have an actuator piston either control swashplate movement directly or control it through a linkage. If it is a bent axis type of pump, the actuator piston will connect to the cylinder block with a pin. As the actuator piston moves, so does the swashplate or cylinder block, which will change the output of the pump.

Here's one example of how a pump control valve works in an excavator: To change the pump output, oil will be directed to the actuator piston from the pump control valve. A linkage connected to the actuator piston will pivot on a pin with the other end of the link, moving a spool or sleeve over a spool that is part of the pump control valve. This will give the spool some feedback from the swashplate. See **FIGURE 32-38** for a cross-sectional view of an excavator pump assembly.

Pump control valves that are part of electrohydraulic systems can have position sensors that send a signal back to the ECM to tell it where the valve spool is. The sleeve is moved by the actuator piston to close off a drain passage to keep oil trapped behind the actuator piston until another part of the regulator valve either adds more oil or drains it.

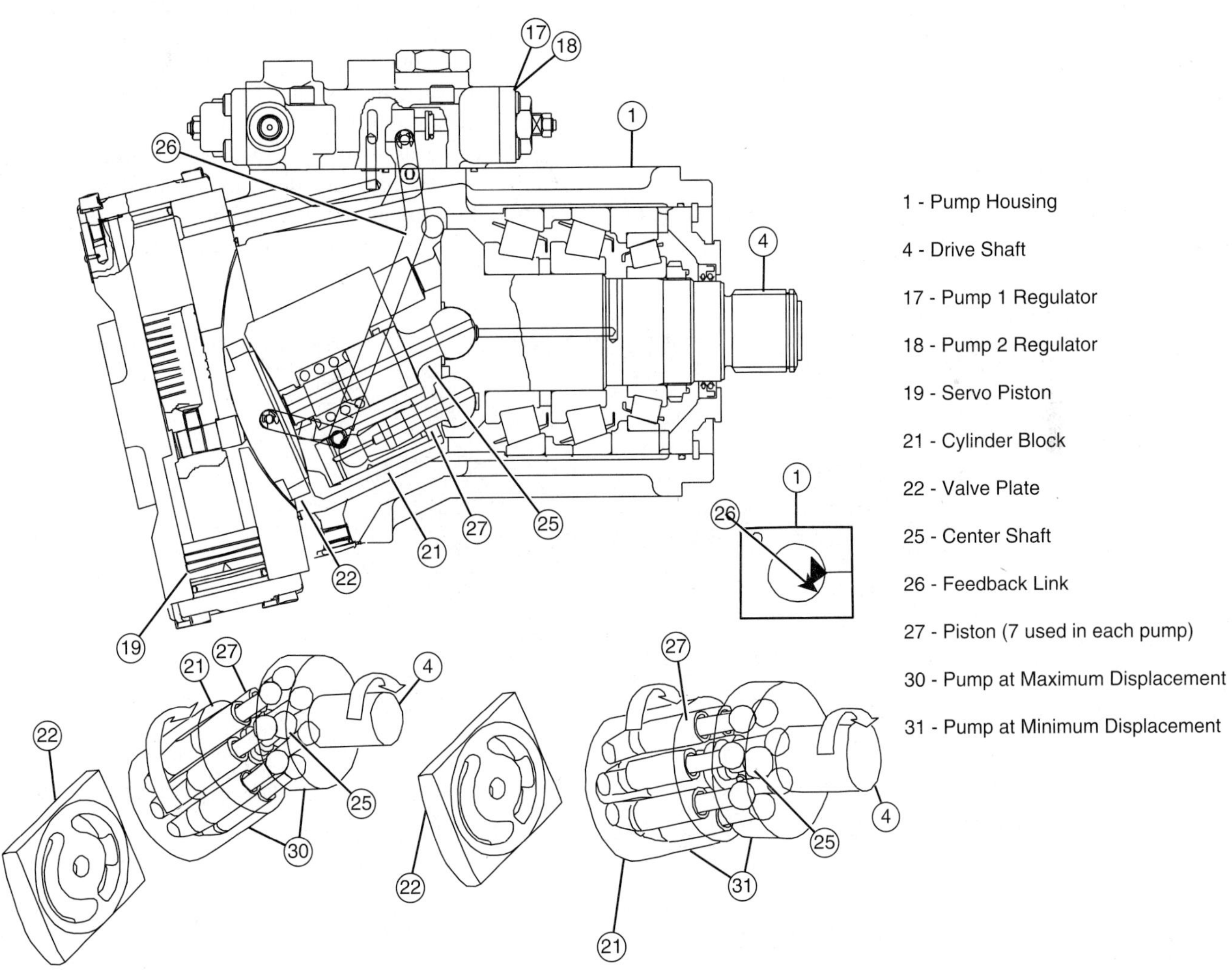

FIGURE 32-38 Cross-sectional view of excavator pump assembly.

Image Provided As Courtesy of John Deere.

The goal of the pump control system is to make the pump(s) supply just enough oil to meet system demands and to limit the amount of oil output of the pumps so the engine doesn't go into a lug condition. This is done by monitoring engine speed, operator input, pump output pressure, and pump displacement with sensors. Pump control valves can have one or two spools that are moved by oil pressure and direct oil to the pump displacement actuator. See **FIGURE 32-39** for a cross section of a pump control valve. See **FIGURE 32-40** for an exploded view of the actual valve.

Any pump control valve will always be in one of three states:

1. Upstroking—changing the pump to a higher displacement. See **FIGURE 32-41** for the pump control valve in an upstroking state.
2. Downstroking—changing the pump to a lower displacement.
3. Constant flow—metering oil pressure to the pump displacement actuator to maintain a steady pump flow.

An example of how an excavator's pump control system will keep its prime mover in its most efficient rpm range follows: a medium to large excavator will typically have an engine that operates most efficiently in a speed range of 1,900 to 2,000 rpm. If the hydraulic load increases and starts to drop the engine rpm to close to 1,900, then the pump controls will destroke the pumps to lessen the load on the engine. The engine rpm will then increase to 2,000, and the pumps can then upstroke to supply more oil if the operator wants to. In real time, as the machine is working, this upstroking and destroking action is taking place constantly and quickly to meet flow demands and to keep the engine from lugging.

Excavator Main Control Valve(s)

A typical arrangement for excavator main control valves is to have one pump supply a five-spool main control valve and have the other pump supply a four-spool main control valve. The five valve spool will supply one travel motor, auxiliary circuit, stick cylinder, boom combiner valve, and swing motor. The four valve spool will supply the other travel motor, bucket cylinder, boom cylinders, and stick combiner valve. See **FIGURE 32-42** for a typical main control valve arrangement.

There are many other features/circuits that a hydraulic excavator could have as part of its hydraulic system. The following are a few examples.

Combiner Valves

The combiner circuits are activated to enable both pumps to supply oil for high-flow circuits, like the stick and boom. There will be an extra spool, which will be activated based on extra movement of the joystick, which creates a higher pilot oil pressure.

Regeneration Circuits

Some excavator functions will move with the force of gravity faster than the pump can supply oil to them. When this happens, there is a possibility of cylinder cavitation: a destructive force that can damage components. The cylinder is also not in control, which is a safety concern.

A regeneration circuit allows the return oil from a cylinder or motor that would normally be directed to the tank to be sent to the opposite side of the cylinder piston. An example of this is when an excavator has its stick extended with the bucket in the air and the operator wants to bring the stick in. The cylinder needs to extend, which will require a large volume of oil. Since the pump can't supply the required oil fast enough, gravity will try to pull the stick and bucket down, which could create a void in the cylinder and cause a cavitation condition.

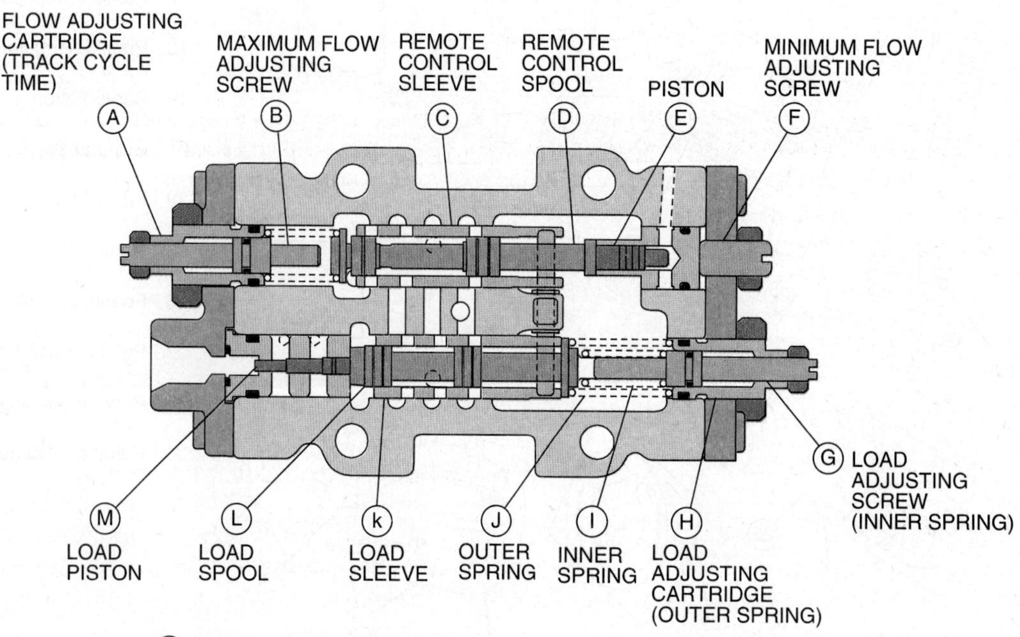

FIGURE 32-39 Cross section of pump control valve.

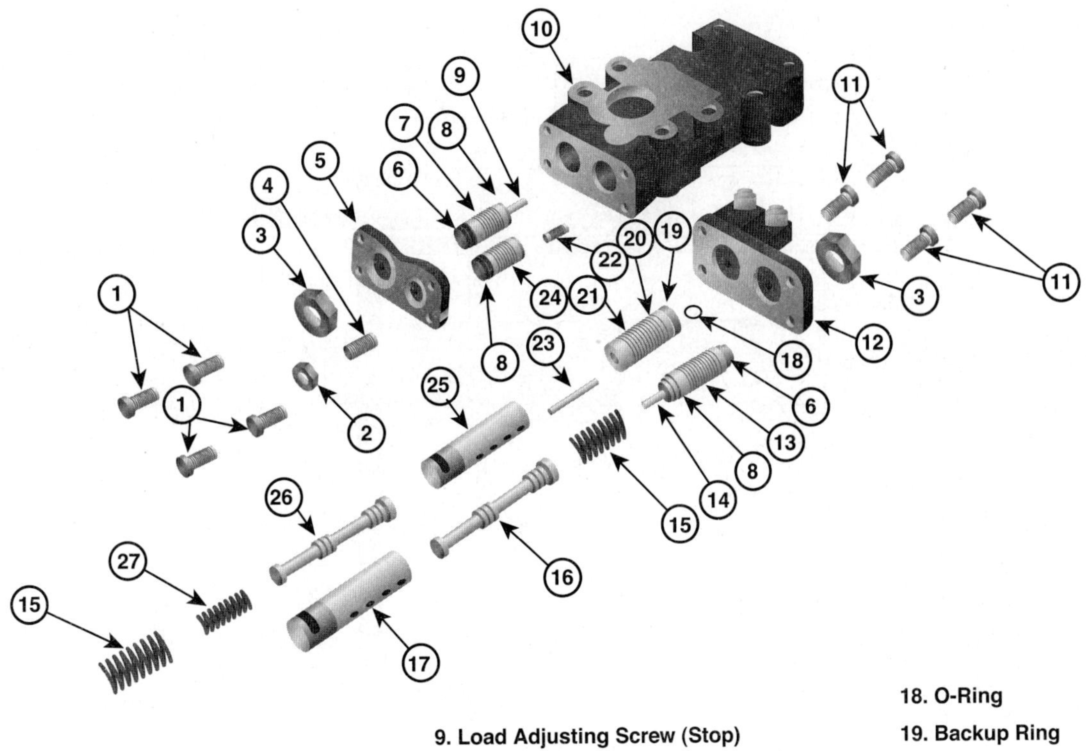

1. Cap Screw (four used)
2. Nut
3. Nut (two used)
4. Minimum Flow Adjusting Screw
5. Cover
6. Nut (two used)
7. Load Adjusting Cartridge
8. O-Ring (three used)
9. Load Adjusting Screw (Stop)
10. Regulator Body
11. Cap Screw (four used)
12. End Plate
13. Flow Adjusting Cartridge
14. Maximum Flow Adjusting Screw (Stop)
15. Spring (two used)
16. Remote Control Spool
17. Remote Control Sleeve
18. O-Ring
19. Backup Ring
20. O-Ring
21. Cylinder
22. Piston
23. Load Piston
24. Cylinder
25. Load Sleeve
26. Load Spool
27. Inner Spring

FIGURE 32-40 Exploded view of actual valve.

Image Provided As Courtesy of John Deere.

The regeneration valve will combine the oil leaving the rod end of the cylinder with pump supply oil to give the required volume that is needed to prevent cavitation.

A regeneration circuit could be part of the main control valve spool or the spool could be used in combination with an electrically controlled solenoid valve. Regeneration circuits can also be used to supply oil from one circuit to another under certain conditions. For example, when an excavator is booming up and moving the stick in the rod end, oil from the boom cylinders can go to the stick cylinder head end in combination with pump oil. See **FIGURE 32-43** for a regeneration circuit schematic.

Auxiliary Circuits

Excavators can have many different attachments put in place or in addition to their bucket, such as hydraulic hammers, swivel buckets, tampers, thumbs, and wood chippers.

There will be an extra spool valve in the main control valve that will likely be shifted with pilot oil and controlled electrically. The operator will start this function operating with a button, trigger, or foot pedal. Some machines will have an electronic auxiliary flow controller that can be used to match pump flow to the attachment's flow requirements.

There will be hoses and lines from the main control valve to shutoff valves and quick couplers that are used to connect to the attachment.

Straight Travel Function

Many excavators will have a feature that will allow the operator to easily make the machine travel in a straight line if another circuit is activated. Normally, each travel motor is fed oil from one of the main pumps. If another function is activated while the machine is traveling, there would be a decrease of flow to one travel motor, which could make the machine turn. The straight travel function will dedicate one pump to drive both motors to prevent an unwanted turn if there is another circuit activated.

Work/Power Modes

Most excavators produced today will feature operator-selectable hydraulic power modes. There are usually three or four different

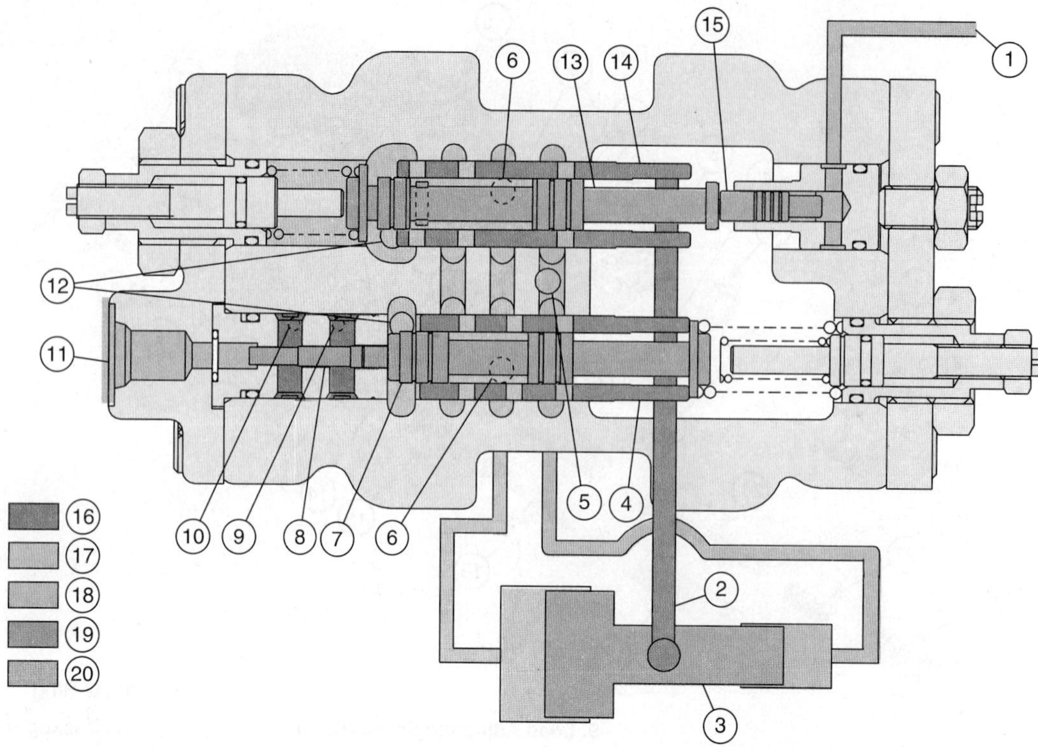

1 - From Pump 1 or Pump 2 Flow Rate Pilot Valve (SA or SB)
2 - Feedback Link
3 - Servo Piston
4 - Load Sleeve
5 - Pilot Oil Inlet
6 - To Large End of Servo Piston
7 - Load Spool
8 - Load Piston
9 - Pump 1 Pressure Inlet
10 - Pump 2 Pressure Inlet
11 - Torque Sensing Port
12 - Return to Pump Housing
13 - Remote Control Spool
14 - Remote Control Sleeve
15 - Piston
16 - Supply Oil
17 - Pilot Oil
18 - Flow Rate Valve Pilot Oil
19 - Torque Sensing Pilot Oil
20 - Return or Pressure-Free Oil

FIGURE 32-41 Control valve in an upstroking state.

settings that the machine can work in. If the machine has selectable power modes, the operator could choose a power mode to match the type of job being done. If the machine is working in light-soil conditions, it won't need full hydraulic power. If the machine is being used for heavy lifts, then it will likely have a dual stage main relief valve that will get shifted to increase the maximum system pressure, and the pump flow will be limited. See **FIGURE 32-44** for an excavator working mode control.

These modes could also prioritize different circuits to get more pump flow than others. If there is a need to swing the machine a lot, then a swing priority mode could be chosen to give more flow to the swing circuit.

Backup Modes

If the machine has a major problem with its hydraulic/electronic control system, there needs to be a way to keep the machine running to enable the operator to get the machine off the jobsite or just out of the way.

Most excavators will have a backup or limp-home mode that bypasses the normal operation of the electronic control system to allow the engine to provide just enough power to drive the hydraulic system so that the machine can be moved. There will likely be one or more switches that the operator needs to move to change into backup mode.

Overload Warning

An excavator is sometimes used for lifting heavy objects. For example, if it is being used on a sewer and water main job, it will typically dig a trench and then place a length of pipe as it is going. There may be pressure sensors that will alert the operator to overload conditions.

Auto Idle

Most of today's excavators feature a function called auto idle or a similarly named system designed to save fuel, reduce noise, and increase engine life when there is no demand for a hydraulic

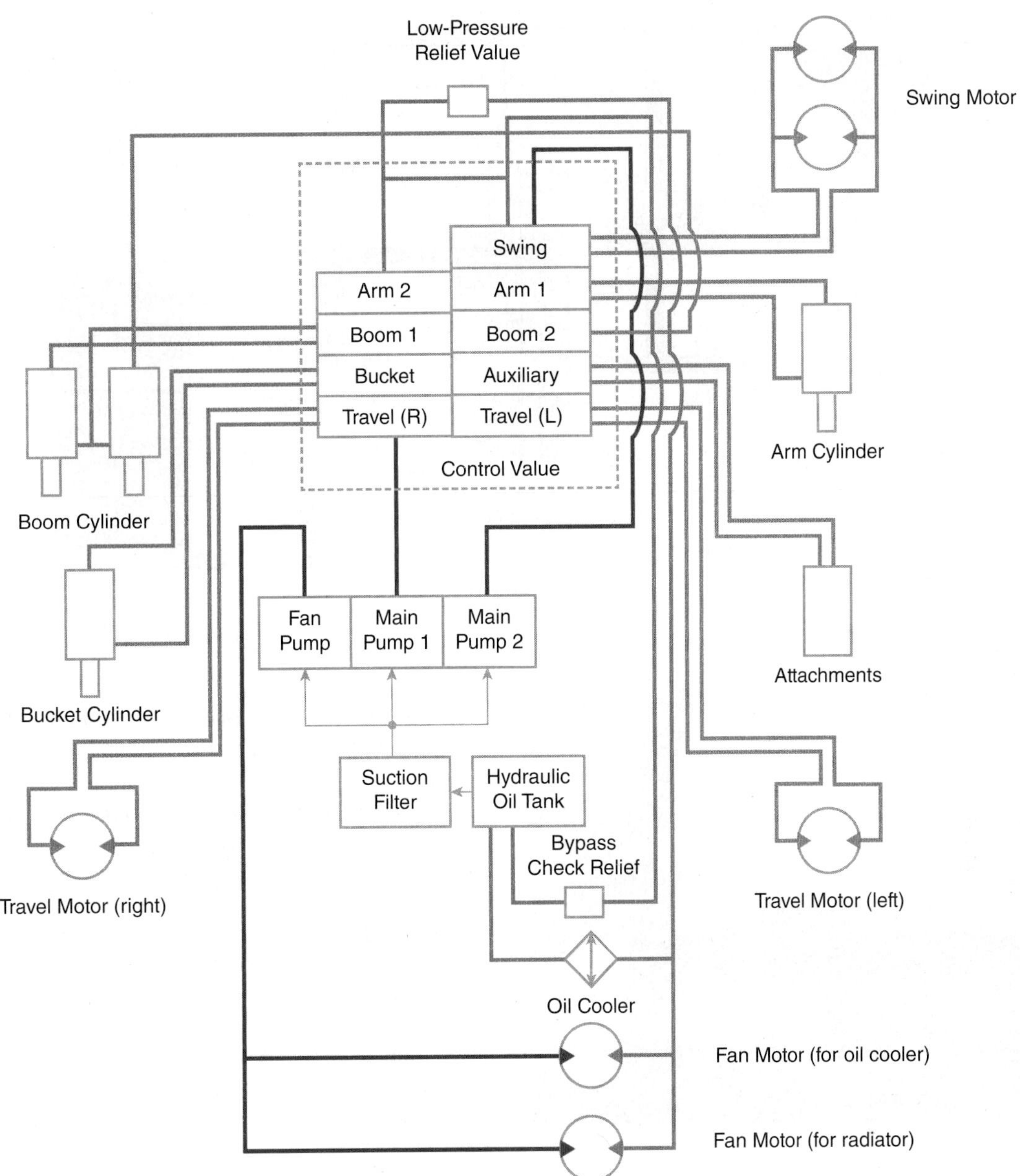

FIGURE 32-42 A typical main control valve arrangement.

Image Provided As Courtesy of John Deere.

system. This is a feature that will detect when the hydraulic system is not being used for a few seconds and automatically reduce the engine speed.

Most of these systems will operate by having a pressure sensor in either the pump outlet, the main control valve, or the pilot oil system to detect when the system pressure drops to a minimum value. This pressure sensor or switch will send a signal to an ECM, which will then send a signal to the engine fuel system control. This will reduce engine speed to save fuel. When there is an increase in pressure, the engine rpm will raise to where it originally was, and then the machine will work as it was.

Swing and Travel Circuits

Excavators use motors for both travel and swing circuits, and these circuits will likely have a couple of unique valves in them. Both motors will likely incorporate brakes, which will need a brake release valve and circuit. The motors could be one of several designs and may be dual displacement to give a two-speed function. Smaller excavators could use cam lobe motors or bent axis motors, while medium to large excavators could use bent axis or axial piston motors. Most large excavators will use two swing drives, each with its own swing motor. See **FIGURE 32-45** for a swing motor for a large excavator.

Makeup valves are required in travel and swing circuits to eliminate the ability of the load to overcome the pump flow capacity. In other words, if an excavator is traveling downhill, there would be a tendency for the machine to freewheel out of control. The pump flow could not keep up to the travel motor flow requirement and a cavitation condition would occur. This would mean the operator could not control the machine travel speed, which would be a huge safety concern. In this

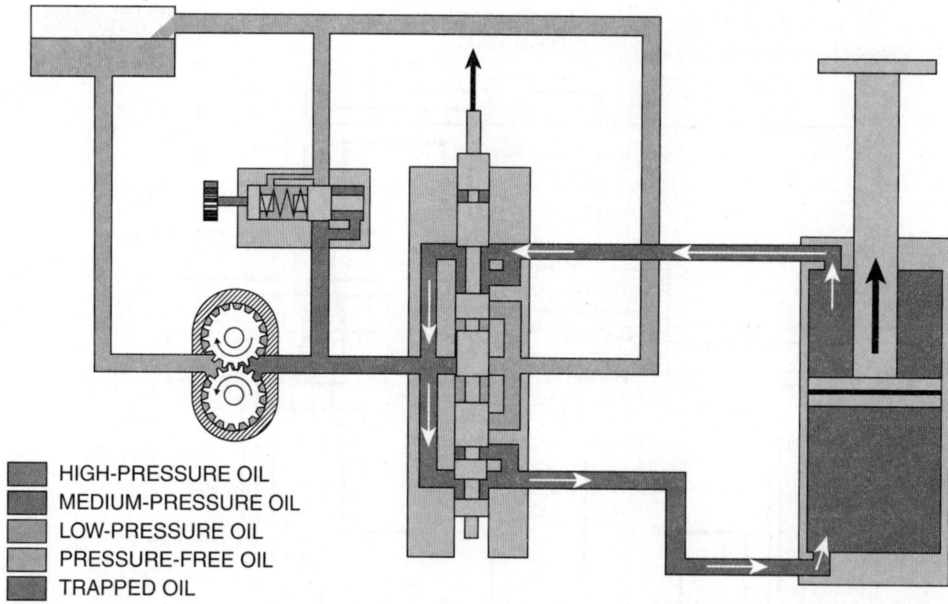

FIGURE 32-43 Regeneration circuit schematic.

Image Provided As Courtesy of John Deere.

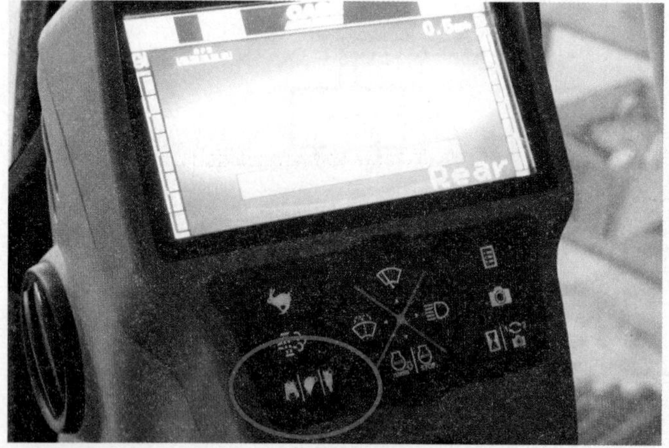

FIGURE 32-44 An excavator working mode control.

FIGURE 32-45 Swing motor for a large excavator.

valve, a spring will hold a poppet closed and be assisted by the pressure that builds on the outlet of the loaded actuator. The poppet stays closed until enough pressure is built up to overcome the spring pressure. This will mean the actuator will move only if there is pressure applied to the inlet side of the actuator.

Swing circuits will also need crossover relief valves. These normally closed valves will open when the upper structure is in motion and the control lever is returned to neutral. The oil will be trapped in the circuit between the main control spool and the motor. The inertia of the upper structure will want to keep it turning, which is why the crossover relief is needed.

It will open when pressure builds during a swing stop condition and let oil go to the opposite side of the motor to prevent cavitation. This forces oil through an orifice in the relief valve and provides a braking action. This valve will also provide a cushion when starting and stopping a swing function.

▶ Construction Features of Electronically Managed Hydraulic Systems

S32001

The following section will help you identify the construction features of some of the main electrohydraulic components.

CAN Wiring and Connectors

All of the electrical/electronic components in a typical electrohydraulic system need to be connected either with each other, with an ECM, or with both. The integrity of the wiring system that goes along with a typical electrohydraulic system is as important as the components that are connected to it. The wires and wiring harness for an electrohydraulic system need to be secured and protected from damage. Most manufacturers will secure a harness every 12–18 inches, and this requirement should be maintained when repairs are made. CAN wiring consists of either a two-wire or a three-wire group twisted in a continuous spiral formation with a specific number of turns per inch.

Most machine sensors, solenoids, and switches will have 14–18 gauge wires coming out of them that lead to a connector. Some types of different connectors are Weatherpack, Deutsch Transportation (DT), Sure-Seal, Metri-Pack, and Packard.

Connectors will be crimped, soldered, or crimped and soldered to the wire. (Some manufacturers will recommend that wires not be soldered.) Most crimping procedures will require a specific type of crimper to do the job properly, and you should follow the specific instructions for the crimpers you use. One part of the connector will be the male or pin, and the other part will be the female or socket. There will be some kind of seal to prevent dirt and moisture from getting into the mating area and starting corrosion. Special extractor tools are needed to remove wire ends from connector plugs. When the connectors are mated together, they will allow current flow. Connectors could be for a single wire or grouped together with 70 or more wires being secured to the male and female junctions. There will be bulkhead connectors when harnesses go through cab walls or firewalls. See **FIGURE 32-46** for a typical bulkhead wiring connector.

Sensor Construction

Electrohydraulic sensors are a permanently assembled device. When they are found to be defective, they will need to be replaced. Sensors that are exposed to working system fluid (temperature or pressure) will have male threads to fasten them to a component. Typical thread styles include straight thread-O-ring (STOR), NPT, and metric. New O-rings should always be used when installing a sensor, and they should be lubricated prior to installation.

Joysticks and Pedals

There are many variations of joysticks, from simple two-axis (forward/back, left/right) controls to joysticks that could include a third axis (twist clockwise/counter-clockwise) and a wide variety of buttons, triggers, thumbwheels, and paddles. All of these features are part of a position sensor that sends a signal to an ECM. See **FIGURE 32-47** for a joystick that controls the blade functions on a dozer.

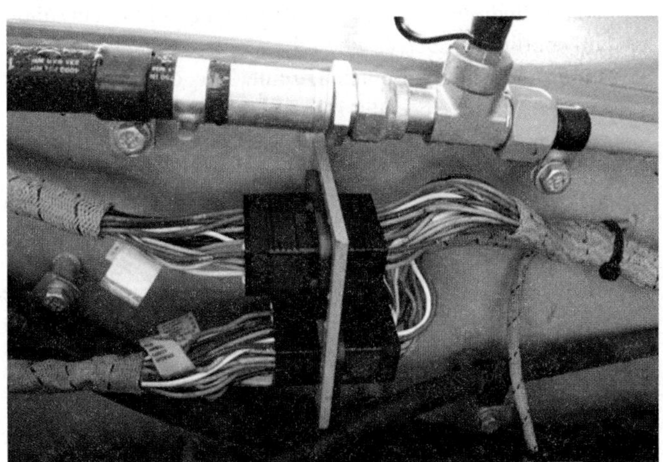

FIGURE 32-46 A bulkhead wiring connector.

FIGURE 32-47 A joystick that controls the blade functions on a dozer.

Some joystick assemblies will even incorporate ECMs in them. They are typically a permanent assembly that must be replaced as a unit if found to be defective. A pedal can be an assembled unit that includes a position sensor or a pedal and separate position sensor. Both joysticks and pedals are connected to the machine's wiring harness with electrical connectors to make them "plug and play."

Pump Control Valves

Due to there being a wide variety of types of pump control valves, it is difficult to describe each one in great detail. Generally speaking, they will have one or two spool-type valves that are moved with oil pressure against spring pressure. They will send oil pressure to an actuator in the pump that adjusts the pump displacement. Spring pressure will be adjustable with either a threaded adjuster or shims. They will need to be sealed with O-rings at several locations to prevent oil leakage. Pump control valves could also have solenoids mounted to them, which could either meter oil flow between sections of the valve or block/allow flow between sections.

Solenoids

Solenoids are an electromagnetic device used to convert current flow into a linear mechanical movement. They can be used for controlling oil flow in hydraulic control and any other strong, short, linear action.

A solenoid is a permanent assembly made up of a coil of wire surrounding an iron core. The iron core (armature) is the movable part or plunger that moves when the coil winding is energized. For solenoids in an electrohydraulic system, the armature is connected to a spool that blocks or allows oil flow between two or more ports.

The armature either pulls in or pushes out depending on the way the current flows through the windings. Solenoids will usually have to overcome spring pressure when they are energized. The spring will reverse the motion created by the magnetic field. One type of solenoid will only travel full distance both ways without stopping in between, which is called an on/off or bang/bang solenoid. This type of solenoid usually has a removable coil and simply slips over the valve assembly. If the coil is defective, it can be replaced separately.

Another type of solenoid is a proportional type. These solenoids are usually used in a hydraulic system where a pressure needs to be varied, such as a pilot oil control system or a pump control valve. Proportional solenoids will receive a PWM signal and will move in proportion to the signal. This type of solenoid is a one-piece assembly. See **FIGURE 32-48** for examples of some proportional solenoids.

Operator displays

All machines produced today that have an electrohydraulic system will have an interactive operator display. This means there will be a way to retrieve and display information related to the machine systems, including its electrohydraulic system. It could also provide a means to adjust system parameters, such as flow and pressure limits for auxiliary circuits.

Some displays will incorporate an ECM into them. Other displays will have a series of push buttons to navigate through the menus and enable system value adjustments. Yet other displays will be touch screens that require using a finger to navigate and enter inputs. But they will all be a sealed assembly with no serviceable internal parts, which means any defect they have will necessitate replacement. See **FIGURE 32-49** for a dozer's operator display.

FIGURE 32-48 Examples of some proportional solenoids.

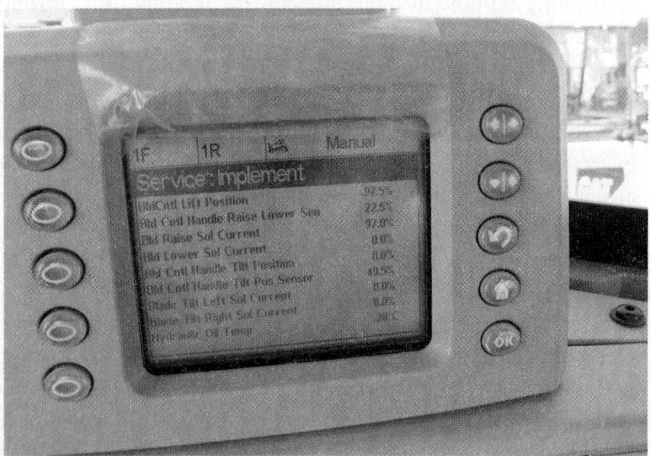

FIGURE 32-49 A dozer's operator display.

Inspect, Test, and Diagnose an Electronically Managed Hydraulic System

S32002

Just like all other machine systems, electrohydraulic systems will at some point require the attention of a MORE technician. This will result from one or more operator complaints of poor performance:

- slow—one function or entire system
- weak—one function or entire system
- cylinder drifting
- overheating hydraulic fluid
- hydraulic fluid won't warm up
- unusual noise
- excessive vibration
- one or more functions or entire system not operable.

Troubleshooting an Advanced Hydraulic System Problem

Troubleshooting an advanced hydraulic system problem isn't really any different than trying to solve problems with other systems. A systematic approach needs to be taken to efficiently troubleshoot an advanced hydraulic system problem.

You should first verify the operator complaint. This may require you to get familiar with how the machine is supposed to work unless you are already knowledgeable about the machine. This could mean reading the operator's manual or asking someone who is familiar with the machine how it should normally work. The best information source will be the most current service information for the exact machine you are working on. Referring to machine service information from similar machines could lead to misdiagnosing the problem. The key point is that you won't be able to know whether there is a problem if you don't know how the system is supposed to work. At this point, you should also determine that there are no other hydraulic system problems and try to define whether the problem is with only one part of one circuit, one complete circuit, or the complete system.

Many hydraulic system problems will only occur under certain conditions, such as when the oil is a certain temperature or when there is a load on the circuit. This can be difficult to replicate at times, especially if the machine is at the shop and not on the jobsite.

Advanced Hydraulic System Inspection

Once you understand the system and can verify that there is a problem, you should then perform a visual inspection, which for any hydraulic system problem will include the following:

1. Check for external leaks.
2. Check the hydraulic fluid level, the visual appearance, and the temperature (it should be clear and have no foam).

3. Check for damaged hydraulic components (bent cylinder rod, dented tank, crushed tube, and/or hose damage).
4. Check for fault codes. If a machine has an operator display that will show diagnostic information, you should access this and record any related fault codes or any other related information, such as pressures, flows, and ECM input/output values.

Now since you know the problem and know the system, you should be able to put together a list of possible causes for the problem. Most service information manuals will have a diagnostic troubleshooting process that should be followed. The list of possible causes can then be prioritized in order of the easiest and quickest to be tested first and the hardest and most difficult tested last.

Hydraulic System Problems

There are five common types of problems that are possible when dealing with hydraulic systems. The root cause of most of these problems is often system contamination.

Low or High Pressure

If an operator complaint is related to the lack of force a hydraulic circuit has, this directly relates to the pressure or lack thereof in the circuit. An example of a typical operator complaint would be that the machine's bucket won't fill as easily as it used to.

It is rare that a MORE technician will receive a complaint that leads to a high-pressure problem. However, if the prime mover rpm is lower than it should be or implements are being repeatedly damaged, there could be an excessive pressure problem.

Inadequate or Excessive Flow

If an operator complaint is related the slow speed of an actuator, this is a lack-of-flow problem. A simple saying summarizes this: "Flow makes it go." There is a possibility of an excessive flow problem wherein functions are jerky and hard to control.

Excessive Fluid or Component Heat

Hydraulic systems transfer energy to either heat or motion. If too much heat is being created, it is likely a result of a loss of motion, and if the hydraulic oil cooling system can't manage this excessive heat, the system will overheat. Problems with the hydraulic cooling system will also cause an overheating condition.

Leakage

External leaks are usually obvious, but what isn't obvious is that contamination can enter the system if fluid can leak out. Internal leaks aren't so obvious, but keep in mind that fluid takes the path of least resistance. Many components will seal oil internally, and if this seal is compromised, then an internal leak will occur. This could show up as a cylinder drift, excessive pump or motor case drain flow, or an overheated system. See **FIGURE 32-50** for a hydraulic leak.

Noise and vibration

Hydraulic systems will create a certain amount of noise and vibration due to oil flow and pressure pulses. Some hydraulic systems will use an attenuator on the pump outlet to reduce pump pulsations. As components wear, there may be an increase in noise and/or palpable vibrations.

FIGURE 32-50 A hydraulic leak.

> ▶ TECHNICIAN TIP
>
> When working on advanced hydraulic systems, you may need to open the system, which might lead to a hydraulic fluid leak. You must do everything possible to avoid contaminating the environment with hydraulic fluid. There is environmentally friendly hydraulic fluid available that can be used to reduce the impact of hydraulic leaks.

Hydraulic System Testing

The testing procedures for hydraulic system troubleshooting will likely require some special tools. Proper diagnosis of problems cannot be accomplished if the proper tools aren't available and aren't used properly.

> SAFETY TIP
>
> When testing advanced hydraulic systems, you will be tapping into hot hydraulic fluid that has the potential to seriously injure or kill you. You need to be aware of this potential and take steps to protect yourself and others from this hazard. Use only recommended pressure gauges, fittings, hoses, and flow meters to perform testing. Any adapter fittings needed for hooking up test equipment must be certified to handle the system pressure applied to them. If you are handling test equipment that has high pressure and/or flow in them, be aware of the potential for serious injury if it failed.
>
> If testing requires you to operate a machine in a shop, ensure that the machine's engine is adequately ventilated and that all other personnel are kept out of the danger area surrounding the machine.

Most tools for testing hydraulic systems are precision instruments that should be handled with care and stored properly. The following tools are for hydraulic testing.

Pressure Gauges

Pressure gauges can be either analog or digital. See **FIGURE 32-51** for a variety of analog pressure gauges.

You should be aware of the normal operating pressure and maximum system pressure of the system you are about to test and use the appropriate gauge so that you don't damage gauges or connecting hoses/fittings. The maximum working pressure of the system should be 75% of the maximum pressure of the gauge. You will be measuring pressures from a negative pressure to 7,500 psi.

Unless a gauge indicates it is showing pressure in psia, you should assume the pressure you read is adding atmospheric pressure—which is called psig, or psi "gauge." This will matter only for lower pressure readings. In other words, if the gauge reads 75 psi and it's an absolute gauge, the pressure is 75 psi minus the atmospheric pressure at that location and elevation. If there were no markings on it, then the pressure would be considered to be a psig gauge, and therefore the reading would actually mean 75 psi plus 14.7 psi.

The easiest way to think of this is if you have two gauges—one that reads absolute and the other psig—and you were standing on a beach beside the ocean on a summer day, the absolute gauge would read 14.7 psi and the other one would read 0 psi.

Analog gauges will have a curved tube (Bourdon tube) inside that will try to straighten out as the system pressure is applied to it. As the tube moves, it will turn a gear rack that will move a pinion gear, which will mechanically move the gauge's needle. The needle will move according to how much pressure is applied to it. Ideally, an analog gauge should be selected so that the needle will be in the 10 o'clock to 2 o'clock position for the pressure range being tested.

Digital pressure gauges consist of pressure transducers and a display unit. The transducers will have test pressure applied to them and convert this pressure into a variable electrical signal. The transducer sends this signal to the display unit through a wire. The display will then give a readout in psi or kPa on the display. There are three different pressure ranges of transducers that can be used, which are identified by colors: blue—500 psi; red—5,000 psi; and orange—10,000 psi. Always use a transducer that is rated for a pressure higher than the system pressure. Digital pressure meters can be used to easily give pressure differentials between two pressure sources. This is a common test for measuring margin pressure on a variable displacement pump. See **FIGURE 32-52** for a digital pressure gauge transducer and display.

FIGURE 32-51 A variety of analog pressure gauges.

FIGURE 32-52 Digital gauge and transducer.

Digital pressure meters are safer to use because the display unit has no pressurized oil in it. One downfall of them is that if the pressure fluctuates, it may not be able to give an accurate reading. An analog gauge would be better suited for this task. Calibrating pressure gauges on a regular basis will give you confidence that the pressure you are reading is accurate. Most gauges are accurate within 2%.

Flow Meters

Flow meters are used to measure the rate of oil movement through a hose or tube. This is usually measured close to the pump outlet, but they could be used anywhere in a circuit. Depending on the unit, they can measure 1–1,000 gpm and can withstand pressures of several thousand psi.

There are a few variations of flow meters. Some are simple mechanical inline meters used to measure flow through the meter. These are relatively inexpensive and robust units that don't require any additional hardware. However, they are unidirectional and not highly accurate. This type of simple flow meter uses magnetism to show flow by having a disc move according to the amount of flow, and the disc then magnetically moves a follower that has a line on it. When the line matches with a scale on the outside of the flow meter, it indicates the amount of oil flowing through the flow meter.

Some are equipped with an adjustable restriction that can be used to put a load on the pump. This will increase system pressure and is a true test of how the pump will operate in a working system. The flow meter reading with this type of unit

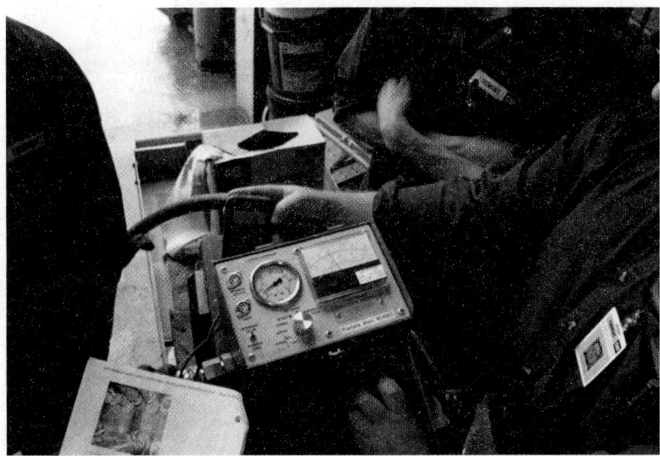

FIGURE 32-53 A flow meter with an adjustable restriction.

will be compared to specifications that will give a minimum amount of flow at a certain pressure. As the pressure increases, the flow will decrease. This type of flowmeter will have a burst disc to protect the unit and connecting hoses from rupturing if the flow is restricted too much. See **FIGURE 32-53** for a flow meter with an adjustable restriction.

Other flow meters will measure flow with a turbine wheel that generates an electrical signal sent to a digital readout.

Test Fittings and Hoses

You may need a variety of test fittings and/or hoses to connect gauges and flowmeters. You must be sure the threads match and that any type of seal used is compatible with system fluid type and pressure levels. Always check for leaks on any test fittings before pressure, flow, and temperature levels rise. See **FIGURE 32-54** for a kit with test fittings and gauges.

Stopwatch

A typical test for a hydraulic function is to measure how fast a cylinder rod cycles. A digital stopwatch is necessary to measure these speeds, in what are called measuring cycle times. You can also test the speed of a rotary actuator with a stopwatch.

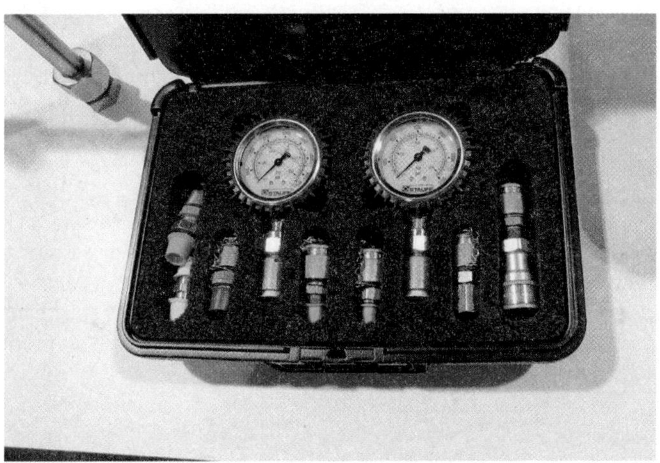

FIGURE 32-54 A kit with test fittings and gauges.

Tachometer

Hydraulic motor speed may need to be measured and a digital tachometer can be used to do this. A good digital tachometer can also measure length and velocity which may be useful for checking cylinder rod speed.

Portable Hydraulic Hand Pump (Electric or Air)

Some problems can be diagnosed with a "porta-power" by applying pressure to a component and seeing if it will hold pressure. This is called leakage testing. This type of pump can also be used occasionally to release parking brakes.

Temperature Probe or Heat Gun

A critical condition of hydraulic fluid is its temperature. A thermocouple adapter connected to a multimeter is a valuable tool to measure this with. The probe needs to be placed in the hydraulic fluid, so caution needs to be taken if the tank is pressurized and because the oil can get hot enough to cause severe burns. Most hydraulic systems will have oil coolers that are needed to regulate oil temperature. To check temperature drop across the oil cooler, an infrared heat gun can be used for this.

Some problems, like failed cylinder seals, can be detected with a heat gun by checking along a cylinder barrel and looking for abnormal temperature changes. A failed seal is similar to an orifice, and if oil flows through an orifice, it will generate heat. See **FIGURE 32-55** to see an infrared heat gun.

Testing and Adjusting Advanced Hydraulic Systems

There are some common testing and adjusting procedures that may need to be occasionally performed to keep advanced

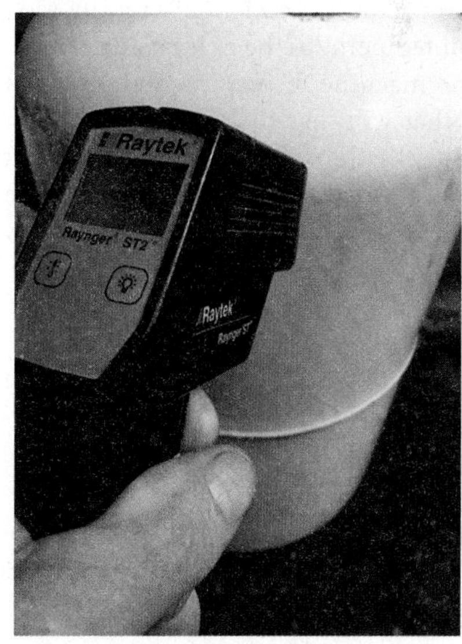

FIGURE 32-55 An infrared heat gun.

hydraulic systems running at their most efficient level, producing the necessary flow and pressure, and being responsive to the operator's input. These procedures are sometimes part of a hydraulic system tune-up. With the increasing popularity of electronic controls, hydraulic tune-ups may be required less frequently since the control system can compensate for wear and flow losses to a certain extent. Hydraulic tune-ups will require the technician to measure flows, pressures, temperatures, and cycle times while comparing them to specifications and then making adjustments if needed.

One test is to set the minimum flow for a variable displacement pump. This requires a flow meter to be hooked up to the pump outlet and a way to measure engine speed. There will be a minimum displacement screw that can be adjusted to match the pump flow with the specification. If the pump control valve is electronically controlled, the pump output can be adjusted with a laptop computer.

Other tests are for pressure relief valve settings that control pressures like main system, pilot system, or line relief settings.

Calibration of Functions

Some machine electrohydraulic systems will require a calibration procedure to set function limitations, adjust the operation of the input for operator preference, or compensate for component wear. Some calibrations can be made through the machine's operator display (a password will be required), while others will require connecting a laptop computer through a communication adapter. See **FIGURE 32-56** to see a communication adapter connected to a machine.

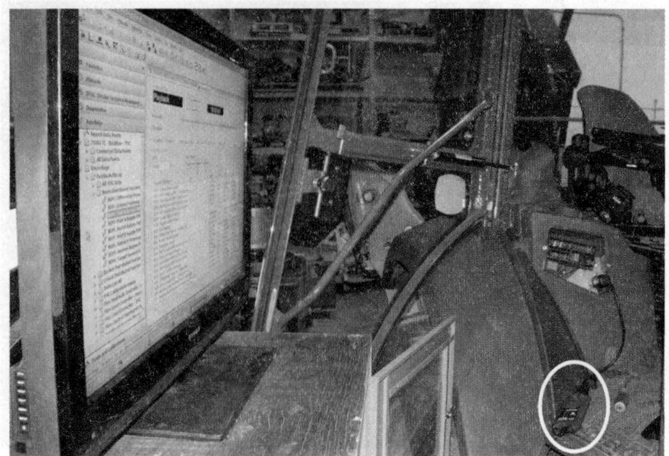

FIGURE 32-56 A communication adapter connected to a machine.

An example would be the swing function calibration for the previously described John Deere backhoe. If the operator didn't like how the swing function reacted to joystick movement—in other words, the operator thought it was too slow/lazy or too fast/jerky—then a calibration of the joystick would change the reaction time.

The calibration of a function typically requires that the hydraulic oil temperature be at least 125°F. Then the service mode on the machine display is entered, and a set of steps is followed that will match the joystick movement to when the operator sees the swing function work. This can then be fine-tuned to give the swing function the exact desired relationship between joystick movement and swing cylinder movement.

Another example would be for a machine that incorporates a weight scale into its electrohydraulic system. A wheel loader that loads highway trucks needs to be as close as possible to the truck's maximum payload without going over. To keep this weighing function accurate, the system should be calibrated regularly. This will require the machine to lift a known weight and the operator to go through a series of instructions shown on the machine's display. The first step to this is to get an empty bucket weight that allows the operator to zero the scale. There will be pressure transducers that translate hydraulic cylinder pressure into an electrical signal, which is then interpreted by an ECM. At this point, the value of the known weight is entered by the operator into the machine keypad. This step tells the ECM that the electrical signal coming out of the pressure transducer equates to the weight in the bucket. This is the end of the calibration procedure. To become familiar with procedures for test and adjusting an electrohydraulic system, follow the steps in **SKILL DRILL 32-1**.

▶ TECHNICIAN TIP

Don't rely on a machine's electronic system to troubleshoot problems for you.

A technician was called to a wheel loader with an electrohydraulic system that had an intermittent hydraulic problem. When trying to verify the complaint the technician ran the large wheel loader, and every fifth or sixth bucket load, the boom would reset to an unusual level. It normally would lower to a preset level when the boom lever was set to float after dumping. There were no active or logged fault codes related to the problem displayed.

Relying on previous experience, the technician checked the boom location sensor and found that the return spring on its lever was broken. There was nothing wrong electrically, but because the sensor's arm couldn't follow the ramp properly because of the broken spring, it was sending a false signal to the ECM.

In other words, the ECM didn't know where the boom was in its travel. The only way to know if there was a problem with this was to visually inspect the sensor.

SKILL DRILL 32-1 Testing and Adjusting an Electrohydraulic System

The following procedure will get you familiar with testing and adjusting procedures for an electrohydraulic system.

1. Perform a pre-start check on the machine.
2. Barricade the surrounding area to keep the machines danger zone clear.
3. Connect a laptop to the machine with a communication adapter.
4. Turn on the main power for the machine, but don't start the engine.
5. Enable the laptop to communicate with the machine.
6. Look for a menu related to the hydraulic system.
7. Make a note of all viewable values related to the hydraulic system.
8. Look for any logged or active codes.
9. Record all codes found.
10. Start the machine and warm up the hydraulic system as per machine service information (have at least one spotter watching blind spots around the machine and keeping the area clear).
11. Stall one implement and record maximum pressure.
12. Perform cycle time testing for one implement and record results.
13. Cool down machine and shut off.
14. Compare results to specifications.
15. If results were out of specification, determine what adjustments could be made to bring them back into acceptable range.

▶ Wrap-Up

Ready for Review

- Open center hydraulic systems are usually paired with fixed displacement pumps, while closed center hydraulic systems have variable displacement pumps supply flow to them.
- Simple open center hydraulic systems are inherently inefficient because of unnecessary flow and heat.
- Hydraulic system design goals include increasing machine efficiency, reducing operator fatigue, and increasing hydraulic power and speed.
- Heat generated in a hydraulic system through flow losses equates to an inefficiency.
- Flow losses occur when fluid flows past internal pump components, internal valve components, and internal actuator components.
- Variable displacement pumps with pump control valves will make a system much more efficient by producing only the flow needed for the current working condition.
- A pump control valve will control the displacement of a variable displacement pump. It will move the swashplate of an axial piston pump and the cylinder block of a bent axis pump.
- Pump control valves receive signals (hydraulic or electrical) from other parts of the hydraulic system and produce an output based on its setting and the input's values.
- A load-sensing hydraulic system is one that monitors the hydraulic circuit loads and sends the highest pressure to a control valve or ECM.
- Standby pressure is the low pressure produced by a variable displacement pump when there is no demand for flow.
- Load-sense check valves are used to send the highest work port pressure to the pump control valve.
- Margin pressure is created by spring pressure and ensures that the pump always produces 300–500 more psi than required.
- Electronic load sensing is done with pressure sensors in work ports and will be part of an electrohydraulic system.
- Pressure compensation is a monitoring and control system that maintains a level of flow output that will always satisfy the demands of the operator up to maximum pressure and flow output levels.
- A high-pressure compensator will reduce pump flow when pressure levels start to reach a predetermined maximum.
- Upstroking is when a variable displacement pump's displacement is changing to a higher displacement.
- A torque limiter valve reduces pump displacement when demands for flow and pressure are high simultaneously.
- Load-sensing and pressure-compensated systems will have lower pressure drops across their valve spools. This reduces operator effort and keeps actuator speed consistent.
- Some main control valves will incorporate extra valves for each circuit, such as pressure and flow compensators.
- Pilot controls use a low-pressure and low-flow system controlled by hand levers or foot pedals manipulated by the operator, and they will in turn control the machine's main high-pressure and high-flow system.

- An electronically managed hydraulic system uses an ECM to manage or control hydraulic functions and operator input. System monitoring is also managed by the ECM. The ECM compares the input signals to stored information and produces output signals to control electrohydraulic devices like pumps and valves.
- A CAN system provides a means for two or more ECMs to communicate with each other.
- Input devices convert temperatures, pressures, and motion into electrical signals.
- Output devices convert electrical signals from the ECM into motion (solenoids) or visual information (operator displays).

Key Terms

CAN (controller area network) system An electronic system that allows communication between two or more ECMs on a machine.

closed center hydraulic system A type of hydraulic system that blocks pump flow when its spool(s) are in neutral, which is usually paired with a variable displacement pump.

downstroking A term that describes the action that occurs when a pump reduces its displacement.

ECM (electronic control module) A module that gathers information, processes it, and produces output signals.

electronically managed hydraulic system A hydraulic system that uses sensors and switches for inputs to an ECM. The ECM then sends out signals to solenoids that control hydraulic components like valves and pumps.

electrohydraulic system See electronically managed hydraulic system.

fluid power system efficiency A measure of how much usable energy is produced by a hydraulic system compared to how much energy is consumed by it.

flow losses The fluid flow from a pump that is not used to produce output power. This is wasted energy or the inefficient part of a fluid power system.

high-pressure compensator A part of the pump control valve that reduces pump flow when a maximum set pressure value is reached.

input components Components such as sensors, switches, joystick controls, and touch screens that provide electrical signals to the ECM.

load sensing A hydraulic system that monitors the load on the pump through different circuits is considered to be load sensing.

margin spring pressure This spring in the pump control valve will maintain a higher pump output pressure than the highest work port pressure.

open center hydraulic system A type of hydraulic system that has a main control valve that allows pump flow through its center at all times.

output components Components, such as solenoids and displays, that are used to control hydraulic system flow and pressure.

pilot controls A low-pressure hydraulic system that is metered by the operator to actuate the main control valves.

poppet valves A type of valve used with pilot control systems to meter oil to main control valves.

pressure/flow compensator A part of a pump control valve that ensures pump flow will maintain a system pressure that is always higher than the highest load-sense signal.

proportional solenoid valves Solenoids that will move a certain amount based on the level of electrical signal delivered to them.

pump control valves Valves that can change the displacement of a variable displacement pump.

torque limiter A third type of pump control valve that reduces pump flow at times of both high flow and high pressure.

unloading valve A valve that can be used when two fixed displacement pumps are used.

upstroke The term used when a pump is changing to a higher displacement in order to supply fluid to one system.

variable displacement pump A more efficient type of pump that can be set up to produce only slightly more flow than what is needed for any condition, up to maximum flow design limits.

Review Questions

1. An open center system differs from a closed center system mainly by ______________.
   a. the size of the actuator the system can handle
   b. the maximum speed the actuators can move
   c. the maximum pressure the actuators receive
   d. the type of directional control valve the system uses
2. A closed center type of system will most likely feature ______________.
   a. a gear pump
   b. a variable displacement pump
   c. an accumulator
   d. no relief valve
3. A bent axis type of pump will vary its displacement by ______________.
   a. having its shaft speed change
   b. changing the swash plate angle
   c. rotating its camplate
   d. moving its cylinder block
4. Margin pressure is used in order to ______________.
   a. ensure that the pump flow output will always be slightly greater than the minimum required
   b. replace the main relief pressure setting
   c. keep system pressure at 0 psi when no flow is required
   d. match pump output to the lowest circuit pressure demand
5. A hydraulic system that uses a pilot oil system will ______________.
   a. use lower pressure pilot oil to move the actuators slower
   b. always have a pilot oil pump
   c. use lower pressure oil to move the main control valve spools
   d. always have its relief valve set 1,000 psi lower than main system pressure

6. An example of an input to an ECM that is part of an electrohydraulic system is ________________.
   a. proportional solenoid
   b. pump control solenoid
   c. a variable relief valve sensor
   d. a pump speed sensor
7. To prevent stiction from occurring to a valve, the ECM will ________________.
   a. pulse an electrical signal to the valve
   b. use a lower viscosity hydraulic fluid
   c. use a higher voltage signal to the valve
   d. reduce the main relief pressure setting
8. One advantage of using a digital pressure gauge to test hydraulic systems is that ________________.
   a. they can withstand higher pressures
   b. there is no high-pressure oil in the handheld display
   c. they can read quickly fluctuating pressures
   d. they are cheaper than analog gauges
9. If an operator complains that the hydraulic system is slow, you would be looking for a/an ________________ problem.
   a. overheating
   b. excessive pressure
   c. reduction of flow
   d. vibration and noise
10. A flow meter is used for testing ________________.
   a. maximum circuit pressure
   b. flow output of a pump
   c. speed of rotary actuators
   d. speed of the pump flow

ASE Technician A/Technician B Style Questions

1. Technician A says a fixed displacement pump usually sends flow to an open center valve. Technician B says a closed center valve must be used with a variable displacement pump. Who is correct?
   a. Technician A
   b. Technician B
   c. Both Technician A and Technician B
   d. Neither Technician A nor Technician B
2. Technician A says a large amount of internal leakage is normal in any hydraulic system. Technician B says all heat generated in a hydraulic system is put to work. Who is correct?
   a. Technician A
   b. Technician B
   c. Both Technician A and Technician B
   d. Neither Technician A nor Technician B
3. Technician A says load sensing will make a system more efficient. Technician B says a pump control valve will always be found on a fixed displacement pump. Who is correct?
   a. Technician A
   b. Technician B
   c. Both Technician A and Technician B
   d. Neither Technician A nor Technician B
4. Technician A says margin pressure is the maximum pressure a variable pump will produce. Technician B says a torque limiter reduces pump flow when both pressure and flow demands are high. Who is correct?
   a. Technician A
   b. Technician B
   c. Both Technician A and Technician B
   d. Neither Technician A nor Technician B
5. Technician A says pilot control hydraulic systems originated on commercial aircraft. Technician B says a pilot oil system meters low-pressure oil to control a high-pressure system. Who is correct?
   a. Technician A
   b. Technician B
   c. Both Technician A and Technician B
   d. Neither Technician A nor Technician B
6. Technician A says proportional solenoids will only be in two states (on or off). Technician B says the CAN system allows two or more ECMs to communicate. Who is correct?
   a. Technician A
   b. Technician B
   c. Both Technician A and Technician B
   d. Neither Technician A nor Technician B
7. Technician A says joysticks and pedals used for an electrohydraulic system are inputs to the ECM. Technician B says temperature and pressure sensors are outputs from an ECM. Who is correct?
   a. Technician A
   b. Technician B
   c. Both Technician A and Technician B
   d. Neither Technician A nor Technician B
8. Technician A says a regeneration circuit uses an accumulator to store energy. Technician B says a pump control valve could have a position sensor as part of it. Who is correct?
   a. Technician A
   b. Technician B
   c. Both Technician A and Technician B
   d. Neither Technician A nor Technician B
9. Technician A says CAN wiring will use wires that are twisted. Technician B says electrohydraulic harnesses should be secured every 12–18 inches. Who is correct?
   a. Technician A
   b. Technician B
   c. Both Technician A and Technician B
   d. Neither Technician A nor Technician B
10. Technician A says an initial inspection of an electrohydraulic system includes testing main relief pressure. Technician B says digital pressure gauges are safer than mechanical gauges. Who is correct?
   a. Technician A
   b. Technician B
   c. Both Technician A and Technician B
   d. Neither Technician A nor Technician B

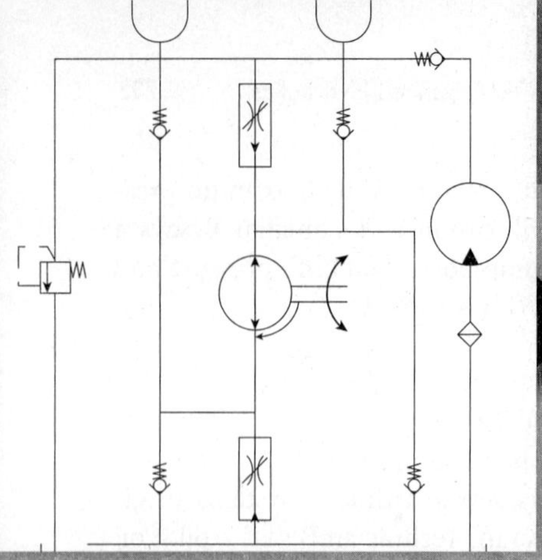

CHAPTER 33

Graphic Symbols and Schematics

Knowledge Objectives

After reading this chapter, you will be able to:

- **K33001** Explain and interpret a manufacturer's schematic legends.

Skills Objectives

After reading this chapter, you will be able to:

- **S33001** Draw a basic hydraulic system using graphic symbols.

▶ Introduction

Hydraulic systems found in many types of industrial and heavy equipment applications are represented on drawings called hydraulic system diagrams. Different types of diagrams are used to represent hydraulic systems. For instance, **pictorial diagrams** use sketches to illustrate what the components in the system look like and how they are connected. This type of diagram provides a way to easily recognize the system components, but it does not necessarily depict the actual locations of the components (**FIGURE 33-1**).

Cutaway diagrams show internal parts of the components in the system to help illustrate how the components function (**FIGURE 33-2**).

Schematic diagrams use symbols and lines to represent the components and how they are connected (**FIGURE 33-3**). These schematic diagrams are the ones most commonly used by service technicians to troubleshoot problems in hydraulic systems.

In order for service technicians to maintain and troubleshoot hydraulic systems, they must be able to accurately read and interpret schematic diagrams. This chapter identifies and describes common symbols used on schematic diagrams and examines how those symbols represent the components, connections, and operation of a hydraulic system.

▶ Schematic Legends and Symbols

K33001, S33001

A hydraulic system schematic is basically a line drawing that uses symbols and connecting lines to represent the components in a hydraulic system. The symbols used on schematic diagrams have been developed over the years by different standards organizations:

- The International Standards Organization (ISO)
- The American National Standards Institute (ANSI)
- The American Standards Association (ASA)
- The Joint Industry Conference (JIC)

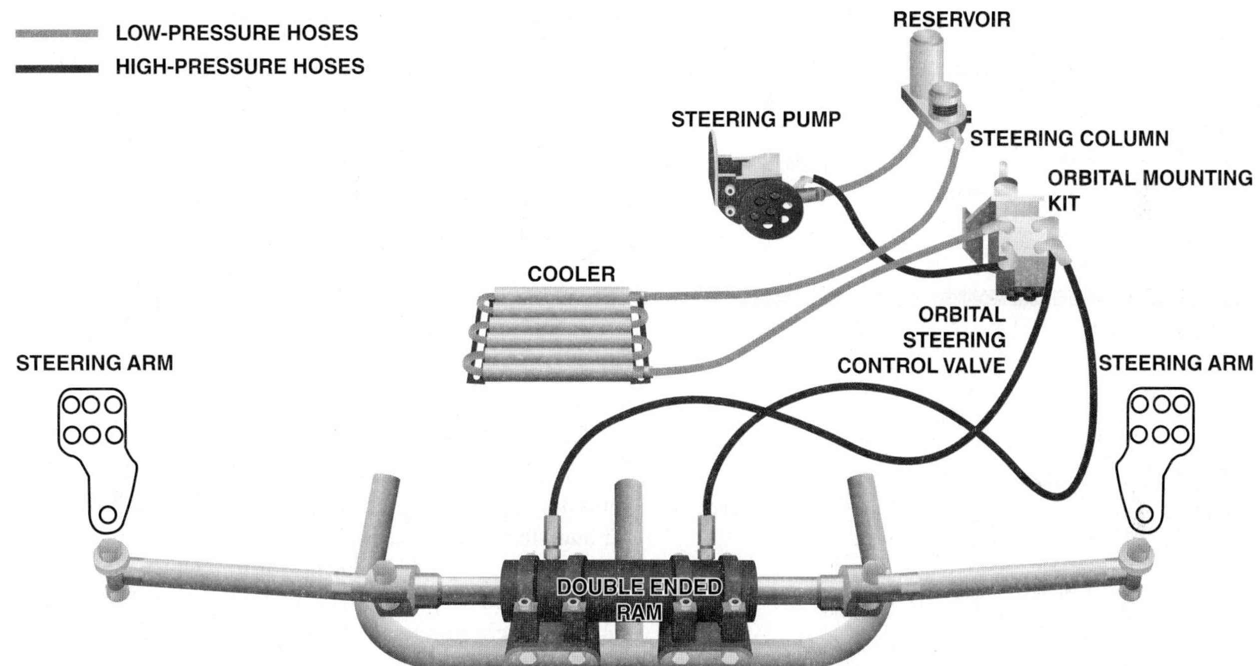

FIGURE 33-1 Pictorial diagram of hydraulic steering system.

You Are the Mobile Heavy Equipment Technician

You are called to troubleshoot a problem in the hydraulic system for a wheel loader. The customer who calls you is simply relaying a message from one of their equipment operators, so they don't have a lot of detailed information. When you arrive at the customer's place of business, you have some factors to consider.

1. Since you are troubleshooting the system, what type of system diagram might be best for showing the components and connections in the system?
2. If the customer is unable to provide any manufacturer manuals or drawings, where might you look to find helpful information?
3. How could locating and identifying components in the system, such as the reservoir, the hydraulic pump, and check valves, help you determine things like the direction of fluid flow through the system?
4. What might you assume if the schematic diagram shows a section of the system bordered by a line with long and short dashes?

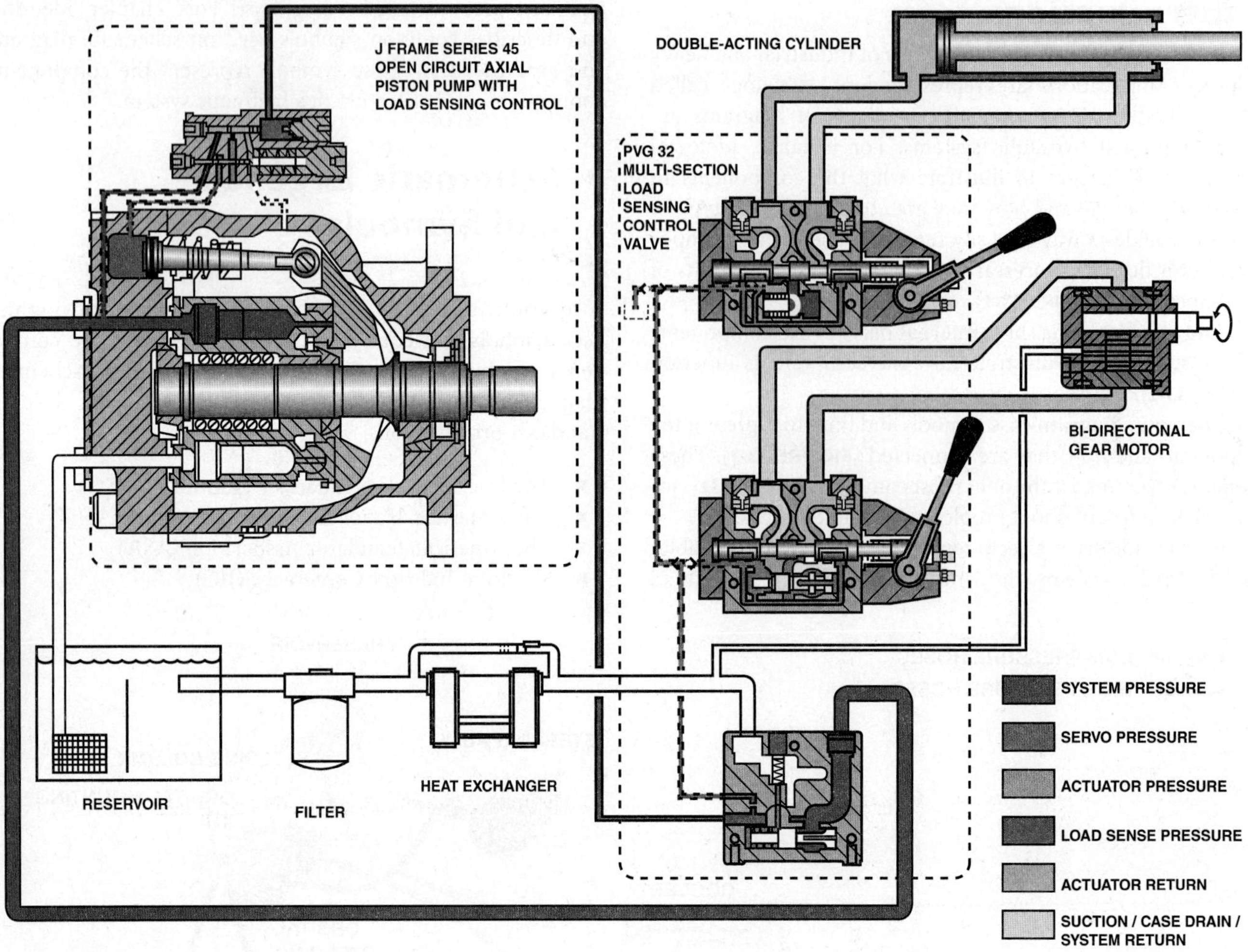

J FRAME SERIES 45 OPEN CIRCUIT AXIAL PISTON PUMP WITH LOAD SENSING CONTROL
DOUBLE-ACTING CYLINDER
PVG 32 MULTI-SECTION LOAD SENSING CONTROL VALVE
BI-DIRECTIONAL GEAR MOTOR
RESERVOIR
FILTER
HEAT EXCHANGER
SYSTEM PRESSURE
SERVO PRESSURE
ACTUATOR PRESSURE
LOAD SENSE PRESSURE
ACTUATOR RETURN
SUCTION / CASE DRAIN / SYSTEM RETURN

FIGURE 33-2 Cutaway diagram of hydraulic system components.

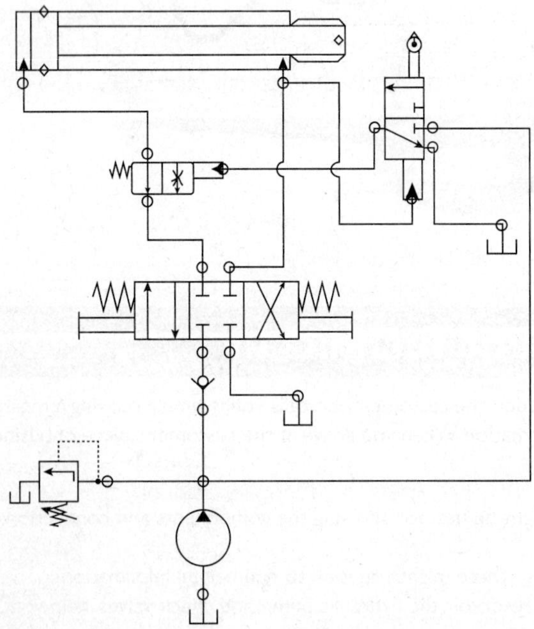

FIGURE 33-3 A schematic diagram of a hydraulic system.

While there are subtle differences among some of the symbols used by these organizations, most of the symbols are similar enough for service technicians to recognize and interpret them. The same can be said about the form in which a hydraulic system schematic appears. A schematic found in a manufacturer's manual might differ somewhat from one displayed on an electronic screen, but a technician who is familiar with schematic symbols should be able to discern any differences. To help alleviate concerns about variations in graphic symbols, schematic diagrams often include a section called a legend that provides explanatory information about the symbols and other features on the schematic.

▶ TECHNICIAN TIP

If you are uncertain about the meaning of a particular symbol on a hydraulic system schematic, you should search online to find applicable charts and graphics or look through hydraulic system books, magazines, and manuals for clarification. Schematic symbols are generally easy to locate, and accurately interpreting symbols is always better and safer than guessing.

Legends

To ensure that technicians can accurately interpret schematic drawings, most manufacturers include some type of legend to identify the symbols used on the drawing. A legend is a section of a schematic that provides information about the symbols, lines, colors, and other features that represent components and fluid flows in a hydraulic system.

Schematic legends can vary a great deal, depending on the complexity of the schematic with which they are associated. A simple legend may be all that is necessary for a small hydraulic circuit that contains only a few basic components (**FIGURE 33-4**).

Large hydraulic systems with many components and connections require a much more detailed legend (**FIGURE 33-5**). Detailed legends are commonly divided into sections to help further clarify symbols for categories like pumps, valves, actuators, and connecting lines.

Regardless of the simplicity or complexity of a hydraulic system's schematic legend, the basic purpose is the same: accurately identify the symbols used on the schematic so that technicians can interpret them and use that knowledge to troubleshoot and repair hydraulic system problems.

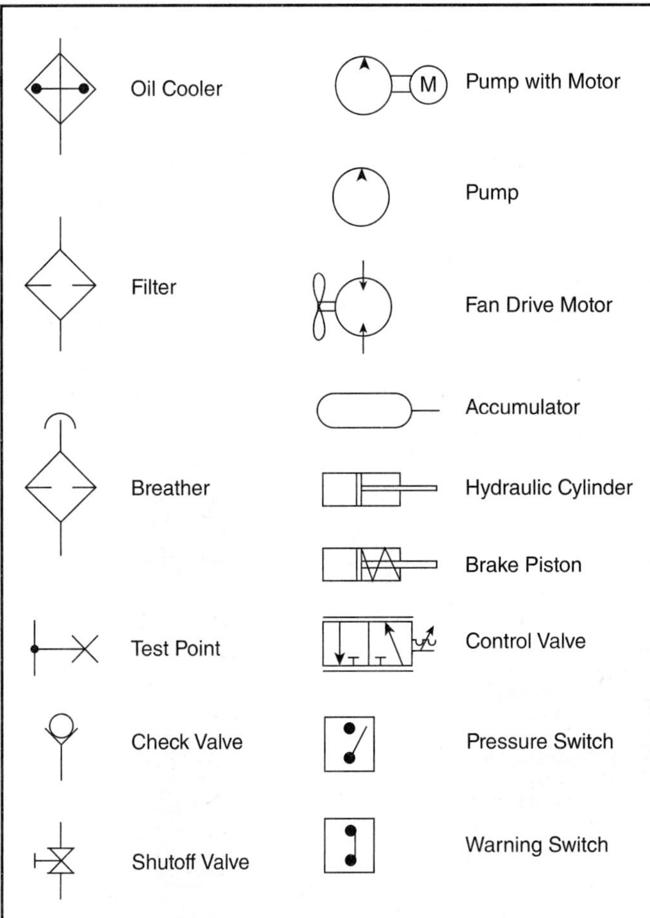

FIGURE 33-4 Simple legend for small hydraulic system.

SAFETY TIP

Always follow all company and manufacturer safety guidelines when troubleshooting, repairing, and maintaining any hydraulic system. Service technicians must be aware of high temperatures and high pressures maintained in the system. Use caution around hydraulic system components and be on the lookout for leaks.

Symbols

The symbols used on hydraulic system schematics typically include those used to represent one or more of the following components:

- Reservoirs (tanks)
- Fluid conditioners (such as strainers and filters, heaters and coolers, and separators)
- Valves (such as pressure relief, directional, flow, and check)
- Valve actuators
- Hydraulic pumps
- Hydraulic motors
- Hydraulic cylinders
- Connecting lines (such as fluid suction and return lines, pilot lines, and drain lines) and arrows

There can be, of course, other components in a hydraulic system, but these basic types are likely to appear in many of the hydraulic systems that MORE (mobile off-road equipment) service technicians encounter.

Reservoirs

A reservoir, or tank, is a vessel that stores the hydraulic fluid used in a hydraulic system. Two symbols are commonly used to represent a reservoir in a schematic drawing: one that appears to be open at the top for **vented reservoirs** and one that appears to be closed at the top for **pressurized reservoirs** (**FIGURE 33-6**).

Reservoir symbols also show when hydraulic fluid suction, and return lines terminate at the reservoir (**FIGURE 33-7**). These connecting lines show whether the lines terminate above the fluid level or below the fluid level in the reservoir.

▶ TECHNICIAN TIP

On some schematics, connecting lines are shown entering or leaving the bottom of a reservoir. Keep in mind that such a configuration is an exception to the rule and is used only when a bottom connection is critical to how the hydraulic system functions.

Fluid Conditioners

Fluid conditioners are components that affect the physical characteristics of the hydraulic fluid. For example, strainers and filters are used to remove impurities in the hydraulic fluid; heaters and coolers are used to change the temperature of the fluid; and separators are used to remove water from fluid (**FIGURE 33-8**).

The basic symbol for a fluid conditioner is a square turned on its corner to look like a diamond. Additional lines and shapes

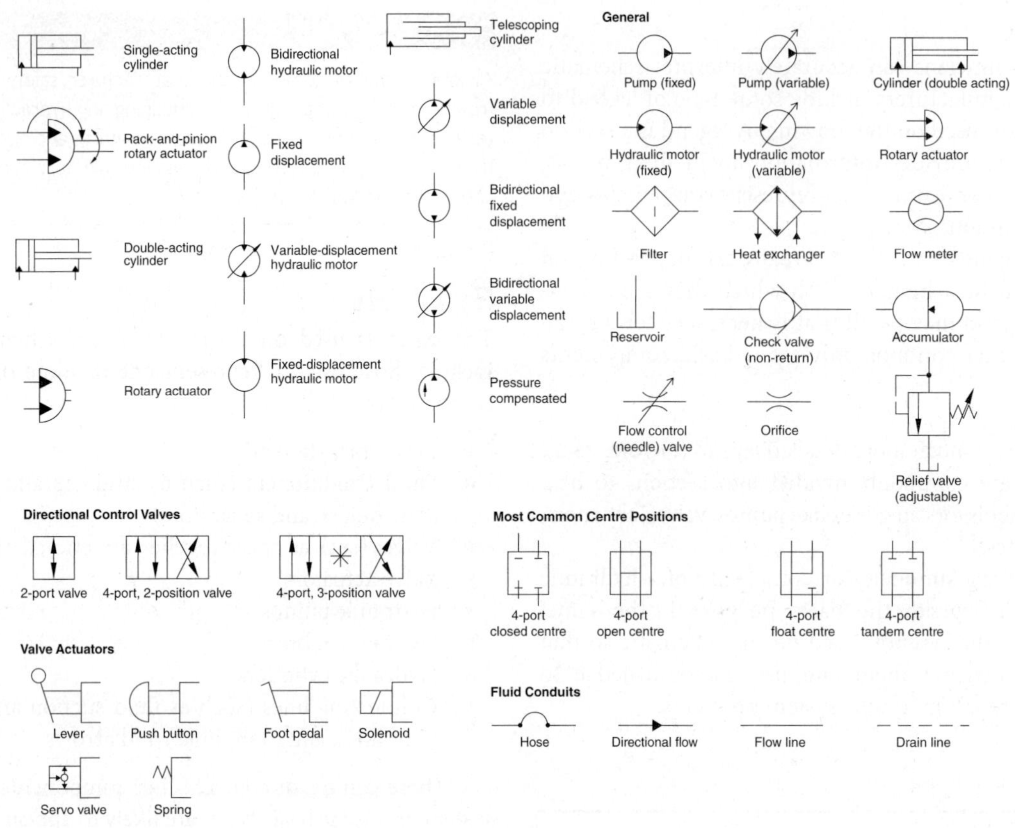

FIGURE 33-5 Detailed legend for hydraulic system.

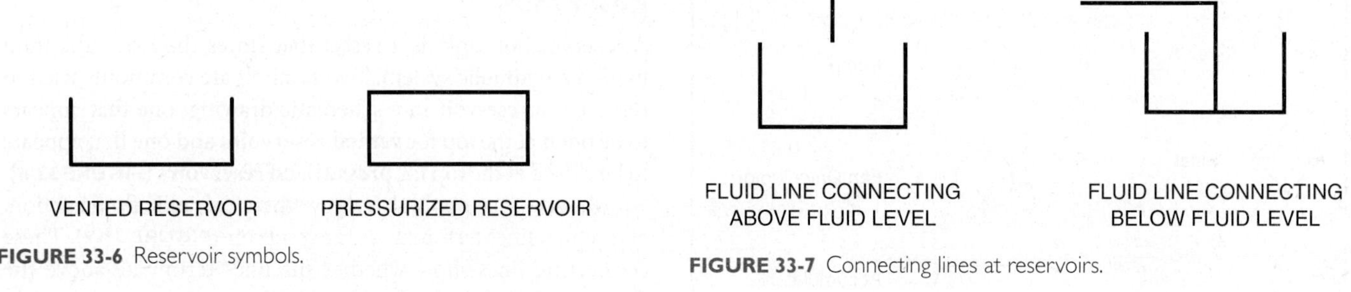

FIGURE 33-6 Reservoir symbols.

FIGURE 33-7 Connecting lines at reservoirs.

FIGURE 33-8 Hydraulic fluid conditioners.

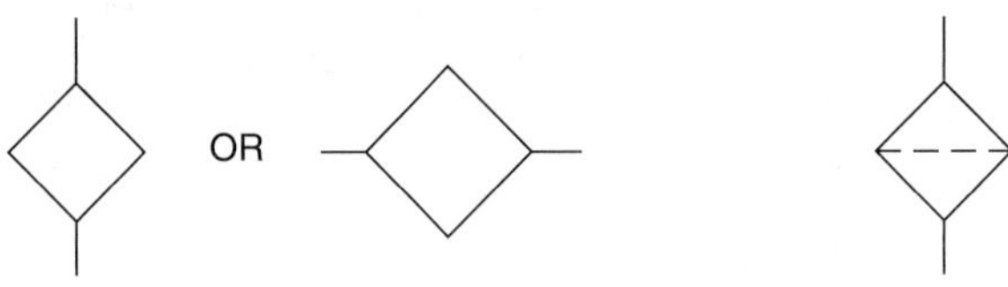

FIGURE 33-9 Basic fluid conditioner and strainer/filter symbols.

are added to the basic symbol to represent specific types of fluid conditioners. For example, a dashed line across the diamond symbol represents a strainer or filter (**FIGURE 33-9**).

Hydraulic heat exchangers use arrows on the basic fluid conditioner diamond to indicate whether they are heaters or coolers and what type of heating or cooling medium is being used (**FIGURE 33-10**).

Separators in a hydraulic system are depicted using lines at the bottom of the diamond symbol (**FIGURE 33-11**).

Valves

Different types of valves are used in hydraulic systems to control conditions such as the pressure, direction, and flow of hydraulic fluid. Valve symbols can be among the most complex of all schematic symbols. But being able to accurately interpret a valve symbol can provide a service technician with a great deal of information about the valve, including the type of valve, the valve position(s), and the direction of fluid flow into and out of the valve.

Pressure control valves and directional control valves are represented on schematic diagrams using one or more square boxes called **envelopes** (**FIGURE 33-12**). The number of envelopes used for the symbol indicates the number of valve operating positions. A one-position valve symbol is typically used to represent pressure-relief and pressure-reducing valves, while two- and three-position valve symbols are used to represent directional control valves.

Lines, arrows, and other symbols are added to the basic envelopes to represent line connections, flow paths, and valve functions. For instance, lines that connect to the outside of the envelopes represent valve ports, which are passages that hydraulic fluid can pass through the valve (**FIGURE 33-13**).

A pressure-relief valve symbol includes a single envelope with an arrow to represent the direction of flow, a jagged line to represent the valve spring, and a dashed line to represent the pilot line sensing pressure in the system (**FIGURE 33-14**). The flow arrow is offset from the inlet and outlet ports to indicate that this is a **normally closed valve**. In other words, the valve spring holds the valve closed until pressure in the system overcomes the force of the spring. A reservoir symbol is included underneath the relief valve to illustrate that pressure in the system is relieved by directing hydraulic fluid back to the tank.

A similar pressure control valve symbol that has the directional flow arrow in line with the inlet and outlet ports is used for a **normally open valve** (**FIGURE 33-15**). In this case, the valve spring holds the valve open until pressure in the system overcomes the force of the spring. This type of valve is commonly called a pressure-reducing valve.

Another type of normally open valve used in hydraulic systems is a pressure-reducing valve (**FIGURE 33-16**). Unlike a pressure-relief valve that senses inlet pressure, a pressure-reducing valve senses outlet pressure. When outlet pressure increases, it eventually overcomes the force of the valve spring

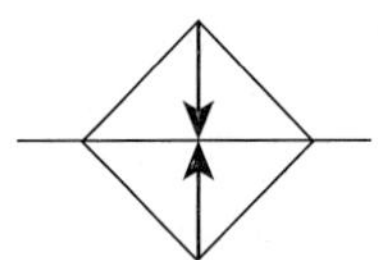

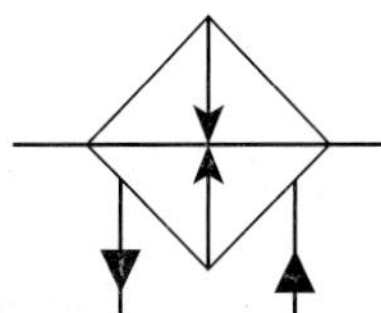

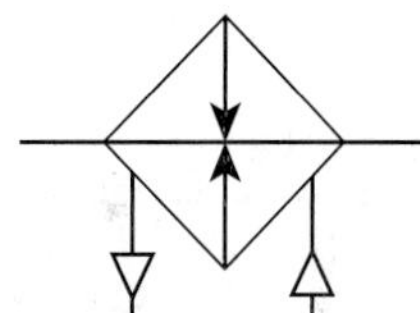

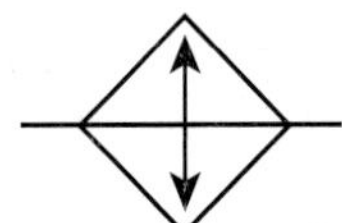

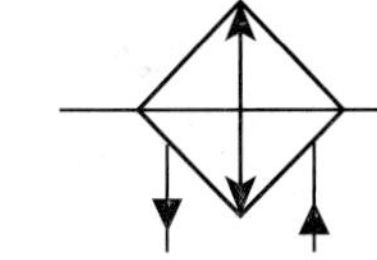

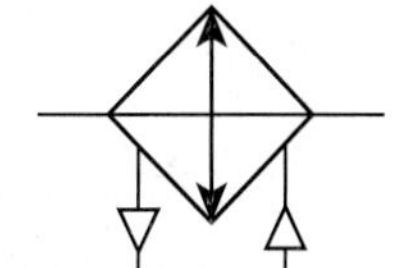

FIGURE 33-10 Heat exchanger symbols.

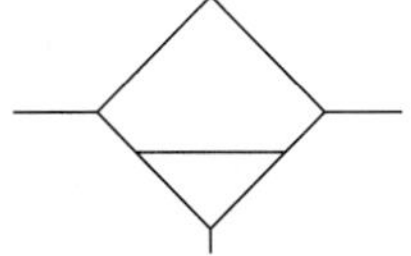

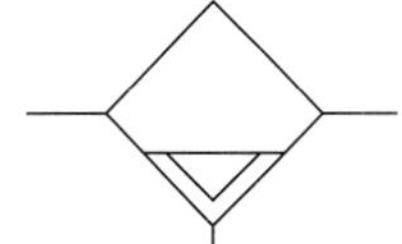

FIGURE 33-11 Separator symbols.

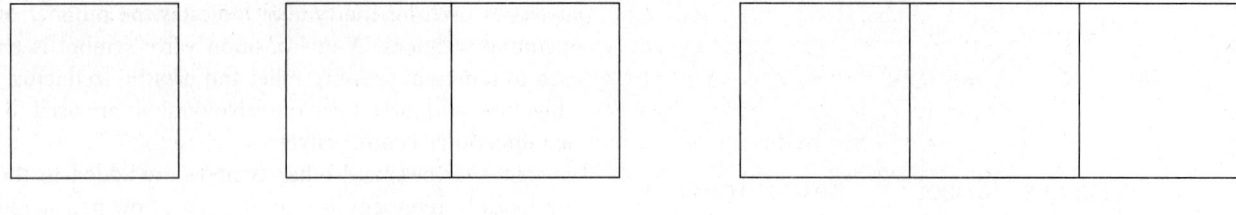

FIGURE 33-12 Basic pressure and directional control valve envelopes.

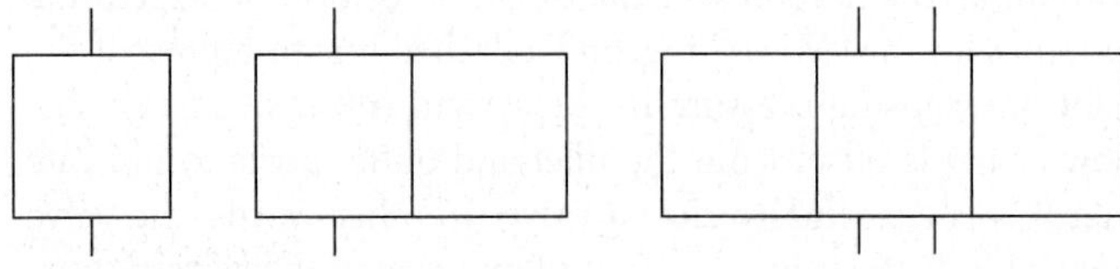

FIGURE 33-13 Valve port symbols.

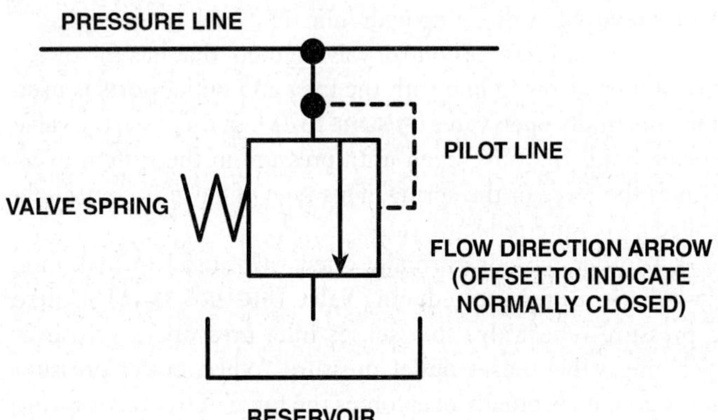

FIGURE 33-14 Symbol for normally closed pressure-relief valve.

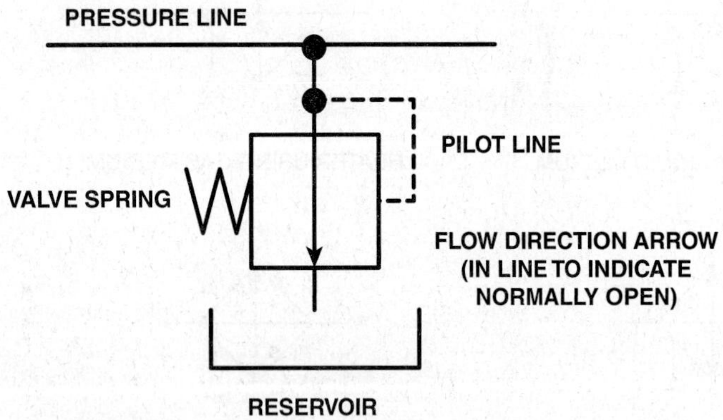

FIGURE 33-15 Symbol for normally open pressure control valve.

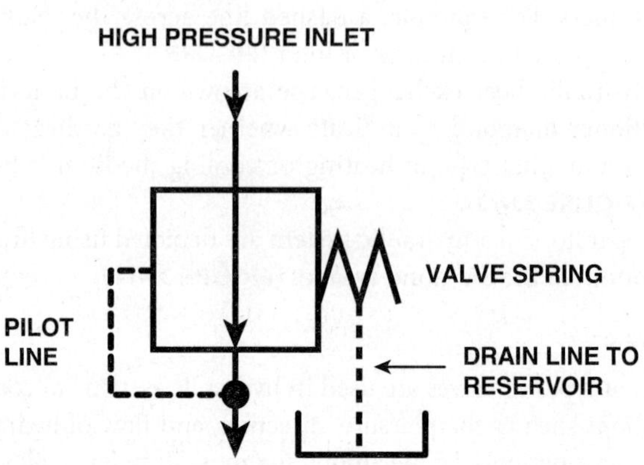

FIGURE 33-16 Symbol for normally open pressure-reducing valve.

and decreases or stops flow through the valve. A dotted line indicates that pressure is reduced by draining hydraulic fluid back to the tank.

Directional control valves use arrows and other symbols inside the envelopes to indicate flow direction (**FIGURE 33-17**). For instance, one double-headed arrow inside an envelope indicates that fluid can flow in either direction through a single line. Two separate arrows inside an envelope indicate that fluid can flow in either direction, but through two separate lines. Two arrows that cross diagonally indicate two lines of flow that cross over inside the valve.

One or more symbols that look like Ts are often used inside a directional control valve envelope. These T-shaped figures indicate that the ports of the valve are blocked internally (**FIGURE 33-18**).

If valve ports are connected internally—that is, not blocked—the T-shaped symbols are replaced with connected lines that resemble an H (**FIGURE 33-19**).

There are many possible configurations for directional control valves. In a typical example, a three-position valve has three

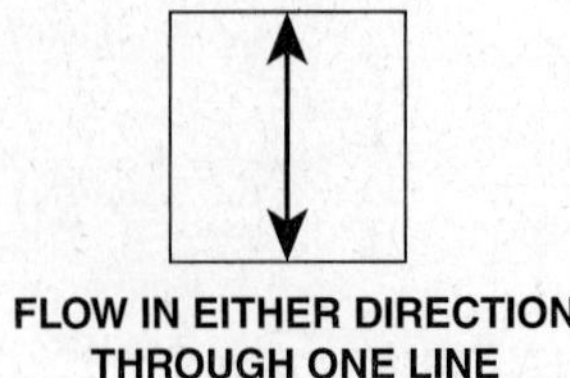

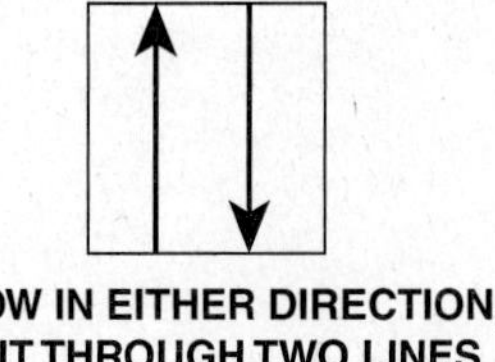

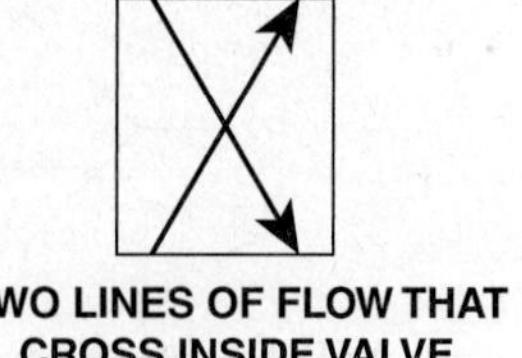

FIGURE 33-17 Fluid flow arrows inside envelopes.

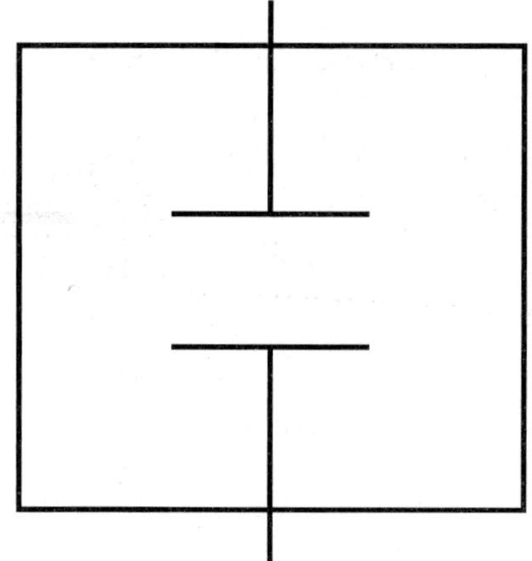

FIGURE 33-18 Two ports of a directional control valve blocked internally.

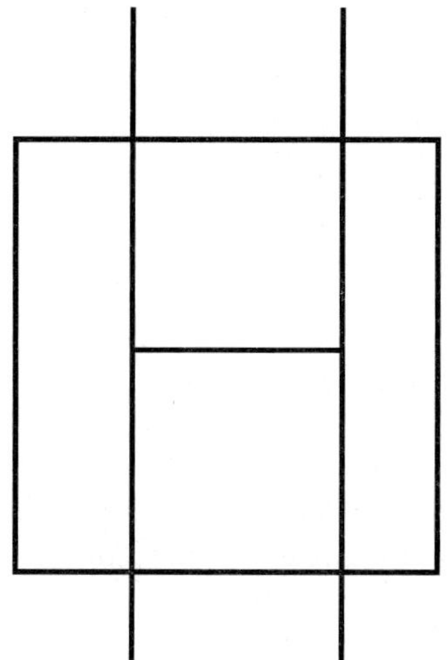

FIGURE 33-19 Four ports of a directional control valve connected internally.

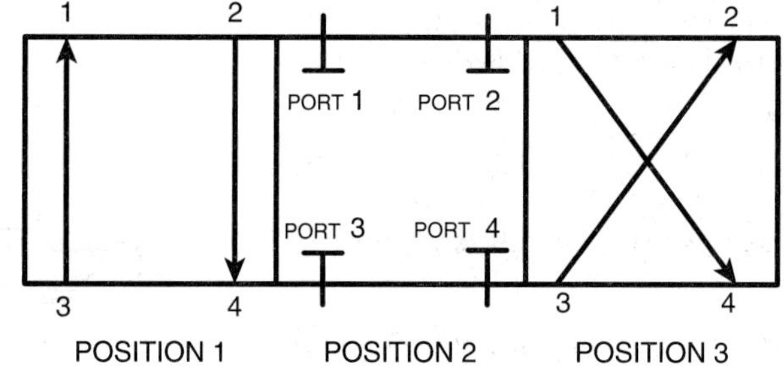

FIGURE 33-20 Four-port, three-position valve.

envelopes, along with arrows and symbols in each envelope, to indicate the direction and flow when the valve is in that position (FIGURE 33-20). The center position in this type of valve indicates the flow path of the fluid while the valve is centered or in neutral.

Three common valve center configurations are **closed center**, **tandem center**, and **open center** (FIGURE 33-21). When a closed center valve is in the neutral position, all four ports are blocked, so there is no pathway for the fluid through the valve. When a tandem center valve is in the neutral position, fluid flows from the

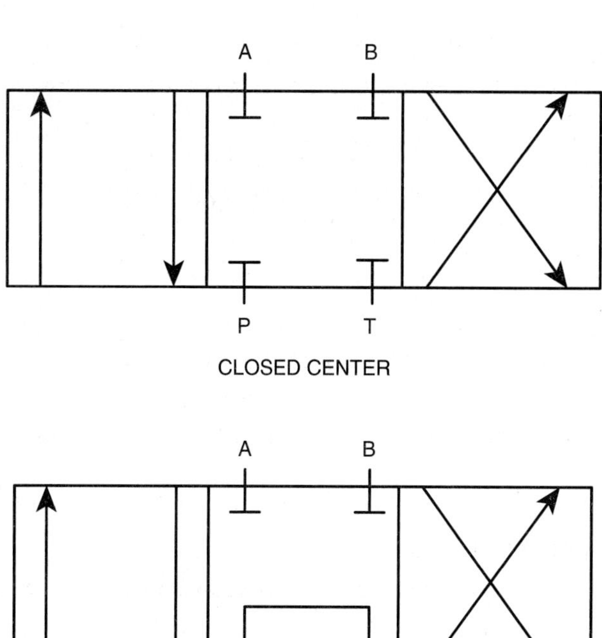

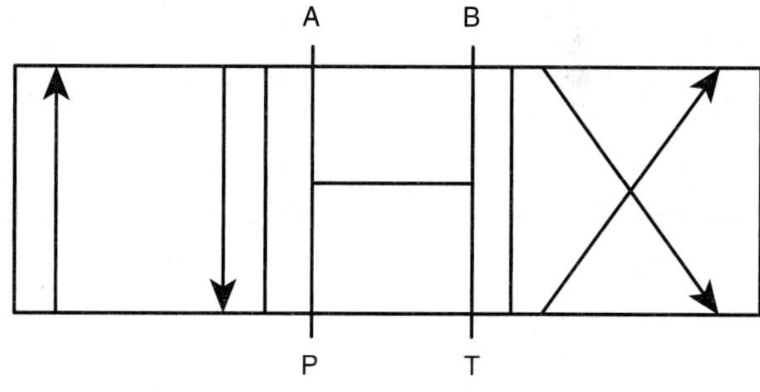

FIGURE 33-21 Four-port, three-position valve configurations.

pump (P), through the valve, and back to the tank (T). When an open-center valve is in the neutral position, fluid flows between all four ports. This is often referred to as the **float position**.

Another type of valve used in hydraulic systems is a flow control valve. A flow control valve is used to restrict the flow of oil. On a schematic diagram, a flow control valve has an upper arc above the connecting line and a lower arc below the line (FIGURE 33-22). This symbol represents a fixed orifice in the line. An angled arrow across the arcs and connecting line indicates that the orifice is adjustable.

Other types of valves commonly found in hydraulic systems include check valves, bypass valves, and on/off (manual shutoff) valves (FIGURE 33-23). Check valves permit flow in only one direction. A bypass valve symbol looks much like a check valve symbol, except it includes a spring on the ball end of the symbol. This symbol indicates that a pressurized flow is needed to overcome the force of the spring and allow flow

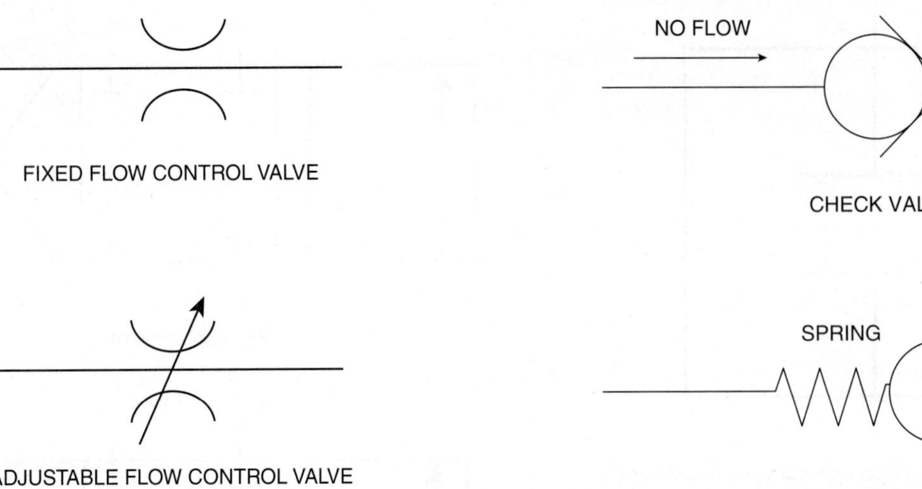

FIGURE 33-22 Hydraulic flow control valves.

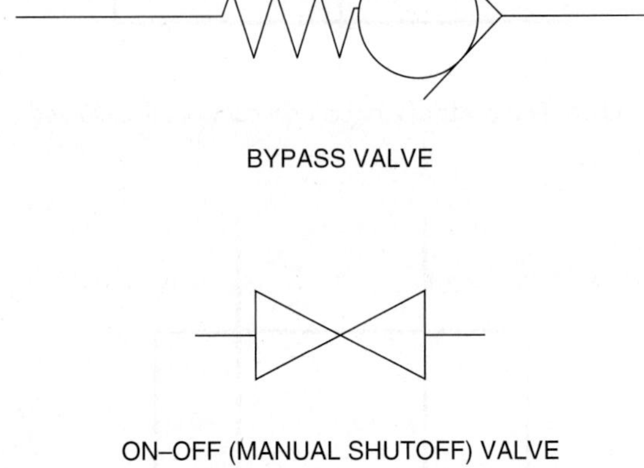

FIGURE 33-23 Check, bypass, and on/off valves.

around the ball. The symbol for an on/off (manual shutoff) valve looks like a bowtie placed over the connecting line.

Valve Actuators

In order for control valves in a hydraulic system to operate, there has to be some type of manual or automatic actuating mechanism. A valve actuator is essentially a component used for opening and closing a valve. Some common actuating mechanisms include pushbutton, pedal, spring, lever, mechanical, and solenoid actuators (**FIGURE 33-24**).

Hydraulic Pumps

A hydraulic pump is the component in a hydraulic system that generates the system pressure needed by hydraulic motors to drive another component or other components. In most cases, a hydraulic pump is driven by the engine of the equipment on which it is used. On a schematic diagram, hydraulic pump symbols are circles with solid black triangles pointing outward, away from the center of the circle. A unidirectional, or nonreversible, hydraulic pump has one black triangle, while a bidirectional, or reversible, hydraulic pump has two triangles (**FIGURE 33-25**). Both of these types of hydraulic pumps are **fixed displacement** pumps; that is, they deliver the same volume of hydraulic fluid with each cycle.

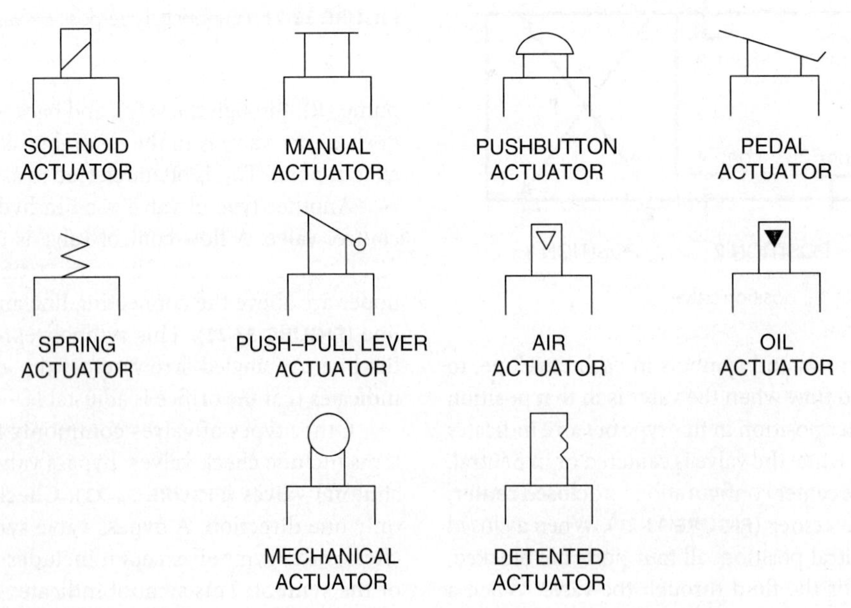

FIGURE 33-24 Hydraulic valve actuator symbols.

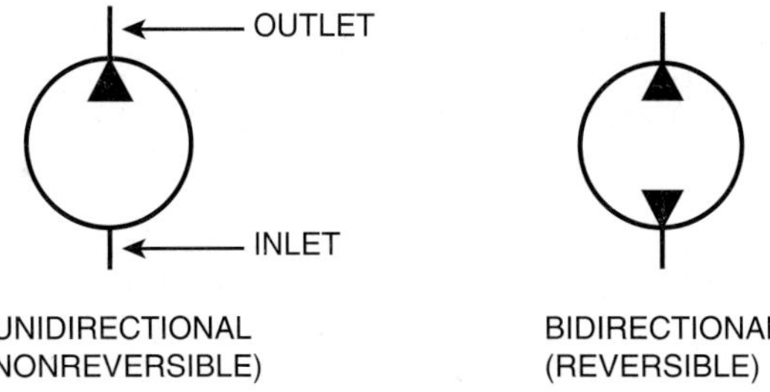

FIGURE 33-25 Fixed displacement hydraulic pump symbols.

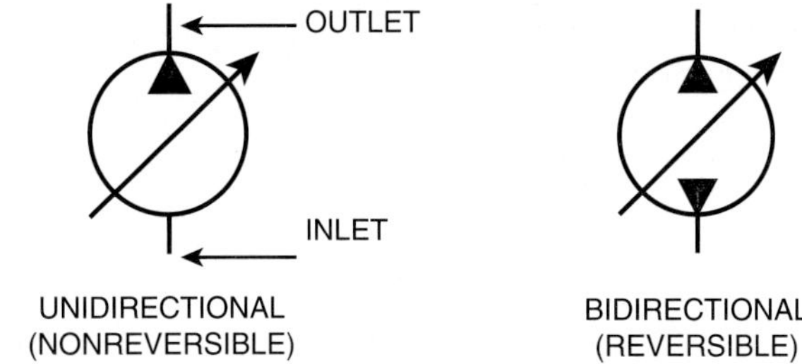

FIGURE 33-26 Variable displacement hydraulic pump symbols.

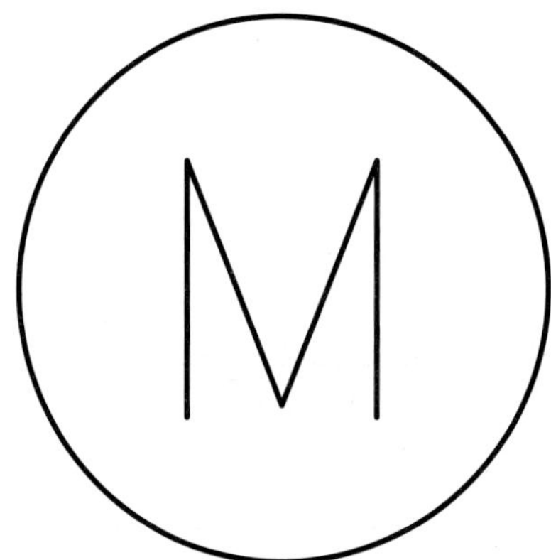

FIGURE 33-27 Electric motor symbol.

The symbols for **variable displacement** hydraulic pumps use the same basic circles and black triangles, but they also include an angled arrow across the middle of the circle (**FIGURE 33-26**).

In some applications, an electric motor might be used to drive a hydraulic pump. When this is the case, a circular symbol with the letter M inside of it will appear beside the hydraulic pump symbol (**FIGURE 33-27**).

Hydraulic Motors

A hydraulic motor is a component that receives pressurized fluid from a hydraulic pump and converts that pressure and flow to rotation and torque to drive some component(s) in the system. Hydraulic motor symbols are circles with solid black triangles pointing inward, toward the center of the circle. A unidirectional, or nonreversible, hydraulic motor has one black triangle, while a bidirectional, or reversible, hydraulic motor has two triangles (**FIGURE 33-28**). Both of these types of hydraulic motors are fixed displacement motors.

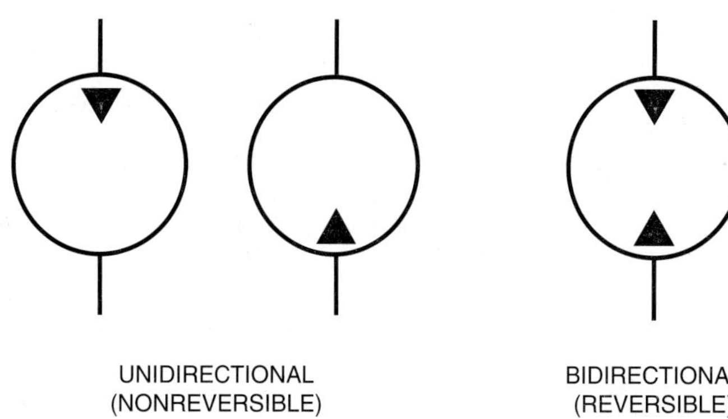

FIGURE 33-28 Fixed displacement hydraulic motor symbols.

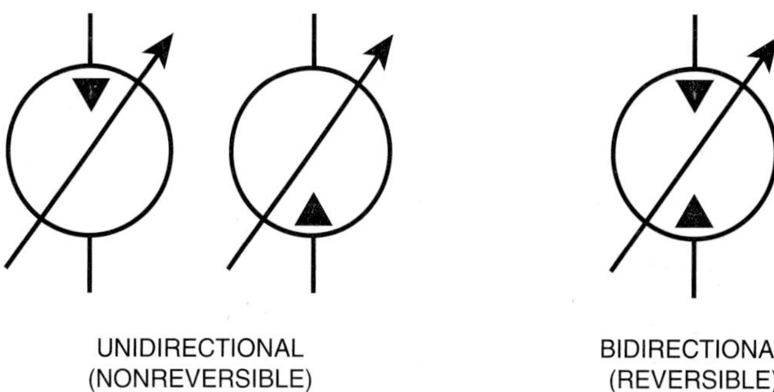

FIGURE 33-29 Variable displacement hydraulic motor symbols.

The symbols for variable displacement hydraulic motors use the same basic circles and black triangles, but they also include an angled arrow across the middle of the circle (**FIGURE 33-29**).

Hydraulic Cylinders

Hydraulic cylinders, which are sometimes referred to as **linear actuators**, are commonly used in hydraulic systems to move loads. For instance, hydraulic cylinders are used on loaders to lift and lower the loader arms and to extend and retract the loader bucket.

There are different types of hydraulic cylinders, including **single-acting cylinders** and **double-acting cylinders**. Single-acting cylinders can apply force in only one direction, while double-acting cylinders can apply force in two directions. Each type of hydraulic cylinder has its own schematic symbol (**FIGURE 33-30**). These symbols basically consist of a rectangle that represents the cylinder housing, short lines that represent the ports, and a T-shaped line that represents the piston rod.

Some hydraulic cylinders have cushions to dampen the piston's movement and reduce shock during operation. Symbols for these types of hydraulic cylinders show the cushions and indicate whether the cushions are fixed or adjustable (**FIGURE 33-31**).

Lines and Arrows

Line and arrow symbols are prevalent on schematic diagrams. Different types of line symbols are used to help technicians distinguish between flow lines, pilot lines, drain lines, and other

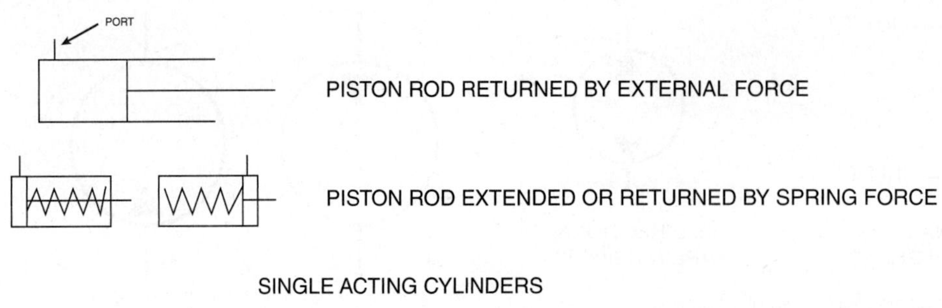

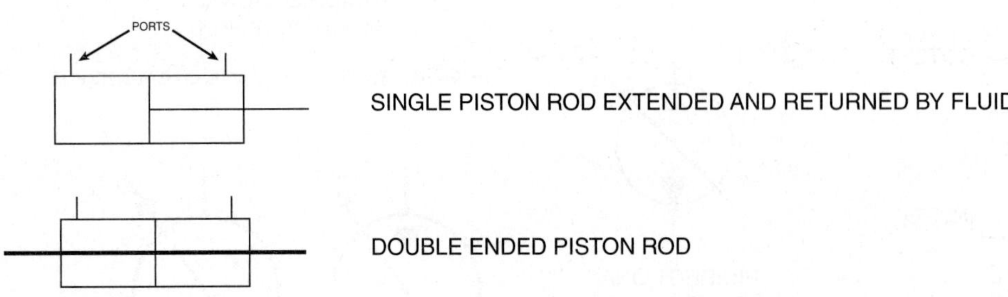

FIGURE 33-30 Hydraulic cylinder symbols.

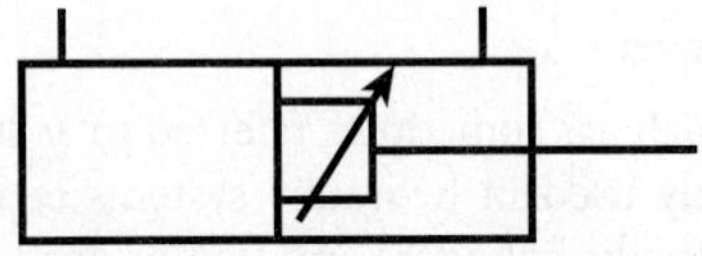

FIGURE 33-31 Hydraulic cylinder cushion symbols.

connections. For instance, a solid line represents a working fluid line, a dashed line represents a pilot line, a dotted line represents an exhaust or drain line, and a line made up of long and short dashes represents the outline of an enclosure (**FIGURE 33-32**).

Arrows are often used with lines to indicate the direction of flow for the liquid or gas being pumped through the system (**FIGURE 33-33**).

A special symbol is used to represent a flexible line in a hydraulic system. This symbol is a solid arced line with a black dot at each end (**FIGURE 33-34**). This symbol is often used to represent a hose that is connected to some type of moving part.

When fluid lines intersect in a hydraulic system schematic, there must be a way to illustrate whether those lines simply cross over each other or whether they actually join. Otherwise, it could be impossible for service technicians to understand the hydraulic fluid's flow through the system. For this reason, special line symbols have been developed to distinguish between lines that cross and lines that join (**FIGURE 33-35**).

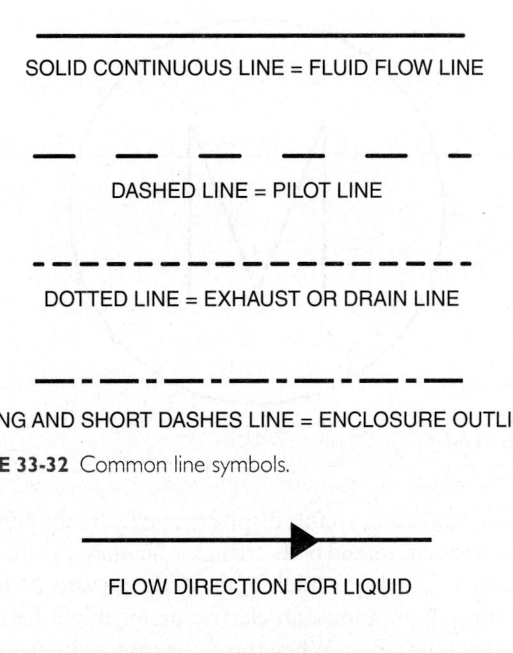

FIGURE 33-32 Common line symbols.

FIGURE 33-33 Line symbols with arrows for flow direction.

Miscellaneous Symbols

Some schematic diagrams include symbols for components that can be uncommon in many hydraulic systems. While MORE service technicians may not see these symbols on a regular

FIGURE 33-34 Flexible line symbol.

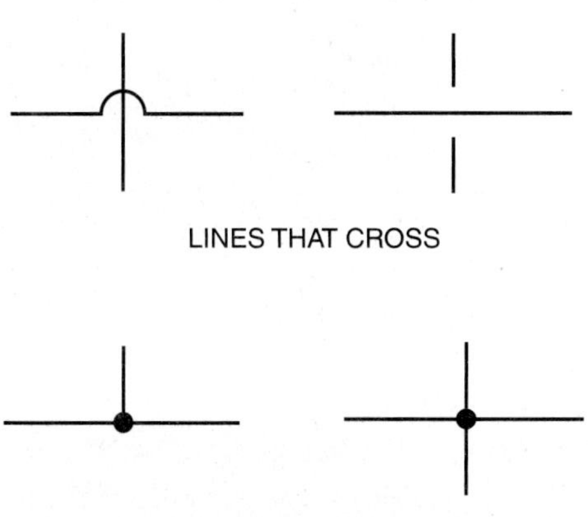

FIGURE 33-35 Intersecting line symbols.

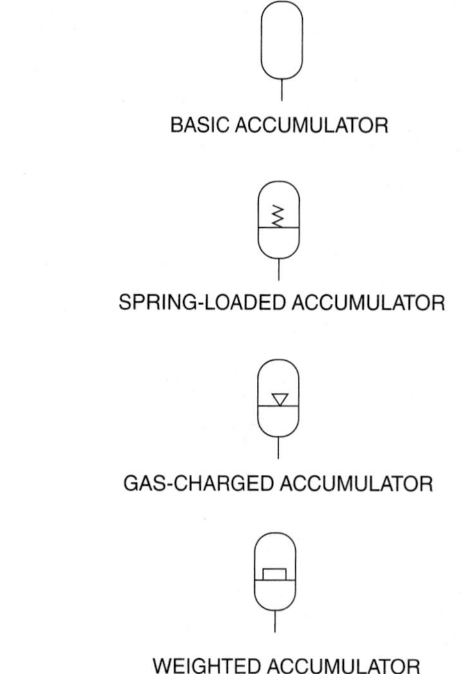

FIGURE 33-36 Common accumulator symbols.

basis, it is still important to be able to recognize and understand what these symbols mean.

One device found in some hydraulic systems is an accumulator. An accumulator is a storage device that holds hydraulic fluid under pressure. The use of an accumulator enables a hydraulic system to absorb shock, supplement pump delivery, and maintain pressure while the system is in a holding pattern. Since the pressure applied to the fluid in an accumulator comes from an external source, there are numerous symbols used to identify the accumulator in use (**FIGURE 33-36**).

Other hydraulic system components sometimes found on schematic diagrams include pressure and temperature indicators, quick disconnect couplings, mechanical connections, and springs (**FIGURE 33-37**).

Service technicians should keep in mind that electronic displays of hydraulic system schematics can vary somewhat from hardcopy versions. For one, software used to create schematic diagrams typically provides a great deal of user control over naming and identifying components used in a schematic. In addition, simply mousing over or clicking on a graphic symbol might reveal additional information about a component, such as real-time values of operating parameters (**FIGURE 33-38**). The same mouse action might also call up a pictorial or cutaway image of the component to further clarify the component's identity and its operating conditions. As technology continues to advance, service technicians will need to become more familiar with, and take advantage of, these enhanced capabilities.

To draw a basic hydraulic system schematic diagram using graphic symbols, follow the steps in **SKILL DRILL 33-1**.

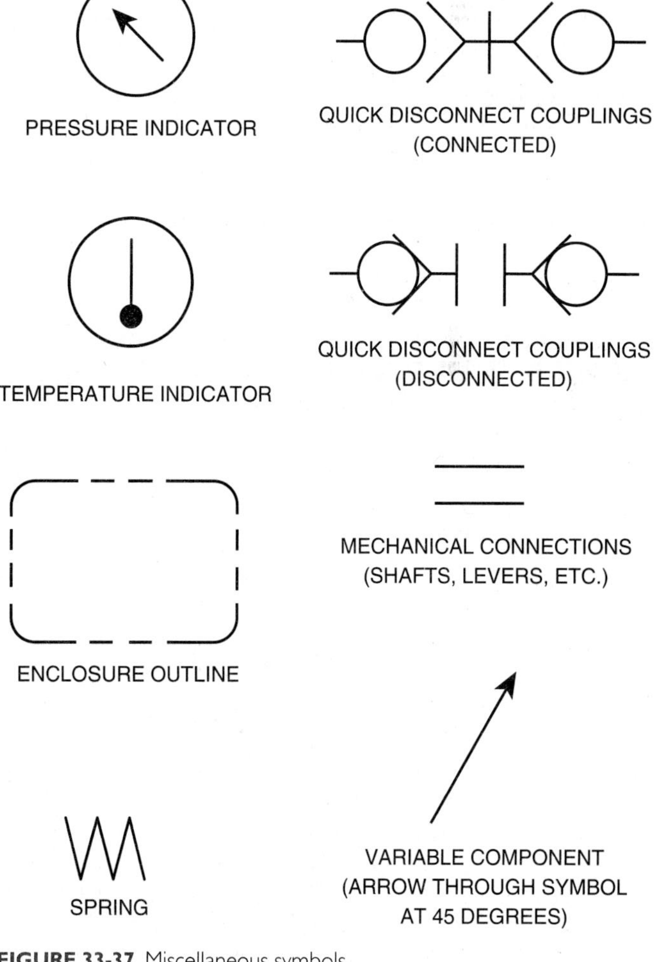

FIGURE 33-37 Miscellaneous symbols.

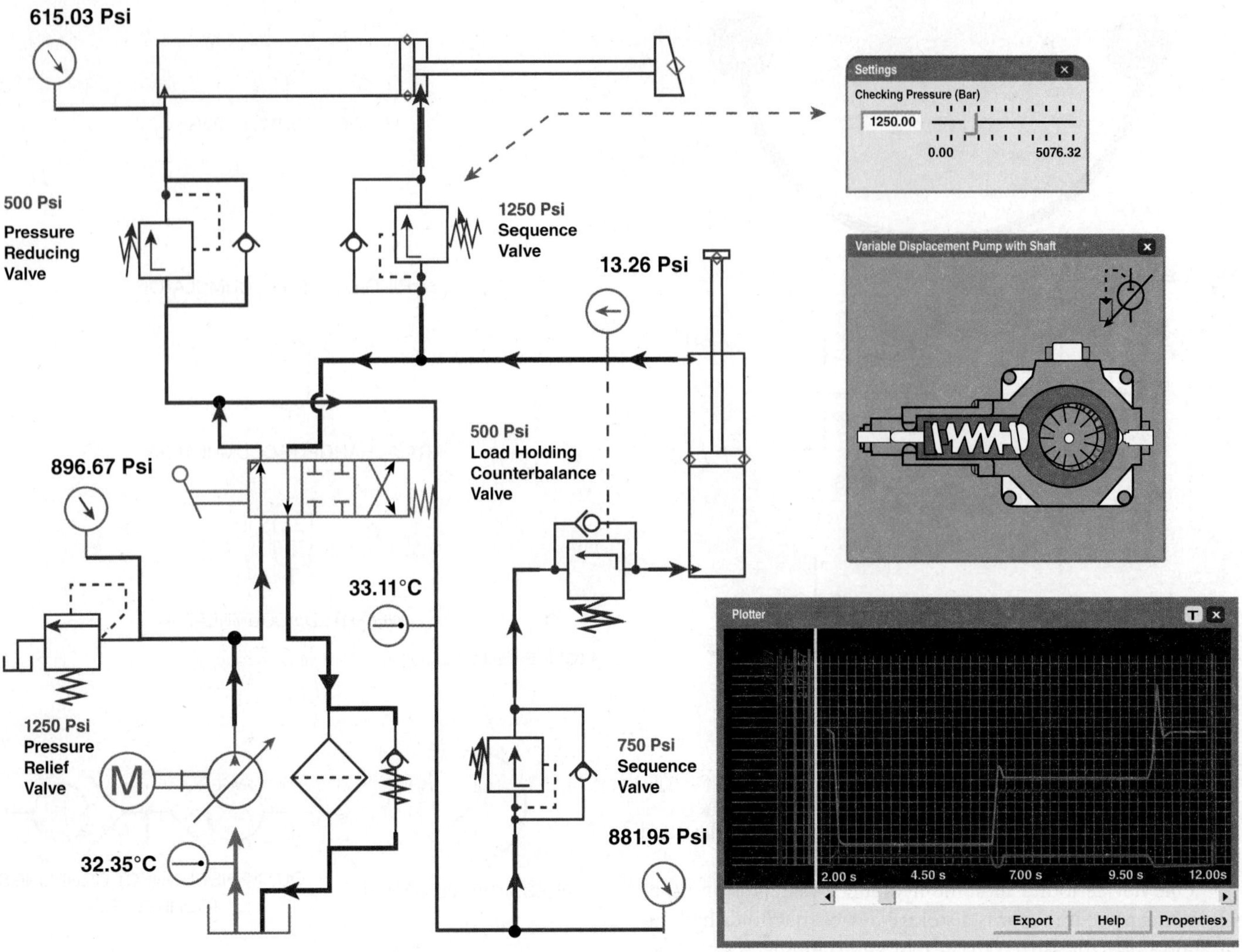

FIGURE 33-38 Electronic display of hydraulic system schematic.

SKILL DRILL 33-1 Drawing a Basic Hydraulic System Schematic Using Graphic Symbols

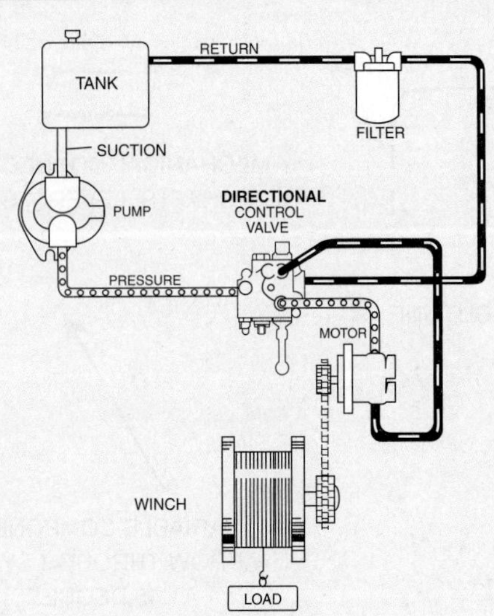

1. Identify the components that make up the hydraulic system and determine how the components are connected. In this case, use the pictorial drawing of the hydraulic system that controls a dozer winch. The system includes a pressurized reservoir; a unidirectional fixed displacement pump; a four-port, three-position, open-center directional control valve; a bidirectional, or reversible, motor that turns a chain to drive the winch; a filter; and connecting lines.

SKILL DRILL 33-1 Drawing a Basic Hydraulic System Schematic Using Graphic Symbols (Continued)

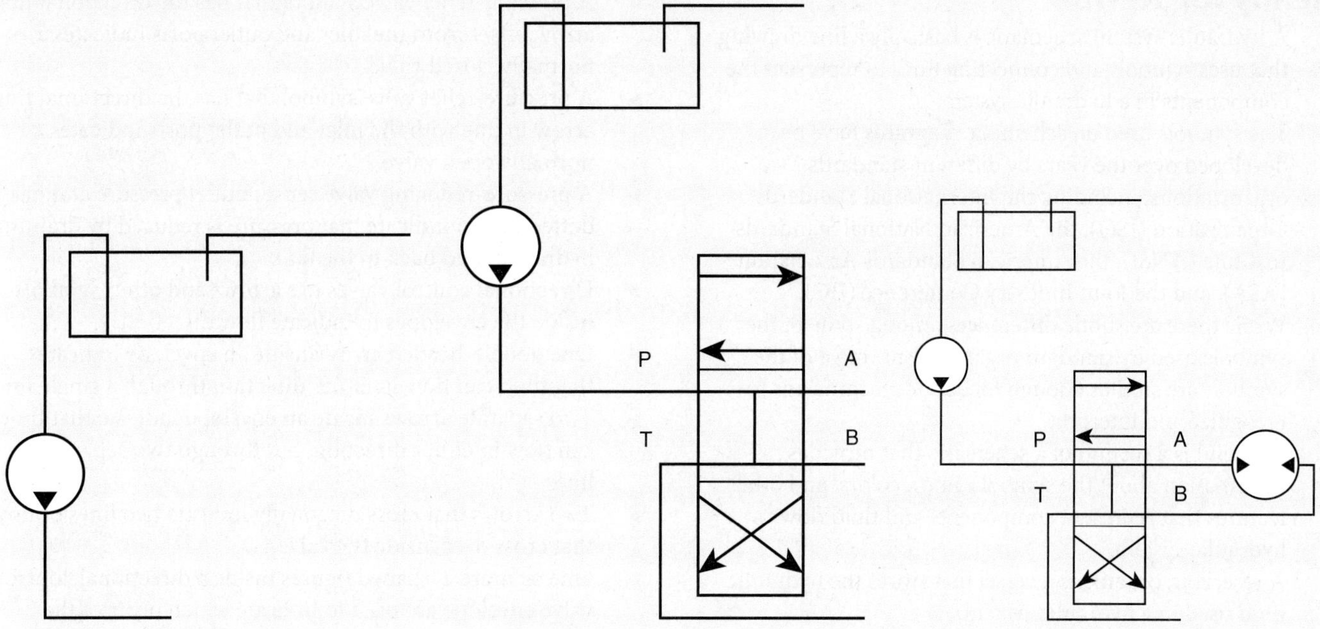

2. Begin the schematic diagram by drawing the symbols for the pressurized reservoir, the unidirectional fixed displacement pump, and the pressure and return lines leading to and from the components. Draw the suction line below the oil surface at the reservoir. Draw the return line above the oil surface at the reservoir.

3. Continue the schematic diagram by adding symbols and lines for the four-port, three-position, open-center directional valve. Draw the valve in the neutral position.

4. Continue the schematic diagram by adding the symbol for the bidirectional (reversible) motor, along with the appropriate connecting lines.

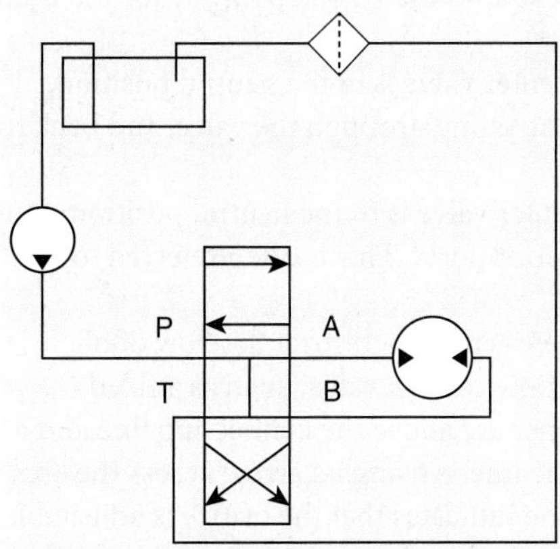

5. Complete the schematic diagram by adding the symbol for the filter and the remaining section of the return line.

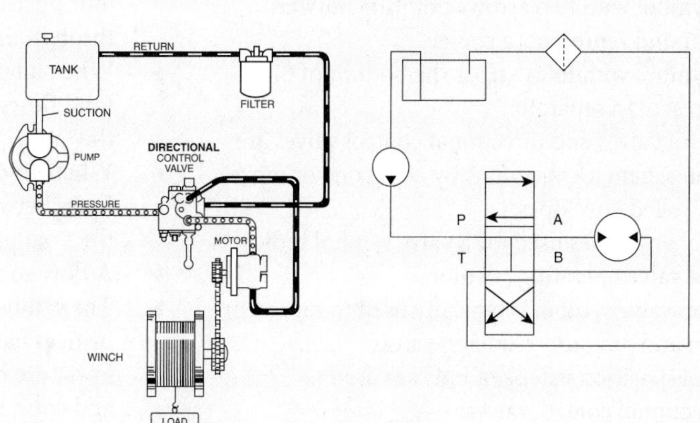

6. Compare the completed schematic diagram with the pictorial reference drawing to ensure that the proper symbols and connecting lines were used to represent the hydraulic system.

Wrap-Up

Ready for Review

- A hydraulic system schematic is basically a line drawing that uses symbols and connecting lines to represent the components in a hydraulic system.
- The symbols used on schematic diagrams have been developed over the years by different standards organizations, including the International Standards Organization (ISO), the American National Standards Institute (ANSI), the American Standards Association (ASA), and the Joint Industry Conference (JIC).
- While there are subtle differences among some of the symbols used by standard organizations, most of the symbols are similar enough for service technicians to recognize and interpret.
- A legend is a section of a schematic that provides information about the symbols, lines, colors, and other features that represent components and fluid flows in a hydraulic system.
- A reservoir, or tank, is a vessel that stores the hydraulic fluid used in a hydraulic system.
- The symbol used to represent a vented reservoir in a schematic drawing appears to be open at the top, while the symbol for a pressurized reservoir appears to be closed at the top.
- Fluid conditioners—such as strainers and filters, heaters and coolers, and separators—are components that affect the physical characteristics of the hydraulic fluid.
- A diamond symbol with a dashed line across it represents a strainer or filter.
- A diamond symbol with two arrows pointing inward inside the diamond represents a heater.
- A diamond symbol with two arrows pointing outward inside the diamond represents a cooler.
- A diamond symbol with lines across the bottom of the diamond represents a separator.
- Pressure control valves and directional control valves are represented on schematic diagrams by using one or more square boxes, called envelopes.
- The number of envelopes used for a valve symbol indicates the number of valve operating positions.
- A one-position valve symbol is typically used to represent pressure-relief and pressure-reducing valves.
- Two- and three-position valve symbols are used to represent directional control valves.
- Lines, arrows, and other symbols are added to the basic envelopes to represent line connections, flow paths, and valve functions.
- A pressure-relief valve symbol includes a single envelope with an arrow to represent the direction of flow, a jagged line to represent the valve spring, and a dashed line to represent the pilot line that is sensing pressure in the system.
- A pressure-relief valve symbol that has the directional flow arrow offset from the inlet and outlet ports indicates a normally closed valve.
- A pressure-relief valve symbol that has the directional flow arrow in line with the inlet and outlet ports indicates a normally open valve.
- A pressure-reducing valve senses outlet pressure and has a dotted line to indicate that pressure is reduced by draining hydraulic fluid back to the tank.
- Directional control valves use arrows and other symbols inside the envelopes to indicate flow direction.
- One double-headed arrow inside an envelope indicates that fluid can flow in either direction through a single line.
- Two separate arrows inside an envelope indicate that fluid can flow in either direction, but through two separate lines.
- Two arrows that cross diagonally indicate two lines of flow that cross over inside the valve.
- One or more T-shaped figures inside a directional control valve envelope are used to indicate which ports of the valve are blocked internally.
- There are many possible configurations for directional control valves. A typical three-position valve has three envelopes, along with arrows and symbols in each envelope, to indicate the direction and flow when the valve is in that position. The center position in the valve indicates the flow path of the fluid while the valve is centered or in neutral.
- Three common valve center configurations are closed center, tandem center, and open center.
- When a closed center valve is in the neutral position, all four ports are blocked, so there is no pathway for the fluid through the valve.
- When a tandem center valve is in the neutral position, fluid flows from the pump, through the valve, and back to the tank.
- When an open-center valve is in the neutral position, fluid flows between all four ports. This is often referred to as the float position.
- A flow control valve is used to restrict the flow of oil.
- The symbol for a flow control valve (such as a fixed orifice) has an upper arc above the connecting line and a lower arc below the line. An angled arrow across the arcs and connecting line indicates that the orifice is adjustable.
- A check valve permits flow in only one direction.
- A bypass valve symbol includes a spring on the ball end of the symbol.
- The symbol for an on/off (manual shutoff) valve looks like a bowtie placed over the connecting line.
- Common actuators used in order to open and close valves include pushbuttons, pedals, springs, levers, mechanical mechanisms, and solenoids.

- A hydraulic pump generates the system pressure needed by hydraulic motors to drive another component or other components.
- Hydraulic pump symbols are circles with solid black triangles pointing outward, away from the center of the circle.
- A unidirectional, or nonreversible, hydraulic pump has one black triangle.
- A bidirectional, or reversible, hydraulic pump has two triangles.
- Fixed displacement pumps deliver the same volume of hydraulic fluid with each cycle.
- The symbols for variable displacement hydraulic pumps use circles and black triangles, but they also include an angled arrow across the middle of the circle.
- If an electric motor is used to drive a hydraulic pump, a circular symbol with the letter M inside of it will appear beside the hydraulic pump symbol.
- A hydraulic motor is a component that receives pressurized fluid from a hydraulic pump and converts that pressure and flow to rotation and torque to drive some component(s) in the system.
- Hydraulic motor symbols are circles with solid black triangles pointing inward, toward the center of the circle.
- A unidirectional, or nonreversible, fixed displacement hydraulic motor has one black triangle.
- A bidirectional, or reversible, hydraulic motor has two black triangles.
- The symbols for variable displacement hydraulic motors use the same basic circles and black triangles, but they also include an angled arrow across the middle of the circle.
- Hydraulic cylinders, which are sometimes referred to as linear actuators, are commonly used in hydraulic systems to move loads.
- Single-acting hydraulic cylinders can apply force in only one direction, while double-acting cylinders can apply force in two directions.
- Hydraulic cylinder symbols consist of a rectangle that represents the cylinder housing, short lines that represent the ports, and a T-shaped line that represents the piston rod.
- Symbols for hydraulic cylinders that have cushions to dampen the piston's movement and reduce shock during operation show the cushions and indicate whether the cushions are fixed or adjustable.
- A solid line symbol represents a working fluid line.
- A dashed line symbol represents a pilot line.
- A dotted line symbol represents an exhaust or drain line.
- A line symbol made up of long and short dashes represents the outline of an enclosure.
- Arrows used on line symbols indicate the direction of flow for the liquid or gas being pumped through the system.
- A solid arced line with a black dot at each end represents a flexible line, such as a hose that is connected to some type of moving part.
- Symbols for fluid lines that intersect in a hydraulic system schematic are different for lines that simply cross over each other and those that actually join.
- An accumulator is a storage device that holds hydraulic fluid under pressure to enable the hydraulic system to absorb shock, supplement pump delivery, and maintain pressure while the system is in a holding pattern.
- Accumulator symbols vary depending on the external source of the pressure applied to the fluid inside.
- Hydraulic system schematics often include symbols for pressure and temperature indicators, quick disconnect couplings, mechanical connections, and springs.

Key Terms

closed center A control valve center configuration in which when the valve is placed in the neutral position, all four ports are blocked and there is no pathway for the fluid through the valve.

cutaway diagram A type of sketch in which the internal parts of components in a hydraulic system are exposed to help illustrate how the components function.

double-acting cylinder A type of hydraulic cylinder that can apply force in two directions.

envelopes Square box symbols used to represent pressure control valves and directional control valves on a schematic diagram; the number of envelopes equates to the number of valve operating positions.

fixed displacement A type of pump or motor in which the amount of flow displaced by each cycle of rotation remains the same.

float position A control valve center configuration in which when the valve is placed in the neutral position, fluid flows between all four ports; it is often referred to as open center.

linear actuator A type of device, such as a hydraulic cylinder, that when activated, moves a load in a straight direction.

normally closed valve A type of valve, such as a pressure-relief valve, that remains closed during normal operating conditions but will open if the system becomes overpressurized.

normally open valve A type of valve, such as a pressure-reducing valve, that remains open during normal operating conditions but will close if the system becomes overpressurized.

open center A control valve center configuration in which when the valve is placed in the neutral position, fluid flows between all four ports; it is often referred to as the float position.

pictorial diagram A type of sketch used to illustrate what the components in a hydraulic system look like and how they are connected.

pressurized reservoir A type of reservoir used to store hydraulic fluid that is closed at the top to maintain pressure in the reservoir.

schematic diagram A type of diagram that uses symbols and lines to represent the components in a hydraulic system and how they are connected.

single-acting cylinder A type of hydraulic cylinder that can apply force in only one direction.

tandem center A control valve center configuration in which when the valve is placed in the neutral position, fluid flows from the pump, through the valve, and back to the tank.

variable displacement A type of pump or motor in which the flow rate and outlet pressure can be changed during operation.

vented reservoir A type of reservoir used to store hydraulic fluid that is open or vented at the top.

Review Questions

1. One way for service technicians to get information about the symbols, lines, colors, and other features shown on a hydraulic system schematic is to look at the _________.
   a. gateway
   b. float
   c. envelope
   d. legend
2. The symbol shown here represents a _____________.
   a. drain line pulling oil from the bottom of a reservoir
   b. fluid line connecting below the oil level in a reservoir
   c. pilot line being grounded at the bottom of a cylinder
   d. blocked port on a single-acting hydraulic cylinder

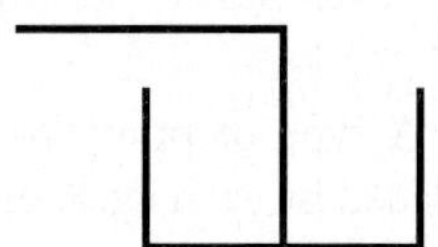

3. Which of these statements about hydraulic heater and cooler symbols is true?
   a. Both heater and cooler symbols have arrows that point inward, toward the center of the diamond.
   b. Heater symbols have arrows that point outward; cooler symbols have arrows that point inward.
   c. Heater symbols have arrows that point inward; cooler symbols have arrows that point outward.
   d. Both heater and cooler symbols have arrows pointing outward from the center of the diamond.
4. The number of envelopes in a directional control valve symbol is equivalent to the number of _____________.
   a. valve operating positions
   b. separators needed in the system
   c. ports in the valve body
   d. float positions needed for the pump
5. The symbol shown here represents a _____________.
   a. manual shutoff valve
   b. check valve
   c. normally closed pressure-relief valve
   d. pushbutton actuator

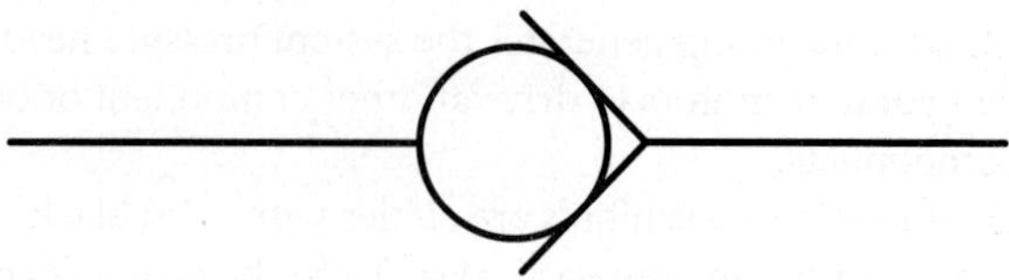

6. On a schematic diagram, a nonreversible hydraulic pump symbol is a _____________.
   a. circle with a solid black triangle pointing inward, toward the center
   b. square with a solid black arrow pointing outward, toward the center
   c. square with a solid black arrow pointing inward, toward the center
   d. circle with a solid black triangle pointing outward from the center
7. The symbol shown here represents a _____________.
   a. unidirectional, variable displacement hydraulic motor
   b. bidirectional, fixed displacement hydraulic pump
   c. multidirectional, fixed displacement pneumatic motor
   d. unidirectional, variable displacement hydraulic pump

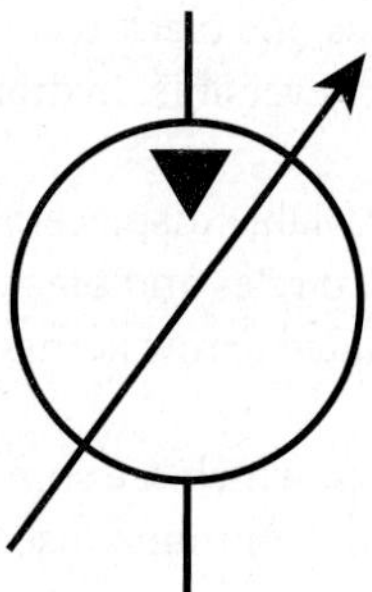

8. The symbol shown here represents a _____________ _____________.
   a. double-acting cylinder with a single piston rod and an adjustable cushion on one end
   b. single-acting cylinder with a bidirectional piston and a cushion
   c. double-acting cylinder with a single piston rod and a fixed cushion on both ends
   d. single-acting linear valve with an adjustable cushion on one port

9. A symbol that shows a solid arced line with a black dot at each end represents a ____________.
   a. fuel suction line
   b. flexible line or hose
   c. exhaust or drain line
   d. pilot line crossing a flow line
10. The symbol shown here represents a ________________.
   a. pressure indicator
   b. variable component
   c. single exit port in a motor
   d. temperature indicator

ASE Technician A and Technician B Style Questions

1. Technician A says the section of a schematic that provides information about the symbols, lines, colors, and other features that represent components and fluid flows in a hydraulic system is called a legend. Technician B says it is called a pictorial. Who is correct?
   a. Technician A
   b. Technician B
   c. Both Technician A and Technician B
   d. Neither Technician A nor Technician B
2. Technician A says the symbol on the left represents a vented reservoir. Technician B says the symbol on the right represents a pressurized reservoir. Who is correct?
   a. Technician A
   b. Technician B
   c. Both Technician A and Technician B
   d. Neither Technician A nor Technician B

3. Technician A says only heaters and coolers are considered to be fluid conditioners in a hydraulic system. Technician B says fluid conditioners can include strainers and filters, heaters and coolers, and separators. Who is correct?
   a. Technician A
   b. Technician B
   c. Both Technician A and Technician B
   d. Neither Technician A nor Technician B
4. Technician A says this symbol represents a strainer or filter. Technician B says the symbol represents a separator with an automatic drain. Who is correct?
   a. Technician A
   b. Technician B
   c. Both Technician A and Technician B
   d. Neither Technician A nor Technician B

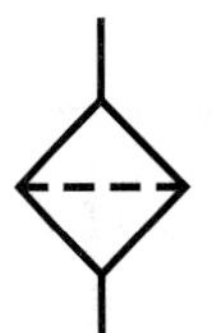

5. Technician A says a symbol with two square boxes joined together represents a pump and motor combination. Technician B says the symbol represents a two-stage filter. Who is correct?
   a. Technician A
   b. Technician B
   c. Both Technician A and Technician B
   d. Neither Technician A nor Technician B
6. Technician A says this symbol represents an adjustable flow control valve. Technician B says the symbol represents a normally open pressure-relief valve. Who is correct?
   a. Technician A
   b. Technician B
   c. Both Technician A and Technician B
   d. Neither Technician A nor Technician B

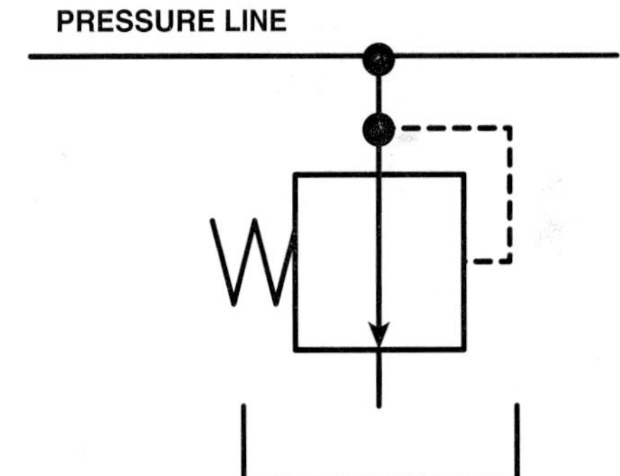

7. Technician A says this symbol represents two ports of a directional control valve that are blocked internally. Technician B says the symbol represents a valve spool in which two ports are converted to four ports internally. Who is correct?
   a. Technician A
   b. Technician B
   c. Both Technician A and Technician B
   d. Neither Technician A nor Technician B

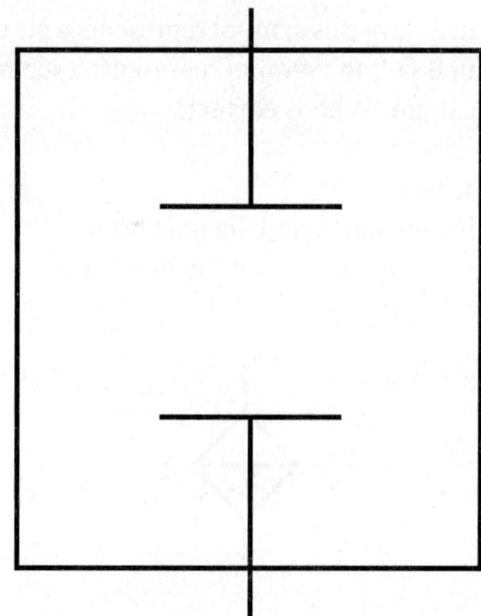

8. Technician A says this symbol represents a reversible pump. Technician B says the symbol represents a reversible motor. Who is correct?
   a. Technician A
   b. Technician B
   c. Both Technician A and Technician B
   d. Neither Technician A nor Technician B

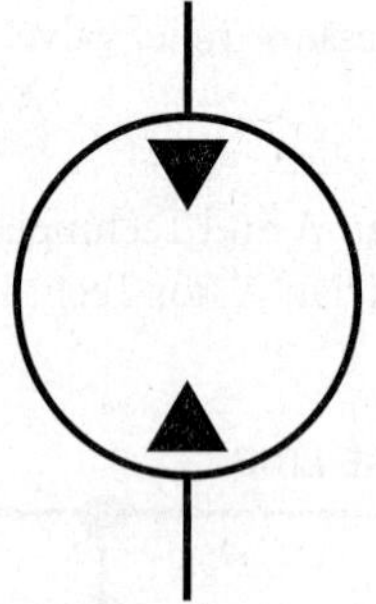

9. Technician A says this symbol represents a double-acting hydraulic cylinder. Technician B says the symbol represents a hydraulic cylinder with a single piston rod that is extended and returned by fluid. Who is correct?
   a. Technician A
   b. Technician B
   c. Both Technician A and Technician B
   d. Neither Technician A nor Technician B

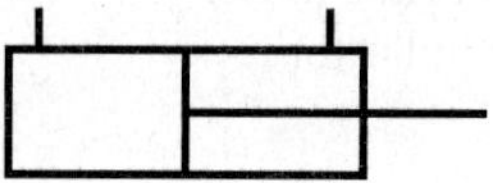

10. Technician A says a pilot line in a hydraulic system is represented on a schematic with a dotted line. Technician B says any type of pilot line should be represented with a line made up of long and short dashes. Who is correct?
    a. Technician A
    b. Technician B
    c. Both Technician A and Technician B
    d. Neither Technician A nor Technician B

CHAPTER 34
Preventive Maintenance

Knowledge Objectives

After reading this chapter, you will be able to:

- **K34001** Explain the fundamentals of regular hydraulic system maintenance service.

Skills Objectives

After reading this chapter, you will be able to:

- **S34001** Complete maintenance procedures following manufacturer's recommendations for hydraulic systems.

▶ Introduction

Hydraulic systems are a critical part of virtually every piece of heavy equipment used in construction, forestry, mining, and agricultural applications. Without a properly performing hydraulic system, basic equipment functions such as locomotion, steering, and braking, as well as machine-specific functions such as lifting, lowering, tilting, extending, and retracting can become greatly diminished or inoperable. One of the most effective means of ensuring the reliability and longevity of hydraulic systems is through regular **preventive maintenance**.

To help preserve the performance of hydraulic systems and reduce operating and repair costs over the lifespan of the equipment, service technicians must understand and be able to perform regular maintenance service on hydraulic systems. This chapter explains the importance of routine hydraulic system maintenance and describes the fundamentals of establishing and following a preventive maintenance program.

▶ Regular Hydraulic System Maintenance

K34001, S34001

Heavy equipment of virtually every type and size relies extensively on numerous hydraulic circuits to carry out basic functions. The hydraulic systems found in modern heavy equipment are more complex and operate under tougher parameters than those used in years past. As a result, repairs to these systems are likely to take longer and cost more than ever before. Regular maintenance is absolutely essential to the dependability and longevity of hydraulic systems and the equipment itself.

The Case for Regular Maintenance

Failing to perform regular preventive maintenance on a heavy equipment hydraulic system is the leading cause of component failures within the system. Simply stated, a lack of preventive maintenance, or planned maintenance (PM) as it is sometimes called, can quickly lead to the need for **corrective maintenance** and all the costs associated with it. Another way of thinking about this is the difference between following a proactive approach to maintenance versus a reactive approach. Being proactive toward maintenance—that is, identifying abnormal conditions before they become problems—is more efficient and cost-effective than being reactive to problems that have already occurred. To better understand the importance of regular hydraulic system maintenance, it helps to identify some of the effects and costs associated with *not* performing preventive maintenance.

All of the components in a hydraulic system—the reservoir, hydraulic fluid, pumps, motors, valves, cylinders, hoses, lines, filters, and accessories—work closely together (**FIGURE 34-1**). So, a problem with one component can easily affect other components in the system.

A simple example of this complex interaction involves the hydraulic fluid. The hydraulic fluid is the lifeblood of the entire system. Problems with the hydraulic fluid, such as improper fluid levels, contamination, and overheating, can affect the operation of every component in the system. Seals, O-rings, and hoses can break down and cause leaks. Gears, pistons, and vanes in hydraulic pumps and motors can be damaged by contaminants and fail to maintain system pressure and flow.

Something as simple as a slow hydraulic fluid leak can have a costly domino effect on system performance, unnecessary downtime, and environmental consequences. Not only is there the cost associated with replenishing the fluid itself, there are also many other related costs, including but not limited to the following:

- personnel time needed for cleanup,
- possible system component damage,
- unplanned repairs,
- equipment downtime,
- productivity losses,
- spill cleanup supplies,
- possible regulatory agency fines for environmental damage.

Together, the costs associated with a seemingly insignificant problem (a minor fluid leak) can add up to thousands of dollars in unplanned expenses. And more serious problems that are not identified during routine maintenance have even costlier consequences. This is why prevention is at the heart of any preventive maintenance program for hydraulic systems. Identifying and correcting potential issues in a hydraulic system before they become problems helps maximize equipment performance and service life while minimizing equipment failures and operating costs. Avoiding system problems provides numerous long-term benefits:

- greater productivity
- increased reliability
- improved planning
- less downtime
- lower costs for replacing equipment.

You Are the Mobile Heavy Equipment Technician

You are preparing to perform preventive maintenance on the hydraulic system of a wheeled loader. There have been no reports of problems on the machine, but before you begin, you want to collect some information.

1. What sources of information might you check before beginning the preventive maintenance procedure?
2. Where might you look to find any historical data on the equipment?
3. Will you need any diagnostic equipment? If so, what types of equipment would you want to have available?

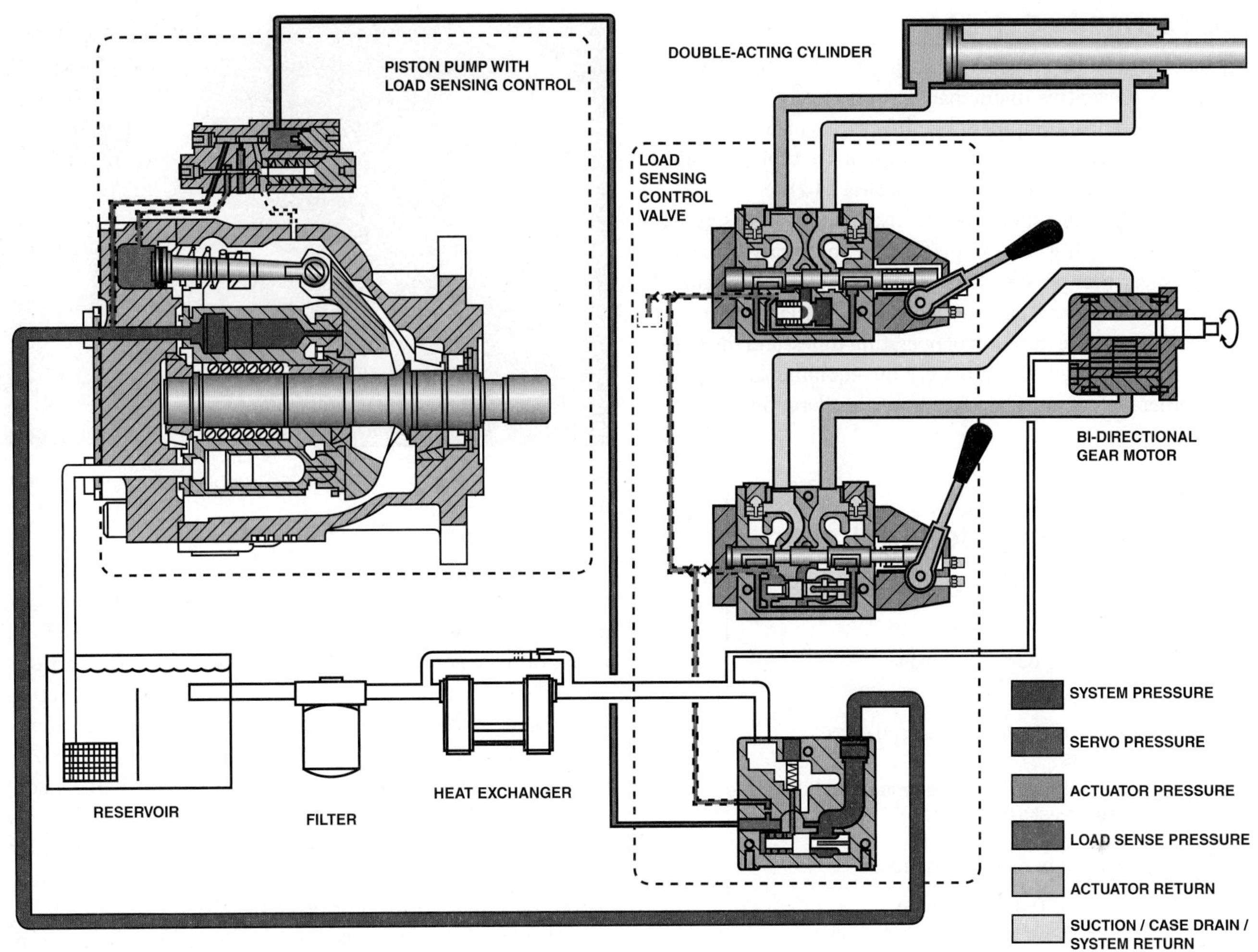

FIGURE 34-1 Cutaway diagram of hydraulic system components.

Another way to understand the significance of a preventive maintenance program is to examine the general types of failures that occur in hydraulic systems. There are three basic categories of malfunctions or failures in a hydraulic system—most of which can be attributed to contaminated hydraulic fluid.

- **Degradation failures** tend to occur gradually over long periods of time. They are commonly associated with basic wear and tear and manifest as diminished flow rates, decreased cylinder speeds, valve leakage, and similar symptoms of general deterioration. Problems with fluid contamination can hasten these types of failures.
- **Transient failures** are intermittent. They may appear and disappear, but they typically indicate an underlying problem that will need to be addressed. For example, particles in contaminated fluid might temporarily affect the gears in a pump. If the particles dislodge themselves, the pump might return to normal operation temporarily. Ultimately, however, the fluid contamination will have to be addressed to avoid component failures.
- **Catastrophic failures** represent a complete component or system malfunction. They occur suddenly and without warning. Most often, catastrophic failures occur when transient failures are neglected over time. They are typically the most time-consuming and costly failures to repair.

While a carefully developed preventive maintenance program can resolve many of these hydraulic system issues, the truth is that no maintenance program will detect and correct every problem ahead of time. Components wear out over time and can't always be diagnosed to the extent that they can be replaced before they fail. But developing and following a preventive maintenance program is the best way to minimize problems before they become costly failures.

Establishing and Using a Preventive Maintenance Program

Despite the complexity of modern hydraulic systems, the goal of a preventive maintenance program for hydraulic systems should be simplicity. Preventive maintenance is an ongoing process that spans the life of the equipment. It must be performed with regularity, and it should be set up to be as routine and unobtrusive as possible.

Input Factors to Consider

Many factors must be considered during the development and practice of a preventive maintenance program for a hydraulic system. For instance, equipment manufacturers provide routine inspection and maintenance guidelines that are typically based on hours, days, or months of usage (**FIGURE 34-2**).

Service technicians should always use manufacturer's guidelines when developing and/or performing preventive maintenance. However, they must keep in mind that these recommended guidelines do not always take into consideration factors such as climate conditions, the duration of operating times, and the manner in which equipment operators use the equipment. For those reasons, other factors must be taken into consideration.

Recommended hydraulic system service intervals

10-Hour or daily inspection

- Check hydraulic fluid level
- Check hydraulic cylinders and pumps for leaks
- Check hoses, lines, and hydraulic tank area for leaks or damage

250-Hour or monthly inspection

- Perform 10-hour preventive maintenance checks
- Check hydraulic oil cooler for leaks or plugging
- Check all hydraulic lines for damaged, missing, or loose connections

500-Hour or quarterly inspection

- Perform 10- and 250-hour preventive maintenance checks
- Perform oil sample testing and analysis
- Change hydraulic filter
- Check hydraulic pumps and mountings for loose or missing hardware

1,000-Hour or six-month inspection

- Perform 10-, 250-, and 500-hour preventive maintenance checks
- Check pump weep holes for leaks

2,000-Hour or annual inspection

- Perform 10-, 250-, and 1,000-hour preventive maintenance checks
- Check hydraulic system pressure
- Check hydraulic system cycle times and drift rates

FIGURE 34-2 Typical hydraulic system service interval recommendations.

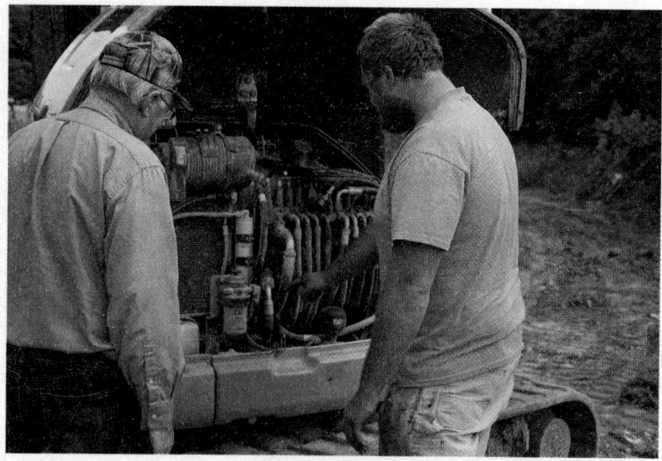

FIGURE 34-3 Equipment operator relaying information to service technician.

One of the most important sources of information about a hydraulic system is the equipment operator. Typically, the operator is responsible for doing a walk-around inspection before and, in some cases, after each shift. This inspection is performed on the entire piece of equipment and includes checks of the hydraulic system for leaks, fluid levels, and other visible signs of problems. In addition, the operator is the best source of information about the performance of the hydraulics on the equipment. Any degradation and transient problems can often be detected by the operator and passed on to service technicians before system failures occur (**FIGURE 34-3**).

Historical data that has been collected on the equipment can also be a valuable source of information. If known problems with the hydraulic system have occurred in the past, service technicians might be able to avoid failures by responding early to similar symptoms. In addition, technicians can compare current conditions with those recorded in the past.

Many pieces of heavy equipment are equipped with onboard computer systems that display and record abnormal conditions that suggest potential problems. Service technicians can use this information to help troubleshoot potential problems. Some onboard systems allow technicians to connect a laptop computer to a USB port on the system, much like how automobile mechanics attach code readers to cars to troubleshoot problems (**FIGURE 34-4**).

By using these and other available inputs, not only can technicians familiarize themselves with a particular piece of equipment, but they can also fine-tune a preventive maintenance program to stay ahead of problems by analyzing current and past conditions and symptoms.

Preventive Maintenance Procedures

The exact steps and the order in which those steps are performed during a preventive maintenance program for a hydraulic system can vary according to the company, the equipment manufacturer, and technician preferences. The primary objective of the procedure is to carefully follow the established maintenance program so that every task is accurately performed.

FIGURE 34-4 Technician accessing data from equipment's onboard computer.

FIGURE 34-5 Equipment for fluid analysis.

▶ TECHNICIAN TIP

Always read the preventive maintenance guidelines before performing any of the tasks. In many cases, the guidelines will include information about safety precautions that need to be followed; tools, equipment and replacement parts that might be needed; and environmental factors that might need to be considered.

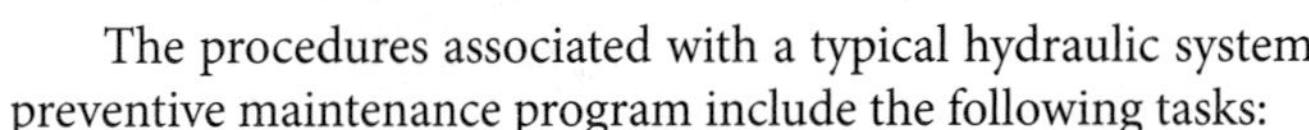

SAFETY TIP

Hydraulic systems operate under high pressures and high temperatures. Service technicians must be constantly aware of the dangers associated with these hydraulic fluid conditions. If a hydraulic line or hose bursts, the hot fluid can cause severe burns and it can be injected into the body. Always follow safe work practices when working around any parts of a hydraulic system.

The procedures associated with a typical hydraulic system preventive maintenance program include the following tasks:

1. Check, analyze, and (if necessary) replace the hydraulic fluid.

   By far, the majority of hydraulic system problems originate with the hydraulic fluid. For this reason, technicians should always check fluid levels and the condition of the fluid. Contaminated hydraulic fluid can sometimes be detected because of discoloration and/or an odor of something that has been burned. But to be certain about the condition of the fluid, a sample of the fluid should be obtained and analyzed using oil-testing equipment (**FIGURE 34-5**).

   Different methods are used to obtain hydraulic fluid for testing. Whichever method is used must be able to provide a sample that is representative of the fluid's condition in the system during operation. To help ensure that an accurate sample can be obtained, technicians should start the equipment and let it reach normal operating temperature and pressure before shutting down the equipment to collect a sample.

FIGURE 34-6 Remote hydraulic testing port.

Sampling points in the system are also important. Simply extracting fluid from the reservoir will not provide an accurate sample, because many of the contaminants in the fluid that should be tested for will have settled to the bottom of the reservoir. For this reason, hydraulic systems are often equipped with sampling ports to enable technicians to collect fluid from designated areas of the system (**FIGURE 34-6**).

Sometimes, fluid is sampled from a low-pressure circulating line, such as a drain line. In this case, the fluid should be collected from a point where the fluid would typically collect, such as the underside of a horizontal line. Often, because of the low-pressure condition, a vacuum pump is needed to help extract the fluid.

Ideally, hydraulic fluid should be sampled from a point in the circulating line that has the following characteristics:

- It is in a highly turbulent area in which **laminar flow** is not present, such as at an elbow or a sharp bend in the line.

- It is downstream from the major components in the system, such as pumps, motors, actuators, and cylinders.
- It is upstream from filters located in the return line to the reservoir.

A sampling point that meets these criteria is said to be in a **live zone**. A live zone sample is the most representative sample of the fluid, because it has been taken from an area where the fluid is well mixed, likely to contain wear particles from the system components, and upstream from any return line filters that would remove contaminants (**FIGURE 34-7**).

Hydraulic fluid analysis detects chemical impurities and particle contaminants in the fluid. The results of this analysis can often identify the type and source of the contamination, which service technicians can use to remedy the problem (**FIGURE 34-8**). For instance, the presence of **wear metals** such as iron, aluminum, and copper can indicate wear on components such as cylinders, gears, bearings, and bushings. Silicon contamination could be an indicator of worn seals and/or dirt intrusion into the system. Other contaminants, such as calcium, coolant, and water, can indicate leaks in the heat exchanger of a hydraulic system. Technicians should be knowledgeable about the types of contaminants being measured and the possible sources of those contaminants.

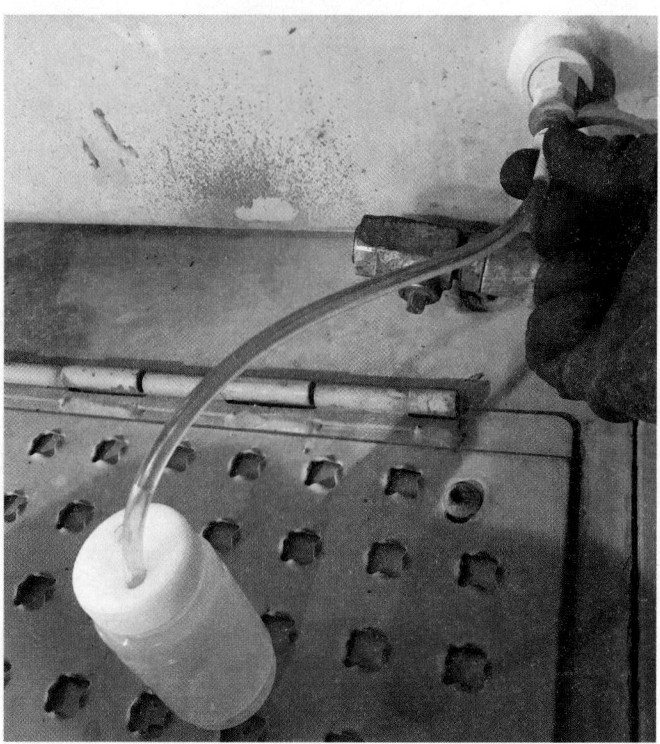

FIGURE 34-7 Taking a hydraulic oil sample from a live zone.

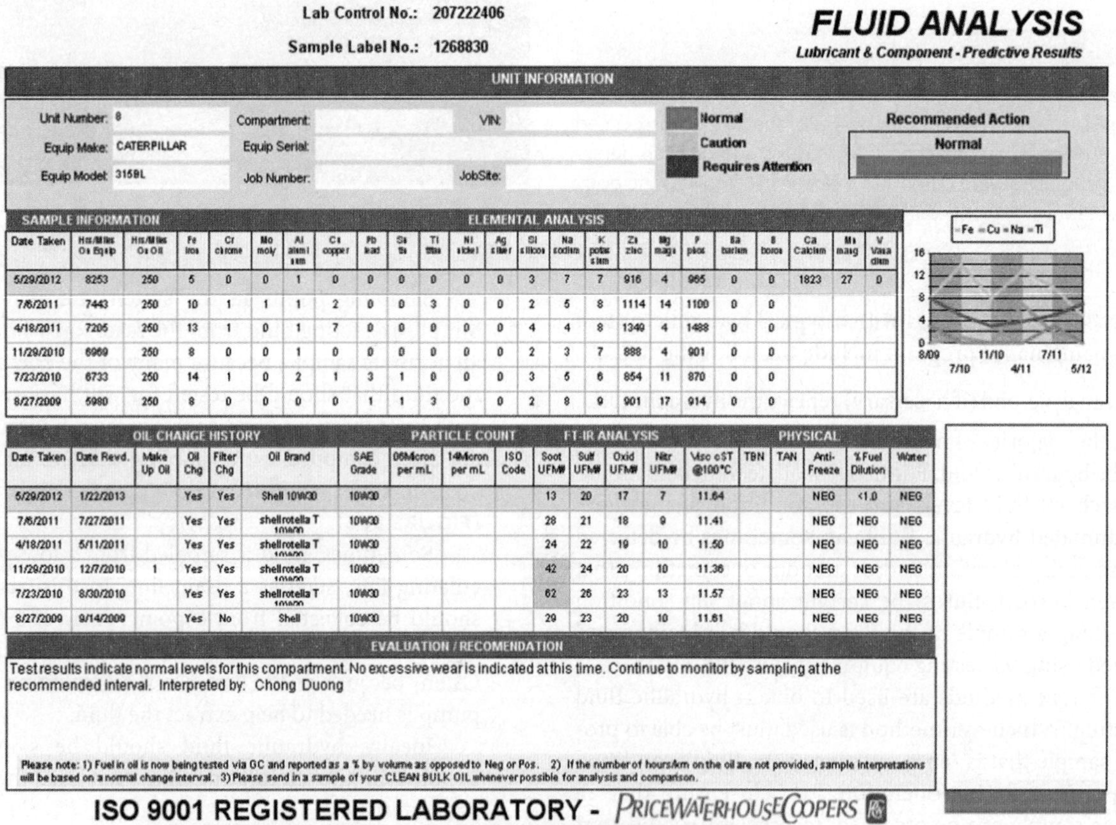

Lab Control No.: 207222406
Sample Label No.: 1268830

FLUID ANALYSIS
Lubricant & Component - Predictive Results

UNIT INFORMATION

Unit Number: 8 | Compartment: | VIN:
Equip Make: CATERPILLAR | Equip Serial:
Equip Model: 315BL | Job Number: | JobSite:

Normal / Caution / Requires Attention

Recommended Action: Normal

SAMPLE INFORMATION / ELEMENTAL ANALYSIS

Date Taken	Hrs/Miles On Equip	Hrs/Miles On Oil	Fe iron	Cr chrome	Mo moly	Al aluminium	Cu copper	Pb lead	Sn tin	Ti titan	Ni nickel	Ag silver	Si silicon	Na sodium	K potassium	Zn zinc	Mg magn	P phos	Ba barium	B boron	Ca Calcium	Mn mang	V Vanadium
5/29/2012	8253	250	5	0	0	1	0	0	0	0	0	0	3	7	7	916	4	965	0	0	1823	27	0
7/6/2011	7443	250	10	1	1	1	2	0	0	3	0	0	2	5	8	1114	14	1100	0	0			
4/18/2011	7205	250	13	1	0	1	7	0	0	0	0	0	4	4	8	1340	4	1488	0	0			
11/29/2010	6969	250	8	0	0	1	0	0	0	0	0	0	2	3	7	888	4	901	0	0			
7/23/2010	6733	250	14	1	0	2	1	3	1	0	0	0	3	5	6	854	11	870	0	0			
8/27/2009	5980	250	8	0	0	0	0	1	1	3	0	0	2	8	9	901	17	914	0	0			

OIL CHANGE HISTORY / PARTICLE COUNT / FT-IR ANALYSIS / PHYSICAL

Date Taken	Date Revd.	Make Up Oil	Oil Chg	Filter Chg	Oil Brand	SAE Grade	06Micron per mL	14Micron per mL	ISO Code	Soot UFM#	Sulf UFM#	Oxid UFM#	Nitr UFM#	Visc cST @100°C	TBN	TAN	Anti-Freeze	%Fuel Dilution	Water
5/29/2012	1/22/2013		Yes	Yes	Shell 10W30	10W30				13	20	17	7	11.64			NEG	<1.0	NEG
7/6/2011	7/27/2011		Yes	Yes	shellrotella T	10W30				28	21	18	9	11.41			NEG	NEG	NEG
4/18/2011	5/11/2011		Yes	Yes	shellrotella T	10W30				24	22	19	10	11.50			NEG	NEG	NEG
11/29/2010	12/7/2010	1	Yes	Yes	shellrotella T	10W30				42	24	20	10	11.36			NEG	NEG	NEG
7/23/2010	8/30/2010		Yes	Yes	shellrotella T	10W30				62	26	23	13	11.57			NEG	NEG	NEG
8/27/2009	9/14/2009		Yes	No	Shell	10W30				29	23	20	10	11.61			NEG	NEG	NEG

EVALUATION / RECOMENDATION

Test results indicate normal levels for this compartment. No excessive wear is indicated at this time. Continue to monitor by sampling at the recommended interval. Interpreted by: Chong Duong

Please note: 1) Fuel in oil is now being tested via GC and reported as a % by volume as opposed to Neg or Pos. 2) If the number of hours/km on the oil are not provided, sample interpretations will be based on a normal change interval. 3) Please send in a sample of your CLEAN BULK OIL whenever possible for analysis and comparison.

ISO 9001 REGISTERED LABORATORY - PRICEWATERHOUSECOOPERS

Toromont Cat Fluids Analysis Lab - 548 Edgeley Blvd, Concord, Ontario L4K 1B6 - (416)667-5937 - Fax (416)667-5969
website: www.toromontcat.com/sos_oilanalysis.asp toll-free phone: 1-866-9-SOS-LAB

This Analysis is intended as an aid in predicting mechanical wear. No guarantee, expressed or implied, is made against failure of this component.

FIGURE 34-8 Hydraulic fluid analysis results.

Contaminants will always find their way into a hydraulic system, but they can be minimized by keeping the areas around dipsticks, filters, and filler plugs as clean as possible. It also helps to keep fluid containers clean before pouring fluid into the hydraulic system.

▶ TECHNICIAN TIP

Since contamination is such a problem for hydraulic systems, it is always a good idea to wash equipment on a regular basis. Washing equipment helps minimize sources of contamination, reduce hydraulic system temperatures, and improve visibility around hoses and other system components so that operators and technicians can see leaks and component damage.

While one or more hydraulic filters are used to help minimize contaminants in the hydraulic fluid, they alone are unable to remove every particle and impurity that enters the system. In addition, when fluid collects in the hydraulic reservoir, contaminants can settle there over time. To help further purify the hydraulic fluid, special equipment is sometimes used as part of a preventive maintenance program. One example of this type of equipment is an **off-line kidney loop system** (**FIGURE 34-9**).

An off-line kidney loop system connects to the fluid reservoir and consists of a motor, a pump, and one or more high-efficiency filters. This system is independent of the equipment's hydraulic system and can be set to operate continuously or periodically. Off-line kidney loop systems are very effective at removing particulates that have passed through the system filters, particles that have found their way into the reservoir, and, in some models, water that has contaminated the hydraulic fluid. Not only can using this type of equipment improve the quality of the hydraulic fluid, but it can also extend the usable life of the filters and reduce wear and other problems with hydraulic system components.

FIGURE 34-9 Off-line kidney loop system.

FIGURE 34-10 Portable dehydrator.

Another piece of special equipment that is sometimes used during preventive maintenance procedures to remove particle contamination and water from the hydraulic fluid is a **dehydrator** (**FIGURE 34-10**). A portable dehydrator attaches to the fluid reservoir of a piece of equipment and directs some of the fluid through a vessel. There, the fluid cascades downward through a stream of filtered dry air. The air absorbs moisture from the fluid and is directed out of the equipment while the dewatered fluid is returned to the reservoir.

Another step that technicians should perform during hydraulic fluid testing is to check the temperature of the hydraulic fluid while the equipment is being operated. Fluid that is too hot could indicate a problem with an oil cooler or obstructed air flow around the reservoir.

Use the data from the fluid analysis, the manufacturer's recommendations, and the preventive maintenance program guidelines to determine whether the hydraulic fluid should be changed. If so, flush and clean the inside of the fluid reservoir before adding new fluid.

2. Replace all hydraulic fluid filters.

   Hydraulic systems use one or more filters to help reduce fluid contamination (**FIGURE 34-11**). These filters may be located on the suction line that leaves the reservoir and/or the return line leading back to the reservoir.

▶ TECHNICIAN TIP

Always refer to the manufacturer's literature to ensure that the correct replacement filters are used when changing hydraulic filters. In addition, ensure the filter housing is clean before putting the new filter(s) in place. Filter mounting areas are a common source of hydraulic fluid contamination.

FIGURE 34-11 Hydraulic filter on tractor wheel loader.

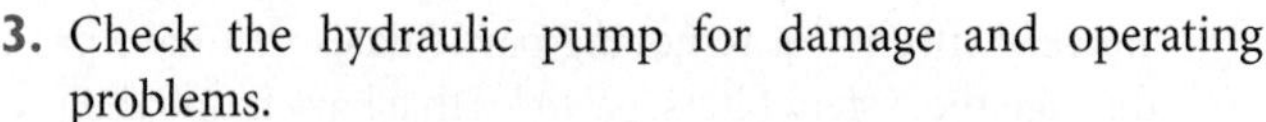

FIGURE 34-12 Hydraulic cylinder leak.

3. Check the hydraulic pump for damage and operating problems.

   Technicians should visually inspect the hydraulic pump for any obvious signs of wear or damage. In addition, they should listen to the pump while the hydraulic system is operating. Abnormal sounds, such as banging, rattling, or churning rocks, could be an indication of air in the hydraulic fluid, **cavitation**, or other problems. All hydraulic lines entering and leaving the pump should be checked for tightness and leaks. If damage to the pump is suspected, it should be removed and repaired or replaced.

4. Check the hydraulic motor for damage and operating problems.

   The internal components of a hydraulic motor can be scored or scraped by contaminants in the hydraulic fluid, which can result in a loss of pressure. Technicians should take pressure readings while the motor is operating at the normal rpm and compare them to the normal pressure range to determine whether there might be damage to the motor. They should also check the motor's drive shaft for any obvious damage or fluid leakage.

5. Check all hydraulic valves for damage and operating problems.

   Directional control valves in a hydraulic system have O-rings, spools, springs, and other close-fitting components that direct flow through the system. As with the internal parts of pumps and motors, these components can be damaged by contaminants in the hydraulic fluid. One of the main symptoms of internal valve damage is low hydraulic pressure. Technicians should check hydraulic system valves for any obvious damage or fluid leakage and take pressure readings while the system is operating, in order to identify possible problems.

6. Check the hydraulic cylinders for leaks and damage.

   Hydraulic cylinders are susceptible to leaks around the cylinder rod seals and rings caused by contaminated hydraulic fluid or excess system pressure (**FIGURE 34-12**). Technicians should carefully check each cylinder for leaks and inspect the cylinder rod for scratches, dents, and other visible damage. If leaks or rod damage is found, it may be necessary to rebuild or replace the cylinder.

7. Check all hydraulic lines and hoses for leaks, wear, and loose connections.

   All hydraulic lines and hoses must be checked on a regular basis to ensure that they are not dented, worn, leaking, or loosely connected. Tubing lines can be damaged from contact with other equipment or objects, which can lead to fluid leaks, restricted flow, and pressure leaks. If hoses make contact with other components or structures, they can be pinched or worn by friction (**FIGURE 34-13**). They can also become kinked or entangled if they are improperly routed in the system. All fittings and couplings used on lines and hoses must be checked regularly for tightness and leaks. Any line or hose that has physical damage should be replaced.

FIGURE 34-13 Worn hydraulic hose.

8. Record all actions performed and all data collected during the preventive maintenance procedure.

   Technicians should clearly note what takes place during a preventive maintenance procedure. Any replacement parts used and adjustments made should be recorded. All data collected during the procedure, such as fluid analysis results and temperature, pressure, and flow readings, should be logged as well. This way, all pertinent information will be available to review prior to the next maintenance activity.

To complete routine maintenance procedures on a hydraulic system, follow the steps in **SKILL DRILL 34-1**.

SKILL DRILL 34-1 Complete Routine Maintenance Procedures on a Hydraulic System

1. Check, analyze, and (if necessary) replace the hydraulic fluid. Also, check the temperature of the hydraulic fluid while the equipment is being operated. If fluid is replaced, flush and clean the inside of the reservoir first.

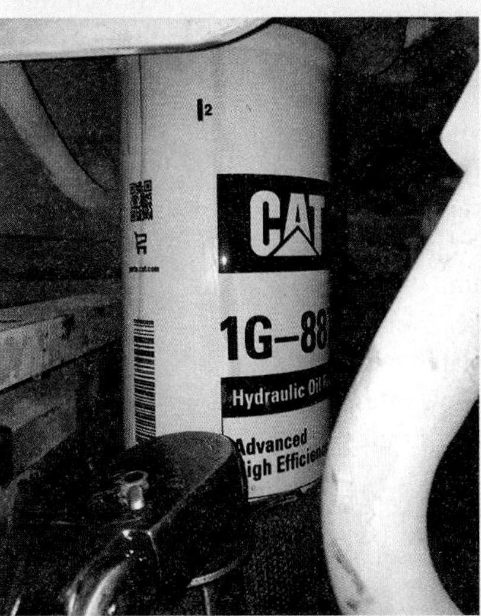

2. Replace all hydraulic fluid filters with the proper types and sizes for the system. Also, clean around the filter housing(s) to help prevent contamination from entering the system.

3. Check the hydraulic pump, hydraulic motor, and hydraulic valves for damage and operating problems. Look for leaks and listen to each component for abnormal sounds that could indicate a problem. Take temperature, pressure, and flow readings and compare them to the normal range for the components.

4. Check the hydraulic cylinders for leaks and inspect the cylinder rods for scratches, dents, and other visible damage.

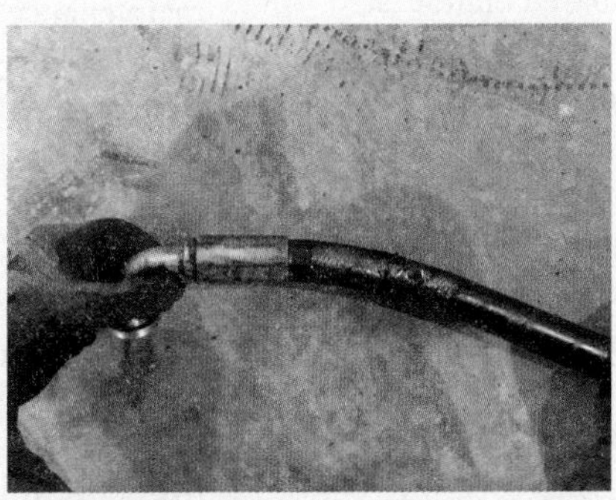

5. Check all hydraulic lines and hoses for leaks, dents, wear, tangling, kinks, and loose connections.

6. Record all actions performed and all data collected during the preventive maintenance procedure.

▶ Wrap-Up

Ready for Review

- Heavy equipment of virtually every type and size relies extensively on many hydraulic circuits to carry out basic functions.
- Failing to perform regular preventive maintenance on a heavy equipment hydraulic system is the leading cause of component failures within the system.
- Being proactive toward maintenance—that is, identifying abnormal conditions before they become problems—is more efficient and cost-effective than being reactive to problems that have already occurred.
- All of the components in a hydraulic system—the reservoir, hydraulic fluid, pumps, motors, valves, cylinders, hoses, lines, filters, and accessories—work closely together. So, a problem with one component can easily affect other components in the system.
- Degradation failures tend to occur gradually over long periods of time. They are commonly associated with basic wear and tear and manifest as diminished flow rates, decreased cylinder speeds, valve leakage, and similar symptoms of general deterioration.
- Transient failures are intermittent. They may appear and disappear, but they typically indicate an underlying problem that will need to be addressed.
- Catastrophic failures represent a complete component or system malfunction. They occur suddenly and without warning—most often when transient failures are neglected over time.
- Preventive maintenance is an ongoing process that spans the life of the equipment. It must be performed with regularity, and it should be set up to be as routine and unobtrusive as possible.
- Many factors must be considered during the development and practice of a preventive maintenance program for a hydraulic system.
- Equipment manufacturers provide routine inspection and maintenance guidelines that are typically based on hours, days, or months of usage.
- One of the most important sources of information about a hydraulic system is the equipment operator.
- Historical data that has been collected on the equipment can also be a valuable source of information.
- Many pieces of heavy equipment are equipped with onboard computer systems that display and record abnormal conditions that suggest potential problems. Service technicians can use this information to help troubleshoot potential problems.
- One of the procedures in a typical preventive maintenance program for a hydraulic system is to check, analyze, and (if necessary) replace the hydraulic fluid.
- By far, the majority of hydraulic system problems originate with the hydraulic fluid.
- Contaminated hydraulic fluid can sometimes be detected because of discoloration and/or an odor of something that has been burned.
- To be certain about the condition of the fluid, a sample of the fluid should be obtained and analyzed using oil-testing equipment.
- Samples of hydraulic fluid should be collected from a live zone area, where the fluid is well mixed, likely to contain wear particles from the system components, and upstream from any return line filters that would remove contaminants.
- Hydraulic fluid analysis detects chemical impurities and particle contaminants in the fluid. The results of this analysis can often identify the source of the contamination, which service technicians can use to remedy the problem.
- Contaminants will always find their way into a hydraulic system, but they can be minimized by keeping the areas around dipsticks, filters, and filler plugs as clean as possible.
- An off-line kidney loop system connects to the fluid reservoir and is very effective at removing particulates that have passed through the system filters, particles that have found their way into the reservoir, and, in some models, water that has contaminated the hydraulic fluid.
- A portable dehydrator attaches to the fluid reservoir of a piece of equipment and directs some of the fluid through a vessel, where it cascades downward through a stream of filtered dry air. The air absorbs moisture from the fluid and is directed out of the equipment while the dewatered fluid is returned to the reservoir.
- Technicians should check the temperature of the hydraulic fluid while the equipment is being operated. Fluid that is too hot could indicate a problem with an oil cooler or obstructed air flow around the reservoir.
- Technicians should use fluid analysis data, the manufacturer's recommendations, and the preventive maintenance program guidelines to determine whether the hydraulic fluid should be changed.
- If hydraulic fluid is being replaced, flush and clean the inside of the fluid reservoir first.
- During preventive maintenance, replace all hydraulic fluid filters.
- Check the hydraulic pump for damage and operating problems. Listen to the pump while the hydraulic system is operating. Abnormal sounds, such as banging, rattling, or churning rocks, could be an indication of air in the hydraulic fluid, cavitation, or other problems.
- Check the hydraulic motor for damage and operating problems. Take pressure readings while the motor is operating at the normal rpm and compare them to the normal pressure range to determine whether there might be damage to the motor.

- Check all hydraulic valves for any obvious damage or fluid leakage and take pressure readings while the system is operating, in order to identify possible problems.
- Check all hydraulic cylinders for leaks and inspect the cylinder rod for scratches, dents, and other visible damage.
- Check all hydraulic lines and hoses for leaks, wear, and loose connections. All fittings and couplings used on lines and hoses must be checked regularly for tightness and leaks.
- Record all actions performed and all data collected during a preventive maintenance procedure. Any replacement parts used and adjustments made should be recorded. All data collected during the procedure, such as fluid analysis results and temperature, pressure, and flow readings, should be logged as well.

Key Terms

catastrophic failure A type of hydraulic system failure that occurs suddenly and without warning and represents a complete component or system malfunction.

cavitation The formation of air bubbles in the hydraulic fluid as a result of low pressure at the pump inlet.

corrective maintenance A type of maintenance that is performed after a system or equipment failure to identify and repair the problem and enable the system or equipment to be restored to its normal operating condition.

degradation failure A type of hydraulic system failure that occurs gradually over a long period of time, which is commonly associated with basic wear and tear.

dehydrator A piece of equipment that can be connected to the reservoir of a hydraulic system and used to remove particle contamination and water from the hydraulic fluid.

laminar flow A smooth, streamline flow pattern that occurs when fluid flows in parallel layers.

live zone An area in a hydraulic system that is highly desirable for fluid sampling because the flow there is highly turbulent, downstream from major components in the system, and upstream from filters in the return line to the reservoir.

off-line kidney loop system A piece of equipment that can be connected to the reservoir of a hydraulic system and used to remove particulates that have passed through the system filters, particles that have found their way into the reservoir, and, in some models, water that has infused the hydraulic fluid.

preventive maintenance A type of routine maintenance performed on a regular basis to help identify and correct problems to minimize system or equipment failures, which is sometimes referred to as planned maintenance (PM).

transient failure A type of hydraulic system failure that is intermittent but typically indicates an underlying problem that will need to be addressed to avoid a catastrophic failure.

wear metal Any one of several different types of metal (such as iron, aluminum, or copper) that when detected in hydraulic fluid, can indicate component wear in the hydraulic system.

Review Questions

1. The leading cause of component failures in a heavy equipment hydraulic system comes from ________.
   - **a.** operating the equipment for more than one shift per day
   - **b.** ignoring the need for transient equipment maintenance
   - **c.** failing to allow for hydraulic fluid expansion in the system
   - **d.** failing to perform regular preventive maintenance
2. Identifying and correcting potential issues in a hydraulic system before they become problems helps ________.
   - **a.** maximize equipment performance while minimizing equipment service life and operating costs
   - **b.** maximize equipment performance and service life while minimizing equipment failures and operating costs
   - **c.** maximize equipment service life while minimizing equipment performance and efficiency
   - **d.** minimize equipment performance and service life while maximizing equipment failures and operating costs
3. A basic category of hydraulic system failures commonly associated with wear and tear is called ________.
   - **a.** catastrophic failures
   - **b.** acute failures
   - **c.** degradation failures
   - **d.** transient failures
4. Transient failures in a hydraulic system that are neglected over time are most likely to lead to ________.
   - **a.** catastrophic failures
   - **b.** chronic failures
   - **c.** degradation failures
   - **d.** mitigation failures
5. Routine inspection and maintenance guidelines provided by equipment manufacturers are typically based on ________.
   - **a.** operating parameters and climate conditions
   - **b.** hours, days, or months of usage and calendar time
   - **c.** operator knowledge and skill
   - **d.** historical data collected from the machine
6. One reason equipment operators are good sources of information about hydraulic systems is because they ________.
   - **a.** were, in most cases, service technicians before they became operators
   - **b.** typically operate many different types of equipment over their careers
   - **c.** are usually responsible for making all other types of equipment repairs
   - **d.** can often detect degradation and transient problems before failures occur
7. The part of a hydraulic system from which most of the problems in the system originate is the ________.
   - **a.** hydraulic fluid
   - **b.** suction hose lining
   - **c.** filter assembly
   - **d.** electro hydraulic motor

8. If a hydraulic pump sounds like it has rocks churning inside of it, the mostly likely problem is ________________.
   a. low aeration
   b. segmentation
   c. cavitation
   d. high pressurization
9. A problem with a hydraulic system oil cooler or an obstruction in the air flow around the fluid reservoir is most likely to manifest itself as a ________________.
   a. strong vibration in the hydraulic motor
   b. higher-than-normal hydraulic fluid temperature
   c. sluggish cycling of the hydraulic cylinder rods
   d. lower-than-normal hydraulic fluid temperature
10. The most logical thing to do at the end of a preventive maintenance procedure is ________________.
   a. provide the operator with a concise list of what must be done to the equipment
   b. repair all transient failures, but simply note any degradation failures for later
   c. remove a similar piece of equipment from service to do a comparison check
   d. record all the actions performed and all the data collected during the procedure

ASE Technician A/Technician B Style Questions

1. Technician A says a lack of preventive maintenance can lead to the need for corrective maintenance. Technician B says being proactive toward maintenance is more efficient and cost-effective than being reactive to problems that have already occurred. Who is correct?
   a. Technician A
   b. Technician B
   c. Both Technician A and Technician B
   d. Neither Technician A nor Technician B
2. Technician A says the costs associated with a minor fluid leak can add up to thousands of dollars in unplanned expenses. Technician B says minor fluid leaks are inexpensive and simply a part of equipment operation. Who is correct?
   a. Technician A
   b. Technician B
   c. Both Technician A and Technician B
   d. Neither Technician A nor Technician B
3. Technician A says a transient failure is a problem that happens once, but then goes away completely. Technician B says transient failures are intermittent and typically indicate an underlying problem that will need to be addressed. Who is correct?
   a. Technician A
   b. Technician B
   c. Both Technician A and Technician B
   d. Neither Technician A nor Technician B
4. Technician A says the most time-consuming and costly failures to repair are degradation failures. Technician B says the most time-consuming and costly failures are transient failures. Who is correct?
   a. Technician A
   b. Technician B
   c. Both Technician A and Technician B
   d. Neither Technician A nor Technician B
5. Technician A says the goal of a preventive maintenance program for a hydraulic system should be simplicity. Technician B says a preventive maintenance program should be as routine and unobtrusive as possible. Who is correct?
   a. Technician A
   b. Technician B
   c. Both Technician A and Technician B
   d. Neither Technician A nor Technician B
6. Technician A says equipment manufacturer guidelines are all you need when performing preventive maintenance. Technician B says manufacturer guidelines are only one source of input material because they do not always take into consideration factors such as climate conditions, the duration of operating times, and the manner in which equipment operators use the equipment. Who is correct?
   a. Technician A
   b. Technician B
   c. Both Technician A and Technician B
   d. Neither Technician A nor Technician B
7. Technician A says one of the most important sources of information about a hydraulic system is the equipment operator. Technician B says the most important source is the shift supervisor since the supervisor is responsible for doing a walk-around inspection before and after each shift. Who is correct?
   a. Technician A
   b. Technician B
   c. Both Technician A and Technician B
   d. Neither Technician A nor Technician B
8. Technician A says the majority of hydraulic system problems have to do with the hydraulic hoses. Technician B says most hydraulic system problems can be traced to the hydraulic pump. Who is correct?
   a. Technician A
   b. Technician B
   c. Both Technician A and Technician B
   d. Neither Technician A nor Technician B
9. Technician A says a thorough hydraulic fluid analysis will detect chemical impurities in the fluid. Technician B says a hydraulic fluid analysis can reveal particle contaminants in the fluid. Who is correct?
   a. Technician A
   b. Technician B
   c. Both Technician A and Technician B
   d. Neither Technician A nor Technician B
10. Technician A says that during preventive maintenance, you should drain all of the hydraulic filters in the system. Technician B says you should replace all of the filters. Who is correct?
   a. Technician A
   b. Technician B
   c. Both Technician A and Technician B
   d. Neither Technician A nor Technician B

CHAPTER 35
Troubleshooting and Diagnostics

Knowledge Objectives

After reading this chapter, you will be able to:

- **K35001** Explain the fundamentals of diagnosing hydraulic systems.
- **K35002** Identify primary causes of failures for hydraulic systems.
- **K35003** Describe the procedures to inspect and test the hydraulic system.
- **K35004** Inspect, test, and diagnose a hydraulic system following the manufacturer's recommended procedures.
- **K35005** Recommend reconditioning or repairs following the manufacturer's recommended procedures.

Skills Objectives

After reading this chapter, you will be able to:

- **S35001** Troubleshoot and diagnose hydraulic pump problems.
- **S35002** Perform system temperature tests.
- **S35003** Perform system pressure, flow, and cycle time tests.
- **S35004** Test a relief valve.
- **S35005** Test a cylinder for internal leakage.

▶ Fundamentals of Diagnosing Hydraulic Systems

K35001

Knowing how to troubleshoot and diagnose problems in hydraulic systems is an important part of being a MORE (mobile off-road equipment) technician. This chapter discusses how to distinguish the cause of a problem from its symptom and offers general guidelines for troubleshooting hydraulic systems, as well as an overview of essential and optional equipment. A wide range of specific problems, and their remedies, are covered—from inoperative systems, erratic operation, overheating, and foaming fluid to excessive pump noise and leaking control valves. Common diagnostic procedures are also included.

▶ Troubleshoot Hydraulic Systems

K35002

Symptom Versus Root Cause

When **troubleshooting**, you will need to be able to distinguish the cause of a problem from its symptoms so that you can treat the root cause and effectively correct the problem. In a hydraulic system, a witnessed malfunction (such as slow speed, fluid leakage, or hot hydraulic oil) is known as the symptom. The reason for the specific malfunction is known as the root cause. In the workshop or in the field, troubleshooting a problem will enable you to match the symptom with its possible cause and then rectify the situation by treating the root cause to correct the symptom.

General Guidelines

There is no one set of steps that can be used for troubleshooting all types of hydraulic equipment. The following steps provide general guidelines:

1. Know the system. Read and understand the operator's manual for the machine to find out how the machine should be operated. Knowing what is normal and how the machine should be operated can many times highlight nonexistent problems due to lack of awareness on the operator's part. Reading and understanding machine service information is also key to understanding how the system functions. Communicate with coworkers, supervisors, or the equipment dealer's technical staff to gain knowledge about the system.
2. Discuss the malfunction with the operator. Ask questions:
   a. What is the system doing that is not normal?
   b. What warning signs preceded the problem?
   c. What previous work has been done on the system?
   d. Has this trouble happened before?
3. Inspect the system and note any discrepancies, such as low oil level, leaks, or unusual wear.
4. Verify the complaint by operating the system, if possible, and note what is happening when the malfunction occurs. This can be done only if the technician is qualified to operate the machine in a safe manner and in a safe environment.
5. List possible causes of the malfunction by using past experience or referring to the machine's service information.
6. Following machine service information eliminates possible causes by testing the system and starting with the easiest fixes first. Reach a conclusion on what you believe to be causing the malfunction.
7. Fix the problem or problems.
8. Operate the system to determine whether the malfunction has been corrected.

▶ TECHNICIAN TIP

Hydraulic system test equipment should be inspected prior to use and taken out of service if you suspect that it may be defective. High-pressure and high-temperature hydraulic fluid can escape from test equipment, with dangerous results.

▶ Hydraulic Systems Testing Equipment

K35003

When identifying issues that need to be resolved on hydraulic systems, you will need certain items of *essential* testing equipment. *Optional* testing equipment consists of additional items that may be useful but are not required.

You Are the Mobile Heavy Equipment Technician

You are working for a small general contractor that has a small fleet of older small to medium sized machines. The aging fleet has recently had a rash of hydraulic system problems that don't seem to have a common root cause.

The company owner had been getting the machine dealer to diagnose and repair the hydraulic system problems. He has realized this is a very expensive way to get his machines fixed and now wanting you to diagnose and repair all hydraulic system problems.

He has asked you to put together a list of tooling and information that you will need.

1. List all the tooling and service information you would need to be able to diagnose a hydraulic system problem.
2. List in order the first five steps you would perform to start diagnosing a "hydraulic system won't function" complaint.

Essential Testing Equipment

Pressure testing hydraulic systems is a common part of diagnosing hydraulic system problems. Any shop or service truck should have a selection of pressure gauges with coupler fittings on them to provide connection to the machine. Most machines will provide test ports at critical areas on the machine, such as pumps and valves. It may be necessary to install pressure taps in order for pressures to be read. Always select a gauge with a maximum value that is higher than the maximum expected pressure that would be found in the system.

Analog gauges will have a sweeping needle that moves from low pressure to high pressure over a face that reads in a range of psi, bar, kg/cm^2, or H_2O. Small diameter hoses are used between the test point fitting and the gauge and can come in a wide variety of lengths. Analog pressure gauges can be seen in **FIGURE 35-1**.

Digital pressure gauges are safer to use since there are no hoses and fittings involved, because all that is needed is a pressure transducer that threads into a system port. An electronic display similar to a multimeter is connected to the transducer with a cable. Pressure transducers come in a variety of pressure ranges and are usually color coded. Ensure the maximum pressure limit for the transducer is higher than the maximum expected pressure to be tested.

Flow meters are used occasionally for hydraulic system testing, primarily to measure pump flow; however, they can be plumbed into a system anywhere to measure flow, if needed. They will usually incorporate a variable restriction so that the technician can simulate putting a load onto the pump. Extra care must be taken when increasing the restriction to avoid excessive pressures. Remember that pressure is created by a restriction to flow. See **FIGURE 35-2** for an example of a flow meter.

Reading temperatures throughout a hydraulic system can give valuable information when diagnosing certain hydraulic problems. Digital infrared thermometers are relatively inexpensive and accurate. See **FIGURE 35-3** for an example of a temperature gauge.

Occasionally, it may be necessary to read pump inlet pressure, which could be a negative pressure. A vacuum gauge (**FIGURE 35-4**) will be capable of only low pressure readings.

FIGURE 35-1 Example of pressure gauges.

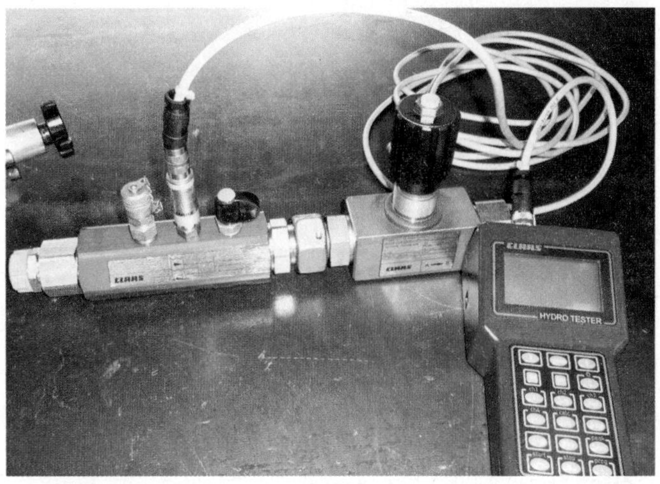

FIGURE 35-2 Example of a flow meter.

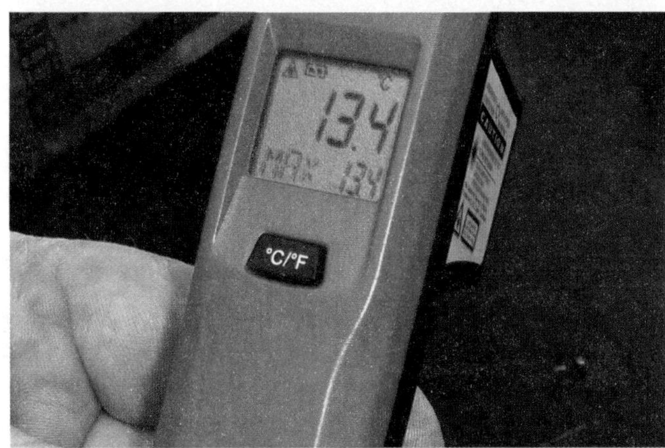

FIGURE 35-3 Example of a temperature gauge.

FIGURE 35-4 Example of a vacuum gauge.

Optional Testing Equipment

Using a tachometer is necessary to measure the speed of rotary actuators. Photo tachometers are the most common type and work by reading the reflection of light generated by the unit. A piece of reflective tape must be secured to the motor shaft or the component that it is driving. See **FIGURE 35-5** for an example of a tachometer.

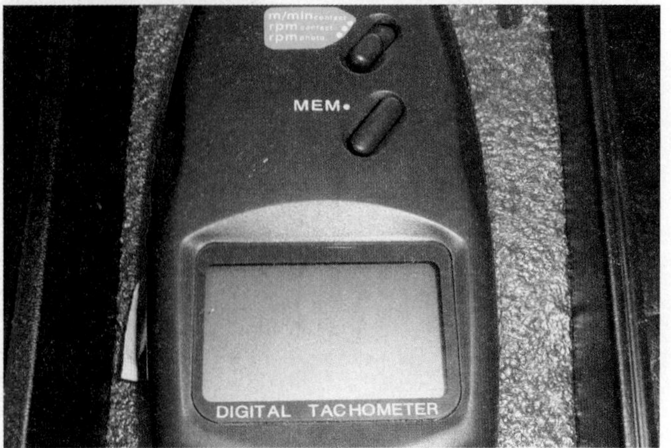

FIGURE 35-5 Example of a tachometer.

SAFETY TIP

When using a tachometer, you will be exposed to rotating parts. Use extreme caution to avoid getting caught or tangled up in rotating parts. Using a tachometer will likely be a two-person task, and clear communication must be maintained at all times.

▶ TECHNICIAN TIP

Familiarize yourself with the operation of the circuit by studying technical manuals and circuit diagrams on how the system works.

▶ Hydraulic System Problems and Remedies

K35004

This section provides descriptions of common problems encountered in hydraulic systems and their remedies.

Inoperative Systems

Typical problems that can cause inoperative systems and their remedies are shown in **TABLE 35-1**.

Low or Erratic System Pressure

Typical problems that can cause low or erratic system pressure and their remedies are shown in **TABLE 35-2**.

TABLE 35-1 Problems and Remedies for Inoperative Systems

Problem	Remedy
No oil in system	• Fill to the full mark (**FIGURE 35-6**). • Check the system for leaks and damage.
Oil low in reservoir	• Check the fluid level and fill to the full mark. • Check the system for leaks.
Oil of wrong viscosity	• Refer to specifications for the proper fluid viscosity.
Filter dirty or plugged	• Try to find the source of contamination. • Replace the filter.
Restriction in system	• The pump supply oil lines could be dirty or collapsed, or the pump outlet hoses could have inner walls that are collapsing and cutting off the oil supply. • Clean or replace the lines.
Air leaks in pump suction line	• Check for loose fittings. • Check that the suction filter is tightened correctly. • Repair or replace the lines.
Badly worn pump	• Repair or replace the pump. • Check for problems that cause pump wear, such as misalignment, contaminated oil, or cavitation.
Badly worn components	• Examine and test valves, motors, cylinders, etc. for external and internal leaks. If the wear is abnormal, try to locate the cause. • Draw fluid samples for analysis.
Oil leak in pump outlet line(s)	• Tighten the fittings or replace defective lines. • Examine the mating surfaces on the couplers for irregularities.
Relief valve defective	• Check the main relief valve to ensure it isn't stuck open (**FIGURE 35-7**). • Clean the main relief valve and check for broken springs, worn poppet seat, missing poppet valve, etc.
Slipping or broken pump drive	• Repair the pump drive and adjust the tension.
Pump not operating	• Check the pump coupling and shaft. • Check to determine whether the prime mover is operating. • Replace the pump.

FIGURE 35-6 Sight glass.

FIGURE 35-7 Typical main relief valve.

TABLE 35-2 Problems and Remedies for Low or Erratic System Pressure

Problem	Remedy
Low relief valve setting	• Reset the relief valve to its proper setting. • Test to make sure relief valves are operating at their rated pressures.
Worn pump	• Repair or replace the pump. • Check for problems that cause pump wear, such as misalignment, contaminated oil, or cavitation.
Pump compensator set too low or sticking	• Reset the pump compensator to the proper setting. • Clean the pump compensator and change the fluid if necessary. • Check for a worn or bent pump compensator. • Repair or replace any binding parts.
Contamination in relief valves	• Clean the relief valves. • Check the source of contamination and correct the problem.
Aerated fluid	• Check the suction line for leaks. • Tighten the fittings or replace the suction line. • Check the reservoir level and fill if necessary.

Systems That Operate Erratically

Typical problems that can cause systems to operate erratically and their remedies are shown in **TABLE 35-3**.

TABLE 35-3 Problems and Remedies for Systems That Operate Erratically

Problem	Remedy
Air in system	• Examine the suction side of the system and check for leaks. • Make sure the oil level is correct. Note: Oil leaks on the pressure side of the system could account for loss of oil.
Cold oil	• The viscosity of the oil may be too high at the start of the warm-up period. • Allow the oil to warm up to operating temperature before using hydraulic functions.
Components sticking or binding	• Check for dirt or gummy deposits. If the dirt is caused by contamination, try to find the source. • Check for worn or bent parts.

(Continued)

TABLE 35-3 Problems and Remedies for Systems That Operate Erratically (Continued)

Problem	Remedy
Pump damaged	• Check for broken or worn parts and determine the cause of the pump damage.
Dirt in relief valves	• Clean the relief valves.
Restriction in filter or suction line	• The suction hose could be dirty or have inner walls that are collapsing and cutting off the oil supply. • Clean or replace the suction line. • Check the filter line for restrictions.
Hydraulic cylinder leaking internally	• Repair or replace the cylinder packing.

Systems That Operate Slowly

Typical problems that can cause systems to operate slowly and their remedies are shown in **TABLE 35-4**.

TABLE 35-4 Problems and Remedies for Systems That Operate Slowly

Problem	Remedy
Cold oil	• Allow the oil to warm up before operating the machine.
Oil viscosity too high	• Use the oil recommended by the manufacturer.
Insufficient engine speed	• Refer to the operator's manual for the recommended engine speed.
Low oil supply	• Check the reservoir, and add oil if necessary. • Check the system for leaks that could cause loss of oil.
Flow control valve not set properly	• Check the machine specifications for the proper setting. • Adjust the flow control valve.
Air in system	• Check the suction side of the system for leaks.
Badly worn pump	• Check for problems that cause pump wear, such as misalignment, contaminated oil, or cavitation. • Repair or replace the pump.
Restriction in suction line or filter	• The suction hose could be dirty or could have inner walls that are collapsing and cutting off the oil supply. • Clean or replace the suction line. • Examine the filter for plugging.
Relief valves not properly set or leaking	• Test the relief valves to make sure they are opening at the proper pressure. • Examine the relief valves for damaged seats that could leak.
Badly worn components	• If the wear is abnormal, determine the cause. • Replace components as necessary.
Valve or regulators plugged	• Check the source of the dirt and correct the problem. • Clean dirt from the components.
Oil leak in pressure lines	• Tighten the fittings or replace defective lines. • Examine the mating surfaces on the fittings for irregularities.
Components not properly adjusted	• Refer to the machine technical manual for the proper adjustment of components.

Systems That Operate Too Fast

Typical problems that can cause systems to operate too fast and their remedies are shown in **TABLE 35-5**.

TABLE 35-5 Problems and Remedies for Systems That Operate Too Fast

Problem	Remedy
Pump control valve not adjusted properly	• Adjust pump control according to machine service information (**FIGURE 35-8**).
Obstruction or dirt under seat of flow control valve	• Remove the foreign material and readjust the valve.
Prime mover operating too fast	• Lower prime mover speed.

FIGURE 35-8 Pump control valve.

Systems That Overheat

Typical problems that can cause systems to overheat and their remedies are shown in **TABLE 35-6**.

TABLE 35-6 Problems and Remedies for Systems That Overheat

Problem	Remedy
Using incorrect oil	• Use the oil recommended by the manufacturer. • Be sure the oil viscosity is correct.
Low oil level	• Fill the reservoir. • Look for leaks.
Dirty oil	• Check that filters are installed. • Check that filters are intact. • Look for the source of contamination. • Install new filters that meet the manufacturer's recommendations.
Incorrect relief valve pressure	• Reset the relief valve to the proper setting. • Replace the relief valve if necessary.
Internal component oil leakage	• Examine and test valves, cylinders, motors, etc. for internal leaks. Note: If the wear is abnormal, try to locate the cause.
Restriction in pump suction line	• Clean or replace the pump suction line.
Dented, obstructed, or undersized oil lines	• Replace the defective or undersized oil lines. • Remove the obstructions.
Oil cooler malfunctioning	• Clean or repair the oil cooler.
Control valve stuck in partially or fully open position	• Free all spools so that they return to the neutral position.
Heat not radiating properly	• Clean dirt and mud from the reservoir, oil lines, coolers, and other components.
Automatic unloading control inoperative (if equipped)	• Replace the valve.
Clogged or dirty heat exchanger	• Clean the component. • Look for the source of contamination.

Foaming Fluid

Typical problems that can cause foaming fluid and their remedies are shown in **TABLE 35-7**.

TABLE 35-7 Problems and Remedies for Foaming Fluid

Problem	Remedy
Low fluid level	• Fill the reservoir and look for leaks.
Water in fluid	• Drain and replace the fluid.
Wrong kind of fluid being used	• Use the fluid recommended by the manufacturer.
Air leak in line from reservoir to pump	• Tighten or replace the suction line.
Kink or dent in fluid lines (restricts fluid flow)	• Replace the fluid lines.
Worn seal around pump shaft	• Clean the sealing area, replace the seal, and check the fluid for contamination or the pump for misalignment.

Excessive System Noise

Typical problems that can cause excessive system noise and their remedies are shown in **TABLE 35-8**.

TABLE 35-8 Problems and Remedies for Excessive System Noise

Problem	Remedy
Loose pump mount bolts	• Check and tighten the pump mount bolts according to the manufacturer's specifications.
Pump noise	• Refer to Table 35-9.
Amplified pump pulsations (**pump ripple**)	• Check pressure flow and pump performance to ascertain the severity of the condition.
Noisy prime mover (especially electric motor fan noise)	• Check all fan drives and fan blades for integrity and security.
Leakage in valves and actuator seals	• Clean or replace the valves and seals as needed.
Valves too small for system flow rate	• Replace the valves with correctly rated replacements.
Binding or dragging cylinder rod	• Check the cylinder rods for wear. • Check the cylinder seals for damage. • Check associated control valves.
Improperly secured lines allowing vibration	• Tighten or replace the fittings.
Fluid hammer caused by valves opening and closing too quickly	• Check operational pressures.

Note: Some of the problems listed are design problems. Never assume that the system has been designed properly or that components that have been replaced were replaced with the correct parts.

Excessive Pump Noise

Typical problems that can cause excessive pump noise and their remedies are shown in **TABLE 35-9**.

TABLE 35-9 Problems and Remedies for Excessive Pump Noise

Problem	Remedy
Low fluid level	• Fill the reservoir. • Check the system for leaks.
Fluid viscosity too high	• Change the fluid to one with the correct viscosity.
Pump speed too fast	• Operate the pump at the recommended speed.
Suction line plugged or pinched	• Clean or replace the line between the reservoir and the pump.
Sludge and dirt in pump	• Check the filters. • Clean the hydraulic system. • Determine the source of the dirt.

TABLE 35-9 Problems and Remedies for Excessive Pump Noise (Continued)

Problem	Remedy
Reservoir air vent plugged	• Remove the breather cap, then flush and clean the air vent.
Air in fluid	• Check the suction line for leaks. • Tighten the fittings or replace the suction line. • Check the reservoir level and refill if necessary.
Worn or scored pump bearings or shafts	• Determine the cause of the scoring. • Replace the worn parts or the complete pump if the parts are badly worn or scored.
Inlet screen plugged	• Clean the screen to prevent cavitation in the pump.
Broken or damaged pump parts	• Look for the cause of the damage—for example, contamination or too much pressure. • Repair or replace the pump.
Sticking or binding parts	• Clean the parts and change the fluid if necessary. • Repair or replace the binding parts.

Leaking Pumps

Typical problems that can cause leaking pumps and their remedies are shown in **TABLE 35-10**.

TABLE 35-10 Problems and Remedies for Leaking Pumps

Problem	Remedy
Damaged pump shaft seal	• Replace the seal. • The trouble may be caused by contaminated oil. Check the oil for abrasives and clean the entire hydraulic system. Try to locate the source of contamination. • Check the pump drive shaft. Misalignment could cause the seal to wear. If the shaft is not aligned, check the pump for other damage.
Loose or broken pump parts	• Tighten or replace the parts. Make sure all bolts and fittings are tight. • Check the gaskets. • Examine the pump castings for cracks. If the pump is cracked, look for a cause, such as too much pressure or a clogged case drain line.
Loose or broken connections	• Tighten or repair the connections.

Load Drop with Control Valve in Neutral Position

Typical problems that can cause load drop when the control valve is in the neutral position and their remedies are shown in **TABLE 35-11**.

TABLE 35-11 Problems and Remedies for Load Drop with Control Valve in Neutral Position

Problem	Remedy
Leaking or broken oil lines from control valve to cylinder	• Check for leaks. • Tighten the fittings or replace the lines. • Examine the mating surfaces on the fittings for irregularities.
Oil leaking past cylinder packings or O-rings	• Replace any worn parts. Note: O-rings must be compatible with the type of fluid. • If the wear is caused by contamination, clean the hydraulic system and determine the source.
Oil leaking past control valve or relief valves	• Clean or replace the valves. • Wear may be caused by contamination. Clean the system and determine the source of contamination.
Control lever not centering when released	• Check the linkage for binding. • Make sure the valve is properly adjusted and has no broken or binding parts, such as spools or detent springs.

Control Valve Sticking

Typical problems that can cause the control valve to stick and their remedies are shown in **TABLE 35-12**.

TABLE 35-12 Problems and Remedies for a Control Valve That Sticks

Problem	Remedy
Misalignment or seizing of control linkage	• Realign as required. • Lubricate as required.
Tie bolts too tight (on valve stacks)	• Check the manufacturer's specifications and adjust as needed (**FIGURE 35-9**).
Valve broken or scored internally	• Determine the cause of the scoring. • Replace the worn or damaged valve.
Contaminated oil (the most common cause)	• Check that filters are installed. • Check that filters are intact. • Look for the source of contamination. • Install new filters that meet the manufacturer's specifications.

FIGURE 35-9 A main control valve with tie bolts.

FIGURE 35-10 A leaking control valve.

Leaking Control Valve

Typical problems that can cause a control valve to leak (**FIGURE 35-10**) and their remedies are shown in **TABLE 35-13**.

TABLE 35-13 Problems and Remedies for a Leaking Control Valve

Problem	Remedy
Tie bolts too loose (on valve stacks)	• Check the manufacturer's specifications and adjust as needed.
Worn, damaged, or incompatible O-rings	• Replace as required.
Broken valve parts	• Check for the source of the damage. • Replace parts as required.
Excessive wear between a select-fit spool and valve	• Check for the source of the damage. • Replace parts as required.
Seals damaged or missing on valve stacks or manifolds	• Check for the source of the damage. • Replace parts as required.

Leaking Cylinder

Leaking cylinders are shown in (**FIGURE 35-11**), Typical problems that can cause a cylinder to leak and their remedies are shown in **TABLE 35-14**.

FIGURE 35-11 Leaking cylinders.

TABLE 35-14 Problems and Remedies for a Leaking Cylinder

Problem	Remedy
Damaged cylinder barrel	• Check for the source of the damage. • Replace parts as required.
Rod seal leaking	• If contamination has caused the seal to wear, look for the source. Wear may be caused by external and internal contaminants. • Check the piston rod for scratches or misalignment. • Check for source of damage. • Replace parts as required.
Loose parts	• Tighten all loose fastening devices.
Piston rod damage	• Check for the source of the damage. • Replace parts as required.
Worn or incorrectly installed piston seals	• Check for the source of the damage. • Replace parts as required.

▶ Diagnostic Procedures

K35005, S35001

To properly diagnose hydraulic system problems, a technician needs a combination of knowledge, experience, service information, and tooling. Some problems can be difficult to diagnose, but when equipped with a good understanding of hydraulic system fundamentals and machine-specific information, no problem is insurmountable. The following Skill Drills will allow a technician in training to practice some troubleshooting procedures.

Troubleshooting and Diagnosing Hydraulic Pump Problems

To troubleshoot and diagnose hydraulic pump problems, follow the guidelines in **SKILL DRILL 35-1**.

Performing System Temperature Tests

S35002

To perform system temperature tests, follow the guidelines in **SKILL DRILL 35-2**.

Performing System Pressure, Flow, and Cycle Time Tests

S35003

To perform system pressure, flow, and cycle time tests, follow the guidelines in **SKILL DRILL 35-3**.

SKILL DRILL 35-1 Troubleshooting and Diagnosing Hydraulic Pump Problems

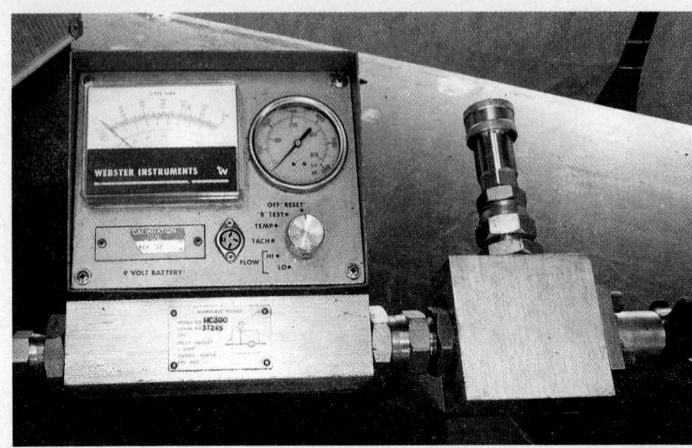

For this procedure, you will need the following tools, materials, and equipment:

- training stand with facilities for the instructor to build in various pump problems
- wrenches and spanners of appropriate sizes
- appropriate test equipment (pressure gauge, vacuum gauge, flow meter, etc.)
- safety glasses or goggles
- gloves.

1. Put on gloves and safety glasses or goggles.
2. Observe the operation of the stand and the pump malfunctions.
3. Select and install the appropriate test equipment to diagnose the problem, depending on the malfunction observed.
4. Suggest the solution to the problem and correct it if possible.
5. Clean the work area, and return tools and equipment to their proper storage area.

SKILL DRILL 35-2 Relating System Leakage to Hydraulic Fluid Temperature

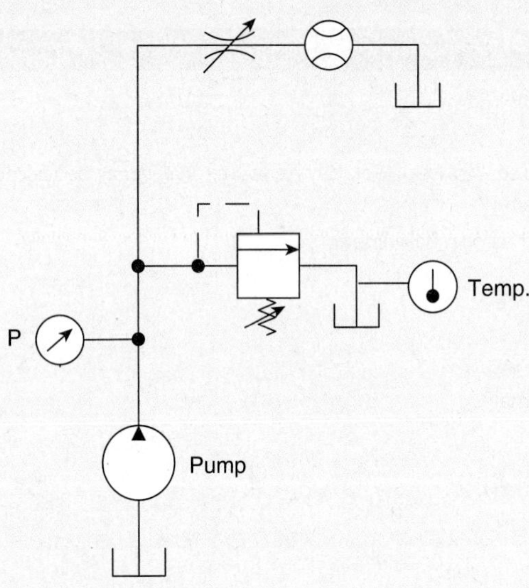

For this procedure, you will need the following tools, materials, and equipment:

- training stand
- wrenches and spanners of appropriate sizes
- components to assemble the hydraulic circuit shown
- temperature gauge to install as shown
- safety glasses or goggles
- gloves.

1. Put on gloves and safety glasses or goggles.
2. Assemble the circuit as shown in the circuit diagram.
3. Open the relief valve completely by backing off the knob.
4. Open the flow control valve completely.
5. Start the stand.
6. Close the flow control valve completely.
7. Using the relief valve, set the system pressure to 41.37 bar (600 psi).
8. Open the flow control valve completely.
9. Record the pressure and oil temperature.
10. Close the flow control valve to reduce the flow through that valve to three-quarters of the flow, with the valve fully open. (Where is the rest of the flow going?)
11. After five minutes of operation at this setting, record the pressure and oil temperature.
12. Close the flow control valve to reduce the flow through that valve to half the original flow, with the valve fully open.
13. After five minutes of operation at this setting, record the pressure and oil temperature.
14. Close the flow control valve to reduce the flow through the valve to one-quarter of the original flow, with the valve fully open.
15. After five minutes of operation at this setting, record the pressure and the oil temperature.
16. Close the flow control valve completely.
17. After five minutes of operation at this setting, record the pressure and the oil temperature.
18. Shut down the stand.
19. Clean the work area, and return tools and equipment to their proper storage area.
20. What conclusions can you draw between fluid temperature and oil flowing past a relief valve?

SKILL DRILL 35-3 Performing System Pressure, Flow, and Cycle Time Tests

For this procedure, you will need the following tools, materials, and equipment:

- training stand

  Note: To be able to gather the data for this test, a relatively large cylinder will be required so that cycle times will be long enough to allow the instrument to be read.
- wrenches and spanners of appropriate sizes
- components to assemble the hydraulic circuit shown
- safety glasses or goggles
- gloves.

1. Put on gloves and safety glasses or goggles.
2. Assemble the partial circuit as shown in the circuit diagram.

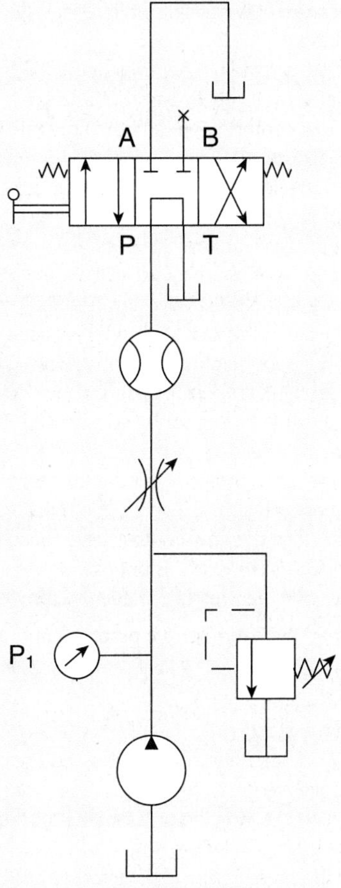

3. Set initial pressure and flow rate.
   a. Open the relief valve and the flow control valve completely.
   b. Start the stand.
   c. Establish a flow rate of 3.78 lpm (0.2 gpm) through the flow meter with a pressure of 13.79 bar (200 psi) on pressure gauge P_1.
   d. From this point on, *make no additional adjustments to the flow control valve.*
4. Assemble the complete circuit shown in the circuit diagram.

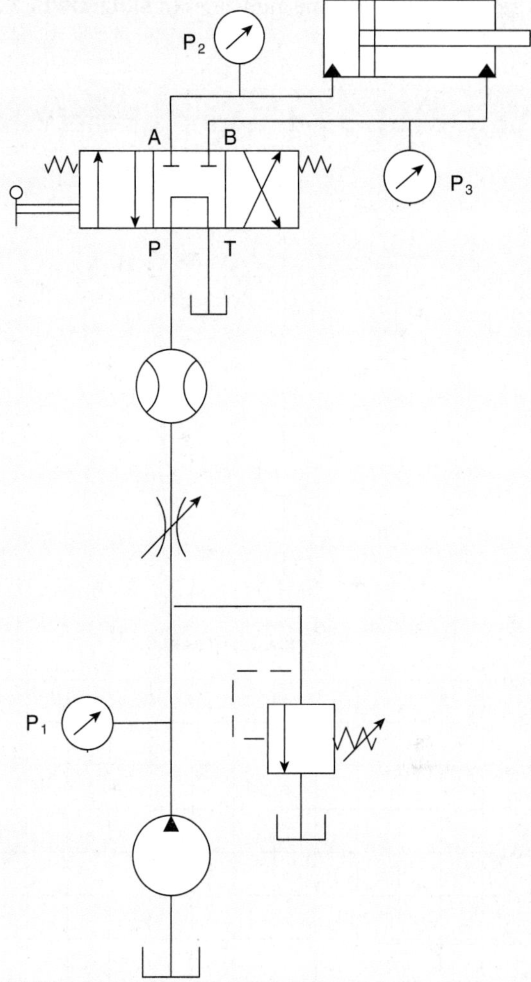

5. Conduct pressure, flow, and cycle time tests.
   a. Start the stand.
   b. Start with the cylinder fully retracted.
   c. Extend the cylinder. While the cylinder is moving, record the pressures on gauges P_1, P_2 and P_3, the flow rate (*Q*, in lpm), and the time to extend the cylinder fully.
   d. Retract the cylinder.
   e. Increase the pressure on P_1 to 27.58 bar (400 psi). (Do this by adjusting the relief valve, not the flow control valve.)
   f. Repeat steps 3 and 4, recording the same data.
   g. Increase the pressure on P_1 in 13.79-bar (200 psi) increments to 68.95 bar (1,000 psi) or until the limits of the stand are reached, whichever comes first. Repeat steps c and d at each setting and record the same data.
   h. Shut down the stand.
   i. Clean the work area, and return tools and equipment to their proper storage.
   j. Create a table, graph, or other visual presentation to show the relationship between the pressure drop across the flow control valve, the flow rate through that valve, and the cylinder cycle time. This may require more than one table or graph. What can you say about the pressures on P_2 and P_3 and why they do what they do?

Testing a Relief Valve

S35004

To test a relief valve, follow the guidelines in **SKILL DRILL 35-4**.

SKILL DRILL 35-4 Testing a Relief Valve

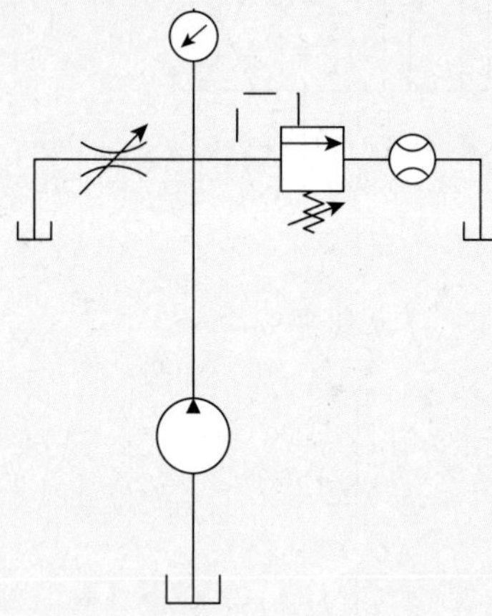

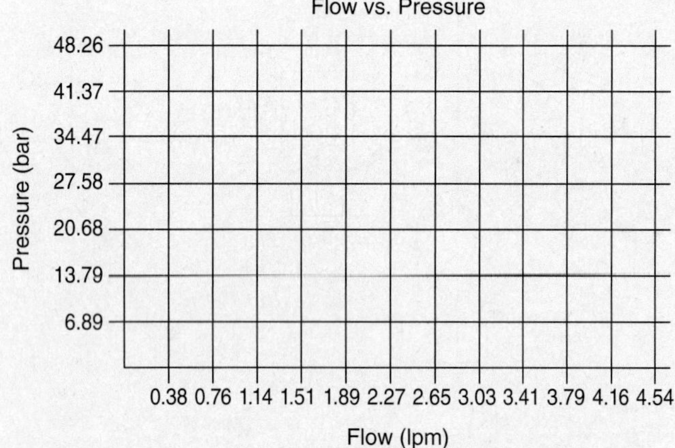

For this procedure, you will need the following tools, materials, and equipment:

- training stand
- wrenches and spanners of appropriate sizes
- components to assemble the hydraulic circuit shown
- safety glasses or goggles
- gloves.

1. Put on gloves and safety glasses or goggles.
2. Assemble the partial circuit as shown in the circuit diagram.
3. Check for leakage at low pressure.
   - **a.** Open the flow control valve completely.
   - **b.** Remove the drain line from the relief valve. Alternatively, install a clear plastic tube on the relief valve drain port.
   - **c.** Start the stand.
   - **d.** Check for any oil coming out of the relief valve drain port.
   - **e.** Shut down the stand.
   - **f.** Replace the drain line on the relief valve if it was removed.
4. Check the pressure/flow profile of the relief valve.
   - **a.** Start the stand.
   - **b.** Close the flow control valve completely.
   - **c.** Set the relief valve to 68.95 bar (1,000 psi).
   - **d.** Open the flow control valve until the flow rate through the flow meter drops to 0.0 lpm.
   - **e.** Slowly close the flow control valve until you get the first indication of flow through the flow meter.
   - **f.** Record the pressure at which the first flow occurs. (This is the cracking pressure of the relief valve. It should occur between 60% and 70% of the relief valve setting—41.37 to 48.26 bar (600 to 700 psi) in this case—for a direct-acting relief valve. A cracking pressure below 60% probably indicates a weak or broken spring. A cracking pressure above 70% probably indicates either the wrong spring or a broken spring that is jamming the mechanism.)
   - **g.** Close the flow control valve until the flow through the flow meter reaches 0.76 lpm (0.2 gpm), and record the pressure.
   - **h.** Continue to close the flow control valve to increase the flow in 0.76 lpm (0.2 gpm) intervals until the valve is completely closed, recording the pressure at each increment.

     (*Note*: To keep the exercise to a practical time, it may be necessary to adjust the flow increments to your particular equipment.)
   - **i.** Shut down the stand.
   - **j.** Clean the work area, and return tools and equipment to their proper storage area.
   - **k.** Create a graph showing the pressure versus the flow rate through the valve. (Show pressure on the vertical axis.) This represents the pressure/flow characteristics of the valve.

Testing a Cylinder for Internal Leakage

S35005

To test a cylinder for internal leakage, follow the guidelines in **SKILL DRILL 35-5**.

SKILL DRILL 35-5 Testing a Cylinder for Internal Leakage

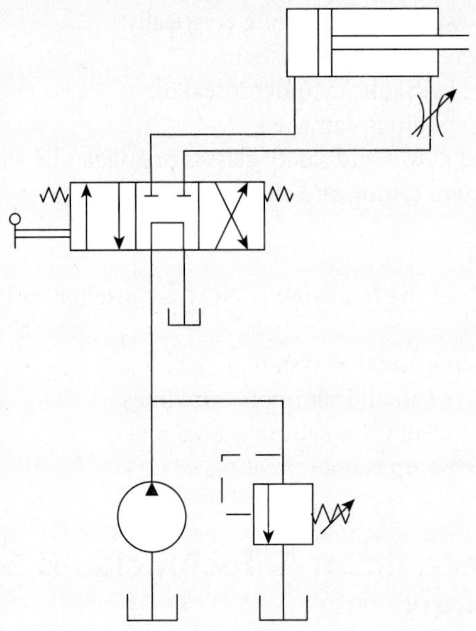

For this procedure, you will need the following tools, materials, and equipment:

- training stand
- wrenches and spanners of appropriate sizes
- components to assemble the hydraulic circuit shown
- safety glasses or goggles
- gloves.

1. Put on gloves and safety glasses or goggles.
2. Assemble the partial circuit as shown in the circuit diagram.
3. Check for internal leakage.
   - **a.** Start the stand.
   - **b.** Set the system pressure to 68.95 bar (1,000 psi).
   - **c.** Open the flow control valve completely.
   - **d.** Retract the cylinder completely.
   - **e.** Close the flow control valve completely.
   - **f.** Hold the directional control valve in the position to extend the cylinder.
   - **g.** Watch for any cylinder drift. Also, observe the pressures on both ends of the cylinder. Why is the pressure on the rod end higher?
   - **h.** Open the flow control valve slightly to allow the cylinder to extend a small amount.
   - **i.** Close the flow control valve and again watch for cylinder drift.
   - **j.** Repeat these actions at several points along the complete stroke of the cylinder so that leakage at any spot along the barrel can be detected.
   - **k.** Report any excessive leakage and list possible causes.
   - **l.** Shut down the stand.
   - **m.** Clean the work area, and return tools and equipment to their proper storage area.

▶ Wrap-Up

Ready for Review

- The witnessed malfunction in the operation of a system is termed the symptom.
- The reason for the malfunction is the root cause.
- When troubleshooting, treat the root cause to correct the symptom.
- When identifying issues that need to be resolved, the following are *essential* testing equipment:
  - pressure gauge
  - flow meter
  - temperature gauge
  - vacuum gauge.
- When identifying issues that need to be resolved, the following are *optional* testing equipment:
  - tachometer
  - load valve (needle valve) suitable for use at the maximum system pressure and flow rate
  - stopwatch
  - ultrasonic leak detector
  - oil can or heavy bearing grease for vacuum leak detection.
- You should be able to troubleshoot and diagnose the following issues (always follow the manufacture's recommended procedures):
  - inoperative systems
  - low or erratic system pressure

- systems that operate erratically
- systems that operate slowly
- systems that operate too fast
- systems that overheat
- foaming fluid
- excessive system noise
- excessive pump noise
- leaking pumps
- load drop with control valve in neutral position
- control valve sticking or working hard
- leaking control valve
- leaking cylinder.

▶ You should know the procedures to troubleshoot and diagnose the following issues (always follow the manufacturer's recommended procedures):
- troubleshooting and diagnosing hydraulic pump problems
- performing system temperature tests
- performing system pressure, flow, and cycle time tests
- testing a relief valve
- testing a cylinder for internal leakage.

Key Terms

pump ripple An effect that is common with positive displacement pumps and is the result of small fluctuations in flow. These ripples can lead to structural vibration of pipework and associated components and hence result in audible noise.

troubleshooting A systematic and logical approach to determining the causes of and solutions to malfunctions.

Review Questions

1. All of the following are essential testing equipment except ______________.
   a. pressure gauge
   b. stopwatch
   c. flow meter
   d. vacuum gauge
2. All of the following are optional testing equipment except ______________.
   a. tachometer
   b. ultrasonic leak detector
   c. heavy bearing grease
   d. temperature gauge
3. The witnessed malfunction in the operation of a system is termed the ______________.
   a. root cause
   b. symptom
4. The reason for the malfunction is the ______________.
   a. root cause
   b. symptom
5. When troubleshooting, treat the ______________.
   a. root cause
   b. symptom
6. Which of the following is a root cause, not a symptom?
   a. The system is inoperative.
   b. There is air in the fluid.
   c. The pump is leaking.
   d. The system is operating slowly.
7. Which of the following is a root cause, not a symptom?
   a. The fluid is foaming.
   b. There is excessive pump noise.
   c. The control valve is leaking.
   d. The cylinder rod is binding
8. Which of the following is a symptom, not a root cause?
   a. The system is operating erratically.
   b. There is air in the system.
   c. The hydraulic cylinder is leaking.
   d. The pump is damaged.
9. Should gloves and safety glasses or goggles be worn during all system testing and checking procedures?
   a. Yes.
   b. No.
10. Which of the following is NOT a cause for an inoperative system?
    a. There's no oil in system.
    b. There's an oil leak in pressure lines.
    c. The relief valve setting is low.
    d. The pump is not operating.

ASE Technician A/Technician B Style Questions

1. The system is operating erratically. Technician A says there is air in the system. Technician B says there is water in the system. Who is correct?
   a. Technician A
   b. Technician B
   c. Both Technician A and Technician B
   d. Neither Technician A nor Technician B
2. The system is not operating. Technician A says there may be no oil in the system. Technician B says the pump is not operating. Who is correct?
   a. Technician A
   b. Technician B
   c. Both Technician A and Technician B
   d. Neither Technician A nor Technician B
3. The system is operating slowly. Technician A says the flow control valve is installed backwards. Technician B says the flow control valve is just not set properly. Who is correct?
   a. Technician A
   b. Technician B
   c. Both Technician A and Technician B
   d. Neither Technician A nor Technician B
4. There is excessive system noise. Technician A says there is a kink in the pump inlet line, restricting fluid flow. Technician B says the hydraulic oil is dirty. Who is correct?
   a. Technician A
   b. Technician B
   c. Both Technician A and Technician B
   d. Neither Technician A nor Technician B

5. The control valve is leaking. Technician A says the tie bolts on the valve stacks are too loose. Technician B says the tie bolts on the valve stacks are too tight. Who is correct?
   a. Technician A
   b. Technician B
   c. Both Technician A and Technician B
   d. Neither Technician A nor Technician B
6. The system is operating too fast. Technician A says the flow control valve is installed backward. Technician B says the pump control valve is not set properly. Who is correct?
   a. Technician A
   b. Technician B
   c. Both Technician A and Technician B
   d. Neither Technician A nor Technician B
7. The system is overheating. Technician A says the oil viscosity is incorrect. Technician B says the relief valve pressure is set incorrectly. Who is correct?
   a. Technician A
   b. Technician B
   c. Both Technician A and Technician B
   d. Neither Technician A nor Technician B
8. The oil is foaming. Technician A says there is leakage in the valves and actuator seals. Technician B says the seal around the pump shaft is worn. Who is correct?
   a. Technician A
   b. Technician B
   c. Both Technician A and Technician B
   d. Neither Technician A nor Technician B
9. The pump is leaking. Technician A says there are loose or broken pump parts. Technician B says there are loose or broken valve connections. Who is correct?
   a. Technician A
   b. Technician B
   c. Both Technician A and Technician B
   d. Neither Technician A nor Technician B
10. The control valve is sticking. Technician A says there is misalignment or seizing of the control linkage. Technician B says the O-rings are worn, damaged, or incompatible. Who is correct?
   a. Technician A
   b. Technician B
   c. Both Technician A and Technician B
   d. Neither Technician A nor Technician B

KOMATSU
“WE GAVE THE D61i A TRY.
IT'S THE BEST DOZER
E'VE EVER RUN.”
KOMATSU

SECTION IV

Wheeled Equipment and Attachments

CHAPTER 36

Wheels, Tires, and Hubs

Knowledge Objectives

After reading this chapter, you will be able to:

- **K36001** Describe wheel types, operation, functions, and mounting designs.
- **K36002** Describe tire purposes, functions, construction, applications, and classifications for MORE; describe and perform tire maintenance and service.
- **K36003** Describe the functions, types, and construction of hubs, bearings, and seals.

Skills Objectives

After reading this chapter, you will be able to:

- **S36001** Explain procedures for wheel maintenance.
- **S36002** Explain procedures for tire maintenance.
- **S36003** Explain procedures for hub maintenance.

Introduction

Many important safety concerns must be kept in mind when working with the wheels, tires, and hubs of heavy equipment machines. The weight of rubber-tired heavy equipment machines is supported by tires that contain enormous potential energy in the form of air pressure that can vary from as low as 15 psi to well over 100 psi. Many deaths and serious injuries have resulted from mishandling tires during heavy-equipment servicing or when performing repairs. Tires should *always* be deflated when a technician performs any type of servicing or repairs on wheel assemblies. If you remove the valve core to do this, ice can form in the valve as air rushes out. To be sure that all air pressure drains down in the tire, carefully run a piece of wire or small screwdriver into the valve stem.

A tire explosion is a *very violent* event and can easily cause death if anyone is close by when it happens. An explosion happens when the temperature of the air inside the tire or the tire itself reaches 250°C (482°F). The resulting reaction is called **pyrolysis**. The use of nitrogen to inflate a tire can prevent the explosion from happening. A **tire explosion** is different from a **blowout**. Blowouts occur if a tire fails while the machine is traveling or because of overinflation. Tire explosions can occur when a tire starts to burn on the inside and pressure eventually rises high enough to explode the tire. Excessive heat on a rim from welding or cutting, a brake that is dragging, or a machine that has caught fire can cause this. If you notice a burning rubber smell or see smoke from a tire, do not approach the machine. Evacuate the area immediately. Exploding tires can propel debris more than 1,500 feet. Wait at least eight hours before approaching the machine, to allow the tire to cool down.

Technicians must take care *never* to apply excessive heat to wheels and tires, as heat increases pressure, and increased pressure can cause component failure. Never use torches, welding equipment, or any other type of heat source near tires or wheels.

Technicians must handle large tires and wheels properly to avoid crushing or pinching injuries. In most cases a heavy-duty equipment technician is wise to call a tire technician to deal with tire issues. Tire technicians have the proper tools and equipment as well as the necessary training to handle machine tires safely.

Never leave a machine on hydraulic jacks alone when servicing the machine. Hydraulic jacks are only meant for lifting and lowering and not for holding the machine in place. Lower the machine onto jack stands or wooden cribbing after lifting it.

Some machines may have the main parts of the rim bolted together, unlike most rims that are welded together when they are manufactured. If this is the case, you must take special care not to loosen the fasteners that hold the two pieces (inner and outer) together. If this happens and the tire is pressurized, the rim halves could separate, and the pieces could cause serious injury or death.

Wheels

K36001, S36001

Rubber-tired heavy-equipment machines can have several different types of wheels. (Wheels are also called rims.) Small equipment such as skid steers and backhoe loaders have **one-piece rims** (**FIGURE 36-1**). Sometimes called disc-type wheels, one-piece rims are automotive-style rims made from two pieces of stamped, pressed, and rolled steel welded together with a center hole that fits over the hub and with several holes drilled around the hub hole for wheel studs or bolts. Their outer circumference has rolled lips for the tire bead to seat against air. Toward the inside of the wheel on the surface that is exposed to air pressure, the wheel steps down (**FIGURE 36-2**). This allows

FIGURE 36-1 One-piece rim on machine.

You Are the Mobile Heavy Equipment Technician

You are working for a large gold mine that owns a fleet of 320 ton haul trucks. The mine's equipment manager is concerned about a recent decline in tire life and has asked you to investigate. The tire budget for the mine is in the multi million dollar range and any way to get more life out of the trucks' tires will lead to significant savings.

You first need to find out if the right specification of tires are being used for the application. You then need to know if the correct tire pressure is being maintained. All trucks have tire pressure monitoring systems.

Answer the following questions based on the scenario presented above.

1. where would you find the correct information to know what the correct tire specification is (tire size, ply rating, tread pattern etc.)?
2. where would you find the correct tire inflation specification?
3. how could you confirm that the tire pressure monitoring system is working properly?
4. what are three possible causes of reduced tire life?

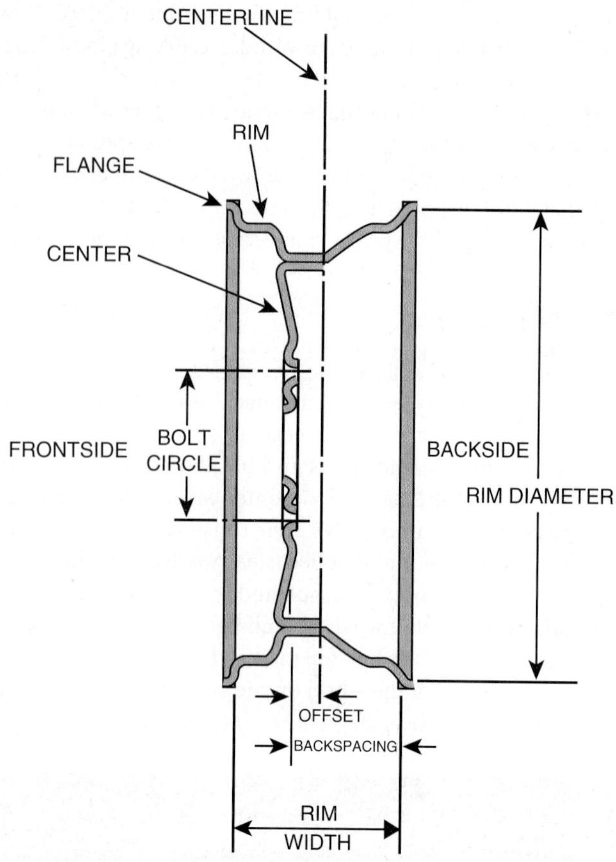

FIGURE 36-2 Cross section of a one-piece rim.

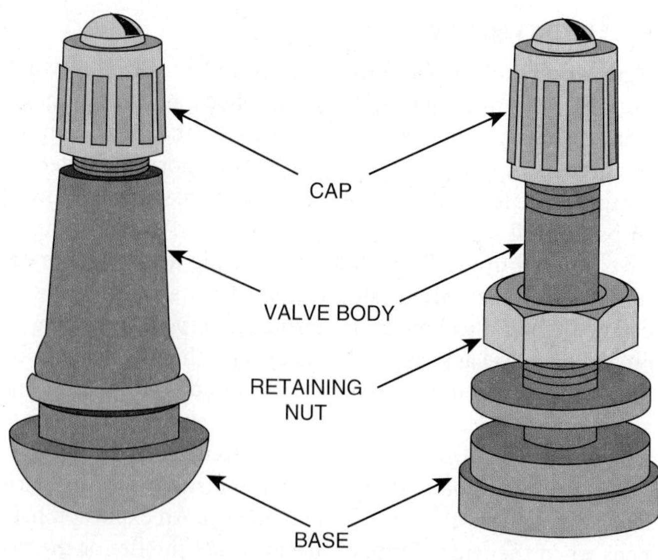

FIGURE 36-3 Two types of valve stems.

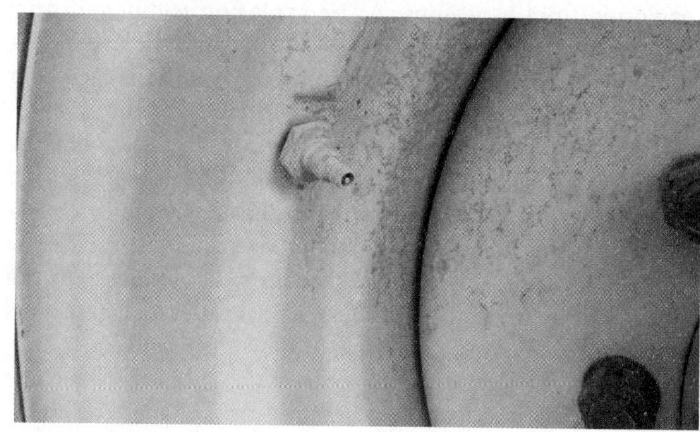

FIGURE 36-4 A typical valve stem on a heavy machine.

the tire bead to drop into a smaller circumference area when the technician installs or removes the tire.

Some road-worthy rubber-tired cranes use aluminum rims forged as one piece and then finished to make an attractive and functional wheel. These machines can travel at close to highway speeds and require a wheel similar to a highway truck's wheel.

Heavy-equipment wheels are a tubeless design. This means the valve stem is not part of a tube and fits to the rim base. Valve stems are simply one-way check valves that feature a removable core. Remove the cap to inspect the valve stems for damage on a regular basis. Always reinstall the cap.

In the past, most tires had to have an inner tube to hold air. This meant the tube's valve stem would protrude through a hole in the rim. Today, most wheel and tire assemblies for heavy equipment are tubeless. Tubeless tire/wheel assemblies must have a valve stem that seals to the rim. Light-duty tubeless tires have a valve stem that pulls through the wheel from the inside (**FIGURE 36-3A**) while heavy-duty tubeless tires have a valve stem assembly that has a seal on both sides of the rim and then a washer and nut that tightens onto it from the outside to complete the seal (see **FIGURE 36-3B** and **FIGURE 36-4**).

When installing rims onto a hub, always make sure the mating surfaces are clean and free of dust, dirt, and grease. Install fasteners properly, and torque to specification with a calibrated torque wrench.

Tighten and torque wheel fasteners in a star pattern. In other words, move to the opposite side of the rim to tighten the next fastener. If you need to draw the rim in over the hub, make sure to draw it in evenly so it doesn't get distorted. Clean the rim and hub before installing. To install a rim, follow the steps in **SKILL DRILL 36-1**.

Inspecting a One-Piece Rim

Because these rims are simple by design, they usually do not require any maintenance outside of a good visual inspection. When inspecting one-piece rims, check for rust, cracks, and bending. Pay close attention to the hub-mounting area, wheel-fastener hole area, and bead-seat area.

Installing and Removing a Tire with a One-Piece Rim

The installer installs the tire onto a one-piece rim by forcing the inside tire bead over the outside wheel bead first and then forcing the outside tire bead over the outside wheel bead. This can be a challenge because the installer needs to deform the tire bead slightly to do this. Once the tire is on the rim, the installer spreads a rubber lubricant around the wheel bead area and feeds air into the tire valve.

Seating the bead can also be a challenge, and the installer should take extra caution while doing this because the job will likely require higher than specified operating air pressure.

SKILL DRILL 36-1 Installing a Rim

1. Locate a light-duty rim and hub.
2. Clean rim and hub of dust, dirt, and grease.
3. Clean mating surfaces of dust, dirt, and grease.
4. Draw the rim in over the hub evenly, so it does not become distorted
5. Tighten the fasteners in a star pattern; in other words, move to the opposite side of the rim to tighten the next fastener.
6. Torque fasteners in a star pattern to specification, using a calibrated torque wrench.

To remove a tire from a one-piece rim, first deflate the tire and remove the valve core. All valve stems have a core that threads into the stem. The core is sometimes called a Schrader valve.

> **TECHNICIAN TIP**
>
> Any time you remove a wheel assembly from a machine, deflate the tire first to reduce the chance of an accident. The easiest way to deflate a tire is to remove the valve core. Wear gloves and safety glasses when doing this. Check the empty valve stem for blockage with a piece of wire, as it is common for ice to form in the stem from the air rushing out.

Multipiece Rims

As tires get larger, they become more difficult to remove and install from a rim. This is why manufacturers use **multipiece rims** for larger tire sizes. Multipiece rims provide a way for a technician to disassemble the rim, which in turn allows the tech to remove the tire without having to deform the tire bead to get it over top of the rim bead seat area.

Multipiece rims have O-rings to seal the areas between their base and removable bead seats. Multipiece rims may also feature bead locks or keys that prevent bead seats from spinning on the rim's base, which can happen when the machine is under high-load, low-speed working conditions.

When inspecting a multipiece rim, include the basic visual inspections for one-piece rims, but also inspect lock rings and rim locks for cracks, bends, and damage.

Three- and Five-Piece Rims

Medium-size rubber-tired machines likely use a **three-piece rim** (**FIGURE 36-5**). These rims have a main rim base with an inner bead seat flange as one piece, and an outer bead seat and locking ring that make up the other two pieces.

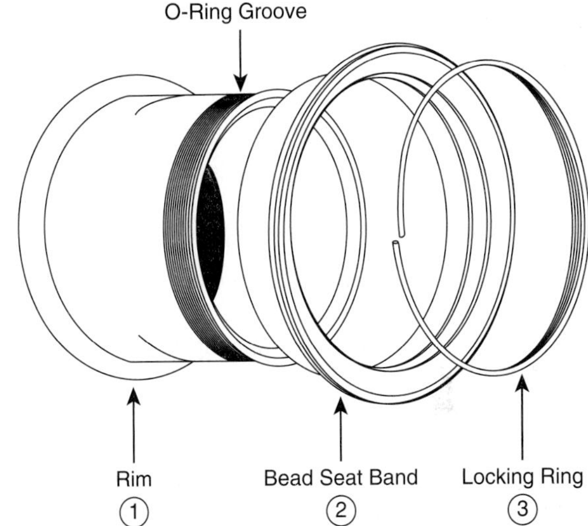

FIGURE 36-5 Three-piece rim.

Manufacturers use **five-piece rims** on large wheeled machines (**FIGURE 36-6**). These rims are similar to three-piece rims but have an additional separate inner bead seat and a bead seat band for the outer flange.

Installing a Multipiece Rim

To install a tire on a three-piece rim, fit the tire over the rim base, and then install the outer bead and lock ring.

> **SAFETY TIP**
>
> The tire and rim assembly is at its most dangerous while it is being inflated. The components of the rims can become projectiles if the lock does not hold. Before inflating the tire and rim assembly, place it in an inflation cage, or use a chain wrapped through and around the rim as a restraint to prevent the rim components from flying outward. When you inflate the tire, the outer bead pushes out, and this pushes out the outer rim bead against the lock ring. The lock ring then seats in a groove in the rim base. Always ensure the lock ring is completely seated after inflation before removing the restraint or taking the assembly out of the inflation cage.

▶ Tires

K36002, S36002

The tires on heavy equipment machines represent a large portion of maintenance and running costs. If they are abused or not maintained properly, the replacement cost and downtime can be very expensive. Tires for the biggest haul trucks can cost over $100,000 each.

For wheel-type machines, tires are the contact point between the machine and the ground on which the machine travels. The tread pattern and sidewall construction play a huge

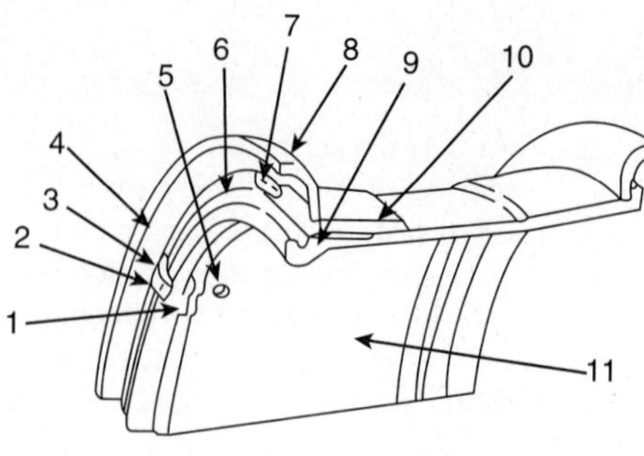

1. Locator - Demountable Rim Only
2. Lock Ring Driver
3. Gutter Notch For Lock Ring Driver
4. 5° Bead Seat Band, Tapered Ring
5. Tubeless Valve Hole
6. Lock Ring
7. Pry Bar Slot
8. Flanges
9. O-Ring Gasket
10. Bead Seat Band Toe
11. Rim Base

O-Ring Groove

Key

Rim ① Flanges ② ③ Bead Seat Band ④ Locking Ring ⑤

FIGURE 36-6 Five-piece rim.

part in how the machine performs and feels to the operator. Tire size, type, condition, and air pressure greatly affect the operating characteristics of a machine.

Manufacturers make tires mostly from rubber-based compounds, which they reinforce with steel cords and layers (also called belts or plies) made of materials like nylon, fiberglass, polyester, and rayon.

Pneumatic Tires

Most tires on machines are pneumatic, meaning they are hollow and must be filled with pressurized air to support the load of the machine and its payload or bucket full of material. Think of a **pneumatic tire** as a cushioning container for the air pressure needed to keep the machine from riding on its rims.

Solid Rubber Tires

Certain machine applications require **solid rubber tires**, for example, those used in a scrap yard, where there is a constant threat of tire punctures. The downfall of solid rubber tires is that there is very little flex to them, which makes for a rough ride for the operator. They also heat up if the machine travels fast for long periods. This is in contrast to an air-filled tire, where the air inside provides a cooling effect.

Tire Longevity

The main factors that affect tire life are listed here:

- Operating conditions
- Operator abuse
- Proper tire selection for worksite conditions
- Proper inflation

Most of these factors are out of the technician's control except for proper inflation. Proper inflation is based on the weight on the tires and the speed at which the machine travels. Tire manufacturers provide inflation information in cases where the machine manufacturer does not make the information available.

One of the biggest enemies of tires is heat. If heat builds up in a tire from overloading or underinflation, the structure of the rubber starts to break down.

If a tire is underinflated, its sidewalls flex excessively, which causes heat buildup. Some tire manufacturers set limits as to how far a tire should travel in 1 hour at a certain load. If the tire exceeds this distance, the tire starts to run hot. Tire manufacturer sometimes provide charts to inform the user of a tire's maximum TMPH (ton-mile per hour). Excessive loading and speed takes life out of the tire in direct proportion to how much the limit is exceeded.

▶ TECHNICIAN TIP

Some tire manufacturers suggest that if a tire runs with less than 80% of its proper pressure at any time, it may be permanently damaged. The tire's sidewalls may have flexed excessively, which causes cord damage, or the tire may have overheated, which causes rubber degradation. In these cases, you should inspect the tire for possible replacement.

The two main types of tires on machines today are radial tires and an earlier design called bias ply tires.

Tire Construction

The construction of a tire starts with loops of metal cords that form the base for each tire bead. The **tire bead** is the area that contacts the rim and must form an airtight seal with it. **Sidewalls** are the areas between the tread area and the bead area. The multiple layers, or **plies**, of material that form a base for the tire from bead to bead are called the **carcass** or **casing** (**FIGURE 36-7**). With radial tires, these plies run at 90 degrees to the tread, which gives the tire more flexible sidewalls and results in a smoother ride and bigger contact patch. The plies run at angles to the tread and the sidewall in bias ply tires. Manufacturers make plies from

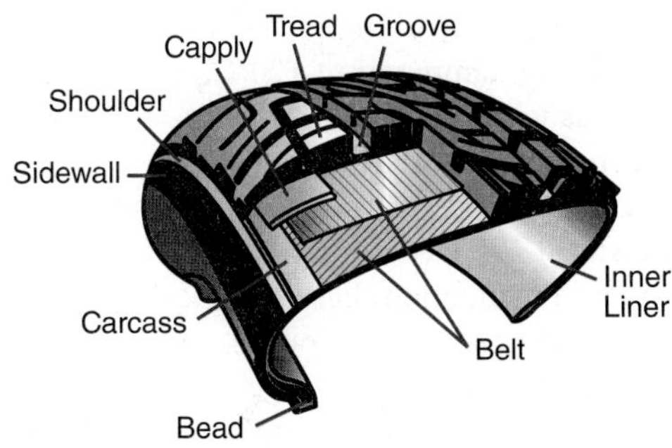

FIGURE 36-7 Tire carcass cross section.

many different types of materials to give the tires their different characteristics, such as higher strength, smoother ride, or less rolling resistance. The inside of a tubeless tire is a smooth rubber layer to seal the air on the inside. Before tubeless tires became the norm, an inner tube sealed the air and gave the effect of having a separate bladder on the inside of the tire.

The industry rates tires according to the number of plies that a tire has tire. Generally, the more plies a tire has, the stronger it is. **Ply ratings** for heavy-equipment tires range from 12 to 78. Some tire manufacturers use a star rating to indicate the strength of a radial tires carcass.

Tread

Tread designs offer an almost endless variety of different patterns. The most common working conditions and traction needs dictate the best tread design for an application. **FIGURE 36-8** shows various thread designs.

The rubber compound for the tread is based on the type of operating conditions the machine typically works in, such as highly abrasive material, or whether the machine is travelling at high speed for long distances. Letter and number combinations such as A, A4, B, B4, C, and C4 allow you to identify tread compounds.

Manufacturers also classify tread depth and design with letters and numbers. For example, machine-type C-compactor; G-grader; E-earthmover; L-loader, and tread style/depth S-smooth, 1-ribbed, 2-traction, 3-rock, 4-deep rock, 5-extra deep rock, 7-floatation.

> TECHNICIAN TIP

The value of tires becomes apparent when replacement tires are unavailable. Several years ago, when the world economy was running at full capacity, there was a shortage of large tires for heavy equipment. This not only drove the price of tires through the roof but there were many stories of machines sitting idle because of there were no tires available to put on them. Manufacturers were shipping some new machines to customers with no tires. Many companies were forced to find any tire that could hold air to keep machines running, and limiting top speeds to make the tires last as long as possible. This also prompted many companies to install tire pressure monitoring systems. Not only was this a major frustration to the end user, it put a major emphasis on maintaining tires on working machines.

To illustrate the importance of making tires last as long as possible some companies send operators home if they spin tires. Many machines come with traction-control systems to prevent tire spin as well.

FIGURE 36-8 Various thread designs.

Tire Sizes

There are three important dimensions used to determine a tires size. The first dimension is the bead diameter, which manufacturers measure in inches. The second diameter is the section width. The industry measures section width in inches (millimeters for smaller tires) at the widest part of the tire if you were looking directly at the tire tread face. The third dimension is the sidewall height. The industry does not measure it in inches but as a ratio of the height of the sidewall compared to the section width. If these two dimensions are the same it means the ratio is one to one or 100%, which indicates the tire has a normal aspect ratio. (If a tire has a one to one aspect ratio there is no indication of this in the tire sizing.) However, if the sidewall height is shorter than the tread face width, then this ratio is included with the tire size and indicates a low-profile tire. The industry identifies this ratio as a percentage of the sidewall dimension in comparison to the tread face (**FIGURE 36-9**).

Also, if the tire size includes an "R," this indicates the tire is a radial design. For example, a tire size of 27.00-49 indicates a bead diameter of 49 inches and a tire section width of 27 inches. It also tells you that the section width and the sidewall height are equal. A tire size of 33.25 R 29 indicates the section width is

FIGURE 36-9 This tire has a 40-inch section width and a 57-inch bead.

33.25 inches wide, it is a radial tire, and the rim diameter that it fits on is 29 inches.

Another example is 45/65 R 45. This indicates a bead diameter of 45 inches, a section width of 45 inches, and a sidewall dimension that is 65% of the section width. This example can be related to automotive tires that are sometimes termed "low-profile tires." An extreme example of low-profile tires is 290/35 R 17. This is a low-profile tire for a high-performance car.

Some tire section widths are indicated in metric dimensions, for example 800/65 R 29. This means the tire's section width is 800 mm wide; it is a radial; and it has an aspect ratio of 65. To determine tread pattern and tire size, follow the steps in **SKILL DRILL 36-2**.

Proper inflation

As mentioned previously, proper tire inflation is one of the major contributors to determining tire life. An underinflated tire allows the sidewall to flex excessively as the machine travels while loaded. This causes excessive heat buildup in the tire casing and can weaken the rubber. To avoid breaking down the tire, the critical temperature of the air inside the tire should not exceed 80°C, or 176°F.

An overinflated tire can cause bulging in the tread face and excessive wear on the center of the tread. It may be acceptable to overinflate a tire in certain circumstances to compensate for an overloaded machine, but you should normally inflate tires as closely as possible to the recommended "cold" psi specification. Ideally, check tire pressure when tires are cold for a more consistent reading. Cold means that the machine has not been working for at least 6 hours and should be close to room temperature (20°C, or 68°F). Once the machine begins to operate, its tires warm up, and this causes an increase in tire pressure.

A rule of thumb is that a 10°F temperature change changes the tire pressure 1 psi. Underinflation is much more damaging to tires than overinflation because excessive sidewall flex dramatically increases tire temperature.

Ideally, inflate tires with nitrogen, which is an inert gas. This helps maintain a more stable pressure, keeps moisture outside of the tire, and reduces the risk of an explosion, as there is no oxygen to support combustion. Because nitrogen comes in bottles that are charged with over 2,000 psi, only properly trained technicians should inflate tires with nitrogen. In reality, most technicians inflate tires with air from shop or mobile air compressors, which is fine for most applications.

As mentioned earlier, proper tire inflation is critical to getting maximum life from machine tires. Small machine tires may cost as little as $250, but large mining machines, like haul trucks and rubber-tired loaders, use tires that cost close to $100,000 each. If an improperly inflated tire reduces tire life by 20%, the cost of a technician monitoring tire pressure is a wise investment.

Companies equip many machines with tire pressure monitoring systems to provide a constant watch on tire pressures. These become very cost effective with tire prices in the several-thousand-dollar range. The systems have pressure monitors mounted to the machine's rims that send tire pressure information wirelessly to a display unit in the machine's cab. To inflate a tire, follow the steps in **SKILL DRILL 36-3**.

SKILL DRILL 36-2 Determining Tread Pattern and Tire Size

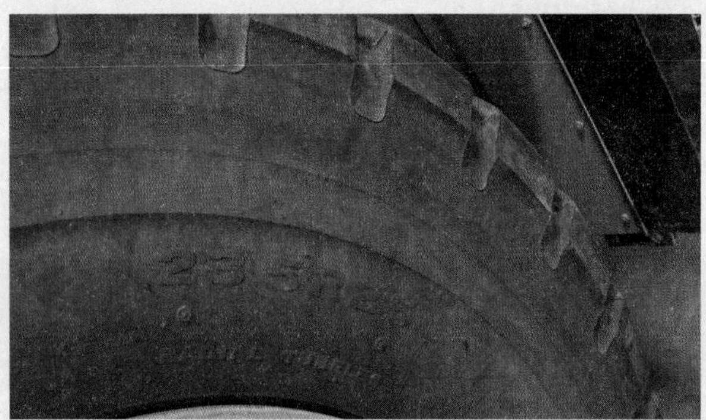

1. On a tire's sidewall, locate the letter that indicates the rubber compound the manufacturer used to make the tread.
2. Next, locate the letters and/or numbers that indicate the tread depth and design.
3. Finally, determine the tire's size and type by locating the letter/number combinations for bead diameter, section width, aspect ratio, and whether or not the tire is a radial.

SKILL DRILL 36-3 Inflating a Tire

1. Locate a light- or medium-duty heavy-equipment tire. If the tire is mounted on a machine, deflate the tire and dismount it from the machine.
2. Place the tire in a tire cage or wrap chains around it.
3. Stand to the side of the tire, and use a pressure monitor and inflator to inflate the tire to the manufacturer's specification.

Tire Pressure Monitoring Systems

Maintaining proper tire pressure is essential for the safety and performance of a vehicle. **Tire inflation pressure** is the level of air in the tire that provides it with load-carrying capacity and affects overall vehicle performance. It also plays a significant role in decreasing fuel consumption, reducing CO_2 emissions, and extending tire life. All tires lose inflation over time, and as many modern machines have extended service intervals, tires can become dangerously underinflated if a service Technician does not check inflation regularly.

In addition to increased fuel consumption and tire wear, driving with low tire pressures can cause additional stress on the tire sidewalls. This results in increased operating temperatures that can lead to premature tire failure. Tires operating with low pressures can also affect the machine's handling and performance. In a worst-case scenario, underinflation can lead to a tire blowout or tread separation.

The automated **tire pressure monitoring system (TPMS)** provides a means of reliable and continuous monitoring of the vehicle tire pressure and is designed to increase safety, decrease fuel consumption, and improve vehicle performance. A TPMS monitors the tires for low air pressure and alerts the operator when one or more tires are lower than (or in some cases, higher than) the designated thresholds. This alert can be an illuminated warning lamp or a chime. With most TPMS systems, operators can monitor the tire pressures and temperatures from the cab to ensure that their tires are properly inflated under all operating conditions. The TPMS is designed to ignore normal pressure variations caused by changes in ambient temperature.

The TPMS measures the tire pressure via a sensor installed inside each wheel, which helps protect the TPMS from damage. Each wheel sensor has an antenna that wirelessly relays the information it senses to receivers within the machine. The receivers send the signal to the control unit. The control unit sends an appropriate signal to the on-board computer, which in turn illuminates a display on the machine's information screen to warn the operator of low tire pressure in a certain wheel. An audible and visual warning alerts the operator to the problem. These systems can also be added to older machines and can be very cost effective when the machine's tires cost thousands of dollars each.

An internal battery designed to last between 5 and 10 years powers the sensors. A **centrifugal switch** in the sensor allows the sensor to go to sleep when the machine stops, which extends battery life. When this battery goes dead, it has to be replaced, which usually means that the entire sensor must be replaced, because the battery is typically sealed inside the sensor.

A TPMS can be of two types: one-way communication or two-way communication. In one-way communication, the TPMS sensor can only transmit to the receiver; it cannot receive any information. In this type of system, the sensors usually use a centrifugal switch to turn themselves on and off to conserve the battery energy. In a two-way communication TPMS, the sensor can receive signals as well as transmit signals. This allows the control unit to send signals to wake up or cause the sensor to sleep, thus extending the sensor's battery life. The two-way communication system is more complex and expensive than the one-way system (**FIGURE 36-10**).

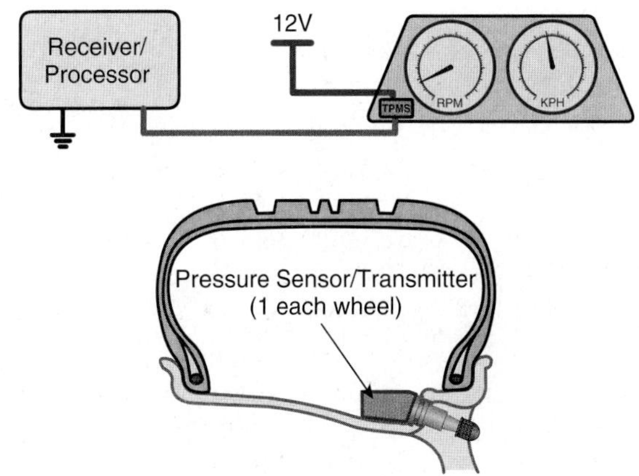

FIGURE 36-10 A TPMS is a cost-effective way of protecting the machine's tires.

Inspecting, Diagnosing, and Calibrating the TPMS

Technicians need to inspect, diagnose, and calibrate the TPMS in several general situations. Inspect whenever you have dismounted the tires from the wheels. In some cases, you need to replace the TPMS sensor batteries and inspect the sensor mounts. When the system detects a fault and turns on the warning light, you need to diagnose system faults. One or more tires that are not at the proper pressure can cause this, and it requires that you inspect for leaks or incorrect pressures. It could also be a system fault requiring use of a scan tool capable of communicating with the TPMS. Calibrate the system whenever you have replaced a sensor, wheel, or tire so that the TPMS knows on which wheel each sensor is located.

To inspect, diagnose, and calibrate the TPMS, follow the guidelines in **SKILL DRILL 36-4**.

▶ TECHNICIAN TIP

Technicians must always exercise caution when both checking and inflating tires. Only stand beside the sidewall of a tire when absolutely necessary, such as when checking pressures or connecting an air chuck. The ideal tire-inflator tool clips onto the valve stem and has a long enough hose extension to allow the technician to get away from the sidewall of the tire. It also has a gauge and a hand-operated valve (**FIGURE 36-11**).

If you inflate a tire off the machine, place the tire in a tire cage or wrap chains around the tire to create containment if the tire or rim comes apart while you are inflating it.

Dual Tires

Single drive-axle haul trucks for use in mining operations have dual tire arrangements on the rear drive axle. As is the case with on-highway trucks, the payload capacity of the truck is increased by running dual tires on the rear axle. It is important

SKILL DRILL 36-4 Inspecting, Diagnosing, and Calibrating the TPMS

1. Turn the ignition key to the run position, and observe the TPMS warning light. If the light indicates low tire pressure at any wheel, check the pressure of that wheel with an accurate tire pressure gauge. If incorrect, adjust the pressure using compressed air (or compressed nitrogen, if indicated).
2. If the light indicates a system fault, connect an appropriate scan tool to the system and read any diagnostic trouble codes (DTCs). Since TPMS systems are not standardized, research DTCs in the appropriate service information, and follow the diagnostic steps it lists to identify the cause of the fault.

FIGURE 36-11 An extended tire inflator keeps the technician out of the line of fire if a tire explodes while being inflated.

FIGURE 36-12 Rock ejectors keep the space between dual tires free from debris and rocks.

that tires are identical in size, the same type and model of tire, and are closely matched for wear. Most trucks with dual tires have rock ejectors between the tires in case a rock becomes wedged between the tires while the machine is operating. If not ejected, the rock becomes a serious safety hazard and will severely damage the tire sidewalls. **Rock ejectors** are metal bars that hang down from the truck's box (**FIGURE 36-12**).

Tire Handling

When the heavy-equipment technician needs to remove and install tire assemblies as a part of other repair procedures, the tech needs to understand the safe and unsafe methods of working with tires. Proper tire handling methods are based on tire size, machine type, and available equipment and tooling.

Technicians should handle medium and large tires with an appropriate-sized forklift and rigging, or a truck with a tire clamp arm. The tech should only handle extremely large tires with the proper equipment: specialty machines that are sometimes converted wheel loaders or forklifts. If a machine is in the shop and you need to remove one or more or its tires, you can use the shop crane with tire slings or chains if overhead access is available. Manually working with heavy tires is dangerous if not impossible. The tires shown in **FIGURE 36-13** can weigh between several pounds to several thousand pounds.

Always deflate tires by removing the valve core before removing the tires from a machine.

FIGURE 36-13 The tires pictured can weigh anywhere from several hundred to well over ten thousand pounds.

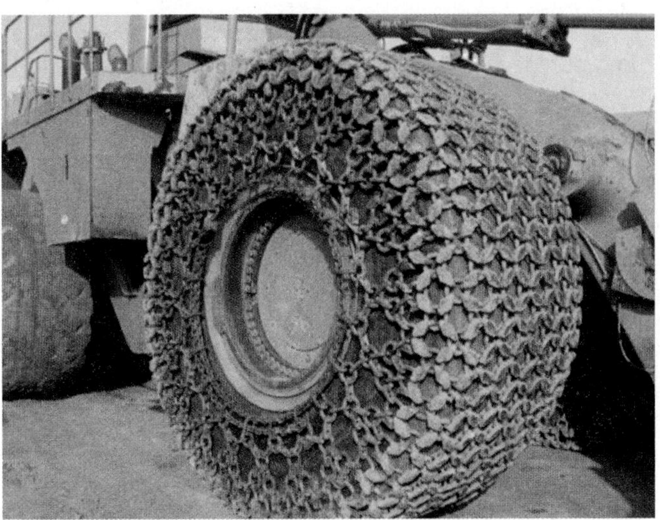

FIGURE 36-14 Tire chains are used to protect expensive tires from slip damage and to provide added traction.

FIGURE 36-15 Plain wheel hub on the front axle of a two-wheel drive backhoe.

Tire Chains

Some worksites can be damaging to rubber tires. Machines that work in quarries where sharp rocks are present require extra protection to prolong tire life. **Tire chains** are good extra protection because they completely surround the tire forming a protective barrier (**FIGURE 36-14**).

Tire chains can also improve traction. Some forestry machines use tire chains to improve the machine's maneuverability. They are a more open design and can have a variety of different patterns.

Tire chains wear over time and therefore require extra maintenance. This involves tightening the chains to maintain a proper tension on them. If the chains become too loose, they can cause damage to the machine. Chains also require extra work if the technician needs to remove a tire from the rim, as the tech must remove the chains first.

Tire Repair

To save money, because tires can be expensive to replace, companies can repair damaged tires to give them a second life. The repair process requires a specialized tire repair facility. Even if a tire is severely damaged, it may be possible to repair it by putting a new section in the tire's casing. Worn-down treads can be retreaded providing the casing is in good shape.

▶ Wheel Hubs

K36003, S36003

In rubber-tired machines, the wheel assembly fastens to the hub assembly. The hub allows smooth wheel rotation while it supports part of the weight of the machine. **Wheel hubs** can vary a great deal among different types of machines; **FIGURE 36-15** shows a plain wheel hub. Many wheel hubs transfer torque from the drivetrain to the wheel; in these a final drive planetary gear set is incorporated into the wheel hub.

Non-drive axles, or dead axles, have plain wheel hubs that are supported by a set of two tapered roller bearings the axles spindle shaft. When the machine's wheels are fastened to plain wheel hubs, the hubs allow wheel rotation on a stationary axle spindle.

Some plain wheel hubs also connect to the machine's brake system to transfer braking torque from the rotating wheel to the stationary axle spindle. **FIGURE 36-16** shows a cross section of a plain wheel hub. Plain wheel hubs have inner and outer tapered roller bearings. The roller bearing cones (inner race) rest on the axle's spindle, and their cups (outer race) press into the rotating wheel hub. The inside of the wheel hub also has a lip-type seal that presses into it to retain lubricating oil or grease inside the wheel hub and to keep contamination out. The lip of the seal rotates on a smooth metal sleeve or surface on the spindle shaft. When the hub is installed, the inner bearing cone slides over the shaft and stops against a step on the shaft. The outer bearing is then installed and held in place with a washer and nut.

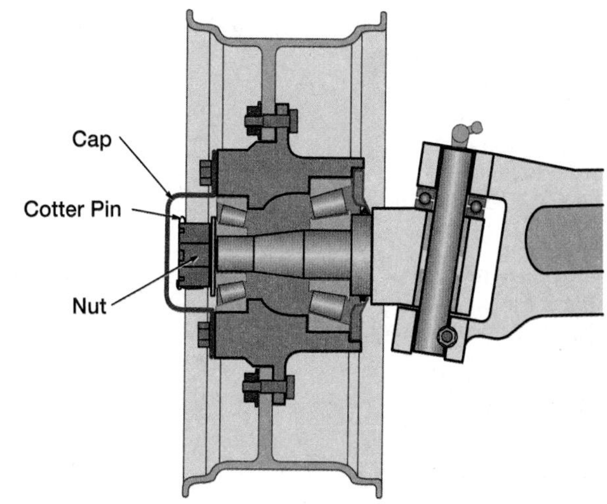

FIGURE 36-16 Plain wheel hub cross section.

Bearings and Adjustments

The technician must secure the bearing adjusting nut in place because there is no clamping force to hold it. You can secure the nut in several ways, including by using:

- a castellated nut and a cotter pin or lock wire that goes through a hole in the spindle;
- a locking washer that has an internal tab to hold it to the spindle and then bending a tab over one flat of the nut;
- or a double nut arrangement with a locking washer between them.

Some plain wheel hubs do not require any adjustment procedure and rely on machined steps on the spindle and the accurately manufactured specifications of the tapered roller bearings to give the correct bearing freeplay.

Grease lubricates the bearings of light-duty wheel hubs on machines that don't travel very fast. The manufacturer applies the grease to the bearings upon assembly (this is called "packing the bearings"). There is also extra space in the wheel hub for grease. The hub has a grease fitting so that the tech can apply some grease during servicing. *Note:* Take care not to over-grease wheel hubs, as this blows out the grease seals.

Wheel bearing adjustment for larger wheel hubs is usually based on measuring the rolling resistance of the wheel.

If a machine has an axle with an inboard final drive arrangement, the wheel hub is part of the axle shaft and a set of bearings supports the shaft. The bearing cones are on the axle shaft and the bearing cups press into the hub assembly. This type of axle can use two types of seals. Lighter duty axles use a lip seal installed on the inside of the hub assembly, and the lip rides on the axle shaft. This seal keeps the axle's lubricating fluid from leaking out. Higher capacity axles use metal face–type seals (duo-cone) to seal between the axle housing and hub assembly. **FIGURE 36-17** shows an axle hub, which is part of an inboard final drive axle assembly.

If a wheel hub incorporates a final drive, there may be a procedure that uses shims to set the bearing preload in order to get the correct rolling torque of the hub. This may require some special tools such as a hub turning tool, depth micrometer, dial-type torque wrench, fish scale, and outside micrometer. After the HDET assembles the hub onto the spindle with new bearings and with or without the wheel seal (check manufacturer's procedure), the HDET measures the rolling resistance. If it is within specification, the HDET can complete final assembly.

If the rolling torque is out of specification, the HDET must make a shim adjustment to adjust the bearing preload. See **FIGURE 36-18** to find where the shim pack is located.

Wheel assemblies are fastened to wheel hubs with some type of threaded fasteners. Some hubs may be tapped so the wheels can be fastened with bolts, but usually wheel studs provide a way for wheel nuts and/or washers to secure the wheel to the hub. The studs may have a serrated shoulder that grabs the hole they are driven into when they are installed, or they may have a clipped head that rests against a step in the back of the hub. Both styles prevent the stud from turning once they are installed (**FIGURE 36-19**).

Wheel Hub Servicing

In hubs for larger machines or those that travel at higher speeds, gear oil is used to lubricate their bearings. The technician must change this oil on a regular basis with oil that is the proper viscosity for the machine's operating ambient temperatures. The oil level will likely be about halfway up the hub housing. Do not overfill: this can also lead to seal failure because the oil expands after it warms up.

A typical oil viscosity for wheel hubs is SAE 30 or GL 80W90; a typical oil change interval is 1,000 hours.

Take care when removing the plug to check the level. If the machine has been running and the oil is warm, pressure builds up in the hub cavity. This pressure can force oil out of the plughole when you remove the plug (**FIGURE 36-20**). Use gloves

A. Face-Type Oil Seal
B. Outer Bearing
C. Dipstick
D. Axle Shaft
E. Spanner Nut
F. Planetary Carrier/Brake Hub
G. Thrust Washer
H. Locking Tab or Pin
I. Axle Housing
J. Sun Gear and Pinion Shaft
K. Snap Ring
L. Final Drive Ring Gear
M. Planet Pinion (3 used)
N. Thrust Washer (6 used)
O. Needle Roller
P. Planet Pinion Shaft (3 used)
Q. Pinion Shafts Retaining Snap Ring

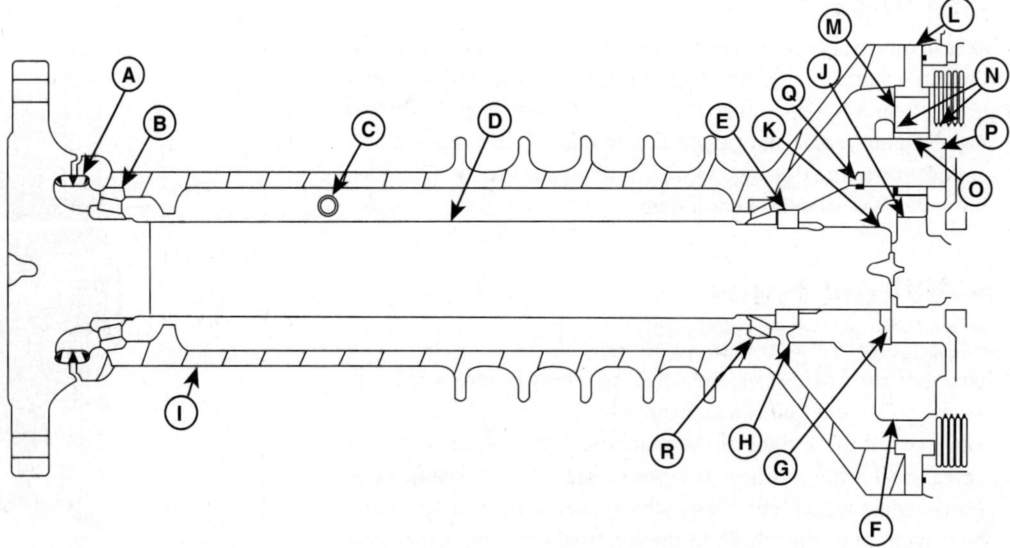

FIGURE 36-17 Inboard axle hub with duo-cone or face-type (A) seals.

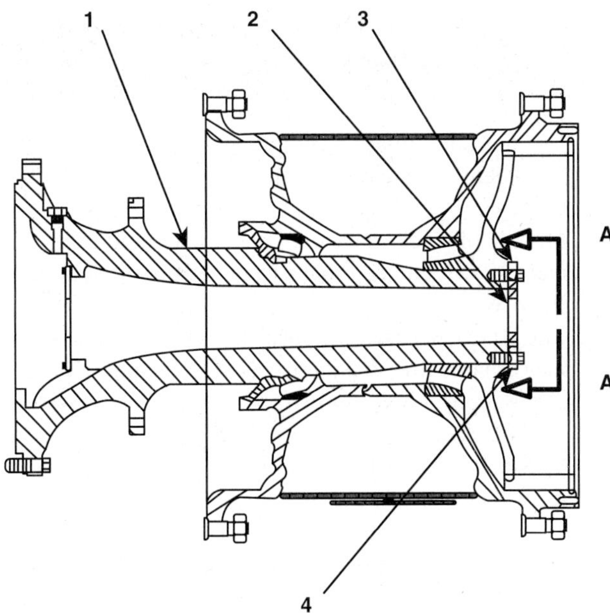

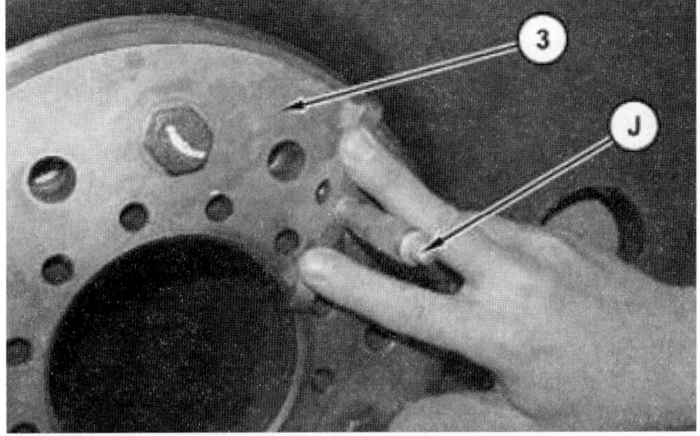

FIGURE 36-18 Shim pack thickness being measured for rolling torque wheel bearing adjustment.

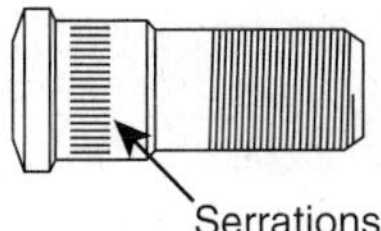

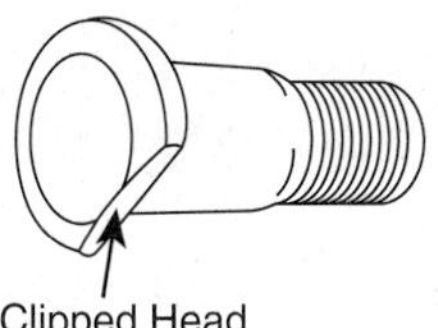

FIGURE 36-19 Studs are prevented from rotating when they are installed.

FIGURE 36-20 Oil-level check/fill plug.

and/or a rag to protect yourself when you check hub oil levels. Some hubs may have a magnetic drain plug that collects metal wear particles. Always clean this off at service time.

Wheel hub repairs usually start as a result of a fluid leak. The cause can be a seal failure only or from a seal that failed as a result of a wheel bearing failure. If a wheel bearing fails, major damage can occur to the hub, axle shaft, axle housing, and/or final drive components. To check the oil on an oil-filled hub, follow the steps in **SKILL DRILL 36-5**.

SKILL DRILL 36-5 Check the Oil on an Oil-Filled Hub

1. Locate a machine that has oil-filled wheel hubs.
2. With an experienced operator position the machine with the hub oil level plug in the correct position.
3. Lock out the machine and chock the wheels.
4. Wearing gloves or using a rag, carefully remove the plug for checking the oil level.

   Caution: If the machine has been running and the oil is warm, pressure builds up in the hub cavity, which can force oil out of the plughole when you remove the plug.
5. Check the oil level, and inspect the hub for defects (leaks, damage).
6. If the hub has a magnetic drain plug, check it for metal wear particles.
7. Record the type and viscosity of oil the manufacturer recommends.

▶ Wrap-Up

Ready for Review

- ▶ Use extreme caution when handling and working near tires and rims on heavy equipment. If the tire overheats, an explosion can occur, suddenly releasing tremendous energy.
- ▶ One-piece steel rims on light-duty machines are similar to those on commercial heavy- duty pickup trucks
- ▶ *Always* deflate tires before starting to remove them from a machine.
- ▶ Lighter duty machines use one-piece rims, which are similar to automotive style rims.
- ▶ Multipiece rims allow the technician to change the tire without deforming it while the tech positions the bead over the bead flange.
- ▶ Medium-duty machines use three-piece rims with a lock ring to hold one removable flange in place.
- ▶ Large, heavy-duty rims are five-piece assemblies with lock lugs that prevent the bead flange from slipping on the rim's base.
- ▶ Tires are a major cost of operating heavy equipment.
- ▶ The technician can view a tire on heavy equipment as a container for pressurized air that supports the weight of the machine. The tire can also assist with providing a smoother ride because the sidewalls flex.
- ▶ Some tires do not use air pressure and are either solid rubber or have voids in the sidewall to allow some flex.
- ▶ Proper inflation pressure is a big factor in getting maximum life from tires. The HDET is responsible for checking and maintaining air pressure in tires.
- ▶ Most tires on machines today are radial design. Older design types are called bias ply, which refers to the arrangement of the supporting plies of the carcass.
- ▶ Tire ply rating refers to how many layers of supporting plies manufacturers use for the carcass. Generally, the more plies, the stronger the tire. Some tires have over 70 plies.
- ▶ Tires have many different composition and design ratings such as rubber compound, tread depth, and tread design.
- ▶ Tread designs vary greatly, and machine application dictates which design is best.
- ▶ Tire sizing is based on rim diameter, tread face width, and aspect ratio.
- ▶ Aspect ratio is a comparison of sidewall height to tread face width. Low-profile tires have an aspect ratio—80, 70, or 65, for example.
- ▶ Check tire inflation when the tire is cold (not at operating temperature).
- ▶ The technician can use nitrogen to inflate tires, which is preferable to air because it is a pure inert gas and therefore is more stable. In addition, nitrogen does not support combustion.
- ▶ Tire pressure monitoring systems are becoming popular and can alert equipment operators and owners if a tire is losing pressure.
- ▶ Using proper inflating equipment prevents an HDET from being in a dangerous area when the HDET inflates tires.
- ▶ Most haul trucks have dual rear wheels and rock ejectors, which keep rocks from getting stuck between the tires.
- ▶ The HDET needs to use special machines or trucks to handle large tires during tire installation and removal.
- ▶ Some applications require tires with chains to preserve the tires (rock quarry loaders for example).
- ▶ Wheel hubs allow the rotation of wheel assemblies on axles. They usually use two sets of tapered roller bearings and can incorporate planetary final drives.
- ▶ Wheel bearing adjustment can involve shims or nut adjustment procedures.

Key Terms

blowout Failure of a tire because of damage or overinflation.

carcass (or casing) Multiple layers or plies of material that form a base for the tire from bead to bead.

centrifugal switch A switch in the sensor of a TPMS that allows the sensor to go to sleep when the vehicle stops, which extends the TPMS's battery life.

five-piece rims Similar to three-piece rims but have an additional separate inner bead seat and a bead seat band for the outer flange.

multipiece rims Rims that have O-rings to seal the areas between their base and removable bead seats; may also feature bead locks or keys that prevent bead seats from spinning on the rim's base.

one-piece rims Automotive-style rims made from two pieces of stamped, pressed, and rolled steel welded together with a center hole that fits over the hub, and with several holes drilled around the hub hole for wheel studs or bolts; also called disc-type wheels.

plies Cords made of materials like nylon, fiberglass, polyester, or rayon that make up the carcass or casing.

ply rating A rating the industry assigns to tires based on the number of the number of plies that the tire has. Generally, the more plies a tire has, the stronger it is.

pneumatic tires Tires that must be filled with pressurized air to support the load of a machine and its payload.

pyrolysis An explosive reaction that can occur when the temperature of the air inside the tire or the tire itself reaches 250°C (482°F).

rock ejector A metal bar that hangs down from the truck's box and ejects rocks from between dual tires, helping to prevent tire damage.

sidewall The area between the tread area and the bead area.

solid rubber tires Tires that are not filled with pressurized air.

three-piece rims Rims that have a main rim base with the inner bead seat flange as one piece, and an outer bead seat and locking ring that make up the other two pieces.

tire bead The area that makes contact with the rim and that must form an airtight seal with it.

tire chains Installed on heavy-duty machines to prevent damage to tires from sharp objects.

tire explosion When a tire starts to burn on the inside and pressure eventually raises high enough to explode the tire.

tire inflation pressure The level of air in the tire that provides it with load-carrying capacity and affects overall vehicle performance.

tire pressure monitoring system (TPMS) An automated system that provides a means of continuous monitoring of the vehicle tire pressure.

wheel hub What the wheel and tire fastens to.

Review Questions

1. Tire explosion occurs when ________________.
   - a. a machine is overloaded for too long
   - b. a sharp object punctures the tire
   - c. a reaction inside the tire causes extreme pressures
   - d. the machine runs over a gas line
2. If a tire has the numbers 750/65 R 25 on its sidewall, it means ________________.
   - a. the rim is 750 mm in diameter
   - b. the tire section is 750 mm wide
   - c. the rim is 65 in. tall
   - d. the tire is 25 in. wide
3. When is the safest time to weld a rim?
   - a. In the dark
   - b. On the weekend
   - c. Any time as long as the tire is deflated
   - d. Never
4. The purpose of a locking key or driving lug on multipiece rims is to ________________.
   - a. prevent the tire slipping on the flange
   - b. prevent the flange from slipping on the rim base
   - c. protect the valve stem
   - d. keep the locking ring from coming out
5. Most machines that feature dual wheels use this to save the tires:
   - a. Sidewall cleaners
   - b. Sidewall covers
   - c. Rock ejectors
   - d. Mud flaps
6. Non-drive wheel hubs have this type and quantity of wheel bearings:
   - a. Two plain bearing
   - b. Two self-aligning bearings
   - c. One tapered roller bearing
   - d. Two tapered roller bearings
7. Wheel hubs that transfer drive from inboard final drives are ________________.
   - a. part of the axle shaft
   - b. driven by the ring gear
   - c. only lubricated by grease
   - d. only used to drive dual wheels
8. Which of the following are true about plies in heavy equipment tires?
   - a. Plies are the layers of material in a tire.
   - b. The more plies a tire has, the stronger it is.
   - c. Ply ratings range from 12 to 78.
   - d. All of the above
9. Which of the following is true about the tread on heavy equipment vehicle tires?
   - a. The compound manufacturers use to make the tread is based on the operating conditions in which the machine typically works.
   - b. The compound manufacturers use to make tread is based solely on the load-carrying capacity of the machine.
   - c. The letters K, K4, L, L4, M, and M4 help the technician identify tread compounds.
   - d. Manufacturers use a set of numbers to classify tread design and depth.
10. Which of the following statements about rims is *not* true?
    - a. Smaller equipment such as backhoe loaders and skid steers have one-piece rims.
    - b. One-piece rims have two pieces of steel welded together.
    - c. Aluminum rims are forged as one piece.
    - d. Most heavy equipment wheels are made for tires that require a tube.

ASE Technician A/Technician B Style Questions

1. When preparing to service a light-duty wheel assembly, Technician A says you need to deflate the tire first before removing the assembly. Technician B says remove the wheel assembly and then deflate the tire. Who is correct?
   - a. Technician A
   - b. Technician B
   - c. Both A and B
   - d. Neither A nor B
2. Technician A says that while inspecting a multipiece rim, you should look for the same issues as with a one-piece rim. Technician B says inspecting a multipiece rim means also inspecting the lock rings and rim locks. Who is correct?
   - a. Technician A
   - b. Technician B
   - c. Both A and B
   - d. Neither A nor B
3. Technician A says the rims used on medium-sized rubber-tired machines are the same as those on large rubber-tired machines, only larger. Technician B says rims on large rubber-tired machines are similar but usually have additional parts. Who is correct?
   - a. Technician A
   - b. Technician B
   - c. Both A and B
   - d. Neither A nor B

4. Technician A says machine owners use solid rubber tires on machines that will travel frequently on the highway. Technician B says machine owners install solid rubber tires specifically on machines where the machine will encounter sharp objects. Who is correct?
   a. Technician A
   b. Technician B
   c. Both A and B
   d. Neither A nor B
5. Technician A says the biggest enemy that affects tire life on heavy-duty equipment is cool weather. Technician B says the biggest enemy is improper work-site application. Who is correct?
   a. Technician A
   b. Technician B
   c. Both A and B
   d. Neither A nor B
6. Technician A says the tire industry rates tires according to the number of plies the tire has. Technician B says the industry rates tires according to the strength of the rubber compound it uses to manufacture the tire. Who is correct?
   a. Technician A
   b. Technician B
   c. Both A and B
   d. Neither A nor B
7. Technician A says a tire pressure monitoring system (TPMS) monitors tire pressure and temperature. Technician B says a TPMS only monitors pressure. Who is correct?
   a. Technician A
   b. Technician B
   c. Both A and B
   d. Neither A nor B
8. Technician A says when the battery goes dead on a TPMS unit, it usually means that you must replace the sensor. Technician B says you only need to replace the battery. Who is correct?
   a. Technician A
   b. Technician B
   c. Both A and B
   d. Neither A nor B
9. Technician A says a rock ejector's main purpose is to protect property and people against damage and injury. Technician B says the main purpose of a rock ejector is to protect a vehicle's tires. Who is correct?
   a. Technician A
   b. Technician B
   c. Both A and B
   d. Neither A nor B
10. Technician A says wheel hub repairs usually start as a result of a seal failure. Technician B says wheel hub repairs usually start as a result of a bearing failure. Who is correct?
    a. Technician A
    b. Technician B
    c. Both A and B
    d. Neither A nor B

CHAPTER 37
Operators Station

Knowledge Objectives

After reading this chapter you will be able to:

- **K37001** Explain the purpose and fundamentals of operator stations.
- **K37002** Describe the function and operation of typical controls and warning devices in the operator station.
- **K37003** Explain the purpose and fundamentals of ROPS and FOPS protection systems.
- **K37004** Describe the purpose and fundamentals of operator station suspension systems.
- **K37005** Explain the function and operation of operator station HVAC systems.

Skills Objectives

After reading this chapter, you will be able to:

- **S37001** Perform testing and repair procedures on operator station HVAC systems.

▶ Introduction

The operator station or cab of a piece of off road-equipment is the place where an operator will spend long days working and fulfilling the purpose of the machine in question. If that operator is not comfortable, those days will seem interminable. Cabs have come a long way from the days of the leather-necked machine operator baking in the sun all day with very little creature comforts, if any. Today's cabs are designed for comfort and ease of operation. Safety on the job site is a huge concern to all: whether you are an operator, a foreman, or a business owner, safety is everyone's responsibility. Today's cabs have many integrated safety features to protect operators from harm and their bosses from litigation resulting from accidental injuries.

SAFETY TIP

Operator safety features have to be checked for integrity. For example, the rollover protective structure has to be structurally sound; seat belts have to be checked on a regular basis; machine interlock systems have to be checked for correct operation; and windows and mirrors have to be in good condition. If a machine is equipped with supplemental vision systems (cameras) and/or object warning systems (radar), these systems must be verified to be working correctly before the machine is released back to the operator.

When working on the outside of a machine's operator station, you should be careful to not fall off the machine. For larger machines, you may need to wear a fall arrest apparatus.

Air-conditioning systems can produce extreme temperatures. There is always a risk of frostbite or burns when working near an operating air-conditioning system.

▶ Fundamentals of Operator Stations

K37001

Operator stations, the interface between the machine and the operator, also more commonly called cabs, have changed a great deal in the last 50 years of machine development. Older machines didn't have any operator protection from machine rollover, bad weather, or falling objects. The machine controls started as big and heavy levers and pedals that were connected to mechanical linkages that transferred operator effort into powertrain and hydraulic system control movement. Operator seats were lightly padded or not padded, and were not very comfortable.

Machine system monitoring consisted of the operator having to keep an eye on mechanical gauges if there were any. All these factors meant long days in the operator seat were hot or cold, dusty, windy, and/or wet, and generally tiring, unhealthy, and unsafe. **FIGURE 37-1** depicts an operator's station of an older machine.

The need to make operators safer and more comfortable in order to keep them more productive for longer periods of time has changed the design and complexity of operator stations over the years. Creature comforts such as heating and air-conditioning; sealed cabs; seats with suspension; music-playing devices; and smaller, lighter fingertip controls have made operator cabs much more user friendly.

Increasing visibility out of the cab is always a desire and challenge for designers. The better an operator is able to see what the machine is doing, the more productive the machine will be. Awareness of other machines and people near the machine will also be improved, which increases the safety factor of the worksite. To improve visibility, the glass area of the cab

FIGURE 37-1 Older machine's operator station.

You Are the Mobile Heavy Equipment Technician

You are given the task of testing the air-conditioning system on a CAT 272D skid steer loader. The operator has complained that the system is not cooling the cab effectively. You visually inspect the system and find that it is a CCOT (cycling clutch orifice tube) system. You do a quick performance test by operating the machine at 1,400 rpm for 10 minutes with the A/C controls in the maximum cool position. You find that the outlet temperature from the vents is high. You further check the system and find that the inlet tube to the evaporator is cool and the outlet tube is warm. What do you do next?

1. Install the manifold gauge set to check system pressures.
2. Recover the refrigerant, and evacuate and recharge the system.
3. Inspect for leaks.
4. Add refrigerant to the system.

has increased, which makes the efficiency of the machine's HVAC (heating, ventilation, and air-conditioning) system even more critical. A common feature of new machines is to have cameras mounted around the machine, with a display in the cab. This allows the operator to view hidden blind spots, to reduce the chance of the machine contacting other machines, people, or objects. One roadblock to better visibility lately is the extra hardware that has been added to the low-emission diesel engines, which has added a lot of bulk to machines. Compare the profile of any engine compartment of two similar-sized machines that are 10 years apart, and you'll see how machine design has changed.

Machine systems monitoring has also vastly improved with **electronic displays** (also called electronic monitoring systems, or EMSs) and gauges being the norm now. Most machines can be equipped with a remote monitoring system that can communicate a wide variety of information to owners and service personnel anywhere in the world.

▶ Machine Controls

K37002

The operator station is the interface between the operator and the machine. Older machine controls were mainly mechanical linkages that started with levers and pedals that connected to rod ends, rods, bell cranks, cables, and shafts. Motion was transferred through these mechanisms to engine, drivetrain, brake, steering, and hydraulic components. Many of these mechanisms required lubrication and adjustment regularly. See **FIGURE 37-2** for an older machine with mechanical controls.

These mechanisms were replaced by maintenance-free components that would last longer. This included components that were made of higher-quality metals and other materials that would resist wear and corrosion better.

The next step was to replace mechanical controls for hydraulic systems with hydraulic or pilot controls. Pilot controls are covered in detail in the hydraulics section of this book.

FIGURE 37-3 Hydraulic leak in a cab.

These controls required less effort for the operator to move and eliminated a lot of mechanical wear points. However, the possibility of hydraulic leaks in or near the cab was introduced. See **FIGURE 37-3** for an illustration of a hydraulic leak in a cab.

Brake controls also upgraded from mechanical to hydraulic. See the chapter on hydraulic braking systems for more details on hydraulic brake controls.

To get away from hydraulic leaks in cabs and decrease the effort required to manipulate a machine the next step was to feature electric and/or electronic controls in cabs. Many machines now have controls for drivetrain, engine, and hydraulics that are electrical devices such as switches and/or dials that either directly control machine systems or are inputs to ECMs (electronic control modules), which in turn send outputs to the various machine systems. This is where the term "fly by wire," borrowed from the airline industry, is applied to newer heavy equipment. **FIGURE 37-4** illustrates a set of electronic operator controls. Many of these operator inputs require very little effort. For example, with one finger an operator could control the hydraulic system for a wheel loader that is capable of lifting 50 tons of material!

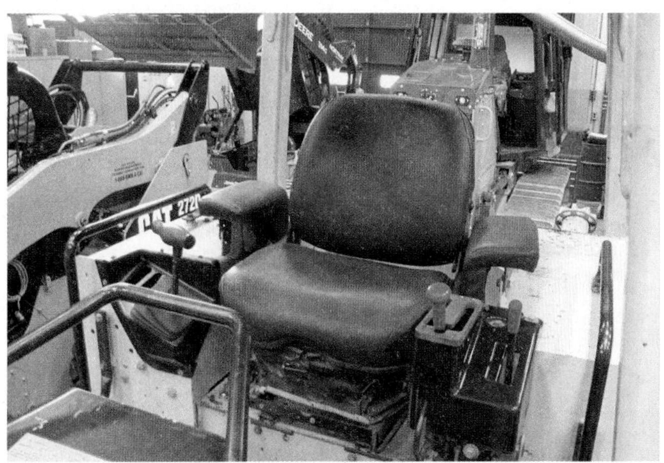

FIGURE 37-2 Mechanical controls.

FIGURE 37-4 Electronic controls.

> **TECHNICIAN TIP**
>
> Did you know some machines don't need an operator on the machine? Bobcat has a remote control system that allows an operator to run the machine from a safe distance away from the machine (up to 1,500 ft.). This may be necessary if the machine must work in hazardous environments that aren't safe for a human being.

Other machines can run on their own with the help of GPS and/or cell phone technology that links the machine to a remote command center. Machines such as haul trucks, drills, track-type dozers and loaders can also be operated without an operator.

The term **autonomous machine** is often used when describing a machine that can function without an operator, and refers to a smart machine that can learn the worksite and function with very limited assistance. Search the Internet to see the latest developments on autonomous machines.

FIGURE 37-5 An example of mechanical gauges.

Operator Displays/Machine Gauges

Throughout the day, when a machine is working, its various systems have to be monitored to ensure they stay within predetermined safe temperatures and pressures and that there are no faults. The different devices for doing this can be as simple as a warning light or as sophisticated as a complicated electronic monitoring system that can inform the operator with progressive updates on the status of the machine.

Mechanical Gauges

Older machines used mechanical gauges to monitor, for example, engine coolant temperature and oil pressure. This type of gauge had a needle that moved mechanically across a range of colors or numbers to inform the operator about a system's fluid temperature, pressure, or level. **FIGURE 37-5** provides an example of mechanical gauges.

A line connected to mechanical pressure gauges is plumbed into the component whose pressure is being monitored. An engine oil pressure gauge, for example, would be fed oil pressure through a small hose that is connected to the main oil gallery of the engine. The gauge is then able to sense the pressure. The gauge's needle moves as a result of the pressure acting on a thin tube that is normally curved. As more pressure is applied to the tube, it tries to straighten out, and an attached linkage moves the needle. This type of gauge is called a Bourdon tube. The numbers on the gauge are calibrated to match the needle movement, and give the operator an accurate reading of engine oil pressure. **FIGURE 37-6** shows a Bourdon tube gauge.

The line between the engine and the gauge has to be protected and secured because a failure will cause a pressurized engine oil leak that could be disastrous.

Some low-pressure fuel systems have a mechanical gauge that displays fuel pressure, as seen in **FIGURE 37-7**. Mechanical

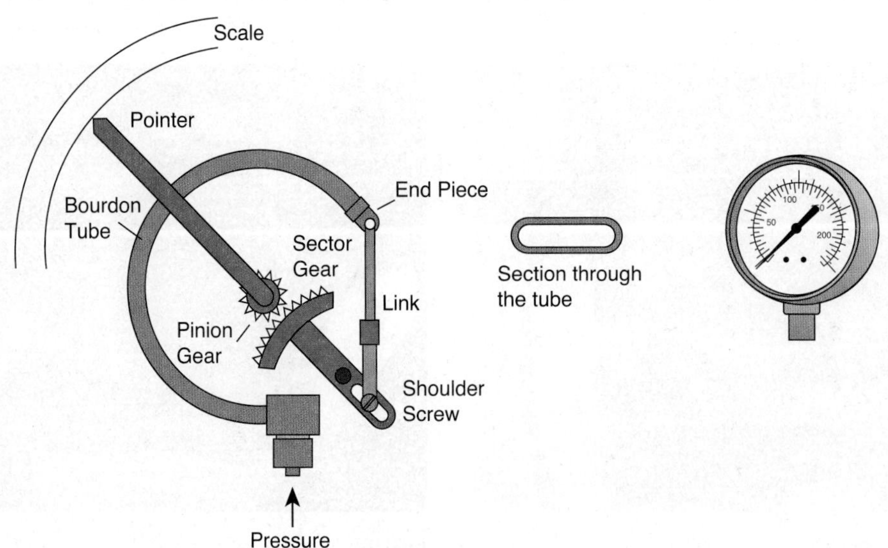

FIGURE 37-6 Bourdon tube gauge.

FIGURE 37-7 Mechanical low-pressure fuel gauge.

FIGURE 37-8 Murphy gauge.

temperature gauges use a temperature-sensing bulb that is exposed to the fluid it is meant to monitor. The bulb is sealed to a tube that is connected to a Bourdon tube at the gauge. Inside that tube is a fluid such as alcohol that will expand easily when heated. Because the tube is sealed, the heated fluid expands and acts on the Bourdon tube to make the gauge's needle move. An example is a gauge used to monitor engine coolant temperature; its bulb is usually placed in the water jacket of the engine, near the engine's thermostat housing.

Great care should be taken not to kink or pinch the line between the bulb and gauge, as this will make the gauge inoperable, and it will have to be replaced as an assembly.

Mechanical level gauges use a float that raises and lowers with the fluid level, and this movement is transferred mechanically into needle movement. An example is a fuel tank that has a gauge on its side to allow the person filling the tank to see how full the tank is.

▶ TECHNICIAN TIP

Machines can be equipped with a different type of gauge that is sometimes called a **Murphy gauge**. Although Murphy is a manufacturer of many different types of gauges and operator displays, the gauges they make as part of a warning/shutdown system are seen as a standard for this type of gauge.

These are normal-looking gauges in that there is a moving needle, but they feature integrated switches that are used either to turn on a warning system or to shut the engine down if an extreme condition exists.

The switch closes when the gauge needle moves too far, triggering a warning or disabling the engine's fuel system, thereby causing it to shut down. These gauges are found on many stationary engine applications, as these engines are usually only monitored briefly when someone starts them. **FIGURE 37-8** displays a Murphy gauge.

Operator Warning Systems

It soon became obvious to machine manufacturers that an operator couldn't be expected to constantly monitor the gauges for a machine. This led to the manufacturers adding a warning system that would alert the operator if operating parameters exceeded normal ranges. An alerting system turns on a light and/or buzzer to grab the operator's attention and make him or her aware of what is happening with a machine system. Some machines have different levels of warning systems that change depending on the severity of the problem.

An example of this is Caterpillar's EMS. If there is a minor problem, like the engine air filter being plugged, then a small red light will start flashing on the EMS display. It is then the operator's responsibility to find out why the light is flashing, as soon as it is convenient to do so. The operator should then either report the problem, take action to correct the problem, or stop operating the machine—and possibly shut down the engine. **FIGURE 37-9** shows an EMS warning display. If a more severe problem exists, such as the transmission starting to overheat, then a higher-level warning is actuated. This includes the small light in the EMS display and a larger "Master Fault" light. The larger light is placed in a more direct line of vision than the smaller light, and the operator is expected to change operating methods or worksite conditions to make the problem stop.

The third level of warning includes both lights and a loud audible warning. This buzzer or horn should indicate to the

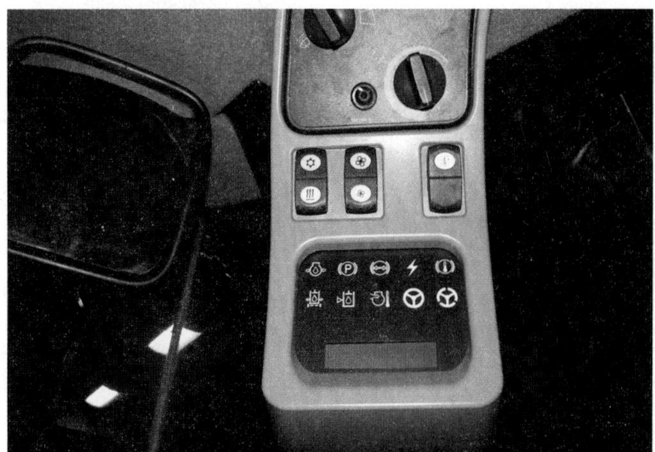

FIGURE 37-9 EMS display.

operator that immediate action is needed or else severe machine damage will occur. An example of this type of problem is low engine oil pressure.

Electric Gauges

Electrically actuated gauges look similar to mechanically actuated versions, but the needle movement is created by changing electrical signals. These variable signals start at the sender unit (sensing device) as a varying resistance. The sender unit is grounded to the machine, and the wire connecting the sender to the gauge provides a variable resistance to ground for the gauge assembly. The variable resistance changes current flow to the gauge, which in turn creates needle movement. Needle movement can be created by varying the current flow through two coils of wire in the gauge or by changing current flow through a bimetal strip that bends as it heats up or cools. The amount of current flowing through the strip changes its temperature.

In a balancing coil-type electric gauge, two coils are on either side of the gauge's needle. As the current flow through these coils changes, their magnetic strength changes, which in turn makes the needle move. System voltage is fed to one side of both coils. The other end of one coil goes directly to ground; in the second coil, the sender's variable resistance to ground is placed in series with it. The variable ground value creates a variable current flow through one coil that creates a variable strength magnetic field, and this is what changes the position of the gauge's needle. **FIGURE 37-10** illustrates a balancing coil type of electric gauge using three different sending units.

Diagnosing and repairing faulty electrical gauges requires a good understanding of the basic principles of Ohm's law and electrical troubleshooting procedures. The gauge circuit's sender is exposed to system fluid for pressure, temperature, level monitoring, or a sender that is close to a moving component for speed monitoring.

An electric pressure gauge sender has a diaphragm that is exposed to the system's fluid pressure. As the diaphragm is deflected by system pressure, a contact moves across a variable resistance that goes to ground. As the sender's resistance value changes, a wire from the sender sends this changing resistance to ground value to the gauge assembly. A common type of electrical pressure gauge is one used to measure engine oil pressure. See **FIGURE 37-11** for an example of a diaphragm-type pressure sender.

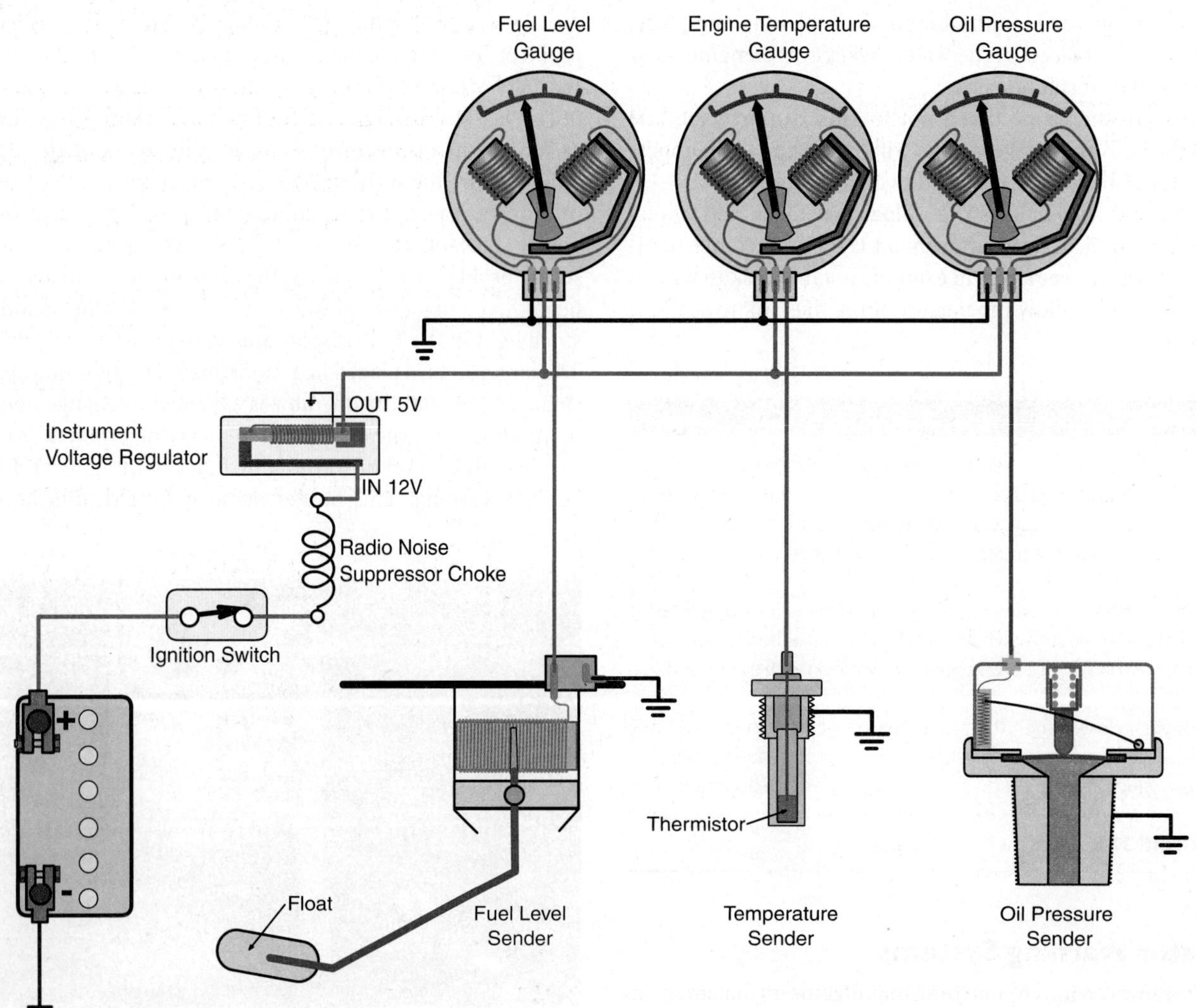

FIGURE 37-10 Balancing coil–type gauge.

FIGURE 37-11 Diaphragm-type pressure sender.

FIGURE 37-12 LCD gauge.

An electric temperature gauge sender changes its resistance when the fluid it is exposed to changes temperature. The most common type of temperature sender is a thermistor that contains a type of material that changes its resistance based on its temperature. There are two types of thermistors: NTC (negative temperature coefficient) that decreases resistance as temperature increases, and PTC (positive temperature coefficient) that increases resistance as temperature increases.

Another less common type of temperature sender has a bimetal strip that bends with temperature changes. As the strip bends a contact moves across a variable resistance to ground and this changing value is sent to the gauge assembly through a wire. This changing value creates gauge needle movement in the same manner as the electric pressure gauge.

An electric level gauge has its needle move as a reaction to the level sender. The sender has a float that raises and lowers with fluid level and this action is changed into a variable resistance to ground value through a contact that moves across a variable resistor. There is a single wire leaving the sender to carry the resistance value to the gauge. The movement of the gauge is the same as the previously explained pressure and temperature gauges.

Electronic Gauges

Electronic gauges are ones that use the output of an ECM to create needle movement. Different types of senders send inputs to the ECM such as variable resistance, variable capacitance, Hall effect, and piezo resistive. These senders were explained in detail in the electrical/electronics section of this book. Once the ECM receives input values, it compares this information to data that are stored in the ECM memory and an output is sent to an electronic gauge.

Different types of electronic gauges exist. Some are similar to electric gauges and have real moving needles; others are part of an LCD display that could show one or more separate gauges. **FIGURE 37-12** demonstrates an LCD gauge arrangement.

Many machines today feature an interactive display that allows the operator to scroll through different menus, as well as view virtual gauges. The menus could include pressure and temperature readings in numerical form, payload information or could be used as a display for blind spot cameras. See **FIGURE 37-13** for an electronic display.

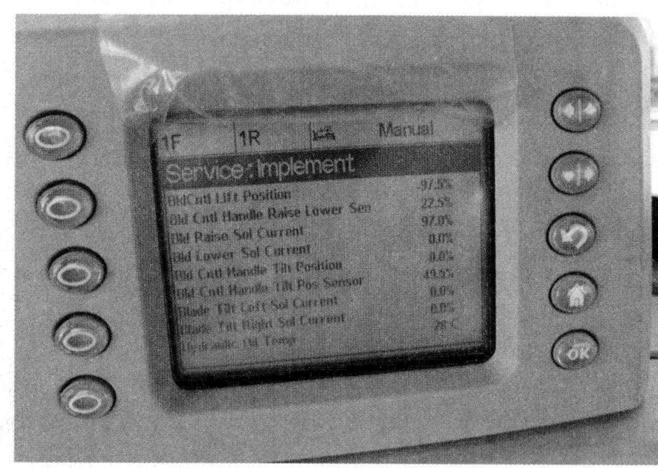

FIGURE 37-13 Electronic display.

▶ Telematic Systems and GPS Guided Machines

K37003

The word "telematic" comes from "telecommunication," which refers to wireless communication, and informatics refers to the exchange of information. Telematics refers directly to mobile equipment and the wireless exchange of information between them and a remote device.

Many of today's machines are equipped with electronic communication systems that allow the machine to be monitored from remote locations, allow partial control of the machine, or allow full control of the machine. These systems are sometimes called telematic systems and are based on cell phone and/or satellite communication systems that allow either one- or two-way transfer of data to and from a machine to anywhere in the world that has access to the Internet or is within range of a cell phone tower.

The machine requires certain hardware to be telematics capable, such as a system controller that contains an ECM, modem and GPS chipset, a SIM plug to enable cellular communication, and a GSM/GPS antenna. To communicate with a machine that is equipped with the proper hardware, the machine owner needs the compatible software, a subscription, and an Internet connection. Subscriptions are usually for 3- to 5-year terms and are either sold outright or hidden in the cost of a machine.

Typically, different levels of communication are possible with telematic systems. A base level allows the machine owner to monitor where the machine is, whether it is running, and some basic data like fuel consumption and hours. There could also be a "**geo fence**," an electronically limited operational area, constructed by software that allows the owner to stop the engine from starting if the machine is outside of the selected area. If the machine is moved outside of the selected area, a text message is sent to the owner. If the machine owner has access to the machine manufacturer's electronic service information system, then a remote link to that machine's CAN network is available through the telematics system. This allows viewing of live data, checking fault codes, and monitoring machine systems.

A higher level of service communication sends alerts to the machine owner for events such as active fault codes, new fault codes or aborted DPF, diesel particulate filter, and regenerations. Sometimes customers can even download and install flash files into the machine ECM when updates become available. Machine production reports can be created and downloaded on a regular basis. This can be a very valuable tool for machine management if used properly. **FIGURE 37-14** shows one of the screens for John Deere's JD link system.

Dealer access allows all of the previous functions, plus they are able to change parameters that are stored in the machine's ECM, such as increasing or decreasing engine horsepower.

Telematic systems are a huge benefit to machine owners with medium to large fleets because of their ability to track machines easily. This was made even easier recently when most major manufacturers got together and standardized the format for the wireless transfer of commonly requested machine data. For example, machine location, machine hours, fuel consumption, and whether or not the machine is running can all be monitored and downloaded to the same spreadsheet, even though the machine owner might own several different makes of machines. Close-range wireless communication is also possible with Bluetooth technology.

GPS Material Leveling Systems

In many machines, a GPS (global positioning system) system has been added onto their hydraulic control system to provide automatic capability for material leveling. These systems can be installed at the factory or added on at the dealership. Some examples of machines using this technology are graders, excavators, and dozers. See **FIGURE 37-15** to see a dozer GPS material-leveling system.

These GPS systems allow an operator to feed information to the machine's control system, and the machine will follow the preprogrammed instruction as to grade angle, position, and height, with accuracies to within fractions of an inch. The operator inputs all the data required through a large graphical interface screen in the machine and selects "Start." The computer screen will follow and show the machine's progress. All the operator has to do is observe and make sure that the machine does not hit any cross traffic or other obstacles.

▶ Operator Protection Systems

K37004

Several systems are put into place to protect the operator from danger and also to ensure operator comfort. When the operator is comfortable, he or she is more productive and happier in the work environment. This section deals with some of these systems, such as roll over protection systems, falling object protection systems, and the most basic protection—seatbelts.

Seat Belts

One of the most critical safety features that a machine has is its operator restraint or seat belt. All operator manuals will recommend that the operator wear a seat belt any time the machine is being operated. Because wearing a seat belt or

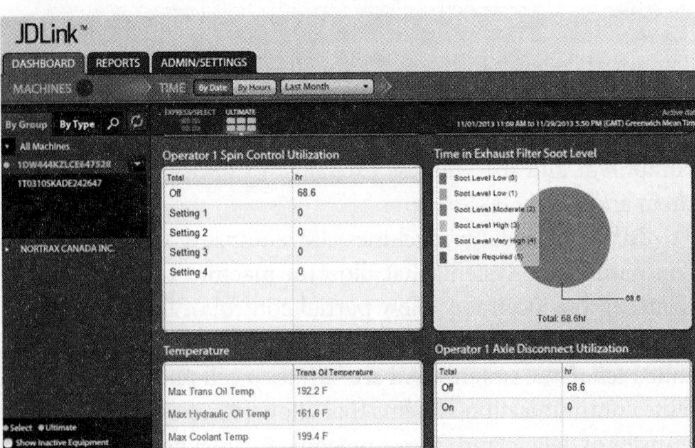

FIGURE 37-14 JD link.

Image Provided As Courtesy of John Deere.

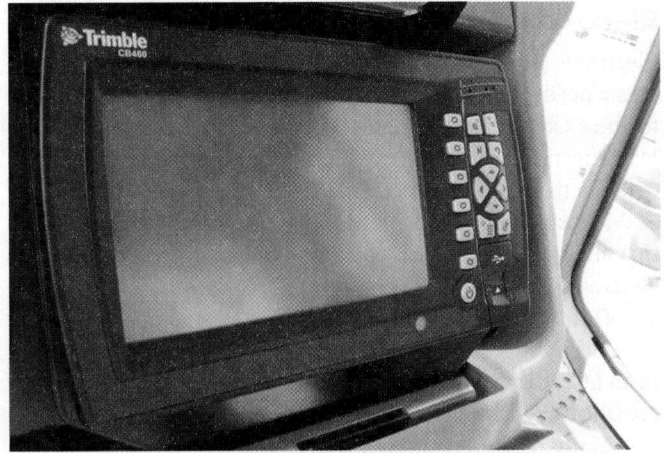

FIGURE 37-15 Bull dozer equipped with a GPS material-leveling system.

FIGURE 37-16 A 2-point belt.

FIGURE 37-17 Machine with a ROPS canopy.

restraint while operating a machine is not enforced by law, as it is in on-highway vehicle operation, it is up to the individual employer to thoroughly educate the operators in the use of and necessity for these devices. Most machine seat belts are adjustable lap belts, but some machines feature three-point belts with shoulder restraints just like those found in automobiles, or even four-point systems with dual shoulder straps. In **FIGURE 37-16**, a two-point seat belt is depicted.

Seat belts *must* be inspected on a regular basis for tears, rips, and others defects to the material, and *must* be replaced in accordance with the machine's operating manual. Their retracting and adjusting mechanisms must be inspected as well. The seat belt anchor and latching mechanism *must* also be inspected for proper torque and proper operation.

ROPS/FOPS/Canopies

Rollover protection systems (ROPS) are designed to keep the cab intact when the machine either turns on its side or completely upside down. The ROPS is usually an external frame that surrounds the cab at four corners. It can also be an integral part of the machine's cab structure. It can be compared to a roll cage found in a racing vehicle. It is designed to support several times the weight of the machine. The ROPS is fastened to the machine's main frame with large high-grade fasteners. The ROPS is a complete structure and should not be compromised in any way. You must *never* drill holes in it to mount accessories, and it must not be welded on or have any excessive heat applied to it. It should be inspected on a regular basis and be kept free of rust, and any impact or structural damage must be repaired at once. Any compromise of the structure could lead to its failure in a rollover situation. It is important to note that ROPSs are designed with the premise that the operator will be secured by the seat belt. If a rollover occurs while the operator is not belted, the safety offered by the ROPS will be severely diminished. A machine with a ROPS canopy is featured in **FIGURE 37-17**.

A **falling object protection system (FOPS)** is a reinforced roof or canopy structure, either added to the operator station or integrated with it, designed to protect the operator from heavy objects that may fall on the machine's cab. Again, as with the ROPS, no holes should be drilled into the FOPS, and no welding on the structure is allowed as such activities may compromise the structures integrity.

ROPS and FOPS structures must always be inspected at *all* service intervals. The torque on their fasteners should also be checked at intervals, as recommended in the maintenance guide for the machine.

Radar Warning/Vision Supplement Cameras

Radar warning systems use a transponder device to detect objects that are close to the machine and in its path of travel. This system is capable of warning the operator of a collision about to happen, with enough notice that an avoidance maneuver should be possible.

Another common feature on newer machines is to have one or more video cameras mounted on the machine that feed a signal to a display in the cab. The operator is then able to see blind spots around the machine to determine whether any object or person is in its path of travel.

These camera systems could be standard equipment already installed on many large machines or an option that could be requested and installed by the dealer before machine delivery. **FIGURE 37-18** shows an operator display for a blind spot camera.

Operator Seating

Older machines had very basic operator seats; some did not even have padded cushions. Today's machine seats are meant to keep operators as comfortable as possible and support their spine and lower torso completely.

Seats could be mounted to the cab frame or mounted to a suspension mechanism, to reduce operator fatigue and the occurrence of health problems such as sore backs. Fast traveling machines, such as scrapers and rock trucks, that have to cross rough terrain have suspended seats, but these seats can also be found on any type of machine.

The seat suspension systems could be simple linkages utilizing springs and a damping mechanism and/or air bag suspension systems also with a damping mechanism. Some older

FIGURE 37-18 Blind spot camera and display.

scrapers used a linkage system with hydropneumatic suspension and damping.

Most suspended seats are height adjustable, and the ones with dampened suspension can have adjustable damping for added operator comfort.

Cab Noise Prevention

Recently manufacturers have started to put more focus on noise level reduction inside cabs. Part of the motivation for this has been tighter noise restriction regulations imposed by governing bodies. Decreasing noise also reduces operator fatigue and increases safety.

This is accomplished by installing more and thicker insulating material on the interior surfaces of the cab, including floor mats. What this means to technicians is that if panels are removed in a cab or on a machine, they must be replaced; otherwise, sound levels inside the cab could exceed safe levels.

Cab Suspension Systems/Mounts

Many cabs are mounted on isolating mounts that separate the cab from machine-generated vibrations and noise. These mounting systems can be as simple as hard rubber mounts between the cab and the machine, which are designed to merely dampen vibration from the rest of the machine and prevent it from being transferred to the cab and therefore the operator. Some cabs have two-point spring suspension support. These cabs are typically mounted so that one part of the cab (either the front or the rear) is attached to pivot pins, and the opposite end is supported by springs and hydraulic shock absorbers to reduce oscillations. Other systems can consist of four-point, fully independent suspension systems using spring and shock absorbers to control cab movement. Spring suspension systems are used where cost or the lack of a pneumatic system is a factor, so they are usually found on lower-priced machines. Higher-end machines, especially those used in rough terrain, can be equipped with air spring shock absorber modules that can be individually computer controlled to fine-tune the suspension system, and automatically control cab leveling. Some machines are now equipped with hydropneumatic systems with active dampening control that can sense the cab oscillation and control dampening to maintain cab level, thus greatly increasing operator comfort. Of course as these systems become more sophisticated, their cost is impacted as well, so these automatic systems are typically found on only the most expensive machines.

Automatic cab leveling suspension systems can usually be adjusted and/or diagnosed using OEM computer software. Cab suspension system maintenance is similar to regular suspension system maintenance: check for loose fasteners, broken springs, interference between the cab and rest of the machine, pneumatic or hydraulic leaks, worn or leaking shock absorbers, and/or loose or broken linkage components. If it is necessary to remove the cab for any reason, ensure that all of the suspension components and isolating mounts are correctly reinstalled and/or replaced. Many times a faulty cab mount can be misdiagnosed as a drivetrain issue.

Tilting and Removing Cabs

Many machine repair procedures require the cab to be tilted or removed. Some machines allow the cab to be tilted for access to drivetrain components. Some track loaders, track dozers, and articulated trucks are examples of machines with tilting cabs. There will likely be a hydraulic cylinder on the machine to hoist one side of the cab as it pivots on the other. *Never* get under a tilted cab unless it is mechanically locked in place.

Cab removal can be necessary for larger repairs such as transmission and/or pump removal. It can also be part of a complete machine reconditioning process. Make sure *all* wiring, hoses, tubing, and linkages are disconnected before starting to hoist the cab away from the machine. See **FIGURE 37-19** to see a machine with its cab tilted.

▶ HVAC Systems

K37005

Heating, ventilation, and air-conditioning (HVAC) systems can be found in varying forms and are standard equipment on most machines that have an enclosed cab sold today. They are a key part in keeping the operator comfortable and therefore more productive. Both cold winter mornings and hot sunny days present challenges to HVAC systems, but if they are designed and maintained properly, they can overcome any heat, cold, or moisture influences from weather or from heat created by the machine itself.

FIGURE 37-19 Tilted cab.

Cab Heater and Pressurizer

The most basic version of an HVAC system is one that pressurizes a sealed cab to keep the dust out and provides heat to keep the inside temperature at a comfortable temperature. Pressurizing the cab prevents outside air, which may be dirty, dust filled, and possibly hazardous, from entering the cab.

Air is drawn in past a cab filter by a fan that is controlled by the operator. The fan usually has three or four speeds to allow the operator to vary the amount of airflow through the cab. **FIGURE 37-20** shows a cab filter.

A simple electrical circuit to operate a fan motor starts with a protected power supply (fused or circuit breaker). This lead then goes to a switch that sends voltage out one of two to four terminals on the back of the switch. Wires connect these leads to a stepped resistor. The stepped resistor has two to four input terminals and one output terminal, and the resistance is different between each input and the output terminal. As the switch is turned through various positions, different outputs of the switch leads connect to corresponding different input terminals on the stepped resistor. The output of the stepped resistor is connected to the feed terminal on the fan motor. The differing amount of resistance between the different terminals in the stepped resistor determines how much current goes to the motor and therefore how fast the motor

FIGURE 37-20 Cab filter.

and therefore the fan turns. See **FIGURE 37-21** for a schematic of an electric fan with a stepped resistor. Many larger machines use more than one fan and motor. This increases the airflow through the cab to ensure it stays pressurized. Most fans are the squirrel cage style. See **FIGURE 37-22** to see a squirrel cage fan motor.

Some newer machines have electronically controlled fan motors. The fan switch is an input to an ECM, and the output from the ECM is likely a voltage signal that either goes directly to the fan motor or to a relay coil that, once energized, allows current flow to the fan motor.

All simple HVAC systems have a means to vary the amount of airflow in the cab, but some may not have the means to reroute the airflow direction from the fan motor. These systems may just have one outlet from the fan through a heater core and out into

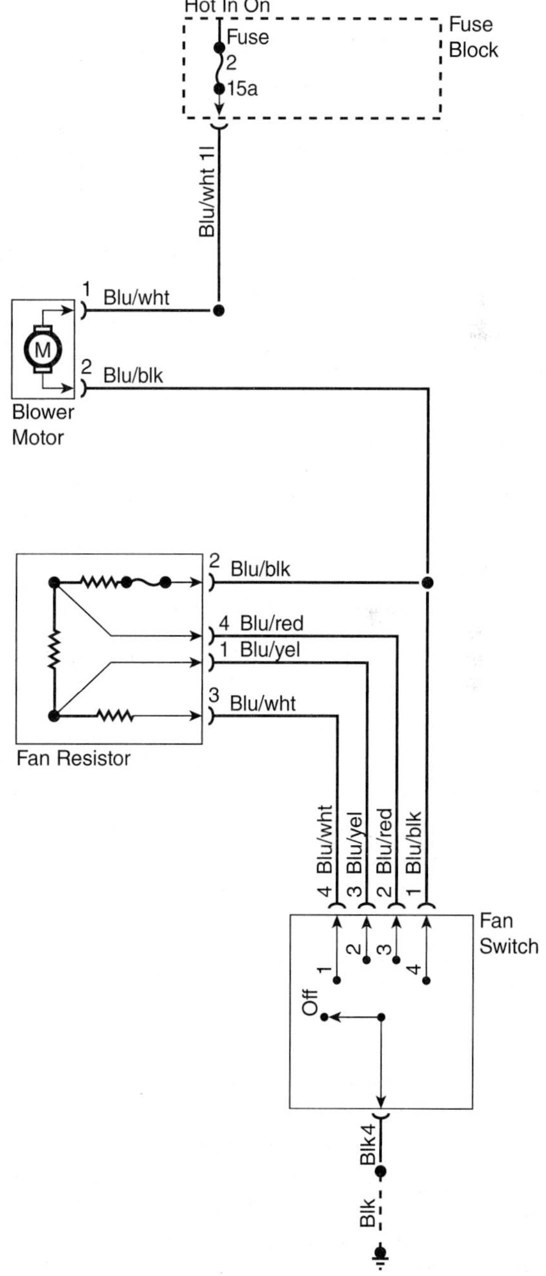

FIGURE 37-21 Fan with stepped resistor schematic.

FIGURE 37-22 Squirrel cage fan motor.

FIGURE 37-23 Heater control valve.

the cab interior. Other machines have ventilation systems, similar to those in cars and pickup trucks, that will allow the operator to change the airflow to different parts of the cab. The use of ducts and doors makes this possible. Most HVAC vent doors are moved by sliding levers that are connected to cables. The inner wire of the cable gets moved to make the door pivot. Some machines with electronically controlled HVAC systems use stepper motors to move the vent doors. These systems are most often controlled by a sealed touch pad; they will likely have their own ECM that may or may not be multiplexed with the other machine ECMs and will be able to generate fault codes to help with diagnosing problems.

Because all windows and doors are sealed with weather stripping, the air in the cab is pressurized as it tries to escape through a small ventilation opening that also has a filter over it.

The cab air filter is an often overlooked maintenance item that has to be cleaned and/or replaced on a regular basis. If it becomes plugged with dust, the pressurizing effect won't work, and the cab air becomes stale. All windows and doors must be closed, and their weather stripping must be intact for this pressurization to take place. If a machine is operated with the doors and/or windows open, it won't be long before the cab is coated in dust. Besides being messy, this could also become a health concern.

A cab heater uses warm engine coolant to add heat to the cab air. Coolant is routed to a heat exchanger (heater core), where cab air is blown across it to warm the cab up. The coolant flows through a pair of heater hoses that typically have a ½" or ⅝" (13 or 17 mm) inside diameter. The inlet to the heater core starts from the higher-pressure side of the cooling system (water pump outlet), and the outlet of the heater core returns to the low-pressure side of the cooling system (engine block usually).

The amount of coolant flowing through the heater core is directed by a valve that is controlled by the operator. A rotary knob or slide mounted in the cab can be moved, and this increases or decreases the amount of coolant flow to increase or decrease the heat coming out of the heater core. Some controls move a cable that turns a ball-type valve; some move a plunger in and out; and others send an electrical signal to an ECM. The ECM then sends an electrical signal to a motor that turns a rotary valve through a set of gears. **FIGURE 37-23** illustrates a heater control valve.

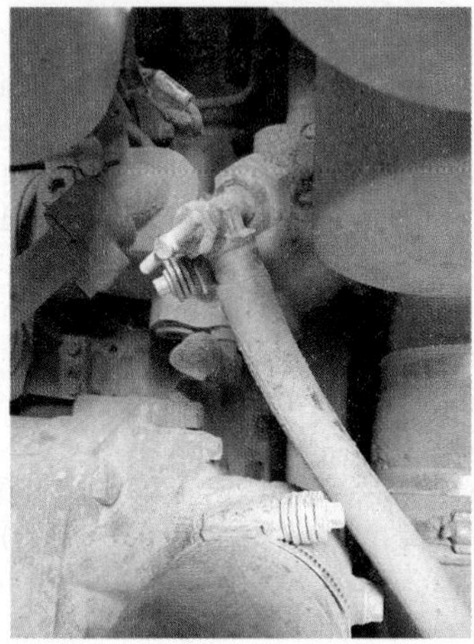

FIGURE 37-24 Heater shutoff valve.

Some machines use a separate set of shutoff valves to allow the system flow to be disabled no matter the position of the control valve. These valves are typically used in the summer to stop any heat from entering the cab or when servicing the system to prevent excessive loss of coolant. They are usually located where the hoses are connected to the engine. **FIGURE 37-24** shows a heater shutoff valve.

Air-conditioning

Most machines with cabs have large areas of glass. On sunny days, the cab may seem like a greenhouse because the heat load from the sun creates a great deal of heat inside the cab. Even in underground mining machines, the cab will eventually heat up just from the heat transferring from other machine systems into the cab.

The heat can accumulate to make unbearable operating conditions for the operator. If the windows and/or doors are opened to allow some cooler air into the cab, then the cab will likely become dusty and unhealthy. Unlike automobiles, operators of heavy equipment machines can't roll down the windows and get cooled by the air rushing by at highway speeds. It is not uncommon for a machine operator to refuse to operate a machine on a hot, sunny day because the air-conditioning system isn't working properly. Air-conditioning systems also dehumidify and clean the air inside the cab. As the system removes heat, the moisture in the warm air passing over the cool evaporator condenses on its surface, and dust and pollen in the air is trapped in the water. This again makes the operator more comfortable and reduces the possibility of the glass fogging up in high-humidity conditions.

For these reasons understanding air-conditioning system operation and diagnostic procedures to correct air-conditioning problems is a vital part of what a technician needs to know.

> ▶ TECHNICIAN TIP
>
> For an excellent visual demonstration of how a refrigeration system works, search for a U.S. Department of Education 1944 video *Principles of Refrigeration*. It explains the fundamentals different pressures and temperatures involved in a refrigeration process, and their change of states. Many similar principles are involved in a mobile air-conditioning system.

Air-Conditioning Overview

To understand how an air-conditioning system works, you must understand how the cab air is cooled. You need to know how heat is transferred out of the cab air, and realize that the air-conditioning system doesn't add cold air to the cab; it *removes heat* from it. To understand this, you should know that heat energy always travels from hot to cold.

An air-conditioning system is a closed loop fluid system that uses a fixed quantity of refrigerant sealed inside hoses, lines, and other main components. Like any fluid system, it needs a pump to make the fluid flow. The pump for an air-conditioning system is called a compressor. When the operator turns on the system's compressor, the refrigerant starts to flow through the system and does so in a continuous loop as long as the compressor is running.

Heat

Heat is described in a number of ways, but in air-conditioning systems we are concerned about two types of heat. The first of these is **sensible heat**, which is the heat that you can measure with a thermometer, and for the operator it is the most important. If it is too hot or too cold, the operator will not be comfortable. The second type of heat—and the most important to the function of an air-conditioning system—is **latent heat**. Latent heat, which cannot be measured with a thermometer, is the amount of heat required to make a substance change state. Any matter can exist in only three states: solid, liquid, or gas (there is actually a fourth state, plasma, which is only important to us in physics or space travel, and not necessary here, so we will ignore it). Latent heat is the amount of heat energy that must be added to make a substance change state from a solid to a liquid, or a liquid to a gas, or the amount of heat energy we must remove to cause the change from a gas to a liquid, or a liquid to a solid. To understand latent heat, we must have a measure of heat energy. The most commonly used measurement of heat energy is the **BTU**, or **British thermal unit**, the amount of heat required to raise the temperature of 1 pound of water 1 degree Fahrenheit. Another measure of heat energy is the **calorie**, the amount of heat energy required to raise the temperature of 1 gram of water 1 degree Celsius. One BTU is the equivalent of 252 calories. Because most air-conditioning systems use BTUs as the heat energy unit, we use it here. Recall that 1 BTU equals the amount of energy required to raise the temperature of 1 pound of water 1 degree; the latent heat required to change state is much more. For example, we can raise the temperature 1 pound of water from 211°F to 212°F (99°C to 100°C) (boiling point of water at sea level), using 1 BTU, but to cause that pound of water to vaporize or turn into steam without raising its temperature requires 970 BTUs. Although the latent heat of vaporization is much less for common refrigerants such as R-134a, less than 100 BTUs, air-conditioning systems take advantage of the large amount of latent heat required to change state to function. **FIGURE 37-25** portrays the latent heat required for water to change state.

An air-conditioning system basically uses pressure to increase the temperature of low-pressure gaseous refrigerant, it

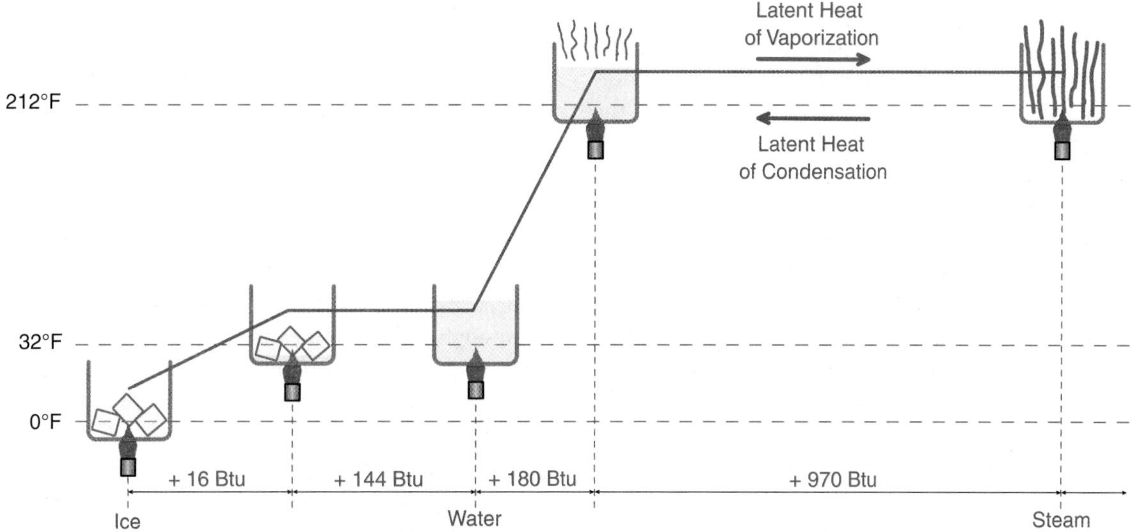

FIGURE 37-25 When a substance changes state, much more heat is required than changing its temperature a few degrees.

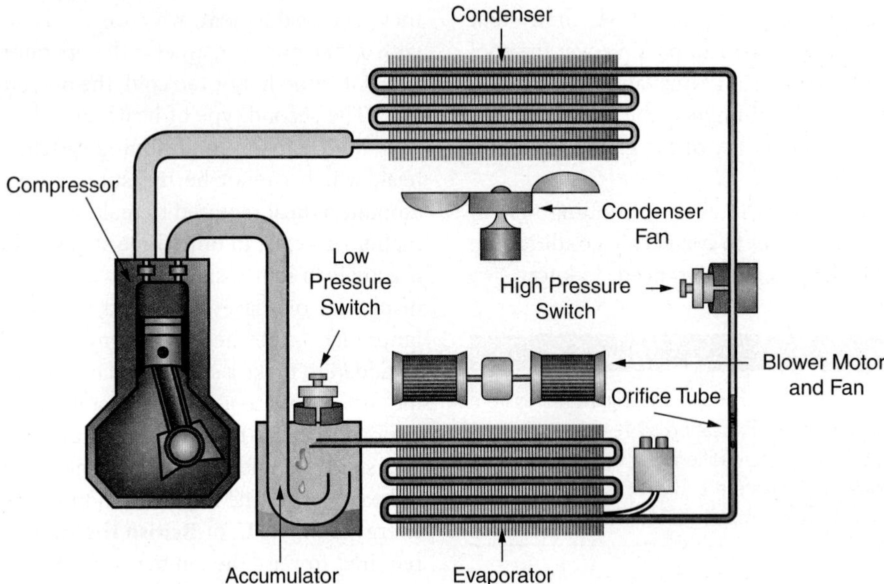

FIGURE 37-26 The components of an air-conditioning unit.

then passes the gas through a heat exchanger that dissipates that heat to the ambient air; this loss of heat cause the high-pressure gas to change state to a high pressure-liquid giving off a tremendous amount of heat to the ambient air. The high-pressure liquid is then sent through a restriction, which causes its pressure and temperature to drop dramatically. The low-pressure liquid is then sent through a second heat exchanger, the evaporator, and the warm air from the cab is blown over it. The low-pressure liquid absorbs a massive amount of heat from the cab air and changes state, vaporizing to a low-pressure gas, then the refrigeration cycle repeats. See **FIGURE 37-26** to see the basic layout of an air-conditioning system.

Besides the two heat exchangers all air-conditioning systems have the following components: a compressor, a restriction, hoses, tubes, fittings, controls, either an accumulator or a receiver drier (depending on the type of system), and of course the refrigerant and some oil. Two fans move air past both the evaporator and the condenser. The cab fan is part of the cab pressurization system and moves air past the evaporator. The condenser may have its own fan(s) or may use the engine cooling fan to move air past it. These two fans are critical to the proper operation of any A/C system.

Air-conditioning system types

Two main types of air-conditioning systems are found on a heavy equipment machine. They are defined by the type of restriction used in the system. An air-conditioning system is a sealed fluid system, and as mentioned in the section on hydraulics, all fluid systems need a pump, in this case a compressor and a restriction to build pressure and make the fluid flow.

Both types of restrictions are located downstream from the compressor outlet, near the inlet to the evaporator.

The first type of system is the **cycling clutch orifice tube** or **CCOT system**, this system uses a small orifice in the evaporator inlet line to create the restriction. This system can be identified by the presence of an accumulator located between the evaporator outlet and the compressor inlet. This system meters refrigerant into the evaporator at a fixed rate and uses a low-pressure-sensing switch to control compressor operation in order to prevent the evaporator from becoming too cold and freezing. The main components of an orifice tube system are shown in **FIGURE 37-27**.

The second type of restriction is the **thermostatic expansion valve (TXV) system**. The TXV is the restriction in the system, which is identified by the presence of a receiver drier between the condenser and the TXV located at the evaporator. This type of system meters refrigerant to the evaporator at a variable rate. The TXV may use an external capillary tube to vary the orifice, based on the evaporator temperature, or it may be the H type, which uses an internal sensing device that measures evaporator outlet temperature to vary the orifice. Both of these TXVs prevent **evaporator freezing** (a condition in which excess refrigerant floods the evaporator) by reducing refrigerant flow if the temperature is too low. They may also cut out the compressor if pressure is too low. See **FIGURE 37-28** for a TXV system.

Refrigerant and Oil

Many different substances are used as refrigerants. Household air conditioners, commercial air conditioners, and huge cold-food storage facilities all use different refrigerants in their systems, with slightly different properties that make them ideal for their application. An ideal refrigerant is one that can mix with lubricating oil, has a boiling point of less than 32°F, (0°C) at atmospheric pressure, and is noncorrosive, nonpoisonous, and nonexplosive.

In the early 1990s, the refrigerant used in almost all vehicles and mobile equipment was R-12, a **chlorofluorocarbon** (a chlorine-based fluorocarbon compound), which is devastating to the earth's ozone layer. The use of R-12 ceased in 1996.

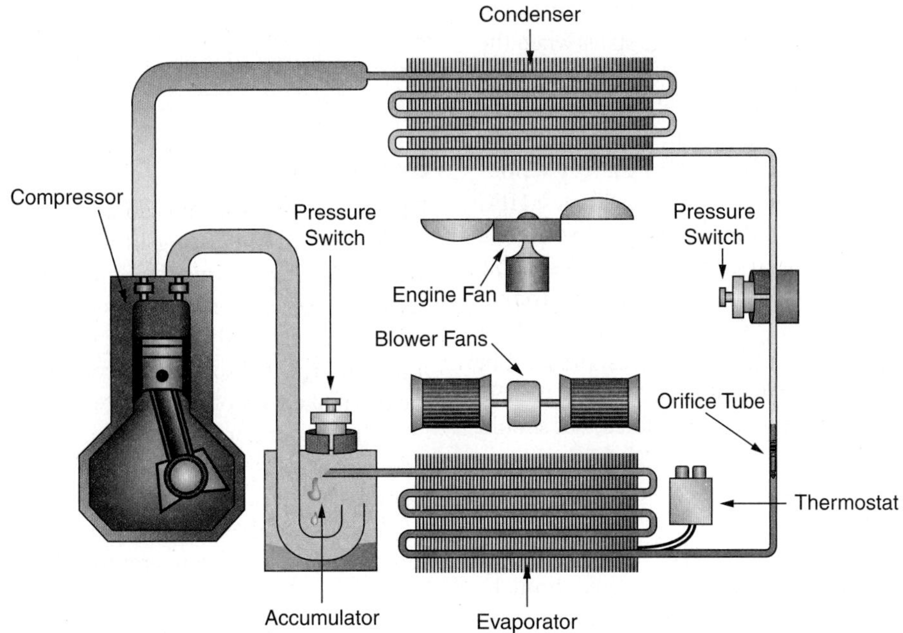

FIGURE 37-27 Orifice tube system.

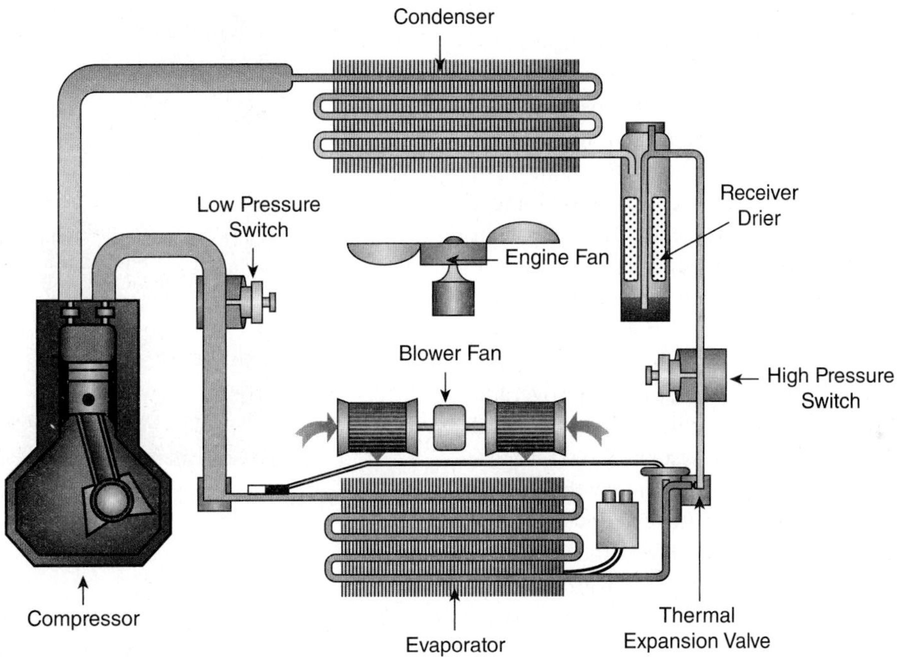

FIGURE 37-28 TXV system.

> **TECHNICIAN TIP**
>
> In 1987, a conference in Montreal, attended by representatives from 22 countries, was held to decide how to move forward with better refrigerants to establish better refrigerant handling practices. The Montreal Protocol had several significant outcomes. The main ones affecting all technicians were as follows:
>
> - R-12 production would cease, and its replacement (R-134a) would start to be used in 1996.
> - All technicians that service or repair mobile air-conditioning systems *must* be properly trained and certified by an accredited organization.
> - Refrigerant recovery and recycling equipment must be properly approved.
>
> Each jurisdiction in North America has its own certification processes and standards that must be adhered to when working on mobile air-conditioning systems and handling refrigerant. Make sure you are compliant with these standards before working on any air-conditioning system; otherwise, severe fines and/or jail time could be incurred.

A replacement refrigerant, R-134a, was found that is not harmful to the ozone layer. The properties of R-134a give it a low boiling point of −14.9°F (−26°C). Even when it is pressurized to 20 psi in the evaporator, it will still easily change states when the cab air temperature is transferred into it. R134a is a hydrofluorocarbon (HFC) that does not contain the chlorine responsible for ozone depletion, so it does not damage the ozone layer. Subsequent study, however, discovered that HFCs are a very serious contributor to greenhouse emissions. By some estimates, HFC is 10,000 times worse than carbon dioxide gas, and so its use and emission to the atmosphere is strictly controlled. A suitable replacement for R-134a is being sought now, and the production and consumption of R-134a is to be phased out by 2024 according to the latest amendment to the Montreal protocol in October 2016. Although this amendment is agreed to by the 197 participants involved, it is not yet officially in force, but should be soon.

Refrigerant Oil

All air-conditioning systems have a specific type and amount of oil that is mixed in with the refrigerant and gets circulated throughout the system. Unless there is a leak or the system is connected to test equipment, there is no way that oil can escape. If service or repairs are needed to the system and oil has to be added, it is *very* important that the correct amount and type of oil be used. Air-conditioning systems require lubricant for several reasons. The first reason is to reduce friction between moving surfaces and bearings inside the compressor in order to ensure a long service life. Additionally, thermostatic expansion valves must be lubricated to operate freely. Lubricant also coats the inside of the air-conditioning system to prevent any corrosive substances from attacking the internal system components. Oil is helpful in keeping the system's seals soft and pliant, which reduces seepage from the system and increases compressor efficiency. In reciprocating piston compressors, the 90–120W viscosity lubricant helps the piston rings seal tightly against their cylinder walls to prevent leakage and apply maximum pressure to the refrigerant. Refrigerant oil used in early systems was made from mineral oil specially formulated for air-conditioning systems. That refrigeration oil was free of sulfur, so it would not form corrosive substances. It was also nonfoaming and wax-free to allow free flow through the system. Any water was removed from the oil to prevent contamination. However, as refrigerant oil is hygroscopic, it will absorb moisture from the air if the system is open or the storage container is not sealed. The refrigerant acts as a solvent for the oil and carries it through the system. Two types of synthetic oils are commonly used in today's systems: **polyalkylene glycol (PAG)** and **polyalphaolefin (PAO)**. PAG is used in all R-134a systems, as it mixes with R-134a better than straight mineral oil. PAO oil is used in systems converted from R-12 refrigerant or special blends of refrigerant because the seals in these systems can be broken down by PAG oil. See **FIGURE 37-29** for an example of one type of air-conditioning oil.

> **TECHNICAN TIP**
>
> Never attempt to hot-wire the operation of an air-conditioning compressor in a system low on refrigerant. Pressure switches within the air-conditioning system disable the compressor to protect it from a loss of lubricant, which is carried through the air-conditioning system by the refrigerant. Extreme damage to the compressor can occur if it is operated without sufficient oil.

Evaporator

The **evaporator** is in the cab and is usually next to the heater core so that the circulating air will blow through it and then the heater core. It performs the opposite function of a heater core in that it absorbs heat from the cab by blowing the warm cab air through the external fins of the evaporator; the refrigerant that flows through it absorbs heat from the air. **FIGURE 37-30** shows the thermal effects of an evaporator.

The evaporator is a tube that contains the refrigerant. The tube weaves back and forth to allow enough time for the refrigerant to absorb cab heat and vaporize.

Because of the different properties of the system refrigerant it boils at a low temperature. This is made easier because

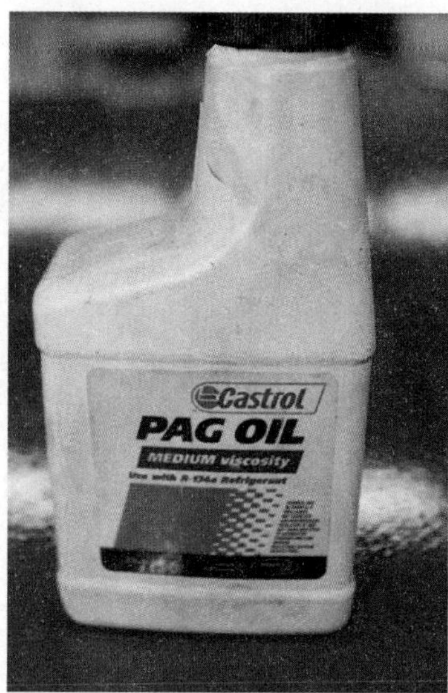

FIGURE 37-29 A/C oil.

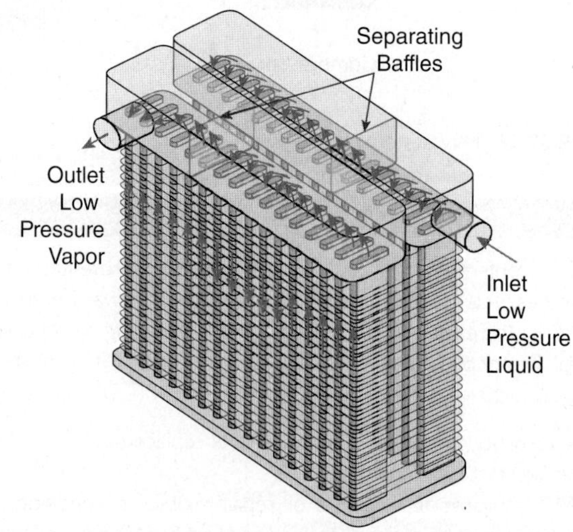

FIGURE 37-30 The evaporator removes heat from the cab air.

it is also under low pressure because it has just flowed past the restriction (orifice tube or TXV valve). It enters the evaporator as a low-pressure, low-temperature liquid. As the warm air flows past the cool evaporator, its heat gets transferred through the evaporator to the refrigerant. The refrigerant absorbs the heat and changes state from a liquid to a vapor. In other words, it boils or evaporates. Remember that heat always travels from hot to cold, and this is what happens with the warm cab air. It transfers its heat into the cold refrigerant. About two-thirds of the way through the evaporator, the refrigerant should have changed from a liquid to a gas.

The low pressure in the evaporator is usually between 15 and 30 psi. The R-134a refrigerant used in the system will easily vaporize, or boil, at this pressure, absorbing tremendous heat as it does so.

When any liquid reaches its boiling point temperature, it changes state to a gas. Think of what you see coming out of a kettle when the water starts to boil. The steam seen rising from the kettle is vaporized water that was liquid water just moments before. This change of state takes a great deal of heat energy, and this massive transfer of heat is what can remove heat from the cab air with great efficiency.

The low-pressure, low-temperature liquid that entered the evaporator leaves as a low-pressure vapor. Its temperature at this point will be similar to the inlet temperature.

▶ TECHNICIAN TIP

BTU is a measure of the amount of heat required to raise the temperature of 1 pound of water 1°F at sea level. For example, if you wanted to heat 1 pound of water from 50°F to 150°F (10°C to 66°C), it would take 100 BTUs. However, once that water is heated to its boiling point of 212°F (100°C) it then takes 970 BTUs to change its state. The same amount of heat has to be removed to change the steam back into water. These two processes are called **vaporization** (liquid to vapor) and **condensation** (vapor to liquid).

Compressor

The pump for the system is called the **compressor**, because the refrigerant is in a gaseous state when it reaches the compressor and is therefore compressible. Most compressors are the reciprocating piston type and use an angled swashplate to allow the pistons to travel up and down in their bores as they rotate inside the compressor housing. This is a similar action to a hydraulic piston pump with a swashplate. **FIGURE 37-31** depicts an air conditioner compressor.

Check valves in the compressor ensure refrigerant flow continues in the proper direction. The low-pressure, high-temperature vapor is drawn into the compressor inlet as it leaves the evaporator outlet. This gas is then compressed in the compressor when the piston pushes it out the outlet of the compressor. The resistance to flow that creates the higher pressure is the restriction downstream of the condenser. The oil mixed in with the refrigerant keeps all the moving parts in the compressor lubricated.

FIGURE 37-31 A/C compressor.

Compressor Drive

The compressor is belt driven, and the belt could be a V-belt or multi-rib belt. Belt tension is critical to proper operation of the air conditioner system because the compressor must turn at the proper speed to get the proper refrigerant flow. The compressor operation is controlled electrically through the use of a magnetic clutch that allows the compressor to be driven only when it is required, and can cycle on and off repeatedly.

The compressor pulley rides on a large bearing on the front of the compressor and is not directly connected to the compressor driveshaft. The compressor shaft is keyed to the center of a drive plate that sits just in front of the drive pulley. The drive plate is actually two plates: an outer circular ring that is then connected to the center plate by drive straps. Inside the drive pulley is a large stationary electromagnet. When the magnet is energized, the outer circular ring of the drive plate is pulled against the drive pulley by the magnetic field, and it drives the center plate through the drive straps. **FIGURE 37-32** shows the drive plate of a compressor magnetic clutch.

Electrical power to the magnetic clutch coil is controlled by the air-conditioning systems controls. As the compressor cycle on and off, it can cause a noticeable load on the engine that can be easily heard, especially on small machines.

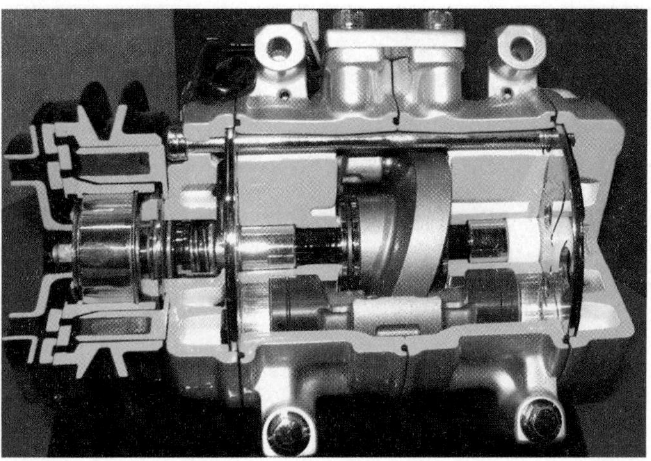

FIGURE 37-32 Cutaway of a magnetic clutch.

Condenser

When a gas is compressed, it heats up. This is the same principle that applies to diesel or compression ignition engines. These engines compress air in the cylinder so much that its temperature gets hot enough to ignite diesel fuel.

Refrigerant pressure in a normally operating system usually reaches 250–300 psi, depending on ambient temperature and heat load, as it is pushed out from the compressor against the system restriction to the **condenser**. As its pressure rises, its temperature also rises. At 250 to 300 psi, the temperature of the R-134a will be 150–160° F (65–70°C). The engine fan draws ambient air across the condenser to dissipate the heat.

The condenser is a tube that contains the refrigerant, and light fins attached to it allow easy heat transfer. The tube weaves its way back and forth across the condenser assembly to allow enough time for the refrigerant's heat to be exposed to the air in order to shed heat. Once again it is the principle of heat traveling from hot to cold that transfers heat in the refrigerant through the condenser to the outside air, because the outside air is much cooler than the high-pressure, high-temperature refrigerant.

About two-thirds of the way through the condenser, the refrigerant should change state and return to liquid form, giving up a tremendous amount of heat.

The condenser is usually located near the engine cooling fan because it requires air flowing past it to get rid of the heat in the refrigerant. **FIGURE 37-33** depicts a typical air-conditioning condenser. In some machines, the condenser is located elsewhere and has one or more fans, driven with electric motors, dedicated to moving air past it. **FIGURE 37-34** depicts a condenser with its own fans. As the heat leaves the refrigerant, it cools down, changes state, and condenses back to a liquid. It then flows to the system restriction, where its pressure drops.

Thermostatic Expansion Valve

As mentioned previously, two different devices can be used to make a restriction in the system. One of these is a variable restriction, called a **thermostatic expansion valve**. There are again two types of TXV. The first type has a capillary tube with a sealed bulb at its end. The bulb is placed on the evaporator

FIGURE 37-33 Condenser.

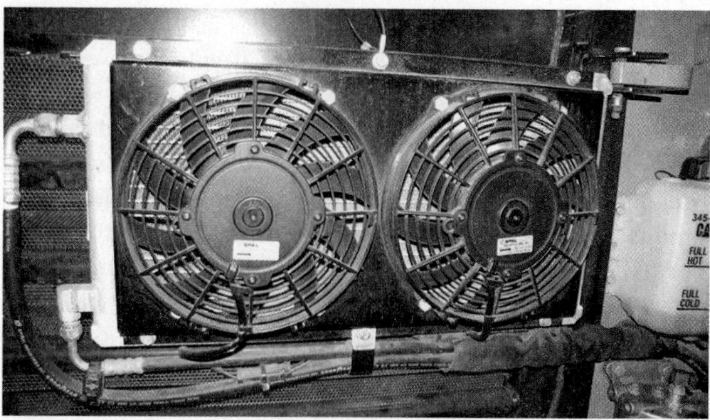

FIGURE 37-34 Condenser with electric fans.

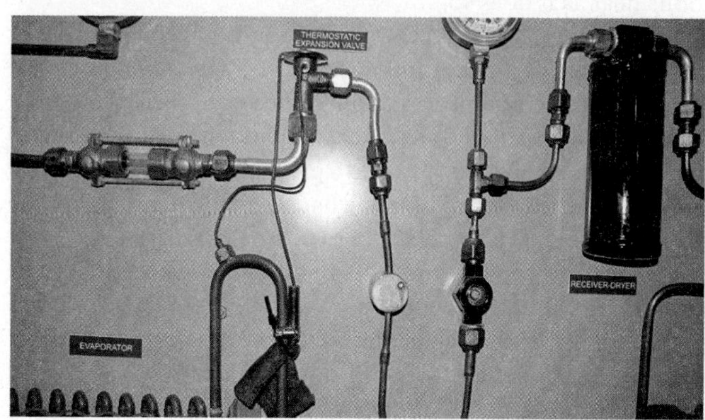

FIGURE 37-35 TXV valve with a sensing bulb.

outlet line and filled with a gaseous refrigerant, usually the same as the system refrigerant. The bulb senses the temperature of the outlet line and is connected to one side of the expansion valve diaphragm. The other side of the TXV diaphragm is exposed to the refrigerant pressure at the evaporator inlet. The refrigerant in the bulb expands and contracts in reaction to the evaporator outlet line temperature. **FIGURE 37-35** illustrates a TXV valve with a sensing bulb.

In the expansion valve, a movable rod controls the valve orifice. Spring force and the refrigerant pressure at the evaporator inlet moves the rod to close the orifice. As evaporator outlet temperature increases, the sensing bulb refrigerant expands, forcing the orifice to open and thus increasing refrigerant flow. This variable orifice controls the flow of refrigerant through the evaporator and therefore its temperature.

▶ TECHNICAN TIP

The sensing bulb on a conventional TXV systems is attached to the evaporator outlet, using a special insulating tape. It is essential that this tape is not disturbed or damaged as it could lead to the bulb being affected by ambient or engine compartment temperatures. If this tape is removed or damaged, it can lead to the evaporator being flooded with refrigerant and condensation freezing on the evaporator, stopping the airflow.

The other type of thermal expansion valve is called an H-block valve. **FIGURE 37-36** shows an H-block valve mounted

FIGURE 37-36 H-block on an evaporator.

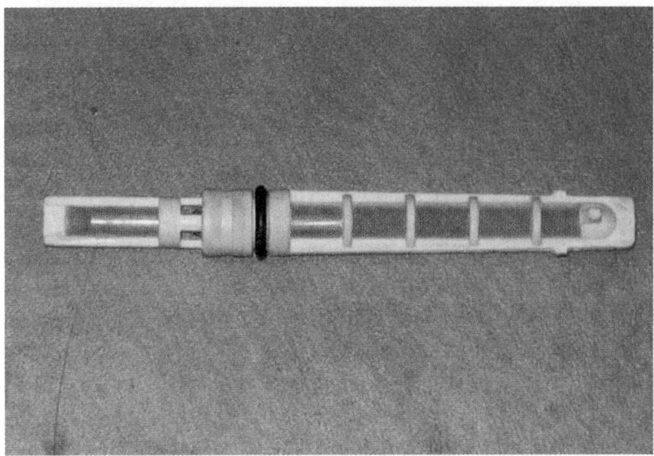
FIGURE 37-38 Orifice tube.

on an evaporator. It works on the same principle as the valve previously described, except there is no remote sensing bulb. Both the lines going into and leaving the evaporator are attached to the valve, and the temperature-sensing element is in the top of the valve, where it senses the outlet temperature directly. It also works with a spring and diaphragm to move a pushrod that in turn varies the orifice in the line leading into the evaporator. In **FIGURE 37-37**, we see an H-block valve.

Orifice Tube

The second main type of mobile air-conditioning system is called a cycling clutch orifice tube, or CCOT, system. It uses a fixed restriction that is placed in the line between the condenser outlet and evaporator inlet. It is usually incorporated with a screen to stop any contamination from entering the evaporator. This type of system uses the low-pressure switch to cycle the compressor on and off; this regulates the evaporator outlet temperature to prevent flooding and freezing of the evaporator. **FIGURE 37-38** illustrates an orifice tube.

▶ TECHNICAN TIP

One method of quickly assessing whether a CCOT system is fully charged or not is to feel the temperature of the evaporator inlet tube, after the orifice tube, and compare it to the temperature of the tube leaving the evaporator. On a fully charged and properly functioning system, they should be close to the same temperature.

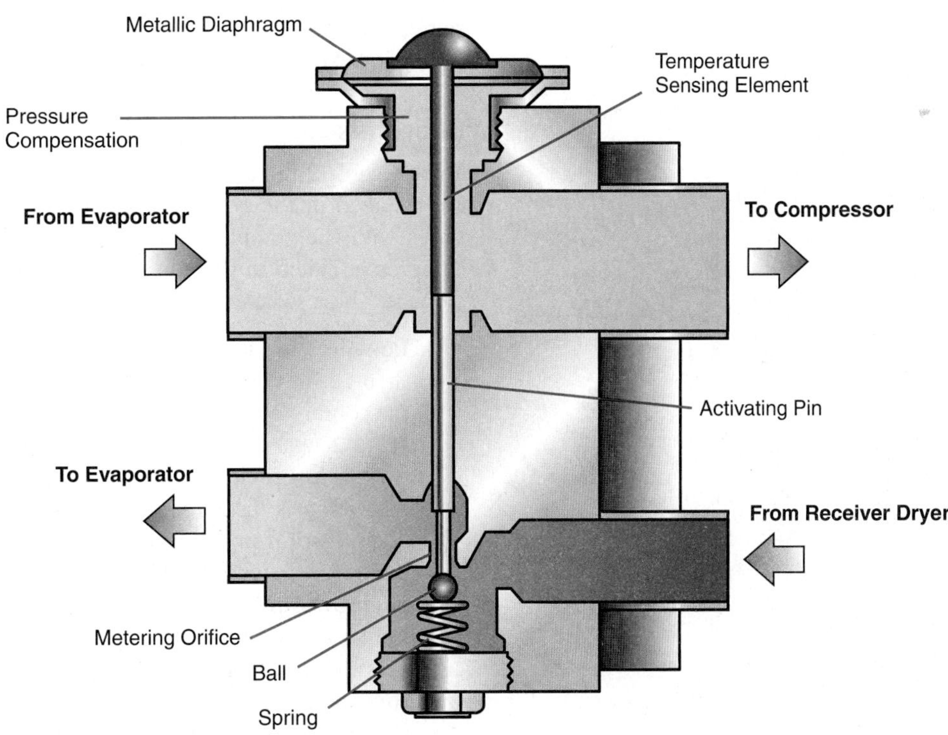

FIGURE 37-37 H-block valve.

Accumulator

Orifice tube systems use accumulators, and they can be found between the outlet of the evaporator and the inlet of the compressor. The **accumulator** prevents any liquid refrigerant from getting into the compressor. Because the compressor will only pump vapor, any liquid reaching it would cause it to lock and possibly cause permanent damage. During operation at high engine speeds and low heat load in the cab, the evaporator can flood, allowing liquid refrigerant to exit. The accumulator stores any liquid refrigerant, ensuring that only vapor reaches the compressor.

The accumulator also serves as a reservoir of refrigerant and contains desiccant that removes any moisture (water) in the system. An accumulator is shown in **FIGURE 37-39**.

Receiver Drier

Air-conditioning systems with expansion valves use a **receiver drier** to serve as storage for liquid refrigerant and to remove any water moisture from the system. The receiver dryer is located in the line past the condenser and before the expansion valve. Like the accumulator, it contains a desiccant packet to remove moisture. **FIGURE 37-40** depicts a cutaway of a receiver drier.

Many receiver driers have a sight glass on them to allow a technician to view refrigerant flow when the system is operating. By observing the color and consistency of the refrigerant, the technician can gain useful knowledge of the system operation, as shown in **FIGURE 37-41**.

Hoses, Lines, and Fittings

Because the air-conditioning system is a sealed pressurized system, the refrigerant inside must be positively contained in the system. A combination of hoses, lines, and fittings connect all system components.

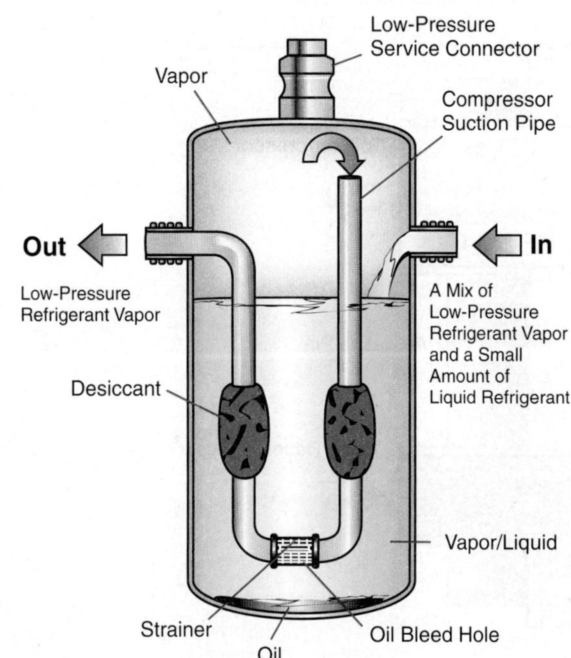

FIGURE 37-39 Accumulator.

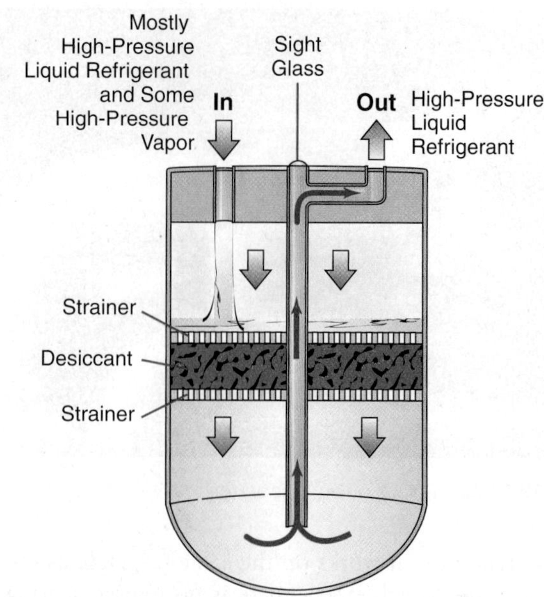

FIGURE 37-40 Receiver drier.

Hoses allow some movement between components and are constructed of layers of rubber and fabric. The rubber compound must be compatible with R-134 refrigerant and the oil used for the system. Lines are made of aluminum tubing and formed to fit the machine contours. There should be several clamps to hold all lines and hoses secure from vibration.

When hoses, lines, and fittings connect to each other or other components, O-ring seals are used to ensure no leakage occurs. These seals must also be compatible with the refrigerant and oil. Some components, like receiver driers, have quick couplers to allow for easier servicing. System hoses and lines are shown in **FIGURE 37-42**.

Switches

To help control and monitor air-conditioning systems, switches are installed in the system refrigerant lines and are wired in series with the compressor clutch. If the switches open, the compressor clutch won't drive the compressor shaft to prevent damage. These switches are listed here:

- **Low-pressure switch:** If the refrigerant pressure is lower than 10 to 20 psi, this switch opens and does not allow the compressor clutch to energize. A pressure lower than 10 to 20 psi indicates there is a leak. At this pressure, there is insufficient refrigerant and therefore insufficient oil, which is dissolved in the refrigerant to protect the compressor from damage. This switch prevents the compressor from working without proper lubrication.
- **High-pressure switch:** If system pressure exceeds safe limits, a high-pressure switch will open. When the high-pressure switch opens, it again cuts power to the compressor protecting the system. The typical high-pressure limit is 385 psi. **FIGURE 37-43** provides examples of pressure switches.

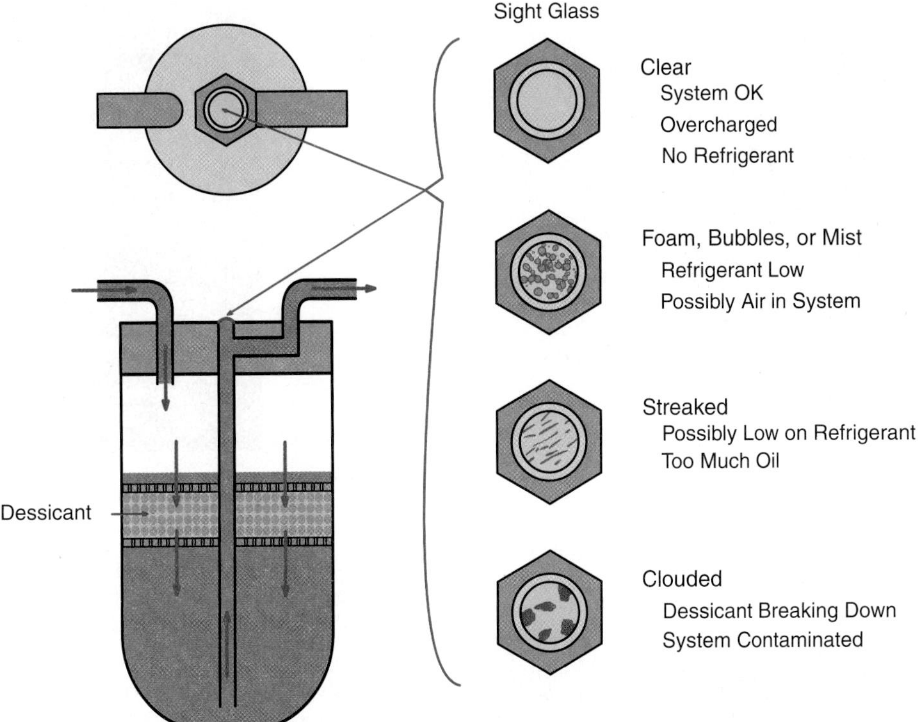

FIGURE 37-41 The color and consistency of the refrigerant is an indicator of the degree to which it is degraded.

FIGURE 37-42 A complete A/C system uses many hoses and tubes to connect its components.

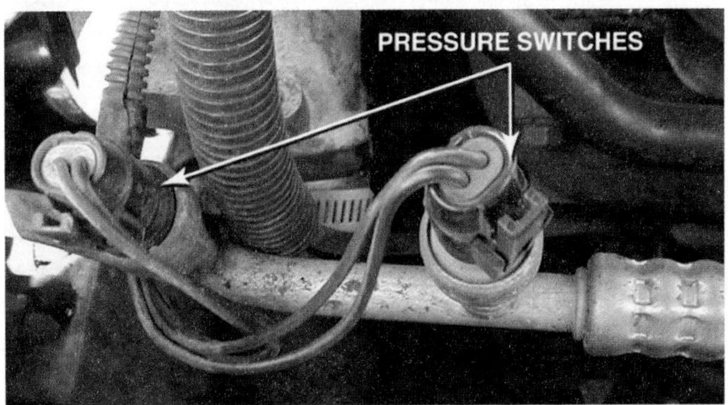

FIGURE 37-43 Different systems use different pressure switches.

The system may also have a high-pressure switch that separately controls the operation of electric condenser fans when the machine is so equipped.

Humidity Reduction

Cab humidity is also controlled with an A/C system. This occurs when the cab air is moved past the cold evaporator, and the moisture in the air condenses on the outside of the evaporator as shown in **FIGURE 37-44**. It will drain off the evaporator and should be channeled outside of the cab, where it drains on the ground. You'll notice this action on a hot, humid summer day if your vehicle is sitting stationary with the A/C system running. A puddle of water accumulates on the pavement under the vehicle; this is the moisture that has been removed from the air inside your vehicle.

Cab drains must be checked for plugging because dust will collect on the drain tube and form mud, which then closes off the drain. A plugged drain can also cause unpleasant odors in the cab.

Electronic Climate Control

As mentioned earlier, some HVAC systems have electronic controls. These are usually part of a touch pad that the operator uses to select different fan speeds, temperature, and ventilation modes. One other feature that HVAC systems may have is climate control. This feature allows the operator to simply set the

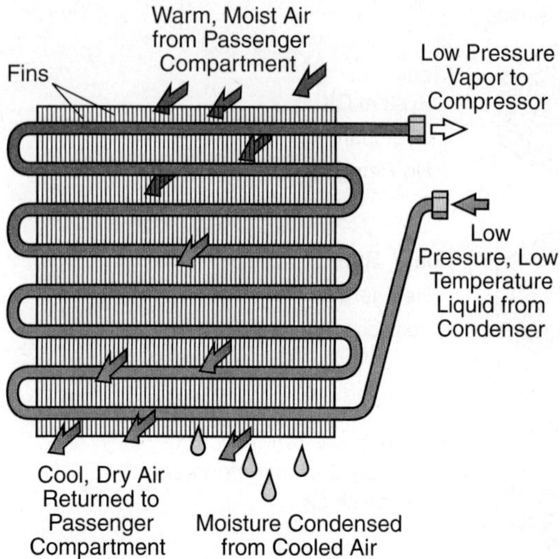

FIGURE 37-44 Moisture in the air condenses on the cold evaporator, drying out the air.

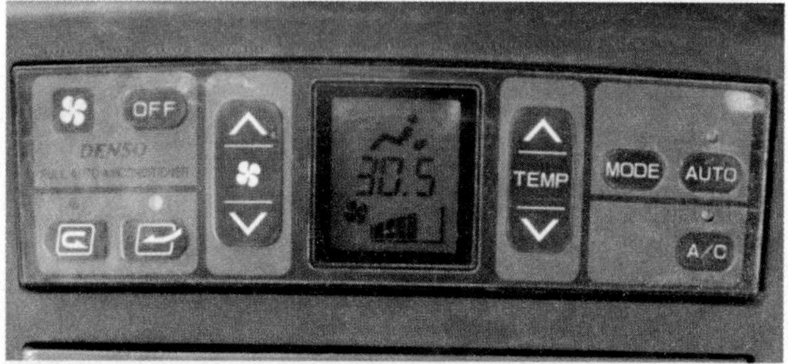

FIGURE 37-45 Electronic HVAC control.

temperature in the cab, after which an ECM takes control of the system and tries to reach and maintain the set temperature. It controls the entire HVAC system. Ambient air temperature sensors, in-cab temperature sensors, and sunlight sensors send input information to the system ECM. Outputs from the ECM are the compressor clutch coil, heater control valve actuator, fan speed, ventilation duct doors actuators, and the control display. This system is usually capable of displaying fault codes. In **FIGURE 37-45**, we see an electronic control for an HVAC system.

▶ Servicing and Repairing HVAC Systems

S37001

Although HVAC systems are not critical to the productive operation of a machine, a great deal of a technician's time will be spent resolving HVAC system problems because many operators place their comfort level ahead of machine productivity. It is understandable that if the HVAC system isn't keeping the cab warm in the winter and cool in the summer, then the operator won't be happy.

One of the simplest repair procedures when dealing with A/C systems is changing the cab filters. This is often overlooked and can easily be the root cause of many HVAC complaints, as good airflow is critical to proper operation. Although there may be suggested hourly intervals for changing these filters, their cleanliness mainly depends on the operating conditions of the machine. These filters can be cleaned by blowing low-pressure air through them in the reverse direction, but they are usually inexpensive enough to make changing them an easy choice. **FIGURE 37-46** portrays a dirty cab filter.

FIGURE 37-46 Dirty cab filter.

Cab Heater Diagnosis

Cab heaters use a heat exchanger (heater core) to get heat from hot engine coolant transferred into the cab. A fan blows cold air across the hot heater core to warm the cab air. If a complaint is about a lack of heat in the cab, these steps should be taken:

1. Verify the complaint. Make sure all the controls are in the right place.
2. Make sure the engine is reaching proper operating temperature.
3. Ensure that the fan is working.
4. Check to see that the air-conditioning system isn't working as well.
5. If the system is part of a climate control system, check for related fault codes.
6. Check the condition of any air filters in the cab.
7. If all previous checks don't reveal any problems, carefully feel the heater hoses going into and coming out of the heater core. They should be too hot to touch. If they are, the heater should be hot as well, and there is an air circulation problem. If the hoses aren't hot, there is a coolant circulation problem that must be addressed. Look for any shutoff valves that may be off or restricting flow. The machine's service information will likely guide you through a troubleshooting exercise to find the cause.
8. Find the root cause of the problem and perform the repair.
9. Verify that the repair has corrected the problem.

A/C Service and Repair

Regular maintenance of A/C systems is fairly straightforward. It includes thorough visual inspections of all A/C components that are easy to see when performing other machine servicing.

The A/C service and repair processes consist of the following basic tasks:

1. Carrying out a *performance test* of the air-conditioning system is the first step in the diagnostic process. **Performance testing** is the term used to describe the standard air-conditioning testing process. You need to look at all of the components and compare how the air-conditioning unit is functioning versus how it is designed to function. Typically, it consists of turning on the air conditioner to its maximum setting, with the windows closed, and raising the engine revolutions per minute (rpm) to 1,100–1,500. The vent temperature in the cab is checked and compared to the temperature and humidity specifications on the manufacturer's temperature chart.
2. After the performance test is complete, the next step is *diagnosing any faults* that are causing the system to operate incorrectly. This could be as simple as a slipping belt or it could be any of the components not working properly or a leak in the system. The next step depends on the diagnosis.
3. If the diagnosis determines that a component of the air-conditioning system is not working properly, then leak testing is not needed at this point. If the diagnosis is that the refrigerant is low, you need to perform a leak test next. The electronic leak detector and dye leak tester require the air-conditioning system to be relatively full of refrigerant. If there is insufficient refrigerant in the system, then reclaim the refrigerant and pressurize the system with nitrogen to check for leaks.
4. *Leak testing* is the next step. If the system is charged, then electronic leak detectors or fluorescent dye testing are good methods. If the refrigerant has leaked out of the system, then nitrogen testing is a good method of leak testing. Use the three-step method listed in the Leak Testing section to determine whether there is a leak, and take the appropriate action. Do not forget to vent the nitrogen to the atmosphere on completion.
5. *Reclaiming* the air-conditioning system before any repair or nitrogen testing is required by the Environmental Protection Agency (EPA), section 609 of the Clean Air Act. Reclaiming involves first checking the system to see if there has been any sealant added to it. The second step is identifying the refrigerant and removing all of it, using an approved machine, then measuring and recording both the amount of refrigerant and oil that was removed from the system. Compare the amount of reclaimed refrigerant to the amount listed on the OEM decal in the engine compartment, and determine whether the air-conditioning system may have been under- or overcharged. If undercharged, suspect a leak, and leak check with nitrogen. Check the amount of oil removed with the refrigerant, and be sure to reinstall the same amount when recharging. If a significant amount of oil is removed (more than 30 mL), then the system should be flushed, removing all of the oil. Then recharge the system with the amount of oil listed on the information label.
6. *Repair* the air-conditioning problem. Now that the air-conditioning system has been diagnosed and tested, the system fault can be repaired. Take the appropriate action and precautions that the repair requires. At this point, the air-conditioning system can be flushed and the base oil installed if needed. In small systems, if less than 1 ounce (30 mL) of base oil has to be added to the system, this step can wait until after the evacuation is complete. Finish the repair and continue to the evacuation.
7. *Evacuation* of the air-conditioning system is the next step after all repairs are made. Evacuation is the process of creating a low pressure or vacuum in the air-conditioning system, using a vacuum pump and gauges. Water boils and turns into a gas at normal ambient temperatures when placed in a vacuum, so this process can remove any moisture that entered the system. This process usually requires a strong vacuum for a minimum of 15 minutes for removal of all the moisture. Follow the proper procedure for evacuation with a mechanical gauge, or use a more accurate micron gauge. When the evacuation is complete, the oil for the air-conditioning system can be added, after which the vehicle is ready for the charging process.
8. *Charging* the air-conditioning system to the proper refrigerant level is an important process of the air-conditioning repair. When adding refrigerant to the system, be sure that you add the correct amount. After the refrigerant has been charged into the air-conditioning system, rotate the compressor shaft by hand to push out any liquid that may have entered the compressor during the charge process.
9. *Post-testing* of the air-conditioning system is recommended to catch any masked problems that did not appear when the original problem was diagnosed. It is a repeat of the performance test to ensure that all moisture is removed and a recheck of the pressure gauges to be sure the high- and low-side pressures are as specified. All readings should be checked against a diagnostic chart. If you used an electronic leak detector or dye leak testing method, it is a good idea to confirm that there are no leaks. If the vehicle passes the post-test and the air-conditioning system is in good functioning order, then you are ready to contact the customer.

Determining Refrigerant Type

The only way to determine the type of refrigerant in a system is with the aid of a refrigerant identifier (**FIGURE 37-47**). This easy-to-use device connects to the low-side air- conditioning fitting and takes a reading of the refrigerant. It will give a readout such as 100% R-134a, or if the system is contaminated, you may see a reading such as 60% R-134a, 40% R-12, meaning that two different types of refrigerant have been mixed in the system. As long as the refrigerant is pure, it can be recycled, using a reclaiming machine, and reused. If it is contaminated by the wrong refrigerant or the wrong oil, then it is considered a hazardous waste and must be put in a separate unit and disposed of according to state law. The air-conditioning decal in the engine compartment lists the type of refrigerant and how much should be in the system.

Air Conditioner Capacity

The proper **charge** (amount of refrigerant) of the air-conditioning system is important because if the amount of refrigerant is too low or too high, the resulting change in system operating pressure will change the boiling point of the

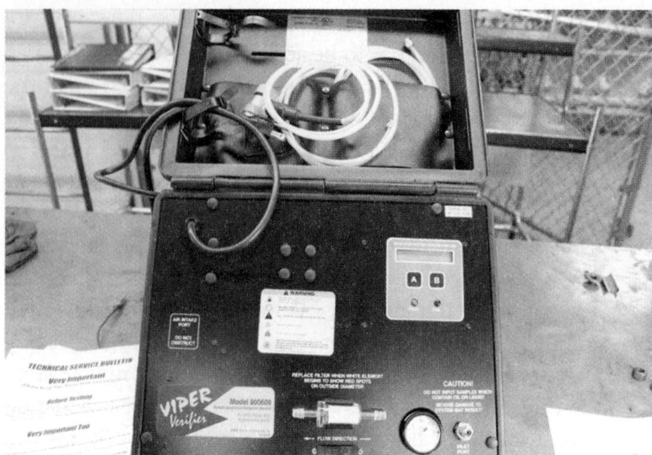

FIGURE 37-47 Refrigerant identifier.

refrigerant, making it unable to effectively remove heat in the evaporator. Safety features are built into the air-conditioning system. For example, the low-pressure safety switch turns the compressor off if the pressure drops too low due to a low charge of refrigerant, and the high-pressure safety switch turns the compressor off if the pressure gets too high due to an overcharge. Because the system pressures vary greatly during operation, the switches are designed to allow operation within a wide window. Thus, they should not be used as indicators of a proper charge.

The proper charge for the air conditioner can be found listed on the OEM A/C decal or label on the system (**FIGURE 37-48**). The label should detail the oil type, charge amount, and type of refrigerant. The type of refrigerant must remain the same because cross-contamination will create a hazardous substance.

There are different ways to measure the refrigerant to be added. Systems may give you the charge amount in kilograms, pounds, pounds with ounces, or straight ounces. The machine that you use to charge the system determines the type of measurement you need or the one you will need to convert to. If the sticker is not located in the engine compartment, you should turn to service information or industry literature. Charging a system without knowing the correct amount of refrigerant is playing a guessing game and is likely to lead to a poor-performing system and customer dissatisfaction.

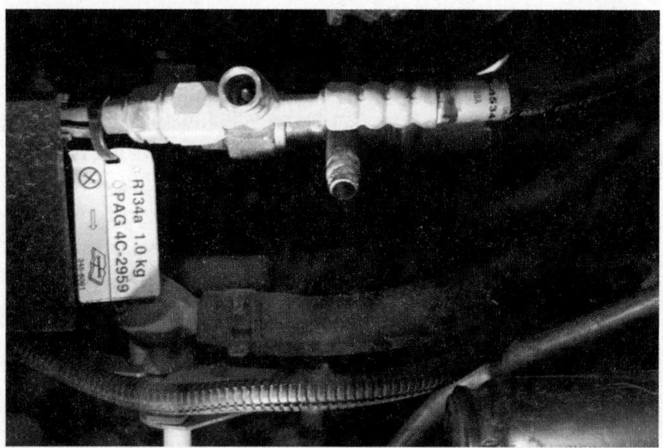

FIGURE 37-48 An air-conditioning identification label.

State of Charge

State of charge in the air-conditioning system refers to the amount of refrigerant in the system compared to how much should be in the system. It is best tested by removing all the refrigerant from the air-conditioning system, comparing that amount to the manufacturer's specifications, and then recharging the system with the proper amount of refrigerant as specified by the service information. If the air conditioner cannot be discharged for any reason, and the state of charge has to be determined, then you need to start your diagnosis by performance testing the air-conditioning system on the vehicle.

Undercharge

An undercharged air-conditioning system contains less refrigerant than the system calls for. For example, if the system is designed to hold 1.5 lb (0.7 kg) of refrigerant, but only 0.75 lb (0.34 kg) are removed during the system evacuation, then the state of charge is half of what it should be. This air-conditioning system would be referred to as undercharged. Systems become undercharged for two primary reasons: (1) There is a leak in the system, or (2) the system was incorrectly charged. Either way, you should plan on leak testing the system to verify that there is not a leak. The following two sections discuss how each type of system responds to an undercharged condition.

Orifice Tube System

In a typical orifice tube system, an undercharge of refrigerant causes a rapid cycle time (rapid turning on and off) of the air-conditioning clutch. The excessive cycling frequency is caused by inadequate flow of refrigerant into the evaporator. What little liquid refrigerant enters the evaporator quickly turns to vapor, causing evaporator pressures to increase as well. The pressure cycling switch used to regulate evaporator pressure responds to the rapid pressure changes by rapidly cycling the compressor clutch on and off. The air from the ducts will feel warm to the hand instead of cold, and the air-conditioning gauge readings will be lower than normal.

Thermal Expansion Valve System

An undercharged thermal expansion valve (TXV) system operates with below normal high- and low-system pressures. A low-pressure switch, located in the trinary or binary switch, or in the evaporator, disables the A/C system. The low-pressure switch typically disables the A/C system if pressures fall below 10 psi (69 kPa). In an undercharged TXV system, the A/C will under-cool as well.

Overcharge

Overcharging the air-conditioning system will affect the orifice tube and TXV systems in the same manner. Both the low- and the high-side gauges will be running higher than normal. The air in the ducts will feel slightly cool, and the compressor clutch will run for a few seconds and then turn off for a long period of time. This behavior is caused by flooding of the evaporator with excessive refrigerant or opening the high-pressure switches, thus disabling the A/C system.

Diagnosis

The most common air-conditioning problem is simply that the air conditioner is not performing. Usually the root cause is leaks in the system. Other issues that could cause the same complaint are compressor failure, debris causing system blockages on the high or low side, or system blockages caused by moisture freezing in the system. These problems occur far less often than leaks, but they do happen. Normally, a check of the gauge pressures will indicate what is going on. Normal system operating pressures vary with ambient temperature, but they typically range between 25 and 45 psi (172 and 310 kPa) on the low side and 150 and 170 psi (1,034 and 1,172 kPa) on the high side at 70°F (70°C). When both gauges read low pressure, the system may be low on refrigerant. If the gauges read low pressure on the high side, high pressure on the low side, or about equal pressures, it usually means that the compressor is not working. If the low side reads as a vacuum, such as in the TXV system, the valve is blocked and refrigerant cannot flow into the evaporator. Extremely high-pressure readings on the high side indicate that there is a blockage on the high side or an airflow restriction across the condenser.

On occasion, the problem of not blowing cold air is not the air-conditioning system at all; rather, the blend door or heater control valve is not closing adequately to keep air or hot coolant from passing through the heater core. This can be identified by checking pressures and determining that the air-conditioning system is performing correctly and moving on to the next logical cause, a heater that is not turning off.

Another operator complaint is unusual smells when running the air conditioner. The air-conditioning evaporator box has a drain tube that allows removal of water collected from the moist air as it condenses on the cold evaporator and drips into the box. If the drain is plugged, then the water will provide a breeding ground for bacteria, and the smell will be distributed throughout the cab. This problem is fixed by clearing the drain, spraying the system with a disinfectant and allowing it to sit, then running the system on high to blow everything out.

▶ TECHNICIAN TIP

If the duct temperature is warmer than the ambient temperature, then the heater control valve is stuck open, or the blend door is not positioned properly. Use hose pinch pliers to shut off the flow to the heater core, and then retest the air-conditioning system.

When diagnosing air-conditioning systems, you need to look at all of the factors involved. Always refer to service information, precautions, history, and service bulletins. Some of the variable factors in air-conditioning are the weather, air moisture content, and temperature. Obviously, the temperature is important, as the hotter or colder the outside air, the harder it is to heat or cool it. Moisture in the air, through either humidity or precipitation, can stick to the fins of the evaporator and freeze. Because the evaporator is used during air-conditioning and on the defrost setting to dry the air, a frozen evaporator can affect both the heating and the cooling systems. If a machine is running badly, the air-conditioning may be turned off to try to correct the issue. Slipping belts will cause the compressor to spin slowly or not at all. Any leaks in doors or windows will cause outside air to enter, which will have to be conditioned. A cloudy day will decrease the heat load on the vehicle, increasing the air-conditioning system's efficiency and possibly giving the impression that the system is cooling fine.

▶ TECHNICIAN TIP

The one rule for diagnosis of an air-conditioning system is "When in doubt, suck it out." This means if you cannot find the problem while diagnosing, remove all refrigerant and start over from a base charge. Starting with a known base charge will remove any question as to whether the refrigerant is too low or too high, or whether there is any moisture causing a problem in the system.

Performance Testing

The pretest and inspection of the air-conditioning system are the first step in the diagnostic process. *Performance testing* is the term used to describe the standard air-conditioning testing process. You need to look at all of the components and compare how the air-conditioning unit is functioning to how it is designed to function. When testing the air-conditioning system, make sure to have all the controls at the maximum settings. The heater fan has to be on the highest speed. The heater control knob should be on the coldest setting. The airflow should be set to the dash vents.

Before testing the air-conditioning system, let the system stabilize for a few minutes to allow the refrigerant to equalize and the temperatures to reach the proper level. To performance test an air-conditioning system, follow the steps in **SKILL DRILL 37-1**.

▶ TECHNICIAN TIP

Performance testing the air-conditioning system must be done before and after the repair. Doing so helps ensure that you identify any faults before starting the repairs, as well as verify that the faults are completely repaired.

Inspecting the Evaporator Housing Water Drain

As the air-conditioning system is running, the evaporator will sweat water throughout the day. The water collected has to be drained from the evaporator housing. A drain hose is connected to the evaporator housing, allowing moisture to exit. Checking that the drain is not plugged is a common diagnostic procedure.

To inspect the evaporator housing water drain, follow the steps in **SKILL DRILL 37-2**.

Electronic Leak Detection Testing

The use of an SAE-compliant electronic leak detector is considered the safest and most accurate method for locating a

SKILL DRILL 37-1 Performance Testing an Air-Conditioning System

1. Start the machine and let it reach normal operating temp.
2. Close all windows if the vehicle is so equipped.
3. Turn the air conditioner to its maximum setting.
4. Raise the engine rpm to 1,200–2,000.
5. Check the vent temperature in the cabin, using a thermometer. Compare the temperature recorded to the diagnostic chart in the manufacturer's service manual.

SKILL DRILL 37-2

1. Determine that the drain tube is clogged by allowing the air-conditioning system to run while observing the drain tube for water drops. In the case of a plugged drain, no water or very few drops are found.
2. Carefully use low-pressure air and an air nozzle to blow air into the drain tube. Note that water will come out of the drain tube when the clog is removed and will result in a large discharge of malodorous water.
3. When the water has completely drained, the task has been performed. Advise the operator to keep an eye out for normal water discharge while the machine is operating, if possible. A lack of water could indicate the problem's reoccurrence.

refrigerant leak. The latest SAE standard, the J-2791 electronic refrigerant leak detector, accurately detects refrigerant leaks down to 0.1 oz (3 g) per year. Three sensitivity levels are typically available on the detector, to identify large and small leaks. The detector will beep, activate a light, or do both when a leak is found.

To obtain the most accurate results, leak detection must be performed with the system under pressure with no less than 50% refrigerant charge in the system. Finding smaller leaks, however, may require that the system refrigerant pressure be increased above normal before the leaks can be located.

The detector needs to be moved slowly and evenly around the components and lines. Starting with the sensitivity on a high setting and turning down the sensitivity as the alarms and lights get louder and brighter will help you pinpoint the problem. Moving with a steady hand and taking your time is critical to using this device.

When using the detector, be sure there is no wind or draft on the machine. A draft or air movement over the machine could cause the refrigerant not to enter the detector.

To test for leaks using a sniffer device, follow the steps in **SKILL DRILL 37-3**.

Dye Testing

Using ultraviolet (UV) light and refrigerant dye is a common way to test for leaks in an air-conditioning system. Some equipment manufacturers add dye during the manufacturing process. When using dye for the first time on an air-conditioning system, the dye has to be injected as a concentrate into the system. Most machines have a special port for this purpose. Injecting concentrated dye into the low side of the air-conditioning system should be done with the machine off. When installing dye for the first time, the air-conditioning system has to be operated so that the dye is distributed throughout all parts of the air-conditioning system.

SKILL DRILL 37-3 Testing for Leaks Using an Electronic Leak Detector

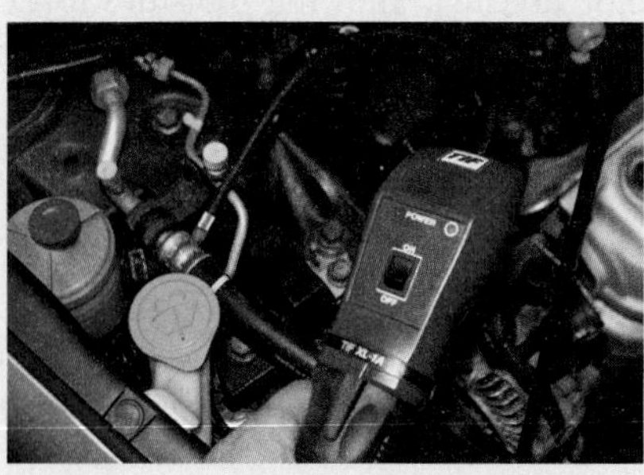

1. Make sure the air-conditioning system has refrigerant by installing a pressure gauge set and checking the readings against the PT chart.
2. Select a fairly sensitive setting for the detector. Slowly move the wand around and under all of the air-conditioning lines and components. If a leak is detected, turn the sensitivity down, and pinpoint the exact location of the leak. Once the leak is located, move the wand tip from the leak to outside the machine. This allows the detector to "breathe" clean air, cleaning out its sensors and stopping the alarm.
3. Reclaim the refrigerant, and repair the leak.
4. Always recheck for a leak after the system has been properly recharged.

If the machine already has dye installed, or after operating the machine's A/C system for several minutes after injecting dye, locating the leak requires using a UV light. When using a UV light, make sure all safety precautions are followed, including wearing UV safety glasses. Finding leaks with a UV light is easier in the dark; installing a cover over the area of the machine being tested will help you to find the leak.

To perform a dye test to find a leak, follow the steps in **SKILL DRILL 37-4**.

Reclaiming and Recovering the Air-Conditioning System

Any time the air-conditioning system has to be opened up, the refrigerant must be removed so that refrigerant will not be released into the atmosphere. Removing refrigerant is called **reclaiming** or **recovering**. The reclaiming process uses the air-conditioning machine to remove refrigerant from the system. It is also a good method of measuring the existing refrigerant charge in a machine, which will verify whether the system was undercharged, overcharged, or properly charged. The air-conditioning machine can measure the amount of refrigerant recovered from the machine. Comparing the amount removed to the specified capacity allows you to determine the charge status.

To perform the reclaim process, follow the steps in **SKILL DRILL 37-5**.

> **TECHNICAIN TIP**
>
> Service valves allow testing and refilling equipment to be connected to the high and low sides of the system. R-134a systems will have one small (high-pressure) and one large (low-pressure) cap that are threaded on and sealed with an O-ring. They are a type of quick coupler and are different sizes from each other to prevent mixing up low and high sides.
>
> R-12 systems also had service valves but had threads on their outside to allow test equipment connection. There is no way of interchanging R-12 and R-134 test or refill equipment. See **FIGURE 37-49** to see the service connections for an R-134a system.

FIGURE 37-49 Service connections.

SKILL DRILL 37-4 Testing for Leaks Using Dye

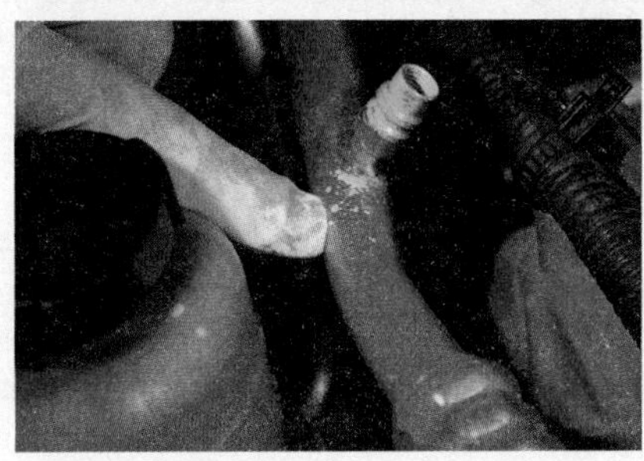

1. Check system pressure to be sure there is enough refrigerant to turn on the compressor. Turn on the compressor. If the compressor does not come on, add refrigerant in small increments until the compressor runs.
2. Add the dye through the low-pressure port, using a dye injection system. Run the air-conditioning system to circulate the dye. The system may have to run for several minutes or even several days, depending on the size of the leak.
3. Using a black light, follow the lines, hoses, components, and compressor seal, looking for the orange or green glow of the dye, which indicates a leak. If a leak is not found in the lines or hoses, it may be in the evaporator; the blower motor resistor may have to be removed to see into the air-conditioning box.
4. Recover the refrigerant in the system, and repair the leak. Then evacuate and recharge the refrigerant, and recheck for leaks.

SKILL DRILL 37-5 Reclaiming and Recovering the Air-Conditioning System

1. Identify the refrigerant using the refrigerant identifier, and verify that there is no sealer in the system.
2. Start the reclaim process by hooking up the air-conditioning machine to the low- and high-side service ports.
3. Open the valves and turn on the air-conditioning machine. Select the reclaim mode and follow the prompts on the screen.
4. When the refrigerant has been removed, record the amount and compare it to the sticker or label on the machine.
5. The air-conditioning machine drains any excess oil that might have been reclaimed. The refrigerant oil that is drained should be minimal or nonexistent. Record the amount of oil that is discharged, and install the same amount if the total oil removed is less than 30 mL. If the oil drain discharges more than 30 mL, the air-conditioning system will have to be flushed using a flush machine, removing all of the oil from the system.
6. After the old oil is flushed, reinstall the proper amount of new oil to the system.

Wrap-Up

Ready for Review

- Safety concerns related to operator stations include checking all safety-related features that are part of the operator station to ensure their proper operation (e.g., seat belt, mirrors, steps, handrails, machine controls). Fall arrest apparatus may also be required, and air-conditioning systems can produce extreme temperatures, so burn and frostbite are possibilities.
- Operator stations or cabs have changed a great deal in the past decades to ensure operators can be comfortable, to reduce fatigue, and to increase production.
- Machine controls have evolved from heavy levers and pedals to small electronic joysticks.
- Operator displays provide the operator information related to how the machine systems are reacting to the operating conditions under which the machine is working.
- Displays can be simple mechanical gauges in which the needle moves with a Bourdon tube to show temperatures, levels, and pressures
- Dash display warning systems alert the operator to machine system conditions that are outside of normal parameters. This should prompt the operator to change how the machine is being operated, or component damage is likely to occur.
- Electrical gauges use sending units to send variable electrical signals that make their needle move.
- In electronic gauges, the needle moves in reaction to an ECM output. The ECM receives an input from a sending unit.
- Machines can be equipped with telematic systems that transmit live and stored data from the machine to a remote location. They can be Bluetooth, cell-based, or satellite-based systems.
- Machines used to grade material may have a GPS integrated into the machine hydraulic system.
- Operator stations have to protect the operator from falling objects (FOPS) or rollover (ROPS). These structures have to be inspected regularly for damage and *cannot* be welded on or drilled into or modified in any way.
- Many machine displays now incorporate blind spot display systems that use one or more cameras to show operators what they normally can't see around the machine.
- Operator seats can have suspension systems with air compressors.
- Seat belts are a critical safety feature and require regular inspection and replacement.
- If a cab must be tilted, the proper lock must be in place before anyone goes under the cab.
- HVAC (heating, ventilation, air-conditioning) systems should pressurize the cab and keep heat and humidity levels to a comfortable level.
- Cab fans draw outside air past a filter to give the inside a slightly higher than atmospheric pressure in order to keep out dust. Cab fans usually have three speeds and may use a stepped resistor to give it different speeds.
- Cab heaters circulate engine coolant through a heat exchanger, and a fan pushes air past it to heat the cab up on cold days. Heater control valves can regulate the amount of coolant running through the heater.
- Air-conditioning systems remove heat from cab interiors on hot days. They will also remove humidity.
- An A/C compressor moves a refrigerant through a sealed system that has two heat exchangers. The properties of the refrigerant allow it to boil when exposed to warm cab air in the evaporator. The refrigerant then moves to the condenser, where it condenses as it cools down. The cycle continues as long as the compressor moves the refrigerant and air moves past the heat exchangers.
- Two main types of HVAC systems are orifice tube and thermal expansion valve (TXV). These components create a pressure drop in the system.
- Presently, machines use R-134a for refrigerant, but this will change to a more environmentally friendly refrigerant in the future. Technicians *must* be aware of *all* government regulations related to handling refrigerants and servicing A/C systems.
- A/C systems require a specific type and amount of oil.
- HVAC evaporators are located in the cab, usually with the cab heater and fan, and have a filter to prevent their fins from getting dirty.
- HVAC compressors have an electromagnetic clutch that is belt driven and engaged when the HVAC controls send an electric current to it.
- HVAC condensers are usually located near the engines cooling fan to use the airflow from the fan to shed heat. They sometimes have their own fans that use electric motors.
- TXV valves are variable orifices with a temperature-sensing bulb, an orifice tube is a fixed restriction with a screen.
- Orifice tube systems use accumulators to trap liquid refrigerant and a desiccant to absorb any water.
- TXV systems use receiver driers with a desiccant to absorb any water.
- HVAC hoses, lines, and fittings have to be compatible with the refrigerant and withstand heat and temperature changes.
- A pressure switch in the clutch circuit opens if system pressure gets too high.

- HVAC systems with climate control allow the operator to set a temperature and an ECM will control the system to achieve it.
- HVAC systems must have regular maintenance to operate properly. This includes filter cleaning/changing and belt tension adjustment.
- Cab heater problems can include no heat, too much heat, no air movement, and leaks.
- Heater diagnostics includes a thorough visual inspection, coolant level check, control valve check, filter check, and fan check.
- A/C problems include the cab being too hot or too cold, or no air movement.
- A/C diagnostics include a thorough visual check; setting A/C to maximum and checking clutch engagement; and venting air temp and airflow at evaporator and condenser.
- Refrigerant leaks must be found and repaired before recharging. The system can be pressurized with nitrogen and dye injected to assist in finding a leak.
- Recovery and recycling of refrigerant is mandatory and easy to perform with proper equipment and training.
- The system must be recharged with the correct amount and type of refrigerant and oil.

Key Terms

accumulator Prevents any liquid refrigerant from getting into the compressor.

autonomous machine A smart machine that can function without an operator in the cab.

British thermal unit (Btu) The amount of energy required to heat or cool 1 pound of water 1°F.

calorie The unit of energy that reflects the amount of energy required to raise the temperature of 1 gram of water by 1°C.

chlorofluorocarbon A chlorine-based fluorocarbon compound.

compressor The pump for the A/C system.

condensation Change of state from a vapor to a liquid such as the moisture that collects on a cool surface.

condenser A component of the HVAC system that transfers heat from the system to the atmosphere.

cycling clutch orifice tube (CCOT) A fixed-orifice tube with pressure control obtained by cycling the compressor clutch on and off.

electronic display An electronic monitoring system; also known as EMS.

evaporator The cold surface of the air-conditioning system that absorbs heat from a cab or vehicle

evaporator freezing A condition in which excess refrigerant floods the evaporator.

FOPS Falling object protection system.

"geo fence" An electronically limited operational area.

heater core An in-cab heat exchanger that regulates heating by circulating engine coolant.

heating, ventilation, and air-conditioning (HVAC) system The system in the vehicle responsible for heating and cooling the air.

latent heat The quantity of heat required to produce a change of state from a solid to a liquid, or a liquid to a gas.

latent heat of condensation The process of removing heat energy from matter to effect a change of state from vapor to liquid.

latent heat of vaporization The process of adding heat energy to matter to effect a change of state from liquid to vapor.

Murphy gauge A type of gauge with an integrated switch that can shut off the machine or trigger a warning.

operator station The interface between the operator and the machine; also called a cab.

polyalkylene glycol (PAG) Synthetic oil used in all R-134a systems.

polyalphaolefin (PAO) Oil used in R-12 systems and those converted from R-12.

receiver-dryer A storage reservoir for refrigerant that also absorbs moisture from the air-conditioning system.

ROPS Roll-over protection system.

sensible heat Heat that can be sensed or felt.

suspension seat An operator seat suspended by springs and/or compressed air.

thermostatic expansion valve (TXV) An expansion device used in commercial vehicle air-conditioning systems.

vaporization Change of state from a liquid to a gas.

Review Questions

1. If a cab is pressurized, it means which of the following?
   a. The cab has pilot controls.
   b. The machine has power brakes.
   c. There is negative pressure inside the cab.
   d. There is positive pressure inside the cab.
2. The stepped resistor that is used in some fan motor circuits will do which of the following?
   a. Turn the motor on and off
   b. Provide reverse rotation
   c. Provide different fan speeds
   d. Make the motor last longer
3. An air-conditioning system is a ________ system.
   a. sealed fluid
   b. open liquid
   c. sealed gas
   d. open gas
4. What is the name of the heat exchanger that removes heat from the refrigerant?
   a. Evaporator
   b. Condenser
   c. Receiver drier
   d. Accumulator
5. The refrigerant that was formerly used in mobile air-conditioning systems and had its production stopped

because of its ozone-destroying properties is called which of the following?
a. H-12
b. R-12
c. H-134a
d. R-134a

6. At an ambient temperature of 70°F (21°C) normal pressure range on the high side of an air-conditioning system is which of the following?
a. 15–30 psi
b. 30–50 psi
c. 100–150 psi
d. 150–200 psi

7. An air-conditioning system is called a(n) __________ system if a fixed restriction is part of it.
a. TXV
b. H-block
c. accumulator
d. CCOT

8. This would *not* be one method/tool of finding a refrigerant leak in the system:
a. Black light
b. Smell
c. Electronic sniffer
d. Soapy water

9. This air-conditioning component ensures no liquid refrigerant reaches the compressor inlet:
a. Thermal expansion valve
b. Evaporator
c. H-block valve
d. Accumulator

10. What is the stage of an air-conditioning repair process where a strong vacuum is applied?
a. Evacuation
b. Leak detection
c. Refrigerant identification
d. Recharge

ASE Technician A/Technician B Style Questions

1. Technician A says that a ROPS protects the operator from roll over. Technician B says that the ROPS is a good place to weld on some brackets for lights and other accessories, as it is the highest point on the machine usually. Who is correct?
a. Technician A
b. Technician B
c. Both A and B
d. Neither A nor B

2. Technician A says that a balancing coil-type gauge uses a sending unit with a variable resistor. Technician B says that a Bourdon-type gauge uses a sending unit with a variable resistor. Who is correct?
a. Technician A
b. Technician B
c. Both A and B
d. Neither A nor B

3. Technician A says that heat, like all forms of energy, can be transferred from one place to another. Technician B says that the air-conditioning system's condenser removes heat from the cab and transfers it to the atmosphere via the evaporator. Who is correct?
a. Technician A
b. Technician B
c. Both A and B
d. Neither A nor B

4. Technician A says that a British thermal unit, or Btu, is a common term for heating and air-conditioning. Technician B says that 1 BTU is the amount of heat required to change the temperature of 1 pound of water by 1 degree Fahrenheit. Who is correct?
a. Technician A
b. Technician B
c. Both A and B
d. Neither A nor B

5. Technician A says that simply changing the pressure of a liquid will allow a change of state to take place. Technician B says that changing a refrigerant back and forth between a gas and liquid state is accomplished by compressing a gas refrigerant or lowering the pressure of a liquid refrigerant. Who is correct?
a. Technician A
b. Technician B
c. Both A and B
d. Neither A nor B

6. Technician A says that air-conditioning and refrigeration systems transfer heat from the cab to the air stream outside the machine. Technician B says that air-conditioning and refrigeration systems also remove moisture from the air passing through the evaporator and channel it to a drain leading outside the machine. Who is correct?
a. Technician A
b. Technician B
c. Both A and B
d. Neither A nor B

7. Technician A says that outside air flows over the fins of the condenser and absorbs heat from the refrigerant as it converts from a gas to a liquid. Technician B says that the condenser typically consists of coiled tubing mounted in a series of thin cooling fins. Who is correct?
a. Technician A
b. Technician B
c. Both A and B
d. Neither A nor B

8. Technician A says that the thermostatic expansion valve controls refrigerant flow by the action of a spring-loaded control valve. Technician B says that the H-type TXV is internally balanced. Who is correct?
a. Technician A
b. Technician B
c. Both A and B
d. Neither A nor B

9. Technician A says that the low-pressure cutout switch is connected in the compressor clutch electrical circuit. Technician B says that when a predetermined low pressure is sensed, the switch stops compressor operation. Who is correct?
   a. Technician A
   b. Technician B
   c. Both A and B
   d. Neither A nor B

10. Technician A says that the pressure-cycling switch is used on CCOT (orifice-tube) systems and usually located on the accumulator. Technician B says that it is not possible to remove and replace the switch without having to discharge the system. Who is correct?
   a. Technician A
   b. Technician B
   c. Both A and B
   d. Neither A nor B

CHAPTER 38
Machine Frames and Suspension Systems

Knowledge Objectives

After reading this chapter, you will be able to:

- K38001 Describe the purpose and fundamentals of frames used with MORE.
- K38002 Identify the different construction, types design, and features of frames used with MORE.
- K38003 Explain the purpose of suspension systems used with MORE.
- K38004 Identify the different construction, types, design, and features of suspension systems used with MORE.
- K38005 Describe the principles of operation and construction of tracked vehicle suspension systems.

Skills Objectives

After reading this chapter, you will be able to:

- S38001 Describe the recommended procedure for frame repair.
- S38002 Describe manufacturers' recommended procedures for inspection and testing of suspension systems used with MORE.
- S38003 Recommend reconditioning or repairs of suspension systems used with MORE.

▶ Introduction

All heavy equipment machines have some type of main frame. The frame of the machine is its backbone and serves as the mounting point for all other systems and components that the machine must have to function as it is designed to. Main frames vary greatly in their construction, depending on the type of machine. Main frames are a welded and machined assembly that starts out as plate steel and/or cast sections. Large presses are used to cut and form the plate steel into box sections, and the separate pieces are welded together to form frame sections. These individual box and cast (if used) sections are then welded together to form a strong structure. Once the assembled frame is completed, it is painted to prevent rust from weakening it. **FIGURE 38-1** features the main frame of a track loader.

▶ Fundamentals of Off-Road Equipment Frames

K38001

Engineering a frame would seem very simple if all that was required of the frame was to support the components attached to it, but there are many more stresses that the frame is subject to. When engineering a frame, all these other forces have to be considered. Shock loading and bumps to the machine while encountering rough terrain can more than quadruple the forces acting on the frame, so a frame must have a large safety margin in terms of strength. The frame must allow some flexibility and twisting as the machine travels over bumps and dips, but must always return to its original shape without permanent deformation. A frame that is too rigid would fail due to fracture. The frame must also allow for this flexing without succumbing to fatigue failure. The ideal frame, then, must be strong enough to support anticipated loading, flexible enough to allow some flexing without permanent damage or deformation, and resilient enough to handle the forces acting on it millions of times during its expected life. To accomplish all of the above goals, the frame design, materials, and construction are very carefully selected.

FIGURE 38-1 This track loader has been stripped down to its main frame.

Machine manufacturers design the main frame to withstand the most severe forces that may normally be applied to it, and it should be able to last the expected life of the machine without any type of failure. If the design limits are exceeded, a variety of failures could occur. A frame will get overstressed from overloading, rollover, traveling over extremely rough ground, or operator abuse. Any of these events could lead to a frame failure.

Frame failures usually start out as small cracks or slight bending and will likely progress to larger cracks and possibly complete failures, where the frame completely breaks. Most frames can be repaired with straightening and/or welding procedures that may include adding reinforcing.

Frame Design

Although frame design is not a necessary skill for technicians, an understanding of frame design helps when diagnosing frame damage and deciding on frame modifications and/or repair strategies. Three basic terms are used by engineers when discussing frame design and strength: resist bending moment, section modulus, and yield strength.

Resist Bending Moment

The first of the terms used in frame design is resist bending moment, or RBM. A moment is the torque or twisting/bending force applied to any component around a pivot point. The use of the word "moment" may seem strange, but it is based on an older meaning of the word. In days long gone by, one of the meanings of "moment" was "of great significance or importance," such as in "this was a discovery of great *moment*," so the use of "moment" to describing a force refers to the importance of the force in terms of where it is acting on the component. When we use this in the context of a frame, the resist bending moment is the ability of the frame to support the force trying

You Are the Mobile Heavy Equipment Technician

You are asked to investigate the cause of a strange, loud, banging noise from an excavator. You observe the machine as the operator uses it to dig into a trench. Every time the operator uses the bucket to pry into the trench, there is a loud banging noise. You investigate further and notice rust streaks on the machine's upper frame, but you do not see an obvious problem. You know that downtime for this machine is a serious problem, and want to clear it back to work ASAP.

1. What do you do next?
2. What, if anything, could be the significance of the rust streaks?
3. Do you think this noise could be normal for this machine?

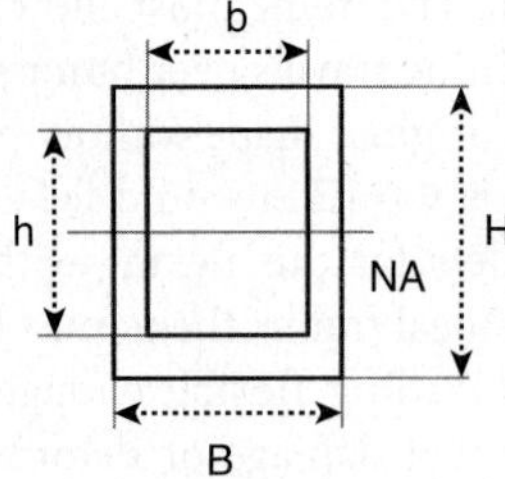

$$SM = \frac{B \times H2}{6} - \frac{b \times h3}{6H}$$

FIGURE 38-2 Box channel section modulus.

to bend it at the point where this bending force is greatest. The RBM of a frame is the actual measure of the strength of the frame, and it is calculated from two other terms that are used in designing frames: section modulus and yield strength.

Section Modulus

Section modulus is an engineering term used to describe the strength of the *shape* of a certain component and has absolutely no connection to the material the component is made of. For example, the section modulus calculation for a box channel (a hollow rectangular box shape) made of plastic and a section modulus for the exact same size box channel made from high carbon steel are identical. Section modulus is a measure of the strength of the design shape, not the material. The section modulus calculation result is in the units used for the calculation; the actual measurement units do not matter. Section modulus can be therefore stated as inches, centimeters, and so on. There are actually two section modulus calculations; one is for elastic section modulus, and the other is for plastic section modulus. Elastic section modulus is used for frame design, so we use that calculation here. See **FIGURE 38-2** for the box channel section modulus calculation, where B is the overall width of the channel; H is the overall height of the channel; b is the width of the inside of the channel; and h is the height of the inside of the channel.

So the calculation does not take in to account the material used to create the channel and will not change as long as the shape is the same. The calculation for section modulus will change only if the shape of the component changes.

If you play around with the section modulus calculation for box channel, you can quickly see that the height of the box has a much larger effect on the outcome than the width of the box. For example, suppose we use the following numbers for the box channel:

B = 12
H = 18
b = 10
h = 16

The calculation will be as follows:

$$SM = \frac{12 \times 18 \times 18}{6} - \frac{10 \times 16 \times 16 \times 16}{6 \times 18}$$

$$= 648 - 379.26 = 268.76$$

If we switch the numbers so that the box is wider than it is high, the calculation will be different.

B = 18
H = 12
b = 16
h = 10

The calculation is as follows:

$$SM = \frac{18 \times 16 \times 16}{6} - \frac{10 \times 16 \times 16 \times 16}{6 \times 12}$$

$$= 768 - 568.88 = 199.12$$

By the above calculations, we see that the height of the component is much more important than the width, and this makes sense. Imagine a typical 2 × 6 wooden beam used in construction. If that beam is placed on its narrow edge between two supports, it will hold a much larger load than if we place the board on its wider flat side between the two supports. The same is true in the context of a box channel: making the box taller will enable it to carry a bigger load than making the box wider.

Different formulas are used to find the section modulus of flat plate and/or I-beams and so forth, as shown in **FIGURE 38-3**.

Yield Strength

The second number required to calculate RBM is the yield strength of the material the frame is constructed from. Yield

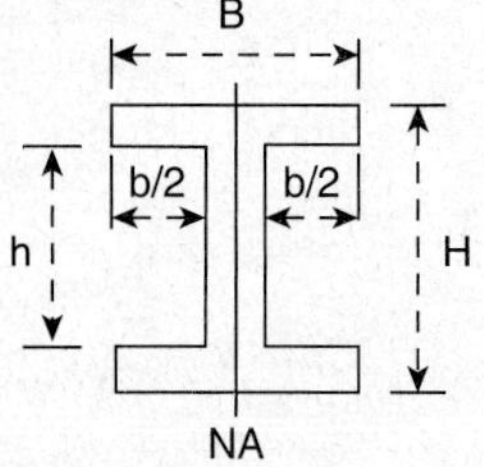

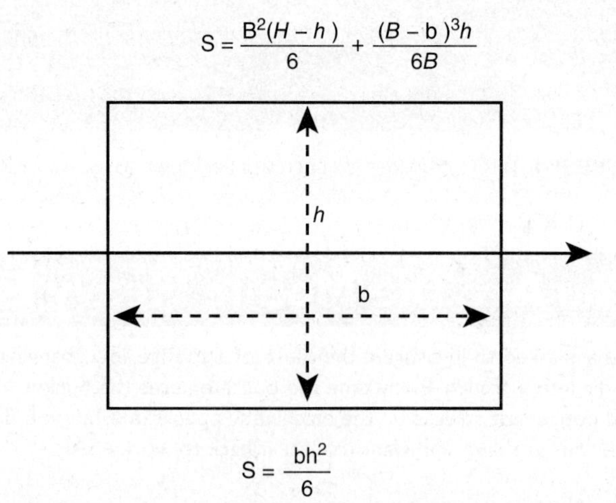

FIGURE 38-3 Different shapes have different section modulus calculation formulas.

strength is the amount of force required to permanently deform the material. Until the yield strength is reached, the material can deform, but it will return to its original shape when the load is removed. Once we surpass the yield strength, the deformation is permanent. Yield strength is determined by placing a piece of the material with a specific cross-sectional area (typically 1 square inch) in a machine that gradually exerts increasing force as it stretches the material, trying to pull it apart. When the material reaches its yield strength, the material shape will permanently deform. This is also known as the elastic limit of the material, where it has stretched to the point that it can no longer rebound to the original shape. Yield strength changes depending on the material being tested, but here are some typical yield strengths: medium carbon, high-tensile steel yields and deforms at approximately 50,000 psi, whereas heat-treated alloy steel yields at 110,000 psi or higher. Most machine frames today use steel frames with around 50,000 psi yield strength. Heat-treated alloy is difficult to repair without decreasing its yield strength. Using a thicker but lower yield-strength steel makes repairing the frame easier, but the frame will still have to have the required RBM, or structural strength.

Actual Frame Strength

The actual amount of load a frame can withstand is listed as the RBM and is calculated by multiplying the yield strength of the material by its section modulus. As an example, for a box channel like the one just mentioned, utilizing steel rated at 50,000 psi, yield strength would be multiplied by its section modulus of 268.74 that we calculated above. This would result in an RBM of 13,437,000 inch-pounds. In order to recommend this frame for a particular application, the maximum force acting on the frame has to be found and then compared to the RBM of the frame design. The force the frame must be capable of supporting is determined by finding the maximum load on the frame and then multiplying that by the distance in inches from the load point to the frame support point. This distance is the length of the lever arm, or "moment" arm, trying to bend or twist the frame. This point is called the maximum bending moment. Typically, a frame has an RBM high enough to support three times the expected maximum force or more.

▶ Types of Frames

K38002

Machine frames can be one-piece assemblies but can also be multipiece as well. A bulldozer has a main frame and two separate track frames, as shown in **FIGURE 38-4**. The track frames have a pivot point and a connection to an equalizer, allowing the track frame to oscillate as the machine moves over uneven terrain. **FIGURE 38-5** shows the connection to the equalizer and the rubber block "spring" suspension. An articulating wheel loader uses a two-piece frame, whereas a wheeled tractor-scraper uses a three-piece frame. Pivot points between the main frame sections for a multipiece frame use pins and bearings to allow movement and hold the sections together. The pins and bearings must be lubricated according to the machine's maintenance manual. An articulated truck must also allow rotation between the front and rear sections of the truck in case the box flops over while it is dumping. A pair of large bearings allow this rotation.

FIGURE 38-4 A bulldozer usually has a main frame and two-track frames like this one.

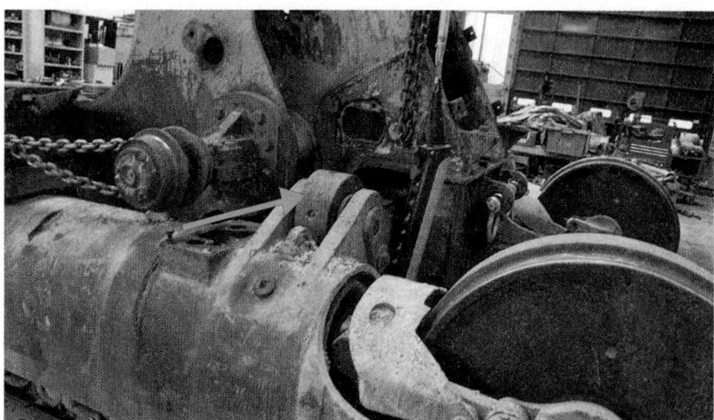

FIGURE 38-5 The transverse equalizer bar allows the track frames to oscillate independently of the main frame.

An excavator has upper and lower frames that are held together with one large bearing. This bearing is usually called the swing bearing but is sometimes called the rotex bearing. Part of the bearing has teeth that allow the machine's swing motor to turn the upper structure.

Machine frame design flaws may appear at some point during the machine's life. If this happens, the manufacturer should create an update to the frame that could include a welding procedure and/or adding reinforcements to repair and improve the frame.

Whenever a technician is working on a machine, he or she should consider where the high-stress areas of the frame are and perform visual inspections on these areas. Typical high stress areas are where:

- main component mounts are located such as transmission, engine, or track frames;
- a cast section to box section weld is located;
- threaded holes have been cut into the frame;

- main boxed sections are welded together;
- suspension components are mounted;
- anywhere stresses are concentrated such as cylinder mounting points; and
- any point where there is a change in section modulus, that is, where the frame gets thicker or thinner.

To perform a thorough main frame inspection, it is necessary to remove all covers and wash the frame. Part of a complete machine reconditioning includes stripping the machine down to the main frame in order to check it for cracks. Some types of nondestructive test methods for frame defects are magnetic particle testing, dye penetrant testing, fluorescent liquid testing, and X-ray imaging. Any defects found must be repaired with industry-accepted welding and fabricating procedures and equipment.

▶ Frame Repair

S38001

Frames tend to fail at stress concentration points. These points can be where the maximum bending moment occurs on the frame, but they can also occur anywhere there is a change in section, meaning a place where the frame material thickness or shape changes. Another common place for cracks or failures is places where components are attached with bolted-on brackets or welds. These concentration points create what are known as **stress risers**, and fatigue failures of most metal components typically occur at a stress riser. This kind of failure can be seen in other components such as pinion shafts and other shafts. Fatigue failure of these components usually occurs where the section (shape and size) of the component changes, as it does, for example, when a spline is machined into the shaft or when a shaft from a raised section that supports a bearing reduces to a smaller diameter; these are typical breakage points because the stress is concentrated where the shaft widens or narrows, and its ability to flex is changed. In shaft manufacturing, attempts are made to reduce the stress concentration by gradually increasing or decreasing the size, using a radius transition from the thinner to thicker part. This has the tendency to spread out the effects of the stress concentration through the area of the radius. The same thinking is used when dealing with a frame. To limit the stress concentration, we try to spread out the change in section to make it more gradual and therefore reduce the effects of stress risers. For technicians, it is important to understand the frame construction and avoid causing or increasing stress risers during repair. Quite commonly, a frame repair requires reinforcement around the repair area. Sometimes the entire frame can be reinforced, but when this is impossible, it is incumbent upon the technician not to create a stress riser. The secret to successful reinforcement is tapering, that is, angling or rounding the edges of the reinforcing plate to spread out the stress concentration. The tapering or rounding spreads out the change in the section modulus and therefore the stress riser. See **FIGURE 38-6** for an example of a main frame repair.

FIGURE 38-6 Main frame repair.

SAFETY TIP

Read and understand these welding precautions before attempting any welding procedure on the frame or vehicle:

- Avoid welding near the fuel tank, fuel lines, or brake lines.
- Any components near the welding area that may be damaged by excessive heat must be removed or adequately protected.
- Always disconnect the battery's (or batteries') positive and negative terminal posts.
- Check the manufacturer's recommendation to protect the vehicle electronics (this may include disconnecting computer module grounds).
- Take precaution to ensure the electrical system or components are not damaged.
- Protect vehicle components from electrical brinelling caused by arc welding. Ensure grounding is sufficient.
- Keep the ground connection of the arc welding machine as close to the work area as possible.
- Do not allow the welding cables to run across or along any vehicle wiring, to prevent induction current that may damage electronic modules.
- Before welding the frame, the paint and/or powder coating must be removed from the weld area.
- After welding, apply an anticorrosion finishing compound to the weld and surrounding area.

Frame Crack Repair

In general, a welded repair will have the same fatigue life as the original equipment. However, if the weld is performed under less than optimum conditions (poor accessibility, awkward welding position, adverse environmental conditions, etc.), the repair is likely to have a much shorter operational life. Following is a general procedure for a crack repair. Always follow the manufacturer's procedures, if available. Most MORE manufacturers will publish documents that detail frame repair procedures. These procedures must followed as laid out to ensure a quality repair. For general instruction on crack repair, follow the steps in **SKILL DRILL 38-1**.

SKILL DRILL 38-1 Crack Preparation

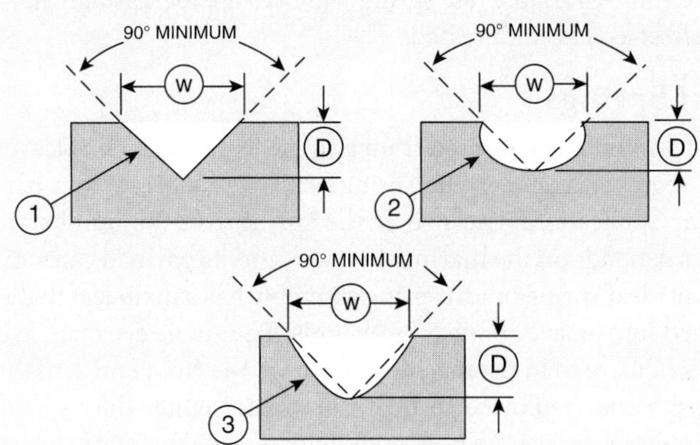

1. In order to repair a crack, the entire crack must be positively removed with an air carbon arc torch or similar tool.

2. When a crack is completely removed, use a penetrating dye to make sure that the crack is fully gouged out down to solid metal.

3. Open the area around the crack to at least 90 degrees, using one of the patterns above.

4. When filling the crack, use the recommended electrode for the base steel.

5. The width of the fill area, W, must be twice the depth, D.

6. Apply reinforcement plates as necessary, using the techniques outlined above to avoid stress concentrations.

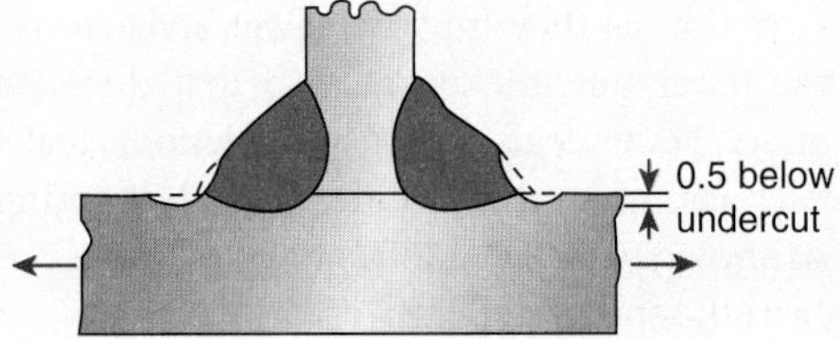

7. If the crack area is at a butt or lap joint, toe grinding is recommended to reduce stress concentration at the weld.

8. The procedure should produce a smooth concave. Toe grinding can improve the fatigue strength of the weld by as much as 30%.

▶ Suspension System Fundamentals

K38003

Some heavy equipment machines must have suspension systems to provide a smoother ride for the operator and to allow the machine to travel faster over rough roads and terrain. This makes the machine more productive and lengthens its lifetime, as there is less jarring and vibration to its frame-mounted machine systems. There will also be less stress on the machine's frame if some independent movement is allowed between the machine's wheels or tracks and its frame. A wheel-type machine with no suspension must rely on the cushion its tires give as the machine travels over rough ground. See **FIGURE 38-7** for an example of an off-road suspension system.

As the name implies, suspension systems are intended to suspend some of the machine and allow relative movement

FIGURE 38-7 Most large off-road equipment uses suspension cylinders like these on a Terex rock truck.

between two or more main parts of the machine. This motion is mainly between the machine's axles or tracks and its frame, but can also be between two other parts of the machine, such as the tractor and scraper frames of a wheel tractor-scraper. Movement occurs when the machine travels over anything other than flat, hard ground and when the machine accelerates and brakes.

Suspension systems vary greatly depending on the type of machine they are on and what they are intended to do. They can be simple mechanical devices like springs or complex electrohydraulic systems that include ECMs and sensors.

A machine with a suspension system that isn't working properly will not likely be as productive as it should be, as the operator will likely slow down over rough terrain. It may also cause damage to other parts of the machine because of the extra shock loads placed on machine components. For this reason, it is important to understand how different types of suspension systems work, why they need to be maintained, and what may be required to diagnose problems and repair them.

▶ Off-Road Equipment Suspension Types

K38004

Many types of off-road equipment and machines do not require suspension systems, but instead rely on the flexibility of rubber tires to provide some cushioning. There are, however, several types of suspension systems that can be used on mobile equipment, especially if the machine has to travel long distances and/or at speed. Following are some of the most common suspensions that a heavy equipment technician may come across.

Springs

The simplest type of suspension system is one that uses springs. Older rock trucks and some small utility equipment manufactured today use springs to allow movement between the machine's frame and its drive axles or steering axles. The types of springs most commonly found on heavy equipment are leaf, coil, and rubber springs. They may or may not be combined with shock absorbers to control axle and wheel movement. The springs allow movement by flexing under compression, and the shock absorbers control the movement hydraulically.

Steel springs, leaf or coil, are made from a high alloy content spring steel that should meet the SAE 5160 specification that refers to the specific metal's composition. This alloy is formed into flat bars or wires (round bars) that then are formed into leaf or coil springs.

The load-carrying characteristics of coil and leaf springs are related to their **spring rate**, which is a measure of the ability of a spring to resist deflection. It is usually measured as the amount of force required to change the length of the spring 1 inch. Spring rate is governed by Hooke's law, which states that the amount a spring will compress or stretch is directly proportional to the force applied to the spring. In other words, a spring that has a rate of 500 pounds means it takes 500 pounds of force to change the spring's length 1 inch. Hooke's law refers to a spring with a fixed or linear spring rate. Springs can be designed with fixed (linear) or a variable rate. A spring with a linear spring rate will compress at the same predictable rate throughout its normal deflection. A variable rate spring will become increasingly hard to deflect as it is compressed.

Leaf Springs

Leaf springs can be formed from a single leaf or a stack of leaves held together to match the spring's capacity and rate to a particular application. The size of the spring and the number of leaves depends on the machine's weight and its payload capacity. A multi-leaf spring or leaf spring assembly has a main leaf that is formed into an eye at one or both ends. The single eye main leaf is then anchored to the machine's frame at the front end, and the opposite end is allowed to float on a pad. Lighter-duty spring assemblies have eyes on both ends, with one end being anchored and the opposite end being allowed to move because it is connected to the machine's frame through a **spring shackle**. This is necessary because as the spring deflects, its length changes. **FIGURE 38-8** depicts a machine that uses front leaf springs.

The spring eye(s) gives the spring a second function of locating the attached axle in relation to the machine's frame.

The main leaf has one or more shorter leafs stacked beneath it, and they are all held together with one long bolt. Each leaf is progressively shorter as they are stacked below the main leaf. Older multi-leaf springs, as shown in **FIGURE 38-9**, created considerable interleaf friction as they moved; newer styles of leaf springs tend to use fewer but thicker leafs so that there not as many are required. Fewer leafs mean less friction created between them, which can give a better ride. Some leaf springs use tapered leafs, as shown in **FIGURE 38-10**, to give a more progressive spring rate as the spring deflects.

Usually, band straps or U-bolts and brackets keep the multi-leafs aligned with the main leaf. They wrap around the spring assembly at the mid-points between the axle and the ends of the assembly.

Leaf springs are made with an arch that counteracts the weight of the machine and its payload. The arch gets straightened as the load is increased, and stops limit the amount of

FIGURE 38-8 This machine uses front leaf springs and a solid mount walking beam rear suspension.

FIGURE 38-9 Multi-leaf springs generate substantial interleaf friction while oscillating, leading to a rougher ride.

FIGURE 38-11 Axle lock cylinders.

FIGURE 38-10 A tapered leaf spring.

FIGURE 38-12 Large coil spring.

deflection in the spring assembly caused by the load or by the machine traveling over rough terrain. The amount of arch in a spring assembly is determined when the spring is manufactured and stays in the spring as a "memory." The spring may lose this memory over time, reducing the spring arch. The spring will then start to sag, and the axle stops will be contacted more easily.

The top of the axle housing will contact stops if the spring is fully compressed. Stops shouldn't normally make contact, but as the spring starts to sag, then it becomes easier to contact the stops.

All the leaves of the assembly are bolted together with a long bolt going through their center. This bolt then serves to locate the axle to the spring assembly. U-bolts fasten the axle to the spring assembly through brackets.

▶ TECHNICIAN TIP

Some heavy equipment machines that use leaf springs have a system to eliminate spring action when the machine is digging. In the case of rubber-tired excavators that travel at fairly high road speeds, the springs are needed to allow the axles to conform to road imperfections as the machine travels. However, when the machine is stationary and digging, spring action would be counterproductive. This machine has hydraulic cylinders that lock the axle in place and eliminate the springs from deflecting. See **FIGURE 38-11** for axle lock cylinders.

Coil Springs

Coil springs can be used to provide for movement between the machine's frame and axles and as with leaf springs these aren't used for suspension much anymore except for small equipment. Coil springs only provide tension to suspend the machine and its payload weight and don't help to locate the axle to the machine's frame unlike leaf springs. Some older small straight frame haul trucks used large coil springs in the front end. See **FIGURE 38-12** for an illustration of a heavy-duty coil spring.

In this case, the coil spring is located between the machine's frame and a pivoting trailing arm. In cases where they are used on machines for suspending drive axles, the axles will need links to keep the axle located relative to the frame but still allow it to move up and down.

Coil springs are formed from spring steel wire into spirals. As they are compressed, the wire twists and the resistance of it twisting give the spring its strength.

Coil spring capacity increases with an increase in the diameter of the coil, the diameter of the wire, the length of the coil, and the number of coils.

Walking Beam Suspension

Walking beam suspension systems use leaf springs or rubber springs to help cushion the load, or they can be solid mounted. A walking beam suspension is a unique style of suspension. The beam is connected to both axles of a tandem axle arrangement and attached to the frame of the machine by a trunnion at the center of the beam. The trunnion may be attached directly to the frame or indirectly through rubber or leaf springs. Walking beams have a series of linkages that hold the rear axles in place but also allows them to move in relation to the machine's frame. These linkages are called **torque rods** The suspension may also have a **panhard rod** or **transverse torque rod**. Torque rods control suspension movement fore and aft, and panhard rods control suspension movement from side to side.

As the machine encounters a bump, one axle goes over the bump first. As it does so, it pushes the end of the walking beam up, but because the beam is attached to the machine frame near its center, the effect of the bump on the machine is reduced by 50%. As the front of the beam moves up, the beam acts as a lever pivoting around the beam connection point of the rear axle, and the center of the beam only moves half the distance of the axle. This action reduces the shock to the machine. **FIGURE 38-13** shows a solid mount walking beam suspension arrangement used on a Gradall 4100.

Rubber springs can be used with walking beams suspensions. Rubber springs can be made of single blocks of rubber or several layers of rubber stacked together. Typical rubber springs have a fixed spring rate but using different layers or types of rubber in a stack or different shapes of rubber block can give the rubber spring a variable spring rate. Walking beam suspensions on articulated trucks typically use rubber springs. **FIGURE 38-14** shows examples of rubber spring used in suspension systems.

FIGURE 38-13 The lever action of the walking beam suspension reduces shock loads by 50%.

FIGURE 38-14 Several types of rubber springs are used in suspension systems.

Rubber springs can be very susceptible to chemical damage. Take care that no volatile solvents or lubricants come in contact with rubber springs, as this can cause the springs to fail.

Shock Absorbers

Some machines use shock absorbers to reduce the suspension oscillations created when they travel over rough ground. Shock absorbers are usually used in combination with springs to provide a dampening effect, and they are sometimes called dampers. If there weren't shock absorbers, the machine would move up and down in a series of slightly decreasing rebounds and slowly come back to rest. If a machine uses multi-leaf springs, sometimes the interleaf friction is sufficient to stop uncontrolled spring oscillation, but shocks are a more reliable oscillation damper. A cutaway of a typical shock absorber is seen in **FIGURE 38-15**.

A shock absorbers is a sealed and oil-filled device with a movable piston inside. The piston is connected to a rod that extends out of the barrel, past seals. The rod is fastened to the frame of the machine while the barrel is fastened to the axle or steering arm. The two parts of the machine are allowed to move in relation to each other and are limited to the maximum amount of travel by axle stops.

The piston on shock absorbers has one or more valves and/or orifices that allow the transfer of oil from one side of the piston to the other. This happens as the rod is pulled out or pushed into the barrel. As the oil moves through a restriction in the piston, it is slowed, and this action makes the suspension travel slow down.

▶ TECHNICIAN TIP

If you have ever driven on a multi-lane highway and noticed a vehicle with one wheel that moves up and down rapidly and uncontrollably, then you have seen a vehicle with a failed shock absorber. This is not only unsafe, as the wheel spends as much time in the air as it does on the road, but it is also very hard on suspension and/or drive axle components.

Heavy equipment machines that have one or more failed shock absorbers will experience the same problems as an automobile with a failed shock absorber.

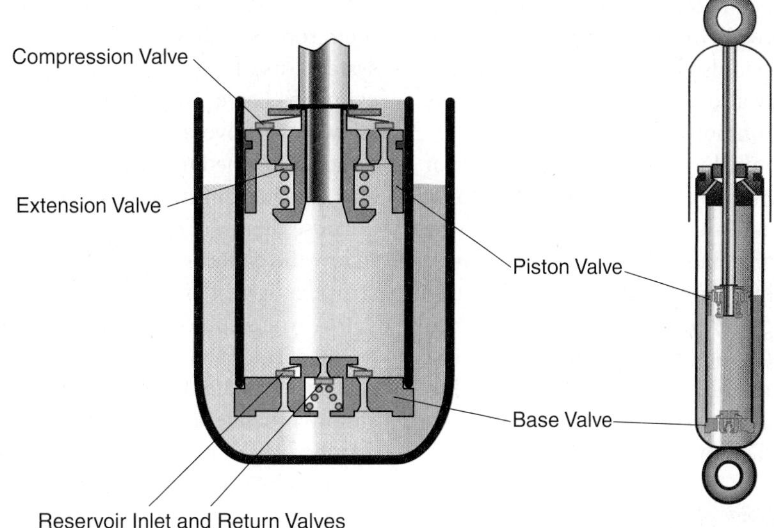

FIGURE 38-15 Shock absorber valves.

Oscillating Axles

All recently made wheel loaders have an oscillating rear axle, and all backhoe loaders have an oscillating front axle. The axle is mounted to the machine's main frame through a pivot at its center. This allows the axle to oscillate or tilt a few degrees either way from being parallel to the machine's frame. When the machine travels over uneven terrain, this helps to keep the machine level longer and keeps all the tires on the ground, where they can get traction and move the machine.

In the front axle of a backhoe, a raised portion of its housing machine is bored to provide for the installation of two plain bushings. The machine's frame has two crossmembers with holes machined into them. The axle is held to the frame by a pin that is held stationary to the crossmembers with a bolt. The bushings are drilled to accept grease fittings, and as grease is applied to them, it forms a lubricating barrier between the pin and bushings. Lip-type seals on both sides of each bushing assist in keeping grease in while keeping dirt out. The relative rotational movement between the bushings and pin is what allows the axle to pivot. The amount that it can pivot is limited by stops on the axle housing that contact the bottom of the machine's frame. **FIGURE 38-16** demonstrates how much the front axle of a tractor loader backhoe will oscillate.

FIGURE 38-16 Tractor loader backhoe front axle oscillating.

This oscillation makes the axle operate similar to a walking beam, but from side to side rather than front to back. However, the shock impact to the machine is lessened by 50% (until the axle contacts the stop) because of the lever action of the axle. This is the same as the lever principle used in walking beam suspensions mentioned previously.

Wheel loader rear axles pivot on trunnions that are mounted to the front and rear of the center axle housing. The front trunnion is a smooth machined surface that is on the outside of the pinion shaft housing. The rear trunnion is bolted to the main axle housing and also has a machined surface on its outer surface. Two trunnion supports (front and rear) are bolted to the machine's main frame. Each trunnion support is fastened to the bottom of each side of the main frame. In **FIGURE 38-17**, you can see how the trunnion is mounted to the frame.

FIGURE 38-17 Rear axle trunnion mounting.

The trunnion supports have plain bushings or sleeves that allow movement between the axle trunnion and the machine's frame. Grease fittings on each trunnion support allow grease to create a lubricating barrier between the trunnions and trunnion supports. The trunnion supports also have grease seals on each side of the bushing. There may also be a thrust plate that limits the fore and aft travel of the trunnions in the supports.

Rear axle oscillation is limited to a few degrees because of stops on the axle housing that contact the main frame. Some rubber-tired excavators feature an oscillating axle that can be locked in place to make the machine more stable when it is in digging mode. The grease fittings for these oscillating axles usually have hoses or tubes going to them to allow the operator to grease the bushings easily from a convenient location. Because of the high forces applied to them, the pins and trunnions have to be lubricated on a regular basis. Always check to find the correct greasing interval in the manufacturer's service information.

> **TECHNICIAN TIP**
>
> An important part of any service interval on a machine that has an oscillating axle is to ensure the pin and bushing for the axle pivot is getting greased regularly. Moist grease should be visible either around the pivot bushing or coming out of a grease relief valve. Another check on these machines is to examine the axle stops to see whether they are getting contacted frequently. This could be an indication that the machine is being abused.

Suspension Cylinders

Several types of machines use suspension cylinders to provide both a spring action and a damping function for the machine. One machine that uses them is the straight frame haul truck. It has one suspension cylinder at each corner of the machine to allow movement between the frame and the machine's axles, wheels, and tires. Suspension cylinders can also be used for articulated trucks, either for the front wheels only or for front and rear suspension of the truck. Another common term for this suspension component is "suspension strut" or just "strut."

There are two main types of suspension strut systems: active and passive. An active **strut** is part of the machine's main hydraulic system and has a remote accumulator. Passive struts are sealed units that contain gas and oil.

Passive Suspension Cylinder

Each passive suspension cylinder uses a combination of oil and gas to act as a spring and to provide a damping or shock absorber effect. Struts have three main parts: a barrel, a rod, and a piston. They are similar to a hydraulic cylinder or a shock absorber because the rod moves in and out of the barrel.

The gas inside the strut is precharged to a certain pressure, and when compressed under load by either suspension action or payload, it acts like a spring. The precharge pressure value usually extends the strut's rod a little more than halfway out of the barrel when the machine is empty. When the machine is loaded, the gas is compressed, and the rod is pushed into the barrel. Damping is needed to reduce the oscillations caused by the compression and expansion of the gas as the machine moves over rough ground.

In some machines, the front suspension cylinders uses their rod as a kingpin, similar to how conventional steering systems use kingpins as pivots for the steering knuckle. The cylinder's barrel is fixed to the machine's frame, and its rod is allowed to move in and out. These haul trucks have a steering knuckle attached to the rod of the suspension cylinder. The rod and knuckle can turn in the barrel of the cylinder for steering purposes, and the rod can also move in and out of the barrel to follow the contours of the haul road. See **FIGURE 38-18** to see a strut that is part of the steering system.

A wheel spindle is attached to the steering knuckle, as well as a steering arm that has a tie rod and steering cylinder to move it to rotate the rod. For most other applications, the strut simply provides a suspension function. The rod and barrel are attached to the machine with pins that go through self-aligning bearings held in the strut, and the ends of the pins are held to the machine's frame and axle or suspension component. These bearings have to be greased regularly because they take the weight of the machine and its payload.

Another manufacturer of haul trucks has the front suspension cylinder's rods attached to trailing arms that pivot on large tubes fastened to the bottom of the machine's frame just behind the front bumper. **FIGURE 38-19** shows a trailing arm suspension system.

The struts that are used with trailing arms suspend the machine weight between the trailing arm and the frame. For all types of suspension cylinders, the barrel is sealed at the rod

FIGURE 38-18 Strut with steering knuckle.

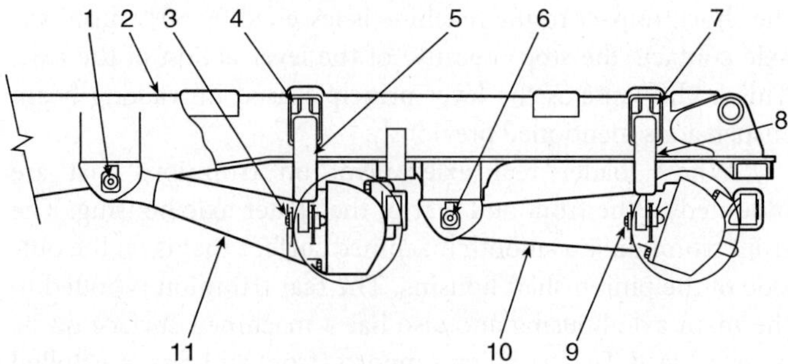

FIGURE 38-19 Trailing arm suspension.

to keep oil and gas in and dirt and other contamination out. A piston is fastened to the rod, and like a hydraulic cylinder, it has seals around its outer diameter to create a seal between the piston and the inside of the barrel. There could be as many as four seals, and they usually have backup rings to support them.

A cavity inside the rod is open to the head end of the cylinder. A check valve and orifices allow oil to move from the rod cavity to the opposite side of the piston. The nitrogen at the top of the piston gives a spring effect to the strut while the oil lubricates the moving rod and gives a damping effect. This will slow the movement of the rod and reduce the oscillations created by the gas spring effect as the machine travels over rough terrain.

The damping effect is accomplished with the check valve and orifices. Oil is forced to move from inside the rod to the top of the rod, either past the check valve or through the orifices. The way the rod is moving (in or out) determines which way the oil has to move and opens and closes the check valve. If the oil opens the check valve, it will flow freely past it to allow the rod to move quickly when the rod is moving into the barrel. If the oil reverses flow, it will close the check valve, forcing the oil to travel through the orifices in the rod, which slows the travel of the rod back out of the barrel. **FIGURE 38-20** demonstrates how oil moves in a passive strut.

The majority of suspension struts use **nitrogen** gas as a precharge and SAE transmission oil. Some manufacturers, however, use helium as a precharge gas. These struts also use a different type of fluid, called **neo-con**, which is a silicon-based fluid that is exclusive to Hitachi truck suspension cylinders.

Strut gas precharge is sometimes given as a fixed pressure, and other times based on the proper amount of extension of the strut rod. Total strut travel is usually only a few inches.

Active Struts

Active struts can use oil from an external source to extend or retract the rod. This is done to adjust the machine's ride height based on the load it is carrying. See **FIGURE 38-21** for a cross section of a typical active suspension cylinder or strut.

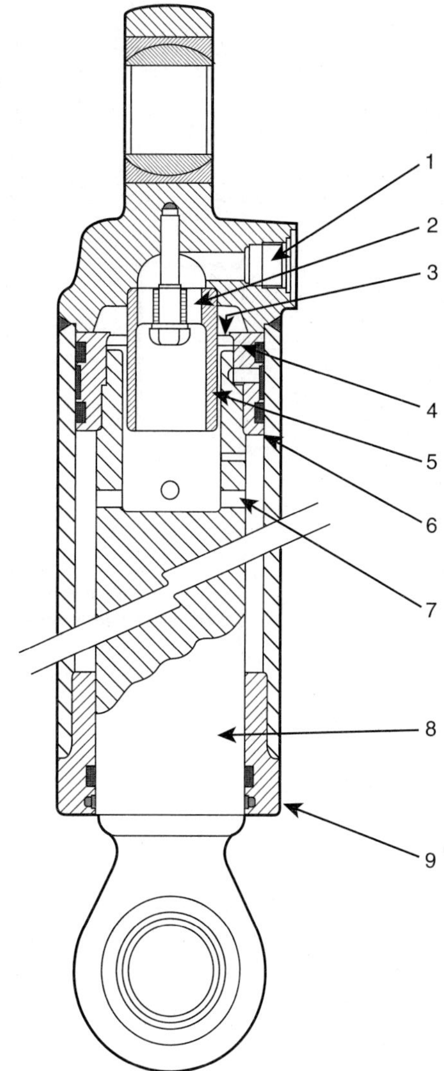

FIGURE 38-21 A typical suspension cylinder. (1) Inlet port. (2) Holes. (3) Holes. (4) Valve ring. (5) Damper. (6) Piston. (7) Holes. (8) Piston rod. (9) End cap.

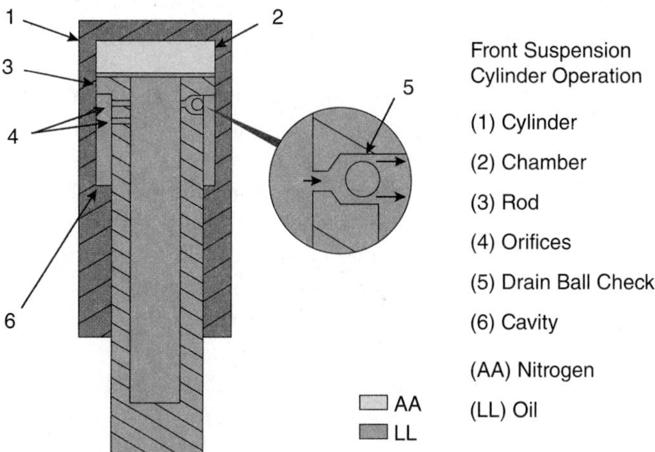

FIGURE 38-20 When the oil movement is slowed down, it performs a damping effect to reduce suspension oscillations.

A typical application is an articulated truck that has suspension cylinders for only the front suspension. Such a truck sometimes features a separate accumulator to give the strut a spring effect; otherwise, part of the strut has a nitrogen charge in it. A manifold with electronically actuated solenoids directs main pump oil into the bottom of the strut, and ride height sensors send a signal to the chassis ECM. The ECM then sends electrical signals to the solenoids, based on preprogrammed information, and attempts to keep the struts extended within a certain range. See **FIGURE 38-22** to see the schematic for an active suspension system.

Leveling Systems

Some machines such as telehandlers must be kept as level as possible. This is necessary if the machine is used for lifting materials in a safe manner. Hydraulic suspension cylinders are at each corner of these machines.

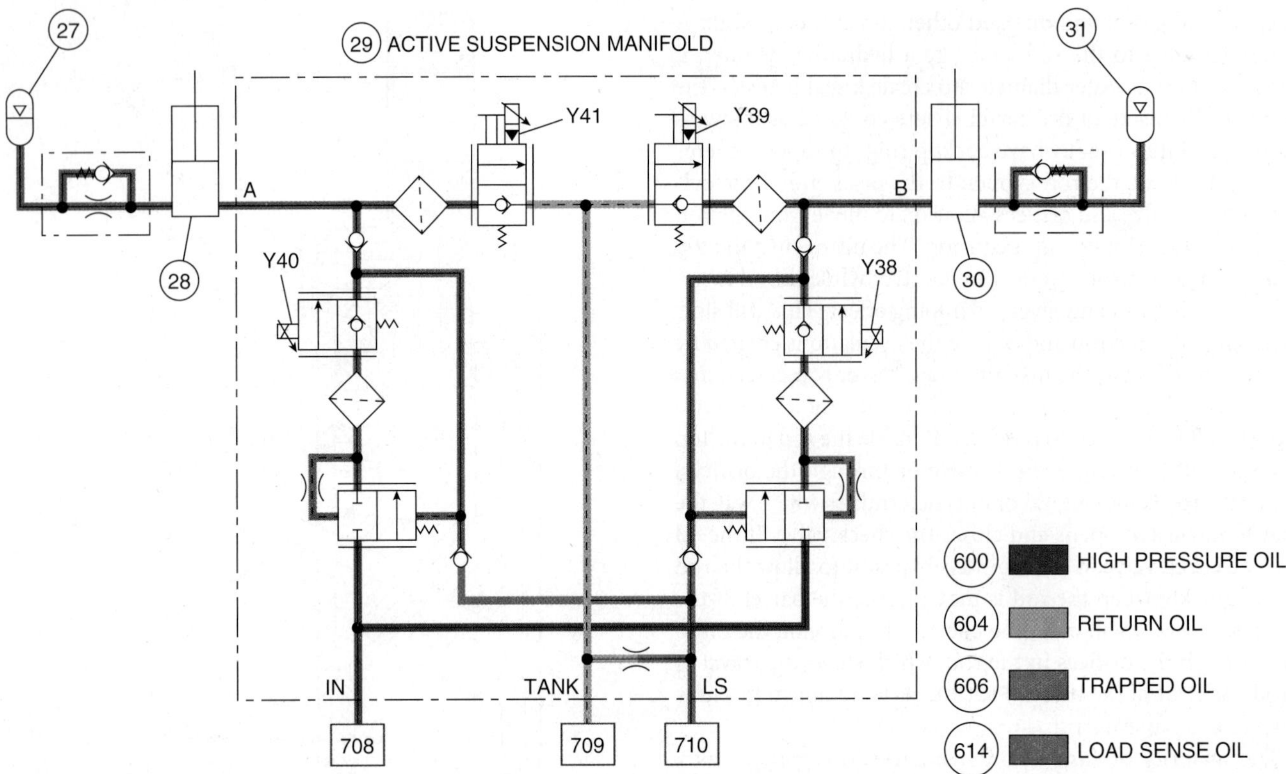

FIGURE 38-22 Schematic for active suspension.
Image Provided As Courtesy of John Deere.

An electronic control system adjusts the height of the struts to keep the machine level when lifting a load. The control system can change the rod extension for the suspension cylinders by adding or draining oil to the suspension cylinder as required.

Ride Control

A variation of a suspension system that has recently become popular is one called ride control, which is found on many machines with loader booms. This system allows the boom cylinder rods to move and give a cushion effect to the loader boom when the machine is traveling.

One or more accumulators are teed into the head end of the boom cylinder circuit. When ride control is actuated, the boom cylinder head end circuit oil is exposed to the bottom of the accumuluator's piston, with nitrogen gas on the other side. The nitrogen acts like a spring to allow the rod of the boom cylinder to move in and out freely as the gas is compressed.

As the machine travels over rough ground, the ride control system allows the loader boom to move up and down. For backhoe loaders that are traveling fast, either on jobsites or on public roads, this keeps the front tires on the road longer, which makes the machine safer to operate. It also gives the operator a much smoother ride, and for wheel loaders it saves a lot of jarring and shock loads throughout the machine.

Ride control must be disabled when the machine is digging; otherwise, the accumulator/s will not allow positive upward movement of the loader frame because the nitrogen gas will compress.

Some systems can have electronics incorporated into them to only allow ride control to be enabled if the machine is traveling over a certain speed.

Cushion Hitch

Wheel-type tractor/scraper machines (scrapers) can travel fast (up to 35 mph) with heavy loads and usually work on uneven ground. Scrapers have a suspension system to allow the two main parts of the machine to move independently of each other in order to reduce operator fatigue and machine damage. A pair of H-bar linkages allow vertical movement between the two main parts of the machine, and a hydropneumatic system controls this movement. **FIGURE 38-23** shows the cushion hitch arrangement for a scraper.

The main components of the system include a cushion hitch pump, control valve (leveling valve), load cylinder, and accumulator(s). The **load cylinder** looks like a typical double-acting hydraulic cylinder with a barrel, head, rod, piston, and seals. The barrel is fastened to the tractor part of the machine, and the rod is pinned to the scraper **gooseneck**, the protruding part of the scraper. The rod supports the front of the scraper section and moves in and out of the barrel to provide suspension between the two main parts of the machine.

The cushion hitch pump is driven by the transmission and uses the machine's main hydraulic system oil. Pump output is sent to the leveling valve that controls oil flow to the head end of the load cylinder.

To control the cushion system, newer scrapers have a switch in the cab that the operator uses to send an electrical signal to

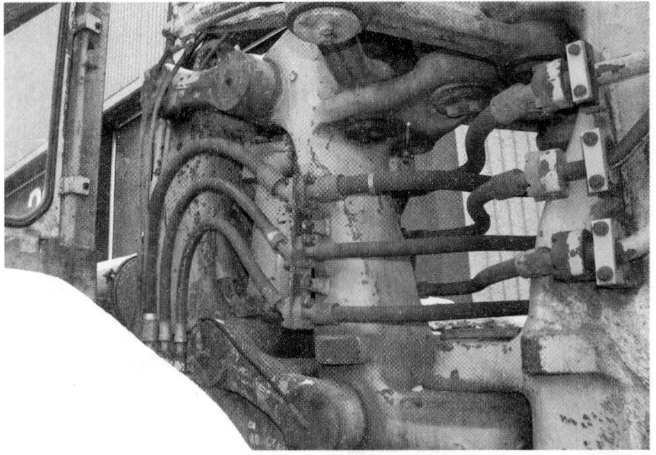

FIGURE 38-23 Cushion hitch for a scraper.

FIGURE 38-24 Leveling valve.

a solenoid on the leveling valve. When the switch is moved to actuate the cushion hitch system, the solenoid is energized, causing the spool to move in the leveling valve. This position of the spool sends pump oil to the bottom of the load cylinder and the bottom of the accumulator. Older scrapers used a pilot oil valve that was moved by the operator and sent oil to the leveling valve. The leveling valve is mounted on the cushion hitch assembly and is a single-circuit directional control valve.

When the machine is first started, the load cylinder piston is bottomed out in the load cylinder. When the machine is running and the operator wants the cushion hitch to provide suspension, the operator shifts the leveling valve spool either by electric control or by a remote pilot valve in the cab. When the spool shifts, pump oil is directed to the head end of the load cylinder, and it pushes the rod out the load cylinder. A leveling system shifts the valve back to neutral when the load cylinder rod is extended approximately halfway through its travel. At this point, pump oil flow is diverted to the tank, and the head end of the cylinder is opened to the oil end of the cushion hitch accumulator. Now, when the machine is traveling and runs over some rough ground, the accumulator acts like a spring because its precharged gas compresses to allow its piston to move, which in turn allows the load cylinder rod to move in and out.

The oil is free to flow between the accumulator and load cylinder but is slowed down by an orifice. The orifice gives a damping effect to slow down the cushion hitch oscillations.

The **leveling valve** has a leaf spring assembly attached to the leveling valve spool at one end and to the scraper part of the cushion hitch frame at the other end. As the scraper part of the machine is raised, because of the load cylinder rod extending, the tension of the leaf spring changes. The point at which the change of tension shifts the valve spool occurs when the pump oil flow stops raising the load cylinder and opens the accumulator to the cylinder. Now, as the machine travels over rough ground, the leveling valve tries to maintain a specific ride height between the tractor and scraper. After the machine is loaded, the extra weight of the load is automatically compensated for by the leveling valve because it allows more oil into the head end of the circuit before the valve is shifted back to neutral. As the load is dumped, the load cylinder rod extends because of the reduced weight, but the leaf spring shifts the leveling valve and drains some oil from under the load cylinder piston. This maintains a rod extension that allows the load cylinder to provide a cushion between the main frame sections because of the accumulator action. **FIGURE 38-24** illustrates a leveling valve.

When the machine is getting loaded, the load cylinder must be locked down to prevent movement between the tractor and scraper. The leveling valve will create a hydraulic lock on the rod side of the cylinder's piston to keep the rod retracted for this part of machine operation.

Although loading only occurs at low speed, the forces involved in loading the bowl means the rod would get full extended if it wasn't locked down. This could damage the load cylinder. The control valve creates a hydraulic lock on top of the load cylinder piston.

One or two accumulators could be used for these cushion hitch systems, and they are precharged with nitrogen gas to a specific pressure. **FIGURE 38-25** illustrates the accumulator for a cushion hitch.

FIGURE 38-25 Cushion hitch accumulator.

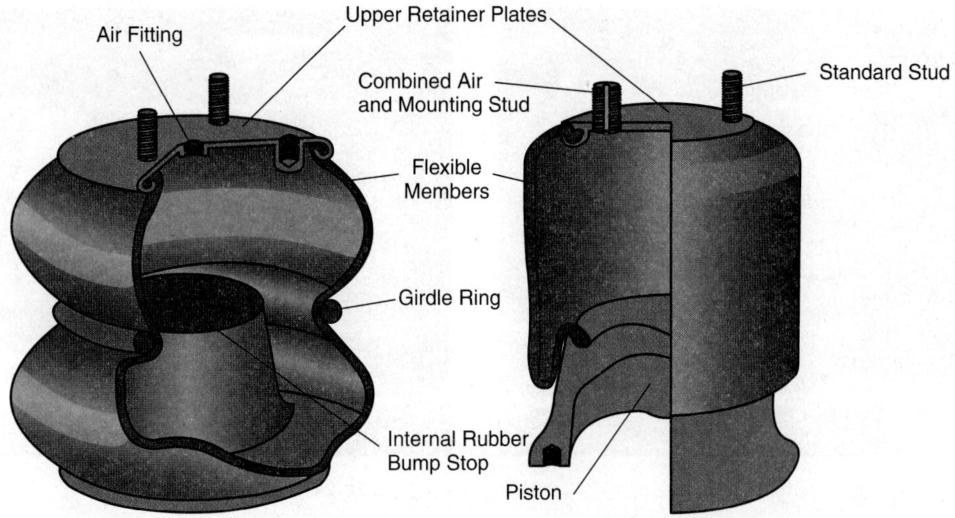

FIGURE 38-26 Two types of air bags are generally used: the convoluted bellows type (left) and the rolling lobe type (right).

Air Bags

Some lighter-duty machines and over-the-road cranes use air bags for suspension. The machine's pneumatic system fills a reinforced rubber bag with air, up to a certain pressure, which pressure is determined by a leveling valve that is mounted to the machine's frame. The valve has an arm with linkage going to the axle the air bags are attached to. When the air bags fill, the frame rises from the axle, and the leveling valve arm moves to stop the air supply to the bags, which in turn limits air pressure to the bags. In some machines, the cab is suspended on air bags. Air bags are usually either a rolling lobe design or a convoluted bellows design; both types are depicted in **FIGURE 38-26**.

Electronic Controls for Suspension Systems

Some machine suspension systems incorporate an electronic control system, which allows the operator to adjust or change modes of suspension. It also allows the technician to carry out some diagnostic functions. The system can also be part of the machine's CANbus network and can integrate suspension operation with other machine systems.

Payload Scale

An added benefit of some machines with hydropneumatic suspension systems is that an electronic scale can be incorporated into the system. The most common use for this is with haul trucks used for mining operations.

All that is required is for a pressure sensor (transducer) to be added to each suspension strut, and the signal from these sensors is then sent to an ECM. Once the system has been calibrated to zero with an empty box and then with a known weight, it can accurately measure the payload of a truck. The weight that accumulates in the truck as the truck is loaded is displayed to the loader operator by an LED readout. The display should be monitored to prevent overloading the truck. The ECM can also record all loads and total weights for each shift. **FIGURE 38-27** shows a payload scale display.

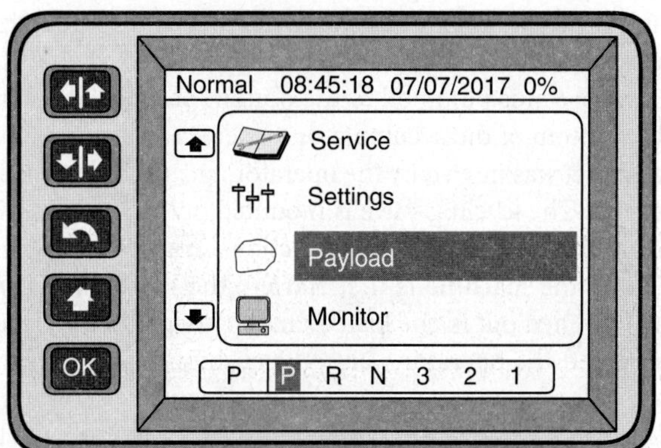

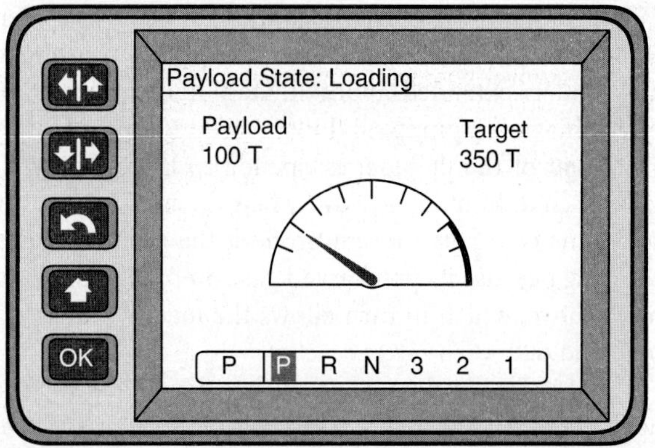

FIGURE 38-27 Payload scale.

▶ Track Machine Suspension Systems Track Roller Bogie Systems

K38005

Some track-type dozers feature a bogie suspension system that uses rubber blocks and pivoting track roller assemblies to allow the machine's undercarriage to conform to uneven terrain. This

FIGURE 38-28 Bogie suspension system.

FIGURE 38-29 Equalizer bar.

not only provides a smoother ride for the operator but also reduces the shockload on the track rollers and the rest of the machine. In most other large track drive machines, the track rollers are mounted directly to the track frame so that any shock caused by the machine traveling over uneven ground is transferred directly to the machine's frame. **FIGURE 38-28** depicts a track machine with a bogie suspension system.

Larger high-drive track dozers use this system and have a pair of bottom rollers mounted to a bracket that can swivel on pins at one end of a large bracket. The large bracket pivots on a pin at one end that is held in the track frame. The top of the opposite end of the large bracket rests on a rubber block that is held to the bottom side of the track roller frame. The compression of the rubber block, as well as the pivoting of the roller assembly small bracket, provides some suspension as the machine is traveling.

Some smaller (100 Hp and under) track loader machines feature rollers that are suspended on springs to give a smoother ride.

Equalizer Bar

Most track machines have a basic form of suspension that allows the track frames to pivot a few degrees. Looking at the side of a track machine, the front idler can be seen to move up and down slightly in order to keep the track engaged longer with the ground. This system can be used for track loaders and dozers.

In some machines that don't feature high-drive track arrangements, the track frames pivot on a shaft that extends out from the main frame. Older, low-drive machines may have that pivot at two points at the rear of the machine. One is a large bearing that extends from the final drive, and the other is a shaft at the rear bottom center of the machine.

These machines also use an equalizer bar that extends across the frame under the engine and pivots in the center on a pin. Each end of the equalizer bar rests on a pocket in each track frame. This is where the weight of part of the machine is transferred to the track frames.

The equalizer bar limits the maximum up and down movement of the track frames, and when one side moves up, it makes the other side tilt down an equal degree. An example is a large track loader that allows for a maximum of 6 inches of up and down travel at the idler. The travel is limited by stops on the equalizer bar that contact the bottom of the main frame.

The center pivot for equalizer bars is a plain or self-aligning bearing that has to be greased regularly. **FIGURE 38-29** shows an equalizer bar.

Pivot shafts support the track frame on large plain bushings that are usually lubricated with gear oil. This oil may have its own separate reservoir and has to be checked regularly. Seals keep the oil in place, and if these seals leak, causing a loss of oil, an expensive and time-intensive repair will follow.

▶ Diagnosing Suspension Systems

S38002

Operator complaints that stem from suspension system faults include the following:

- The machine is rough riding.
- The machine is not level.
- The machine continues to bounce after it hits a bump.
- There are noises when the machine travels over rough ground.

A thorough visual inspection of all suspension components will reveal the cause of many problems. All components should be fastened securely to the machine's frame or other components. Any loose suspension component should be repaired immediately.

Because suspension system operation requires moving parts, lubrication must be applied regularly to allow free movement and to keep wear to a minimum. Look for any signs of dry joints that should have grease.

If a machine with a suspension system is not sitting level on level ground when unloaded, you can make a few simple checks, based on the type of its system. A rubber-tired machine should first be checked to see whether it is equipped with the proper size of tires; then look for broken springs or leaking suspension cylinders. Also look for dry pivot joints that should have grease in them.

Fault codes related to the malfunction may be set in an electronically controlled suspension system. This is a good place to start if there is a complaint related to the suspension system.

SAFETY TIP

When working on a machine's main frame and suspension system, you have to pay attention to safety-related concerns such as the ones following:

- Be aware of all hazards related to cutting and welding on machine frames, such as the buildup of pressure in closed vessels.
- Be aware of the potential for uncontrolled machine and/or component movement when working on frame and suspension systems. Use proper lifting and blocking procedures.
- Be sure not to mix different types of gases when filling suspension cylinders or accumulators.
- Make sure any stored energy in accumulators is released before opening a system they are part of.
- Make sure spring tension is released slowly and in a controlled manner.
- Use proper lifting and blocking equipment and procedures.
- Some suspension systems use high-pressure gas and/or fluid. Be aware of the safety concerns related to working with these high-pressure systems.

▶ Servicing Suspension Systems

S38003

Regular lubrication of many suspension components is necessary because of their many moving parts, including torque rod ends, strut mounts, and leaf spring shackle bushings. Always check with the machine manufacturer's service information for the correct type of lubrication to use and the proper frequency of greasing intervals. In many machines, automatic greasing systems are installed, which must be checked to ensure grease is getting to all the places where it should. If the machine does not have an automatic greasing system, it will be equipped with remote grease lines to feed lubricant to hard-to-reach components. **FIGURE 38-30** illustrates a remote grease line.

FIGURE 38-30 Remote grease lines on a machine.

Some track machines may have pivot oil reservoirs that are often overlooked. Be sure to check the oil level in the reservoir.

Strut Recharge Procedure

A common service and/or repair procedure performed on suspension systems is a strut recharge. This is necessary when the nitrogen precharge inside the strut has leaked down. If a strut has a low charge, it will cause the machine to ride unevenly and could lead to the strut bottoming out when traveling over rough ground. If there are signs of oil leakage from a strut, it will have to be removed and resealed, at a minimum, and may have more damage, such as a scored barrel or piston, which would require machining or parts replacement. To recharge a strut follow the procedure in **SKILL DRILL 38-2**.

SKILL DRILL 38-2 Suspension Strut Servicing

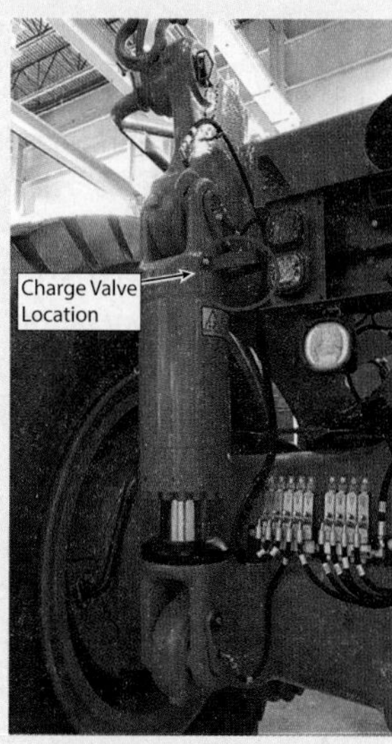

1. First, measure the rod extension of a strut. Before doing this, the unloaded machine must be allowed to coast to a stop on firm, level ground. This ensures an accurate reading. Some machines require special tooling to measure the rod extension, and the proper dimension can be found in the machine's service information. Follow all Lock out Tag out and wheel chocking procedures that are required.
2. If the measured dimensions are correct and there are no visual leaks or damage, nothing else has to be done unless there is an operational complaint. If so, this will require further troubleshooting.
3. The technician may be able to purge the old oil from some struts. This could be part of a regular service procedure, as the oil is under a great deal of stress inside the strut and will eventually break down.
4. The nitrogen gas charge in a strut has to be at a specified pressure for the strut to work properly and for the machine to have the proper ride height. Always refer to the machine's service information to find the correct precharge pressure.

SKILL DRILL 38-2 Suspension Strut Servicing (Continued)

5. An accumulator charging kit is the special tooling needed for a strut recharge. If the oil level has to be adjusted or the oil has to be purged, then additional oil pumping tooling is also required. Some procedures suggest using the machine's brake system to purge the oil; extra fittings and hoses are needed for this.
6. For most machines, this procedure requires both struts on one end to be charged at the same time providing the struts on the other end of the machine are charged properly. The tooling to do this will tee together both struts into one valve assembly that is fed the gas precharge from a that is fastened to a gas bottle. Pressure from the bottle is regulated to around 400 psi and a gate valve can be opened to allow gas to flow into the struts.
7. Drain the struts of their precharge gas. The strut charging tooling is fastened to the struts charging valves and the precharge pressure is bled out through the tee before the gas line is attached. This should fully retract the rods of the struts. A measurement from the top and bottom mounting pin of both cylinders will confirm this.
8. Next step is to charge the struts. The gate valve is opened and when both struts reach the specified extension height the valve is closed and the tooling is removed. The machine should then be sent to work, loaded through a normal work cycle and then return to have the strut extension measured. Another charge pressure adjustment may be required at this point.
9. Oil viscosity is an important consideration when servicing struts since the damping effect is dependent on oil flowing through orifices. Having the wrong viscosity oil in a strut will make the strut rod to move in and out either too fast or too slow. Make sure the specified viscosity and oil type is used for the strut oil. This is usually 10W.

Repairing Suspensions Systems

Suspension systems will need repairs as their components wear past acceptable limits. Components that need oil and gas sealed in them may need to be resealed on occasion if they start to leak either internally or externally. Caution needs to be taken when disassembling struts since there may still be pressurized oil and/or gas in them.

Suspension system components that need to be greased regularly will need to be repaired if they run dry and have normal wear accelerated. Most repairs to greaseable suspension components are fairly straightforward procedures.

Checking and repairing walking beam type suspensions is a fairly simple procedure to inspect and test walking beam suspension follow the steps in **SKILL DILL 38-3**.

SKILL DRILL 38-3 Inspecting Rear Beam Suspension Components

1. Locate and follow the appropriate procedure in the service manual.
2. Complete the accompanying job sheet or work order with all pertinent information.
3. Remove all grease and dirt from suspension area using a high pressure washer.
4. Identify whether suspension is spring type (a) or rubber cushion type (b), then follow the corresponding instructions below.
   a. If the suspension is a spring type, inspect the spring hanger, forward spring hanger pin, and spring eye bushings for excessive wear or damaged parts.
   b. If the suspension is a rubber cushion type, visually inspect the rubber pads or cushions for cuts or damage.

   Note: The load cushions are made of butyl and natural rubber and are not resistant to petroleum products. If the cushions become saturated with these products, they will split and disintegrate.
5. On rubber spring suspensions with frame mounted drive pins, check all the frame hangers for cracks, paying particular attention to the drive pin hangers. These will usually appear between bolt holes or from a bolt hole to the edge of the hanger bracket as shown.
6. Check carefully for signs of rust emanating from the rubber spring mounting area or from the drive pins and bushings. Rust streaks can indicate cracks or movement between components.
7. Using a jack, raise the frame slightly. If the drive pin or hanger bracket is cracked through, it will separate and it can be easily detected during this check.

   Note: Issues with any of the items checked in steps 4–7 will require hanger replacement.
8. Inspect equalizer beam for cracks, gouges, or other damage.
9. With the vehicle loaded, check the equalizing beam rubber end bushings. The bushings are under compression on the top side. The bottom of the rubber is relaxed, so the ends of the rubber will show a gap in the mounting bracket. This is normal.
10. Check the bushings for wear by placing a small jack under the beam end. Place a soft material between the beam and the jack to protect the beam from scratches. Try to raise the beam. If the inner sleeve of the bushing moves, the bushing must be replaced. Remember that the bushing is rubber mounted. Compression of the rubber is expected, but the inner sleeve should not move. Check rubber center bushings by placing a jack under the saddle cap of the beam. If the saddle raises 1/8" (3.1 mm) before the beam is raised, the bushing is worn and must be replaced.
11. Check torque on all attaching hardware according to manufacturer's recommendations.
12. List the test results and recommendations on the job sheet or work order, clean the work area, and return tools and materials to their proper storage.

Wrap-Up

Ready for Review

- Safety-related concerns when working with machine frames and suspension systems include using proper equipment and procedures for torch cutting on sealed vessels, lifting and blocking equipment, and bleeding accumulator pressures before disassembly. High-pressure oil could also be present and must be handled with care.
- Machine frames are the backbone of the machine, and all machine systems are mounted to it. The frame must be strong enough to withstand the extreme forces that will be applied to it.
- Frames are constructed from welded-together plate steel and cast steel sections.
- Frames will likely fail at one of the welds if the frame is pushed past design limits or the weld is defective.
- Articulated machines have two-piece frames, and excavators have an upper and lower frame held together with a rotex bearing.
- Frame inspection should be part of regular maintenance, and focus should be concentrated on welds and threaded holes.
- Frames can be repaired and reinforced to prevent recurring failures. Frames should always be covered with paint to prevent rust.
- Any welding repairs should not create stress risers by angling and curving reinforcements.
- Suspension systems allow movement between a machines frame and its drivetrain. This gives the operator a smoother ride and keeps the tires or tracks engaged with the ground longer.
- Some older and/or small machines will use springs for suspension. Springs can be leaf type, coil type, or rubber.
- Leaf-type springs are stacked up in shortening multiples and held stationary at one end. The other end pivots in a shackle, and an axle is held to the spring assemblies' center with U-bolts.
- Coil springs can be for axle suspension but the axle needs to have links to keep it in place.
- A sprung axle usually has a set of two shock absorbers mounted to it. The other end will be mounted to the frame. Shock absorbers use a hydraulic piston, oil, and an orifice to reduce spring oscillations.
- Front axles on backhoe loaders and rear axles on wheel loaders oscillate. This is a simple type of suspension that allows the axle to pivot a few degrees on a center pin or bolt on trunnions. These moving parts need regular greasing.
- Suspension cylinders act like springs and shock absorbers and are mostly found on trucks to give a smooth ride and allow the machine to travel fast over rough ground.
- Most suspension cylinders use nitrogen gas for the spring effect and hydraulic oil for the damping action. They must be precharged to a certain pressure or to make the rod extend a certain length.
- Oil can be fed into or drained out of active suspension cylinders to change ride height or level the machine.
- Ride control is a form of suspension for backhoe loaders and wheel loaders that introduces an accumulator to the head end of the boom circuit. This gives a spring action to the boom when the machine is traveling fast and/or over rough ground.
- Scrapers have cushion hitches that allow some movement between the tractor section and the scraper section of the machine. A load cylinder and linkage allows movement between the frame sections, and an accumulator provides spring action.
- Walking beam suspension can be found on the rear tandem axles of articulated rock trucks and allows a few degrees of oscillation between all four wheels. Travel is cushioned with rubber blocks, and axles are located with torque rods.
- Payload scale systems can use suspension components to translate pressures into payload weights.
- Track-type machines may have suspension systems to increase operator comfort. Equalizer bars allow track frames to pivot a few degrees, and track rollers may have a bogie system to allow them to follow the underfoot profile.
- Operator complaints related to machine frames and suspension systems include rough ride, noises, excessive oscillation, machine not level.
- Diagnostic procedures start with knowing the system and a thorough visual inspection.
- Most suspension components that allow movement require regular greasing.
- Adjustments could be made to accumulator or strut precharge pressures. This requires a charging kit that includes special tools.

Key Terms

gooseneck The protruding part of the scraper.

leveling valve A valve that controls suspension height.

load cylinder A typical double-acting hydraulic cylinder with a barrel, head, rod, piston, and seals.

neo-con A special fluid used in Hitachi suspension struts.

nitrogen An inert gas used in struts.

panhard rod Controls suspension movement fore and aft; also known as a transverse torque rod.

spring rate The amount a spring will deflect when loaded.

spring shackle A movable connection for a leaf spring, allowing length changes.

stress riser A point of stress concentration.

strut A cylinder charged with gas and oil used in suspensions.

torque rod A rod that is used to position an axle fore and aft.

transverse torque rod Controls suspension movement from side to side.

Review Questions

1. Why should you use extreme caution when servicing suspension cylinders?
   a. Because they get extremely hot
   b. Because they can contain high pressures
   c. Because they contain extreme vacuum
   d. Because they are extremely expensive
2. A payload system uses what type of information obtained from suspension cylinders to provide a payload reading to the operator?
   a. Height
   b. Weight
   c. Temperature
   d. Pressure
3. A cushion hitch suspension system has a leveling valve that does which of the following?
   a. Keeps the suspension cylinders level
   b. Diverts pump flow away from the load cylinder when the proper rod extension is reached
   c. Diverts pump flow to the nitrogen side of the accumulator when the proper precharge is reached
   d. Charges the accumulator to the proper pressure to achieve the proper load cylinder rod extension
4. A machine that is equipped with ride control allows this component to move up and down to provide a suspension effect:
   a. Loader boom
   b. Ripper
   c. Bucket
   d. Cab
5. Ride control should only be activated on a machine under which of the following conditions?
   a. It is reversing.
   b. It is digging from a bank.
   c. It is leveling rough ground.
   d. It is traveling fast.
6. A machine with front leaf springs also has which of the following?
   a. Suspension cylinders
   b. Coil springs
   c. Rubber blocks
   d. Spring shackles
7. The term "spring rate" refers to which of the following?
   a. The price per pound that a spring costs
   b. The amount of stretch a spring provides
   c. The amount of force needed to deflect a spring a certain distance
   d. The amount of distance a spring will deflect when a certain weight is applied
8. Oscillating axles are most commonly found on which types of machines?
   a. Wheel loaders and backhoe loaders
   b. Scrapers and track loaders
   c. Haul trucks and drills
   d. Excavators and dozers
9. Which of the following are the two types of gases used in suspension cylinders?
   a. Helium or oxygen
   b. Helium or nitrogen
   c. Nitrogen or acetylene
   d. Butane or propane
10. Which of the following provides a damping effect in a suspension cylinder?
    a. Nitrogen gas
    b. Helium gas
    c. Orifice
    d. Seals

ASE Technician A/Technician B Style Questions

1. Technician A says that all multi-leaf spring packs are variable rate. Technician B says that taper leaf springs are variable rate. Who is correct?
   a. Technician A
   b. Technician B
   c. Both A and B
   d. Neither A nor B
2. Technician A says a shock absorber is effective in minimizing suspension oscillation. Technician B says interleaf friction in leaf springs is not effective in minimizing suspension oscillation. Who is correct?
   a. Technician A
   b. Technician B
   c. Both A and B
   d. Neither A nor B
3. Tech A says that most frame fatigue cracks are caused by overloading the frame. Tech B says that cracks often occur at a section change, where the frame becomes less flexible. Who is correct?
   a. Technician A
   b. Technician B
   c. Both A and B
   d. Neither A nor B
4. Tech A says that actual frame rail strength can be calculated by multiplying the section modulus by the yield strength. Tech B says that to determine actual rail strength, the RBM is multiplied by the section modulus. Who is correct?
   a. Technician A
   b. Technician B
   c. Both A and B
   d. Neither A nor B
5. Technician A says that an incorrectly installed reinforcement can cause a stress riser for a frame. Technician B

says that stress risers can occur anywhere there is a section change. Who is correct?

a. Technician A
b. Technician B
c. Both A and B
d. Neither A nor B

6. Technician A says that when weld repairing a crack, you must grind out the crack until there is no visible rust left. Technician B says that you must completely remove all trace of the crack before welding. Who is correct?

a. Technician A
b. Technician B
c. Both A and B
d. Neither A nor B

7. Technician A says that when reinforcing a frame after a weld repair, the reinforcement material should be made from the highest quality heat-treated steel. Technician B says that the material should be the same as the original material. Who is correct?

a. Technician A
b. Technician B
c. Both A and B
d. Neither A nor B

8. Technician A says that a frame reinforcement should be angled as much as possible to avoid a stress concentration. Technician B says that a weld repair should have the weld toe ground to relieve stress. Who is correct?

a. Technician A
b. Technician B
c. Both A and B
d. Neither A nor B

9. Technician A says that all walking beam suspensions use rubber springs. Technician B says that walking beam suspensions reduce shock load to the machine, using the lever principle. Who is correct?

a. Technician A
b. Technician B
c. Both A and B
d. Neither A nor B

10. Technician A says that active strut suspension systems have a leveling system to maintain ride height. Technician B says that active strut systems can be equipped with a payload scale. Who is correct?

a. Technician A
b. Technician B
c. Both A and B
d. Neither A nor B

CHAPTER 39

Conventional Steering Systems

Knowledge Objectives

After reading this chapter, you will be able to:

- **K39001** Describe the different types of steering systems used for wheeled machines.
- **K39002** Describe the purpose, construction, applications, and operation of manual steering gears.

Skills Objectives

After reading this chapter, you will be able to:

- **S39001** Perform troubleshooting, diagnosis, and repair of power steering system.

▶ Introduction

Although the concept of controlling vehicle direction by turning a steering wheel is familiar to every vehicle operator, steering is a "life and limb" system that has significant consequences for safety. The responsibility of technicians to choose safe work practices is needed not only to protect the operator and vehicle but others as well. To assume these responsibilities properly, technicians need to be knowledgeable about the purpose, construction, and operation of the components of various types of steering systems. Equipped with this knowledge, technicians can properly choose the correct service practices and tools when performing inspection, maintenance, or repairs on steering systems.

SAFETY TIP

Some machines can travel up to 40 mph, with enormous payloads, and will be near other machines and people. They may even travel on public roads to go between jobsites. Safe machine operation relies on a properly operating steering system as a steering system failure could have deadly results for the operator and others.

The technician working on a machine's steering system must be familiar with the system before performing any service or repairs and must always confirm that the system operates properly before the machine is put back into service.

Whenever you are working on an articulated machine and are near the pivot point, the steering lock must be in place to prevent the machine from turning. You should also use wheel chocks to prevent the machine from rolling. **FIGURE 39-1** shows a technician installing a steering lock.

Heavy equipment machines are grouped into two general categories, depending on how they are propelled: tracks or tires. There are different ways to steer the two types of machine. Machines that travel on wheels can change direction or steer in one of four different ways:

- Skid steering (the wheels do not pivot)
- Articulated steering
- Conventional steering
- All-wheel steering

This chapter discusses how articulated, conventional, and all-wheel systems steer machines. Most machines that are steered with conventional steering systems have a one-piece frame (straight frame); articulated graders are the exception to this.

Conventional steering systems have many similarities to heavy-duty automotive steering system principles. A few light-duty machines, backhoe loaders, and straight frame haul trucks have components and principles that are similar to heavy-duty automotive steering systems.

In **conventional steering** systems, also known as standard steering systems, both front wheels pivot left and right to guide the front of the machine in the direction the operator wishes. As the steering angle increases to provide a smaller turning radius, the left and right wheels turn at different angles because the inside wheel turns through a smaller radius than the outside wheel. **FIGURE 39-2** shows conventional steering during cornering.

Some older straight frame wheel loaders and many current forklifts use a non-steering drive axle at the front and a steering axle at their rear to make a rear-wheel conventional steer system. **FIGURE 39-3** shows a machine with a rear steering axle.

Some other types of straight frame machines use **all-wheel steer** systems, which means they have front and rear steerable axles. Examples include telehandlers, forklifts, and rough terrain cranes. Some large cranes that have multi-axle arrangements have two or more axles at each end of the machine that are steer axles. **FIGURE 39-4** shows a crane with many steering axles.

Articulated steering machines have a two-piece frame and a steering system that makes the two-piece frame pivot on a center hinge pin arrangement. This pivoting action enables the machine to turn in the direction that it pivots, and the greater the pivot angle, the smaller turning radius it travels through. **FIGURE 39-5** shows the turning radius of an articulated machine.

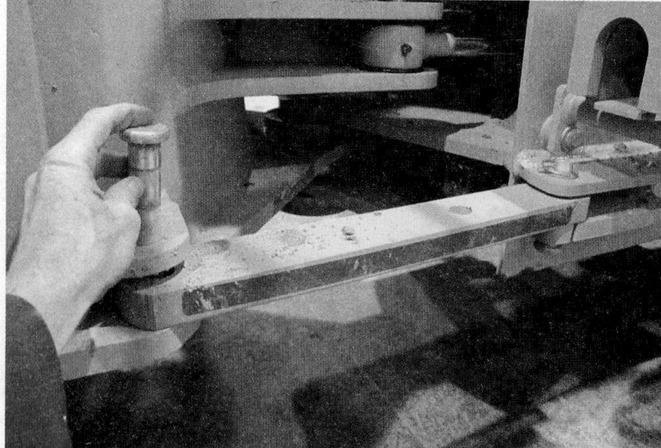

FIGURE 39-1 Steering locks positively prevent the machine from articulating.

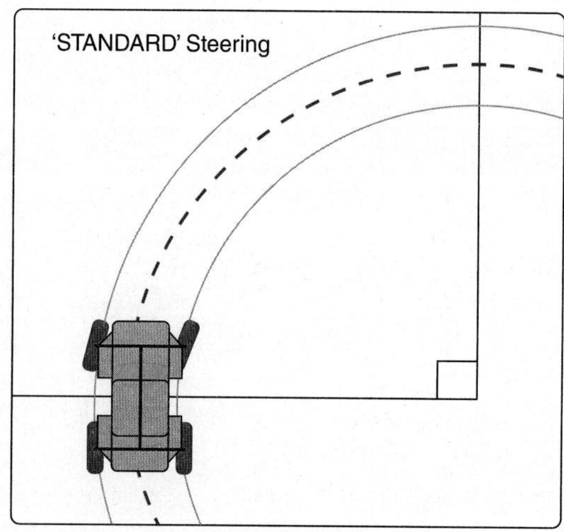

FIGURE 39-2 Conventional steering during cornering.

FIGURE 39-3 Fork lifts like this one use rear steering.

FIGURE 39-4 Crane with multiple steering axles.

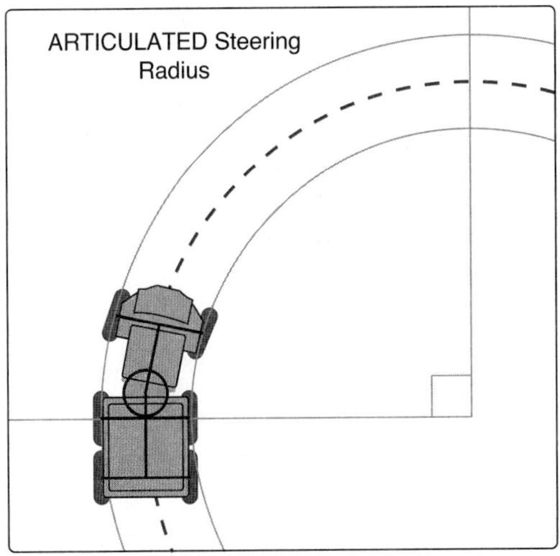

FIGURE 39-5 Turning radius of an articulated machine.

Both types of steering systems (conventional and articulated) have some similar control section components, and except for very small machines that use all mechanical systems or boosted mechanical systems, they are operated by hydraulic systems.

The greatest stress on a machine's steering system is when the machine is loaded; it is stationary; brakes are applied; and it sits on soft terrain. Once the machine starts to move, or once it is on a hard surface or is unloaded, the energy required to steer the machine is greatly reduced. Many steering complaints result from problems associated with the system being under load.

Tires for heavy equipment are very expensive, and improper steering geometry shortens their life. Worn or improperly adjusted components cause this, which results in the scrubbing of tires and grinding rubber off their treads.

It is important for an HDET to have a good understanding of machine steering systems. In the remainder of this chapter, we discuss different types of steering systems for wheel-type machines in more detail.

▶ Types of Conventional Steering Systems

K39001

The primary purpose of any steering system is to allow the driver to guide the machine's direction. Mechanical steering is the collection of components, linkages that allow the machine to follow the desired course. Hydraulic steering is also called power steering because it provides additional power to assist the driver of the machine to steer by directing power to swiveling the steered road wheels about their steering axes.

Mechanical Steering Systems

Only very small or very old small machines use mechanical steering systems, but a brief look at their operation and components is a good starting point for the other more common steering systems of today. A machine with this type of steering system uses mechanical components to transfer operator input to pivoting the wheels that turn the machine. The most conventional steering arrangement is to turn the front wheels using a hand-operated steering wheel positioned in front of the driver, via the steering column, which may contain universal joints that allow it to deviate somewhat from a straight line. Tracked vehicles such as bulldozers use differential steering where the tracks are made to move at different speeds or even in opposite directions, using clutches and brakes, to bring about a change of course or direction.

The operator input starts at the steering wheel. The steering wheel fastens to a shaft (keyed or splined) that is suspended by bearings in a tube called a steering column. The shaft connects to a steering box (or steering gear) that transfers rotary motion into partial rotary motion, and this motion comes out of the steering box on a splined shaft called the sector shaft. The direction of power flow changes 90 degrees through the steering box. The two main types of steering boxes are the worm and roller gear type and the recirculating ball type. These steering boxes usually mount to the machine's frame rail and are filled with oil to keep all internal moving parts lubricated. **FIGURE 39-6** shows

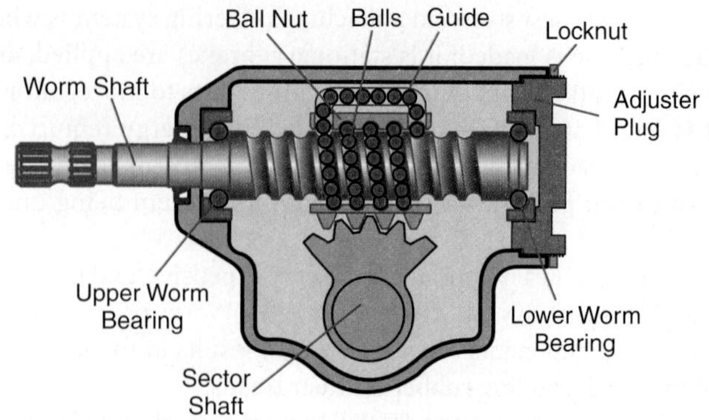

FIGURE 39-6 Typical manual worm–type steering box.

a manual steering box. Only very light-duty and older machines use a manual steering box.

From the steering box output, a lever called a pitman arm attaches to the steering box's splined output shaft that transfers motion to a drag link. The drag link may be adjustable in length and has a ball joint on each end of it. The opposite end of the drag link connects to a steering arm. The steering arm connects to a steering knuckle that has a spindle as part of it. The spindle swivels on a pivot point at the end of the axle housing. The pivot is either a one-piece kingpin or upper and lower kingpins. Attached to the bottom of one of the spindles is a tie-rod arm and attached to that through a ball joint is a tie-rod end. The tie rod threads to the left and right tie-rod ends and provides a connection between left and right spindles as well as a means of adjustment for toe angle.

The spindle has two tapered roller bearings on it that allow the hub, wheel, and tire to rotate on it. The hub is either oil or grease filled. A dynamic seal on the inside of the hub and a cover with a gasket or seal on the outside retains the grease or oil. **FIGURE 39-7** shows the major components of a medium- to heavy-duty steering axle.

▶ TECHNICIAN TIP

Ball joints have many uses on heavy equipment (**FIGURE 39-8**). Any time a part of linkage has to transfer motion to a component or another linkage and there must be an allowance for some rotary motion, manufacturers use a ball joint. For control linkages that move spool valves, this is a simple swivel ball that moves inside a housing. The swivel ball either has a stud protruding from it or a hole drilled in it to allow a bolt through. Some small ball joints are dry, but others have a grease fitting to allow lubrication of the swivel.

Ball joints that are part of steering linkages provide the same functions as smaller ball joints but need to be more robust to handle the high turning and shock loads. They sometimes thread to hydraulic cylinder rod ends. When used for steering, they are almost always greaseable.

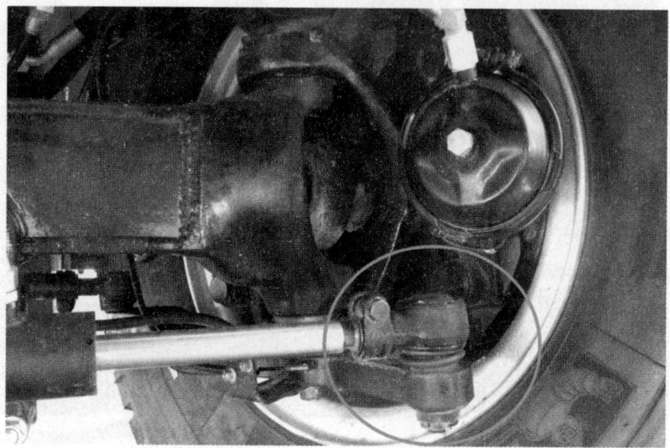

FIGURE 39-8 Ball joints are used at most connection points on steering systems, as they allow rotary motion of the connection.

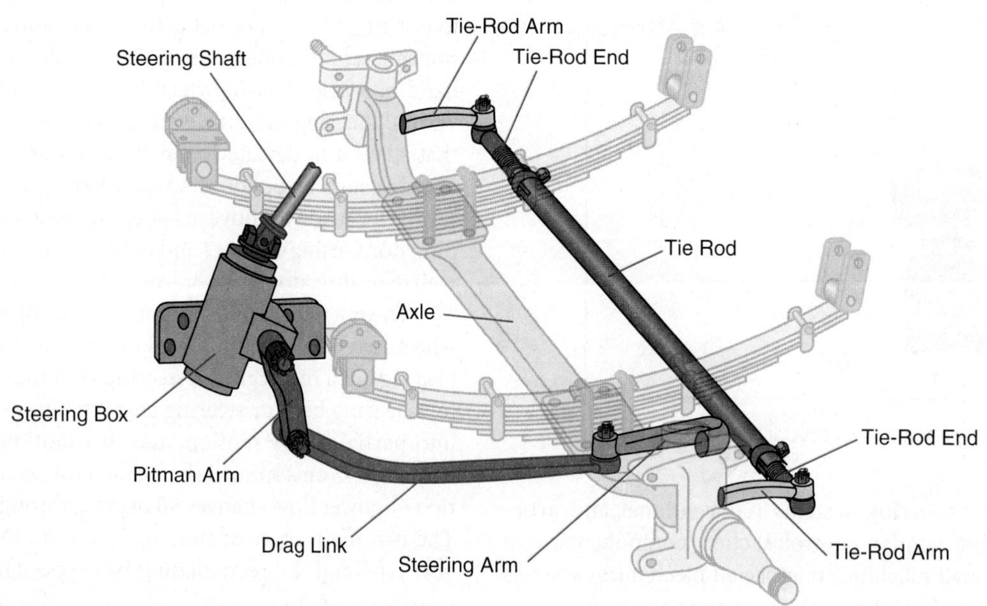

FIGURE 39-7 Typical components of a heavy-duty steering system.

Steering axles can simply steer and carry some of the machine's weight, but they can also provide drive. Most steering axles on machines today drive and steer. Non-drive steer axles have a plain steering knuckle at each end that pivots, a shaft called a **kingpin** that is stationary in the steering axle, and a steering knuckle that has pressed-in upper and lower bushings and allows movement between the knuckle and axle. Another arrangement calls for a knuckle that pivots on upper and lower kingpins in the knuckle and protrudes into bushings that are pressed into the axle housing. Lighter-duty axles use plain bushings, and other axles use tapered roller bearings. **FIGURE 39-9** shows a steering knuckle with upper and lower kingpins. This arrangement is typically found on a steer axle that is also a drive axle, where the upper and lower kingpins allow room for the drive shaft.

Grease fittings allow grease to fill the clearance between the bushings and the kingpin. The steering knuckle and axle have stops to limit the number of degrees that the knuckle can turn.

A tie-rod arm attached to the bottom of the knuckle with the steering arm allows a connected tie rod to transfer the steering movement to the other side's steering knuckle. The tie rod has threaded tie-rod ends that include ball joints on either end to allow toe adjustment and pivoting.

Steering axles that also drive transfer torque from the differential to the wheel hub. An axle shaft connects the hub and differential side gear inside the drive axle. **FIGURE 39-10** shows a heavy-duty oscillating steer/drive axle.

In light-duty machines, the axle shaft drives the hub directly. In almost all steer/drive axles, the shaft drives another gear reduction that is part of the steering knuckle called a final drive. This is a planetary gear set filled with oil. See Chapter 15 for a complete explanation of drive/steer axles. **FIGURE 39-11** shows a drive/steer axle drive shaft going through the steering knuckle.

FIGURE 39-10 Steer axles can also be drive axles.

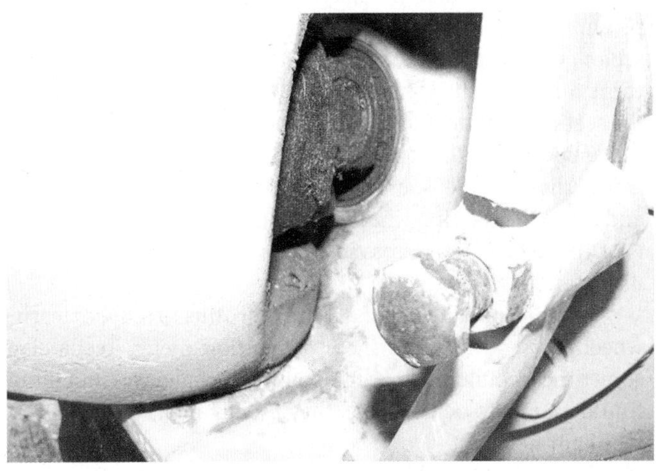

FIGURE 39-11 Using upper and lower kingpins in this steering knuckle allows the driveshaft to pass through to the wheel hub.

Hydraulic Assist Steering Systems

As size and weight increase, a machine needs a hydraulic assist system to help the operator turn the steering wheels. There are two types of power steering systems: hydraulic and electric/electronic. Electric or electronic steering is not current used for industrial applications. Hydraulic assist steering uses hydraulic pressure supplied by an engine-driven pump to assist the motion of turning the steering wheel. The hydraulic pump must run constantly to supply the fluid pressure for the assist.

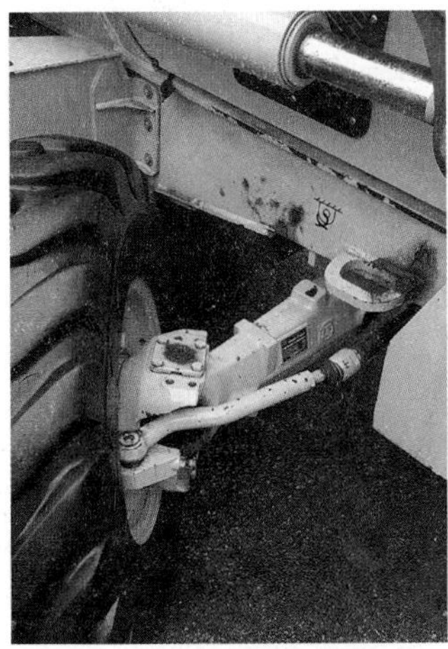

FIGURE 39-9 Upper and lower kingpins allow the axle to be driven.

This system integrates into the steering box that then moves all the normal steering components past it with greater force. **FIGURE 39-12** shows a steering box with hydraulic assist. Adding an hydraulic cylinder to the steering linkage accomplishes the same objective.

This steering arrangement first evolved into a power-assisted steering system with the addition of a low-pressure hydraulic pump, reservoir, and the replacement of the manual steering box with a power steering unit. The hydraulic steering box uses pump oil flow to apply pressure to a piston inside the unit. A rotary valve that the operator turns controls the oil flow. The piston then moves up or down, depending on which

FIGURE 39-12 Power steering box.

way the operator turns the steering wheel. On the outside of the piston, a rack of teeth machined on the outside engages with a sector gear and turns the sector gear as it moves. The sector gear turns a splined shaft that extends outside of the steering box; the section shaft turns the pitman arm. The system's oil pressure is usually limited to 1,500 psi, but this provides plenty of power assist, allowing the operator to turn the steering wheel easily and make the steering wheel turn on a heavily loaded machine. **FIGURE 39-13** shows a cross section of a power steering box and its hydraulic system.

Technicians adjust manual steering units to reduce steering wheel play, and they test them with a flow meter. Technicians sometimes rebuild manual and power steering boxes, but if they find the units to be defective, they usually replace them with a rebuilt or new unit.

Most rubber-tired machines do not allow many adjustments to the geometry of steering axle components. However, the following are a few terms you should understand when it comes to steering geometry:

- **Caster**: If you look at the side of a machine and draw a straight line through the center of the kingpin(s), you see that the angle where the line intersects with a line drawn between the bottoms of the front and rear wheels (road surface) is less than 90 degrees. This angle actually compares to the 90-degree angle from the road surface and is usually a few degrees positive when the top of the kingpin normally leans back. This helps self-center the wheels after a turn and makes the machine more stable as speed increases. The only time you adjust caster angle on a heavy-duty steering axle is if it has a provision to put tapered shims between the axle and its leaf springs. It is this part of steering geometry that makes one side of a vehicle lift as the operator turns the wheels. **FIGURE 39-14** shows an example of negative, zero, and positive caster
- **Camber**: If you look at a one of the machine's steering axle wheels from the front, you see that it may lean slightly at the top one way or the other. For an extreme example of camber, think of oval track racing cars that only turn left when racing. Their right front wheel has a noticeable camber angle to counteract the weight transfer when turning left hard. Most machines have a 0- to 1-degree camber angle, and this is nonadjustable. **FIGURE 39-15** shows positive and negative camber.
- **Toe angle**: If you were able to look down on the steering axle from high up, you might notice that the forward inside edge of the tires is closer together than the rear inside edge.

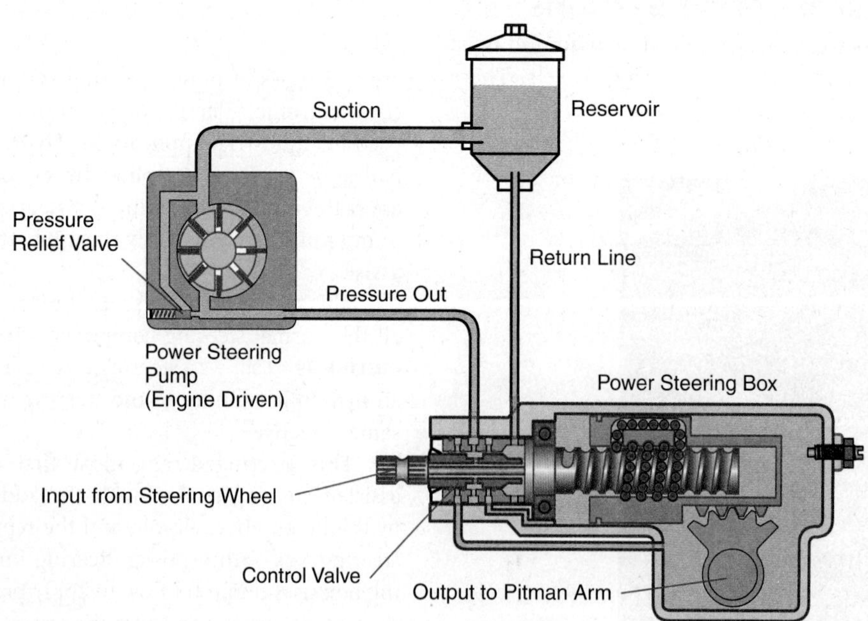

FIGURE 39-13 Power steering hydraulic system.

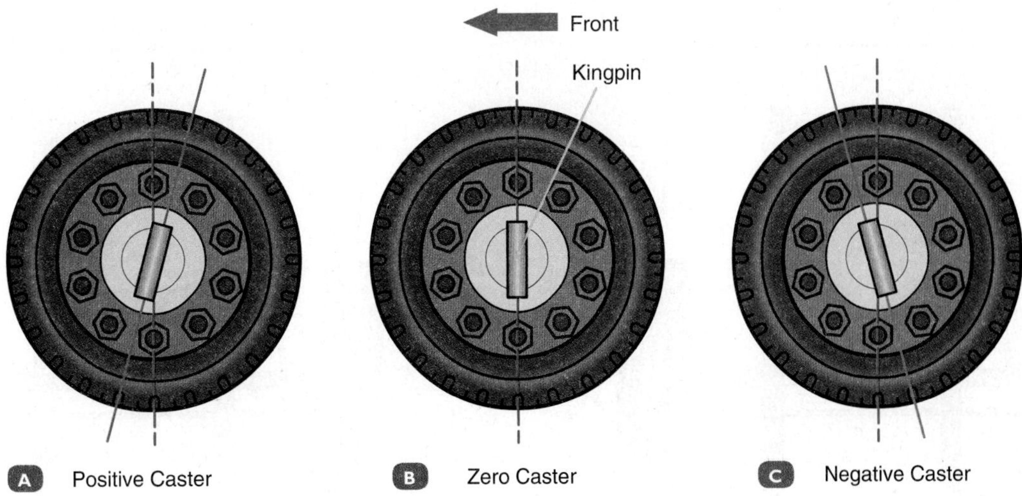

FIGURE 39-14 **A.** Positive caster. **B.** Zero caster. **C.** Negative caster.

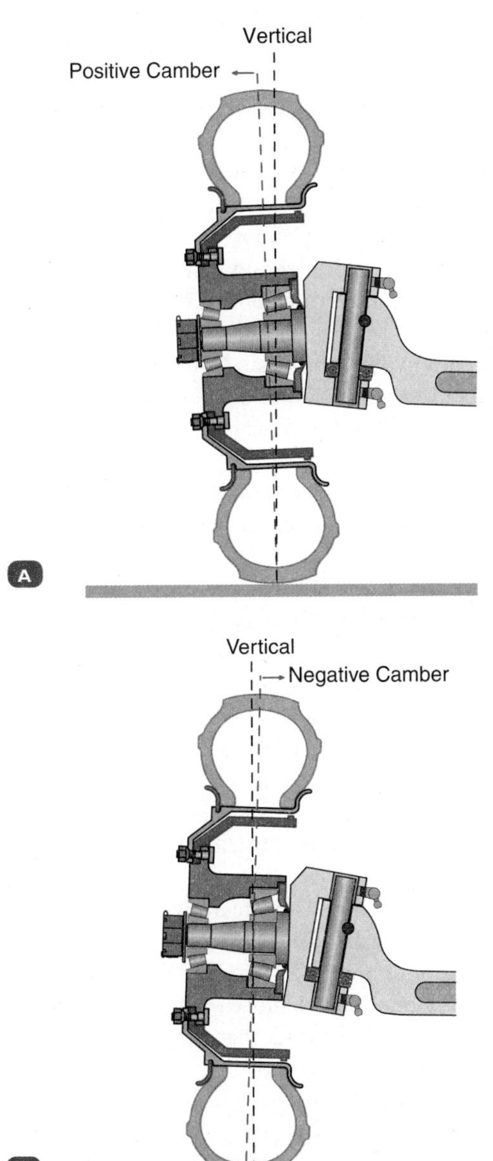

FIGURE 39-15 **A.** Positive camber. **B.** Negative camber.

This is called a toe-in dimension. As the machine's speed increases, there is a tendency for the wheels to toe out. A slight toe-in is the most common setting. This is one angle that the technician can adjust on heavy-duty steering axles by changing the length of the tie rod(s). **FIGURE 39-16** shows toe angle.

- **Ackerman angle**: This is the angle between an imaginary point that extends from the centerline of the rear axle to the steering, or tie rod, arms or from a point midway between the rear axles of a tandem to the steering arms. As a machine with a steering axle turns, the steering arms that pivot the wheels turn each wheel at differing individual angles because of the Ackerman angle. The Ackerman angle ensures that the wheel on the inside of a curve, because it has a shorter distance to travel, turns at a sharper angle than the wheel on the outside. In this way, both wheels follow the curve without scuffing the tires **FIGURE 39-17** shows the Ackerman angle for a single and a dual rear axle truck.

As the steering wheels turn farther, the geometry between the tie rod and tie-rod or steering arms naturally provides differing angles between the left and right steering wheels. This forces the wheels to travel through different arcs as the machine moves through a turn, which decreases tire scrub to lengthen tire life. If the steering components are designed, adjusted, and functioning properly, the Ackerman angle intersection points meet during all points of left and right turns.

Conventional Steering: Full Hydraulic

Almost all steering systems on machines today that have a conventional steering system (straight frame with front wheels pivoting) use a hydraulic system to either control it and/or actuate it. The steering axle is hydraulically assisted any time the engine is running. Hydraulic oil pressure is provided by a transmission-mounted pump that is shared by the mast, pivot/shift assembly, and steering system. No mechanical linkages are generally used between the steering column and the steering

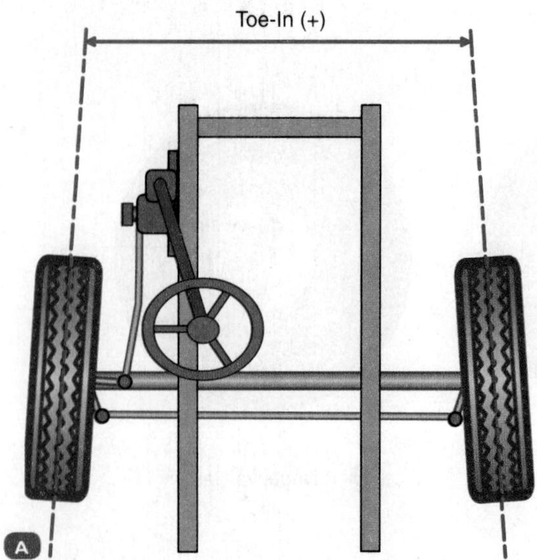

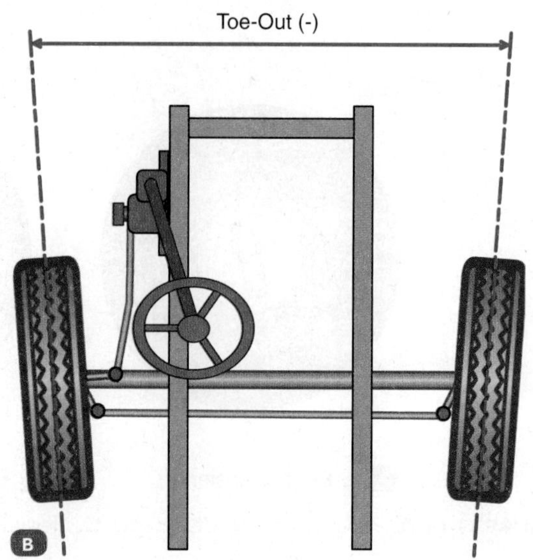

FIGURE 39-16 **A.** Toe-in angle. **B.** Toe-out angle.

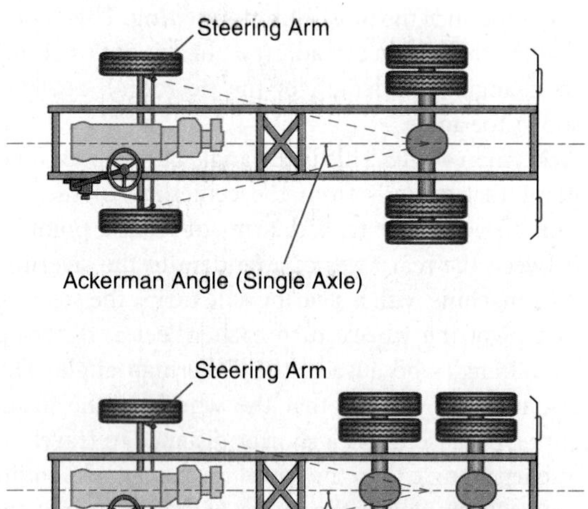

FIGURE 39-17 The Ackerman angle allows each wheel to follow a different curve on turns.

axle for control of the steer axle. A valve is connected to the steering column and controls fluid flow from the pump to the steer axle.

The steering system is likely part of the machine's main hydraulic system, which is designed to ensure the steering circuit always has sufficient oil flow to allow the operator to steer the machine safely under any condition. The system's flow divider valve is sometimes called a priority valve because it gives priority to the steering circuit. **FIGURE 39-18** shows a hydraulic schematic for a forklift that has a flow divider valve to ensure the steering circuit always has oil.

Larger machines like mining haul trucks have a separate hydraulic system for steering (tank, pump, valve, filter, lines). The full hydraulic steering system replaces the steering box, pitman arm, and steering arm of older conventional steering systems. **FIGURE 39-19** shows the steering axle from a 300-ton rock truck with conventional steering—full hydraulic.

The full hydraulic steering system starts with the steering wheel that turns a steering control valve. This valve has several different names such as hand metering unit (HMU), metering pump, **orbital valve**, and Char-Lynn® valve. It is a valve with a rotary spool valve section and a gerotor pump/motor section. **FIGURE 39-20** shows a steering control valve.

The valve directs steering-pump oil flow to one or two steering cylinders. The amount and speed with which the cylinder(s) moves depends on how fast and far the operator turns the steering wheel.

If the machine has one steering cylinder, it will have a **double-rod cylinder**, where each of its rods attaches to a tie rod. The tie rods attach to the steering knuckles that pivot on the outer ends of the axle housing. As oil arrives in the cylinder from the steering valve, the rods move left or right, which causes the wheels to steer left or right. Oil must also leave the cylinder, and it returns to tank through the steering valve. This is a common arrangement for backhoe loaders, rough terrain cranes, and telehandlers. **FIGURE 39-21** shows a double-rod steering cylinder.

If a machine has two steering cylinders, the machine's steering control valve feeds them oil. It sends oil to one cylinder's head end and one cylinder's rod end. This moves one rod in and one rod out to move each wheel. A mechanical link between the wheels ensures that they move together and that the Ackerman angle stays correct. This can be a one-piece tie rod or a two-piece tie rod that attaches to a center pivoting link. **FIGURE 39-22** shows the steering cylinder and tie-rod arrangement for one side of the steering axle of a 300-ton rock truck. This is a common arrangement for a large straight-frame haul truck and some larger rough terrain cranes.

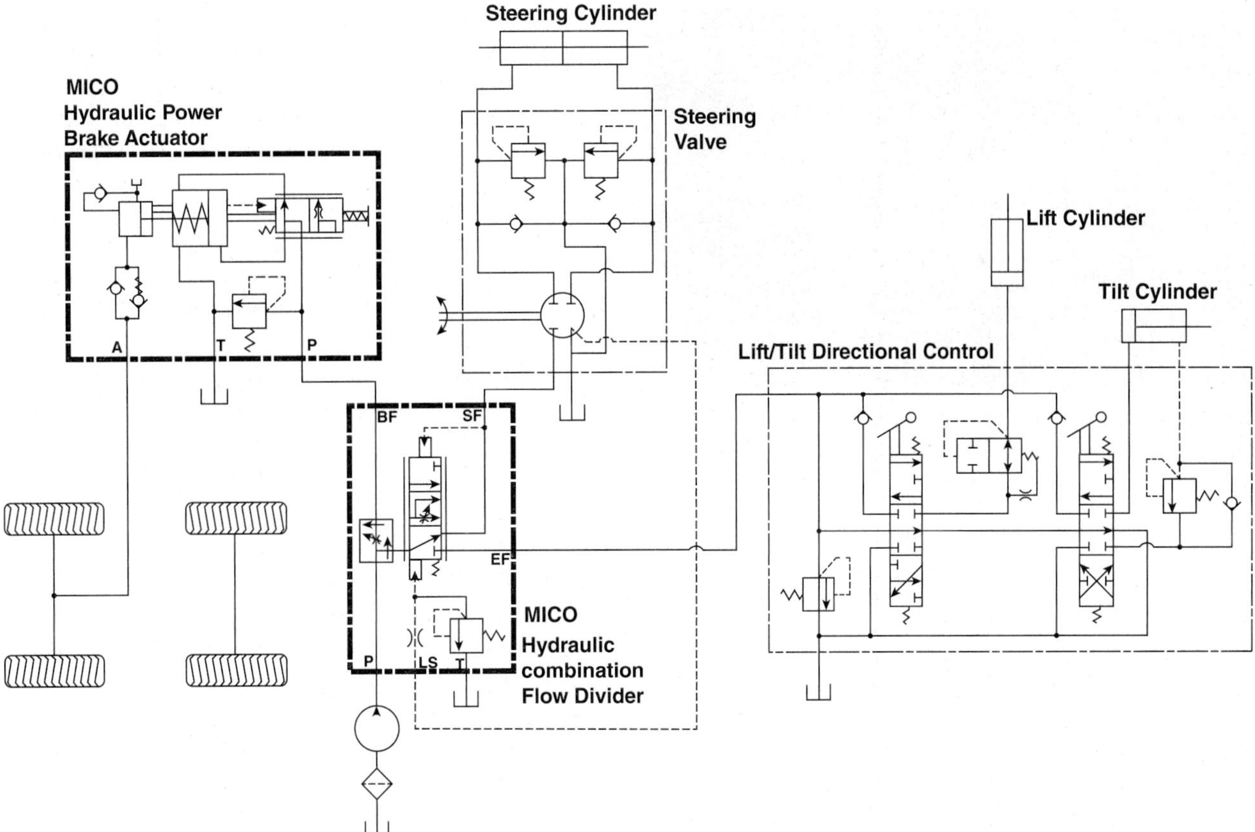

FIGURE 39-18 Forklift hydraulic system with a flow divider.

FIGURE 39-19 Full hydraulic steering system.

FIGURE 39-20 Typical steering control valve.

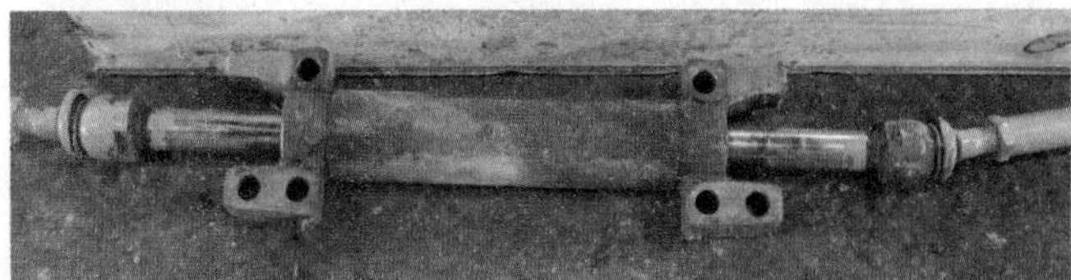

FIGURE 39-21 A double-rod steering cylinder.

Articulated Steering Systems

Articulated steering is a directional system that allows for easier navigation of vehicles in tight spaces. Articulated steering systems separate the vehicle into a front half and a back half, with a pivot point directly in the middle. Hydraulic pistons on each side of the vehicle allow the operator to rotate the body about the pivot point, which in turn steers the vehicle. Because the entire body rotates, not just the front wheels, the front axle remains solid and can handle a heavier payload than a comparable vehicle with standard steering. Yet operators must be wary when adjusting the angle of the body with an elevated payload, as articulated steering systems are more prone to tipping. Many machines use two-piece main frames, such as wheel loaders, articulated truck, graders, skidders, forwarders, feller/bunchers, and compactors.

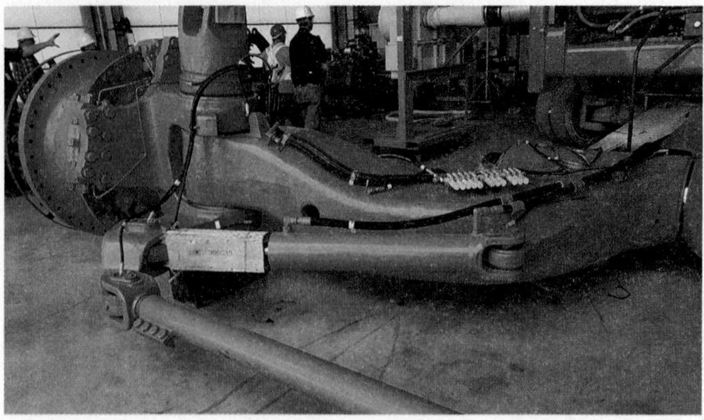

FIGURE 39-22 Notice the double-acting cylinder controlling the steering arm position on this 300-ton rock truck axle.

The two-piece frame for these machines has a pivot point that can be as simple as a top and bottom stationary pin supported by two plain bushings, or the system can use a more complicated arrangement with top and bottom pins supported by tapered roller bearings. These pins require regular lubrication.

The steering systems for today's articulated machines turn the machine by pivoting the front and rear frames to the left or right. Some small machines use a single cylinder to do this, but the majority of machines use two steering cylinders. The head end fastens to the rear frame, and the rods attach to the front frame. A left steer sends oil to the left cylinder's rod end and the right cylinder's head end. Reversing oil flow to the cylinders pivots the machine in the opposite direction. **FIGURE 39-23** shows an articulated machine frame and steering cylinders. On both sides of the machine's turning pivots, a **neutralizer valve** is mounted that acts to stop the turning effort when the pivots are contacted.

Machines with a steering wheel use a steering control valve that is identical to the one in conventional steering systems. The valve meters oil to the steering cylinders.

FIGURE 39-23 Steering cylinder and pivot point for an articulated steering machine.

Some machines feature joystick-controlled steering. The joystick control can be a valve that the machine's low-pressure system supplies with pilot oil and which it then meters to a main control valve. How far the operator moves the joystick determines the metered oil. The main control valve then sends oil to the steering cylinders.

Another version of joystick steering uses a joystick to send proportional electrical signals to an ECM. The ECM then sends a proportional signal to an electrohydraulic control valves solenoid(s). When the solenoid(s) energizes, it shifts a spool that sends oil to the cylinders.

Some machines are steered by either a steering wheel or joystick. The two modes are changed by an electrical solenoid-actuated valve. Some older systems had a mechanical follow-up linkage moved by the pivoting frames to recenter the spool.

All-Wheel Steering

In an all-wheel steering system, all four wheels turn at the same time when the driver steers. In some systems, the rear wheels are steered by a computer and actuators. The rear wheels generally cannot turn as far as the front wheels. All-wheel steering minimizes ground disturbance, with less damage on fragile surfaces like grass or paver. The machine may change position with less yaw and improved buildup of the lateral acceleration, enhancing straight-line stability.

Some types of machines with straight frames, such as telehandlers, backhoe loaders, and rough terrain cranes, feature all-wheel steering. This means that both the front and rear axles can steer. These machines are usually able to switch to one of four modes:

- Conventional steering: The front axle wheels steer only.
- All-wheel steering: Both axles steer at the same time in the opposite direction to make the machine turn in a smaller radius.
- **Crab steering**: Both axles steer at the same time in the same direction to make the machine move diagonally.
- Rear axle steering: Some cranes steer with only the rear axle wheels.

FIGURE 39-24 shows the different modes of all-wheel steering.

A three- or four-position, four-way, solenoid-operated directional control valve installed between the front and rear steering cylinders allows switching between steering modes. When the valve's two solenoids are not energized, the springs center the valve spool. This position blocks oil flow to the rear axle steering, and the system performs steering in the conventional mode.

When one of the valves, solenoids is energized, it shifts the spool and allows oil flow to go to both axles for steering. This steers both axles in the opposite direction for all-wheel steer. When the other solenoid is energized, the spool shifts to the farthest opposite position; this forces all wheels to turn in the same directions for crab steering (see **FIGURE 39-25**).

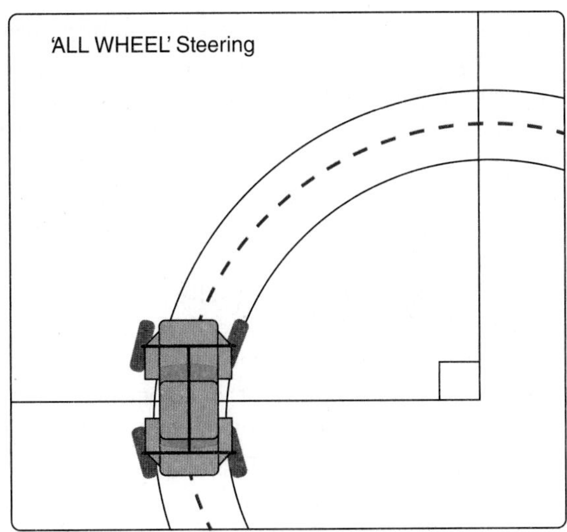

FIGURE 39-24 All-wheel steering.

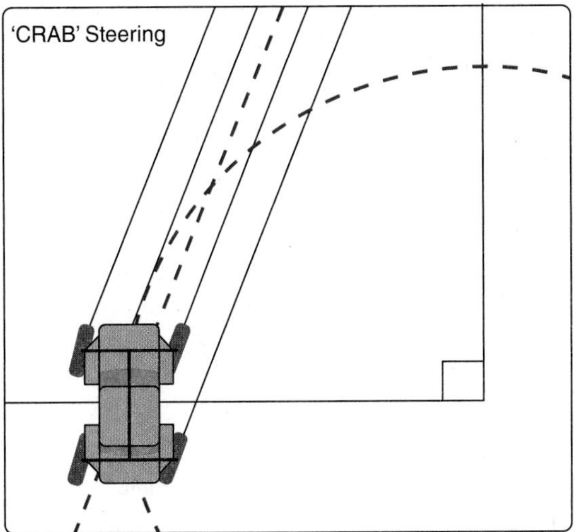

FIGURE 39-25 Crab steering turns the wheels on both axles in the same direction.

The operator control for this could be as simple as a three-position toggle switch or a switch that is an input to an ECM. The machine may also have wheel-position sensors in the ECM that determine whether the wheels are straight ahead when they are supposed to be.

Secondary Steering

A **secondary steering** system can be used to back up a hydraulic steering system in emergency situations. The secondary system includes a fluid accumulator for storing system fluid under pressure and a valve for regulating flow of such fluid in response to system pressure. Above a predetermined pressure level, fluid is diverted from the main system to the accumulator until a fully charged condition exists therein. Under this pressure level, fluid is released from the accumulator to the main system by selective actuation of the valve and by operation of the conventional steering controls.

Many medium to larger systems have a secondary steering system that serves as a backup oil supply if the machine's regular steering system oil supply fails. The system uses a different pump that is either mechanically ground driven or electrically driven. A secondary steering is a safety backup to ensure that the operator can steer the machine to a parked position.

The shaft of a **ground-driven pump** turns whenever the machine is moving. Part of the machine's driveline, driven by the wheels, also drives the pump, which usually mounts on the transfer case.

Because this type of pump is driven any time the machine is moving, the pump's flow goes to a secondary steering valve, where it is routed back to tank. Inside the secondary steering valve, the primary steering valve holds a check valve closed. The check valve opens when the primary pump flow stops, allowing the secondary pump flow to move into the system and supply flow until the machine stops moving.

The other type of secondary steering system has an electric-driven pump that works when a test switch activates it or when a pressure or flow switch changes state when primary pump flow stops. The motor is similar to a starter motor, but it drives a pump instead of a pinion gear.

Load-Sensing Hydraulic Steering Systems

A hydraulic steering system for an industrial machine uses a variable displacement pump operatively connected to a system that senses the hydraulic pressure in the steering cylinder. The system automatically varies the stroke and pressure of the hydraulic pump in accordance with steering requirements. Most hydraulic steering systems on machines today are part of a load-sensing hydraulic system. The pump is a pressure-compensated, variable-displacement type and usually an axial piston pump. A load sense line going to the pump displacement control changes pump flow based on steering demands. This reduces energy waste when there is little or no need for oil flow because the pump destrokes to near zero, which minimizes pump output. When the steering control valve senses a steering function, it sends a signal to the pump control valve, and the pump upstrokes to supply slightly more oil flow than is needed for the steering function.

▶ Steering System Components and Operation

K39002

Hydraulic steering system components and operations vary from machine to machine, but in general all machines with an hydraulic steering system have the following:

- **A pump that creates oil flow.** The pump can be a dedicated steering pump, which is the case for most large machines, or steering oil flow can be shared with the main hydraulic system pump flow. If the steering system uses pump flow from the main pump, a priority valve ensures that the steering circuit flow requirements are satisfied before any other circuits.

- **A method to direct oil flow to the steering cylinder(s).** A rotary steering-control valve that a steering wheel turns can do this, or a steering wheel or a joystick that either sends pilot oil to a main control valve or an electrical signal to an ECM, which the ECM then sends oil to a solenoid-operated directional control valve. The valve also directs return oil back to tank.
- **One or more linear actuators (cylinders) to convert pump oil flow into movement.**
- **Other components that normally constitute a complete hydraulic system.** These include fluid, one or more filters, a tank and lines, fittings, gaskets, and seals.

FIGURE 39-26 shows an articulated truck's hydraulic system.

Hydraulic Steering Pump

For simple systems, the steering system may share oil flow with another machine hydraulic circuit, as steering flow is usually not very high even in high-demand steering situations. The pump may be a fixed displacement gear or a vane pump, but most systems use a variable displacement pump that gets a load sense signal from the steering valve.

Rotary Steering Valve Operation

As mentioned above, this valve has several different names, such as hand metering unit, steering control unit, orbital valve, and Char-Lynn valve. Manufacturers use the valve in many types of steering systems. In general, it sends steering pump oil to one or two steering cylinders and returns oil back to the tank. It is a rotary directional control valve that the operator controls by turning its input shaft. The input shaft is splined to a shaft turned by the machine's steering wheel, such as a steering column; or the steering wheel mounts directly to the valve, depending on the machine.

Several variations of this type of valve exist, depending on where in the system the manufacturer uses it. The valve can be used with fixed displacement pumps or in a load-sensing, pressure-compensated system. Most variations of these valves allow the operator to steer the machine manually if there is no pump flow. This happens if the engine quits running or the pump fails.

The input to the valve is through the inner section of the rotary valve. The inner section is allowed to turn a few degrees inside of an outer sleeve. These two pieces always try to stay centered with each other because of a set of leaf springs that link them. The inner and outer valve sections of this unit are part of the rotary valve and can stop or allow oil flow between them based on their rotational relationship to each other. This is similar to the action between a spool and body in a spool-type directional control valve.

Inside the inner sleeve is a shaft that transfers drive from the outer sleeve down to the inner rotor of the gerotor pump/motor. When the steering wheel turns continuously, the inner sleeve, outer sleeve, and gerotor all turn together inside the

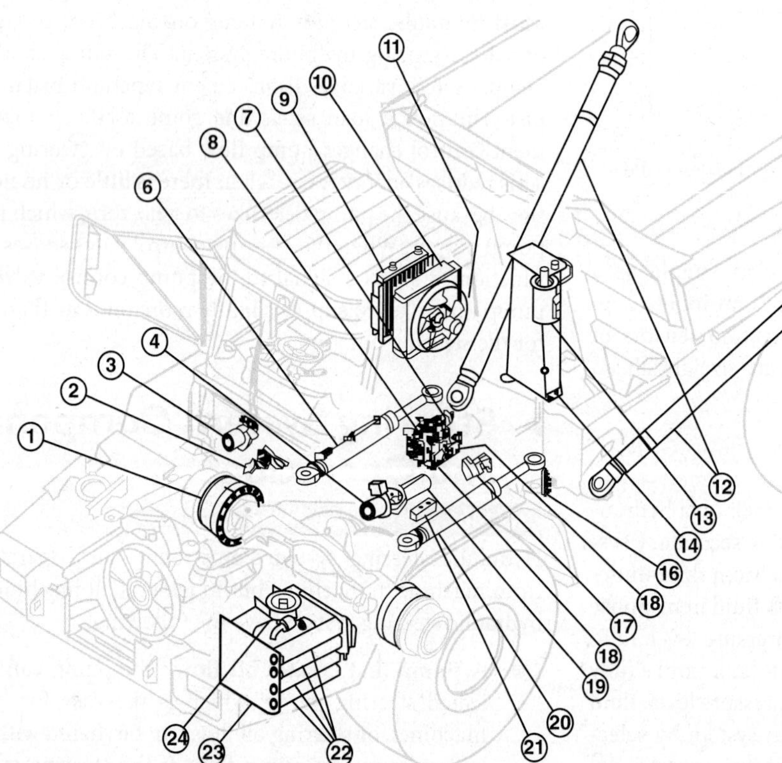

3 - Steering Valve
4 - Main Hydraulic Pump
5 - Right Steering Cylinder
6 - Hydraulic System Manifold
9 - Hydraulic Oil Cooler
10 - Hydraulic Fan Motor
14 - Test Ports
16 - Secondary Steering Pump
20 - Left Steering Cylinder
21 - Hydraulic Reservoir Return Manifold
23 - Hydraulic Reservoir
24 - Return Filter

FIGURE 39-26 The hydraulic system of an articulated truck's hydraulic system.

valve's outer housing. The outer housing has four threaded ports to accept hydraulic lines for the following:

- P-pump
- T-tank
- A-left
- B-right

If the valve is part of a load-sensing system, it has a fifth port to send a load-sense signal to the pump.

To understand how oil flows through one of these valves, see the closed-center type of valve in **FIGURE 39-27**.

The steering valve (O) consists of a spool (I) inside a sleeve (H) within a housing. When the steering wheel is not moving, the valve is in the neutral (A) position. In neutral, the spool and sleeve align to block the oil flow through the valve. Trapped oil in the left and right work ports hold the steering cylinders (B) stationary.

When the steering valve turns to the right, the spool rotates relative to the sleeve and opens passages, which allow pump flow through the spool and sleeve assembly. Oil flows to the gerotor (E), causing the gerotor gear to rotate. Oil flow from the gerotor flows back into the valve, where it is directed out the right work port to the respective ends of the steering cylinders.

A bypass orifice is machined into the spool and sleeve assembly. It is a variable orifice that introduces a small leak into the pressure side of the steering valve. Its purpose is to dampen the initial pressure surge when the steering wheel is partially turned. When the steering wheel is fully turned, the leak closes off.

Return oil flows back in through the left work port by way of the spool and sleeve assembly. A load-sensing orifice between the sleeve and the gerotor orifice feeds the load-sensing pressure to the priority valve.

When the rotation of the steering wheel stops, the gerotor gear continues to move, turning the sleeve until the sleeve stops the flow to the gerotor. At this point, the valve is back in the neutral position and remains there until the steering wheel moves again.

The valve provides a variable steering rate proportional to the speed at which the operator rotates the steering wheel. A variable orifice bypasses oil around the gerotor. Turning the steering wheel from full lock to lock takes approximately 1.5–4.5 turns, depending on the model of machine. Four anti-cavitation balls inside the spool/sleeve prevent cavitation in the system.

Crossover relief valves in the steering valve protect the steering circuit from spikes sudden excessive loads may cause. For example, if an external force tries to move the machine and the steering valve is in neutral, the crossover relief valve opens and lets the oil pressure relieve to the tank. This may happen if a stuck machine is being towed out.

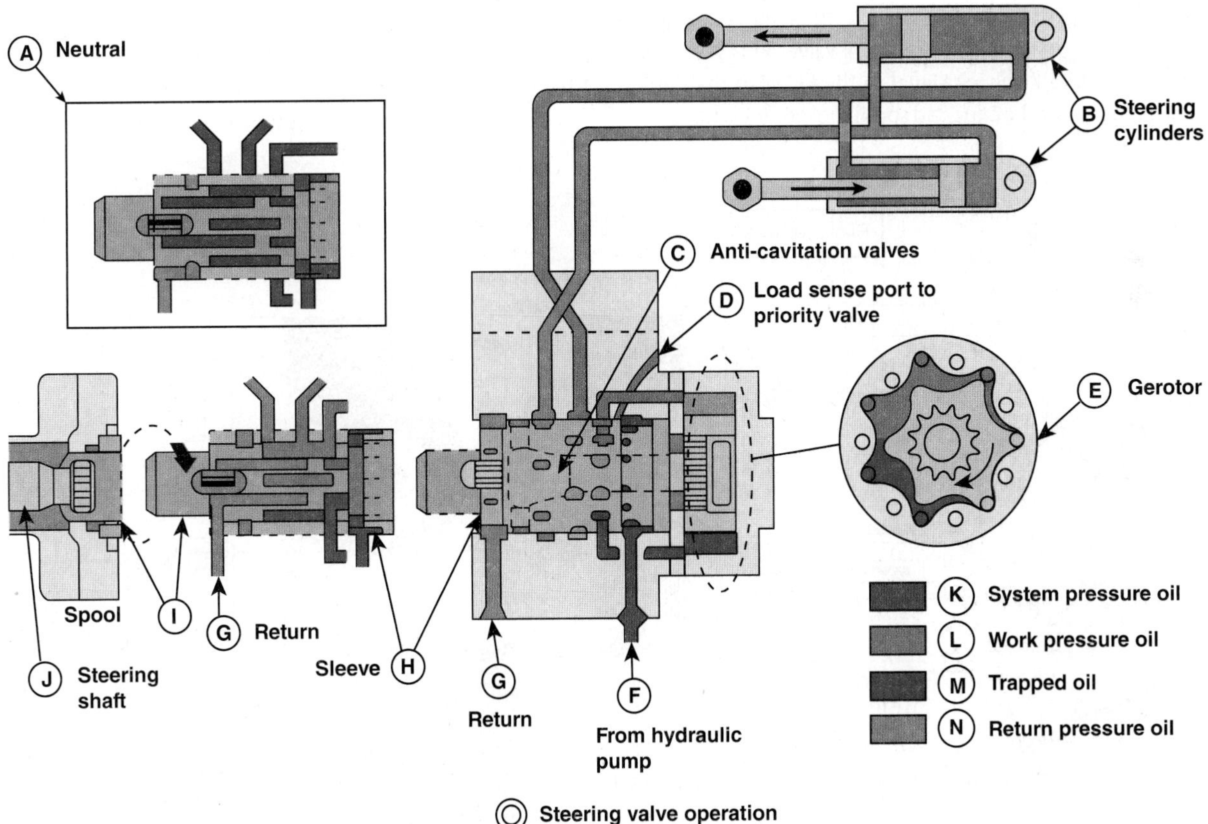

FIGURE 39-27 Steering valve oil flow.

> ▶ TECHNICIAN TIP
>
> Rotary steering valves can be rebuilt. However, unless you have experience with reconditioning these valves, it is recommended that you replace a faulty unit with either a rebuilt or new valve assembly. Proper reconditioning requires patience, some special tools, and a clean, well-lit work area.

It is better if you leave some tasks to technicians who specialize in one area and only work on a limited number of components on a regular basis. Reconditioning hand metering units is an example of a component that you should leave to someone else to perform.

Joystick Steering Controls

Some articulated machines provide an option to steer the machine with a joystick in addition to a steering wheel or by joystick only. **FIGURE 39-28** shows a large wheel loader that only uses a joystick for steering. If the joystick is on a machine equipped with a power shift transmission, it will also have a switch for FNR and two switches for upshifting and downshifting, as well as other switches.

Joystick steering may also actuate the steering wheels on a conventional steering axle for a slow-moving machine like a man lift or for slow maneuvering with a wheel-type excavator. Joysticks for steering may be poppet-type pilot oil controls that send a proportional oil pressure signal to a main control valve, or they may be electrical position sensors that send a proportional signal to an ECM, which processes the signal and then sends an output signal to the joystick steering control valve. **FIGURE 39-29** shows an electronically controlled joystick steering control valve. This valve has the capability to send a feedback signal to the ECM so that fault codes can be generated if the expected spool movement is not met.

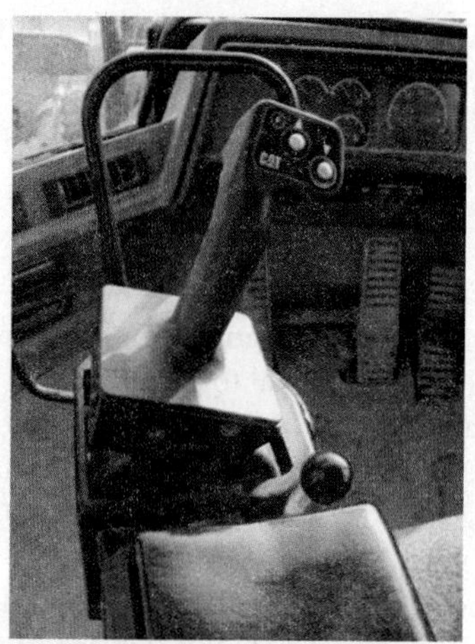

FIGURE 39-28 Joystick steering.

Steering Cylinders

Steering cylinders are no different than those used for other purposes on a machine. One variation of a steering cylinder that is not common, however, is the double-rod type that may be used for a steering axle's wheels. Double-rod cylinders feature one piston with a rod attached to each end. **FIGURE 39-30** shows a system with a double-rod cylinder.

There are often snubbers on the end of steering cylinder rods in articulated machines to prevent the cylinders from bottoming out.

Electronic Steering Controls

Electronic components that are part of an electrohydraulic system control some steering systems. Manufacturers usually use

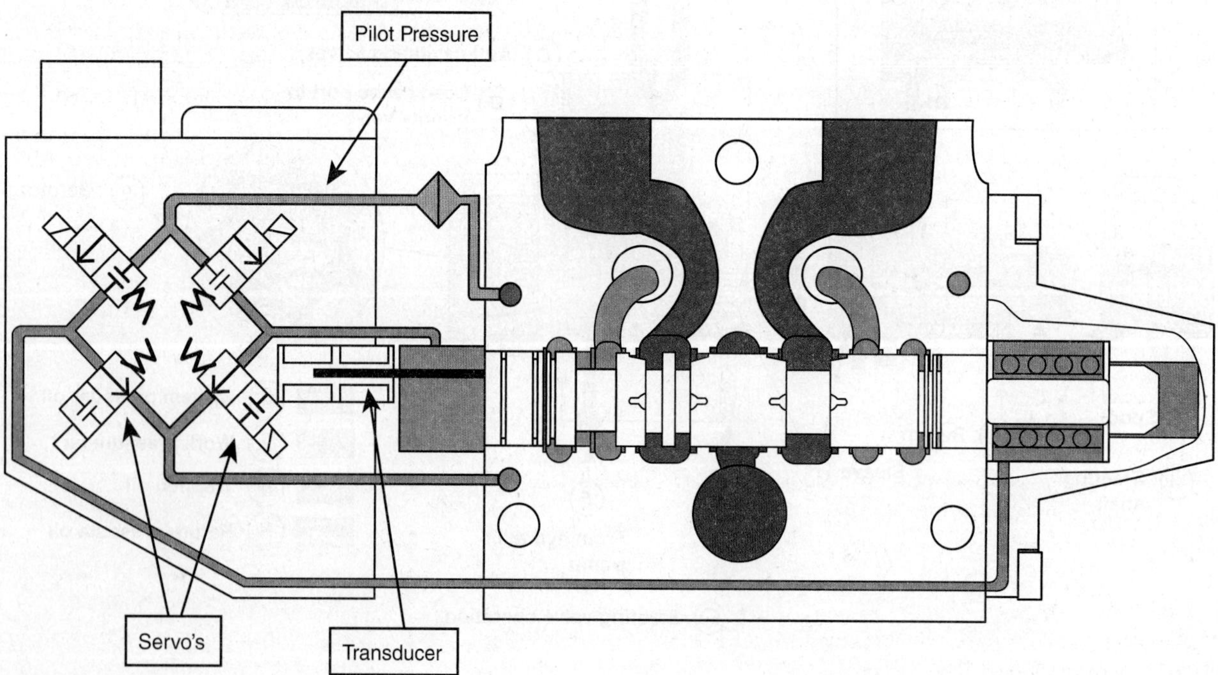

FIGURE 39-29 Joystick steering control valve.

FIGURE 39-30 Double-rod steering cylinder.

FIGURE 39-31 This loader can be switched from all-wheel steer to skid steer electronically.

these for articulated and all-wheel steering machines, but these systems may be part of conventional steering systems as well.

For example, one machine manufacturer makes a skid steer that switches between normal skid steering and all-wheel steering. An electronic system that has input sensors, an ECM, and output actuators controls these functions. **FIGURE 39-31** shows an all-wheel steer skid steer loader.

The main inputs are the operator controls that include a steering-mode switch and electronic joystick, and wheel position sensors that tell the ECM to what angle the wheels are turned.

The ECM processes this information and sends one or more signals to a set of solenoid valves. These valves then direct oil to the four steering cylinders individually. This system can steer the four wheels totally independently of each of other; therefore, it relies on the wheel position sensors for feedback so the machine can turn smoothly and as the operator desires.

The system may have to be calibrated by the technician. A port on the machine allows the HDET to connect to a laptop for this purpose and to diagnose problems.

▶ TECHNICIAN TIP

Search the Web to find a video of a machine that features different steering modes, such as all-wheel steering, crab steering, and rear-wheel steering. Does it show how the operator selects the modes? Do you think there are any sensors on the machine to determine wheel position?

▶ Steering Service

S39001

Servicing steering systems is an important part of any maintenance procedure. This ranges from simple inspections such as looking at oil levels, checking for leaks, and inspecting for excessive wear and damage, to changing oil and filters and taking an oil sample. Greasing all steering-related grease points is critical to ensuring safe operation of the machine and longevity of the components. Some machines have an automatic greaser that should be inspected to make sure it has the correct grease level. The HDET should check all steering-related grease points to see that grease is reaching them, as many grease points are hard to reach.

The HDET should inspect steering systems for proper operation when the machine is serviced, to ensure the machine works smoothly and evenly. If the steering system has different modes, the HDET should make sure they are operating properly. The HDET should also check secondary steering systems for proper operation, as secondary systems are not actuated very often.

Checking for Wear

The HDET can examine mechanical steering components for excessive wear to see whether they are within acceptable specification. Examples of these components are: kingpins and bushings, tie-rod ends, and steering columns. This may be a simple process such as working the steering wheel back and forth slightly and watching for excessive wear at all moving joints, or it may require unweighting components to check for wear.

Also, a machine's steering wheel should have a specific amount of resistance, which the HDET can measure with a fish weighing scale to see whether the resistance is within specification.

Steering Diagnostics

TABLE 39-1 lists common steering operational symptoms, problems, and possible solutions:

Tools that may be required for diagnosing steering system complaints include pressure gauges, flow meter, heat gun, stopwatch, fish scale, filter cutter, and tape measure.

Steering System Adjustments

Toe-angle adjustments may be required on occasion if you notice excessive tire wear. You can do this easily if the machine has a double-rod steering cylinder because you can turn the rod in the cylinder to change the toe dimension. For other types of steering arrangements, you need to rotate the tie-rod tube.

TABLE 39-1 Common Steering Issues, Causes, and Corrections

Symptom	Problem	Solution
Slow or No Steering Function	Articulation locking bar installed	Disconnect articulation locking bar and put in storage position.
	Oil level low	Check oil level in hydraulic reservoir.
	Steering load sense relief valve pressure setting too low or malfunctioning	Check steering load sense relief valve pressure. Inspect steering load sense relief valve.
	Steering lines damaged	Inspect and replace lines.
	Priority valve in hydraulic system manifold	Check priority valve operation. Remove priority valve and inspect.
	Steering valve	Disassemble steering valve and inspect.
	Steering cylinder piston seals	Check steering cylinders for leakage. Replace piston seals as needed.
	Secondary steering system not functioning properly	
Constant Steering to Maintain Straight Travel	Air in steering system	Check for foamy oil. Tighten loose fitting. Replace damaged lines.
	Steering cylinder piston seals	Check steering cylinders for leakage. Replace piston seals as needed.
	Steering valve	Disassemble steering valve and inspect.
Erratic Steering	Air in steering system	Check for foamy oil. Tighten loose fitting. Replace damaged lines.
	Oil level low	Check oil level in hydraulic reservoir. Add hydraulic oil.
	Cylinder piston loose	Disassemble cylinder and inspect.
	Steering valve	Disassemble steering valve and inspect.
Spongy or Soft Steering	Air in steering system	Check for foamy oil. Tighten loose fitting. Replace damaged lines.
	Oil level low	Check oil level in hydraulic reservoir. Add Hydraulic Oil.
Free Play at Steering Wheel	Steering wheel-to-shaft nut loose	Tighten nut.
	Splines on steering shaft or valve worn or damaged	Inspect and replace worn or damaged parts.
Steering Locks Up	Large particles of contamination in steering valve	Inspect return filters for contamination. Repair cause of contamination. Flush hydraulic system. Disassemble steering valve and inspect.
Abrupt Steering Wheel Oscillation	Steering valve gerotor not timed correctly	Time gerotor gear.
Steering Wheel Turns by Itself	Lines connected to wrong ports	Connect lines to correct ports.
Machine Turns in Opposite Direction	Lines to steering cylinders connected to wrong ports at steering valve	Connect lines to correct ports.
Machine Turns When Steering Valve Is in Neutral	Steering valve leakage	Disassemble steering valve and inspect.

Its female threaded ends mate with tie-rod ends. **FIGURE 39-32** shows a toe-in and toe-out angle. The angle should be measured at the center of the tire tread and at the center of the tire vertically as well.

Steering Cylinder Leakage Check

If a steering problem relates to a possibility of the steering cylinder leaking, you can perform a procedure to check for cylinder leakage or bypass. This involves turning the wheel all the way one way, turning the machine off, removing the hose on the cylinder that returns oil to tank, and installing a hose on the cylinder that directs any bypassing oil into a measuring container. You then start the machine and turn the steering wheel to send oil into the hose that is still attached to the cylinder, for a specific amount of time. There should be very little oil going into the container; for example, the specification for a backhoe loader is no more than 5 mL/min. To check for steering cylinder leakage, follow the steps in **SKILL DRILL 39-1**.

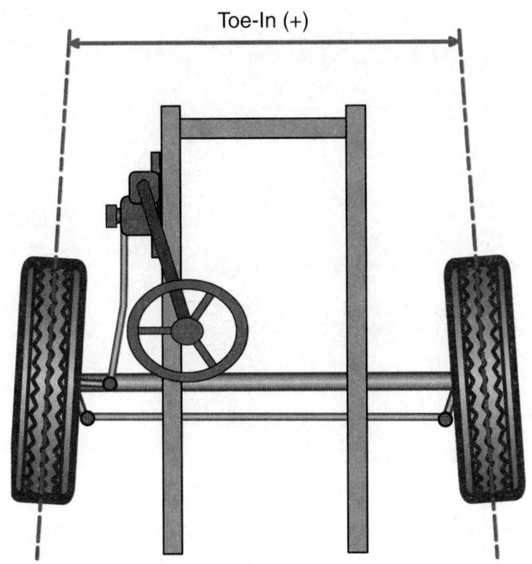

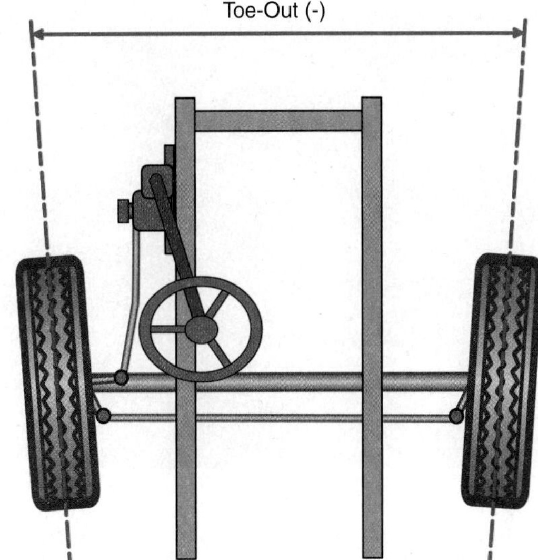

FIGURE 39-32 Toe angle.

SKILL DRILL 39-1 Steering Cylinder Leakage or Bypass Check

1. Turn the steering wheel all the way in one direction.
2. Turn the machine off.
3. Remove the hose on the cylinder that returns oil to tank.
4. Install a hose on the cylinder that directs any bypassing oil into a measuring container.
5. Start the machine and turn the steering wheel to send oil into the hose that is still attached to the cylinder for a specific amount of time.
6. Very little oil should be going into the container, for example, a backhoe loader should be no more than 5 mL/min.

Steering System Repair

Steering system repairs vary from simple mechanical repairs to hydraulic component repairs, to electrical repairs. We present an example of each here.

Tie rods take a lot of stress. If a machine is moving along a rough road, shock loads transfer into the tie rod, eventually wearing it out. HDETs need to grease most tie rods regularly; if they don't, the tie rods wear out quickly. Tie rods taper fit to the steering knuckle and are held in place with a lock nut or castellated nut and cotter pin. The other end of the tie rod threads into a tie-rod tube or a steering cylinder, depending on the machine. Either a jam nut holds it in place in the rod, or a clamp locks it in the tie-rod tube.

You can use one of several methods to separate the tapered end of the tie rod from the steering knuckle. For smaller tie rods, use a simple tool called a pickle fork. It's always a good idea to mark the old tie rod's threads into the tie rod, or count the ones showing so you know where to locate the new one. For large tie rods, the tapered end may have to be pressed out; when they have been in place for many hours, they are rusted into place. Although it may be tempting to apply heat to the steering knuckle to aid in removing it, *do not* use any form of heat. Use proper pressing tools to remove any tie rod.

Once the tapered end is loose, loosen the threaded end of the tie rod and remove it. **FIGURE 39-33** shows the pickle fork tool used to remove smaller tie-rod ends.

Install the new tie rod with the same amount of threads exposed as the old one; then install the tapered end into the steering knuckle, and torque the nut to specified torque. Before locking the tie-rod tube or rod end, check the toe-in dimension according to the service manual. To replace a tie-rod end, follow the steps in **SKILL DRILL 39-2**.

Steering System Hydraulic Repair

One common repair for a steering system's hydraulic system is to replace the HMU (hand metering unit). These valves are very susceptible to contamination, easily becoming damaged if any contamination gets in between their moving parts. It is mandatory that you thoroughly diagnose the problem to ensure this valve is faulty because many of these valves have been replaced for no good reason.

Once you have determined that the valve is faulty, proceed with the usual steps taken for any hydraulic repair. These include releasing pressure and having oil drain buckets and floor dry handy.

It is very important to mark the lines going to the valve before removing, as you can easily confuse them. Taking a couple pictures at this time is a good idea as well. Do not leave the lines open any longer than necessary, to avoid contaminating the replacement valve.

Replacing the valve itself can sometimes be a challenge, depending on its location, but patience and the right tools enable you to do the job correctly.

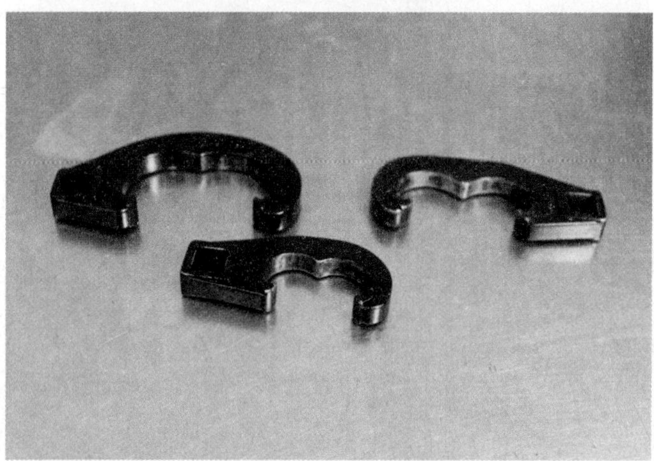

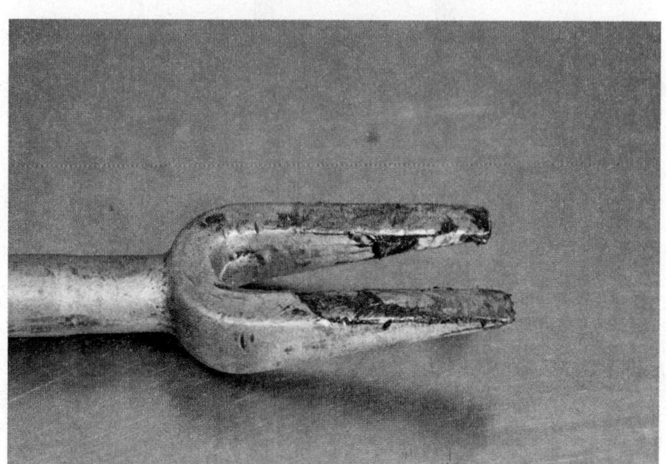

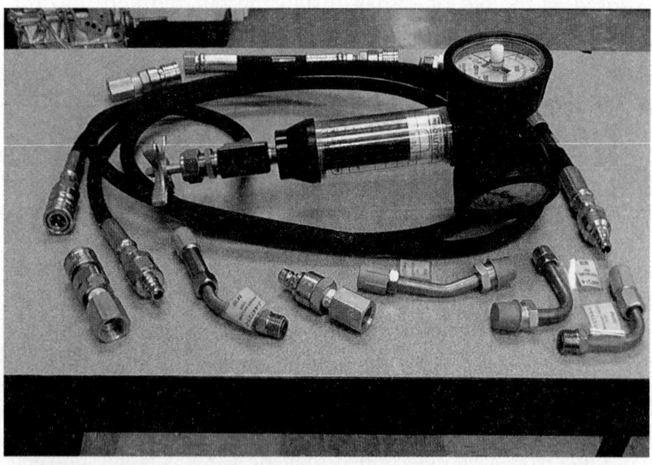

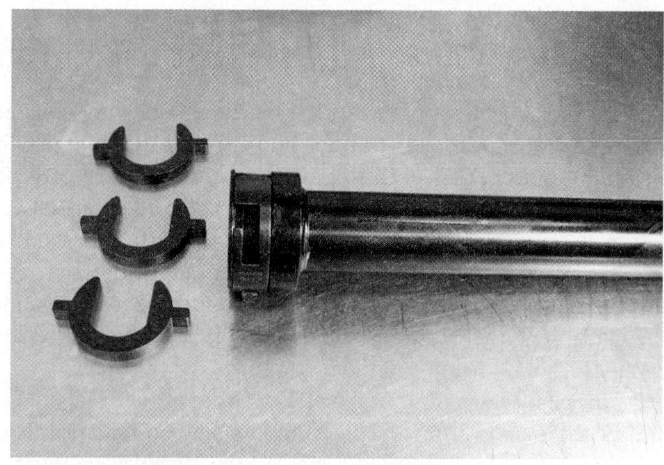

FIGURE 39-33 This tool is hammered between the tie-rod end and the steering arm to separate them.

Filter replacement should be a standard part of this procedure. Make sure the hydraulic oil level is correct before starting the machine. Start the engine; leave it at low idle; and slowly work the steering wheel back and forth just short of a full turn a few times to remove all the air from the system. Do this until the steering system seems to react normally to steering wheel input.

After the oil has warmed up a little, you can operate the machine to see if the steering works properly. When the oil is up to operating temperature, you can perform cycle time checks to see whether the system is working within specified cycle times. If the system fails the testing, further test is required, and eventually it may be necessary to replace the HMU valve. If this is the case, follow the procedure in **SKILL DRILL 39-3** to replace the valve.

SKILL DRILL 39-2 Remove and Replace a Tie-Rod End

For smaller tie rods, you can use a "pickle fork" for this job. For larger tie rods, the tapered end may have to be pressed out.

1. Mark the old tie rod's threads or count the threads showing, so you know where to locate the new part.
2. Use a proper pressing tool to remove the tie rod. *Do not* use any form of heat to help remove the tie rod.
3. Once the tapered end is loose, loosen the threaded end of the tie rod and remove it.
4. Install the new tie rod with the same amount of thread showing.
5. Install the tapered end into the steering knuckle.
6. Torque the nut to specification.
7. Before locking the tie rod tube or rod end, check the toe dimensions according to the service manual.

SKILL DRILL 39-3 Replacing the HMU Valve

The HMU can easily become contaminated if any foreign materials get in between any of its moving parts. Thoroughly diagnose the problem before replacing this valve, to make sure it requires replacement.

1. Release hydraulic pressure.
2. Mark the hydraulic lines going to the valve before removing them, or take pictures of the lines. Do not leave the lines open any longer than necessary, to avoid contaminating the replacement valve.
3. Use proper tools to remove and install the new valve.
4. Replace any filters.
5. Make sure the hydraulic oil level is correct before starting the machine.
6. Start the engine and run at low idle.
7. Work the steering wheel back and forth just short of a full turn a few times to remove all the air from the system. Do this until the system reacts normally to steering wheel input.
8. After the oil has warmed up, operate the machine to determine if the steering works properly.
9. Perform cycle time checks to see whether the system is working within specified cycle times.

Steering System Electrical Repair

Some steering systems include electrohydraulic components. Most of these systems have solenoid valves that occasionally fail. To diagnose a solenoid you suspect is faulty, it is helpful if there is more than one solenoid that is the same, which enables you to swap solenoids fairly easily when troubleshooting, in order to isolate the problem. A light-duty nut loosely holds the solenoids onto the solenoid valve assembly. Replacing a faulty solenoid is easy because of this.

▶ TECHNICIAN TIP

- Go to a machine with a conventional steering system, and check whether there is a toe adjustment.
- Go to a machine with a double-rod steering cylinder, and describe how the cylinder mounts to the machine.
- Go to a machine that has articulated steering, and draw a schematic of the steering cylinders and HMU valve.

▶ Wrap-Up

Ready for Review

- Some safety concerns related to wheeled machine steering systems include:
  - Confirmation of proper steering system operation after service or repair work
  - Steering lock being in place for articulated machines during service or repair
- Wheeled steering machines can be steered four different ways:
  - Skid steer (wheels do not pivot)
  - Articulated steering
  - Conventional steering
  - All-wheel steering
- Articulated machines have two-piece frames that pivot to allow steering.
- Straight frame or one piece-frame machines can have one or more steering axles.
- Some light-duty machines may have mechanical steering boxes that transfer operator input from a steering wheel to a steering linkage that pivots the wheels on a steering axle.
- Steering box output travels to a pitman arm, then on to a drag link that moves a steering arm. The steering arm turns one steering knuckle.
- Both steering knuckles connect together with tie rods that have ball joints on each end.
- Spindles on steering knuckles allow wheel bearings and wheels to turn on them. Steering knuckles pivot on kingpins or tapered roller bearings.
- Steering axles can be non-drive or they can provide drive for all-wheel drive arrangements.
- Hydraulic assist steering features a power-assist steering box that uses hydraulic pressure from a pump to multiply operator effort.

- Steering geometry terms include:
  - Caster (lean of kingpin when seen from the side)
  - Camber (lean of kingpin when viewed from front)
  - Toe angle (turn in between two wheels)
- Full hydraulic steering systems feature a steering valve that a steering wheel turns, a hydraulic pump, steering cylinder(s), and lines. The steering cylinders move the wheels through mechanical linkage.
- Articulated steering systems feature a steering valve that is inputted by the steering wheel. Then oil is sent to a pair of steering cylinders that pivot the two-piece frame.
- Machines with joystick steering feature a pilot valve that sends oil to a main control valve, and the pump oil goes to the steering cylinders.
- All-wheel steering machines can have up to four steering modes: conventional steer, crab steer, all-wheel steer, and skid steer. The operator selects the mode with a switch that shifts a spool valve. The spool valve redirects oil to the steering cylinders.
- Hydraulic steering system DCVs are called orbital valves, Char-Lynn valves, rotary valves, or hand metering units. They are a combination of rotary DCV, gerotor pump/motor, and pressure relief valve.
- Steering cylinders can be conventional differential type when manufacturers use them in pairs for articulated steering, or double-rod type when they use them for a steering axle.
- Secondary steering systems provide a backup oil flow in case the primary pump fails or stops turning. This system can be a ground-driven or electrically driven pump.
- Manufacturers use neutralizer valves on articulated machines to stop the turning action when the machine is fully turned.
- Steering system service includes:
  - Thorough visual inspection
  - Greasing ball joints and steering linkages
  - Checking fluid levels for hydraulic system
  - Changing oil and filters
  - Check operation of system
- Steering system–related complaints include:
  - Slow or no steering
  - Abnormal tire wear
  - No steer one way
  - Not changing steering mode
  - Drifting
  - Stiff steering wheel
- Steering linkage can be adjusted to correct some problems such as toe-in adjustment with tie-rod adjustments.
- Steering system repairs can include:
  - Worn component replacement
  - Hydraulic system leaks and component replacement
  - Electrical circuit repairs

Key Terms

Ackerman angle The angle between an imaginary point that extends from the centerline of the rear axle to the steering, or tie-rod, arms; or from a point midway between the rear axles of a tandem to the steering arms. As a machine with a steering axle turns, the steering arms that pivot the wheels turn each wheel at differing individual angles because of the Ackerman angle.

all-wheel steer The type of steering system that has front and rear steerable axles.

articulated steering A system that makes the vehicle's two-piece frame pivot on a center hinge pin arrangement.

camber Looking at one of the machine's steering axle wheels from the front, it is the slight lean you see at the top in one direction or the other.

caster Looking at the side of a machine and drawing a straight line through the center of the kingpin(s), it is the angle where the line intersects with a line drawn between the bottoms of the front and rear wheels (road surface).

conventional steering A system in which both front wheels pivot either left or right to direct the front of the machine in the direction that the operator desires. As the steering angle increases to provide a smaller turning radius, the left and right wheels turn at different angles since the inside wheel turns through a smaller radius than the outside wheel.

crab steering When both axles steer at the same time in the same direction to make the machine move diagonally.

double-rod cylinder If the machine has one steering cylinder, it has this device where each of its rods attaches to a tie rod.

ground-driven pump Part of the machine's driveline that the wheels drive also drives this pump, which usually mounts on the transfer case.

kingpin A shaft that is stationary in the steering axle on a non-drive axle.

neutralizer valve Manufacturers use this valve on articulated machines to stop the turning action when the machine is fully turned.

orbital valve Another name for a steering control valve.

secondary steering A safety backup to ensure the operator can steer the machine to a parked position.

toe angle The inward or outward angle of the wheels, measured at the front.

toe-in When the forward inside edge of the tires are closer together than the rear inside edge.

Review Questions

1. All of these machines feature conventional steering, but which one of them can also have articulated steering?
   a. Tractor loader backhoe
   b. Mining haul truck
   c. Fork lift
   d. Grader
2. An articulated machine features ________________.
   a. a two-piece main frame
   b. a steering box
   c. a pitman arm
   d. four steering knuckles

3. The greatest load is placed on steering components when ________________.
   a. the machine is stationary and there is a steering action
   b. the machine is loaded going uphill
   c. the machine is loaded going downhill
   d. the machine is reversing with a full load
4. If you were measuring a machine's toe angle, you would ________________.
   a. measure the lean in or out of the steering wheels
   b. measure the difference in distance between the front and the back of the steering wheels level with the wheel spindle
   c. measure the tilt of the kingpin
   d. measure the pitman arm angle at full turn
5. This is *not* one mode of steering for an all-wheel steer machine:
   a. Articulated
   b. Crab
   c. Conventional
   d. Rear axle
6. This is *not* one other name for a Rotary steering valve:
   a. Hand metering unit
   b. Electrohydraulic valve
   c. Char Lynn valve
   d. Orbital valve
7. Which component tries to keep the two moving parts of a rotary steering valve centered?
   a. Coil spring
   b. Leaf spring
   c. Heavy-duty O-ring
   d. Proportional solenoid
8. Joystick steering can use these *two* different ways to control the main steering control valve:
   a. Mechanical linkage and pilot oil
   b. Position sensors and poppet valves
   c. Mechanical linkage and poppet valves
   d. Poppet valves and rotary valve
9. Neutralizer valves are used as part of hydraulic steering systems to ________________.
   a. destroke the pump when no steering occurs
   b. stop the flow of power through the drivetrain when the machine is turning
   c. stop the machine from turning further
   d. upstroke the pump during a steer function to improve response
10. If a machine needs to have tie-rod ends replaced, this is one method that the technician should *not* use:
   a. Heat with acetylene torch
   b. Mechanical puller
   c. Hydraulic puller
   d. Soft hammer

ASE Technician A/Technician B Style Questions

1. Technician A says heavy equipment machines steer according to how they are propelled. Technician B says the number of wheels determines the type of steering a machine has.
   a. Technician A
   b. Technician B
   c. Both A and B
   d. Neither A nor B
2. Technician A says heavy equipment machines can steer by means of skid steer or articulated steering. Technician B says they can steer with conventional steering or all-wheel steering.
   a. Technician A
   b. Technician B
   c. Both A and B
   d. Neither A nor B
3. Technician A says straight frame machines can have all-wheel steering. Technician B says machines with articulated steering have a two-piece frame.
   a. Technician A
   b. Technician B
   c. Both A and B
   d. Neither A nor B
4. Technician A says many steering problems become evident when the machine is under load. Technician B says many steering complaints occur mostly because of tire problems.
   a. Technician A
   b. Technician B
   c. Both A and B
   d. Neither A nor B
5. Technician A says manufacturers still make heavy equipment machines with conventional steering. Technician B says only older machines have conventional steering.
   a. Technician A
   b. Technician B
   c. Neither A nor B
   d. Neither A nor B
6. Technician A says most steering axles on today's machines only provide steering ability. Technician B says most steering axles provide steering and drive.
   a. Technician A
   b. Technician B
   c. Both A and B
   d. Neither A nor B
7. Technician A says a hydraulic assist steering system helps the operator steer the wheels. Technician B says adding a hydraulic cylinder to a conventional steering system can help the operator steer the wheels.
   a. Technician A
   b. Technician B
   c. Both A and B
   d. Neither A nor B

8. Technician A says toe-in is when you look at the steering axle from the front and see that it leans slightly at the top one way or the other. Technician B says toe-in is when you are looking down at the steering axle and you notice the forward inside edge of the tires is closer than the rear inside edge.
   a. Technician A
   b. Technician B
   c. Both A and B
   d. Neither A nor B
9. Technician A says the steering control valve can also be called an HMU (hand metering unit) or an orbiting valve. Technician B says the steering control valve has no other names.
   a. Technician A
   b. Technician B
   c. Both A and B
   d. Neither A nor B
10. Technician A says most articulated machines have two hydraulic cylinders that pivot the rear frame left or right to steer. Technician B says most of these machines have one hydraulic cylinder that pivots the rear frame left or right.
    a. Technician A
    b. Technician B
    c. Both A and B
    d. Neither A nor B
11. Technician A says the joystick on a machine meters the amount of hydraulic oil for steering. Technician B says the joystick controls the amount of electrical energy needed for steering.
    a. Technician A
    b. Technician B
    c. Both A and B
    d. Neither A nor B
12. Technician A says a secondary steering system is needed on heavy equipment machines to supplement power. Technician B says the system is needed to increase loading ability.
    a. Technician A
    b. Technician B
    c. Both A and B
    d. Neither A nor B

CHAPTER 40
Wheeled and Tracked Drive Working Attachments

Knowledge Objectives

After reading this chapter, you will be able to:

- **K40001** Describe the construction, design, types, function, and operation of blades and frames, buckets, booms and arms, rippers and arms, hydraulic cylinders, tampers, rock breakers, and grapples.
- **K40002** Describe adjustment, lubrication, operational testing, and scheduled maintenance of attachments for wheeled equipment.
- **K40003** Perform operational tests of working attachments.
- **K40004** Outline recommended procedures for working attachment component inspection, removal, and replacement.

Skills Objectives

After reading this chapter, you will be able to:

- **S40001** Lubricate and make adjustments to commonly used working attachments.
- **S40002** Recommend service to working attachments.

Attitude

After reading this chapter, you will be able to:

- **A40001** Locate and follow OEM service procedures for servicing.
- **A40002** Justify component replacement and service based on OEM guidelines.

▶ Introduction

Most types of heavy equipment, whether they are wheel- or track-driven machines, are designed to perform certain basic functions. For example, dozers are used to clear areas and push soil or aggregate; graders are used to smooth, slope, and ditch roadways; and excavators are used to dig, trench, and load material. But these same machines can be fitted with a vast array of specialty attachments to greatly expand their versatility. For instance, excavators can be fitted with attachments that enable them to break rocks, demolish buildings, drive posts, grab bundles of logs, and fulfill many other construction, mining, forestry, and agricultural needs.

MORE service technicians are responsible for working not only on heavy equipment but on the many equipment attachments as well. For this reason, technicians must be familiar with the types of attachments that are commonly used on heavy equipment and understand how these attachments work and are maintained. This chapter describes many of the attachments used on heavy equipment and examines how those attachments are adjusted, tested, and maintained.

▶ Attachment Types and Functions

K40001

Heavy equipment of virtually every type and size can be fitted with different attachments that expand the equipment's function. Some of these attachments are made by the equipment manufacturer, and others are made by third-party, or aftermarket, companies. Among the more common attachments used on heavy equipment are specialty blades, buckets, booms, rippers, hydraulic cylinders, tampers, rock breakers, and grapples.

Blades and Frames

Blades are critical components of dozers, graders, and some loaders and excavators. There are so many blade options available that it can be difficult to identify a typical "standard" blade for a particular piece of equipment. In general, though, a few types of blades are used in most dozing and grading applications.

> **▶ TECHNICIAN TIP**
>
> Dozer blades are sometimes categorized as general-purpose blades, production blades, and special application blades. Each of these basic categories includes numerous types of blades. For example, general-purpose blades are used for routine construction jobs that require soil stripping and basic site development. Production blades are used in large-scale applications involving big loads, such as land reclamation and stockpiling material. Special application blades are used for jobs that require a particular type of blade to meet a specific application. These blades might be used for moving trash in a landfill, uprooting and moving trees in a forestry environment, and removing rocks and brush in land clearing operations. It is important for technicians to recognize the type of blade being used and refer to the proper equipment and attachment manuals to ensure that the blade is suitable for use on the equipment.

One common type of dozer blade is a straight blade, or **S blade** (**FIGURE 40-1**). The S blade is essentially a short, horizontally straight blade with no side wings to prevent material from spilling off the sides of the blade. For this reason, an S blade is not particularly suitable for gathering and pushing large amounts of material. It is better equipped for fine grading, dozing compacted surface material, backfilling, and ditching.

S blades are often attached to a dozer with low-mounted arms, called **push arms**, that provide great strength for pushing material. Older dozers did not always allow for blade angling (**FIGURE 40-2**).

FIGURE 40-1 Dozer with straight blade (S blade).

You Are the Mobile Heavy Technician

You are told that an operator is having trouble with a hydraulic breaker attachment on one of the company's excavators. The operator reports that it seems to be taking longer and longer to break up the rocks and other material that he is working on. You have some ideas about what might be causing the problem, but before you jump to a conclusion, you want to investigate the issue.

1. What sources of information might you check before you start troubleshooting the problem?
2. What might you do once you have gathered and reviewed all the source information?
3. How might the equipment operator help you during testing?
4. What actions might you want the attachment to perform during testing?

FIGURE 40-2 Straight blade (S blade) connections to old dozer.

FIGURE 40-3 S blade connections for angling.

FIGURE 40-4 Dozer with universal blade (U blade).

Modern dozers that use S blades typically have hydraulic cylinders that enable the blade to be angled and, in some cases, tilted on the ends (**FIGURE 40-3**).

Another common dozer blade is a universal blade, or **U blade** (**FIGURE 40-4**). This blade is tall and has a basic U shape that enables it to scoop up large amounts of material and move that material over long distances without spilling it off the sides. A U blade mounts to a dozer much like an S blade, with heavy push arms that provide strength and stability and hydraulic cylinders to lift, angle, and tilt the blade.

FIGURE 40-5 Dozer with semi-universal blade (SU blade).

A semi-universal blade, or **SU blade**, basically combines the features of an S blade and a U blade (**FIGURE 40-5**). An SU blade is mostly straight like an S blade and less curved than a U blade. It has small side wings to help prevent spillage off the sides of the blade. This type or blade is commonly used for pushing rocks and for crowning and ditching roads.

Many dozers use so-called angle blades for working in softer soils and stripping, shaping, and ditching jobs An angle blade is actually a typical straight blade that is mounted onto a pivoting point at the center of the mounting mechanism between the blade and the dozer.

In many cases, the mounting mechanism used on an angle blade is called a **C frame**. The C frame attaches to the dozer and has connection points for hydraulic cylinders to lift the blade, angle it to the left or right, and tilt the blade ends upward or downward. Some blades can also be tipped or pitched so that the top of the blade and the cutting edge can be leaned forward and backward for better ground penetration. Other mounting mechanisms, such as those used on other types of heavy equipment, might only allow the blade to be lifted and angled

A **PAT blade** (or power, angle, and tilt blade) is similar to an angle blade in that it is used on many dozers to add greater flexibility in how the blade can be moved (**FIGURE 40-6**).

A PAT blade is actually a straight blade that is attached to the dozer with a C frame that has a center **blade ball** that allows the blade to be raised and lowered, angled to the left or right, and tilted on each end using hydraulic cylinders.

Many types of specialty blades can be used on dozers to meet specific needs. Listed here are several types of specialty blades that service technicians might encounter:

- Rake blades that are used to remove roots, rocks, and brush
- V blades for clearing brush, cutting trees, and, in some configurations, pushing snow
- Coal blades for moving huge amounts of coal
- Landfill blades for pushing large amounts of debris while still providing a viewing area for operators

FIGURE 40-6 Dozer with PAT blade.

- Cushion blades, or push plate blades, that are reinforced to push other pieces of equipment
- Sidewall blades for pushing large amounts of woodchips or similar material
- Folding blades that can be turned inward to scoop material or outward to disperse material on each side; and
- Sloping blades that can cut and clean ditches and grade slopes.

▶ TECHNICIAN TIP

Other specialty blades exist for dozers, graders, loaders, and excavators. Always identify the type of blade that you are working on. Ask for manufacturer literature on the blade, if necessary. And check with the equipment operator to verify that you understand how the attachment functions before attempting any type of inspection or maintenance on the blade.

A blade that resembles a dozer straight blade, known as a **backfill blade**, is commonly used on smaller types of excavators to push excavated material back into trenches and holes or around building foundations (**FIGURE 40-7**). Backfilling is a common task for wheeled and mini-excavators.

FIGURE 40-7 Small backfill blade on a mini excavator.

Buckets

Buckets are common attachments used on numerous types of loaders, backhoes, excavators, and even cranes. Many types and sizes of buckets are available, but most of them are used to perform the basic task of digging, moving, and loading material. Other buckets are used for trenching, removing pavement, and removing rocks or other debris from soil. The specific type of bucket used depends on the equipment being used and the material being handled.

Many buckets used on wheel loaders and front end loaders have smooth cutting edges along the front (**FIGURE 40-8**). These types or buckets are sometimes called **utility buckets** and are designed to lift and load loose soil or other material. The buckets do not require special teeth along the front edge because they are typically not used to dig deep into the ground.

Excavators and other digging machines commonly use buckets that have cutting teeth along the front edge (**FIGURE 40-9**). These buckets are used for digging soil during excavation work and for cutting trenches.

FIGURE 40-8 Loader utility bucket with smooth cutting edge.

FIGURE 40-9 Excavator bucket with cutting teeth.

The width of a bucket and the number of cutting teeth can vary depending on the size of the machine and the type of digging or trenching being done.

Common types of buckets are attached to the stick and boom of excavators and backhoes so that they can be maneuvered as needed. Hydraulic cylinders enable the operator to lift, swing, and extend and retract the stick and boom to position the bucket. Hydraulic cylinders mounted on the stick provide a way to tilt the bucket so that it can be pulled back to dig into the soil. Loaders use hydraulic cylinders to lift, lower, and tilt the bucket so that it can be pushed forward to fill it and moved to a different location to unload it.

In addition to the more common types of buckets found on excavating equipment, specialty buckets are available to handle almost any uncommon application. For instance, a V ditching bucket for a backhoe is designed to cut ditches in one pass, with the proper slopes and bottom width. Because of their shape, V ditching buckets are sometimes called trapezoidal buckets.

Buckets are also designed for cleaning ditches. A ditch-cleaning bucket typically has a smooth front edge (rather than cutting teeth) and numerous holes to allow water to drain from the bucket during use.

Another specialty bucket that is used to move large amounts of lightweight material is a sand bucket (**FIGURE 40-10**). Sand buckets are basically high-strength, oversized buckets used on excavators and loaders to move material such as grain, wood chips, fertilizer, and similar material that weighs less than soil.

Some buckets are designed to pick up and hold material in place. For instance, cranes are often fitted with clamshell buckets to easily grab and hold a variety of materials such as loose soil, chemicals, coal, and ores (**FIGURE 40-11**). These types of buckets are opened wide, dropped into the material to be moved, and then closed to secure the material while the boom is swung to the spot for unloading.

Buckets are designed for every conceivable function and can be equipped with numerous ground engagement tool options. **FIGURE 40-12** shows just some of the optional (teeth) or ground engagement tools available.

FIGURE 40-10 Loader with a sand bucket.

FIGURE 40-11 Clamshell bucket.

FIGURE 40-12 Different types of ground engagement tools (teeth).

> **TECHNICIAN TIP**
>
> When working on or around any type of standard or specialty bucket, make sure that you can accurately identify the type of bucket and understand how the bucket is used. It may be necessary to ask for manufacturer literature on the bucket or speak with the equipment operator to verify that you understand how the attachment functions before attempting any type of inspection or maintenance on the bucket.

Booms and Arms

Different types of heavy equipment, including cranes, excavators, loaders, and even dozers used in certain applications, have some type of boom that allows the equipment to maneuver and use buckets, blades, and other attachments. In a typical configuration, for instance, an excavator has a boom with a stick, or dipper stick, that connects the bucket to the excavator's rotating platform (**FIGURE 40-13**). Hydraulic cylinders are used to raise and lower the boom, and extend and retract the stick and the bucket. A linkage connects the hydraulic bucket cylinder and the stick to the bucket itself to allow the bucket to be manipulated.

FIGURE 40-13 Typical hydraulic excavator boom, stick and bucket cylinders.

> **SAFETY TIP**
>
> Any special boom and/or stick attachment must be carefully matched to the equipment on which it is being used. Overweight or oversized attachments can damage the equipment and cause the equipment to overturn. Additional counterweights are likely to be needed to help offset the additional weight of the special boom and/or stick. Always refer to the manufacturers' recommendations on the acceptable sizes and weights of any special attachments being used.

Wheeled excavators that can be driven on the highway or over rough terrain commonly have a **telescoping boom** (**FIGURE 40-14**). Telescoping booms can typically be extended, retracted, and rotated. This type of equipment is relatively compact and is commonly used on highway projects.

Other types of booms can be used on an excavator to enable it to perform different functions. For example, excavators can be fitted with long-reach booms and sticks to extend the reach of the bucket or other attachment being used.

Another attachment that can be used to extend the reach of an excavator is an **extension jib**. The extension jib attaches to the end of the excavator's stick to extend the reach of the bucket. It has a built-in hydraulic cylinder to control the bucket movement.

A similar type of boom attachment that is sometimes used on excavators is a special **telescopic dipper** stick attachment. In this configuration, the excavator has a typical boom section, but instead of a solid stick connecting the boom to the bucket, a telescoping stick is used. A common application for this type of attachment is when an excavator needs to dig and move material from below grade. The telescopic dipper enables to bucket to be extended far beyond what a standard stick can reach. Telescopic dippers are also sometimes used with blades for grading tall embankments and demolition attachments for tearing down tall buildings.

The boom configuration on a backhoe loader is very similar to what is found on an excavator (**FIGURE 40-15**). There is a boom, a dipper stick, and a bucket, each with its corresponding hydraulic cylinder for controlling movement. A swing cylinder at the mounting point of the boom enables an operator to move the entire backhoe mechanism to the left and right.

If a backhoe needs additional reach capability, it can be equipped with a special long-reach boom. A long-reach boom is similar to a standard boom, but with added length. Also, the boom is narrower and curved to improve the operator's visibility.

Another boom attachment that is used with backhoes and loaders is a truss boom attachment. Truss boom attachments mount onto the end of a dipper stick to extend the reach of the equipment for applications such as lifting and positioning rafters and trusses for buildings, and loading trees and other objects onto trucks. These attachments are available in different sizes and capacity ratings, but they are not capable of lifting enormous loads. Some truss boom attachments are fitted with hydraulic winches to increase their versatility.

As with other heavy equipment attachments, booms can vary a great deal. Although most booms are **lattice booms** or telescoping booms, some cranes are equipped with a combination of the two. For instance, large truck-mounted cranes sometimes use a telescoping boom at the base, with lattice boom extensions to maximize the crane's reach (**FIGURE 40-16**).

Some booms are designed for very specific applications. One example of such a boom is a dozer-mounted side boom (**FIGURE 40-17**). Side booms are commonly used for pipe-laying applications, but they can also be used for railroad work and

FIGURE 40-14 Wheeled excavator with telescoping boom.

FIGURE 40-15 Backhoe boom and dipper stick cylinder configuration.

FIGURE 40-16 Truck-mounted crane with telescoping boom and lattice boom extensions.

FIGURE 40-18 Dozer with five-shank ripper attachment.

FIGURE 40-17 Dozer-mounted side boom for pipe laying.

FIGURE 40-19 Motor grader with three-shank ripper attachment.

other tasks. In a typical configuration, the boom and hook are controlled using winches. Counterweights on the opposite side of the dozer offset the load being lifted and manipulated.

Rippers and Arms

Rippers are attachments mounted onto heavy equipment, primarily dozers and motor graders, to help break up rocky and/or compacted soil (**FIGURE 40-18**). A ripper consists primarily of one or more steel shanks, each with a cutting tooth mounted onto its end. Each ripper shank is attached to a metal frame that is connected to the rear of the equipment. Hydraulic cylinders enable the operator to raise and lower the ripper attachment as needed. Depending on the size of the equipment being used, rippers can vary from a single shank to several shanks.

Rippers used on motor graders are typically smaller in size than the ones used on dozers, and they can have more or less shanks per attachment (**FIGURE 40-19**). On most ripper attachments, the shanks can be removed and added to the frame as needed to meet the specific need.

Another type of ripper attachment that is often used on motor graders is a **scarifier**. Scarifiers are usually mounted near the front of a motor grader (ahead of the blade) to help loosen compacted soil. The shanks and teeth of a scarifier are smaller than those of a ripper, as they are used primarily to break up the soil surface and not to cut deep into the soil.

Ripper attachments can also be used on the front of skid steer loaders and on the end of excavator booms (**FIGURE 40-20**). In any of these applications, the basic purpose of the ripper is the same: to break up hard and compacted soil to make excavation and grading easier.

SAFETY TIP

Hydraulic cylinders operate at very high pressures. Always use caution when working on or around hydraulic cylinders and their connecting hoses and/or piping to avoid injury. Refer to the manufacturers' recommendations to determine the operating conditions for any hydraulic cylinder being serviced.

Tampers

Tampers, or compactors as they are often called, are hydraulic attachments most often used on excavators to compact soil or

FIGURE 40-20 Ripper tooth attachment on excavator.

FIGURE 40-22 Hydraulic breaker attachments and chisels for excavators.

FIGURE 40-21 Vibrating plate compactor attachment for an excavator.

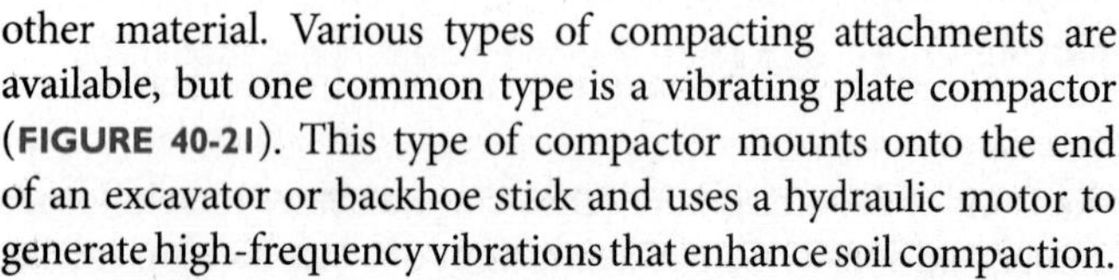

FIGURE 40-23 Excavator with hydraulic breaker attachment.

other material. Various types of compacting attachments are available, but one common type is a vibrating plate compactor (**FIGURE 40-21**). This type of compactor mounts onto the end of an excavator or backhoe stick and uses a hydraulic motor to generate high-frequency vibrations that enhance soil compaction.

Another use for a vibrating plate compactor is driving various types of sheeting and, in some cases, posts and pilings. It should be noted, however, that most vibrating compactors used for driving posts and similar objects have a cylinder-like addition on the bottom of the vibrating plate to help hold the post in place.

Another type of tamper that is sometimes used on excavators and backhoes, especially for compacting backfill soil in trenches, is a compaction wheel. This attachment relies on the static weight of the excavator or backhoe and the sheepsfoot-like pads of the wheels to compact the soil.

Rock Breakers

Rock breakers are attachments that are typically mounted onto the end of an excavator stick and used to break rocks, concrete, pavement, walls, or other hard material (**FIGURE 40-22**). Many different names are used to describe these attachments, including rock hammers, hydraulic hammers, and, most commonly, **hydraulic breakers**.

Hydraulic breakers are like jack hammers in that they rely on the reciprocating motion of a chisel to rip through rock, concrete, or similar material. These attachments come in different sizes, and the chisels are typically interchangeable to meet the requirements of the work being performed (**FIGURE 40-23**).

Grapples

Grapples are jaw-like attachments used on excavators, loaders, tractors, and other equipment to grab and pick up objects such as rocks, debris, brush, logs, and other material (**FIGURE 40-24**). These attachments come in many shapes and sizes and are commonly found in construction, demolition, agricultural, and forestry applications.

A typical grapple attachment mounts onto the end of a dipper stick or onto a loader mounting plate and has two or more grapple arms (jaws) that can be opened and closed with one or more hydraulic cylinders. A rotating connection enables a boom-mounted grapple to be rotated 360 degrees so that the load can be positioned as needed.

Skid steer loaders are often fitted with grapple attachments to collect and remove debris (**FIGURE 40-25**).

FIGURE 40-24 Excavator grapple attachment.

FIGURE 40-25 Skid steer with grapple attachment.

FIGURE 40-26 This grapple/bucket has hydraulic cylinders to adjust the grappling jaws.

FIGURE 40-27 Remotely adjustable fork attachment.

▶ Attachment Adjustments and Maintenance

K40002, S40001

MORE service technicians are responsible for inspecting, testing, adjusting, and maintaining many types of heavy equipment. They are also responsible for performing the same maintenance-related tasks on whatever attachments are used on the equipment. This means service technicians must be thoroughly familiar with how many types of equipment attachments perform and how they are tested and serviced.

Adjustments

Some of the attachments used on wheeled equipment can be adjusted based on the specific tasks being performed. For instance, some grapple fork attachments used on skid steer loaders have different mounting holes for the rod end of the grapple's hydraulic cylinder. Changing the mounting hole for the cylinder increases or decreases the amount of opening or closing that the grapple can do. Service technicians might be asked to adjust the cylinder mounting if the equipment operator is not seeing satisfactory results during use of the attachment.

Some excavator grapples have a similar adjustment, but one that is done with an adjustable stabilizer bracket instead of a hydraulic cylinder mount. Other grapple-type attachments use individual hydraulic cylinders to adjust the position of the grappling jaws (**FIGURE 40-26**). In this case, the position of the rear section of the grapple can be adjusted by choosing from several mounting holes in the bracket.

Some fork attachments used on heavy equipment can be adjusted remotely by the operator because they have hydraulic cylinders that can move the forks closer together or farther apart (**FIGURE 40-27**). This alleviates the need for an operator to leave the cab and manually move the forks.

Other adjustments that service technicians might be involved with on wheeled equipment attachments include measuring and adjusting the positions of blade and bucket cutting edges, modifying (when possible) the hydraulic fluid pressure being supplied to an attachment, and adjusting the depth of ripper and scarifier teeth.

Lubrication

One of the most important maintenance procedures that can be performed on any heavy equipment attachment is regular lubrication (**FIGURE 40-28**). Nearly every attachment has numerous pivoting points, and many of these points have bushings and sleeves that absorb wear to protect the more expensive housings. Others simply have pivot holes without bushings. In both cases, it is absolutely critical that these pivoting points are lubricated on a regular basis. Otherwise, unnecessary wear will occur and quickly lead to expensive repairs and downtime.

Look for grease fittings, and follow the equipment manufacturer's guidelines for how often to grease the components. A typical lubrication plan might call for greasing every day or every 8-hour shift. Some plans are even stricter, recommending greasing every 4 hours.

Keep in mind that grease attracts dust and contaminants. Always wipe away excess grease to minimize the risk of dirt getting into the components being lubricated.

The level of hydraulic fluid in the equipment's system is also critical. All attachments rely on hydraulic fluid to operate, and some attachments require more fluid than others. For these reasons, the hydraulic fluid level should be checked at least every 40 hours and whenever two attachments are switched.

SAFETY TIP

Hydraulic attachments operate at very high pressures and temperatures. Always use caution when working on or around hydraulic hoses, piping, and cylinders to avoid injury. Refer to the manufacturers' recommendations to determine the operating conditions for any attachment being serviced.

Operational Testing

If an attachment appears to be having problems, it is often necessary to test the attachment under normal operating conditions to see how it is performing. Service technicians can sometimes perform operational testing on their own, but it may be necessary to have the equipment operator use the attachment while the technician observes the activity from the ground. In either case, any operational testing should be performed after the equipment has reached its normal operating temperatures and pressures.

FIGURE 40-28 Technician greasing hydraulic breaker attachment.

Some of the typical problems to watch for on heavy equipment attachments during operational testing are listed here:

- Blades that do not raise, lower, angle, or tilt properly
- Buckets that do not raise, lower, or tilt properly
- Booms that do not raise, lower, extend, or retract properly
- Rippers that do not raise, lower, or tip properly
- Hydraulic cylinders that leak or do not activate properly
- Tampers that do not vibrate or roll properly
- Hydraulic breakers that do not reciprocate the chisel properly
- Grapples that will do open, close, or rotate properly

If any unusual operation is observed, the equipment should be taken out of service, inspected in greater detail, and repaired or replaced as needed.

Scheduled Maintenance

Heavy equipment attachments require routine maintenance just like the equipment itself. Many attachments are manufactured by the equipment manufacturers, but just as many are designed and built by aftermarket companies. Regardless of the manufacturer, it is critical that service technicians follow the attachment manufacturer's recommended maintenance schedule.

The exact scheduled maintenance plan for an attachment varies according to the attachment itself. Most plans, however, call for a walk-around inspection at the beginning of every shift or least once a day. These visual inspections include checking for loose or missing mounting hardware; hydraulic cylinder leakage; hydraulic hose damage; excessive dirt that might be interfering with the attachment's operation; and worn or damaged cutting edges, teeth, shanks, and similar components. Technicians should pay close attention to all high-wear areas, such as pivoting points, blade edges, and bucket teeth.

Attachment manufacturers provide recommendations for the frequency of inspecting and maintaining their equipment. Some recommendations, such as lubrication, may be based on hours of usage. Other recommendations may be based on a time schedule, such as every two weeks or every month. Technicians should be aware of these recommendations and follow them closely to avoid serious problems and unexpected downtime.

In order to properly lubricate and adjust commonly used working attachments, follow the steps in **SKILL DRILL 40-1**.

▶ Locating and Following OEM Service Procedures

A40001

Before inspecting, testing, adjusting, or servicing any mobile equipment attachment, it is important for technicians to be familiar with the equipment. This includes locating and reading any operator manuals and service manuals that may exist on-site. Find out where those manuals are normally kept, and take action to obtain the proper manuals for the equipment. Remember, many

SKILL DRILL 40-1 Lubricating and Adjusting Commonly Used Working Attachments

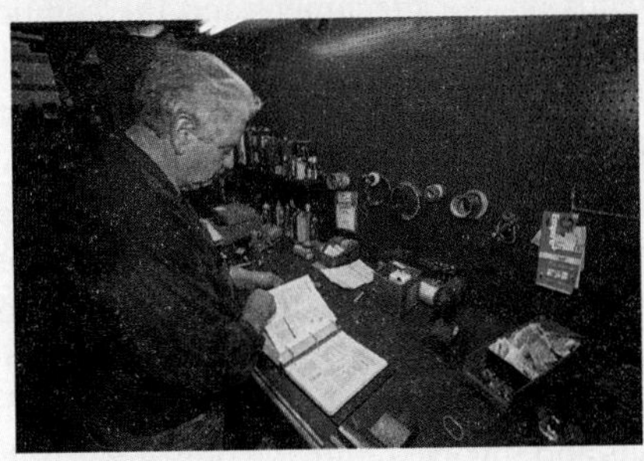

1. Obtain the attachment manufacturer's recommended guidelines that cover regular lubrication and adjustment procedures.

2. Locate all lubrication points on the attachment that correspond to the recommended points in the manufacturer's guidelines.

3. Apply the recommended type and amount of grease to each lubrication point fitting. Wipe away any excess grease to minimize the risk of dirt contamination.

4. Locate all adjustment points on the attachment that correspond to the recommended points in the manufacturer's guidelines.

5. Carefully examine the adjustment points, and make any adjustments to the attachment that are deemed necessary.

6. Record all actions performed during the lubrication and adjustment procedure on the appropriate service form or into an electronic database.

attachments are built by manufacturers other than the equipment manufacturer. If printed manuals are not available for the attachment, try to find electronic versions either from the client or online through the equipment manufacturer's website. It might also be possible to find the appropriate material by searching online. In some cases, it might be necessary to call the equipment manufacturer to get the needed information. Some attachments might have stickers on them that provide service-related information Whatever the means, it is important to ensure that the resource material being used matches the attachment being worked on.

▶ Performing Operational Tests

K40003

Operational testing of equipment attachments can be a form of troubleshooting or an evaluation that might be conducted on a scheduled basis, such as annually. For example, if an attachment is performing properly, a service technician might only perform an operational test in the timeframe suggested by the attachment manufacturer's guidelines. The need for and frequency of testing typically depends on the attachment itself or the equipment on which it is used. A properly operating grapple attachment on a skid steer loader, for instance, might not present a critical need for operational testing on a regular basis, whereas a similar attachment on a large mobile crane could require more frequent monitoring and testing to minimize hazards.

Whatever the need for operational testing, the process should follow some general rules. For example, the first step should be to gather information. Talk to the operator or equipment owner to determine whether there are noticeable problems during the operation of the attachment, and have the operator describe in as much detail as possible when and how the problem occurs. Locate and read all manuals and guidelines provided by the attachment manufacturer. It is difficult to identify a problem if you are not sure how the attachment is designed to work in the first place. Also, check for existing inspection and repair records on the attachment to determine whether similar problems might have occurred in the past.

> **▶ TECHNICIAN TIP**
>
> Keep in mind that equipment attachments are controlled by the same hydraulic system that controls the equipment itself. So, a problem such as a low hydraulic fluid level or a faulty hydraulic pump affects both the equipment and any attachments mounted on the equipment. For this reason, it is a good idea to examine the equipment for leaks or obvious signs of damage that might affect the attachment.

After collecting information about the problem, examine the attachment for obvious signs of damage or other problems. Something as simple as a hose leak or a loose connecting pin might be the cause of the problem. Do not stop inspecting the attachment after the first sign of a problem. There could be other obvious damage that could affect the attachment as well.

If no obvious problems are observed during the attachment inspection, check for common issues that could cause the problem described by the operator. Start with the simplest possible causes first, such as low fluid levels, leaks, and loose fasteners. Be careful not to jump to conclusions about possible causes and neglect other possible causes. For instance, simply topping off the hydraulic fluid level could have a positive effect on the problem, but it might not be the root of the problem.

At this point, it is time to observe the attachment in use. Some pieces of heavy equipment require special training to operate. If you are unable or disinclined to operate the equipment, ask the operator to do so while you observe. Make sure that the equipment is started up in the proper manner and allowed to reach normal operating conditions. Have the operator make all of the normal movements with the attachment without any load. Carefully observe the movements, and note the cycle times for opening and closing or extending and retracting the attachment. Listen for any unusual noises during operation, and check for unusual odors that might suggest overheating. If the problem is still unclear, have the operator use the attachment under load.

Once the problem has been observed and diagnosed, determine the best approach to repairing the attachment. Some repairs can be done on the spot, but others might have to be scheduled. Of course, in some cases, repairs can be so costly and time consuming that it might make more sense to simply replace the attachment. Either way, be sure to document the inspection and testing that took place, as well as the repairs.

▶ Component Inspection, Removal, and Replacement Procedures

K40004, S40002

Attachment components are subject to wear and damage because of the harsh environments in which they are used. For example, blade cutting edges wear; bucket teeth break; boom pivoting points deteriorate; and hydraulic cylinders develop leaks. Attachment manufacturers understand that certain components will wear out over time, and they publish guidelines for inspecting, removing, and replacing these components. Part of a service technician's job is to be familiar with these guidelines and utilize them to develop procedures for inspecting, removing, and replacing these components.

Many attachment components that are subject to wear can be seen during an operator's daily walk-around inspection. The operator should notify the service department when components like cutting edges, bucket teeth, bushings, and hoses appear worn or damaged. Service technicians inspect these same components during their routine maintenance procedures, based on the manufacturer's guidelines. With some components, premature wear can be delayed by following strict lubrication recommendations and keeping the components as clean as possible. Eventually, however, high-usage components will have to be removed and replaced.

Removing attachment components for replacement can be relatively simple or difficult and time consuming. The complexity and effort depends on the attachment and the components being removed. It is always best to perform these tasks in a shop environment where tools and equipment are available for hoisting the attachment and securing it for safety purposes.

To identify the proper component removal procedures, always refer to the attachment manufacturer's literature. Most operation and maintenance manuals include drawings or photos of how the attachment is assembled. Safety warnings and procedural details are noted as well. In some cases, component removal may be obvious and involve removing only a few bolts or pins. Other cases can involve heating components with a torch to free them for removal.

The steps to use for replacing worn components are commonly described in the attachment manufacturer's manuals. Make sure that the correct replacement components are available, and follow the guidelines for installing the new parts. In some specific cases, such as repairing worn pivoting points, it may be necessary to weld additional metal into the pin holes and then drill out new holes of the original size and shape. Once the components have been properly installed, test the attachment to ensure that it operates properly.

To perform service on working attachment components, follow the steps in **SKILL DRILL 40-2**.

1. Obtain and review the attachment manufacturer's recommended guidelines for inspecting, removing, and replacing worn or broken attachment components.
2. Talk to the equipment operator to get input about any suspected worn or damaged components on the attachment.
3. Inspect all components on the attachment for wear or obvious damage.
4. Follow the manufacturer's guidelines for removing any worn or damaged components.
5. Ensure that the correct replacement parts are obtained, follow the manufacturer's guidelines for replacing the components, and then test the attachment for proper operation.
6. Record all actions performed during the inspection, removal, and replacement of attachment components on the appropriate service form or into an electronic database.

▶ Justifying Component Replacement and Service

A40002

Equipment attachments are built to last a long time, especially if they are operated in the correct manner and routinely inspected and maintained. Failure to regularly lubricate, adjust, and service an attachment will shorten its workable lifespan. Attachment manufacturers provide guidelines that specify how often to perform routine inspections and maintenance. Service technicians should always follow these guidelines to ensure that the attachment functions effectively for as long as possible.

Because of the harsh environments in which equipment attachments operate, there will always be wear and tear on

SKILL DRILL 40-2 Performing Component Inspection, Removal, and Replacement Procedures

1. Obtain and review the attachment manufacturer's recommended guidelines for inspecting, removing, and replacing worn or broken attachment components.

2. Talk to the equipment operator to get input about any suspected worn or damaged components on the attachment.

3. Inspect all components on the attachment for wear or obvious damage.

4. Follow the manufacturer's guidelines for removing any worn or damaged components.

5. Ensure that the correct replacement parts are obtained, follow the manufacturer's guidelines for replacing the components, and then test the attachment for proper operation.

6. Record all actions performed during the inspection, removal, and replacement of attachment components on the appropriate service form or into an electronic database.

components. It is important for operators, owners, and technicians to understand that, even with the most stringent maintenance schedule, components will always wear out or break. The most effective means of addressing component failure is to recognize the need to make adjustments along the way and understand when to replace worn-out parts. Doing this enables service technicians to schedule maintenance ahead of time to prevent unnecessary downtime. After all, scheduling a time to replace a relatively inexpensive bushing or hose before it fails is much more efficient than replacing an expensive housing or hydraulic cylinder after the equipment breaks down unexpectedly.

Another important aspect of component replacement and service is that the attachment will perform at its highest level when all of its parts are in good shape. Dull blades, broken teeth, and leaking cylinders slow down the operation of the equipment and may lead to additional problems later on. For all these reasons, it is better to spend some money up front to maintain attachments than to wait until failures occur and spend a lot more money and time trying to repair them.

Wrap-Up

Ready for Review

- Heavy equipment of virtually every type and size can be fitted with different attachments that expand the equipment's function.
- A straight blade, or S blade, is essentially a short, horizontally straight blade with no side wings to prevent material from spilling off the sides of the blade.
- S blades are often attached to a dozer with low-mounted arms, called push arms, that provide great strength for pushing material.
- A universal blade, or U blade, has a basic U shape that enables it to scoop up large amounts of material and move that material over long distances without spilling it off the sides.

- A semi-universal blade, or SU blade, is mostly straight like an S blade and less curved than a U blade.
- An angle blade is basically a straight blade that is mounted onto a pivoting point at the center of the mounting mechanism, between the blade and the dozer, to make it more adjustable.
- A C frame is a mounting mechanism that attaches to the dozer and has connection points for hydraulic cylinders to lift the blade, angle it to the left or right, and tilt the blade ends upward or downward.
- A PAT blade is similar to an angle blade in that it is used on many dozers to add greater flexibility in how the blade can be moved.
- A PAT blade is actually a straight blade attached to the dozer with a C frame that has a center blade ball that allows the blade to be raised and lowered, angled to the left or right, and tilted on each end, using hydraulic cylinders.
- A backfill blade is commonly used on smaller types of excavators to push excavated material back into trenches and holes or around building foundations.
- A utility bucket, which is commonly used on wheel loaders and front end loaders, has a smooth cutting edge along the front to lift and load loose soil or other material.
- Excavators and other digging machines commonly use buckets that have cutting teeth along the front edge to dig soil during excavation work and to cut trenches.
- The width of a bucket and the number of cutting teeth can vary depending on the size of the machine and the type of digging or trenching being done.
- A sand bucket is basically a high-strength, oversized bucket used on excavators and loaders to move material such as grain, wood chips, fertilizer, and similar material that weighs less than soil.
- A clamshell bucket is sometimes used on a crane to easily grab and hold a variety of materials such as loose soil, chemicals, coal, and ores.
- A telescoping boom can typically be extended, retracted, and rotated.
- Long-reach booms and sticks are used to extend the reach of the bucket or other attachment being used.
- An extension jib attaches to the end of an excavator's stick to extend the reach of the bucket; a built-in hydraulic cylinder controls the bucket movement.
- A telescopic dipper stick attachment is used in place of a solid stick to connect the boom to the bucket and enables the bucket to be extended far beyond what a standard stick can reach.
- Truss boom attachments mount onto the end of a dipper stick to extend the reach of the equipment for applications such as lifting and positioning rafters and trusses for buildings and loading trees and other objects onto trucks.
- A typical track-mounted, or crawler, crane has a lattice boom made up of one or more sections.
- Rippers are attachments mounted onto dozers and motor graders that consist primarily of one or more steel shanks with teeth to help break up rocky and/or compacted soil.
- Scarifiers are smaller ripper attachments that are usually mounted near the front of a motor grader (ahead of the blade) to help loosen compacted soil.
- Tampers, or compactors as they are often called, are hydraulic attachments most often used on excavators to compact soil or other material.
- A vibrating plate compactor mounts onto the end of an excavator or backhoe stick and uses a hydraulic motor to generate high-frequency vibrations that enhance soil compaction.
- A compaction wheel is a type of tamper that relies on the static weight of an excavator or backhoe and sheepsfoot-like pads on the wheels to compact the soil.
- Rock breakers, or hydraulic breakers, are attachments that are typically mounted onto the end of an excavator stick and used to break rocks, concrete, pavement, walls, or other hard material.
- Grapples are jaw-like attachments used on excavators, loaders, tractors, and other equipment to grab and pick up objects such as rocks, debris, brush, logs, and other material.
- Some grapple fork attachments on skid steer loaders have different mounting holes for the rod end of the grapple's hydraulic cylinder that can be changed to increase or decrease the amount of opening or closing that the grapple can do.
- One of the most important maintenance procedures that can be performed on any heavy equipment attachment is regular lubrication.
- If an attachment appears to be having problems, it is often necessary to perform operational testing of the attachment under normal operating conditions.
- Attachment manufacturers provide recommendations for the frequency of inspecting and maintaining their equipment, and technicians should follow these recommendations closely to avoid serious problems and unexpected downtime.
- Operational testing of an attachment should begin by gathering information about the suspected problem.
- Attachment manufacturers understand that certain components will wear out over time, and they publish guidelines for inspecting, removing, and replacing these components.

Key Terms

backfill blade A type of blade that is commonly used on smaller types of excavators to push excavated material back into trenches and holes or around building foundations.

blade ball A pivoting point on some dozer blade mounting frames that enables the blade to be raised and lowered, angled to the left or right, and tilted on each end, using hydraulic cylinders.

C frame A mounting mechanism used on an angle blade that attaches to the dozer and has connection points for hydraulic cylinders to lift the blade, angle it to the left or right, and tilt the blade ends upward or downward.

extension jib A device that attaches to the end of an excavator's stick to extend the reach of the bucket.

grapple A jaw-like attachment used on excavators, loaders, tractors, and other equipment to grab and pick up objects such as rocks, debris, brush, logs, and other material.

hydraulic breaker An attachment, commonly called a rock breaker, that functions much like a jackhammer by using the reciprocating motion of a chisel to rip through rock, concrete, or similar material.

lattice boom A basic type of boom, used on many crawler cranes, that consists of one or more sections of interlaced steel rods that provide strength and support.

PAT blade A straight blade, sometimes called a power, angle, and tilt blade, that is attached to a dozer with a C frame and uses hydraulic cylinders to be raised and lowered, angled to the left or right, and tilted on each end.

push arms Low-mounted arms used to connect a dozer blade to a dozer and provide great strength for pushing material.

ripper An attachment that is commonly mounted onto the rear of a dozer or motor grader that consists of one or more steel shanks with cutting teeth to help break up rocky and/or compacted soil.

S blade A short, horizontally straight blade with no side wings to prevent material from spilling off the sides of the blade.

scarifier A type of ripper attachment that is mounted near the front of a motor grader (ahead of the blade) to help loosen compacted soil.

SU blade A semi-universal blade that is mostly straight like an S blade and less curved than a U blade, with side wings to help prevent spillage off the sides of the blade.

tamper One of several types of attachments used on excavators and loaders to compact soil using vibrating plates or rolling pads.

telescopic dipper A device that is used in place of a normal dipper stick on an excavator to extend the reach of the bucket, especially in applications where material needs to be removed from below ground level or high above ground level.

telescoping boom A type of boom that is commonly used on wheeled excavators and cranes that can be extended, retracted, and rotated.

U blade A universal dozer blade that is tall and has a basic U shape that enables it to scoop up large amounts of material and move that material over long distances without spilling it off the sides.

utility bucket A type of bucket used on wheel loaders and front end loaders that has a smooth cutting edge along the front to lift and load loose soil or other material.

Review Questions

1. S blades need great strength for pushing material, so they are often attached to a dozer with low-mounted _____.
   a. universal joints
   b. ball frames
   c. tamper rods
   d. push arms
2. A device on a C frame that allows a dozer blade to be raised and lowered, angled to the left or right, and tilted on each end using hydraulic cylinders is called a(n) _____.
   a. extension jib
   b. blade ball
   c. hydraulic breaker
   d. PAT rod
3. Cushion blades are reinforced so that they can be used to _____.
   a. cut tree roots during excavation
   b. backfill trenches and around foundations
   c. push other pieces of equipment
   d. move rocks without breaking them
4. A type of blade that is commonly used on mini-excavators to push excavated material back into trenches is called a(n) _____.
   a. backfill blade
   b. SU blade
   c. landfill blade
   d. folding blade
5. A trapezoidal bucket is most likely to be used for _____.
   a. separating rocks from surrounding soil
   b. cutting shaped ditches in one pass
   c. scooping up and holding soft material
   d. removing slabs of concrete or pavement
6. One of the most common applications for a dozer-mounted side boom is _____.
   a. trenching
   b. demolition
   c. ditching
   d. pipe laying
7. A common type of tamper is a _____.
   a. vibrating plate compactor
   b. post hole grapple
   c. hydraulic sheepsfoot breaker
   d. mechanical rock hammer
8. After routinely greasing an attachment, it is important to _____.
   a. perform an operational test on the attachment
   b. wait five minutes and then grease again
   c. wipe away excess grease to minimize contaminants
   d. use a ballast tamper to secure the seals
9. During operational testing of an attachment, a service technician should always _____.
   a. apply a heavier-than-normal load to the attachment
   b. make sure the equipment is at normal operating conditions
   c. disregard unusual noises or odors for the time being
   d. isolate the attachment from the equipment's hydraulic system
10. Procedures for inspecting, removing, and replacing attachment components can typically be found in _____.
   a. most heavy equipment service manuals
   b. OSHA and/or state regulations
   c. most metalworking handbooks
   d. the attachment manufacturer's literature

ASE Technician A/Technician B Style Questions

1. Technician A says an S blade is not particularly suitable for gathering and pushing large amounts of material. Technician B says an S blade has no side wings to prevent material from spilling off the sides of the blade. Who is correct?
   a. Technician A
   b. Technician B
   c. Both A and B
   d. Neither A nor B
2. Technician A says a universal blade, or U blade, is tall and has a basic U shape. Technician B says a U blade cannot be used to move material over long distances. Who is correct?
   a. Technician A
   b. Technician B
   c. Both A and B
   d. Neither A nor B
3. Technician A says a C frame is a ripper-like attachment used on motor graders. Technician B says a C frame attaches to a dozer and has connection points for hydraulic cylinders to lift, angle, and tilt the blade. Who is correct?
   a. Technician A
   b. Technician B
   c. Both A and B
   d. Neither A nor B
4. Technician A says another common name for a V ditching bucket is a triangular bucket. Technician B says a V ditching bucket is commonly called a skeleton bucket. Who is correct?
   a. Technician A
   b. Technician B
   c. Both A and B
   d. Neither A nor B
5. Technician A says an extension jib attaches to the end of an excavator's stick to extend the reach of the bucket. Technician B says a telescopic dipper stick attachment can be used in place of a solid stick when an excavator needs to dig and move material from below grade. Who is correct?
   a. Technician A
   b. Technician B
   c. Both A and B
   d. Neither A nor B
6. Technician A says a scarifier is a type of grapple used for loading logs onto a truck. Technician B says a scarifier is usually mounted near the front of a motor grader (ahead of the blade) to help loosen compacted soil. Who is correct?
   a. Technician A
   b. Technician B
   c. Both A and B
   d. Neither A nor B

7. Technician A says most hydraulic cylinders used on heavy equipment are welded cylinders. Technician B says most hydraulic cylinders used on heavy equipment attachments are tie-rod cylinders. Who is correct?
   a. Technician A
   b. Technician B
   c. Both A and B
   d. Neither A nor B
8. Technician A says a typical lubrication plan for an attachment suggests greasing the components no more than once a month. Technician B says most attachments use sealed bearings and sleeves that do not require greasing. Who is correct?
   a. Technician A
   b. Technician B
   c. Both A and B
   d. Neither A nor B
9. Technician A says that before performing any operational testing on an attachment, a service technician should first locate and read all manuals and guidelines about the attachment. Technician B says a service technician should talk to the equipment operator before doing operational testing. Who is correct?
   a. Technician A
   b. Technician B
   c. Both A and B
   d. Neither A nor B
10. Technician A says that if a pin mounting hole at an attachment pivoting point becomes worn and oversized, the best way to repair it is to weld the pin to the perimeter of the hole. Technician B says you should weld additional metal into and around the pin hole and then machine out a new hole of the original size and shape. Who is correct?
    a. Technician A
    b. Technician B
    c. Both A and B
    d. Neither A nor B

SECTION V

Track Drive Undercarriage & Working Attachments

CHAPTER 41

Track Drive Undercarriage Systems

Knowledge Objectives

After reading this chapter, you will be able to:

- **K41001** Identify and describe types of steel and rubber track drive undercarriage and major features of each track drive system.
- **K41002** Explain the advantages, operating principles, and major features of track drive undercarriage systems.
- **K41003** Identify and describe major features of steel track drive systems.
- **K41004** Identify and describe common causes of accelerated undercarriage wear and normal progression of track wear.
- **K41005** Explain principles of differential steering systems.
- **K41006** Describe developmental stages of track drive system technology.

Skills Objectives

There are no Skills Objectives for this chapter.

▶ Introduction

Track drive undercarriage systems enable off-road equipment to travel and operate over soft, uneven, rugged ground conditions encountered working in farm fields, forests, mines, quarries, or earth moving. Track systems not only enable machines to maneuver well but also supply extra traction force for pushing or pulling heavy loads without sinking or allowing significant traction slip. In this chapter, technicians are introduced to important operating principles and construction features of track drive systems. Understanding the function, operation, and construction of track components provides the foundation to identify wear factors, analyze wear patterns through various inspections, perform services, and recommend track maintenance.

▶ What Is Track Drive Undercarriage?

K41001

The term "undercarriage" is the generic name given to all the components making up the propulsion mechanism or travel system for track drive equipment. With its conveyor belt-like propulsion system, track drive **undercarriage** is the most recognizable feature on countless variations of dozers, farm tractors, excavators, cranes, compact skid steer loaders, road building equipment, and even military tanks (**FIGURE 41-1**). What makes this undercarriage system so popular is that it uses a continuously revolving belt made of either rubber or steel plates that enables machines to move or crawl over ground surfaces where wheeled equipment cannot be satisfactorily used (**FIGURE 41-2**). Because track drives have more ground contact area to distribute machine weight, tracked equipment will not sink into soft ground surfaces where wheeled equipment would easily become stuck. More ground surface contact with moving track belts containing cleat-like features also translates into superior traction force compared to wheeled equipment. Superior traction capabilities; greater pulling, digging, or pushing force to move material; and a rugged track drive undercarriage give off-road equipment enhanced working capabilities that no other propulsion system can match.

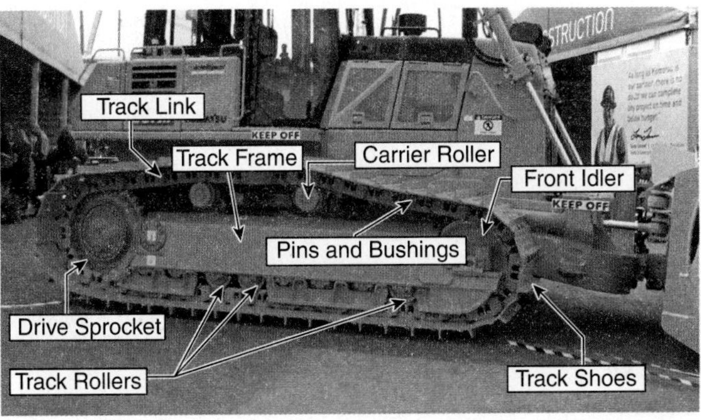

FIGURE 41-1 "Undercarriage" refers to all the components making up the track drive system used by countless types of off-road machinery.

FIGURE 41-2 Rubber track drive is an alternative to steel track and provides smoother, quieter operation at higher speeds.

Because track drive undercarriage makes up 20% of the initial cost of a machine and approximately 50% of the lifetime maintenance costs, according to manufacturer estimates, it's critical for technicians to not only understand the construction and operation of track drive systems but also to be aware of factors affecting the service life of track drive undercarriage. A good working knowledge of track drive systems is necessary to make the best service recommendations and develop proper maintenance practices to extend the life of tracked equipment. Given the high cost of track replacement parts, equipment downtime, and labor-intense service work, it is important for technicians to be capable of properly inspecting track drive components and efficiently performing replacement procedures, using safe work practices outlined in this chapter.

Development of Track Drive Machines

Over a century ago, a solution to the problem encountered by heavy steam-powered wheeled tractors sinking into the rich topsoil of California farmland was to place wooden boards, one after another, in front of large tractor tires. Rather than concentrating the machine weight and drive torque on a small contact patch below the wheel, boards distributed the machine weight over a larger surface area and provided superior traction force to grip the ground surface for moving farm equipment. By bolting chains to link the boards into a continuously moving belt, driven by the wheels, the machine's weight was more effectively distributed, which not only helped to prevent equipment from sinking but also gave equipment exceptional traction and maneuverability. Observers noted that the slow steady movement of ground-hugging equipment using movable chained wooden tracks resembled the crawl of a caterpillar. Subsequently, this caterpillar-like movement of equipment built by the enterprising **Benjamin Holt**, the industrialist who first developed the practical use of crawler-type track drive systems in North America, became synonymous with products built by his original company, the **Holt Manufacturing Company**. The name "caterpillar" stuck to Holt's machines when the company later merged with Best Manufacturing, and the combined

FIGURE 41-3 Benjamin Holt, the industrialist who first developed the practical use of crawler-type track drive; his Holt Manufacturing Company and Best Manufacturing merged to form Caterpillar in 1925.

enterprise incorporated into the Caterpillar Tractor Company in 1925, just 18 years after patenting his continuous track drive system (**FIGURE 41-3**). Today the principle of using a movable steel track or crawler drive traction systems is incorporated into many types of off-road equipment that works in locations where soft, uneven ground surfaces and sharp debris such as rocks or scrap metal are regularly encountered. Its high traction force enables it to outperform wheeled equipment at the difficult work of pulling stumps, ripping concrete or asphalt, digging, or pushing massive amounts of earth while working at very steep angles.

FIGURE 41-4 Steel track shoes with **A.** a single and **B.** triple grouser bars. The cleat-like bars penetrate the ground to provide better traction.

Advantages of Track Drives

The superior traction ability of tracked undercarriage is enhanced by using one or more **grousers** in track plates. Grousers are wedges or bars on steel track that function like cleats on athletic shoes. These steel bars penetrate the ground surface, providing even more surface area to push or pull against the ground (**FIGURE 41-4**). Wheeled vehicles are much more likely to spin tires if the rolling resistance in soft ground becomes excessive (**FIGURE 41-5**). However, the superior traction capabilities of track drives are demonstrated when bulldozers pull wheel loaders or other vehicles become stuck in mud or soft

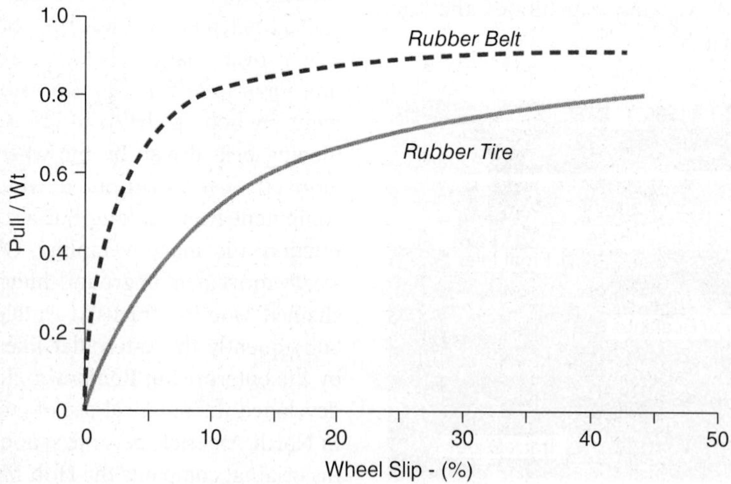

FIGURE 41-5 Comparing the traction capabilities of a rubber belt track with wheeled equipment tires. Track machines pull more weight with less track slippage.

ground. The same traction capabilities enable bulldozers to operate on slopes with much steeper angles because the traction capabilities, combined with a track drive machine's lower center of gravity, can overcome greater rolling resistances when excavating, pushing, or pulling heavy loads. In fact, maximum side slope and fore-aft working angles are typically between 30 and 45 degrees. In contrast, side slope work for wheel loaders is typically limited to 15 degrees. When climbing, tracked machines can ascend a hill as steep as 60 degrees compared to 30 degrees for wheel loaders.

Because track drives use a steering mechanism that changes the drive torque applied to each track, they are more maneuverable. By driving the tracks at different speeds, the operator can steer the machine in any direction. Smaller turning radius is obtained by driving the tracks in opposite directions, which enables the machine to rotate around its own center point without forward or backward movement (**FIGURE 41-6**). Long tracks also help smooth out the rough bumps and small obstacles for even better maneuverability. Tracks also enable machines to cross ditches or trenches and highly uneven terrain. In fact, driving a long, fast tracked machine feels more like riding in a boat over heavy swells. When steel track is used rather than rubber tires, the track cannot be punctured or torn by sharp hard objects struck with high-impact loads. And if a track is broken, with the correct tools it can be repaired without the need to move it to a specialized facility—a feature that is crucial in military tracked tanks.

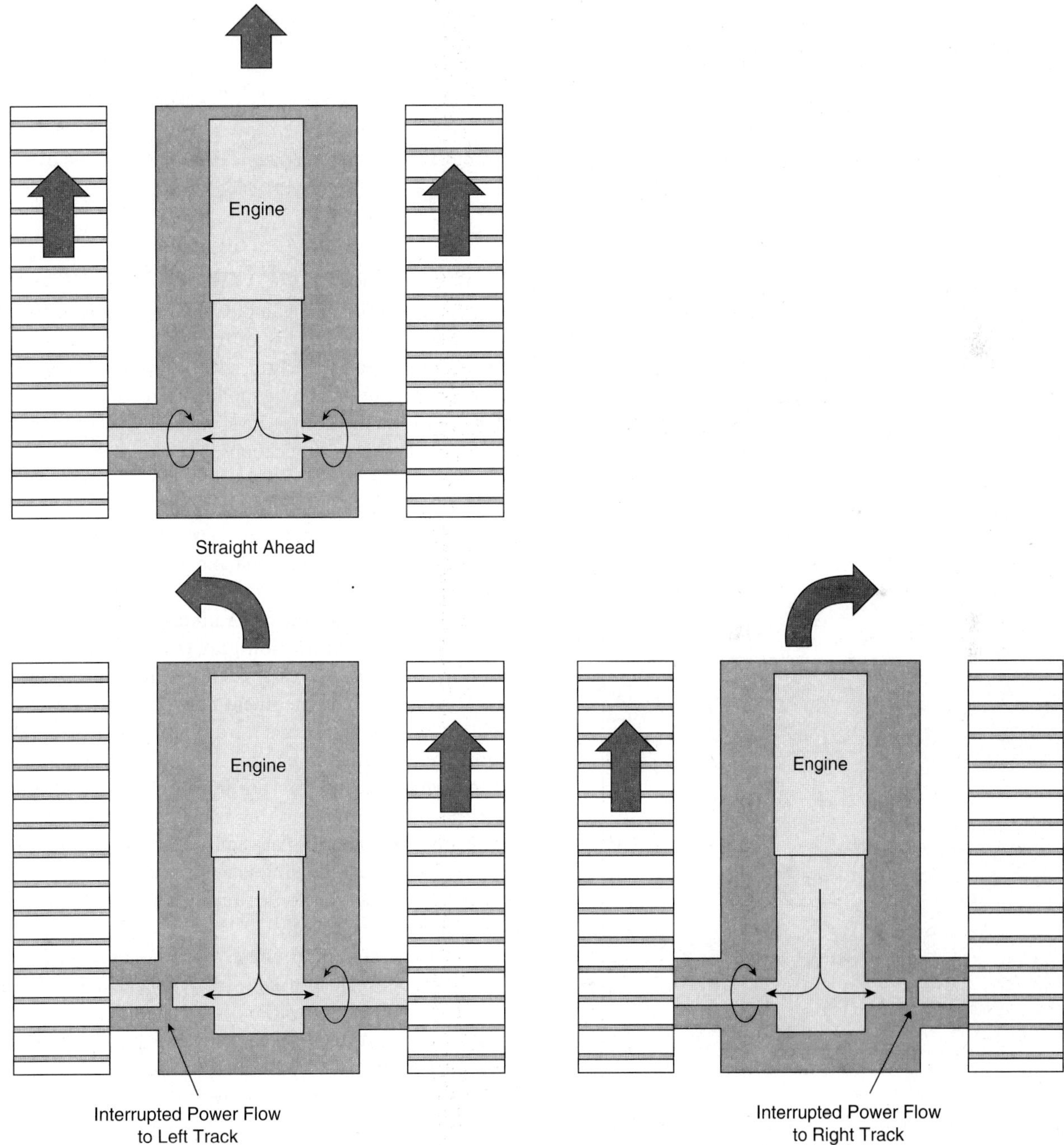

FIGURE 41-6 Principles of skid steering used by track drive equipment. Driving tracks at different speeds turns the machine.

Low Ground Pressure Track

Ground pressure is the force exerted by the tires or track of a machine. It is drastically lowered with the use of track by giving equipment a larger contact patch to distribute weight and grip ground surface in order to pull, push, or carry heavy loads (**FIGURE 41-7**). Ground pressure exerted by track varies with the length of track and width of the track shoe. Measured in pascals or pounds per square inch, the ground pressure exerted by track drive systems allows an average mid-sized dozer weighing 22,270 kg (49,096 lb) to exert as little as 4.7 psi ground pressure while pulling or pushing as much as 80,000 pounds (350,000 N·m) of material. This compares with the ground pressure of an average man's footprint of 8 psi ground pressure or a 70-ton Abrams M1 tank track of 15 psi. Some rubber-tracked vehicles have less than 1 psi of ground pressure. On average, wheeled loaders have between 35 and 45 psi ground pressure. More importantly, for greater traction the larger ground contact of tracked equipment produces an increased amount of friction between the tracks and the ground surface. This means a track can transmit or push off with more force against ground surface before slipping, which makes high traction preferable to low traction for any machine. Tracked equipment provides the greatest tractive effort to perform work when moving earth, removing tree stumps, or pulling multiple shank rippers through concrete.

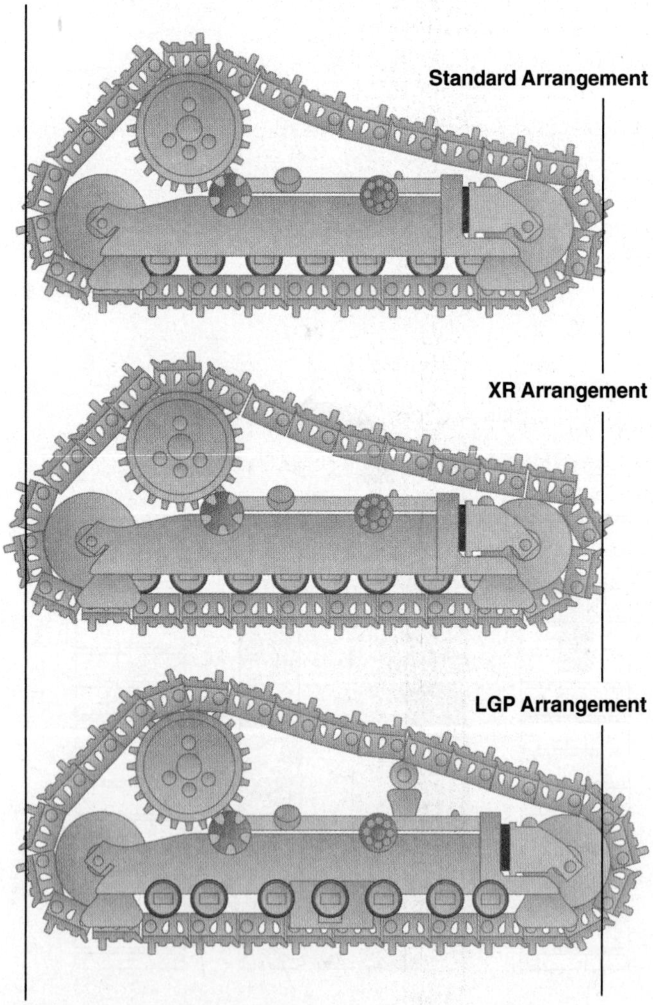

FIGURE 41-7 The ratio between the area of track in contact with the ground and machine weight varies ground pressure. Note that the longer track on the lower image has the lowest ground pressure.

> **TECHNICIAN TIP**
>
> Track drive machines are commonly classified and rated by the ground pressure produced by the track as it supports machine weight. Ground pressure rating is significant because it affects a machine's mobility, and rate of track wear. Ground pressure is defined as the load exerted by a machine's contact points with the ground and is measured in pounds per square inch (psi), or kilopascals (kPa). By changing the width and length of a machine's tracks, its ground pressure changes.
>
> Ground pressure is calculated by using the total vehicle weight and dividing that by the track (or tire) contact area. To calculate ground pressure of machine track, use the following equation:
>
> Ground pressure = Operating weight/Ground contact area
>
> Ground contact area = Width of track shoe × Length of track on ground × 2

Disadvantages of Track Undercarriage

The greater mechanical complexity and weight of steel tracks are the primary weaknesses of tracked machines. In comparison to wheeled machines, track drives have a lower top speed and a much shorter service life before requiring costly, labor-intensive overhaul. Slower travel speeds means the machine is not as productive in applications where a lot of machine travel on a worksite is required. Increasing speed results in accelerated track wear. More significantly, increased machine speed means the maximum **drawbar capacity**—that is, the amount of weight a track drive can pull at a given speed—falls off with increased travel speed (**FIGURE 41-8**). Drawbar capacity drops because track rolling resistance increases proportionally with speed while the transmission gear reduction ratio simultaneously drops in higher gears, resulting in reduced torque output. Moving tracked equipment between worksites is another problem. Rather than drive a tracked machine over a road to a worksite like wheeled equipment, the machines are typically floated which means transporting using a specialized trailer. **Floating** is the term describing the transfer of a heavy machine between worksites on a flat semi-trailer or specialized gooseneck trailers. While floating is cumbersome, it is necessary to speed up machine transfer between job sites and reduce unnecessary undercarriage wear.

Packing, a condition where, ground materials can stick and accumulate between sprockets, track, rollers, and other mating components during operation, is inevitable in many worksite applications (**FIGURE 41-9**). Not only does packing prevent parts from engaging correctly, it causes tracks to tighten, which in turn accelerates track wear and requires more engine power to maintain machine speed. Daily cleaning of track components, regular inspection of track tension or track adjustment can minimize the detrimental effects of packing.

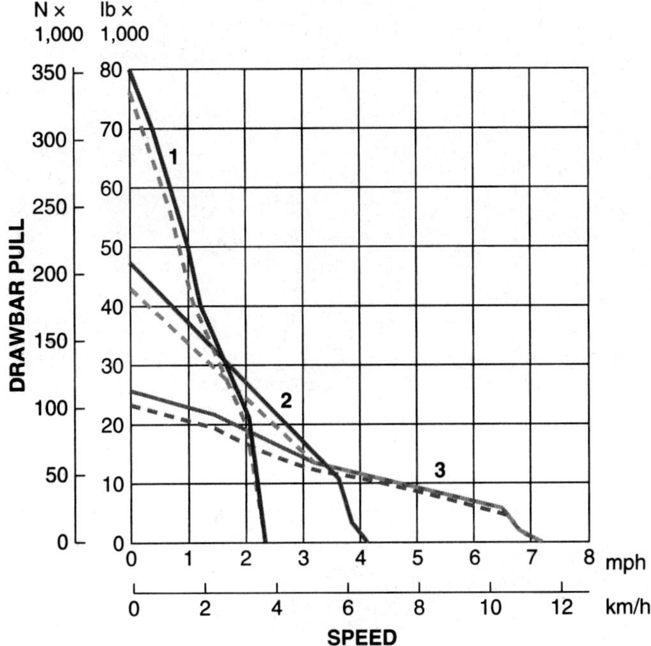

FIGURE 41-8 Tracked machines quickly lose the ability to move heavy loads as machine speed increases.

FIGURE 41-9 A machine with packed undercarriage.

The use of steel rather than rubber track enables track to withstand high-impact forces encountered working on rock or hard concrete. But steel track grousers damage asphalt and other sensitive surfaces traversed by tracks. Rubberized pads can be attached to track shoes to minimize damage while allowing smoother, quieter, and faster movement on paved surfaces.

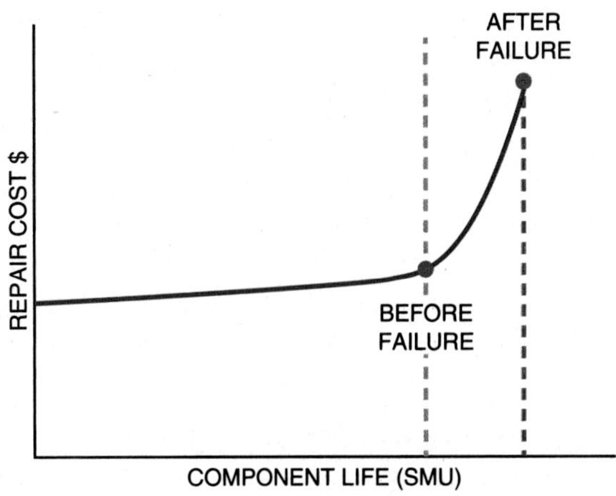

FIGURE 41-10 Inspection and repair before failure is a more economical maintenance strategy than repair or run to failure.

Although exceedingly tough, steel or rubber track drives may not be as reliable as wheeled equipment. The loss of a tire, or even more than one tire, may allow a wheeled machine to move, but a track drive is completely immobilized if even a track link or pin becomes broken. A condition called a **thrown track** can also occur when tracks ride off worn rollers wheels, chains, idlers, or sprockets. Tracks can also become jammed to the point where it requires labor-intensive work to separate before undertaking a repair. Pins and chains on older track can rust and seize if allowed to sit and will require downtime, a lot of lubricant, and labor-intensive work to free (**FIGURE 41-10**). On lubricated sealed pins, heating torches cannot be used to loosen seized track without damaging oil and grease seals. See **TABLE 41-1** to compare the advantages of track and wheeled equipment.

▶ Track Drive Components and Operation

K41002

Track drive equipment uses two types of drive systems to transfer engine torque to the track. One system, called the **friction drive**, uses friction between the track and a rubberized drive

TABLE 41-1 Choosing Track or Tire Undercarriage

Job Requirement	Preferred
High traction force	Track
Low traction force	Tire
Stable, firm ground condition	Tire
Short push or travel distance	Track
Long push or travel distance	Tire
Muddy, soft, unstable ground condition	Track
Steep side slope	Track
Lifting and loading heavy unstable product (dump truck)	Track
High maneuverability in confined place	Tire
Fast travel speed	Tire

wheel to rotate the track, which in turn moves the machine. The drive wheels on friction drive systems operate like a tire to rotate the track. Friction drives are potentially able to travel faster and more smoothly and quietly, and are commonly used with rubber track belt systems.

The other major category of drive is a **positive drive** system, which uses a gearlike sprocket to engage a drive lug or bushing in the track. Positive drive systems are common in earth-moving equipment where very high drive torque is required. Both rubber and steel track can use positive drive systems.

Simple Sprocket Drive Operation

The operation of a positive drive system like those used by steel track undercarriage system has a lot in common with a simple bicycle chain drive mechanism (**FIGURE 41-11**). On a bicycle, the front gear sprocket turned by the cyclist transmits drive torque to a chain that engages a sprocket on the rear wheel. Likewise, a track drive system also has a drive sprocket that engages a chain used to transmit drive torque supplied by an engine. The chain of a track drive isn't as visible as it is on a bicycle, though, because the chain bolts directly to metal plates called track shoes. Turning the sprocket engaged with the track chain pulls the chain that is securely attached to track shoes. Moving the track shoes produces the crawler-like track travel to take place. The combination of chain and track shoe operates like both a self-laying rail system and a road for the machine to crawl over. The lower rollers on the track frame transfer machine weight to the chain links and in turn onto the track shoes in contact with the ground.

Steel track shoes can be replaced by a rubber belt, where the simple sprocket drive principle of metal track still applies to rubber track operation (**FIGURE 41-12**). Either a drive sprocket engages indentations in the belt called cams to produce belt rotation, or a drive wheel transfers torque through friction with the inside surface of the belt.

To create a continuous return of chain to the drive sprocket, a large idler wheel or idler sprocket is located opposite the drive sprocket (**FIGURE 41-13**). It's important to note that the idler is at the front of the track drive, whereas the drive sprocket is at the rear in terms of forward travel direction (**FIGURE 41-14**). The idler sprocket or wheel is non-driving and functions to create an oval track loop. Looping the chain around the large idler wheel or non-driving idler sprocket creates a return path for the track chain. At least one idler sprocket or wheel is used on a track

FIGURE 41-11 The operation of a steel track undercarriage resembles a simple bicycle chain drive mechanism.

FIGURE 41-12 A rubber track belt contains drive lugs that can be driven by a sprocket.

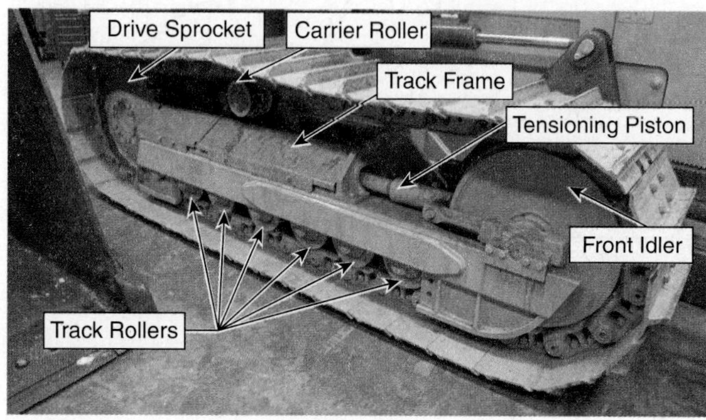

FIGURE 41-13 Typical components of a dozer's dozers track drive system.

FIGURE 41-14 The idler wheel is the reference point for machine travel. The idler leads forward track travel.

drive. The size of the idler may be the same or smaller than the drive sprocket depending on a variety of factors such as the position of the drive sprocket, the machine operators need to maintain site lines and the machine's ground clearance. A track tensioning mechanism is attached to the idler sprocket that is used to adjust and maintain some track slack. Without the track tensioner, the track can become too loose from wear and may run off the guide rollers and the sprocket. The track can also become too tight in some circumstances and require loosening using the tensioning mechanism (**FIGURE 41-15**). A tight track adds additional friction or drag force into the chain, which in turn increases the amount of power required by the engine to move the machine. With increased friction, wear in all track components accelerates while travel speed and the power to perform work drops (**FIGURE 41-16**).

FIGURE 41-15 The recoil spring is part of a track tensioning mechanism attached to the front idler. The tensioner absorbs shock loads and is used to adjust track tension.

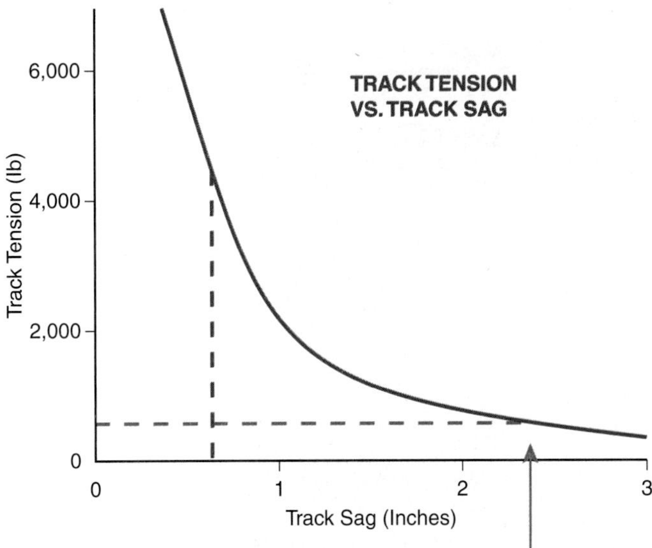

FIGURE 41-16 As track tension increases, friction increases exponentially. Some track sag is desirable, with 2" sag indicating an optimal track tension.

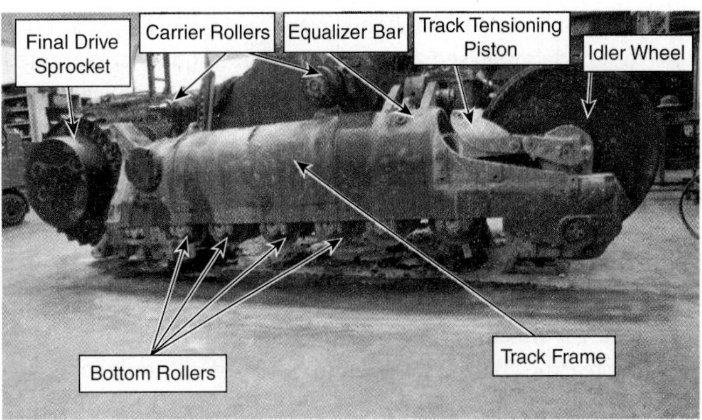

FIGURE 41-17 There are more bottom rollers than top or carrier rollers. Bottom rollers transfer machine weight to the track chain and then into the track shoe.

Rollers located on the inside radius of the track loop guide and support the weight of the track and transfer machine weight to the ground. Top rollers are often called idler or carrier rollers because they only guide and support the weight of the top track chain loop to keep it from drooping. Fewer top idler rollers are used compared to the lower track rollers that transfer machine weight to the ground (**FIGURE 41-17**).

Track Drive Steering

There is no steering wheel or steering linkage in track drive machines. Instead, one track is driven faster than the other, pushing the machine in the direction toward the slower or stopped track. Because the leading and trailing edges of the track slide sideways to steer the machine, that sliding action lends the name **skid steering** to this type of steering principle. However, the more accurate term for track steering principle is **differential steering**. Several methods are used to steer machines using skid steer principles. The simplest system used on older, mid-sized machines incorporates a brake and clutch mechanism at each final drive. Hand levers and/or a set of foot-operated pedals control the clutch and friction brake on side of the machine (**FIGURE 41-18**). The clutch and brake mechanism either brakes the final driveshaft or applies torque. The planetary gear outputs in the final drives either speed up or slow down in response to

FIGURE 41-18 Older machines like this one used pedal or lever steering.

movement of foot pedals or hand levers, also called **laterals**. With both foot pedals released, clutches transmit torque that is applied evenly to each track. Partially depressing a pedal disengages the drive clutch; fully depressing the pedal applies the brake, effectively locking the transmission output shaft to the frame. If one pedal is partially or fully depressed, releasing the opposite pedal applies torque to track with the released pedal and starts a turn; applying a brake through a lateral lever or foot pedal brake also slows one track and causes the machine to turn.

In larger machines, a **cross-drive transmission** is used to control steering. Because there are three differentials incorporated into the transmission, skid steering is also called **triple differential steering** (**FIGURE 41-19**). A cross-drive transmission is the most contemporary type of track drive transmission enabling precise, energy-efficient steering function. It connects track to the engine, continuously operating at working speed while varying road speeds and amount of torque applied to the left or right final drive sprocket. The transmission has two input shafts—one from the engine flywheel and another from a hydraulic or electric motor used for a steering input. Two output shafts connect the transmission to the final drive sprockets. Turning the steering input shaft either clockwise or counterclockwise controls the torque supplied to each final drive. If no input is received from the steering input shaft, both tracks turn at the same speed. A clutch engages and disengages the engine when no drive is requested, such as when the machine is parked or stopped.

A cross-drive transmission can completely stop the machine track movement, lock the speed of both tracks together, increase the speed of one track, or stop one track and turn the other. A **pivot turn** of a tracked machine stops one track while driving the opposite.

Caterpillar's diesel electric D7E steers its track using two 3-phase electric motors. Caterpillar claims that the electric drive system achieves 50% better maneuverability because the D7E can perform both pivoting stop-track turns. This takes place when one track completely stops while the other pivots the dozer around the stopped track. It can also perform counterrotating turns, where the two tracks turn in opposite directions.

Most midrange larger machines today use electronically controlled **hydrostatic, or "hystat," drive systems**. Whether it is using a hystat drive or cross-drive transmission, steering input can be controlled several ways. The most contemporary method is "arcade" steering that uses a joystick with electronic outputs (**FIGURE 41-20**). Also called a **tiller**, the lever's outputs are connected to an engine control module which in turn controls one or two hydraulic servo motors regulating power flows through the cross-drive transmission. An arcade type stick controls electrohydraulic valves at hydraulic pumps and motors of a hystat steering system (**FIGURE 41-21**). The operator controls machine speed and direction with a joystick, with the neutral stick center placing the machine in a stopped position.

▶ Steel Track Undercarriage

K41003

Two major sections of a track undercarriage include the track frame, or side frame as it is sometimes called, and the track components themselves. Depending on the application—whether it is used as a dozer, asphalt spreader, excavator, or farm tractor in heavy, medium, or light duty—there is considerable variation in the configuration of track components to best adapt a machine for the work it performs. However, the following is a brief description of steel track components common to all track machinery. After identifying the common components in the next section, this chapter takes a more detailed look at various design and operating features of steel track.

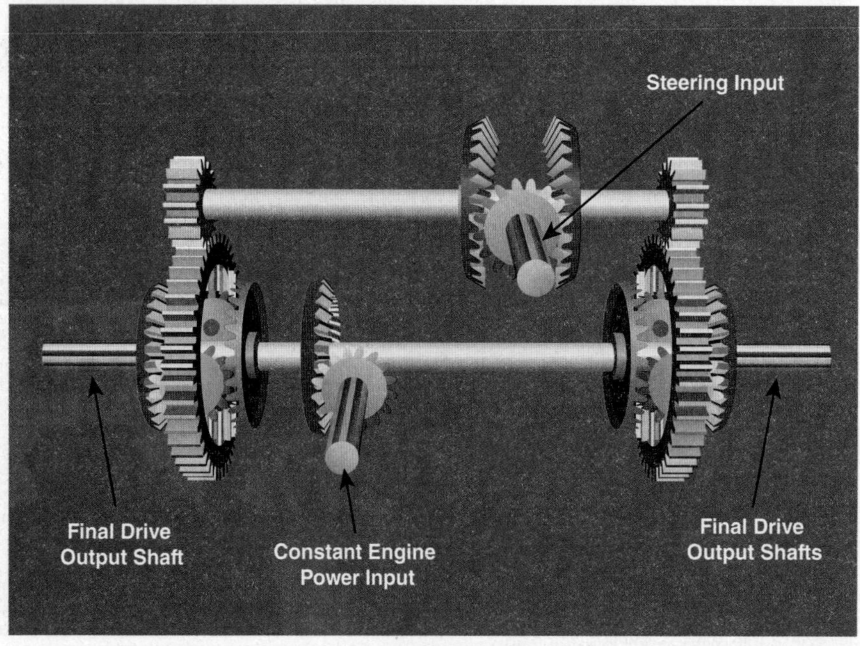

FIGURE 41-19 A cross-drive transmission with three differentials and two planetary gear sets controls track drive travel and steering.

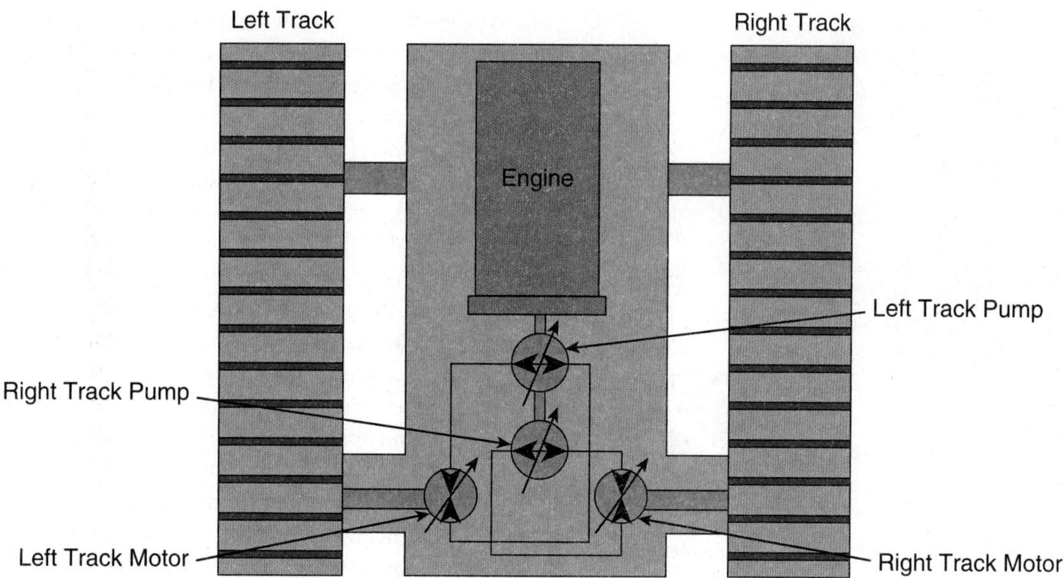

FIGURE 41-20 Hydrostatic drive systems use a hydraulic pump and motor for each track, to control machine direction, using skid steer skid-steer principles.

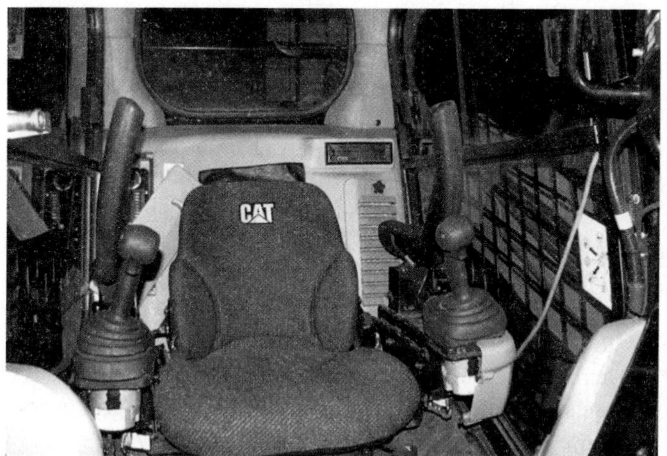

FIGURE 41-21 Arcade-style steering uses a joystick to control machine speed and direction. A gear change requires twisting the stick.

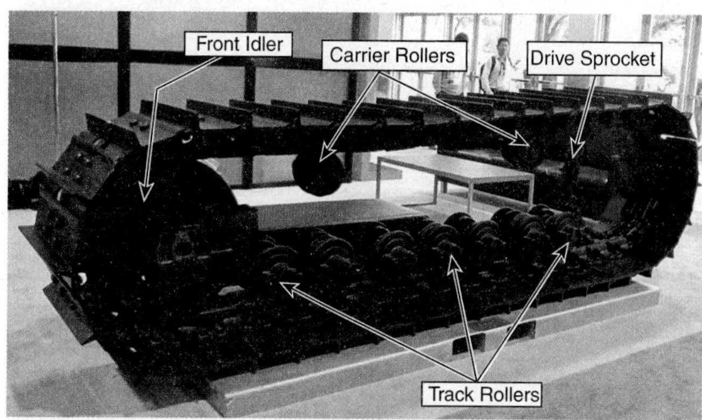

FIGURE 41-22 Basic structure of an excavator undercarriage.

FIGURE 41-23 Track frame, inverted to see roller attachment points.

Major Track Components

To differentiate a track drive system on excavators from other machines, the undercarriage and associated components on excavators are referred to as the **travel system**. However, excavators and other track drive machines share similar track system construction (**FIGURE 41-22**). For all track machines, the undercarriage backbone is the track frame. Also called a roller frame, as track rollers are attached to it, the track frame is essentially two, relatively large, forged cast steel or fabricated steel frame components located on each side of the main chassis (**FIGURE 41-23**). A track tensioning mechanism that acts through the idler wheel is usually located inside the hollow track frame. The type of attachment between the track and the machine's main frame varies with the application. Some track frames are rigidly attached to the main frame of the machine, whereas others allow some oscillation or vertical articulation—that is, some up and down movement of the track frame at the front of the track. The frame also provides an attachment point for all the track drive components except the final drive unit and drive sprocket (**FIGURE 41-24**). The

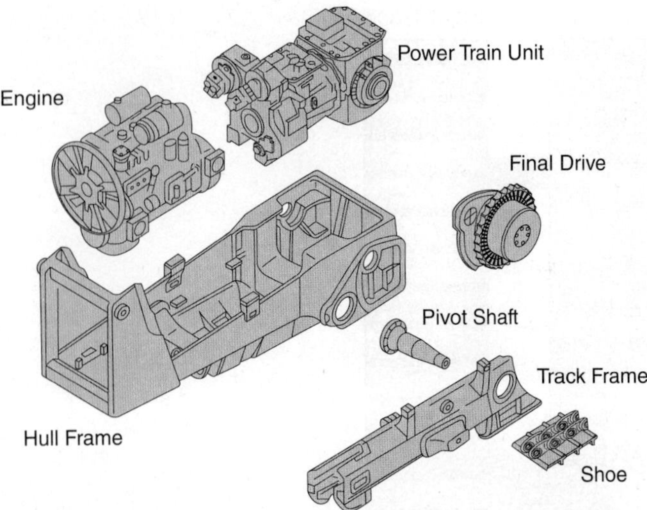

FIGURE 41-24 Arrangement of major track and chassis components for a dozer.

FIGURE 41-25 Examples of two types of track chain. Both chains have links connected together with pins and bushings.

track itself is made of several separate components assembled together and includes the following common elements:

1. Track chains are the foundational component of a track drive system. Chains essentially transmit torque to the track from the machine's drive sprocket and provide an attachment point for track shoes. The chain also functions like a self-laying rail system or road over which the machine crawls. Each chain segment is assembled from two track links connected in parallel to form two rows (**FIGURE 41-25**). The links on each side of the chain are connected using hardened steel pins. Track rollers make contact with the links to transfer machine weight through the link to track shoes also bolted to the links. A section of chain consists of four links forming each side of the chain, plus a pin and a cylindrical bushing that covers each of the pin. The longer pin passes through the ends of each pair of links locking together the two outside links. The shorter bushing is typically pressed into two ends of the inside links and cannot rotate in conventional track. Although the track pin supplies the hinge or articulation point for the track links, it is the chain bushing, made from tough, hardened steel, that contacts the chain's drive sprockets. Track pins rotating inside the bushings enable each chain section to turn or articulate inside the bushing. On all systems, the flat surface on the link rails enables track rollers to contact and guide the chain as it rotates around the frame. Like other track parts, steel links are alloyed with metals such as boron or manganese and undergo various hardening and heat treatment such as flame carburizing and quenching to give chains optimum strength and abrasion resistance. A link rail Rockwell hardness of 58–62 is typically achieved through specialized hardening techniques, which makes the link harder than most materials it should encounter.

   On lighter machines such as excavators with minimal travel distance, a combined pad-link-type track chain combines a chain link and a track pad into single unit. Sprocket drive forces are directly transferred from the sprocket into the massive pad-link unit.
2. Track shoes are the most visible parts of track drive equipment. Shoes are steel plates bolted to the track chain to form one continuous belt of plates. Shoes are made from alloyed steel because it has the ability to resist wear and cutting and to withstand high-impact forces encountered working in hard concrete, rock, or even scrap metal. Track shoe grousers are steel projections used to increase the track grip over a loose ground surface.
3. Track pin bushings are hardened steel sleeves wrapped around the track pins and often have a lubricating film of either oil or grease between the track pin and bushing. It is the bushing wrapped around the track pin that engages the sprocket teeth to transfer the drive torque from the final drive sprocket to the track chain. Although bushings are traditionally not designed to rotate as they move around the drive sprocket, some newer track systems have alloy bushing rotation.
4. Drive sprockets are a toothed wheel mounted on the final drive assembly. It functions to turn the track chain by engaging the track bushing wrapped around the track pins. Drive torque supplied to the sprocket is developed by the engine and transmitted to the final drive through a transmission. There is one drive sprocket for each side of the track, which is located near the rear of the oval-shaped track.
5. Rollers directly contact the track chain links and are used to guide and support the track chain as it revolves around the frame. Most machine weight is transferred to the chain through the rollers. Bottom rollers are attached to the lower side of the frame and support the weight of the machine

on the track through the rail of the chain links. Because there is a tremendous amount of weight to support, there are more bottom rollers than top rollers. Upper rollers, also called **carrier** or **idler rollers**, are located on the top side of the track frame. These rollers guide the track and prevent track "whipping" and excessive track sag from contacting the frame while the machine is moving. A rock or roller guard—that is, a steel plate—is often bolted to the track frame to prevent rocks from entering the roller and idler wheel area and jamming the track.

6. **Idler wheels** or **idler sprockets** are large non-driving wheels or sprockets with at least one on each side of the machine and located opposite the drive sprocket on the track frame. The idler is much larger than a roller and shapes the tracks into an oval loop by creating a return path back to the drive sprocket. Working in combination with a track tensioner, the idler also helps minimize transmission of shock loads to the drive sprocket and maintain track tension.
7. Track tensioners, as the name suggests, are used to maintain track tension to prevent the track from running off the rollers if it becomes too loose. The tensioner is connected to the idler wheel and also absorbs some shock loading of the track chain. Tensioners are necessary to compensate for changes to chain length due to wear. Together, rollers, idler wheels, sprockets drives, chains, and chain-tensioning mechanisms are used to stabilize track, that is, to keep the track running straight, and form suspension mechanisms.

FIGURE 41-26 A rigid track frame used by this excavator does not move or allow any frame articulation.

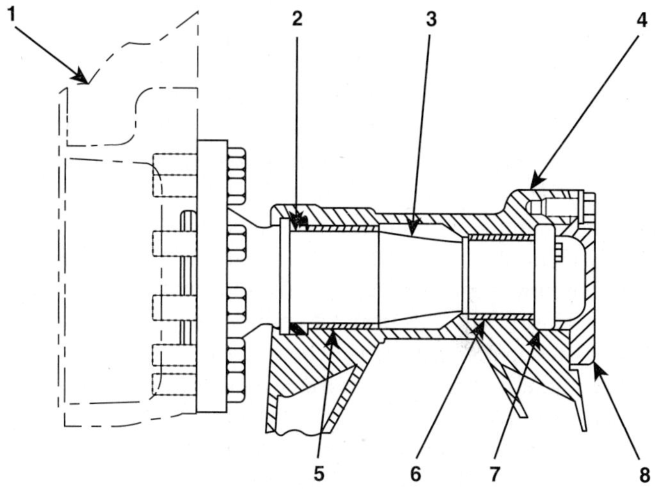

Pivot shaft (Section Taken Through Track Roller Frame) 1. Tractor main frame. 2. Seal. 3. Pivot shaft. 4. Track roller frame. 5. Bushing. 6. Bushing. 7. Retainer. 8. Cover pivot shaft (3) is fastened to the side of tractor main frame (1). Roller frames (4) are connected to the pivot shaft by sintered metalbushings (5) and (6). Each roller frame can oscillate (turn) at the pivot shaft. The roller frames oscillate on the sintered metalbushings in a sealed oil compartment in each roller frame.
Retainer (7) is fastened to the end of pivot shaft (3) and prevents axial movement of the track roller frame on the pivot

FIGURE 41-27 The pivot shaft enables the suspended-type track frame to rotate around the shaft. An oil-filled bearing housing typically supports plain-type sintered metal bearings.

Track Frame Systems

The track frame is the backbone of the track system by providing attachment points for almost all the track system components. The frame is shaped like a hollow tube with internal reinforcements. Frame designs are adapted to specific applications. For example, excavators use a longer track frame to provide the machine with better stability when digging. The width of the frame may be wider or narrower, depending on where the machine is working or digging. For example, frames for dozers and excavators are available in three configurations: standard, extended, and narrow, each with different types of shoes and track lengths.

Track frames may be either suspended or rigid type. **Rigid frames** have solid attachment points to the main frame and allow no movement between the two (**FIGURE 41-26**). This means there is no relative movement between the track frame and main frame. Neither is movement allowed between any lift arm attached to the main frame and the track frame of a rigid-mounted undercarriage. Smaller track drive machines use rigid mount, unlike larger dozers that allow some movement. Rigid mount configurations give a machine's blade or attachments considerably more stability and are best used for machines such as those mostly used for grading or those having a frame attachment such as pipe layers. The rigid mount frame offers simplicity with fewer parts, increasing durability while potentially lowering maintenance cost.

Suspended track frames allow some oscillation of the two frames relative to one another. A three-point attachment system is used. Near the rear of the frame but ahead of the final drive, a **pivot shaft** runs from one frame to the other through the machine's main frame in order to connect the track frames to one another. Shock loads from the track are transmitted through the pivot shaft throughout the case of the machine's main frame. This setup minimizes the bending stresses applied to just the sides of a machine's main frame in rigid mount systems. The pivot shaft typically has an oil-filled plain-type bearing at each end of the track frame to enable free vertical movement of the front of the track (**FIGURE 41-27**). The pivot shaft also functions to help keep the track frames properly aligned.

At the front of each track frame is also a connection point to an **equalizer bar** pinned in the center to the main frame

FIGURE 41-28 The pivot shaft located just in front of the final drive sprocket enables the suspended track frame to rotate around the pivot shaft.

FIGURE 41-29 Segmented sprocket teeth are easy-to-handle sections of sprocket teeth that are bolted onto the final drive.

(**FIGURE 41-28**). A heavy bushing or bearing connects the track frame to the equalizer bar. If one side of the track is lifted passing over an obstacle, some of the weight is transferred to the opposite track frame by the pivoting equalizer bar. This lever-like weight transfer through the equalizer bar minimizes the tendency of the machine to excessively roll when encountering large bumps or ground depressions, which helps maintain machine stability. However, blades and other attachments move with the track frame, using suspended frames. Side thrust loads against the track frames are absorbed by large steel track guide plates on the main frame. These contact points keep track frames properly aligned during frame oscillation. Thus the ability of track frames to oscillate up or down enables track to better match ground contours while providing for improved traction, slightly faster travel speeds, and better operator comfort.

FIGURE 41-30 One piece sprocket.

Track Undercarriage Arrangements

Track drives can be classified several other ways in addition to the method of frame attachment systems. Other classifications include:

- Drive sprocket arrangement
- Track chain and bushing configuration
- Track roller configuration.

Drive Sprocket Design

The type and position of the drive sprocket influence weight distribution, rates of track wear, and service procedures used in maintaining undercarriage systems. The primary function of the sprocket is to transfer drive torque to the track chain through teeth on the sprocket circumference. The sprocket and final drive are never mounted on the track frame. This arrangement minimizes transmission of shock loads into the final drive from the track. Contemporary sprockets are made from wear-resistant hardened steel segments that are bolted to the final drive in order to enable a rapid parts change-out. This eventually happens as sprocket teeth become excessively worn due to the continual grinding of abrasives between the sprocket and chain bushings. **Segmented sprockets**, which are formed by bolting segments of sprocket teeth made of between three and six teeth, form an entire drive sprocket (**FIGURE 41-29**). Considerable downtime and labor is saved using segmented sprockets. Rather than using a hydraulic puller to pull a splined drive sprocket from the final driver, or cutting off an older one-piece sprocket and rewelding another in its place, a segmented sprocket simply bolts to the final drive plate. Updating older sprockets to new segmented types is also possible. By welding an adapter ring in place of an old, single-piece sprocket, new segmented sprockets are bolted to the adapter ring (**FIGURE 41-30**).

Sprockets commonly use what is termed a **hunting tooth arrangement** of teeth. By using an odd number of sprocket teeth to match an even number of track chain bushings, there is a change in tooth-to-bushing contact with every sprocket revolution. With a hunting tooth arrangement, the same sprocket tooth and chain bushing will not make contact together until all other chain bushings have passed over the same tooth or at least until after several sprocket rotations. This design enables an even distribution of wear among the sprocket teeth.

▶ TECHNICIAN TIP

Track drive sprockets use a hunting gear ratio. A hunting ratio for the sprocket means that the sprocket will have an odd number of drive teeth and the chain will have an even number of links. For example, a drive sprocket may have 31 teeth where the number of track links is 40. In this case, a bushing and sprocket tooth will not match up together again until many other bushings have made contact with the sprocket tooth. In a sense, the two parts are looking for one another, or hunting. A non-hunting sprocket has the same number of teeth or an even multiple of track links to sprocket teeth. Because a track using a hunting tooth ratios doesn't allow track bushings to make contact with the same drive sprocket tooth each time it contacts the sprocket, wear pattern is evenly distributed over the sprocket.

Elevated Drive Sprockets

Oval-shaped track has been the traditional track configuration where a single drive sprocket is placed at the rear and idler wheel at the front. However, in the 1970s, Caterpillar introduced an **elevated sprocket** that places the drive sprocket above the track frame, giving the track a triangular shape (**FIGURE 41-31**). More commonly referred to as a high-drive track, the design uses two large idler wheels, instead of a single idler, but stretches the bottom section of track between the two idlers to enable better contact between the track and ground. The track remains tighter between the two idlers, unlike oval track drives that allow track to loosen when moving in a reverse direction (**FIGURE 41-32**).

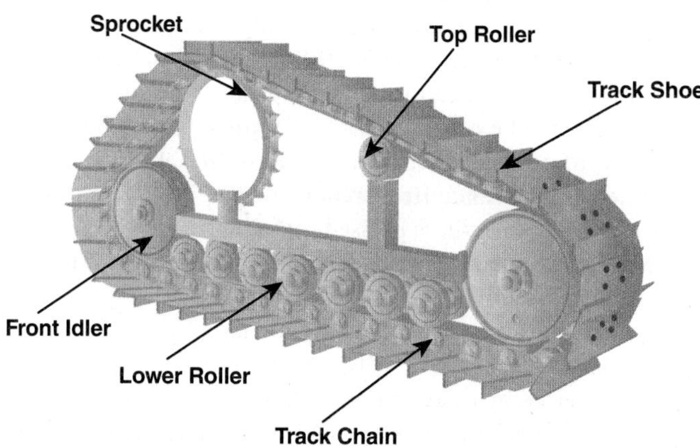

FIGURE 41-31 Elevated or high-drive sprocket design requires the use of two idlers and a separate roller frame for the front and rear.

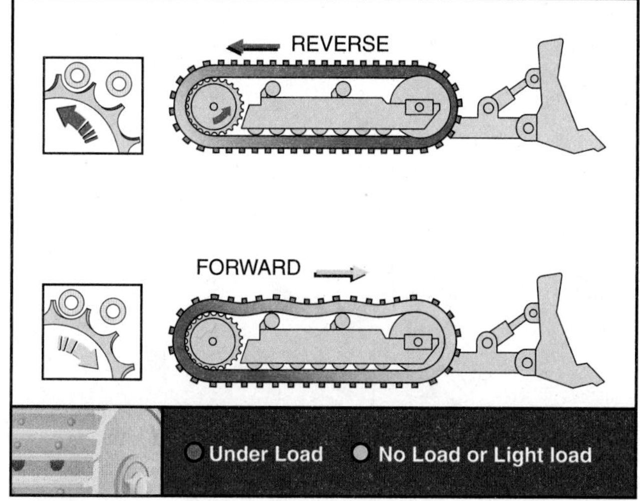

FIGURE 41-32 In oval track designs, only a single idler wheel is used to loop track.

When in reverse, backing up a steep hill or embankment, drive sprocket torque on oval tracks tightens the top section of track and allows the excess slack to move to the bottom. The track is at a greater risk of running off the rollers and drive sprocket, particularly when turning as side thrust forces push against the track and rollers. Elevated drive sprocket keep tracks tight on the ground, whether in reverse or forward, because the loose section of track is either in front of or behind the high drive sprocket. The track remains tight between the front and rear idler sprockets. Removing the transmission is much easier on high-drive track, as is servicing the final drive assembly that is more open. Mud and dirt do not as easily pack a high-drive sprocket, and it shed debris more quickly, so wear is reduced. Operators also have better lines of sight with the triangular track shape.

Most manufacturers have adopted the use of an elevated sprocket design, even though the track needs an additional track segments and another idler sprocket. These slight disadvantages are compensated by greater flexibility to distribute machine weight using different track frames with the elevated sprocket. High-drive sprockets enable the use of different lengths of track frame and flexible positioning of track frame relative to the main machine frame, to minimize the rate of wear on different components. For example, loading using a bucket, dozing, and pushing loads usually shift the machine weight toward the front, increasing weight and wear rates on the front rollers and idlers. Using a ripper or pulling with a drawbar shifts the weight toward the rear, accelerating wear on the rear rollers, idlers, and drive sprockets. When a machine carries loads in both a bucket and dozes, and then changes to a task shifting weight from the front to the rear, less wear occurs on the center rollers and more on the front and rear rollers. The ability to move the track frame without repositioning the final drive sprocket or transmission provides a greater flexibility to adjust weight distribution using different track positions.

Three common track frame configurations are used with high-drive sprockets. The first is a standard arrangement. This general-purpose undercarriage balances machine weight evenly on a track frame center aligned with the mid-center point of the machine. A second configuration, the XR arrangement, moves the track frame rearward, which in turn movies the tractor's weight forward to enhance traction and stability for drawbar, skidding, and ripping applications. A third setup, the low ground pressure (LGP) arrangement, moves the frame forward and increases track frame length, along with wider shoes. This track is designed to work in soft and spongy conditions, with better floatation capabilities. The width of the machine is increased with wider shoes, which means it has a wider gauge. Wide track shoes, long track frames, and a wider gauge increase track contact area and reduce ground pressure for improved stability, providing excellent floatation in swampy conditions.

On elevated track, the location of the drive sprocket and idler size can be adapted not only to achieve better weight distribution but also to improve operator sight lines, change the ride characteristics, and improve maneuverability. For example, smaller idler wheels, which provide a sharper curve at the end of the track, can make sharper turns. The disadvantage of a smaller idler is that the track may penetrate softer ground materials farther. The diameter of the front idler changes a dimension called the angle of approach

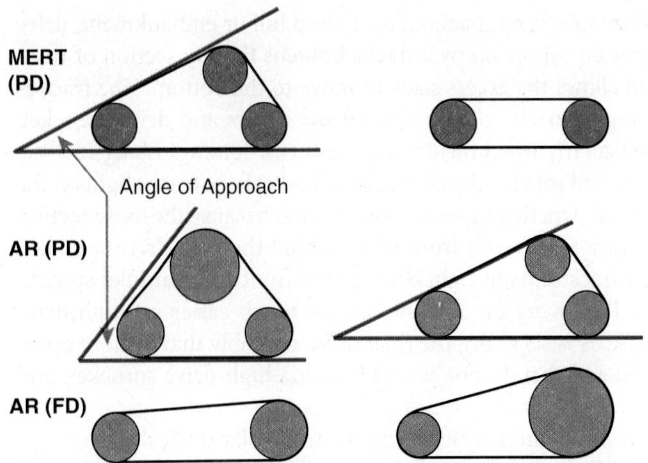

FIGURE 41-33 The position of the angle of approach influences maneuverability, sight lines, and ground penetration. The use of the elevated drive sprocket can change weight distribution by altering the machine to track frame relationship.

or **attack angle.** These angles are formed between an imaginary line along the top track and the point where it intersects with the ground. The angle should be greater for agricultural applications to prevent machines sinking in soft dirt or mud (**FIGURE 41-33**). Snowplows use a smaller attack or angle of approach to better penetrate snow and lower machine ground clearance.

▶ Track Chains

K41004

The most essential component of a track drive system is the track chain. As already mentioned, a segment of track chain consists of two links, a pin, and a cylindrical bushing that wraps around the pin (**FIGURE 41-34**). Between 30 and 50 segments of links make up a typical track chain on mid to large dozers or loaders. Chains function to transfer final drive torque to the track, provide a connection point for track shoes, supply a surface for rollers to transfer machine weight to the track while guiding the track, and enable smooth track articulation and flexibility. Because very high driving forces are transmitted through the chain parts when it is continuously exposed to abrasive dirt, sand, and mud, the chain is sensitive to wear and deterioration. What differentiates various chain designs are the construction techniques used to minimize chain wear and assemble the chain. Tractors and excavators have different construction because they have different jobs to perform. Most modern chain systems use lubricant between the pin and bushing. But the type of lubricant, how the lubricant is retained, and the assembly method used to connect the chain segments together are unique to each manufacturer, reflecting different approaches used to reduce chain wear and track maintenance. Four basic chain construction techniques are used, with several variations among different manufactures:

1. Sealed track chain (SLT nonlubricated)
2. Sealed and greased track chain (SAGT)
3. Sealed and lubricated track (SALT)
4. Rotating bushing track.

Sealed Track Chain (Nonlubricated)

Sealed track chain (**SLT**), the earliest type of chain assembly technique, uses a nonlubricated track pin and bushing design (**FIGURE 41-35**). A solid steel alloy pin rotating inside a cylindrical bushing connects the opposite sides of the chain links together. The pin operates like a hinge inside the bushing, fixed to a different set of links. Pins and bushings use a machined **interference fit** to retain the pin and bushings in the track links. The pin is pressed into one pair of links while the bushing is pressed into the counterbore area of another pair of adjacent links of the track. An interference fit means the pin and bushing diameter is slightly larger than the counterbore in the track link. With an interference fit assembly technique, large hydraulic presses, either portable or stationary, are used to press pins and bushings out of track links when track is rebuilt.

Sealed-type track chain earns its name from the use of two cone-shaped spring-steel washers located at each end of the pin in the link counterbore area. Also called **Belleville washers,**

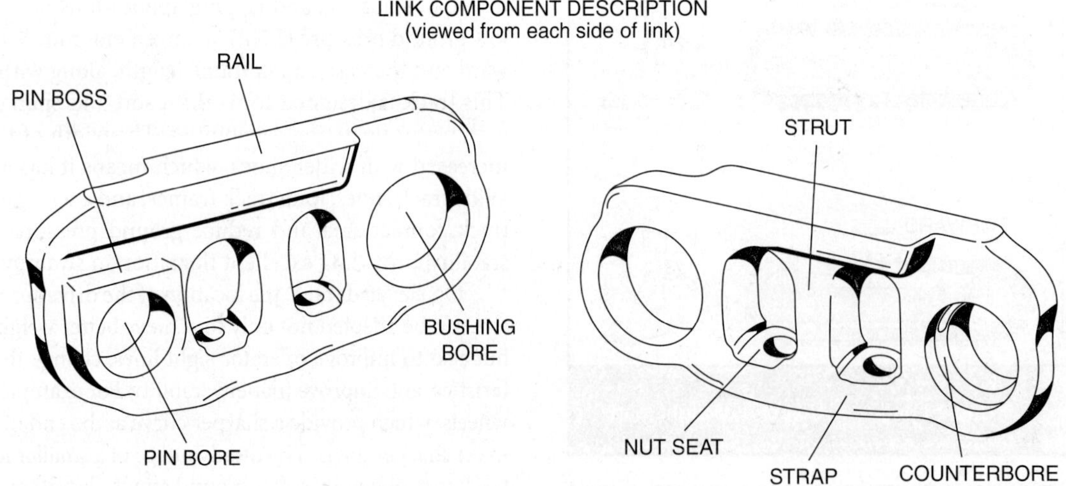

FIGURE 41-34 Features of a track link.

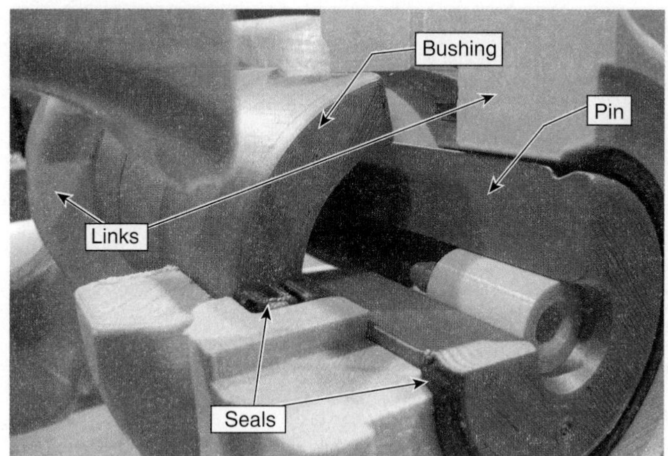

FIGURE 41-35 A sealed track chain segment consists of two links, a pin, bushing, and seals.

these hardened, spring-like metal seals are used to keep abrasive dirt particles from entering the clearance between the pin and bushing (**FIGURE 41-36**). No lubricant is used between the pin and bushing because grease and oil can attract and hold abrasive dirt, which rapidly accelerates wear between the pin and bushing. When this track has worn out, pins and bushings are pressed out of the links, and new pins and bushing kits are pressed into the links.

SLT chain is ideally used where machine travel is not a priority and is a low-cost alternative to lubricated pins. For example, excavators do not travel as far pushing or pulling heavy loads compared to say a bulldozer, sealed nonlubricated track can be used.

Track Pin and Bushing Wear

As already mentioned, in conventional chain design the chain bushing is pressed into a pair of track links, locking it in position between links using an interference fit. The fixed bushing design means that when the track chain revolves around the sprocket and front idler, the track pins and bushings rotate independently in the opposite direction of each other. This relative movement between parts is due to the curvature of the round drive and idler sprockets (**FIGURE 41-37**). Pin and bushing rotation takes place twice during one chain revolution. The first rotations happen as the chain prepares to leave the idler or drive sprockets, where it

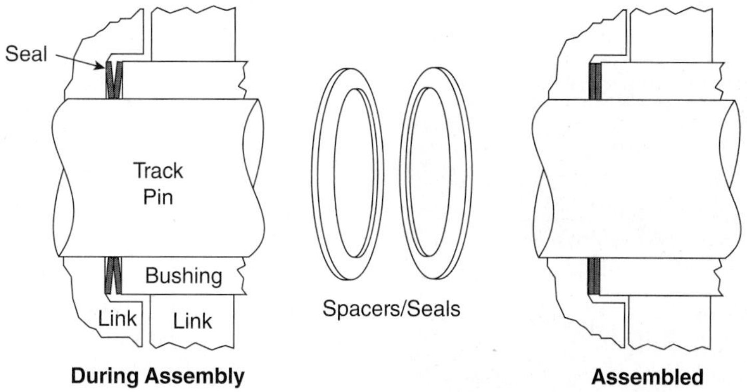

FIGURE 41-36 Sealed track links use conical-shaped washers, which are compressed by the link bushing during assembly. The seals keep out dirt from between the pin and bushing.

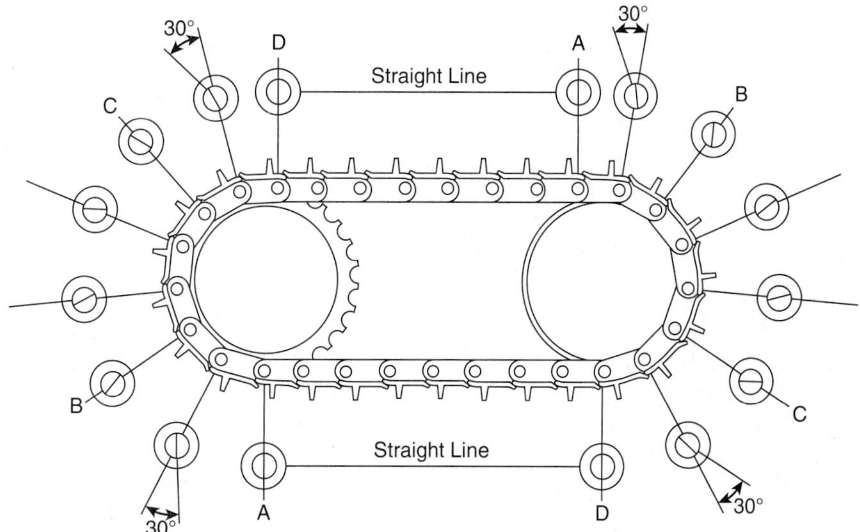

FIGURE 41-37 Because the track pin and bushing only move through a 30-degree motion when moving through the sprockets, wear takes place on one side of the pin and bushing takes place on the other.

will leave a round sprocket or wheel and straighten out. Entering either sprocket will curve the track links again, resulting in rotation of the pins and bushing. This movement sweeps back and forth through 30 degrees of motion four times for every track revolution when only a single drive and idler sprocket are used. A back-and-forth pin movement takes place two times as the chain swivels around the bottom and top of the drive sprocket and twice through its rotation around the front idler. This swiveling motion occurs the same way in a forward and reverse track direction. Similarly, as the bushing engages the bottom of the track or idler sprocket, it does not remain exactly in the same place inside the sprocket tooth. Instead, the bushing scrubs or rotates 30 degrees relative to the tooth position at the top and bottom of the idler and drive sprocket.

Under torque, the tremendous amount of friction produced while the bushing turns in the root of the sprocket tooth is further aggravated by the presence of abrasive dirt. This explains why external bushing wear takes place on only part of the outer bushing surface (**FIGURE 41-38**). Internally, pin and bushing wear takes place only on one side of each part **FIGURE 41-39**. **Root or radial wear** is the name given to the outside diameter bushing

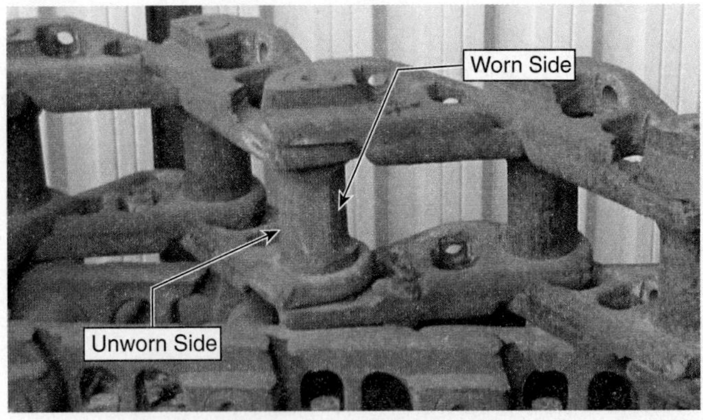

FIGURE 41-38 Track bushings wear only on one side due to the scrubbing action of the heavily loaded pin through 30 degrees of sprocket rotation.

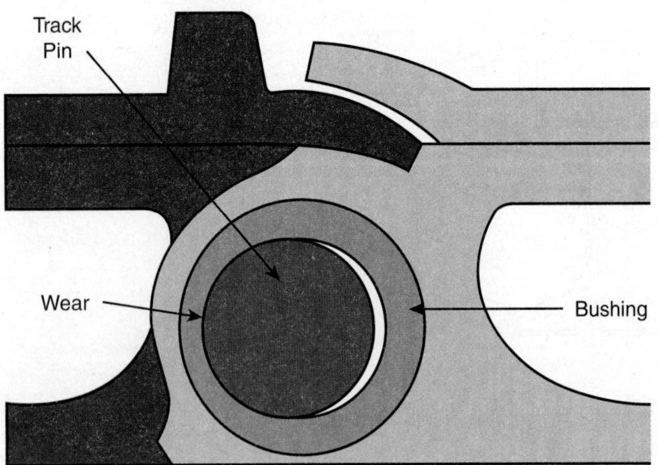

FIGURE 41-39 The track pin bushing wear takes place only on an outer third and internally on an inner third.

FIGURE 41-40 Drive sprocket wear takes place as the bushing scrubs the sprocket tooth with abrasives while under high load as it rotates around the sprocket.

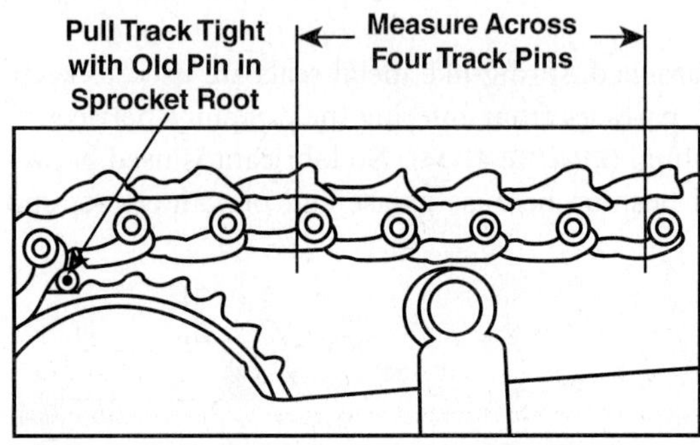

FIGURE 41-41 Track pitch is the measured distance between track pins after the track is stretched. Generally the distance between four pins is measured.

wear as it scrubs through the sprocket root (**FIGURE 41-40**). When bushing and pin wear takes place, the distance between the track pins lengthens. The dimension between the pins is known as **track pitch** (**FIGURE 41-41**). Pitch is measured between one, two, or even three sets of track segments and is a critical dimension used to evaluate track wear. Worn bushings and pins extend track pitch.

Sealed and Greased Track

Without the use of lubricant, nonlubricated track chain is noisy during operation and can wear rapidly. When it wears out, pins, bushings, and sometimes chain links require replacement. To improve chain life and reduce noise and maintenance cost, most manufacturers use chain that is sealed and lubricated with either oil or grease to extend track life. Similar to nonlubricated sealed chain construction, lubricated track chain minimizes friction between the pin and bushing using grease. Pins are typically cross-drilled and filled with grease, with a second drilled passage intersecting the axial drilled passage that supplies a reservoir of grease for the pin-to-bushing clearance (**FIGURE 41-42**). Steel Belleville washers are replaced with polyurethane type seals to prevent grease from leaking out and dirt from entering into the pin-to-bushing clearances (**FIGURE 41-43**). Lubricated and sealed chains using molybdenum or lithium grease to extend chain life approximately 20–40% compared with nonlubricated track chain.

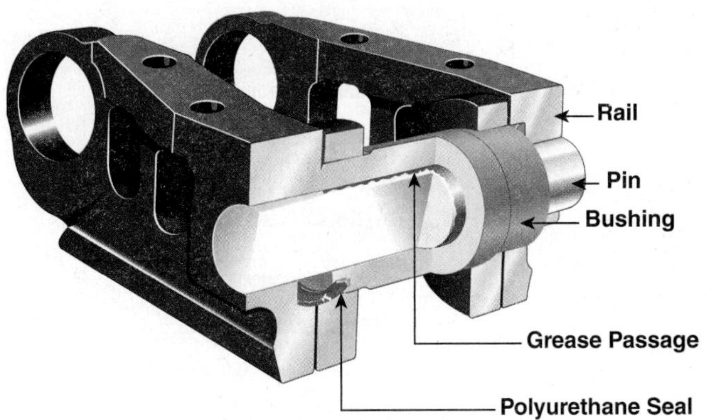

FIGURE 41-42 Sealed and greased type track pins use a polyurethane seals and drilled pins to retain grease.

Not only does greased chain lower travel resistance and noise levels, but also maintenance costs are reduced since this chain can reuse pins and bushings even after they are worn out. A service procedure called **pin turning** enables reuse of pins and bushings if the machine has been used in a non-impact conditions. If track has encountered rocky and rough ground, pins can bend and become unsuitable for turning. Turning can be performed on nonlubricated track but is less common since components reach maximum wear limits much faster and it is often more economical to replace pins and bushings than perform a turn. In that situation, track is operated to destruction and simply replaced.

Greased Turns

The service practice of turning takes place after track is dissembled and both pins and bushings are pressed out of the track links. Since most track pin and bushing wear typically takes place on only one side of each component, rotating or turning the bushings and pins 180 degrees can restore proper operating clearances, and the track is reassembled and returned to service. During a turn, the pin and bushing receive a coat of fresh grease that lends the name **greased turn** to this service procedure. No provision exists on SAG track to force grease into the clearances after track reassembly. If bushings and pins are too worn out or damaged, the alternative is to replace all pins and bushings instead of only turning the parts. The economics of either procedure can vary depending on labor cost, the number of dry or bent pins, condition of track links, and whether the edges of the grease seals have worn deep grooves in the links which prevents them from effectively sealing grease again after a turn only procedure. Older loaders, dozers, and excavators or equipment that does not travel far will most commonly use sealed and greased track.

> **TECHNICIAN TIP**
>
> As track bushings and pins wear, the seals retaining grease will wear too and allow grease to leak from a track joint. Dry joints result when lubricant is lost leading to rapid wear and a lengthening of the track pitch. (Pitch is the length of track measured across three or four track segments.) To check for a dry joint in order to perform maintenance, allow a machine track to first work for a few hours. Wet your hand and touch the end of each track pin after the machine has stopped. Dry joints will be very hot. Alternatively, use an infrared thermometer to measure the temperature of each pin. The hotter pins will indicate a dry pin needing maintenance.

Rotating Bushing Track

A track design enabling both the bushing and pin to rotate is the biggest advancement to extend chain life since bushing and sprocket wear takes place more evenly over the surfaces of these parts, and the mechanical factors causing wear are dramatically reduced.

Two design methods help minimize wear common to sealed lubricated and nonlubricated track. One method uses a two-piece bushing called a Rotating Bushing Track (RBT). Komatsu pioneered this design, which is called **PLUS (parallel**

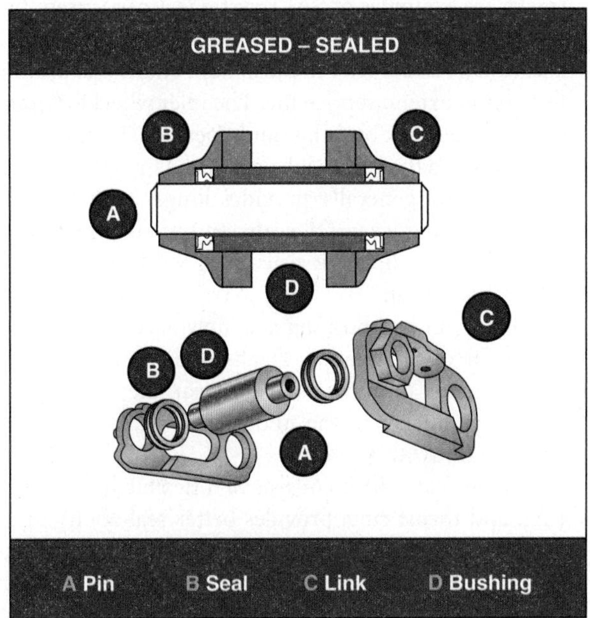

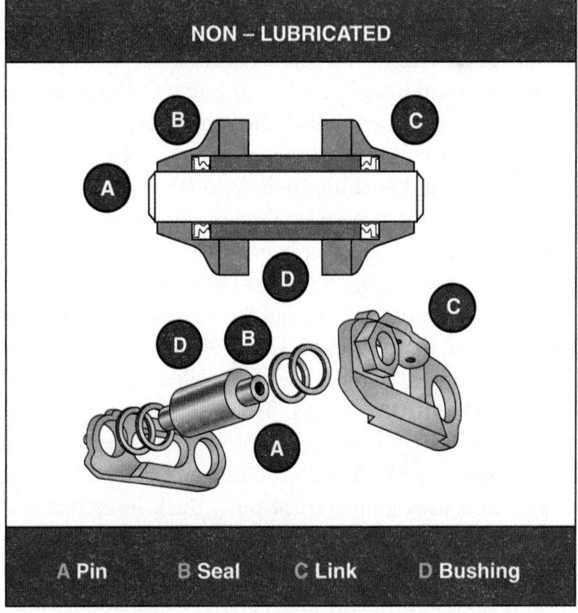

FIGURE 41-43 Comparing sealed and grease type pin construction. The primary difference is the seal arrangement.

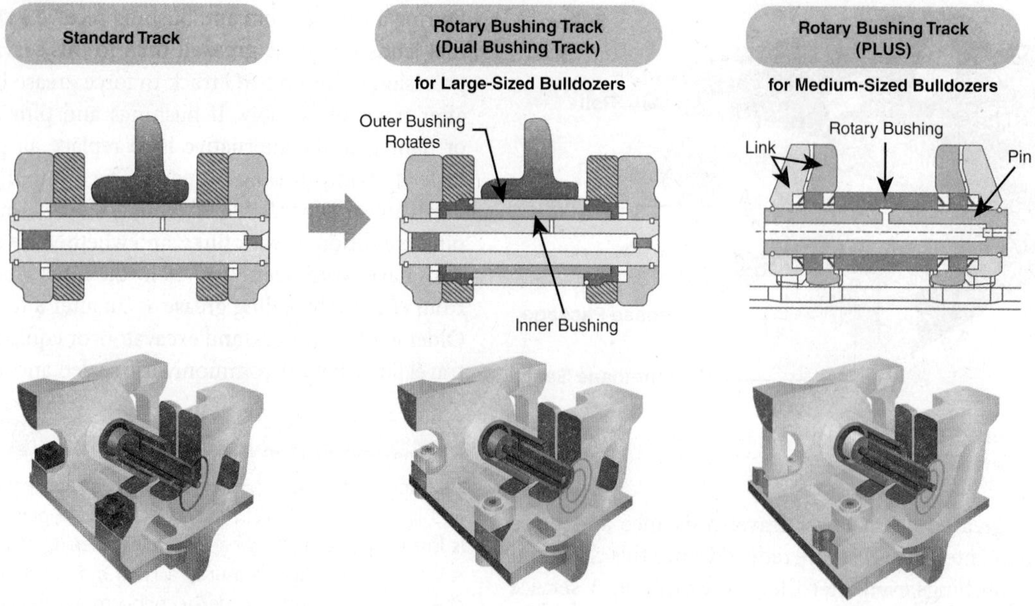

FIGURE 41-44 Komatsu's dual bushing track pin designs.

link undercarriage system), a track system developed for medium-sized bulldozers and introduced in 2008. A second one for larger machines is called the **dual bushing track (DBT)** (**FIGURE 41-44**). The dual bushing track also uses a double bushing construction in which a hardened outer bushing rotates freely around the inner bushing. Unlike the PLUS system, no lubricant is present between the two outer bushings. However, rotating inside the inner bushing is an oil lubricated track pin. Komatsu field-testing observed that the dual bushing system enabled bushing and sprocket life to increase to over 3,500 hours of operation from 700 hours using standard track configuration. This translates into a 46% increase in track life that compensates for the additional cost of an RBT track system.

The Komatsu PLUS system used on lighter machines does not use dual bushings, but instead enables the bushing to rotate in an oil-lubricated track link counterbore. Since neither the bushing or pin use and interference fit to retain the parts in the link, only a snap ring is used to lock the pin in place to prevent it from sliding out from between the track links. The use of oil to lubricate the pins and bushings in link counterbores requires four, rather than two, separate oil seals: a pair to keep dirt from entering the oil cavity and another pair to prevent oil from leaking out of the pin operating clearances. Enabling the bushing to rotate in an oil-lubricated link counterbore minimizes tooth to bushing friction to the point where 50–70% less wear is achieved. Case also uses a similar system, called **case extended life track (CELT)** (**FIGURE 41-45**). This dual bushing system doubles track life, using a second, hardened bushing over an inner bushing and pin. To obtain even longer service life, both track systems also uses longer track pins, track links that are wider and have a taller rail on which the rollers ride. Because the bushings rotate, relative motion between the bushings and the sprocket teeth is almost eliminated. Any wear that does take place distributes evenly around the bushings. This means no bushing turns are required to reestablish correct track pitch, and sprocket segment wear is dramatically reduced.

Sealed and Lubricated Track Tractors

The newest track chains on machines doing a significant amount of traveling use oil lubrication in the pin and bushing joint and allow the bushing to rotate. This design enabling the bushing to rotate is the biggest recent advancement to extend chain life since bushing and sprocket wear is dramatically reduced. Enabling the bushing to rotate in an oil lubricated link counterbore minimizes tooth to bushing friction to the point where 50–70% less wear is achieved. Caterpillar's System One, introduced in the early 2000s, and Komatsu's Plus tracks are examples of SALT systems. Cat's System One uses a simpler box-shaped track link that is less vulnerable to damage. Rollers and track links also have additional premium track features to extend service life. The idler wheel for example only runs on the track bushings and does not sit on track link rails. Compared to the grease lubricant used in sealed and lubricated track, the oil generally provides longer service life with less pin-to-bushing wear. Oil seals tend to last longer than grease seals since the lip-type seals used with oil lubricant receive better lubrication.

Each pin and bushing assembly is sealed and has its own cavity for oil lubrication that is often synthetic oil. Polished bushing ends minimize seal lip wear. Stepped-type bushings, which are thicker in the middle, provide more external wear material (**FIGURE 41-46**).

Rigid seal, which consists of a flexible load ring, rigid seal ring, and thrust ring, provides better seal ability in all underfoot conditions, reducing the effects of impact on track joints that cause premature seal failure. The rotating pin and bushing design means there is little internal wear on the joint. And if significant wear does take place, the interval for the turning of the

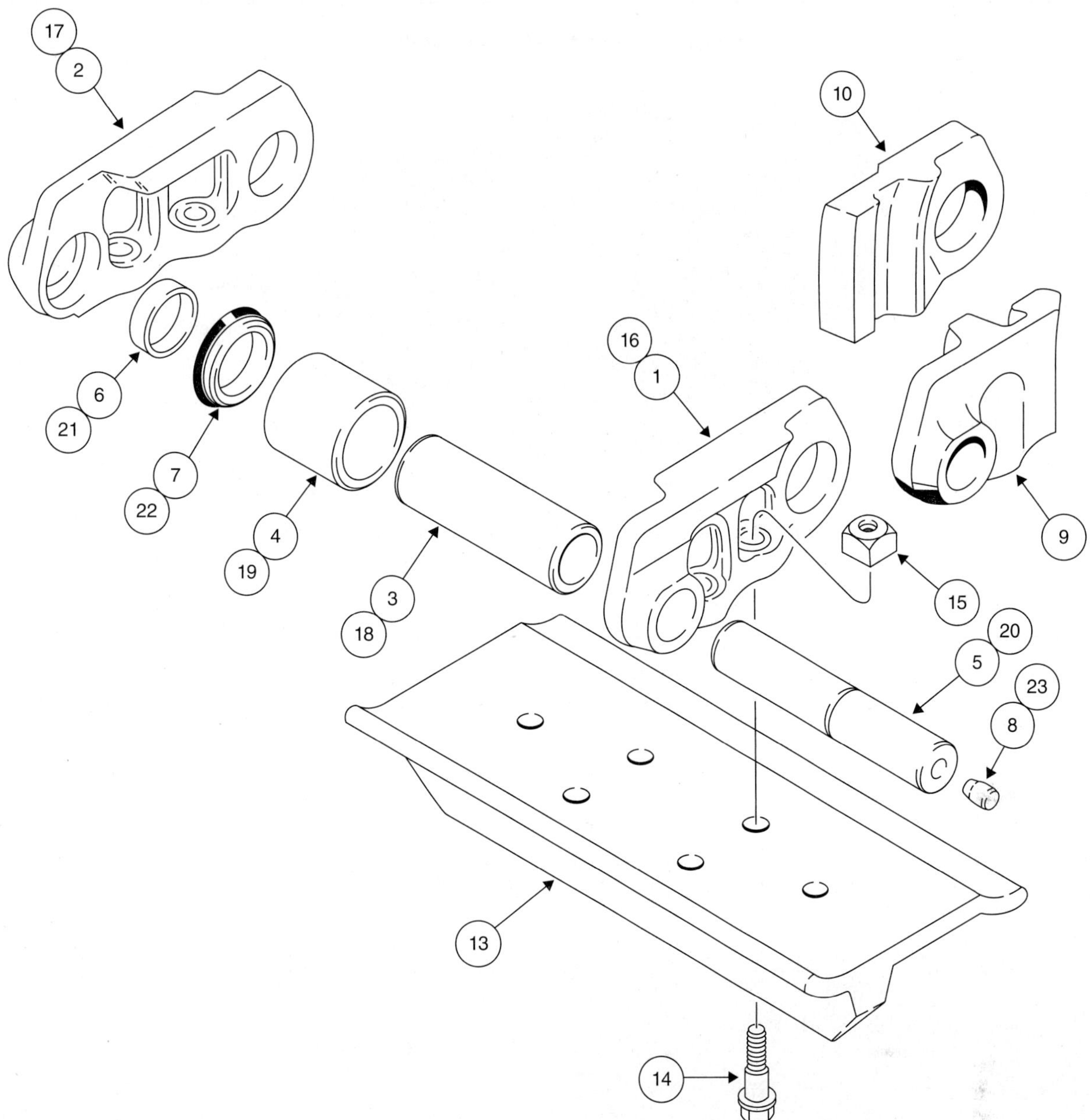

FIGURE 41-45 The arrangement of track pins and dual bushing design used by Case CELT System.

track pins and bushings is much longer because most wear will be on the outside of the bushings and in the track links.

When external bushing wear approaches 50% after measuring track pitch and comparing with specifications, a **wet turn** is a service option on SALT track with fixed bushings. The procedure is called a wet turn because oil rather than grease is used as a lubricant. Like a grease turn, a wet turn involves pressing the bushings and pins out of the track and rotating the parts 180 degrees or flipping pins end for end. During a wet turn, refilling the oil cavity uses a method that involves a vacuum pump to draw new oil into the pin through a self-sealing plug in the end of the pin (**FIGURE 41-47**). New oil seals must be installed during a wet turn. Worn or damaged seals prevent pulling a vacuum that indicates the pin seals will leak.

SALT track has plugs, which can be removed to fill pin cavities with oil. The clear plastic plug appears dark when filled with oil, and light when oil has drained from the pin. Oil is retained in the track pin by a rubber stopper and polyurethane plug. The oil is installed in the pin through a hole in the center of the rubber stopper. When the pin oil cavity is filled, the plug is reinstalled in the stopper.

Quad and Tri-Link Track

Tri-Link Track and Quad-Link Track is a track system developed by Caterpillar for the most severe impact working conditions, such as in forestry (**FIGURE 41-48**). In addition to the two parallel links of conventional track, a third or even fourth track link is bolted onto the track shoe, and an additional chain called an outrigger is formed. The outrigger chain is not driven by a

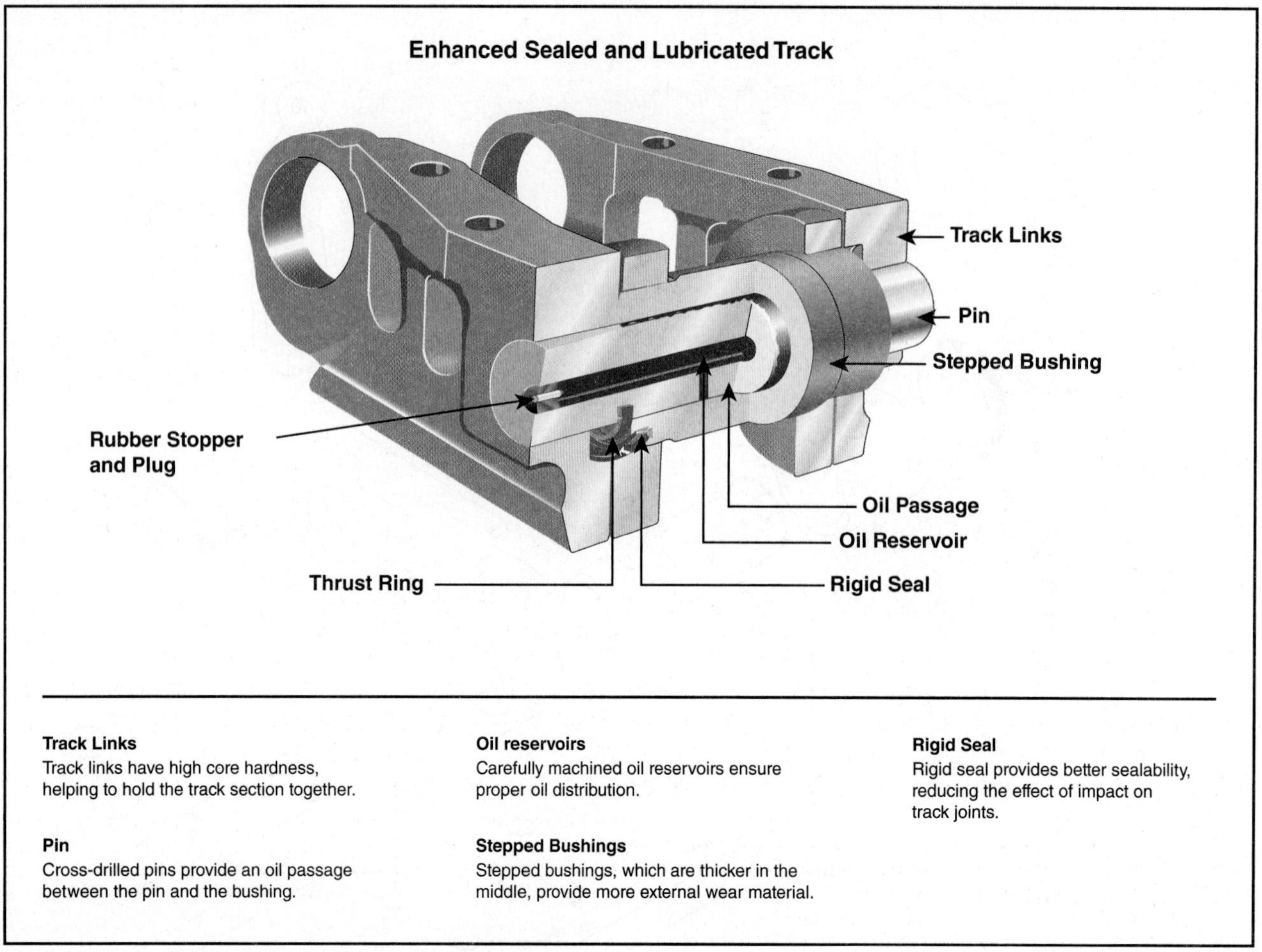

Enhanced Sealed and Lubricated Track

Track Links
Pin
Stepped Bushing
Rubber Stopper and Plug
Oil Passage
Oil Reservoir
Thrust Ring
Rigid Seal

Track Links
Track links have high core hardness, helping to hold the track section together.

Pin
Cross-drilled pins provide an oil passage between the pin and the bushing.

Oil reservoirs
Carefully machined oil reservoirs ensure proper oil distribution.

Stepped Bushings
Stepped bushings, which are thicker in the middle, provide more external wear material.

Rigid Seal
Rigid seal provides better sealability, reducing the effect of impact on track joints.

FIGURE 41-46 Cat System One track pin and bushing features.

FIGURE 41-47 The oil fill plug for a Cat System One SALT track system.

sprocket but only provides more support for the shoe. The effect is that less shoe damage takes place in any application where shoe deflection is high. Other benefits include improved load distribution and track pin lubrication, producing longer joint life with fewer dry joints, and greater system reliability. Using Tri- or Quad-Link Track in high-impact applications has a higher initial cost, but with less shoe damage; overall operating costs per hour are lower.

> ▶ TECHNICIAN TIP
>
> Neglecting undercarriage maintenance can be costly. Waiting until a failure, such as a broken chain on a job site, requires unscheduled work stoppage and more expensive field service call. Failures often involve working in more difficult conditions that take more time to complete. Lifting and shoring up a heavy tractor or excavator out of muddy conditions also requires additional labor-intense work. Proactive maintenance, such as periodic inspection and measurement of track components, is always a more convenient and less expensive approach to maintenance.

Track Master Links

To disassemble any type of track, it must first be separated at a track link. Some track is disassembled by removing a track pin to separate two adjoining links. One type of master link, a pin type, uses a pin with a dimple in each end for identification purposes, but the other pins do not (**FIGURE 41-49**). The pin has a slightly smaller diameter than the other pins, and the bushing in that pin is shorter than the other bushings. This type of pin is driven out of the link after either removing a snap ring from one side or driving out small spring pins, instead of removing a snap ring. Some lighter machines use a dimpled pin on one end only, to center a driving tool along with a wider pin head on one end.

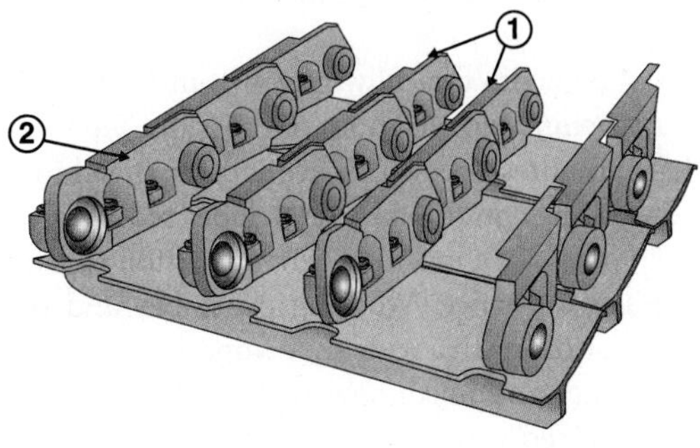

FIGURE 41-48 Tri- and Quad-Link Track resist shoe bending and support higher machine weights in high-impact working conditions.

> ▶ TECHNICIAN TIP
>
> It's important to install the dimpled master pin with the dimpled end facing outward on the track. Failure to do so will make it difficult to identify the master pin if removed again. If the pin is installed backward, use a flashlight to inspect the bushings, and locate the pin in the track link with a shorter bushing.

The majority of tracks use a unique track link, known as a master link, that enables track chain to be quickly disconnected for service. The split link is the most common master link and is often called an alligator or crocodile link because of the five or so serrated teeth that latch onto one another (**FIGURES 41-50** and **41-51**). Two bolts passing through the track shoes hold the link halves together, which are removed first. Striking the link with a hammer separates the link halves used on both the left and right sides of the chain. A newer, revised version of this serrated link uses a single hook-like tooth engagement to replace the multiple serrations and is also bolted together. The bolts are first removed before the link is struck and separated. Remember, during track assembly, that there is a right and a left link, which are different depending on which side of the frame the link is used to form a rail. To prevent the master link loosening, always clean any dirt or paint between the tooth serrations before assembly, and torque the connecting bolts.

Track Shoes

Track shoes are formed metal plates bolted to the track chain. Machine weight distributes over the ground contact patch surface area of the shoe plate. Cleat-like protrusions, called the grip grouse or grouser, penetrate the ground to increase the shoe's

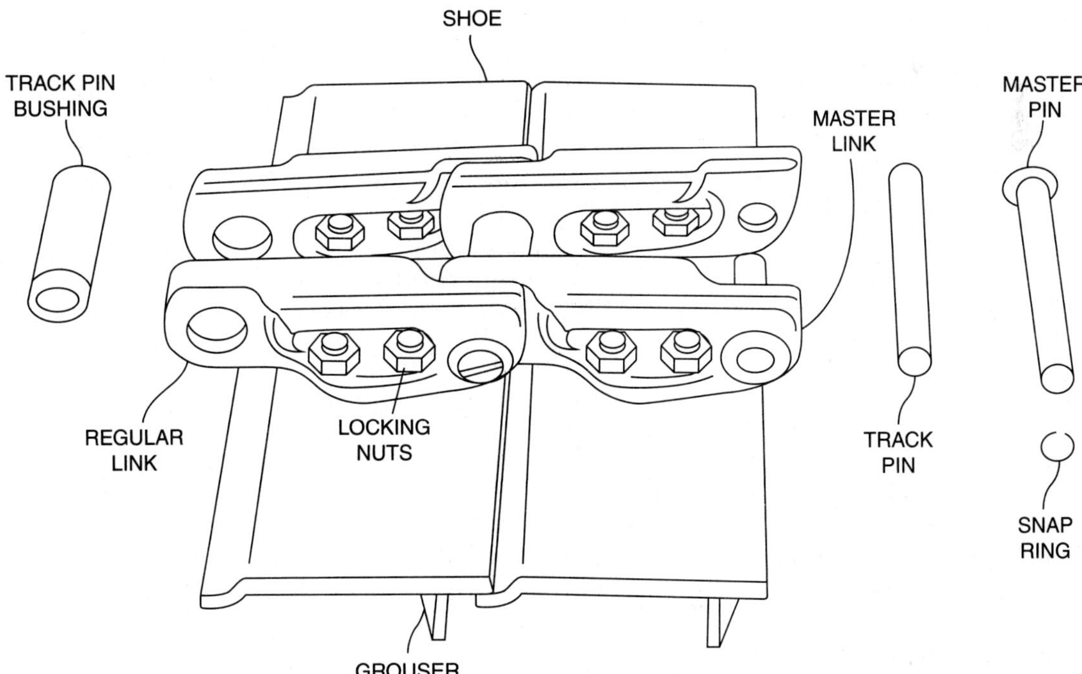

FIGURE 41-49 Track link using a master pin with positive pin retention using a snap ring.

FIGURE 41-50 Features of a single-tooth master link.

New Single Tooth Master Link **Former Five Tooth Master Link**

FIGURE 41-51 Comparing a single-tooth and older serrated tooth master link.

traction capabilities. Grousers also provide shoes greater bending resistance. More grousers provide the greatest resistance to bending needed in high-impact working conditions, defined as exposure to rock or concrete bumps of 6 inches or more. Holes in the shoes are designed to allow mud, snow, soil, or other material to squeeze through the shoe, and clean material as the track rotates. The forward edge of the shoe overlaps the shoe ahead of it on the track. A curve built into this leading edge opens when the shoe rotates around the idler or drive sprocket to help clear material buildup.

Shoe design naturally depends on the operational requirements of the machine. For example, a typical standard dozer shoe uses a deep, single grouser to adequately penetrate the ground and provide the traction force necessary to push or pull a load. A more highly maneuverable loader with a hydrostatic drive, enabling operators to turn rapidly and in a small radius, uses two or three low-profile grousers. In this application, smaller grouser profiles allow the track to slip more and reduce stress on track components as the track undergoes tremendous side loading when turning. Ground disturbance is also minimized by low-profile grousers. If a shoe encounters high turning resistance, it may bend or even crack and break. Offsetting the advantage of low-profile grousers is that increased plate wear takes place.

Shoes are rated according to their wear resistance. Although most shoes are heat treated and made from alloyed steel to increase hardness and reduce abrasive wear, faster wear rates are encountered in severe working conditions. Shoes for extreme conditions are made for applications such as ripping in hard ground and working in rocky soil and over concrete. The extreme-service shoes have thicker plates with greater hardness, plus they have taller grousers to compensate for rapid abrasive wear. Thicker, hardened plates impart greater impact resistance.

Chemical effects from soils can undermine the effectiveness of severe-service shoes. For example, salt, calcium and other corrosive minerals accelerate corrosion in hardened steel. Pitting in the shoes creates stress risers that are points where shoes can more easily fracture.

Ground conditions that are extremely soft or in extremely soft or completely penetrable material, such as loose soil, sand, or muddy conditions, is classified as low-impact condition equipment.

Track shoe width typically ranges from 12" to 36", depending on the machine model. Shoe width is adjusted to provide an optimal ground pressure, which depends on matching machine weight to working conditions. Wider shoes reduce ground pressure, which provides a machine better flotation capabilities and less ground disturbance. Working on slopes and performing grading operations with a wide shoe improve blade control. The ride is smoother and machine stability is better. Grouser penetration is reduced with lower ground pressure, which in turn reduces traction.

> **TECHNICIAN TIP**
>
> Over 50 different combinations of track shoes are available on medium- and large-track machines. When recommending track shoe width, always select the narrowest track shoes possible to obtain flotation or adequate ground pressure. Wide shoes can reduce chain life by 50% and accelerate wear to all components by placing an increased load on the track–chain pin and bushing joints, especially in rough terrain. Wider shoes also increase bending forces applied to idlers and rollers. Drive torque transmitted through sprockets increases with increased track width.

Openings in the shoes and changes in the direction or shape of grousers are designed to match ground conditions. Holes in the shoes allow materials to be extruded or squeezed through plates for improved self-cleaning. However, closed centered shoes are standard unless more self-cleaning properties of shoes are required. A drawback of single or double open-centered shoes on some track designs is that they can leave more material deposited onto sprockets, rollers, and idlers, leading to more track packing, which accelerates track wear.

Moderate-Service Track Shoes Options

Moderate-service track shoe options include:

- **Single-grouser shoes:** Considered an all-purpose shoe, and recommended for any general application, these shoes are best used in low- to medium-abrasive materials conditions and low- to moderate-impact conditions. A single grouser bar provides adequate ground penetration and traction while resisting wear and bending (**FIGURE 41-52**).

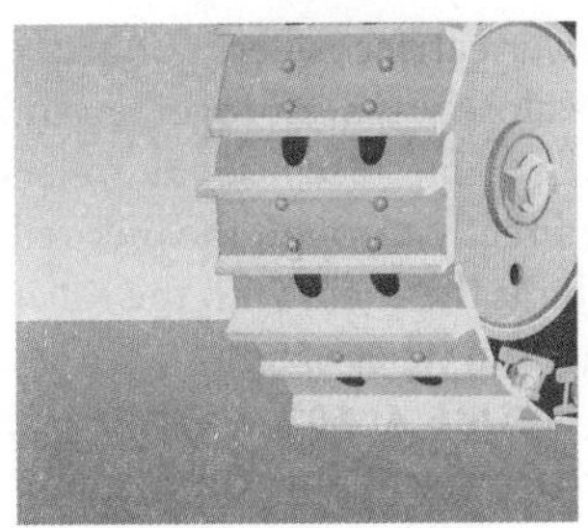

FIGURE 41-52 Single grouser shoe.

- **Center hole shoes:** With a single center hole, these shoes are intended for applications where packing causes the track to tighten, accelerating pin and bushing wear. Reducing the amount of material stuck to the shoes minimizes packing between the shoe and the bushing because the sprocket action can push dirt and debris out through the large center hole, giving the material another place to go. Center hole shoes are also used by double-grouser and chopper-type shoes (**FIGURE 41-53**).
- **Multi-grouser shoes:** Use two or three short grousers instead of one tall grouser. These shoes are recommended for applications that require high turning capability and minimal ground disturbance. Traction is compromised as there is less penetration by the smaller grouser bars.

With a smaller grouser bar height, the shoe wears quickly in abrasive conditions and are best adapted for low usage on medium-size track-type machines (**FIGURE 41-54**).

Centre Hole Shoes
(Moderate and Extreme Service Shoes)
• Work best in applications where packing causes the track to tighten, accelerating pin and bushing wear
• Recommended for applications where large amounts of debris tend to pack in the track
• Reduce extrudable packing between the shoe and the bushing due to sprockets that punch out dirt and debris
• Also available for Double-Grouser and Chopper Shoes

FIGURE 41-53 Double-grouser track shoe with a large open-center hole.

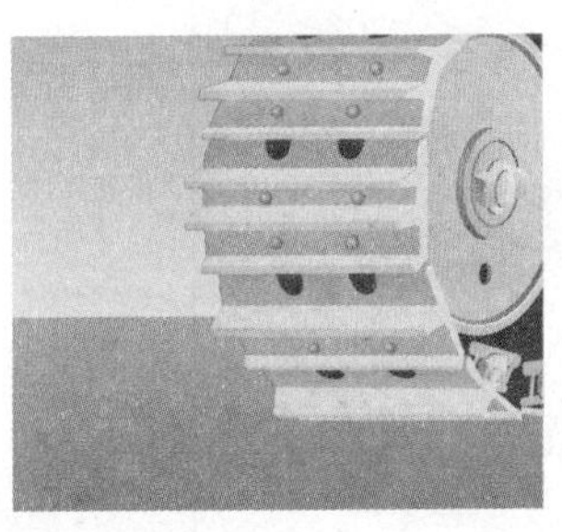

FIGURE 41-54 A multi-grouser shoe with two center holes.

Extreme Service Shoes

Hard working surfaces, such as broken rock, concrete, or asphalt, can quickly damage or wear out shoes. Other operating conditions such as working in highly acidic soils or fine abrasives can accelerate shoe wear. To prolong service intervals before needing to replace track shoes, several features are incorporated into track shoe design to match shoes with extreme working conditions.

Single-Grouser Shoes

Unlike the moderate service shoe, these extreme-service shoes are thicker and are more deeply hardened to withstand use in moderate- to high-impact conditions. If track shoes are wearing out before the track chain links, extreme-service shoes are recommended.

Self-Cleaning, Low Ground Pressure Shoes

Very soft soils, such as peat, muskeg, and volcanic ash, lower machine floatation capabilities, causing traction problems. One show option is to use a track shoe with a V-shaped cross section forming a pair of thick sidewalls, which also curve into a trough-like shape on either side of the V. The shoes are also shaped to separate from each other as they move around the sprocket, ejecting dirt and debris as they turn. These shoes should not be used in high-abrasive or high-impact working conditions (**FIGURE 41-55**).

Chopper Shoes

A track shoe that helps compact material as the machine travels uses additional diagonal grouser bars. These shoes are recommended for landfills, waste transfer stations, and demolition applications where debris tends to stick in the shoes or requires compaction. The shoe also features a large trapezoidal center hole for increased self-cleaning capabilities (**FIGURE 41-56**).

Self-Cleaning, Low Ground Pressure Shoes
• Work best in soft underfoot conditions; should not be used in highly abrasive or high-impact conditions
• Recommended for applications where flotation is a problem (LGP only)
• Separate from one another as they move around the sprocket and idler, allowing dirt and debris to fall out

FIGURE 41-55 Low ground pressure shoes.

Chopper Shoes
• Work best in applications where debris tends to stick in the shoes
• Recommended for landfills, transfer stations, and demolition applications
• Feature a full-length grouser to resist bending, diagonal side grouser for increased chopping ability and a large trapezoidal center hole for increased material extrusion

FIGURE 41-56 Chopper-type shoe for landfill work.

Rubber Track Pads

Attaching rubber track pads to steel tracked machines is one solution for preventing ground damage by heavy equipment on finished roads and sensitive ground surfaces. Pads made from rubber or polypropylene can expand a machine's versatility while providing a quieter, smoother ride. Pads may be bolted on or clipped on, or may use a combination of both attachment mechanisms. They are also used as direct replacements for steel track in applications over smooth concrete roadways and floors to provide adhesive-like traction. On larger machines where a rubber track is not available, rubber track pads can be used instead.

▶ Track Guidance System

K41005

Track rollers and the idler wheel have several functions, but together they maintain track alignment—that is the straight-line movement of the track. Bottom rollers riding over the track chain ensure the track does not squirm around, and top rollers prevent track sag under normal conditions and whipping at high speed. Track guards or roller guards, which are steel plates attached to the track frame on both sides of the bottom rollers, also guide the track and prevent it from slipping off the rollers. The guards function primarily to keep the rocks and foreign debris from getting between the track rollers and track links. But positioned next to the track chain, the guards also help guide the track chain (**FIGURE 41-57**). Guards are especially critical for track guidance and stability when working on side hill operation. It's important to note here that good work practice requires that the area around the track guards be regularly cleaned, particularly after operating in muddy conditions, to prevent accelerated track wear.

Track Rollers

Track rollers are differentiated according to their location and function. When installed on the bottom of the track frame or roller frame, the rollers support the weight of the equipment and distribute it evenly over the section of track contacting the ground. Rollers supporting the weight of the top half of track are called idler or carrier rollers. Because the carrier rollers do not bear as much weight, there are fewer carrier rollers compared to bottom rollers, which are more closely spaced together and mounted to the bottom of the track frame. Because the rollers contact only the track chain links directly through the link rail, a flange on the side of the rollers aligns the chain with the roller.

Most track designs use two different types of bottom rollers: single flange and double flange (**FIGURE 41-58**). Single-flange rollers are used closest to the sprockets or idler wheel, allowing some slight track movement only at those points, to enable smoother engagement of the idler wheel and drive sprocket. With single-flange rollers, the flange is located on the inside edge of the track chain. Double-flange rollers maximize track stability and alignment by minimizing any side-to-side movement of the track link. Twin flanges on both sides of the track link force the track chain to move only in a straight-line direction through the roller flanges. Typically, a combination of single- and double-flanged rollers is arranged alternately on the bottom of track frames (**FIGURE 41-59**). For example, on a Cat D5, the bottom rollers are arranged like this:

On Standard Undercarriage

No. 1 Single-flange roller (front nearest idler wheel)
No. 2 Double-flange roller

FIGURE 41-57 Track guide and rock guard.

FIGURE 41-58 Single-flange. **A.** and double-flange **B.** track rollers.

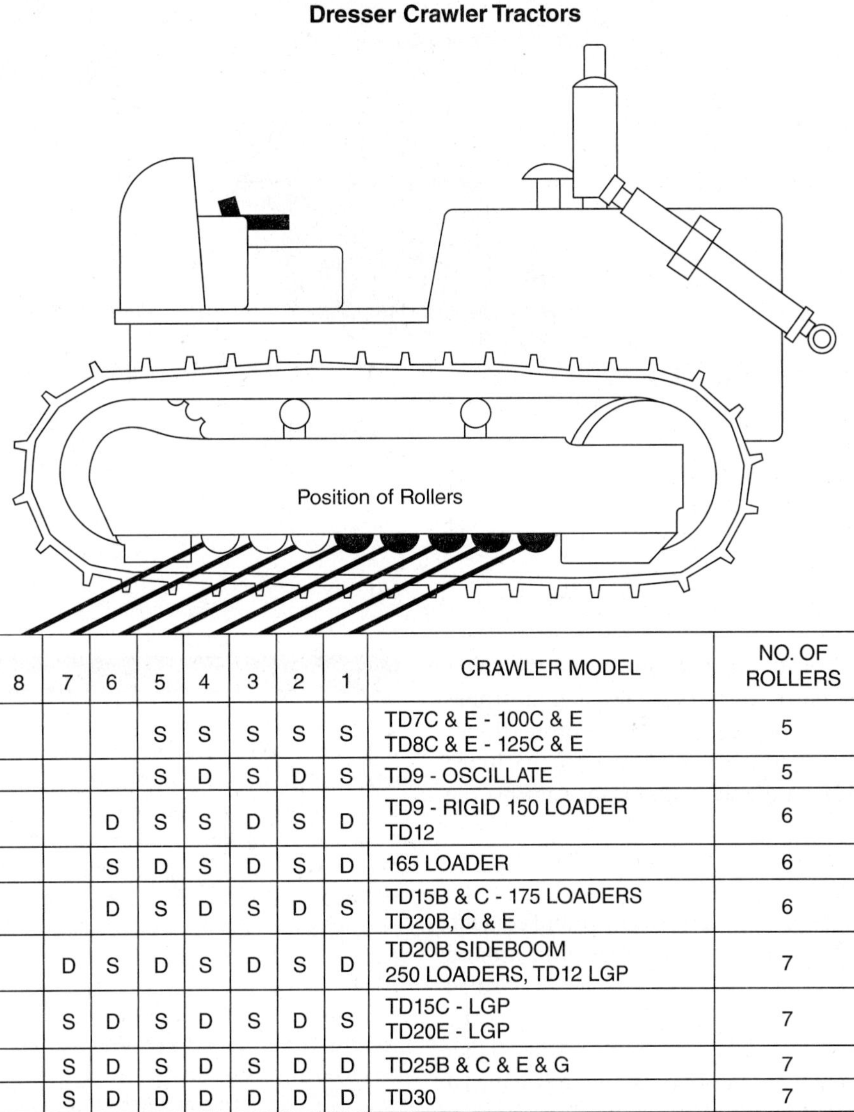

8	7	6	5	4	3	2	1	CRAWLER MODEL	NO. OF ROLLERS
			S	S	S	S	S	TD7C & E - 100C & E TD8C & E - 125C & E	5
			S	D	S	D	S	TD9 - OSCILLATE	5
		D	S	S	D	S	D	TD9 - RIGID 150 LOADER TD12	6
		S	D	S	D	S	D	165 LOADER	6
		D	S	D	S	D	S	TD15B & C - 175 LOADERS TD20B, C & E	6
	D	S	D	S	D	S	D	TD20B SIDEBOOM 250 LOADERS, TD12 LGP	7
	S	D	S	D	S	D	S	TD15C - LGP TD20E - LGP	7
	S	D	S	D	S	D	D	TD25B & C & E & G	7
	S	D	D	D	D	D	D	TD30	7
	S	D	D	S	D	D	S	TD40	7
S	D	S	D	S	D	S	D	TD25B SIDEBOOM	8

FIGURE 41-59 The arrangement of single- and double-flanged rollers generally alternates one with another with single flange rollers located immediately after the drive sprocket.

No. 3 Single-flange roller
No. 4 Single-flange roller
No. 5 Double-flange roller
No. 6 Single-flange roller (rear nearest drive sprocket)

On an LGP Undercarriage

No. 1 Single-flange roller
No. 2 Double-flange roller
No. 3 Single-flange roller
No. 4 Double-flange roller
No. 5 Double-flange roller
No. 6 Single-flange roller
No. 7 Double-flange roller
No. 8 Single-flange roller

Because abrasive dirt, rocks, and gravel get between the roller and track chain, roller surfaces are hardened at least to the same degree as the track links. Stainless steel alloys are used to form the replaceable roller shell and also to minimize corrosion from chemical action of soils and water. Inside the roller are oil-lubricated bearings that help transfer heat from the bearing to the bearing shell (**FIGURE 41-60**). Rollers are commonly filled with synthetic SAE 30 or SAE 40 weight oil, which can be added or drained through a fill plug located in the roller body. If a roller does lose oil through leaking seals, it will seize and develop a **"flatted" condition**. Flattening is evident when one side of the roller is worn away from continual sliding friction with the chain link rail. If severe packing has taken place, the roller may also seize and become flatted.

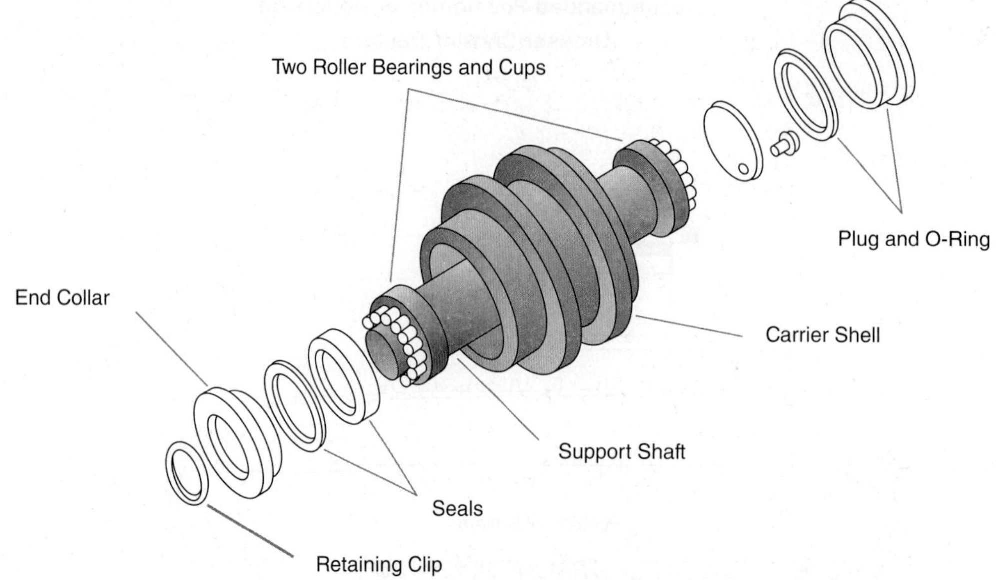

FIGURE 41-60 Construction details of a track roller.

When worn to 75% of its original dimension, the roller shell must be replaced, the roller rebuilt, or the entire roller replaced. Extreme flange roller wear takes place on machines regularly moving across the sides of slopes. All the machine's weight will be applied against the side of the flange against the track.

Roller Bogies

To provide a smoother ride and improve track ground contact, the bottom roller can be arranged in pairs that pivot around a single frame connection point. These roller pairs are called bogies. Pivoting roller bogies allow the track to move vertically over ground irregularities, keeping more of the track in contact with the ground, resulting in improved traction and reduced impact loading (**FIGURE 41-61**). Track bogies may be spring loaded to enable both pivoting and scissor movement around a central fulcrum point. Because track rollers are always in contact with track links, undercarriage durability is improved because of better control of track chain alignment with track rollers.

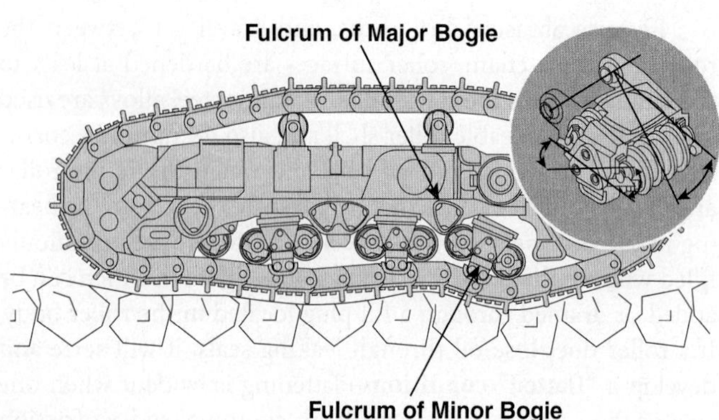

FIGURE 41-61 Track rollers can be assembled into bogies that provide improved ground contact and a smoother ride.

> **TECHNICIAN TIP**
>
> Seals in track drive systems encounter the most severe operating conditions because of abrasives and extreme side loading encountered when turning. To retain pin lubricant and keep dirt out, seals are double lipped, with a very rugged design. A typical track pin seal configuration like Duo-Cone® double-faced steel seal includes the following: two mating seal halves, with each seal half incorporating a metal seal ring and an elastomeric (rubber) ring. The metal seal rings act as the primary seals, and the rubber ring acts as the energizer and secondary (static) seal. These types of seals are designed for installation in the counterbores of the links and are lubricated with oil from the pin cavity. The rubber ring pushes the metal seal rings against the end of bushing and the link in order to provide a positive seal between the bushing and the link counterbore. The use of the rubber ring against the metal seals gives a specific amount of compression to the seal assemblies and controls the end play (free movement) of the joint. The result is that foreign materials are kept out of the joint and the oil in the joint (**FIGURE 41-62**).

FIGURE 41-62 Duo-Cone seals are used in SALT links to keep dirt out and seal oil in. Metal faces of the two ring halves provide a positive seal.

> ▶ TECHNICIAN TIP
>
> Always park a machine on level ground. If machine track is parked sideways on an incline or uneven terrain, the weight of the machine applied against the roller flanges will compress oil seals inside the bottom rollers. If that takes place, the roller seals can become deformed or damaged due to excessive side loading of the roller, resulting in lubricant loss. Without lubricant, the internal parts of a roller are destroyed within hours.

Track Idler Wheel

Idlers are the track larger wheels that are placed opposite the drive sprocket in an oval track configuration. In an elevated sprocket design, two idlers are used on each track to redirect and align the track loop along the track rollers. A front and back idler designates the position of idlers in an elevated sprocket design. Depending on the position of the idler, it will support part of the weight of the equipment, along with the bottom rollers. The bearing block assembly used on the idler shaft and shell is a plain bimetal bearing with better load and wear characteristics than a ball bearing (**FIGURE 41-63**). A retainer ring holds the end collar to the idler shell. The end collar holds the oil seals and the other components inside the idler hub assembly. A guide plate connects the idler to a **recoil spring mechanism**, which is used to absorb shock loads and tension the track. Guides located on each side of the raised center flange of the idler sit on the chain link rails. Track chain is guided by the raised center flange moving between the link rails.

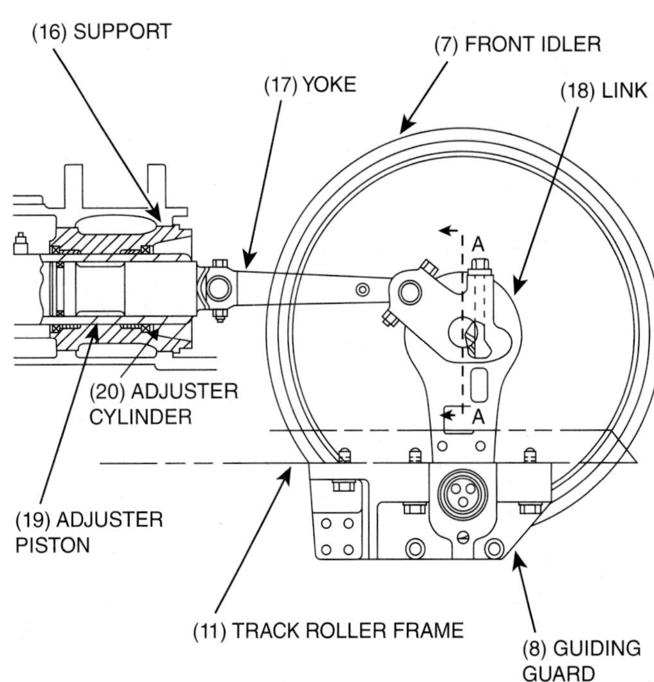

FIGURE 41-63 Arrangement of the tensioner and idler wheel.

One other major function idlers perform is to maintain the correct track tension, along with the track tensioner, also called a recoil mechanism. Track tension or slack is adjusted by moving the idler back and forth on the track frame (**FIGURE 41-64**).

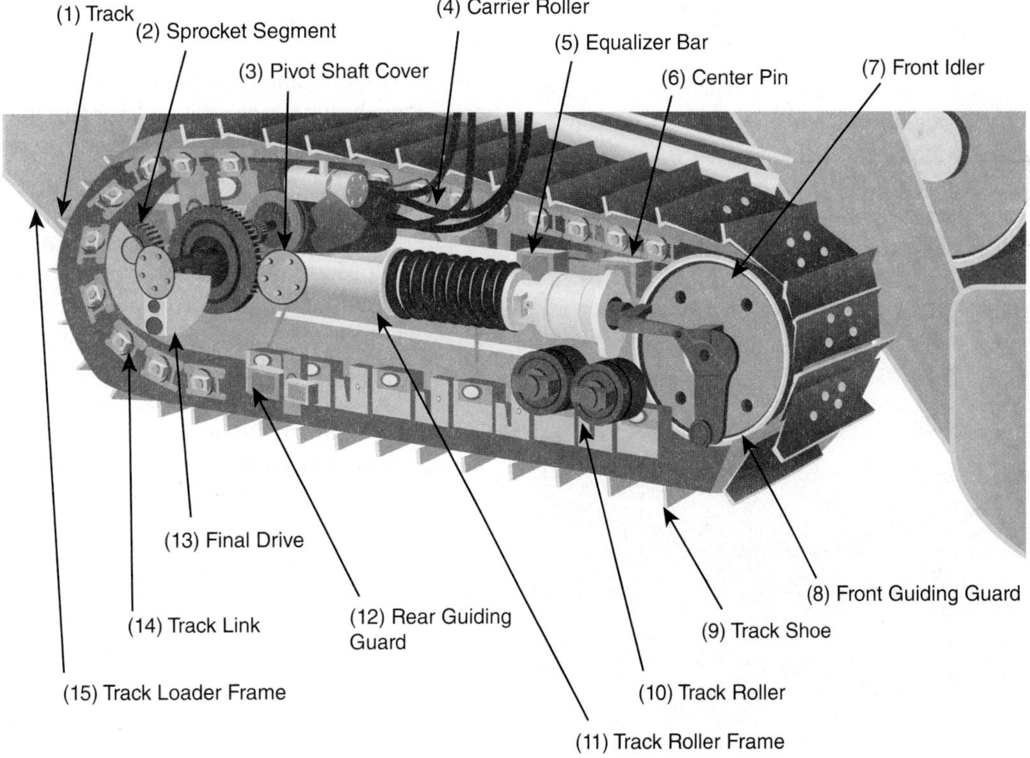

FIGURE 41-64 The tensioning mechanism is used to adjust the chain to obtain the correct slack or track tension.

Alignment of the idler is critical during service to prevent continuous contact between the chain link rail and idler. Selective shims are used on the idler guide plate to establish correct idler-to-track-link alignment (**FIGURE 41-65**). The recoil tensioning mechanism contains a large heavy spring that acts like a shock absorber. High-impact shock loads to the track, caused by large rocks or uneven terrain, have the potential to break the chain. The tensioning mechanism absorbs shock loads by compressing the tensioning spring and allowing the idler wheel to retract inside the tensioning mechanism.

Equipment with oval tracks may use a two-position idler: one position that is used when ripping work or drawbar is required, and another when heavy front implements are attached.

When heavy front-mounted equipment is operated, the idler is placed in a lower position. This places more track in contact with the ground, making the equipment more stable. The opposite takes place when the rear-mounted drawbar is used. The idler is moved up to a higher initial position, placing less track in contact with the ground. The bar, however, tends to lift the rear of the machine, tipping the front track forward. A more even distribution of weight takes place over the track when the idler is moved up.

Track Tension Adjustment

The most significant and controllable factor in undercarriage wear is the establishment of correct track tension. Track tension is easily estimated by observing the amount of track slack or sag (**FIGURE 41-66**). Measured on the top track section, track sag is checked by placing a straightedge between the highest point, above the carrier roller and the next contact point, usually the front idler or a second carrier roller. The track sag is the distance from the straightedge to the track at its lowest point between the two contact points. Correct track sag for conventional oval track is 2 inches (±¼"). Track that is too tight because of packing or maladjustment accounts for 20–50% of wear on track parts due to increased friction between moving parts. Tight track multiplies the friction and force required to move track. The result is more wear on the track bushings, sprocket teeth contact areas, and idler roller contact areas. One manufacturer has

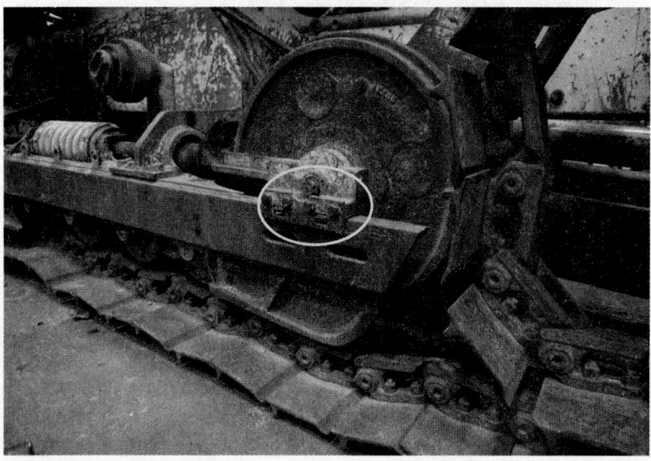

FIGURE 41-65 Location of the shims used to adjust the idler wheel.

FIGURE 41-66 Track sag should be checked on a daily basis.

calculated that a crawler tractor with an 80-horsepower engine using a ½-inch track–chain sag results in approximately 5,600 pounds of chain tension when measured at the track adjuster. The same machine with a correct 2-inch track sag reduces track tension to approximately 800 pounds. Increased friction translates into the need for greater engine power output and higher fuel consumption.

Alternatively, when the tracks are too loose, they can buckle, jam, and jump the drive sprocket teeth or idler wheel, resulting in a thrown track that will require several hours to reinstall.

Track adjustment is necessary as a result of track pin, bushing, and roller wear. Track tension will also change with the condition of the soil in which the machine works.

Track Recoil Spring and Tensioner

To adjust and maintain correct track tension, the track assemblies of all early (very old) tracked machines, such as Allis-Chalmers, Caterpillar, and International Harvester Tractors, an adjusting screw on a threaded coil spring retainer was turned. This difficult mechanical procedure required two workers; a long, heavy wrench with a lever bar; and an average time of approximately 1.5 hours. The adjusting screw was connected to the front idler wheel of the machine while the retainer held a heavy recoil spring to the track frame. In1951, a hydraulic means of adjusting and holding the tension on crawler tractors was developed, eliminating a labor-intensive procedure with the use of a simple hand-operated grease gun, enabling track adjustment on any size of machine in 2–3 minutes (**FIGURE 41-67**). This mechanism, called a Hydra-Juster®, enables the machine operator to both tighten and loosen the track chain, as required, by either adding grease or opening a bleeder screw to release grease pressure inside the recoil mechanism (**FIGURE 41-68**).

The Hydra-Juster uses a stepped piston device to multiply the force of a standard grease gun with 10,000 psi to 30,000 psi used to compress the recoil spring. Recoil spring force is as high as 40 tons when compressed by the Hydra-Juster. Forcing semisolid grease into the recoil tensioner mechanism compresses the recoil spring and forces the idler forward to increase track tension. The grease is trapped in a cylinder until the track adjustment requires changing. During track operation, the pressure on the Hydra-Juster piston may exceed 100 tons as a result of idler recoil spring tension. However, no grease is lost because

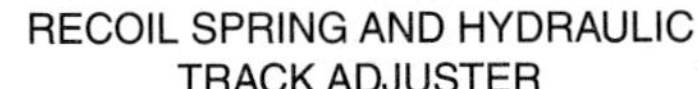

FIGURE 41-67 A track tensioner with a grease-type fill and relief valve used to adjust spring tension.

of the design of the special grease-retaining seal. Because grease is a semisolid and cannot be compressed, track adjustment will remain stable. However, if excessive shock loading takes place, a pressure relief valve may vent some grease to compensate for extreme track loads. Afterward, it may be necessary to recharge the Hydra-Juster mechanism after one the travel cycle to restore correct track tension. Opening the bleeder screw at the base of the Hydra-Juster cylinder relieves recoil spring tension and loosens the track tension.

To enable a more consistent recoil force over a longer idler wheel travel, a gas accumulator piston located behind the recoil spring is incorporated into heavier track tensioning systems. The spring rate is changed by simply altering the gas pressure inside the cylinder. A typical gas charge pressure is between 1,500 psi and 2,000 psi when charged with dry nitrogen (**FIGURE 41-69**).

TECHNICIAN TIP

The track tensioning mechanism contains a hydraulic accumulator that acts as a spring to maintain track tension. Check the accumulator pressure whenever the track is adjusted or repaired.

SAFETY TIP

Hydraulic accumulators for track tensioners contain gas and oil under high pressure. *Do not* disconnect lines or disassemble any component of a pressurized accumulator. All precharge gas pressure must be removed from the accumulator, as instructed by the service manual, before servicing the accumulator or any accumulator component. Failure to follow the instructions and warnings could result in personal injury or death. Only use dry nitrogen gas—*never* oxygen—to recharge accumulators; oxygen will cause an explosion (**FIGURE 41-70**).

Rubber Track

K41006

Rubber track drive systems, replacing linked steel plates with a single-piece, metal-reinforced rubber belt, are an increasingly popular alternative to steel track systems (**FIGURE 41-71**). Like

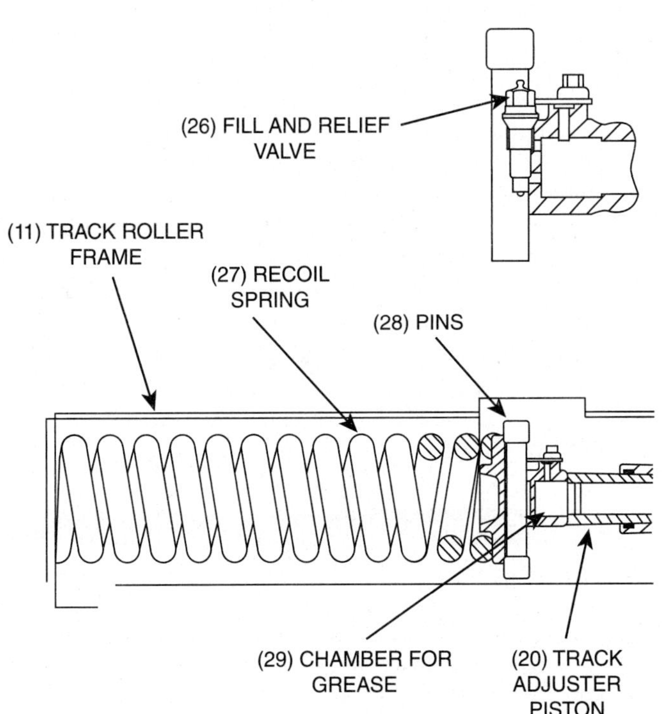

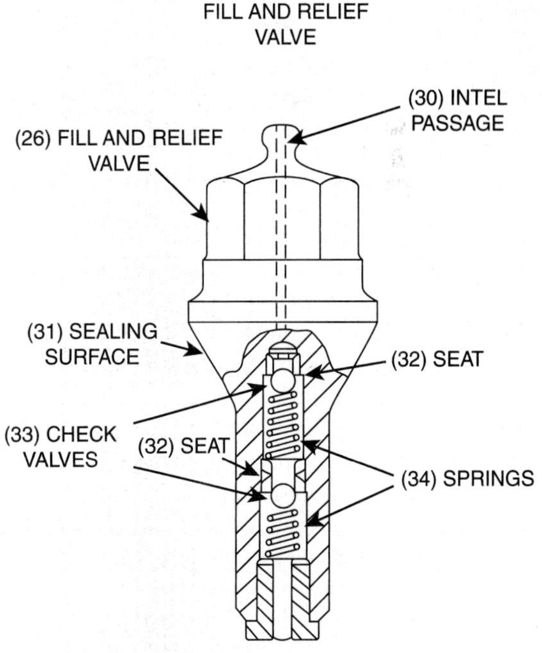

FIGURE 41-68 Cross-sectional view of a Hydra-Juster track tensioner.

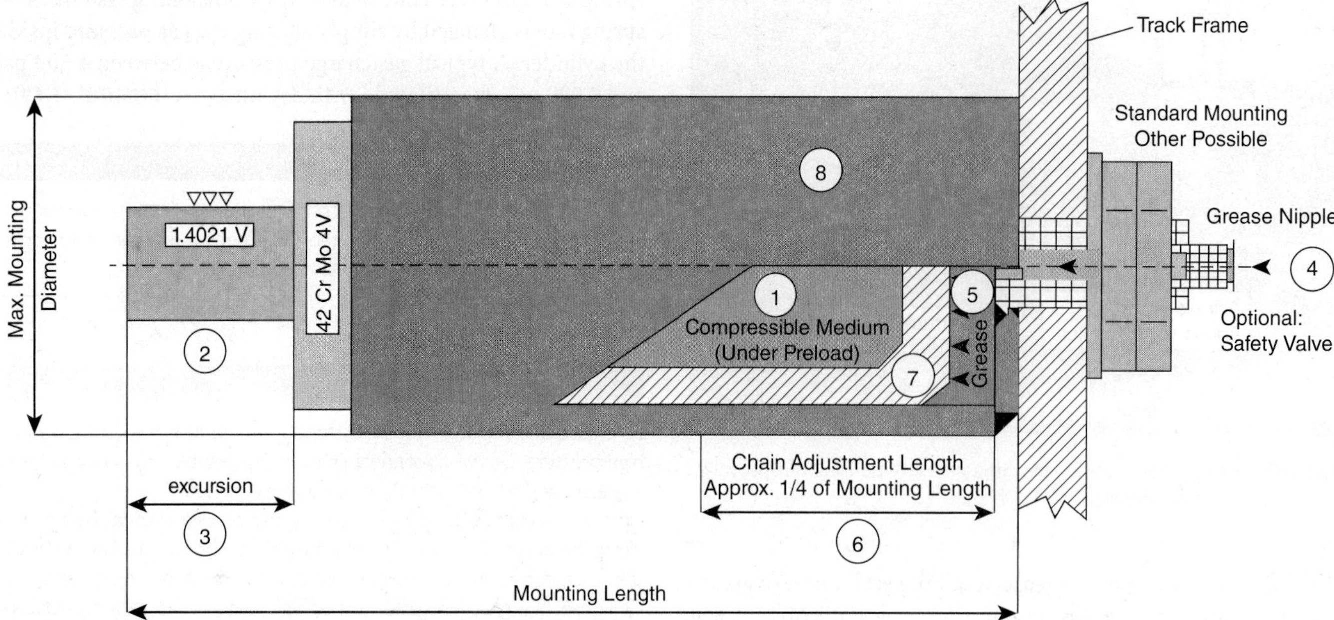

FIGURE 41-69 Cross section of a gas accumulator–type track tensioner.

FIGURE 41-70 Safely disposing of a gas accumulator–type track tensioner.

steel track, rubber track has better traction and lower ground pressure than wheeled equipment and is ideal for working in loose, muddy, and irregular ground. But rubber's performance is improved over steel track because it uses significantly fewer components, has a less complex design, and disturbs ground much less than steel. Compared to a wheeled machine, rubber track is approximately 15% more expensive to purchase, but long-term maintenance costs are about the same. Rubber tracks are lighter in weight, using a single-piece belt construction that is far less damaging to sensitive surfaces such as lawns, sidewalks, and road surfaces. Rubber tracks are also preferred by operators for their lower vibration and noise levels. In operating conditions where ground chemicals can attack steel track, rubber tracks are more resistant to deterioration. In comparison to steel tracks, machines using rubber tracks are lighter and make less noise when traveling. Manufacturers boast that the latest rubber track systems can last 3,000–5,000 hours and double the life of a wheeled machine performing the same work under the same working conditions. The primary disadvantage of rubber track is that it can be damaged in high-impact, highly abrasive operating conditions, such as rock quarries, demolition sites, or when working with scrap metals. Although rubber track systems can travel faster than steel with less wear, they still should be floated between distant worksites. A cooldown period of 30 minutes is needed when doing continuous or extensive travel over concrete and asphalt.

Rubber track systems have been more slowly adopted by equipment operators, accounting for less than 10% of the wheeled and steel track market. In the agriculture market, rubber track systems have as much as 30% of market share of large horsepower tractors. Part of the explanation for the poor take-up is previous belt-like systems, such as those used for half-tracks in World War II, were not as strong and during military actions were easily damaged. Machines in the agricultural market often use four tracks for better weight distribution and traction in muddy, wet soil. They have between a 14% and 22% higher cost premium in initial purchase price (**FIGURE 41-72**).

▶ TECHNICIAN TIP

Rubber track systems are becoming more popular for military applications because of the rubber's ability to withstand damage from blasts from land mines. Rubber tracks are more easily repaired in the field with track repair kits than are steel track systems. Quieter, faster operation provides even more advantages for rubber track over steel.

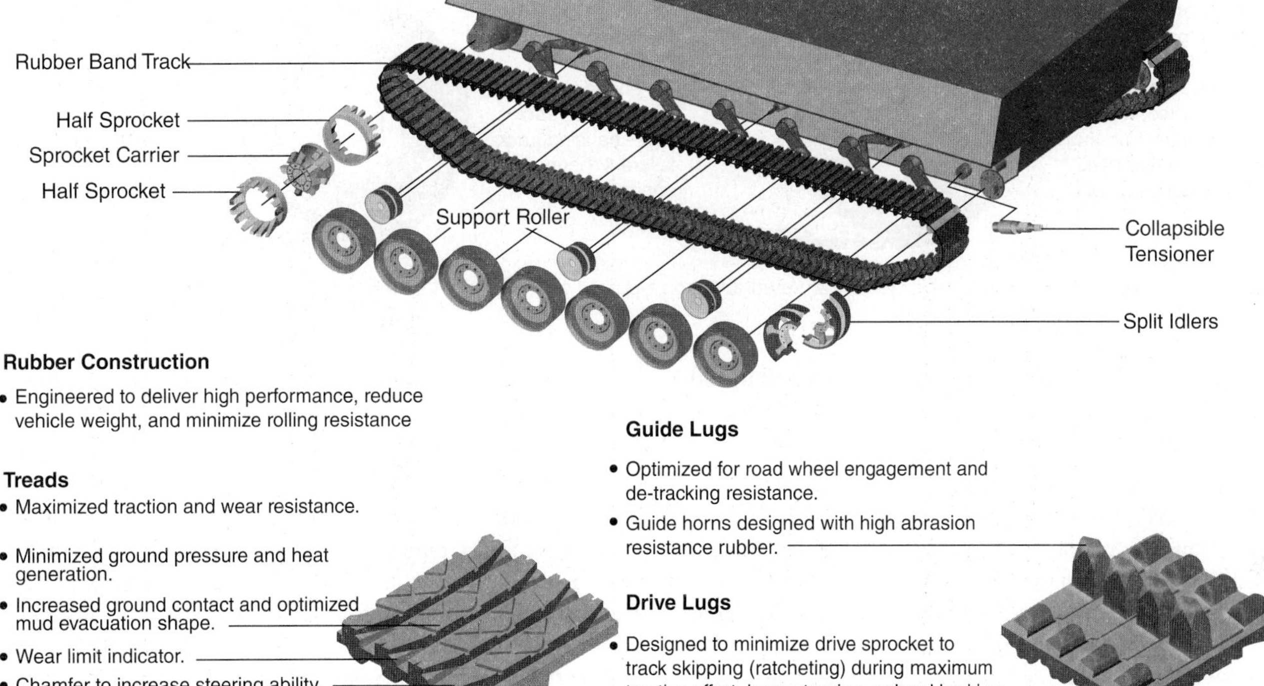

TRACK FEATURES
Rubber Band Track
Half Sprocket
Sprocket Carrier
Half Sprocket
Support Roller
Collapsible Tensioner
Split Idlers
Rubber Construction
• Engineered to deliver high performance, reduce vehicle weight, and minimize rolling resistance
Treads
• Maximized traction and wear resistance.
• Minimized ground pressure and heat generation.
• Increased ground contact and optimized mud evacuation shape.
• Wear limit indicator.
• Chamfer to increase steering ability.
Guide Lugs
• Optimized for road wheel engagement and de-tracking resistance.
• Guide horns designed with high abrasion resistance rubber.
Drive Lugs
• Designed to minimize drive sprocket to track skipping (ratcheting) during maximum tractive effort, heavy turning, or hard braking.

FIGURE 41-71 Components of a typical rubber track undercarriage with a positive drive sprocket.

FIGURE 41-72 Agriculture applications account for the largest use of rubber track machines.

Types of Rubber Track System

Rubber track drives use one of two types of drive systems. The simplest system, called a friction drive, only uses the adhesive friction between the rubber track and a rubberized or pneumatic drive wheel to rotate the track. Belts run at very high tension to maintain drive friction between the driving wheel and track. In fact, as much as 15,000 pounds of belt tension is typically applied to the belt, using a hydraulic tensioning mechanism. A center lug in the underside of the tread guides the track between grooves in the idler and drive wheels. John Deere, Allis Chambers, and Agco are three popular manufacturers of friction drive track (**FIGURE 41-73**).

Positive drive rubber tracks use a drive method similar to steel track where a final drive sprocket engages the drive lug or track cog in the tread. Drive motors independently rotate drive sprockets on the left and right side of the undercarriage. Friction and wear between drive sprockets and track lugs can be minimized through the use of two-piece track pins or with rotating steel sleeves on drive sprocket rollers. Wheel-to-track slip found in friction drive track is eliminated in the positive drive system. However, this track and drive system requires more precise manufacturing and tensioning system. Positive drive systems are better adapted to aggressive work requiring high-drive torque such as dozing and using drawbars in agricultural work. Choosing a friction drive over a positive drive system is determined by other factors such as operating cost, travel speed, weight, duty cycle, ground pressure, traction needs, machine life expectation and the machine's application (agricultural, construction, forestry, etc.).

Rubber Track Construction

One set of rubber track, driven by the machine's final drive, is used on each side of a machine to support and drive the machine. Although the construction of rubber track systems and components is different from steel track, there is complete

Friction Drive Vs. Positive Cog Drive

Friction Drive allows track to dissipate stress to over 50% of the wheel surface area - also, with no, drive bars, track lugs stay damage free, increasing track life.

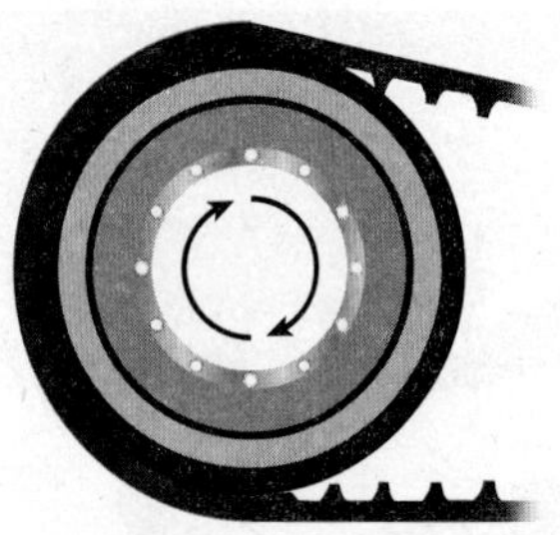

Positive Cog Drive creates stress points on only the engaging & disengaging track lugs - causing track failure & 'bouncy' operation.

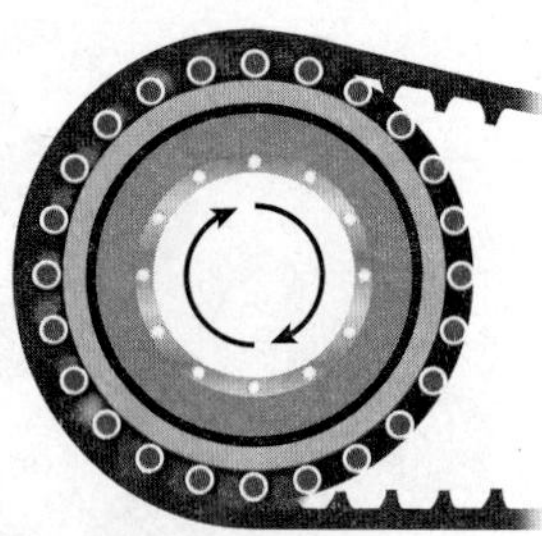

FIGURE 41-73 Two types of rubber belt drive systems are used: a friction type and a positive drive system, which uses a sprocket-like mechanism to turn the belt.

commonality between rubber and steel track operation and function. Like steel track, six basic components are used in rubber track systems:

- Rubber track is a single-piece continuous belt.
- Drive wheels transmit torque to the track.
- Mid-rollers to maintain track alignment and transmit machine weight through the track; Rubber track rollers often use a suspension system to maintain good ground contact and provide a smoother ride.
- A front idler supports track weight, aligns track, and works with a tensioning mechanism to maintain track belt tension.
- A belt tensioning mechanism is used to adjust belt tension and absorb shock loads to the track.
- A track frame is a major frame component that supports track parts.

All these parts together make up the rubber track undercarriage system.

Rubber Track Belts

If only rubber were used to construct a track, it would quickly stretch, break, or rapidly wear out. To provide the 3,000- to 5,000-hour life that is double that for tires, rubber track uses specialized construction features. Track strength, durability, and stability are achieved primarily through heavily reinforcing the track carcass with steel cables and wire plies. This kind of construction lends the name **metal-reinforced rubber** or **metal-embedded rubber tracks (MERT)** to rubber track belts (**FIGURE 41-74**). Like tires, the carcass may have several plies of rubber and metal belts. Steel links are embedded into positive drive tracks to provide a solid foundation for track rollers to

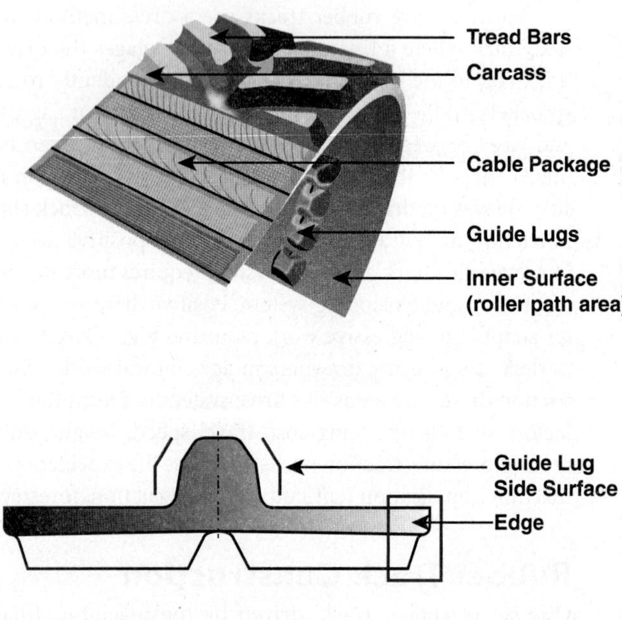

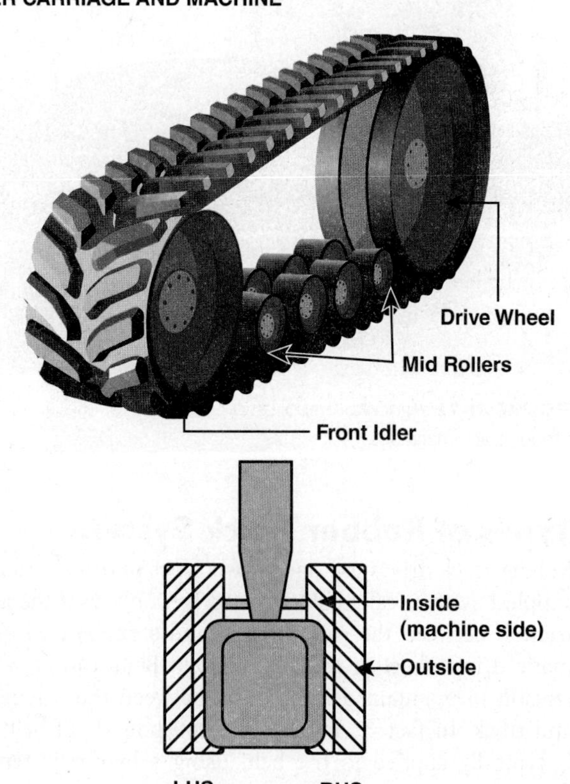

FIGURE 41-74 Construction of a metal-reinforced rubber drive belt.

FIGURE 41-75 A friction drive system uses an elastomer or plastic-type drive wheel along with high belt tension to drive the belt. Belt cogs are used to guide the belt through the drive wheel.

travel across, plus a point for a drive sprocket to grasp the belt. Thick tread lugs provide maximum traction and long belt service before needing replacement. Tractions lugs may be directional or nondirectional, which means technicians must observe whether the track should be installed in a particular way. A series of guide lugs on the side of the track maintain alignment with the drive wheel, rollers, and idler wheel as it rotates around the track frame. In positive drive systems, traction or drive lugs are also used to transfer torque to the belt. In friction drive system the lugs merely guide the track. Friction drive systems are common in paving applications (**FIGURE 41-75**).

It's important to observe a proper break in period and procedure for new track. Working new track at high speed and aggressive maneuvering will overheat the track, resulting in permanent damage. Track has to be gradually "broken in" by using talcum powder and even dust and dirt to act as a dry lubricant, which minimizes heat buildup and reduces rubber stickiness.

It is normal for rubber track to develop scuffs, cracks, and cuts and to lose rubber chunks in any application. This type of wear does not necessarily degrade the performance of the machine. However, criteria that determine track serviceability include the following:

- The track must have the ability to maintain proper tension: If track is torn or damaged to the point where it cannot be properly tensioned, it will require replacement.
- Track drive lugs should not constantly jump over sprocket cogs or ratchet when the track is properly tensioned. Excessively worn lugs will continually ratchet or slip under load, which requires belt replacement. In some instances, track lugs wear only on one side because of roller or drive wheel force concentrated on one side of the lug if it continuously operated on a side slope. In some cases, though, the track can be turned 180 degrees and reinstalled on the same side to extend its life.
- Replace the rubber track if the metal cable package is exposed. Replacement is recommended if tread depth is less than 10 mm.

Drive Wheels

On all rubber track machines, the drive wheel supplies torque to the track through the machine's final drive. The outer rim of the friction-type drive wheel uses a polyurethane or bonded rubber wheel, often capable of retreading, to provide friction for power transfer to the rubber track. A drive wheel configuration for a positive drive system in some Caterpillar machines uses a two-piece rotating roller sleeve to minimize friction as the rollers engage track lugs on either side of the drive wheel. Like the Cat SALT track used by the system One steel track, a roller bushing sleeve rotates over a stationary inner roller pin. When pin-to-bushing wear does increase, the inner pin will normally wear only on one side because it is locked in the drive wheel. The free-rotating outer sleeve will evenly wear around its circumference. Cat recommends that when the outer bushing sleeves are replaced, the inner pins should be rotated 180 degrees to "double" their service life. Only one turn is permissible, though. A second replacement cycle requires new pins and bushing.

Mid-Rollers

The mid-rollers, made of polyurethane or rubber bonded to steel wheels, are mounted on the track frame to support machine weight. They are relatively small and close together to provide consistent ground pressure on the track as it revolves and engages the ground. Normally there are two rows of rollers, one row on each side of the guide lugs. A suspension system attached to the mid-rollers enables the track to articulate over uneven surfaces to further improve ground contact and traction. Roller wheels are a wear item and require periodic replacement. Generally, though, worn wheels can continue to function if they have a minimal amount of rubber surface (**FIGURE 41-76**).

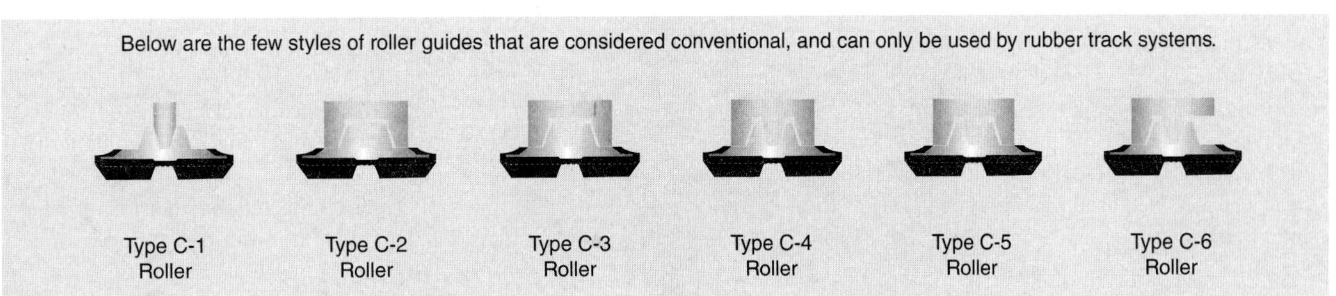

FIGURE 41-76 Mid-rollers provide guidance to the rubber belt.

Front Idlers and Tensioning Systems

The front idler wheel supports the track as it revolves around the track frame. With the idler is a track tensioning mechanism that operates to absorb shock loads and adjust track tension. The tensioning mechanisms may resemble the grease-operated servo piston types found on steel track or may use simpler spring-type adjustment mechanisms or a gas accumulator hydraulic system, providing a constant, flexible tension on the track (**FIGURE 41-77**).

FIGURE 41-77 This rubber track system uses a track tensioner connected to the elevated-type sprocket to tension the belt.

▶ Wrap-Up

Ready for Review

- Undercarriage is the generic name given to all the components making up the propulsion mechanism for track drive equipment.
- Track drive machines have more ground contact area to distribute machine weight. Tracked equipment will not sink into soft ground surfaces where wheeled equipment would easily become stuck.
- Tracked equipment has superior traction force compared to wheeled equipment and can operate at much steeper working angles due to its low center of gravity.
- Track undercarriage makes up 20% of the initial cost of a machine and approximately 50% of the lifetime maintenance costs, according to manufacturer estimates.
- A track drive's high traction force enables the machine to outperform wheeled equipment at the difficult work of pulling stumps, ripping concrete or asphalt, digging or pushing massive amounts of earth.
- Track drives use a differential steering mechanism that changes the drive torque applied to each track. Changing the torque applied to each track changes machine direction.
- Pivot turns are accomplished by driving track in the opposite direction. Pivoting a machine rotates it around its own center point without forward or backward movement.
- Ground pressure is defined as the load exerted by a machine's contact points with the ground and is measured in pounds per square inch (psi), or kilopascals (kPa).
- Changing the width and length of a machine's tracks changes its ground pressure. Ground pressure exerted by track varies with the length of track and width of the track shoe.
- Drawbar capacity, which is the amount of weight a track drive can pull at a given speed, falls off with increased travel speed. Increased machine speed means the maximum drawbar capacity is lowered.
- Packing is a condition that occurs during operation when ground materials stick and accumulate between sprockets, track, rollers, and other mating components. Packing increases track tension.
- A tight track adds additional friction or drag force into the chain that in turn increases the amount of power required by the engine to move the machine.
- The use of steel rather than rubber track enables track to withstand high-impact forces encountered working on rock or hard concrete.
- Loose track causes a condition called a "thrown track," which can also occur when tracks ride off worn rollers wheels, chains, idlers, or sprockets.
- Two types of track drive systems are used friction and positive drive.
- A friction drive system uses a rubberized drive wheel to rotate the track, which in turn moves the machine. Friction drives are potentially able to travel faster, more smoothly, and more quietly, and are commonly used in rubber track systems.
- A positive drive system uses a gearlike sprocket to engage a drive lug or bushing in the track. Positive drive systems are common in earth-moving equipment where very high drive torque is required.
- The idler sprocket or wheel is non-driving and functions to create an oval track loop. Looping the chain around the large idler wheel or non-driving idler sprocket creates a return path for the track chain.
- A track tensioning mechanism that acts through the idler wheel is usually located inside the hollow track frame. The tensioner is connected to the idler wheel and can also absorb some shock loading of the track chain. Tensioners are necessary to compensate for changes to chain length due to wear.
- Links, bushings, and pins connected together form track chain systems. Chains transmit torque to the track from

the machine's drive sprocket and provide an attachment point for track shoes. The chain also functions like a self-laying rail system or road, over which the machine crawls.

- Track pitch is measured between one, two, or even three sets of track segments and is a critical dimension used to evaluate track wear. Worn bushings and pins extend track pitch.
- Four basic chain construction techniques are used, with several variations among different manufacturers:
  - Sealed track chain (SLT nonlubricated)
  - Sealed and greased track chain (SAGT)
  - Sealed and lubricated track (SALT)
  - Rotating bushing track.
- Track pin bushings are hardened steel sleeves wrapped around the track pins, and often have a lubricating film of either oil or grease between the track pin and bushing.
- Track pin and bushing wear typically takes place on only one side of each component. Rotating or turning the bushings and pins 180 degrees can restore proper operating clearances during a pin and bushing turn.
- Drive sprockets are a toothed wheel mounted on the final drive assembly. Segmented sprockets are sprockets formed by bolting together segments of teeth, consisting of between three and six teeth, to form an entire drive sprocket.
- Track frames may be either suspended or rigid type. Rigid frames have solid attachment points to the main frame and allow no movement between the two.
- Suspended track frames allow some oscillation of the two frames relative to each other. A three-point attachment system is used.
- Oval-shaped track has been the traditional track configuration where a single drive sprocket is placed at the rear and idler wheel at the front.
- Elevated sprockets use two idler wheels and place the drive sprocket above the track frame, giving the track a triangular shape. Elevated drive sprocket keeps tracks tight on the ground, whether in reverse or forward.
- Rubber track drive systems, replacing linked steel plates with a single-piece, metal-reinforced rubber belt, are an increasingly popular alternative to steel track systems.

Key Terms

attack angle The angle formed between an imaginary line drawn across the top track and it's intersection point on the ground; also called angle of approach.

Belleville washers Cone-shaped spring-steel washers. Belleville washers are located at each end of the track pin in the link counterbore area.

Benjamin Holt The industrialist who first developed the practical use of crawler-type track drive systems in North America.

carrier or idler rollers Rollers that do not support machine weight but carry the track at the top.

case extended life track (CELT) A dual bushing system doubles track life using a second hardened bushing over an inner bushing and pin. It also uses longer track pins, track links that are wider and have a taller rail on which the rollers ride.

cross-drive transmission A type of transmission that incorporates a steering mechanism with the drive system. Because there are three differentials incorporated into the transmission, skid steering is also called triple differential steering.

differential steering A steering mechanism in which one track is driven faster than the other in order to control machine direction.

drawbar capacity A tracked machine's performance measurement of the amount of weight a track drive can pull at a given speed.

dual bushing track (DBT) Refers to a construction technique using a double bushing with a hardened outer bushing rotating freely around the inner bushing. No lubricant is present between the two outer bushings. However, an oil-lubricated track pin rotates inside the inner bushing.

elevated sprocket A track system using two idler wheels and a drive sprocket located above the level of the idler wheels. An elevated sprocket system forms a triangular, rather than oval-shaped, track.

equalizer bar A bar connecting two opposite track frames that functions as a weight transfer lever connection point between the two frames. Because the equalizer bar pinned in the center to the main frame it causes a weight transfer from one track to the other as it lifts and passes over an obstacle.

"flatted" condition Flattening is evident when one side of a track roller is worn away from continual sliding friction with the chain link rail.

floating Term describing the transfer of a heavy machine between worksites on a flat semitrailer or specialized gooseneck trailers.

friction drive A track drive systems using only adhesive friction between a rubber track and a rubberized or pneumatic drive wheel to rotate the track.

greased turns Involve lubricating track pins with grease during a pin turning service operation.

ground pressure The force exerted by the tires or track of a machine. It is a function of the machine weight divided by the surface area below the tire or track. Ground pressure is measured in pounds per square inch.

grousers Wedges or bars on steel track that function like cleats on athletic shoes. These steel bars penetrate the ground surface, providing even more surface area to push or pull against the ground.

Holt Manufacturing Company The company that merged with Best Manufacturing and incorporated into the Caterpillar Tractor Company.

hunting tooth arrangement A final drive tooth pattern using an odd number of sprocket teeth to match an even number of bushing. In track systems, the odd–even change in the ratio between the tooth sprocket and track chain bushings ensures there is a change in tooth-to-bushing contact with every sprocket revolution.

hydrostatic, or "hystat," drive systems Machines using hydraulic motors to propel a machine. Hydraulic motors are typically located in the wheel ends or in the final drive assemblies. The motors are driven by hydraulic pumps connected to an engine or electric motor.

idler wheels or idler sprockets Large non-driving wheels or sprockets used to loop the track around the track frame. At least one idler wheel or sprockets is used on each side of the machine and located opposite the drive sprocket on the track frame.

interference fit A machinist's term describing an assembly technique where a machined part has a slightly larger diameter than the diameter of the bore where it's installed. On track systems, an interference fit exists between the track bushing and counterbore of the track link.

laterals Hand-operated levers used by early differential steering systems to apply a brake to one or both tracks of a machine in order to steer the machine.

metal-reinforced rubber or metal-embedded rubber tracks (MERT) A rubber track construction technique that adds strength, durability, and stability to rubber track, using heavily reinforced track carcass with steel cables and wire plies.

packing A condition where ground materials stick and accumulate between sprockets, track, rollers, and other mating components during operation. Packing increases track tension and track component wear.

pin turning A service procedure where track pins and bushings are disassembled and turned 180 degrees apart before reassembling. Turning can restore proper operating clearances between pins and bushings.

pivot shaft A large weight-bearing shaft that runs from one suspended track frame to the other through the machine's main frame to connect the track frames to one another. Shock loads from the track are transmitted through the pivot shaft to the opposite track.

pivot turn A special movement of a track machine where it turns around its own center point by allowing one track to drive while braking the opposite track.

PLUS (parallel link undercarriage system) The Komatsu PLUS system used on lighter machines does not use dual bushings, but instead enables the bushing to rotate in an oil-lubricated track link counterbore. Because neither the bushing nor the pin uses an interference fit to retain the parts in the link, only a snap ring is used to lock the pin in place to prevent it from sliding out from between the track links. The use of oil to lubricate the pins and bushings in link counterbores requires four rather than two separate oil seals.

positive drive A category of track drive system that uses a gearlike sprocket to engage a drive lug or bushing in the track. Positive drive systems are common in earth moving equipment where very high drive torque is required.

recoil spring mechanism A mechanism used to adjust track tension and absorb shock loads applied to the track.

rigid frames An undercarriage track frame arrangement that uses solid attachment points of the track frame to the main frame that allows no movement between the two frames.

root or radial wear The name given to sprocket tooth wear caused by the outside diameter of a bushing as it scrubs through the sprocket tooth root.

sealed track chain A track pin and bushing assembly technique using a nonlubricated track pin and bushing design. The pin operates like a hinge inside the bushing, and washers at each end of the pin prevent dirt from entering the space between the pin and bushing.

segmented sprockets A type of final drive sprocket formed by bolting pieces or segments of sprocket teeth together. Segments consist of between three and six teeth that, when bolted together with other pieces, form an entire drive sprocket.

skid steering Refers to a steering principle where one track is driven faster than the other, pushing the machine in the direction toward the slower or stopped track. Since the leading and trailing edges of the track will slide sideways to steer the machine, that sliding action lends the name skid steering.

suspended track frames An undercarriage track frame that allow some oscillation of the two track frames relative to one another. A three-point attachment system is used.

thrown track A condition when tracks separate from a machine by riding off worn rollers wheels, chains, idlers, or sprockets.

tiller A joystick used to control the steering functions of a track machine.

track pitch The dimension between the track pins.

travel system An alternative term used to describe a track drive system on excavators. The term "travel system" is used to differentiate the propulsion system from the undercarriage and associated components used on other machines.

triple differential steering Another name for a cross-drive transmission that incorporated three different drive differentials to transmit power to track and steer the machine.

undercarriage The generic name given to all the components making up the propulsion mechanism or travel system for track drive equipment.

wet turn Lubricating track pins with oil, rather than grease, during a pin turning service operation.

Review Questions

1. Which of the following is the most significant advantage track-type undercarriage has in comparison to wheeled machines that use tires?
   a. It has better maneuverability.
   b. It will have better flotation on soft ground.
   c. It has a longer service life,
   d. Tracked equipment is less expensive to purchase and maintain.
2. Which of the following conditions can take place when track packing is excessive?
   a. Track can be more easily thrown.
   b. Track wear is reduced.
   c. Track tension increases.
   d. Track pins and bushings will seize.

3. Which of the following components transfers machine weight to the track shoe?
   a. The track frame
   b. The track idler wheel
   c. Lower track rollers
   d. The final drive
4. When a machine with steering clutches and brakes has its left steering clutch released and left brake applied, what is the result?
   a. No movement takes place.
   b. The machine turns right.
   c. The machine turns left.
   d. The machine performs a pivot turn.
5. What would cause a crawler tractor with a clutch and brake steering system to track to the left all the time?
   a. A worn right side steering clutch friction disk
   b. A worn left side steering clutch friction disk
   c. A worn right side steering brake
   d. A worn left side steering brake
6. A bulldozer with a hydrostatic steering system will only make pivot turns to the left whenever the operator tries to move the machine in either forward or reverse direction. What could be causing this problem?
   a. Low battery voltage
   b. Failed left side motor
   c. Poor wiring connection at the motor for the left track
   d. Poor wiring connection at the pump for the left track
7. What causes track chain pitch to increase?
   a. Sprocket tooth wear
   b. Track tension adjustment
   c. Internal bushing and pin wear
   d. External bushing and chain wear
8. A smaller front idler on an elevated sprocket track will __________.
   a. increase the angle of approach or attack angle allowing deeper track penetration in soft soil
   b. decrease the angle of approach or attack angle, allowing deeper track penetration in soft soil
   c. increase the angle of approach or attack angle, preventing deeper track penetration in soft soil
   d. more likely block the sight line of an operator
9. Bushing and pin wear on sealed track pins and bushings __________.
   a. takes place evenly around the track pin
   b. takes place only on the outside of a track bushing
   c. takes place on mostly on only one side of the track pin and bushing
   d. takes place evenly around the track bushings inside diameter
10. How is track tension reduced when adjusting track tension using a Hydra Juster?
    a. Nitrogen gas is added to a hydraulic accumulator.
    b. An adjusting screw is loosened to relive spring tension.
    c. A grease bleeder screw is opened.
    d. Oil pressure is relieved from the hydraulic accumulator.

ASE Technician A/Technician B Style Questions

1. Technician A says that Caterpillar Company invented track-type undercarriage. Technician B says that track-type undercarriage was first used in California farm fields before the Caterpillar Company was incorporated. Who is correct?
   a. Technician A
   b. Technician B
   c. Both A and B
   d. Neither A nor B
2. Technician A says that track equipment can work while traveling sideways on slopes steeper than wheeled machines can travel on. Technician B says the advantage applies only when ascending and descending steep slopes. Who is correct?
   a. Technician A
   b. Technician B
   c. Both A and B
   d. Neither A nor B
3. While evaluating a low power complaint, Technician A says that inability of a bulldozer to push the same load at high speed as it can at low speed demonstrates that there is a problem with the engine or powertrain. Technician B says that drawbar capacity normally falls as machine travel speed increases. Who is correct?
   a. Technician A
   b. Technician B
   c. Both A and B
   d. Neither A nor B
4. Technician A says that a friction-type drive system is best used when more traction force is required because there is less potential for drive slippage. Technician B says that positive drive systems can travel faster, more smoothly, and with less noise. Who is correct?
   a. Technician A
   b. Technician B
   c. Both A and B
   d. Neither A nor B
5. According to Technician A, an excessively tight track will result in power loss. Technician B says that tight tracks can be loosened by releasing grease from a track tensioning mechanism. Who is correct?
   a. Technician A
   b. Technician B
   c. Both A and B
   d. Neither A nor B
6. Technician A says rigid track frames use an equalizer bar and pivot shaft to transmit shock loads to the main frame of a crawler. Technician B says that guide plates are used by suspended track frames to absorb side thrust loads. Who is correct?
   a. Technician A
   b. Technician B
   c. Both A and B
   d. Neither A nor B

7. Technician A says elevated track sprocket design enables track to stay tighter and is less likely to be thrown. Technician B says that elevated track sprockets clear dirt and debris better, which prevents packing and excess tightening of the track. Who is correct?
   - a. Technician A
   - b. Technician B
   - c. Both A and B
   - d. Neither A nor B
8. Technician A says that track shoes are heat treated and made from steel alloys to resist wear. Technician B says that severe service shoes are made thicker, which prolongs shoe life before needing replacement. Who is correct?
   - a. Technician A
   - b. Technician B
   - c. Both A and B
   - d. Neither A nor B
9. Technician A says that when recommending track shoes, the narrowest shoe permissible for an application should be used because there is reduced load on track components and chain wear is reduced. Technician B says the use of wider shoes reduces ground pressure and track component wear. Who is correct?
   - a. Technician A
   - b. Technician B
   - c. Both A and B
   - d. Neither A nor B
10. Technician A says that more roller wear takes place on the upper carrier rollers because there are fewer of them compared to lower rollers. Technician B says the lower rollers wear more than upper rollers because lower rollers support the machine weight. Who is correct?
   - a. Technician A
   - b. Technician B
   - c. Both A and B
   - d. Neither A nor B

CHAPTER 42
Undercarriage Inspection and Maintenance

Knowledge Objectives

After reading this chapter, you will be able to:

- **K42001** Identify factors accelerating track component wear and lifecycle cost.
- **K42002** Evaluate track component wear, and make recommendations to minimize wear.
- **K42003** Describe track drive undercarriage inspection, adjustment, and repair procedures.
- **K42004** Recommend service and maintenance procedures for track drive undercarriage.

Skills Objectives

There are no Skills Objectives for this chapter.

▶ Introduction

When asked about undercarriage maintenance, track specialists often begin with an observation about its cost: track accounts for 20% of a machine's purchase price, and an investment equivalent to 50% of the machine's initial value is spent repairing and maintaining track over a typical lifecycle. The cost of parts and labor are included in that summary, but the investment in terms of per hour operating cost can be substantially lowered by extending track life. So although technicians can do little to reduce lifecycle operating costs, they are instrumental in extending a machine's service life, thereby reducing costs in terms of hourly operation or machine productivity. By using best practices for routine inspection and maintenance procedures, understanding and minimizing wear factors affecting track life, and incorporating good judgment about when and how to replace worn components, maintenance cycles are extended, and greater service life is obtained from track components. This chapter's purpose is to help technicians implement effective work practices by identifying and analyzing various types of track problems. These include the following:

- Track wear factors
- Track tension and adjustment
- Track and frame alignment
- Track runoff

Service and inspection procedures of common work routines associated with track drive undercarriage include the following:

- Turning pins and bushings
- Replacing pins and bushings
- Disassembling and reassembling track
- Replacing track components such as shoes, rollers, and sprockets
- Cleaning track
- Scheduling inspection procedures
- Using specialized tools to evaluate track wear
- Evaluating wear in track components such as chains, bushings, pins, idlers, sprockets, rollers, and shoes
- Inspecting oil level in sealed and lubricated pins and replacing lubricated pins and bushings
- Inspecting track frame alignment
- Following safety precautions while working around track undercarriage

▶ Undercarriage Wear Factors

K42001

A large number of variables affects undercarriage life, maintenance schedules, and procedures. But after sorting through the causes of wear determining undercarriage system life, wear factors can be categorized into three major groups. The first set of variables consists of those variables under the technician's control. These include inspecting and adjusting items such as track tension, alignment of undercarriage components, machine weight balance, and appropriate matching of machine parts such as track shoe type and width to working conditions.

The second groups of variables are factors out of the technician's control and include machine worksite conditions such as soil type and condition—whether it is abrasive, hard or soft, rocky, muddy, corrosive, or wet (**FIGURE 42-1**). Those variables exert significant influence on component durability.

Variables that a technician has partial control over are the third group. These factors include how a machine is operated and whether tracks are kept clean. Wear rate changes due to the use of working attachments and machine balance: whether the machine is worked in gullies or on slopes, whether digging is taking place over final drives, the type and frequency of turns the machine makes, travel speed, and whether productive movement is taking place in forward or reverse machine direction (**FIGURE 42-2**).

FIGURE 42-1 Track wear is affected by factors such as worksite or underfoot conditions, operator skill, and maintenance practices.

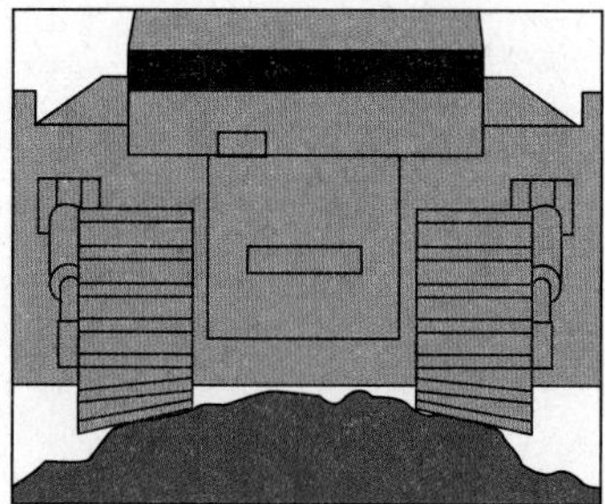

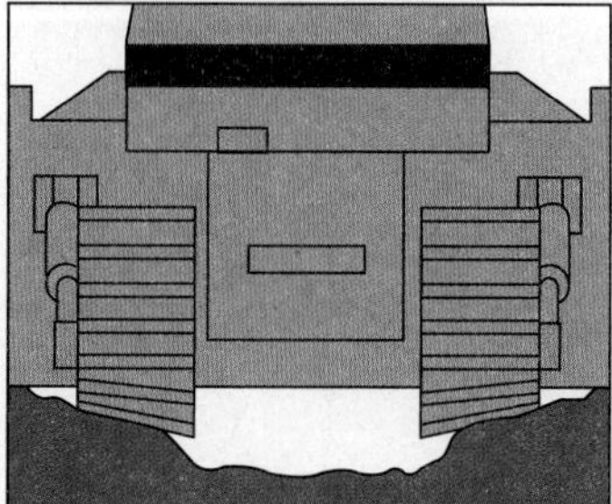

FIGURE 42-2 The shape of work terrain can influence patterns of undercarriage wear. **A.** Crowns wear tracks inside. **B.** Depressions wear tracks outside.

Despite every effort of technicians to recommend good operating practices and ensure every inspection and adjustment procedure is correctly followed, undercarriage wear is unavoidable. The simple fact is that movement in track components means wear takes place. Rolling, rotating, and sliding friction are the three most common wear-related actions. An example of **rolling friction** is encountered as the track rollers and idlers move across chain rails formed by the track links or segments. The hardened wear surfaces of each component are gradually ground away through rolling contact. Wear due to **rotating friction** is observed as track pins and bushings, making up a hinge joint for track shoes, turn to enable track chain and shoes to bend and travel endlessly around the track frame (**FIGURE 42-3**). External wear due to **sliding friction** takes place on bushings because they do not always remain motionless in sprocket teeth as they are pulled around the sprocket (**FIGURE 42-4**). Instead, bushings can scrub the sprocket gear root between each sprocket tooth in addition to the internal wear taking place between pins and bushings as they rotate relative to one another. When coupled with high machine weight, drive torque, abrasive soil conditions, high track tension, mud, and water, undercarriage wear accelerates even faster (**FIGURE 42-5**).

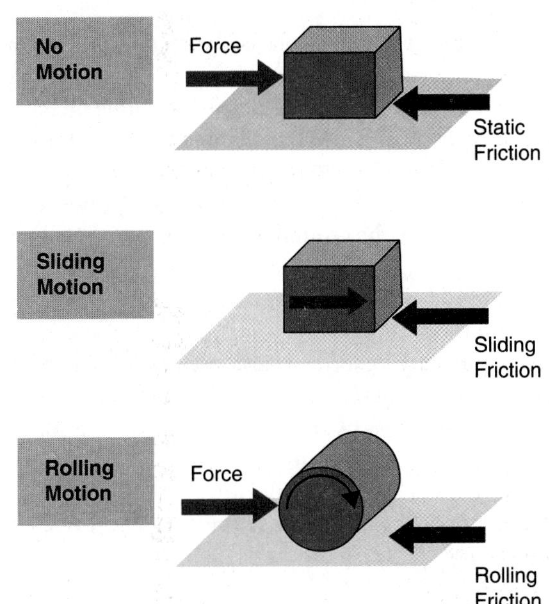

FIGURE 42-3 Example of rolling versus sliding friction.

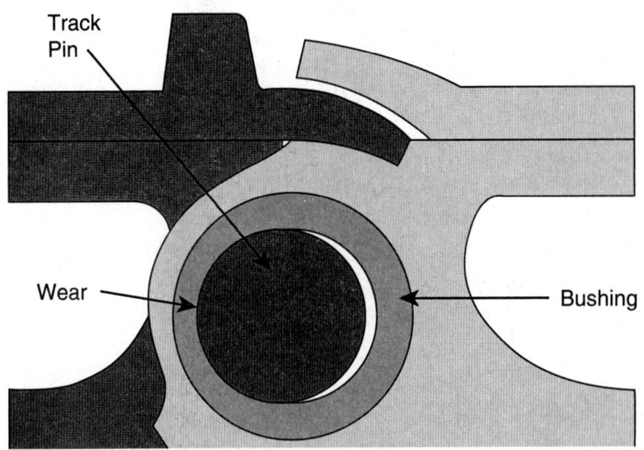

FIGURE 42-4 Track pins and bushings rotate relative to one another and undergo wear on internal and external surfaces.

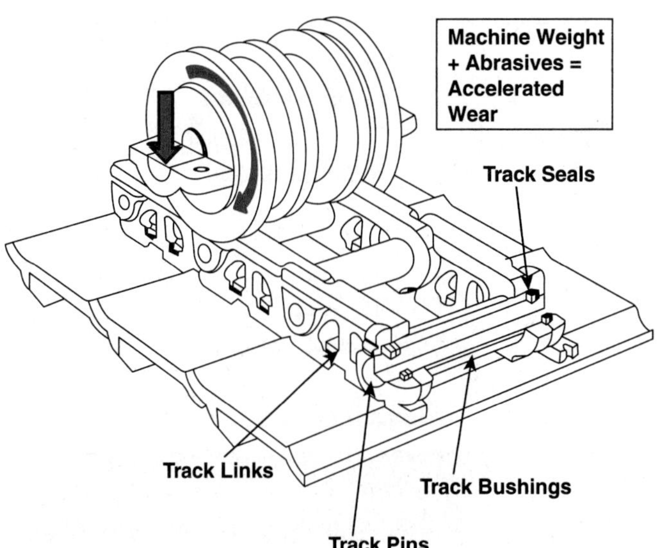

FIGURE 42-5 Track and other undercarriage wear takes place due to friction between moving parts, which is accelerated by machine weight, water, and abrasive dirt.

Although a large number of conditions can affect the rates of wear and accelerate wear in specific components, and many factors affecting track wear are out of the technician's control, a good track technician should recognize the causes of unusual wear patterns in order to make proper operational recommendations or implement service practices to extend track life. To understand more specifically unique features of track wear, a starting point is a review of the important dynamics of normal track operation as the track moves in a forward and reverse direction.

Wear During Forward Drive Cycle Operation

The least amount of track wear takes place during forward machine movement. To understand this, consider simple oval track operation. Track grouser bars grip the ground and create traction while the drive sprocket pulls chain bolted to track shoes. Torque needed to move the chain transfers through the drive sprocket to the track bushings located along the track chain. In the forward direction, track is only tensioned between the drive sprocket and along the bottom section of track where grouser bars on track shoes grip the ground (**FIGURE 42-6**). This means only about 25% of the track pins and bushings are in contact with the drive sprocket and under load with motion. Track is pulled toward the bottom of the sprocket, and almost all torque applied to the chain is through the bottom two bushings located near the sprockets 6 o'clock position. Scrubbing movement between the drive sprocket and the chains bushings

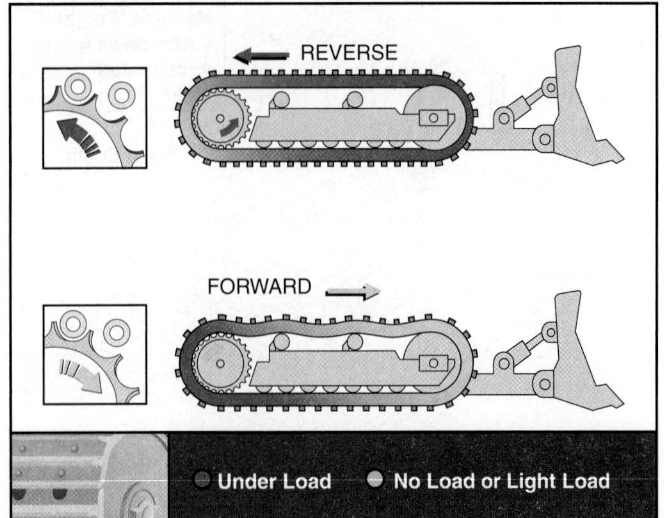

FIGURE 42-6 Most of the track is under tension during reverse travel, which increases wear rates. Only 25% is tensioned in forward travel. During reverse travel, 75% of the track is tensioned.

outside diameter is minimal at the 6 o'clock position because little track bending has taken place. As the track rotates around the sprocket, about 30 degrees of track pin and bushing rotation take place between the sprocket's 6 and 9 o'clock positions. However, because drive torque transmits only through just a couple of bushings and only at the bottom, relatively little scrubbing wear caused by sliding friction takes place on the outside diameter of bushings and in the root of sprocket teeth (**FIGURE 42-7**). When bushings reach the 7 o'clock position, torque applied through the sprocket is only enough to overcome the upper chain track weight and friction of rollers, the forward idler and bending forces needed to push the chain around for another rotation. This explains why the top section of track chain is slack at it moves along to the idler wheel.

Track pin-to-bushing joints make four bending motions per track revolution in either a reverse or a forward direction. Each time the chain links bend or flex while moving around the drive sprocket or front idler, it turns 30 degrees—twice; two times on the drive sprocket and the other two times time on the idler wheel. On the drive sprocket, the first bend takes place as a track joint made up of a pin and bushing moves from the 6 o'clock position to the 9 o'clock position. Moving from the 9 o'clock to 12 o'clock position at the top of the sprocket, the track straightens out again as it travels onto the front idler (**FIGURE 42-8**). The same oscillation of pins and bushings takes place around a single idler wheel. Internal pin and bushing wear is produced by the rotating friction between the inside diameter of the bushing and outside diameter of the pin as they both rotate around the sprocket and idler wheel, or even around a third idler such as those used by high-mounted sprockets that use two idler wheels.

Wear During Reverse Drive Cycle Operation

The greatest track wear takes place when a machine operates in reverse. To understand this, note that during reverse machine travel, when the drive sprocket leads the machine direction, the transfer of drive torque into the chain takes place at the top of the sprocket, or the 12 o'clock position. This is unlike forward direction travel where torque transfers through the section of track in contact with the ground. Reverse drive torque transmits through the track all the way from the bushing at the top of the sprocket, around the front idler, and finally to track shoes in contact with the ground.

More pin and bushing joints are tensioned in reverse drive cycle than in forward drive cycle. In fact, during reverse operation, about 75% of track pins and bushing joints tensioned, including those having contact with the drive sprocket and forward idler wheel, while under load. More external bushing wear takes place because reverse drive cycle travel is

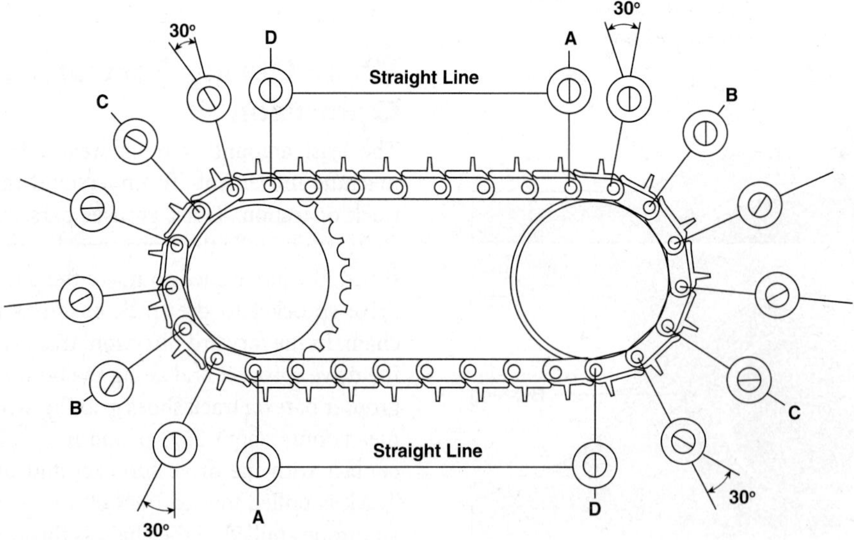

FIGURE 42-7 Rotation of track pins and bushing during forward machine motion. The pivoting of bushings and pins takes place four times with each rotation of the track.

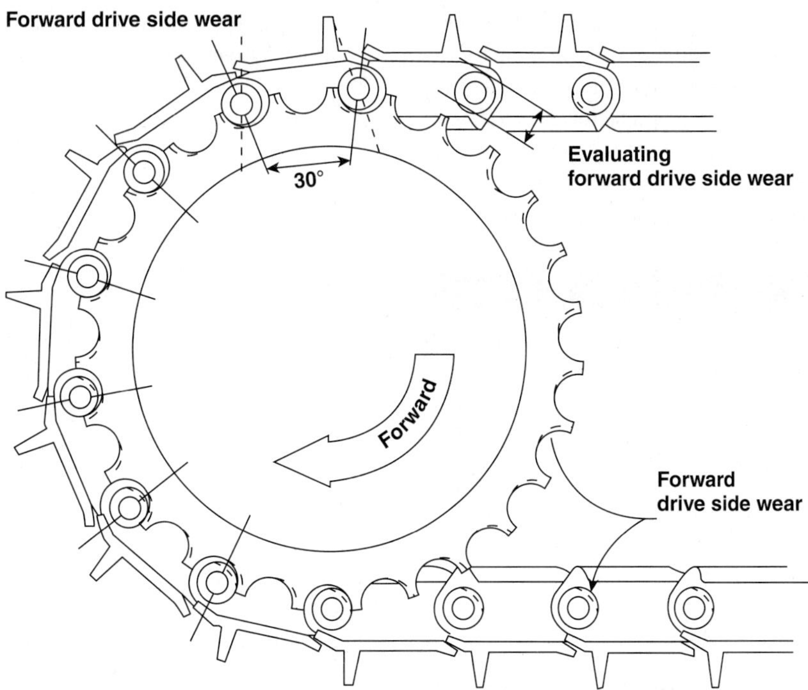

FIGURE 42-8 Rotation of bushing in the sprocket teeth taking place during forward machine travel. The bottom couple of bushings transmit the most torque to the track chain during forward travel. The top section of track is only lightly loaded when bushings rotate.

the only time bushings rotate or twist against sprocket teeth under load (**FIGURE 42-9**). Additional chain, front idler, and drive sprocket wear also take place, as the chain is pulled under load against the front idler. Increased wear to track links, pins, and bushings, both internal and external, takes place as more of the chain is tensioned while bending.

During reverse travel, the drive sprocket geometry involved in engaging the bushing at the 12 o' clock position while pulling

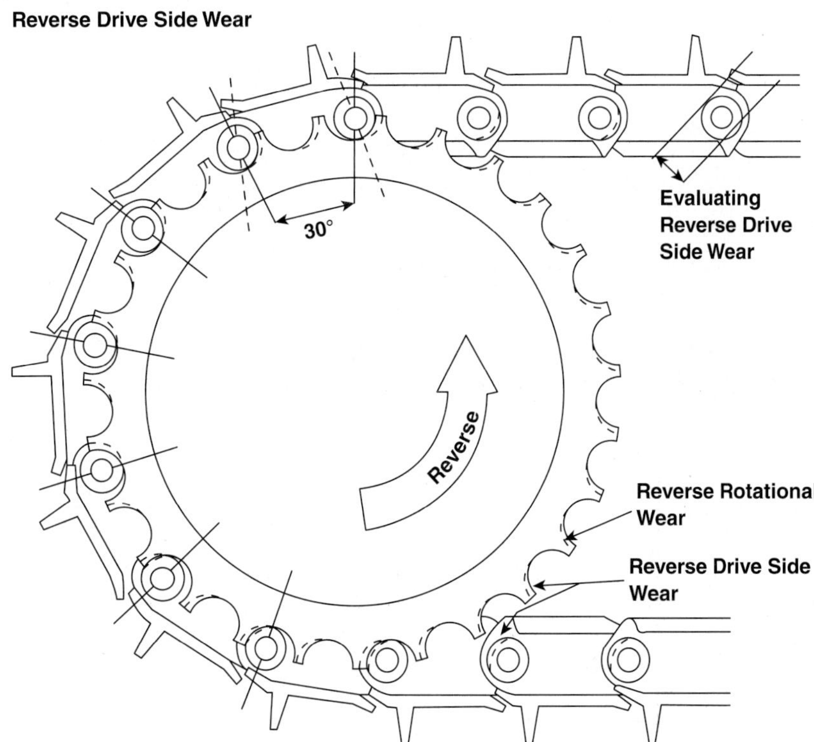

FIGURE 42-9 Bushings at the top of the sprocket are heavily tensioned during reverse travel. Since the bushings rotate in the sprocket teeth at this position, more wear takes place.

on the heavily loaded bushing causes the bushing's outside diameter to scrub through a 30-degree twisting motion inside the tooth root of the sprocket gears. The bushings motion, plus machine weight or load, multiplies the tooth wear by a factor of two times, according to track experts. In reverse, since the top section of track is under tension rather than having slack, it has the additional effect of increasing idler roller or carrier roller wear.

▶ TECHNICIAN TIP

A doubling of the amount of wear takes place when tracked machines travel in reverse. Not only is wear accelerated in track pins and bushings, but telltale wear patterns are observed in drive sprockets and other track parts when machines are productive in reverse operation rather than just in forward travel. To extend track life and reduce maintenance costs, it is always recommended that tracked machines move heaviest loads while operating in a forward rather than in a reverse direction.

Track Pitch and Chain Wear

With any track chain, either lubricated or dry sealed, the relative motion between pins and bushings eventually produces wear on one side of the track pin and the surface of the inner diameter of the bushing (Figure 42-9). Bushings that have substantial external wear are good indicators that track also has internal wear and is nearing the end of its service life. Lubricated and greased pins are more durable, but internal wear takes place in all pins and bushings (**FIGURE 42-10**). As both parts wear against each other, the result is a lengthening of the track chain. Because wear is also internal and not immediately visible, it is observed by measuring a change in the track length. Increasingly, worn clearances between pin and bushing surface allow the distance between pin centers to lengthen as wear progresses.

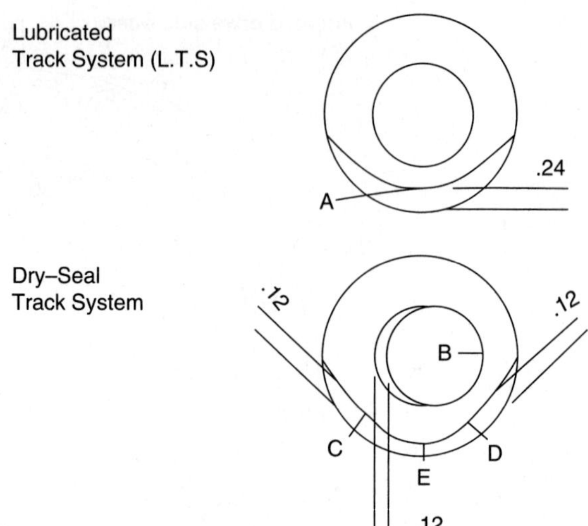

FIGURE 42-10 Wear takes place in both lubricated and non-lubricated track pin and bushing assemblies but wear patterns are different. Less internal pin to bushing wear takes place in lubricated pins.

A measurement between pin centers, known as track pitch, is an important indicator of track pin-to-bushing wear (**FIGURE 42-11**). When track pitch length becomes excessive

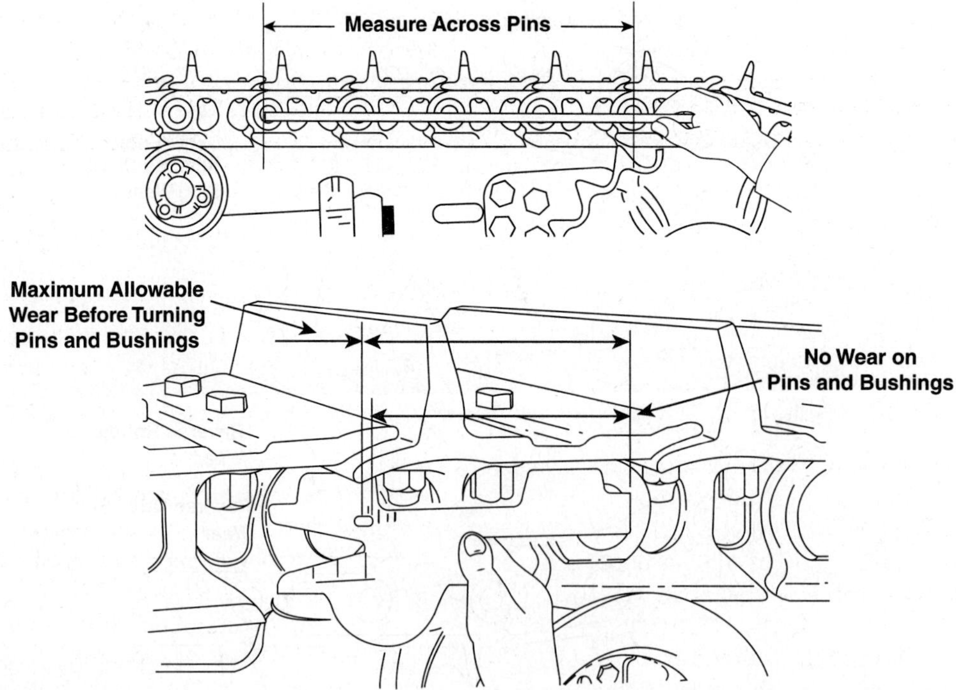

FIGURE 42-11 A steel measuring tape is used to evaluate track pitch. The distance between pin centers of a tensioned track is measured and recorded to provide an indication of pin-to-bushing wear.

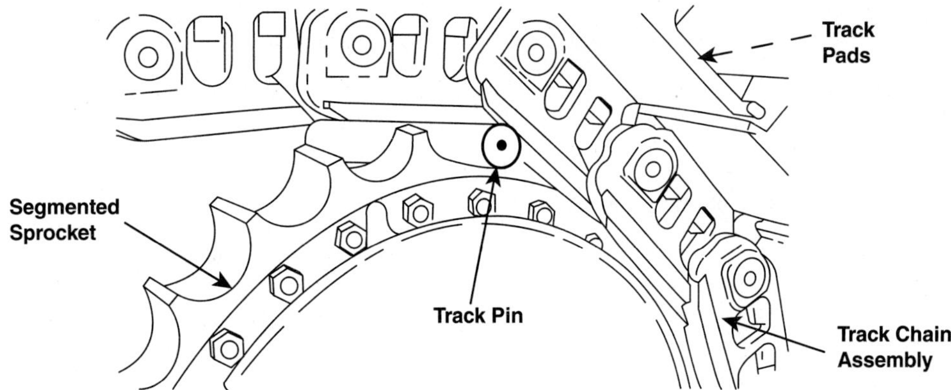

FIGURE 42-12 To measure pitch, the track must be tensioned. One method is to place a track pin between the drive sprocket and track while the machine is slowly moved in reverse.

after comparing worn dimensions to OEM specifications, the track is at the end of its service life and should be rebuilt, pins and bushings turned or replaced. Track pitch is measured with a ruler or measuring tape after tensioning the upper section of track chain (**FIGURE 42-12**). Bushing diameters are measured using an outside caliper.

To measure track pitch, follow the steps in **SKILL DRILL 42-1**.

> ▶ TECHNICIAN TIP
>
> **Evaluating Track Service Life**
>
> Track bushings that have significant external wear are good indicators of inner pin-to-bushing wear that is nearing maximum manufacturer limits. Wear in this area increases track pitch, that is, the distance from pin to pin. When pitch has reached its maximum limits, the track should be rebuilt and pins and bushings turned or replaced. To determine whether the track should be removed for rebuilding or replacement, measure the outside diameter of the bushings and the track pitch. Pitch is measured when the track is tensioned. A ruler or measuring tape is used to measure the distance between a specific number of pins. Before measuring pitch, the track is tensioned by placing a pin between the drive sprocket and track chain while gently reversing the machine. After a dimension for pitch is obtained, an outside caliper is a common measure to inspect and record bushing diameter. All dimensions are then compared with OEM specifications.

Track Sag

Because pitch extension allows the track to lengthen, an increase in the amount of **track sag** becomes evident with increasing wear. Generally speaking, sag is the distance measured between the lowest and highest points of the top of the track (**FIGURE 42-13**). Maintaining correct track sag is the most critical controllable factor in undercarriage wear. If allowed to become too loose so that sag is excessive, track becomes snake-like in operation and causes a number of track problems. First, loose track allows the section of track in contact with the ground to move or twist back, and back and forth when the machine travels, which results in steering instability and the track running off the rollers or throwing the track.

Modern hydrostatic drive machines, which enable operators to rapidly turn in a small radius, allow machines to more easily throw loose track. This condition is not as much of an issue in elevated sprocket design because the track remains relatively tight between two idler wheels. However, on oval track, machines, turning the machine with loose track may suddenly allow the track rollers to run off the chain links. Loose track may also prevent proper engagement of bushings with the drive sprocket, allowing bushings to climb or skip sprocket teeth, which causes reverse tip wear. Popping and loud banging sounds will originate from track because drive sprocket teeth and the space between bushings prevent proper synchronization of contact. Track will also drag along the frame, and whip at higher travel speeds.

Tight tracks cause another set of problems. Most importantly, excessively tight tracks increase wear up to 50%. One example provided by an OEM found that a crawler tractor in the 80-horsepower range with ½-inch track-chain sag produced 5,600 pounds of chain tension when measured at the track adjuster. When adjusted to obtain the recommended 2"+ ¼" track chain sag, only 800 pounds of chain tension was measured at the track adjuster. A tight track having high chain tension amplifies friction between track components, which results in more wear for track bushings, sprocket teeth contact areas, track link to front idler, and roller contact areas. Tight track also robs a machine of useful horsepower and increases fuel consumption (**FIGURE 42-14**). Maneuverability of the machine improves when tight tracks are adjusted to the correct tension. Heat generated from increased friction at track pins also damages the sealing system, resulting in loss of lubrication from sealed pins, bushings, and rollers. For rubber-tracked machines, tracks that are too tight may stretch or break track, in addition to causing excessive roller and idler wear.

Track sag is another way of expressing how much tension is applied to the track to keep it stretched over the rollers, idler, and guidance system components. Maintaining the proper amount of track sag is the single most important adjustment made on tracks. Tight tracks can reduce the service life by more

SKILL DRILL 42-1 Measuring Track Pitch

A measurement between track pin centers, known as track pitch is an important indicator of track pin-to-bushing wear. When track pitch length becomes excessive, the track is at the end of its service life and should be rebuilt, or replaced.

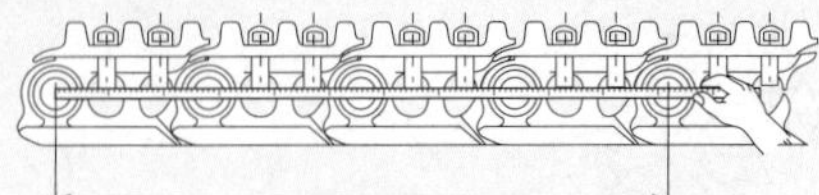

1. Track pitch is measured with a ruler or measuring tape after tensioning the upper section of track chain.

2. A used track pin can be inserted between the drive sprocket and track while moving the machine slightly to roll the track onto the tensioning bushing. On excavators the drive sprockets should be facing the back of machine to identify left and right sides of the machine relative to the operator's seat in the cab.

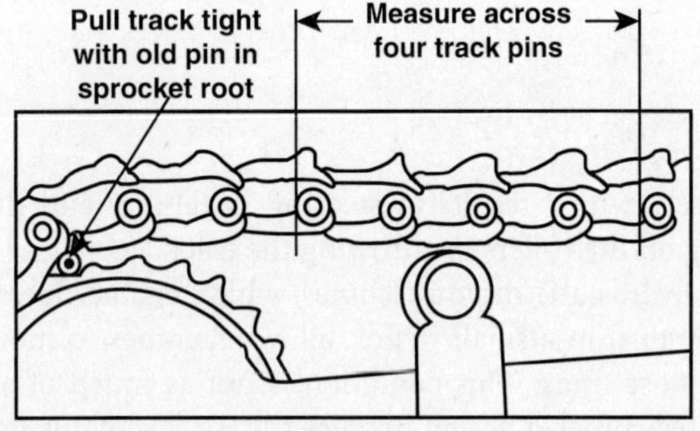

3. Measurement is typically made across the span of 4 track pins.

Crawler Model	Pitch (New)	25% Wear	50% Wear	75% Wear	100% Worn
A-1	622 mm 24.48"	625 mm 24.6"	628 mm 24.71"	632 mm 24.87"	637 mm 25.07"
A-2	1042 mm 41.03	1046.5 mm 41.20"	1053 mm 41.45"	1060 mm 41.73"	1070 mm 42.14"

4. Compare actual measurements with OEM specifications.

FIGURE 42-13 Track sag is measured with a straight edge and ruler. The distance below the straight edge and the track shoe at the lowest point of the track is used to measure sag.

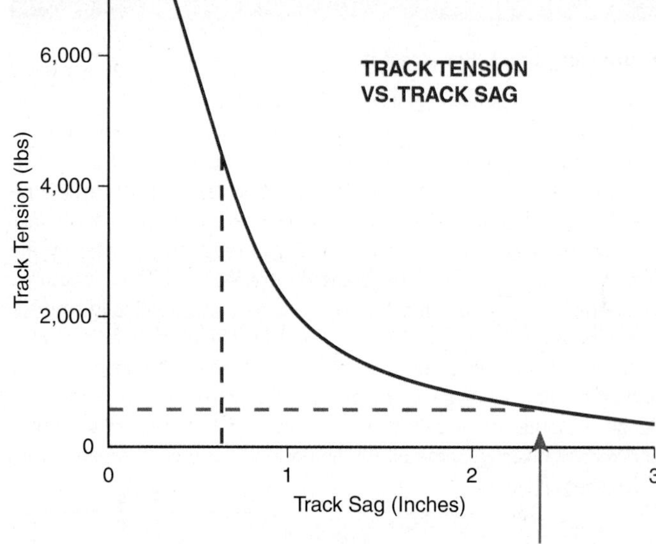

FIGURE 42-14 Increasing track tension causes track wear to increase exponentially.

than 50% compared with tracks that are properly tensioned. Worn and loose tracks produce too much sag in the tracks. Loose track allow the machine to throw track in soft ground or under extreme pivot turns.

Always refer to the manufacturer's manual for specific information about procedures and specifications for correct track sag. Excavators often measure sag from the machine frame to the bottom of the lower track shoe. The number of carrier rollers and where track sag is measured will change the amount of allowable sag and how it is calculated. Generally, correct track sag for smaller mini excavators should be about 2.5 cm, whereas correct tension on larger rubber track machines should be about 5 cm.

To measure track sag, follow the steps in **SKILL DRILL 42-2**.

Track Packing and Adjustment

Packing, the condition where mud, snow, and debris stick to track components and sprockets, also excessively tightens track (**FIGURE 42-15**). This happens because debris caught between the sprocket, idlers, and bushings causes the bushings to ride and seat higher in the sprocket tooth. If worksite

SKILL DRILL 42-2 Measuring Track Sag

1. Move the machine forward and let it coast to a stop without applying the brakes. Then park the machine and turn off the engine.

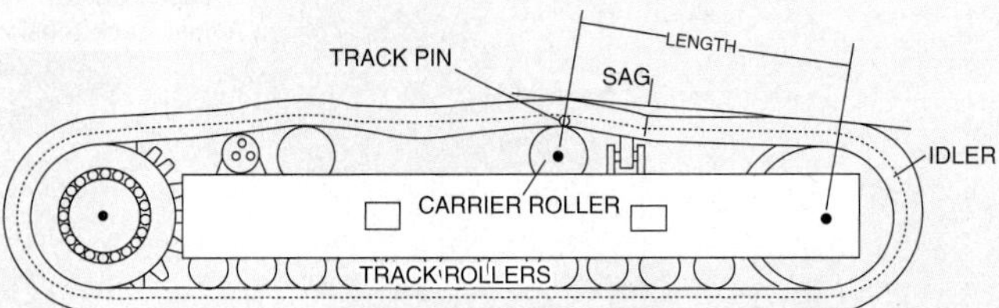

2. Make sure track slack is observable between the sprocket and front idler.

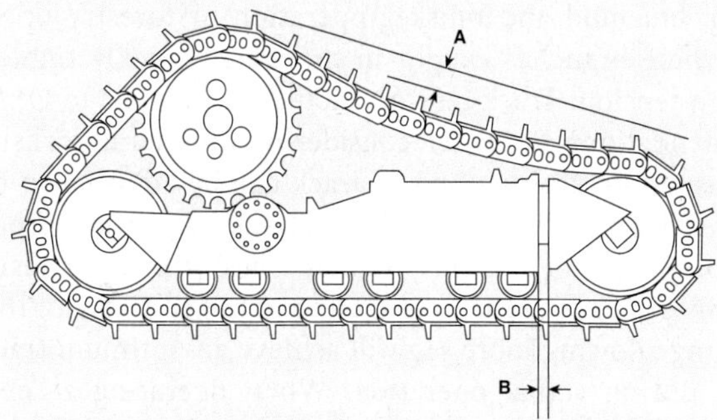

3. Center the track pin over the carrier roller.

4. Place a straight edge or a tight line over the track shoe grouser tip at the sprocket end of the track to the front idler.

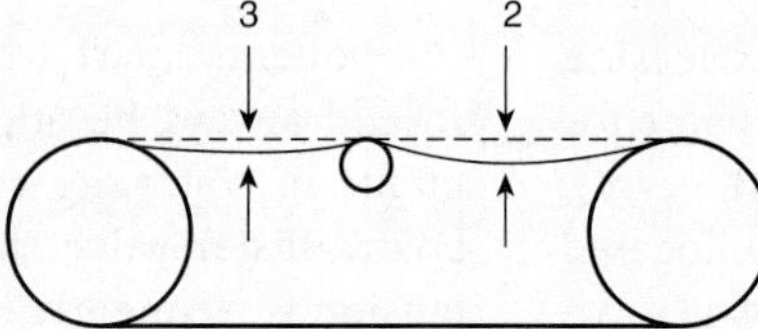

5. For machines without carrier rollers, measure the distance from the line or straight edge to the grouser tip at the lowest point of sag.

6. For machines with a single carrier roller, measure the distance from the line to the grouser tips in two places: one at the lowest point of sag between the front idler and carrier, and the second between the line and the rear section of track. Add the distance between two points, and then average the two measurements.

7. If sag requires adjustment, perform the adjustment, operate the machine in forward and reverse, and then remeasure track tension.

Working Conditions—Key Owning & Operating (0&0) Cost Factors

	Application	Operating Techniques	Underfoot Conditions	Maintenance Practices
1—Excellent	Snow Material Handling Turf/Sod	Trained Operators One Operator 3 Point Turns	Snow Turt Concrete	**Daily** Cleaning, Track Tension Check, Inspection
2—Good	Digging Grading Trenching	Stop Track turn Pivot Turns Up & Down Slopes	Dirt Mud Clay	**Weekly** Cleaning, Track Tension Check, Inspection
3—Poor	Dozing Cold Planning Focestry (Mulching)	Counter-rotating Loaded Turning Spinning Tracks	Milled Asphall Rock 2° Dirt with 10–20% rock	**Monthly** Cleaning, Track Tension Check, Inspection Loosely Follow OMM
4—Bad	Recycling Demoltion	Transition Turning Travel over Curbs at Speed	Stone _° Dirt with 20–50% rock	**Rare** Cleaning, Track Tension Check, Inspection Do Not Know OMM

Increasing Impact on 0&0 (rows, downward)

Increasing Impact on 0&0 (columns, rightward)

FIGURE 42-15 Underfoot conditions and machine operation have a major influence on track wear.

material dries and hardens or continues to accumulate in the spaces between the frame and track, links eventually wear as they are dragged across the concrete-like material. Proper daily cleaning to remove debris is necessary, depending on working conditions. Dry sand offers the least likelihood of packing, but mud and muskeg operation or forestry operation, where branches caught in the track, quickly tighten the chain tension. Track tension should be adjusted to OEM recommendations. But when considering whether a worksite will cause more packing or not, track can be adjusted to be slightly tighter for rock and looser for sand and snow. Rock does not pack, and a slightly tighter track will better resist track run-off. Snow, sand, and mud tend to pack, and an initial setting allowing more sag will achieve an optimum track tension during actual operation. When operating at new worksites, track sag should be checked and adjusted after 1 or 2 hours of operation. However, sag is typically adjusted every 50 hours or after 1 week of operation. Adjustment of most track systems is performed by adding or releasing pressurized grease from the Hydra-Juster®, a brand name for the grease-operated tensioning mechanism (**FIGURE 42-16**). Track tension is released by opening a bleeder valve located at the base of tensioning of the cylinder (**FIGURE 42-17**). An adjusting force of approximately 8,000–10,000 psi can be obtained using a hand-operated grease gun to expand a piston inside the tensioning cylinder. When multiplied by the area of the cylinder piston, the tensioning cylinder can adjust track with a force of as much as 30,000 lb. Grease pumped into the grease fitting expands the tensioning cylinder piston outward, which pushes on the front idler and stretches track components apart from each other (**FIGURE 42-18**). Grease should always be added slowly because even small adjustments in track sag can have a big impact on tension. The Hydra-Juster valve should be inspected for leakage if track tension is frequently lost.

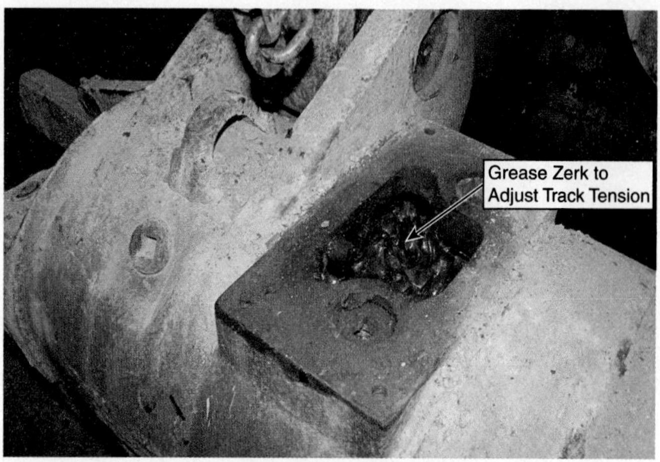

FIGURE 42-16 Components of a Hydra-Juster that tensions track, using a hand-operated grease gun.

A conventional oval track typically has approximately 2" of sag measured at the top section of track between the track's lowest and highest points. But each manufacturer's method is different. Depending on the arrangement of the top idler rollers, track sag may be calculated by measuring the sag between two points on the track, instead of one, and adding the numbers together (**FIGURE 42-19**). Another technique used on

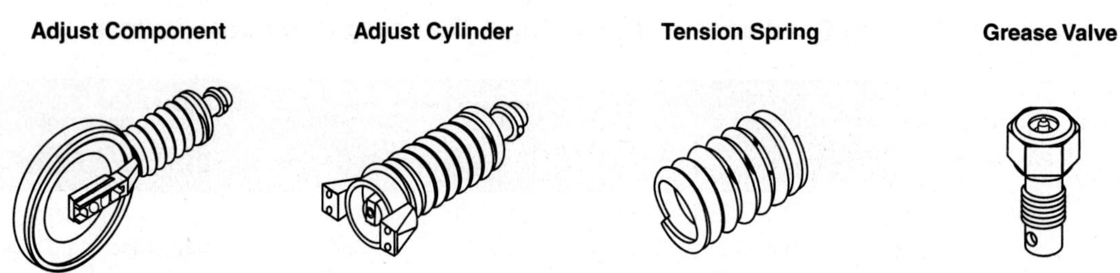

FIGURE 42-17 Components of the track tensioning mechanism.

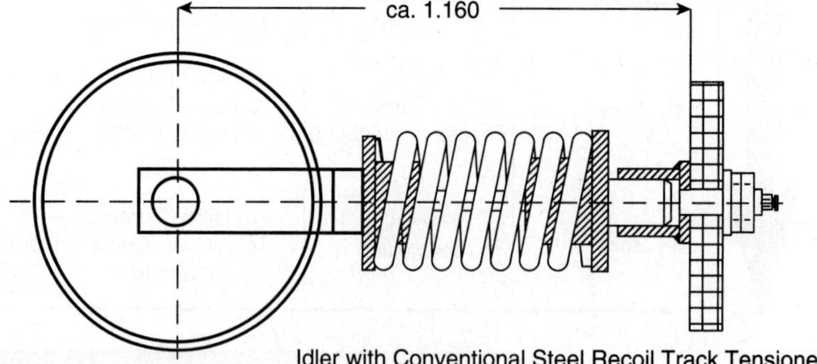

FIGURE 42-18 In a Hydra-Juster track tensioner, a grease-filled column is used to tension the recoil spring, which in turn exerts pressure against the idler wheel tensioning the track.

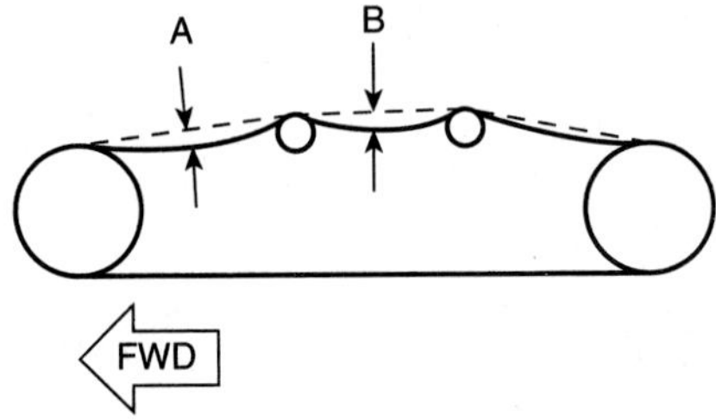

FIGURE 42-19 This track drive machine measures sag by combining "A" and "B" distances. Because there are differences between OEM tracks, always consult specifications before making adjustments.

some excavators involves using a tape to measure the distance between the upper face of the track shoe on the top track, at its lowest point, and the bottom of the track frame. Elevated sprocket drives have greater variation in measurement of track sag, so it's vital to check specifications anytime sag is measured.

SAFETY TIP

Adjusting Track Sag

Grease inside the track tensioning cylinder is under very high pressure. Always wear proper personal protection equipment, such as gloves and safety glasses, when adjusting track tension. Never remove the grease fitting to release the grease. If grease does not immediately drain from the tensioning cylinder vent hole when the grease check valve nut is loosened, slowly drive the machine in forward and reverse directions until grease escapes. Never disassemble any part of the tensioning mechanism unless you are thoroughly familiar with the correct procedure and have access to the recommended tools.

Adjusting Track Tension

After measuring the amount of track sag, track may either need tightening or loosening. If too loose, a machine throws a track in soft ground or under extreme pivot movements. Too much tension will increase wear rates.

To adjust track tension, follow the steps in **SKILL DRILL 42-3**.

SAFETY TIP

When adjusting track sag using the grease-type track tensioner, never directly visually inspect the vent holes or valves on the tensioner to see whether grease or oil is coming out of them. High-pressure grease can easily penetrate skin and cause severe personal injury. Make sure the vent holes are clean before the chain tension is released on the track. To check whether the tension is released, watch the front idler roller or roller frame to see that it moves instead of checking for the venting of grease from the track tensioner adjusting valve (**FIGURE 42-20**).

SKILL DRILL 42-3 Tightening Track

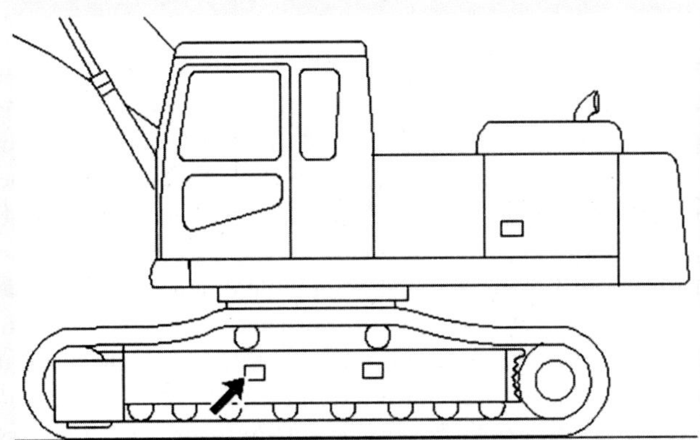

1. Remove the cover for the Hydra-Juster tensioning mechanism.
2. Identify the grease nipple and release fitting on the mechanisms.
3. Wipe and clean the grease fitting before you add grease.
4. Using only a hand-operated grease gun, add grease to the mechanism until the correct amount of sag is obtained by moving the idler in the forward direction.
5. Duplicate the procedure on the opposite track.
6. Operate the machine in forward and reverse directions in order to equalize the pressure in both track-adjusting mechanisms.
7. Reinspect by measuring the amount of track sag.
8. Readjust the track as needed.

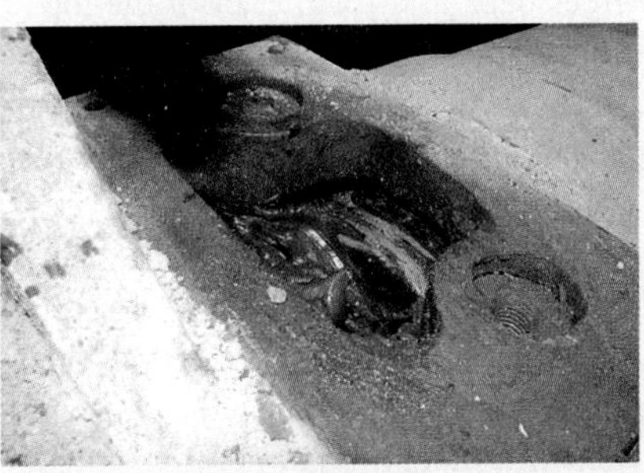

Loosening the Track

1. Remove the cover for the Hydra-Juster tensioning mechanism.
2. Loosen relief valve carefully until the track begins to loosen. One turn should be the maximum rotation needed to open the release valve.
3. Tighten the relief valve after the desired track tension is reached.
4. Duplicate the procedure on the opposite track.
5. Operate the machine in forward and reverse directions in order to equalize the pressure in both track-adjusting mechanisms.
6. Reinspect by measuring the amount of track sag. Readjust the track, as needed.

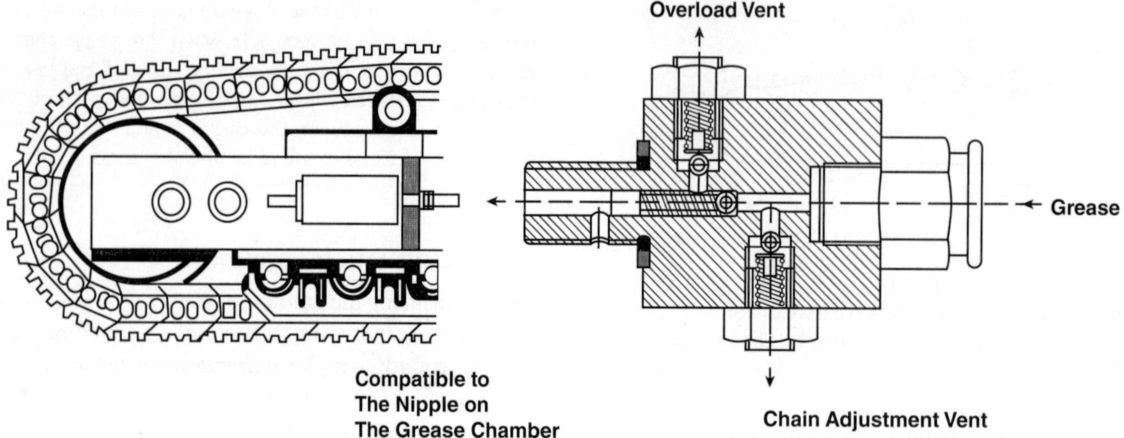

FIGURE 42-20 The track tensioning adjuster valve uses grease to move a piston back and forth in the track frame. Grease is released when the track is loosened. Grease is forced into the piston cavity to increase track tension.

▶ Track Component Wear

K42002

After looking at factors that contribute to overall track wear, this next section examines wear patterns at a component level. Unique operating conditions can accelerate wear in components that technicians should familiarize themselves with when performing inspection and maintenance checks.

Sprocket Wear

After looking at the dynamics of conventional oval track movement that causes wear in pins, bushings, and other moving track parts, it's important to examine sprocket drive wear patterns. Each side of the drive sprocket tooth develops a particular wear pattern while making contact with the track bushing (**FIGURE 42-21**). Wear on the forward tooth face takes place when torque transfers to the bushing in forward direction of travel. Similarly, wear on the tooth back side, or reverse side, takes place when torque transmits in a reverse travel direction. Depending on whether the bushing scrubs or rotates in the root tooth under load, another wear pattern is established. Root wear and radial wear are interchangeable terms given to describe sprocket tooth wear caused by the twisting motion and sliding friction of bushings in sprocket teeth produced by either reverse or forward drive wear.

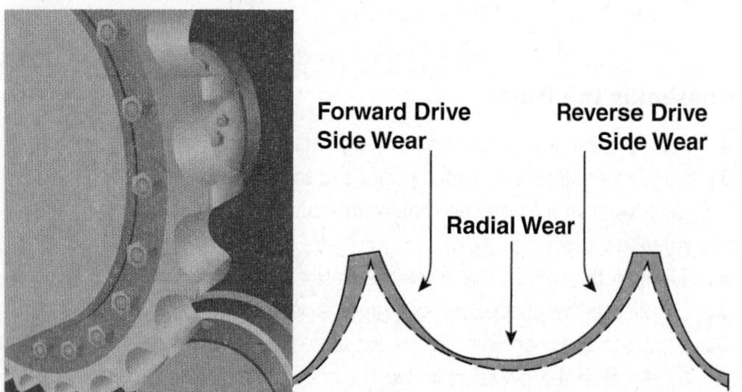

FIGURE 42-21 Sprocket wear corresponds to the direction of machine travel and dominant machine operating practices.

To determine when track component service and part replacement should be performed, specific wear patterns have to be identified, as well as an analysis of the degree of wear and whether normal or abnormal wear conditions exist, in order to make the proper service recommendations. Technicians should be able to identify these five common types of bushing and sprocket wear track:

- Forward drive side wear
- Reverse drive side and rotational wear
- Root or radial wear
- Side wear
- Reverse tip wear

Forward Drive Side Wear

Forward drive side wear is produced by sprocket and bushing contact on the forward side of the sprocket tooth. Because drive torque transfers to the bushing with the sprocket at the 6 o'clock position, and diminishes rapidly as the sprocket pulls the bushing around the sprocket curvature to the 9 o'clock position, forward wear or the outside bushing diameter and sprocket tooth is not as substantial compared to other causes of bushing and sprocket tooth wear. Additionally, during forward machine travel, the bushing will not rotate very much in the tooth root until the 11 or 12 o'clock position, when relatively little torque is transmitted to the bushing and pin. The pin, however, will rotate 30 degrees back and forth at both the top and bottom of the sprocket. The most outside diameter pin wear and inside diameter bushing wear take place in dry-sealed pins. Much less wear takes place in greased or wet-lubricated pins.

Reverse Drive Side and Rotational Wear

These two types of wear patterns, reverse and drive side rotation, are produced during reverse travel operation. While the bushing and sprocket wear is not substantial in normal operation when the machine is operated unloaded, increased reverse drive side wear accelerates during high-speed reverse travel operations. At high travel speeds, machine operation accelerates wear on both the sprocket tooth and the reverse side of the bushing (**FIGURE 42-22**).

As the name suggests, **reverse drive wear** produced during reverse drive cycles is observed by examining the sprocket tooth. Each side of the tooth wears specifically from either forward or reverse drive cycle operation. A tooth that is not symmetrically worn or has more root wear on its reverse drive side indicates excessive reverse drive cycle operation. This wear is even more exaggerated if travel speed is high and the machine loaded, or productive in reverse. In addition to reverse drive wear on the tooth face, a pocket can form on the tooth of the reverse drive side of the sprocket (**FIGURE 42-23**). The wear pocket forms on the reverse side of the sprocket tooth where the bushing twists and scrubs against the tooth face. Wear that forms a pocket on the reverse drive side of the tooth is called **reverse rotational wear** and is different from reverse drive wear that simply wears

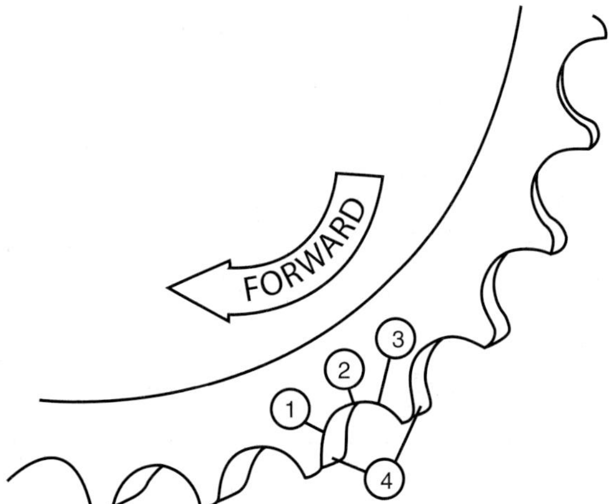

FIGURE 42-22 Wear surfaces on a sprocket that correspond to wear caused by bushing movement or tooth contact with the bushing.

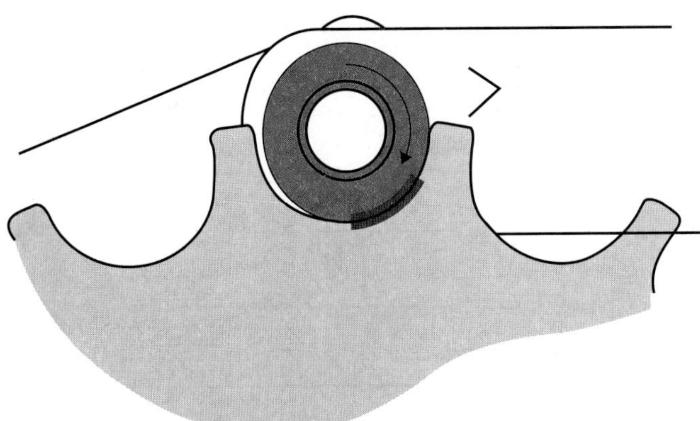

FIGURE 42-23 Reverse pocket wear takes place during high-speed reverse machine travel. Reverse pocket wear is one of the more severe and preventable types of sprocket wear.

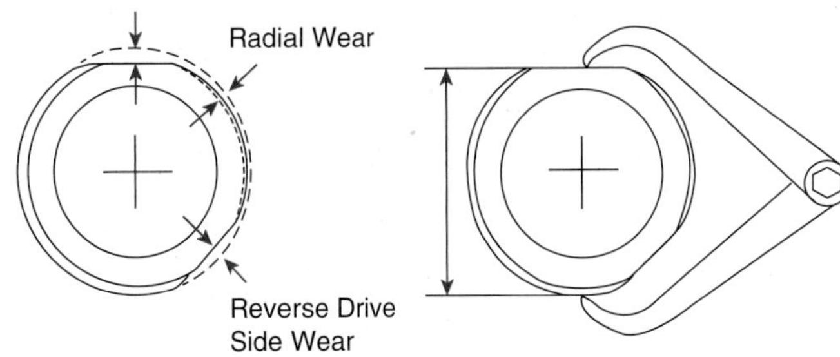

FIGURE 42-24 Bushing wear corresponds to the dominant machine operating mode. Contact between the drive sprocket and bushing produces wear in both the sprocket tooth and on the OD of the bushing.

one side of the sprocket tooth. Both reverse drive and rotational wear are evident together, but rotational wear does not always appear with reverse drive wear because it is the more severe of the two wear patterns.

Just as there are both forward and reverse drive side wears on sprocket teeth, there is corresponding wear on the outside diameter of bushings. Forward drive cycle wear erodes only a portion of one side of the bushing's external diameter, whereas reverse drive cycle wears the section 60–120 degrees opposite to the bushing's outside diameter (**FIGURE 42-24**).

Because more external and internal wear of the bushings and pins takes place, such as in a dry-seal track, the bushing has a tendency to seat deeper in the root tooth and roll even more inside the tooth root as it is carried around the sprocket curvature from the 6 o'clock position to the 12 o'clock position. With greater pin and bushing wear, the bushing both slides and rolls from the initial contact on the tooth face, into the tooth root, and then moves to the tooth face opposite the side of initial contact. Greased or wet-lubricated pins, which minimizes OD pin and ID bushing wear, do not prevent transfer of torque deep in the sprocket tooth root. Root or radial wear results in wear of the outside diameter of the bushing and the sprocket tooth root (**FIGURE 42-25**).

▶ TECHNICIAN TIP

Forward Versus Reverse Travel Wear

Reverse drive side and rotational wear bushing, which accelerates wear by a factor of at least two times more than forward operational wear in normal track operation, explains why it is preferable to operate the machine's productive cycle in the forward travel direction as much as possible. The least amount of drive sprocket, pin, and bushing wear takes place during forward travel because high torque is applied to the chain bushings only as they enter the bottom of the sprocket. The highest forward drive torque force is applied to track bushings and sprocket teeth only for a short duration of sprocket rotation when little bushing rotation takes place in the sprocket's tooth. In reverse drive, most of the chain link joints are tensioned, starting from the top of the drive sprocket, around the forward idler, and then to track that is in contact with the ground. Heavy loading of joints and bushings while they scrub the root of the drive sprocket accelerates both sprocket and chain wear.

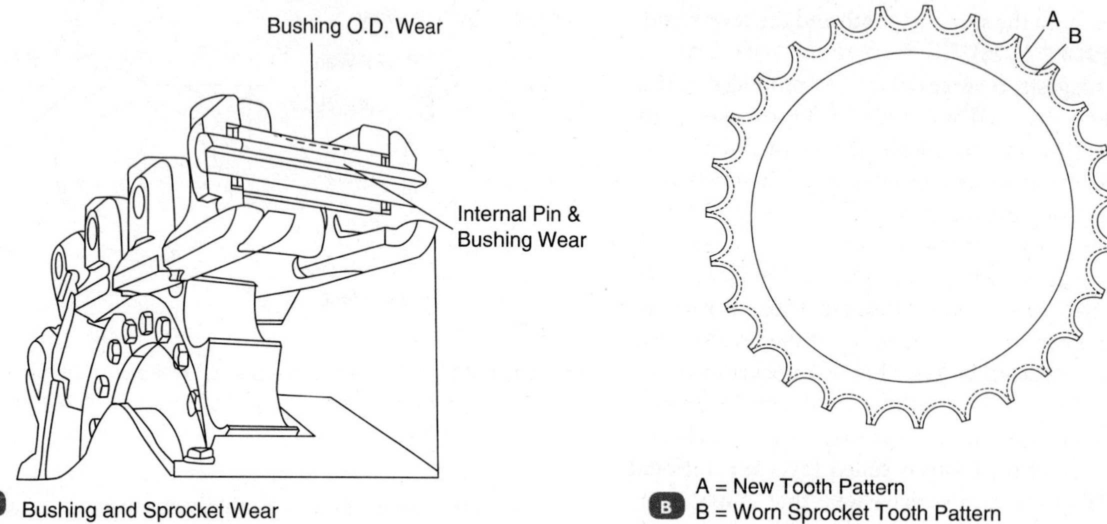

FIGURE 42-25 A. Contact between the drive sprocket and bushing produces wear in both the sprocket tooth and on the OD of the bushing. **B.** The tooth root becomes deeper due to radial wear. A worn sprocket becomes slightly smaller in diameter, and the tooth tip becomes thinner.

Side Wear of Sprocket Teeth

Side wear of a drive socket, also called corner gouging of sprocket teeth, is caused by contact of the sides of sprocket teeth with track links (**FIGURE 42-26**). When correctly aligned and operating, track should move evenly from the center of the rear roller and not rub or make contact with the sides of the sprocket (**FIGURE 42-27**). This means the clearances between either side of the track links and rear roller should be the same and maintain that clearance as the track leads from rear roller onto the drive sprocket. Several problems can exist if the alignment is not observed (**TABLE 42-1**). First, the drive sprocket may be misaligned with the track. If this is the case, the hub of the final drive sprocket requires inspection for any hub damage and should be re-shimmed with selective shims to move the sprocket out or in (**FIGURE 42-28**).

A second cause of side tooth wear is misalignment between the track frame and sprocket. Any misalignment angle created

FIGURE 42-26 Some side wear is normal; however, misalignment between the sprocket and bushings accelerates side wear.

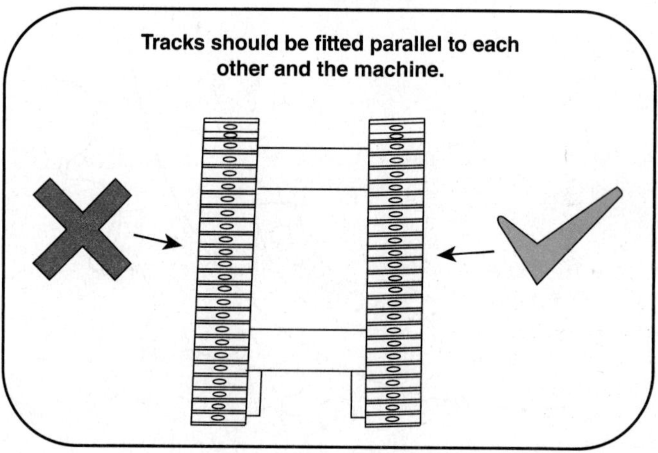

Tracks should be fitted parallel to each
other and the machine.

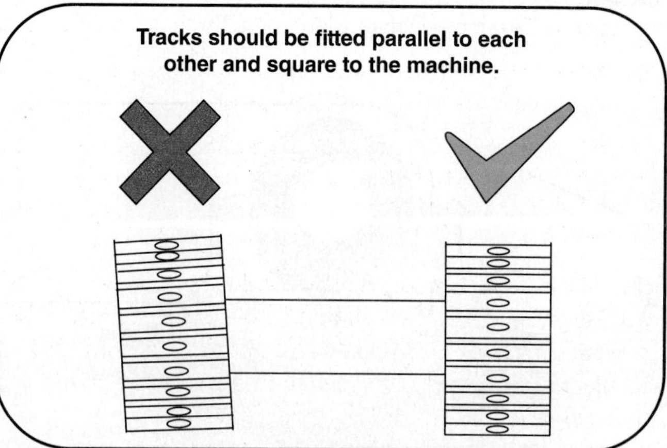

Tracks should be fitted parallel to each
other and square to the machine.

FIGURE 42-27 Misalignment between the sprocket teeth and the roller frame produces sprocket tooth side wear and accelerates wear of other track components.

TABLE 42-1 Causes of Side Sprocket Wear

Wear	Possible Causes
Sprocket side wear	Misalignment between track frame
	Cracked equalizer bar
	Improperly shimmed final drive sprocket
	Worn or damaged final drive sprocket hub
	Worn equalizer bushings and bearings
	Improper shim adjustment from side to side on final drive sprocket
	Worn or damaged pivot shaft bearing
	Bent track frame
	Worn or damaged diagonal brace
	Improperly shimmed diagonal brace

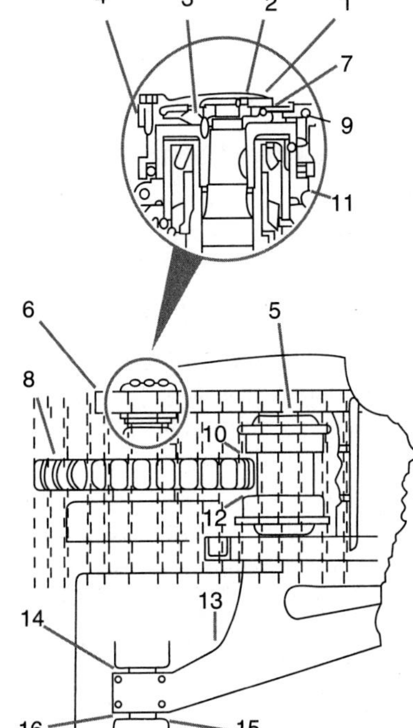

FIGURE 42-28 The final drive sprocket must be centered between the flanges of the rear track roller to prevent sprocket side tooth wear. Shims in the final drive hub are used to center the sprocket. The diagonal brace also uses shims to align the track frame with the machine frame.

between the drive sprocket and the chain will also produce side wear. Most commonly, this action takes place when track is loose; the track chain is misaligned; or the track frame is misaligned with the machine frame. Track frames are required to operate parallel to each other and the machine. If alignment is not within specification, the sprocket that is attached to the machine, not to the track frame, will operate at an angle to the sprocket.

One method to inspect frame-to-machine alignment is to measure the distance between the bottom track rollers on each side of the machine. The distance between the front and rear ends of the roller shafts must be the same, typically within ±¼". Shims located on either side of the diagonal brace in larger machines are used to correct misalignment (**FIGURE 42-29**). Keep in mind that top-to-bottom alignment of the track is not the same, and a slight angle between the top and bottom of the track exists. When unloaded, a slight vertical angle is formed between the track frame and machine so that the top of the track tilts out slightly compared to the bottom. This tilt of 1 or 2 degrees produces a small positive camber angle relative to the main frame, with zero vertical load on the roller frames. The camber angle cycles back and forth between negative and positive angles during machine loading of the roller frames. Without the angle, the slight flexion in the pivot shafts would cause more wear on the inboard side of bottom rollers and links. When loaded, the wear is evenly distributed because the links and rollers are flat. When roller frame misalignment is present, there is generally a large difference between wear patterns observed on each side of the machine.

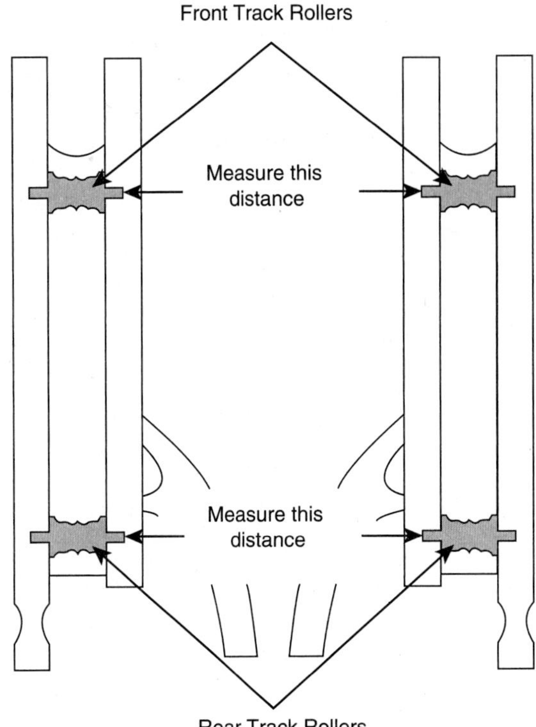

FIGURE 42-29 To inspect the track frame–to-machine alignment, measure the distance between the ends of the bottom roller pins. All dimensions should be the same ±¼".

When track frames are rebuilt and inspected for straightness on larger track frames, the concentricity, or alignment of the pivot shaft bore with the frame, should be inspected (**FIGURE 42-30**). A bent track frame does not have a perpendicular or square alignment between the pivot shaft and the track or main frame. A guide bar bolted to the track frame is used to check the pivot shaft bore for straightness, using a framing square and level. When installed in the bore, the straightness of the guide bar is checked with a level.

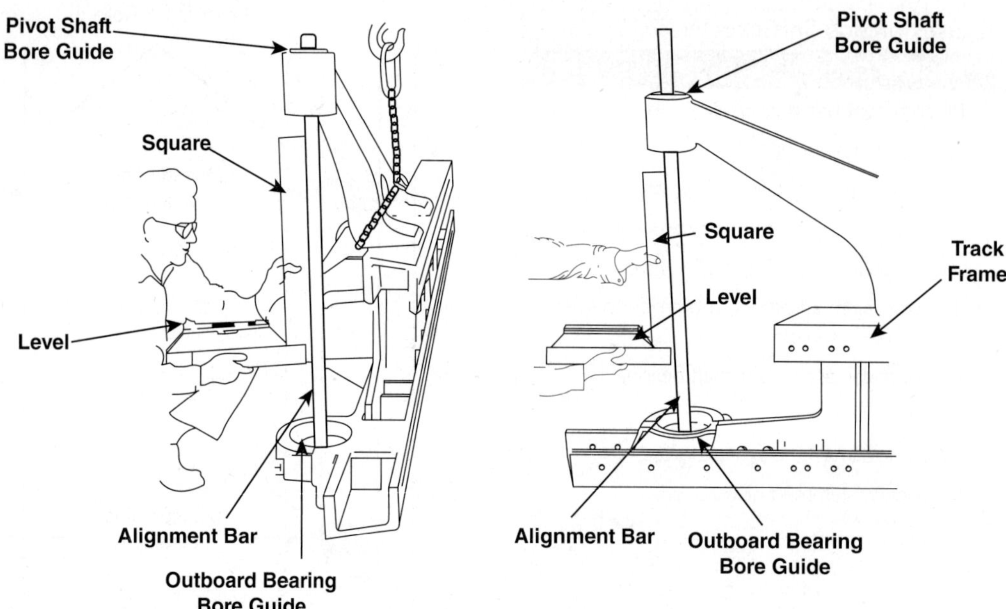

FIGURE 42-30 Alignment of the pivot shaft bearing bore and track frame is checked for squareness during a rebuild.

Reverse Tip Wear

Reverse tip wear is not like reverse drive side wear, which takes place traveling in the reverse direction. Reverse tip wear occurs during forward travel when the sprocket teeth make direct contact with the track bushings rather than the gap between the bushings. This condition is caused by a mismatch between the sprocket teeth spacing and the gap between the track bushings. A precondition for reverse tip wear is significant wear between track pins and internal diameter of the bushings. When pin-to-bushing wear takes place, it allows the distance between each pin to lengthen. This extension of track length or pin-to-pin distance, which is known as track pitch, is greatest when the track is tensioned, such as when it is packed with debris and mud. When track pitch lengthens, the result is a mismatch between the drive sprocket teeth spacing and the distance between track bushings. Rather than have the sprocket tooth contact the forward drive side of the bushing, as it does when track pitch is within normal limits, sprocket teeth make contact with the reverse side of the bushing while the track is operating in forward direction of travel. Instead of smooth engagement of the sprocket and track bushings, the tips of sprocket teeth contact the top of the bushing and slide off the bushing, producing a popping or banging noise. The front idler also moves back and forth to compensate for the sudden changes in chain tension whenever the teeth mismatch occurs. Because the chain is tight when packing takes place, reverse tip wear rapidly accelerates outside diameter bushing wear between the 11 o'clock and 12 o'clock sprocket positions when the bushing is twisting 30 degrees and the pin is turning 30 degrees.

Extreme wear is the result of the improper contact between the sprocket teeth and chain. Due to the forces involved during track operation, combined with the unusual tooth-to-bushing contact pattern, reverse tip wear is unquestionably the most severe type of wear on drive sprockets and on the outside diameter of track bushing.

Evaluating Sprocket Tooth Wear

Sprocket wear can be difficult to evaluate accurately because, under normal operating conditions, the original tooth outline can be completely worn away. However, several techniques are used to provide accurate assessment.

1. Measuring across sprocket teeth. Sprocket wear can be determined by measuring the distance across the tips of several sprocket teeth, usually three. Using a straight edge or measuring tape, the distance is measured between the drive side tooth tip of one tooth to the drive side of a sprocket tooth tip located three teeth away. The measurement should be performed on the same segment if the drive sprocket is segmented (**FIGURE 42-31**).
2. Using a wear gauge. Tooth wear is evaluated using a gauge that has an outline or template of the original sprocket tooth profile to compare against used part dimensions. The gauges can combine measurements of the grouser height, pitch, carrier roller wear, roller radius, front idler radius, and link wear. Sprockets on tank track drives may have a profile engraved in the sprocket identifying wear limits, or a template may be used to inspect sprocket wear (**FIGURE 42-32**).

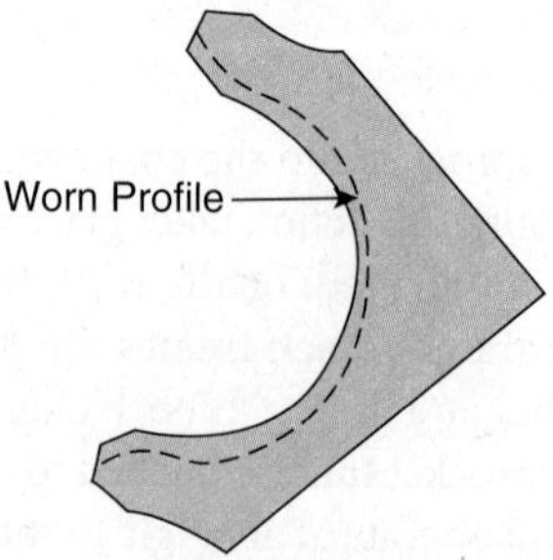

FIGURE 42-31 Sprocket wear can be determined by measuring the smallest distance across the tips of several sprocket teeth; usually three are measured.

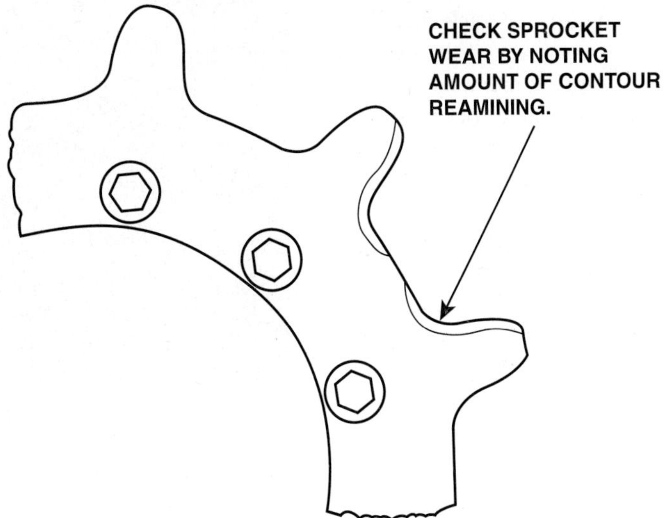
DRIVE SPROCKET WEAR CHECK
FOR NEW DESIGN SPROCKET
CHECK SPROCKET
WEAR BY NOTING
AMOUNT OF CONTOUR
REAMINING.
NOTE. Wear indicator contour must be
visible. Bottom of contour indicates
limit of wear allowable.
If not visible replace sprocket.
A

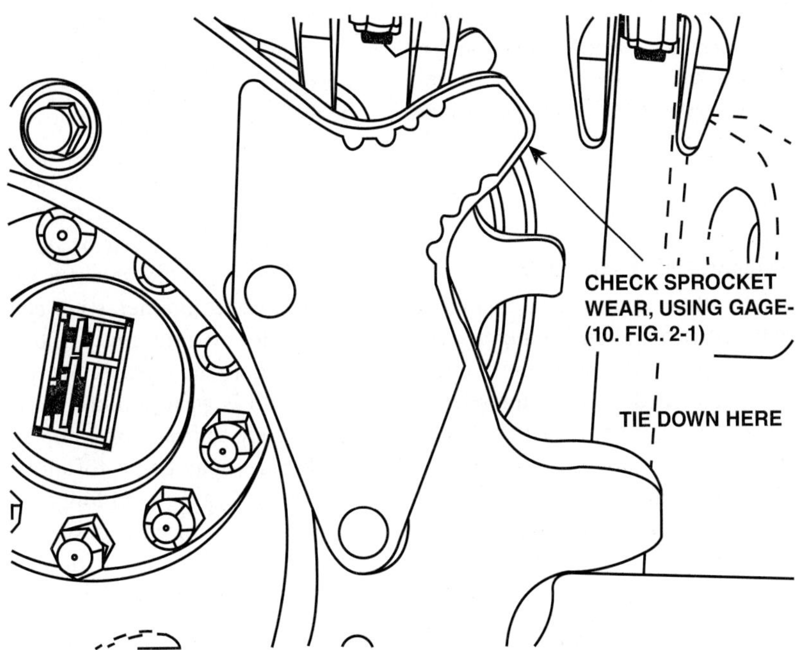
DRIVE SPROCKET WEAR CHECK
CHECK SPROCKET
WEAR, USING GAGE-
(10. FIG. 2-1)
TIE DOWN HERE
NOTE. SPROCKET EDGE CONTOUR MUST EXTEND BEYOND EDGE OF
GAGE. BOTTOM OF NOTCHES IN GAGE INDICATE MAXIMUM
WEAR LIMIT. IF ANY EDGE OF SPROCKET FALLS BEHIND
GAGE, REPLACE OR REVERSE SPROCKET (FIG. 2 - 186).
B

FIGURE 42-32 **A.** The sprocket of this tank track drive has a wear limit engraved on the sprocket face. **B.** This tank drive sprocket is checked using a gauge placed over the face of the sprocket.

Replacing Sprockets

Track specialists recommend replacement of drive sprocket wheels or segments anytime a bushing turn or track chain link assembly replacement takes place. Because wear on the sprocket is typically the same percentage of outside diameter wear on the bushings, bushings at wear limits indicate sprocket replacement. If components are not replaced at the same time, matching worn components to new ones will accelerate the wear of new components, shortening service life.

Segmented sprockets are simply replaced by unbolting and replacing with new segments (**FIGURE 42-33**). The track need not be separated to do this. The machine can be moved to rotate the sprocket segment to the inside section of the track loop that is not engaged with the track.

Sprocket wheels replacement requires separating the track and replacing the sprocket with a new bolt-on wheel. Older sprocket wheels may have a tapered fit onto the final drive hub, requiring the setup and use of a portable hydraulic puller to separate the sprocket from the drive hub.

FIGURE 42-33 Replaceable drive sprocket is unbolted and removed after the track is separated.

> TECHNICIAN TIP

Replacing Specialized Sprocket Segments

To minimize the increased tension and packing encountered working in conditions with mud or snow underfoot, a special sprocket segment is designed for soft, extrudable packing materials. The segments have reduced contact with bushings in the tooth root to allow the underfoot material to squeeze out of the segment teeth rather than bind and pack the track chain. These should only be used in the constant presence of mud, snow, and other soft, extrudable conditions. Used in any other materials, the segments will cause accelerated bushing wear due to reduced contact area in the sprocket root.

Track Drive Wear Limit Factors

Before examining component replacement, calculating remaining service life or **wear factor** is useful when making determinations about replacement or providing inspection reports. Because most track parts are hardened, wear factor refers to the amount of hardened material in each component before the hardening is removed. Manufacturers assign a wear factor to components based on the depth of hardening. In other words, the wear factor is important in calculating the exact percentage of remaining service life and can vary for each component. To determine the remaining service life using a wear factor, consider the following example of a grouser bar height on a track shoe. A new shoe height is 0.75", or has 100% remaining service life, and the manufacturer's maximum wear limit with 0% service life is 0.25". To calculate the wear factor, the minimum height is subtracted from the maximum height. This means maximum height of 0.75" – minimum height of 0.25" = 0.50" or 0.50" wear factor. If an in-service grouser bar height is measured to have 0.40" height, what is the remaining service life? To calculate this, subtract the wear limit of 0.25" from 0.40". The result is 0.15". Divide this number by the wear factor of 0.50" previously calculated. 0.15/0.50" = 0.30 × 100% is 30% remaining service life or wear remaining (**FIGURE 42-34**). This same procedure can be used to report component wear or remaining service life for any track part.

The wear charts for components display track component wear measurements to 100% and 120% worn. One hundred percent worn or 0% service life is considered the typical service replacement maintenance point. However, only a few track components are commonly replaced when 100% worn. More commonly, a 120% wear point is used, which is described as the **destruction point**. In the field, the destruction point is wear condition reached when the component is most likely to break or completely fail. As guideline, various track parts may begin to fail or break near the 120% worn, with some lasting even longer, depending on worksite conditions. To minimize the cost per hour, machines are frequently operated to the point of destruction, or 120% worn, leaving track parts untouched for as long as possible. At 120% wear, parts are replaced.

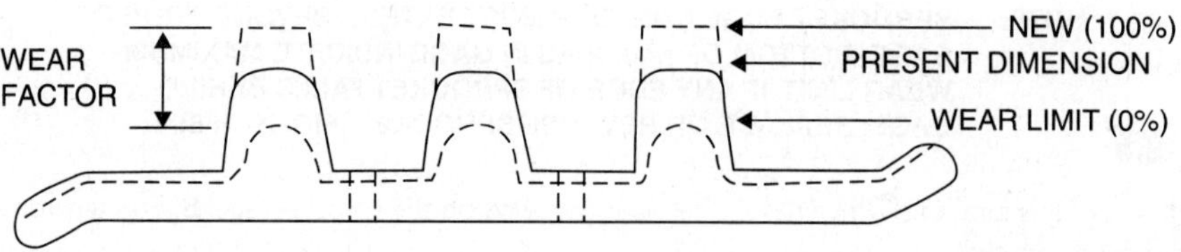

FIGURE 42-34 To calculate the remaining service life, the measured wear is multiplied by a wear factor and then converted to a percentage.

▶ Track Drive Undercarriage Inspection, Adjustment, and Repair

K42003

In this next section, specific inspection and repair procedures commonly performed by track technicians are discussed.

Service Tools—Ultrasonic Wear Indicator

Measuring the thickness of various track components is critical to undercarriage inspection. A variety of measuring tools typically used include outside calipers, measuring tapes, straight edges, and depth gauges. One particularly useful tool used to perform fast but accurate, nondestructive thickness measurements is an ultrasonic wear indicator. These electronic service tools can measure the thickness of bulldozer blades, bucket base and cutting edges, track bushings, idler center flange, and roller and shoe thicknesses. Although calibrated primarily for measuring the thickness of steel, the tool can be used to measure thickness of other materials like aluminum, plastic, copper, and glass. The ultrasonic tester is especially helpful measuring the thickness of parts where the opposite side is not accessible to a caliper.

Various devices are available with differing features and capabilities, but they all operate to measure part thickness by transmitting high-frequency sound waves through the material being measured. After a sound wave passes through a part and reaches its opposite side, the sound is reflected back like an echo, where it is sensed by a special probe, which can slide along a part surface. Like a sonar or radar, the device calculates the difference between the time required for the sound to travel through the part and reflect back again in order to measure the part's thickness. A microprocessor in the ultrasonic tester converts the transmission time into a thickness value for display and recording.

The device offers the advantages of being capable of ignoring paint and dirt on parts unless the part is very small. Track parts do not require cleaning to use ultrasonic testing, which eliminates errors of other direct measure techniques caused by dirt packed around parts. Ultrasonic testers are especially useful for accurately measuring bushing wear after turning. Uploading data to a PC enables software to analyze measured values and prepare a cost-per-hour estimate for various track service options.

Evaluating Pin and Bushing Wear

Track bushings are the most important component in the undercarriage for the technician to accurately measure and correctly interpret wear. Monitoring bushing wear is important not only because it predicts track service life but also because the bushing wear rate doubles after the surface hardening is completely worn through. Sealed and lubricated track (SALT) pins have 50% more service life than sealed pins because of decreased internal pin to bushing wear. However, extended service life does require external bushing wear also be minimal because external bushing wear is a service-limiting factor. To maintain minimal external wear, proper track adjustment is necessary, along with the absence of severe and frequent packing. Underfoot working conditions can also increase external bushing wear.

Three measurement techniques based on the type of measuring tool are commonly used. The techniques measure outside diameter wear using an ultrasonic wear indicator, calipers, or a depth gauge that measures vertical wear only.

Ultrasonic Wear Indicator Method

This method is considered the most reliable and accurate measure of the most critical track dimension, which is bushing wall thickness. What makes the technique even more versatile is that it can be used to measure bushings wall thickness before and after a bushing turn. After an ultrasonic probe is calibrated, the probe measures metal thickness approximately 20 times a second by slowly sliding the probe over the bushing's reverse and forward drive sides. Wear is determined using the smallest dimension actually measured. Using a wear factor, the amount of wear or service life is calculated using OEM reference charts.

Caliper Method

The caliper method uses an outside caliper or Vernier dial gauge to measure bushing diameter in three dimensions: forward and reverse drive plus a vertical measure. Before measuring, the bushing surfaces must be carefully cleaned, and the proper measuring technique must be used to make accurate, reliable observations. Without proper technique, the measurement will have errors. Squeezing the caliper too tightly can distort readings, so can using the caliper at the wrong angle or at incorrect spots on the bushings. See **FIGURE 42-35**.

Depth Gauge Method

A third method for measuring bushing wear compares the depth of worn spots on the bushings with a known nominal or

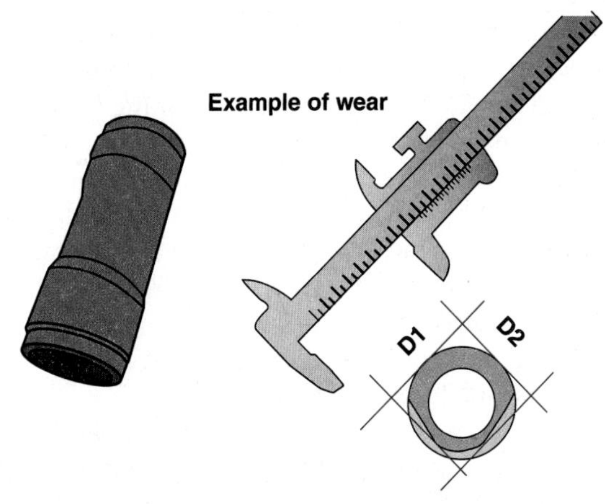

FIGURE 42-35 Two dimensions of a track bushing are measured with a caliper or ultrasonic tester to evaluate wear.

new dimension. The measuring tool used is a depth gauge that can only record the vertical height or depth of worn spots on the bushing. This technique cannot measure reverse or forward drive wear and is prone to error caused by incorrect measuring techniques or improperly cleaned parts. One advantage is the technique enables measurement of the bushing dimension after a bushing turn.

Bushing Turns

Rather than replace track pins and bushings, track service life is extended by removing the bushings and turning them both 180 degrees to reorientate worn internal and external pin-to-bushing surfaces. This technique, called "turning," places an unworn internal bushing diameter against the unworn track pin, and an unworn external surface against the sprocket drive teeth. Turning bushings restores track pitch to its original length and extends undercarriage service life by deferring chain link replacement until slower wearing links and rollers need service. Although it is a labor-intensive process to separate track and then press out bushings and pins either on-site or at a track rebuild facility, savings are achieved by reusing rather than replacing the bushings. A bushing turn can be expected to provide service life equal to the service before turning. Keep in mind, some operations have determined the economics of turns is not viable and run the track to destruction. At that point, the entire track chain assembly, including links, bushings, pins, and seals, is replaced (**FIGURE 42-36**).

During turns, the pins and bushings are pressed out of the track links with either a portable hydraulic press, or the track is separated, removed from the machine, and bushings are pressed out using a stationary track press. A turn can either be a dry, greased, or wet type, depending on whether bushings are lubricated and the type of lubricant used. During a turn of sealed bushings that are the dry type having no lubricant, both the bushings and pins are pressed out of the track. Track links, pins, and bushings are inspected according to reuse guides. Cracked, bent, excessively worn, or otherwise damaged parts are replaced, and the track is reassembled after turning the bushings 180 degrees. Pin-to-bushing seals, which are intended to keep out dirt, are usually reused as well. Any cracked or excessively worn thrust washer used in sealed track must be replaced to prevent end play, which causes the link bushing bore to wear into an oval shape of interlocking links, using a counterbore for the bushing. Worn seals also allow contact between the end of the bushings and track link counterbore, which wears links beyond reuse (**FIGURE 42-37**). On oval track machines, a turn typically takes place after about 2,000 hours of service or when wear exceeds 50% of the bushing's external diameter. Sealed-type chains are most commonly used on older models of excavators and dozers.

With sealed and greased track (SAGT), service life is approximately 20–42% longer than sealed (nonlubricated) track chain. During a SAGT turn, the major difference between procedures used with a dry turn is that the pins are coated with a layer of grease, and the track is assembled with new polyurethane-type seals between the pins and bushings.

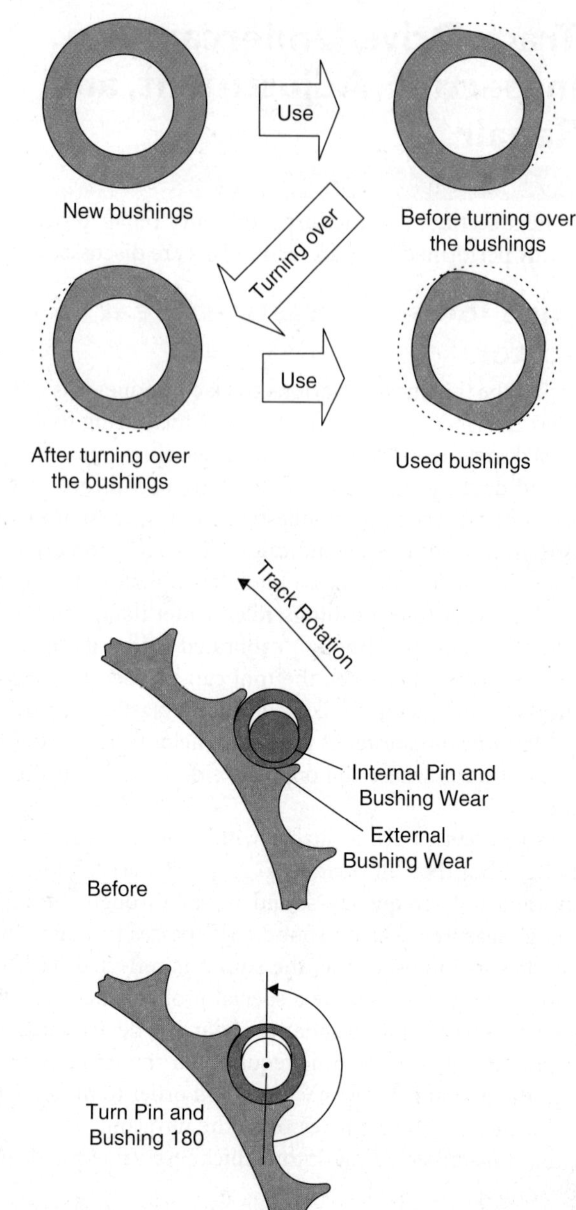

FIGURE 42-36 A bushing turn flips the bushing end for end and places both the internal and external unworn section of the bushing against the pin and drive sprocket.

When performing turns of SALT pins and bushings, the pins' internal reservoirs are refilled with oil using a unique technique that involves pulling oil into clearances using a vacuum pump. A rubber sealing plug is placed in the end of the pin to keep oil from leaking from the pin (**FIGURE 42-38**). Next, a vacuum pump is connected to the pin, using a needle that is pushed through the pin's rubber sealing plug. A vacuum is applied to the pin and pulls any air from the cavities around the pin (**FIGURE 42-39**). If the vacuum holds in the pin, which means there is no leak path for the oil around seals and other clearances, pressurized oil is injected into the pin. Using a hand pump, oil is added to the reservoir that is located along the pin axis center. Oil is then pulled into the internal or annular clearances between the pin and bushing, as any air in these

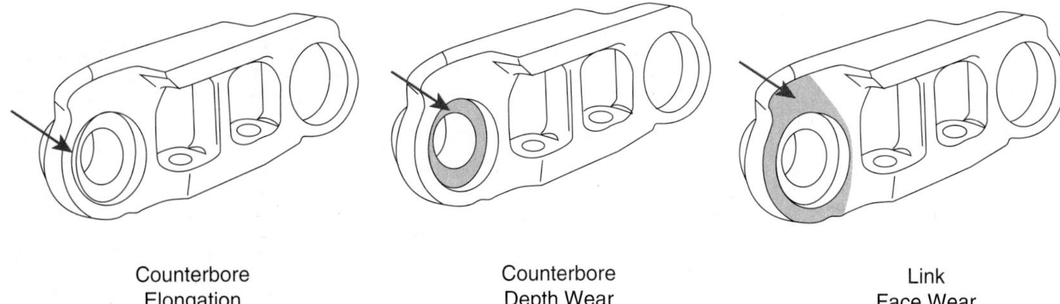

FIGURE 42-37 Counterbore elongation and depth wear is caused by loose bushings combined with abrasives making contact with the track links. High side thrusts, such as hill work, and frequent turning accelerate counterbore depth wear. Worn bushings with counterbore wear eventually cause face wear on links as the link faces are allowed to make contact.

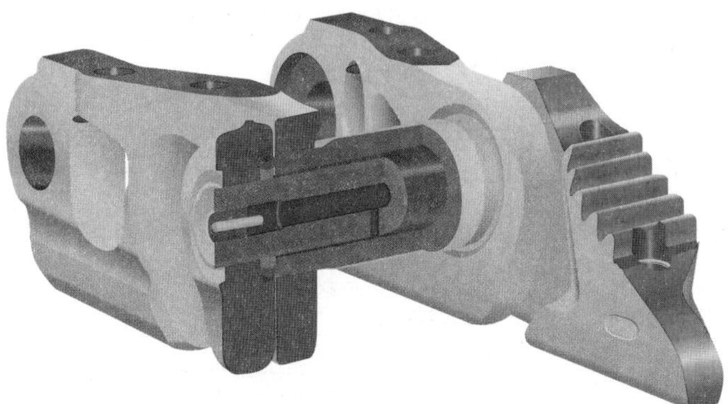

FIGURE 42-38 Cross section of a sealed and lubricated-type track pin and bushing joint. Note the presence of the rubber sealing plug.

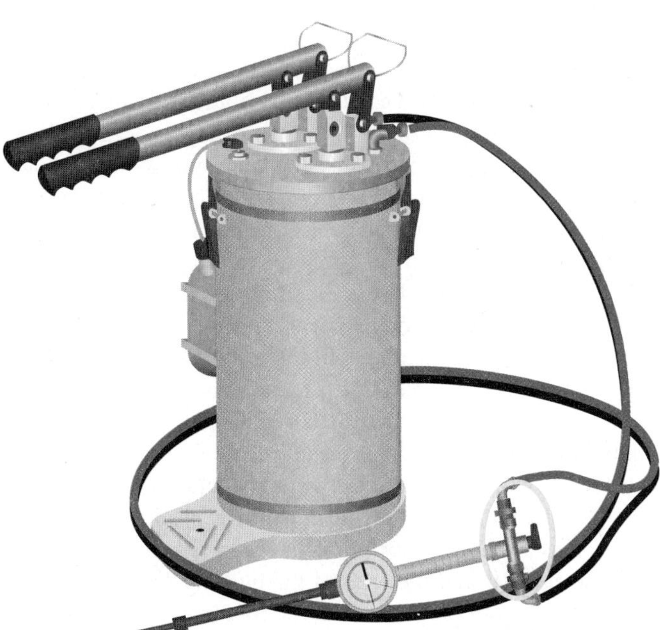

FIGURE 42-39 A mobile device used to create a vacuum, perform a leak test, and fill the joints of oil-lubricated track pins. Two manual pumps control vacuum and pressurization of the joint. The gun has a valve that selects either vacuum or injection of oil into the pin of the chain.

clearances was removed by the vacuum pump. Pin and bushing assemblies that do not build up a vacuum likely have leaking oil seals. Often, SALT seals may be defective, or grooves are worn into the seal bore areas that allow air into the joint. The eventual result is an oil leak from the pin that produces a rapidly wearing or seized dry pin condition.

▶ TECHNICIAN TIP

Maintenance After a Bushing Turn

A bushing turn does not end the need for close inspection of track components and following good operating practices. Any external damage due to extreme abusive service conditions (for example, use of excessive track pad widths or lack of routine maintenance procedures) that occurs to the links, bushings, or link rail assemblies causes a loss of lubrication between the pin and bushing and will void a warranty of a track rebuilder.

The Economics of Pin and Bushing Turns

Although turning pins and bushings was a frequent maintenance practice in the past, the use of SALT pins and high labor costs is making the practice obsolete. With SALT track, internal wear can lengthen track pitch by as much as 40% before the external wear on bushings justifies turning. In that case, many other parts will require replacement because joints will have leaked oil, and pins and bushings will be excessively worn.

If there are many dry joints causing excessive pin and bushing wear, additional replacement pin and bushing kits are needed, which may increase both parts and labor costs to near the cost of new track chain. Turning SALT assumes that sealing surfaces on track links remain in good condition and won't leak after new seals are installed. Some shops take SALT tracks and perform turns using grease lubricant instead. Track seals, pins, and bushings are reused at substantially less cost. Today, track chain with new pins, links, and bushings are commonly used when track wear exceeds 120%, or is at its destructive limit. Ultimately, the deciding factors about turning versus outright chain replacement depends on the size of the tractor, its age, current condition, application, cost of components, and how the operator anticipates using the machine in the future.

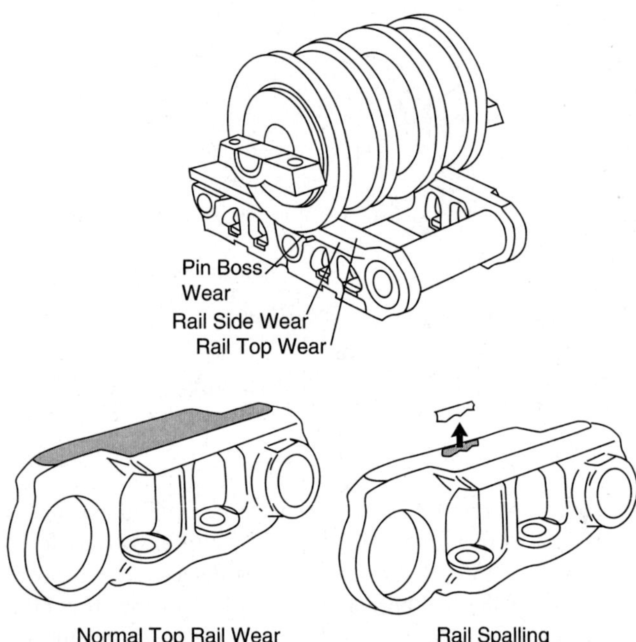

FIGURE 42-40 The rail on the top of the link experiences wear due to rolling and sliding friction combined with abrasive materials. High loading causes fatigue failure of the hardened rail material.

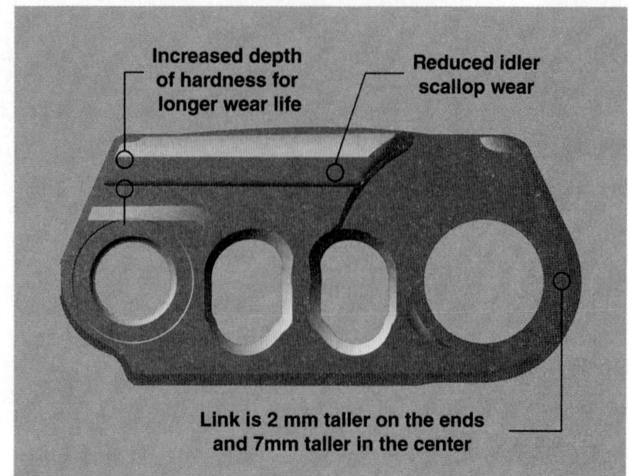

FIGURE 42-41 Features of SALT-type track links to extend track link durability.

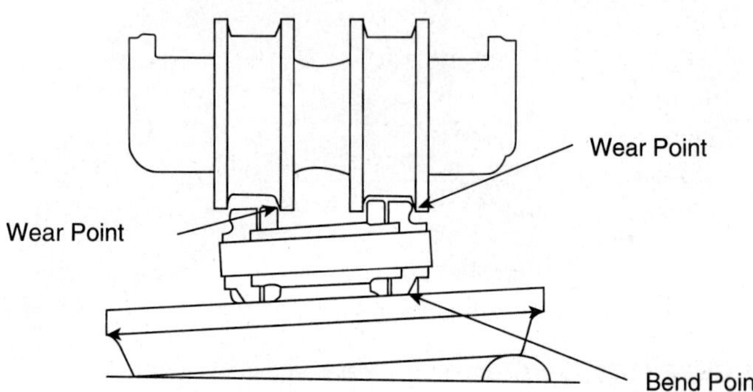

FIGURE 42-42 Wide shoes act like a lever to multiply shock loads and heavy machine force against the track link. Wide shoes accelerate roller and link rail wear.

▶ TECHNICIAN TIP

Dry chains may be preferable in two different working conditions. One is in areas with underfoot conditions where there are many rocks and trees. Another is where extreme low-ground-pressure environments require extra-wide track shoes. In both these areas, underfoot conditions, combined with severe lateral forces generated by high shoe widths, weaken the joint between the pin and track link, causing damage to wet-type seals. In that case, lubricant can leak out and produce premature dry track joints.

Similarly, excavators that use wide track shoes and have high lateral forces produced while the "stick" is digging over the track tend to more often damage the seals in lubricated pins and bushings. Given the low number of travel hours an excavator track has compared to a dozer that's generally moving all the time, the additional expense of sealed and lubricated chain does not justify its use in these applications.

Evaluating Link Wear

Track links are designed to withstand a tremendous amount of weight and twisting in service. Normal wear is caused by roller friction between the rail and roller (**FIGURE 42-40**). Because the weight of the machine is transmitted through the rollers into the narrow links, the link shape is reinforced and constructed of materials alloyed to resist wear from the rollers grinding away with abrasive materials between them. For extended service life, link rail surfaces have additional heat treating to harden them to resist abrasive wear and rolling friction (**FIGURE 42-41**).

Top rail wear is accelerated by increased machine weight and ground conditions such as soil abrasiveness or chemical action of soil. Operating conditions such as these accelerate rail wear on the link and can lead to spalling and link cracking. Spalling is the separation of the hardened layers of the link rail due to fatigue failure caused by the continuously loading and unloading of the rollers. Cracking takes place when the heavily loaded link is twisted on rough terrain and operated with excessively wide shoes, which multiply the force applied to the pins and bushings (**FIGURE 42-42**). Side rail wear takes place during hill work when the machine is perpendicular to the hill slope and when turning a machine. In these situations, roller flanges place heavy lateral forces against the links. Once again, wide track shoe width multiplies the lateral force transmitted to the links from on the outside or inside edges of a track shoe when working in gullies or on high crowns (**FIGURE 42-43**).

Constant rotation of the link hinge produces link face wear. This is the contact point between two interconnected links. Wear between the ends of the bushing pressed into one pair of links takes place between the rotating ends of interconnected links. In flush type links, the bushing does not protrude beyond the edge or face of the link. In **interconnected-type track links**, the bushings have a second precision counterbore machined into the interconnected link, allowing the bushing to protrude into the interconnected link (**FIGURE 42-44**). This counterbore acts like a barrier to prevent dirt, water, and abrasive materials from entering the clearances between the pin and bushing. A seal in this area further minimizes abrasive intrusion. Because the bushing is longer, and less dirt enters the pin-to-bushing clearances, interconnected links have a longer service life.

When links worn 100% operate with an identically worn roller, it is normal for the roller flanges to make contact with either the link pin bosses or the bushing on double-flange rollers. The link pin boss may even get jammed against the roller flange when both parts are worn. As wear continues beyond 100%, wear on the link pin boss reduces the link's ability to remain tight and hold the track pin and bushing with an interference fit (**FIGURE 42-45**). Weakened pin bosses may allow pins and bushings to begin popping out of worn track links.

Additionally, wear of the roller flanges against the bushings ends may cause cracking of the bushing or link itself. This explains why it is important to inspect links for cracks in the area of the strut and pin bores. Any cracking in these areas requires link replacement. Pin and bushing bores or counterbores that are worn out of round or have worn from excessive end play require replacement.

Link height is the most critical determining factor of remaining chain service. It follows then that when evaluating the serviceability or remaining life of a link, the most important measurement is link height. Link wear limits are determined by setting the allowable wear equal to some fraction of the clearance between the link and the roller. On some tracks using single rollers, this clearance is between the link pin boss and the roller flange. On other tracks using double rollers, the clearance is between the bushing and the inner flanges of the double-flange roller.

SALT-type track uses wider and higher link rail height to match the longer pin and bushing life. But generally, in sealed chains, links are replaced when bushings have reached a wear limit following a bushing turn. Stated another way, links wear at 50% the rate of a sealed bushing. Once the wear of the link reaches the maximum wear limit, it should be replaced even if the roller shell is not worn to a maximum limit.

Operating conditions produce specific wear patterns in the track that can be observed and interpreted by technicians during track evaluation.

Measuring Track Link Height

Track links are measured using a depth gauge or with an ultrasonic wear indicator. The depth gauge measures link height from the links' rail surface in contact with rollers to the track

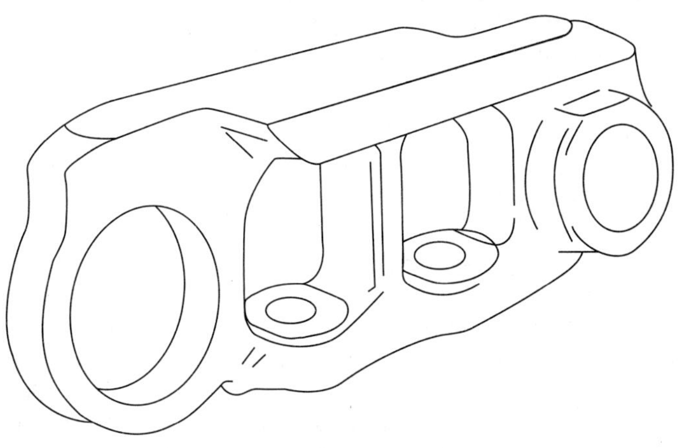

FIGURE 42-43 Side rail wear is caused by high lateral forces, such as working on hills, crowns, or gullies.

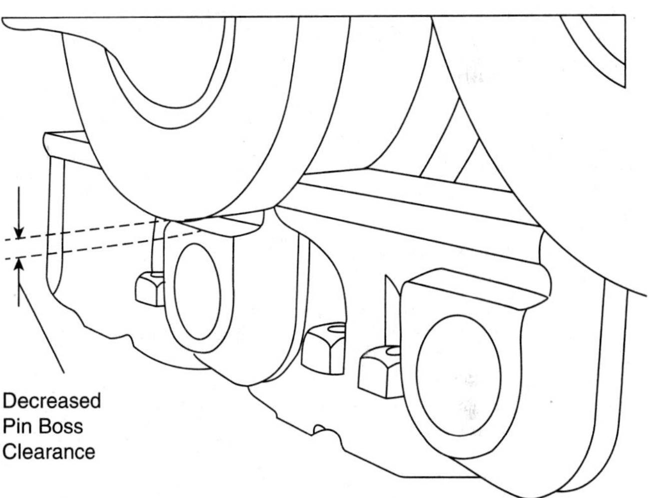

FIGURE 42-45 When the rail is worn, the pin boss around the track pin is worn down, which leads to lower retention force on the pin.

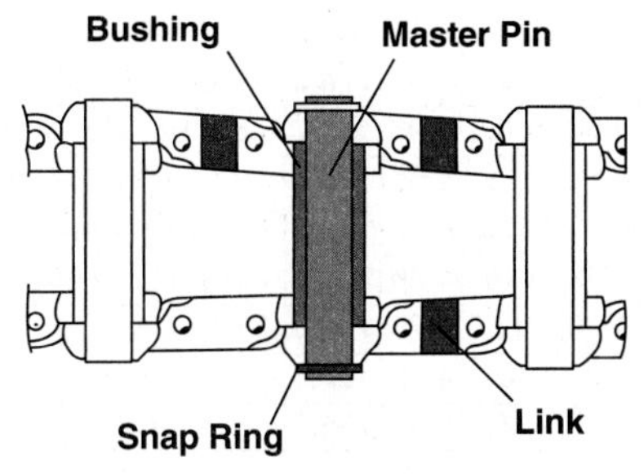

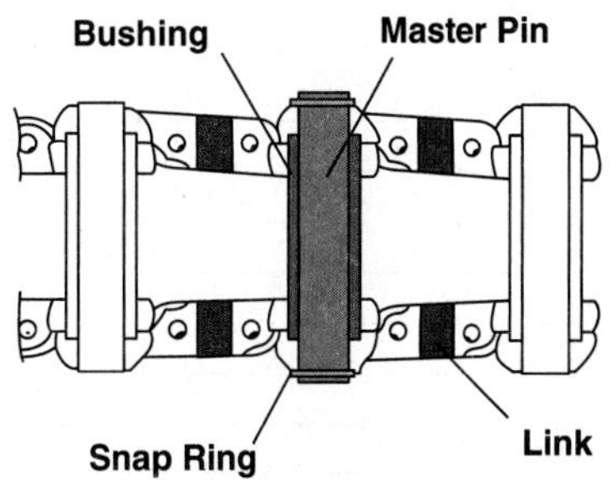

FIGURE 42-44 Interconnected links have a precision-machined counterbores in the link end they attach to.

shoe. The best location for track link measurement is the outside edge of the links at the end closest to the track pin, as link thickness is thinnest there and receives the greatest wear from the rollers. Contact between the track rollers and the links produces more wear on the thin end of the links, where they overlap with the adjacent link. However, contact on the links' wider center is mostly from the idler wheel. If a large difference exists between the height of the two wear spots, track-excited vibration will be noticeable on smooth underfoot conditions because a scalloped wear pattern forms on each track link (**FIGURE 42-46**).

When using a depth gauge, first clean the link and track shoe surface. Next, position the T bar close to the pin end. The gauge's bar must be positioned to lie flat across the link rails (**FIGURE 42-47**). The longer extension piece should also be perpendicular to the shoe surface (**FIGURE 42-48**). When an ultrasonic wear indicator is used, it measures the depth between the link rail and bushing bore (**FIGURE 42-49**). The probe of the ultrasonic tester should slide along the link above the pin bore. With both tools, measure and record the smallest dimension.

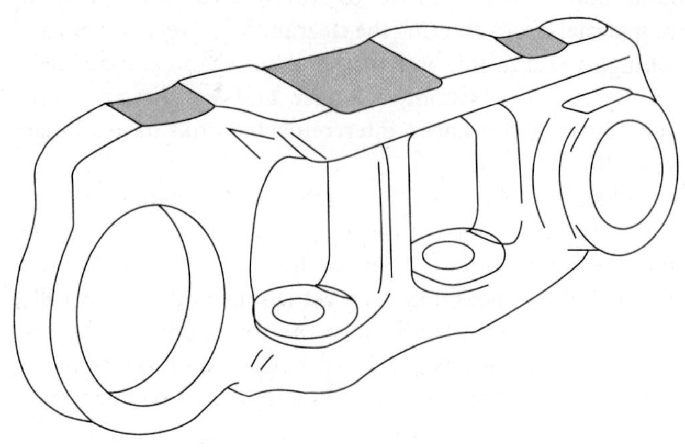

FIGURE 42-46 Scallop wear patterns are caused by contact of different track parts with the link. The thin end will wear due to contact with the rollers, and the thicker middle section wears from contact with the large flange of the idler.

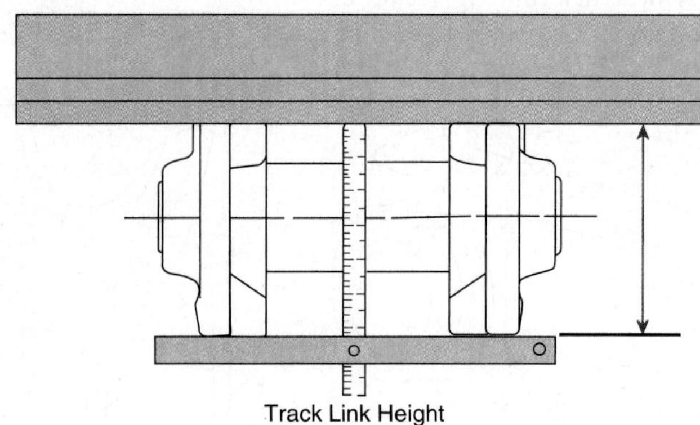

Machine Model	New		Wear Percentage							
			25%		50%		75%		100%	
	mm	in	mm	in	mm	in	mm	in	mm	in
	76	3.00	**75.2**	2.95	**74**	2.90	**72.8**	2.87	**71**	2.79
A	**76.2**	3.00	**75.3**	2.95	**74**	2.90	**72.5**	2.85	**70.5**	2.78
B	**81.3**	3.20	**80.2**	3.15	**79**	3.10	**77.5**	3.04	**75.5**	2.96
C	**85.7**	3.37	**84.5**	3.32	**83**	3.26	**81.2**	3.20	**79**	3.10
	97.5	3.84	**96.2**	3.78	**94.6**	3.73	**92.6**	3.64	**90**	3.54
	104.8	4.12	**103.2**	4.06	**101.3**	4.00	**99**	3.89	**96**	3.78
	118.1	4.55	**116.6**	4.59	**114.8**	4.53	**112.6**	4.43	**110**	4.32
	101.6	4.00	**100.3**	3.93	**98.8**	3.89	**96.5**	3.79	**94**	3.70
	117.5	4.62	**116**	4.56	**114**	4.48	**111.5**	4.39	**108.5**	4.26
	120.5	4.73	**118.5**	4.67	**116.3**	4.57	**113.5**	4.46	**110.5**	4.34
	117.5	4.62	**116**	4.56	**114.2**	4.50	**112**	4.40	**109.5**	4.31
	122	4.79	**120.5**	4.73	**118.5**	4.67	**116**	4.56	**113**	4.45
	127	5.00	**125**	4.92	**122.5**	4.82	**119.5**	4.70	**116**	4.56
L	**139.7**	5.50	**137.6**	5.41	**134.5**	5.29	**131.5**	5.18	**127.7**	5.03

FIGURE 42-47 Track link height is measured from the track shoe to the top of the rail. A chart with wear limits is used to determine remaining service life.

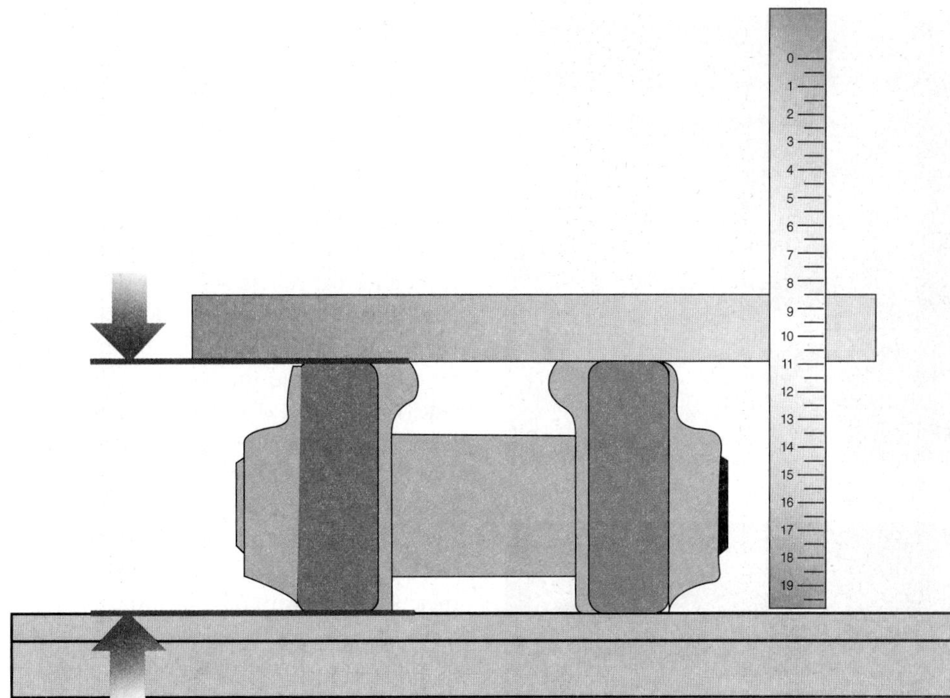

FIGURE 42-48 Measuring link height with a depth gauge and ruler.

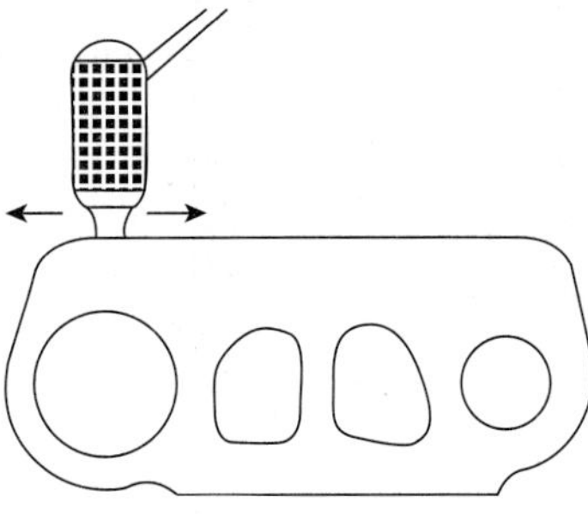

Measuring Track Links

1. Measure distance from tread surface to bushing bore.
2. Place probe over the center line of the bushing.
3. Slide the probe along the tread surface and take the smallest reading.

FIGURE 42-49 Steps involved when measuring link thickness with an ultrasonic tester.

Track Chain Seizure

Sealed track chains may seize if they remain stationary for more than a few days. Seized chains kink, causing the recoil adjuster mechanism to move back and forth each time the kink rotates around the front idler track. Track sag cannot be properly adjusted, and excessive friction resists drive sprocket movement. Kink formation can be prevented by daily moving the machine back and forth 50–100m. If kinks do form due to rusted pins and bushings, it may be possible to loosen the seized track joint by applying penetrating fluid or lubricant to the seized pin, then allowing it to seep into the joint for several hours. Afterward, the machine can be moved back and forth. If penetrating lubricant does not loosen the joint, the seized link can be cut out and replaced with a new repair link having two new links with pins, seals, and bushings. With multiple seized joints on a track chain, track removal is recommended. The track can then be disassembled and the joints repaired using a specialized track press to remove and reinstall pins and bushings after they are cleaned of rust. Note, greased or sealed and lubricated track should never be heated with a torch because the seals will be damaged and the lubricant burned.

▶ TECHNICIAN TIP

Operating a machine on a slope or hill with the same side of the machine facing downhill all the time produces tremendous lateral pressure on roller flanges and links. This means a machine operating on side-hill applications will have the link side working constantly against the roller flanges, which accelerates wear on both the links and on the roller flange Good practice in order to minimize wear uses the machine for half the time with a different side facing down the slope. Similarly, always park the machine on level ground. If parked on an incline or uneven terrain, the roller seals can deform, resulting in lubricant loss (**FIGURE 42-50**). A skilled technician will be able to identify whether a machine is operating incorrectly and make a service recommendation to adjust operating practice.

Roller Wear Measurement

Rollers make direct contact with sliding track chain links. Their work of transmitting machine weight to the track or supporting the upper section of moving track chain is done in the

FIGURE 42-50 A seized upper or carrier roller destroyed the roller shaft.

presence of abrasive and often wet materials. It's not surprising that roller wear takes place rapidly—and unevenly, depending on the operating conditions. In this next section, techniques for inspecting and measuring roller wear are examined to help technicians make sound recommendations for repair and maintenance of rollers.

Evaluating Roller Wear

Upper carrier rollers and lower track rollers wear due to rolling friction as the roller tread, which is the center part of the roller, contacts the chain link rails. As wear increases, the roller diameter becomes smaller, and flanges begin to make contact with the pin and bushing bosses of the track links. To minimize wear and extend service life, the roller shell or case is made of the same hardness of material as the rail. The typical manufacturing procedure involves hot forging medium carbon steel containing various amounts of boron, manganese, chromium, and other hardening alloys, then machining the mating surface. The metal is then either induction hardened or heat treated with a carburizing flame.

Chemical conditions of soils can cause the bottom roller surfaces to corrode, which accelerates the effect on wear due to abrasion. This corrosion cannot be reduced by hardening the steel, so manufactures are experimenting with powder coating rollers with metal alloys made up from at least 60% by weight of iron, cobalt, nickel, or other corrosion-resistant alloys.

Roller wear varies with the position of the roller. For example, upper carrier rollers, which support only the weight of the top section of track, have less wear than the lower rollers, although there are fewer upper rollers in comparison to lower rollers. Depending on the work performed by the machine, front and rear rollers will wear differently if the machine has a bucket or a rear ripper (**FIGURE 42-51**). Either adds more weight to one end of the track. To extend service life, some rollers can be rotated around the track—such as back to front or side to side (**FIGURE 42-52**). However when swapping rollers, the cost of labor must be included into the calculations comparing the cost savings through extending roller service life (**FIGURE 42-53**). An industry rule of thumb suggests roller swapping is economical when the wear percentage of the most worn rollers exceeds the wear percentage of the least worn rollers by a ratio of 1:3. This means a roller with 65% or more wear can be swapped with a roller worn 50% (50% × 1.3 = 65%). Roller swaps should only be considered when the average percentage of wear is between 50% and 60% (**FIGURE 42-54**). Swaps should take place between the most worn and least worn having the same flange type. Next, a swap can take place between the second most worn with the second least worn of same flange type, and so on. Rollers can be interchanged between each side of a machine as well.

A roller that stops rotating due to packing undercarriage will drag along and wear the track chain (**FIGURE 42-55**). Rock guards bolted to the track frame are used to guide track roller and links to help protect rollers from rocks, stones, gravel, and other debris, which can jam rollers and damage track. These guards help prevent track runoff when track sag is excessive.

Measuring Roller Wear

Track roller wear is evaluated using three measurements:

1. Tread diameter
2. Flange height
3. Rim thickness

Carrier roller tread wear can be measured with either a large caliper and steel ruler or an ultrasonic wear indicator. The calipers are positioned so the tips are contacting the tread in its most worn position. Measurements are made to the closest 0.01 inch (0.25 mm) (**FIGURE 42-56**).

When the ultrasonic wear indicator measurement technique is used, special precautions are necessary to prevent interference from the varying thickness of tapered roller bearings inside the rollers. The rim thickness of carrier rollers is measured by sliding the probe around to find the location with the smallest thickness reading. However, the probe should be placed only on the outer half of the tread surface on the side of the roller opposite the roller shaft where the bearing is located.

Track roller wear is difficult to measure because roller guards interfere with access to the rollers.

Terrain Conditions

Working on Sidehill

Shifts weight balance to the downhill side of the machine. This Increases the wear rate on components on the downhill side of the machine. It also increases wear on rail sides, roller and idler flanges, bushing ends, and grouser ends.

Working Downhill

Shifts weight balance forward causing relatively high wear on front track rollers and idlers and on the reverse drive side of the sprocket and bushing.

Working Uphill

Shifts weight balance to the rear causing relatively higher wear on rear track rollers and idlers and on the forward drive side of the sprocket and bushing.

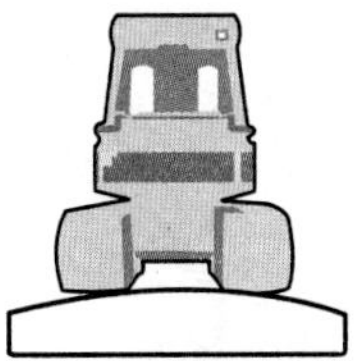

Working on a Crown

The side of components that is nearer the center of the machine carries heavier loads. This results in increased wear on the inside wear surface of links, rollers, idler treads and grouser ends. In extreme cases, the inner bushing-to-sprocket contact surfaces also may experience greater wear.

Working in a Depression

Causes loads to be carried by the side of components that is on the outside of the machine. This increases wear on the outside wear surface of links, rollers, idler treads, and grouser ends. In extreme cases the outer bushing-sprocket contact surfaces also may experience greater wear.

FIGURE 42-51 The operation of the machine produces specific wear patterns in the track components.

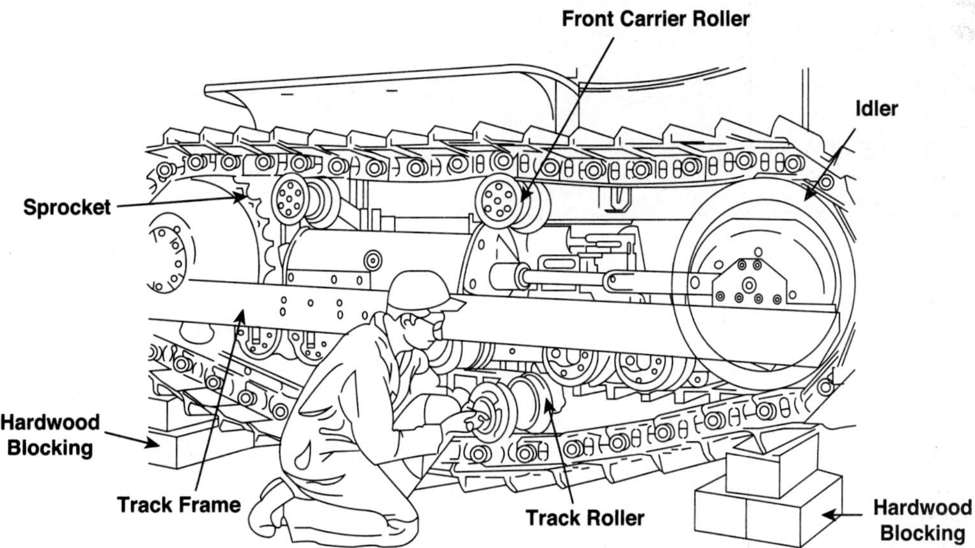

FIGURE 42-52 A roller "swap" can be performed after loosening the track tension, blocking, and supporting the track with blocks. The rollers can be removed because enough track clearance is available.

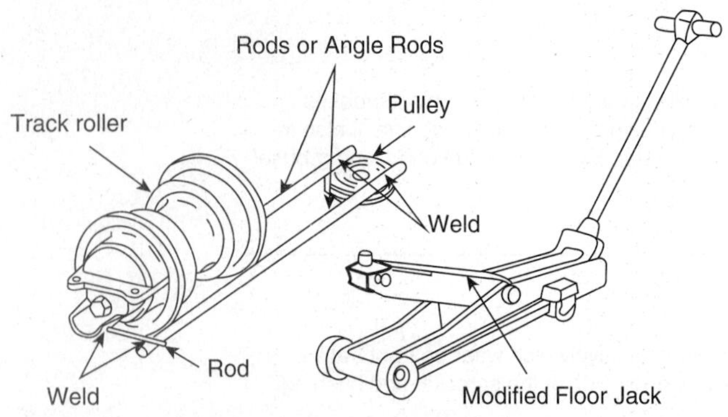

FIGURE 42-53 An example of a purpose-made adapter to be used to remove and reinstall heavier rollers with a floor jack.

FIGURE 42-54 Comparing roller wear of **A.** a double-flange roller to the wear of **B.** a single-flange roller.

To measure roller thread with a caliper, follow the steps in **SKILL DRILL 42-4.**

Ultrasonic Wear Indicator Measurement

The ultrasonic wear indicator measures the depth of the wear surface of the roller to the inside diameter of the roller. It is important *not* to measure tread thickness over the bearing retainer bolt holes of the roller in order to obtain an accurate measurement. On rollers with retaining bolts, note the location of the retainer bolts, and place the probe between the bolts when probing the tread thickness.

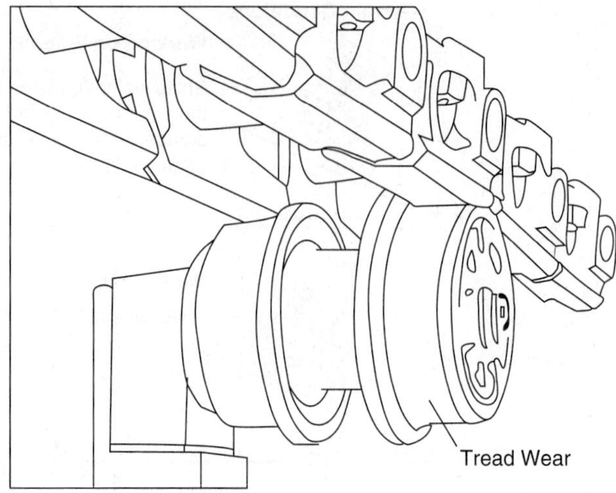

FIGURE 42-55 Tread wear takes place because of rolling and sliding friction of the roller tread against the track link rail.

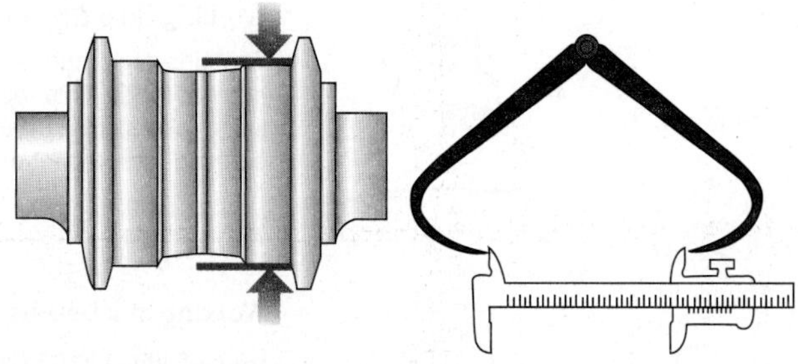

FIGURE 42-56 Measuring a roller with a set of large calibers and a ruler.

▶ TECHNICIAN TIP

Front and Rear Roller Wear

Front and rear rollers typically are most worn and therefore are the most important rollers to measure wear in order to make service decisions. If roller guards interfere with measurement of all bottom rollers, then the rear roller is the most important roller to estimate wear. Next is the front roller. These two rollers should be inspected by whatever method is safely possible.

Idler Wear and Adjustments

Depending on the track design, the equipment can have one or two idlers per track section. Elevated track use two idler wheels—a front and a rear one—whereas conventional oval track use only one. Idlers function to guide the track through track rollers while supporting some of the machine's

SKILL DRILL 42-4 Caliper Measurement of Roller Tread

1. Remove the track guards, if necessary, and clean all track components with a pressure washer.
2. Using a pair of large calipers, position the caliper tips so they are touching the tread in its most worn position on the tread diameter.
3. Move the caliper back and forth across the tread to determine an accurate minimum diameter.
4. Measure and record the tread thickness while noting the roller position.

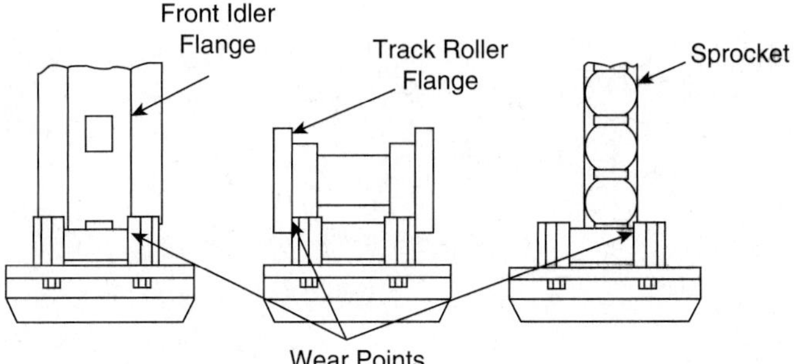

FIGURE 42-57 Points of wear when the idler is not properly centered and aligned.

weight. This means idler alignment is critical to proper track operation. Front idler misalignment will accelerate wear on all track components. Technicians can inspect for alignment by observing the wear patterns on the bottom rollers, carrier rollers, and front idlers. Edge wear takes place on these parts when the idler is not running parallel with the track (**FIGURE 42-57**). Technicians can also can stand at the front and rear of the machine and carefully observe to inspect whether the idler is parallel with the track and track frame. This means track idlers must align in exactly the same direction as track to prevent wear of other undercarriage components (**FIGURE 42-58**).

Oval track machines may have a two-position idler, with one position raising the idler higher, such as when a drawbar is used. In these circumstances, the area of track in contact with the ground is reduced, which in turn, results in less track wear. If heavy working attachments are connected to the front of the machine, the idler position can be lowered to place more track in contact with the ground for better machine balance and weight distribution. Increased track footprint improves machine stability but causes more track wear.

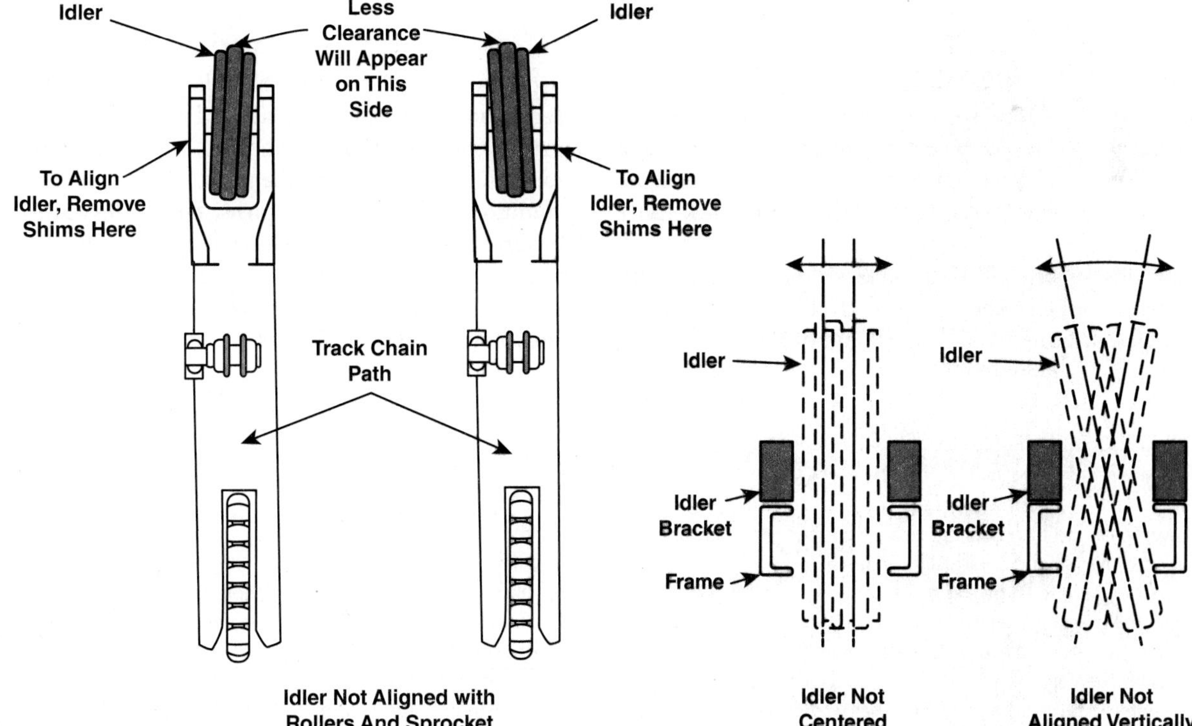

FIGURE 42-58 Idler adjustments are performed to ensure the flange is centered and parallel with the track.

Idler Wear Measurement Technique

The difference between tread and center flange height are positions on idlers to measure wear. Tread wear is evaluated by using a depth gauge to measure from the idler center flange to the tread surface. An average depth taken from both sides of the center tread is reported. Idler tread wear depth increases as tread wear takes place and decreases as center flange wear occurs. If the idler wear on the center flange has taken place on a conventional idler, it will distort the reference point. If it is suspected that center flange wear has taken place, some correction can be made to compensate for the wear. Measurement of wear depth on the tread surface is done first; then center flange wear is added to the depth gauge measurement before determining percent worn.

Center flange wear on solid steel idlers cannot be measured using an ultrasonic wear indicator because there is no ability to measure the depth differences in the solid structure. An ultrasonic wear indicator can be used on some fabricated types of idlers only. This tool measures the thickness of the center flange and should be taken directly over the metal band attached to the idler wheel (**FIGURE 42-59**).

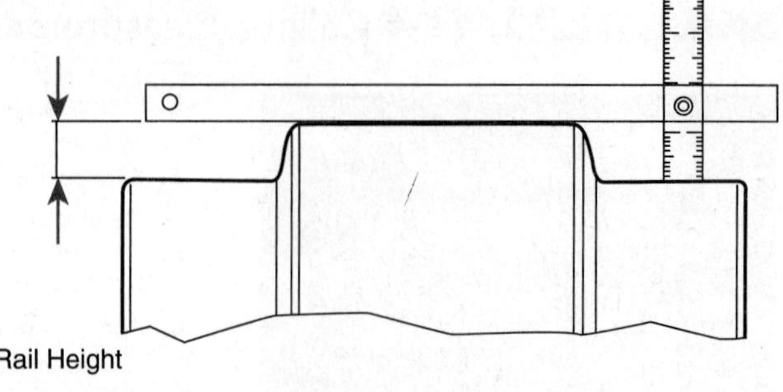

FIGURE 42-59 Measuring the idler flange height with a protrusion gauge and ruler.

Idler tread and center flanges can be successfully rebuilt by welding and machining to original diameter if they are not worn beyond service limits.

The following check is for an oval track Caterpillar System One undercarriage that uses center tread idler with track.

The Caterpillar System One undercarriage requires shim adjustment when the wear on the track links and the roller system is at 25%, 50%, and 75%. The shim adjustment lowers the idler to compensate for wear on the idler and track chain.

To adjust front idler height, follow the steps in **SKILL DRILL 42-5**.

Idler Centering Adjustment

After adjusting or checking idler height, measure the gap between the idler side shims and the idler block. The same number of shims on both the left and right side must be installed so the idler will remain centered in the track roller frame (**FIGURE 42-60**).

FIGURE 42-60 Shims located beneath the bearing block on either side of the idler are used to adjust idler alignment.

Add shims to both side shim packs until the total amount of gap between the block and idler on each side is even, which is typically between 4 mm (0.160") and 8 mm (0.320").

Track Shoe Wear and Replacement

Two wear points of a track shoe limiting service life are the track plates and grousers. Plate and grouser wear is caused by normal contact with the ground. Although underfoot conditions influence shoe wear the most, it is excessive **slipping**—a condition where the track turns, but no forward or reverse movement takes place—that leads to accelerated wear. Hard ground or rocky conditions increase grouser wear. Severe-service shoes with thicker plates can extend shoe life. These shoes have additional plate hardness and thicker grouser bars.

SKILL DRILL 42-5 Adjusting Front Idler Height

1. Power wash the track with a pressure washer.
2. Park the machine on a hard, flat surface.
3. Raise the blade to 3" off the ground.
4. Move the machine in reverse until a track shoe grouser bar is directly below the center of the front idler shaft.
5. Measure the height from the flat ground surface to the grouser tip centered below the track idler shaft. Compare this distance with specifications. A typical specification is a clearance between the grouser and ground ranging from 0.5 mm (0") to a maximum of 4 mm (0.160").
6. If the grouser height is not acceptable, relocate idler shims to the lower the idler. For example, move a 4.5 mm (0.180") shim from the bottom of the idler bearing block, and relocate it to the top of the block. After the idler is lowered, reinspect the shim adjustment after moving the 4.5 mm (0.180") shim.

It is important to note that the correct selection of shoe type and width has a major impact on the service life of other track components. The tendency is to use wider track shoes because they provide better flotation or lower ground pressure to work in both hard and softer underfoot conditions. Shoe width has a substantial influence on wear rates, with the use of too wide a shoe causing increased bending stress on shoes and track linkage. Bending stress increases proportionately with shoe width, as wider shoes lengthen the mechanical leverage of bending stress against track parts. Most affected is the track pin and bushing joint, which flexes more with wider shoes. A wide shoe shortens the service life of pins and bushing seals, leading to loss of lubricant because the joint tends to "open up," or loosen, as clearance in the joint increases. Track links crack more easily; roller flange wear increases; and bushing wear accelerates with wider shoe width. Wide track shoes can increase turning resistance, making the machine difficult to maneuver. Shoes will crack, bend, and have loosening hardware issues as shoe width increases (**FIGURE 42-61**). Track specialists' rule of thumb for shoes is to specify the narrowest shoe possible that will provide adequate flotation or ground pressure that prevents a machine from sinking in underfoot conditions, and provide traction without excessive track slippage.

To replace track bushings or other components, it is necessary to separate the track. A master pin located in the track is the point to separate track requiring service. When separating track, it cannot be emphasized enough to follow all manufacturer guidelines and recommended procedure, as steel track is very heavy and can cause not only body damage but also lethal crush injuries.

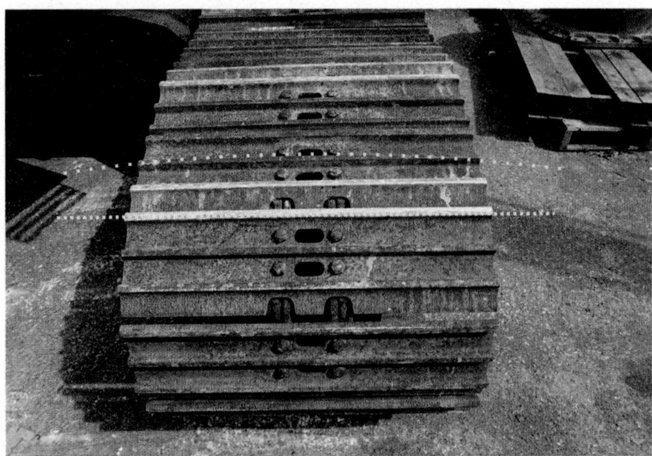

FIGURE 42-61 Excavator track shoes can bend easily because they are wider. Although these shoes are fine, a dotted red line shoes the direction bent shoes will take.

To separate steel track, follow the steps in **SKILL DRILL 42-6**.

Track Shoe Measurement Technique

Track shoe wear is evaluated by measuring grouser bar height and plate thickness (**FIGURE 42-62**). The dimensions are measured with either a T-bar type of depth gauge or an ultrasonic wear indicator. When using the ultrasonic wear indicator, it should measure the distance from the tip of the grouser to the bottom of the shoe plate. Measurements are made one-third of the way in from the outer edge of the shoe, and the probe can be moved along either on the top or bottom of the shoe.

SKILL DRILL 42-6 Separating Steel Track

1. Position the tracked machine on a hard level surface, with sufficient room to work.
2. Loosen track by releasing grease from track adjuster or idler. Most machines have a separate pressure release valve. Extremely pressurized grease released from the fitting may cause bodily damage and death.
3. Locate the master pin. Master pins often have a dimple machined into the end of the pin.
4. Move the machine to position the master pin about 20–30 degrees from the vertical center line of the front idler. At the same time, block the track just under the idler high enough to keep the track from falling to the ground when the master track pin is removed.
5. Remove two pads, one on each side of the master pin.
6. If the pin is retained by a snap ring, remove the snap ring.
7. Select the correct anvil for the size of pin being pressed.
8. If using a portable hydraulic press, follow the manufacturer's setup procedures, and center the press over the master pin, with the press's hydraulic cylinder aligned in parallel with the link and pin. The press anvil should also be centered over the pin at the opposite end.
9. Begin pressing out the track pin with a starter pin, and close any protective cage to surround the pin and bushing assembly. When pressing out a pin, always stay away from the exit area until pin is fully removed.
10. Severely rusted pins may require the link to be heated to get them started.
11. After the pin is removed, pull the two ends of the track together with a chain puller, choker chains, or purpose-made straps while the track is separated.
12. Realign the bores of the links with a pry bar or chain puller when reinstalling a master pin.
13. When installing the pin, the master pin is correctly in place if there is approximately 1/8" of the pin extending out of each side of the link.

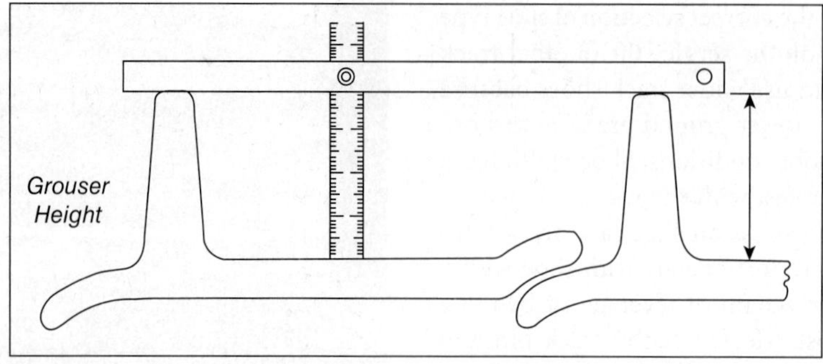

Shoe Part No.	New Shoe mm	Wear Percentage 25%	50%	75%	100%
		mm			
SBG 505	43.0	41	39.5	38	36.5
SBG 510	47.0	45.5	44	42.5	41
SBG 014	52	50.5	49.0	47.5	46.0
SBG 070	55.5	54.0	52.5	51.00	49.5

FIGURE 42-62 Measuring a single-grouser bar shoe.

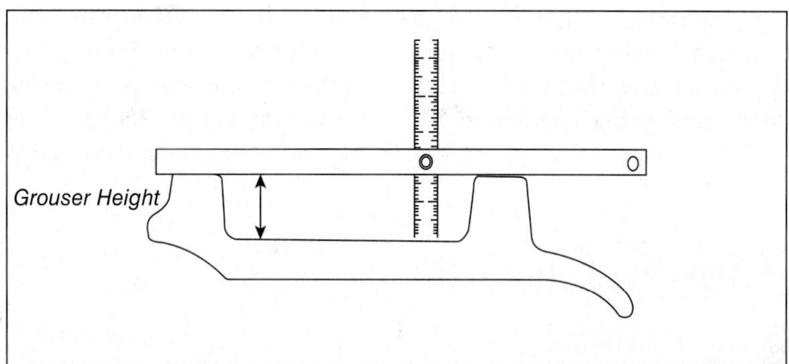

Shoe Part No.	New Shoe mm	Wear Percentage 25%	50%	75%	100%
		mm			
DBG 014	30.0	29.2	28.4	27.6	26.7
DBG 020	31.0	30.7	30.4	30.1	29.7
DBG 026	34.5	33.9	33.3	32.7	32.0
DBG 070	35.0	34.4	33.8	33.2	32.5

FIGURE 42-63 Measuring a double-grouser bar shoe.

When measuring grouser height on double grouser and triple grouser shoes, the rear grouser is not measured because it is not representative of shoe thickness because of a thinner trailing edge (**FIGURES 42-63** and **42-64**). With shoes that have had the grouser rebuilt by welding, the ultrasonic tester may measure only the thickness of the original grouser bar (**FIGURE 42-65**).

When measuring with a depth gauge, the bar is set across two adjacent grousers, and measurement is made to the plate.

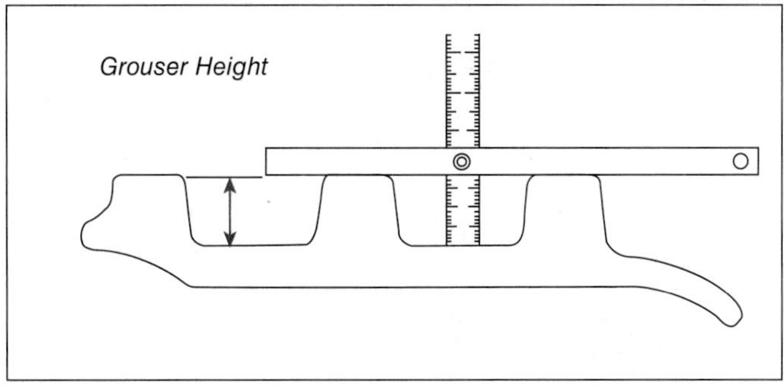

Shoe Part No.	New Shoe mm	Wear Percentage			
		25%	50%	75%	100%
		mm			
TBG 010	14	13.5	13.1	12.6	12.2
TBG 5L5	14	13.5	12.9	12.4	11.8
TBG 505	18	17.4	16.8	16.2	15.6
TBG 510	22	21.2	20.4	19.6	18.8
TBG 014	25	24.2	23.4	22.6	21.8
TBG 020	25.3	25	24.7	24.4	24.1
TBG 070	26	25.4	24.8	24.2	23.6
TBG 026	26.5	25.9	25.3	24.7	24.1
TBG 027	26.5	25.9	25.3	24.7	24.1
TBG 080	30	29.3	28.5	27.8	27

FIGURE 42-64 Measuring a triple-grouser bar shoe.

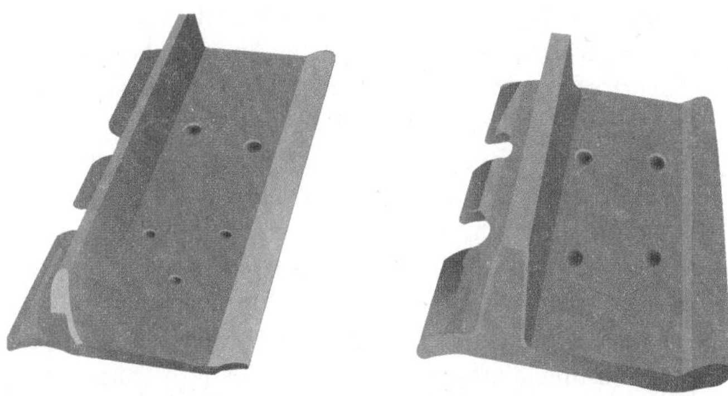

FIGURE 42-65 An extreme-service shoe is much thicker than a moderate-service shoe.

Again, the position of the depth gauge should be one-third of the way in from the outer edge of the shoe. When measuring single grousers, two shoes are spanned with the T-bar over a straight section of track. Plate thickness is also measured and compared with the new dimension to determine wear.

Shoes must be cleaned before measuring, and measurement must not be made over areas where the shoe is chipped. The difference between the actual height and 0% wear limit is obtained by subtracting the actual dimension from the wear limit dimension. The result is then divided by a wear factor and reported as a percentage.

Track shoes are bolted to the links using special hardware (**FIGURE 42-66**). Bent or damaged shoes can be replaced individually as needed (**FIGURE 42-67**). It is important to replace bent shoes quickly, as the stress of a bent shoe is transmitted to the surrounding shoes, causing them to bend as well. The primary cause of loose shoes is improperly tightened shoe hardware. Technicians must follow OEM instructions for assembly, torque sequence, and other procedures for periodic retightening of track shoe bolts.

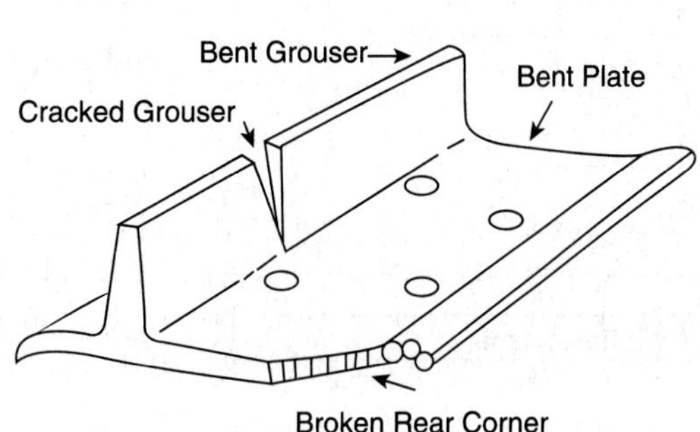

FIGURE 42-66 Inspection points of a track shoe indicating a mismatch between the shoe and operating conditions.

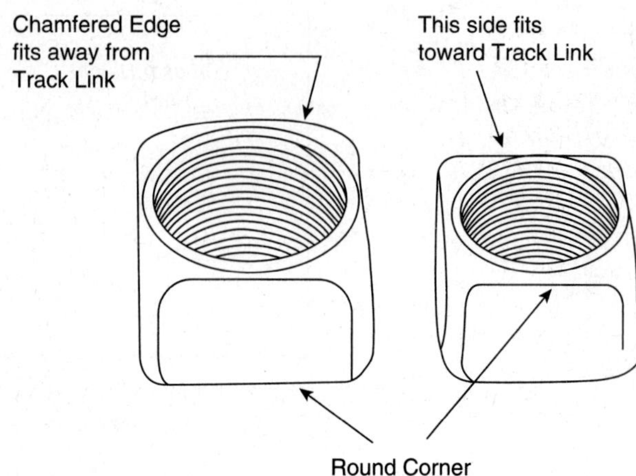

FIGURE 42-67 Track nuts have a chamfered edge that must be installed toward the track link. If the sharper edge is installed toward the link, vibration and movement in the bolts will loosen the nuts.

SKILL DRILL 42-7 Replacing Track Shoe

1. Remove all rust and paint from mating surfaces of links and shoes, to obtain accurate preload of bolts.
2. Lubricate the bolt threads and bolt washer faces.
3. Install nuts with the chamfered face away from the track links.
4. Tighten the bolts to the specified torque.
5. Turn each bolt an additional one-third turn to apply a proper preload or bolt stretch to ensure proper retention and adequate clamping force.

To replace the track shoe, follow the steps in **SKILL DRILL 42-7**.

▶ Track Technician Consultation

K42004

Although a track technician makes observations during an inspection, data about track and other machine conditions should be recorded for reference when conferring with the equipment owner or to make service recommendations. A technician should be capable of outlining options for maintenance or replacement procedures, based on a through track inspection. An analysis of wear patterns should also provide the data necessary to advise machine operators to change operating practices in order to extend service life of track components.

Common repair options for track systems include the following:

- Bushing turns on wet or sealed-type track joints. These may be done in the field or the track may be removed and a bushing turn performed in a specialized shop.
- Roller reshelling of worn rollers, which involves replacing the roller shell or case with a service part where available and if it is economical to do so.
- Roller swapping is performed when rollers are worn at least more than 50%. The most worn roller is switched with the roller with the least amount of wear. The second most worn roller is switched with the roller with the second least amount of wear, and so on.
- Idler resurfacing is a rebuild procedure where the worn idler surfaces are welded and the part is remachined to original dimensions. The bearings are also replaced, and the idler returned to service.
- Track shoe regrousering is a procedure where the track shoe grouser bars are welded and machined to return the shoe to original dimensions. Shoe rebuilding is performed at a much lower cost than replacement with a new shoe.
- Track frame rebuilds are performed in specialty shops where the entire frame is removed, cleaned, sandblasted, and inspected for cracks. Any replaceable parts, such as rollers, links, track shoes, and all pin bushings or bearings, are replaced or rebuilt and reinstalled. The entire is returned to service for much shorter machine turnaround time.
- Sprocket or segment replacement is performed whenever the sprocket drive is worn. Often the replacement is performed in the field at the same time when bushing turns are done, or track chain is replaced to reduce wear when mismatched parts are assembled together.
- Chain replacement is performed whenever the pin-to-bushing joints are damaged or excessively worn. A new or completely rebuilt chain is installed that has new or reconditioned links and new bushings, pins, and seals.

Operating Practices

Operating practices impact track wear characteristics and can substantially reduce the service life of track components. Technicians should familiarize themselves with wear patterns

TABLE 42-2 The Type of Soil Influences Track Wear Rate

	Description	Soil Type
High-abrasive soil	Saturated wet soil containing a majority of hard, angular or sharp sand particles	Wet sand, sea sand, wet clay
Medium-abrasive soil	Slightly damp soil containing low portion of hard, angular or sharp particles	Dry clay
Low-abrasive soil	Dry soil or rock containing a very low portion of hard, angular sharp sand	Soil rich in lime

having the most significant impact on wear rates (**TABLE 42-2**). The following are typical operating practices that are correctable or controllable and dramatically influence track life:

1. Machine travel speed and direction of travel influence wear rates and impact damage from shock loading increase. Likewise friction increases exponentially, and the amount of wear is far greater over the same distance traveled when a machine travels at higher speeds. As noted earlier, high speed and reverse traveling are especially damaging to track bushings and sprocket teeth. Technicians should encourage operators travel in the forward position, with the sprockets at the rear end of the machine, and limit nonproductive, high-speed travel, particularly in reverse, to extend undercarriage service life and reduced operating costs.

   Tracked excavators sometimes travel continuously, which can cause heat buildup inside the track roller and idlers. In these cases, heat will damage seals inside rollers and idlers and eventually cause oil leakage. Operators should avoid continuous traveling on hard or uneven ground for more than half an hour and on moderate flat ground for more than 2 hours. Pausing to allow track components to cool will extend component life.
2. Increased turning frequency produces high lateral load forces between track links and rollers, idlers, and sprockets. This especially affects the track link rail side, roller flanges, and idler flange. The effects of constantly turning in one direction should be avoided by taking larger gradual turns, and balanced by changing the turning direction from one side to the other side when turning the machine. When turning using hydrostatic drive systems, use both tracks, as applying power to only one track causes the opposite track to drag, increasing component wear.
3. The profile of the terrain also influences wear life. Working on a crown places the load of machine weight on the inner ends of the track shoes. This in turn transfers the load to the inside of track links, roller, idler tread surfaces, bushing ends, and sprocket contact areas. Similarly working in a depression places the load of machine weight on the outer ends of the track shoes. Machine weight is unequally supported by the outside track links, outside roller, idler tread surfaces, bushing outside ends, and sprocket contact areas. Continual work in a depression accelerates wear on the outer track link surfaces, just as working continually on a crown increases wear on the inside track link surfaces. Too wide a shoe exaggerates the effects of unequal loads even more.
4. Use track guards selectively. Full-length rock guards are not required in normal working conditions and can in fact trap more dirt between the rollers and track chain. However, using rock guards while working in rocky material prevents larger rock and material from packing or getting caught between the sprocket teeth and track bushings or between the track links and idler tread. Rock guards also help prevent track runoff in extreme hillside work by guiding the track movement.
5. Track slippage and spinning accelerate track shoe grouser wear and reduces productive work. Heavy contact between the sprocket teeth and track bushings, between the track links and rollers, and between idler tread surfaces accelerates wear.
6. Perform regular maintenance by daily inspecting the undercarriage. Track should be cleaned at the end of each working day, and the track tension regularly checked. Soil condition influences wear rates, depending on its abrasiveness and chemical properties (**TABLE 42-3**).

TABLE 42-3 Abnormal Wear Patterns and Operating Complaints for Steel Track Drives

Problem	Possible Cause
Accelerated wear is on one side of the final drive sprocket teeth.	• Track misalignment • Loose track • Sprocket misalignment due to improper installation
Accelerated wear is on one side of the idler(s) or rollers.	• Track misalignment • Idler misalignment due to improper installation
There is accelerated wear to track pins, bushings, and track links.	• Track adjustment too tight • Misaligned track • Excessively worn sprocket teeth • Excessive high-speed operation
There is excessive wear to the final drive bearing.	• Track adjustment too tight • Misaligned track

(Continued)

TABLE 42-3 Abnormal Wear Patterns and Operating Complaints for Steel Track Drives (Continued)

Problem	Possible Cause
Operator complains of loss of drawbar power.	• Improper track adjustment • Track adjustment too tight
Operator complains that the dozer drifts either to the right or left while being driven in a straight direction.	• Improper track adjustment • One track is tighter than the other • Track misalignment
There is frequent packing of the track during operation.	• Improper track adjustment • Track adjusted too loose
The track is noisy during operation.	• Improper track adjustment • Track adjustment too loose
The track whips excessively during operation.	• Improper track adjustment • Track adjusted too loosely • Idler seized in the retracted position
The track is thrown off during operation.	• Improper track adjustment • Track adjustment too loose

Wrap-Up

Ready for Review

- Fifty percent of the machine's initial value is spent repairing and maintaining track over a typical lifecycle. Track drive systems account for 20% of a machine's purchase price.
- Maintenance variables under the technician's control that influence wear rates include track tension adjustment, alignment of undercarriage components, machine weight balance, and appropriate matching of machine parts such as track shoe type and shoe width to working conditions.
- Variables affecting track wear that are out of the technician's control include worksite conditions such as soil type and condition—whether the soil is abrasive, hard or soft, rocky, muddy, corrosive, or wet.
- Three types of friction encountered by track components are rolling friction such as between rollers and idlers moving across chain rails; rotating friction that takes place between track pins and bushings; and sliding friction that takes place between bushings and drive sprocket teeth.
- Internal pin and bushing wear is produced by the rotating friction between the inside diameter of the bushing and the outside diameter of the pin as they both rotate around the sprocket and idler wheel.
- The least amount of track wear takes place during forward machine movement, and the most amount of wear takes place during reverse machine movement.
- Track pin-to-bushing joints make four bending motions per track revolution in either a reverse or a forward direction.
- During reverse machine travel, the transfer of drive torque into the chain takes place at the top of the sprocket, or the 12 o'clock position. Reverse drive increases wear because 75% of track pins and bushings joints are under tension. During reverse drive conditions, torque transmits through the track all the way from the bushing at the top of the sprocket, around the front idler, and finally to track shoes in contact with the ground.
- Less than a third of the track is under tension during forward machine travel.
- Bushings that have substantial external wear are good indicators that track also has internal wear and is nearing the end of its service life.
- Lubricated and greased pins are more durable, but internal wear takes place in all pins and bushings.
- A measurement between track pin centers, known as track pitch, is an important indicator of track pin-to-bushing wear. The track chain lengthens with increased wear. Because wear is also internal and not immediately visible, it's observed by measuring a change in the track length. Increasingly, worn clearances between pin and bushings surface allow the distance between pin centers to lengthen as wear progresses.
- When track pitch length becomes excessive, which is ascertained after comparing worn dimensions to OEM specifications, the track is at the end of its service life and should be rebuilt or replaced.
- Track pitch is measured with a ruler or measuring tape after tensioning the upper section of track chain.
- Because pitch extension allows the track to lengthen, an increase in the amount of track sag will become evident with increasing wear.
- If track is allowed to become too loose and excessively sag, track becomes snake-like in operation and causes a number of track problems. Loose track allows the machine to move or twist back and back-and-forth, resulting in steering instability. Loose track allows the track to run off the rollers or throw the track.

- Modern hydrostatic drive machines that enable operators to rapidly turn in a small radius also allow machines to more easily throw loose track. Elevated sprocket design minimizes the problem of thrown track because the track remains relatively tight between two idler wheels.
- Loose track can also prevent proper engagement of bushings with the drive sprocket, allowing bushings to climb or skip sprocket teeth, which causes reverse tip wear. Popping and loud banging sounds originate from track as drive sprocket teeth and the space between bushings prevents proper synchronization of contact. Track also drags along the frame and whips at higher travel speeds.
- Packing, the condition where mud, snow, and debris stick to track components and sprockets, can excessively tighten track.
- Excessively tight tracks increase wear up to 50%. Tight tracks also rob a machine of useful horsepower and increase fuel consumption.
- Track sag is adjustable by releasing or adding grease to a track tensioning mechanism.
- When adjusting track sag using the grease-type track tensioner, never directly visually inspect the vent holes or valves on the tensioner to see whether grease or oil is coming out of them. High-pressure grease can easily penetrate skin and cause severe personal injury.
- Root and radial wear of a sprocket are interchangeable terms given to describe sprocket tooth wear caused by the twisting motion and sliding friction of bushings in sprocket teeth produced by either reverse or forward drive wear.
- Forward drive side wear is created by sprocket and bushing contact on the forward side of the sprocket tooth.
- A sprocket tooth that is not symmetrically worn or that has more root wear on the reverse drive side of the tooth indicates excessive reverse drive cycle operation. This wear is even more exaggerated if travel speed is high and the machine loaded, or productive in reverse.
- Reverse tip wear occurs during forward travel when the sprocket teeth make direct contact with the track bushings rather than the gap between the bushings. This condition is caused by a mismatch between the sprocket teeth spacing and the gap between the track bushings.
- Sprocket wear that forms a pocket on the reverse drive side of the tooth is called reverse rotational wear and is different from reverse drive wear that simply wears one side of the sprocket tooth. Both reverse drive and rotational wear are evident together, but rotational wear does not always appear with reverse drive wear because it is the more severe of the two wear patterns.
- Side wear, also called corner gouging of sprocket teeth, is caused by contact of the sides of sprocket teeth with track links, which in turn is caused by misalignment between the drive sprocket and track. A second cause of side tooth wear is misalignment between the track frame and sprocket.
- Track frames are required to operate parallel to each other and the machine. If alignment is not within specification, the sprocket that is attached to the machine and not the track frame will operate at an angle to the sprocket.
- When track frames are rebuilt, they are inspected for straightness. On larger track frames, the concentricity or alignment of the pivot shaft bore with the frame should be inspected during rebuild.
- The term "wear factor" is useful when making determinations about replacement or providing inspection reports. A component's wear factor is important for calculating the exact percentage of remaining service life and varies for each component. A wear factor is based on the depth of component hardening.
- Ultrasonic wear indicators are primarily used for measuring the thickness of steel. Like a sonar or radar, the device calculates the difference between the time required for the sound to travel through the part and to reflect back again, to measure the part's thickness. The inspection tool can be used to measure thickness of other materials like aluminum, plastic, copper, and glass.
- Techniques used to measure track wear include:
  - Ultrasonic wear indicator method
  - Caliper method
  - Depth gauge method
- Rather than replace worn track pins and bushings, track service life is extended by removing the bushings and turning them both 180 degrees to reorientate worn internal and external pin-to-bushing surfaces.
- The technique of rotating pins and bushing 180 degrees is called "turning" and places an unworn internal bushing diameter against the unworn track pin, and an unworn external surface against the sprocket drive teeth. Turning bushings restores track pitch to its original length and extends undercarriage service life by deferring chain link replacement until slower wearing links and rollers need service.
- With SAGT, service life is approximately 20–40% longer than sealed (nonlubricated) track chain.
- Top rail wear is accelerated by increased machine weight and ground conditions such as the degree of soil abrasiveness or chemical action of the soil.
- Track link heights are measured using a depth gauge or with an ultrasonic wear indicator.
- Track roller wear is evaluated using three measurements:
  - Tread diameter
  - Flange height
  - Rim thickness
- Idlers function to guide the track through track rollers while supporting some of the machine's weight. This means idler alignment is critical to proper track operation. Front idler misalignment accelerates wear on all track components. Tread wear of an idler wheel is evaluated by using a depth gauge to measure from the idler center flange to the tread surface.
- Two wear points of a track shoe limiting service life are the track plates and grousers. Excessive slipping—a condition where the track turns, but no forward or reverse movement takes place—leads to accelerated wear.

- Wider track shoes increase track stress on track parts. Bending stress increases proportionately with shoe width as wider shoes lengthen the mechanical leverage of bending stress against track parts. Most affected is the track pin and bushing joint, which flexes more with wider shoes.
- Shoes will crack, bend, and have loosening hardware issues as shoe width increases. Track specialists' rule of thumb for shoes is to specify the narrowest shoe possible that will provide adequate flotation or ground pressure that prevents a machine from sinking in underfoot conditions, and provide traction without excessive track slippage.
- Track shoe wear is evaluated by measuring grouser bar height and plate thickness. The dimensions are measured with either a T-bar type of depth gauge or an ultrasonic wear indicator.

Key Terms

destruction point Wear condition reached when the component is most likely to break or completely fail. The point of destruction is considered to be 120% wear. This is 20% more than the maximum limit of wear when component replacement is required.

forward drive side wear Produced by sprocket and bushing contact on the forward side of the drive sprocket tooth.

interconnected-type track links A category of links using a track bushing have a second precision counterbore machined into the link, allowing the bushing to protrude further into the link to help seal the leak path into the pin-to-bushing clearance.

reverse drive wear Wear formed on the reverse side of the drive sprocket, produced during reverse drive cycles. Reverse drive wear may form a pocket on the reverse drive side of the tooth.

reverse rotational wear Wear on the drive sprocket, but different from reverse drive wear in that the wear is only on one side of the sprocket tooth.

reverse tip wear Wear occurring during forward travel when the sprocket teeth tips make direct contact with the track bushings rather than the gap between the bushings.

rolling friction Resistance encountered between parts that roll against one another. An example of rolling friction is the movement of track rollers and idlers across chain rails formed by the track links or segments.

rotating friction Resistance between a stationary component and a rotating component. An example of rotating friction is track pins and bushings. The bushings turn to enable the track chain and shoes to bend while the pin remains stationary in the link.

side wear of a drive sprocket Caused by contact of the sides of sprocket teeth with track links; also called corner gouging of sprocket teeth.

sliding friction Resistance between two components moving across one another or one component being dragged across a stationary component.

slipping A track operating condition where the track turns, but no forward or reverse movement takes place. Slipping leads to accelerated wear.

track sag The distance measured between the lowest and highest points of the top of the track.

wear factor A number used to calculate the percentage of component service life remaining. It is based on the depth of hardening of a component.

Review Questions

1. Which of the following variables contributing to track wear is under the control of a technician?
   a. Soil conditions
   b. Machine balance
   c. How the machine is operated
   d. Track tension
2. Under which of the following conditions are track components under tension?
   a. Reverse drive operation up a hill
   b. Forward drive operation on a flat grade
   c. Side slope work
   d. Working in a gully or on a high crown
3. Which of the following changes takes place when track pitch increases?
   a. Track sag decreases.
   b. Track length increases.
   c. The distance between track pins shortens.
   d. There is increased packing.
4. Which of the following changes takes place when pin-to-bushing wear increases?
   a. Track pitch lengthens.
   b. Track packing increases.
   c. There is increase in track tension.
   d. There is little to no track sag.
5. Which of the following tools is best used to measure track sag?
   a. An ultrasonic wear indicator
   b. A caliper and measuring tape
   c. A micrometer and dial indicator
   d. A straight edge and measuring ruler
6. Which of the following procedures is best used to decrease track tension?
   a. Release grease from a track tension mechanism.
   b. Perform a pin and bushing turn.
   c. Shim the idler wheel.
   d. Replace worn track links.
7. Which of the following is observed of track drives during forward machine travel?
   a. The upper section of track is under tension.
   b. Increased track component wear takes place compared to other operating conditions.
   c. The bottom section of track nearest the drive sprocket is under tension.
   d. A slight vertical angle is formed between the top and bottom of the track.

8. A new track shoe grouser has 1.00" thickness. At 0% service life, it has a thickness of 0.50". If the grouser bar is measured to have 0.75" thickness, what is its remaining service life?
   a. 20%
   b. 40%
   c. 50%
   d. 75%
9. After servicing a SALT-type track pin, a vacuum pump is used to perform a test. During the test, the vacuum pump is shut off, and the vacuum gauge does not change after waiting for several minutes. Which of the following best explains this condition?
   a. There is a leak in a seal around the track pin.
   b. The bushing is worn,
   c. The rubber plug in the track pin is missing,
   d. There are no leak paths between the pin and bushing for fluid to leak out of the joint.
10. What is the most likely cause of a thrown track?
   a. The track is packed with dirt and debris.
   b. The track is too tight.
   c. Track sag is excessive.
   d. Track links are excessively worn.

ASE Technician A/Technician B Style Questions

1. Technician A says that track drive undercarriage accounts for 20% of the purchase cost of a machine. Technician B says that track is very expensive to maintain, adding up to 50% of the machines initial cost over the life of the equipment. Who is correct?
   a. Technician A
   b. Technician B
   c. Both A and B
   d. Neither A nor B
2. A loud popping and banging sound is originating from one side of a steel track. Technician A says it is likely caused by a worn sprocket tooth. Technician B says it is likely the sprocket tooth tip contacting the bushing rather than the tooth entering between the track bushings. Who is correct?
   a. Technician A
   b. Technician B
   c. Both A and B
   d. Neither A nor B
3. Technician A says that link height is the most critical factor limiting track chain service. Technician B says that track pitch is the best indicator of track wear. Who is correct?
   a. Technician A
   b. Technician B
   c. Both A and B
   d. Neither A nor B
4. While inspecting for possible causes for an operator complaint that a crawler tractor machine is difficult to turn and maneuver, Technician A says the most likely cause is tight track. Technician B says that loose track makes a machine more difficult to turn. Who is correct?
   a. Technician A
   b. Technician B
   c. Both A and B
   d. Neither A nor B
5. While inspecting track rollers, Technician A says that the top rollers supporting the track will have more wear because there are fewer top than bottom rollers. Technician B says that most wear takes place on the bottom rollers because they support the machine's weight. Who is correct?
   a. Technician A
   b. Technician B
   c. Both A and B
   d. Neither A nor B
6. While examining excessive side tooth wear of a drive sprocket, Technician A says that it is likely due to a misaligned or bent track frame. Technician B says that the drive sprocket is not shimmed correctly. Who is correct?
   a. Technician A
   b. Technician B
   c. Both A and B
   d. Neither A nor B
7. To evaluate the remaining service life of a drive sprocket, Technician A says the distance between three sprocket teeth should be measured with a ruler or measuring tape and compared with specifications. Technician B says that tooth wear patterns indicate remaining service life. Who is correct?
   a. Technician A
   b. Technician B
   c. Both A and B
   d. Neither A nor B
8. To achieve the lowest cost per hour of machine operation, Technician A says that component wear is allowed to run to its destruction point of 120% wear. Technician B says that components should be replaced as close to 100% wear as possible, to reduce operating costs. Who is correct?
   a. Technician A
   b. Technician B
   c. Both A and B
   d. Neither A nor B
9. Technician A says that using the widest track shoes will ensure shoes last longer and increase track component life because less weight is applied per square inch of track. Technician B says that the narrowest track shoe is the best option to reduce track wear. Who is correct?
   a. Technician A
   b. Technician B
   c. Both A and B
   d. Neither A nor B
10. Technician A says that idler wheels are shimmed to properly align the idler with the track. Technician B says that idler wheels are shimmed to adjust the height of the idler to change the amount of track contact with the ground. Who is correct?
   a. Technician A
   b. Technician B
   c. Both A and B
   d. Neither A nor B

Greyhill
Smarter. Sleeker. Safer.
Drive and Motion
SPICER
brevini
YAMAHA
Support
SPICER

SECTION VI
Power Transfer Systems

CHAPTER 43
Friction Clutches

Knowledge Objectives

After reading this chapter, you will be able to:

- **K43001** Explain the function and fundamentals of the various clutches and flywheels used with mobile off-road equipment.
- **K43002** Identify the composition, construction, types, and applications of clutches and flywheels used with mobile off-road equipment.
- **K43003** Identify and describe the various clutch linkage systems used with mobile off-road equipment clutches.
- **K43004** Describe the principles of operation of clutches and flywheels used with mobile off-road equipment.
- **K43005** Explain the fundamentals and operation of ancillary (PTO) clutches used with mobile off-road equipment.

Skills Objectives

After reading this chapter, you will be able to:

- **S43001** Outline the inspection, testing, and diagnostic procedures for clutches, flywheels, and linkages used with mobile off-road equipment.
- **S43002** Identify and describe failures or root causes of failures and recommend necessary reconditioning or repairs.

▶ Introduction

In automotive and truck applications, the clutch is an indispensable part of most power systems. It is the link between the power plant (the engine) and the rest of the machine driveline. In heavy equipment, however, clutches are used for a variety of jobs: They are used to connect and disconnect the engine from the driveline in some applications, but they are also used to connect and disconnect various power take-off devices to drive pumps and various types of implements. Many different types of clutches are used in heavy equipment, such as disc, expanding shoe and drum, over-center, centrifugal, electromagnetic, band, and cone. An early cone-type clutch is shown in **FIGURE 43-1**.

The proper functioning of these clutches is essential to the operation of the machine. This chapter will introduce the various types of clutches used in heavy equipment. Technicians need to fully understand the functioning, maintenance, and (when necessary) the replacement of these vital components.

▶ Fundamentals of Clutches

K43001

The origin of the simple friction clutch dates back to the middle of the 1800s, circa 1835–1845. At that time, clutches were used for the same purposes that we use them for today: to connect and disconnect a power device from a mechanical system. In those days, however, clutches were typically connecting and disconnecting machinery from a steam engine. Today, of course, the power source or prime mover in off-road equipment is almost always a diesel engine.

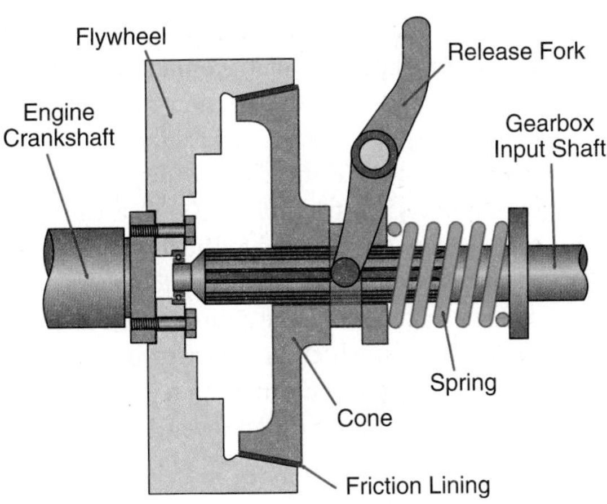

FIGURE 43-1 Early cone-type clutch.

Prior to the invention of the clutch, machinery was typically directly connected to the power source, usually a steam engine. The machinery was started by closing a valve, which allowed the steam pressure to build up and provide the necessary power to drive the machine. Heavy loads would hinder the start of the machinery. The innovation of the clutch allowed the engine to be started and to build up momentum in its flywheel before the load was applied. The clutch also allowed the driven machinery to be stopped quickly without shutting down the engine.

Modern Clutches

The dictionary definition of "clutch" is to "grab or hold tightly," which is exactly what we need a clutch to do: to grab onto a component from a running engine and transfer its power to the driven machinery of the machine. Most people understand this to be the essential function of a clutch, but if the only purpose of a clutch were to connect two components, the machine could be built more simply with just a solid connection from the engine to the driven equipment. The clutch could be eliminated altogether.

The real purpose of the clutch is to enable the engine to be disconnected from the driven machinery, whether it is the actual driveline of the machine or accessory equipment so that the operation of the machine can be stopped without having to stop the engine. (The clutch does have other important functions. We will discuss those functions later in this chapter.)

The clutch accomplishes its job by using friction to connect one or more driven members or discs attached to the driveline or driven equipment and a flywheel or other component driven by the engine.

The Role of Friction

The clutch performs its duty by using friction. **Friction** is the relative resistance to motion between any two bodies in contact with one another. In simple terms, the more friction that there is between two bodies, the harder it will be to move the bodies in contact relative to each other. The **coefficient of friction (CoF)** is a measure of the friction that exists between two particular materials in contact. As illustrated in **FIGURE 43-2** the coefficient of friction is related to the force required to move an object across a given surface, divided by the weight of the object.

You Are the Mobile Heavy Equipment Technician

A wood-chipper is brought to your shop, and the operator complains that the machine won't stay engaged. As soon as they start to send wood through the chipper, the clutch disengages and the machine stops working. You investigate, but you do not have any wood to put through the machine to check it under load properly, so when you engage the **over-center clutch** to operate the machine, it seems to function normally.

1. What would you suspect could be the cause of the problem?
2. How would you test the engagement of the over-center clutch?
3. Could something other than the clutch be causing this problem?

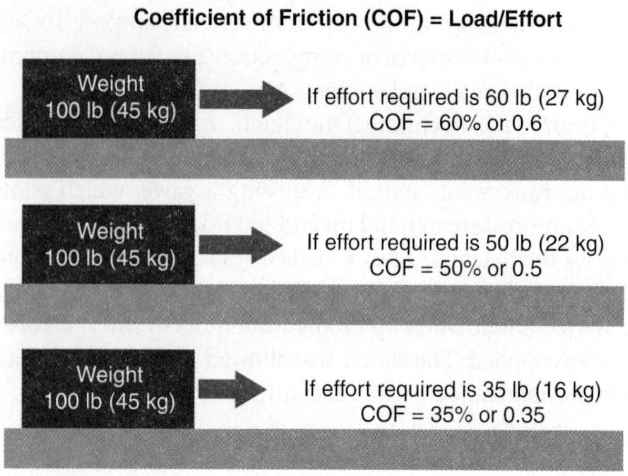

Coefficient of Friction (COF) = Load/Effort

Weight 100 lb (45 kg) — If effort required is 60 lb (27 kg) COF = 60% or 0.6

Weight 100 lb (45 kg) — If effort required is 50 lb (22 kg) COF = 50% or 0.5

Weight 100 lb (45 kg) — If effort required is 35 lb (16 kg) COF = 35% or 0.35

FIGURE 43-2 The coefficient of friction is the force required to move the object divided by the object's weight.

Engineers carefully select material so that the coefficient of friction will give the desired result. The clutch should engage smoothly and not slip when transmitting torque. Several factors affect the coefficient of friction, such as the surface conditions of the objects. For example, rough surfaces have different coefficients of friction than smooth surfaces, as do wet and dry surfaces. Two blocks of smooth steel in contact will be easier to move than two rough-surfaced concrete bricks of the same weight. When lubricating oil is placed between the two steel blocks, they move even more easily.

Basic Clutch Functions

As mentioned previously, clutches do more than just connect and disconnect the engine to the driveline. A clutch must allow a certain amount of slippage at engagement while the load is being taken up. That calculated slippage is known as **kinetic friction** and helps to prevent shock loads to the driven components. The kinetic friction also gives the operator a feel for the clutch engagement. A clutch must also offer a long service life and perform hundreds of thousands of engagements and disengagements.

An important function of most clutches is to absorb damaging torsional vibrations. **Torsional vibrations** are powerful vibrations caused by the engine firing impulses. Every time a cylinder fires, the force from the firing actually twists and accelerates the crankshaft. It is part of the clutch's job to help mitigate these vibrations before they are passed on to the rest of the driveline or equipment.

Clutch Capacity

Clutch capacity is the amount of torque a clutch can transmit before it starts to slip. Generally speaking, clutch capacity is affected by three factors: coefficient of friction of the materials used in the clutch's manufacture, surface area of the materials in contact, and **clamp load** (the force that squeezes or pushes the components of the clutch together). Most clutches are manufactured with cast iron flywheels and **pressure plates**, which have similarly rough surfaces at the microscopic level, so the coefficient of friction of the cutch disc facing material is the important element here. The larger the surface area of the components in contact with each other, the more torque that can be transmitted. That is the reason that many clutches are manufactured with dual or multiple friction discs.

The clamp load is the next factor in clutch capacity. The greater the force pushing or squeezing the clutch components together, the more torque that the clutch can handle without slipping.

▶ Types and Design of Clutches

K43002

As mentioned earlier in this chapter, there are many types of clutches used in heavy equipment applications. Automotive flywheel-style clutches are now almost obsolete in new machines. These have given way to torque converters, which can be used to engage and disengage the driveline (torque converters are covered in Chapter 47). However, the automotive flywheel-style clutch, as can be seen in **FIGURE 43-3**, is still used in a few applications and was commonly used for this purpose in the past.

The automotive flywheel type of clutch consists of two or more driving components—the flywheel and the pressure plate—which transmit torque to one or more driven friction discs attached to the transmission **input shaft** or the components to be driven. The **flywheel** is a heavy, round metal disc bolted to the end of the engine crankshaft. It provides one of the friction surfaces for the clutch disc(s). The **clutch cover** is the outside part of the clutch typically bolted to the flywheel and which holds all of the other clutch components, except the clutch disc. It is mistakenly, but commonly, called the pressure plate. The pressure plate is actually contained inside the clutch cover. The pressure plate is the friction surface in the clutch cover that squeezes the clutch disc against the flywheel. Together, these components squeeze the friction disc(s) between them. That action connects the friction disc(s) to the engine output, allowing torque to be transmitted to the driveline.

Two basic types of automotive clutches are used in the industry: the push type and the pull type. "Push" and "pull" refer to the direction in which the release fingers or levers have to be moved to disengage the clutch. In a push-type clutch, the release fingers or levers are pushed toward the engine flywheel

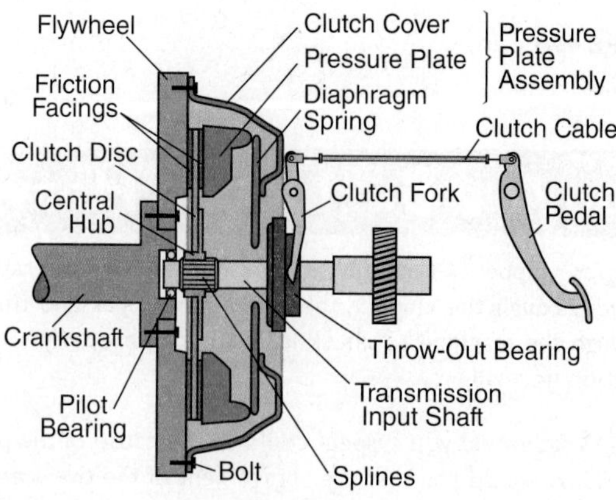

FIGURE 43-3 A standard vehicle clutch.

to release the clutch; in the pull-type clutch, the levers are pulled away from the flywheel to disengage.

Push-type clutches are also available with dual or multiple friction discs for more severe-duty applications. Using multiple friction discs allows the clutch capacity to be increased without changing the clamp load or the diameter of the clutch, if a clutch has more than one friction disc, it will have a driven **intermediate plate** between each pair of discs so that each friction surface of the discs is transmitting torque. The single-disc push-type clutch illustrated in Figure 43-3 is typical of a light-duty application.

Pull-type clutches, such as the one shown in **FIGURE 43-4**, are not very common in MORE but are sometimes used in heavier applications with unsynchronized transmissions.

Using a pull-type clutch allows the use of a **clutch brake** to slow and stop the transmission gearing when first or reverse gear is being selected. We will explain clutch brakes in greater detail a little later in the chapter. Pull-type clutches are also available in dual or multiple disc designs for increased clutch torque capacity.

Automotive flywheel-type clutches are further broken down by the type of clutch cover used. The clutch cover is the component that houses the functioning parts of the clutch, the actuating levers, the springs, and the pressure plate. The clutch cover is sometimes referred to simply as the pressure plate; however, the pressure plate is just one of its components. There are three broad design categories for clutch covers:

1. The coil spring style, available in push or pull type, uses a set of coil springs perpendicular to the pressure plate to apply **clamp force**.
2. The diaphragm spring style, available in push or pull type, uses a single one-piece diaphragm spring to apply clamp force.
3. The angle spring style, available in pull type, uses multiple angle-mounted coil springs and levers to apply the clamp force.

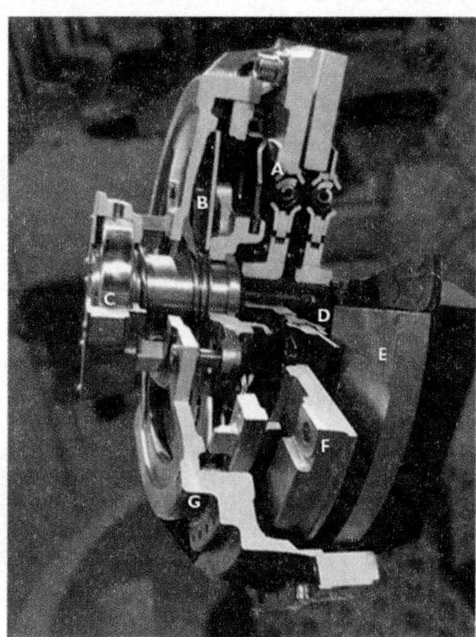

FIGURE 43-4 Dual disc pull-type clutch. **A.** Torsional dampening springs. **B.** Diaphragm spring (supplies clamp load). **C.** Integral (attached) release bearing. **D.** Friction discs. **E.** Intermediate plate. **F.** Pressure plate. **G.** Clutch cover.

These clutches are available in self-adjusting versions of each design category as well.

Coil Spring Clutch

The **coil spring–style clutch** uses perpendicular coil springs that act directly against the back of the pressure plate to supply clamping force. In a push-type coil spring clutch, such as the one illustrated in **FIGURE 43-5**, a series of levers are attached to a pivot point, which is in turn attached to the clutch cover. The outer edges of the levers are attached to the pressure plate.

When disengagement is required, the release bearing is pushed against the inner surface of these levers. The **release bearing** is a hollow bearing that the shaft passes through and that allows the pushing or pulling of clutch release levers to release the clutch. The levers actually pull the pressure plate away from the flywheel, caging (or collapsing) the pressure springs. The same method is used in a pull-type coil spring clutch, except that in that case, the pivot point and contact point of the levers are merely reversed. The pivot point of the levers is now at the levers' outer edge, and the attachment point to the pressure plate is further inboard. In both push and pull types, in order to compensate for the discs wearing, the pressure plate moves closer to the flywheel. This causes the coil springs to extend in order to keep contact with the pressure plate.

Hooke's law states that the force delivered by a spring to an object is directly related to its compression or extension. That means that the more the spring is compressed, the more force it delivers to the pressure plate. As the friction disc wears, the coil springs extend. That extension of the springs reduces the force against the pressure plate. Therefore, the more that the clutch disc wears, the less clamping force and therefore clutch capacity it has. To compensate for less clamp force as the discs wear, coil spring clutches are built with very strong springs. The strong springs can make coil spring clutches more difficult for the driver to disengage when the clutch is new.

In any clutch, the clutch cover is the component that is bolted to the flywheel, so the driving torque must be transferred from the cover to the pressure plate. Coil spring–style clutches

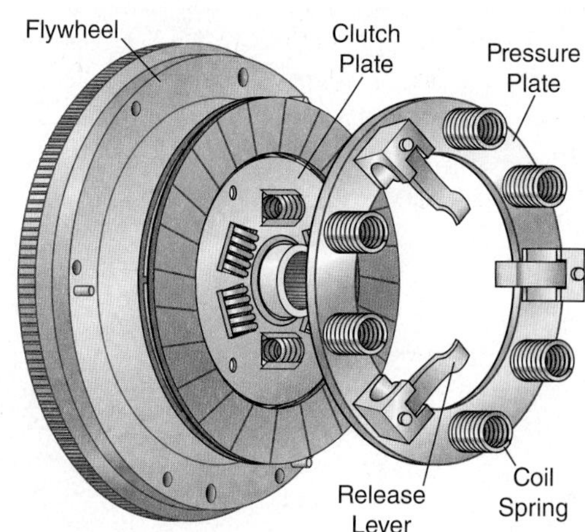

FIGURE 43-5 The coil spring pressure plate uses coil springs to create the clamping pressure and uses release levers to release the clutch disc.

transfer this torque to the pressure plate in one of two ways, depending on whether the cover is cast iron or aluminum or formed from stamped steel. The stamped steel version normally has pockets or notches formed in the stamped steel cover and drive lugs cast into the pressure plate, as shown in **FIGURE 43-6**.

This allows positive torque transfer while allowing the pressure plate to move forward and backward as it engages and disengages. The cast cover version may use a similar arrangement to transfer torque to the pressure plate, or it may have cutouts in the cover that engage notches in the pressure plate, as can be seen in **FIGURE 43-7**.

Coil spring clutches have mostly given way to diaphragm spring clutches or **angle spring clutches** as the first choice of machine manufacturers.

Diaphragm Spring Clutch

The **diaphragm spring clutch** uses a single diaphragm spring (or Belleville spring) to provide the clamping force. A diaphragm spring clutch may have a stamped steel, cast iron, or aluminum cover. The cover is bolted to the engine flywheel and therefore turns with it. Normally, in both the push-type and pull-type diaphragm style, driving torque is transmitted to the pressure plate through a series of drive straps attached to both the clutch cover and the pressure plate.

These straps are made from laminated spring steel and have two functions. The first is to linearly transfer the driving torque to the pressure plate, as mentioned above. The second function of the straps is to act as return springs and move the pressure plate away from the clutch disc when it is disengaged.

In their normal, relaxed position, the drive straps are straight. As the clutch is engaged, the pressure plate moves toward the flywheel, and this movement bends the straps slightly. When the clutch is disengaged, the straps straighten out and pull the pressure plate back. Drive straps are shown in **FIGURE 43-8**.

These straps must be strong enough to withstand maximum engine torque with a safety margin. If the drive straps are overloaded, they can permanently deform, causing poor clutch release symptoms. Some diaphragm spring clutches will have small coil springs or metal links attached to the pressure plate to pull it back when the clutch is disengaged. A diaphragm spring clutch is illustrated in **FIGURE 43-9**.

A diaphragm spring clutch creates clamp load with the use of a single diaphragm spring pushing on the pressure plate. The diaphragm spring is a single cone-shaped steel spring. Its outer edge rests against the pressure plate, and the inner part of the spring is cut into segments called fingers. These fingers act as the release levers. A pivot ring is installed inside the clutch cover between the outside edge of the spring and the fingers.

To disengage the push-type diaphragm clutch, the release bearing is pushed against the release fingers. The pivot ring acts as a fulcrum, and the outer edge of the spring is pulled away from the pressure plate. The plate drive straps return to their normal straight shape, pulling the pressure plate away from the clutch disc. A diaphragm spring is shown in **FIGURE 43-10**.

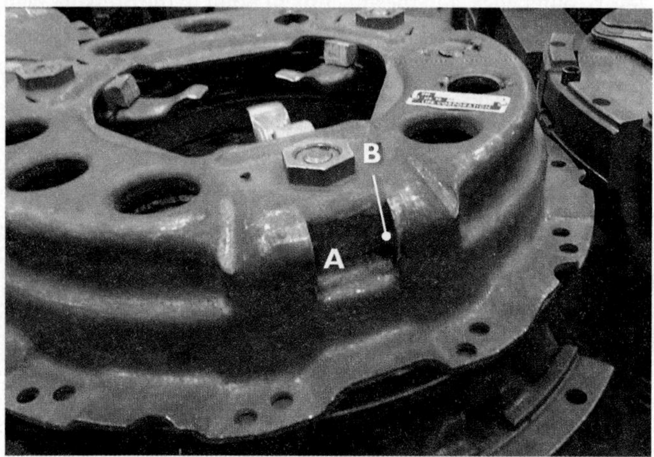

FIGURE 43-6 The driving force must be transferred from the clutch cover to the pressure plate. **A.** Formed notches in the stamped steel cover engage the cast iron pressure plate to transfer driving torque. **B.** Lugs on the pressure plate.

FIGURE 43-7 The pressure plate protrudes through the large cutouts in the clutch cover for positive torque transfer.

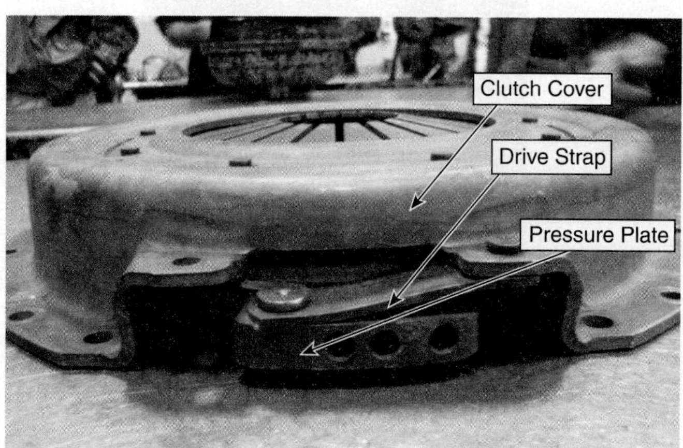

FIGURE 43-8 The drive straps serve two purposes: They drive the pressure plate, and they pull the plate away from the flywheel when the clutch is disengaged.

Driven Unit Disengaged

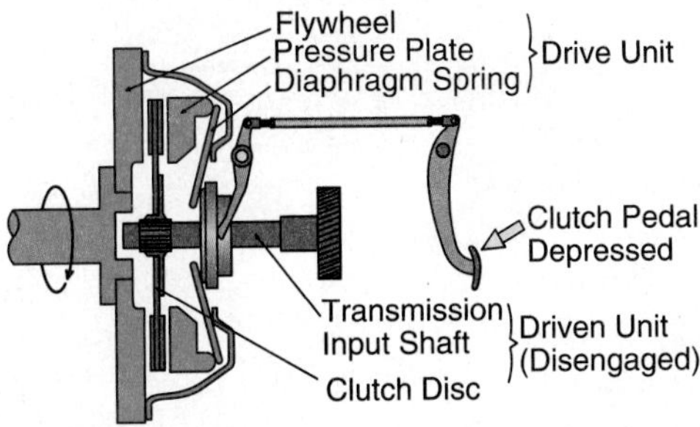

Driven Unit Engaged

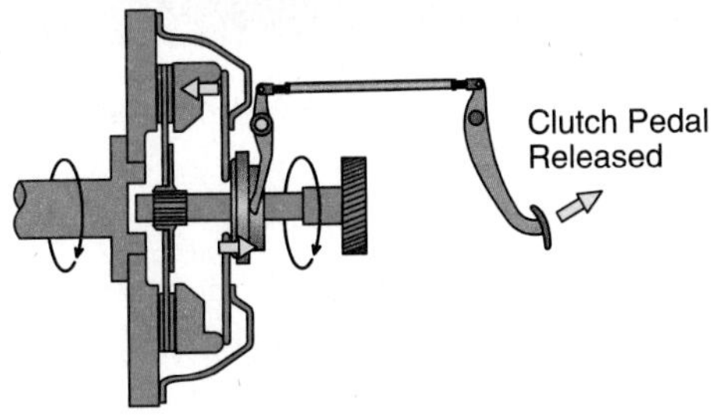

FIGURE 43-9 Releasing the clutch pedal reapplies the clamping force and reconnects the engine and transmission, firmly clamping them together to continue rotating as a unit.

FIGURE 43-10 A diaphragm spring.

Rather than lose pressure as disc wear occurs (which happens in the coil spring type), the diaphragm spring clutch is designed to actually increase loading on the pressure plate as disc wear occurs until it is approximately 50% worn. At that point, the pressure gradually decreases again for the second 50% of wear until the pressure returns to the original loading. This varying clamp load is accomplished through the changing contact point of the diaphragm spring with a specially designed lobe on the pressure plate and the pivot ring, which changes the effective lever length of the diaphragm spring. The pull-type version of the diaphragm spring style clutch, shown in **FIGURE 43-11**, arranges the diaphragm spring differently.

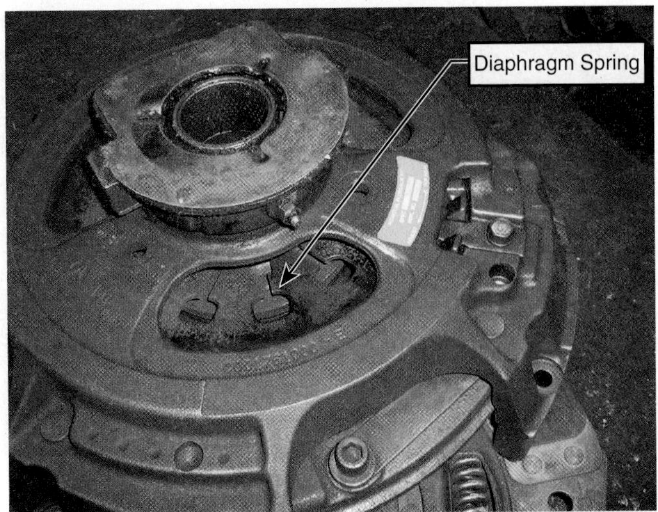

FIGURE 43-11 Pull-type diaphragm spring clutch.

The pivot point changes to the outer edge, and it engages the pressure plate further in toward the center. This has the effect of reversing the release direction. In the pull-type diaphragm spring–style clutch, the drive torque may be transferred to the pressure plate through either drive straps or pockets in the cover and lugs on the pressure plate. If the clutch does not have drive straps, the pressure plate will be drawn away from the friction disc by several small springs or metal links when the clutch is disengaged.

Angle Spring Clutch

The angle spring clutch uses three pairs of angled springs that push against the levers to supply the clamp load. The angle spring pull-type clutch manufactured by Eaton is very popular in heavy-duty on-highway trucks. The angle spring design allows for a near constant clamp load throughout the life of the clutch discs as long as the adjustment is correct. Six angle-mounted coil springs push axially against the bearing retainer. In turn, the bearing retainer pushes against the inner edge of six equally spaced levers. These levers multiply the pressure of the springs and press against the pressure plate to create clamp load. Driving torque is transferred to the pressure plate by lugs and pockets.

The use of the levers in the clutch design allow increased clamp load with a decreased pedal effort to disengage the clutch. The Eaton angle spring clutch, shown in **FIGURE 43-12**, also uses three assist springs that function to reduce pedal effort on clutch release.

The three assist springs are arranged so that as the clutch releases, the springs help to hold the clutch in the release position. In fact, once the clutch is released, only 30% of the pedal effort required for disengagement is needed to hold the clutch pedal down. For that reason, this type of clutch is known as the "easy pedal clutch."

To disengage the clutch, the integral (attached) release bearing pulls the inner edge of the release levers toward the transmission. The release levers are pivoted off the clutch cover at their outer edge and contact the pressure plate at a point closer

FIGURE 43-12 Eaton "Easy Pedal" angle spring clutch. **A.** Angled pressure springs. **B.** Disengagement assist (Easy Pedal) springs. **C.** Clutch cover. **D.** Integral release bearing. **E.** Quick adjust mechanism for internal clutch adjustment. **F.** Pressure plate return springs (1 of 4).

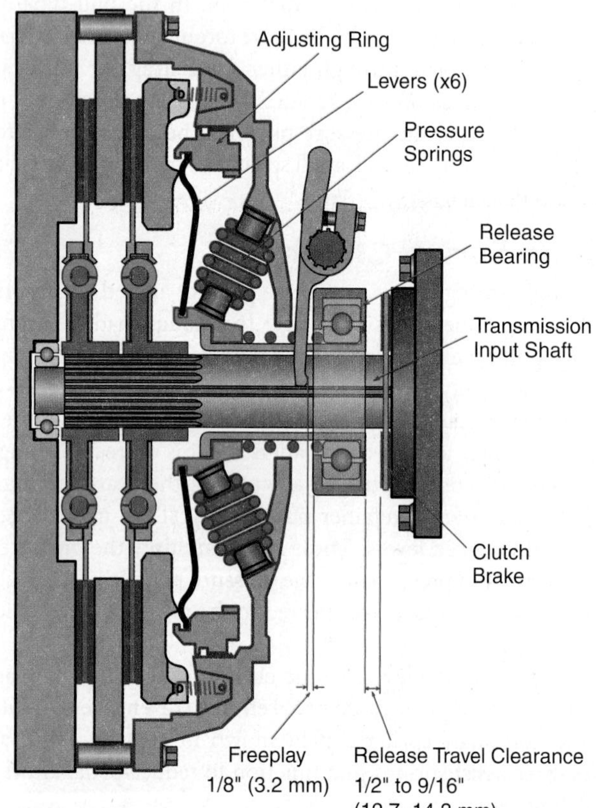

FIGURE 43-13 An angle spring clutch.

to the center of the clutch cover. Pulling the levers back takes the pressure off the pressure plate and allows small return springs to pull the pressure plate away from the clutch disc. **FIGURE 43-13** shows a cutaway drawing of an angle spring pull-type clutch.

As mentioned previously, flywheel clutches can have a single clutch disc; two clutch discs, like the angle spring clutch illustrated in Figure 43-13; or more than two discs, multidisc oil-cooled (wet) clutches are used in some applications. **FIGURE 43-14** shows the pressure plate used in this type of clutch.

FIGURE 43-14 This particular clutch uses oil as a cooling medium to protect the clutch.

Wet Clutches

When the clutch duty cycle is high, multiple engagement and disengagements can lead to extreme heat in the clutch components. Wet clutches either are submerged in oil inside the bell housing or will have oil pumped through to the clutch components. Submerged clutches typically have a bell housing that is partially filled with oil because the oil helps to cool and lubricate the clutch components. Other wet clutches, such as the one illustrated in Figure 43-14, have pressurized oil delivered to the clutch, usually through the transmission input shaft. The oil flows through center and cross drillings in the shaft and lubricates and cools the discs and the other clutch components. The oil drains from the housing and is returned to the transmission sump to circulate again.

Components of Automotive Flywheel Clutches

Clutches include several components critical to their function, including friction discs, flywheels, intermediate plates, pilot and release bearings, and clutch brakes. Additionally, regardless of type, every clutch has an actuation system that is mechanically, hydraulically, or automatically controlled.

Clutch Friction Discs

Clutch friction discs are the only driven member of the clutch assembly. The friction discs must transfer all of the engine torque to the driveline without slipping. Today's clutch discs must also absorb damaging engine torsional vibrations, cushion shock loads, and prevent gear rattle at idle. The clutch disc must do all this for many years of machine operation. For those reasons, the clutch discs can be thought of as the heart of the clutch. They are essential to successful clutch operation. Different types of clutch discs contribute varying benefits to the clutch system.

The friction facings on the clutch discs come in two distinct categories: organic and ceramic. Both are available in rigid and/or dampened disc styles. The dampened disc style provides vibration control.

Organic Facings

Organic facings are made of various natural materials, such as cotton fibers, rubber material, aluminum, glass fibers, copper or brass fibers, and carbon material. These materials are blended together and formed into solid discs, such as the ones shown in **FIGURE 43-15**, which are then bonded or riveted to the outermost edge of the friction disc.

Organic friction discs are made from a variety of carefully selected materials to give them the correct coefficient of friction. Organic facings are usually attached to what are called cushion segments or marcels. The cushion segments are waved to create a slight space between the front and rear friction facing, as shown in **FIGURE 43-16**.

On clutch engagement, these segments compress, allowing a gradual increase in friction. That gradual increase gives the machine a smoother engagement. As their name suggests, cushion segments cushion the engagement of the clutch and assist in releasing the discs on clutch disengagement. Cushion segments are not normally used in heavier applications.

Organic facings are full-face linings. That means that the outer area of the disc is completely covered by the facing material. Organic facings normally have grooves cut into the facing, from the central hub to the outside edge, to allow for heat dissipation and removal of debris by centrifugal force. Although a clutch facing (clutch lining) is very thin when new, less than ⅛ inch (3–4 mm), quite a large amount of dust and debris will be present on the facing when the clutch has worn out.

FIGURE 43-15 An organic friction disc.

Dangers of Organic Facings

Asbestos has been used as the material of choice in the production of friction materials because of its high heat resistance; however, since the late 1970s, it has been banned from use in friction materials in North America. It is important to note that friction materials manufactured overseas and installed on imported new machines may still contain various amounts of asbestos. Use of imported clutches or brake linings may also expose a technician to asbestos. Exposure to asbestos fibers is known to cause asbestosis, which affects the lungs and is a precursor to lung cancer. Asbestos exposure is also a known cause of mesothelioma, a rare and almost always fatal condition affecting the outer lining of the lungs or the lining of the chest cavity. Asbestos can also affect the peritoneum, the lining of the stomach cavity.

Much debate surrounds the long-term effects of exposure to the newer organic friction material that contains no asbestos but may contain other fine fibers such as glass. Some critics argue that new materials are even worse than asbestos. The long-term effects of exposure to ceramic friction material dust is also not fully understood.

The safest bet for technicians is to protect themselves when servicing any machine by always wearing a respirator approved by the National Institute of Occupational Safety and Health (NIOSH), as shown in **FIGURE 43-17**, and coveralls that protect street clothes from being contaminated by dust.

FIGURE 43-16 The cushion segments or marcels allow a gradual clamping and therefore a smoother engagement.

FIGURE 43-17 Always wear an approved respirator when dealing with dusty components.

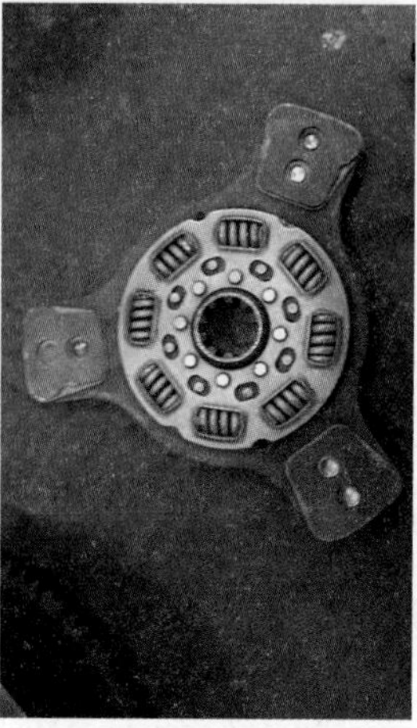

FIGURE 43-18 Ceramic linings are rarely full faced, because they have a higher coefficient of friction.

FIGURE 43-19 Dampened friction discs are designed to absorb damaging engine torsional vibrations before they are sent to the rest of the vehicle.

Always wear an approved respirator when dealing with dusty components. Technicians should also vacuum any dust before working on clutches or brakes.

Ceramic Clutch Facings

In most medium-to-heavy applications, organic clutch discs have been replaced by discs with ceramic facings, such as the one shown in **FIGURE 43-18**

Ceramic friction facings are made mostly of artificial materials specifically designed to produce desirable characteristics. Specifically, ceramic facings have a much higher coefficient of friction and tend not to have a full-face lining.

Ceramic facings are made by mixing the materials together and then forming the material into the shape required and baking it. The material is then attached to a steel backing plate before being riveted to the disc. Ceramic facings have a much higher coefficient of friction and therefore do not usually require full-face linings to give satisfactory clutch torque capacity. Consequently, ceramic discs have several pads or buttons around the disc surface, with spaces in between. The spaces allow for excellent cooling and better debris removal. Ceramic facings are not attached to cushion segments in the way that some organic facings are. The lack of attachment to a cushion segment combined with their higher coefficient of friction results in a more abrupt clutch engagement when ceramic facings are used.

Rigid and Dampened Friction Discs

Both ceramic and organic discs are available in rigid and or dampened disc styles. **FIGURE 43-19** shows a dampened disc, and **FIGURE 43-20** shows a rigid disc. Dampened discs have a set of torsional dampening springs around their center hub. The springs are designed to absorb engine torsional vibrations.

Vibration Control

Engine torsional vibrations are caused by the acceleration of the engine crankshaft that occurs on each cylinder firing. Torsional vibrations can be responsible for severe driveline damage, including wearing of the input shaft spline, transmission input gear set, and drive axle gearing, as well as leakage of the transmission gasket and pinion seal.

FIGURE 43-20 Rigid discs are not capable of absorbing engine torsional vibrations.

A dampened disc is actually constructed of several components attached together. The central hub is splined to the transmission input shaft, but it is not driven directly by the friction discs. Another disc, called the driven plate, sits around the central hub. The driven plate has a large slot that will rotate around the central hub. This driven plate has slots for the torsional springs. Usually, the coaxial, which is a spring inside a spring, and the friction material are attached to this plate.

Sandwiched on both sides of the drive plate are two or more spring cage plates that hold the torsional springs in place. These plates are rigidly attached to the central hub and contact the springs in the driven plate. The power flow for this arrangement then flows from the flywheel and pressure plate to the friction material attached to the driven plate. The flow continues through the coaxial torsion springs to the spring cage plates and onto the central hub and the input shaft.

This means that the drive goes through the springs before it reaches the input shaft. The springs compress to absorb the

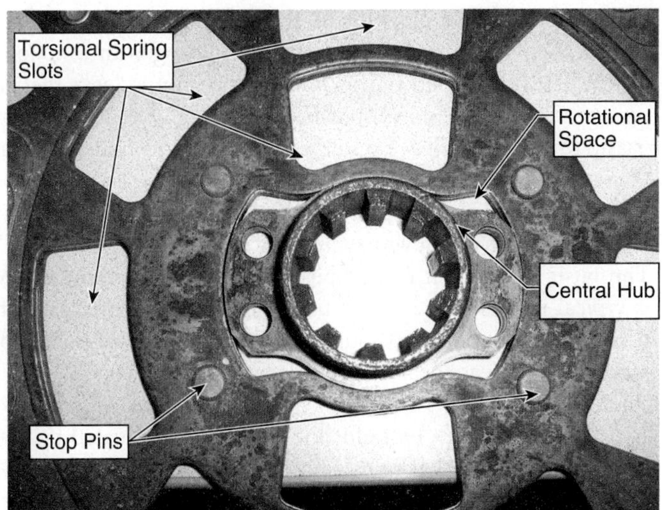

FIGURE 43-21 Torque is transferred to the input shaft through the torsional dampening springs. Note that the springs and their cage plates have been removed for clarity.

FIGURE 43-22 Flat-type flywheel.

FIGURE 43-23 The pot-type flywheel will have most of the clutch components mounted inside the "pot" area of the flywheel.

acceleration of the crankshaft due to the firing pulses, effectively dampening the oscillations before they reach the driveline. Notice in **FIGURE 43-21** that the cutout in the clutch disc for the splined hub is quite a bit larger than the central hub.

This allows the torsional springs to be compressed as they transfer drive to the hub, thereby absorbing torsional vibrations. There are stop pins that limit how far the driven plate can move around the central hub to protect the torsional springs.

Flywheels

As defined earlier in this chapter, a flywheel is a heavy, round metal disc attached to the end of the crankshaft. One of the flywheel's several purposes is to smooth out vibrations from the crankshaft assembly. Flywheels provide this torsional dampening because of their mass. The accelerations of the crankshaft are somewhat subdued by the energy required to accelerate and decelerate the heavy flywheel.

Flywheels carry inertia as they rotate. That is, once they are rotating at a certain speed, they tend to keep rotating such that the engine runs smoothly in between firing cycles.

The flywheel will provide one of the friction surfaces for a clutch disc used on manual transmission applications. It forms the surface against which the friction disc is clamped. It will also usually have a ring gear attached to its outside edge to provide a means to crank the engine for starting.

Flywheels come in two basic designs. **Flat-type flywheels**, such as the one in **FIGURE 43-22**, have all of the clutch components inside the clutch cover and the cover bolts to the flywheel.

The second type is the **pot-type flywheel**, shown in **FIGURE 43-23**.

In the pot-type flywheel, the clutch friction discs and the intermediate plate are installed into the "pot" shape of the flywheel, and the clutch cover containing the pressure plate bolts to the flywheel like the lid of a pot. If the flywheel has a raised bolt circle where the clutch cover mounts, it is extremely important that when the pot-type flywheel face is resurfaced, the raised bolt circle is machined the same amount in order to maintain the correct clamp load. If the bolt circle is not ground down the same amount, the flywheel friction surface will be further away from the clutch pressure plate. That distance will cause the springs to extend, reducing clamp load.

Intermediate or Spacer Plates

The intermediate plates are the plates that sit between the friction discs on multiple disc clutches. These plates create a "friction sandwich" of flywheel clutch discs, intermediate plates, and the pressure plate. In dual disc clutch designs that using flat-type flywheels, driving torque is transferred to the intermediate plate directly by notches or slots in the clutch cover, as shown in **FIGURE 43-24**, or the intermediate plates may be splined to a drive ring.

Dual disc clutches with pot-type flywheels drive the intermediate plate with drive lugs or splines in the flywheel.

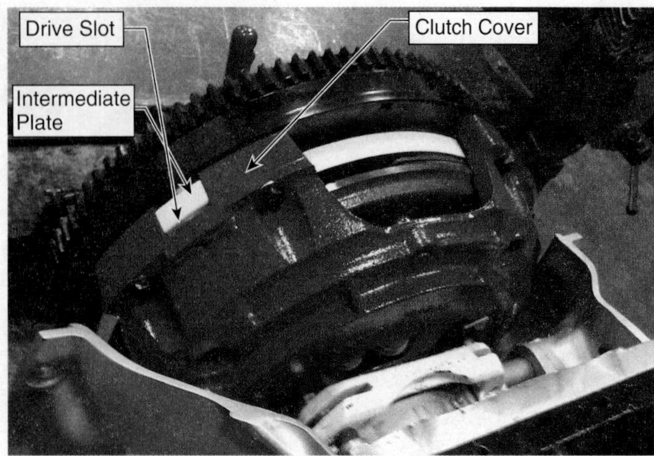

FIGURE 43-24 The intermediate plate is typically driven by slots in the clutch cover.

Pilot Bearings and Release Bearings

Pilot bearings are called so because they carry the pilot end of the input shaft. This often overlooked bearing is extremely important. It allows the input shaft to be supported straddle style. That is, the front of the shaft in the pilot bearing and the rear of the shaft in the transmission input bearing are mounted in the transmission case. This holds the shaft solidly when the clutch discs are disengaged and ensures the shaft remains centered. This bearing is typically a ball bearing mounted in the center of the flywheel, as shown in **FIGURE 43-25**.

It is recommended that the pilot bearing be replaced when the clutch is replaced, even if it seems fine. The added cost to replace it during a clutch servicing is incidental compared to the costs that would be incurred to replace the bearing separately at a later date if it fails.

Release Bearing

As its name implies, the release bearing is used to release the clutch discs. This bearing allows a stationary clutch fork to apply pressure to a rotating clutch's release levers or fingers. The pressure allows the clutch to cage the pressure plate spring(s) and interrupt power flow to the transmission. In a push-type clutch, the release bearing is part of a housing with a hollow center. The hollow part of this housing rides on a sleeve that is part of the transmission input bearing cover. The input shaft passes through this sleeve, and the release bearing housing is on the outside of the sleeve.

The release bearing itself is a ball bearing that is specially designed so that it can withstand both axial and radial loading. The push-type clutch release bearing shown in **FIGURE 43-26** is typical in that it is a sealed unit. That means that it cannot be lubricated periodically, but there may be a grease fitting to lubricate the release bearing housing where it slides on the input shaft sleeve.

The **release fork (yoke)** is the lever that is actuated by the clutch linkage and that moves the release bearing. The release fork engages a groove in the release bearing housing. The release fork is mounted on a pivot in the clutch bell housing so that when the driver pushes the clutch pedal down the release bearing and its housing move toward the clutch release levers or fingers. The release bearing in a push-type clutch does not actually rotate until it comes in contact with the release fingers or levers of the pressure plate. This is important to remember when diagnosing clutch noise complaints. Once the bearing is pushed against the fingers or levers with sufficient force, the pressure plate spring(s) are caged and the clutch is disengaged. Even though the push-type clutch release bearing is more expensive than a pilot bearing, the release bearing should always be replaced when a clutch is replaced. Like the flywheel ball bearing, replacing the release bearing during a clutch replacement is less expensive than doing it separately because of failure later.

The release bearing in a push-type clutch is designed only for periodic rotation when disengaging the clutch. If the driver rides the pedal or if the clutch adjustment is incorrect, the bearing will be constantly rotating. That constant rotation will cause it to overheat and cause the permanent lubricating grease to liquefy and run out of the bearing, leading to premature bearing failure.

In a pull-type clutch, the release bearing performs the same function as in a push-type clutch—that is, to release the

FIGURE 43-25 A typical pilot bearing.

FIGURE 43-26 Release bearing for a push-type clutch.

FIGURE 43-27 A release bearing for a pull-type clutch is integral to (attached to) the clutch.

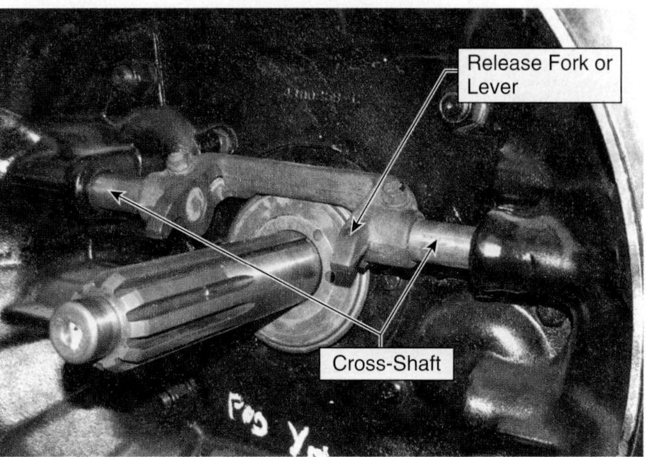

FIGURE 43-28 A pull-type clutch release fork or lever.

clutch—but the pull type's design is quite different. The pull-type clutch release bearing is integral to the clutch. That means it is attached to the clutch cover and in most cases is not serviced separately. See **FIGURE 43-27**. The release bearing for a pull-type clutch is integral to (attached to) the clutch.

The release bearing again is usually a ball bearing designed to handle axial and radial thrust loads. The transmission input bearing cover used with a pull-type clutch does not have a sleeve as it does in the push-type clutch. Instead, the release bearing is encompassed in a hollow housing. The outer race of the bearing is attached to the housing itself, and the inner race is attached to a sleeve. Inside the sleeve, there are two bronze bushings that allow the sleeve to ride on the transmission input shaft. This sleeve, in turn, attaches to what is commonly referred to as a retainer. It is the retainer that actually engages the release levers. Release bearings for pull-type clutches usually require periodic lubrication. It is important to not overlook this service procedure.

Release Fork

The release fork or lever in a pull-type clutch is U shaped and is attached to a cross-shaft that is mounted inside the clutch bell housing as shown in **FIGURE 43-28**. The shape of the fork fits closely over the outside of the release bearing housing from the top, holding it stationary.

As noted earlier in this section, the inner race of the release bearing is attached to the sleeve and the retainer. The retainer is fixed to the release levers, so all three turn with the clutch. Consequently, the inner race of the release bearing rotates any time the engine is running.

To disengage the clutch, the driver actuates the clutch pedal. Actuating the pedal causes the cross-shaft and the U-shaped fork to rotate the ends of the U-shaped contact wear pads located on the front of the release bearing housing and push the bearing to the rear. This action pulls the retainer and the release levers to the rear, which cages the pressure plate spring(s) disengaging the clutch. Most pull-type clutch release bearings need to be lubricated as part of regular maintenance procedures and are equipped with a grease fitting to allow this. There are, however, some permanently lubed designs as well. In some installations, a tube is attached to the release bearing and connected to a grease zerk, or grease nipple, on the outside of the bell housing so that the bearing can be lubricated more easily.

Clutch Brakes

Pull-type clutches may be used with machines with non-synchronized transmissions. The input shaft, the countershafts, and all of the main shaft gearing are rotating when these machines are idling in neutral with the clutch engaged. When the operator wants to select a gear, they first depress the clutch pedal to disengage the engine. The inertia of the rotating components tends to keep them rotating, however, so if the operator were to try to engage a gear, the difference in speed between the rotating gear and the stationary main shaft would cause tremendous clashing. The rotating components have no load on them and little resistance to rotation, so they may continue to rotate for some time before a clash-free shift can be made.

Pull-type clutches facilitate the use of a clutch brake that can alleviate this problem. A clutch brake is a small frictional brake usually mounted on the transmission input shaft and designed to slow down or stop the transmission rotation when the driver wishes to engage first or reverse from a neutral position. The clutch brake is mounted on the input shaft between the release bearing and the transmission input bearing housing, as can be seen in **FIGURE 43-29**.

The input shaft has two splines that run its entire length, and the cutch brake has two matching teeth that fit into the splines. The rear of the release bearing housing has a smooth surface, as does the front of the transmission input bearing cover. The clutch brake has friction material on the front and back that will contact these smooth surfaces.

As the operator disengages the clutch, the release bearing moves backward toward the transmission. If the clutch pedal is pushed all the way to the floor, the clutch brake will be squeezed between the release bearing housing and the transmission input bearing cover so that the input shaft rotation will be stopped. This allows the operator to select a gear without gear clash. The clutch brake is actuated within the last 1 inch (2.5 cm) of clutch pedal travel. If the operator pushes the clutch pedal to the

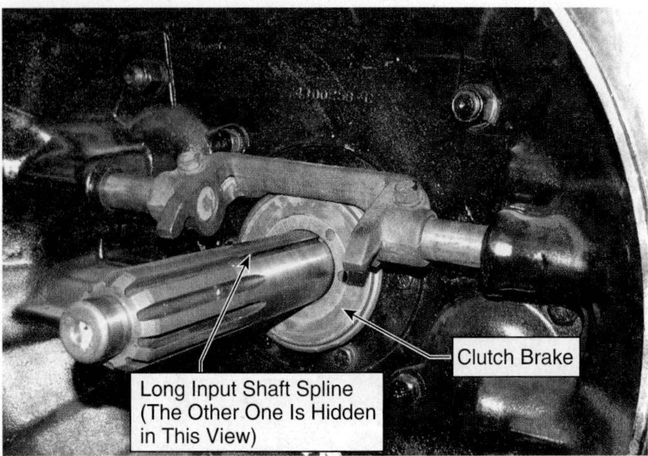

FIGURE 43-29 A clutch brake allows the operator to slow the rotating components in the transmission when shifting from neutral to gear.

FIGURE 43-31 A torque-limiting clutch brake is designed to slip internally when a certain torque is reached, protecting the brake from an inexperienced driver.

floor when the machine is moving in gear, the clutch brake will be destroyed very quickly. In this situation, the clutch brake is attempting to stop the entire machine, not just the transmission rotating components.

There are two types of clutch brakes that are commonly used the conventional and the torque-limiting clutch brake: the conventional clutch brake and the torque-limiting clutch brake.

Conventional Clutch Brake

The conventional clutch brake is a solid piece of metal with friction material on either side. To install a conventional clutch brake, the transmission must be removed. To avoid the associated labor costs, aftermarket versions of this brake are made in a two-piece design that allows them to be replaced without removing the transmission. When installing a two-piece clutch brake, the original clutch brake is carefully cut off of the input shaft by using an oxyacetylene torch. The two pieces are then put into place and connected together. **FIGURE 43-30** shows various clutch brakes.

Extreme caution must be taken to not damage the input shaft when using an oxyacetylene torch inside the clutch bell housing. An accumulation of grease, oil, and clutch dust can also result in a fire. Therefore, always clean the area first, and be prepared with a fire extinguisher to douse any flames if fire erupts.

FIGURE 43-30 Various clutch brakes.

Torque-Limiting Clutch Brake

The torque-limiting clutch brake, like that shown in **FIGURE 43-31**, is the brake of choice of most manufacturers. A torque-limiting clutch brake is designed to slip internally when a certain torque is protecting the brake from an inexperienced driver.

It is preferred because it is designed to slip when the torque applied exceeds its setting, typically 25 ft-lb (34 N·m). The brake consists of an outer housing. Attached to the housing are the friction material and a separate inner hub that is splined to the input shaft. Two Belleville-type (diaphragm spring–type) spring washers are placed inside the housing on either side of the inner hub to exert pressure against the hub. The brake is designed so that when approximately 25 ft-lb (34 N·m) of torque is twisting against the inner hub, the hub will slip inside the housing protecting the clutch brake. This design allows a modicum of tolerance for an inexperienced driver who hits the clutch brake while upshifting. The key advantage of the torque-limiting clutch brake is that it will last longer than the conventional clutch brake if the driver actuates the brake while the machine is moving. If the driver abuses the clutch brake repeatedly, however, even this design will fail. Therefore, driver training on the proper use of clutch brakes is essential.

▶ Clutch Actuation Systems

K43003

Clutches can use a variety of different systems: actuation, mechanical linkage, hydraulic, air-assisted hydraulic, automatic, centrifugal, and electrical. Most driveline clutches (automotive-style clutches) will use either mechanical or hydraulically actuated clutches.

Mechanical Linkage

The mechanical actuation system starts with the clutch pedal. The pedal is usually a first- or second-class lever that helps the operator to overcome the tremendous clamp loads associated

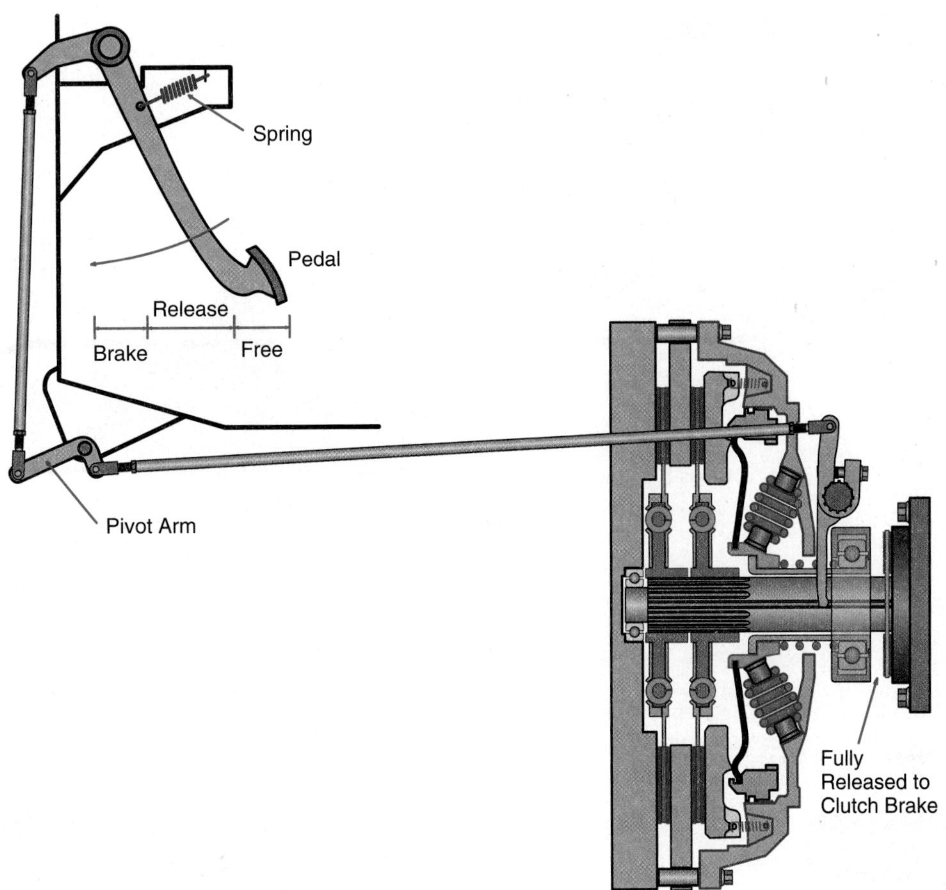

FIGURE 43-32 A typical clutch linkage system.

with modern clutches. Clamp loads can be more than 4,000 lb (1,814 kg)! Without leverage, it would be impossible to release the clutch. As illustrated in **FIGURE 43-32**, the clutch pedal attaches to a series of rods, bell cranks or pivot arms, and levers to operate the clutch. Those components are, in turn, attached to the **cross-shaft** in the clutch bell housing and the release fork is actuated by the cross-shaft.

The levers in the linkage and in the clutch itself compound the force exerted by the operator on the clutch pedal. That leverage allows a force of around 50 to 60 lb (22 to 27 kg) to cage the 3,200 lb or 4,000 lb (1,451 kg or 1,814 kg) clutch clamping force. But, as always when we use levers to compound force and gain mechanical advantage, travel distance is reduced.

When pushing the pedal through 10 inches or 11 inches (25–28 cm) of travel, the release bearing will move only 0.5 inches (1.3 cm) or so. The pressure plate inside the clutch cover will usually move only 0.15–0.20 inches (0.381–0.508 cm), and this in turn in a dual disc clutch allows approximately 0.050 inches (0.127 cm) of clearance on each side of each clutch disc in order for it to spin freely. With such a small amount of clearance for the discs, it is clear that any warping or damage to the discs could cause the discs to stay partially pressed against the flywheel or pressure plate when disengaged, which could cause clashing shifts. In some cases, the rods, levers, and bell cranks of a mechanical linkage system can be replaced by a cable, as illustrated in **FIGURE 43-33**.

Hydraulic Actuation Systems

Hydraulically actuated clutches, such as the one as illustrated in **FIGURE 43-34**, consist of a clutch master cylinder and push rod that will be connected to the clutch pedal.

A clutch **slave cylinder** will be mounted at the transmission to actuate the cross-shaft, and a hydraulic circuit will push the cross-shaft lever. Mechanical advantage is gained in two ways: first by the effective lever length of the pedal and second by using a piston in the slave cylinder that is larger than the one in the master cylinder. Hydraulically controlled actuation allows much more design freedom in the location of components.

▶ Clutch Operation

K43004

Clutches are usually engaged by spring force, meaning that when an operator approaches a machine, the clutch will be engaged and the operator must disengage the clutch before the machine is started. Use the previous figures in the chapter to visualize the basic operation of the clutch, which follows:

1. First, the operator will disengage the clutch by pushing the clutch pedal. This action moves the release fork through either the mechanical or the hydraulic linkage system discussed above.

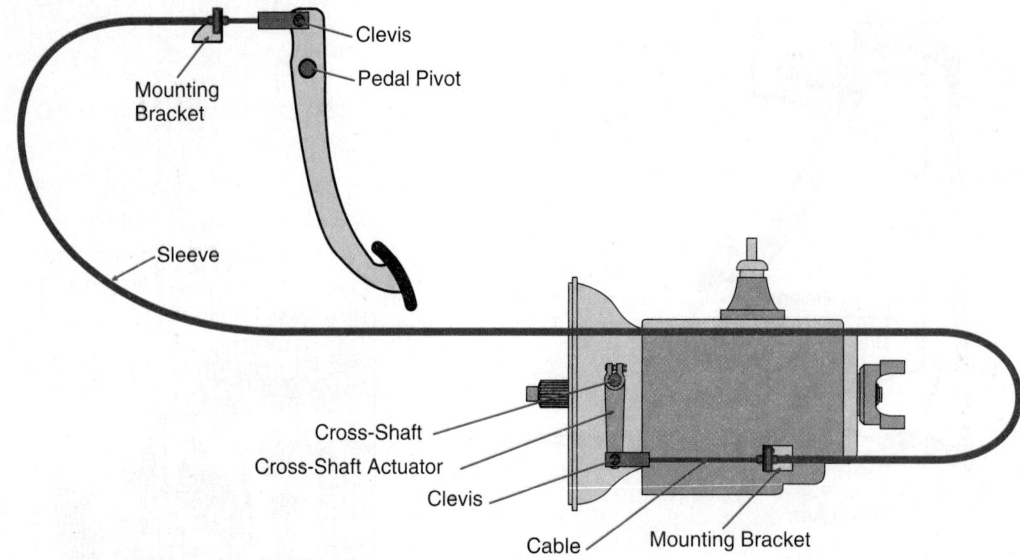

FIGURE 43-33 Cable linkage allows more flexibility in locating and connecting components.

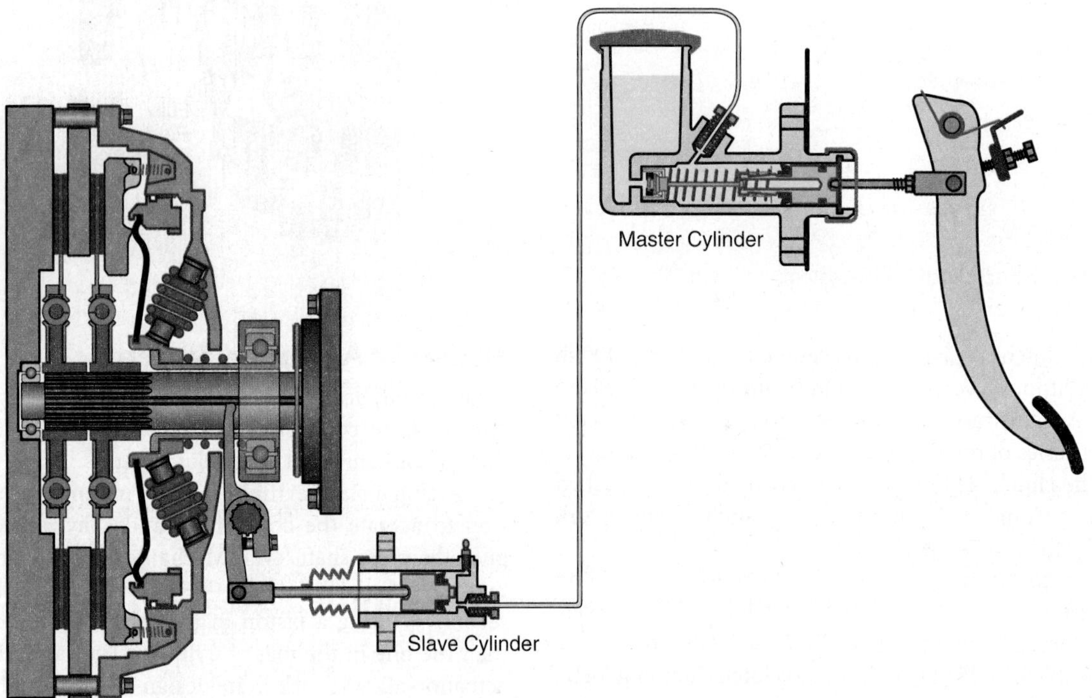

FIGURE 43-34 Hydraulic linkage, although more complex than the other systems, allows maximum flexibility in mounting.

2. The release fork then pushes or pulls the release bearing toward or away from the clutch assembly, depending on whether the clutch is a push or pull type.
3. As the release bearing moves, it pushes or pulls the levers inside the clutch that will release the force applied by the coil or diaphragm springs clamping the pressure plate against the friction disc and locking it to the flywheel.
4. As the levers are moved, the spring clamping force is caged (collapsed), and either drive straps or small springs will pull the pressure plate away from the friction disc or discs, allowing the disc or discs (if it is a multiple plate clutch) to be free between the pressure plate and the flywheel.
5. As the disc is splined to the transmissions input shaft, this action disconnects the engine and the transmission. The operator can now start the machine safely because the clutch disengaged and there is no contact between the friction disc and the flywheel or pressure plate.
6. To engage the clutch and operate the machine, the operator slowly engages the clutch by letting up on the clutch pedal. This is the most critical time in the operation of any clutch, because the point of engagement of the clutch is the only time that clutch friction disc wear occurs unless of course the clutch is slipping when it should not be.

Because friction disc wear is the primary reason for clutch replacement, minimizing wear is crucial, and the operator is the only one who can help in this situation. If the operator engages the clutch too slowly, there will be a lot of slippage and disc wear, leading to short clutch life and premature clutch replacement. If the operator engages the clutch too quickly, however, it can shock load the driveline of the equipment, causing other problems. Proper training of the operator in the use of the clutch is essential to long clutch and machine life. As the clutch engages, there will be a significant speed difference between the pressure plate and flywheel (traveling at engine speed) and the clutch friction disc (usually stopped at initial engagement).

When the clutch is engaged correctly, not too slowly and not too quickly, the dampening springs in the clutch hub will absorb the initial engagement shock. Once the clutch is fully engaged again, no friction disc wear will occur. When the clutch is engaged and the machine is in operation, the clutch functions as the connection point between the engine and the transmission. The dampening springs in the clutch friction disc will be absorbing shocks from acceleration and deceleration and absorbing the torsional vibrations created by the engine firing pulses, ensuring that they are not transmitted to the rest of the driveline. Depending on the skill of the operator and the utilization of the machine, clutches can last almost the entire effective life of the equipment, but with operator abuse and/or misuse, misapplication, or overloading of the machine, clutches can wear out in a very short time.

Remember that a clutch does not wear while it is engaged and not slipping. It wears only when the operator is engaging the clutch, so a bad operator can destroy a clutch very quickly. Although the operation of clutches as described above is typical of most clutches, there can be differences in some clutch designs, but they will still be similar. There are other problems and operator errors that can occur with clutches that can lead to premature failure of the friction disc, such as the operator riding the clutch pedal, causing reduced clamp load and slippage and possible damage to the linkage, the release bearing, and the release fork. This and other issues are discussed in the next section on clutch maintenance.

▶ Preventive Maintenance of Clutches

S43001

Clutch inspection and maintenance should be performed according to the manufacturer's maintenance schedule. This schedule will vary depending on the machine and its **vocation** but is usually every 250 to 300 hours. Clutch preventive maintenance involves three basic elements:

1. *Clutch inspection*: Inspection of the clutch and its actuating system can allow a technician to prevent costly downtime by preventing potential problems. All linkages should be inspected for wear and repaired as necessary.
2. *Lubrication*: During a machine service, all moving components of the clutch actuation system should be lubricated, as should the release bearing if possible and clutch release fork and cross-shaft. Note that some systems will have **sealed release bearings**. Those do not require lubrication, but they still require inspection.
3. *Clutch adjustment*: Timely adjustment of the clutch is essential to its longevity. The clutch should be adjusted as necessary when the machine is in the shop for maintenance.

The following are the adjustment procedures for various types of medium- and heavy-duty clutches.

Clutch Adjustment Procedures

Many factors can affect the useful life of a clutch. Loading, operator skill, and duty cycle are all important factors, but one of the most important is correct and timely clutch adjustment.

Push-Type Clutch Adjustment

A properly adjusted push-type clutch will usually have a certain amount of free play between the clutch release levers, or the diaphragm spring fingers, and the release bearing.

As the clutch friction disc(s) wear, the pressure plate must move toward the flywheel to compensate. Therefore, the outer edge of the release levers or diaphragm spring fingers must also move in order to follow the pressure plate. This causes the inner edge of the release levers to move toward the transmission and the release bearing. Eventually, their travel will be stopped by the release bearing. Any further wear after this point will cause clutch clamp load to be lessened, leading to clutch slippage and early clutch failure.

In a push-type clutch, this adjustment is accomplished by adjusting the cable or mechanical linkage in such a way as to gain approximately 0.125 inches of clearance between the release bearing and the release levers or fingers.

This adjustment typically leads to approximately 1–2 inches of free travel at the clutch pedal. Clutch adjustment should be performed as often as necessary when the pedal-free travel is reduced by half because of disc wear to re-establish normal clearance at the release bearing and free pedal in the cab. Push-type clutches with hydraulic actuation systems may have an adjustable slave cylinder pushrod to re-establish the 0.125 inches of clearance. However, some hydraulic systems may operate with no clearance at all. In that case, there will be light contact between the bearing and the release levers. Always check the manufacturer's specifications to be sure of the correct adjustment setting.

▶ TECHNICIAN TIP

Note that the specification of 0.125 inches of clearance may vary by OEM (original equipment manufacturer). Be sure to consult the manufacturer's documentation for the clutch you are working on.

Pull-Type Clutch Adjustment

A properly adjusted pull-type clutch has a certain clearance between the tips of the release fork and the wear pads on the release bearing. In a pull-type clutch, as the disc(s) wear, the pressure plate also moves toward the flywheel to compensate. However, because the release levers or diaphragm spring

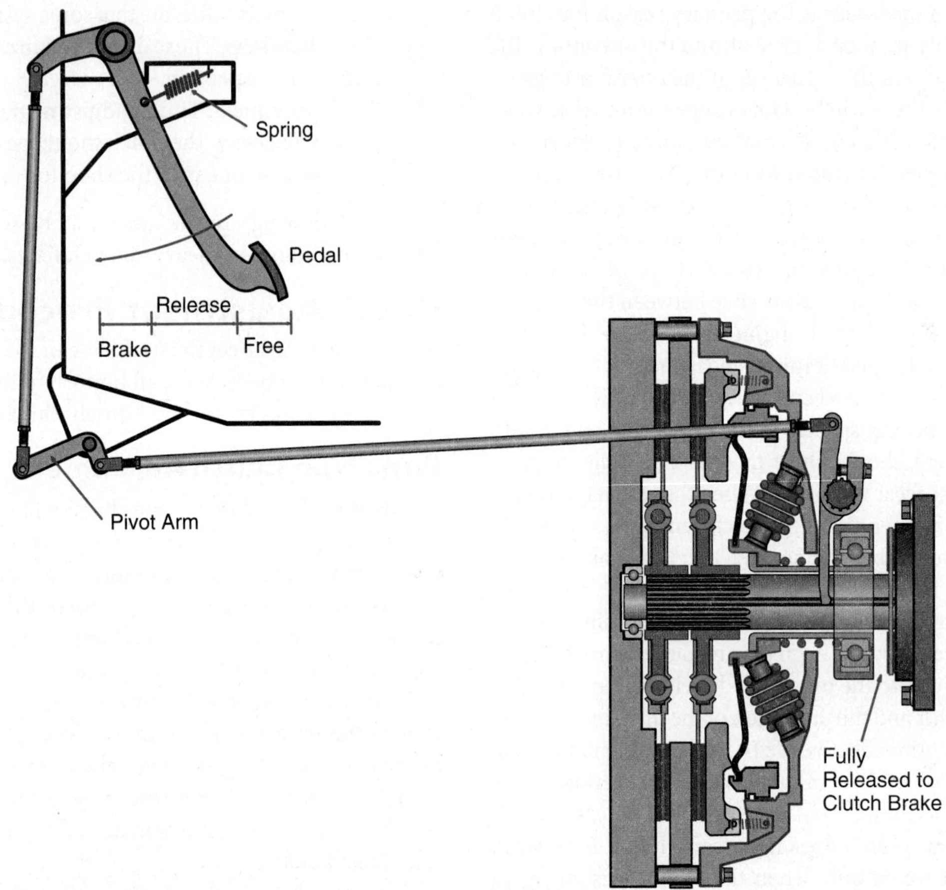

FIGURE 43-35 Pull type clutch adjustment accomplishes three things, pedal free play, release travel and clutch brake squeeze.

pivot points are on their outer edge, the inner edge of the levers or fingers and the integral release bearing move toward the flywheel. The clutch release fork is in front of the release bearing. Eventually, therefore, it will stop the **release bearing travel**. Any further wear will cause decreased clamp load, which can lead to slippage and early clutch failure. Clutch adjustment re-establishes the correct free play of the release bearing and ensures the plate load is not affected by disc wear.

Pull-type clutch adjustment as shown in **FIGURE 43-35**, is significantly different from the push-type adjustment and must accomplish three things:

1. Release bearing travel. This ensures that the release bearing moves far enough to completely disengage the clutch.
2. Free play between the release fork and the release bearing. This establishes pedal-free travel in the cab and ensures that the clamp load is not affected by disc wear.
3. Clutch brake squeeze (if equipped). **Clutch brake actuation or squeeze** is affected by the total pedal travel and is adjusted by using the clutch linkage.

SAFETY TIP

Clutch linkage adjustment should never be performed to compensate for clutch disc wear on a pull-type clutch. Adjusting the clutch with the linkage will lead to a loss of clutch brake actuation and eventual clutch failure! Linkage adjustment should be performed only to correct the clutch brake squeeze dimension. Pull-type clutches are adjusted internally with the large **adjusting ring** threaded into the clutch cover or externally with a threaded release bearing sleeve, never with the clutch linkage.

Release Bearing Travel

Release bearing travel is the distance that the release bearing moves as the clutch pedal is depressed to the floor. As the discs wear, the release bearing moves toward the flywheel with the pressure plate and the release levers. This increases release bearing travel at the same time that it reduces free play at the release fork. Release bearing travel is typically 0.5–0.5625 inches (1.25–1.4 cm) and is set by adjusting the clutch internally to move the release bearing back to where it started from.

The most common form of internal adjustment involves turning a large adjusting ring inside the clutch cover. Clockwise movement of this adjusting ring moves the lever or diaphragm spring pivot points closer to the pressure plate. That movement causes their inner edges and the integral release bearing to move toward the transmission. That resets the release bearing travel to 0.5–0.5625 inches (1.25–1.4 cm), and if no linkage adjustment has been made, the release fork free play is re-established also.

There are two adjustment systems for the angle spring clutch. As shown in **FIGURE 43-36**, the first system uses a

FIGURE 43-36 In this angle spring clutch, the locking tang **A.** is removed and the large adjusting ring **B.** turned clockwise to adjust for wear.

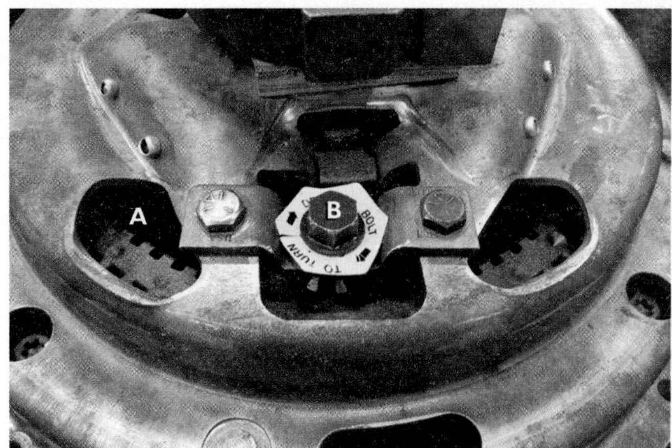

FIGURE 43-37 Quick-adjustment device. **A.** Adjusting ring. **B.** Quick adjust device.

locking tang that is bolted to the clutch cover and that rests between two of the square lugs formed on the adjusting ring.

SAFETY TIP

The clutch pedal must be depressed and the clutch disengaged in order to turn the large adjusting ring. Doing so relieves the clamp load and allows the ring to turn. Trying to turn the adjusting ring with the clutch engaged can destroy the clutch and or the adjusting mechanism.

To adjust the clutch, the engine must be rotated until the locking tang is at the bottom and accessible through the clutch inspection plate. The locking tang is then removed, and an adjusting tool is bolted to the same hole as the tang bolt. Next, the clutch pedal is depressed to remove the clamp load, and the adjusting tool is used to turn the adjusting ring. The ring is turned clockwise when looking from the rear, to compensate for worn clutch discs.

The second adjusting system is exclusive to Eaton/Spicer angle spring clutches and uses a "**quick adjust**" device shown in **FIGURE 43-37**.

This device consists of 5/8 inch bolt attached to a small pinion gear that meshes with internal teeth on the large adjusting ring. The 5/8-inch bolt has a spring-loaded locking system that prevents it from moving by itself. The quick adjust device is bolted to the clutch cover. **FIGURE 43-38** illustrates a properly adjusted pull-type clutch with release bearing travel of 0.5–0.5625 inches (12.4–14.2 mm).

To adjust the clutch with this system, the engine must again be rotated until the quick adjust is at the bottom and accessible through the clutch inspection cover. The clutch pedal is depressed to remove the clamp load, and the technician uses a wrench or socket first to depress the locking bolt and then to turn the quick adjust, which rotates the large adjusting ring in the clutch cover. The quick adjust is rotated clockwise from the rear to adjust for worn clutch discs. One turn of the quick adjust will equate to approximately 0.125–0.2 inches (3.2–5 mm) of difference in release bearing travel.

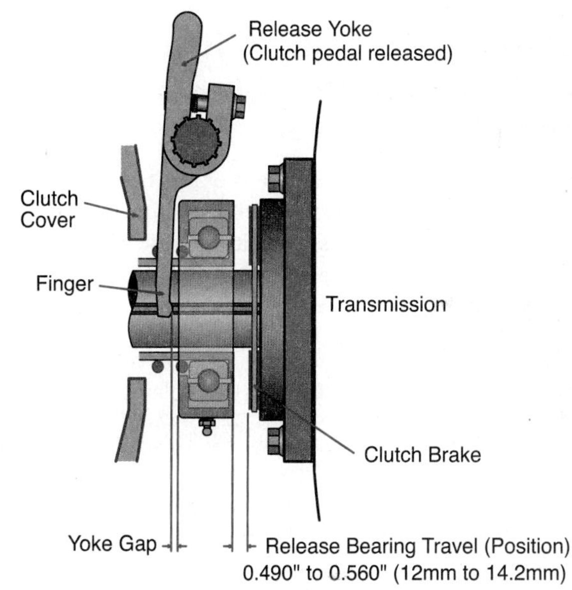

FIGURE 43-38 A properly adjusted threaded release sleeve type of clutch.

▶ TECHNICIAN TIP

Remember that in most cases, linkage adjustment shouldn't be required. The internal adjustment is normally all that is needed to achieve proper adjustment of the clutch.

SAFETY TIP

Failure to depress the clutch pedal prior to trying to rotate the adjusting ring in a pull-type clutch will cause damage to the quick adjust mechanism. It must only be rotated with the clutch pedal fully depressed.

Linkage Adjustment, or Clutch Brake Squeeze Adjustment

The need for linkage adjustment is normally caused by wear in the linkage system. Once the worn components are replaced, adjustment is unnecessary. Linkage adjustment controls the total movement of the release fork and therefore when the fork will push the release bearing against the clutch brake. This should occur in the last half to 1 inch of pedal travel. A worn clutch brake may necessitate the need for linkage adjustment, but a better fix is to replace the worn clutch brake. To check clutch brake squeeze, insert a 0.010-inch feeler gauge between the clutch brake and the release bearing, and have a colleague push the clutch pedal as far as it will go. While clamping the feeler gauge between the brake and the bearing, note the clutch pedal position with a tape measure. Now have the colleague raise the pedal slowly and stop when the feeler gauge can be removed. Measure the height of the clutch pedal at this point. It should be ½–1 inch higher than the end of pedal travel noted previously. If that is not the case, the clutch linkage should be adjusted to gain proper brake squeeze. Lengthening the linkage will lower the squeeze point, and shortening the linkage will raise the squeeze point.

▶ Troubleshooting Clutch Failures and Problems

S43002

The primary cause of clutch failure is excess heat. Excess heat causes the surface of the friction materials to liquefy, so they can no longer transfer torque. As a result, the disc starts slipping, which in turn causes more heat. At that point, complete failure occurs very rapidly.

Shock loads can also cause severe damage to a clutch and must be avoided. Proper operator education is essential to a long and trouble-free clutch life, but the operator and the technician must work together to get the maximum life from the clutch. **TABLE 43-1** lists various common clutch complaints and their causes. This table is by no means a comprehensive list of clutch complaints, though, so always check the manufacturer's service literature when diagnosing clutch system problems.

▶ Other Clutch Types Used with Mobile Off-Road Equipment

K43005

Mobile off-road equipment and machines use a variety of other types of clutches to operate various power take-off devices: over-center disc-type clutches, over-center expanding shoe clutches, cone clutches, centrifugal clutches, and electromagnetic clutches. The following section will discuss each of these types and explain their use and operation.

Over-Center Clutches

Over-center clutches are very similar to automotive-style flywheel clutches in that they use friction to transmit torque. However, they have one major difference: they are not engaged by a spring-loaded pressure plate but rather by mechanical

TABLE 43-1 Common Clutch Complaints, Causes, and Corrections

Symptom	Cause	Correction
Clutch slips on engagement or during operation	Insufficient release bearing clearance; no free play Riding the pedal Clutch worn out	Readjust clutch to gain correct clearance Instruct driver on proper techniques Replace worn out clutch
Pedal hard to depress	Linkage binding Release bearing wear pads grooved	Repair or replace linkage Replace release bearing or clutch assembly
Clutch does not release completely	Insufficient release bearing free travel Worn or damaged input shaft splines; discs hanging up Warped clutch disc or pressure plate Intermediate plate binding	Readjust clutch Replace input shaft Replace clutch as necessary Correct binding intermediate plate check drive pin on 14" (36.6 cm) clutch and drive slots on 15.5" (39.4 cm) clutch repair or replace as necessary
Clutch chatters on engagement	Starting in too high a gear for the load Oil-soaked discs Warped or damaged pressure plate, flywheel, or clutch disc	Instruct the driver on proper operating techniques Repair source of oil contamination and clean or replace discs Replace warped or damaged components
Clutch noisy on disengagement	Worn or damaged release bearing Worn or damaged pilot bearing; noisy only when fully disengaged Clutch adjustment incorrect on pull-type clutch	Replace release bearing Release pilot bearing If adjustment was made with linkage instead of internal adjustment, it can cause bearing retainer to contact clutch cover—readjust correctly
Gear clash on shifting	Too much free play at pedal (push-type clutch) Not enough release bearing free travel (pull-type clutch) Discs warped or damaged Pilot bearing binding	Adjust clutch linkage Adjust clutch internally Replace damaged components Replace pilot bearing

FIGURE 43-39 Over-center clutches are commonly used to drive PTOs (power take-offs) to send power from the engine to ancillary equipment.

clamping force. The operator will (usually) move a hand lever to engage the clutch, and once moved to the engaged position, it will lock there until the operator moves the lever to the disengage position. An over-center clutch is shown in **FIGURE 43-39**.

These types of clutches are typically used for power take-off applications to drive various types of equipment, screeners, rock crushers, etc., but they have been used to engage the driveline for bulldozers and other mobile equipment in the past. In these applications, the clutch would typically input a standard transmission with a forward/reverse shuttle. (A forward/reverse shuttle allows the transmission to switch from forward to reverse without disconnecting from the power source; it will be covered in more detail in Chapter 48.) To use the machine, the operator sets the throttle, chooses the transmission speed range, and then engages the over-center clutch and operates the unit through forward and reverse cycles using the shuttle until they disengage the clutch.

Over-center clutches typically have friction material that is directly driven by a splined flywheel, such the one shown in **FIGURE 43-40**. The over-center clutch may have one or two friction discs sandwiched between the two driven plates, which in turn are attached to the output. Over-center clutches have a mechanism that when activated mechanically squeezes the friction disc(s) between two driven plates. The mechanism used to apply the force to the friction disc(s) can be moved to an over-center position. The mechanism is shown as released in **FIGURE 43-41a** and as engaged in **FIGURE 43-41b**. Notice that the links in the mechanism have moved beyond the perpendicular to the output shafts axis. This is the "over-center" position.

FIGURE 43-40 The flywheel for an over-center clutch has splines like this one that directly drive the friction material.

"Over-center" here means that the mechanism is moved to squeeze the friction disc and then a little bit further, and it will lock in that position until the operator physically pulls the lever for the mechanism back toward its starting position. The greatest amount of clamp force occurs when the links are in the perpendicular position. As they move past this position, they slightly lose clamp load, but they have sufficient force to carry the load. To understand the over-center position, think of a clasp-type buckle or clamp closing a tool box, as shown in **FIGURE 43-42**.

As you move the clasps lever toward the closed position, the lever pivots through an arc and the force required to move

FIGURE 43-41 **A.** The over-center mechanism links in the disengaged position. **B.** The engaged or locked position.

FIGURE 43-42 This type of clasp uses the over-center principle to hold tension on the closure and lock the clasp lever in the closed position.

it increases until it reaches a point (the center of the arc) where the required force suddenly diminishes. The lever then snaps into the closed position and stays there until you pull it back toward the open position. This is what an over-center mechanism does when applying force to its clutch disc. The clamp load on the friction disc increases until the center point and then slightly diminishes as the mechanism moves past center, locking it in place.

To increase capacity, over-center clutches are available in dual or multiple disc designs, and as with flywheel-type clutches, multiple discs will require intermediate or separator plates in between each set of two frictions discs. Over-center clutches usually will have the friction disc(s) splined directly to an internally splined flywheel, making the disc(s) the driving element(s), and the clamping plates will be attached to the output, making them the driven elements. This arrangement is shown in **FIGURE 43-43**.

Expanding Shoe Clutch

Over-center clutches are also available in expanding shoe type. Expanding shoe clutches have a drum attached to the prime mover rather than a flywheel with a flat friction surface. The expanding shoes contact the inner surface of this drum to engage the clutch. This type of over-center clutch is typically engaged either hydraulically or by air and can be used to allow controlled raising and free-fall lowering of a hoist or winch. Expanding shoe clutches can also be engaged by a lever being placed in the over-center position by an operator. An expanding shoe clutch can also be applied hydraulically, like the one shown in **FIGURE 43-44**.

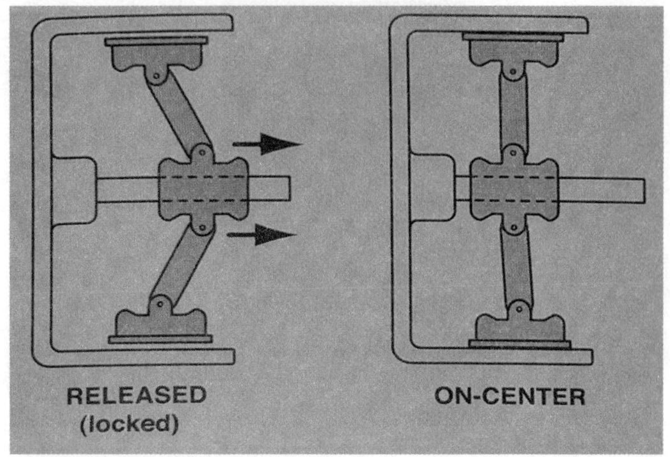

FIGURE 43-44 An expanding shoe clutch.

Cone-Type Clutch

A cone-type clutch consists of a male cone and female cup, one of which will be lined with friction material. Either component of the cone clutch can be the drive or driven member, depending on the application. A cone clutch is shown in **FIGURE 43-45**.

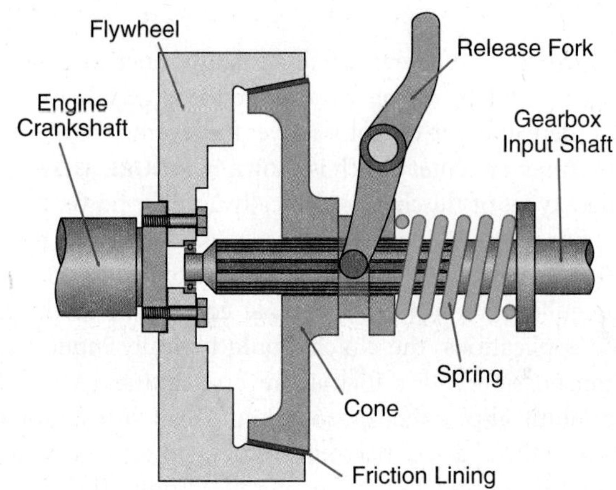

FIGURE 43-45 A cone-type clutch can have either the cone or the cup as the driven member.

The cone clutch can be engaged and disengaged by using conventional clutch linkages, but in heavy equipment, it is normally an over-center-type design, again manually engaged by an operator. Cone-type clutches can transmit large amounts of torque but can lock together and be difficult to disengage if the cone angle is less than 20 degrees.

FIGURE 43-43 The two friction discs of this dual disc over-center clutch spline directly to the inside of the flywheel, and the clamping plates are the driven members of the clutch.

Maintenance of Over-Center Clutches

Over-center clutches require the same periodic maintenance as flywheel clutches: lubrication of the actuation linkage and inspection of the friction material and operation. Over-center actuated clutches will also require periodic adjustment to maintain clamp load and prevent slippage and also to ensure that the clutch stays in the desired position when placed there by the operator. Adjustment of the over-center clutch requires checking the torque required to move the lever to the over-center position and then tightening or loosening the engagement method. (A typical way to measure the torque required is to weld a socket or a bolt to the linkage lever and use a dial-type torque wrench to determine the torque required to engage the clutch.)

Centrifugal Clutches

Centrifugal clutches are clutches that are engaged by centrifugal force caused by the engine's rotation, which are available in several designs. Some centrifugal clutches will have conventional friction discs, usually multiple discs. Other types of centrifugal clutches will have brake-shoe-type friction material that when engaged will press against a drum to transfer torque. Shoe-type centrifugal clutches are typically driven by the engine or power source, while the drum that the shoes will press against is attached to the component we wish to drive. As the engine rpm increases, the shoes are thrown outward by centrifugal force, so they contact the drum and transmit torque to the driven component. A series of centrifugal clutches are shown in **FIGURE 43-46**.

Centrifugal clutches allow a certain amount of slip and rarely achieve a full engagement; they are therefore used only in specialized, usually light-duty, applications.

Centrifugal clutches can be tailored to a specific application, but by their nature, they have a specific engagement rpm. That is to say, the weighted components will engage when the sufficient rpm is achieved for centrifugal force to overcome the hold-off springs or the weight of the shoes. Because of this, if they are operated at an rpm close to this point, excessive slippage will occur, generating significant amounts of heat and wear. Consequently, these clutches are typically used in an on/off-type operation where the engine will be running at rated speed or at idle. Servicing these clutches typically involves replacing worn friction material or friction surfaces. There may be an adjustment to change the engagement rpm, but that is usually the only adjustment. As always, check the equipment manufacturer's literature for directions.

Electromagnetic Clutches

Electromagnetic clutches are usually constructed with a stationary electromagnetic coil mounted inside a rotating assembly, quite often a pulley that is driven by an engine or motor. The pulley will have a flat engagement surface on the front. An engagement plate or disc attached to the input shaft of the component to be driven by the clutch will be mounted very closely in front of the pulley, typically less than 0.050 inches. The engagement plate will be mounted in such a way that the plate can move toward the pulley when required. Usually, the plate is connected to the input shaft of the component through flexible drive straps and is therefore the driven member. To engage the clutch, a current is sent to the electromagnetic coil, which pulls the engagement plate against the pulley, causing it and the shaft attached to it to rotate with the pulley. A partially cutaway electromagnetic clutch is shown in **FIGURE 43-47**.

A typical use of an electromagnetic clutch is to drive an air-conditioning compressor. Service of electromagnetic clutches is typically limited to checking and adjusting the air gap between the driven plate and the pulley, replacing worn components or replacing the electromagnetic coil.

FIGURE 43-46 Shoe-type centrifugal clutches.

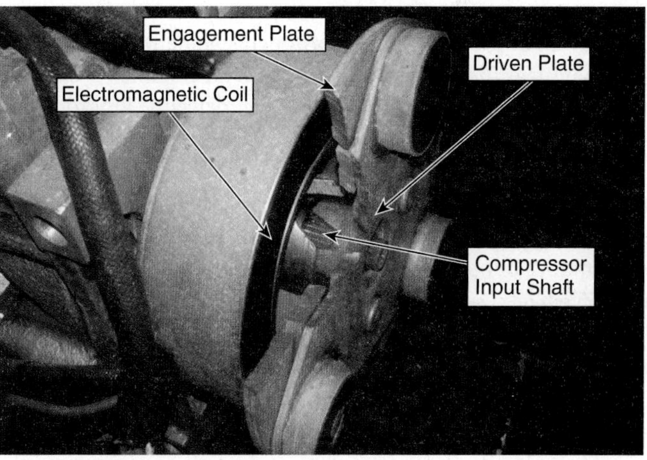

FIGURE 43-47 An electromagnetic clutch.

▶ Wrap-Up

Ready for Review

- Mobile off-road equipment (MORE) uses many different types of clutches: traditional, single, dual, and multiple disc flywheel clutches and several types of PTO clutches.
- A flywheel friction clutch has two basic functions. The first function is to transmit torque from the engine to the driveline; the second is to allow the engine and the driveline to be disconnected when required.
- Clutches operate by using friction, which is the resistance of motion between two bodies in contact to transmit torque.
- Clutches must deal with increasingly powerful engine torsional vibrations that can damage driveline components every time a cylinder fires.
- Clutch capacity, or the amount of torque a clutch can handle without slipping, is affected by the coefficient of

friction of the material used, the surface area in contact, and the clamp load.

- Flywheel clutches can be push type or pull type. This refers to the direction a clutch release bearing moves while the clutch is being disengaged.
- Coil springs can be used to supply clamping load for the clutch. As the clutch discs wear, they lose clamping force.
- Diaphragm spring clutches are a better choice in most applications, because their clamp load is not diminished as the disc wears.
- The easy-pedal angle spring pull-type clutch design prevents a reduction in clamp load as long the clutch is correctly adjusted.
- Pull-type clutches allow the use of clutch brakes. Clutch brakes are splined to the input shaft of a non-synchronized transmission.
- For years, clutch friction facings were made with asbestos, which is a known carcinogen. Today, clutches manufactured in North America don't contain asbestos. The long-term effects of exposure to clutch dust from modern facing materials is unknown. Technicians should always wear NIOSH-approved respirators when working in any dust-laden environment.
- Two general types of friction materials are used today: organic and ceramic. Ceramic facings have higher coefficients of friction than organic facings have, but provide a more abrupt engagement. Today's manufacturers of clutches have developed clutch systems that are very good at smoothing out driveline vibrations caused by engine torsional vibrations, both under load and at idle.
- Engine flywheels have several important functions. They offer a friction surface for the clutch, provide inertia, and smooth out power pulsations from the engine.
- Flywheels come in two predominate designs: a flat-type flywheel and a pot-type flywheel.
- Dual disc clutches use an intermediate plate that provides a friction surface for the rear of the front friction disc and the front of the rear disc.
- Multiple disc clutches used on mobile off-road equipment require a separator plate between each pair of friction discs and are typically oil cooled.
- Pilot bearings support the front end of the transmission input shaft and should be replaced when the clutch is replaced.
- The release fork (yoke) is the lever that actually moves the release bearing to disengage the clutch.
- The release bearings in push-type clutches slide on a sleeve that surrounds the input shaft and rotate only when the clutch is being disengaged.
- The release bearings in a pull-type clutch are integral, and the inner bearing rotates whenever the engine is rotating.
- Clutches can be actuated by mechanical linkage, cable, or hydraulics in mobile off-road equipment.
- Proper and timely clutch maintenance can go a long way to extending clutch life. Clutches should be inspected and adjusted as per the manufacturer's maintenance schedule.
- Adjusting push-type clutches involves adjusting the clutch actuating mechanism to re-establish free pedal or release fork clearance.
- Adjusting pull-type clutches usually does not require any linkage adjustment. The clutch is adjusted internally to re-establish release bearing travel and release fork clearance.
- Release bearing travel is the distance that the release bearing moves while releasing the clutch on a pull-type clutch. This dimension gets smaller as the clutch discs wear.
- The most common cause of premature clutch failure is excessive heat. While a clutch is engaged and not slipping, heat is basically nonexistent, but if the clutch slips or the driver allows the clutch to slip too much during engagement and disengagement, the clutch will fail rapidly.

Key Terms

adjusting ring A large threaded ring in the clutch cover of a pull-type clutch used to adjust the clutch internally.

angle spring clutch A clutch that uses three pairs of angled springs pushing against levers to supply the clamp load.

ceramic friction facings Friction facings made mostly of artificial materials specifically designed to produce desirable characteristics.

clamp force The force that squeezes the clutch disc(s) between the pressure plate and the flywheel; also called clamp load.

clamp load The force that squeezes the clutch disc(s) between the pressure plate and the flywheel; also called clamp force.

clutch brake A small frictional brake usually mounted on the transmission input shaft, which is designed to slow down or stop the inertia of the transmission gearing so that shifts into first or reverse can be made without clashing.

clutch brake actuation or squeeze The point of clutch pedal actuation on a pull-type clutch when the clutch brake is being actuated or squeezed, which is adjusted by linkage.

clutch capacity The amount of torque that the clutch can safely handle without slipping.

clutch cover The outside part of the clutch that is bolted to the flywheel and that holds all of the clutch components except the clutch disc. It is mistakenly but commonly called the pressure plate.

coefficient of friction (CoF) The amount of force required to move an object while in contact with another, divided by its weight.

coil spring–style clutch A clutch that uses coil springs mounted perpendicular to the pressure plate to provide the clamp load.

cross-shaft A rotating shaft that holds the release fork. In a pull-type clutch, there are actually two cross-shafts: a left and a right.

dampening disc A disc with a ring of torsional dampening springs around its hub designed to absorb engine torsional vibrations.

diaphragm spring clutch A clutch that uses a single diaphragm spring, also known as a Belleville spring, to provide the clamp force.

drive pin A pin used in a pot-type flywheel to drive the intermediate plate.

flat-type flywheel A flywheel that is predominately flat, with all of the clutch components inside the clutch cover.

friction The relative resistance to motion between any two bodies in contact with one another.

flywheel A heavy, round metal disc attached to the end of the crankshaft to smooth out vibrations from the crank-shaft assembly and provide one of the friction surfaces for a clutch disc used on a manual transmission.

Hooke's law A law of physics that states that force delivered by a spring to an object is directly related to its compression or extension; the greater the spring is compressed, the more force the spring delivers.

input shaft The component to which the clutch discs are splined.

intermediate plate/separator plate A plate driven by the flywheel or the clutch cover, separating two friction discs.

kinetic friction The friction between two surfaces that are sliding against each other.

locking tang A small flat piece of metal that stops the large internal adjusting ring from moving when the clutch is operating.

organic facings Friction facings made of various natural materials, such as cotton fibers, rubber, aluminum, glass, copper or brass fibers, and carbon material.

over-center clutch A clutch that engages by using clamp force rather than spring force.

quick adjust A small mechanism used to turn the large adjusting ring in the clutch cover when adjustment is required.

pilot bearing A bearing that supports the front of the transmission input shaft, which is mounted in the flywheel or the rear of the crankshaft.

pot-type flywheel A flywheel shaped like a deep pot, inside of which all of the components of the clutch are housed, with the exception of the clutch cover.

pressure plate The friction surface of the clutch cover and the plate that squeezes the clutch disc against the flywheel.

pull-type clutch A clutch with an integral release bearing, which is pulled toward the transmission to disengage the clutch.

push-type clutch A clutch in which the release bearing is pushed toward the engine to release the clutch.

release bearing A hollow bearing through which the input shaft passes, which pushes or pulls against rotating clutch release levers to release the clutch.

release bearing travel The distance that the release bearing moves while releasing the clutch in a pull-type clutch.

release fork (yoke) The actuator that moves the release bearing.

sealed release bearing A release bearing with no grease nipple or zerk.

slave cylinder The hydraulic cylinder used to release the clutch in hydraulically actuated clutch systems.

torsional vibrations Powerful vibrations caused by the firing force twisting and accelerating the crankshaft every time a cylinder fires.

vocation The type of service a machine is involved in.

Review Questions

1. Which of the following clutch types has an integral or attached release bearing?
   a. Push-type clutch
   b. Diaphragm-type clutch
   c. Lever-type clutch
   d. Pull-type clutch
2. What are the components found inside a clutch that allow us to release it with less pedal effort and also amplify clutch application pressure when it is engaged?
   a. Pressure plates
   b. Torsional springs
   c. Levers
   d. Pivot rings
3. The function of coaxial or cushion springs in a clutch disc hub concerns which of the following?
   a. Increase clutch clamp load
   b. Make the disc stronger
   c. Absorb torsional vibrations
   d. All of the above.
4. The function of most types of clutch brakes concerns which of the following?
   a. Slowing down or stop the input shaft while shifting to first gear or reverse
   b. Allowing for easier upshifting
   c. Absorbing engine torque
   d. All of the above.
5. What is the primary reason that pull-type clutches are used?
   a. Pull-type clutches will last longer.
   b. Pull-type clutches are less expensive to manufacture.
   c. Pull-type clutches require less pedal effort than push-type clutches.
   d. Pull-type clutches allow the use of a clutch brake.
6. Which of the following affects the capacity of the clutch to handle engine power without slipping?
   a. The coefficient of friction of the clutch disc material
   b. The surface area of the friction discs
   c. The number of friction discs
   d. All of the above.
7. Over-center clutches are usually operated by which of the following methods?
   a. Manually with a lever
   b. Hydraulically
   c. Mechanically with a foot pedal
   d. Electronically

8. Which of the following should not usually be necessary during a routine adjustment of a pull-type clutch?
   a. An internal adjustment
   b. A check of clutch brake squeeze
   c. A check of linkage free play
   d. A linkage adjustment
9. Which of the following clutch types never have less than the original pressure plate clamp load throughout the life of the clutch as long as adjustment is correct?
   a. Coil spring–style clutch
   b. Diaphragm spring clutch
   c. Coaxial spring clutch
   d. None of the above.
10. Where would you most likely find an electromagnetic clutch?
    a. On an engine flywheel
    b. Driving a PTO
    c. Driving an air-conditioning compressor
    d. Connecting the transmission to the driveline

ASE Technician A/Technician B Style Questions

1. Technician A says that angle spring pull-type clutches are adjusted by turning the large adjustment ring in the clutch cover. Technician B says that the adjustment will change the clutch brake squeeze dimension. Who is correct?
   a. Technician A
   b. Technician B
   c. Both Technician A and Technician B
   d. Neither Technician A nor Technician B
2. Technician A says that clutch brake squeeze should occur in the last inch of clutch pedal travel near the floor. Technician B says that clutch brake squeeze can be altered by a linkage adjustment. Who is correct?
   a. Technician A
   b. Technician B
   c. Both Technician A and Technician B
   d. Neither Technician A nor Technician B
3. Technician A says that coil spring clutches are the best because the heavy coil springs provide exceptional clamp load. Technician B says that diaphragm spring clutches are a better choice because they do not lose clamp load. Who is correct?
   a. Technician A
   b. Technician B
   c. Both Technician A and Technician B
   d. Neither Technician A nor Technician B
4. Technician A says that the release bearing in pull-type clutches rotates only when disengaging the clutch. Technician B says that the release bearing in push-type clutches continuously rotates while the engine is running. Who is correct?
   a. Technician A
   b. Technician B
   c. Both Technician A and Technician B
   d. Neither Technician A nor Technician B
5. Technician A says that using dual discs in a clutch doubles the clutch capacity. Technician B says that increasing clamp load can increase clutch capacity. Who is correct?
   a. Technician A
   b. Technician B
   c. Both Technician A and Technician B
   d. Neither Technician A nor Technician B
6. Technician A says that a pull-type clutch with mechanical linkage should have ⅛ inch (3.2 mm) free play between the release fork and the release bearing. Technician B says that a pull-type clutch release bearing travel dimension should be at least ½ inch (1.27 cm). Who is correct?
   a. Technician A
   b. Technician B
   c. Both Technician A and Technician B
   d. Neither Technician A nor Technician B
7. Technician A says that clutch brakes help the operator to shift without clashing. Technician B says that clutch brakes can be replaced without removing the transmission. Who is correct?
   a. Technician A
   b. Technician B
   c. Both Technician A and Technician B
   d. Neither Technician A nor Technician B
8. Technician A says that an over-center clutch friction material is usually splined to the flywheel. Technician B says that diaphragm spring clutches are found only in light-duty machines. Who is correct?
   a. Technician A
   b. Technician B
   c. Both Technician A and Technician B
   d. Neither Technician A nor Technician B
9. Technician A says that the clutch should be adjusted when the pedal-free play is reduced by half. Technician B says that free play is not used to check whether an over-center clutch requires adjustment. Who is correct?
   a. Technician A
   b. Technician B
   c. Both Technician A and Technician B
   d. Neither Technician A nor Technician B
10. Technician A says that over-center clutches are usually used to drive a PTO. Technician B says that over-center clutches do not require adjustment. Who is correct?
    a. Technician A
    b. Technician B
    c. Both Technician A and Technician B
    d. Neither Technician A nor Technician B

CHAPTER 44
Gearing Basics

Knowledge Objectives

After reading this chapter, you will be able to:

- **K44001** Explain the purpose and fundamentals of gears used in mobile off-road equipment.
- **K44002** Identify the construction features, composition, types, and application of gears used in mobile off-road equipment.
- **K44003** Describe the fundamentals and principles of both the operation and the power flows of planetary gears used in mobile off-road equipment.

Skills Objectives

After reading this chapter, you will be able to:

- **S44001** Calculate conventional gear ratios, gear speed, and torque multiplication.
- **S44002** Calculate planetary gear ratios.

▶ Introduction

In order to properly diagnose and repair gear systems, technicians must have a fundamental knowledge of gearing concepts. Gears are essential to the operation of any piece of equipment. Gears are found in engines, transmissions, final drives, and drive hubs. The correct functioning of those gears makes the machine operate. The basic function of a gear is to transfer torque and motion to gain mechanical advantage to increase either output power or output speed. **Torque** is the twisting force generated by the engine. Mechanical advantage is anything that allows us to travel greater distances and/or move more weight with less effort.

There are many different types of gears, but all of them share common basic terms and principles. **FIGURE 44-1** shows a cutaway of a transmission exposing the gearing.

▶ Gear Basics

K44001

The first gears were simple wooden peg gears. As illustrated in **FIGURE 44-2**, one wheel of wood would have pegs installed perpendicular to its axis, and these pegs would mesh with another wheel of wood on which the pegs were installed in parallel to its axis. The intermeshed pegs of the driving wheel would cause the driven wheel to turn. Motion could be transferred in this way.

As the pegs begin to mesh, however, the outer end of the driving peg contacts the driven peg first. As they continue

FIGURE 44-1 A six-speed fuller single countershaft transmission.

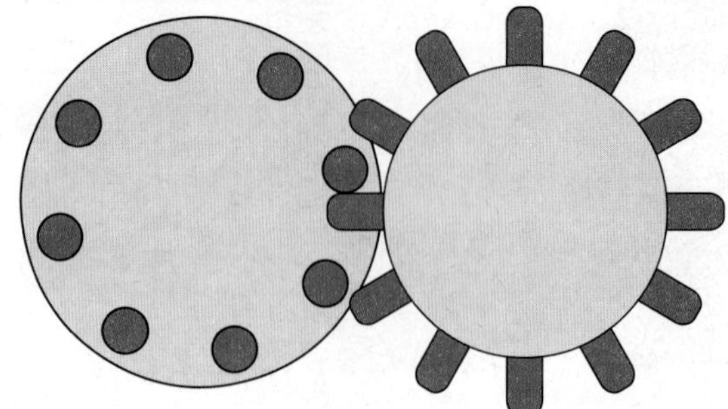

FIGURE 44-2 Wooden peg gears cause irregular speed of the driven gear.

through mesh, the driving peg will slide along the driven peg until the centers of the two wheels align. At that point, the driving peg will slide back out until it leaves mesh.

With pegs sliding in and out of mesh, the distance from the center of the driving wheel's axis to the point of contact of the driven wheel's pegs is constantly changing. The constant change causes the driven wheel to turn faster at the longer contact points and slower at the shorter contact points. As a result, the speed of the driven wheel is also constantly changing.

Changing speeds would have little effect on a system such as a grain miller's grindstone being turned with a slow-moving water wheel. As speed increases, however, the constantly changing speed would become a serious vibration. Imagine what that would mean for a machine. It would be totally unacceptable! The whole powertrain would be trying to speed up and slow down constantly. Imagine the vibration that would result!

Modern gears are specially formed to eliminate this anomaly, so the driven gear operates at a consistent speed. This chapter will discuss basic gearing terminology and explain the construction and operation of gears in basic, universal terms.

Fundamentals of Gears

Because gears are such a foundational part of the mechanics of any machine or vehicle, it is important to understand how they are designed and made, how they interact, and how their ratios determine their functionality.

Gear Design

Gears can be made from a variety of metals. In medium- and heavy-duty applications, gears are typically made from **cast ductile iron**. "Ductile" means that it is bendable rather than

You Are the Mobile Heavy Equipment Technician

You are asked to inspect a tractor that has a significant vibration felt throughout the machine. When the operator starts off in first gear, the vibration seems to get worse as they speed up the machine. The vibration is not present if the machine is operated in neutral only while it is in first gear. Once the shift is made into second gear, the vibration goes away. You first check the transmission fluid, and although the level is correct, you notice the fluid has a silvery look. What would you recommend as the next step for diagnosing this machine?

1. Would you recommend replacing the transmission bearings?
2. Would you inspect the gearing for wear?
3. What would you look for in the transmission to find the root of this problem?

hard and brittle. Gears can also be made of steel. All gears undergo various methods of surface hardening. **Hardening** is a manufacturing process that makes the surface of a gear much harder than its core. Typically, the surface is hardened to a depth of no more than 0.050 inches (1.2 mm). The idea is to produce a gear with a surface hard enough to withstand the extreme pressures that come from the sliding and then rolling contact that gear teeth are subjected to. Although the exterior of the gear must be extremely hard, the gear's core must be more ductile so that it can resist fracture and absorb shock loads.

Gear Nomenclature

All gears can be described with a core set of terminology. As you read this section, consult the labeled illustration of gears shown in **FIGURE 44-3**.

The basic structure of the gear is its teeth, which, as you might imagine, are the protrusions around the gear's circumference. The apex of the tooth is called the **top land**. The **tooth face** is the area that actually comes into contact with a mating gear. The tooth faces of the gears in Figure 44-3 are parallel to the gear's axis of rotation. The upper portion of the tooth contact area is called the **addendum**, and the lower portion of this area is called the **dedendum**.

The **root** (also called **fillet radius**) of a gear is the bottom of the valley formed between two teeth. The precise design of the fillet radius provides a gradual change in section and determines the shape of the formed tooth. The root minimizes stress risers (possible break points) to make the tooth stronger. The **root diameter** of a gear is the smallest circle of the gear measured at the fillet radius, or root, of the teeth.

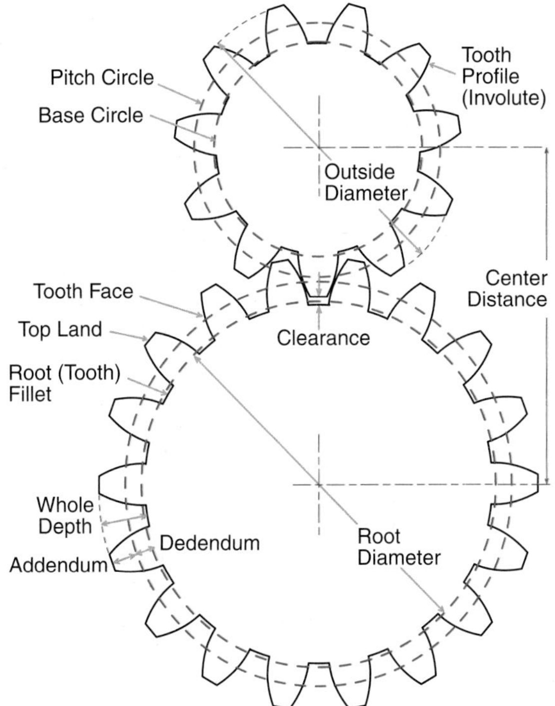

FIGURE 44-3 Anatomy of a gear.

Gear Face Contact During Mesh

As teeth on a gear engage, or mesh, with a mating gear, the contact starts at the addendum of the driven gear tooth and the dedendum of the driving gear tooth. The gears then slide into full mesh, where the sliding motion stops and only rolling motion occurs between them. Then the gears slide out of mesh. At that point, contact ends between the dedendum of the driven gear tooth and the addendum of the driving tooth. The average contact point of a given tooth is its **pitch diameter** (also called the pitch circle). The **pitch circle** is the theoretical point where only rolling motion exists. The pitch diameter is usually a point approximately half way up the tooth face from the fillet radius to the top land.

A gear's **pitch** is determined by the number of teeth per unit of diameter measured at the pitch circle of the gear. For example, a gear with 60 teeth and a pitch diameter of 10 inches (25.4 cm) is a six-pitch gear. This is important because only gears of the same pitch can mesh together properly. That means our example gear could be in mesh only with another six-pitch gear.

Involute Tooth Shape

Modern gears are designed with a special tooth shape called an **involute**, which compensates for the changing point of contact between gears as they rotate through mesh. On an involute tooth, the dedendum (the lower part of the tooth) is thicker than the addendum (the upper part of the tooth). This special shape is how we eliminate the speed changes noted in the introduction. Let's follow two teeth in contact through mesh and see how this is done. **FIGURE 44-4** illustrates this process.

As the driving tooth comes into mesh with the driven tooth, the dedendum (thicker part) of the driving tooth comes in contact with the addendum (thinner part) of the driven tooth. As the meshing continues, the driving tooth slides down the face of the driven tooth. That slide shortens the distance from the axis of the driving gear to the point of contact of the driving tooth—just as it did in the peg wheel example described in the introduction. As the driving tooth slides into mesh, the point of contact is moving toward the thicker part of the driven tooth. The thickening causes a minute acceleration of the driven gear, canceling out the deceleration caused by the changing point of contact.

This action continues until the point of contact reaches the pitch line, where there is no more sliding contact, only rolling contact. As mesh continues, the reverse happens. The point of contact slightly lengthens. As the contact point of the driving tooth slides up to its addendum (thinner part), a minute deceleration cancels out the acceleration caused by the increasing distance from the driving gear centerline.

What does all that mean? It means that, as the teeth go through mesh, the speed of the driven gear will remain consistent rather than speeding up and slowing down.

It is important for the technician to understand that any change in the involute shape or axial positioning of the gears caused by wear may cause this speed oscillation of the driven gear. In high-speed equipment (such as a vehicle), this speed

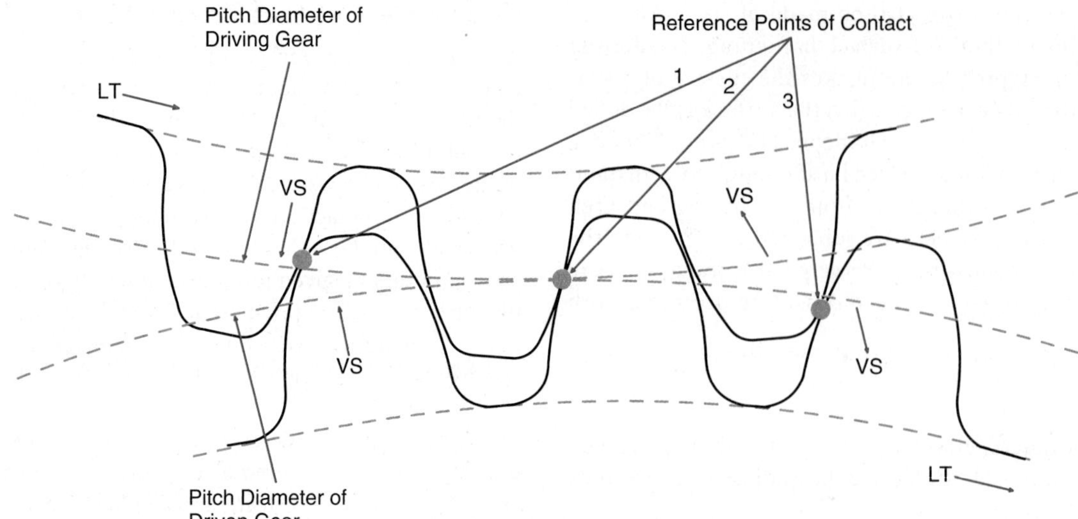

FIGURE 44-4 Involute tooth during mesh.

oscillation will manifest as a vibration. Left unchecked, that vibration can cause catastrophic damage to the component and probably to any component connected to it because of the constant torsional stress caused by the speed fluctuations.

Direction of Rotation

Gear rotation is described based on how the gear is moving when the flat face of the gear is viewed from the top. Rotation is normally referred to as clockwise when the viewed face on the gear moves to the right from the top. Rotation is counterclockwise when the viewed face on the gear moves to the left from the top. **Clockwise** rotation is usually referred to as forward rotation and **counterclockwise** rotation as reverse rotation.

When two externally toothed gears, such as the ones shown in **FIGURE 44-5**, are in mesh with each other, the driven gear will turn in the opposite direction to the drive gear.

Not all gears are externally toothed, however. Some gears have internally facing teeth and are called **ring gears** or internal gears. When a gear with external teeth is in mesh with a ring or internal gear, the driven gear will rotate in the same direction as the drive gear, as shown in **FIGURE 44-6**.

Gear Interaction

Gears can be mounted in many positions to accomplish the desired result. In transmissions, the most common mounting of gear sets is side by side on parallel axes. A notable exception to this is bevel gears, which are normally mounted at 90 degrees to each other. Gears must be mounted so that they have a certain amount of backlash. "**Backlash**" means the clearance between the teeth of gears in mesh. As shown in **FIGURE 44-7**, backlash allows for a thin layer of lubricant between the tooth contact surfaces and for expansion of the gears due to heat.

Backlash must be closely controlled. Too little backlash will not allow lubricant in between teeth, which will lead to failure. Too much backlash can allow the gears to climb out of mesh and

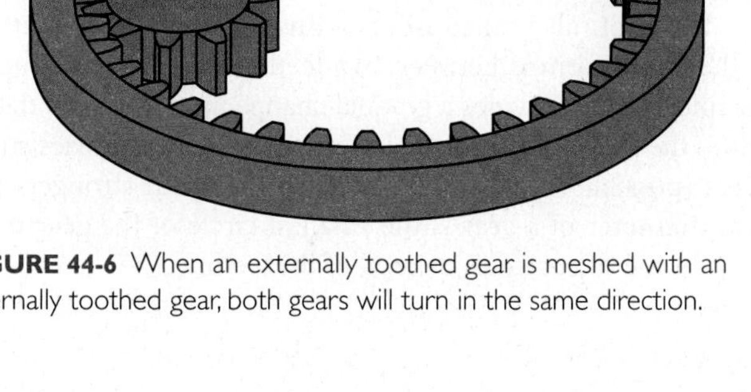

FIGURE 44-6 When an externally toothed gear is meshed with an internally toothed gear, both gears will turn in the same direction.

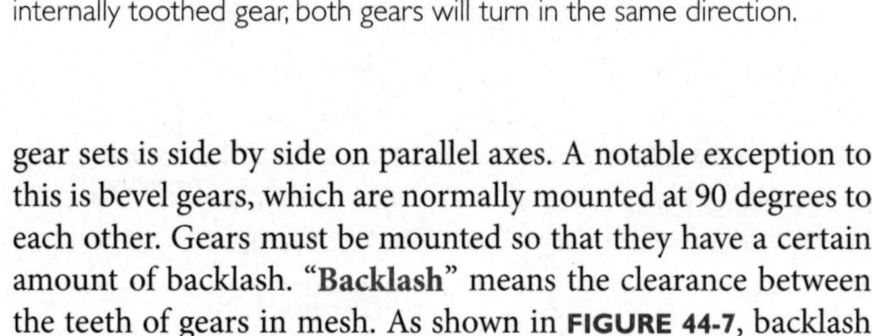

FIGURE 44-5 Two externally toothed gears in mesh will rotate in opposite directions.

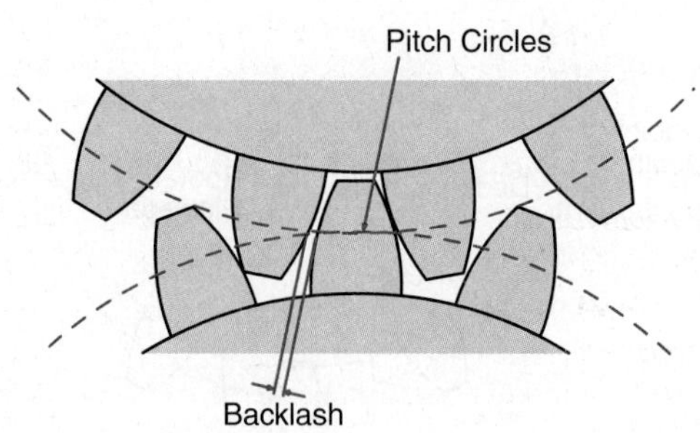

FIGURE 44-7 Backlash clearance in meshing gears.

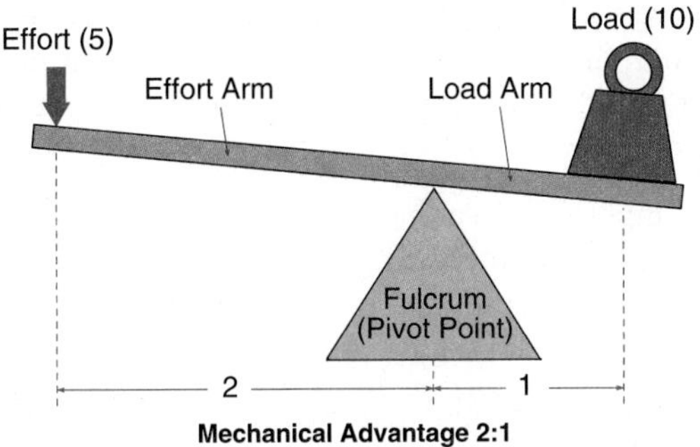

FIGURE 44-8 Lever.

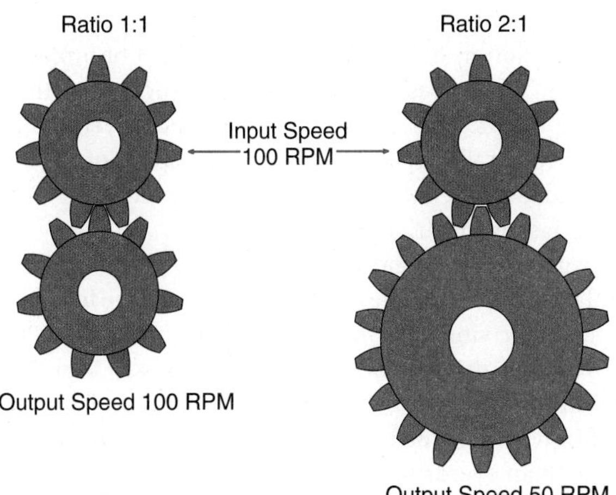

FIGURE 44-9 Two gear sets: one with a 1:1 gear ratio and the other with a 2:1 ratio.

skip a tooth, which will again lead to failure. Backlash is controlled by moving the gears' axes closer together or farther apart.

A **lever**, as shown in **FIGURE 44-8**, is a simple machine that allows a large object to be moved with less force. **Simple machines** are the simplest mechanisms that allow us to gain mechanical advantage. A first-class lever has an effort arm, a load arm, and the fulcrum in the middle. Gears are essentially rotating levers and the effort arm is the distance from the tooth face to the center of the gear's axis of rotation.

Gears have clearly evolved since the lever. As two gears in mesh rotate, the driving gear applies force or effort to each of the gear teeth in sequence. If we look at just one tooth through the body of the gear, we see that the distance from the tooth to the center of the gear or shaft becomes the effort arm of the lever. The center of the gear, or shaft, is the fulcrum. The load is represented by the weight on the gear or shaft that is resisting its rotation. The driving gear is, of course, a lever also, but with the position of the load reversed.

In practice, different lengths of these "levers" provide different levels of output. That is, we can use the different lengths either to gain mechanical advantage—for example, by increasing torque and decreasing speed. Likewise, the different lengths can allow a loss of mechanical advantage by decreasing torque and increasing speed. Gears can also be used to transfer speed and torque unchanged.

▶ Gear Ratio Calculations

S44001

The sizing of the gears and the relationship between them is known as the **gear ratio**. One way to calculate the ratio between gears uses lever length (the distance from the center of the gear's axis to the tooth contact point). A much simpler method uses the number of gear teeth. Simple gear ratios are the relationship between one driving gear and one driven gear, while **compound ratios** involve more than one set of gears. Once the ratio is calculated, we can use it to calculate the torque and speed increase or decrease.

Simple Gear Ratios

Imagine a driving gear that has 15 teeth in mesh with a driven gear that has 30 teeth. Every time the driving gear rotates one complete turn, it will move the driven gear 15 teeth, or one-half of the driven gear's total teeth. Therefore, to move the driven gear one full turn, the driving gear must move 30 teeth, or two complete revolutions. The two gears in our example have a gear ratio of 2:1. Two turns of the driving gear equal one turn of the driven gear. This ratio is illustrated in **FIGURE 44-9**.

The formula to calculate this ratio is simple. Divide the number of teeth on the driven gear by the number of teeth on the drive gear:

$$30/15 = 2$$

The ratio is always compared to one revolution of the driven gear. Therefore, the two revolutions of the driving gear becomes 2 to 1 and is expressed 2:1.

What does this ratio accomplish? The ratio does two things. First, it is responsible for slowing down the speed of the driven gear. The speed of the driven gear will be the speed of the driving gear divided by the ratio. In our example, that means the driven gear will turn only half as fast as the driving gear. Second, and more importantly, gear ratios are responsible for producing mechanical advantage. The mechanical advantage is the effort applied by the driving gear multiplied by the ratio. For example, a driving gear torque of 100 ft-lb (136 N·m) passing through a gear set with a 2:1 ratio becomes 200 ft-lb (271 N·m) at the driven gear. Any ratio with a first number greater than one is known as a **gear reduction** or **underdrive ratio**. The speed of the driven gear will be reduced by the ratio, but available torque will be increased by the same proportion.

But what happens if we reverse the two gears in our example and have the 30-tooth gear driving the 15-tooth gear? Every rotation of the 30-tooth driving gear will turn the 15-tooth driven gear 30 teeth, or two complete revolutions. The formula for calculating the ratio remains the same. That is, the ratio is still calculated by dividing the number of teeth on the driven gear (in this case, 15) by the number of teeth on the driving gear (in this case, 30):

$$15/30 = 0.5$$

As with our earlier example, the ratio is always compared to one revolution of the driven gear. The 0.5 becomes 0.5 to 1 or 0.5:1. What does this ratio accomplish? Again, the ratio does two things. First, it now speeds up the driven gear. That is, the speed of the driven gear will be the speed of the driving gear divided by the ratio. That means the driven gear will turn twice as fast as the driving gear.

By gaining speed, however, we give up mechanical advantage. The torque available at the driven gear is the torque available at the driving gear multiplied by the ratio. So, 100 ft-lb (136 N·m) of driving torque becomes 100 × 0.5 or 50 ft-lb (68 N·m) of torque at the driven gear. Any ratio in which the first number is less than one is known as an **overdrive ratio**. In gears with an overdrive ratio, the speed of the driven gear will be increased by the ratio, but available torque will be decreased by a corresponding amount.

Let's walk through the basic ratio, gear speed, and torque calculations for a simple gear arrangement. As we go through the calculations, we will make the following assumptions:

- The drive gear has 20 teeth.
- The driven gear has 60 teeth.
- The input torque on the drive gear is 100 ft-lb (136 N·m).
- The input speed is 300 rpm.

Let's begin finding the gear ratio by dividing the number of teeth on the driven gear by the number of teeth on the drive gear:

$$60/20 = 3$$
$$3:1$$

That means the gear ratio is 3:1. Because 3 > 1, 3:1 is a reduction, or underdrive, ratio.

Next, let's calculate the torque available at the driven gear by multiplying the input torque by the gear ratio:

3 × 100 = 300 ft-lb (407 N·m) of torque available to the driven gear

Notice how the calculations prove the basic premise that reduction gears increase output torque. The gear ratio of 3:1 is a reduction ratio, and the torque output is higher than the torque input.

The next calculation we perform is one to find the speed of the driven gear. To accomplish that, we need to divide the input speed by the ratio:

$$300 \text{ rpm}/3 = 100 \text{ rpm}$$

As we would expect, our underdrive gear ratio has caused a decrease in output speed.

Compound Ratios

In most applications, there will be more than one set of gears involved in the transfer of speed and torque. When we have a ratio with more than one pair of gears involved, it is called a compound ratio.

Let us examine briefly how compound ratios work. Consider the first gear power flow in a typical transmission. In this transmission, we will assume the input gear has 27 teeth, and it drives a countershaft driven gear with 51 teeth. The countershaft first gear has 13 teeth, and it drives the main shaft first gear, which has 64 teeth. The following is a summary of this power flow:

- The input drive gear has 27 teeth.
- The driven countershaft gear has 51 teeth.
- The countershaft first drive gear has 13 teeth.
- The driven main shaft gear has 64 teeth.

Following our formula, we divide the first driven gear by the first driving gear.

$$51/27 = 1.8888/1$$
$$1.89:1$$

Our gear ratio, therefore, is 1.89:1. This means that the input gear has to turn 1.89 times to turn the countershaft once. Next, we calculate the ratio for the second set of gears. The second driven gear has 64 teeth, and its driving gear has 13 teeth.

$$64/13 = 4.9230/1$$
$$4.92:1$$

So, the countershaft has to turn 4.92 times to turn the main shaft one complete turn. If the input shaft has to turn 1.89 times to turn the countershaft once and the countershaft has to turn 4.92 times to turn the main shaft once, then to find the overall ratio, we have to multiply how many times the input shaft must turn by how many times the countershaft must turn.

$$\text{Therefore, } 1.89 \times 4.92 = 9.30$$

We see then that in order to turn the main shaft one complete revolution, the input shaft must turn 9.30 times. That means the total (compound) ratio of this scenario is 9.30:1. Compound ratios can often involve four, six, or even more gears in the transfer of power. Calculating ratios with that many gears is more simply done by dividing the product of all of the driven gears (all of the driven gears multiplied together), D, by the product of all of the drive gears (all of the drive gears multiplied together), d. The formula for six gears would look like this:

$$\frac{D1 \times D2 \times D3}{d1 \times d2 \times d3}$$

Let's apply our ratio formula to a transmission where the input gear has 27 teeth and it drives a countershaft driven gear with 51 teeth; the countershaft first gear has 13 teeth; and it drives the main shaft first gear, which has 64 teeth.

To calculate the compound ratio for that setup, we first multiply together the number of teeth on each of the driven gears:

$$51 \times 64 = 3{,}264$$

Next, we multiply together the number of teeth on each of the driving gears:

$$27 \times 13 = 351$$

Finally, we divide the product of the driven gears multiplied together by the product of the driving gears multiplied together.

$$3264 / 351 = 9.299$$
$$9.3:1$$

Ratios are usually rounded after two decimals, so this result would be a compound ratio of 9.30 to 1, or 9.30:1.

Because 9.3 > 1, this compound ratio is a reduction or underdrive. Therefore, the input shaft must turn 9.30 times for every one turn of the transmission main shaft. Available torque at the main shaft will be input torque multiplied by the ratio. That means the available torque at the main shaft will be 9.30 times greater than the input torque. The output speed on the main shaft, however, will be the input speed divided by the ratio, or 9.30 times slower.

The same formula can be used no matter how many gear sets are involved in a ratio. It simply becomes a larger calculation, with the number of teeth on each driven gear multiplied together divided by the number of teeth on each of the drive gears multiplied together. **FIGURE 44-10** shows a typical transmission arrangement that uses compound ratios.

Gear sets are used in combination to produce the desired gear ratio for the job required. For example, any underdrive or overdrive ratio through a transmission will have at least two ratios working together:

1. the ratio of the input gear to the countershaft driven gear
2. the ratio of the countershaft speed, or range gear, to its corresponding main shaft speed or range gear.

Those two gears ratios combine to create a compound ratio. Off-road equipment commonly uses compound ratios to achieve the desired torque multiplication.

Not all gear ratios are overdrive or underdrive, however. When gears with exactly the same number of teeth are meshed, the resulting ratio is 1 to 1 (or 1:1). In this case, the gears transmit the exact speed of rotation, and torque remains unchanged.

Idler Gears

The gears used in most manual transmissions are almost exclusively externally toothed gears meshed together. When two externally toothed gears are in mesh, the driven gear will turn in the reverse direction to the drive gear. That direction change suits our purpose well for all gear ratios, with the exception of reverse.

By following the power flow, we can see how this works for us. The engine usually turns clockwise when viewed from the front. So too does the transmission input shaft, because it gets its input from the engine. Inside the transmission, the input shaft gear drives the countershaft driven gear counterclockwise. (That's why we call it a countershaft.) The countershaft first gear is part of the countershaft, and so, it is also turning counterclockwise. Countershaft first gear is in mesh with the main shaft (output shaft) first gear. Therefore, the main shaft gear is driven in a clockwise direction, and the powertrain moves the machine forward. These flow directions are repeated for the rest of the transmission forward gear ratios.

In reverse, however, we must turn the output shaft counterclockwise to move backward. To do this in most transmissions, we use an idler gear. The purpose of the **idler gears** is to act as a bridge between two gears and reverse the direction of rotation without changing the ratio. Idler gears are used in transmissions to drive a vehicle backward. As shown in **FIGURE 44-11**, an idler gear is placed in the power flow between the countershaft reverse drive gear and the main shaft

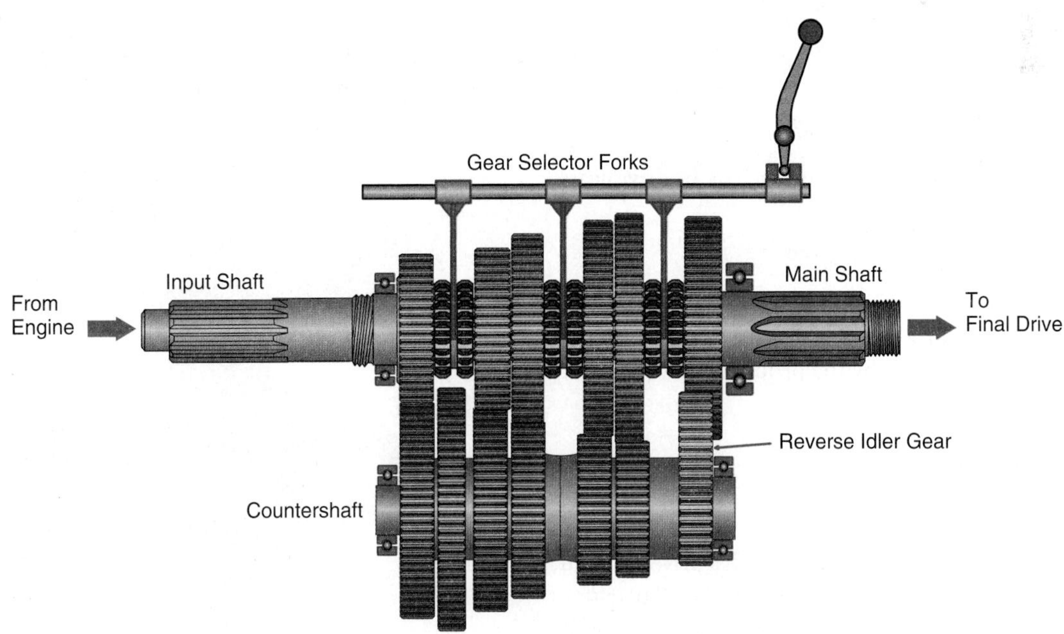

FIGURE 44-10 Most power flows from this transmission will be compound ratios.

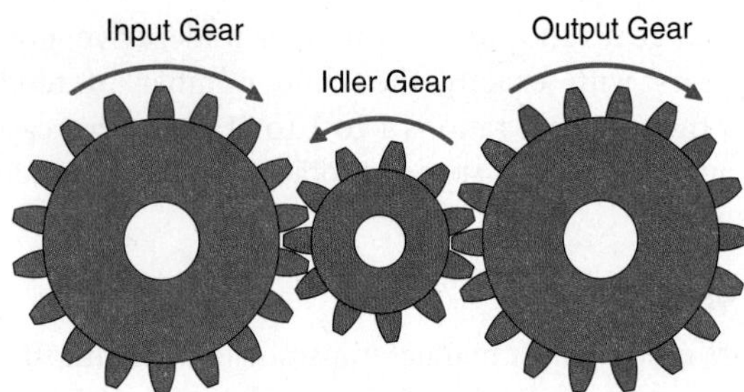

FIGURE 44-11 An idler gear.

reverse gear. The input shaft of the transmission will usually be turning clockwise when viewed from the front, so the countershaft driven gear will be turning counterclockwise. When the machine is put into reverse, the counterclockwise rotation of the countershaft reverse drive gear causes the reverse idler gear to turn clockwise, which as a result makes the output (reverse gear on the main shaft) turn counterclockwise. The equipment then moves backward.

An idler is both a driven gear and a drive gear. The idler gear in our scenario above is driven by the countershaft reverse gear, and the idler gear drives the main shaft reverse gear. Because the idler gear functions in both of those capacities, it has no bearing on gear ratios.

To illustrate this point, let's use the same numbers we used for first gear ratio calculation in the Gear Ratio Calculation section. This time, however, we will insert a nine-tooth idler gear into the first gear power flow and make it reverse.

Recall our assumptions:

- The input drive gear has 27 teeth.
- The driven countershaft gear has 51 teeth.
- The countershaft first drive gear has 13 teeth.
- The driven main shaft gear has 64 teeth.
- Our newly introduced idler gear has 9 teeth.
- The reverse gear main shaft has 64 teeth.

First, we take the number of teeth on each of the driven gears and multiply them together:

$$51 \times 9 \times 64 = 29{,}376$$

Next, we take the number of teeth on each of the drive gears and multiply them together:

$$27 \times 9 \times 13 = 3{,}159$$

Remember that the idler gear drives the main shaft reverse gear, so it is also a drive gear. Now we divide the product of all the driven teeth by the product of all the drive teeth. That is,

$$29{,}376 / 3{,}159 = 9.299$$
$$9.3{:}1$$

That result, 9.30:1, is the exact same ratio that we had in the earlier calculation. Because an idler gear is both a drive gear and a driven gear, it cancels itself out in the calculation. Therefore, idler gears do not need to be included when calculating gear ratios. An idler gear is shown in Figure 44-11.

▶ Types of Gears

K44002

MORE uses many different types of gears in its various systems and powertrains. In this section, we will discuss idler, spur, helical, herringbone, bevel, worm, rack-and-pinion, and planetary gears.

Spur Gears

Spur gears are the simplest of modern gears used in vehicles today. As shown in **FIGURE 44-12**, a spur gear has teeth that are cut parallel to the gears axis of rotation. The advantages of spur gears are numerous. Spur gears are simpler and therefore less expensive to manufacture. Their shafts can be mounted on simple ball or roller bearings, which allows for less expensive manufacture of components. In addition, spur gears do not produce any axial thrust when they are in operation. **Axial thrust** is thrust that tries to move the gears apart along their axis. Spur gears in mesh merely produce **radial thrust**. That is, they tend to want to push away from each other radially, or perpendicular to their axis.

Spur gears do, however, have some disadvantages. First, they tend to be noisy in operation. As spur gear teeth come into mesh with each other, their meshing teeth tend to impact each other, causing a clicking sound. At higher speeds, the clicking becomes a high-pitched whine. Spur gear whine may be heard when a car with a typical standard transmission is operated in reverse. Despite the whine, spur gears are commonly used for reverse gear in automobiles because the reverse gear train is usually operated for only short periods and at relatively slow speeds.

Another disadvantage of spur gears is that only one or two teeth are in mesh at any given time. That causes all of the torque transfer to be carried by those one or two teeth. Consequently, the gear must be made larger or thicker so that one tooth can carry the load alone.

Helical Gears

Helical gears have teeth that are cut at an angle to their axis of rotation. The tooth will actually have a slight spiral shape to it

FIGURE 44-12 Spur gears.

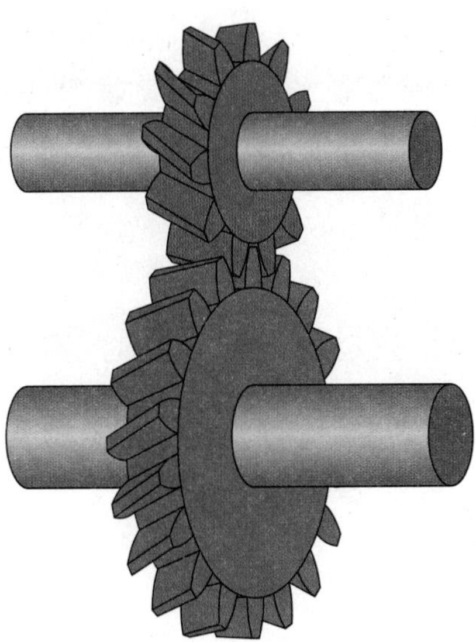

FIGURE 44-13 Helical gears.

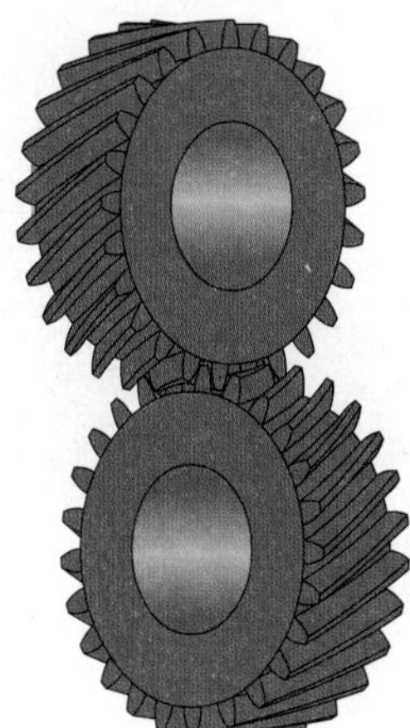

FIGURE 44-14 When mounted at right angles, two like-handed helical gears will mesh.

because the angle must remain constant as the gear turns, so it is actually a spiral cut. The design of a helical gear, such as the one shown in **FIGURE 44-13**, comes with some advantages. First, when helical gears mesh, there is always more than one tooth in mesh at a time. As a result, helical gears do not make the characteristic whining noise that spur gears do. As the next set of teeth is coming into mesh, they do not click together. The effect is more of a sliding motion as the teeth engage. Consequently, helical gears are much quieter in operation than spur gears are.

Another advantage of helical gears is their strength. Because more than one or two teeth are in mesh at once, the individual teeth on a helical gear do not have to carry as much torque. Therefore, helical gears are stronger than equivalently sized spur gears. Furthermore, the design of helical gears allows gear width to be reduced with no loss of torque capacity. Helical gears are manufactured with either a left-hand helix or a right-hand helix. To determine the hand, look at a helical gear from the top. A left-hand helix appears to move down to the left, and a right-hand helix appears to move down to the right.

When used together in side-by-side applications, a left-hand gear must mesh with a right-hand gear. When mounted at right angles to each other, however, two right-hand or two left-hand helices will mesh, as shown in **FIGURE 44-14**. This arrangement allows the power to turn a 90-degree corner.

The main disadvantage of helical gears is that they cause axial thrust. Axial thrust can be extreme under load and must be counteracted by tapered roller bearings and/or thrust bearings and washers. Another disadvantage of helical gears is their expense. Helical gearing is more expensive and more complicated to manufacture, leading to increased costs for components.

Herringbone Gears

Herringbone gears, such as those shown in **FIGURE 44-15**, have opposite helices on each side of their face. That is, one half of the tooth face is cut with a right-hand helix, and the other half of the tooth face is cut with a left-hand helix. Usually there is a groove cut at the apex of the "V" formed by the two helices, to allow trapped lubricant to escape.

FIGURE 44-15 Herringbone gears.

The advantages of herringbone gears are the same as helical gears, with one key difference. The dual-cut helices on herringbone gears cause all axial thrust to be canceled out.

These gears are obviously much more expensive to manufacture and, consequently, are not found in most applications. These gears can carry extreme loads and operate very quietly with no axial thrust. Herringbone gears are used in specialized equipment, such as large turbines for generating electricity.

Bevel Gears

Bevel gears are gears cut on an angle and designed to allow the flow of power to turn a corner, usually 90 degrees. Therefore, bevel gears are primarily used in drive axles to send rotating force to the drive wheels.

Bevel gear sets can be designed to allow for any degree of turning up to 90 degrees. Bevel gears consist of a cone-shaped **pinion gear** (a pinion gear is a term used to describe a small driving gear) and a ring, or "crown," gear. True bevel gearing is similar to spur-type gearing in that the teeth are straight cut.

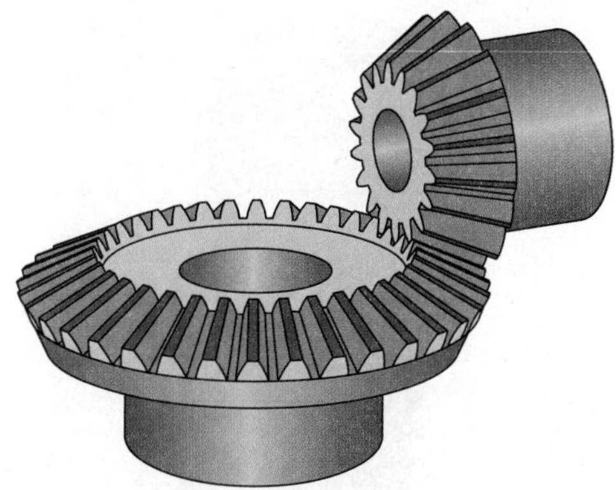

FIGURE 44-16 Bevel gears.

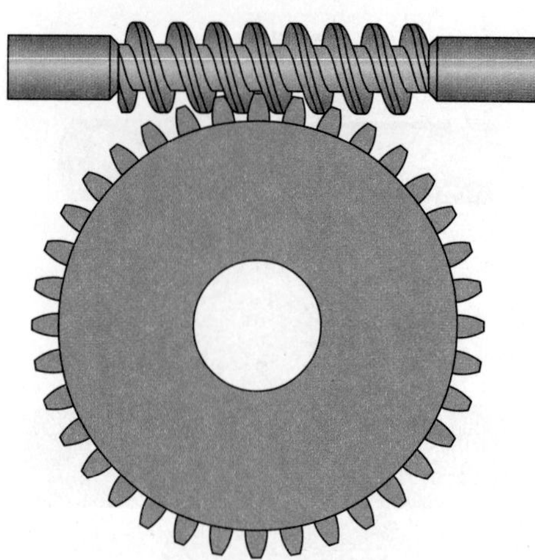

FIGURE 44-18 Worm gear.

FIGURE 44-17 Spiral bevel gears offer the same advantages over plain bevel gears as helical gears offer over spur gears.

Bevel gears have the same inherent advantages and disadvantages of spur-type gearing: bevel gears are noisy and generally weaker but cheaper to manufacture. **FIGURE 44-16** shows bevel gears.

Spiral bevel gearing attempts to minimize the disadvantages of bevel gears by using helically cut teeth. The spiral bevel's helical tooth configuration imparts the advantages of helical gearing to the bevel gear set, making them stronger and quieter, but they are more expensive to manufacture. **FIGURE 44-17** shows spiral bevel gears.

Worm Gears

Worm gears, such as the one illustrated in **FIGURE 44-18**, are another type of gear that allows the flow of power to turn a 90-degree corner. Worm gears consist of the worm shaft or screw, which meshes with the crown wheel. The outer edges of the crown wheel's teeth are scooped out at the center to allow for the shaft of the worm gear. That recess cut makes the wheel somewhat resemble a crown. Compared to bevel gearing systems, worm drive systems are more capable of very large speed reductions with much smaller gears.

The ratio of worm gears is set by changing the number of tooth leads or starts on the worm. With a single-start worm, the driven crown wheel will advance only one tooth with each revolution of the worm. So, a 20-tooth crown gear produces a ratio of 20:1. To achieve that reduction with bevel gears using a 12-tooth pinion, the crown gear would have to have 240 teeth. (Just imagine the size of such a gear!)

Most worm gears will have a worm with three or four starts, which will advance the crown gear three of four teeth per revolution, respectively. Worm gears are usually found in various types of machinery that require large reduction ratios.

One interesting feature of these gears is that when a high ratio is used, the worm can drive the crown wheel easily, but extremely high resistance prevents the crown wheel from driving the worm. An example of this feature is the self-locking effect of the machine heads used for adjusting guitar strings.

Rack-and-Pinion Gears

Rack-and-pinion gears consist of a flat rack with either spur or helically cut teeth on one side and a meshing circular pinion gear. Rotation of the pinion causes the rack to move linearly or horizontally. Rack-and-pinion gears can be used in a variety of applications. See **FIGURE 44-19** for a rack-and-pinion gear arrangement.

FIGURE 44-19 Rack-and-pinion gears convert rotary motion to linear motion.

▶ Planetary Gears

K44003

Planetary gears are called so because of the way they are designed and how their components interact with each other. Planetary gear operation and ratios are quite different from the conventional gearing discussed so far. Planetary gearing is used extensively in off-road equipment in power-shift transmissions and in final drive hubs, where they can be used to create large gear reductions and great torque multiplication. Quite often, a heavy bull dozer may be powered by a seemingly too small power plant, but by using combinations of interconnected planetary gears, it is possible to multiply the available torque, making it possible for that small engine to do tremendous amounts of work. Here we will explain the rules and laws of simple planetary gears, their ratios, and how compound planetary gears (interconnected planetary gears) interact with each other.

Fundamentals of Planetary Gearing

The simple planetary gear set consists of three components. First is the central externally toothed sun gear. Second is the externally toothed planet pinions held in a component called the carrier. The pinions revolve around the **sun gear** like planets in our solar system. The internally toothed ring gear surrounds the pinion gears, as illustrated in **FIGURE 44-20**.

The three different gear components are in constant mesh with one another. Planetary gears are also known as **epicyclical gears**. "Epicyclical" means that they are arranged to revolve around a common centerline.

Planetary gears are extremely versatile. They allow several ratios from one set of gears. One simple planetary gear set can be arranged to produce the following ratios:

- two different forward reduction ratios to increase output torque while decreasing output speed
- two different forward overdrives that increase output speed but decrease output torque
- one reverse reduction ratio
- one reverse overdrive ratio.

The planetary gear set can also be used to create a direct drive, allowing torque and speed to pass through the gear set

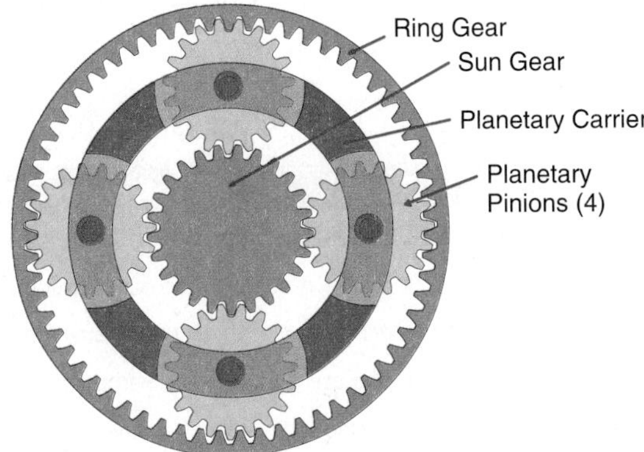

FIGURE 44-20 The simple planetary gear set is versatile and strong.

unchanged. Although all planetary gear sets can produce the same seven general ratios, the actual number of teeth on the sun gear and ring gear will determine the actual ratio numbers for the particular gear set. Planetary gear sets have excellent torque-carrying capabilities when compared to conventional gearing. This is because of the number of teeth involved to actually transfer the power. In conventional gearing, only two or three teeth are involved in torque transfer. However, in planetary gearing, many sets of teeth are involved in transmitting torque. The epicyclical design of planetary gears also allows them to cancel out most radial thrust loads.

Planetary gear sets are not without drawbacks, however. Planetary gears are normally helically cut for strength and noise reduction, but that means that they create a serious amount of axial thrust under load. Several components must be used to deal with that thrust, such as thrust washers and bearings. The devices that control planetary gears are operated hydraulically, usually by multi-plate clutches. It is easy to supply hydraulic pressure to a stationary hydraulic clutch; however, when the clutch must rotate, it presents more of a challenge.

Rules of Planetary Gears

The planetary gear set can be designed with straight-cut spur-type gears or with stronger and quieter helical-cut gears. Spur-cut gears will be noisier in operation, but they create no axial thrust. Helical-cut gears are stronger and quieter but create axial thrust that must be dealt with.

Planetary gears are very strong for their size. Consider a single countershaft transmission gear train. All the torque is transmitted through one or two sets of teeth in mesh at any given time. In a planetary gear set, there are at least three sets of teeth (the three pinions) transmitting the torque. In heavier applications, the number of pinions is increased, giving even more teeth in contact. Helical planetary gears also have the benefit of increased strength that helical gears bring to conventional gears. Because of this, planetary gears can be made very compact and yet still transmit great amounts of torque. In order for planetary gears to transmit torque, the following three criteria, known as the rules of planetary gears, must be met:

1. One of the three planetary gear components must be inputted from the power source.
2. One of the planetary gear components must be held stationary.
3. One of the planetary gear components must be connected to an output.

The only exception to the rules above occurs when we want a direct drive, or 1:1 ratio, through the gear set. To obtain a 1:1 ratio, two members of the gear set are inputted at the same speed. That causes the third component to turn with them. The third component would be connected to the output so the result is direct drive. If these three rules are not met and any of the planetary gear components is free to turn, it will do so. The result will be neutral, and no torque or rotational output can be transmitted.

All simple planetary gears can produce the same seven ratios, regardless of size. The actual reductions and overdrives will vary, however, based on the number of teeth on the components. The key to figuring out which ratio will be achieved is the carrier. Recall that the carrier is the component that holds the planetary pinions. The pinions merely connect the carrier to the gear set. The active component is the carrier itself. Knowing which one of the rules of planetary gears applies to the carrier—that is, whether the carrier is the input, the output, or the held member—will allow the resulting power flow to be determined.

The Role of the Carrier

The **carrier** is the key to planetary gear power flows; provided that the rules of planetary gears are met, the following holds true:

1. If the carrier is the **output member** of the gear set, the resulting power flow will always be a forward (same direction as input) reduction, or underdrive, ratio.
2. If the carrier is the **input member** of the gear set, the result will always be a forward overdrive ratio.
3. If the carrier is the held or reaction member of the gear set, then the result will always be reverse (opposite direction of input).

Once it is known what the carrier is doing, figuring out what the other two planetary components are doing becomes easier.

If the carrier is output, which always gives a forward (same direction as input) gear reduction (increased out-put torque and decreased output speed), then to satisfy the three rules of planetary gears, the sun gear and the ring gear must be either the input or the held component.

If the carrier is input, the result is always a forward overdrive. That is, the direction is the same as the input, and there is decreased torque and increased output speed. In that case, to satisfy the three rules of planetary gears, the sun gear and the ring gear must be either the output or the held component.

If the carrier is the held component, the result will always be a reverse gear. That is, the direction will be opposite to input. To satisfy the rules of planetary gears, the sun gear and the ring gear must be either input or output. If the sun gear is input, the result will be a **reverse reduction**; if the ring gear is input, the result will be a **reverse overdrive**.

▶ Planetary Gear Power Flows

S44002

The roles and results of planetary gear sets are organized in **TABLE 44-1**.

Note that if any two planetary gear set members are input at the same speed, the third will become the output at the same speed and direction for a 1:1 ratio or direct drive.

Throughout the sections on planetary gear power flows, planetary gear motion is described using the simplified planetary gear drawings. Each diagram uses the following legend:

- The input component and direction is indicated by a red arrow.
- The output component and direction is indicated by a green arrow.
- The held component is indicated by a black line and ground symbol.
- The reaction direction of the planet pinions is indicated by a brown arrow.

Let's examine in greater detail the seven possible ratios from planetary gears, maximum and minimum forward reduction, maximum and minimum forward overdrive, reverse reduction, and reverse overdrive. Remember that even though all planetary gear sets are capable of the same seven general ratios, the number of teeth on the sun gear and ring gear of the individual gear set will vary the ratios.

Maximum Forward Reduction

The lower or **maximum forward reduction**, shown in **FIGURE 44-21**, will be obtained if the sun gear is the input, because a smaller input gear always gives a lower output speed. Therefore, the ring gear would have to be the held component. In Figure 44-21, we see that the input (red arrow) turns the sun gear clockwise, and the ring gear is held. This turns the carrier in a clockwise direction for the output (green arrow). Notice the reaction direction on the carrier pinion gear (brown arrow). It has to walk around the stationary ring gear in a counterclockwise direction. This means that the carrier pinions against which the sun gear is pushing are moving away from the sun gear's teeth. That movement by the sun gear reduces its effort to move the carrier. The sun gear has to turn one complete turn plus the number of teeth on the ring gear to drive the carrier one turn. Consequently, this power

TABLE 44-1 Roles and Results of Planetary Gear Sets

Sun Gear	Carrier	Ring Gear	Speed	Torque	Direction
Input	Output	Held	Max reduction	Increase	Same as input
Held	Output	Input	Min reduction	Increase	Same as input
Output	Input	Held	Max increase	Decrease	Same as input
Held	Input	Output	Min increase	Decrease	Same as input
Input	Held	Output	Reduction	Increase	Reverse
Output	Held	Input	Increase	Decrease	Reverse

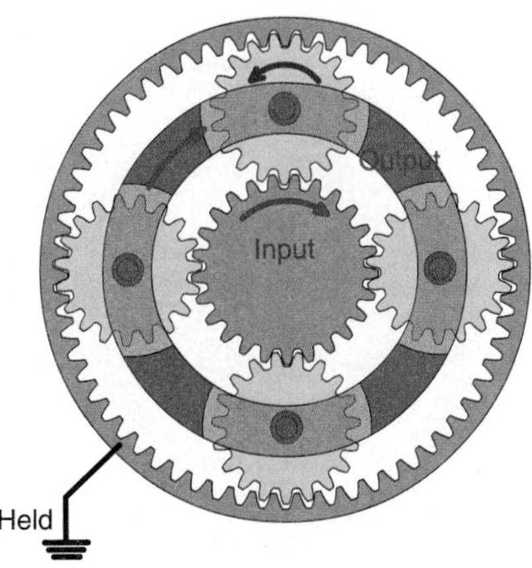

FIGURE 44-21 Maximum forward reduction is obtained with the sun gear as input, the ring gear held, and the carrier as output.

flow gives the maximum forward reduction in speed but the maximum increase in torque.

Minimum Forward Reduction

To obtain the higher of the two forward gear ratios, the roles of the ring gear and the sun gear are reversed. The ring gear becomes the input component, and the sun gear becomes the held component. This results in the **minimum forward reduction** (or higher ratio of the two) that results in a torque increase and a speed decrease.

In **FIGURE 44-22**, we see clockwise input on the ring gear (red arrow). The ring gear tries to turn the carrier in a clockwise direction, as can be seen by the green arrow. However, notice the reaction direction of the carrier pinion gear (brown arrow). It has to walk around the stationary sun gear, which causes it to rotate clockwise as well. The teeth of the carrier pinion gear are moving away from the input of the ring gear, thus reducing its effort to move the carrier. In this power flow, the ring gear has to turn one complete revolution plus the number of teeth on the sun gear in order to drive the carrier one full turn. This results in a smaller speed reduction and a smaller torque increase than the maximum forward reduction power flow.

In a typical planetary gear set, the maximum or greater forward reduction (lower ratio) is around 3.4:1, and the minimum or lesser forward reduction (higher ratio) would be around 1.4:1—although actual ratios will depend upon the number of teeth on the sun gear and ring gear.

Maximum Forward Overdrive

If the carrier is the input component, the result is always a forward overdrive; that is, there is decreased output torque and increased output speed. For forward overdrive to occur, the sun and the ring gear must either be the output component or the held component. Logically, the carrier would drive the sun gear faster than it would the ring gear, because the sun gear is smaller and has fewer teeth. When the sun gear is the output component, we achieve the **maximum forward overdrive** (highest output speed), and to satisfy the rules of planetary gears, the ring gear must become the held component.

Following the motion in **FIGURE 44-23**, the carrier is input (red arrow), and the ring gear is held stationary. The carrier rotation forces the sun gear to rotate clockwise with it (green arrow). But notice the reaction direction of the carrier pinion gear (brown arrow): it is forced to rotate counterclockwise by the ring gear teeth. The pinion gears transfer this rotation to the sun gear and therefore add to its output speed. In this power flow, one rotation of the carrier will drive the sun gear one complete turn plus the number of teeth on the ring gear.

Minimum Forward Overdrive

To achieve the slower overdrive speed, or the **minimum forward overdrive**, the carrier is still the input component. The roles of the sun gear and the ring gear, however, are reversed. The ring gear becomes the output component, and the sun gear becomes the held component.

To follow this power flow, see **FIGURE 44-24**. The carrier is the input (red arrow), the sun gear is held stationary, and the carrier's rotation forces the ring gear to rotate with it in a clockwise direction (green arrow). Again, notice the reaction direction of the carrier pinion gear (brown arrow) as it is forced to rotate around the stationary sun gear. The carrier pinion must

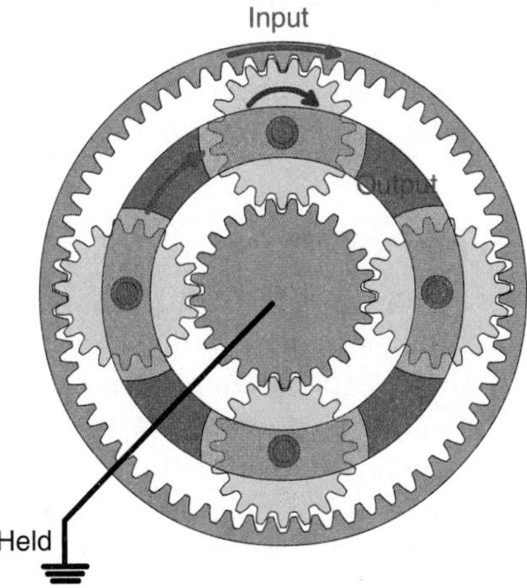

FIGURE 44-22 In the minimum forward reduction power flow, the ring gear is input and the sun gear is held, making the carrier output again.

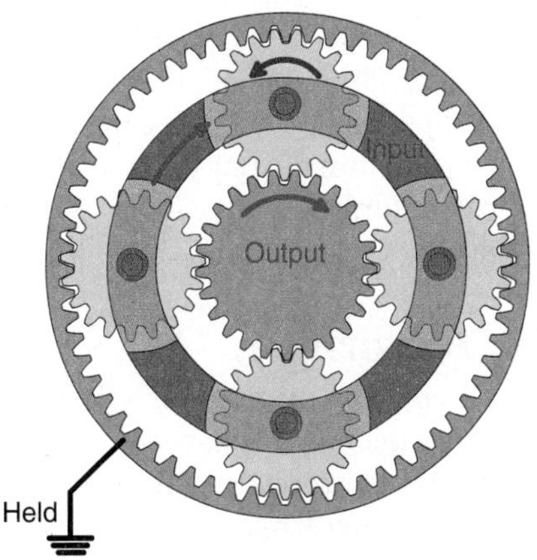

FIGURE 44-23 A maximum forward overdrive power flow. When the carrier is the input member, the result is always an overdrive ratio.

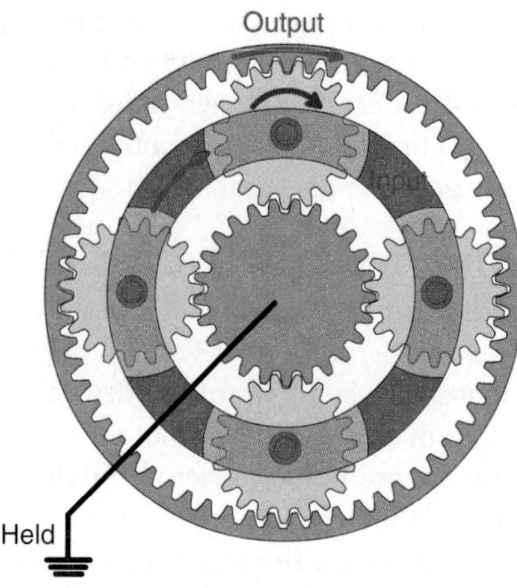

FIGURE 44-24 A minimum forward overdrive power flow. The carrier is still input, but now the sun gear becomes the held member.

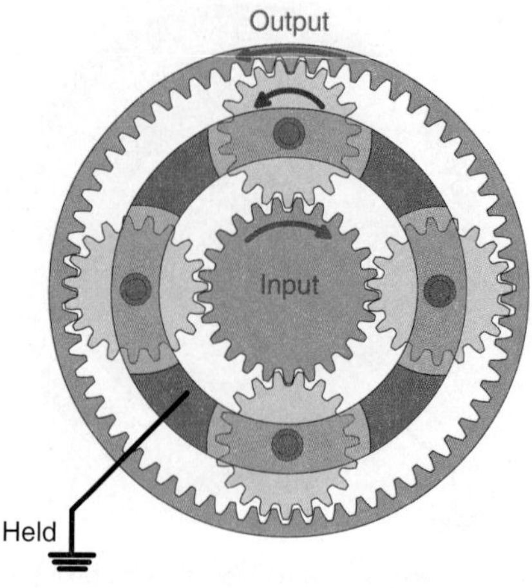

FIGURE 44-25 In reverse, the carrier is the held member of the planetary gear set. If the sun gear is input, the result is a reverse underdrive.

turn clockwise. The pinion transfers this clockwise rotation to the ring gear, therefore adding to its speed. In this power flow, one complete rotation of the carrier will drive the ring gear one complete turn plus the number of teeth on the sun gear. The result is a slower overdrive than the previous power flow.

In a typical planetary gear set, the maximum forward overdrive ratio would be around 0.29, and the minimum forward overdrive would be around 0.76:1.

Reverse Reduction or Underdrive

If the carrier is the held component, the result is always reverse. One combination produces a reverse overdrive and one a reverse reduction. To complete this power flow according to the rules of planetary gears, the ring gear and the sun gear must be either the input or the output component. Logically, a small gear as input will always result in a slower output speed. Therefore, when the sun gear is the input component and the ring gear is the output, the result will be a reverse reduction; that is, there will be a torque increase and a speed decrease. The power flow through the planetary gear set when the carrier is held is very straightforward; the carrier pinions merely act as idler gears.

In **FIGURE 44-25**, we see clockwise input on the sun gear, as shown by the red arrow. This causes the carrier pinion gears to rotate counterclockwise, as shown by the brown arrow. The pinion gear acts as an idler gear and transfers this motion to the ring gear, causing it to rotate counterclockwise as well, as shown by the green arrow. To turn the ring gear one complete turn, the sun gear will have to turn exactly the same number of teeth that are on the ring gear.

Reverse Overdrive

What happens, then, when the ring gear is the input component and the sun gear is the output component? Switching the sun and ring gear roles with the carrier still being the held member will result in a reverse overdrive.

In **FIGURE 44-26**, we see the ring gear is clockwise input, as shown by the red arrow, and the carrier is held. This rotation causes

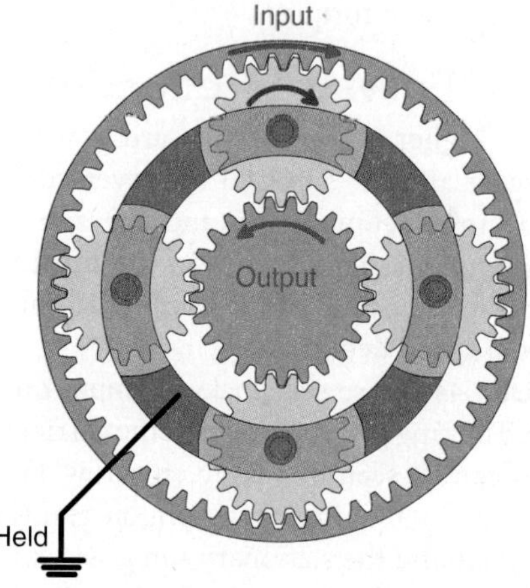

FIGURE 44-26 If the ring gear is the input member and the carrier is held, the sun gear turns in reverse at an overdrive speed.

the carrier pinion gears to rotate clockwise as well, as shown by the brown arrow. Again the pinion gear acts merely as an idler gear and transfers this motion to the sun gear. The sun gear then turns counterclockwise, as shown by the green arrow. One rotation of the ring gear will drive the sun gear the same number of teeth that are on the ring gear, leading to a reverse overdrive.

In a typical planetary gear set, the reverse reduction ratio would be around 2.5:1, and the reverse overdrive ratio would be around 0.42:1.

Direct Drive, or 1:1

To achieve the seventh possible ratio—that is, direct drive, or 1:1—any two of the planetary gear components are inputted at the same speed. For our example, the sun gear and ring gear are input, as illustrated in **FIGURE 44-27**, but any two of the three components could be the inputs. Because the ring gear and the sun gear are turning at the same speed, the carrier pinions cannot rotate, and the carrier must turn at the same speed as well. In this power flow, the planetary gear set is basically locked together, and the third component will be

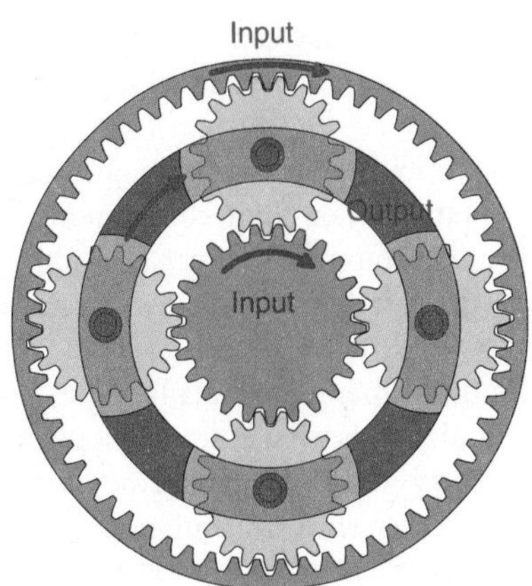

FIGURE 44-27 When any two members of the planetary gear set are input at the same speed and direction, the third member will output at the same speed.

connected to the output. What results is a 1:1, or direct drive, ratio that allows torque and speed to travel through the gear set unchanged.

Ratio Calculations for planetary Gears

Planetary gear ratios depend on the role of the carrier in the power flow, and therefore, there are some unique formulas used to calculate them. We still use driven over drive as the basic ratio formula. The carrier, however, will impact the ratio if it is the output or the input member, because of its reaction. First, we need to know the number of teeth on the ring gear and on the sun gear. Let's assume we have a planetary gear set with the following number of teeth on the gears:

- sun gear (S) = 36 teeth
- ring gear (R) = 84 teeth.

Because they are simply connecting the ring and the sun gear, the pinion gears act as idler gears. The number of teeth on the pinions will have no bearing on the ratios.

If the carrier is the output member of the planetary gear set and the sun gear is input, the ring gear will be the held member. During this power flow, the carrier reacts against the stationary ring gear, and its teeth have a negative effect on the output. The sun gear must therefore rotate once plus rotate the number of teeth on the ring gear as well. The ratio can be found by using the following formula:

$$\begin{aligned} \text{Ratio} &= \frac{R+S}{S} \\ &= \frac{84+36}{36} \\ &= \frac{120}{36} \\ &= 3.33:1 \end{aligned}$$

This is the maximum forward underdrive or speed reduction.

If the carrier is the output member of the planetary gear set and the ring gear is input, the sun gear will be the held member. The formula changes to accommodate the fact that the sun gear with fewer teeth is the **reaction member**. In that case, the formula looks like this:

$$\begin{aligned} \text{Ratio} &= \frac{S+R}{R} \\ &= \frac{36+84}{84} \\ &= \frac{120}{84} \\ &= 1.43:1 \end{aligned}$$

This is the minimum forward underdrive or speed reduction.

If the carrier is the input member and the sun gear is the output, the ring gear must be held to satisfy the rules of planetary gears. The carrier will turn the sun gear one revolution plus the number of teeth on the stationary ring gear. That amount of rotation is due to the ring gear being the reaction member and the carrier pinions walking around the ring gear and adding their rotation to the sun gear's output. The formula in this scenario is as follows:

$$\begin{aligned} \text{Ratio} &= \frac{S}{S+R} \\ &= \frac{36}{36+84} \\ &= \frac{36}{120} \\ &= 0.3:1 \end{aligned}$$

This is the maximum forward overdrive or speed increase.

If the carrier is the input member and the ring gear is the output, then to satisfy the rules of planetary gears, the sun gear must be held. The carrier will turn the ring gear one revolution plus the number of teeth on the stationary sun gear, because it is the reaction member. The pinions are walking around the sun gear and adding their rotation to the ring gear's output. The formula in this scenario is as follows:

$$\begin{aligned} \text{Ratio} &= \frac{R}{S+R} \\ &= \frac{84}{36+84} \\ &= \frac{84}{120} \\ &= 0.7:1 \end{aligned}$$

This is the minimum forward overdrive or speed increase.

When the carrier is the held member, the result is always reverse and the carrier pinions merely act as idler gears. Because there is no reaction motion from the carrier, the ratio in that case is simply a matter of driven over drive, as described below.

If the sun gear is the input and the ring gear is output,

$$\text{Ratio} = \frac{R}{S} = \frac{84}{36} = 2.33{:}1$$

This ratio is the reverse underdrive.

If the ring gear is input and the sun gear is output, again there is no reaction motion from the carrier, and the formula is as follows:

$$\text{Ratio} = \frac{S}{R} = \frac{36}{84} = 0.43{:}1$$

This ratio is the reverse overdrive.

The preceding formulas can be used to calculate simple planetary gear ratios only. Most machines, however, will have power flows that involve more than one planetary gear set, making them compound power flows. In some **compound planetary gear sets**, rather than components actually being held stationary, the component may be "acting as the held member," even though they are actually rotating slowly. In order for this to work, the acting-as-held member must turn slower than the input member. Calculating ratios like these is much more difficult and is usually unnecessary. We will discuss compound planetary gears set arrangements in greater detail in the section on power-shift transmissions in Chapter 48 and final drives in Chapter 52.

▶ Wrap-Up

Ready for Review

- Gears are essential to the operation of any mechanized equipment.
- The involute gear tooth design compensates for the natural tendency of two gears in mesh to turn at a constantly changing ratio of speed.
- Gear teeth spacing is known as gear pitch. Only gears of the same pitch can run in mesh with each other.
- Gears can have externally or internally cut teeth. When externally toothed gears are in mesh, they rotate in opposite directions. A gear with internally cut teeth is known as a ring gear, and when in mesh with a gear with externally cut teeth, both gears turn in the same direction.
- Backlash is the clearance between the teeth of gears in mesh. Backlash is essential for lubrication and expansion but must be tightly controlled to prevent gears slipping over each other's teeth.
- Gear design evolved from the lever of one of the six simple machines. Simple machines allow us to gain mechanical advantage to accomplish a task.
- Gear ratio is the comparison of the input to the output result of gears in mesh. The formula to calculate ratio is the number of teeth on the driven gear divided by the number of teeth on the drive gear. If input torque is known, output torque can be calculated by multiplying input torque by the ratio. Output speed can be calculated by dividing input speed by the gear ratio.
- Compound gear ratios are those that involve more than one set of gears. All ratios where the power flows through a transmission's countershaft are compound ratios. These can be calculated by multiplying all of the driven gears together and dividing that figure by the product of all the drive gears.
- Idler gears are used to change the direction of rotation. They have no influence on gear ratio, because they are both a driven gear and a drive gear.
- Spur gears are the simplest gears to manufacture. They have only radial thrust, but they are inherently noisy while in operation.
- Helical gears are quieter and stronger than spur gears.
- Helical gears create both radial and axial thrust, and they are more complex to manufacture. Helical gears can be left handed or right handed.
- Herringbone gears have a left-hand helical cut on one side of the tooth surface and a right-hand helical cut on the other side of the tooth surface. These gears cancel out the axial thrust common to helical gears. Because herringbone gears are complex to manufacture, they are expensive and uncommon.
- Bevel gearing is used wherever a power flow must turn a corner—usually 90 degrees at the drive axle, for example.
- Straight bevel gearing has the same problem as spur gears in that they are noisy while in operation. Spiral bevel gearing is quieter and stronger while in operation than bevel gearing is.
- Many different types of spiral bevel gears have been developed over the years and are all improvements to basic spiral bevel design.
- Worm gears are capable of extremely large reductions in a very small package. Reductions of 40:1 or even 50:1 can be achieved in a relatively small space.
- Rack-and-pinion gears change rotary motion to linear.

- Planetary gears are very versatile. They provide up to seven possible ratios from one simple planetary gear set: two forward reductions, two forward overdrives, two reverse ratios, and a one-to-one (direct) ratio.
- Planetary gears are epicyclical gears. That is, they revolve around a common centerline and thereby cancel out radial thrust.
- Helical planetary gears operate very quietly and are very strong for their size because they have multiple sets of teeth involved in their power flows.
- According to the rules of planetary gears, in order to have a power flow, one component must be inputted, one component must be held, and one component must be connected to an output.
- The carrier is the key to planetary gear power flows. If the carrier is output, the result is a forward reduction. If the carrier is the input, the result is a forward overdrive. If the carrier is the held component, the result will always be reverse.
- To produce a one-to-one ratio, two components of the planetary gear set are input at the same speed, and the third component is connected to the output.
- When calculating planetary gear ratios, the number of teeth on the stationary or reaction member of the planetary gear set is either added to or subtracted from the output.
- Compound power flows are those that use more than one planetary gear set to produce the power flow.
- An important aspect of planetary gears is that the held component in a particular power flow does not actually have to be stationary. The component can be moving as long as it is not moving faster than the input component; this is known as acting as a held component.

Key Terms

addendum The top, thinner part of an involute tooth contact area.

axial thrust Thrust that tries to move the gears apart along their axis.

backlash The clearance between teeth in mesh with each other.

bevel gear Gear cut on an angle, allowing a power flow to turn a corner.

carrier The housing that holds the pinion gears of a planetary gear set and their shafts.

cast ductile iron Cast iron that is ductile (bendable), not brittle.

clockwise The clockwise direction of rotation of a gear as you look at it corresponding to the motion of the clock; also known as forward.

compound planetary gear set Planetary gear power flow that utilizes more than one gear set to produce the ratios.

compound ratio Any gear ratio that involves more than one pair of gears.

counterclockwise The counterclockwise direction of rotation of a gear as you look at it corresponding to the motion of the clock; also known as backward.

dedendum The lower, thicker part of an involute tooth contact area.

epicyclical gear Gears that revolve around a common centerline.

fillet radius The radius shape between the bottoms of two teeth; also called root.

gear ratio The relationship between two gears in mesh as a comparison to input versus output.

gear reduction Any gear set that reduces output speed while it at the same time increases output torque; also known as underdrive ratio.

hardening A manufacturing process that makes the surface of a gear much harder than its core: typically, the surface is hardened to a depth of no more than 0.050 inches (1.2 mm).

helical gear A gear with teeth cut on an angle or spirally to its axis of rotation.

herringbone gear A gear cut with opposite helices on each side of the face.

idler gear Gear used to change direction.

input member The element of the planetary gear set inputted from the power source.

involute A gear design shape that compensates for the changing point of contact between gears as they rotate through mesh.

lever A simple machine that can allow a large object to be moved with less force.

mechanical advantage Anything that allows us to move greater distances or weight with less effort.

maximum forward overdrive The highest (fastest) ratio possible in a planetary gear set.

maximum forward reduction The lowest (slowest) ratio possible in a planetary gear set.

minimum forward overdrive The second highest (fastest) ratio possible in a planetary gear set.

minimum forward reduction The second lowest (slowest) ratio possible in a planetary gear set.

output member The element of the planetary gear set that is connected to the output shaft.

overdrive ratio A ratio that provides a speed increase and output torque decrease.

pinion gear A small driving gear.

pitch The number of teeth per unit of pitch diameter on a gear.

pitch circle The theoretical point on the tooth face halfway between the root and the top land, where only rolling motion exists; also called the pitch diameter.

pitch diameter The theoretical point on the tooth face halfway between the root and the top land, where only rolling motion exists; also called the pitch circle.

planetary gear A gear arrangement consisting of a ring gear with internal teeth, a carrier with two or more small pinion gears in constant mesh with the ring gear, and an externally toothed sun gear in the center in constant mesh with the planetary pinions.

rack-and-pinion gear A gear consisting of a flat rack with either spur-cut or helically cut teeth on one side and a meshing circular pinion gear.

radial thrust Thrust that tries to push gears in mesh apart perpendicular to their axis.

reaction member The element of the planetary gear set that is held stationary.

reverse overdrive A reverse direction overdrive ratio through the planetary gear set.

reverse reduction A reverse direction underdrive ratio through the planetary gear set.

ring gear An internally toothed gear that surrounds the pinion gears.

root The radius shape between the bottoms of two teeth; also called fillet radius.

root diameter The smallest circle of the gear measured at the fillet radius (root) of the teeth.

simple machine The simplest mechanism that allows us to gain mechanical advantage.

spiral bevel gearing Bevel gears that are cut helically, making the gear set stronger and quieter.

spur gear A gear with teeth cut parallel to its axis of rotation.

sun gear The small, externally toothed gear at the center of the planetary gear set.

tooth face The area that actually comes into contact with a mating gear and is parallel to the gear's axis of rotation.

top land The apex of a gear tooth.

torque The twisting force applied to a shaft that may or may not result in motion.

underdrive ratio Any ratio that decreases output speed while increasing output torque; also known as a gear reduction.

worm gear A gear arrangement capable of large reductions in a small space.

Review Questions

1. The input gear in a transmission has 24 teeth, the countershaft driven gear has 40 teeth. First gear countershaft has 12 teeth, and main shaft first gear has 36 teeth. What is the first gear ratio?
   - **a.** 1:5
   - **b.** 0.55:1
   - **c.** 1.8:1
   - **d.** 5:1
2. If input torque is 1,000 ft-lb (1,356 N·m), how much torque will be present at the output shaft when an input gear having 24 teeth is driving a countershaft driven gear with 48 teeth, and a counter shaft second gear with 45 teeth is driving a main shaft gear with 60 teeth?
   - **a.** 1,750 ft-lb (2,373 N·m)
   - **b.** 2,670 ft-lb (3,620 N·m)
   - **c.** 666 ft-lb (903 N·m)
   - **d.** 571 ft-lb (774 N·m)
3. A gear having 48 teeth that is rotating at a speed of 400 rpm is driving another gear that has 78 teeth. Approximately how fast is the gear with 78 teeth rotating?
   - **a.** 120 rpm
   - **b.** 400 rpm
   - **c.** 246 rpm
   - **d.** None of the above.
4. What does gear pitch refer to?
   - **a.** The number of teeth per inch (25.4 mm) of pitch diameter
   - **b.** The angle of the gear teeth
   - **c.** The contact point of the gear teeth
   - **d.** The shape of the gear teeth
5. What is the purpose of the involute tooth shape on a gear?
   - **a.** To make the gear contact smoother
   - **b.** To add strength to the gear tooth
   - **c.** To make the gear teeth last longer
   - **d.** To make the driven gear turn at a steady speed
6. Why is backlash required between meshing gears?
   - **a.** It limits coasting whine.
   - **b.** It controls climbing.
   - **c.** It allows for heat expansion and the lubrication of gears.
   - **d.** All of the above.
7. Which of the following will produce a direct ratio from a planetary gear set?
   - **a.** Sun gear input, carrier held, ring gear output
   - **b.** Ring gear input, carrier output, sun gear held
   - **c.** Carrier input, ring gear held, sun gear output
   - **d.** Carrier input, sun gear input, ring gear output
8. If a simple planetary gear set has 24 teeth on the sun gear and 60 teeth on the ring gear, what will be the ratio if the sun gear is input, the ring gear is held, and the carrier is output?
   - **a.** 2.5 to 1
   - **b.** 0.4 to 1
   - **c.** 4 to 1
   - **d.** 3.5 to 1
9. The power flow through two interconnected planetary gear sets is best described as which kind of power flow?
   - **a.** double reverse
   - **b.** versatile
   - **c.** reverse
   - **d.** compound
10. What power flow will result from a planetary gear set if the carrier is the input member, the ring gear is held, and the sun gear is the output?
    - **a.** Maximum forward reduction
    - **b.** Minimum forward reduction
    - **c.** Maximum forward overdrive
    - **d.** Minimum forward overdrive

ASE Technician A/Technician B Style Questions

1. Technician A says that the gear attached to the input shaft on a countershaft transmission is a drive gear and that the gear it meshes with on the countershaft is a driven gear. Technician B says that all the countershaft speed gears

are drive gears and that all the main shaft speed gears are driven gears. Who is correct?
   a. Technician A
   b. Technician B
   c. Both Technician A and Technician B
   d. Neither Technician A nor Technician B
2. Technician A says a ratio that involves more than one set of gears is known as a compound ratio. Technician B says that the formula to calculate ratio is drive over driven. Who is correct?
   a. Technician A
   b. Technician B
   c. Both Technician A and Technician B
   d. Neither Technician A nor Technician B
3. Technician A says that all modern gearing uses an involute tooth shape. Technician B says the involute compensates for differing points of contact as a gear goes through mesh. Who is correct?
   a. Technician A
   b. Technician B
   c. Both Technician A and Technician B
   d. Neither Technician A nor Technician B
4. Technician A says that to calculate gear compound ratios, you add all the driven gears together and divide by all the drive gears added together. Technician B says that idler gears are not used in gear ratio calculations. Who is correct?
   a. Technician A
   b. Technician B
   c. Both Technician A and Technician B
   d. Neither Technician A nor Technician B
5. Technician A says that externally toothed gears in mesh turn in opposite directions. Technician B says that idler gears are used to change the direction of rotation of the driven gear compared to the driving gear. Who is correct?
   a. Technician A
   b. Technician B
   c. Both Technician A and Technician B
   d. Neither Technician A nor Technician B
6. Technician A says that the meshing of peg gears causes an uneven speed in the driven gear. Technician B says that the distance between the contact point and the center of peg gears in mesh is constantly changing. Who is correct?
   a. Technician A
   b. Technician B
   c. Both Technician A and Technician B
   d. Neither Technician A nor Technician B
7. Technician A says that an underdrive ratio increases torque. Technician B says that an underdrive ratio creates a speed increase at the output. Who is correct?
   a. Technician A
   b. Technician B
   c. Both Technician A and Technician B
   d. Neither Technician A nor Technician B
8. Technician A says that a simple planetary gear set can produce seven different ratios. Technician B says that planetary gears are epicyclical. Who is correct?
   a. Technician A
   b. Technician B
   c. Both Technician A and Technician B
   d. Neither Technician A nor Technician B
9. Technician A says that if the planetary carrier is the output member, a reverse will be the outcome if the rules of planetary gears are satisfied. Technician B says that if the carrier is output, a forward overdrive will be the result if the rules of planetary gears are satisfied. Who is correct?
   a. Technician A
   b. Technician B
   c. Both Technician A and Technician B
   d. Neither Technician A nor Technician B
10. Technician A says that helical planetary gears do not produce any thrust. Technician B says that epicyclical gears cancel out radial thrust. Who is correct?
   a. Technician A
   b. Technician B
   c. Both Technician A and Technician B
   d. Neither Technician A nor Technician B

CHAPTER 45
Manual Transmissions

Knowledge Objectives

After reading this chapter, you will be able to:

- **K45001** Explain the purpose and fundamentals of manual transmissions.
- **K45002** Identify the construction, composition, types, and applications of manual transmissions.
- **K45003** Describe the operation of manual transmissions.
- **K45004** Explain the power flows of manual transmissions.
- **K45005** Identify the construction and types of power take-offs (PTOs) used on mobile off-road equipment (MORE).
- **K45006** Outline the installation procedures for PTOs.
- **K45007** Explain the purpose fundamentals and basic operation of transfer cases.

Skills Objectives

After reading this chapter, you will be able to:

- **S45001** Recommend necessary reconditioning or repairs on manual transmissions.
- **S45002** Recommend repair or service procedures for PTOs.

▶ Introduction

In order to diagnose and repair manual transmissions, a technician must have a firm grasp of basic transmission operating principles and power flows. Transmissions are not overly complex in their design, but they do have a certain mystique about them, because their operating components are hidden from view inside the transmission case. In most mobile off-road equipment (MORE), the prime mover will be a diesel engine typically producing only 100 to 400 hp, yet the machines themselves will weigh more than 25,000 lb and as much as 100,000 lb or even more, not to mention the work that they must accomplish pushing, pulling, or lifting.

So how does a relatively small engine move such large equipment and accomplish all that work? By using mechanical advantage. **Mechanical advantage** simply means giving up speed to multiply available torque. Mechanical advantage can be achieved in many ways, but in mobile equipment, gear ratios or hydraulics are usually used to multiply available torque.

Transmissions are just one of the places where this mechanical advantage is used. The primary role of any mechanical transmission is to provide a selection of gear ratios that will allow the machine or vehicle to move and complete the tasks required of it. Several different types of transmissions are used in MORE, such as manual transmissions, multiple countershaft power-shift transmissions, and planetary power-shift transmissions. In this chapter, we will look at the inner workings of clutch-driven manual transmissions and forward/reverse shuttle transmissions.

▶ Fundamentals of Transmissions

K45001

The transmission allows us to move extremely heavy loads by using torque multiplication. However, a transmission must also allow us to move loads at speeds that are appropriate to the situation. For example, a bulldozer may need to move at only a maximum of 7 mph (11 kph) to accomplish its function, while an articulated truck may require speeds of 25 mph (40 kph) or greater. **FIGURE 45-1** shows a typical transmission.

Careful selection of the transmission and its ratios can allow us to have the best of both worlds: low-speed pulling or pushing power and higher speed operation when required.

FIGURE 45-1 Transmissions are tailored to their specific vocation.

Transmissions are tailored to the machine they are installed in to accomplish these goals. Very few mobile off-road machines manufactured today will be equipped with purely manual transmissions; instead, they are more likely to be equipped with power-shift gearboxes or other automated types of gearboxes. However, it is important for any technician to have a good grasp of the functioning of manual transmissions because their basic operating principles are used in almost all transmissions.

Transmission Shafts

As illustrated in **FIGURE 45-2**, a basic transmission will have at least four shafts running parallel to each other and installed in a housing known as the transmission case: the input shaft, the countershaft, the main shaft or output shaft, and the reverse idler shaft. Engine torque is introduced to the transmission through the clutch disc or discs, which are splined to the input shaft.

Input shaft and countershaft

The **input gear** is part of, or splined to, the input shaft. The **input shaft** is the input to the transmission driven by the clutch friction disc. The **countershaft** is the shaft inside the transmission, driven by the input gear. The countershaft is a shaft with various sizes of gears attached to it.

You Are the Mobile Heavy Equipment Technician

An owner/operator complains that the transmission in their John Deere 870 tractor jumps out of third gear when under heavy loads. You investigate the complaint and find that this model is equipped with a three-speed synchronized transmission with three ranges. You operate the machine and just as the owner said, the gear select transmission jumps out of third gear when loaded. What issues do you think could cause this situation? Could the fault have be caused by the operator? Which of the following steps should you proceed with?

1. Check the shift lever mechanism for proper operation.
2. Check the transmissions shift tower and pivot.
3. Remove and overhaul the transmission.
4. Convince the operator to hold the lever in place while in third gear.

FIGURE 45-2 All transmissions have at least four shafts.

The input gear is in constant mesh with the countershaft driven gear. That is, the gears are always in mesh. The countershaft range gears are part of, or keyed to, the countershaft. Consequently, when the input gear turns the countershaft driven gear, all of the countershaft gears turn with it.

Main Shaft

The **main shaft** is the shaft that carries the range or speed gears that are driven by the countershaft, and it provides output for the transmission. For this reason, the main shaft is also called the output shaft. It shaft usually supports the range or speed gears on bushings or bearings. The speed gears on the countershaft and the main shaft create the transmission's ratios. **Ratios** are the speed and torque relationship between two or more gears in mesh and can increase torque and decrease speed, decrease torque and increase speed, or transfer power without changing speed and torque.

Most modern transmissions will have all of the main shaft gears in constant mesh with their mating countershaft gears and are therefore known as constant mesh transmissions. The speed gears are usually not splined to the shaft and therefore are free to turn. In order for rotational power to flow through the transmission, the main shaft gears must be driven by the corresponding countershaft gears, and they then must transfer this power to the main shaft.

There are several different systems used to connect the main shaft gears to the main shaft, which we will discuss later on, in the section on transmission types.

Reverse Idler Shaft

The final shaft essential for transmission operation is the **reverse idler shaft**, which supports the reverse idler gear. This gear is in mesh or is slid into mesh (depending on the particular transmission) between the countershaft reverse gear and the main shaft reverse gear to provide a means to move the vehicle backward. Recall from the previous chapter, on gearing basics, that the engine and the transmission input gear typically both turn clockwise when viewed from the front. The input gear turns the countershaft counterclockwise, and the countershaft gears then turn the main shaft gears clockwise. The result is forward motion. Sliding the idler gear in between the countershaft reverse gear and the main shaft reverse gear means the countershaft reverse gear turns the idler clockwise. Then, the idler turns the main shaft reverse gear counterclockwise to achieve reverse.

▶ Transmission Types

K45002

Transmissions are generally typed according to the gear selection method they use. The three main types of transmission gear selection systems are the sliding gear transmission, the sliding clutch or sliding collar transmission, and the synchronized transmission.

Sliding Gear Transmission

The first type is the **sliding gear transmission**. In sliding gear transmissions, a main shaft gear that is splined to the main shaft is slid into and out of mesh with a corresponding countershaft gear to create the ratio. These transmissions are also known as "crash boxes" because shifting them can be quite difficult to accomplish without gear clash. The image in Figure 45-2 shows a sliding gear transmission.

Sliding clutch or sliding collar transmissions

The second gear selection method is the sliding clutch, also known as the sliding collar or simply a collar shift transmission. A **collar shift transmission** uses sliding collars or clutches to select gear ratios. In this type of transmission, the main shaft speed gears are in constant mesh with the countershaft speed gears. The main shaft gears are not splined to the main shaft. The speed gears are connected to the main shaft to create a ratio by sliding collars or clutches that are splined to the main shaft. These collars or clutches slide along the main shaft to engage "dog" teeth, or clutching teeth, on the gears to lock them to the shaft.

The terms "sliding clutch" and "sliding collar" are used synonymously. However, to be correct, a sliding clutch will have internal splines to connect it to the main shaft and external clutching teeth to engage the internal clutching teeth of the main shaft gear, whereas a sliding collar will have only internal clutching teeth. The collar slides on an externally splined hub, which is in turn splined to the main shaft and held in place by snap rings. The internal clutching teeth of the collar will engage external clutching teeth, also known as dog teeth, on the main shaft gear to lock the gear to the main shaft. A sliding clutch and a sliding collar are shown in **FIGURE 45-3**.

Synchronized Transmissions

The third method of gear selection is the **synchronizer**. The **synchronized transmission** is again a constant-mesh transmission, meaning that the main shaft and countershaft speed gears are always in mesh. This transmission uses synchronizers to match shaft and gear speeds. Synchronized transmissions, like the collar shift transmission, use sliding clutches or collars for gear selection. The sliding clutches and collars, however, are fitted over synchronizer hubs that are splined to the main shaft. **FIGURE 45-4** shows a cutaway of a synchronized transmission.

The synchronizers in these transmissions match shaft and gear speeds before gear engagement to prevent grinding of the gears and the sliding clutches or collars, known as gear clash. Some transmissions will use a combination of one or more of these gear selection systems. We will discuss each type in more detail later in the chapter.

Shift Controls

Regardless of type, transmissions use many of the same basic types of controls. The transmission operator interface with a manual transmission is better known as the shift lever. The **shift lever** is a shift control the operator uses to change transmission gear position. The shift lever is the only part of the transmission shift mechanism that the operator sees on a daily basis.

FIGURE 45-3 A. Sliding clutch. **B.** Sliding collar.

FIGURE 45-4 Synchronizers match gear and shaft speeds to prevent gear clash.

There is much more to shifting the gears than just the lever, however. The **shift pattern** (the direction in which the lever must be moved to select a given gear) may be displayed on or near the shift lever or in another prominent location. The shift pattern is usually shaped like an H for a four-gear selection transmission or an H with an extra upright line if there are more than four gears.

The lever can usually be moved forward and back and side to side to engage the various ranges. The lever itself is mounted in a **shift tower**, a raised section on the transmission with a pivot into which the shift lever fits. The shift tower or pivot is not usually visible to the operator of the machine. The shift tower has a spring-loaded pivot point just above the transmission shift bar housing, and it may be part of or bolted to the shift bar housing of the transmission. The spring tends to return the shift lever to the neutral position when the transmission is not in gear. In many machines, the shift lever is remote from the transmission and connects to the transmission shift tower through linkages.

Below the pivot point in the shift tower is the **shift finger**, a flat-sided piece that sits into the shift gates. The shift finger can be part of the shift lever or it can be just connected to the linkage the shift lever operates. Note that because of the pivot point, moving the lever forward will cause the shift finger to move back. Moving the lever to the right causes the finger to move left.

The **shift gates** are rectangular notches either formed into or attached to the shift rails (the bars that control shift fork position), and the shift finger fits into these gates. **FIGURE 45-5** shows typical shift gates and the shift finger.

Shift rails have the shift forks that actually select a particular range attached to them. **Shift forks** are rounded, U-shaped components that move the sliding clutches or sliding collars in the transmission to actually select gear ranges. Each rail, and

FIGURE 45-5 The shift finger sits in the shift gates, and each of these gates is attached to a shift rail. **A.** First and reverse gate. **B.** Spring-loaded reverse lock out. **C.** Second and third gate. **D.** Fourth and fifth gate.

therefore each fork, is usually responsible for two ranges: one in the rearward position and one in the forward position. In a typical five-speed transmission, the rail on the right-hand side will control the selection of first and reverse ranges, the center rail will control the selection of second and third ranges, and the left-hand side rail will control the selection of fourth and fifth ranges.

Shifting Gears

With the transmission in neutral, the shift gates all line up with each other and the finger can be moved side to side in the gates. To select first gear in the shift gates, shown in Figure 45-5, the operator pulls the lever toward the left. That action moves the finger to the right-side gate.

The operator then pulls the lever rearward, which moves the right shift rail to the front, engaging first range. Selecting reverse involves the same basic motion, except that the operator would push the lever forward, thereby moving the rail back. **FIGURE 45-6** shows shift forks attached to shift rails.

FIGURE 45-6 Shift forks attached to shift rails move the sliding clutches to engage the main shaft gears.

To change gears, the operator would depress the clutch, move the lever back to neutral, and then select the appropriate gate, move the lever to the desired gear, and then release the clutch again.

As the operator makes the shifts, the power flows through the transmission change. **Power flow** is the path that power takes from the beginning of an assembly to the end. In a transmission, the power flow changes as different gears are selected by the operator. This is true for all transmissions.

Shift Rail Interlock

If the operator were to move more than one shift rail at once, the transmission would be in two ranges at once. In other words, the countershaft would be trying to drive the main shaft at two different speeds. That would cause the transmission to lock up and experience catastrophic failure. To prevent this from happening, the shift rails have an interlock system that prevents two rails from being moved from the neutral position at once. The **shift rail interlock** system also prevents the other two rails from moving if one rail is not in neutral. This action positively prevents two gears from being selected at one time. One of the simplest forms of interlock uses two balls and a pin, illustrated in **FIGURE 45-7**.

The shift rails are positioned parallel and close to one another. The two outside rails will have a semicircular indent on their inside surfaces. Two steel balls are placed in the shift bar housing so that they fit into each indent. The center shift rail has a semicircular indent on both sides. In the neutral position, these indents line up with the indents on the outside shift rails. The center rail also has a small cross-drilled hole that extends from one indent to the other. Inside this hole is a sliding pin. The steels balls are particularly sized so that for one rail to move, it must force the ball over slightly.

In operation, if the center rail is moved either forward or backward, the two balls are moved out of its indents and are pushed farther into the indent on the outside rails. The new position blocks any movement of the outside rails. If either outside rail is moved forward or backward, its ball is forced farther into the indent of the center rail, preventing the center rail from moving. This action also forces the pin in the center rail to move toward the other outside rail. The corresponding ball is forced into the outside rail indent so that it cannot move either.

In addition to these basic components, there may be other components in the shift bar housing as well. For example, mistakenly selecting reverse while moving forward could be very detrimental to the transmission. Various methods are used to discourage this. These methods may be as simple as a spring-loaded system that requires an extra effort to select reverse, as was shown in Figure 45-5, or there may be a complex reverse interlock system that positively prevents reverse from being engaged when moving forward. Most shift bar housings will also have spring-loaded detent balls that engage notches on the shift rails. By engaging the notches, the detent balls keep the shift rails in position when a shift is made to prevent vibration from moving the shift lever back to a neutral position.

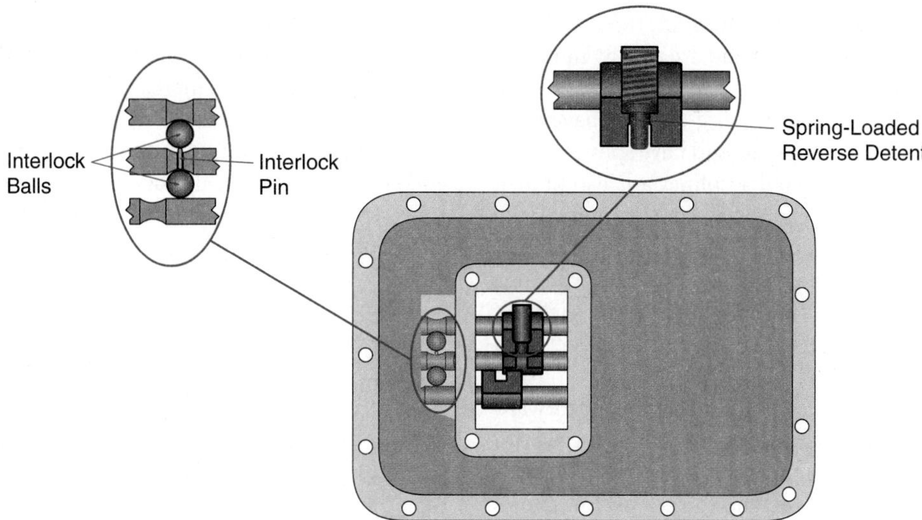

FIGURE 45-7 The shift rail interlock positively prevents two gears from being selected at the same time.

▶ Operation and Power Flows of Manual Transmissions

K45003

As mentioned above, transmissions are classified by the method of gear selection or engagement. Sliding gear transmissions are generally obsolete and have been replaced by constant-mesh transmissions. Technicians may, however, still find sliding gears used for low and reverse range (or gear) in some transmissions, so it is important to know how they function. In this section, we will explain the operation of all three general types of transmissions in detail, the sliding gear, the constant-mesh collar shift (also known as sliding collar or sliding clutch), and the constant-mesh synchronized transmission.

Sliding Gear Transmissions

In a sliding gear transmission, the main shaft gears are splined to the main shaft. In the neutral position, they are not in mesh with their matching countershaft gear. The main shaft gear will have a groove cut into one side, and a shift fork is installed in the groove. In order to select a range, the operator uses the shift fork to slide the gear along the main shaft until its teeth mesh with the teeth of the corresponding countershaft gear. (Refer back to Figure 45-2 for a diagram of a sliding gear transmission shaft.) The power flows from the clutch disc to the input gear, to the countershaft driven gear, to the countershaft range gear, and finally to the main shaft range gear. From there, power flows to the main shaft, which doubles as the transmission output shaft, and then on to the driveshaft and the wheels. This transmission type works very well from a standing start when nothing inside the transmission is moving.

Selecting a range when driving down the road, however, becomes a challenge because all the gears and shafts will be rotating at different speeds. In order to shift ranges when this type of transmission is moving, the operator must use a double-clutch technique to synchronize gear and shaft speed. To double-clutch, the operator first disengages the clutch and moves the shift lever to neutral position. Next, the operator re-engages the clutch and allows the engine speed to decrease to slow down the countershaft gears. That allows the speed of the countershaft gear to match the speed of the next higher range gear. The operator then disengages the clutch again, makes the shift, and then engages the clutch again.

Sliding gear transmissions have a few disadvantages. For example, when downshifting, the countershaft gear would be turning slower than the next lower main shaft range gear. So, after re-engaging the clutch in the neutral position, the operator would accelerate the engine to speed up the countershaft gears to match the vehicle speed. Although that might sound simple, it actually involves considerable skill for the operator to get it right.

Another problem with sliding gear transmissions is that they can use only spur-cut gears and not quieter helical gears. (Helical gears cannot slide into mesh with each other when they are rotating.) As a result, sliding gear transmissions tend to be noisy in operation and not as strong as they could be because of the spur gears.

Even though sliding gear transmissions are, for all intents and purposes, considered obsolete today, some constant-mesh transmissions do use a sliding gear power flow for low range and reverse. As both these ranges are initiated from a stopped position, nothing inside the transmission case is turning, so these shifts can be made without clashing.

Constant-Mesh Collar Shift Transmissions

In a constant-mesh collar shift transmission, the main shaft gears are constantly in mesh with their corresponding countershaft gears. All of the main shaft gears are turning at different speeds whenever the countershaft is turning. The differing speeds are based on the ratio between the range gears and their corresponding countershaft gears. Consequently, the main shaft gears cannot be splined to the main shaft. Otherwise, it would be trying to turn at several different speeds at once, which of course is impossible.

Instead, in a **constant-mesh transmission**, the main shaft gears are free to turn on the main shaft and are usually mounted on bearings or bushings. In order to select a range, sliding clutches or sliding collars are used. Sliding clutches have their inside surfaces splined to the main shaft and have splines cut on their outside surface as well. The outer splines are also known as clutching teeth. The sliding clutches have a circumferentially cut groove in the center that is engaged by the shift fork. Sliding clutches are splined to the main shaft in between two range gears and are used to lock one of the two gears to the shaft. As shown in **FIGURE 45-8**, there will be a sliding clutch between each pair of main shaft gears.

To make a gear selection, the sliding clutch is moved forward or backward, and its outside spline is brought into mesh with matching internal splines in the main shaft gear. The main shaft gear is then locked to the main shaft, and the power flow comes from the countershaft gear to the selected main shaft gear. The power flow then travels through the sliding clutch to the main shaft and out to the driveshaft.

The terms "sliding clutch" and "sliding collar" are used interchangeably, and some manufacturers refer to the sliding clutches discussed above as sliding collars. "Sliding collar," though, also refers to a ring that is splined on the inside surface of the collar. The sliding collar slides along a hub that is itself splined to the main shaft. There will be a sliding collar and hub between each pair of main shaft gears. The outside of the sliding collar has a groove to accept the shift fork.

To make a shift, the collar is moved by the shift fork, and its internal splines slide over external teeth that are cut on the main shaft gears. The external teeth are also called "dog" teeth because of their pointed shape. The movement of the shift fork and the internal splines of the collar lock the main shaft gear to the main shaft through the sliding collar's hub. The power flows from the countershaft gear to the main shaft gear, through the shift collar to the collar's hub, then to the main shaft, and finally out to the drive train. Sliding gear constant-mesh transmissions and sliding clutch or sliding collar constant-mesh transmissions are both unsynchronized. That is, in order to perform a proper clash-free shift, both types of transmissions still need to be double-clutched to match gear speeds.

FIGURE 45-8 Sliding clutches (indicated) are splined to the main shaft.

The constant-mesh design of these transmissions allows for helical gears to be used. Helical gearing makes the transmission stronger because of the increased tooth contact. In addition, the wiping action of helical gears makes the transmission quieter in operation. Overall, transmission length can also be shortened because the helical gears do not need to be as wide as the spur-type gears to carry the same load. Transmission weight is reduced as a result.

Constant-Mesh Synchronized Transmissions

A synchronized transmission is, again, a constant-mesh transmission. Synchronization eliminates the need for double-clutching techniques. The synchronizer is an assembly that matches shaft and gear speeds as a shift is being made for a clash-free engagement. The synchronizers are very similar to the sliding collar shift system described in the Constant-Mesh Collar Shift Transmissions section. A key exception is the addition of the synchronizer components that match the speeds. There are four basic types of synchronizers: plain type, block or insert type, pin type, and disc-and-plate type. All of the types rely on friction and some sort of shift delay system to synchronize the gear speeds.

Plain-Type Synchronizer

The plain-type synchronizer, illustrated in **FIGURE 45-9**, has a central hub splined to the main shaft and a sliding collar splined

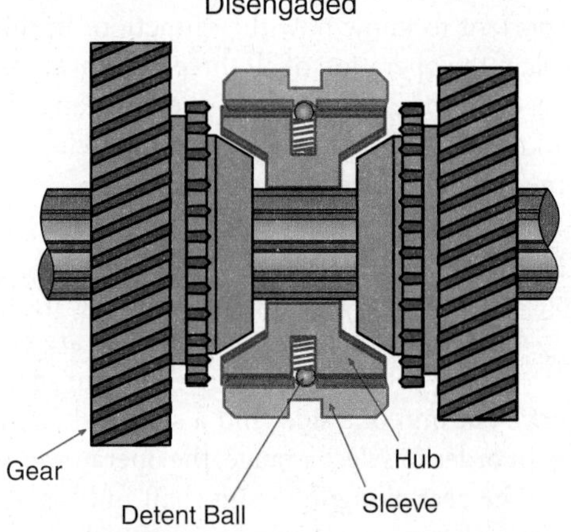

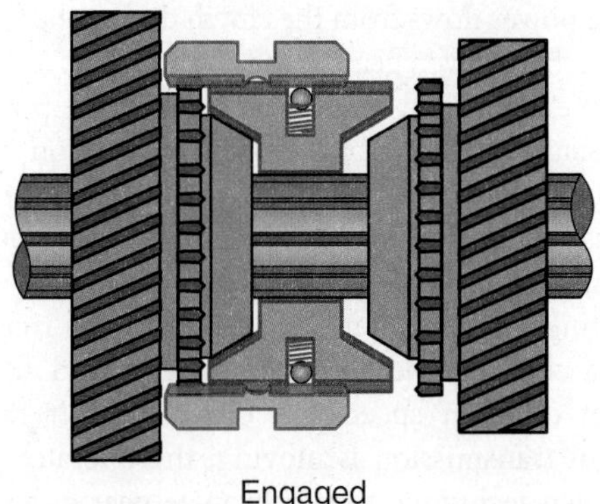

FIGURE 45-9 Plain-type synchronizer.

to the hub. Several springs located in the hub force detent balls into a groove cut into the center of the collar's internal splines. These detent balls tend to stop the collar from moving past the center or neutral position.

The main shaft gears have smooth, cone-shaped areas and a series of clutching teeth machined on their engagement side. Inside the plain-type synchronizer are two bronze cups that engage the cone-shaped machined area on the gear as the shift is initiated. The detent balls inside the sliding collar ensure that sufficient pressure is applied between the bronze cup and the smooth cone of the gear before the collar can slide over the clutching teeth on the main shaft gear. Ensuring the proper pressure beforehand allows the speeds to match before engagement, thereby eliminating gear clash.

Block- or Insert-Type Synchronizer

The block-type synchronizer, illustrated in **FIGURE 45-10**, is very similar to the plain-type synchronizer, but the block type has a more positive speed-matching system and a few more parts. The block-type synchronizer also has a central hub and a sliding collar, like the plain type has. Block-type synchronizers also have two bronze blocking rings (also known as blocker rings or balk rings), parts that increase or decrease a gear's speed to match shaft speed so that the synchronizer sleeve can lock the gear to the shaft.

Blocking rings have dog teeth on their outside circumference that are identical to the ones on the main shaft gear. (Bronze or a similarly soft metal is usually used for blocking rings to prevent damage to the main shaft gear.) The block-type synchronizer also has three floating spring-loaded blocks (inserts) set into grooves in the central hub. The blocks, or inserts, have a raised center that engages a groove in the internal splines of the collar. This engagement tends to keep the collar in the neutral position.

The block-type synchronizer positively blocks gear engagement until the speeds match. As a shift is initiated, the shift fork moves the shift collar toward the intended gear. The groove in the moving collar drags the three blocks with it. The ends of the blocks engage three rectangular notches in the bronze blocker rings. These notches are specially sized so that the blocker ring can rotate slightly clockwise or counterclockwise in relation to the blocks or inserts. The pressure on the blocker rings forces them to contact the smooth cone-shaped surface of the main shaft gear. The inside of each blockers ring is machined with sharp ridges that help cut through the film of lubricating oil on the gear's cone.

Pressure on the blocker ring causes friction between the two components. The friction causes the blocker ring to rotate slightly left or right, depending on whether the gear is turning faster or slower than the main shaft and synchronizer. The size of the notches in the blocker rings allows this rotation to continue until the notch contacts the block. The rotation is equivalent to approximately one half of the thickness of one dog tooth. When the notch contacts the block, the dog teeth on the blocker ring no longer line up with the splines on the sliding collar. Therefore, the teeth block any further movement of the collar. Blocking action continues until the gear is speeded up or slowed down sufficiently. Once the gear has sufficiently accelerated or decelerated, its momentum carries the blocker ring in the opposite direction, allowing the dog teeth to align with the splines in the collar again. The collar then slides over the blocker ring dog teeth and the dog teeth of the main shaft gear. The result is a positive clash-free shift.

Pin-Type Synchronizer

A pin-type synchronizer uses a sliding clutch or collar as its engagement device. The sliding clutch is splined to the main shaft and has a groove or a disc that is engaged by the shift fork. The pin-type synchronizer is positioned between a pair of main shaft gears and has two cone-shaped synchronizer friction rings. The surface of the friction rings can be made of bronze, aluminum, or a variety of synthetic materials. Grooves or notches are cut into the friction material to channel away lubricant and ensure contact with the gear.

The synchronizer friction rings have pins that are stepped. One section of each pin has a larger diameter, and the other has a smaller diameter. A chamfer bridges the large and the small dimension. The pins fit into chamfered holes in the sliding clutch, and springs keep tension on the pins. A pin-type synchronizer is shown in **FIGURE 45-11**.

In the neutral position, the small dimension of each pin is held against the edge of the holes in the sliding clutch by spring

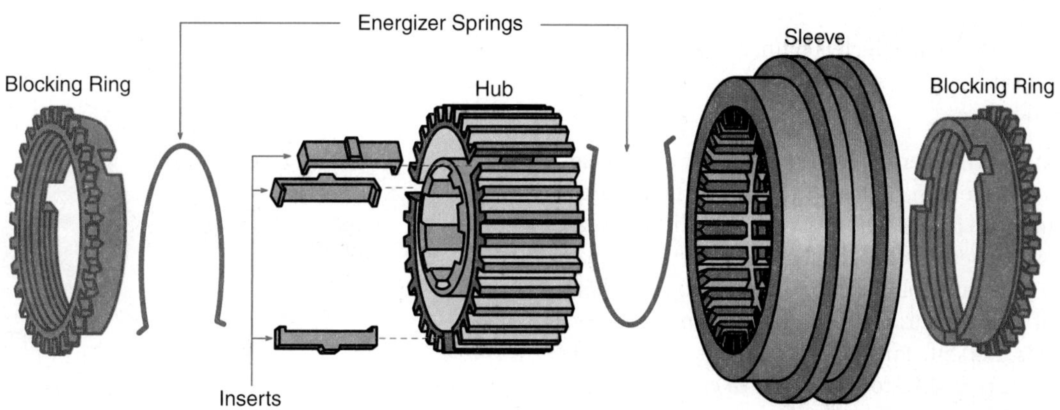

FIGURE 45-10 Block-type synchronizer.

FIGURE 45-11 A pin-type synchronizer.

tension. The main shaft gear that the synchronizer controls may have a removable cup splined to its clutching teeth. The cup may either exactly match the synchronizer cone or simply have a surface machined to match the cone. When a shift is initiated, the sliding clutch is moved toward the intended main shaft gear. The clutch pushes against the chamfered shoulder of the synchronizer ring pins, and that movement forces the ring to contact the mating cup on the gear.

The spring tension stops the sliding clutch from moving up onto the large diameter of the pin until sufficient pressure is applied to overcome the spring tension. Pressure causes enough friction to be generated at the main shaft gear that the gear slows down or speeds up until it synchronizes with the sliding clutch. Further pressure causes the sliding clutch to force its way up onto the large diameter shoulders of the synchronizer pins and engage the main shaft gear with its clutching teeth.

There are several varieties of the pin-type synchronizer, with slight differences in their construction, but they all essentially operate in the manner just described.

Disc-and-Plate-Type Synchronizer

The disc-and-plate-type synchronizer has several components:

- the synchronizer gear
- the input gear we want to engage
- the blocker, which is splined to and turns with the synchronizer gear
- the synchronizer drum, which is splined to and turns with the output gear
- the discs and plates.

Several plates with external tangs, called separator plates, are placed into corresponding notches in the synchronizer drum and therefore turn with it. Disc-and-plate-type synchronizers are rarely seen today. Between each set of plates are the synchronizer discs, which are internally splined to the blocker ring and therefore turn with it. The synchronizer drum has a circumferential groove that holds the shift fork. When a shift is initiated, the synchronizer drum is pushed toward the blocker and the input gear. In theory, this should move the blocker up the splines of the input gear.

The blocker, however, has a spring-loaded detent ball pushing into a groove on the splines of the input gear, so the blocker resists moving. That resistance causes the synchronizer discs to be squeezed between the separator plates. The resulting friction between the plates and discs causes the synchronizer gear to match speeds with the output gear. Further pressure overcomes the tension in the detent springs, and the blocker slides forward on the splines of the input gear. The splines in the synchronizer drum can now slide onto the input gear splines. Because the synchronizer drum splines are also still in mesh with the output gear, the gear is now engaged.

▶ Single and Multiple Countershaft Transmissions Power Flows

K45004

As its name suggests, the single-countershaft transmission has only one countershaft. Many transmissions are designed with more than one countershaft, for a variety of reasons. In truck applications, twin and triple countershafts are used as a way to increase the torque's carrying capacity of a transmission without significantly increasing its length. **FIGURE 45-12A** and **45-12B** shows double- and triple-countershaft arrangements.

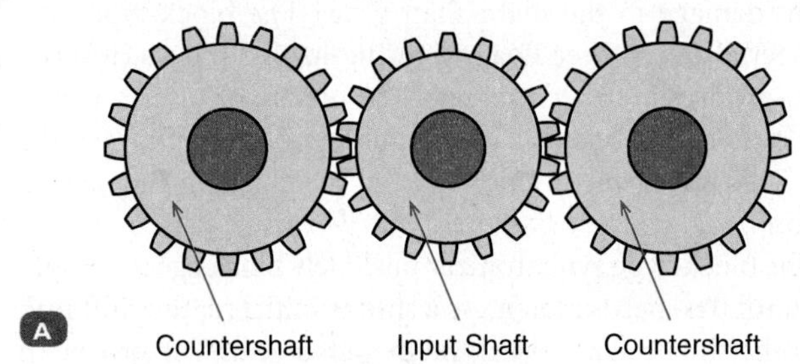

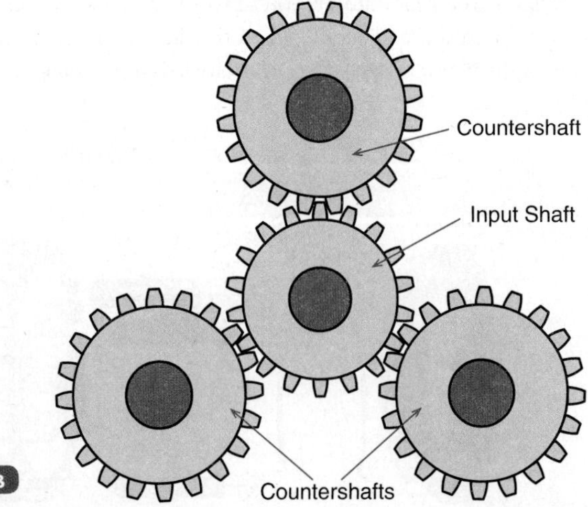

FIGURE 45-12 A. Transmissions with two countershafts split the torque load between the countershafts. **B.** The triple-countershaft transmissions split input torque between three countershafts.

FIGURE 45-13 By using multiple countershafts in series, this type of transmission is capable of very large gear reductions.

In heavy equipment, multiple countershafts are used to compound gear ratios to get deep reductions and massive torque multiplication. Countershafts can be arranged so that the power flows from gears on one countershaft to the gears on the next in series so that gear reduction and torque multiplication is compounded (multiplied). **FIGURE 14-13** shows a multiple countershaft transmission designed to compound gear ratios.

All countershaft transmissions multiply torque and supply gear selection in a very similar fashion, and because the single-countershaft transmission is the simplest design, we will study the power flow of a typical five-speed single-countershaft transmission.

Single-Countershaft Transmission Power Flows

Most single-countershaft transmissions are constant-mesh and synchronized. They may, however, still use a sliding gear for first range and reverse. We will now explain the power flows for a simplified version of a single-countershaft transmission. The transmission depicted in **FIGURE 45-14** is a simplified version of a five-speed single-countershaft transmission.

This five-speed transmission uses sliding clutches to engage all of the main shaft gears, and for clarity, it is depicted as unsynchronized. In unsynchronized transmissions, the operator will have to double-clutch when shifting gears to match the gear and shaft speeds because there is no system installed to do so. To engage the gears, the operator slides a sliding clutch that is splined to the main shaft into mesh with main shaft gears, which are not splined to the main shaft.

Neutral Power Flow

In neutral, as shown in Figure 45-14 below, with the engine running and the clutch engaged, engine power is transmitted through the clutch to the transmission input shaft and the input gear. The input gear transmits the rotating power to the countershaft, and the countershaft gears transmit the power to the main shaft, but because no main shaft gears are engaged, the power flow stops there.

Reverse Power Flow

As illustrated in **FIGURE 45-15**, the reverse power flow begins when the operator depresses the clutch and moves the shift lever to the far left and then forward. This action moves the first and reverse shift fork and slides the first and reverse sliding clutch into reverse gear on the main shaft. This locks the gear to the main shaft, and the power flows from the input shafts drive gear to the countershaft driven gear then through the countershaft reverse gear, the reverse idler gear, the main shaft reverse gear, and finally through the first and reverse sliding clutch onto the main shaft.

First Gear Power Flow

To engage first gear, the operator depresses the clutch and moves the shift lever to the left and backward. This causes the first and reverse sliding clutch to slide into the first gear main shaft, locking it to the shaft, as shown in **FIGURE 45-16**. When the operator releases the clutch pedal, the power flows from the input shafts drive gear to the countershaft driven gear, then through the countershaft first gear, the main shaft first gear, and through the first and reverse sliding clutch onto the main shaft.

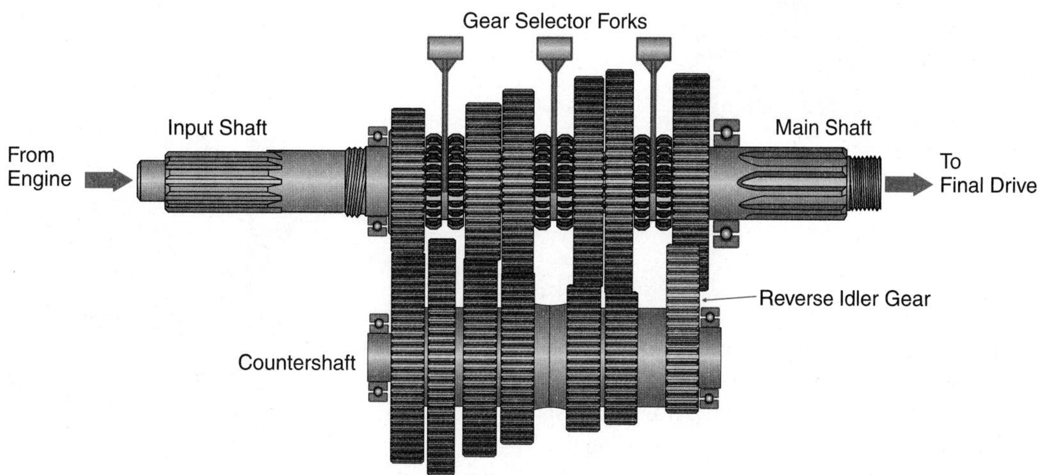

FIGURE 45-14 A five-speed single-countershaft transmission in neutral.

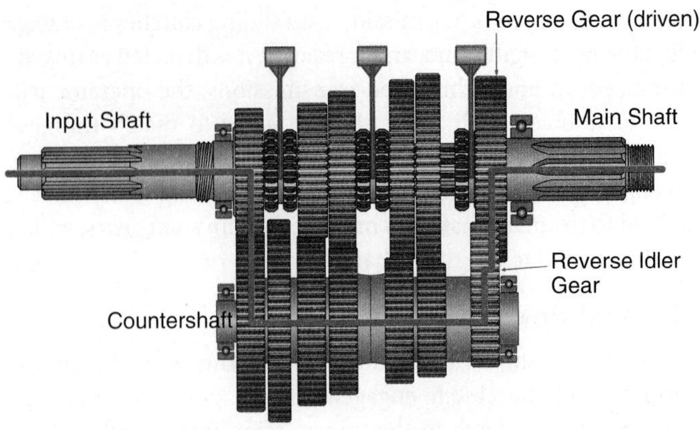

FIGURE 45-15 Reverse gear power flow for a single-countershaft, five-speed transmission.

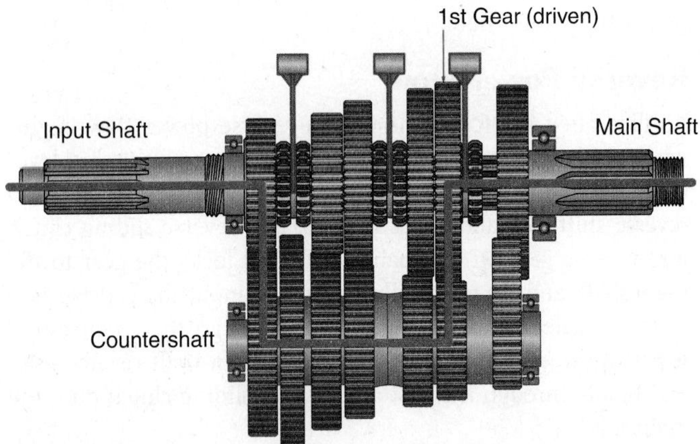

FIGURE 45-16 First gear power flow for a single-countershaft, five-speed transmission.

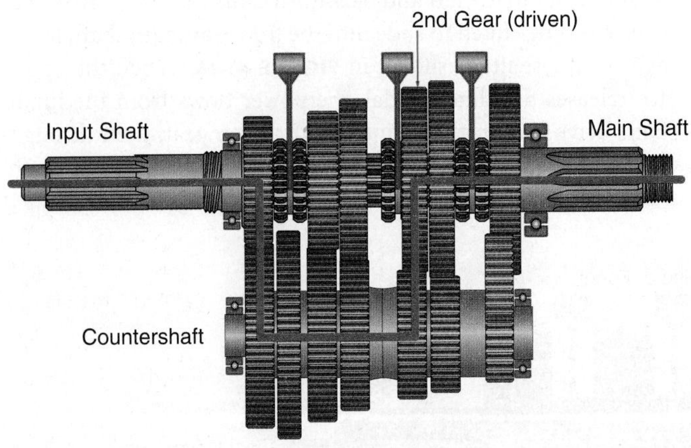

FIGURE 45-17 Second gear power flow for a single-countershaft, five-speed transmission.

Second Gear Power Flow

To engage second gear, as shown in **FIGURE 45-17**, the operator depresses the clutch pedal and moves the shift lever to the neutral position, pulling the first and reverse sliding clutch from the first gear main shaft and then selects the middle shift gate, moving the shifter forward. This causes the second and third sliding clutch to slide into the second gear main shaft, locking it to the shaft. When

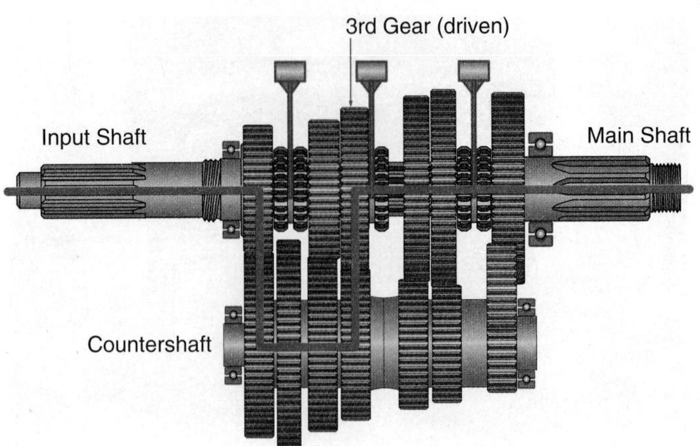

FIGURE 45-18 Third gear power flow for a single-countershaft, five-speed transmission.

the operator releases the clutch pedal, the power flows from the input shafts drive gear to the countershaft driven gear, then through the countershaft second gear, the main shaft second gear, and through the second and third sliding clutch onto the main shaft.

Third Gear Power Flow

To engage third gear, as shown in **FIGURE 45-18**, the operator pulls the shift lever rearward in the center shift gate. This disengages the two/three sliding clutch from the second gear main shaft and engages it to the third gear main shaft. When the clutch is re-engaged, the power then flows from the input shaft to the third gear countershaft then to the third gear main shaft, through the two/three sliding clutch, onto the main shaft.

Fourth Gear Power Flow

To engage fourth gear, as shown in **FIGURE 45-19**, the operator moves the shifter to the neutral position and then to the far-right shift gate and forward to the fourth gear position. This action moves the four/five sliding clutch rearward to engage the fourth gear main shaft and lock it to the main shaft. The power now flows from the input shaft to the countershaft fourth gear to the main shaft fourth gear, through the four/five sliding clutch, and then on to the main shaft.

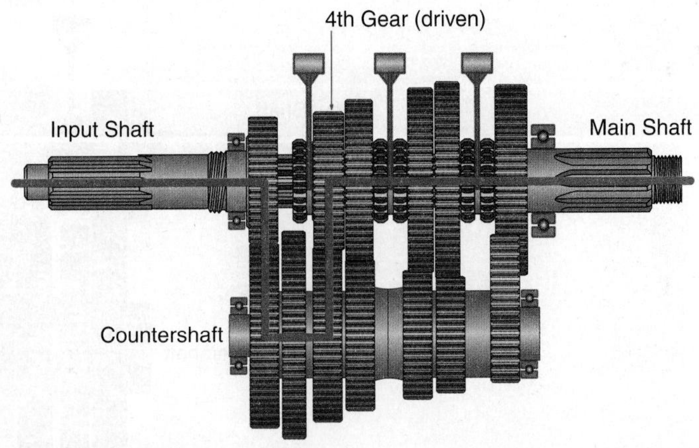

FIGURE 45-19 Fourth gear power flow for a single-countershaft, five-speed transmission.

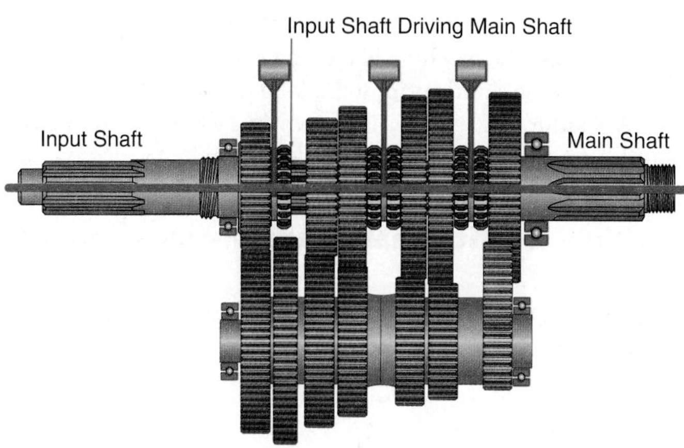

FIGURE 45-20 Fifth gear power flow for a single-countershaft, five-speed transmission.

Fifth Gear Power Flow

To engage fifth gear, as shown in **FIGURE 45-20**, the operator depresses the clutch and then pulls the shifter rearward in the far-right shift gate into the fifth gear position. This action moves the four/five sliding clutch forward, causing it to disengage the main shaft fourth gear and engage the clutching teeth in the back of the input shaft, effectively connecting the input shaft to the main shaft. The power flow now flows directly from the input shaft through the four/five sliding clutch to the main shaft. Power is still available through the countershaft to the main shaft gears. No main shaft gears are engaged, however, so the flow stops there.

Forward/Reverse Shuttles

In some applications, such as bulldozers and wheeled loaders, it is advantageous to have the same number of forward and reverse gears. These types of machines will typically perform the same task repetitively during their workday, such as digging into a dirt pile, then carrying it to a dump truck and dumping the load, and then returning to the pile again. To accommodate this cyclic work load, manufacturers commonly use a forward/reverse shuttle either before the actual standard transmission or integral with it. The shuttle uses two multidisc clutches. **FIGURE 45-21** shows a forward reverse shuttle.

The forward/reverse shuttle is a set of two multi-plate hydraulic clutches, one of which inputs the transmission gearing in a forward (clockwise) direction when it is applied, and the other of which inputs the transmission in a reverse (counterclockwise) direction when it is applied. This arrangement can increase the machine's cycle rate by allowing fast changes between forward and reverse without the need to change the mechanical gear ratio. Although these shuttles can be shifted on the fly, it is highly recommended that the vehicle come to a stop before a direction change is made. In these types of transmissions, input power is typically delivered to the shuttle through a torque converter. A torque converter is a type of hydraulic coupling that can cushion the quick direction changes and shock loads to the machine's driveline. Torque converters will be more fully discussed in Chapter 47.

The multi-plate clutches used in the shuttle are composed of several friction discs sandwiched between an equal number of steel reaction plates. Typically, the friction discs are splined to the component we will want to drive. For the forward direction clutch, this will be the input shaft of the mechanical transmission, and the reaction plates will be splined or lugged to the housing of the clutch. The clutches are spring released, so until they are actuated, the two sets of plates remain apart and can rotate independently of each other. The clutches are activated by sending hydraulic pressure to a piston in the clutch housing that squeezes the stack of plates together, causing them to turn as one and creating the input. The reverse clutch receives its input through an idler gear arrangement, so when the reverse clutch is

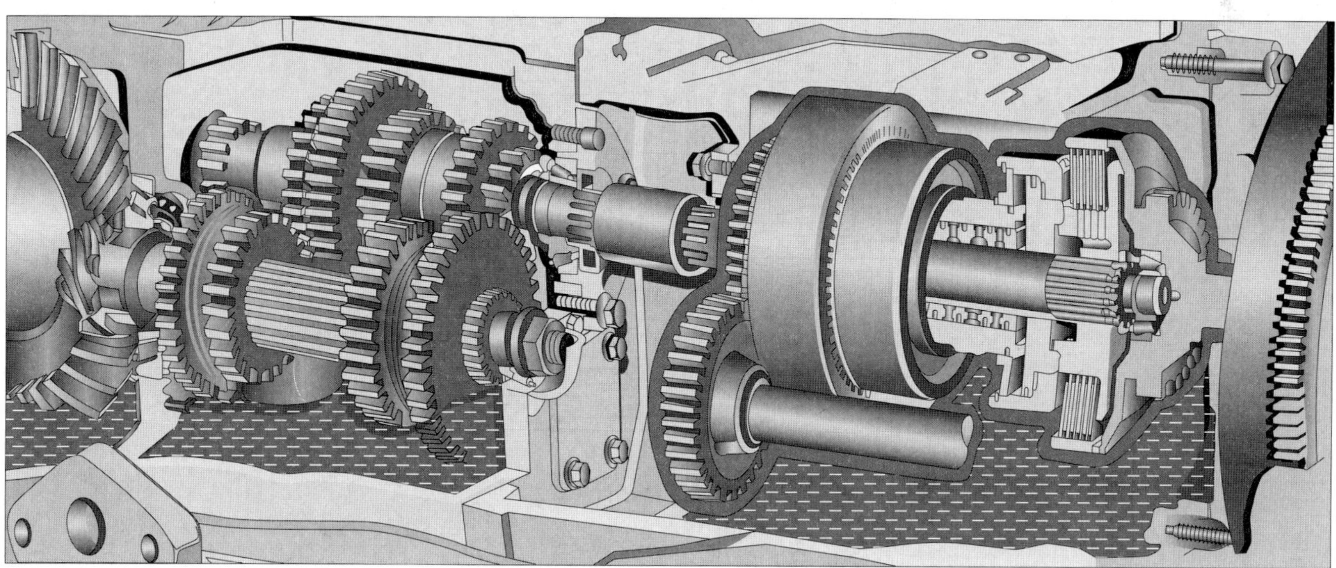

FIGURE 45-21 A forward/reverse shuttle uses two multidisc clutches.

applied, it turns the input shaft counterclockwise. **FIGURE 45-22** shows the forward power flow through a shuttle.

There are many different arrangements for forward/reverse shuttles. The preceding is merely one of them, but they all function in a similar fashion. **FIGURE 45-23** shows the reverse power flow through the shuttle. Typically, the hydraulic clutches are controlled by an electric solenoid that when actuated will move a valve that sends hydraulic pressure to the clutch.

Please note that if the forward/reverse shuttle is engaged before the main transmission is put into gear, the machine will not move. Selecting a gear after the shuttle has been engaged would cause severe gear clash, causing transmission damage. Shifting while the machine is moving can be accomplished by disengaging the shuttle prior to making the shift.

A shuttle shift control is shown in **FIGURE 45-24**. Power shuttles are discussed in more detail in Chapter 48.

Multiple Countershaft Transmissions Power Flows

As mentioned previously, there are two basic types of multiple countershaft transmissions: those that are designed to spread

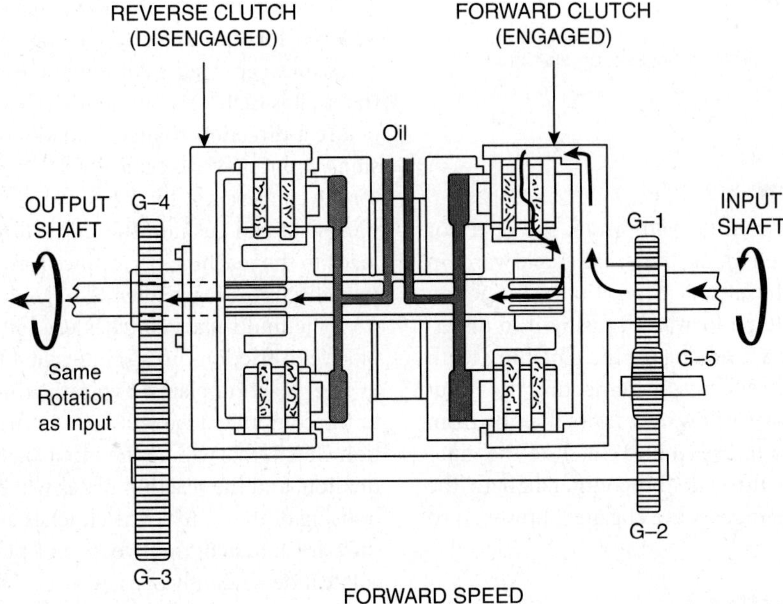

FIGURE 45-22 One of the two clutches will engage a gear that drives the transmission clockwise, and the other will drive an idler to drive the transmission counterclockwise.

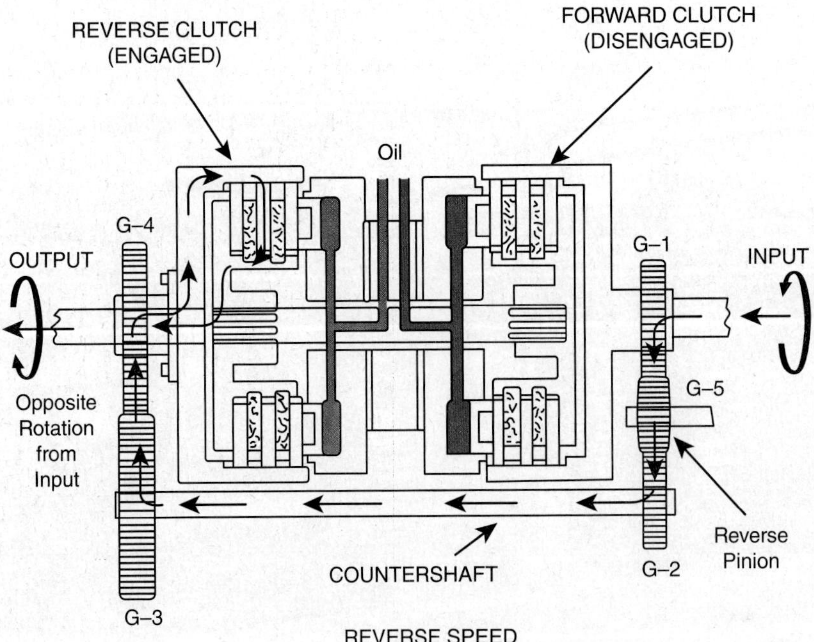

FIGURE 45-23 In reverse the power flows through the idler gear reversing output direction.

FIGURE 45-24 Shuttle shift allows direction changes without having change gears leading to faster cycle times.

the torque load over more than one countershaft and those that use multiple countershafts to gain larger torque multiplication. The first of these types is the double- and triple-countershaft designs commonly found in heavy trucks, the most common being the Eaton Fuller line of double-countershaft transmissions and the Volvo/Mack line of triple-countershaft transmissions. The truck that brings machines to the jobsite will likely have one or the other of these transmissions. **FIGURE 45-25** shows a double-countershaft transmission.

In both the double- and triple-countershaft types of these transmissions, the countershafts are installed parallel to each other and are all driven by the same input gear. Arranging the countershafts in this way allows the input torque to be divided between the two or three countershafts. This allows the transmission's gears to be smaller and yet still carry heavy loads, because instead of one set of teeth carrying the entire load, several sets of teeth divide the load equally. In turn, this allows the transmissions to be relatively more compact. In both of these transmission designs, the countershafts have to be timed at installation,

FIGURE 45-25 This transmission uses two countershafts to double its torque carrying capacity.

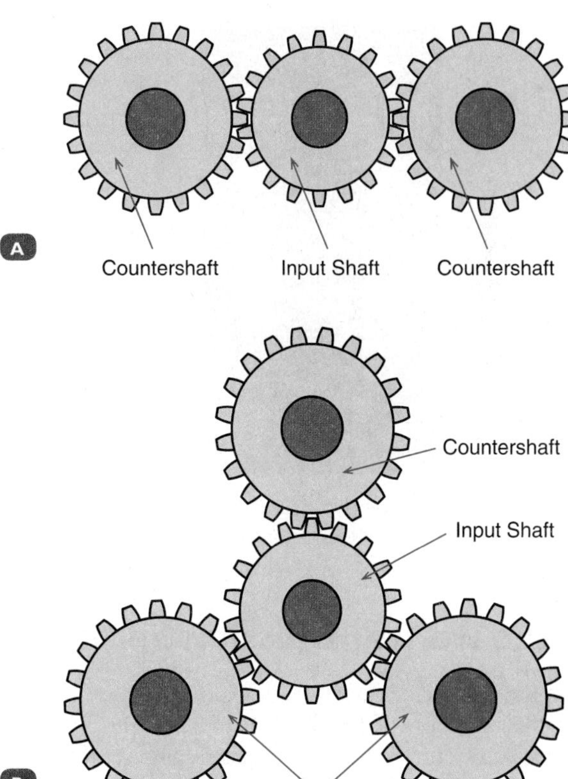

FIGURE 45-26 Timing the twin **A.** and triple **B.** countershafts ensure that the load is equally distributed and that the main shaft is supported properly by the two or three countershafts.

as shown in **FIGURE 45-26A** and **45-26B**. These transmissions are equipped with auxiliary sections to provide more usable ranges. An auxiliary section is simply a second transmission bolted to the back of the main transmission, which can multiply the number of available ranges by two, three, or even four. These types of transmissions are not often found in off-road machinery. Power flows for multiple countershaft transmissions are identical to those for the five-speed single-countershaft transmission described above, except that the torque load is split between two countershafts instead of one.

The second type of multiple countershaft transmissions are those that use the countershafts to gain more torque multiplication and/or more usable gear ratios. In this type, again the countershafts are installed parallel to each other, but only one of them is connected to the input gear. Power is then transferred from gears on one countershaft to the other, compounding ratios with each transfer. Sliding clutches, synchronizers, and/or power-shift multidisc clutch packs will be located on the countershafts to select different gear ratios. Power-shift transmissions will be discussed in Chapter 48.

FIGURE 45-27 shows a ZF multiple countershaft power-shift transmission that uses multidisc clutch packs to select gear ratios. The power flows through these types of transmissions is at first glance a little more complicated, but it is merely a matter of transferring power sequentially from one countershaft to the next through various gears to complete the flow.

FIGURE 45-27 This ZF power-shift transmission uses multiple countershafts to gain torque multiplication and increase available ratios.

▶ Standard Transmission Servicing

S45001

It is not the intention of this book to describe in detail the repair procedures for individual transmissions used in off-road equipment. The following procedures and skill drills are therefore general in nature and not specific to any one machine. Once the particular problem has been identified, the technician should consult the appropriate manufacturer's documentation for that machine in order to perform the repairs required. Perhaps one of the most common service procedures on transmissions is a fluid change. **SKILL DRILL 45-1** lists the procedure for oil and filter service on a typical transmission.

Lubrication

Before diving into a transmission maintenance or service procedure, it is critical that you understand the fundamentals of lubrication. Today's machines are designed to give exceptional service and longevity. The only way this equipment can give this kind of service is with careful operator training and proper lubrication. Lubrication is the lifeblood of any mechanical component, and a transmission is no different. It is absolutely essential that the correct type and quantity of lubricant is used. Note that most manual transmissions rely on the rotation of the countershaft to move oil around the inside of the transmission case to lubricate the internal components. Because of this fact, it is essential that the lubricant is kept at the correct level. Any less than the correct amount of lubricant inside the transmission can cause areas of the transmission to be starved for oil and lead to failure.

SKILL DRILL 45-1 Changing Transmission Oil

1. Operate the machine for a few minutes to warm the transmission oil, the machine should be on level ground for the procedure.
2. Lower the machine bucket if equipped, engage the parking brake and shut off the engine.
3. Locate and remove the transmission drain plug and allow the fluid to drain, when complete clean and reinstall the drain plug.
4. Locate and remove the transmission oil filter element, if equipped, with a strap-type wrench.
5. Clean the mounting base for the filter element.
6. Ensure that the old seal or gasket is completely removed.
7. Apply a light coat of clean oil to the gasket or seal of the new filter.
8. Install the new filter, and after the seal comes in contact with the base, tighten by hand an additional 1/2 to 3/4 turn.

   Note: Check the service manual for the particular machine to ensure that the filter is tightened correctly.
9. If the transmission's magnetic strainer cover is equipped, remove it.
10. Carefully remove the magnets from the strainer housing. Do not drop or damage the magnets, because sharp knocks can cause them to lose their effectiveness.
11. Remove the screen from the housing.
12. Wash the screen in a clean, nonflammable solvent.

    Note: Never use flammable solvent, such as gasoline, for cleaning.
13. Clean the magnets with a cloth rag or a stiff bristle brush.
14. Reinstall the screen and the magnets.
15. If necessary, replace the strainer cover seal and reinstall the cover. Tighten the bolts to the manufacturer's specification.
16. Check and, if necessary, remove and clean the transmission breather from the top of the transmission case. Clean the breather with solvent. Dry and reinstall the breather.
17. Open the machine's access door, remove the transmission dipstick or fill cap, and fill the transmission with the correct type and quantity of lubricant (check the manual from the original equipment manufacturer (OEM) for the correct fluid and amount).
18. Replace the dipstick or fill cap and operate the machine for a few minutes, and then shut it off.
19. Carefully inspect the oil filter's magnetic strainer cover and the drain plug for leakage and repair as necessary.
20. Check and adjust the transmission fluid level. Usually, the dipstick will have markings for hot and cold fluid levels, but check the OEM documentation to be sure.

Manufacturers produce specific oils and lubricants for each component of the machine: the engine, the transmission, the brakes, and the hydraulic systems. Many companies produce equivalent lubricants; however, technicians must ensure that the lubricant they use meets or exceeds the manufacturer's requirements. Synthetic-based lubricants and semisynthetic-based lubricants are becoming more popular, and in most cases, they should not be mixed with non-synthetic blends. Be sure to follow the manufacturer's recommendations and service schedule when servicing a particular machine. John Deere's recommended lubricant is shown in **FIGURE 45-28**.

The key to keeping any transmission in working order is following regular maintenance procedures. Preventive maintenance is the first step. As mentioned previously, the proper lubricant is essential to transmission operation. A regularly scheduled maintenance program should be followed to ensure the lubricant is doing its job. The transmission should also be visually inspected for oil leaks every day and repaired as necessary. In addition to daily checks, the following preventive maintenance checks are recommended for every service, typically every 50 hours of operation. Machines may have a decal with the manufacturer's recommended maintenance schedule, or it may be found in the operator's manual. **FIGURE 45-29** shows a maintenance schedule affixed to a John Deere backhoe.

The following is a partial list of typical preventive checks to be performed on a machine with a standard (manual) transmission. Note that this list is not comprehensive and is not intended to supersede the manufacturer's recommended preventive checks.

Clutch pedal shaft and mechanism: Use a pry bar on the clutch release mechanism shafts to check for wear. If excessive movement is found, remove the clutch release mechanism and check bores and shafts on all bushings for wear. Check OEM documentation for correct clearances.

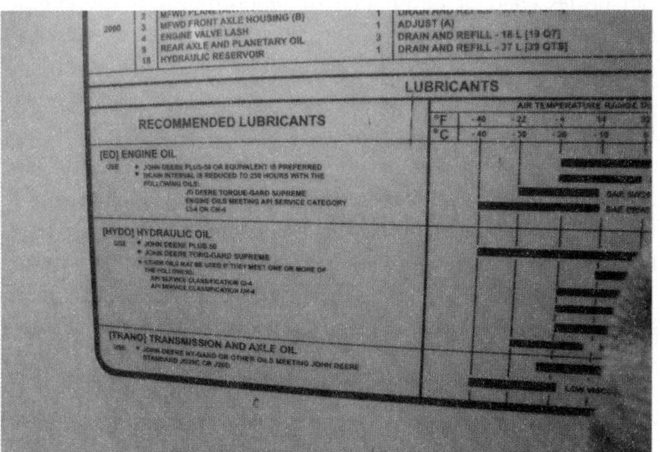

FIGURE 45-28 In John Deere's transmissions, the company recommends using their own brand, Hy-Gard lubricant, or one that meets John Deere's specifications.

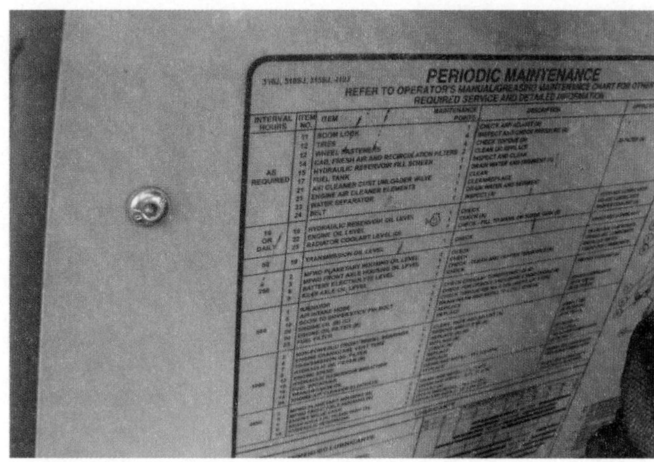

FIGURE 45-29 Maintenance schedules may be found directly on the machine, in the operator's manual, or by contacting the OEM.

Lubricant: Check the lubricant level. Always top off fluid levels with the correct lubricant. Never mix different types or brands. Checking the fluid level of a manual transmission is discussed in **SKILL DRILL 45-2**.

Oil filter: Inspect oil filter (if equipped) for damage or rust. Replace as necessary. Inspect oil filter adapter for damage or leakage. Replace as necessary. Most manufacturers recommend changing the filter at the same time as the transmission oil change intervals. Check the OEM manual.

Drain plugs: Check for leaks and tighten drain plugs securely.

Mounting and attaching bolts and gaskets: For applicable models, check all bolts, especially those on power take-off (PTO) covers and rear bearing covers, for looseness, which might cause oil leakage. Check PTO opening and rear bearing covers for oil leakage due to faulty gaskets.

Troubleshooting Transmission System Problems

The first step in any maintenance activity is to diagnose the problem. It does little good to start dismantling components without an idea of what could be causing the trouble! Diagnosing problems is a systematic activity that involves looking for and interpreting basic signs. As a technician, you will have to diagnose common transmission complaints, such as oil leaks, noise, vibration, hard shifting, and gear slip. Skill Drill 45-2 lists the steps to follow to check the transmission fluid level and inspect for leaks.

Oil Leaks

Oil leaks are, of course, a cause for concern with any mechanical component because they lead to a decrease in lubricant. Still, many unnecessary repairs are performed when there is only a slight weeping. An oil leak is different from an oil weep. An oil weep is a very minor oil seepage, usually caused by a wicking effect, and is not usually a reason for repair. Oil weep can be recognized by a slight wetting of an area on the component. The area

SKILL DRILL 45-2 Checking Transmission Fluid Level and Inspecting for Leaks

The following instructions are for a machine with a manual transmission that has a forward reverse shuttle:

1. To begin the test, the engine must be running at low idle and the oil must be at normal operating temperature.
2. During these checks, a magnet can be used to detect the presence of ferrous particles.
3. Check the oil level in the transmission by removing the dipstick.
   Note: Some machine transmissions may have a visual indicator (a sight glass) for the transmission oil level.
4. Look for air (bubbles) or water on the dipstick. Many transmission problems can be caused by low oil level, air in the oil, or oil contamination.
5. Add oil to the transmission if it is needed.
   Note: Air (bubbles) can be caused by a loose suction tube or a damaged casting that allows air to enter the suction side of the system, along with allowing oil to leak out.
6. Check all oil lines, hoses, and connections for leaks and damage. Look for oil on the ground under the machine. Check all gaskets and seals for leaks.
7. If the oil is found to be contaminated, drain the oil from the transmission case. Use a magnet to determine whether the contamination material is ferrous or not.
   a. Rubber particles can indicate seal or hose failure.
   b. Shiny or silvery steel particles indicate mechanical failure or gear wear of the transmission or pump.
   c. A heavy accumulation of black fibrous material can indicate worn clutch discs in the shuttle.
   d. Aluminum particles indicate failure in a clutch piston or torque converter.
   e. Iron or steel chips indicate broken components in the transmission.

around the weep appears damp, and oil has soaked in to any dirt accumulated there—but there is no dripping of fluid.

An oil weep is usually not a cause for concern. If an oil weep is discovered at a gasket, however, re-torque the attaching bolts and monitor the machine through its next few services. Depending on the state of the weep, it may not require a repair.

By contrast, a leak will always be associated with oil dripping and/or an extremely wet area. Oil leaks must always be repaired. It may be difficult to see the actual path of the leak. Accumulated dirt and/or oil flow patterns may obstruct visibility. Nonetheless, it is essential that the actual leak path is determined before deciding on a repair. Remove the excess dirt and clean the affected area with an approved degreaser. Refill the transmission lube to the proper level (even with the bottom of the fill hole). Operate the machine until it reaches normal operating temperatures and re-inspect the suspect area. Ensure that that area is not being contaminated by oil leaking elsewhere and splashing on the area. Once the source of the leak has been identified and repaired, repeat the process to verify the repair. Poor investigation into the actual source of a leak can cause considerable wasted effort, so take the time to properly diagnose any leak.

Transmission Noise

A certain amount of noise is expected from a transmission as it does its job. Excessive or unusual noises, however, are indications of a problem. And remember that noises that appear to be coming from the transmission may actually be originating elsewhere in the machine driveline systems. Before undertaking transmission repairs, eliminate all other possible sources of the noise before condemning the transmission.

Common noises in transmissions include the gears rattling at idle, knocking sounds, whining, and growling.

Gear Rattle at Idle

A rough idling engine can cause gear rattle at idle. The small torsional vibrations set up by rough running can cause the gears in a transmission to strike each other, resulting in rattle. This can be lessened or eliminated by smoothing out the engine operation. A certain amount of gear rattle is to be expected and normal.

Knocking

Gears are sometimes damaged before or on installation. Gears can be damaged from some other cause as well, such as something that has impacted the gear teeth. Damaged gears can have bumps or swells on the teeth, as illustrated in **FIGURE 45-30**. These can cause a knocking or thudding sounds as the gears go through mesh. Knocking is usually more pronounced when under load.

Bearings that have worn spots on the bearing races or damaged rollers or balls can cause a similar noise. A gear that is cracked or broken from shock loading can have the same type of noise at low speeds. The noise changes to a howling sound as speed increases.

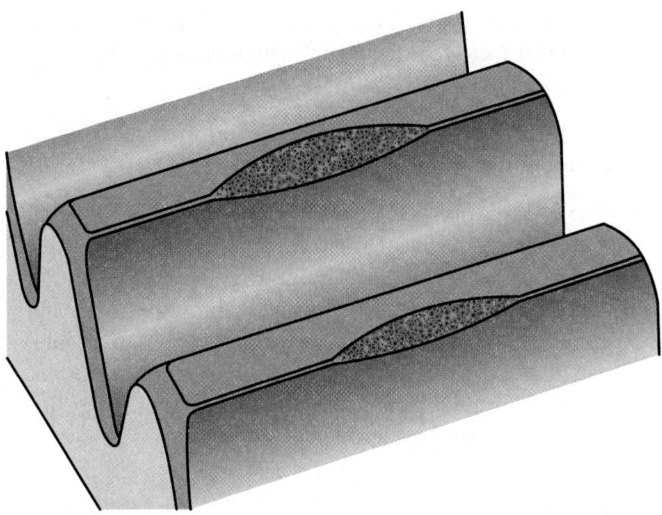

FIGURE 45-30 Swells or bumps on gear teeth can cause a knocking sound.

Whining

Spur-type gears have a natural tendency to whine, and a certain amount of whining noise is normal with these gears. Regardless, when gear teeth wear and pitting occurs, whining will start. As the gear teeth continue to deteriorate, the whining will become a louder howling. Whining can also be caused by lack of backlash between gears. In addition, bearings that are improperly installed or "squeezed" (have insufficient clearance) can also cause a whining noise.

Growling

A growling noise can be caused by bearings that are worn and badly damaged. Bearings can wear due to lube contamination. When this is the case, bearing damage has occurred throughout the transmission, so growling can be an indication that a complete overhaul will be necessary. Gears that are extremely spalled or pitted can cause this type of noise as well.

Vibration

In addition to noise, another problem that technicians must commonly diagnose is vibration. Vibration can be caused by many things in a machine, but vibration originating in the transmission is usually a sign of extreme wear in the bearing and/or the gear teeth themselves. Transmission vibration is usually preceded by whining, growling, or knocking and indicates failure to have the machine repaired in a timely fashion. To diagnose noise or vibration in a backhoe, follow the steps in **SKILL DRILL 45-3**.

Hard Shifting

Hard shifting can be caused by several factors, so it is important to first find out whether the issue is inside or outside of the transmission. If the transmission has remote shift linkage, where the shift linkage is not directly on top of the shift cover, the remote shift linkage could be the culprit. To confirm that is the case, disconnect the remote shift linkage from the shift cover and try to move the shift rails inside the transmission. If the rails move freely, the problem is with the remote shift linkage. Hard shifting can also have internal causes, such as a sliding clutch, collar, or synchronizer that is binding. The shift yoke for a particular gear can be bent and therefore restrict the sliding clutch or synchronizer. Hard shifting can also be the result of the shift rails binding in the shift housing because of a cracked housing or a sprung (bowed) shift rail.

Gear Slip Out

Gear slip out, or jump out, occurs when an engaged gear's sliding clutch, collar, or synchronizer moves out of engagement while the vehicle is pulling a load, causing the transmission to go into neutral. If the clutching teeth on the sliding clutch, collar, or the gear are badly worn from excessive gear clashing, slip out is very likely. **FIGURE 45-31** shows the clutching teeth on a synchronizer sliding collar.

Gear slip out can also occur because of worn shift forks, worn shift fork wear pads, as shown in **FIGURE 45-32**, or sliding

SKILL DRILL 45-3 Diagnosing Noise or Vibration

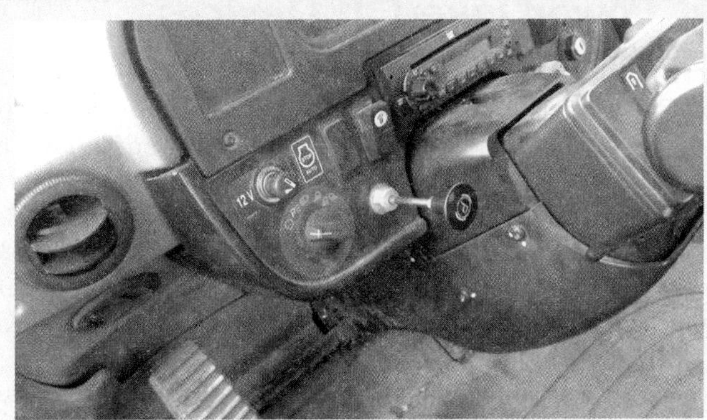

1. Position the machine on level solid ground.
2. Start the engine and allow it to warm up for a few minutes.
3. Lower the backhoe stabilizers and raise the rear wheels just off the ground, approximately 150.0 mm (6.0").
4. Lower the bucket and lift the front wheels until they too are approximately 150.0 mm (6.0") off the ground.
5. Set engine speed to low idle.
6. With the engine running and park brakes on, move the lever for the forward/reverse shuttle and the shift lever for the transmission speeds.
7. Operate the machine in each direction and in all gear ranges. Take note of any noises that do not seem normal and try to locate their source. If the machine operation is not correct in all speed ranges and directions, consult the manufacturer's troubleshooting documentation to narrow down and ultimately isolate the possible problems and their causes.

FIGURE 45-31 Always carefully inspect the clutching teeth of synchronizer collars, because worn teeth can lead to gear slip out.

FIGURE 45-32 These wear pads on a shift fork can wear out, leading to partial gear engagement and possible slip out.

clutch/collar grooves that will not allow the sliding clutch or collar to fully engage with the main shaft gears. Other causes of slip out include worn shift rail detents and weak or broken detent ball springs.

Transmission Overhaul

The information required to successfully rebuild a transmission is very precise and unique to the model being worked on. For that reason, we will focus our discussion on general procedures for several transmission-related tasks. Information on overhauling or rebuilding particular transmissions is available from the equipment manufacturer.

As with any repair, it is critical that your work area be staged, orderly, and complete. Before beginning any maintenance or repair procedure on a transmission, ensure that the following items are on hand and organized in your work area:

- the correct overhaul manual for the transmission model being serviced
- a clean dust-free area large enough to complete the repair
- all of the recommended tools found in the overhaul manual
- replacement parts (i.e., gaskets, seals and/or bearings, snap rings, etc.) for parts that will definitely be or may be destroyed during disassembly.

Before attempting any repair on any transmission, read and understand the following precautions and procedures:

- Remove bearings with appropriate pullers. Carefully clean and inspect the bearings for damage and wear. Check races and balls or rollers for pitting, heat discoloration, and other damage. If there is any doubt as to the bearing's condition, replace it. If the bearing is to be reused, lubricate it and wrap in protective material until ready to use. Before reinstallation, always check that the bearings fit in the bore and on its shaft.
- Regarding assemblies, when disassembling various components, lay the pieces out on a clean surface in the order that they come apart and protect them from dirt and damage.
- Always remove snap rings with pliers designed for the job. Remember that even when they are removed correctly, snap rings are quite commonly distorted. Any distortion requires that the snap ring be replaced. Never reuse a sprung snap ring.
- Check all gear teeth for frosting or pitting. Frosting is a slight discoloration of the gear tooth face caused by tiny pits that occur naturally as the gears run together and find a common pitch line. Frosting and light pitting are usually not a cause for concern. As the gears continue to run together, frosting is usually replaced by a shiny smooth surface in a process known as healing. Moderate and heavy pitting, however, will require gear replacement, especially if it is concentrated at the pitch line of the gear teeth.
- Check for cracks in the gears, and carefully inspect the clutching teeth for excessive wear from clashing. If clutching teeth are significantly worn, replace the gear.
- Check all shaft splines for wear, and replace as necessary.
- Check all cast iron components for cracks and/or leaks, and replace as necessary.

▶ Power Take-Off Devices

K45005

PTO devices allow power to be rerouted to operate other equipment on the machine. A PTO device, such as the one shown in **FIGURE 45-33**, is basically a device attached to the transmission that is gear driven and can be used to run accessories.

A PTO, then, is a gearbox that is driven by the engine to power another mechanical or hydraulic component. PTOs attached to the transmission are bolted to one of two SAE (International Society of Automotive Engineers) standard size openings: a six-bolt or an eight-bolt opening. A PTO can also be driven by the engine flywheel or even by the front gear train of the engine. There are several different designs used in the manufacture of PTOs. One of the more common is the two-gear design. The two-gear design typically contains two shafts (the idler shaft and the output shaft) in the unit and three gears

FIGURE 45-33 A transmission-mounted PTO.

FIGURE 45-34 This PTO is engaged by a cable actuated lever, but PTOs can also be actuated electrically. **A.** Constant mesh gears. **B.** Sliding collar.

(the input gear, the drive gear, and the output gear). The PTO input gear is mounted on the idler shaft and is in constant mesh with the transmission countershaft gear or part of the engine gear train. The output gear, also called the ratio gear, is attached to the output shaft of the PTO. The drive gear is usually mounted on the input shaft, but not splined to it. A sliding clutch or collar splined to the input shaft is used to engage the drive gear, which is in constant mesh with the output gear. When the sliding clutch or collar engages the drive gear, power is transmitted to the output gear to drive the PTO output shaft. The PTO output shaft can be connected directly to a hydraulic pump or to a drive shaft to power a remote hydraulic or mechanical system. The sliding clutch can be moved mechanically or by an electric or air solenoid to engage the PTO. A typical PTO is shown in **FIGURE 45-34**.

The ratio gear may be fixed to the idler shaft or free to rotate on it. If the ratio gear is freely rotating, the sliding clutch will lock it to the idler shaft to engage the PTO. (In some spur-tooth input gear PTOs, the input gear is splined to the idler shaft and slid into mesh with the countershaft gear to engage the PTO. Those types are less common, however.) The second shaft is the PTO output shaft, which has the PTO-driven gear keyed or splined to it. The PTO is generally engaged by moving the sliding clutch to lock the input gear to the shaft. Some models use a different configuration and have a sliding gear on the output shaft for PTO engagement. **Power take-offs (PTOs)** can directly or indirectly drive hydraulic pumps, air compressors/vacuum pumps, pneumatic blowers, or other mechanical components. They can also drive components, such as a high-pressure water pump, through a driveshaft.

There are several other types of PTOs, such as front-mount belt-driven hydraulic pumps and PTOs provided by transfer cases. One type of PTO common in mobile off-road equipment is sandwiched between the engine and the transmission.

▶ PTO Installation

K45006

When installing a transmission-mounted PTO, care must be taken to provide the correct running clearance, or backlash, between the countershaft gear and the PTO drive gear. In most cases, this clearance runs between 0.006 inches and 0.018 inches (0.15 mm and 0.46 mm). A PTO mounted too tightly will run noisily and ultimately fail. It can also damage the transmission in the process. Conversely, a PTO mounted too loosely (with too much backlash) runs the risk of skipping teeth under load. It also may cause catastrophic damage from pieces of metal that have broken off the gears running through the transmission and the PTO.

Deciding which type and size of PTO is correct for a given application is better left to the PTO manufacturer, who can give advice on PTO speed, horsepower capability, and the suitability for a given vocation. Regardless of type, PTOs are a simple and effective way to use the powertrain of the vehicle to operate accessory devices when necessary.

▶ PTO Service and Repair

S45002

PTO equipment is subject to constant and occasionally severe torsional vibrations. Because of this, a set maintenance schedule for inspections is required. Failure to correct loose bolts or to repair leaks could result in PTO or transmission damage. Therefore, periodic PTO maintenance is necessary to ensure proper, safe, and trouble-free operation.

Daily inspections:

- Check all air, hydraulic and working mechanisms before operating PTO and repair as necessary.
- Check PTO for correct operation, noise, looseness etcetera.

Monthly inspections:

- Check for leaks and tighten all air, hydraulic, and mounting hardware, if necessary.
- Torque all bolts, nuts, and mounting hardware to specifications.

- Check and lubricate splined shafts, as necessary. The nearly constant torsional vibrations that these units are subject to can lead to lubricant being forced out of direct splined shafts, and they will eventually fail. A high-temperature, high-pressure grease is required to protect these areas from fretting wear. Fretting wear will appear as rusting and streaking at the shaft spline area. High cycle units may require more frequent greasing.
- Perform maintenance as required.

▶ Transfer Cases

K45007

A **transfer case** is a gearbox arrangement that is either attached to the back of the main transmission or connected to it by a short drive shaft. The transfer case allows the torque from the transmission to be split between the front and rear driving axles of a vehicle. The transfer case may also provide a lower gear ratio and PTO options. A transfer case is pictured in **FIGURE 45-35**. Transfer cases are sometimes called drop boxes because their design allows the front drive shaft to clear the bottom of the transmission in order to go to the front axle.

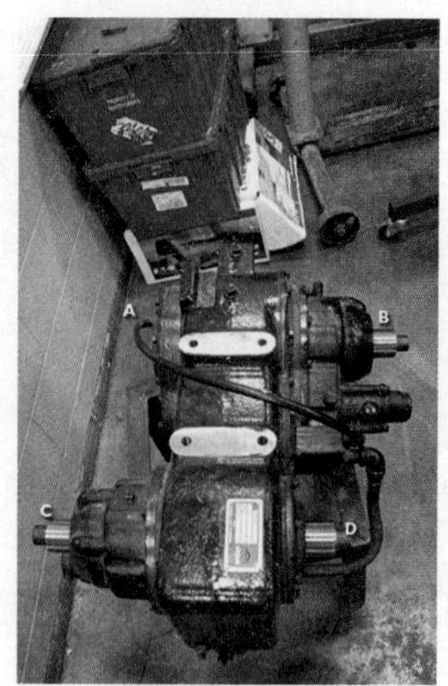

FIGURE 45-35 Transfer case: **A.** PTO shaft. **B.** Input from transmission. **C.** Rear drive axle. **D.** Front drive axle.

The transfer case will usually have at least four shafts (illustrated in **FIGURE 45-36**):

1. the input shaft
2. the countershaft
3. the front axle drive shaft
4. the rear axle drive shaft.

The transfer case may also contain reduction gearing to allow two speeds (low and high) through the case when desired. A two-speed transfer case will have two sets of gears that can drive the output shafts. The operator can select these gear sets by using a sliding clutch splined to the input shaft. The transfer case may or may not contain an inter-axle differential gear set to allow for speed changes between the front and rear drive axles. Speed differences between the front and rear drive axles can be induced by turning and/or unequal road conditions. If a vehicle is classified as all-wheel drive, it typically means that it is in front and rear axle drive mode at all times. Therefore, the vehicle must have an inter-axle differential. If the vehicle only uses the front drive axle in off-road or poor traction conditions, the vehicle is said to have part-time front-wheel drive. In that situation, an inter-axle differential is not always required. If an inter-axle differential is present, it will normally have a lockout to prevent the differential from operating in poor traction conditions.

The front axle engagement, the two-speed shift control, and the inter-axle differential lockout are all controlled by the operator through a series of control valves on in the operator station.

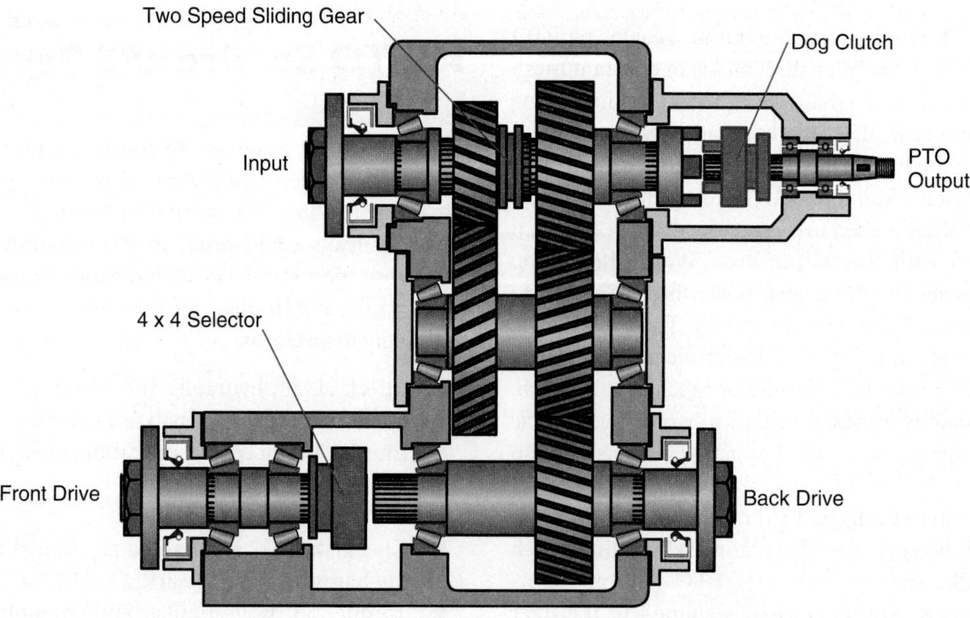

FIGURE 45-36 Schematic of a transfer case with a PTO option.

Transfer cases come in a variety of designs. Some come equipped with one or two PTO outputs that can be used to drive accessories on the machine. Transfer can use splash lubrication systems in which the lower gears rotate in a bath of lubricant and splash a steady stream of lube onto the higher gears. Some systems will use an externally filtered lube pump to supply pressurized oil to critical areas, such as the input shaft needle bearing and gears. This lubricant will fall down through the transfer case and lubricate the other gears and shafts on the way down.

▶ Wrap-Up

Ready for Review

- Transmissions are designed with sufficient ratio steps or increases so that they can be operated under the necessary conditions for which the machine is designed.
- All transmissions will have at least four shafts: an input shaft, a countershaft, a main or output shaft, and a reverse idler shaft.
- Transmissions are classified by the method they use to select gear ratios.
- A sliding gear transmission will use only spur gears and have all of the speed gears splined to the main shaft. The spur gears must be slid into mesh with their corresponding countershaft gears to select a ratio.
- Constant-mesh transmissions have all of their main shaft speed gears and corresponding countershaft gears in mesh at all times. All of the main shaft gears turn freely on the main shaft until they are locked to it either by a sliding clutch, a sliding collar, or a synchronizer.
- Double-clutching is a technique to provide clash-free shifting. The operator disengages the clutch, shifts to neutral, and then re-engages the clutch again. The operator then tries to match the engine speed to the speed of the desired main shaft gear. The operator once again disengages the clutch, selects the gear, and re-engages the clutch. Double-clutching is used with sliding gear transmissions and unsynchronized transmissions.
- Sliding clutches are internally splined to the transmission main shaft. To select a ratio, the clutch's external clutching teeth engage internal clutching teeth on the main shaft gears. This arrangement is an unsynchronized transmission.
- Sliding collars are splined to a hub that in turn is splined or keyed to the main shaft. To select a ratio, the internal splines of the sliding collar slide over external clutching (dog) teeth on the main shaft gear. This arrangement is a unsynchronized transmission.
- Synchronizers eliminate the need for double-clutching and simplify transmission operation to the point that anyone could operate a manual transmission. Synchronizers use friction to match shaft and gear speed.
- Shift mechanisms include the shift lever, shift tower, shift cover, shift gates, shift rails, and shift forks.
- The shift rail interlock prevents two gears from being selected at once.
- The shift detents, usually spring-loaded balls, help the shift rail stay in gear.
- All transmission power flows, except direct, will be compound flows. That is, more than one set of gears is involved in the ratio. Usually, four gears are involved to create all ratios.
- Direct drive, or 1:1, does not use gears to change a ratio.
- Multiple countershaft transmissions split the input torque between two or three countershafts. They use many more teeth on the main shaft gears to transmit torque to the main shaft and allow the transmission to handle greater overall torque.
- Lubricant is the lifeblood of transmissions. It is essential that the quality and level be maintained for long transmission service life.
- Transmission model number nomenclature can give the technician valuable information about the transmission being serviced or repaired.
- Transmission preventive maintenance typically involves a visual inspection of the transmission for leakage, checking the mounting components for integrity, and checking the shift mechanisms for correct operation.
- Some manufacturers recommend full synthetic or synthetic blend lubricants for their machines.
- Noise from the transmission can come from a variety of causes. The type of noise—knocking, growling, whining, or rattling—can help the technician isolate the cause.
- Gear slip out or jump out can occur if components such as sliding clutches or shift forks are worn. Wear on these components is frequently caused by operator error or abuse.
- PTO devices are used to power auxiliary devices on a vehicle, such as hydraulic pumps and conveyor systems. PTOs can be connected to the engine, the transmission, or the transfer case. The position of the PTO is usually dependent on when the auxiliary power is needed with the vehicle stationary, when the auxiliary power is needed with the vehicle moving, and how much power is required.
- Transfer cases can be used to supply power to the front and rear drive axles of a wheeled machine and to provide take-off power connections.

Key Terms

collar shift transmission A transmission that uses sliding collars or clutches to select gear ratios.

constant-mesh transmissions Transmissions that have all of the main shaft gears in constant mesh with their mating countershaft gears.

countershaft A shaft with various sizes of gears attached to it and driven by the input gear.

input gear The gear part of or attached to the input shaft that delivers power to the countershaft.

input shaft The input to the transmission driven by the clutch friction disc.

main shaft The shaft that carries the speed gears that are driven by the countershaft; also called the output shaft.

mechanical advantage Advantage gained when a mechanism is used while transferring force.

power flow The path that power takes from the beginning of an assembly to the end.

power take-offs or PTOs Devices that allow power to be rerouted to operate other equipment on the machine.

ratios The speed and torque relationship between two or more gears in mesh.

reverse idler shaft A shaft that supports the reverse idler gear.

shift gates Rectangular notches either formed into or attached to the shift rails.

shift finger A flat-sided piece that sits into the shift gates.

shift forks Components that move the sliding clutches or collars in the transmission to actually select gear ranges.

shift lever A shift control that the operator uses to change transmission gear position.

shift pattern The direction that the lever must be moved to select a given gear.

shift rail interlock A system that prevents two shift rails from being moved from the neutral position at once.

shift rails The bars that control shift fork position.

shift tower A raised section on the transmission with a pivot into which the shift lever fits.

sliding gear transmission A transmission that has sliding gears splined to the main shaft that slide in and out of mesh with the countershaft gears.

synchronized transmission A transmission that uses synchronizers to match shaft and gear speeds to avoid clashing on shifts.

synchronizer An assembly that matches shaft and gear speeds as a shift is being made for a clash-free engagement.

transfer case A gearbox arrangement that allows the torque from the transmission to be split between the front and rear driving axles of a vehicle.

Review Questions

1. A synchronizer assembly is used to do which of the following?
   a. Reduce gearshift lever effort
   b. Match gear and shaft speeds
   c. Reduce main shaft speed
   d. Shorten gearshift lever travel

2. What is the purpose of an idler gear in most transmissions?
   a. To provide counter clockwise output
   b. To increase gear ratios and provide more torque
   c. To provide an overdrive ratio
   d. To turn the reverse gear clockwise

3. Which of the following is a correct statement about a constant-mesh transmission's helical main shaft gears when the transmission is in neutral?
   a. They are splined to the main shaft
   b. They are keyed to the main shaft
   c. They are free to turn on the main shaft
   d. They are keyed to the synchronizer hub

4. When a sliding gear is used in the transmission, it is connected to the main shaft by which of the following?
   a. Splines in the sliding gear
   b. A sliding clutch
   c. A synchronizer
   d. A shift fork

5. Which of the following is responsible for lubricating most standard transmissions?
   a. A gear pump
   b. An electric pump
   c. All components are submerged in the fluid
   d. The splash caused by the countershafts rotation

6. When synchronizers are used, the power flow is connected to the transmission output shaft by which of the following components?
   a. The countershaft
   b. The input shaft
   c. The synchronizer sliding collar or clutch and hub
   d. The synchronizer blocker ring

7. In order to rotate a countershaft transmission driven gear in the same direction of rotation as the drive gear, which of the following is a requirement?
   a. The drive gear must be larger in diameter than the driven gear.
   b. There must be two gears, and both must have external teeth.
   c. There must be an idler gear between the drive and driven gears.
   d. This will happen whenever two gears are in mesh and one of them is driving.

8. If a transmission is described as being unsynchronized, which of these is the *recommended* operating technique?
   a. Double-clutching
   b. Having a good ear
   c. Feathering the clutch
   d. Rapid gear engagements

9. What is the purpose of the shift rail interlock system?
   a. To allow two gears to be selected at once
   b. To allow the transmission to be locked in gear
   c. To prevent the transmission from going into gear by mistake
   d. To prevent the selection of two gears at once

10. What is the minimum number of shafts in a typical five-speed mechanical transmission?
   a. Three
   b. Four
   c. Five
   d. Six

ASE Technician A/Technician B Style Questions

1. Technician A says that torque multiplication means the same thing as mechanical advantage. Technician B says that mechanical advantage reduces output speed in a transmission. Who is correct?
   a. Technician A
   b. Technician B
   c. Both Technician A and Technician B
   d. Neither Technician A nor Technician B
2. Technician A says that the input gear drives the countershaft in a mechanical transmission. Technician B says that the main shaft is turned by the countershaft whenever the input shaft turns. Who is correct?
   a. Technician A
   b. Technician B
   c. Both Technician A and Technician B
   d. Neither Technician A nor Technician B
3. Technician A says that all transmissions use sliding gears. Technician B says that sliding gears are splined to the main shaft. Who is correct?
   a. Technician A
   b. Technician B
   c. Both Technician A and Technician B
   d. Neither Technician A nor Technician B
4. Technician A says that a synchronizer uses friction to help prevent gear clash. Technician B says that synchronizers match the shaft and gear speeds before engagement. Who is correct?
   a. Technician A
   b. Technician B
   c. Both Technician A and Technician B
   d. Neither Technician A nor Technician B
5. Technician A says that the reverse idler gear allows the main shaft to be turned in the same direction as the input shaft. Technician B says that the reverse idler turns in the opposite direction as the input shaft. Who is correct?
   a. Technician A
   b. Technician B
   c. Both Technician A and Technician B
   d. Neither Technician A nor Technician B
6. Technician A says that the input shaft is splined to the engine. Technician B says that the output shaft is the same as the main shaft. Who is correct?
   a. Technician A
   b. Technician B
   c. Both Technician A and Technician B
   d. Neither Technician A nor Technician B
7. Technician A says that when the operator moves the gear shift lever forward, the sliding clutch it controls moves in the opposite direction. Technician B says that sliding clutches have internal and external splines. Who is correct?
   a. Technician A
   b. Technician B
   c. Both Technician A and Technician B
   d. Neither Technician A nor Technician B
8. Technician A says that multiple countershafts in a transmission can be used to increase the torque carrying capability of a transmission. Technician B says that multiple countershafts in a transmission can be used to compound ratios. Who is correct?
   a. Technician A
   b. Technician B
   c. Both Technician A and Technician B
   d. Neither Technician A nor Technician B
9. Technician A says that a power flow must always go through the countershaft in a five-speed transmission. Technician B says that a sliding clutch or sliding collar will normally control two gears. Who is correct?
   a. Technician A
   b. Technician B
   c. Both Technician A and Technician B
   d. Neither Technician A nor Technician B
10. Technician A says that the transmission service schedule for a machine can usually be found on a decal on the machine. Technician B says that service information can usually be found in the operator's manual. Who is correct?
    a. Technician A
    b. Technician B
    c. Both Technician A and Technician B
    d. Neither Technician A nor Technician B

CHAPTER 46
Automated Transmissions

Knowledge Objectives

After reading this chapter, you will be able to:

- **K46001** Explain the purpose and fundamentals of automated transmissions.
- **K46002** Identify the types and applications of automated transmissions.
- **K46003** Explain the operation and power flows of automated transmissions.

Skills Objectives

After reading this chapter, you will be able to:

- **S46001** Troubleshoot automated transmissions.

▶ Introduction

The heavy-duty equipment technician (HDET) will seldom be called on to repair automated transmissions, commonly known as AMTs, because these types of transmissions are typically not found in mobile off-road equipment. However, more and more vocational trucks used in grading and other construction jobs and the trucks that bring equipment to the jobsite will be running an automated transmission, so a general knowledge of their operation can only benefit the HDET. There are also several transmission variations being used in the mobile off-road equipment field that don't quite fit into the normal transmission or automated transmission label. These transmissions have not been covered in previous chapters. In this chapter, we will cover the basics of the most popular automated transmissions and transmission variants that are combinations of technologies, such as **constant velocity transmissions** (CVTs) and dual-clutch transmissions.

▶ Fundamentals of Automated Transmissions

K46001

Automated transmissions are fast becoming the transmission of choice for the heavy truck market for a number of reasons, primarily fuel economy. These transmissions are capable of optimizing shift points, which leads to a realized savings of approximately 5–7% in fuel usage. This increases the **thermal efficiency** of the vehicle's engine, meaning more of the fuel it uses is actually doing work. By being more fuel-efficient, they also reduce their output of **carbon dioxide**, a contributor to the greenhouse gas effect and therefore global warming. These transmissions, however, offer other benefits: They lessen driver fatigue since the driver no longer has to constantly shift the transmission, which in turn allows the driver to pay more attention to the road and their surroundings, improving safety. The ease of operating vehicles equipped with these transmissions also addresses another problem in the trucking industry: the availability of trained drivers to operate the truck. Driver training is easier, and so driving a truck for a living is appealing to a broader range of the population because the operation is easier.

The extra upfront cost of these transmissions is offset by the fuel saving, reduced downtime caused by driver error or abuse and increased resale value when the truck is eventually sold. In North America, the automated transmission market is dominated by Eaton Fuller's **AutoShift** and **UltraShift** transmissions. However, Detroit Diesel's DT-12, shown in **FIGURE 46-1**, and Volvo's I-Shift/Mack's mDrive are big competitors. We will concentrate on these AMTs in this chapter.

The Role of Torque Break in Shifting

For years, experienced drivers have been shifting truck transmissions without using the clutch pedal except for starting from a stop. Although not recommended by any transmission manufacturer, this "**gear jamming**" technique is the basis for most electronically automated manual transmissions (AMTs). Essentially, what drivers were doing when making a shift was breaking torque by letting up on the accelerator in order to pull the gear stick to a neutral position. (Without breaking torque, the load on the gear shift components would make them impossible to move.) The driver would then carefully select the next gear as the engine rpm and the transmission main shaft speeds synchronized. They would complete the shift by jamming the transmission into the next gear.

Performing this technique properly requires great skill and experience, and even the best drivers cause some damage to the shift collar or sliding clutch teeth when the speeds of the collar and gear don't match. Matching the shaft and gear speeds involved making a best guess, and a less-experienced driver

FIGURE 46-1 Detroit Diesel's DT-12 transmission.

You Are the Mobile Heavy Equipment Technician

A truck that has just dropped off a large backhoe at the mine where you are employed will not start. The manager asks you to have a look to see if you can get it going. You assess the vehicle and find that it is an Eaton Fuller two-pedal 10-speed UltraShift transmission. While checking out the problem, you turn the key to the on position and discover that the shift control gear display has two asterisks showing in the window that normally would tell you what range the vehicle is in. You cycle the key on and off two times, but no codes are displayed, just the same two asterisks. What would be your next move?

1. Do you use a scan tool to diagnose the transmission?
2. Do you check the fuses for the transmission?
3. Do you check the connectors to the shift control?
4. What do you think could cause this problem?

could destroy a transmission in very little time. Most automated transmissions use this gear jamming technique but use computer controls to break torque. Matching the shaft speeds is achieved with precision. The computer uses sensors to monitor the shaft speeds and then moves the shift forks with electric motors or air cylinders. Gear jamming is done automatically, without gear clash, and results in no damage to the transmission.

Most automated shift transmissions still use the conventional method of shifting. Before a shift can be made, the driver must unload the drivetrain or "**break torque**." Breaking torque means that the engine must be throttled back and that the throttle must be reapplied when the shift is complete. Changing the throttle position causes a delay in overall vehicle acceleration. The deceleration and acceleration required when changing the throttle position also causes a reduction in fuel economy. Several manufacturers are now producing **dual-clutch transmissions** (transmissions with two inputs). Dual-clutch transmissions are capable of shifting without breaking torque, thereby improving fuel economy. Dual-clutch transmissions have two separate inputs controlled by two separate clutches. These transmissions can select the next gear range while still in gear. To shift, the transmission control simply switches to the other input clutch, so shifting occurs much faster and with no torque break.

FIGURE 46-2 Eaton UltraShift 10-speed transmission.

▶ Types of Automated Transmissions

K46002

The North American market for AMTs is dominated by the Eaton Fuller Corporation. Therefore, this chapter will focus its discussion primarily on Eaton's range of automated transmissions. There are, however, other entries into this market, and we will discuss them as well.

Eaton Fuller's Automated Transmissions

The first fully automated standard transmission to hit the North American market was the Eaton AutoShift. It was introduced in 1996/1997 and featured the first generation of computer control. The AutoShift was a 10-speed model and had a standard dry double-disc clutch that was used only when starting from a standstill. Once the vehicle was moving, its transmission was capable of automatic shifting through the vehicle's entire operating range, all the way to tenth gear and back down again as necessary. **FIGURE 46-2** depicts an Eaton Fuller UltraShift 10-speed transmission. Note the orientation of the shift motors. Older generations had the rail select motor oriented on the right-hand side of the transmission. The present location on the left allows more room for complicated exhaust systems.

Since the debut of the AutoShift, Eaton Fuller has introduced several other models of automated transmissions, ranging from 6 to 18 speeds and with or without clutch pedals.

Detroit Diesel's DT-12

Detroit Diesel has recently released a new transmission onto the North American market. The DT-12, pictured in Figure 46-1, is a 12-speed automated transmission. It is the same transmission marketed by Mercedes in Europe in its Actros trucks. The design of the DT-12 single-countershaft transmission is common to a number of transmissions produced in Europe. The DT-12 is a single-countershaft design with three speed gears on the main shaft. The input to the transmission goes through a two-range splitter gear set, then through one of the main shaft speed gears, and then through a planetary high–low-range gear set at the rear of the transmission.

The splitter gear set and the planetary range set both multiply the ratios available on the actual main shaft by two, resulting in a 12-speed transmission. The DT-12 system does not use a clutch pedal. Instead, it relies on an air-actuated release bearing to control a large single- or dual-disc organic clutch. Shifting is accomplished by an electric-over-air shift controller system. The DT-12 is available in two sizes: the A model, or "large transmission," capable of input torque up to 2,050 ft-lb and the B, or "small transmission," capable of input torque up to 1,650 ft-lb. Both are available as direct models—DT-12-DA or DT-12-DB—or overdrive models—DT-12-OA or DT-12-OB.

Volvo Trucks' I-Shift/Mack's mDrive

Volvo Trucks introduced the I-Shift automated transmission series in North America in 2004. As shown in **FIGURE 46-3**, the **I-Shift** is a 12-speed, two-pedal design with electric-over-air actuation controlled by the TCU (transmission control unit).

The I-Shift is similar to the Detroit DT-12 in design in that it uses a two-range splitter input and a two-range planetary output. The I-Shift uses only one countershaft and its power flows are identical to the DT-12's. The I-Shift is available in four models, including two with overdrive, and is capable of handling up to 2,300 ft-lb (3,118 N·m) of input torque. The Mack mDrive shown in **FIGURE 46-4** is basically identical to the I-Shift; only the available software vocations are different.

Volvo's latest addition to its transmission line is the new dual-clutch I-Shift. The 12-speed overdrive transmission has been available as an option in Volvo trucks in Europe since September 2014. The Volvo dual-clutch transmission uses two

FIGURE 46-3 Volvo's I-Shift.

FIGURE 46-4 Mack's mDrive.

dry-friction disc clutches. Plans to introduce this transmission into North America have not been announced as yet.

▶ Operation and Power Flows of Automated Manual Transmissions

K46003

Automated manual transmissions (AMTs) have unique operations and power flows when compared to standard transmissions. And different makes and models of AMTs operate slightly differently from one another as well. Although each type of automated transmission will have its own control systems, they are all relatively similar. This section will cover the operation of the Eaton Fuller AutoShift and UltraShift in detail and explain the operation of the Detroit Diesel DT-12 and the Volvo I-Shift/Mack mDrive.

Eaton Fuller AutoShift and UltraShift Operations

Eaton has two basic lines of automated transmissions available for the North American truck market. The three-pedal AutoShift line is now available in 10- and 18-speed models. The two-pedal UltraShift line is available in 5-, 6-, 10-, 11-, 13-, 16-, and 18-speed models, with either an electronically actuated clutch or a data mechanical (DM) clutch. DM clutches are operated centrifugally. The operating systems for the two lines are of such similar design that we will discuss them together. We will point out the differences between each as we go. The base transmission on each model is almost identical to a standard Eaton Fuller transmission. Additional components that make the transmission automated include the following:

- transmission controller
- shaft speed sensors
- driver interface (electronic shifter)
- start enable relay
- MEIIR (momentary engine ignition interrupt relay)
- electric shift assembly, including the shift motors and the position sensors
- electronically controlled range valve
- electronically controlled splitter valve
- inertia brakes
- clutches used with electronically automated transmissions
- shift strategies.

Transmission Controller

The transmission control used with the first generation (Gen. 1) of these transmissions consisted of a shift control keypad or lever module, like the one shown in **FIGURE 46-5A**, connected to a system manager ECU (engine control module), comparable to the one shown in **FIGURE 46-5B**. The **system manager** ECU was connected to the shift control ECU, like the one shown in **FIGURE 46-5C**, on the transmission.

In second generation (Gen. 2) AutoShift transmissions, the system manager and the shift lever (or push-button pad) were combined. The number of electronic modules was reduced to two, one at the shift control and one at the transmission itself. Gen. 1 transmissions communicated with the **engine control module (ECM)** over the **J-1587** datalink, which communicates slowly at 9600 bits/second. Gen. 2 models, launched in 1999, use the much faster **J-1939** datalink for communication. The SAE J-1939 communication protocol features data transmission at a rate of at least 250,000 bits/second and up to 500,000 bits/second.

Shift initiation is handled by the shift control module at the driver interface. The shift control can be either push button or lever type. The controller communicates with the ECM to request a torque break to allow the shift. Shifts are initiated based on engine rpm and load factors. The transmission software monitors engine rpm and predicts an expected rpm decrease during the shift, identifying a target rpm at which to select the next gear. If the engine rpm does not decrease quickly enough, the software can wait or initiate braking with either the engine brake or an inertia brake, if one is installed. When the rpm falls to the target rpm of the shift, the shift controller tells the transmission controller to make the shift. Upon completion of the shift, the ECM resumes normal rpm control. As more

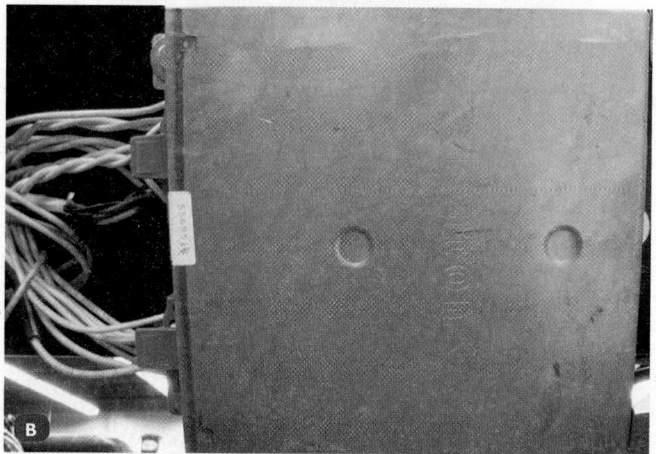

FIGURE 46-5 First-generation Eaton AMTs had three modules: **A.** The shift control. **B.** The system manager. **C.** The transmission controller.

and more shifts are initiated, the transmission shift control will learn the predictable rpm drop and respond accordingly. The driver can also request shifts to occur by pushing the push buttons on the shift controller or operating the transmission in the hold mode. The software will then only shift when requested by the driver. The Gen. 3 software, introduced in 2006, has only one module. As shown in **FIGURE 46-6**, it is mounted on the transmission.

FIGURE 46-6 Gen. 3 transmissions have only one module mounted on the transmission.

The driver interface is merely a series of switches that input to the controller, but the shift process is similar to previous generations. The software has advanced with each generation. Gen. 3 software is capable of **adaptive learning**, meaning that the software can learn and change strategy based on different factors. The software also has several preprogrammed operating modes for performance and fuel economy. The transmission control learns the terrain, the load, and the driving style of the driver and constantly adapts the shift strategies on the fly. The **transmission control unit (TCU)** has **self-diagnostic** capabilities. It will log diagnostic fault codes and produce a data snapshot of each incident. A data **snapshot** records all the relevant TCU data before and after a diagnostic code is set to ease diagnoses. The controller is programmed to protect the transmission by prohibiting driver-initiated shifts that may damage the transmission, such as high-speed direction changes, high rpm shifts from neutral to range, or shifts that would place the engine outside of its normal rpm operating range. The controller also has a fallback strategy that actuates when a problem is detected. Fallback strategies include shift inhibits, hold in gear, down shift to last held gear, and many others. Each fallback strategy permits failsafe but limited operation if necessary.

Shaft Speed Sensors

For clash-free shifts to occur, the transmission control software must know the precise speed of the input shaft, the countershaft, the main shaft gears, and the main shaft itself. The transmission has three speed sensors, like those shown in **FIGURE 46-7**, to accomplish this.

The input speed sensor is at the front right corner of the transmission shift cover and targets the upper countershaft power take-off (PTO) gear. When the speed of the countershaft and the transmission ratios are known, the software can calculate the input shaft speed and the main shaft gear speeds. The main shaft speed sensor is located at the left rear side of the transmission shift cover and targets the auxiliary countershaft driven gear. The main shaft speed sensor monitors the speed of the auxiliary countershaft and sends that information to the

FIGURE 46-7 The AutoShift and UltraShift transmissions have three speed sensors that input shaft speed information to the transmission controller. **A.** Output shaft speed sensor. **B.** Main shaft speed sensor. **C.** Input shaft speed sensor.

transmission controller. The transmission controller can calculate the speed of the main shaft and of the sliding clutches used to engage the main shaft gears. The controller uses all of that information to tell the ECM to synchronize the speeds to perform a clash-proof shift. The output speed sensor is in the support housing of the output shaft bearing. The output speed sensor targets a tone wheel mounted on the shaft. The controller uses this sensor to detect output shaft speed and confirm that shifts have been made.

Driver Interface

The driver shift control in Gen. 1 and 2 software versions contained an electronic module responsible for shift scheduling while the transmission controller actually handled the shifting. In Gen. 3, these modules have been combined into a single module located on the transmission. The shift control can be push button or lever style. Single-module Gen. 3 transmission controllers require only a series of switches for driver input. The design of the switches varies depending on the original equipment manufacturer (OEM). **FIGURE 46-8** shows a push-button control.

Every shifter, regardless of the OEM, has several components to it. Each control has a display that alerts the driver to gear range and shifting status and that will display diagnostic fault codes. The display can be integral to or remotely mounted from the shift control. The display indicates to the driver what gear the transmission is in. During a shift, the display indicates the target range as a solid number. As the transmission shifts to neutral, the target range will start flashing. Once the shift completes, the range number will go back to being solid.

The control has up and down buttons for driver-initiated shifts and usually has five positions or push-button choices—R for reverse, N for neutral, D for drive, M for manual (or H for hold), and L for low range. Drive is the position used for fully automatic operation. Selecting M will cause the transmission to remain in the current gear range. In manual, the driver can initiate shifts by using the up and down buttons. Selecting low when decelerating will allow maximum engine breaking. The driver can also use the up or down arrows in drive to select a different start-up gear than the one selected by the software. The control usually has a service light to alert the driver to transmission malfunctions. Some UltraShift transmission installations will use an OEM-supplied shift control that may differ from the Eaton type. OEM shift controls are either resistive ladder-type controllers or J-1939 controllers. J-1939 controllers have communication capabilities and can interface directly with the transmission ECM. The transmission controller also uses multiplexing to communicate with all other vehicle modules through the CAN-bus line. **FIGURE 46-9** shows an OEM control.

Start Enable Relay

The **start enable relay** is an OEM-supplied relay usually mounted in the dash that is controlled by the transmission TCU. The start enable relay interrupts the circuit to the starter solenoid when it is not activated, preventing the vehicle from starting. When the driver turns on the key, the transmission controller goes through an initiation and self-check process. Next, the controller will check for neutral; when it has verified that the transmission is in a neutral position, it will turn on the start enable relay, allowing the vehicle engine to be started. The controller

FIGURE 46-8 Push-button control.

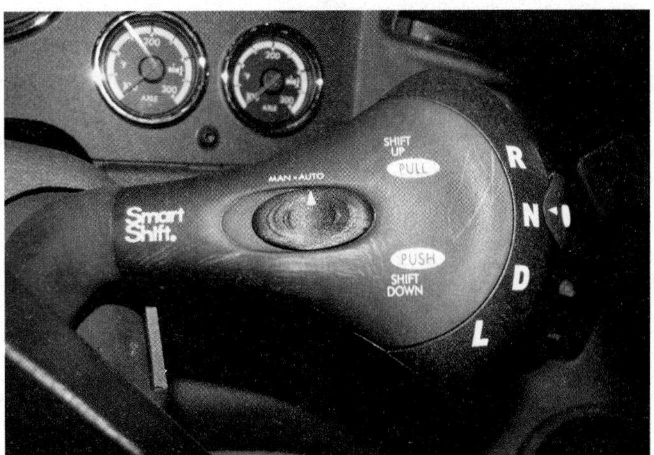

FIGURE 46-9 Freightliner shift control.

will turn on the start enable relay only after the system initiation completes and after it has verified that the transmission is not in any gear and that the transmission is in fact in neutral.

Momentary Engine Ignition Interrupt Relay

The **momentary engine ignition interrupt relay** (MEIIR) is a relay supplied by the OEM and is usually installed in the dash. This relay is supplied only when the vehicle has an UltraShift transmission with a DM clutch. The relay is controlled by the transmission controller, and it will interrupt the engine ignition (or fuel supply on diesel engines) in the event of a catastrophic failure of the DM clutch. That typically occurs when the DM clutch fails to disengage. The interruption of fueling or ignition is designed to break torque to allow the transmission shift controller to pull to neutral. The relay is activated when the following occurs:

1. when the driver has selected neutral
2. when neutral is not been achieved
3. after 2.5 seconds have passed since the driver selected neutral
4. when engine rpm is greater than 850 or when engine torque is more than 200 ft-lb (271 N·m)
5. when the vehicle has an active J1939 fault.

When these conditions have been met, the TCU will activate the relay, momentarily shutting off engine ignition/fueling to break torque in order to allow the shift control to pull to neutral. If neutral is not achieved, the system will activate the relay again and again until the conditions no longer exist.

Electric Shift Assembly

The **electric shift assembly** consists of two shift motors: the shift finger and the shift finger position sensors. The shift motors perform the actual gear selection inside the AutoShift or UltraShift main box. There are two of these motors mounted on the top of the transmission shift cover. When shifting a normal standard transmission, the driver moves the shift lever in one of four different directions: left, right, backward, or forward. The twin shift control motors are responsible for moving the shift finger side to side to select the correct shift rail and forward and back to select the desired gear. This mechanism is shown in **FIGURE 46-10**.

At the bottom of the shift lever is a shift finger that engages one of the three shift rails when the lever is moved left to right. Each shift rail controls the position of one shift fork inside the transmission. Shift rail gates are shown in **FIGURE 46-11**. The shift fork engages with a sliding clutch that will lock one gear to the transmission main shaft, depending on whether the driver moves the rail lever forward or backward. The right rail moves the first and reverse shift fork. The center rail moves the second and third shift fork. The left rail moves the fourth and fifth gear shift fork.

In the Eaton automated transmission, the two shift motors accomplish the same thing. A shift finger is mounted on a shift shaft. One motor moves the shift finger from left to right to select the correct rail, which is called the rail select motor. The other motor moves the shift finger forward and back to select the correct gear. It is called the gear select motor. The motors are reversible DC motors, and they both drive a worm shaft that controls the position of a recirculating ball nut. This type of nut is used because it provides very smooth and precise movement and longevity. A recirculating ball nut has a series of ball bearings running in the groove of the worm shaft. When in use, the bearings complete several circuits around the shaft. Their circuit is determined by the width of the ball nut. The bearings are returned to the beginning of the ball nut by a tube attached to the nut. The recirculating ball nuts move the shift finger from side to side and front to back to complete a shift. **FIGURE 46-12** shows recirculating ball nuts with a shift rail nut.

FIGURE 46-10 The electric shift assembly moves the shift finger.

FIGURE 46-11 Three shift rail gates. **A.** Left. **B.** Center. **C.** Right.

FIGURE 46-12 **A.** Shift rail nut. **B.** Recirculating balls.

The electric shift assembly on the earlier model of Auto-Shift transmissions was oriented with the rail motor mounted laterally. The body of the motor protruded to the right side of the transmission case, and the gear select motor protruded toward the front of the transmission. In contrast, Gen. 3 Auto-Shift transmissions are oriented with the rail motor protruding toward the left side of the transmission case to allow more room for the installation of exhaust components on the right side.

Position Sensors

The precise positioning of the shift finger is essential to the proper operation of an automated transmission. Therefore, two position sensors are used: the rail select position sensor and the gear select position sensor. Both sensors are shown in **FIGURE 46-13**. The rail select motor moves the shift finger left to right.

The gear select motor will move the shift finger forward and back. In both cases, the travel distance is just over 1 inch (2.54 cm) in total, so exacting control is necessary. The two position sensors are Hall-effect sensors that produce a digital signal and send it to the transmission control module. Every time the transmission is powered down, the shift motors and the position sensors work in concert to map the shift gate area. First, the sensors move across the gate to measure the total distance from the left shift rail to the right shift rail. Next, the sensors push against the shift rail interlocks by trying to move the center and the light rail together, forward and back, and then by trying to move the center and the left-side shift rail together, forward and back. This recalibration procedure gives the transmission ECU a precise map of exactly where the gates and the rails are. Once the procedure is complete, the transmission is ready for the next power-up and drive cycle. **FIGURE 46-14** illustrates the sequence of the recalibration process.

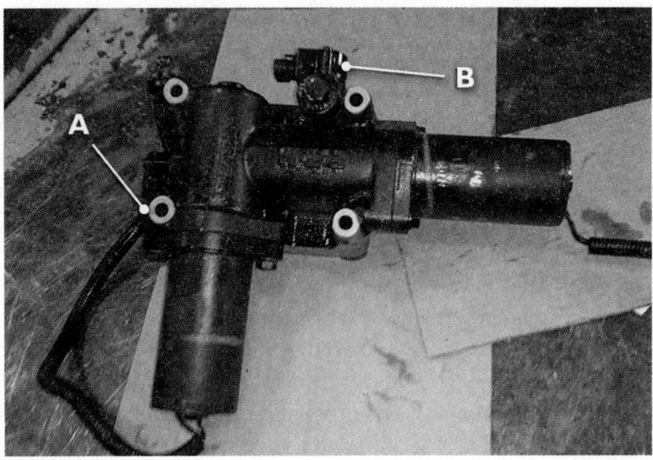

FIGURE 46-13 Position sensors provide extremely accurate shift finger position data to the transmission control unit. **A.** Gear position sensor. **B.** Rail position sensor.

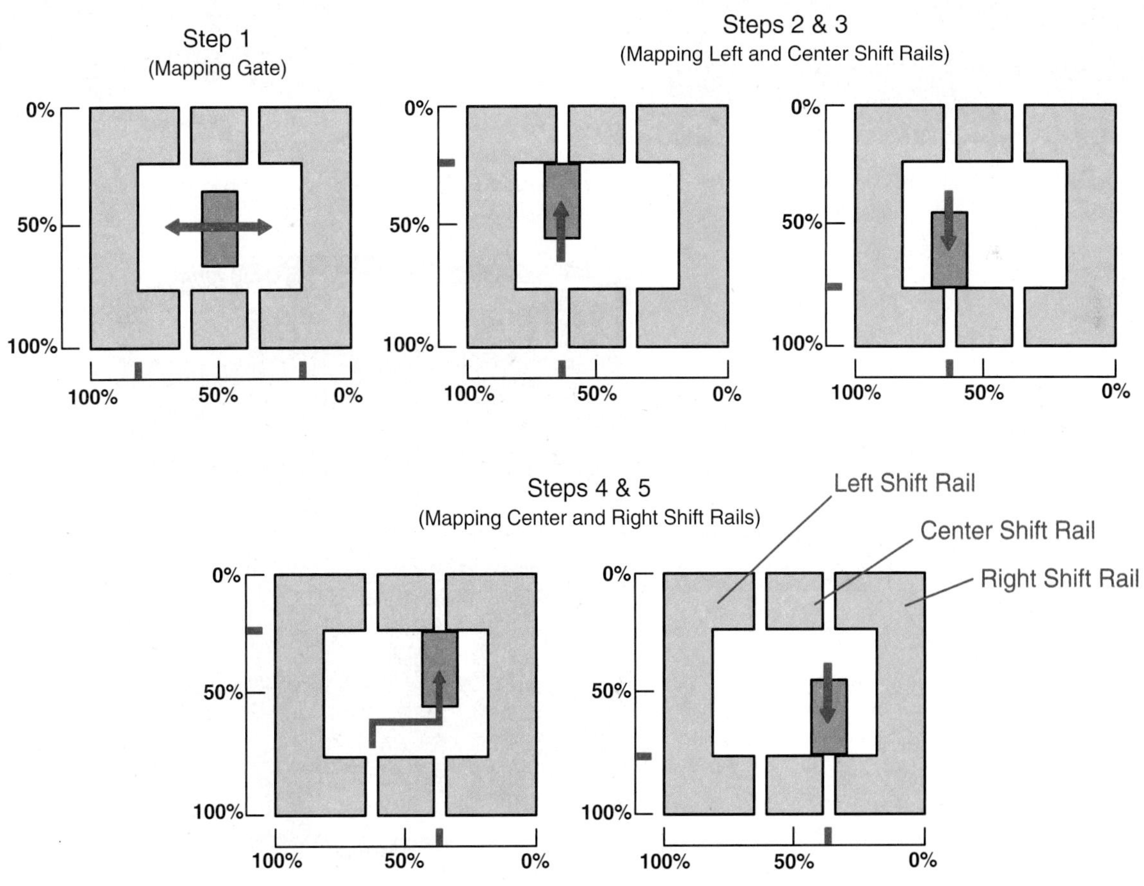

FIGURE 46-14 An inertia brake assembly.

Auxiliary Section Power Flows

Eaton twin countershaft AMTs use auxiliary sections to multiply the available ratios. An auxiliary section is basically a second transmission bolted to the back of the main transmission so that the output of the main transmission becomes the input to the auxiliary section. The auxiliary section can have two, three, or even four different ratios that are used to multiply the available ratios from the five-speed main transmission, resulting in transmissions that have 9, 10, 13, 15, and 18 speeds. The auxiliary section can supply very low deep reduction gearing for off-road operation (9 speed and 15 speed), or it can merely be arranged so that the ratio steps are closer together for high fuel economy on highway operation. Here we will discuss the power flow for a 13-speed auxiliary section and a 10-speed auxiliary section.

Although they are different, the auxiliary section for 10- and 13-speed transmissions have the same low-range, high-range system. **FIGURE 46-15** shows a 10-speed auxiliary section.

The range gear is a large gear on the auxiliary section countershaft, and the power from the main box can be directed through the range gear (low range), or it can be passed directly to the auxiliary section main shaft (high range or direct). In low range, the range synchronizer is moved to the rear by an air piston–controlled shift fork. The synchronizer sliding clutch engages the clutching teeth of the range gear, locking it to the auxiliary section main shaft. The output of the main box main shaft is splined to the auxiliary section drive gear. The power flows from the auxiliary section drive gear to the countershafts and back to the engaged range gear, as shown in **FIGURE 46-16**.

In high range, the range synchronizer is moved forward and locks the auxiliary drive gear directly to the auxiliary main shaft, and the power flows straight through the auxiliary, as shown in **FIGURE 46-17**. The range system allows the main box power flows to be multiplied by two.

FIGURE 46-15 A 10-speed auxiliary section has two speeds: low range and direct.

FIGURE 46-16 An auxiliary section in low range.

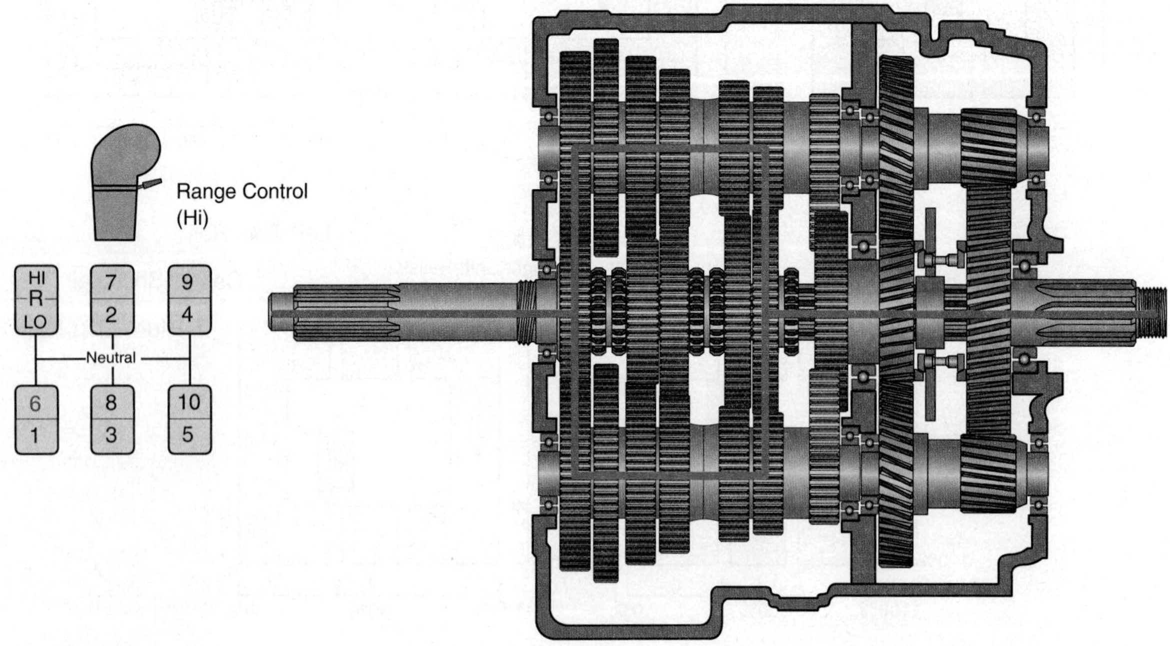

FIGURE 46-17 In high range, the power flows straight through the auxiliary unchanged.

FIGURE 46-18 The 13-speed auxiliary has another set of gears at the front, called the splitter gears.

In the 13-speed auxiliary section, the range system works the same way, but this auxiliary has an extra set of gears, called the splitter gears, mounted in front of the range gear set. This gives the auxiliary section two possible inputs from either the front auxiliary drive gear or the rear auxiliary drive gear. A 13-speed auxiliary is pictured in **FIGURE 46-18**.

The output shaft of the main box is splined to the splitter sliding clutch mounted on the shaft between the two auxiliary drive gears. The air-actuated splitter shift fork can move forward to select the front auxiliary drive gear (low-split position) or rearward to select the rear auxiliary drive gear (high-split position). When the auxiliary section is in low range, the splitter sliding clutch remains in the forward position so that the power enters the auxiliary from the front auxiliary drive gear and flows to the countershafts and the engaged range gear and out, as shown in **FIGURE 46-19**.

In high range, the range synchronizer locks to the back of the rear auxiliary drive gear. In low split, the splitter sliding clutch is forward and the power enters the auxiliary through the front auxiliary drive gear, flows to the countershafts, and down to the rear auxiliary drive gear and out, as shown in **FIGURE 46-20A**. In high split, the splitter sliding clutch is moved rearward and engages the front side of the rear auxiliary drive gear, and because the range synchronizer is still engaged to the back of the rear auxiliary drive gear, power flows directly from the main box output shaft to the auxiliary section output shaft, as shown in **FIGURE 46-20B**. An 18-speed transmission's auxiliary section functions in exactly the same way, except that the splitter sliding clutch can be used in low range as well as in high range.

Electronically Controlled Range Valve

AutoShift and UltraShift models with 10 or more forward ranges will have an auxiliary section and can be operated in high or low range, depending on the operating conditions. In the AutoShift and UltraShift models, the shifting is controlled by the transmission ECU. The range cylinder cover is modified to accept the electrically operated air-control solenoid valve, as shown in **FIGURE 46-21**. The **air-control solenoid valve** has two electric solenoid valves that control the flow of air from the air filter/pressure regulator to the range cylinder piston. That is, the two electric solenoids direct air to the low- and high-range side

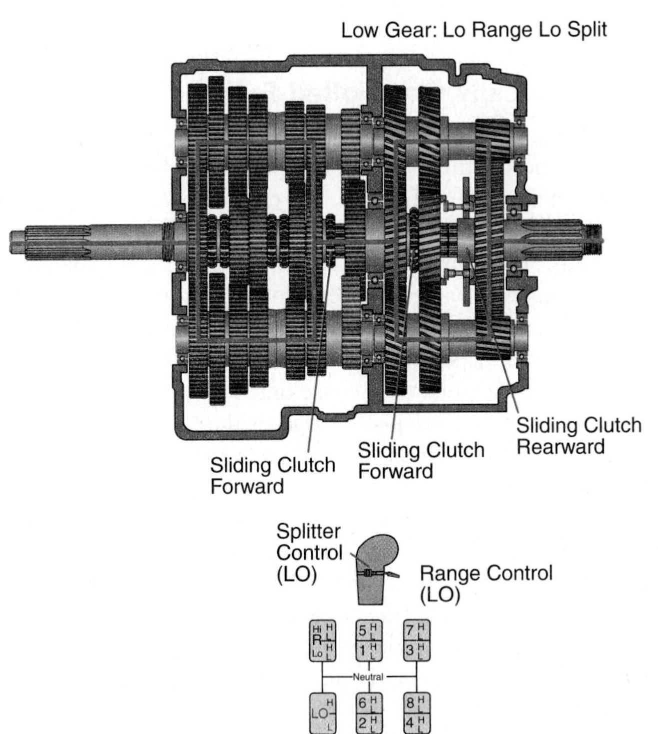

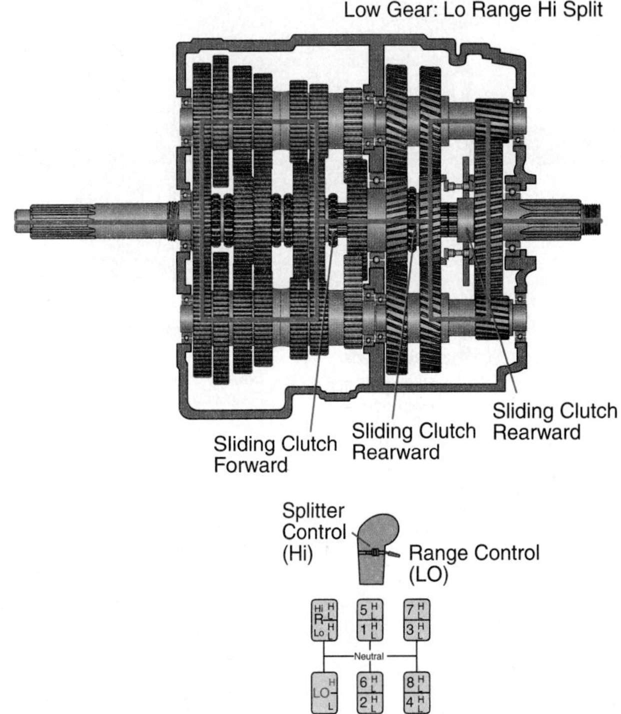

FIGURE 46-19 In low range, the 13-speed auxiliary is always in low split.

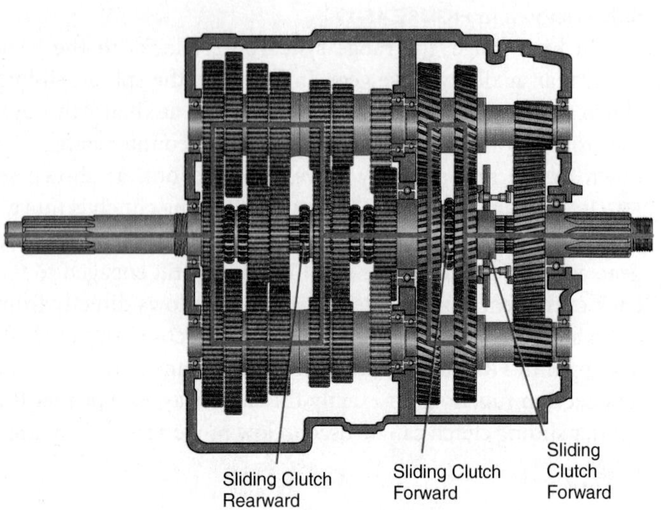

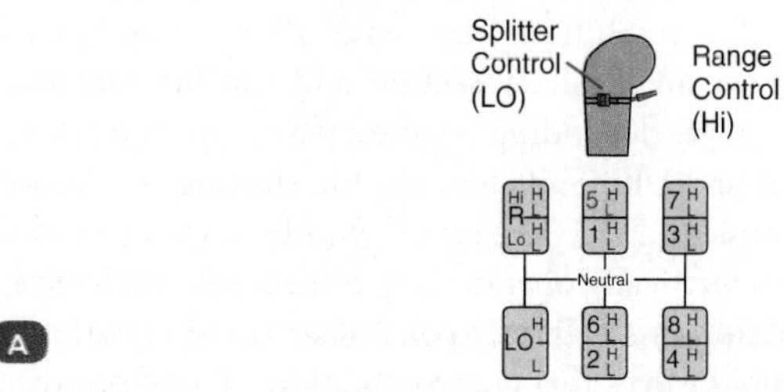

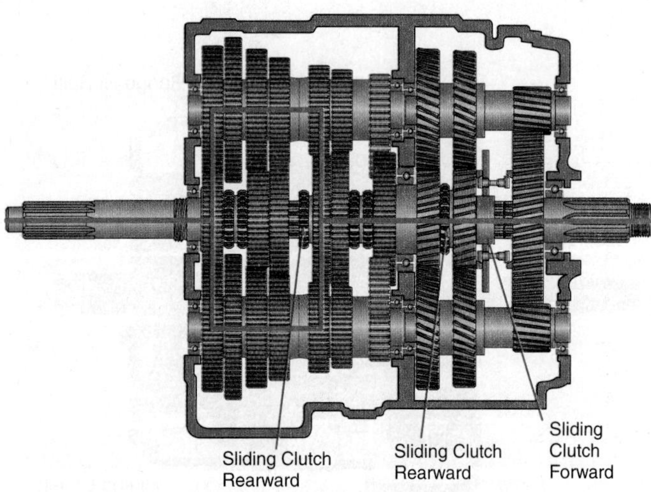

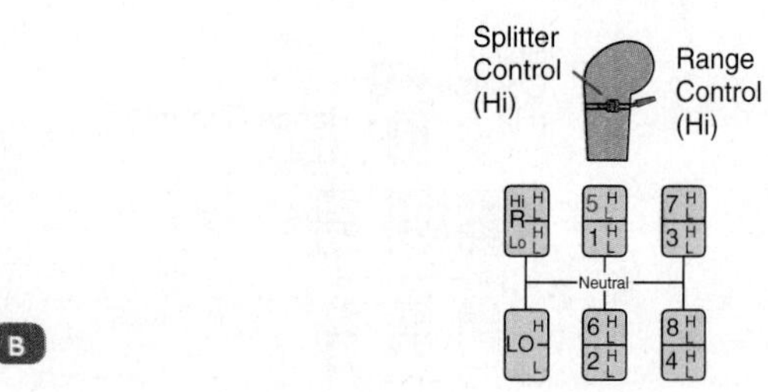

FIGURE 46-20 **A.** High-range low split. **B.** High-range high split.

FIGURE 46-21 Electric solenoids in a range cylinder. **A.** Low range port. **B.** High range port. **C.** Solenoid pack.

of the cylinder piston as required by the control unit. The regulator holds the pressure between approximately 58 and 63 psi (400 and 434 kPa).

The operation of these valves is rather simple. To achieve low range, the transmission ECU energizes the low solenoid. Doing so allows air to flow to the front side of the range cylinder piston. The piston and its attached yoke move rearward to engage the low-range gear. The air behind the piston exhausts through the high-range solenoid. When a shift to high range is required, the ECU deenergizes the low-range solenoid and energizes the high-range solenoid. Doing so exhausts air from the low side of the range cylinder piston through the low-range solenoid. Pressurized air is directed to the back of the piston, forcing it and the yoke forward. High range is then engaged.

Electronically Controlled Splitter Valve

On AutoShift and UltraShift models with more than 10 forward speeds, there will be a splitter cylinder that controls the position of the splitter sliding clutch. In AMTs, the splitter cylinder cover has been modified to hold the splitter shift solenoids. The splitter shift solenoids are electric solenoids over air-control valves, are controlled by the transmission, and are identical to the valves used for the range control. The ECU controls the solenoids to direct air supplied from the air filter/pressure regulator to cause one of two splits. The front of the splitter cylinder piston engages the high-split position, or to achieve low split, air is directed to the rear of the splitter cylinder piston.

Inertia Brake

Medium-duty AutoShift and UltraShift transmissions and heavy-duty UltraShift transmissions use an **inertia brake** to slow input and countershaft speed on engagement from neutral to reverse or a forward range. Slowing the input and speed helps prevent gear clash. As shown in **FIGURE 46-22**, inertia brakes are typically mounted on the lower PTO opening of the transmission.

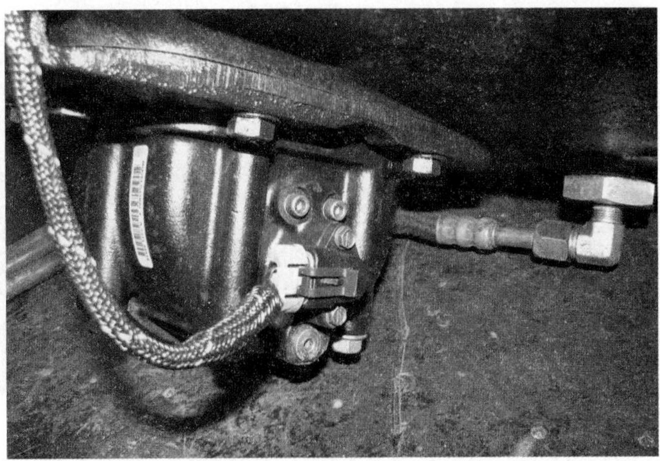

FIGURE 46-22 The inertia brake slows the countershaft and therefore the main shaft gearing.

FIGURE 46-24 Eaton's electronically actuated clutch. **A.** Inertia brake. **B.** Clutch fork. **C.** Actuator.

The inertia brake can also be used to assist in gaining synchronicity of the transmission shafts and gears during upshift events. Synchronizing shafts and gears allows for slightly faster shift times. Fuller claims that an 18-speed UltraShift transmission can shift through all its gear ranges while pulling 160,000 lb (72,575 kg) on a 15% grade by using the inertia brake during upshifts. While climbing a hill under heavy load, the transmission main shaft can slow faster than the engine and the main shaft gears due to the loading. The inertia brake can reduce the main shaft gear rpm more quickly, allowing faster shifts. Even the most skilled driver would be hard-pressed to match such a feat. The inertia brake is attached to the lower left side of the case. The brake's gear engages the lower main box countershaft. As illustrated in **FIGURE 46-23**, inside the brake are two rotating ramps separated by steel balls, called the ball ramp. An electromagnetic coil and a friction clutch pack are attached to the gear, so the gear rotates with the countershaft.

The electromagnetically operated ball ramp in the inertia brake assembly applies pressure to the friction plates to slow the transmission gearing. The transmission ECU actuates the inertia brake by energizing the electromagnetic coil. This slows one half of the ball ramp, which causes the balls to roll up the ramps. As the balls roll upward, the forward ramp is forced against the friction clutch pack. The gear slows, and because it is splined to the countershaft, both the countershaft and the transmission gearing are slowed. The ECU is then able to speed up the synchronization process and, therefore, also speed up the upshift. The newer model of UltraShift heavy-duty transmissions uses an electric clutch actuator. Instead of an inertia brake mounted on the countershaft, a large inertia brake, called a low capacity inertia brake, is installed on the input shaft between the clutch release bearing and the transmission front bearing cover. Notice in **FIGURE 46-24** that the location is where a clutch brake used to be.

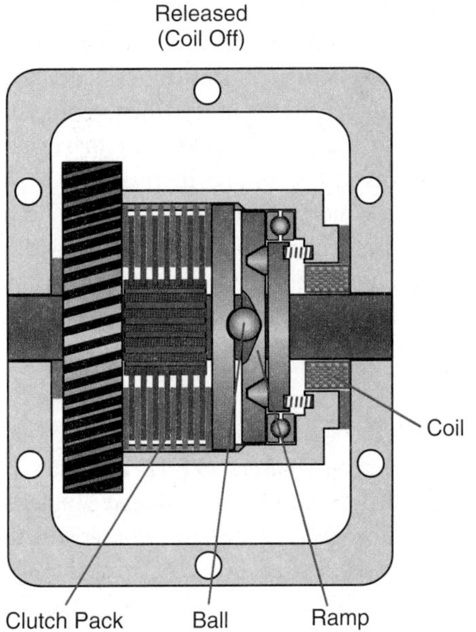

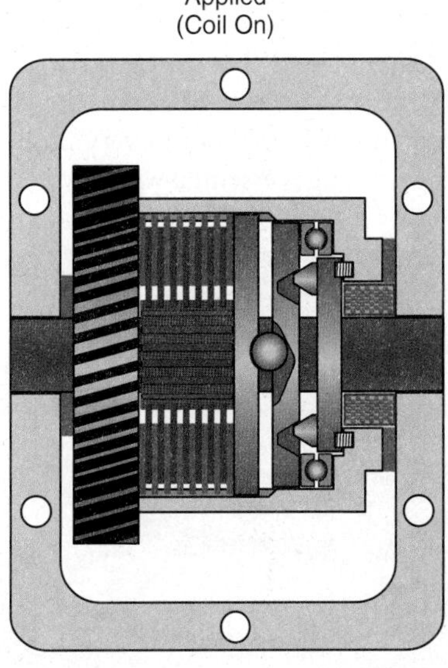

FIGURE 46-23 An inertia brake assembly.

The inertia brake serves the same purpose as a clutch brake. That is, the inertia brake stops the input shaft while the transmission is shifting into first gear or reverse gear. The inertia brake can also be used during upshifts when warranted by the operation of the vehicle. The electric clutch actuator is not normally used while shifting, but in certain operating conditions, it is used to reduce engine rpm during upshifts under heavy loads.

Clutches Used with Electronically Automated Transmissions

Three different clutches are used by Eaton Fuller in its line of double-countershaft electronically automated transmissions: the SOLO, DM, and the electronically actuated SOLO.

The SOLO self-adjusting clutch is the only manually actuated clutch supplied in the AutoShift line of transmissions. SOLO clutches are used with the AutoShift three-pedal systems. They have a clutch pedal, and the driver must use the clutch when starting off shifting from neutral to reverse or forward only. The rest of the shifting is handled automatically by the transmission. **FIGURE 46-25** shows an Eaton SOLO self-adjusting clutch.

The DM clutch is centrifugally applied by increasing engine rpm. The DM clutch is used with both medium- and heavy-duty models of the UltraShift line of transmissions. DM clutches use a two-pedal system with no clutch pedal. Four centrifugal weights apply the DM clutch as engine rpm increases. As the weights move out, they push against ramps built into the back of the pressure plate. That is what creates the clamp load. **FIGURE 46-26** shows the four weights in a DM clutch. The DM clutch starts engagement at approximately 800–850 rpm. From there, it ramps up to full clamp load at approximately 1,350 rpm. On disengagement, full clamp load remains until rpm has dropped to approximately 900 rpm. At that point, the clutch starts to release. By the time approximately 800 rpm has been reached, the clutch is fully released.

The DM clutch can be subject to abuse by an unskilled driver. If the driver tries to hold the vehicle on an incline by feathering the throttle to around 800–850 rpm, the clutch will be constantly slipping and will burn out in very little time. As always, proper driving training is essential with any new system!

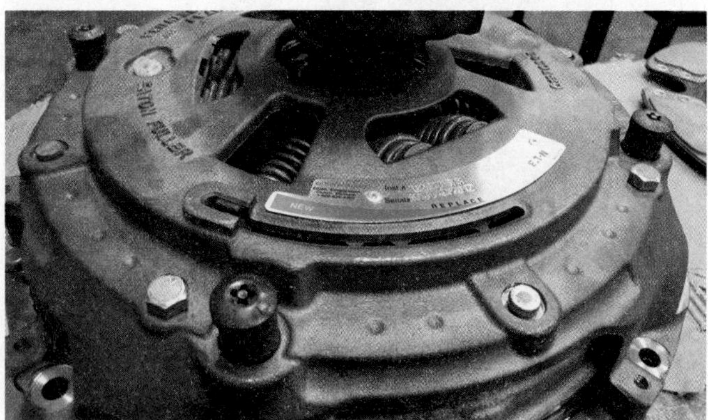

FIGURE 46-25 Eaton SOLO self-adjusting clutch.

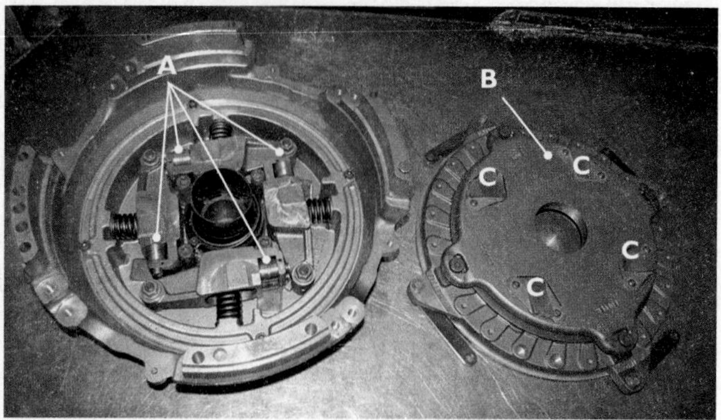

FIGURE 46-26 The four large weights fly out with centrifugal force to apply the clutch.

The third type of clutch used on two-pedal models of Eaton Fuller AMT models is called an electronic clutch actuation device. The actuator can be seen in Figure 46-24 above. An electronically actuated clutch contains an electronic module with an integrated electric motor to operate a standard SOLO self-adjusting clutch. Eaton calls this the ECA (electric clutch actuator). Typically, the clutch actuator is used only for starting off, but occasionally, the system controller will actuate the clutch during shifting to aid in synchronization. This is similar to the double-clutching technique discussed in the Manual Transmissions chapter (Chapter 45).

Shifting Strategies

The transmission ECU can be programmed to allow a range of shift strategies, depending on the requirement. Most transmission controllers in use today are capable of sensing engine load, vehicle weight, and road grade or incline. The transmission controllers monitor the fueling demand and other parameters over the J-1939 CAN-bus line and adjust shifting strategies based on this information. The ability to change shifting as needed optimizes performance and fuel economy. All automated transmissions have a manual shift mode that allows the driver complete control over shift points when required. Still, failsafe fallback modes exist to compensate for driver error. Automated transmissions are becoming increasingly popular. As their software becomes more sophisticated, it will become nearly impossible to find a driver capable of shifting with the skill and accuracy of an automated transmission while still reaching fuel economy targets. Most automated transmissions will employ these same strategies.

Detroit Diesel's DT-12

The Detroit Diesel's DT-12 automated transmission, shown in **FIGURE 46-27**, is a 12-speed single-countershaft transmission. The DT-12's design is based on the 12-speed Mercedes transmission used in its Actros trucks in Europe. The DT-12 is currently built in Germany by Mercedes for Detroit Diesel, but plans are in the works to have a version of this transmission designed and built in North America. That will allow the

FIGURE 46-27 Detroit's single-countershaft DT-12.

FIGURE 46-28 The CPCA actuates the clutch.

transmission to be better tailored to the North American market. The DT-12 is available as a direct drive model, DT-12D, or as an overdrive model, DT-12O.

The DT-12 is a single-countershaft, heavy-duty transmission. It comes equipped with a 17-inch (432 mm) organic-faced, single-disc clutch or a 14.7-inch (400 mm) dual-disc clutch that is operated by the transmission electronic controller. The transmission controller controls the flow of air to a self-contained air-actuated release bearing, known as a concentric pneumatic clutch actuator (CPCA), that actuates the clutch, as shown in **FIGURE 46-28**. The CPCA controls clutch adjustment. The clutch has two modes of operation: a slow actuation mode and a fast actuation mode. The TCM (transmission control module) selects the mode based on the operating conditions. The transmission has a clutch learn routine that must performed when the clutch, transmission, or the TCM is replaced.

The state of clutch adjustment is monitored every time the clutch is disengaged and engaged. The DT-12 transmission uses a three-module design, as illustrated in **FIGURE 46-29**, and includes the following:

- a two-speed splitter gear input section
- a two-speed main shaft gear box module
- a planetary range section for a low- and high-range output.

The transmission has an internal tilt sensor to aid the TCM in determining terrain and vehicle loading. This sensor aids in using the hill-start feature, where the vehicle brakes are held on by the transmission controller until the clutch engages when starting on a hill. There are three selectable operating modes for the transmission: (1) automatic economy, (2) automatic performance, and (3) manual. The automatic economy mode is the default.

DT-12 Operation

Engine power is delivered by the clutch to the input shaft and is channeled through a splitter gear set at the front of the

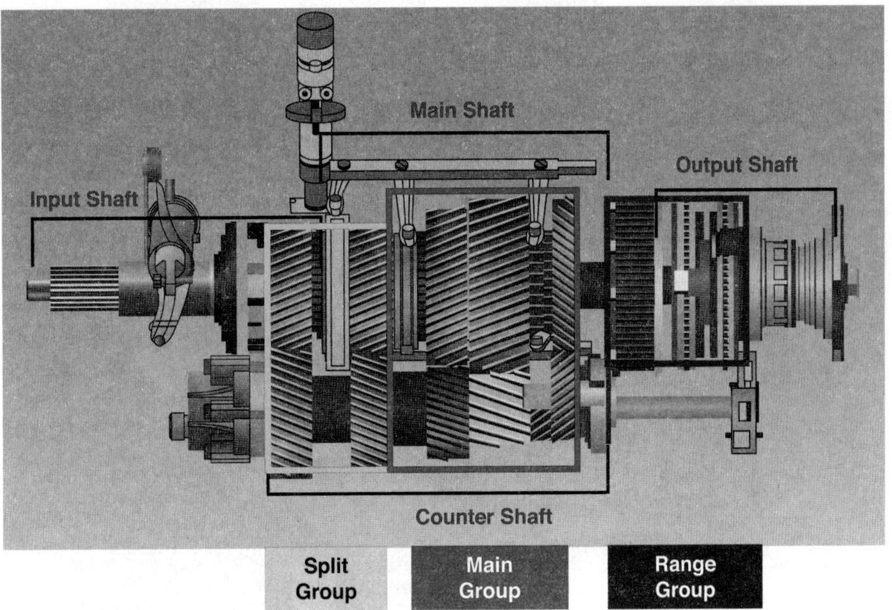

FIGURE 46-29 The DT-12 has three modules or groups.

transmission. The shift control will determine whether the power flows through the high or the low splitter gear set. In **direct drive** models, the front splitter gear is low split, and in overdrive models, the front splitter is high or overdrive split. After the splitter gear set, the power is delivered to the countershaft. The main shaft has only two forward speed gears plus direct, for a total of three ranges and one reverse. From the countershaft, the power is delivered to the engaged main shaft gear. From the main shaft, the power is delivered to a planetary range gear set in the rear of the transmission. The range planetary gear set provides low range by inputting the sun gear, holding the ring gear, and the carrier of the planetary gear set becomes output. In high range, the power passes through the planetary gear set unchanged. The range is selected by an air cylinder, which is in turn controlled by the transmission shift control.

The DT-12 transmission, illustrated in **FIGURE 46-30**, uses each main shaft gear four times by using the splitter gear set twice in low range and twice in high range, for a total of 12 forward speeds. Power flows in the DT-12 are relatively simple; as mentioned previously, each main shaft gear is used four times. See Figure 46-30 to follow the transmissions power flows.

First Range In first range, power is delivered to the countershaft through the front, low-split gear set and is delivered to the first main shaft speed gear. Power then passes through the planetary range gear set in low range.

Second Range To move to second range, the splitter gear set is shifted to the rear high-split gear set. Power flows from the rear splitter gear set to the countershaft, back to the same main shaft speed gear, and through the planetary range set in low range.

Third Range During third range, the input once again shifts to the low-split gear set. The power flows to the countershaft and back to the now selected second main shaft speed gear. Power flows once again through the planetary gear set in low range.

Fourth Range For fourth range, the splitter gear is shifted to high split again. Power flows to the countershaft, back to the second main shaft speed gear, and again through the planetary range set in low range.

Fifth Range For fifth range, again the splitter gear set is shifted to low split. This time, however, the main shaft is connected to the back of the rear splitter gear set and the countershaft speed gears are not used. Power flows to the countershaft through the low-split gear set, back down to the main shaft through the rear high-split gear set, and from there directly to the main shaft. Once more, the power flows through the planetary range set in low range.

Sixth Range For sixth range, the splitter gear is shifted to the rear (high split). This puts the splitter section and the main shaft sections of the transmission into direct range. In other words, the input is connected to the front side of the rear splitter gear, and the main shaft is connected to the rear of the gear. The power, however, is still flowing from the main shaft through the low range of the planetary section.

Seventh Range For seventh range, the planetary range section is put into high range, or direct. At that point, power passes through the range section unchanged. The front section of the transmission repeats the exact same sequence as above from first to sixth range, ending up with 12 forward ranges in total.

The power flow of the overdrive model, DT-12, is identical to the power flow explained above, with one exception: the splitter gear sequence. In the overdrive models, the splitter gear set at the front of the transmission is arranged so that when the power flows from the front splitter gear set to the rear set, it creates an

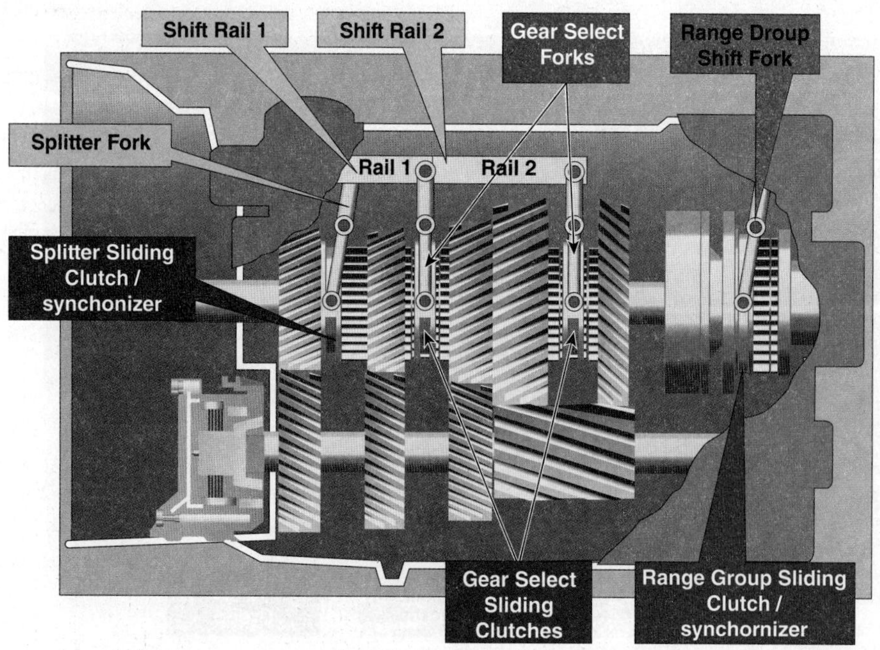

FIGURE 46-30 Each main shaft gear position is used four times in the DT-12 power flow.

overdrive through the four gears involved. Shifting for the overdrive model starts with the splitter gears in the direct position, which means that in first gear, the countershaft is driven by the rear splitter gear set. As the transmission shifts to second again, the splitter is the only sliding clutch that moves, but it now sends the power through the front splitter and then back to the rear splitter and the input to the countershaft is slightly faster. Other than the reversal of the splitter's position, the power flow follows the sequence described previously and again creates 12 forward speeds, which ends with an overdrive in 12th.

The DT-12 uses an air-operated countershaft brake to control shaft and gear speeds in the transmission to enable it to synchronize speeds for shifting. The countershaft brake is a multidisc clutch attached to the front end of the countershaft inside the clutch housing of the transmission. The countershaft brake can be seen in **FIGURE 46-31**.

The brake is controlled by the transmission ECU and can speed up shift times by being able to slow the countershaft and therefore the main shaft gearing, when necessary.

These transmissions use a two-pedal design, so there is no clutch pedal. Therefore, the transmission can operate totally automatically or can be switched to manual by the driver if desired. As with all automated transmissions, though, the transmission has mechanisms to prevent abusive operation by the driver. The DT-12 transmission works to optimize shifting strategies for all road, load, and driver conditions.

Volvo Trucks' I-Shift/Mack's mDrive

The Volvo I-Shift and the Mack mDrive are essentially the same transmission. The mDrive can have several different software variations that suit the more common vocational operations of Mack trucks, but other than that, the design is identical. For that reason, we will only discuss the Volvo I-Shift here. The Volvo I-Shift, shown in **FIGURE 46-32**, automated transmission is a two-pedal dry clutch design.

The transmission uses a 17-inch (43.2 cm) single organic disc clutch. The clutch is actuated by a self-contained

FIGURE 46-31 The multidisc countershaft brake is used by the transmission controller to synchronize shaft and gear speeds for clash-free shifting.

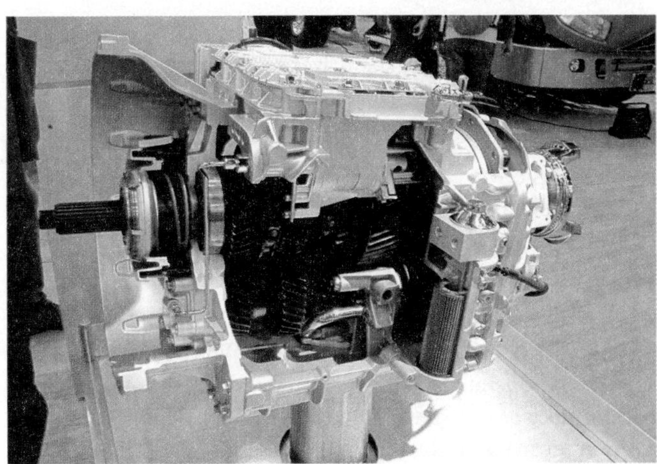

FIGURE 46-32 Similar in function to the DT-12, the Volvo I-Shift uses only one countershaft.

FIGURE 46-33 The large organic disc clutch used by Volvo allows smooth engagement.

air-actuated release bearing controlled by the TCU. The Volvo I-Shift clutch is shown in **FIGURE 46-33**.

The transmission design is very similar to the DT-12 transmission. One difference is that the countershaft is located directly below the mainshaft, whereas in the DT-12, the countershaft is mounted to the side of the mainshaft. Like the DT-12, the Volvo transmission has a two-speed input splitter section, a three-speed main shaft section, and a planetary range section. Therefore, the main shaft gears are used four times each in total: twice in low range through the planetary range section and twice in high range, for a total of 12 forward speeds. Shifting is accomplished by electric solenoids controlling air shifters that are integral to the transmission shift cover. The power flows are identical to the DT-12, with the exception of the extra countershaft, and so, it will not be repeated here. The I-Shift transmission is available in four different models, two of which have overdrive and two of which do not:

1. AT2512C—direct drive for Volvo D11 and D13 engines
2. ATO2512C—overdrive for Volvo D11 and D13 engines
3. AT2812C—direct drive for Volvo D16 engines
4. ATO3112C—overdrive for Volvo D16 engines.

The transmission has adaptive shift control. Several selectable shift strategies allow the driver to optimize either performance or fuel economy—or combinations of the two—using the following strategies:

- B = basic
- EB = enhanced basic
- FE = fuel economy
- P = performance
- CO = comprehensive.

As with all automated transmissions, Volvo's transmissions can also be operated in manual mode if desired. The I-Shift driver interface is shown in **FIGURE 46-34**. Notice the "M" position for manual control.

The latest version of the Volvo I-Shift and the Mack mDrive offer an optional "crawler" or "creeper gear." This option adds a deep reduction feature to the transmissions. This is accomplished by lengthening the transmission by approximately 4.5 inches (12 cm) and installing a new input gear on the input shaft in mesh with a selectable crawler gear on the countershaft. The countershaft crawler gear is engaged by a sliding clutch when desired.

This crawler or creeper gear allows much lower reductions than the original I-Shift does. To operate in crawler mode, the driver first must select it from their shift control by selecting drive or manual and then pressing the downshift button two to three times (depending on the vehicle normal start gear) until the operator sees C-1 (crawler 1) on the dash display. This operation moves a sliding clutch to lock the crawler gear to the countershaft so that the crawler gear on the input shaft inputs the countershaft of the transmission.

The driver can select crawler 1 or crawler 2. The crawler 1 position engages first gear on the main shaft to complete the power flow and creates a ratio through the transmission of 32:1, allowing the vehicle to operate as low as 0.6 mph. In the crawler 2 position, the second gear on the main shaft is engaged, and the ratio changes to 19:1. If the driver selects crawler 1 and leaves the transmission in automatic mode, the transmission will shift normally from crawler 1 to crawler 2, then to first gear, etc. The driver can also switch the transmission to manual mode, in which case it will remain in crawler 1 until the driver requests a shift with the shift control buttons. If the driver selects the crawler 1 position in reverse, the ratio is 37:1. According to Volvo Europe, these ratios allow the truck to start a load of 325 tons from a standstill, a whopping 650,000 pounds! In North America, crawler gear–equipped trucks are rated to pull 220,000 pounds.

FIGURE 46-34 Volvo I-Shift driver interface.

Dual-Clutch Transmissions

Volvo has recently released the new 12-speed overdrive dual-clutch I-Shift in Europe. Introduced in September 2014, this new transmission has two dry-friction input clutches. Each of the transmission's two clutches drive a separate input shaft, a solid inner shaft, and a hollow outer shaft.

Gear selector synchronizers are used alternately on the output shaft and on the countershaft. The two main shaft gears are driven by the countershaft, either through the primary or the secondary input shafts. That allows for four different ratios. A fifth ratio can be achieved when the main shaft is driven directly by the primary input shaft when the output shaft is connected to it.

Several manufacturers are developing or have developed dual clutch transmissions. Eaton, for example, has a dual wet clutch transmission available for their mid-range class five and six trucks, which they call the Procision. **FIGURE 46-35** depicts the Procision dual clutch transmission.

Dual clutch transmissions save fuel by shifting without breaking torque and shifting much faster than a normal automated transmission does. Shift speeds are lowered from 100 to 200 milliseconds to as quick as 6 to 12 milliseconds.

Because dual clutch transmissions have two separate input power paths, the solid inner input shaft and the hollow outer input shaft, the transmission controller can select the next gear range while it is still in the first. To change ranges, the transmission simply switches the input clutch to drive the other input shaft, making the shift much quicker.

With the primary input shaft connected to the output shaft, the transmission can reach a sixth ratio by switching to the secondary input clutch and driving the primary input shaft through the secondary input shaft and the countershaft. All of those ratios pass through a planetary range gear system. That makes for six forward ratios in the low range of the planetary range system. The same six ratios are repeated in high range when the planetary range system allows the power flow to pass through unchanged. That brings the total to 12 forward ratios. All of the transmission shifts are power shifts with no torque brake, except for the range shift between sixth and seventh. Compared to its traditional I-Shift, Volvo claims that the new I-Shift has increased cycle time from faster shifts and improved fuel economy. Volvo's dual-clutch model number is the SPO2812. It is capable of handling up to 2,065 ft-lb (2,800 N·m) of torque.

Continuously Variable Transmissions

Several machine manufacturers are offering continuously variable transmissions (CVTs) as standard or optional equipment. A CVT or continuously variable transmission is a transmission

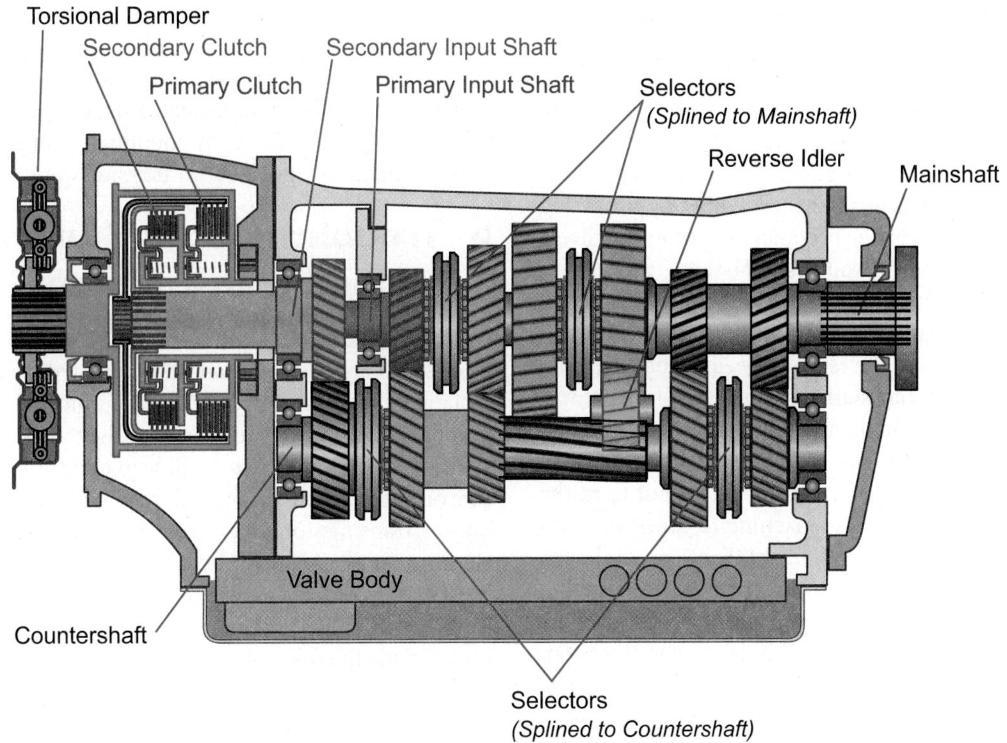

FIGURE 46-35 Dual-clutch transmissions have gear selectors on both the mainshaft and the countershaft.

FIGURE 46-36 Dual-clutch transmissions have two input shafts.

in which the ratios are continuously and almost limitedly variable. This type of transmission offers several advantages to an operator. The biggest advantage is that the engine can be operated at its single best rpm in terms of fuel economy and engine efficiency.

CVTs are not new; they have been around for many years and come in many designs. The simplest design is one that uses two variable sheave pulleys and a drive belt. The drive sheave starts out with a wide groove and the driven sheave with a narrow groove. To change the ratios, the drive sheave must narrow as the driven sheave gets wider. If you have ever driven a snowmobile, you have used this type of drive system. In the snowmobile, the sheaves change by centrifugal force, but more sophisticated systems use computer controls and actuators to change the sheaves. Automobiles using this type of CVT use steel drive belts for longevity.

Although these CVTs are functional, they are not commonly seen in off-road equipment. The popular design for CVTs' use in off-road machines typically uses a dual input system that uses a direct input from the prime mover to a planetary gear set sun gear and a second input to the planetary ring gear from hydraulic motor. Case's Magnum CVT uses this arrangement. This transmission allows the engine of the tractor to be run at a near constant rpm while using the transmission to vary output speed. The transmission is a combination of a four-speed power-shift transmission with a compound planetary gear input.

The engine input drives both the planetary sun gear and a hydraulic pump that powers a hydraulic motor along with auxiliary pumps and the PTO. The planetary gear set is arranged so that the sun gear is input from the engine through either the forward or reverse clutch, and the ring gear of the planetary is connected to the hydraulic motor. The machine's ECM will control the speed of the planetary ring gear by using the hydraulic motor. In forward, the forward clutch is applied by inputting the sun gear of the planetary gear set in a clockwise direction. At a stop gear, the ring gear of the planetary is driven backward by the hydraulic motor to compensate for the engine input to the sun gear. The speed of the ring gear will depend on the rpm that the operator has selected. This situation is called active stop or power neutral by Case.

The combination of the sun gear input and the ring gear's reverse rotation together hold the machine at a stop without the need for a service brake application. When the operator moves the propulsion lever to go forward, the transmission control starts slowing the reverse rotation of the ring gear, and so the machine starts moving. The sun gear of the planetary gear is input, and the ring gear acts as the held member by providing resistance. The planetary carrier becomes output and delivers power to the four-speed power-shift transmission.

The four-speed power-shift transmission has four clutches: one for each of its four ranges. From a standing start, the first clutch is applied. By slowing the reverse speed of the ring gear, the transmission control can start to speed up the machine. As acceleration continues, the hydraulic motor will eventually bring the ring gear to a stop and then will start to turn it in the same direction as the sun gear, causing the output from the planetary carrier and therefore the machine to speed up even more. As the power-shift transmission shifts into second gear, the process repeats: The ring gear will turn in reverse at first and then forward. This allows the engine speed of the machine to remain at a relatively constant rpm while accelerating from a stop to transport speed, leading to optimum fuel economy. In reverse, the reverse clutch is applied and the entire system works backward, with the input to the sun gear traveling in the opposite direction. Shifting in reverse is limited to first gear and second gear only.

This arrangement has some similarities to the power divider concept used by Caterpillar. See Chapter 47, on torque converters and power dividers, for more information on power dividers. A similar arrangement is used by a number of manufacturers to provide CVTs by coupling a split planetary input in front of manual or power-shift transmissions.

▶ Troubleshooting Automated Manual Transmissions

S46001

In order to service or repair an automated transmission, technicians must be able to decipher the nomenclature (the model number) for the transmission that they are going to work on. **TABLES 46-1**, **46-2**, and **46-3** will help to decipher the nomenclature on Eaton Fuller automated transmissions. As the company's line of transmissions has become more varied, new nomenclature is now used to reflect the variety of models available. **TABLE 46-4** contains an example of Eaton Fuller's new nomenclature. The specific changes to Eaton Fuller's new nomenclature include the following:

- "E" or "F" has been added to the prefix to identify the brand as "Eaton" or "Fuller."
- "M" has been added to the prefix to identify this transmission is approved for use with multi-torque engines.

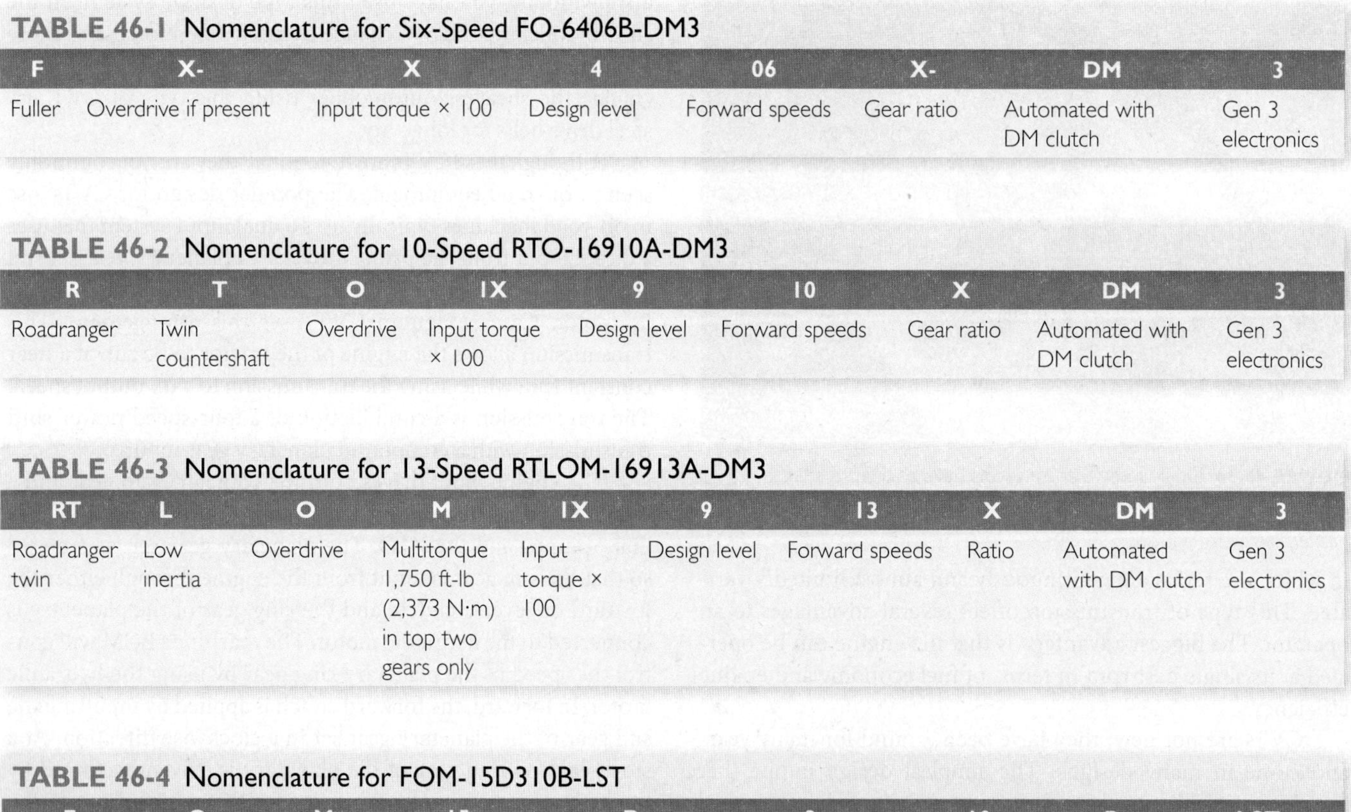

TABLE 46-1 Nomenclature for Six-Speed FO-6406B-DM3

F	X-	X	4	06	X-	DM	3
Fuller	Overdrive if present	Input torque × 100	Design level	Forward speeds	Gear ratio	Automated with DM clutch	Gen 3 electronics

TABLE 46-2 Nomenclature for 10-Speed RTO-16910A-DM3

R	T	O	1X	9	10	X	DM	3
Roadranger	Twin countershaft	Overdrive	Input torque × 100	Design level	Forward speeds	Gear ratio	Automated with DM clutch	Gen 3 electronics

TABLE 46-3 Nomenclature for 13-Speed RTLOM-16913A-DM3

RT	L	O	M	1X	9	13	X	DM	3
Roadranger twin	Low inertia	Overdrive	Multitorque 1,750 ft-lb (2,373 N·m) in top two gears only	Input torque × 100	Design level	Forward speeds	Ratio	Automated with DM clutch	Gen 3 electronics

TABLE 46-4 Nomenclature for FOM-15D310B-LST

F	O	M	15	D	3	10	B	LST
Brand Eaton or Fuller	Overdrive	Multitorque	Input torque × 100	Clutch configuration	Design level	Forward speeds	Ratio	Application and value

The following are configurations, which denote the type of clutch the transmission uses:

- D—dry mechanical
- E—electronic clutch actuator
- S—wet shifting clutch.

The design level is now a combination of the gearbox design and automation platform.

The final suffix contains the application and value code. The following are the application and value codes:

- L—line-haul
- H—highway (and high in second position)
- P—performance (and PTO in second position)
- S—severe duty
- ST—standard
- V—vocational (and value in second position)
- M—multipurpose (and mixer in second position)
- C—construction
- X—extreme duty
- R—recreational (motor home)
- G—generator
- P—PTO
- U—utility
- E—efficient.

The following tables list the nomenclature for the Eaton Fuller line of automated transmissions.

TABLE 46-5 explains the Volvo I-Shift model number nomenclature; it is essential that the technician knows the correct model number of the transmission before diagnoses are carried out as each model will have slightly different operating parameters.

Troubleshooting an automated transmission fault should be done in a logical sequence. First, find as much information as you can about the complaint from the driver. Then, verify the complaint. Overlooking this step has sent many a technician on a wild goose chase to find nonexistent complaints! Once you have established that the complaint does exist, rule out any mechanical causes for the complaint, such as air system problems or transmission mechanical problems.

Most AMTs will have a way to manually display fault codes. To retrieve fault codes in an Eaton Fuller AMT, start by enabling the system's self-diagnostic mode. Alternatively, use an OEM or aftermarket electronic service tool, such as Eaton's PC-based service tool, ServiceRanger, or MPSI Pro-Link. Ensure that the appropriate cartridge is installed. Note that on Eaton Fuller's Gen. 1 and Gen. 2 transmissions, electronics do not flash the service transmission light for system codes, only for component codes. Examples of system codes are the front box control system, the splitter control system, or the engine control system. System codes may or may not be associated with a recognizable symptom when they are set, but the check transmission light will not flash. Component codes are set for component problems, such as the range valve, a speed sensor, and a rail position sensor. Those codes will cause the check transmission light to flash. To enable the system's self-diagnostic mode and retrieve codes through the check transmission light, follow the steps in **SKILL DRILL 46-1**.

You can clear inactive fault codes by using an OEM or aftermarket electronic service tool, such as Eaton's PC-based service tool, ServiceRanger, or MPSI Pro-Link, with the appropriate cartridge installed. To manually clear all inactive fault codes from the ECU's memory, follow the guidelines in **SKILL DRILL 46-2**.

Although Skill Drill 46-1 and Skill Drill 46-2 are specific to Eaton Fuller, most manufacturers of automated transmissions have similar procedures for reading and clearing fault code information. If the transmission is displaying a fault code, consult the manufacturer's fault code listing in the troubleshooting manual. Follow the fault code trouble tree. The fault code trouble tree is a step-by-step method of diagnosing and repairing the fault. The Eaton Fuller fault code chart lists 54 separate codes, so trying to go through them here would simply take up too much space.

Manufacturers have spent millions of dollars setting up trouble trees and fault- and symptom-based diagnostic systems for their products. The best method of troubleshooting complaints is to follow the manufacturer's recommendations. Failure to follow the trouble tree to the letter, or skipping steps, is simply a waste of your time and the vehicle owner's time. Do not be tempted to jump ahead when using a trouble tree. If you do, it is more than likely that you will end up having to start all over again.

▶ TECHNICIAN TIP

You can find the OEM manuals, troubleshooting manuals, and fault code guides for Eaton Fuller transmissions on the company website: www.roadranger.com. Information on Volvo I-Shift/Mack mDrive can be found on Volvo's website: https://volvotrucks.vg-emedia.com. For other automated transmissions, contact the manufacturer. There is no substitute for the OEM manual. If you cannot access one, then you would be advised not to take on the repair job.

TABLE 46-5 Nomenclature for Volvo ATO2512C

AT	O	XX	12	C
Automated mechanical transmission	Overdrive No letter = Direct	Max input torque N·m (ft-lb) 25 = 2,500 (1,850) 28 = 2,800 (2,050) 31 = 3,100 (2,300)	Twelve-speed	Design level

SKILL DRILL 46-1 Enabling the Self-Diagnostic Mode and Retrieving Codes

1. Place the transmission in neutral.
2. Set the parking brake.
3. Retrieve the active codes:
   a. Start with the key in the ON position.
   b. Turn the key off and on two times within five seconds.
   c. End with the key in the ON position.
   d. After five seconds, the service lamp should begin flashing two-digit fault codes. If no faults are active, the service light will flash code 25 (no codes).

   Note: A code 88 may show up in the dash at key ON. That is a normal power-up test of the display.
4. Retrieve the inactive codes:
   a. Start with the key in the ON position.
   b. Turn the key off and on four times within five seconds.
   c. End with the key in the ON position.
   d. After five seconds, the service lamp should begin flashing two-digit fault codes. If there are no inactive faults, the service light will flash code 25 (no codes).
5. Two-digit fault codes may be read directly from the gear display or by observing the flashing service transmission light, if equipped. Observe the sequence of flashes on the service light, and record the codes. The flash codes are displayed as follows: one flash, a short pause, and then three flashes equals code 13. There is a long pause of three to four seconds between codes. Then the next code will be flashed. For example, three flashes, a short pause, and then two flashes equals code 32. Another long pause would follow and the two codes would repeat once more.

SKILL DRILL 46-2 Clearing Inactive Codes

1. Place the shift lever in neutral.
2. Set the parking brake.
3. Turn the ignition key on, but do not start the engine.
4. Clear the inactive codes:
   a. Start with the key in the ON position.
   b. Turn the key off and on six times within five seconds.
   c. End with the key in the ON position.

   Note: If the codes have been successfully cleared, the service lamp will come on and stay on for five seconds. The gear display will show code 25 (no codes).
5. Turn the key off and allow the system to power down.

Using a Diagnostic (Scan) Tool to Diagnose Transmissions

Using electronic diagnostic equipment to troubleshoot components has become a necessity in today's industry. Because you will work with many different diagnostic tools, it is important to locate the correct service manual procedure before attempting to retrieve trouble codes. A laptop computer, a hand-held diagnostic tool, and an onboard diagnostic component are the most common diagnostic trouble code retrieval systems. To use a scan tool to diagnose automated transmissions, follow the procedure in **SKILL DRILL 46-3**.

The two types of trouble codes are active and inactive. These two types of codes tell the technician what has taken place in the system. A digital multimeter is normally used to test the area where the fault code indicates that the malfunction has occurred. As you can see, it is important that a technician in today's high-tech world be proficient at using electronic diagnostic tools to retrieve trouble codes and at troubleshooting electronic systems.

Every technician's toolkit should contain the basic hand tools for the tasks to be undertaken, such as appropriately sized wrenches and socket sets, screwdrivers, hammers, and pliers. These items let technicians undertake the normal day-to-day activities associated with their position. In addition, special tools are always required to perform particular tasks on a specific manufacturer's equipment. These are normally

SKILL DRILL 46-3 Using a Scan Tool to Diagnose Transmissions

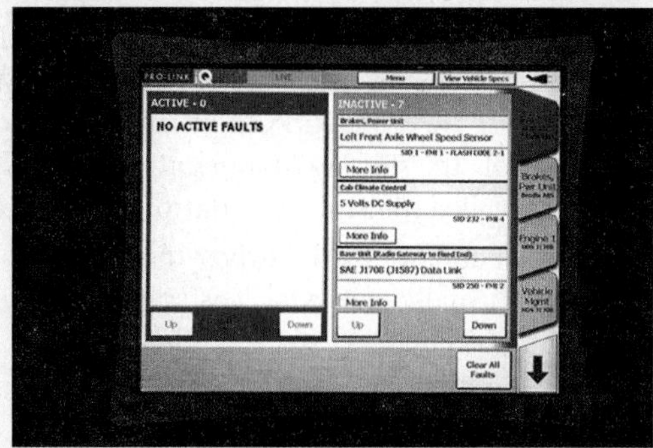

1. Locate and follow the appropriate procedure in the service manual.
2. Complete the accompanying job sheet or work order with all pertinent information.
3. Move the vehicle into the shop and park it on level ground.
4. Apply parking brakes, chock the vehicle wheels, and observe lockout/tag-out procedures.
5. If the vehicle has a manual transmission, place it in neutral; if it has a park position, place it in park.
6. Check for active and inactive trouble codes by using the appropriate service manual procedure and diagnostic tool.
7. Record any displayed trouble codes on the job sheet or work order.
8. Use a multimeter to verify the problem(s) associated with the trouble code(s).
9. Record all diagnostic readings.
10. Repair or replace the affected systems or components.
11. Clear all inactive and active trouble codes.
12. List the test results and/or recommendations on the job sheet or work order, clean the work area, and return tools and materials to their proper storage area.

provided by the company that the technician works for and may be, in some cases, hired in from tool suppliers because of their specialist nature. Whatever the case, before starting to work on a specific task, you should have access to the following:

- common technician hand tools
- the correct OEM manual
- diagnostic equipment
- tachometer
- temperature gauge
- job ticket—use appropriate one provided at your facility
- wheel chocks
- safety glasses
- shop towels
- diagnostic trouble code retrieval tool
- multimeter.

▶ Wrap-Up

Ready for Review

- The Volvo I-Shift AMT has a power flow that is similar to the one in the Detroit DT-12.
- Automated manual transmissions (AMTs) are standard mechanical transmissions adapted to computer control.
- AMTs were developed to reduce carbon dioxide emissions and to reduce fuel consumption, and their development was driven by EPA-mandated reductions in exhaust emission.
- AMTs optimize shift points, leading to increases in fuel economy.
- AMTs are also a draw for new drivers because of their ease of operation and reduction in driver fatigue.
- AMTs can come in a three-pedal design, where the clutch is used by the driver for starting and stopping, or a two-pedal design, with no clutch pedal at all.
- Some newer AMTs have dual clutches that even further improve fuel economy.
- AMTs reduce driver training requirements, vehicle downtime, and vehicle driveline abuse by the driver.
- Most AMTs still require torque to be broken to complete a shift, but the newer dual-clutch models do not. Breaking torque costs fuel.
- Dual-clutch AMTs allow very quick, full-power shifting, leading to even greater fuel economy than that of traditional AMTs.
- Eaton Fuller's lineup of AMTs includes the AutoShift and the UltraShift. These are the most popular models of AMT found in North America.
- The computer controller that commands the shift process is the brains of the AMT. Depending on the manufacturer, this computer is called the TCU (transmission control unit) or the transmission engine control unit (ECU).
- In 2014, Detroit Diesel launched its own version of the Mercedes 12-speed AMT popular in Europe and called it the DT-12.
- The DT-12 has a single-countershaft main box with a planetary range section and has power flows very similar to those in Volvo I-Shift.

- AMT shifting is usually accomplished by electric motors and/or electric-over-air solenoids.
- AMT software has become increasingly sophisticated and is now capable of adaptive electronic control based on driver, load, terrain, and other operating conditions, thereby optimizing shifting strategies and fuel economy.
- To shift without gear clash, AMTs use software to read shaft and gear speeds inside the transmission.
- AMT controllers are capable of self-diagnosis and will set diagnostic fault codes, alerting the driver to problems.
- AMT software is capable of initiating failsafe strategies to protect the transmission while still allowing limited operation.
- Eaton AMTs use air solenoids to control shifting of the range and the splitter sliding clutches in their transmissions that are equipped with auxiliary sections.
- Inertia or countershaft brakes are used by the AMTs to control transmission shaft speeds for shifting to first or reverse from neutral and to increase shift speed synchronization when required.
- AMTs still require clutches, although there may be no clutch pedal. The clutches can be standard mechanical versions (Eaton AutoShift), a centrifugally operated clutch (some Eaton UltraShift models), an electrically operated clutch (some Eaton UltraShift models), an air-operated clutch (used on the DT-12 and the I-Shift), or dual clutches as either dry or wet (the new Volvo I-Shift uses a dual dry clutch).
- AMT TCUs record active and inactive diagnostic fault codes that can assist the technician in diagnosing complaints. These codes can usually be retrieved manually and/or by using an electronic service tool to access them.
- All manufacturers have detailed troubleshooting strategies and trouble-tree sequences listed in their service manuals to assist the technician in their diagnosis.

Key Terms

adaptive learning Software that can learn and change strategy based on different factors.

air-control solenoid valve An electric-over-air solenoid used to control shifting by controlling the flow of air from the air filter to the range cylinder piston.

automated manual transmission (AMT) A standard manual transmission operated by electronic control.

AutoShift Eaton's first shift-by-wire transmission.

break torque The unloading of the driveline to allow a shift to occur.

carbon dioxide One of the resulting gases produced when burning a hydrocarbon fuel, which contributes to global warming.

CVT A continuously variable transmission.

direct drive A dual-clutch transmission from John Deere.

DT-12 A 12-speed AMT manufactured by Detroit Diesel.

dual-clutch transmission A transmission with two shafts controlled by two separate clutches.

electric shift assembly The shift actuation system for an Eaton AutoShift or UltraShift transmission that contains two shift motors, the shift finger, and the shift finger position sensors.

electronic control module (ECM) An electronic control module can control a transmission or an engine or Anti-lock braking systems. In this chapter we are talking about an electronic control module that controls the shifting in an electronically automated transmission; also called transmission control unit (TCU).

gear jamming An attempt by the driver to shift without using the clutch, which usually causes at least some damage to the transmission sliding clutches; also called float shifting.

I-Shift The Volvo AMT; Mack trucks use the same transmission.

inertia brake A component used to control the speed of the transmission countershaft and main shaft gears.

J-1587 An older SAE communication protocol, which is quite slow in terms of data transmission at 9,600 bits/second.

J-1939 A newer SAE communication protocol, which transmits data at a rate of at least 250,000 bits/second and up to 500,000 bits/second.

momentary engine ignition interrupt relay (MEIIR) A relay controlled by the TCU that cuts the engine ignition or fueling in the event that a DM clutch will not disengage.

self-diagnostic The TCU's capability to analyze its own functions.

shift by wire Shifting controlled completely by the transmission electronic control.

snapshot A snapshot records all the relevant TCU data before and after a diagnostic code is set to ease diagnoses.

start enable relay The start enable relay is controlled by the TCU and interrupts the circuit to the starter solenoid unless the TCU passes a self-check and verifies that the transmission is in neutral.

system manager A transmission control module used with older Gen. 1 and Gen. 2 Eaton AutoShift transmissions.

thermal efficiency A measurement of how much of the fuel that has been used has actually turned into power to drive the vehicle.

transmission control unit (TCU) The unit that controls the shifting in an electronically automated transmission; also called transmission engine control module (ECM).

UltraShift A two-pedal AMT from Eaton that is completely shift by wire with no clutch pedal.

Review Questions

1. Which of the following is NOT one of the reasons that AMTs are becoming more popular?
   - **a.** They have better fuel economy.
   - **b.** They are less expensive than standard transmissions.
   - **c.** They lead to reduced carbon dioxide emissions.
   - **d.** They reduce driver training requirements.
2. The transmission shift tower is replaced by which of the following on an Eaton AMT?
   - **a.** A shift motor
   - **b.** A rail select motor
   - **c.** An electric shift fork
   - **d.** An electric shift assembly

3. Before a vehicle with an Eaton Fuller AMT can be started, which of the following must happen?
   a. The transmission controller must conduct and pass an initiation and self-check.
   b. The transmission controller must verify a neutral position.
   c. The transmission controller must turn on the start enable relay.
   d. All of the above.
4. Each time the vehicle is shut down, which of the following occurs in the Eaton Fuller AMTs?
   a. The transmission controller conducts a self-check diagnostic.
   b. The range and splitter air shift cylinders are moved to neutral.
   c. The transmission controller maps and records the shift rail gates.
   d. All of the above.
5. The Eaton Gen. 3 AutoShift transmission has which of the following electronic modules?
   a. A shifter module, a system manager ECU, and a shift control ECU
   b. A shifter module with a built-in system manager and a shift control ECU
   c. A single TCU on the transmission
   d. A shifter module with a built-in, single-transmission control ECU
6. How is the auxiliary section high- and low-range shift accomplished on a 10-speed Eaton Fuller UltraShift transmission?
   a. By air, using two control solenoids
   b. By air, using one control solenoid
   c. Electrically, using one electric motor
   d. Electrically, using two electric motors
7. In an Eaton Fuller UltraShift transmission, what must the transmission controller do in order to make a shift?
   a. It must request the ECM to break torque.
   b. It must assume control of the engine.
   c. It must ask the driver to depress the clutch.
   d. All of the above.
8. The rail select sensor on an Eaton Fuller UltraShift transmission is a(n) ______________.
   a. induction pulse generator
   b. potentiometer
   c. rheostat
   d. Hall-effect sensor
9. The output speed sensor on an Eaton Fuller UltraShift transmission is a(n) ______________.
   a. induction pulse generator
   b. potentiometer
   c. rheostat
   d. Hall-effect sensor
10. What must the driver do to select high range while driving forward in an UltraShift transmission?
   a. Preselect the range by moving the range lever to high while the transmission is in gear
   b. Preselect the range shift by pushing the up arrows
   c. Select range after the transmission shifts to neutral
   d. The driver cannot select high or low range only gear numbers.

ASE Technician A/Technician B Style Questions

1. Technician A says that two-pedal AMTs still require a clutch. Technician B says that in three-pedal AMTs, the driver uses the clutch only for starting off and stopping the vehicle. Who is correct?
   a. Technician A
   b. Technician B
   c. Both Technician A and Technician B
   d. Neither Technician A nor Technician B
2. Technician A says that all AMTs use a standard dry disc clutch. Technician B says that the Volvo I-Shift uses a large wet disc clutch. Who is correct?
   a. Technician A
   b. Technician B
   c. Both Technician A and Technician B
   d. Neither Technician A nor Technician B
3. Technician A says that the John Deere direct drive transmission uses two multi-plate wet clutches. Technician B says that the direct drive transmission has two sets of input gears. Who is correct?
   a. Technician A
   b. Technician B
   c. Both Technician A and Technician B
   d. Neither Technician A nor Technician B
4. Technician A says that the DT-12 transmission from Detroit Diesel uses a splitter gear at the input to double the ratios in the front box section. Technician B says that the rearward split in the splitter section of the DT-12 is the low-split position. Who is correct?
   a. Technician A
   b. Technician B
   c. Both Technician A and Technician B
   d. Neither Technician A nor Technician B
5. Technician A says that the 12-speed Volvo I-Shift transmission has the same basic power flows as the 12-speed DT-12 from Detroit Diesel. Technician B says the 12-speed Volvo I-Shift has only one countershaft. Who is correct?
   a. Technician A
   b. Technician B
   c. Both Technician A and Technician B
   d. Neither Technician A nor Technician B
6. Technician A says that the planetary gear set in Case's Magnum CVT has two inputs. Technician B says that the ring gear of the planetary gear set in Case's Magnum CVT always turns clockwise. Who is correct?
   a. Technician A
   b. Technician B
   c. Both Technician A and Technician B
   d. Neither Technician A nor Technician B
7. Technician A says that an Eaton Fuller 18-speed UltraShift transmission uses two air solenoids to control the splitter

shift in the auxiliary section. Technician B says that an Eaton Fuller 18-speed UltraShift transmission uses two air solenoids to control the range shift in the auxiliary section. Who is correct?

a. Technician A
b. Technician B
c. Both Technician A and Technician B
d. Neither Technician A nor Technician B

8. Technician A says that the MEIIR relay is controlled by the ECM. Technician B says that the MEIIR relay is actuated only when there is catastrophic clutch failure. Who is correct?
   a. Technician A
   b. Technician B
   c. Both Technician A and Technician B
   d. Neither Technician A nor Technician B
9. Technician A says that the John Deere direct drive transmission does not need to break torque while shifting. Technician B says that the John Deere direct drive transmission has only four gears on the output shaft. Who is correct?
   a. Technician A
   b. Technician B
   c. Both Technician A and Technician B
   d. Neither Technician A nor Technician B
10. Technician A says that the DT-12 transmission has an overdrive gear in the range section. Technician B says that the Volvo I-Shift can have an overdrive in the splitter section. Who is correct?
    a. Technician A
    b. Technician B
    c. Both Technician A and Technician B
    d. Neither Technician A nor Technician B

CHAPTER 47
Torque Converters

Knowledge Objectives

After reading this chapter, you will be able to:

- **K47001** Explain the purpose and fundamentals of torque converters, torque dividers, and fluid couplings.
- **K47002** Identify the construction, types, and applications of the various torque converters, torque dividers, and fluid couplings used with MORE.
- **K47003** Describe the operation of torque converters and torque dividers.
- **K47004** Describe torque converter and torque divider hydraulic circuits.
- **K47005** Describe and explain common failures and the root causes for torque converters, torque dividers, and fluid couplings.
- **K47006** Describe the purpose and fundamentals of retarders.
- **K47007** Explain the operation of hydraulic retarders.

Skills Objectives

After reading this chapter, you will be able to:

- **S47001** Explain testing procedures for torque converters and torque dividers.
- **S47002** Recommend reconditioning or repairs following manufacturer's procedures on torque converters and torque dividers.
- **S47003** Explain common problems with hydraulic retarders and recommend reconditioning or repairs.

▶ Introduction

Although machines are produced that have disconnect clutches, the most likely configurations that you come across will be machines that have torque converters or torque dividers that will allow the engine to be disconnected from the driveline to stop and start the machine. Fluid couplings have also been used for this function, but because of their lack of efficiency under heavy loads, they are rarely used in mobile equipment. A fluid coupler can transmit torque to a drive system hydrodynamically (by using fluid as the power transfer medium), but a torque converter is a hydrodynamic drive that is also capable of multiplying available engine torque to help get the machine moving. This can be very handy when trying to move a machine that can weigh several hundred thousand pounds. Most torque converters are capable of multiplying available engine torque by two to three times and in some applications by much more. Using hydrodynamic drive systems to connect and disconnect the engine also reduces shock loads to the rest of the driveline on starting off and especially on directional changes, because the fluid can absorb the shock loads better than a conventional disconnect clutch can.

Certain machines will use a special type of torque converter called a torque divider. A torque divider is a type of torque converter that incorporates a planetary gear set that can multiply torque in two ways: one through the planetary gear set and the other through the torque converter. Torque dividers can insulate the driveline from shocks and multiply torque to an even greater extent than a regular torque converter can. In this chapter, we will look at the operation of fluid couplings, torque converters, and torque dividers and their use in mobile off-road equipment (MORE).

▶ Fundamentals of Fluid Couplers, Torque Converters, and Torque Dividers

K47001

All equipment that uses a transmission must have a means of disconnecting the engine power from the driveline when the vehicle is stopped. Otherwise, the engine would stall when the machine is brought to a stop. This function can be handled by a standard disconnect clutch. The clutch physically disconnects the transmission input shaft from the engine when the clutch is disengaged. Most machines, however, use a torque converter or torque divider to perform this function. The torque converter is a sophisticated type of **fluid coupling** that allows the vehicle to slow down and stop without any disconnection of components. The torque converter is able to accomplish this because the engine power is transmitted to the driveline through a fluid, rather than a physical, connection. The easiest way to visualize this power transmission is to imagine two electric fans facing each other. Turn one fan on, and observe the other fan. The air being pushed out by the powered fan strikes the blades of the unpowered fan. As illustrated in **FIGURE 47-1**, the blades of the unpowered fan start to turn even though there is no physical connection between them. The air acts as a fluid that transmits the power from the first fan to the second fan. This is the basic principle of the fluid coupler: power can be transmitted through a fluid to drive another component.

For a functioning fluid coupler to work, however, you need more than just the two fans mentioned above. Because air is easily compressed, the fans could not transmit very much torque. In addition, the fans are open at the sides, so at the first sign of resistance, the fluid (air) would merely deflect to the side. To make a proper fluid coupling, you first need to use a liquid. The reason is that most liquids are essentially uncompressible. In a fluid coupler, hydraulic oil is used to transmit the power. Second, you must stop the fluid from being deflected to the side when the torque increases. To accomplish this, the fans in a fluid coupler are encased in a circular housing. Third, as shown in **FIGURE 47-2**, the fans are placed very close to one another, and the blades of the fans

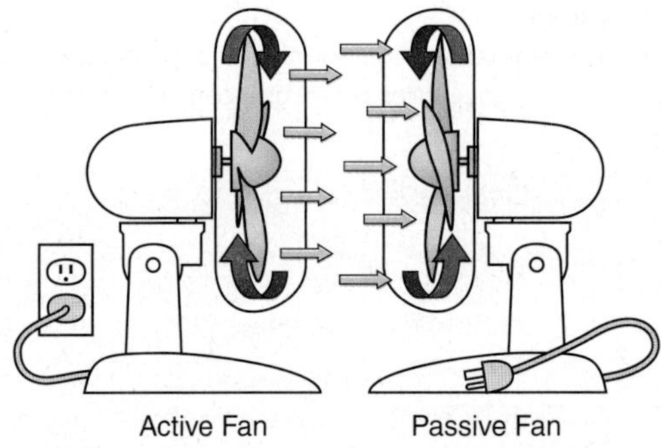

FIGURE 47-1 Air driven by the powered fan drives the blades of the unplugged fan.

You Are the Mobile Heavy Equipment Technician

An operator complains that their machine, a Caterpillar 980K wheeled loader, seems to be a lot slower on cycle time than they are used to. The operator says that during the normal cycle, they load the bucket, carry it some distance down the jobsite and dump it, and then return. The operator says that for some reason, the machine does not seem to get from one end of the site to the other as quickly as before.

1. What would you initially check on this machine to investigate?
2. Could the engine be the cause of the complaint?
3. Could the driveline be the issue?
4. If you suspect the driveline, what specifically could cause this complaint?

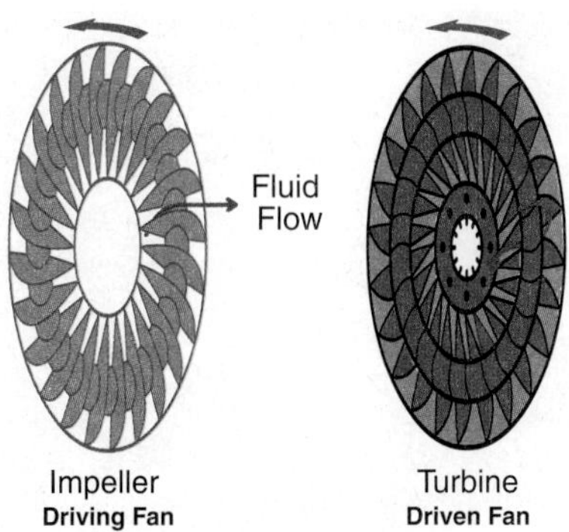

FIGURE 47-2 A simple fluid coupling has only two elements: the driving "fan" and the driven "fan" inside a sealed shell.

are slightly angled to optimize power transfer. Then the driving fan is attached to the power source and the driven fan to the output to create a functioning fluid coupler.

Using a fluid coupler can yield many advantages. A fluid coupling allows equipment to start up virtually load-free. When an electric motor starts up, it tends to accelerate very rapidly. A fluid coupling allows the drive to slip as the motor speed ramps up. That slippage reduces the start-up shock load, the current draw, and the potential for overheating.

A fluid coupler can also cushion the shock from overloads, machinery that jams up, or sudden speed changes by allowing the driven fan to slip. Fluid couplers are used in many applications where low-speed start-up torque is not a significant issue, including conveying systems, processing equipment, and assembly-line systems, such as filling and packaging operations. Power can be supplied by electric motors, industrial engines, or power take-off units on mobile equipment, such as tractors in agricultural applications. The fluid coupler is simply designed, and it can achieve nearly 100% efficiency at high speeds as long as the applied load is not too great.

The main disadvantage of the fluid coupler is that it is quite inefficient at starting speeds, when the input is much faster than the output. The coupler is also incapable of multiplying torque. During start-up operation, the driven element of the coupler is much slower than the speed of the driving element. A lot of power is wasted and dissipated as heat, caused by the shearing force and turbulence of the oil inside the coupler, which is imparted into the fluid because of the difference in speed. Because of this, a fluid coupler is not suitable for uses where heavy loads must be moved from a standing start.

The torque converter, on the other hand, uses the advantages of the fluid coupler to allow the vehicle to be stopped while the engine is still running, and it still allows a power transfer efficiency of 90–95% when conditions are correct. The torque converter also has a huge advantage over the fluid coupler in that the converter can multiply torque. When starting out from a stop, the torque created by the typical internal combustion engine is quite low because the engine speed is also quite low. The torque converter multiplies this available torque to allow quicker throttle response. Depending on the torque-converter design, this multiplication can be two to four or even more times the torque than the engine is producing. Although most torque converters will multiply torque by two or three to one, the torque converter will never operate at 100% efficiency. The driven element (the **turbine**) can be accelerated only to approximately 95% of the speed of the driving element (the **impeller**). This is due to the turbulence caused by the other element in the converter, the **stator**, and by the design of the turbine itself.

Today, torque converters address this inadequacy by using a **lockup clutch**. When conditions are correct, the lockup clutch locks the turbine to the converter shell, and the engine power is transmitted one to one to the driveline, eliminating any loss in efficiency. We will look at how the converter accomplishes this as we continue this chapter.

Torque Dividers

A torque divider uses the same elements as a torque converter, but it also uses a planetary gear set to provide a split drive input to the driveline. This split drive input allows even greater torque multiplication and provides further cushioning to the driveline against shock loads. More information of the functioning of torque dividers will be found later in the chapter, in the section covering torque dividers operation. **FIGURE 47-3** shows a torque divider.

▶ Components of Fluid Couplers, Torque Converters, and Torque Dividers

K47002

In the section on the fundamentals of torque converters, we referred to the driving and driven fans in a fluid coupler because they enable us to explain the basic concept most simply. Of course, the components of a fluid couple are not actually called fans. Their correct names are the impeller (pump), which is the driving "fan," and the turbine, which is the driven "fan." These are the only components inside the housing of a fluid coupler.

FIGURE 47-3 The torque divider has two inputs both driven by the flywheel one to the torque converter and the other to a planetary gear set.

FIGURE 47-4 The modern torque converter housing contains all of the elements involved in power transfer and lock-up clutch operation.

FIGURE 47-6 This type of torque converter has an output flange that will connect to a transmission through a short drive shaft.

The modern torque converter, shown in **FIGURE 47-4**, includes several components. The shell, or housing, contains all of the component parts. The impeller (pump) is the driving member and is part of or attached to the shell. The turbine, which is the driven member; the stator, which is the reaction member; and the two halves of the split guide ring are the final components of the torque converter. The modern torque converter housing contains all of the elements involved in power transfer and lockup clutch operation.

Converter Mounting Positions

In MORE, the torque converter can be mounted in a number of different configurations. Traditionally, the torque converter is mounted to the engine flywheel through a flex plate, a strong flexible plate or plates that allow some movement between the converter and flywheel. The rear of the torque converter enters and is supported by the front pump of the transmission. In a lot of MORE installations, the converter is splined directly to a pot-style flywheel and supported by the transmission. **FIGURE 47-5** shows a splined torque converter.

FIGURE 47-5 A splined torque converter fits into the front of the transmission.

In some equipment, however, this arrangement is changed. The converter can be mounted in its own housing, which is attached to the engine flywheel housing, and again the converter is directly driven by splines in a pot-style flywheel. The output from the converter does not go directly to a transmission but instead connects to it with a short drive shaft. **FIGURE 47-6** shows this type of torque converter.

Torque dividers will be mounted so that both the planetary sun gear and the torque-converter housing/impeller are driven by the flywheel. Figure 47-3 shows a torque divider.

The converter also houses the components that make up the lockup clutch if so equipped. Lockup clutches are usually standard for any modern machines that travel significant distances, because they increase fuel economy and decrease emissions. Components of the lockup clutch include a gear or spline attached to the turbine, a friction disc that fits the spline or gear, the clutch actuation piston, and the backing plate attached to the converter housing that the piston squeezes the friction disc against. We will discuss these components individually at first and then explain how they interact with each other.

Because fluid couplers are rarely seen in MORE, from this point onward, we will concentrate mostly on torque converters and torque dividers.

Converter Shell or Housing

The converter shell is composed of two halves. The rear half has the shape of a hollowed-out donut, as shown in **FIGURE 47-7**. The donut shape is called a **torus**.

Depending on the positioning of the torque converter in the driveline, the rear half of the converter housing may have a hollow stub attached to its center. This is called the pump drive hub. When installed in the transmission, the pump drive hub drives the transmission oil pump gears. The front of the converter housing is usually flat on the outside to accommodate the placing of the lockup clutch components when equipped. In some cases, it may have a rounded shape, especially if the converter does not have a lockup clutch. The front half of the shell of traditionally mounted torque converters normally has

FIGURE 47-7 The rear half a traditional torque converter is shaped like a hollowed-out donut and has the pump drive attached to it.

FIGURE 47-9 The impeller is responsible for the fluid movement in the torque converter. **A.** Impeller blades. **B.** Split guide ring.

FIGURE 47-8 The front half of the traditional torque converter is typically flat and has a pilot that supports the converter in the flywheel.

a protruding pilot that will engage the rear of the crankshaft or the engine flywheel to help support the converter weight, as shown in **FIGURE 47-8**.

Typically, the torque-converter halves are bolted together to ease the overhaul process; however, lighter-duty torque converters may have to two halves welded together.

Impeller or Pump

Both impeller and pump are used to name the driving member in the torque converter. We will use the term impeller to avoid confusion with the transmission hydraulic pump or other pumps driven by the torque converter. The impeller is a series of vanes. The vanes can be cast as part of the rear half of the converter shell or they may be welded to it, as seen in **FIGURE 47-9**. One-half of the **split guide ring** is attached to the middle of the impeller's blades to provide strength to the blades and create a circular passage for fluid flow.

The torque-converter shell or housing is physically attached, though not directly, to the engine crankshaft. As a result, the shell and the impeller turn with the engine. During operation, the torque converter is filled with fluid. The impeller blades generate centrifugal force that flings the fluid outward. The curved torus shape of the rear half of the shell then forces the fluid forward toward the engine.

Turbine

The turbine sits just in front of the impeller inside the converter housing. The turbine is also shaped like a donut (torus), as shown in **FIGURE 47-10**. When the turbine is installed in front of the impeller, the torus shape of the rear converter housing and the turbine combine to form a complete donut shape. The turbine has a series of curved blades that are designed to catch the oil being thrown forward by the rotating impeller. The second half of the split guide ring is attached to the middle of the turbine blades; again, to strengthen the blades and to help form a circular fluid flow between the impeller and the turbine and back again.

The turbine sits very close to the front of the impeller. The turbine does not, however, touch the impeller. Clearances may

FIGURE 47-10 The turbine's design, along with the impeller, completes the hollowed-out donut shape that the fluid travels through in the torque converter. **A.** Split guide ring. **B.** Turbine blades.

be as tight as 0.060 inches to 0.080 inches (1.5 to 2.0 mm), but the two components will not touch. The turbine is supported by thrust bearings or washers that locate it axially and is not connected to anything in the torque converter. The turbine is splined to the input shaft of the transmission, which enters the torque converter from the rear or to the output shaft of the converter. The forward end of the input shaft or the front of the turbine is usually supported by a bushing inside the torque-converter housing that serves to locate the turbine radially.

Stator or Reaction Member

The outside edges of the turbine and the impeller are very close together inside the torque converter. In contrast, the inner edges are a fair distance apart. The stator sits between the turbine and impeller to take up that space. The stator is shaped like a wheel with curved blades for spokes. The outer edge of the "wheel" is positioned very close to the inner edge of the two halves of the split guide ring, as shown in **FIGURE 47-11**.

When the converter is assembled, the two halves of the split guide ring and the outer edge of the stator wheel create an almost complete circular ring. The fluid can flow from the impeller, around the ring, thorough the turbine, and back to the impeller. This ring helps to reduce fluid turbulence inside the converter. In most heavy equipment, but not all, the stator will be mounted on a one-way clutch.

The stator usually has three components: the inner hub; the **over-running clutch**, or (**one-way clutch**); and the actual stator wheel. The inner hub of the stator is splined to the **stator support** (**ground shaft**), which is either part of the transmission or part of the converter housing if the transmission is remote mounted. The stator support shaft enters the converter from the rear. The stator support (ground shaft) is fixed, so neither it nor the inner hub of the stator can ever turn. The over-running (one-way) clutch sits on the stator inner hub and supports the stator wheel. That clutch will allow the stator wheel to turn in only one direction. The stator wheel's axial position is usually controlled by thrust bearings or washers. Note that if the torque converter has a fixed stator, there will be no one-way or over-running clutch. This can be the case for machines that require high torque but not high-speed operation.

FIGURE 47-11 The outer edge, or wall, of the stator wheel completes the ring formed by the two halves of the split guide ring around which the fluid revolves during vortex flow. **A.** Stator. **B.** Split guide ring. **C.** Outside edge of stator wheel.

Lockup Clutch Assembly

No matter how sophisticated the design, all torque converters allow some inherent slippage between the impeller and the turbine. That is, the impeller can never drive the turbine at engine speed. Speed loss varies but is usually in the neighborhood of 5%. In the past, that level of speed loss was acceptable. The primary focus was on torque multiplication rather than fuel economy and emission control. Today, even that small level of speed loss is not tolerated by both government regulators and equipment operators. Most of today's torque converters are equipped with a lockup clutch designed to lock the turbine to the torque-converter shell and thereby eliminate this slippage and improve fuel economy and emissions.

Lockup clutches usually have the following components:

- A backing plate that is either part of the front of the torque-converter shell or bolted to the shell
- A hydraulic piston that is usually located in the front half of the converter shell
- A friction disc that sits between the backing plate and the piston, as shown in **FIGURE 47-12**

The friction disc will be splined to the turbine. When the piston is actuated hydraulically, it squeezes the friction disc between the piston and the backing plate. That action locks the turbine to the shell, eliminating all slippage.

Torque Dividers

Torque dividers will have all of the same components as torque converters, but they also contain a planetary gear set that allows a split torque input. The torque-converter housing, and therefore the impeller, is driven by the engine flywheel, as it is in a normal torque converter, but the sun gear of the planetary gear set is also driven by the engine flywheel. The turbine in the torque divider is not directly splined to the input shaft of the transmission but rather to the ring gear of the planetary gear set. The carrier of the planetary gear set is connected to the

FIGURE 47-12 A typical lockup clutch used in a truck torque converter. **A.** Disc splines. **B.** Piston. **C.** Friction disc. **D.** Backing plate.

torque-converter output or directly to the transmission input shaft. This gives the torque divider two separate inputs. We will discuss how this operates in detail after we discuss basic torque-converter operation.

▶ Operation of Torque Converters and Torque Dividers

K47003

The first thing we must understand about torque-converter operation is that the converter must be completely filled with fluid to work properly. Any air inside the converter will cause aeration, excess heat, and very poor torque transmission. The torque converter and/or transmission oil-pressure circuits prioritize fluid delivery to the torque converter to ensure it is always full. We will look at the oil-pressure circuits that involve the torque converter a little later on in this chapter.

Rotary Flow and Vortex Flow

The torque-converter shell is driven by the engine crankshaft. Any time the engine is turning, so is the torque-converter shell. Remember that the impeller blades are directly connected to the rear half of the shell, so they also turn with the shell. The blades of the impeller are relatively straight (that is, they are not curved very much). The reason for that shape is that the impeller's job is to act on the mass of transmission fluid inside the torque converter and force the fluid toward the outside of the shell. The rotation of the shell causes **centrifugal force**: the apparent force by which a rotating mass tries to move outward away from its axis of rotation, which acts on the fluid and the blades of the impeller. **FIGURE 47-13** illustrates this centrifugal effect. The rear half of the split guide ring attached to the impeller blades helps to direct and smooth the flow of fluid toward the outside of the housing or shell.

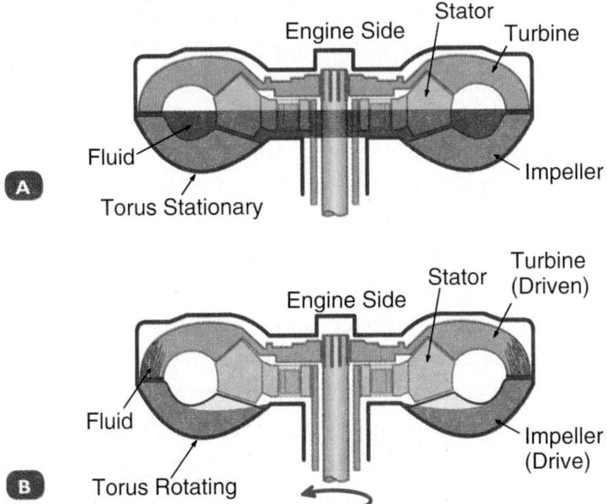

FIGURE 47-13 A. At rest, the converter shell is full of fluid. **B.** As the torque converter shell starts to turn, the centrifugal force throws the oil outward and the torus shape of the impeller forces it forward, toward the turbine.

FIGURE 47-14 Unlike the blades of a fluid coupler or the blades in the impeller, the turbine blades are very sharply angled in order to take advantage of as much of the force from the fluid striking them as possible. **A.** Inlet. **B.** Stator. **C.** Input shaft spline. **D.** Inside edge of outlet.

The torus shape of the rear half of the torque-converter shell uses centrifugal force to redirect the fluid thrown outward by sending the fluid forward toward the blades of the turbine. The blades in the torus-shaped turbine are curved significantly to catch the fluid. The force created by the impeller's rotation is directed against these curved blades, as shown in **FIGURE 47-14**. The curve of the turbine blades and the front half of the split guide ring attached to them help to direct the fluid back toward the center of the impeller.

The turbine is not attached to anything inside the torque converter, but the turbine is splined to the transmission input shaft or the torque converter output. When a machine is fired up in neutral or park, the input shaft will not be physically connected to the driveline. On initial start-up, then, there is no load on the turbine of the torque converter. Consequently, the force of the fluid striking the turbine blades quickly spins the turbine up to almost the speed of the impeller. Both of these elements will turn at close to the same speed because there is nothing to resist the turbine's motion.

The mass of fluid in the torque converter in this scenario would be rotating as a solid circle of fluid traveling in the same direction. The impeller and turbine would be rotating with the converter. This type of fluid dynamic in the torque converter is known as **rotary flow**, which is illustrated in **FIGURE 47-15B**. As soon as a load is placed on the turbine, however, the situation changes. For example, putting the transmission in gear connects the turbine to the machine driveline. Assuming that the machine is at a standstill and the engine is at idle speed, the turbine will immediately come to a stop because it now has a significant load attached to it. That greatly changes the fluid dynamic inside the torque converter. What was a smooth rotary flow instantly changes to a much more turbulent flow, known as **vortex flow**. Vortex flow is the tornado-like flow of oil between the impeller to the turbine through the stator and back again, as illustrated in **FIGURE 47-15A**.

In vortex flow, the fluid being thrown outward by the centrifugal force is again thrown forward by the torus shape of the rear half of the shell. With the turbine stopped, the fluid must

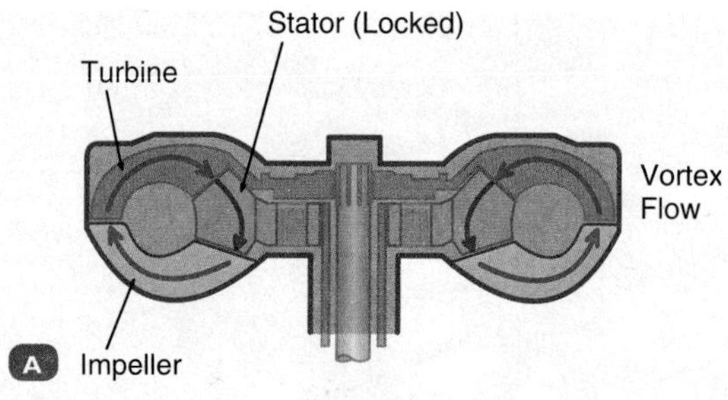

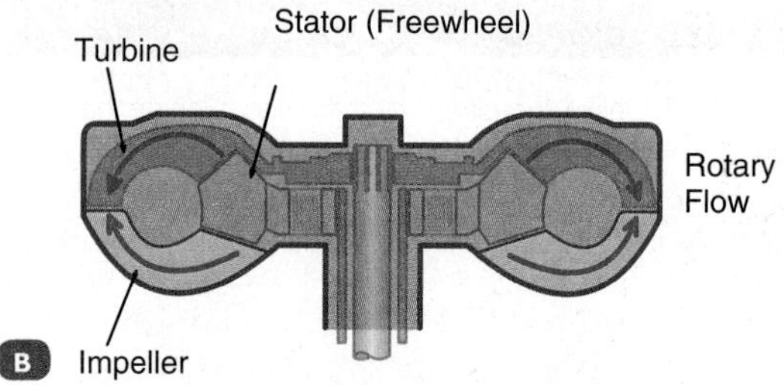

FIGURE 47-15 A. During vortex flow, the fluid flows from the impeller, around the split guide ring, to the turbine, then around the turbine's split guide ring, through the stator, and back to the impeller. **B.** During rotary flow, the fluid travels in a circle that follows the rotation of the converter shell.

flow through the curves of the turbine blades and return to the impeller. The front half of the split guide ring attached to the turbine blades helps to smooth the semicircular flow through the turbine.

The actual flow is as follows. First, the fluid enters the impeller near its center and flows behind the split guide ring to the outside edge, due to the impeller's rotation and centrifugal force. The fluid is then forced forward by the torus shape of the rear housing of the torque converter and enters the turbine at its outside edge. Fluid continues to flow around the curved blades and behind the front half of the split guide ring. The torus forces the fluid rearward, causing the fluid to exit the turbine near the center of the converter and flow back toward the impeller. Because of the sharp curvature of the turbine blades, the fluid exiting the turbine is now flowing in a direction that opposes the impeller's rotation, as shown in **FIGURE 47-16**. In effect, the fluid exiting the turbine is trying to stop the impeller from rotating.

With the machine's transmission in gear and at idle speed, the centrifugal force generated by the rotating impeller is very low. Therefore, the force of the fluid exiting the turbine is also very low and has little effect on the impeller's rotation. Still, as the engine accelerates, both the centrifugal force and the turbine exit force increase greatly. Increasing these forces causes extreme turbulence, excess heat, and very inefficient power transfer, because the engine is trying to drive the impeller at the same time that the fluid exiting the turbine is trying to stop the impeller. To prevent this, the fluid exiting the turbine needs to be redirected so that it helps the power transfer instead of hindering it, as shown in **FIGURE 47-17**. To accomplish this, the center of the torque converter contains a stator placed between the exit area of the turbine and the inlet area of the impeller.

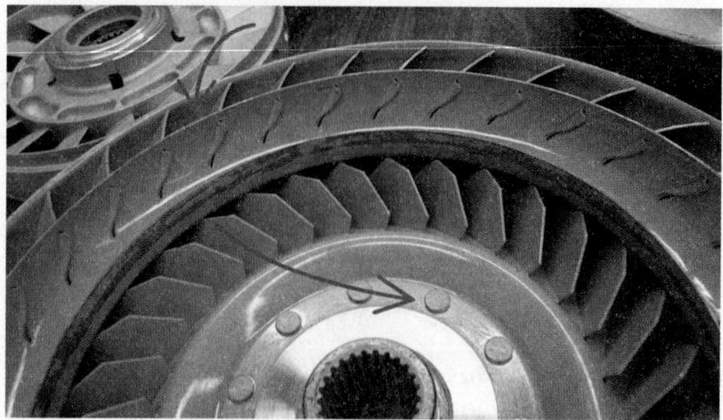

FIGURE 47-16 Fluid exiting the turbine flows in the opposite direction of the impeller's rotation.

FIGURE 47-17 The stator redirects fluid flow so that it re-enters the impeller in the same direction as the impeller rotation. This redirection adds to the effort applied to the turbine.

The stator is a wheel with blades instead of spokes. The outer edge of the wheel completes the inner edge of the circular fluid path formed by the two halves of the split guide rings. The fluid flow corkscrews around this circular tube. The **stator inner hub** is splined to the stator support (ground) shaft, which is part of the transmission front pump assembly. That means that the inner hub cannot turn. The outer hub or wheel of the stator is mounted on an over-running (one-way) clutch that allows the wheel to turn in only one direction. Some equipment applications use fixed stators that do not turn in either direction, but usually the stator is mounted on a one-way clutch.

The "spokes" of the stator wheel are very sharply curved or angled blades. The converter is designed to cause the fluid exiting the turbine during vortex flow to strike the faces of the stator blades. The converter tries to turn the stator with it, but fluid striking the blades in this direction causes the stator wheel to lock on its one-way clutch. The stator remains stationary. The stator blades then sharply redirect the fluid exiting the turbine and cause the fluid to enter the impeller in the same direction that the impeller is turning. The force of the fluid assists the impeller's rotation and increases the amount of torque that the engine is sending to the transmission and driveline.

It is important to realize that the torque converter does not produce torque out of thin air. The torque increase is based on three things: the angles of the turbine blades and the stator blades, and the speed differential between the impeller and the turbine. The angle of the blades in the turbine will determine the exit angle of the fluid and its speed. The angle of the stator blades will determine how much force the fluid will impart on the impeller when it is redirected. The speed difference between the impeller and the turbine will also affect the torque multiplication. Of these three, the speed difference between the impeller and the turbine is the most significant factor in torque multiplication. In a standard transmission, when we gear down, we sacrifice speed for increased torque. In an automatic transmission, the torque converter does the same to increase torque; the impeller must rotate faster than the turbine.

Torque-Converter Operational Phases

Torque converters have two significant operational phases: the torque multiplication phase and the coupling phase. As its name suggests, the torque multiplication phase involves increasing torque output, and there is a significant difference in the high vortex flow and the speed of the impeller and turbine. The coupling phase occurs when the impeller and turbine are close to the same speed and the flow has changed to rotary. Let's examine these phases in more detail.

Torque Multiplication Phase

The **torque multiplication phase** occurs any time the torque converter is increasing the engine's torque output to the transmission's input shaft. Maximum torque multiplication occurs when the engine is accelerated to the maximum speed, at which point it can turn the impeller while the turbine remains stationary. That maximum speed is also known as the torque converter's **stall speed**. The engine cannot turn any faster, because of the resistance provided by the stationary turbine. Reaching the stall speed rarely occurs in normal operation, because the machine will usually start to move before maximum torque multiplication is reached.

Normally, the torque converter will stall only during a stall test procedure where the machine brakes are applied to prevent it from moving or if the machine becomes severely overloaded. Most torque converters are set up to have a torque multiplication factor of around 2:1 to 3:1. Recall that torque multiplication is primarily based on speed difference between the turbine and the impeller. Therefore, torque converters with higher torque multiplication typically have higher stall speeds. Within certain limitations, stall speeds and the torque multiplication factor can be manipulated in the design stage by changing the size of the torque-converter elements, the angle of the turbine blades, the angle of the stator blades, and the clearance between the elements. A high-stall or high-torque-multiplication torque converter can be excellent for picking up heavy loads. A lower-stall torque converter is usually more suitable for high-speed operation.

Over the years, manufacturers have used many torque-converter designs to optimize vehicle operation. For example, converters with **variable pitch stators** allow the angle of the stator blades to be changed hydraulically to benefit both starting-off and high-speed operation. Converters with twin stators achieve much the same effect, and converters with two or even three turbines fine-tune torque-converter performance and produce the optimal torque multiplication for the application.

In normal operation, starting from a stop with the machine in gear, the impeller is turning at engine speed. At this idle speed, the force of the fluid striking the turbine blades is insufficient to start turning the turbine very much. The force may be enough to start turbine creep, causing the machine to move forward slightly and the operator to apply the brakes to hold the vehicle stationary. As the operator increases the throttle, the speed of the impeller increases, as does the fluid force pushing against the turbine blades. This force is redirected by the stator to assist the impeller's rotation, increasing the force again. This force will continue to increase with engine speed. The torque converter will multiply the torque from the engine within its design limitations until the machine starts to move. The amount of torque actually necessary to move the machine will depend on grade, load, and other factors. It is important to note that, as soon as the turbine starts to turn and the vehicle begins moving, the torque multiplication factor starts to drop. It will continue to drop as the turbine speed increases and the speed difference between the impeller and turbine becomes smaller.

Vortex oil flow—the flow of fluid from the impeller, through the turbine, through the stator, and then back to the impeller—occurs at all times during torque-converter operation but is greatest at peak torque multiplication. That is, vortex flow is greatest at the converter stall speed, as illustrated in **FIGURE 47-18**. As the turbine speed increases, vortex flow—and therefore torque multiplication—decreases. In effect, while in operation, the torque converter has an almost unlimited number of torque multiplication ratios—from its design maximum to zero torque multiplication.

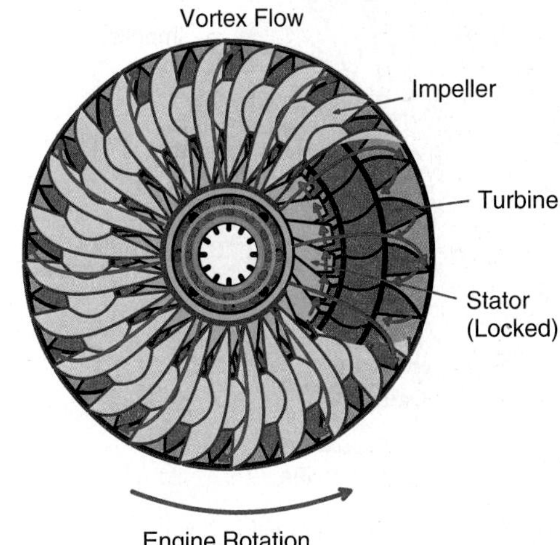

FIGURE 47-18 Vortex flow is greatest at full stall and decreases as the turbine speed catches up to the impeller's speed.

Coupling Phase

During the torque multiplication phase of torque-converter operation, vortex fluid flow kept the stator held stationary on its one-way clutch to help multiply torque. As the speed of the turbine approaches the speed of the impeller, the fluid flow changes. Most of the fluid no longer exits the turbine near its center. In fact, the turbine starts to impart centrifugal force on the fluid present in its torus and starts to force the fluid back the way it came toward the impeller. At this stage, the vortex fluid flow slows down and nearly stops in the converter. Very little fluid is flowing through the turbine blades. Most of the fluid follows the rotation of the torque-converter shell. Torque-converter operation has now entered the **coupling phase**, illustrated in **FIGURE 47-19**. The fluid inside the converter is basically a solid donut-shaped mass of fluid rotating in the same direction and at nearly the same speed as the converter itself (that is, rotary fluid flow). In the coupling phase, however, the stationary stator we used in the torque multiplication phase would now be in the way and would restrict this rotary flow and cause extreme turbulence.

This is the reason that the stator is mounted on an over-running (one-way) clutch. When rotary flow starts to take over inside the converter, the flow of fluid starts to hit the stator blades from the back, which unlocks the stator one-way clutch and allows the stator to turn freely in the direction of the fluid. The stator is mounted on either a sprag-type one-way clutch, as shown in **FIGURE 47-20A**, or a roller-type one-way clutch, as shown in **FIGURE 47-20B**, so that it locks in one direction and can freewheel in the other. A sprag-type one-way clutch uses a series of peanut-shaped sprags that are specially designed so that they allow rotation in only one direction. A roller-type one-way clutch uses rollers and ramps that cause the rollers to jam and lock up if they try to turn in the reverse direction.

The stator wheel is unlocked only during the coupling phase. During the coupling phase, the impeller, the turbine, the stator, and the fluid are all turning together at essentially the same speed. Also in this phase, vortex flow in the converter has almost ceased, and rotary flow is at maximum. There is always some fluid flowing around with the converter shell, so some rotary flow is always present, but it is at its maximum level at the coupling phase and at its minimum level at converter stall.

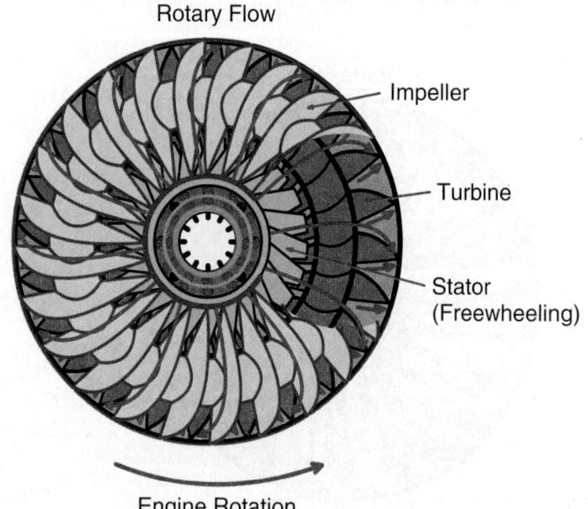

FIGURE 47-19 Rotary flow is greatest during the coupling phase, when the fluid and the three converter elements—the turbine, the stator, and the impeller—are all turning in the same direction at nearly the same speeds.

FIGURE 47-20 A. Sprag-type one-way clutch with sprags showing. **B.** Roller-type one-way clutch with rollers and ramps.

The coupling phase is related to torque demand and not to speed. That means the coupling phase can happen at any speed. For example, consider a normal operation cycle. An operator moves off from a standstill, and is aggressive on the throttle. What happens? The torque-converter impeller speeds up instantly with the engine, and the converter enters the torque multiplication phase. Vortex flow is high because there is a significant difference between the impeller and the turbine speed. Even though vortex flow and torque multiplication are very high, it is not at maximum torque multiplication, because the turbine starts to turn right away to move the machine. Remember that maximum torque multiplication occurs only at the torque-converter stall speed. The stator is locked and redirecting fluid to contribute to the torque multiplication.

The operator continues to increase speed when they remember that they forgot lunch, so the operator reduces throttle immediately. The engine speed and the impeller speed will decrease until both are close to the turbine speed. The torque converter will enter the coupling phase of operation in which the impeller and turbine will be turning at close to the same speed. Torque multiplication and vortex flow will have all but ceased, and rotary flow is now predominant in the converter. The stator will be freewheeling with the fluid. The operator realizes they can go back for their lunch later, so they push hard on the throttle once again, and then the impeller speed instantly increases, locking the stator and returning the converter to high vortex flow and torque multiplication.

As you can imagine, this scenario changes constantly, based on the demand for torque or acceleration. In most operating cycles, the torque converter will be constantly switching from the torque multiplication phase to the coupling phase and back again. The torque converter, then, is an automatic device that changes the torque multiplication factor within its design limit based on operator demand.

Note that converters in some slow-moving machines will use a fixed stator that does not freewheel and is always stationary. In these machines, high-speed operation is not a concern, so the stator is solidly mounted to the stator support shaft and cannot turn in either direction. The torque-converter elements in such machines are designed for high torque multiplication and low-speed operation only.

Flex Plates

Engine flywheels have several important functions: They provide inertia to keep the engine running between its power impulses; the weight of the flywheel helps to absorb torsional vibrations from the engine; and they provide a place to mount the ring gear to start the engine. Some lighter applications will use the mass of the converter to replace a traditional flywheel, while heavier applications will still require a flywheel. Regardless, the torque converter cannot be coupled directly to the engine crankshaft or to the flywheel.

When the torque converter is under heavy loads (while multiplying torque), its shell actually swells and contracts slightly. The fluid exerts a force over the large surface area of the converter shell to create these expansion-and-contraction cycles. The swelling is very slight, but over time the constant fatigue or bending forces caused by this swelling would cause the converter shell or the mounting bolts to fracture and break if it were mounted solidly to the flywheel or crankshaft. To avoid that type of failure, the converter can be bolted to an individual flex plate or a series of flex plates, as shown in **FIGURE 47-21**, which in turn are bolted to the crankshaft or flywheel. Alternately, the torque converter is not bolted to the flywheel at all and instead is driven by splines inside a pot-shaped flywheel.

In lighter machines, the flex plate can be a single plate of flexible steel bolted directly to the crankshaft. The single flex plate may also have the ring gear for starting the engine welded to it. (If the ring gear is not on the flex plate, it may be attached to the converter itself.) The converter will be bolted to the outside of the flex plate. The weight of the converter supplies the inertia to keep the engine running and smooth out the power pulses.

FIGURE 47-21 Flex plates bolted to a flywheel for use in heavy-duty vehicles.

In heavier applications, the engine flywheel is still used to create sufficient inertia, and the ring gear is attached to it. The torque converter is typically bolted to a stack of several flexible steel plates, which in turn are bolted to the flywheel. Both methods allow the converter to flex as necessary during its operation.

If the torque converter is not bolted to the flywheel, the torque converter will be entirely supported by its housing and merely splined to the engine flywheel, as shown in **FIGURE 47-22**. This allows the converter to move in the splines as necessary.

Lockup Clutch Operation

A torque-converter impeller is incapable of driving the turbine at 100% of impeller (engine) speed. There will always be some amount of slippage involved. The amount of slippage is determined by many factors: The design of the turbine and impeller blades, the clearance between the torque-converter elements, the viscosity of the fluid, and more can affect the amount of slippage. That slippage can cause speed differences from 5% to 10%. To compensate for that slippage, most modern torque converters are equipped with a lockup clutch to lock

FIGURE 47-22 This type of torque converter is driven directly by matching splines on the engine flywheel.

FIGURE 47-23 The three components of a lockup clutch assembly. **A.** Backing plate. **B.** Piston. **C.** Clutch disc.

the turbine to the converter shell. Such locking eliminates the inherent slippage and provides a 1:1 drive between the impeller and the turbine.

The lockup clutch usually consists of the three basic components, as shown in **FIGURE 47-23**:

- A hydraulic clutch piston is secured to the torque-converter shell so that it cannot rotate.
- A friction disc is splined to the converter turbine. (Note that in some lighter applications, the lockup clutch friction disc and piston may be combined as one unit.)
- A backing plate is also secured, usually by bolts, to the converter shell. (In some models, the backing plate is a machined surface on the inside of the front half of the converter shell.)

When lockup is desired, hydraulic pressure is directed to the back of the piston to squeeze the friction disc against the backing plate. All slippage is stopped, and the turbine turns at the same speed as the shell (that is, at engine speed). **FIGURE 47-24** contains a cross-sectional view of a lockup clutch system.

FIGURE 47-24 A cross section of a lockup torque converter. **A.** Backing plate. **B.** Turbine. **C.** Impeller. **D.** Piston. **E.** Friction disc. **F.** Stator.

There are two basic control strategies for lockup. The first is **programmed (systematic) lockup**. The second is **modulated lockup**. In the first type of lockup strategy, the transmission controller engages lockup every time the transmission reaches a certain gear range. That occurs whether the transmission controller is hydraulic or electronic. The achieved gear range may be as low as second range. Lockup will then be engaged in every range except first. For that reason, the programmed lockup strategy is usually the best regarding fuel economy and, therefore, carbon dioxide emission. This is the most common strategy used in MORE.

The second strategy, namely modulated lockup, is performance based. With this strategy, the transmission will enter lockup at any time—even in first range—as long as certain criteria are met. For example, the transmission usually must be in second range or higher. The operator should not be trying to accelerate rapidly, and the torque converter should be nearing coupling phase. (In other words, the turbine speed is close to the impeller speed.)

When these criteria have been met, the controller may engage the lockup clutch. If any of these criteria changes—for example, if the operator increases throttle to accelerate the machine or if there is a demand for more torque—the lockup clutch will usually disengage. Torque multiplication will then be allowed to occur again. Modulated lockup is not commonly found in off-road machines, but it may sometimes be available in emergency equipment. With modulated lockup, there is no specific time when the lockup clutch will always be engaged.

One of the functions of lockup clutches is to reduce operational waste. That reduction is increasingly important because the Environmental Protection Agency (EPA) has mandated reducing limits for noxious emissions. The next challenge for engine and equipment manufacturers is to reduce the emission of carbon dioxide. The only way to reduce the production of carbon dioxide while burning hydrocarbon fuels is to reduce the amount of fuel consumed. So, manufacturers are pulling out all the stops in terms of maximizing engine thermal efficiencies and minimizing any parasitic load on the engine. Lockup clutches are one way to minimize wasted energy in the driveline.

Torque Divider Operation

As mentioned earlier, a torque divider is a torque converter with a planetary gear added to split the input torque to the transmission. At the front of the torque divider, there are two splines in series: the first spline inputs the sun gear of the planetary gear in the torque divider, and the second spline drives the housing of the torque-converter component of the torque divider. **FIGURE 47-25** shows the sun gear removed from the torque divider.

At the front of the torque divider is the planetary carrier of the gear set, which is the only part of the torque divider actually connected to the input shaft of the transmission (it is the output from the torque divider). The planetary ring gear is also at the front of the torque divider housing and is attached to the turbine of the torque-converter portion of the divider. Other than the addition of the planetary gear set, the torque divider has the same components as a regular torque converter: the impeller,

FIGURE 47-25 The engine flywheel has internal splines that drive both the torque-converter portion and the planetary sun gear of a torque divider.

turbine, and stator. The stator of the torque divider can be fixed, or it can be mounted on a one-way clutch. Most torque dividers use a fixed stator that does not rotate. The divider can also be equipped with a torque-converter lockup clutch, though it is not common. The function of the torque-converter part of the divider is almost identical to the regular torque converter, but there are a couple of significant differences, which will be discussed in the following paragraphs. **FIGURE 47-26** shows a cutaway drawing of a torque divider.

The torque divider functions as follows: on start-up with the machine in park or neutral, the internal spline on the engine flywheel inputs both the sun gear of the torque divider's planetary gear and the housing of the torque converter. Because there is no load, the output of the torque divider, the planetary sun gear, the carrier, the ring gear, the torque-converter impeller, the turbine, and the stator (if it is mounted on a one-way clutch) will all be turning at close to the same speed.

In this scenario, the torque-converter part of the torque divider is in coupling phase with the turbine turning at close to engine speed and because the turbine is connected to the ring gear of the planetary gear set it is also turning at approximately engine speed. The sun gear of the planetary gear set is splined to the engine flywheel so that it too is turning at engine speed. This gives the planetary gear set two inputs at or near engine speed, which causes the carrier of the planetary gear to also turn at engine speed. And because the carrier is connected to the output of the torque divider, the input shaft of the transmission will be turning at close to engine speed. Because the transmission is not in gear, the power does not go further than the input shaft. The oil flow in the torque converter is almost 100% rotary at this time. This dynamic may change slightly if the stator in the torque divider is fixed. The stationary stator will cause some turbulence, and the turbine may be slightly slower than engine speed. When the operator selects a gear, there is an immediate load placed on the transmission's input shaft, because it is now connected to the driveline of the machine, and the fluid flows inside the torque divider change right away.

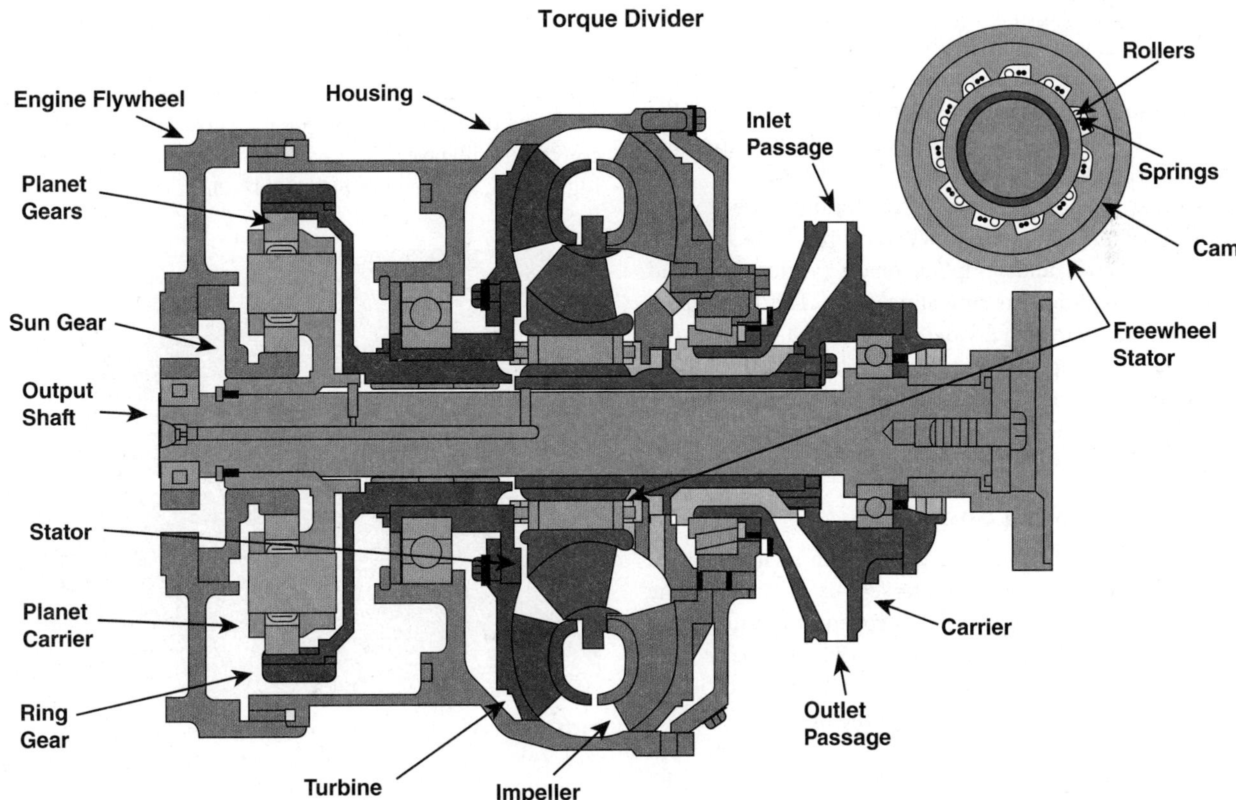

FIGURE 47-26 In a torque divider, both the torque converter shell and the sun gear of the planetary gear set are driven by the flywheel.

First, the planetary carrier of the gear set will stop because it is connected directly or indirectly to the transmission input. This places a heavy load on the ring gear of the gear set and therefore the turbine of the torque converter, causing the turbine to stop and changing the oil flow to vortex. The vortex flow will cause the stator to stop on its one-way clutch (if equipped). Because the input to the planetary gear set of the divider is mechanical with the carrier stopped by the vehicle weight, the ring gear and therefore the turbine of the converter attached to it will be turning in reverse at approximately one-third to one-half engine speed. The planetary pinions in the carrier will be turning counterclockwise. Because the converter's oil flow gives little resistance to the counter-rotating turbine (because the engine is at idle), the machine will typically not move, depending on the exact circumstances.

As the operator applies the throttle, the impeller will increase the force of the oil acting against the turbine, which will slow its rotation and therefore the ring gear's rotation. The increasing effort required to turn the ring gear counterclockwise (caused by the oil forces pushing against the turbine) causes the ring gear to start acting as the held member of the planetary gear set, making the carrier become the output member. Because the carrier is connected to the output of the torque converter, this causes the machine to move. As the throttle increases, the ring gear slows and then starts to turn in the normal direction (usually clockwise from the front).

This then gives the planetary gear set two inputs: one from the sun gear and the other from the turbine/ring gear, causing the carrier to speed up. This arrangement gives the driveline two inputs: a mechanical one through the gear set and a hydrodynamic one through the torque converter. The overall power output of the power divider is typically 30% mechanical and 70% hydrodynamic. Like all other torque-converter systems, there will always be some loss of output speed and power through the power divider, so when conditions are correct, the lockup clutch (if equipped) will apply in order to eliminate losses.

Depending on the operating conditions, the torque divider's torque converter will switch back and forth between torque multiplication and coupling phase (vortex flow and rotary flow) throughout the operating cycle. The two inputs and the ability of the torque divider's turbine and therefore the planetary gear sets ring gear to turn backward when required to give the torque divider very smooth operating characteristics, especially when the machine changes the direction and/or encounters heavy loads.

Torque Divider Stall Speed

Because the turbine in the torque divider can turn backward before enough force—as rpm increases—is created by the oil flow to turn it clockwise, the stall speed of the machine/torque divider combination can be elusive. The true stall speed of these combinations occurs just as there is sufficient force on the fluid to turn the turbine in the normal direction. The stall speed of a torque divider will be the engine rpm when the turbine first starts to turn clockwise. This can be difficult to determine in the field unless there is a sure-fire way to determine turbine speed.

▶ Torque-Converter and Torque-Divider Hydraulic Circuits

K47004

Any torque converter, including the torque-converter portion of a torque divider, must be completely full of fluid in order to operate properly. The transmission hydraulic system prioritizes fluid delivery to the converter. In most torque-converter installations, manufacturers take advantage of the direct connection between the torque converter and the transmission. The hydraulic pump at the front of the transmission is driven by the pump drive hub that is attached to the back of the torque converter. As soon as the engine turns, the pump starts pressurizing fluid. As pressure builds, one of the first places the fluid is directed to is the torque converter. Directing fluid from a stationary transmission to a rotating torque converter is accomplished by using a passage that is formed between the pump drive hub attached to the converter shell and the stator support or ground shaft, which enters the converter from the rear. This passage is shown in **FIGURE 47-27**. Fluid is sent through this passage and enters at the center of the torque converter behind the stator. There, it fills the impeller blades and flows forward toward the turbine to fill its blades as well. The exit passage for the fluid is formed between the inside of the stator support shaft and the outside of the input or turbine shaft. The space between these two shafts provides the exit passage for the fluid.

As the fluid pressure from the transmission pump builds in the torque converter, the fluid is delivered to the point where the input shaft exits the stator support shaft. That point is just behind the splines that fit into the turbine. The fluid exits through the inside of the stator support shaft.

In other torque-converter arrangements where the torque converter is remote from the transmission, either the fluid is delivered directly to the torque-converter housing or the torque converter will have a designated oil reservoir and its own pumping system, as shown in **FIGURE 47-28**.

FIGURE 47-27 The arrangement of the different shafts that enter the torque converter from the transmission form passageways that can be used to deliver fluid to and from the converter and to the lockup clutch. **A.** Lockup clutch apply passage. **B.** Converter out passageway. **C.** Converter in passageway.

FIGURE 47-28 This torque converter has its own pump and designated inlet and outlet passages for the fluid.

FIGURE 47-29 The lockup clutch components. **A.** The hydraulic passageway for clutch application. **B.** The turbine front support bushing. **C.** The lockup clutch disc spline that connects to the turbine. **D.** The lockup clutch piston is splined to the converter shell. **E.** The lockup clutch backing plate is bolted to the converter housing.

In most conventional torque converters where the converter is attached to the transmission directly, the fluid pathway in the transmission that leads to the torque converter has a pressure-relief valve to restrict converter maximum working pressure. The fluid pathway also features **anti-drain-back check valves** that ensure the fluid does not drain back out of the torque converter when the vehicle is shut off. The exit passage from the converter also includes check valves to try to keep the converter full of fluid even when the machine is not running. The torque converter places enormous load and shear forces on the transmission fluid that in turn create tremendous amounts of heat.

That heat must be dissipated, so the first place the fluid goes on exiting the torque converter is usually the **transmission oil cooler**. In the transmission oil cooler the fluid flows through oil passages or tubes that are surrounded by recirculating engine coolant. As the fluid flows through the cooler, the heat is absorbed by the coolant. The fluid then exits the cooler and is returned to the transmission sump for recirculation. The converter in and out hydraulic circuits normally supply the transmission lubrication circuits. Typically, the front components of the transmission are lubricated from a passage intersecting the converter fluid-in circuit. A third passage is usually needed in the converter in order to supply the hydraulic pressure for the lockup clutch piston application if equipped. Most manufacturers use a drilled hole in the center of the input shaft to create this passage. The input shaft is usually cross-drilled at a point where it passes through the rear of the hydraulic pump. That point will be sealed between two nylon or steel sealing rings.

The apply pressure for the lockup clutch is delivered to this point and then travels up the input shaft center drilling to the hydraulic passageway for clutch application, as shown in **FIGURE 47-29**. This apply pressure flows to the front of the **lockup clutch piston**, pushing it rearward so that it squeezes the **lockup clutch disc** between the piston and the backing plate. That action locks the disc to the converter shell and thereby eliminates turbine slip.

The process just described is the most common method for hydraulic circuits to apply lockup clutches in heavy-duty applications. Lighter-duty machines may use a different method of applying the lockup clutch. In these transmissions, the lockup clutch piston and the friction disc are combined, as shown in **FIGURE 47-30**. This saves manufacturing costs associated with forming a cylinder inside the torque converter in which the lockup clutch apply piston can operate.

The transmission fluid flows from the input shaft and around the outside of the lockup clutch/piston assembly to the rear of the torque converter. This flow of fluid is sufficient to push and hold the **lockup clutch/piston assembly** rearward and away from the front of the converter housing, keeping the lockup clutch disengaged. To engage the lockup clutch, the transmission control system reverses the converter fluid flow direction. With the fluid flowing from the back of the torque converter to the front, the fluid catches the formed edge of the lockup clutch/piston assembly and pushes it forward. The fluid pressure squeezes the lockup clutch/piston assembly against the inside of the converter shell. That motion locks the turbine to the shell. While the torque converter is in lockup mode, the

FIGURE 47-30 A converter that uses a combination piston and clutch plate. **A.** Lockup clutch/piston assembly. **B.** Front housing. **C.** Friction material.

FIGURE 47-31 Lockup clutch disc with torsional dampening.

fluid does not circulate through the converter—it only applies pressure to the lockup clutch. Turning off converter fluid flow when it is not required reduces parasitic loss due to pumping the fluid through the torque converter. Remember that in lockup mode, the converter is not generating any heat. To disengage the clutch, the control system again reverses the flow and the piston/clutch assembly releases.

Most of the lockup clutches in use today incorporate a spring-loaded torsional damper hub to absorb the damaging torsional vibrations created by power pulsations from the engine. These can be very simple spring dampers or more elaborate models that use coaxial springs, as shown in **FIGURE 47-31**. Some dampers even use internal friction dampening similar to those used on mechanical clutches. Without dampers, the power pulsations from the engine would be transmitted directly to both the transmission and the rest of the driveline when the torque-converter lockup clutch is applied. Those torsional vibrations can cause catastrophic damage to driveline components.

▶ Troubleshooting Torque-Converter Failure

K47005

Torque converters are ruggedly constructed and should last the expected service life of the machine. Torque converters will not, however, stand up to serial abuse, such as high-speed direction changes and severe overloading.

Both the transmission and the torque converter are hydraulic devices, and they will not function without fluid. Before trying to diagnose any problem with the converter or the transmission, ensure that fluid level is correct.

There are a number of failures that can occur in the torque converter alone, and they usually fall into three categories: noise, lockup clutch issues, and performance. Noise complaints are usually caused by bearing or thrust washer failures. Lockup clutch complaints are usually precipitated by either failure to engage or failure to disengage or shudder on engagement. Performance complaints, such as no power on take-off or the machine being sluggish at speed, usually indicate stator problems. Regardless of the complaint, confirm that the engine performance is not to blame before condemning a torque converter.

Converter noise complaints are relatively easy to diagnose because they tend to show up only when the machine is placed in gear. When the transmission is in neutral or park, the converter elements are typically rotating at or near the same speed because there is no load on the turbine. As soon as a load is connected to the torque-converter output, the turbine will come to a stop. At that point, its supporting bearings will start to turn. If the noise begins at that point, the bearings are likely the source of the complaint. During converter operation, if the noise ceases when the lockup clutch engages, this could indicate failed thrust bearing or washers. Whining noises that seem to emanate from the converter but that do not change usually indicate one or more of the following:

- Transmission front pump problems (direct-mounted torque converters)
- Wear in the converter pump drive hub bushing (excessive wear here is normally accompanied by a transmission fluid leak from the front pump seal)
- Wear in the front pump gearing (direct-mounted torque converters)
- Aeration problems that can cause cavitation and rapid destruction of the converter or the transmission oil pump

Aeration of the transmission fluid can be caused by one of two extremes. On the one hand, when the fluid level is too low, air is drawn in to the pump. On the other, when the fluid level is too high, the rotating components of the transmission can contact the fluid. What happens is like a kitchen mixer—the rotating components churn up the fluid and mix in significant amounts of air. Proper fluid level is always essential.

▶ TECHNICIAN TIP

Aeration of the fluid or cavitation of the front pump cause an extremely loud whining that can be mistaken as front pump or bushing failure. The sound is similar to a power steering system that is low on fluid. If you hear whining, always check the fluid level and condition before condemning any components.

On some machines, lockup clutch engagement and disengagement can be monitored by carefully observing engine rpm during an operation cycle. As the lockup clutch engages, engine rpm will drop on clutch engagement and increase when the clutch disengages. Failure of the lockup clutch or disc will normally cause the transmission fluid to discolor from excessive heat and burned clutch material.

Manufacturers use specific fluids for their transmissions and torque converters. These fluids may include friction modifiers, and using the wrong fluid can cause converter clutch issues and can also cause the power-shift transmission's hydraulic clutches to not engage properly. Always use the fluid recommended by the original equipment manufacturer (OEM) or its equivalent. If lockup clutch disengagement is the problem, it will manifest itself as a stall condition or almost stall as the machine is brought to stop. In that case, careful examination of the lockup control circuit must be conducted to determine whether the problem is on the control side or is an internal torque-converter problem. To diagnose torque-converter complaints that may involve stator operation, both a stall test and an operation cycle test are required.

▶ Torque-Converter and Torque-Divider Testing

S47001

The most common diagnostic test on torque converters and/or torque dividers is the stall test. The stall test procedure can be used to determine engine, torque converter, and transmission performance. It is very commonly the first test a technician will perform when diagnosing transmission or converter complaints. The stall test procedure is very straightforward, but there are some preparatory steps that must be undertaken. Also, prior to conducting a stall test, check the particular manufacturer's specifications for the specific transmission model so that the test is carried out properly. The following stall test procedure is from Caterpillar and used on their 980K wheel loader, but most manufacturers will have similar guidelines to stall test their machines. To conduct a stall test, follow the guidelines in **SKILL DRILL 47-1**.

▶ Servicing Torque Converters

S47002

Light-duty torque converters are not designed to be serviceable, since the two halves of the converter shell are welded together. It is common, however, in the aftermarket for these converters to

SKILL DRILL 47-1 Conducting a Stall Test

Refer to the factory test procedure to determine the proper specification for the machine that is being tested. If the machine that is being serviced not within the range of listed engine stall speed, the powertrain components should be checked to determine the proper corrective action. Stall test specifications should not be used to reset engine power output of the machine. If engine output power is deemed to be the problem, the engine should be tested to determine the low-power issue.

The torque-converter stall test helps ascertain whether the engine is producing the correct power output and whether the torque converter is functioning as designed. The torque-converter stall test provides an engine speed that should be obtained with the torque converter at stall and is set at the factory. The engine stall speed should be in the listed range shown for the particular machine.

The parking brake must be applied when the tests are performed. Make sure that the parking brake is fully operational before starting the stall test.

The service brakes must be applied when the tests are performed. Ensure that the service brakes are fully operational before starting the stall test.

Ensure that the transmission oil is at the normal operating temperature of 75–105°C (167–220°F) when the stall test is performed.

Sudden movement of the machine could lead to personal injury or the death of the technician and/or other personnel near the machine. To prevent such injury or death, ensure that the area around the machine is clear of personnel and obstructions before operating the machine.

Use the following procedure to conduct a stall test:

1. Move the machine to a smooth horizontal location.
2. Engage the parking brake and shift the transmission to the NEUTRAL position.
3. Start the machine's engine and warm the transmission oil to normal operating temperature: approximately 75–105°C (167–220°F).
4. Check and, if necessary, adjust the fluid level.
5. Ensure that the work tool is positioned on the ground.
6. Fully depress the right-side service brake pedal. (The left-side brake pedal is used to neutralize the transmission clutches and should not be used for this test.)
7. Shift the transmission direction control and speed control to the FOURTH SPEED FORWARD position. Hold the brake pedal in the depressed position for the duration of the test.
8. Fully depress the throttle control pedal. Allow the engine rpm to stabilize. Then, observe the tachometer. The correct torque-converter stall speed for the 980K wheel loader is 2185 ± 65 rpm.
9. Shift the transmission direction control and speed control to the NEUTRAL position.

   Note: Allow the engine coolant and the transmission oil to cool. Wait at least two minutes between tests in order to allow the transmission oil to cool. If the oil fails to cool, other conditions could exist: the stator may be seized in the converter, or the engine cooling system may be compromised.

   If the torque-converter stall speed is too high, the engine power output could be too high or a hydraulic clutch in the transmission could be slipping.
10. If the torque-converter stall speed is too low, the engine may not be developing full power. There may be a parasitic load on the engine.
11. If stall speed is very low—600–800 rpm lower than specification—the stator could be freewheeling in the converter. This condition can cause extreme turbulence in the converter, resulting in very low engine speed.

be overhauled by cutting them open and then re-welding them after replacing worn components. This is not recommended by most manufacturers.

Servicing these welded shell torque converters is limited to checking turbine end play and clearances to specification and to testing for leaks. If the welded converters meet these specifications, they can probably be reused, but unfortunately, most automatic transmission failures tend to be catastrophic. So the converter may be full of debris from the failure. Almost no amount of flushing will completely remove this debris; therefore, most manufacturers recommend that light-duty converters that cannot be disassembled for cleaning be replaced during transmission overhaul.

In contrast, heavy-duty torque converters are designed to be rebuilt and are bolted together to facilitate this process. The overhaul procedures described in this section are general in nature and refer to most—but not all—heavy-duty torque converters. Always consult the manufacturer's manual for the correct procedure. The end play and leakage tests performed on heavy-duty torque converters are the same as those performed on light-duty torque converters.

▶ TECHNICIAN TIP

Removing the torque converter can be as simple as pulling it forward out of the front of the removed transmission. Some transmissions, though, have the torque converter bolted to or otherwise fastened to the transmission. Allison transmissions, for example, have a bolt located under a plug in the front cover pilot of the torque converter, as shown in **FIGURE 47-32**. This bolt must be removed in order to remove the torque converters. Always have the correct service procedure for the torque converter/transmission being serviced.

The torque converters used in large machines can be extremely heavy. Care must be taken when removing them from

FIGURE 47-32 The bolt that secures the torque converter turbine to the input shaft in the Allison World Transmission.

the transmission. Use a crane and a sling when possible, to avoid injury. To disassemble a torque converter, follow the steps in **SKILL DRILL 47-2**. To inspect the parts after disassembly, follow the guidelines in **SKILL DRILL 47-3**.

Reassembling the Torque Converter

After all of the components have been checked and verified to be in working order, clean all components and reassemble the torque converter by reversing the order of disassembly. Replace the lockup clutch piston seal and the converter shell O-ring seal, as shown in **FIGURE 47-33**. It is also a good idea to replace the roller bearings that axially locate the turbine because it is far cheaper than having to redo the job at a later date.

Special care is needed while reinstalling the lockup piston. Most pistons have locating pins or splines that stop the piston

SKILL DRILL 47-2 Disassembling a Torque Converter

1. Place the torque converter on a bench with a drainage system. When the converter is disassembled, there will be a significant amount of transmission fluid inside, so be prepared for that.
2. Before removing the bolts, mark the two halves of the shell so that it can be reassembled in the exact same location. The converter elements are usually individually balanced, but it always makes sense to reinstall the halves the way that they came apart.
3. Check the turbine end play dimension before disassembly. This will allow you to correct any deficiencies when you have it apart. This is accomplished by inserting a special tool that grabs the turbine and allows you to lift it. Measure the total movement and calculate the shims required to bring it to specification.
4. Remove the converter bolts (there may be as many as 50). Remove the rear half from the rest of the converter. Although it is the lighter half, it is still quite heavy, so be careful. You may need to tap the shell with a dead-blow hammer to separate the halves. When they are apart, discard the sealing O-ring. Remove the stator and the thrust washers/bearings that support it, and then remove the turbine.
5. Next, remove the lockup clutch backing plate, if equipped. It may be sandwiched between the front and the rear half of the shell, or it may be bolted into the front half of the converter housing. Remove the lockup clutch disc, and finally remove the lockup clutch piston. It should be marked in a way that indicates its position in the converter shell. To remove the piston, apply a small amount of air pressure to the piston apply side.

SKILL DRILL 47-3 Inspecting Torque-Converter Components

1. Inspect both the impeller and the turbine for damaged or loose blades. Inspect the two halves of the split guide ring to ensure that they are firmly attached to the impeller and the turbine blades. Any looseness in the blades fails the component. Further inspect the turbine, locating bearing surfaces for any signs of wear or damage. If necessary, replace the turbine.
2. Check the bushing in the front cover of the converter shell that supports the turbine or the end of the input shaft (depending on converter). Replace as necessary. Inspect the turbine thrust washers or bearings and replace as necessary.
3. Inspect the rear half of the converter shell. Look for any impact damage or leaks. Inspect the pump drive hub surface for wear where it is supported in the front pump of the transmission. If wear is present, it usually means that the shell and the front pump bushing need to be replaced. Pay particular attention to the surface of the hub where the front pump seal runs. The seal can cut a groove into the hub, which may cause a leak. Wear here will usually require replacement of the shell.
4. Inspect the bearing surface between the turbine and the front of the converter shell. Damage here would require replacing the parts.
5. Inspect the roller bearing or washers behind the turbine that locate it axially and replace as necessary.
6. Check the stator for movement. It should move freely in one direction and not at all in the other (unless it is a fixed stator). If it moves even slightly in the opposite direction, it must be repaired or replaced.
7. Remove the one-way clutch cover from the stator and inspect the rollers, the springs, and the ramp surfaces. Also, inspect the inner hub for scoring and the bearing thrust faces. Replace components as necessary. Carefully inspect the roller ramp area of the one-way clutch for cracks or surface damage caused by high-speed direction changes.
8. Inspect the lockup clutch piston and backing plate for signs of overheating, bluing, heat checks, etc. Inspect the clutch disc by measuring the remaining friction material and comparing it to the manufacturer's specifications. If the disc has a dampened hub, check the dampening springs for looseness.

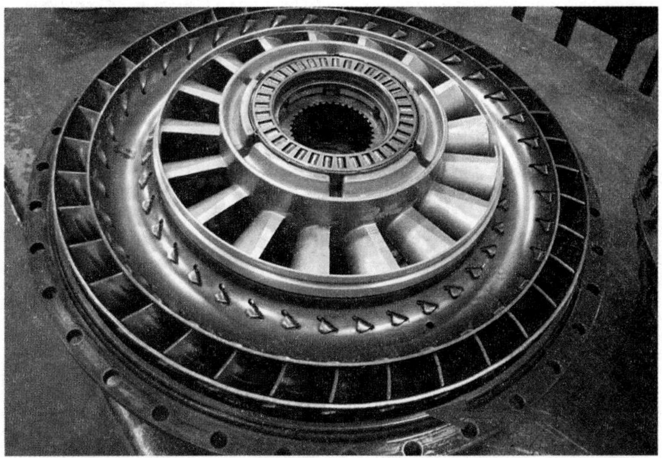

FIGURE 47-33 Take extra care to ensure the O-rings (indicated) are not damaged during installation.

FIGURE 47-34 This special tool locks to the turbine so that it can be pulled up against a dial indicator to measure the end play.

from rotating when the clutch applies. Ensure that the piston fits over the locating pins properly. Note the manufacturer's recommend reassembly without the use of any grease, because some greases could clog fluid passages or interfere with valve action in transmission control. Only a light coating of the fluid type being used for the transmission should be used.

Turbine End Play and Torque-Converter Leak Checks

After reassembly, there are two checks that should be made. The first check is turbine end play. Two methods are commonly used to check this. In the first method, the torque converter is placed face down on a bench, and a special tool that expands to grab the splines of the turbine is installed, as shown in **FIGURE 47-34**. A dial indicator is then used to measure turbine movement as the tool is pulled upward.

This measurement must be checked against the manufacturer's specification. If adjustment is needed, it usually requires a new thrust washer in the converter. Overall, turbine end play usually ranges from 0.060 inches to 0.080 inches (1.5 to 2.0 mm) in most converters, but some will have larger or smaller end play dimensions. Always check the specification.

Note that the converter end play is manipulated by some manufacturers to change converter stall speed. A larger end play would result in a higher stall speed. Always check OEM literature for the correct dimension.

The second check on the newly reassembled torque converter is a leak check. A special adapter is clamped into the hole formed by the pump drive hub, and air pressure is applied to the inside of the converter. Leak checks are then made either by submersing the converter in water or by using a soapy water solution to check the seams of the converter housing. Pay particular attention to the weld joint of the pump drive hub.

▶ Retarders

K47006

The brake systems of many machines that are capable of high-speed travel—25–50 mph/50–80 kph—can become extremely overburdened if those machines are in a situation that encounters multiple stops on steep grades. The use of retardation systems can reduce the load on the brakes enormously. Retardation systems come in many forms:

- *Engine brakes* basically turn the diesel engine into an air compressor by using the energy required to compress air on each compression stroke to slow the machine.
- *Exhaust brake systems* throttle the exhaust from the engine to slow the machine.
- Electrical driveline retarders slow the machine by using powerful electromagnets designed to slow the driveline.
- Hydraulic retarders use hydraulics at pressure to slow the machine.

Hydraulic Retarders

Machines can use one or two or a combination several of the systems mentioned in the previous section to slow the machine when necessary. Using retardation systems greatly extends the service life of brake systems and increases the available braking horsepower of the machine. Hydraulic retarders are capable of very high braking power in mobile applications: typical ranges are from 350 to over 800 hp. A typical hydraulic retarder installation is shown in **FIGURE 47-35**. It is important to note, however, that all of the above retardation systems with the exception of the exhaust brake system merely convert kinetic energy into heat, so keeping the retarder cool is essential, and if it is overused, its braking capability will be greatly diminished.

In this section, we will concentrate on the hydraulic retarder. A hydraulic retarder is usually but not always at the input to a power shift (automatic shifting transmission) or more commonly at the output of a power-shift transmission. There are hydraulic retarders that are mounted on the driveline, but we will focus on more common designs. If a retarder is located ahead of the transmission's torque converter, then the torque converter will have a lockup clutch that must be activated for the retarder to provide driveline braking.

Most hydraulic retarders are located at the transmission outlet, as shown in Figure 47-35, and in that case, a lockup clutch is not a requirement. A hydraulic retarder uses principles similar to a fluid coupling or torque converter, but instead of transmitting or multiplying torque, the retarder absorbs torque from the drive system. Its purpose is to slow the machine down without the use of wearable service brakes. The retarder functions by using oil under pressure in a chamber that consists of one or two stationary elements, called stators. The stators will have vanes, more commonly called cups, cast into them. Next to or between the two stators is a rotor, which is a bladed wheel rotor that is connected to either the input or the output shaft of the machine's transmission. **FIGURE 47-36** shows the rotor and one of the stationary stators from a typical retarder. Notice how the cups or vanes on the rotor and the stator face opposite directions to optimize braking effort.

The clearance between the rotor and the stators is very small similar to the clearance between the impeller and the turbine in a torque converter. During normal operation, the space

FIGURE 47-35 The large rotor in this retarder turns with the output shaft.

FIGURE 47-36 The hydraulic retarder consists of a vaned rotor splined to the transmission output shaft and two stationary vaned elements in the housing.

between the stators and the rotor is empty. When braking effort is required, the space is filled with oil under pressure. The rotor drives the oil against the stationary stator cups, and the resistance slows the rotor and therefore the driveline. Retarders greatly reduce the load on the machine service brakes and are ideal for holding a machine at a steady speed when going down a long grade without using service brakes. As mentioned above, however, retarders will generate a great deal of heat because they are simply an energy conversion device. The retarder coverts the kinetic energy of a moving machine into heat. This heat will be absorbed into the oil in the retarder, oil which then must be cooled down. A properly functioning oil cooling system is a must for a machine with a retarder. A retarder will usually have a dedicated oil-to-engine coolant cooling system. This requires a machine with a retarder to have excess to the cooling system capacity in order to deal with the heat created by the retarder.

▶ Retarder Operation

K47007

The operator controls for the retarder can vary from machine to machine: The retarder may have its own dedicated foot pedal that the operator can press, or there may be a lever on the steering wheel that the operator can pull. The level of retardation can be controlled automatically by the machine's electronic control, or there may be switches on the control panel that the operator can use to select the level of retardation. When the operator or engine control module (ECM) wants the retarder to slow the machine down, a valve will be activated that will send oil to the retarder housing. The oil may be forced into the retarder housing by an accumulator, by using air pressure, or by a pump alone. The housing is normally empty, so as oil enters the housing, the stator cups will try to keep the oil stationary. As the oil contacts the moving rotor, the rotor will be slowed down. Since the rotor is part of the driveline, the machine will be slowed down. The horsepower equivalent of a retarder on a 300 hp machine could be as high as 800 hp. To achieve a higher retarding effect, the control system merely increases the pressure in the retarder housing. For a schematic of a typical oil circuit for a retarder, see **FIGURE 47-37**.

The retardation will cause the oil to absorb the energy in the form of heat, so the oil will be sent to a heat exchanger/cooler when it leaves the housing. The oil-to-water heat exchanger transfers heat to the engine's cooling system, which in turn dissipates it into the atmosphere. The control for the retarder is typically electronically controlled, and if the heat level increases too much, the control will restrict retardation or stop it altogether. Without proper cooling, the retarder will not function.

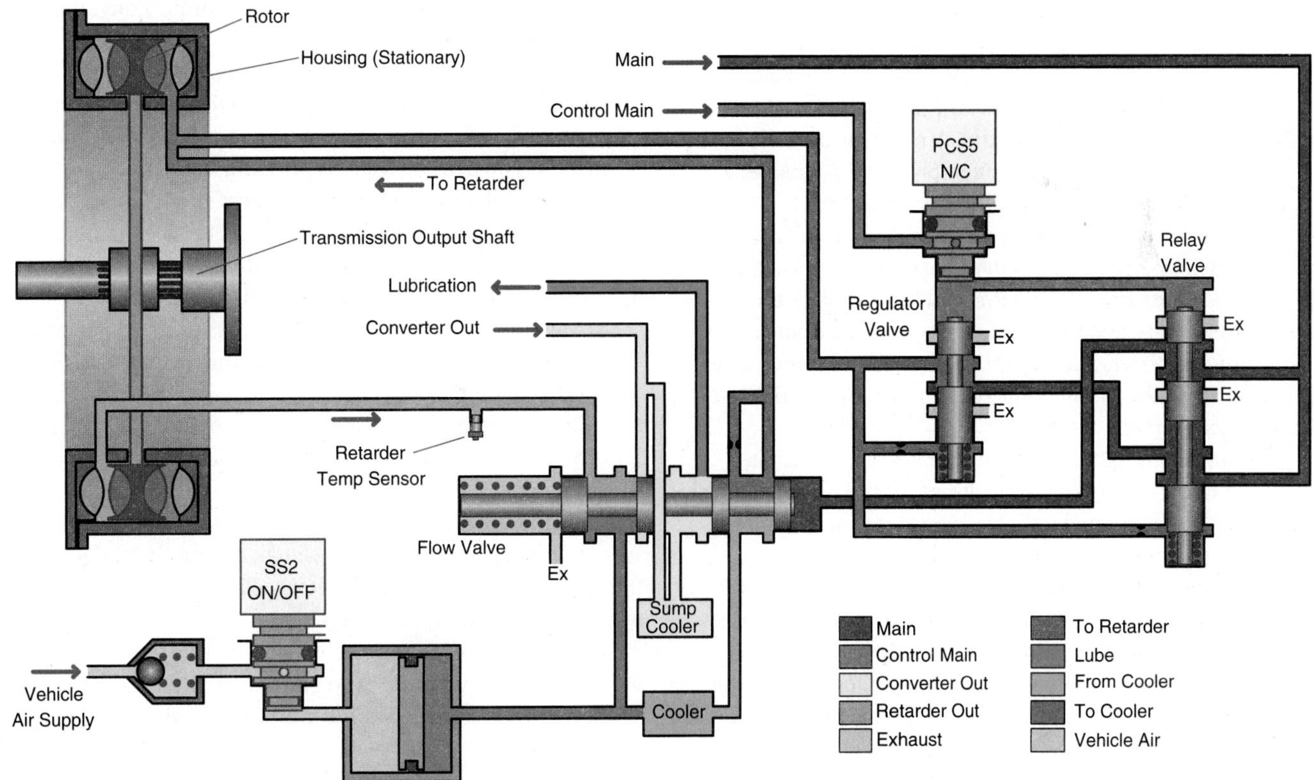

FIGURE 47-37 Retardation is controlled by filling the space that the rotor occupies with transmission fluid under pressure.

▶ Common Retarder Problems

S47003

The most common operator complaint that could indicate a retarder problem is that the retarder isn't slowing the machine as well as it should. Before condemning the system, ensure the operator is using the system properly. Most newer machines will have fail-safes that prevent improper operation, though. After the complaint has been verified, first check for fault codes if the machine is electronically controlled. Oil condition should also be checked. Aerated oil will not provide good retarder function.

The next common problem with retarders is that the oil is overheating. If this is the case after you confirm the system is being operated correctly, then a few checks with a heat gun may find that the oil isn't reaching the cooler, that it isn't circulating, or that the cooler is plugged either internally or externally. A good visual inspection should determine whether the cooler is plugged externally.

Finally, the retarder control valving and/or the accumulator could cause a non-functioning complaint. The retarder control valve, the accumulator, and (if equipped) the air supply system should be checked for proper function.

Retarder Repair or Replacement

Since the retarder is a simple device, it will be rare that something goes wrong with it. If it is part of the transmission or torque converter, then it should be inspected and reconditioned if necessary when these components are repaired or reconditioned. Reconditioning the retarder will involve inspecting and cleaning the elements, the rotor, the stators, and the rotor support bearings. Check the input and output fluid passageways. Inspect and, as necessary, replace the sealing O-rings and shaft seals (replacement of all seals is recommended practice). On reassembly, ensure that rotor-to-stator clearances are correct.

▶ Wrap-Up

Ready for Review

- ▶ Torque converters are able to multiply torque at the expense of output speed.
- ▶ Fluid couplings are similar to torque converters in that they transfer power from the source to a driveline through fluid. A fluid coupling cannot multiply torque.
- ▶ Both torque converters and fluid couplings have an impeller or pump and a turbine inside a shell that is shaped like a hollowed-out donut. This shape is called a torus.
- ▶ Torque converters have an extra element inside, called a stator, which is the primary component that enables a torque converter to multiply torque.
- ▶ A torque converter's torque multiplication factor can be controlled by changing the curvature of the blades of the elements (the turbine, the stator, and the impeller), the sizing of the elements, and the clearance between the elements.
- ▶ Torque converters can be equipped with multiple turbines to fine-tune the torque multiplication factor and fluid flow in the converter.
- ▶ The impeller is part of the converter housing, which is bolted to the engine, and so it always turns with the engine.
- ▶ The turbine is splined to the transmission input shaft to deliver power to the transmission.
- ▶ The stator is (usually) mounted on a one-way clutch and can freewheel in one direction, but it will lock up if it tries to turn in the opposite direction. The stator inner hub is supported by the stator ground shaft or stator support shaft.
- ▶ A torque converter's impeller can drive the turbine to approximately only 90–95% of impeller speed. This speed difference is known as slippage. Torque converters may be equipped with a lockup clutch to eliminate the 5–10% slippage.
- ▶ The torque-converter fluid flow can be rotary or vortex. Rotary flow in the torque converter is fluid that follows the rotation of the converter housing. Vortex flow is the flow of fluid from the impeller, through the turbine, through the stationary stator, and back to the impeller.
- ▶ Rotary flow is always present in the torque converter but is greatest at the converter's coupling phase, when the turbine speed is within 10% of impeller speed.
- ▶ Vortex flow is always present in the torque converter (unless the torque converter is in lockup) but is greatest at full stall, when the engine is driving the impeller as fast as it can while the turbine is stationary.
- ▶ The torque converter has two distinct phases of operation: the torque multiplication phase and the coupling phase.
- ▶ The torque multiplication phase occurs anytime the converter is multiplying torque (that is, when the impeller is turning significantly faster than the turbine). It is not related to vehicle speed.
- ▶ The coupling phase occurs anytime the turbine and the impeller speeds are within 10% of each other. It is not related to vehicle speed.
- ▶ During the torque multiplication phase, the stator is held stationary by the one-way clutch; during the coupling phase, the stator will be freewheeling.
- ▶ Variable pitch stators can alter a torque converter's multiplication factor by changing their blade angles.
- ▶ Torque-converter lockup clutches will typically apply once a certain gear range is attained and conditions are correct.
- ▶ Stall testing can help determine whether the engine, the transmission, or the torque converter is the source of an operator complaint.

- A stall test rpm that is significantly lower than specification (600 to 800 rpm lower) could indicate a freewheeling stator.
- Transmission fluid that does not cool down during the cool down phase of a stall test could indicate a stuck stator.
- A light-duty torque converter should be replaced with a new one when a transmission overhaul is required. Rebuilt aftermarket torque converters are available, but they are not recommended by OEMs.
- Heavy-duty torque converters should be overhauled when the transmission requires an overhaul.
- During torque-converter overhaul, pay particular attention to the turbine end play and positioning washers or bearings. The turbine position in relation to the impeller can affect the torque multiplication factor of the torque converter.
- Hydraulic retarders reduce the load on service brakes and increase overall braking capacity.
- Hydraulic retarders control retardation by varying fluid pressure in the retarder.
- Hydraulic retarders can be at the transmission inlet, the transmission outlet, or elsewhere on the driveline.
- Hydraulic retarders are capable of retardation exceeding 800 hp.
- Retarder oil can be fed into the retarder by accumulators, by using air pressure, or by pump pressure alone.

Key Terms

centrifugal force The apparent force by which a rotating mass tries to move outward, away from its axis of rotation.

coupling phase A torque-converter operating phase when the turbine and the impeller are at close to the same speed.

electrical driveline retarders Retarders that use electromagnetic force to slow the driveline.

engine brakes A brake retardation system that turns the engine cylinders into a compressor to slow the machine.

exhaust brakes A brake retardation system that throttles the exhaust to slow the machine.

flex plate A flexible plate used to connect the torque converter to the engine.

fluid coupling A power transfer device that uses fluid to transmit power to the driveline.

ground shaft A stationary shaft that holds the inner hub of the stator one-way clutch; also called stator support shaft.

hydraulic retarder A system that uses hydraulic oil under pressure to slow the machine.

impeller The bladed element in a torque converter or fluid coupling that is fixed to the housing and therefore rotates with it.

lockup clutch The lockup clutch locks the turbine to the converter shell when conditions are correct for 100% efficiency.

lockup clutch disc The friction disc used in a lockup clutch.

lockup clutch/piston assembly A combination lockup clutch disc and piston assembly, which is used in light-duty vehicles.

lockup clutch piston The hydraulically actuated piston that applies the lockup clutch.

one-way clutch A roller- or sprag-type device that allows rotation in one direction but locks in the opposite direction; also called over-running clutch.

over-running clutch A roller- or sprag-type device that allows rotation in one direction but locks in the opposite direction; also called one-way clutch.

rotary flow Fluid flow inside the torque converter that follows the rotation of the housing.

rotor The rotating element in a hydraulic retarder

split guide ring A ring that attaches to the impeller and the turbine blades and creates a circular fluid passage.

stall speed The maximum speed the engine can drive the torque-converter impeller with the turbine held stationary.

stator (torque converter) The element inside a torque converter most responsible for torque multiplication.

stator (hydraulic retarder) The stationary element in the retarder that tries to slow oil flow.

stator support shaft A stationary shaft that holds the inner hub of the stator one-way clutch; also called ground shaft.

stator inner hub The inner race of the stator one-way clutch, which splines to the stator ground shaft.

transmission oil cooler A series of oil tubes or passages that are cooled by engine coolant.

torque converter A type of fluid coupling that is also capable of multiplying torque.

torque multiplication phase A phase that occurs whenever the impeller is turning significantly faster than the turbine.

torus The hollowed-out donut shape of the rear of the converter housing and the turbine.

turbine The torque-converter element that is splined to the transmission input shaft.

variable pitch stator A stator with blades that can change the angle to alter the torque-converter multiplication factor.

vortex flow The flow of fluid from the impeller, through the turbine, through the stator, and back to the impeller.

Review Questions

1. What is meant when a torque converter is said to have a modulated lockup strategy?
   a. The lockup clutch will apply as early as possible during the drive cycle.
   b. The lockup clutch will apply only when the driver requests it.
   c. The lockup clutch will apply only in high range.
   d. The lockup clutch will apply based on a number of factors, including throttle request.
2. A stall speed slightly lower than specified would typically indicate which of the following problems?
   a. A slipping clutch
   b. A stuck stator
   c. A freewheeling stator
   d. Engine power is lower than normal

3. What are the two phases of torque-converter operation?
   a. The torque multiplication phase and the lockup phase
   b. The torque multiplication phase and the coupling phase
   c. The lockup phase and the torque multiplication phase
   d. The stator phase and the lockup phase
4. The stall test can be used to determine which of the following?
   a. The condition of the engine only
   b. The condition of the torque converter only
   c. The condition of the transmission only
   d. The condition of the engine, torque converter, and the transmission
5. Which of the following is likely the problem if a stall speed is lower than specification by 600 rpm or more?
   a. A stuck stator in the torque converter
   b. A freewheeling stator in the torque converter
   c. A torque converter that is not full of fluid
   d. A transmission that has a seized clutch
6. During peak torque multiplication in a torque converter, which of the following would be occurring?
   a. Vortex oil flow is high.
   b. The stator is held stationary by the one-way clutch.
   c. Rotary oil flow is low.
   d. All of the above.
7. A lockup clutch in the torque converter does which of the following?
   a. It provides 100% efficiency between the impeller and turbine.
   b. It increases rotary oil flow in the torque multiplication phase.
   c. It allows a higher stall speed.
   d. It increases vortex oil flow in the coupling phase.
8. When the engine is idling and you are in park or neutral, which of the following is happening in the torque converter?
   a. The impeller is turning, the stator is locked, and the turbine is stopped.
   b. Both the impeller and the turbine are turning, and the stator is locked.
   c. Both the impeller and the turbine are stopped, and the stator is turning.
   d. The impeller, the stator, and the turbine are all turning at close to the same speed.
9. What is the main purpose of a hydraulic retarder?
   a. to reduce service brake wear
   b. to reduce machine heat load
   c. to increase machine torque capability
   d. None of the above.
10. Retarders can be in which of the following locations?
   a. in the engine
   b. at the transmission input
   c. at the transmission outlet
   d. All of the above

ASE Technician A/Technician B Style Questions

1. Technician A says that a fluid coupler is capable of transmitting torque to a driveline as long as the load is not too great. Technician B says that a fluid coupling can multiply torque up to four to one. Who is correct?
   a. Technician A
   b. Technician B
   c. Both Technician A and Technician B
   d. Neither Technician A nor Technician B
2. Technician A says that the primary key to torque multiplication in a torque converter is the stator. Technician B says that the angle of the blades in the turbine affects the torque multiplication. Who is correct?
   a. Technician A
   b. Technician B
   c. Both Technician A and Technician B
   d. Neither Technician A nor Technician B
3. Technician A says that the stator locks up during the torque-converter coupling phase. Technician B says that the stator freewheels during the torque multiplication phase. Who is correct?
   a. Technician A
   b. Technician B
   c. Both Technician A and Technician B
   d. Neither Technician A nor Technician B
4. Technician A says that vortex flow in the torque converter is highest during full stall. Technician B says that vortex flow follows the rotation of the converter housing or shell. Who is correct?
   a. Technician A
   b. Technician B
   c. Both Technician A and Technician B
   d. Neither Technician A nor Technician B
5. Technician A says that the torque multiplication factor of a torque converter is affected by the angle of the stator blades. Technician B says that the turbine end play can affect the torque converter's multiplication factor. Who is correct?
   a. Technician A
   b. Technician B
   c. Both Technician A and Technician B
   d. Neither Technician A nor Technician B
6. Technician A says that when a torque converter is multiplying torque, the stator is freewheeling. Technician B says the impeller can drive turbine at approximately only 90–95% of engine speed. Who is correct?
   a. Technician A
   b. Technician B
   c. Both Technician A and Technician B
   d. Neither Technician A nor Technician B

7. Technician A says that when a torque divider is used and the machine is stopped in gear, the turbine is stationary. Technician B says a torque divider has two inputs from the engine. Who is correct?
   a. Technician A
   b. Technician B
   c. Both Technician A and Technician B
   d. Neither Technician A nor Technician B
8. Technician A say that when a machine equipped with a torque divider first starts to move, the turbine may actually be turning slightly counterclockwise. Technician B says that the lockup clutch for a torque converter usually locks up only at top speed. Who is correct?
   a. Technician A
   b. Technician B
   c. Both Technician A and Technician B
   d. Neither Technician A nor Technician B
9. Technician A says that a torque divider has a planetary gear set. Technician B says that a torque divider's turbine is attached to a planetary gear set ring gear. Who is correct?
   a. Technician A
   b. Technician B
   c. Both Technician A and Technician B
   d. Neither Technician A nor Technician B
10. Technician A says that a hydraulic retarder adds only a small amount of braking effort to a machine. Technician B says that the retardation force in a hydraulic retarder is controlled by the fluid pressure. Who is correct?
   a. Technician A
   b. Technician B
   c. Both Technician A and Technician B
   d. Neither Technician A nor Technician B

CHAPTER 48
Power-Shift Transmissions

Knowledge Objectives

After reading this chapter, you will be able to:

- **K48001** Explain the purpose and fundamentals of power reversers (power shuttles).
- **K48002** Explain the construction of power shuttles.
- **K48003** Describe the power flows of power shuttles.
- **K48004** Explain the purpose and fundamentals of countershaft and planetary power-shift transmissions.
- **K48005** Identify the construction, types, and applications of the different types of power-shift transmissions used in MORE.
- **K48006** Describe the power flows of countershaft and planetary power-shift transmissions.
- **K48007** Explain the function and operation of hydraulic clutch control systems used with power-shift transmissions.
- **K48008** Describe the shift control logic of computer-controlled power-shift transmissions.
- **K48009** Describe the common failures of power-shift transmissions and power shuttles and their root causes.
- **K48010** Explain the overhaul procedures for power-shift transmissions and power shuttles.

Skills Objectives

After reading this chapter, you will be able to:

- **S48001** Perform recommended maintenance on power-shift transmissions and power shuttles.

▶ Introduction

Mobile off-road equipment used in construction, mining, forestry, and agricultural applications is designed to withstand harsh working environments while enabling operators to control the equipment safely, comfortably, and effectively. These machines must also be productive and efficient at moving material. Two major drivetrain components used in off-road equipment that can satisfy these fundamental requirements are power reversers—or, as they are more commonly called, **power shuttles**—and **power-shift transmissions**. Power shuttles can be considered to be a type of power-shift transmission.

Power shuttles allow operators to make forward and reverse directional changes on a piece of equipment while on the go and under load without having to use a foot clutch, stop the movement of the equipment, and manually shift into a forward or reverse gear. Power-shift transmissions go a step further: they allow operators to shift speed ranges up or down and to change directions on the go and under load without having to use a foot clutch. There are many configurations of power shuttles and power-shift transmissions. They are built by numerous manufacturers, and they are referred to by a variety of names.

To effectively maintain and service power shuttles and power-shift transmissions, MORE (mobile off-road equipment) service technicians must have a thorough understanding of how these major components function. This chapter identifies different types of power shuttles and power-shift transmissions, describes common applications for each type, and describes how the internal mechanisms and power flows enable each of these components to perform. Common problems that affect power-shift transmissions and power shuttles are identified, and maintenance and overhaul procedures for each component are described.

▶ Power Shuttle Fundamentals

K48001

This type of transmission is a combination of power-shift and manual shift transmission and is used in combination with a torque converter that is driven by the engine's flywheel. The power shuttle transmission is popular with many makes of backhoe loaders but could be found in other light-duty machines, such as fork lifts. The power-shift part of this transmission will only control forward and reverse directional clutches and is sometimes in a separate housing from the speed range section. This simple type of power-shift transmission allows the operator to quickly shift from forward to reverse and under load for increased machine productivity. There could be two- to five-speed ranges that will be selected manually with a floor-mounted shifter that is connected to shift forks in the transmission. The forks move synchronizers to provide smoother speed range changes. The speed range section of the shuttle shift is very similar to manual mechanical transmissions.

The forward/reverse power shuttle part of this transmission will use two hydraulically actuated clutches controlled by a hydraulic control valve. Older versions of shuttle shift control valves were mechanically controlled, but most newer versions are electrically or electronically controlled. The electrical system will incorporate a safety interlock system to prevent the machine from starting or starting in gear unless certain conditions are met, such as the controls being in neutral and the parking brake being applied. There could also be an electronic fault-code display and storage system integrated, as well as oil temperature monitoring and overheat warning systems provided.

There will usually be a transmission neutralizer function that uses operator-controlled switches to send current to a solenoid. The solenoid will get energized to cut power flow through the transmission so that a speed range shift can be made smoothly. The neutralizer simply drains any clutch apply pressure to disengage a clutch and interrupt power flow.

▶ TECHNICIAN TIP

MORE technicians should be aware that other names are frequently used incorrectly to describe power shuttles. For example, terms like "shuttle transmission," "non-synchronized shuttle," and "synchronized shuttle" describe transmission types that perform similarly to power shuttles, but unless they are equipped with a power shuttle unit, they still require the use of a foot clutch. In addition, people often confuse power shuttles (as well as power-shift transmissions) with **hydrostatic transmissions (HST)**, **continuously variable transmissions (CVT)**, and **infinitely variable transmissions (IVT)**. HSTs, CVTs, and IVTs are types of automatic transmissions that use pressurized fluid and/or some other means to transfer power from the engine to the axles and wheels and provide infinitely variable speed.

Because of the confusion surrounding power shuttle and power-shift transmission terminology, service technicians must be able to accurately identify the type of transmission being serviced before they perform any work on the transmission. To ensure accuracy, always look for data plates or other equipment identifying stickers on the equipment and/or locate and review the manufacturer's manuals and guidelines that pertain to the equipment transmission.

Service technicians are still likely to encounter this type of transmission during their work.

You Are the Mobile Heavy Equipment Technician

A start-up construction company owner comes into your shop and says they are having problems with a used loader that they recently purchased. It ran fine for several months, but now it takes a long time to change from forward to reverse and vice versa when they use the power shuttle's directional control lever. They say that they checked the lever linkages and the fluid level for the transmission and that both seemed fine.

1. Should you check the type and condition of the oil being used in the transmission and power shuttle? Why or why not?
2. Should you check the pressure settings for the power shuttle?
3. Should you assume there are internal problems and simply overhaul the power shuttle? Explain.

Power Shuttle Purpose

Power shuttles were developed to help reduce the burdens of operating manual transmissions in older mobile off-road equipment (MORE). Having to depress the foot clutch, bring the piece of equipment to a complete stop, and manually shift gears and/or speed ranges was a tiring exercise for operators during jobs that required frequent changes in forward and reverse direction. The advent of power shuttles greatly simplified this process.

A good example of a piece of equipment that benefits from the use of a power shuttle is a tractor loader backhoe. In many work applications, such as loading, this equipment would need to make constant forward and reverse directional changes during a typical loading cycle. Instead of having to routinely clutch and shift gears in a manual transmission, the operator can accomplish the same thing by simply moving a directional shift lever on the steering column (**FIGURE 48-1**). This method of directional shifting greatly increases machine production and reduces operator fatigue.

Other types of MORE equipment that benefit from the use of power shuttles include small wheel loaders, forklifts, utility tractors, and small dozers. The following are some of the advantages provided by a power shuttle, regardless of the equipment on which it is installed:

- Ease of operation. The operator experiences less fatigue by not having to use the clutch, stop the equipment, and make gear changes in the manual transmission.
- Reduced wear and tear. The foot clutch does not have to be used for shifting between forward and reverse, and it therefore experiences less wear.
- Improved efficiency. The engine rpm and equipment speed can be maintained while changing direction.

Power Shuttle Hydraulic System

To enable the power shuttle transmission to perform directional shifts under power, the transmission must have a hydraulic system that is controlled by the operator and that supplies oil to one of two clutches. To understand the operation of a typical power shuttle hydraulic system, we'll look at the John Deere 310E backhoe transmission.

FIGURE 48-1 Power shuttle control lever on steering column.

The transmission pump is driven at engine speed by the transmission input shaft and takes oil from the bottom of the transmission housing and supplies flow to the hydraulic control valve. It is an external gear-type pump and provides an oil supply for the hydraulic control section of the transmission for clutch application, cooling, and lubrication.

Next we'll look at the transmission control valve. See **FIGURE 48-2** for a cross-sectional view of the valve and a schematic representation to see how the oil flow and pressure are regulated.

The following is a list of the components that make up the control valve:

1. The pressure-regulating valve (6) controls maximum system pressure at 230–275 psi and is set by adjusting shims behind a spring. This is the pressure that will be applied to the clutch piston when a forward or reverse shift is made.
2. The converter relief valve (5) controls maximum pressure to the torque converter, which should be 116–125 psi.
3. Modulation valve (7) controls rate of clutch fill time.
4. Forward and reverse shift valve (10) is a spool-type valve that sends oil to the forward or reverse clutches.
5. Neutral shift valve (11) will dump or drain clutch apply pressure.
6. Pressure-reducing valve (12) reduces pressure oil made available to the solenoid valves and should be 123–152 psi.
7. Forward, neutral, and reverse solenoids (2, 3, and 4) direct reduced pressure to the shift valves. These solenoid valves are on-or-off valves that allow oil to flow past them when energized. To describe them hydraulically, you would say they are two-position, three-way, electrically actuated directional control valves.

The forward and reverse shift valve (10) is a spring-loaded spool valve that engages the directional clutches. The neutral shift valve (11) is a spring-loaded spool valve that must also be shifted to allow pressure oil to be directed to the selected directional clutch. The forward or reverse shift valve solenoids (2 or 4) are activated by the forward/neutral/reverse (FNR) lever. The neutral solenoid (3) is controlled by the park brake switch and must be energized before forward or reverse clutches can be engaged. The loader and shift lever disconnect switches (sometimes called neutralizers) also control the neutral solenoid.

It may be hard to understand how oil flows through the transmission control valve by looking at the cross-sectional diagram, and even if you have an actual valve in your hand, it would be hard to follow the passages through the valve. To better understand how the solenoids control the oil flow, see **FIGURE 48-3.**

The transmission pump gets oil from the sump and sends the oil through the filter. The filter has a bypass valve that will open if the filter gets plugged. The pump flow has its maximum pressure limited by the pressure regulator. As not much oil flow is needed to actuate the clutches (maybe a few ounces), there

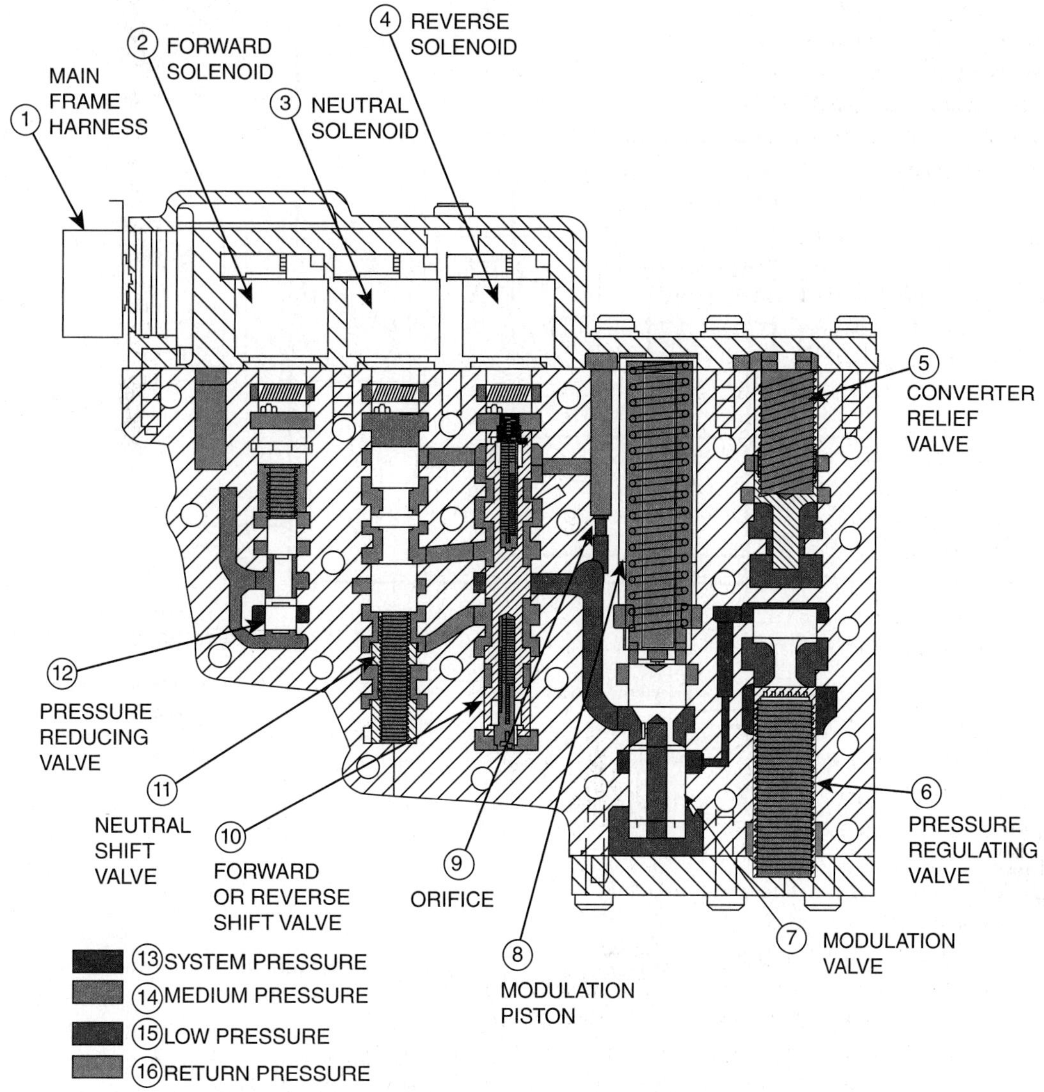

(1) MAIN FRAME HARNESS
(2) FORWARD SOLENOID
(3) NEUTRAL SOLENOID
(4) REVERSE SOLENOID
(5) CONVERTER RELIEF VALVE
(6) PRESSURE REGULATING VALVE
(7) MODULATION VALVE
(8) MODULATION PISTON
(9) ORIFICE
(10) FORWARD OR REVERSE SHIFT VALVE
(11) NEUTRAL SHIFT VALVE
(12) PRESSURE REDUCING VALVE
(13) SYSTEM PRESSURE
(14) MEDIUM PRESSURE
(15) LOW PRESSURE
(16) RETURN PRESSURE

FIGURE 48-2 Cross-sectional view of 310E transmission control valve.

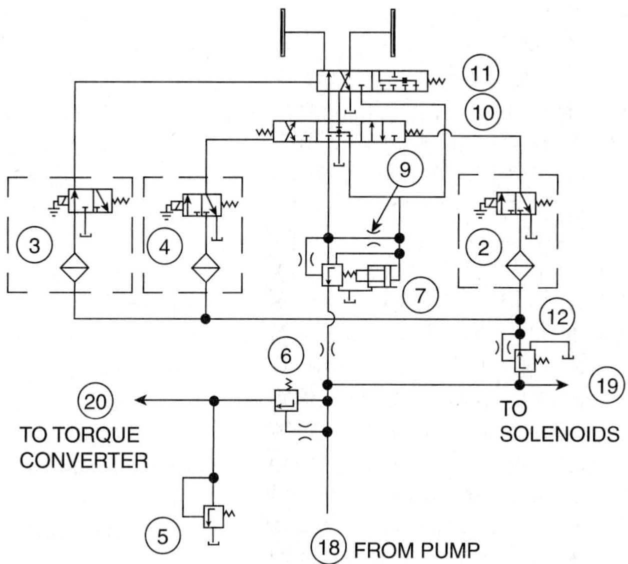

FIGURE 48-3 310E transmission control valve in schematic form.

will be plenty of excess oil from the pump that is then directed to the torque converter. Its pressure is limited by the converter relief valve.

The oil is then routed to the oil cooler. A portion of the oil returning from the cooler provides lubrication oil to the shaft bearings and cooling oil to the clutches. The remaining oil goes to sump or to the bottom of the transmission case, where it is picked up by the pump again.

The pressure-reducing valve supplies medium pressure oil to the solenoid valves (neutral, reverse, and forward). In neutral, with park brake OFF, the forward and reverse solenoids are deenergized (open), and medium pressure oil is not directed to the ends of the forward/reverse shift valve. The neutral solenoid valve is energized (closed), and medium pressure oil is routed to the end of the neutral shift valve. The neutral shift valve in this position allows oil at the forward and reverse clutches to drain through the forward/reverse shift valve. See **FIGURE 48-4** for the schematic of the control valve when forward is selected.

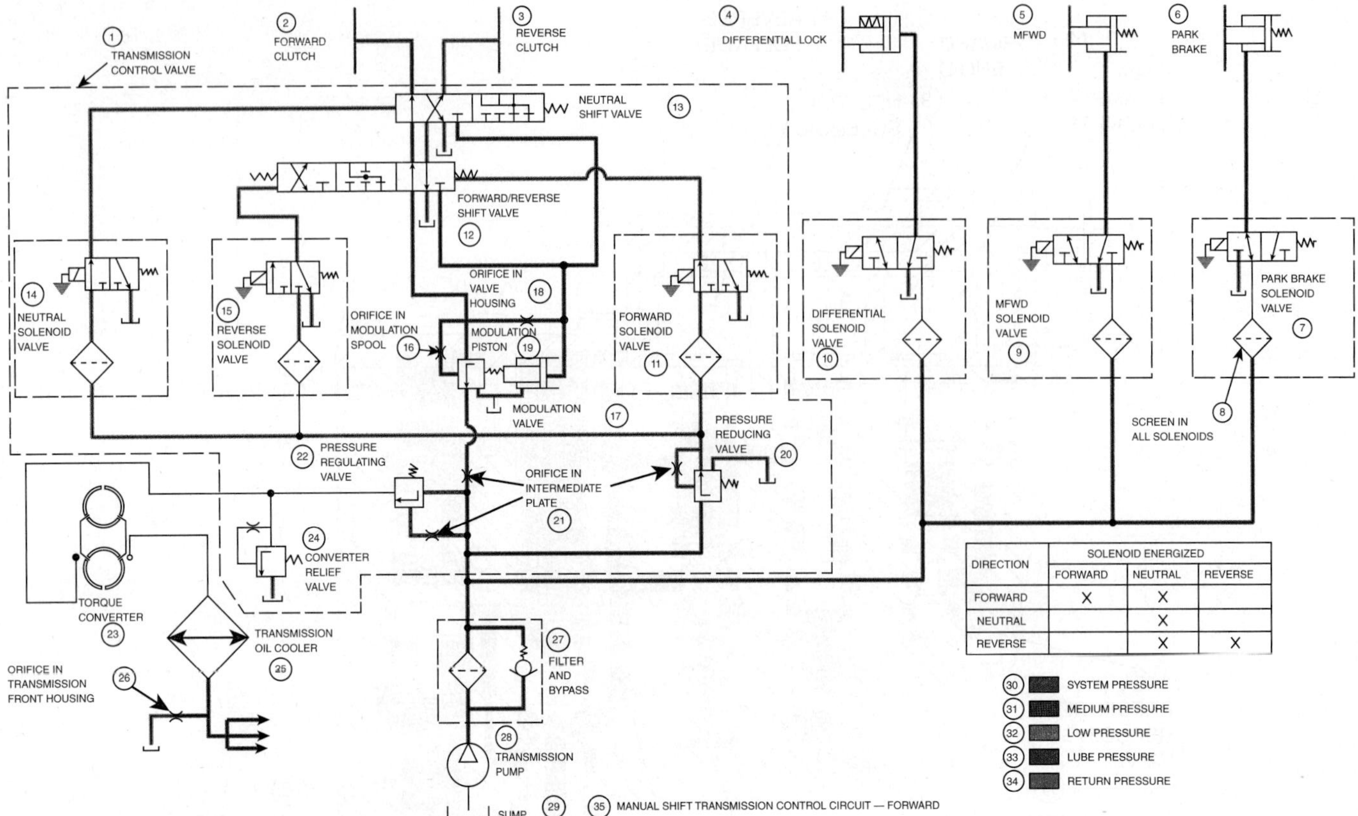

DIRECTION	SOLENOID ENERGIZED		
	FORWARD	NEUTRAL	REVERSE
FORWARD	X	X	
NEUTRAL		X	
REVERSE		X	X

FIGURE 48-4 310E transmission control valve in forward.

To control the hydraulic portion of this transmission, the operator will move the FNR lever, which is an electrical switch by the steering wheel or the transmission neutralizer switches on either the speed range lever or the loader control lever.

There are three other switches used to control transmission oil flow used for other functions: the park brake switch, the differential lock switch, and the MFWD (mechanical front wheel drive) switch. The switches will send an electrical current to solenoid valves. When energized, the solenoid valves will direct reduced pressure oil to perform various functions.

If the operator moves the FNR lever forward, battery voltage will be given a path to the forward and neutral solenoid valves (11 and 14) to energize them. The neutral solenoid valve (14) sends reduced pressure oil (31) to the neutral shift valve (12) and moves the spool to the right against spring pressure. The energized forward solenoid (11) sends reduced pressure oil to the forward/reverse shift valve (12), moving the spool to the left against spring pressure. Clutch apply oil modulation now starts to provide a smooth transition from disengaged to engaged. Shifting of the forward/reverse spool also blocks the flow of oil downstream of the orifice in the valve housing from returning to the tank and allows the pressure in the modulation valve to build. As pressure builds, the balance between orifice size and spring load in the modulation valve controls the rate of shift and pushes the modulation piston to the left. The force from the modulation piston pushes on the modulation springs, which move the modulation spool to the fully open position. In the fully open position, high-pressure oil (30) from the pressure-regulating valve (22) forces the clutch piston against the clutch discs and plates to engage the clutch. See **FIGURE 48-5** for a cross-sectional view of the modulation valve and a graph to show the different stages of modulation and how pressure rises at a controlled rate.

The rate of shift from neutral into forward or reverse is controlled by the movement of the modulation valve and modulation piston during a shift. By regulating the amount of oil flow being sent to engage the direction pack, the time required is extended to ensure a smooth shift. The time for a normal smooth shift is one and a half to two seconds. This time allows the clutch discs and plates to be squeezed together relatively slowly to provide a cushion effect for the drivetrain. If the modulation was too slow, too much clutch slippage and overheating would occur, possibly followed by premature clutch failure. An operator complaint in this case may be lazy, unresponsive shifting. If the clutch engaged too fast because of too little modulation, there would be shock loading of the drivetrain and possibly broken universal joints and other related damage. Some operator complaints would be harsh shifting, banging, clunking, or jerking as the transmission shifts. See **FIGURE 48-6** for examples of driveline component damage caused by shockloading. Some transmission control valves allow for adjustment of clutch modulation by adding or removing shims to change modulation valve spring pressure.

Refer to Figure 48-5 to visualize the four modes of modulation. Neutral (A): System pressure oil (K) bleeds by the edge of the modulation spool (J). This (low-pressure) oil (M) flows

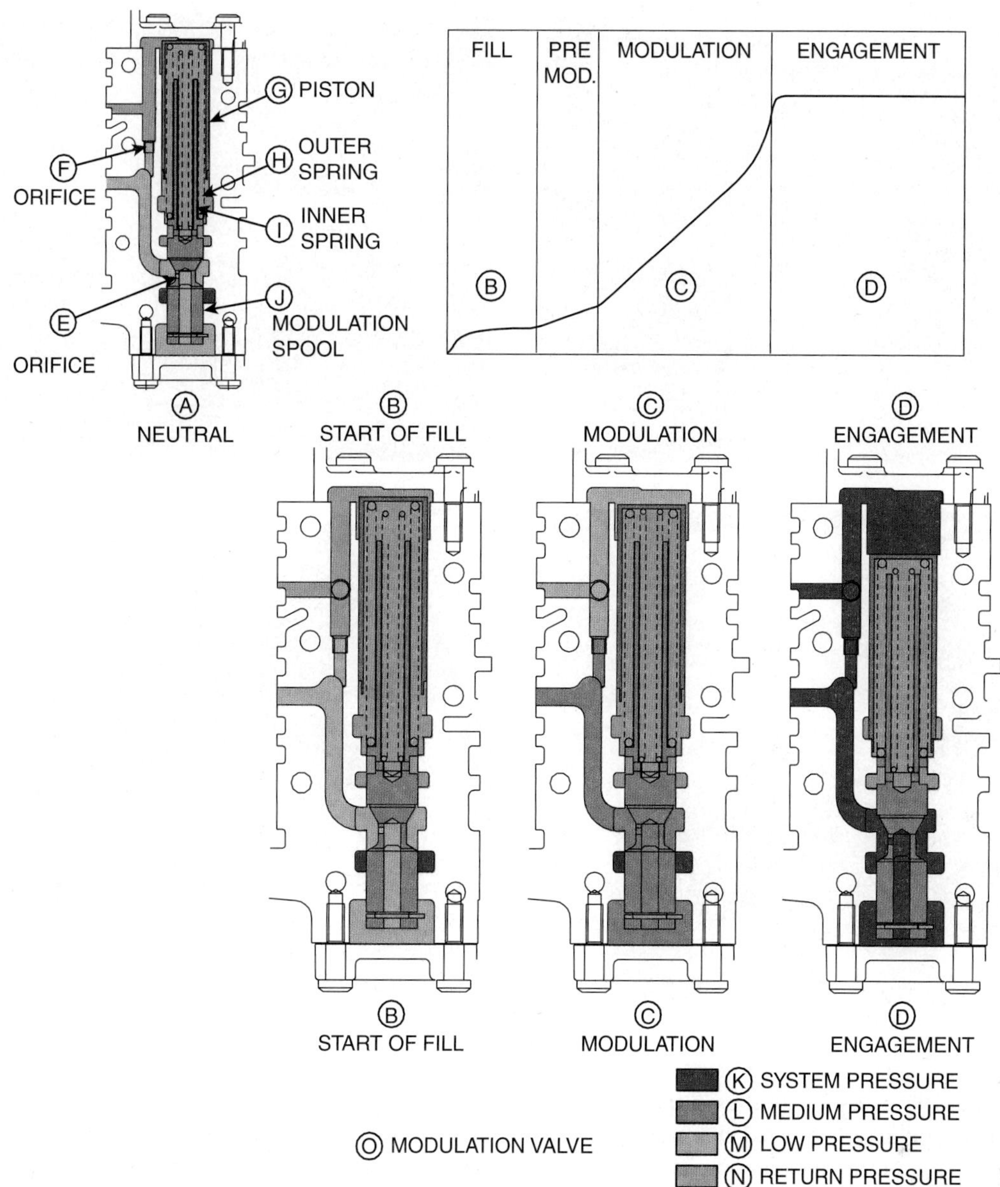

FIGURE 48-5 Modulation valve and how pressure rises at a controlled rate.

through orifice (F), and this passage is open to return. Low-pressure oil (M) also flows through orifice (E) to the bottom side of modulation spool (J). This oil applies sufficient force on the spring to hold the spool up against spring pressure on the edge of the pressure port opening. Forward/reverse clutch packs are also open to sump when in neutral.

Start of fill (B): Mode begins when a shift to forward or reverse occurs. Shifting of the forward/reverse spool allows oil to flow from the modulation valve to the neutral shift valve and fill the clutch pack. Shifting of the forward/reverse spool also blocks the flow of oil downstream of the orifice (F) from returning to tank and allows the pressure in the modulation valve to build. The clutch pack fills rapidly at the low-pressure level.

Modulation (C): This begins as pressure in the clutch pack begins to rise (L). The pressure is also being sensed through orifice (F). Pressure on the back side of orifice (F) is building to low pressure (M). This pressure starts moving the piston (G), springs (H and I), and modulation spool (J) down. There are two small orifices toward the top of the piston (G) (not shown). The orifices allow return oil to dump to sump during the start of fill and halfway through modulation mode. This helps control the rate of shift. The orifices in the piston close off as the piston moves down. An equalization of spring and pressure forces on the modulation valve regulates the rate of clutch engagement during modulation.

Final engagement (D): When this is reached, the modulation spool (J) is in the fully open position, and the two small orifices (not shown) in the modulation piston (G) are closed off. With the spool in the fully open position, high-pressure oil from the pressure-regulating valve maintains the downward force on the modulation piston and keeps the clutch engaged until the next shift.

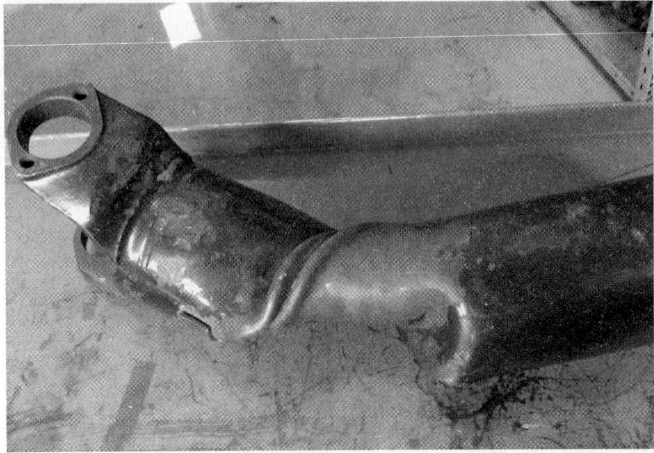

FIGURE 48-6 Driveline components such as driveshafts, u-joints and gears can be severely damaged by shock loading.

Cycling the forward/reverse spool or the neutral shift spool allows the high-pressure oil in the engaged clutch and between the orifice (F) and the top of the modulation piston to vent to the tank. The resulting loss in pressure allows the modulation valve to reset to begin the next shift sequence.

Basically, the rate of pressure rising is controlled by the balancing act between the oil pressure on the piston plus spring pressure, on the one hand, and the oil pressure acting on the modulation spool, on the other. This oil pressure is also controlled by the effect of the orifices. This modulation process by springs, spools, and orifices has almost completely been replaced by electric/electronic modulation. This will be discussed in a later section of this chapter.

Now that you understand how the hydraulic system works and how clutch apply oil is modulated, take a look at the clutch cross section in **FIGURE 48-7** to see how the oil flows in the clutch pack.

You can also see how the oil is directed through the shaft to the piston. Pressure oil (D) from the control valve forces the clutch piston (G) to compress the plates (C) and discs (A). The plates are splined to the clutch drum (B) and the discs are splined to hub (E), locking them together. The hub is splined to the drive shaft. All gears are constantly meshed and supported by anti-friction bearings. The bearings and clutches are lubricated with cooled lubrication oil (I). Spring discs push back the piston when the clutch pack (J) is disengaged, thus releasing the multidisc clutch.

The operation of this hydraulically applied clutch is identical, if not very similar, to most other clutches used in power-shift transmissions.

▶ Power Shuttle Construction

K48002

Power shuttle construction, mounting, and operation can vary considerably according to the manufacturer and the age and type of equipment. To better understand how a typical power shuttle is constructed, start by looking at a cutaway illustration of a transmission to see the major components.

John Deere uses this type of transmission in the 310E backhoe loader. We'll start by identifying the main components inside the transmission. See **FIGURE 48-8** for a cross-sectional look at the 310E transmission mechanical components.

Its output could be to the rear axle only or to both front and rear axles. The output to the front axle is out the MFWD shaft.

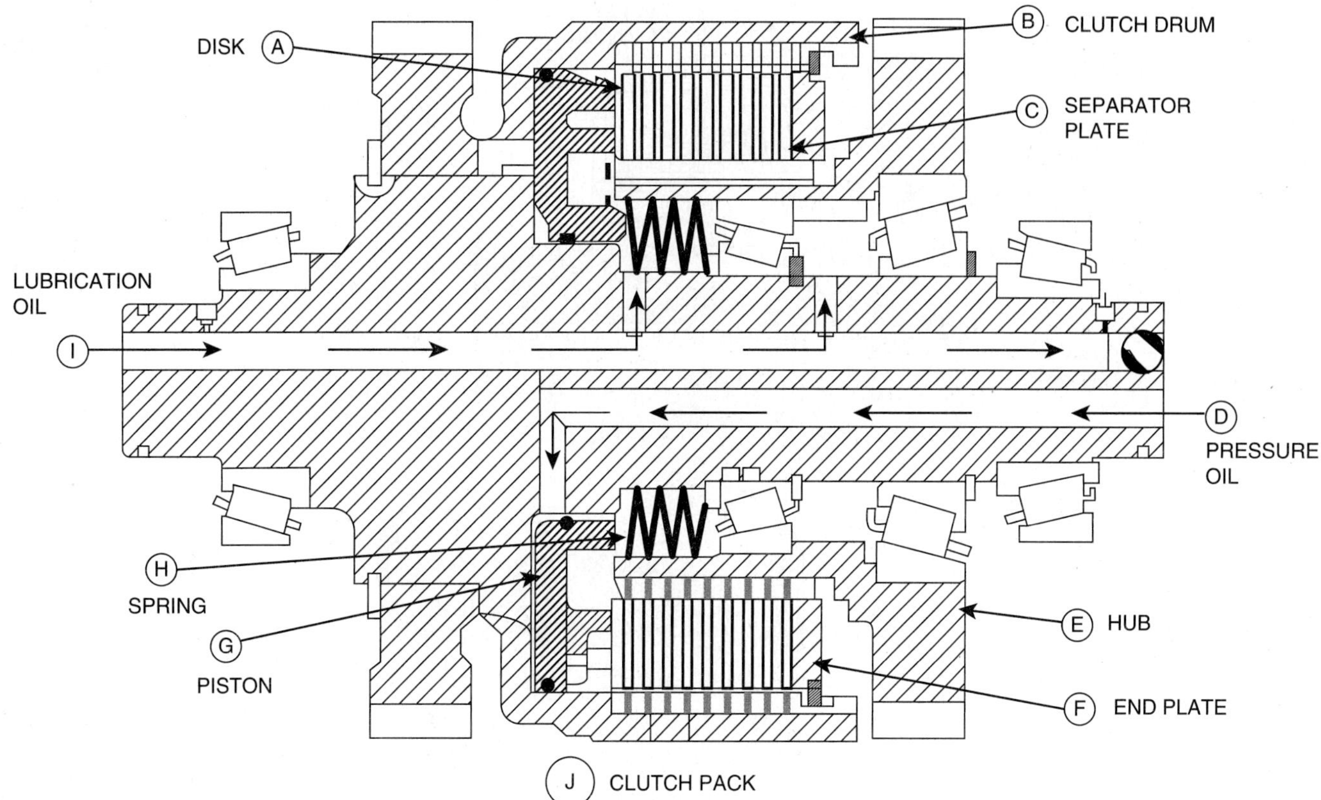

FIGURE 48-7 How the oil flows inside a clutch housing.

This four-speed transmission's direction and speed range gears are in constant mesh. The torque converter (A) is driven by the engine, and its output comes out the turbine shaft, which is coupled to the transmission input shaft. The input shaft drives both the direction clutch pack (K and B) and the floating drive hubs. If neither clutch is actuated, this is as far as the torque is transferred to. When either forward (K) or reverse (B) clutch is filled with oil through drilled passages in the shafts, the discs and plates are squeezed together and torque is sent to the intermediate shaft (J).

▶ Power Shuttle Power Flows

K48003

This four-speed transmission's direction and speed range gears are in constant mesh. The torque converter (A) is driven by the engine and its output comes out the turbine shaft, which is coupled to the transmission input shaft. The input shaft drives both direction clutch pack (K and B) floating drive hubs. If neither clutch is actuated, this is as far as the torque is transferred to. When either forward (K) or reverse (B) clutch is filled with oil through drilled passages in the shafts, the discs and plates are squeezed together and torque is sent to the intermediate shaft (J). See **FIGURE 48-9** for how the power flows through the transmission in first-speed forward.

Input shaft (B) is always driving the forward clutch hub (D) and the reverse clutch hub. Until one of the direction clutches is pressurized, there is no power flow through the transmission. If oil is directed through the drilled passage in the clutch shaft (O), this causes the piston (M) to move, compressing the plates and discs (E), causing the forward clutch gear (N) to be driven. This gear is in constant mesh with intermediate gear (L) and shaft (F). If first speed is selected by the operator by moving the gear shift lever for the manually selected part of the transmission, torque will transfer from the intermediate shaft to the output shaft, where it is sent either to the rear axle or to both front and rear axles. See **FIGURE 48-10** for how power flows through the transmission in third-speed reverse.

What is not apparent in this diagram is that the reverse clutch output gear (N) and forward clutch output gear (M) are in constant mesh. The gears appear to be not in mesh, so that the illustration is less confusing. If oil is directed through reverse clutch shaft (P) to engage the reverse clutch, then gear (N) will drive forward output gear (M). This gear acts like an idler gear to reverse rotation to the intermediate shaft (G). Torque can now be sent through the manually shifted part of the transmission, and all gears selected will be in reverse rotation.

▶ Power-Shift Transmission Fundamentals

K48004

A power-shift transmission is a type of transmission that was developed to allow operators to shift speed ranges up or down and change directions on the go and under load without a

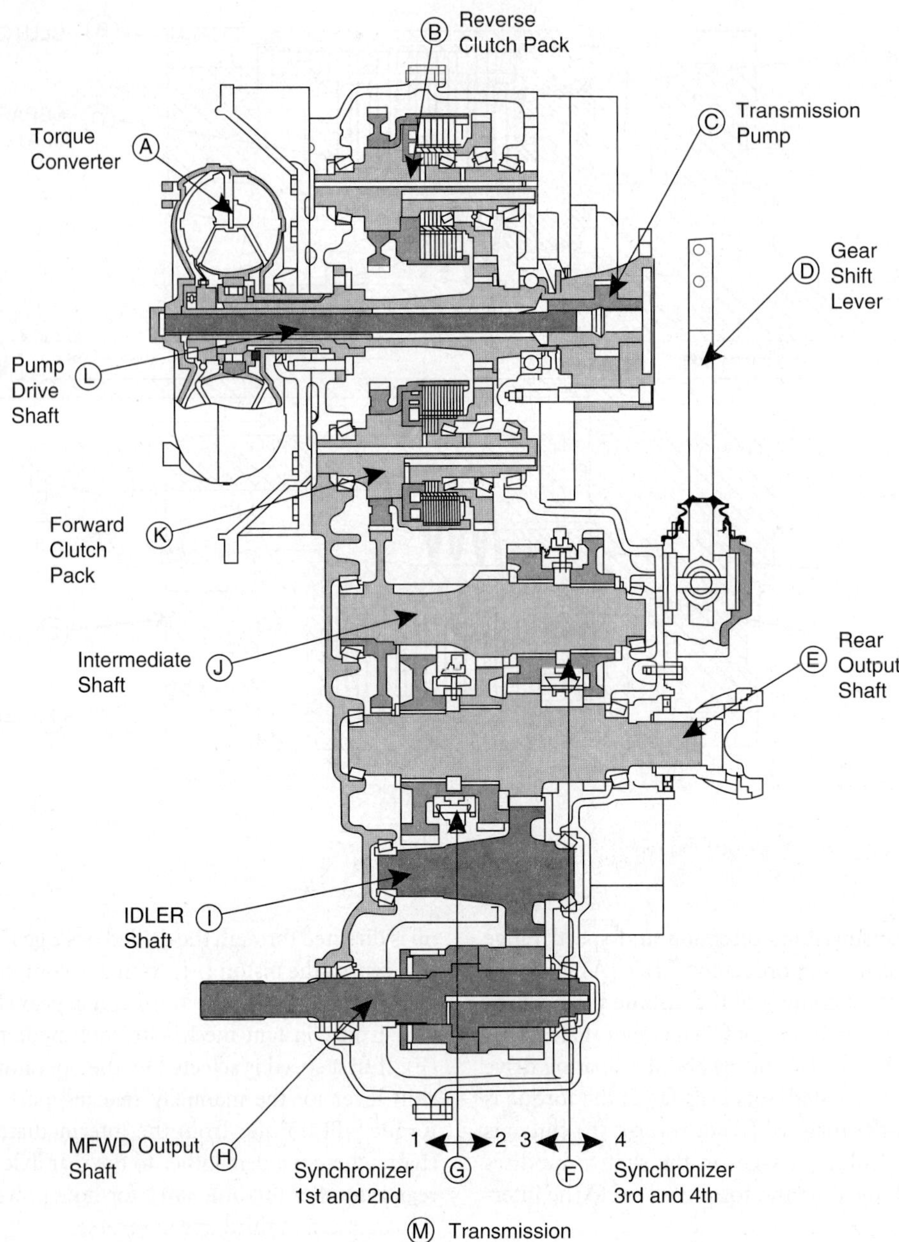

FIGURE 48-8 A cross-sectional look at the 310E transmission mechanical components.

loss in acceleration or torque and without having to use a foot clutch. More specifically, a power-shift transmission takes the torque output from the engine flywheel or torque converter and changes the speed, torque, and direction of rotation through different gear ratios. It then passes those changes on to the rest of the machine's drivetrain, which can include a differential, a set of axles, or steering clutches (**FIGURE 48-11**).

Power-Shift Transmission Purpose

The need for power-shift transmissions became apparent quite early in the evolution of heavy equipment. Initially, mobile heavy equipment used standard manual-type transmissions with flywheel clutches. This meant that if a directional change needed to be made on a machine with this type of transmission or if upshifting or downshifting needed to occur, the operator would first have to slow the machine, push in the clutch, wait for the machine to stop, select a different gear, and then carefully ease out the clutch. This process of changing gears took a lot of extra time and effort, which reduced the machine's productivity and fatigued the operator. It was soon obvious to equipment owners, operators, and equipment manufacturers that an improved transmission was needed. To enhance machine productivity and ease operator effort, the power-shift transmission was created.

A power-shift transmission, coupled with a torque converter, enabled operators to shift to different speed ranges without having to bring the equipment to a full stop and to make directional changes much faster with very little shock through

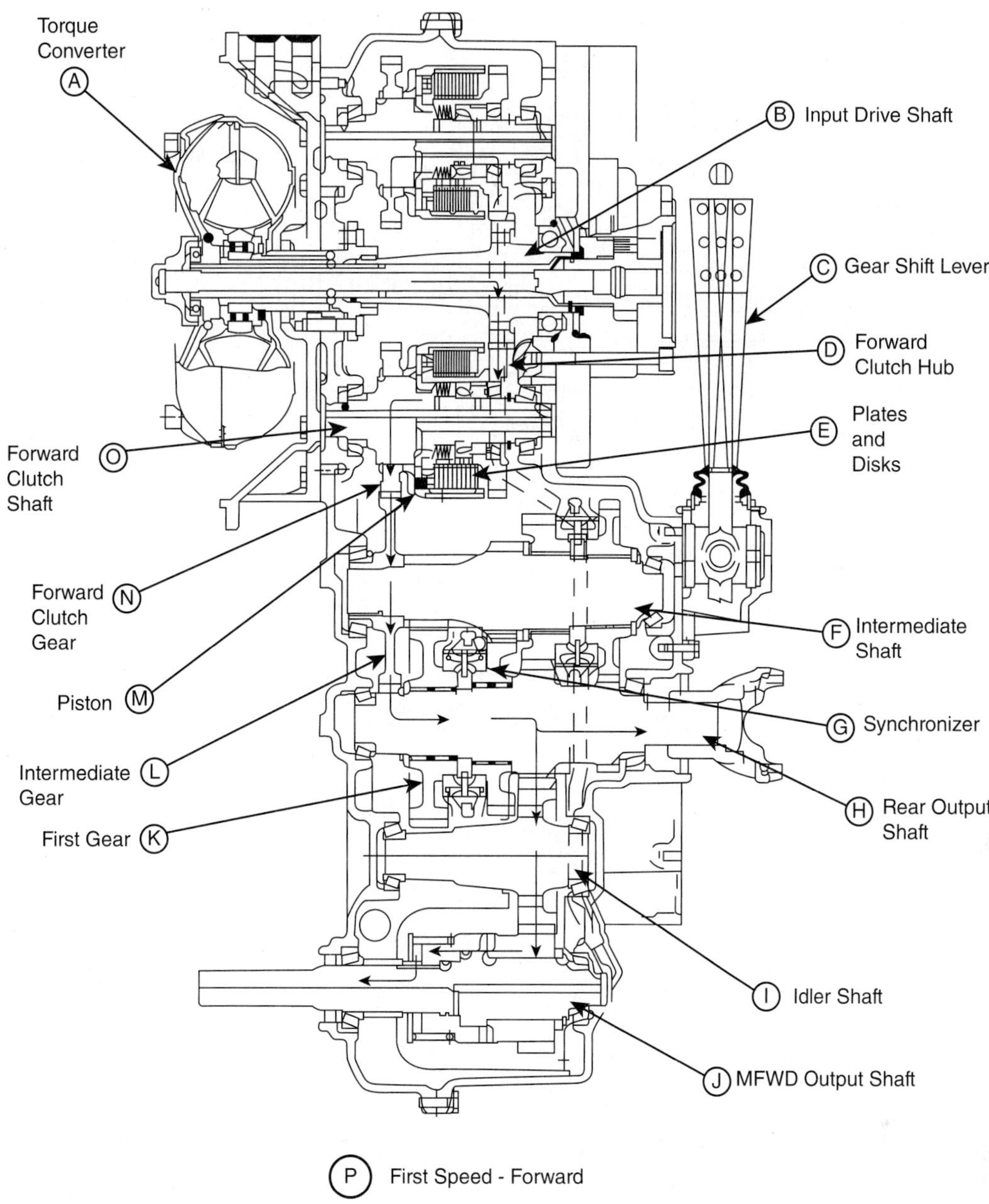

FIGURE 48-9 Power flow in first-speed forward.

the drivetrain. In a typical application, an operator selects the proper gear, speed range, and engine rpm for the work being performed. If the load on the equipment changes, the operator can manually upshift or downshift as needed by moving the shifter without depressing the foot clutch. This type of transmission makes it possible to transfer power from the engine to the axles and wheels more efficiently.

Power-Shift Transmission Operating Fundamentals

The ability of a power-shift transmission to shift under power is accomplished by hydraulic clutch packs that engage and disengage a series of gears and are controlled by a hydraulic system. The specific operator controls that are used for power-shift transmissions have changed over time (**FIGURE 48-12**).

Originally, power-shift transmissions were controlled by the operator through mechanical linkages in which a series of rods, levers, and ball joints transferred the motion of two gearshift levers from the cab to a series of spool valves in the transmission control valve. This mechanical control system eventually gave way to cables. Today, most power-shift transmissions are controlled electronically, where the operator is merely actuating electrical switches that control electric solenoids for both speed ranges and direction. Machines with power-shift transmissions today typically have one control lever that combines both direction and speed range control (**FIGURE 48-13**). Many modern power-shift transmission control systems give the operator

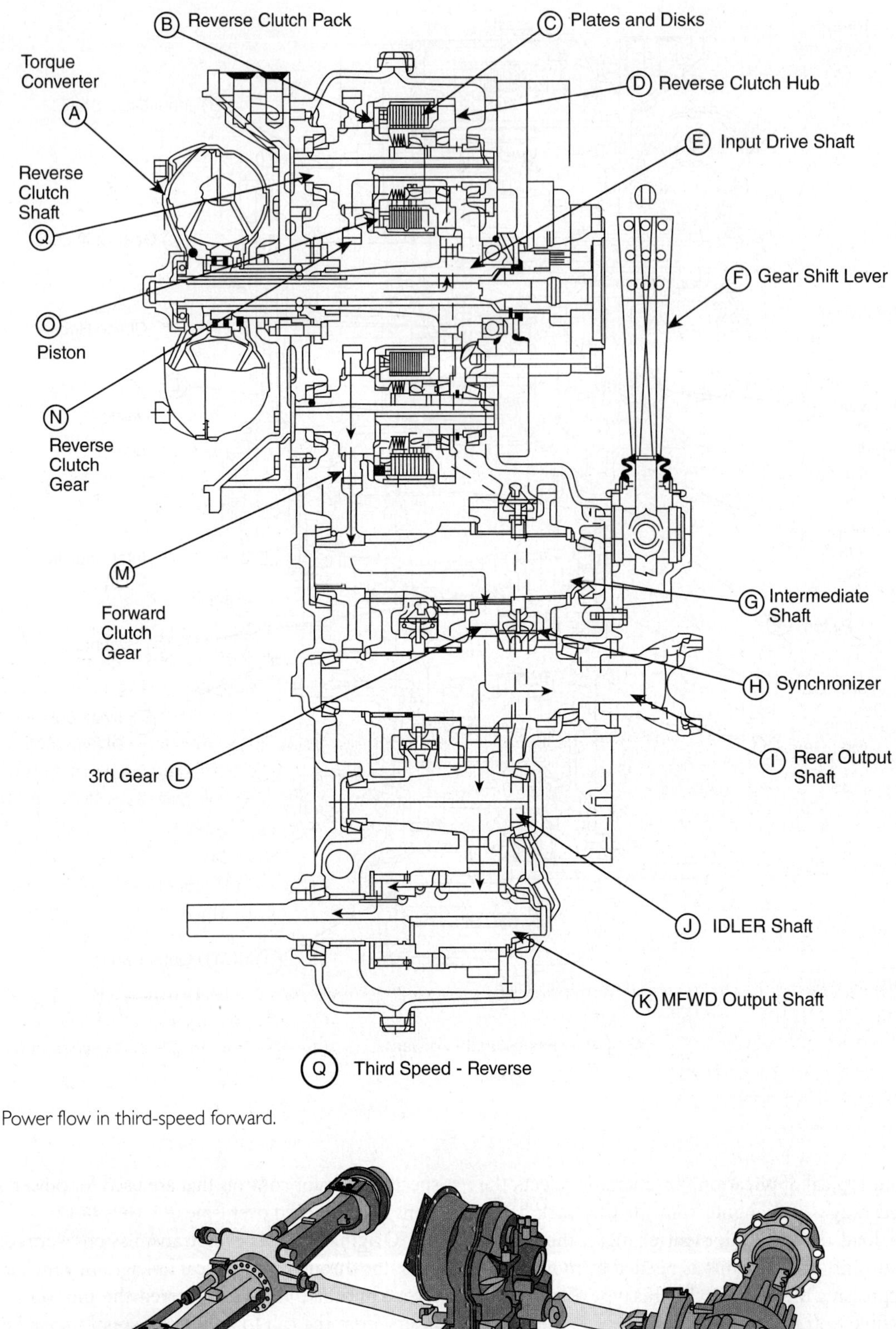

(B) Reverse Clutch Pack
(C) Plates and Disks
Torque Converter
(A)
(D) Reverse Clutch Hub
(E) Input Drive Shaft
Reverse Clutch Shaft
(Q)
(F) Gear Shift Lever
(O)
Piston
(N)
Reverse Clutch Gear
(M)
Forward Clutch Gear
(G) Intermediate Shaft
(H) Synchronizer
(I) Rear Output Shaft
3rd Gear (L)
(J) IDLER Shaft
(K) MFWD Output Shaft
(Q) Third Speed - Reverse

FIGURE 48-10 Power flow in third-speed forward.

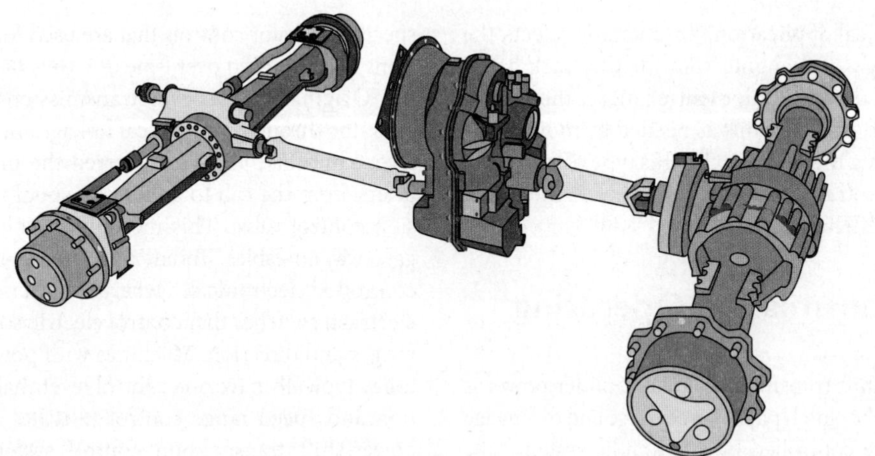

FIGURE 48-11 Typical powertrain arrangement with power-shift transmission.

FIGURE 48-12 Evolution of power-shift transmission controls.

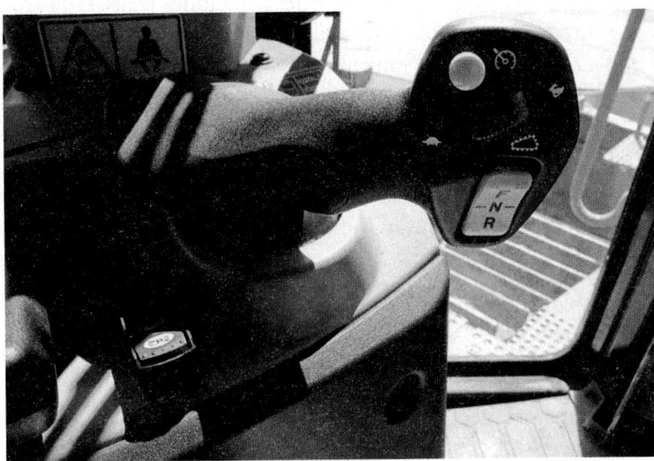

FIGURE 48-13 Multifunction power-shift control lever.

the option of being in control or letting an electronic control module (ECM) control transmission shifting.

In order to optimize equipment efficiency in terms of torque, fuel economy, and exhaust emissions, different gear ratios need to be available for each type of machine and each kind of work to be performed. For this reason, manufacturers

TABLE 48-1 Speed Ranges for Various Machines

Machine Type	Forward Speeds	Reverse Speeds
Track-type tractors	3	3
Wheel loaders	3–5	3–4
Motor graders	5–8	5–8
Mining trucks	6–8	1–2
Articulated trucks	5–8	1–2
Track loaders	3	3
Scrapers	6–18	1
Backhoe loaders	3–5	2–4
Skidders	4–8	3–4

offer transmissions with a variety of gear ratios. For instance, power-shift transmissions used in heavy equipment might have 2 to 18 forward speed ranges, or "gears," and 1 to 8 reverse speeds (TABLE 48-1).

Power-Shift Transmission Types

There are two main types of power-shift transmissions: countershaft and planetary. These terms refer to the type of gear arrangement used to transfer torque through the transmission. Both types are constant-mesh transmissions, which means that each of the gears inside the transmission is always in mesh with another gear. When one or more gears are locked to a shaft by a hydraulic clutch, torque is transferred through the transmission.

In a **countershaft power-shift transmission**, the hydraulic clutches control counter-rotating shafts by using meshed gears. This type of power-shift transmission is typically found in small- to medium-sized wheel loaders, graders, trucks, and other machines that are in the 100–400 hp (75–298 kW) range.

In a **planetary power-shift transmission**, the hydraulic clutches control sets of planetary gears to transfer power. Planetary power-shift transmissions can be found in any type or size of machine, from less than 100 hp to 1,000 hp (75 kW to 746 kW) or more.

▶ Power-Shift Transmission Construction

K48005

There are some similarities between countershaft and planetary power-shift transmissions. For example, both types of transmissions use hydraulically actuated clutches to change speeds and directions by engaging gears to shafts. The main difference between the two types involves the mechanical components that transfer torque from the input to the output.

Both types of power-shift transmissions can be found in tractors and earth-moving equipment such as dozers, graders, loaders, and scrapers. Some of these types of equipment are used in excavation work, where soil and aggregate material are pushed during grading operations. The loads handled by these types of equipment vary constantly. For example, an operator might use a dozer to grade a roadway. As the dozer moves forward, more and more soil accumulates in front of the blade. During such an operation, the operator might find it necessary to downshift to a lower gear to accommodate the increased load. The opposite situation can occur if the dozer is being used to spread large amounts of soil or gravel over an area. The operator might begin a pass by pushing a large pile of material. As the material is spread, the load at the front of the dozer blade decreases, enabling the operator to upshift to a higher gear to improve efficiency. A power-shift transmission provides a way for the operator to easily downshift and upshift—as well as change direction—under load with little to no loss of power flow to the final drive components.

Countershaft Power-Shift Transmissions

A countershaft power-shift transmission provides an operator with the ability to change speed and direction under full power because all gear changes are done with hydraulic clutches. The gear arrangement is a countershaft constant-mesh design with two clutches per shaft. To transfer torque from the input shaft to the output shafts, at least two hydraulic clutches must be engaged.

Most power-shift transmissions today are electronically controlled. By integrating electronics into the transmission controls, the operator will sometimes have different options or shift modes, such as autoshift, which automatically shifts the transmission ranges according to inputs to the transmission's ECM. These inputs are usually provided by sensors that monitor engine speed, transmission input shaft speed, transmission output speed, transmission oil temperature, and engine boost pressure. ECM outputs are likely to include fault-code logging and diagnostic systems. There might also be shift calibration or shift logic capabilities based on a machine's current operating conditions.

The countershaft power-shift transmission used in a John Deere 872D grader serves as a good example of how this type of transmission is arranged in a machine's drivetrain (**FIGURE 48-14**).

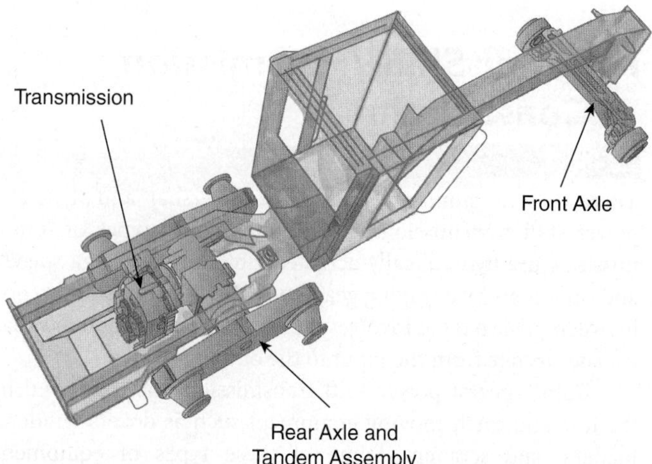

FIGURE 48-14 Countershaft power-shift transmission arrangement in a grader drivetrain.

This countershaft transmission is driven directly from the engine flywheel. In other words, there is no torque converter. The input shaft is driven at a 1:1 ratio from the engine through a **torsional damper**. There are eight forward and eight reverse gear ratios available. Each gear selection actuates two clutches: one for speed and one for direction. Each clutch is engaged hydraulically and controlled by an individual electronically controlled proportional solenoid valve. The rate of pressure rise behind each clutch piston is determined by the transmission control unit (TCU) that provides the solenoids with a 24V **pulse-width modulated (PWM)** signal to each valve.

The transmission's output shaft drives a differential assembly that contains planetary final drives. These final drives power the tandem drive, which in turn drives the grader's wheels and tires.

The operator inputs include the transmission shift control lever, an inching pedal, and an autoshift button. The transmission is shifted from neutral when the operator moves the shift lever to any of eight forward or reverse detents in the transmission shift switch. The inching pedal will neutralize the transmission and simulate a mechanical clutch to the operator. If autoshift is selected, the TCU will select upshift and downshift points only from fifth to eighth gear if the selector is in the eighth position. The shift points will depend on engine speed, throttle position, and engine load inputs. These inputs, along with several speed and temperature values gathered from sensors, are sent to the TCU that will control clutch engagement by energizing proportional solenoid valves with a PWM signal.

Planetary Power-Shift Transmissions

Planetary power-shift transmissions are used in many types and sizes of heavy equipment machines, including track-type tractors, graders, wheel loaders, and trucks. They can provide from 2 to 12 forward speed ranges and up to 5 reverse speeds. Planetary power-shift transmissions use a gear arrangement with one or more planetary gear sets, a combination of hydraulic clutches, and a control system.

Planetary gear sets consist of a combination of three main components that are used to transfer torque (**FIGURE 48-15**):

1. a sun gear
2. a planetary pinion carrier (driven or held by planetary pinion gears)
3. a ring gear.

Planetary gear sets have several advantages over conventional gear sets:

- a more balanced load on gears, shafts, and bearings
- the ability to change gear ratios and directions easily
- a more compact design.

In a planetary gear set, holding one component while driving another will result in an output from the third component (**FIGURE 48-16**).

Planetary gear sets can provide an increase in speed and a decrease in torque, a decrease in speed and an increase in

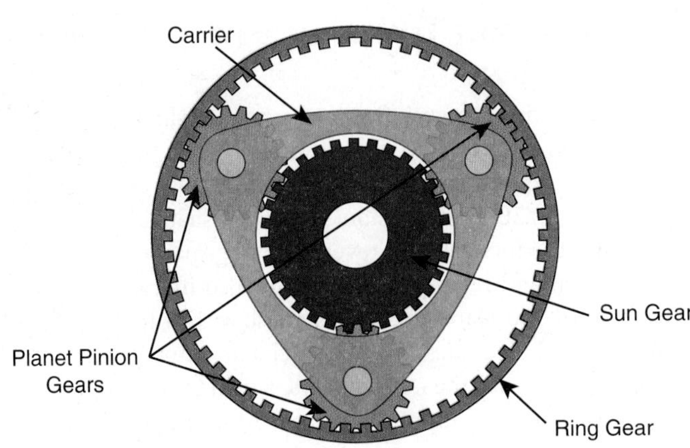

FIGURE 48-15 Planetary gear set.

torque, a direct drive ratio of 1:1, or reverse rotation. More specifically, this type of gear set can provide seven combinations when one member is driven while one member is held, or when two members are locked together (**TABLE 48-2**).

This planetary power-shift transmission can be found in an articulated truck and features three sets of planetary gears and five hydraulically actuated clutches (**FIGURE 48-17**). The transmission receives its input from the engine flywheel, through a torque converter, and into the input shaft. After two clutches have been engaged, power can then flow through the transmission and out to the output shaft. The output shaft is connected to a transfer case, which drops the power flow down and makes it available to the front axle and back to the rear tandem axles.

The three sets of planetary gear sets provide torque flow through the transmission, depending on which combination of planetary gear set members are held and which are allowed to freewheel. This is determined by the five clutches that are attached to various gear sets. As these clutches are engaged or disengaged at the maximum of two at a time, torque flow will be transferred through the gear sets.

The five clutches used in order to change input torque, speed, and direction are called C1, C2 (both rotating clutches), C3, C4, and C5 (stationary clutches, or brakes). The torque converter turbine provides input to both the C1 and C2 clutches. When the C1 clutch is engaged, it will drive the transmission main shaft at the speed of the torque converter turbine. When the C2 clutch is engaged, it will drive the P2 planetary carrier

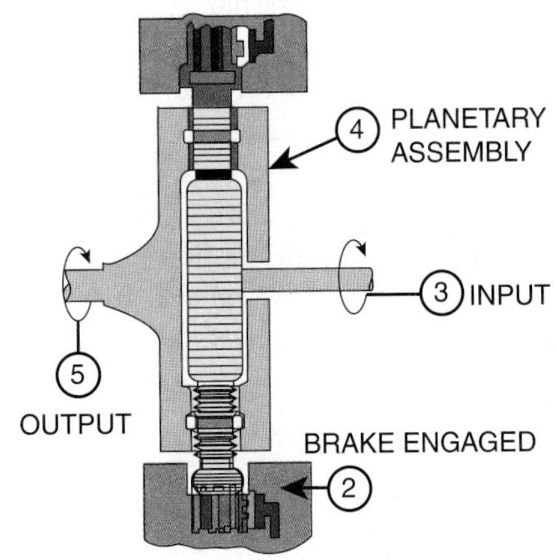

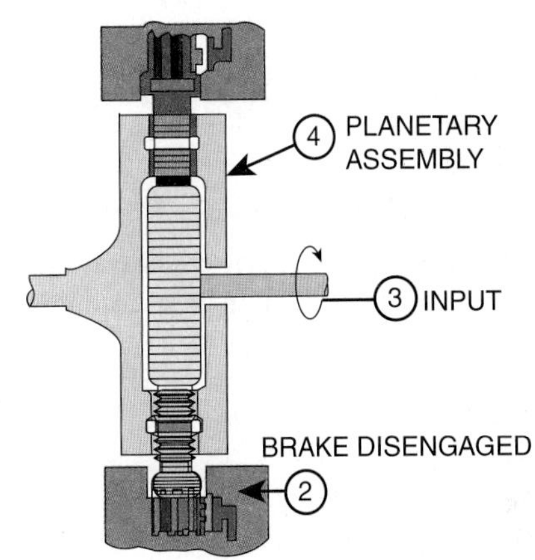

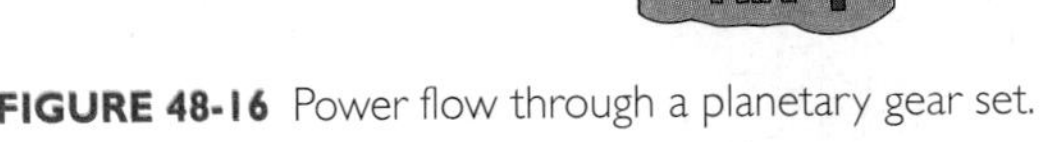
FIGURE 48-16 Power flow through a planetary gear set.

TABLE 48-2 Power Flow Combinations Through a Planetary Gear Set

	Sun	Carrier	Ring	Speed	Torque	Direction
1	Input	Output	Held	Maximum reduction	Increase	Same as input
2	Held	Output	Input	Minimum reduction	Increase	Same as input
3	Output	Input	Held	Maximum increase	Reduction	Same as input
4	Held	Input	Output	Minimum increase	Reduction	Same as input
5	Input	Held	Output	Reduction	Increase	Opposite of input
6	Output	Held	Input	Increase	Reduction	Opposite of input
7	When any two members are held together, speed and direction are same as input; ratio is 1:1.					

If the carrier is

1 - then the output, under drive results, or speed decrease
2 - then the input, overdrive results, or speed increase
3 - then the held member or output direction is reversed.

FIGURE 48-17 Planetary power-shift transmission components.

at the speed of the torque converter turbine. When the C3, C4, or C5 clutches are engaged, they will lock the ring gears of the P1, P2, or P3 planetary gear sets to the transmission housing, respectively. The P2 ring gear is also connected to the P1 planetary carrier, and the P3 ring gear is connected to the P2 planetary carrier.

▶ Power-Shift Transmission Power Flows

K48006

The way that power flows through a power-shift transmission depends on whether the transmission is a countershaft power-shift transmission or a planetary power-shift transmission.

Countershaft Transmission Power Flows

To understand the power flows of a countershaft power-shift transmission, it helps to first examine how the shafts are arranged in the transmission housing (**FIGURE 48-18**). In this John Deere 872D transmission, the input shaft is in constant mesh with the forward and reverse input gears on their shafts. The forward and reverse hub gears are also in constant mesh. The forward hub gear is in constant mesh with both of the speed clutch input hub gears. The speed clutch output gears are in constant mesh with the output gears, which in turn are in constant mesh with the output shaft gear. The output yoke is driven by the output shaft.

When the transmission control lever is placed in first-speed forward, clutches C and D are engaged (**FIGURE 48-19**). The solenoids controlling the transmission clutches are energized by a signal that produces proportional pressure and flow changes.

Engine power comes into the input shaft (A), where it drives the four input floating gears on the directional clutch shafts. If one of the forward clutches is engaged, it will send torque to the two speed clutch cylinders. When system pressure oil is applied to clutch C, the piston moves to apply pressure to the clutch plates. This clutch can now transfer torque out through the external gear on its cylinder. The cylinders are the common drum for the two clutches on each shaft. As soon as any one of the four directional clutches is engaged, torque will be transferred to that clutch's output gear. This gear will then transfer torque down to the bottom shafts and out through the output shaft. In this case, the first gear clutch is engaged (D) and torque flows out its shaft gear to drive gear E, which in turn drives gear F and turns gear G on the output shaft, which turns yoke H.

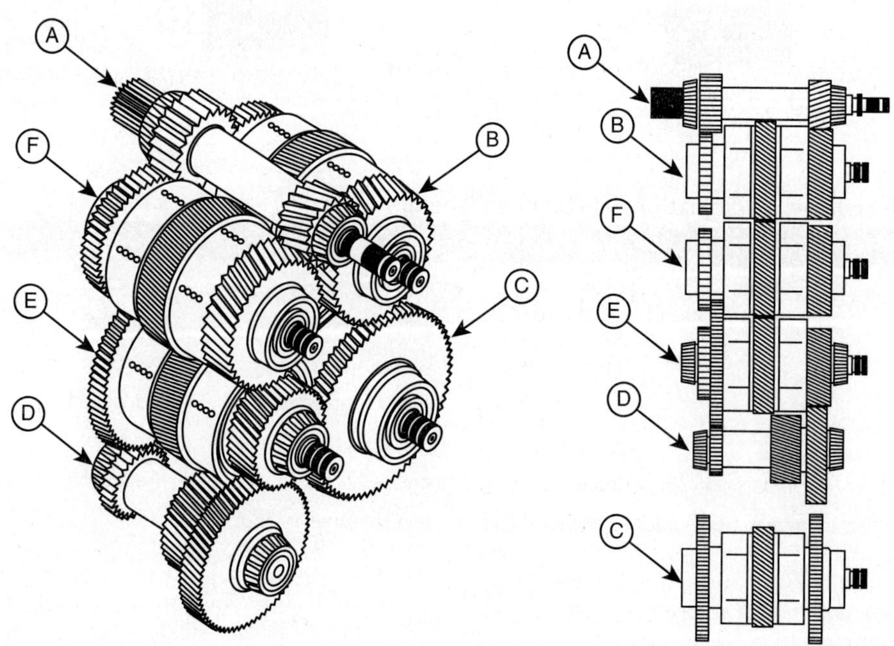

FIGURE 48-18 Arrangement of shafts in countershaft power-shift transmission.

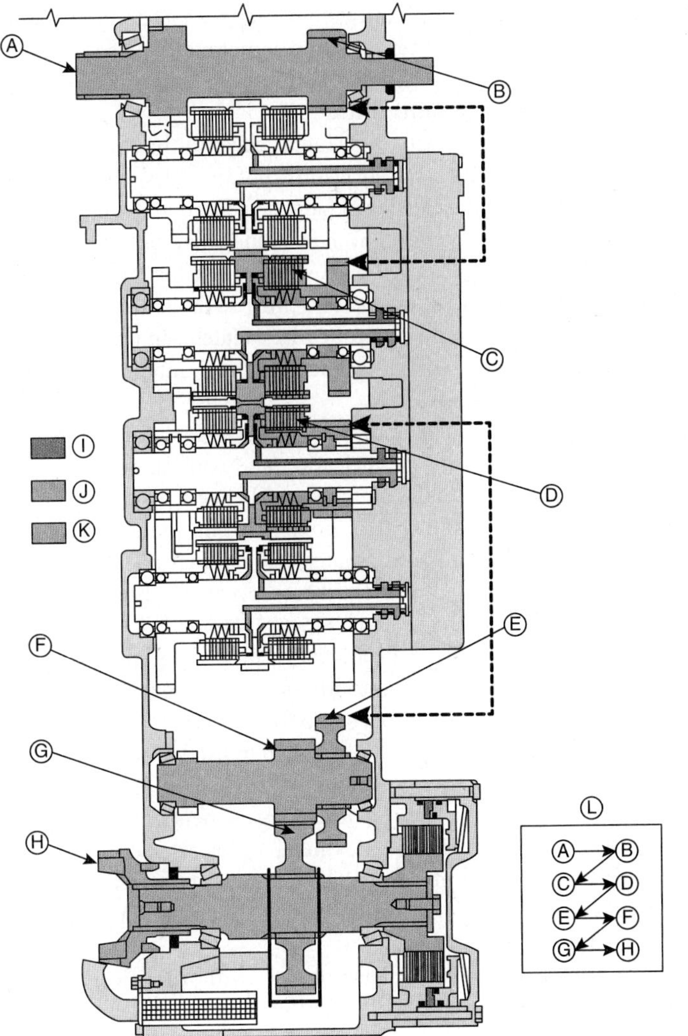

FIGURE 48-19 Power flow in first-speed forward.

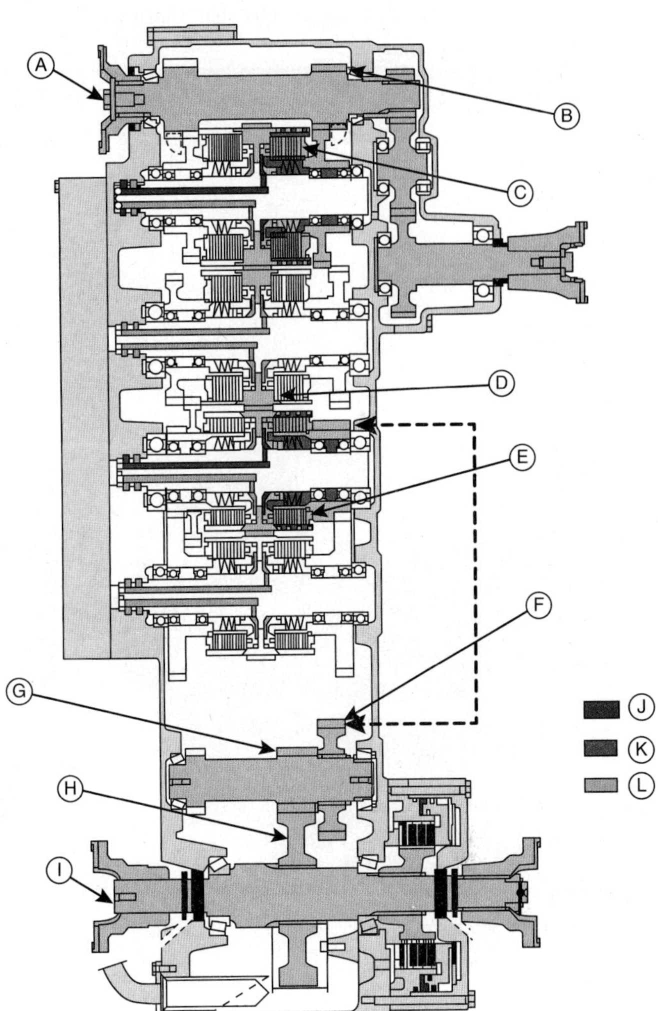

FIGURE 48-20 Power flow in first-speed reverse.

If one of the reverse range directional clutches is engaged, it will transfer torque from the transmission's input shaft to its cylinder, and since this cylinder is in mesh with only the forward cylinder, the torque will flow through that cylinder. This will reverse the rotation from the reverse shaft, and when any speed clutch is engaged, its rotation will be transferred out the transmission in reverse rotation. The forward shaft then acts as a reverse idler.

Power flow through the countershaft power-shift transmission can also be visualized for the reverse direction. When the transmission control lever is placed in first-speed reverse, clutches C and E are engaged (**FIGURE 48-20**). The solenoids controlling the transmission clutches are energized by a signal that produces proportional pressure and flow changes.

Engine power comes into the input shaft (A) to the first-stage gear (back) (B). Power flow is directed to the third-stage direction clutch C, through the second-stage cylinder gear D to the fourth-stage speed clutch E, and on through the transmission to the sixth-stage gear F and middle gear G. Power then flows to the seventh-stage output gear H and out through the output stage (I).

Planetary Transmission Power Flows

Trying to visualize the power flows for a planetary power-shift transmission can be difficult because of the complexity involving torque transfer through planetary gear sets. Often, a better way to understand the power flows through this type of transmission is with a chart that shows which clutches are engaged for each speed and direction range (**TABLE 48-3**).

▶ Hydraulic Clutch Control Systems

K48007

The key component for enabling a power-shift transmission to shift speed ranges and directions under full power is the hydraulically applied, spring-released clutch (**FIGURE 48-21**). The development of this type of clutch has made the power-shift transmission a widely used and reliable powertrain component. Because these components are so prevalent, MORE service technicians need to understand how hydraulic clutches are constructed, how they operate, and how they are controlled.

TABLE 48-3 Clutch Engagement for Planetary Power-Shift Transmission

Transmission Gear	Clutches Engaged
Neutral	C5
First forward	C1, C5
Second forward	C1, C4
Third forward	C1, C3
Forth forward	C2, C3
Fifth forward	C2, C4
Reverse	C3, C5

FIGURE 48-21 Hydraulically applied, spring-released clutch.

Hydraulic Clutch Components

The basic purpose of a hydraulic clutch used in any type of power-shift transmission is to either lock two rotating components together, such as one gear to another gear, or stop a rotating component by locking it to a stationary component. A hydraulic clutch accomplishes these tasks by applying pressurized fluid from the powertrain hydraulic system to a piston that squeezes plates and discs together.

> **TECHNICIAN TIP**
>
> When a hydraulic clutch is used to lock a rotating component to a stationary housing, the clutch is sometimes referred to as a brake. This can sometimes be confusing, but the action is the same. That is, it uses a hydraulically actuated piston to squeeze discs and plates together to lock two components together.

The torque transfer components inside a hydraulic clutch are plates (sometimes called **separator plates**) and discs (sometimes called **friction discs**) that are alternately stacked together in groups of 2 to 10. The clutch plates are thin, round slices of steel or cast iron that have teeth on either the inside or the outside diameter or tangs on the outside diameter. The teeth or tangs are used to lock the plates to a component, such as a gear hub, a ring gear, or a housing.

The clutch discs are sandwiched between the clutch plates and have teeth on their inside diameter or, in some cases, their outside diameter. Each clutch plate and disc can be up to ¼ of an inch (6 mm) thick.

The torque capacity of a clutch relates to the surface area of the discs. The greater the surface area of the discs, the higher the torque load that the clutch can handle. Consequently, clutch discs and plates for low-horsepower machines may only be 4 inches (102 mm) in diameter, while the ones used for large machines could be as big as 36 inches (914 mm) in diameter. To increase the maximum amount of torque that a clutch can transfer, transmission manufacturers either increase the number or the size of the plates and discs.

The clutch plates and discs are designed to operate in a hydraulic fluid bath for lubrication and cooling purposes. The plates inside a hydraulic clutch should have a relatively smooth surface, but not one that is polished. The plate surfaces are usually ground with a crosshatch pattern that enables them to retain a film of hydraulic fluid to prevent overheating during clutch application or release (**FIGURE 48-22**). Whenever plates are removed during a disassembly procedure, they must be inspected for heat checks, tooth wear, grooving, and discoloration, and they must be measured for flatness.

The discs in a hydraulic clutch must be able to absorb huge amounts of energy when a shift is made. There is a brief period between the start of clutch engagement and full engagement when these clutch discs need to tolerate some slippage. This slippage generates heat. The discs' ability to withstand this heat and engage smoothly depends on the type of material from which they are made.

Clutch discs have a base of steel with a friction material bonded to both sides. This friction material can be made of various compounds:

- sintered metal combinations of bronze, iron, and copper
- paper-based or cellulous materials (sometimes called organic materials)
- elastomeric materials containing a mixture of rubber, inorganic fibers, and friction particles.

FIGURE 48-22 Clutch plate showing signs of overheating.

FIGURE 48-23 Different types of clutch discs.

Transmission manufacturers determine the type of friction material by determining the loads and temperatures that the clutch must withstand and the shift characteristics desired (**FIGURE 48-23**). When the clutch is engaged under load, the type of friction material used will affect how the shift feels to the operator and how much shock load is transferred through the drivetrain.

Hydraulic Clutch Operation

When a hydraulic clutch needs to be engaged, pressurized fluid from the hydraulic system is routed through a control valve past a solenoid controlled by the operator. The clutch apply oil is fed through a bore in the transmission housing that the clutch shaft rotates in and enters a cross-drilling in the shaft. The cross-drilling is sealed with O-rings, and the oil then travels through the clutch shaft to another cross-drilling at the piston housing. Here the oil is then applied to the face of the piston. This pressure forces the piston to clamp the plates and discs together (**FIGURE 48-24**). Seals along the oil flow path and around the piston prevent the oil from leaking out.

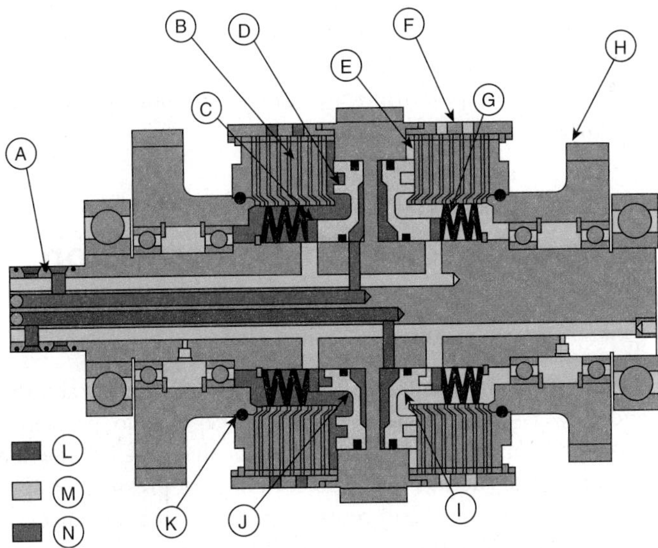

FIGURE 48-24 How oil moves a hydraulic clutch piston (I and J).

FIGURE 48-25 Clutch release spring.

Once a hydraulic clutch is disengaged, springs in the clutch retract the clutch piston and allow the plates and discs to rotate independently (**FIGURE 48-25**). Clutch release springs are usually one of two types: a series of coil springs spaced around the circumference of the piston or one or more Belleville springs. A Belleville spring is shaped like a dished washer and can be used singly or stacked in multiples. Either way, the spring or springs push on the piston to keep it in the released position.

Hydraulic Clutch Control

K48007

The way that hydraulic clutches in a power-shift transmission are controlled depends on factors such as the type of transmission, the equipment manufacturer, and the type of control system being used. To better understand the basic principles of hydraulic clutch control, it helps to start by looking at a block diagram of an electronic transmission control system (**FIGURE 48-26**).

The transmission control system in this example consists of the following components:

- transmission control unit (TCU)
- engine control unit (ECU)
- accelerator position sensor
- transmission speed sensors
  - input speed sensor
  - turbine speed sensor
  - output speed sensor
- transmission shift control
- transmission control module (TCM)
  - pressure switch
  - temperature sensor
  - oil level sensor
  - solenoid valves
  - retarder control
- diagnostic data connector.

In this transmission, the accelerator position sensor, the transmission speed sensors, and the transmission shift control send information via wiring harnesses to the transmission control unit (TCU). The TCU processes this information and sends electrical signals to actuate specific solenoid valves. Energizing and deenergizing these solenoid valves controls the oncoming and off-going clutch pressures to enable transmission shifts that match engine speed and operating conditions to protect the transmission from damage.

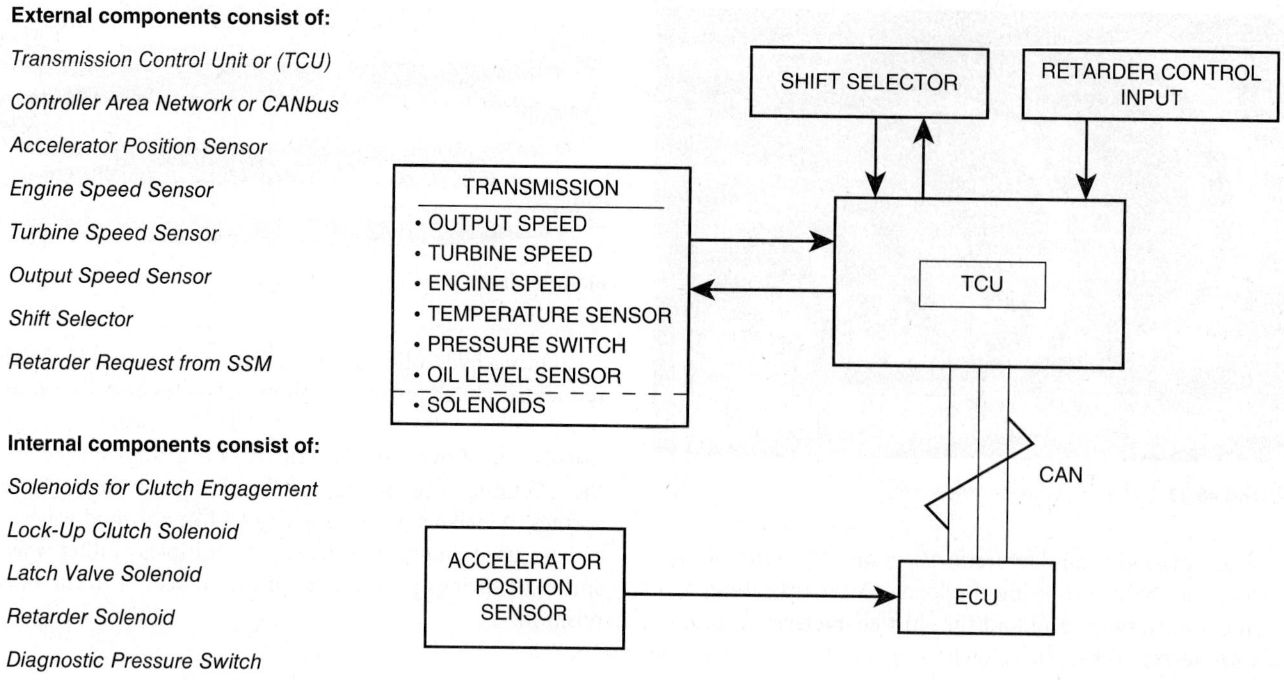

External components consist of:

Transmission Control Unit or (TCU)

Controller Area Network or CANbus

Accelerator Position Sensor

Engine Speed Sensor

Turbine Speed Sensor

Output Speed Sensor

Shift Selector

Retarder Request from SSM

Internal components consist of:

Solenoids for Clutch Engagement

Lock-Up Clutch Solenoid

Latch Valve Solenoid

Retarder Solenoid

Diagnostic Pressure Switch

SHIFT SELECTOR
RETARDER CONTROL INPUT
TRANSMISSION
• OUTPUT SPEED
• TURBINE SPEED
• ENGINE SPEED
• TEMPERATURE SENSOR
• PRESSURE SWITCH
• OIL LEVEL SENSOR
• SOLENOIDS
TCU
CAN
ACCELERATOR POSITION SENSOR
ECU

FIGURE 48-26 Transmission control system.

A controller area network (CAN) data line signal is used to communicate between the TCU and the chassis control unit (CCU). The CCU provides a signal that prevents the TCU from upshifting the transmission above first gear. The TCU also provides the CCU with a signal to activate the neutral start circuit and the backup alarm circuit.

See (**FIGURE 48-27**) to see a typical example of a power shift transmission hydraulic system that is electronically controlled. Five proportional solenoids are used to control the flow of pressurized hydraulic fluid to the clutches. Clutch application pressure is typically regulated between 145 and 300 psi (1,000 and 2,068 kPa), depending on the value of the PWM signal from the TCU to the solenoids. Each solenoid and regulator valve assembly controls one clutch apply circuit. The solenoids receive a signal from the TCM and ECM to control both incoming and off-going clutch pressures. The output pressure from the solenoids is proportional to the current supplied by the TCM, so the solenoids are commonly known as pressure control solenoids (PCS).

As is the case with most clutch pack solenoids, the ones in this system are variable bleed solenoids. Two of the solenoids are normally open, and the rest are normally closed. The normally open solenoids provide a "limp home" mode if there is an electrical failure.

▶ Power-Shift Transmission Shift Control Logic

K48008

The software in the TCU of a power-shift transmission provides numerous features that relate to shift control. For instance, the software enables the TCU to adapt or "learn" while it operates. Each shift is measured and stored by the TCU so that the optimum shift rate is adapted for present operating conditions.

Another feature of the software is referred to as event-based shifting (EBS). EBS is designed to provide optimum shift quality. This feature automatically adjusts clutch engagement based on the load that the TCU senses. The TCU uses sensors on the transmission, along with information from other controllers and sensors via the CAN, to aid in this operation. Transmission shift duration and timing may vary based on these inputs.

When the operator selects a gear, the TCU follows a standard shift logic paradigm that incorporates clutch protection, speed matching, downshift inhibiting, inching pedal use, shuttle shifting, and autoshift. After a gear is determined by the shift logic, the engagement of that gear is governed by the EBS portion of the software. The EBS software may "feather" a clutch to provide a smooth, soft shift, such as during transport, or it may provide a rapid, firm shift to maintain momentum when the machine is under load.

▶ Common Power Shuttle and Power-Shift Transmission Failures

K48009, S48001

As with any component used in a piece of MORE, power shuttles and power-shift transmissions are susceptible to problems. Both components contain many parts that can be affected by conditions such as heat, lubrication, and pressure. Proper operating techniques and routine preventive maintenance are essential to prolonging the life of the equipment. Since many types of power shuttles and power-shift transmissions are used

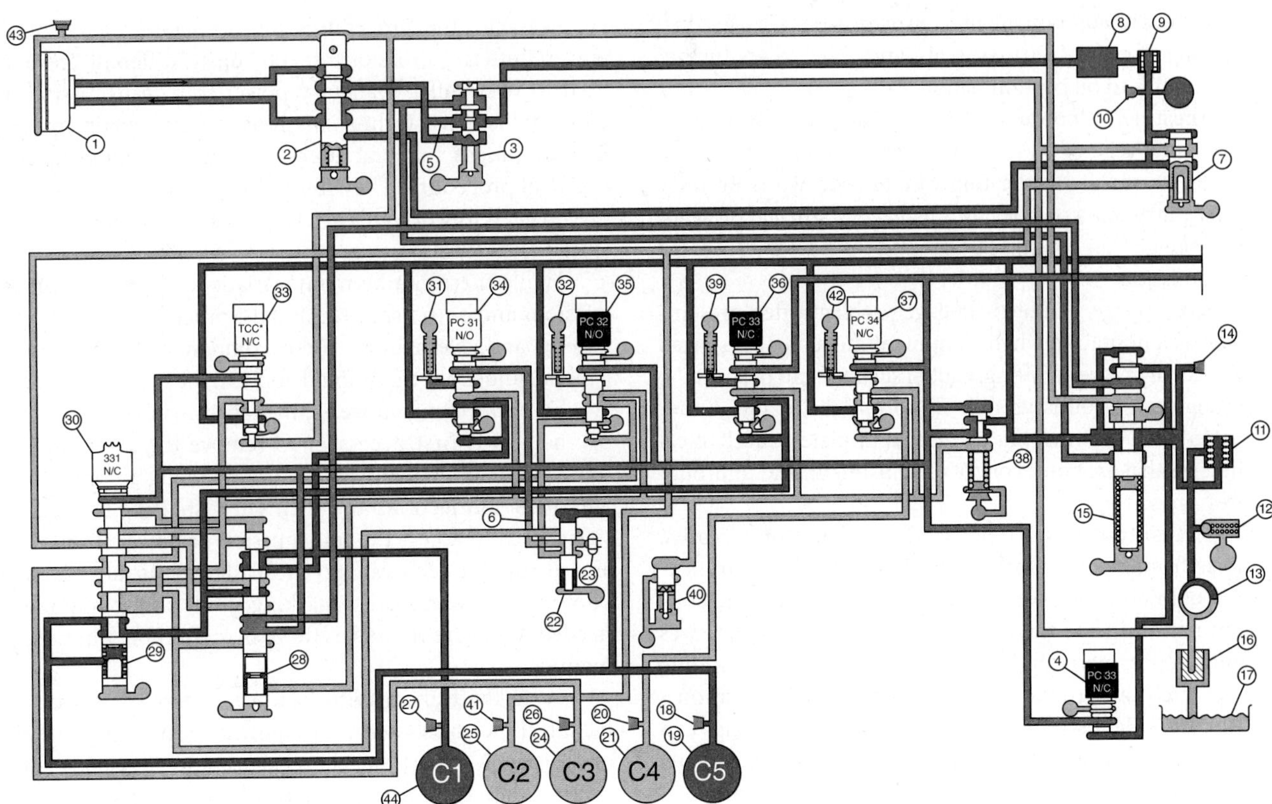

FIGURE 48-27 Transmission hydraulic system schematic.

in MORE, technicians should always follow the specific manufacturer's guidelines for maintaining, troubleshooting, and repairing these components.

SAFETY TIP

When testing a machine to diagnose a power shuttle or power-shift transmission problem, it may be necessary to make the machine travel. This action can have the potential for accidents and injury unless some basic safety precautions are followed. Ensure that the area around the machine is clear of people and objects that could be injured or damaged by machine movement. Also, be aware of all hazards and follow all traffic rules and company policies regarding machine movement. In some cases, it can be helpful to have a spotter assist you while you are testing the equipment.

▶ TECHNICIAN TIP

During any power shuttle or power-shift transmission troubleshooting, it is important to bring the hydraulic fluid to its normal operating temperature, which is typically around 180°F (82°C). This is important because the change in the fluid viscosity can greatly affect how transmission controls and clutches respond to operator input.

Power Shuttle Problems

Since the purpose of a power shuttle is to allow an operator to easily change the direction of the equipment, most problems relate to the inability of the power shuttle to perform that basic task. Common power shuttle problems and failures involve sluggish or absent forward and/or reverse movement. The following are the primary causes of forward and reverse problems:

- low oil level, contaminated oil, and/or the wrong type of oil
- worn or dirty solenoid valves
- improper pressure settings
- worn clutch discs and plates
- bound or improperly adjusted linkages between the directional shift lever and the power shuttle (for mechanically controlled power shuttles)
- electrical issues (for electrohydraulically controlled power shuttles).

Power-Shift Transmission Problems

Problems related to power-shift transmissions can range from hydraulic fluid leaks to worn or broken gears and other internal components. Both countershaft transmissions and planetary transmissions have hydraulic clutches with multiple plates and discs, as well as a large array of shafts, gears, bearings, and seals. Always follow the manufacturer's recommendations for troubleshooting and identifying problems in the specific transmission being worked on.

The following are some of the more common problems that can affect nearly any type of power-shift transmission:

- Hydraulic oil-related problems. Oil problems such as low oil level, contaminated oil, the wrong type of oil, and debris in the hydraulic oil filter can damage or destroy nearly every component in a transmission. The gradual wearing of gears, bearings, seals, and clutch discs further contributes to oil contamination.

- Overheating. A power-shift transmission can overheat if the wrong type of oil is used or if the oil level is too low. Other causes of overheating can include worn or dirty relief valves and control valves, worn or damaged oil seals, and plugged oil cooling devices and oil flow paths in the transmission.
- Clutch slippage. A clutch slippage problem often presents itself as a hesitation when equipment movement is started and during power-shifting. Clutch slippage can occur if the wrong type of oil is used or if the oil level is low. Other causes include worn clutch discs and plates, mechanical linkages that are bound or out of adjustment, and improper pressure settings.
- Abnormal transmission noise. Unusual and/or excessive noise from a power-shift transmission can be an indication of low oil level, worn gears and/or bearings, and contamination inside the transmission. Improper pressures and temperatures can lead to **cavitation** of the hydraulic oil, which can produce unusual noise during operation.
- Vibration. Bent shafts and damaged gears or bearings can affect the rotation of parts inside the transmission and are, therefore, among the most likely causes of vibration.
- Oil leaks. Worn or damaged oil seals and gaskets are common causes of leaks from a transmission.
- Gear selection, shifting, and directional change issues. Problems or failures related to gear shifting and/or directional changes can be caused by many factors, including oil-related issues, dirty or damaged solenoids or regulator valve assemblies, and problems in any of the electrohydraulic components of the TCU.

Many common power shuttle and power-shift transmission failures can be avoided by establishing and following a regular preventive maintenance program. Equipment manufacturers provide information about routine checks and adjustments, fluid and filter changes, and guidelines for proper operation. Following these recommendations can reduce unnecessary downtime and extend the life of these components.

To perform recommended maintenance on power-shift transmissions and power shuttles, follow the steps in **SKILL DRILL 48-1**.

▶ Power-Shift Transmission and Power Shuttle Overhauls

K48010

Specific procedures used during any power-shift transmission or power shuttle overhaul will vary according to the equipment, the manufacturer, and, in some cases, company guidelines. For example, the procedures for overhauling a countershaft power-shift transmission are obviously different from those used to overhaul a planetary power-shift transmission. Consequently, service technicians must always obtain and follow the equipment manufacturer's recommendations during any overhaul procedure. They must also follow all company guidelines related to work area safety, personal protective equipment (PPE), and cleanliness.

While there can be many variations in power-shift transmissions and power shuttles, and the procedures used for maintaining and overhauling these components, there are some general guidelines that should apply in most cases.

To perform any power-shift transmission or power shuttle overhaul, it is first necessary to remove the component from the equipment. This involves disconnecting all wiring, hoses, and other connections and then safely splitting the equipment (if needed) to access the transmission or power shuttle. Before and during the removal and overhaul, technicians should take photographs, use match marking, and label components as needed to ensure that everything is reassembled in the proper manner.

Once the transmission has been removed and disassembled, technicians should thoroughly inspect each part for wear or damage. Any part that shows signs of wear, damage, or overheating should be replaced. Normal wear parts such as seals, bearings, O-rings, and gaskets should always be replaced. The same basic rule applies to parts like clutch plates and discs. Other components, such as valves, can sometimes be rebuilt separately and reused. Always use the manufacturer's service information to ensure that all replacement parts correctly match the originals. Also, keep track of all the parts used during the overhaul.

Manufacturer guidelines must also be followed during reassembly and reinstallation of the components. Be sure to properly lubricate all O-rings and install all match-marked components to their original positions. In addition, follow all manufacturer recommendations for torquing bolts.

Once the transmission has been reinstalled in the equipment, double-check that all wiring, tubing, and hoses are properly reconnected. Fill the transmission with the proper type and amount of hydraulic fluid based on the manufacturer's recommendations, and check for leaks. The equipment should then be started and allowed to reach normal operating conditions for temperatures and pressures. Verify these values using the manufacturer's guidelines.

Test the equipment to ensure that the overhaul was successful. Verify that all shifting and directional changes are taking place as designed. Check again for leaks or any signs of unusual operating conditions.

To complete the procedure, carefully log what was done and list the parts that were used during the overhaul. Save this information in a database so that it can be referenced for future maintenance, repairs, and overhauls.

SKILL DRILL 48-1 Power-Shift Transmission and Power Shuttle Recommended Maintenance

1. Obtain and review the manufacturer's guidelines that cover recommended maintenance procedures for the specific equipment.

2. Locate and secure the equipment in an area where maintenance can occur safely and contamination can be minimized.

3. Perform a visual inspection to check for fluid leaks, damaged or broken piping and/or hoses, and other obvious problems.

4. Change the hydraulic fluid and filters, and have the fluid analyzed to identify contaminants or characteristics that might indicate pending problems.

5. Lubricate and adjust (if necessary) any mechanical connections that might exist, based on the manufacturer's recommendations.

6. Start the equipment, allow it to reach normal operating conditions, and test the shifting and directional change performance.

7. Record all actions performed during the maintenance procedure on the appropriate service form or into an electronic database.

Wrap-Up

Ready for Review

- A power shuttle is an addition or improvement to a transmission that enables an operator to easily change the direction of the equipment between forward and reverse while maintaining the same speed and engine rpm.
- Other common names for a power shuttle are power reverser and hydraulic shuttle.
- Power shuttles were developed to help reduce the burdens of having to depress a foot clutch, bring a piece of equipment to a complete stop, and manually shift gears and/or speed ranges.
- Power shuttles are commonly used on equipment, like loaders, that need to make constant forward and reverse directional changes during operation.
- Directional changes in a power shuttle are accomplished electrohydraulically. Moving the directional shift lever activates proportional solenoid valves that engage two multidisc wet clutches (one for forward direction and one for reverse direction).
- A power-shift transmission allows operators to shift gears up or down and change directions on the go and under load without a loss in acceleration or torque and without having to use a foot clutch.
- The ability of a power-shift transmission to shift under power is accomplished by hydraulic clutch packs that engage and disengage a series of gears and are controlled by a hydraulic system.
- Today, most power-shift transmissions are controlled electronically, where the operator is merely actuating electrical switches that control electric solenoids for both speed ranges and direction.
- There are two main types of power-shift transmissions: countershaft and planetary.
- In a countershaft power-shift transmission, hydraulic clutches control counter-rotating shafts with meshed gears.
- A countershaft power-shift transmission is typically found in small- to medium-sized wheel loaders, graders, trucks, and other machines that are in the 100–400 hp (75–298 kW) range.
- In a planetary power-shift transmission, hydraulic clutches control sets of planetary gears to transfer power.
- Planetary power-shift transmissions can be found in any type or size of machine, from less than 100 hp to 1,000 hp (75 kW to 746 kW) or more.
- The key component for enabling a power-shift transmission to shift speed ranges and directions under full power is a hydraulically applied, spring-released clutch.
- The basic purpose of a hydraulic clutch used in any type of power-shift transmission is to either lock two rotating components together, such as one gear to another gear, or stop a rotating component by locking it to a stationary component.
- The torque transfer components inside a hydraulic clutch are plates and discs that are alternately stacked together in groups of 2 to 10.
- The torque capacity of a clutch relates to the surface area of the discs. The greater the surface area of the discs, the higher the torque load that the clutch can handle.
- When a hydraulic clutch is engaged, pressurized fluid from the hydraulic system is routed through a control valve or solenoid that is controlled by the operator, fed through a bore on the clutch piston housing, and applied to the face of the piston to clamp the plates and discs together.
- Once a hydraulic clutch is disengaged, springs in the clutch retract the clutch piston and allow the plates and discs to rotate independently.
- The way hydraulic clutches in a power-shift transmission are controlled depends on factors such as the type of transmission, the equipment manufacturer, and the type of transmission control system being used.
- The software in a power-shift transmission control unit (TCU) enables the TCU to "learn" while it operates so that an optimum shift rate can be adapted for present operating conditions.
- Event-based shifting (EBS) is a TCU software feature designed to automatically adjust clutch engagement based on the load that the TCU senses.
- Common power shuttle problems include those associated with the hydraulic oil, worn or dirty solenoid valves, improper pressure settings, worn clutch discs and plates, bound or improperly adjusted linkages between the directional shift lever and the power shuttle (for mechanically controlled power shuttles), and electrical issues (for electrohydraulically controlled power shuttles).
- Common power-shift transmission problems include those associated with the hydraulic oil; overheating; worn or dirty relief valves and control valves; worn or damaged oil seals; clutch slippage; abnormal transmission noise; vibration; oil leaks; and gear selection, shifting, and directional change issues.
- Many common power shuttle and power-shift transmission failures can be avoided by establishing and following a regular preventive maintenance program.
- Specific procedures used during any power-shift transmission or power shuttle overhaul will vary according to the equipment, the manufacturer, and, in some cases, company guidelines.
- Some general guidelines that apply to most power-shift transmission and power shuttle overhauls include removing

the transmission from the equipment and disassembling it; inspecting and replacing worn or damaged components; reassembling and reinstalling the transmission; refilling the transmission with the proper type and amount of hydraulic fluid; testing the equipment to ensure that the overhaul was successful; and carefully logging what was done and listing the parts that were used during the overhaul.

Key Terms

axial forces Forces applied along the longitudinal, or lengthwise, axis of a component such as a transmission shaft.

cavitation The formation and subsequent collapse of bubbles in a liquid caused by a decrease in pressure.

continuously variable transmission (CVT) A type of automatic transmission that uses a belt or chain between two variable-diameter pulleys instead of gears to provide a continuous range of gear ratios.

countershaft power-shift transmission A type of power-shift transmission that uses hydraulic clutches to control counter-rotating shafts with meshed gears.

friction discs Components inside a hydraulic clutch that are coated with a friction material to help transfer torque.

hydrostatic transmission (HST) A type of automatic transmission that uses pressurized fluid instead of gears to transfer power from an engine to axles and wheels and provide infinitely variable speed.

infinitely variable transmission (IVT) A type of continuously variable transmission that is sometimes coupled to a planetary gear train to achieve an infinite gear ratio range.

multidisc wet clutch A type of hydraulic clutch that contains multiple plates and discs and operates in a bath of hydraulic oil.

planetary power-shift transmission A type of power-shift transmission in which hydraulic clutches control sets of planetary gears to transfer power.

power-shift transmission A type of transmission that allows operators to shift gears up or down and change directions on the go and under load without a loss in acceleration or torque and without having to use a foot clutch.

power shuttle An addition or improvement to a transmission that enables an operator to easily change the direction of the equipment between forward and reverse while maintaining the same speed and engine rpm; also called a power reverser or a hydraulic shuttle.

pulse-width modulated (PWM) A type of digital signal commonly used to control the power supplied to electrical devices.

separator plates Thin, round slices of steel or cast iron inside a hydraulic clutch that sandwich friction discs and lock to components such as gear hubs, ring gears, or housings to transfer torque.

solenoid valve A type of electromechanically operated valve that uses an electric current to control fluid flow.

torsional damper A device mounted onto a rotating shaft to minimize vibration.

Review Questions

1. A good example of a piece of equipment that benefits from the use of a power shuttle is a machine that needs to make ________________.
   - **a.** regular upshifts on the go
   - **b.** constant speed range changes
   - **c.** regular downshifts on the go
   - **d.** constant direction changes
2. The primary components in a power shuttle that enable a piece of equipment to make directional changes at any speed are the ________________.
   - **a.** axial thrust bearings
   - **b.** hydraulic clutch assemblies
   - **c.** event-based shifters
   - **d.** planetary pinion gears
3. When the directional shift lever for a power shuttle is placed in the forward position, the applicable solenoid valve is activated to supply pressure to ________________.
   - **a.** move the piston in the forward clutch assembly
   - **b.** an annular piston in the planet carrier's braking device
   - **c.** the transmission's torsional damper
   - **d.** move the cylinder in the reverse clutch assembly
4. The two main types of power-shift transmissions are ________________.
   - **a.** hydrostatic and continuous
   - **b.** countershaft and planetary
   - **c.** infinite and countershaft
   - **d.** planetary and synchronous
5. One advantage that planetary gear sets have over conventional gear sets is a ________________.
   - **a.** greatly reduced need for hydraulic oil
   - **b.** much larger linear design footprint
   - **c.** more balanced load on gears, shafts, and bearings
   - **d.** significantly longer service life
6. Power enters a countershaft power-shift transmission through the ____________.
   - **a.** reverse clutch drum
   - **b.** planetary shaft
   - **c.** output shaft
   - **d.** input shaft
7. In a newer power-shift transmission, hydraulic clutch control is most likely to be provided by the ________________.
   - **a.** transmission control unit (TCU)
   - **b.** diagnostic data connector
   - **c.** transmission speed sensor
   - **d.** shuttle input analyzer
8. If a piece of equipment is under heavy load, the event-based shifting (EBS) software may provide a rapid, firm shift in order to ________________.
   - **a.** shorten the transport time
   - **b.** bypass the torque converter
   - **c.** maintain the machine momentum
   - **d.** feather the engine rpm

9. Improper oil viscosity in the hydraulic oil of a power-shift transmission can lead to ______________.
   a. clutch slippage
   b. cavitation
   c. modulation
   d. synchronizing
10. Because there are so many types and models of power shuttles and power-shift transmissions available, it is critical during any overhaul procedure to ______________.
   a. select as many generic replacement parts as possible
   b. consult OSHA (Occupational Safety and Health Administration) and/or state regulatory agencies for a list of steps
   c. minimize the extent of the overhaul to avoid confusion
   d. obtain and follow the equipment manufacturer's recommendations

ASE Technician A/Technician B Style Questions

1. Technician A says power shuttles were developed to allow operators to change directions easily on a piece of equipment. Technician B says power shuttles were developed so that operators could upshift and downshift on the go. Who is correct?
   a. Technician A
   b. Technician B
   c. Both Technician A and Technician B
   d. Neither Technician A nor Technician B
2. Technician A says the two clutch assemblies in a power shuttle are spring applied. Technician B says the two clutches will never both be applied at the same time. Who is correct?
   a. Technician A
   b. Technician B
   c. Both Technician A and Technician B
   d. Neither Technician A nor Technician B
3. Technician A says when the directional shift lever of a power shuttle is placed in the neutral position, both of the solenoid valves are activated. Technician B says when the lever is placed in neutral, neither of the forward and reverse clutches are locked up. Who is correct?
   a. Technician A
   b. Technician B
   c. Both Technician A and Technician B
   d. Neither Technician A nor Technician B
4. Technician A says a power-shift transmission allows an operator to shift gears up or down while on the go and under load without having to use a foot clutch. Technician B says a power-shift transmission allows an operator to change directions on the go and under load without having to use a foot clutch. Who is correct?
   a. Technician A
   b. Technician B
   c. Both Technician A and Technician B
   d. Neither Technician A nor Technician B
5. Technician A says to transfer torque from the input shaft to the output shafts in a countershaft power-shift transmission, at least five hydraulic clutches must be engaged. Technician B says only two clutches need to be engaged. Who is correct?
   a. Technician A
   b. Technician B
   c. Both Technician A and Technician B
   d. Neither Technician A nor Technician B
6. Technician A says it is easier to understand the power flows through a planetary power-shift transmission by using a chart that shows which clutches are engaged for each speed and direction range. Technician B says power flows through planetary gear sets are simple and easy to plot. Who is correct?
   a. Technician A
   b. Technician B
   c. Both Technician A and Technician B
   d. Neither Technician A nor Technician B
7. Technician A says the torque capacity of a hydraulic clutch relates to the number of release springs used. Technician B says torque capacity depends entirely on the flow rate of the hydraulic oil through the friction discs. Who is correct?
   a. Technician A
   b. Technician B
   c. Both Technician A and Technician B
   d. Neither Technician A nor Technician B
8. Technician A says event-based shifting (EBS) is a synonym for manual shifting. Technician B says EBS automatically adjusts clutch engagement based on the load that the TCU senses. Who is correct?
   a. Technician A
   b. Technician B
   c. Both Technician A and Technician B
   d. Neither Technician A nor Technician B
9. Technician A says a common problem that affects both power shuttles and power-shift transmissions is contaminated oil. Technician B says oil is not a factor in the operation of a power shuttle. Who is correct?
   a. Technician A
   b. Technician B
   c. Both Technician A and Technician B
   d. Neither Technician A nor Technician B
10. Technician A says before and during the removal and overhaul of a power shuttle or a power-shift transmission, you should take photographs of the components to ensure that everything gets reassembled in the proper manner. Technician B says match marking and labeling components helps ensure proper reassembly. Who is correct?
   a. Technician A
   b. Technician B
   c. Both Technician A and Technician B
   d. Neither Technician A nor Technician B

CHAPTER 49
Drivelines

Knowledge Objectives

After reading this chapter, you will be able to:

- **K49001** Explain the purpose and fundamentals of driveshafts, power take-off shafts, and universal joints.
- **K49002** Identify the construction features, composition, types, and applications of driveshafts, power take-off shafts, safety shields, and universal joints.
- **K49003** Describe the principles of operation of driveshafts, power take-off shafts, and universal joints.

Skills Objectives

After reading this chapter, you will be able to:

- **S49001** Inspect and adjust driveline angularity as necessary.
- **S49002** Perform the inspection, testing, and diagnostic procedures by following the manufacturers' recommendations for driveshafts, shafts, and universal joints.
- **S49003** Recommend reconditioning or repairs of driveshafts, power take-off shafts, and universal joints.

▶ Introduction

A machine's driveline consists of several components clutches, torque converters, retarders, transmissions, transfer cases, axles, power dividers, and final drives. See **FIGURE 49-1** for the components that make up a wheel loader driveline.

Most of the time, because of the location and/or height of the driveline components, they are not directly connected to each other. Torque is usually transferred between the components by driveshafts and universal joints. Mechanical drive may also need to be sent from the engine or one of the other driveline components to an auxiliary system such as a hydraulic pump drive. This auxiliary drive will also be connected to the source of power by using a driveshaft. Because the individual components of the driveline are covered in individual chapters, driveshafts and universal joints will be the main topic of this chapter. The job of transferring torque from an engine to the rest of the driveline was originally done with chains and sprockets or sometimes cables and pulleys.

FIGURE 49-2 shows an old chain drive system. This particular drive system drove a differential gear set that sent power to both wheels. The system was inherently noisy, dirty, and notorious for failing. Chain drives were okay for lighter loads and slower speeds, but they required a lot of maintenance, including adjustments and lubrication.

In 1903, Clarence Spicer was issued a patent for an encased **Cardan joint** for use in vehicle driveshafts. At that time, he was the only manufacturer of these so-called **universal joints** for this purpose. Cardan joint is the original name for a universal joint. As seen in **FIGURE 49-3**, it consists of a cross with four machined end posts called **trunnions**, over which are installed four bearing caps with needle roller bearings. These bearing caps are installed into two yokes attached to two shafts: an input or driving shaft and an output or driven shaft. The universal joint and the yokes connect the two shafts together, and the joint allows the driven shaft to operate at an angle to the driving shaft.

Mr. Spicer soon had orders from most of the automotive manufacturers of the day for his universal joint driveline system.

FIGURE 49-1 The machine "driveline" consists of many components connected together.

FIGURE 49-2 Chain drives like this one were notoriously unreliable.

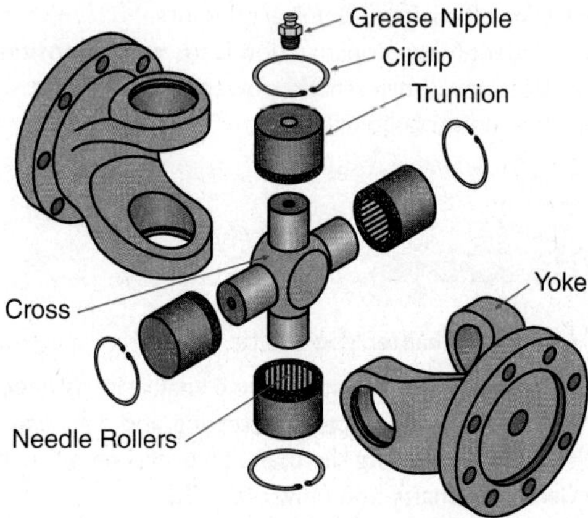

FIGURE 49-3 An exploded view of a typical U-joint.

You Are the Mobile Heavy Equipment Technician

You are called upon to lubricate the universal joints on a wheeled loader. You park the machine on a level surface in the shop, and using a creeper, you start the service procedure. While you are lubricating one of the U-joints, you notice brown rust streaks around one of the bearing caps. As you continue to pump the grease gun, a couple of drops of brownish water escape from the bearing cap. Then grease purges from the cap.

1. Would you be concerned about the rust streaks?
2. Is a small amount of water escaping the U-joint cap normal?
3. What would be your recommendation for this machine?

FIGURE 49-4 Originally universal joints were completely enclosed, as shown, for protection from the elements.

The actual Cardan, or universal joint, that Mr. Spicer used in his patented "Casing for A Universal Joint" had been around for a long time before he considered its use in automobiles. The original universal joints were enclosed as seen in **FIGURE 49-4** to protect them from the elements, but improved sealing and manufacturer made the enclosure unnecessary.

Heavy-duty equipment technicians (HDETs) will be very familiar with Mr. Spicer's universal joints as they are used in almost all machines, even machines with hydrostatic drive will sometimes use driveshafts with universal joints to drive hydraulic pumps and accessories.

The invention of the universal joint is generally attributed to the Italian mathematician Gerolamo Cardano (hence the name Cardan joint), who described the operation of the joint in detail in 1545 but did not produce it. Cardano died in 1576. The concept was studied by Robert Hooke between 1667 and 1675, so in some countries, the Cardan joint is known as a **Hooke joint**. Hooke was the first to document that the joint produced **non-uniform velocity** when operated at an angle. That is, the driven shaft turns at a constantly changing speed. The Non-uniform Velocity section in this chapter discusses the concept in greater detail.

The scientific community actually traces the universal joint back to the **gimbals** used by the ancient Greeks, as early as 220 B.C.E., and some suggest the use of gimbals began in China even farther back. Two-axis gimbals have an object suspended on the center axis of a circle that, in turn, is suspended on the center axis of a second circle. That construction allows the object to stay horizontal no matter the angle of the support. For example, gimbals allow a gyroscope or compass on a ship to be kept at the exact same position, even when rough seas toss the ship around. The universal joint operates on the same principle as gimbals, but the pivot points for the circles are on the inside of the joint (the cross), and the circles are actually the two shafts that the joint connects. Whatever the definitive origin of the joint, its use today in the mechanical world is attributed to Clarence Spicer's patent. The universal joint is essential to the operation of most modern equipment.

This chapter will explain the principles of the operation, construction, and types of driveshafts and joints used in the mobile off-road equipment (MORE) field. Included in the chapter will be discussions on the theory of non-uniform velocity, driveline angularity, Cardan joints, and support bearings. The chapter will also cover troubleshooting driveshaft problems and typical failures, as well as the inspection and maintenance of driveshafts.

▶ Fundamentals of Driveshaft Systems

K49001

Although there are many aspects to a driveshaft, such as the one shown in **FIGURE 49-5**, any driveshaft must perform the following three basic functions:

1. It must be strong enough to withstand the maximum torque from the power source.
2. It must allow the shaft to change length due to oscillating components.
3. It must transmit torque while allowing the angle of drive to change.

Strength

The primary function of a driveshaft is to provide the strength needed to withstand the peak torque delivered from the engine while providing an ample safety margin. It might seem that increasing strength can be achieved simply by increasing the weight of the driveshaft. As the driveshaft is made heavier to carry more load, however, the shaft's maximum speed of rotation is affected. The heavier the shaft is, the lower its maximum speed will be.

As a driveshaft's rotational speeds goes up, centrifugal force acting on its weight will tend to move the shaft off its axis of rotation, causing a whipping action. The speed at which the centrifugal force causes the shaft to move off its axis is known as **critical speed**. If a shaft operates at or above this speed, the

FIGURE 49-5 A typical machine driveshaft.

resultant vibration will destroy the shaft. This problem can be compensated for by making the shaft lighter, larger in diameter, or shorter in length, but careful consideration should be given to adjusting the dimensions. The overall shaft dimensions must be carefully selected to match the machine and its vocation.

Length Changes

The second function of a driveshaft is that it must allow the shaft to change in length due to the varying distance between the driveline components caused by axle oscillations. As the machine maneuvers over rough terrain, its suspension moves. This movement typically changes the distance between the driveline components, such as the transfer case and the drive axle. Torque effects that occur as the machine is put under load, or in some cases braking, can also cause variations in the driveshaft length. For these reasons, it is essential that the operating length of the driveshaft can change.

Rigid Joint Driveshaft

A rigid joint driveshaft can be used to connect two components that are both rigidly mounted, such as the torque converter at the back of the engine and a remotely mounted transmission. This type of driveshaft does not allow for length changes, because it connects two components that cannot move relative to each other.

Angle of Drive

The engine, transmission, transfer case, etc. are fixed to the machine frame and so are always on the same plane when the machine is operated. This is not always the case, however, for the drive axles of the machine. The drive axles articulate according to the operating conditions, so the position of the drive axle relative to the transmission will change. A driveshaft must, therefore, be capable of transmitting torque while operating through changing drive angles. This is the third essential function of the driveshaft.

Driveshaft Series

Driveshafts are made by many different manufacturers, and one of the most common driveshafts used in heavy equipment built in North America is the Spicer 10 Series—1610, 1710, and 1810—driveshaft. The Spicer series number depicts the shaft's capacity. Driveshaft capacity is the maximum torque that the shaft can handle. This capacity has to be carefully matched to the particular machine so that the driveshaft is capable of transferring the required torque without failure. **TABLE 49-1** shows some of the recommended limits for the various Spicer shaft series numbers. Please note that the chart is a guideline only; always consult the manufacturer for accurate and up-to-date recommendations.

Spicer has introduced the Life Series driveshaft to replace the 10 series. **TABLE 49-2** shows the cross-reference between the 10 Series and the Life Series. The Life Series for MORE is available in torque capacities of up to 25,000 N·m (18,439 ft-lb). **FIGURE 49-6** shows a machine driveline using the Spicer Life Series driveshafts.

Spicer has two other series for the heavy equipment market: the 2000 Series, with capacities of up to 35,000 N·m (25,814 ft-lb); and the Wing Series, using heavy-duty wing-type U-joints, with capacities of up to 120,000 N·m (88,507 ft-lb).

Strength alone, however, is not the only limiting criteria for a driveshaft. There are several other limitations on the shaft design, such as maximum shaft length, maximum rpm, maximum **torsional excitation**, and maximum inertial excitation. The last two of these are extremely complicated calculations, based on the diameter, length, and weight of the shaft. Torsional excitation refers to the inherent vibration effects caused by the acceleration and deceleration of the rotating driveshaft. As such, calculating excitation levels is better left to the engineers. Driveshaft vibrations are not as critical an issue with MORE as they are with on-highway vehicles, because of the lower operational speed of off-road machines. It would be difficult for an HDET to

TABLE 49-1 Recommended Limits for Driveshafts by Series

Series	Tube Diameter	Maximum Shaft Length	Maximum Shaft Torque	Max Speed at 3.0° U-joint Angle
1610	4.00" × 0.134" (101.6 × 3.4 mm)	70" (177.8 cm)	5,700 ft-lb (7,728 N·m)	4,000 rpm
1710	4.00" × 0.134" (101.6 × 3.4 mm)	70" (177.8 cm)	7,700 ft-lb (10,440 N·m)	4,000 rpm
1710 HD	4.09" × 180" (103.9 × 4.6 mm)	70" (177.8 cm)	10,200 ft-lb (13,829 N·m)	4,000 rpm
1760	4.0" × 0.134" (101.6 × 3.4 mm)	70" (177.8 cm)	10,200 ft-lb (13,829 N·m)	4,000 rpm
1760 HD	4.09" × 0.180" (103.9 × 4.6 mm)	70" (177.8 cm)	12,200 ft-lb (16,541 N·m)	4,000 rpm
1810	4.5" × 0.134" (114.3 × 3.4 mm)	75" (190.5 cm)	12,200 ft-lb (16,541 N·m)	3,400 rpm
1860 HD	4.59" × 0.180" (116.6 × 4.6 mm)	75" (190.5 cm)	16,500 ft-lb (22,371 N·m)	3,400 rpm

TABLE 49-2 10 Series Equivalents in Life Series of Spicer Driveshafts

Older Spicer 10 Series Driveshafts	Equivalent Spicer Life Series Driveshaft
1710 is replaced by ⟶	SPL-140
1760 is replaced by ⟶	SPL-170
1810 is replaced by ⟶	SPL-250

FIGURE 49-6 The Spicer Life Series driveshafts are typically permanently lubricated.

feel a vibration issue, because of the rough terrain. Because of the slower rotational speed, machine driveline operating angles can be much larger than what is found in highway applications. Excessive vibration, however, can lead to early U-joint and driveshaft support bearing failure and for that reason must be avoided.

▶ Components of Driveshafts/ Drivelines

K49002

Depending on the machine and the installation requirements, many components can be used to make up a driveline. Certain manufacturers will have a propensity for using different types of yokes, universal joints, and shaft support systems. In heavy equipment installations, a driveline can consist of a torque converter, transmission, transfer case, and two drive axles connected by driveshafts between each component. A machine may have other driveshafts driving auxiliary pumps or mechanisms. All driveshafts, however, will use several common components, such as the driveshaft tube, driveshaft yokes, slip joints, coupling shafts, universal joints, and fastening systems.

Driveshaft Tube

The driveshaft tube used in off-road equipment is typically made from steel because of its strength. Steel tubing can be manufactured in several ways. A flat piece of steel can be bent into the shape of a tube and the seam welded. Another method of manufacture is by extrusion, where a solid bar is pierced with a die and a hollow tube is created. This method will form a seamless tube: it has no seam weld. A drawn-over-mandrel (DOM) tube is a welded tube drawn over a mandrel (a die the size and shape of the finished tube). DOM construction provides an extremely consistent wall thickness and smoothness for increased strength and stability. **FIGURE 49-7** shows a typical DOM tube. Regardless of the method of construction, driveshaft tubes are hollow. Consequently, they tend to amplify any sounds, like a bell does. To combat this, sound deadeners made of a variety of materials, even cardboard, are usually placed into the tube at manufacture to stop the shaft from conducting noise.

FIGURE 49-7 Driveshaft tubing may be forged or manufactured by using the DOM method, which produces consistent wall thickness and strength. Then the tube is welded to the yokes.

Driveshaft Yokes

All driveshafts have yokes. Three types of yoke are prevalent in heavy-duty applications: tube, end, and flange.

Tube Yokes

Tube yokes, such as the one shown in **FIGURE 49-8**, are pressed into the tube at manufacture and welded into place. Tube yokes

FIGURE 49-8 Tube yokes are welded to the tube and have two bores to accept the U-joint bearing caps.

have full-round bores that accept two of the pressed-in U-joint bearing caps. There are several sizes of tube yokes to accommodate different universal joint sizes. Universal joint bearing caps are retained in the tube yoke ears by internal or external snap rings or circlips (also known as C-clip), bolt-in bearing caps, or bolted spring clips.

End Yokes

End yokes are designed to be installed over the splined output shaft of the transmission; the splined input shaft of the drive axle; other driveline component, as shown in **FIGURE 49-9**; or a splined shaft that is part of the driveshaft itself. End yokes are usually bolted to their respective shafts. End yokes can come in wing type, full-round or half-round designs. The wing type allows the bearing caps to be bolted directly to the yokes. This arrangement uses a notch and key way in the connection that increases torque capacity. The full-round design allows the bearing caps to be retained by internal or external snap rings or circlips, bolt-in bearing caps, or bolted spring clips. Half-round designs use attaching hardware such as U-bolts, wing-shaped bearing caps bolted to the yoke, or bolted half-round straps. Half-round yokes using straps as attaching hardware will usually have small metal tangs cast into the yoke to prevent the universal joint bearing caps from moving outward.

Flange Yoke

A **flange yoke**, shown in **FIGURE 49-10**, will hold two of the universal joint bearing caps and incorporate a flat flange with a series of mounting holes so that the flange can then be attached to a component. Universal joint bearing caps are retained in the flange yoke ears by internal or external snap rings or circlips, bolt-in bearing caps, or bolted spring clips. A flange yoke is designed to be bolted to a matching flange mounted on the component, called a companion flange.

Sometimes, a **companion flange** is matched with a flange yoke and used instead of an end yoke. The flange yoke and the companion flange bolt together when the driveshaft is installed. See **FIGURE 49-11** for a companion flange. A companion flange is splined to the output shaft of the transmission or the input shaft of the driveline component. A companion flange does not have bores to accept the universal joint bearing caps and so must be used with a flange yoke. The flange will be held in place on the shaft by a large nut or bolt. The companion flange can be round or square in shape but must match the shape of the flange yoke that will bolt to it.

FIGURE 49-9 End yokes are usually splined to a component. This end yoke is of the wing design.

FIGURE 49-10 A flange yoke connects to a driveline component with a matching companion flange.

FIGURE 49-11 A companion flange can be used in place of an end yoke.

Slip Joint

A **slip joint** is a two-piece splined component consisting of a splined shaft fitted into a splined sleeve. **FIGURE 49-12** shows a slip joint. A slip joint allows the driveshaft to lengthen or shorten and is essential in a non-rigid driveline to accommodate length changes caused by suspension oscillation. Some, but not all, slip joints will have a master spline so that they cannot be reassembled incorrectly. If they do not have a master spline, the technician must mark the mating position of the two halves of the slip joint before removal, as shown in **FIGURE 49-13**. Otherwise, a serious driveline vibration could result.

Most slip joints used on newer Spicer driveshafts will have a coating called Glidecoat. This blue nylon coating is designed to reduce friction in the slip joint. Care must be

FIGURE 49-12 A slip joint allows the driveshaft to change in length as required to accommodate suspension oscillation.

FIGURE 49-14 Spicer Life Series driveshafts have a sealed slip yoke.

FIGURE 49-13 Failure to correctly reinstall a separated slip joint will lead to vibration. Always mark the joint before removal.

FIGURE 49-15 A hanger bearing is a rubber-encased or solid bearing bolted to the vehicle frame that supports the driveshaft.

taken not to damage the coating while removing or installing the yoke. The blue Glidecoat can be partially seen in Figure 49-12. Some slip joints will have a threaded-on seal cap, or gland nut, that must be removed before the joint can be separated. Still others will have a pressed-on seal cover that needs to be popped off to separate the joint. Spicer Life Series driveshaft slip yokes are permanently lubricated and feature a flexible boot that covers the slip joint, as seen in **FIGURE 49-14**.

Coupling Shaft

A **coupling shaft** is usually a short driveshaft without a slip joint that is used in a multiple shaft driveline. A coupling shaft may also be known as a **jack shaft**. When a coupling shaft is used, the driveline must also have a hanger or support bearing to support the non-drive end of the coupling shaft.

A **center bearing**, also called a **hanger bearing**, is shown in **FIGURE 49-15**. The center bearing is used to support a multi-piece driveshaft. The center bearing consists of a bearing pressed onto a machined surface past the splined area of the coupling shaft. The bearing is supported in a molded rubber cushion bracket that is, in turn, bolted to the vehicle framework. The rubber cushion can be slotted rubber or solid, depending on the severity of the expected duty cycle of the driveline. Center bearings are typically permanently lubricated. A bulkhead support bearing is necessary when a driveshaft has to pass through machine bulkheads. Typically, a flanged bearing or pillow block type of bearing is used for this purpose. Pillow block support bearings can also be used when driveshaft length is excessive. Breaking a long driveshaft into two or more shorter sections supported by a bearing reduces the shaft's tendency to bow out or flex under load. A pillow block support bearing is shown in **FIGURE 49-16**.

Universal Joints

The universal (Cardan) joint is essential to the operation of today's motor vehicles. It consists of a cross with four finely machined round trunnions equally spaced 90 degrees apart. The trunnions hold the four bearing caps, which are fitted with long needle bearings to distribute the load.

The cross of the joint is drilled with passages that connect the center of the four trunnions with a grease fitting that is installed in the cross at the center or on the outside of one or two of the bearing caps. The purpose of the passage is to supply lubricating grease to all the trunnions and bearing caps. **FIGURE 49-17** shows a u-joint grease fitting or zerk.

FIGURE 49-16 A pillow block support bearing supports a multi-piece driveshaft.

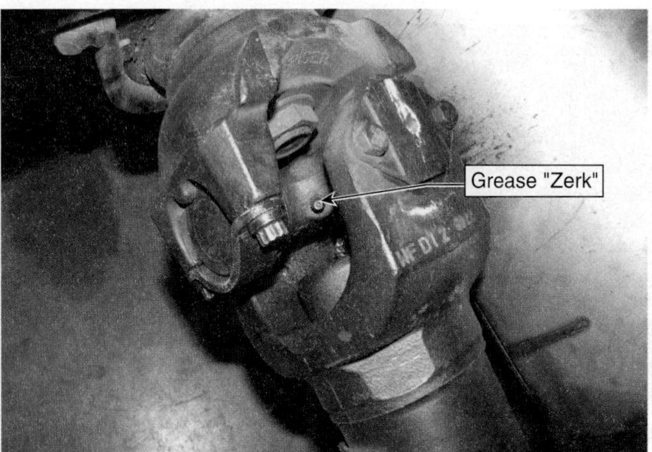

FIGURE 49-17 Lubrication is essential to U-joint longevity. Grease fittings, or zerks, and drilled passageways are provided to ensure that the lubricant reaches all four trunnions and bearing caps.

Some U-joints will have a standpipe incorporated into the lube passages. The standpipe acts as a check valve to retain the lubricant.

The bearing caps fitted over the trunnions contain thrust washers or hardened thrust surfaces to resist axial movement of the cross. A seal keeps grease in and dirt out. The seals are specially designed to allow grease to purge from the seals when the joint is lubricated, but they do not allow water or dirt to enter.

Two of the bearings are fitted into a yoke that is welded to a driveshaft component. The other two bearings are fitted to a second yoke either attached to another shaft or fitted into an end yoke that is connected to a transmission or a drive axle. The U-joint allows the two connected yokes to rotate at different angles to each other. Note that some U-joints are permanently lubricated and do not have grease fittings.

Fastening Systems

The universal joint can be attached to the driveshaft components in several ways. The caps can be press fit into the shaft yoke and be retained with snap rings or clips. Alternatively, the caps can be held in place with straps and bolts or U-bolts and nuts. Finally, the bearing caps themselves may have a machined flange that, in turn, bolts directly to the yoke. **FIGURE 49-18** shows two popular types of attaching the joint to the driveshaft components. Bolt-on, semicircular straps hold the joint to the half-round end yoke. Note the small cast lugs in the yoke used to prevent axial movement of the joint. In addition, the bearing caps on the tube yoke have flanges that are bolted directly to the yoke.

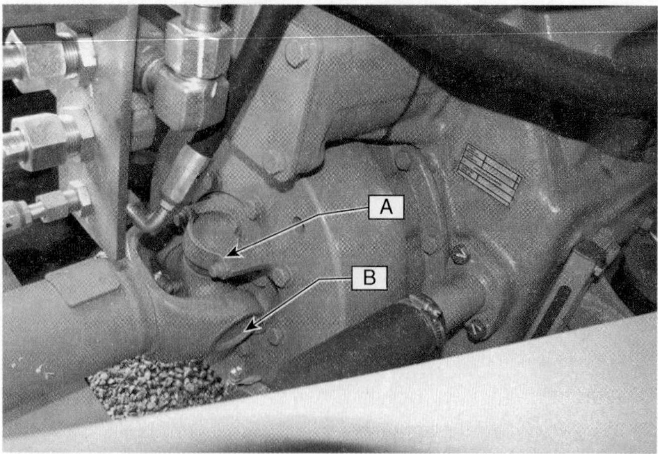

FIGURE 49-18 U-joint fastening system using bolt-on straps in the half-round end yoke A, and the bearing caps are retained in the tube yoke by circlips B.

Manufacturers recommend that most fastening devices not be reused when servicing universal joints. Spicer states that reusing the fastening hardware may cause failure of the driveline and lead to catastrophic damage to the vehicle and even personal injury or death. Spicer Life Series driveshafts use bolt-on spring-tab retainers for their bearing caps, like the ones shown in **FIGURE 49-19**. These caps must be replaced, along with their bolts, every time they are removed. The Life Series driveshaft uses cold-formed semicircular retaining straps, such as those shown in **FIGURE 49-20**. On quick release half-round end yokes, these straps may be reused, but not the bolts that attach them.

FIGURE 49-19 The spring-tab bearing cap retainers on this Spicer Life Series driveshaft and the attaching bolts must be replaced any time they are removed.

FIGURE 49-20 These cold-formed semicircular straps on the Spicer Life Series driveshafts may be reused, but the attaching bolts must be replaced.

FIGURE 49-21 Wing series U-joints provide greater torque capacity.

Wing-Type U-Joints

Wing-type U-joints that use specially shaped bearing caps with "wings" that are bolted to the yokes are very popular in MORE. This type of U-joint will have a keyway as part of the U-joint bearing cap that fits into a notch in the yoke. This notch and keyway provide much greater torque capacity to the connection. This type of U-joint is the type used in Spicer's high-torque-capacity Wing Series driveshafts, with torque capacities as high as 120,000 N·m (88,507 ft-lb). **FIGURE 49-21** shows a wing joint connection.

▶ Principles of Operation of Driveshafts and Universal Joints

K49003

When a driveshaft is considered for a certain application, several things must be considered. For example, it is critical to know how much load the shaft must be capable of transmitting without failure, how fast the shaft must rotate, what angle it must operate at, and how long the shaft must be.

Shaft Mass and Critical Speed

The driveshaft and driveline must obviously be made strong enough to carry the torque load that will be transmitted through them. The crudest calculation of the peak torque that the shaft must carry is the product of the engine's peak torque multiplied by the transmission's or the transfer case's lowest gear ratio. If equipped with a torque converter, engine peak torque must be multiplied by the torque-converter stall ratio or torque multiplication factor. Manufacturers choose the strength of a driveshaft to match the machine's configuration.

Maximum driveshaft torque can be calculated by multiplying the following figures:

- net engine torque (or 95% of gross engine torque)
- transmission lowest gear ratio
- transmission efficiency (0.8 for power-shift transmission; 0.85 for standard)
- torque-converter stall ratio or peak torque multiplication, if applicable.

Mathematically, that looks like the following:

$$\text{net engine torque} \times \text{transmission lowest gear ratio} \times \text{transmission efficiency} \times \text{torque-converter stall ratio}$$

Manufacturers may also have to figure in the torque multiplying effect of a transfer case and its efficiency factor of about 95%.

The driveline will also have a significant amount of extra strength built in as a safety margin. Recall from the Fundamentals of Driveshaft Systems section that critical speed is an issue in trying to increase the strength of a driveshaft. As the mass of the shaft increases, the centrifugal force acting on it as it rotates increases. As a result, the shaft's critical speed decreases. **FIGURE 49-22** illustrates the bow related to critical speed. Critical-speed issues are not usually a concern in off-road equipment, because driveshaft rotational speed is typically between 100 and 800 rpm, but speed can be a problem in certain applications.

As the shaft approaches critical speed, it will start to vibrate violently. The intensity of the vibration will increase until it reaches critical speed. At critical speed, the shaft will usually fail catastrophically. One way to combat critical-speed problems is to reduce the mass of the driveshaft. Doing so, however, will decrease its torque carrying capability. A second way is to decrease the shaft length. A longer shaft has more of a tendency to sag, while a shorter shaft reduces this tendency. Using a shorter shaft will decrease the overall mass of the shaft but will

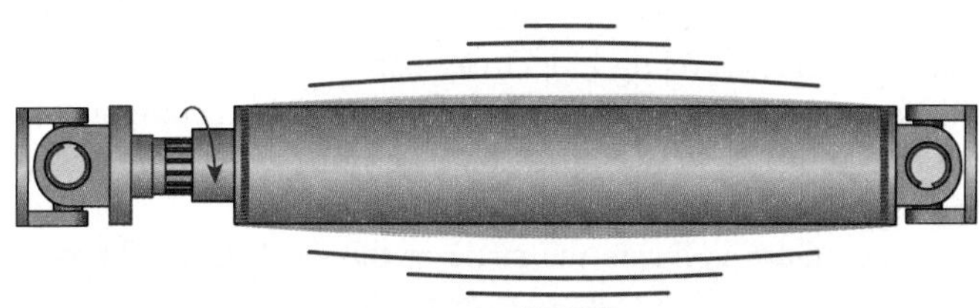

FIGURE 49-22 As the rotating shaft approaches critical speed, its mass causes the shaft to bow off its axis, which in turn causes imbalance and vibration.

require the use of a multi-piece driveshaft to reach the required length. Multi-piece driveshafts can lead to vibration problems caused by non-canceling universal joint operating angles. This in turn can lead to premature failures of the U-joints. A third way is to increase the diameter of the shaft tube. The larger diameter makes the shaft stronger and less likely to sag, but the larger diameter carries a weight penalty.

In addition to certain failure, another phenomenon called a harmonic vibration is associated with a driveshafts critical speed. A **harmonic vibration** is an inherent vibration that occurs at exactly half critical-speed rpm and creates a vibration that will cause damage to the universal joints and, indeed, the whole driveline. Although not as severe as critical-speed vibration, harmonic vibration must still be avoided for a driveline to provide worry-free service.

So, carefully selecting tubing type, length, and driveline components is essential when the machine is being designed, so that the shaft will not be operating at or near critical speed or half critical speed during normal use. The bottom line is that a driveshaft is usually constructed to be as light as possible but as strong as necessary to do the job required of it.

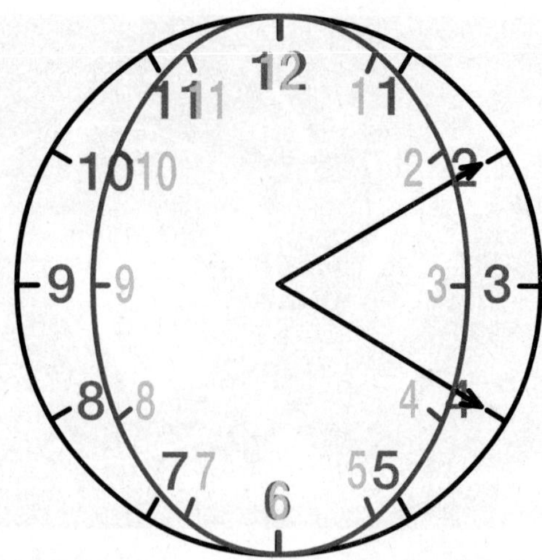

FIGURE 49-23 Notice that the hand of the clock is ahead of the two on the ellipse as it points to the two on the circle. That difference in location indicates that the driven shaft, the ellipse, had to speed up. When the hand points to four on the circle, it is before four on the ellipse, indicating that the driven shaft had to slow down.

Non-uniform Velocity

All driveshafts have a natural tendency to vibrate because of a phenomenon called non-uniform velocity. Non-uniform velocity happens when any shaft with a universal joint operates at an angle different from the axis of rotation of the drive component. This concept must be understood in order to understand the dynamics of a driveshaft.

The universal joint allows a shaft to deliver torque through an angle. That is, the input or driving component of the shaft is at one angle and the output component is at a different angle. That relationship causes the output component to turn at a velocity that is not constant. In fact, the driven shaft component will accelerate and decelerate twice during each revolution even though it is physically attached to the input.

It can be difficult to visualize this concept. Consider the input component of a universal joint as turning in a circle. The output component of the joint, because of the angle, will then be turning not in a circle but in an ellipse. To help you visualize the difference, imagine looking at a coin straight on. The coin forms a circle. If you were to turn the coin at an angle, the coin would seem to be elliptical or oval shaped. That is exactly what is happening with the driven component of the shaft. The yoke ears of the drive and driven parts of the joint are rotating in different planes because of the angle. One of the best ways to explain non-uniform velocity is to consider the input component of the shaft, which is traveling in a circle, as the face of a clock with the hours marked on it and then to take the driven component, which is traveling in an ellipse, and superimpose its motion over the clock face, as illustrated in **FIGURE 49-23**.

The ellipse is inside the circle of the clock face. The two shafts are physically connected together, so they revolve around a common center point and will meet at the 3, 6, 9, and 12 o'clock positions. Now, draw an arrow from the center to the two o'clock position on the outer circle, and look where the line intersects the inner ellipse. The line on the ellipse is at some time past two o'clock. That difference indicates that the output member (the ellipse) has accelerated in relation to the input member (the circle).

At the three o'clock position, the timing of the circle and the ellipse will coincide. But that changes at the five o'clock position. An arrow pointing to the five o'clock position on the circle (the input member) will bisect the ellipse (the output member) at some time before five o'clock. That means that the driven member has now slowed down in relation to the input member.

The process is then repeated as the input component moves toward the nine o'clock and then the 12 o'clock position. The output component must again speed up and slow down to match it. If we divide the motion into quadrants, as the input component rotates through a complete circle of 360 degrees, the driven component accelerates for the first 90 degrees of rotation, or the first quadrant; then decelerates for the next 90 degrees of rotation, or the second quadrant; then accelerates for the third quadrant; and finally decelerates for the fourth quadrant. The rate of acceleration and deceleration is entirely based on the severity of the angle of drive. In other words, the higher the working angle, the greater the speed fluctuations will be. **FIGURE 49-24** shows typical yoke speed variations.

Consider that a driveshaft has to transmit rotating power to a driveline component. If we were to connect the shaft directly to a component with this non-uniform velocity unchecked, the acceleration and deceleration would be transmitted to the component and to the whole driveline. The machine's driveline would be trying to accelerate and decelerate constantly. Left uncorrected, this would lead to U-joint and driveline component failure. In order to connect the shaft to a component, then, we must first correct the non-uniform velocity by using another universal joint with an equal, or very close to equal, operating angle, which will cancel out the changing velocity and deliver a constant rotational speed to the drive axle, as is illustrated in the graph in **FIGURE 49-25**.

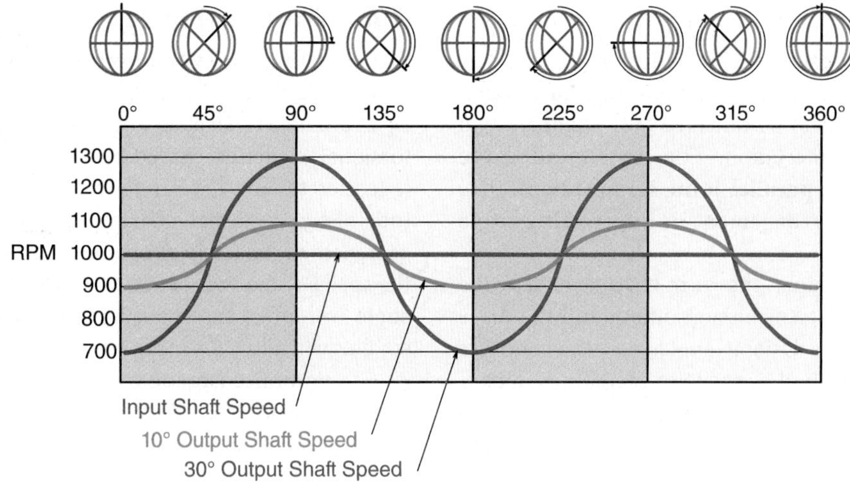

FIGURE 49-24 The frequency of the accelerations and decelerations are constant, each occurring twice per revolution. The amplitude or intensity of the speed fluctuations is based on the severity of the drive angle.

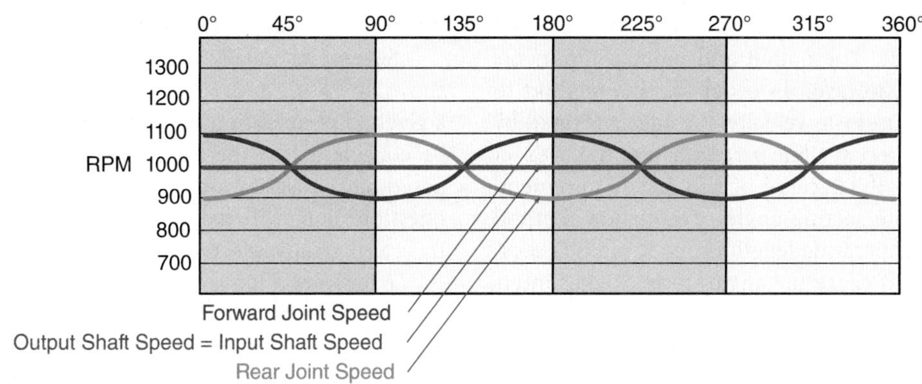

FIGURE 49-25 Installing a second universal joint with an equal and opposite angle at the other end of the driven shaft serves to cancel out the non-uniform velocity.

There is more to the story, however. This phenomenon of non-uniform velocity can lead to driveshaft vibrations even if we cancel out the speed fluctuations with a second universal joint. The inertial forces caused by the acceleration and deceleration of the driveshaft's mass can, by themselves, lead to vibrations as overall shaft speed increases. The intensity of the speed fluctuations is a direct result of the severity of the operating angles and the shaft rotational speed. This means that the safe rotational speed of a shaft decreases as shaft operating angles increase. These inertial forces caused by the shaft accelerating and decelerating are hard to calculate, but they must be taken into consideration when designing a driveline.

Driveshaft Angle Cancelation

The non-uniform velocity of a universal joint working through an angle must be canceled out by installing another joint with an equal and opposite working angle at the other end of the shaft. When working with Cardan joint angularity, there are three basic rules to follow:

1. There must be some working angle at the joint—at least one-half to one degree.
2. Operating angles at either end of a driveshaft must be equal to within one degree to obtain acceptable **cancelation** of the non-uniform velocity created by joint working angles.
3. Working angles should be kept as small as possible to minimize vibrations caused by shaft inertial excitation.

Rule Number One

All Cardan joints use needle roller bearings to carry the torque load exerted on a driveshaft. These needles require lubrication if they are to survive. If a joint works with no angle at all, the needle rollers will remain stationary in the caps and will eventually squeeze all of the lubricant out of the contact points in the caps and the trunnions. Without the lubricant, the needles will start to dig into the trunnions. This causes an effect known as **false brinelling**, which is the wearing away of the trunnion in the shape of the needles. False brinelling leads to joint failure. When the joint works at least a slight angle, for example one-half to one degree minimum, the needles will roll during operation. The rolling motion distributes the lubricant each time the needles move, so false brinelling is less likely to occur.

Rule Number Two

The operating angles at each end of a driveshaft must be kept equal to within one degree if the non-uniform velocity caused by the joint angle is to be canceled out. There are two ways of achieving this cancelation. The first is called the **waterfall arrangement** or **parallel joint arrangement**. The other is the **broken back arrangement** or **intersecting angle arrangement**.

In the parallel arrangement, shown in **FIGURE 49-26A**, the side-view centerline of the transmission output and the drive axle input are parallel. The U-joint angles at either end are equal to within one degree and opposite to each other. This is the preferred method of cancelation because the two joints will remain equal during suspension oscillation and shaft-length changes.

The broken back or intersecting angle method, shown in **FIGURE 49-26B**, is used when the proximity of the two components would lead to extreme operating angles if a waterfall or parallel arrangement were used. In the broken back method of cancelation, the U-joint operating angles must still be equal at each end of the shaft. The output and input components are no longer parallel, however. In order for this method to effectively cancel non-uniform velocity, the angles formed by the U-joints must intersect at a line perpendicular to the exact center of the shaft length. Because of this last requirement, the broken back or intersecting angles cancelation method cannot be used where operating length changes can be excessive, because this would cause the angles to no longer intersect at the center of the shaft and lead to vibration. Broken back installations appear usually only where driveshaft length changes are minimal.

Rule Number Three

The operating angles of universal joints should be kept as small as possible. Because of the phenomenon of non-uniform velocity of a shaft driven at an angle, all driveshafts have an inherent torsional excitation caused by the inertial forces of the shaft as it accelerates and decelerates twice per revolution. The magnitude of this torsional excitation is directly proportional to the acuteness of the angle of operation, the weight of the shaft, and the speed of the shaft. **FIGURE 49-27** shows how joint operating angle will affect the expected life of the joint. Keeping angles smaller will allow for maximum working life.

To minimize vibration, one of three things must occur: The angle has to be lessened, the shaft must turn at a lower speed, or the shaft must become lighter. The shaft speed must be consistent with the machine system for which it is transmitting torque. Therefore, limiting shaft speed is not one of the favored options. The weight of the shaft material can be altered, but that will have a direct impact on the shaft's torque carrying capabilities. The best solution to deal with inertial and torsional excitation is to keep the operating angle as small as possible.

Several manufacturers produce charts, such as the one shown in **TABLE 49-3**, specifying maximum rotational speed for a given joint operating angle. The weight of the shaft must also be considered, so the maximum operating angle will change based on the "series" or load-carrying capability of the shaft in question, along with its rotational speed. Universal joint longevity is also greatly affected by large joint working angles.

A universal joint operating at an angle of three degrees can be expected to last 90% or more of its normal wear life. As angles increase, this wear life reduces drastically. A joint that has a normal wear life of 10,000 hours will likely last for only

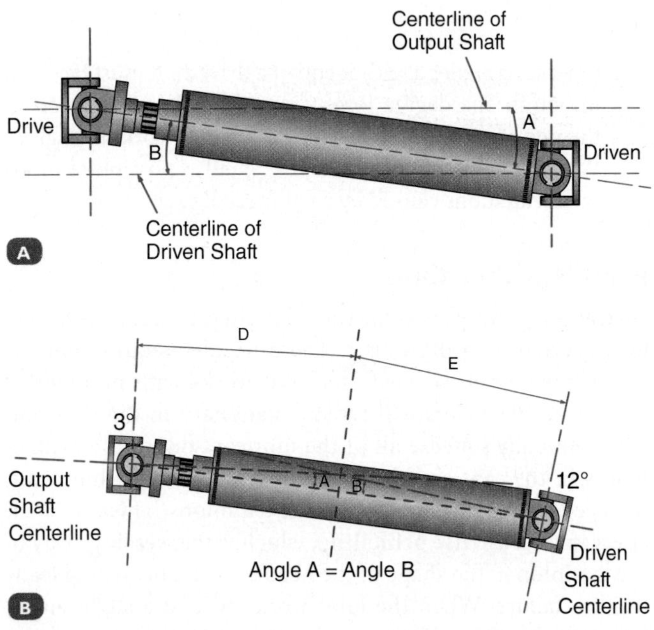

FIGURE 49-26 A. The parallel or waterfall (or parallel joint) arrangement is the preferred arrangement. **B.** The intersecting angle (or broken back) arrangement can be used when length changes are not excessive.

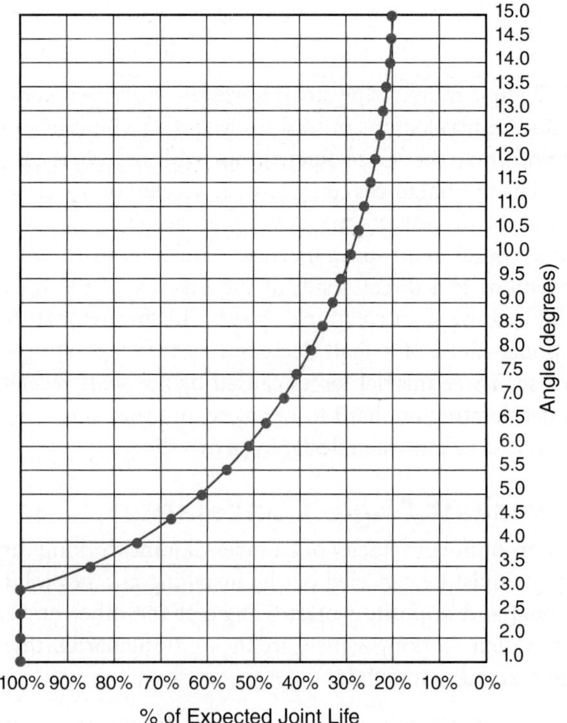

FIGURE 49-27 Relationship of joint life to operating angle.

TABLE 49-3 U-Joint Operating Angles and Shaft Speeds

Driveshaft rpm	Maximum Normal Operating Angles
5000	3° 15'
4500	3° 40'
4000	4° 15'
3500	5° 0'
3000	5° 50'
2500	7° 0'
2000	8° 40'
1500	11° 30'

6,000 hours when operated at an angle of five degrees and for only 3,000 hours at a 10-degree working angle. Smaller working angles reduce the chance of vibration and allow the longest wear life for universal joints.

Phasing

The working angles of a driveshaft system must be very carefully selected in order to prevent unacceptable vibration of the rotating shaft. However, there is another element to the story. In order for cancelation to occur and for vibrations to be eliminated, the canceling joint angle must be in the same phase in terms of rotation.

As we discussed in the Non-uniform Velocity section, if we divide a circle into quadrants of 90 degrees each, the driven shaft accelerates for the first 90 degrees, decelerates for the second 90 degrees, etc. **Phasing** of the universal joint operating angles means that the output yoke of the joint doing the cancelation of the non-uniform velocity has to be doing exactly the opposite of the driven yoke of the input universal joint, meaning that it must decelerate for the first 90 degrees of rotation and accelerate for the second 90 degrees in order to deliver a uniform velocity to the component it is connected to. To accomplish this, the inboard yoke ears on either end of the driven shaft must line up. This will place their respective joints in phase with each other, as in **FIGURE 49-28**. An out-of-phase driveshaft causes the accelerations and decelerations of the joints on either end of the shafts to be out of sync with each other. The result can be seen in **FIGURE 49-29**. Failure to correctly phase the universal joints will worsen the vibration rather than cancel it.

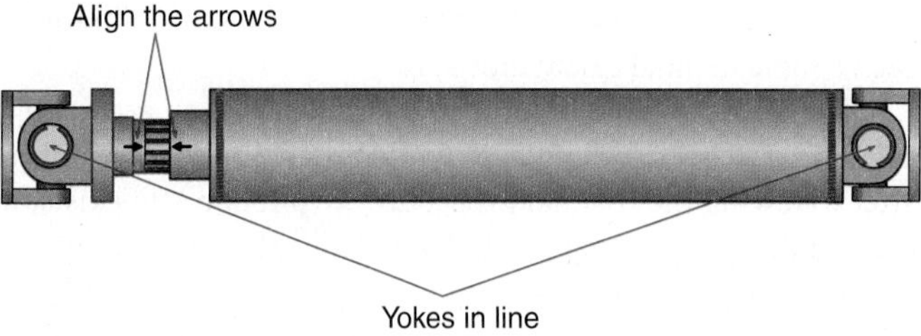

FIGURE 49-28 An in-phase driveshaft will have its inboard yoke ears in line.

The most common cause of out-of-phase problems is a failure by the technician to mark the slip yoke of a split driveshaft before disassembly. Always mark the slip yoke position before removal so that it can be reinstalled correctly.

Driveline Angularity

Driveline angularity simply refers to the angles at the universal joints. For the most part, driveline angles should not need to be reset in the field. However, if a driveline failure occurs that could be attributed to vibration, such as cracked tube welds or repeated U-joint failures, it may be necessary to check the driveline angles. Unless the vehicle or the driveline has been obviously tampered with, problems other than driveline angles are more likely to be the cause of driveline vibration failure, so always check for signs of significant changes to the driveline system arrangement.

▶ Measuring and Calculating Driveline Angles

S49001

Most driveline manufacturers offer a computer-based program to analyze driveline angle. Software can determine whether vibration is likely to occur. These programs take into account driveline weight and length to determine torsional and inertial

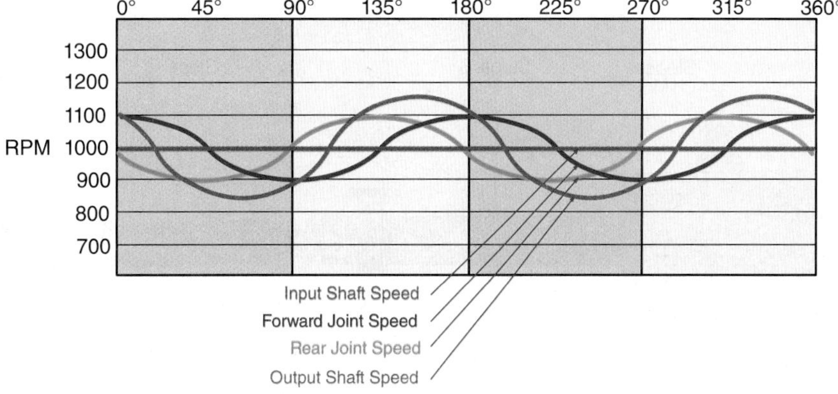

FIGURE 49-29 Failure to phase the driveshaft will mean the cancelation is occurring at the wrong time in terms of shaft rotation and lead to extreme vibration.

excitations and are much more accurate at predicting vibrations than simple manual calculations are.

A manual calculation procedure, however, is an acceptable preliminary check for angle issues that may cause vibration. If, after following the manual procedure, a vibration still exists, it may be due to torsional inertial vibrations that should be calculated using a computer-based program. Driveline angles are best measured with an electronic angle gauge or inclinometer, such as the Spicer Anglemaster, to ensure that readings are accurate. Readings should be accurate to within one-quarter of a degree.

The process is relatively simple when the components of the driveline have angles only in the side view. Some vehicles, however, have angles that occur in more than the side plane. In these drivelines, the shaft may move to the right or left along its length when viewed from above. That side-to-side variance is called the **plan angle**. Components that have slopes in two planes (side-view angle and plan angle) create a compound angle, and they must be calculated differently.

To calculate side-view-only angles, the angle of slope of each component in the driveline is measured and the operating angle between any two components is calculated. When a driveline is observed from the side, any slope that goes lower as it moves toward the rear of the machine is a down slope and is expressed as a positive angle. If the component slope goes higher as it moves to the back of the machine, it is an upward slope and recorded as a negative angle. To begin the process, ensure that the machine is on a level surface and that the tires, if equipped, are properly inflated. Operate the machine until the yokes to be measured are in the vertical position.

Driveshaft manufacturers may supply worksheets, similar to the one shown in **FIGURE 49-30**, that can be used to record the angles that will correspond to the driveline being worked on. If no worksheet is available, simply write down all of the components and record their slopes. We will use a two-piece driveshaft with a single single-axle drive for our example for a total of three operating angles.

The first measurement is the transmission slope. This measurement can usually be taken from any flat surface of the transmission that is parallel to its centerline, as illustrated in **FIGURE 49-31**. Alternatively, the transmission angle can be measured from its end yoke bearing caps using adapters supplied with the Spicer Anglemaster tool. Note that if you are measuring from the end yoke, the yoke ears must be positioned vertically.

Next, measure the slope of the first driveshaft, shown in **FIGURE 49-32**, which may be a coupling shaft. Shaft slope measurements can be taken on any clean and smooth section of the

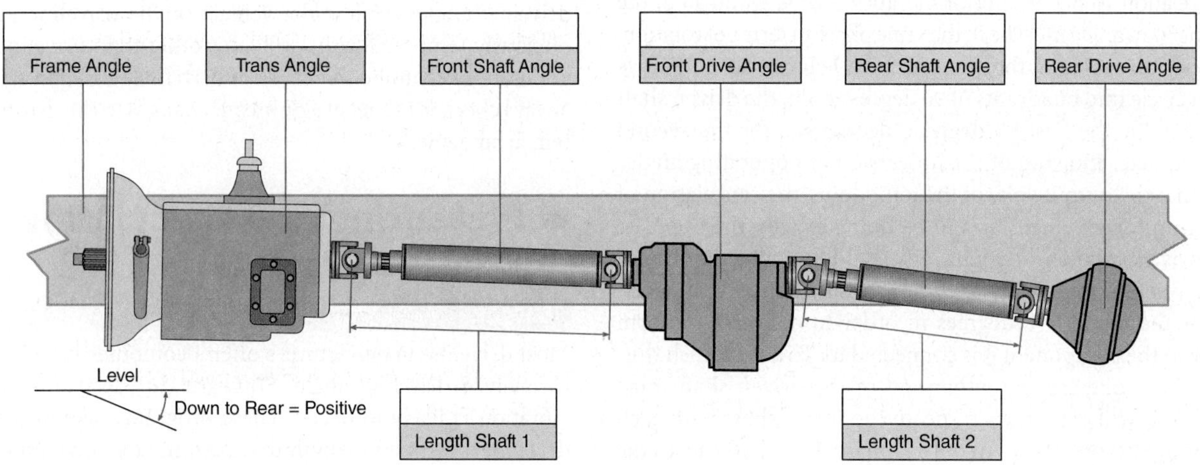

FIGURE 49-30 A work sheet is a helpful aid when recording angles, but it is not absolutely necessary.

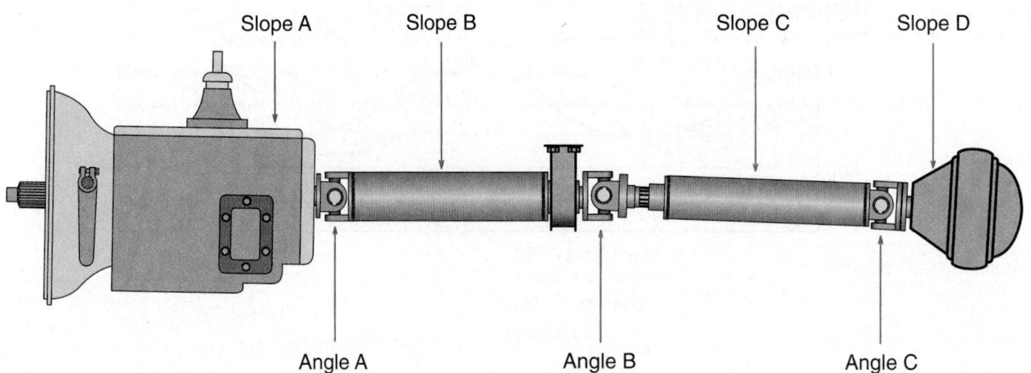

FIGURE 49-31 Measure the transmission slope from any flat surface parallel to its centerline.

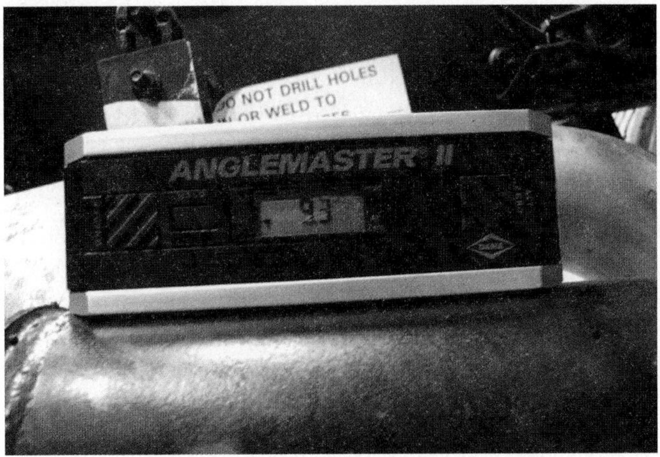

FIGURE 49-32 Measuring the slope of the first driveshaft.

driveshaft tube. Then, measure the slope of the next shaft and, finally, measure the slope of the drive axle.

The drive axle slope is usually measured at the flat section near the spring-mounting hardware or from its input yoke ears by using the adapter. Again, the yoke ears should be vertical. If all slopes are down and all readings are positive, then to calculate the working angle of each joint, simply subtract the smaller number from the larger number: that is the U-joint working angle.

Driveline Angle Examples

Consider the following example. The transmission's slope is four degrees down, the coupling shaft is five degrees down, the second driveshaft is six degrees down, and the drive axle is seven degrees down. Given those parameters, the following are true:

- The calculation for the first U-joint angle is 5 degrees – 4 degrees = 1 degree.
- The calculation for the second U-joint is 6 degrees – 5 degrees = 1 degree.
- The third U-joint angle is 7 degrees – 6 degrees = 1 degree.

These angles satisfy the three rules for universal joint angles:

1. Rule One states that there must be at least one-half to one degree of operating angle so that the needle bearings rotate.
2. Rule Two states that the angles at opposite ends of a shaft must be equal to within one degree.
3. Rule Three states that working angles be kept as small as possible.

Given the angles and their conformance to the rules, the driveline in this example should not cause a vibration because of driveline angles.

Now, let's consider another example. This time, we will use a driveline with a two-piece main driveshaft and tandem drive axles with a one-piece rear driveshaft. That makes a total of five operating angles, as illustrated in **FIGURE 49-33**.

Here are the parameters for this driveshaft:

- The transmission measures one degree down.
- The coupling shaft measures one degree up or minus one degree.
- The second driveshaft measures two degrees down.
- The first drive axle measures 0.5 degrees down.
- The rear driveshaft measures three degrees down.
- The rear-rear drive axle measures three degrees down.

Given those conditions, the operating angles are as follows:

- For the first U-joint angle, the transmission and the first shaft slopes are in different directions, so the degrees have to be added rather than subtracted— one degree down for the transmission and one degree up for the first shaft. The operating angle is two degrees.
- The calculation for the second joint angle is one degree up for the coupling shaft and two degrees down for the second shaft, so the operating angle is three degrees.
- The third operating angle is two degrees down for the second shaft and 0.5 degrees down for the front rear axle, so the operating angle is 2.5 degrees.
- The fourth operating angle is 0.5 degrees down for the power-divider and 3 degrees down for the rear driveshaft, so the operating angle is 2.5 degrees.
- The fifth operating angle is three degrees down for the rear driveshaft and three degrees down for the rear-rear drive axle, so the operating angle is zero degrees.

This second example meets the three rules of driveline angles for all the operating angles, except for the fifth one. The fifth operating angle fails Rule Two because it is not within one degree of the fourth operating angle. Therefore, it will not cancel out the non-uniform velocity in the rear driveshaft and thus will cause vibration. The fifth operating angle also fails Rule One in that the operating angle must be at least one-half to one degree. This angle is zero degrees, so by itself, it will cause the U-joint to wear out prematurely because the needle bearings will not rotate.

This problem can be corrected by shimming the rear-rear axle spring mounts to rotate the axle until it is only 0.5 degrees down. This would make the fifth operating angle 2.5 degrees and satisfy all three rules.

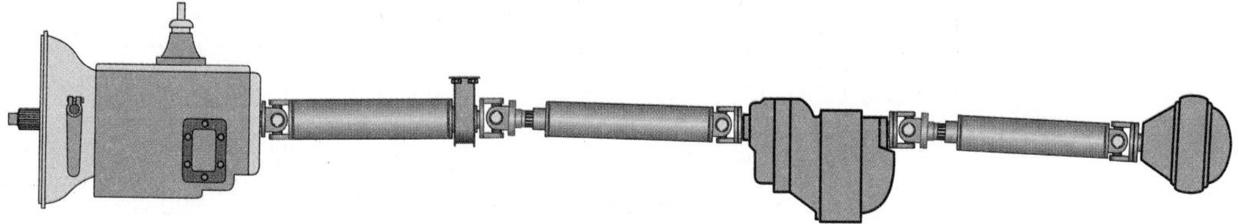

FIGURE 49-33 A five-angle driveshaft system.

Compound Driveline Angles

Compound driveline angles involve angles in two planes—the side view and the plan or top view, as illustrated in **FIGURE 49-34**. When compound angles are encountered, we must still take the same measurements as in our previous examples. However, with compound angles, we must also calculate the true operating angle by combining the measured side-view angle with the plan-view angle.

The only way to obtain the plan or top-view angle is through careful calculation or by using a plan-view angle chart, such as the one shown in **FIGURE 49-35**. The chart's *x* axis is the driveshaft length in inches, and the *y* axis is the number of inches the shaft is offset over its length. The point of intersection is marked on the chart and then a line is drawn from the corner, where the *x* and *y* axes meet, to a circular line on the right-hand side of the chart that is graduated in degrees. This is then the plan- or top-view angle.

Once you have determined the plan-view angle, use the following formula to obtain the true U-joint operating angle:

$$C = \sqrt{S^2 + T^2}$$

where

C = true operating compound angle
S = side-view angle
T = top-view angle

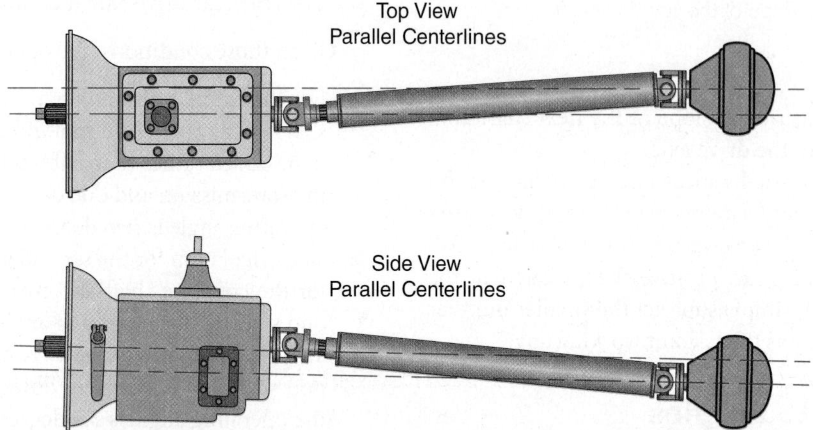

FIGURE 49-34 Compound angles are angles that exist in two planes, both from the side view and from the top view (the plan angle). These must be calculated differently.

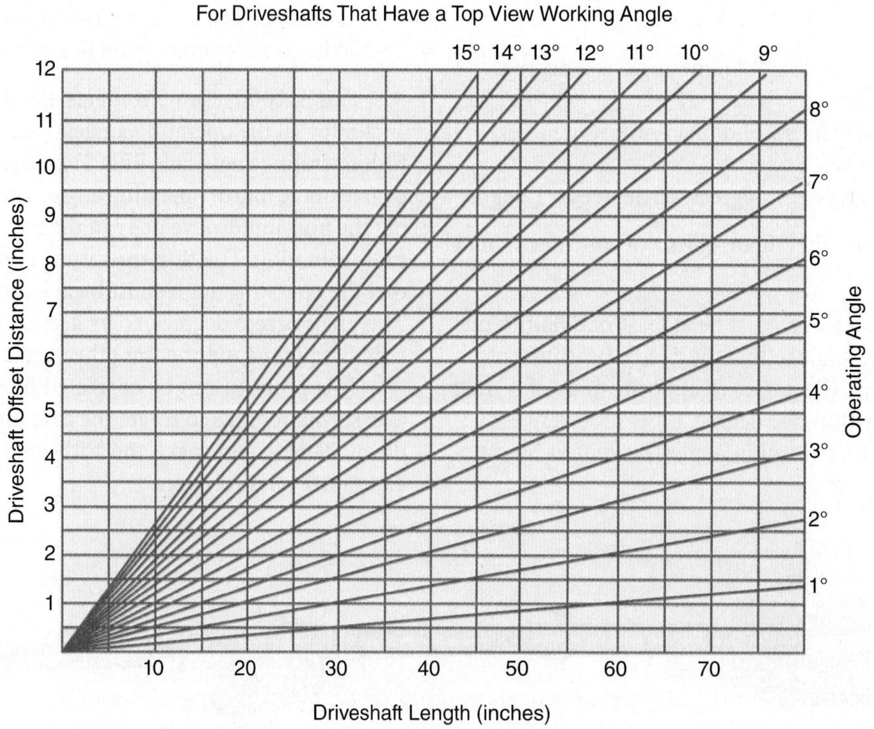

FIGURE 49-35 Plan-view angle calculation chart.

For example, if the side-view or measured angle is 2.5 degrees and the top-view or calculated angle is 1.5 degrees, then the compound angle would be as follows:

$$C = \sqrt{2.5^2 + 1.5^2}$$
$$= \sqrt{8.5}$$
$$= 2.92$$

When calculating the true U-joint operating angles for both ends of the shaft, the resultant angles must meet the same three rules for all driveline angles, to avoid vibration and premature wear out: They must be at least one-half to one degree; they must be equal to within one degree; they should be as small as possible.

Compound angles can be very common in machine drivelines. They are especially common in power take-off (PTO) or auxiliary drivelines.

Calculating driveline angles to solve vibration problems is a limited answer to a sometimes very complex issue. These simple measurements do not take into account inertial excitations and critical-speed issues. Computer programs that analyze driveline angle take shaft diameter, length, and weight into consideration, meaning these programs consider these other sources of vibration. When possible, the technician should use these programs to eliminate the need for complex calculations and ensure much greater accuracy in determining the source of a vibration.

Troubleshooting Vibrations and Failures

Even though driveline vibration can be a common source of driveline component failures, it is necessary to eliminate all other possibilities before condemning the driveshaft. Vibrations from other systems, such as the engine, clutch, or other sources, can mimic driveshaft-caused problems. The HDET will usually have to rely on their knowledge of failure causes to be capable of discerning driveline vibration issues. Understanding the various causes of vibrations, measuring driveshaft runout, checking angularity, and analyzing driveshaft failure are all critical aspects to troubleshooting this system.

Driveline Vibration Diagnostics

There are different causes of driveline vibrations caused by driveshafts. This section explains the types and causes of the different driveshaft vibrations.

Transverse vibrations are caused by an out-of-balance driveshaft or system, and they occur once per shaft revolution. Always check shafts for missing balance weights. These shafts are very heavy, so even small imbalances can cause large vibrations. Balance weights are shown in **FIGURE 49-36**.

FIGURE 49-36 Check shaft for missing balance weights.

There are two causes of **torsional vibrations** in the driveline. One source originates from the power impulses from the engine caused by the forces on the crankshaft during each power stroke. With today's engines that produce high torque at low speed, these impulses cause a twisting force to be placed on the crankshaft up to 20 times a second at rated speed. If these impulses are not properly muted by the clutch or powertrain system, they can be transmitted throughout the driveline.

The other cause of driveline torsional vibrations is the U-joint angles or phasing. Remember that a U-joint working at an angle causes the driven yoke to accelerate and decelerate twice per revolution. If proper cancelation is not achieved by correct angles and phasing, the driveshaft will be subjected to twisting forces. Just as a coat hanger that is bent back and forth snaps in two, enough torsional forces in the driveshaft will lead to driveshaft or U-joint failure. Vibrations from this source will occur at twice driveshaft speed.

Inertial excitation stems from the operating angles of the U-joint at the drive end of the driveshaft and is caused by the sheer weight of the driveshaft being accelerated and decelerated twice per revolution. These vibrations are hard to pinpoint. There are only two possible solutions for inertial excitation. The first is to decrease the operating angle and thereby reduce the magnitude of the acceleration and decelerations. The second is to reduce the driveshaft weight, which is seldom practical. Even though the driveline angles may be correctly canceling each other out, the larger the angle at the drive end, the more severe the inertial excitation will be.

Secondary couple vibrations are vibrations that are passed through or coupled through the hanger bearing in a heavy-duty driveshaft. These vibrations are then passed along the entire length of the driveline. Secondary couple vibrations occur at twice driveshaft speed frequency and can affect the whole driveline. They are most often observed by failure of the hanger bearing rubber support. Secondary couple vibrations can be lessened by making sure the U-joint angle at the front of the coupling shaft is as small as possible.

Critical-Speed Vibrations

Critical-speed vibrations occur if the driveshaft is operated at or faster than its critical speed. Recall that critical speed is the speed at which the centrifugal force acting on the rotating shaft becomes stronger than the shaft itself; if this occurs, the shaft will start to bow off its centerline. Critical-speed vibrations occur at driveshaft speed frequency and will always eventually cause shaft failure. It is not common for a machine's driveline to operate at or above the driveshaft's critical speed.

Diagnosing Vibrations

To begin diagnosing vibration-caused failures, gather as much information as possible about the failures and find out whether they are recurring. After gathering all the information necessary to narrow down the problem, if the driveshaft is isolated as the cause of the vibration, the shafts must be carefully inspected for missing balance weights or any buildup of foreign material, which could be the cause of vibration from imbalance. Dents in the driveshaft tubing displace shaft mass toward the center rather than the outside, where it was when the shaft was initially balanced. Dents are a common cause of vibration and also weaken the tube's section modulus (strength). Dented tubing should be replaced.

Measuring Driveshaft Runout

Shaft runout is another possible cause of vibration. Driveshaft runout can be caused by a bent driveshaft, damaged yokes, or worn U-joints. A dial indicator is normally used to measure driveshaft runout. Before measuring runout, first sand and clean around the front, center, and rear of the driveshaft to remove any uneven buildup of paint or rust. This will give the dial indicator a smooth surface for accurate measurements. Mount the dial indicator perpendicular to the shaft. The indicator base must be placed on a rigid surface; the machine frame is a good choice. The driveshaft must *not* be at a sharp angle during runout measurement.

With the transmission in neutral, turn the driveshaft. Measure runout at the front, center, and rear of the shaft, as shown in **FIGURE 49-37**. Compare your measurements to specs. Generally, driveshaft runout should not exceed 0.010–0.015 inches (0.25–0.38 mm), but always check the manufacturer's specification. If driveshaft runout is beyond specs, try removing and rotating the shaft 180 degrees in the rear yoke. Make sure the universal joints are in good condition and that the yokes are not damaged. If shaft runout is okay after all other causes of possible vibration have been eliminated, then try rotating the shaft 180 degrees in the rear yoke to possibly lessen vibration caused by an out-of-balance driveshaft. If there is still a vibration present, the driveshaft should be sent out for balancing.

Driveline angles can be measured, as was discussed in the Measuring and Calculating Driveline Angles section. Measuring the angles in that way does not take inertial excitations into consideration, however. The best way to eliminate a driveline vibration is to use one of the computerized programs offered by driveshaft manufacturers that analyze driveline angle. These programs take driveshaft weight, length, and angles into consideration and are much better at eliminating driveshaft inertial excitations and angle vibration problems.

Analyzing Driveshaft Failure

Driveshafts can fail for a number of reasons, including brinelling, spalling, galling, fractured or broken U-joints, accelerated wear, twisted tubing, or failure of the hanger bearings.

Brinelling and False Brinelling

Brinelling occurs when the rollers in the universal joint are hammered into the trunnions, leaving indentations. This can happen for several reasons. Excess torque can lead to brinelling, as the trunnion metal is repeatedly overloaded. The perpetual hammering will eventually lead to brinelling. Brinelling can also occur if the slip yoke is seized. In that case, brinelling will appear on the front and rear of the trunnion rather than on the torque faces (the sides of the trunnion). As the shaft tries to lengthen or shorten, the seized slip yoke causes the front and back of the trunnions to be hammered. Brinelling can also result after a long service life through the normal wearing of the universal joint.

If the U-joint operates at a zero angle, the rollers do not rotate and the lubrication is squeezed out between the rollers and trunnions. This leads to brinelling-like wear on the trunnions, called false brinelling. The operating angle must be adjusted to have a least one-half to one degree; otherwise, this failure will occur over and over again. Over-tightening of retaining straps or distorted or damaged end yokes can cause the same problem by restricting the roller's rotation. **FIGURE 49-38** shows brinelling on a trunnion.

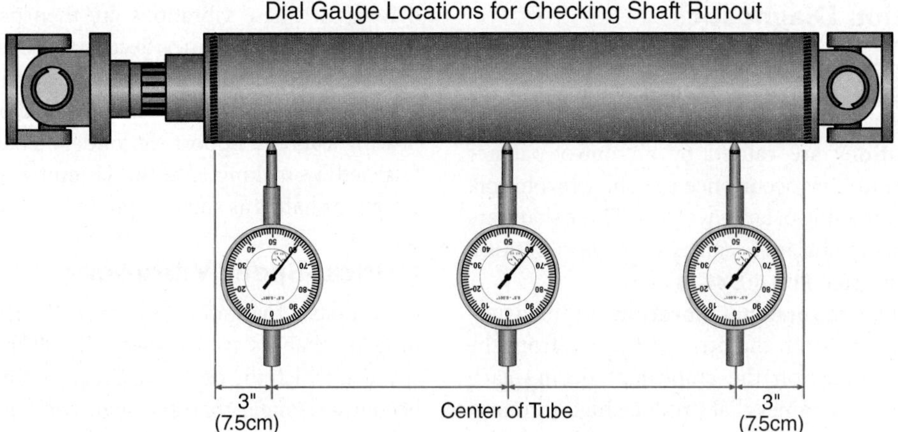

FIGURE 49-37 Runout should be checked at least 3 inches (7.5 cm) from the ends of the shaft and in the center.

FIGURE 49-38 Brinelling causes wear on the trunnions in the shape of the roller bearings.

FIGURE 49-40 U-joint breakage is usually caused by shock loading, as is the case in this image of a broken U-joint cross. Notice the uniform roughness of the break.

Spalling or Galling

Spalling and galling are the transfer of metal from one surface to the other, caused by excessive friction between them. **FIGURE 49-39** shows an example of extreme spalling.

This is normally caused by either a lack of joint lubricant or contamination of the joint lubricant. Water and dirt are the most likely contaminants. Lack of lubricant indicates poor maintenance practices. Either reason can lead to burned trunnions. End galling of the trunnions is usually caused by excessive joint operating angles.

U-joint Fractures and Breakage

Fractures and breakage, as shown in **FIGURE 49-40**, are usually the result of shock loads sending excessive torque through the joint. This type of breakage is more common in highway applications but can occur when the machine's driveline is severely overloaded.

Fractures may also occur at weld seams because of fatigue, which may be caused by excessive working angles introducing torsional stresses on components. Welding on the tube near the weld seams can also weaken the metal and lead to weld seam failures. Never weld balance weights within one inch of a weld seam.

FIGURE 49-39 Contaminated lubricant or lack of lubricant leads to spalling. This image is an extreme case of spalling.

Accelerated Wear

Any joint that operates at an angle of more than three degrees will suffer reduced wear life. (Recall that the life expectancy is directly related to the size of the angle.) Excess torque and overloading will contribute to a shortened wear life as well.

Reusing attachment hardware can lead to wear, specifically in the end yoke. Attachment hardware is designed to stretch as it is torqued so that it effectively clamps the U-joint caps in the yoke. Hardware that is reused can be deformed enough to allow the U-joint bearing cap to move. The increased motion causes wear. Always replace attaching hardware when reinstalling a U-joint. One exception to this rule is the Spicer Life Series formed-metal hardware.

Twisted Tubing

Twisted tubing, like that shown in **FIGURE 49-41**, is usually caused by excessive torque loading of the driveline. Excessive torque loading is typically caused by operator error. If twisting occurs, a check should be made to determine whether the driveline is capable of transferring the available driveline torque.

Hanger Bearing Failures

Hanger bearing failures are actually quite rare because the bearing is sealed and permanently lubricated. The stamped steel cavity surrounding the hanger bearing does need to be packed with water-proof grease at installation. If this procedure is overlooked, the bearing will fail prematurely.

Failure of the hanger or "center" bearing is depicted in **FIGURE 49-42**. This type of failure usually occurs in the rubber support block and is most often caused by excessive angles at the coupling shaft drive end. This angle should be less than one and a half degrees if possible. Remember that it must also have at least one-half degree so that the rollers will turn.

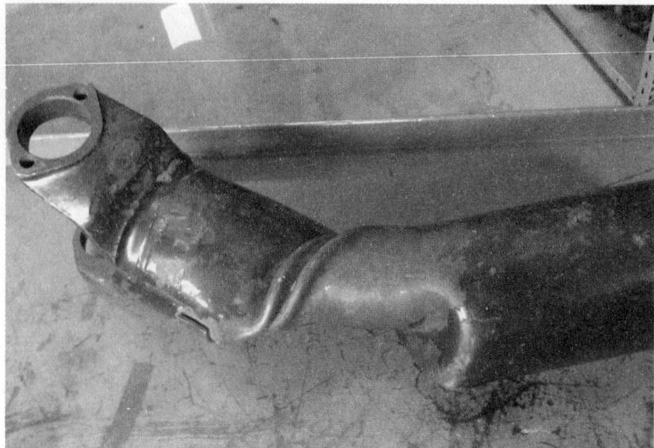

FIGURE 49-41 Twisted tubing from overloading.

FIGURE 49-42 Failed hanger bearing.

This problem will usually manifest as black rubber dust surrounding the hanger bearing. On every revolution, the coupling shaft will try to straighten out its angle, and the rubber block must absorb this motion. Some large coupling shafts can weigh in excess of 100 lb (45.35 kg). The rubber support must be strong enough for the shaft that it is attached to. Hanger bearing failure is usually caused by shaft imbalance or excessive torsional vibrations that lead to failure of the rubber mount. Because they are permanently lubricated, bearing failure is normally attributed to external damage to the bearing or its seals. Pillow block bulkhead support bearings can fail due to excessive vibrations and/or lack of periodic lubrication.

▶ Inspection Diagnoses and Maintenance of Driveshafts

S49002

Regular driveshaft maintenance is usually limited to inspecting the shaft and components for wear or damage and properly lubricating the driveshaft following the manufacturer's recommended procedures. Any inspection for wear *must* be done prior to lubricating the components. The reason is simple: the lubricant itself may mask wear in the universal joints and make it hard to detect.

Begin with a careful visual inspection of the driveshaft. Look for any broken or loose fasteners. Pay particular attention to the attaching hardware for the universal joint and the center bearing support bracket if equipped. Look for broken yoke tabs or missing spring clips or locks. Check the tubes for damage, dents, or missing balance weights, all of which can cause vibration problems. Also make sure that there is no foreign material stuck to the shafts because this can also result in balance vibrations. **FIGURE 49-43** illustrates how problems with the shaft can produce various vibrations.

Look for any unusual rust streaking or rust patterns at or near the universal joints, the end yoke attaching bolts or nuts, and the center bearing hanger bolts. Rust streaking at any of these components can be a telltale sign of wear or looseness. Carefully check the center bearing rubber support. Rubber dust here is an indicator of excessive movement either from wear or from vibration.

Next, check all of the universal joints for wear. Grasp both sides of each joint and try to rotate them in opposite directions to each other, checking for radial play. There should be no perceptible movement between the trunnions and the caps. Even slight movement here fails the joint, and it should be replaced. Next, grasp the shaft side of the joint and move it vertically and horizontally, to check for end play between the joint bearing caps and the ends of the trunnions. For most manufacturers, this end play cannot exceed 0.006 inches (0.15 mm). Although some manufacturers recommend universal joint replacement if there is any noticeable end play, check the original equipment manufacturer (OEM) manual to be sure.

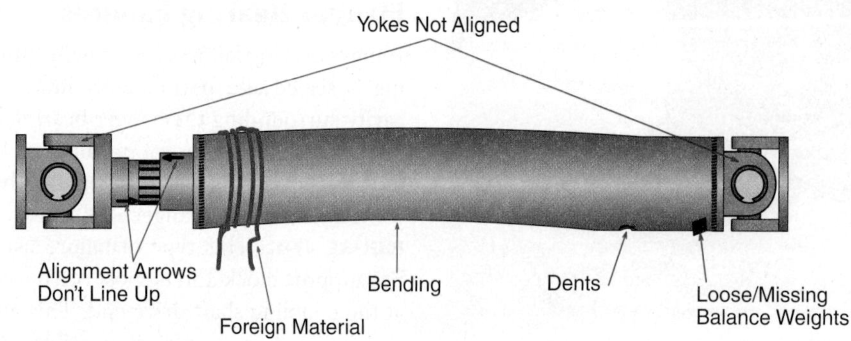

FIGURE 49-43 Any of the problems indicated in the diagram can cause driveshaft vibrations.

Next, grasp each of the end yokes where they enter the transmission and the driveline component pinion(s) and rotate them back and forth and up and down to check for looseness. There should be no perceptible free play at these components. If play is present, consult the transmission manual or the manufacturer's manual for instructions on how to repair the situation. Consult the manufacturer's manual for specifications if necessary.

Grasp the slip yoke and move it up, down, and radially to check splines for looseness and radial play. Maximum play should be no more than 0.012 inches (3 mm), but measurable play exceeding 0.004–0.006 inches (0.1–0.15 mm) should be investigated and corrected. Play in the slip joint components can cause driveshaft vibration because the play will allow the shaft to move away from its centerline while it is rotating.

Lubrication

Lack of proper lubrication is one of the most common causes of universal joint and driveshaft failures. Regular lubrication with high-quality grease that meets or exceeds the manufacturer's specifications will assist in achieving maximum joint wear life. Although each manufacturer will have its own recommendations, the lubricant used should meet the following minimum specifications:

- The grease should be good quality EP (extreme pressure) grease.
- The grease should meet National Lubricating Grease Institute (NLGI) Grade 2 specification.
- The grease should have an operating range of at least 325°F to –10°F (163°C to –21°C).
- The grease should be compatible with commonly used multipurpose greases. When lubricating universal joints, it is essential to purge grease from all four caps until the new grease is visibly exiting the cap seals. This will eliminate the old grease and lessen compatibility issues.

Knowing the correct lubricant is only one aspect of proper lubrication. In addition, the components must be lubricated at the correct intervals. Lubricating intervals vary by manufacturer and by driveshaft design. Most mobile off-road equipment will have a lubrication chart decal on the machine with the intervals. A typical service interval for driveshaft and U-joint lubrication would be 1,000 hours or six months.

Some of the Spicer series of driveshafts can come with permanent lubrication or extended interval lubrication schedules, but the driveshaft system should still be inspected on a regular basis.

Probably the most important advice for technicians performing lubrication service on a driveshaft is to ensure that the universal joints purge grease from all four universal joint caps. If one cap fails to purge after all attempts have been made, the joint must be disassembled to find the cause.

Using a hand-operated or an air-powered grease gun fully lubricates each of the universal joints. As the grease is being forced into the joint, watch the bearing caps for any water or rust that purges from them. Sometimes a very small amount of clear water, one or two drops from condensation, may be present. The presence of one or two water droplets is acceptable unless there is any sign of water contaminating the lube, any sign of rust-colored

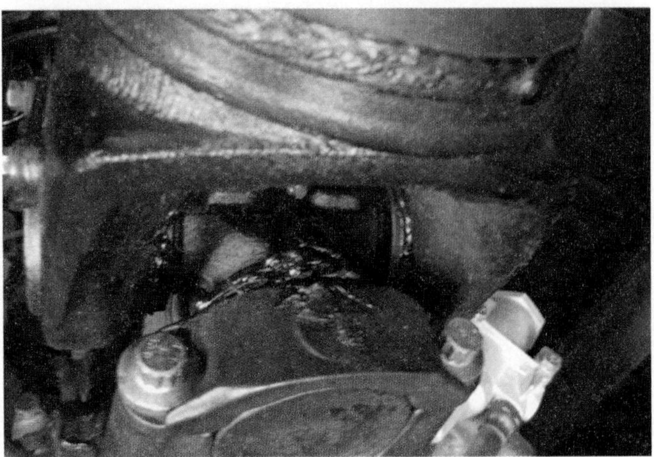

FIGURE 49-44 New grease should purge from all four bearing caps when lubricating new or in-service U-joints. If a cap fails to purge grease, it is essential to investigate the cause.

material, or any sign of dirt purging from the caps. In that case, the joint must be replaced. Ensure that grease is pumped into the joint caps until they are completely purged and that only new grease is coming out of the caps, as shown in **FIGURE 49-44**. This ensures that there is sufficient grease in each cap and that there will not be any compatibility issues with dissimilar greases.

If one or more of the caps do not purge grease immediately, try to lessen the pressure on the cap that will not purge by using a jack with slight pressure to push the opposite cap against its trunnion while trying to get grease to purge. If this is unsuccessful and the universal joints have bolt-in caps, try loosening the bolts on the problem cap a couple of turns each, and then try to purge the cap again. If these methods fail, the shaft or the joint must be removed so that you can investigate and remedy the situation. A universal joint bearing cap that does not purge grease while being lubricated. It will most certainly fail, so keep at it until it purges or replace the joint. After all caps have been purged with fresh grease, wipe up the excess grease, to protect the environment and keep the vehicle underside clean.

Next, you will need to lube the slip joints. Most slip joints have a Welch plug pressed into the end of the sliding tube. Where the tube turns into the yoke, the plug will have a small hole in the center for air to escape, as shown in **FIGURE 49-45**.

Apply grease until it purges from the Welch plug hole and, again, watch for any signs of contamination. Even though contamination here is not as critical as with universal joint bearing caps, serious contamination should be investigated. When grease purges from the Welch plug hole, cover the hole with a finger and continue to pump the grease into the joint until it purges from the seal end. Again, purge until fresh grease is visibly exiting the seal.

After completion, clean up the excess grease. If the machine is to be parked outside in colder climates for a significant amount of time, it is a good idea to operate the machine so that the slip joint will reciprocate a bit and purge any excess grease. In cold weather, the grease can solidify while the machine is parked. When finally operated, the solid plug of grease can sometimes force the Welch plug out of the joint. During continued

FIGURE 49-45 When lubricating a slip yoke, block the bleed hole in the welch plug until new grease purges from the slip yoke.

operation the grease will start to soften, and eventually all of the grease will be thrown out of the joint. This will lead to premature slip joint failure.

SAFETY TIP

If you use an air-powered grease gun to lube a slip yoke, use a piece of rubber gasket to seal the Welch plug hole in the end of the slip yoke. The rubber acts as a precaution to prevent grease from being injected into the skin. An air grease gun may be capable of piercing the skin. Grease injection can lead to severe tissue damage.

▶ Repairing Driveline Systems

S49003

Drivelines will require repairs from time to time, and 90% of these repairs will involve removing the driveshaft and/or replacing universal joints. The following section covers several common driveshaft repair procedures.

Replacing a Universal Joint

Replacing a universal joint may or may not require that the driveshaft be removed from the machine. If it does, the shaft must be separated from the end yokes before being taken to a work bench or press to complete the joint replacement.

The following are general steps for universal joint replacement procedures. Each driveline system will have individual attaching hardware styles (bolts and straps, clips, etc.), and most manufacturers insist that attaching hardware be replaced if it is removed. Therefore, before attempting to remove the shaft or any components, ensure that the correct parts are on hand to complete the job. There are several different pulling and pushing tools available to replace universal joints. Regardless of the type of tool used, the same basic instructions apply when working with all driveshafts.

The most important aspects of universal joint replacement are being careful not to damage the shaft and using as little force as possible when removing the joint. Take extreme care not to damage the shaft itself, because dents in the shaft will cause vibrations and lead to premature joint failure. Scratches and gouges can lead to localized stress risers, which weaken the shaft. The yokes can be damaged in several ways as well, so take care when working with them. The ears can be expanded by stretching them apart and be distorted or twisted by hammering and indiscriminate use of excessive force. Remember to use as little force as possible while removing universal joints. It is not recommended to use torches to heat components to ease removal, because the heat can change the metallurgy of the shaft and/or yoke material.

Removing the Driveshaft

Driveshaft manufacturers recommend that none of the attaching hardware be reused; any bolts, straps, or clips should be replaced because they are torqued to yield when installed correctly and may not secure the driveshaft if they are used again. Therefore, before removing any driveshaft hardware, ensure that replacement hardware is readily available.

The first step in removal of a universal joint is to always attach slings, hangers, or jacks to support the shaft before removing the attaching hardware. Be sure to use enough supports so that the shaft does not fall when one end or the other is removed. If working on a driveline with more than one shaft, each section of the shaft will require at least two slings or hangers. When removing a multi-piece shaft, start at the drive axle end and work toward the transmission.

▶ TECHNICIAN TIP

Heavy-duty driveshafts can weigh well over 100 lb (45.35 kg), and removing the attaching bolts before supporting the shaft can lead to personal injury and/or damage to the shaft. Always use a sling or other support to hold the shaft weight securely before removing any of the attaching bolts.

Before removing the sections of a multi-shaft driveline, always mark the slip joints with paint or a marking pencil so that they can be reinstalled correctly. (White correction fluid used in office supplies makes a good marking compound.) If the universal joint is bolted to a half-round end yoke, then after installing the correct support slings, remove the attaching hardware that holds the joint bearing caps into the end yoke. Remove the shaft to the bench to complete joint removal. Before removing the attaching bolts, as shown in **FIGURE 49-46**, always use a sling to support the driveshaft before removing the attaching bolts.

There are several commercially available pullers that can be used to remove the bearing caps from shafts that have a full-round end yoke. Using pullers such as the Tiger Tool U-joint puller, shown in **FIGURE 49-47**, is the manufacturers' recommended procedure to prevent damage to the yoke and/or shaft.

The attaching hardware on the full-round end yoke caps should be removed and the puller installed according to the manufacturer's procedure. The puller will remove the cap using a steady pulling action that pushes against one yoke ear and pulls against another. No damage to the yoke itself will occur during this process. When the first cap is removed, the tool is reinstalled

FIGURE 49-46 Heavy-duty driveshafts are extremely heavy, so always use a sling to support the driveshaft before removing the attaching bolts.

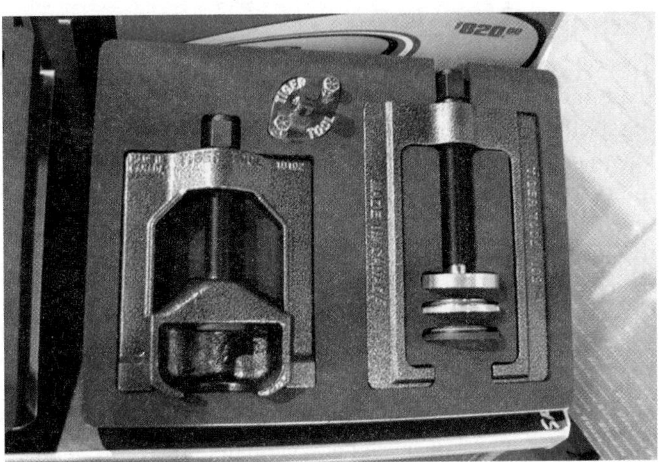

FIGURE 49-47 Aftermarket U-joint removal tools from the Tiger Tool Company.

to remove the other cap. The shaft is then taken to the bench to remove the other caps. If a universal joint is to be reused, ensure that the correct bearing caps are reinstalled on their original trunnions. In some repair facilities a popular method of removing the U-joint caps is to use a jack and a hammer. The joint cap to be removed is placed in the vertical position, and a jack is positioned close to the joint under the yoke. The jack is operated, and the weight of the vehicle is used to remove the cap. Sometimes a hammer is used to try to break the cap loose if it is seized. No matter how common, THIS METHOD IS NOT RECOMMENDED BY ANY MANUFACTURER. We mention the process here only to try to avoid damage to equipment and/or injury to technicians. It is *not* recommended.

Using the weight of the machine to force the cap out can cause several problems. First, the bearing cap can let go suddenly if it is seized. The jack can slip, causing the machine to drop quickly, resulting in crush injuries and other damage. The jack itself can cause damage to the shaft by bending it or gouging at the point of contact. The yoke ears can be spread by the uneven forces being applied, and using hammers can cause damage to the shaft or yoke.

Using the proper pulling tools avoids all of these dangers and is the only procedure that should be followed. If only one universal joint is being replaced, the entire removal procedure can be accomplished with the shaft still in place on the vehicle and supported. Simply remove one cap at a time with the puller. If more than one joint is to be replaced, the shaft can be taken to the work bench, and the work can be completed there, using either the puller or a suitable hydraulic press. Alternatively, if the shaft has a slip joint, the joint may be separated to remove one section of the shaft. When separating a slip joint, be sure to mark the position of the slip joint so that it can be reinstalled correctly.

Some slip joints have a threaded seal cap that must be unscrewed before the slip joint can be separated, as depicted in **FIGURE 49-48**. Remember that a heavy-duty driveshaft can weigh well over 100 lb (45.35 kg), so get assistance when removing the shaft. There are several different pullers available for universal joints, and the method described above can be adapted to use with any one of them. The relatively low cost of these pullers should mean that all shops will use them. Unfortunately, however, some will not and will instead resort to the jack method. Remember that the jack method is likely to cause injury and/or shaft damage and therefore should not be used.

After the joint has been removed, the yoke ears should be checked for wear and for damage from removal. Slight burrs can be removed with a small rat-tail file. Remove heavy rust with an emery cloth to make the reinstallation process easier.

Finally, check the yokes for distortion by using a yoke alignment bar. Slide the bar through both yoke ears. If the bar does not go through, it indicates that the yoke has been twisted due to excessive torque or disassembly damage. In that case, the yoke should be replaced.

Inspecting and Installing Universal Joints

As mentioned previously, most manufacturers recommend that all driveshaft attaching hardware bolts, nuts, straps, and lock

FIGURE 49-48 It may be necessary to unscrew the seal cap on a slip joint to separate it. Be sure to mark both halves so that they can be reassembled correctly.

plates be replaced after being removed and never be reused. When hardware is installed properly, straps and bolts are usually torqued to yield and may be distorted. Consequently, reusing hardware may allow bearing caps to move or cause attachment to loosen.

Before installing a new universal joint, carefully inspect the new joint by removing all of the bearing caps and checking the rollers and the cap seals. Check for any debris or dirt in the joint, and ensure that the grease zerk is in good order. Also note the location of the grease zerk. If the grease zerk is mounted on one side (for example, toward the front or back) of the universal joint cross, that side should be installed toward the driveshaft tube. Doing so ensures that the zerk is accessible by a grease gun after installation. In some cases, it may still be possible to grease the joint if the zerk is installed toward the end yoke, but it is always better to be safe than sorry.

Remember that new universal joints are packaged with just enough lubricant to hold the rollers in place and stave off rusting. The joints *must* be fully lubricated after installation. When installing universal joint caps, it is essential that the cap and bearings be on the trunnion before forcing the cap back into the yoke ears. Otherwise, one or more of the rollers can fall between the cap and the trunnion end. Preventing that involves positioning the trunnion through the yoke, installing the cap on the trunnion, and then forcing the cap and trunnion back into the yoke ear. Universal joints should be removed and installed by using steady controlled pressure only and using the proper pulling and pushing tools. A dead-blow or brass hammer may be used to help seat bearing caps, but be very careful not to damage the shaft, the yokes, and/or the universal joint itself. To disassemble and inspect a Wing Series U-joint with a bolted end, follow the steps in **SKILL DRILL 49-1**. To install universal joints, follow the guidelines in **SKILL DRILL 49-2**.

▶ TECHNICIAN TIP

It cannot be stressed enough how easy it can be to "drop a roller" (when one of the roller bearings falls into the bearing cap unseen by the technician) while installing universal joints. Take extreme care to avoid this scenario. If it is suspected that a roller has dropped, be sure to recheck the joint carefully. A dropped roller will cause a new joint to fail very quickly.

▶ TECHNICIAN TIP

New universal joints only have enough lube to retain the roller bearing and prevent rust. It is essential that they are completely lubricated after installation with new grease purging from all four bearing caps or failure will likely occur!

Inspecting and Replacing Center (Hanger) Bearings

The center (hanger) bearing supports the end of a split driveshaft and is a very important part of any driveline. The bearing itself is usually sealed. It cannot be lubricated, but if it does have a grease zerk, it will actually require lubrication at the same interval as the rest of the driveline.

The center support bearing is mounted in a rubber support to allow flexibility as the driveline moves up and down. Failure of the center bearing can cause vibration and noise in the driveline. The rubber support can become damaged by being in contact with petroleum products, which swell the rubber. Excessive vibration will weaken the rubber. The rubber can also be damaged simply by age and weathering, which will eventually cause the rubber to break down and disintegrate. Follow the procedure in **SKILL DRILL 49-3** to remove and reinstall the driveshaft and center support bearing and mounts. Follow the procedure in **SKILL DRILL 49-4** to inspect and, if necessary, replace the center bearing.

SKILL DRILL 49-1 Disassembling and Inspecting a Wing Series U-Joint with a Bolted End

1. Locate and follow the appropriate procedure in the service manual.
2. Complete the accompanying job sheet or work order with all pertinent information.
3. Remove the U-joint from the driveshaft:
   a. Bend tangs of lock plates, if equipped, away from cap screw heads.
   b. Remove cap screws and lock plates.
   c. Remove bearing caps from flange and U-joint.
4. Inspect Wing Series U-joint:
   a. Clean all U-joint parts.
   b. Check bearing journals for evidence of wear or heat damage; also, check ends of cross trunnions.
   c. Ensure lubricant passages in cross are clean.
   d. Check for missing, worn, or damaged needle bearings.
   e. Apply the recommended lubricant to rollers in caps.
   f. Turn caps on journals to check for wear.

   Note: If any parts are worn or damaged, replace the entire U-joint.
5. List the test results and/or recommendations on the job sheet or work order, clean the work area, and return tools and materials to their proper storage area.

SKILL DRILL 49-2 Installing a Universal Joint with Full-Round Yokes and Bolt-in Caps

1. With all of the caps removed from the cross, position it in the tube yoke with one of the trunnions protruding above the yoke ear. Install the cross in the yoke, one trunnion at a time.
2. Place the bearing cap over the trunnion, ensuring that the rollers remain properly seated in the cap. Then, slide the cap into position while holding the cross, so that the rollers remain engaged with the trunnion. If the cap binds in the yoke, tap it lightly with a dead-blow hammer until it is flush. Always tap the center of the cap only, not the edges.
3. Install the cap retaining bolts with the lock strap, if equipped, but do not fold the lock strap tangs to secure the bolt at this time. (Wait until the joint is properly lubricated.)
4. With one cap installed correctly, turn the yoke over and raise the cross sufficiently to engage the rollers of the second cap with its trunnion. Do not raise the cross so high that the other trunnion comes out of its cap. Then, push the second cap into position and secure it.
5. Rotate the joint on its bearing to be sure there is no binding. If it binds, the joint should be disassembled to find the cause.
6. If the shaft is being installed into a half-round end yoke, place the two other caps on their trunnions and tie the exposed caps together with electrical tape so that they do not fall off when positioning the shaft for installation. Install the shaft and the attaching hardware.
7. If installing the shaft into a full-round yoke, repeat the installation instructions used on the bench by lifting the first trunnion through the end yoke then installing its cap so that the rollers are seated. Push the cross into place. Depending on the type of joint, it may be necessary to use a pushing installation tool to install the caps. Lift the last trunnion through the end yoke just enough so that the rollers of the bearing cap are held in place by the trunnion as the cap is installed. Push it into position.
8. After the shaft is installed, follow the lubricating instructions in the Lubrication section of this chapter. It may be necessary to loosen the attaching bolts during the lubrication procedure. If your U-joint bolts have locking straps, wait to fold over the lock strap tabs until after you have correctly lubricated the U-joints. After lubricating the joints, correctly fold up the lock strap tangs, if equipped, to secure the attaching bolts.

SKILL DRILL 49-3 Removing and Reinstalling the Driveshaft

1. Locate and follow the appropriate procedure in the service manual.
2. Complete the accompanying job sheet or work order with all pertinent information.
3. Position the machine on a level surface and apply parking brakes. Observe lockout/tag-out procedures.
4. Place the transmission in park (if equipped) or neutral.
5. Raise the machine and support it with jack stands if necessary.
6. Mark all slip joints and yokes with a paint marker to retain correct orientation and phasing.
7. Support the driveshaft with a suitable sling, and remove the driveshaft attaching bolts. Study the driveshaft to determine how it is fastened.
8. Remove heavy driveshafts in sections.
9. Remove the center support bearing if a two-piece driveshaft is used. Check between center support and mounting for shims. If shims are used, they must be replaced when the driveshaft is reinstalled.
10. Remove the driveshaft. Wrap tape around the U-joint bearing caps so that they don't fall off, in order to prevent loss of needle bearings. The slip yoke should also be protected to prevent damage during removal. When removing, replacing, or servicing a driveshaft, careless handling can damage the shaft and U-joints.
11. Service the driveshaft according to the service manual.
12. Reinstall the driveshaft:
    a. Place in position and check alignment marks. All mounting surfaces should be clean and free of nicks before assembly.
    b. Replace all fasteners and tighten evenly to correct torque.
    c. Replace fasteners in center support bearing, if used.
13. Grease each U-joint. Continue to grease until the air is removed and grease comes from all four bearing cap seals. Continue to lubricate until all old grease is purged from the cups, wipe seals of all grease with a shop towel.
14. Raise the machine and remove jack stands.
15. Lower the machine to the floor.
16. List the test results and/or recommendations on the job sheet or work order, clean the work area, and return tools and materials to their proper storage area.

SKILL DRILL 49-4 Inspecting and Servicing Center Support Bearings

1. Safely raise the machine and support it on stands. Inspect the center bearing components for any major defects, such as looseness or noises.
2. Inspect the center bearing for proper mounting.
3. Inspect the bearing mount rubber insert for dry rotting and cracking.
4. If the bearing must be replaced, follow the manufacturer's specifications and procedures for proper installation of a new bearing. Typical bearing replacement may proceed as follows:
   - **a.** Mount the driveshaft in an approved vice.
   - **b.** Mark the shafts so that they may be properly phased when put back together.
   - **c.** Separate the two driveshafts.
   - **d.** Remove the metal mounting bracket.
   - **e.** Remove the rubber mount from around the center bearing.
   - **f.** Remove any snap rings or circlips that may be holding the bearing in place.
   - **g.** Use an appropriate puller or press to remove the bearing from the driveshaft.
   - **h.** Check for any defects in the splines of the slip yoke.
   - **i.** Check the slip yoke on the mating shaft for wear and defects.
   - **j.** Press on a new bearing.
   - **k.** Reinstall any necessary snap rings or circlips.
5. Install a new rubber mount around the new bearing. Reinstall the mounting bracket.
6. Put the two shafts back together, paying attention to driveshaft phasing.
7. Remove the driveshaft from the vice, and reinstall it the machine.

▶ Wrap-Up

Ready for Review

- Most, if not all, heavy machine drivelines consist of one or more driveshafts coupled by universal joints, also known as Cardan joints.
- Robert Hooke discovered that a shaft driven at an angle through a universal joint accelerates and decelerates twice per revolution. In some places, universal joints are known as Hooke joints because of this.
- Most driveshafts must meet three criteria:
  - They must be strong enough to transmit the maximum engine torque without failure.
  - They must allow the shaft length to change due to suspension oscillation and torque wind up.
  - And they must be able to operate at constantly changing operating angles.
- The Spicer Life Series driveshaft is a sealed driveshaft system now being installed in some heavy equipment.
- Driveshaft tubing can be seamed or seamless and constructed by being welded, being forged, or using a welded tube drawn over mandrel. The drawn-over-mandrel (DOM) design is very consistent in tube strength and thickness.
- Driveshafts are connected to the machine's components and to each other using various yokes. Yokes have two openings, called ears, to accept two of the universal joint bearing caps. These ears can be full-round (circles), which use circlips to secure the caps, or half-round, which require bolt-on straps to secure the caps.
- Tube yokes are welded to the tube ends. End yokes are splined to components such as drive axles. Both will have full-round or half-round ears.
- Flange yokes are splined to components and have a flat flange that, in turn, is bolted to a companion flange with two full-round yoke ears.
- Machine drivelines may have more than one driveshaft, requiring the use of a center (hanger) or other support bearing.
- Slip yokes allow the driveshaft length to change.
- Most manufacturers recommend that driveshaft attaching bolts and most hardware be replaced and not reused.
- The critical speed of a driveshaft is the speed at which it will bow off its centerline due to centrifugal force. If operated at or beyond its critical speed, a driveshaft will fail catastrophically.
- Critical speed can be raised by reducing the shaft weight, increasing shaft diameter, or by shortening the shaft's length.
- The shaft on the driven side of a universal joint operating at an angle accelerates and decelerates twice per revolution. The rate of this non-uniform velocity increases as the operating angle of the universal joint increases.
- The intensity of the acceleration and deceleration causes inertial excitation of the shaft, leading to vibration. As the operating angles increase, maximum shaft speed must decrease; otherwise, the U-joint will fail. So the speed of the shaft is restricted by its angle of operation.

- The non-uniform velocity of the universal joint must be canceled out by a second universal joint with an equal and opposite angle at the other end of the shaft.
- This cancelation can be effected in two ways: with a parallel joint arrangement (also known as a waterfall arrangement) or with an intersecting angle arrangement (also known as a broken back arrangement).
- Driveshafts with universal joints must be phased so that the velocity cancelation occurs during the correct quadrant of rotation.
- Driveline angles should be at least one-half degree to ensure lubricant distribution in the joint, the angle at each end of a driveshaft should be equal to within one degree, and the angles should be kept as small as possible (three degrees or less) to minimize inertial excitation of the driveshaft.
- Driveline vibration can be caused by a bent or dented driveshaft, foreign material buildup on the shaft, worn U-joints or slip yokes, driveshaft imbalance, driveline angles out or too steep, or a driveshaft being out of phase.
- When lubricating U-joints, it is crucial that new grease purges all four caps. Otherwise, the joint should be replaced.
- Universal joints should always be replaced using proper tooling only.

Key Terms

brinelling A condition that occurs when extreme torque indents the bearing surface of the trunnion with the shape of the needle rollers.

broken back arrangement A method of angle cancelation in which the U-joint angles will intersect at a point exactly at the middle of the shaft length; also known as an intersecting angle arrangement.

cancelation The act of canceling the non-uniform velocity in a driveshaft.

Cardan joint A joint with four trunnions and four bearing caps; also known as a Hooke joint or a universal joint.

center bearing A bearing pressed onto a machined surface after the splined area of a driveshaft's slip yoke spline, which is used to support a multi-piece driveshaft; also called a hanger bearing.

companion flange A splined flange attached to a vehicle component, such as a drive axle pinion shaft, that bolts to a flange yoke on a driveshaft.

coupling shaft A short shaft usually at the front of a driveline; also called a jack shaft.

critical speed The rotational speed at which a driveshaft starts to bow off its centerline due to centrifugal force, leading to vibration and shaft failure.

driveline A series of driveshafts, yokes, and support bearings used to connect a transmission to the rear axle.

driveline angularity The angles at the universal joints.

end yoke A splined yoke attached to a component, a component such as a transmission output shaft.

false brinelling A condition where lubricant is squeezed out from between the needles and the trunnions of a U-joint, leading to wear, which is caused by too small of an angle or no angle at the joint, so lubricant is not distributed.

flange yoke A yoke with two ears to hold a U-joint and a flat flange to bolt to a companion flange.

gimbals Two or more concentric circles used to support an item; while the circles can move, the supported object will remain stationary.

hanger bearing A bearing pressed onto a machined surface after the splined area of a driveshaft's slip yoke spline, which is used to support a multi-piece driveshaft; also called a center bearing.

harmonic vibration An inherent vibration that occurs at precisely 50% of a shaft's critical speed.

Hooke joint A joint with four trunnions and four bearing caps; also known as a Cardan joint or a universal joint.

inertial excitation The force caused by the speeding up and slowing down of the shaft driven through an angle. These stem from the operating angles of the U-joint at the drive end of the driveshaft and are caused by the sheer weight of the driveshaft being accelerated and decelerated twice per revolution.

intersecting angle arrangement A method of angle cancelation in which the U-joint angles will intersect at a point exactly at the middle of the shaft length; also known as a broken back arrangement.

jack shaft A short shaft usually at the front of a driveline; also known as a coupling shaft.

non-uniform velocity The phenomenon that a shaft driven through an angle will accelerate and decelerate twice per revolution.

parallel joint arrangement Two or more universal joint arrangements where the joint angles form parallel lines; it is a method of angle cancelation for use with parallel angles; also known as the waterfall arrangement.

phasing Lining up the inboard yoke ears of a two-piece driveshaft so that the non-uniform velocity cancelation occurs in the proper quadrant of the circle.

plan angle An angle where the driveshaft moves toward the side of a vehicle when viewed from above.

secondary couple vibrations Vibrations, caused by U-joint angles, that travel the length of the driveshaft.

slip joint A splined shaft and tube assembly that allows driveshaft length changes.

torsional excitation Twisting forces caused by inertial excitation.

torsional vibrations Vibrations caused by twisting forces on the driveshaft; these occur twice per revolution.

transverse vibrations Vibrations caused by shaft imbalance; these occur once per revolution.

trunnion The smooth ends of the U-joint cross that accepts the bearing caps.

tube yoke A yoke with two ears that accept a U-joint and which is welded to the driveshaft tube.

universal joint A cross-shaped joint with bearings on each leg, where one set of parallel legs is connected to the end of one shaft and the other set of parallel legs is connected to the end of a second shaft. This arrangement allows the shafts to operate at shallow angles to each other; also called a U-joint, a Cardan joint, or a Hooke joint.

waterfall arrangement Two or more universal joint arrangements where the joint angles form parallel lines, which allows for a method of angle cancelation for use with parallel angles; also called parallel joint arrangement.

Review Questions

1. The expected life of a universal joint operating at 3 degrees is 10,000 hours. What would its expected life be if its operating angle were changed to 10 degrees?
   a. 7,000 hours
   b. 5,000 hours
   c. 3,000 hours
   d. 1,000 hours
2. The broken back driveshaft arrangement cannot be used in which of the following situations?
   a. When operating length changes are excessive
   b. Between the two drive axles on a tandem
   c. When operating length changes are minimal
   d. When slip joints are used
3. A parallel joint arrangement driveshaft has which of the following?
   a. Two U-joints in phase
   b. Operating angles within 1 degree
   c. A slip yoke
   d. All of the above
4. The working angle of a U-joint is restricted by which of the following?
   a. The torque it must transmit
   b. The speed at which it must operate
   c. The diameter of the driveshaft
   d. The size of the U-joint
5. U-joint working angles must be equal to within which of the following limits?
   a. 5 degrees
   b. 3 degrees
   c. 2 degrees
   d. 1 degree
6. What is the minimum U-joint operating angle that manufacturers recommend?
   a. 1/4 degree
   b. 1/2 degree
   c. 1 degree
   d. 3 degrees
7. The critical speed of a driveshaft can be increased by ________________.
   a. shortening the shaft length
   b. increasing the tube diameter
   c. decreasing the shaft weight
   d. All of the above
8. What percentage of expected life would a universal joint have if it operates at 15 degrees?
   a. 10%
   b. 20%
   c. 30%
   d. 40%
9. If a driveshaft has a plan angle and a side-view angle, what must you do to determine the true operating angle?
   a. Add the two angles together and divide by two.
   b. Add the squares of the two angles and get the square root of the total.
   c. Add the two angles, square the result, and then get the square root of the answer.
   d. None of the above.
10. How much radial clearance is allowed at the universal joint?
    a. zero clearance
    b. 0.006 inch clearance
    c. 0.012 inch clearance
    d. 0.010–0.030 inch clearance

ASE Technician A/Technician B Style Questions

1. Technician A says that when a driveshaft operates at an angle, the driven shaft accelerates and decelerates once per revolution. Technician B says that using a U-joint at the front and back with equal angles cancels the non-uniform velocity. Who is correct?
   a. Technician A
   b. Technician B
   c. Both Technician A and Technician B
   d. Neither Technician A nor Technician B
2. Technician A says that a driveline is always made up of more than one driveshaft. Technician B says that multi-shaft drivelines must have a center or other support bearing. Who is correct?
   a. Technician A
   b. Technician B
   c. Both Technician A and Technician B
   d. Neither Technician A nor Technician B
3. Technician A says that that driveline attaching bolts should not be reused. Technician B says that Spicer Life Series spring clips can be reused as long as they are not bent. Who is correct?
   a. Technician A
   b. Technician B
   c. Both Technician A and Technician B
   d. Neither Technician A nor Technician B
4. Technician A says that all driveshaft slip yokes have a master spline. Technician B says that when a driveshaft slip yoke is removed, you should mark its position so that it is reassembled correctly in phase. Who is correct?
   a. Technician A
   b. Technician B
   c. Both Technician A and Technician B
   d. Neither Technician A nor Technician B

5. Technician A says that critical speed is when a driveshaft starts to bow off its centerline due to centrifugal force. Technician B says that a driveshaft operating at or above critical speed will vibrate violently. Who is correct?
   a. Technician A
   b. Technician B
   c. Both Technician A and Technician B
   d. Neither Technician A nor Technician B
6. Technician A says that driveshaft angularity is the first thing to check when diagnosing driveshaft vibration problems. Technician B says that a driveshaft out of phase will vibrate. Who is correct?
   a. Technician A
   b. Technician B
   c. Both Technician A and Technician B
   d. Neither Technician A nor Technician B
7. Technician A says that as long as a driveshaft has canceling angles, it will not vibrate. Technician B says that driveshaft operating angles are limited by the speed at which the shaft must rotate. Who is correct?
   a. Technician A
   b. Technician B
   c. Both Technician A and Technician B
   d. Neither Technician A nor Technician B
8. Technician A says that a dent in a driveshaft may cause the shaft to vibrate. Technician B says that foreign material on the driveshaft may cause vibration. Who is correct?
   a. Technician A
   b. Technician B
   c. Both Technician A and Technician B
   d. Neither Technician A nor Technician B
9. Technician says that small amounts of rust purging from the U-joint while greasing it is expected and that you should keep greasing the joint until all the rust is gone. Technician B says that a couple of drops of water escaping the U-joint grease seals while lubricating the joint is normal. Who is correct?
   a. Technician A
   b. Technician B
   c. Both Technician A and Technician B
   d. Neither Technician A nor Technician B
10. Technician A says that when checking U-joints, end play between the U-joint trunnions and the bearing cap should be no more than 0.006 inches (0.15 mm). Technician B says that slip yoke radial play should not exceed 0.030 inches (0.76 mm). Who is correct?
   a. Technician A
   b. Technician B
   c. Both Technician A and Technician B
   d. Neither Technician A nor Technician B

CHAPTER 50 Drive Axles

Knowledge Objectives

After reading this chapter, you will be able to:

- **K50001** Explain the purpose and fundamentals of drive axles.
- **K50002** Identify the construction features, types, and applications of drive axles used in MORE.
- **K50003** Explain the purpose of differential gearing.
- **K50004** Describe the principles of operation and differential gearing.
- **K50005** Explain the operation and function of controlled traction and locking differentials.
- **K50006** Explain the fundamentals and operation of multispeed and double-reduction drive axles.
- **K50007** Explain the operation and function of interaxle differentials and locks.
- **K50008** Outline the overhaul procedures common to drive axles and differentials.

Skill Objectives

After reading this chapter, you will be able to:

- **S50001** Perform maintenance on drive axles according to manufacturers' procedures.
- **S50002** Analyze failures of drive axle and differential gearing, and determine the root cause of failure.
- **S50003** Recommend repairs for drive axles and differentials.

▶ Introduction

This chapter explains the principles, operation, and construction of different types of drive axles used in the off-road equipment market. The chapter focuses on single reduction and double-reduction, single-speed drive axles, and multispeed drive axles. It also discusses differential gears, controlled traction differentials, locking differentials, tandem-drive systems, interaxle differentials, and interaxle differential locking systems.

▶ Fundamentals of Axles

K50001

Three distinct types of axles are used in equipment applications. **Steering axles** allow a wheeled machine to turn. Not all machines will use a steering axle at the front; articulated machines do not require a steer axle. Some axles just support some of the machine's weight and may or may not steer. If an axle doesn't steer and is just for supporting weight, it is called a **dead axle** or tag axle. These are rarely used for heavy equipment because of the adverse traveling conditions machines usually work in; therefore, if an axle doesn't steer, it will likely drive. A steering axle is shown in **FIGURE 50-1**.

Steering axles are also most often drive axles when used on machines with straight frames. Some heavy-duty machines, such as mobile cranes, may use dual, triple, or multiple steering axles; even rear axles on these machines can be steer axles. All axles support part of the weight of the machine because they are attached to the machine's frame.

The third type of axle is the **drive axle** (or **live axle**), so called because it contains the gearing necessary to drive or propel the machine. Drive axles can be single or two speed and single or double reduction, meaning that the overall ratio is the result of two separate gear reductions in the axle. They can also be arranged as a **tandem** drive, where the driving force is divided between two drive axles, or **tridem**, in which three drive axles split the driving force. Drive axles are mounted at the rear or at the front, and in most cases both the front and the rear axles of a machine are drive axles. In this last case, the machine may have four-wheel drive, with one drive axle at the front and one at the back; or six-wheel drive, with one drive axle at the front and a tandem drive at the rear. Still other machines have multiple front and rear drive axles. **FIGURE 50-2** shows a tandem rear drive axle arrangement.

Drive Axle Design

Internal combustion engines usually produce rotating power in a clockwise direction (viewed from the front) and send it through a transmission and a driveline to the rear of the machine. Here, the power must turn a corner in order to drive the wheels or tracks and propel the machine. The primary function of a drive, or live, axle, therefore, is to allow the rotational power to turn 90 degrees in order to drive the machine. **FIGURE 50-3** shows a typical tandem-drive axle.

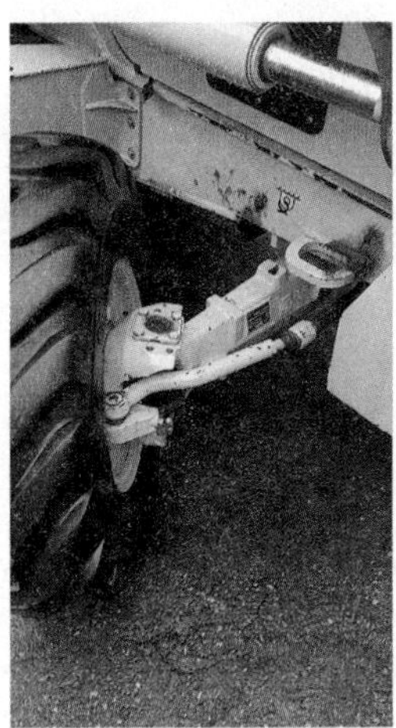

FIGURE 50-1 Off-road equipment is about functionality, so if an axle does not steer, it will likely drive the machine or, like this axle, it will both steer and drive.

FIGURE 50-2 A tandem rear drive axle.

You Are the Mobile Heavy Equipment Technician

An operator of a John Deere backhoe loader complains that his machine gets stuck in low-traction situations. He says that he engages the differential lock, but the lock does not seem to work. He tells you that he still sees one wheel spinning even though the lock is engaged. He also complains of a small hydraulic fluid leak at the drive axle.

1. What would you need to know about the machine before staring your diagnoses?
2. What type of differential lock does this machine have?
3. Would the hydraulic leak have anything to do with the complaint?

FIGURE 50-3 Drive axles allow the rotational power from the engine to turn 90 degrees to propel the machine.

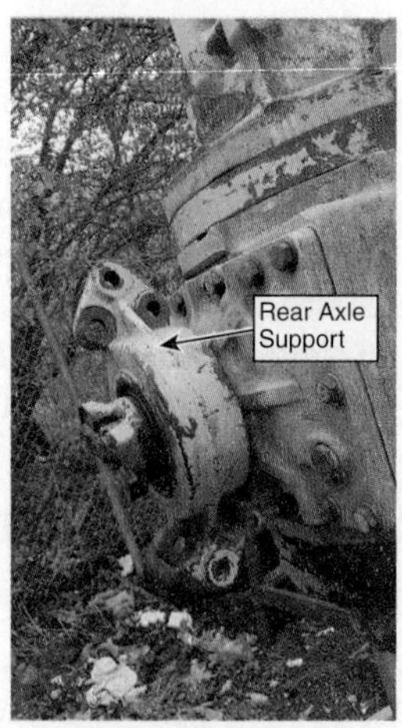

FIGURE 50-5 Supports like this one, at the front and back of the drive axle, allow the axle to oscillate. An arrow shows the support bracket.

FIGURE 50-4 The axles on this articulated wheel loader are solidly bolted to the frame.

FIGURE 50-6 This axle oscillates on a mounting pin. An arrow shows the oscillation point.

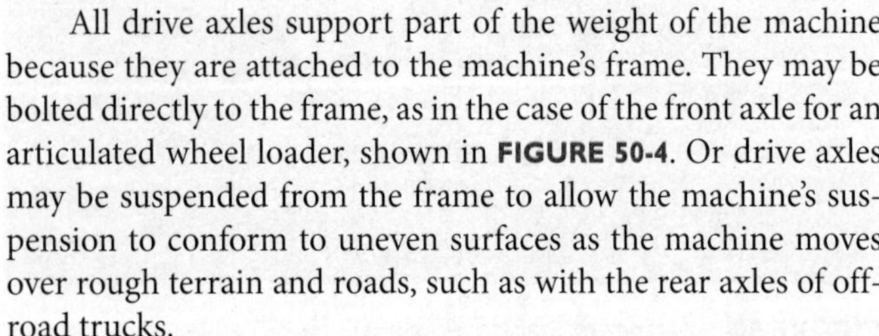

All drive axles support part of the weight of the machine because they are attached to the machine's frame. They may be bolted directly to the frame, as in the case of the front axle for an articulated wheel loader, shown in **FIGURE 50-4**. Or drive axles may be suspended from the frame to allow the machine's suspension to conform to uneven surfaces as the machine moves over rough terrain and roads, such as with the rear axles of off-road trucks.

Machine suspension systems are relatively simple and are designed to allow a few degrees of axle movement with some damping, or in some cases no damping.

The axle may also be mounted to a pivot point that allows the axle to pivot at its center and rotate a few degrees. This is called an oscillating axle and is typical for the rear axle of a rubber-tired wheel loader or the front axle of a backhoe loader. See **FIGURE 50-5** for the oscillation arrangement of the rear axle of a medium wheel loader.

Oscillation joints may be a simple pin that protrudes from the top of the axle housing and is parallel to the centerline of the machine. The axle housing has plain bushings pressed into a bore in which the pin pivots. The bushings have grease seals to keep grease in and dirt out. The pin also fits into two bores that are part of one of the machine's main frame crossmembers, and is held in place with a bolt that goes through the pin ear. This is a typical arrangement for a backhoe loader front axle and other machine axles. See **FIGURE 50-6** for the front axle oscillation joint of an axle.

On larger machines, such as wheel loaders, a short trunnion shaft is bolted to the rear of the axle housing and rides in a support that is bolted to the main frame of the machine. The input yoke is centered in a large opening in the front support for the axle. Both supports have plain bushings that require regular greasing. The front support is also bolted to the main frame, similar to the support in Figure 50-4.

The drive axle usually also provides a significant gear reduction, or even two gear reductions, to provide a torque increase in a powertrain. The drive axle also contains the **differential gears**, which allow for speed differences between the two axle shafts of a wheeled machine drive axle when turning. Differential gears are discussed in the Fundamentals of Differential Gearsets section later in this chapter.

▶ Types of Drive Axle Gearing and Housings

K50002

Drive Axle Gearing

Generally speaking, all of today's machines use **bevel gears** that intersect at an angle to make the power turn the corner at a point 90 degrees to the driveline. **FIGURE 50-7** shows bevel gears.

Bevel gears consist of a relatively small driving gear known as the **pinion gear** and a large gear known as the **crown gear** or **ring gear**. The teeth in bevel gears are cut at a 45-degree angle from their axis, allowing them to mesh at 90 degrees to one another. The pinion gear is rotated by the driveline and in turn drives the crown gear. The crown gear is usually attached to the **differential case**, which houses the differential gears. The differential gears connect to the axle shafts. Although their basic design is the same, several different types of bevel gears are used on heavy-duty machines.

Plain Bevel Gears

Plain bevel gears, shown in Figure 50-7, have straight-cut teeth. Consequently, plain bevel gears are inherently noisy and only have one set of teeth in mesh at any time. That is, one tooth must carry the entire torque load. Because the power flow is turning a 90-degree corner through the bevel gearset, the load and friction created at the intersection of the bevel gear teeth is extreme.

A special lubricant must be used to combat the extreme friction created by bevel gears This lubricant has extreme pressure (EP) additives to prevent metal-to-metal contact of the bevel gear teeth. The plain bevel pinion gear is mounted at the centerline of the crown gear.

Spiral Bevel Gears

The next development in bevel gears was the **spiral bevel gear**. The teeth of a spiral bevel gear are cut in a spiral design.

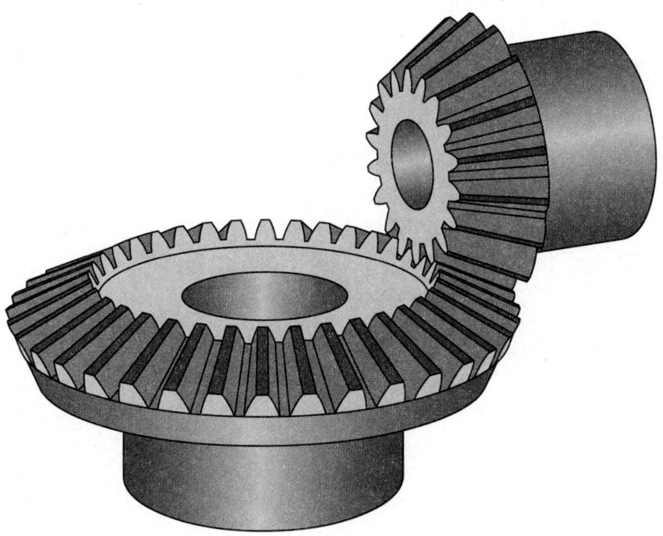

FIGURE 50-7 Plain bevel gears.

FIGURE 50-8 Spiral bevel gears provide the same benefits to bevel gears that helical gears do for spur gears.

The spiral cuts improved upon bevel gearsets much as helical gears improved upon spur cut gears. That is, the design of spiral bevel gears increased torque capacity because more than one set of teeth were involved in torque transfer. Spiral bevel gearing can be seen in **FIGURE 50-8**.

Spiral bevel gears also reduce the noise associated with plain bevel gearing because of the wiping or sliding effect of the tooth contact. Spiral bevel gears still have the pinion gear mounted at the centerline of the crown gear. In spiral bevel gearsets, the pinion, when moving forward, drives the crown gear on the convex side of the teeth.

Hypoid Gearing

Hypoid gearing is another form of bevel gearing. Hypoid gearing was developed to increase the strength of a normal spiral bevel gear. Hypoid bevel gears also allow the driveline of the machine to be lowered. The hypoid gearset looks very similar to a spiral bevel set, with one notable exception: on hypoid gears, the pinion gear is mounted below the centerline of the crown wheel, as can be seen in **FIGURE 50-9**. That difference explains how the teeth of hypoid gears achieve a deeper engagement on

FIGURE 50-9 In a hypoid gearset, the pinion is mounted below the centerline of the crown gear.

the pinion. More teeth are in contact, greatly increasing the strength of the gearset.

The hypoid gearset is very popular, but it is not without its issues. The primary drawback to hypoid gearsets is that the deeper mesh of the pinion gear leads to even higher friction between the gear teeth. The point at which the teeth of the crown gear and the pinion mesh is subjected to extreme pressure under load. That pressure necessitates the pinion and the crown gear to be rigidly supported. Even then, they still try to push each other apart.

To counteract this force, sometimes a thrust screw and block are mounted in the carrier at the back of the crown wheel at the point of the gearset contact. The thrust block is adjusted so that under normal conditions it has a slight clearance from the back side of the crown gear. As the load is increased and the crown gear starts to flex away from the pinion, the crown gear contacts the thrust block, stopping its flexing so that it remains in mesh with the pinion. As with spiral bevel gearsets, when moving forward, the hypoid pinion drives the crown gear on the convex side of the teeth.

Amboid Gears

At first glance, **amboid gears** resemble hypoid, but on further inspection, it is clear that, on amboid gears, the pinion gear is mounted above the centerline of the crown gear. A second notable difference between amboid and hypoid is that the teeth on the crown gear are spiraled in the opposite direction. An amboid gearset is shown in **FIGURE 50-10**.

Both designs have their pinion gear teeth cut in the same direction. In the hypoid, the drive side of the crown gear teeth is the convex side. The opposite is true on amboid gears: the drive side of the crown gear teeth is the concave side. Like hypoid gearing, amboid gearing uses more than two teeth in contact to carry the torque load.

Amboid gearing was developed for use in special applications and is typically only found in applications requiring a higher input from the driveline to the drive axle. Using an amboid gearset in these applications can lead to smaller operating angles used on the connecting driveshaft universal joints.

Drive Axle Housings

Two general housing types are used for drive axles. The housings have one key point of differentiation: whether the carrier is removable. The **carrier** is the component that holds the support bearings for the drive axle gearing. In most drive axles, the pinion gear is supported by two opposed tapered roller bearings whose races are pressed into a housing that is part of integral housing, or bolted to the carrier (removable carrier). The crown gear is bolted to the differential case of the drive axle, which in turn is supported by two side bearings. Again, the races of the side bearings are held in the housing (integral housing) or in the carrier (removable carrier). **Integral carrier housings** can be found in smaller equipment. These axle housings are similar to what would be found in a light-duty automotive type of truck. In the integral carrier type, all of the bearing supports are machined into the housing, which means that the carrier is part of, or integral to, the housing. The drive axle gearing and bearings are accessed through a removable pan bolted to the back of the housing. Most equipment, however, has the second type of housing, known as the **removable carrier type**.

In this style, the entire carrier, with all of the gears and bearings, is bolted into the front of the housing. To access the gearing or bearing for repair, the entire carrier is removed from the housing. **FIGURE 50-11** shows a removable carrier design for a Caterpillar axle.

Almost all drive axles used for heavy equipment have a second gear reduction between the differential and the wheels. This is called the final drive and is typically a planetary gearset. Some final drives are incorporated into the differential housing. These axles are said to be equipped with inboard final drives. If the final drives are located at the wheel ends of the axle, they are considered outboard final drives. The drive axle may also have brakes near the center of the axle housing; this is said to be an axle with inboard brakes.

FIGURE 50-10 The amboid gearset has the pinion mounted above the crown gear centerline, and, unlike the hypoid design, the tooth drive face of the amboid crown gear is on the concave side, not the convex side.

FIGURE 50-11 Most mobile off-road equipment (MORE) has drive axles with removable carriers similar to this one.

Some drive axles provide two gear ratios that are selectable, and these are called two-speed axles. Depending on the machine type, most drive axles are driven by a drive shaft, but they could have a hydrostatic motor providing input torque directly to them as well. Some telehandlers and small wheel loaders have this arrangement.

In machines that use four- or six-wheel drive, all of the drive axles are interconnected by power dividers that split the torque between the available drive axles. In machines with front-wheel drive, the front drive axle is connected by a transfer case that splits the power and torque between the front and rear drive axles.

▶ Fundamentals of Differential Gearsets

K50003

The term "differential" is used mistakenly by some technicians as a synonym for a drive axle, because that is where the **differential gearset** is housed. The drive axle gearing, as we know, is used to turn the power from the engine 90 degrees and to provide a final gear reduction. The differential gears are a set of gears integral to the drive axle that are for a completely different purpose from that of the drive axle gearing. A differential gearset is shown in **FIGURE 50-12**.

To illustrate the operation of a differential gearset, let's consider a rear drive machine with four wheels, two steering and two driving. If the machine is traveling in a straight line, then all of the wheels will be turning at the same speed. (For the moment, we are ignoring any discrepancies in the tire sizes or irregularities in the terrain.)

When the machine starts to turn, however, the situation changes. As the machine moves through a turn, the wheels on the inside of the turn revolve more slowly than the wheels on the outside of the turn because the wheels on the inside are closer to the apex of the turn than the wheels on the outside. This phenomenon can be seen in **FIGURE 50-13**. The inside wheels follow a smaller curve than the outside wheels, and therefore a shorter distance.

FIGURE 50-12 The differential gearset is held in the differential case inside the drive axle. Arrows point to the differential gears.

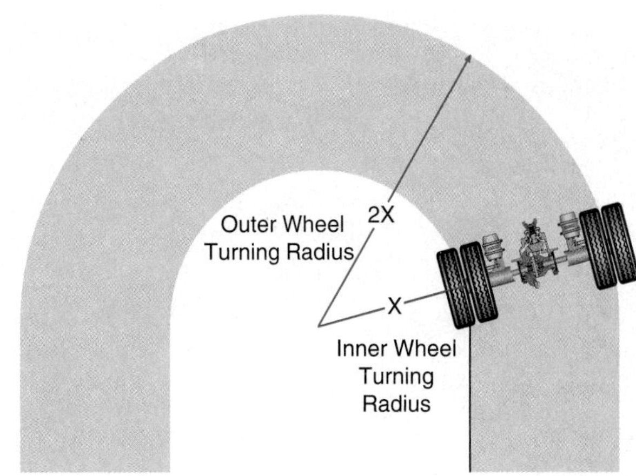

FIGURE 50-13 The wheel on the outside of an axle has to travel further than the wheel on the inside during a turn.

The difference in turning radius presents no problems for the wheels on the steering axle, as they are not connected to each other and turn freely on their bearings. It is a different story for the rear wheels, however, because they are connected to the machine's driveline. Provisions must be made for them to turn at unequal speeds. This is where the differential gears come into play.

▶ Differential Gear Operation

K50004

Differential gears allow for the wheels to turn at unequal speeds. The differential gearset is a gear arrangement that allows the available power being delivered to the crown gear to be split exactly equally between two drive wheels. The differential gearset simultaneously allows one wheel to turn faster or slower than the other when required. The need for unequal speeds is caused by turning, tire size or inflation mismatch, and uneven terrain. The differential gears are contained inside the differential case, which is bolted or riveted to the drive axle crown gear. When the drive axle pinion gear turns the crown gear, the case must turn with it. The case is made up of two halves—the flange half and the plain half—bolted together. The flange half is the side that is attached to the crown gear. In heavy-duty machines, a four-legged **differential cross** (or **differential spider**) is sandwiched between the two halves of the differential case. The cross legs are fitted into four holes bored into the differential case, as shown in **FIGURE 50-14**. Therefore, the cross always rotates with the differential case and the crown wheel.

Inside the differential case are the actual differential gears. The typical differential gearset consists of four beveled **spider gears** (sometimes referred to as **differential pinion gears**) and two beveled **side gears**. The spider gears are fitted to the four legs of the differential cross, so they must rotate with it. The side gears are splined to the two axle shafts to drive the wheels. The side gears are in constant mesh with the differential spider gears. The differential spider gears and side gears normally have thrust washers between them and the differential case.

FIGURE 50-14 The differential cross is sandwiched between the two case halves and therefore must turn with the case.

As the machine moves in a straight direction, the crown gear and the differential case rotate. As the case rotates, the spider gears basically drag the side gears along as the cross tumbles end over end with the case. In this kind of operation, the differential gears are stationary in relation to the differential case. The differential gears are not rotating inside the case. They are merely acting as a connection between the differential case and the two side gears.

The situation changes when the machine starts to turn. When negotiating a turn, it helps to think of the centerline of the machine as the arc the machine must follow through the turn. Think of the arc in terms of the speed of the differential case as it goes through the turn. The wheel on the inside of the turn and its axle shaft and side gear are on a smaller arc and must turn more slowly than the differential case. At the same time, the wheel on the outside and its axle shaft and side gear must turn faster than the case. **FIGURE 50-15** illustrates these differences. As the machine operates through a turn, the side gear splined to the axle on the inside of the turn slows down and causes the spider gears to turn counterclockwise by the same amount that the side gear slows. The spider gear is now forced to rotate, and it then transfers that motion to the other side gear, and pushing it forward by the same amount therefore causing it to speed up by the exact same amount that the inside side gear slowed down.

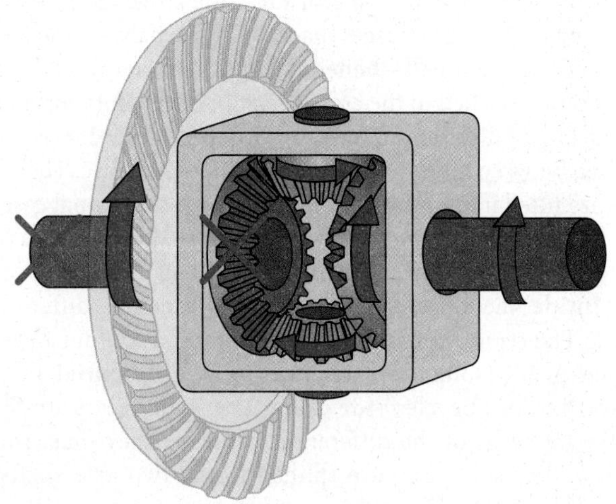

FIGURE 50-15 As the machine turns, the inside side gear slows down and causes the spider gears to turn. The spider gears then transfer that motion to the other side gear, causing it to speed up.

The differential gearset allows this to happen because the spider gears can turn not only *with* the cross but *on* the cross as well. As the inner wheel starts to slow down during the curve, its axle shaft and side gear turn more slowly than the case and the spider gears. The spider gears start to walk around the slower moving inner side gear. As they do so, the spider gears' walking motion is transferred to the outer side gear, causing it to speed up by the exact same amount. This means the outer wheel speeds up by the same amount that the inner wheel slows down. The power being sent to each side gear is still exactly equal, but they can turn at different speeds when required.

In any operational situation, when we add the speed of the two axles or side gears together, the total will always equal 200% of case speed, no matter how much the difference in speed is. For example, on negotiating a turn, if the inner axle shaft and side gear slow down to 96% of the differential case speed, that means that the outer axle shaft and side gear must increase in speed to 104% of case speed to compensate. This compensation is automatic and occurs without any operator input.

If a machine were built without a differential, the difference in wheel speeds during a turn would cause one or the other wheel and axle to scuff, or be dragged through the turn. The resultant twisting forces could lead to serious fatigue failures of the axle shafts. It is important to note that the difference in wheel speed encountered in normal operation is usually very slight. In a normal operating day, the side gears would only rotate inside the differential case around 400 or 500 revolutions, depending on conditions, and would do so at very low rotational speeds. Because of the relatively slow speed and small distance that they turn, side gears and spider gears do not have to be supported by bearings and instead run steel on steel. Certain models may have friction bearings (bushings) to support the spider gears, but in most cases the spider gears are simply made of hardened steel and have no bushings. In operation the outward thrust placed upon the differential side and spider (pinion) gears is very substantial as the gears would rather move outward than carry the load, so they will normally have steel thrust washers separating them from the differential case, as shown in **FIGURE 50-16**.

The advantage of using a differential gearset, however, is also its primary disadvantage. Because the differential gearset allows one wheel to turn faster than the other, this can lead to a machine becoming stuck easily when low traction terrain is encountered. A wheel with good traction can remain stationary while the wheel with poor traction merely slips, and the machine doesn't move. For this reason, most heavy equipment differentials are equipped with differential gearsets that resist slippage or ones that can prevent differential action from taking place at all.

FIGURE 50-16 Thrust washers absorb the heavy thrust loads caused by the bevel differential gears.

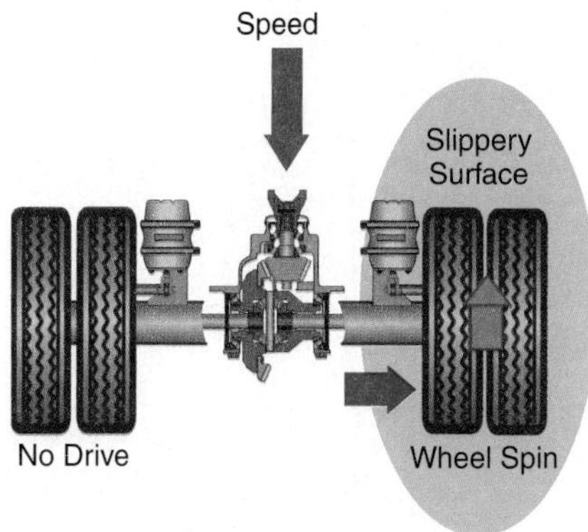

FIGURE 50-17 A wheel on a slippery surface does not provide much resistance, so little torque is generated. In a wheel slip condition, the spinning wheel, its axle shaft, and its side gear will be turning twice as fast as the differential case.

▶ Controlled Traction and Locking Differential Gearset Types

K50005

All differential gearsets perform the same function—that is, to allow wheel speed differences when required. However, because they perform the same function does not mean that all differentials are identical. The differential discussed above is known as an "open differential"; this type has no control over differential action when wheel slip occurs. Other differentials are available that can either control or eliminate differential action and therefore wheel slip. Controlled traction and locking differentials are the main other types of differential gearsets. This section describes these types in more detail.

Controlled Traction and Locking Differentials

The major benefit of a differential is that it allows wheels to rotate at different speeds when necessary. Unfortunately, that benefit is also its major drawback. During low-traction conditions, the wheel that has the least traction will spin uncontrolled, as mentioned in the previous section. When this wheel slip condition is observed, it can lead an observer to think that the differential is sending all of the power to one wheel only, but this is not the case. Think of it this way: if a bolt is loosely installed and the technician attempts to torque it to specification with a torque wrench, it will quickly become apparent that it is impossible to build any torque until the bolt starts to tighten in its bore. Without resistance, the bolt will merely turn freely.

The same is true for the powertrain of a machine. In order for the engine to build torque, there must be some resistance to motion. When a wheel is on a slippery surface, the engine can only build as much torque as is required to make the wheel slip. Once the wheel loses traction, the torque required to keep it spinning is even less, as illustrated in **FIGURE 50-17**.

The differential gearset will still be dividing the available torque equally between the two driving wheels, but the small amount of torque needed to keep the wheel spinning is not sufficient for the wheel with good traction to move the machine. In order to overcome this drawback of differential gears, engineers have developed several controlled traction and locking differentials.

Controlled Traction and Locking Differentials Operation

A **controlled traction differential** allows the engine to build more torque before the wheels can slip. There is some form of resistance that must be overcome before the side gears can move inside the differential case. Most commonly, this resistance to motion is provided by a spring-loaded clutch pack.

In a controlled traction differential, such as shown in **FIGURE 50-18**, a series of friction plates are splined to a movable sliding clutch that slides along one axle shaft. The sliding clutch has teeth to engage matching teeth on one of the side gears. There is also a series of reaction plates, which are splined or lugged to the differential case. These two sets of plates are interleaved to form a clutch pack similar to the clutch packs found in automatic transmissions. These clutch packs can be permanently loaded by springs that pressurize the clutch pack. The sliding clutch can also be made to engage the side gear by using an air or electric shifter. This allows the controlled traction to be engaged or disengaged as required. Some installations have the controlled traction permanently engaged.

The purpose of this controlled traction arrangement is to provide resistance that must be overcome before the side gear can rotate inside the case. This resistance is easily overcome by the twisting forces on the axle shafts during turns. In slippery conditions, the resistance causes more torque to build before a wheel can start slipping. The controlled traction differential is carefully designed so that the amount of torque necessary to cause the wheels to slip is more than is required

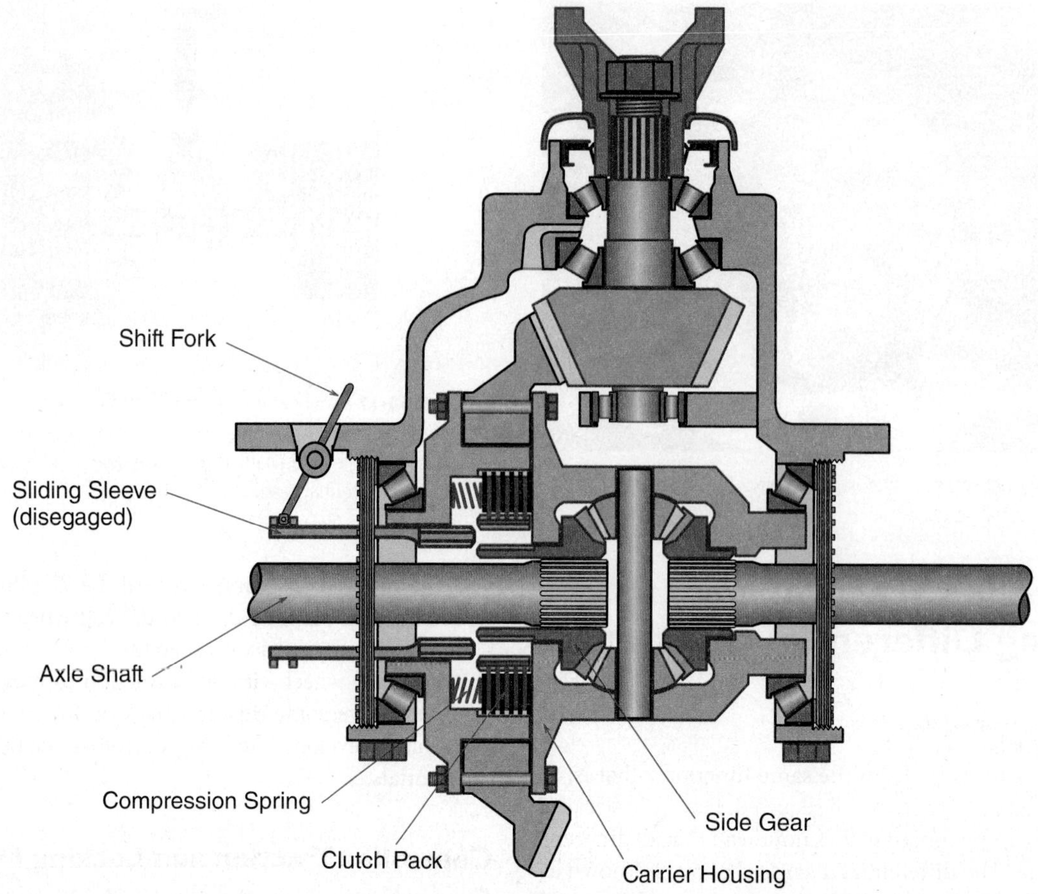

FIGURE 50-18 Controlled traction differentials, when used, only allow wheel slip after the engine builds enough torque to cause the clutch plates to slip. This torque is enough to move the loaded machine as long as one wheel has sufficient traction. Some controlled traction differentials are operator selectable, like the one illustrated here.

for one wheel with good traction to overcome the machine's load and move the machine. Other designs of controlled traction differentials use a similar spring-loaded clutch pack that is permanently connected to one or both side gears, meaning that the controlled traction is always engaged. There are many designs of controlled traction differentials. Eaton has recently developed a controlled traction differential called the Suretrac™ for wheel loaders and other off-road machines that is capable of biasing torque to the wheel with good traction. The Suretrac uses clutch packs on each side gear and a unique diamond shape at the ends of the differential cross or spider. The diamond-shaped cross is fitted into two actuators inside the differential case. The actuators are lugged to the differential case but can move outward and inward. When wheel slip starts to occur, the forces acting to rotate the differential pinion gears cause the diamond shape of the cross legs to push against the actuators, which forces the actuator on the side that is not slipping to increase the pressure on its clutch pack, resulting in up to 72.5% of the available torque being sent to the wheel with good traction. **FIGURE 50-19** shows a cross section of this design; note the diamond shape on the cross (spider) legs and the corresponding V-shape where they fit into the actuators.

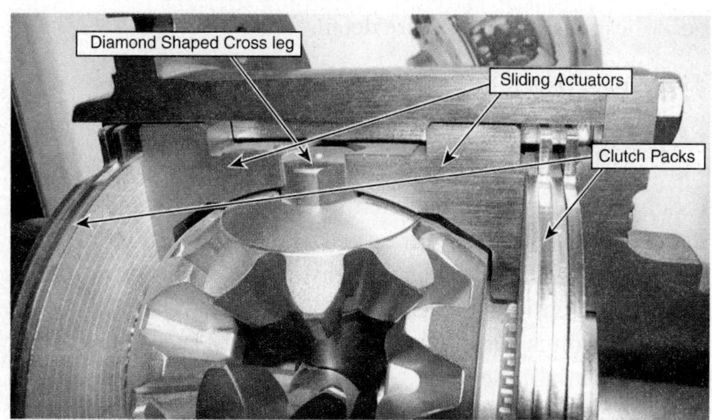

FIGURE 50-19 This controlled traction differential can bias the torque applied to each wheel with up to 72.5% going to the wheel with good traction.

No-Spin Differential

A no-spin type of differential is a mechanical unit that replaces the side gears, cross, and bevel pinion gears with other mechanical pieces to lock the two axle shafts together under certain conditions. The no-spin differential consists of a central spider assembly that replaces the normal differential cross or spider,

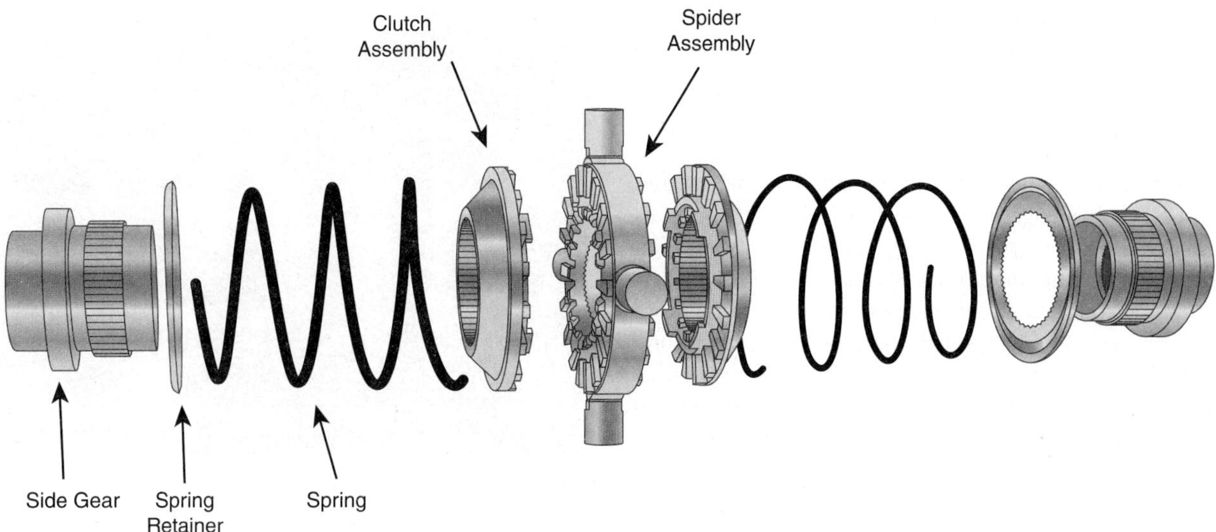

FIGURE 50-20 The no-spin differential.

two spring-loaded jaw or dog clutches that engage the central spider, and two "side gears" that spline to the jaw clutches (on the outside) and the axle shafts (on the inside). **FIGURE 50-20** shows a blow-up of the no-spin differential, also known as a Detroit Locker. These differentials can directly replace most standard open differentials and are an option available for most machines. It is recommended to use only one no-spin differential on a machine.

This type of differential mechanically keeps the left and right axles driving together unless one wheel starts to speed up, as it would when turning in a high traction situation. The faster wheel is then unlocked and allowed to freewheel. In simple terms, the no-spin differential is a relatively simple device with two spring-engaged dog clutches that are normally engaged until one wheel starts to turn faster than the crown gear. In operation, this keeps the differential locked unless the machine turns a corner, and then only the slower wheel is driven. In other words, when the machine encounters slippery conditions, both wheels continue to drive, but when the machine turns on good footing, differential action is allowed, and one wheel disengages to allow the wheels to travel at different speeds. This eases turning and reduces tire wear.

Operation of the No-Spin Differential

The crown gear drives the differential case, which in turn drives the central spider. The spider has dogteeth on each side that engage the teeth of the spring-loaded clutches. **FIGURE 50-21** shows the components of a no-spin differential.

The spring-loaded clutches are splined to the side gears, which in turn are splined to the axles. In straight-ahead operation, the spider drives the dog clutches at equal speeds, and there can be no differential action and therefore no slippage. As the machine starts to turn, the outer wheel must rotate faster than the inner wheel. The central spider has a cam ring with a series of teeth at the center, and the dog clutches have teeth to match. When the outer wheel and therefore the outer dog clutch starts to turn faster, the dog clutch cam teeth ride up the cam teeth of the spider, and the clutch becomes disconnected from the central spider. This action allows the outside axle and wheel to freewheel as the machine moves through a turn. One hundred percent of engine torque is now delivered to the inner wheel during the turn. When the turn is completed and both wheels are again turning the same speed, the springs force the outer dog clutch inboard to re-engage the spider, and both wheels are driven once again. It is important to note that no-spin differentials only allow the outside wheel to turn faster when it has sufficient traction to cause the unlocking process. In low traction conditions, the outside wheel will merely slip. For this reason, manufacturers recommend only using a no-slip differential in one drive axle of a four-wheel-drive machine. If a no-spin was used in both axles, the machine's steering could be severely compromised in low-traction conditions. It is also critical that

FIGURE 50-21 The no-spin differential positively prevents differential action until a turn is made.

tire size on both ends of an axle be perfectly matched when a no-spin differential is used; unmatched tires cause severe strain on the axles and components.

Locking Differentials

Locking differential systems actively prevent differential action from occurring when engaged. Heavy-duty locking differentials can be engaged or disengaged by the machine operator when required. These locking differentials should only be used when the machine encounters a low-traction condition that allows one wheel to spin. When activated, these systems prevent one side gear from turning in relation to the differential case, which stops any movement of the spider gears in the differential. Because the spider gears can no longer rotate, the second side gear cannot move either.

One common design of locking differential incorporates the following features:

- One axle shaft has a second spline after the spline that engages the side gear.
- Mounted on this spline is a sliding clutch or collar.
- The sliding clutch or collar has clutching teeth on the side that faces the differential case.
- The differential case has clutching teeth that match those on the sliding clutch or collar.

When conditions require the lock to be engaged, the sliding clutch is moved into position over the clutching teeth on the differential case, locking the axle, and therefore the side gear it is splined to, to the differential case.

There are a few different ways of locking a differential: mechanical, air pressure, and hydraulic pressure. Let's explore these different mechanisms.

Mechanical

This used to be common for use in backhoe loaders. The operator steps on a pedal in the cab. The pedal is mechanically linked to a lever on the side of the axle housing. The lever pivots and, inside the housing, mechanically moves the sliding clutch that locks one of the side gears to the differential housing. This eliminates the differential action. When the pedal is released, spring force is enough to move the sliding clutch away and release the side gear from being locked to the housing.

Because one of the side gears is locked to the differential housing and the bevel pinion gears (or spider gears) are carried around with the differential housing, the opposite side gear also has to rotate at the same speed as the differential housing.

This type of clutch could also be actuated by an air cylinder. The operator steps on a valve in the cab that sends air to the cylinder. The cylinder's piston then extends and actuates a lever that moves the sliding clutch. From there the action is the same as for the mechanically actuated locking differential. **FIGURE 50-22** shows a locking differential.

Pneumatically Actuated Locking Differential

This differential is locked with air pressure only. An air signal goes to a piston that moves out and applies pressure to a clutch.

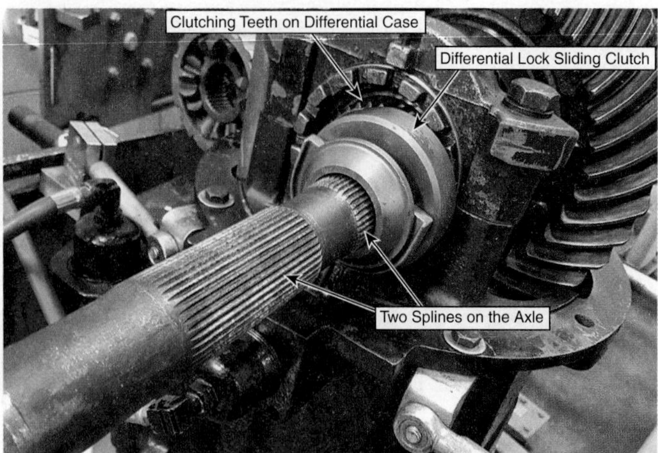

FIGURE 50-22 The differential lock locks one axle, and therefore its side gear to the differential case, preventing differential action. Arrows point to the two splines on the axle shaft, the sliding clutch, and the differential case clutching teeth.

A rotating seal must seal the air pressure between the rotating part of the differential and the stationary housing.

When air pressure is sent to the piston, the piston locks one of the side gears to the differential housing to make the axle shafts turn at the same speed. The air signal comes from a valve in the operator's cab and is usually foot actuated. This type of locking differential is used for some Caterpillar scraper differentials.

Hydraulically Actuated Locking Differential

Many locking differentials use a hydraulic signal to move a piston and squeeze a set of plates and discs together. When engaged, the multidisc clutch locks one of the side gears to the differential housing and prevents any differential action.

As with the pneumatically locking differential, there has to be a rotating seal assembly to allow the oil pressure to transfer from the stationary axle housing to the rotating section of the differential.

Similar to an axle assembly with inboard brakes, this type of locking differential could create cross-contamination if the seal for the piston failed.

This system is usually controlled electrically by a switch in the cab. It could even be part of the machine's CAN. A solenoid energizes and sends oil pressure through steel tubes or hoses to the axle housing, where it passes through the housing and is fed into the differential through a rotating seal. See **FIGURE 50-23** for a cross section of a hydraulic locking differential.

When a differential with a hydraulic locking function is reconditioned, the piston should be checked for leaks with air pressure after differential installation. Provided there is no difference in wheel speed, the differential lock can be engaged at any time, whether the machine is moving or not. The operator should only engage the lock during times of poor traction. In high-traction conditions, the operator should disengage the lock to allow the differential to resume its function of compensating for wheel speeds in turns.

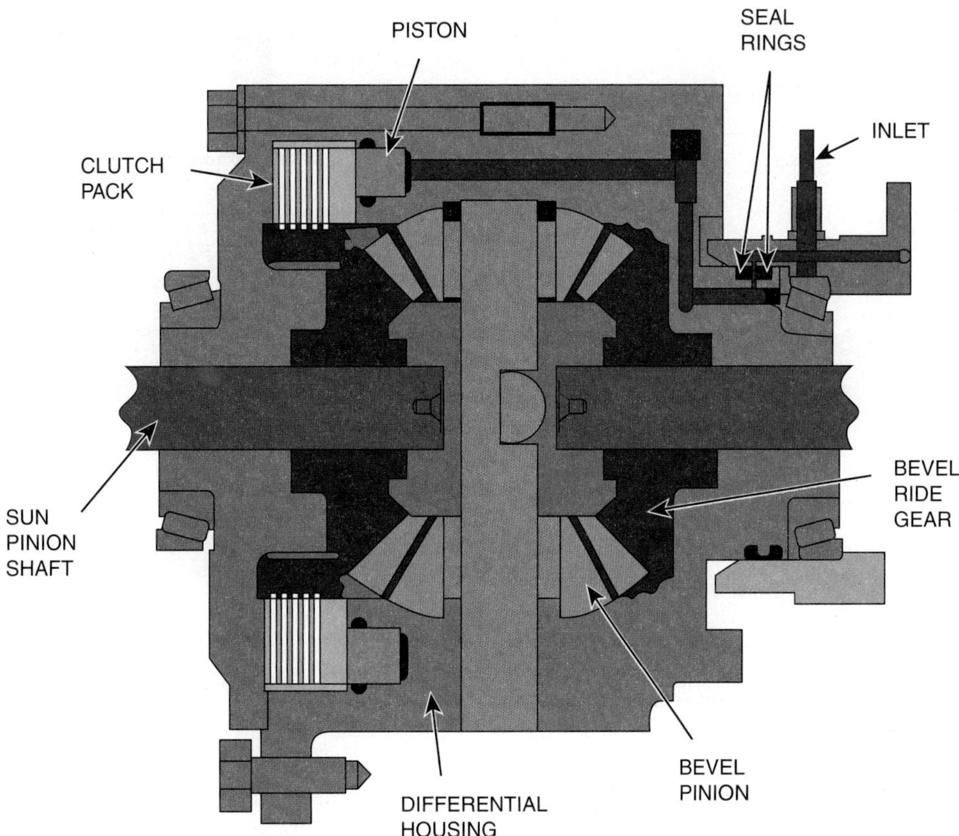

FIGURE 50-23 The locking differential above can be hydraulically locked. A similar arrangement can be used for a pneumatically locked differential.

▶ Double-Reduction and Multi-Speed Drive Axles

K50006

Double-reduction drive axles use two gear reductions at all times. Double-reduction drive axles come in two styles—helical double reduction and planetary double reduction.

Helical Double-Reduction Drive Axles

A **helical double-reduction drive axle** is a double-reduction drive axle that uses a helical gearset for the second gear reduction. Helical double-reduction axles were developed for two reasons. First was to reduce the size of the crown gear and make it less likely to flex under load. The drive axle could then handle higher torque loads. The second reason was to reduce the overall size of the drive axle housing while still achieving a large overall reduction.

The first reduction in a helical double-reduction drive axle consists of a small conventional crown and pinion gearset. The second reduction is accomplished by a set of helical gears. By using the two reductions together, we can achieve a large overall gear ratio with a much smaller drive axle package. Large crown gears tend to flex under heavy load as they try to move away from the pinion gear. A smaller crown gear helps to prevent this. The pinion is mounted in the drive axle as is normal, but the crown gear is not attached to the differential case. Instead, the crown wheel drives a cross shaft to which a small helical gear (called the helical pinion gear) is attached. The helical pinion gear meshes with a much larger helical gear that is bolted to the differential case.

In this arrangement, the power flow goes through two reductions: one with the crown and pinion gearset and the other with the helical gearset. This compounds the overall reduction through the axle. A compound gear ratio is one where two or more reductions are used to increase the overall ratio. The final drive axle ratio is the product of the two reductions (the ratios are multiplied together).

Double-reduction helical drive axles are available in front-mount or top-mount designs depending on the needs of the application. In a top-mount design, the crown and pinion gearset is mounted above the differential case. In a front-mount design, the differential case is mounted in line with and directly behind the crown and pinion gears.

Helical Double-Reduction Two-Speed Drive Axles

Helical double-reduction drive axles are also available as two-speed models. **Helical double-reduction two-speed drive axles**

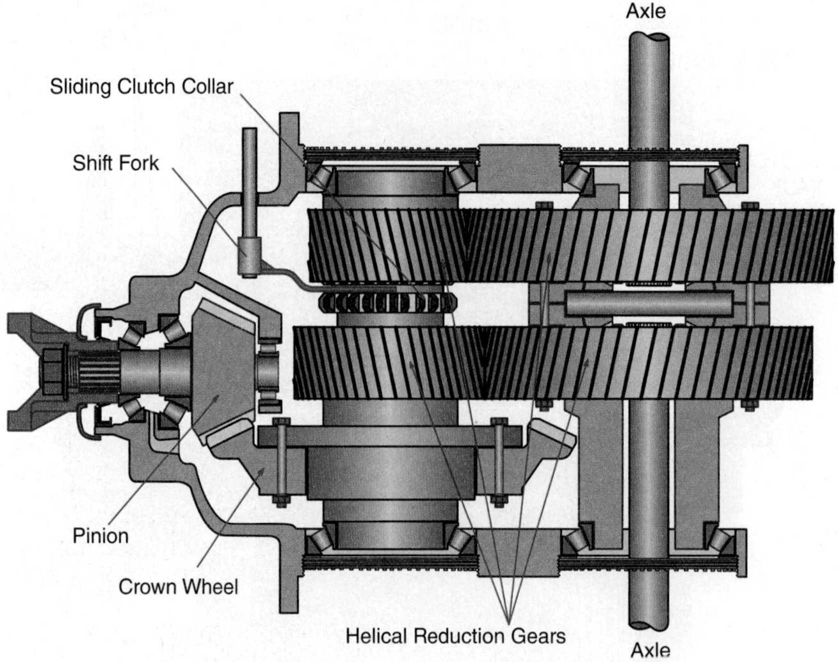

FIGURE 50-24 A helical two-speed axle uses two reductions whether in high or low range.

use two selectable sets of helical gears as the second gear reduction. A helical double reduction two-speed drive axle is illustrated in **FIGURE 50-24**.

A helical two-speed axle uses two reductions, whether in high or low range. The overall reduction is selectable by the operator, effectively extending the operating ranges of the machine. This is accomplished by installing two different-sized helical pinion gears on the cross shaft driven by the crown gear.

These helical pinion gears are in constant mesh with two large helical gears bolted to either side of the differential case. The helical pinions are not splined to the cross shaft and therefore are free to rotate on it. Between the two helical pinions is a sliding clutch collar that is splined to the cross shaft. When the shift fork moves the clutch collar from one side to the other, it disengages one of the helical gearsets and engages the other. The fork is moved by an electric motor or an air shifter controlled by the driver.

Adding two-speed capability to a double-reduction drive axle effectively doubles the transmission ranges available to the operator. Regardless of whether the double reduction two-speed is in high or low range, it always uses two reductions through the drive axle. The first reduction is through the crown and pinion gears and the second is through whichever helical gearset is engaged at the time.

Planetary Two-Speed and Planetary Double-Reduction Axles

A **planetary two-speed drive axle**, as shown in **FIGURE 50-25**, uses a double reduction to achieve a low-range ratio through the drive axle, and a single reduction in high range. The first reduction in low range is the normal crown and pinion gear. The second reduction is a planetary gearset built into the crown wheel and the differential case. For high range, only the crown and pinion gears are used to achieve the ratio. As with double-reduction helical drive axles, this setup allows transmission ranges to be split and doubles the number of gear ratios available to the operator.

In a planetary drive axle, the crown gear has a set of internal teeth machined on its inner circumference. This becomes the ring gear of the planetary gearset. A housing is bolted to the crown gear instead of the differential case, so the differential case is able to rotate inside this housing.

The planetary two-speed drive axle differential case, shown in **FIGURE 50-26**, has four legs to hold the planetary pinion gears. The differential case, then, actually becomes the carrier of the planetary gearset. The sun gear is a hollow gear mounted in such a way that its teeth are constantly in mesh with the planetary pinions held on the differential case legs. Bolted to the side of the differential case on the outside of the planetary pinions is the high-speed plate. Teeth cut on its inside surface match the teeth on the sun gear, which has another set of clutching teeth machined on its outer edge. These clutching teeth match a set of clutch teeth machined into the inside circumference of the side bearing adjuster on that side of the drive axle. The sun gear also has a groove to accept a shift fork, which can move the sun gear in or out, using a hydraulic, air, or electric shift motor.

The operation of the two-speed planetary drive axle is quite simple. When low range is selected by the operator, the shifter fork moves the sun gear to an inboard position, shown in **FIGURE 50-27A**. This causes its clutching teeth to engage with the clutching teeth on the bearing adjuster and hold the sun gear stationary. The power flow is as follows:

- The drive axle pinion gear brings rotational input to the crown gear.

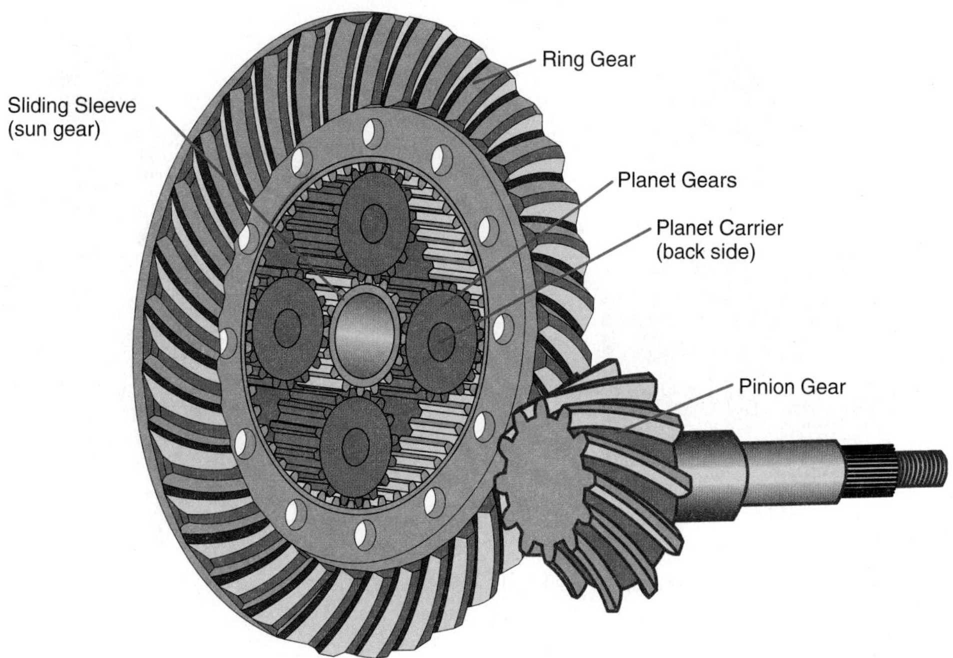

FIGURE 50-25 Planetary drive axles use a planetary gear to create two-speed capability.

FIGURE 50-26 A planetary two-speed drive axle differential case and sun gear.

FIGURE 50-27 A. The sun gear is moved inboard for low range, locking the sun gear's clutching teeth to the bearing retainer so it cannot turn. **B.** For high speed, the sun gear is moved outward so the sun gear engages the teeth in the high-speed plate.

- The ring gear, machined on the inner circumference of the crown gear, transfers the input to the planetary pinion gears attached to the legs of the differential case.
- The planetary pinions are forced to rotate around the stationary sun gear.
- They drive the carrier (the differential case) at a speed roughly one-third slower than the crown gear's rotation.

In high range, the shift fork moves the sun gear outward, as shown in **FIGURE 50-27B**, which disengages the clutching teeth from the bearing adjuster and slides the outer end of the sun gear teeth into mesh with the high-speed plate bolted to the carrier (the differential case). The sun gear teeth are still in mesh with the planetary pinions as well.

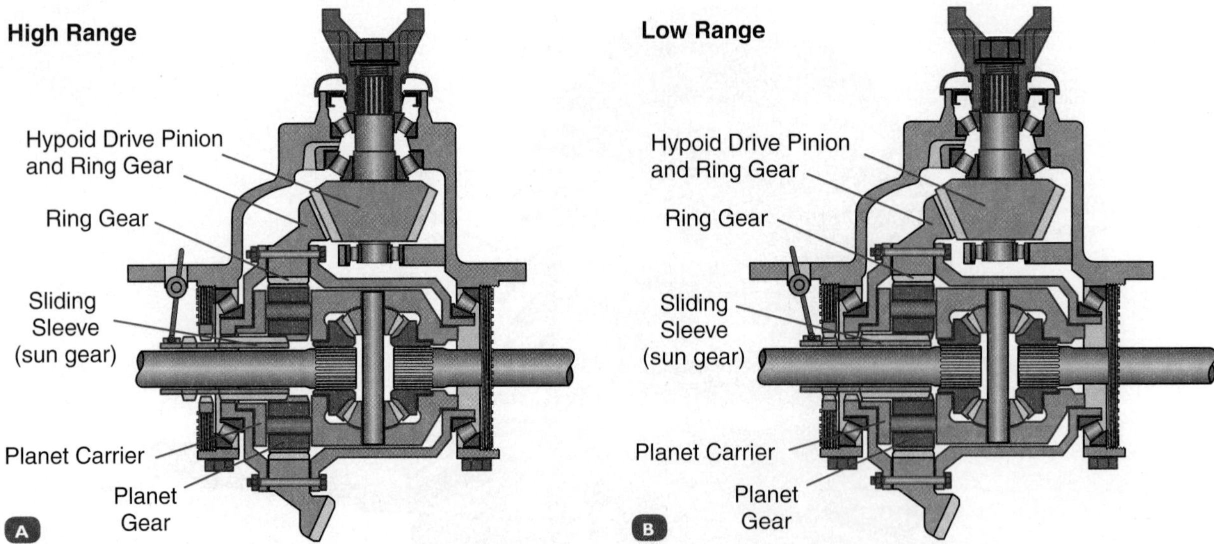

FIGURE 50-28 Power flow through a planetary drive axle. **A.** High range with the sun gear outward and locked to the high-speed plate. **B.** Low range with the sun gear inward and locked stationary to the bearing retainer clutch plate.

The power flow through a planetary two-speed drive axle is shown in **FIGURE 50-28**. The high-range power flow is as follows:

- The drive axle pinion gear brings rotational power to the crown gear.
- The ring gear machined on its inner circumference transfers that rotation to the planetary pinions mounted to the differential case.
- The sun gear is now splined to the carrier through the high-speed plate.
- The planetary pinions cannot rotate, so the ring gear drives the carrier (the differential case) at the same speed as the crown gear.

In certain vocations, a planetary drive axle may be permanently fixed in low range by replacing the shift motor with a holding plate. This axle then becomes known as a **planetary double-reduction drive axle**. The planetary double reduction always uses the two reductions through the drive axle, hence the "double-reduction" in its name.

Air Shift Control

Two-speed drive axles in vocational off-road trucks are typically controlled by air. Air shift systems, like the one shown in **FIGURE 50-29**, are very simple. Air shift systems consist of a shift motor unit attached to the drive axle. The shift unit contains a piston, a strong return spring, and a mechanism to engage the shift fork in the drive axle.

External to the shift unit are the following components:

- Air lines
- Air control switch (usually attached to the shift lever)
- Control solenoid
- Quick-release valve

The control solenoid is turned on when the ignition switch is on, allowing air to flow into the control circuit from the machine air tanks. Air flows to the control switch on the shift lever. When the operator places the control switch in the low-range position, airflow is stopped at the control switch. When the operator selects high range, air flows through the switch and the quick-release valve to the shift unit. Air pushes against the piston, and the piston then moves the mechanism attached to the shift fork. The drive axle shifts to high range.

When the operator shifts back to low range, the air flowing through the control valve is cut off. The air in the line to the quick release valve exhausts at the control switch. This causes the quick release valve to exhaust the air going to the shift control unit such that the return spring forces the piston and the shift mechanism back to the low-range position. The key-on control solenoid ensures that the drive axle shifts to low range when the key is turned off.

▶ Power Dividers (Interaxle Differentials)

K50007

Power dividers are used when a machine has a tandem-drive axle arrangement. A power divider splits the available torque and delivers 50% to the front rear-drive axle of the tandem and 50% to the rear rear-drive axle. In order to do this the power divider has a differential gearset called an **interaxle differential**. A power divider combines an interaxle differential and a regular crown and pinion gear drive axle with a wheel differential.

The interaxle differential is similar to the drive axle, or wheel differentials discussed previously; however, this differential splits the torque between two drive axles not two wheels and can allow for speed differences between the axles when necessary. The front rear axle of the tandem drive will contain the interaxle differential gearset consisting of a differential cross that is driven directly by the input shaft of the forward drive axle.

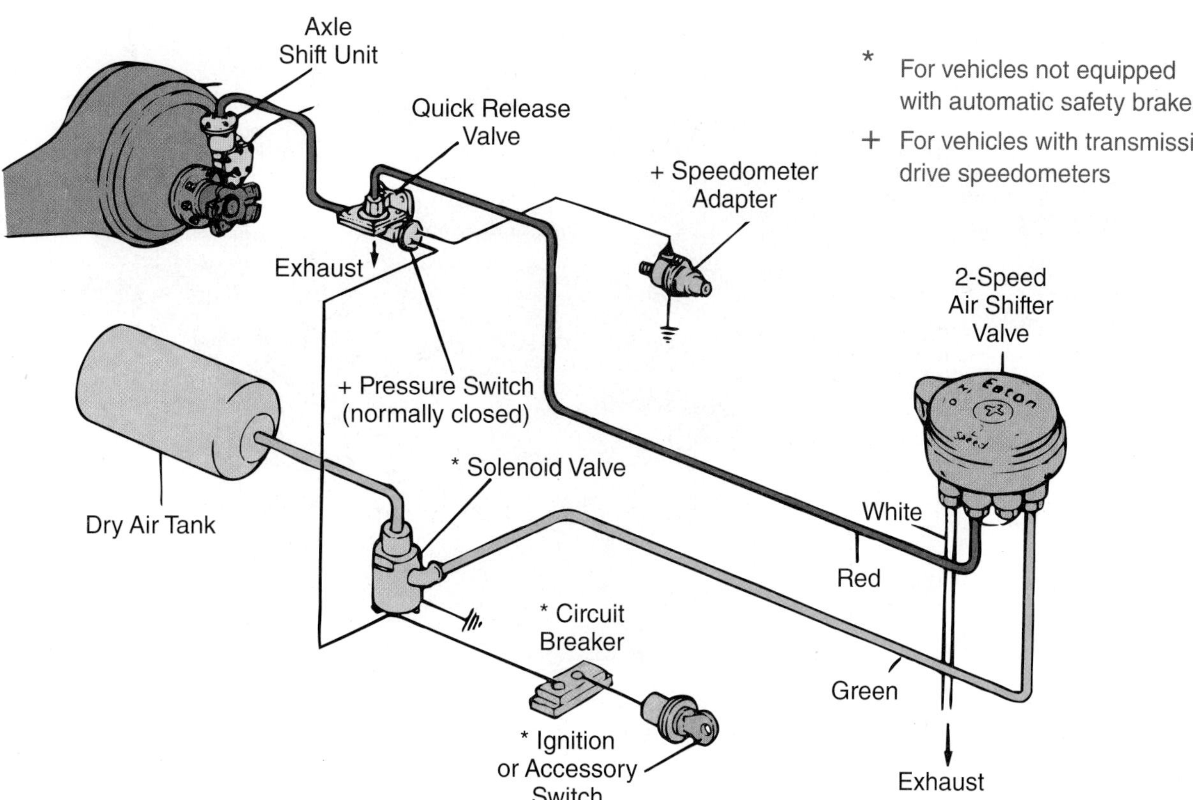

FIGURE 50-29 Air shift systems usually contain a quick release valve so that shifts occur faster.

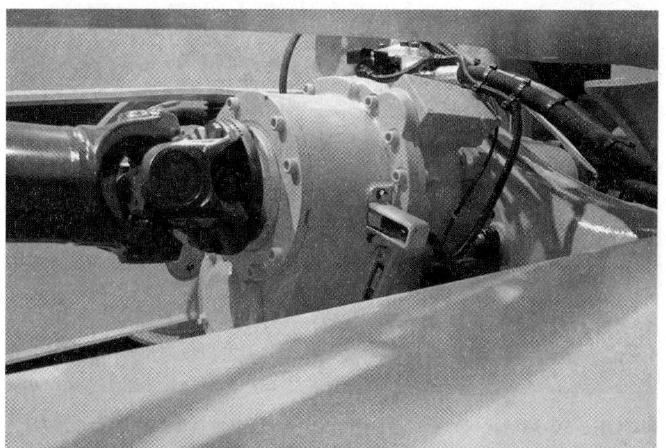

FIGURE 50-30 Power divider for an articulated truck.

FIGURE 50-31 A tandem-drive axle.

The front side gear of the interaxle differential will be part of or attached to a gear that will drive the pinion gear of the forward drive axle. The rear side gear of the interaxle differential will drive a through shaft that connects to the interaxle drive shaft and from there to the input pinion of the rear-rear axle of the tandem set. **FIGURE 50-30** shows the power divider for an articulated truck.

As its name suggests, the power divider allows the power from the machine driveline to be equally split between the front-rear drive axle and the rear-rear drive axle of a tandem. Even as it splits the power, the power divider allows the axles to rotate at different speeds. The final, or rear-rear, drive axle of the tandem has a normal drive axle arrangement with a regular differential for wheel speed differences. **FIGURE 50-31** shows a tandem-drive arrangement.

Power Divider Components

The power divider has several components, as illustrated in **FIGURE 50-32**:

- Input shaft
- Helical or spur gears

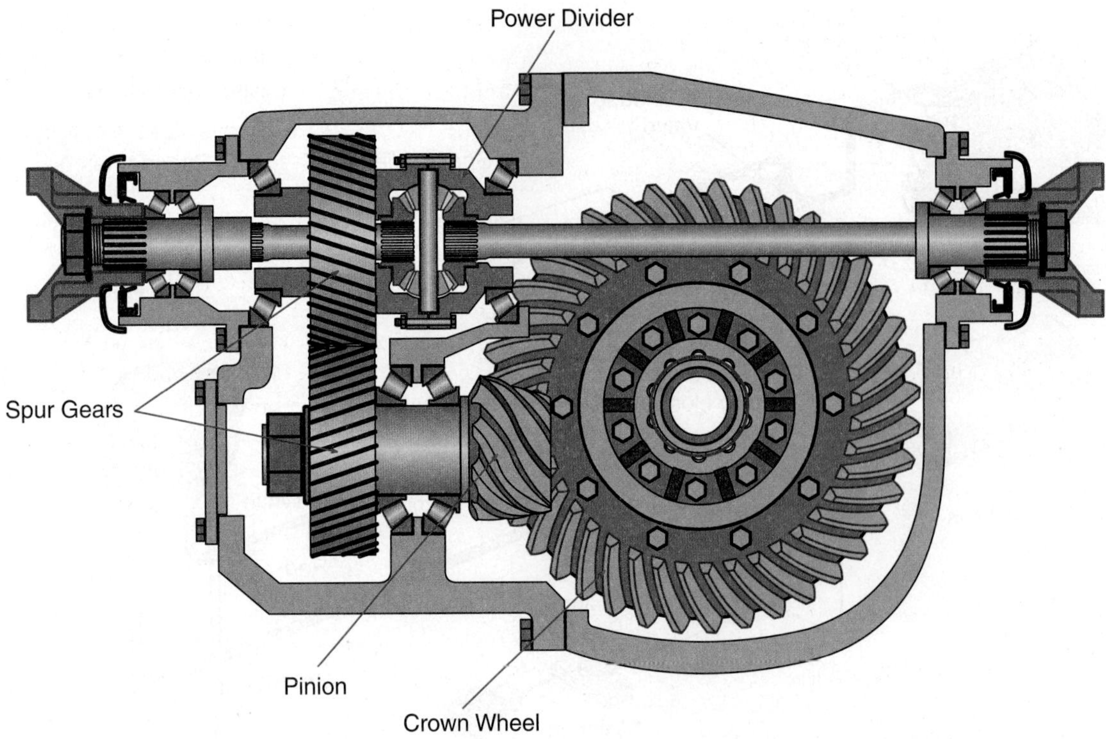

FIGURE 50-32 The major power divider components.

- Front side gear (usually part of one of the helical or spur gears)
- Rear side gear (usually part of the output shaft)
- Output or through shaft
- Interaxle differential with its case as well as cross and spider gears
- Crown and pinion gearset (driven by the helical or spur gears)
- Wheel differential and case with its side and spider gears

In addition, the power divider is also usually equipped with a lube pump and an interaxle differential locking mechanism. These components work together. The machine's drive shaft is connected to the input shaft of the power divider and is splined to the cross of the interaxle differential. The cross rotates with the input shaft and delivers power in equal quantities to the front and rear side gears of the interaxle differential. The front side gear is part of one of the helical or spur gears, like the one pictured in **FIGURE 50-33**. The helical gear drives the pinion gear of the front drive axle of the tandem. The input shaft passes through this gear but is not attached to it. The gear rides on a bushing or bearing on the input shaft. The gear is in mesh with another gear, which in turn is splined to the pinion gear of the front drive axle of the tandem. When the axle rotates, power is transferred to the crown gear and then to the wheel differential case. At that point, the power is split again, through the differential gears, between the two drive wheels of the axle.

The rear side gear is part of or splined to the **output shaft** (or **through shaft**), like the one pictured in **FIGURE 50-34**. Half of the power from the interaxle differential cross is transferred to the rear side gear and the output shaft. The output shaft exits the rear of the power divider housing and connects to a short driveshaft, which in turn connects to the rear-rear drive axle pinion gear.

FIGURE 50-33 Notice the spline in the interaxle differential cross. All of the input torque is delivered through the hollow front side gear to the cross.

The power is then split at the rear-rear drive axle differential to the rear two driving wheels. In this way, each of the four driving wheels receives exactly 25% of the available power.

In straight-ahead driving with tires of equal size, that is the extent of the power divider operation. As the machine turns or when tire sizes are mismatched, however, the situation changes. The power divider must allow each drive axle to turn at different speeds. The power divider therefore performs two functions.

FIGURE 50-34 The rear side gear of the interaxle differential is splined to the through shaft, so half the available torque is sent to the rear drive axle of the tandem.

It allows two drive axles to rotate at different speeds when necessary while still splitting the available torque and power between them equally.

The interaxle differential of the power divider is the key to this ability. The input shaft of the power divider is splined to the cross of the interaxle differential only. The cross contains the four differential spider gears, one on each cross leg. The gears and the cross are assembled into a case. As the cross rotates, the spider gears essentially drag the two side gears along. The spider gears are also capable of rotating on the cross when necessary, allowing the two side gears to rotate at different speeds when required by the driving situation. When one of the two axles of the tandem is turning more slowly than the other because of mismatched tires, turning, or terrain variations, the side gear driving the slower moving axle slows down slightly, and the spider gears in the interaxle differential begin to turn. The rotation of the spider gears causes the side gear that drives the other axle of the tandem to speed up. The differential still splits power equally, but the drive axles are allowed to turn at different speeds when required. Remember that, by design, there should be only a very slight speed difference between the two axles. For that reason, it is important that tires be matched between the front and rear drive axles of the tandem.

Power dividers typically have an interaxle differential lock similar to the ones found in the main differential. The lock can be engaged by the operator during low-traction situations.

FIGURE 50-35 shows the power flow through a power divider's interaxle differential with and without the interaxle differential lock engaged.

Preventing Interaxle Differential Spinout

Spinout is a situation in which one wheel of a drive axle (or one drive axle of a tandem) loses traction and spins uncontrolled while the other remains stationary. Spinout can occur under slippery or poor traction conditions.

The interaxle differential lock can avoid spinout. In a tandem drive, spinout usually occurs when one drive axle's wheels lose traction and spin at twice normal speed while the second drive axle's wheels remain stationary. **FIGURE 50-36** illustrates this concept.

In a tandem-drive axle spinout, the interaxle differential case rotates at driveshaft speed, or up to three to five times faster than a wheel differential. Therefore, one side gear will be turning at twice driveshaft speed, and the spider gears will be going approximately twice as fast as that again!

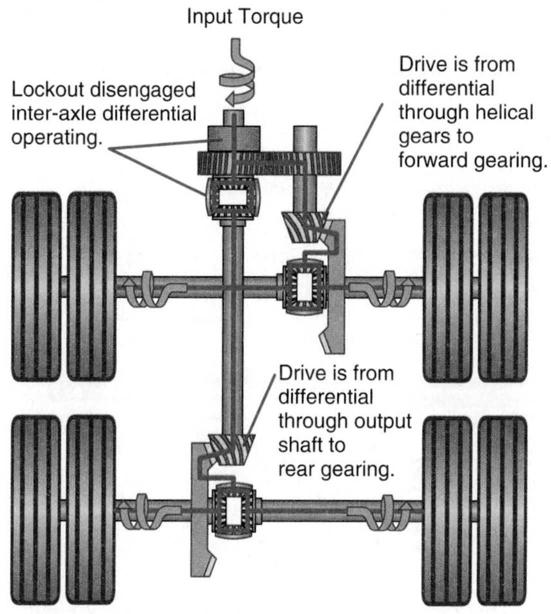

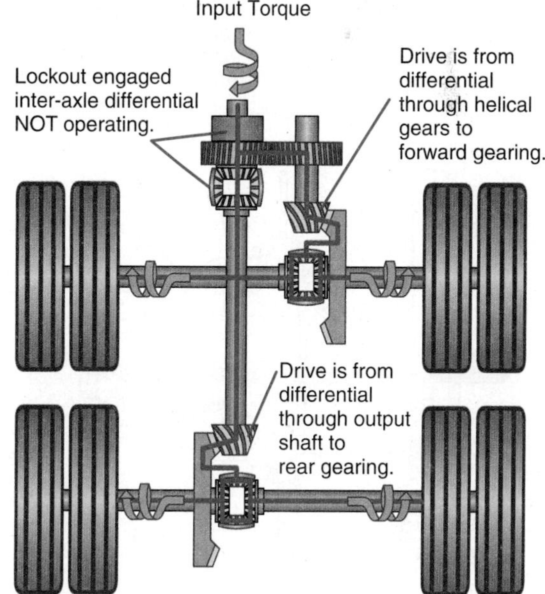

FIGURE 50-35 Power flow through the interaxle differential. Each wheel receives 25% of the available torque.

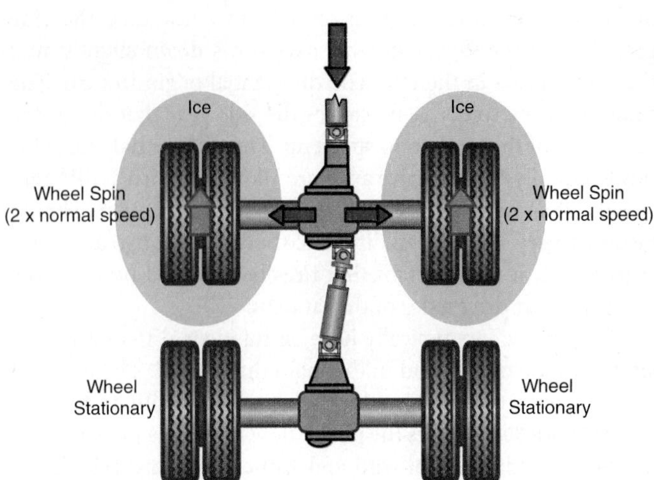

FIGURE 50-36 Tandem axle spinout can occur with one drive axle stationary and the other drive axle spinning at double normal speed.

FIGURE 50-37 The interaxle differential lock is a sliding clutch that is splined to the input (indicated) shaft of the power divider. When engaged, it locks the front side gear to the input shaft.

As a result, most if not all interaxle differentials are equipped with an interaxle differential lock similar to the one shown in **FIGURE 50-37**, to prevent interaxle spinout.

The lock is a sliding clutch splined to the input shaft. The lock has a series of clutching teeth that match another series of clutching teeth on the helical or spur gear. Remember that the gear is splined to or part of the front side gear of the interaxle differential. The sliding clutch is typically moved by an air motor that the operator controls. When the operator engages the lock, the sliding clutch locks the front side gear to the input shaft. The input shaft is splined to the interaxle differential cross as well, so the cross and the front side gear must now turn at the same speed. This means that the spider gears cannot rotate; because the spider gears can no longer turn, the rear side gear cannot turn either and must "go along for the ride." All interaxle differential action stops, positively preventing spinout from occurring.

The interaxle differential lock can be engaged at any speed provided no wheels are spinning. It is essential that the wheels are not slipping while engaging the lock or else damage will occur.

Types of Axle Shafts

Off-road machines have many different type of axles, depending on whether they drive the wheels directly or input final drives on the way to the wheels. There are, however, two basic types of axles: semi-floating, shown in **FIGURE 50-38A**, and full-floating, shown in **FIGURE 50-38B**. **Semi-floating axle shafts** are so called because the outer end of the axle shaft supports the machine's weight at the wheel end, as the wheel is bolted directly to the axle shaft flange. The inner end of the semi-floating axle shaft "floats" in the side gear. That is, the inner end of the axle carries none of the machine weight, hence the name "semi-floating." Semi-floating axle shafts are used on

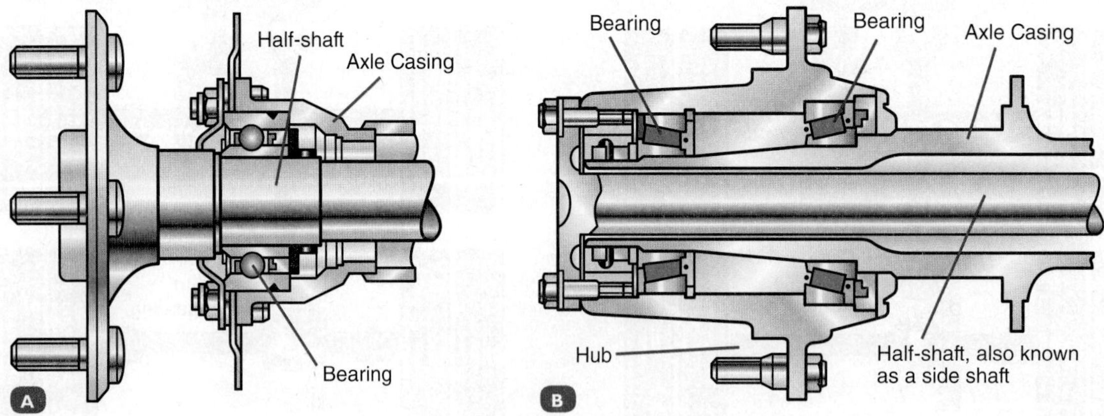

FIGURE 50-38 The two most common types of axle shafts are the full-floating and the semi-floating types. **A.** A semi-floating axle shaft carries the machine weight on the outside end of the axle shaft while the inside end carries no weight. **B.** A full-floating axle shaft carries none of the machine weight.

lighter machines only because they would be unable to carry the weight of a large machine.

Heavier machines including most articulating trucks, use full-floating axle shafts exclusively. A **full-floating axle shaft** does not carry any of the machine's weight on either end on the shaft. The inner end of a full-floating axle shaft floats in the side gear and the outer end is bolted to the wheel hub. The wheel hub is mounted on two opposing tapered roller bearings. Those bearings are supported by the spindle, which is attached to the drive axle housing. The machine's weight is transmitted through the frame to the axle housing and then through the bearing to the wheel hub and through the tire to the ground. Machine torque is transmitted to the wheel hub through the axle shaft. Because the shaft carries none of the weight, it is known as a full-floating axle shaft. A lot of machines have planetary wheel hubs; in these machines, the axle merely transmits power from the drive axle gearing the planetary gearset in the wheel hub.

▶ Drive Axle Maintenance

S50001

Axle maintenance should be performed as recommended by the manufacturer. What follows here is a rough outline of some of the usual maintenance procedures on typical drive axles used in off-road equipment.

SAFETY TIP

Care should be taken when axle oil level is checked on a warm axle because there could be pressure built up. When the plug is almost ready to be free of its threads, you should place a rag over the plug and stay as far back as possible to avoid having hot fluid sprayed on you.

Axle Lubrication

Axles could use a wide range of fluid for lubrication and cooling. The term "fluid" is sometimes used instead of "oil" because there are non-mineral-based fluids that are required, such as synthetic, but most axle fluid is mineral-based oil. For the balance of this chapter, we refer to axle oil as "axle fluid" or "lubricant." Axle fluid also lubricates differentials and power dividers.

In some drive axles, lubrication is effected by the movement of the crown wheel. A fluid level plug is threaded into the drive axle housing or the rear cover (on lighter-duty models) and the fluid is to be filled to the level of the plug, as illustrated in **FIGURE 50-39**. Some drive axles may have more than one level plug. In those instances, both must be filled to the level of the plugs. Always consult the manufacturer's manual to determine the proper filling sequence on these axles.

With fluid at approximately halfway up the differential case, the fluid bathes the differential gears and the side bearings. As the crown wheel rotates through this fluid, its teeth throw the fluid upward in the drive axle. The fluid then follows the curvature of the housing and is directed by channels formed in the carrier housing and/or stamped metal slingers and troughs to the pinion bearings. The fluid also splashes all around the inside of the housing onto the side bearings as well. The flowing and splashing movement allows the fluid to complete its purpose of lubricating, cooling, and carrying away foreign material from components that are in contact with each other. This type of lubrication is known as splash lubrication and is similar to what occurs in most standard transmissions.

Splash lubrication can also be used in the power divider of a tandem drive. The interaxle differential creates a unique problem for this type of lubrication system, however. The interaxle differential component can be lubricated in the same fashion, with formed channels bringing essential lube to its components.

Drive axles and power dividers can also be equipped with an internal or external lube pump, similar to the one pictured in **FIGURE 50-40**.

Axle Fluid Cooling and Filtration

Many axles have a system to cool the lubricating fluid. With the high levels of torque created and the action of meshing gears and rotating bearings constantly shearing and stressing the fluid, a lot of heat is generated in the fluid. If the temperature of the fluid is allowed to climb too high, it will start to degrade the lubricating fluid, which could lead to component failure.

Fluid cooling is even more critical if the axle has inboard brakes. Inboard brakes rely on axle oil to dissipate heat. The brakes transfer heat to the fluid, and this heat has to be removed. Smaller machines and machines that have axles that don't have inboard brakes may rely on the transfer of heat

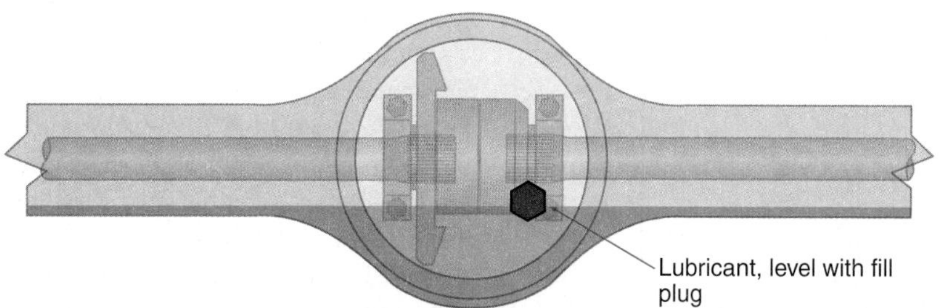

FIGURE 50-39 Most drive axles are lubricated by splash caused by the rotation of the crown wheel. It is essential that the correct fluid level be maintained.

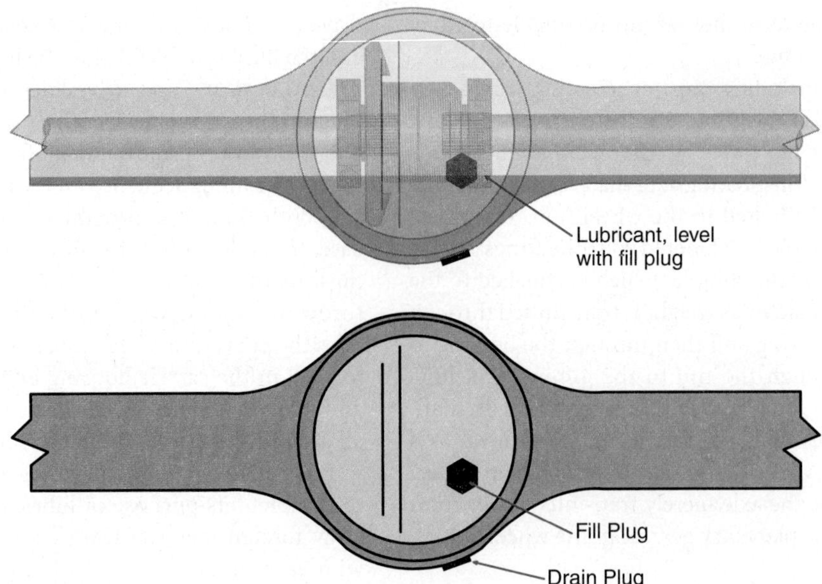

FIGURE 50-40 Axle and power dividers can be equipped with a gear-driven lubrication pump (indicated) to supply vital lubrication to the components.

from the oil to the axle housing, where it can transfer to the surrounding air.

Axle cooling circuits are simple systems that use a pump to circulate axle lubricant from the axle housing to a cooler where the heat in the fluid is transferred to the air flowing by the cooler.

The cooler is usually located near the engine cooling fan, but it could also have its own fan. Some machines have separate cooling systems for each axle. There are a combination of hoses and steel tubes to connect the axle, pump, and coolers. There could also be fittings that enable live oil sampling.

Some axle fluid circulation systems include one or more filters that clean the fluid as it is pumped around the system. See **FIGURE 50-41** for an axle oil cooling system.

The axle housing contains all the required oil for cooling and lubrication unless the axle uses a cooling system. Axles rarely use a remote reservoir for their oil because the axle housing contains more than enough volume needed for lubrication.

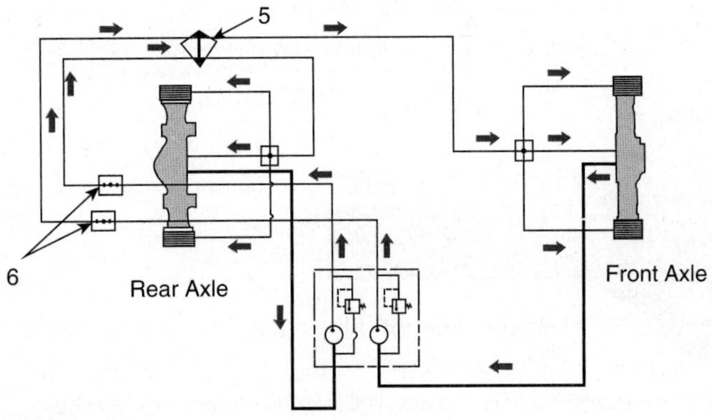

FIGURE 50-41 Axle cooling system.

Maintenance Schedules

Drive axle maintenance should be done on a regular basis, as described in the machine's maintenance manual. Oil levels for the axle and final drive are normally required to be checked every month.

This is usually done by removing a level plug; the oil level should be right at the bottom of the threads. Some axles have a plug on top, with a dipstick attached to it.

It's important for the machine to be parked on a level surface when checking axle oil levels.

There may be a breather for the axle housing that should be cleaned or replaced on a regular basis. This is quite often overlooked and could result in the housing getting overpressurized, and axle fluid leaks could result.

A visual inspection should also be done any time a machine is serviced. Any leaks should be noted, and if they are minor, they can be repaired when convenient. Major leaks should be repaired as soon as possible because otherwise the oil level will not be properly maintained, and if oil leaks out, then water, dirt, and other contaminants will be able to leak in.

Axle oil changes should normally take place at 2,000-hour intervals. A good practice in between oil changes is to take oil samples to monitor oil condition. Axle oil changes should ideally be done after the oil has been circulated and warmed up.

Proper oil refill type and quantity is important to get the maximum longevity of the axle. Cold-weather operation can be harmful to differentials because the axle oil is normally thick to start with, and if the oil isn't allowed to warm up and flow before heavy loads are encountered, meshing teeth and bearings can be damaged from lack of lubrication. If the oil is thick enough, the crown gear will cut a path through it; this is called channeling. With the oil this thick, not much lubrication will take place.

▶ Drive Axle Diagnostics and Repair Recommendations

S50002

SAFETY TIP

When working on final drives, drive axles, and power dividers, you must be aware of the potential for a machine to roll away. If a machine has inboard or driveline parking brakes, then any disconnection of mechanical drive at the final drive will allow the machine to roll uncontrolled. Wheel chocks must be used to prevent this.

You will be working with components that are heavy. The proper use of lifting devices is critical for staying safe.

You may be required to release or disassemble brakes that have heavy springs as part of them. Take precautions outlined in the machine's service information section to prevent uncontrolled release of spring tension.

As always, proper use of appropriate PPE will go a long way toward keeping you safe.

Operator complaints related to drive axles could include noises, vibrations, no drive, intermittent drive, unusual smell, pull to one side while traveling, and leaks.

The first step in diagnosing a drive axle problem is to gather from the operator information related to the problem. This includes the conditions under which the problem happens, when the problem started, how often it occurs, and whether there are any other problems that may be related. Next, you should get to know the type of drive axle on the machine; for example, if it has a locking differential, then how is it actuated and what types of brakes are on it? If the machine is operational, you should operate the machine to verify the complaint.

You would then perform a visual inspection including looking for leaks, checking the fluid level, and perhaps taking an oil sample. If the machine has an axle oil filtration system, you could take the filter off, cut it open, and inspect it for contamination.

For an axle with a no-drive problem, it may be fairly easy to remove an axle shaft to see whether it has broken or to remove a final drive carrier to see if the problem is with the final drive.

Drive Axle Removal

Many times it will be easier to repair an axle if it is removed from the machine. This requires proper lifting and blocking equipment. You may also need another machine to pull the axle out from under the machine. A typical axle removal procedure involves securing the machine, draining the axle fluid, removing brake lines, undoing axle mounts, and then supporting the axle. The machine would then be supported by its frame, and the wheels would be removed so the axle could be lowered. Depending on the weight of the axle, it could be pulled out from under the machine, or the machine could be moved away from the axle.

Drive Axle Diagnostics

Some drive axle troubleshooting procedures stem from an operator complaint such as the machine will not drive; it gets stuck more easily than it used to; there are leaks, noises, or vibrations; or the machine is hard to turn. These complaints should lead to the technician performing a diagnostic procedure to determine the cause of the problem.

The first step is to verify the complaint. If you are going to operate the machine, make sure that you are familiar with how to operate it safely and that there is plenty of room to run the machine.

One of the first things to do is a visual inspection for damage; then check the oil level and take an oil sample while doing this.

"No drive" means you would need to see whether the drive shaft input to the differential is turning. This would eliminate the need to check all other preceding driveline components.

If the machine gets stuck more easily than it used to, you need to check and see whether the machine has either a limited slip differential or a locking differential and then check to see if it is working properly.

A leak at the pinion shaft seal should be fairly easy to diagnose. You may need to clean the area first and top up the axle fluid to see if that is where the leak is originating. If this is the leak location, then you could start a repair process to replace the seal and install a wear sleeve on the pinion yoke. Don't forget to check the axle breather to see if it's plugged and causing the housing to overpressurize and leak.

Noises and vibrations are going to be hard to narrow down to the drive axle. It may be necessary to remove the drive shaft and axle shafts for that drive axle in order to determine whether the drive axle is the source of the vibration. Oil sample reports that show a high metal content, or just a visual inspection of the oil after it's drained, could lead you to suspect a failed drive axle. Be careful not to jump to conclusions because some wear is normal, and if the axle oil hasn't been changed, it could look a lot worse than it is. However, if chunks of teeth come out with the oil, this means without a doubt that the drive axle must be removed.

If a machine is hard to turn, it could be a problem with the limited slip or locking differential not releasing. If it is a locking differential, the control for it should be checked for proper operation. If this isn't the problem, then it will require the differential be removed to confirm and repair the problem. This could be a sticking piston, a sticking disc, or a part of the mechanical linkage not returning inside the housing.

You need to be certain the problem lies with the differential because this will require the differential to be removed, and this is usually a big job.

Once a problem has been diagnosed to be an internal drive axle problem, you must determine whether the repair can be made with the axle in the machine or whether the axle has to be removed.

Some axle repairs that can be done with the axle left on the machine are differential carrier removal and repair, final drive removal and repair, wheel bearing and seal replacement, axle shaft replacement, and leaks.

Outboard final drive problems can usually be fixed without removing the axle from the machine, but inboard final drive problems require the axle to be removed and disassembled.

Once an axle is removed, it can be disassembled, inspected, and repaired with new parts. The extent to which it must be

FIGURE 50-42 This axle is ready for disassembly.

disassembled depends on the type of repair needed. The following procedures assume the axle must be completely disassembled.

Smaller axles could be mounted to a stand or even put on top of a large bench. FIGURE 50-42 shows an axle with inboard final drives mounted on a stand and ready for disassembly.

Larger axles should be supported on stands where they can be disassembled. Axle shafts are removed, and if the axle has outboard final drives, they should be removed next. The differential can then be removed and disassembled if required.

The axle housing should be inspected for cracks and can be measured for straightness.

For smaller axles, it makes economic sense to replace all bearings, seals, and gaskets. Larger axles will have larger and more expensive bearings. They could be reused if no signs of wear or damage are present, but if there is any doubt, then they must be replaced.

▶ TECHNICIAN TIP

Many driveline components use tapered roller bearings to support shafts or other parts. A tapered roller bearing assembly consists of two parts. The outside diameter of the outer race (also called the cup) is usually pressed into a bore. Its inner surface is tapered, and the tapered rollers ride on it. The inner race is also tapered and the rollers are held onto it with a light-gauge framework called a cage. The cage also spaces the rollers evenly around the race. This assembly is called the cone because of its shape. Tapered roller bearing assemblies are almost always used in pairs and usually have to be preloaded. **Preloading** ensures that the rollers are seated on the races properly and will align the parts that are being suspended or supported by them. Tapered roller bearings control both axial and radial movement once properly preloaded.

▶ Common Drive Axle Repair Procedures

S50003

Wheel bearing adjustment is a critical part of axle rebuilding. There are two general ways to set the preload for the tapered roller bearings: shims and lock nuts.

Shim adjustment: If a drive axle wheel bearing adjustment is done with shims, the following generic procedure is likely to be followed. This is a procedure for an axle that has outboard final drives.

1. Install the inner axle bearing cone and metal face wheel seal on the axle spindle. Bearing cone installation may require heating the bearing. *Do not* overheat.
2. Apply axle oil to the bearing and wheel seal face.
3. Install wheel bearing cups and a metal face seal in the wheel hub, and apply axle oil. Bearing cup installation may require cooling the cups.
4. Place the wheel hub over the spindle. It may be necessary to pull in the hub and support it in order to center it on the bearing.
5. Install the outer bearing cone on the ring gear hub.
6. Install the ring gear hub onto the splines of the spindle.
7. Measure the thickness of the retainer plate.
8. Install the hub retaining plate onto the end of the spindle, and tighten bolts in the specified pattern and to the specified torque.
9. Rotate the wheel hub at least one revolution to seat the bearings.
10. Measure the distance from the outside of the retainer plate to the outside surface of the spindle.
11. Calculate the distance from the bottom of the retainer plate to the outside of the spindle.
12. Use the calculated distance for a reference to install the proper thickness of shims under the retainer plate. This should give the correct amount of preload to the wheel bearings. The specification may require a greater or lesser thickness of shims than the present gap dimension. For example, if the gap is 0.056 in. and the specification requires 0.004 in. more, then the correct thickness of shims would be 0.060 in.
13. Adjust the retainer plate fasteners to their final torque.

Lock nut adjustment: If a drive axle wheel bearing adjustment is done with a nut, the following generic procedure is likely to be followed. If the axle has an outboard final drive, the bearing will be behind the final drive ring gear hub and be part of a full-floating axle, whereby the axle shaft merely transfers torque to the sun gear of the final drive. If the axle has an inboard final drive, then the axle shaft supports weight and will have the bearings mounted on the shaft. The bearing nut-type adjustments are similar for both types of axles, but the following is for an inboard final drive semi-floating type of axle. This requires the outer axle housing to be removed.

1. The outer bearing cone and half of the metal face seal is installed on the axle shaft at the wheel end. This may require heating the bearing. The bearing and seal should be lubricated with axle oil.
2. The bearing cups are installed in the axle housing. This may require cooling the cups. The other half of the metal face seal is installed as well.
3. The housing is then installed over the axle shaft onto the axle shaft bearing and seal.

4. The inner bearing is lubricated and installed along with the adjusting nut on the axle shaft.
5. With the nut left slightly loose, a measurement of the torque it takes to turn the axle housing is taken. This needs to be considered when the rolling torque is measured.
6. The adjusting nut is then tightened while the housing is turned, and the torque is measured that is required to turn the housing. A specification indicates the proper rolling torque. This can be measured with a torque wrench or a string and scale. The seal drag torque is subtracted from the measured torque to find the actual rolling torque. The adjusting nut is then tightened or loosened to meet the specified torque, and the nut is locked in place if it is not a locknut. Sometimes a second check is done to see if there is end play between the axle and the housing.

Whatever the procedure is, it must be followed to a tee, and the preload must be confirmed and reset if it is found to be outside of specifications.

One way to check the wheel bearing setting when the axle is assembled on the machine is to check the vertical movement of the wheel in relation to the axle housing. When the weight is taken off the wheel by jacking the axle or using the machine blade or bucket, a dial indicator is mounted to the end of the axle housing and zeroed with its pointer resting against the wheel or axle shaft. The axle is then lowered to put the machine's weight back on it (with brakes applied), and the dial indicator is read. An allowable maximum reading might be 0.015 in. If the reading is more than this, it indicates a misadjusted, worn, or damaged bearing.

Differential Carrier Removal

If a defective drive axle is suspected from your diagnostic procedure, the only option is to remove the differential carrier and repair it. Some differential carriers can be removed without taking the axle assembly out of the machine. This depends on the clearance available ahead of the axle because it has to come ahead quite a distance for the crown gear to clear the axle housing. Most often there is not sufficient room to allow this. Even if there is room to do this, it will likely be more time efficient and safer to remove the entire axle assembly and then remove the differential carrier.

The axle shafts have to be removed first, and you may be able to lift the differential carrier straight out, or it may be lifted up after the axle housing is turned on its back.

A ring of bolts or nuts must be removed, and then usually two or three forcing bolts are installed to push the differential carrier away from the housing. **FIGURE 50-43** shows a typical removable carrier in a drive axle.

Differential Carrier Repair

Once the differential carrier is removed, it is easiest to repair it if it is installed on a rotating stand or a fixed stand. The type of stand used depends on the size of the unit and what is available at the shop where you are working. A rotating stand enables you to rotate the carrier to any position to make the repair easier.

FIGURE 50-43 To remove the carrier, first the axles are removed, and then the ring of bolts holding the carrier to the housing. Arrows point to the axle and the carrier bolts.

FIGURE 50-44 Check backlash before disassembly to ensure correct reassembly.

Any time a differential carrier is removed, its components should be thoroughly inspected for wear and damage before it is disassembled. The ring gear should be closely inspected to see if its wear pattern is normal. It's always a good idea to measure **backlash**; measure pinion shaft end play if it's supposed to be there; and check the tooth wear pattern before disassembly. You should also take several pictures with a digital camera to keep for reference and evidence if there is a warranty issue. **FIGURE 50-44** shows backlash being checked.

As there are many variations of drive axles, here a rebuild procedure is highlighted from a medium-duty wheel loader with an open differential. This is a typical process that may be close to the differential carrier that you are rebuilding but in no way should be used as a guideline for any specific unit. *Always* consult the proper service information for the differential carrier you are working on because there could be changes to parts and procedures even within a close serial number range of machines.

This procedure should be carried out in a clean, well-lit area with plenty of bench space. Some special tools are required, so it's a good idea to check that you have the required tools and that they are in proper working condition before starting the procedure.

Mark all mating components of the differential carrier before disassembly, to aid in reassembly. A paint stick, permanent marker, or carefully placed punch marks can be used for this. To remove bearings, follow the steps in **SKILL DRILL 50-1**.

SKILL DRILL 50-2 is a generic disassembly procedure for the differential carrier; there can be several differences to the procedure depending on the carrier involved. As always, the correct OEM service manual is essential for successful completion of the overhaul procedure.

> **TECHNICIAN TIP**
>
> It may be easier to remove the side bearings after the differential case is disassembled.

> **TECHNICIAN TIP**
>
> Some differential carrier thrust screws have a thrust block swaged to the end of the screw. During the disassembly, do not remove the thrust screw completely on this type; doing so will force the block off the end of the screw.

SKILL DRILL 50-1 Removing the Differential Carrier

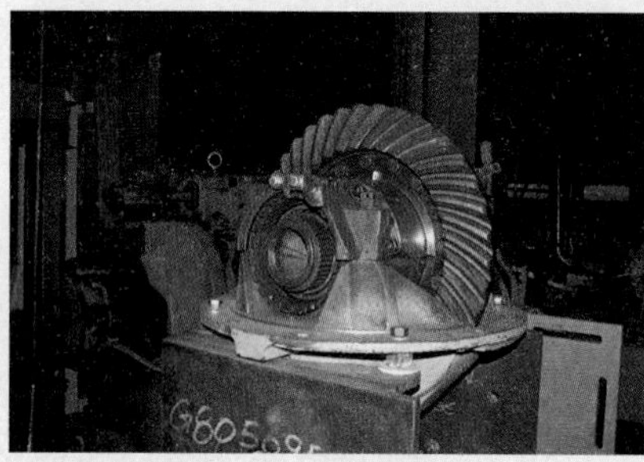

1. Safely raise the machine to a sufficient level that allows enough room to work beneath it, and securely block the machine. Remove the differential carrier without interference from the frame and/or other components.
2. Remove the driveshaft from the drive axle, and ensure it is sufficiently out of the way to allow differential carrier removal.
3. Drain the axle fluid into a suitable container. The fluid can be an important indicator of the axle's condition. Watch for evidence of metal contamination, indicating extreme wear, or sludge, usually caused by overheating or lack of lubricant.
4. Remove the wheels.
5. Remove the planetary wheel hubs if the machine is so equipped.
6. Remove the axles and mark them as either right or left.
7. Support the differential carrier with a suitable lifting device, and secure it to the device. The rear side of the carrier is much heavier than the front and will try to roll off as it is removed. Before removing the differential carrier attaching bolts, ensure the carrier is securely supported.
8. Remove the differential carrier, retaining cap screws or stud nuts, leaving the top two loose to hold the weight while the carrier mounting flange is loosened.
9. Loosen the differential carrier-to-housing mounting flange by using forcing bolts in the holes provided or by moving the front of the housing back and forth.
10. Remove the top two retainers and pull the differential carrier forward and out from under the machine.
11. Mount the differential carrier in a suitable stand for overhaul.

SKILL DRILL 50-2 Disassembling the Differential Carrier

1. Mark with punch marks one of the differential **side bearing bore** legs (the bore in the casting that holds the side bearing races) and the bearing retaining caps (semicircular caps that clamp the side bearing into the casting). This allows the caps to be reinstalled on the correct side.

2. If the differential carrier has a **thrust screw**, loosen the jamb nut, and back out or remove the thrust screw. The thrust screw (circled) will be located on the ring gear side of the differential carrier housing.

3. Remove the **bearing adjuster locks** (cotter pins, lock plates, and so on that stop the adjusters from turning) and loosen the four (or more) bearing cap retaining cap screws. Back out the **bearing adjusters** (threaded rings that position the side bearings) two to three turns. Remove the bearing caps crews (A), support caps (B), and the adjusters (C). Keep each side together as a set to ensure you will be able to reinstall them in the correct location.

SKILL DRILL 50-2 Disassembling the Differential Carrier (Continued)

4. Using a sling and a hoist, remove the differential case and crown gear as an assembly, and place it on a work bench. Remove the taper roller bearings from either the differential case or the pinion gear, using a wedge-type bearing puller. Place the assembly in the press with the puller vertical at first.

5. After the bearing has been loosened, retighten the wedge-type puller, and install the assembly into the press horizontally to finish the removal procedure.

6. Remove the crown gear, if replacing, by removing the retaining cap screws or drilling and punching out the rivets. The crown gear may have to be pressed off or lightly tapped off the differential case with a soft hammer. Always protect the crown gear from falling, so it is not damaged.

SKILL DRILL 50-3 is a generic version of a drive axle carrier assembly process. *Always* use pinion gears and crown gears as a matched set. Use clean oil of the type that will be used in the axle housing to lubricate bearings as they are installed.

The differential carrier is now ready for installation into the axle housing.

Contact Pattern

After assembly of any drive axle, it is essential to check the contact pattern. All conventional drive axles using hypoid gearing have the same desired hand-rolled contact pattern. Study the names of the tooth surfaces shown in **FIGURE 50-45** to ensure

SKILL DRILL 50-3 Assembling a Drive Axle Carrier

1. Install inner tapered roller bearing onto pinion shaft: This will likely require heating and pressing the bearing on. The race of the cone will seat against a shoulder on the pinion shaft.

2. Adjust pinion preload: The pinion may rotate in a separate housing that bolts to the differential carrier or in the carrier itself. The pinion shaft is supported by two tapered roller bearing assemblies. In the pinion shown in step 1, the pinion bearing cups are supported in the integral drive axle housing. The preloading of these bearings can be done with a spacer, shims, or a lock nut.

3. Lock nut adjustment: Other differentials have pinion preload adjusted with a lock nut on the pinion shaft. The lock nut puts pressure on the outer pinion bearing cone. This is similar to a wheel bearing adjustment. Sometimes the nut is under the yoke, or it can be the retaining nut for the yoke. Preload of the bearing on this type of pinion is measured with an inch-pound torque wrench. On heavier equipment, it is more common, however, to see the pinion bearings supported in a removable cage.

(Continued)

SKILL DRILL 50-3 Assembling a Drive Axle Carrier (Continued)

4. Preload on this type of pinion arrangement can be checked before reassembly. A hydraulic press is used to simulate the clamping force created when the yoke is installed and torqued on the pinion shaft. Then the rotating torque required to turn the pinion is measured. To get the rotating torque, the press is set to the correct number of pounds force that represents the pinion nut torque. Next a string is wrapped around the pinion bearing cage, and a fish scale is used to rotate the pinion. The pounds pull required to rotate the pinion is multiplied by the number of inches from the center of the pinion cage to the point where the string is attached, resulting in the inch-pound rotating torque. To increase the torque, a thinner spacer is used between the pinion bearings, and a thicker spacer is used to decrease the dimension. An example of a proper amount of preload is typically rotating torque with no seal, 9–18 in.-lb. This should be done without the pinion seal installed to get a more accurate reading. Once the proper preload is set, then the seal is installed.

5. Install yoke: The drive shaft yoke is installed, and its fastener is torqued to specification. Recheck rolling torque. Sometimes a dimension is given for checking shaft end play. An example is to apply 50 lb of force and measure end play. A proper dimension might be 0.00–0.001 in.

6. Pinion depth: This can be a calculated dimension that relates to how far the pinion protrudes in to the differential carrier, and is sometimes called the cone point adjustment (this refers to the shape of the pinion gear).

7. Cone point adjustment: A measurement should be taken in the differential carrier that relates the centerline of the ring gear to the face of the surface that the inner pinion bearing rests on or the face of the surface that the pinion housing rests on. This dimension will then have the dimension of the inner bearing cup and the dimension marked on the pinion gear subtracted from it. The dimension that is left is the thickness of the shim pack that will be installed under the inner bearing cup.

8. Pinion housing adjustment: The pinion depth dimension could also be changed by adjusting the thickness of the shims under the pinion bearing cage flange when it is installed in the differential carrier.

9. Install pinion assembly: Install O-ring seal, if equipped, and torque the ring of bolts to specification to hold the pinion assembly to the differential carrier. Remove yoke and install pinion seal in housing. Install yoke and torque nut to specification. This may require special tools to hold the yoke while torquing the nut. This could be several hundred foot-pounds of torque.

10. Assemble differential housing: One side of the housing is placed on a bench with the opening facing up. One side gear is installed into housing. The bevel pinion gears are installed on to the cross and then the thrust washers are installed on the ends of the gears. The assembled cross is placed in the slots in the housing. The second side gear is laid on top of the bevel pinions, and then the other half of the housing is installed with ring of fasteners that are torqued to specification. The crown gear is then installed on the housing with a ring of fasteners and torque to specification. If the differential has a limited slip device, the clutch packs would be installed at this stage. If it was a locking differential, the locking mechanism would be installed now.

11. Install differential side bearings: The bearing cones are pressed onto the housing. Sometimes heating the bearings eases installation. Be sure to not overheat bearings.

12. Back out thrust screw: If the differential carrier has a thrust screw, it should be backed out to avoid interfering with differential installation.

13. Install differential assembly into carrier: The proper lifting device needs to be used to carefully lift the assembly into the carrier.

14. Install outer bearing races and trunnion caps: With the differential assembly hanging freely from a hoisting device, install bearing cups, caps, and adjusting nuts. The adjusting nuts are specifically designed to push on the bearing cups and usually have a series of lugs protruding from the outside face that allow the nut to be turned with a pry bar or a special socket. The nut has fine threads that mate with threads in the differential carrier and the bearing caps. The caps have to be left slightly loose when adjusting the nuts. Care must be taken not to damage the threads in the carrier or caps at this point. Remove the lifting device.

15. Remove axial end play: Adjusting nuts should be tightened at this point to remove any end play in the differential assembly. Always rotate the crown gear to rotate the bearings when adjusting bearing preload, to help seat the rollers. It may be required to turn the adjusting nuts an additional few notches to add some preload to the bearings.

16. Adjust backlash (clearance between crown and pinion gears): With the pinion gear locked in place, use the adjusting nuts to adjust backlash according to specification. An example of this is 0.011–0.013 in. This is measured with a dial indicator that has its pointer resting on one tooth of the crown gear. Backlash is necessary to allow the gears to have clearance to allow lubrication between the meshing teeth. It can be adjusted by tightening one adjusting nut and loosening the opposite side the same amount. This moves the crown gear closer to or farther away from the pinion gear while maintaining preload.

SKILL DRILL 50-3 Assembling a Drive Axle Carrier (Continued)

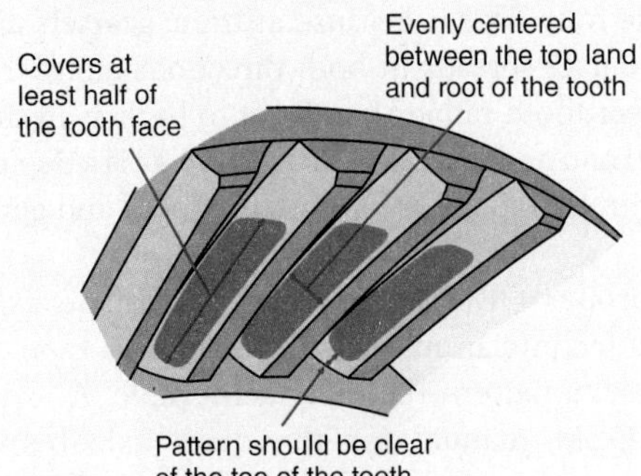
Correct Contact Pattern (for new gears)
Covers at least half of the tooth face
Evenly centered between the top land and root of the tooth
Pattern should be clear of the toe of the tooth

17. Check gear **contact pattern**: This step checks to see whether the crown and pinion gears are meshing properly. With marking paste, Prussian blue or red lead, or other paint-like liquid applied to the teeth, rotate the pinion in both directions while applying a slight load on the ring gear. Compare the mark left on the ring gear tooth drive side to the contact pattern. If necessary, adjust backlash and pinion depth to obtain correct pattern. This can take a while; be patient and try to anticipate how much or little an adjustment has to be made before making one. Use Table 50-1 to determine the correct adjustment. More information on setting contact pattern follows this drill.

18. Install adjusting nut locks: There are different ways to lock the adjusting nuts. Roll pins or bolt on locks are two examples.

19. Adjust thrust screw: The thrust screw needs to be close to the back of the crown gear; this is done by turning it in until it contacts crown gear and then backing it off slightly. A lock nut is tightened to hold it in place.

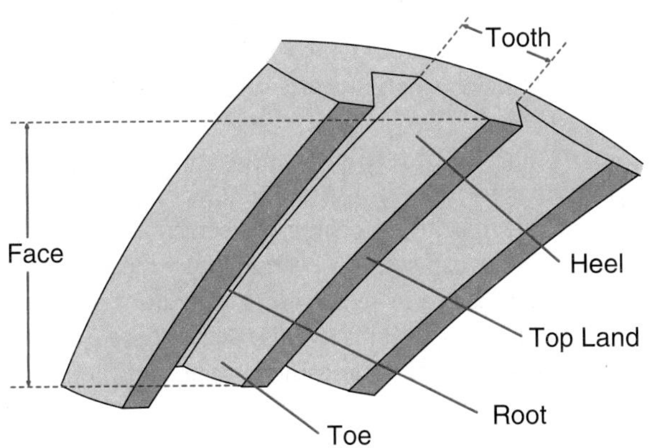
Tooth
Face
Heel
Top Land
Root
Toe

FIGURE 50-45 Proper gear tooth nomenclature.

the contact pattern check is performed correctly and the results can be properly interpreted.

The contact pattern itself consists of a **lengthwise bearing** along the **tooth face** from the **toe** to the **heel** and a **profile bearing** between the **top land** and the **root**. The correct contact pattern ensures that as the gearset is loaded, the contact will spread toward the heel of the tooth, along its face width, so the whole tooth can carry the load. If the contact pattern runs off the tooth face at any point, the gearset will make noise. A whining noise will be heard on acceleration or deceleration, depending on where the pattern runs off the tooth. This type of contact also weakens the gearset as less than the entire tooth is involved in carrying the load.

The pattern is typically checked on the drive side of the crown gear teeth. To check contact pattern, six or more teeth of the crown gear are lightly marked on their drive side with a tooth marking compound. The crown gear is then turned in a reverse direction while a resistance load is applied to the pinion by having an assistant hold the pinion. The load increases the chance of getting a good view of the pattern. Rotate the marked teeth through mesh in one direction a couple of times; then bring the marked teeth to the top to read the pattern.

A good, conventional hypoid pattern has the following three elements:

1. The pattern must start near but clear of the toe of the tooth.
2. The pattern should cover at least 50% of the crown gear tooth face width.
3. The pattern should be centered between the top land and the root of the tooth.

The diagram shown in step 16 of Skill Drill 50-3 illustrates the correct pattern for new hypoid gearing.

FIGURE 50-46 shows an actual correct contact pattern for new conventional gearing. Notice that the pattern is more oval

FIGURE 50-46 Actual gear contact patterns are slightly different than the theoretical pattern depicted in Skill Drill 50-3, step 16. The contact is more oval in shape, as shown here.

but meets the three criteria of being clear of the toe, covering half of the tooth face, and being centered between the top land and the root.

The difference in pattern shape is caused by the slight crowning of new teeth. The pattern will flatten out as the gears wear together. As a gearset increasingly wears, it creates a pattern with more of a pocket (or V) shape toward the heel end of the tooth. Nonetheless, the gearset will still have the same three elements of starting near the toe, having 50% or more of the tooth covered, and being centered between the top land and the root.

The two elements of drive axle assembly that affect contact pattern are the gearset backlash and the pinion depth setting. The gearset backlash affects the positioning of the pattern along the face width of the tooth. Increasing backlash moves the pattern along the tooth face toward the heel of the tooth, and decreasing backlash moves the pattern along the tooth face toward the toe of the tooth. The pinion depth setting affects the position of the contact pattern between the top land and the root of the tooth. Moving the pinion gear mounting closer to the axial center of the crown gear moves the pattern down the tooth face toward the root of the tooth; moving the pinion further away from the axial center of the crown gear causes the pattern to move up the tooth face toward the top land of the tooth. The adjustments are somewhat interrelated in that if the pinion gear is moved closer to the crown gear's center, it will decrease backlash, and if it is moved further from the center, backlash will increase. When a pattern adjustment is necessary, always adjust the pinion position first, if necessary, and then readjust backlash. **TABLE 50-1** shows incorrect patterns and what has to be done to correct them. Take caution, though, if you have to move the pinion toward the crown gear's center. This action decreases backlash, so the crown gear should be moved away from the pinion before the pinion gear is repositioned. If this is not done, there may not be sufficient clearance for the deeper meshed pinion. This could cause damage to the gear faces.

Most gearsets that a technician comes across use the conventional pattern described previously. Some bevel gears, however, use a centralized contact pattern. This type of gearing is commonly known as **generoid** gearing. Generoid gearing has a hand-rolled contact pattern centered along the face of the crown gear tooth. The generoid pattern is also centered between the top land and the root. This is because as these gearsets are loaded, the tooth contact spreads in both directions along the face of the crown gear tooth rather than front to back as in the conventional hypoid and amboid gears. **FIGURE 50-47** is a depiction of a correct centralized pattern for both durapoid and generoid gearsets.

Without the proper OEM documentation for the axle being worked on, a technician may be fooled by this type of gearing and try to set a pattern that is unachievable. Always have the correct OEM manual for the drive axle being worked on.

Diagnosing Component Failures in Drive Axle Systems

Failure analysis is a very important component of a technician's skill set. The ability to determine what, specifically, caused a failure to occur is essential to performing a complete repair and not having a repeat failure. If a power divider is disassembled and a broken interaxle differential cross is discovered, as shown in **FIGURE 50-48**, it cannot be simply said that the cross itself was the cause of the failure. That is where the failure happened, but what caused it?

All other parts of the axle must be examined and a determination made as to the root cause of the failure. Several things must be considered when deciding the cause of failure: the machine's function, the duty cycle, operator experience, operating conditions, maintenance records, and an accurate report as to how and when the failure occurred. If the technician simply replaces the broken components without finding the cause, the machine will likely experience the same or a similar failure in the future.

The true cause of a failure can usually be determined by knowing what to look for. Most manufacturers make guidebooks available to help the technician decide on a the root cause of a failure. Drivetrain systems are frequently the subject of premature failures caused by overloading, operator error or abuse, or poor maintenance practices. This section covers a methodical five-step process for diagnosing failures and then discusses the most common types of drive axle failure.

Process for Diagnosing Failures

There are five steps to diagnosing a component failure:

1. Record all the known details of the failure.
2. Investigate the machine history and condition.
3. Inspect the components carefully.
4. Determine the cause of the failure.
5. Ensure the cause has been corrected.

Step 1—Record Details of the Failure

Step 1 of diagnosing drive axle failures is to record all the known details of the failure. Start by checking the machine's

TABLE 50-1 Troubleshooting Tooth Patterns

Incorrect Pattern	Problem	Solution
Pattern too close to toe	Pattern too close to edge of tooth toe	Move ring gear away from pinion to increase backlash
Pattern too close to heel	Pattern too far along tooth toward tooth heel	Move ring gear toward pinion to decrease backlash
Pattern too close to tooth root	Pattern too close to tooth root	Move pinion away from ring gear
Pattern too close to top land	Pattern too close to tooth top land	Move pinion toward ring gear

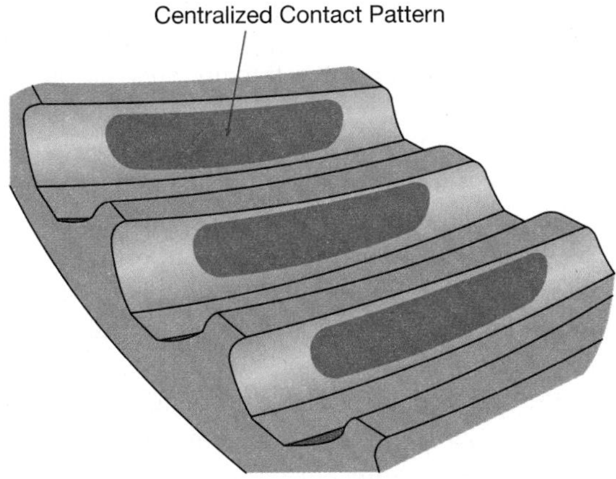

FIGURE 50-47 A centralized contact pattern is used for generoid gearsets, under load the contact spreads in both directions along the tooth face width.

FIGURE 50-48 Reassembling a failed component without discovering the cause of failure usually means the failure will reoccur.

service history. Then, talk to the operator and ask the following questions:

- What is the machine's normal use?
- Is this problem a repeat failure or the first occurrence?
- How was the machine operating when the failure occurred?
- Did the operator notice anything unusual at the time of the failure?
- Were there any noises or vibrations?
- Was the machine or any of its components overheating?

Step 2—Investigate the Machine's History and Condition

The second step in the diagnosis process is to investigate the machine's history and its condition. Start this step by looking for any leaks, cracks, or other damage that may have contributed or caused the failure. Does the machine look like it receives regular maintenance, or is it in poorly maintained condition? Record anything noteworthy that could be a contributing factor to the failure. Something small at this point may help once the component is disassembled!

Step 3—Inspect the Failed Components Carefully

Step 3 of the diagnosis process is to inspect the failed components carefully. While disassembling a unit, try to disturb as little as possible until the exact failed piece is discovered. Do not aggressively clean the parts, as vital evidence may be washed away. Wait until disassembly is complete. Examine the lubricant. Is it full of metal shavings? Is the level and quality of the lubricant sufficient? Once the failed component is found, carefully examine it and all the parts it interacts with to determine what type of failure occurred. For example, was it fatigue failure, shock load failure, or was it a defect in the component?

Step 4—Determine the Cause of the Failure

Replacing a failed component without knowing why it failed is a recipe for disaster. It is up to the technician to determine what actually happened to the failed part and decide how to prevent reoccurrence.

When examining gears and shafts, remember the following: gears and shafts are typically made of ductile iron and are usually case- or induction-hardened, typically to a depth of no more than 0.050" (1.27 mm). The hardening allows the components' surface to resist wear, but the ductile core allows them to flex as they are loaded so that they can absorb some shocks. This flexibility allows them to bend before they break, a characteristic that provides insight into the actual cause of a failure.

Step 5—Ensure That the Cause Has Been Corrected

The final step is to ensure that the cause has been corrected. Merely finding out what actually happened to a component may not be sufficient in proper failure analysis. For example, while examining a failed gear tooth, it can be clearly seen that a gas pocket makes up a large percentage of the break site. It would be safe to assume that the failure is a defect in material and that replacing the components and rebuilding the unit will solve the problem. However, if a broken tooth is found and there is evidence of a fatigue failure, for example, beach marks, a determination must be made as to the cause of the constant overloading that led to the break. Is the machine being used for a purpose that it is not capable of? If so, repairing the problem just means the machine will eventually be back with a repeat failure. When a shock load failure is discovered, it is necessary to investigate why it happened. Was it abuse? Would an operator education program help? If a lubrication failure occurred, does the machine's maintenance program have to be revamped? It is essential that the root cause of the problem be determined and repaired, or at least documented on the work order, before a machine is returned to service. This protects the reputation of the technician and the service facility and allows the machine owner to consider what steps he or she must take to prevent reoccurrence of the failure.

Types of Drive Axle Failure

Drive axles can fail in several different ways. The principal types of drive axle failure include:

- Shock load failures
- Fatigue failures
- Abuse failures
- Lubrication failures

Proper maintenance of drive axle involves recognizing the characteristics of each type of failure.

Shock Load Failures

Shock load failures occur when a component is momentarily overloaded to a level that surpasses the base strength of the material, causing it to fail immediately. A shock load failure results in a broken component. Figure 50-48 shows an extreme shock load failure.

If it is a shaft that breaks, the failure usually occurs at a **section break**, a point where the shaft changes in shape, thereby changing its section modulus (a measure of its load-carrying capability). For example, where a spline or thread begins is a section break. So is the point where the shaft is suddenly thicker or thinner. Shock failure breakage leaves a relatively flat and uniformly rough surface at the fracture area, as can be seen in **FIGURE 50-49**. Notice how the break follows the contour of the groove in the shaft. This groove constitutes a section break. Sometimes a shaft will break on an angle, leaving the fractured surface uniformly rough. If the shaft has turned after the failure, the break surface may have smoothened out somewhat.

Shock load failure on a gear usually results in a broken gear tooth. The tooth surface is, again, uniformly rough, and there is typically a raised area on the compression side of the break. If the gear is operated after breaking, this area may be worn down. Sometimes a defect in the manufacturing process leads to gear tooth fracture. Small imperfections known as **gas pockets** or **stringers** can occur. Gas pockets (stringers) occur during the casting process when the metal of the entire tooth

FIGURE 50-49 Shock failures are recognizable by the uniform roughness **A.** of the surface areas where a break has occurred. However, if a component is run after the break, there will be some areas that are smoothed out **B**.

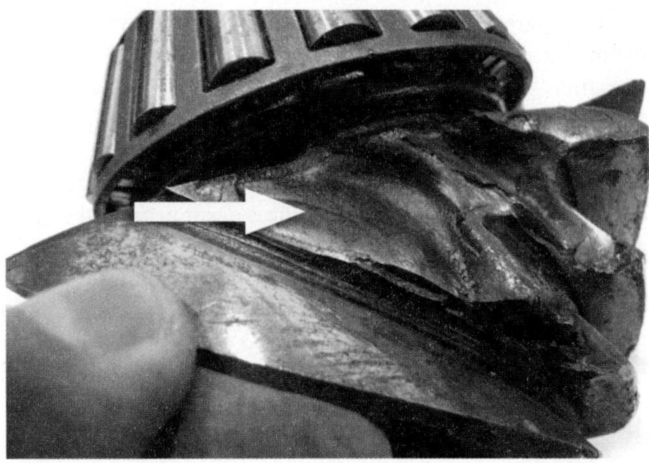

FIGURE 50-50 Gear teeth fatigue fractures are characterized by beach marks (indicated).

is not uniformly fused together with the metal of the rest of the gear. This type of imperfection significantly weakens the gear tooth. Gas pockets can be identified by a difference in texture and shape of the fracture surface. Some of the break area will be rough, as in a normal shock load failure, but other parts of the break area will have an unusual texture. For example, it could be smooth or even hollowed out. This change in texture will be quite obvious to the technician.

Fatigue Failures

Fatigue failures occur as the result of the component simply wearing out. They occur gradually and progress until the component fails. Fatigue can be classed into three separate types of failures: bending stresses, torsional or twisting stresses, and surface fatigue.

In bending failures, the component is stressed by load sufficient to crack the component but insufficient to break it outright. The stress occurs repeatedly until the component finally does break. Bending fatigue usually occurs with gear teeth, and the break area is characterized by **beach marks**. Beach marks are semicircular marks that indicate repeated cracking of the component. The crack will continue to progress until the part fails, leaving telltale beach marks in the fracture, as can be seen in **FIGURE 50-50**. A fatigue failure indicates repeated overloading of the component, so the technician must take steps to prevent the overloading. Otherwise, the component will fail again.

Twisting or torsional failures usually occur with shafts that are constantly exposed to twisting forces sufficient to crack the material but insufficient to break it outright. Torsional failures generally result in either a scalloped or star-type fracture. As shown in **FIGURE 50-51**, a scalloped-shaped fracture shows beach marks similar to a bending failure. In a star-type fracture, such as the one shown in **FIGURE 50-52**, some of the break area was smoothed out by the shaft spinning after the break occurred.

Surface fatigue is the final type of fatigue failure. Surface fatigue is caused by overloading to such a degree that the hard surface of gear teeth breaks down and starts flaking away. This type of failure leads to pitting and spalling as the flaking progresses, resulting in eventual failure. There are many situations when minor pitting of a gear tooth is not cause for concern. As

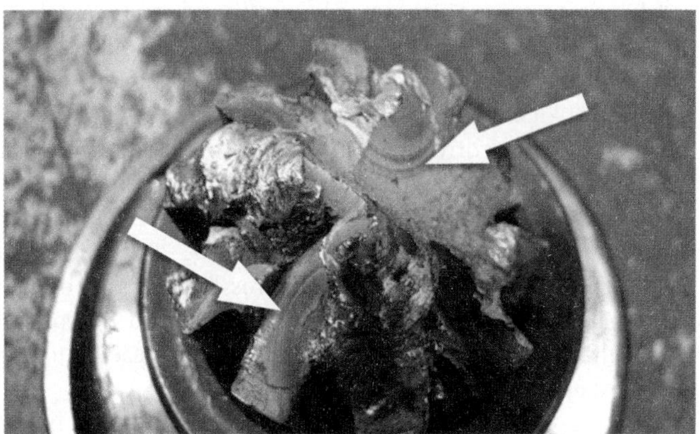

FIGURE 50-51 This shaft shows classic beach marks indicative of a torsional fatigue failure.

FIGURE 50-52 This shaft shows a star-type fracture caused by repeated fatigue stresses.

pitting progresses and the tooth surface breaks down, however, the involute shape of the tooth will be lost, leading to noise and vibration.

Abuse Failures

Several failures are the result of poor operator training and/or outright abuse. So-called **abuse failures** occur because the operator is ill prepared to operate a particular machine, or he or she simply didn't care. Shock loading a machine is a common form of operator abuse. For example, when the operator rams a machine's bucket into a pile, a stress load is placed on the entire driveline. Common failures that occur from this abuse are twisted shafts, driveshaft torsional failure, and/or broken universal joints.

Spinout, whether in a main differential or an interaxle differential is another common source of operator abuse that can cause damage. When the operator allows the wheels to spin, the differential side and spider gears are rotating at high speeds. This can lead to severe shock loads if the spinning wheels suddenly gain traction. Spinout can be a common source of failure in haulage trucks with single or tandem axles. Spinout is always an operator abuse situation and is 100% avoidable by using differential locks and/or waiting for a tow. Spinout damage can be devastating to a drive system. **FIGURE 50-53** shows a side gear shattered by a sudden shock load caused by a spinning wheel suddenly gaining traction. **FIGURE 50-54** shows the damage that can occur when spinout is allowed to continue. This differential spider gear has become welded to the cross leg and then broken free again. The wildly spinning components in a differential throw the lubricant away from where it is needed leading to this type of damage.

The preceding is by no means a comprehensive list of failures that can occur due to abuse. It is merely a sampling of common driver-caused failures that are totally preventable with proper training.

Lubrication Failure

Lubrication failures are normally due to poor maintenance, incorrect lubrication, lack of lubrication, and/or contaminated lube. Driveline lubricants are the lifeblood of components, so any lubricant failure can lead directly to component failure. **FIGURE 50-55** shows an input gear from a standard transmission that basically melted during operation due to lack of lubricant. Think of the heat required to do that to a component!

Contaminated lubricant is a serious problem. Lubricant can become contaminated in several ways. One way is by mixing the wrong type of lubricants. Contamination also occurs when dirt is ingested through improperly filtered vents during normal component breathing. (All drivetrain components are vented to the atmosphere to allow components to breathe as the lubricant heats up and cools down.) Lubricant can also be contaminated by the introduction of foreign material during poor maintenance practices or because of component breakdown. Water can also contaminate lubricant. If the machine is operated in a wet area in which water rises above the component vent level, water ingestion could occur.

FIGURE 50-54 This differential spider gear had become welded to the differential cross and then broken free again.

FIGURE 50-55 It is hard to imagine the amount of heat that can be generated when components have insufficient lube, but results like this burned input gear from a Fuller transmission are commonplace when lubrication is absent.

FIGURE 50-53 Sudden shock when a spinning wheel hits dry pavement can lead to shock failures such as this broken differential side gear.

▶ Wrap-Up

Ready for Review

- Axles can be divided into three categories—steer axles, dead axles, and live or drive axles.
- Dead axles merely support the machine weight.
- Live axles actually drive the machine, so they are also called drive axles.
- Drive axles allow the power from the engine to turn a 90-degree corner to send that power to the wheels.
- Drive axles provide a gear reduction in a drivetrain
- All drive axle gears are bevel gears, meaning that they intersect at an angle (in this case, 90 degrees).
- Bevel gearsets usually consist of a large crown (or ring) gear and a smaller pinion gear.
- Bevel gears are subdivided into several types, including plain bevel, spiral bevel, hypoid, and generoid.
- Plain bevel gears are similar to spur gears and have the same problems with noise and weakness. Plain bevel gear pinions are mounted at the crown gear's centerline.
- Spiral bevel gears are quieter and stronger than plain bevel and their pinion gears are mounted at the centerline of the crown gear.
- Hypoid gears are a type of spiral bevel gear that mounts the pinion below the centerline of the crown gear.
- Amboid gears are a type of spiral bevel gearing in which the pinion gear is mounted above the centerline of the crown gear.
- Generoid gears have asymmetrical tooth flanks for extra strength.
- The drive axle is commonly misnamed the differential because the differential gearset is inside the drive axle. The drive axle and the differential are, however, different.
- The differential gear arrangement allows the power from the engine to be split equally between two axle shafts while allowing the axle shafts to turn at different speeds when required.
- The differential gearset consists of two side gears, four pinion or spider gears, and a differential spider or cross.
- The differential gears are contained in the differential case.
- As a wheeled machine turns a corner, the inner wheel must slow down and the outer wheel must speed up. The differential gearset allows this to happen.
- The differential always splits the available torque equally between the two wheels.
- Controlled traction differentials allow the engine to build more torque before a wheel can spin in low traction situations.
- Bias torque differentials can send more torque to the wheel with good traction.
- Differential locks are used during low traction situations only.
- Double reduction drive axles use two gear reductions at all times.
- Planetary two-speed drive axles use a planetary gearset to produce two ratios through the drive axle.
- Tandem systems use interaxle differentials to divide the torque between the two axles.
- An interaxle differential splits the available torque between two drive axles, not the wheels.
- Axle shafts on lighter duty machines are called semi-floating.
- Heavier machines use full-floating axle shafts.
- Drive axle lubrication can effected by splash from the rotation of the crown wheel or by lube pump
- Power dividers typically will have a gear pump to ensure adequate lubrication of the interaxle differential gears.
- Proper maintenance, as with all other components, is essential to the service life of a drive axle. Timely fluid checks and changes can go a long way to protecting the equipment.
- Always check for metal particles in the drive axle lubricant during service. This can be a good indicator of a failing drive axle.
- When filling or topping up drive axle lubricant, always use the correct fluid, and be aware that some drive axles require fluid to be added in more than one location.
- All drive axles require the same four adjustments during overhaul: pinion bearing preload, pinion depth setting, side bearing preload, and the gearset backlash adjustment.
- Always mark the components, such as the side bearing retaining caps and the differential case halves, during disassembly so they can be reassembled correctly.
- The differential gears, the spider gears, and the side gears run on thrust washers. These and the surfaces they contact should be carefully inspected for wear.
- All components in the axle should be checked for wear and damage—not just the obviously failed pieces.
- While rebuilding a drive axle, remember that the cost of replacement parts is small compared to having to redo the job. Replace all questionable parts.
- Crown and pinion gears are replaced as a set only.
- Contact pattern is controlled by pinion depth and gearset backlash.
- Pinion and side bearing preload ensures rigidity in the gearset.
- After reassembling a drive axle, it is essential to check and, if necessary, correct the contact pattern.
- A conventional contact pattern should have three elements: close to but clear of the toe of the tooth, centered between the top land and the root, and extended across at least 50% of the tooth face.
- Generoid gearsets have a centralized tooth contact pattern.
- After the contact pattern is correct, the thrust screw, if present, should be adjusted.

- Component failures occur because of four basic issues: shock load failures, fatigue failures, lubrication failures, and abuse failures.
- When a component fails, it is essential to determine the correct cause to prevent reoccurrence.

Key Terms

abuse failure Failure directly attributed to driver or other person's actions.

amboid gear A bevel gear arrangement with the pinion gear mounted above the centerline of the crown gear.

backlash The required clearance between two meshing gears

beach mark Semicircular mark in a fracture indicating repeated overload.

bearing adjuster Threaded wheel used to tighten the side bearing races.

bearing adjuster lock Lock to secure the bearing adjusters.

bevel gears Gears that intersect at an angle—usually 90 degrees.

carrier The component that holds the support bearings for the drive axle gearing.

contact pattern The contact area between two gear teeth in contact.

controlled traction differential A differential that allows the engine to build more torque before the wheels can slip.

crown gear A large bevel gear that is driven by a smaller pinion gear in the bevel gearset; also known as a ring gear.

dead axle An axle that supports machine weight only.

differential case The housing that holds the differential gears.

differential cross The mechanism that holds the differential pinion or spider gears; also known as the differential spider.

differential gear A gear arrangement that splits the available torque equally between two wheels while allowing them to turn at different speeds when required.

differential gearset Consists of two side gears, four pinion gears, and a cross; allows for speed difference between the two axle shafts of the drive axle when turning.

differential pinion gear A beveled gear that is a component of the differential gearset; it is fitted to the four legs of the differential cross and rotates with it; also known as a spider gear.

differential spider The part that holds the differential pinion or spider gears; also known as the differential cross.

double-reduction drive axle A drive axle that uses two gear reductions at all times.

drive axle The axle that drives the machine by turning the power from the driveshaft 90 degrees to deliver it to the wheels; also known as a live axle.

fatigue failure Failure of components due to repeated overload.

full-floating axle shaft An axle that carries none of the machine weight.

gas pocket Imperfection in the adhesion of molten metal during the casting or forming process.

generoid An asymmetrical tooth design it gives added strength to the hypoid and amboid gearsets.

heel The end of a crown gear tooth furthest from the center of its axis.

helical double-reduction drive axle A double-reduction drive axle that uses a helical gearset for the second gear reduction.

helical double-reduction two-speed drive axle A double-reduction drive axle that uses two selectable sets of helical gears as the second gear reduction.

hypoid gearing A type of spiral bevel gearset that mounts the pinion gear below the centerline of the crown gear.

integral carrier housing A drive axle housing that does not have a removable carrier.

interaxle differential A differential gearset that splits the available torque equally between two drive axles; also called a power divider.

lengthwise bearing The contact pattern along the tooth face from the toe toward the heel.

live axle The axle that drives the machine by turning the power from the driveshaft 90 degrees to deliver it to the wheels and providing the final gear reduction in the drivetrain; also known as a drive axle.

locking differential A system that actively prevents differential action from occurring when engaged.

lubrication failure Failure caused by incorrect lubricant, contaminated lubricant, or lack of lubricant.

output shaft The output shaft of an interaxle differential. The rear side gear is part of or splined to the output shaft; also known as the through shaft.

pinion depth The mounting position of the pinion in relation to the crown gear center of axis.

pinion gear A small driving gear.

plain bevel gear A bevel gearset with straight-cut teeth.

planetary double-reduction drive axle A drive axle that incorporates two planetary gearsets to achieve two gear reductions.

planetary two-speed drive axle A two-speed drive axle that uses a planetary gearset for the low range.

power divider A differential gearset that splits the available torque equally between two drive axles; also called an interaxle differential.

preload Negative end play, or less than zero clearance.

profile bearing Contact pattern between the root and the top land of the tooth.

removable carrier type A drive axle housing with a removable carrier.

ring gear A large bevel gear that is driven by a smaller pinion gear in the bevel gearset; also known as a crown gear.

root The radius shape between the bottoms of two teeth; also called fillet radius.

section break A point where the diameter of a shaft or thickness of a component changes.

semi-floating axle shaft An axle shaft that carries the entire weight of the machine on its outer end.

shock load failure Fracture caused by one sudden shock.

side gears Part of the differential gearset; the side gears are splined to the axles.

spider gear A beveled gear that is a component of the differential gearset; it is fitted to the four legs of the differential cross and rotates with it; also known as a differential pinion gear.

spinout A low-traction situation where one drive wheel or one drive axle spins wildly while the other remains stationary.

spiral bevel gear A bevel gearset with spirally or helically cut gears.

steering axle An axle that allows the machine to turn.

stringer Small inclusion in a cast or formed metal that weaken it.

tandem Two drive axles connected by a power divider.

through shaft The output shaft of an interaxle differential. The rear side gear is part of, or splined to, the through shaft; also known as output shaft.

thrust screw A screw that stops the crown gear from flexing under load.

toe The end of a crown gear tooth closest to the center of its axis.

tooth face The area that actually comes into contact with a mating gear and is parallel to the gear's axis of rotation.

top land The apex of a tooth.

tridem A driving arrangement where three drive axles split the driving torque.

Review Questions

1. In a single-speed drive axle, the differential case always travels at which of the following speeds?
   - **a.** 50% of crown gear speed
   - **b.** 200% of crown gear speed
   - **c.** 0% of crown gear speed
   - **d.** 100% of crown gear speed
2. In a normal or nonlocking differential, if one axle is turning at 96% of case speed, at what speed is the other axle turning?
   - **a.** 96% of case speed
   - **b.** 100% of case speed
   - **c.** 104% of case speed
   - **d.** 92% of case speed
3. Which of the following describes a double-reduction drive axle?
   - **a.** The axle has two speeds.
   - **b.** It has a helical gear mounted on either side of the differential case.
   - **c.** It uses two reductions (a compound reduction) through the axle at all times.
   - **d.** It is a special axle used in low-floor buses.
4. When a machine is moving and no differential action is taking place, which of the following is a correct statement about the spider and side gears?
   - **a.** They are stationary inside the differential case.
   - **b.** They are moving opposite to the case direction.
   - **c.** They are each turning opposite directions.
   - **d.** They are freewheeling in the same direction.
5. Which of the following axle types normally results in wheel loss should the axle shaft break?
   - **a.** Semi floating
   - **b.** Full-floating
   - **c.** 3/4 floating
   - **d.** Nonfloating
6. Which of the following gears are responsible for differential action?
   - **a.** The ring and pinion gears
   - **b.** The ring and side gears
   - **c.** The spider and pinion gears
   - **d.** The spider and side gears
7. Which of the following are two critical adjustments of a rear drive axle assembly not related to tooth contact pattern?
   - **a.** Pinion depth and gearset backlash
   - **b.** Crown gear depth and pinion depth
   - **c.** Side bearing and pinion bearing preload
   - **d.** Crown gear and pinion torque
8. If a drive axle's contact pattern is too close to the toe, which of the following must be done to correct it?
   - **a.** Increase backlash.
   - **b.** Decrease backlash.
   - **c.** Move the pinion toward the crown gear.
   - **d.** Move the pinion away from the crown gear.
9. If a drive axle tooth contact pattern is too low on the tooth (at the root), which of the following must be done to correct it?
   - **a.** Increase backlash.
   - **b.** Decrease backlash.
   - **c.** Move the pinion toward the ring gear.
   - **d.** Move the pinion away from the ring gear.
10. You examine a pinion gear that has broken and see beach marks clearly present at the break point. Which of the following likely caused the break?
    - **a.** A sudden shock the drivetrain
    - **b.** A repeated overloading of the drivetrain over a period of time
    - **c.** A failure of the axle lubrication system
    - **d.** Spinout

ASE Technician A/Technician B Style Questions

1. Technician A says that a hypoid gearset has the pinion gear mounted above the centerline of the crown wheel. Technician B says that a generoid gearset uses a stronger tooth design. Who is correct?
   - **a.** Technician A
   - **b.** Technician B
   - **c.** Both A and B
   - **d.** Neither A nor B
2. Technician A says that a differential gearset allows for drive axle wheel speed difference in turns. Technician B says that a differential gearset allows a single wheel on a drive axle to spin wildly while the other wheel remains stationary. Who is correct?
   - **a.** Technician A
   - **b.** Technician B

c. Both A and B
d. Neither A nor B

3. Technician A says that a controlled traction differential allows the engine to build more torque in poor traction conditions. Technician B says that controlled traction differentials prevent any differential action from occurring while engaged. Who is correct?
   a. Technician A
   b. Technician B
   c. Both A and B
   d. Neither A nor B
4. Technician A says that in a tandem-drive machine most of the driving effort is provided by the front-rear axle. Technician B says that the rear-rear drive axle only receives 50% of the available driving torque. Who is correct?
   a. Technician A
   b. Technician B
   c. Both A and B
   d. Neither A nor B
5. Technician A says that two-speed drive axles offer more speed ranges to a machine operator. Technician B says that two-speed helical axles use a smaller crown gear so are less apt to flex under load. Who is correct?
   a. Technician A
   b. Technician B
   c. Both A and B
   d. Neither A nor B
6. Technician A says that an amboid gearset has the pinion mounted below the centerline of the crown gear. Technician B says that the crown gear teeth of an amboid gearset are concave on the drive side. Who is correct?
   a. Technician A
   b. Technician B
   c. Both A and B
   d. Neither A nor B
7. Technician A says that a drive axle must be filled from the plug at the rear of the housing to the correct level. Technician B says that some drive axles have more than one fill plug. Who is correct?
   a. Technician A
   b. Technician B
   c. Both A and B
   d. Neither A nor B
8. Technician A says that the pinion depth adjustment influences the drive axle's contact pattern. Technician B says that the gearset backlash influences the drive axle's contact pattern. Who is correct?
   a. Technician A
   b. Technician B
   c. Both A and B
   d. Neither A nor B
9. Technician A says that side gear support bearings should always be changed when overhauling a drive axle. Technician B says that spinout damage is usually visible as excess heat stress on the differential components. Who is correct?
   a. Technician A
   b. Technician B
   c. Both A and B
   d. Neither A nor B
10. Technician A says that side bearing preload causes a slight flexing of the bearing mounts. Technician B says that gearset backlash is set after side bearing preload. Who is correct?
    a. Technician A
    b. Technician B
    c. Both A and B
    d. Neither A nor B

CHAPTER 51

Track-Type Machine Steering Systems

Knowledge Objectives

After reading this chapter, you will be able to:

- **K51001** Understand the fundamentals of track machine clutch and brake steering systems.
- **K51002** Explain the fundamentals of track machine differential steering systems.

Skills Objectives

After reading this chapter, you will be able to:

- **S51001** Discuss track machine steering system diagnostics.
- **S51002** Describe track machine general steering system repair.

▶ Introduction

Tracked machines, such as dozers, track loaders, drills, and many other types of machines, have unique needs when it comes to steering arrangements. Because the tracks on almost all track-type machines stay parallel to each other, the only way to steer most track-type machines is to change the speed of the tracks in relation to each other. Some track machines have a two-piece frame and use articulated steering systems similar to those on wheeled machines with articulated steering (articulated steering is covered in the Conventional Steering Systems chapter). This chapter covers track machines that have one-piece main frames (straight frame) and are steered with mostly mechanical components. There are three different systems to do this.

One way to steer a straight frame track–type machine is by stopping the drive to one track and driving the opposite track around it with a mechanical-drive arrangement. This is done by disconnecting the drive to one track with a clutch and/or applying a brake to it while the other track drive stays connected and continues driving. This is sometimes called skid steering because of the stopped track skidding on the ground. See **FIGURE 51-1** to see a simple illustration of a how a track machine turns.

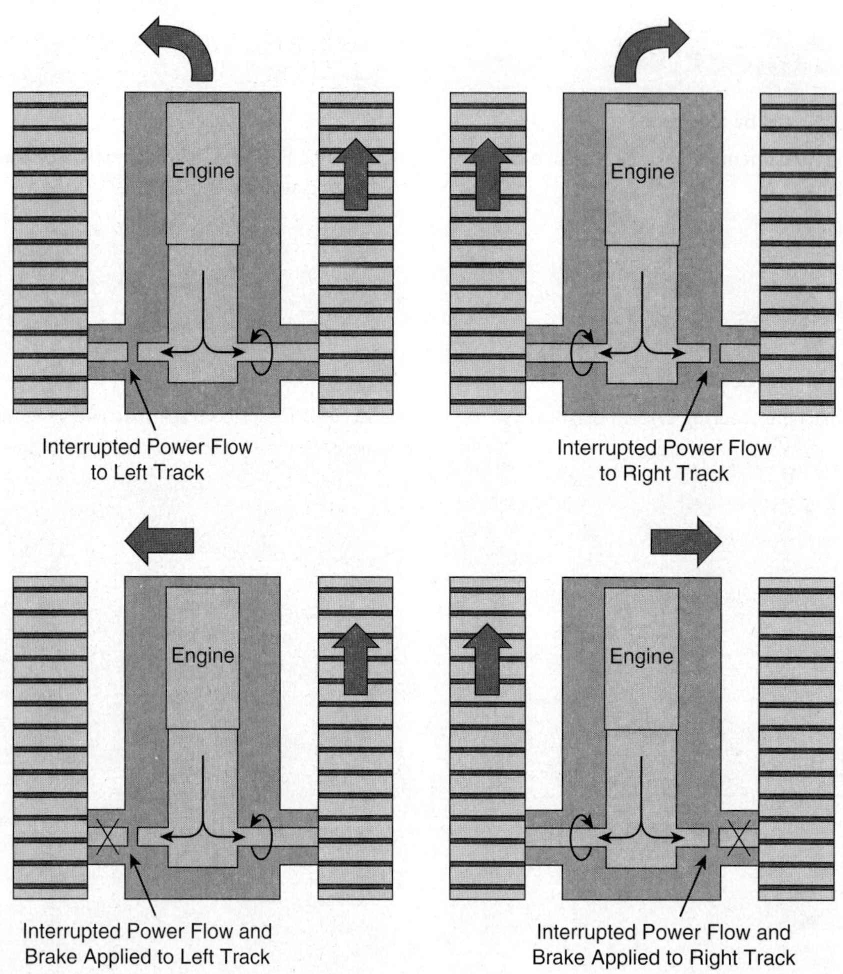

FIGURE 51-1 How a track machine turns.

You Are the Mobile Heavy Equipment Technician

You are asked to investigate an operator complaint on a John Deere 450G dozer. The operator says that the machine works fine in a forward direction and turning right, but when he turns left, there is a significant grabbing or jerking. You question the operator about the situation and determine that this jerking happens only on sharper turns and not as much on gradual turns. You operate the machine and verify that the operator complaint is valid.

1. What type of steering system is on this type of machine?
2. Do you think the problem is on the mechanical side or the control side?
3. What would you check first to determine the cause of the issue?
4. Could this problem be caused by lack of or improper maintenance?

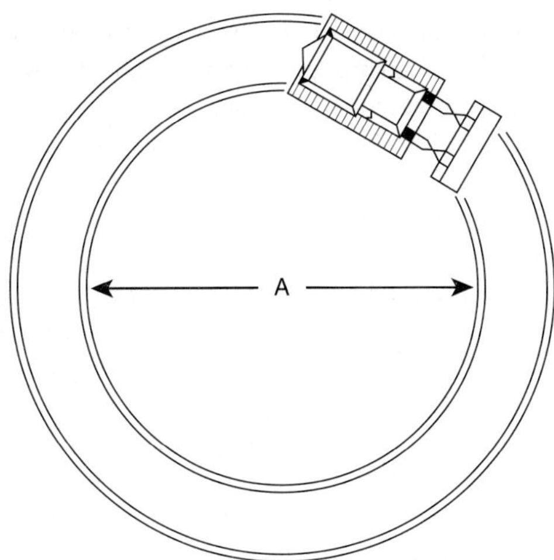

FIGURE 51-2 Differential steer machine turning.

The second way to do it is to use a differential steering arrangement to adjust the speeds between the two tracks to make the machine turn. With differential steering, both tracks are driven when the machine is turning through a gradual turn. Differential steering uses a combination of gears and a hydraulic drive to drive the tracks at different speeds relative to each other. It is also possible to make the tracks turn in opposite directions or **counterrotate** with differential steering systems. This enables the machine to perform on-the-spot turns for turning in tight quarters. **FIGURE 51-2** provides an illustration of a differential steer machine turning.

A third way to steer a track-type machine is to incorporate a two-speed mechanical drive system for the left and right tracks. This gives the operator a way to turn the machine without stopping the drive to one track. The downfall is that the steering will be a fixed arc because of the fixed speed differential between high and low. With this system. when the operator wants to turn while driving with both tracks, one track is put in low range and the other is put in high range. A machine with this steering feature also has steering clutches and brakes to provide one-track drive for sharp turns (skid steering turn). Because track drive machines control or drive the tracks individually, there is no need for a conventional differential gearset in the driveline as in wheeled equipment.

Two other drive systems for track machines are hydrostatic and electric. Hydrostatic drive uses a hydraulic motor to drive each of the track sprockets individually. Electric-drive systems either use an electrical motor to power the machines driveline or, like the hydrostatic system, use two electric motors to drive the track sprockets individually. Both of these hydrostatic- and electric sprocket–drive systems are capable of driving both tracks at the same speed: one track slower than the other for gradual turns and one track only for sharp turns, and they are also capable of turning the tracks in opposite directions for an on-the-spot turn. Hydrostatic and electrical drives provide infinitely variable speed changes between the two tracks for turns of varying degrees. Caterpillar uses a combination of electric drive and differential steering to steer one of its dozers. This particular drive system also provides infinitely variable speeds and counterrotation. In this chapter, we concentrate on the clutch and brake steering systems and differential steering systems.

SAFETY TIP

Concern for your safety and of those around you is paramount in any work environment. Follow these safety tips:

- You may be required to lift heavy components when repairing a steering system. Make sure you are competent with proper lifting methods and use only approved and inspected lifting devices.
- Machine cabs may have to be tilted to allow access to steering components. *Do not* work under a raised cab unless it is securely held in place.
- Some friction material may contain asbestos fibers. Treat any dust that has been created from friction material wear as if it contains asbestos. This will include wearing appropriate breathing protection and hand protection.
- Some steering systems use extremely high hydraulic pressures. Take caution and wear appropriate PPE before working on high-pressure steering systems.
- Always refer to the manufacturer's service information before working on steering systems.
- A malfunctioning steering system has the potential to make the machine a safety hazard. If the operator is unable to control the machine when it is traveling, then it could put the operator or any workers close by at risk. For this reason, the technician must always confirm the steering system operates properly before the machine is put back into service.

▶ Track Machine Clutch and Brake Steering System Fundamentals

K51001

Track-type machines that may use mechanical steering systems are track-type tractors (crawler dozers/bulldozers) and track loaders.

The power flow for older track-type machines that use mechanical methods to steer the machine is as follows: diesel engine flywheel to clutch or torque converter, to transmission (manual or power shift), to pinion gear, to bevel gear, to steering clutches, to final drives, to sprockets, to tracks. Between the steering clutches and final drives there are also brakes to stop the tracks from turning. See **FIGURE 51-3** to see the pedal controls of a machine that uses linkage controlled steering clutches and brakes.

The drive to each sprocket can be connected and/or disconnected by its steering clutch. Steering clutches allow the operator to stop or drive each track individually. The steering clutches use friction material that is squeezed against a smooth metal surface to transfer torque through them. Springs or oil pressure can provide the squeezing force. Some slippage is acceptable as the clutch is engaged or disengaged, but when the clutch is fully engaged, there shouldn't be any slipping between the input and output of the clutch.

Although there are several variations of steering clutches, currently they are mostly based on a multidisc-type clutch that can be either a spring-applied/oil-released or a hydraulically applied type of clutch.

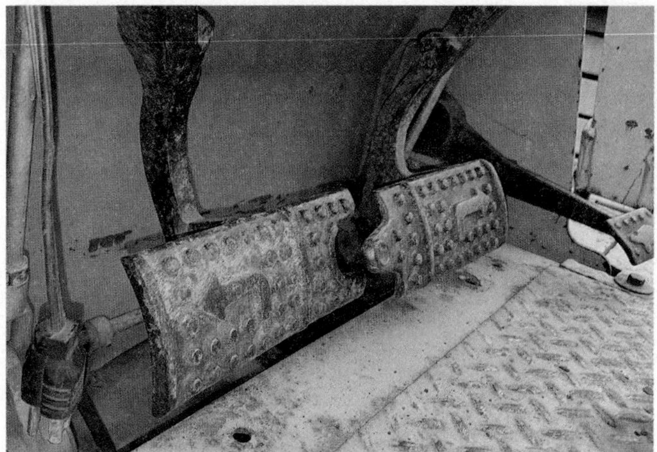

FIGURE 51-3 Brake pedals of a machine that uses steering clutches and brakes.

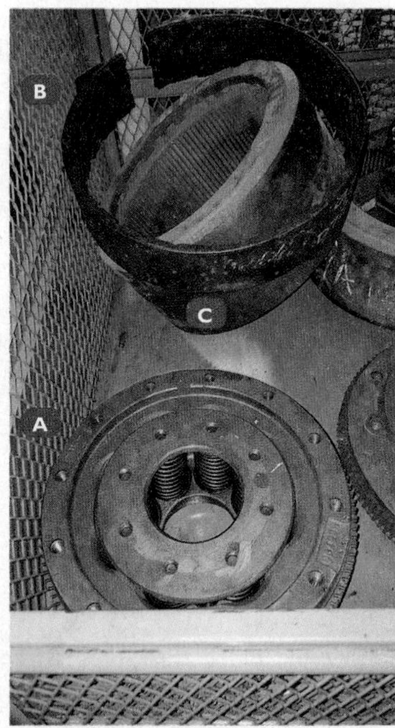

FIGURE 51-4 **A.** Steering clutch. **B.** Brake band. **C.** brake drum.

Steering brakes also use friction to stop one track from turning so that the machine can pivot on the stopped track while the other track continues to drive. Steering brakes may be either a band-type brake that is squeezed around a rotating drum or multidisc-type brakes. **FIGURE 51-4** shows one of the steering clutches and brake bands of a dozer using this steering system.

As machine horsepower increases for larger machines, steering clutch and brake torque capacity must also increase so that they can handle the load without slipping. Clutch and brake torque capacity is directly related to the frictional surface area in contact and the clamping force squeezing the components together. To increase torque capacity of brakes, the manufacturers either increase the diameter or number of discs in a multidisc brake or clutch, or the width and diameter of the brake band friction material and drum. Clamping force and/or the friction material's coefficient of friction could also be increased to increase clutch capacity. To increase the clamping force when the clutch or brake is spring applied, the number or the strength of the springs is increased. To increase the capacity of a hydraulically applied clutch or brake, either the oil pressure and/or the piston surface area is increased.

When the operator wants to steer a machine with steering clutches and brakes, he or she releases one steering clutch to stop driving one track. This could give a partial turn, depending on the ground conditions and the load on the machine's blade, bucket, or ripper. For a more positive turn, the operator applies the brake to the track that has no power flow to it and continues to drive the opposite track.

The original way for the operator to control this was to move mechanical levers or pedals in the operator station that would be connected by linkages to the steering clutches and brakes. This evolved into hydraulically actuated clutches and brakes that are controlled by the operator moving a mechanical lever. Eventually, electronic controls replaced all mechanical controls for hydraulically actuated clutches and brakes. This allows the operator of a very large track-type machine, Caterpillar's 850 HP D11, for example, to steer it with the strength of one finger.

▶ TECHNICIAN TIP

In steering brakes and clutches that have multiple discs, different terms are used for the wear parts that transfer torque through the clutch or brake. One set of discs has friction material bonded to their face, and they will be squeezed against another set of smooth steel plates. Following is an example of some different terms you may see used.

- Discs: friction linings, fiber plates, clutch facing discs, clutch discs
- Metal plates: steel plates, reaction plates, steels

Discs and plates have either internal or external teeth or tangs to hold them to one part of the clutch or brake assembly.

Spring-Applied Steering Clutches

Spring-applied steering clutches can be found in small to large older dozers and track loaders and are still used to steer some small current dozers. They rely on spring pressure to squeeze a stack of friction discs and steel plates together to transfer torque through them. The discs are squeezed between a smooth-faced hub and a smooth-faced movable pressure plate. Their operating principles are similar to the spring-applied flywheel clutches. **FIGURE 51-5** shows a spring-applied multidisc steering clutch.

The clutch is driven by a flanged hub (input) that is driven by a bevel gear that is driven by the transmission output pinion gear. The bevel gear and the left and right clutch drive hubs are fastened to a shaft that is supported by bearings that are supported in the machine's frame. This assembly is located roughly under the operator's seat inside the machine's main frame. Usually, three compartments are part of the machine's frame that houses the bevel gear and the left and right steering clutches. Each clutch assembly drives a brake drum (output) that is bolted to a flange that in turn drives a final drive pinion gear. The brake drum is surrounded by a band-type brake. **FIGURE 51-6** shows a brake drum and band with the steering clutch splines inside.

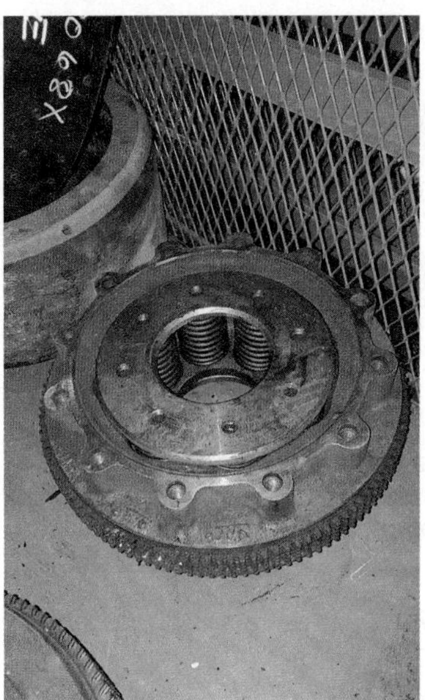

FIGURE 51-5 Spring-applied multidisc steering clutch.

FIGURE 51-6 Steering clutch housing and brake drum with band.

The flanges (clutch input and final drive input) are usually pressed onto tapered and splined shafts (bevel gear and final drive input), with 5 to 50 tons of force, before a large nut and locking device is installed. This is necessitated because of the extreme torque forces and shock loads that are transmitted through the flanges as the machine is stopped, started, and steered. The flanges are fastened to the steering clutch with a ring of threaded fasteners.

For a spring-applied clutch, one of two types of springs is used to create the necessary clamping force: one is a Belleville type of spring (dished washer shape) that is either singular or stacked back to back; the other is a coil spring type that is arranged in multiples around the outside circumference of the clutch assembly. Both types of springs apply pressure to a series of alternating friction discs and plates by squeezing the drive hub and a pressure plate together. The plates have internal splines or tangs that are driven by the drive hub. The discs have friction material bonded to a metal plate that is externally splined. The external splines drive the brake drum that then drives the input to the final drive.

Oil for cooling and lubrication circulates past most steering clutches and brakes, but not all. The friction material on the discs or bands is grooved to allow passage for oil flow, letting heat be carried away from the discs/band. **FIGURE 51-7** shows the grooves in a wet brake band.

When oil circulates through a steering clutch housing and around the clutches and brakes, they are considered to be "wet" steering clutches and brakes. In machines equipped with wet steering clutches, all compartments usually use the same oil. The oil flow originates from one section of a multi-section powertrain oil pump and flows through passages in the steering clutch and brake housing. Once it flows past the clutches and brakes, it drains into the machine's steering clutch case. Another section of the multi-section pump moves the oil through an oil cooler to transfer heat into the engine's coolant. When the machine uses a dry steering clutch arrangement, the bevel gear housing has its own oil that is sealed from the steering clutch compartments.

Overheated clutch and brake components quickly deteriorate, becoming worn out or damaged and nonfunctional. Wet-type clutches handle higher horsepower applications and almost always have the oil cooled to keep the clutch temperatures below damaging levels to ensure longevity. Dry-type clutches and brakes are used on low-horsepower machines and are not usually subject to high temperatures.

Operation of Spring-Applied Steering Brakes and Clutches

For mechanically controlled spring-applied steering clutches, a mechanism called the release bearing pulls the pressure plate away from the drive hub against spring pressure when moved by the clutch release linkage. When the pressure plate is moved

FIGURE 51-7 The hydraulic line supplies cooling oil to the brake band.

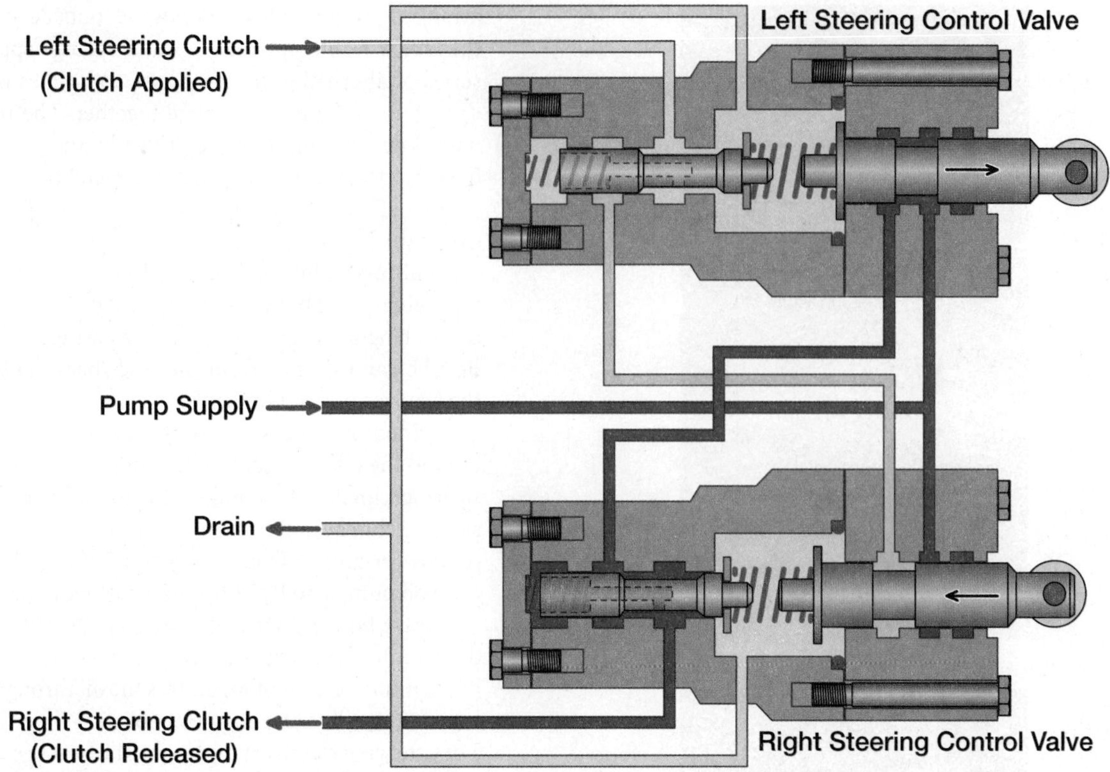

FIGURE 51-8 Oil-assisted clutch release valve.

away, it allows the plates and discs to turn independently of each other, and therefore torque transfer through the clutch is stopped. Linkage connects the operator control (lever or pedal) to a pivoting yoke that moves the release bearing cage with the release bearing inside it. The release bearing outer race does not rotate and is moved sideways while the inner race rotates with the clutch and acts on the pressure plate.

Further advancements in design for this type of clutch was to use hydraulic assist to cage the springs and release the pressure from the clutch pack. This advancement lessens the operator effort required to control clutch release. This system uses a mechanical linkage to actuate a spool valve that sends oil to a cylinder. The cylinder pushes on the release bearing yoke to release the clutch. See **FIGURE 51-8** to see an oil assisted clutch release mechanism.

The oil pressure for this type of clutch assist is sourced from the transmission control system and is usually fairly low at around 300 psi. This oil is most often prioritized in the transmission system to be available to the clutch and/or brake system first.

Oil-Applied Steering Clutches

Spring-applied steering clutches are always engaged until released by oil pressure or mechanical movement. Oil-applied clutches are disengaged until there is oil pressure applied to a piston. They are similar in design but don't have any springs. As oil pressure builds behind the piston it pushes on the clutch plates and discs and torque will be transferred between the clutch's drive hub (input) and the brake drum (output). See **FIGURE 51-9** to see an illustration of an oil-applied steering clutch.

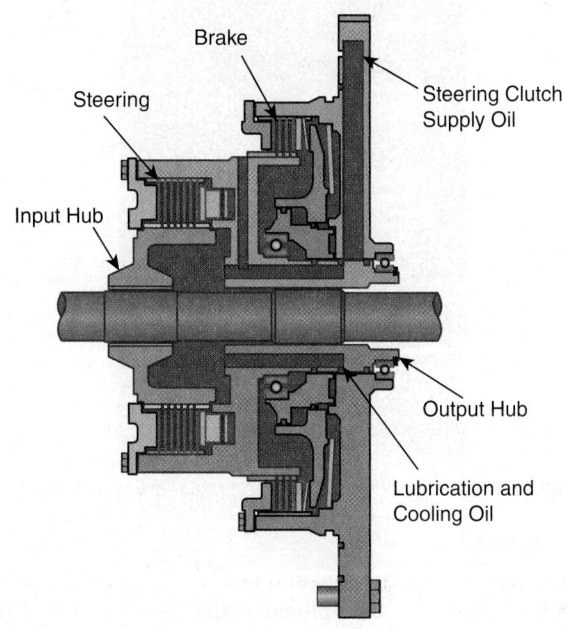

FIGURE 51-9 Oil-applied steering clutch.

This type of clutch can be found on all sizes of track-type machines. The typical power flow for a machine that uses this style of steering clutch is as follows: the machine's transmission output pinion drives a ring gear that drives the clutch shaft. The clutch shaft drives the left and right clutch hubs that are splined externally to drive the clutch discs. When the clutch is engaged, the discs drive the steel plates through friction; tangs on the plates' outer circumference transfer drive into the brake drum, and the brake drum sends torque to the final drive. This arrangement typically uses a band-style brake to stop the drum for tighter turns.

Oil-applied steering clutches can also be used in conjunction with multidisc-type brakes to slow or stop the tracks. In this case, then, the discs will drive a housing that is the output of the clutch and is in turn splined to accept the splines of the brake discs.

Operation of Oil-Applied Steering Clutches

When no oil pressure is applied to the steering clutch piston, the discs and plates are able to rotate independently. Oil is sent to the piston through a rotating seal from a spool type valve that is moved by operator-actuated linkage. Oil pressure is normally present at the clutch to provide drive torque to the final drive, but when the operator wants to steer the machine, the spool valve is moved, and oil is drained from the clutch. With the clutch released, the machine makes a gradual turn until the brake is applied on the same side to lock the track, and then the machine makes a sharp turn.

Like oil-assisted clutches, oil-applied clutches receive their oil from the transmission control system. **FIGURE 51-10** depicts the hydraulic system for powertrain controls of a typical dozer with hydraulically actuated steering brakes and clutches.

Steering Brakes—Band Type

Older machines with steering clutches and brakes used band-type brakes to slow down or to lock one track up when steering the machine. These brakes also often double as parking brakes. Smaller and older machines used mechanical linkage from the operator input (levers or pedals) to apply the left and right brake bands. The brake bands surround the brake drums and are lined with friction material. The friction material is riveted and/or bonded to a flexible seven-eighths of a circle metal band. The friction material is likely in multiple pieces and may or may not have grooves in its contact face. The grooves allow oil to circulate around the friction material to cool and clean it. See **FIGURE 51-11** for an example of a **band brake**.

Operation of Band-Type Steering Brakes

To operate band-type steering brakes, the open part of the band is squeezed together, and the friction material grabs the smooth exterior surface of the brake drum and slows it or stops it from turning. After the steering clutch is released, the brake is applied to stop the final drive pinion shaft, which stops the track. When the brake is released, a support screw or a couple of light springs hold the brake away from the drum so it doesn't drag.

For larger and/or newer machines, the band brake actuation was updated to either a spring-applied/oil-released or oil-applied

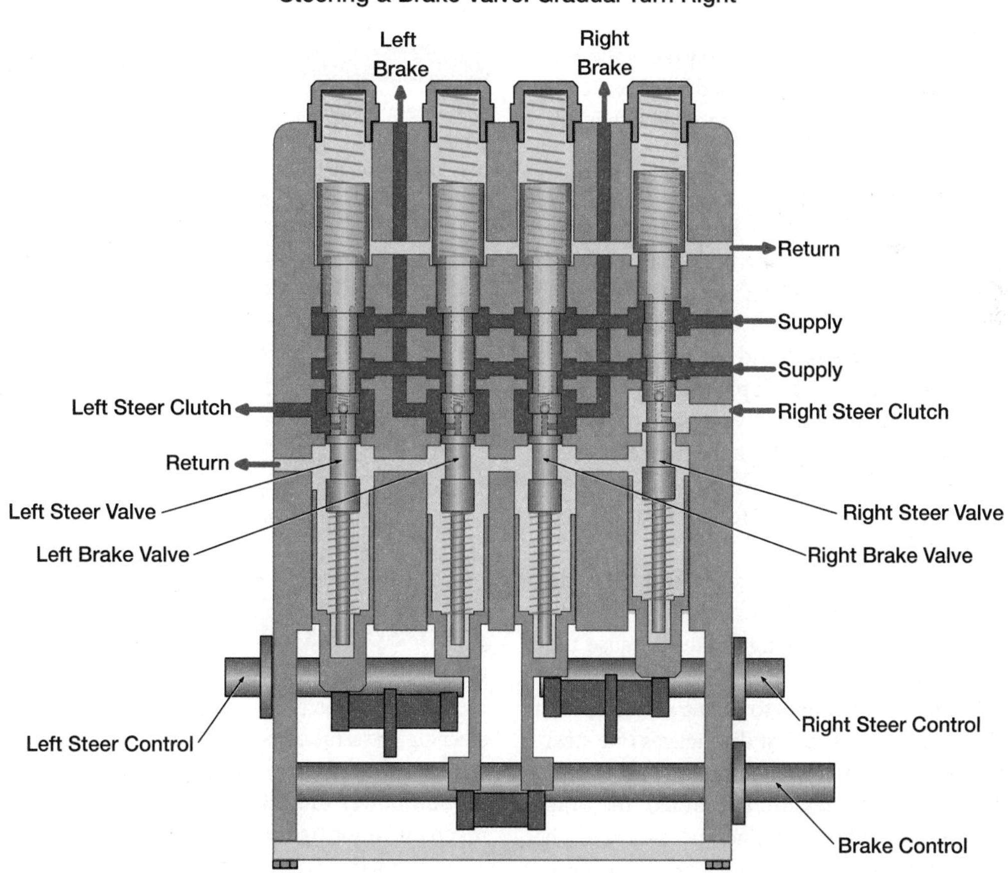

FIGURE 51-10 Hydraulic system.

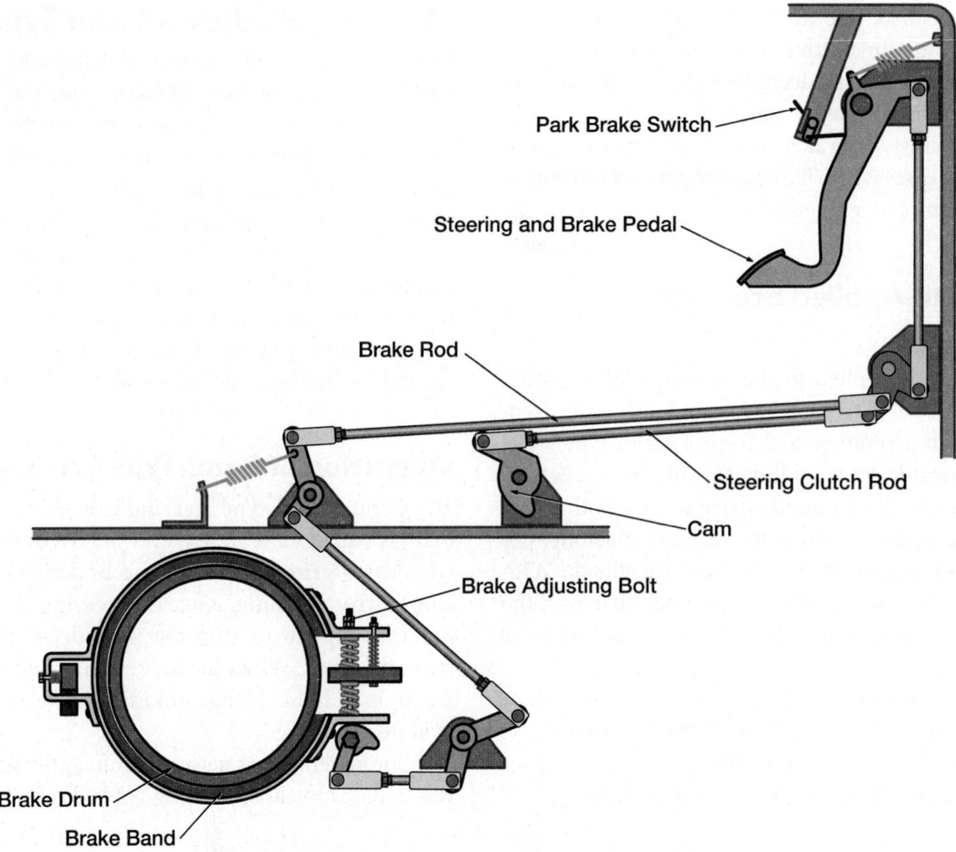

FIGURE 51-11 Band brake system.

brake that uses a booster piston or cylinder to apply the brake. This arrangement provides a way to use spring applied band brakes for parking brakes when oil is drained away from the brake cylinder.

Multidisc Steering Brakes

Most new, medium to large track-type machines that use steering clutches and brakes use multidisc type brakes. Just like the band-type brakes, they are also between the steering clutch output and the final drive input in the driveline torque transfer sequence. They are spring applied and oil released with a Belleville washer type of spring used to apply them. The spring pushes directly on the piston, and the opposite side of the piston pushes on the discs and plates. The appearance of these brakes could be mistaken for a clutch unless you are able to see where they are located in the drivetrain. **FIGURE 51-12** shows a multidisc steering brake.

The machine has a steering and brake control valve that sends oil to the clutches and the brakes in order to steer the machine. These brakes double as parking brakes because they are spring applied.

When the machine operator wants to turn a machine with this type of steering brake, he or she first disengages one steering clutch, and then drains the oil from behind the brake piston on the same side. Once the oil pressure is drained, the brake applies, and the track on that side of the machine is locked. The track on the opposite side continues driving, and the machine is turned.

▶ TECHNICIAN TIP

Dry steering clutches and brakes are only used for the smallest and lightest-duty applications. Clutches and brakes that are "dry" means they don't run in oil. All steering clutches and brakes today use friction material that is capable of being run in oil. The friction material is just a different formulation that allows it to be compatible with oil.

The oil also carries away contamination and wear particles. where they are trapped in the powertrain oil filter. The main purpose of having clutches run in oil is to have the oil absorb heat from the friction material so it doesn't break down and fail prematurely.

The heat in the oil is then transferred into an oil cooler, which then transfers the heat to engine coolant, where it is ultimately dissipated to the atmosphere.

A variety of friction material can be used for steering clutches and brakes. Generally, this includes paper-based, elastomer-based, or sintered metal–based materials. Added to these base materials are binders, glass fibers, friction modifiers, fillers, and curatives.

Two-Speed Steering

Currently the heavy equipment manufacturer Dressta produces medium to large (160–515 hp) dozers that feature a two-speed steering system consisting of a two-speed planetary geared steering module that provides gradual turns while maintaining full power to both tracks with a conventional clutch-brake mechanism for tight or pivot turns.

Coupled to a three-speed transmission, the two-speed steering module provides six speeds forward and six reverse.

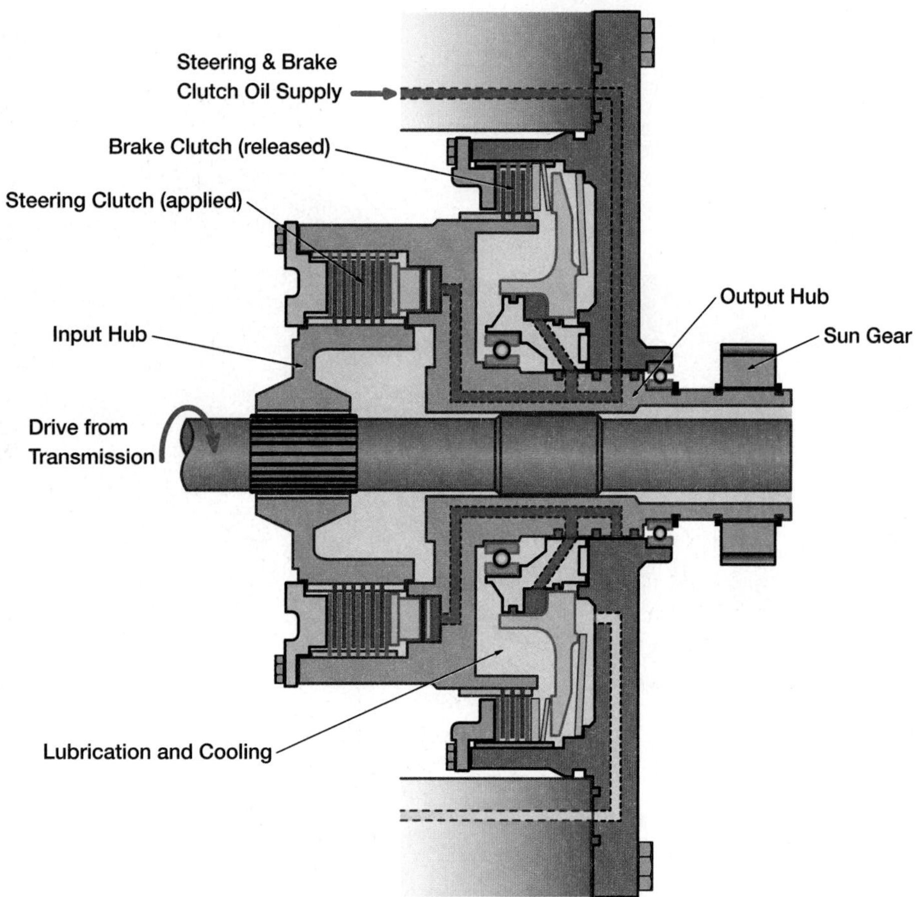

FIGURE 51-12 Multidisc steering brake.

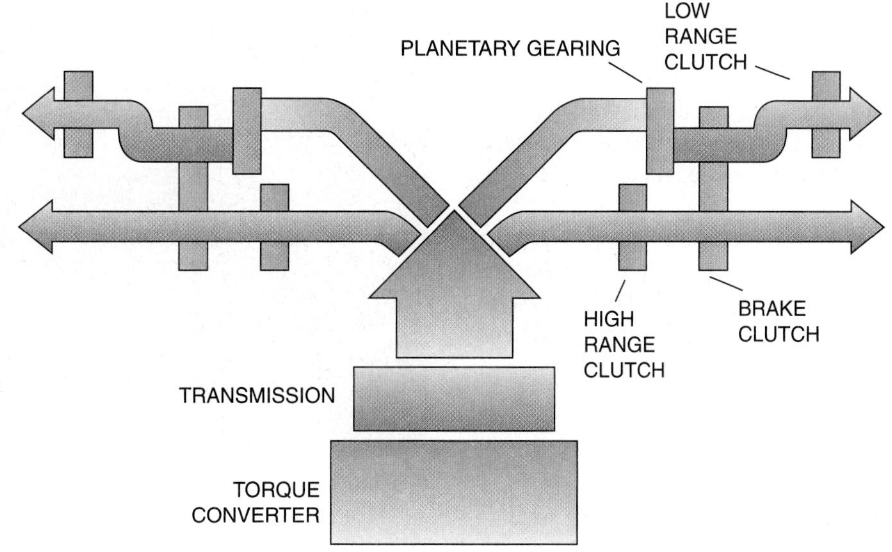

FIGURE 51-13 Two-speed steering system.

The steering module contains a planetary gearset; a wet multidisc, low-range steering clutch; a high-range steering clutch; and brake clutches. See **FIGURE 51-13** for a two-speed steering system schematic.

When one track is driven in high range and the other at low range, there is a 30% speed difference between the two tracks. For example, if the machine is traveling straight ahead in second gear high range, it travels at 4.2 mph. If the operator wants a gradual turn to the left, then the right track is switched to low range and it slows down 30% to 3.2 mph. See **FIGURE 51-14** for a cross-section illustration of one side of the steering module.

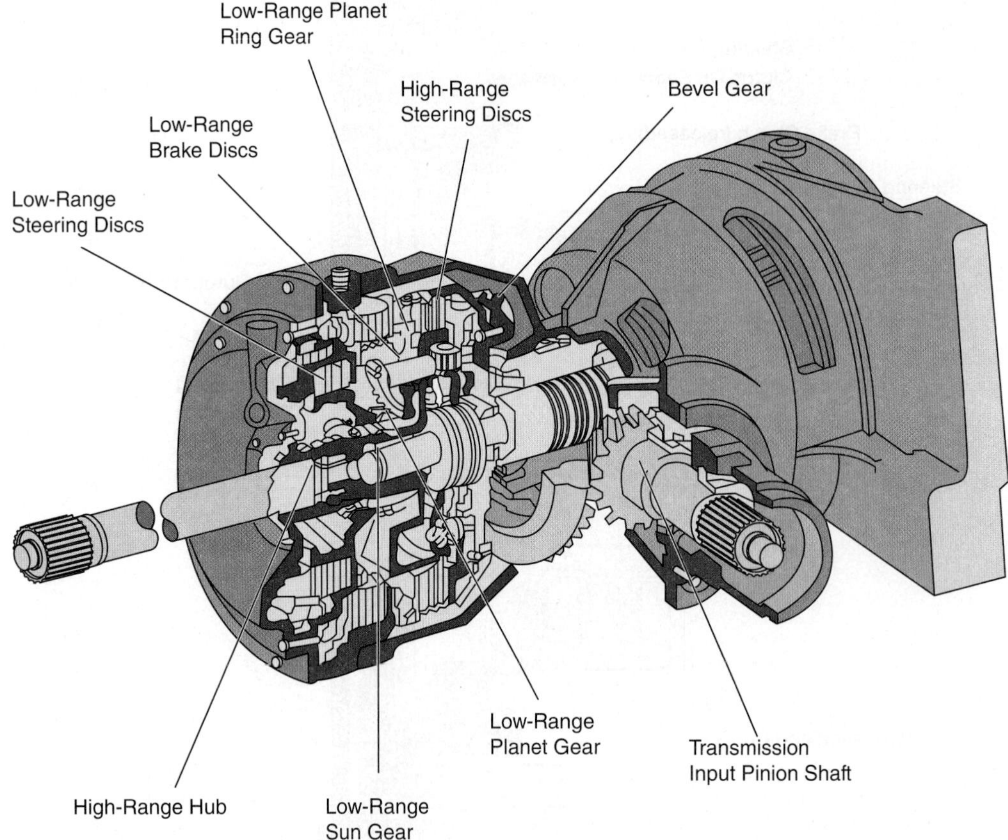

FIGURE 51-14 Cross section of a two-speed steering module.

If a turn sharper than 30% must be made, the operator disengages the steering clutch and applies the brake to one track while the opposite track drives. This is just like a conventional steering clutch/brake arrangement that only has one track driving during turning. The two-speed steering system only gives a fixed amount of turning radius for two-track drive power turns.

The left-hand joystick controls transmission and steering drive for up and down shifting, steering, Hi/Lo selection and LH/RH gradual geared turn. Foot pedals apply both brakes for parking and downhill control. Brakes are spring applied and hydraulically released.

Steering Controls

Older machines originally used a combination of levers and pedals to steer a machine that had steering clutches and brakes. The levers would disengage the clutches and the pedals applied the brakes. This evolved into either two pedals or two levers to actuate the clutches and brakes. See **FIGURE 51-15** for an illustration of an older machine that uses foot pedal steering.

The switch to two pedals or two levers incorporated the use of hydraulic pressure to assist the operator. When differential steering machines (discussed in the next section) were introduced, a single lever called a tiller could be used to steer the machine by pushing or pulling it. It moved a pilot control valve spool that directed oil to a main control valve spool. This changed to the tiller moving a position sensor that sends a signal to an ECM. The ECM then sends an electrical signal to the steering pump displacement control. **FIGURE 51-16** shows an electronically controlled steering "tiller."

FIGURE 51-15 Foot pedal steering controls.

The newest machines that use steering clutches and brakes use fingertip levers that move electronic position sensors. The position sensors then send an electrical signal to an ECM, and the ECM generates an output signal to two or more solenoids. The solenoids then direct oil to the steering clutches and

FIGURE 51-16 Tiller steering.

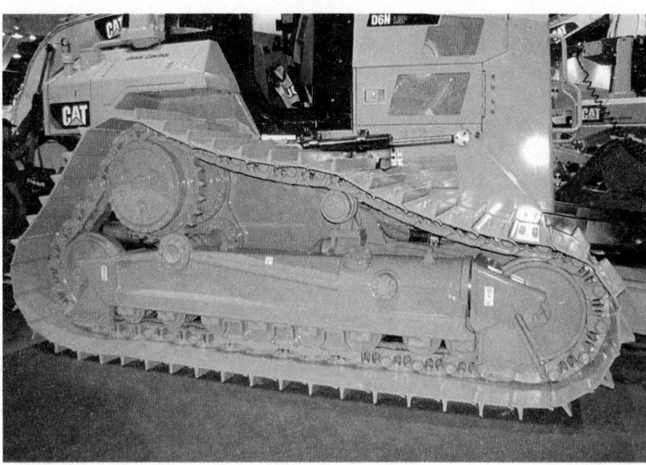

FIGURE 51-17 Differential steering machine.

brakes to steer the machine. A 200,000 lb machine can easily be steered with one finger if it has electronically controlled steering clutches and brakes.

Two-speed turning systems are controlled with two levers that are pulled back to achieve low range and then pulled back farther to release the clutch and apply the brake.

▶ Fundamentals of Differential Steering Systems

K51002

As mentioned earlier, track-type machines that use steering clutches and brakes can only drive one track when they are turning. This is a big disadvantage when the machine is under load and trying to make a smooth turn. A machine that uses a differential steering system, on the other hand, always drives both tracks and allows the machine to make smooth turns easily. A differential steering machine can even turn the tracks in opposite directions for extremely tight maneuvering.

A track-type machine with differential steering operates in a similar principle to a wheeled machine's drive axle with a differential, although it does not use a conventional differential. When a machine with wheels turns a corner, the wheels must follow two different arcs. If the machine turns left, the left wheel must slow down and the right wheel must speed up to follow the different arcs. The average speed between the two wheels is the speed that the machine is traveling.

Similarly, for a track-type machine, the differential steering action slows down one track and speeds up the opposite track to make the machine turn. In other words, it creates a speed differential between the two tracks. Again, the average speed of the two tracks is the speed of the machine.

Differential steering has been around for a long time but was not widely used for heavy equipment until the late 1980s. Currently Caterpillar's medium to large track-type tractors (D6–D9) use differential steering. In **FIGURE 51-17**, a track-type dozer with differential steering is shown.

The electric-drive dozer mentioned earlier also incorporates differential steering where two electric motors take the place of a power shift transmission in the drivetrain. Differential steering uses a combination of gears and a hydraulic system to make the machine turn.

▶ TECHNICIAN TIP

For an excellent visual demonstration of planetary gears, do an Internet search for the 1953 U.S. Army video "Planetary Gears Principles of Operation," which explains the interaction of the gears of a single set of planetary gears as well as how multiple sets can be used to steer a tank by using planetary gears as a differential.

The main components of differential steering systems are the transmission output pinion, which supplies forward, reverse, and three-speed range inputs to the system; the planetary differential assembly; a hydraulic steering pump and motor; and the steering controls. The **steering motor** is controlled by the operator, and as it rotates it turns the machine left or right. The speed of the motor determines how sharp the turn will be, and the direction the motor turns determines the direction the machine turns. In other words, there are two possible inputs to a differential steering system: the input from a power shift transmission and from the steering motor.

In electric-drive machines, the input to the differential steering system comes from a gear driven by two electric motors to give infinitely variable speed and direction changes and from the steering motor.

The planetary differential assembly consists of three sets of planetary gearsets. Refer to **FIGURE 51-18** to see the differential assembly.

One set (furthest left) has its ring gear driven by the steering motor and is called the **steering planetary**. Another set (furthest right) is called the **equalizing planetary**, and its ring gear is held stationary at all times. The third set, in the center, is called the drive planetary. The drive planetary carrier is attached to the ring gear of the conventional pinion and the ring gear that is driven from the transmission, so the drive planetary carrier becomes the input to the differential steering. The outputs from

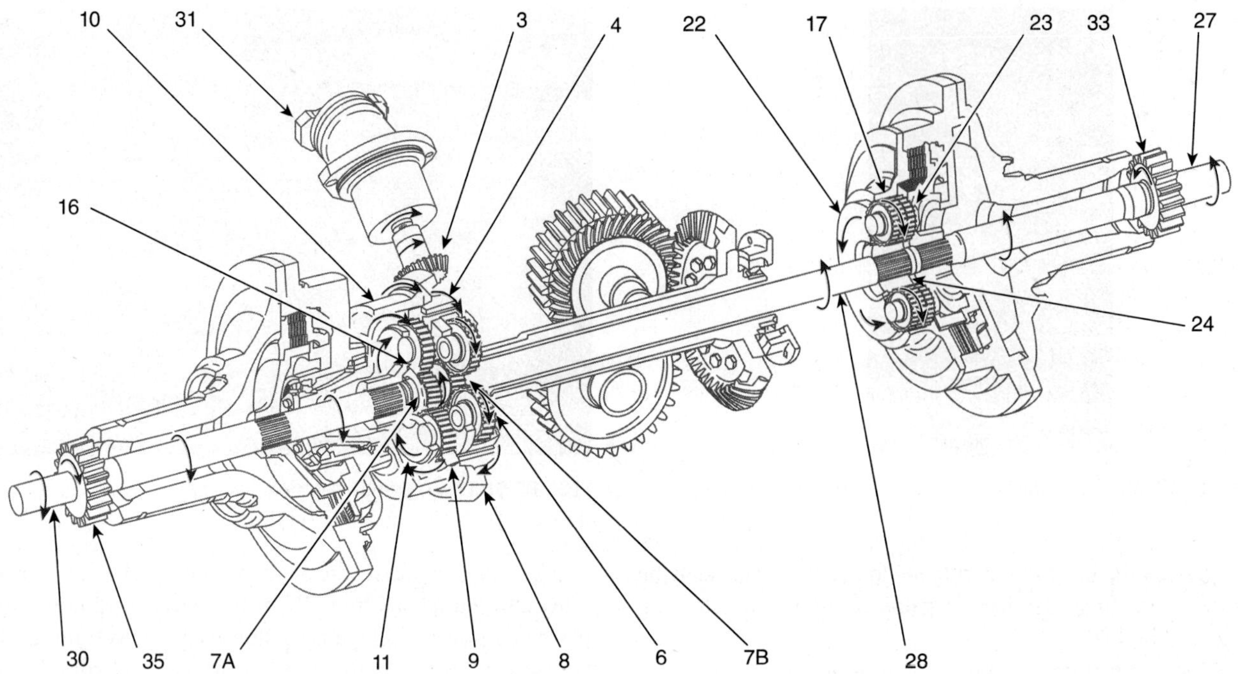

FIGURE 51-18 Differential steering assembly.

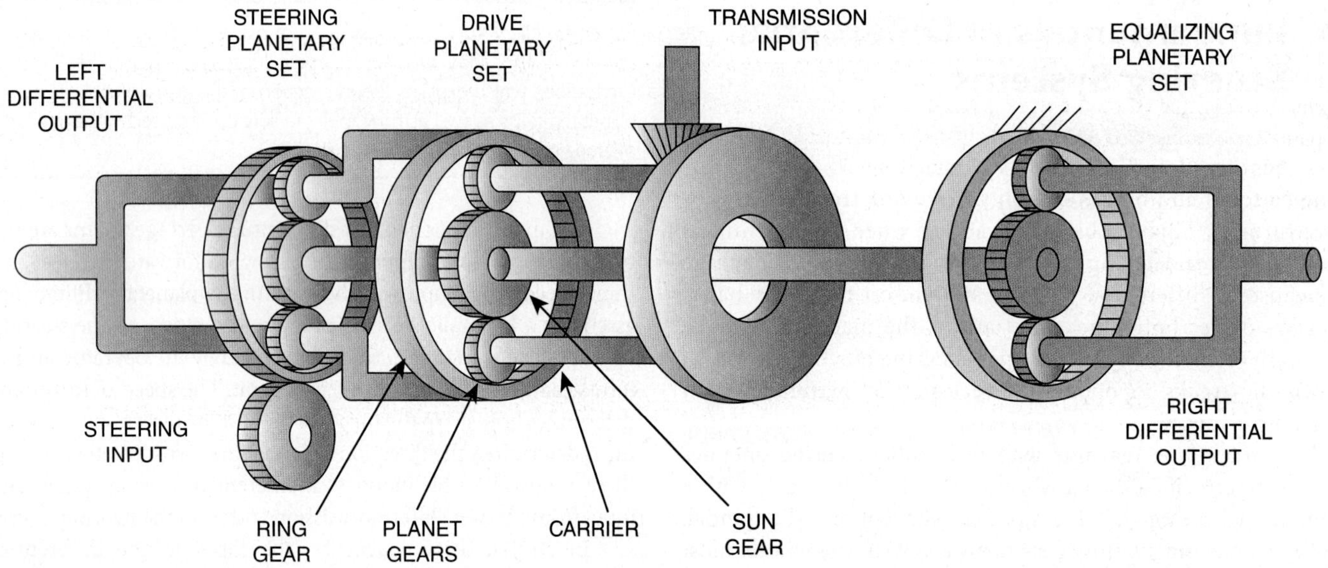

FIGURE 51-19 Differential steering system.

the differential assembly are the steer planetary, whose planet carrier drives an axle shaft that drives the left final drive; and the equalizing planetary, whose planet carrier drives an axle shaft that drives the right final drive. The interaction of these three planetary gearsets and the two inputs (from the transmission to the drive planetary carrier and the steering motor to the steering planetary ring gear) makes the machine's final drives, sprockets, and tracks drive and turn the machine. **FIGURE 51-19** shows the differential steering system in schematic form.

> **TECHNICIAN TIP**
>
> A planetary gearset consists of three elements: a sun gear, a planetary carrier with the planetary pinion gears, and a ring gear. To transfer drive through this combination, one element or member is the input (drive); one member is held stationary; and the third member is the output (driven). By holding and driving different members, a combination of seven different gear ratios and rotation directions result. See Chapter 45 to refresh your knowledge of planetary gears.

Operation of Three Planetary Differential Steering Systems

When traveling straight, the steering motors pinion gear does not turn and therefore it holds the steering planetary ring gear stationary. In this situation, the differential steering system splits the input from the transmission between the left and right final drive axle shafts and both final drives are driven at the same speed with the same torque. See **FIGURE 51-20** to see how the system works in a straight line.

The only input for straight travel is the transmission pinion, and whether it turns clockwise or counterclockwise, for forward or reverse, the torque and speed output is always divided evenly between the left and right tracks.

Straight Driving Operation

The transmission pinion drives the drive planetary planet carrier as the input to the drive planetary; the drive planetary sun gear acts as a held member because it is attached to the sun gear input for the equalizing planetary, and therefore the right final drive. The ring gear of the drive planetary then becomes the output. The drive planetary ring gear is attached to the steering planetary carrier and to the left final drive. The left final drive is therefore driven directly by the drive planetary ring gear.

The pinion gear of the steering motor holds the steering planetary ring gear stationary. Because the steering planetary carrier is being driven by the drive planetary ring gear, the steering planetary sun gear becomes the output of the steering planetary set. The steering planetary sun gear, the drive planetary sun gear, and the equalizing planetary sun gear are all connected to the same shaft, so all three sun gears always turn at the same speed.

The rotation of the sun gear in the drive planetary set reduces the reaction of the drive carrier's pinion gears, which are being input from the transmission, and thereby slows the output of the drive planetary ring gear. The equalizing planetary sun gear inputs the equalizing planetary gearset. This ring gear of the gearset is permanently held and can never rotate, and its carrier becomes the output to the right-side final drive axle. Engineers have designed this system with planetary gears sized so that, with the three sun gears connected together and the ring gear output in the drive planetary being slowed by the rotation of the drive planetary sun gears, the resulting power flows to the pinions of the final drive axles are equal on both sides of the machine, and the tracks turn at the same speed.

Operation While Turning Left or Right

To turn the machine while it is moving under power, the steering motor rotates the ring gear of the steering planetary gearset in one direction or the other. Rotating the steering ring gear in the same direction as the drive planetary ring gear, along with the rotation of the steering planetary carriers, slows the output on the steering differential sun gear, and therefore the input on the equalizing planetary sun gear, causing the right-side track to slow down. The rotation of the ring gear in the same direction of the steering planetary carrier adds to the carrier's speed and causes the left-side track to speed up.

Turning the steering ring gear opposite to the drive planetary ring gear and the steering planetary carrier causes the steering planetary sun gear to speed up. Because they are connected, this means that the speed of the drive planetary sun gear speeds up, which in turn slows down the ring gear output of the drive planetary and its connected steering planetary carrier, and therefore the left final drive. The equalizing planetary sun gear is also connected to the steering and drive sun gears, so its speed is increased as well. The increased speed on the sun gear inputting the right-side equalizing planetary gearset causes the equaling carrier and therefore the right-side final drive to speed up.

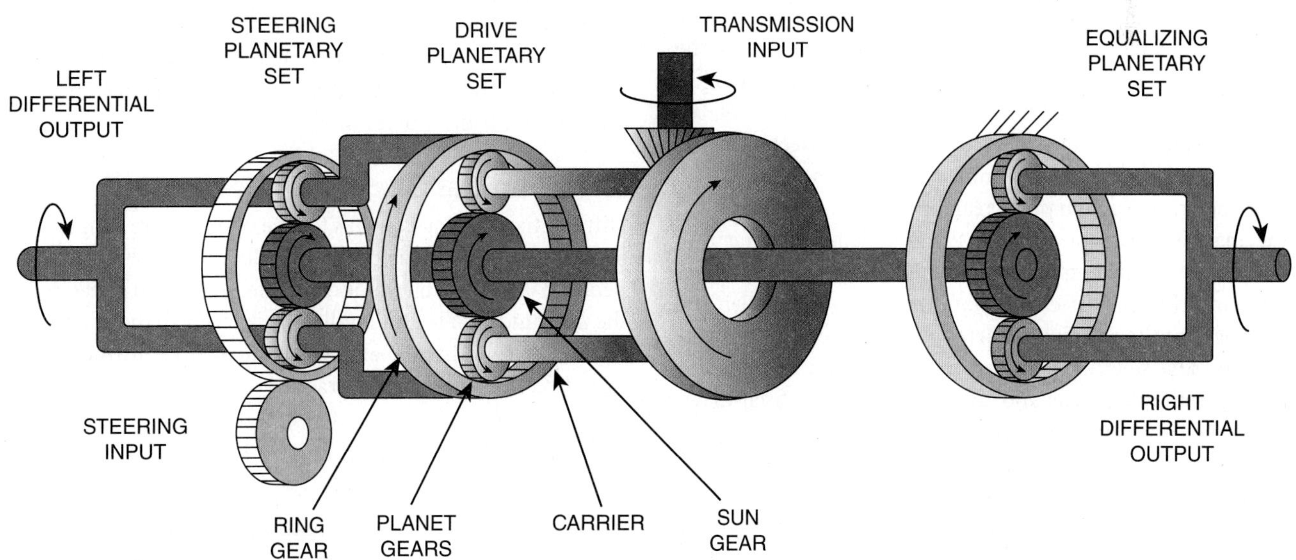

FIGURE 51-20 Differential steer, straight.

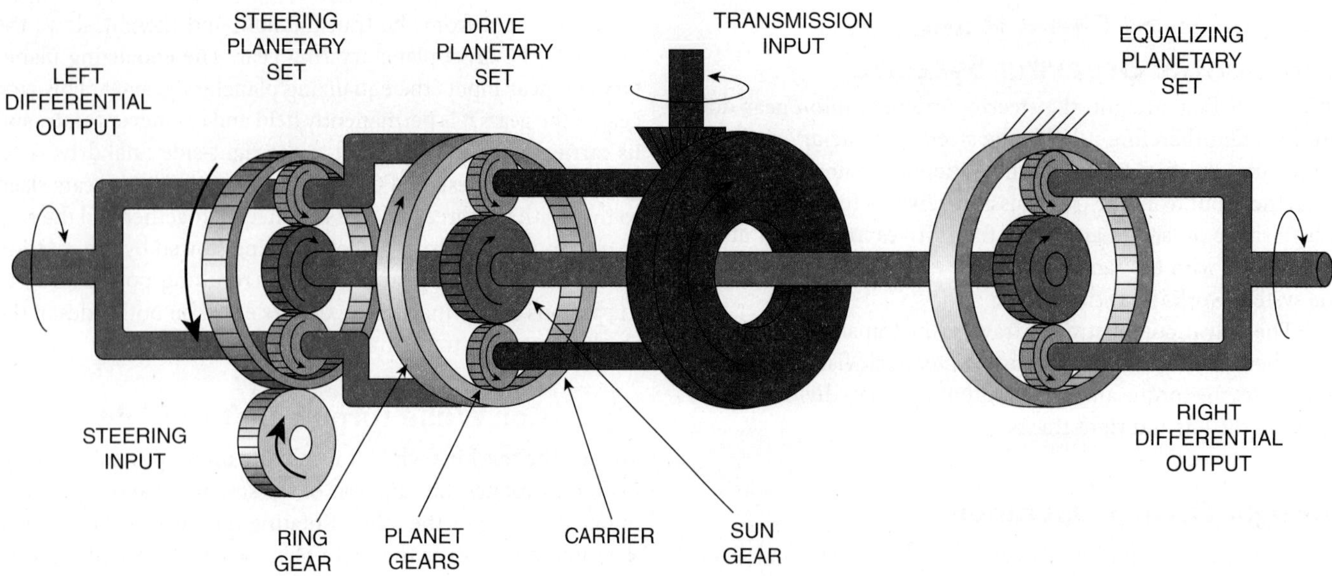

FIGURE 51-21 Gradual turn.

The sharpness of the turn can be controlled by the speed of the steering motor, from very gradual to quite tight depending on how fast the motor turns the steering planetary ring gear. The faster the steering motor turns, the sharper the machine's turn will be. See **FIGURE 51-21** for an illustration of a gradual turn.

An example of a gradual turn is when a machine is driving straight ahead at 3 mph and the operator moves the steering control to turn the machine to the left, the left track will slow to 2 mph, and the right track will speed up to 4 mph.

Spot Turn Operation

The extreme opposite of straight travel and gradual turns is a spot turn where the machine's tracks counterrotate. This type of turn occurs when the transmission is in neutral and there is no transmission input to the differential steering system. The operator moves the steering control lever, which makes the steering motor rotate the steering ring gear either left or right. The steering planetary carrier acts as a held member of the planetary gear, as the left-side final drive is connected to the carrier, so the weight of the machine resists its motion.

The steering planetary sun gear, however, is also connected to the machine's weight through the equalizing planetary, so it too acts as a held member. When the steering motor rotates the steering ring gear, it causes both the planetary carrier and the sun gear of the steering planetary to rotate, but in opposite directions. The steering planetary carrier rotates in the same direction as the ring gear and drives the left-side final drive, again in the direction of the ring gears rotation. The steering sun gear rotates in the opposite direction of the steering ring gear, and because it is connected to the equalizing planetary sun gear, it in turn drives the right-side final drive through the equalizing planetary gearset, again in a direction opposite to the rotation of the steering ring gear. This causes the machine's tracks to turn at the same speeds, but in opposite directions, and the machine turns on the spot. The faster the motor turns with no transmission input, the faster the tracks counterrotate, (a counterrotation only turns the tracks relatively slowly), and the direction the motor turns determines which direction the tracks will actually turn. See **FIGURE 51-22** for an illustration of a counterrotation maneuver.

The power transferred to the final drives is provided by the transmission or electric drive in all cases except a spot turn. Also, the direction of rotation of the axle shafts is controlled by the transmission when its output pinion is turning to make the machine travel forward or backward.

The amount of speed difference between the axle shafts and the direction of the machine's turn is controlled by the steering motor. The speed of the motor shaft determines the tightness of the turn, with a faster motor speed causing a sharper turn. The direction of rotation of the steering motor controls the direction of the turn. Refer to **TABLE 51-1** for the direction of rotation during the various operations.

Differential Steering Controls

Differential steering controls for the operator are simple. A lever to the left of the seat is called the tiller and it pivots on a short pedestal at the left end of it. The tiller is pushed ahead to make the machine turn left and pulled back to make the machine turn right. The tiller handle also has controls to shift the transmission direction and/or speed range.

Differential Steering Hydraulic System

In some differential steering machines, the differential steering motors get their oil supply from a steering control valve that is part of the implement hydraulic system. This system uses one

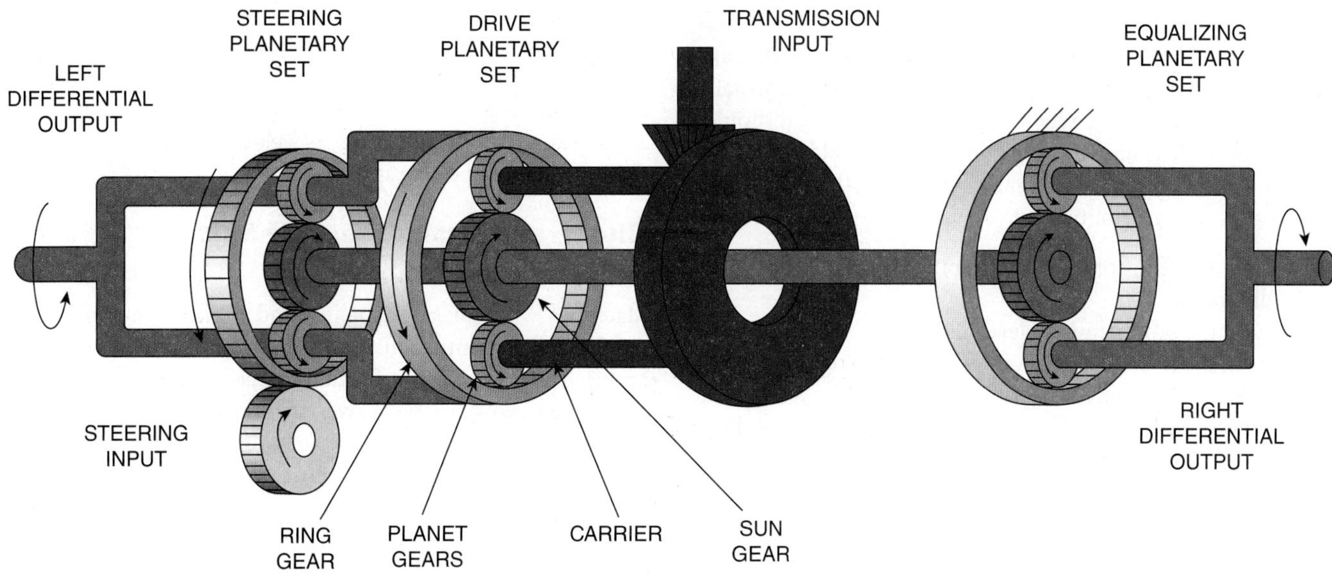

FIGURE 51-22 Differential steer counterrotation.

TABLE 51-1 Steering Motor Direction of Rotation

	Left Turn Forward	Left Turn Reverse	Right Turn Forward	Right Turn Reverse
Rotation of steering motor input (1)	Clockwise	Counterclockwise	Counterclockwise	Clockwise
Rotation of transmission pinion (3)	Clockwise	Counterclockwise	Clockwise	Counterclockwise
Position of steering control lever	Pushed forward	Pulled back	Pulled back	Pushed forward

pump as part of a load-sensing pressure-compensated system for all hydraulic functions (blade, ripper, and steering). Because the steering section is first in the main control valve assembly, the steering system has priority over other functions (blade, ripper). However, when other functions are activated, steering slows down because the oil flow of the pump is divided between steering and other circuits. The steering control valve spool can be shifted by direct linkage or by pilot oil from a pilot control valve.

The motor for newer differential steering systems is part of a hydrostatic closed-loop system. A dedicated steering pump for this system maintains a consistent steering speed whether the implement functions are used or not. This means the pump supplies flow to the motor directly and not through a directional control valve. The return flow from the motor goes directly to the pump inlet. The direction and speed that the motor turns is determined by the output of the pump. A charge pump replenishes any oil lost in the loop due to normal internal leakage and from losses created by the motor flushing valve. Although the steering pump/motor is a separate system from the rest of the machine's hydraulic system, they share a common reservoir.

For older hydrostatic steering differential systems, the operator control shifts a pilot valve that sends oil to the pump's swashplate control. Newer systems replace the pilot oil system with an electronic/electrical system to control the pump. The system pump is a bidirectional variable displacement pump with a swashplate control piston. The operator moves the control lever to make the swashplate move, which makes the pump oil flow out of either of two pump ports and to one of two motor ports. If one port receives oil, the motor will turn clockwise; and if the opposite port receives oil, it turns counterclockwise. This in turn makes the machine turn left or right. The motor is a fixed-displacement bent axis type, and its output shaft drives a pinion gear. The pinion gear is the input for the steering planetary and drives the ring gear.

▶ Steering System Diagnostics

S51001

Track machine steering systems that are working properly should allow the operator to steer the machine left and right either in forward or reverse with ease and consistency. Depending on the type of steering system the machine uses, this could be a seamless power turn with a differential steer system; a fixed arc power turn, as with the two-speed system; or a turn that is made in two steps to drive one track around the other one that is either not driving or is locked up, as with the clutch and brake system. Because these systems operate quite differently, we look at diagnostic procedures for each separately.

Steering Clutch and Brake Diagnostics

When diagnosing a problem with a steering clutch and brake system, you need to know how it should operate normally before you can figure out why it isn't working the way it should. Unless you are familiar with how the system should work, you need to read the operator's manual. After that, there are some basic checks to perform initially:

- Check that the controls are operating smoothly and with full motion.
- Check the powertrain oil level and condition.
- Check the track tension. A track that is too tight is hard to drive and could affect steering operation.
- If the machine has electronic controls, check for fault codes.
- Check for oil leaks and obvious damage.

If these initial checks don't reveal any problems, then proceed to confirm the complaint by operating the machine. Make sure you are familiar with all safety features of the machine, and find a flat and open area with a consistent surface material where you can check its operation. The machine steering controls should turn the machine in a smooth and consistent manner equally left and right. You should be able to tell when the steering clutch is disengaged and when the brake is applied. If the brake comes on too soon after the clutch is released, the machine will jerk. There should be a noticeable space in the control travel between clutch release and brake application.

For older machines without hydraulic assist clutches or brakes, specifications for dimensions should be checked and measured for the control pedal and/or lever linkage. You may find that to restore proper operation an adjustment is needed to either a stop screw or a linkage length. Be aware that you may need to perform a series of adjustments in a specific order. For example, the following is a list of adjustments that must be done in this specified order to reset the **steering pedal** linkage on a John Deere 450G dozer:

1. Loosen brake bands
2. Adjust linkage inside transverse housing
3. Adjust stops
4. Adjust linkage
5. Adjust steering valve
6. Adjust brakes.

Some operational problems you may have to trouble shoot:

- The machine only steers one way.
- The machine doesn't steer either way.
- The machine steers erratically.
- The machine steers slowly one way.
- The machine won't travel.

For machines with hydraulic steering systems, you may need to install pressure gauges to check apply or release pressures. These pressures usually come from the transmission oil control system and are limited to around 250 psi. You may also need to check that pressure drains to zero when it is supposed to. If the oil is supplied from the transmission oil circuit and you suspect there is a problem, you should check to see whether there are any operational problems with the transmission as well. This could lead you to an oil pump or oil supply problem. The oil system filter and/or suction screen should be removed and inspected for excessive wear particles and contamination. An oil sample should be taken as well if there are doubts about the state of the oil in the system.

Clutch and Brake Steering System Adjustments/Calibrations

Machines with steering clutches and brakes sometimes need regular adjustments. This could be adjustment to the band brakes to compensate for friction material wear. Generally, this means removing a small cover and turning an adjuster that moves the ends of the band brake closer together. The proper adjustment is determined by pedal travel and should be referenced to a specification in the machine's service information. If the pedals travel too far and don't stop the tracks, then an adjustment or repair is needed.

A calibration procedure may have to be done for a steering system that has electronic controls. Calibrations could be required when a system isn't working right, or sometimes it may be necessary to calibrate a new sensor when one is installed. This ensures the sensor is sending the proper information to the ECM. Calibration procedures could be part of other repairs and may include calibrating steering position sensors, pump control solenoids, and articulation sensors. Calibrating procedures can sometimes be performed from the machine display or from a connected EST (electronic service tool). A calibrating procedure matches an ECM input either from an operator input or a machine sensor to a physical dimension or speed. This serves as a reference point or a zero point for the ECM to then provide proper control of the machine component. It requires the technician to perform a series of actions that must be followed in a specific sequence. Calibration keeps the operator input controls matched to what is happening with the actuators or pistons and cylinders on the machine.

Two-Speed Steering Diagnostics

The same initial checks should be performed for this steering system as for the steering clutch and brake checks. The technician operating the machine should also verify the complaint. Because this system relies on oil pressure applied to its clutches and brakes, the hydraulic control system pressures may have to be checked. Pressure taps are available to install gauges for these pressure checks. This system gets its oil supplied from the powertrain hydraulic system, and the entire system should be checked to see whether it is operating properly. There may be steering system problems that are common to another powertrain hydraulic problem.

If a mechanical problem with the system's planetary gears is suspected, you should drain the steering case oil and look for metal flakes or pieces. Oil and filter condition could also be checked.

Differential Steering Diagnostics

The same initial instructions apply to diagnosing a differential steering machine problem as with the steering clutch and brake machine. Familiarize yourself with how it should operate. Some operational problems you may have to trouble shoot are:

- The machine only steers one way.
- The machine doesn't steer either way.
- The machine steers erratically.
- The machine won't counterrotate.
- The oil overheats.

Because this steering system uses a hydraulic system to steer the machine, there are some additional initial checks to perform when troubleshooting:

- Check oil level for hydraulics.
- Check for leaks.
- Check for fault codes.
- Check to see whether there are other hydraulic system problems.

If the machine is older and shares pump flow to the steering motor with other implements, make sure the other functions are working properly if there is a steering problem. This should eliminate the pump and its control system as the source of the problem.

▶ General Steering System Repair

S51002

Steering system repairs can vary from fairly simple mechanical repairs to hydraulic component repairs, to electrical repairs.

A simple mechanical repair is one that involves repairing the control linkage. This could be as easy as applying penetrating fluid to a rod end or greasing a pivot shaft, as any binding of linkages will affect steering operation.

If excessive wear is found in this linkage, the worn parts should be replaced. You will have to reset the manufacturer's linkage dimensions whenever any linkage components are replaced.

If a steering system has clutches and brakes that are hydraulically actuated, their seals can occasionally fail, causing pressure loss. This would entail, at a minimum, removing the clutch or brake assembly and reconditioning the assembly, including replacing all seals and bearings.

A hydraulic component repair could be a simple leak repair or a total pump or motor recondition. Whenever the steering hydraulic system is opened up, it is critical for the technician to practice extreme cleanliness. Cleanout filters are sometimes used after a hydraulic system repair for an extra bit of insurance against a repeat failure. A cleanout filter has a smaller micron rating and is only designed for short-term use as it will plug up faster than a regular filter.

An electrical repair related to a steering system could be the replacement of a wiring harness, solenoid, or position sensor.

Steering Clutch and Brake Reconditioning

If a steering clutch or brake is found to be defective, it can be reconditioned. The main reason for reconditioning a steering clutch is that the friction material has been reduced to less than specified minimum dimension. There has to be a certain thickness of friction material on the steering and brake discs and the brake band. The teeth or tangs on the discs should be checked for excessive wear. **FIGURE 51-23** shows a multidisc steering clutch.

FIGURE 51-23 Multidisc steering clutch.

Friction discs that are worn too thin have to be replaced; brake bands, on the other hand, have friction material that can be replaced as part of a reconditioning procedure. Discs and plates must be replaced if any cracks or excessive warpage are found. The steel plates can be reconditioned if there aren't deep grooves in them or they aren't warped or dished. They can be ground slightly to renew the surface finish as long as the minimum thickness isn't exceeded, and they should be ground to a specified roughness so they can retain oil. They are checked for straightness with a straightedge on a flat surface.

Differential Steering Operational Checks

Manufacturers give specifications for steering performance. The operational checks listed in **SKILL DRILL 51-1** are general in nature but follow a typical testing procedure. As always, it is critical that you have the correct specifications for the machine you are testing, as specifications vary with different machines.

If your results do not match the manufacturer's specification, the problem will have to be investigated. Common problems are misadjusted or broken steering linkages, hydraulic failures, (steering pump, steering motor, fluid levels, hoses, and valves), or mechanical problems in the drivetrain, such as the parking brakes applied or dragging while in the released position.

Most manufacturers provide detailed troubleshooting guides to determine the problem. These should be followed to the letter to find the specific cause.

There are test procedures for mechanical clutch and brake steering systems to ascertain whether the brakes and steering are working properly. In newer machines, the steering clutches and brakes will be electrohydraulically controlled and will have a calibration procedure. Older pedal steer machines may require mechanical adjustment when necessary. **SKILL DRILL 51-2** is a general check procedure for testing steering clutch and brake operation of a pedal steer crawler-type machine.

SKILL DRILL 51-1 Differential Steering Operational Testing

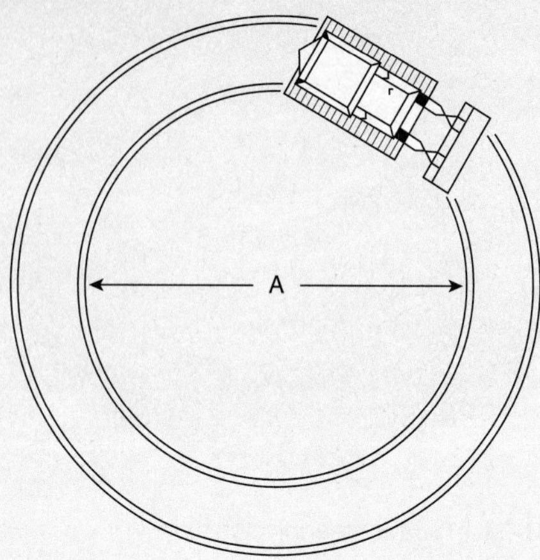

The steering operational checks indicate whether the steering mechanical and hydraulic circuit operation are normal. Measure the steering circle diameter shown in the diagram and compare it to specifications.

Caution: Before conducting any tests where the machine must be operated, it must be communicated to all personnel that there will be a potential risk should something go wrong. Ideally, testing should take place in a barricaded area, with signage informing all others to keep out.

Any other personnel that are needed for the test procedure must be in full view of the machine operator at all times.

Turn Diameter Check

This test determines the functionality of the track steering system.

1. Operate the machine in an area that has solid enough ground so that there is little or no track slip during the test. Slipping tracks can alter the turn circle dimension.
2. Secure the machine implements in the fully raised position.
3. Set the throttle to high idle.
4. Operate the machine in low gear.
5. Operate the tiller to turn hard right.
6. Turn the machine one complete circle right; then bring the machine to a stop and engage the parking brake.
7. Lower the implements to the ground, and measure the inside diameter of the machine's turning circle.
8. Repeat this procedure while turning the machine to the left, and again measure the inside diameter of the turning circle.
9. Compare your results to the manufacturer's specification; results may be not turning one direction, a larger diameter turn in one direction, or no turning at all.

SKILL DRILL 51-2 Steering clutch adjustment check procedure on pedal steer machine

The following procedure is general in nature for a steering clutch adjustment check procedure on pedal steer machine. In the field, you must use the correct manufacturer's procedure for the particular machine you are testing.

1. Position machine on a hard, flat surface against an immovable object.
2. Run engine at low idle speed.
3. Depress power control pedal.
4. Shift to first gear.
5. Depress left pedal approximately 25 mm (1 in.) or 35 mm (1.4 in.), depending on the machine (check OEM manual).
6. Slowly increase engine rpm until right track starts moving.
7. The left track must not move.
8. Depress power control pedal again
9. Release the left pedal.
10. Depress right pedal approximately 25 mm (1 in.) or 35 mm (1.4 in.), depending on the machine (check OEM manual).
11. Slowly increase the engine rpm until left track starts moving. The right track must not move.

If test is good, no further action is needed. If either of the tracks moves when it shouldn't, the steering linkage must be adjusted according to manufacturer's specifications.

Steering Brake Operation Check

1. Position the machine on a flat surface with room to maneuver the machine
2. Operate engine at slow idle.
3. Place transmission in first gear.
4. While the machine is moving, push left pedal until increased effort is felt. The left track should stop, and the machine should turn left
5. Resume straight-ahead operation, and push right pedal until increased effort is felt. The right track should stop, and the machine should turn right.

If the check is good, no further action is required. If the test fails, adjust the brakes according to manufacturer's specifications.

Wrap-Up

Ready for Review

- Safety concerns related to track machine steering systems include the following:
  - Proper lifting methods must be used, and equipment should be used for heavy components.
  - Friction material can contain hazardous material and should be treated with care.
  - High-pressure oil may be present, and appropriate precautions must be taken when working near it.
  - Proper steering operation must be confirmed before a machine is put back into service.
- Track-type machines with one-piece frames can only steer by having their two tracks drive at different speeds. Three ways to do this are by steering clutches and brakes, differential steering, or two-speed gearing.
- In track-type machines, steering clutches and brakes are located past the ring gear shaft and before the final drives. Disengaging one steering clutch stops drive. Then applying the steering brake locks the track; the other track can still drive, and this turns the machine.
  - Most steering clutches are multidisc, spring applied, and oil released. Steering brakes can be external band and drum type or multidisc.
- Steering clutches and brakes can be controlled with mechanical linkage, oil-assisted mechanical linkage, or electrohydraulic systems.
- A steering clutch is driven by a flange that is driven by a bevel gear shaft that is driven by the transmission output pinion gear.
- The steering clutch output is its friction discs that have external teeth that mesh with a brake drum. The brake drum has a smooth outer surface and drives an input flange to the final drive.
- Clutch apply pressure can come from springs (Belleville or coil type) or oil pressure.
- Most clutches are wet type that run in oil to transfer heat away from friction material.
- Clutch release devices remove clamping pressure from the friction discs to stop torque transfer. They compress springs or drain oil pressure.
- Newer machines that use steering clutches use multidisc steering brakes that are spring applied and oil released. These brakes can also function as parking brakes.
- One machine manufacturer uses a two-speed steering system that can provide drive to both tracks while the machine steers. Two planetary gearsets along with steering clutches and brakes are used.
- If one track is driven in high range and the other in low, there is a 30% speed difference, which makes the machine turn.
- Differential steering systems for track machines use the same principle as drive axle differentials to provide a speed differential for the tracks, which in turn makes the machine turn.
- Larger track-type dozers can feature differential steering, and in these machines the transmission output pinion drives through three planetary gearsets, which sends drive toward each track's final drive. A hydraulic motor is also used in conjunction with the steering planetary to provide a speed difference between the left and right tracks.
- For straight travel with differential steering, the motor doesn't turn. To steer the machine, oil is sent to the motor, and when the motor rotates, its output gear turns the ring gear of the steering planetary, which changes the speed between the two tracks.
- Differential steering systems can provide track counterrotation and steering is controlled with movement of a tiller lever.
- Track-type machine steering system operator concerns can include no steering, no drive on one side, rough engagement, slipping, overheating, and strong odor.
- Diagnostics start with knowing the system, thorough visual inspection, verifying the complaint, and performing tests.
- Inspections include checking oil level and condition, looking for leaks, and checking control operation, and track tension.
- Adjustments may be required to restore proper clutch and brake operation because wear of friction material changes clearances.
- Oil pressure checks are common and detect seal failure or valve issues.
- Differential steering system diagnostics include hydraulic pressure and flow testing.
- Steering system repairs include friction disc replacement, plate replacement, brake band relining, and hydraulic motor replacement.

Key Terms

band brake A type of brake that utilizes a steel band lined with friction material that wraps around a brake drum to slow the drum.

counterrotate When the tracks of a machine turn in opposite directions to complete a fast turn.

equalizing planetary The planetary gearset on a differential steer machine attached to the left-side final drive.

steering motor The hydraulic motor responsible for turning the tracks at different speeds to cause a turn.

steering pedal The pedals used to steer older track machines one pedal steers left and the other right.

steering planetary A planetary gearset in a differential steer machine drive axle that is used to steer.

Review Questions

1. A track machine that uses steering clutches and brakes to steer will *never* use which of the following?
   a. A differential
   b. Final drives
   c. Foot controls
   d. Hand controls
2. If a track machine with clutch and brake steering turns sharply left, the operator must actuate controls that will do which of the following?
   a. Release the right clutch and apply the left brake.
   b. Release the left clutch and apply the left brake.
   c. Release the left clutch and apply the right brake.
   d. Release the left clutch and release the release the left brake.
3. If the left band brake used on a track machine for steering is adjusted to be too loose, what would be the likely result?
   a. The machine would roll away if parked on a slope.
   b. The left clutch would burn out.
   c. The left track would not lock up.
   d. The left control would bind up.
4. If a piston seal failed for a hydraulically released steering clutch, the result would be which of the following?
   a. A slipping clutch
   b. The clutch not disengaging
   c. Broken release springs
   d. The brake locking up
5. Which of the following is the power flow for a track machine with steering clutches and brakes?
   a. Transmission to torque converter, to steering clutch, to final drive
   b. Hydrostatic motor to steering clutch, to final drive
   c. Transmission to differential, to steering clutches, to final drive
   d. Torque converter to transmission, to pinion, to ring gear, to steering clutches, to final drive
6. In a track machine that can "counterrotate," which of the following will be likely?
   a. It will use an HMU.
   b. It will use a lock-up torque converter.
   c. It will have a differential steering system.
   d. It will have double reduction final drives.
7. A differential steer machine that is performing a fast counter rotation turn will have which of the following?
   a. Its left and right steering clutches turning opposite
   b. Its transmission output gear turning at maximum speed
   c. Its steering motor turning at maximum speed and transmission output stationary
   d. Its left and right brakes turning opposite
8. Which of the following would allow a track machine to counterrotate?
   a. Having planetary final drives
   b. Having two-speed track steering
   c. Having hydraulically actuated steering clutches
   d. Having either hydrostatic drive or differential steer
9. An operator running a track machine is complaining that the machine is hard to steer to the left. Which of the following would be a good first troubleshooting step?
   a. Run the machine to verify the complaint.
   b. Check the air filter.
   c. Check left track tension.
   d. Check the powertrain oil filter.
10. A machine with a differential steering system uses how many planetary gearsets to steer the machine?
   a. 1
   b. 2
   c. 3
   d. 4

ASE Technician A/Technician B Style Questions

1. Technician A says that a dozer with clutch and brake steering has one steering clutch. Technician B says that a dozer with clutch and brake steering has two steering brakes. Who is correct?
   a. Technician A
   b. Technician B
   c. Both A and B
   d. Neither A nor B
2. Technician A says that a clutch on a brake steering machine uses multidisc clutches only for the clutch and brake. Technician B says that clutch and brake steering offer the best control for tracked machine steering. Who is correct?
   a. Technician A
   b. Technician B
   c. Both A and B
   d. Neither A nor B
3. Technician A says that clutch and brake steering systems use spring-applied brakes. Technician B says that clutch and brake steering systems can use a spring-applied steering clutch. Who is correct?
   a. Technician A
   b. Technician B
   c. Both A and B
   d. Neither A nor B
4. Technician A says that machines with clutch and brake steering systems prioritize oil supply to the steering system so the machine is always under control. Technician B says that most heavier machines with clutch and brake steering use oil as a cooling medium for the brakes. Who is correct?
   a. Technician A
   b. Technician B
   c. Both A and B
   d. Neither A nor B
5. Technician A says that in differential steering machines, a differential gearset is attached to the engines ring gear. Technician B says that counter rotating can occur with the transmission in neutral. Who is correct?
   a. Technician A
   b. Technician B
   c. Both A and B
   d. Neither A nor B

6. Technician A says that differential steering systems use two planetary gearsets to control the machine's direction. Technician B says that machines with differential steering systems are turned by using the output of a hydraulic motor. Who is correct?
   a. Technician A
   b. Technician B
   c. Both A and B
   d. Neither A nor B
7. Technician A says that in a differential steering system, the ring gear of the drive planetary and the carrier of the steering planetary are connected and turn together. Technician B says that the sun gears of the planetary gearsets in the differential steering system all turn at the same speed. Who is correct?
   a. Technician A
   b. Technician B
   c. Both A and B
   d. Neither A nor B
8. Technician A says that the steering motor in the differential steering system turns the sun gear of the equalizing planetary gearset. Technician B says the left-side final drive is directly connected to the steering planetary ring gear. Who is correct?
   a. Technician A
   b. Technician B
   c. Both A and B
   d. Neither A nor B
9. Technician A says that when the steering motor turns as the machine is moving forward with a differential steering system that one track speeds up and the other track slows down by the same amount. Technician B says that differential steering allows more precise control of the machine when compared to using steering clutches and brakes. Who is correct?
   a. Technician A
   b. Technician B
   c. Both A and B
   d. Neither A nor B
10. Technician A says that the equalizing planetary ring gear in a differential steering system is fixed and never rotates. Technician B says that the sun gear of the drive planetary in a differential steering system always rotates if the machine is moving. Who is correct?
    a. Technician A
    b. Technician B
    c. Both A and B
    d. Neither A nor B

CHAPTER 52

Final Drives

Knowledge Objectives

After reading this chapter, you will be able to:

- **K52001** Describe the purpose and fundamentals of final drives used with MORE.
- **K52002** Explain the function of the various types of final drives used with MORE.
- **K52003** Describe the construction and features of the various final drives used with MORE.
- **K52004** Outline the maintenance procedures on final drives.

Skill Objectives

After reading this chapter, you will be able to:

- **S52001** Identify common failures of final drives and recommend repairs or reconditioning.

▶ Introduction

The term **final drive** is somewhat self-explanatory: it refers to the final drive system of a machine before the wheels or tracks, but final drives are much more than that. When we look at off-road equipment, we see machinery that is capable of huge amounts of work, but the prime mover or engine that powers this equipment usually seems relatively small. For example, consider a Caterpillar D8N dozer. This particular machine weighs 83,000 pounds (37,500 kg), and can push 11.5 yards of material while cutting to a depth of 23 inches (58.42 cm); 11.5 yards of wet soil can weigh as much as 35,200 pounds (15,900 kg). So this machine is moving almost 120,000 pounds (545,00 kg) with a diesel engine that produces 306 horsepower at 2,100 rpm and 1,200 ft-lb of torque at 1,650 rpm.

How can an engine with that torque output power this machine? The answer is: by using **torque multiplication**—that is, using gears to slow down output speed while multiplying the available torque, thus gaining mechanical advantage. **Mechanical advantage** occurs when we reduce the speed output of a torque-producing prime mover, like a diesel engine, through the use of gear reduction. This particular machine has a top speed of 6.7 mph (10.8 kph), with the engine running at approximately 2,100 rpm. At that speed, the track drive **sprocket** (the toothed wheel that drives the track) is rotating at approximately 80 rpm, meaning that the overall **gear reduction** (torque increase) through the driveline in third gear is around 26:1; in first gear, the ratio could be as high as 100:1. We could use the transmission and the drive axle to achieve this large gear reduction, but that would mean that the components would have to be much larger to handle the multiplied torque. This machine and others like it use final drives with gear arrangements like double planetary gears to achieve the large torque multiplication (mechanical advantage).

By allowing most of the driveline to operate at lower torque levels, most of the driveline components can be lighter and smaller. Only the final drive components are subjected to the increased torque. The machine's driveline is subjected to only three to five times the engine's maximum torque, and the final drives multiply that torque by over nine times to get the necessary torque output at the drive sprockets or tires.

This provides other benefits as well. The machine's brakes are installed before the final drives, meaning that they take advantage of the torque multiplication to stop and hold the machine, so the brakes can be smaller and more compact.

▶ Purpose and Fundamentals of Final Drives

K52001

As mentioned in the introduction, the final drive on a machine is the last or final gear reduction in the machine's drive system. Final drives can refer to several different types of drive systems: pinion drives, bull drives, planetary drives, chain drives, worm drives, and simple drive axles. The final drive can be driven mechanically, hydraulically, or in some cases electrically. In some machines, usually lighter models, the drive axle is the last reduction in the driveline or the final drive. Drive axles are covered in their own chapter, so they aren't discussed here. All medium- and large-sized machines and most smaller machines have one or the other of the above-mentioned final drive systems. Final drive reductions in most mobile machines range between a low of 3 or 4 to 1 to a high of 25 to 1, although in certain applications much larger reductions can be found. The Bonfiglioli F-1300 hydraulically powered final drive shown in **FIGURE 52-1** has as many as seven planetary gears creating a reduction of several hundred to one and an incredible torque output capacity of 1,300 kilonewton meters (kN·m), or 950,000 ft-lb of torque.

Even larger final drives are available for specialty applications such as tunnel boring rigs. Pinion-type final drives can be

FIGURE 52-1 Multiple planetary gear final drives such as this one are available for special applications.

You Are the Mobile Heavy Equipment Technician

You are asked to inspect a CAT 953 track loader that is being prepped for sale. You start the machine and bring it into the repair shop for the inspection. The machine seems to operate fine, and though it is an older model, you are certain that it can still provide many thousands of hours of service. You start your inspection by checking fluid levels and find that the drive axle oil level is down significantly, but you do not see any leaks around the axle.

1. Could this low level be caused by poor service procedures?
2. Is there anywhere else where the axle oil could have leaked out?
3. What would you check next?

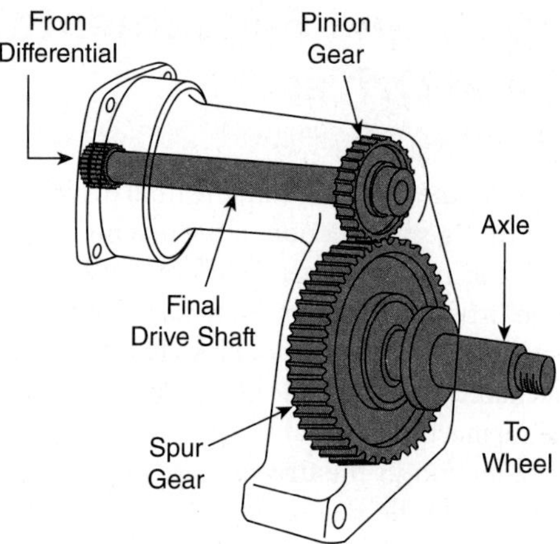

FIGURE 52-2 A drop-type bull and pinion gear.

internal to a drive axle or external in their own housing. When they are internal, they are known simply as **pinion drives**, and when in their own housing, they are called bull drives or **bull and pinion drives**. Bull and pinion drives can be used to drop the power flow closer to the ground, which allows greater operating clearance for the machine's driveline. **FIGURE 52-2** shows a drop-type of bull and pinion gear arrangement.

Planetary final drives can use single or multiple planetary gearsets to achieve the necessary reduction. These drives can be found on many different types of machines because of their versatility. Chain drives are very common in motor graders and other equipment that use more than one set of wheels or track drives to propel the machine. Chain drives are an economical and relatively simple final drive that can be used when speeds are lower. Chain drives use smaller drive sprockets than driven sprockets to achieve their reductions. In some machine applications, combinations of final drives are used, meaning that the final drive may have a bull and pinion arrangement to achieve the first part of the overall reduction, and then a planetary hub or wheel end may be used to multiply the reduction. Or a planetary final drive can be used to drive a chain sprocket, and again the overall reduction is multiplied. **FIGURE 52-3** shows a planetary final drive driving a chain sprocket.

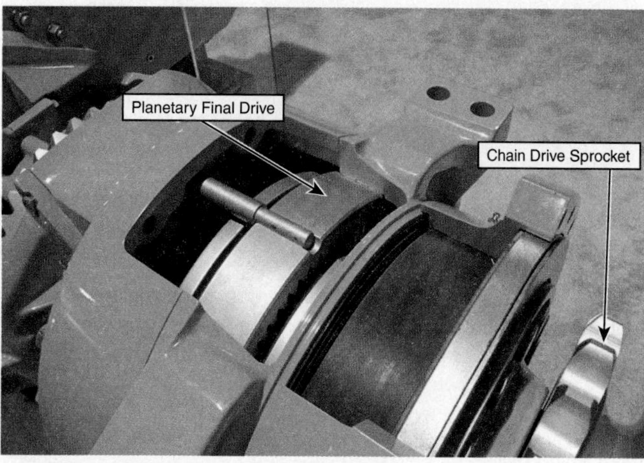

FIGURE 52-3 Final drives can be a combination of reductions such as a planetary drive turning a chain sprocket.

▶ Operation and Function of Final Drives

K52002

Without final drives, a machine's driveline would have to be able to create enormous gear reductions through the transmission and the drive axle. Imagine trying to fashion a driveline that by itself could produce a reduction ratio of several hundred to one as the Bonfiglioli final drive mentioned in the previous section. This would create two big problems immediately. The transmission itself would have to be enormous to create the necessary ratios, and the driveline of the machine would have to be built strong enough to handle the resulting multiplied torque. To carry the torque that the Bonfiglioli drive is capable of, 950,000 ft-lb of torque (1,300 kN·m), the driveline and drive axle would have to be huge. The driveshaft alone would likely have to be several feet in diameter and weigh several tons. Final drives allow us to reduce the loads on the rest of the drive systems, the transmission, the driveline and the drive axle while still giving us the required result, getting the necessary torque to the wheels or the track sprockets of the machine. Although final drives all have the same basic purpose, that is, to provide that final gear reduction in the driveline, they function in unique ways. In this section, we examine each of them.

Pinion-Type Final Drives

Pinion-type final drives are typically part of the drive axle housing assembly. These drives utilize a small gear driving a larger gear to gain the reduction required. Because they are internal to the drive axle, they do not require a separate lubrication system, but are lubricated by the flow of the drive axle lubricant. These drives are typically found on smaller tractors and agricultural equipment. Because of the location, this drive system is more compact and relatively easy to service. The pinion gear or gears, as shown in **FIGURE 52-4**, drive larger spur gears that are splined to and drive the axles.

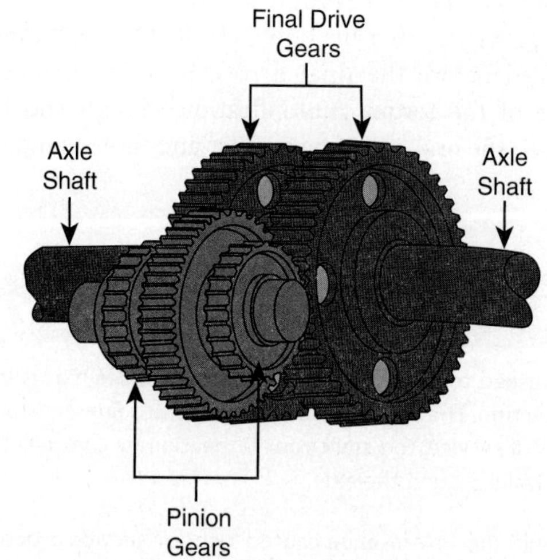

FIGURE 52-4 Pinion drives are typically integral to the drive axle housing.

The axles are attached to the machine's wheel ends, which are typically supported by two tapered roller bearings that carry the weight of the machine. Tapered roller bearings are used because they can carry heavy loads and absorb axial (side) thrust loading. Preload or end play of the bearings (depending on the manufacturers specification) is typically adjusted by shims or by adjusting and locking nuts. Maintenance on this type of drive is usually part of the normal drive axle maintenance recommended by the manufacturer.

Bull and Pinion Drives

Bull and pinion drives are typically located in their own separate housing at the end of the machine's steering clutch housing. These drives use a small pinion gear driving a larger "bull" gear to produce the final gear reduction. This is a very common type of drive on older dozers. The steering clutch output drive of the machine or a hydraulic motor supply rotation to the pinion gear, which in turn drives the larger bull gear. The pinion and bull gears may be spur cut or helical, but using spur gears reduces axial loading of the drive system. Helical gears inherently cause axial thrust loading, and accommodation must be made to deal with it. This arrangement is also handy to drop the power flow to a lower center. The machine driveline can be at a relatively high level, and as it goes through the pinion and bull gear, the centerline of the power flow is dropped. This allows more ground clearance to the machine and keeps the driveline away from mud, dirt, and rocks, thereby protecting it. This arrangement is known as a drop axle housing. A pinion and bull gear arrangement can be seen in **FIGURE 52-5**.

When this type of drive is used, it may share the transmission lubrication system, or the housing may be filled to a certain level with lubricant that is separate from the machine's drive axle lubrication system. In this case, the gears are lubricated by the oldest from of lubrication—the splash method. As the bull gear churns through the lubricant, the oil is splashed around the housing and lubricates the gears and their support bearings. This lubricant has to be changed on a regular schedule, just as with any other lubrication system. Maintenance is a simple matter of draining and refilling the oil with the correct lubricant to the specified level. While draining, the fluid should be carefully monitored for signs of metal or other contamination, which could indicate the need for further investigation. Both the drive pinion and the bull gear are supported by bearings, typically tapered roller bearings as they can absorb both radial and axial load. Even when spur gears are used, the machine's operation causes a certain amount of side loading, so bearings must be able to deal with both axial and radial loads. The bearing endplay or preload is adjustable by shims and/or adjusting and locking nuts.

Double-Reduction Pinion and Bull Drives

Bull and pinion final drives can be single reduction, as depicted above, but they can also be double reduction, utilizing two sets of bull and pinion gears to achieve the overall ratio. This arrangement can be used for one of two reasons: first, simply to increase the final drive ratio; and second, to make the drive more compact. By using two pinion and bull gears to get the final ratio, the drive housing "package" can be smaller. **FIGURE 52-6** shows a double-reduction helical pinion and bull gear arrangement used on a wheeled machine.

These drives use the splash method of lubrication, although newer machines using double-reduction gearing like this use pressurized lubrication systems. In some cases, double-reduction drives have the first reduction inside the drive axle housing ends and the second reduction in a separate housing that bolts to the axle housing. This is the case in large dozer applications. The machine's brakes and/or steering clutches are incorporated into the interior section of the reduction gearing. Double-reduction final drives may use a combination of gearing systems in certain applications. Planetary gear arrangements can be used to drive the pinion of the pinion and bull gearset. This will provide overall reduction or the bull gear may drive a planetary hub, again multiplying the total reduction.

Planetary Final Drives

Planetary gearing was discussed in an earlier chapter. Please reference that chapter to refresh your knowledge of planetary

FIGURE 52-5 Bull and pinion gears in a drop-type housing allows the machine to have greater center ground clearance.

FIGURE 52-6 This double-reduction bull and pinion gear arrangement multiplies, or compounds, the final gear ratio.

gear power flows. Planetary final drives are used in a multitude of machines for very good reasons. Planetary gearing is very compact, a large reduction can be accomplished in a very small space. Planetary gearing is extremely strong when compared to typical power transfer gearing. In standard or conventional gearing, only one or two teeth are used to transmit torque.

Planetary gears, on the other hand, have several sets of teeth in contact at once to transmit the torque, making them inherently stronger. A planetary final drive wheel end is shown in **FIGURE 52-7**. Planetary gearing also eliminates the radial thrust loading that convention gear transfer systems are subject to. These types of final drives are typically found in the wheel end hubs of wheeled machines and/or in the sprocket hubs of tracked machines, although they can also be found in many other locations such as winch drives and swing drives for machine upper structures; in fact they can be utilized in any location on any machine where a torque multiplication or speed reduction is required. Recall that a planetary gearset has three elements, a ring gear, a planetary carrier with planet pinion gears, and a sun gear. Planetary final drives are typically arranged so that the input to the drive from a mechanical drive system or from a hydraulic motor drives the sun gear of the planetary gearset. The ring gear of the set will be held stationary and the carrier of the planetary gearset will be the output element. This power flow equates to the maximum forward reduction from a planetary gearset. In the chapter that included planetary gearing fundamentals, we discovered that planetary gears are capable of seven different ratios, two forward reductions, two forward overdrives, and two reverses; the seventh power flow is 1 to 1 or direct. The actual ratio for the maximum forward reduction from a planetary gearset will depend on the number of teeth on the ring gear and the sun gear but is typically around 3.5 to 1.

Double- and Multiple-Reduction Planetary Final Drives

The Bonfiglioli final drive mentioned previously would not be capable of the large reduction it has without the use of multiple planetary gearsets. It uses five or more interconnected planetary gears arranged so that the first sun gear is input, the ring gear held, and the carrier is output. The carrier from the first planetary gearset drives the sun gear of the next gearset, and this pattern repeats through all of the planetary sets that are used in the drive. If you consider that one planetary gearset can create approximately a 3.5:1 ratio, each set would then compound the reduction, meaning that the ratio of each gearset output would multiply together to get the final ratio. For example, let us just say that each of five interconnected planetary gearsets in this particular drive have a reduction ratio of 3.5:1. To get the overall ratio, then, we have to multiply them all together. So $3.5 \times 3.5 \times 3.5 \times 3.5 \times 3.5 = 525.22:1$—a massive reduction ratio multiplying the torque supplied by its hydrostatic motors.

Chain-Type Final Drives

Chain-type final drives are used as an alternate way of driving a wheel end or sprocket over a significant distance between the drive and driven components. For example, an articulated truck has a tandem wheel arrangement with the rear wheels spaced behind the front wheels at the rear of the machine. A chain drive can be used to connect the truck's front rear wheels to the back rear wheels. Chain drives are also a convenient and relatively inexpensive way to drive tandem wheel ends on a machine. A motor grader, for example, uses a double-drive sprocket at the output from the machine's drive axle, which drives two chains, one connected to each of the actual wheel ends of the graders tandem drive, as shown in **FIGURE 52-8**. The tandem drive can use a gear arrangement to transfer the power, as shown in **FIGURE 52-9**, but transferring torque with a chain drive is much simpler.

Tandem chain drives are also used in skid steer machines with either wheel or track drives. Tandem chain drives can also be the last reduction in the power flow by using sprockets of differing sizes. When a smaller sprocket drives a larger one, there is a reduction ratio, just as there is with gears. Chain drives are also very reliable as long as they are kept adjusted, lubricated, and clean. Some smaller skid steer machines use drive belts in place of chains. These systems are basically identical to the

FIGURE 52-7 Planetary gears can achieve large reductions in a relatively small space.

FIGURE 52-8 This chain-type final drive drives two chains: the red chain drives the rear wheel of the grader, and the black chain drives the front wheel.

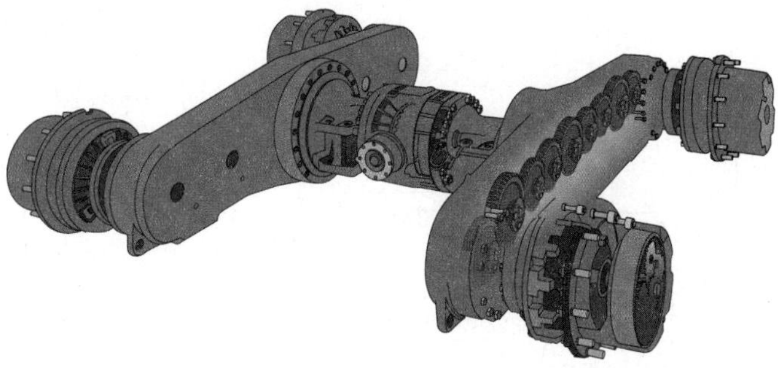

FIGURE 52-9 Gears can be used to transmit torque to two drive wheels in a tandem drive arrangement.

chain drive with the exception that they use toothed drive belts, similar to engine drive belts, and sprockets/gears to transmit the torque to the wheel end.

▶ Final Drive Construction

K52003

Final drives can be driven in several ways—mechanically, hydraulically, and electrically—and their output can be sent on to drive tracks or wheels. This section describes the details of the construction, design, and features of various final drive systems found on mobile equipment.

Construction of Bull and Pinion–Type Final Drives

Bull and pinion–type final drives are commonly found on bulldozers and may be driven by hydraulic motors or by mechanical drive axles. The final drive shown in **FIGURE 52-10A**, front view, and **52-10B**, rear view, from a caterpillar dozer is driven hydraulically. The shape of the bull and pinion gear arrangement can be clearly seen by the shape of the housings in the picture. See **FIGURE 52-11** for the internal components of the drive.

A hydraulic motor drives the pinion gear through the brake assembly, shown in Figure 52-10B. The pinion gear meshes with the bull gear. The pinion and bull gear reduce the speed and increase the torque coming from the hydraulic motor significantly. The pinion gear is supported by two taper roller bearings inside the housing, as is the bull gear. Although the pinion and bull gears are the final reduction, in some machines torque is further increased by using a planetary gearset. The bull gear drives the sun gear of the planetary gearset. The ring gear of the planetary gearset is fixed to the housing and cannot rotate. The carrier of the planetary gearset becomes the output, and it is connected to the drive sprocket. The addition of the planetary gearset multiplies the final gear ratio of the bull and pinion gears by approximately 3.5 times before the power reaches the drive sprocket. The final drive, including the pinion and bull gear and the planetary gearset, is lubricated by the splash method so the sprocket housing is filled to a particular level with oil. Pinion and bull–type final drives can also be driven mechanically directly from the machine's clutch shafts. In this arrangement, the clutch output shafts are splined to the final drive pinions. In this case, the final drive shares its lubrication system with the clutches and bevel gear. Other than those differences, the construction is similar to that mentioned above.

FIGURE 52-10 A. Front view and **B.** Rear view of a bull and pinion final drive.

Double-Reduction Pinion and Bull Gears

Double-reduction pinion and bull gears use two sets of spur or helical gears to create the final reduction. The input is similar to that mentioned in the previous section, but the first pinion drives a cluster gear. In the cluster gear, the first bull gear is in mesh with the input pinion, and a small pinion drives a second bull gear that is attached to the drive wheel or sprocket. This type of final drive is depicted in **FIGURE 52-12**.

The input pinion, the cluster gear, and the second bull gear are all supported in the housing by tapered roller bearings, as can be seen in Figure 52-12. The use of the two bull and pinion gears compounds the final gear ratio. This type of drive may be splash lubricated as well and will hold oil in the housing at a certain level to facilitate this. Newer machines using **double-reduction bull and pinion drives** are pressure lubricated.

Planetary Final Drive Construction

Planetary gears are used in wheel end final drives for many applications. Planetary final drives may also be installed inboard, that is, toward the bevel gearset of the drive axle. An inboard planetary final drive is shown in **FIGURE 52-13**.

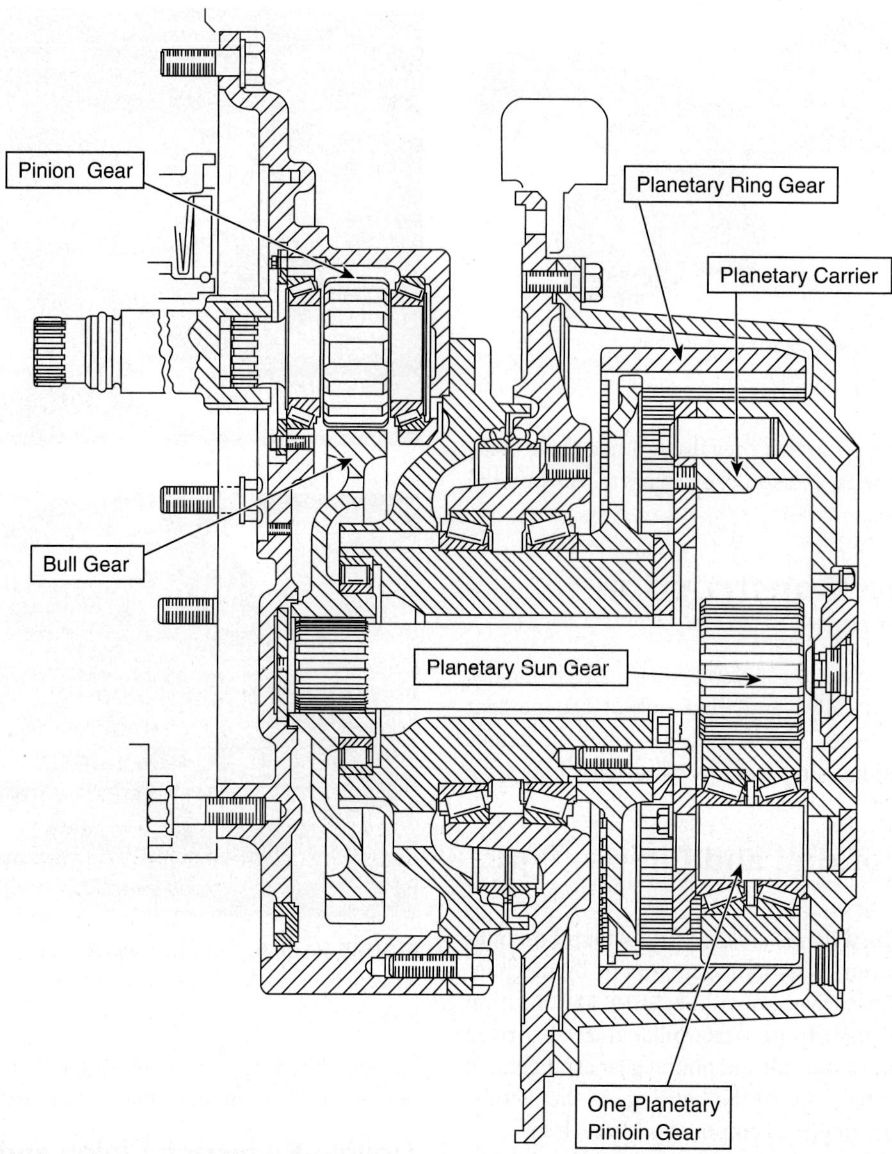

FIGURE 52-11 An internal view of a bull and pinion final drive using a planetary gear to multiply the ratio.

These drives are very common in machines but can also be found in trucks and industrial machinery. The construction of these drives is relatively simple. In almost all machine applications, the planetary power flow is the same: sun gear input, ring gear held, and the carrier is the output. This power flow results in the maximum reduction possible from a planetary gearset. The planetary wheel end final drive is typically a self-contained system that can be removed, overhauled, and replaced without disassembling any other part of the machine other than removing the track or wheel. The planetary gearset can be made with spur gears or helical gears. However, most final drives use spur-cut gears to avoid axial thrust loads. Although there can be slight variations in different **planetary drives**, their construction is generally as follows. The ring gear of the planetary gearset is part of or bolted to the wheel end mounting (axle stub) so it cannot turn. The sun gear will be input by the drive system, whether hydraulic or mechanical. The carrier, containing the pinion gears will be splined or bolted to the rotating wheel end. The carrier and the rotating wheel end will be supported by tapered roller bearings.

Double- and Multiple-Reduction Planetary Final Drives

Double- and/or multiple-reduction planetary final drives are constructed in the same way as single-reduction planetary drives, with the exception that the output from the first planetary carrier is connected to the sun gear of the next planetary gear. **FIGURE 52-14** shows a multiple-reduction planetary wheel end.

Because planetary gears are epicyclical—that is, they revolve around a common centerline—they cancel out all radial thrust and therefore do not require bearings to support them. Only the input and the final carrier and the rotating wheel end must be supported. Because of their compact size, multiple planetary gears can be arranged in a single wheel end to achieve

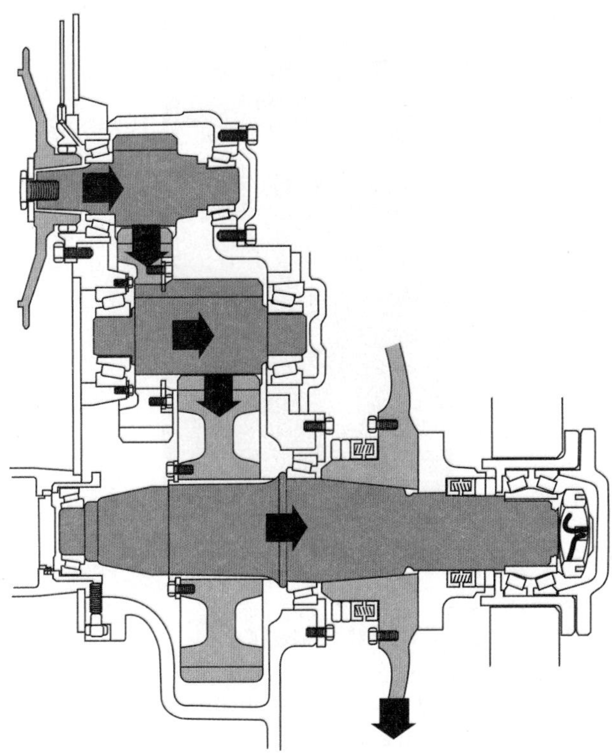

FIGURE 52-12 A double-reduction bull and pinion final drive.

FIGURE 52-13 This planetary final drive is mounted inboard close to the bevel gears of the drive axle.

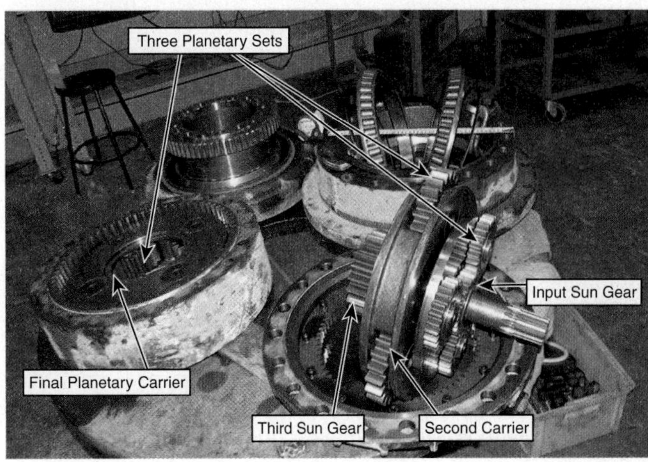

FIGURE 52-14 Multiple planetary gears can be used to achieve the necessary reduction.

the reduction necessary. As many as seven planetary gearsets can be used in a single wheel end. Most planetary drives used with mobile equipment have ratios between 9:1 and 25:1; however, multiple planetary final drives for special applications are available with drive ratios as high as 1500:1!

Chain Drive Construction

Chain final drives are relatively simple. Anyone who has owned or ridden a bicycle has seen a chain drive system in action. There are however some intricacies to chain drives. In chain drive systems, it is important that the same links on the chain do not contact the same teeth on the sprocket over and over again, for this reason the sprockets are usually made with an uneven number of teeth, and the chain has an even number of links. This way, the wear is spread out equally.

Chain final drives use roller chains—that is, the links are actually rollers, so there is no relative motion between the rollers and the sprocket teeth as the chain is driven. This means that friction wear between the link roller and the sprocket teeth is minimized. There are actually two different links in the chain: the roller link and the pin link. The roller link contains the rollers and the roller bushings, which are flanked by two side bars. The roller links fit inside the pin links. The pin links have two pins through their side bars that fit through the roller bushings. One pin link is at each end of a roller link. See **FIGURE 52-15** to view the roller and pin links.

The pin link is the part that actually connects the chain's rollers together. Usually one of the pin links is a master link that

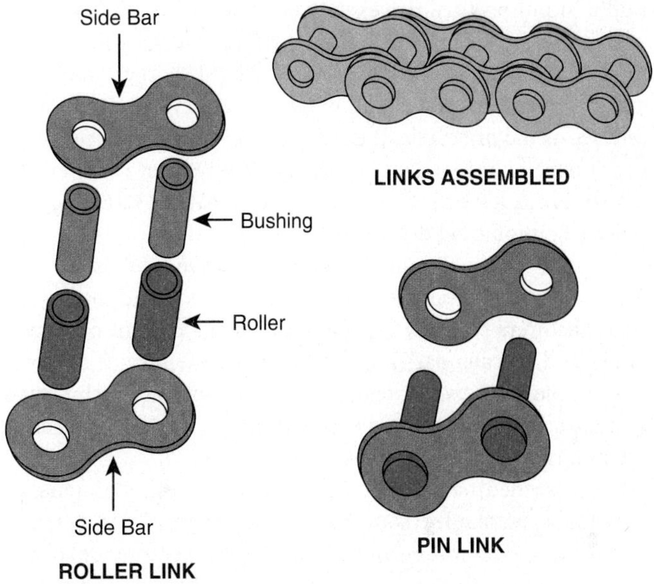

FIGURE 52-15 A roller chain is made up of two types of links connected together.

can be disassembled to remove or install the chain. If the chain does not have a master link, then a chain-breaking tool has to be used to disassemble the chain. The rollers on the chain contact the sprocket teeth, and because they are free to turn on their bushings, there is little or no friction between the chain and the sprocket. Chains are manufactured to a certain size, called pitch. The chain pitch is the distance between the rollers from center to center. Common chain pitch sizes used in off-road equipment are 1.75" (44.5 mm) to 3.0" (76.2 mm). As the chain wears, this pitch dimension elongates or stretches, necessitating replacement. Chain final drives are typically lubricated by the splash method; there is a level of oil in the chain case or housing. Some chain drives use an idler sprocket to control chain tension on the chain's normally slack side, although not all. Belt-drive machines usually use an idler pulley belt tensioner on the normally slack side of the belt. Belt-drive systems run dry with no lubricant in the tandem housing.

FIGURE 52-16 A bull and pinion final drive being serviced.

▶ Maintenance Procedures on Final Drives

K52004

Final drive maintenance is relatively simple. Most manufacturers have an inspection and lubrication regimen for their final drives that should be followed. Technicians should be aware of the functioning of the final drive and what maintenance procedures can be successfully accomplished in the field. Wheel end final drives support the entire weight of the machine and are subject to massive torque loads, so proper and timely maintenance is essential. The following is a basic listing of the minimum maintenance procedures for various final drives.

Bull and Pinion Final Drive Maintenance

Bull and pinion final drives may be attached to the drive axle of the machine or may be in their own separate housings. If the final drive is part of the drive axle, it will likely share the drive axle's lubrication system, and it should be serviced at the same interval as the drive axle. If the drive has its own separate housing, it usually has its own lubricant and reservoir, whether it is splash lubricated or pressure lubricated. **FIGURE 52-16** shows a bull and pinion final drive being serviced.

The service interval for both of these drive systems can vary greatly depending on the machine's application and load cycle. Manufacturers typically recommend a fixed amount of service hours and or calendar time to determine the service interval. Oil samples are usually taken at all machine service intervals and especially when the oil is changed. A typical oil change interval is every 2,000 hours or yearly.

When the final drive requires more in-depth maintenance or must be overhauled, some normal checks are pinion gear end play and rotating torque and bull gear (wheel end) endplay and rotating torque checks. Backlash between the bull and pinion gear must also be checked. The unit will normally require bearing and/or seal replacement during overhaul.

Final Drive Maintenance

Planetary final drive maintenance again will be relatively simple. As with the bull and pinion drives discussed above, planetary drives can be part of the drive axle, as is the case with inboard final drives previously depicted in Figure 52-13. In this case, the lubrication system must be serviced with the drive axle. Planetary drives that are self-enclosed at the wheel or sprocket end of the drive system have to be serviced individually by simply draining and replacing the lubricant in the wheel end. During more in-depth maintenance, bearings and/or seals will require replacement.

Chain Final Drive Maintenance

Chain final drives typically are splash lubricated by oil in the chain case or housing. Chains can provide long service life if the lubricant is kept clean and free of contaminants. Regular scheduled replacement of the chain lubricant is recommended. The **chain case** of a motor grader is shown in **FIGURE 52-17**.

FIGURE 52-17 The oil in the chain case or housing should be changed on a regular basis.

TABLE 52-1 Caterpillar Procedure and Elongation Limits for Chain Drives

Motor Grader Model #	Chain Pitch	Number of Chain Links	New Measurement	Measurement of Maximum Wear	Chain Tension(1)
120H	44.5 mm (1.75")	14	622.3 mm (24.50 inch)	641.1 mm (25.24 inch)	173 kg (381 lb)
135H					
12H, 140H, 143H, 160H, 163H	50.8 mm (2.00")	12	609.6 mm (24.00")	628.7 mm (24.72")	277 kg (610 lb)
14H	57.2 mm (2.25")	11	628.7 mm (24.75")	647.7 mm (25.50")	286 kg (630 lb)
16H	63.5 mm (2.50")	10	635 mm (25")	654.1 mm (25.75")	354 kg (780 lb)
24H(2)	76.2 mm (3.00")	10	762 mm (30")	773.4 mm (30.45")	782 kg (1724 lb)

(1) The chain is tensioned in order to displace oil between the links of the chain. This ensures metal-to-metal contact between the components so that the measurement is accurate.
(2) Caterpillar recommends maximum chain elongation of 1.5% for the 24H motor grader.

Chains must also be kept carefully aligned. Any misalignment of the chain will cause rapid wear of both the chain and the sprocket. Chain alignment should be checked regularly for side loading of the chain and sprocket. On some chain drive systems, chain slack has to be adjusted, but in most cases the chain must be checked only for stretching or elongation. Stretching the chain is actually caused by the wear between the rollers and the bushing, not actual stretching of the material, but it causes the pitch of the roller links to elongate, meaning that they no longer match the tooth spacing of the sprocket. This "stretching" then causes rapid wear at the sprocket. The chain is checked by tensioning the chain and measuring the distance across a certain number of links from the center of one roller to the center of the roller at the correct number of links for that chain. **TABLE 52-1** shows the chain-checking procedure and elongation limits set by Caterpillar for the chain drives on their motor graders. **FIGURE 52-18A** and **52-18B** shows the sprockets and chains of a motor grader.

When a chain has stretched beyond the limit, it is necessary to replace the chain. New links should never be used with an old chain, as the new link's pitch will be shorter, leading to shock loads as the chain runs. The sprockets should also be changed at the same time as the chain to ensure the tooth pitch is correct. Using an old sprocket with a new chain commonly causes rapid wear of both the sprocket and the chain. In some cases, the sprocket can be removed and installed backward to give a new tooth surface in the primary direction of chain travel but this is not commonly recommended.

Belt drive machines will need to have the drive belt inspected regularly for cracks and wear and should be replaced as necessary. Drive belt tension is usually controlled by a spring loaded idler and is not normally adjustable on these machines.

FIGURE 52-18 It is recommended that chains **A.** and sprockets **B.** be changed at the same time.

▶ Common Final Drive Problems and Repair Procedures

S52001

As mentioned above final drives usually carry the entire weight of the machine and transmit heavy torque loads to do this successfully for many hours of operation the drive must be in top operating condition. Loss of lubrication is the number one cause of final drive failures. Oil leaks at the final drive can lead to costly and time-consuming failures.

When servicing final drives, it is essential to use the correct type and quantity of lubricant. Incompatibility of different lube types can lead to lubrication breakdown and failure, causing wear to components. Final drive housings can also contain the machine brakes, and using the wrong lubricant can lead to brake failure or weakness. Care must be taken that the service is performed correctly, with the lubricant at the correct operating temperature to ensure proper draining. When removing oil drain plugs, check to see whether any metal has accumulated (a lot of manufacturers use magnetic drain plugs), excessive metal on the plug can be an indicator of imminent failure. Several machine manufacturers are using synthetic lubricants, and these should not be mixed with nonsynthetics. As with any type of service, strict adherence to the manufacturer's recommendations is required.

Leaks

Leaks are a serious problem for final drives because they must be repaired as soon as practical. A leaking final drive may have to be removed from the machine for proper servicing. The following procedure is by necessity very general in scope. The particular manufacturer's procedure should be followed for the machine you are working on. To remove the final drive on a tracked loader, follow the steps in **SKILL DRILL 52-1**.

Grader Tandem Drive Oil Change

The oil in the chain drive housing should be changed according to the manufacturer's recommendations. A typical change interval is 2,000 hours or one year. To change the oil in the chain drive, follow the steps in **SKILL DRILL 52-2**.

SKILL DRILL 52-1 Removing the Final Drive

Perform all required lock-out/tag-out procedures to reach zero energy before proceeding with any repairs. First, the track has to be separated to clear the final drive. Follow the manufacturer's procedure for separating and securing the track.

1. Remove the guard to access the parking brake lines.
2. Disconnect the parking brake lines from their connectors, and plug both ends.
3. Remove the clips that hold the brake lines to the machine frame.
4. Remove the bolts and the lock for the spanner nut that holds the parking brake manifold to the frame.
5. Remove the spanner nut; check and discard as necessary the o-ring seal on the back of the spanner nut.
6. Remove the bolts that hold the bottom of the final drive case to the frame.
7. Remove two bolts on opposite sides of the top of the final drive case and install two guide studs at least 6" (15 cm) long.
8. Remove one or two sprocket segments to gain clearance from the track roller.
9. Attach a sling and lifting device to the final drive between the sprocket and the case to take the weight of the drive.
10. Remove the remaining bolts attaching the final drive case to the frame, and install forcing screws into the appropriate threaded holes in the case.
11. Use the forcing screws to push the case away from the frame.
12. When the final drive is removed, oil will leak from the opening in the track motor for the driveshaft of the final drive. Install a plug to stop this leak.
13. Repair the drive as necessary, following the manufacturer's procedures.

SKILL DRILL 52-2 Changing the Oil in the Chain Drive

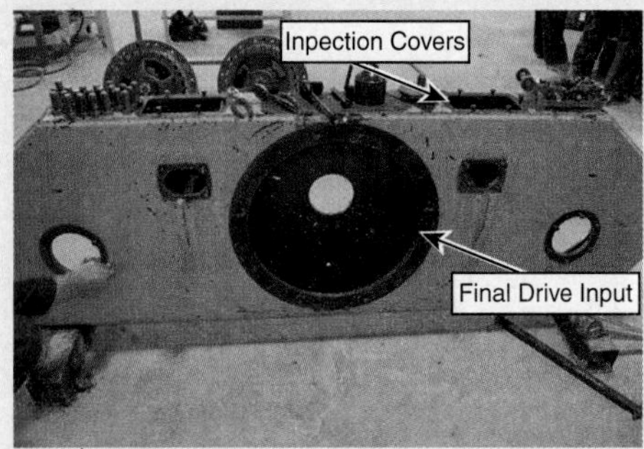

1. Operate the machine long enough to warm the oil.
2. Place a suitable container under the drain plug for the tandem drive. Note that the tandem drive can contain as much as 17 to 21 gallons (65 to 80 liters) of lubricant.
3. Remove the drain plug and the level check plug, and allow the lubricant to drain.
4. Check the lubricant closely for signs of metal wear, contamination, and/or sludge. If there is evidence of contamination, it may be necessary to flush the tandem housing with diesel fuel.
5. Clean the area around one of the cover plates, and remove it from the top of the housing.
6. Clean and replace the drain plug, and fill the tandem through the cover plate opening to the correct level with the recommended lubricant. Clean and replace the level check plug.
7. Clean and replace the top cover.
8. Operate the machine for a few minutes. Then stop and recheck the oil level. The oil level should be even with the bottom of the level plughole; adjust as necessary.
9. Reinstall the level check plug.

Wrap-Up

Ready for Review

- Final drives provide the final reduction in a drive system.
- Machines use large reductions to gain mechanical advantage to do the work required of them.
- Using final drives reduces the load on the other drive system components.
- Transmissions, driveshafts, and drive axles can be smaller.
- In smaller machines, the drive axle can be the final drive.
- Pinion-type final drives are typically part of the drive axle housing.
- Bull and pinion–type final drive can be part of the drive axle or in a separate housing.
- Bull and pinion drive can be single or double reduction.
- Planetary final drives are probably the most common type.
- Planetary drives can be single, double, or even multiple reduction.
- Planetary final drives all use the sun gear input, ring gear held, and carrier for output planetary power flow.
- Chain-type final drives are commonly used to drive tandem machines like graders.
- Planetary drives can be combined with bull and pinion and/or chain drives to create the necessary reduction.
- A typical gear reduction, or torque multiplication through a single planetary gearset, is 3.5:1.
- Multiple planetary gears can be used to create reductions of 9:1 to 25:1 in typical machines.
- Multiple planetary final drive reductions can be as high as 1500:1 in special applications.
- Chain elongation, or "stretching," should be checked regularly.
- Chain "stretching" is actually caused by wear at the rollers and bushings.
- Leaks are a common and serious problem for final drives.
- Final drive lubricants should not be mixed.
- On some machines, the brakes are part of the final drive housing, and these drives require particular lubricants specific to brake application.

Key Terms

bull and pinion drive A drive that uses a small pinion gear driving a larger "bull" gear usually in a separate housing.

chain case The housing that the chain drive runs in.

chain-type final drive A drive system that uses a chain to transmit the torque from a drive sprocket to a sprocket at the wheel end.

double- or multiple-reduction planetary drive A drive that uses more than one planetary gearset.

double-reduction bull and pinion drive A drive that uses two sets of bull and pinion gears in its own housing.

final drive The last reduction in a drive system.

gear reduction A torque increase.

mechanical advantage Occurs when we give up either speed or torque to increase either torque or speed through a machine.

pinion drive A drive that uses a small gear driving a larger gear usually integral to the drive axle.

planetary drive A drive using a planetary gearset.

sprocket A toothed wheel that drives a chain or the track of a crawler machine.

torque multiplication An increase in torque that corresponds to a decrease in speed.

Review Questions

1. What is the main purpose of a final drive?
   a. To connect the drive axle and the wheel end
   b. To provide the last gear reduction in a driveline system
   c. To reduce torque at the wheel or sprocket
   d. To increase the load on the drive axle
2. What speed approximately is the drive sprocket turning on a D8N dozer at 2,100 rpm in top gear?
   a. 200 rpm
   b. 150 rpm
   c. 100 rpm
   d. 80 rpm
3. Which of the following is *not* one of the ways a final drive unit can be driven?
   a. Pneumatically
   b. By hydraulics
   c. By electricity
   d. By a mechanical drive
4. Pinion-type drives are typically located where?
   a. In their own housing
   b. Inside the drive axle
   c. Inboard close to the bevel gearset
   d. Inside the wheel end
5. A bull and pinion drive is typically located in which of the following locations?
   a. Inside the wheel end
   b. Inboard near the bevel gearset
   c. In their own housing
   d. None of the above
6. Bull and pinion final drives can have which of the following?
   a. A single reduction
   b. A double reduction
   c. A planetary gearset as well
   d. All of the above
7. In some machines, the final reduction is from which of the following?
   a. The engine
   b. The transmission
   c. The drive axle
   d. The hydraulic pump

8. The largest planetary gear final drives can have as much as which of the following reductions?
   a. 1500:1
   b. 500:1
   c. 250:1
   d. 25:1
9. Chain drive final drives typically have which of the following lubrication systems?
   a. Pressurized lubrication systems
   b. Splash lubrication from oil in the chain's tandem housing.
   c. The chains are permanently lubed and do not need further lubrication.
   d. Grease fittings to lubricate the chain
10. What must you do before chain elongation or stretch can be measured?
   a. The chain must be tensioned.
   b. The chain should be thoroughly cleaned first.
   c. The chain should be soaked in the proper lubricant.
   d. The chain should be lying on a table at rest.

ASE Technician A/Technician B Style Questions

1. Technician A says that a final drive is the last reduction in a drive system. Technician B says that a final drive may have more than one reduction. Who is correct?
   a. Technician A
   b. Technician B
   c. Both A and B
   d. Neither A nor B
2. Technician A says that a final drive is only capable of increasing torque by three or four times at the wheel end. Technician B says that certain final drives are capable of reductions in the range of several 100 to 1. Who is correct?
   a. Technician A
   b. Technician B
   c. Both A and B
   d. Neither A nor B
3. Technician A says that chain-type final drives are economical when used to drive a set of tandem wheels. Technician B says that chain drives are capable of transmitting torque over significant distance. Who is correct?
   a. Technician A
   b. Technician B
   c. Both A and B
   d. Neither A nor B
4. Technician A says that a final drive reduces the stress on driveline components. Technician B says that final drives allow the use of smaller engines? Who is correct?
   a. Technician A
   b. Technician B
   c. Both A and B
   d. Neither A nor B
5. Technician A says that bull and pinion gears can be used to drop the power flow to the ground from a relatively higher drive axle such as in a crop sprayer. Technician B says that bull and pinion gears are always attached directly to the drive axle housing. Who is correct?
   a. Technician A
   b. Technician B
   c. Both A and B
   d. Neither A nor B
6. Technician A says that planetary final drives use the ring gear in, carrier held, and sun gear output planetary gear power flow. Technician B says that planetary final drives can have multiple planetary gears. Who is correct?
   a. Technician A
   b. Technician B
   c. Both A and B
   d. Neither A nor B
7. Technician A says that a typical reduction from one planetary gear is approximately 9:1. Technician says that most planetary final drive gears are spur gears to prevent axial loading. Who is correct?
   a. Technician A
   b. Technician B
   c. Both A and B
   d. Neither A nor B
8. Technician A says that there can be significant friction between the driven sprocket and the chain in a chain final drive. Technician B says that pins in the pin links of the chain are what contacts the sprocket teeth. Who is correct?
   a. Technician A
   b. Technician B
   c. Both A and B
   d. Neither A nor B
9. Technician A says that all bull and pinion final drives use the lubricant from the drive axle and don't require service. Technician B says that all planetary final drives are pressure lubricated. Who is correct?
   a. Technician A
   b. Technician B
   c. Both A and B
   d. Neither A nor B
10. Technician A says that leaks are one the most common problems with final drives. Technician B says that to repair a leaking final drive, the drive must usually be removed from the machine. Who is correct?
   a. Technician A
   b. Technician B
   c. Both A and B
   d. Neither A nor B

CHAPTER 53
Electric-Drive Systems

Knowledge Objectives

After reading this chapter, you will be able to:

- **K53001** Describe the common safety-related practices for working on electric-drive systems.
- **K53002** Explain how DC switches back to AC to drive propulsion motors.
- **K53003** Describe how an inverter works.
- **K53004** Explain what three-phase AC output is.
- **K53005** Describe the operation of electric-drive cooling systems.
- **K53006** Explain how an induction motor works.
- **K53007** Explain how an electric-drive system can provide machine braking.
- **K53008** Describe a typical maintenance procedure for an electric-drive system.

Skills Objectives

There are no skills objectives in this chapter.

Attitude Objectives

After reading this chapter, you will be able to:

- **A53001** Acquire correct service information for testing and maintenance of batteries.

▶ Introduction

Electric-drive systems have been around for a long time. In the early 1900s, a battery-powered car was developed and produced for public use. During the last few years, electric-drive has started to become accepted in the mainstream automotive world because of the movement to reduce internal combustion engine emissions.

▶ Safety First

K53001

Be aware of some very serious safety concerns when working with a machine that has any type of high-voltage electric propulsion system on it.

Just like machines with high-pressure hydraulic systems, machines that use high voltage have hidden dangers that can cause serious injury or death. Similarly, use common sense and follow the manufacturer's service information, including the cautions, warnings, and procedures. If you anticipate the potential for danger, you can safely work on these systems. **FIGURE 53-1** shows a warning symbol for high voltage.

High-voltage electric propulsion means any system that moves the entire machine, whether it has tracks or wheels, or any system that moves part of a machine, such as the swing function of an excavator with electrical energy, as the power source. Electric propulsion systems require a diesel engine running and driving a generator to create the electrical energy. They may have energy storage such as batteries or a **capacitor**, a passive two-terminal electrical component that stores electrical energy in an electric field, to supplement the generator at certain times.

If the machine has capacitors or batteries built into the system, it may store a potential voltage high enough to injure or kill you. Even if a machine does not have proper electrical storage devices, a possibility for dangerous high voltages exist in conductors and components for some time after the generator and motors stop turning. Many electric propulsion systems normally operate at 480 V, and under certain conditions, over 1,000 V may be present.

Safety experts highly recommend that before anyone works on a machine with a high-voltage system, the person should be aware of any workplace or government regulation that requires specific training or licensing.

Never work on a machine's electrical propulsion system with the generator or motors turning.

If a machine has a high-voltage electrical storage device (batteries or capacitors), to consider it safe, you must isolate it from the system you are working on or deplete its energy level to below 50 V.

You *must always* confirm that the voltage of any conductor or component is under a safe limit of 50 V before proceeding with service or repairs. Do this with a CAT III-rated multimeter, which is a multimeter designed to a **CAT III** standard (CAT is an abbreviation for "category") and is resistant to much higher energy transients than one designed to CAT II standards. You should also wear proper PPE (personal protective equipment). **FIGURE 53-2** shows a CAT III multimeter.

Always consult the machine's service information and follow the procedures it describes to confirm that no more than 50 V are present in any part of the machine's electrical system.

Until you can confirm that less than 50 V are present, *always* wear the appropriate PPE that the machine's service information describes. This includes gloves that meet or exceed ASTM D120-09 specifications, OSHA 29C FR 1910.269 regulations, and NFPA 70E-certified gloves that are rated for 1,000 VAC or 1,500 VDC. Inspect the gloves before use. Take extra care when you inspect the gloves visually, and avoid handling sharp objects. In addition to visual inspection, perform an air test before each day's use. Perform the test per American Society for Testing and Materials (ASTM) Standard Guide F1236-96. **FIGURE 53-3** shows a class 0 glove.

Retest gloves electrically within six months of putting the gloves into service. Gloves that are not in service have a shelf life of 12 months. If gloves have been on the shelf for 12 months and have not been in service, you must retest the gloves electrically before putting them into service. When old gloves are beyond their service date, retest them or shred and dispose of them.

FIGURE 53-1 High-voltage warning.

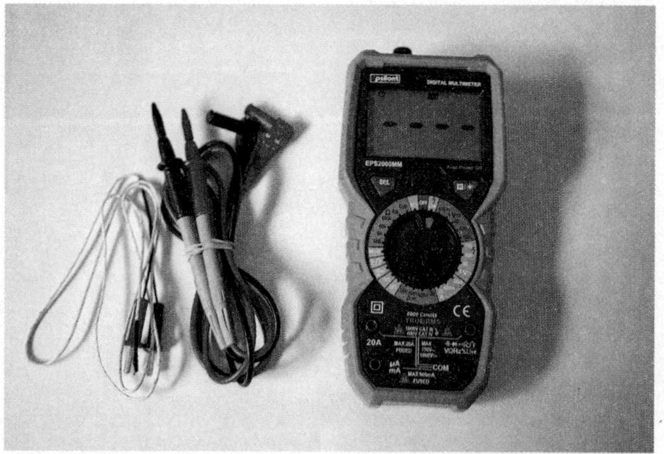

FIGURE 53-2 A CAT III multimeter.

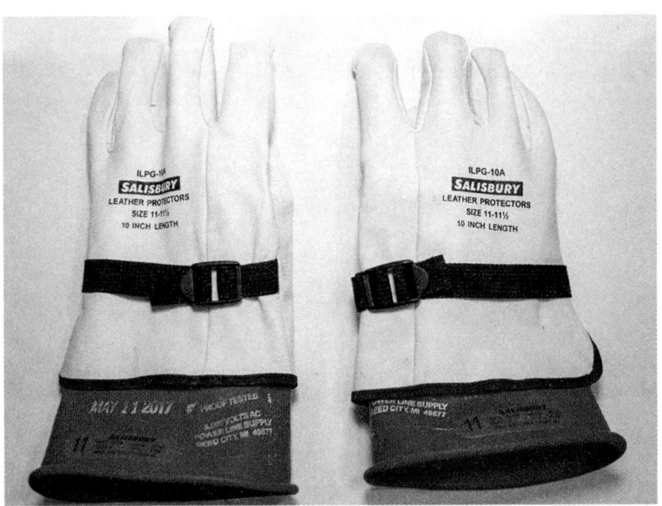

FIGURE 53-3 A class 0 glove.

Until the generator and motors stop turning, *never* remove covers that are part of the machine's electric propulsion system.

Orange insulation on larger conductors indicates high voltage is normally present when the generator or motors are turning, or that high voltage could be present any time an electrical storage device is on the machine.

Never perform any type of service/repair on any orange conductors while the generator or motors are turning. **FIGURE 53-4** shows orange high-voltage cables.

You must properly connect any grounding wires that are part of the machine's electrical propulsion system to where they originally were on the machine. All high-voltage connectors *must* be clean and dry when you assemble them, and you *must* torque all threaded fasteners to specification. You *must* install all original clamps to secure high-voltage cables.

Some electric-drive machines have a hazardous-voltage warning lamp to alert anyone working on the machine that dangerous levels of voltage are present. There are also safe shutdown procedures the technician should follow to ensure that no dangerous voltage is present.

There may be unique ways to lock out and tag out machines with high-voltage systems. Always refer to the manufacturer's service information when performing lockout and tag-out procedures. **FIGURE 53-5** shows a machine's battery disconnect and unsafe voltage light.

FIGURE 53-4 Orange high-voltage cables.

FIGURE 53-5 Locked disconnect and an "Unsafe Voltage" light.

Service personnel should take extra care when using pressure-washing machines with high-voltage drive systems so that they *do not* direct high-pressure water at any high-voltage components or cables.

If you are unsure or uncomfortable working on any part of an electric-drive machine's electric system, do not feel pressured into doing something you are not totally sure about. You need to be confident that you are perfectly safe doing any kind of work on a system that has a potential to cause serious injury or death.

SAFETY TIP

The following is a summary of steps you *must* follow when servicing the electric-drive system:

1. **De-energize.** Eliminate or isolate any electrical system from producing potentially hazardous voltage.
2. **Secure (lock out).** Ensure that the machine does not generate potentially hazardous voltage without knowledge of service personnel.
3. **Verify.** Ensure that potentially hazardous voltage is no longer present.
4. **Proceed.** Perform service to the electric-drive system. Be aware of hazard and warning decals.
5. **Restore.** Ensure that all protective equipment is back in place before resuming operation.

▶ Electric-Drive Systems in Heavy Equipment Machines

K53002

Heavy equipment machines have used diesel electric-drive systems for decades. LeTourneau was the first major equipment manufacturer to embrace electric-drive technology fully when the company produced the first all-wheel drive electric machine for the construction industry in the 1940s.

Underground mines utilize full electric-drive machines because they do not create diesel exhaust emissions. The limiting factor is that the machine has to have either an umbilical cord or a trolley cable system, both of which limit range.

Manufacturers have used diesel electric-drive systems in large mining trucks and some wheel loaders and scrapers since the 1950s.

Diesel electric machines have recently become more popular and either are expected to continue to become a drivetrain option or will replace some models of diesel/mechanical drivetrain machines as time moves on.

Some machines have certain functions or components that high-voltage circuits or electrical energy storage devices power. A few manufacturers have experimented with true hybrid drive systems. These systems take braking or hydraulic energy that is normally wasted and turn it into stored electrical energy that the machine can use for acceleration or operating hydraulic systems. This is the principle behind the hybrid system manufacturers' use for the on-highway vehicles we see now. Several manufacturers have made prototype hybrid drive machines where either batteries or capacitors provide energy storage. Battery technology is the limiting factor in making a true electric hybrid machine practical today.

▶ TECHNICIAN TIP

A true hybrid electric-drive system has the capability to store energy and release it whenever needed. The energy is created by braking action that was typically lost energy in the form of heat. The machine can store energy electrically in batteries or capacitors, hydraulically in accumulators, or mechanically in flywheels.

Some "hybrid" systems can recover braking energy, but not store it, and therefore the system must use the energy instantaneously. When a device such as a blade or excavator stick is lowered, return hydraulic flow can also be converted to electrical energy and stored.

Some electric propulsion systems power the swing mechanism for giant electric shovels. These systems, however, use grid-fed high voltage (they require a massive extension cord!), and only qualified electrical technicians should service them. One massive shovel uses fourteen 700 hp AC motors just to swing the upper structure! **FIGURE 53-6** shows an electric shovel. Notice the wire that feeds power to it.

Any electric-drive machine can use its drive motors for braking. The motor reverses its purpose and becomes a generator that puts a load on the wheels and creates a braking effect. The machine usually sends this heat energy to a resistor grid, where it is dissipated. This is unlike hybrid vehicles that use the drive motors to convert braking energy into electrical energy to recharge the vehicle's batteries.

John Deere recently began selling an electric-drive wheel loader that recycles the energy that slows the machine, to assist turning the engine. In turn, this turns the machine's hydraulic pump. For example, if the machine is coasting with a full bucket and the operator applies the brakes, the propulsion drive motor acts like a generator, and the power it produces feeds into the generator, which is now acting like a motor to assist in driving the diesel engine. If the operator needs to raise the boom when decelerating, this recycled braking energy helps turn the engine that is also turning the hydraulic pumps. The machine saves the fuel that it normally needs to perform this function.

FIGURE 53-6 An electric powered dragline excavator.

This machine reportedly shows an improvement of 25% in fuel economy compared to the same machine that has a conventional drivetrain (torque converter and powershift transmission). This wheel loader is called a hybrid because it can recycle braking energy for instantaneous use, but is not able to store any energy. A diesel engine drives a generator that drives a single motor. The motor then drives a three-speed powershift transmission that does not need directional clutches because the motor changes directions electrically. The transmission then outputs its torque to drive shafts and axles in a conventional manner.

The latest generation of LeTourneau loaders also uses braking energy to drive the engine. LeTourneau currently produces large electric-drive wheel loaders and wheel dozers. **FIGURE 53-7** shows an electric-drive loader.

John Deere is also about to introduce a large electric-drive wheel loader that has an electric motor for each wheel.

For several years, Komatsu has sold a production excavator that features an electric-drive swing system. It captures the

FIGURE 53-7 Electric-drive loader.

FIGURE 53-8 Komatsu hybrid excavators.

FIGURE 53-9 An electric-drive track-type tractor.

energy the machine uses to stop the upper structure when it is swinging and stores it in ultracapacitors. The ultracapacitor can release up to 60 hp instantly to drive the upper structure. Also, a generator/motor between the engine flywheel and hydraulic pumps can charge the ultracapacitor when necessary, and the motor can use stored energy to keep the engine rpm from dropping too far due to sudden load changes. **FIGURE 53-8** shows the Komatsu hybrid excavator. This system reportedly saves 25% in fuel compared to the same-size machine with a regular hydraulic-drive swing function.

Many manufacturers today use electric-drive systems for their large haul trucks in mining applications. AC drive motors eliminate the need for complex drive transmissions using clutches and gear technology. They provide smoother acceleration with highest torque output from 0 rpm. Faster machine speeds accompany improved fuel efficiency when AC drive motors are used. These trucks are in the 150-ton and higher payload class and typically feature a diesel engine–driven generator that outputs to a rectifier that converts the AC generator output to DC capable of charging batteries or capacitors. A wave inverter converts the DC back to AC, which the machine then sends to a pair of drive motors. Motor speed and torque is regulated by frequency control of the AC current supplied to the motor. Three-phase AC electric motors send torque to final drives, which then drive the dual wheels at the rear of the truck. The wheel motors can also provide braking by switching to generator mode. In generator mode, the machine sends electric energy generated by the motors to a brake resistor, where it converts to heat radiated to the atmosphere.

Caterpillar recently came out with an electric-drive track-type tractor. This electric-drive system uses a diesel engine–driven generator whose output electronically changes from AC to DC and then to AC, where it drives two identical AC motors. These motors drive a common bull gear that drives a set of planetary gears. The planetary gears along with a hydraulic steering motor provide a left-to-right track speed differential that steers the machine based on operator commands. Torque then leaves the planetary steering section and goes out to a planetary final drive for each track. **FIGURE 53-9** shows an electric-drive track-type tractor.

▶ TECHNICIAN TIP

Search the Internet for manufacturers that produce electric-drive heavy equipment. See who makes them and what types of machines they are currently producing. Check to see whether any new machines and manufacturers are coming along.

▶ AC Electric-Drive

K53003

Manufacturers use a wide variety of configurations for AC electric-drive systems for machine propulsion. In most systems, the diesel engine's flywheel drives the generator directly, but one machine uses a gearbox that is between the engine's flywheel and the generator. The output shaft of the gearbox transmits torque to the generator's input shaft. **FIGURE 53-10** shows a generator gear drive. For this machine, the engine's speed multiplies three times to increase the speed of the generator to 5,400 rpm when the engine runs at 1,800 rpm. The gearbox also drives the machine's hydraulic pump.

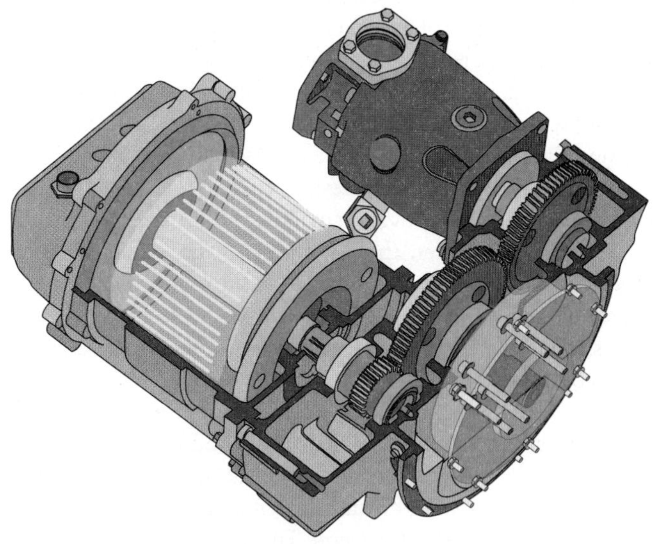

FIGURE 53-10 Generator-drive gearbox.

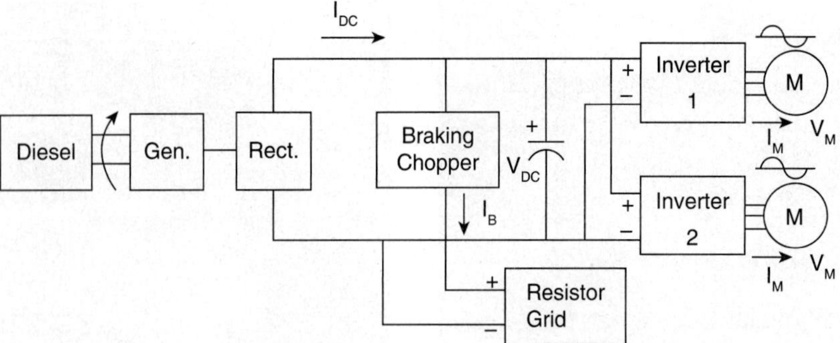

FIGURE 53-11 A block diagram of an electric-drive transmission system.

The main differences between the systems are the type and number of generators, and the type and number of drive motors and how they are controlled. Almost all machines employ one generator to feed one or more electric motors. There are, however, machines that use two generators.

A diesel engine–driven generator produces three-phase AC that supplies a current rectifier converting AC to DC current. To supply more than one AC electric motor with current from an AC alternator, the current has to be converted to DC first before it can be divided to supply AC voltage to two or more traction motors. This DC voltage from the generator is filtered and supplied to AC wave inverters, each of which powers one motor at each wheel end. You may wonder, why not just send the AC power from the generator to the AC motors directly? To change the speed of an AC motor, the frequency of the AC voltage has to change. To do that without converting the generator output to DC would require the speed of the generator to fluctuate because AC frequency is controlled by generator speed. Electronic controls can precisely control the inverter output to the AC motors to match operator demands for speed and direction while having the engine-driven generator turn at a constant rpm (**FIGURE 53-11**).

Advances in the use of AC traction motors have been enabled by the development of insulated gate bipolar transistors (IGBTs) used in the inverters. IGBT are transistors that invert DC current to AC current used by the motors. They are also used to change the speed of the motors by varying the frequency of AC current supplying each motor phase. In contrast to conventional transistors, IGBTs operate at very high currents (>1,000 A) and can switch the frequency of the AC current three to four times faster. High-frequency switching capability not only reduces the AC current resistance, and therefore the heat generated, but it also provides smoother motor acceleration.

From the inverter, the AC flows to the induction-type, asynchronous-drive motors, where it sets up opposing magnetic fields that create an output torque through the motor's shaft. Gears then multiply the motor's output torque to drive either tracks or tires.

This briefly explains the electric propulsion system for most electric-drive machines. Komatsu produces an excavator that has an electric-drive swing system that captures the energy from slowing the swing down, stores it briefly, and reuses it to start the machine swinging again. This energy also assists with keeping the engine rpm steady.

▶ Three-Phase AC Voltage Generation

K53004

If a generator has a rotating magnetic field inside of a housing that has one stator winding formed into two coils, its output is single-phase AC. **FIGURE 53-12** shows a single-phase voltage generator.

This means that at two points throughout each revolution of the rotor, there is zero voltage output. This occurs when the magnetic fields are parallel to the stator winding. At two other points, there is maximum voltage created and in alternating polarities. As the magnetic field rotates between the stator coils, the lines of magnetic flux induce current flow in the stator. The polarity changes each time the poles alternate.

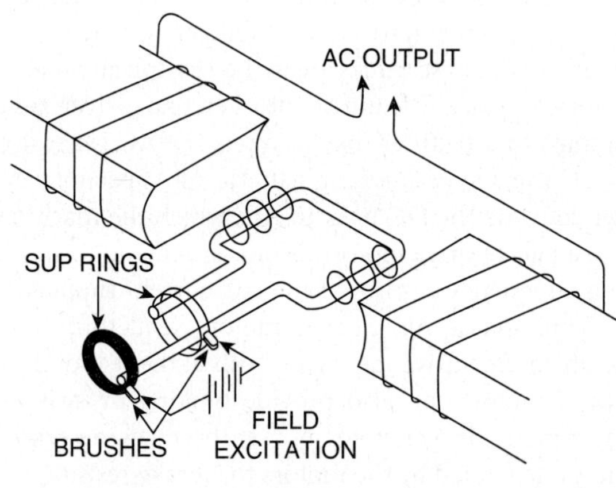

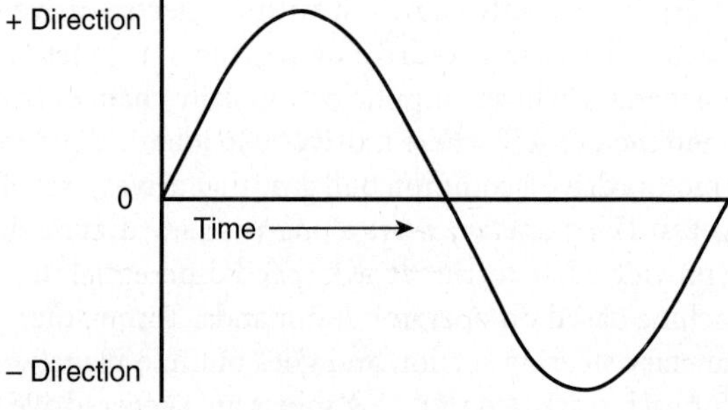

FIGURE 53-12 Single-phase generation.

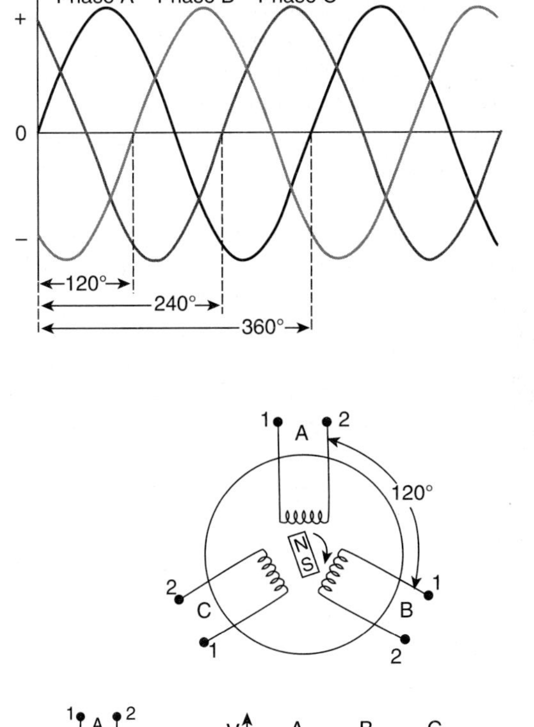

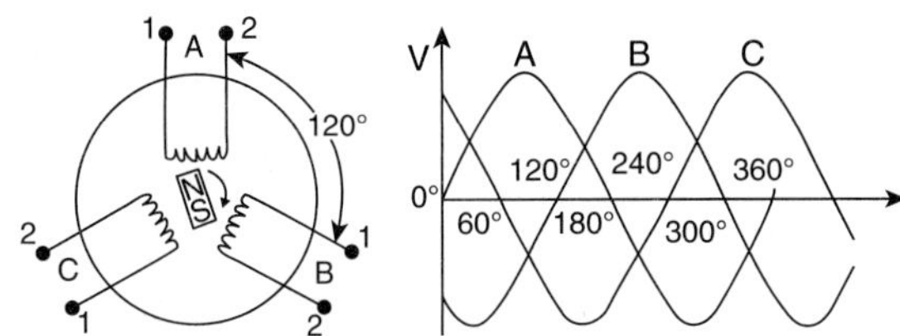

FIGURE 53-13 Three-phase voltage output.

This single-phase output may be alright for a light-duty generator that puts out 120 V AC, but it is not effective for a heavy-duty application. To make a more efficient, stable, and consistent power source, generators must have three separate stator windings. This means for every revolution of the rotor, there are three power outputs. When these combine, a much more stable power supply is created, and the generator actually gains a large amount of efficiency compared to a single-phase generator. This type of generator output is called **three phase**. **Phase**, technically the timing between each point in time (an instant) on a waveform cycle, refers to the timing that occurs between each phase. The **windings** are spaced evenly at 120 degrees around the generator housing. **FIGURE 53-13** shows the output of a simple three-phase AC generator.

▶ TECHNICIAN TIP

The principle behind how a generator works originated with Faraday's law of magnetic induction. If a magnetic field passes over a stationary conductor or piece of wire, and the wire is connected to a load, then a current flow is induced in the wire. Likewise, if the same piece of wire moves over a stationary magnet, then again current flows in the wire. It is the magnetic lines of flux that move past the wire that induce a current flow.

A more practical and effective way of producing voltage is to arrange the magnetic field on a shaft and spin it past the stationary wire, as well as make loops in the wire. Because a magnet has two opposite poles as the alternating north and south poles move past the stator coil, the current flow changes direction in the stator. This is how AC is produced.

To increase the frequency of the AC voltage, the shaft is spun faster. Having more loops in the stator wire or increasing the magnetic field strength increases the amount of current flow.

Generators

The main parts of a typical three-phase AC generator are the rotor, stator, and enclosure. The **stator** is a stationary series of copper-insulated wires that are wound in place in the generator housing. The **rotor** is driven by the diesel engine and creates a series of magnetic poles that spin very close to the stator windings. **FIGURE 53-14** shows a three-phase AC generator.

All generators on electric-drive systems create three-phase voltage. Think of this as one unit making three separate power outputs. This results from three separate windings for the stator assembly. These windings are staggered evenly around the stator frame, which spreads each phase out evenly to create a more even total power output. Each winding wraps around a series of poles that make up the stator frame. The frame is housed in the enclosure and surrounds the rotor.

The generator's three individual stator windings are heavy insulated copper wire that is looped into coils and placed into slots in a laminated soft iron core or pole. The stator leads go to some type of threaded terminal where heavy conductors transfer the generator output to an inverter.

Most heavy-duty generators have a rotor that spins on a bearing at each end of its shafts. These usually run in oil for lubrication and cooling. Some bearings have temperature sensors that initiate a fault code if temperatures exceed a specified limit. The rotors have to be balanced to eliminate any vibration that might make the bearings fail and cause contact with the stator, because there is little clearance between the rotor and stator.

FIGURE 53-14 The main parts of a three-phase generator.

When generators are producing power, they create heat. If the heat level rises too high, permanent damage can occur to stator windings or rotor bearings. All generators on heavy equipment electric-drive machines require some type of cooling. Two common cooling mediums are air and oil.

Because of the unfavorable environment, off-road machines usually work in generators that are sealed from the elements. For air-cooled generators, a pressurized and filtered cooling air system supplied from a central fan ensures generator cooling. Other generators have oil circulating through them for cooling purposes.

Because there is really only one moving part in a generator, not much maintenance is necessary other than changing the cooling oil when required. A generator's biggest enemies are heat and dust.

Manufacturers use three basic types of generators in electric-drive machines: permanent magnet, excited rotor, and switched reluctance.

Permanent Magnetic Generator

A permanent magnet generator is the simplest because the rotor is just a series of spinning magnets. The magnets are arranged to alternate north and south poles past the stator windings as the prime mover (diesel engine) drives the rotor.

Remember: It takes movement of magnetic lines of force (flux lines) to induce current flow in a conductor. The generator's stator is the conductor, and its rotor creates the moving magnetism that induces current flow in the stator.

In these types of generators, as the strength of the magnet is fixed; the output is variable only by fluctuating rotor rpm. **FIGURE 53-15** shows a permanent magnet generator.

A three-phase permanent magnet generator has three separate windings to create three-phase output as the rotor spins inside the stator.

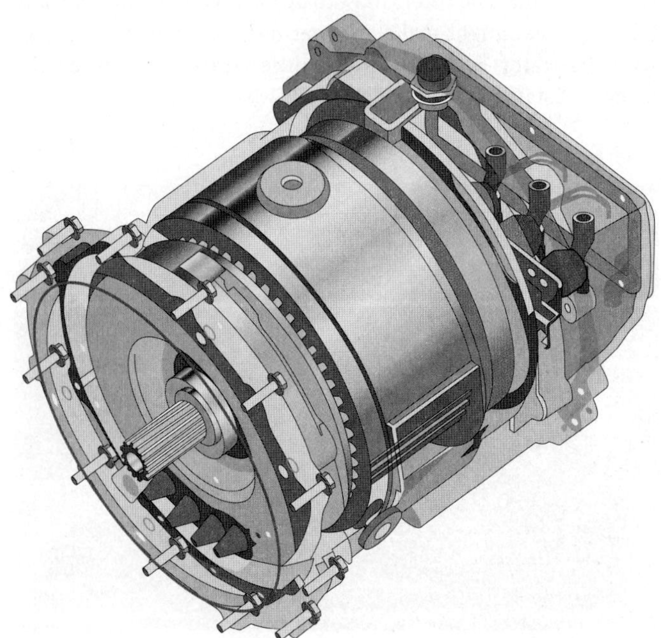

FIGURE 53-15 Permanent magnetic generator.

Excited Rotor Generator

This type of generator most closely resembles the alternator design for the charging system of a machine because the rotor has to become energized to control the output of the generator. In the rotor, a coil of wire, arranged in a series of loops, wraps around a laminated iron core. The energized rotor creates a series of alternating north and south poles that induce voltage into the main generator stator windings as the rotor spins. A rotating exciter coil also energizes the rotor coil, however, and a stator energizes the exciter coil. When the exciter stator is energized and the exciter coil rotates past it, voltage is induced in the coil. Rotating diodes that are part of the rotor assembly then rectify this AC voltage into DC voltage that flows to the main rotor winding to create a strong electromagnet and induce voltage in the main stator. This assembly does the same thing as the permanent magnet rotor except that its strength is controlled with a signal from an ECM (electronic control module). **FIGURE 53-16** shows the rotor of an excited rotor generator.

The generator's output can be closely regulated by controlling the current flow in the exciter stator winding. For example, in a large mining truck, the exciter is controlled electronically at 144V AC and varies current flow from 0 to 20 amps. This in turn varies generator output voltage from 0 VAC to over 2,000 VAC, and output amperage to over 1,000 amps.

Switched Reluctance Generator

A third type of generator is the switched reluctance. It uses a rotor made of a stack of iron laminations and projections or salient poles extending out from a base circle. The diesel engine drives a shaft, which in turn drives this assembly. The rotor's poles and the gaps between them create a changing magnetic reluctance that makes this type of generator work. Reluctance describes how easily magnetic lines of flux can pass through a material. Air has high reluctance, whereas iron has low reluctance.

In the generator's stator are a series of pole pairs with a coil of wire wound around each pair. These poles act as an electromagnet to start the generation process, and are induced with magnetism to create voltage in them. **FIGURE 53-17** shows a switched reluctance generator.

FIGURE 53-16 Excited rotor.

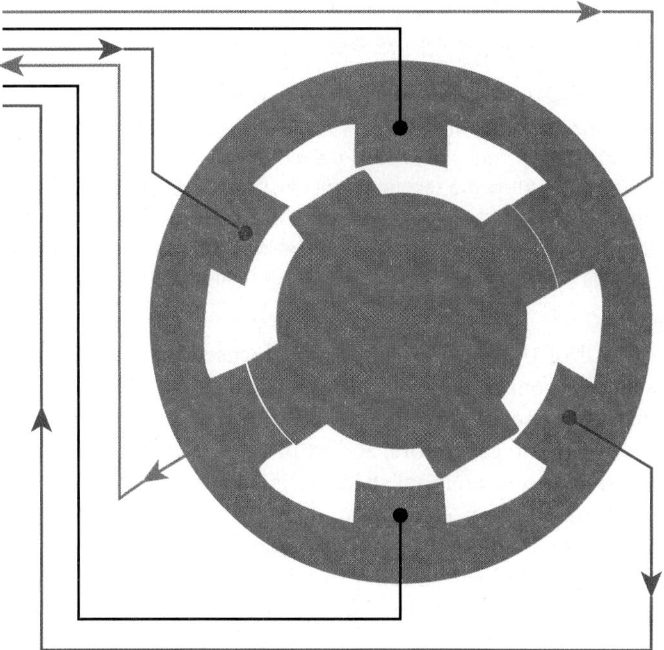

FIGURE 53-17 Switched reluctance generator.

There are more stator poles than rotor poles. A pair of stator poles that are opposite each other are wired in series with a loop of wire. This is called a phase. Electronic controls can switch pole pairs on and off quickly. A popular arrangement for a switched reluctance generator is one that has six stator poles (three phases) and four rotor poles. This type of generator requires sophisticated electronic controls to time the switching of stator poles exactly right to produce the optimum output from the generator.

Switching on a stator pole when it aligns with the rotor directs a magnetic field through the rotor. The mechanical input on the rotor pulls the magnetized poles apart, which increases the stored energy in the magnetic field. When the electronic switch controlling the phase winding turns off the phase, a voltage is induced in the phase winding. The outputs of the individual phase combined with the two other phases make the three-phase output of the generator.

LeTourneau machines use switched reluctance generators in combination with switched reluctance drive motors.

Generator Ratings

All generators are rated by their output in kVA (1,000 volt amps) at a given rpm. This rating for three-phase generators represents the product of their voltage and amperage output multiplied by a power factor that relates to the type of load to which the generator feeds power. **FIGURE 53-18** shows a generator's rating tag.

To calculate the power output of a generator, multiply its maximum amperage output by its maximum voltage output. This gives the output in watts, which you then divide by 1,000 to get its output in kilowatts. Find the equivalent horsepower value by dividing kilowatts by 0.746, because 746 watts equals 1 hp.

FIGURE 53-18 Generator rating tag.

▶ Electric-Drive Cooling

K53005

Most large mining trucks and wheel loaders have an air cooling system that provides pressurized, filtered air for the major parts of the electric-drive system. This is a critical system that keeps the generator, motors, and inverters cool and clean. The system starts with one or more electrically or hydraulically driven fans that draw air through a filter and push it through ducting to the major components of the system. The pressurized air keeps dust and other contaminants out of sensitive electrical/electronic components. Other electric-drive machines have oil-cooled generators or motors in which drivetrain oil circulates through the components to transfer heat away.

Natural convection cools some inverter assemblies, whereas others have their own closed system loop with coolant flowing through it. **FIGURE 53-19** shows a cooling system for an inverter assembly.

▶ Motors

K53006

Electric-drive systems require motors in order to perform work, and they do this by transforming electrical energy into mechanical rotation. They create the necessary torque to propel the machine or to perform other work such as the swing function in the Komatsu excavator. Older electric-drive systems used DC motors that were more difficult to control and required more maintenance. Almost all high-voltage electric motors on machines today are AC motors.

In reality, magnetism moves all loads that electric motors transport. The purpose of every component in a motor is to help harness, control, and use magnetic force to create torque. When attempting to understand an AC drive system, it helps to remember that the machine is actually creating and using magnetic fields to move a load. To move a load quickly requires moving the magnetic fields. To move a heavier load or accelerate faster, stronger magnetic fields (more torque) are needed. This is the basis for all AC motor applications. **FIGURE 53-20** shows an electric motor driving a wheel loader wheel.

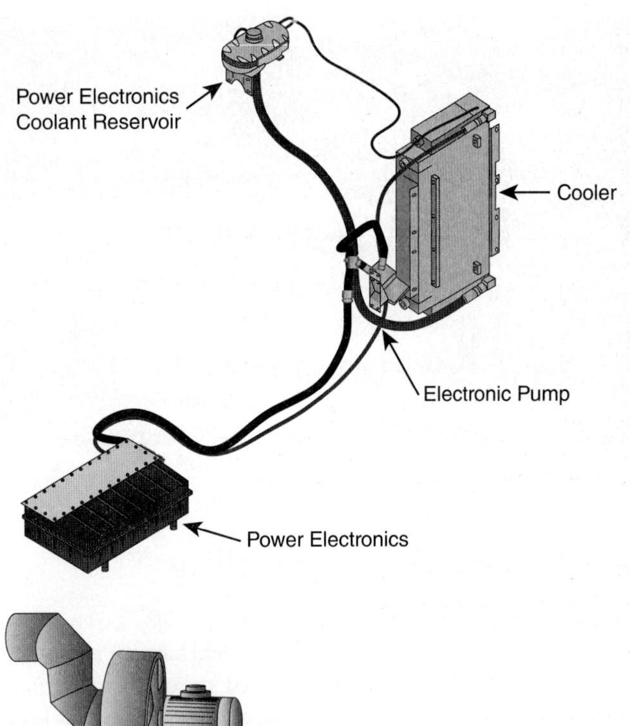

FIGURE 53-19 Cooling system for an inverter assembly.

FIGURE 53-20 AC wheel motor.

> **TECHNICIAN TIP**
>
> Imagine two small, rectangular-shaped permanent magnets sitting in the bottom of a plastic pipe that is cut in half and is several feet long. If you place the two magnets in the slot, with like poles facing each other, and slowly push one toward the other, there is a constant distance between them. If you push the first magnet faster, the second magnet moves faster, as the distance stays the same between them (assume friction is not a big factor here).
>
> If you put an eraser in front of the second magnet to represent a load and push the first one, the distance between the two magnets decreases because of the extra load. A fixed distance between them still exists, but it is just shorter. If you double the size of the first magnet, the distance between the two magnets increases, even with the extra load on it.
>
> This example is similar to the principle of what happens in a motor. If you move the pushing magnet faster, the second magnet moves faster. This changes the output speed of the motor.
>
> If the load on the second magnet increases, then by increasing the strength of the first magnet the load can be overcome and can still be moved. This changes the torque of the motor. These principles apply to the magnetic forces that keep an electric-drive motor turning.

All of the previous discussion focused on the motor as a power consumer that creates torque. Most electric-drive machines also use their motors to perform braking. In this role, they turn into generators, and by producing power, their output shaft is now an input shaft driven by the moving machine. The output of an electric "motor" can charge a battery or capacitor. It can travel to the generator, where it becomes a motor to help loads, similar to what happens with hydraulic pumps; or it can travel to a large resistor, where the power gets converted into heat.

Most AC motors that generate electric propulsion are one of three types:

- Induction-type (squirrel cage) asynchronous motors (the most common)
- Synchronous motors
- Switched reluctance–type motors (used by LeTourneau)

Induction Motors

Induction motors use a stationary stator that creates rotating magnetic fields when it is energized with three-phase AC voltage. The interaction of the three-phase voltage with the three sets of stator windings naturally produces a constantly rotating set of alternating magnetic poles. The speed and strength of these magnetic poles changes with the changing output of the machine's inverter. As the frequency of the AC voltage going to the motor increases, the speed of the rotating field increases, and therefore the speed of the rotor increases. As the level of voltage increases, the strength of the magnetic field increases, and therefore the torque of the motor increases.

The stator's opposing magnetic fields rotate the motor's rotor magnetic fields, and its shaft is the output of the motor. The short explanation of the induction motor is that the rotating magnetic field of the stator produces pushes the rotor around ahead of it.

One type of induction, or asynchronous, motor uses a rotor called a squirrel cage. This term derives from the aluminum conductor bars around its laminated frame, which resemble a squirrel cage. AC voltage that flows through the stator windings induces current in these conductor bars. The induced current in the rotor's individual conductor bars then creates separate magnetic fields around them, which interact with the stator's magnetic fields and constantly try, without success, to work toward a balance of magnetic forces. This is not possible because of the changing stator magnetic fields. This constant offset of magnetic fields keeps the rotor turning. Think of a dog

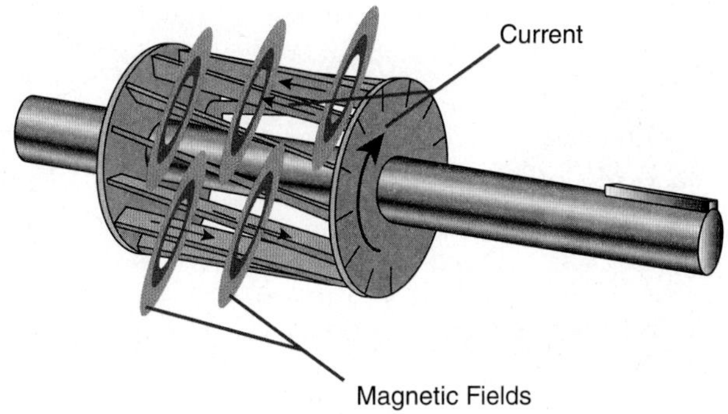

Squirrel Cage Rotor

When the stator's moving magnetic field cuts across the rotor's conductor bars, it induces voltage in them. This voltage produces current, which circulates through the bars and around the rotor end ring. This current in turn produces magnetic fields around each rotor bar. The continuously changing stator magnetic field results in a continuously changing rotor field. The rotor becomes an electromagnet with continuously alternating poles, which interract with the stator's poles.

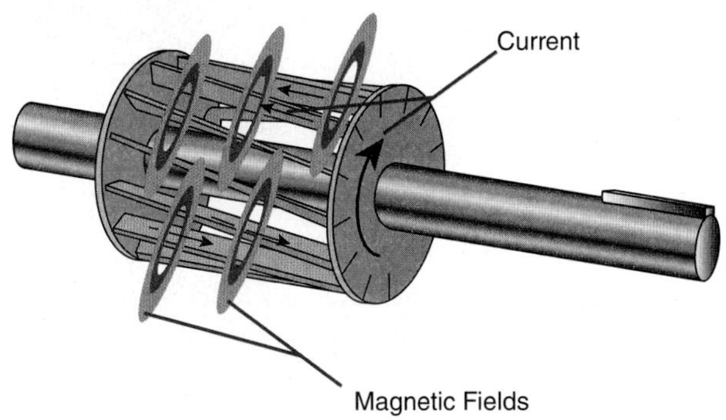

FIGURE 53-21 Rotor of a squirrel cage motor.

chasing its tail. As hard as it tries and no matter how fast the dog moves, it will never quite catch its tail. **FIGURE 53-21** shows a cutaway view of a squirrel cage motor.

An example of the specification of an AC induction motor used for propelling a 240-ton mining truck is presented here:

- The three-phase windings are connected in a wye configuration.
- Maximum rotational speed is 3,180 rpm.
- Full-load travel mode voltage is 1,960 VAC.
- Full-load retarding mode voltage is 2,060 VAC.
- Maximum stall current is 1,300 amps.
- Maximum torque output is 35,523 N·m (26,200 ft-lb).
- Nominal power in travel mode is 1,206 kW.
- Nominal power in retarding mode is 2,430 kW.
- Weight of each motor is 4,100 kg (9,039 lb).

This type of motor has slip between the rotor and stator magnetic fields. Slip is the difference in speed between the rotor and the rotating magnetic fields of the stator. An increase in load causes the rotor to slow down, which creates a higher slip and more torque, exactly what the motor needs to overcome the higher load. A smaller load means a lower slip value. Slip is necessary in this type of motor, to induce current in the rotor windings.

If the operator needs to change the direction of machine travel, a signal is received from the Forward, Neutral, and Reverse (FNR) switch and sent to the drivetrain ECM. The drivetrain ECM sends the signal to the motor control ECM, which then electronically switches two of the three-phase outputs for each traction motor. This phase switch results in the drive motor reversing the direction of rotation.

Permanent Magnet Motors

A permanent magnet motor is the simplest design, and manufacturers use it for low kilowatt applications. Its rotor is made up of a series of magnets spaced equally around the rotor shaft. When three-phase voltage arrives at the stator's three windings, a rotating set of magnetic fields sets up around the perimeter of the rotor. These fields interact with the permanent magnets on the rotor, and because like poles repel, the rotor turns. The rotor shaft is the output of this motor and then goes on to a gear reduction. **FIGURE 53-22** shows a permanent magnet motor.

There is no slip with a permanent magnet because the rotor speed matches the speed of the rotating magnetic fields of the stator. Because of this, they are also called synchronous motors.

Switched Reluctance Motors

In construction, the switched reluctance motor (SRM) is the simplest of all electrical machines. Only the stator has windings.

FIGURE 53-22 Permanent magnet motor.

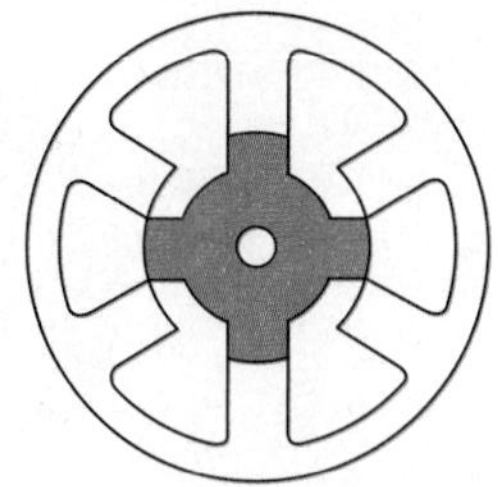

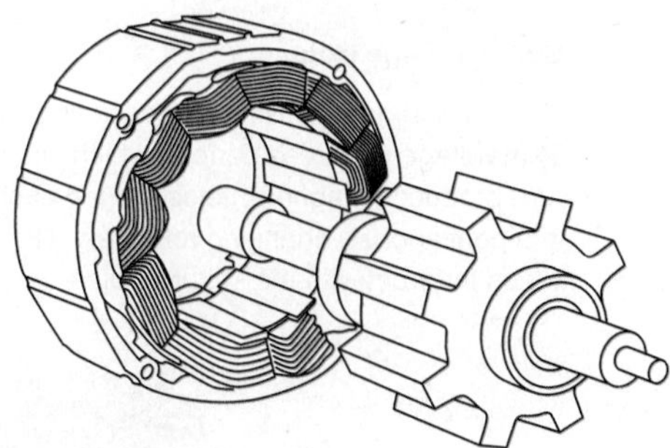

FIGURE 53-23 SRM motor and stator.

The rotor contains no conductors or permanent magnets. It consists of steel laminations stacked onto a shaft that are shaped into poles (sometimes called salient poles).

The two previous types of motors (induction and synchronous) rely on two opposing magnetic fields in the stator and rotor to create shaft rotation. The switched reluctance creates shaft rotation as a result of the variable reluctance in the air gap between the rotor and the stator. When a stator winding is energized, producing a single magnetic field, the tendency of the rotor is to move to its minimum reluctance position, which produces reluctance torque. Basically, the magnetic field occurring between two opposite coils of the stator wants to align with a set of the rotor's poles because that provides the least reluctance. This is a similar action to the force that attracts iron or steel to permanent magnets. In those cases, reluctance is minimized when the magnet and metal come into physical contact. **FIGURE 53-23** shows an SRM rotor and stator.

The direction of torque this configuration generates is a function of the rotor position with respect to the energized phase and is independent of the direction of current flow through the phase winding. Intelligently synchronizing each phase's excitation with the rotor position can produce continuous torque. An SRM has more stator windings than rotor poles.

An SRM achieves rotation by the sequential energizing of stator poles. When the stator pole winding is energized, the nearest rotor pole is attracted into alignment with that stator pole. The rotor follows this sequence, attempting to align rotor poles with energized stator poles. However, as the rotor and stator poles align, the stator poles switch off and the next group of stator poles switches on, continuing the rotation of the rotor.

The SRM generates continuous movement by switching the currents on and off consecutively, thus ensuring that the poles on the rotor continually chase the stator current. The movement achieved is a function of the current flowing through the winding and the characteristics of the iron in the rotor.

SRMs must have their rotor speeds accurately monitored to give feedback to the ECM so it can switch the poles at precise times. Hence, similar to switched reluctance generators, these motors require sophisticated electronics to precisely control the three-phase power to them.

The simplicity of SRMs is one of their main advantages. The downside is the sophisticated electronics and software that must accompany these motors, which have prevented their more widespread popularity.

▶ Braking Resistor

K53007

Electric-drive machines have the benefit of using their drive system to create a braking force. They can turn their motors into generators. The way this happens differs depending on the type of drive motor. Once again the ECM controls this, based on what the operator requests and the stored information in the ECM. This newly created voltage generated by the drive motors has to be dispersed and is sent to a braking resistor.

The most common type is a simple resistor element that is similar to a diesel engine intake heater, only much larger. Think of this as a large toaster grid. This retarder grid usually has a fan mounted to it so that when it heats up, the fan can help dissipate the heat. Sometimes the engine fan does this or a dedicated retarder grid fan that has its own motor to drive it does it. The ECM also controls this motor.

The second type of braking resistor is one that uses engine coolant as a medium to absorb braking heat when needed. **FIGURE 53-24** shows a resistive-type brake resistor.

FIGURE 53-24 Brake resistor.

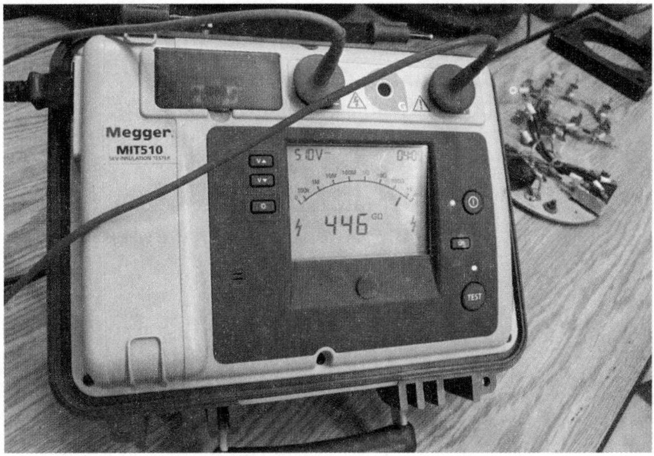

FIGURE 53-25 A megohmmeter.

▶ Maintenance

K53008

A thorough visual inspection of the electric-drive system on a regular basis is very important. Look for any missing or damaged covers or damaged insulation on the high-voltage conductors.

One of the benefits of electric-drive components is their low maintenance requirements. Motors and generators really only have one moving part, and as long as the bearings are lubricated, they should last a long time.

As mentioned before, heat and dust are the biggest enemies of electric-drive components. The technician must check the cooling system for proper operation to ensure that it provides clean, pressurized air to the components. Look for filters that you need to change regularly; they keep the cooling system working well.

Insulation Testing and Maintenance

You can sometimes trace electrical device and cable failures to insulation failure. New electrical insulation deteriorates over time because of the effects of mechanical vibration; excessive heat or cold, dirt, or oil; corrosive vapors; or even humidity on a muggy day. As pinholes or cracks develop, moisture and foreign matter penetrate the surfaces of the insulation, which provides a low resistance path for current to leak to ground, causing a fault. You generally will not notice insulation breakdown visually, but the megohmmeter test can better determine when insulation is starting to fail.

The Megohmmeter Test

The job of insulation is to keep current flowing along its path in the conductor. Ohm's law can help you better understand how to quantify and measure insulation's value. The law states that the voltage in an electrical circuit must equal current multiplied by resistance, or $V = I \times R$. Resistance represents the insulation value of a device or cable as it is tested with a megohmmeter, more commonly known as a megger. This test basically applies a voltage to a conductor and its insulation, and measures the amount of current that "leaks" through the insulation of the device or cable. Good insulation has a high resistance to current flowing through it.

The megohmmeter insulation tester is a small, portable instrument that reads insulation resistance in ohms or megohms directly. Good insulation readings are normally in the megohm range. This testing method is nondestructive to the insulation. The megohmmeter develops a high DC voltage that causes a small current to flow through and over the surfaces of the insulation you are testing. The megohmmeter reads and records the current. If you take readings at scheduled intervals, you can establish trends to help determine when equipment requires replacement or servicing.

FIGURE 53-25 shows a megohmmeter. Technicians should conduct megohmmeter tests under the same conditions each time so the tests provide accurate trending over the life of the cable or device. Temperature, humidity, and other atmospheric conditions can have a huge effect on the results of the megohmmeter test outcome. The megohmmeter test also requires that you remove the power from the cable or device during the testing period, so proper scheduling is an important part of the test procedure. Conduct the test annually unless the cable or device is exposed to the atmosphere, in which case conduct the test quarterly.

When a cable or device fails a megger test, clean, repair, or replace the cable or device.

▶ Electric-Drive Diagnostics and Repairs

A53001

Manufacturer, employee, and government regulations and policies may prevent you from working on high-voltage systems. Attending a manufacturer-backed and dealer-provided service training course is highly recommended before you attempt any repairs on a high-voltage system.

Always start troubleshooting electric-drive systems with simple checks. These include visual inspection and checking for fault codes. Troubleshooting *never* includes removing protective covers on a running unit.

You *must* make yourself familiar with how the system operates, how to check for high voltage, the proper PPE to use when doing this, and the proper test equipment to use. The correct electrical schematic should be available as a reference as well. *Never* proceed with working on a high-voltage electrical system until you are completely familiar with all related safety concerns.

If you find fault codes, a step-by-step procedure exists to help you find the root cause of the problem. A common procedure is to reflash ECM software if updates are available.

If you suspect the power transistors are faulty, special testing tools exist to test their operation. Once you find that an electric-drive major component (generator, inverter, motor) is defective, you will likely replace it as an assembly. The replacement may be a brand-new or exchange unit from a dealer, or a reconditioned unit from a third-party vendor.

It is highly unlikely that a heavy-duty equipment technician (HDET) will disassemble the main components of an electric-drive system unless his or her employer is set up with specialized tooling and provides the proper training to allow this.

▶ Wrap-Up

Ready for Review

- Safety concerns related to electric-drive systems include these:
  - Follow lockout tag-out (LOTO) procedures to prevent high-voltage shock injuries or death.
  - Do not expose high-voltage components when the machine is operating.
  - Use proper lifting procedures to avoid heavy-lifting injuries.
  - Proper PPE usage is critical.
  - CAT III multimeters must be used.
- Orange wires that are part of the electric-drive system indicate high-voltage conductors.
- The five steps to follow when working on an electric-drive system are as follows:
  1. De-energize.
  2. Secure.
  3. Verify.
  4. Proceed.
  5. Restore.
- There are many types of electric-drive machines, such as haul trucks, wheel loaders, dozers, and swing drives for excavators.
- Electric-drive machines allow the prime mover (diesel engine) to run at a steady speed, which translates into greater efficiency.
- A typical electric-drive arrangement is as follows: diesel engine drives a generator; generator output of AC current is rectified to high voltage DC; DC current is converted to AC in an inverter. The operator controls the speed of a motor through the inverter, which varies the frequency of AC current supplied to the AC motors that drive final drives.
- Electric motors have high torque characteristics.
- The AC generator output is three phase for a smoother total current flow.
- An inverter changes DC output to AC; it also regulates the frequency of the AC current to vary motor speed.
- AC generators have two main parts: the rotating rotor and the stationary stator.
- Three main types of generators are permanent magnet, excited rotor, and switched reluctance.
- Permanent magnet generators use magnets on the rotor to induce voltage into the stator when it is rotated inside the stator.
- Excited rotor generators have a rotor with coils of wire wrapped around iron cores. When the coils are energized, the generator produces current. A rotating exciter coil sends current to the main rotor coil.
- A switched reluctance generator has a laminated iron rotor with a series of projections called salient poles. Its stator is a series of pairs of coiled wire arranged in equal spacing around the outside of the generator housing. Sophisticated electronics switch on stator windings at the right moment, which creates a magnetic field in the rotor.
- Generators are rated in kVA units.
- High-voltage conductors are sized in gauge sizes, and MCM and high-voltage connectors must be clean, dry, and secure.
- Larger electric-drive machines have a cooling system for components. This could be a fan and ducting moving air past components or liquid cooling system that circulates oil or coolant through components.
- Inverter assemblies change generator output from AC current to DC current. Then heavy-duty electronic components change the DC back to three-phase AC current. AC voltage and frequency can then be changed to vary the torque output of the motor.
- Electronic controls allow faster and more precise management of electric-drive systems. ECMs can control insulated gate bipolar transistors (IGBTs) that vary the motor output to satisfy operator needs and overcome loads. Electronic controls can easily control machine travel speed and direction.
- Electronic control systems require sensor inputs such as speed, temperature, pressure, position, voltage, and current. An ECM processes these data and sends signals to output devices such as transistors to control the electric-drive system.

- Electric motors change electric energy into mechanical energy. Electric motors have a rotor that rotates inside its housing. The stator is a series of wire loops arranged around the inside of the housing. Electric voltage and current sent to the stator create magnetic fields that rotate the motors shaft. The shaft then drives powertrain components to make the machine travel.
- An increase in current flow increases the torque output of the motor. An increase in frequency increases the speed of the motor.
- Electric motors can also perform braking because they can act like generators when needed.
- Three types of electric motors are induction, synchronous, and switched reluctance.
- Three-phase current sent to an induction motor creates a rotating set of magnetic fields in their stator, which interacts with the rotor to keep it rotating.
- High-voltage systems have to be properly grounded and bonded to prevent stray voltage and injuries related to it.
- Braking resistors dissipate heat from motors when they are used for braking. They resemble large toaster grids, and fans work to cool them down.
- Electric-drive maintenance consists of the following:
  - Complete, thorough visual inspections of all system components and conductors
  - Generator and motor bearing lubrication
  - Cooling system inspection
- Conductor insulation integrity is part of maintenance and consists of using a megger tester. High voltage is applied to the conductor insulation, and excessive leakage is displayed on the test unit.
- Operator complaints lead to a diagnostic procedure to resolve the problem. Technicians must be familiar with all safety-related procedures related to diagnosing electric-drive systems and components. Strict adherence to service information and successful completion of training courses related to diagnosing electric-drive systems will ensure no injuries occur.
- Technicians have to replace most major electric-drive components (generators, motors, inverters) if they find these components are defective.

Key Terms

capacitor A passive two-terminal electrical component that stores electrical energy in an electric field.

CAT III A multimeter designed to a CAT standard (CAT is an abbreviation for "category") that measures high energy levels.

high-voltage electric propulsion Any system that moves the entire machine, whether it has tracks or wheels, or any system that moves part of a machine, such as the swing function of an excavator with electrical energy as the power source.

phase The timing between each point in time (an instant) on a waveform cycle.

rotor A device the diesel engine drives, which creates a series of magnetic poles that spin very close to the stator windings.

stator A stationary series of copper-insulated wires that are wound in place in the generator housing.

three phase Electrical output from every revolution of the rotor in a generator, from three separate windings.

windings Electrical conductors that are wrapped around a magnetic material.

Review Questions

1. This component would *not* be part of an electric-drive system:
   a. Generator
   b. Torque converter
   c. Motor
   d. Inverter
2. When working on a high-voltage system, you should use a multimeter that is rated ________.
   a. SAE III
   b. ISO III
   c. CAT III
   d. API III
3. One type of generator that is *not* used on electric-drive machines:
   a. Switched inductance
   b. Permanent magnet
   c. Excited rotor
   d. Switched reluctance
4. If you were monitoring an AC voltage on an oscilloscope, it would ___________.
   a. be a flat line and negative
   b. be a flat line and positive
   c. be an oscillating line that is positive and negative
   d. be an oscillating line that is positive
5. Three-phase voltage is created by ____________.
   a. having a reversible rotor
   b. having a stator with three sets of windings
   c. having a rotor with three sets of windings
   d. rectifying the single-phase output
6. An induction motor has its conductor bars turned into electromagnets by ________.
   a. commutators and brushes
   b. stator phases being energized
   c. variable reluctance
   d. permanent magnets
7. This color identifies high-voltage conductors:
   a. White
   b. Black
   c. Red
   d. Orange
8. A switched reluctance motor has ____________.
   a. a series of permanent magnets
   b. a series of winding
   c. a series of salient poles
   d. a set of commutator bars

9. You would find an IGBT in this electric-drive component:
   a. The motor
   b. The inverter assembly
   c. The generator
   d. The cooling system
10. Technicians commonly use a megohmmeter to test __________.
    a. the generator stator windings
    b. the motor rotor windings
    c. the retarder grid
    d. the insulation on high-voltage conductors

ASE Technician A/Technician B Style Questions

1. Technician A says you should retest PPE class 0 gloves within six months of putting the gloves into service. Technician B says you should retest gloves that have not been in service for 12 months. Who is correct?
   a. Technician A
   b. Technician B
   c. Both A and B
   d. Neither A nor B
2. Technician A says red insulation on large conductors indicates that high voltage is normally present when the generator or motors are turning. Technician B says orange insulation indicates this high voltage. Who is correct?
   a. Technician A
   b. Technician B
   c. Both A and B
   d. Neither A nor B
3. Technician A says an inverter converts AC generator output to DC then back to AC voltage. Technician B says an inverter converts DC generator output to AC. Who is correct?
   a. Technician A
   b. Technician B
   c. Both A and B
   d. Neither A nor B
4. Technician A says electric-drive machines allow the engine to run at a constant rpm. Technician B says electric-drive machines make the engine run more efficiently. Who is correct?
   a. Technician A
   b. Technician B
   c. Both A and B
   d. Neither A nor B

5. Technician A says that electric-drive machines originally had a generator that produced AC voltage that the machine rectified to DC to drive DC motors. Technician B says these early machines produced DC voltage that the machine rectified to AC to drive AC motors. Who is correct?
   a. Technician A
   b. Technician B
   c. Both A and B
   d. Neither A nor B
6. Technician A says almost all machines employ one generator to feed one or more electric motors. Technician B says almost all machines use two generators. Who is correct?
   a. Technician A
   b. Technician B
   c. Both A and B
   d. Neither A nor B
7. Technician A says single-phase generator output is best for heavy equipment applications. Technician B says three-phase output is best. Who is correct?
   a. Technician A
   b. Technician B
   c. Both A and B
   d. Neither A nor B
8. Technician A says a generator's biggest enemies are water and air. Technician B says they are dust and cold. Who is correct?
   a. Technician A
   b. Technician B
   c. Both A and B
   d. Neither A nor B
9. Technician A says the main parts of a typical three-phase AC generator are the windings, the housing, and the rotor. Technician B says the main parts are the rotor, the stator, and the enclosure. Who is correct?
   a. Technician A
   b. Technician B
   c. Both A and B
   d. Neither A nor B
10. Technician A says the ECM increases power to the brakes to control traction on some heavy equipment. Technician B says the ECM decreases the output to the rotor to control the traction. Who is correct?
   a. Technician A
   b. Technician B
   c. Both A and B
   d. Neither A nor B

SECTION VII

Braking Systems

CHAPTER 54

Off-Road Heavy-Duty Hydraulic Brakes Fundamentals

Knowledge Objectives

After reading this chapter, you will be able to:

- K54001 Explain the purpose and fundamentals of hydraulic braking systems.
- K54002 Describe the principles of operation of hydraulic brake system components.
- K54003 Describe the components of an off-road heavy-duty hydraulic foundation brake.
- K54004 Describe the actuation components of an off-road hydraulic brake system.

Skills Objectives

After reading this chapter, you will be able to:

- S54001 Describe the steps to test and diagnose the brake system.
- S54002 Describe the steps for hydraulic brake circuit inspection.
- S54003 Troubleshoot and repair hydraulic brake systems and components.
- S54004 Describe bleeding of a brake system to remove air in the system.

▶ Introduction

Heavy-duty equipment technicians working on machine braking systems must be fully aware that the braking system/s on any piece of heavy equipment machinery could be considered the most important safety feature of that machine. If a technician fails to repair a brake system fault properly, there are huge potential negative consequences, from monetary damage to machines and surrounding equipment, to injury and death of operators and workers. The machine's brake system must be fully functional as it is designed to be. From simple things like properly checking brake fluid level to brake system air bleeding, many crucial checks and procedures must be carefully followed to ensure maximum brake performance is available. Several videos available on the Internet demonstrate the serious results of brake system failure. Machines usually have a fail-safe brake system so that if there is a major failure of the service brake system, a secondary brake system will bring the machine to a controlled, safe stop. This should happen automatically, and the secondary system could also have a backup system as well; this would be called a triple redundant system. This chapter introduces the technician to the various types of hydraulic braking systems used on MORE and the service and maintenance required for those systems.

▶ Fundamentals of Hydraulic Braking Systems

K54001

The automotive industry has had a mostly consistent configuration for frictional/hydraulic braking systems. Generally, **hydraulic calipers** and rotors are used for the front wheel braking action, and the same arrangement or drum brakes are used for the rear wheel brakes. The brake components that actually perform the braking action are called the foundation brakes. These systems are usually vacuum boosted to create a more powerful brake system. Vehicles larger than a standard half-ton pickup truck could use deviations from this standard, and most highway trucks that are five tons and larger use an air brake system that generally uses air chamber–actuated S-cam drum brakes for the foundation brakes.

These are general statements that overlook the recent influence of electronics being incorporated into brake systems to give antilock, stability, and traction control. Antilock brake systems, or ABS, were rarely seen in the MORE market due to the relatively slow speeds of these machines. However, these systems are now being offered in a variety of equipment. Traction control systems are becoming increasingly popular on wheeled machines for stability while negotiating turns. The machine's electronic controls sense wheel slip and selectively apply the brakes on the slipping wheel to regain control. Traction control gives the operator a more stable machine. Perhaps the most important reason, however, for a traction control system is to protect the expensive tires on these machines from damage caused by wheel slip. The tires on a loader can be worth thousands of dollars each, and when these tires slip on jagged rocks, severe damage can ensue. Traction control helps to avoid early tire failure. Advancements in electronics, such as the addition of more sensors, ECMs, and proportional control valves, have made brake systems more effective, efficient, and smarter. Brake bias (front to rear proportioning) can be adjusted by the ECM to give more effective braking. Brake wear can also be compensated for by electronic control systems.

Making general statements like this in relation to heavy equipment brake systems is impossible. Because of the diversity in design of MORE, almost every conceivable method of slowing or stopping a machine is likely already being used in one form or another in the braking systems of heavy equipment. As many as four different types of brake systems may be used to slow a machine down, stop it, and hold it in place. This chapter focuses mainly on hydraulically actuated, spring-released as well as spring-actuated, hydraulically released types of brakes that are used on wheeled machines. Brakes are used for different functions on heavy equipment, such as for steering the machine and for controlling winches, but this chapter deals with brakes that are used for slowing and stopping moving machines (dynamic braking) and holding machines stationary (static braking). MORE brake systems are required to control extremely heavy equipment, such as the 100-ton rock truck shown in **FIGURE 54-1**.

Brakes that are used to slow a moving machine under normal conditions are called service brakes; brakes used to stop a machine in an emergency or to hold a parked machine stationary are called secondary brakes.

Brakes systems use different energy sources such as air, hydrodynamic, electromagnetic, and engine exhaust, but this chapter only discusses brake systems that use hydraulic and spring pressure.

You Are the Mobile Heavy Equipment Technician

You are asked to visually inspect the hydraulic brake system on a Caterpillar 725C articulated rock truck and determine the following:

1. What type of foundation brakes does it use?
2. What type of fluid does the system use?
3. How is the brake fluid level checked?
4. Is there any brake system malfunction operator warning system in the cab?
5. What type of parking brake does the machine use?
6. Are there any adjustments that can be made to the braking system?

FIGURE 54-1 A robust braking system is required to stop machines such as this 100-ton rock truck.

FIGURE 54-2 Hybrid electric drives like this one from John Deere are making inroads in the heavy equipment market.

The kinds of machines that use these types of brake systems are listed here:

- Track-type machines: for steering and static braking
- Wheel loaders: for service and parking brakes
- Mining trucks: for service and parking brakes
- Articulated trucks: for service and parking brakes
- Graders: for service and parking brakes
- Forestry machines: for service and parking brakes
- Backhoe loaders: for steering, service and parking brakes
- Fork lifts: for service and parking brakes.

Braking Fundamentals

Any brake system used to slow down (dynamic braking) and stop (static braking) a vehicle in motion is merely an energy conversion machine. The law of conservation of energy states that energy can't be destroyed; it only changes states. For a heavy equipment machine, an energy source (usually diesel fuel) gets converted into heat energy by the machine's drivetrain to create motion, and once the machine is moving, its momentum or inertia wants to keep it moving. This is called kinetic energy. If the machine were to continue to coast on a level surface, frictional losses in the drivetrain would overcome the kinetic energy, and the machine would eventually stop moving. To allow the operator to bring the machine to a controlled stop or decelerate on command, there has to be a frictional brake system to convert the kinetic energy back into heat energy. This heat energy is ultimately dissipated to the atmosphere on most machines. Hybrid drivetrain systems try to recycle the braking energy that was previously lost by using the kinetic energy to charge a capacitor or battery pack. The stored energy is then used to power the machine (**FIGURE 54-2**).

The kinetic energy of a moving machine is converted into heat energy by friction. A simple example of how friction is turned into heat is by imagining what you do if your hands are cold. By rubbing your hands together, you are creating friction and heat. The faster you rub and the harder you press them together, the more heat you create. This is the same principle used for the dynamic braking system of a machine. As mentioned, brake systems are designed to create heat. However, if this heat isn't dissipated properly, it becomes excessive and will then transfer into the brake system and other related components. Premature failure of these components is likely to occur soon after.

The operating concept of hydraulic brake applications is the use of fluid as a transmitter of power. This concept is well known to the MORE technician. One of the main principles of hydraulic systems is that they can be designed to apply significant stopping pressure through mechanical advantage (leverage), using the fluid as the transfer medium. This means that few mechanical linkages are necessary, as tubes and flexible hoses can be used to transfer the required force from the **master cylinder** exerting the initial application force to the **wheel cylinders** exerting the activating force to apply braking pressure. Off-road heavy-duty hydraulic braking systems are closed-loop systems. The basic hydraulic system, shown in **FIGURE 54-3**, pressurizes hydraulic fluid at the master cylinder when the operator steps on the brake pedal. That pressure is then transmitted through the system lines (tubes and hoses) to the wheel cylinders. There is very little fluid movement in the system—only enough to move the pistons in the wheel cylinders. When the brake pedal is released, springs in the wheel cylinders return the fluid to the lines.

Advantages of Hydraulic Braking Systems

Hydraulic braking has the advantage of having fewer mechanical parts that can wear and break down. Hydraulic braking systems are compact and rely on the multiplication of hydraulic force applied to the **brake shoes** or **brake pads**, meaning a small force can control large forces. The following list summarizes the main advantages of hydraulic systems:

- **Simplicity:** Hydraulic braking systems do not require complicated systems of gears, cams, cables or linkages, and the wear and distortions associated with these components is eliminated.
- **Precise control:** Brake application control must be very accurate and repeatable.

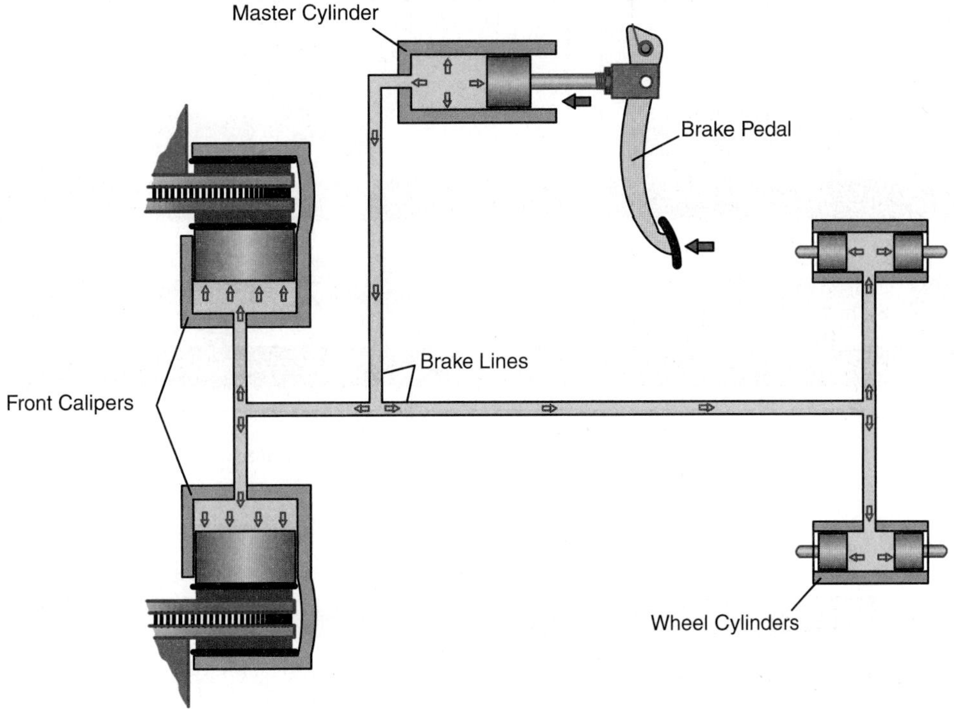

FIGURE 54-3 Basic closed-loop brake system.

- **Multiplication of force:** Hydraulic braking systems allow for relatively small actuators at the point of force application compared to other types of systems.
- **Flexibility:** Components can be located at widely separated points.
- **Construction:** Although numerous components may be required, the actual construction of the system is fairly simple.
- **High control ratios:** Very large forces can be controlled by very small forces.
- **Ability to turn corners:** Fluid conduits are designed to transmit fluids up, down, and around corners without significant losses in efficiency.

Disadvantages of Hydraulic Braking Systems

There are disadvantages to hydraulic systems, such as the potential for equipment failure when hoses fail and the hydraulic fluid leaks. However, the disadvantages are far outweighed by the advantages of these systems.

The following list summarizes the main disadvantages of hydraulic systems:

- **Cleanliness requirements:** To ensure long life and best efficiency, hydraulic fluids must be kept clean and free of contaminants.
- **Safety:** High-pressure fluids can be a safety hazard in the case of hose or tubing breaks.
- **Fire hazard:** All hydraulic fluids will burn under certain circumstances. Fluids must not be exposed to open flames or high-temperature heat sources.
- **Leaks:** Fluid leaks and spills can be hazardous.

Braking Effort

Brake effort is usually measured in inch-pounds and can be thought of as the opposite force to the one created by an engine's crankshaft, which is measured in foot-pounds. If a heavy-duty diesel engine can produce 2,000 ft-lb of torque at the flywheel, the opposite but equal value of brake effect would be 24,000 in.-lb. The crankshaft of an engine twists or rotates a load at the start of the machine's drivetrain in order to move the machine from a stop or accelerate it to a higher speed, and the brake system slows or stops rotation at the opposite end of the drivetrain to slow or stop the machine's motion.

The brake effort that is discussed in this chapter is created by the force applied to a component with attached friction material being pushed against another component usually made from steel or cast iron. One of the two components has to be stationary and one rotating; as pressure is applied, friction increases and the speed of the rotating components diminishes.

Braking effect can also be measured in horsepower. The amount of horsepower consumed when slowing a moving machine is massive when compared to its engine's horsepower. Horsepower is calculated based on the amount of rotational force (torque) created and the speed (rpm), or rate of time, at which that force is spinning.

To stop a machine from full speed in a very short distance requires a huge braking effort. For example consider a rock truck loaded with 400 tons of material and traveling at a top speed of 42 mph. The total weight of the vehicle is 1,375,000 lb, and it uses a 4,000 hp engine to propel the machine. Its total brake surface area is just over 52,000 square inches. The torque of a 4,000 hp engine is sent through the machine's drivetrain and is able to take the loaded truck from 0 to 42 mph in 60 seconds. If the truck is

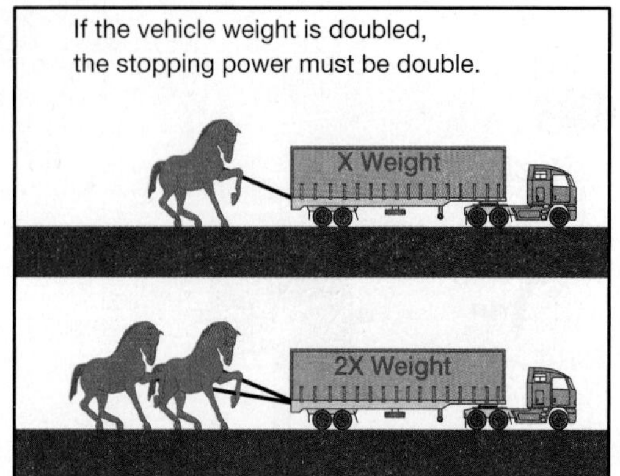

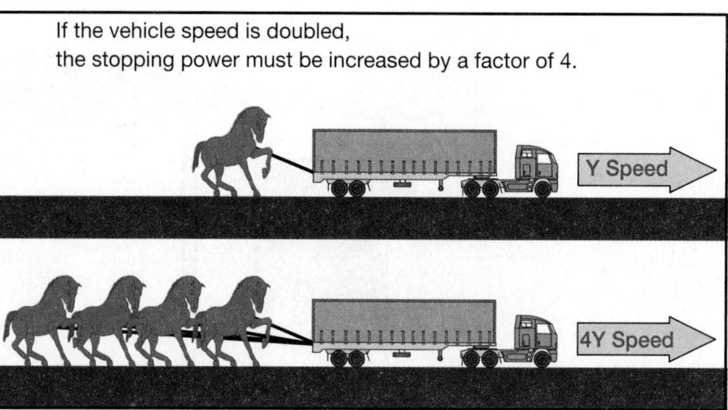

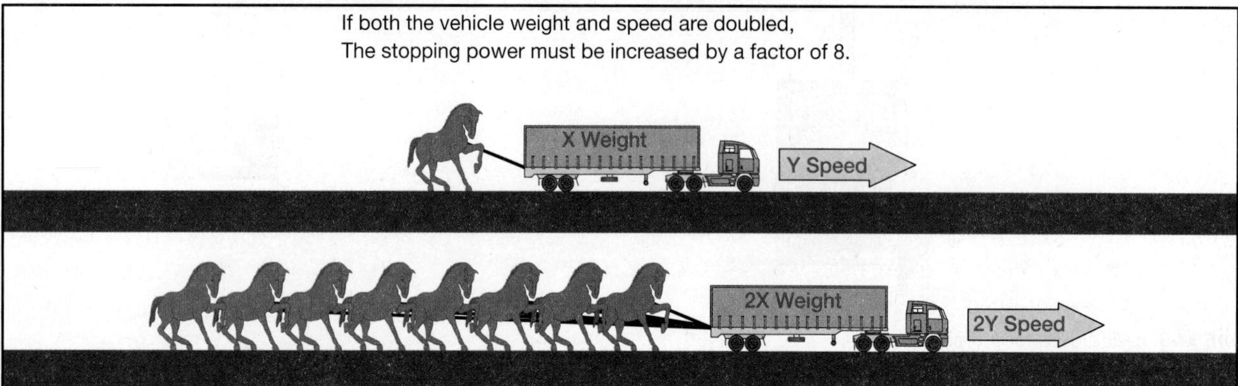

FIGURE 54-4 How speed and weight affect stopping distances.

required to stop from this speed in less than 6 seconds, the brake system must be capable of converting 40,000 hp worth of kinetic energy back into heat. Although the amount of heat energy created is massive and hard to fathom, it is still just created by the friction of the brake material against steel or cast iron.

The forces involved in decelerating a machine are considerable. Looking more closely at the factors influencing brake system capabilities, it is important to note increasing amounts of energy are required as a machine's weight and speed increase. Using the engineering formula used to calculate the energy of motion, kinetic energy, it can be demonstrated that as the weight of the machine is doubled, the kinetic energy required to be converted into heat energy to stop it is also doubled. Doubling the speed of the machine, however, requires four times the braking effort. **FIGURE 54-4** shows the influence of vehicle speed and weight on required braking force. When weight and speed are both doubled, braking force must increase by a factor of eight.

Increasing speed therefore has a greater effect than weight on the required braking system power. Figure 54-4 shows how speed and weight affect stopping distances. In older, very primitive brake systems, the effect was created by forcing a stationary piece of wood against a rotating steel rim. See **FIGURE 54-5** for an illustration of a primitive braking system.

The amount of braking effect created by these two materials is determined by their coefficient of friction and the clamping force applied to the block of wood. Coefficient of friction is a major factor in determining the rate of deceleration a braking system can create. The amount of force applied is determined by mechanical advantage, spring pressure, hydraulic pressure, or air pressure. Coefficient of friction is defined as the force required to move a material of a certain weight across the surface of another material. See **FIGURE 54-6** for an example of this.

FIGURE 54-5 A primitive friction brake system.

If it takes 35 lb of force to move the 100 lb block of hardwood across a steel plate, then the hardwood and is said to have a coefficient of friction of 0.35 to that surface. If another type of material (that also weighs 100 lb) takes 50 lb of force to move it across the same steel plate, then its coefficient of friction is 0.50.

If the friction material is intended to be used in a dry state and a lubricant is introduced, this will lower the coefficient of

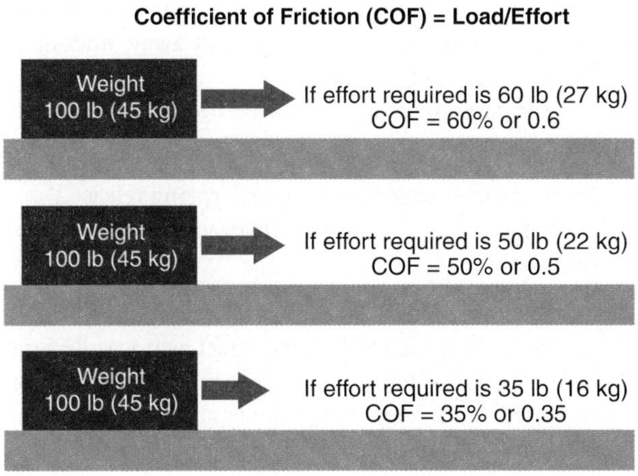

Coefficient of Friction (COF) = Load/Effort

Weight 100 lb (45 kg) → If effort required is 60 lb (27 kg) COF = 60% or 0.6

Weight 100 lb (45 kg) → If effort required is 50 lb (22 kg) COF = 50% or 0.5

Weight 100 lb (45 kg) → If effort required is 35 lb (16 kg) COF = 35% or 0.35

FIGURE 54-6 Different coefficients of friction.

FIGURE 54-7 Friction material COF is tailored to the specific use.

friction. For example, this happens if there is a leak from the brake hydraulic system onto the friction material. Some friction material is designed to be operated wet or to have oil circulate around it. The oil circulating around the brake material carries heat away from the friction-creating components.

Brake friction material manufacturers test their materials and list their products with a coefficient of friction. The higher the value, the higher the force required to move the material across a steel surface and therefore the better braking effect for that material. The trade-off for this is usually a shorter lifespan for the friction material and more heat generated.

Brake friction materials consist mainly of non-asbestos organic and/or metallic materials (fiberglass, Kevlar, ceramic, etc.), friction modifiers (alumina or silica), and a resin binding agent that keep these compounds together. The materials are combined and cured in a baking process and formed into different shapes. These shaped friction materials are then attached to a metal backing that makes a disc, shoe, or pad assembly. They are either chemically bonded (glued), riveted, or attached by both methods to the metal backing. These assemblies are then connected to the machine as part of a stationary or moving component of the brake system. Friction material can withstand intense high temperatures, but if the operating temperature gets close to the manufacturing temperature of the materials, the material will start to break down. If you have ever watched a car race at night and observed the action at a hard-braking zone, you may have noticed the brake rotors glowing red soon after the driver applies the brakes. This is a good example of the heat energy that has been created by the brake system to slow down the speeding racecar. The friction material for racing applications must be formulated to withstand these extreme temperatures.

In Europe there is a racing series that features large highway trucks that are highly modified and reach high speeds. To keep the friction material from melting, the teams install a water spray system to help cool the brakes after a heavy application. You can view several videos of these trucks in action and see the steam coming off the brakes as the truck is braked hard into a corner.

Generally, softer organic friction material has a higher coefficient of friction (COF) but will not last as long as harder material, which usually has a lower coefficient of friction. Ceramic, or inorganic friction materials, will have the highest coefficient of friction (**FIGURE 54-7**).

▶ TECHNICIAN TIP

Here's an example of what can happen when excessive heat builds up from a malfunctioning brake system:

I worked at a limestone quarry where a large wheel loader had a leak at the front axle. I was asked to determine where the leak originated and how to fix it. When the machine was closely inspected, it was found to be leaking at both front wheel seals. When the axle was filled up, the oil leaked out fairly steadily, so I reported that both wheel seals had to be replaced. I also noticed that the axle oil smelled burnt. The foreman wanted the machine to go back to work, so the axle was topped up, and the machine was given back to the operator. I noticed when the operator pulled the machine out of the shop and went from reverse to forward that it rocked more than usual. I asked the operator to stop, and then I got in the cab myself. Upon further investigation, I found that the brake pedal was sticking down slightly because of a mud buildup on the floor of the cab.

The sticking pedal caused the brakes to always be slightly applied, and the longer the machine was run this way, the more heat built up. This excessive heat eventually caused the wheel seals to fail, which resulted not only in a repair that cost several thousand dollars but also in the machine being down for unplanned maintenance.

Factors That Affect Braking

Braking effort can be changed by changing any of the following four factors:

- **Braking leverage:** The further away the friction material is from the centerline of the component being braked, the higher the brake torque that will be generated, meaning more effective braking. For example, if the friction material is forced against a rotating component 12 inches from its axis of rotation, instead of 6 inches, braking effort on the component will be much higher. This factor is part of the design of the machine and is determined by engineers in order to give the brake system enough torque to properly slow and stop the machine. An automotive example is the larger-diameter brake rotors, installed on high-performance cars, that increase braking leverage and therefore braking performance.

- **Total swept area:** The brake swept area is the total surface area that the friction material has in contact with its opposing brake surface. An increase in the swept area means more friction surface area creating the brake effect and therefore more powerful brake function. This is also determined by engineers and is not an item to be modified. Some articulated rock trucks use as many as three sets of calipers per rotor in order to increase the braking effort by increasing the swept area of friction material exposed to the rotor. See **FIGURE 54-8** to see a rotor and dual caliper brake arrangement used on a rock truck.
- **Coefficient of friction:** If the friction material has a higher value, this means more grab or more brake effect. This is another item that is not typically changed from what the engineers originally designed to be used for a particular machine. When friction material lasts for less than its expected life, it may be possible to buy another type of material, but this isn't very common for heavy equipment machines.
- **Higher clamping force:** More force applied to the friction material means more brake effect. Whether this force comes from springs or a hydraulic system, it must be as high as originally designed or the machines brakes will not perform as they should. This part of the brake system is the one area where a technician will have the most influence.

For the service brake system, the clamping force must be infinitely variable from zero pressure to maximum system pressure as requested by the operator. If the operator can't control the clamping force as he or she should, there will be complaints like the brakes locking up or not slowing the machine as much as desired.

For the parking or secondary brake system, the clamping force has to be as high as originally designed. Anything less than this means the parking or secondary braking system will not work properly, and the machine may roll away, uncontrolled, after the parking brake is applied.

FIGURE 54-8 Rotor and dual caliper.

The clamping force applied to the friction material comes from three sources:

- Mechanical linkage (lever applied, spring released)
- Hydraulic fluid pressure (hydraulic applied, spring released)
- Spring force (spring applied, hydraulic released).

The key to keeping the braking effect as it was designed is to keep the brake system components relatively cool, use the recommended fluid, keep components adjusted properly, and keep them in good condition.

▶ Machine Hydraulic Brake Systems

K54002

To apply or release a machine's dynamic hydraulic brake system, the operator controls the flow of hydraulic fluid to do one of two things. The fluid will either force a friction material against a steel component to slow down and stop a machine, or it will release (drain) fluid pressure to allow spring pressure to force a friction material against a steel component. If the operators braking action sends fluid to move a component against spring pressure, this fluid is being modulated to differing pressures by the operator. If the operators braking action releases fluid pressure or drains it, this is called a reverse modulating system.

A reverse modulating system has spring-applied brakes, fluid pressure is used to compress the spring and release the brakes when the brakes are not applied. When the operator applies the brakes, this pressure is then released, allowing the spring(s) to apply the brakes. This is one way to provide a fail-safe type of brake because if the hydraulic system fails, then the brakes are automatically applied by spring pressure.

For a machine that uses a hydraulic system for its parking brakes, the operator directs fluid to release a spring-applied brake in order to move the machine. These brake hydraulic systems can be very simple or very complicated, and many machines now incorporate electronics into their brake systems.

Service brake application usually starts with pedal movement. **FIGURE 54-9** shows a typical hydraulic system brake pedal and valve.

Machine brake systems usually use mineral-based oil, but sometimes automotive-type brake fluid is specified. These fluids are virtually noncompressible, and this will give the brake system an immediate and powerful response to the operator's input. Air, however, is compressible and is not something you want in a brake hydraulic system. If a hydraulic brake system is suspected to have air in it, then a proper bleeding procedure should be followed to remove all traces of air from inside the system. If air does get into a brake hydraulic system, the brake pedal will feel spongy, and the brake performance will not be as responsive or effective as it should. This can lead to a dangerous brake failure situation and should be corrected ASAP.

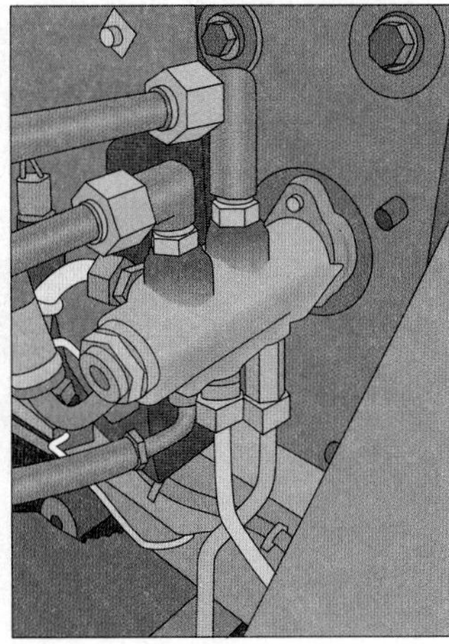

FIGURE 54-9 Brake pedal and valve.

Use of Hydraulic Systems for Machine Braking

As mentioned previously, early primitive friction-type brake systems relied on strictly mechanical linkage to provide the force needed to create enough friction to slow and stop the machine. The limiting factor to the required brake effect was how much force the operator could apply to the linkage and how much this could be multiplied by the mechanical advantage that was created through the use of levers.

Today, only very small machines use strictly mechanically actuated service brakes, and some still use mechanically applied parking brakes, as shown in **FIGURE 54-10**.

Machine braking systems evolved many years ago to include a hydraulic system in order to create more braking effect and eliminate the maintenance involved with the mechanical linkages. As described in Chapter 22 on the basics of hydraulics, hydraulic pressure is created by the resistance to flow. Because a hydraulic brake circuit ends at the foundation brake actuator (caliper, wheel cylinder, piston), the moment the friction material comes into contact with its opposing member fluid, flow virtually stops and pressure rises quickly. Very little flow is needed to move the actuators—maybe a few cubic inches—which is a very small amount. A U.S. gallon has 231 cubic inches. This makes brake applications quick and powerful when needed, as the control system has to move so little fluid. It is also much easier to route pressurized hydraulic fluid through hoses and steel tubes than to use mechanical linkages and cables to transfer force.

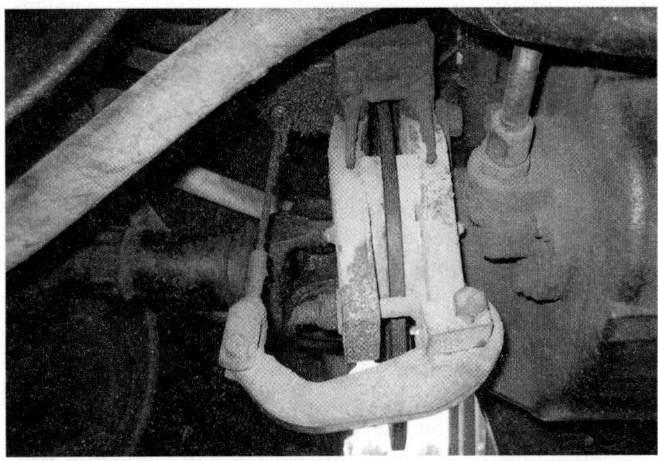

FIGURE 54-10 Mechanical parking brake.

Although some smaller equipment and some graders use glycol-based automotive-type brake fluid (DOT Type 3 or 4), most heavy-duty brake systems use mineral-based oil. **FIGURE 54-11** presents a view of a backhoe loader brake system that uses a simple hydraulic system to actuate the brakes.

This backhoe loader uses two master cylinders to transfer operator effort to the friction brakes. This system allows the operator to use the brakes individually to assist with steering in tight quarters. Because hydraulic brake systems rely on some type of fluid, these systems require fluid maintenance and must stay sealed to prevent contamination.

▶ Components of Hydraulic Brake Systems

K54003

Hydraulic systems are made up of several components that interact with each other to form the complete system. The following sections identify the various components and describe their functions within a hydraulic system.

Friction-Type Foundation Brakes

The term "foundation brake" refers to the business part of the brake system or the part that provides the actual brake effect. A foundation brake assembly has one or more rotating members and one or more stationary members. As brake application pressure is applied, the rotating member is slowed down to try to match the state of the stationary member. This is done by creating friction between the two members.

Friction Material

Brake friction materials are mainly non-asbestos organic and/or metallic materials (fiberglass, Kevlar, ceramic, etc.). Friction modifiers (alumina or silica) and a resin binding agent keep these compounds together.

The materials are combined and cured in a baking process and formed into different shapes. These shaped friction materials are then attached to a metal backing that makes a shoe or pad assembly. The pads or shoes are chemically bonded (glued) or riveted to the metal backing, or both methods are used for attaching them to the backing.

Foundation Brake Actuators

The foundation brakes have an actuator component (piston) to convert the hydraulic pressure that is created by the brake system supply components into mechanical movement. This mechanical movement is used to squeeze two or more components together to create friction. All actuators have a means to bleed air from them so that only brake fluid is in the system.

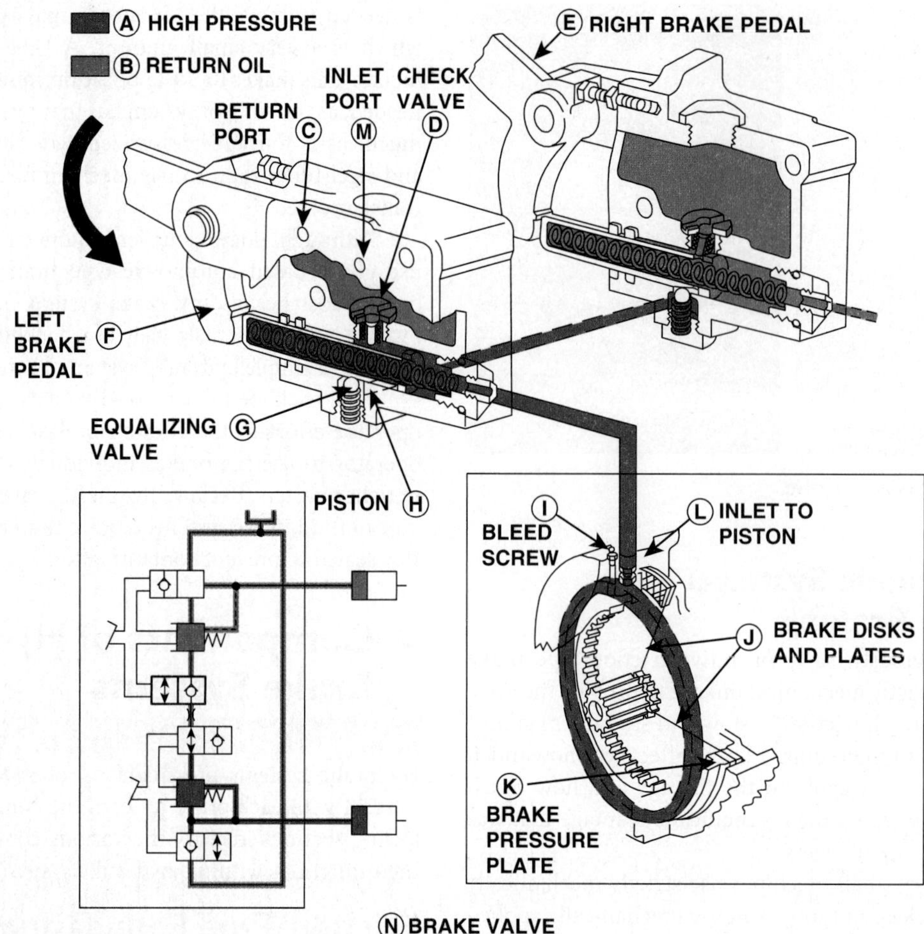

FIGURE 54-11 A simple hydraulic brake system.

There are a few different types of foundation brakes:

1. Expanding shoe and drum
2. Caliper and rotor: fixed, sliding, multi-caliper, multidisc
3. Single and multi wet disc
4. Bladder type.

Expanding Shoe and Drum

More commonly called drum brakes, this type of brake is becoming less popular for heavy equipment machines. A drum brake assembly consists of two half-moon-shaped "shoes" that match the internal radius of the rotating drum they fit inside. The shoes are moved by one or more hydraulic actuators (pistons). There is also an adjustment mechanism and related hardware to keep everything in place. The shoes are stationary (they don't rotate) and are lined on their external surface with a friction material. They are anchored to the axle housing, and as they are expanded inside the rotating drum by the wheel cylinders, their friction material grabs the drum and provides a braking action.

Because the drum is attached to the rotating wheel, this slows the machine down, providing there is good traction between the tire and the roadway surface. These brakes work best when they are dry and therefore are not as favorable as other types of brakes for most types of heavy equipment because of the muddy and wet conditions in which most machines work. To prevent the drum brakes from being affected by moisture and mud, the brakes are usually covered as much as possible. This creates another problem because the covers do not allow air circulation to cool the brakes down. When excessive heat is created in drum-type brakes, the drum expands, which means the shoes have to travel farther to maintain the same amount of force against the drum. The friction material can also become overheated and lose some of its coefficient of friction. This results in a phenomenon called brake fade, where the braking effect decreases even though the apply pressure stays the same or increases. See **FIGURE 54-12** to view a typical drum/expanding shoe–type brake.

Drum-type brakes are also used for static braking (parking brake) on a machine's driveline, where they are typically spring applied but sometimes mechanically applied with a cable and ratchet mechanism.

Drum type static brakes are applied with a lever that turns a cam to expand the brakes against the drum. The lever can also be moved to apply the brake with spring pressure and may be released with air or hydraulic pressure.

Hydraulic drum brakes are broken down into two types, servo and non-servo, and both can be actuated by one or two

FIGURE 54-12 A typical expanding shoe and drum-type brake.

hydraulic wheel cylinders that are mounted to the stationary axle housing. These cylinders receive hydraulic fluid from a master cylinder that is controlled by the operator and usually started with moving a foot pedal. As fluid enters the cylinder, it acts on a piston or pistons that move out of the cylinder housing and in turn act on the brake shoes to move them into the brake drum. The amount of piston movement and the force it creates depends on the amount of fluid flow and pressure that is sent to the wheel cylinder. This is determined by how far and how hard the operator pushes the brake pedal or moves a lever. Maximum brake pressure can range from 750 to 2,500 psi, depending on the mechanical advantage of the pedal or lever and whether or not the master cylinder is boosted.

The wheel cylinder piston has at least one seal on its outside diameter to keep the brake fluid from leaking out past the piston. This is usually a lip-type seal that has the lip facing toward the fluid. There is also a seal and/or rubber boot to keep dirt away from the piston seal. See **FIGURE 54-13** for an example of a typical wheel cylinder.

To return the piston and brake shoes to the released position after the brake pedal is released, usually return springs are attached to the shoe and axle hub. As the shoe is pulled back to the released position, it also bottoms the piston back in the housing.

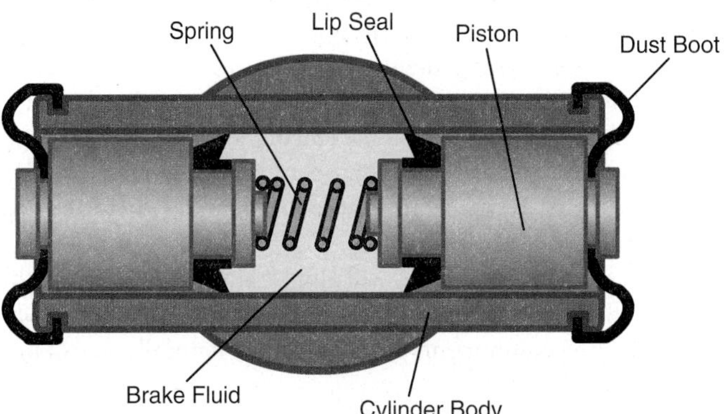

FIGURE 54-13 A typical wheel cylinder.

Drum-type brakes have to be adjusted to compensate for shoe and drum wear, and typically have some type of threaded adjuster that can be automatically or manually adjusted.

Non-servo type: In this type of drum brake, the wheel cylinder acts on the toe of each shoe, and the heel of each shoe pivots on a common anchor pin. This provides a sturdy platform for the shoes and is a very simple arrangement. There is one return spring to bring the toes of the shoes back away from the drum and an adjuster mechanism to provide a means of keeping the shoes fairly close to the drum. As the friction material wears off the shoes, the gap between the shoes and drum gets bigger, and this delays the start of braking and also decreases the effective braking. The adjuster can be used to minimize the gap between the shoes and drum; the clearance between them should be checked to ensure it is within specification.

Because with this type of drum brake there is one leading and one trailing shoe for each direction of machine travel, only one shoe is being self-energized.

Self-energizing occurs when the friction of the drum against the shoes tries to pull the shoe with it. Because the shoe is stopped by its anchor, this has the effect of pulling the shoe tighter against the drum, thus increasing brake effort. The trailing shoe is not nearly as effective because it relies strictly on the wheel cylinder to push the shoe into the drum against the direction of rotation.

Servo Type

Lighter-duty drum brakes are usually the servo type, which means they use two shoes that are joined together with an adjuster and work together as one shoe. This arrangement allows one shoe to increase the braking effort of the other shoe. See **FIGURE 54-14** to understand how servo type brake shoes get self-energized.

Wedge Type

A less popular hydraulically actuated drum brake is the wedge type. A hydraulic cylinder is used to push out a wedge that moves a roller out; in turn, this moves the toe end of the shoes out to the inside diameter of the drum.

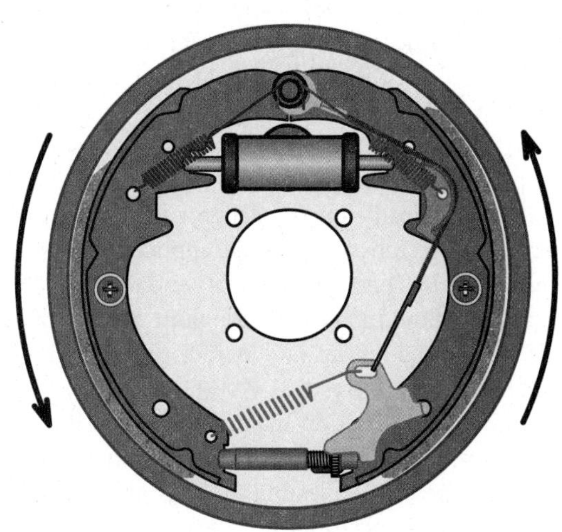

FIGURE 54-14 How a brake shoe gets energized.

Caliper and Rotor Brakes

This type of brake is very common in the automotive world and is also the most common type of hydraulically actuated "dry" brake. The term "dry" relates to the friction material that is not running in oil.

Caliper and rotor brakes create friction by clamping a stationary friction material (brake pad) against a rotating steel, or cast iron, rotor. The rotor is attached to a wheel hub that, when slowed down, transfers the braking action to the machines tires, which then slows the machine down.

For heavy equipment applications, it is not uncommon that these brakes can be used as multi-caliper per wheel arrangements or even multi-rotor per wheel in order to improve the overall effective braking results. Once again, the multiple-caliper or multiple-rotor arrangement provides more swept area to create a higher braking effect.

Caliper brakes are mostly oil applied, but they can also be spring applied and oil or air released. Spring-applied caliper brakes are usually found as a driveline brake for static or parking brake purposes. The SAHR (spring-applied hydraulic release) type of caliper has springs behind the caliper pistons, and oil moves the piston back to release the brake.

When used for service braking, this type of brake is less susceptible to brake fade because as the rotor heats up, it expands into the brake pad and actually improves the brake effect. The brake components are also much more exposed and therefore cool down faster than drum brakes. This of course depends on the application, and if the machine is normally working in a lot of wet, muddy conditions, there are usually covers to try to protect the brakes, which also reduces the cooling effect.

Rotor and caliper brakes can be broken into two types: sliding and fixed caliper. Sliding caliper brakes are not very common on heavy equipment, as they are usually single or double piston and therefore are used for light-duty applications. The term "sliding caliper" refers to how the caliper is mounted to the machine's axle or spindle. Because the piston(s) are only on one side of the caliper, the housing must float or slide to allow for even brake pad wear.

The fixed caliper brake is more popular because it uses pistons on both sides of the rotor to apply force to the brake pads. Because of this, the pads should wear evenly, and there is no need to allow the caliper to slide. There are up to eight pistons in fixed calipers. **FIGURE 54-15** illustrates a view of a fixed caliper type of brake.

Some hydraulically applied calipers have springs to assist in retracting the pistons after a brake application, but most rely on the piston seals. These square seals bend to allow the pistons out and seal the fluid in, but after the fluid pressure is released, the seals will straighten up and retract the pistons back into the caliper. This also gives this type of brake a self-adjusting effect because as the friction material and/or rotor wears, the piston keeps moving out past the seal slightly to compensate for the wear. The caliper sealing O-rings are square cut, and as the piston moves out to push the pad against the rotor, the square O-ring flexes. When the brakes are released, the O-ring returns to its normal shape, retracting the piston slightly. This retraction and a slight movement of the rotor, plus the cooling down of the friction material, provide the necessary clearance between the brake pads and rotor.

FIGURE 54-15 A fixed caliper type of brake.

The rotors have a relatively rough surface when new, which will **burnish** (make smooth or polish) the friction material after the first few brake applications. Until this burnishing process is complete, the friction material has about half its designed coefficient of friction. Caution must be taken when new brake material is installed, and a machine's brakes are applied the first few times. The rotor will also take on a polished appearance after the burnishing process.

Most rotors are ventilated to allow them to cool faster. Ribbed vents between the braking surfaces give the rotor more exposed surface area to improve cooling. However, once the vents get filled with mud, which easily happens if the machine works in less than ideal conditions, this cooling effect is negated.

Single and Multidisc Foundation Brakes

Single and multidisc foundation brakes are likely the most common type of brake you will find on medium- to large-size heavy equipment. They can be used for both spring-applied, oil-released and oil-applied, spring-released brakes. You will find them used for service and parking brakes as well. Some machine applications use the same multidisc foundation brakes for both service and parking brakes. They can be used for steering track machines as well as for braking other functions like winches and the swing function of an excavator. See **FIGURE 54-16** to view a multidisc brake arrangement.

If these disc-type brakes are used for a wheeled machine, they could be mounted out at the end of the axle near the wheels, in which case they are called outboard brakes, or they could be mounted close to the center of the differential, where they are called inboard brakes.

These Disc-type brakes will almost always be wet type, this means they will be running in oil and the oil will carry away heat from the components to be dissipated naturally or to a heat exchanger.

The friction material used for this type of brake is designed to be run in oil and still provide its designed coefficient of friction. A series of grooves formed into the friction material of

FIGURE 54-16 A multidisc brake arrangement.

the discs allows the oil to remove heat from them. Another big advantage of this type of brake is that these brakes run in a sealed compartment and thus are not exposed to the environment. These two factors mean this type of brake will last a long time. It is not uncommon for a set of multidisc brakes to last well over 15,000 hours if properly maintained and used.

The main components of these disc brakes are one or more discs (lined with friction material), one or more steel plates that are sometimes called reaction plates, a spring or springs to apply or release the brake, and a piston to transfer hydraulic pressure to apply or release the brake. The piston applies even pressure as it is a similar shape and size to the discs and plates. In multidisc brakes, the plates and discs alternate with each other to make the brake assembly, whereas a single disc brake employs a single disc that rotates and is squeezed by a pair of stationary plates.

The discs and plates have either internal or external teeth or tangs to hold them to another component, which is either a rotating wheel hub or a stationary axle member.

If the discs are the rotating member of the brake assembly and either spring pressure or hydraulic pressure is applied to the stationary plates, then the discs will slow or stop as the friction between the plates and discs increases.

Bladder Type

Bladder-type brakes were used on some older models of Caterpillar equipment and were basically a different way of forcing brake shoes out against a rotating drum. The bladder was similar to an inner tube that would expand as hydraulic fluid flow and pressure was applied to the inside of it. As the bladder expanded, it pushed the friction material out against the drum. This type of brake system was prone to bladder failure and was soon replaced by other more reliable brake systems.

▶ Hydraulic Brake Actuation Components

K54004

Hydraulic brake application systems can be broken into three categories: non-boosted, boosted, and full power. Machine designers choose one of the three types based on the weight and travel speed of the machine and the braking energy required for slowing and stopping it.

A **non-boosted hydraulic brake system**, that is, a system that does not have any power assist to increase application pressure, consists of a master cylinder, brake lines (hoses or steel lines), wheel cylinders (actuators), foundation brakes, and brake fluid. The master cylinder receives an input force from the operator, usually through a foot pedal, but in some cases a hand lever could be used.

Boosted brake systems have a boost mechanism incorporated into the master cylinder assembly between the brake pedal and the master cylinder. The foot pedal pushes on a lever that uses the boost system to multiply the force input to the master cylinder. The master cylinder moves fluid out through the brake lines to the wheel cylinders, and their pistons move as a result. The wheel cylinder piston movement is transferred to the foundation brakes, and a brake application is made. When the brake pedal is released, the wheel cylinders are withdrawn, and the master cylinder and foot pedal return to their starting position and are ready for the next application.

A **full power system** has brake lines and wheel cylinders as well but has a hydraulic system and modulating valve that are capable of creating higher pressures. The operator actuates the modulating valve to make a brake application with pressurized fluid movement.

▶ TECHNICIAN TIP

As with any hydraulic system, all hydraulic brake systems transfer energy through a fluid to create work. Brake fluid is moved through lines to actuators, and the actuators convert the fluid movement into mechanical movement that actuates the foundation brakes. Pressure is created in the system by resistance to flow, which is produced by the foundation brakes. For example, if a brake caliper piston pushes a brake pad onto a brake rotor, the application pressure rises as soon as contact between the pad and rotor is made. As more force is applied to the fluid at the master cylinder end, the pressure increases, which increases the braking action.

Brake Controls

Some brake controls are combined with powertrain controls. Most medium- to large-size wheel loaders have two brake pedals. The right pedal is usually just for brake application, and the left one is a combination drivetrain neutralizer and brake. For wheel loaders that use a power shift transmission, the first part of the left brake control movement quite often neutralizes the transmission. This is sometimes called an inching or de-clutch function. **FIGURE 54-17** shows a typical three-pedal arrangement.

Non-Boosted Hydraulic Brake Systems

This type of system is only found on very light-duty equipment, because the brake application pressure is limited to the maximum force the operator can apply to the brake pedal plus any gain through a mechanical lever or levers between the pedal and the master cylinder. Maximum pressure that is sent to the brake actuators is around 1,000 psi.

The operator's input is transferred to a master cylinder that forces brake fluid out to the foundation brake actuators. A master cylinder has a rod that is pushed into its bore by the

FIGURE 54-17 Typical three-pedal arrangement.

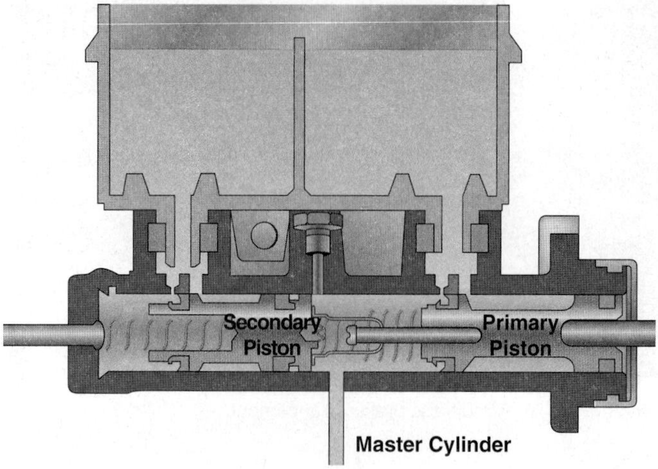

FIGURE 54-18 A dual-circuit master cylinder.

operator, and the rod pushes on a piston that has brake fluid sealed in front of it with a cup or seal. The size of the bore determines how much pressure is created in the system. For example, if 500 pounds of force is created by the operator pushing the brake pedal through a mechanical advantage, and this force is then used to push a cup that has a 1 sq. in. diameter, there will be 500 psi of oil pressure in the system. If the same force acts on a 2 sq. in. cup, then 250 psi of pressure will force the foundation brakes to work (remember F = P/A).

The master cylinder can be a single-circuit system but will more likely be a dual-circuit system, meaning the brake system is split into two circuits, either front and rear or left front–right rear and right front–left rear. The dual-circuit master cylinder depicted in Figure 54-18 has two pistons, each with two lip seals. The primary piston controls braking for one circuit, and the secondary piston controls braking for the other circuit. When the brake pedal is pushed, the rod pushes on the primary piston. This piston then forces the brake fluid out of the master cylinder, through hoses and/or tubes, and on to the foundation brake actuators in order to create braking action in the primary circuit. The pressure created in the master cylinder also pushes against the secondary piston, and it in turn pressurizes the secondary circuit, sending pressure to the brakes in the secondary circuit.

If a leak occurs in the primary circuit, the secondary circuit will be mechanically actuated by the pedal and the push rod. If there is a leak in the secondary circuit, the primary circuit will still operate. Brake fluid is always available to the pistons from the reservoir. After the fluid has been pushed out of the master cylinder and the operator releases the brake pedal, a return spring pushes the piston back into the master cylinder, where it will be ready for the next application. The returning actuator piston also returns the brake fluid back to the reservoir.

If the master cylinder has its own reservoir, it will have a vented cap to allow air on top of a diaphragm. This keeps atmospheric moisture from getting into the fluid but still allows the fluid level to lower slightly without creating a vacuum on top of it.

There may be a sensor in the reservoir that will turn a warning light on if the fluid level gets too low. **FIGURE 54-18** shows a non-boosted master cylinder.

The master cylinder may have its own fluid reservoir or a remote reservoir, or it may use fluid from another machine hydraulic system like the steering or implement systems. The master cylinder will also likely incorporate one or more additional valves. One may be a residual check valve that keeps a small amount of pressure in the brake lines to ensure responsive brake action. Another may be a pressure differential valve that senses any pressure loss in one-half of the dual-circuit system and closes that circuit off. It will also turn on a warning light in the cab to warn the operator of a brake system problem. These additional valves may be in the master cylinder or housed separately in a combination valve that is between the master cylinder and the wheel cylinders.

Boosted Hydraulic Brake Systems

To increase the brake fluid apply pressure, many brake systems are boosted. This term refers to a system that has an additional force besides the operator's foot or hand pressure applying input force to the master cylinder. This is most common with small- to medium-size machine brake systems and some older haul trucks. If more force is exerted on the master cylinder, more pressure can be applied to the foundation brakes. This in turn creates a higher braking effect.

The boost is provided from an air system or a hydraulic system. An **air-boosted brake system** uses an air over oil master cylinder. Air systems are covered in depth in Chapter 55. An air-boosted, also known as an air over hydraulic, master cylinder receives regulated air from a treadle valve that the operator pushes on with foot pressure or from a hand-operated lever (spike) that regulates air. This air pressure acts on a diaphragm in the air section of the master cylinder, which in turn pushes a plunger into the master cylinder. The master cylinder operation after that point is basically the same as that for a non-boosted master cylinder. If the diaphragm of the air chamber has a surface area of 10 sq. in. and 100 psi is applied to it, 1,000 pounds of force will be applied to the master cylinder. The master cylinder can multiply this force to create up to 2,000 psi brake application pressure. **FIGURE 54-19** shows an air over oil master cylinder.

A **hydraulic-boosted brake system** works in a similar manner to that of the air over hydraulic system, except that the hydraulic oil is supplied at a much higher pressure and therefore doesn't need as big an area to work on to increase force being delivered to the master cylinder piston.

FIGURE 54-19 Air over oil master cylinder.

A hydraulically boosted master cylinder uses operator input to push a plunger that will seat a valve. When this valve closes, hydraulic boost pressure acts on a larger piston that in turn pushes on the master cylinder piston. From there, the master cylinder works like any other master cylinder to send oil pressure to the wheel brakes. There is a pressure relief valve in the boost section to limit boost pressure from getting too high. When the operator stops pushing the brake pedal farther, the valve comes off the seat, and the master cylinder doesn't get moved any farther. When the brake pedal is released, return springs return the spool and piston to their starting positions. See **FIGURE 54-20** for a schematic of a simple hydraulic brake system for a forklift that uses drum-type foundation brakes with a hydraulically boosted master cylinder. In this case, the forklift brake boost system uses common oil that is shared with the steering and implement systems.

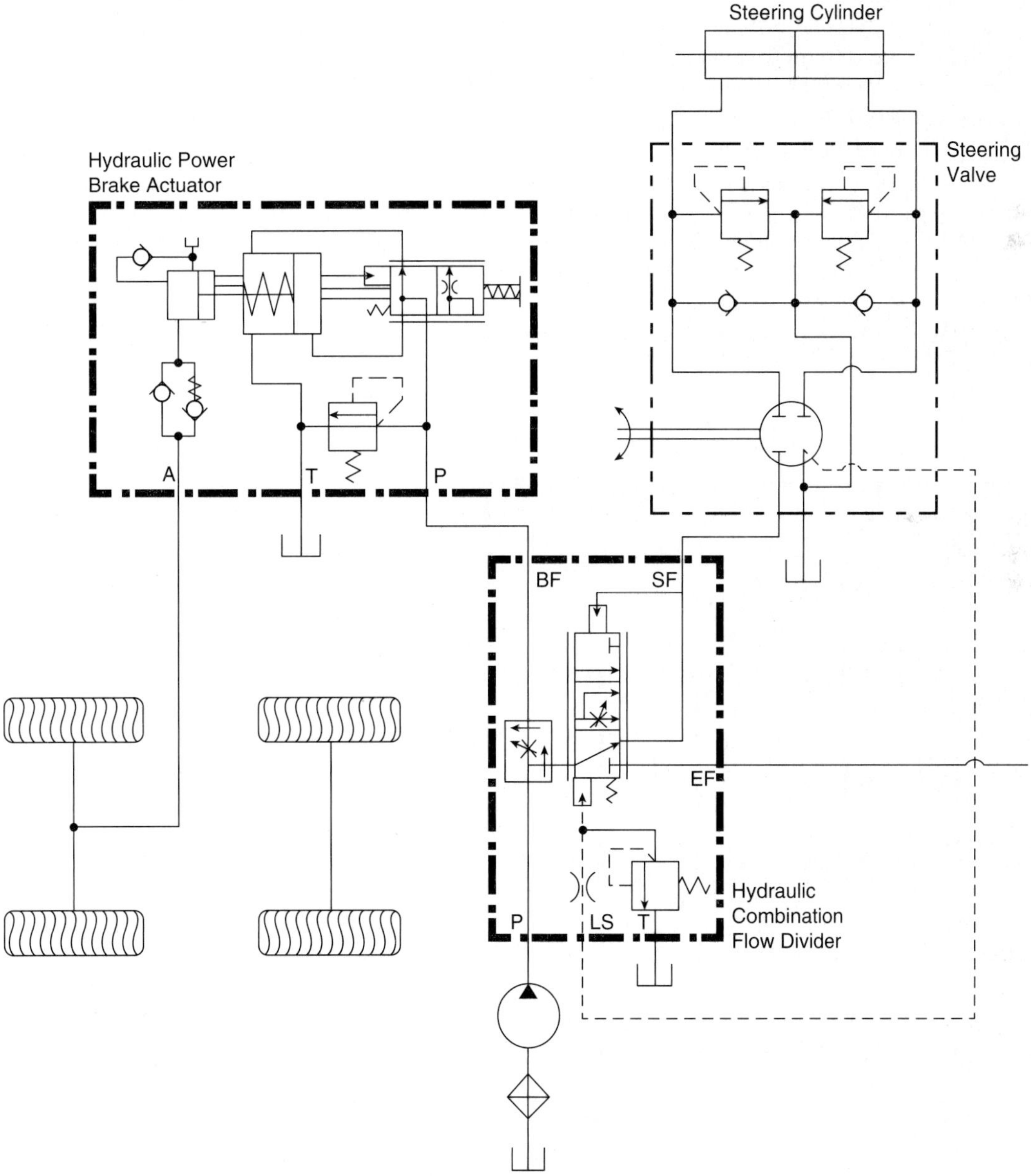

FIGURE 54-20 A simple hydraulic brake system used on a small forklift.

All hydraulically boosted system master cylinders can provide brake application without boost pressure if the boost system fails or the engine is off. In this case, brake pedal movement is transferred directly to the master cylinder piston(s) without boost assist and provides some brake pressure to slow the machine.

Supplementary boost systems provide boost pressure if the normal boost system fails. This safety backup feature is usually an electrically driven pump that is powered from the machines 12 or 24 VDC electrical system. There are flow and/or pressure sensors that turn on the supplementary system if the sensors detect a pressure or flow loss. This important safety feature should be checked on a regular basis.

Full Power Hydraulic Brake Systems

Full power hydraulic brake systems only require the operator to create a small amount of force at the operator input valve, thus reducing operator fatigue. Full power systems usually create higher apply pressures and therefore more effective braking. The apply pressure is created by a hydraulic system that could be dedicated to brakes or part of another machine hydraulic system. These systems use an accumulator to store hydraulic pressure to supplement pump supply and/or supply brake apply pressure if the supply pump stops producing flow. There are a specific minimum number of full brake applications that the system should be capable of when there is a power-off (dead engine) situation, and this should be verified whenever a brake system is serviced or repaired. **FIGURE 54-21** depicts a full power brake system schematic.

This hydraulic brake supply system is usually only used with rotor and caliper, or disc-type, brakes. The main components of a typical full power hydraulic brake supply and control system are the pump (fixed or variable displacement), accumulator charging valve, accumulator(s), modulating or reverse modulating valve, lines, and foundation brakes.

The system shown in Figure 54-21 is a dual circuit that provides brake application to two separate circuits. If this were used on a wheel loader, it could be one circuit for each axle or a diagonal front left–right rear and right front–left rear arrangement. This system uses a dual-charging valve to keep two accumulators charged up and keep them charged within a high- and low-pressure range. These pressures are called the cut-in and cutout pressures. Sometimes these pressures are adjustable, and a typical setting is 2,100 psi cutout and 1,700 cut in. In other words, the accumulator pressure should stay within this range if the accumulator charge valve is working properly. If there are enough brake applications made to drop the accumulator charge pressure to 1,700 psi, then the charge valve should direct pump oil flow to the accumulators and stop it when it reaches 2,100 psi.

Accumulator Charging Valve

The accumulator charging valve is a combination valve that diverts some pump flow from another systems pump to the accumulator(s) when the cut in pressure is reached. This is done with an unloading spool. A check valve in the charge valve also keeps the oil charge in the accumulators from draining away

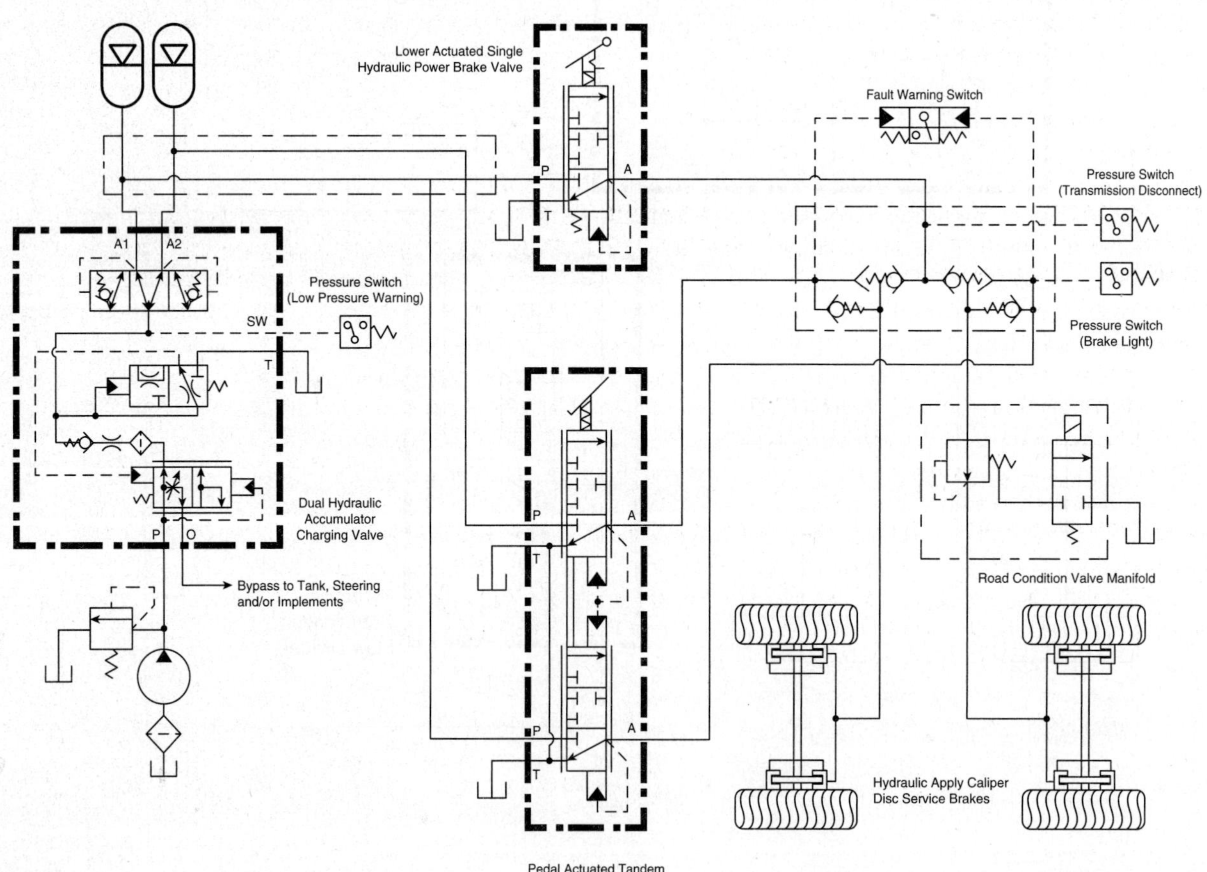

FIGURE 54-21 A full power brake system.

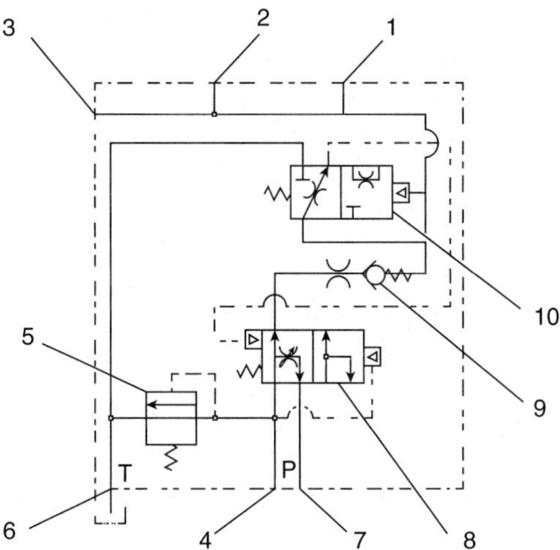

FIGURE 54-22 An accumulator charging valve.

and available for use by the modulating valve. The last part of the charging valve is the cut-in/cutout spool. This determines at what point oil is sent to the accumulators and when oil is diverted away from them. See **FIGURE 54-22** to view an accumulator charging valve.

An open-center-type accumulator charge valve is used with a fixed displacement pump.

If the charging valve uses a variable-type pump, then it will have a load sense section that sends a signal to the pump to upstroke the pump if flow to the accumulator(s) is needed. A dual charging valve also has poppet valves that always charge the lowest charged accumulator first. Some charging valves also incorporate a system relief pressure valve.

Full power brake systems need modulating valves to allow the operator to use the available built-up accumulator pressure for applying the brakes with as much or as little force as required. They also give the operator a feedback feel to give him or her a sense of how much application pressure they are sending to the wheel ends. **FIGURE 54-23** shows a modulating valve.

Modulating valves are usually floor mounted for foot operation but could also be lever operated or remotely operated to allow operation from a different location.

A typical dual-circuit modulating valve has four main moving parts and four ports that connect lines to it. One line supplies accumulator pressure; one is a drain line that allows return oil to go to tank; and the other two supply oil to the brake circuits to actuate the wheel end brakes.

The main moving parts inside are the compensating spring that receives pressure from the operator through a pedal or lever, the upper and lower spools, and a bias spring at the bottom of the spools.

The spools meter application oil from the supply port to the work port, based on compensator spring pressure. The apply pressure combines with bias spring pressure to oppose compensator spring pressure and give the operator feedback that directly relates to how much pressure is going to the brakes. In other words, the harder the pedal is pushed, the more pressure is sent out to the brakes and the harder the pedal is to push. This gives the pedal a natural feel. When the pedal is held partway down, the spool is balanced between the two springs, and the apply

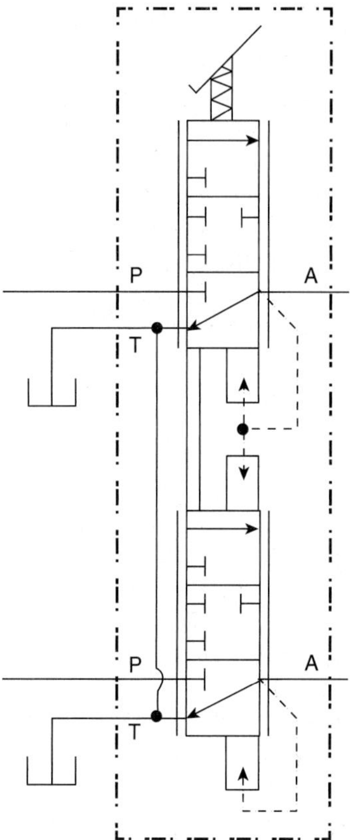

FIGURE 54-23 A modulating valve.

pressure is trapped in the line to the brake. If the pedal is released, then the spool moves up, and the trapped oil is allowed to go to tank through the return port. This allows the brakes to release.

Reverse Modulating Valves

Reverse modulating valves are used with spring-applied, oil-released brakes. This type of brake is termed a "fail-safe brake," as it will apply whenever pressure is lost. The most common type of foundation brake used with this system is the multidisc type. The reverse modulating valve works the exact opposite way of the modulating valve that was just explained. When the machine is first started, oil is sent through the valve to the spring applied brakes to release them. Then as the pedal pressure is applied, this oil is drained away to apply the brakes. A full brake pedal application will completely drain the brake and fully apply it.

Other Hydraulic Brake Components

A number of other components may or may not be found on off-road hydraulic brake systems. Following are some of these. Note that this list does not cover all of the possible components and accessories on these systems, just some of the more common ones.

Slack Adjusters

A slack adjuster is used to hydraulically compensate for wear in the foundation brakes. It always ensures that the quantity of brake application oil only has to be the minimum amount required to move the foundation brakes in order to make an application. This is done in the slack adjuster with the use of two different diameter pistons and a check valve. If the friction material wears enough that the large piston is allowed to travel to

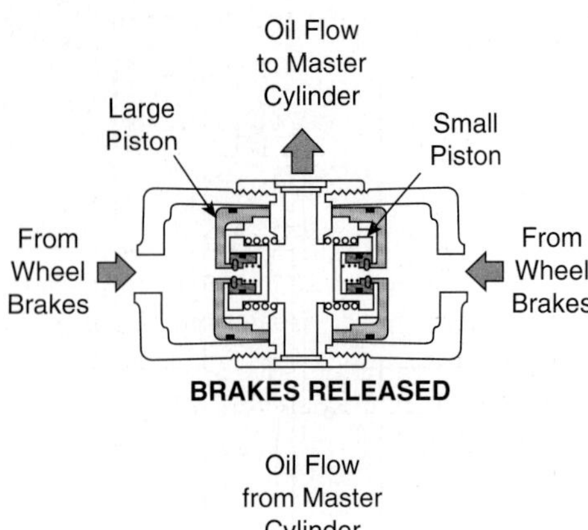

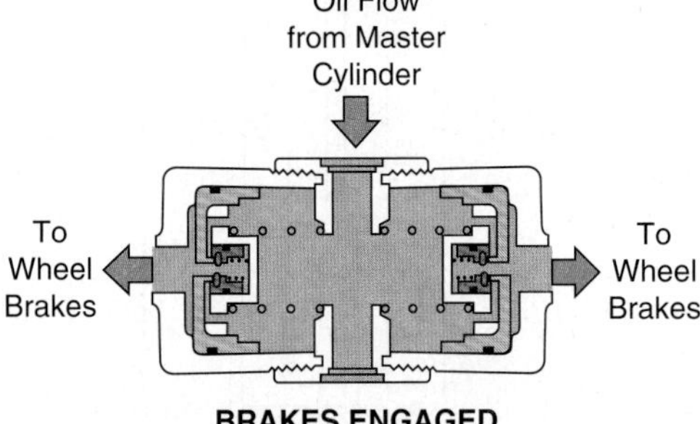

FIGURE 54-24 The hydraulic slack adjuster automatically compensates for wear in high-volume hydraulic brake systems.

the end of the slack adjuster housing, the check valve will open, and when the oil pressure is released, the large piston will reset or move back to the bottom of the slack adjuster. **FIGURE 54-24** shows a hydraulic slack adjuster.

Relay Valve

A relay valve is sometimes used on larger machines to make the brakes more responsive. The relay valve is located close to the foundation brake that it is actuating, and it is similar in operation to an air relay valve. The oil from the modulating valve is used as a signal that then sends oil on from the relay valve to apply the brakes.

Brake Release Pump

Some larger machines are equipped with a brake release system to be used in the event that the machine loses hydraulic pressure. If the machine has to be towed, then an electrically driven pump can supply hydraulic pressure to release the spring-applied parking brake.

Brake Cooling Systems

Many medium- to large-size machines that travel fast and use multidisc foundation brakes have a brake oil cooling system that circulates oil around the brake friction components, absorbs the heat generated by them into the oil, and sends the oil to a cooler. These systems can be simple, with a minimum of hoses, a pump, and an oil-to-air heat exchanger; or they may be more complex, with diverting valves being controlled by an ECM that uses temperature sensors as inputs.

The ECM turns on a warning light and alarm if the brake temperature gets too high, and a fault code will be set.

▶ Testing Brake Operation

S54001

Like all other machine systems, you need to know how a machine's brake system should work properly before you can determine whether there is a problem with it. Because of the importance of the safe operation of the brake system and the negative consequences that could occur if the brakes are not operating properly, you should also test a machine's braking performance and operation as part of any routine maintenance check.

Always check the machine's manual for the proper procedure to test the braking system. Some examples of machine brake system tests are covered in **SKILL DRILL 54-1**.

Some test procedures ask that you park the machine on a slope of a certain degree of angle, apply the parking brake, and see whether the machine stays stationary. Another example of a test for a grader's brakes is to put the machine into second gear and get the machine moving at high idle. While that machine is moving, put it in neutral and apply the parking brake. If the parking brakes are working properly, the wheels should skid.

Again, these are general test procedures, and you should always consult the manual for the machine and follow the exact test method.

SKILL DRILL 54-1 Testing Brake Systems

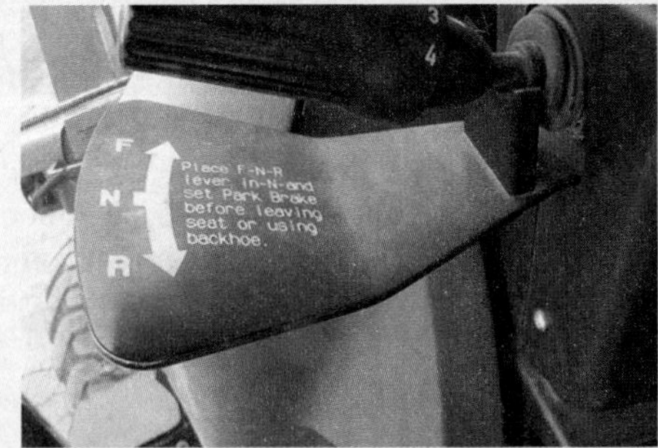

If the machine has a powershift transmission, follow these steps.

1. Put the machine in its highest speed range, forward or reverse.
2. Apply the service brakes, and slowly increase engine RPM to high idle. The machine should not move.

If the machine has a hydrostatic drivetrain, follow these steps.

1. Disable the parking brake release.
2. Try to move the machine with the park brake applied.

   Note: Some machines should be left at low idle and others at high idle for this test. The machine should not move.

For a machine with a driveline parking brake, follow these steps.

1. Apply the parking brake.
2. Try to move the machine in high-speed range. The machine should not move.

For machines with reverse-modulated spring-applied brakes follow these steps.

1. Depress the brake pedal fully.
2. Try to drive the machine. The machine should not move.

If you are checking brake performance on any machine, you should make sure the machine stops straight, with no drifting to one side, and that the machine does not demonstrate any unusual noises or vibrations when the brakes are applied.

Service and parking brakes should also be checked to ensure they release fully, because a dragging brake will waste fuel and can cause major drivetrain component damage by overheating.

▶ Brake Servicing

S54002

The importance of servicing machine brakes regularly and thoroughly cannot be overstated. As mentioned, it can easily be argued that the brake system is the most important safety-related system on the machine, and proper servicing will lead to ensuring maximum brake performance.

Part of machine servicing is to service the brake system. Depending on the type of brake system, servicing can be a simple process or a complex procedure.

If the machine is newer and has an electronic fault code logging system, a good place to start a brake service is to check for any brake-related fault codes that have been logged or are still active.

On the hydraulic supply and control section of any brake system, there are some common service procedures that should be performed. The most basic of these procedures is a general inspection of the system. To perform a general brake system inspection, follow the procedures in **SKILL DRILL 54-2**.

Foundation Brake Servicing

Following are some examples of brake servicing procedures for different types of foundation brakes:

1. **Drum and shoe:** This type of brake could require an adjustment to ensure proper operation. This adjustment keeps the shoes close to the drum, with a minimum clearance to provide quick positive brake action and ensure there is no brake drag. If there is an automatic adjuster mechanism for a drum and shoe brake, it should be checked to ensure it isn't seized, and it could also require lubrication.

   Drum and shoe brakes could require manual adjustment as well as friction material measurements to ensure the drums don't get damaged if there is metal-to-metal contact. Shoe adjustments could include special tools that are needed to turn the adjusting mechanism to set the proper shoe to drum clearance. A visual inspection is performed to check for damaged components and unusual wear patterns.

   Sometimes a service requires the wheel to be rotated with the axle raised to see whether the brakes drag.
2. Rotor and caliper: Servicing rotor and caliper brakes is fairly simple in that it usually only requires inspection. Some machines that use this style of brake require a measurement of the pads to ensure they get replaced before too much friction material is gone, which creates the possibility of the metal backing contacting the rotors. Measuring involves using a steel rod that is inserted through a hole in the caliper casting that measures the thickness of the pad.

   Rotors should be inspected for discoloration (indicating overheating), cracks, warping, grooves, and glazing. **FIGURE 54-25** provides an example of a large brake rotor.
3. Multidisc: Because these brakes are sealed, there is little that can be done for a service procedure. Some machines have an access hole that allows the technician to perform a measuring procedure to warn when friction material is getting worn enough to need replacement.

Brake Fluid Service

If automotive brake fluid is used, it will occasionally have to be replaced. This type of fluid is hygroscopic, which means that it absorbs moisture. Over time, the fluid's water content increases and starts to allow rust to form inside the system. A higher water content also means a lower boiling point for the brake fluid. If the foundation brakes get too hot and transfer enough heat into the fluid, it will boil or vaporize. This will result in poor brake pressure because the fluid now has gas in it.

SKILL DRILL 54-2 Inspecting a Brake System

1. Check the fluid level. This could involve looking at a sight glass, pulling a dipstick, or looking at a transparent reservoir.
2. Check the fluid condition. There should be no air visible, and the fluid should appear clean, with no burnt smell.
3. Check the brake system malfunction warning system. This could involve turning the key to a certain position and looking for a warning light or pushing a button or toggle switch.
4. Check for fault codes related to the brake system.
5. Check for leaks.
6. Check for any damage to seals or boots at the calipers or wheel cylinders.
7. Check for proper operation of the service brake system.
8. Check for proper operation of the parking brake system.
9. Perform a visual inspection of the controls for the brake system.
10. Check any brake lights the machine may have for proper operation and/or damage.
11. Check any brake cooling system for proper operation.
12. Check for any unusual or excessive wear of friction materials on drums or rotors.
13. Check for loose or missing covers around foundation brakes.

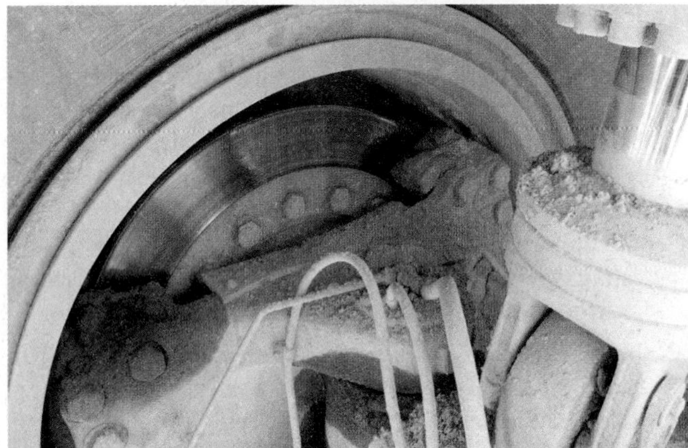

FIGURE 54-25 A large brake rotor.

If the system requires glycol-based automotive fluid (DOT 3 or DOT 4) or silicone-based fluid (DOT 5), make sure that no mineral-based fluid (hydraulic oil) gets mixed with it, and vice versa.

New automotive brake fluid has a boiling point much higher than water. For example a typical **DOT 3** fluid has a minimum dry (new) boiling point of 400°F (204°C); **DOT 4**, a boiling point of 450°F (232°C); and **DOT 5**, a boiling point of 500°F (260°C). See **FIGURE 54-26** to view different types of automotive brake fluid.

▶ Brake System Troubleshooting

S54003

Some general troubleshooting tips can be applied to all hydraulic brake systems, but because of the diversity of differing systems, there is no way to cover even a fraction of the procedures you may use to find the root cause of a brake system malfunction. Here are some general tips:

- Verify the complaint. This will involve performing brake performance tests, so make sure you are comfortable with running the machine and that you know the proper test procedure.
- Know the system. Because of the great variety of systems, don't assume you know how the system works. Read the operator's manual and/or service manual to familiarize yourself with it.

FIGURE 54-26 Different types of brake fluid.

- Check the simple stuff first (fluid level/condition, leaks, damage, control operation, fault codes), and check any recent repair history. One simple test is to use a heat gun to compare the heat buildup between individual foundation brakes (both wheels on the same axle should be close to the same temperature).
- Determine whether it's a complete system problem or an individual or multi-foundation brake problem. If a machine is pulling one way when the brakes are applied, it is likely the brake on the side the machine is pulling to is working too soon or that the opposite side brake is not working as it should.
- Perform instrument testing. You may need to install pressure gauges to assess the hydraulic brake system. Some checks could include application pressures, boost system pressure, accumulator precharge pressure, and accumulator cut in/cutout pressure.

▶ Brake Repairs

S54004

Brake repairs are performed when either an operational problem is found or the friction material is found to be at or near its wear limit. Some examples of typical brake repairs are listed here:

- Leak repairs: Any hydraulic brake system leaks have to be repaired ASAP. These include seals, hoses, tubes, valves, actuators, and accumulators. These components should be repaired and/or replaced as necessary.
- Friction material replacement: For rotor and caliper type brakes, this is a relatively easy repair. After the wheel is removed, some calipers allow the brake pads to be replaced without removing the caliper. You may have to remove some retainer clips or bolts, and the pads can be replaced after the piston is pushed back into the caliper bore. Other calipers may have to be removed to enable the pads to be removed. Care must be taken whenever a caliper is removed, in order not to damage the flex lines or hoses that connect the caliper to the brake hydraulic system.

- For Shoe and drum brakes that require friction material replacement, you need to remove the wheel and drum to allow access to the shoes. Depending on the axle configuration, this task could include sliding the drum over the wheel studs or removing the final drive assembly and wheel bearings. For some larger brake shoes that are riveted only to their backing, the technician is able to reline the shoes. This process requires the technician to drill all rivets out, remove the old friction material (sometimes called blocks), clean the shoe mounting surface, and rivet the new material on.
- Replacing the friction material on single and multidisc brakes requires the most time and skill, mainly because they are inside a sealed compartment, and the process will likely involve removing a wheel, final drive, and hub assembly for a wheeled machine, and possibly dismantling the axle assembly if the brakes are the inboard type. Once the discs and plates are exposed, they should be measured and inspected, and can be reused if they meet certain criteria. Generally, the friction discs should not show signs of discoloration, nor have any teeth or tangs missing, nor be warped or cracked, and they must be a certain minimum thickness. The same goes for the steel plates, and there should be no grooves worn into them.

Wheel Cylinder Resealing or Replacement

If a wheel cylinder seal is found to show signs of leakage, it must be resealed or replaced. After the wheel cylinder is removed, it is disassembled and checked for damage to its bore. If there is light scoring, these marks can be removed with a brake cylinder hone, and the cylinder is then reassembled with new seals. If there is heavy scoring or rust, the cylinder should be replaced. Pistons are also inspected and replaced if found to be damaged. Care must be taken when installing new piston seals to ensure the lip is pointing in the right direction.

Caliper Resealing or Replacement

For caliper resealing or rebuilding, the process is much the same as for rebuilding wheel cylinders. When rebuilding or replacing a master cylinder, it may have to be resealed, and this involves disassembly, inspection, cleaning, possible honing, resealing, and reassembly. Some valves in the master cylinder may have to be replaced as well. The master cylinder is then bench bled to remove all air before it is installed.

Other Component Repair or Replacement

- Modulating valve repair/replacement: Most modulating valves are mounted on the floor of a machine, where they are subject to mud, dirt, and moisture. There is usually a protective boot that keeps this contamination away from the valve spool, but if this boot fails, valve replacement or resealing must soon follow.
- Accumulator repair or replacement: Most larger accumulators can be resealed and put back into service if there is no damage to the bore or piston. Care must be taken to release all pressure before removing and disassembling any accumulator.
- Other brake valves: Many brake valves can be resealed, but if the valve body or seat is damaged, they must be replaced. If there is any doubt about the integrity of a brake valve's condition, it is better to err on the side of caution and replace it. This point also applies to any brake component.
- Brake bleeding: One of the last steps of any brake system repair is to remove all air from the system. Always refer to the machines service manual for the proper procedure to bleed the brake system.

In general, you always start with the wheel cylinder/caliper/disc that is farthest away from master cylinder. Pressure is built in the brakes lines by either an assistant working the brake control or by some tooling. When pressure is built, the bleeder valve is opened, and any air in the system is purged out into a container through a hose attached to the bleeder. The procedure is repeated until nothing but clean, air-free fluid comes out of the bleeder. This is then repeated for the rest of the brake actuators. The brake reservoir must be monitored and maintained to ensure no new air is introduced into the system. To bleed the brakes, follow the procedure in **SKILL DRILL 54-3**.

SKILL DRILL 54-3 Bleeding the Brakes

Clear communication between you and the assistant is required for successful bleeding.

1. Ask an assistant to slowly push the brake pedal down.
2. Starting with the bleeder screw that is the farthest from the master cylinder, attach a clear bleeder hose to the bleeder screw and insert the tube into a clear plastic container. Then open the bleeder screw one-quarter to one-half turn.
3. Observe any old brake fluid and air bubbles coming out of the bleeder screw.
4. When the brake fluid stream stops, close the bleeder screw lightly, and have the assistant slowly release the pedal. This allows

(Continued)

SKILL DRILL 54-3 Bleeding the Brakes (Continued)

the master cylinder to pull a fresh charge of brake fluid from the reservoir.

5. Repeat the previous three steps until there are no more air bubbles coming out of the brake unit.
6. Close off the bleeder screw, and tighten it to the manufacturer's specifications. Be sure that you *do not* bleed the system so much that the reservoir runs dry and admits air into the hydraulic braking system.
7. Check the level in the master cylinder reservoir, top it off, and reinstall the reservoir cap.
8. Repeat this procedure for each of the wheel brake units, moving closer to the master cylinder, one wheel at a time, until all of the air has been removed and the brake pedal is not spongy.
9. Start the engine and ensure the proper functioning of the brakes with the power assist operational.

▶ Wrap-Up

Ready for Review

- Some safety concerns related to hydraulic frictional brake systems include hot pressurized oil, strong compressed springs, defective test equipment, and friction material dust. Brake systems should be tested for proper operation before the machine is put back to work.
- A wide variety of braking systems are used for heavy equipment machines. Hydraulic fluid pressure and its application to friction material is the most common method to slow down and/or hold a machine in place.
- Brakes that are used to slow down a machine are usually called service brakes. This is called dynamic braking.
- Brakes that are used to hold a machine in place are usually called parking brakes but are sometimes called secondary brakes. This is called static braking.
- Brake systems that slow down machines do so by converting kinetic energy into heat energy. This is called static braking.
- Braking effort is the resistance to rotating torque and can be measured in ft-lb or N·m.
- A heavily loaded machine that is traveling fast needs a massive amount of braking effort to slow it down.
- Friction brake effort is influenced by the coefficient of friction of the friction material, the surface area of the friction material, and the amount of pressure applied to the friction material.
- The coefficient of friction of a material is determined by measuring the force it takes to move a certain weight of material across the surface of a second material. A higher coefficient of friction for a material means it grabs better.
- Manufacturers of friction material use different chemical formulas to arrive at the composition of materials that can be used for brake components.
- Hydraulic systems needed for braking have to create a varying amount of pressure and not much flow. The pressure is used to either apply or release brake friction components.
- The type of fluid used in the hydraulic system can be the same as that used in any hydraulic system or can be automotive-type glycol-based brake fluid.
- Foundation brake assemblies are found near wheel assemblies and consist of rotating components and frictional components. As brake application pressure is applied to the rotating component, its speed will start to match the stationary component.
- Some examples of types of foundation types of brakes are: expanding shoe and drum; caliper and rotor: fixed, sliding, multi-caliper, multidisc, single and multi wet disc, and bladder type.
- Expanding shoe and drum foundation brakes feature a rotating drum and nonrotating shoes. When actuated, the shoes move out against the drum. Shoes are moved with hydraulic pistons at one end and can pivot on an anchor on the other.
- Drums expand when heated, which decreases the brake effort.
- Drum brakes can be used for static or dynamic braking.
- Return springs pull the shoes back away from the drum, and there is an adjusting mechanism to allow the shoe-to-drum clearance to be kept within a specified tolerance.
- Caliper and rotor brakes consist of a rotating steel disc (rotor) and a stationary caliper. The caliper has one or more movable pistons that squeeze friction material (pads) against the rotor.
- Caliper and rotor brakes can be hydraulically applied or spring applied, and can be used for static or dynamic braking.
- Piston seal design provides the means to return the pistons after an application to keep a slight clearance between the pad and rotor.
- Single and multidisc brakes can be used for static or dynamic braking. They are sealed in a housing, and oil pressure applied to a piston moves one rotating component toward a stationary component. They are almost always "wet" brakes, which means they have oil circulating around them to dissipate heat.
- The two main components are discs (friction material) and plates (steel discs). They can have either external or internal teeth or tangs to lock them to either a stationary or rotating component.

- Hydraulic brake application systems can be one of three types: non-boosted, boosted, and full power.
- Non-boosted are only found on very light-duty machines; in these systems, the operator pedal input goes directly to a master cylinder that transfers oil pressure to a piston or caliper. They usually only develop 1,000 psi maximum.
- Boosted systems have a master cylinder that combines a second energy source with the operator input to create a higher apply pressure. It uses vacuum, air pressure, or low-pressure oil and usually has an electric backup pump to provide boost in case of engine failure.
- Full power systems use a dedicated hydraulic circuit with an operator-actuated modulating valve to meter apply pressure. These systems use an accumulator to store a quantity of pressurized oil in case of engine failure. An electric- or ground-driven pump supplies oil flow in emergencies.
- Some multidisc brake systems incorporate a cooling system that circulates oil past the brake friction components. The oil pulls heat away and then transfers the heat to the engine cooling system.
- Testing brake operation should be part of regular maintenance checks, and any deficiencies should be corrected. Check the machine's service information to ensure the proper procedure is used.
- Brake system maintenance may include thorough visual inspection, adjustments to shoes, adjustments to linkages or cables, checking fluid levels, and changing oil and filters.
- Brake system complaints can include no brakes, weak brakes, brakes pulling, brakes grabbing, overheating, or brakes not releasing.
- Brake system troubleshooting involves knowing the system, verifying the complaint, listing possible causes, repairing the root cause, verifying the repair, and testing the brake system operation.
- Brake system repairs include friction material replacement, piston resealing, drum reconditioning, rotor replacement, valve resealing, valve replacement, accumulator repair or recharging, brake line repair, and brake system bleeding.

Key Terms

air-boosted brake system Use air to push on a diaphragm that pushes on the master cylinder pistons to increase applied brake pressure.

brake cylinder Both the pressure actuating component (in the master cylinder) and the mechanism that actuates the pad or shoe to apply friction pressure to the wheel.

brake pads The flat metal casting and the bonded friction material in a disc brake system.

brake shoes The arched metal castings and the bonded friction material in a drum brake system.

burnish To make smooth or polish.

DOT-3, DOT 4, and DOT 5 Brake fluid standards.

full power brake system Brake system capable of supplying fluid to a range of both small- and large-volume service brakes with actuation that is faster than air brake systems.

hydraulic boosted brake system A power brake system that uses a hydraulic pump to boost the master cylinder output force.

hydraulic calipers Linear actuators.

master cylinder A control device that converts mechanical pressure from a driver's foot into hydraulic pressure.

non-boosted brake hydraulic system A system that does not have any power assist to increase application pressure.

wheel cylinders Located inside drum brakes or outside brake calipers in order to push the brake shoes or pads toward a surface that rotates with the wheel, creating friction against that rotating surface to slow or stop the wheel.

Review Questions

1. Ideally, secondary or parking brakes will always be ___________.
   a. oil applied
   b. spring applied
   c. air applied
   d. air released
2. When vehicle speed doubles, its braking force must increase ___ times to stop in the same distance.
   a. 4
   b. 8
   c. 10
   d. 12
3. If it takes 33 pounds of force to move a 100-pound block of friction material across a surface, it is said to ___________.
   a. need 33 psi applied to it to stop it
   b. have a surface coefficient of friction of 0.33
   c. need more force to keep it going than to stop it
   d. have a surface coefficient of friction of 3.3
4. If a machine has a faulty service brake system, this will be the result:
   a. The machine's brakes are overheating.
   b. The machine will roll on a hill when the parking brakes are applied.
   c. The machine will slow down normally.
   d. The machine will not slow down normally.
5. This is one factor that will *not* increase a machine brake system braking effect:
   a. Increasing the clamping force on the friction material
   b. Increasing the friction material coefficient of friction
   c. Increasing the brake fluid viscosity
   d. Increasing the swept area of friction material
6. This would *not* normally be found in a hydraulic brake system.
   a. Mineral oil
   b. Brake fluid
   c. Air
   d. Hydraulic oil

7. Brake fade is a condition that typically happens to this type of brake.
   a. Shoe and drum
   b. Rotor and caliper
   c. Multidisc
   d. Bladder
8. This caliper component returns the brake pads away from the rotor.
   a. Piston seal
   b. Air pressure
   c. Adjuster spring
   d. Hydraulic pressure
9. This type of brake is *never* spring applied.
   a. Drum
   b. Rotor caliper
   c. Multidisc
   d. Bladder
10. One main advantage that multidisc type brakes have over other types of hydraulically applied foundation brakes is that ___________.
   a. they will apply faster
   b. they are easier to repair
   c. they are air cooled
   d. they are sealed from the environment

ASE Technician A/Technician B Style Questions

1. Technician A says the secondary or parking brakes are usually spring applied. Technician B says the secondary or parking brakes are usually air applied. Who is correct?
   a. Technician A
   b. Technician B
   c. Both A and B
   d. Neither A nor B
2. Technician A says if a machine has a faulty service brake system the machine will roll on a hill when the parking brakes are applied. Technician B says a service brake fault will not affect parking brakes. Who is correct?
   a. Technician A
   b. Technician B
   c. Both A and B
   d. Neither A nor B
3. Technician A says increasing brake fluid viscosity does not affect braking effectiveness. Technician B says increasing brake fluid viscosity increases the clamping force on the friction material. Who is correct?
   a. Technician A
   b. Technician B
   c. Both A and B
   d. Neither A nor B
4. Technician A says hydraulic fluid power is used to transmit pressure to one or more actuators to slow or stop a load. Technician B says hydraulic fluid power is used to transmit energy to one or more actuators to provide a force to move a load. Who is correct?
   a. Technician A
   b. Technician B
   c. Both A and B
   d. Neither A nor B
5. Technician A says hydraulic systems allow multiplication of force. Technician B says hydraulic components are conveniently located at widely separated points. Who is correct?
   a. Technician A
   b. Technician B
   c. Both A and B
   d. Neither A nor B
6. Technician A says fluid conduits operate around corners without loss of efficiency. Technician B says all hydraulic fluids burn under certain circumstances. Who is correct?
   a. Technician A
   b. Technician B
   c. Both A and B
   d. Neither A nor B
7. Technician A says hydraulic brake systems they can be designed to apply significant stopping pressure through mechanical advantage using the fluid as the transfer medium. Technician B says hydraulic brake systems use a small force to control large forces. Who is correct?
   a. Technician A
   b. Technician B
   c. Both A and B
   d. Neither A nor B
8. Technician A says Pascal's law states that pressure exerted on a fluid in a confined system is the same at any point in the system. Technician B says Pascal's law states that pressure exerted on a fluid in a confined system is exerted equally to the walls of the container. Who is correct?
   a. Technician A
   b. Technician B
   c. Both A and B
   d. Neither A nor B
9. Technician A says ABS prevents wheel lockup lock up by automatically and rapidly pumping the brakes whenever the system detects a wheel that is near a lock up state. Technician B says if the ABS does not function the brakes will still work, but have less stopping power. Who is correct?
   a. Technician A
   b. Technician B
   c. Both A and B
   d. Neither A nor B
10. Technician A says OBD fault codes will cause a warning light on the dash panel to illuminate. Technician B says indicate leaks in the hydraulic brake system. Who is correct?
   a. Technician A
   b. Technician B
   c. Both A and B
   d. Neither A nor B

CHAPTER 55

Pneumatic Brake Systems

Knowledge Objectives

After reading this chapter, you will be able to:

- **K55001** Explain the fundamentals of pneumatics in off-road heavy-duty braking systems.
- **K55002** Describe the components of an off-road heavy-duty air brake circuit and their functions.
- **K55003** Describe the advantages and disadvantages of air brake systems.
- **K55004** Define and describe off-road heavy-duty air brake components and control circuits.
- **K55005** Describe how S-cam foundation brakes work.
- **K55006** Describe the fundamentals and functions of pneumatic accessory systems.

Skills Objectives

After reading this chapter, you will be able to:

- **S55001** Describe the steps to diagnose and inspect the brake system.
- **S55002** Describe the steps for servicing and repairing an air brake circuit inspection.

▶ Introduction

MORE (mobile off-road equipment) machines can sometimes be found with pneumatic brake systems. Although the majority of machines use one or more variations of hydraulic brake systems, some manufacturers use pressurized air as the energy source for their machines' braking system.

Although there are similarities between MORE pneumatic brake systems (air brake systems) and on-highway truck brake systems, the versions used on MORE machines are very basic. While today's on-highway truck brake systems incorporate electronics to provide antilock braking and traction control and include extra valves and components for one or more trailers, MORE air brake systems are fairly simple.

Pressurized air can also be used for other systems, such as for powering starting motors, powering rock drill hammers, and actuating air horns.

There is a good chance a MORE technician will be asked to service or repair a pneumatic brake or accessory system at some point in his or her career, and a good basic knowledge of pneumatic system operation is important.

▶ Pneumatic Brake Systems

K55001

Pneumatics is a general term applied to the use of a gas—typically compressed air—to transfer power to one or more actuators that in turn can create a mechanical force to perform work. In that sense, a pneumatic system is a type of hydraulic system, with the main difference being that air is the medium used for energy transfer, as opposed to a liquid.

Pneumatic brake systems, otherwise called air brake systems, use compressed air as an energy source to actuate service brakes and release parking brakes. There are variations of these systems, such as service brakes only, service and parking brakes, and air-boosted hydraulic brake systems.

Service brakes are used to slow down and stop the machine, and parking brakes are used to hold the machine in place after it has been stopped.

▶ Basic Air Brake System Components

K55002

As shown in **FIGURE 55-1**, the basic air brake system contains the following components:

- **Compressor**—compresses atmospheric air to provide air pressure for the system.
- **Governor**—controls compressor duty cycle and sets maximum system pressure.
- **Air dryer**—removes excessive moisture from the air after it leaves the compressor.
- **Secondary and primary reservoirs**—store pressurized air produced by the compressor.
- **Foot valve**—allows the operator to meter air pressure to the brake system from the reservoir (can also be called a treadle valve).

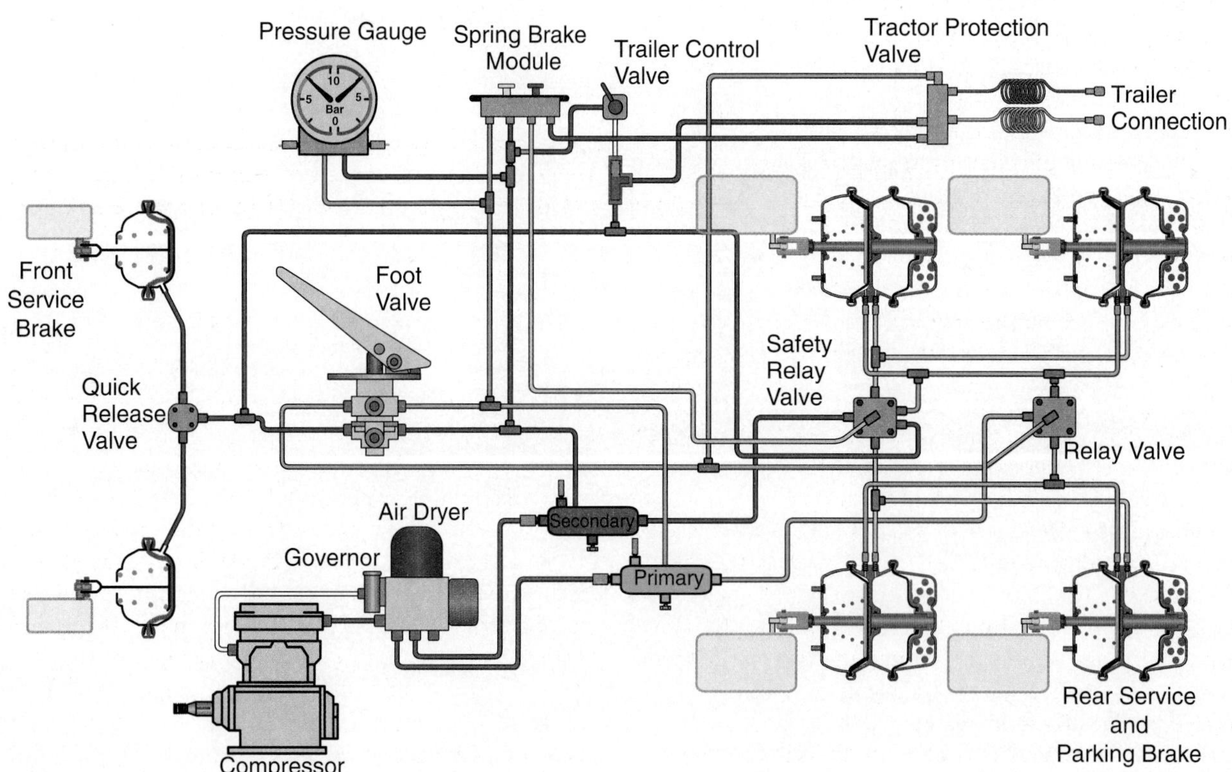

FIGURE 55-1 Example of a basic pneumatic (air) braking system.

- Pressure gauge—indicates air pressure available in the reservoirs.
- **Brake chamber**—actuator used to convert the pressurized air into mechanical action to actuate the foundation brakes.
- **Relay valves**—provide faster brake actuation.
- **Quick-release valve**—prevents delay of brake release.
- **Spring brake module**—delivers air pressure to spring brake chambers to release parking brakes.

Additionally, there are:

- **Air lines**—connect all components and allow transfer of air from the compressor throughout the system.
- **Foundation brakes**—use friction materials attached to brake shoes (drum) or pads (disc) that are forced against the rotating component (brake drum or rotor) by the action of the brake chambers; these are located at each wheel end.
- **Slack adjusters**—adjust (taking the slack out of) the clearance between the brake drum and brake linings or brake pad and rotor; these adjusters can be either automatic or manual.

▶ Advantages and Disadvantages of Pneumatic Braking Systems

K55003

One major advantage of air brakes is its low operating pressure, roughly 105–125 **psi** (pounds per square inch) compared to a hydraulic brake system that can generate line pressures of 1,500 to 2,500 psi. This low pressure, along with the fact that the "working fluid" is air, makes it a much safer system to work with and easier to use as an energy source for other systems on the vehicle, like air horns and air-cushioned seats.

Air is the medium of choice for transferring and multiplying force, as compared to hydraulic fluid or brake fluid, is also in an endless supply and an environmentally friendly alternative. Air pressure can be stored in one or more simple reservoirs anywhere on the machine.

Air brake systems multiply and transfer brake pedal force using the energy of safe compressed air. Air brake systems have several other advantages:

- The supply of air is limitless, which allows for minor leaks without the loss of braking. If small leaks do occur, the air can be replenished without a loss of braking.
- Air lines can be disconnected without major consequence. Hydraulic systems require bleeding of air each time they are opened.
- Air brakes can maintain brake pressure at high altitudes because an air compressor multiplies atmospheric air pressure. Vacuum boosters used with hydraulic brakes lose effectiveness with increased altitude.
- Other vehicle systems may also use the supply of compressed air. For example, air suspension, transmission controls, or differential locks might use compressed air.

Air brake systems do have some disadvantages:

- The pressurized air must be dried and stored in relatively large tanks.
- **Brake lag** occurs between driver application and brake actuation because of the nature of compressed air (it has a spring effect). This compares to hydraulic force transmission which has little or no delay.
- Control of air pressure through air brake circuits requires more valves and components, which adds complexity and cost to the air brake system.
- There is a delay when an air system has leaked down and has to build up pressure after the machine is started.
- There is little positive feedback from the brake pedal during braking application.
- Air systems operate at lower pressures than hydraulic systems, so larger brake system components, and lines with larger diameters are needed to achieve equivalent braking forces.
- Air can become contaminated with moisture and cause brake valves and other components to freeze up in cold weather operation.

▶ Air Brake Subsystems and Control Circuits

K55004

Pneumatic brake systems can be divided into four distinct systems:

- Air supply system
- Air delivery system
- Foundation brake system
- Park-emergency/supply brake system

Compressed Air Supply System

Pneumatic brake systems require a sufficient supply of pressurized dry air to operate effectively. Components such as the compressor, governor, air dryer, air tanks, air lines, and safety valves make up the air supply system.

Air Compressor

Air compressors can be belt driven, but most are gear driven directly from the engine's timing gears. Most compressors used for air brake systems are the reciprocating piston type. The compressors usually have one or two cylinders. However, if the system needs a large airflow, V-four or inline four-cylinder compressors are available.

The compressor crankshaft moves the connecting rods and pistons up and down inside a cylinder bore. Some compressors can be used to drive other engine or machine pumps such as fuel or steering oil pumps. Check valves in the compressor head control the flow of air in and out of the compressor.

Compressors are usually cooled by engine coolant and are lubricated with engine oil. Inlet air to the air compressor is usually sourced from the engine's inlet air once it has been cleaned by the engine air filter. See **FIGURE 55-2** for an air compressor mounted to a diesel engine.

FIGURE 55-2 Air compressor on engine.

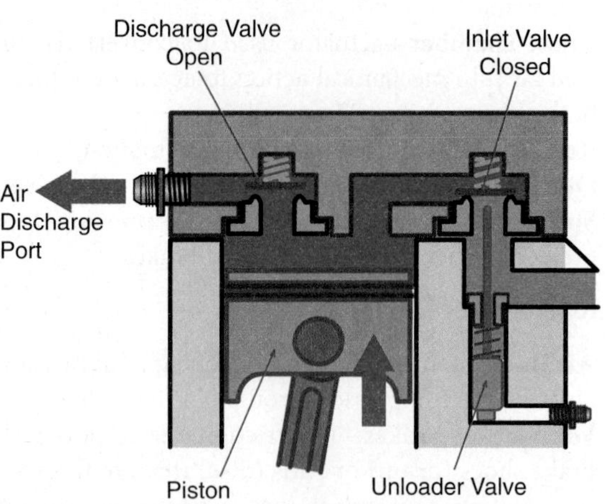

FIGURE 55-4 Compressor components when piston is moving up.

Coolant from the engine flows through the head to keep it cool, because compressing air generates heat. Pressurized engine oil is fed to the bearings for the crankshaft in order to create a film of oil between the crankshaft and the bearings. This oil also goes through the crankshaft to journals where the connecting rods are attached to it. The oil keeps the connecting rod bearings from making direct contact with the crankshaft journals. The oil then drains back to the engine sump, either through a drain line or through an opening in the compressor body, and into the oil sump of the engine.

The connecting rods transfer rotary torque from the crankshaft to the pistons in order to drive them up and down. The pistons are similar to combustion engine pistons in that they have metal piston rings to create a seal between the piston and its cylinder bore.

As the air compressor piston is drawn down by the crankshaft, air moves in past the inlet check valve and fills the void on top of the piston. The discharge valve (check valve) is held closed by the pressure in the outlet line.

See **FIGURE 55-3** for an illustration of the compressor components when the piston is moving down.

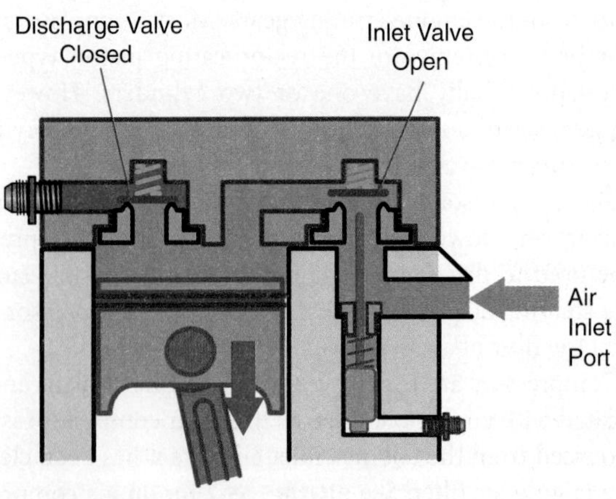

Intake Stroke

Discharge Valve
Closed

Inlet Valve
Open

Air
Inlet
Port

FIGURE 55-3 Compressor components when piston is moving down.

As the piston then travels up in the bore, the inlet valve is closed, and air is pushed past the discharge valve that is now open. **FIGURE 55-4** shows how the compressor components react when the piston is moving up.

Because the engine timing gears constantly drive the air compressor when the engine is running, there must be a way to regulate system air pressure. The governor has an air line connected to the supply air tank that allows the governor to sense system pressure. System pressure works on a plunger inside the air governor, which is held in place with spring pressure. As system pressure rises, it pushes the plunger against spring pressure, which opens a passage in the governor. The air pressure then leaves the governor and goes to the compressor unloader valve, a normally closed valve that is held in place by a spring and controlled by the system's governor. A small rod pushes against the inlet check valve when the unloader valve is moved up. The inlet check valve is then held open to unload the compressor, and the piston just pushes air in and out of the inlet line or back and forth between the two compressor pistons, depending on the type of compressor. This pressure setting is called cut-out pressure. See **FIGURE 55-5** for a look at compressor components when the unloader valve is actuated. A check valve in the outlet line of the compressor stops pressure from returning into the compressor when it is in the unloaded mode.

Compressors are sized by the volume of air they can pump at a certain pressure level. An example of a compressor used to supply air for an air brake system is 15 **cfm** (cubic feet per minute) @ 100 psi. They are usually sized so that they move air only 25% of the time that the compressor crankshaft is turning. This constitutes a 25% **duty cycle**, and the other 75% of **run time** gives the compressor time to cool down. The amount of time that compressors are pumping is controlled by the governor, which determines this by monitoring system pressure.

If there is an air leak downstream and the duty cycle increases to compensate for the air loss, the compressor will likely overheat. Air lines for the compressor outlet must be heat resistant. For example, they could be copper- or stainless

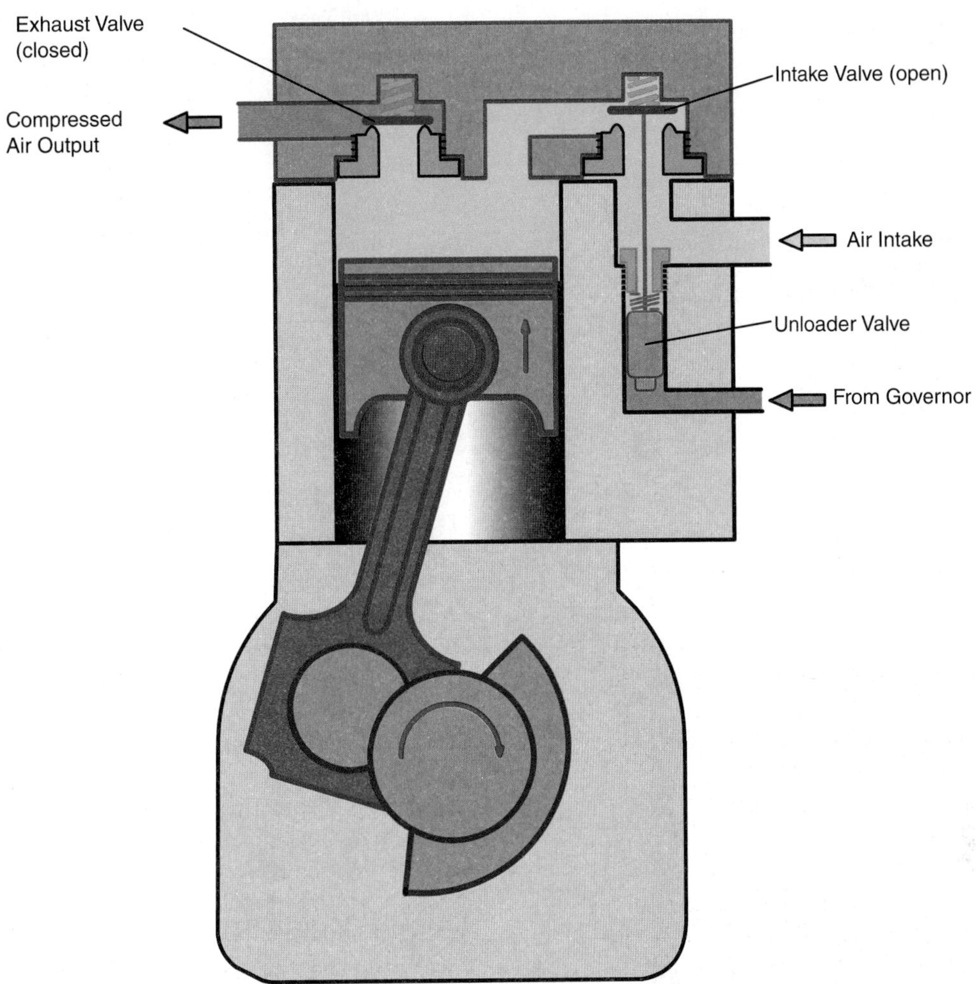

FIGURE 55-5 Compressor components when the unloader is actuated.

steel–reinforced nylon hose. Other air lines could be rubber or plastic, and their ends could have a variety of different types of connectors.

Pneumatic System Governor

To control maximum system pressure and cycle the compressor on and off, every pneumatic system requires a governor to perform these functions. Governors are usually mounted on the compressor but can be mounted remotely as well. See **FIGURE 55-6** for an example of a governor mounted to a compressor.

Spring tension in the governor is adjustable, so by varying spring tension the technician can set maximum system pressure. As system pressure drops, the governor plunger rises and blocks off the outlet to the unloader valve, and the compressor starts pushing air out the discharge line. This pressure is called cut-in pressure and is not adjustable, but is a fixed difference below the cut-out pressure, usually between 20 and 30 psi. **FIGURE 55-7** depicts a cutaway illustration of a governor.

A typical value for maximum pressure is 120 psi, which would make cut-in pressure 100 psi. Typically, a dash gauge displays the supply air pressure.

FIGURE 55-6 Governor mounted to a compressor.

Air Dryer

Airflow from the compressor outlet goes to an air dryer next, to get most of the moisture removed from the air. As shown in **FIGURE 55-8**, an air dryer is a canister that contains desiccant (A), which is a substance that absorbs moisture. A purge valve

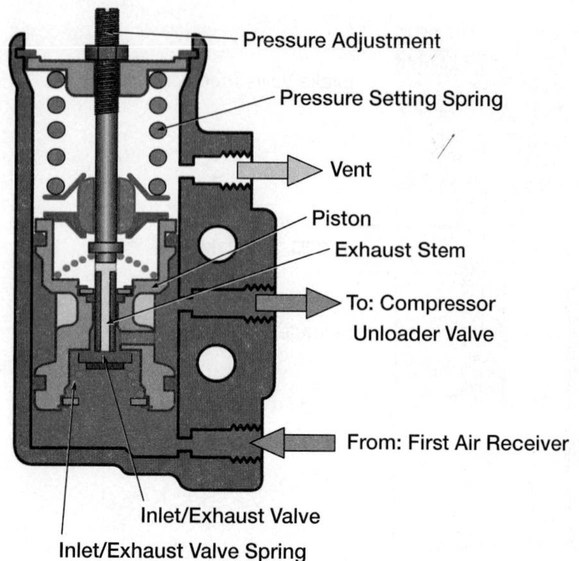

FIGURE 55-7 Cutaway illustration of a governor.

FIGURE 55-8 Typical air dryer.

(B) at the bottom of the air dryer opens when cut-out pressure is reached and exhausts any accumulated moisture from inside the air dryer. An air line going from the governor to the bottom of the air dryer unseats the purge valve.

Air Tanks

Once the mostly dry air leaves the air dryer, it goes to the supply tank, which has a **wet side** and a **dry side**, as shown in **FIGURE 55-9**. The compressed air enters the tank hot, and when it cools down in the wet side of the tank, any moisture left in the air condenses and collects in the bottom of the tank. This makes it necessary to drain the wet tank on a daily basis in order to purge any collected moisture.

Some systems use a separate wet tank, and depending on the amount of pressurized air storage required, there could be several air tanks on one machine.

Some systems have automatic drain valves on the supply tank. Air pressure that is stored in the supply tank can now be used for a variety of uses, as mentioned earlier.

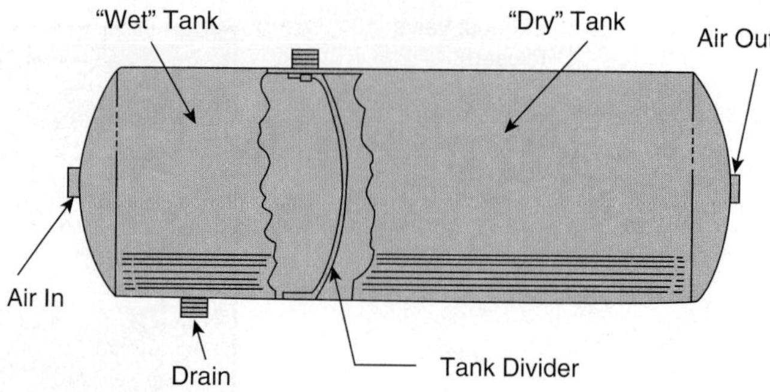

FIGURE 55-9 Wet/dry tank.

Safety Valves

There should be **safety valves** in all components of the supply system. In case the governor doesn't limit pressure and there is a blockage somewhere downstream from the governor, a safety valve will open and release air pressure. Safety valves are usually set for 250 psi and should only open if system pressure reaches dangerous levels.

Air Delivery System

The air delivery system takes the dry, pressurized air from the air supply system and transfers it to actuators downstream that convert the pneumatic energy into mechanical energy to apply brakes. The air delivery system is mainly controlled by the operator, but some functions occur automatically.

Dual-Circuit Brake System

Some machines have a dual-circuit brake system with **primary brakes** working the rear **service brake** system and the secondary brake system applying the front service brake system. This dual-circuit system, shown in **FIGURE 55-10**, improves air brake system safety, as the split systems minimize the chance of complete brake failure.

The air supply system includes a supply **reservoir** that supplies air to the primary and secondary air reservoirs. From there, it is available to one or more valves that the operator can use to meter pressurized air to brake actuators.

Treadle Valve

Primary and secondary air tanks supply the **foot pedal treadle valve** shown in **FIGURE 55-11**. The secondary tank supplies air to one section of the treadle valve, and the primary tank supplies the other. When the brake pedal is pushed down, air is metered out of both valve sections to the front and rear service brake chambers.

The treadle valve is capable of controlling the air application pressure from as little as 4 psi up to the full 100+ psi that may be in the tanks.

The air brake system is a "full power" system that requires no driver effort to apply the brakes—no ratio of foot power to brake power. To give the driver a sense of the amount of pressure being applied, some "feedback" is built into the treadle valve. This feedback is not as strong as the feedback in a hydraulic brake system, but it does provide the driver a gauge of brake application.

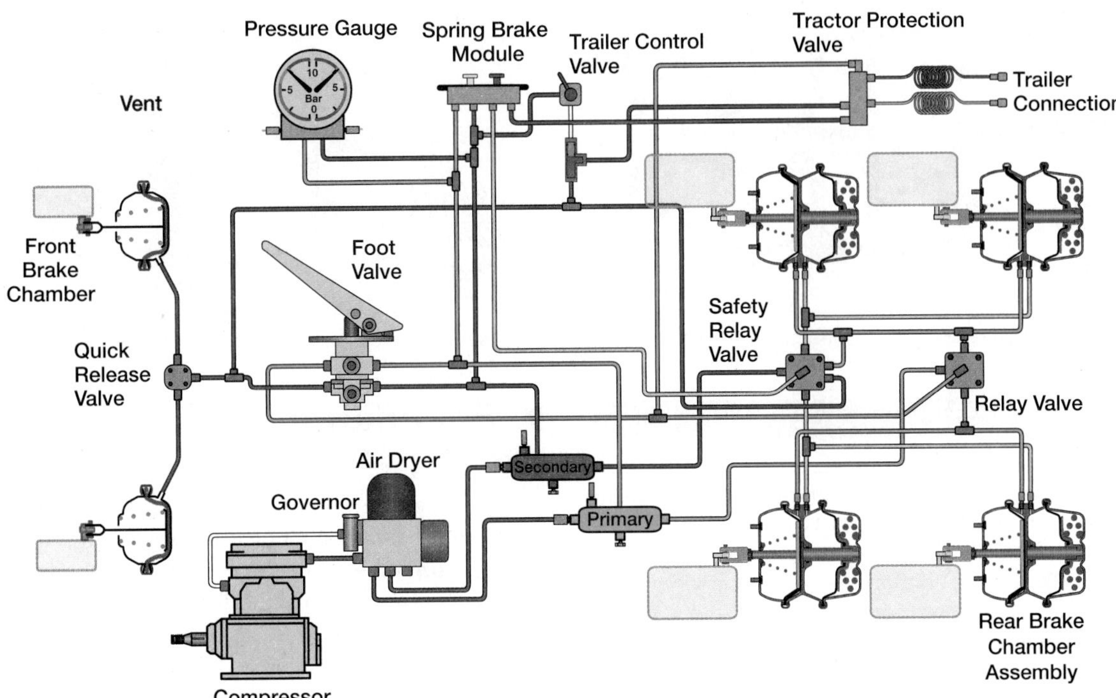

FIGURE 55-10 Dual circuit brake system.

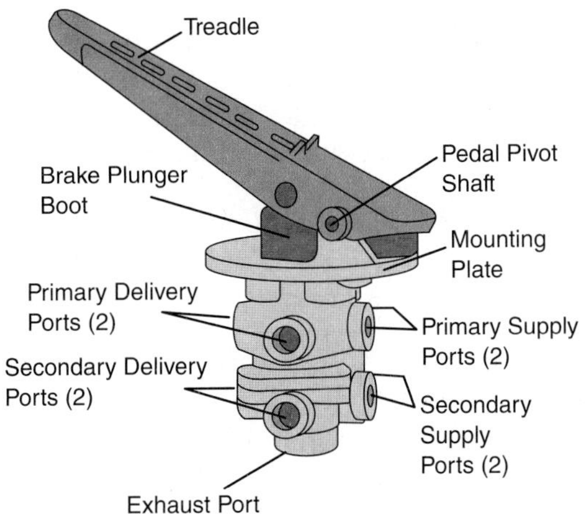

FIGURE 55-11 Foot pedal treadle valve.

Another difference in the "feel" of air brakes compared to hydraulic brakes is that air brakes are both "force sensitive" (the built-in feedback against the brake pedal) and "travel sensitive." When the operator applies air brakes, both resistance felt in the pedal and the distance the pedal travels give the operator an indication of how much power is being sent to the brake chambers.

Service Brake Chambers

When the treadle valve is opened and air pressure is released into the brake lines, the brake chambers at each wheel begin to sense the pressure rise, and inside the brake chamber, as shown in **FIGURE 55-12**, air pressure pushes on the **diaphragm** against spring pressure on the opposite side of the diaphragm.

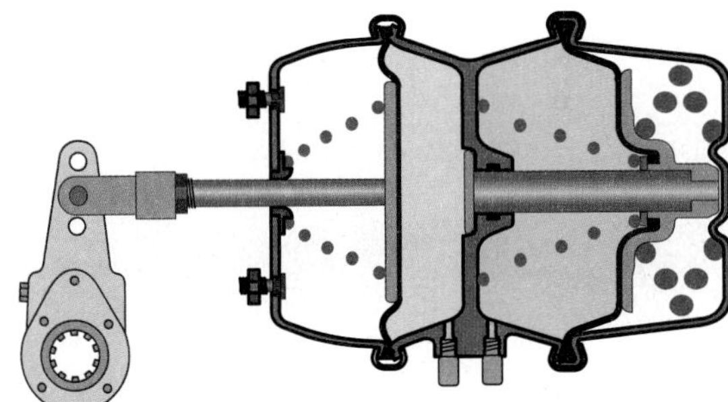

FIGURE 55-12 Service brake chamber (left section) with air applied to its diaphragm.

The diaphragm then pushes on a plate that pushes the brake rods out of the brake chamber that in turn mechanically actuates the foundation brakes. Service brake chambers are considered to be air applied and spring released.

Parking Brake Chambers

All parking brakes on an air brake–equipped MORE machines are spring applied. This ensures the brakes are applied if air pressure is lost. Parking brake chambers are typically only on the rear brakes. The rear brake system has two chambers (service and parking brake) stacked together and actuate the same rod coming out of it.

A very strong spring in the **spring brake** (parking) chamber, shown in **FIGURE 55-13**, keeps the rod pushed out and the brake shoes applied until the parking brake release valve sends air to it. Air pressure on the diaphragm compresses the spring, which in turn pulls the rod in to release the brake. The service brake chamber is then able to push the rod out to apply the brakes when air pressure is modulated to it. A pressure of 80 psi will release and hold the parking brake.

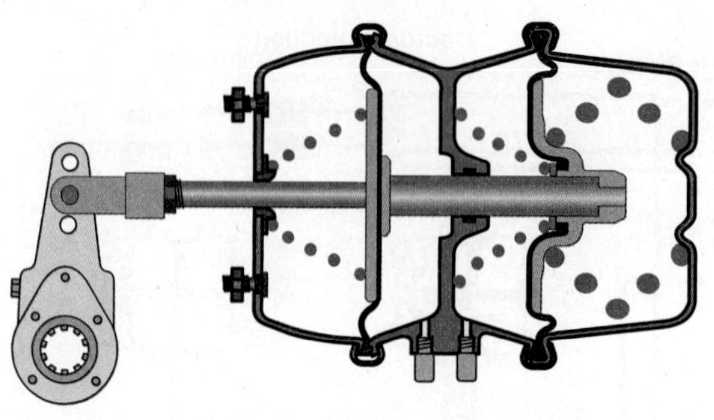

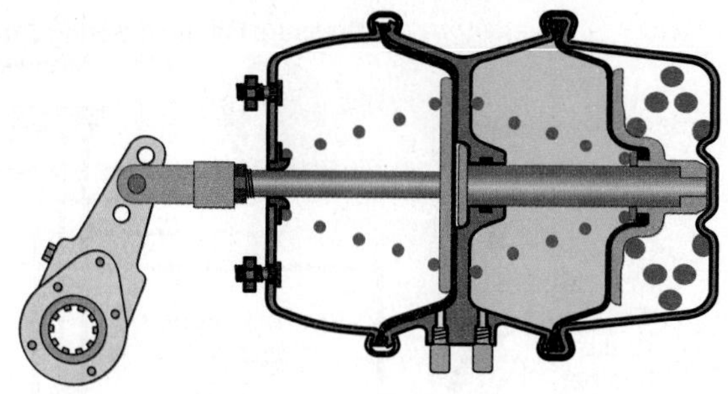

FIGURE 55-13 Parking brake chamber (right section) shown both applied (left illustration) and released (right illustration).

> ▶ TECHNICIAN TIP
>
> Some service procedures require spring brakes to be caged. This means that they are held in a released position mechanically. To do this, a spring brake tool (caging bolt), shown in **FIGURE 55-14**, is inserted through the back of the brake chamber. Two small pins protrude from the end of it that, when turned 180 degrees, locks into the plate of the spring brake. Next, a nut and washer is tightened against the housing, and as the nut is turned, the tool pulls the plate back into the chamber housing as if air pressure was being applied to the opposite end of the diaphragm. This is done whenever there is a need to release the parking brakes mechanically.
>
> Be extra cautious whenever a brake is caged because the spring-applied feature is now defeated.

FIGURE 55-14 Brake release tool.

▶ Foundation Brakes

K55005

There are several variations of air-actuated foundation brakes, but the most common for off-road heavy-duty equipment is the **S-cam drum brake**. The (S-cam) refers to the shaft that forces the shoes outward against the drum, which is shaped like an "S." The S-cam design provides adjustment to compensate for wear of the brake linings and brake drums.

When air is applied to the service brake chambers, the rod attached to the diaphragm plate pushes on the slack adjuster, which is splined to the S-cam shaft. The shaft has an "S" shaped cam on its opposite end that will push against a pair of rollers that are hooked onto one end of each brake shoe. As shown in **FIGURE 55-15**, as the rollers ride up the S-cam profile, they spread the brake shoes. Braking action takes place when the brake shoes are pushed out against the inner surface of the brake drum.

Because the brake shoes are anchored to the axle housing and the brake drum rotates at wheel speed, the friction material on the brake drums tries to make the brake drum match the speed of the axle housing (0 rpm).

The amount of braking action is directly proportional to the force applied by the brake shoes to the brake drum. This force increases as air pressure applied to the service brake chamber increases, which is metered by the operator's foot on

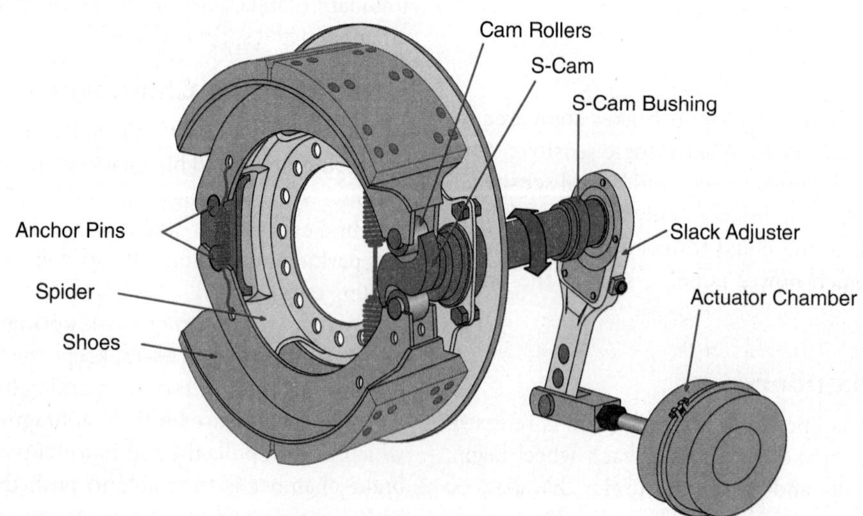

FIGURE 55-15 S-cam foundation brake.

the brake pedal. Normally, the only variable is the air pressure that gets metered to the chamber because the size of the brake chambers and the length of the **slack adjusters** are determined by the engineers who design the machine.

Slack Adjusters

Connecting the brake chamber rod and the S-cam shaft is a lever, called a slack adjuster, with a mechanism that allows adjustment to maintain the proper clearance between the brake drum and brake shoe; MORE machines usually have manually adjusted slack adjusters, but most highway air brake systems have automatic slack adjusters. **FIGURE 55-16** shows a manual slack adjuster. Slack adjuster mechanisms that are automatic will maintain the proper clearance between shoe and drum without a technician's attention.

The service brake **chamber rod** pushes on the end of a slack adjuster, which causes the adjuster to pivot about the center of the S-cam shaft. The opposite end of the slack adjuster has a large female spline that mates with one end of a shaft. So, as the slack adjuster is moved by the brake chamber it rotates the shaft.

Manually adjusted slack adjusters allow the technician to maintain the specified clearance between the brake shoe and the drum. They are adjusted by pushing down a lock ring and turning an adjusting screw. **FIGURE 55-17** shows how a manual slack adjuster can be adjusted.

Rotochamber

Another type of brake chamber used for S-cam type foundation brakes that is particularly common with MORE machines, is called the **rotochamber**, as shown in **FIGURE 55-18**.

It is similar to the previously mentioned brake chambers except that it uses a different style of diaphragm that allows it to produce a longer stroke and maintain a constant force throughout the entire stroke. The rolling-type diaphragm also provides long life.

Rotochambers may also have a different parking brake apply-and-release mechanism instead of a separate spring-applied chamber. A series of balls work on the rod of the chamber to hold the rod in place. The balls are held in place by a wedge-type mechanism and released with air pressure.

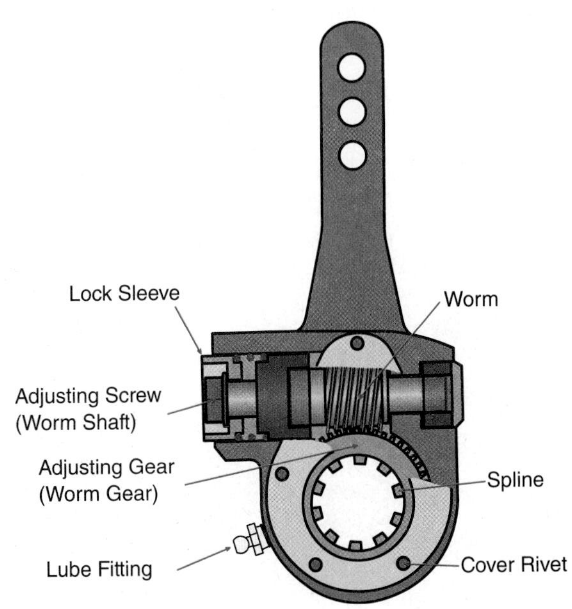

FIGURE 55-16 Slack adjuster mechanism.

FIGURE 55-17 To adjust, a **A.** locking ring is pushed down, and the **B.** adjusting screw is turned to obtain the correct stroke or brake shoe–to-drum clearance.

▶ Pneumatic Accessory Systems

K55006

MORE machines can use pneumatic energy for other applications besides applying and releasing brakes. Other uses include actuating air horns, air seat suspensions, differential locks, and main hydraulic control valves, and cranking diesel engines. All of the previous examples use the same low-pressure (125 psi) supply system that is used for the pneumatic brake system described above.

High-pressure and high-volume pneumatic systems can be found on many drilling machines. Certain functions on rock drills need high pressure (300–500 psi) and high volume (200–1,500 cfm) such as: to operate the drill hammer and to flush out the muck as the drill progresses through the material it is working in. Large screw-type air compressors provide the necessary pressure and volume. Some drills have the compressor on the machine and driven directly by the prime mover, whereas others use a stand-alone compressor with its own prime mover and connect to it with a high-pressure hose. Some stand-alone air compressors require prime movers with over 1,000 hp to drive them, and the air compressor has its own lubrication systems and cooling system. **FIGURE 55-19** depicts a horizontal rock drill, that needs a standalone air compressor and **FIGURE 55-20** shows a stand-alone high-pressure/high-volume air compressor.

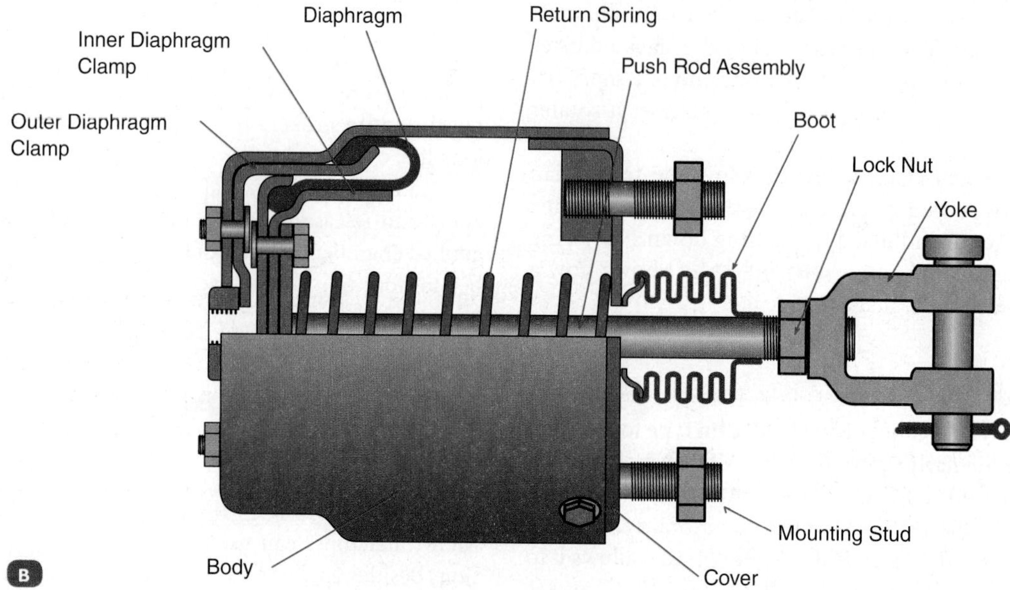

FIGURE 55-18 **A.** Rotochambers are brake chamber actuators with a different style of diaphragm that "unrolls" during operation. **B.** The construction of a rotochamber provides consistent output pressure regardless of brake pushrod position.

FIGURE 55-19 Horizontal rock drill.

FIGURE 55-20 Stand-alone high-pressure/high-volume air compressor.

Diagnosing and Inspecting Air Brake Systems

S55001

Some air brake system problems are listed here:

- No air pressure
- Low air pressure
- Air compressor cycling too fast
- Too much moisture in the air
- Air leaks

As with any other diagnostic procedure, start by verifying the complaint.

Park the machine on level ground and chock the wheels. Leave the engine running, and allow the air compressor governor to raise the system's air pressure. Depress the parking brake button; then listen for the sound of escaping air or unfamiliar noises coming from the compressor.

Then move on to performing a walk-around inspection, looking and listening for air leaks, checking the wet tank for oil, checking system pressure, checking the air dryer for purging, and timing the compressor cut-in/cut-out cycle.

Check for water in the air-brake system, a byproduct of the condensed air. Water in the system, especially in colder climates, may turn to ice and block air from reaching the brake chambers. This could cause the wheels to lock up. To prevent this problem, regularly inspect the drain valves in each air tank.

Also:

- Make sure the minimum operating pressure for a vehicle air-brake systems is no less than 100 psi.
- Check that it takes no longer than 2 minutes for air pressure to rise from 85 psi to 100 psi at 600–900 rpm. (This is called the air pressure buildup rate.)
- Confirm that the correct cut-out governor pressure for the air compressor is between 120 psi and 135 psi. Cut-in pressure is 20 psi to 25 psi below cut-out pressure.
- Have someone operate the brake pedal, and visually check the operation of the service chambers at each wheel.

Servicing Air Brake Systems

S55002

To keep an air brake system operating properly, a few simple service steps should be regularly performed. Drain valves should be drained daily to make sure water is removed. Otherwise, air systems will accumulate moisture, which leads to operational problems; excessive moisture in air brake systems can also lead to rust and corrosion on internal components.

Some systems have an alcohol injector for the pneumatic system. The injector meters alcohol into the system, which prevents freezing, but it has to be topped up on a regular basis. Brake chamber stroke should be kept within specification.

Perform a brake performance check as per machine service information instructions. For example: put the machine in third speed forward, apply the brakes, and increase engine RPM to high idle. The brakes should hold the machine stationary. If not, investigate further.

Air Brake System Repairs

Air line leaks can be repaired by replacing the entire line assembly or by using a line repair kit. The valves of a pneumatic system can be rebuilt, but it may be cheaper to replace the entire valve assembly. The deciding factor with valve replacements may be the condition of the air lines connected to the valve body. If the lines are corroded or they are steel lines that can't be moved easily, it may be more time efficient to rebuild the valve in place, if that's possible.

An air compressor that has to be repaired is usually replaced as an assembly. If the air compressor has had a major failure, then a system cleanout may be required. In some machines, air compressors that drive other components such as fuel pumps or small hydraulic pumps. In this case, the air compressor replacement becomes more complicated.

Air tanks that show signs of corrosion should be replaced because air tank failures can be deadly. The same strategy of replacement rather than repair should also apply to faulty service brake chambers. Although the diaphragms and other components are typically replaceable, corrosion of the chamber housing is common. A service chamber showing signs of corrosion should be replaced.

SAFETY TIP

Use extreme caution when working on or near spring brake chambers. If the brake chamber housing or retaining ring fails, the spring contained inside will be released with deadly force. When these springs are compressed, they have a potential of several thousand pounds of force waiting to be released.

To adjust cut-out pressure, follow the steps in **SKILL DRILL 55-1**.

SKILL DRILL 55-1 Adjusting Cut-Out Pressure

- PPE required: safety glasses, gloves, safety boots, and hearing protection
- Equipment required: machine with pneumatic brake system
- Tools required: 7/16" wrench, straight screwdriver

1. Open all air tank drain valves to reduce system air pressure to below 60 psi.
2. Start the machine and build air pressure.
3. Read air pressure when you hear the air dryer purge (this should also be when the pressure stops rising).
4. Stop the machine and bleed off air pressure, as in step 1.
5. Adjust the governor adjuster screw counterclockwise a half turn.
6. Repeat steps 2 and 3. How much did the maximum pressure change?
7. Repeat step 4 and then adjust cut-out pressure to 120 psi.

Wrap-Up

Ready for Review

- A pneumatic system governor in cut-out mode will send air pressure to the unloader plunger.
- As long as the compressor is working, the supply of air is limitless, which allows for minor leaks without the loss of braking. If small leaks do occur, the air can be replenished without a loss of braking.
- Air lines can be disconnected and nothing but air is lost. Hydraulic systems would require bleeding of air each time they are opened.
- Air brakes can maintain brake pressure at high altitudes because an air compressor multiplies atmospheric air pressure. Vacuum boosters used with hydraulic brakes lose effectiveness with increased altitude.
- Other vehicle systems may also use the supply of compressed air. For example, the air suspension, transmission controls or interaxle differential lock may use compressed air.

Key Terms

air dryer A canister that contains desiccant to absorb moisture.

air lines Carry the pressurized air to each brake chamber.

brake chambers At each wheel convert the pressurized air into mechanical action.

brake lag The delay between driver application and brake actuation.

cfm Cubic feet per minute is a measure of the flow rate of a gas.

compressor Provides airflow for the system.

diaphragm Component inside the brake chamber that converts air pressure to mechanical actuation.

dry side The side of the reservoir tank where cooled air is stored after leaving moisture in the tank wet side.

duty cycle The amount of time a compressor is actually pumping air (a percentage of run time).

foot pedal treadle valve Activated by the operator meters air out of both valve sections to the front and rear service brake chambers.

foundation brakes At each wheel are made up of friction materials attached to brakes shoes (drum) or pads (disc) that are forced against the rotating component by the action of the brake chambers.

governor Controls compressor duty cycle and sets maximum system pressure.

pneumatics A general term applied to the application of compressed air to transmit power.

primary brakes The part of a dual brake system that works the rear brakes of a vehicle.

psi Pressure measurement-pounds per square inch.

quick-release valve Prevents delay of brake release.

relay valves Provide faster brake actuation.

reservoir Provides stored, pressurized air.

rotochamber Produces a longer stroke and maintains a constant force throughout the entire stroke.

run time The total time the compressor is running (includes duty cycle and unloaded time).

safety valves Open and release air pressure in case of a blockage in the system.

S-cam drum brake The cam that forces the shoes outward against the drum is shaped like an "S."

secondary and primary reservoirs Store pressurized air from compressor.

service brake The rear brakes of a dual brake system.

slack adjusters Levers with either automatic or manual means of adjusting the brake linings.

spring brake A very strong spring that applies the parking brakes.

spring brake module Delivers air pressure to spring brake chambers to release parking brakes.

wet side The side of the reservoir tank where compressed air cools down and any moisture in the air will condense and collect in the bottom on this side of the tank.

Review Questions

1. The air that leaves the compressor of a pneumatic brake system will ________.
   - **a.** be cool and moist
   - **b.** be under negative pressure
   - **c.** be hot and dry
   - **d.** be hot and pressurized
2. Oil is circulated in an air compressor so that ________.
   - **a.** rotating parts stay separated
   - **b.** the compressor stays cool
   - **c.** the air gets lubricated before it leaves the compressor
   - **d.** the check valves stay lubricated
3. Governor cut-in pressure is ________.
   - **a.** determined whenever the machine starts
   - **b.** adjusted at the governor
   - **c.** nonadjustable but related to the cut-out pressure
   - **d.** higher than cut-out pressure sometimes
4. Rotochambers will always ________.
   - **a.** be used with automatic slack adjusters
   - **b.** not last as long as regular brake chambers
   - **c.** have a set of balls that lock the rod out
   - **d.** have square diaphragms

5. Slack adjusters are meant to ________________ for foundation brakes.
   a. make the brakes apply harder
   b. multiply the air pressure in the brake chamber
   c. make the brakes release faster
   d. allow an adjustment to reduce clearances between the shoe and drum
6. An air dryer uses this to remove moisture from air by using a(n) ________.
   a. electric heater
   b. desiccant
   c. diesel heater
   d. hot coolant
7. The governor sends air to the ______________ to stop the air compressor pumping air.
   a. inlet valve
   b. outlet valve
   c. toploader valve
   d. unloader valve
8. The treadle valve's purpose in a pneumatic brake system is to ________________.
   a. apply the parking brake
   b. apply the service brakes
   c. give feedback after the brakes are applied
   d. quickly release the service brakes
9. Compressor duty cycle refers to ________________.
   a. the time it takes to reach cut-out pressure
   b. the time it takes to reach 80 psi
   c. the amount of time it isn't pumping air
   d. the amount of time it is pumping air
10. Air lines that are used for the compressor outlet must ________________.
    a. be solid steel tube
    b. be rubber for flexibility
    c. be heat resistant
    d. be insulated to keep out the heat

ASE Technician A/Technician B Style Questions

1. Technician A says the unloader plunger acts on the inlet valve when the governor is in cut-out mode. Technician B says the unloader plunger acts on the outlet valve when the governor is in cut-out mode. Who is correct?
   a. Technician A
   b. Technician B
   c. Both A and B
   d. Neither A nor B
2. Technician A says the parking brake chamber used with S-cam brakes is spring actuated and air released. Technician B says the service brake chamber used with S-cam brakes is air actuated and spring released. Who is correct?
   a. Technician A
   b. Technician B
   c. Both A and B
   d. Neither A nor B
3. Technician A says service brakes slow down and stop machines. Technician B says the parking brakes hold the machine stationary after it is stopped. Who is correct?
   a. Technician A
   b. Technician B
   c. Both A and B
   d. Neither A nor B
4. Technician A says off-road heavy-duty air brake systems typically use S-cam shoe–type foundation brakes. Technician B says off-road heavy-duty air brake systems may also use disc-type foundation brakes. Who is correct?
   a. Technician A
   b. Technician B
   c. Both A and B
   d. Neither A nor B
5. Technician A says pneumatic systems can be found on machines for brake systems, starting systems, or other systems controls. Technician B says that pneumatic systems have higher pressures than hydraulic systems. Who is correct?
   a. Technician A
   b. Technician B
   c. Both A and B
   d. Neither A nor B
6. Technician A says air compressors use reciprocating pistons to compress air and charge the supply circuit where pressure is typically maintained between 100 and 120 psi. Technician B says safety valves are usually set for 250 psi and should only open if system pressure reaches dangerous levels. Who is correct?
   a. Technician A
   b. Technician B
   c. Both A and B
   d. Neither A nor B
7. Technician A says the governor that turns the compressor on and off controls air compressor pressure. Technician B says a check valve in the outlet line of the compressor stops pressure from returning into the compressor when it is in the unloaded mode. Who is correct?
   a. Technician A
   b. Technician B
   c. Both A and B
   d. Neither A nor B
8. Technician A says compressed air enters the tank hot, and when it cools down in the wet side of the tank, any moisture left in the air condenses and collects in the bottom of the tank. Technician B says air dryers are needed to remove moisture from the air after it has been compressed and cools down. Who is correct?
   a. Technician A
   b. Technician B
   c. Both A and B
   d. Neither A nor B

9. Technician A says brake chambers use S-cams to move their diaphragms. Technician B says the diaphragm in the service brake chamber compresses the parking brake spring to apply the brakes when air pressure is modulated to it. Who is correct?
   a. Technician A
   b. Technician B
   c. Both A and B
   d. Neither A nor B

10. Technician A says parking brakes on off-road heavy-duty vehicles are typically only on the wheels of one rear axle. Technician B says an air pressure of at least 120 psi is required to release the parking brake. Who is correct?
    a. Technician A
    b. Technician B
    c. Both A and B
    d. Neither A nor B

APPENDIX A

AED FOUNDATION 2014 STANDARDS FOR CONSTRUCTION EQUIPMENT TECHNOLOGY

Task List	Chapter
SAFETY	
Use of Hand Tools	
Can identify and correctly name the basic hand tools.	Chapter 05
Demonstrates the proper use of the designed application and safe operating procedure for each.	Chapter 05
Demonstrates a proper source for calibration of precision hand tools.	Chapter 05
Use of Electric Tools	
Can identify and correctly name the electrical tool.	Chapter 11
Demonstrates the proper use of the designed application and safe operating procedure for each.	Chapter 11
Demonstrates the proper inspection, care and storage for electric hand tools.	
Understands and exhibits the safe and proper use of ground fault circuits.	
Use of Air Tools	
Can identify and correctly name the basic air tool.	Chapter 05
Demonstrates the proper use of the designed application and safe operating procedures for each.	Chapter 05
Demonstrates the proper inspection, care, maintenance, and storage for cleaning equipment.	Chapter 05
Use of Hydraulic Tools	
Can identify and correctly name the basic hydraulic tools.	
Demonstrates the proper inspection, care, maintenance, and storage as applicable.	
Demonstrates the proper use of the designed application and safe operating procedure as applicable.	
Use of Lifting Equipment	
Can identify and correctly name the various types of lifting equipment.	Chapter 1, 2, 8
Demonstrates the proper inspection, care, maintenance, and storage for each.	Chapter 8
Demonstrates the proper use of the designed application and safe operating procedure for each.	Chapter 2
Students understand current regulations and standards for use, inspection and certification of lifting equipment.	Chapter 8
Use of Various Cleaning Equipment	
Can identify and correctly name the basic cleaning equipment used in our industry.	
Demonstrates the proper use of the designed application and safe operating procedures for each.	
Demonstrates the proper inspection, care, maintenance, and storage for cleaning equipment.	
Can identify the various solvents and solutions used in the cleaning process.	
Can identify the risks, hazards and precautions for cleaning materials, both personal and environmental.	Chapter 3
Demonstrate an understanding of Safety Data Sheets (SDS) and requirements to meet OSHA standards.	Chapter 3
Use of Fluid Pressure Testing Equipment	
Can identify and correctly name the various types of fluid pressure test equipment and the accessories required for proper testing.	
Can explain the proper use of the designed application and safe operation of each type of equipment.	
Demonstrates a proper source for calibration of precision test equipment and accessories.	

(Continued)

Task List	Chapter
Can identify, correctly name and demonstrate the use of the personal protective equipment required for the various types of fluid pressure testing equipment.	
Can explain at least three dangers of working with fluids under pressure.	Chapter 3
Environment of Service Facility	
Can identify the various types of exhaust systems used in repair facility.	
Demonstrates the proper use of the designed application and safe operation of each type of system.	
Demonstrates the proper inspection, care, maintenance and storage of the systems and the equipment required for operation.	
Can explain why carbon monoxide and diesel smoke can be hazardous to your health and the precautions required for eliminating injury or death.	Chapter 3
Recognize symptoms of exposure to carbon monoxide, diesel smoke and other hazardous materials.	Chapter 3
Machine Identification and Operation	
Can identify the various types of construction equipment and forklifts, using the standard industry names accepted by equipment manufacturers.	Chapter 1, 2
Demonstrates and can explain the proper, safe and fundamental operation of the various types of machinery.	Chapter 2
Can understand from a user's perspective the importance of and reasons for caution/warning lights, backup alarms, seat belts, safety instructions, decals and other customer-related safety information.	Chapter 17
Recognize hybrid systems and/or machines as they relate to safety concerns.	
Mandated Regulations	
Can identify and correctly name the various types of equipment required for these regulations.	
Can exhibit and explain the principles and procedures for each of the regulations.	
Demonstrates the operation, inspection, proper care and maintenance of the various equipment required for conforming with federal and state OSHA and MSHA regulations.	
Identify the different types of fire extinguishers and know the applications and correct use of each type.	Chapter 3
Demonstrates how to find, explain and use an SDS for a product.	Chapter 3
Understand and identify underground utility hazard marking that would commonly be encountered on a job site.	
Can explain why working safely is important, and explain the procedures for reporting unsafe working conditions and practices.	Chapter 3
Shop and In-field Practices	
Can identify safe work practices in each situation.	Chapter 3
Can demonstrate safe work practices in the shop or in the field.	Chapter 3
Can identify proper lifting and pulling techniques to avoid personal injury.	Chapter 3
Demonstrate proper lifting and pulling techniques.	Chapter 3
Demonstrate proper shop/facility cleanliness/appearance to dealer standards.	Chapter 3
Hazard Identification and Prevention	
Demonstrate safe mounting and dismounting practices on construction machinery.	
Explain proper types of chains and binders used in securing loads.	
Demonstrate proper lock out tag out procedures.	Chapter 3
Demonstrate understanding of the HazCom standard and how to use Safety Data Sheets and Chemical Labels.	Chapter 3
Write about or discuss from personal or team experience (shop, workplaces, etc.,) co mmon safety hazards and what you would have done to eliminate them.	
Demonstrate proper work procedures in handling wheel assemblies. Refer to industry standard procedures.	Chapter 36
Know when tethering is necessary and proper use of the fall protection equipment.	

Task List	Chapter
Comprehend Basic Academic Functions	
Exhibit the ability to use parts and service reference/technical materials, and safety materials in print or computer format.	Chapter 3
Exhibit the ability to follow written instructions.	Chapter 3
Exhibit the ability to complete forms, time cards, work orders, accident reports, sales leads, technical bulletins, parts requisitions, and other related written forms of communication.	
Exhibit the ability to perform basic math functions, including measurement in both U.S. and metric, calculations, conversions, and currency.	
Utilize Industry Software and Electronic Communications Systems and Reference Resources	
Develop and exhibit good listening skills.	
Exhibit the ability to use a computer, and related hardware, current software, Internet, and technology currently in use.	
Demonstrate efficient, effective, correct and timely communications to a customer and co-worker utilizing telephone, fax, computer, word processing and E-mail.	
Using a computer, demonstrate the ability to retrieve specifications, part numbers, bulletins, schematics, produce reports, and similar types of information using manufacturers' software and internet based resources.	
Awareness of Dealership Goals, Objectives and Policies	
Exhibit the ability to work toward achieving established goals while in a diversified environment.	
Recognize organizational chart.	
Demonstrate understanding of how product support activities contribute to the overall profitability of the company.	
Identify expense control requirements.	
Maintain awareness of sexual harassment policy, safety rules, environmental regulations, disciplinary action policy, and equal opportunity policy.	Chapter 3
Explain the need for performance reviews and the impact of different performance levels.	
Maintain confidentiality as required.	
Define Basic Business Practices	
Explain the need for quality performance and the impact on customer satisfaction and profitability.	
Demonstrate a positive attitude towards the company and other contacts.	
Define impact of not meeting the customers' needs in a timely manner.	
Recognize customer retention policies and procedures.	
Exhibit the ability to communicate to coworkers and customers in a courteous, professional manner.	
Demonstrate time management and organizational skills.	
Develop an awareness of stressful situations, and the ability to handle and resolve problems with difficult internal and external customers.	
Exhibit the ability to listen and follow verbal and written instructions.	
Respect authority and accept the responsibilities of the position.	
Demonstrate proper appearance to dealer standards.	
Describe Functions of the Dealership Service Department; Explain Department Goals and Procedures	
Identify and establish both short and long-term goals and the requirements to achieve them (business and personal).	
Describe parts inventory control, procurement and accountability.	
Demonstrate knowledge of factors that can determine shop labor rates.	

(Continued)

Task List	Chapter
Demonstrate the ability to accurately complete work orders/repair orders and other related reports, including parts and consumables.	
Demonstrate the ability to write a thorough and comprehensive service report.	
Describe tool procurement procedures.	
Describe time tracking.	
Demonstrate the ability to use correct industry terminology.	
ELECTRONICS/ELECTRICAL SYSTEMS	
Fundamental Knowledge	
Know the basic structure of conductors, insulators, and semi-conductors.	Chapter 09
Know the reaction of like and unlike charges.	Chapter 09
Describe the differences of conventional and electron theory current flow.	Chapter 09
Define resistance and its effect on current flow.	Chapter 09
Demonstrate the principles of operation and the correct usage of the various types of meters to measure volts, amps, and ohms.	Chapter 09
Demonstrate ability to convert between kilo, milli, and micro units.	
Demonstrate knowledge of the laws governing permanent magnets, electromagnets, and magnetic fields.	Chapter 09
Demonstrate knowledge of the effects of magnetic forces on current carrying conductors.	Chapter 09
Know the basic parts and operation of the basic types of storage batteries.	Chapter 12
Understand remote monitoring systems and the ability to remotely diagnose electrical/electronic issues.	
Ohm's Law	
Demonstrate the mathematical relationship of the various terms in ohms law as they pertain to series, parallel, and series-parallel circuits.	Chapter 10
Demonstrate the ability to set-up and measure the voltage, amperage, and resistance values in series, parallel, and series/parallel DC circuits.	Chapter 10
12/24 Volt Cranking Circuits	
Know the basic components that make up the various types of 12/24 volt cranking systems.	Chapter 14
Demonstrate the sequence of operation of the components contained within a cranking system. The emphasis is on how each component effects the system's overall operation.	Chapter 14
Demonstrate the ability to isolate problems using voltage drops and other diagnostic methods. The proper use of testing equipment is paramount.	Chapter 14
Demonstrate the ability to properly test, evaluate and replace the following components using manufacturers' service publications and specifications. **1.** Conductors **2.** Relays/ Solenoids **3.** Starters	Chapter 14
12/24 Volt Charging Circuits	
Know the basic components that make up the various types of 12/24 volt charging systems.	Chapter 10, 15
Demonstrate the sequence of operation of the components contained within a charging system. The emphasis is on how each component effects the system's overall operation.	Chapter 15
Demonstrate the ability to isolate problems using voltage drops and other diagnostic methods. The proper use of testing equipment is paramount.	Chapter 15
Demonstrate the ability to properly test, evaluate and replace the following components using manufacturers' service publications and specifications. **1.** Conductors **2.** Alternators **3.** Regulators	Chapter 15

Task List	Chapter
Lighting, Accessory and Control Systems	
Know the basic components that make up the various types of lighting, accessory and control systems.	
Demonstrate the sequence of operation of the components contained within various lighting, accessory and control systems. The emphasis is on how each component effects the system's overall operation.	
Demonstrate the ability to isolate problems within various lighting, accessory and control systems using voltage drops and other diagnostic methods. The proper use of testing equipment is paramount.	
Demonstrate the ability to properly disassemble, test, assemble, replace, or repair lighting, accessory and control system components using manufacturers' service publications and specifications. Examples of the components are as follows: **1.** Wiring harness/connectors **2.** Fuses/circuit breakers **3.** Lights/bulbs **4.** Electromagnetic devices **5.** Gauges **6.** Meters **7.** Horns and buzzers **8.** Relays **9.** Diodes **10.** Resisters **11.** Potentiometers **12.** Solenoids **13.** Rheostats **14.** Switches **15.** Electric motors **16.** Transformers/converters **17.** Pre-heat devices - ie Glow plugs, intake heaters **18.** Sensors **19.** Monitors **20.** Controllers **21.** HID/LED **22.** Transducers **23.** Transistors	
Electrical Schematics/Diagrams	
Demonstrate the ability to identify basic electrical/electronic symbols.	
Demonstrate the ability to trace various circuits using wiring schematics/diagrams.	
Demonstrate a working knowledge of diagnosing and troubleshooting electrical systems using schematics/diagrams.	
SAE Computer Can-Buss Standards	
Demonstrate the knowledge of the different systems used to communicate on computer controlled machinery. SAE J1587 & J1939.	Chapter 19, 20
Understanding the importance of twisted and shielded wire systems.	Chapter 19
Demonstrate the knowledge of the codes to identify errors within the different systems.	Chapter 20
Diagnostics Systems Troubleshooting	
Understand the complaint prior to beginning diagnostic tests.	Chapter 20
Demonstrate the ability to perform a diagnostic procedure.	Chapter 19
Demonstrate the ability to reason with regard to a specific malfunction in the system.	Chapter 20
Demonstrate mastering the use of all test equipment including digital volt ohm meter (D.V.O.M.), lap top computers, and other system specific troubleshooting devices.	
Demonstrate the ability to use schematic diagrams and follow troubleshooting flow charts in selected techncial manuals.	

(Continued)

Task List	Chapter
Utilize an interactive equipment diagnostic program.	
Demonstrate technical write-up competency	
Demonstrate logic and critical thinking in identifying, evaluating and diagnosing customer complaint.	
Identify the root cause of failure	
Correction procedure	
Machine inspection	
HYDRAULICS/HYDROSTATICS	
Theory and Operation, Hydraulic and Hydrostatic	
Demonstrate knowledge that fluids have no shape of their own, are practically incompressible, apply equal pressure in all directions, and provide great increases in work force.	Chapter 22, 28
Understand Hydraulic Theory	
Demonstrate the understanding of the function of a reservoir, pump, filters, relief valve, control valve, and cylinder in relation to each other.	Chapter 23, 24, 25, 26, 28
Know that open and closed center systems are determined by one or all of the following: **a.** the type of control valve **b.** the type of pump **c.** use of unloading valve **d.** path of oil return to reservoir from pump.	Chapter 23, 32
Describe a basic, but complete, open center hydraulic system, explaining the operation of the system, the route of fluid during the use of a function, and the route of the fluid while the machine is running when no hydraulic function is being used.	Chapter 32
Describe a basic, but complete, closed center load sensing hydraulic system, explaining the operation of the system, the route of fluid during the use of a function, and the route of the fluid while the machine is running when no hydraulic function is being used.	Chapter 32
Be able to identify applications, and the benefits of those applications on construction equipment.	Chapter 32
Understand Hydrostatic Theory	
Demonstrate knowledge of hydrostatic systems, including closed-loop and open-loop systems.	Chapter 23
Understand the various types of cooling circuits.	Chapter 30
Understand the purpose of a charge circuit and how charge pressure relates to hydrostatic system efficiency.	
Explain the differences between hydraulic and hydrostatic systems.	
Be able to identify applications, and the benefits of those applications on construction equipment.	
Explain the different characteristics between various types of pumps, exhibit the ability to follow the oil flow through each pump both while using a hydraulic function and with no hydraulic function being used.	Chapter 23, 25, 31
Pump identification and Operation	
Be able to identify a gear pump, name all parts, follow the oil flow through a gear pump, identify inlet and outlet ports, and identify the direction of rotation of the pump.	Chapter 23, 25, 31
Be able to identify a vane pump, name all parts of a vane pump, follow the oil flow through a vane pump, identify inlet and outlet ports of a vane pump, and identify the direction of rotation of the pump. Explain how a vane pump can be changed to operate in the opposite direction, when applicable.	Chapter 23, 25, 31
Be able to identify various piston pumps, name all parts of a piston pump, follow the oil flow through a piston pump, identify inlet and outlet ports of a piston pump (both variable and fixed), and identify the direction of rotation of the pump.	Chapter 23, 25, 31
Identify types of swash plate control (manual, servo piston, electronic, etc.).	Chapter 31
Motor Identification and Operation	
Explain the different characteristics between the various motors; exhibit the ability to follow the oil flow through each motor while using a hydraulic function.	
Be able to identify a gear motor, name all parts of a gear motor, follow the oil flow through a gear motor, identify inlet and outlet ports of a gear motor, and identify the direction of rotation of the motor.	Chapter 23, 25, 31

Task List	Chapter
Be able to identify a vane motor, name all parts of a vane motor, follow the oil flow through a vane motor, identify inlet and outlet ports of a vane motor, and identify the direction of rotation of the motor.	Chapter 23, 25, 31
Be able to identify radial and axial piston motors, name all parts of these piston motors, follow the oil flow through these piston motors, identify inlet and outlet ports of these piston motors (both variable and fixed), and identify the direction of rotation of the motors.	Chapter 23, 25, 31
Be able to identify a gerotor motor, name all parts, and understand its operation.	Chapter 25, 31
Function and Operation of Hydraulic Valves	
Exhibit the differences between these three major types: **a.** Pressure control valves **b.** Directional control valves **c.** Volume control valves	Chapter 26
Exhibit knowledge of the uses and functions of the following valves: **a.** Direct acting relief valves **b.** Pilot operated relief valves **c.** Cartridge relief valves **d.** Pilot operated valves **e.** Sequence valves **f.** Unloading valves **g.** Multi-function valves **h.** Counterbalance valves **i.** Pressure reducing valves **j.** Pressure limiting valves	Chapter 26
Electro-Hydraulics	
Exhibit knowledge of the uses and functions of the following valves: **a.** Check valves **b.** Rotary valves **c.** Spool valves **d.** Pilot controlled poppet valves **e.** Electro-hydraulic valves **f.** Electro-hydraulic control systems **g.** Pulse width modulated valves	Chapter 32
Exhibit knowledge of the uses and functions of the following valves: **a.** Flow control valves **1.** Compensated **2.** Non-compensated **b.** Flow divider valves **1.** Priority **2.** Non-priority **3.** Proportional	Chapter 26, 31, 32
Cylinder Identification and Operation	
Explain the uses and movements of the two types of cylinders.	Chapter 27
Be able to identify a single acting cylinder, name all of its parts, and follow the oil flow through the cylinder.	Chapter 27
Understand operation of a cushioned cylinder.	Chapter 33
Be able to identify a double acting cylinder, name all of its parts, and follow the oil flow through the cylinder. (deleted in sentence ie. vane type cylinder - rotary actuator)	Chapter 27
Accumulator Identification and Operation	
Explain how accumulators store energy, absorb shocks, build pressure, and maintain a constant pressure within a system.	Chapter 30
Explain where and why gas, pneumatic, spring loaded, and weighted accumulators are used.	Chapter 30
Explain and practice all accumulator safety practices.	Chapter 30

(Continued)

Task List	Chapter
Fluids, Transfer Components and Filtering	
Exhibit the ability to select the proper hose for a given function, taking into consideration the flow needed, pressures to be used, routing, clamping, fittings required and pulsating of lines.	Chapter 29
Exhibit knowledge of the understanding of hydraulic fittings, the importance of selecting the proper fitting, and their relationship to noise and vibration.	Chapter 29
Demonstrate the ability to identify various fittings and thread styles, examples: o-ring boss, NPT, NPTF, British Metric, o-ring flange, ORFS, etc. Proper procedure to torque fittings and flanges.	Chapter 29
Demonstrate the ability to crimp hydraulic fittings onto hose.	Chapter 29
Know the Construction and Function of Filters used in Hydraulic/Hydrostatic Systems	Chapter 28, 31
Describe the use of various filters in hydraulic and hydrostatic systems.	Chapter 28, 31
Demonstrate an understanding of the concept of auxiliary by-pass filtration and its benefits to total system cleanliness.	
Maintenance Procedures	
Demonstrate familiarity with, and practice good hydraulic maintenance/safety practices.	Chapter 22, 34
Perform all hydraulic functions and repairs in a clean atmosphere.	Chapter 34
Exhibit the ability to follow the proper flushing procedure using the correct technical manual/service information.	
Exhibit the proper maintenance techniques to prevent internal and external leaks.	Chapter 27
Demonstrate the procedure for cleaning hoses after cutting and crimping.	
Demonstrate knowledge of overheating conditions. Prevent overheating by keeping the oil at the proper levels, cleaning dirt and mud from around lines and cylinder rods, keep relief valves adjusted properly, do not overload or overspeed systems, and do not hold control valves in a position longer than necessary.	Chapter 35
Recognize the root causes of "blistering" or frayed hoses and procedures to avoid these problems.	
Component Repair and Replacement	
Following the proper technical manual/service information, exhibit the ability to remove, disassemble, diagnose failure, evaluate, repair or replace/reinstall, and test operate any given component including but not limited to: • Gear, vane, and piston pumps • Gear, vane, and piston motors • Pressure control valves • Directional control valves • Volume control valves • Single acting, double acting cylinders (If OEM recommends or allows: gas, pneumatic, spring, and weight loaded accumulators.	Chapter 25, 26, 27, 30
Following the proper technical manual/service information, exhibit the ability to remove and replace any given component including but not limited to: • Gear, vane, and piston pumps • Gear, vane, and piston motors • Pressure control valves • Directional control valves • Volume control valves • Single acting, double acting cylinders • Gas, pneumatic, spring, and weight loaded accumulators • Hoses, steel lines, and fittings • Oil coolers • Reservoirs	Chapter 25, 26, 27, 30
Hydraulic Schematics	
Exhibit knowledge of symbol identification through demonstration.	Chapter 23, 33
Given a selected schematic, exhibit your knowledge of schematics by using JIC, ISO and various symbols to identify locations of various components.	Chapter 23, 33

Task List Diagnostics Systems and Component Troubleshooting	Chapter
Exhibit the ability to reason with regard to a specific malfunction.	Chapter 35
Exhibit mastering the use of all test equipment including flow meters, pressure gauges, vacuum gauges, and temperature measuring devices, in both the metric and standard scales.	Chapter 32, 35
Demonstrate the ability to use schematic diagrams and follow a troubleshooting flow chart using a selected technical manual.	Chapter 35
Demonstrate the ability to follow an operational check procedure using a selected technical manual.	Chapter 35
Troubleshooting of load-sensing hydraulics.	Chapter 32
Demonstrate technical write-up competency • Demonstrate logic and critical thinking in identifying, evaluating and diagnosing customer complaint. • Identify the root cause of failure • Correction procedure • Machine inspection	Chapter 35
Understand Hydraulic Theory	
Demonstrate knowledge that fluids have no shape of their own, are practically incompressible, apply equal pressure in all directions, and provide great increases in work force.	Chapter 22, 28
Demonstrate the understanding of the function of a reservoir, pump, filters, relief valve, control valve, and cylinder in relation to each other.	Chapter 23, 24, 25, 26, 28
Know that open and closed center systems are determined by one or all of the following: **a.** the type of control valve **b.** the type of pump **c.** use of unloading valve **d.** path of oil return to reservoir from pump.	Chapter 23, 32
Describe a basic, but complete, open center hydraulic system, explaining the operation of the system, the route of fluid during the use of a function, and the route of the fluid while the machine is running when no hydraulic function is being used.	Chapter 32
Describe a basic, but complete, closed center load sensing hydraulic system, explaining the operation of the system, the route of fluid during the use of a function, and the route of the fluid while the machine is running when no hydraulic function is being used.	Chapter 32
Be able to identify applications, and the benefits of those applications on construction equipment.	Chapter 32
Understand Hydrostatic Theory	
Demonstrate knowledge of hydrostatic systems, including closed-loop and open-loop systems.	Chapter 23, 31
Understand the various types of cooling circuits.	Chapter 31
Understand the purpose of a charge circuit and how charge pressure relates to hydrostatic system efficiency.	Chapter 31
Explain the differences between hydraulic and hydrostatic systems.	
Be able to identify applications, and the benefits of those applications on construction equipment.	Chapter 31
Pump Identification and Operation	
Explain the different characteristics between various types of pumps, exhibit the ability to follow the oil flow through each pump both while using a hydraulic function and with no hydraulic function being used.	Chapter 23, 25, 31
Be able to identify a gear pump, name all parts, follow the oil flow through a gear pump, identify inlet and outlet ports, and identify the direction of rotation of the pump.	Chapter 23, 25, 31
Be able to identify a vane pump, name all parts of a vane pump, follow the oil flow through a vane pump, identify inlet and outlet ports of a vane pump, and identify the direction of rotation of the pump. Explain how a vane pump can be changed to operate in the opposite direction, when applicable.	Chapter 23, 25, 31
Be able to identify various piston pumps, name all parts of a piston pump, follow the oil flow through a piston pump, identify inlet and outlet ports of a piston pump (both variable and fixed), and identify the direction of rotation of the pump.	Chapter 23, 25, 31
Identify types of swash plate control (manual, servo piston, electronic, etc.).	Chapter 31

(Continued)

Task List **Motor identification and Operation**	Chapter
Explain the different characteristics between the various motors; exhibit the ability to follow the oil flow through each motor while using a hydraulic function.	
Be able to identify a gear motor, name all parts of a gear motor, follow the oil flow through a gear motor, identify inlet and outlet ports of a gear motor, and identify the direction of rotation of the motor.	Chapter 23, 25, 31
Be able to identify a vane motor, name all parts of a vane motor, follow the oil flow through a vane motor, identify inlet and outlet ports of a vane motor, and identify the direction of rotation of the motor.	Chapter 23, 25, 31
Be able to identify radial and axial piston motors, name all parts of these piston motors, follow the oil flow through these piston motors, identify inlet and outlet ports of these piston motors (both variable and fixed), and identify the direction of rotation of the motors.	Chapter 23, 31
Be able to identify a gerotor motor, name all parts, and understand its operation.	Chapter 25, 31
Function and Operation of Hydraulic Valves	
Exhibit the differences between these three major types: **a.** Pressure control valves **b.** Directional control valves **c.** Volume control valves	Chapter 26
Exhibit knowledge of the uses and functions of the following valves: **a.** Direct acting relief valves **b.** Pilot operated relief valves **c.** Cartridge relief valves **d.** Pilot operated valves **e.** Sequence valves **f.** Unloading valves **g.** Multi-function valves **h.** Counterbalance valves **i.** Pressure reducing valves **j.** Pressure limiting valves	Chapter 26, 32
Electro-hydraulics	
Exhibit knowledge of the uses and functions of the following valves: **a.** Check valves **b.** Rotary valves **c.** Spool valves **d.** Pilot controlled poppet valves **e.** Electro-hydraulic valves **f.** Electro-hydraulic control systems **g.** Pulse width modulated valves	Chapter 32
Exhibit knowledge of the uses and functions of the following valves: **a.** Flow control valves **1.** Compensated **2.** Non-compensated **b.** Flow divider valves **1.** Priority **2.** Non-priority **3.** Proportional	Chapter 26, 31, 32
Cylinder Identification and Operation	
Explain the uses and movements of the two types of cylinders.	Chapter 27
Be able to identify a single acting cylinder, name all of its parts, and follow the oil flow through the cylinder.	Chapter 27
Understand operation of a cushioned cylinder.	Chapter 33
Be able to identify a double acting cylinder, name all of its parts, and follow the oil flow through the cylinder.	Chapter 27

Task List	Chapter
Accumulator Identification and Operation	
Explain how accumulators store energy, absorb shocks, build pressure, and maintain a constant pressure within a system.	Chapter 30
Explain where and why gas, pneumatic, spring loaded, and weighted accumulators are used.	Chapter 30
Explain and practice all accumulator safety practices.	Chapter 30
Fluids, Transfer Components and Filtering	
Exhibit the ability to select the proper hose for a given function, taking into consideration the flow needed, pressures to be used, routing, clamping, fittings required and pulsating of lines.	Chapter 29
Exhibit knowledge of the understanding of hydraulic fittings, the importance of selecting the proper fitting, and their relationship to noise and vibration.	Chapter 29
Demonstrate the ability to identify various fittings and thread styles, examples: o-ring boss, NPT, NPTF, British Metric, o-ring flange, ORFS, etc. Proper procedure to torque fittings and flanges.	Chapter 29
Demonstrate the ability to crimp hydraulic fittings onto hose.	Chapter 29
Know the Construction and Function of Filters used in Hydraulic/Hydrostatic Systems	
Describe the use of various filters in hydraulic and hydrostatic systems.	Chapter 28, 31
Demonstrate an understanding of the concept of auxiliary by-pass filtration and its benefits to total system cleanliness.	
Maintenance Procedures	
Demonstrate familiarity with, and practice good hydraulic maintenance/safety practices.	Chapter 34
Understand the Importance of Maintenance	
Perform all hydraulic functions and repairs in a clean atmosphere.	Chapter 34
Exhibit the ability to follow the proper flushing procedure using the correct technical manual/service information.	
Exhibit the proper maintenance techniques to prevent internal and external leaks.	Chapter 27, 34
Demonstrate the procedure for cleaning hoses after cutting and crimping.	
Demonstrate knowledge of overheating conditions. Prevent overheating by keeping the oil at the proper levels, cleaning dirt and mud from around lines and cylinder rods, keep relief valves adjusted properly, do not overload or overspeed systems, and do not hold control valves in a position longer than necessary.	Chapter 35
Recognize the root causes of "blistering" or frayed hoses and procedures to avoid these problems.	
Know the Characteristics of Oils	
Understand oils and show familiarity with various fluids and their effects on hydraulic systems.	Chapter 4
Understand the effects of mixing oil types.	
Fluid Cleanliness	
Understand ISO cleanliness code principles.	Chapter 28, 35
Identify key elemental categories.	
Understand the proper way to obtain fluid samples from a system.	
Identify key elements found in oil analysis and the types of failures related to each.	
Identify key indicators on a fluid analysis report that illustrate: **1.** The proper fluid type is being used. **2.** Fluid types have not been mixed. **3.** Indicators of fluid degradation. **4.** Trend analysis.	
Be able to identify aeration and determine the root cause.	

(Continued)

Task List	Chapter
Understand the Usage and Types of Seals and Gasket Materials	
Show understanding of how reactions of some sealant materials differ among types of hydraulic fluids.	
Describe the applications of various types of sealants.	Chapter 4
Ensure safety practices are followed.	Chapter 4
Component Repair and Replacement	
Following the proper technical manual/service information, exhibit the ability to remove, disassemble, diagnose failure, evaluate, repair or replace/reinstall, and test operate any given component including but not limited to: • Gear, vane, and piston pumps • Gear, vane, and piston motors • Pressure control valves • Directional control valves • Volume control valves • Single acting, double acting cylinders (If OEM recommends or allows: gas, pneumatic, spring, and weight loaded accumulators.	Chapter 25, 26, 27, 30
Following the proper technical manual/service information, exhibit the ability to remove and replace any given component including but not limited to: • Gear, vane, and piston pumps • Gear, vane, and piston motors • Pressure control valves • Directional control valves • Volume control valves • Single acting, double acting cylinders • Gas, pneumatic, spring, and weight loaded accumulators • Hoses, steel lines, and fittings • Oil coolers • Reservoirs	Chapter 25, 26, 27, 30
Describe proper system flushing/cleanup procedures to achieve ISO cleanliness code.	Chapter 28
Proper bleeding and priming procedures.	
Hydraulic Schematics	
Exhibit knowledge of symbol identification through demonstration.	Chapter 23, 33
Given a selected schematic, exhibit your knowledge of schematics by using JIC, ISO and various symbols to identify locations of various components.	Chapter 23, 33
Diagnostics - Systems and Component Troubleshooting	
Exhibit the ability to reason with regard to a specific malfunction.	Chapter 35
Exhibit mastering the use of all test equipment including flow meters, pressure gauges, vacuum gauges, and temperature measuring devices, in both the metric and standard scales.	Chapter 32
Demonstrate the ability to use schematic diagrams and follow a troubleshooting flow chart using a selected technical manual.	Chapter 35
Demonstrate the ability to follow an operational check procedure using a selected technical manual.	Chapter 35
Troubleshooting of load-sensing hydraulics.	Chapter 32
Demonstrate technical write-up competency: • Demonstrate logic and critical thinking in identifying, evaluating and diagnosing customer complaint. • Identify the root cause of failure • Correction procedure • Machine inspection	
THE STANDARDS - POWER TRAINS	
Theory and Operation	
Demonstrate knowledge of basic power train components and how those components, as a whole, relate to one another. Demonstrate by following a power flow chart from flywheel to ground.	
Recognize hybrid systems and/or machines as they relate to safety concerns.	

Task List	Chapter
Basic Principles of Power Train	
Demonstrate knowledge by identifying the various types of gears using a matching test.	
Explain the benefit of one type of gear versus other types of gears using factors such as cost, strength, quietness, bulkiness, and capability of ratios.	
Identify types of bearings through matching tests.	
Demonstrate understanding of various types of bearings and proper adjustment procedures.	Chapter 4
Identify components of a torque converter and describe the relationship of those components to one another.	Chapter 47
Describe the operation of a given torque converter and various stages of operation.	Chapter 47
Use OEM manuals/service information to test a torque converter unit and determine if operation is within specifications.	Chapter 47
Theory and Principles of Manual Transmissions	
Exhibit your understanding of "sliding gear" transmissions by identifying components, explaining operation, and demonstrating power flow through all gear sets.	Chapter 45
Same as above substituting "collar shift."	Chapter 45
Same as above substituting "syncromesh."	Chapter 45
Identify shifting control components and explain their operation.	Chapter 45
Demonstrate ability to perform adjustments to transmissions as instructed in the OEM service manual/information.	Chapter 45
Theory and Principles of Powershift Transmissions	
Demonstrate your understanding of the operation of powershift transmissions by explaining which clutches and/or brakes are engaged, and which planetary gear sets are being used during a specific gear selection.	Chapter 45, 48
Explain the differences, advantages and disadvantages of planetary and countershaft transmissions.	Chapter 45, 48
Theory and Principles of Clutches	
Use service manual/information to test and/or troubleshoot a powershift transmission (on-highway truck transmissions do not qualify), and verify if it is within OEM specifications.	Chapter 48
Demonstrate ability to set and measure preload, endplay and backlash for a specific component using OEM manuals/service information.	
Identify all components in a single and multiple disc and plate-type clutch, including flywheel, pilot and release bearings, disc and pressure plate parts, and power train input shaft. Also, explain differences and benefits of solid and button-type clutches.	Chapter 43
Explain operation of a selected clutch.	Chapter 43
Demonstrate knowledge and operation of single and multiple-disc clutches by explaining the relationship of the clutch components to each other and their roles in the transfer of power.	Chapter 43
Describe the relationship of the number of discs, types of discs (wet or dry), and type of clutch material to the transfer of torque and horsepower to the ground.	Chapter 43
Demonstrate understanding of overrunning clutches by identifying the different types of clutches, their operation and various applications.	
Explain the operation of magnetic clutches and name various applications.	Chapter 43
Explain operation and applications.	Chapter 43
Theory and Principles of Electronic-Controlled Transmissions	
Exhibit knowledge of electronic control systems by identifying components used on a specific unit.	Chapter 46
Demonstrate understanding of a specific unit's operation by explaining the functions of all components and their relationships to one another.	Chapter 46
Demonstrate ability to follow flow and troubleshooting charts to correctly identify the operation of a specific unit's system and troubleshooting methods used by the OEM.	

(Continued)

Task List	Chapter
Theory and Principles of Hydrostatic Transmissions	
Demonstrate understanding of theory and principals of hydrostatic systems by explaining, in writing, how a basic hydrostatic system functions.	Chapter 31
Exhibit knowledge of hydrostatic transmission operation by explaining the flow of fluids through the charge circuit, pump, motor, control and loop circuits.	Chapter 31
Explain the differences between fixed and variable pumps and motors, and the effects of their various combinations.	Chapter 31
Driveshaft Function and Construction	
Demonstrate knowledge of driveshafts by recognizing components, realizing the effects of driveline angle and studying why driveline failures occur.	Chapter 49
Theory and Principles of Differentials	
Exhibit understanding of basic differential operation by identifying the components and explaining how pinion, ring and bevel gears operate in relationship to each other.	Chapter 50
Identify each type of differential locking device and explain in detail how each one operates.	Chapter 50
Given a specific component and proper manuals/information, perform all adjustments on a differential with a new ring and pinion, and also perform all adjustments with original ring and pinion but with new bearings.	Chapter 50
Identify the most common root causes of failure with differentials.	Chapter 50
Theory and Principles of Final Drives	
Exhibit knowledge of final drives by identifying the different types, and the components that make up final drives.	Chapter 52
Perform adjustments according to OEM standards.	Chapter 52
Fundamental Theory of Hydraulic and Pneumatic Braking Systems	
Fundamental theory, adjustments and repair of hydraulic and pneumatic braking systems used primarily in mobile construction equipment.	Chapter 54,55
Demonstrate knowledge of basic brake components, both wet internal and dry external.	Chapter 54, 55
Explain and sketch hydraulic and pneumatic brake systems, internal and external.	Chapter 54, 55
Understanding Maintenance Practices in Power Trains	
Describe, in writing, procedures to follow in keeping a work area and the parts worked with clean.	
Describe proper flushing procedures, including when components are replaced.	
Describe scheduled oil sampling and cite several reasons why it is necessary.	
Power Train Schematics and Flow Diagrams	
Be able to identify all electrical/hydraulic, pneumatic and mechanical symbols used in power train units.	
Demonstrate ability to use schematics and flow diagrams to follow both control circuits and power flow of a given piece of equipment using the corresponding OEM manual/service information.	
Troubleshooting and Failure Analysis	
Describe steps in solving a problem related to a power train system, decisions required to perform work and analysis as to why problem occurred and how it could have been prevented.	
Failure Analysis	
Describe common reasons for parts failure and be able to discuss symptoms of wear, corrosion, etc., of actual parts.	
Demonstrate ability to follow reference information, test, and determine if unit is within specifications for a hydraulic/hydrostatic trainer or equipment with a hydrostatic drive using service manuals/information/software; demonstrate ability to follow a diagnostic troubleshooting chart for a specific system.	Chapter 31
Troubleshooting	
Demonstrate technical write-up competency: • Demonstrate logic and critical thinking in identifying, evaluating and diagnosing customer complaint • Identify the root cause of failure • Correction procedure • Machine inspection	

Task List	Chapter
THE STANDARDS - DIESEL ENGINES	
Safety	
Safety instruction specifically related to engine applications, including OSHA regulations.	
Identification and Use of Basic Tools	
Review assignments, evaluation of identification exercises. Written exams that will determine the competency on many items unable to check by hands-on exercises. Emphasis on safety should be demonstrated with all tool usage.	
Performance testing of tool/equipment to check comprehension. Demonstrate all torque and de-torque methods with hands-on exercises.	
The student should be able to read accurately all precision measuring tools and gauges.	
Be able to demonstrate the ability to convert standard to and from metric measurements, both pressure and distance.	
Be able to determine engine speed and pulses per revolution.	
Tasks related to measuring, understanding and recording pressure, flows and temperature.	
Tasks related to measuring specific gravity of fuel, coolant and electrolyte.	
Theory and Operation	
Competency demonstrated in the application of engine theory of operation. Written tests designed for this purpose. Possible task list.	
Understanding and comprehension of formulas to calculate engine performance criteria.	
Understand the relationship between engine HP and torque.	
Know the differences between spark ignited and compression ignition engines.	
Determine engine/component motion and speed ratios.	
Be able to explain diesel 4-stroke engine cycle.	
Memorize the order of strokes. Identify the specific stroke of each cylinder during engine rotation.	
Determine the number of degrees between power strokes on various engines.	
Understand diesel combustion principles, and the effects of pre-ignition, detonation and misfire.	
Demonstrate glow plug operation & testing.	
Determine engine rotation by valve overlap.	
Identify the various combustion chambers and know the advantages/disadvantages of each type.	
Perform basic valve and injection timing tasks.	
Understand the theory of injection pump timing.	
Understand the functions of various cooling system components.	
Understanding measurement and properties of the engine fluids. Understand cross contamination root causes and effects of each.	Chapter 4
Understand the functions and components of diesel engine lubrication systems and the effects of machine operating angle.	
Understand effects of lubrication system levels (over and under).	
Understand the functions and components of diesel engine fuel and governing systems, including mechanical, electronic and computer controlled systems.	
Understand common rail fuel systems.	
Understand the functions and components of emission control systems and governmental regulations (i.e. EPA).	
Understand penalties for non-compliance to emission regulations to the dealer, equipment owner and the technician.	
Understand how emissions impact engine life and repairs.	

(Continued)

Task List	Chapter
Maintenance Practices	
Be able to locate maintenance specifications including fluid change intervals, fluid specifications (SAE/API, etc.), fuel specifications, filter replacement intervals, proper filter replacement procedures, other maintenance guidelines, etc.	Chapter 4
Understand commonly used methods for maintenance records keeping and their importance.	
Hands on experience in how to obtain proper oil, fuel and coolant samples.	
Practical understanding in how to interpret fluid analysis results.	
Hands on experience in how to inspect used filters for early warning signs of potential problems.	
Preventive maintenance tasks performed to industry standards; completion of an inspection task sheet.	
Component repair - Understanding Proper Component Repair Procedures	
Practical exercises in parts reusability procedures and guidelines.	
Understanding industry remanufactured component guidelines and how to determine when to use remanufactured components.	
Be able to remove and replace commonly serviced external components. Know the inspection, service, and cleaning techniques associated with replacement of these items.	
Engine Subsystems - Engine Identification of External Components	
Locate and identify various external components.	
Knowledge of vibration fundamentals. • Linear characteristics • Rotational characteristics	
Understanding of the basic theory of exhaust after treatment systems like: • Diesel Particulate Filters (DPF) • Diesel Oxidation Catylist (DOC) • Selective Catalytic Reduction (SCR) • Diesel exhaust fluid (DEF) • Regeneration process	
Understanding Internal Engine Components	
Demonstrate comprehension of the removal, inspection and installation tech-niques associated with basic internal com-ponents.	
Perform identification and inspection of all internal components.	
Tasks associated with the removal, inspection and installation of internal engine components (i.e., cylinder packs).	
Understand bearing "roll-in" and tasks associated with in-frame overhauls.	
Valve and injector adjustments. Timing and idler gear installations.	
Understanding Basic Engine Subsystems	
Knowledge of hydraulic accessories driven or operated by the engine.	
Understanding of cold weather starting aids and block heaters.	
Fuel and Governing Systems, Mechanical and Electronic Systems - Understanding Basic Fuel Systems	
Perform basic maintenance and diagnosis of the different fuel delivery systems avail-able today. Demonstrate a basic under-standing of the adjustment and repair of various governing systems used by the major manufacturers.	
Understand basic hydraulic principles and fluid transfer technology.	
Measure specific gravity of fuel and deter-mine proper grade and/or contamination. Understand the use of fuel conditioners, fuel coolers and heaters. Recognize waste oil/fuel blends.	
Measure fuel pressure/volume with correct diagnostic tools and compare to specifications. Determine and understand the problems with the basic supply systems. Understand the affects of air, moisture and contamination on the basic fuel system.	
Proper replacement of fuel transfer pumps, filters, lines, and hoses including proper bleeding/priming procedures.	

Task List	Chapter
Identify misfiring cylinders with appropriate tooling. Emphasis on cleanliness and safety.	
Replacement and timing of various injection pumps including inline, distributor and unit injector pumps.	
Understanding Governor Fundamentals	
Tasks associated with troubleshooting, adjusting and replacing governor components.	
Identification exercises and demonstrations of system operation.	
Inspection and testing of proper mechanical governor operation. Rack settings and low idle adjustments should be emphasized.	
Troubleshoot hydraulic/servo governors.	
Troubleshooting and programming principles of electronic governors should be emphasized. Use of scantools and PCs should be demonstrated to illustrate the self-diagnosing capabilities of this system.	
Be able to demonstrate the ability to locate and test the following sensors: boost pressure, engine position, engine speed, throttle position, manifold pressure, fuel pressure, and high pressure oil sensor.	Chapter 16
Diagnostics - Understand Proper Diesel Engine Diagnostic Procedures	
Tasks associated with troubleshooting emission controls and basic adjustments.	
Visual basic exhaust analysis; white, gray or black; as applicable.	
Practical exercises in identification of common diesel engine problems using proper diagnostic tools and procedures.	
Determine root causes of failure, establish reusability, and know the recommended repair options available.	
Demonstrate proper use of special tools and equipment utilized in engine repair.	
Tasks using technical service manuals, service information, bulletins and special instructions. Proficient use of service manuals, desktop PCs, and laptops for retrieval of specifications and service procedures.	
Troubleshooting common problems caused by a malfunctioning engine subsystem.	
Have a basic understanding of EGR, SCR, DEF, DPF and exhaust after-treatment systems and how their use affects performance.	
Testing of the engine cooling system, including overheating issues and testing procedures; especially the flow through the radiator; correct temperature drops.	
Demonstrate technical write-up competency • Demonstrate logic and critical thinking in identifying, evaluating and diagnosing customer complaint. • Identify the root cause of failure • Correction procedure • Machine inspection	
THE STANDARDS - AIR CONDITIONING /HEATING	
Fundamental Knowledge	
Demonstrate knowledge of heat sources, types of heat transfer, and how humidity affects heat transfer. Emphasis will be placed on factors that affect heat transfer and how to measure heat energy.	Chapter 37
Demonstrate knowledge of the following terms: **1.** Sensible heat **2.** Change of state **3.** Saturation temperature **4.** Latent heat (Hidden heat) **5.** Latent heat of fusion **6.** Latent heat of evaporation **7.** Latent heat of condensation **8.** Super heated **9.** Sub-cooled **10.** Vapor **11.** Gas	Chapter 37

(Continued)

Task List	Chapter
Demonstrate the knowledge to measure and calculate the effects of pressures on liquids. Emphasis will be placed on understanding and using pressure and temperature (P/T) charts.	
Demonstrate knowledge of refrigerant characteristics in relation to environmental damage. Emphasis will be placed on identification, labeling, and handling of refrigerants in accordance with EPA regulations.	
Demonstrate knowledge of the types of oils used in AC systems.	Chapter 37
Demonstrate knowledge on handling and storing of refrigerant oils.	
Demonstrate knowledge on recovery, recycle, and reclaiming of refrigerants with respect to the amounts of oil, water and particulates that are removed.	Chapter 37
Demonstrate knowledge of the following system components: **1.** Compressor **2.** Condenser **3.** Metering device **4.** Evaporator **5.** Service valves **6.** Schrader valves **7.** Receiver-drier **8.** Accumulator **9.** Lines	Chapter 37
Demonstrate knowledge of refrigerant flow through an AC system.	Chapter 37
Demonstrate the knowledge of the state (super heated vapor, saturated mixture, and sub-cooled liquid) of the refrigerant at various points in an AC system. Emphasis will be placed on the locations in the system that the refrigerant exists as a saturated mixture.	
Servicing AC Systems	
Demonstrate knowledge of how to identify various types and refrigerant capacities of AC systems. Emphasis will be placed on the ability to identify types and capacities by using manufacturers' service publications along with equipment tags, labels, and specifications.	
Demonstrate the ability to properly connect and disconnect gauge manifold sets. Emphasis will be placed on using proper procedures to purge hoses to prevent cross-contamination and introduction of non-condensables.	
Demonstrate the ability to connect gauge sets to systems having either Schrader or Stem type service valves.	
Demonstrate the ability to properly evacuate and dehydrate an AC system.	Chapter 37
Demonstrate knowledge of the damage caused to AC systems by non-condensables and moisture. Emphasis will be placed on having knowledge of using micron gauges and establishing minimum and maximum evacuation time periods to completely dehydrate AC systems.	
Demonstrate the ability to properly recover and charge AC systems with refrigerants.	
Emphasis placed on properly connecting and operating gauge manifold sets, recovery and charging equipment.	
Demonstrate the knowledge and ability to describe the conditions that need to exist to charge AC systems with refrigerant existing as a liquid or vapor into the high or low side.	
Demonstrate the ability to add oil, dye, and refrigerants to operating AC systems.	Chapter 37
Testing, Troubleshooting, Diagnosing, and Repairing AC Systems	
Demonstrate the ability to perform a visual inspection of an AC system. **a.** Loose or missing service caps. **b.** Oily spots – connections – evaporator drain tube. **c.** Belt tension **d.** Condensor condition **e.** Determine refrigerant type.	Chapter 37
Demonstrate the ability to visually identify the type of AC system and determine the amount of refrigerant charge. **a.** TXV(H-Block) – Receiver/drier **b.** Metered orifice - accumulator	
Demonstrate the ability to identify control systems and components.	

Task List	Chapter
Demonstrate the ability to troubleshoot and diagnose AC systems by converting system pressures to saturated mixture temperatures and comparing this to temperature readings taken at key points in the system.	
Demonstrate the ability to troubleshoot and diagnose metering devices and limit switch malfunctions.	
Demonstrate the ability to detect refrigerant leaks.	
Demonstrate the knowledge and/or ability to replace or repair AC system components i.e. compressor, compressor clutch, seals, metering valves, condenser, receiver-drier, accumulator, limit switches and lines.	
Demonstrate the ability to test the cooling capabilities of an AC system including controls. Emphasis will be placed on demonstrating the knowledge to determine the operational conditions needed to validate a performance test.	
Demonstrate technical write-up competency • Demonstrate logic and critical thinking in identifying, evaluating and diagnosing customer complaint. • Identify the root cause of failure • Correction procedure • Machine inspection	
Heating System Operation	
Demonstrate knowledge of the following system components: **1.** Water pump **2.** Heater core **3.** Coolant control valve **4.** Coolant lines **5.** Engine thermostat	
Demonstrate knowledge of how water pumps work.	
Demonstrate knowledge of coolant flow direction.	
Demonstrate knowledge of the function of thermostats.	
Servicing Heating Systems	
Demonstrate knowledge of how to correctly remove and install heater core and coolant lines.	
Demonstrate knowledge of how to correctly remove and install heater system control valves.	
Demonstrate knowledge of how to correctly remove, test and install engine thermostats.	
Pressurized Cabs	
Demonstrate knowledge of the purpose and function of pressurized cab systems.	Chapter 37
Demonstrate knowledge of how to correctly remove, clean, and install cab air filters.	

GLOSSARY

Absorbed Glass Mat (AGM) battery A type of lead-acid battery that uses a thin fiberglass plate to absorb the electrolyte; this prevents the solution from sloshing or separating into layers of heavier acid and water.

abuse failure Failure directly attributed to operator or other person's actions.

AC ripple A pattern produced by voltage fluctuations from the alternator that create differences between the peak voltage of an AC sine wave and the minimum voltage found in the trough between sine waves.

access covers Necessary to gain access to the inside of a hydraulic tank.

accumulator Prevents any liquid refrigerant from getting into the compressor.

Ackerman angle The angle between an imaginary point that extends from the centerline of the rear axle to the steering, or tie-rod, arms; or from a point midway between the rear axles of a tandem to the steering arms. As a machine with a steering axle turns, the steering arms that pivot the wheels turn each wheel at differing individual angles because of the Ackerman angle.

active fault A fault that is currently taking place and uninterrupted in action.

active sensor A sensor that uses a current supplied by the ECM to operate.

actuator The component of a machine that is responsible for transferring hydraulic pressure to move or control a mechanism.

adaptive learning Software that can learn and change strategy based on different factors.

adaptor plates An accessory for bearing removal and installations tools. The plates surround a shaft, and provide a surface for puller jaws to attach while also ensuring all the forces are placed at the inner press-fit race of the bearing.

addendum The top, thinner part of an involute tooth contact area.

additives Chemical compounds added to the base hydraulic fluid intended to combat many fluid degrading conditions (foaming, rust, corrosion, viscosity breakdown).

adhesion The bonding property that occurs when two metals are joined together using molten filler metal to fill the gap between them.

adjusting ring A large threaded ring in the clutch cover of a pull-type clutch used to adjust the clutch internally.

AEMP telematics data standard A communication protocol enabling telematic end users with the freedom to use only one telematics service provider for different brands or makes of machinery.

aeration A condition caused by excessive air in the system fluid.

air drill A compressed-air–powered drill.

air dryer A canister that contains desiccant to absorb moisture.

air hammer A tool powered by compressed air with various hammer, cutting, punching, or chisel attachments. It's also called an air chisel.

air lines Carry the pressurized air to each brake chamber.

air nozzle A compressed-air device that emits a fine stream of compressed air for drying or cleaning parts.

air ratchet A ratchet tool for use with sockets powered by compressed air.

air tools A tool that is powered by compressed air, also called pneumatic tools.

air-boosted brake system Use air to push on a diaphragm that pushes on the master cylinder pistons to increase applied brake pressure.

air-control solenoid valve An electric-over-air solenoid used to control shifting by controlling the flow of air from the air filter to the range cylinder piston.

air-impact wrench An impact tool powered by compressed air designed to undo tight fasteners. It's also called a rattle gun, or impact gun.

Allen head screw Sometimes called a hex head screw, it has a hexagonal recess in the head that fits an Allen key. This type of screw usually anchors components in a predrilled hole.

Allen wrench A type of hexagonal drive mechanism for fasteners.

all-wheel steer The type of steering system that has front and rear steerable axles.

alternating current (AC) A type of current flow that continuously changes direction and polarity.

alternator ripple The top of the waveform.

ambient temperature The temperature of the surrounding environment.

amboid gear A bevel gear arrangement with the pinion gear mounted above the centerline of the crown gear.

American National Standards Institute (ANSI) An organization that oversees the creation, promulgation, and use of norms and guidelines that impact U.S. businesses.

ammonia sensor A sensor used in selective catalyst reduction (SCR), which provides data to the ECM that is used to determine whether ammonia values are out of anticipated range.

amperage The measurement of the quantity of electrons in electric current movement.

ampere (amp) The unit for measuring the quantity or numbers of electrons flowing past one point in a circuit per unit of time.

amp-hour A measure of how much amperage a battery can continually supply over a 20-hour period without the battery voltage falling below 10.5 volts.

analog meter A meter that uses a sweeping needle that continuously measures electrical values.

analog signal An electric current that is proportional to a continuously changing variable.

analog to digital (AD) conversion The process when an analog waveform is sampled and measured many times a second to generate a digital representation of the waveform.

angle spring clutch A clutch that uses three pairs of angled springs pushing against levers to supply the clamp load.

angular Consisting of, or forming, an angle.

anticavitation valves Check valves that allow tank oil to flow into an actuator if pressure falls below tank pressure.

API (American Petroleum Institute) An organization in the United States that sets standards and standardized tests for petroleum products.

arbitration The process of deciding which messages have priority to transmit over the network to prevent data collision between positive and negative signals canceling one another.

arbor press A small hand operated press that uses mechanical leverage to apply a compressive force to a ram.

armature The only rotating component of the starter; has three main components: the shaft, windings, and the commutator.

articulated frame A type of equipment frame that has a permanent hinge, or pivoting point, in the frame to enhance maneuverability.

articulated steering A system that makes the vehicle's two-piece frame pivot on a center hinge pin arrangement.

asynchronous motor A category of AC motors, also known as an induction motor where the rotor speed and apparent speed of the magnetic field in the stator winding are not synchronized. Asynchronous motors operating speed is always less than maximum speed.

attack angle The angle formed between an imaginary line drawn across the top track and it's intersection point on the ground; also called angle of approach.

automated external defibrillator (AED) A portable device that checks the heart rhythm and can send an electric shock to the heart to try to restore a normal rhythm. AEDs are used to treat sudden cardiac arrest (SCA).

automated manual transmission (AMT) A standard manual transmission operated by electronic control.

automatic disengagement lockout (ADLO) A device that prevents the starter motor from operating if the engine is running.

automatic mode The machine's hydraulics are electronically controlled with no driver intervention to make blade or implement adjustments.

automation The use of control systems that reduce or eliminate human intervention to operate machinery.

autonomous machine A smart machine that can function without an operator in the cab.

auto-ranging multimeter A multimeter that has fewer positions on its range selection knob and will automatically select the correct range when meter test leads are connected to a circuit.

AutoShift Eaton's first shift-by-wire transmission.

auxiliary motor A motor that drives auxiliary devices using a belt or gear drive or that is directly coupled.

aviation snips A scissor-like tool for cutting sheet metal.

axial (thrust) Axial, or thrust, loads always act along the centerline of a shaft. So, they can only apply a force that moves a shaft in or out along its axis.

axial forces Forces applied along the longitudinal, or lengthwise, axis of a component such as a transmission shaft.

axial piston The style of pump that is most commonly used for hydrostatic drives.

axial thrust Thrust that tries to move the gears apart along their axis.

back brace A piece of PPE that protects the back by bracing, which is used when heavy or frequent lifting is involved.

backfill blade A type of blade that is commonly used on smaller types of excavators to push excavated material back into trenches and holes or around building foundations.

backhand welding A welding technique (also called the rightward technique, backward welding, drag angle welding, and pull welding) best suited for thick metals in which the welding torch is held in the right hand, the filler rod is held in the left hand, and the welding direction moves from the left side of the seam toward the right side of the seam.

backlash The required clearance between two meshing gears.

baffle Partitions in tanks to help slow down the return oil before it gets to the suction tube.

balancers A device designed to adjust battery voltage to compensate for unequal charges in multiple batteries; also called battery equalizers.

ball bearings A type of bearing which uses spherical balls as the rolling elements within a raceway, to reduce friction between moving parts. They are typically mounted between a shaft and stationary housing.

ballast The addition of weight inside a pneumatic tire that's used to give the machine additional stability and traction force. A common ballast material is a water and calcium chloride mixture.

ball-peen (engineer's) hammer A hammer that has a head that is rounded on one end and flat on the other, which is designed to work with metal items.

band brake A type of brake that utilizes a steel band lined with friction material that wraps around a brake drum to slow the drum.

barrier cream A cream that looks and feels like a moisturizing cream but has a specific formula to provide extra protection from chemicals and oils.

battery equalizers A device designed to adjust battery voltage to compensate for unequal charges in multiple batteries; also called balancers.

battery isolator systems A system designed to separate the main starting battery and the auxiliary battery; also called a split charge relay.

battery management system (BMS) A system of electrical devices used to manage battery performance.

baud rate The rate at which serial data is transmitted.

beach mark Semicircular mark in a fracture indicating repeated overload.

bead The deposit of filler metal and/or base metal along a joint or seam that results from a welding process.

bearing A machine element that constrains movement to only the desired direction and reduces friction between moving parts.

bearing adjuster Threaded wheel used to tighten the side bearing races.

bearing adjuster lock Lock to secure the bearing adjusters.

bearing driver A tool used to install bearings, and sometimes seals, that applies a uniform amount of force to a targeted area of the bearing to drive the press-fit surface of a bearing onto a shaft or into a housing.

Belleville washers Cone-shaped spring-steel washers.

bench vice A device that securely holds material in jaws while it is being worked on.

Benjamin Holt The industrialist who first developed the practical use of crawler-type track drive systems in North America.

bent axis Piston centerlines are at an angle to the pump shaft.

bent axis motor One type of hydraulic motor that has a set of pistons and cylinder block inside it that receive oil flow and create torque.

bevel gears Gears that intersect at an angle—usually 90 degrees.

bidirectional communication Two-way multiplex communication.

bimetallic gauge A gauge in which two dissimilar pieces of metal are bonded together and expand at different rates when heated, thereby converting the heating effect of electricity into mechanical movement.

binocular cameras Elements of an object detection system required to measure depth or provide stereo vision using the principle of parallax.

bit The smallest piece of digital information, which is either a 1 or 0.

bladder An inflatable bag, or sack, that contains fluids or gas.

blade ball A pivoting point on some dozer blade mounting frames that enables the blade to be raised and lowered, angled to the left or right, and tilted on each end, using hydraulic cylinders.

blind hole bearing puller A bearing removal tool that is used when the outer bearing race is press fit into a housing and can only be removed by placing a tool through the center, or blind, hole and pulling from the inside.

blind rivet A rivet that can be installed from its insertion side.

blink code A method of providing fault code data for a specific system, which involves counting the number of flashes from a warning lamp and observing longer pauses between the light blinks.

blocking Includes blocking, cribbing, jack stands, timbers, dunnage, and any other devices or equipment designed to support a load in a stationary position.

blocking devices Also referred to as blocking and cribbing. These include blocking, cribbing, jack stands, timbers, dunnage, and any other devices or equipment designed to support a load in a stationary position.

blowout Failure of a tire because of damage or overinflation.

Bluetooth A short-range wireless technology that can automatically connect a device to a network.

bolt A type of threaded fastener with a thread on one end and a hexagonal head on the other.

bolt cutters Strong cutters available in different sizes, designed to cut through non-hardened bolts and other small-stock material.

bore The inside diameter of a tube.

bottoming tap A thread-cutting tap designed to cut threads to the bottom of a blind hole.

boundary lubrication When two moving components come into contact occasionally by breaking through the fluid film.

brake chambers At each wheel convert the pressurized air into mechanical action.

brake cylinder (piston) Both the pressure actuating component (in the master cylinder) and the mechanism that actuates the pad or shoe to apply friction pressure to the wheel.

brake lag The delay between driver application and brake actuation.

brake pads The flat metal casting and the bonded friction material in a disc brake system.

brake shoes The arched metal castings and the bonded friction material in a drum brake system.

brake valve A valve used to limit motor speed when a load tries to overrun it.

break torque The unloading of the driveline to allow a shift to occur.

brinelling A condition that occurs when extreme torque indents the bearing surface of the trunnion with the shape of the needle rollers.

British thermal unit (Btu) The amount of energy required to heat or cool 1 pound of water 1°F.

broken back arrangement A method of angle cancelation in which the U-joint angles will intersect at a point exactly at the middle of the shaft length; also known as an intersecting angle arrangement.

bull and pinion drive A drive that uses a small pinion gear driving a larger “bull” gear usually in a separate housing.

burnish To make smooth or polish.

burst pressure The extreme pressure (typically six times more than working pressure) where a conductor may be expected to fail.

bypass valve A valve used in filter bases or near coolers that will open to provide flow when pressure become too high. This will occur when a filter becomes plugged or cold fluid can’t flow through a cooler.

byte A unit of 8 bits.

C frame A mounting mechanism used on an angle blade that attaches to the dozer and has connection points for hydraulic cylinders to lift the blade, angle it to the left or right, and tilt the blade ends upward or downward.

cable clip A device consisting of a U-bolt, a saddle, and two nuts, used to bind a loop at the end of a wire rope.

calibration A procedure performed to match electronic input and output values to ECM software.

calorie The unit of energy that reflects the amount of energy required to raise the temperature of 1 gram of water by 1°C.

cam lobe motor A type of motor, sometimes called a radial piston motor. A series of pistons ride around an inside cam and create torque from fluid flow.

cam ring In a balanced vane pump the cam ring is elliptical in shape and makes the vanes move.

camber Looking at one of the machine’s steering axle wheels from the front, it is the slight lean you see at the top in one direction or the other.

CAN A distributed network control system in which no single central control module is used. When two or more ECMs are connected, they can communicate over a network.

CAN (controller area network) system An electronic system that allows communication between two or more ECMs on a machine.

CANbus A two-wire network typology that connects modules in parallel.

cancelation The act of canceling the non-uniform velocity in a driveshaft.

Canopy A part of the body of an off-road truck that extends above the cab to protect the operator from any falling material.

capacitance touch screen A display screen that uses two transparent plates, one of which is electrically charged.

capacitor A passive two-terminal electrical component that stores electrical energy in an electric field.

capacitor-start motor A motor using a capacitor in series with the starter winding to put the starter winding 90 degrees out of phase with the main winding. Capacitor-start systems are required to begin rotor movement.

capillary action The ability of a liquid, such as molten filler metal, to flow into narrow gaps between two objects. The adhesive properties of a metal’s surface for dissimilar metals are directly related to capillary action.

carbon dioxide One of the resulting gases produced when burning a hydrocarbon fuel, which contributes to global warming.

carburizing flame A torch flame that has an excess of acetylene in the oxyacetylene fuel mix and is characterized by a sootier flame using an inner flame cone that is longer and less defined than that of a neutral flame.

carcass (or casing) Multiple layers or plies of material that form a base for the tire from bead to bead.

Cardan joint A joint with four trunnions and four bearing caps; also known as a Hooke joint or a universal joint.

carrier The component that holds the support bearings for the drive axle gearing.

carrier or idler rollers Rollers that do not support machine weight but carry the track at the top.

cartridge assembly Another term for the pumping assembly inside a vane pump.

cartridge filters Filters that have replaceable elements that are sealed in reusable housings.

cartridge valve A type of preassembled valve that is easily serviceable; two types are thread-in and slip-in valves.

cartridge-type directional control valves A style of DCV that has a thread-in or slip-in cartridge that is part of a solid block of machined steel or aluminum.

case drain Another name for internal leakage oil that piston pumps have drained away.

case extended life track (CELT) A dual bushing system doubles track life using a second hardened bushing over an inner bushing and pin. It also uses longer track pins, track links that are wider and have a taller rail on which the rollers ride.

cast ductile iron Cast iron that is ductile (bendable), not brittle.

castellated nut A nut with slots, similar to towers on a castle, that is used with split pins; it is used primarily to secure wheel bearings.

caster Looking at the side of a machine and drawing a straight line through the center of the kingpin(s), it is the angle where the line intersects with a line drawn between the bottoms of the front and rear wheels (road surface).

CAT III A multimeter designed to a CAT standard (CAT is an abbreviation for “category”) that measures high energy levels.

catastrophic failure A type of hydraulic system failure that occurs suddenly and without warning and represents a complete component or system malfunction.

caution Indicates a potentially hazardous situation, which, if not avoided, may result in minor or moderate injury.

cavitation The formation and subsequent collapse of bubbles in a liquid caused by a decrease in pressure.

C-clamp A clamp shaped like the letter C; it comes in various sizes and can clamp various items.

center bearing A bearing pressed onto a machined surface after the splined area of a driveshaft’s slip yoke spline, which is used to support a multi-piece driveshaft; also called a hanger bearing.

center of gravity (CG) Also called the center of balance. The center of gravity, or CG, of an object is the point, or position, at which the item's weight is evenly dispersed, and all sides are in balance. If the item were to be supported in a direct vertical axis from the center of gravity, it would balance perfectly.

centrifugal force The apparent force by which a rotating mass tries to move outward, away from its axis of rotation.

centrifugal start switch Used by split-phase motors to place a starter winding in series with the main winding during initial motor start-up when no rotor speed is present.

centrifugal switch A switch in the sensor of a TPMS that allows the sensor to go to sleep when the vehicle stops, which extends the TPMS's battery life.

ceramic friction facings Friction facings made mostly of artificial materials specifically designed to produce desirable characteristics.

cfm Cubic feet per minute is a measure of the flow rate of a gas.

chafing Abrasion caused by mechanical friction.

chain blocks A chain block is a piece of equipment used to lift heavy items. The typical block, also known as chain falls, consists of two grooved wheels with a chain wound around them in the same fashion as a block and tackle. The chain wound around the two wheels creates a simple machine that uses the leverage and the increased lifting ability created by the two wheels to lift heavy weights.

chain case The housing that the chain drive runs in.

chain trencher A track-mounted trencher with a hydraulically controlled boom that uses a chain with cutting bits that travel around the boom to cut through hard soil and rock.

chain-type final drive A drive system that uses a chain to transmit the torque from a drive sprocket to a sprocket at the wheel end.

charge pressure Controlled pressure for the charge pump outlet that can feed the low-pressure side of the closed loop.

charge pump A fixed displacement pump that is needed to replenish the fluid that leaves the loop due to component leakage and due to cooling and cleaning intentional leakage.

check valve A simple valve that allows flow in one direction but blocks it in reverse flow.

chlorofluorocarbon A chlorine-based fluorocarbon compound.

chocks Blocks of material placed against a wheel to prevent undesired rolling movement.

circuit (wire) tracer An electronic service tool used to trace a single wire over a distance where multiple wires are bundled, shorted, or open.

circuit breaker A device that trips and opens a circuit, preventing excessive current flow in a circuit. It is resettable to allow for reuse.

clamp force The force that squeezes the clutch disc(s) between the pressure plate and the flywheel; also called clamp load.

clamp load The force that squeezes the clutch disc(s) between the pressure plate and the flywheel; also called clamp force.

clevis An eye in a hydraulic mount, which secures with a bolt.

clockwise The clockwise direction of rotation of a gear as you look at it corresponding to the motion of the clock; also known as forward.

closed center A control valve center configuration in which when the valve is placed in the neutral position, all four ports are blocked and there is no pathway for the fluid through the valve.

closed center hydraulic system A type of hydraulic system that blocks pump flow when its spool(s) are in neutral, which is usually paired with a variable displacement pump.

closed end A wrench with a closed or ring end to grip bolts and nuts.

closed loop A hydraulic system that has the pump outlet flow going directly to the motor and the return fluid from the motor going directly to the pump inlet.

closed-loop control A process where the operation of an output device is monitored and controlled by a sensor that provides feedback directly to an electronic control unit.

club hammer The club hammer is like a small mallet, with two square faces made of high-carbon steel. It is the heaviest type of hammer that can be used one-handed.

clutch brake A small frictional brake usually mounted on the transmission input shaft, which is designed to slow down or stop the inertia of the transmission gearing so that shifts into first or reverse can be made without clashing.

clutch brake actuation or squeeze The point of clutch pedal actuation on a pull-type clutch when the clutch brake is being actuated or squeezed, which is adjusted by linkage.

clutch capacity The amount of torque that the clutch can safely handle without slipping.

clutch cover The outside part of the clutch that is bolted to the flywheel and that holds all of the clutch components except the clutch disc. It is mistakenly but commonly called the pressure plate.

coalescence The fusing together of two or more metals that occurs when the metals are heated to a point of liquefaction and, after cooling, are bonded together to form one continuous solid.

Code 61 The standard series flange connector.

Code 62 The "6,000 psi" series flange connector.

coefficient of friction (CoF) The amount of force required to move an object while in contact with another, divided by its weight.

coil spring–style clutch A clutch that uses coil springs mounted perpendicular to the pressure plate to provide the clamp load.

cold cranking amps (CCAs) A measurement of the load, in amps, that a battery can deliver for 30 seconds while maintaining a voltage of 1.2 volts per cell (7.2 volts for a 12-volt battery) or higher at 0°F (−18°C).

collar shift transmission A transmission that uses sliding collars or clutches to select gear ratios.

combination (series-parallel) circuit A circuit that uses elements both of series and parallel circuits.

combination pliers A type of pliers for cutting, gripping, and bending.

combination valves Pressure relief valves and check valves in one housing. They can open to relieve high pressure to prevent damage or open to allow fluid in to the closed loop if pressure drops too low.

combination wrench A type of wrench that has an open end on one end and a closed-end wrench on the other.

companion flange A splined flange attached to a vehicle component, such as a drive axle pinion shaft, that bolts to a flange yoke on a driveshaft.

complicated fracture A fracture in which the bone has penetrated a vital organ.

composite Composed of several substances.

compound planetary gear set Planetary gear power flow that utilizes more than one gear set to produce the ratios.

compound ratio Any gear ratio that involves more than one pair of gears.

compressor Provides airflow for the system.

computer vision A more difficult challenge of recognizing and interpreting the significance of objects using binocular cameras.

computer-aided earth-moving system (CAES) Integrates GPS data into the machine's hydraulic controls and guidance to autonomously operate a machine's hydraulic implements, such as buckets, shovels, booms, sticks, and blades. As the worksite features change, the machine transmits data about the work it's completed to enable software to update worksite maps, rendering the latest terrain and site conditions.

condensation Change of state from a vapor to a liquid such as the moisture that collects on a cool surface.

condenser A component of the HVAC system that transfers heat from the system to the atmosphere.

conductance test A type of battery test that determines the battery's ability to conduct current.

conductor (electrical) A material that easily allows electricity to flow through it. It is made up of atoms with very few outer-shell electrons, which are loosely held by the nucleus.

conductors (hydraulics) A pipe, tube or hose that carries fluids.

confined space An enclosed area that has limited space and accessibility and requires special safety procedures for entering, working, and exiting.

connectors A device that joins two pieces of pipe, tubing, or hose together.

constant current The ability of a system to maintain a consistent current output even when there are voltage variations in the load.

constant-current charger A battery charger that automatically varies the voltage applied to the battery to maintain a constant amperage flow into the battery.

constant-mesh transmissions Transmissions that have all of the main shaft gears in constant mesh with their mating countershaft gears.

constant-voltage charger A direct current (DC) power that is a step-down transformer with a rectifier to provide the DC voltage to charge.

contact pattern The contact area between two gear teeth in contact.

contamination Anything (solid, liquid, air, heat or chemical) that is not a part of the original fluid formulation.

continuously variable transmission (CVT) A type of automatic transmission that uses a belt or chain between two variable-diameter pulleys instead of gears to provide a continuous range of gear ratios.

controlled area networks (CAN) A distributed network control system in which no single central control module is used.

controlled traction differential A differential that allows the engine to build more torque before the wheels can slip.

conventional current theory The theory that the direction of current flow is from positive to negative.

conventional steering A system in which both front wheels pivot either left or right to direct the front of the machine in the direction that the operator desires. As the steering angle increases to provide a smaller turning radius, the left and right wheels turn at different angles since the inside wheel turns through a smaller radius than the outside wheel.

corrective maintenance A type of maintenance that is performed after a system or equipment failure to identify and repair the problem and enable the system or equipment to be restored to its normal operating condition.

counterclockwise The counterclockwise direction of rotation of a gear as you look at it corresponding to the motion of the clock; also known as backward.

counter-electromotive force (CEMF) An electromagnetic force produced by the spinning magnetic field of the armature, which induces current in the opposite direction of battery current through the motor.

counterrotate When the tracks of a machine turn in opposite directions to complete a fast turn.

countershaft A shaft with various sizes of gears attached to it and driven by the input gear.

countershaft power-shift transmission A type of power-shift transmission that uses hydraulic clutches to control counterrotating shafts with meshed gears.

coupling phase A torque-converter operating phase when the turbine and the impeller are at close to the same speed.

coupling shaft A short shaft usually at the front of a driveline; also called a jack shaft.

crab steering When both axles steer at the same time in the same direction to make the machine move diagonally.

cranking amps (CAs) A measurement of the load, in amps, that a battery can deliver for 30 seconds while maintaining a voltage of 1.2 volts per cell (7.2 volts for a 12-volt battery) or higher at 32°F (–0°C).

crescent wrench The open-ended adjustable wrench, or crescent wrench, which has an adjustable thumb wheel that moves the lower jaw to grip smaller or larger fasteners.

cribbing Also referred to as blocking. This includes blocking, cribbing, jack stands, timbers, dunnage, and any other devices or equipment designed to support a load in a stationary position.

critical speed The rotational speed at which a driveshaft starts to bow off its centerline due to centrifugal force, leading to vibration and shaft failure.

cross-cut chisel A type of chisel for metal work that cleans out or cuts key ways.

cross-drive transmission A type of transmission that incorporates a steering mechanism with the drive system. Because there are three differentials incorporated into the transmission, skid steering is also called triple differential steering.

crossover relief valves Valves in the system that will relieve high pressure on one side of the loop if pressure gets too high.

cross-shaft A rotating shaft that holds the release fork. In a pull-type clutch, there are actually two cross-shafts: a left and a right.

crown gear A large bevel gear that is driven by a smaller pinion gear in the bevel gearset; also known as a ring gear.

crumber bar A device on a chain trencher that follows the digging chain to prevent loose soil from collecting in the trench.

current clamp A device that claps around a conductor to measure current flow. It is often used in conjunction with a digital volt-ohmmeter (DVOM).

curved file A type of file that has a curved surface for filing holes.

cutaway diagram A type of sketch in which the internal parts of components in a hydraulic system are exposed to help illustrate how the components function.

cycle time A measure of the time it takes a cylinder rod to travel one full stroke.

cycling clutch orifice tube (CCOT) A fixed-orifice tube with pressure control obtained by cycling the compressor clutch on and off.

cylinder pressure gauge The gauge on an oxygen or acetylene regulator that shows how much pressure is in the cylinder.

cylindrical roller bearings Bearings that feature cylindrical rolling elements to reduce friction between moving parts. Roller bearings will have an inner race, outer race, bearing cage, and rollers. The axis of the rollers is parallel to the shaft. They are designed to carry heavy radial loads, not axial loads.

D'Arsonval gauge A type of electromagnetic gauge that moves a pointing needle directly proportional to current flow through an electromagnet attached to the pointer.

dampening disc A disc with a ring of torsional dampening springs around its hub designed to absorb engine torsional vibrations.

danger Indicates an immediately hazardous situation, which, if not avoided, will result in death or serious injury.

danger zone Area of a machine where if a person were to have a body part during the machine cycle would incur injury.

data The typology that forms the communication pathway of modules in a network.

data inline package (DIP) switches A small slide switch located at the rear of the speedometer head placed in either an on or off (1 or 0) position.

data link adapter A device used to translate serial data from the DLC into a format readable by a desktop or laptop computer.

dead axle An axle that supports machine weight only.

dead reckoning systems Are a navigation system that depends on only vehicle sensors such as speed, steering angle, and even a magnetic compass to guide a machine. A radio-operated node or signal transmitter may provide a reference point.

dead-blow hammer A type of hammer that has a cushioned head to reduce the amount of head bounce.

deaeration The removal of excess air from the fluid.

dedendum The lower, thicker part of an involute tooth contact area.

deep cycle battery A battery used to deliver a lower, steady level of power for a much longer time.

degradation failure A type of hydraulic system failure that occurs gradually over a long period of time, which is commonly associated with basic wear and tear.

dehydration The removal of water from the fluid.

dehydrator A piece of equipment that can be connected to the reservoir of a hydraulic system and used to remove particle contamination and water from the hydraulic fluid.

delta windings Stator windings in which the windings are connected in the shape of a triangle.

delta-wound stators A three-phase stator wiring configuration where the stator windings are connected at each end to form a triangle resembling the Greek letter delta.

demulsibility The ability of a fluid to separate water from itself.

depth micrometers A micrometer that measures the depth of an item such as how far a piston is below the surface of the block.

destroking The action a variable pump makes to reduce its displacement.

destruction point Wear condition reached when the component is most likely to break or completely fail. The point of destruction is considered to be 120% wear. This is 20% more than the maximum limit of wear when component replacement is required.

diagnostic link connector (DLC) The connection point for electronic service tools used to access fault codes and other information provided by chassis electronic control modules.

diagnostic trouble code (DTC) A code logged by the electronic control module when electrical faults or system problems occur in commercial vehicle control systems.

diagonal-cutting pliers Pliers for cutting small wire or cable.

dial bore gauge A gauge that is used to measure the inside diameter of bores with a high degree of accuracy and speed.

dial indicator A device for precision measurements used to measure small variations, such as end play, movement in a bearing, or run-out.

diameter nominal (DN) Tubing dimensions specified in metric.

diaphragm Component inside the brake chamber that converts air pressure to mechanical actuation.

diaphragm spring clutch A clutch that uses a single diaphragm spring, also known as a Belleville spring, to provide the clamp force.

die stock handle A handle for securely holding dies to cut threads.

differential Refers to the voltage difference on a wire pair when one wires voltage is the mirror opposite voltage. A wide separation between the voltage pulses represents a 1 and a narrow separation represents a 0.

differential case The housing that holds the differential gears.

differential cross The mechanism that holds the differential pinion or spider gears; also known as the differential spider.

differential gear A gear arrangement that splits the available torque equally between two wheels while allowing them to turn at different speeds when required.

differential gearset Consists of two side gears, four pinion gears, and a cross; allows for speed difference between the two axle shafts of the drive axle when turning.

differential mode transmission A situation in which network modules detect the voltage difference between two wires to determine if a signal is a 1 or a 0.

differential pinion gear A beveled gear that is a component of the differential gearset; it is fitted to the four legs of the differential cross and rotates with it; also known as a spider gear.

differential spider The part that holds the differential pinion or spider gears; also known as the differential cross.

differential steering, or skid steering A steering principle where one track will turn at a different speed than the other, providing even the largest track-type machines with exceptional maneuverability.

differential voltage A signal processing technique used on CANs to transmit serial data with the least amount of signal noise.

digital multimeters An electronic test instrument

digital signals Electrical signals that represent data in discrete, finite values. Digital signals are considered as binary, meaning it is either on or off, yes or no, high or low, 0 or 1.

direct current (DC) Movement of current that flows in one direction only.

direct current electrode positive (DCEP) Also referred to as a reverse polarity connection. The flow through an electrical circuit that is formed when an electrode cable is connected to the positive terminal of a power source and the work cable is connected to the negative terminal of the power source.

direct drive A dual-clutch transmission from John Deere.

direct-acting relief valve A simple normally closed valve that opens when oil pressure overcomes its spring pressure.

directional control valves, DCVs Direct the fluid to and from the actuators.

dislocation The displacement of a joint from its normal position, which is caused by an external force stretching the ligaments beyond their elastic limit.

displacement The volume rating used for pumps and motors that determines how much fluid it takes to create one rotation of a motor and how much fluid a pump moves per revolution, measured in cubic inches per revolution (CIR) or cubic centimeters per revolution (CCR).

DOT-3, DOT 4, and DOT 5 Brake fluid standards.

double flare A seal that is made at the end of metal tubing or pipe.

double- or multiple-reduction planetary drive A drive that uses more than one planetary gearset.

double-acting cylinder A type of hydraulic cylinder that can apply force in two directions.

double-insulated tools or appliances that are designed in such a way that no single failure can result in a dangerous voltage coming into contact with the outer casing of the device.

double-reduction bull and pinion drive A drive that uses two sets of bull and pinion gears in its own housing.

double-reduction drive axle A drive axle that uses two gear reductions at all times.

double-rod cylinder If the machine has one steering cylinder, it has this device where each of its rods attaches to a tie rod.

downstroking A term that describes the action that occurs when a pump reduces its displacement.

drawbar capacity A tracked machine's performance measurement of the amount of weight a track drive can pull at a given speed.

drift punch A type of punch used to start pushing roll pins to prevent them from spreading.

drill vice A tool with jaws that can be attached to a drill press table for holding material that is to be drilled.

D-ring A ring shaped higher in the middle and lower on the ends to eliminate performance degradation as the valve cycles in the reverse direction.

drive axle The axle that drives the machine by turning the power from the driveshaft 90 degrees to deliver it to the wheels; also known as a live axle.

drive pin A pin used in a pot-type flywheel to drive the intermediate plate.

driveline A series of driveshafts, yokes, and support bearings used to connect a transmission to the rear axle.

driveline angularity The angles at the universal joints.

dross Oxidized and molten metal waste (slag) that is left over during oxyacetylene cutting and welding operations.

dry side The side of the reservoir tank where cooled air is stored after leaving moisture in the tank wet side.

DT-12 A 12-speed AMT manufactured by Detroit Diesel.

dual bushing track (DBT) Refers to a construction technique using a double bushing with a hardened outer bushing rotating freely around the inner bushing. No lubricant is present between the two outer bushings. However, an oil-lubricated track pin rotates inside the inner bushing.

dual path hydrostatic systems A drive system that uses two pumps and two motors to drive either two sets of tracks or wheels.

dual-clutch transmission A transmission with two shafts controlled by two separate clutches.

duty cycle The amount of time a compressor is actually pumping air (a percentage of run time).

dynamic Objects that are dynamic are moving or changing.

dynamic machine braking Hydrostatic drive machines provide natural braking because of the closed-loop system.

ear protection Also called hearing protection. Protective gear worn when the sound levels exceed 85 decibels, when working around operating machinery for any period of time, or when the equipment you are using produces loud noise.

ECM (electronic control module) A module that gathers information, processes it, and produces output signals.

ecology drain valve A type of drain that provides a way to control the oil flow when draining the tank.

effective area The area of a piston that fluid pressure can act on to move a load

e-fuse A software-controlled fuse that uses field effect transistors for the circuit control device. Also called *virtual fuses*.

elasticity The amount of stretch or give a material has.

elastomeric A natural or synthetic material that returns to its original shape after a deforming force is removed.

electric shift assembly The shift actuation system for an Eaton AutoShift or UltraShift transmission that contains two shift motors, the shift finger, and the shift finger position sensors.

electrical driveline retarders Retarders that use electromagnetic force to slow the driveline.

electrical polarity The direction of current flow in an electrical circuit based on the fact that current flows from the positive pole, or terminal, to the negative pole.

electrical resistance A material's property that reduces voltage and amperage in an electrical current.

electrically erasable read-only memory (EEPROM) Nonvolatile memory technology that is used to store operating instructions or programming for an ECM.

electrohydraulic system See electronically managed hydraulic system.

electrolysis The use of electricity to break down water into hydrogen and oxygen gases.

electrolyte An electrically conductive solution.

electron theory of current movement The movement of negatively charged electrons to a positive charge.

electronic display An electronic monitoring system; also known as EMS.

electronically managed hydraulic system A hydraulic system that uses sensors and switches for inputs to an ECM. The ECM then sends out signals to solenoids that control hydraulic components like valves and pumps.

electrostatic theory The idea that like charges repel one another and unlike electrical charges attract.

elevated sprocket A track system using two idler wheels and a drive sprocket located above the level of the idler wheels. An elevated sprocket system forms a triangular, rather than oval-shaped, track.

end termination The way the end of a wire rope is treated, usually by forming an eye that becomes the attachment for the wire rope.

end yoke A splined yoke attached to a component, a component such as a transmission output shaft.

energy conversion A pump converts mechanical energy into fluid energy.

engine brakes A brake retardation system that turns the engine cylinders into a compressor to slow the machine.

engine hoist A small crane used to lift engines.

entrained air Air that has mixed with hydraulic fluid and is circulated through the system.

envelopes Square box symbols used to represent pressure control valves and directional control valves on a schematic diagram; the number of envelopes equates to the number of valve operating positions.

Environmental Protection Agency (EPA) A U.S. federal government agency that deals with issues related to environmental safety.

epicyclical gear Gears that revolve around a common centerline.

equalizer bar A bar connecting two opposite track frames that functions as a weight transfer lever connection point between the two frames.

equalizing planetary The planetary gearset on a differential steer machine attached to the left-side final drive.

evacuation routes A safe way of escaping danger and gathering in a safe place where everyone can be accounted for in the event of an emergency.

evaporator The cold surface of the air-conditioning system that absorbs heat from a cab or vehicle.

evaporator freezing A condition in which excess refrigerant floods the evaporator.

exhaust brakes A brake retardation system that throttles the exhaust to slow the machine.

extension jib A device that attaches to the end of an excavator's stick to extend the reach of the bucket.

external bleeding The loss of blood from an external wound, where blood can be seen escaping.

external gear pump A simple design that features one drive gear meshed with a driven gear. Oil is transferred from the pump inlet to its outlet between adjacent gear teeth and the inside of the housing.

failure mode identifier (FMI) The type of failure detected in the SPN, PID, or SID.

false brinelling A condition where lubricant is squeezed out from between the needles and the trunnions of a U-joint, leading to wear, which is caused by too small of an angle or no angle at the joint, so lubricant is not distributed.

fasteners Devices that securely hold items together, such as screws, cotter pins, rivets, and bolts.

fatigue failure Failure of components due to repeated overload.

feeler gauges Also called feeler blades. Flat metal strips used to measure the width of gaps, such as the clearance between valves and rocker arms.

field effect transistor (FET) A unipolar transistor that uses an electric field to control the conductivity of a semiconductor material.

filler cap Allows oil to be added to the tank.

fillet radius The radius shape between the bottoms of two teeth; also called root.

filter media The material that the filter element is made from, which can be cellulose or synthetic.

filters Component that removes damaging contaminants from the hydraulic fluid.

final drive The last reduction in a drive system.

finished rivet A rivet after the completion of the riveting process.

fire blanket A safety device designed to extinguish incipient (starting) fires. It consists of a sheet of fire retardant material that is to be placed over a fire in order to smother it.

fire-resistant fluids Three main types are water/glycol, water emulsion, and synthetic based fluids.

first aid The immediate care given to an injured or suddenly ill person.

first aid kit A kit containing items needed to apply emergency first aid, such as bandages, gauze, medical tape, and other items.

first-degree burns Burns that show reddening of the skin and damage to the outer layer of skin only.

fittings Components that couple conductors. Fittings are categorized by shape and function, such as tees, unions, and elbows.

five-piece rims Similar to three-piece rims but have an additional separate inner bead seat and a bead seat band for the outer flange.

fixed displacement A type of pump or motor in which the amount of flow displaced by each cycle of rotation remains the same.

fixed displacement motor Simple hydrostatic drive systems use a motor that will only produce a constant rotational speed if a constant supply of fluid is sent to it.

fixed displacement pumps Produce the same volume of flow per revolution.

flange A ring or collar that increases strength and provides a place to attach other objects.

flange yoke A yoke with two ears to hold a U-joint and a flat flange to bolt to a companion flange.

flare-nut wrench A type of closed-end wrench that has a slot in the box section to allow the wrench to slip through a tube or pipe. It's also called a flare-tubing wrench.

flash point The lowest temperature at which vapors of a volatile material will ignite when given an ignition source.

flashback An unintentional ignition of oxygen and acetylene inside a torch handle that, if left unimpeded, can travel backward through the torch, hoses, and regulators into the cylinders.

flashback arrestor A spring-loaded valve installed on oxyacetylene equipment as a safety device to prevent flame from entering the torch hoses and traveling backward to the cylinders.

flashing Reprogramming or recalibrating the ECM. Information is stored in the ECM's memory.

flat tip screwdriver A type of screwdriver that fits a straight slot in screws.

flat washers Spread the load of bolt heads or nuts as they are tightened and distribute it over a greater area. They are particularly useful in protecting aluminum alloy.

flat-nosed pliers Pliers that are flat and square at the end of the nose.

flatted condition Flattening is evident when one side of a track roller is worn away from continual sliding friction with the chain link rail.

flat-type flywheel A flywheel that is predominately flat, with all of the clutch components inside the clutch cover.

flex plate A flexible plate used to connect the torque converter to the engine.

float A fourth DCV position that allows free flow between an actuator's A and B ports.

float position A control valve center configuration in which when the valve is placed in the neutral position, fluid flows between all four ports; it is often referred to as open center.

floating Term describing the transfer of a heavy machine between worksites on a flat semitrailer or specialized gooseneck trailers.

flooded lead-acid battery A lead-acid battery in which the plates are immersed in a water-acid electrolyte solution.

flow Hydraulic pumps create fluid flow. The movement of fluid in a hydraulic system is measured in gpm or lpm.

flow control valves Control the flow rate of the fluid to the actuators so they operate at the proper speed.

flow divider A component used to split one source flow into two or more separate flows.

flow losses The fluid flow from a pump that is not used to produce output power. This is wasted energy or the inefficient part of a fluid power system.

flow meter A tool used to measure fluid flow in a hydraulic system.

flow pattern Each DCV center section has a certain flow pattern type based on whether flow is allowed between P, T, A, and B or blocked between them.

fluid A substance, such as liquid or gas, that flows and easily changes shape.

fluid cleanliness code An ISO-established code to accurately measure solid particle contamination.

fluid conditioning Refers to filtering, cooling, and heating of hydraulic fluid.

fluid conductors Another term for tubes, hoses, and fittings that hydraulic system fluid flows through and that connects components.

fluid coupling A power transfer device that uses fluid to transmit power to the driveline.

fluid power Both air and hydraulic systems that transfer power to machine implements and accessories performing work.

fluid power system efficiency A measure of how much usable energy is produced by a hydraulic system compared to how much energy is consumed by it.

fluid properties There are several properties of hydraulic fluid that have to be considered before adding fluid to a system.

flushing valve A valve usually on the motor that allows a small amount of fluid out of the system for cleaning purposes.

flux A material that is used during brazing and soldering operations to prevent oxidation and remove impurities from the metals.

flywheel A heavy, round metal disc attached to the end of the crankshaft to smooth out vibrations from the crankshaft assembly and provide one of the friction surfaces for a clutch disc used on a manual transmission.

foot pedal treadle valve Activated by the operator, it meters air out of both valve sections to the front and rear service brake chambers.

FOPS Falling object protection system.

force multiplication The force advantage that can be gained at the actuator in a hydraulic system.

forehand welding A welding technique (also called the leftward technique, forward welding, push welding, puddle welding, and ripple welding) best suited for relatively thin metals in which the welding torch is held in the right hand, the filler rod is held in the left hand, and the welding direction moves from the right side of the seam toward the left side of the seam.

forward drive side wear Produced by sprocket and bushing contact on the forward side of the drive sprocket tooth.

foundation brakes At each wheel are made up of friction materials attached to brakes shoes (drum) or pads (disc) that are forced against the rotating component by the action of the brake chambers.

free air Air is a contaminant in a hydraulic system, and free air is not mixed with the fluid.

free water Water that hasn't combined with hydraulic oil and will settle to the bottom of the tank.

frequency The number of events or cycles that occur in a period, usually 1 second.

frequency-sensing relay A relay connected to the alternator that detects alternating current only when the alternator is charging.

friction The relative resistance to motion between any two bodies in contact with one another.

friction bearing A plain bushing, or friction bearing, also called a plain bearing is a mechanical element used to reduce friction between rotating shafts and stationary support members or housings. They contain no rolling elements and are often lubricated with pressurized lubricant.

friction discs Components inside a hydraulic clutch that are coated with a friction material to help transfer torque.

friction drive A track drive systems using only adhesive friction between a rubber track and a rubberized or pneumatic drive wheel to rotate the track.

friction fit An interference fit, also called a press fit or friction fit, is a means of fastening two parts together so that they are in direct contact with one another and are held in place only by friction or by the tightness of the fit.

full fielding Making the alternator produce maximum amperage output.

full film lubrication When two moving components are separated by a thin film oil fluid.

full power brake system Brake system capable of supplying fluid to a range of both small- and large-volume service brakes with actuation that is faster than air brake systems.

full-floating axle shaft An axle that carries none of the machine weight.

fully autonomous A machine control system capable of sensing its environment and navigating without human input.

gallons per minute (gpm) The flow rate of a fluid measured in the number of gallons through a conductor in a minute.

gallons per minute or liters per minute Two common units of measure used to quantify fluid flow in a hydraulic system.

galvanic reaction A chemical reaction that produces electricity when two dissimilar metals are placed in an electrolyte.

galvanized Steel that has been coated with a layer of zinc to protect it from corrosion.

gantry crane A crane similar to an overhead crane except that the bridge for carrying the trolley or trolleys is rigidly supported on two or more legs running on fixed rails or other runway.

gas A state of matter characterized by low density, easy compressibility, and a tendency to diffuse readily and uniformly.

gas pocket Imperfection in the adhesion of molten metal during the casting or forming process.

gas welding goggles Protective gear designed for gas welding, which provide protection against foreign particles entering the eye and are tinted to reduce the glare of the welding flame.

gasket scraper A broad, sharp, flat blade to assist in removing gaskets and glue.

gassing A situation that occurs when overcharging or rapid charging causes some gas to escape from the battery.

gateway module A module that translates communication between different networks that operate with the use of different protocols or speeds.

gear jamming An attempt by the driver to shift without using the clutch, which usually causes at least some damage to the transmission sliding clutches; also called float shifting.

gear pullers A tool with two or more legs and a cross-bar with a center forcing screw to remove gears.

gear pumps Two types—internal and external gear hydraulic pumps.

gear ratio The relationship between two gears in mesh as a comparison to input versus output.

gear reduction A torque increase.

gel cell battery A type of battery to which silica has been added to the electrolyte solution to turn the solution to a gel-like consistency.

generoid An asymmetrical tooth design, it gives added strength to the hypoid and amboid gearsets.

geo fence An electronically limited operational area.

geofencing A feature provided by a telematic service supplier to alert a subscriber to movement of a machine outside a particular geographical area or during expected operating hours.

gerotor A variation of an internal gear pump.

gimbals Two or more concentric circles used to support an item; while the circles can move, the supported object will remain stationary.

gland A recess, or gap, in a part where a seal or O-ring is placed to form a seal when two parts are brought together.

global positioning system (GPS) Also called the global navigation satellite system (GNSS). A worldwide radio-navigation system using satellites to communicate with earth-based radio receivers.

gooseneck The protruding part of the scraper.

gooseneck boom A curved boom used on some types of equipment that connects to a dipper stick and bucket.

governor Controls compressor duty cycle and sets maximum system pressure.

gpm Gallons per minute (usually U.S. gallons).

graphing meter An electrical test instrument used to analyze waveforms and graphically plot an electrical value of a signal over time.

grapple A jaw-like attachment used on excavators, loaders, tractors, and other equipment to grab and pick up objects such as rocks, debris, brush, logs, and other material.

grease gun A device used to force grease into an item, usually a grease fitting. It can be powered by hand, compressed air, or electricity.

greased turns Involve lubricating track pins with grease during a pin turning service operation.

grooves The smaller diameter part of a valve spool that allows oil to flow past it and through the valve when it is shifted.

ground The pathway through the chassis components, rather than insulated wiring for electrical current to move through a machine.

ground pressure The force exerted by the tires or track of a machine. It is a function of the machine weight divided by the surface area below the tire or track Ground pressure is measured in pounds per square inch.

ground shaft A stationary shaft that holds the inner hub of the stator one-way clutch; also called stator support shaft.

ground-driven pump Part of the machine's driveline that the wheels drive also drives this pump, which usually mounts on the transfer case.

grounded circuit A circuit characterized by an unwanted low-resistance connection between battery positive power and chassis ground.

grousers Wedges or bars on steel track that function like cleats on athletic shoes. These steel bars penetrate the ground surface, providing even more surface area to push or pull against the ground.

hall-effect sensor A sensor commonly used to measure the rotational speed of a shaft; they have the advantage of producing a digital signal square waveform and have strong signal strength at low shaft rotational speeds.

hanger bearing A bearing pressed onto a machined surface after the splined area of a driveshaft's slip yoke spline, which is used to support a multi-piece driveshaft; also called a center bearing.

hardening A manufacturing process that makes the surface of a gear much harder than its core: typically, the surface is hardened to a depth of no more than 0.050 inches (1.2 mm).

harmonic vibration An inherent vibration that occurs at precisely 50% of a shaft's critical speed.

hazard Anything that could hurt you or someone else.

hazard control measures Actions taken to reduce, eliminate, or lessen the possible damage from hazards.

hazardous environment A place where hazards exist.

hazardous material Any material that poses an unreasonable risk of damage or injury to persons, property, or the environment if it is not properly controlled during handling, storage, manufacture, processing, packaging, use and disposal, or transportation.

head pressure The pressure created by the weight of a liquid.

headgear protective gear that includes items like hairnets, caps, or hard hats.

heat buildup A dangerous situation that occurs when the glove can no longer absorb or reflect heat and heat is transferred to the inside of the glove.

heat exchanger A device that transfers heat from one fluid to another without allowing the fluids to mix.

heater A device for adding heat to hydraulic fluids.

heater core An in-cab heat exchanger that regulates heating by circulating engine coolant.

heating, ventilation, and air-conditioning (HVAC) system The system in the vehicle responsible for heating and cooling the air.

heel The end of a crown gear tooth furthest from the center of its axis.

helical double-reduction drive axle A double-reduction drive axle that uses a helical gearset for the second gear reduction.

helical double-reduction two-speed drive axle A double-reduction drive axle that uses two selectable sets of helical gears as the second gear reduction.

helical gear A gear with teeth cut on an angle or spirally to its axis of rotation.

HEPA (high-efficiency particulate absorption) A type of particulate air filter, which is effective at filtering out fine particles and dust.

herringbone gear A gear cut with opposite helices on each side of the face.

hertz (Hz) The unit for electrical frequency measurement, in cycles per second.

high-impedance multimeter A meter that samples very little of a circuit's own current to take a measurement.

high-pressure compensator A part of the pump control valve that reduces pump flow when a maximum set pressure value is reached.

high-voltage electric propulsion Any system that moves the entire machine, whether it has tracks or wheels, or any system that moves part of a machine, such as the swing function of an excavator with electrical energy as the power source.

historical fault A fault that took place at one time but that is now corrected and no longer active.

hoisting The action of lifting a load using cables or ropes.

holt manufacturing company The company that merged with Best Manufacturing and incorporated into the Caterpillar Tractor Company.

hooke joint A joint with four trunnions and four bearing caps; also known as a Cardan joint or a universal joint.

hooke's law A law of physics that states that force delivered by a spring to an object is directly related to its compression or extension; the greater the spring is compressed, the more force the spring delivers.

hot mounting A method of bearing installation in which heat is used to expand a bearing, and then the bearing is placed onto a shaft, where it cools and contracts. The bearing will then have a transverse interference fit.

housing An enclosed case for a mechanism.

Humans in the Loop (HITL) People who provide assistance with autonomous function or other machine support, such as a repair technician.

hunting tooth arrangement A final drive tooth pattern using an odd number of sprocket teeth to match an even number of bushings. In track systems, the odd–even change in the ratio between the tooth sprocket and track chain bushings ensures there is a change in tooth-to-bushing contact with every sprocket revolution.

hydraulic accumulator A pressure storage reservoir in which a noncompressible hydraulic fluid is held under pressure, which an external source applies.

hydraulic boosted brake system A power brake system that uses a hydraulic pump to boost the master cylinder output force.

hydraulic breaker An attachment, commonly called a rock breaker, that functions much like a jackhammer by using the reciprocating motion of a chisel to rip through rock, concrete, or similar material.

hydraulic calipers Linear brake actuators.

hydraulic cylinder, or ram A device that uses hydraulic fluid flow and converts it to linear mechanical movement.

hydraulic fluid The medium that flows through any hydraulic system. There are many types of hydraulic fluid that can be found in MORE machines.

hydraulic fluid power A specific area of hydraulics in which a liquid is used to transmit energy.

hydraulic hoist A type of hoist that the vehicle is driven onto that uses two long, narrow platforms to lift the vehicle.

hydraulic jack A type of vehicle jack that uses oil under pressure to lift vehicles.

hydraulic motor Creates rotary motion when it receives oil flow.

hydraulic press A machine that uses a hydraulic cylinder to generate a compressive force.

hydraulic retarder A system that uses hydraulic oil under pressure to slow the machine.

hydraulic schematic A paper or electronic drawing that uses symbols to represent components; together they represent a machine's hydraulic system.

hydraulic system An energy conversion systems that uses a hydraulic fluid to transfer power output from a prime mover to actuators that perform work.

hydrodynamic A system that converts kinetic energy contained in hydraulic fluid flow into mechanical movement.

hydrodynamics The study of hydraulic systems where a high volume of fluid is in motion at a high velocity.

hydrolysis The use of electricity to break down water into its oxygen and hydrogen gas components.

hydrostatic Fluid at rest and is the term associated with hydraulic closed-loop drive systems.

hydrostatic transmission (HST) A type of automatic transmission that uses pressurized fluid instead of gears to transfer power from an engine to axles and wheels and provide infinitely variable speed.

hydrostatic, or "hystat," drive systems Machine's using hydraulic motors to propel a machine. Hydraulic motors are typically located in the wheel ends or in the final drive assemblies.

The motors are driven by hydraulic pumps connected to an engine or electric motor.

hydrostatics The study of fluid in an enclosed system where the fluid is at rest.

hypoid gearing A type of spiral bevel gearset that mounts the pinion gear below the centerline of the crown gear.

idle validation switch (IVS) A circuit used for safety reasons that is used to verify throttle position.

idler gear Gear used to change direction.

idler wheels or idler sprockets Large non-driving wheels or sprockets used to loop the track around the track frame. At least one idler wheel or sprockets is used on each side of the machine and located opposite the drive sprocket on the track frame.

impact driver A tool that is struck with a blow to provide an impact turning force to remove tight fasteners.

impedance An electrical term to describe resistance in an AC circuit.

impeller The bladed element in a torque converter or fluid coupling that is fixed to the housing and therefore rotates with it.

incipient fault A fault that is the result of system or component deterioration.

incompressible The property of a hydraulic fluid that is desirable to make the system responsive (hydraulic fluid is slightly compressible).

indicate-only mode A computer-aided earth-moving technique that supplies machine data to a cab terminal, providing feedback about the position of a blade or implement.

induction motor The most common type of AC motor, where the rotor current flow is induced by the stator's moving magnetic field; also called asynchronous motors.

inductive amp clamp A device that measures amperage by measuring a conductor's magnetic field strength, which is proportional to amperage.

inert gas A gas that does not undergo chemical reactions or change under different sets of conditions, such as temperature change.

inertia brake A component used to control the speed of the transmission countershaft and main shaft gears.

inertial excitation The force caused by the speeding up and slowing down of the shaft driven through an angle. These stem from the operating angles of the U-joint at the drive end of the driveshaft and are caused by the sheer weight of the driveshaft being accelerated and decelerated twice per revolution.

inertial guidance systems A type of machine navigation that uses a known starting point, orientation, and velocity to guide a machine. Inertial guidance systems use onboard sensors or instruments that measure speed, direction, and rate of acceleration.

inertial measurement units (IMU) sensors Sensors attached to the body of the machine, blade, or implement. When attached to the machine body, the positioning or spatial data and the known dimensions of the machine enable the system to precisely calculate the position of a cutting blade at all times.

infinitely variable transmission (IVT) A type of continuously variable transmission that is sometimes coupled to a planetary gear train to achieve an infinite gear ratio range.

inhibitors Additives used to prevent the degrading of system fluid under normal circumstances.

inlet port An opening in the housing that allows oil in from the tank.

input components Components such as sensors, switches, joystick controls, and touch screens that provide electrical signals to the ECM.

input gear The gear part of or attached to the input shaft that delivers power to the countershaft.

input member The element of the planetary gear set inputted from the power source.

input shaft The input to the transmission driven by the clutch friction disc.

inside diameter (ID) The wall-to-wall measurement on the inside of a conductor.

inside micrometer A micrometer that measures inside dimensions.

insulator A material that holds electrons tightly and prevents electron movement.

integral carrier housing A drive axle housing that does not have a removable carrier.

intelligent charger A battery charger that varies its output according to the sensed condition of the battery it is charging.

interaxle differential A differential gearset that splits the available torque equally between two drive axles; also called a power divider.

interconnected-type track links A category of links using a track bushing have a second precision counterbore machined into the link, allowing the bushing to protrude further into the link to help seal the leak path into the pin-to-bushing clearance.

interference fit A machinist's term describing an assembly technique where a machined part has a slightly larger diameter than the diameter of the bore where it's installed. On track systems, an interference fit exists between the track bushing and counterbore of the track link.

intermediate plate/separator plate A plate driven by the flywheel or the clutch cover, separating two friction discs.

intermediate tap also called a plug tap—one of a series of taps designed to cut an internal thread.

intermittent circuit A circuit characterized by uneven current flow.

intermittent fault A fault that is not ongoing and can be both active and historical.

internal bleeding The loss of blood into the body cavity from a wound, where there is no obvious sign of blood.

internal gear pumps Another type of gear pump used for low flow and lower pressure applications.

intersecting angle arrangement A method of angle cancelation in which the U-joint angles will intersect at a point exactly at the middle of the shaft length; also known as a broken back arrangement.

inverter A device that changes direct current into alternating current. Also called a *wave inverter.*

involute A gear design shape that compensates for the changing point of contact between gears as they rotate through mesh.

I-Shift The Volvo AMT; Mack trucks use the same transmission.

ISO (International Organization for Standards) An international body which sets standards for members, typically in engineering, mechanical, automotive, and aerospace areas.

ISO 4406 A fluid cleanliness code used to determine the level of contamination in system fluid.

ISO viscosity ratings A viscosity rating at 40°C (104°F) that ranges from 22 to 68 for common fluids.

ISO 11783 Also called ISO-bus. A network protocol developed in Germany and used primarily by European agriculture and forestry machines.

J-1587 An older SAE communication protocol, which is quite slow in terms of data transmission at 9,600 bits/second.

J-1939 A newer SAE communication protocol, which transmits data at a rate of at least 250,000 bits/second and up to 500,000 bits/second.

J-1939-2 An SAE network protocol used by agricultural and forestry vehicles.

jack shaft A short shaft usually at the front of a driveline; also known as a coupling shaft.

jack stands Metal stands with adjustable height to hold a vehicle once it has been jacked up.

JIC 37-Degree Flare (SAE J514) Society of Automotive Engineers standard for flare connectors (male and female). Both the JIC male and JIC female components have a 3-degree flare seat and straight threads. The male and female flare seats seal when the 37-degree faces of the same size and thread style are engaged.

joystick A term used to describe hand levers that could be used to control hydrostatic systems.

keep alive memory (KAM) Memory that is retained by the ECM when the key is off.

key-off electrical loads Machine electrical loads drawing battery current when the ignition is off.

kidney loop An external filtration machine that is sometimes connected to a hydrostatic drive system to clean contamination out of the fluid.

kidney loop filtration A separate filter machine that is connected to the hydraulic system to perform an extra cleaning.

kinematic One method of testing fluid viscosity.

kinetic friction The friction between two surfaces that are sliding against each other.

kingpin A shaft that is stationary in the steering axle on a non-drive axle.

Kirchhoff 's law A law that states that the sum of the current flowing into a junction is the same as the current flowing out of the junction.

ladder logic The designed-in logic of a circuit that determines what activates a specific circuit.

laminar flow A smooth, streamline flow pattern that occurs when fluid flows in parallel layers.

lands The larger part of a valve spool that creates a seal in the valve body.

latent heat The quantity of heat required to produce a change of state from a solid to a liquid, or a liquid to a gas.

latent heat of condensation The process of removing heat energy from matter to effect a change of state from vapor to liquid.

latent heat of vaporization The process of adding heat energy to matter to effect a change of state from liquid to vapor.

laterals Hand-operated levers used by early differential steering systems to apply a brake to one or both tracks of a machine in order to steer the machine.

lattice boom A basic type of boom, used on many crawler cranes, that consists of one or more sections of interlaced steel rods that provide strength and support.

leak test solution A soapy liquid that, when placed on oxyacetylene equipment connections, can indicate leaks by bubbling.

lengthwise bearing The contact pattern along the tooth face from the toe toward the heel.

Lenz's law A law of electromagnetism stating that the current induced in a circuit due to a change or movement of a magnetic field will create a magnetic field having a polarity opposite to the magnetic field of the original inducing current.

leveling valve A valve that controls suspension height.

lever A simple machine that can allow a large object to be moved with less force.

lidar An acronym for light detection and ranging, which uses pulsed laser beams rather than radio waves to measure distances.

lifting equipment Also known as lifting gear, any equipment or devices used to lift a load vertically. This can include jacks, a block and tackle, vacuum lift, hydraulic lift, hoist, gantries, windlasses, cranes, forklifts, slings or lifting harnesses, rigging, wire rope/cables, and any other items used to lift a load vertically.

line relief valves Valves that limit system pressure in one section of a circuit.

linear Extending or moving in one dimension only.

linear actuators Receive oil from the directional control valve and convert oil flow into linear motion.

linear voltage differential transformer (LVDT) A linear hydraulic control sensor that supplies a voltage signal corresponding to a change in actuator length. When proportional electrohydraulic valves are used, the movement of the spool valve is proportional to the amount of electrical current passed though the sensor's armature coils.

liquid A fluid that has a definite volume, but no shape. Liquid takes on the shape of its container, up to that volume. For most practical purposes, liquid is incompressible.

live axle The axle that drives the machine by turning the power from the driveshaft 90 degrees to deliver it to the wheels and providing the final gear reduction in the drivetrain; also known as a drive axle.

live zone An area in a hydraulic system that is highly desirable for fluid sampling because the flow there is highly turbulent, downstream from major components in the system, and upstream from filters in the return line to the reservoir.

load A device in an electrical circuit with resistance.

load check valve A valve used to hold or lower a load in a controlled manner that is supported by a cylinder. Different types of counterbalance valves include counterbalance valves, vented counterbalance valves, brake valves, and pilot-operated check valves.

load cylinder A typical double-acting hydraulic cylinder with a barrel, head, rod, piston, and seals.

load sensing A hydraulic system that monitors the load on the pump through different circuits is considered to be load sensing.

load test A battery test that subjects the battery to a high rate of discharge; the voltage is then measured after a set time to see how well the battery creates current flow.

load-dumping A feature that allows temporary suppression of high-voltage spikes.

locking differential A system that actively prevents differential action from occurring when engaged.

locking pliers A type of plier where the jaws can be set and locked into position.

locking tang A small flat piece of metal that stops the large internal adjusting ring from moving when the clutch is operating.

lockup clutch The lockup clutch locks the turbine to the converter shell when conditions are correct for 100% efficiency.

lockup clutch disc The friction disc used in a lockup clutch.

lockup clutch piston The hydraulically actuated piston that applies the lockup clutch.

lockup clutch/piston assembly A combination lockup clutch disc and piston assembly, which is used in light-duty vehicles.

LOTO (Lock Out Tag Out) A system that must be adhered to that ensures a machine is safe to work on. The machine's energy sources are neutralized, and the machine is prevented from starting.

low-voltage burnout A damaging condition for starter motors in which excess current flows through the starter, causing the motor to burn out prematurely.

low-voltage disconnect (LVD) A device that monitors battery voltage and disconnects noncritical electrical loads when battery voltage level falls below a preset threshold value.

lpm Liters per minute.

lubrication failure Failure caused by incorrect lubricant, contaminated lubricant, or lack of lubricant.

machine screw A screw with a slot for screwdrivers.

magnetic pickup tools An extending shaft, often flexible, with a magnet fitted to the end for picking up metal objects.

main relief valves Valves that limit system pressure in a complete system.

main shaft The shaft that carries the speed gears that are driven by the countershaft; also called the output shaft.

makeup valves Valves in the system that allow charge fluid into the closed loop if the pressure on the low side drops below the charge pressure setting.

mandrel The shaft of a pop rivet.

manual-ranging multimeter A multimeter that must first be set to the correct range based on anticipated values measured.

margin spring pressure This spring in the pump control valve will maintain a higher pump output pressure than the highest work port pressure.

master cylinder A control device that converts mechanical pressure from a driver's foot into hydraulic pressure.

material safety data sheet (MSDS) Same as safety data sheet (SDS).

maximum forward overdrive The highest (fastest) ratio possible in a planetary gear set.

maximum forward reduction The lowest (slowest) ratio possible in a planetary gear set.

mechanic's mirror A small mirror on a stick that can be adjusted to view leaks, identify tags, and find dropped parts and tools. It can be placed into areas that are difficult to view or access.

mechanical advantage Advantage gained when a mechanism is used while transferring force.

mechanical bearing packer A tool that uses mechanical force to push grease into all a bearing's external and internal parts. Used to easily *pack* bearings with grease.

mechanical fingers Spring-loaded fingers at the end of a flexible shaft that pick up items in tight spaces.

mechanical jack A type of jack that utilizes mechanical power to provide lifting. A screw jack is a type of mechanical jack.

message identifier (MID) Also called module identifier. The electronic control module that has identified a fault. J-1587 protocols use MIDs.

metallic Composed of metal

metal-reinforced rubber or metal-embedded rubber (MERT) tracks A rubber track construction technique that adds strength, durability, and stability to rubber track, using heavily reinforced track carcass with steel cables and wire plies.

metering notches Grooves or notches in lands of spool valves that allow gradual metering of oil to or from an actuator when a valve is shifted.

MFA A shortened term for multiple flame acetylene torch tip, which is a type of oxyacetylene torch tip used for heating metal.

microcontroller A special-purpose processor with limited capabilities, designed to perform a set of specific tasks.

micron A unit of distance measurement for microscopic particles. One micron is equivalent to one-millionth of a meter.

mineral oil A type of base fluid derived from crude oil.

minimum forward overdrive The second highest (fastest) ratio possible in a planetary gear set.

minimum forward reduction The second lowest (slowest) ratio possible in a planetary gear set.

mobile off-road equipment (MORE) Mobile equipment designed specifically for off-highway use. Examples are front-end loaders, back-hoes, haul trucks, trenchers, mining equipment, etc.

momentary engine ignition interrupt relay (MEIIR) A relay controlled by the TCU that cuts the engine ignition or fueling in the event that a DM clutch will not disengage.

MOSFET A field effect transistor made from metal-oxide semiconductor material.

MSHA (Mine Safety and Health Administration) A U.S. federal government agency created to provide safety and regulatory enforcement in mining activities.

multidisc wet clutch A type of hydraulic clutch that contains multiple plates and discs and operates in a bath of hydraulic oil.

multipiece rims Rims that have O-rings to seal the areas between their base and removable bead seats; may also feature bead locks or keys that prevent bead seats from spinning on the rim's base.

multiplexing A concept where the transmission of more than one electrical signal or message takes place over a single wire or pair of wires.

Murphy gauge A type of gauge with an integrated switch that can shut off the machine or trigger a warning.

National Institute for Automotive Service Excellence (ASE) An independent, nonprofit organization that seeks to improve the quality of automotive repair by testing and certifying automotive service professionals.

national pipe taper (NPT) A standard for tapered thread of a pipe.

national pipe-taper fuel (NPTF) A type of thread designed to provide a leak-free seal in pipe connections; also called dryseal.

needle bearings Bearings that are characterized by their thin (small diameter), long, and numerous roller elements.

needle-nosed pliers Pliers with long tapered jaws for gripping small items and getting into tight spaces.

neo-con A special fluid used in Hitachi suspension struts.

network node A point on a network.

neutral flame A torch flame that has the correct proportions of oxygen and acetylene and is characterized by one or more inner cones, which are light blue in color, surrounded by a darker blue outer flame envelope.

neutralizer valve Manufacturers use this valve on articulated machines to stop the turning action when the machine is fully turned.

nickel-metal hydride (NiMH) battery A battery in which metal hydroxide forms the negative electrode and nickel oxide forms the positive electrode.

nippers Pliers designed to cut protruding items level with the surface.

nitrogen An inert gas used in struts.

NLGI (National Lubricating Grease Institute) An industry organization in the United States that sets standards and rating for grease products.

nominal tube size (NPS) Tubing dimensions specified in inches.

non-boosted brake hydraulic system A system that does not have any power assist to increase application pressure.

noncompressibility A fluid, unlike air, does not compress under pressure.

nonpositive displacement Types of pumps that have loose-fitting internal components and use centrifugal force to move fluid at low pressure.

non-uniform velocity The phenomenon that a shaft driven through an angle will accelerate and decelerate twice per revolution.

non-volatile memory Memory that is not lost when power is removed or lost.

normally closed valve A type of valve, such as a pressure-relief valve, that remains closed during normal operating conditions but will open if the system becomes overpressurized.

normally open valve A type of valve, such as a pressure-reducing valve, that remains open during normal operating conditions but will close if the system becomes overpressurized.

NOx sensor A sensor that detects oxygen ions originating from nitric oxide (NOx) from among the other oxygen ions present in the exhaust gas.

N-type material Semiconductor material able to hold a small amount of extra electrons.

nut A fastener with a hexagonal head and internal threads for screwing on bolts.

nyloc nut Keeps the nut and bolt done up tightly; it can have a plastic or nylon insert. Tightening the bolt squeezes it into the insert, where it resists any movement. The self-locker is highly resistant to being loosened.

OBD manager Software that identifies fault codes and ensures emissions systems are operating correctly.

object or collision avoidance systems Systems that identify objects such as a boulder or a deep hole capable of damaging or even swallowing a machine.

occupational safety and health A multidisciplinary field concerned with the safety, health, and welfare of people in the workplace.

Occupational Safety and Health Administration (OSHA) The agency that assures safe and healthy working conditions by setting and enforcing standards and by providing training, outreach, education, and assistance.

off-board diagnostics Procedures to isolate a fault based on fault code information, including retrieving fault code information, monitoring system operation, performing actuator tests and pinpoint electrical tests, and inspecting components.

off-line kidney loop system A piece of equipment that can be connected to the reservoir of a hydraulic system and used to remove particulates that have passed through the system filters, particles that have found their way into the reservoir, and, in some models, water that has infused the hydraulic fluid.

offset screwdriver A screwdriver with a 90-degree bend in the shaft for working in tight spaces.

offset vice A vice that allows long objects to be gripped vertically.

ohm The unit for measuring electrical resistance.

Ohm's law A law that defines the relationship between amperage, resistance, and voltage.

oil cooler A device that reduces the temperature of the hydraulic fluid in the system.

oil-filter wrench A wrench used to grip and loosen an oil filter. Not to be used for tightening an oil filter.

onboard diagnostics (OBD) Self-diagnostic capabilities of electronic control modules that allow them to evaluate voltage and current levels of circuits to which they are connected and determine whether data is in the correct operational range.

one-piece rims Automotive-style rims made from two pieces of stamped, pressed, and rolled steel welded together with a center hole that fits over the hub, and with several holes drilled around the hub hole for wheel studs or bolts; also called disc-type wheels.

one-way clutch A roller- or sprag-type device that allows rotation in one direction but locks in the opposite direction; also called over-running clutch.

open center A control valve center configuration in which when the valve is placed in the neutral position, fluid flows between all four ports; it is often referred to as the float position.

open center hydraulic system A type of hydraulic system that has a main control valve that allows pump flow through its center at all times.

open fracture A fracture in which the bone is protruding through the skin or there is severe bleeding.

open loop Hydraulic system that has the pump inlet fluid supplied from the tank and fluid leaving the DCV (directional control valve) returning to tank.

open-circuit voltage (OCV) The difference of the electrical potential between the two terminals of a battery when the battery is disconnected from any circuit.

open-end wrench A wrench with open jaws to allow side entry to a nut or bolt.

open-ended adjustable wrench The open-ended adjustable wrench, or crescent wrench, has an adjustable thumb wheel that moves the lower jaw to grip smaller or larger fasteners.

operating cycle The time that a machine requires to perform a specific operation such as fill and dump one bucket of material.

operating manual A manual published by an equipment manufacturer with information on how to safely and properly operate equipment.

operator protection systems Safety systems and devices designed to protect the operator of machinery from injury.

operator station The interface between the operator and the machine; also called a cab.

orbital valve Another name for a steering control valve.

organic facings Friction facings made of various natural materials, such as cotton fibers, rubber, aluminum, glass, copper or brass fibers, and carbon material.

O-ring A ring that has a round cross section designed to be seated in a groove and compressed during assembly between two or more parts, creating a seal at the interface.

O-ring boss (ORB) A connector that has an O-ring on the male half of the connector and a chamfer on the female half to accept the O-ring. When the connection is tightened, the O-ring is compressed into the chamfer, making the seal, and the applied torque holds the connection together.

O-ring face seal (ORFS) The ORFS connector has the O-ring at the end of the male half of the connector and a straight thread. The female contact has a flat surface and a straight thread. A seal is formed when the O-ring in the face of the male end is compressed onto the machined flat surface female seat. The female nut mechanically holds the connection.

outlet port An opening in the housing that allows oil to leave the pump and move downstream through the system.

out-of-range monitoring Validating sensor data to verify that a system is operating within an expected range for a given operating condition.

output components Components, such as solenoids and displays, that are used to control hydraulic system flow and pressure.

output force Resulting force from a linear actuator that comes from the working pressure applied to the surface area of its piston, expressed as pounds, newtons, or kilograms.

output member The element of the planetary gear set that is connected to the output shaft.

output shaft The output shaft of an interaxle differential. The rear side gear is part of or splined to the output shaft; also known as the through shaft.

outside diameter (OD) The measurement of a cylindrical tube between opposite points on the external surface.

outside micrometer A micrometer that measures the outside dimensions of an item.

over-center clutch A clutch that engages by using clamp force rather than spring force.

over-crank protection (OCP) thermostat A thermostat that monitors the temperature of the starter motor and opens a relay circuit to interrupt the current to the solenoid if prolonged cranking causes the motor temperature to exceed a safe threshold.

overdrive ratio A ratio that provides a speed increase and output torque decrease.

overhead crane A crane with a movable bridge carrying a movable or fixed hoisting mechanism and traveling on an overhead fixed runway structure.

overrunning alternator decoupler (OAD) A pulley that uses an internal spring and clutch system that allows it to rotate freely in one direction and provide limited, spring-like movement in the other direction.

over-running clutch A roller- or sprag-type device that allows rotation in one direction but locks in the opposite direction; also called one-way clutch.

oxidation A condition that results from the combination of hydraulic fluid and oxygen and heat.

packing A condition where ground materials stick and accumulate between sprockets, track, rollers, and other mating components during operation. Packing increases track tension and track component wear.

panhard rod Controls suspension movement side to side; also known as a transverse torque rod.

parallel circuit A circuit in which all components are connected directly to the voltage supply.

parallel joint arrangement Two or more universal joint arrangements where the joint angles form parallel lines; it is a method of angle cancelation for use with parallel angles; also known as the waterfall arrangement.

parameter group number (PGN) A package of serial data transmitted over the CAN network that includes SPN, source addresses, and FMI, as well as commands, data, requests, acknowledgments, negative acknowledgments, and fault codes.

parameter identifier (PID) A value or identifier of an item being reported with fault data.

parasitic draw An electrical load similar to a key-off electrical load except that the current draw is usually unintended or unwanted.

Pascal's law The law of physics that states that pressure applied to a fluid in one part of a closed system will be transmitted equally to all other areas of the system.

passive sensor A sensor that does not use a current supplied by the ECM to operate.

PAT blade A straight blade, sometimes called a power, angle, and tilt blade, that is attached to a dozer with a C frame and uses hydraulic cylinders to be raised and lowered, angled to the left or right, and tilted on each end.

peening A term used to describe the action of flattening a rivet through a hammering action.

personal protective equipment (PPE) Safety equipment designed to protect the technician, such as safety boots, gloves, clothing, protective eyewear, and hearing protection.

phase The timing between each point in time (an instant) on a waveform cycle.

phasing Lining up the inboard yoke ears of a two-piece driveshaft so that the non-uniform velocity cancelation occurs in the proper quadrant of the circle.

Phillips screwdriver A type of screwdriver that fits a head shaped like a cross in screws. It's also called a Phillips head screwdriver.

pi The ratio of the circumference of a circle to its diameter; represented by the Greek letter π.

pictorial diagram A type of sketch used to illustrate what the components in a hydraulic system look like and how they are connected.

piezoresistive sensor A sensor that uses a piezoresistive crystal arranged with a Wheatstone bridge to measure the change in resistance of the piezo crystal; these sensors are adapted to measuring vibration and dynamic or continuous pressure changes.

pilot bearing A bearing that supports the front of the transmission input shaft, which is mounted in the flywheel or the rear of the crankshaft.

pilot controls A low-pressure hydraulic system that is metered by the operator to actuate the main control valves.

pilot oil A term to describe a low-pressure oil system used to actuate the spools in a DCV.

pilot pressure A lower pressure hydraulic system that controls a higher-pressure and higher-flow hydraulic system.

pilot-operated relief valve A two-stage relief valve that provides a narrow pressure override.

pin punch A type of punch in various sizes with a straight or parallel shaft.

pin turning A service procedure where track pins and bushings are disassembled and turned 180 degrees apart before reassembling. Turning can restore proper operating clearances between pins and bushings.

pinion depth The mounting position of the pinion in relation to the crown gear center of axis.

pinion drive A drive that uses a small gear driving a larger gear usually integral to the drive axle.

pinion gear A small driving gear.

piston A solid disk that moves within a tube (or cylinder) under fluid pressure.

piston pumps The most complex type of pump, and can be either fixed or variable displacement. Swashplate angle determines pump displacement.

pitch The number of teeth per unit of pitch diameter on a gear.

pitch circle The theoretical point on the tooth face halfway between the root and the top land, where only rolling motion exists; also called the pitch diameter.

pitch diameter The theoretical point on the tooth face halfway between the root and the top land, where only rolling motion exists; also called the pitch circle.

pivot shaft A large weight-bearing shaft that runs from one suspended track frame to the other through the machine's main frame to connect the track frames to one another. Shock loads from the track are transmitted through the pivot shaft to the opposite track.

pivot turn A special movement of a track machine where it turns around its own center point by allowing one track to drive while braking the opposite track.

plain bearing A plain bushing, or friction bearing, also called a plain bearing is a mechanical element used to reduce friction between rotating shafts and stationary support members or housings. They contain no rolling elements and are often lubricated with pressurized lubricant.

plain bevel gear A bevel gearset with straight-cut teeth.

plain bushings A plain bushing, or friction bearing, also called a plain bearing is a mechanical element used to reduce friction between rotating shafts and stationary support members or housings. They contain no rolling elements and are often lubricated with pressurized lubricant.

plain spherical bearings The plain spherical bearing consists of an inner spherical ring, placed within an outer spherical ring and locked together so that the inner ring is held captive within the outer ring in the axial direction only.

plan angle An angle where the driveshaft moves toward the side of a vehicle when viewed from above.

planetary double-reduction drive axle A drive axle that incorporates a planetary gearset to achieve two gear reductions through the drive axle.

planetary drive A drive using a planetary gearset.

planetary gear A gear arrangement consisting of a ring gear with internal teeth, a carrier with two or more small pinion gears in constant mesh with the ring gear, and an externally toothed sun gear in the center in constant mesh with the planetary pinions.

planetary gear reduction drive A type of gear reduction system in which a planetary gear set reduces the starter output speed to multiply motor torque to the pinion gear.

planetary power-shift transmission A type of power-shift transmission in which hydraulic clutches control sets of planetary gears to transfer power.

planetary two-speed drive axle A two-speed drive axle that uses a planetary gearset for the low range.

platooning A method of controlling the operation of multiple machines performing the same tasks in a farm field with a single lead machine. Platooning is enabled through machine-to-machine communication or an inter-vehicle communication system and uses only a single operator to control the operation of multiple machines in an agriculture field operation.

pleated Describes how filter media is folded when it is formed into an element

pliers A hand tool with gripping jaws.

plies Cords made of materials like nylon, fiberglass, polyester, or rayon that make up the carcass or casing.

PLUS (parallel link undercarriage system) The Komatsu PLUS system used on lighter machines does not use dual bushings, but instead enables the bushing to rotate in an oil-lubricated track link counterbore. Because neither the bushing nor the pin use an interference fit to retain the parts in the link, only a snap ring is used to lock the pin in place to prevent it from sliding out from between the track links. The use of oil to lubricate the pins and bushings in link counterbores requires four rather than two separate oil seals.

ply rating A rating the industry assigns to tires based on the number of the number of plies that the tire has. Generally, the more plies a tire has, the stronger it is.

pneumatic jacks A type of vehicle jack that uses compressed gas or air to lift a vehicle.

pneumatic tires Tires that must be filled with pressurized air to support the load of a machine and its payload.

pneumatics A general term applied to the application of compressed air to transmit power.

polarity The state of charge, positive or negative.

policy A guiding principle that sets the shop direction.

polyalkylene glycol (PAG) Synthetic oil used in all R-134a systems.

polyalphaolefin (PAO) Oil used in R-12 systems and those converted from R-12.

polymeric positive temperature coefficient (PPTC) device (resettable fuse) A thermistor-like electronic device used to protect against circuit overloads. Also called *resettable fuse*.

poppet valves A type of valve used with pilot control systems to meter oil to main control valves.

pop-rivet gun A hand tool for installing pop rivets.

port plate Component in piston pumps that directs oil in and out of the barrel to and from the housing.

portable lifting hoists A type of vehicle hoist that is portable and can be moved from one location to another.

positive displacement pumps Hydraulic pumps that have close internal clearances and will always move oil when they are turning.

positive drive A category of track drive system that uses a gearlike sprocket to engage a drive lug or bushing in the track. Positive drive systems are common in earth moving equipment where very high drive torque is required.

potentiometer A variable resistor with three connections: one at each end of a resistive path, and a third sliding contact that moves along the resistive pathway.

pot-type flywheel A flywheel shaped like a deep pot, inside of which all of the components of the clutch are housed, with the exception of the clutch cover.

pounds per square inch or kilograms per square centimeter Two common units of measure used to quantify pressure in a hydraulic system.

power divider A differential gearset that splits the available torque equally between two drive axles; also called an interaxle differential.

power flow The path that power takes from the beginning of an assembly to the end.

power shuttle An addition or improvement to a transmission that enables an operator to easily change the direction of the equipment between forward and reverse while maintaining the same speed and engine rpm; also called a power reverser or a hydraulic shuttle.

power source A component in an arc welding system that converts AC input power into an AC or DC output at the appropriate voltage and current levels needed for the welding task.

power take-offs or PTOs Devices that allow power to be rerouted to operate other equipment on, or off, the machine.

power-shift transmission A type of transmission that allows operators to shift gears up or down and change directions on the go and under load without a loss in acceleration or torque and without having to use a foot clutch.

precision farmer techniques Farming strategies that use technology such as automated machinery to precisely cultivate, seed, fertilize, and harvest crops.

preload Negative end play, or less than zero clearance.

press fit An interference fit, also called a press fit or friction fit, is a means of fastening two parts together so that they are in direct contact with one another and are held in place only by friction, or the tightness of the fit. There is negative clearance between the interference fit parts, so they must be pressed or forced together.

pressure The result of resistance to fluid flow.

pressure control valves Used to manage pressure levels in hydraulic circuits or systems.

pressure differential The pump creates a pressure differential at its inlet and once it is pushed out of the pump it flows toward the tank which is another pressure differential.

pressure override The difference in pressure between a relief valve opening (cracking) pressure and its fully open pressure.

pressure plate The friction surface of the clutch cover and the plate that squeezes the clutch disc against the flywheel.

pressure rating Pumps must withstand maximum system pressure plus a safety factor.

pressure ratio A term used to describe the difference in pressure required to open a valve versus the pressure locked behind it.

pressure relief valves Valves that limit pressure in one part of a circuit or a complete system.

pressure/flow compensator A part of a pump control valve that ensures pump flow will maintain a system pressure that is always higher than the highest load-sense signal.

pressure-compensated flow control valves Valves that maintain a constant pressure drop and flow across them.

pressure-reducing valve A valve that provides a lower pressure for part of a hydraulic system.

pressurized reservoir A type of reservoir used to store hydraulic fluid that is closed at the top to maintain pressure in the reservoir.

pressurized tank Hydraulic tank that has positive internal pressure.

preventive maintenance A type of routine maintenance performed on a regular basis to help identify and correct problems to minimize system or equipment failures, which is sometimes referred to as planned maintenance (PM).

prick punch A punch with a sharp point for accurately marking a point on metal.

primary battery A battery using chemical reactions that are not reversible, and the battery cannot be recharged.

primary brakes The part of a dual brake system that works the rear brakes of a vehicle.

prime mover The initial source of energy in a system; a machine that transforms energy from thermal, electrical, or pressure form to mechanical form.

procedure A list of the steps required to get the same result each time a task or activity is performed.

productivity A measurement of machine power. Productivity is calculated by measuring the amount of work performed by a machine and dividing that by the time it takes to perform the work. Units for productivity vary and could range from tons of material moved per hour or how many trees are moved a minute.

profile bearing Contact pattern between the root and the top land of the tooth.

programmable read-only memory (PROM) Memory that stores programming information and cannot be easily written over.

proportional solenoid valves Solenoids that will move a certain amount based on the level of electrical signal delivered to them.

prove-out sequence A sequence in which the warning lights come on for several brief seconds with the key on and engine off or during key-on engine cranking.

pry bars (crowbars) A high-strength carbon-steel rod with offsets for levering and prying.

psi Pressure measurement- pounds per square inch.

P-type material Semiconductor material having electron deficiency or a place to hold additional electrons.

pull-down switch A switch connected between the ECM and a negative ground current potential.

pullers A generic term to describe hand tools that mechanically assist the removal of bearings, gears, pulleys, and other parts.

pulling plates An accessory for bearing removal and installations tools. The plates surround a shaft and provide a surface for puller jaws to attach to while also ensuring all the forces are placed at the inner press-fit race of the bearing.

pull-type clutch A clutch with an integral release bearing, which is pulled toward the transmission to disengage the clutch.

pull-up switch A switch connected between the ECM and a battery positive.

pulse-type charger A battery charger that sends current into the battery in pulses of 1-second cycles; used to recover sulfated batteries.

pulse-width modulated (PWM) A type of digital signal commonly used to control the power supplied to electrical devices.

pump The component in a hydraulic system that receives power from a prime mover and produces fluid flow.

pump control valves Valves that can change the displacement of a variable displacement pump.

pump displacement Volume of fluid a pump can move in one revolution.

pump drive Some hydrostatic drive systems that have more than one pump may use a pump drive to rotate their pumps.

pump output flow The amount of flow a pump produces for a given amount of time.

pump ripple An effect that is common with positive displacement pumps and is the result of small fluctuations in flow. These ripples can lead to structural vibration of pipework and associated components and hence result in audible noise.

pump unloading valve A valve used to divert pump oil flow during high pressure periods to reduce heat and load on the prime mover.

punches A generic term to describe a high-strength carbon-steel shaft with a blunt point for driving. Center and prick punches are exceptions and have a sharp point for marking or making an indentation.

push arms Low-mounted arms used to connect a dozer blade to a dozer and provide great strength for pushing material.

push-type clutch A clutch in which the release bearing is pushed toward the engine to release the clutch.

pyrolysis An explosive reaction that can occur when the temperature of the air inside the tire or the tire itself reaches 250°C (482°F).

quick adjust A small mechanism used to turn the large adjusting ring in the clutch cover when adjustment is required.

quick-release valve Prevents delay of brake release.

race, also called a raceway The area in which the rolling elements on a rolling bearing ride.

rack A bar with teeth; used with a pinion to convert circular to linear motion.

rack-and-pinion gear A gear consisting of a flat rack with either spur-cut or helically cut teeth on one side and a meshing circular pinion gear.

radar An acronym for radio detection and ranging. It detects objects and determines their distance, angle, and velocity relative to the radio transmitter.

radial Radial loads act from the center of a circle or shaft outwards. So, the load, or force, is always at a right angle to the circumference of the circle they are acting from.

radial shaft seals Also called lip seals. A seal are used between cylindrical moving elements such as a shaft and a bore or housing.

radial thrust Thrust that tries to push gears in mesh apart perpendicular to their axis.

radiator A device that transfers heat from a fluid within to a location outside.

random access memory (RAM) A temporary storage place for information that needs to be quickly accessed.

ratchet A generic term to describe a handle for sockets that allows the user to select the direction of rotation. It can turn sockets in restricted areas without the user having to remove the socket from the fastener.

ratcheting closed-end wrench A closed-end wrench that has a ratcheting mechanism so that the tool does not have to be removed, to continue turning.

ratcheting open-end wrench An open-end wrench that can be moved slightly and then repositioned so that the tool does not have to be completely removed in order to continue turning it.

ratcheting screw driver A screwdriver with a selectable ratchet mechanism built into the handle that allows the screwdriver tip to ratchet as it is being used.

ratios The speed and torque relationship between two or more gears in mesh.

reaction member The element of the planetary gear set that is held stationary.

reactivity The rate at which a substance will undergo a chemical reaction. The higher the reactivity, the faster it will chemically react.

read-only memory (ROM) Memory used for permanent storage of instructions and fixed lookup table values used by the ECM that control the microprocessor.

real-time kinematic (RTK) Or dual frequency receivers. GPS receivers that use a subscription-based signal correction for satellite GPS. RTK can provide positional accuracy to the centimeter or less than ½ inch on a year-to-year basis.

receiver-dryer A storage reservoir for refrigerant that also absorbs moisture from the air-conditioning system.

recoil spring mechanism A mechanism used to adjust track tension and absorb shock loads applied to the track.

rectification A process of converting alternating current (AC) into direct current (DC).

rectifier A device that converts alternating current (AC) to direct current (DC).

reduction gear drive A starter motor drive system in which the motor multiplies torque to the starter pinion gear by using an extra gear between the armature and the starter drive mechanism.

reference datum line (RDL) The arbitrary reference point from where the center of gravity is measured. Determined by the equipment manufacturer.

reference voltage (Vref) A precisely regulated voltage supplied by the ECM to sensors; the value is typically 5 VDC, but some manufacturers use 8 or 12 volts.

regenerative Another type of DCV position that allows return oil from the actuator to join pump oil going to the other side of the actuator.

relay valves Provide faster brake actuation.

release bearing A hollow bearing through which the input shaft passes, which pushes or pulls against rotating clutch release levers to release the clutch.

release bearing travel The distance that the release bearing moves while releasing the clutch in a pull-type clutch.

release fork (yoke) The actuator that moves the release bearing.

remote control A machine control system where an operator can use a set of controls that electronically duplicates actual machine controls, enabling the operator to work at a distance.

remote sensing Referencing the battery positive connection through an input terminal that is used for the regulator reference voltage.

removable carrier type A drive axle housing with a removable carrier.

repair and maintenance manual A manual published by an equipment manufacturer with information on how to safely and properly maintain, repair, and troubleshoot equipment.

reserve capacity Refers to the length of time, measured in minutes, that a battery discharges under a specified load of 25 amps at 26.6°C (80°F) before battery cell voltage drops below 1.75 volts per cell (10.5 volts for a 12-volt battery).

reservoir Provides stored, pressurized air.

residual magnetism The small amount of magnetism left on the rotor after it has been initially magnetized by the coil windings' magnetic field.

resistance-start motors A type of split-phase motor with a starter winding used to initiate rotor rotation. A resister placed in series with the starter winding is used to unbalance motor magnetic fields to initiate rotor movement.

resistive circuit A circuit in which grounds and power connections cannot properly function due to overly high resistance.

resistive touch screen A display screen composed of two flexible, transparent sheets lightly coated with an electrically conductive yet slightly resistive material.

resistor A component designed to produce electrical resistance.

resolver A Hall-effect sensor used to measure the rotor position and speed for a motor controller in order to properly manage the motor operation in three-phase traction motors.

respirator Protective gear used to protect the wearer from inhaling harmful dusts or gases. Respirators range from single-use disposable masks to types that have replaceable cartridges. The correct types of cartridge must be used for the type of contaminant encountered.

restraint criteria Used to determine the proper amount of restraint that must be applied to a piece of cargo to prevent movement in the forward, rearward/aft, lateral, and vertical directions.

return filter A filter used to clean oil before it returns to the tank.

return screen Coarse screen that stops large contaminants from entering the tank with the return oil.

reverse drive wear Wear formed on the reverse side of the drive sprocket, produced during reverse drive cycles. Reverse drive wear may form a pocket on the reverse drive side of the tooth.

reverse idler shaft A shaft that supports the reverse idler gear.

reverse overdrive A reverse direction overdrive ratio through the planetary gear set.

reverse polarity Also referred to as a direct current electrode positive (DCEP) connection. The flow through an electrical circuit that is formed when an electrode cable is connected to the positive terminal of a power source and the work cable is connected to the negative terminal of the power source.

reverse reduction A reverse direction underdrive ratio through the planetary gear set.

reverse rotation Hydrostatic drives provide reverse by reversing the flow of the pump.

reverse rotational wear Wear on the drive sprocket, but different from reverse drive wear in that the wear is only on one side of the sprocket tooth.

reverse tip wear Wear occurring during forward travel when the sprocket teeth tips make direct contact with the track bushings rather than the gap between the bushings.

RFID technology Electromagnetic fields that automatically identify and track objects with tags attached. Information about the object, such as a blade or machine, is electronically stored on the tag and can be read by an RFID reader.

rheostat A variable resistor constructed of a fixed input terminal and a variable output terminal, which vary current flow by passing current through a long resistive tightly coiled wire.

rigger A person who specializes in lifting and moving heavy objects.

rigging/rigging gear All the components used to attach the mechanical hoisting equipment to the load being lifted. This can include rope, wire rope/cables, slings, shackles, eyebolts, eye nuts, links, rings, turnbuckles, rigging hooks, compressions hardware, rigging blocks, load-indicating devices, and precision load positioners.

rigid frames An undercarriage track frame arrangement that uses solid attachment points of the track frame to the main frame that allows no movement between the two frames.

ring gear A large bevel gear that is driven by a smaller pinion gear in the bevel gearset; also known as a crown gear.

ripper An attachment that is commonly mounted onto the rear of a dozer or motor grader that consists of one or more steel shanks with cutting teeth to help break up rocky and/or compacted soil.

risk Exposing a person or a valuable item to danger, harm, or loss.

risk controls Measures or actions taken to reduce and control risk.

rock ejector A metal bar that hangs down from the truck's box and ejects rocks from between dual tires, helping to prevent tire damage.

rod The moving part of a cylinder

rod speed A measure of how fast a linear actuators rod moves. Usually measured in fps (feet per second) or mps (meters per second).

roller bearings Bearings which feature cylindrical rolling elements to reduce friction between moving parts. Roller bearings will have an inner race, outer race, bearing cage, and rollers. They may be straight or tapered roller bearings.

rolling friction Resistance encountered between parts that roll against one another. An example of rolling friction is the movement of track rollers and idlers across chain rails formed by the track links or segments.

root The radius shape between the bottoms of two teeth; also called fillet radius.

root diameter The smallest circle of the gear measured at the fillet radius (root) of the teeth.

root mean square (RMS) A measurement method for AC voltage providing a comparable measurement of AC current to DC current. The RMS value of AC voltage refers to the effective value of AC voltage or current and not the wave peak positive-to-wave peak negative difference in voltage.

root or radial wear The name given to sprocket tooth wear caused by the outside diameter of a bushing as it scrubs through the sprocket tooth root.

ROPS Roll-over protection system.

rosebud A type of torch tip with numerous holes in the end that produce multiple flames with a wide pattern suitable for heating metal.

rotary Turning, or capable of turning, on an axis.

rotary flow Fluid flow inside the torque converter that follows the rotation of the housing.

rotating friction Resistance between a stationary component and a rotating component. An example of rotating friction is track pins and bushings. The bushings turn to enable the track chain and shoes to bend while the pin remains stationary in the link.

rotating ring laser angle sensors A positional type IMU sensor integrated into the machine's body, boom, stick, and bucket. There are a variety of IMU sensors, but are generally a rotation ring laser combined with mirrors and a specialized laser light sensor or catcher that detects movement.

rotochamber Produces a longer stroke and maintains a constant force throughout the entire stroke.

rotor A device the diesel engine drives, which creates a series of magnetic poles that spin very close to the stator windings.

run time The total time the compressor is running (includes duty cycle and unloaded time).

S blade A short, horizontally straight blade with no side wings to prevent material from spilling off the sides of the blade.

SAE J-3016 The SAE standard that classifies the level of autonomous control of on-highway vehicles.

SAE viscosity ratings A viscosity rating at 212°F (100°C) and 0°F (−18°C). SAE 20 and SAE 10W are common ratings.

safe working load (SWL) The maximum safe lifting load for lifting equipment.

safety The condition of being protected from or unlikely to cause danger, risk, or injury to yourself or others.

safety data sheets (SDS) Also called material safety data sheets. Sheets that provide information about handling, use, and storage of materials that may be hazardous.

safety valves Open and release air pressure in case of a blockage in the system.

Saybolt Viscosimeter A test instrument used to measure fluid viscosity.

S-cam drum brake The cam that forces the shoes outward against the drum is shaped like an "S."

scarifier A type of ripper attachment that is mounted near the front of a motor grader (ahead of the blade) to help loosen compacted soil.

schematic diagram A type of diagram that uses symbols and lines to represent the components in a hydraulic system and how they are connected.

scored Notched, scratched, or incised.

screen A coarse filter that can be used for pump inlet, return, or pressure filtration.

screw extractor A tool for removing broken screws or bolts.

screws Usually smaller than bolts and are sometimes referred to as metal threads. They can have a variety of heads and are used on smaller components. The thread often extends from the tip to the head so they can hold together components of variable thickness.

seal Something used to completely close a gap, seam, or opening.

sealed release bearing A release bearing with no grease nipple or zerk.

sealed track chain A track pin and bushing assembly technique using a nonlubricated track pin and bushing design. The pin operates like a hinge inside the bushing, and washers at each end of the pin prevent dirt from entering the space between the pin and bushing.

secondary and primary reservoirs Store pressurized air from compressor.

secondary batteries A battery that produces electricity using reversible chemical reactions, allowing the battery to be recharged.

secondary couple vibrations Vibrations, caused by U-joint angles, that travel the length of the driveshaft.

secondary steering A safety backup to ensure the operator can steer the machine to a parked position.

second-degree burns Burns that involve blistering and damage to the outer layer of skin.

section break A point where the diameter of a shaft or thickness of a component changes.

segmented sprockets A type of final drive sprocket formed by bolting pieces or segments of sprocket teeth together. Segments consist of between three and six teeth that, when bolted together with other pieces, form an entire drive sprocket.

self-diagnostic The TCU's capability to analyze its own functions.

self-exciting alternator An alternator that relies on the residual magnetism found in the rotor after operating as a way to switch on the voltage regulator and supply current to the rotor.

self-tapping screw A screw that cuts its own thread as it goes.

semiconductor A material that can have properties of both conductors and insulators and that can switch back and forth between either state, using small electrostatic charges.

semi-floating axle shaft An axle shaft that carries the entire weight of the machine on its outer end.

sensible heat Heat that can be sensed or felt.

sensing The voltage reference point the alternator uses for regulation of the output.

separator plates Thin, round slices of steel or cast iron inside a hydraulic clutch that sandwich friction discs and lock to components such as gear hubs, ring gears, or housings to transfer torque.

sequence valve A valve to ensure two or more cylinders connected in series operate in a specific sequence.

sequentially Operating in a series, or in logical order.

serial communication Communication using 0s and 1s to transmit data in a series, one bit after another in sequence.

serial data Pieces of data sent by the master module.

series circuit The simplest type of electrical circuit, with multiple loads but only one path for current to flow.

series-type hybrid electric drive A powertrain configuration where an engine drives only an electric generator, which in turn powers an electric motor.

serrated-edge shake-proof washer A washer that is used to anchor smaller screws.

service brake Brakes used to slow down or stop the machine in motion.

servo control valves Valves that are electronically controlled by the operator and in turn control a pump servo piston that changes pump output.

servo pistons Pistons used to hydraulically adjust swashplate angle.

shedding A process that reduces the plate surface area and therefore reduces capacity. Shedding may also produce short circuits between the bottom of positive and negative plates.

shift by wire Shifting controlled completely by the transmission electronic control.

shift finger A flat-sided piece that fits into the shift gates.

shift forks Components that move the sliding clutches or collars in the transmission to actually select gear ranges.

shift gates Rectangular notches either formed into or attached to the shift rails.

shift lever A shift control that the operator uses to change transmission gear position.

shift pattern The direction that the shift lever must be moved to select a given gear.

shift rail interlock A system that prevents two shift rails from being moved from the neutral position at once.

shift rails The bars that control shift fork position.

shift tower A raised section on the transmission with a pivot into which the shift lever fits.

shims Thin round pieces of metal used to adjust spring tension in a hydraulic valve.

shock Inadequate tissue oxygenation resulting from serious injury or illness.

shock load failure Fracture caused by one sudden shock.

short circuit An electrical circuit that is formed between two points, allowing current to flow through an unintended pathway.

shunts Internal conductors with small calibrated resistance and that direct current flow into the meter while measuring amperage.

shuttle check valve A type of check valve with three ports that sends the higher of two pressures to another component.

side gears Part of the differential gearset; the side gears are splined to the axles.

side wear of a drive sprocket Caused by contact of the sides of sprocket teeth with track links; also called corner gouging of sprocket teeth.

sidewall The area between the tread area and the bead area.

sight glass A feature of a hydraulic tank to visually check fluid level.

simple fracture A fracture that involves no open wound or internal or external bleeding.

simple machine The simplest mechanisms that allow us to gain mechanical advantage.

sine wave The shape of an AC waveform as it changes from positive to negative, graphed as a function of time.

single flare A sealing system made on the end of metal tubing.

single-acting cylinder A type of hydraulic cylinder that can apply force in only one direction.

single-path hydrostatic systems Hydrostatic drive systems that use one pump to drive one motor.

single-phase current AC current that peaks two times during a cycle.

skid steering Refers to a steering principle where one track is driven faster than the other, pushing the machine in the direction toward the slower or stopped track. Since the leading and trailing edges of the track will slide sideways to steer the machine, that sliding action lends the name skid steering.

slack adjusters Levers with either automatic or manual means of adjusting the brake linings.

slag Oxidized and molten metal waste that is left over from welding operations.

slave cylinder The hydraulic cylinder used to release the clutch in hydraulically actuated clutch systems.

sliding friction Resistance between two components moving across one another or one component being dragged across a stationary component.

sliding gear transmission A transmission that has sliding gears splined to the main shaft that slide in and out of mesh with the countershaft gears.

sliding T-handle A handle fitted at 90 degrees to the main body that can be slid from side to side.

slip The difference between the speed of the rotating stator field and the rotor speed.

slip fit A slip fit is when two parts fit together with positive clearance between them so that they will slip over one another.

slip joint A splined shaft and tube assembly that allows driveshaft length changes.

slip joint pliers Adjustable pliers with parallel jaws that allow you to increase or decrease the size of the jaws by selecting a different set of channels.

slipping A track operating condition where the track turns, but no forward or reverse movement takes place. Slipping leads to accelerated wear.

smart charger A battery charger with microprocessor-controlled charging rates and times.

smart-iron Off-road equipment integrating some level of telematic, semis autonomous, or fully autonomous machine control.

snap ring pliers A pair of pliers for installing and removing internal or external snap rings.

snapshot A snapshot records all the relevant TCU, or ECU, data before and after a diagnostic code is set to ease diagnoses.

Society of Automotive Engineers (SAE) A U.S.-based, globally active professional association and standards developing organization for engineering professionals in various industries, including automotive; mobile, off-road equipment; commercial truck; and aerospace. It sets industry standards and regulations.

socket An enclosed metal tube commonly with 6 or 12 points to remove and install bolts and nuts.

soft-face steel hammers A type of hammer featuring a drop forged head specifically designed to mushroom when striking hard base materials are gaining popularity for added safety against chipping and spalling causing injury.

solenoid valve A type of electromechanically operated valve that uses an electric current to control fluid flow.

solid rubber tires Tires that are not filled with pressurized air.

source address (SA) The field that designates which control module is sending the message.

spats A type of PPE, often made of leather, worn over the laces and tongue of work boots to protect workers from hot metal.

speed brace A U-shaped socket wrench that allows high-speed operation. It's also called a speeder handle.

speed nut A nut usually made of thin metal; it does not need to be held when started, but it is not as strong as a conventional nut. It's a fast and convenient way to secure a screw.

spherical roller bearings Bearings that are characterized by their barrel-shaped rollers. The rollers are narrow at the ends, and they bulge in the middle like a wooden barrel. They will handle some axial load and can tolerate misalignment of the two separated components.

spider gear A beveled gear that is a component of the differential gearset; it is fitted to the four legs of the differential cross and rotates with it; also known as a differential pinion gear.

spill kit A kit or container containing items needed to clean up and control liquid and hazardous material spills.

spin on-type filters One-piece filter assembly.

spinout A low-traction situation where one drive wheel or one drive axle spins wildly while the other remains stationary.

spiral bevel gear A bevel gearset with spirally or helically cut gears.

spiral-wound cell battery A type of AGM battery in which the positive and negative electrodes are coiled into a tight spiral cell with an absorbent microglass mat placed between the plates.

split ball gauge (small hole gauge) A gauge that is good for measuring small holes where telescoping gauges cannot fit.

split charge relay A system designed to separate the main starting battery and the auxiliary battery; also called a battery isolator system.

split guide ring A ring that attaches to the impeller and the turbine blades and creates a circular fluid passage.

split-phase motor A single-phase motor with a starting winding used to initiate rotor movement.

spool The name for the movable part of a DCV valve that blocks oil flow and allows oil flow when shifted.

spot turns A machine whose left and right tracks or tires rotate in opposite directions.

sprain An injury in which a joint is forced beyond its natural movement limit.

spring brake A very strong spring that applies the parking brakes.

spring brake module Delivers air pressure to spring brake chambers to release parking brakes.

spring rate The amount a spring will deflect when loaded.

spring shackle A movable connection for a leaf spring, allowing length changes.

spring washer A washer that compresses as the nut tightens; the nut is spring-loaded against this surface, which makes it unlikely that it will work loose. The ends of the spring washer also bite into the metal.

spring-loaded accumulator A type of hydraulic fluid energy storage device that uses a spring to provide mechanical energy.

sprocket A toothed wheel that drives a chain or the track of a crawler machine.

spur gear A gear with teeth cut parallel to its axis of rotation.

square file A type of file with a square cross-section.

square thread A thread type with square shoulders used to translate rotational to lateral movement.

squirrel cage induction motor An AC motor with a rotor having solid conductor bars connected at each end with a shorting ring

squirrel cage rotor The type of construction used for rotors in an induction motor. In a squirrel cage rotor, the conductor bars are placed parallel to one another in a rotor cylinder. Ends of the conductor bar are connected with a shorting ring.

stall speed The maximum speed the engine can drive the torque-converter impeller with the turbine held stationary.

STAMPED A system of hose selection which stands for size, temperature, application, material conveyed, pressure, ends, delivery.

standard (imperial) Bolts, nuts, and studs can have either metric or imperial threads. They are designated by their thread diameter, thread pitch, length, and grade. Imperial measures are in feet, inches, and fractions of inches. Most countries use metric.

start enable relay The start enable relay is controlled by the TCU and interrupts the circuit to the starter solenoid unless the TCU passes a self-check and verifies that the transmission is in neutral.

state of charge test A test that indicates how complete the battery state of charge is, expressed as a percentage of a full charge.

static Objects that are static are not moving or are not changing.

static working pressure The force acting on a conductor inner surface.

stator A stationary series of copper-insulated wires that are wound in place in the generator housing.

stator (hydraulic retarder) The stationary element in the retarder that tries to slow oil flow.

stator (torque converter) The element inside a torque converter most responsible for torque multiplication.

stator inner hub The inner race of the stator one-way clutch, which splines to the stator ground shaft.

stator support shaft A stationary shaft that holds the inner hub of the stator one-way clutch; also called ground shaft.

steel ruler A ruler that is made from stainless steel.

steering axle An axle that allows the machine to turn.

steering motor The hydraulic motor responsible for turning the tracks at different speeds to cause a turn.

steering pedal The pedals used to steer older track machines one pedal steers left and the other right.

steering planetary A planetary gearset in a differential steer machine drive axle that is used to steer.

step-down transformer A component that converts high-voltage, low-current AC power from a wall outlet (or engine) to a lower-voltage, higher-current AC or DC output.

straight edges A measuring device generally made of steel to check how flat a surface is.

strain An injury caused by the overstretching of muscles and tendons.

stress riser A point of stress concentration.

stringer Small inclusion in a cast or formed metal that weakens it.

strut A cylinder charged with gas and oil used in suspensions.

stud A type of threaded fastener with a thread cut on each end, as opposed to having a bolt head on one end.

SU blade A semi-universal blade that is mostly straight like an S blade and less curved than a U blade, with side wings to help prevent spillage off the sides of the blade.

suction screen Coarse screen that stops large contaminants from entering the pump inlet.

sulfation Refers to a process where sulfate, originally contained in the electrolyte, becomes chemically bound to both battery plates

sun gear The small, externally toothed gear at the center of the planetary gear set.

suspect parameter number (SPN) A numerical identifier that defines the data in a fault message and the priority of the fault.

suspended track frames An undercarriage track frame that allows some oscillation of the two track frames relative to one another. A three-point attachment system is used.

suspension seat An operator seat suspended by springs and/or compressed air.

swashplate Component in an axial piston pump that creates reciprocating piston motion.

synchronized transmission A transmission that uses synchronizers to match shaft and gear speeds to avoid clashing on shifts.

synchronizer An assembly that matches shaft and gear speeds as a shift is being made for a clash-free engagement.

synchronizing shaft Part of a bent axis motor that connects its cylinder block to the output shaft.

synchronous motor A category of AC motors where the rotor and stator magnetic field revolve together at the same time.

synthetic hydraulic fluid Created from a manmade chain of molecules that result in a high-viscosity index, which is excellent cold weather use.

system identifier (SID) A fault code used by J-1587 protocols that identifies which subsystem has failed.

system manager A transmission control module used with older Gen. 1 and Gen. 2 Eaton AutoShift transmissions.

tab washer A washer that gets its name from the small tabs that are folded back to secure the washer. After the nut or bolt has been tightened, the washer remains exposed and is folded up to grip the flats and prevent movement.

tamper One of several types of attachments used on excavators and loaders to compact soil using vibrating plates or rolling pads.

tandem Two drive axles connected by a power divider.

tandem center A control valve center configuration in which when the valve is placed in the neutral position, fluid flows from the pump, through the valve, and back to the tank.

tandem scraper A type of scraper that has separate engines for the tractor section and the scraper section to provide greater power and traction for rough terrain.

tap A term used to generically describe an internal thread-cutting tool.

tap handle A tool designed to securely hold taps for cutting internal threads.

taper tap A tap with a taper; it is usually the first of three taps used when cutting internal threads.

taper-current charger A battery charger that applies either constant voltage or constant amperage to the battery through a manually adjusted current selection switch.

tapered roller bearings Bearings that are characterized by the conical (cone-shaped) rollers that are arranged in at a *tapered* angle to the shaft, so that the rollers form a cone shape around the shaft.

technical manual A collection of information (paper or electronic) containing specific technical data regarding how to properly operate, maintain, repair, or troubleshoot a piece of equipment. Technical manuals may also contain technical data on how to complete a task or procedure.

technical safety bulletins Documents periodically published and distributed by an equipment manufacturer that identify a safety risk or hazard and how to properly control the risk or hazard.

telematics The transmission and reception of information from remote objects. Typically, GPS signals and onboard network data are transmitted over cell phone or satellite communication systems. The data are analyzed to supply machine information through a web portal.

telescopic dipper A device that is used in place of a normal dipper stick on an excavator to extend the reach of the bucket, especially in applications where material needs to be removed from below ground level or high above ground level.

telescoping boom A type of boom that is commonly used on wheeled excavators and cranes that can be extended, retracted, and rotated.

tensile strength The amount of force required before a material deforms or breaks.

terrain compensation An important consideration for autoguidance systems to compensate for the effect that varying terrain altitudes can have on the machine's position as measured by the GPS receiver. The effect of roll can be very significant when the GPS antenna is mounted on the cab roof. If uncorrected, rolling and changes in altitudes can become a major source of steering error.

test certificate A certificate issued when lifting equipment has been checked and deemed safe.

test light The simplest piece of electrical test equipment, which consists of an incandescent lightbulb connected to an insulated lead and a sharpened metal probe.

theoretical flow rate A calculated value that uses pump displacement and pump speed to determine a 100% efficient pump's output.

thermal efficiency A measurement of how much of the fuel that has been used has actually turned into power to drive the vehicle.

thermal fuse A type of fuse opened by heat produced from resistance caused by high-amperage flow.

thermistor A temperature-sensitive variable resistor commonly used to measure coolant, oil, fuel, and air temperatures.

thermostat An automatic device for regulating temperature.

thermostatic expansion valve (TXV) An expansion device used in commercial vehicle air-conditioning systems.

third-degree burns Burns that involve white or blackened areas and damage to all skin layers and underlying structures and tissues.

thread chaser A device similar to a die that cleans up rusty or damaged threads.

thread pitch The coarseness or fineness of a thread as measured by the distance from the peak of one thread to the next, in threads per inch.

thread repair A generic term to describe a number of processes that can be used to repair threads.

threaded adjuster A mechanism used to adjust spring tension in a hydraulic valve.

three phase Electrical output from every revolution of the rotor in a generator, from three separate windings.

three-body wear Occurs between two moving components and solid contamination.

three-coil gauge A gauge in which three field coils are wound in series, with a coil at minimum reading, one at maximum reading, and one between the two.

three-piece rims Rims that have a main rim base with the inner bead seat flange as one piece, and an outer bead seat and locking ring that make up the other two pieces.

threshold limit value (TLV) The maximum allowable concentration of a given material in the surrounding air.

through shaft The output shaft of an interaxle differential. The rear side gear is part of, or splined to, the through shaft; also known as output shaft.

thrown track A condition when tracks separate from a machine by riding off worn rollers wheels, chains, idlers, or sprockets.

thrust loads Axial, or thrust, loads always act along the centerline of a shaft. So, they can only apply a force that moves a shaft in or out along its axis.

thrust screw A screw that stops the crown gear from flexing under load.

tiller A joystick used to control the steering functions of a track machine.

time division multiplexing (TDM) A type of multiplexing used in onboard networks and that works by dividing the time available to each network module or device.

tin snips A cutting device for sheet metal, which works in a similar fashion to scissors.

tire bead The area that makes contact with the rim and that must form an airtight seal with it.

tire chains Installed on heavy-duty machines to prevent damage to tires from sharp objects.

tire explosion When a tire starts to burn on the inside and pressure eventually raises high enough to explode the tire.

tire inflation pressure The level of air in the tire that provides it with load-carrying capacity and affects overall vehicle performance.

tire pressure monitoring system (TPMS) An automated system that provides a means of continuous monitoring of the vehicle tire pressure.

toe The end of a crown gear tooth closest to the center of its axis.

toe angle The inward or outward angle of the wheels, measured at the front.

toe in When the forward inside edge of the tires are closer together than the rear inside edge.

tooth face The area that actually comes into contact with a mating gear and is parallel to the gear's axis of rotation.

top land The apex of a tooth.

torque The twisting force applied to a shaft that may or may not result in motion.

torque angle A method of tightening bolts or nuts based on angles of rotation.

torque converter A type of fluid coupling that is also capable of multiplying torque.

torque limiter A third type of pump control valve that reduces pump flow at times of both high flow and high pressure.

torque multiplication An increase in torque that corresponds to a decrease in speed.

torque multiplication phase A phase that occurs in the torque converter whenever the impeller is turning significantly faster than the turbine.

torque rod A rod that is used to position an axle fore and aft.

torque specification Describes the amount of twisting force allowable for a fastener or a specification showing the twisting force from an engine crankshaft, which is supplied by manufacturers.

torque wrench A tool used to measure the rotational or twisting force applied to fasteners.

torque-to-yield (TTY) A method of tightening bolts close to their yield point or the point at which they will not return to their original length.

torque-to-yield (TTY) bolts Bolts that are tightened using the torque-to-yield method.

torsional damper A device mounted onto a rotating shaft to minimize vibration.

torsional excitation Twisting forces caused by inertial excitation.

torsional vibrations Vibrations caused by twisting forces on the driveshaft; these occur twice per revolution.

torus The hollowed-out donut shape of the rear of the torque converter housing and the turbine.

torx bolt A type of screw with an internal or external six point star shaped head.

towing equipment and devices Equipment or devices used to pull, or tow, a load horizontally.

toxic dust Any dust that may contain fine particles that could be harmful to humans or the environment.

track pitch The dimension between the track pins.

track sag The distance measured between the lowest and highest points of the top of the track.

track shoes Metal plates linked together to form the tracks of a track-type undercarriage system.

traction batteries A type of battery construction, commonly used in hybrid electric vehicles, designed to deliver high-amperage loads to electric traction motors.

traction motors Electric motors used in a propulsion drive system.

transfer case A gearbox arrangement that allows the torque from the transmission to be split between the front and rear driving axles of a vehicle.

transient failure A type of hydraulic system failure that is intermittent but typically indicates an underlying problem that will need to be addressed to avoid a catastrophic failure.

transient voltage suppression (TVS) diodes Specialized diodes in the rectifier bridge that become resistive rather than conductive at a specific voltage level.

transmission control unit (TCU) The unit that controls the shifting in an electronically automated transmission; also called transmission electronic control module (ECM).

transmission oil cooler A series of oil tubes or passages that are cooled by engine coolant.

transverse torque rod Controls suspension movement from side to side

transverse vibrations Vibrations caused by driveshaft imbalance; these occur once per revolution.

travel system An alternative term used to describe a track drive system on excavators. The term "travel system" is used to differentiate the propulsion system from the undercarriage and associated components used on other machines.

triangulation A method using three or more satellite signals to locate position. Triangulation works when a receiver connects with signals transmitted from each satellite at precisely the same time. Since the satellites are located at different distances from the receiver, the signals will arrive at slightly different times.

trickle charger A battery charger that charges at a low amperage rate.

tridem Three drive axles that split the driving force.

triple differential steering Another name for a cross-drive transmission that incorporates three different differentials to transmit power to track and steer the machine.

troubleshooting A systematic and logical approach to determining the causes of and solutions to malfunctions.

trunnion The smooth ends of the U-joint cross that accepts the bearing caps.

tube yoke A yoke with two ears that accept a U-joint and which is welded to the driveshaft tube.

tube-flaring tool A tool that makes a sealing flare on the end of metal tubing.

tubing A fluid conductor that may be bent and shaped to accommodate the installation on the machine. Tubing dimensions are typically available in 1/16-inch increments from 1/8 inch up to 1 inch outside diameter (OD) and in ¼-inch increments above 1 inch.

turbine The torque-converter element that is splined to the transmission input shaft.

turbulence A disturbed moving stream of fluid flow.

twin-line hose Oxygen and acetylene hoses that are connected together for most of their length.

two-body wear Describes wear between two moving components that break through the fluid film barrier.

type 1 circuit breaker A cycling circuit breaker that automatically resets.

type 2 circuit breaker A noncycling circuit breaker.

type 3 circuit breaker A circuit breaker that requires manual reset.

type K thermocouple A low-cost, general-purpose, temperature-sensing element connected to the same meter terminals for measuring DC millivolts.

typology The manner in which modules are connected to one another.

U blade A universal dozer blade that is tall and has a basic U shape that enables it to scoop up large amounts of material and move that material over long distances without spilling it off the sides.

ultracapacitor A new generation of high-capacity, high-energy density capacitors.

UltraShift A two-pedal AMT from Eaton that is completely shift by wire with no clutch pedal.

undercarriage The generic name given to all the components making up the propulsion mechanism or travel system for track drive equipment.

underdrive ratio Any ratio that decreases output speed while increasing output torque; also known as a gear reduction.

universal joint A cross-shaped joint with bearings on each leg, where one set of parallel legs is connected to the end of one shaft and the other set of parallel legs is connected to the end of a second shaft. This arrangement allows the shafts to operate at shallow angles to each other; also called a U-joint, a Cardan joint, or a Hooke joint.

unloading valve A valve that can be used when two fixed displacement pumps are used.

upstroke The term used when a pump is changing to a higher displacement in order to supply fluid to one system.

utility bucket A type of bucket used on wheel loaders and front end loaders that has a smooth cutting edge along the front to lift and load loose soil or other material.

vacuum breaker/pressure relief valves Used on a pressurized tank to minimize vacuum and pressure levels in the tank.

valve A component that changes the condition of the hydraulic fluid it comes in contact with, in terms of pressure, flow, or direction.

valve-regulated lead-acid (VRLA) batteries A battery design using a gas-tight case that does not permit battery gases or electrolyte to leak from the battery except through a pressure-sensitive safety valve.

vane pumps Have multiple sliding vanes that are carried around in a rotor that is driven by the pump shaft.

vanes The movable part of a vane pump the creates fluid flow.

vaporization Change of state from a liquid to a gas.

variable capacitance pressure sensor An active sensor that measures both dynamic and static pressure.

variable displacement A type of pump or motor in which the flow rate and outlet pressure can be changed during operation.

variable displacement bidirectional A term that describes the type of pump used for hydrostatic drive systems.

variable displacement pumps A type of pump that can vary its displacement independently of its shaft speed.

variable pitch stator A stator with blades that can change the angle to alter the torque-converter multiplication factor.

variable reluctance sensor A sensor used to measure rotational speed, including wheel speed, machine speed, engine speed, and camshaft and crankshaft position.

vehicle hoist A type of vehicle lifting tool designed to lift the entire vehicle.

velocity The speed of a fluid in a specified direction.

vent An opening that releases or discharges a fluid or gas.

vented reservoir A type of reservoir used to store hydraulic fluid that is open or vented at the top.

vented tank Hydraulic tank that allows atmospheric pressure in.

vernier caliper An accurate measuring device for internal, external, and depth measurements that incorporates fixed and adjustable jaws.

virtual fuse A software-controlled fuse that uses field effect transistors for the circuit control device A circuit protection strategy that monitors circuit amperage with software and shuts off the circuit when amperage exceeds a predetermined threshold. Also called *e-fuses*.

virtual terminal A screen mounted in the tractor used so that the operator can control connected implements. Modules on ISO-bus machines can transmit what are called virtual objects along the CANbus to be displayed on the virtual terminal.

viscosity The quality of a fluid's thickness and resisting tendency to flow.

viscosity chart Can be found in the maintenance guide to show the proper fluid viscosity for hydraulic fluid according to ambient temperature.

viscosity index The measure of the rate of change in a fluid's viscosity as its temperature changes.

vocation The type of service a vehicle is involved in.

volatile memory A type of data storage that is lost or erased when the ignition power is switched off.

volt The unit used to measure potential difference, or electrical pressure.

voltage The pressure that makes electrons flow, it controls the speed at which electrons travel from atom to atom.

volumetric efficiency A calculated value using the actual flow output of a pump and its theoretical output value that determines how efficient the pump is.

vortex flow The flow of fluid from the impeller, through the turbine, through the stator, and back to the impeller.

wad punch A type of punch, which is hollow, used for cutting circular shapes in soft materials, such as gaskets.

warding file A type of thin, flat file with a tapered end.

warning Indicates a potentially hazardous situation, which, if not avoided, could result in death or serious injury.

waterfall arrangement Two or more universal joint arrangements where the joint angles form parallel lines, which allows for a method of angle cancelation for use with parallel angles; also called parallel joint arrangement.

Watt's law A law that defines the relationship between power, amperage, and voltage.

ways A term used to describe the number of ports that one section of DCV has on its external surface. A four-way valve is commonly used for MORE (ports for pump, tank, A, and B).

wear factor A number used to calculate the percentage of component service life remaining. It is based on the depth of hardening of a component.

wear metal Any one of several different types of metal (such as iron, aluminum, or copper) that when detected in hydraulic fluid, can indicate component wear in the hydraulic system.

wear sleeve The wear sleeve is a thin piece of hardened steel placed over a rotating shaft that is designed to wear over time, and it should be replaced when the seal is replaced.

welding helmet Protective gear designed for arc welding; it provides protection against foreign articles entering the eye, and the lens is tinted to reduce the glare of the welding arc.

wet side The side of the reservoir tank where compressed air cools down and any moisture in the air will condense and collect in the bottom on this side of the tank.

wet turn Lubricating track pins with oil, rather than grease, during a pin turning service operation.

wheel cylinders Located inside drum brakes to push the brake shoes toward a drum that rotates with the wheel, creating friction against the drum to slow or stop the wheel.

wheel hub What the wheel and tire fastens to.

wheel trencher A type of trencher that uses a large wheel with teeth to dig through pavement or hard soil.

wide-range planar sensor A type of sensor technology that uses a current pump to calculate relative concentrations of oxygen, nitric oxide, and ammonia in exhaust gases.

winch A mechanical device used to reel in (pull) or wind out (let out) horizontally a length of wire rope or chain.

windings Electrical conductors that are wrapped around a magnetic material.

wire rope clips Fitting for clamping parts of wire rope to each other.

wireless CAN bridge A connection between the controlled area network of one machine and another. Platooning uses the CAN bridge for machine-to-machine communication, collecting data from the CANbus in one machine and wirelessly transmitting the information to the CANbus in the trailing machine.

working pressure The normal operating pressure of a system or component.

working pressure gauge The gauge on an oxygen or acetylene regulator that shows how much pressure is in the hose, or line.

worm gear A gear arrangement capable of large reductions in a small space.

wrench A generic term to describe tools that tighten and loosen fasteners with hexagonal heads.

wye windings Stator windings in which one end of each phase winding is taken to a central point where the ends are connected together.

wye-wound stator A three-phase stator wiring configuration shaped like the letter "Y." Each end of a stator's three windings is connected to a neutral junction point. The other ends are connected to power leads.

yield point The point at which a bolt is stretched so much that it deforms; it is measured in pounds per square inch (psi) or kilopascals (kPa) of bolt cross-section.

INDEX

A

C

E

G

H

I

J

K

L

N

O

T

Y